CATALOGUE OF THE
GOLDSMITHS' LIBRARY

II

UNIVERSITY OF LONDON LIBRARY

CATALOGUE OF
THE GOLDSMITHS' LIBRARY OF
ECONOMIC LITERATURE

COMPILED BY

MARGARET CANNEY
DAVID KNOTT
AND
JOAN M. GIBBS

VOLUME II
PRINTED BOOKS 1801-1850

CAMBRIDGE UNIVERSITY PRESS
FOR THE UNIVERSITY OF LONDON LIBRARY
1975

Published by the Syndics of the Cambridge University Press
Bentley House, 200 Euston Road, London NW1 2DB
American Branch: 32 East 57th Street, New York, N.Y.10022

Library of Congress Catalogue Card Number: 70–121364

ISBN: 0 521 07376 6

First published 1975

Printed in Great Britain
at the University Printing House, Cambridge
(Brooke Crutchley, University Printer)

CONTENTS

PREFATORY NOTE

The arrangement of the second volume of the catalogue follows that of the first, but there is one major change in the material to be found in it: British Parliamentary Papers, as printed for the two Houses of Parliament, have been excluded after the year 1801. However, notable Reports published by H.M. Stationery Office, by commercial firms or reprinted by societies are included. There is also a greater number of local, as distinct from private, Acts than was originally intended when the catalogue was planned. This is because it has been decided to include entries for the original printed texts of, for instance, early Railway Acts which were only published in an abbreviated form with the collections of Public General Acts.

The first half of volume II is the work of the same compilers as volume I. Thereafter, upon Mr David Knott's appointment to another University, his place has been taken by Miss Joan M. Gibbs. We are grateful that Mr Knott has however maintained his connection with the catalogue by giving much help with the reading of the proofs of this volume. During the temporary absence of Miss Gibbs for the session 1973–74, her part in this task has been taken over by Miss Pamela Baker. To her, and to other colleagues who have given us help, the thanks of the compilers are once more due.

ADDITIONAL ABBREVIATIONS USED IN VOLUME II

Agar Ellis: Pamphlets published between 1812 and 1831 which belonged to George Agar Ellis, first Baron Dover (1797–1833).

Black: Black, R. D. G. A catalogue of pamphlets on economic subjects published between 1750 and 1900 and now housed in Irish libraries. *Belfast,* 1969.

BMC: British Museum general catalogue of printed books. Photolithographic edition to 1955. *London,* 1965–66. (Used throughout the catalogue, but only quoted in volume II.)

1801

GENERAL

18114 AITCHISON, T. The Edinburgh and Leith directory for 1801, containing an alphabetical arrangement of noblemen, private gentlemen, merchants, traders and others, in the city and suburbs of Edinburgh and Leith... 231p. *12°. n.p.* [1801]

18115 [BAILLIE, J.] An impartial history of the town and county of Newcastle upon Tyne and its vicinity, Comprehending an account of its origin, population, coal. coasting, & foreign trade. Together with an accurate description of all its public buildings, manufactories, coal works, &c. 610p. *8°. Newcastle upon Tyne*, 1801.

18116 BARBADOS. *Laws, etc.* The public Acts in force; passed by the legislature of Barbados, from May 11th, 1762 to April 8th, 1800, inclusive...a digested abridgment of the said Acts; and, an index: with a table of...all the Acts...By Samuel Moore... 435, 79p. *8°.* 1801.

18117 BENSEN, C. D. H. Materialien zur Polizei- Kameral- und Finanzpraxis für angehende praktische Staatsbeamten. Vols. 1–2. *8°. Erlangen*, 1801–2[–3]. *The title-page of part 1, volume 1 is dated 1800 and those of parts 2 and 3 of volume 2 are dated 1803.*

18118 [BLODGET, S.] Thoughts on the increasing wealth and national economy of the United States of America. [The preface is signed: Observator.] 40p. *8°. Washington*, 1801.

18119 BOURBON-BUSSET, G. DE, called **BOURBON-LEBLANC.** Introduction à la science de l'économie politique et de la statistique générale; ouvrage élémentaire...Par Gabriel Leblanc. 203p. *8°. Paris*, 1801.

18120 BROADLEY, J. Pandora's box, and the evils of Britain; with effectual, just, and equitable means for their annihilation; and for the preservation of the peace, happiness and prosperity of the country. 51p. *8°.* 1801.

18121 —— [Another issue. With 'Supplement to Pandora's box'.] 64p. *8°.* 1801.

18122 CANARD, N. F. Principes d'économie politique, ouvrage couronné par l'Institut National...15 nivôse an IX (5 janvier 1801); et depuis revu, corrigé et augmenté par l'auteur. 236p. *8°. Paris*, 1801.

18123 CAPPER, B. P. A statistical account of the population and cultivation, produce and consumption, of England and Wales, compiled from the accounts laid before the House of Commons, and the reports of the Board of Agriculture; together with observations thereupon, and hints for the prevention of a future scarcity. 119p. *8°. London & Edinburgh*, 1801.

18124 CHAPMAN, THOMAS, *printer*. Chapman's Birmingham directory, or, alphabetical list of the merchants, tradesmen, and principal inhabitants, of... Birmingham, and its vicinity...Also, the departures and arrivals of the...mails...stage coaches...and a list of carriers...[With an appendix.] 134, 10p. *8°. Birmingham*, [1801]

18125 CLARKE, THOMAS B. A survey of the strength and opulence of Great Britain; wherein is shewn, the progress of its commerce, agriculture, population, &c.

before and since the accession of the House of Hanover... With observations by Dean Tucker, and David Hume, Esq. in a correspondence with Lord Kaimes; now first published. 240p. *8°.* 1801. *See also* 1802.

18126 COBBETT, W. Porcupine's works; containing various writings and selections, exhibiting a faithful picture of the United States of America... 12 vols. *8°.* 1801.

18127 DIXON, JOSHUA. The literary life of William Brownrigg, M.D. F.R.S. To which are added an account of the coal mines near Whitehaven: and observations on the means of preventing epidemic fevers. 239p. *8°. London, Dublin, &c.*, 1801. *Presentation copy, with inscription, from the author to 'Mr. Bateman'; with manuscript additions and corrections.*

18128 ENGLAND. *Treaties, etc.* Convention between His Britannick Majesty, and the Emperor of Russia. Signed at St. Petersburgh, the 5/17 June 1801... 17p. *4°.* 1801. *The text is printed in English and French in parallel columns.*

18129 —— —— Preliminary articles of peace, between His Britannick Majesty, and the French Republick. Signed at London, the 1st of October 1801... 8p. *4°.* 1801.

18130 FELL, R. A tour through the Batavian Republic during the latter part of the year 1800. Containing an account of the revolution and recent events in that country. 395p. *8°. London, Edinburgh, &c.*, 1801.

18131 [FESQUET, J. L.] Voyage de Paris à Strasbourg, et principalement dans tout le Bas-Rhin, pour s'assurer de l'état actuel de l'agriculture et des ressources de ce département, depuis la fondation de la République française. Publié en l'an IX, après le traité de Lunéville, par J. L. F***, du Gard. 44, 112p. *8°. n.p.* [1801]

18132 FOX, CHARLES J. The speech of the Honorable Charles James Fox, on the motion for an enquiry into the state of the nation, on the 25th of March, 1801. To which is added an appendix, illustrating some passages of the speech, and contributing to the means of forming a full judgment upon the most momentous questions that agitate the public in the present crisis. 76p. *8°.* 1801.

18133 FRANCE. *Ministère de l'Intérieur.* Instruction sur la manière de rectifier les tables de comparaison entre les anciennes et les nouvelles mesures, calculées d'après le mètre et le kilogramme provisoires, pour les rendre conformes à la détermination définitive du mètre et du kilogramme; suivie de l'Arrêté des Consuls du 13 brumaire an 9. Publiée par ordre du Ministre de l'Intérieur. 12p. *8°. Paris, an IX* [1801]

18134 —— *Napoleon Bonaparte, First Consul.* Nos. 1167, 1305, 1392...Arrêtés relatifs aux biens des émigrés. Des 29 messidor an VIII, 16 pluviôse et 24 thermidor an IX. [1°. Arrêté relatif aux demandes en restitution des fruits et revenus ou du prix de la vente des biens séquestrés... 2°. Arrêté additionnel à celui du 29 messidor...3°. Arrêté qui ordonne la formation d'un etat des bois et forêts actuellement sous la main de la nation.] 3p. *4°. Paris*, 1801.

18135 HOECK, J. D. A. Aperçu statistique des états de l'Allemagne, sous le rapport de leur étendue... population, de leurs productions, de leur industrie...

commerce et de leurs finance...Publié en français par Ad. Duquesnoy. [140]p. *fol. Paris*, an IX [1801] *Translated by A. G. Griffet de la Beaume.*

18136 [**JENKINSON**, C., *1st Earl of Liverpool.*] A vindication of the convention lately concluded between Great Britain and Russia. In six letters. 124p. *8°.* 1801.

18137 KEMP, J. Observations on the Islands of Shetland, and their inhabitants; and, on the climate, soil, state of agriculture, fisheries, &c. of that country: with hints for their improvement. 39p. *8°. Edinburgh*, 1801.

18138 LEQUINIO, J. M. Voyage pittoresque et physico-économique, dans le Jura... 2 vols. *8°. Paris*, an IX [1801]

18139 [**LESPARAT**, J. F.] Métrologies constitutionelle et primitive [*sic*] comparées entre elles et avec la métrologie d'ordonnances. 2 vols. *4°. Paris*, 1801.

18140 MORTIMER, THOMAS (1730–1810). Lectures on the elements of commerce, politics, and finances; intended as a companion to Blackstone's Commentaries on the laws of England... 442p. *8°.* 1801. *For other editions, see* 1772.

18141 [**ORIANI**, B., *Conte.*] Istruzione su le misure e su i pesi che si usano nella Repubblica Cisalpina. Pubblicata per ordine del comitato governativo. 128p. *8°. Milano*, 1801. *See also* 1806.

18142 PLAYFAIR, W. The statistical breviary; shewing...the resources of every state and kingdom in Europe; illustrated with...charts, representing the physical powers of each distinct nation...To which is added, a similar exhibition of the ruling powers of Hindoostan. 64p. *8°.* 1801.

18143 [**REMNANT**, W.] A sketch of Hambourg, its commerce, customs and manners. With some account of the laws respecting bills of exchange and bankrupts. By an English resident here. 131p. *8°. Hambourg*, 1801. *Attributed to 'Wm. Remnant' in a manuscript note on the title-page.*

18144 ROTH, J. F. Geschichte des Nürnbergischen Handels. Ein Versuch...Zweyter Theil. *8°. Leipzig*, 1801.

18145 ROYAL DUBLIN SOCIETY. The royal charter of the Dublin Society. To which is added the society's by-laws and ordinances, for the good government of the corporation. 42p. *8°. Dublin*, 1801.

18146 SEMPERE Y GUARINOS, J. Biblioteca Española económico-política. Vols. 1–3. *8°. Madrid*, 1801–4.

18147 SILVESTRE, A. F., *Baron de.* Essai sur les moyens de perfectionner les arts économiques en France ...Ouvrage approuvé par l'Institut National et par la Société d'Agriculture du Département de la Seine. Imprimé par ordre du Préfet du Département. 176p. *8°. Paris*, an IX [1801]

18148 SMITH, ADAM. An inquiry into the nature and causes of the wealth of nations. [With 'Reflections on the formation and distribution of riches. By Mr. Turgot'.] 4 vols. *8°. Basil & Paris*, 1801. *For other editions, see* 1776.

18149 SONNENFELS, J. VON. Grundsätze der Staatspolizey, Handlung und Finanzwissenschaft...Zum Gebrauche bey akademischen Vorlesungen ausgearbeitet von Franz Xav. v. Moschamm...Zweyte verbesserte und vermehrte Auflage. 557p. *8°. München*, 1801.

18150 The **SOUND** and Baltic, considered in a political, military, and commercial view: intended to illustrate the relative connections, and maritime strength, of the northern powers. To which are added, observations upon Egypt, and the trade of India, as connected with the Baltic, or East Sea. Translated from a German pamphlet published at Berlin... 89p. *8°.* 1801.

18151 STORCH, H F. VON. The picture of Petersburg. From the German. 591p. *8°.* 1801.

18152 —— Tableau historique et statistique de l'empire de Russie à la fin du dixhuitième siècle...Edition française, avec cartes. 2 vols. *8°. Basle & Paris*, 1801.

18153 T., R. The dark cloud in the political hemisphere broken, and a bright beam of consolation issuing therefrom, in favor of His Majesty's ministers and depressed stockholders...Respectfully addressed to the Right Hon. William Pitt... By an old naval officer. 25p. *8°.* 1801.

18154 A short **VIEW** of the Preliminaries of peace, signed at London, October 1, 1801. 36p. *8°.* 1801.

18155 WILLIAMS, H. M. Sketches of the state of manners and opinions in the French Republic, towards the close of the eighteenth century. In a series of letters. 2 vols. *8°.* 1801.

18156 YOUNG, ARTHUR (1741–1820). Voyage en Irlande...Traduit de l'anglais, par Ch. Millon...Avec des recherches sur l'Irlande, par le traducteur. Seconde édition, augmentée d'un essai sur le commerce d'Irlande... 2 vols. *8°. Paris*, 1801. *For other editions, see* 1780.

AGRICULTURE

18157 AGRICULTURE SOCIETY, *Manchester.* Manchester Agricultural Society. A general meeting of this society will be held at the Unicorn Inn, in Altrincham, on Monday the nineteenth day of October next...[Dated: Sep. 23, 1801.] *s.sh.fol. Manchester*, [1801] *The Sheffield copy.*

18158 ARCHER, J. Statistical survey of the County Dublin, with observations on the means of improvement; drawn up for the consideration, and by order of the Dublin Society. 276p. *8°. Dublin*, 1801.

18159 BARTLEY, N. To the printer of the Bath Chronicle. [*Begin.*] Desirous of contributing in some sort to the general benefit of society...[A letter on the cultivation of potatoes, dated: Bath, Feb. 1801.] *s.sh.4°. Bath*, [1801] *The Sheffield copy.*

18160 COOTE, SIR C., *Bart., of Donnybrook.* General view of the agriculture and manufactures of the Queen's County, with observations on the means of their improvement, drawn up in the year 1801, for the consideration... of the Dublin Society. [With 'Index (by Daniel Bagot, Esq.)'.] 236, [36]p. *8°. Dublin*, 1801. *The half-title reads: Statistical survey of the Queen's County, being the first volume of the statistical surveys of Ireland.*

18161 —— General view of the agriculture and manufactures of the King's County, with observations on the means of their improvement, drawn up in the year 1801. For the consideration...of the Dublin Society. 242p. *8°. Dublin*, 1801. *The half-title reads: Statistical survey of the King's County, being the second volume of the statistical surveys of Ireland.*

18162   COTES, J. Thoughts on the means of affording an efficient supply to the country, addressed to Lord Carrington, President of the Board of Agriculture. In two letters [dated: December 30, 1800 and January 28, 1801]. 4p. *fol.* [*London*, 1801] *The Sheffield copy.*

18163   DALRYMPLE, W. A treatise on the culture of wheat, with an appendix; containing an account of the growth of beans with wheat, and a plan of improved seed harrows...Second edition. 76p. *8°*. 1801. *The Sheffield copy. For another edition, see* 1800.

18164   DIXON, JOHN, *of Kensington.* Improvement of the fisheries; letter II. Or, a plan for establishing a nursery for disbanded seamen and soldiers, and increasing the strength...of the British Empire. 8p. *4°*. 1801. *For the first part, see* 1800, *and for the third, fourth and fifth parts, see* 1802, 1803 *and* 1804 *respectively.*

18165   DRURY, D. Thoughts on the precious metals, particularly gold...With directions and hints to travellers, captains of ships, &c. for obtaining them, and selecting other natural riches that mankind have universally agreed to deem valuable; from the rough diamond, down to the pebble-stone. 59, [5]p. *8°*. 1801.

18166   ENGLAND. *Laws, etc.* [*Endorsed:*] An Act for dividing, allotting, and inclosing a certain tract of common or waste land, called Kentismoore, within the manor and parish of Kentisbeere in the county of Devon. 41 Geo.III. 1801. 28p. *fol. n.p.* [1801]

18167 —— —— An Act for dividing, allotting, and inclosing all the commons, and waste lands, within the manor and parish of Dunkeswell in the county of Devon. 29p. *fol.* [*London,*] 1801.

18168   FRASER, R. General view of the agriculture and mineralogy, present state and circumstances of the County Wicklow, with observations on the means of their improvement, drawn up for the consideration of the Dublin Society... 284p. *8°. Dublin,* 1801.

18169   FULLARTON, W. A letter, addressed to... Lord Carrington...[On the conversion of grass lands into tillage.] 100p. *8°*. 1801. *The Sheffield copy.*

18170   GLEANINGS from books, on agriculture. 196p. *8°*. 1801.

18171   GOUBE, I. J. C. Traité de la physique végétale des bois, et des principales opérations forestières, avec le modèle des actes à rédiger; terminé par le tableau des proportions que doivent avoir les bois de construction pour la marine, rapportées au calcul décimal. 326p. *8°. Paris,* 1801.

18172   HESLOP, L. A comparative statement of the food produced from arable and grass land, and the returns arising from each; with observations on the late inclosures, and the probable effect of a general Act for inclosing commons or wastes, heaths, &c.; together with other matters... 18p. *4°*. 1801.

18173   HOWLETT, J. An enquiry concerning the influence of tithes upon agriculture...Together with some thoughts respecting their commutation. To which are added, Remarks upon the animadversions of Mr. A. Young and his correspondents relative to the subject of tithes... 120p. *8°*. 1801.

18174   JOHNSTONE, JOHN (*fl.* 1797–1834). An account of the mode of draining land, according to the system practised by Mr. Joseph Elkington. Second edition, corrected and enlarged... 164p. *8°. London, Edin-*

burgh, *&c.*, 1801. *The copy that belonged to Arthur Young. For other editions, see* 1797.

18175   [LAWRENCE, J.] The modern land steward; in which the duties and functions of stewardship are considered and explained...By the author of the New farmer's calendar... 415p. *8°*. 1801. *See also* 1806.

18176   [——] The new farmer's calendar; or, monthly remembrancer, for all kinds of country business...By a farmer and breeder. Second edition, with considerable additions. 554p. *8°*. 1801.

18177   [——] Third edition. 556p. *8°*. 1801. *For other editions, see* 1800.

18178   LETTER from a solicitor to a country gentleman, on the report of the Committee of the House of Commons, to consider of facilitating the inclosure of wastes and commons, which was ordered to be printed the 9th July, 1800. 19p. *4°. Shrewsbury,* 1801. *The Sheffield copy.*

18179   MARSHALL, W. On the appropriation and inclosure of commonable and intermixed lands: with the heads of a Bill for that purpose: together with remarks on the outline of a Bill, by a Committee of the House of Lords, for the same purpose. 88p. *8°*. 1801. *Author's presentation copy.*

18180   MOORE, THOMAS, *of Maryland.* The great error of American agriculture exposed: and hints for improvement suggested... 72p. *8°. Baltimore,* 1801.

18181   NEEDWOOD FOREST. Case of the freeholders. 3p. *4°*. [*London,* 1801] *The Sheffield copy.*

18182   NETHERLANDS. *Batavian Republic.* Publicatie van het Uitvoerend Bewind...houdende ordonnantiën en maatregelen, concerneerende het vangen, zouten, havenen, kenren...van den haring; enz. Gearresteerd den 28 july 1801... 50p. *8°. den Haag,* 1801.

18183   PARKER, T. N. An essay, or practical inquiry concerning the hanging & fastening of gates and wickets. With plates. 57p. *8°*. 1801. *See also* 1804.

18184   PICTET, C. Traité des assolemens, ou de l'art d'établir les rotations de récoltes. 284p. *8°. Genève,* 1801.

18185   PROVIS, J. Tables, of the most useful kind, to facilitate business in several branches of the copper trade ...and which will apply to almost every individual concerned therein; from original calculations... 263p. *4°. Truro,* 1801. *See also* 1832.

18186   REY DE PLANAZU, . Œuvres d'agriculture et d'économie rurale...enrichies de trente planches enluminées, précédées d'un tableau annuel de la régie, administration et comptabilité des revenus d'une terre, où l'on découvre au premier coup-d'œil...les produits de toutes les parties d'un bien quelque considérable qu'il puisse être. Nouvelle édition, revue, corrigée et augmentée. 205, [65]p. *4°. Paris,* 1801.

18187   SIMONDE DE SISMONDI, J. C. L. Tableau de l'agriculture toscane. 327p. *8°. Genève,* 1801.

18188   SINCLAIR, SIR JOHN, *Bart.* Hints as to the advantages of old pastures, and on the conversion of grass lands into tillage. 8p. *4°. n.p.* [1801] *Presentation copy, with inscription, from the author; from the Sheffield Collection.*

18189 —— Observations on the means of enabling a cottager to keep a cow, by the produce of a small portion of arable land...Drawn up for the consideration of the Board of Agriculture... 18p. *4°*. 1801.

18190 —— [Another edition.] 16p. *4°. 1801.*

18191 SUSSEX AGRICULTURAL SOCIETY. At a meeting of the Committee of subscribers... appointed to arrange the prizes and premiums for the present year, held at the Star Inn, Lewes, April 18, 1801...the following resolutions were agreed to. *s.sh.fol. Lewes,* [1801] *The Sheffield copy. See also* 1804, 1805, 1807, 1808.

18192 SUTTON, ROBERT. A complete guide to landlords, tenants, and lodgers; being a methodical arrangement of the whole law...respecting the taking or letting lands, houses...With...directions for making a distress for rent, &c....The third edition. 104p. *8°. 1801.*

18193 TAPLIN, W. The gentlemen's stable directory; or, modern system of farriery...The fourteenth edition. 2 vols. *8°.* 1801, 1799. *The second volume is of the fifth edition.*

18194 TATHAM, W. National irrigation, or the various methods of watering meadows; affording means to increase the population, wealth, and revenue of the kingdom, by an agricultural, commercial and general economy in the use of water. 427p. *8°. 1801.*

18195 WASHINGTON, G., *President of the USA.* Letters from His Excellency General Washington, to Arthur Young, Esq., F.R.S. Containing an account of his husbandry, with a map of his farm; his opinions on various questions in agriculture; and many particulars of the rural economy of the United States. 172p. *8°.* 1801. *See also* 1847.

18196 YOUNG, ARTHUR (1741–1820). An inquiry into the propriety of applying wastes to the better maintenance and support of the poor...Being the substance of some notes taken in a tour in the year 1800. 160p. *8°. Bury* [*St. Edmunds*] & *London,* 1801.

POPULATION

18197 HEBERDEN, W. Observations on the increase and decrease of different diseases, and particularly of the plague. [Based on the statistics in the Bills of Mortality during the eighteenth century.] 96p. *4°. 1801.*

18198 SPAIN. *Secretaria de Estado.* Censo de la poblacion de España de el año de 1797, executado de orden del Rey en el de 1801. [6]p., 47 tables. *fol. Madrid,* [1801]

TRADES & MANUFACTURES

18199 ACKERMANN, SUARDY & CO. Analytical hints relative to the process of Ackermann, Suardy & Co's. manufactories for waterproof cloths, and wearing apparel...[With 'Rain defied...Health preserved', an advertisement.] 27, [3]p. *8°.* [1801]

18200 [COCHRANE, ARCHIBALD, *9th Earl of Dundonald.*] [*Begin.*] Kent produces the best wool for the worsted and hosiery trade of any county in England... [An announcement that the author has 'engaged Mr. Callaway's worsted mill, for some years, late in the possession of Messrs. Fellows and Myers in London'.] *s.sh.4°. n.p.* [1801 ?] [*Br.* 672] *The Sheffield copy. The attribution to 'Lord Dundonald' is in pencil at the head of the text, probably in Lord Sheffield's hand.*

18201 COMPANY OF CABINET AND CHAIR MAKERS, *Norwich.* The Cabinet & Chair Makers' Norwich book of prices; containing the piece-prices of all the newest cabinet and chair work ever yet published. The second edition, with additions; revised and corrected by a Committee of Journeymen Cabinet and Chair Makers. 160, 75, [64]p. *8°. Norwich,* 1801.

18202 DESMOND, W. Directions for tanning all sorts of hides and skins, according to the new process introduced by Mr. W. Desmond. Fourth edition. [With 'Letter from Mr. Desmond to A. Tilloch, Esq.'.] 24p. *12°.* 1801.

18203 FREDERIC, MR., *coal-dealer, pseud.* A short essay on the composition of œconomical fuel, and of various mixtures that may be used with coal, to produce a clear saving of one-third part of the expense of keeping up fires in general, by the patentee of the coal manufactory, Millbank-Street, Westminster. 42p. *12°. n.p.* [1801] *A manuscript note on the title-page identifies 'Mr. Frederic' as the Marquis de Chabannes.*

18204 JAUBERT, P. Dictionnaire raisonné universel des arts et métiers, contenant l'histoire, la description, la police des fabriques et manufactures de France et des pays étrangers...nouvelle édition, corrigée et considérablement augmentée d'après les mémoires et les procédés des artistes... 5 vols. *8°. Lyon,* 1801. *For another edition, see* 1773.

COMMERCE

18205 ANDERSON, JAMES (1739–1808). A calm investigation of the circumstances that have led to the present scarcity of grain in Britain: suggesting the means of alleviating that evil, and of preventing the recurrence of such a calamity in future... 94p. *8°. 1801.*

18206 —— The second edition. 94p. *8°. 1801.*

18207 An **APPEAL** to a humane public, for the poorer millers and bakers, respecting the high price of bread; and the injury sustained by them from the establishment of the London Flour, Meal & Bread Company. With an account of the effect...this new chartered company had

in immediately raising, instead of lowering, the price of corn. By an attentive observer. 24p. *8°.* [1801 ?] *Attributed to Francis Chalmer, in a manuscript note in the copy in Kress, tentatively dated 1800.*

18208 ATWOOD, G. Review of the Statutes and ordinances of Assize, which have been established in England from the fourth year of King John, 1202, to the thirty-seventh of His present Majesty. [With an appendix.] 44, xvi, [6]p. *4°. 1801.*

18209 B., W. Observations on the commerce of Great Britain with the Russian and Ottoman Empires, and on the projects of Russia against the Ottoman and British dominions. 59p. *8°.* 1801.

18210 A COLLECTION of public acts and papers, relating to the principles of armed neutrality, brought forward in...1780 and 1781. 278p. *8°.* 1801.

18211 CROKE, Sɪʀ A. Remarks on Mr. Schlegel's work, upon the visitation of neutral vessels under convoy. 157p. *8°.* 1801.

18212 DUNDAS, H., *Viscount Melville.* Letter from the Right Honourable Henry Dundas to the Chairman, Deputy Chairman, and Court of Directors of the East-India Company. 82p. *8°.* 1801.

18213 EAST INDIA COMPANY. Papers respecting the trade between India and Europe. Printed, by order of the Court of Directors, for the information of the proprietors. 83p. *4°.* [*London,*] 1801.

18214 —— Private trade. Hasty sketch of the debate at the East India House on the subject of the private trade... May 28, 1801...Reported by William Woodfall. 44p. *4°.* [*London,*] 1801.

18215 EDWARDS, Gᴇᴏʀɢᴇ. Radical means of counteracting the present scarcity, and preventing famine in future; including the proposal of a maximum founded on a new principle; to which is prefixed, an address to the legislature, on a plan for meliorating the condition of society at large. 153p. *8°.* 1801.

18216 ENGLAND. *Commissioners of Customs.* An account of the quantity of Portugal and Madeira wines imported into the several ports of England in the years 1798, 1799, and 1800; distinguishing each year. [A table, signed by W. Irving, Inspector General of the Imports and Exports of Great Britain, and dated: 2d May 1801.] *s.sh.fol. n.p.* [1801] [*Br.* 465]

18217 —— *Parliament.* [*Endorsed:*] No. 1. (Copy.) Accounts from the London Company [for the Manufacture of Flour, Meal and Bread], laid before both Houses of Parliament, on the 1st April, 1801. Ordered to be printed 24th June, 1801. 11p. *8°. n.p.* [1801] *The Sheffield copy.*

18218 —— ——. A Bill for repealing the several Acts now in force "for preventing the combination of coal owners, lightermen and masters of ships to advance the price of coals, and for preventing the frauds and abuses committed in the admeasurement of coals within the city of London and the liberties thereof..." and for preventing the impositions practised on coalheavers on the river Thames by coal undertakers. Ordered to be printed 16th March, 1801. 49p. *fol. n.p.* [1801]

18219 GIOJA, M. Sul commercio de' commestibili a caro prezzo del vitto. Opera storicao-teorico-popolare. 2 vols. *12°.* Milano, anno x [1801–2]

18220 GLASGOW. *Town Council.* Table of dues to be levied at the Broomie-law for fish sold there, and to be paid to the tacksmen of the Town's Fish Market and Water Officer, established by acts of the magistrates and town council of Glasgow, dated the 4th. of September and 14th. of October, 1801. *s.sh.fol.* Glasgow, [1801]

18221 HENCHMAN, T. Observations on the Reports of the Directors of the East India Company, respecting the trade between India and Europe...To which is added, an appendix, containing the papers referred to in the work. 229p. *4°.* 1801. *The copy that belonged to Augustus Frederick, Duke of Sussex, with his book-plate. See also 1802.*

18222 JENKINSON, C., *1st Earl of Liverpool.* A discourse on the conduct of the government of Great Britain in respect to neutral nations. A new edition. 111p. *8°.* 1801. [*Higgs* 1675*n*]

18223 —— A new edition. xlix, 108p. *8°.* 1801. *For other editions, see 1758.*

18224 LAWN, B. The corn trade investigated, and the system of fluctuations exposed: with a proposition... offered for the consideration of the Legislature, which will effectually remedy the alarming fluctuating prices of bread corn. And an investigation of the import and export laws ...A new edition, with large additions. 112p. *8°.* Salisbury & London, 1801. *For another edition, see 1800.*

18225 LE MOINE DE L'ESPINE, J. De koophandel van Amsterdam, en andere Nederlandsche steden, naar alle gewesten der waereld...Ontworpen, door de l'Esping [*sic*], vermeerderd, door le Long...Tiende druk. 4 vols. *8°.* Amsterdam, Dord., *&c.,* 1801–2. *Edited and enlarged by R. Arrenberg. For other editions, see 1710.*

18226 MACNAB, H. G. A letter, addressed to John Whitemore, Esq. M.P. member of the Committee of the House of Commons on the coal trade. Pointing out the impolicy of the proposed measure of obtaining a supply of coal from the manufacturing districts to the Metropolis; the causes of the high price of coal, and the means of an immediate and continued reduction of price. 52p. *4°.* 1801. *The copy that belonged to William Vaughan (1752–1850).*

18227 —— Observations on the probable consequences of even attempting by legislative authority to obtain a large supply of coal from Staffordshire to the Metropolis; on the iron trade in Staffordshire and Shropshire in the large way, on the iron and copper trades at Birmingham in the small way; on the price of coal to the inhabitants of London and Westminster; on the collieries in the north; on the carrying trade of Sunderland and Shields; and on the Navy of Great Britain. In a letter to William Manning ...112p. *4°.* 1801. *See note to no. 18226, above.*

18228 A MAXIMUM; or, the rise and progress of famine. Addressed to the British people, by the author of A residence in France, during the years 1792, 1793, 1794, 1795... 62p. *8°.* 1801. *A residence in France is described as 'a series of letters from an English lady...Prepared for the press by John Gifford' (pseudonym for John Richards Green). The present work also appears to have been written by a woman, but is attributed in the BMC to John Gifford, Tory pamphleteer, apparently a different person from J. R. Green.*

18229 OBSERVATIONS on the enormous high price of provisions: shewing...that the overgrown opulence of the husbandman or farmer...if not salutarily corrected, will be the perpetual bane and misery of the country. By a Kentish clergyman. 54p. *8°.* London, Dorchester, *&c.,* 1801.

18230 OBSERVATIONS on the importance of a strict adherence to the navigation laws of Great Britain. 16p. *8°.* 1801.

18231 PAINE, T. Compact maritime, under the following heads: ɪ. Dissertation on the law of nations. ɪɪ. On the Jacobinism of the English at sea. ɪɪɪ. Compact Maritime for the protection of neutral commerce, and securing the liberty of the seas. ɪᴠ. Observations on some passages in the discourse of the Judge of the English Admiralty. 24p. *8°.* Washington, 1801.

18232 PLAYFAIR, W. The commercial and political atlas, representing, by means of stained copper-plate charts, the progress of the commerce, revenues, expenditure and debts of England, during the whole of the eighteenth century. The third edition, corrected and brought to the end of last year. 96p. *8°.* 1801. *For other editions, see* 1785.

18233 REMARKS on the present high price of grain, and on the expediency of farther legislative restrictions in order to effect its reduction. 22p. *8°.* 1801.

18234 A brief **REVIEW** of the causes which have progressively operated to enhance the price of provisions, but particularly of bread-corn. With suggestions as to the best means of alleviating the present distress, and preventing the recurrence of a similar calamity. 91p. *8°.* 1801.

18235 STEEL, D. The ship-master's assistant and owner's manual...The ninth edition, very considerably improved and enlarged...[With 'Steel's tables of the British custom and excise duties...The second edition'; and 'The duties payable upon importation of goods into the United States of America'.] 414, 136, 24p. *8°.* 1801. *For other editions, see* 1790.

18236 SULPICIUS, *pseud.* Letters of Sulpicius, on the northern confederacy. With an appendix, containing the treaty of armed neutrality, together with other documents relative to the subject. 48, xxiiip. *8°.* 1801.

18237 VERZEICHNISS der vorzüglichsten russischen Produkte, welche von St: Petersburg 1800 ausgeschift worden sind. [A table, printed in Russia, of the number of British and American ships engaged in the export trade from Russia, their destinations, and the amount of each commodity carried.] *obl.s.sh.fol. n.p.* [1801 ?] *See also* 1802 (MARCHANDISES...). *For earlier examples of these tables see* 1792 (LIST *of the principal Russian products*...).

18238 WARD, afterwards **PLUMER WARD,** R. A treatise of the relative rights and duties of the belligerent and neutral powers, in maritime affairs: in which the principles of armed neutralities, and the opinions of Hubner and Schlegel are...discussed. 172p. *8°.* 1801.

18239 —— An essay on contraband: being a continuation of the Treatise of the relative rights and duties of belligerent and neutral nations, in maritime affairs. p.[173]–255. *8°.* 1801. *Signed and paginated in sequence with the author's earlier work.*

COLONIES

18240 *BARRINGTON, G. A voyage to Botany Bay with a description of the country, manners, customs, religion, &c. of the natives...To which is added his life and trial. 120p. *12°.* [1801] *See also* 1803.

18241 *—— A sequel to Barrington's voyage to New South Wales, comprizing an interesting narrative of the... behaviour of the convicts; the progress of the colony... 88p. *12°.* 1801.

18242 CUNHA DE AZEREDO COUTINHO, J. J. DA, *Bishop of Elvas.* A political essay on the commerce of Portugal and her colonies, particularly of Brasil in South America...Translated from the Portuguese. 198p. *8°.* 1801. *For other editions, see* 1794.

18243 DUFOUR DE PRADT, D., *Archbishop of Mechlin.* Les trois âges de colonies, ou de leur état passé, présent et à venir... 3 vols. *8°.* Paris, 1801–2.

18244 EAST INDIA COMPANY. Abuse of patronage. The debates held at the East India House on

...the 17th December, 1800. And on...January 20, 1801. On which latter day the following resolution was moved: "That it be the opinion of this Court that the enquiry into the alledged abuse of patronage ought to be continued." ...Reported by William Woodfall. 96p. *4°.* [*London,*] 1801.

18245 —— The debate at the East India House, on... the 15th of January, 1801, when a motion was made to confirm the...resolution of the Court of Directors to request the Marquis of Wellesley to accept an annuity of 5,000 l...for the term of twenty years...Reported by William Woodfall. 39p. *4°.* [*London,*] 1801.

18246 MACKENZIE, SIR ALEXANDER. Voyages from Montreal, on the River St. Laurence, through the continent of North America, to the frozen and Pacific Oceans, in...1789 and 1793. With a preliminary account of the rise, progress, and present state of the fur trade of that country...By Alexander Mackenzie...[assisted by W. Combe]. cxxxii, 412p. *4°.* 1801.

FINANCE

18247 ALLARDYCE, A. A second address to the proprietors of Bank of England stock. 53p. *4°.* 1801.

18248 [ANDERSON, WILLIAM (*fl.* 1797–1832).] The iniquity of banking; or bank notes proved to be an injury to the public, and the real cause of the present exhorbitant [*sic*] price of provisions. Fifth edition. Part I. [With 'Part II...Third edition'.] 41, 64p. *8°.* 1801. *For other editions, see* 1797.

18249 ARNAUD, . Proposition aux Consuls de la République Française, d'une monnaie de haute-billon pour remplacer les monnaies de cuivre... 20p. *8°.* Paris, 1801.

18250 —— Réponse aux observations du Cen. Mongey,

sur le billon; insérées dans le numéro 134 du Journal de Paris. 28p. *8°.* Paris, 1801.

18251 BALDASSERONI, A. Delle assicurazioni marittime...Seconda edizione nuovamente riordinata e notabilmente accresciuta e corretta dall' autore...Vols. 1–2, 4–5. *4°.* Firenze [*Livorno*], 1801–4.

18252 BANK OF ENGLAND. A list of the names of all such proprietors of the Bank of England, who are qualified to vote at the ensuing election...March 24th, 1801. 18p. *fol.* [1801] *See also* 1738, 1749, 1750, 1789, 1790, 1791, 1792, 1793, 1794, 1795, 1796, 1797, 1798, 1799, 1803, 1804, 1808, 1809, 1812, 1816, 1819, 1836, 1843.

18253 BARING, SIR F., *Bart.* Observations on the

publication of Walter Boyd, Esq. M.P. 31p. 8°. 1801. *The copy that belonged to Francis Horner (1778–1817), with his signature on the half-title.*

18254 [——] A twelve-penny answer to a three shillings and six-penny pamphlet, intituled A letter on the influence of the stoppage of issues in specie at the Bank of England, on the prices of provisions, and other commodities. 29p. 8°. 1801.

18255 [——] A second twelve-penny answer to a new (and five shillings) edition of a three shillings and six-penny pamphlet, intituled "A letter on the influence of the stoppage of issues in specie at the Bank of England, on the prices of provisions and other commodities; with additional notes and a preface." 56p. 8°. 1801.

18256 BATTYE, T. Strictures upon the church-wardens and overseers of Manchester, with some introductory remarks on public abuse, parochial taxes, &c.... 110p. 8°. *Manchester,* 1801.

18257 BOYD, WALTER. A letter to the Right Honourable William Pitt, on the influence of the stoppage of issues in specie at the Bank of England; on the prices of provisions, and other commodities. 112p. 8°. 1801.

18258 —— The second edition, with additional notes; and a preface, containing remarks on the publication of Sir Francis Baring, Bart. lvi, 87, 48p. 8°. 1801. *See also* 1811.

18259 BUESCH, J. G. Johann Georg Büsch's... sämtliche Schriften über Banken und Münzwesen. Theils vom Verfasser neu bearbeitet, theils nach seinem Tode gesammlet. 768p. 8°. *Hamburg,* 1801. *Edited by C. D. Ebeling.*

18260 —— Johann Georg Büsch's...zusammengedrängter Vortrag über Münzen...Ein Vorbereitungsbuch zu den Comtoirgeschäften. 93p. 8°. *Hamburg,* 1801.

18261 An **ENGLISH MEMENTO,** being hints of circumstances which appear favourable for procuring a repeal of the duties on coals carried coastways in England (after the mode adopted in Scotland in 1793)... 48p. 8°. [*London,* 1801 ?]

18262 FENNING, D. The ready reckoner: or, trader's most useful assistant in buying and selling all sorts of commodities, either wholesale or retail...The twelfth edition, with additions on board and timber measure, brick work, and guaging by the pen and slip-rule. Carefully revised and corrected, by Joseph Moon. [276]p. 12°. *London & Salisbury,* 1801. *For another edition, see* 1767.

18263 FORTUNE, E. F. THOMAS. Historia breve e authentica do Banco de Inglaterra, com dissertações sobre os metaes, moeda, e letres de cambio, e a carta de incorporaçaõ...Traduzida da segunda ediçaõ de Londres... 97p. 4°. *Lisboa,* 1801. *For other editions, see* 1797.

18264 FRANCE. *Napoleon Bonaparte, First Consul.* No. 1305...Arrêté additionnel à celui du 29 messidor an VIII, relatif aux demandes en restitution de fruits et revenus. Du 16 pluviôse an IX de la République Française ...[With the text of the Arrêté of 29 messidor.] 2p. 4°. *Paris,* [1801]

18265 —— —— No. 1323...Loi qui proroge, en faveur des créanciers d'individus inscrits sur la liste des émigrés, le délai accordé pour l'inscription des droits d'hypothèque ou de privilége. Du 16 ventôse an IX de la République Française... 4p. 4°. *Paris,* [1801]

18266 FREND, W. The effect of paper money on the price of provisions: or, the point in dispute between Mr. Boyd and Sir Francis Baring examined; the Bank paper money proved to be an adequate cause for the high price of provisions; and constitutional remedies recommended. 27p. 8°. 1801.

18267 GALLATIN, A. Views of the public debt, receipts, & expenditures of the United States...Second edition. 72p. 8°. *Philadelphia,* 1801.

18268 GWILLIM, *Sir* H. A collection of Acts and records of Parliament, with reports of cases argued and determined in the courts of law and equity, respecting tithes. 4 vols. 8°. 1801.

18269 LIPSIUS, J. G. I. G. Lipsii bibliotheca numaria sive catalogus auctorum, qui usque ad finem seculi XVIII. de re monetaria aut numis scripserunt. Praefatus est brevi commemoratione de studii numismatici vicissitudinibus Christ. Gottl. Heyne. 2 vols. 8°. *Lipsiæ,* 1801. *The copy that belonged first to Matthew Young, numismatist, then to Thomas Burgon (1787–1858), Turkey merchant and numismatist, and thirdly to Churchill Babington (1821–1889). There are manuscript notes and additions in several hands.*

18270 [**M'ARTHUR,** JOHN (1755–1840).] Financial facts of the eighteenth century; or, a cursory view, with comparative statements, of the revenue, expenditure, debts, manufactures, and commerce of Great Britain. 88p. 8°. 1801. *For an enlarged edition, see* 1803 (GENERAL).

18271 [**MARNIÈRES,** J. H., *Marquis de Guer.*] Essai sur le crédit commercial considéré comme moyen de circulation; et prospectus de la traduction de l'Histoire des finances de la Grande-Bretagne, de Sir John Sinclair... Par J. H. M. 133p. 8°. *Hambourg & Paris,* 1801.

18272 MONGEZ, A. Résumé des notions simples sur les monnaies, insérées dans le Journal de Paris depuis un an. 8p. 8°. *n.p.* [1801 ?]

18273 MORGAN, W. A comparative view of the public finances, from the beginning to the close of the late administration. 75p. 8°. 1801. *See also* 1803.

18274 MORTIMER, THOMAS (1730–1810). Every man his own broker; or, a guide to the Stock-Exchange... The thirteenth edition, considerably improved. 257p. 12°. 1801. *For other editions, see* 1761.

18275 NETHERLANDS. *Batavian Republic.* Gelykheid, vryheid, broederschap. Extract uit het register der decreten van de Tweede Kamer van het Vertegenwoordigend Lichaam des Bataafschen Volks. Saturdag den 14. maart 1801...[Containing an address on the projected 'free-will loan' signed: K. Hovens, J. H. Siccama, P. Linthorst.] 12p. 8°. *n.p.* [1801]

18276 —— —— Prys-courant van obligatien en andere effecten; zo als de pryzen waren op Vrydag den 1sten mey 1801. Geformeerd op last van het Uitvoerend Bewind... [4]p. *fol. den Haag,* 1801. *See also* 1796, 1797, 1800, 1802, 1803, 1804.

18277 —— —— Publicatie van het Uitvoerend Bewind ...houdende vernieuwing der belasting, onder de naam van het Borkumsche vuur- en bakengeld. Gearresteerd den 5. february 1801... 4p. 8°. *den Haag,* 1801.

18278 —— —— Publicatie van het Uitvoerend Bewind ...houdende prolongatie van den termyn van betaaling van drie per cent der inkomsten, tot den eersten April.

Gearresteerd den 15 february 1801... [41]p. *8°. den Haag*, 1801.

18279 —— —— Publicatie van het Uitvoeren Bewind ...houdende bepaligen omtrent de conversie der recepissen gesproten uit de heffing van 4. en 1. ten honderd... Gearresteerd den 20 maart 1801... 4p. *8°. den Haag*, 1801.

18280 —— —— Publicatie van het Uitvoerend Bewind ...houdende, 't besluit des Vertegenwoordigenden Lichaams, om de vrywillige negotatie op de nationale domeinen, uitgeschreven 20. febr. LL. werkelye te doen plaats hebben. Gearresteerd den 20. maart 1801... 3p. *8°. den Haag*, 1801.

18281 —— —— Publicatie van het Uitvoerend Bewind ...wegens de heffing van twee proCent op de bezittingen als don gratuit, onder eenige bepaaligen. Gearresteerd den 19 juny 1801... 16p. *8°. den Haag*, 1801.

18282 —— —— Publicatie van het Uitvoerend Bewind ...houdende bepaalingen wegens de heffing van 4 procent op de inkomsten over den jaare 1800, als een don gratuit. Gearresteerd den 5 september 1801... 13p. *8°. den Haag*, 1801.

18283 —— —— Publicatie van het Staats-Bewind... Houdende continuatie der bepaalingen tot weering der sluikeryen van den impost op de wynen en gedisteleerde wateren, uit den lande van Ysselstein in de voormalige gewesten van Holland en Utrecht. Geärresteerd den 11 december 1801. 4p. *8°. den Haag*, 1801.

18284 NEWBERY, F. Observations on the Income Act; particularly as it relates to the occupiers of land: with some proposals of amendment. To which is added, a short scheme for meliorating the condition of the labouring man. 44p. *8°.* 1801.

18285 Brief **OBSERVATIONS** on a late letter addressed to the Right Hon. W. Pitt, by W. Boyd, Esq. &c. on the stoppage of issues in specie by the Bank of England, &c.&c. 35p. *8°.* 1801. *Sometimes attributed to Sir Francis Baring or to William Combe.*

18286 OBSERVATIONS on Mr. Dundas's letter, of the 30th of June, 1801, to the Chairman, and Deputy Chairman, of the East India Company. 32p. *8°.* 1801. *The copy that belonged to William Cobbett.*

18287 P., A. Aanmerkingen op het plan van eene vrywillige negotiatie, gevestigd op de nationaale domeinen, gearresteerd by de Eerste Kamer van het Vertegenwoordigend Lichaam...op 19 february 1801, briefswyze medegedeeld. [Signed: Uwen welmeenenden medeburger, A. P.] 16p. *8°. den Haag, Amsterdam, &c.*, [1801]

18288 PIET, P. Les arbitrages simplifiés, ou recueil des arbitrages de changes de la France avec les principales places de commerce de l'Europe; contenant un répertoire de vingt-huit tableaux d'arbitrages...une table de logarithmes... 96, 23p. *8°. Paris*, an IX [1801]

18289 PLAN, by which the tax upon income may be rendered unnecessary to the continuation of the war; and taxes in general greatly diminished, without lessening the warlike power of the United Kingdom. 24p. *8°.* 1801.

18290 REMARKS on Mr. Morgan's Comparative view of the public finances... 80p. *8°.* 1801.

18291 RICHARDSON, GOODLUCK & CO. [*Begin.*] The only office that ever sold, in shares, two prizes of thirty thousand pounds...The tickets in the Irish and English state-lotteries are on sale...at their licensed state-lottery offices, the corner of Bank-Buildings, Cornhill... *s.sh.8°. n.p.* [1801]

18292 SIDNEY, J. A. A scheme for improving small sums of money: shewing that great part of the national specie which now lies hidden...may be employed to the greatest uses of Government, trade, and private persons ...[Recommending the establishment of a fund for investment of small sums upon government security.] 45p. *8°. Rochester*, 1801.

18293 [SLACK, T.] The British negotiator: or, foreign exchanges made perfectly easy. Containing tables for all the various courses of exchange...Arbitrations of exchanges...Several mercantile tables...And an essay on ...exchanging in general, is prefixed...The sixth edition, corrected and much enlarged. By S. Thomas merchant. 346p. *long 12°. London & Newcastle*, 1801. *For other editions, see 1759.*

18294 SOCIETY FOR EQUITABLE ASSURANCES. The deed of settlement of the Society for Equitable Assurances on Lives and Survivorships...With the bye laws of the society. And three addresses...by Mr. Morgan, the actuary. 170p. *8°.* 1801. *See also 1833.*

18295 SOUTON, J. B. Exposition de la saine doctrine monétaire, suivie d'observations sur quelques opinions accréditées sur cette matière, et sur la proposition de démonétiser l'or. Nécessité d'une refonte générale des monnaies...Eclaircissemens sur ce qui s'est passé au sujet des cloches converties en monnaie. Par P.[sic] B. Souton, ex-directeur de la Monnaie de Pau. 46p. *8°. Paris*, 1801.

18296 SURR, T. S. Refutation of certain misrepresentations relative to the nature and influence of bank notes, and of the stoppage of issues in specie, at the Bank of England, upon the prices of provisions, as stated in the pamphlets of Walter Boyd, Esq. and Mr. William Frend. 44p. *8°.* 1801. *The copy that belonged to William Cobbett.*

TRANSPORT

18297 CARY, JOHN (d. 1835). Cary's new guide for ascertaining hackney coach fares and porterage rates: being an actual and minute admeasurement of every street which is a carriage way throughout the metropolis...To which are also added, abstracts of the hackney coach and porterage acts...list of coach stands... 256 cols. *8°.* 1801.

18298 ENGLAND. *Laws, etc.* An Act for enabling the Company of Proprietors of the Grand Junction Canal more effectually to provide for the discharge of their debts, and to complete the whole of the works to be executed by them...and for altering and enlarging the powers and provisions of the said Acts. 22p. *fol. n.p.*, 1801.

18299 —— —— Anno quadragesimo primo Georgii III. Regis. [Local & Personal.] Cap. 32. An Act for enabling Charlotta Bethell widow, to make...a navigable canal from the River Hull...in the parish of Leven...in the East Riding of the county of York, to Leven Bridge in the said Riding. ⟨21st May 1801.⟩ p.461–476. *fol.* 1801.

18300 HUTTON, C. The principles of bridges: containing the mathematical demonstrations of the properties of the arches, the thickness of the piers, the force of the water against them, &c....The second edition, with corrections and additions. 104p. *8°. 1801. For another edition, see 1772.*

18301 LANCASTER CANAL NAVIGATION. [*Begin.*] At a general meeting of the Company of Proprietors of the Lancaster Canal Navigation, held...the 7th...of July, 1801...[The resolutions passed, with 'Extract from the report of the committee' and, on the verso, 'Extract from the report of William Jessop and John Rennie Esquires'.] [2]p. *s.sh.fol. Lancaster,* [1801]

18302 —— Lancaster Canal Navigation, second call on the new shares. [4]p. *4°. n.p.* [1801] *Addressed in manuscript to 'Richd. Shawe Esq.', with an additional manuscript note.*

18303 —— Third call on the new shares. [4]p. *4°. n.p.* [1801] *Addressed in manuscript to 'Richd. Shawe Esq.', with a manuscript receipt from Cox, Merle and Co., for the sum requested.*

18304 —— Fourth call on the new shares. *s.sh.fol. n.p.* [1801] *See note to no. 18303, above.*

18305 —— Fifth call on the new shares. [4]p. *4°. n.p.* [1801] *See note to no. 18303, above.*

18306 RENNIE, JOHN (1761–1821). ⟨Copy.⟩ Additional report of John Rennie, Esq. engineer. [Addressed to the Lord Provost of Edinburgh, and dated July 27, 1801. On the alternative route, known as the 'North Line', for the Canal between Edinburgh and Glasgow.] 2p. *4°. n.p.* [1801] *The Rastrick copy.*

18307 STEUART, SIR H. S., *Bart.* Letter, addressed to James Dunlop, Esq. on his late remarks on the proposed plan for the better supplying the city of Edinburgh with coal. 12p. *8°. Edinburgh & London,* 1801.

18308 TELFORD, T. and DOUGLASS, . An account of the improvements of the Port of London, and more particularly of the intended iron bridge, consisting of one arch, of six hundred feet span. 20p. *8°.* 1801.

SOCIAL CONDITIONS

18309 ASSOCIATION FOR DISCOUNTENANCING VICE, *Dublin.* The bye laws of the Association incorporated...A.D.1800... 14p. *8°. Dublin,* 1801.

18310 CALONNE, C. A. DE. Projet pour obvier aux vols de grand chemin dans les environs de Londres; ou, exposé de ce qu'étoit en France la Maréchaussée; et examen de ce qu'on pourroit faire en Angleterre, pour y avoir un établissement de pareille utilité...Proposal for preventing highway robberies in the environs of London ... 81p. *4°.* 1801. *The title, in French and English, is printed in columns on the title-page; the French and English texts on opposite pages.*

18311 The CASE of the new House of Correction, in Cold-Bath Fields, and that of the new prison, in Clerkenwell...fairly and impartially stated; in a letter to ******* *********, Esq. one of His Majesty's Justices of the Peace...for the county of Middlesex. By a brother-magistrate. 63p. *8°. Brentford & London,* 1801.

18312 EDEN, SIR F. M., *Bart.* Observations on friendly societies, for the maintenance of the industrious classes during sickness, infirmity, old age, and other exigencies. 30p. *8°.* 1801.

18313 HARROW SCHOOL. Orders, statutes and rules made and set forth the 18th day of January, in the three and thirtieth year of the reign of our Sovereign Lady Elizabeth...by me John Lyon...founder of the free grammar school in Harrow...to be observed and kept by the governours of the lands...and possessions of the said free grammar school... 10p. *fol.* [*London,* 1801]

18314 HILL, JOHN (1760?–1807). The means of reforming the morals of the poor, by the prevention of poverty; and a plan for meliorating the condition of parish paupers, and diminishing the enormous expence of maintaining them. 157p. *8°.* 1801. *With a letter from the author accompanying a presentation copy, presumably to Patrick Colquhoun, to whom it belonged, inserted. There is also a Sheffield copy.*

18315 [LLOYD, , *Rector of Montgomery.*] Letters to John Probert ... upon the advantages and defects of the Montgomery and Pool House of Industry. By an Honorary Director. 54p. *8°. Shrewsbury & London,* 1801. *The Sheffield copy, attributed to 'Revd. Mr. Jones, Rector of Montgomery' on the title-page. Attributed to Lloyd in vol. 4 of the Reports of the Society for Bettering the Condition of the Poor, 1805, p. 119.*

18316 MASSEY, W. Hints, relative to Mr. Owen Jones's Charity, or serious reflections, in consequence of a letter from J. Bramwell Esq. late chief magistrate of the City of Chester. 25p. *8°. Chester,* 1801. *See note to no. 16807.*

18317 MILE END NEW-TOWN CHARITY SCHOOL. Rules and orders for governing the Mile-End, New-Town, Stepney Charity-School, for educating and cloathing sixty poor children...Instituted in the year 1785. 24p. *8°.* 1801.

18318 MURRAY, THOMAS A. Remarks on the situation of the poor in the Metropolis, as contributing to the progress of contagious diseases; with a plan for the institution of houses of recovery for persons infected by fever... 47p. *8°.* 1801. *The Sheffield copy.*

18319 NOSTITZ UND JAENCKENDORF, G. A. E. VON. Versuch über Armenversorgungsanstalten in Dörfern in näherer Beziehung auf das Markgrafthum Oberlausitz. 214p. *8°. Görlitz,* 1801.

18320 Further OBSERVATIONS on the improvements in the maintenance of the poor, in the town of Kingston-upon-Hull. 44p. *8°. Hull, London, &c.,* 1801.

18321 Practical ŒCONOMY: or a proposal for enabling the poor to provide for themselves; with remarks on the establishment of soup houses: and an investigation of the real cause of the present extravagant consumption of fine wheaten bread by the people of this country. By a physician. 55p. *8°.* 1801.

18322 SHEPHERD, SIR S. [*Endorsed:*] Copy. Serjᵗ Shepherd's opinion on perversion of charities, and misapplication of poor's rates. Vide 43 Eliz. Cap.4. [Dated: 9th December 1801. On the possibility of the funds of the ancient Charity-School at Mortlake being diverted to benefit the new School of Industry.] 3p. *fol.* [London, 1801]

18323 SHIPTON MOYNE. Rules for the better management of the poor of the parish of Shipton Moyne; agreed to at a vestry of the said parish, held on Friday the 27th day of February, 1801. 20p. *8°.* 1801.

18324 *[SMITH, THOMAS W.] A proposal on behalf of the married poor. 52p. *8°.* 1801. *Attributed to 'Thos. Woodrofe Smith' in a manuscript note on the title-page. The copy that belonged to Augustus De Morgan.*

18325 SOCIETY FOR BETTERING THE CONDITION OF THE POOR, London. Extract from an account [by Sir Thomas Bernard] of what is doing to diminish the present scarcity, and to restore plenty in this country. With observations. 15p. *8°.* 1801.

18326 SOCIETY FOR THE DISCHARGE AND RELIEF OF PERSONS IMPRISONED FOR SMALL DEBTS, London. A summary view of the money annually expended by the Society for relief of debtors, from the institution in 1772, to the 31st of March, 1801. *s.sh.fol.* Southwark, [1801]

18327 SOCIETY OF SCHOOLMASTERS. The address and rules of the Society of Schoolmasters, instituted 1798. [Containing a scheme to establish a fund for the widows and orphans of schoolmasters.] 24p. *8°.* London, 1801.

18328 THOUGHTS on the best modes of carrying into effect the system of economy recommended in His Majesty's Proclamation [enjoining 'the greatest economy and frugality in the use of every species of grain'. With the text of the Proclamation of 3 December 1800.] xvi, 46p. *8°.* 1801. *With a manuscript note on the verso of the title-page entitled 'Advertisement, omitted by the Printer' which reads: 'The profit which may arise from the sale of this Pamphlet will be supplied to the subscription for soup shops, now opened at Lloyds Coffee House'.*

18329 W., I. Democracy the cause of the present dearth, and sufferings of the poor. 34p. *8°.* 1801.

18330 WANSEY, H. Thoughts on poor-houses, with a view to their general reform, particularly that of Salisbury, comparing it with the more improved ones of Shrewsbury, Isle of Wight, Hull, Boldre, &c.... To which is added, an account of the population of Salisbury, with observations thereon. 48p. *8°.* 1801.

18331 WESTERN DISPENSARY, London. Plan of the Western Dispensary in Charles-Street, Westminster, instituted in the year 1789, for administering advice and medicines to the poor inhabitants of the City of Westminster...at the Dispensary, or at their own habitations. 36p. *8°.* 1801.

18332 WESTMINSTER HOSPITAL. Plan of the Committee of Management of the Westminster Hospital; framed...in pursuance of a resolution of a quarterly General Board of Trustees...30th of October, 1800. With an explanatory preface. 33p. *8°.* 1801.

SLAVERY

18333 BARCLAY, D. An account of emancipation of the slaves of Unity Valley Pen, in Jamaica. 20p. *8°.* 1801. *The copy that belonged to William Cobbett.*

18334 —— Second edition, with an appendix. 19p. *8°.* 1801. *See also* 1825.

POLITICS

18335 BANNANTINE, J., *comp.* Opinions of His Majesty's ministers, respecting the French Revolution, the war, &c. from 1790 to 1801, chronologically arranged. Selected from their speeches in Parliament. With extracts from the speeches of the opposition... 159p. *8°.* 1801.

18336 BOWLES, J. Reflections at the conclusion of the war: being a sequel to "Reflections on the political and moral state of society, at the close of the eighteenth century". The second edition, with additions. 102p. *8°.* 1801. *For another edition, see* 1800.

18337 [CANNING, GEORGE (1770–1827), and others.] Poetry of the Anti-Jacobin. Fourth edition. 256p. *4°.* 1801.

18338 The CASE of conscience solved; or, Catholic emancipation proved to be compatible with the coronation oath, in a letter from a casuist in the country to his friend in town... 36p. *8°.* 1801.

18339 —— [Another edition.] With a supplement in answer to Considerations on the said oath, by John Reeves, Esq. 89p. *8°.* 1801.

18340 CONSIDERATIONS on the present state of Europe, with respect to peace, or, a further prosecution of the war. 80 p. *8°.* 1801.

18341 DILLON, afterwards **DILLON LEE,** H. A., *Viscount Dillon.* Short view of the Catholic question, in a letter to a counsellor at law in Dublin. 50p. *8°.* 1801. *The copy that belonged to William Cobbett.*

18342 [DILLON, SIR JOHN J.] The question, as to the admission of Catholics to Parliament, considered, upon the principles of existing laws. With supplementary observations on the coronation oath. By a barrister. 79p. *8°.* 1801.

18343 —— [Another edition.] To which is annexed a further supplement, occasioned by the second edition of Mr. Reeves's considerations... 79, 53p. *8°.* 1801.

18344 Political ESSAYS on popular subjects. Containing dissertations on first principles; liberty; democracy; and the party denominations of Whig and Tory... Third edition. 142p. *8°.* 1801.

18345 FABIUS, *pseud.* The letters of Fabius, to the Right Hon. William Pitt, on his proposed abolition of the Test, in favour of the Roman Catholics of Ireland. With an appendix, containing Mr. Pitt's speech in the debate of 1790. 71p. *8°.* 1801. *The copy that belonged to William Cobbett.*

18346 FRANCE. *Napoleon Bonaparte, First Consul.* No. 1464. Arrêté relatif à l'élimination de ceux qui ont été mis en prévention d'émigration par une inscription ou par le séquestre, et dont les noms ne sont pas inscrits ou sont inscrits, avec des désignations incertaines, sur la liste générale des émigrés. Du 13 frimaire an x de la République Française... 2p. 4°. Paris, [1801]

18347 GODWIN, WILLIAM (1756–1836). Thoughts occasioned by the perusal of Dr. Parr's Spital sermon, preached at Christ Church, April 15, 1800: being a reply to the attacks of Dr. Parr, Mr. Mackintosh, the author of an Essay on population, and others. 82p. 8°. 1801. *The copy that belonged to George Birkbeck (1776–1841), from the library of Dr. [Thomas?] Garnett (1766?–1802).*

18348 HUNTER, WILLIAM (*fl.* 1801). A short view of the political situation of the northern powers: made during a tour through Russia, Sweden and Denmark, in...1800... 111p. 8°. 1801.

18349 MARSH, H., *Bishop of Peterborough.* The history of the politicks of Great Britain and France vindicated from a late attack of Mr. William Belsham. 136p. 8°. 1801. *Presentation copy from the author to William Pitt.*

18350 The **OPINION** of an old Englishman: in which national honour, and national gratitude, are principally considered. Humbly offered to his countrymen & fellow-citizens, on the resignation of the late ministry. 20p. 8°. 1801.

18351 REEVES, J. Considerations on the coronation oath, to maintain the protestant reformed religion, and the settlement of the Church of England as prescribed by Stat.1, W. and M., c.6 and Stat.5, Ann, c.2. 44p. 8°. 1801.

18351A —— Second edition, with additions. 69p. 8°. 1801. *The copy that belonged to William Cobbett.*

18352 SÉGUR, L. P. DE, *Comte.* Politiques de tous les cabinets de l'Europe, pendant les règnes de Louis XV et de Louis XVI; contenant des pièces authentiques sur la correspondance secrète du Cte de Broglie; un ouvrage sur la situation de toutes les puissances de l'Europe, dirigé par lui et exécuté par M. Favier;—les doutes sur le traité de 1756, par le même;—plusieurs mémoires du Cte de Vergennes, de M. Turgot...Seconde édition...augmentée de notes...et d'un mémoire sur le pacte de famille, par L. P. Ségur... 3 vols. 8°. Paris, 1801.

18353 WINDHAM, W. The speech of the Right Honourable William Windham, delivered in the House of Commons...Nov. 4, 1801, on the report of an address to the throne, approving of the Preliminaries of peace with the Republick of France. 79p. 8°. 1801. *See also 1802.*

18354 WYVILL, C. A letter to John Cartwright, Esq. [on Parliamentary reform]. 19p. 8°. York, 1801.

SOCIALISM

18355 SPENCE, T. The restorer of society, to its natural state, in a series of letters to a fellow citizen. With a preface, containing the objections of a gentleman who perused the manuscript, and the answers by the author. 41p. 8°. 1801. *The preface is signed in manuscript by the author.*

MISCELLANEOUS

18356 February 11, 1801. **CONSIDERATIONS** and a plan proposed for removing the live stock, &c. from the coast of Great Britain, and for rendering the body of the people instrumental in the defence of the country. 16p. 8°. Newport, [1801]

18357 DIGGES, T. A briefe discourse what orders were best for repulsing of forraine force, if at any time they should invade us by sea in Kent, or elsewhere. [Reprinted from an edition said to have been printed in 1590.] 18p. 8°. 1801.

18358 ENSOR, G. The principles of morality. 357p. 8°. 1801.

18359 *LONDON. Livery Companies. *Salters.* A list of the Master, Wardens, Court of Assistants, and Livery of the Worshipful Company of Salters. 11p. 8°. 1801. *See also 1784, 1787, 1790, 1792, 1794, 1797, 1799, 1803, 1806, 1809, 1812, 1815, 1818, 1821, 1824, 1827, 1830.*

18360 MURRAY, afterwards **MURRAY-PULTENEY,** SIR J., *Bart.* The substance of a speech made by Sir James Pulteney, Bart. in the House of Commons...19th February, 1801, on a motion for an enquiry into the cause of the failure of the expedition to Ferrol. 39p. 8°. 1801.

18361 SMITH, ADAM. The theory of moral sentiments...To which is added, a dissertation on the origin of languages...The ninth edition...2 vols. 8°. London & Edinburgh, 1801. *For other editions, see 1759.*

1802

GENERAL

18362 An **ADDRESS** to the people of Ireland, with a brief report of parliamentary proceedings on Irish affairs: containing a summary view of the principal measures discussed, and an abstract and index of all the statutes passed, for that part of the United Kingdom, in the second session of the first united Parliament, 42 Geo. III. 1802. 94p. *8°*. 1802.

18363 **ADVICE** to the labourer, the mechanic, and the parent. With remarks on the late conduct of magistrates, monopolizers & volunteer corps, &c....By a tradesman. 12p. *12°*. [*London*, 1802]

18364 **ANNALS** of public economy: containing reports on the state of agriculture, commerce and manufactures, in the different nations of Europe. Vol. I. Collected by Henry Redhead Yorke, Esq. 543p. *8°*. 1802.

18365 An **APPEAL** to experience and common sense, by a comparison of the present with former periods. 50p. *8°*. 1802.

18366 **BALGUERIE**, . Tableau statistique du Département du Guers...Publié par ordre du Ministre de l'Intérieur. 61p. *8°*. *Paris, an x* [1802] *This and other works in the same series, set out below, belonged to the third Marquis of Lansdowne* (1780–1863).

18367 **BARANTE**, C. I. B. DE. Statistique du Département de l'Aude...Publiée par ordre du Ministre de l'Intérieur. 26p. *8°*. *Paris, an x* [1802] *See note to no.* 18366, *above*.

18368 **BELL**, B. Essays on agriculture, with a plan for the speedy and general improvement of land in Great Britain. 549p. *8°*. *Edinburgh, London, &c.*, 1802. *An enlarged edition of* Three essays on taxation, *1799* (*q.v.* FINANCE).

18369 **BONNAIRE**, F., *Baron*. Statistique du Département des Hautes-Alpes...Publiée par ordre du Ministre de l'Intérieur. 113p. *8°*. *Paris, an x* [1802] *See note to no.* 18366.

18370 **BORIE**, N. Y. Statistique du Département d'Ille-et-Vilaine...Publiée par ordre du Ministre de l'Intérieur. 56p. *8°*. *Paris, an x* [1802] *See note to no.* 18366.

18371 **BRUSLE DE VALSUZENAY**, C. L., *Baron*. Tableau statistique du Département de l'Aube... Publié par ordre du Ministre de l'Intérieur. 116p. *8°*. *Paris, an x* [1802] *See note to no.* 18366.

18372 **CATTEAU-CALLEVILLE**, J. P. W. Tableau des États Danois, envisagés sous les rapports du mécanisme social...avec une carte... 3 vols. *8°*. *Paris*, 1802.

18373 **CAVENNE**, . Statistique du Département de la Meuse-Inférieure...Approuvée pour être presentée au Ministre de l'Intérieur, par le citoyen Loysel, préfet... 131p. *8°*. *Paris, an x* [1802] *See note to no.* 18366.

18374 **CHALMERS**, G. An estimate of the comparative strength of Great-Britain; and of the losses of her trade from every war since the Revolution...A new edition, corrected and continued to 1801. To which is now annexed Gregory King's celebrated State of England.

[With 'Notices of the life of Gregory King'.] 449p. *8°*. 1802. *For other editions, see* 1782.

18375 **CHANLAIRE**, P. G. and **HERBIN DE HALLE**, P. E. Tableau général de la nouvelle division de la France, en départemens, arrondissemens communaux et justices de paix, d'après les lois des 28 pluviôse an 8 et 8 pluviôse an 9; indiquant la population, l'étendue territoriale et le nombre des communes, par chaque justice de paix et arrondissement communal...Avec une table alphabétique des nouveaux cantons, et un atlas de 102 cartes... 114p. *obl.4°*. *Paris*, 1802. *For a supplement, see* 1803.

18376 **CLARKE**, THOMAS B. Coup d'œil sur la force et l'opulence de la Grande-Bretagne...On y a joint une correspondence inédite du doyen Tucker et de David Hume, avec le lord Kaims, concernant le commerce... Traduit de l'anglois par J. Marchéna. 342p. *8°*. *Paris & Strasbourg*, 1802. *For another edition, see* 1801.

For **COBBETT'S ANNUAL REGISTER**, 1802–35, *see* vol. III, *Periodicals list*, Cobbett's political register.

18377 **COLIN**, . Statistique du Département de la Drôme...Publiée par ordre du Ministre de l'Intérieur. 48p. *8°*. *Paris, an x* [1802] *See note to no.* 18366.

18378 **DAUCHY**, L. J. E. Statistique du Département de l'Aisne...Publiée par ordre du Ministre de l'Intérieur. 144p. *8°*. *Paris, an x* [1802] *See note to no.* 18366.

18379 **DELAISTRE**, G. J. N. Statistique du Département de la Charente...Publiée par ordre du Ministre de l'Intérieur. 42p. *8°*. *Paris, an x* [1802] *See note to no.* 18366.

18380 **DESGOUTTES**, Z. H. Statistique du Département des Vosges...Publiée par ordre du Ministre de l'Intérieur. 111p. *8°*. *Paris, an x* [1802] *See note to no.* 18366.

18381 **DESMOUSSEAUX**, A. F. E. M. C., *Baron*. Statistique du Département de l'Ourthe...Publiée par ordre du Ministre de l'Intérieur. 54p. *8°*. *Paris, an x* [1802] *See note to no.* 18366.

18382 **DUPIN**, C. F. E., *Baron*. Statistique du Département des Deux-Sèvres...Publiée par ordre du Ministre de l'Intérieur. 177p. *8°*. *Paris, an x* [1802] *See note to no.* 18366.

18383 **EDEN**, SIR F. M., *Bart*. Eight letters on the peace; and on the commerce and manufactures of Great Britain. 132p. *8°*. 1802.

18384 —— The second edition, with considerable additions. 210p. *8°*. 1802. *The copy that belonged to William Cobbett.*

18385 **EDWARDS**, GEORGE. An attempt to rectify public affairs, and promote private prosperity...by means arranged in one comprehensive...design; which will enable the wealth and power of Great Britain to increase at least in proportion with those of France...Part I. [With 'Appendix, no. 1. Outlines of a plan for the agricultural society of the circle of Barnard Castle' and 'Appendix, no. 2. Extracts from the author's works'.] 420, 58p. *8°*. 1802.

18386 ENGLAND. *Treaties, etc.* The definitive treaty of peace, between His Britannick Majesty, and the French Republick, His Catholick Majesty, the Batavian Republick, signed at Amiens, the 27th of March 1802... 19p. *4°. 1802. The text is printed in English and French in parallel columns.*

18387 —— —— Definitive treaty. The articles of the definitive treaty of peace; between His Majesty the King of the United Kingdom of Great Britain and Ireland, (on the one part:) and the French Republic, His Majesty the King of Spain and the Indies, and the Batavian Republic, (on the other part.)... 22p. *8°.* [1802]

18388 FAUCHET, J. J. A. Statistique du Département du Var...Publiée par ordre du Ministre de l'Intérieur. 121p. *8°. Paris, an* x [1802] *See note to no.* 18366.

18389 FRANCE. *Conseil d'Etat.* No. 1502...Extrait des registres des délibérations des Consuls de la République. Du 5 germinal an x de la République Française... Avis du Conseil d'Etat, relatif aux ascendans des émigrés. [With 'No. 379*. Loi relative à levée du séquestre mis sur les biens de pères et mères d'émigrés. Du 9 floréal an III'.] 8p. *4°. Paris,* [1802]

18390 —— —— No. 1628. Avis...relatif aux ascendans des émigrés. Du 24 thermidor an x de la République Française...Approuvé par les Consuls le 25. 2p. *4°. Paris,* [1802]

18391 —— *Treaties, etc.* The concordat between Bonaparté, Chief Consul of the French Republic, and His Holiness Pope Pius VII. Together with the speech of Citizen Portales...on presenting it to the legislative body. Translated from the official documents. 79p. *8°. 1802.*

18392 —— —— Recueil général des traités de paix, d'alliance et de commerce, de neutralité...conclus par la République Française...depuis le premier traité conclu avec le Grand-Duc de Toscane, jusqu'aux deux derniers, l'un de Campo-Formio, l'autre...avec la République Cisalpine... 368p. *12°. Paris,* [1802 ?]

18393 HENDERSON, GEORGE, *Esq.* A short view of the administrations in the government of America, under the former presidents, the late General Washington, and John Adams, and of the present administration, under Thomas Jefferson: with cursory observations on the present state of the revenue, agriculture, commerce, manufactures and population of the United States. 71p. *8°. 1802. The copy that belonged to William Cobbett.*

18394 HERBOUVILLE, C. J. F. D'. Statistique du Département des Deux-Nèthes...Publiée par ordre du Ministre de l'Intérieur. 131p. *8°. Paris, an* x [1802] *See note to no.* 18366.

18395 HUGUET, J. A. Statistique du Département de l'Allier...Publiée par ordre du Ministre de l'Intérieur. 68p. *8°. Paris, an* x [1802]. *See note to no.* 18366.

18396 IRVINE, A. An inquiry into the causes and effects of emigration from the Highlands and western islands of Scotland, with observations on the means to be employed for preventing it. 158p. *8°. Edinburgh & London,* 1802.

18397 JERPHANION, G. J. Statistique du Département de la Lozère...Publiée par ordre du Ministre de l'Intérieur. 79p. *8°. Paris, an* x [1802] *See note to no.* 18366.

18398 LABRETONNIÈRE, P. L. C. Statistique du Département de la Vendée, contenant la description topographique, et l'histoire naturelle de son bocage, de son marais et de sa plaine...Publiée par ordre du Ministre de l'Intérieur. 130p. *8°. Paris, an* x [1802] *See note to no.* 18366.

18399 LAUMOND, J. C. J. Statistique du Departement du Bas-Rhin...Publiée par ordre du Ministre de l'Intérieur. 284p. *8°. Paris, an* x [1802] *See note to no.* 18366.

18400 LUÇAY, J. B. C. L. DE, *Comte.* Statistique du Département du Cher...Publiée par ordre du Ministre de l'Intérieur. 84p. *8°. Paris, an* x [1802] *See note to no.* 18366.

18401 LYCÉE D'ALENÇON. Statistique du Département de l'Orne; redigée par le Lycée d'Alençon, sur la demande du Cn. Lamagdeleine, préfet. Publiée par ordre du Ministre de l'Intérieur. 56p. *8°. Paris, an* x [1802] *See note to no.* 18366.

18402 MARTENS, G. F. VON. A compendium of the law of nations...To which is added, a complete list of all the treaties, conventions...from...1731 to 1788... Translated, and the list of treaties, &c. brought down to June, 1802, by William Cobbett. 454p. *8°. 1802.*

18403 [MICOUD D'UMONS, C. E., *Baron.*] Sur les finances, le commerce, la marine et les colonies... 2 vols. *8°. Paris,* 1802.

18404 NECKER, J. Dernières vues de politique et de finance, offertes à la nation française. 475p. *8°. n.p.,* 1802.

18405 [PERCIVAL, THOMAS (1740–1804).] Biographical memoirs of the late Thomas Butterworth Bayley, Esq. F.R.S. &c.&c. of Hope Hall, near Manchester. 12p. *4°. Manchester,* 1802.

18406 PIÈYRE, J., *Baron.* Statistique du Département de Lot-et-Garonne...Publiée par ordre du Ministre de l'Intérieur. 64p. *8°. Paris, an* x [1802] *See note to no.* 18366.

18407 QUESTIONS statistiques sur l'Italie, pour parvenir à rassembler, dans les tables méthodiques, les notions les plus intéressantes sur son état actuel, sur ses richesses et ses ressources en tout genre. 108p. *8°. Milan,* 1802. *The Sheffield copy.*

18408 ROBERTSON, WILLIAM (1721–1793). An historical disquisition concerning the knowledge which the ancients had of India; and the progress of trade with that country prior to the discovery of the passage to it by the Cape of Good Hope. With an appendix, containing observations on the civil policy—the laws and judicial proceedings...of the Indians...The fourth edition. 369p. *12°. London & Edinburgh,* 1802. *For other editions, see* 1791.

18409 ROERGAS DE SERVIEZ, E. G. Statistique du Département des Basses-Pyrénées...Publié par ordre du Ministre de l'Intérieur. 140p. *8°. Paris, an* x [1802] *See note to no.* 18366.

18410 SAUZAY, A. DE. Statistique du Département du Mont-Blanc...Publiée par ordre du Ministre de l'Intérieur. 125p. *8°. Paris, an* x [1802]. *See note to no.* 18366.

For **SCIENCE OF SOCIETY** *and Gnomian review, see vol.* III, *Periodicals list.*

18411 SMITH, ADAM. An inquiry into the nature and causes of the wealth of nations...The tenth edition. 3 vols. *8°. 1802.*

18412 —— Recherches sur la nature et les causes de la richesse des nations...Traduction nouvelle, avec des notes et observations; par Germain Garnier... 5 vols. 8°. Paris, an x —— 1802. For other editions, see 1776.

18413 SOCIÉTÉ D'AGRICULTURE, COMMERCE, SCIENCES ET ARTS DU DEPARTEMENT DE LA MARNE. Description topographique du Département de la Marne; redigée par la Société d'Agriculture, Commerce, Sciences et Arts du Département...Publiée par ordre du Ministre de l'Intérieur. 129p. 8°. Paris, an x [1802] See note to no. 18366.

18414 [THORNTON, HENRY (1760–1815).] On the probable effects of the peace, with respect to the commercial interests of Great Britain: being a brief examination of some prevalent opinions. 75p. 8°. 1802. The copy that belonged to William Cobbett.

18415 VERGNES, . Statistique du Département de la Haute-Saône...Publiée par ordre du Ministre de l'Intérieur. 24p. 8°. Paris, an x [1802] See note to no. 18366.

18416 WOLLSTONECRAFT, afterwards **GODWIN,** M. Letters written during a short residence in Sweden, Norway, and Denmark. Second edition. 262p. 8°. 1802. The first edition, 1796, is also in the Goldsmiths' Library (q.v. vol. III, Addenda.

AGRICULTURE

For the **AGRICULTURAL MAGAZINE,** 1802–6, see vol. III, Periodicals list.

18417 AINSLIE, J. The gentleman and farmer's pocket companion and assistant: consisting of tables for finding the contents of any piece of land by pacing, or by dimensions taken on the spot...Likewise, various other tables, of great use to every gentleman and farmer in Scotland. 180p. 4°. Edinburgh, Glasgow, &c., 1802.

18418 AMORETTI, C. Della coltivazione delle patate a loro uso. Istruzione. 36p. 8°. Roma, 1802.

18419 AMOS, W. Second edition. The theory and practice of the drill husbandry...Containing I. A dissertation on the natural food of plants...IV. Full directions for making two different kinds of drill machines...VI. Full directions for making several kinds of horse and hand hoes... 244p. 4°. London & Boston [Lincs.], 1802.

18420 BARTLEY, N. Some cursory observations on the conversion of pasture land into tillage, and, after a certain course of crops, relaying the same into pasture... To which is added, a copy of a letter...on the...measure of permitting starch manufactured from potatoes to be exempted from the revenue duties, with occasional remarks. Also, some interesting hints on the utility of applying the potatoe as food for sheep, particularly at the present juncture; from practical observations. 42p. 8°. Bath & London, 1802.

18421 COOTE, SIR C., Bart., of Donnybrook. Statistical survey of the county of Cavan, with observations on the means of improvement; drawn up in the year 1801... under the direction of the Dublin Society. 304p. 8°. Dublin, 1802.

18422 DIXON, JOHN, of Kensington. Improvement of the fisheries; letter III. Or, a plan for establishing a nursery for disbanded seamen and soldiers, and increasing the strength...of the British Empire. 43p. 4°. 1802. For the first part, see 1800; for the second, fourth and fifth parts, see 1801, 1803 and 1804 respectively.

18423 DUFOUR DE PRADT, D., Archbishop of Mechlin. De l'état de la culture en France, et des améliorations dont elle est susceptible... 2 vols. 8°. Paris, 1802.

18424 DUTTON, H. Observations on Mr. Archer's Statistical survey of the county of Dublin. [With 'Appendix. Extracts from Doctor Rutty's Essay towards a natural history of the county of Dublin, printed in...1772'.] 182, 127p. 8°. Dublin, 1802.

18425 ENGLAND. Commissioners and Trustees for Improving Fisheries and Manufactures in Scotland. Directions for raising flax: published by order of the Commissioners...for the benefit of the country. 34p. 8°. Edinburgh, 1802. A modernized and rewritten version of an eighteenth-century manual. For one edition of this, see 1781.

18426 FINDLATER, C. General view of the agriculture of the county of Peebles, with various suggestions as to the means both of the local and general improvement of agriculture... 413p. 8°. Edinburgh & London, 1802. Not published by the Board of Agriculture.

18427 FRANCE. Napoleon Bonaparte, First Consul. No. 1410...Arrêté qui annulle un jugement rendu par le ci-devant tribunal civil du département du Nord, qui révoque une contrainte décernée pour le paiement des fermages des biens appartenant à l'ascendant d'un prévenu d'émigration, objet de la compétence de l'autorité administrative. Du 27 fructidor an IX de la République Française ... 2p. 4°. Paris, [1801]

18428 FRASER, R. Gleanings in Ireland; particularly respecting its agriculture, mines, and fisheries... 88p. 8°. 1802.

18429 HALL, CHARLES, gardener. A concise treatise on the most effectual method of destroying heath, an turning the soil into good pasture; with an infallible mode of covering rocks, barren hills, &c. with verdure. Also a new mode of turning waste and marshy land into good pasture. Likewise a new method of improving moss, &c. Together with valuable receipts for destroying vermin... 228p. 8°. Edinburgh, 1802.

18430 [LAWRENCE, J.] The new farmer's calendar; or, monthly remembrancer for all kinds of country business...By a farmer and breeder. Fourth edition. 554p. 8°. 1802. For other editions, see 1800.

18431 M'PARLAN, J. Statistical survey of the county of Mayo, with observations on the means of improvement; drawn up in the year 1801...under the direction of the Dublin Society. 168p. 8°. Dublin, 1802.

18432 MAWE, J. The mineralogy of Derbyshire: with a description of the most interesting mines in the north of England, in Scotland, and in Wales; and an analysis of Mr. Williams' work, intituled "The mineral kingdom". Subjoined is a glossary of the terms and phrases used by miners in Derbyshire. 211p. 8°. London & Derby, 1802.

18433 MUNNINGS, T. C. An account of some experiments for drilling and protecting turnips, in...1800, 1801, and 1802, together with some miscellaneous observations on agricultural subjects. 84p. 8°. Norwich, London, &c., [1802]

18434 OBSERVATIONS, particularly addressed to the adventurers in Tincroft Mine; and submitted to the consideration of the lords, adventurers, merchants, and landholders, in the mining parts of Cornwall. By a Cornishman. 38p. *8°. Exeter, 1802.*

18435 SAMPSON, G. V. Statistical survey of the county of Londonderry, with observations on the means of improvement; drawn up...under the direction of the Dublin Society. 509, 42p. *8°. Dublin, 1802.*

18436 SINCLAIR, Sir John, *Bart.* Essays on miscellaneous subjects. 467p. *8°. 1802.*

18437 [——] Hints regarding cattle. [Drawn up with a view to its insertion in the *Analysis of the statistical account of Scotland*.] 16p. *4°. [London, 1802] The Sheffield copy.*

18438 —— Hints regarding certain measures calculated to improve an extensive property, more especially applicable to an estate in the northern parts of Scotland. [With two appendixes.] 47p. *4°. [London, 1802] Two copies, one the copy presented by the author, with inscription, to P.*

Colquhoun; the other in a volume that belonged to Lord Sheffield.

18439 —— [Another edition of Appendix I.] Hints regarding the fisheries... 8p. *4°. [London, 1802]*

18440 —— Sketch of an introduction to the proposed Analysis of the statistical account of Scotland. As drawn up for the consideration of a few intelligent friends. 17p. *4°. [1802] The Sheffield copy.*

18441 The **SUBSTANCE** of the leases, granted on the Lovat estate, 1802, with their clauses arranged under their respective heads. 32p. *4°. Inverness, 1802. The Sheffield copy.*

18442 THOMPSON, Robert. Statistical survey of the county of Meath, with observations on the means of improvement; drawn up...under the direction of the Dublin Society. 49p. *8°. Dublin, 1802.*

18443 TIGHE, W. Statistical observations relative to the county of Kilkenny, made in the years 1800 & 1801. 644, 119p. *8°. Dublin, 1802.*

CORN LAWS

18444 KEITH, G. S. A general view of the corn trade and corn laws of Great Britain...From the Farmer's magazine for August 1802. 20p. *8°. Edinburgh, 1802.*

18445 VERRI, P., *Conte.* Sulle leggi vincolanti principalmente del commercio de' grani riflessioni adattate allo stato di Milano coll'occasione, che l'anno 1769. trattavasi di riformare il sistema d'annona... Seconda edizione. 219p. *8°. Roma, 1802.*

POPULATION

18446 EDEN, Sir F. M., *Bart.* Recherches sur le nombre des habitans de la Grande-Bretagne et de l'Irlande. 60p. *4°. Paris, [1802]. The copy sent to Sir Frederick Eden by the translator, A. C. Duquesnoy, through the good offices of Jeremy Bentham, with a manuscript note by Bentham, dated '22d. November 1802', on a slip facing the title-page. For another edition, see 1800.*

18447 SINCLAIR, Sir John, *Bart.* Hints on longevity. 12p. *4°. [London, 1802] Presentation copy, with*

inscription, from the author to William Eden, Baron Auckland (1744–1814).

18448 UNITED STATES OF AMERICA. *Department of State.* Return of the whole number of persons within the several districts of the United States: according to "An Act providing for the second census...of the United States", passed February the 28th, one thousand eight hundred. 88p. *8°. Washington City, 1802.*

TRADES & MANUFACTURES

18449 The **BUILDER'S** price book; containing a correct list of the prices allowed by the most eminent surveyors in London, to the several artificers concerned in building. Including the journeymen's prices. A new edition, corrected. By an experienced surveyor. 139p. *4°. 1802.*

18450 COMMITTEE OF MASTER CHAIR-MANUFACTURERS AND JOURNEYMEN. The London chair-makers' and carvers' book of prices for workmanship. As regulated and agreed to by a Committee ...With the methods of computation adopted in the work... 111, 26p. *4°. 1802. For another edition, see 1823; for the first and second supplements, see 1808 and 1811, and for the third supplement, 1844 (SOCIETY OF CHAIR-MAKERS AND CARVERS).*

18451 DALRYMPLE, Sir John, *4th Bart.* Advantages of public washing houses, in or near great towns,

conducted by steam instead of fuel and the hand. 3p. *fol. n.p. [1802] The Sheffield copy.*

18452 FENWICK, T. Four essays on practical mechanics. The first on water wheels; the second on the common and improved steam engine; the third on mills; and the fourth on the simplification of machinery, on the equalising of powers applied in turning machinery, and on the thrashing machine. The second edition. 102p. *8°. Newcastle upon Tyne & London, 1802.*

18453 GARCES Y EGUIA, J. Nueva teórica y práctica del beneficio de los metales de oro y plata por fundicion y amalgamacion... 168p. *4°. Mexico, 1802.*

18454 MOIR, W. Brewing made easy; being a compendium of all the directions...hitherto...published... With full directions for the management of the cellar, &c., and instructions respecting the making and preservation of British wines. 40p. *12°. 1802.*

18455 PRICES of carpenter's work, adjusted by the actual cost of the materials. 88p. *8°. 1802. A printed list, with the prices added in manuscript.*

For the **REPERTORY OF ARTS, MANUFACTURES AND AGRICULTURE,** second series, 1802–25, *continued as* the Repertory of Patent Inventions, 1825–62, *see vol.* III, *Periodicals list,* Repertory of Patent Inventions.

COMMERCE

18456 **ATCHESON,** N. A letter addressed to Rowland Burdon, Esq. M.P. on the present state of the carrying part of the coal trade, with tables of several of the duties on coals received by the Corporation of the City of London. 33p. *8°. 1802. The Sheffield copy.*

18457 **BLANC DE VOLX,** J. Du commerce de l'Inde, comparé dans ses effets advantageux ou nuisibles, et de la nécessité de le confier à une compagnie. 82p. *4°. Paris,* 1802. *The copy that belonged to William Cobbett.*

18458 **BORDEAUX.** *Conseil de Commerce.* Mémoire du Conseil sur le commerce de l'Inde. 28p. *4°. Bordeaux,* [1802]

18459 —— —— Mémoire du Conseil...adressé aux Consuls de la République Française; contre le rétablissement du droit exclusif, ci-devant accordé aux villes de Lorient et Toulou, pour le déchargement des navires revenant de l'Inde. [Dated: le 26 pluviôse an 10.] 12p. *4°. Bordeaux,* [1802]

18460 —— —— Mémoire du Conseil...au Citoyen Ministre de l'Intérieur. [On merchant shipping. Dated: le 26 pluviôse, an 10.] 27p. *4°. Bordeaux,* [1802]

18461 —— —— Mémoire du Conseil...sur les Compagnies d'Afrique et du Sénegal. [Dated: 26 pluviôse, an 10.] 27p. *4°. Bordeaux,* [1802]

18462 —— —— Mémoire du Conseil...sur nos relations maritimes avec les puissances du nord. [Dated: le 26 pluviôse, an 10.] 29p. *4°. Bordeaux,* [1802]

18463 —— —— Mémoire du Conseil...sur la seconde des questions proposées le premier frimaire an 10 [1802], par le Ministre de l'Intérieur. [On relations with former French colonies in America. Dated: 27 germinal, an 10.] 10p. *4°. Bordeaux,* [1802]

18464 **BROOKE,** C. Proceedings of the Court of King's Bench, Guildhall on...April 28, 1802, before Mr. Justice Grose, and a special jury of London merchants, in an action, brought by Charles Brooke, wool-broker, versus Henry Guy, clothier, for a libel. Taken in short-hand by Mr. Gurney. The second edition. 122p. *8°. Chippenham, London, &c.,* 1802.

18465 **CAINES,** G. An enquiry into the law merchant of the United States; or, lex mercatoria Americana, on several heads of commercial importance...Vol. I. [With an appendix.] *8°. New-York,* 1802.

18466 **DALLAS,** SIR G., *Bart.* A letter to Sir William Pulteney, Bart. Member for Shrewsbury, on the subject of the trade between India and Europe. 102p. *4°.* 1802.

18467 **EAST INDIA COMPANY.** The debate at the East India House, at a special General Court, held on...April 8, 1802. On the subject of the private trade; when Mr. Twining made the following motion: "That this Court...approve the proceedings of the Court of Directors upon the subject of the private trade of India... but that the Court of Directors be authorised to take such further steps as may appear...necessary for the defense of those rights...solemnly sanctioned to the Company by their Charter..." which was carried...Reported by William Woodfall. 98p. *4°.* 1802.

18468 —— Papers respecting the trade between India and Europe. Printed, by order of the Court of Directors, for the information of the proprietors. 141p. *4°.* [*London,*] 1802.

18469 —— Further papers respecting the trade between India and Europe. Printed, by order of the Court of Directors, for the information of the proprietors. [With an appendix.] 36, 190p. *4°.* [*London,*] 1802. *The copy that belonged to William Cobbett.*

18470 **ENGLAND.** *Court of Admiralty.* Formulare instrumentorum: or, a formulary of authentic instruments, writs, and standing orders...Perused...by Sir James Marriott... 388p. *8°.* 1802.

18471 The **ENGLISHMAN'S** letters relative to the trade between Great Britain and the East-Indies. In which the exclusive rights of the East India Company, and the rights of the private merchants, under the Act of 1793, are discussed. 79p. *8°.* 1802.

18472 **FRANCE.** *Laws, etc.* Projet de code du commerce, présenté par la Commission nommée par le Gouvernement le 13 germinal an 9. xcxiv, 202p. *8°. Paris,* 1802.

18473 **HENCHMAN,** T. Observations on the reports of the Directors of the East India Company, respecting the trade between India and Europe...To which is added, an appendix...Second edition, considerably enlarged. 259, 201p. *8°.* 1802. *For another edition, see* 1801.

18474 **LAMPREDI,** G. M. Du commerce des neutres en tems de guerre, ouvrage élémentaire, destiné à fixer les principes des conventions maritimes et commerciales entre les nations; traduit de l'italien...par Jacques Peuchet... 527p. *8°. Paris,* 1802.

18475 A **LETTER** to the proprietors of East India stock, respecting the present situation of the Company's affairs both abroad and at home; in answer to the statements given in the latter part of the third report of the special committee, of the Court of Directors respecting private trade, dated the 25th of March, 1802. 113p. *8°.* 1802.

18476 **MARCHANDISES** exportées de St. Petersbourg, 1801. [A table, printed in Russia, of the number of British, American, Swedish and Portuguese ships engaged in the export trade from Russia, their destinations, and the amount of each commodity carried.] *obl.s.sh.fol. n.p.* [1802 ?] *See also* 1801 (VERZEICHNISS...).

18477 **NEVEU,** J. J. C. J. Cours pratique de commerce, à l'usage des agriculteurs, fabricans et négocians... 2 vols. *8°. Paris,* 1802. *The copy that belonged to the Société de Lecture de Genève.*

18478 **SARTORIUS VON WALTERHAUSEN,**

G. F. C., *Freiherr*. Geschichte des Hanseatischen Bundes. 3 vols. *8°. Göttingen*, 1802–8.

18479 SPAIN. *Laws, etc.* Arancel general de los frutos, generos y efectos prohibidos extraer del Reyno, de los que en su extraccion son libres de todos los derechos: de los que se permite sacar con pago de ellos; y de los que tienen premios señalados para su salida. 49p. *fol. n.p.* [1802]

COLONIES

18480 BARRINGTON, G. The history of New South Wales, including Botany Bay, Port Jackson, Pamaratta [*sic*], Sydney, and all its dependancies, from the original discovery of the island: with the customs and manners of the natives; and an account of the English colony, from its foundation, to the present time... 505p. *8°.* 1802. *The last plate is dated: Jan. 21. 1803.*

18481 FALCONBRIDGE, A. M. Narrative of two voyages to the river Sierra Leone, during...1791–2–3... With...every interesting particular relating to the Sierra Leone Company. Also the present state of the slave trade in the West Indies, and the improbability of its total abolition. The second edition. 287, [5]p. *12°.* 1802. *A reissue of the second edition of* Two voyages to Sierra Leone, *1794, (q.v.) with a new title-page.*

18482 FRANCE. *Napoleon Bonaparte, First Consul.* No. 1652 ..Arrêté qui supprime les listes locales d'émigrés formées dans les colonies. Du 28 brumaire an XI de la République Française... 2p. *4°. Paris,* [1802]

18483 GALE, SAMUEL (1783–1865). Reply to the report of the Executive Council of the Province of Lower Canada...to the Lords of His Majesty's Most Honourable Privy Council, of the 28th of November, 1800, in behalf of his constituents, applicants for grants of various tracts and parcels of the waste lands of the Crown in that Province. To which is prefixed, a copy of the said memorial, and of the report... 58p. *4°.* [1802]

18484 MALOUET, P. V. DE, *Baron.* Collection de mémoires et correspondances officielles sur l'administration des colonies, et notamment sur la Guiana française et hollandaise. 5 vols. *8°. Paris,* an x [1802]

18485 MARTIN, SAMUEL, *of Antigua.* Three tracts on West-Indian agriculture, and subjects connected therewith; viz. An essay upon plantership; by Samuel Martin...The sugar-cane, a didactic poem...and, an essay on the management and diseases of negroes...the two latter by James Grainger...[With 'Practical notes, and a Linnæan index, by William Wright'.] 95, 170, 98p. *8°. Jamaica,* 1802. *Presentation copy from the editor to 'Dʳ. Wright Edinb.'.*

18486 A fair and candid **REVIEW** of the proceedings of the House of Assembly of the Province of New-Brunswick in their late session; addressed to the loyal inhabitants and electors of the Province. By a spectator. 32p. *8°. n.p.,* 1802. *The copy that belonged to William Cobbett.*

18487 [**STEPHEN,** J.] The crisis of the sugar colonies; or, an enquiry into the objects and probable effects of the French expedition to the West Indies...To which are subjoined, sketches of a plan for settling the vacant lands of Trinidada. In four letters to...Henry Addington... 222p. *8°.* 1802. *The copy that belonged to Jeremy Bentham, with his signature on the title-page.*

FINANCE

18488 ANGOT DES ROTOURS, N. F. M. Mémoire sur la nécessité d'une refonte générale. 60p. *4°. Paris,* fructidor an x [1802]

18489 [**ATKINSON,** JASPER.] Considerations on the propriety of the Bank of England resuming its payments in specie at the period prescribed by the Act 37th George III. By ———— ———— ————. 110p. *8°.* 1802.

18490 BORDEAUX. *Conseil de Commerce.* Conseil de Commerce de Bordeaux. Mémoire en réponse à la cinquième question, présentée le 1er frimaire dernier... par le Ministre de l'Intérieur. [On the customs tariff. Dated: le 26 pluviôse, an 10.] 26p. *4°. Bordeaux,* [1802]

18491 CORBAUX, F. Dictionnaire des arbitrages simples, considérés par rapport à la France, dans les changes entre les villes commerçantes... 2 vols. *4°. Paris,* 1802.

18492 CRAUFURD, G. A letter to the Right Honourable Henry Addington, on the finances of Great Britain. 29p. *8°.* 1802 .

18493 Public **CREDIT** in danger; or, frauds on the revenue, private wrongs, and public ruin. To which are added hints on the best means to provide for a peace establishment without increasing the national burthens... By a member of the Honourable Society of the Inner Temple. 84p. *8°.* 1802. *The copy that belonged to William Cobbett.*

18494 FAIRMAN, WILLIAM. The stocks examined and compared: or, a guide to purchasers in the public funds. Containing an account of the different funds...to the year 1802...With...tables...including a new table for shewing the comparative value of deferred stock, for every half-year...Also, statements of the National Debt ...The fourth edition, considerably improved. 171p. *8°.* 1802. *For other editions, see* 1795.

18495 FORTUNE, E. F. THOMAS. A concise and authentic history of the Bank of England. With dissertations on metals & coin, bank notes and bills of exchange. To which is added, their charter...Third edition, with considerable additions. 134p. *12°.* 1802. *For other editions, see* 1797.

18496 ———— An epitome of the stocks & public funds... Sixth edition, with additions. 88p. *12°.* 1802. *For other editions, see* 1796.

18497 FRANCE. *Napoleon Bonaparte, First Consul.* No. 1594...Arrêté qui annulle un arrêté par lequel le préfet de l'Eure avait envoyé l'épouse de l'émigré Vaudemont en possession d'une partie des biens de son mari, pour la remplir de ses créances. Du 7 thermidor an x de la République Française... 2p. *4°. Paris,* [1802]

18498 GERBOUX, Fr. Discussion sur les effets de la démonétisation de l'or, relativement à la France. 98p. *4°*. [*Paris*, 1802]

18499 GRAY, John, *LL.D.* The income tax scrutinized, and some amendments proposed to render it more agreeable to the British Constitution. 84p. *8°*. 1802.

18500 GRISWOLD, R. Speech of Mr. Griswold, on the Bill for the repeal of the internal taxes; delivered in the House of Representatives of the United States, on... the 18th of March... 27p. *8°*. *Philadelphia*, 1802.

18501 GUINEAS an unnecessary and expensive incumbrance on commerce; or, the impolicy of repealing the Bank Restriction Bill considered. 123p. *8°*. 1802. *See also* 1803.

18502 The **IMPOLICY** of returning bankers to Parliament in the ensuing General Election. Including strictures on the productions under the signature of Common Sense, &c.&c.&c.... By a friend to the poor, the commerce, and the constitution of England. 34p. *8°*. 1802.

18503 [**MARNIÈRES,** J. H., *Marquis de Guer.*] Considérations sur la facilité d'établir à Paris une banque égale à celle de Londres. 43p. *8°*. *Paris*, [1802 ?]

18504 MOORE, John (1742–1821). Case respecting the maintenance of the London-clergy, briefly stated and supported by reference to authentick documents. 54p. *8°*. 1802.

18505 NETHERLANDS. *Batavian Republic.* Pryscourant van obligatien en andere effecten, zo als de pryzen waren op Dingsdag primo juny 1802. Geformeerd op last van het Staats-Bewind... [4]p. *fol. den Haag*, 1802. *See also* 1796, 1797, 1800, 1801, 1803, 1804.

18506 —— —— Publicatie van het Staats-Bewind... Wegens eene vrywillige negotiatie van dertig millioenen; enz. Geärresteerd den 11 february 1802. 10, [4]p. *8°*. *den Haag*, 1802.

18507 —— —— Publicatie van het Staats-Bewind... houdende bepalingen van uitzondering in de inschryvingen der vrywillige negotiatie van dertig millioenen, voor de ingezetenen van Holland en Utrecht, enz. Geärresteerd den 18 february 1802. [4]p. *8°*. *den Haag*, 1802.

18508 —— —— Publicatie van het Staats-Bewind... wegens eene heffing van vier percent op de bezittingen, en zestien percent op de inkomsten, te betalen in acht jaren. Geärresteerd den 26 february 1802. 16p. *8°*. *den Haag*, 1802.

18509 —— —— Publicatie van Thesaurier-Generaal en Raaden van Financien...houdende: nadere bepalingen opzichtelyk de inschryvingen en fournissementen in de vrywillige negotiatie...van den 11den february 1802, als ook een nader plan van loterye, aan dezelve negotiatie geaccrocheerd. Geärresteerd den 5den mey 1802. 7p. *8°*. *den Haag*, 1802.

18510 —— —— Publicatie van Staats-Bewind...betrekkelyk de wyze, waarop de agtjarige heffing van ½ perCt. op de bezittingen, en 2 perCt. op de inkomsten, bepaald by publicatie van de 26 february dezes jaars, zal werden geëffectueërd, enz. Geärresteerd den 15 juny 1802. 24p. *8°*. *den Haag*, 1802.

18511 —— —— Publicatie van het Staats-Bewind... houdende vrylating aan de ingezetenen, om binnen drie maanden hun nog verschuldigde in onderscheidene heffingen aantebetalen...Geärresteerd den 1 july 1802. 4p. *8°*. *den Haag*, 1802.

18512 —— —— Publicatie van het Staats-Bewind... houdende bepalingen betrekkelyk de opbrengst van 5 per cent in de 25 jarige heffing, enz. Geärresteerd den 8 july 1802. 4p. *8°*. *den Haag*, 1802.

18513 —— —— Publicatie van het Staats-Bewind... houdende verbod wegens het verkoopen van heele of gedeelten van loten in de vrywillige negotiatie lotery... den 11 february dezes jaars...Geärresteerd den 13 augustus 1802. 4p. *8°*. *den Haag*, 1802.

18514 —— —— Publicatie van het Staats-Bewind... betrekkelyk eenige alteratiën in de publicatie van den 26 february dezes jaars, wegens de agtjarige heffing op de bezittingen en inkomsten. Geärresteerd den 16 augustus 1802. 4p. *8°*. *den Haag*, 1802.

18515 —— —— Publicatie van het Staats-Bewind... houdende prolonguatie [*sic*] der termynen van betaling in de respective agt- en vyf-en-twintig jarige heffingen, geduurende dit jaar. Geärresteerd den 20 september 1802. 3p. *8°*. *den Haag*, 1802.

18516 POPE, S. Considerations, political, financial, and commercial, relative to the important subject of the public funds. Addressed to stock-holders in general, and more particularly to the holders of omnium. 33p. *8°*. 1802.

18517 PROFUSION of paper money, not deficiency in harvests; taxation, not speculation, the principal causes of the sufferings of the people. With an appendix, containing observations on the Report of the Committee of the House of Commons appointed to enquire into the high price of provisions...By a banker. 32p. *8°*. 1802.

18518 The **READY RECKONER;** or trader's sure guide: adapted for the use of all persons, who buy or sell ...wholesale or retail. Shewing, at one view, by exact tables, the amount or value of any number or quantity of goods...from one farthing...to twenty shillings; either by the ounce, pound, yard, or ell, hundred, half hundred, or quarter. With tables of interest... [240]p. *12°*. *Air*, 1801 [1802]

18519 Serious **REFLECTIONS** on paper money in general, particularly on the alarming inundation of forged bank notes...In which are included observations on Mr. Thornton's Enquiry concerning the paper credit of Great Britain. 62p. *8°*. 1802.

18520 ROSE, George. Considerations on the debt on the Civil List. 40p. *8°*. 1802. *Two copies that belonged to William Cobbett.*

18521 SANDERUS, P. Beredeneerd vertoog over de vorderingen van contributie, op de eigenaars, afladers, of geconsigneerden van verlorene goederen, als avarijegrosse, over schip en lading; en over de thans daaromtrent plaats hebbende practijk bij de Hollandsche assurantiekameren. 18op. *8°*. *Amsterdam*, 1802.

18522 SOCIETY FOR EQUITABLE ASSURANCES. A short account of the Society for Equitable Assurances on Lives and Survivorships, established by deed, inrolled in His Majesty's Court of King's Bench, at Westminster. 18, [2]p. *8°*. 1802. *For other editions, see* 1762.

18523 SPAIN. *Laws, etc.* Recopilacion de todas las providencias respectivas a vales reales expedidas desde M.DCCLXXX... 2 vols. *8°*. *Madrid*, 1802.

18524 TAXATIO ecclesiastica Angliæ et Walliæ auctoritate P. Nicholai IV. Circa A.D. 1291. Printed by command of...King George III...[Edited by T. Astle,

S. Ayscough and J. Caley.] 448p. *fol.* [*The Record Commission,*] 1802.

18525 **TESCHEMACHER**, J. R. Tables calculated for the arbitration of exchanges, both simple and compound; with an account of the currencies and monies of the principal commercial cities of Europe. Taken from the latest and best authorities. 56, [46], 13p. *4°.* 1802.

18526 **THORNTON**, HENRY (1760–1815). An enquiry into the nature and effects of the paper credit of Great Britain. 320p. *8°.* 1802. *A second, imperfect, copy belonged to Sir Robert Peel. See also 1803.*

18527 **UNITED STATES OF AMERICA.** *Treasury Department.* The report of Mr. Gallatin on the

finances, January 1802: likewise, the report of the Committee of Ways and Means making provision for the redemption of the public debt; and that of the Committee of Investigation. 72p. *12°. Bennington,* 1802.

18528 The **UTILITY** of country banks considered. 86p. *8°.* 1802. *The copy that belonged to William Cobbett.*

18529 **WOLCOTT**, O. An address, to the people of the United States, on the subject of the report of a Committee of the House of Representatives, appointed to "examine and report, whether monies drawn...have been faithfully applied to the objects for which they were appropriated...". Which report was presented on the 29th of April, 1802. [With an appendix, containing the report.] 70p. *8°. Hartford,* 1802.

TRANSPORT

18530 **BORDEAUX.** *Conseil de Commerce.* Mémoire du Conseil...en réponse à la septième question du Ministre de l'Intérieur, du 1er frimaire, an 10. [On suggested improvements to the port of Bordeaux. Dated: le 26 pluviôse, an 10.] 8p. *4°. Bordeaux,* [1802]

18531 **BRISTOL.** *Corporation.* Explanation of the plan proposed for the improvement of the harbour of Bristol; and also a scheme and proposals for raising the sum necessary to carry the plan into effect. Published by order of the Corporation of the City, and the Society of Merchant Venturers. 18p. *4°. Bristol,* 1802.

18532 **CONSIDERATIONS** on the probable commerce and revenue, that may arise on the proposed canal, between Newcastle and Maryport. Published in 1796; now reprinted, with a preface, shewing the great national utility of the proposed canal. 21p. *8°. Newcastle, Hexham, &c.,* 1802.

18533 **ENGLAND.** *Laws, etc.* Copies of the several Acts of Parliament, passed for making and repairing the roads, belonging to Fisherton Turnpike. 130p. *12°. Salisbury,* 1802.

18534 —— *Post Office.* Twopenny Post-Office. The enclosed has been opened by the proper officer, and is returned to you for the reason assigned thereon.

[Signed: C. Walcot, Comptroller. E. Johnson, Depy. Comptroller. A list of regulations and charges is appended, dated: January 6, 1802.] *s.sh.4°. n.p.* [1802] [*Br.* 466] *The copy addressed in manuscript to Lord Sheffield.*

18535 **GRAND JUNCTION CANAL COMPANY.** Substance of the report of the general committee of the Grand Junction Canal Company, to the general assembly of proprietors, on the 2d of November, 1801... 21p. *8°.* 1802.

18536 **LANCASTER CANAL NAVIGATION.** Lancaster Canal Navigation, sixth call on the new shares. [4]p. *4°. Lancaster,* [1802]. *Addressed in manuscript to 'Richd. Shawe Esq.', with a manuscript receipt from Cox, Merle and Co., for the sum requested.*

18537 **SUTHERLAND**, A. Reports, with estimates, plans, and sections, &c. first, of the proposed canal through the Weald of Kent, intended to form a junction of the rivers Medway and Rother...secondly, of a branch from the canal by the river Teise to...Lamberhurst... thirdly, of a branch from the canal to...Hedcorn; and fourthly, of a branch from the canal to the town of Cranbrook...Together with some general observations on their great local and national importance. 28p. *4°.* 1802.

SOCIAL CONDITIONS

18538 [*Begin.*] The following **ACCOUNT** of outrages lately committed will shew the distracted state of the clothing districts in this neighbourhood... *s.sh.fol. n.p.* [1802] *Headed in manuscript 'Bath 1802'; with a further manuscript note, 'Several other outrages have been committed since this account was sent to the Press'. The Sheffield copy.*

18539 **ACCOUNTS** of the soup house in West Street, Seven-Dials, for the year 1801. [With a list of subscribers.] 20p. *8°.* 1802.

18540 **ALEXANDER**, L. Answer to Mr. Joshua Van Oven's Letters on the present state of the Jewish poor in London; in which some of his hasty mistakes are rectified, with a word to P. Colquhoun Esq. on the subject of the Jews as treated in his Police of the Metropolis, with...an exact copy of the Bill now before Parliament for bettering the state of the indigent Jews. 44, 8p. *8°.* 1802. *The copy that belonged to James Colquhoun.*

18541 **BATE**, H., afterwards **DUDLEY**, SIR H. B., *Rev., Bart.* A few observations respecting the...state of the poor; and the defects of the poor laws: with some remarks upon parochial assessments, and expenditures. 36p. *8°.* 1802. *The Sheffield copy.*

18542 —— Third edition. 36p. *8°.* 1802. *The copy that belonged to William Cobbett.*

18543 **BENTHAM**, J. Letter to Lord Pelham, &c.&c.&c. Giving a comparative view of the system of penal colonization in New South Wales, and the home penitentiary system, prescribed by two Acts of Parliament of the years 1794 & 1799. [With 'Second letter to Lord Pelham, &c.&c.&c. In continuation of the comparative view of the system of penal colonization in New South Wales...'.] 80, 72p. *8°. n.p.* [1802] *Presentation copy, with inscription from the author to Lord Sheffield on the introductory circular, addressed to the Lord Chancellor and the judges.*

18544 CONSIDERATIONS on the late election for Westminster and Middlesex; together with some facts relating to the House of Correction in Cold Bath Fields. 86p. *8°. 1802.*

18545 FRIENDLY SOCIETY OF THE SHOE-MAKERS OF THE ABBEY OF CAMBUS-KENNETH. Articles of the Friendly Society... 8p. *8°. Stirling, 1802.*

18546 HAMPSTEAD PAROCHIAL BENE-FIT SOCIETY. Plan of the Parochial Benefit Society, proposed to be established at Hampstead, under the patronage and protection of the principal inhabitants, for the benefit of the sober and industrious of all descriptions. 16p. *8°. 1802.*

18547 —— [Another edition.] Plan of the Parochial Benefit Society established at Hampstead, on Tuesday the ninth day of February 1802...[With an account of the inaugural meeting and a list of elected officers.] 16p. *8°. 1802.*

18548 [HANKIN, E.] A letter to the Right Hon. Henry Addington...on the establishment of parochial libraries, for the benefit of the clergy. By a Kentish clergyman. 33p. *8°. 1802.*

18549 HEVEY, J. Third edition. Trial by nisi prius, in the Court of King's Bench, Ireland, in the case wherein Mr. John Hevey was plaintiff, and Charles Henry Sirr, Esq. was defendant, on an action for an assault, and false imprisonment... 61p. *8°. Dublin, [1802?]*

18550 [JACKSON, WILLIAM (*fl.* 1802) and **CARTE, S.]** An account of the many and great loans, benefactions & charities, belonging to the City of Coventry, to which is annexed, a copy of the decretal order, of the Court of Chancery. Relating to the memorable charity of Sir Thomas White. [The dedication signed: AB, CD, EF, GH, &c.] A new edition. 216p. *8°. Coventry & London, 1802.*

18551 MAGDALEN HOSPITAL. By-laws and regulations of the Magdalen Hospital, instituted...1758 ...[With a list of officers and committee.] 63p. *8°. 1802.*

18552 MORAES, I. P. DE. Dissertaçaõ sobre o melhor methodo de evitar, e providenciar a pobreza, fundamentada nas memorias, que a' Sociedade de Bath offereceraõ Ricardo Pew, o senador Gilbert, e Joaõ Me. Farlan [*sic*], augmentada com huns novos estatutos, e apropriada ao reino de Portugal... 71p. *8°. Lisboa, 1802.*

18553 The **NAMES** of parishes and other divisions maintaining their poor separately in the county of Westmorland; with the population of each, on a plan which may facilitate the execution of the poor laws, and the future ascertainment of the number of inhabitants in England. By a justice of the peace for the counties of Westmorland and Lancaster. 17p. *8°. Kendal & London, 1802.*

18554 NEILD, J. An account of the rise, progress and present state of the Society for the Discharge and Relief of Persons imprisoned for Small Debts throughout England and Wales. 359[363]p. *8°. [London,] 1802. See also 1808.*

18555 [NELSON, W.] The duty of overseers of the poor. To be delivered to them at their appointment, being first signed and sealed, by the justices, in their Petty Sessions...By a country magistrate. 27p. *8°. 1802. The copy that belonged to James Colquhoun. For another edition, see 1792.*

18556 ROBERTSON, E. F. Who are the swindlers? A query...[An account of the author's case against dishonest tradesmen.] Second edition, with additions. 46p. *8°. London & Huntingdon, [1802?]*

18557 ROUEN. Ordonnance du Maire de la ville de Rouen. Police des inhumations. 6p. *4°. [Rouen, 1802]*

18558 SAUNDERS, ROBERT. An abstract of Observations on the poor laws; with a reply to the remarks of the Rev. James Nasmith, D.D. 43p. *8°. 1802. The Sheffield copy, presented by the author. For an edition of* Observations on the poor laws, *see 1799.*

18559 SOCIETY FOR BETTERING THE CONDITION OF THE POOR, London. The following report of a select committee of the Society upon some observations on the late Act respecting cotton mills, and on the account of Mr. Hey's visit to a cotton mill at Burley, are printed by order of the Society... 22p. *8°. [London, 1802]*

18560 —— The reports of the Society...[first to the eighteenth, edited by Sir T. Bernard]. The third edition. 3 vols. *12°. London, York, &c., 1802, 1800. For the original editions of the 1st–30th reports, see Vol. III, Periodicals list, Reports of the Society for bettering the condition...of the poor. See also 1805, 1811.*

18561 VAN OVEN, J. Letters on the present state of the Jewish poor in the Metropolis; with propositions for ameliorating their condition by improving the morals of the youth of both sexes, and by rendering their labour useful and productive in a greater degree... 36p. *8°. 1802. The copy that belonged to James Colquhoun.*

18562 WAKEFIELD, EDWARD (1774–1854). A letter to the land owners and others contributors to the poor's rates, in the Hundred of Dangye, in Essex. 67p. *8°. London & Chelmsford, [1802].*

18563 [WESTON, CHARLES (*fl.* 1802).] Remarks on the poor laws and on the state of the poor. 163p. *8°. Brentford, London, &c., 1802. The copy that belonged to William Cobbett.*

18564 —— [Another issue.] 163p. *8°. Brentford, London, &c., 1802. The title-page, bearing the author's name, is a cancel.*

SLAVERY

18565 FRANK, L. Mémoire sur le commerce des nègres au Kaire, et sur les maladies auxquelles ils sont sujets en y arrivant. 52p. *8°. Paris, 1802.*

18566 PETERS, C. Two sermons, preached at Dominica, on the 11th and 13th of April, 1800...To which is added, an appendix, containing minutes of three trials which occurred at Roseau in the spring of the preceding year; together with remarks and strictures on the issue of those trials, as well as on the slave trade, and the condition of slaves in general in our West-Indian colonies. 82p. *8°. 1802. The Sheffield copy.*

POLITICS

18567 BOND, SIR T., *Bart.* The prosperity of Ireland, with respect to its civil and religious interests, considered [*sic*] and promoted. 31p. *8°. Dublin*, 1802.

18568 BOWLES, J. Thoughts on the late general election. As demonstrative of the progress of Jacobinism. 97p. *8°.* 1802.

18569 BUONAPARTE'S confession of the massacre of Jaffa. *s.sh.fol.* [*London*, 1802]

18570 COBBETT, W. Letters to the Right Honourable Lord Hawkesbury, and to the Right Honourable Henry Addington, on the peace with Buonaparte, to which is added, an appendix, containing a collection...of... documents...Second edition. 259, xcvip. *8°.* 1802. *Presentation copy, with inscription, from the author to John Penn (1760?–1834).*

18571 COPIES of the addresses to Mr. Burdon, with the names subscribed thereto, and of letters...relative to his late election as one of the representatives in Parliament, for the county of Durham. 91p. *8°. London, Durham, &c.,* 1802.

18572 [CURRIE, J.] Observations on the present relative situation of Great Britain and France. November the 16th, 1802. 16p. *8°. Liverpool,* 1802.

18573 L'EMPIRE Germanique réduit en départements, sous la préfecture de l'Electeur de ********** [Brandebourg]. Traduit de l'allemand. 89p. *8°. Londres,* 1802. *The translation into French is conjecturally attributed to J. G. Peltier.*

18574 FOX, CHARLES J. The letter of the Honourable Charles James Fox to the electors of Westminster, dated January 23d, 1793. [On his conduct in the House of Commons.] With an application of its principles to subsequent events. By Robert Adair, Esq. M.P. 120p. *8°.* 1802. *For another edition, see* 1793.

18575 FRANCE. *Napoleon Bonaparte, First Consul.* No. 1508. Senatus-Consulte relatif à l'amnistie accordée pour fait d'émigration. Du 6 floréal an x de la République Française... 8p. *4°. Paris,* [1802]

18576 —— —— No. 1589...Extrait des registres des délibérations des Consuls de la République. Du 9 thermidor an x. Avis sur différentes questions relatives à l'exécution du Sénatus-Consulte portant amnistie pour fait d'émigration, donné par le Conseil d'Etat le 8 thermidor. 3p. *4°. Paris,* [1802]

18577 A correct **LIST** of the knights, citizens, and burgesses, elected to serve in the Parliament...1802... To which are added, the names of the candidates where the elections were contested, and the numbers polled...With the addresses of the Hon. C. J. Fox, Mr. Baker, Mr. Coke, Sir James Astley, and Sir Francis Burdett. 76p. *8°.* 1802.

18578 M⸦CARTHY, F. Sir Francis Burdett, and Parliamentary reform. 20p. *8°.* [*London,* 1802 ?]

18579 REVIEW of public affairs since the commencement of the present century. 99p. *8°.* 1802.

18580 WINDHAM, W. Substance of the speech of the Right Honourable William Windham, delivered in the House of Commons...Nov. 4, 1801, on the report of an address to the throne, approving of the Preliminaries of peace with...France. Second edition, with notes. 109p. *8°.* 1802. *The copy that belonged to William Cobbett. For another edition, see* 1801.

SOCIALISM

18581 SPENCE, T. Spence's songs. 12, [8], [4]p. *8°.* [1802 ?] *See also* 1812.

MISCELLANEOUS

18582 FOX, CHARLES J. Substance of the speech of the Honourable Charles James Fox, on moving a new writ for the borough of Tavistock, March 16, 1802... [on the character of the late Duke of Bedford.] 18p. *8°.* 1802.

18583 HALL, RICHARD, *M.D.* Elements of botany; or an introduction to the sexual system of Linnæus; to which is annexed an English botanical dictionary... 219p. *8°.* 1802.

18584 [HOWELL, T. B.] Observations on Dr. Sturges's pamphlet respecting non-residence of the clergy; in a letter to Mr. Baron Maseres. 63p. *8°.* 1802.

18585 KIPLING, T. The Articles of the Church of England proved not to be Calvinistic. 91p. *8°. Cambridge, London, &c.,* 1802. *The copy that belonged to William Cobbett.*

18586 LAICUS, CHRISTIANUS, *pseud.* A letter, addressed to the Hon. Charles James Fox, in consequence of a publication, entitled, "A sketch of the character of the most noble Francis Duke of Bedford." 28p. *8°. Bath & London,* [1802] *The copy that belonged to M. T. Sadler.*

18587 —— A letter addressed to the Hon. Charles James Fox, in consequence of his speech in the House of Commons, on the character of the late most noble Francis Duke of Bedford. The second edition. To which are added, observations on a sermon preached in...Woburn, March 14, 1802...by Edmund Cartwright...Prebendary of Durham. 57p. *8°.* [*London,* 1802] *The copy that belonged to William Cobbett.*

18588 A **LETTER** addressed to a member of the House of Commons, on the stat. 21. Hen. VIII, c. 13 and on the grievances to which the clergy are exposed in consequence of it; with hints and observations respecting a new Bill. [Signed: A resident parish priest.] 41p. *8°. Truro,* 1802.

18589 A **LETTER** to the Hon. Charles James Fox, on the death of His Grace the late Duke of Bedford. 32p. *8°.* 1802.

18590 SCOTT, WILLIAM, *Baron Stowell.* Substance of the speech of the Right Honourable Sir William Scott, delivered in the House of Commons...April 7, 1802, upon a motion for leave to bring in a Bill, relative to the non-residence of the clergy, and other affairs of the Church. 58p. *8°.* 1802. *The copy that belonged to William Cobbett.*

18591 STURGES, J. Thoughts on the residence of the clergy and on the provisions of the Statute of the twenty-first year of Henry VIII, c. 13. The second edition, with additions. 74p. *8°. Winchester & London,* 1802. *The copy that belonged to William Cobbett.*

1803

GENERAL

18592 AUSWAHL neuer Erfindungen, Entdeckungen und Verbesserungen in der Oekonomie, Stadt- und Landwirthschaft, Feldbau, Viehzucht, Gärtnerey, Bräuerey &c. für Künstler, Fabrikanten, Handwerker, Güterbesitzer und Haushälater aller Gattung...[Vol. 1.] 368p. *8°. Stadtamhof,* 1803.

18593 BENTHAM, J. A plea for the Constitution: shewing the enormities committed to the oppression of British subjects, innocent as well as guilty, in breach of Magna Charta, the Petition of Right, the Habeas Corpus Act, and the Bill of Rights; as likewise of the several transportation acts; in and by the design, foundation and government of the penal colony of New South Wales: including an enquiry into the right of the Crown to legislate without Parliament in Trinidad, and other British colonies. 68p. *8°.* 1803. *Published as part of the author's* Panopticon versus New South Wales *in 1812, q.v.* (SOCIAL CONDITIONS).

18594 BLANC DE VOLX, J. Etat commercial de la France, au commencement du dix-neuvième siècle; ou du commerce français, de ses anciennes erreurs et des améliorations dont il est susceptible. 3 vols. *8°. Paris & Strasbourg,* 1803.

18595 BURNEY, J. A chronological history of the discoveries in the South Sea or Pacific Ocean. Part I. Commencing with an account of the earliest discovery of that sea by Europeans, and terminating with the voyage of Sir Francis Drake, in 1579. Illustrated with charts. 5 vols. *4°.* 1803–17. *Volume 1 only belongs to the Goldsmiths' Library.*

18596 CHANLAIRE, P. G. and **HERBIN DE HALLE,** P. E. Tableau de la division des six nouveaux départemens...avec une table alphabétique des cantons, et 7 cartes... 8p. *obl.4°. Paris,* 1803. *For* Tableau général de la nouvelle division de la France, *of which this is a supplement, see* 1802.

18597 CUSTODI, P., *Barone, ed.* Scrittori classici italiani di economia politica. 50 vols. *8°. Milano,* 1803–16.

18598 EDWARDS, GEORGE. Reasons why a true or genuine system of public and private welfare, adapted to the present crisis...should be laid before Parliament... 56p. *8°.* 1803.

18599 ENGLAND. *Parliament.* The Parliamentary register; or, a history of the proceedings and debates of the Houses of Lords and Commons...during the first session of the second Parliament of the United Kingdom... Vols. 1–3. *8°. J. Debrett,* 1803–4. *Wanting the three volumes for the year 1804.*

18600 —— —— *House of Commons.* Reports from Committees of the House of Commons [which have been printed by order of the House, and are not inserted in the Journals]. Reprinted by order of the House. 16 vols. *fol. n.p.,* 1803–6.

18601 —— *Treaties, etc.* The correspondence between Great Britain and France on the subject of the late negotiation...To which are added, His Majesty's declaration, and copies of the preliminary and definitive treaties of peace. 168p. *8°.* 1803. *The copy that belonged to David Ricardo.*

18602 —— —— Official papers, relative to the Preliminaries of London and the Treaty of Amiens. Published at Paris by authority of the French government. 74, 111p. *8°.* 1803.

18603 FRANCE. *Napoleon Bonaparte, First Consul.* No. 1805. Arrêté relatif aux biens confisqués à raison d'émigration, et aux droits des créanciers d'émigrés. Du 3 floréal an XI... 3p. *4°. Paris,* [1803]

18604 FRASER, A. C., *of Lovat.* Tracts. 39, 51p. *8°. Inverness,* 1803.

18605 FRASER, R. A letter to the Rt. Hon. Charles Abbot...containing an inquiry into the most effectual means of the improvement of the coasts and western isles of Scotland, and the extension of the fisheries. With a letter from Dr. Anderson to the author, on the same subject. 104p. *8°.* 1803.

18606 GARDINER, JOHN. Essays, literary, political, and œconomical... 2 vols. *8°. Edinburgh & London,* 1803.

18607 HERBIN DE HALLE, P. E., *ed.* Statistique générale et particulière de la France et de ses colonies, avec une nouvelle description topographique, physique, agricole, politique, industrielle et commerciale de cet état... Avec un atlas grand...contenant...tableaux, et...cartes enluminées...dressées par J. B. Poirson...Par une société de gens de lettres et de savans... 8 vols. *8° & 4°. Paris,* 1803–4.

18608 HINTS submitted to the consideration of the Select Committee, to whom the survey and report of the coasts and central Highlands of Scotland, made by the command of the Commissioners of His Majesty's Treasury, has been referred; including some observations on the advantages of domestic colonization. 11p. *4°.* [*London,* 1803] *Possibly by Sir John Sinclair, who presented this copy to Lord Sheffield.*

18609 M'ARTHUR, JOHN (1755–1840). Financial and political facts of the eighteenth and present century; with comparative estimates of the revenue, expenditure, debts, manufactures and commerce of Great Britain... Fourth edition. With an appendix of...documents. The whole revised, corrected, and...enlarged. lxxxix, 294p. *8°.* 1803. *For an earlier version, see* 1801 (FINANCE).

18610 MALISSET D'HERTEREAU, J. B. A. La boussole des spéculateurs, contenant un traité complet et méthodique de la science du commerce, et des connoissances les plus utiles aux diverses classes de la société, et particulièrement aux négocians, armateurs, navigateurs ...Tome premier... 2 vols. *8°. Paris, 1803.*

18611 MEYER, E. Die Kunst sich glücklich als Kaufmann oder Fabrikant zu etabliren, oder Belehrungen fur jünge Kauflente [*sic*] und Fabrikanten, welche sich etabliren und diesen... Schritt nicht zu ihrem und anderer Menschen Unglück thun wollen... 532p. *8°. Weimar, 1803.*

18612 ORR, G. The possession of Louisiana by the French, considered, as it affects the interests of those nations more immediately concerned, viz. Great Britain, America, Spain, and Portugal. 45p. *8°. 1803.*

18613 PLAN of national improvement, pointing out the means to render Great Britain independent of supplies of corn from abroad, to extend the British fisheries, and augment the military and naval strength of the Empire... To which are added... an exposition of Bonaparte's grand project to conquer Great Britain and Ireland... 154[164]p. *8°. Brunswick & London, 1803.*

18614 POLO Y CATALINA, J. Censo de frutos manufacturas de España ó islas adyacentes... aumentado con las principales reflexiones sobra la estatística de cada una de las provincias... 104l. *fol. Madrid, 1803.*

18615 RAGOUNEAU, A. M. Recherches sur l'état actuel des sociétés politiques, ou jusques à quel point l'économie intérieure des états modernes leur permet-elle de se rapprocher de la liberté et de l'égalité? 313p. *8°. Paris & Strasbourg, 1803.*

18616 SAY, J. B. Traité d'économie politique, ou simple exposition de la manière dont se forment, se distribuent, et se consomment les richesses... 2 vols. *8°. Paris, 1803. See also 1814, 1817, 1819, 1821, 1826, 1827, 1830, 1834, 1836.*

18617 SIMONDE DE SISMONDI, J. C. L. De la richesse commerciale, ou principes d'économie politique, appliqués à la législation du commerce... 2 vols. *8°. Genève, 1803.*

18618 SLADE, R. Narrative of a journey to the north of Ireland, in the year 1802. [The report of Robert Slade 'to the... Governor and Assistants of the New Plantation in Ulster' with 'Report of J. C. Beresford... as to the state of timber'.] 96p. *8°. 1803.*

18619 [SMITH, ADAM.] Compendio de la obra inglesa intitulada Riqueza de las naciones, hecho por el Marques de Condorcet, y traducido al castellano con varies adiciones del original, por Don Carlos Martinez de Irujo ... 300p. *8°. Madrid, 1803. For editions of the complete work, see 1776.*

18620 WATSON, RICHARD, *Bishop of Llandaff*. The substance of a speech, intended to have been spoken in the House of Lords, November 22d, 1803. 46p. *8°. 1803. The copy that belonged to William Cobbett.*

18621 —— The second edition. 52p. *8°. Kendal, Manchester, &c., [1803] Presentation copy, with inscription, from the author to the Duke of Bedford.*

AGRICULTURE

18622 BOARD OF AGRICULTURE. List of the members... 38p. *4°. 1803. Two copies from the Sheffield Collection, one with manuscript additions and corrections. See also 1793, 1796.*

18623 COCHRANE, ARCHIBALD, *9th Earl of Dundonald*. A treatise, shewing the intimate connection... between agriculture and chemistry. Addressed to the cultivators of the soil, to the proprietors of fens and mosses, in Great Britain and Ireland; and to the proprietors of West India estates... A new edition. 252p. *4°. 1803. A reissue of the sheets of the 1795 edition (q.v.), with a new title-page.*

18624 CULLYER, J. The gentleman's & farmer's, assistant; containing, first, tables for finding the content of any piece of land... Second, tables, shewing the width required for an acre, in any square piece of land, from one to five hundred yards in length. Third, tables, shewing the number of loads that will manure an acre of land... Fourth, a table for measuring thatcher's work... The fourth edition. 148p. *24°. Norwich & London, [1803] See also 1848.*

18625 DAVY, SIR H., *Bart*. An account of some experiments and observations on the constituent parts of certain astringent vegetables; and on their operation in tanning... From the Philosophical Transactions. 41p. *4°. 1803. Presentation copy, with inscription, from the author to Lord Sheffield.*

18626 —— Outlines of a course of lectures on the chemistry of agriculture. To be delivered before the Board of Agriculture, 1803. 14p. *4°. 1803. The Sheffield copy.*

18627 DIXON, JOHN, *of Kensington*. Improvement of the fisheries; letter IV. Or, a plan for establishing a nursery for disbanded seamen and soldiers, and increasing the strength... of the British Empire. 18p. *4°. 1803. For the first part, see 1800; for the second, third and fifth parts, see 1801, 1802 and 1804 respectively.*

18628 FORSYTH, WILLIAM (1737–1804). A treatise on the culture and management of fruit trees... Together with observations on the diseases... in all kinds of fruit and forest trees; as also, an account of a... cure, made public by order of the British Government... To which are added, an introduction and notes, adapting the rules of the treatise to the climate... of the United States of America. By William Cobbett. 280p. *8°. Albany, Boston, &c., 1803. For another edition, see 1791.*

18629 HUNTER, A., *ed*. Georgical essays. 6 vols. *8°. York, 1803–4. For other editions, see 1773.*

18630 LEFEBVRE D'HELLENCOURT, A. M. Aperçu général des mines de houille exploitées en France, de leurs produits, et des moyens de circulation de ces produits... Extrait de tome XII du Journal des Mines. 139p. *8°. Paris, 1803. With the book-plate of the Marquis of Lansdowne.*

18631 MARSHALL, W. Agriculture-pratique des différentes parties de l'Angleterre. *8°. Paris, 1803. A translation and systematization by P. A. Paris of Marshall's works on the rural economy of Norfolk, Yorkshire, Gloucestershire and the Midlands.*

18632 NICOL, W. The practical planter, or, a treatise on forest planting; comprehending the culture and management of planted and natural timber...also on the culture and management of hedge fences, and the construction of stone walls, &c. Second edition, corrected and improved. 306p. *8°*. 1803.

18633 PERTHUIS DE LAILLEVAULT, DE. Traité de l'aménagement et de la restauration des bois et forêts de la France, ouvrage rédigé sur les manuscrits de feu M. de Perthuis...par son fils... 384p. *8°*. *Paris*, 1803.

18634 PLYMLEY, J. General view of the agriculture of Shropshire: with observations. Drawn up for the consideration of the Board of Agriculture... 366p. *8°*. *London, Edinburgh, &c.*, 1803. *See also* 1813.

18635 SINCLAIR, SIR JOHN, *Bart*. A sketch of the improvements, now carrying on by Sir John Sinclair...in the county of Caithness, North Britain. 16p. *4°*. 1803. *The Sheffield copy.*

18636 SMITH, ROBERT, *Baron Carrington*. The speech of the Right Hon. Lord Carrington, delivered at the Board of Agriculture, on...March 15, 1803. Printed by order of the Board. [An account of the Board, during his three years' presidency.] 18p. *4°*. 1803. *The Sheffield copy.*

18637 SPAIN. *Laws, etc.* Real ordenanza para el gobierno de los montes y arbolados de la jurisdiccion de marina. 265, [16]p. *4°*. *Madrid*, 1803.

18638 THOMPSON, THOMAS, *banker*. Reasons for giving land to cottagers, to enable them to keep cows... 16p. *8°*. *Hull*, [1803]

18639 WHATELY, G. N. Hints for the improvement of the Irish fishery. 45p. *8°*. 1803.

POPULATION

18640 MALTHUS, T. R. An essay on the principle of population; or, a view of its past and present effects on human happiness; with an inquiry into our prospects respecting the future removal or mitigation of the evils which it occasions. A new edition, very much enlarged. 610p. *4°*. 1803. *For other editions, see* 1798.

18641 REMARKS on a late publication, entitled, "An essay on the principle of population; or, a view of its present and past effects on human happiness. By T. R. Malthus"... 62p. *8°*. 1803.

TRADES & MANUFACTURES

18642 ANSTIE, J. Observations on the importance and necessity of introducing improved machinery into the woollen manufactory; more particularly as it respects the interests of the counties of Wilts, Gloucester, and Somerset; with general remarks on the present application to Parliament, by the manufacturers, for the repeal of several of the existing laws. In a letter, addressed to...Lord Henry Pettey. 99p. *8°*. 1803.

18643 BANKS, JOHN. On the power of machines, etc. Including Doctor Barker's mill, Westgarth's engine, Cooper's mill...With the method of computing their force. Description of a simple instrument for measuring the velocity of air out of bellows...Observations on wheel carriages, on lathes...Experiments on the strength of oak, fir, and cast iron; with many observations respecting the form and dimensions of beams for steam engines... 127p. *8°*. *Kendal & London*, 1803.

18644 CLOTHIERS BILL. In the Right Honourable the House of Lords. Case of the woollen weavers, in ...Gloucester, Somerset, and Wilts. [4]p. *fol*. [*London*, 1803] *Endorsed: Case of the woollen weavers.*

18645 COLLIER, JOHN D. An essay on the law of patents for new inventions. To which are prefixed, two chapters, on the general history of monopolies...With an appendix, containing...an arranged catalogue of all the patents granted from January 1, 1800, to the present time. 116p. *8°*. 1803.

18646 CONSIDERATIONS upon a Bill now before Parliament, for repealing (in substance) the whole code of laws respecting the woollen manufacture of Great Britain:

and for dissolving the ancient system of apprenticeship... 57p. *8°*. 1803.

18647 OBSERVATIONS on woollen machinery. 24p. *8°*. *Leeds*, 1803.

18648 PAIN, W. The carpenter's pocket directory; containing the best methods of framing timber buildings ...With the plan and sections of a barn...A new edition. [28]p., xxiv plates. *4°*. 1803.

18649 S., J. A view of the cotton manufactories of France...Together with some political & national remarks thereon. Embellished with the translation of a very interesting memorial [signed: A. D. F.], presented to the Minister of the Interior of the French Republic, by a merchant and manufacturer of Rouen, in Normandy, at the conclusion of the late war, on the subject of the treaty of commerce concluded with Great Britain in the year 1786. 49p. *8°*. *Manchester*, 1803.

18650 SOCIETY FOR BETTERING THE CONDITION OF THE POOR, *London*. Hints for those who may be desirous of introducing the manufacture of split straw in country towns, villages, schools, workhouses, &c. 8p. *16°*. [*London*, 1803]

18651 TAYLOR, J., *bookseller*. A catalogue of modern books on architecture, theoretical, practical, and ornamental; books of plans and elevations for cottages, farmhouses, mansions, &c....bridges...Books of use for carpenters, bricklayers, and workmen in general...which ...are...on sale at J. Taylor's Architectural Library, No. 59, High Holborn, London. 16p. *8°*. *n.p.* [1803]

COMMERCE

18652 ATCHESON, N. Case of the owners of the British ships which were let on freight during the late peace to merchants respectively subjects of the Batavian Republic. 21p. *8°*. 1803. *The Sheffield copy.*

18653 CHAPMAN, WILLIAM (1749–1832). Observations on the prevention of a future scarcity of grain, by means contributive to the benefit of the landed, commercial, and manufacturing interests. 31p. *8°*. 1803.

18654 CLARKE, THOMAS B. An historical and political view of the disorganization of Europe: wherein the laws and characters of nations, and the maritime and commercial system of Great Britain and other states, are vindicated against the imputations and revolutionary proposals of M. Talleyrand and M. Hauterive... 208p. *8°*. 1803.

18655 [*Endorsed:*] A **COLLECTION** of affidavits relating to the coal trade in the north of England; including several letters from the agents of the proprietor to the agents of the surviving lessee of High Flatworth Colliery. These papers were sent to the Committee of the House of Commons, in the year 1800, and are now published in consequence of a second demand made five years after the expiration of the lease... 11p. *fol.* [*London*, 1803]

18656 EAST INDIA COMPANY. Proceedings relative to ships tendered for the service of the United East-India Company, from the twenty-fourth of September, 1800, to the thirteenth of April, 1803. ⟨Printed, agreeably to the resolution of the General Court of Proprietors.⟩ With an appendix. 2 vols. *fol.* 1803.

18657 EDINGTON, R. An essay on the coal trade, with strictures upon the various abuses now existing; commencing with the shipping of coals in the principal ports in the north, and proceeding with the carrying trade, the delivery &c., more especially in the Port of London...

With hints and suggestions for the amelioration of the trade.... 101p. *8°*. 1803.

18658 FRANCE. *Napoleon Bonaparte, First Consul.* No. 1795...Arrêté relatif aux marins portés sur la liste des émigrés. Du 28 germinal an XI... 2p. *4°*. *Paris*, [1803]

18659 HUNT, ROWLAND. An address to the merchants and owners of the mercantile navy of the United Kingdom, on the advantages of maritime volunteer service... 25p. *8°*. *Shrewsbury* [& *London*], 1803.

18660 JACOBSEN, F. J. Handbuch über das practische Seerecht der Engländer und Franzosen in Hinsicht auf das von ihnen in Kriegszeiten angehaltene neutrale Eigenthum, mit Rücksicht auf die englischen Assecuranz-Grundsätze über diesen Gegenstand. 2 vols. *8°*. *Hamburg*, 1803–5.

18661 MERCATOR, *pseud.* A third letter to the inhabitants of Manchester, on the exportation of cotton twist. 20p. *8°*. *Manchester*, 1803. *For the first and second letters, see* 1800.

18662 MONTEFIORE, J. A commercial dictionary: containing the present state of mercantile law, practice, and custom. Intended for the use of the cabinet, the counting-house and the library. [657]p. *4°*. 1803.

18663 STEEL, D. The ship-master's assistant and owner's manual...The tenth edition...improved and enlarged... [With 'Steel's tables of the British custom and excise duties...Third edition...improved', and 'The duties of scavage, package, baillage, and portage'.] 450, 128, 39p. *8°*. 1803. *For other editions, see* 1790.

18664 WALKER, GEORGE (*fl.* 1803). Observations, founded on facts, upon the propriety or impropriety of exporting cotton twist, for the purpose of being manufactured into cloth by foreigners. 64p. *8°*. 1803.

COLONIES

18665 BARRINGTON, G. An account of a voyage to New South Wales...To which is prefixed a detail of his life, trials, speeches... 467p. *8°*. 1803. *For another edition, see* 1801.

18666 BROUGHAM, H. P., *Baron Brougham and Vaux.* An inquiry into the colonial policy of the European powers... 2 vols. *8°*. *Edinburgh & London*, 1803.

18667 CHARPENTIER-COSSIGNY DE PALMA, J. F. Moyens d'amélioration et de restauration, proposés au gouvernement et aux habitans des colonies; ou mélanges politiques, économiques, agricoles, et commerciaux, etc., relatifs aux colonies... 3 vols. *8°*. *Paris*, 1803.

18668 DALLAS, ROBERT C. The history of the Maroons, from their origin to the establishment of their chief tribe at Sierra Leone: including the expedition to Cuba...and the state of the island of Jamaica for the last

ten years: with a succinct history of the island... 2 vols. *8°*. 1803.

18669 FRANCIS, SIR PHILIP. Mr. Francis's speech on the affairs of India; delivered in the House of Commons, on...the 29th of July, 1803. 23p. *8°*. 1803. *The copy that belonged to William Cobbett.*

18670 KERR, RICHARD H. A letter to the Hon. Court of Directors, for conducting the affairs of the East India Company of England; with copies of various documents, submitted to the Hon. Court...January 19, 1803. xi, 59p. *4°*. 1803.

18671 *WINTERBOTTOM, THOMAS. An account of the native Africans in the neighbourhood of Sierra Leone; to which is added, an account of the present state of medicine among them... 2 vols. *8°*. 1803. *The copy that belonged to Beilby Porteus, Bishop of London.*

FINANCE

18672 ADDINGTON, H., *Viscount Sidmouth.* The substance of the speech of the Right Honourable Henry Addington, in the Committee of Ways and Means, on Friday, December the 10th, 1802. 35p. *8°.* 1803.

18673 —— Second edition. 35p. *8°.* 1803.

18674 BANK OF ENGLAND. A list of the names of all such proprietors of the Bank of England, who are qualified to vote at the ensuing election...March 22d, 1803. 18p. *fol.* [1803] *See also* 1738, 1749, 1750, 1789, 1790, 1791, 1792, 1793, 1794, 1795, 1796, 1797, 1798, 1799, 1801, 1804, 1808, 1809, 1812, 1816, 1819, 1836, 1843.

18675 BOSC D'ANTIC, J. A. Corps législatif. Discours prononcé...sur le projet de loi relatif aux monnoies. Séance du 7 germinal an 11. 18p. *4°. Paris,* germinal an 11 [1803]

18676 BURN, JOHN I. A brief treatise, or summary of the law relative to stock-jobbing. 91p. *8°.* 1803. *The copy that belonged to David Ricardo.*

18677 COAD, J. The true interest of the United Kingdom proved; in two beneficial plans of finance: to take off all the taxes, prior to 1803; and provide thirty millions for the present emergency, without the income & property taxes, &c.... 15p. *4°.* 1803.

18678 COSTAZ, L., *Baron.* Tribunat. Opinion de Costaz. Sur la peine à infliger pour le crime de faux-monnoyage. Séance du 12 germinal an 11. 6p. *4°.* [*Paris,*] germinal an 11 [1803]

18679 COURTENAY, T. P. Observations upon the present state of the finances of Great Britain; suggested by Mr. Morgan's supplement to his "Comparative View", and by Mr. Addington's financial measures. 95p. *8°.* 1803.

18680 CRAUFURD, G. The doctrine of equivalents; or an explanation of the nature, value and power of money: together with their application in organising public finance...In two parts. 280p. *8°.* Rotterdam, 1803. *Presentation copy from the author to William Spence. For another edition of Part 1, see* 1794.

18681 DARU, P. A. N. B., *Comte.* Tribunat. Discours ...sur le système monétaire. Séance du 3 germinal an 11. 105p. *4°. n.p.* [1803]

18682 ELSE, R. An explanation of the Property and Income Act, passed August 11, 1803; wherein the intricacies of that voluminous Act are clearly explained, clause by clause, and made intelligible to the meanest capacities, and at one-third the expence of the Act itself. 71p. *8°. Bath,* 1803.

18683 An **ESSAY** on the funding system. With a view to determine its limits. 40p. *8°.* 1803.

18684 An **EXPOSITION** of the Act for a contribution on property, professions, trades, and offices; in which the principles and provisions of the Act are fully considered, with a view to facilitate its execution...Part the first. 66p. *8°.* 1803. *The copy that belonged to William Cobbett.*

18685 FAIRMAN, WILLIAM B. A letter addressed to the Right Honourable William Windham...on the expediency of allowing a drawback of the duties upon wines for the consumption of the army. Interspersed with observations on the insufficiency of military pay, and the present situation of subaltern officers...The second edition. 88p. *8°.* 1803.

18686 FRANCE. *Administration des Monnaies.* Instruction pour les fonctionnaires des monnaies. [Signed: Dibarrart, and others.] 10p. *4°. Paris,* fructidor an XI [1803]

18687 —— —— Tarif du prix auquel doivent être payés, au change, les écus de six livres rognés ou altérés, en conformité de la loi du 7 germinal an XI, qui ordonne que les nouvelles pièces d'argent seront fabriquées au titre de neuf cents millièmes...[Signed: Dibarrart, and others.] [4]p. *4°. Paris,* 1803.

18688 —— —— Tarif du prix auquel doivent être payés, au change, les louis fabriqués en vertu de la déclaration du 30 octobre 1795, en conformité de la loi du 7 germinal an XI, qui ordonne que les nouvelles pièces d'or seront fabriquées au titre de neuf cents millièmes... [4]p. *4°. Paris,* 1803.

18689 —— —— 1730 bis. Tarifs des monnaies d'or et d'argent, en exécution de la loi du 7 germinal en [*sic*] XI. [Signed: Dibarrart, and others.] 2p. *4°. Paris,* [1803]

18690 —— *Conseil d'Etat.* Extrait du registre des délibérations du Conseil d'Etat. Séance du premier germinal, an 11...Exposé des motifs du projet de loi sur la refonte des monnoies altérées... 3p. *4°.* [*Paris,*] germinal an 11 [1803]

18691 —— —— Extrait du registre des délibérations du Conseil d'Etat. [Séance du 18 ventôse, an 11...Exposé des motifs du projet de loi sur les monnoies.—Séance du 14 ventôse...(No. 153.) Projet de loi sur les monnoies.] 6p. *4°.* [*Paris,*] ventôse an 11 [1803]

18692 —— *Ministère des Finances.* No. 1765 bis. Circulaire du Ministre des Finances, relative à l'admission au change ou dans la circulation des pièces d'or de 24 et 48 livres, et des écus de 6 livres Tournois. Du 6 messidor an XI...[Signed: Gaudin.] 2p. *4°. Paris,* [1803]

18693 —— *Napoleon Bonaparte, First Consul.* Arrêté qui règle le mode de comptabilité des caissiers des ateliers monétaires. Du 10 floréal, an 11... 3p. *4°. Paris,* prairial an XI [1803]

18694 —— —— No. 1826...Arrêté relatif à la liquidation des rentes viagères possédées par les individus non prévenus d'émigration, sur la tête et pendant la vie d'un individu maintenu ou à maintenir sur la liste des émigrés. Du 15 prairial an XI... 2p. *4°. Paris,* [1803]

18695 —— —— No. 1872...Arrêté relatif à l'échange des ecus de trois livres et des pièces de vingt-quatre sous, douze et six sous, qui n'ont conservé aucune trace de leur empreinte. Saint-Cloud, le 6 fructidor an XI... 2p. *4°. Paris,* [1803]

18696 —— —— Extrait des registres des délibérations du Gouvernement de la République. Paris, le 4 prairial, an 11...[With 'Tarif des frais d'affinage qui seront perçus aux changes des monnaies, en exécution de l'article XII de la Loi du 7 germinal an 11'.] [4]p. *4°. Paris,* prairial an XI [1803]

18697 —— —— Extrait des registres des délibérations du Gouvernement de la République. Le 17 prairial an

11...[With 'Or. Tarif du prix...en conformité de la Loi du 7 germinal an XI' and 'Argent. Tarif'.] 19p. *4°. Paris, prairial an XI* [1803]

18698 —— —— Extrait des registres des délibérations du Gouvernement de la République. Le 17 prairial, an 11...[Authorising the exchange rates, established under the law of 7 germinal an 11. With tables of the rates annexed, drawn up by the Administration des Monnaies, and signed Dibarrart, and others.] 20p. *4°. Paris, messidor an XI* [1803]

18699 —— —— Loi sur la fabrication et la vérification des monnaies. Du 7 germinal, an 11... 4p. *4°. Paris, prairial an XI* [1803]

18700 —— —— Loi relative aux pièces d'or et d'argent rognées ou altérées. Du 14 germinal, an 11... [2]p. *4°. Paris, messidor an XI* [1803]

18701 —— *Tribunat.* Rapport fait au nom de la section des finances, sur le projet de loi relatif aux monnaies, par Joachim Lebreton. Séance du 2 germinal an XI. 22p. *4°. Paris, germinal an XI* [1803]

18702 —— —— Rapport fait au nom de la section des finances, sur le projet de loi relatif à la refonte des monnoies, par J. B. Say. Séance du 9 germinal an 11. 8p. *4°.* [*Paris,*] *germinal an 11* [1803]

18703 GUINEAS an unnecessary and expensive incumbrance on commerce; or, the impolicy of repealing the Bank Restriction Bill considered. The second edition. To which is added an appendix, shewing the influence that the Restriction Bill has upon our foreign exchange and commerce. 123, 22p. *8°.* 1803. *The copy that belonged to William Cobbett. For another edition, see* 1802.

18704 HARRISON, GEORGE, *barrister.* Observations on the nature and extent of the advantages resulting to the public, and to the landed proprietor, from the redemption of the land tax. 20p. *8°.* 1803.

18705 HATCHETT, C. Experiments and observations on the various alloys, on the specific gravity, and on the comparative wear of gold: being the substance of a report made to...the Committee of Privy Council, appointed to take into consideration the state of the coins of this Kingdom, and the present establishment and constitution of His Majesty's Mint...From the Philosophical Transactions. 154p. *4°.* 1803.

18706 [**HERRIES,** J. C.] A reply to some financial mistatements [*sic*] in and out of Parliament. 68p. *8°.* 1803.

18707 HOWISON, W. An investigation into the principles and credit of the circulation of paper money, or bank notes, in Great Britain...Together with a discussion of the question, whether the restraining law in favour of the Bank of England from paying notes in money, ought or ought not to be continued as a measure of the State? 75p. *8°.* 1803. *The copy that belonged to William Cobbett.*

18708 KEARSLEY, G. All the new taxes. Kearsley's correct tax tables, for the years 1803 and 1804...Containing the new assessed taxes, payable from April 5, 1804 ...210p. *12°.* [1803] *For other editions, see* 1786.

18709 KEITH, G. S. A general view of the taxes on malt, as imported both in England and in Scotland. 25p. *8°. Edinburgh,* [1803] *The Sheffield copy.*

18710 KING, PETER, *7th Baron King.* Thoughts on the restriction of payments in specie at the Banks of England and Ireland. 106p. *8°.* [1803] *See also* 1804.

18711 LABROUSTE, F. M. A. Corps Législatif.

Discours...sur le projet de loi relatif à la refonte des monnoies. Séance du 14 germinal an 11. 6p. *4°.* [*Paris,*] *germinal an 11* [1803].

18712 LETTER addressed to the Commissioners of Supply, and landholders in the County of Stirling: containing an historical sketch of the malt laws: with observations illustrative of the inferiority of Scots to English malt, and the causes which produce that inferiority. 38p. *8°. Edinburgh & Stirling,* 1803.

18713 LOWNDES, THOMAS, *of Liverpool.* The duties, drawbacks, and bounties of customs and excise payable in Great Britain, on merchandise...as settled by various Acts of Parliament passed prior to the tenth of November, 1803. In which is comprised, an account of such goods as are absolutely or circumstantially prohibited to be imported, or exported... 164p. *8°. Liverpool & London,* 1803.

18714 MORGAN, W. A comparative view of the public finances, from the beginning to the close of the late administration...Second edition, with a supplement, containing an account of the management of the finances to the present time. 114p. *8°.* 1803. *The copy that belonged to William Cobbett. For another edition, see* 1801.

18715 NETHERLANDS. *Batavian Republic.* Pryscourant van obligatien en andere effecten, zo als de pryzen waren op Saturdag primo january 1803. Geformeerd op last van het Staats-Bewind... [4]p. *fol. den Haag,* 1803.

18716 —— —— Prys-courant van obligatien en andere effecten, zoo als de dezelven den 1sten augustus 1803 ter Beurse van Amsteram zyn geweest, opgemaakt naar aanleiding der tauxatie daarvan door de beëedigde makelaars G. W. van Ophoven, J. A. Jourdany, J. Jarman, J. D. Mercker, B. Everard, S. en D. Saportas, J. Groeneboer en G. Blancke, gedaan. [1 Sept. 1803.] [4]p. *fol. den Haag,* 1803. *See also* 1796, 1797, 1800, 1801, 1802, 1804.

18717 —— —— Publicatie van het Staats-Bewind... betrekklyk de wyze van invordering en onderzoek naar den opbrengst der agt en vyf-en-twintigjarige heffingen, over dit en de volgende jaren. Geärresteerd den 17 february 1803. 31p. *8°. den Haag,* 1803.

18718 —— —— Publicatie van het Staats-Bewind... wegens eene vrywillige geld-negotiatie, als mede eene loterye in nationale schuldbrieven. Geärresteerd den 22 february 1803. 22p. *8°. den Haag,* 1803.

18719 —— —— Publicatie van het Staats-Bewind... houdende eene ampliatie der publicatie van den 17 february 1803, wegens de fournissementen in de 8 en 25 jarige heffingen, in qualiteit. Geärresteerd den 24 juny 1803. 4p. *8°. den Haag,* 1803.

18720 —— —— Publicatie van het Staats-Bewind... betrekkelyk het heffen eener buitengewoone belasting van twee ten honderd op de bezittingen, als don gratuit. Geärresteerd den 8 augustus 1803. 27p. *8°. den Haag,* 1803.

18721 —— —— Publicatie van het Staats-Bewind... houdende ampliatie en alteratie der publicatie van den 8 augustus dezes jaars, betrekkelyk de buitengewoone belasting van twee ten honderd, als don gratuit. Geärresteerd den 10 november 1803. 7p. *8°. den Haag,* 1803.

18722 —— —— Publicatie van het Staats-Bewind... houdende bepaligen wegens te doene fournissementen by anticipatie, onder Korting, in de 2 per Cts. heffing op de bezittingen, gearresteert den 8 augustus, 1803. Geärresteerd den 19 december 1803. 8p. *8°. den Haag,* 1803.

18723 NOTITIE van alle de geld-heffingen, die door de ingezetenen van Holland en vervolgens met de verdere ingezetenen der Bataafsche Republiek betaald zyn...in de onderstaande jaaren [1788–1803]. Tweede druk verbeterd. *s.sh.fol. Amsterdam*, [1803]

18724 OBSERVATIONS sur le compte rendu de l'Administration des Finances de la France pour l'an x.— 1801, 1802. 64p. *8°. Londres*, 1803. *With a manuscript attribution to 'Mr. Getz', i.e. F. von Gentz? In a volume that belonged to William Cobbett.*

18725 PRICE, RICHARD. Observations on reversionary payments; on schemes for providing annuities for widows, and for persons in old age...The whole new arranged, and enlarged by the addition of algebraical and other notes...and a general introduction. By William Morgan. Sixth edition. 2 vols. *8°.* 1803. *For other editions, see* 1771.

18726 PRICE, THEOPHILUS. Interest tables, calculated from two and a half to eight per cent. To which are added...instructions for dealing in the streets; and a summary of the duties on bills, notes and receipts. 383p. *16°.* 1803. *For another edition, see* 1786.

18727 REED, W. Improved interest tables, at five per cent. for every day in the year...Also, tables for calculating commissions on the sale of goods...To which is prefixed, a table of compound interest...With a table of salaries, wages, &c. [738]p. *8°.* 1803.

18728 RICHE DE PRONY, G. C. F. M., *Baron.* Rapport fait à la classe des sciences mathématiques et physiques, de l'Institut National, sur diverses inventions de Jean-Pierre Droz, relatives à l'art du monnoyage... 59p. *4°. Paris, an* XI [1803]

18729 SINCLAIR, SIR JOHN, *Bart.* The history of the public revenue of the British Empire. Containing an account of the public income and expenditure from the remotest periods...to Michaelmas 1802. With a review of the financial administration of the Right Honorable William Pitt...The third edition. 3 vols. *8°. London, Edinburgh, &c.,* 1803–4. *For other editions, see* 1785.

18730 [SLACK, T.] The banker's sure guide; or, monied man's assistant. In three parts, viz. I. Tables of interest...II. Sundry tables shewing the value of annuities certain, and annuities on lives...III. A large and accurate table of commission or brokerage...To which is prefixed ...A new and comprehensive treatise on decimals...The eighth edition, enlarged and corrected. By S. Thomas. 328p. *4°. London & Newcastle,* 1803. *For other editions, see* 1762.

18731 THORNTON, HENRY (1760–1815). Recherches sur la nature et les effets du crédit du papier dans la Grande-Bretagne...Traduit de l'anglais. 270p. *8°. Genève & Paris,* 1803. *For another edition, see* 1802.

18732 WHEATLEY, J. Remarks on currency and commerce. 262p. *8°.* 1803.

TRANSPORT

18733 LANCASTER CANAL NAVIGATION. [*Begin.*] At the adjourned general meeting of the Company of Proprietors of the Lancaster Canal Navigation, held... on...the 2d...of August, 1803...[The resolutions passed, with a covering letter concerning a proposed temporary loan.] [4]p. *4°. Lancaster,* [1803]. *Addressed in manuscript to 'Richd. Shawe, Esq.'.*

18734 MARSHALL, R. An examination into the respective merits of the proposed canal and iron railway, from London to Portsmouth. 20p. *8°.* 1803.

18735 PHILLIPS, JOHN (*fl.* 1785–1807). A general history of inland navigation, foreign and domestic: containing a complete account of the canals already executed in England; with considerations on those projected. Abridged from the quarto edition, and continued to the present time...The fourth edition. 598p. *8°.* 1803. *For other editions, see* 1792.

18736 RENNIE, JOHN (1761–1821). Report and estimate of a canal proposed to be made between Croydon and Portsmouth. By means of which, and the Croydon canal, an inland navigation will be opened between London and Portsmouth. 22p. *fol.* 1803.

18737 —— Specification of the locks proposed to be built on the Royal Canal of Ireland, on the lands of Porterstown, Riverstown, Grehanstown, and Cushionstown. [Dated: November 29, 1803.] *s.sh.fol. Dublin,* [1803]

SOCIAL CONDITIONS

18738 [BERNARD, SIR T., *Bart.*] Society for Bettering the Condition of the Poor. The cottager's religious meditations. 84p. *8°. London, York, &c.,* [1803]

18739 COLQUHOUN, P. A treatise on the functions and duties of a constable; containing details and observations interesting to the public, as they relate to the corruption of morals, and the protection of the peaceful subject against penal and criminal offences. 90p. *8°.* 1803. *Presentation copy, with inscription, from the author to Lord Sheffield.*

18740 DIMSDALE, W. P. Extract from an account of cases of typhus fever, in which the affusion of cold water has been applied in the London House of Recovery. 15p. *8°. Society for Bettering the Condition of the Poor: London, York, &c.,* [1803]

18741 EDINGTON, R. A descriptive plan for erecting a penitentiary house for the employment of convicts; to which are added, plans for the prevention of frauds and thefts, so far as respects His Majesty's dock-yards, public works, and stores...Likewise a plan of a rail-way from London to Portsmouth... 85p. *4°.* [1803 ?].

18742 GILPIN, W., *and others.* An account of a new poor-house erected in the parish of Boldre, in New Forest, near Lymington. Printed at the desire of the Society for Bettering the Condition and Increasing the Comforts of the Poor. [Signed: John Walter, Thomas Robins, William Gilpin. With an 'Advertisement' describing later developments, signed by William Gilpin.] 34p. *12°. London & Lymington,* 1803.

18743 HARRISON, GEORGE, *Quaker.* Education

respectfully proposed and recommended, as the surest means, within the power of government, to diminish the frequency of crimes. 24p. *8°*. 1803. *See also* 1810.

18744 HILL, ROWLAND (1744–1833). Village dialogues, between Farmer Littleworth, Thomas Newman, Rev. Mr. Lovegood, and others...Fourth edition. Corrected by the author. 4 vols. *8°*. 1803–4. *See also* 1826, 1833.

18745 LANCASTER, JOSEPH. Improvements in education, as it respects the industrious classes of the community; containing a short account of its present state, hints towards its improvement, and a detail of some practical experiments conducive to that end. 66p. *8°*. 1803. *The copy that belonged to William Allen.*

18746 *—— Second edition, with additions. 80p. *8°*. 1803. *See also* 1805.

18747 MARTIN, MATTHEW. Letter to the Right Hon. Lord Pelham, on the state of mendicity in the Metropolis. 30p. *8°*. [*London,*] 1803. *See also* 1811.

18748 MORAYSHIRE FARMER CLUB. A draft of the proposed rules and regulations of the Morayshire Farmers Fund, for the benefit of widows, orphans and decayed members. 20p. *8°*. *Inverness,* 1803.

18749 SOCIETY FOR THE SUPPRESSION OF VICE. Part the first, of an address to the public from the Society...instituted, in London, 1802... 106p. *8°*. 1803. *For Part the second, see* 1804.

18750 WILLAN, R. Society for Bettering the Condition of the Poor. Extract from an account of the dreadful effects of dram-drinking; with directions for those who are desirous of returning to sobriety and health. 14p. *16°*. [1803]

SLAVERY

18751 LETTER from a gentleman in Barbadoes, to his friend in London, on the subject of manumission from slavery, granted in the City of London, and in the West India colonies. 35p. *8°*. 1803.

18752 SANCHO, I. Letters of the late Ignatius Sancho, an African. To which are prefixed, memoirs of his life, by Joseph Jekyll, Esq. M.P. The fifth edition. 310p. *8°*. 1803. *For another edition, see* 1783.

POLITICS

18753 APOLOGIE des emigrés françois contre la Proclamation diffamatoire rendue sous le nom d'amnistie, le 26 avril 1802, le nommé Napoleone Buonaparté... s'appelant le Gouvernement de France. 31p. *8°*. *Londres,* 1803.

18754 [BENTLEY, THOMAS R.] A few cursory remarks upon the state of parties, during the administration of the Right Honourable Henry Addington. By a near observer. Second edition. 81p. *8°*. 1803.

18755 [——] The third edition, corrected. 84p. *8°*. 1803.

18756 [COBBETT, W.] Important considerations for the people of this kingdom...[Reprinted from the *Political Register* 30 July, 1803.] 16p. *12°*. *Association for Preserving Liberty and Property,* [1803]

18757 [CODE, H. B.] The insurrection of the twenty-third July, 1803. [An account of the trials of Robert Emmet and others. The preface is signed: H. B. C.] 110p. *8°*. *Dublin,* [1803]

18758 [COURTENAY, T. P.] A plain answer to the misrepresentations and calumnies contained in the Cursory remarks of a near observer. By a more accurate observer. 83p. *8°*. 1803. *See also* 1804.

18759 DOYLE, F. A report of an interesting case, wherein Mr. Francis Doyle of Carrick-on-Suir, merchant and cloth-manufacturer, was plaintiff, and Sir Thomas Judkin Fitzgerald, High-Sheriff of the County of Tipperary, in the year 1798, was defendant. Tried...at Clonmel Spring Assizes...1801, before Lord Avonmore. [An action for damages, consequent upon the flogging of the plaintiff by the defendant, who accused him of being a rebel.] 46p. *8°*. *Dublin,* 1803.

18760 EMMET, R. Adjournment of a special commission of oyer and terminer. The trial of Robert Emmet, Esq. for high treason...On the 19th...of September, 1803... 56p. *8°*. *Dublin,* 1803.

18761 ENGLAND. *Treaties, etc.* [Diplomatic correspondence between England and France, 1802–3. With an appendix.] 117, 25p. *fol. n.p.* [1803?] *Wanting the title-page.*

18762 FITZ-ALBION, *pseud.* Fitz-Albion's letters to the Right Hon. William Pitt, and the Right Hon. Henry Addington, on the subject of the ministerial pamphlet entitled Cursory remarks on the state of parties, by a near observer: first published in the True Briton, and now re-published, revised, and corrected, with the addition of notes, &c. 128p. *8°*. 1803.

18763 [HEYWOOD, S.] Serious considerations, addressed to British labourers and mechanics, at the present crisis. 19p. *8°*. 1803.

18764 HUNTER, WILLIAM (*fl.* 1801). A vindication of the cause of Great Britain; with strictures on the insolent and perfidious conduct of France, since the signature of the Preliminaries of peace...The second edition. 84p. *8°*. 1803.

18765 IVERNOIS, SIR F. D'. Les cinq promesses. Tableau de la conduite du Gouvernement Consulaire envers la France, l'Angleterre, l'Italie, l'Allemagne, et surtout envers la Suisse. Seconde édition. Augmentée d'un supplément à l'introduction, et d'un appendice sur la Suisse. lxxvi, 279p. *8°*. *Londres & Hambourg,* 1803.

18766 LONDON, July 26, 1803. The declaration of the merchants, bankers, traders, and other inhabitants of London and its neighbourhood. [The report of a meeting and text of the declaration of loyalty there issued. Signed: Jacob Bosanquet.] *s.sh.fol.* [1803] [*Br.* 467]

18767 PITT, WILLIAM M. Thoughts on the defence of this kingdom, &c. Part III. p.101–156. *8°*. 1803. *Paginated in sequence with parts 1 & 2, for which see* 1796 *and* 1797.

18768 PUBLICOLA, *pseud.* Publicola's addresses. To the people of England; to the soldiers; and to the sailors. To which is added his postscript to the people of England. 22p. *12°*. 1803.

18769 [**SMITH**, SIR WILLIAM CUSACK, *2nd Bart.*] A letter to the Right Honourable William Wickham, Chief Secretary...of Ireland...on the subject of Mr. Scully's advice to his Catholic brethren...By a yeoman. 59p. *8°*. *Dublin*, 1803.

18770 **STEWART**, JOHN (1749–1822). The tocsin of social life: addressed to all the nations of the civilized world; in a discovery of the laws of nature relative to human existence. 96p. *8°*. 1803.

18771 **THOUGHTS** on the military relations of Great Britain and Ireland. 32p. *8°*. *Dublin*, 1803.

18772 [**WILLIAMS**, DAVID (1738–1816).] Regulations of parochial police; combined with the military and naval armaments to produce the energy and security of the whole nation. The fourth edition, corrected and enlarged. 43p. *8°*. 1803.

18773 A few **WORDS** to the friends of the poor, concerning an address to the labouring part of the community... 12p. *8°*. 1803.

SOCIALISM

18774 **SPENCE**, T. Dh'e 'imp'ort'ant tri'al ŏv T'om'is Sp'ens f'or a p'ol'it'ik'al p'amfl'et 'entitld "Dhĕ Rĕstorr ŏv sosiĕte tw ĭts nătĕŭrăl stat," on Ma 27th, 1801, 'at W'estm'instr H'o'ol, b'efor L'ord K'ene'un ănd a spĕshăl jwre. [With an edition of *The restorer of society*, which was read by Spence at the trial as part of his defence.] 84p. *12°*. 1803. *See also* 1807.

18775 —— Dh'e K'onst'itush'un 'ov Sp'ensone'a, a kŭntre ĭn Fare Lănd, sĭtuatĕd bĕtwen Utope'a' and Oshean'a: brŏŏt from dhĕns bi K'apt Sw'alo. 'And prĭntĕd ĭn dhĕ Spensoneăn mănr. 27p. *12°*. *n.p.* [1803 ?]

18776 —— Something to the purpose. A receipt to make a millenium or happy world. Being extracts from The constitution of Spensonia. *s.sh.fol.* [1803]

MISCELLANEOUS

18777 A **DIGEST** of the whole law now in force relating to volunteer corps in Great-Britain, Aug. 25, 1803. By a volunteer. 23p. *8°*. 1803. *The copy that belonged to David Ricardo.*

18778 **ENGLAND**. *Laws, etc.* A complete abstract of the Act for the general defence of the country...With an index...Passed the 17th of July, 1803. 23p. *8°*. *Leeds*, [1803]

18779 —— *Secretary of State for War and the Colonies.* Circular. [To Lords Lieutenant on the organization of the Militia. Signed: Hobart, i.e. Robert Hobart, Lord Hobart, afterwards 4th Earl of Buckinghamshire.] *s.sh.fol.* [*London*, 1803]

18780 [**HANKIN**, E.] Observations on the speech of Sir William Scott, and other matters relating to the Church; in which the fatal consequences of permitting the clergy to hold farms are stated, in a letter to a Member of Parliament. By a Kentish clergyman... 91p. *8°*. 1803.

18781 **HINTS** on a revisal of the statute 21st Hen. 8, ch. 13 concerning the residence of the clergy. Addressed to the members of both Houses of Parliament. By a clergyman in Hampshire. 21p. *8°*. *Salisbury, Winchester, &c.*, 1803.

18782 *****LONDON**. Livery Companies. *Salters.* A list of the Master, Wardens, Court of Assistants, and Livery, of the Worshipful Company of Salters. 11p. *8°*. 1803. *See also* 1784, 1787, 1790, 1792, 1794, 1797, 1799, 1801, 1806, 1809, 1812, 1815, 1818, 1821, 1824, 1827, 1830.

18783 **POOLE**, J. An account of moulds for casting Roman coins, found at and near Edington, in the county of Somerset...in a letter to C. J. Harford. Read [before the Society of Antiquaries] May 14, 1801. [From *The Archaeologia*, Vol. 14.] 6p. *4°*. [*London*, 1803]

18784 **RIVERS**, D. A discourse on patriotism, or the love of our country...The third edition, with additions and corrections. 20p. *8°*. 1803. *The copy that belonged to David Ricardo.*

1804

GENERAL

18785 **ADAMS**, JOHN Q., *President of the USA.* Letters on Silesia, written during a tour through that country in the years 1800, 1801...In two parts: Part I. Containing a journal of a tour through Silesia...in... 1800...Part II. Containing a complete geographical, statistical, and historical account of Silesia... 387p. *8°*. 1804.

18786 [**ASTON**, J.] The Manchester guide. A brief historical description of the towns of Manchester &

Salford, the public buildings, and the charitable and literary institutions. Illustrated by a map, exhibiting the improvements and additions made since the year 1770. 290p. *8°*. *Manchester & London*, 1804. *See also* 1816.

18787 **BELL**, ROBERT (*fl.* 1804). A description of the condition and manners as well as of the moral and political character, education, &c. of the peasantry of Ireland, such as they were between the years 1760 & 1790 ... 43p. *8°*. 1804.

18788 CHALMERS, G. An estimate of the comparative strength of Great Britain; and of the losses of her trade, from every war since the Revolution...A new edition, corrected and continued to 1803. To which is now annexed, Gregory King's celebrated State of England, with notices of his life. 367, 73p. *8°. 1804. For other editions, see 1782.*

For **COBBETT**, W. and **WRIGHT**, JOHN (1770?–1844), *eds.* Cobbett's Parliamentary debates [1803–12], *continued as* The Parliamentary debates, *ed. T. C. Hansard* [1812–29], *continued as* Hansard's Parliamentary debates [1829→], 1804→, *see vol.* III, *Periodicals list*, Hansard's Parliamentary debates.

18789 CORRY, JOHN. The life of Joseph Priestley... 60p. *12°. Birmingham, 1804.*

18790 COXE, W. Account of the Russian discoveries between Asia and America. To which are added, the conquest of Siberia, and the history of the transactions and commerce between Russia and China...The fourth edition, considerably enlarged. 380p. *4°. 1804.*

18791 DIEUDONNÉ, C. Statistique du Département du Nord... 2 vols. *8°. Douai, 1804.*

18792 DUTENS, J. M. Analyse raisonnée des principes fondamentaux de l'économie politique. 207p. *8°. Paris, 1804.*

18793 An **EAST-INDIA** register and directory, for 1804; corrected to the 1st January, 1804. Containing... lists of the Company's servants... Together with lists of the Europeans, mariners, &c. not in the service of the... Company; and merchant vessels employed in the country trade. Compiled...by John Mathison & Alexander Way Mason... p. 1–350. *12°. [1804] See also 1805, 1808, 1809, 1810, 1814, 1815, 1816, 1817, 1818, 1819, 1820, 1821, 1822, 1823, 1824, 1826, 1827, 1828, 1831, 1832, 1837, 1841, 1844.*

18794 EVANS, JOHN (*fl.* 1792–1812). Letters written during a tour through South Wales, in the year 1803, and at other times; containing views of the history, antiquities, and customs of that part of the Principality...with observations on its scenery, agriculture...trade and manufactures. 449p. *8°. 1804.*

18795 FRANCE. *Laws, etc.* Code civil des Français. Edition originale et seule officielle. 579p. *4°. Paris, 1804.* [*Binding 63*] *With the arms of Napoleon I stamped on the upper cover. See also 1808.*

18796 —— *Napoleon I, Emperor of the French.* No. 49 ...Décret impérial relatif à la compétence des tribunaux pour le jugement des contestations sur l'exercice des droits dans lesquels les émigrés rayés, éliminés ou amnistiés ont été restitués...Le 30 thermidor an XII. 3p. *4°. Paris,* [1804]

18797 GENTZ, F. VON. On the state of Europe before and after the French Revolution; being an answer to the work entitled De l'état de la Frence à la fin de l'an VIII [by Count A. M. Blanc de Lanautte]...Translated from the German by John Charles Herries, Esq. The fifth edition. cxxiv, 397p. *8°. 1804.*

18798 HOLCROFT, T. Travels from Hamburg, through Westphalia, Holland, and the Netherlands, to Paris. 2 vols. *4°. 1804.*

18799 *KENT'S directory: for 1804. Being an alphabetical list of the names and places of abode of the merchants & traders of London...To which is added, lists of the Lord Mayor & Court of Aldermen...directors of the Bank of England; East India, South Sea, Hudson's Bay, Russia, and London and West-India Dock Companies...Seventy-second edition. [With 'The shopkeeper's & tradesman's assistant: for 1804. Being a new... alphabetical list of all the stage coaches, carriers, coasting vessels, &c....'] 232, 154p. *8°. [1804] See also* 1740, 1816 (*Kent's original London directory*), 1825, 1826, 1827.

18800 The intercepted **LETTERS** taken on-board the Admiral Aplin East-Indiaman, translated from the Moniteur of the 16th of September: to which is prefixed the French official account of the engagement of Linois' squadron with the East-India fleet. 94p. *8°. 1804.*

18801 MAITLAND, JAMES, *8th Earl of Lauderdale.* An inquiry into the nature and origin of public wealth, and into the means and causes of its increase. 482p. *8°. Edinburgh & London, 1804. See also* 1808, 1819.

18802 —— Observations by the Earl of Lauderdale, on the review [by Lord Brougham] of his Inquiry into the nature and origin of public wealth, published in the VIIIth number of the Edinburgh Review. 88p. *8°. Edinburgh & London, 1804.*

18803 NECKER, J. Manuscrits de Mr. Necker, publiés par sa fille. [With 'Du caractère de Mr. Necker et de sa vie privée'. By Madame de Staël.] 153, 354p. *8°. Genève, an XIII* [1804]

18804 O'CONNOR afterwards **CONDORCET O'CONNOR**, A. Etat actuel de la Grande-Bretagne. 168p. *8°. Paris, 1804.*

18805 [**PARNELL**, W.] An inquiry into the causes of popular discontents in Ireland. By an Irish country gentleman. 74p. *8°. 1804.*

18806 RIDER'S British Merlin: for...1804...With notes of husbandry, fairs, marts, high roads...Compiled ...by Cardanus Rider. 60p. *12°. [1804] For other editions, see* 1693.

18807 ROBERTSON, WILLIAM (1721–1793). An historical disquisition concerning the knowledge which the ancients had of India; and the progress of trade with that country prior to the discovery of the passage to it by the Cape of Good Hope. With an appendix containing observations on the civil policy—the laws...of the Indians ...The fourth edition. 384p. *8°. London & Edinburgh, 1804. For other editions, see* 1791.

18808 The **ROYAL KALENDAR**: or, complete and correct annual register, for England, Scotland, Ireland, and America, for...1804...[With 'Debrett's Arms of the Peers'.] 87, xvi, 363p. *12°. [1804] For other editions, see* 1779.

18809 —— ⟨With additions.⟩ A companion to The royal kalendar, for...1804: being a list of all the changes in administration, from...1760...The seventy-ninth edition, carefully corrected. 120p. *12°. [1804] For another edition, see* 1791.

18810 [**SCHLOEZER**, A. L. VON.] Theorie der Statistik. Nebst Ideen über das Studium der Politik überhaupt. Erstes Heft. Einleitung. (*Stats Gelartheit.* Zweiter Theil. *Allgemeine Statistik,* 1.) 150p. *8°. Göttingen, 1804.*

18811 [**SILVA LISBOA**, J. DA.] Principios de economia politica, para servir de introducção a' tentativa economica do author dos Principios de direito mercantil. 202p. *4°. Lisboa, 1804.*

18812 SMITH, ADAM. A complete analysis, or abridgment of Dr. Adam Smith's Inquiry into the nature and causes of the wealth of nations. By Jeremiah Joyce... The second edition. 324p. *8º. Cambridge*, 1804. *For editions of the complete work, see* 1776.

18813 SVEDENSTIERNA, E. T. Resa, igemon en del af England och Skottland, åren 1802 och 1803. 329p. *8º. Stockholm*, 1804.

18814 TIGHE, R. S. Observations and reflections on the state of Ireland: respectfully submitted to the consideration of the British nation. 83p. *8º.* 1804.

18815 WAKEFIELD, DANIEL (1776–1846). An essay upon political œconomy; being an inquiry into the truth of the two positions of the French œconomists; that labour employed in manufactures is unproductive; and that all taxes ultimately fall upon...land...Second edition. [With 'Appendix: being a review of the Réflexions sur la formation et la distribution des richesses de M. Turgot'.] 120p. *8º.* 1804. *For another edition, see* 1799 (Inquiry into the truth of the two positions of the French œconomists...).

18816 YORKE, H. R. Letters from France, in 1802... 2 vols. *8º.* 1804.

AGRICULTURE

18817 AMOS, W. Minutes in agriculture and planting ...Illustrated with specimens of...natural grasses, and ...drawings and descriptions of ...practical machines... 92p. *4º. Boston [Lincs.] & London*, 1804.

18818 BARTLEY, N. A series of letters on the national importance, as well as the individual benefit, of extending the growth of fine clothing wool, by interbreeding with Spanish rams and British ewes... 84p. *8º. Bath, London, &c.*, 1804.

18819 BATH AND WEST OF ENGLAND SOCIETY. Rules, orders, and premiums, of the Bath and West of England Society...With a list of the members of the Society, and of the premiums granted in 1803. 76p. *8º. Bath*, 1804. *See also* 1777.

18820 BOARD OF AGRICULTURE. Communications to the Board of Agriculture; on subjects relative to the husbandry, and internal improvement of the country. Vol. I. [–Vol. II.] The second edition. *4º. London, Edinburgh, &c.*, 1804–5. *A new edition of the first two volumes only of the* Communications, *printed 1797–1800* (*q.v.* 1797). *In a set with second copies of Vols. 3–6, 1802–8.*

18821 —— Premiums offered by the Board...1804. 16p. *8º.* [1804] *The Sheffield copy. See also* 1808, 1809, 1810, 1812, 1816, 1818.

18822 COOTE, SIR C., *Bart., of Donnybrook.* Statistical survey of the county of Armagh, with observations on the means of improvement; drawn up in the years 1802, and 1803...under the direction of the Dublin Society. 395, 33p. *8º. Dublin*, 1804.

18823 DIXON, JOHN, *of Kensington.* Improvement of the fisheries; letter V. Or a plan for establishing a nursery for disbanded seamen and soldiers, and increasing the strength...of the British Empire. 51p. *4º.* 1804. *For the first part, see* 1800; *for the second, third and fourth parts, see* 1801, 1802 *and* 1803 *respectively.*

18824 ESTCOURT, T. An account of the result of an effort to better the condition of the poor in a country village [Long Newnton]: and some regulations suggested, by which the same might be extended to other parishes... Presented to the Board of Agriculture. 16p. *4º.* 1804.

18825 FORSYTH, R. The principles and practice of agriculture, systematically explained...being a treatise compiled for the fourth edition of the Encyclopædia Britannica, and revised and enlarged. 2 vols. *8º. Edinburgh & London*, 1804.

18826 FRANCE. *Conseil des Mines.* Extrait des registres des délibérations du Gouvernement de la République. Paris, le premier germinal an 12...[A grant of a mining concession in the Département de Vaucluse.] *s.sh.fol. Avignon*, [1804]

18827 HARRISON, E. An inquiry into the rot in sheep; and other animals; in which a connection is pointed out between it, and some obscure and important disorders, in the human constitution. 56p. *8º.* 1804.

18828 MARSHALL, W. On the landed property of England, an elementary and practical treatise; containing the purchase, the improvement, and the management of landed estates. 444p. *4º.* 1804. *See also* 1806.

18829 March 9. 1804...**MEMORIAL** for John Gray, Esq. of Scotstown, defender in the original action... against Colonel John Spens of Stenlaw, Robert Gray for Westmuir Coal Company, James M'Nair of Greenfield, James Farie younger of Farm, and William Dixon for Govan Coal Company, pursuers of the original action. [Concerning mining rights on the property of John Gray. Signed: Ar. Fletcher. With an appendix.] 18, 7p. *4º. n.p.* [1804]

18830 PARKER, T. N. An essay on the construction, hanging, and fastening of gates; exemplified in six quarto plates. Second edition; improved and enlarged. 116p. *8º.* 1804. *For another edition, see* 1801.

18831 A PROJECT for extending the breed of fine-wooled Spanish sheep, now in the possession of His Majesty, into all parts of Great Britain, where the growth of fine clothing wools is found to be profitable. 3p. *4º.* [*London*, 1804] *Attributed to Sir Joseph Banks by C. P. Lasteyrie in his* An Account of the introduction of merino sheep into...Europe, *1810* (*q.v. p. 122*). *The Sheffield copy.*

18832 SUFFOLK. A plan, offered to the consideration of the publick, for letting farms, in order to avoid hazardous speculation. 18p. *8º. Ipswich*, 1804.

18833 SUSSEX AGRICULTURAL SOCIETY. At a general meeting of the subscribers of the ...Society, to arrange the prizes and premiums for the present year, held at the White-Hart Inn, Lewes, May 19, 1804, the following resolutions were agreed to. *s.sh.fol. Lewes*, 1804. *The Sheffield copy. See also* 1801, 1805, 1807, 1808.

18834 UNITED STATES OF AMERICA. *Congress.* Report of the committee, to whom it was referred, on the fifteenth of November last, the report of a select committee made at the last session of Congress, on the subject of the fisheries of the United States, with instruction to enquire and report whether any, and if any, what measures are necessary for the encouragement of the whale and cod-fisheries... 8, [4]p. *8º. n.p.* [1804]

18835 —— *Treasury Department*. Letter from the Secretary of the Treasury, addressed to William Lattimore, on the subject of lands south of the State of Tennessee. Accompanying a Bill, further to amend an Act, intituled, "An Act, regulating the grants of land... south of the state of Tennessee;" presented, the 31st of December, 1804. 8p. *8°. Washington City, 1804.*

18836 Oeconomisch-praktisches **WIRTSCHAFTS-BUCH** für Haus- und Landwirthe auf jeden Monath des Jahres...Neue verbesserte Auflage. 260p. *4°. Nürnberg,* 1804.

18837 WISSETT, R. On the cultivation and preparation of hemp; as also, of an article, produced in various parts of India, called sunn, which...may be introduced as a substitute for many uses to which hemp is...applied. Compiled from various authorities, by Robert Wissett... 221p. *4°. 1804. See also 1808.*

18838 YOUNG, ARTHUR (1741–1820). The farmer's calendar: containing the business necessary to be performed on various kinds of farms during every month of the year...A new edition, greatly enlarged and improved. 575p. *8°. 1804. For other editions, see 1771.*

18839 —— General view of the agriculture of Hertfordshire. Drawn up for the consideration of the Board of Agriculture...By the Secretary to the Board. 236p. *8°. London, Edinburgh, &c., 1804. See also 1813.*

18840 —— General view of the agriculture of the county of Norfolk. Drawn up for the consideration of the Board of Agriculture...By the Secretary of the Board. 532p. *8°. London, Edinburgh, &c., 1804.*

18841 —— General view of the agriculture of the county of Suffolk; drawn up for the consideration of the Board of Agriculture...By the Secretary to the Board. Third edition. 432p. *8°. London, Edinburgh, 1804. For other editions, see 1794.*

CORN LAWS

18842 COMMITTEE OF MERCHANTS OF WATERFORD. Observations by the Committee... on the Report of the Committee of the House of Commons of the 14th instant, on the petitions of six counties respecting the corn laws of Great Britain. [Dated: May 30, 1804, and signed in manuscript, Rob*t*. Hunt, chairman.] [4]p. *fol. n.p.* [1804] *The Sheffield copy, sent through the post from Waterford.*

18843 [**GIDDY,** afterwards **GILBERT,** D.] Cursory observations on the Act for ascertaining the bounties, and for regulating the exportation and importation of corn. By a Member of Parliament. 16p. *8°. 1804.*

18844 SMITH, CHARLES. Tracts on the corn-trade and corn-laws...A new edition [by George Chalmers]. With additions from the marginal manuscripts of Mr. Catherwood. To which is now added a supplement of interesting pieces on the same subject. With some account of the life of Mr. Smith. 323, 54p. *8°. 1804. For other editions, see 1766.*

TRADES & MANUFACTURES

18845 COMBRUNE, M. The theory and practice of brewing...A new edition. Corrected and greatly enlarged by the author. 367p. *8°. 1804. For another edition, see 1762.*

18846 MAXWELL, JOHN I. The victuallers advocate. With remarks upon the discretionary power of magistrates, in granting licences, and a late resolution of the sessions; with observations relative to brewers leases, particularly interesting to publicans and the consumers of porter... 46p. *8°. 1804.*

18847 PENNSYLVANIA SOCIETY FOR THE ENCOURAGEMENT OF MANUFACTURES AND THE USEFUL ARTS. A communication from the Pennsylvania Society... 28p. *8°. Philadelphia,* 1804.

18848 PLOMER, T. The speech of Thomas Plomer, Esq. addressed to the Committee of the House of Commons, to whom a Bill to repeal certain regulations & restrictions, contained in various Acts of Parliament, relating to the woollen trade, had been referred; on his opening the case of the manufactures...on the 24th and 25th of May 1803... 90p. *8°. Glocester & London,* 1804.

18849 RHYND, M. The third edition, considerably enlarged, and very much improved. Rhynd's printers' guide: being a new and correct list of master printers, in London and its vicinity: together with the letter-founders, joiners, printers' smiths, &c. To which are added, the Greek, Hebrew, and Arabic alphabets, the scales of prices, schemes for imposing, and other important information. 40p. *12°. 1804.*

18850 SAINT VINCENT, PHILO, *pseud.* A reply to a pamphlet intituled "A brief enquiry into the present condition of the Navy of Great Britain": wherein is clearly demonstrated the force of the enemy, and what was opposed to it by the late Board of Admiralty; as well as the actual strength possessed by the King's dock-yards, and their ability to keep up and encrease the Navy without the aid of merchant builders. 36p. *8°. 1804.*

COMMERCE

18851 ABBOTT, C., *Baron Tenterden.* A treatise of the law relative to merchant ships and seamen...The second edition, with additions. 463p. *8°. 1804.*

18852 [**BENTLEY,** THOMAS R.] A brief appeal to the honour and conscience of the nation, upon the necessity of an immediate restitution of the Spanish plate ships...By the author of the "Cursory remarks". 39p. *8°. 1804.*

18853 CHILD, SIR J., *Bart.* A new discourse of trade ...A new edition. 224p. *12°. 1804. For other editions, see 1690.*

18854 COCK, S. An answer to Lord Sheffield's pamphlet, on the subject of the navigation system; proving, that the Acts deviating therefrom...were beneficial to our trade and navy, in the last war, and ought to be renewed in the present. 74p. *8⁰.* 1804.

18855 COWELL, JOHN and G. West India Dock Company. The important trial John and George Cowell versus George Smith, Esquire, Treasurer to the said Company, upon the question of cooperage on rums. Tried...March 7th, 1804. In which Mr. Garrow's speech ...is given verbatim. 29p. *8⁰.* 1804.

18856 DUBOST, D. The merchants' assistant, or a treatise on exchanges and arbitrations of exchanges, bullion and dollars; and merchandise. Containing every information on the commerce of London with the principal places of Europe. 208p. *8⁰.* 1804.

18857 GARONNE, . Réflexions sur le commerce de France... 134p. *8⁰. Paris,* 1804.

18858 HOLROYD, J. B., *Earl of Sheffield.* Strictures on the necessity of inviolably maintaining the navigation and colonial system of Great Britain. 65p. *8⁰.* 1804. *Presentation copy, with inscription, from the author to George Chalmers. See also 1806.*

18859 JACKSON, JOHN (*d.* 1807). Reflections on the commerce of the Mediterranean...Containing a particular account of the traffic of the kingdoms of Algiers, Tunis, Sardinia, Naples & Sicily; the Morea, &c....With an impartial examination into the manners and customs of the inhabitants, in their commercial dealings. And a particular description of the British manufactures properly adapted for each country... 192p. *8⁰.* 1804.

18860 LIVERPOOL BREAD COMMITTEE. Report from the Liverpool Bread Committee, met with a view to prevent the measures recommended by a Committee of the House of Commons, for an advance in the price of corn, from passing into law. And also to point out measures for procuring, at all times, a constant, regular, and cheap supply of foreign corn, when wanted, without detriment to the British farmer. 36, [4]p. *8⁰. [Liverpool,* 1804]

18861 [MILL, JAMES.] An essay of the impolicy of a bounty on the exportation of grain; and on the principles which ought to regulate the commerce of grain... 70p. *8⁰.* 1804.

18862 MONTEFIORE, J. The trader's and manufacturer's compendium; containing the laws, customs, and regulations, relative to trade; intended for the use of wholesale and retail dealers... 2 vols. *8⁰. London, Liverpool, &c.,* 1804.

18863 NEWMAN, S. A collection of mercantile tables, upon a new...method...Adapted to the use of the public offices, bankers, merchants, lawyers &c. Containing ...universal buying and selling tables...Simple interest tables...Commission brokerage, or discount tables... Wine table...Annuity and compound interest tables... Tables of Irish exchanges... 367, [79]p. *8⁰.* [1804]

18864 Some general **OBSERVATIONS** on the present practice of carrying on the coal-trade in the Metropolis, by persons who are well acquainted with the subject...also pointing out to the public those means which the existing laws have provided for the prevention of fraud in the admeasurement... 29p. *8⁰.* 1804.

18865 *RAYNAL, G. T. F. A philosophical and political history of the settlements and trade of the Europeans in the East and West Indies...With a new set of maps...and a copious index. 6 vols. *12⁰. Edinburgh & Glasgow,* 1804. *The De Morgan copy. For other editions, see* 1773.

18866 REINHARD, C. Ueber die Wichtigkeit des englischen Handels im gegenwärtigen Kriege... 63p. *8⁰. Hamburg,* [1804]

18867 —— Observations on the present state of the British commerce; including strictures on the extent, importance, influence, advantages, and probable increase of the trade of Great Britain, with all parts of the world. Translated from the German...With notes and considerable additions, by the editor. [Translator's preface signed: J. W. H.] 58p. *8⁰.* 1804. *See also* 1805.

18868 WALLACE, A., & CO. Another important trial with the West-India Dock-Company! A. Wallace & Co. versus G. Smith, Esq. Treasurer to the said company, tried March 7, 1804...relative to an order, dated October 25, 1803, prohibiting brokers & agents from following their accustomed business, including the substance of Mr. Garrow's speech. 18p. *8⁰.* 1804.

COLONIES

18869 [COLEBROOKE, H. T.] Remarks on the husbandry and internal commerce of Bengal. 198p. *8⁰. Calcutta,* 1804. *See also* 1806.

18870 COLLINS, DAVID (1756–1810). An account of the English colony in New South Wales, from its first settlement in January 1788, to August 1801: with remarks on the dispositions, customs...&c. of the native inhabitants of that country. To which are added, some particulars of New Zealand; compiled...from the MSS. of Lieutenant-Governor King: and an account of a voyage performed by Captain Flinders and Mr. Bass...Abstracted from the journal of Mr. Bass...The second edition [abridged and edited by M. Collins]. 562p. *4⁰.* 1804.

18871 PERCIVAL, R. An account of the Cape of Good Hope; containing an historical view of its original settlement by the Dutch, its capture by the British in 1795 ...Also a sketch of its geography, productions, the manners and customs of the inhabitants, &c.&c. With a view of the political and commercial advantages which might be derived from its possession by Great Britain. 339p. *4⁰.* 1804.

18872 PICTON, SIR T. A letter addressed to the Rt. Hon. Lord Hobart...106p. *8⁰.* 1804. *Written in reply to* A statement, letters and documents respecting the affairs of Trinidad, including a reply to Col. Picton's Address to the Council of that island, *by W. Fullarton.*

18873 [STEPHEN, J.] The opportunity; or, reasons for an immediate alliance with St. Domingo. By the author of "The crisis of the sugar colonies". 156p. *8⁰.* 1804.

FINANCE

18874 BANK OF ENGLAND. A list of the names of all such proprietors of the Bank of England, who are qualified to vote at the ensuing election...March 20th, 1804. 18p. *fol.* [1804] *See also* 1738, 1749, 1750, 1789, 1790, 1791, 1792, 1793, 1794, 1795, 1796, 1797, 1798, 1799, 1801, 1803, 1808, 1809, 1812, 1816, 1819, 1836, 1843.

For **BANQUE DE FRANCE,** Assemblée-Générale des actionnaires de la Banque de France...1804–1900, *see* vol. III, *Periodicals list,* Assemblée-Générale.

18875 —— Recueil des pièces relatives au régime de la Banque de France. 234p. *4°. Paris,* 1804. *A collection of laws, comptes-rendus, and annual lists of the 200 actionnaires qualified to form the Assemblée générale in each of the years 1800–1803. Parts of this volume appear to have been reissued in 1839 with the annual comptes-rendus, etc., of the years 1804–1839, with the general title:* Recueil des discours et comptes rendus depuis 1800 jusques et compris 1839. *A copy of this reissue, from the library of the Duc de Broglie, is catalogued with the annual comptes-rendus in vol. III.*

18876 BLEWERT, W. Tables, formed on a new and easy principle, for calculating the value of stocks and annuities, and for a ready dispatch of business in the public funds...The second edition, improved. 409p. *16°.* 1804.

18877 BOASE, H. A letter to the Right Hon. Lord King, in defence of the conduct of the Directors of the Banks of England and Ireland, whom his Lordship (in a publication entitled "Thoughts on the restriction of payments in specie", &c.&c.) accuses of abuse of their privilege. With remarks on the cause of the great rise of the exchange between Dublin and London, and the means of equalizing it. 52p. *8°.* 1804.

18878 BOSSE, R. H. B. Grundzüge des Finanzwesens im römischen Staate... 2 vols. *8°. Braunschweig & Leipzig,* 1804.

18879 CHETTLE, J. The public taxes of England & Scotland, for the year ending 5th January, 1804; shewing, at one view, what each article produced, expence of management, &c.... 16p. *8°.* 1804.

18880 A candid **COBLER'S** cursory and critical conjectures on ex-change and small-change, on balance of trade, on balance of remittance, on circulating medium and kite-flying...[A series of four letters, signed with various pseudonyms, addressed to *The Hibernian Journal* during March 1804.] 46p. *8°. n.p.,* 1804.

18881 EURE-ET-LOIR, *Département d'.* Chartres, ce 6 fructidor an 12. Le préfet du département d'Eure et Loir, aux maires. [*Begin.*] Messieurs, afin de faire cesser les difficultés qui s'élèvent chaque jour pour l'admission ...des monnaies de 3 livres, 24 sous, 12 sous & 6 sous, qui ne conservent que de légères traces de leur empreinte primitive, le gouvernement vient d'ordonner... [2]p. *4°. n.p.* [1804]

18882 FOSTER, JOHN L. An essay on the principle of commercial exchanges, and more particularly of the exchange between Great Britain and Ireland: with an inquiry into the practical effects of the bank restrictions. 209p. *8°.* 1804.

18883 FRANCE. *Napoleon Bonaparte, First Consul.* Arrêté portant réglement sur l'Administration des Monnaies. Du 10 prairial an XI. 12p. *4°. Paris,* thermidor an XII [1804]

18884 —— —— No. 1931...Loi relative aux maisons de prêt sur nantissement. Paris le 16 pluviôse an XII... 10p. *4°. Paris,* [1804]

18885 —— *Napoleon I, Emperor of the French.* No. 20... Decret impérial concernant les monts-de-piété et les maisons de prêt sur nantissement. Au Palais de Saint-Cloud, le 24 messidor an XII. 3p. *4°. Paris,* [1804]

18886 —— —— Décret impérial relatif aux pièces de trois livres, vingt-quatre sous, douze sous et six sous... le 25 thermidor an 12. [2]p. *4°. Paris,* [1804]

18886A —— [Another edition.] 2p. *4°.* [*Paris,* 1804]

18887 FREND, W. The principles of taxation... in which it is shewn, that if every man pays in proportion to the stake he has in the country, the present...system of taxation, the Custom House, and the Excise Office, may be abolished, and the National Debt gradually and easily paid off. 72p. *8°.* 1804. *For another edition, see* 1799.

18888 HEGEWISCH, D. H. Historischer Versuch über die römischen Finanzen. 385p. *8°. Altona,* 1804.

18889 HUIE, J. An abridgment of all the Statutes now in force, relative to the revenue of excise in Great Britain...The second edition, revised, and brought down to the end of...1803. 654p. *8°. Edinburgh & London,* 1804.

18890 KING, PETER, *7th Baron King.* Thoughts on the effects of the bank restrictions...The second edition, enlarged, including some remarks on the coinage. 178p. *8°.* 1804. *Interleaved, with extensive manuscript notes by Henry Thornton, M.P. These were printed in the 1939 edition of Thornton's* An Enquiry into the nature and effects of the paper credit, 1802. *For another edition of Lord King's work, see* 1803.

18891 LONDON. Livery Companies. *Goldsmiths' Company.* Assay Office, Goldsmiths' Hall, London. [A table of duty payable on silver and gold on and after 10th October 1804. Signed: Thomas Lane, accomptant.] *s.sh.fol.* [*London,* 1804] *See note to no.* 13563.

18892 MAGENS, M. D. An inquiry into the real difference between actual money, consisting of gold and silver, and paper money of various descriptions. Also, an examination into the constitutions of banks; and the impossibility of their combining the two characters of bank and exchequer. 68p. *8°.* 1804.

18893 NETHERLANDS. *Batavian Republic.* Prys-courant van obligatien en andere effecten, zoo als dezelven op den 2den january 1804 ter Beurze van Amsterdam zyn geweest. Opgemaakt naar aanleiding der tauxatie daar van door de beëedigde makelaars G. W. van Ophoven, J. A. Jourdany, J. Jarman, J. D. Mercker, B. Everard, S. en D. Saportas, J. Groeneboer, G. Blanken en F. Huskus, gedaan. [4]p. *fol. den Haag,* 1804.

18894 —— —— Prys-courant van obligatien en andere effecten, zoo also dezelven op den 2den july 1804 ter Beurze van Amsterdam zyn geweest. Opgemaakt naar aanleiding der tauxatie daar van door de beëedigde makelaars G. W. van Ophoven, J. A. Jourdany, J. Jarman, J. D. Mercker, B. Everard, S. en D. Saportas,

J. Groeneboer, G. Blanken en F. Huskus, gedaan. [4]p. *fol. den Haag,* 1804. *See also* 1796, 1797, 1800, 1801, 1802, 1803.

18895 —— —— Publicatie van het Staats-Bewind der Bataafsche Republiek, houdende het plan eener vrywillige geld-negotiatie. Geärresteerd den 19 maart 1804. 35p. *8°. den Haag,* 1804.

18896 —— —— Publicatie van het Staats-Bewind der Bataafsche Republiek, bepalende eenige straffen en boeten, wegens met splitsen en verkoopen van heele of gedetten van loten in de vrywillige negotiatie-lotery, gearresteerd den 19 maart 1804, door, daar toe, onbevoegden. Geärresteerd den 23 april 1804. 4p. *8°. den Haag,* 1804.

18897 —— —— Publicatie van het Staats-Bewind... tegen het verlaten dezer Republiek, door einige ingezetenen, alvorens genoegzame borgtocht voor derzelver verschuldigde in de onderschiedene gearresteerde en nog te arresteeren geldheffingen te hebben gesteld. Geärresteerd den 27 april 1804. 4p. *8°. den Haag,* 1804.

18898 —— —— Publicatie van het Staats-Bewind der Bataafsche Republiek, wegens eene voorbetaling in den eersten termijn der buitengewoone belasting op de bezittingen en inkomsten, gearresteerd den 9 july 1804, onder genot van Korting. Geärresteerd den 30 augustus 1804. 7p. *8°. den Haag,* 1804.

18899 —— —— Publicatie van het Staats-Bewind der Bataafsche Republiek, wegens eene voorbetaling in den tweeden termijn der buitengewoone belasting op de bezittingen en inkomsten, gearresteerd den 9 july 1804, onder genot van Korting. Geärresteerd den 17 november 1804. [4]p. *8°. den Haag,* 1804.

18900 Desultory **OBSERVATIONS** on the Act of the last session of Parliament, entitled, "An Act for granting to His Majesty...a contribution on the profits arising from property, professions, trade, and offices "... By a landholder. 55p. *8°. London & Edinburgh,* 1804.

18901 **OBSERVATIONS** on the exchange between London and Dublin. By a merchant of Dublin. 14p. *8°. Dublin,* 1804.

18902 **PARNELL**, H. B., *Baron Congleton.* Observations upon the state of currency in Ireland, and upon the course of exchange between Dublin and London. 59p. *8°. Dublin,* 1804.

18903 —— The second edition... 63p. *8°. Dublin,* 1804.

18904 —— Third edition...[With an additional appendix.] 92p. *8°.* 1804. *See also* 1805.

18905 **PLUNDER** and partition! As practised on the continental neighbours of France, by Napoleon I. Explained to the British public, by an Englishman. 63p. *8°.* 1804.

18906 A **REFUTATION** of some doctrines relating to the Sinking Fund, &c.&c. contained in a work lately published by the Earl of Lauderdale; with original remarks on different subjects of political economy. By a member of the Middle-Temple. 51p. *8°.* 1804.

18907 [**ROSNY**, A. J. N. DE.] Histoire secrète d'un écu de six livres; transformé en une pièce de cinq francs; contenant sa naissance et son entrée dans le monde sous Louis XIV; ses aventures sous Louis XVI; ses malheurs... sous le règne de la terreur; son émigration...sous Robespierre...et sa métamorphose sous le consulat de Bonaparte. Par l'auteur du Péruvian à Paris. 163p. *12°. Paris,* 1804.

18908 **SOULET**, P. Traité des changes et arbitrages, précédés des autres calculs relatifs au commerce, par des méthodes neuves, simples et expéditives... 454p. *8°. Paris,* an XII [1804] *See also* 1808.

TRANSPORT

18909 **ANDREOSSI**, A. F., *Comte.* Histoire du Canal du Midi, ou Canal de Languedoc, considéré sous les rapports d'invention, d'art, d'administration, d'irrigation, et dans ses relations avec les étangs de l'intérieur des terres qui l'avoisinent...Nouvelle édition, mise dans un nouvel ordre, et considérablement augmentée... 2 vols. *4°. Paris,* 1804.

18910 **BERTRAND**, P. M. Mémoire et discussion sur les moyens de rendre le Doubs navigable, pour opérer la jonction du Rhône au Rhin, suivant le projet imprimé en mars 1792, avec application à plusieurs autres rivières, ou système de navigation fluviale...Seconde édition. 31p. *4°. Paris,* 1804.

18911 **ENGLAND.** *Commissioners appointed for Improving and Completing the Navigation of the Rivers Thames and Isis.* Bye-laws, rules, orders, and regulations, to be observed and kept, by the barge-masters, costbearers, barge-men, pound-keepers, lock-shutters, horse-towers and all persons concerned in the navigation, of the rivers Thames and Isis...made...at a general meeting of the Commissioners...the 18th day of August...1804. — And also the fines and penalties...appointed to be inflicted for breach of...the said bye-laws... 18p. *12°. Henley,* [1804]

18912 **Q.**, P. Observations on the West India Dock salaries, in a letter addressed to Randle Jackson, Esq.... 16p. *8°.* 1804.

18913 **THOUGHTS** on the propriety of granting a pecuniary remuneration to the West India Dock directors; with a view of the situations of the directors of the Bank of England, of the East India Company, and the Imperial Assurance Office, as far as they apply to that proposition. 31p. *8°.* 1804. *Presentation copy from the anonymous author to Lord Sheffield.*

SOCIAL CONDITIONS

18914 **ACCOUNT** of the Lying-in Charity for Delivering Poor Married Women at their own Habitations [later the Royal Maternity Charity]. Instituted 1757. 62p. *8°.* 1804. *For another edition, see* 1770.

18915 **CUMING**, R. An address to the people of the United Kingdoms on the cow pox inoculation, setting forth the manifold advantages it enjoys over the small-pox inoculation...with a variety of important observations...

relative to government, the Royal Navy, Army, &c....
44p. *8°. Romsey, London, &c.*, [1804 ?]

18916 FILKES, J. A sermon, in behalf of those useful and benevolent institutions, called friendly societies; preached at Navestock, Essex, August, 1802... The second edition. 22p. *8°. London & Oxford,* 1804.

18917 FRANCE. *Conseil d'Etat.* No. 12...Extrait des minutes de la Secrétairerie d'Etat...Le 18 prairial an XII. Avis du Conseil d'Etat, sur les actes de divorce faits pendant la disparition des émigrés ou absens; du 11 prairial an XII. 2p. *4°. Paris,* [1804]

18918 GREEN, WILLIAM (*fl.* 1788–1818). Plans of economy; or the road to ease and independence...The sixth edition, considerably improved. 86p. *8°.* [1804 ?] *See also* 1806, 1812.

18919 GREGORY, JAMES. Review of the proceedings of the Royal College of Physicians in Edinburgh, from 1753 to 1804, both inclusive; with respect to separating the practice of medicine from the practice of pharmacy, and preventing any of their own fellows or licentiates residing in Edinburgh, from keeping an apothecary's shop or practising pharmacy by himself, his copartners or his servants. 32p. *4°. Edinburgh,* 1804. *Presentation copy from the author to Henry Stewart of Allanton.*

18920 HORSLEY, S., *Bishop of St. Asaph.* Substance of the Bishop of St. Asaph's speech, in the House of Peers, on Monday, July the 23d, 1804, upon the motion for the third reading of the Bill entituled An Act for the relief of certain incumbents of livings, in the City of London. 40p. *8°.* 1804.

18921 INCORPORATION OF BAKERS, *Edinburgh.* Contract by the Incorporation of Bakers of the City of Edinburgh. [Concerning a fund for annuities to the widows of members.] 16p. *8°. Edinburgh,* 1804.

18922 KING, JOHN (*fl.* 1783–1805). Remarks on imprisonment for debt, on the recent progress of the law and increase of lawyers. The second edition. 39p. *8°.* 1804.

18923 LOVELASS, P. A proposed practicable plan, for such a speedy easement of the poor rates throughout England; as that in...few years the parishes may be eased of one fourth, if not of one third, part of their present burthens... 32p. *8°.* 1804.

18924 ⟨Bill Chamber.⟩ February 28, 1804...**MEMORIAL** for David George, Alexander Cowie, James Anderson, William Aitken, and William Fleming, for themselves, and the other compositor-printers of the City of Edinburgh; against Mr. David Ramsay, printer in Edinburgh, for himself, and in behalf of the other master printers in Edinburgh [that the Court may adjudicate in a wages dispute. Signed: George Jos. Bell. With an appendix.] 26, 16p. *4°.* [*Edinburgh,* 1804]

18925 —— ⟨Bill Chamber.⟩ May 12, 1804...Additional memorial for David George, Alexander Cowie [and others]...for themselves and the other compositor-printers of the City of Edinburgh; against Mr. David Ramsay, printer in Edinburgh, for himself, and in behalf of the other master-printers in Edinburgh. [Signed: George Jos. Bell. With an appendix.] 9, 2p. *4°.* [*Edinburgh,* 1804]

18926 The **MEMORIAL** of the journeymen calico printers, and others connected with their trade. [Praying Parliament that masters may be restrained by law from taking too many apprentices, and thereby preventing journeymen from finding employment.] 23p. *8°.* 1804. *Addressed in manuscript to the Hon. Edward Phipps.*

18927 [**MILBURNE,** H.] An inquiry into the causes which produce...febrile contagious diseases, in Newcastle and Gateshead; with a detail of interesting facts, relative to the fever which prevailed in the months of October and November last...By a Member of the College of Surgeons in London, &c., &c., &c. 72p. *8°. Newcastle, Durham, &c.,* 1804. *Presentation copy, with inscription, from the author to J. H. Frere.*

18928 PITT, WILLIAM M. A plan for the improvement of the internal police of prisons. 16p. *8°.* 1804.

18929 November 20, 1804...**REPORT** in the process, the journeymen compositor printers in Edinburgh, against the master printers. [Signed: Robert Bell, and dated, September 5, 1804. Containing tables of wages paid in Edinburgh printing houses in the 1770's, in 1791 and 1802.] 30p. *4°.* [*Edinburgh,* 1804]

18930 ROSS, JOHN. A few loose remarks on the advantages of friendly societies; and also, on a scheme for supporting the widows and orphans of teachers. 32p. *8°. Edinburgh,* 1804.

18931 SOCIETY FOR BETTERING THE CONDITION OF THE POOR, *London.* Extract from an account of the Ladies Society for the education and employment of the female poor. 32p. *8°. London, York, &c.,* 1804.

18932 SOCIETY FOR THE SUPPRESSION OF VICE. An address to the public, from the Society... instituted, in London, 1802, part the second, containing an account of the proceedings of the Society from its original institution. 98p. *8°.* 1804. *For* Part the first, *see* 1803.

18933 TROTTER, T. An essay, medical, philosophical, and chemical, on drunkenness, and its effects on the human body. 203p. *8°.* 1804. *The Turner copy.*

18934 —— The second edition, corrected and enlarged. 211p. *8°.* 1804. *The Turner copy. See also* 1810.

SLAVERY

18935 BRITANNICUS, *pseud.* A letter to the Right Hon. William Pitt, containing some new arguments against the abolition of the slave trade. 33p. *8°.* 1804.

18936 [**BROUGHAM,** H. P., *Baron Brougham and Vaux.*] A concise statement of the question regarding the abolition of the slave trade. [With 'Appendix to the concise statement'.] 108p. *8°.* 1804.

18937 [——] Second edition. 108p. *8°.* 1804. *The Sheffield copy.*

18938 [**HARRISON,** GEORGE, *Quaker.*] Notices on the slave-trade: in reference to the present state of the British Isles. 20p. *8°.* 1804.

18939 *Addressed to the serious consideration of the peers. No **SLAVES**—no sugar. Containing new and irresistible arguments in favour of the African trade. By a Liverpool merchant. 64p. *8°.* 1804. *The copy that belonged to Beilby Porteus, Bishop of London.*

POLITICS

18940 ADRESSE à tous les souverains de l'Europe. Le 5 février 1804. [On revenging the death of the Duc d'Enghien.] 34p. *8°. Londres*, 1804.

18941 A short **APPEAL** to the good sense of the people of the United Kingdom...occasioned by reading A plain answer to the misrepresentations and calumnies contained in the Cursory remarks of a near observer. 63p. *8°.* [1804]

18942 BURDETT, SIR F., *Bart.* A full report of the speeches of Sir Francis Burdett at the late election...The legal arguments upon the last day of the election, particularly the admired speech of Mr. Plumer, are given at full length: together with a selection of the papers published during the election; and a preface. 94p. *8°. London, Nottingham, &c.*, 1804.

18943 CARRET, M. Tribunat. Opinion de Carret... sur la motion d'ordre relative au gouvernement héréditaire. Séance extraordinaire du 11 floréal an 12. 7p. *8°.* [*Paris*,] an 12 [1804]

18944 CATHOLIC POLITICS, including some hints for tranquillizing Ireland. In a dialogue between a Popish priest and a Roman Catholic gentleman. By a Milesian. 27p. *4°. Dublin*, 1804.

18945 The **CONDUCT** and character of the late and present administration considered by a national observer. 70p. *8°.* 1804.

18946 [**COURTENAY**, T. P.] A plain answer to the misrepresentations and calumnies contained in the Cursory remarks of a near observer. By a more accurate observer. Fifth edition. 88p. *8°.* 1804. *For another edition, see* 1803.

18947 DAVIES, B. and **NORTH**, RICHARD. The petition of Benjamin Davies and Richard North [against the forfeiture of their recognizances on behalf of William Cobbett], to the Senate and Representatives of the Commonwealth of Pennsylvania; together with a statement of the case, and sundry documents relating thereto. 28p. *8°. n.p.* [1804?] *The copy that belonged to William Cobbett.*

18948 ESSAI sur le principe de la souveraineté. Par un grand vicaire. 196p. *8°. Londres*, 1804.

18949 ESSAI sur les relations politiques de la Russie avec la France. 45p. *8°. Londres*, 1804.

18950 EVANS, JOHN (*d.* 1832). War not inconsistent with Christianity. A discourse...intended to have been delivered at the parish Church of St. Augustine, Bristol. 47p. *8°. Bristol, London, &c.*, 1804.

18951 GRAGLIA, J. A. The speeches of a Jacobin and a Royalist: including their respective arguments whether or not Napoleon Bonaparte should resign his dignity of First Consul. 47p. *8°.* 1804.

18952 HAMILTON, LORD ARCHIBALD (1770–1827). Thoughts on the formation of the late and present administrations. 69p. *8°.* 1804.

18953 —— [Another edition.] 70p. *8°.* 1804.

18954 IVERNOIS, SIR F. D'. Immenses préparatifs de guerre qui eurent lieu en France d'abord après le Traité d'Amiens. Fragment d'un exposé historique des événemens qui ont amené la rupture de ce Traité. 48p. *8°. Londres*, 1804.

18955 LETTER to Lord Archibald Hamilton, on the occasion of his late pamphlet, in which the fatal consequences of the King's melancholy state of health are particularly considered. [With appendixes.] 42, [10]p. *8°.* 1804.

18956 A **LETTER** to the freeholders of Middlesex; containing an examination of the objections made to the return at the close of the late Middlesex election; and remarks on the political character and connexions of Sir Francis Burdett, Bart. By an attentive observer. Second edition. 107p. *8°.* 1804.

18957 MACLEOD, A. Letters on the importance of the present war... Letter I.—The question stated. 22p. *8°.* [1804?]

18958 —— Letter II. Strictures on the constitution resumed... 32p. *8°.* [1804?]

18959 MIDDLESEX FREEHOLDERS' CLUB. Declaration and regulations of the Middlesex Freeholders' Club. Instituted in...1804. 24p. *8°.* 1804.

18960 MITFORD, JOHN F., *Baron Redesdale.* Correspondence between the Right Hon. Lord Redesdale... and the Right Hon. the Earl of Fingall...from the 28th of August, to the 26th of September, 1803; and the narrative of the Rev. P. O'Neil...referred to in the correspondence. To which is added, a letter from Dr. Coppinger to Lord Redesdale. Second edition. 51p. *8°.* 1804.

18961 O'——, P. Letters to the farmers, tradesmen, shop-keepers and labourers of Ireland. By P. O'—— parish priest of ——. 55p. *8°. Dublin*, 1804.

18962 PETRE, R. E., *Baron Petre.* Reflections on the policy and justice of an immediate and general emancipation of the Roman Catholics of Great-Britain and Ireland ...to which are added some strictures on the same subject, by the editor [Felix M'Carthy]... 57p. *8°.* 1804.

18963 A **REPLY** to Lord Archibald Hamilton's Thoughts on the formation of the late and present administrations. 45p. *8°.* 1804.

18964 RUSSELL'S observations on some late publications, with remarks on the epithets of invader and plunderer on the Orange societies, and fraternities of United Irishmen, with a concise account of the religious & civil government of a few states in Germany, and a few observations on the second edition of Mr. Scully's essay, as revised and corrected by the author... 73p. *8°. Dublin*, 1804. *With a manuscript note on the title-page, 'For J. H. Brown, Esq., from the Author, E. N.' [i.e. Sir Edward Newenham?], and manuscript notes throughout.*

18965 SIMEON, J. J., *Comte.* Tribunat. Discours prononcé par Siméon, sur la motion d'ordre relative au gouvernement héréditaire. Séance extraordinaire du 10 floréal an 12. 11p. *8°. Paris*, an 12 [1804]

18966 [**SMITH**, SIR WILLIAM CUSACK, *2nd Bart.*] The yeoman's second letter to the Right Honourable William Wickham...Occasioned by the second edition of an Irish Catholic's advice to his brethren. Second edition. 98p. *8°. Dublin*, 1804.

18967 A **VINDICATION** of Mr. Pitt, for having moved the previous question on the motion of Colonel Patten [concerned with the conduct of ministers, 3rd June, 1803]; with a view of the conduct of that statesman, from that period to the present. 43p. *8°. 1804.*

18968 [**WARD**, afterwards **PLUMER WARD**, R.] A view of the relative situations of Mr. Pitt and Mr. Addington, previous to, and on the night of, Mr. Patten's motion. By a Member of Parliament. 127p. *8°. 1804.*

18969 **WYVILL**, C. Considerations on the twofold mode of election adopted by the French. 40p. *8°. York & London,* 1804.

18970 **YATE**, W. H. A serious & impartial address, to all the independent electors of the United Kingdoms, upon the recent Middlesex election... 47p. *8°. Glocester, London, &c.,* 1804.

MISCELLANEOUS

18971 **AUDI ALTERAM PARTEM:** or the real situation of the Navy of Great Britain at the period of Lord St. Vincent's resignation; being a reply to the mistatements of "An answer to Mr. Pitt's attack upon Earl St. Vincent and the Admiralty"; also containing the substance of a suppressed pamphlet on the same subject; by an officer of His Majesty's Navy. [With an appendix consisting of a letter addressed to the Earl St. Vincent, entitled 'The ship builders', signed: John Wells.] 68p. *8°. 1804.*

18972 **BARTELL**, E. Hints for picturesque improvements in ornamented cottages, and their scenery: including some observations on the labourer and his cottage... 140p. *8°. 1804.*

18973 **BERKELEY**, HON. SIR G. C. The trial of James Whiting, John Parsons, and William Congreve, for a libel against the Hon. G. C. Berkeley, Rear Admiral of the Red...June 27th, 1804. Taken in short hand by Mr. Gurney... 132p. *8°. Buckingham [& London],* 1804.

18974 **BUTLER**, JOHN (*fl.* 1804). A letter to the Right Honorable William Pitt, on the defence of the country, with a detail of improvements in the construction and use of fire-arms, great and small... 24p. *8°. Dublin,* 1804.

18975 **ENGLAND**. *Laws, etc.* Abstract of an Act (passed June 29, 1804) including the latest amendments, for establishing and maintaining a permanent additional force for the defence of the realm...and for the gradual reduction of the militia of England. 20p. *8°. 1804.*

18976 **HANGER**, G., *4th Baron Coleraine.* Reflections on the menaced invasion, and the means of protecting the capital, by preventing the enemy from landing in any part contiguous to it. A letter to the Earl of Harrington, on the proposed fortifications round London. A defence of the volunteer system, and the means of employing it to the greatest advantage. And a correct military description of Essex and Kent, with the military roads and strong positions in those counties. 207p. *8°. 1804.*

18977 **HARDINGE**, G. N. [*Begin.*] Scorpion, April 1804. My ever dearest friend...[A letter containing an account of the cutting out of the Dutch brig *Atalante* in the Texel in March 1804.] *s.sh.4°. n.p.* [1804] [*Br.* 468]

18978 **HATFIELD**, J. F. Outlines of rational patriotism and a plea for loyalty. Intended to promote the love of our country. With a concluding address to young volunteers. 87p. *8°. London & Newbury,* 1804. *The copy that belonged to M. T. Sadler, with a presentation inscription from the author, dated 1829(?), on a slip preceding the title-page.*

18979 **IZOUARD**, J. B. C., calling himself J. B. C. **DELISLE DE SALES**. De la philosophie de la Nature, ou, traité de morale pour le genre humain, tiré de la philosophie et fondé sur la Nature. Septiéme édition, et la seule conforme au manuscrit original. [With 'Préliminaires de la philosophie de la Nature; par J. Courvoisier'.] 10 vols. *8°. Paris,* 1804.

18980 Some **OBSERVATIONS** on the propriety of effectually employing our present military forces against France: and a few cursory remarks on the threatened invasion. 56p. *8°. 1804.*

18981 **THOUGHTS** on the national defence. [With an appendix.] 137, [5]p. *8°. 1804. The copy that belonged to John Calcraft (1765–1831).*

18982 **TRINDER**, W. M. Nine letters on military subjects, published in the True-Briton, in the year 1803 ... 52p. *8°.* [1804] *Presentation copy, with inscription, from the author to William Pitt.*

18983 **WILSON**, SIR ROBERT T. An enquiry into the present state of the military force of the British Empire, with a view to its re-organization... 106p. *8°.* 1804. *The copy that belonged to David Ricardo.*

18984 **WINDHAM**, W. The substance of the principal speeches of the Right Honourable William Windham, delivered in the House of Commons, in the late and present sessions of Parliament, on measures connected with the defence of this country. To which is added, the substance of a speech, delivered...on the second day of the present session. 46p. *8°. Norwich,* [1804]

1805

GENERAL

18985 BARRY, G. The history of the Orkney Islands: in which is comprehended an account of their present as well as their ancient state; together with the advantages they possess for several branches of industry, and the means by which they may be improved... 509p. *4°. Edinburgh & London, 1805. See also 1808.*

18986 BOYDELL, JOSIAH. Suggestions towards forming a plan for the encouragement, improvement, and benefit, of the arts and manufactures in this country, on a commercial basis. In two letters addressed to Robert Udney, Esq. dated December 22 and 23, 1801. 20p. *4°. [London, 1805] The Sheffield copy. There is also in the Library what is probably a proof copy, without the printer's imprint.*

18987 BRIDSON, P. and **STOWEL,** W. Isle of Man. Letter to their colleagues... [Attacking the activities of the House of Keys in opposing the measures in favour of the Duke of Atholl.] 20p. *8°. 1805.*

18988 [BROUGHAM, H. P., *Baron Brougham and Vaux.*] Thoughts suggested by Lord Lauderdale's observations upon the Edinburgh Review. 93p. *8°. 1805.*

18989 [CHRISTIAN, JOHN and **QUAYLE,** T.] Observations on the measure of creating, by authority of Parliament, an hereditary rent-charge, payable out of the revenue of the Isle of Man, in favour of the Duke of Atholl. On behalf of the House of Keys... 23p. *8°. [London, 1805]*

For **COBBETT'S SPIRIT OF THE PUBLIC JOURNALS** *see vol. III, Periodicals list.*

18990 DENINA, C. G. M. Tableau historique, statistique et moral de la Haute-Italie, et des Alpes qui l'entourent; précédé d'un coup d'œil sur le caractère des empereurs, des rois et autres princes qui ont regné en Lombardie, depuis Bellovèse et César jusqu'à Napoléon premier... 412p. *8°. Paris, 1805.*

18991 DONNANT, D. F. Statistical account of the United States of America... Translated from the French, by William Playfair: with an addition on the trade to America... 72p. *8°. 1805.*

18992 DOUGLAS, T., *Earl of Selkirk.* Observations on the present state of the Highlands of Scotland, with a view of the causes and probable consequences of emigration. 22p. *8°. London & Edinburgh, 1805. See also 1806.*

18993 The **EAST-INDIA** register and directory, for 1805; corrected to the 8th November, 1804. Containing ...lists of the Company's servants... Together with lists of...mariners, &c. not in the service of the...Company; and merchant vessels employed in the country trade. Compiled...by John Mathison & Alexander Way Mason ... 388p. *12°. [1805] For other editions, see 1804.*

18994 [EDWARDS, GEORGE.] Proposals, through means of a subscription of 2d. or the least mite...for carrying into effect, in a loyal, constitutional and unexceptionable manner, a discovery that has been lately made of the complete and divine plan of human prosperity... [A circular, with blanks for names to be filled in.] *s.sh.fol. Barnard Castle, [c. 1805 ?] [Br. 673(1)]*

18995 ENGLAND. *Parliament.* The Parliamentary register; or, an impartial report of the debates that have occurred in the two Houses of Parliament in the course of the third session of the second [-first session of the third] Parliament of the United Kingdom. 5 vols. *8°. J. Stockdale, 1805–7. Wanting vol. 2 of 1805.*

18996 FERRIER, F. L. A. Du gouvernement considéré dans ses rapports avec le commerce. 400p. *8°. Paris, 1805. See also 1821, 1822.*

18997 [HUTTON, W.] A brief history of Birmingham: intended as a guide to the inhabitant & stranger... Third edition: containing all subsequent changes &c. 44p. *8°. Birmingham & London, 1805. An abridgment of Hutton's History of Birmingham, 1781 (q.v.).*

18998 KAUFFMAN, C. H. The dictionary of merchandize, and nomenclature in all languages, for the use of counting houses: containing the history, places of growth, culture, use, and marks of excellency, of such natural productions as form articles of commerce; with their names in all European languages...Second edition. 380p. *8°. 1805. See also 1814.*

18999 KRUENITZ, J. G. D. Johann Georg Krünitz's ökonomisch-technologische Encyclopädie... Zuerst fortgesetzt von Friedrich Jakob Floerken, nunmehr von Heinrich Gustav Flörke...Sieben und neunzigster Theil, welcher den Artikel Münze und Münzwissenschaft enthält... 994p. *8°. Berlin, 1805. For another edition of part 17, see 1779.*

19000 MACPHERSON, DAVID. Annals of commerce, manufactures, fisheries, and navigation...Containing the commercial transactions of the British Empire and other countries from the earliest accounts to... January 1801; and comprehending...part of...Mr. Anderson's History of commerce, viz. from the year 1492 to the end of the reign of George II... 4 vols. *4°. London & Edinburgh, 1805.*

19001 MAITLAND, JAMES, *8th Earl of Lauderdale.* Hints to the manufacturers of Great Britain, on the consequences of the Irish Union; and the system pursued, of borrowing in England, for the service of Ireland. 51p. *8°. Edinburgh, London, &c., 1805. The copy that belonged to William Cobbett.*

19002 MANGOURIT, M. A. B. DE. Voyage en Hanovre, fait dans les années 1803 et 1804; contenant la description de ce pays sous les rapports politique, religieux, agricole, commercial, minéralogique, etc.... 500p. *8°. Paris, 1805.*

19003 The **PICTURE** of Liverpool; or, stranger's guide. 156p. *8°. Liverpool, 1805. A different work from that published with the same title in 1832 (q.v.).*

19004 PLAYFAIR, W. An inquiry into the permanent causes of the decline and fall of powerful and wealthy nations, illustrated by...engraved charts...Designed to shew how the prosperity of the British Empire may be prolonged. 301p. *4°. 1805. See also 1807.*

19005 POPHAM, Sir H. R. A description of Prince of Wales Island, in the Streights of Malacca: with its real and probable advantages and sources to recommend it as a marine establishment. 72p. 8°. 1805.

19006 The **POST-OFFICE** annual directory for the year 1805...By Messrs. Ferguson, Sparke, and Critchett. The sixth edition. 326p. 12°. [1805] *The earliest edition, entitled: The new annual directory for the year 1800, is in the Goldsmiths' Library (q.v. vol. III, Addenda, no. 17852·2). See also 1810, 1813, 1814, 1820 (Post Office London directory), 1823, 1825, 1830, 1832, 1834, 1836, 1841.*

19007 SABATIER, J. J. Tableaux comparatifs des dépenses et des contributions de la France et de l'Angleterre; suivis de considérations sur les ressources des deux états, et servant en même temps de réfutation à l'ouvrage de M. Gentz. 504p. 8°. *Paris & Bordeaux*, 1805.

19008 SCHUMMEL, J. G. Kleine Welt-Statistik. 422p. 8°. *Berlin*, 1805.

19009 SMITH, Adam. An inquiry into the nature and causes of the wealth of nations...The eleventh edition; with notes, supplementary chapters, and a life of Dr. Smith, by William Playfair. 3 vols. 8°. 1805. *For other editions, see 1776.*

19010 STEUART, Sir J., *Bart*. The works, political, metaphisical and chronological, of the late Sir James Steuart...now first collected by General Sir James Steuart...from his father's corrected copies. To which are subjoined anecdotes of the author... 6 vols. 8°. 1805.

19011 TALLEYRAND-PÉRIGORD, C. M. de. Mémoire sur les relations commerciales des Etats-Unis avec l'Angleterre...Suivi d'un essai sur les avantages à retirer de colonies nouvelles dans les circonstances présentes... 47p. 8°. *Londres*, 1805. *See also 1806.*

AGRICULTURE

19012 BAILEY, John and **CULLEY**, G. General view of the agriculture of the county of Northumberland; with observations on the means of its improvement. Drawn up for the consideration of the Board of Agriculture...The third edition. [With 'General view of the agriculture of the county of Cumberland' by the same authors, and 'General view of the agriculture of the county of Westmoreland...By Mr. A. Pringle'.] 361p. 8°. *London, Edinburgh, &c.*, 1805. *Each of the reports in this collection was printed separately for the first time in 1794 (q.v.), and published in 1797 (q.v.).*

19013 BANKS, Sir Joseph, *Bart*. A short account of the cause of the disease in corn, called by farmers the blight, the mildew, and the rust. With two plates. 14, [2]p. 4°. 1805.

19014 BECHER, W. A statement. Rate of rents and various charges on arable farms, previous to...1790, in the western part of Norfolk. Rate of rents and various charges on arable farms, at this time, in the same district. 3p. *fol.* [*London, c.* 1805]

19015 Ueber den **BERGBAU** Chursachsens auf Gold, ein Beitrag zur Geschichte seiner Bergwerke. 168p. 8°. *Penig*, 1805.

19015A BOYS, J. General view of the agriculture of the county of Kent; with observations on the means of its improvement. Drawn up for the consideration of the Board of Agriculture...from the original report...with additional remarks of several respectable country gentlemen and farmers. To which is added, a treatise on paring and burning...Second edition, with amendments and additions. 293p. 8°. *London, Canterbury, &c.*, 1805. *For other editions, see 1794.*

19016 DAVY, Sir H., *Bart*. On the analysis of soils, as connected with their improvement. 17p. 4°. 1805. *The Sheffield copy.*

19017 DICKSON, R. W. Practical agriculture; or, a complete system of modern husbandry: with the methods of planting, and the management of live stock. 2 vols. 4°. 1805. *See also 1810, 1813.*

19018 DUNCUMB, J. General view of the agriculture of the county of Hereford; drawn up for the consideration of the Board of Agriculture... 173p. 8°. *London, Hereford, &c.*, 1805. *See also 1813.*

19019 FINESCHI, A. M. Della stima dei frutti pendenti teorie legali ridotte alla pratica per uso del foro e degli stimatori...Edizione quarta. 112p. 8°. *Siena*, 1805.

19020 GREENWICH HOSPITAL. A report of the proceedings of Sir John Colpoys, K.B., Sir William Bellingham, Bart. and John Harrison, Esq. three of the directors of the Royal Hospital for Seamen at Greenwich, on a view of the estates belonging to the Hospital in the counties of Cumberland, Northumberland and Durham, in...August, September and October 1805. 257p. *fol.* [*London*, 1805]

19021 [HORNE, Thomas H.] The complete grazier; or, farmer and cattle-dealer's assistant. Comprising instructions for the buying, breeding, rearing, and fattening of cattle...The general economy of a grass-farm... The economy and general management of the dairy... Together with a synoptical table of the different breeds of neat cattle, sheep, and swine...By a Lincolnshire grazier... 510p. 8°. *London, Newark, &c.*, 1805. *See also 1830, 1833, 1846.*

19022 HOYTE, H. An essay, on the injury done to landed property, and the community at large; where a looseness of covenants forms a loop hole for peculation. 21p. 4°. *Newbury*, 1805.

19023 An **INQUIRY** into the causes of the present high rent of farms, in the neighbourhood of Glasgow and Paisley; addressed to the landed proprietors of these vicinities, for their investigation. By a Renfrewshire heritor. 20p. 8°. *Glasgow*, 1805.

19024 LAWRENCE, J. A general treatise on cattle, the ox, the sheep, and the swine: comprehending their breeding, management, improvement and diseases... 639p. 8°. 1805.

19025 LUCCOCK, J. The nature and properties of wool, illustrated: with a description of the English fleece. 360p. 12°. *Leeds & London*, 1805. *See also 1809.*

19026 La petite **MAISON** rustique, ou cours théorique et pratique d'agriculture, d'économie rurale et domestique. D'après Rozier, Parmentier, Duhamel-Dumonceau, de la Bretonnerie...Gilbert, Tessier, Lafosse...Chaptal... Valmont de Bomare...Cadet-de-Vaux...Seconde édition, refondue, corrigée et considérablement augmentée ... 2 vols. 8°. *Paris*, 1805.

19027 MALCOLM, JAMES. A compendium of modern husbandry, principally written during a survey of Surrey made at the desire of the Board of Agriculture... In which is comprised an analysis of manures...Also an essay on timber... 3 vols. *8°*. 1805.

19028 PARKINSON, RICHARD (1748–1815). The experienced farmers' tour in America: exhibiting...the American system of agriculture and breeding of cattle, with the recent improvements...To which are added, Sketches, published by J. B. Boadley... 735p. *8°*. 1805.

19029 —— Dedicated, by permission, to His Royal Highness the Duke of York. Proposals for publishing by subscription...The experienced farmer's tour in America ...[With 'Outlines of this work' and 'Subscribers'.] 4p. *4°*. [*London*, 1805 ?] *The Sheffield copy.*

19030 February 20. 1805...Unto the Right Honourable the Lords of Council & Session, the **PETITION** of John Gray, Esquire of Scotstown. [Concerning mining rights on his property. Signed: Tho. Thomson. With an appendix.] 17, 7p. *4°*. [*Edinburgh* ? 1805]

19031 PONTEY, W. The forest pruner; or, timber owner's assistant: being a treatise on the training or management of British timber trees...including...their general diseases and defects...also...the properties of English fir timber...the management of oak woods... 277p. *8°*. *Huddersfield, London, &c.*, [1805]

19032 PRIZES for stock, 1805–6. [Offered by Lord Somerville.] *s.sh.fol.* [*London*, 1805] [*Br.* 470]

19033 SEMPERE Y GUARINOS, J. Historia de los vinculos y mayorazgos. 451p. *8°*. *Madrid*, 1805.

19034 SMITH, JOHN (1747–1807). General view of the agriculture of the county of Argyle; with observations on the means of its improvement. Drawn up for the consideration of the Board of Agriculture... 347p. *8°*. *London, Edinburgh, &c.*, 1805. *For another edition, see* 1798.

19035 SOMERVILLE, R. General view of the agriculture of East Lothian; drawn up for the consideration of the Board of Agriculture...from the papers of the late Robert Somerville, Esq. surgeon in Haddington. 326p. *8°*. *London, Edinburgh, &c.*, 1805.

19036 SPEECHLY, W. A treatise on the culture of the vine, exhibiting new and advantageous methods of propagating, cultivating and training that plant, so as to render it abundantly fruitful. Together with new hints on the formation of vineyards in England. The second edition with additions. 300p. *8°*. [1805] *For another edition, see* 1790.

19037 SUSSEX AGRICULTURAL SOCIETY. At a general meeting of the subscribers of the...Society, to arrange the prizes and premiums for the present year, held at the Star Inn, Lewes, April 20, 1805, the following resolutions were agreed to. *s.sh.fol. n.p.* [1805] *The Sheffield copy. See also* 1801, 1804, 1807, 1808.

19038 WOBURN, 1805. Premiums given to promote the improvement of live stock, &c.&c. 4p. *4°*. [1805] *The Sheffield copy.*

CORN LAWS

19039 COMMITTEE APPOINTED TO FORWARD A PETITION TO THE HOUSE OF COMMONS FOR THE REPEAL OF THE CORN BILL, *Nottingham.* A reply to the vindication of the writer of a pamphlet called Sober considerations; by the Committee...[Signed: J. Blackner, secy.] 12p. *8°*. *Nottingham*, 1805.

19040 COMMON SENSE, *pseud.* Strike! but read. Vindication of the writer of "Sober considerations," &c. 15p. *8°*. *Nottingham*, 1805.

19041 OBJECTS of the Norfolk land-owners and barley-growers. *s.sh.fol.* [*London, c.* 1805]

19042 OBSERVATIONS on the corn laws, shewing that they can never benefit the farmer, but are most detrimental to commerce and manufacture. Also, the advantages of the free importation and exportation of corn are pointed out, &c. 24p. *12°*. *Glasgow*, [1805]

19043 REASONS in support of the petition of the land-owners and barley-growers of the county of Norfolk, for an alteration in the Corn Act of 1791, in respect to the import and export of corn, and other matters relative to the corn trade of this kingdom. 3p. *fol.* [*London, c.* 1805] *Endorsed: Reasons in support of the Norfolk land-owners' and corn-growers' petition to Parliament.*

POPULATION

19044 NEWENHAM, T. A statistical and historical inquiry into the progress and magnitude of the population of Ireland. 360p. *8°*. 1805.

19045 TINSEAU D'AMONDANS, . A statistical view of France, compiled from authentic documents ...Second edition; to which are annexed supplementary tables for Piedmont... 188, [2]p. *8°*. 1805.

19046 WHITELAW, J. An essay on the population of Dublin. Being the result of an actual survey taken in 1798...To which is added, the general return of the District Committee in 1804, with a comparative statement of the two surveys...[With 'Population tables of...the city of Dublin, A.D. 1798'; and 'An alphabetical list of the streets'.] 66, [74], 24p. *8°*. *Dublin*, 1805.

TRADES & MANUFACTURES

19047 DUNDAS, H., *Viscount Melville.* Speech delivered by Lord Viscount Melville, in the House of Peers, on Friday the 24th May, 1805, in answer to Lord Darnley's motion respecting the state of the Navy. 111p. *8°*. 1805.

19048 The **EDINBURGH** book of prices, for manufacturing cabinet-work. With various tables, as mutually agreed upon by the masters and journeymen. 126p. *8°*. *Edinburgh*, 1805. *For the supplement to this work, see* 1825 (Supplement to the cabinet-makers book of prices).

19049 EDLIN, A. A treatise on the art of bread-making. Wherein the mealing trade, assize laws, and every circumstance connected with the art is particularly examined. 221p. *12°. 1805.*

For **IRELAND.** *Trustees of the Linen and Hempen Manufactures*, Minutes of the proceedings of...the Trustees, 1805–1806, *continued as* Proceedings of the Trustees, 1806–1823, *see vol.* III, *Periodicals list*, Proceedings of the Trustees...

19050 NICHOLSON, P. The carpenter and joiner's assistant; containing practical rules for making all kinds of joints, and various methods of hingeing them together; for hanging of doors...for fitting up windows...To which are added, examples of various roofs...Also extracts from M. Belidor, M. du Hamel, M. de Buffon, &c. on the strength of timber...Illustrated with seventy-nine plates...The second edition. 79p. *4°. 1805.*

19051 —— The carpenter's new guide: being a complete book of lines for carpentry and joinery...Including some observations and calculations on the strength of timber...The fourth edition. 76p. *4°. 1805. See also 1825.*

19052 OBSERVATIONS on brick bond, as practised at various periods; containing an investigation of the best disposition of bricks in a wall, for procuring the greatest possible strength; with figures representing the different modes of construction. 15p. *8°. 1805.*

19053 A few **OPINIONS** of some great and good men, and sound lawyers, on the apprentice laws of Queen Elizabeth; applicable to the æra of 1805. *s.sh.fol.* [1805] [*Br.* 469]

19054 SOCIETY OF MANUFACTURERS OF SILK, *London.* Rules and orders of the Society of Manufacturers of Silk, and silk mixed with other materials, dyers, and other persons concerned in the manufactory, established in October, 1791 and amended and enlarged in October, 1805; for the purpose of forming general regulations and punishing embezzlements, combinations & other offences in the silk manufacture. [With a list of officers for 1805.] 12p. *8°. 1805.*

19055 SOUFFLOT DE MEREY, . Considérations sur le rétablissement des jurandes et maîtrises. Précédées d'observations sur un rapport fait à la Chambre de Commerce du Département de la Seine sur cette importante question, et sur un Projet de statuts et règlemens de MM. les Marchands de Vin. 167p. *8°. Paris,* 1805.

COMMERCE

19056 [ANTHOINE, A. I., *Baron de Saint Joseph.*] Essai historique sur le commerce et la navigation de la Mer-Noire, ou voyage et entreprises pour établir des rapports commerciaux et maritimes entre les ports de la Mer-Noire et ceux de la Méditerranée... 300p. *8°. Paris,* 1805. *See also 1820.*

19057 An **ARGUMENT** upon the justice and expediency of the order issued by Government, for the detaining all ships bound to the ports of Spain, freighted with treasure or warlike stores. 63p. *8°. 1805.*

19058 CLAUDIUS, G. C. Der Rathgeber bey den vorzüglichsten Geschäfts- und Handelsangelegenheiten für Manufacturisten, Fabrikanten, Handelsleute, Krämer und alle...welche die Handlung erlernen wollen. In Verbindung einiger...Kaufleute herausgegeben von G. C. Claudius. 2 vols. *8°. Leipzig,* 1805.

19059 DUBOST, C. The elements of commerce; or, a treatise on different calculations,—operations of exchange...Operations of specie...practical speculations in merchandize...Being a complete system of commercial calculations... 2 vols. *8°.* [1805] *See also 1818.*

19060 ETON, W. A concise account of the commerce and navigation of the Black Sea: from recent and authentic information. 53p. *8°. 1805.*

19061 MALLET, PAUL H. De la Ligue Hanséatique, de son origine, ses progrès, sa puissance et sa constitution politique jusqu'à son déclin au seizième siècle. 339p. *8°. Genève,* 1805.

19062 MONBRION, . De la prépondérance maritime et commerciale de la Grande-Bretagne, ou des intérêts des nations relativement à l'Angleterre et à la France. 368p. *8°. Paris,* 1805.

19063 Le grand **NÉGOCIANT** des Pays-Bas, ou le marchand fidèle et éclairé tant dans le calcul des monnoies, intérêts, répartitions, &c. que des prix de toutes sortes de marchandises en gros en détail...Nouvelle édition, revue... 591p. *8°. Gand,* [*c.* 1805]

19064 ODDY, J. J. European commerce, shewing new and secure channels of trade with the continent of Europe; detailing the produce, manufactures, and commerce of Russia, Prussia, Sweden, Denmark, and Germany... With a general view of the trade, navigation, produce, and manufactures of the United Kingdom of Great Britain and Ireland...With a canal and river map of Europe. 651p. *4°. London & Hamburg,* 1805.

19065 REINHARD, C. A concise history of the present state of the commerce of Great Britain. Translated from the German...With notes, and...additions relating to the principal British manufactures by J. Savage. The second edition. 74p. *8°. 1805. For other editions, see 1804.*

19066 [STEPHEN, J.] War in disguise; or, the frauds of the neutral flags. 215p. *8°. 1805.*

19067 [——] The second edition. [With an appendix.] 252p. *8°. 1805. See also 1806.*

19068 TARGA, C. Ponderazioni sopra la contrattazione marittima, ricavate dalla legge civile e canonica, dal Consolato del Mare e dagli usi marittimi... 163p. *4°. Trieste,* 1805. *For another edition, see 1692.*

19069 [WINTER, W. H.] A defence of the principle of monopoly; of corn-factors, or middle-men; and, arguments to prove that war does not produce a scarcity of the necessaries of life. 30p. *8°. London & Bristol,* 1805.

COLONIES

19070 ABEILLE, J. Essai sur nos colonies, et sur le rétablissement de Saint Domingue, ou considérations sur leur législation, administration, commerce et agriculture. 154p. *8°. Paris*, 1805.

19071 BEAVER, P. African memoranda: relative to an attempt to establish a British settlement on the island of Bulama, on the western coast of Africa, in...1792. With...some observations on the facility of colonizing that part of Africa...particularly as the means of gradually abolishing African slavery. 500p. *4°.* 1805.

19072 FRANCIS, SIR PHILIP. Speeches in the House of Commons, on the war against the Mahrattas. 94p. *8°.* 1805. *The copy that belonged to William Cobbett.*

19073 HUDLESTON, J. Substance of a speech, delivered in the House of Commons, on...April 5, 1805 ...on the motion of Philip Francis, Esq. "That this House adheres to...its unanimous resolution on the 28th of May, 1784...that to pursue schemes of conquest...in India is repugnant to...the policy of this country." 50p. *8°.* 1805.

19074 JAMAICA. *Assembly.* Report from a committee of the House of Assembly of Jamaica, appointed in a session, which began on the 23d of October, 1804, to inquire into the proceedings of the Imperial Parliament... relative to the slave trade, [equalisation of the duties on sugar imported from the East Indies,] &c.... 40p. *4°.* 1805.

19075 LEITH, SIR G., *Bart.* A short account of the settlement, produce, and commerce, of Prince of Wales Island in the Straits of Malacca. 94p. *8°.* 1805.

19076 LINDLEY, T. Narrative of a voyage to Brasil; terminating in the seizure of a British vessel...by the Portuguese. With general sketches of the country, its natural productions, colonial inhabitants, &c. and a description of the city and provinces of St. Salvadore and Porto Seguro... 298p. *8°.* 1805.

19077 OBSERVATIONS on Lord Castlereagh's speech of the 19th of July 1804, and on the state of the East India Company's affairs. 55p. *8°.* 1805. *The copy that belonged to William Cobbett.*

19078 ORME, R. Historical fragments of the Mogul Empire, of the Morattoes, and of the English concerns in Indostan; from the year M.DC.LIX. Origin of the English establishment, and of the Company's trade, at Broach and Surat; and a general idea of the government and people of Indostan...To which is prefixed, an account of the life and writings of the author. lxvii, 472p. *4°.* 1805.

19079 SCOTT, DAVID. Some observations on the subject of the debate in the House of Commons, on Indian affairs, on the 5th of April, 1805. 24p. *8°.* 1805. *The copy that belonged to William Cobbett.*

FINANCE

19080 [BIRD, J. B., *ed.*] The laws respecting tithes. Comprising all the cases and statutes on...tithes... Together with all other matter necessary for the information of clergyman, farmers, and country solicitors. The third edition...enlarged. By the author of the Laws of landlord and tenant... 97p. *8°.* 1805.

19081 CONSIDERATIONS on the silver currency, relative to both the general evil as affecting the Empire, and the present...evil in Ireland. With an appendix containing a report of Sir Isaac Newton on the state of the gold and silver coin, in the year 1717; and also some tables relative to the same subject. 58p. *8°. Dublin*, 1805.

19082 [DAWSON, WILLIAM (*fl.* 1805–1814).] Thoughts on public trusts. 203p. *12°. Edinburgh & London*, 1805. *The copy that belonged to Francis Place, with his signature on the title-page.*

19083 ENGLAND. *Commissioners of Customs.* General instructions for the landing-waiters and king's-waiters, in the Port of London. [With 'Additional instructions for the landing-surveyors...Containing I. Rules for their attendance...II. Rules about East India goods...III. Rules about tobacco. IV. Rules about linen. V. Rules about the wood-farm...VI. Rules about jerquing or passing their accounts' and 'Instructions for gauging wine'.] 15, 8, 5, 9, 14, 14, 40, 14, 3, 6p. *4°.* [*London*,] 1805.

19084 FRANCE. *Ministère de la Justice.* Circulaire. Ministère du Grand-Juge. [*Begin.*] Nous, Grand-Juge, Ministre de la Justice...en vertu de l'article 3 du décret impérial du 29 ventôse dernier...chargeons...le Sieur Tiolier...d'exécuter les timbres et sceaux à l'usage de toutes les autorités judiciaires de l'Empire...le 9 vendémiaire, an XIV. Signé Regnier. [With a printed letter, addressed and signed in manuscript, from Tiolier to Monsieur Lamouque, Juge de Paix du sixième arrondissement, asking him to indicate his requirements.] [4]p. *4°. n.p.* [1805]

19085 —— *Napoleon Bonaparte, First Consul.* Arrêté relatif aux piastres destinées à être converties en monnaies nationales. Du 26 prairial an 11. [2]p. *4°. Paris*, jours complémentaires an XIII [1805]

19086 —— Arrêté relatif au change des écus de trois livres et des pièces de vingt-quatre, douze, et six sous qui n'ont conservé aucune trace le leur empreinte. Saint-Cloud, le 6 fructidor an 11. [2]p. *4°. Paris*, jours complémentaires an XIII [1805]

19087 —— *Napoleon I, Emperor.* No. 183...Décret impérial concernant la clôture des maisons de prêt existantes à Paris. A Saint-Cloud, le 8 thermidor an XIII. 3p. *4°. Paris*, [1805]

19088 —— —— No. 184...Décret impérial contenant réglement sur l'organisation et les opérations du Mont-de-Piété de Paris. Au Palais de Saint-Cloud, le 8 thermidor an XIII. 16p. *4°. Paris*, [1805]

19089 —— —— No. 185. Extrait des minutes de la Secrétairerie d'Etat. A Paris, le 8 thermidor an XIII. Avis du Conseil d'Etat relativement à la liquidation des dettes de l'ancien Mont-de-Piété de Paris. 2p. *4°. Paris*, [1805]

19090 FRYER, W. Fryer's second edition on finance, with additions: addressed to the Right Honourable Lord

Sidmouth. With an appeal to the proprietors of lands, houses, builders, and occupiers of houses. 26[27]p. *8°*. 1805.

19091 GRELLIER, J. J. The terms of all the loans which have been raised for the public service: with observations on the rate of interest...And an account of Navy and Exchequer Bills...The third edition, considerably enlarged and improved. 92p. *8°*. 1805. *Presentation copy, with inscription, from the author to 'Mr. Baily' [i.e. Francis Baily?]. For other editions, see* 1799.

19092 [HESLOP, L.] Observations on the duty on property, &c. 37p. *8°*. *Buckingham*, [1805]. *The preface is signed in manuscript by the author. The Sheffield copy.*

19093 HOLLAND. *Provinciaal Bestuur.* Waarschouwing...betreffende den opbrengst van de 4de en volgende termijnen der vastgestelde buitengewone belasting, ingevolge publicatie van den 9 julij 1804. Geärresteerd den 23 julij, 1805. 4p. *8°*. *den Haag*, 1805.

19094 —— *Raad van Finantien.* Waarschouwing... betreffende den opbrengst van den 5de termijn der buitengewone belasting. Geärresteerd den 14 october 1805. 4p. *8°*. *den Haag*, 1805.

19095 IVERNOIS, SIR F. D'. Les recettes extérieures. 269p. *8°*. *Londres*, 1805.

19096 JENKINSON, CHARLES, *1st Earl of Liverpool.* A treatise on the coins of the realm; in a letter to the King. 268p. *4°*. *Oxford & London*, 1805. *This copy contains a letter from Sir Francis Burdett returning it to an unidentified owner. For the letter, see vol. III, A.L.* 459. *See also* 1846.

19097 JOHNSTONE, HON. A. J. C. Correspondence between the Honourable Colonel Cochrane Johnstone and the departments of the Commander in Chief, and the Judge Advocate General, during the period, from September, 1803, to August, 1804. [Relating to charges made by Colonel Cochrane Johnstone against an officer under his command in the West Indies.] 128p. *8°*. 1805.

19098 —— Defence of the Honourable Andrew Cochrane Johnstone; including a view of the evidence produced on his trial [for fraudulently converting to his own use sums destined for paying his regiment, and for other offences]; with the sentence and varied commentaries thereon by the Judge Advocate General... cxix, 1, 8, 280p. *8°*. 1805.

19099 LA CROIX, , *Chef de Bataillon au 108e. Régiment d'Infanterie de Ligne.* Réflexions sur la combinaison métallique des monnaies, en général, et particulièrement de celles françaises. 75p. *8°*. *Bruxelles*, 1805.

19100 A LETTER from an Irish Member of Parliament, upon the Report of the Select Committee of the House of Commons appointed...1804, to take into consideration the circulating paper, the specie, and current coin of Ireland; and also the exchange between that part of the United Kingdom and Great Britain. 52p. *8°*. 1805.

19101 LOWRIE, W. The conveniences, principles and method of keeping accounts with bankers in the country and in London; with...tables adapted to the calculating of interest accounts...To which is added, a... practical treatise on bills of exchange and promissory notes... 308p. *8°*. *Sheffield & London*, 1805. *See also* 1809.

19102 MACLEOD, A. Strictures on the tenth Report of the Commissioners of Naval Enquiry...To which are subjoined, an appendix, containing the substance of that Report; and Lord Melville's letter of 28th March, 1805,

to the Commissioners, together with their answer. 96p. *8°*. 1805. *The copy that belonged to William Cobbett.*

19103 MAITLAND, JAMES, *8th Earl of Lauderdale.* Thoughts on the alarming state of the circulation, and on the means of redressing the pecuniary grievances in Ireland. 122p. *8°*. *Edinburgh & London*, 1805. *The copy that belonged to William Cobbett.*

19104 MARSHALL, S. A treatise on the law of insurance. In four books. I. Of marine insurances. II. Of bottomry and respondentia. III. Of insurance upon lives. IV. Of insurance against fire...First American, from the English edition... 759p. *8°*. *Boston, Portland, &c.*, 1805.

19105 MÉMOIRE pour les ajusteurs et monnoyeurs de la Monnoie de Paris et du Royaume. 7p. *4°*. [*Paris, c.* 1805?]

19106 NETHERLANDS. *Batavian Republic.* Publicatie van het Staats-Bewind...wegens eenen te heffen derden termijn der buitengewoone belasting, gearresteerd bij publicatie van den 9 julij 1804. Geärresteerd den 22 januarij 1805. 4p. *8°*. *den Haag*, 1805.

19107 —— —— Publicatie van het Staats-Bewind... houdende nadere bepalingen wegens den opbrengst in de agt- en vijf-en-twintig-jarige heffingen en buitengewoone belasting, volgens publicatie van 9 julij 1804 en 22 januarij 1805. Geärresteerd den 11 maart 1805. 6p. *8°*. *den Haag*, 1805.

19108 —— —— Publicatie van het Staats-Bewind... wegens eenen te heffen vierden, vijfden en zesden termijn der buitengewoone belasting, geärresteerd by publicatie van den 9 julij 1804. Geärresteerd den 25 maart 1805. 5p. *8°*. *den Haag*, 1805.

19109 —— —— Publicatie van hun Hoog Mogende, vertegenwoordigende het Bataafsch Gemeenebest, houdende ordonnantie eener belasting op het regt van successie, alömme in het Bataafsch Gemeenebest intevorderen. Geärresteerd den 4den october 1805. 36p. *8°*. *den Haag*, 1805.

19110 —— —— Publicatie van hun Hog Mogende vertegenwoordigende het Bataafsch Gemeenebest. Houdende nadere bepaling, opzigtelijk den opbrengst van de zesde termijn der buitengewone belasting op de bezittingen en imkomsten. Geärresteerd den 19 december 1805. 3p. *8°*. *den Haag*, 1805.

19111 —— *Departement van Finantien.* Notificatie van den Secretaris van Staat voor de Finantien... geärresteerd den 4den december 1805. Behelzende bepalingen ter executie van de ordonnantie der belasting op het regt van successie, gearresteerd bij hun Hoog Mogende, vertegenwoordigende het Bataafsch Gemeenebest, den 4den october 1805. 16p. *8°*. *den Haag*, 1805.

19112 OBSERVATIONS on the nature and properties of a metallic currency. 56p. *8°*. *n.p.* [1805?]

19113 PARIS. *Cour Impériale. Cour de Justice Criminelle et Spéciale.* Acte d'accusation contre Aubin Quartier, négociant [and 22 others, accused of counterfeiting gold pieces and other currency. Signed: Gérard, Procureur-Général-Impérial]... 8p. *4°*. [*Paris*, 1805]

19114 PARNELL, H. B., *Baron Congleton.* Fourth edition. The principles of currency and exchange illustrated by observations upon the state of the currency of Ireland, the high rates of exchange between Dublin and London, and the remittances of rents to Irish absentees. 186p. *12°*. 1805. *An enlarged and revised version of Obser-*

vations upon the state of the currency in Ireland, *1804 (q.v.). The copy that belonged to Edward Wakefield (1774–1854), with his signature on the title-page and notes in his hand.*

19115 SAEZ, L. Demostracion histórica del verdadero valor de todas las monedas que corrian en Castilla durante el reynado del Señor Don Enrique IV., y de su correspon-dencia con las del Señor D. Cárlos IV.... 580p. *4°. Madrid,* 1805.

19116 STATEMENT of the case of the Duke of Atholl, claiming a compensation out of the surplus revenues of the Isle of Man. [With an appendix.] 21, 33p. *4°.* 1805.

TRANSPORT

19117 ALLNUTT, Z. Considerations on the best mode of improving the present imperfect state of the navigation of the river Thames from Richmond to Staines ... 46p. *8°. Henley, London, &c.,* 1805.

19118 DAWSON, HON. *and* REV. WILLIAM. Plan for a complete harbour at Howth-town, for the use of His Majesty's mail packet-boats, merchants ships...and fishing vessels...with remarks on all the plans for the improvement of the harbour or bay of Dublin for the shipping... 23p. *12°. Dublin,* 1805.

19119 ENGLAND. *Laws, etc.* [*Endorsed:*] An Act for altering, amending, and enlarging the powers of certain Acts for making and maintaining the Grand Junction Canal. 17p. *fol. n.p.* [1805]

19120 ——— ——— Anno quadragesimo quinto Georgii III. Regis. [Local & Personal.] Cap. 63. An Act to authorize the advancement of further sums of money out of the Consolidated Fund, for completing the canal and other works directed to be made by an Act...intituled, An Act for...better regulating the Port of London. ⟨27th June 1805.⟩ p. 1097–1104. *fol.* 1805.

19121 HISTOIRE du Canal de Languedoc, rédigée sur les pièces authentiques conservées à la Bibliothèque Impériale et aux archives du canal, par les descendans de Pierre-Paul Riquet de Bonrepos. 399p. *8°. Paris,* 1805.

SOCIAL CONDITIONS

19122 February 9, 1805...**ANSWERS** for the journeymen compositors, to the petition of the master printers of Edinburgh. [With an appendix, containing an offer of the journeymen compositors to bring the dispute to an end, dated June 2d, 1804.] 10, 2p. *4°. n.p.* [1805]

19123 *BELL, ANDREW. An experiment in education, made at the male asylum at Egmore, near Madras... Second edition; to which is prefixed the scheme of a school on the above model...and a Board of Education and poor-rates suggested. 84p. *8°.* 1805. *See also* 1807. **The first edition, 1797, is in the Quick Memorial Library see vol.* III, *Addenda.*

19124 [**BERNARD**, SIR T., *Bart.*] Society for Bettering the Condition of the Poor. Outline of measures proposed for the improvement of the character and condition of the English poor. [Signed: B., and dated, 18 Jan. 1805.] 19p. *8°. n.p.* [1805]

19125 BONE, J. Outline of a plan, for reducing the poor's rate, and amending the condition of the aged and unfortunate; including those of the naval and military departments: in a letter to the Right Hon. George Rose, occasioned by his Observations on the poor laws, &c. 61p. *8°.* 1805.

19126 GREGORY, JAMES. Censorian letter to the President and Fellows of the Royal College of Physicians in Edinburgh. 142p. *4°. Edinburgh,* 1805.

19127 HUNTINGFORD, G. I., *Bishop of Hereford.* A sermon preached before the incorporated Society for the Propagation of the Gospel in Foreign Parts; at their anniversary meeting...February 15, 1805. [With 'An abstract of the charter, and...proceedings of the Society ...1804, to...1805'.] 80p. *4°.* 1805.

19128 [**JOURDAN**, C. F.] Réflexions sur les moyens de détruire entièrement la mendicité, et de contribuer en même temps à la restauration des mœurs. Par C. F. J. 59p. *8°.* [*Paris,* 1805]

19129 LANCASTER, JOSEPH. Improvements in education, as it respects the industrious classes of the community, containing...an account of the institution for the education of one thousand poor children, Borough Road, Southwark...Third edition, with additions. 211p. *8°.* 1805. *For another edition, see* 1803.

19130 ——— A letter to John Foster, Esq., Chancellor of the Exchequer for Ireland, on the best means of educating and employing the poor in that country. 44p. *8°.* 1805. *The Sheffield copy.*

19131 NOLAN, M. A treatise of the laws for the relief and settlement of the poor... 2 vols. *8°.* 1805. *See also* 1825.

19132 PELHAM, HON. G., *Bishop of Lincoln.* A sermon preached...on...May 30, 1805, being the time of the yearly meeting of the children educated in the Charity-Schools, in and about the cities of London and Westminster...To which is annexed an account of the Society for Promoting Christian Knowledge. 15, 178p. *4°.* 1805. *The copy that belonged to Patrick Colquhoun.*

19133 January 23. 1805...Unto the Right Honourable the Lords of Council and Session, the **PETITION** of David Ramsay printer in Edinburgh, for himself and in behalf of the other master printers in and about Edinburgh [praying for an alteration in the interlocutor of the Lords of Council and Session granting a rise of wages to the journeymen compositors of Edinburgh. Signed: John Burnett.] 13p. *4°. n.p.* [1805]

19134 PRESTAT, , *the elder.* Mémoire sur l'indigence, et sur les moyens d'éteindre, sans retour, la mendicité. 104p. *12°. Paris,* 1805.

19135 ROSE, George. Observations on the poor laws, and on the management of the poor, in Great Britain, arising from a consideration of the returns now before Parliament. 44p. *8°*. 1805. *The copy that belonged to William Cobbett.*

19136 —— The second edition. 44p. *8°*. 1805.

19137 SCOTLAND. *Court of Session.* Interlocutor pronounced by the Lords of Council and Session in the process the journeymen compositor printers in Edinburgh against the master printers, for a rise of wages, so as to make them conform to the preceding scale. [Signed: Ilay Campbell, I.P.D. and dated December 22, 1804, with two later Interlocutors, dated 29 January and 19th February 1805.] 3p. *4°*. [*Edinburgh*, 1805] *The scale of prices referred to is printed on p.1.*

19138 SOCIETY FOR BETTERING THE

CONDITION OF THE POOR, *Clapham.* Rules and regulations of the Society for Bettering the Condition of the Poor, at Clapham, Surrey, instituted February 11, 1799. To which is prefixed, an account of the origin and designs of the Society. Second edition. 30p. *8°*. *London & Clapham*, 1805. *See also* 1829.

19139 SOCIETY FOR BETTERING THE CONDITION OF THE POOR, *London.* The reports of the Society...The fourth edition. [Edited by Sir T. Bernard.] 6 vols. *8°*. *London, York, &c.*, 1805, 1802–14. *For other editions, see* 1802.

19140 SOCIETY OF ASSOCIATED HOUSEWRIGHTS, *Boston.* The constitution of the Associated Housewright Society of the town of Boston. Instituted October, 1804. [With a list of members.] 15p. *8°*. *Boston*, 1805. *See also* 1820.

SLAVERY

19141 The HORRORS of the Negro slavery existing in our West India islands, irrefragably demonstrated from official documents recently presented to the House of Commons. 36p. *8°*. 1805.

19142 —— Second edition. 36p. *8°*. 1805. *The Sheffield copy.*

19143 —— [Another edition.] Horrors of West India slavery. 12p. *12°*. [*London*, 1805]

19144 SHARP, G. Serious reflections on the slave trade and slavery. Wrote in March, 1797. 46p. *12°*. 1805.

POLITICS

19145 CARTWRIGHT, J. The state of the nation; in a series of letters to His Grace the Duke of Bedford. [With a list of the author's works.] 173p. *8°*. *Harlow & London*, 1805.

19146 CAWTHORNE, J. A short defence of the Right Honorable Lord Viscount Melville, in a letter to a distinguished Member of Parliament. 126p. *8°*. *Deptford* [*& London*], 1805.

19147 DUIGENAN, P. The speech of Doctor Duigenan, delivered in the House of Commons...May 10, 1805, in the debate on a petition presented in the name of the Roman Catholics of Ireland, by the Hon. Charles James Fox. 95p. *8°*. 1805.

19148 DUNDAS, H., *Viscount Melville.* The substance of the speech of Lord Viscount Melville, in the House of Commons, on the 11th June, 1805... 104p. *8°*. 1805.

19149 FRANCE. *Conseil d'Etat.* No. 230...Avis du Conseil d'Etat sur l'époque à compter de laquelle sont valables les actes faits par des émigrés amnistiés par le Sénatus-consulte du 6 floréal an x, et sur la compétence, en matière de contestations élevées entre eux et leurs parens républicoles avant la délivrance du certificat d'amnistie. (Séance du 18 fructidor.) Le 26 fructidor an XIII. 2p. *4°*. *Paris*, [1805]

19150 The GHOST of Dean Swift, to the British people, upon the persecution of Lord Melville. [Consisting of excerpts from *A discourse of the contests and dissensions between the nobles and commons of Athens and Rome.*] 46p. *8°*. 1805.

19151 JAUBERT, F., *Comte. Tribunat.* Motion d'ordre de M. Jaubert...tendant à ce que le Tribunat

émette le vœu qu'un édifice soit destiné à perpétuer le souvenir des actions mémorables du siècle de Napoléon-le-Grand. Séance extraordinaire du 9 nivôse an 14. 8p. *8°*. [*Paris*, 1805 ?]

19152 JENKINSON, R. B., *2nd Earl of Liverpool.* Speech of the Right Honourable Lord Hawkesbury, in the House of Lords, on...the 10th of May, 1805, on the subject of the Catholic petition. 38p. *8°*. 1805.

19153 On the LAWFULNESS of hostility before a declaration of war. 76p. *8°*. [*London, c.* 1805.]

19154 M'KENNA, T. Thoughts on the civil condition and relations of the Roman Catholic clergy, religion and people in Ireland. 223p. *8°*. *Dublin*, 1805.

19155 —— [Another edition.] 193p. *8°*. 1805. *The copy that belonged to William Cobbett.*

19156 MACLEOD, A. Reflections on the proceedings of the House of Commons on the nights of the 8th and 10th April, 1805, embracing a view of the conduct of Mr. Whitbread and the Whig opposition...To which is annexed, a verbatim copy of the Act [25 Geo. III, c. 31] for regulating the office of the Treasurer of his Majesty's Navy. 94p. *8°*. 1805.

19157 MILNER, John, *Bishop of Castabala.* A short view of the chief arguments against the Catholic petition now before Parliament, and of answers to them, in a letter to a Member of the House of Commons. 53p. *8°*. 1805.

19158 OBSERVATIONS on the late and present state of Ireland; in considerations on the correspondence of Lords Redesdale and Fingal: and on the remonstrance of the Reverend Peter O'Neil, parish priest of Ballymacoda. Respectfully addressed to both Houses of Parliament. 99p. *8°. Dublin & London, 1805.*

19159 Brief **REMARKS** on the proceedings in the House of Commons, concerning Lord Melville, on the 8th of April, 1805. 22p. *8°.* 1805.

19160 **THOUGHTS** on the Protestant ascendancy in Ireland. With an appendix. 108p. *8°. London & Dublin, 1805. The copy that belonged to William Cobbett.*

19161 [**WARD,** afterwards **PLUMER WARD,** R.] An enquiry into the manner in which the different wars in Europe have commenced, during the last two centuries: to which are added the authorities upon the nature of a modern declaration. By the author of the history and foundation of the law of nations in Europe. 72p. *8°.* 1805.

19162 **WHEATLEY,** J. Thoughts on the object of a foreign subsidy. 46p. *8°.* 1805.

SOCIALISM

19163 **HALL,** CHARLES (1745?–1825?). The effects of civilization on the people in European states. [With 'Observations on the principal conclusion in Mr. Malthus's Essay on population'.] 349p. *8°.* 1805. *Another copy,*

without the 'Observations', is a presentation copy, with an inscription, from the author to Mr. Curwen. See also 1820, 1850.

MISCELLANEOUS

For the **MORALIST,** by Simon Style [i.e. James Yates, William Parker, and Robert Bill], *see vol.* III, *Periodicals List.*

19164 **NETHERLANDS.** *Batavian Republic.* Publicatie van hun Hoog Mogende, vertegen woordigende het Bataafsch Gemeenebest. Houdende ordonnantie op het middel van het klein zegel binnen de Bataafsche Republiek. Geärresteerd den 28sten november 1805. 53p. *8°. den Haag,* 1805.

19165 **SHARP,** G. An inquiry whether the description of Babylon, contained in the 18th chapter of the Revelations, agrees perfectly with Rome as a city?...[With 'Appendix of notes'.] 69, 43p. *12°.* 1805.

19166 **YATES,** R. An illustration of the monastic history and antiquities of the town and abbey of St. Edmund's Bury...With views of the most considerable monasterial remains; by the Reverend William Yates. 252, 10, 32, 8p. *4°.* 1805.

1806

GENERAL

19167 **BLODGET,** S. Economica: a statistical manual for the United States of America. [With an appendix.] 202, xivp. *8°. City of Washington,* 1806.

19168 **BROWN,** ROBERT (1757–1831). Strictures and remarks on the Earl of Selkirk's Observations on the present state of the Highlands of Scotland... 120p. *8°. Edinburgh & London,* 1806.

19169 **COBBETT,** W. [and **WRIGHT,** JOHN (1770?–1844)], *eds.* Cobbett's Parliamentary history of England. From the Norman conquest, in 1066 to...1803. From which last-mentioned epoch it is continued downwards in the work entitled "Cobbett's Parliamentary debates." 36 vols. *8°.* 1806–20.

19170 **CONSIDERATIONS** on the alliance between Christianity & commerce, applied to the present state of this country. 81p. *8°.* 1806. *Sometimes attributed to Richard Raikes.*

19171 **DANDOLO,** V., *Conte.* Sulla pastorizia, sull' agricoltura e su varj altri oggetti di pubblica economia. Discorsi di Vincenzo Dandolo. 331p. *8°. Milano,* 1806.

19172 **DOUGLAS,** T., *Earl of Selkirk.* Observations on the present state of the Highlands of Scotland, with a view of the causes and probable consequences of emigration...Second edition. 232p. *8°. Edinburgh & London,* 1806. *For another edition, see 1805.*

19173 **ENGLAND.** *Treaties, etc.* The late negociation.

The whole of the correspondence, and official notes, relating to the late negociation with France, as they appeared in the Moniteur of the 26th ult. 85p. *8°.* [1806]

19174 **FILANGIERI,** G. The science of legislation. From the Italian. [Translated by Sir Richard Clayton, Bart.] 2 vols. *8°.* 1806.

19175 **FRANKLIN,** B. The complete works, in philosophy, politics, and morals of the late Dr. Benjamin Franklin, now first collected and arranged: with memoirs of his early life, written by himself. [Edited by — Marshall, assisted by Benjamin Vaughan.] 3 vols. *8°.* 1806.

19176 [**GORDON,** JAMES, *of Craig.*] Eight letters on the subject of the Earl of Selkirk's pamphlet on highland emigration; as they lately appeared under the signature of Amicus in one of the Edinburgh newspapers. 59p. *8°. Edinburgh & London,* 1806.

19177 [——] Second edition, with supplementary remarks. 136p. *8°. Edinburgh & London,* 1806.

19178 **GREGORY,** G. A dictionary of arts and sciences... 2 vols. *4°.* 1806–7.

19179 **GUTHRIE,** W. A new geographical, historical, and commercial grammar; and present state of the several kingdoms of the world. Containing I. The figures...of the planets...IV. The situation and extent of Empires...and colonies. V. Their climate...vegetable productions, metals, minerals...VIII...their...government, revenues, taxes

...x. Their...arts, sciences, manufactures, and commerce ...The astronomical part by James Ferguson, F.R.S. To which have been added the late discoveries of Dr. Herschel ...the twentieth edition. Corrected and considerably enlarged. 1036p. *8°. London & York*, 1806. *For other editions, see* 1790.

19180 MEUSEL, J. G. Litteratur der Statistik... Zweyte, ganz umgearbeitete Ausgabe. 2 vols. *8°. Leipzig*, 1806–7.

19181 [MOLÉ, L. M., *Comte.*] Essais de morale et de politique. 254p. *8°. Paris*, 1806.

19182 [ORIANI, B., *Conte.*] Istruzione su le misure e su i pesi che si usano nel Regne d'Italia. Edizione seconda, corretta ed aumentata della riduzione dei franchi in lire Milanesi. 145p. *8°. Milano*, 1806. *For another edition, see* 1801.

19183 PALEY, W. The principles of moral and political philosophy...The sixteenth edition... 2 vols. *8°.* 1806. *For other editions, see* 1785.

19184 REMARKS on the Earl of Selkirk's Observations on the present state of the Highlands of Scotland... 353p. *8°. Edinburgh & London*, 1806.

19185 SARTORIUS VON WALTERSHAUSEN, G. F. C., *Freiherr.* Abhandlungen, die Elemente des National-Reichthums und die Staatswirthschaft betreffend

...Erster Theil. 519p. *8°. Göttingen*, 1806. *No more published.*

19186 SOCIEDAD ECONOMICA DE MADRID. L'identité de l'intérèt général avec l'intérèt individuel, ou la libre action de l'intérêt individuel est la vraie source des richesses des nations. Principe exposé dans le rapport sur un projet de loi agraire, adressé au Conseil suprême de Castille au nom de la société économique de Madrid. Par Don Guspard [*sic*] Melchior Jovellanos. 282p. *8°. St. Petersbourg*, 1806. *The translator's preface is signed: Rouvier. For other editions, see* 1795.

19187 STARK, John. Picture of Edinburgh; containing a history and description of the city, with a particular account of every remarkable object in, or establishment connected with, the Scottish metropolis... 504p. *12°. Edinburgh & London*, 1806.

19188 TALLEYRAND-PÉRIGORD, C. M. DE. Memoir concerning the commercial relations of the United States with England...Read at the National Institute, the 15th Germinal, in the year v. To which is added an essay upon the advantages to be derived from new colonies in the existing circumstances. By the same author. Read at the Institute the 15th Messidor, in the year v. 87p. *8°.* 1806. *For another edition, see* 1805.

19189 *Provisorische VERFASSUNG des Bauern-Standes in Ehstland. 133p. *8°. St. Petersburg*, 1806. *The copy that belonged to George Grote.*

AGRICULTURE

19190 CROCKER, A. The elements of land surveying, designed principally for the use of schools & students. 279p. *12°.* 1806.

19191 FARMING SOCIETY OF IRELAND. Farming Society of Ireland. Ballinasloe Shew. Monday, October 6th, 1806. [List of winning entries.] *s.sh.fol. n.p.* [1806] *The Sheffield copy. See also* 1808.

19192 FRANÇOIS DE NEUFCHÂTEAU, N. L., *Comte.* Voyages agronomiques dans la Sénatorerie de Dijon, contenant l'exposition du moyen employé avec succès, depuis un siècle, pour corriger l'abus de la désunion des terres, par la manière de tracer les chemins d'exploitation... 260p. *4°. Paris*, 1806.

19193 May [*blank*]. 1806...**INFORMATION** for the Right Honourable James Hope Johnstone, Earl of Hopetoun, in the action of declarator at his instance, and that of the Duke of Queensberry, against the Officers of State [claiming the right to export lead from his mines free of duties imposed by Acts of Parliament before and after the Union. Signed: Alex. Irving]. 45p. *n.p.* [1806]

19194 May 23. 1806...**INFORMATION** for the Officers of State, against His Grace the Duke of Queensberry [who claims the right to export lead from his mines free of duties imposed by Acts of Parliament before and after the Union. Signed: David Monypenny]. 11p. *4°. n.p.* [1806]

19195 May 23. 1806...**INFORMATION** for the Officers of State, defenders, against the Right Hon. James Hope Johnstone Earl of Hopetoun. [Signed: David Monypenny. With 'Appendix. Act of Parliament for furthering the King's commodity by the mines and metals, made in the Parliament holden at Edinburgh the 5th day of June 1592'.] 40, 1–4p. *4°. n.p.* [1806] *The text of the Act is incomplete.*

19196 July 1. 1806...**INFORMATION** for His Grace William Duke of Queensberry and his lessees, pursuers, against the Officers of State, defenders. [Signed: Ad. Gillies.] 34p. *4°. n.p.* [1806]

19197 LAWRENCE, J. The modern land steward; in which the duties and functions of stewardship are considered and explained...Second edition, with additions. 494p. *8°.* 1806. *For another edition, see* 1801.

19198 [——] The new farmer's calendar; or, monthly remembrancer, for all kinds of country business...By a farmer and breeder. Fifth edition. 629p. *8°.* 1806. *For other editions, see* 1800.

19199 LOUDON, J. C. A treatise on forming, improving, and managing country residences...With an appendix, containing an enquiry into the utility and merits of Mr. Repton's mode of shewing effects by slides and sketches, and strictures on his opinions and practice in landscape gardening... 2 vols. *4°.* 1806.

19200 MARSHALL, W. On the management of landed estates: a general work; for the use of professional men; being an abstract from the more enlarged treatise on landed property. 448p. *8°.* 1806. *For* On the landed property of England, *see* 1804.

19201 NAISMITH, J. General view of the agriculture of the county of Clydesdale [Lanark], with observations on the means of its improvement. Drawn up for the consideration of the Board of Agriculture... 252p. *8°. London, Edinburgh, &c.*, 1806. *For other editions, see* 1794.

19202 PARKINSON, Richard (1748–1815). The English practice of agriculture, exemplified in the management of a farm in Ireland, belonging to the Earl of Conyngham, at Slane, in...Meath. With an appendix;

containing...a comparative estimate of the Irish and English mode of culture, as to profit and loss: and...a regular rotation of crops for a period of six years. 338p. *8°*. 1806.

19203 February 5. 1806...Unto the Right Honourable the Lords of Council and Session, the **PETITION** of Mathew Robertson, bookseller in Glasgow...[A dispute about the possession of land adjacent to the petitioner's mill at Milldavie, in the parish of Rutherglen. Signed: John McFarlan.] 11p. *4°*. *n.p.* [1806]

19204 June [*blank*]. 1806...Unto the Right Honourable, the Lords of Council and Session, the **PETITION** of His Grace William Duke of Queensberry [stating his right to grant leases of the entailed Lordship of Neidpath, which

he had inherited. Signed: John A. Murray]. 62p. *4°*. *n.p.* [1806]

19205 July 10. 1806...Unto the Right Honourable, the Lords of Council and Session, the **PETITION** of His Grace William Duke of Queensberry. [Signed: John A. Murray. With an appendix.] 65, 21p. *4°*. *n.p.* [1806]

19206 **SINCLAIR**, SIR JOHN, *Bart.* Address to the Board of Agriculture, on...the 22d April, 1806. 12p. *4°*. [*London*, 1806] *The Sheffield copy.*

19207 **SMITH**, WILLIAM (1769–1839). Observations on the utility, form and management of water meadows, and the draining and irrigating of peat bogs, with an account of Prisley Bog, and other...improvements... 121p. *8°*. *Norwich & London*, 1806.

CORN LAWS

19208 **SHARKEY**, R. F. A proposal for the more speedy relief of the poor of Ireland, in seasons of scarcity; addressed to the Rt. Hon. Sir John Newport, Bart. Chancellor of the Irish Exchequer. 32p. *8°*. *Dublin*, 1806.

POPULATION

19209 **JARROLD**, T. Dissertations on man, philosophical, physiological and political; in answer to Mr. Malthus's "Essay on the principle of population". 367p. *8°*. 1806.

19210 **MALTHUS**, T. R. An essay on the principle of population; or, a view of its past and present effects on

human happiness...The third edition. [With an appendix.] 2 vols. *8°*. 1806. *For other editions, see* 1798.

19211 [——] Reply to the chief objections which have been urged against the Essay on the principle of population. Published in an appendix to the third edition. 36p. *4°*. 1806.

TRADES & MANUFACTURES

19212 **BAADER**, J. VON. Projet d'une nouvelle machine hydraulique pour remplacer l'ancienne machine de Marly; suivi de l'apperçu d'un autre moyen de fournir des eaux à la ville et aux jardins de Versailles, sans employer la force motrice de la rivière. 58p. *4°*. *Paris*, 1806.

19213 **COCHRANE**, ARCHIBALD, *9th Earl of Dundonald*. Introduction to and contents of an intended publication [on improvements in the manufacture of textiles, especially linen]. 13p. *8°*. 1806. *The copy presented to Patrick Colquhoun.*

19214 **FRANCE**. *Ministère de l'Intérieur*. Exposition de 1806. Rapport du jury sur les produits de l'industrie française, présenté à S.E.M. de Champagny, Ministre de l'Intérieur; précédé du procès-verbal des opérations du jury. 304p. *8°*. *Paris*, 1806.

19215 The **FRIEND** of youth; or, candid advice to parents and guardians on the choice of such trades, professions and employments as may be suited to the taste and genius...of their respective children and wards. 419p. *12°*. 1806.

19216 **GRAY**, A. The experienced millwright; or, a treatise on the construction of some of the most useful machines, with the latest improvements. To which is prefixed, a short account of the general principles of mechanics...Illustrated with forty-four engravings...Second edition. 73p. *fol. Edinburgh & London*, 1806.

19217 An analytical **INDEX** to the sixteen volumes of the first series of the Repertory of Arts and Manufactures: being a condensed epitome of that work...To which is added a general index to the first eight volumes of the second series. 232p. *8°*. 1806. *For the Repertory of arts and manufactures, see* vol. III, *Periodicals list*, Repertory of patent inventions...

For **IRELAND**. *Trustees of the Linen and Hempen Manufactures of Ireland*, Minutes of the Proceedings, 1806, *continued as* Proceedings of the Trustees, 1807–10, 1815–23, *see* vol. III, *Periodicals list*, Proceedings of the Trustees.

19218 **JACKSON**, RANDLE. The speech of Randle Jackson, Esq. addressed to the Honorable the Committee of the House of Commons, appointed to consider of the state of the woollen manufacture of England, on behalf of the cloth-workers and sheermen of the counties of Yorkshire, Lancashire, Wiltshire, Somersetshire, and Gloucestershire... 79p. *8°*. 1806.

19219 —— Second edition. 79p. *8°*. 1806.

19220 **OBSERVATIONS** on the proposed tax on pig-iron. By an iron-master. 24p. *8°*. 1806.

19221 **RICHARDSON**, WILLIAM, *surgeon*. Designed chiefly for the use of manufacturers. The chemical principles of the metallic arts; with an account of the principal diseases incident to the different artificers; the means of prevention and cure; and a concise introduction to the study of chemistry. cii, 201p. *8°. Birmingham & London*, 1806. *For another edition, see* 1790.

19222 STOUPE, J. G. A. Mémoire sur le rétablissement de la Communauté des Imprimeurs de Paris; suivi de réflexions sur les contrefaçons en librairie, et sur le stéréotypage. 39p. *8°. Paris*, 1806.

COMMERCE

19223 ALFRED, *pseud.* Observations on the American Intercourse Bill; and on the necessity of adhering strictly to the navigation laws of Great Britain, in order to protect the shipping, landed, and manufacturing interests of the United Kingdom...In a letter addressed to Lord Holland. 20p. *8°.* 1806. *The Sheffield copy.*

19224 ALLEY, J. A vindication of the principles and statements advanced in the Strictures of the Right Hon. Lord Sheffield, on the necessity of inviolably maintaining the navigation and colonial system of Great Britain: with tables, and an appendix. 90p. *8°.* 1806.

19225 BLANCARD, P. Manuel du commerce des Indes, ou exposé de celui que les nations européennes font et peuvent faire aux Indes Orientales, à la Cochinchine, à la Chine, aux Isles Philippines, au Golfe Persique et à la Mer-Rouge... 544p. *fol. Paris*, 1806.

19226 BROWN, JOHN, *of Great Yarmouth.* The mysteries of neutralization; or, the British Navy vindicated from the charges of injustice and oppression towards neutral flags. 156p. *8°.* 1806.

19227 EAST INDIA COMPANY. Proceedings relative to ships tendered for the service of the United East-India Company, from the twentieth of April, 1803, to the twenty-seventh of June, 1806... p. 2205–2652. *fol.* 1806. *See also* 1809.

19228 An EXAMINATION of the alleged expediency of the American Intercourse Bill; respectfully inscribed to Robert Curling, Esq. and the other gentlemen who compose the Committee of Ship-Owners. 30p. *8°.* 1806.

19229 HOLROYD, J. B., *Earl of Sheffield.* Extracted from the Parliamentary Debates. — House of Lords. American Intercourse Bill. [Lord Sheffield's speeches of 6th, 12th & 14th May, 1806.] 3p. *fol.* [*London*, 1806] *Endorsed: Lord Sheffield's protest, &c.&c. against the American Intercourse Bill. The Sheffield copy.*

19230 —— [Another edition, containing the first two speeches only.] 4 col. *s.sh.fol. n.p.* [1806] *The Sheffield copy.*

19231 —— Strictures on the necessity of inviolably maintaining the navigation and colonial system of Great Britain. A new edition very much enlarged, with an appendix, &c. 318p. *8°.* 1806. *For another edition, see* 1804.

19232 [MADISON, J., *President of the USA.]* An examination of the British doctrine, which subjects to capture a neutral trade not open in time of peace. 204p. *8°. n.p.* [1806]

19233 —— [Another edition.] 200p. *8°.* 1806.

19234 MEMORIAL of the merchants of the City of New-York [concerning trade between neutral countries and the colonies of belligerent powers]. 38p. *8°.* [*New York,*] 1806.

19235 [MOORE, C. C.] An inquiry into the effects of our foreign carrying trade upon the agriculture, population, and morals of the country. By Columella. 61p. *8°. New-York*, 1806.

19236 [MORRIS, GOUVERNEUR.] An answer to War in disguise; or, remarks upon the new doctrine of England concerning neutral trade. 76p. *8°. New-York*, 1806.

19237 —— [Another edition.] 76p. *8°.* 1806.

19238 RANDOLPH, J. The speech of the Hon. J. Randolph, representative for the State of Virginia, in the General Congress of America; on a motion for the non-importation of British merchandize, pending the present disputes between Great Britain and America. With an introduction by the author of "War in disguise" [James Stephen]. 31p. *8°.* 1806.

19239 REMARKS on the trade with Germany, respectfully submitted to the merchants and others, both here and abroad, interested in this important branch of commerce. March 1806. 137p. *8°.* 1806. *With a translation into German printed on alternate pages.*

19240 SAUVERAIN, J. B. F. Considérations sur la population et la consommation générales du bétail en France; suivies de réflexions particulières sur l'approvisionnement en bestiaux pour Paris, et sur tout ce qui concerne le commerce et la police des viandes de boucherie dans cette ville. 231p. *8°. Paris*, 1806.

19241 A STATE of the allegations and evidence produced, and opinions of merchants...given, to the Committee of Council; extracted from their report of the 31st of May, 1784...made upon the representation of the West-India planters and merchants, purporting to shew the distressed state of His Majesty's Sugar Colonies by the operation of His Majesty's Order in Council of the 2d of July, 1783...Reprinted by order of the Society of Ship-owners of Great-Britain. 154p. *8°. n.p.*, 1806.

19242 [STEPHEN, J.] War in disguise; or, the frauds of the neutral flags. The third edition. 252p. *8°.* 1806.

19243 —— The fourth edition. 252p. *8°.* 1806.

19244 —— [Another edition.] 215p. *8°. New-York & Philadelphia*, 1806. *For other editions, see* 1805.

COLONIES

19245 [COLEBROOKE, H. T.] Remarks on the husbandry and internal commerce of Bengal. 206p. *8°.* 1806. *For another edition, see* 1804.

19246 DURAND, J. B. L. A voyage to Senegal; or, historical, philosophical, and political memoirs, relative to

the discoveries, establishments, and commerce of Europeans in the Atlantic Ocean, from Cape Blanco to the River of Sierra Leone. To which is added an account of a journey from Isle St. Louis to Galam... 181p. *8°.* 1806.

19247 EAST INDIA COMPANY. Copy of a

proposed dispatch [censuring the conduct of the Governor-General, the Marquis Wellesley] to the Bengal Government, approved by twenty-three of the twenty-four directors of the Hon. East-India Company, dated April 3, 1805, but rejected by the Board of Controul... 82p. *8°*. 1806.

19248 —— Papers ordered to be printed by a General Court of proprietors of East-India stock, the 7th May, 1806. 132p. *4°*. [1806]

19249 FULLARTON, W. November 6th, 1806. Colonel Fullarton's address to the electors of Westminster; containing the grounds of his charges...against Sir Samuel Hood [in connection with the case of Sir Thomas Picton in Trinidad], as an improper person to represent that City. [4]p. *fol*. [*London*, 1806]

19250 GLEANINGS in Africa; exhibiting a...view of the manners and customs of the inhabitants of the Cape of Good Hope...With a full...account of the system of agriculture adopted by the colonists...interspersed with observations...on the state of slavery in the southern extremity of the African continent. In a series of letters from an English Officer during the period in which that colony was under the protection of the British Government... 320p. *8°*. 1806.

19251 A **LETTER** to the Right Honourable C. J. Fox on the subject of his conduct upon the charge made by Mr. Paul, against the Marquis Wellesley. To which are annexed a faithful copy of the first letter from the East India Directors to the Marquis which was sent, and also a faithful copy of the dispatch proposed to be sent to the Marquis from the East India Directors. 107p. *8°*. 1806.

The Dispatch, p. 30–107, is the same as that printed as Copy of a proposed dispatch, no. 19247.

19252 PICTON, Sir T. Evidence taken at Port of Spain, Island of Trinidad, in the case of Luisa Calderon, under a mandamus issued by the Court of King's Bench ...with a letter, addressed to Sir Samuel Hood, K.B. late one of the Commissioners for the government of that colony. xxiv, 139p. *8°*. 1806.

19253 —— The trial of Governor T. Picton, for inflicting the torture on Louisa Calderon, a free mulatto ...in the island of Trinidad. Tried before Lord Chief Justice Ellenborough...and found guilty...on the 24th of February, 1806. 126p. *8°*. *London, Liverpool, &c.*, [1806]

19254 PINCKARD, G. Notes on the West Indies: written during the expedition under the command of the late General Sir Ralph Abercromby: including observations on the island of Barbadoes, and...the coast of Guiana; likewise remarks relating to the Creoles and slaves of the western colonies, and the Indians of South America ... 3 vols. *8°*. 1806.

19255 PONS, F. R. J. DE. Voyage à la partie orientale de la Terre-Ferme dans l'Amérique méridionale, fait pendant les années 1801, 1802, 1803 et 1804: contenant la description de la Capitainerie générale de Caracas... 3 vols. *8°*. *Paris*, 1806.

19256 Cursory **REMARKS** on the administration of the late Governor General of India [Marquis Wellesley]; on the conduct of the Court of Directors; and introductory strictures on a pamphlet by John Hudleston, Esq. M.P. 62p. *8°*. 1806.

FINANCE

19257 An **ACCOUNT** of the South Sea Scheme; and a number of other bubbles; which were encouraged by public infatuation in the year 1720, and which terminated in the ruin of many thousand families. With a few remarks upon some schemes which are now in agitation, intended as a warning to the present age. [Extracted from William Maitland's *History of London*.] 23p. *8°* [*London*,] 1806. *The copy that belonged to William Cobbett.*

19258 ARNOULD, A. M. Histoire générale des finances de la France, depuis le commencement de la monarchie; pour servir d'introduction à la loi annuelle ou Budjet [*sic*] de l'Empire français. 224, 164p. *4°*. *Paris*, 1806.

19259 BAILY, F. The rights of the stock-brokers defended against the attacks of the City of London: or, arguments to show that persons buying or selling stock only, by commission, do not come within the meaning of the word broker mentioned in the 6 Anne, c. 16... 46p. *8°*. 1806.

19260 BONNEVILLE, P. F. Traité des monnaies d'or et d'argent qui circulent chez les différens peuples; examinées sous les rapports du poids, du titre et de la valeur réelle, avec leurs diverses empreintes. 250[270]p. *fol*. *Paris*, 1806.

19261 DUNDAS, H., *Viscount Melville*. Articles exhibited by the...Commons of the United Kingdom of Great Britain and Ireland...against Henry Viscount Melville, in maintenance of their impeachment against him...the answer of Henry Viscount Melville; the

replication of the Commons; and the minutes of evidence taken upon the hearing of the impeachment at the Bar of the House of Lords...[With an appendix.] 19, 268, 255p. *fol. n.p.*, 1806.

19262 —— A compendious report of the trial of Henry Viscount Melville, upon the impeachment of the Commons...in Parliament assembled, for high crimes and misdemeanors. [With an appendix of documents.] 237, 14p. *8°*. 1806. *The copy that belonged to David Ricardo.*

19263 —— The trial of Henry Lord Viscount Melville, before the Right Honorable the House of Peers...for high crimes and misdemeanors, upon an impeachment...by the Commons of the United Kingdom of Great Britain and Ireland...begun the 29th day of April, 1806 and... continued...until the 12th day of June 1806. Published by order of the House of Peers. 413p. *fol*. 1806.

19264 ENGLAND. *Commissioners appointed to Enquire into the Mode of Collecting the Revenue of Ireland*. An abridgment of the report of the Commissioners... Containing...I. The several amendments...proposed by the Commissioners...II. An alphabetical list of all persons who hold offices...in the customs...taken from the returns...III. A list of offices the duty of which appears to be useless. IV. A list of officers who have converted their offices into sinecures. 41p. *8°*. *Dublin*, 1806.

19265 —— *Laws, etc.* An Act (passed 13th June 1806,) for granting to his Majesty, during the present war... further additional rates and duties in Great Britain on profits arising from property, professions, trades, and offices... 295p. *8°.* 1806. *With a 27-page manuscript table of contents.*

19266 —— Parliament. *House of Commons.* Report of the debates in the House of Commons upon the tenth, fifteenth and eighteenth days of July 1806 on the East India budget. 127p. *8°.* 1806.

19267 FRANCE. *Laws, etc.* Recueil général des lois, arrêtés, décisions et instructions concernant la perception des droits réunis. Imprimé par ordre de Monsieur le Conseiller d'État Directeur Général des Droits Réunis. 4 vols. *8°. Paris,* 1806.

19268 —— *Ministère du Trésor Impérial.* Tarif de la valeur pour laquelle un kilogramme ou un marc de chaque espèce de monnaie sera admis dans les caisses publiques, ou dans les bureaux de change des colonies françaises, en conséquence du Décret Impérial du 20 floréal an 13 ⟨10 mai 1805⟩. [With the text of the Decree.] 26p. *4°. Paris,* 1806.

19269 —— *Napoleon I, Emperor.* No. 284. Bulletin des Lois. No. 75. Décret Impérial qui fixe le droit à payer pour les tabacs en feuilles venant de l'étranger. Au Palais des Tuileries, le 25 février 1806. [4]p. *4°. Paris,* [1806]

19270 GANILH, C. Essai politique sur le revenu public des peuples de l'antiquité, du moyen âge, des siècles modernes, et spécialement de la France et de l'Angleterre, depuis le milieu du 15e. siècle jusqu'au 19e.... 2 vols. *8°. Paris,* 1806.

19271 JEFFERYS, N. A review of the conduct of His Royal Highness the Prince of Wales, in his various transactions with Mr. Jefferys...Containing a detail of many circumstances relative to...the Prince and Princess of Wales, Mrs. Fitzherbert, &c.&c.&c. 68p. *8°.* [1806]

19272 MILLIN DE GRANDMAISON, A. L. Histoire métallique de la Révolution Française, ou recueil des médailles et des monnoies qui ont été frappées depuis la convocation des Etats-Généraux jusqu'aux premières campagnes de l'Armée d'Italie. 62p., 36 plates. *4°. Paris,* 1806.

19273 MYTTON, H. Letters on finance and taxation. 100p. *8°. Bridgnorth,* 1806.

19274 Desultory **OBSERVATIONS** on the public securities: and hints on taxation. By a revenue officer. p. 1–54. *8°.* 1806.

19275 PAPION, . Réflexions sur le crédit publique. 56p. *8°. Paris,* 1806.

19276 PLOWDEN, F. The principles and law of tithing, adapted to the instruction and convenience...of all persons interested in tithes; illustrated by references to the most leading and recent tithe cases. 628p. *8°.* 1806.

19277 Del **PREZZO** delle cose tutto mercatabili. Trattato legale-economico ove incidentemente si additano i veri principj della moneta. 190p. *8°. Bologna,* 1806.

19278 PROVIDENT INSTITUTION FOR LIFE ASSURANCE AND ANNUITIES. A short account of the Provident Institution... 31p. *8°.* 1806. *See also* 1809.

19279 [**RENDU,** A. M. M.] Considérations sur le prêt à intérêt. Par un Jurisconsulte. 226, 64p. *8°. Paris,* 1806.

19280 The **REPRESENTATION** of the lease-holders and contractors interested in the houses and buildings in Pickett Street, near Temple Bar; Skinner Street, Fleet Market; and Snow Hill. With the schemes of the City state lottery, and plans and elevations of the different buildings constituting the prizes. 8p. *4°.* [*London,* 1806?]

19281 ROSE, GEORGE. A brief examination into the increase of the revenue, commerce, and navigation, of Great-Britain, during the administration of...William Pitt; with allusions to some of the principal events which occured in that period, and a sketch of Mr. Pitt's character. 109, [11]p. *8°.* 1806. *For other editions, see* 1799.

19282 SMITH, WILLIAM, **& CO.** A list of bankrupts with their dividends, certificates, &c.&c. for the last twenty years and six months, viz. from Jan. 1, 1786, to June 24, 1806 [— June 1811], inclusive...arranged alphabetically... 5 vols. in 2. *8°.* 1806–11.

19283 [**WARE,** S. H.] Remarks on the facility of obtaining commercial credit; or, an exposure of the various deceptions by which credit is procured. 54p. *8°. Manchester,* 1806.

TRANSPORT

19284 CARY, JOHN (d. 1835). Cary's traveller's companion, or, a delineation of the turnpike roads of England and Wales; shewing the immediate route to every market and borough town throughout the kingdom...on a new set of county maps. To which is added, an alphabetical list of all the market towns, with the days on which they are held. [22]p., 43 maps. *8°.* 1806. *See also* 1810, 1822.

19285 ELLESMERE CANAL PROPRIETORS. Report to the general assembly of the Ellesmere Canal Proprietors, held at the Royal Oak Inn, Ellesmere, on the 27th day of November, 1805. To which is annexed, the oration [by Rowland Hunt] delivered at Pontcysylte aqueduct, on its first opening, November 26, 1805. 42, 36p. *4°. Shrewsbury,* 1806.

19286 ENGLAND. *Laws, etc.* Anno tricesimo nono & quadragesimo Georgii III. Regis. [Local & Personal.] Cap. 36. An Act for better enabling the Company of Proprietors of the Rochdale Canal, to raise money for completing the said canal, and to vary the line of the said canal, and...to amend the Act...for making the said canal. ⟨30th May 1800.⟩ p. 743–766. *fol.* 1806.

19287 —— —— Anno quadragesimo sexto Georgii III. Regis. [Local & Personal.] Cap. 92. An Act for improving the Birmingham Canal Navigations. ⟨3d July 1806.⟩ p. 1881–1892. *fol.* 1806.

19288 LONDON. Port of London. Extracts from the several Acts of Parliament relative to compensations [consequent upon the reorganization of the London docks]... 86p. *8°.* 1806.

SOCIAL CONDITIONS

19289 BONE, J. The principles and regulations of Tranquillity; an institution commenced in the Metropolis, for encouraging and enabling...individuals...to provide for themselves...and thus effecting the gradual abolition of the poor's rate, whilst it increases the comforts of the poor. 99p. *8°. 1806.*

19290 BOWLES, J. A dispassionate inquiry into the best means of national safety. [A criticism of the morals of society. With 'Supplementary note on Sunday newspapers'.] 115p. *8°. London & Bath, 1806.*

19291 COLQUHOUN, P. A new and appropriate system of education for the labouring people; elucidated and explained according to the plan...for the religious and moral instruction of...children admitted into the free school, No. 19, Orchard Street...Westminster...To which are added concluding observations on the importance of extending the system generally... 93p. *8°. 1806. The copy that belonged to James Colquhoun.*

19292 —— A treatise on indigence; exhibiting a general view of the national resources for productive labour; with propositions for ameliorating the condition of the poor... by regulations of political economy, calculated to prevent poverty from descending into indigence... 302p. *8°. 1806. The copy that belonged to Sir Robert Peel.*

19293 —— A treatise on the police of the metropolis; containing a detail of the various crimes and misdemeanors by which public and private property...are... injured...and suggesting remedies...The seventh edition, corrected and considerably enlarged. 655p. *8°. 1806. The copy that belonged to Sir Robert Peel. For other editions, see 1796.*

19294 DAMPIER, T., *Bishop of Ely.* A sermon preached before the incorporated Society for the Propagation of the Gospel in Foreign Parts; at their anniversary meeting...February 21, 1806. [With 'An abstract of the charter, and...proceedings of the Society...1805, to... 1806'.] 72p. *8°. 1806.*

19295 DAVENPORT, W., *and others.* The trial of W. Davenport, S. Stubbs, J. Woode, G. Jackson, J. Tittersall alias Tittensall, R. Barnes, A. Tittersall alias Tittensall, and J. Hattersley, journeymen hatters, of Macclesfield: for a conspiracy against their masters, and refusing to work for the wages which they and other workmen were accustomed to receive. Taken in shorthand, by Thomas Molineux... 36[34]p. *8°. Macclesfield & London, 1806.*

19296 ENGLAND. *Laws, etc.* A copy of the clauses of two Acts of Parliament, passed in the 25th and 28th years of the reign of His present Majesty, relating to the election and powers of the Commissioners, appointed to superintend the raising of additional rates for the relief of the poor, of the City and County of Exon... 30p. *8°. Exeter: Corporation of the Poor, 1806. Probably printed with an index to the Statutes here mentioned, with which it is bound. For the text of these Statutes, see 1785.*

19297 —— *Navy.* Regulations and instructions relating to His Majesty's service at sea. Established by His Majesty in Council. [With an appendix of forms.] 440, [174]p. *4°. n.p. [1806] [Binding 27] The copy bound for William IV, as Duke of Clarence, with his autograph inscription on the title-page, 'William Henry Duke of Clarence Admiral of the Red Squadron January 1806'. See also 1766 (COMMERCE), 1772.*

19298 —— *Parliament. House of Commons.* Callico printers. Upon the motion of Mr. P. Moore, the following Committee of the House of Commons was appointed to take the case of the callico printers into their consideration [here follow the names of the members of the Committee] ...Upon the 17th of July, Mr. Moore, as Chairman, presented to the House the following Report, which was ordered to be printed. 12p. *8°. Manchester, [1806]*

19299 GREEN, WILLIAM (*fl.* 1788–1818). Plans of economy; or, the road to ease and independence, both in town and country: illustrated by estimates...A new edition, considerably improved. 109p. *12°. 1806. For other editions, see 1804.*

19300 HALE, WILLIAM. A letter to Samuel Whitbread, Esq., M.P., containing observations on the distresses peculiar to the poor of Spitalfields, arising from their local situation. 35p. *8°. 1806. Presentation copy from the author to Patrick Colquhoun, with accompanying letter. For the letter, see vol. III, A.L. 265. See also 1816.*

19301 KELLY, T. Thoughts on the marriages of the labouring poor; containing instructions for their conduct before and after entering into that important state. With four...stories, illustrating the subject. 89p. *4°. 1806.*

19302 WILSON, RICHARD. A correspondence between Richard Wilson, Esq....the Rt. Hon. William Elliot, principal secretary to his Grace the Duke of Bedford, and the Rt. Hon. George Ponsonby, Lord High Chancellor of Ireland: relative to the persecutions of the Roman Catholics in his district, by a certain description of Orangemen... 63p. *8°. Dublin, 1806.*

19303 WINZER, afterwards WINSOR, F. A. To be sanctioned by an Act of Parliament. A national light and heat company, for providing our streets and houses with light and heat... 37p. *8°. [1806?]*

SLAVERY

19304 *CLARKE, THOMAS. A letter to Mr. Cobbett on his opinions respecting the slave-trade. 113p. *8°. 1806. The copy that belonged to Beilby Porteus, Bishop of London.*

19305 *CLEAVER, W., *Bishop of St. Asaph.* House of Peers, Tuesday, June 24th, 1806. The Bishop of St. Asaph upon Lord Grenville's motion to agree with the House of Commons, in resolutions respecting the slave trade, upon which Lord Hawkesbury had moved the previous question. 13p. *8°. [London, 1806] The copy that belonged to Beilby Porteus, Bishop of London.*

19306 ENGLAND. *Parliament.* Substance of the debates on a resolution for abolishing the slave trade, which was moved in the House of Commons on the 10th June, 1806, and in the House of Lords on the 24th June, 1806. With an appendix, containing notes and illustrations. 216p. *8°. 1806. The Sheffield copy.*

19307 FOREIGN SLAVE BILL. Facts and observations in answer to the statements of counsel, and of the petitions to the House of Lords. 12p. *fol.* [*London*, 1806]

19308 PARRISH, J. Remarks on the slavery of the black people; addressed to the citizens of the United States, particularly to those who are in legislative or executive stations in the...governments; and also to such individuals as hold them in bondage. 66p. *8°. Philadelphia*, 1806.

19309 PINCKARD, G. Interesting narrative of a negro sale at Demarara. [Extracted from *Notes on the West Indies.*] 4p. *8°.* [*London*, 1806] *For the original work, see no.* 19254.

POLITICS

19310 [BROUGHAM, H. P., *Baron Brougham and Vaux.*] An inquiry into the state of the nation, at the commencement of the present administration. 219p. *8°.* 1806.

19311 [——] Third edition. 219p. *8°.* 1806.

19312 [——] Sixth edition, with additions. 218p. *8°.* 1806.

19313 CARTWRIGHT, J. England's ægis: or, the military energies of the constitution...The third edition ... 2 vols. *8°.* 1806. *The copy that belonged to Samuel Whitbread (1758–1816), with his book-plate.*

19314 [GENTZ, F. VON.] Fragmente aus der neusten Geschichte des politischen Gleichgewichts in Europa. 274p. *8°. St. Petersburg*, 1806.

19315 [LANE, JOSEPH.] An answer to the Inquiry into the state of the nation; with strictures on the conduct of the present Ministry. 157p. *8°.* 1806.

19316 Fifth edition. An admonitory **LETTER** to H.R.H. the Prince of Wales, on the subject of the late delicate enquiry; containing anecdotes never before published...[Signed: A friend who is no parasite, and dated, Aug. 6th, 1806.] 30p. *8°.* 1806.

19317 PAULL, J. Mr. Paull's letter to Lord Viscount Folkestone [dated: October 20th, 1806]; as it appeared in the Political Register. [Referring to his attacks on Lord Wellesley's government in India.] 16p. *8°.* [1806 ?]

19318 SHERIDAN, RICHARD B. B. Substance of the speech of the Right Honourable Richd. Brinsley Sheridan, at a meeting of the electors of the city of Westminster, at the Crown-&-Anchor Tavern, Sept. 18, 1806. 19p. *8°.* 1806.

19319 THROCKMORTON, SIR J. C., *Bart.* Considerations arising from the debates in Parliament on the petition of the Irish Catholics. 165p. *8°. London & Oxford*, 1806.

19320 UNIVERSITY OF CAMBRIDGE. The poll for the election of a representative in Parliament for the University of Cambridge...February 7, 1806. Candidates: Lord Henry Petty, Lord Althorp, Lord Viscount Palmerston. By John Beverley, M.A. 34p. *8°. Cambridge & London*, [1806]

19321 The **WAR** as it is, and the war as it should be: an address to the united Administration, urging the necessity of a new species of warfare, and a new basis for a treaty of peace. By a true Englishman. 40p. *8°.* 1806.

MISCELLANEOUS

19322 AA, P. J. B. C. VAN DER. Handleiding tot gebruik der ordonnantie op het middel van het klein zegel, gearresteerd den 28. november 1805...Tweede druk. 20p. *8°. Leyden*, 1806.

19323 Circumstantial **DETAILS** of the long illness and last moments of the Right Hon. Charles James Fox. Together with strictures on his public and private life... The second edition. 79p. *8°.* 1806.

19324 GISBORNE, THOMAS (1758–1846). Observations on the plan for training the people to the use of arms, with reference to the subject of Sunday drilling. 20p. *8°.* 1806.

19325 —— [Another issue.] p. 1–20, 25–36. *8°.* 1806. *The additional pages contain the text of correspondence on Sunday drilling.*

19326 HAWTHORNE, C. S. Mr. Hawthorne's speech in the House of Commons, on Wednesday, the 30th of April 1806, on the proposed repeal of the Additional Force Bill. 8p. *8°.* [*London*, 1806]

19327 HOARE, PRINCE. An inquiry into the requisite cultivation and present state of the arts of design in England. 270p. *12°.* 1806.

19328 LETTERS to the Right Honorable W. Windham...By a field officer of volunteers. [On reforming the organization and recruitment of the British Army.] 82p. *8°.* 1806.

19329 *LONDON.* Livery Companies. *Salters.* A list of the Master, Wardens, Court of Assistants, and Livery, of the Worshipful Company of Salters. 12p. *8°.* 1806. *See also* 1784, 1787, 1790, 1792, 1794, 1797, 1799, 1801, 1803, 1809, 1812, 1815, 1818, 1821, 1824, 1827, 1830.

19330 REMARKS on the Report of the Committee of the House of Peers, relative to the administration of civil justice in Scotland. [With the text of the Report.] 42p. *8°. Glasgow & Edinburgh*, 1806.

19331 SHARP, G. Remarks on the two last petitions in the Lord's Prayer. 25p. *12°.* 1806.

19332 STOWER, C. Typographical marks, employed in correcting proofs, explained and exemplified; for the use of authors...Second edition. 14p. *8°.* 1806. *The copy that belonged to David Ricardo.*

1807

GENERAL

19333 CAPMANY SURIS Y DE MONTPALAU, A. DE. Qüestiones criticas sobre varios puntos de historica economica, politica y militar. 305p. *8°. Madrid, 1807.*

19334 CORRY, JOSEPH. Observations upon the windward coast of Africa, the religion, character, customs, &c. of the natives; with a system upon which they may be civilized, and a knowledge attained of the interior...and upon the natural and commercial resources of the country: made in...1805 and 1806...With an appendix, containing a letter to Lord Howick, on the most simple...means of abolishing the slave trade. 163p. *4°. 1807.*

19335 DEAN, RANDLE and W. Deans' Manchester & Salford directory; for 1808 & 1809, containing an alphabetical list of the merchants, manufacturers, and inhabitants in general... 288p. *12°. Manchester,* [1807]

19336 HALL, JAMES. Travels in Scotland, by an unusual route: with a trip to the Orkneys and Hebrides. Containing hints for improvements in agriculture and commerce... 2 vols. *8°. 1807.*

19337 HEADRICK, J. View of the mineralogy, agriculture, manufacture and fisheries of the Island of Arran. With notices of antiquities, and suggestions for improving the agriculture and fisheries of the Highlands and Isles of Scotland. 395p. *8°. Edinburgh & London,* 1807.

19338 PARNELL, W. An historical apology for the Irish Catholics...Second edition, with additions and corrections. 147p. *8°. Dublin,* 1807.

19339 The **PICTURE** of Newcastle upon Tyne: containing a guide to the town & neighbourhood, an account of the Roman Wall, and a description of the coal mines... 186p. *12°. Newcastle,* [1807] *See also* 1812.

19340 PLAYFAIR, W. An inquiry into the permanent causes of the decline and fall of powerful and wealthy nations, illustrated by...engraved charts...Designed to shew how the prosperity of the British Empire may be prolonged. The second edition. 301p. *4°. 1807. The copy that belonged to James Colquhoun, with his book-plate. For another edition, see 1805.*

19341 RITCHIE, T. E. An account of the life and writings of David Hume, Esq. 520p. *8°. 1807.*

19342 [SCHULZ, J. C. F.] Voyage en Pologne et en Allemagne, fait en 1793, par un Livonien; où l'on trouve des détails...sur la révolution de Pologne, en 1791 et en 1794, ainsi que la description de Varsovie, Dresde, Nuremberg, Vienne, Munich, etc. Traduit de l'allemand ... 2 vols. *8°. Bruxelles & Paris,* 1807. *Translated by J. B. B. Eyriès.*

19343 SPENCE, W. Britain independent of commerce; or, proofs, deduced from an investigation into the true causes of the wealth of nations, that our riches, prosperity and power, are derived from sources inherent in ourselves and would not be affected even though our commerce were annihilated. 85p. *8°. 1807. A second, mutilated copy belonged to William Cobbett.*

19344 —— The second edition. 89p. *8°. 1807. See also* 1808.

19345 TYTLER, A. F., *Lord Woodhouselee.* Memoirs of the life and writings of...Henry Home of Kames... Containing sketches of the progress of literature and general improvement in Scotland during the greater part of the eighteenth century... 2 vols. *4°. Edinburgh & London,* 1807.

19346 WELD, I. Travels through the states of North America, and the provinces of Upper and Lower Canada, during the years 1795, 1796, and 1797...Fourth edition ... 2 vols. *8°. 1807.*

AGRICULTURE

19347 BUDDLE, J. Search for coal in a part of the counties of Roxburgh and Berwickshire, in July, 1806. 40p. *8°. Kelso,* 1807.

19348 CULLEY, G. Observations on live stock; containing hints for choosing and improving the best breeds of the most useful kinds of domestic animals...The fourth edition, with an appendix. 274p. *8°. 1807.*

19349 DRALET, . L'art du taupier, ou méthode amusante et infaillible de prendre les taupes, suivant les procédés d'Aurignac...Treizième édition depuis l'an VII. 24p. *8°. Paris,* 1807.

19350 DRAUGHT of a Bill for...an Act for repealing an Act passed in the tenth year of His present Majesty, entituled "An Act to encourage the improvement of lands ...in that part of Great Britain called Scotland, held under settlements of strict entail"...[With an appendix entitled, 'Minutes of a meeting of proprietors or heirs of entailed estates in Scotland...held...on 16th February 1807...at which Sir George Stewart Mackenzie of Coul, Baronet, was unanimously called to the chair'.] 44p. *8°. Edinburgh & London,* 1807.

19351 ENGLAND. *Laws, etc.* An Act for inclosing lands in the parish of Membury, in the county of Devon. 16p. *fol. n.p.* [1807]

19352 An **ESSAY** on the use and application of patent prepared gypsum as a manure. The second edition. 48p. *8°. The Gypsum Company,* 1807.

19353 The complete **FARMER;** or, general dictionary of agriculture and husbandry: comprehending the most improved methods of cultivation; the different modes of raising timber, fruit, and other trees; and the modern management of live-stock: with descriptions of the most approved implements, machinery, and farm-buildings. The fifth edition, wholly re-written and enlarged... 2 vols. *4°. 1807. For other editions, see* 1767.

19354 FRASER, R. Statistical survey of the county of Wexford, drawn up...by order of the Dublin Society. 156p. *8°. Dublin,* 1807.

19355 HOGG, James. The shepherd's guide: being a practical treatise on the diseases of sheep...with observations on the most suitable farm-stocking for the various climates of this country. 338p. *8°. Edinburgh & London, 1807. With the book-plate of the Earls of Hopetoun.*

19356 February 28. 1807...**MEMORIAL** for His Grace William Duke of Queensberry, and the Right Honourable James Hope Johnston, Earl of Hopetoun, in the action of declarator at their instance, against the Officers of State [claiming the right to export lead from their mines free of duties imposed by Acts of Parliament before and after the Union. Signed: John A. Murray]. 27p. *4°. n.p.* [1807]

19357 MILLER, Philip. The gardener's and botanist's dictionary; containing the best and newest methods of cultivating...the kitchen, fruit, and flower garden, and nursery...By the late Philip Miller, F.R.S....To which are now first added, a complete enumeration and description of all plants hitherto known...The whole corrected and newly arranged...By Thomas Martyn...2 vols. in 4. *fol.* 1807. *For other editions, see* 1735.

19358 MOREL VINDÉ, C. G. T. de, *Vicomte.* Mémoire sur l'exacte parité des laines mérinos de France et des laines mérinos d'Espagne, et sur la vrai valeur que devroient avoir dans le commerce les laines mérinos françoises...Suivi d'un rapport fait à l'Institut de France ...par MM. Huzard, Silvestre, et Tessier, rapporteur. [Extrait des Annales de l'Agriculture françoise, tome XXXI.] 50, 4p. *8°. Paris, 1807.*

19359 NAISMITH, J. Elements of agriculture; being an essay towards establishing the cultivation of the soil, and promoting vegetation on steady principles. 543p. *8°.* 1807.

19360 January 29. 1807...Unto the Right Honourable the Lords of Council and Session, the **PETITION** of James Handyside, merchant in Glasgow, trustee for the creditors of John Hunter bleacher in Dumbrock, and of the said John Hunter... [Concerning a disputed lease. Signed: John Greenshields. With an appendix.] 17, 9p. *4°. n.p.* [1807]

19361 RAWSON, T. J. Statistical survey of the county of Kildare, with observations on the means of improvement; drawn up for the consideration...of the Dublin Society. 237p. *8°. Dublin, 1807.*

19362 RENNIE, R. Essays [I. & II.] on the natural history and origin of peat moss...the means of improving it as a soil; the methods of converting it into a manure... 233p. *8°. Edinburgh & London, 1807. The Sheffield copy.*

19363 RUDGE, T. General view of the agriculture of the county of Gloucester. Drawn up for the consideration of the Board of Agriculture and internal improvement... 408p. *8°. London, Gloucester, &c., 1807. See also* 1813.

19364 SMITHFIELD CLUB. At the meetings of the Smithfield Club, held at the Freemason's Tavern, December 14 and 15, 1807...It was resolved, that the premiums and conditions, for the ensuing Christmas Show ...the 16th, 17th, and 19th of December, 1808, be as follows... [With printed entry form.] *s.sh.fol.* [London, 1807] *The Sheffield copy.*

19365 SUSSEX AGRICULTURAL SOCIETY. At a general meeting of the subscribers of the Sussex Agricultural Society, to arrange the prizes and premiums for the present year, 1807, held at the Star Inn, Lewes... The following resolutions were agreed to. [Dated: Feb. 29, 1807] *s.sh.fol. Lewes,* [1807] *The Sheffield copy.*

19366 —— At a general meeting of the subscribers of the...Society, to arrange the prizes and premiums for... 1808, held at the Star Inn, Lewes...The following resolutions were agreed to. *s.sh.fol. n.p.* [1807] *The Sheffield copy. See also* 1801, 1804, 1805, 1808.

19367 TIBBS, T. The experimental farmer: being strictures on various branches of husbandry and agriculture drawn from...practice in different parts of Great-Britain; containing observations on planting & preserving young trees...Likewise plans for laying-out land, on a five and four field system. Also a new method to bring the most barren land into cultivation, for meadows and sheep walks... 153p. *8°.* 1807. *See also* 1810.

19368 WINDOVER, N. In the press, and shortly will be published...The Englishman's guide to plenty... [A prospectus.] 8p. *8°.* 1807. *The Sheffield copy.*

19369 —— The Englishman's guide to plenty; containing the observations of an old Hampshire farmer on the national produce and consumption and the present prices of the necessaries of life... 109p. *8°.* 1807.

19370 YOUNG, Arthur (1741–1820). General view of the agriculture of the county of Essex. Drawn up for the consideration of the Board of Agriculture...By the Secretary of the Board... 2 vols. *8°.* 1807.

POPULATION

19371 [HAZLITT, William (1778–1830).] A reply to the Essay on population, by the Rev. T. R. Malthus. In a series of letters. To which are added, extracts from the Essay; with notes. 378p. *8°.* 1807.

19372 LIVERPOOL. A general Bill of Mortality for the Town and Parish of Liverpool. Comprising an annual and a monthly table of the births, burials and marriages, from the 1st of January, 1806, to the 1st of January, 1807 ...[Signed: E. Coventry, J. Taylor, parish clerks.] *s.sh.fol.* [*Liverpool,* 1807] [*Br.* 471]

19373 MALTHUS, T. R. An essay on the principle of population...The fourth edition. [With an appendix.] 2 vols. *8°.* 1807. *For other editions, see* 1798.

TRADES & MANUFACTURES

19374 BRITISH PLATE GLASS MANUFACTORY. Tariff of the prices of polished plates of glass. 99p. *8°.* 1807. *For another edition, see* 1794.

19375 CLENNELL, J. Thoughts on the expediency of disclosing the processes of manufactories; being the substance of two papers lately read before the Literary and

Philosophical Society of Newcastle upon Tyne. 32p. *8°*. *Newcastle upon Tyne*, 1807. *Presentation copy, with inscription, from the author to Patrick Colquhoun.*

19376 HUDDART, JOSEPH (1741–1816). Remarks on patent registered cordage, made by Messrs. Huddart & Co. at their manufactory, Limehouse, and on common cordage. 54p. *8°*. 1807.

19377 PHILLIPS, JOHN (*fl.* 1785–1807). Eighth

edit. corrected to Feb. 1807, containing the late great advance on timber, lead, and other materials. Crosby's Builder's new price-book, for 1807. Containing a correct account of all the prices allowed...to bricklayers, carpenters, joiners...carvers, paviers, thatchers, and paper hangers. Shewing the average prices for 20 years past. By John Phillips, assisted by several eminent surveyors and builders. 188p. *8°*. 1807.

COMMERCE

19378 An **ADDRESS** to the auctioneers of the Metropolis, containing proposals for forming an establishment to promote their general accommodation and interest... 27p. *8°*. 1807.

19379 AGG, J. The lamp trimmed. An address to the public of the City of Bristol, occasioned by the publication of a pamphlet entitled "Trim the lamp" [by T. Lee]. 16p. *8°*. *Bristol*, 1807.

19380 BALD, A. The farmer and corn-dealer's assistant; or, the knowledge of weights and measures made easy, by a variety of tables...To which are added tables of all the fiars in Scotland...Also, an extract from the custom-house books of the annual exports and imports of grain in Scotland from the year 1707 to 1777. 254p. *8°*. *Edinburgh*, 1807. *For another edition, see 1780.*

19381 BOSANQUET, C. Thoughts on the value to Great Britain, of commerce in general; and on the value and importance of the colonial trade in particular. 83p. *8°*. [1807]

19382 CONSIDERATIONS upon the trade with India; and the policy of continuing the Company's monopoly. 159p. *4°*. *London & Edinburgh*, 1807.

19383 A **DEMONSTRATION** of the necessity and advantages of a free trade to the East Indies; and of a termination to the present monopoly of the East-India Company. 157p. *8°*. *London & Edinburgh*, 1807.

19384 ENGLAND. *George III.* The Orders of Council, and instructions for imposing the restriction of blockade; and for regulating the navigation of the sea, and the importation and exportation of merchandize, in consequence thereof; with a brief view of the several provisions therein contained. Published 21st December 1807. 51p. *8°*. 1807. *See also 1808.*

19385 —— *Laws, etc.* [*Endorsed:*] An Act for repealing the several Acts for regulating the vend and delivery of coals, within the cities of London and Westminster...and in certain parts of the counties of Middlesex, Surry, Kent, and Essex; and for making better provision for the same. 47 Geo. III. 8th August, 1807. 106p. *fol.* [*Printed for the Corporation of the City of London*, 1807]

19386 FLOWERDEW, D. C. An exposition of the three Orders in Council of the 11th November, 1807, on the trade restricted, permitted, and regulated by the new system of blockade, and also of six other Orders, dated 25th November, 1807... 89p. *8°*. [1807]

19387 FRANCE. *Laws, etc.* Code de commerce. Edition originale et seule officielle. 254p. *4°*. *Paris*, 1807.

19388 —— [Another edition.] 2 vols. in 1. *32°*. *Paris*, 1807. *See also 1808, 1824, 1826, 1836.*

19389 —— Exposé des motifs du Code de commerce,

présenté au Corps Législatif par MM. les orateurs du Gouvernement, dans les séances des 1, 2, 3, 4 et 8 septembre 1807. Pour faire suite et servir de commentaire à l'édition officielle du Code de commerce. 155p. *32°*. *Paris*, 1807.

19390 LEE, THOMAS, *of Bristol.* Trim the lamp! An address to the public of Bristol. [With 'Postscript to "More oil to the lamp"' and 'Postscript to "Trim the lamp"'.] 24, 3p. *8°*. *Bristol*, [1807]

19391 [**MARRYAT,** J.] Concessions to America the bane of Britain; or the cause of the present distressed situation of the British colonial and shippings interests explained, and the proper remedy suggested. 63p. *8°*. 1807.

19392 MEDFORD, M. Oil without vinegar, and dignity without pride: or, British, American and West-India interests considered. [With an appendix.] 87p. *8°*. *London & Philadelphia*, 1807.

19393 PHILOPATRIS, *pseud.* Observations on public institutions, monopolies, joint stock companies, and deeds of trust: shewing the advantages the public derive from competition in trade. With remarks upon the Golden-Lane Brewery, the public distilleries, and the Sun, Imperial, Phœnix, Hope, Globe and other insurance-offices... 42p. *8°*. 1807.

19394 A true **PICTURE** of the United States of America; being a brief statement of the conduct of the government and people of that country, towards Great Britain, from the peace concluded in 1783, to the present time. By a British subject. 84p. *8°*. *London & Liverpool*, 1807.

19395 The **POLICY** of the blockading system refuted, with observations on the present stage of the war! In a letter to a friend. 58p. *8°*. 1807.

19396 PONS, F. R. J. DE. Perspective des rapports politiques et commerciaux de la France dans les deux Indes, sous la dynastie régnante. 292p. *8°*. *Paris & Strasbourg*, 1807.

19397 PROPOSITIONS on Sicilian wines. [On establishing a wine trade with Sicily.] 4p. *fol.* [*London*, 1807 ?] *The Sheffield copy.*

19398 SOCIETY OF SHIPOWNERS OF GREAT BRITAIN. Collection of interesting and important reports and papers on the navigation and trade of Great Britain, Ireland and the British colonies in the West Indies and America. With tables of tonnage and of exports and imports, &c., &c., &c.... 154p. *8°*. 1807.

19399 SPENCE, W. The radical cause of the present distresses of the West-India planters pointed out...with remarks on the publications of Sir William Young, Bart. Charles Bosanquet, Esq. and Joseph Lowe, Esq; relative to the value of the West-India trade. 103p. *8°*. 1807. *See also* 1808.

19400 TAYLOR, SIMON. Facts and observations respecting the sugar trade between Great-Britain and her Old West-Indian colonies...Printed in 1803, for the use of the members of the House of Assembly of Jamaica. 2p. *s.sh.fol. Bath*, [1807] [*Br*. 472]

19401 THORP, J. Considerations on the present state of the cotton and silk manufactories of Great Britain; and the political impropriety of continuing to draw the supply

of materials for the latter from France and Italy; as submitted to the Lords of Trade. 28p. *8°*. 1807.

19402 VINCENT, WILLIAM. The commerce and navigation of the ancients in the Indian Ocean... 2 vols. *4°*. 1807. *Contents: 1. The voyage of Nearchus from the Indus to the Euphrates; 2. The Periplus of the Erythrean Sea.*

19403 YOUNG, SIR WILLIAM, *2nd Bart.* (1749–1815). The West-India common-place book: compiled from parliamentary and official documents; shewing the interest of Great Britain in its sugar colonies, &c.&c.&c. 256p. *4°*. 1807.

COLONIES

19404 AMBROSE, R. L. A letter, on the present crisis of affairs in India, addressed to Edward Parry, Esq. chairman of the honorable Court of Directors. 37p. *8°*. [1807]

19405 BOLINGBROKE, H. A voyage to the Demerary, containing a statistical account of the settlements there, and of those on the Essequebo, the Berbice, and other contiguous rivers of Guyana. 400p. *4°*. [1807] *See also* 1809.

19406 BOSANQUET, C. A letter to W. Manning, Esq. M.P. on the causes of the rapid and progressive depreciation of West India property. Second edition. 54p. *8°*. [1807] *The Sheffield copy.*

19407 CORDINER, J. A description of Ceylon, containing an account of the country, inhabitants, and natural productions; with narratives of a tour round the island in 1800, the campaign in Candy in 1803, and a journey to Ramisseram in 1804... 2 vols. *4°*. 1807.

19408 CUNHA DE AZEREDO COUTINHO, J. J. DA, *Bishop of Elvas.* An essay on the commerce and products of the Portuguese colonies in South America, especially the Brazils. Translated from the Portuguese... 198p. *8°*. 1807. *A re-issue of the sheets of* A political essay on the commerce of Portugal and her colonies, *of 1801* (*q.v.*), *with a new title-page. For another edition, see* 1794.

19409 FARQUHAR, SIR R. T., *Bart.* Suggestions, arising from the abolition of the African slave trade, for supplying the demands of the West India colonies with agricultural labourers. [Urging the introduction of Chinese labour.] 66p. *8°*. 1807.

19410 FRANCIS, SIR PHILIP. A letter from Sir Philip Francis, K.B. to Lord Viscount Howick, on the state of the East India Company. [On the Company's financial difficulties.] Second edition. 21p. *8°*. 1807.

19411 HERIOT, G. Travels through the Canadas... with an account of the productions, commerce, and inhabitants of those provinces. To which is subjoined a comparative view of the manners and customs of several

of the Indian nations of North and South America... 602p. *4°*. 1807.

19412 LAYMAN, W. Outline of a plan for the better cultivation, security, & defence of the British West Indies: being the original suggestion for providing an effectual substitute for the African slave trade, and preventing the dependance of those colonies on America for supplies. 93p. *8°*. 1807.

19413 LOWE, JOSEPH. An inquiry into the state of the British West Indies...Second edition. 160p. *8°*. 1807.

19414 OWEN, JOHN (1766–1822). An address to the Chairman of the East India Company, occasioned by Mr. Twining's letter to that gentleman, on the danger of interfering in the religious opinions of the natives of India, and on the views of the British and Foreign Bible Society, as directed to India...The third edition, to which is added a postscript, containing brief strictures on the "preface" to Observation on the present state of the East India Company. 36p. *8°*. 1807.

19415 RENNY, R. An history of Jamaica. With observations on the climate...trade, productions, negroes ...To which is added, an illustration of the advantages, which are likely to result, from the abolition of the slave trade. 333p. *4°*. 1807.

19416 REVIEW of the affairs of India from the year 1798, to the year 1806; comprehending a summary account of the principal transactions during that eventful period. Second edition. 140p. *8°*. 1807.

19417 TWINING, T. A letter, to the Chairman of the East India Company, on the danger of interfering in the religious opinions of the natives of India, and on the views of the British and Foreign Bible Society, as directed to India...Second edition. 31p. *8°*. 1807.

19418 WILCOCKE, S. H. History of the Viceroyalty of Buenos Ayres; containing the most accurate details relative to the topography, history, commerce, population, government, &c....of that valuable colony... 576p. *8°*. 1807.

FINANCE

19419 Naval **ANECDOTES;** or, a new key to the proceedings of a late naval administration [that of Lord St. Vincent]...Second edition. 192p. *8°*. 1807.

19420 BAILY, F. Tables for the purchasing and renewing of leases, for terms of years certain and for lives;

with rules for determining the value of the reversion of estates...To which is added, an appendix, containing... some remarks on the method adopted by Dr. Price and Mr. Morgan for finding the value of annuities payable half-yearly, quarterly, &c. together with some new formulæ for determining the rate of interest in annuities

...The second edition. 127p. *8°*. 1807. *The copy presented by the author to the London Institution.*

19421 BATTYE, T. An address to the ley-payers in the town of Manchester. [On abuses in the administration of local government funds.] 8p. *8°*. [1807]

19422 [*Begin.*] **BERICHT** van eene negotiatie ten behoeve van het Koningrijk Holland, à 6 perCt. intrest... [Dated: Amsterdam, den 1 april 1807.] [4]p. *4°*. *n.p.* [1807]

19423 BOASE, H. The disadvantages of the new plan of finance, demonstrated, by a comparison of its result, with that of the like supply raised on the present system: together with observations on the Sinking Fund, and war taxes. In a letter to a Member of Parliament...Not published. 21p. *8°*. 1807. *The Sheffield copy.*

19424 BRITISH LINEN COMPANY. Charter erecting, and warrant of a charter confirming and granting new privileges to the British Linen-Company. 30, 13p. *8°*. *Edinburgh*, 1807. *For other editions, see* 1746 (COMMERCE).

19425 COAD, J. A new plan of taxation. This plan will render the custom and excise duties useless, abolish the income tax...and reduce provisions more than seventy per cent...The third edition with additions. 52p. *8°*. 1807.

19426 DARIER, H. Tableau du titre, poids et valeur des différentes monnaies d'or et d'argent, qui circulent dans le comerce...[With a supplement.] 86, 4p. *4°*. *Genève*, 1807.

19427 DAVISON, A. Observations on the third Report of the Commissioners of Military Enquiry. [A defence of his conduct as commission agent for the supply of certain commodities to His Majesty's barracks.] 70p. *8°*. 1807.

19428 *Entry cancelled.*

19429 ELIOT, F. P. Demonstration; or, financial remarks: with occasional observations on political occurrences. 117p. *8°*. 1807.

19430 ENGLAND. *Commissioners of Excise.* Instructions for officers of excise, in the country, concerned in charging the duty on beer. 75p. *8°*. 1807.

19431 *Entry cancelled.*

19432 FRANCE. *Conseil d'Etat.* No. 457...Avis... sur les établissemens de monts-de-piété. (Séance du 6 juin 1807.) [12 July 1807.] 2p. *4°*. *Paris*, 1807.

19433 GLEN, W. A treatise on the law of bills of exchange, promissory notes and letters of credit in Scotland. 348p. *8°*. *Edinburgh & Glasgow*, 1807.

19434 LEMOINE, , and **SAVART,** . Mémoire pour les ouvriers, monnoyeurs, ajusteurs et tailleresses de Paris, à son excellence le Ministre des Finances. [Signed: Lemoine et Savart, commissaires des ouvriers monnoyeurs. With 'Etat appartenant aux ouvriers monnoyeurs de Paris, et par eux réclamés'.] 10, [6]p. *4°*. [*Paris*, 1807]

19435 [**LONG,** CHARLES, *Baron Farnborough.*] Short remarks upon recent political occurrences; and, particularly, on the new plan of finance. 50p. *8°*. 1807.

19436 [——] Second edition. 50p. *8°*. 1807.

19437 MAIR, J. Book-keeping moderniz'd; or, merchant-accounts by double entry, according to the Italian form...The ninth edition. 620p. *8°*. *Edinburgh & London*, 1807. *For other editions, see* 1741.

19438 [**O'BEIRNE,** T. L., *Bishop of Meath.*] A letter from an Irish dignitary to an English clergyman, on the subject of tithes in Ireland. 24p. *8°*. 1807.

19439 PAUL, J. The law of tythes, upon an original and practical plan: comprising the Statutes, adjudged cases, resolutions, and judgments, in equity and the ecclesiastical courts. Originally compiled by John Paul Esq. The second edition, with an appendix, containing a copious abstract of the 43d Geo. 3. c. 84. relative to spiritual persons holding farms, and enforcing residence on their benefices: tythe tables...and a comprehensive index...by John Irving Maxwell. 185p. *8°*. 1807.

19440 November 18, 1807...Unto the Right Honourable the Lords of Council and Session, the **PETITION** of John Gray, miller and grain-merchant at the Town of Glasgow's mills. [Concerning a dispute on the terms for the creditors of the estate of John Blair, bankrupt. Signed: Thos. W. Baird. With an appendix.] 15, 5p. *4°*. [*Edinburgh*, 1807] *With a manuscript note, dated '27 Feb. 1808', attached, containing his notes on the judgment, signed: Ilay Campbell L.P.D. [i.e. Sir Ilay Campbell, Lord Succoth (1734–1823)].*

19441 [**PETTY,** H., afterwards **FITZMAURICE,** H. P., *3rd Marquis of Lansdowne.*] Statement of a plan of finance, proposed to Parliament in the year 1807. [With tables.] 22, [48]p. *4°*. [*London,*] 1807. *The copy sent by Lord Grenville to Earl Spencer, according to HSF note in the volume.*

19442 [——] [Another edition.] 28, [66]p. *8°*. 1807.

19443 [——] [A summary of conclusions.] Finance, 1807. [4]p. *fol.* [*London*, 1807 ?] *Endorsed in a contemporary hand: Lord H. Petty's Scheme of Finance 1807.*

19444 —— The substance of the speech delivered in the Committee of Finance, January 29th, 1807, by the Right Hon. Lord Henry Petty. With the necessary tables, and an appendix, containing the plans of Lord Castlereagh and Mr. Johnstone. 116p. *8°*. 1807. *The copy that belonged to William Cobbett.*

19445 SMITH, THOMAS, *accountant, of London.* Essay on the theory of money & exchange. 231p. *8°*. *London & Edinburgh*, 1807. *See also* 1811.

19446 UNITED STATES OF AMERICA. *Congress. House of Representatives.* Letter from the Secretary of the Treasury, transmitting a report...in relation to the direct tax, specifying the quotas assigned to each state and the arrears...prepared in pursuance of a Resolution of this House, of the eighteenth instant. December 31, 1806. Read, and ordered to lie on the table. [4]p. *8°*. *City of Washington*, 1807.

19447 —— —— —— A letter from the Secretary of the Treasury, transmitting a statement of the amount of duties and drawbacks on goods, wares...imported and exported ...therefrom during the years 1803, 1804 and 1805. January 8, 1807. Ordered to lie on the table. [4]p. *8°*. *Washington City*, 1807.

19448 WHEATLEY, J. An essay on the theory of money and principles of commerce. 2 vols. *4°.* 1807–22.

19449 WINZER, afterwards **WINSOR,** F. A. National deposit bank; or the bulwark of British security, credit and commerce, in all times of difficulty, changes, and revolutions, with the mercantile policy of separating the discounts of merchants and manufacturers, from the law of national interest, as practised in the first commercial cities on the continent... 35p. *12°.* 1807.

TRANSPORT

19450 DEACON, W. Observations on stage-waggons, stage-coaches, turnpike-roads, toll-bars, weighing-machines, &c. occasioned by a Committee of the House of Commons being appointed to enquire into the principles and effects of broad and narrow wheels. 94p. *8°.* 1807.

19451 ENGLAND. *Laws, etc.* [*Endorsed:*] An Act for continuing the term, and altering and enlarging the powers, of two Acts, passed in the fifth and twenty-sixth years of His present Majesty, for repairing the roads from the Little Bridge...in Wisbeach...to the sign of the Bear, in Walsoken, in the county of Norfolk...47 Geo. III. sess. 1806–7. 12p. *fol. n.p.* [1807]

19452 INVESTIGATOR, *pseud.* A letter to William A. Maddock, Esq. M.P. containing...observations on a publication of documents and letters addressed to him relative to the building of a pier, at a cove called Porthdynllaen in Carnarvon Bay. [Setting out the superiority of Holyhead over Porthdynllaen both as refuge and as point of departure for the mail service to Dublin.] 19p. *12°.* *Dublin,* 1807.

SOCIAL CONDITIONS

19453 ASYLUM FOR THE SUPPORT AND EDUCATION OF THE DEAF AND DUMB CHILDREN OF THE POOR. Plan of the Asylum ...including purposes of the institution; rules of the society; and lists of the officers and governors. Situated in the Grange-Road, Bermondsey. Instituted 1792. [With a list of the inmates.] 112p. *8°. Shacklewell,* 1807.

19454 BECKWITH, W. A plan to prevent all charitable donations, for the benefit of poor persons... from loss, embezzlement...and abuse in future. 188p. *8°.* 1807.

19455 BELL, ANDREW. An analysis of the experiment in education, made at Egmore, near Madras. Comprising a system alike fitted to reduce the expense of tuition...and expedite the progress of the scholar, and suggesting a scheme for the better administration of the poor-laws, by converting schools for the lower orders of youth into schools of industry...Third edition. 115p. *8°.* 1807. *The copy that belonged to James Colquhoun. For other editions, see* 1805.

19456 —— Extract of a sermon on the education of the poor, under an appropriate system. Preached at St. Mary's Lambeth...1807: for the benefit of the Boys' Charity-School at Lambeth...Second edition. 30p. *8°.* 1807. *Presentation copy, with inscription, from the author to Patrick Colquhoun.*

19457 BERNARD, SIR T., *Bart.* A letter to...the Lord Bishop of Durham...on the principles and detail of the measures now under the consideration of Parliament, for promoting and encouraging industry, and for the relief and regulation of the poor. 62p. *8°.* 1807.

19458 —— The second edition. 64p. *8°.* 1807.

19459 BONE, J. The friend of the people: or, considerations, addressed principally to persons of small incomes, and members of friendly societies, recommending them to adopt some more effectual measures for securing their own independence than those proposed... by Mr. Whitbread... 31p. *8°.* 1807.

19460 —— The wants of the people, and the means of the Government: or objections to the interference of the Legislature in the affairs of the poor, as recommended by Mr. Whitbread in the House of Commons, on...February 19, 1807. 105p. *8°.* 1807.

19461 BOTT, E. The laws relating to the poor. By Francis Const, Esq....The fifth edition: in which the statutes and cases to Easter term 1807, are arranged under their respective heads, and the whole system...including the collections originally made by E. Bott, Esq....placed in a clear and perspicuous point of view. 3 vols. *8°.* 1807. *For another edition, see* 1793.

19462 BOWLES, J. A letter addressed to Samuel Whitbread, Esq. M.P. In consequence of the unqualified approbation expressed by him...of Mr. Lancaster's system of education: the religious part of which is here shewn to be incompatible with...the Established Church, and in its tendency, subversive of Christianity itself... 64p. *8°. London & Bath,* 1807.

19463 BREWER, J. N. Some thoughts on the present state of the English peasantry. Written in consequence of Mr. Whitbread's motion, in the House of Commons, Feb. 19, 1807, relative to an amendment of the poor laws. 43p. *8°.* 1807.

19464 CARPENTER, D. Reflections suggested by Mr. Whitbread's Bill, and by several publications, lately circulated, on the subject of the poor-laws...together with the outlines of a further plan for bettering the condition of the poor, and for improving the morals of the people. 70p. *8°.* 1807.

19465 COLQUHOUN, P. Traité sur la police de Londres, contenant le détail des crimes et délits qui se commettent dans cette capital, et indiquant les moyens de les prévenir...Traduit de l'anglais sur la sixième édition, par L.C.D.B. 2 vols. *8°. Paris,* 1807. *The copy that belonged to James Colquhoun, with his book-plate. For other editions, see* 1796.

19466 COTTINGHAM, J. A letter to Samuel Whitbread, Esq. M.P. containing some remarks on the poor laws, leading to a description of the peculiar poor situation of...Mile-End New-Town, Stepney. 29p. *8°.* 1807.

19467 DEVERELL, R. A letter to Samuel Whitbread, Esq. M.P. On the subjects of two Bills now pending in Parliament. [On the causes of unrest.] 30p. *8°*. 1807.

19468 ENGLAND. *Parliament.* Substance of a Bill for promoting and encouraging of industry amongst the labouring classes of the community, and for the relief and regulation of the necessitous and criminal poor. 40p. *8°*. 1807. *Introduced by Samuel Whitbread.*

19469 FRAME COPARTNERSHIP. Articles of agreement [dated 5 May 1806], to be observed by a frame copartnership, held at the house of Mr. Rd. Sulley, the sign of the Unicorn, Parliament Street, Nottingham. 12p. *12°. Nottingham*, 1807.

19470 GAUM, F. W. Praktische Anleitung zu vollständigen Armenpolizei-Einrichtungen. Mit besonderer Rücksicht auf das Armenwesen in Mannheim. 295p. *8°. Heidelberg*, 1807.

19471 JARROLD, T. A letter to Samuel Whitbread, Esq. M.P. on the subject of the poor's laws. 32p. *8°*. [1807]

19472 LANCASTER, JOSEPH. An appeal for justice, in the cause of ten thousand poor children... Being a reply to the visitation charge of Charles Daubeny. 'June 6th. 1806'... Third edition, with additions. 58p. *8°. London & Bath*, 1807.

19473 LEE, THOMAS, *of Bristol.* The looking glass of the workmen of the United Kingdom... or, an address to journeymen, manufacturers, & labourers... vindicating their efforts to obtain wherewithal to meet the exactions of the present monstrous system of unequal taxation. To which are added, observations on popular education. 28p. *8°. Bristol*, [1807]

19474 A LETTER on the nature, extent, and management, of poor rates in Scotland: with a review of the controversy respecting the abolition of poor laws. 38p. *8°. Edinburgh & London*, 1807. *Presentation copy from the anonymous author to William Cobbett.*

19475 MAGDALEN HOSPITAL. A short account of the Magdalen Hospital. 12p. *8°*. 1807.

19476 MALTHUS, T. R. A letter to Samuel Whitbread, Esq. M.P. on his proposed Bill for the amendment of the poor laws. 40p. *8°*. 1807. *The copy that belonged to William Cobbett.*

19477 —— The second edition. 40p. *8°*. 1807.

19478 MONCK, J. B. General reflections on the system of the poor laws, with a short view of Mr. Whitbread's Bill, and a comment on it. 44p. *8°*. 1807.

19479 NEW ORDNANCE SOCIETY. Plan of the society for the benefit of widows of persons late belonging to the civil establishment of the Office of Ordnance... Instituted 1st July, 1791. 29p. *8°*. 1807.

19480 PARKINSON, J. Remarks on Mr. Whitbread's plan for the education of the poor; with observations on Sunday schools, and on the state of the apprenticed poor. 33p. *8°*. 1807.

19481 *PRUEN, T. A comparative sketch of the effects of variolous and vaccine inoculation...which will enable the public to form its own judgment on the probable importance of the Jennerian discovery. 102p. *8°*. [*London &*] *Cheltenham*, 1807.

19482 REMARKS upon "A Bill ⟨as amended by the Committee⟩ for promoting and encouraging of industry amongst the labouring classes of the community, and for the relief...of the necessitous and criminal poor. Ordered to be printed, 24th. Feb. 1807." By one of His Majesty's justices of the peace. 31p. *8°*. 1807.

19483 —— The second edition, with additions and corrections. 38p. *8°*. 1807.

19484 *SINCLAIR, SIR JOHN, *Bart.* The code of health and longevity; or, a concise view, of the principles calculated for the preservation of health, and the attainment of long life... 4 vols. *8°. Edinburgh & London*, 1807.

19485 The STATE of the silk-manufacture of Spitalfields. Addressed to the magistrates of Middlesex; and submitted to the consideration of masters and journeymen. 29p. *8°*. 1807.

For **STILLORGAN CHARITABLE INSTITUTION.** [First-Ninth] Reports, 1807–1815, *see* vol. III, *Periodicals list*, Report of the Stillorgan Charitable Institution.

19486 TRANQUILLITY INSTITUTION. The rules and regulations of an Institution called Tranquillity; commenced in the Metropolis as an economical bank, to afford persons of all ages, trades and descriptions, an opportunity of providing for their future wants by the payment of small sums...[By the secretary, William Hone.] 15p. *8°*. 1807.

19487 —— Second edition, corrected, with an introductory address. 15p. *8°*. 1807.

19488 [WEYLAND, J.] A short enquiry into the policy, humanity and past effects of the poor laws, and into the principles upon which any measures for their improvement should be conducted, in which are included few considerations on the questions of political œconomy ...connected with the subject, particularly on the supply of food in England. By one of His Majesty's Justices of the Peace for three inland counties. 382p. *8°*. 1807. *The Sheffield copy.*

19489 —— Observations on Mr. Whitbread's Poor Bill, and on the population of England: intended as a supplement to A short inquiry into the policy, humanity, and past effects of the poor laws, &c. 65p. *8°*. 1807. *Two presentation copies, one from the author to Lord Sheffield, the other to Viscount Melville.*

19490 WHITBREAD, S. Substance of a speech on the poor laws; delivered in the House of Commons, on... February 19, 1807... 107p. *8°*. 1807.

19491 —— Second edition. 107p. *8°*. 1807. *The copy that belonged to William Cobbett.*

19492 [WRIGHT, R.] Letters on capital punishments, addressed to the English judges. By Beccaria Anglicus. 85p. *8°*. 1807.

SLAVERY

For **AFRICAN INSTITUTION.** Report[s] of the committee of the African Institution, 1807–1812, 1814–1827, *see* vol. III, *Periodicals list*. Report of the committee of the African Institution.

19493 The CLAIM for fresh evidence on the subject of the slave trade considered. 16p. *8°*. 1807.

19494 CLARKSON, T. Three letters...to the

planters and slave-merchants, principally on the subject of compensation. 15p. 8°. 1807. *The library also has a 16-page proof copy, with manuscript corrections.*

19495 HIBBERT, G. The substance of three speeches in Parliament on the Bill for the abolition of the slave trade, and on the petition respecting the state of the West-India trade, in February and March, 1807. 138p. 8°. 1807. *The Sheffield copy, with an inscription from the author.*

19496 MERCATOR, *pseud.* Letters concerning the abolition of the slave-trade and other West-India affairs. 32p. 16°. 1807. *The copy that belonged to Stephen Lushington.*

19497 —— Third letter on the abolition of the slave-trade and other West-India affairs. 22p. 12°. 1807. *The copy that belonged to Stephen Lushington.*

19498 REFLECTIONS on the slave-trade; extracted from a work, entitled A compendious dictionary of the Holy Bible, under the article slavery...Extracted by R. R. 12p. 12°. 1807.

19499 SHARP, G. "The system of colonial law" compared with the eternal laws of God; and with the indispensable principles of the English Constitution. 20p. 8°. 1807. *Presentation copy, with inscription, from the author to Francis Broderip.*

19500 SLAVE TRADE. [*Begin.*] It is earnestly submitted to the friends of Abolition...that much yet remains to be done...The following speeches delivered in Parliament on the 24th of February, are presented to the notice of persons who may feel an interest in the approaching election for the county of York...[Two extracts from speeches by Lord Milton and William Wilberforce, in support of the abolition of the slave trade, reprinted from the *Courier* of the same day.] *s.sh.fol.* [*London*, 1807]

19501 SMITH, WILLIAM (1756–1835). A letter to William Wilberforce, Esq. M.P. on the proposed abolition of the slave trade, at present under the consideration of Parliament. 48p. 12°. 1807. *The copy that belonged to Stephen Lushington.*

19502 SPILSBURY, F. B. Account of a voyage to the western coast of Africa; performed by His Majesty's sloop Favourite, in the year 1805. Being a journal of the events which happened to that vessel, from the time of her leaving England till her capture by the French, and the return of the author in a cartel... 43p. 8°. 1807.

19503 [STEPHEN, J.] New reasons for abolishing the slave trade; being the last section of a larger work, now first published, entitled "The dangers of the country". By the author of "War in disguise". 67p. 8°. 1807. *The Sheffield copy. For* The dangers of the country, *see nos.* 19531, 19532.

19504 WILBERFORCE, WILLIAM (1759–1833). A letter on the abolition of the slave trade: addressed to the freeholders and other inhabitants of Yorkshire. 396p. 8°. 1807. *Presentation copy from the author to Simonde de Sismondi, with an inscription in his hand.*

19505 —— [Another edition.] 396p. 8°. 1807. *The Sheffield copy.*

POLITICS

19506 ADDINGTON, H., *Viscount Sidmouth.* Substance of the speech of Lord Viscount Sidmouth, upon the motion of the Marquis of Stafford [for an address to the Crown expressing regret at the recent change in His Majesty's councils], in the House of Lords, on Monday, April 13, 1807. Second edition. 28p. 8°. 1807.

19507 A plain **ADDRESS** to the people of England; in explanation of the secret causes which occasioned the dismissal of His Majesty's late ministers. 24p. 8°. 1807.

19508 [BARRETT, E. S.] All the talents: a satirical poem in three dialogues. By Polypus. Ninth edition. 81p. 8°. 1807.

19509 Sir **F. BURDETT'S** address to the electors of Westminster vindicated; in reply to venal prints. 15p. 8°. 1807.

19510 CRITO, *the Euclidian, pseud.* A letter addressed to Sir Francis Burdett, Bart. on the conduct which the electors ought to pursue in the present awful crisis. 20p. 8°. [1807]

19511 DILLON, SIR JOHN J. An essay on the history and effect of the coronation oath; including observations on a Bill recently submitted to the House of Commons. 63p. 8°. 1807.

19512 —— A memoir concerning the political state of Malta. [Parts I and II.] 28p. 4°. 1807.

19513 EDWARDS, GEORGE. Means adequate to the present crisis, and future prosperity and happiness of the Empire: or proposals for the proper management of public affairs and for procuring an immediate...and permanent peace. 124p. 8°. 1807.

19514 —— A plain speech or address to the Imperial Parliament of Great Britain, to the people...and to all nations; showing them in what manner they may be prosperous and happy...and remain in peace and friendship with one another. 43p. 8°. 1807.

19515 An **EXPOSITION** of the circumstances which gave rise to the election of Sir Francis Burdett, Bart. for the city of Westminster, and of the principles which governed the committee who conducted that election. To which are added some documents not hitherto published. 28p. 8°. 1807.

19516 GREY, CHARLES, *2nd Earl Grey.* Speech of the Right Honourable Viscount Howick, in the House of Commons, on...March 26th, 1807; stating the circumstances which led to the change of administration. The second edition. 26p. 8°. 1807.

19517 HORNE, afterwards **HORNE TOOKE,** J. A letter to the editor of The Times [on the political connection between Sir F. Burdett and James Paull]. 16p. 8°. 1807.

19518 —— A warning to the electors of Westminster from Mr. Horne Tooke. [On the results of the duel between Paull and Sir Francis Burdett.] 37p. 8°. 1807.

19519 HUNT, H. An address to all those who wish to preserve their country from the horrors of a sanguinary revolution...Wherein is introduced, the resolutions entered into, at a meeting, held at the Trout-Tavern,

Bristol, on the 2d of June, 1807, the letter of Sir F. Burdett, Bart. M.P. to the President of the above meeting [Henry Hunt]... 32p. *8°. Bristol*, [1807]

19520 —— Address to the public of the City of Bristol ...in answer to an anonymous letter, signed, Centinel, which appeared in the Bristol Western Star, on Friday, August 21, 1807. 8p. *8°. Bristol*, [1807]

19521 LEE, THOMAS, *of Bristol.* Delicate investigation. The right of Britons to be officially informed upon this subject, vindicated. The question betwixt us and our brethren in America. Original thoughts upon these important topics, wherein...Mr. Cobbett is...alluded to, and addressed. 22p. *8°. Bristol*, [1807]

19522 —— Second edition, with additions. White-Lion Club, late riot and dock tax: an address to the public, wherein these...topics are discussed. 34p. *8°. Bristol*, [1807]

19523 LETTERS addressed to Lord Grenville and Lord Howick upon their removal from the councils of the King, in consequence of their attempting the total repeal of the test laws...with respect to His Majesty's Army and Navy. By a Protestant. 37p. *8°.* 1807.

19524 LOLME, J. L. DE. The constitution of England; or, an account of the English government; in which it is compared both with the republican form of government, and the other monarchies in Europe...A new edition; with...notes and a preface biographical and critical. 535p. *8°.* 1807. *For other editions, see* 1771.

19525 MONTAGUE, M. Substance of the speech of the Honourable Mr. Montague, in the House of Commons, on...January 5, 1807, in the debate on the conduct of the late negotiation with France. 14p. *8°.* 1807.

19526 NON-REVEUR, CASSANDRE, *pseud.* The red book; or, the government of Francis the first, [i.e. Sir F. Burdett] Emperor of the English, King of the Scotch and Irish, &c.&c.&c. A dream. By Cassandre Non-Reveur. 76p. *8°.* 1807.

19527 OBSERVER, *pseud.* A certain way to save our country, and make us a more happy and flourishing people...[Signed: The Observer.] 24p. *8°.* 1807.

19528 —— Appendix, or, a fourth letter of the Observer; and an explanatory answer, by Doctor Edwards. 16p. *8°.* 1807.

19529 REFLECTIONS on the war with Denmark, &c. Extracted from Flower's Political Review. p.xxxvii–lii. *8°. Harlow*, 1807.

19530 [**SAYERS**, J.] Elijah's mantle; being verses occasioned by the death of that illustrious statesman the Right Honourable William Pitt...With a prefatory address. The fifth edition. 19p. *8°.* 1807.

19531 [**STEPHEN**, J.] The dangers of the country. By the author of War in disguise. 227p. *8°.* 1807.

19532 [——] The second edition. 163p. *8°.* 1807.

19533 THOUGHTS on the Catholic question. 49p. *8°.* 1807.

19534 TOMLINE, W. E. P. A speech on the character of the Right Hon. William Pitt, delivered in Trinity College Chapel, Cambridge, Dec. 17, 1806...Third edition. 29p. *8°. London...Cambridge*, 1807.

19535 The **UTI POSSIDETIS** and status quo: a political satire. [A satire in verse on the Cabinet of 'all the talents'. First published in the Anti-Jacobin Review for March, 1807.] 20p. *8°.* 1807.

19536 WHITBREAD, S. Substance of the speech delivered in the House of Commons on Monday Jan. 5, 1807...on the subject of the late negotiation with France. 69p. *8°.* 1807.

19537 WILBERFORCE, WILLIAM (1759–1833). A letter to the gentlemen, clergy, and freeholders of Yorkshire; occasioned by the late election for that county. 37p. *8°.* 1807. *The copy that belonged to M. T. Sadler.*

SOCIALISM

19538 SPENCE, T. The important trial of Thomas Spence, for a political pamphlet, intitled "The restorer of society to its natural state," on May 27th, 1801, at Westminster Hall, before Lord Kenyon and a special jury. Second edition. [With an edition of *The restorer of society*, read by Spence at the trial as part of his defence.] 92p. *12°.* 1807. *For another edition, see* 1803.

19539 —— The jubilee hymn. To be sung an hundred years hence, or sooner. *s.sh.8°.* [*London*, 1807 ?]

19540 —— A new and infallible way to make trade. [With 'The progress of Spensonianism', a political song.] *s.sh.8°.* [*London*, 1807 ?]

19541 —— A suitable companion to Spence's songs. A fable. [4]p. *8°.* [*London*, 1807 ?]

MISCELLANEOUS

19542 An authentic **ACCOUNT** of the siege of Copenhagen by the British, in the year 1807. Containing, the Danish description of the attack and bombardment, with the...proclamations and bulletins of the Danes, and the whole of the official dispatches...as published in the London Gazette. To accompany a plan of the City of Copenhagen... 89p. *8°.* 1807. *In a volume of tracts with the book-plate of John Hale Calcraft, which probably belonged to John Calcraft (1765–1831).*

19543 ADDINGTON, H., *Viscount Sidmouth.* Substance of the speech of Lord Viscount Sidmouth, on the 10th of August 1807, upon the motion for the second reading of the Militia Transfer Bill. 16p. *8°.* [*London*, 1807]

19544 CONSIDERATIONS on the best means of calling forth the general strength of the country, for its present and permanent defence. [Preface signed: Miles et Baronettus.] 31p. *8°.* 1807. *The copy that belonged to John Cartwright, with his signature and the date '1807' on the title-page.*

19545 EVANS, T. A humorous catalogue of Spence's songs. [A song.] *s.sh.8°. n.p.* [1807 ?]

19546 FACULTY OF PROCURATORS, *Glasgow*. Report of the committee of the Faculty of Procurators in Glasgow, respecting the Bill for better regulating the courts of justice in Scotland, and the administration of justice therein; and for establishing trial by jury in certain civil cases. 8p. *4°. Glasgow*, 1807.

19547 GLASGOW. *Town Clerks*. Memorial by the town-clerks of Glasgow, on the improvement of the Corporation Courts of that city. [Signed: Jas. Reddie, Richd. Henderson, Rob. Thomson.] 58p. *4°. Glasgow*, [1807]

19548 IRELAND, J. The claims of the Establishment. A sermon, preached August 30, 1807, at Croydon in Surrey. 8p. *8°.* 1807. *The copy that belonged to William Cobbett.*

19549 [KEIR, W.] A summons of wakening; or the evil tendency and danger of speculative philosophy, exemplified in Mr. Leslie's Inquiry into the nature of heat, and Mr. Malthus's Essay on population...To which is subjoined, a prospectus of An inquiry into the origin of government and law. 259p. *8°. Hawick, Edinburgh, &c.,* 1807.

19550 MENTORIUS, *pseud*. Mentoriana; or, a letter of admonition and remonstrance to His Royal Highness the Duke of York, relative to corruption, oppression... and other subjects connected with the Army. 32p. *8°.* 1807.

19551 P., A., *pseud*. Abraham to Peter; being answers to the letters [on the subject of the Irish Catholics] of Peter Plymley [the Rev. Sydney Smith. A series of five letters purporting to be written to Peter Plymley by his brother Abraham, each signed: A.P.]. 5 vols. *8°. Dublin,* 1807–8.

1808

GENERAL

19552 BARRY, G. History of the Orkney Islands. Including a view of the manners and customs of their ancient and modern inhabitants...the present state of their agriculture; manufactures; fisheries; and commerce; and the means of their improvement...The second edition, with corrections and additions by the Rev. James Headrick. 512p. *4°.* 1808. *For another edition, see 1805.*

19553 BELLEW, R. Thoughts and suggestions on the means apparently necessary...towards improving the condition of the Irish peasantry... 82p. *8°. London, Dublin, &c.,* 1808.

19554 *CAREY, WILLIAM (*fl.* 1808). The stranger's guide through London; or, a view of the British Metropolis in 1808: equally useful in the counting-house and on the road; presenting an historical...sketch of the capital...its civil and military government...commerce and population...With...accurate lists of public offices, London bankers, inns...stage-coaches, wharfs...To which is added, a new commercial directory... 399p. *12°.* [1808]

19555 CHALMERS, T. An enquiry into the extent and stability of national resources. 365p. *8°. Edinburgh & London,* 1808.

19556 COMBER, W. T. An inquiry into the state of national subsistence, as connected with the progress of wealth and population. 323, 59p. *8°.* 1808. *The copy that belonged to Richard Arkwright, according to a note by HSF. See also 1822.*

19557 [CROKER, JOHN W.] A sketch of the state of Ireland, past and present. 64p. *8°. London & Dublin,* 1808.

19558 [——] Second London edition. 64p. *8°. London & Dublin,* 1808. *See also 1822.*

19559 The EAST-INDIA register and directory, for 1808; corrected to the 10th August, 1808. Containing... lists of the Company's servants...Together with lists of ...mariners, &c. not in the service of the...Company; and merchant vessels employed in the country trade. Compiled...by John Mathison & Alexander Way Mason ...Second edition. 420p. *12°.* [1808] *For other editions, see* 1804.

19560 EDWARDS, GEORGE. The true original scheme of human economy, applied to the completion of the different interests, and preservation of the British Empire; or, heads, proposing the establishment of the third, the British dispensation. 136p. *8°. Newcastle upon Tyne,* 1808.

19561 FRANCE. *Laws, etc.* Code Napoléon, suivi de l'exposé des motifs, sur chaque loi, présenté par les orateurs du Gouvernement; des rapports faits au Tribunat au nom de la Commission de Législation; des opinions émises dans le cours de la discussion; des discours prononcés au Corps Législatif par les orateurs du Tribunat; et d'une table analytique et raisonnée des matières tant du Code que des discours...Vol. 1. 584p. *12°. Paris,* 1808. *This volume contains the text of the* Code Civil. *For another edition, see* 1804.

19562 HAMILTON, E. The cottagers of Glenburnie; a tale for the farmer's ingle-nook...Third edition. 408p. *8°. Edinburgh & London,* 1808.

19563 *The HARLEIAN MISCELLANY: a collection of scarce...pamphlets and tracts, as well in manuscript as in print. Selected from the library of Edward Harley, second Earl of Oxford. Interspersed with historical, political, and critical annotations, by the late William Oldys, Esq. and some additional notes, by Thomas Park, F.S.A. [With two supplementary volumes, including pieces not published in the former edition, and a classed catalogue and index by T. H. Horne.] 13 vols. *4°.* 1808–13. *A number of excerpts from this edition are separately bound in the Goldsmiths' Library.*

19564 [HUTTON, W.] A concise history of Birmingham, containing an account of its ancient state, and the latest improvements: together with a statement of the arrival and departure of the mails, stage coaches, waggons, &c....Fourth edition... 78p. *8°. Birmingham,* 1808. *An edition of* A brief history of Birmingham, *1797, abridged from Hutton's* History of Birmingham, *1781 (q.v.).*

19565 INQUIRY into the causes and consequences of continental alienation, written as a sequel to the Inquiry into the state of the nation. Second edition. 48, 160p. *8°.* 1808.

19566 LABOULINIÈRE, P. T. DE. De l'influence d'une grande révolution, sur le commerce, l'agriculture et les arts: discours couronné par l'Académie de Lyon... 312p. 8°. *La Haie*, 1808.

19567 LEMOINE, J. J. Discours qui a obtenu la première mention honorable, sur cette question proposée par l'Institut de France: Quelle a été l'influence des Croisades sur la liberté civile des peuples de l'Europe, sur leur civilisation, et sur le progrès des limières, du commerce et de l'industrie? 189p. 8°. *Paris*, 1808.

19568 MAITLAND, JAMES, *8th Earl of Lauderdale.* Recherches sur la nature et l'origine de la richesse publique, et sur les moyens et les causes qui concourent à son accroissement... Traduit de l'anglais, par E. Lagentie de Lavaïsse. 334p. 8°. *Paris*, 1808.

19569 —— Ueber National-Wohlstand. 106p. 8°. *Berlin*, 1808. *For other editions, see* 1804.

19570 MEYER, H. Das französische Decimal-System in Hinsicht auf Münzen, Maasse und Gewichte... Nebst einer gründlichen Anweisung über die richtige Berechnung der Münzorten gegen einander für Kaufleute und Geschäftsmänner. 80p. 8°. [*Braunschweig* & *Halberstadt*, 1808]

19571 MILL, JAMES. Commerce defended. An answer to the arguments by which Mr. Spence, Mr. Cobbett, and others, have attempted to prove that commerce is not a source of national wealth. 154p. 8°. 1808.

19572 —— Second edition. 154p. 8°. 1808.

19573 O'DONAGHUE, DE C. Sketches of the British Empire, in three letters, addressed to the Right Hon. Henry Grattan. 48p. 8°. *Dublin*, 1808.

19574 PITT, WILLIAM (1759–1806). The speeches of the Right Honourable William Pitt, in the House of Commons. [Edited by W. S. Hathaway.] The second edition... 3 vols. 8°. 1808.

19575 The **REASONER;** an independent publication, comprising a general enquiry into the principles upon which the happiness of society and the security of the British Empire depend. Originally designed as a periodical work... By John Bone. [Being a reissue of nos. 1–15 of *The Reasoner and Statistical Journal* with the addition of a title-page and an index.] [256]p. 8°. 1808. *An imperfect copy of the original issue of no. 13 is bound in a volume of pamphlets that belonged to William Cobbett.*

19576 ⟨Corrected to the 25th of April, 1808.⟩ The **ROYAL KALENDAR:** or, complete and correct annual register, for England, Scotland, Ireland, and America, for... 1808... 387p. 12°. [1808] *For other editions, see* 1779.

19577 SPENCE, W. Agriculture the source of the wealth of Britain; a reply to the objections urged by Mr. Mill, the Edinburgh Reviewers, and others, against the doctrines of the pamphlet entitled, "Britain independent of commerce." With remarks on the criticism of the Monthly Reviewers upon that work. 110p. 8°. 1808. *The copy that belonged to William Cobbett.*

19578 —— Britain independent of commerce; or, proofs deduced from an investigation into the true causes of the wealth of nations, that our riches, prosperity and power are derived from sources inherent in ourselves... The third edition. 96p. 8°. 1808.

19579 —— The fourth edition, corrected and enlarged. 96p. 8°. 1808.

19580 —— The fifth edition, corrected and enlarged. 96p. 8°. 1808.

19581 —— The sixth edition, corrected and enlarged. 96p. 8°. 1808. *For other editions, see* 1807.

19582 STRONG, C. Patriotism and piety. The speeches of His Excellency Caleb Strong, Esq. to the Senate and House of Representatives of the Commonwealth of Massachusetts; with their answers; and other official publick papers of His Excellency, from 1800 to 1807. 202p. 12°. *Newburyport*, 1808.

For the **TRADESMAN;** or, commercial magazine, 1808–15, *see vol.* III, *Periodicals list.*

19583 WILLIAMS, P. Remarks suggested by the perusal of a pamphlet [by William Spence], entitled "Britain independent of commerce". 40p. 8°. 1808.

19584 WOODWARD, R., *Bishop of Cloyne.* A new edition. The present state of the Church of Ireland: containing a description of it's precarious situation and the consequent danger to the public... To which are subjoined, some reflections on the impracticability of a proper commutation for tythes; and a general account of the... insurrections in Munster. 128p. 8°. *Dublin*, 1808.

AGRICULTURE

19585 BAKEWELL, ROBERT (1768–1843). Observations on the influence of soil and climate upon wool; from which is deduced, a certain and easy method of improving the quality of English clothing wools, and preserving the health of sheep... and remarks on the means by which the Spanish breed of sheep may be made to preserve the best qualities of its fleece unchanged in different climates... With occasional notes and remarks, by... Lord Somerville. 157p. 8°. 1808.

19586 BALD, R. A general view of the coal trade of Scotland, chiefly that of the River Forth and Mid-lothian, as connected with the supplying of Edinburgh and the north of Scotland with fuel; to which is added, an inquiry into the condition of these women who carry coals under ground in Scotland, known by the name of bearers. 173p. 8°. *Edinburgh, Glasgow, &c.*, 1808. *See also* 1812.

19587 BATCHELOR, T. General view of the agriculture of the county of Bedford. Drawn up by order of the Board of Agriculture... 636p. 8°. *London, Bedford, &c.*, 1808.

19588 BOARD OF AGRICULTURE. Premiums offered by the Board... 1808. 14p. 8°. [*London*, 1808] *The Sheffield copy. See also* 1804, 1809, 1810, 1812, 1816, 1818.

19589 CORNWALL. *Stannaries.* The laws of the Stannaries of Cornwall; with marginal notes and references to authorities. To which are added, the several Acts of Parliament, schedule of fees, resolution of the judges, referred to in the several constitutions, and a copious index. [The dedication is signed: J. T., i.e. J. Tregoning, editor and publisher.] 130p. 8°. *Truro*, 1808. *For other editions, see* 1753.

19590 COVENTRY, A. Discourses explanatory of the object and plan of the course of lectures on agriculture and rural economy. 188p. *8°. Edinburgh & London,* 1808.

19591 CURWEN, J. C. Hints on the economy of feeding stock, and bettering the condition of the poor. 364p. *8°. London, Carlisle, &c.,* 1808. *See also* 1809.

19592 DUTTON, H. October 1808. [*Begin.*] The great annual fair of Ballinasloe commenced the 5th instant... [From the *Correspondent,* 13th October, 1808.] 4p. *8°. n.p.* [1808] *The Sheffield copy.*

19593 —— [*Begin.***]** The shew of seed wheat was held at the Society's house, Sackville-street, on...the 7th instant...[From the *Hibernian Journal,* Nov. 14, 1808.] *s.sh.fol. n.p.* [1808] *The Sheffield copy. See also* 1806.

19594 —— Statistical survey of the county of Clare, with observations on the means of improvement; drawn up...by direction of the Dublin Society. 369, 13p. *8°. Dublin,* 1808.

19595 FARMING SOCIETY OF IRELAND. Farming Society of Ireland. Ballinasloe Shew. Wednesday, October 5th, 1808. [List of winning entries.] *s.sh.fol. n.p.* [1808] *The Sheffield copy.*

19596 FELLENBERG, P. E. VON. Vues relatives à l'agriculture de la Suisse et aux moyens de la perfectionner...Traduit de l'allemand par Charles Pictet. 138p. *8°. Genève,* 1808.

19597 GRAY, A. The plough-wright's assistant; or, a practical treatise on various implements employed in agriculture... 220p. *8°. Edinburgh & London,* 1808.

19598 HOLLAND, SIR H., *Bart.* General view of the agriculture of Cheshire; with observations drawn up for the consideration of the Board of Agriculture... 375p. *8°. London, Chester, &c.,* 1808.

19599 HOLROYD, J. B., *Earl of Sheffield.* Account of Swedish turnips, produced in a field at Toft, in Cheshire, in 1806. Communicated to the Board of Agriculture. 3p. *4°.* 1808. *The Sheffield copy.*

19600 JOHNSTONE, JOHN (*fl.* 1797–1834). An account of the mode of draining land, according to the system practised by Mr. Joseph Elkington. Third edition, corrected and enlarged... 211p. *8°.* 1808. *For other editions, see* 1797.

19601 LASTEYRIE DU SAILLANT, C. P. DE, *Comte.* Du cotonnier et de sa culture, ou traité sur les diverses espèces de cotonniers; sur la possibilité et les moyens d'acclimater cet arbuste en France; sur sa culture dans différens pays... 446p. *8°. Paris,* 1808.

19602 LOUDON, J. C. An immediate, and effectual mode of raising the rental of the landed property of England; and rendering Great Britain independent of other nations for a supply of bread corn. With an appendix, containing hints to commercial capitalists, and to the tenantry of Scotland. By a Scotch farmer, now farming in Middlesex. 157p. *8°.* 1808.

19603 MARSHALL, W. A review of the reports to the Board of Agriculture; from the northern department of England: comprizing Northumberland, Durham, Cumberland, Westmoreland, Lancashire, Yorkshire; and the mountainous parts of Derbyshire, &c. 536p. *8°. York & London,* 1808.

19604 MOREL VINDÉ, C. G. T. DE, *Vicomte.* Mémoire et instruction sur les troupeaux de progression,

c'est-à-dire, sur le moyen de généraliser les troupeaux de mérinos purs en France...suivi d'un rapport fait à l'Institut de France...par MM. Tessier, Huzard, et Silvestre, rapporteur. 96p. *8°. Paris,* 1808.

19605 The practical **NORFOLK FARMER;** describing the management of a farm throughout the year; with observations founded on experience. Dedicated to Thos. Wm. Coke, Esq. 117p. *8°. Norwich & London,* [1808] *See also* 1809.

19606 PITT, WILLIAM (1749–1823). General view of the agriculture of the county of Stafford; with observations on the means of its improvement...With the additional remarks of...gentlemen and farmers in the county. Drawn up by order of the Board of Agriculture. The second edition. 327p. *8°. London, Edinburgh, &c.,* 1808. *For other editions, see* 1794.

19607 PONTEY, W. The profitable planter. A treatise on the theory and practice of planting forest trees, in every description of soil and situation...Second edition, enlarged. 222p. *8°. Huddersfield & London,* 1808.

19608 RE, F., *Conte.* Dizioniario ragionato di libri d'agricoltura, veterinaria, e di altri rami d'economia campestre... 4 vols. *16°. Venezia,* 1808–9.

19609 ROBERTSON, JAMES. General view of the agriculture in the county of Inverness; with observations on the means of its improvement...Drawn up for the Board of Agriculture... 447p. *8°. London, Edinburgh, &c.,* 1808.

19610 *SANDALIO DE ARIAS Y COSTA, A. Cartilla elemental de agricultura acomodada a nuestro suelo y clima. 212[312]p. *8°. Madrid,* 1808.

19611 SINCLAIR, SIR JOHN, *Bart.* Address to the Board of Agriculture...at the conclusion of the session, on the 7th of June, 1808. 8p. *4°.* [*London,* 1808] *The Sheffield copy.*

19612 SMITHFIELD CLUB. [*Begin.*] At the meetings of the Smithfield Club, held at the Freemason's Tavern, December 19 and 20, 1808...It was resolved, that the premiums and conditions, for the ensuing Christmas Show on...the 15th, 16th and 18th of December, 1809, be as follow...[With printed entry form.] *s.sh.fol.* [*London,* 1808] *The Sheffield copy.*

19613 —— [Another edition.] [2]p. *s.sh.fol.* [*London,* 1808] *The Sheffield copy. The text and the form are printed on recto and verso of a half-sheet, instead of side by side on a single sheet. See also* 1809, 1810.

19614 SUSSEX AGRICULTURAL SOCIETY. 1809...[*Begin.*] At a general meeting of the... Society, to arrange the prizes and premiums for...1809, held at the Star Inn, Lewes...The following resolutions were agreed to. [Dated: Nov. 11, 1808.] *s.sh.fol. Lewes,* [1808] *The Sheffield copy. See also* 1801, 1804, 1805, 1807.

19615 SWITZERLAND. *Tagsatzung.* Bericht an Se. Excell. den Herrn Landammann und an die Hohe Tagsatzung der XIX. verbündeten Stände der Schweiz, über die landwirtschaftlichen Anstalten des Herrn Emanuel Fellenberg zu Hofwyl. 143p. *8°. Zürich,* 1808.

19616 VANCOUVER, C. General view of the agriculture of the county of Devon; with observations on the means of its improvement. Drawn up for the consideration of the Board of Agriculture... 479p. *8°. London, Exeter, &c.,* 1808.

19617 WADE, W. Sketch of lectures on artificial or sown grasses, as lucern, saint-foin, clovers, trefoils, vetches, &c.&c. delivered in the Dublin Society's Botanical Garden, Glasnevin. 51p. *8°. Dublin*, 1808.

19618 —— Sketch of lectures on meadow and pasture grasses, delivered in the Dublin Society's Botanical Garden, Glasnevin. 55p. *8°. Dublin*, 1808.

19619 WALKER, JOHN (1731-1803). An economical history of the Hebrides and Highlands of Scotland... 2 vols. *8°. Edinburgh*, 1808. *See also* 1812.

19620 WHITE, JOHN, *gardener*. An essay on the indigenous grasses of Ireland. 156p. *8°. Dublin*, 1808.

19621 WISSETT, R. A treatise on hemp, including a comprehensive account of the best modes of cultivation and production as practised in Europe, Asia, and America; with observations on the sunn plant of India...With an appendix, on the...means of producing a sufficiency of English grown hemp, by...Lord Somerville. 296p. *4°.* 1808. *For another edition, see* 1804.

19622 WRIGHT, THOMAS, *Rector of Ould*. The formation and management of floated meadows; with corrections of errors, found in the treatises of Messrs. Davis, Marshall, Boswell, Young, and Smith, on the subject of floating. To which is added, a dissertation on the size of farms. 207, 27p. *8°. Northampton & London*, 1808. *The 'dissertation on the size of farms' is the author's* Large farms, recommended in a national view, *originally published in 1796 (q.v.) and here reissued.*

19623 YOUNG, ARTHUR (1769-1827). General view of the agriculture of the county of Sussex. Drawn up for the Board of Agriculture... 471p. *8°. London, Brighton, &c.*, 1808. *For other editions, see* 1793.

POPULATION

19624 INGRAM, R. A. Disquisitions on population; in which the principles of the Essay on population, by the Rev. T. R. Malthus, are examined and refuted. 132p. *8°.* 1808.

TRADES & MANUFACTURES

19625 BUCHANAN, ROBERTSON. An essay on the teeth of wheels, comprehending principles, and their application in practice, to millwork and other machinery ...Revised by Peter Nicholson, architect, &c. 164p. *8°.* 1808.

19626 BUSHE, G. P. A digested abridgment of the laws relating to the linen and hempen manufactures of Ireland...Published by order of the Trustees of the Linen and Hempen Manufactures. 140p. *8°. Dublin*, 1808.

19627 CAMPBELL, JAMES, *surveyor*, and **LESLIE**, JOHN, *surveyor*. The Edinburgh builders new price tables for 1808; containing a correct account of all the prices allowed to masons, wrights, slaters...glaziers... smiths, paviours, &c. Shewing the value of materials when furnished, and the prices of labour only... 24p. *8°. Edinburgh*, [1808]

19628 COMMITTEE OF MASTER CHAIR-MANUFACTURERS AND JOURNEYMEN. Supplement to the London chair-makers' and carvers' book of prices for workmanship; as regulated and agreed to by a Committee...With the method of computation adopted in the work... 120p. *4°.* 1808. *For editions of the original work, see* 1802; *for the second and third supplements, see* 1811 *and* 1844 (SOCIETY OF CHAIR-MAKERS AND CARVERS).

19629 GRANT, JAMES L. The report of James Ludovic Grant, Esq. chairman, and the other acting trustees of the fund for assisting Mr. Winsor in his experiments [to produce lighting by means of hydrocarbonic gas]: to the subscribers of that fund, at a meeting convened by public advertisements...on the 26th of May, 1808. 37p. *8°.* [1808]

19630 OBSERVATIONS on the woollen manufacture, in the West-Riding of the County of York. By a clothier. [Setting out the arguments in favour of the domestic as opposed to the factory system of manufacture.] 41p. *8°. Leeds & London*, 1808.

19631 STOWER, C. The compositor's and pressman's guide to the art of printing; containing hints and instructions to learners, with various impositions, calculations, scales of prices, &c.&c. 140p. *12°.* 1808.

19632 TARIF général des prix moyens des matériaux et des journées d'ouvriers employés dans les batimens à Paris, suivant le cours des six premiers mois de l'an 1808. 35p. *8°. Paris*, 1808.

19633 —— Supplément au Tarif général des prix moyens. 4p. *8°. n.p.* [1808 ?] *Containing variations during the second half of 1808.*

COMMERCE

19634 ADAMS, JOHN Q., *President of the USA*. A letter to the Hon. Harrison Gray Otis, a member of the Senate of Massachusetts, on the present state of our national affairs. With remarks upon Mr. Pickering's letter to the Governor of the Commonwealth. 32p. *8°.* 1808. *See also* 1824.

19635 A short **APPEAL** to the landed interest of this country, lest permanent advantage should be bartered for temporary gain. [Signed: A true friend to my country. A discussion of the intended move to use sugar and molasses in distilleries, instead of barley.] 23p. *8°.* 1808.

19636 ATCHESON, N. American encroachments on British rights; or, observations on the importance of the British North American Colonies. And on the late treaties with the United States: with remarks on Mr. Baring's Examination; and a defence of the shipping interest from the charge of having attempted to impose on Parliament, and of factious conduct in their opposition to the American Intercourse Bill. cxiii, 250p. *8°.* 1808.

19637 BARHAM, J. F. Substance of a speech, delivered in the House of Commons...on...May 23, 1808, on the motion for prohibiting corn, and the substitution of sugar, in the distilleries. 35p. *8°.* 1808.

19638 BARING, A., *Baron Ashburton.* An inquiry into the causes and consequences of the Orders in Council; and an examination of the conduct of Great Britain towards the neutral commerce of America. 179p. *8°.* 1808.

19639 —— Second edition. 179p. *8°.* 1808.

19640 —— [Another edition.] 104p. *8°. New-York,* 1808.

19641 BELL, ARCHIBALD. An inquiry into the policy and justice of the prohibition of the use of grain in the distilleries: including observations on the nature and uses of a vent to superfluous land-produce; and a particular application of the general question to the present situation of the colonial interests. 109p. *8°. Edinburgh, Glasgow, &c.,* 1808. *The copy that belonged to William Cobbett. See also* 1810.

19642 BROUGHAM, H. P., *Baron Brougham and Vaux.* The speech of Henry Brougham, Esq. before the House of Commons, Friday, April 1, 1808, in support of the petitions from London, Liverpool and Manchester, against the Orders in Council... 84p. *8°.* 1808.

19643 [BROWN, C. B.] The British treaty [of 31 December 1806]. With an appendix of State papers; which are now first published [including the text of the Treaty of 1794]. 147p. *8°.* 1808.

19644 BUESCH, J. G. Johann Georg Büsch's ehemahligen Professors in Hamburg theoretisch-praktische Darstellung der Handlung in ihren mannichfaltigen Geschäften. Dritte, vermehrte und verbesserte Ausgabe mit Einschaltungen und Nachträgen von G. P. H. Norrmann... 2 vols. *8°. Hamburg,* 1808. *For another edition, see* 1792.

19645 CHRISTIANI, C. J. R. Bemerkungen über des Herrn Justitzrath C. G. Rafns Einladung an alle Dänen und Norweger, vereinigt die vaterländischen Manufacturen zu unterstützen und dem Feinde zu schaden, indem sie sich feyerlich verpflichten, künftig keine englische Waaren zu kaufen. 62p. *8°. Kopenhagen,* 1808.

19646 [CONSOLAT.] Consulat de la mer, ou pandectes du droit commercial et maritime, faisant loi en Espagne, en Italie, à Marseille, et en Angleterre... Traduit du catalan en français, d'après l'édition originale de Barcelonne, de l'an 1494...par P. B. Boucher... 2 vols. *8°. Paris,* 1808. *For other editions, see* 1539.

19647 [COURTENAY, T. P.] Observations on the American Treaty, in eleven letters. First published in "The Sun", under the signature of Decius. 75p. *8°.* 1808.

19648 —— Additional observations on the American Treaty, with some remarks on Mr. Baring's pamphlet; being a continuation of the letters of Decius. To which is added an appendix of state papers, including the Treaty. 94, lxixp. *8°.* 1808.

19649 CROSBY, B., & CO. Crosby's merchant's and tradesman's pocket dictionary, adapted to merchants, manufacturers, and traders in all...branches of commercial intercourse...By a London merchant, assisted by several experienced tradesmen. 500p. *12°.* 1808.

19650 DAY, H. A defence of joint stock companies; being an attempt to shew their legality, expediency, and public benefit. 76p. *8°.* 1808.

19651 ENGLAND. *George III.* The Orders of Council, and instructions for imposing the restrictions of blockade; and for regulating the navigation of the sea, and the importation and exportation of merchandize, in consequence thereof; with a brief view of the several provisions therein contained. Published 1st January 1808. 51p. *8°.* 1808. *The copy that belonged to Patrick Colquhoun. See also* 1807.

19652 —— —— Orders in Council; or, an examination of the justice, legality and policy of the new system of commercial regulations. With an appendix of state papers, Statutes and authorities [and including the text of the Orders in Council of November and December 1807]. The second edition. 120p. *8°.* 1808.

19653 FAUCHÉ, P. F. Réflexions sur Gottembourg, et sur l'importance commerciale à laquelle cette place semble être destinée, &c....Juin, 1808. 8p. *4°.* [1808] *The text is in French and English, printed in parallel columns.*

19654 FRANCE. *Laws, etc.* Code de commerce, avec le rapprochement du texte des articles du Code Napoléon et du Code de procédure civile, qui y ont un rapport direct, suivi d'une table analytique et raisonnée des matières... Edition stéréotype, d'après le procédé de Firmin Didot. 268p. *12°. Paris,* 1808. *For other editions, see* 1807.

19655 GOODRICH, C. Speech of Mr. Goodrich, in the Senate, December 19th, 1808, on the third reading of the bill making further provisions for enforcing the embargo. 7p. *8°. n.p.* [1808]

19656 HUELLMANN, K. D. Geschichte des Byzantischen Handels bis zum Ende der Kreutzzüge... Preisschrift, gekrönt von der königl. Societät der Wissenschaften zu Göttingen. 144p. *8°. Frankfurt an der Oder,* 1808.

19657 By Authority. **JOINT STOCK COMPANIES** with transferrable shares. Report of the arguments upon the application to the Court of King's Bench for leave to file an information against Mr. Ralph Dodd, upon the Statute of 6 Geo. I., cap. 18 (respecting the intended London Distillery Company, &c.&c.). 106p. *8°.* 1808.

19658 LUSHINGTON, W. The interests of agriculture and commerce, inseparable. 72p. *8°.* 1808.

19659 [MARRYAT, J.] Hints to both parties; or, observations on the proceedings in Parliament upon the petitions against the Orders in Council, and on the conduct of His Majesty's Ministers in granting licenses to import the staple commodities of the enemy. 95p. *8°.* 1808. *The Sheffield copy.*

19660 RANDOLPH, F. A few observations on the present state of the nation; in a letter to His Grace the Duke of Bedford. 99p. *8°.* 1808.

19661 ROMANTSOF, N. P., *Graf.* Tableaux du commerce de l'Empire de Russie. Années 1802, 1803, 1804, 1805...Traduits de l'original & rédigés en forme synoptique par Fr. Pfeiffer...[With 'Supplément. Manifeste de Sa Majesté Impériale concernant l'organisation du commerce dans l'Empire de Russie du 1. janvier 1807'.] [90], xp. *fol. St. Petersbourg, 1808. The text of the Manifesto is in Russian and French.*

19662 SILVA LISBOA, J. DE. Observações sobre o commercio franco no Brazil. Parte I. Pelo author dos Principios do direito mercantil. 89p. *4°. Rio de Janeiro, 1808. The copy presented to Sir Thomas Gage, with inscription signed 'S'.*

19663 SPENCE, W. The radical cause of the present distresses of the West-India planters pointed out...with remarks on the publications of Sir William Young, Bart., Charles Bosanquet, Esq. and Joseph Lowe, Esq; relative to the value of the West-India trade...The second edition. 105p. *8°.* 1808. *For another edition, see 1807.*

19664 UNITED STATES OF AMERICA. Congress. *Senate.* Message from the President of the U. States, transmitting copies of all orders and decrees of the belligerent powers of Europe, affecting the commercial rights of the U. States, passed since 1791. December 28th, 1808. Printed by order of the Senate. 123p. *8°. Washington City,* 1808.

COLONIES

19665 CAMPBELL, L. D. A letter addressed to a member of the present Parliament, on the "articles of charge" against Marquis Wellesley [concerned with his conduct while Governor-General of India], which have been laid before the House of Commons. 236p. *8°.* 1808.

19666 The **CARNATIC QUESTION** stated. 196p. *8°.* 1808. *The copy that belonged to John Calcraft (1765–1831).*

19667 FULLER, A. An apology for the late Christian missions to India: comprising an address to the chairman of the East India Company, in answer to Mr. Twining; and strictures on the preface of a pamphlet by Major Scott Waring; with an appendix... 93, xxvip. *8°.* 1808.

19668 —— An apology for the late Christian missions to India: part the second. Containing remarks on Major Scott Waring's letter to the Rev. Mr. Owen; and on a "Vindication of the Hindoos, by a Bengal Officer" [i.e. J. Scott Waring]. 129p. *8°.* 1808.

19669 —— An apology for the late Christian missions to India: part the third. Containing strictures on Major Scott Waring's third pamphlet; on a letter to the President of the Board of Control; and on the propriety of confining missionary undertakings to the Established Church, in answer to Dr. Barrow; with an appendix... 86p. *8°.* 1808.

19670 NAJEEB, *pseud.* Strictures on the present government, civil, military, and political, of the British possessions, in India; including a view of the recent transactions in that country, which have tended to alienate the affections of the natives. In a letter from an officer, resident on the spot, to his friend in England. 124p. *8°.* 1808. *The copy that belonged to William Cobbett.*

19671 SCOTT, afterwards **SCOTT WARING**, JOHN. A letter to the Rev. John Owen...in reply to the "Brief strictures on the preface to Observations on the present state of the East India Company." To which is added a postscript; containing remarks on a note printed in the Christian Observer for December, 1807. 118p. *8°.* 1808. *The copy that belonged to William Cobbett.*

19672 —— Observations on the present state of the East India Company: with prefatory remarks...as to the general disaffection prevailing among the natives of every rank, from an opinion that it is the intention of the British Government to compel them to embrace Christianity... And a plan...for restoring that confidence which the natives formerly reposed in...the British Government... Fourth edition. 76p. *8°.* 1808. *A second (imperfect) copy belonged to William Cobbett.*

19673 [SHORE, J., *Baron Teignmouth.*] Considerations on the practicability, policy, and obligation of communicating to the natives of India the knowledge of Christianity. With observations on the "Prefatory remarks" to a pamphlet published by Major Scott Waring. By a late resident in Bengal. 101p. *8°.* 1808.

FINANCE

19674 An **ADDRESS** to the proprietors of bank-stock. By a proprietor. 20p. *8°. Bath & London,* 1808.

19675 ANNESLEY, A. A compendium of the law of marine insurances, bottomry, insurance on lives, and of insurance against fire, in which the mode of calculating averages is defined, and illustrated by examples. 197p. *8°.* 1808.

19676 BAILY, F. The doctrine of interest and annuities analytically investigated and explained; together with several useful tables. 144p. *8°.* 1808. **Another copy, which belonged to Augustus De Morgan, has manuscript corrections by the author.*

19677 BANK of England. A letter to the proprietors of Bank stock, in consequence of the result of a general meeting held at the Bank...on...the 21st of January, 1808, on special affairs. 24p. *8°.* 1808. *The copy that belonged to William Cobbett.*

19678 BANK OF ENGLAND. A list of the names of all such proprietors of the Bank of England, who are qualified to vote at the ensuing election...March 29th, 1808. 18p. *fol.* [1808] *See also* 1738, 1749, 1750, 1789, 1790, 1791, 1792, 1793, 1794, 1795, 1796, 1797, 1798, 1799, 1801, 1803, 1804, 1809, 1812, 1816, 1819, 1836, 1843.

19679 BATE, H., afterwards **DUDLEY**, SIR H. B., *Rev., Bart.* A short address to the Most Reverend and Honourable William, Lord Primate of all Ireland; recommendatory of some commutation or modification of the tythes of that country. With a few remarks on the present state of the Irish Church. 30p. *8°. London & Dublin,* 1808.

19680 BISH, T. State lottery begins 13th December, 1808. Scheme. First day, first-drawn prize above £15 will be also a grand prize of 500 whole tickets. Second day, also a grand prize of 500 whole tickets...[A handbill.] *s.sh.8°. [London,* 1808]

19681 —— Tomorrow, April 26th, grand city lottery of freehold houses, (discharged of land-tax), will be drawn in Guildhall, and the whole drawing will be finished that day. The above lottery consists of 20,000 tickets, and contains the following list of capital prizes. The Grand Hotel, No. 9, Skinner-Street, value £25,000...[A handbill.] *s.sh.fol.* [*London,* 1808]

19682 BRANSCOMB, Sir J., **& CO.** Six prizes of £20,000. Grand state lottery begins drawing June 28, 1808 ...[A handbill.] *s.sh.8°.* [*London,* 1808]

19683 BROWN, William R. H. Golden Lane Brewery. The Attorney General, versus Brown, Parry, and others. The whole of the proceedings in this important cause...[On excise allowances.] Also a statement of the origin, rise and progress of the concern... 60p. *8°.* [1808]

19684 CAISSE D'ÉPARGNES. L'administration de la Caisse d'Épargnes, aux actionnaires. [Signed: Lafarge, Mitouflet, Mignien-Duplanier.] 36p. *8°. Paris,* 1808.

19685 [COLLIER, John D.] The life of Abraham Newland, Esq. late principal cashier at the Bank of England; with some account of that great national establishment. To which is added an appendix, containing the late correspondence of the Chancellor of the Exchequer with the Bank, and a list of the Statutes passed relative to it... 172p. *12°.* 1808.

19686 COLSON,　. Description de la machine numismabalique, ou machine propre à emballer de l'argent monnoyé. [Invented by Le sieur Colson.] 2p. *4°. n.p.* [1808 ?]

19687 CORRIE, E. Letters on the subject of the duties on coffee...The second edition. 58p. *8°.* 1808.

19688 ——— The third edition. 67p. *8°.* 1808. *The copy that belonged to William Cobbett.*

19688A EDE, J. A view of the gold and silver coins of all nations, exhibited in...engravings...To which is added in a regular index, the name, assay, weight, and value of each. [Second edition.] Also Sir Isaac Newton's Tables of foreign gold & silver coins...1700...73p. *16°.* [*London,* 1808]

19689 [ELRINGTON, T., *Bishop of Ferns and Leighlin.*] Letters on tythes, published in the Dublin Journal & Correspondent, under the signature of N. In reply to a speech made at the meeting held at Cashell, 22d August, 1807; with a postscript, containing observations on a pamphlet, lately published, in which the subject of tythes is discussed. 44p. *8°. Dublin,* 1808.

19690 ENGLAND. *Laws, etc.* Life annuities. Abstract and explanation of the Act (passed in the last session of Parliament,) for enabling the Commissioners for the Reduction of the National Debt, to grant life annuities, by the transfer of funded property. 48 Geo. III. cap. 142. 16p. *8°.* 1808.

19691 FAIRMAN, William. The stocks examined and compared: or, a guide to purchasers in the public funds. Containing an account of the different funds...to the year 1807...Also, statements of the National Debt, a view of the progress of the Sinking Fund, and an account of the American funds. The fifth edition, considerably improved. 187p. *8°.* 1808. *For other editions, see* 1795.

19692 HORNSBY & CO. Grand state lottery begins drawing 28th of this month, June, 1808...[A handbill.] *s.sh.8°.* [*London,* 1808]

19693 KEARSLEY, G. Enlarged edition. Kearsley's tax tables, for 1808... 162p. *12°.* [1808] *For other editions, see* 1786.

19694 MAGNIEN-GRANDPRÉ, N. (1745–1811). Tarif des droits de douane et de navigation maritime de l'Empire français, suivi d'observations sur tout ce qui a rapport aux perceptions et prohibitions; aux denrées coloniales...et à la taxe sur les sels. 221p. *8°. Livourne,* 1808. *The text in French and Italian.*

19695 ——— [Another edition.] Tariffa de' dazj di degana e della navigazione marittima dell' Impero francese, con l'aggiunta delle osservazione sopra tuttociò, che ha rapporto alle percezioni e proibizioni... 127p. *8°. Livorno,* 1808. *The text in Italian and French.*

19696 MASCALL, E. J. A statement of the duties of customs, and those of the excise...Also, the duties outwards...the duties coastwise...together with tables of scavage, baillage, Levant and Russia dues...to the 5th September 1808. 163p. *8°.* 1808. *See also* 1810.

19697 MASON, James. A brief statement of the present system of tythes in Ireland, with a plan for its improvement. 32p. *8°. Shrewsbury & London,* 1808.

19698 PERCEVAL, S. [Copy of a letter to the Revd. Dr. Mansel, on the subject of the Curates Bill [to provide larger salaries for stipendiary curates].] 39p. *8°.* [1808] *Without a title-page, possibly a proof copy. This copy has the title in manuscript on B1, the first leaf.*

19699 ——— [Another issue.] 39p. *8°.* 1808. *The copy that belonged to William Cobbett.*

19700 RIVERS, C. The appeal of an injured individual to the British nation, on the arbitrary and inquisitorial consequences of the tax on income, commonly called the property tax; and particularly to the manner it is assessed on professions, trades and small incomes. 19p. *8°.* 1808.

19701 SOULET, P. Traité des changes et arbitrages, suivi des autres calculs du commerce, par des méthodes neuves, simples et expéditives...Seconde édition, considérablement augmenté par l'auteur. 547p. *8°. Paris,* 1808. *For another edition, see* 1804.

19702 SWIFT & CO. State lottery begins drawing 13th this month. 1,000 tickets as extra benefits...Tickets and shares are on sale by Swift and Co....No. 12, Charing-Cross, and No. 31, opposite Whitechapel Market ...[A handbill.] *s.sh.8°.* [*London,* 1808 ?]

19703 TOLLER, Sir S. A treatise of the law of tithes; compiled in part from some notes of Richard Wooddeson. 312p. *8°.* 1808.

19704 TORRENS, R. The economists refuted; or, an inquiry into the nature and extent of the advantages derived from trade. 84p. *8°.* 1808.

19705 A brief **VIEW** of the produce system, as connected with the failure of Messrs. Walsh and Nesbitt. With a few remarks on its effect on the character of the Stock Exchange. Addressed to the members of that body. By a Member. 18p. *8°.* 1808.

TRANSPORT

19706 BIRD, J. B., *ed.* The laws respecting travellers and travelling; comprising all the cases and statutes... including the use of hired horses, robbery, accidents, &c....And also, the law relating to innkeepers...By the author of "The laws of land lord and tenant" [James Barry Bird]. Second edition, with additions. 91p. *8°.* 1808.

19707 DARLINGTON. A table of the several tolls appointed to be taken at the several turnpike gates on the road from Darlington to West-Auckland, from the 30th day of April, 1808. [Dated: Darlington 1808.] *s.sh.fol. n.p.* [1808]

19708 ENGLAND. *Laws, etc.* [*Endorsed:*] An Act for amending and enlarging the powers of an Act of His present Majesty, for making and maintaining the Barnsley Canal Navigation, and certain railways and other roads to communicate therewith, and for increasing the rates, tolls and duties thereby granted. ⟨Received the Royal Assent, 28th March, 1808.⟩ 48 Geo. III. sess. 1808. 21p. *fol. n.p.* [1808]

19709 ——— ——— An Act for making a navigable cut from the east side of the river Tees, near Stockton, through the neck of land into the said river near Portrack, in the county of Durham, and for making various other improvements in the navigation of the said river between ...Stockton and the sea. 162p. *8°. Stockton,* 1808.

19710 UNITED STATES OF AMERICA. Congress. *Senate.* Report of the Secretary of the Treasury [A. Gallatin], on the subject of public roads and canals; made in pursuance of a resolution of Senate, of March 2, 1807... 123p. *8°. Washington,* 1808.

SOCIAL CONDITIONS

19711 BELL, ANDREW. Sketch of a national institution for training up the children of the poor in moral and religious principles, and in habits of useful industry... Second edition. 18p. *8°. London & Edinburgh,* 1808. *Presentation copy, with inscription, from the author to Patrick Colquhoun.*

19712 BRITISH ASSURANCE SOCIETY. Rules, orders, and regulations, of a friendly society called the British Assurance Society...which was first formed ...1773...To which is prefixed a preface, containing observations on the utility of benefit societies in general and the advantages to be derived from this Society in particular... 56p. *8°.* 1808.

19713 BURGESS, T., *Bishop of Salisbury.* A sermon preached before the incorporated Society for the Propagation of the Gospel in Foreign Parts; at their anniversary meeting...February 19, 1808. [With 'An abstract of the charter, and...proceedings of the society ...1807, to...1808'.] 74p. *8°.* 1808.

19713A CONSIDERATIONS on the nature...of the intended Light and Heat Company. Published by authority of the committee. 26p. *8°.* 1808.

19714 HENRY, M. Observations on seduction and prostitution and on the evil consequences arising from them; extracted from Matthew Henry's exposition on the Old and New Testament, by Mary Smith, a penitent, late of the Magdalen Hospital, and published for her benefit. With a poem by Mr. Pratt on the same subject. Second edition. To which are prefixed, preliminary observations; and an address to the Legislature, containing...measures for the suppression of seduction and female prostitution. 110p. *12°.* 1808. *The copy presented to Patrick Colquhoun by the editor.*

19715 HOLLOWAY, J. A word to the benevolent: being an humble attempt to prove the practicability of relieving effectually the deserving poor throughout the kingdom. 18p. *8°.* 1808.

19716 MASSACHUSETTS. General Court. *Senate.* The Attorney General's report respecting claims [by N. Waite, A. Davis and E. Bruce] for confiscated debts. 22p. *8°. Boston,* 1808.

19717 MURDOCK, W. An account of the application of the gas from coal to œconomical purposes...read before the Royal Society...25th February, 1808, and printed in the Philosophical Transactions for that year. 8p. *8°.* [1808]

19718 NEILD, J. An account of the rise, progress, and present state of the Society for the Discharge and Relief of Persons, imprisoned for Small Debts throughout England and Wales. [Third edition.] 601p. *8°.* 1808. *For another edition, see* 1802.

19719 NOTTINGHAMSHIRE HOUSE OF CORRECTION. Rules, orders, and regulations, to be observed and enforced as bye laws, for the government of the house of correction, provided and established at Southwell, in and for the county of Nottingham. [Drawn up and presented by the Rev. J. T. Becher.] 55p. *8°. Newark,* 1808.

19720 First Division. Dec. 10. 1808...Unto the Right Honourable the Lords of Council and Session, the **PETITION** of Robert Tod, merchant in Glasgow, trustee on the sequestrated estate of David Strong, merchant there, with concurrence of the following persons, creditors of the said David Strong [24 persons and firms of Glasgow, Edinburgh and Irvine]...[Signed: Henry Cockburn. With an appendix.] 18, 6p. *4°. n.p.* [1808]

19721 SOCIETY FOR THE SUPPRESSION OF VICE. The trial of Joseph Powell, the fortune-teller, at the Sessions-House, Clerkenwell, October 31, 1807. Taken in short-hand by Mr. Gurney. With an appendix and notes, containing various original letters and other documents referred to in the trial. By the Society for the Suppression of Vice. 28p. *8°.* 1808.

19722 WAITHMAN, R. Letter to the Governors of Christ's Hospital, being a refutation of the invectives and misrepresentations contained in a letter from the Rev. Dawson Warren...to William Mellish, Esq. M.P. 54p. *8°.* [1808] *Presentation copy from the author to William Cobbett.*

19723 WEYLAND, J. A letter to a country gentleman

on the education of the lower orders... 176p. 8°. *London & Oxford*, 1808. *The Sheffield copy.*

19724 WILLIS, J. On the poor laws of England. The

various plans and opinions of Judge Blackstone [and others] stated and considered, with proposed amendments of easy execution to give effect to the present laws and to the views of Government. 78p. 8°. 1808.

SLAVERY

19725 CLARKSON, T. The history of the rise, progress, and accomplishment of the abolition of the African slave-trade by the British Parliament... 2 vols. 8°. 1808. *See also 1816.*

19726 ENGLAND. *Parliament.* Substance of the debates on the Bill for abolishing the slave trade, which was brought into the House of Lords on the 2d January, 1807, and into the House of Commons on the 10th

February, 1807, and which was finally passed into a law on the 25th March, 1807. 273p. 8°. 1808.

19727 PORTEUS, B., *Bishop of London.* A letter to the governors, legislatures, and proprietors of plantations, in the British West-India Islands. [On the education of slaves. With 'Appendix: containing a short sketch of the new system of education for the poor; in a letter from... Dr. Bell'.] 48p. 8°. 1808.

POLITICS

19728 BOLAÑOS Y NOBOA, P. Compendio de loss preceptos del derecho de gentes natural infringidos por el gobierno frances, contra cuya iniqua, y abominable conducta se arma la España, y deben armarse todas las naciones del Universo... xlivp. 4°. *Cadiz*, [1808] *The copy that belonged to Richard, Marquis Wellesley (1760–1842), with his autograph signature on the fly-leaf.*

19729 —— El desengaño ó particularidades de la vida publica de Napoleon Bonaparte desde su venida de Egipto, hasta nuestros tiempos: mezcladas con reflexiones politicas y morales, que descubren su verdadero caracter. Vol. 1. 360p. 4°. *Cadiz*, 1808. *Bound with no. 19728 above, in a volume which belonged to the Marquis Wellesley.*

19730 John **BULL.** [An attempt to interpret the career of Napoleon in the light of Biblical prophecies.] 55p. 8°. [*London*, 1808] *The copy that belonged to William Cobbett.*

19731 BURGOYNE, M. A letter from Montagu Burgoyne, Esquire, of Mark Hall, on the present state of public affairs, and the representation of the county of Essex. 78p. 8°. *London & Chelmsford*, 1808. *The copy that belonged to William Cobbett.*

19732 CEVALLOS, P. Exposition of the practices and machinations, which led to the usurpation of the crown of Spain, and the means adopted by Buonaparte to carry it into execution... ⟨Taken from the Times of Monday, October 10.⟩ 29p. 4°. [1808]

19733 DECIUS, *pseud.* On the causes of our late military and political disasters, with some hints for preventing their recurrence. 49p. 8°. 1808. *In a volume of tracts with the book-plate of John Hales Calcraft, which probably belonged to John Calcraft (1765–1831).*

19734 EDWARDS, GEORGE. A plain practical plan, by which Great Britain may extricate herself from her present difficulties, procure the blessings of perfect peace, prosperity and happiness, and dispense them to the whole world. 104p. 4°. 1808. *Presentation copy from the author to the Duke of Portland.*

19735 —— Reasons for circulating A plain practical plan of procuring a peace... that may, at pleasure, be rendered the genuine uniform source of human prosperity and happiness;—accompanied with different printed papers, either sent with the plan, or ready to be supplied, as desired. 4p. 4°. [*London*, 1808]

19736 An **EPISTLE** to a lady. [A poem satirizing the Duke of York. Signed: an Englishman.] 40p. 4°. [1808] *The title is printed on the verso of the first leaf. On the recto there is a half-title which reads: Traits of all the royal dukes, and legal characteristics.*

19737 GOURLAY, R. F. Letter to the Earl of Kellie, concerning the farmers' income tax: with a hint on the principle of representation, &c.&c. 63p. 8°. 1808. *A second, imperfect, copy belonged to William Cobbett. Reissued by the author with other pamphlets in a volume entitled:* Early publications, *in 1831, q.v.* (GENERAL).

19738 HAMILTON, WILLIAM G. Parliamentary logick: to which are subjoined two speeches, delivered in the House of Commons of Ireland, and other pieces... With an appendix, containing considerations on the corn laws, by Samuel Johnson, LL.D. Never before printed. [Edited, with a biographical preface, by E. Malone.] 253p. 8°. 1808.

19739 LECKIE, G. F. An historical survey of the foreign affairs of Great Britain, with a view to explain the causes of the disasters of the late and present wars. 172, 80p. 8°. 1808.

19740 MILES, WILLIAM AUGUSTUS (1753?–1817). A letter to His Royal Highness the Prince of Wales; with a sketch of the prospect before him, appendix and notes. 264p. 8°. 1808. *The copy that belonged to John Calcraft (1765–1831).*

19741 MORE, SIR T. Utopia; or, the best state of a commonwealth. Containing an impartial history of the manners, customs, polity, government, etc., of that island... Translated from the original Latin by... Bishop Burnet. To which is prefixed a life of the author. lvi, 212p. 16°. 1808. *For other editions, see 1750.*

19742 PAULL, J. A letter from Mr. Paull [on the subject of the charges preferred by him against the Marquis Wellesley] to Samuel Whitbread, Esq. M.P. 34p. 8°. 1808. *The copy that belonged to William Cobbett.*

19743 ROSCOE, W. Considerations on the causes objects and consequences of the present war, and on the expediency, or the danger of peace with France. 135p. 8°. 1808.

19744 —— Second edition. 135p. 8°. 1808.

19745 —— Fourth edition. 135p. *8°.* 1808.

19746 RYLANCE, R. A sketch of the causes and consequences of the late emigration to the Brazils [of the Regent and the government of Portugal]. 78p. *8°.* 1808.

19747 [SMITH, SYDNEY (1771–1845).] Letters on the subject of the Catholics, to my brother Abraham, who lives in the country. Eleventh edition. By Peter Plymley. 175p. *8°.* 1808.

19748 STRICTURES on a pamphlet, entitled, A plain statement of the conduct of the ministry and the opposition towards His Royal Highness the Duke of York: with some few remarks on domestic councils and family cabinets. By a friend of the late Right Hon. William Pitt. 46p. *8°.* 1808.

19749 SUBSCRIPTION in aid of the Spanish patriots. [*Begin.*] City of London Tavern, December 9, 1808. At a meeting of the merchants, bankers, traders, and inhabitants of London...[With a list of the subscribers.] 4p. *fol.* [*London,* 1808] *The Sheffield copy.*

SOCIALISM

19750 [FOURIER, F. M. C.] Théorie des quatre mouvemens et des destinées générales. Prospectus et annonce de la découverte. 425p. *8°. Leipzig,* 1808. *Two copies; one a presentation copy, with inscription, from the author; the other the copy which belonged to Victor Considérant.*

19751 SAINT-SIMON, C. H. DE, *Comte.* Lettres de C.-H. Saint-Simon. 75, 23p. *4°. Paris,* [1808] *The first part is bound with two manuscript pieces by Saint-Simon and the printed* Lettre de Henry Saint-Simon, *1818 (q.v.). For the manuscripts, see* vol. III, *A.L. 212. The second part belonged to Victor Considérant.*

19752 —— Lettres de C.-H. Saint-Simon, proposées par souscription. Prospectus. 3p. *4°.* [*Paris,* 1808]

MISCELLANEOUS

19753 BANCROFT, E. N. A letter to the Commissioners of Military Enquiry: containing animadversions on some parts of their fifth Report; and an examination of the principles on which the medical department of armies ought to be formed. 104p. *8°.* 1808. *Presentation copy from the author to John Calcraft (1765–1831), in a volume of tracts with the book-plate of John Hales Calcraft.*

19754 [BEAUMONT, JOHN T. B.] The arcanum of national defence. By Hastatus. Originally printed in the Bedford, Buckingham and Hertford Gazette. 60p. *8°.* 1808.

19755 BENTHAM, J. Scotch reform; considered, with reference to the plan, proposed in the late Parliament, for the regulation of the courts, and the administration of justice, in Scotland: with illustrations from English non-reform...in a series of letters, addressed to the Right Hon. Lord Grenville...with tables... 100p. *8°.* 1808. *Two copies, one complete, one lacking two of the four tables, but which belonged to David Ricardo.*

19756 BIRCH, J. F. Memoir on the national defence. 140p. *8°.* 1808. *Presentation copy from the author, probably to John Calcraft (1765–1831), in a volume of tracts with the book-plate of John Hales Calcraft.*

19757 BRITISH MUSEUM. A catalogue of the Harleian manuscripts, in the British Museum. With indexes of persons, places and matters...[by T. H. Horne. Revised by R. Nares, S. Shaw and F. Douce.] 4 vols. *fol.* 1808–12.

19758 BRITON. Presume not beyond measure: a serio-comic letter of advice, addressed to the editors of all the public papers. 29p. *8°.* 1808.

19759 CARR, SIR J. Liberty of the press! Sir John Carr against Hood and Sharpe [for a libel]. Report of the above case, tried at Guildhall...on...the 25th July, 1808 ...To which are added, several letters on the subject, written by the Earl of Mountnorris, Sir Richard Phillips and the author of "My pocket book" [Edward Dubois]. 39p. *12°.* 1808.

19760 DOUGLAS, T., *Earl of Selkirk.* On the necessity of a more effectual system of national defence, and the means of establishing the permanent security of the kingdom. 179p. *8°. London & Edinburgh,* 1808.

19761 A LETTER on toleration and the Establishment; addressed to the Right Hon. Spencer Perceval, Chancellor of the Exchequer. With some remarks on his projected Bill. 52p. *8°.* 1808. *The copy that belonged to William Cobbett.*

19762 MILNER, JOHN, *Bishop of Castabala.* Supplement. An examination of the articles in the Antijacobin Review for November, January, February, and March last, upon "the substance of Sir John C. Hippisley's Additional observations," &c. on the Catholic question: in four letters to a gentleman of Dublin, by the Rev. J. Milner. 56p. *8°.* [*London,* 1808 ?]

19763 ROMEYN, J. B. Two sermons, delivered in the Presbyterian Church in the City of Albany, on Thursday, Sept. 8, 1808; being the day recommended...for fasting, humiliation and prayer. 80p. *8°. Albany,* 1808. *The copy that belonged to William Cobbett.*

19764 STATEMENTS relating to the measures adopted during the present war, for the augmentation of the military force of the country, previous to the introduction of the system of recruiting for service during a term of years. 34p. *8°.* 1808. *In a volume of tracts with the book-plate of John Hales Calcraft, which probably belonged to John Calcraft (1765–1831).*

1809

GENERAL

19765 BRISTED, J. Hints on the national bankruptcy of Britain, and on her resources to maintain the present contest with France. 688p. *8°. New-York,* 1809.

19766 COBBETT, W. The life of William Cobbett. By himself. Intended as an encouraging example to all young men of humble fortune... Second edition. 61p. *8°.* 1809. *For other editions, see* 1798.

19767 CROSBY, B., **& CO.** Crosby's universal gazetteer in miniature; or, the geographer's and news-reader's pocket dictionary of every empire, kingdom, state ...city...sea, harbour, river, lake, mountain...in the known world...Second edition. 64, [242]p. *32°.* 1809.

19768 DEMIAN, J. A. Tableau géographique et politique des royaumes de Hongrie, d'Esclavonie, de Croatie, et de la grande principauté de Transilvanie... Traduit de l'allemand. Publié par MM. Roth et Raymond... 2 vols. *8°. Paris,* 1809.

19769 DOMESDAY BOOK. Dom Boc. A translation of the record called Domesday, so far as relates to the county of York, including also Amounderness, Lonsdale, and Furness, in Lancashire; and such parts of Westmoreland and Cumberland as are contained in the survey. Also the counties of Derby, Nottingham, Rutland, and Lincoln, with an introduction, glossary, & indexes. By the Rev. William Bawdwen. 31, 628, 61p. *4°. Doncaster & London,* 1809. *For other editions of the whole or part of* Domesday Book, *see* 1783.

19770 The **EAST-INDIA** register and directory, for 1809; corrected to the 15th August, 1809. Containing... lists of the Company's servants...Together with lists of mariners, &c. not in the service of the...Company; and merchant vessels employed in the country trade. Compiled...by John Mathison & Alexander Way Mason... Second edition. 428p. *12°.* [1809] *For other editions, see* 1804.

For the **EXAMINER,** *see vol.* III, *Periodicals list.*

For the **FAMILY GAZETTE,** *see vol.* III, *Periodicals list.*

19771 FRANKLIN, B. The life of Dr. Benjamin Franklin. Written by himself. 202p. *12°. Montpelier,* 1809. *See also* 1838.

19772 GANILH, C. Des systèmes d'économie politique, de leurs inconvéniens, de leurs avantages, et de la doctrine la plus favorable aux progrès de la richesse des nations... 2 vols. *8°. Paris,* 1809. *Presentation copy, with inscription (cropped), from the author to* 'M. Lacretelle, *ainé'. See also* 1812, 1821.

19773 GRASWINCKEL, J. A. Register op de publicatie van Hun Hoog Mogende vertegenwoordigende het Bataafsch Gemeenebest: houdende ordonnantie eener belasting op het regt van successie, alömme in het Bataafsch Gemeenebest intevorderen. Gearresteerd den 4. October 1805. Tweede druk vermeerderd... 106p. *8°. Haarlem,* 1809.

19774 IVERNOIS, SIR F. D'. Effets du blocus continental sur le commerce, les finances, le crédit et la prospérité des Isles Britanniques. 103p. *8°. London, Dublin, &c.,* 1809. *See also* 1810.

19775 JOURNAL of a tour to the western counties of England, performed in the summer of 1807. By the author of a tour in Ireland. [From vol. 10 of *A collection of modern and contemporary voyages and travels,* 1805–9.] 32p. *8°.* 1809.

19776 LABORDE, A. L. J. DE, *Comte.* A view of Spain; comprising a descriptive itinerary, of each province, and a general statistical account of the country... Translated from the French... 5 vols. *8°.* 1809.

19777 MASSACHUSETTS. *General Court.* Address to the people of the commonwealth of Massachusetts [against the policy of the Federal Government which will lead to war with England]. 24p. *8°. n.p.* [1809] *Wanting the title-page.*

19778 NEWENHAM, T. A view of the natural, political, and commercial circumstances of Ireland. [With an appendix of tables.] 333, 60p. *4°.* 1809.

19779 ROBERTSON, WILLIAM (1721–1793). An historical disquisition concerning the knowledge which the ancients had of India; and the progress of trade with that country...The fifth edition. 384p. *8°.* 1809. *For other editions, see* 1791.

19780 Political, commercial and statistical **SKETCHES** of the Spanish Empire in both Indies; reflections on the policy proper for Great Britain at the present crisis; and a view of the political question between Spain and the United States respecting Louisiana and the Floridas, with the claims of Great Britain...to the commercial navigation of the River Mississipi, &c.&c.&c. 156p. *8°.* 1809.

19781 SKETCHES on political economy, illustrative of the interests of Great Britain; intended as a reply to Mr. Mill's pamphlet Commerce defended. With an exposition of some of the leading tenets of the economists. 115, 9p. *8°.* 1809.

19782 SMITH, ADAM. An inquiry into the nature and causes of the wealth of nations...With a life of the author. Also, a view of the doctrine of Smith, compared with that of the French economists; with a method of facilitating the study of his works; from the French of M. Garnier. 3 vols. *8°. Edinburgh,* 1809. *For other editions, see* 1776.

19783 [——] An inquiry into the nature and causes of the wealth of nations; containing the elements of commerce and political economy. [An adaptation.] By William Enfield... 352p. *12°.* 1809.

AGRICULTURE

19784 BOARD OF AGRICULTURE. Premiums offered by the Board...1809. 14p. *8°.* [1809] *The Sheffield copy. See also 1804, 1808, 1810, 1812, 1816, 1818.*

19785 BRIEFE über die Fellenbergerische Landwirthschaft zu Hofwyl. Neue, verbesserte und mit einigen Zusätzen vermehrte Auflage. 76p. *8°. Zürich,* 1809.

19786 CURWEN, J. C. Hints on agricultural subjects, and on the best means of improving the condition of the labouring classes...Second edition, improved and enlarged. 385p. *8°.* 1809. *For another edition, see 1808.*

19787 ENGLAND. *Commissioners appointed to Enquire into the Nature and Extent of the Several Bogs in Ireland.* Drainage of the bogs of Ireland. The secretary of the Commissioners...is directed by the Board to communicate for the information of the engineers who may be employed, and of the proprietors of bogs the mode in which they have been advised to proceed. [Signed: B. M'Carthy, secretary to the Commissioners.] 3p. *fol. n.p.* [1809] *The Sheffield copy.*

19788 —— *Commissioners for the Herring Fishery.* Instructions for an officer of the fishery under the Act 48 Geo. III. cap. 110, intituled, "An Act for the further encouragement...of the British white herring fishery until the first day of June, one thousand eight hundred and thirteen...[With an appendix of forms.] 119p. *8°. Edinburgh,* 1809. *The instructions issued to Hugh Sutherland, Officer of the Fishery for Northumberland &c., with his name filled in in manuscript, signed by the Secretary to the Commissioners, on 17 June 1822. See also 1849.*

19789 —— *Laws, etc.* An Act for inclosing lands in the hamlet and chapelry of Wheatley, in the parish of Cuddesdon, in the county of Oxford. 49 Geo. III. sess. 1809. 25p. *fol. n.p.* [1809]

19790 —— —— An Act for inclosing lands in the parish of Berrynarbor, in the county of Devon. 18p. *fol. n.p.* [1809]

19791 —— —— An Act for inclosing lands in the parish of Ilsington, in the county of Devon. 20p. *fol. n.p.* [1809]

19792 —— —— [*Endorsed:*] An Act for inclosing lands in the parish of Stokeintinhead, in the county of Devon. 49 Geo. III. sess. 1809. 19p. *fol. n.p.* [1809]

19793 FISHERY SOCIETY, *Leith.* Letters upon the subject of the herring fishery [the first letter signed 'B.W.', i.e. Benjamin Waters]; addressed to the Secretary of the Honourable the Board for the Herring Fishery at Edinburgh. To which is added, a petition to the Lords of the Treasury on the same subject [dated: 4th December 1809, and signed, Ben. Waters, secretary to the Fishery Society at Leith]. 29p. *4°. Edinburgh,* 1809.

19794 GREG, T. A letter to Sir John Sinclair, Bart., M.P....containing a statement of the system, under which a considerable farm is profitably managed in Hertfordshire. Given at the request of the Board. 22p. *4°.* 1809. *The copy presented by Sir John Sinclair to Lord Sheffield, with inscription.*

19795 HARDING, JOHN, *bookseller.* Harding's new catalogue of books on agriculture, planting, gardening... and rural affairs in general. 36p. *8°.* [1809]

19796 HUNT, C. H. A practical treatise on the merino and anglo-merino breeds of sheep; in which the advantages to the farmer and grazier, peculiar to these breeds, are clearly demonstrated. 198p. *8°.* 1809.

19797 LUCCOCK, J. An essay on wool, containing a particular account of the English fleece. With hints for its improvement... 360p. *12°.* 1809. *A reissue of* The nature and properties of wool, *1805 (q.v.).*

19798 MAVOR, W. General view of the agriculture of Berkshire. Drawn up for the consideration of the Board of Agriculture... 548p. *8°. London, Abingdon, &c.,* 1809. *See also 1813.*

19799 The practical NORFOLK FARMER; describing the management of a farm throughout the year; with observations founded on experience. Second edition, enlarged... 147p. *8°. Norwich & London,* 1809. *For another edition, see 1808.*

19800 [ORSON, B.] Facts and experiments on the use of sugar in feeding cattle: with hints for the cultivation of waste lands. And for improving the condition of the... peasantry in Great Britain and Ireland. 121p. *8°.* 1809. *Presentation copy, with inscription, from the author to Lord Sheffield.*

19801 PITT, WILLIAM (1749–1823). A general view of the agriculture of the county of Leicester; with observations on the means of its improvement, published by order of the Board of Agriculture...To which is annexed a survey of the county of Rutland, by Richard Parkinson. 2 vols. *8°. London, Leicester, &c.,* 1809.

19802 —— General view of the agriculture of the county of Northampton, drawn up for the Board of Agriculture ... 320p. *8°. London, Northampton, &c.,* 1809.

19803 POTTS, T. The British farmer's cyclopædia; or, complete agricultural dictionary; including every science or subject dependant on, or connected with, improved modern husbandry: with the breeding, feeding, and management, of live stock...the management of bees ...[Second edition.] 42 plates, [625]p. *4°.* 1807[1809]. *With a second engraved title-page, dated 1809, and bearing the words 'second edition'. A printed paper label on the spine bears the date 1808.*

19804 RICHARDSON, WILLIAM (1740–1820). Letter to the Right Hon. Isaac Corry, containing an epitome of some of the most curious and important properties of Irish fiorin, or fyoreen grass... 47p. *8°. Belfast,* 1809. *See also 1810.*

19805 —— Plan for reclaiming the Bog of Allen, and the other great morasses, in Ireland; addressed to the...Earl of Rosse. 32p. *8°. Dublin,* 1809.

19806 RITSON, J. The jurisdiction of the court leet: exemplified in the articles which the jury or inquest for the King, in that court, is charged and sworn...to inquire of and present...Second edition, with great additions. 108p. *8°.* 1809. *See also 1816.*

19807 SEBRIGHT, SIR J. S. The art of improving the breeds of domestic animals. In a letter...to...Sir Joseph Banks... 31p. *8°.* 1809. *Inscribed in manuscript 'For Lord Sheffield'.*

19808 SINCLAIR, SIR JOHN, *Bart.* An account of the systems of husbandry adopted in the more improved districts of Scotland...Drawn up for the consideration of the Board of Agriculture... 12p. *8°. Edinburgh,* 1809.

19809 —— [Another edition.] Sketch of the system of husbandry... 11p. *8°. Edinburgh,* 1809.

19810 —— Result of an inquiry, into the nature and causes of the blight, the rust, and the mildew, which have particularly affected the crops of wheat, on the borders of England and Scotland. With some observations on the culture of spring wheat. 74, 17, 60p. *8°. Edinburgh & London,* 1809.

19811 SMITHFIELD CLUB. At the meetings of the Smithfield Club held at the Freemason's Tavern, December 15 and 18, 1809...It was resolved, that the premiums and conditions for the ensuing Christmas Show, on...the 14th, 15th and 17th of December 1810, be as follow... *s.sh.fol. n.p.* [1809] *The Sheffield copy. See also* 1808, 1810.

19812 SOMERVILLE, J., *Baron Somerville.* Facts and observations relative to sheep, wool, ploughs, and oxen: in which the importance of improving the short-wooled breeds of sheep, by a mixture of the merino blood, is demonstrated from actual practice: together with some remarks on the advantages which have been derived to the author's flock, from the use of salt...Third edition, enlarged. 256p. *8°.* 1809.

19813 SUGDEN, E. B., *Baron St. Leonards.* A series of letters to a man of property, on the sale, purchase, lease, settlement, and devise of estates. 127p. *8°. London & Dublin,* 1809.

19814 TRIMMER, JOSHUA K. A brief inquiry into the present state of agriculture in the southern part of Ireland, and its influence on the manners and condition of the lower classes of the people: with some considerations upon the ecclesiastical establishment of that country. 80p. *8°. London, Dublin, &c.,* 1809.

For **WORKINGTON AGRICULTURAL SOCIETY.** The rules and the proceedings of the anniversary of the Workington Agricultural Society, 1809–20, *see* vol. III, *Periodicals list,* Rules and proceedings of the anniversary of the Workington Agricultural Society...

19815 YOUNG, ARTHUR (1741–1820). The farmer's calendar: containing the business necessary to be performed on various kinds of farms during every month of the year...The eighth edition, greatly enlarged and improved. 663p. *8°.* 1809. *For other editions, see* 1771.

19816 —— On the advantages which have resulted from the establishment of the Board of Agriculture: being the substance of a lecture read to that institution, May 26th, 1809. By the secretary to the Board. 60p. *8°.* 1809.

19817 —— [Another edition.] 70p. *8°.* 1809.

19818 —— View of the agriculture of Oxfordshire. Drawn up for the Board of Agriculture...By the secretary of the Board. 362p. *8°. London, Oxford, &c.,* 1809. *See also* 1813.

POPULATION

19819 MALTHUS, T. R. An essay on the principle of population...First American, from the third London edition. 2 vols. *8°. Washington City,* 1809. *For other editions, see* 1798.

19820 WALLACE, ROBERT (1697–1771). A dissertation on the numbers of mankind in ancient and modern times...Second edition, revised and corrected. 338p. *8°. Edinburgh & London,* 1809. *For other editions, see* 1753.

TRADES & MANUFACTURES

19821 An **ADDRESS** to the landed interest of Scotland, on the subject of distillation: by a Scotch farmer. 201p. *8°. Edinburgh, Perth, &c.,* 1809.

COMMERCE

19822 An **ATTEMPT** to elucidate the pernicious consequences of a deviation from the principles of the Orders in Council. 76p. *8°.* 1809. *Attributed in a manuscript note on the title-page to 'Mr. Hilbers'.*

19823 BAILLIE, G. Interesting letters addressed to Evan Baillie, Esq. of Bristol, merchant, Member of Parliament for that great city, and Colonel of the Bristol Volunteers. [On the author's commercial misfortunes.] 80p. *8°. London, Liverpool, &c.,* 1809.

19824 —— Interesting letters addressed to James Baillie, Esq. of Bedford Square, partner in the House of Baillie, Thornton, and Campbell. 48p. *8°. London, Liverpool, &c.,* 1809.

19825 —— Interesting letters addressed to John Bolton, Esq. of Liverpool, merchant, and colonel of a regiment of volunteers...To which is annexed sundry valuable documents. 67p. *8°. London, Liverpool, &c.,* 1809.

19826 [**BROWN,** C. B.] An address to the Congress of the United States, on the utility and justice of restrictions upon foreign commerce. With reflections on foreign trade in general, and the future prospects of America. [The Advertisement signed: C. B. B.] 97[95]p. *8°. Philadelphia,* 1809.

19827 EAST INDIA COMPANY. Proceedings relative to ships tendered for the service of the United East-India Company, from the second July, 1806, to the twenty-seventh September, 1809, with an appendix. p. 2653–3027, 3713–4013. *fol.* 1809. *See also* 1806.

19828 —— Reports and papers on the impolicy of employing Indian built ships in the trade of the East-India Company, and of admitting them to British registry: with observations on its injurious consequences to the landed and shipping interests, and to the numerous branches of trade dependent on the building and equipment of British-built ships. 276p. *8°.* 1809.

19829 ENGLAND. *War Office.* [Begin.] To all

commanders of His Majesty's ships of war and privateers ...[A licence, signed by Lord Liverpool, 29 October 1809, authorising Messrs. Heyman & Co. of London, merchants, to import certain goods 'from Embden or from Norden or from any port eastward of the island of Juist as far as the river Eyder inclusive, to Heligoland'.] *s.sh.4⁰.* [*London*, 1809]

19830 HILLHOUSE, J. Speeches delivered in the Senate of the United States [by J. Hillhouse and T. Pickering], on the resolution offered by Mr. Hillhouse, for repealing the embargo laws. 45p. *8⁰. Albany*, 1809.

19831 HOLROYD, J. B., *Earl of Sheffield.* The Orders in Council and the American embargo beneficial to the political and commercial interests of Great Britain. 51p. *8⁰.* 1809. *Two copies, one presented by the author to the Earl of Selkirk, the other probably Lord Sheffield's own copy, with manuscript additions, one of which may be in his own hand, possibly for a revised edition.*

19832 JULLIEN DU RUET, D. M. Tableau chronologique et moral de l'histoire universelle du commerce des anciens... 2 vols. *4⁰. Paris*, 1809.

19833 [LOWELL, J.?] American candour, in a tract lately published at Boston, entitled An analysis of the late correspondence between our administration and Great Britain and France. With an attempt to shew what are the real causes of the failure of the negociation. 104p. *8⁰.* 1809.

19834 MAGNIEN-GRANDPRÉ, N. (1745–1811) and **DEU DE PERTHES,** L. J. Dictionnaire des productions de la nature et de l'art, qui font l'objet du commerce de la France, soit avec l'étranger, soit avec ses colonies; et des droits auxquels elles sont imposées... 2 vols. in 3. *8⁰. Paris*, 1809. *With the book-stamp of the Société de Lecture de Genève on the title-pages.*

19835 MEMORIAL to the Board of Trade, from the ship-builders in the Port of London, on the ruinous consequences which will result from the employment of Indian built ships in the service of the East India Company, &c.&c.&c. 14p. *8⁰.* [*London*, 1809] *Wanting the title-page.*

19836 (Second Division.) June 14. 1809...Unto the Right Honourable the Lords of Council and Session, the **PETITION** of James Thomson, merchant in Glasgow ...[A case of damages against Peter Clark, master and part owner of the Brigantine *Perseverance*, who refused to take on board goods that he had contracted to take to America. Signed: Henry Cockburn.] 24p. *4⁰. n.p.* [1809]

19837 PRICE, RICHARD H. Remarks proving the use of tea to be against the interests of Ireland, and shewing that its manufactures and produce would be encreased by substituting coffee. 8p. *8⁰. Dublin*, 1809.

19838 STEPHEN, J. The speech of James Stephen, Esq. in the debate in the House of Commons, March 6, 1809, on Mr. Whitbread's motion relative to the late overtures of the American Government: with supplementary remarks on the recent Order in Council. 126p. *8⁰.* 1809.

19839 UNITED STATES OF AMERICA. Documents accompanying the message of the President of the United States, to the two Houses of Congress, at the commencement of the second session of the eleventh Congress. November 29, 1809. Read, and referred to a Committee of the Whole House on the state of the Union. [Concerning the British Orders in Council.] 88p. *8⁰. City of Washington*, 1809.

COLONIES

19840 BOLINGBROKE, H. A voyage to the Demerary, containing a statistical account of the settlements there, and of those on the Essequebo, the Berbice, and other contiguous rivers of Guyana. 120[220]p. *8⁰.* 1809. *For another edition, see 1807.*

19841 EAST INDIA COMPANY. A list of the names of the members of the United Company of Merchants of England, trading to the East-Indies, who stood qualified as voters on the Company's books the 11th April, 1809... 96p. *8⁰.* [*London*, 1809] *See also* 1690 (COMMERCE), 1708, 1773 (COLONIES), 1795, 1813.

19842 GRAY, H. Letters from Canada, written during a residence there in the years 1806, 1807, and 1808; shewing the present state of Canada, its productions— trade—commercial importance and political relations... 406p. *8⁰.* 1809.

19843 JACKSON, JOHN M. A view of the political situation of the province of Upper Canada, in North America, in which her physical capacity is stated; the means of diminishing her burden, encreasing her value, and securing her connection to Great Britain, are fully considered. With notes and appendix. 79p. *8⁰.* 1809. *The copy that belonged to William Cobbett.*

19844 MAITLAND, JAMES, *8th Earl of Lauderdale.* An inquiry into the practical merits of the system for the government of India, under the superintendence of the Board of Controul. 260p. *8⁰. Edinburgh & London*, 1809.

FINANCE

19845 ALBION FIRE AND LIFE INSURANCE COMPANY. Proposals from the Albion Fire and Life Insurance Company, of London: instituted 1805; and empowered by Act of Parliament. 25th March 1809. [Signed: Warner Phipps, secretary.] [4]p. *fol.* [*London*, 1809]

19846 AMICABLE SOCIETY FOR A PERPETUAL ASSURANCE OFFICE. A list of the members of the corporation of the Amicable Society for a Perpetual Assurance-Office...[With 'A short account of the...Society'.] 48p. *8⁰.* 1809.

19847 ASELLUS, *pseud.* A letter to His Grace the Duke of Richmond, Lord Lieutenant of Ireland, stating the case of certain officers in the Custom Department of Ireland, claiming compensation under the Act...for abolishing fees. 26p. *8⁰. Dublin*, 1809.

19848 BANK OF ENGLAND. A list of the names of all such proprietors of the Bank of England, who are qualified to vote at the ensuing election...March 28th, 1809. 18p. *fol.* [1809] *See also,* 1738, 1749, 1750, 1789, 1790, 1791, 1792, 1793, 1794, 1795, 1796, 1797, 1798, 1799, 1801, 1803, 1804, 1808, 1812, 1816, 1819, 1836, 1843.

19849 BANK OF SCOTLAND. [*Endorsed:*] By-laws & ordinances of the Governor and Company of the Bank of Scotland, for the better distinguishing the Bank's cash and bills at their agencies. Made at a general meeting, on 11th December 1809. 4p. *fol. n.p.* [1809]

19850 BEARBLOCK, J. Observations on a pamphlet written by Richard Flower, recommending the abolition of tithes. 38p. *8°. London, Cambridge, &c.,* 1809.

19851 BERIGT eener geldleening van zes millioenen guldens Hollands courant, tegens den interest van vier ten honderd in het jaar, gevestigd op koninklijke en nationale domeinen...[Dated: Amsterdam den 14den van gras-maand 1809.] [2]p. *s.sh.fol. n.p.* [1809]

19852 [*Begin.*] **BERIGT** van eene negotiatie ten behoeve van het Koningrijk Holland, a 6 perCt. intrest... [Dated: Amsterdam, den 16 januarij 1809.] [4]p. *4°. n.p.* [1809]

19853 BISH, T. [*Begin.*] In the last lottery...the above capital prizes were all sold in shares by Bish...who is selling tickets and shares...for the new lottery...[A handbill.] *s.sh.8°.* [1809?]

19854 BRANSCOMB, SIR J., & CO. One thousand five hundred tickets as a free gift in the present state lottery, which begins drawing 12th of April, 1809...[A handbill.] *s.sh.8°.* [*London,* 1809]

19855 BROGDEN, J. Address to the proprietors of the London Assurance Corporation [on the abuses in the management of the company]. 17p. *8°.* [*London,*] 1809.

19856 CRAUFURD, G. Essai sur les dettes publiques, et sur la possibilité de les éteindre avec le temps, sans rembourser le capital, et sans faire le moindre tort aux créanciers publics. 74p. *8°. Rotterdam,* 1809.

19857 ENGLAND. *Commissioners of Customs.* Instructions for the landing surveyors, at the out ports. 4p. *4°.* 1809. *Addressed in manuscript to William Harbord at Yarmouth, dated '13th Decr. 1811' and signed by G. Wilson, J. Williams and J. Hume.*

19858 —— —— Instructions for the landing waiters, at the out ports. 5p. *4°.* 1809.

19859 —— —— Instructions for the searchers, at the out ports. 11p. *4°.* 1809. *Addressed in manuscript to 'Mr. Harbord at Yarmouth'.*

19860 —— —— Instructions to weighing-porters, in the service of the customs, at the out ports. 8p. *4°.* 1809.

19861 FERRALL, D. A new system of book-keeping, by double entry; demonstrating a plain rule of obtaining the principal object of that art by forming a balance account in the day-books... 28, [200]p. *8°. Dublin,* [1809]

19862 FLOWER, R. Abolition of tithe recommended, in an address to the agriculturists of Great Britain; in which the increasing and unjust claims of the clergy are fully examined and disputed: with some observations on the present construction of the law of tithing, and its dangerous consequences to the landed interest of this country. 43p. *8°. Harlow & London,* 1809.

19863 LOCKER, J. Address to the King, the ministry, and the people of Great Britain and Ireland, on the present state of the money system of the United Kingdom.

With an appendix, containing letters of His Majesty's ministers to the author, and some important documents farther explanatory of the system, and the means of amendment. 65p. *8°.* 1809. *The copy that belonged to William Cobbett.*

19864 LOWNDES, T. and PARKE, T. The duties, drawbacks, and bounties, of customs and excise, payable in Great Britain, on merchandize...as settled by various Acts of Parliament, passed prior to the eleventh of September, 1809; in which is comprised, an account of such goods as are...prohibited to be imported, or exported... 132p. *8°. Liverpool,* 1809.

19865 LOWRIE, W. The principles of keeping accounts with bankers in the country and in London; with accurate tables adapted to the calculating of interest accounts...and to the discounting of bills of exchange... To which is added, a concise and practical treatise on bills of exchange and promissory notes...The second edition. 296p. *8°.* 1809. *For another edition, see* 1805.

19866 MEYER, JONAS D. Essai qui a remporté le prix au concours ouvert par l'Académie du Gard à Nismes sur cette question: Déterminer le principe fondamental de l'intérêt, les causes accidentelles de ses variations, et ses rapports avec la morale. 85p. *8°. Amsterdam,* 1809.

19867 MURHARD, J. C. A. Ueber Geld und Münze überhaupt und in besonderer Beziehung auf das König-reich Westphalen. Eine staatswirthschaftliche Unter-suchung. 104p. *8°. Cassel & Marburg,* 1809.

19868 NETHERLANDS. *Laws, etc.* Beredeneerd register op de wet en de reglementen, betrekkelijk het Grootboek der publieke schuld, ten laste van het Koning-rijk Holland. 139p. *8°. Amsterdam,* 1809.

19869 —— —— Besluit, houdende eene wet, tot daar-stelling van een Grootboek der publieke schuld. Gegeven den 27sten januarij 1809. 13p. *8°. n.p.,* 1809.

19870 —— —— Besluit, houdende een reglement op de primitive inschrijving in het Grootboek. Gegeven den 23sten van sprokkelmaand 1809. 12p. *8°. n.p.,* 1809.

19871 —— —— Besluit, houdende een reglement op de overschrijving van ingeschreven kapitalen in het Groot-boek, mitsgaders op de renten- en interest-betaling derzelven. Gegeven den 23sten van sprokkelmaand 1809. 14p. *8°. n.p.,* 1809.

19872 —— —— Besluit, houdende bepalingen ter voor-koming van alle schade of ongerijf, welke bij de oproepin-gen tot roijering en inschrijving in het Grootboek der publieke schuld, voor de eigenaars van vermiste of andere effecten zoude kunnen voortspruiten. Gegeven den 12den van bloeimaand 1809. 7p. *8°. n.p.,* 1809.

19873 [**PARKER,** .] An attempt to ascertain a theory for determining the value of funded property. 56[55]p. *8°.* 1809.

19874 PARNELL, H. B., *Baron Congleton.* Speech of Henry Parnell, Esq. in the House of Commons, on... April 18, 1809, on a motion to assimilate the currencies of Great Britain and Ireland. 24p. *8°.* 1809. *The copy that belonged to William Cobbett.*

19875 PHILIPS, F. The murder is out! or committee-men fingering cash; being a sequel to "New taxes! Seventy-thousand pounds!" Addressed to every house-holder in the manor of Manchester. Published for the benefit of the soup shops, not by a boroughreeve, a con-stable, a lord, nor a Committee-man. 20p. *8°. Manchester,* [1809]

19876 PROVIDENT INSTITUTION FOR LIFE ASSURANCE AND ANNUITIES. A short account of the Provident Institution...The fifth edition. 39p. *8°.* 1809. *For another edition, see* 1806.

19877 RICHARDSON, GOODLUCK & CO. 20th this month, the state lottery will begin and end drawing. The whole in one day. [A handbill, dated 1st September 1809.] *s.sh.8°.* [1809]

19878 *ROCK LIFE ASSURANCE COMPANY, No. 14, New Bridge Street, Blackfriars. [*Begin.*] Sir, I transmit to you the tables for ordinary assurances on lives...[Signed: William Frend. A prospectus, with tables of premiums.] 4p. [*London,* 1809 ?] *The copy that belonged to Augustus De Morgan, with some manuscript notes. See also* 1816.

19879 —— The principles of life assurance explained: together with new plans of assurance and annuities adapted to the prudent of all classes...by the Rock Life Assurance Company. [By J. Perry.] 47p. *8°.* 1809.

19880 SWIFT & CO. One grand day, the 20th of next month. The state lottery, containing two hundred thousand pounds in prizes, will be drawn all in one day... [A handbill.] *s.sh.8°.* [1809]

19881 SWINTON, A. Report upon the affairs of the York-Buildings Company and their creditors. [Dated: 27th February 1809. With 'Schedule of the funds and debts of the York-Buildings Company, referred to in the preceding report'.] 47, 11p. *4°. n.p.* [1809]

19882 SYPHAX, *pseud.* Syphax's letters on the trial by jury, illustrated in the case of Alexander Davison, Esq. [contractor to the army] as they recently appeared in the British Guardian. 38p. *8°.* 1809.

19883 Korte **UITREKENING** der renten en interessen van een honderd tot duizend gulden kapitaal, gerekend van een en een kwart, tot zeven percent intrest in 't jaar... 15p. *8°. n.p.* [1809]

19884 VANSITTART, N., *Baron Bexley.* Substance of Mr. N. Vansittart's speech, June 20, 1809; on moving certain resolutions on finance. [With the Resolutions.] 14p. *8°. n.p.* [1809]

19885 VIEW of one of the grand prizes in Pickett Street, in the only lottery now on sale. Third and last grand city lottery of freehold houses, will be drawn in Guildhall, 4th December [1809]...[A handbill.] *s.sh.8°.* [*London,* 1809]

19886 WARDLE, G. L. Eleven millions income tax. The statement made by Gwyllym Lloyd Wardle, Esq., M.P. respecting the abolition of the £11,000,000 income tax; in a speech delivered in the House of Commons on the 19th of June, 1809: together with the speech of Wm. Huskisson and the able reply of Henry Parnell. [Edited] by P. F. M'Callum. 44p. *8°.* 1809.

19887 WESTPHALIA. *Ministère des Finances.* Administration des finances du Royaume de Westphalie. An 1808. [Reports with documents annexed. The main report is signed: Bulow.] 321p. *4°. Cassel,* 1809.

TRANSPORT

19888 CALCULATIONS of the probable benefit to the neighbouring country, and to the proprietors, of an iron rail way from Berwick to Kelso, passing by the coal pits and lime works in the north Bishopric of Durham. 20p. *8°. Kelso,* 1809.

19889 COMMUNICATION of the British and Bristol Channels, by means of a canal from Bridgwater to Seaton...[With 'Proceedings of the last meeting at Chard'.] 3p. *fol. Bridgwater,* [1809]

19890 ENGLAND. *Post Office.* [Engraved form, filled in in manuscript, headed 'Saturday evening June 17th 1809, Monday morning June 19th 1809', giving details of the arrival and departure of mail. Signed: Aug⁵. Thesiger President.] *s.sh.obl.fol. n.p.* [1809] *Addressed in manuscript, with an explanatory note, to 'Fran⁵. Freeling Esqr'. From the Sheffield Collection.*

19891 —— General Post Office, Monday, Nov. 27, 1809. No. 3463. Daily statement of the packet boats. [With 'Weekly return of the packet boats'.] *s.sh.fol.* [1809]

19892 MEMORIAL of the petitioners to Parliament, for additional trustees in the management of the Broomielaw Harbour and Navigation of the River Clyde. [With an appendix of petitions.] 19p. *4°. Glasgow,* 1809.

19893 Second Division. November 25. 1809...**PROCEEDINGS** before the Sheriff-Depute of Forfarshire, in the summary application, John Guild, Esq. and others, against Hercules Ross and David Scott, Esquires... [Concerning the failure of Ross and Scott, trustees of the turnpike road from Dundee to Ferryden, to repair the road. Signed: John Nicoll.] 18p. *4°.* [*Edinburgh,* 1809]

19894 WEST INDIA DOCK COMPANY. At a General Court of Proprietors of the West-India Dock Company, held...on...the 6th January, 1809...the chairman read...a report from a committee of directors, on the general conduct of the Company's concerns, to the end of...1808; which was ordered to be printed... 15p. *8°.* [*London,* 1809]

SOCIAL CONDITIONS

19895 BERNARD, Sir T., *Bart.* The new school [the Barrington School, Bishop Auckland]; being an attempt to illustrate its principles, detail, and advantages. [With a list of the publications of the Society for Bettering the Condition of the Poor.] 111p. *8°. The Society for Bettering the Condition of the Poor,* 1809. *The copy that belonged to Patrick Colquhoun. See also* 1812.

19896 BLAIR, W. A letter to Mr. Hodson, on the inadequacy of the poor laws for employing, protecting &

reclaiming unfortunate females destitute of work; in answer to Mr. Hale's Reply. 36p. *8°.* [*London,* 1809] *The copy that belonged to Patrick Colquhoun.*

19897 —— Prostitutes reclaimed and penitents protected: being an answer to some objections made against the principle and tendency of the London Female Penitentiary, with observations on licensed brothel-houses... 91p. *8°.* 1809.

**19898 BROUGHAM, H. P., *Baron Brougham and Vaux*. Speeches...delivered before a Committee of the honourable House of Commons, in opposition to a Bill, for incorporating certain persons by the name of the Gas Light and Coke Company. 31p. *fol.* [1809]

19899 BURGESS, W. Cobbett's oppression!! Proceedings on the trial of an action between William Burgess, a poor labouring man! and William Cobbett, a patriot and reformer!! for employing William Aslett and John Dubber, to assault, and falsely imprison the plaintiff. Tried...at Winchester, on Thursday, the 20th of July, 1809... 26p. *8°.* 1809.

19900 May 24. 1809...CASE for Mr. William Bannerman, schoolmaster of the parish of Fraserburgh; against the Right Honourable Alexander, Lord Saltoun; William Kelman, writer in Fraserburgh, and others. (To be heard at the Bar of the Venerable Assembly [of the Church of Scotland], on the [*blank*] day of May 1809.) [Concerning complaints against the schoolmaster's character. Signed: John Cunninghame.] 15p. *4°. n.p.* [1809]

19901 CHELTENHAM SCHOOL OF INDUSTRY FOR GIRLS. Plan of the Cheltenham School of Industry for Girls: and Association of Married Women... 31p. *8°.* 1809.

19902 ENGLAND. *Parliament.* Debates in both Houses of Parliament in...May and June 1808, relative to the agreement made by Government with Mr. Palmer, for the reform and improvement of the Post-Office and its revenue. With an appendix containing...documents... 130, xxxviiip. *8°.* 1809. *See also* 1811.

19903 FISHER, JOHN, *Bishop of Salisbury*. A sermon preached before the incorporated Society for the Propagation of the Gospel in Foreign Parts; at their anniversary meeting...February 17, 1809. [With 'An abstract of the charter, and...proceedings of the Society...1808, to... 1809'.] 69p. *8°.* 1809.

19904 GAS LIGHT AND COKE COMPANY. Gas Light Bill. Third reading, Friday, June 2, 1809. [A statement by the Company.] 3p. *fol.* [1809]

19905 GAS-LIGHT BILL. In Parliament. [*Begin.*] The following are the grounds upon which the Bill is opposed... 13p. *8°. n.p.* [1809]

19906 HALE, WILLIAM. An address to the public upon the dangerous tendency of the London Female Penitentiary; with hints relative to the best means of lessening the sum of prostitution. 68p. *8°.* 1809.

19907 HANSON, JOSEPH. The whole proceedings on the trial of an indictment against Joseph Hanson, Esq. for a conspiracy to aid the weavers of Manchester in raising their wages...at the Lancaster Spring Assizes, 1809...[With a preface by the defendant.] xiv, 116p. *8°. London, Manchester, &c.,* 1809.

19908 HERDMAN, J. A letter, addressed to...the Lord Bishop of Durham...and the other members of the General Committee of the Society for Bettering the Condition...of the Poor; proposing a plan for improving dispensaries, and the medical treatment of the diseased poor. 22p. *4°.* 1809.

19909 *LANCASTER, JOSEPH. An account of the progress of Joseph Lancaster's plan for the education of poor children, and the training of masters for country schools. [With 'List of annual subscribers', etc.] 7, 11p. *8°. Southwark: Royal Free School Press,* [1809]

19910 LA TOUCHE, J. D., *and others*. A report [by J. D. La Touche, W. Disney and G. Renny] upon certain charitable establishments in the City of Dublin, which receive aid from Parliament. [With appendixes.] 95, cxvp. *4°. Dublin,* 1809.

19911 LONDON FEMALE PENITENTIARY. An account of the London Female Penitentiary, with lists of its officers and subscribers. 74p. *12°.* 1809.

19912 MARINE SOCIETY. The bye-laws and regulations of the Marine Society, incorporated in M,DCC,LXXII. With the several instructions, forms of indentures and other instruments used by it. The fifth edition, containing an historical account of this institution ...To which is added, a sermon preached by...Dr. Glasse, Chaplain to the Marine Society. 180p. *12°.* 1809. *For another edition, see* 1792.

19913 MURDOCK, W. A letter to a Member of Parliament, from Mr. William Murdock, in vindication of his character and claims; in reply to a recent publication, by the Committee for conducting through Parliament a Bill for incorporating a Gas-Light & Coke Company. 15p. *8°.* 1809.

19914 P., O. "What-do-you-want?" explained in a poetical epistle from O. P. [i.e. Old Prices] to all the Aitches [i.e. the supporters of John Philip Kemble], with notes illustrative. [With 'Covent-Garden in an uproar; or, the Managers planet-struck'.] 28p. *8°. London & Bristol,* [1809]

19915 In Parliament. REMARKS on the Gas Light and Coke Bill. [Setting out the advantages of the scheme.] 2p. *s.sh.fol. n.p.* [1809] [*Br.* 473]

19916 In Parliament. REMARKS upon the Bill for incorporating the Gas Light and Coke Company. 19p. *8°.* 1809.

19917 SMITH, FREDERICK. An appeal to the virtue and good sense of the inhabitants of St. Martin in the Fields, and other parishes...on the subject of prostitutes walking the streets...[With accounts of the setting up of parish societies in Coventry Street, Fleet Street and St. Dunstan's in the West to organize the policing of these areas.] 23p. *8°.* 1809.

19918 SOCIETY FOR BETTERING THE CONDITION OF THE POOR, *Liverpool*. Report of the select committee appointed in April, 1809, to consider upon the best mode of establishing a permanent society for bettering the condition and increasing the comforts of the poor in the town and neighbourhood of Liverpool. [Signed: James Gerard, and others. With 'Rules and resolutions of the Society'.] 15p. *8°. [Liverpool,* 1809]

19919 SOCIETY FOR BETTERING THE CONDITION OF THE POOR, *London*. Of the education of the poor; being the first part of a digest of the reports of the Society...and containing a selection of those articles which have a reference to education. [Edited, with a preface, by Sir T. Bernard.] 376p. *8°.* 1809.

19920 TAYLOR, WILLIAM, *of Paisley*. An answer to Mr. Carlile's Sketches of Paisley. 60p. *8°. Paisley,* 1809.

19921 VAN VOORST, J. Gas Light and Coke Company. An address to the proprietors of the intended Gas Light and Coke Company: to which is annexed, an epitome of the evidence taken before the Committee of the House of Commons... 84p. *8°.* 1809.

19922 WARREN, C. Speeches of Charles Warren, Esq. and William Harrison, Esq. delivered before a Committee of the honourable House of Commons, in support of a Bill, to authorise His Majesty to grant a charter of incorporation to certain persons, by the name of the Gas Light and Coke Company. 35p. *fol.* 1809.

SLAVERY

19923 MONTGOMERY, JAMES (1771–1854), *and others.* Poems on the abolition of the slave trade; written by James Montgomery, James Grahame, and E. Benger ...Embellished with engravings from pictures...by R. Smirke. [With short notices of Granville Sharp, Thomas Clarkson and William Wilberforce.] 141p. *4°.* 1809.

POLITICS

19924 BURDETT, SIR F., *Bart.* A correct report of the speech delivered by Sir Francis Burdett, Bart. in the House of Commons, on Monday the 13th of March, 1809, on the conduct of H.R.H. the Duke of York...Second edition. 36p. *8°.* 1809.

19925 —— The plan of reform, proposed by Sir F. Burdett, correctly reported in two speeches delivered in Parliament, recommending an inquiry into the state of the representation. To which are added Mr. Perceval's objections to the motion, and a list of the minority who voted for it...June 15th, 1809. 24p. *8°.* 1809.

19926 COBBETT, W. Elements of reform, or an account of the motives and intentions of the advocates for parliamentary reformation. [Extracts from Cobbett's early anti-reform pamphlets, published to discredit him.] 24p. *8°.* 1809.

19927 The **COUNCIL** of hogs, a descriptive poem; containing a patriotic oration to the swinish multitude. [A satire on William Cobbett's attacks on the Duke of York.] 15p. *8°.* 1809.

19928 HINTS to the leaders of political parties in both Houses of Parliament. [Signed: A friend to good order and constitutional reform.] 15p. *8°.* 1809.

19929 An accurate **REPORT** of the proceedings at the meeting of the Friends of Reform, held at the Crown & Anchor Tavern; on Monday, May 1st, 1809. Sir Francis Burdett, Bart. in the chair. Containing the speeches of Sir F. Burdett, Mr. Maddocks, Colonel Wardle, Lord Cochrane, &c.... 20p. *8°.* [*London,* 1809]

19930 A full **REPORT** of the proceedings of the electors of Westminster, on...the 29th of March, 1809, at a meeting held in Westminster Hall, to express their sentiments on the inquiry into the conduct of H.R.H. the Duke of York; containing the speeches...of Sir F. Burdett and Mr. Whitbread, on the necessity of an immediate reform of the House of Commons. 35p. *8°.* 1809.

19931 RUSSELL, JAMES. The ancient liberties and privileges of the Cinque Ports and Ancient Towns: to which is prefixed an original sketch of constitutional rights ... 172p. *8°.* 1809.

19932 WHARTON, R. Remarks on the Jacobinical tendency of the Edinburgh Review, in a letter to the Earl of Lonsdale. 46p. *8°.* 1809. *The copy that belonged to William Cobbett.*

19933 A **WORD,** &c. [An attack on the policy of the Federal Government, and a justification of the policy of the Commonwealth of Massachusetts.] 14p. *8°. n.p.* [1809] *Wanting the title-page.*

MISCELLANEOUS

19934 *****LONDON.** Livery Companies. *Salters.* A list of the Master, Wardens, Court of Assistants, and Livery, of the Worshipful Company of Salters. 12p. *8°.* 1809. *See also* 1784, 1787, 1790, 1792, 1794, 1797, 1799, 1801, 1803, 1806, 1812, 1815, 1818, 1821, 1824, 1827, 1830.

19935 PERCEVAL, S. The substance of the speech delivered by the Right Hon. Spencer Perceval, in the House of Commons, on the 8th and 9th of March, 1809, in the debate on the enquiry into the conduct of His Royal Highness the Duke of York... 140p. *8°.* 1809.

19936 May 23, 1809...Unto the...General Assembly of the Church of Scotland, presently assembled at Edinburgh, the **PETITION** of Colin Cameron, Alexander Munro, James Dewar, John Fraser, spirit-dealer, and John Fraser, plasterer, for themselves and other residenters in Edinburgh...[Concerning a chapel of ease in Edinburgh where services should be conducted in Gaelic and English. Signed: John Jardine. With an appendix.] 4, 10p. *4°.* [*Edinburgh,* 1809]

19937 PLAYFAIR, W. A fair and candid address to the nobility and baronets of the United Kingdom; accompanied with illustrations and proofs of the advantage of hereditary rank and title in a free country. 101p. *8°.* 1809. *The copy specially bound for presentation to the Princess Elizabeth, daughter of George III.*

19938 POWELL, RICHARD, *Captain, and others.* Proceedings of a general court martial...on the 24th and 27th of March 1792, for the trial of Capt. Richard Powell, Lieutenant Christopher Seton, and Lieutenant John Hall, on several charges preferred against them respectively by William Cobbett, late Serjeant-Major...Together with several letters which passed between...William Cobbett and Sir Charles Gould, Judge-Advocate General... 87p. *8°.* 1809.

19939 —— [Another edition.] 32p. *8°.* 1809. *The copy that belonged to David Ricardo.*

19940 SHARP, G. A tract on the law of nature and principles of action in man...First printed in 1777. Second edition. 467p. *8°. London & Durham,* 1809. *For another edition, see* 1777.

19941 The **STATE** of the Established Church; in a series of letters to the Right Hon. Spencer Perceval, Chancellor of the Exchequer... 88p. *8°.* 1809. *The copy that belonged to William Cobbett.*

19942 VAUGHAN, CHARLES R. Narrative of the siege of Zaragoza...The fourth edition, with corrections and additions. 33p. *8°.* 1809.

1810

GENERAL

19943 BETHUNE, M. DE, *Duc de Sully*. The memoirs of the Duke of Sully, Prime-minister to Henry the Great. Translated from the French by Charlotte Lennox. A new edition, revised and corrected, with additional notes, some letters of Henry the Great, and a brief historical introduction [attributed to Sir Walter Scott]... 5 vols. *8°. 1810. For other editions, see 1638.*

19944 BURGOYNE, M. A letter from Montagu Burgoyne, Esq. of Mark Hall, to the freeholders and inhabitants of the county of Essex, on the present awful crisis of public affairs, the pressing necessity of a reform in Parliament, and a more complete organization of our resources for the internal defence of the empire. 62p. *8°. London & Chelmsford,* 1810. *The copy that belonged to William Cobbett.*

19945 CHALMERS, G. An estimate of the comparative strength of Great Britain; and of the losses of her trade, from every war, since the Revolution...A new edition, corrected, and continued, to 1810. 443p. *8°. 1810. For other editions, see 1782.*

19946 DIXON, WILLIAM, *the younger.* An inquiry into the impolicy of the continuance of the prohibition of distillation from grain, in Great-Britain; in which its injurious effects on agriculture, and its tendency to produce a deficiency of national subsistence, are particularly considered. 110p. *8°. Liverpool & London,* 1810.

19947 —— Second edition. 103p. *8°. Liverpool & London,* 1810.

19948 The **EAST-INDIA** register and directory, for 1810; corrected to the 4th August, 1810. Containing... lists of the Company's servants...Together with lists of the...mariners, &c. not in the service of the Company; and merchant vessels employed in the country trade. Compiled...by John Mathison & Alexander Way Mason ...Second edition. 436p. *12°. London, Dublin, &c.* [1810] *For other editions, see 1804.*

19949 ENGLAND. Parliament. *House of Lords.* Calendar of the Journals of the House of Lords. From the beginning of the reign of King Henry VIII. to 30 August 1642; and from the Restoration in 1660, to 21st January 1808. [With continuation 'from 21st January 1808 to 14th November 1826'.] 2 vols. *fol.* 1810[–30 ?].

**19950 —— ** *Record Commission.* The Statutes of the Realm...From original records and authentic manuscripts [1101–1713]. [Edited by A. Luders, and others.] 11 vols. *fol.* 1810–28.

19951 ESSAI statistique sur le Portugal. 78p. *8°. Bordeaux,* 1810.

19952 GIBSON, JAMES, *merchant.* Memoir of the late Joseph Paice... 30p. *8°. Dorking,* [1810]. *Presentation copy, with inscription, from the author to Henry Thornton.*

19953 IVERNOIS, SIR F. D'. Effects of the continental blockade upon the commerce, finances, credit and prosperity of the British Islands...Translated from the third French edition...To which are added, observations on certain statements contained in a late work entitled: "A view of the natural and commercial circumstances of Ireland, by Thomas Newenham Esq."... 152, xxiiip. *8°.* 1810. *For another edition, see* 1809.

19954 JEFFERYS, N. An Englishman's descriptive account of Dublin, and the road from Bangor Ferry, to Holyhead. Also of the road from Dublin, by Belfast, to Donaghadee, and from Portpatick [*sic*] to Newcastle upon Tyne... 224p. *12°. London, Dublin, &c.,* 1810.

19955 LANDT, J. A description of the Feroe Islands, containing an account of their situation, climate, and productions; together with the manners, and customs, of the inhabitants, their trade, &c....Translated from the Danish. 426p. *8°.* 1810.

19956 LAURIE, D. A project for erecting public markets, and a grand academy...in the Gorbals; and for improving the general establishments of that Barony, contained in an address to the heritors. With a general introduction, illustrating the advantages of instituting a Royal Academical Society in the city of Glasgow. ccviii, 271p. *8°. Glasgow,* 1810. *See also* 1811 (Analysis of a new system of general education).

19957 MACDONALD, JAMES, *traveller.* Travels through Denmark, and part of Sweden, during...1809: containing authentic particulars of the domestic condition of those countries, the opinions of the inhabitants, and the state of agriculture. 88p. *8°.* 1810.

19958 [MAN, J.] The stranger in Reading, in a series of letters, from a traveller, to his friend in London. 207p. *12°. Reading & London,* 1810.

19959 The two **PICTURES;** or a view of the miseries of France contrasted with the blessings of England. Earnestly recommended to the notice of every true Briton. 45p. *12°.* 1810.

19960 PLUMPTRE, A. A narrative of a three years' residence in France, principally in the southern departments, from the year 1802 to 1805... 3 vols. *8°.* 1810.

19961 The **POST-OFFICE** annual directory for 1810...By Critchett & Woods. The eleventh edition. 406p. *12°.* [1810] *See also* 1805, 1813, 1814, 1820 (Post Office London directory), 1823, 1825, 1830, 1832, 1834, 1836, 1841.

19962 [SLACK, A.] The instructor; or, young man's best companion: containing spelling...Also merchants' accompts and a short and easy method of book-keeping... Together with the method of measuring carpenters', joiners'...glaziers', and painters' work...Likewise the practical gauger made easy...By George Fisher, accomptant. The thirtieth edition, corrected and improved throughout. 328p. *12°.* 1810. *See also* 1813.

19963 STATE of Ireland considered, with an enquiry into the history and operation of tithe: and a plan for modifying that system, and providing an adequate maintenance for the Catholic and Presbyterian clergy. Second edition: with an appendix containing the Rev. Mr. Howlett's plan of commutation, and a proposition for taxing absentees... 154p. *8°. Dublin & London,* 1810.

19964 [WALSH, ROBERT (1784-1859).] A letter on the genius and dispositions of the French government, including a view of the taxation of the French empire. Addressed to a friend, by an American recently returned from Europe. Second edition. 114p. 8°. *Boston, Portland, &c.,* 1810.

19965 [——] Fourth edition. 252p. 8°. 1810.

19966 [——] Eighth edition. 252p. 8°. 1810.

AGRICULTURE

19967 ADAMS, GEORGE (*fl.* 1810). A treatise on a new system of agriculture, and feeding of stock... 29p. 8°. *Kidderminster & London,* [1810]

19968 ANTIDOTE to the merino-mania now progressing through the United States; or, the value of the merino breed, placed by observation and experience, upon a proper basis. [Précis of essays by C. H. Parry, Sir G. S. Mackenzie, E. Sheppard and others.] 52p. 8°. *Philadelphia,* 1810.

19969 BAILEY, JOHN. General view of the agriculture of the county of Durham, with observations on the means of its improvement. Drawn up for the consideration of the Board of Agriculture... 412p. 8°. *London, Durham, &c.,* 1810. *See also* 1813.

19970 BOARD OF AGRICULTURE. Premiums offered by the Board... 1810. 15p. 8°. [1810] *Addressed in manuscript to Lord Sheffield. See also* 1804, 1808, 1809, 1812, 1816, 1818.

19971 CALVEL, E. Du melon, et de sa culture dans les serres, sous chassis, sur différentes couches et en pleine terre. Nouvelle édition, suivie d'une notice sur la courge-melone... 71p. 8°. *Paris,* 1810.

19972 CAPEL, afterwards CAPEL CONINGSBY, G., *Earl of Essex.* An account of the trial between George Earl of Essex, plaintiff, and the Hon. & Rev. Wm. Capel, defendant... at the summer assizes holden at Hertford, July 20th, 1809; for trespasses committed in hunting with the Berkeley Fox-Hounds... To which is prefixed, a report of the proceedings of the committee of the Association [for the protection of the proprietors... of land in the district]... February 15th, 1810. 50p. 8°. 1810.

19973 CROOME, T. The customs of the manor of Painswick, contained in a decree made in the High Court of Chancery, in a suit between the lord of that manor, and the copyhold tenants. Examined... Together with observations on the laws respecting copyhold tenures in general ... 97p. 8°. *Stroud,* [1810?]

19974 DAVIES, W. General view of the agriculture and domestic economy of North Wales; containing the counties of Anglesey, Caernarvon, Denbigh, Flint, Meirionydd, Montgomery. Drawn up and published by order of the Board of Agriculture... 510p. 8°. *London, Chester, &c.,* 1810.

19975 DICKSON, R. W. The farmer's companion; being a complete system of modern husbandry: including the latest improvements and discoveries in theory and practice... 946p. 8°. 1810. *Abridged edition of the author's Practical agriculture, 1805 (q.v.).*

19976 ENGLAND. *Laws, etc.* [*Endorsed:*] An Act for inclosing lands in the parish of Fridaythorpe, in the East Riding of the county of York. 50 Geo. III. Sess. 1810. 33p. *fol. n.p.* [1810]

19977 FARISH, J. Treatise on fiorin grass; with a short description of its nature and properties, together with the soils and manures, best adapted to its culture... 46p. 8°. *Dumfries, Edinburgh, &c.,* 1810.

19978 FISCHER, JOHANN B. Auf vierzehnjährige Erfahrungen und Beobachtungen gegründete Anweisung zum Anbau ausländischer Getraidarten und einiger Oelgewächse, dann deren Eigenschaften, Kultur, Nutzen und Gebrauch; mit einer Nachweisung der bisher erfolgten Verbreitung jener Früchte, und den Resultaten vieler agronomischen Freunde. 144p. 8°. *Creilsheim,* 1810.

19979 HARDY, W. The miner's guide or complete miner; containing the articles and customs of the High Peak and Wapentake of Wirksworth, Derbyshire. Selected ... from the works of Hardy and Houghton. To which is added; a new article and a copy of the inquisition taken at Ashburn, Derbyshire, in the 16th year of the reign of King Edward the 1st... [With 'A poem' by E. Manlove.] 150, 10p. 8°. *Wirksworth & London,* 1810. *For another edition, see* 1748.

19980 [HORNE, THOMAS H.] A treatise on the choice, buying, and general management of live stock... Together with an appendix, on the improvement of British wool... Second edition, revised, corrected, and enlarged... By the author of The complete grazier. 232p. 8°. *London, Newark, &c.,* 1810.

19981 JONES, THOMAS. A letter to the proprietors of the Middle and South Levels of the Fens. [On the survey carried out by John Rennie for draining these areas.] 39p. 8°. *Lymington,* 1810.

19982 LASTEYRIE DU SAILLANT, C. P. DE, *Comte.* An account of the introduction of merino sheep into the different states of Europe, and at the Cape of Good Hope... From the French... by Benjamin Thompson. With notes by the translator. 248p. 8°. 1810.

19983 MacKENZIE, SIR GEORGE S., *Bart.* A general view of the agriculture of the counties of Ross and Cromarty; with observations on the means of their improvement: drawn up for the consideration of the Board of Agriculture... 353p. 8°. *London, Edinburgh, &c.,* 1810. *See also* 1813.

19984 MANLEY, E. Remarks on the use and advantages of the expedition plough; with directions for working it, and setting the feet. 24p. 8°. *Exeter,* [1810]

19985 [MUSSET PATHAY, V. D. DE.] Bibliographie agronomique, ou dictionnaire raisonné des ouvrages sur l'économie rurale et domestique et sur l'art vétérinaire; suivie de notices biographiques sur les auteurs... Par un des collaborateurs du Cours complet d'agriculture-pratique. 459p. 8°. *Paris,* 1810.

19986 NIELD, D. Two essays: the one on the fire and choke-damps in coal and other mines; the other on irrigation, containing the cause of the fire-damp... a description of the choke-damp and the means by which it is rendered harmless, the action of water in irrigation... experiments in agriculture... 48p. *12°. Ironbridge, Manchester, &c.,* 1810.

19987 PRIEST, St. J. General view of the agriculture of Buckinghamshire. Drawn up for the Board of Agriculture... With an appendix, containing extracts from a survey of the same county... by Mr. Parkinson. 412p. *8°. London, Buckingham, &c.,* 1810. *See also* 1813.

19988 RENNIE, John (1761–1821). Report and estimate on the improvement of the drainage and navigation of the South and Middle Levels of the Great Level of the Fens. In consequence of a reference from the Honorable Corporation of the Bedford Level, made the 24th May 1809, by John Rennie. 18p. *4°.* 1810.

19989 RICHARDSON, William (1740–1820). Essay on fiorin grass; shewing the circumstances under which it may be found in all parts of England, its extraordinary properties, and great utility, to the practical farmer... 58p. *8°.* 1810.

19990 —— Essay on the culture of salt marshes; the advantages of consigning them to fiorin grass alone, with the improvement they will receive from salt water irrigation. 36p. *12°. Belfast,* 1810.

19991 —— Letter to the most noble the Marquis of Hertford, on fiorin grass; containing the necessary directions for its culture; the periods and modes of laying it down, and saving its crops... 43p. *8°.* 1810.

19992 —— Letter to the Rt. Hon. Isaac Corry, containing an epitome of some of the most curious and important properties of Irish fiorin, or fyoreen grass... To which is added a letter from ... Isaac Corry, to ... Charles Abbot, with notes on the state of Doctor Richardson's crops in 1809. 54p. *8°. [Dublin,* 1810] *For another edition, see* 1809.

19993 ROBERTSON, George (1750?–1832). A general view of Kincardineshire; or, the Mearns; drawn up and published by order of the Board of Agriculture... 477, 63p. *8°. London, Edinburgh, &c.,* 1810.

19994 ROBINSON, George (*fl.* 1810). An address to the proprietors of landed property, respecting some improvements in agriculture. 21p. *8°. Doncaster,* 1810. *The Sheffield copy.*

19995 SINCLAIR, Sir John, *Bart.* Address to the Board of Agriculture, on the progress made by that institution in promoting the improvement of the country, on... the 12th of June, 1810. 8p. *4°.* [1810] *The Sheffield copy.*

19996 SMITHFIELD CLUB. At the meetings of the Smithfield Club, held at the Freemason's Tavern, December 14, 17, and 18 1810... It was resolved, that the premiums and conditions, for the ensuing Christmas Show, on... the 13th, 14th and 16th of December 1811, be... *s.sh.fol.* [1810] *The Sheffield copy. See also* 1808, 1809.

19997 THIÉBAUT DE BERNEAUD, A. Du genêt, considéré sous le rapport de ses différentes espèces, de ses propriétés et des avantages qu'il offre à l'agriculture et à l'économie domestique. 92p. *8°. Paris,* 1810.

19998 TIBBS, T. The experimental farmer: being strictures on various branches of husbandry and agriculture... containing observations on planting and preserving young trees... Likewise plans for laying-out land, on a five and four field system. Also, a new method to bring the most barren land into cultivation... 153p. *8°. [c.* 1810] *A reissue of the edition of* 1807 (*q.v.*).

19999 TOWNSEND, H. Statistical survey of the county of Cork, with observations on the means of improvement; drawn up... by direction of the Dublin Society. 749, 104p. *8°. Dublin,* 1810. *See also* 1815.

20000 TUSSER, T. A hundredth good pointes of husbandrie... Copied from the first edition, 1557. 20p. *4°.* 1810. *A reprint, on large paper, of the edition published in Sir E. Brydges' British bibliographer, vol. 3. For other editions, see* 1574.

20001 VANCOUVER, C. General view of the agriculture of Hampshire, including the Isle of Wight. Drawn up for the Board of Agriculture... 520p. *8°. London, Portsmouth, &c.,* 1810.

20002 [WESTERN, C. C., *Baron Western.*] [*Begin.*] Provided always... [A form of indenture containing an agreement for the variation of rent, according to the current price of wheat.] *s.sh.fol. Witham & Maldon,* [*c.* 1810] *The copy that belonged to Lord Sheffield, with a manuscript attribution to 'Mr. Western'.*

20003 WILLIAMSON, Thomas, *Captain.* Agricultural mechanism; or, a display of the several properties, and powers, of the vehicles, implements, and machinery, connected with husbandry: together with a great variety of improvements and inventions... Dedicated to the Bath and West of England Society. 311p. *8°.* 1810.

TRADES & MANUFACTURES

20004 BUCHANAN, Robertson. Practical and descriptive essays on the economy of fuel, and management of heat. Essay first, in three parts. Part I. On the effects of heat... Part II. On heating mills, dwelling-houses, and public buildings, by steam. Part III. On drying and heating by steam. 253p. *8°. Glasgow, London, &c.,* 1810.

20005 CHAPMAN, Thomas, *manufacturer.* A narrative of the case of Mr. Thomas Chapman, who first discovered the means of making the fur of the seal available, to the manufacturers of hats, shawls & superfine cloths, with the evidence adduced before a Committee of the Honorable House of Commons... 22p. *8°. Southwark* [1810]

20006 LONDON. Livery Companies. *Goldsmiths.* Goldsmiths' Hall, January 15, 1810. [A notice to watchmakers and casemakers that all the parts of gold or silver watches must conform to the standard of wrought plate, which will be strictly enforced. Signed: Thomas Lane, clerk to the Company.] *s.sh.4°.* [1810] *See note to no.* 13563.

20007 UNITED STATES OF AMERICA. Congress. *House of Representatives.* Report of the Secretary of the Treasury [A. Gallatin] on American manufactures, prepared in obedience to a resolution of the House of Representatives, April 17, 1810. 48p. *8°. Brooklyn,* 1810.

COMMERCE

20008 A short **ADDRESS** to the gentlemen of the northern counties, on the prohibition of distillation from grain. By a freeholder of the County of Ross. [With an appendix containing the resolutions of meetings in the Counties of Edinburgh, Fife and Kinross.] 27, 13p. *8°. Edinburgh*, 1810.

20009 **AZUNI**, D. A. Origine et progrès du droit et de la législation maritime, avec des observations sur le Consulat de la mer. 289p. *8°. Paris*, 1810.

20010 **BARHAM**, J. F. Considerations on the late Act for continuing the prohibition of corn in the distillery; addressed in a letter to the Right Hon. Lord Holland. 72p. *8°.* 1810.

20011 **BELL**, ARCHIBALD. An inquiry into the policy and justice of the prohibition of the use of grain in the distilleries…Second edition, with a postscript. 109[119]p. *8°. Edinburgh, Glasgow, &c.*, 1810. *For another edition, see* 1808.

20012 **DIJON**. Arrêté concernant les bouchers et les marchands de bétail. [Dated: le 25 avril 1810.] *s.sh.fol. Dijon*, [1810]

20013 **EAST INDIA COMPANY**. Annals of the Honorable East-India Company, from their establishment by the Charter of Queen Elizabeth, 1600, to the union of the London and English East-India Companies, 1707–8. By John Bruce…historiographer to the…Company… 3 vols. *4°.* 1810.

20014 **FRANCE**. *Napoleon I., Emperor.* Série de [Bordeaux] No. 19… [*Begin.*] Napoléon, Empéreur des Français…Sous la caution de la maison de commerce établie à [*blank*] sous la raison de [Sn. Bonnassée & Lance] …[A licence, with the holograph signature of the Emperor, to permit the importation in an American vessel of rice or flour from Carolina or elsewhere in America, to any one of the ports of Marseilles, Bordeaux, La Rochelle or Nantes. Dated from Amsterdam 19 October 1810.] *s.sh.fol. n.p.* [1810] *The words in brackets have been filled in in manuscript.*

20015 **HYSON**, T. A letter, &c. in answer to Mr. Richard Twining, tea-dealer, and one of the candidates for the present vacancy in the East India Direction, written by an old and independent proprietor of East India stock, and addressed to his brother proprietors. [Dated: January 10, 1810.] 16p. *8°.* [1810]

20016 **ILSLEY**, F. A statement of facts, relating to the prime cost of sugar; with observations in behalf of West India planters. 168p. *8°.* 1810.

20017 **INNES**, JOHN (*fl.* 1810), *and others.* Remarks on the observations of the Chairman and Deputy Chairman of the East India Company, on the evidence given before the Committee of the House of Commons appointed for the consideration of India affairs, on the subject of the private trade with India. [Prefatory letter signed: J. Innes, R. C. Bazett, H. Fawcett, H. Trail.] 92p. *4°.* 1810.

20018 [**LESUR**, C. L.] Mémoire sur la conduite de la France et de l'Angleterre à l'égard des neutres. 243p. *8°. Paris*, 1810.

20019 (Bill Chamber.) Second Division. April 5. 1810 …**MEMORIAL** for James Thomson, merchant in Glasgow, complainer in a Bill of Advocation, against Peter Clark, master…of the Perseverance of Derby, and Alexander Leslie merchant in Glasgow his mandatory… respondents. [A case of damages, arising out of Clark's refusal to take on board goods that he had contracted to take to America. Signed: Henry Cockburn.] 19p. *4°. n.p.* [1810]

20020 Second Division. Bill-Chamber. May 12. 1810… **MEMORIAL** for Peter Clark, of the City of Newhaven in Connecticut, master and part owner of the brigantine Perseverance of Derby; against James Thomson, merchant in Glasgow. [Signed: George Jos. Bell. With an appendix.] 26, 4p. *4°.* [*Edinburgh*, 1810]

20021 **MORTIMER**, THOMAS (1730–1810). A grammar illustrating the principles and practice of trade and commerce; for the use of young persons intended for business. 216p. *12°.* 1810.

20022 **OBSERVAÇÕES** sobre o commercio de Hespanha com as suas colonias no tempo da guerra, per hum hespanhol europeo. Occasionadas pelo decreto de 20 de Abril de 1799, que excluio os navios neutros dos portos da America Hespanhola…[With the text of a regulation issued in Buenos Aires 6 November 1809.] 58p. *4°. n.p.* [1810]

20023 (Bill Chamber.) June 19. 1810…Unto the Right Honourable the Lords of Council and Session, the **PETITION** of James Thomson, merchant in Glasgow …[Signed: Henry Cockburn.] 6p. *4°. n.p.* [1810]

20024 **ROSS, HIGGENS & CO.** Price current. Malta. [April 30] 181[0]. *s.sh.fol. n.p.* [1810] *A printed form, with dates completed in manuscript, and a manuscript paragraph entitled 'General Observations' at the end.*

20025 In the House of Lords. James **THOMSON**, merchant in Glasgow, appellant; Peter Clark, master and part-owner of the American brigantine the Perseverance, of Derby; Colin Gillespie, merchant…Glasgow; Leslie M'Naught and Company, merchants there; and Duncan M'Naught and Company, merchants in Greenock, respondents. The respondents' case. [Signed: William Adam. Fra. Horner. Dated 1810.] 7p. *fol. n.p.* [1810]

20026 **UNITED STATES OF AMERICA**. Congress. *House of Representatives.* Report of the Committee of Commerce and Manufactures, on the petition of Anthony Buck [denying involvement in violations of the embargo laws by the master of a merchantman for whom he stood surety]. 8p. *8°. City of Washington*, 1810.

COLONIES

20027 **LEATHART,** J. A narrative of the grievances and illegal treatment suffered by the British officers of the Bengal military establishment, from the rigorous and coercive measures of the Governors of Bengal, with an account of the imprisonment…of the author, on suspicion of writing an address containing a statement of grievances. 188p. *8°.* 1810. *The copy that belonged to William Cobbett.*

20028 MACPHERSON, Sir John, *Bart.* Letter from Sir John Macpherson, Bart. to Whitshead Keene, Esq., M.P. May 31, 1806 [on his part in the affairs of the East India Company, 1796–1782]. The second edition. 20p. *8°.* 1810.

20029 SCOTT, afterwards **SCOTT WARING,** J. Letter to the editor of the Edinburgh Review...in reply to the critique on Lord Lauderdale's view of the affairs of the East India Company; published in the 30th number of the Edinburgh Review. 77p. *8°.* 1810.

20030 WALTON, William (1784–1857). Present state of the Spanish colonies; including a particular report of Hispañola, or the Spanish part of Santa Domingo; with a general survey of the settlements in the south continent of America, as relates to history, trade, population, customs, manners... 2 vols. *8°.* 1810. *Presentation copy from the author to Lord Sheffield.*

FINANCE

20031 ANALYSIS of the money situation of Great Britain, with respect to its coins and bank-notes. 27p. *8°.* 1810.

20032 ATKINSON, Jasper. A letter to a Member of Parliament; occasioned by the publication of the Report from the Select Committee on the high price of gold bullion. 104p. *8°.* 1810. *The copy that belonged to David Ricardo. See also* 1811.

20033 BAILY, F. An account of the several life-assurance companies established in London. Containing a view of their respective merits and advantages. 43p. *8°.* 1810. *See also* 1811.

20034 BANK OF SCOTLAND. [*Endorsed:*] Regulations of the Governor & Company of the Bank of Scotland, for the greater accuracy and precision of the official correspondence. Appointed by the Court of Ordinary Directors, 16th April, 1810. 2p. *fol. n.p.* [1810]

20035 BARBER, J. T. An address to the members of the Provident Institution for Life Insurance and Annuities, delivered by Mr. Barber, the managing director, at a general court holden on the 16th of May, 1810... 14p. *8°.* 1810.

20036 BISH, T. Bish...tickets and shares are selling ...for the lottery to be drawn the 8th of this month... [A handbill.] *s.sh.8°.* [1810]

20037 —— 15th of this month, the state lottery will be drawn all in one day, containing 44 capital prizes... [A handbill.] *s.sh.8°.* [1810?]

20038 —— New year. New mode of drawing. New state lottery...Tickets and shares cheaper!...No prize under twenty pounds! All to be drawn in one day, 15th of February...[A handbill.] *s.sh.8°.* [1810?]

20039 —— Valentine's Day, 14th February, 1810... [list of winning numbers]. All drawn that day and all shared and sold by Bish... [A handbill.] *s.sh.8°.* [1810]

20040 BLACKADER, J. The rates of the duties of excise on inland and imported commodities, with the allowances, bounties, and drawbacks on exportation. Also tables for calculating duties and drawbacks and other useful tables. 95p. *4°. Edinburgh,* 1810.

20041 BLAKE, W. Observations on the principles which regulate the course of exchange; and on the present depreciated state of the currency. 132p. *8°.* 1810.

20042 BONNET, A. Manuel monétaire et d'orfévrerie, ou, nouveau traité des monnaies et des calculs relatifs aux différentes valeurs des espèces, vaisselles et matières d'or et d'argent de France et étrangères... 501p. *4°. Paris & Rouen,* 1810.

20043 BOSANQUET, C. Practical observations on the Report of the Bullion-Committee. 110p. *8°.* 1810.

20044 —— Second edition, corrected, with a supplement. 134p. *8°.* 1810.

20045 BRANSCOMB & CO. Capital prizes, sold, shared and registered in several past lotteries... [A handbill.] *s.sh.fol.* [London, 1810?]

20046 [BURT, W.] Desultory reflections on banks in general, and the system of keeping up a false capital, by accommodation paper, so much resorted to by monopolists and speculators...By Danmoniensis. 81p. *12°.* 1810.

20047 CAMPBELL, William. The value of annuities, from £1. to £1000. per annum, on single lives, from the age of one to ninety years...With the amount of the several rates of legacy duty payable, according to the Statute, on the value of annuities. 318p. *8°. London & Edinburgh,* 1810.

20048 CAREY, M. Desultory reflections upon the ruinous consequences of a non-renewal of the charter of the Bank of the United States...Third edition. 44p. *8°. Philadelphia,* 1810.

20049 —— Nine letters to Dr. Adam Seybert, representative in Congress for...Philadelphia...2. On the existing scarcity of money. 3. On the effect of the dissolution of the Bank of the United States... 59p. *8°. Philadelphia,* 1810.

20050 [CAREY, P.] The real cause of the depreciation of the national currency explained; and the means of remedy suggested. 45p. *8°.* 1810.

20051 COCK, S. An examination of the Report of the Bullion Committee: shewing that the present high price of bullion, together with the scarcity of gold coin, and also the low rate of the foreign exchanges, are not attributable to the issue of bank paper... 93p. *8°.* 1810.

20052 COMMERCIAL BANK OF SCOTLAND. Abstract of the articles of copartnery of the Commercial Banking Company of Scotland. 18p. *8°. Edinburgh,* [1810]

20053 CONSIDERATIONS on the effect of the Bank Restraining Bill, and its connection with our financial and commercial system. By a merchant of the old school. 27p. *8°.* 1810.

20054 [EHRENTHAL, von.] Ueber das öffentliche Schuldenwesen. Eine staatswirthschaftliche Untersuchung. 164p. *8°. Leipzig,* 1810.

20055 ENGLAND. Parliament. *House of Commons.* The Report of the Select Committee of the House of

Commons, appointed to consider...of the state and means of effecting marine insurances, laid before the House the 18th of April 1810. To which are added, the minutes of evidence, with an appendix of accounts. 268p. *8°*. 1810.

20056 —— —— —— Report, together with minutes of evidence, and accounts, from the Select Committee on the high price of gold bullion. ⟨Ordered, by the House of Commons, to be printed, 8 June, 1810.⟩ [With appendixes.] 78, 237, 115p. *8°*. 1810. *The copy that belonged to David Recardo.*

20057 —— —— —— [Another edition.] 89p. *8°*. *London & Newcastle*, 1810.

20058 ERINACEUS, *pseud*. Remarks on the present state of public credit; and the consequences likely to result from the decease of Mr. A. Goldsmid & Sir F. Baring. In a letter to William Manning, Esq., M.P., Deputy-Governor of the Bank. 48p. *8°*. 1810.

20059 An **EXPOSÉ** of the present ruinous system of town & country banks, and a sketch of a plan for the establishment of district banks, to be founded on principles that must effectually secure them from the risk of bankruptcy. By a British merchant. 40p. *8°*. 1810.

20060 FONBLANQUE, J. Doubts as to the expediency of adopting the recommendation of the Bullion Committee. 36p. *8°*. 1810.

20061 FORTUNE, E. F. Thomas. An epitome of the stocks & public funds...Eighth edition, with considerable additions. 103p. *12°*. 1810. *For other editions, see* 1796.

20062 [**FOSTER**, R.] Observations on the National Debt; with a plan for discharging it, so as to do complete justice to the equitable claims of the stock-holder...with hints towards a financial measure, calculated to yield a net revenue of more than five millions annually... 90p. *8°*. [*c*. 1810] *Presentation copy from the author to William Cobbett.*

20063 FRANCE. *Douanes Impériales*. Perceptions. Circulaire. 19 août 1810...Mr. le Directeur en Chef des Douanes de la Toscane, aux receveurs principaux. [Signed: Collin. Transmitting a copy of the Imperial Decree of 5 August, increasing the duty on colonial produce.] [2]p. *4°*. *Livourne*, [1810]

20064 —— —— Dogane Imperiali. Stato dei bastimenti ottomanni messi sotto il sequestro in Livorno, e l'ammissione de' quali, siccome quella dei loro carichi è autorizzata del Decreto Imperiale dell' 8 Settembre 1810... 2p. *4°*. *Livorno*, [1810]

20065 —— —— [*Begin*.] Le tarif qui fixe la quotité du droit de 50 pour ct. de la valeur imposé par l'article 10 du Decret Impérial du 9 juillet 1810, sur les marchandises et denrées coloniales, qui se trouve en Hollande... [A list of taxable articles, with the charges.] *s.sh.fol. Amsterdam*, [1810]

20066 —— *Napoleon I, Emperor*. Douanes Impériales. Extrait des minutes de la Secrétairerie d'État...le 12 septembre 1810...[A decree enforcing the payment of customs duties on articles mainly of colonial origin.] [2]p. *4°*. *Livourne*, [1810]

20067 —— —— Douanes Impériales. Extrait des minutes de la Secrétairerie d'État...le 23 septembre 1810. [A decree establishing a bonded warehouse at Leghorn.] [5]p. *4°*. *Livourne*, [1810] *Printed in French and Italian in parallel columns.*

20068 —— —— Douanes Impériales. Extrait des minutes de la Secrétairerie d'État...le 10 octobre 1810. [A decree extending the prohibition of import of certain goods to Italy.] 7p. *4°*. *Livourne*, [1810] *Printed in French and Italian in parallel columns.*

20069 —— —— Douanes Impériales. Décrêt Impérial portant création de tribunaux chargés de la répression de la fraude et contrebande en matière de douanes, et contenant diverses dispositions relatives aux saisies et à l'emploi des marchandises de contrebande...le 18 octobre 1810. 9p. *4°*. *Livourne*, 1810.

20070 FRANCIS, Sir Philip. Reflections on the abundance of paper in circulation, and the scarcity of specie. 47p. *8°*. 1810. *The copy that belonged to William Cobbett.*

20071 —— Second edition. 64p. *8°*. 1810.

20072 [**GREGOR**, F.] A short historical sketch and account of the expences incurred under the heads of Civil List, pensions, and public offices; with some observations on the conduct of the modern reformers; in a letter addressed to a friend. By the author of a letter signed: A Freeholder of Cornwall. Second edition, with additions and alterations. 68p. *8°*. 1810. *The copy that belonged to T. P. Courtenay.*

20073 GRELLIER, J. J. The history of the National Debt, from the Revolution in 1688 to the beginning of 1800; with a preliminary account of the debts contracted previous to that æra. 420p. *8°*. 1810.

20074 GRENFELL, J. A defence of bank notes against the opinions which have been published in the Morning Chronicle, Cobbett's Register, and a recent pamphlet entitled The high price of bullion, a proof of the depreciation of bank notes, with observations on the balance of trade, and the course of exchange. [With a postscript.] 32p. *8°*. 1810. *A second, imperfect, copy belonged to David Ricardo.*

20075 —— Second edition, with two letters to Francis Horner, Esq. M.P. chairman of the Bullion Committee. 48p. *8°*. 1810.

20076 HILL, John (*fl*. 1810). An inquiry into the causes of the present high price of gold bullion in England, and its connection with the state of foreign exchanges; with observations on the Report of the Bullion Committee. In a series of letters addressed to Thomas Thompson, Esq. M.P. one of the members of the Bullion Committee. 152p. *8°*. *London & Hull*, 1810.

20077 [**HOARE**, Peter R.] A letter, containing observations on some of the effects of our paper currency, and on the means of remedying its present, and preventing its future excess. [With a postscript.] 83, 3p. *8°*. 1810. *Reissued in* Tracts on our present money system *in 1814*, *q.v.* (GENERAL).

20078 HORNSBY & CO. By authority of the Prince Regent. The grandest state lottery ever introduced in this country, will begin and finish on the 4th of June, the King's Birth-day... [A handbill.] *s.sh.8°*. [*London*, 1810 ?]

20079 —— The only state lottery to be drawn this year. The 19th of this month [October]. Tickets and shares are selling by Hornsby & Co.... [A handbill.] *s.sh.8°*. [1810]

20080 HUSKISSON, W. The question concerning the depreciation of our currency stated and examined. 154p. *8°*. *London, Edinburgh, &c.*, 1810.

20081 —— Second edition. 154p. *8°. London, Edinburgh, &c.*, 1810.

20082 —— Third edition, corrected. 154p. *8°. London, Edinburgh, &c.*, 1810.

20083 —— Fourth edition. 154p. *8°. London, Edinburgh, &c.*, 1810.

20084 —— Fifth edition. 154p. *8°. London, Edinburgh, &c.*, 1810.

20085 —— Sixth edition. 154p. *8°. London, Edinburgh, &c.*, 1810. *See also 1811, 1819.*

20086 JACKSON, RANDLE. The speech of Randle Jackson, Esq. delivered at the General Court of the Bank of England, held on the 20th September, 1810, respecting the Report of the Bullion Committee of the House of Commons; with notes on the subject of that Report. 54p. *8°.* [1810]

20087 [**KOSTER,** J. T.] A short statement, of the trade in gold bullion; with an attempt to shew that bank-notes are not depreciated. 51p. *8°. Liverpool & London*, 1810. *See also 1811.*

20088 A LETTER to Jasper Vaux, Esq. chairman of the meeting at Lloyd's, on...the 29th January last, in which the nature and principles and the...extent of marine assurance are examined, the necessity of a new company to effect marine assurance pointed out; and the opposition...to its establishment, especially by the under-writers at Lloyd's Coffee-house, is considered and refuted. By a subscriber to Lloyd's. Second edition. 75p. *8°.* 1810.

20089 A LETTER to the Right Honourable Spencer Perceval, on the augmentation of a particular class of poor livings without burthening the public. 61p. *8°.* 1810.

20090 LEWORTHY, W. The trial between William Leworthy and the Globe Insurance Company...at Taunton Assizes...April, 1810 [arising out of the Company's refusal to meet a claim by Leworthy following a fire on his premises]... 180p. *8°.* 1810.

20091 LYNE, C. A letter to the Right Hon. George Rose, M.P. Vice President of the Board of Trade, &c.&c. in which the real causes of the scarcity and consequent high price of gold and silver are stated and exemplified. 51p. *8°.* 1810. *The copy that belonged to David Ricardo.*

20092 M'CALLUM, P. F. Le livre rouge; or, a new and extraordinary red-book; containing a list of the pensions in England, Scotland and Ireland; together with a view of the receipts and expenditure of the public money. Designed as a companion to the court calendar... Third edition. 155p. *12°.* 1810.

20093 —— The sixth edition... 155p. *12°.* 1810.

20094 MARRYAT, J. Observations upon the Report of the Committee on marine insurance, with a few incidental remarks on a pamphlet lately published, entitled "A letter to Jasper Vaux, Esq." To which is added, copy of a report proposed as an amendment to the report adopted by the Committee on marine insurance. 64, 28p. *8°.* 1810.

20095 —— Second edition. 64, 28p. *8°.* 1810. *For another edition, see 1824 (The substance of a speech)....*

20096 —— The substance of a speech delivered by Joseph Marryat, Esq. in the House of Commons, on...the twentieth of February, 1810, upon Mr. Manning's motion for the appointment of a Select Committee to consider of

...our present means of effecting marine insurances. Published by the special committee at Lloyd's. 40p. *8°.* 1810.

20097 —— Second edition. 40p. *8°.* 1810. *See also 1824.*

20098 MASCALL, E. J. A digest of the duties of customs, and excise...also, the duties outwards...the duties coastwise...together with tables of scavage, baillage, Levant and Russia dues...to the 5th July 1810. 188p. *8°.* 1810. *For another edition, see 1808.*

20099 MORTIMER, THOMAS (1730–1810). The nefarious practice of stock-jobbing unveiled, with an appendix; containing several extraordinary cases, particularly that in which Mr. Bish, stock-broker, was plaintiff, and D. de Chemant, Esq. defendant...and the Acts of Parliament relative to stock-jobbing. [With a preface by the author's widow.] 120p. *8°.* 1810.

20100 MUSHET, R. An enquiry into the effects produced on the national currency, and rates of exchange, by the Bank Restriction Bill; explaining the cause of the high price of bullion, with plans for maintaining the national coins in a state of uniformity and perfection. 100p. *8°.* 1810. *Two copies, one presented by the author to William Cobbett, the other which belonged to David Ricardo.*

20101 —— The second edition. With some observations on country banks, and on Mr. Grenfell's examination of the tables of exchange annexed to the first edition. 112p. *8°.* 1810. *See also 1811.*

20102 PARNELL, H. B., *Baron Congleton.* Tythes. A corrected report of the speech of H. Parnell, Esq. in the House of Commons, on...the 13th of April, 1810, on a motion for a Select Committee to inquire into the collection of tythes in Ireland. 44p. *8°.* 1810.

20103 PÉRIAUX, P. Tarifs des anciennes monnaies d'or et d'argent...Précédés des Décrets impériaux des 18 août et 12 septembre 1810... 48p. *8°. Rouen*, 1810.

20104 New **PLAN,** with additional and superior advantages. State lottery will be drawn June 8, 1810, with four prizes, of tickets...One ticket may gain £100,000... [A handbill.] *s.sh.8°. n.p.* [1810]

20105 POPE, C. A compendium of the laws of customs and excise, relative to the warehousing and bonding system...Likewise, of the laws for the importation, exportation, and warehousing of tobacco and snuff... With indexes. To which is added, a list of the warehousing ports, distinguishing the...species of goods allowed to be warehoused at each port. The whole completed to the 10th October, 1810. 201p. *8°. London & Bristol*, [1810]

20106 RAUMER, F. L. G. VON. Das brittische Besteuerungs-System, insbesondere die Einkommensteuer, dargestellt, mit Hinsicht auf die in der preussischen Monarchie zu treffenden Einrichtungen. 276p. *8°. Berlin*, 1810.

20107 RICARDO, D. The high price of bullion, a proof of the depreciation of bank notes. 48p. *8°.* 1810.

20108 —— Second edition, corrected. 48p. *8°.* 1810.

20109 —— Third edition, with additions. 56p. *8°.* 1810. *See also 1811.*

20110 ROSE, GEORGE. Observations respecting the public expenditure, and the influence of the Crown. 79p. *8°.* 1810.

20111 —— Second edition. 79p. *8°.* 1810.

20112 —— Third edition. 79p. *8°.* 1810.

20113 SIMON, J. Simon's Essay on Irish coins, and of the currency of foreign monies in Ireland; with Mr. Snelling's supplement... 180, 13p. *4°. Dublin, 1810. For another edition, see 1749, and for Snelling's supplement, 1770.*

20114 SIMONDE DE SISMONDI, J. C. L. Over het papieren geld en de middelen om hetzelve te vernietigen... Uit het Fransch vertaald. 86p. *12°. Amsterdam,* 1810.

20115 SINCLAIR, SIR JOHN, Bart. Observations on the Report of the Bullion Committee. 64p. *8°.* 1810.

20116 —— The second edition. 64p. *8°.* 1810.

20117 —— The third edition. 64p. *8°.* 1810.

20118 —— Political maxims regarding coin & paper currency. 9p. *8°. Edinburgh,* 1810. *See also nos.* 20119–20 *below.*

20119 —— Remarks on a pamphlet intitled, "The question concerning the depreciation of the currency stated and examined." By William Huskisson, Esq. M.P. Together with several political maxims regarding coin and paper currency, intended to explain the real nature and advantages of the present system. 74p. *8°.* 1810.

20120 —— The second edition, corrected. 74p. *8°.* 1810.

20121 SONNESCHMID, F. T. Beschreibung der spanischen Amalgamation oder Verquickung des in den Erzen verborgenen Silbers, so wie sie... in Mexico gebräuchlich ist, mit ausführlicher Darstellung einer neuen Theorie... 408p. *8°. Gotha,* 1810.

20122 STEUART, SIR J., Bart. Principles of banks and banking of money, as coin and paper: with the consequences of any excessive issue on the national currency, course of exchange, price of provisions, commodities and fixed incomes. In four books. 314p. *8°.* 1810. *See also* 1812.

20123 SWIFT & CO. Superior advantages in the present new lottery. Only 4,000 numbers... All to be drawn in one day, October 19, 1810... [A handbill.] *s.sh.8°. [London,* 1810]

20124 TOWNSEND, E. [*Begin.*] To the parishioners of Saint Paul, Covent Garden. [A statement on his financial position, dated: 8th March, 1810.] *s.sh.4°.* [1810]

20125 [TROTTER, C.] The principles of currency and exchanges applied to the Report from the Select Committee of the House of Commons, appointed to inquire into the high price of gold bullion, &c.&c. 79p. *8°.* 1810. *The copy that belonged to David Ricardo.*

20126 —— Second edition. 80p. *8°.* 1810. *See also* 1811.

20127 UNITED STATES OF AMERICA. Congress. *House of Representatives.* Documents accompanying the Appropriation Bill for the year 1810. January 30, 1810. Laid on the table by the chairman of the Committee of Ways and Means... 12p. *12°. City of Washington,* 1810.

20128 —— —— —— Letter from the Secretary of the Treasury, in answer to a letter of the chairman of the Committee of Ways and Means, requesting information as to the most eligible method of obtaining loans, March 21st, 1810... 15p. *8°. Washington City,* 1810.

20129 VASSAR, J. J. Copies from a correspondence ...with Mr. Huskisson, Mr. Perceval, &c.&c. on the subjects of the waste and abuses in the military establishments and expenditure; demonstrating... from reported facts and official admissions, the necessity of an immediate and complete change in the existing system of managing and applying the revenue. 155p. *8°.* 1810.

20130 WHITCOMBE, S. Considerations addressed to the Legislature upon the expediency and policy of authorising the alienation of estates belonging to corporate bodies, particularly bishops, and deans and chapters, for the purpose of raising money to purchase the unredeemed land-tax... 63p. *8°.* 1810.

TRANSPORT

20131 BANKS, E. The report of Edward Banks, on the practicality and expence of a navigable canal, proposed to be made between the Grand Southern Canal, near Copthorne Common and Merstham, to communicate with the river Thames at Wandsworth, by means of the Surry iron railways. 8p. *4°.* 1810.

20132 *CARY, JOHN (d. 1835). Cary's new itinerary: or, an accurate delineation of the great roads... throughout England and Wales: with many of the principal roads in Scotland... Fourth edition, with improvements. [96]p., 866 col., p. 868–936. *8°.* 1810.

20133 *—— Cary's traveller's companion, or, a delineation of the turnpike roads of England and Wales... To which is added, an alphabetical list of all the market towns, with the days on which they are held. [22]p., 43 maps. *8°.* 1810. *For other editions, see* 1806.

20134 ENGLAND. Laws, etc. Anno tricesimo nono & quadragesimo Georgii III. Regis. [Local & Personal.] Cap. 24. An Act for amending the several Acts passed for... completing the canal navigation from Manchester to or near Ashton-under-Lyne and Oldham, and the several cuts and other works authorized to be made... by the Company of Proprietors of the said Canal Navigation; and for granting to the said Company... other powers. ⟨16th May 1800.⟩ p. 557–571. *fol.* 1810.

20135 —— —— Anno quadragesimo quarto Georgii III. Regis. [Local & Personal.] Cap. 9. An Act for enabling the Company of Proprietors of the Rochdale Canal more effectually to provide for the discharge of their debts, and to complete the whole of the works to be executed... ⟨23d March 1804.⟩ p. 109–112. *fol.* 1810.

20136 —— Parliament. *House of Commons.* London Dock Bill. ['Extracts from the Report of & minutes of evidence taken before the Committees appointed by the House of Commons to inquire into the best mode of providing sufficient accommodation for the increased trade and shipping of the Port of London... Ordered to be printed 13th May, 1796, and 25 April, and 7th May, 1799.'] 23p. *8°.* [1810] *For the original Report and Minutes of evidence see respectively* 1796 *and* 1799.

20137 LIST of proprietors of the Strand Bridge. 26p. *4°. [London,* 1810]

20138 LIVERPOOL. Dock Committee. A statement of the grounds upon which the Trustees of the Liverpool Docks propose applying to Parliament, next session, for authority to provide additional dock space, &c.&c. 46p. *8°. Liverpool*, 1810.

20139 MERCATOR, *pseud.* Liverpool and its docks. An address to the inhabitants of Liverpool, on the subject of a new dock bill, intended to be introduced into Parliament this present session. 38p. *8°. Liverpool*, 1810.

20140 ODDY, J. J. A sketch for the improvement of the political, commercial, and local, interests of Britain, as exemplified by the inland navigations of Europe in general, and of England in particular, including details relative to the intended Stamford Junction Navigation. [With an appendix containing 'Mr. Telford's report to the committee at Stamford, of the intended Junction Navigation Company, 1810'.] 141p. *8°.* 1810.

20141 RENNIE, JOHN (1761–1821). New Shoreham harbour. The report of J. Rennie, Esq. 22p. *8°.* 1810.

20142 —— Report and estimate of the Grand Southern Canal, proposed to be made between Tunbridge and Portsmouth: by means of which and the river Medway, an inland navigation will be opened between the river Thames and Portsmouth. 10p. *4°.* 1810.

20143 STATE of inland navigation in Ireland. 39p. *8°. Dublin*, 1810.

20144 VAZIE, R. A report on the intended Shoreham Harbour-docks [in a letter addressed to Robert Wilmott. With a testimonial signed by the pilots of the Port of New Shoreham, and the resolutions passed at a meeting of the inhabitants on 13 September, 1809]. [2]p. *s.sh.fol.* [1810]

SOCIAL CONDITIONS

20145 BATHURST, HENRY, *Archdeacon.* A sermon preached before the incorporated Society for the Propagation of the Gospel in Foreign Parts; at their anniversary meeting...February 16, 1810. [With 'An abstract of the charter, and...proceedings of the Society...1809, to... 1810'.] 76p. *8°.* 1810.

20146 CLAPHAM, S. Friendly societies substitutes for parochial assessments. A sermon, preached at Christ-Church, Hants. on...June 11, 1810. 23p. *12°. London, Christ-Church, &c.*, 1810.

20147 *CORSTON, W. British Leghorn, a new source of industry, introduced into this country for the employment of poor female children. [4]p. *8°. Southwark: Royal Free School Press*, [1810]

20148 [DISNEY, J.] Five letters to Sir Samuel Romilly, M.P. on the subject of his motion respecting the penal laws. By Anti-Draco. 45p. *8°.* 1810.

20149 Important official **DOCUMENTS** relative to the disagreements between the members of the late Army Medical Board [on the subject of hospital accommodation for those wounded on active service], not included among the papers printed by order of the House of Commons. 38p. *8°.* 1810.

20150 An **ESSAY** on the poor laws, as they regard the real interests both of rich and poor. 52p. *8°.* 1810.

20151 FRANCE. *Administration des Postes.* Instruction générale sur le service des postes aux lettres. 419p. *4°. Paris*, 1810. *With a second title-page in Dutch and the Dutch and French texts on opposite pages.*

20152 FRIENDLY BROTHERS. Rules and orders to be observed by the members of a benefit society called The Friendly Brothers, held at the Duke's Head, Great-Peter-Street, Westminster. Instituted, August 16, 1808. 16p. *8°. Southwark*, 1810.

20153 *HARRISON, GEORGE, *Quaker.* Education respectfully proposed and recommended, as the surest means, within the power of government, to diminish the frequency of crimes...Second edition: with an appendix. 28p. *8°. Royal Free School Press...By J. Lancaster*, 1810. *For another edition, see* 1803.

20154 HIGHMORE, A. A letter to William Wilberforce, Esq. M.P. relative to the second Bill introduced by him to the House of Commons...for registering charitable donations, &c....Printed at the desire of the Committees of Governors of the Small Pox Hospitals and City of London Lying-In Hospitals. [With the text of the Bill.] 27p. *8°.* 1810.

20155 —— Pietas Londinensis: the history, design, and present state of the various public charities in and near London. 984p. *12°.* 1810.

20156 The **IMPRESS,** considered as the cause why British seamen desert from our service to the Americans; with a review of the encouragement now held out by the Royal Navy, and the means in our power of abolishing the impress. 29p. *8°.* 1810. *The copy that belonged to William Cobbett.*

20157 *LANCASTER, JOSEPH. The British system of education: being a complete epitome of the improvements and inventions practised at the Royal Free Schools, Borough Road, Southwark. 55p. *8°. Royal Free School*, 1810.

20158 MACGILL, S. Remarks on prisons. 79p. *8°. Glasgow, Edinburgh, &c.*, 1810.

20159 A **METHOD** of improving the condition of the Irish poor. Suggested in a letter to Samuel Whitbread, Esq. M.P. 26p. *8°. Dublin*, 1810.

20160 An **OUTLINE** of a plan for the more easily registering and better securing of charitable donations. 24p. *8°.* 1810.

20161 Bill-Chamber. Second Division. May 24. 1810... Unto the Right Honourable the Lords of Council and Session, the **PETITION** of James Wilkie, mason in Glasgow...[Concerning a dispute between him and the householder with whom he lodged, and with whom he had deposited his wages. Signed: James L'Amy. With an appendix.] 10, 7p. *4°.* [*Edinburgh*, 1810]

20162 REMARKS on impressing seamen. 4p. *12°.* [1810]

20163 REMARKS on the report and rules of the select committee, for bettering the condition & increasing the comforts of the poor. [Signed: A subscriber to the fund of 1809. Dated: Liverpool, 1st Feb. 1810.] 3p. *fol. Liverpool*, [1810]

20164 ROMILLY, SIR S. Observations on the criminal law of England, as it relates to capital punishments, and on the mode in which it is administered. 76p. *8°.* 1810.

20165 RUSSEL STREET FRIENDLY SOCIETY, *Liverpool.* Rules, orders and regulations, of the

Friendly Society. Instituted March 1st, 1810. 16p. *8°*. *Liverpool*, 1810.

20166 SOCIETY FOR BETTERING THE CONDITION OF THE POOR, *London*. The cottager's friend. [The preface signed: B., i.e. Sir Thomas Bernard.] 94p. *12°*. *n.p.* [1810]

20167 —— The history of Betty Thomson, and her family and neighbours; being the first part of a practical commentary on the reports of the Society for Bettering the Condition of the Poor. Second edition. 55p. *12°*. 1810.

20168 SOCIETY FOR MAINTAINING AND EDUCATING POOR ORPHANS OF THE CLERGY. 2d April, 1810. Constitutions, orders, and regulations of the Governors of the Society for Cloathing, Maintaining and Educating Poor Orphans of Clergymen

of the Established Church, in...England, until of age to be put apprentice... 87p. *8°*. [1810] *A manuscript list of members is written on the fly-leaf, on the blank spaces of the title-page, and on the last leaf.*

20169 SOCIETY FOR THE SUPPRESSION OF VAGRANTS, *Bath*. Report of the Bath Society for the Suppression of Vagrants...Relief of occasional distress and encouragement of Industry...With an account of the receipts and disbursements from Jan. 1, 1809, to Jan. 1, 1810... 28p. *12°*. *Bath*, 1810. *See also 1811, 1812, 1813, 1816.*

20170 TROTTER, T. An essay, medical, philosophical, and chemical, on drunkenness, and its effects on the human body...The fourth edition, corrected and enlarged. 230p. *8°*. 1810. *The Turner copy. For other editions, see 1804.*

SLAVERY

20171 ENGLAND. *Laws, etc.* Abstract of the Acts of Parliament for abolishing the slave trade, and of the Orders in Council founded on them. 43p. *8°*. *The African Institution*, 1810.

20172 [TUSSAC, F. R. DE.] Cri des colons contre un ouvrage de M. l'Evêque et senateur Grégoire, ayant pour titre De la littérature des nègres... 312p. *8°*. *Paris*, 1810.

POLITICS

For **BLAGDON'S POLITICAL REGISTER,** 1810–11, *see* vol. III, *Periodicals list*.

20173 BURDETT, SIR F., *Bart*. The address of Sir Francis Burdett to his constituents, in a letter, dated March 23, denying the power of the House of Commons to imprison the people of England. 38p. *8°*. [1810]

20174 BURGOYNE, M. An account of the proceedings in the late election in Essex; with the speeches of the candidates and their friends, &c. and a preface. 151p. *8°*. *London & Chelmsford*, 1810. *The copy that belonged to William Cobbett.*

20175 COBBETT, W. Cobbett's remarks on Sir F. Burdett's letter to his constituents, on the power of imprisonment by the House of Commons; taken from the Weekly Political Register, March 24, 1810; also the Speaker's warrant, and Sir F. Burdett's letter to the Speaker. 18p. *8°*. [1810]

20176 ENGLAND. *Laws, etc.* Magna Charta and the Bill of Rights, with the Petition of Right presented to Charles the First by the Lords and Commons, together with His Majesty's answer; and the coronation oath. 51p. *8°*. *J. Blacklock*, [1810]

20177 —— —— Fairburn's second edition of Magna Charta; with the Petition of Right...also the Bill of Rights of the people of England, together with the coronation oath. With an engraved frontispiece of Sir Francis Burdett...and his letter to the Speaker of the House of Commons concerning the illegality...of the warrant of the Speaker to commit him to the Tower. 40p. *8°*. [1810]

20178 ENSOR, G. On national government. First part. 2 vols. *8°*. 1810.

20179 ERSKINE, T., *Baron Erskine*. The speeches of the Hon. Thomas Erskine (now Lord Erskine), when at the Bar, on subjects connected with the liberty of the press, and against constructive treasons. Collected by James Ridgway... 3 vols. *8°*. 1810.

20180 [FARQUHARSON, G.?] Liberty of the subject and the press. Three letters, addressed to the Right Honourable John Lord Eldon, Lord High Chancellor, on the subject of his having excluded gentlemen who have written for the public journals from the English Bar. By one who was a writer for the newspapers. 27p. *8°*. 1810. *Presentation copy to William Cobbett, inscribed on the half-title: 'Cobbett Esqr. with Geo. Farquharson's Respects'.*

20181 GRENVILLE, W. W., *Baron Grenville*. Letter from the Right Honourable Lord Grenville to the Earl of Fingall [on the political status of Roman Catholics]. 16p. *8°*. 1810. *See also 1812.*

20182 HAGUE, T. Sir Francis Burdett. A letter to his electors, being a vindication of his argument, with the rights and liberties of Englishmen, and the laws of Parliament, taken from the Statutes; and the Attorney-General's opinion denied to be law. 46p. *8°*. [*London*, 1810.]

20183 A LETTER, addressed to the Right Hon. Lord Grenville [on his Chancellorship of the University of Oxford]. By a Briton. 174p. *8°*. *Stockton & London*, 1810.

20184 A LETTER to the Right Honourable Spencer Perceval...upon his reported correspondence with Lord Viscount Melville, in reference to the return of that noble Lord to power. By a country gentleman. 43p. *8°*. 1810.

20185 MEMOIRS of the life of Sir Francis Burdett, Baronet, including a faithful narrative of the whole proceedings in the House of Commons on the question of his commitment to the Tower, for publishing a letter to his constituents... 120p. *8°*. 1810.

20186 REFORM in Parliament. Proceedings of the electors of the City and Liberties of Westminster: including correct reports of the speeches delivered at a public meeting held in New Palace-Yard...9th February, 1810, for the purpose of obtaining a reform in the representation of the people in Parliament. 32p. *8°*. 1810.

20187 ROSCOE, W. Brief observations [on the

continuance of the war] on the address to His Majesty proposed by Earl Grey in the House of Lords, 13th June, 1810. 44p. *8°. Liverpool & London, 1810.*

20188 —— Occasional tracts relative to the war between Great Britain and France, written and published at different periods from the year 1793, including Brief observations on the address to His Majesty, proposed by Earl Grey, in the House of Lords, June 13, 1810. 336p. *8°. 1810. Presentation copy from the author to the Earl of Thanet.*

20189 [**SYMMONS**, J.] Reform without innovation; or, cursory thoughts on the only practicable reform of Parliament consistent with the existing laws and the spirit of the constitution. 23p. *8°. 1810. Wanting the title-page.*

20190 **TARLETON**, B. Substance of a speech intended for the Vote of Credit Bill for 1810. [On the conduct of the war and foreign policy.] 23p. *8°. 1810.*

20191 **VALERIUS**, *pseud.* The letters of Valerius to Samuel Whitbread, Esq. M.P. on the privileges of the House of Commons; with a vindication of the conduct of Sir Francis Burdett. 129p. *8°. 1810. The copy that belonged to William Cobbett. 'Valerius' was used as a pseudonym at this date by William Combe.*

20192 A **WARNING** to the frequenters of debating clubs: being a short history of the rise and progress of those clubs: with a report of the trial and conviction of John Gale Jones, the manager of one of them, called the British Forum... 30p. *12°. 1810.*

MISCELLANEOUS

20193 **HANN**, R. A letter to the Right Reverend the Lord Bishop of London concerning the heresy and imposture of Joanna [Southcott] the prophetess. 28p. *12°. 1810.*

20194 **HIGHMORE**, N. A letter to Henry Bankes, Esq., M.P. on the abolition of sinecures, and the reform of abuses. 5p. *8°. 1810.*

20195 **PARIS**, JOHN A. A memoir on the physiology of the egg, read before the Linnean Society of London, on the 21st of March, 1809. 28p. *8°. 1810. The copy that belonged to David Ricardo.*

20196 **PLAYFAIR**, W. Second address to the British nobility; accompanied with illustrations and proofs of the advantage of hereditary rank and title in a free country. 96p. *8°. 1810. Bound with A fair and candid address to the nobility and baronets of the United Kingdom, 1809 (no. 19937), in a presentation binding.*

20197 **VENAULT DE CHARMILLY**, . A letter from Colonel Venault de Charmilly, Knight of the ...Order of St. Louis, to Lieut. General B. Tarleton, Colonel of the Twenty-First Light Dragoons, and Governor of Berwick. 35p. *8°. 1810. Presentation copy from the author to William Cobbett.*

1811

GENERAL

20198 **ANTIBARBARO**, AMADEO, *pseud.* Ueber die Handels-politik von Grossbrittannien...Aus dem Spanischen übersetzt. 2 vols. *8°. Madrid [Hamburg?], 1811.*

20199 **BALSAMO**, P. A view of the present state of Sicily: its rural economy, population, and produce, particularly in the county of Modica. With an appendix, containing observations on its general character, climate, commerce, resources, &c....To which are added, an examination of the Sicilian volunteer system, and extracts from letters written in Sicily in 1809 and 1810. By Thomas Wright Vaughan, Esq. 253, xciiip. *4°. 1811.*

20200 **BARNES**, GEORGE. A statistical account of Ireland, founded on historical facts. Chronologically arranged and collected. 77p. *8°. Dublin & London, 1811.*

20201 **BOILEAU**, D. An introduction to the study of political economy: or, elementary view of the manner in which the wealth of nations is produced, increased, distributed, and consumed. 406p. *8°. 1811.*

20202 **BRISTED**, J. The resources of the British Empire, together with a view of the probable result of the present contest between Britain and France. 527p. *8°. New-York, Philadelphia, &c., 1811. See also 1812.*

20203 **BUTTE**, W. Grundlinien der Arithmetik des menschlichen Lebens, nebst Winken für deren Anwendung auf Geographie, Staats- und Natur-Wissenschaft... 420p. *8°. Landshut, 1811.*

20204 **C.**, S. Multum in parvo: or, a reform catechism; in three parts: (which appeared in the Times of the 5th, 10th, and 17th May, 1811) with additional notes. To which is added, a bullion catechism; in two parts... 40p. *8°. 1811. Attributed to Stephen Cattley in a manuscript note on the title-page.*

20205 **COURTENAY**, T. P. A view of the state of the nation, and of the measures of the last five years; suggested by Earl Grey's speech in the House of Lords, 13th June, 1810. 180p. *8°. 1811.*

20206 **ENGLAND**. *Record Commission.* Introduction to the authentic collection of the Statutes of the Realm. Official copy for the use of His Majesty's Commissioners on the Public Records of the Realm. Not published. 180p. *4°. 1810 [1811].*

20207 **FISHER**, R. B. A sketch of the city of Lisbon, and its environs; with some observations on the manners, disposition, and character of the Portuguese nation. 95p. *8°. 1811.*

20208 **ISOLA**, F. Instituzioni di commercio e di economia civile. 215p. *8°. Roma, 1811.*

20209 IVERNOIS, Sir F. d'. Histoire des décrets commerciaux de Bonaparte et de leurs effets sur l'agriculture, les manufactures, le commerce et les finances de la France. 94p. *4°. Londres, 1811. A proof copy of 12 chapters of Part I of a work which it seems unlikely was ever published. With a manuscript letter from the author to an unnamed recipient bound in, for which see vol. III, A.L. 246.*

20210 JACOB, W. Travels in the south of Spain, in letters written A.D. 1809 and 1810. [With an appendix.] 407, 36p. *4°. 1811.*

20211 JOLLIE, F. Jollie's Cumberland guide & directory: containing a descriptive tour through the county, and a list of persons in public and private situations, in every principal place in the county...Also a list of the shipping. 84, xxxv, 129p. *8°. Carlisle, 1811.*

20212 LANG, Joseph. Grundlinien der politischen Arithmetik. 216p. *8°. Charkow & Kursk, 1811.*

20213 [LAURIE, D.] Analysis of a new system of general education; in which the Lancastrian principles are discussed and enlarged, in a project for the erection of a grand public academy at Glasgow to be supported by public markets in the suburbs of that city...Addressed to the heritors of the Barony of Gorbals... ccviii, 271p. *8°. 1811. Presentation copy from the author to Thomas Chalmers. For another edition, see 1810 (A project for erecting public markets...).*

20214 LOTZ, J. F. E. Revision der Grundbegreiffe der Nationalwirthschaftslehre, in Beziehung auf Theuerung und Wohlfeilheit, und angemessene Preise und ihre Bedingungen. 4 vols. *8°. Koburg & Leipzig, 1811–14.*

20215 MACGILL, T. An account of Tunis: of its government, manners, customs, and antiquities; especially of its productions, manufactures, and commerce. 187p. *8°. Glasgow & London, 1811.*

20216 MEASE, J. The picture of Philadelphia, giving an account of its origin, increase and improvements in arts, sciences, manufactures, commerce and revenue. With a compendious view of its societies...its police, the public buildings... 376p. *12°. Philadelphia, 1811.*

20217 [PEMBERTON, Thomas.] An attempt to estimate the increase of the number of poor during the interval of 1785 and 1803; and to point out the causes of it:

including some observations on the depreciation of the currency. 131p. *8°. London, Edinburgh, &c., 1811. Presentation copy from the author to David Ricardo.*

20218 PETRI, J. C. Russlands blühendste Handels, Fabrik- und Manufakturstädte n alphabetischer Ordnung. Vorher eine kurze Uebersicht der russischen Gewerbskunde und des Handelszustandes. Vornämlich fur Kaufleute und Fabrikanten, 215p. *8°. Leipzig, 1811.*

For the **PHILANTHROPIST,** 1811–19, *continued as* the Lindfield Reporter, 1835–42, *see* vol. III, *Periodicals list.*

20219 [ROBERTSON, Joseph.] The traveller's guide through Scotland and its Islands...Fifth edition. 570p. *12°. Edinburgh & London, 1811.*

20220 [RUBICHON, M.] De l'Angleterre. [Vol. I.] 509p. *8°. Londres, 1811.*

20221 SCUDERI, S. Dissertazioni economiche riguardanti il regno di Sicilia. 192p. *4°. Catania, 1811.*

20222 SMITH, Adam. An inquiry into the nature and causes of the wealth of nations...With a life of the author. Also, a view of the doctrine of Smith, compared with that of the French economists; with a method of facilitating the study of his works; from the French of M. Garnier... 3 vols. *8°. Edinburgh, 1811.*

20223 —— [Another issue.] 3 vols. *8°. London, 1811.*

20224 —— Compendio da obra da Riqueza das naçoes ...Traduzida do original inglez por Bento da Silva Lisboa. 3 vols. *8°. Rio de Janeiro, 1811–12. For other editions, see 1776.*

20225 STEWART, Dugald. Biographical memoirs, of Adam Smith...of William Robertson...and of Thomas Reid...read before the Royal Society of Edinburgh. Now collected...with some additional notes. 532p. *4°. Edinburgh & London, 1811.*

20226 TURGOT, A. R. J., *Baron de l'Aulne.* Œuvres de Mr. Turgot, Ministre d'Etat. Précédées et accompagnées de mémoires et de notes sur sa vie, son administration et ses ouvrages... 9 vols. *8°. Paris, 1811, 1810.*

For the **WEEKLY REGISTER,** 1811–14, *continued as* Niles' weekly register, 1814–37, *then* Niles' national register, 1837–49, *see* vol. III, *Periodicals List,* Niles' national register.

AGRICULTURE

20227 AITON, W. General view of the agriculture of the county of Ayr; with observations on the means of its improvement: drawn up for the consideration of the Board of Agriculture... 725p. *8°. Glasgow, London, &c., 1811.*

20228 —— A treatise on the origin, qualities, and cultivation of moss-earth, with directions for converting it into manure. Published...under the patronage of the Highland Society. 357p. *8°. Air, Glasgow, &c., 1811.*

20229 BOWLES, William (1705–1780). Tratado sobre el ganado merino, y las lanas finas de España...or a treatise on the merino sheep, and the fine wools of Spain ...Rendered into English by E. D. Edited by T. R. 26p. *4°. 1811. The Spanish and English texts are printed on alternate pages.*

20230 BROWN, Robert (1757–1831). Treatise on

rural affairs; being the substance of the article Agriculture, originally published in the Edinburgh Encyclopædia. With improvements and additions. 2 vols. *8°. Edinburgh & London, 1811.*

20231 COVENTRY, A. Notes on the culture and cropping of arable land. [With 'Abstract & tables' and 'Appendix'.] 46, 31, 8p. *8°. Edinburgh, 1811. Presentation copy, with inscription, from the author to 'The Right Honᵗᵉ. Lord Lynedoch'. See also 1812.*

20232 ESTIMATES of produce & rent of arable lands, varying in the fertility of their soil, and in their climate or height of situation. [With 'Observations explanatory of the table of estimates'.] 15p. *8°. n.p. [1811]*

20233 HENDERSON, Robert, *farmer.* A treatise on the breeding of swine, and curing of bacon; with hints on agricultural subjects. 118p. *8°. Leith, Edinburgh, &c.,* 1811.

20234 HIGGINS, JOHN (*fl.* 1811), *and others.* Report upon the farm of Thomas Greg, Esq. at Coles, in Hertfordshire. [Signed: John Higgins, Thomas Wilson, John Foster.] 23p. *8°. Bedford & London,* 1811.

20235 KEITH, G. S. A general view of the agriculture of Aberdeenshire; drawn up under the direction of the Board of Agriculture... 672p. *8°. Aberdeen, Edinburgh, &c.,* 1811.

20236 LESLIE, W. General view of the agriculture in the counties of Nairn and Moray, with observations on the means of their improvement... Drawn up for the Board of Agriculture... 536p. *8°. London, Edinburgh, &c.,* 1811. *See also* 1813.

20237 LEWIS, P. Historical inquiries, concerning forests and forest laws, with topographical remarks, upon the ancient and modern state of the New Forest... 227p. *4°.* 1811.

20238 LIVINGSTON, R. R. An essay on sheep, intended chiefly to promote the introduction and propagation of merinos in the United States of America... Printed by order of the Legislature of... New York. With a preface and explanatory notes by William Cobbett. 247p. *8°.* 1811.

20239 LULLIN, C. Des associations rurales pour la fabrication du lait, connues en Suisse sous le nom de fruitières. 124p. *8°. Paris & Genève,* 1811.

20240 MacDONALD, JAMES, *A.M.* General view of the Hebrides, or Western Isles of Scotland: with observations on the means of their improvement, together with a separate account of the principal islands... Drawn up under the direction of the Board of Agriculture... 824p. *8°. Edinburgh, London, &c.,* 1811.

20241 MARSHALL, W. A review of the reports to the Board of Agriculture from the eastern department of England: comprizing Lincolnshire, Norfolk, Suffolk, and northeast Essex; with the marshes and fens of Yorkshire, north Lincolnshire, south Lincolnshire, Northamptonshire, Huntingdonshire, Cambridgeshire, Norfolk, and Suffolk. 532p. *8°. York & London,* 1811.

20242 MERINO SOCIETY. First report of the Merino Society, established 4th March, 1811, containing lists of the officers, rules and orders, premiums and certificates, to which are added, an alphabetical list of all the members... and an account of the plans, about to be adopted, for promoting the increase of merino sheep in France. 75p. *8°. Nottingham,* 1811. *The Sheffield copy. See also* 1812, 1813.

20243 [ODDY, J. J.] Prospectus of the Royal Western Fishing Company, to be incorporated by Act of Parliament, to be applied for immediately in the present sessions of Parliament. 1811. [With an advertisement for *The policy and economy practised in the fisheries of... Europe* by J. Jepson Oddy and 'Sketch of the contents'.] 16p. *8°. n.p.* [1811]

20244 PARKINSON, RICHARD (1748–1815). General view of the agriculture of the county of Huntingdon; drawn up for the consideration of the Board of Agriculture... 351p. *8°. London, Huntingdon, &c.,* 1811. *See also* 1813.

20245 PHILARATOR, *pseud.* Agriculture defended: in answer to a "Comparative statement of the food produced from arable and grass land, with observations on the late inclosures, published by the Rev. Luke Heslop, Archdeacon of Bucks." Inscribed to the land-holders of the United Kingdom... 86p. *8°.* 1811.

20246 SCHULTES, H. An essay on aquatic rights; intended as an illustration of the law relative to fishing, and to the propriety of ground or soil produced by alluvion and dereliction in the sea and rivers. 140p. *8°.* 1811.

20247 TROTTER, J. General view of the agriculture of the county of West-Lothian: with observations on the means of its improvement, drawn up for the consideration of the Board of Agriculture... 340p. *8°. Edinburgh, London, &c.,* 1811. *For another edition, see* 1794.

20248 WHYTE, A., and **MACFARLAN,** D. General view of the agriculture of the county of Dumbarton, with observations on the means of its improvement, drawn up for the consideration of the Board of Agriculture... 344p. *8°. Glasgow, London, &c.,* 1811.

20249 [YOUNG, ARTHUR (1741–1820).] On the husbandry of three celebrated British farmers, Messrs. Bakewell, Arbuthnot, and Ducket: being a lecture read to the Board of Agriculture... June 6, 1811. By the Secretary to the Board. 52p. *8°.* 1811. *Arthur Young's own copy.*

TRADES & MANUFACTURES

20250 BAVERSTOCK, J. Practical observations on the prejudices against the brewery; with hints to the sugar colonists. 68p. *8°.* 1811. *The copy that belonged to David Ricardo.*

20251 The **BOOK** of trades, or library of the useful arts... The fourth edition. Vols. 2–3. *12°.* 1811. *Vol. 3 is of a new edition, corrected. See also* 1815, 1821, 1824, 1830.

20252 COMMITTEE OF MASTER CHAIR-MANUFACTURERS AND JOURNEYMEN. Second supplement to the London chair-makers' and carvers' book of prices for workmanship... 19p. *4°.* 1811. *For editions of the original work, see* 1802; *for the first and third supplements, see* 1808 *and* 1844 (SOCIETY OF CHAIR-MAKERS AND CARVERS).

20253 DUPORTAL, A. S. Recherches sur l'état actuel de la distillation du vin en France, et sur les moyens d'améliorer la distillation des eaux-de-vie de tous les pays... 112p. *8°. Paris & Saint-Petersbourg,* 1811.

20254 JACKSON, RANDLE. Report of the speech of Randal Jackson, Esq. before a Committee of the House of Commons, on the Tailors' Regulation Bill, delivered... 29th of April, 1811. 43p. *8°.* 1811.

20255 MONEY, W. T. Observations on the expediency of shipbuilding at Bombay, for the service of His Majesty, and of the East India Company. 73, 14p. *8°.* 1811.

20256 RADCLIFFE, WILLIAM (1760–1841). Exportation of cotton yarns. The real cause of the distress that has fallen upon the cotton trade for a series of years past: with hints, as to the only remedy [a tax on the export of cotton twist]... 45p. *8°. Stockport,* 1811.

20257 SHOLL, S. A short historical account of the silk manufacture in England, from its introduction down to the present time...To which is added a faithful account of the first cause of the introduction of the Grand National Flag. By S. Sholl...To which will be subjoined a sketch of the first 58 years of his life, written by himself... 47p. *8°.* 1811.

COMMERCE

20258 BUESCH, J. G. Grundriss einer Geschichte der merkwürdigsten Welthändel neuerer Zeit in einem erzählenden Vortrage...Neueste Ausgabe, durchgesehen und von 1796 bis 1810 fortgestzt von G. G. Bredow. 2 vols. *8°. Wien,* 1811.

20259 EAST INDIA COMPANY. Report on the negociation, between the Honorable East-India Company and the public, respecting the renewal of the Company's exclusive privileges of trade, for twenty years from March, 1794. [With an appendix.] By John Bruce... 287, xlixp. *4°.* 1811.

20260 EXTRACT from the Morning-Post of the 18th of February 1811. Mr. Jackson. [An account of a dinner given by the Committee of Merchants interested in the Trade and Fisheries of the British North American Colonies, to Francis James Jackson, late minister to the United States.] *s.sh.fol.* [1811] [*Br.* 474]

20261 GERARD DE RAYNEVAL, J. M. De la liberté des mers... 2 vols. *8°. Paris,* 1811.

20262 GOWER, R. H. Remarks relative to the danger attendant on convoys; together with a proposition for the better protection of commerce from sea-risk and capture: earnestly recommended to the attention of all merchants and ship-owners throughout Great Britain. 18p. *8°.* 1811.

20263 HAWKINS, Sir C., *Bart.* Observations on the tin trade of the ancients in Cornwall, and on the "Ictis" of Diodorus Siculus... 80p. *8°.* 1811.

20264 HOLROYD, J. B., *Earl of Sheffield.* Lord Sheffield's Present state of the wool trade [being his report to the Wool Fair held at Lewes on 24 July 1811]. 29p. *8°. Dublin,* 1811. *See also* 1815, 1816, 1819.

20265 An INQUIRY into the state of our commercial relations with the Northern Powers, with reference to our trade with them under the regulation of licences, the advantage which the enemy derives from it, and its effects on the revenue, the course of the foreign exchanges, the price of bullion, and the general prosperity of the British Empire. 110p. *8°.* 1811.

20266 NOVA SCOTIA. *Court of Vice-Admiralty.* The substance of a decision, in the Court of Vice-Admiralty at Halifax, upon a petition from the deputy to the treasurer of Greenwich Hospital, against the prize-agents of the Bermuda, for certain unclaimed shares of prize-money due to the Hospital, delivered on the 8th May, 1811. p. 1–28. *8°. Halifax* [*Nova Scotia*], 1811.

20267 PHILLIMORE, Joseph. Reflections on the nature and extent of the licence trade...Second edition. 100p. *8°. London & Oxford,* 1811. *See also* 1812.

20268 WADDINGTON, S. F. The oriental exposition; presenting to the United Kingdom an open trade to India and China... 184p. *8°.* 1811.

COLONIES

20269 An ACCOUNT of the conquest of the Island of Bourbon; with a plan, explanatory of the military operations; and an appendix, containing observations on the state of population, agriculture, commerce, and finance of the island: intended as a basis for estimating its value, as a territorial acquisition. By an officer of the expedition. 116p. *8°.* 1811.

20270 HENDERSON, George, *Capt.* An account of the British settlement of Honduras; being a view of its commercial and agricultural resources, soil, climate, natural history, &c. To which are added, sketches of the manners and customs of the Mosquito Indians...Second edition, enlarged. 237p. *12°.* 1811.

20271 HUMBOLDT, F. H. A. von, *Freiherr.* Essai politique sur le royaume de la Nouvelle-Espagne. 5 vols. *8°. Paris,* 1811. *See also* 1822.

20272 [MACKENZIE, Charles.] Facts relative to the present state of the British cotton colonies, and to the connection of their interests with those of the mother country. 62p. *8°. Edinburgh, Glasgow, &c.,* 1811. *Presentation copy, with inscription, from the author to Benjamin Hobhouse.*

20273 MATHISON, G. Notions respecting Jamaica, in 1808–1809–1810. 117p. *8°.* 1811.

20274 [PATERSON, G.] The history of New South Wales, from its first discovery to the present time; comprising an accurate...description of that...country; and of the persons, manners, and customs, of the natives; with a succinct detail of the establishment and progress of the English colony; including...the situation and conduct of the convicts: to which is added, a description of Van Dieman's Land and Norfolk Island...Compiled...by a literary gentleman... 624p. *8°. Newcastle-upon-Tyne,* 1811.

FINANCE

20275 A., W. A short investigation into the subject of the alleged superfluous issue of banknotes, the high price of bullion, and the unfavourable state of the foreign exchanges: in two letters extracted from the Times newspaper...To which is added the substance of the Earl of Rosse's speech in the House of Lords, on the exchange and currency of Ireland... 31p. *8°.* 1811.

20276 ATKINSON, Jasper. A letter to a Member of Parliament; occasioned by the publication of the Report from the Select Committee on the high price of gold bullion... The second edition. 104p. *8°*. 1811. *For another edition, see 1810.*

20277 BAILY, F. An account of the several life-assurance companies established in London. Containing a view of their respective merits and advantages... The second edition. 49p. *8°*. 1811. *For another edition, see 1810.*

20278 BANFILL, S. A letter to Davies Giddy, Esq. M.P. in answer to his Plain statement of the bullion-question. 29p. *8°*. 1811.

20279 BANKOFSCOTLAND. Books and accounts of the Bank of Scotland, to be kept at the Bank's offices, under the official administration of its agents, in terms of an act and minute of the Court of Directors, dated 25th February, 1811. 4p. *fol. n.p.* [1811]

20280 —— [*Endorsed:*] Instructions to the accountants of the Bank of Scotland, at and for the agencies thereof. 14th Oct. 1811. *fol. n.p.* [1811]

20281 BINGHAM, ROBERT. The trials of the Rev. Robert Bingham... on a charge of sending an incendiary letter, and of setting fire to his dwelling-house... at Horsham, March 26th, 1811, taken in shorthand by Mr. Adams, by order of the Directors of the Union Fire-Office, London. 239p. *8°*. 1811.

20282 BISH, T. The smallest state lottery ever known. 13,500 tickets... To be all drawn Tuesday, 22d October, 1811. [A handbill.] *s.sh.8°*. [1811] [*Br.* 475]

20283 BOASE, H. Remarks on the new doctrine concerning the supposed depreciation of our currency. 110p. *8°*. 1811.

20284 BOLLMANN, E. Paragraphs on banks... Second edition improved. 122p. *12°*. Philadelphia, 1811. *With the signature 'Francis Baring' on the title-page.*

20285 BOYD, WALTER. A letter to the Right Honourable William Pitt, on the influence of the stoppage of issues in specie at the Bank of England: on the prices of provisions, and other commodities. The second edition, corrected. 112p. *8°*. 1811. *A reissue, not of the second, but of the first edition, 1801 (q.v.).*

20286 CANNING, GEORGE (1770–1827). Substance of two speeches, delivered in the House of Commons... on... the 8th and... 13th of May, 1811, in the Committee of the Whole House; to which was referred the Report of the Committee appointed... "to inquire into the cause of the high price of bullion, and to take into consideration the state of the circulating medium..." 155p. *8°*. 1811.

20287 [**CAREY,** J.] A few facts stated in answer to the Report of the Bullion-Committee... by an annuitant. 27p. *8°*. 1811.

20288 [**CAREY,** P.] A letter to Wm. Huskisson, Esq. M.P. on his late publication. By a proprietor of bank-stock. 42p. *8°*. [*London,*] 1811.

20289 CARROLL, . [*Begin.*] 2 of £40,000. 2 of £30,000. 2 of £10,000 &c.&c.... New state lottery begins 17th September... [A handbill.] *s.sh.8°*. [*London,* 1811 ?]

20290 CATTLEY, S. The speech of Stephen Cattley, Esq. at the Bank of England, on... the 21st of March, 1811, shewing that the present high price of bullion is owing to the indiscriminate grant of licences to foreign ships. To which is added an appendix. 39p. *8°*. 1811.

20291 CHALMERS, G. Considerations on com-merce, bullion and coin, circulation and exchanges; with a view to our present circumstances. 237p. *8°*. 1811.

20292 —— The second edition. 237p. *8°*. 1811. *Presentation copy, with inscription, from the author to 'Mr. T. Thompson' [Thomas Perronet Thompson ?].*

20293 CONSIDERATIONS on the dangers of altering the marine insurance laws of Great Britain, in the manner proposed by a Bill... now depending in the House of Commons... 28p. *8°*. [*London,* 1811]

20294 For the **CONTEMPLATION** of honourable and just legislators. In addition to the laws and facts, stated in the memorial now before the legislature [of the United States], to support the demand for payment of the bills of credit, the creditors offer the following. [Signed: Creditors.] 7p. *8°*. *n.p.* [1811]

20295 COOKE, N. Money, what it is, its value, &c. in reference to Bank of England notes, and any valuable circulating medium. With a few observations applicable to our present state of commerce. 19p. *8°*. 1811.

20296 CRUIKSHANK, JAMES. Observations on money, as the medium of commerce, shewing the present circulating medium of this country to be defective in those requisites which a medium of commerce ought to possess, and pointing out in what manner the defect may be remedied... 137p. *8°*. 1811.

20297 —— Recommended to the particular attention of the Right Honourable the House of Lords. A letter to the Right Honourable Spencer Perceval... on the subject of the Distillery-Bill, now pending before Parliament; shewing that Bill to be most unjust and impolitic; and... demonstrating that no part of the revenue of the kingdom is paid by the West-India planters. 27p. *8°*. 1811.

20298 The **DEPRECIATION** of bank-notes demonstrated; and the assertion, that gold is too dear to make guineas with, proved to be absurd. 35p. *8°*. 1811.

20299 DUPONT, P. S. Sur la Banque de France, les causes de la crise qu'elle a éprouvée, les tristes effets qui en sont résultés, et les moyens d'en prévenir le retour. Avec une théorie des banques. Rapport fait à la Chambre de Commerce par une Commission spéciale. 69p. *8°*. Londres, 1811. *The 'Advertisement' is in English.*

20300 ELIOT, F. P. Observations on the fallacy of the supposed depreciation of the paper currency of the kingdom; with reasons for dissenting from the Report of the Bullion Committee. 171p. *8°*. 1811. *The copy that belonged to David Ricardo.*

20301 —— A supplement to Observations on the fallacy of the supposed depreciation of the paper currency of the kingdom, &c. 28p. *8°*. 1811.

20302 FRANCE. *Cour Impériale. Cour Spéciale de Paris.* Arrêt de la Cour Spéciale de Paris, qui condamne à la peine de mort les nommés Louis-Pierre-Jean-Charles Terrier... et Pierre-Françoïs Bohin... convaincus de contrefaçon et d'émission de monnoies nationales ayant cours. Du 29 juillet, 1811. 4p. *4°*. Paris, [1811]

20303 —— *Ministère des Finances.* Compte de l'administration des finances, en 1809 et en 1810. 342p. *4°*. Paris, 1811.

20304 —— *Ministère du Trésor Impérial.* Comptes du Trésor de l'Empire pour l'année 1809, présentés à S.M. l'Empereur et Roi, par son Ministre du Trésor. 142p. *4°*. Paris, 1811.

20305 —— —— Comptes du Trésor de l'Empire pour l'année 1810... 130p. *4°. Paris,* 1811. *See also* 1813.

20306 **GIDDY**, afterwards **GILBERT**, D. A plain statement of the bullion question, in a letter to a friend. 48p. *8°.* 1811. *See also* 1819.

20307 **H.**, C. R. B. A replication to all the theorists and abstract reasoners on bullion, coins, exchanges, and commerce. In a letter addressed to the Legislature of the United Kingdom. 90p. *8°.* 1811.

20308 **HAUTENVILLE**, H. B. A digest of the duties of customs, payable upon all foreign articles imported into, or exported from Ireland. Also, the duties outwards; the countervailing duties between Great Britain and Ireland; the bounties and allowances on Irish produce, and those on the fisheries. Together with tables for facilitating the passing of entries, &c.&c. 156p. *8°. Dublin,* 1811. *See also* 1813.

20309 [**HERRIES**, J. C.] A review of the controversy respecting the high price of bullion, and the state of our currency. 119p. *8°.* 1811.

20310 **HOARE**, PETER R. An examination of Sir John Sinclair's Observations on the Report of the Bullion Committee, and on the general nature of coin or money, and the advantages of paper circulation. 111p. *8°.* 1811. *The copy that belonged to David Ricardo. Reissued in* Tracts on our present money system *in 1814, q.v.* (GENERAL).

20311 —— Reflections on the possible existence and supposed expedience of national bankruptcy. 76p. *8°.* 1811. *Reissued in* Tracts on our present money system *in 1814, q.v.* (GENERAL).

20312 **HOPKINS**, T. Bank notes the cause of the disappearance of guineas, and of the course of exchange being against us, whilst the balance of trade is in our favour: with practicable means suggested to enable the Bank of England to resume its payments in specie, without sustaining any loss. 74p. *8°.* [1811] *The copy that belonged to David Ricardo.*

20313 **HORNER**, F. Resolutions proposed to the House of Commons, on the Report of the Committee appointed to Inquire into the High Price of Bullion, by Francis Horner, Esquire and the Right Hon. N. Vansittart ...To which is added, a list of publications occasioned by the Report of the Committee. 24p. *8°.* 1811.

20314 **HUSKISSON**, W. The question concerning the depreciation of our currency stated and examined... Seventh edition. 154p. *8°. London, Edinburgh, &c.,* 1811. *For other editions, see* 1810.

20315 [**INGLIS**, J.] Commerce as it was, is, and ought to be. [On the causes of the high price of gold. With 'Appendix. Extract from a pamphlet entitled 'A general view of the corn-trade and corn-laws of Great Britain'. By the Reverend George Skene Keith'.] 59p. *8°.* 1811.

20316 **JOHNSTONE**, GEORGE (*fl.* 1802–1818). The speech of Mr. Johnstone, on the third reading of the Bill for preventing the gold coin of the realm from being paid or accepted for a greater value than the current value of such coin; commonly called Lord Stanhope's Bill. Friday, the 19th of July, 1811. 111p. *8°.* 1811.

20317 **KELLY**, P. The universal cambist and commercial instructor; being a general treatise on exchange; including the monies, coins, weights and measures of all trading nations and colonies: with an account of their

banks and paper currencies... 2 vols. *4°.* 1811. *See also* 1821, 1831, 1835.

20318 **KING**, PETER, *7th Baron King.* Speech of the Right Hon. Lord King, in the House of Lords...July 2, 1811, upon the second reading of Earl Stanhope's Bill, respecting guineas and bank notes. [With 'Tables shewing the gradual fall in the value of bank notes, and the intrinsic value of money-contracts at the different periods of depreciation: being a supplement to Lord King's speech upon Earl Stanhope's Bill'.] 48p. *8°.* 1811.

20319 [**KINGSMAN**, W.] A letter to the Right Honourable Sir John Sinclair, Bart. (author of the history of the revenue, and other fugitive pieces), on the subject of his remarks on Mr. Huskisson's pamphlet. By a country gentleman. 23p. *8°.* 1811.

20320 **KOSTER**, J. T. Short statement, of the trade in gold bullion; shewing the true causes of the general scarcity and consequent high price of that precious metal; also, demonstrating that the notes of the Bank of England are not depreciated. A second edition, enlarged. 119p. *8°. Liverpool & London,* 1811. *For another edition, see* 1810.

20321 **LEHUBY**, J. F. Algemeen tafereel van de berekeningen der hollandsche munten in franken, en van de munten des franschen Keizerrijks, in hollandsche guldens...Naargezien en verbeterd door de Heer Poelman, Inspecteur et Essayeur Generaal der Munten in Holland. 83, 53p. *8°. Amsterdam,* 1811. *With a title in French, and the text in French and Dutch, printed on opposite pages.*

20322 A **LETTER** to John Theodore Koster, Esq. in which the arguments used by that gentleman, to demonstrate that bank notes are not depreciated are considered and refuted; also in which it is contended, that Mr. Huskisson has not determined the extent to which bank notes are depreciated. 63p. *8°. Liverpool & London,* 1811.

20323 **LIEBHOLD**, J. E. Johann Ernst Liebhold's Comptoir-Handbuch zur [Georg Thomas Flügel's] Erklärung der Cours-Zettel und Vergleichung des Gewichts und Ellenmaasses der vorzüglichsten Handelsplätze in Europa...Zweyte ganz umgearbeitete, verbesserte und vermehrte Auflage... 48, 302p. *8°. Frankfurt am Main,* 1811. *For an edition of Fluegel, see* 1820.

20324 **LLOYD'S.** Report of the Committee appointed at a general meeting of the subscribers to Lloyd's, held June 6th, 1811, 'to consider and recommend such regulations as, in their opinion, will tend to the future good management of the concerns of this House;' the rules and regulations annexed and adopted at the general meetings of July 31st, and August 15th, 1811; the proceedings at those meetings; and a list of the new Committee. 38p. *8°.* 1811.

20325 **MARRYAT**, J. Thoughts on the expediency of establishing a new chartered bank, suggested by the application to Parliament for the establishment of a new chartered marine insurance company, and confirmed by the Report of the Bullion Committee. 92p. *8°.* 1811.

20326 **MERCATOR**, *pseud.* Considerations on the present state of bank notes, specie, and bullion; in a series of letters, addressed to the Right Honorable ——. In two parts. 32p. *8°.* 1811.

20327 [**MORRIS**, M. R., *3rd Baron Rokeby.*] An essay on bank-tokens, bullion, &c. By a Briton. 36p. *8°. Stockton,* 1811.

20328 MUSHET, R. An inquiry into the effects produced on the national currency and rates of exchange, by the Bank Restriction Bill; explaining the cause of the high price of bullion... The third edition, corrected and enlarged. With the tables brought down to April 5, 1811; and some remarks on Mr. Bosanquet's Observations on the Bullion Report. 120p. 8°. 1811. *For other editions, see* 1810.

20329 NOWLAN, T. An address to the creditors of Williams and Finn [bankers of Kilkenny], bankrupts: with some reflections on the present administration of the bankrupt code. [With 'Appendix. Copy of the report of Thomas Ellis, Esq. one of the Masters of his Majesty's Court of Chancery in Ireland...the 4th day of December, 1809'.] 18, xvip. 8°. *Dublin*, 1811.

20330 PARSONS, L., *2nd Earl of Rosse.* Observations on the present state of the currency of England. 95p. 8°. 1811.

20331 PITT, WILLIAM (1749–1823). The bullion debate: a serio-comic satiric poem. 88p. 8°. *London & Birmingham*, 1811.

20332 PRENTICE, D. Thoughts on the repeal of the Bank Restriction Law. 79p. 8°. *London, Edinburgh, &c.,* 1811.

20333 RAITHBY, J. The law and principle of money considered; in a letter to W. Huskisson, Esq. M.P. 116p. 8°. 1811.

20334 Plain **REASONING,** on the cause and remedy of the present scarcity of gold, and the increased circulation of paper. 16p. 8°. 1811. *Attributed in a manuscript note on the title-page, to 'the Rev. D. M. Peacock, of Trin. Coll.'*

20335 REED, WILLIAM. The maltster's guide, containing the substance of the several excise laws and regulations to which maltsters are subject; and also a variety of information relating to the excise in general. 131p. 8°. 1811.

20336 REMARKS upon the Report of the Select Committee of the House of Commons, appointed to examine into the petition of South Wales, upon the subject of the duty on coal partially borne, ordered by the House to be printed, June 7, 1810; in which the title of Newport, to a duty free trade, past, and present, is considered; with an examination into the claims made by South Wales, and further suggesting a mode by which to conciliate all parties. 78p. 12°. *Bristol,* [1811]

20337 RICARDO, D. The high price of bullion, a proof of the depreciation of bank notes... The fourth edition, corrected. To which is added, an appendix, containing observations on some passages in an article [by T. R. Malthus] in the Edinburgh Review, on the depreciation of paper currency; also suggestions for securing to the public a currency as invariable as gold, with a very moderate supply of that metal. 97p. 8°. *London, Edinburgh, &c.,* 1811. *The copy that belonged to S. J. Loyd, Baron Overstone, formerly among his papers, for which see vol. III, MS. 804. For other editions, see 1810.*

20338 —— Observations on some passages in an article in the Edinburgh Review, on the depreciation of paper currency; also suggestions for securing to the public a currency as invariable as gold, with a very moderate supply of that metal. Being the appendix, to the fourth edition of the "The high price of bullion," &c. 31p. 8°. *London, Edinburgh, &c.,* 1811.

20339 —— Reply to Mr. Bosanquet's Practical observations on the Report of the Bullion Committee. 141p. 8°. *London, Edinburgh, &c.,* 1811. *The copy that belonged to S. J. Loyd, Baron Overstone, formerly among his papers, for which see vol. III, MS. 804.*

20340 ROSE, GEORGE. Substance of the speech delivered in the House of Commons by the Right Honorable George Rose, on...the sixth of May 1811, in the Committee of the Whole House on the Report of the Bullion Committee. 132p. 8°. 1811.

20341 RUTHERFORD, A. W. Hints from Holland; or, gold bullion as dear in Dutch currency as in bank-notes, in a letter to two merchants. 90p. 8°. 1811. *The copy that belonged to David Ricardo.*

20342 —— Hints from Holland, part the second; or, the influences of the continental ratios on the coinage of England. 42p. 8°. 1811.

20343 [——] The true cause of depreciation traced to the state of our silver currency. 31p. 8°. [1811?] *With a long manuscript note at the end of the text.*

20344 [**SCOTT,** WILLIAM, *Baron Stowell.*] Some observations upon the argument drawn by Mr. Huskisson and the Bullion Committee, from the high price of gold bullion. First published in letters to the editor of the Times. By Civis. 74p. 8°. 1811.

20345 SINCLAIR, SIR JOHN, *Bart.* The speech of the Right Honourable Sir John Sinclair, Bart. on the subject of the Bullion Report, in the House of Commons, on...the 15th of May, 1811. 16p. 8°. 1811. *Presentation copy, with inscription from the author, to 'Sir John M. Murray'.*

20346 SIORDET, J. M. A letter to the Right Hon. Sir John Sinclair, Bart. M.P. supporting his arguments in refutation of those advanced by Mr. Huskisson, on the supposed depreciation of our currency. Including a letter to Sir Charles Price, Bart. M.P. in August last, on the report of the Bullion Committee. 48p. 8°. [*London,*] 1811. *Presentation copy, from the author to David Ricardo.*

20347 —— Second edition. 48p. 8°. 1811.

20348 SIVEWRIGHT, J. & J. Valentine's Day 14th Febry. Great chance! small risk! A whole ticket for only 18 shillings...in the lottery to be drawn on Valentine's Day... [A handbill.] *s.sh.fol.* [*London,* 1811]

20349 SMART, B. A letter addressed to...the House of Commons, on the necessity of an immediate attention to the state of the British coinage. In which a new, prompt and efficacious remedy for its defects is proposed. 21p. 8°. 1811.

20350 SMITH, THOMAS, *accountant, of London.* An essay on the theory of money and exchange. Second edition, with considerable additions, including an examination of the Report of the Bullion-Committee. 248p. 8°. *London & Edinburgh,* 1811. *For another edition, see 1807.*

20351 STEWART, R., *2nd Marquis of Londonderry.* The substance of a speech delivered by Lord Viscount Castlereagh, in a Committee of the House of Commons, May 8, 1811; on the Report of the Bullion Committee. 50p. 8°. 1811.

20352 —— Second edition. 50p. 8°. 1811.

20353 —— The substance of a speech delivered by Lord Viscount Castlereagh, in the House of Commons, July 15,

1811; on the second reading of Earl Stanhope's Bill. 51p. *8°*. 1811.

20354 The **THEORY** of money; or, a practical inquiry into the present state of the circulating medium: with considerations on the Bank of England, on its original charter and constitution, and on its present measures and the effects of those measures on the condition of the United Kingdom. 96p. *8°*. 1811.

20355 **THORNTON**, Sir Edward (1766–1852). Observations on the Report of the Committee of the House of Commons, appointed to inquire into the high price of gold bullion, &c.&c. Together with some remarks on the work of Francis Blake, Esq. F.R.S. entitled, "Observations on the principles which regulate the course of exchange, and on the present depreciated state of the currency." 160p. *8°*. 1811.

20356 **THORNTON**, Henry (1760–1815). Substance of two speeches of Henry Thornton, Esq. in the debate in the House of Commons, on the Report of the Bullion Committee, on the 7th and 14th of May, 1811. 79p. *8°*. 1811.

20357 **TICKLE**, Tim, *pseud*. Letters to a friend, explanative of accommodation paper, and the business of country bankers; with a proposition for a new national bank...By T...... T....., Esq., late banker. Second edition. 28p. *8°*. 1811.

20358 **TOWERS**, J. L. The expediency and practicability of the resumption of cash-payments by the Bank of England; or thoughts on the present serious state of the circulating medium of the kingdom; and a series of measures proposed, whereby sufficient supplies of specie might be introduced into the...circulation... 60p. *8°*. 1811. *Presentation copy from the author to David Ricardo.*

20359 **TOWNSEND**, E. An extraordinary history of a bankruptcy. Committed to print with a view to bring the operation of the existing laws relating to bankruptcies under the consideration of the Legislature...March 18, 1811. 31p. *4°*. 1811.

20360 —— To the creditors of Edmund Townsend, of Maiden Lane, Covent Garden. [Prefatory note dated: July 25th 1811.] 21p. *4°*. [*London,*] 1811.

20361 [**TROTTER**, C.] The principles of currency and exchanges applied to the Report from the Select Committee of the House of Commons, appointed to inquire into the high price of gold bullion, &c.&c. 80p. *8°*. 1811. *For other editions, see* 1810.

20362 **UNITED STATES OF AMERICA**. Con-

gress. *House of Representatives*. Report of the Secretary of the Navy, made in obedience to the resolutions of the House of Representatives of the twenty fourth and twenty seventh ult., respecting several bills of exchange drawn on Degen, Purviance, & Company, navy agents of the United States, at Leghorn, in Italy. January 7, 1811... 40p. *8°*. *Washington,* 1810 [1811]

20363 **VANSITTART**, N., *Baron Bexley*. Substance of two speeches, made by the Right Hon. N. Vansittart, on the 7th and 13th of May, 1811, in the Committee of the Whole House of Commons, to which the Report of the Bullion Committee was referred. With an appendix, containing the Resolutions moved by Francis Horner, Esq. and the Right Hon. N. Vansittart; the amendments moved by F. Horner, Esq. and various accounts... 228p. *8°*. 1811.

20364 **WILSON**, Glocester. Defence of abstract currencies, in reply to the Bullion Report and Mr. Huskisson. 165p. *8°*. *London, Edinburgh, &c.,* 1811.

20365 **WILSON**, Robert, *accountant*. Farther observations on the subject of the supposed depreciation of our currency, and the causes of the diminution in the value of money. 44p. *8°*. *Edinburgh & London,* 1811.

20366 [——] Observations, &c. 1. On the effect of the operation of banking in aiding commercial credit... 34p. *8°*. *n.p.* [1811 ?] *Apparently a proof of the text of p. 1–35 of* Farther observations (*no.* 20365 *above*).

20367 —— Observations on the depreciation of money, and the state of our currency. With sundry relative tables. [With an appendix and 'Supplement. Containing considerations as to the utility, and probable consequences of a repeal of the Bank Restriction Act'.] 103p. *8°*. *Edinburgh & London,* 1811.

20368 **WOODS**, G. Observations on the present price of bullion, and rates of exchange; wherein the objections of Mr. Bosanquet, and others, to the Report of the Bullion Committee, are attempted to be over-ruled. 60p. *8°*. 1811.

20369 [**WORSLEY**, R.] A plain enquiry into the nature, value, and operation of coin and paper money; and the methods whereby nations acquire & lose the precious metals...By Peter Pennyless, Gent. A.S.C. 62p. *8°*. 1811.

20370 **WRIGHT**, Samuel (*fl.* 1810). A report of the cases of the King v. Wright, and the King v. De Yonge, who were severally tried for exchanging guineas for bank notes. To which is added, a copy of the Act of Parliament, 51 Geo. III, c. 127, relative to this subject. By John King, Esq. of the Inner Temple... 106p. *8°*. *London & Dublin,* 1811.

TRANSPORT

20371 **BUCHANAN**, Robertson. Report relative to the proposed rail-way from Dumfries to Sanquhar. 46p. *8°*. *Dumfries,* 1811.

20372 **ENGLAND**. *Laws, etc*. [*Endorsed:*] An Act to enlarge the term and powers of two Acts of His present Majesty, for repairing the roads from the East Gate of King's Lynn, to the north end of Babingley Lane, and to extend the road from thence to Darsingham, in the county of Norfolk. ⟨Royal Assent, 4 April 1811.⟩ 51 Geo. III. 1811. 14p. *fol. n.p.* [1811]

20373 —— —— 1811. An Act to enlarge the term and powers of two Acts of His present Majesty, for repairing

the roads from the South Gate of King's Lynn, into the parishes of East Walton, Narborough, Stoke Ferry, and Downham Market, in the county of Norfolk. ⟨Royal Assent, 4 April 1811.⟩ 12p. *fol. n.p.* [1811]

20374 —— —— Anno quinquagesimo primo Georgii III. Regis. [Local & Personal.] Cap. 105. An Act for enlarging the powers of several Acts of His present Majesty, for making and maintaining the Birmingham Canal Navigations, and for further extending and improving the same. ⟨21st May 1811.⟩ p. 2117–2122. *fol.* 1811.

20375 **OBSERVATIONS** on the General Inclosure Act, and on the expediency of explaining and amending such parts of it as relate to the public carriage roads and highways. With an account of the proceedings in the case of an appeal against the commissioners for the inclosure of the parish of Bourn, in…Cambridge. By one of His Majesty's justices of the peace… 26p. *8°. Cambridge,* 1811.

20376 PATERSON, D. A new and accurate description of all the direct and principal cross roads in England and Wales, and part of the roads of Scotland…The whole greatly augmented and improved by the assistance of Francis Freeling…The fifteenth edition. 540p. *8°.* 1811. *For other editions, see* 1771.

20377 Additional **REMARKS** on an intended asylum-port, near Dunleary, comprizing observations on the last grant made by Parliament of £40,000, British, for Howth Harbour, which, with twenty-five per cent. for collecting, will make the neat sum £50,000. By a seaman. 29p. *8°. Dublin,* 1811.

20378 RICHARDSON, WILLIAM (1740–1820). Memoir on the subjects of making the lower Bann navigable, and restraining the winter redundance of Lough Neagh. 54p. *8°. Belfast,* 1811.

SOCIAL CONDITIONS

20379 The **ABUSE** of prisons; or, an interesting and impartial account of the House of Correction in Cold-Bath-Fields, and the treatment of Mr. Gale Jones, founded upon a minute inspection of the prison and a personal interview with him. 36p. *8°.* 1811.

20380 BENTHAM, J. Théorie des peines et des récompenses…Rédigée en françois d'après les manuscrits, par M. Et. Dumont, de Genève… 2 vols. *8°. Londres,* 1811. *See also* 1825, 1830.

20381 CLARK, Z. An account of the different charities belonging to the poor of the county of Norfolk, abridged from the returns under Gilbert's Act to the House of Commons in 1786; and from the terriers in the office of the Lord Bishop of Norwich. [Edited, with a preface, by Thomas Clarkson.] 296p. *8°. Bury St. Edmund's & London,* 1811.

20382 DAY AND SUNDAY FREE SCHOOL, *Circus Street, Liverpool.* Eighth annual report of the Day and Sunday Free School…from the 1st of July, 1810, to the 1st of July, 1811. [With 'List of annual subscribers', etc.] [4]p. *fol.* [*Liverpool,* 1811] *Addressed in manuscript to 'Mr. Jno. Lang'. See also* 1812, 1813, 1814.

20383 DUMBELL, J. [*Endorsed:*] Employment. [A letter, dated: 19th February, 1811, to the Rev. Richard Formby, recommending a new method, patented by him, of spinning flax by hand as suitable employment for inmates of the proposed Asylum for Penitent Prostitutes in Liverpool.] [4]p. *4°.* [*Liverpool,* 1811]

20384 ENGLAND. *Parliament.* Debates in both Houses of Parliament in…May and June 1808, relative to the agreement made by Government with Mr. Palmer, for the reform and improvement of the Post-Office and its revenue. With an appendix containing…documents… 130, xliip. *8°.* 1811. *For another edition, see* 1809.

20385 FOX, JOSEPH. A comparative view of the plans of education, as detailed in the publications of Dr. Bell and Mr. Lancaster. With remarks on Dr. Bell's "Madras School", and hints to the managers and committees of charity and Sunday schools, on the practicability of extending such institutions upon Mr. Lancaster's plan… The third edition. 67p. *8°.* 1811.

20386 GAUTERON, F. L. Coup-d'œil sur l'influence à espérer des établissemens d'Hofwyl quant au perfectionnement de l'industrie et des mœurs. 27p. *8°. Paris & Genève,* [1811?]

20387 GLASGOW GALLOWAY BROTHERLY SOCIETY. Regulations of the…Society, which commenced on 22d August, 1791, as amended 3d December, 1810, and confirmed 28th February, 1811. 15p. *8°. Glasgow,* 1811.

20388 HACKNEY LITERARY INSTITUTION. Regulations of the Literary and Philosophical Society of Hackney; together with the first year's report of its proceedings, and a catalogue of the Library. 17p. *8°.* 1811. *The title-page and the text of the regulations have been extensively altered in manuscript, possibly to provide copy for a later edition.*

20389 HORNE, M. A sermon preached before the Governors of the London Female Penitentiary, at the parish church of St. Lawrence Jewry, London, on Tuesday, May 7th, 1811…in aid of the funds of that charity…Second edition. 32p. *8°.* 1811.

20390 LANCASTER, JOSEPH. Report of J. Lancaster's progress from the year 1798, with the report of the finance committee for the year 1810. To which is prefixed an address of the committee for promoting the Royal Lancasterian system for the education of the poor. [With a list of subscribers.] 27p. *8°.* 1811. *The copy that belonged to David Ricardo.*

20391 A **LETTER** to the Right Hon. Henry Grattan, on the deplorable consequences resulting to Ireland, from the very low price of spirituous liquors…[Signed: a friend to Ireland.] 20p. *8°. Dublin,* 1811.

20392 LUXMORE, J., *Bishop of St. Asaph.* A sermon preached before the incorporated Society for the Propagation of the Gospel, in Foreign Parts; at their anniversary meeting…February 15, 1811. [With 'An abstract of the charter, and…proceedings of the Society…1810, to… 1811'.] 74p. *8°.* 1811.

20393 MARSH, H., *Bishop of Peterborough.* The national religion the foundation of national education: a sermon preached…on Thursday, June 13, 1811: being the time of the yearly meeting of the children educated in the charity-schools in…London and Westminster… Second edition. 33p. *8°.* 1811.

20394 MARTIN, MATTHEW. Substance of a letter, dated…3d March, 1803, to the Right Hon. Lord Pelham, on the state of mendicity in the Metropolis. 24p. *8°. Society for Bettering the Condition of the Poor,* 1811. *For another edition, see* 1803.

20395 ROYAL LANCASTERIAN INSTITUTION FOR THE EDUCATION OF THE POOR. Address of the Committee for Promoting the Royal Lancasterian System for the Education of the Poor. 8p. *8°. n.p.* [1811]

20396 —— Royal British system of education. [Resolutions of the meeting of subscribers and friends of the Royal Lancasterian System of Education, held on May 11, 1811.] 4p. *8°*. [*London*, 1811] *The copy that belonged to David Ricardo.*

20397 SOCIETY FOR BETTERING THE CONDITION OF THE POOR, *Liverpool*. The first report of the Society...[With 'Appendix no. 1. Rules, orders, & regulations, of the Liverpool Friendly Society'.] xxix, 12, 15p. *8°*. *Liverpool*, [1811] *See also* 1813.

20398 SOCIETY FOR BETTERING THE CONDITION OF THE POOR, *London*. The reports of the Society...The fifth edition. [Edited by Sir T. Bernard.] 6 vols. *12°*. *London*, *York*, &c., 1811, 1802–1815. *For other editions, see* 1802.

20399 SOCIETY FOR THE SUPPRESSION OF VAGRANTS, *Bath*. Report of the Bath Society for the Suppression of Vagrants...With an account of the receipts and disbursements [and a list of subscribers] from Jan. 1, 1810, to Jan. 1, 1811... 30p. *12°*. *Bath*, 1811. *See also* 1810, 1812, 1813, 1816.

SLAVERY

20400 AFRICAN INSTITUTION. Report of the Committee of the African Institution, read to the general meeting on the 15th July, 1807. Together with the rules and regulations which were then adopted for the government of the society. 50p. *8°*. 1811. *For another edition of the first, and for the subsequent reports 1808–1812, 1814–1827, see* vol. III, *Periodicals list*, Report of the Committee of the African Institution.

POLITICS

20401 ARMINIUS, *pseud*. Reinstatement of the commander in chief. [An address in verse to the Duke of York.] 43p. *8°*. *Stockton & London*, 1811.

20402 METHODIST MINISTERS OF THE MANCHESTER DISTRICT. Resolutions of the Methodist Ministers of the Manchester District, assembled at Liverpool, May 23, 1811, on the subject of a Bill introduced into Parliament by...Viscount Sidmouth: to which is annexed, an abstract of the debate in the House of Lords, on Tuesday, May 21st, 1811, when the said Bill was rejected. 22p. *8°*. *Liverpool*, [1811]

20403 [O'CONNELL, D.] Historical account of the laws against the Roman-Catholics of England. 51p. *8°*. *London & Dublin*, 1811.

For the **REFORMISTS' REGISTER,** 1811–1812, *see* vol. III, *Periodicals list*.

20404 VISIONS of Albion: or arguments of consolation and confidence, addressed to the inhabitants of the United Kingdom of Great Britain & Ireland in the unexampled conflict with the Gaulic Empire. 46p. *8°*. 1811. *The copy that belonged to M. T. Sadler.*

MISCELLANEOUS

20405 BURDETT, Sir F., *Bart*. Speech of Sir Francis Burdett, Bt., delivered in the House of Commons on the 28th March, 1811, upon a motion of Lord Folkestone, to examine into the practice of ex-officio informations, filed by the Attorney-General, in cases of libel... 38p. *8°*. 1811.

20406 PHILLIPS, Richard (1778–1851). An experimental examination of the last edition of the Pharmacopoeia Londinensis; with remarks on Dr. Powell's translation and annotations. 148p. *8°*. 1811. *The copy that belonged to David Ricardo.*

20407 RUDGE, J. A sermon on the sacrament of the Lord's Supper...Second edition. 34p. *12°*. 1811.

1812

GENERAL

For the **AMERICAN REVIEW OF HISTORY AND POLITICS,** *see* vol. III, *Periodicals list*.

20408 BRISTED, J. The resources of the British Empire, together with a view of the probable result of the present contest between Britain and France. 527p. *8°*. 1812. *For another edition, see* 1811.

20409 BROUGHAM, H. P., *Baron Brougham and Vaux*. The speech of Henry Brougham, Esq. M.P. in the House of Commons, on Tuesday, the 16th of June, 1812, upon the present state of commerce and manufactures... 59p. *8°*. 1812.

20410 BROWN, Thomas (*fl*. 1812). An account of the people called Shakers: their faith, doctrines, and practice...To which is affixed a history of their rise and progress to the present day. 372p. *12°*. *Troy, Albany*, &c., 1812.

20411 CATTEAU-CALLEVILLE, J. P. G. Tableau de la mer Baltique, considerée sous les rapports physiques, géographiques, historiques et commerciaux, avec une carte, et des notices détaillées sur le mouvement général du commerce, sur les ports les plus importans, sur les monnaies, poids et mesures... 2 vols. *8°*. *Paris*, 1812.

20412 [CROKER, JOHN W.] A key to the Orders in Council [respecting trade with French ports, etc., 7 Jan. 1807 to 21 April, 1812]. 19p. *8°. London, Edinburgh, &c.,* 1812.

20413 DEWAR, D. Observations on the character, customs, and superstitions of the Irish; and on some of the causes which have retarded the moral and political improvement of Ireland. [362]p. *8°.* 1812.

20414 DOMESDAY BOOK. Dom Boc. A translation of the record called Domesday, so far as relates to the counties of Middlesex, Hertford, Buckingham, Oxford, and Gloucester. By...William Bawdwen. 26, 76, 82, 62, 72p. *4°. Doncaster & London,* 1812. *For other editions of the whole or part of* Domesday Book, *see* 1783.

20415 EDWARDS, GEORGE. Prospectus of means, as in the gentry, the respectable inhabitants and the different corporations of the Kingdom. [Dated: November 1, 1812.] 16p. *4°. [London,* 1812]

20416 ENGLAND. Parliament. *House of Commons.* An abstract of the evidence lately taken in the House of Commons, against the Orders in Council, being a summary of the facts there proved, respecting the present state of the commerce, and manufactures of the country. 64p. *8°.* 1812.

20417 —— —— —— Orders in Council. A report of the debate on the Orders in Council in the House of Commons on...May 16, 1812. [Concerning the distresses suffered by the manufacturing districts, particularly Birmingham, owing to their operation.] 2p. *s.sh.fol. Birmingham,* [1812] *See note to no.* 20490.

20418 EUSTAPHIEVE, A. The resources of Russia, in the event of a war with France; and an examination of the prevailing opinion relative to the political and military conduct of the Court of St. Petersburgh, with a short description of the Cozaks...Second edition. 52p. *8°.* 1812. *See also* 1813.

20419 FRANCE. *Laws, etc.* Les cinq codes de l'Empire Français. 1°. Code Napoléon, 2°. Code de procédure civile, 3°. Code de commerce, 4°. Code d'instruction criminelle, 5°. Code pénal...suivis des tarifs des frais et dépens en matière civile et en matière criminelle, etc....Seconde édition, augmentée... 827p. *18°. Paris,* 1812.

20420 —— *Ministre de l'Intérieur.* Arrêté pour l'exécution du Décret impérial du 12 février 1812, concernant l'uniformité des poids et mesures. 4p. *8°. Caen,* 1812.

20421 GALT, J. Voyages and travels, in the years 1809, 1810, and 1811; containing statistical, commercial, and miscellaneous observations on Gibraltar, Sardinia, Sicily, Malta, Serigo, and Turkey. 435p. *4°.* 1812.

20422 GANILH, C. An inquiry into the various systems of political economy; their advantages and disadvantages; and the theory most favourable to the increase of national wealth...Translated from the French by D. Boileau. 492p. *8°. London, Edinburgh, &c.,* 1812. *For other editions, see* 1809.

20423 GATTEY, F. Tables des rapports des anciennes mesures agraires avec les nouvelles, précédées des éléments du nouveau système métrique...Troisième édition, augmentée d'une instruction sur les nouvelles mesures usuelles, et de tables... 328p. *8°. Paris,* 1812.

20424 GREEN, WILLIAM (*fl.* 1788–1818). The merchant and trader's manual: a compilation replete with correct tables; and abounding with valuable and useful information. 156p. *8°.* 1812.

20425 HIGHLAND AND AGRICULTURAL SOCIETY OF SCOTLAND. Report on weights & measures. [By a committee of the Highland Society of Scotland, of gentlemen from the different counties of Scotland, and from the Convention of Royal Burghs. With an appendix.] 20, 11p. *fol.* [*Edinburgh,* 1812] *See also* 1813.

20426 HOARE, PETER R. Further observations on the increase of population, and high price of grain. Being an appendix to Reflections on the possible existence, and supposed expedients, of national bankruptcy. 28p. *8°.* 1812. *Reissued in* Tracts on our present money system *in* 1814 (*q.v.*).

20427 HUME, JOSEPH. Copy of a letter addressed to the Right Honourable the Chancellor of the Exchequer, and the substance of a speech of Mr. Joseph Hume on the third reading of the Bill (Friday, July 21, 1812) for "preventing frauds and abuses in the frame-work-knitting manufacture and in the payment of persons employed therein;" in which the impolicy of attempting by legislative enactments to regulate or controul, the employment of capital and the price of labour is clearly shewn. xiv, 43p. *8°.* 1812.

20428 JERVIS, SIR JOHN J. W., *Bart.* A refutation of M. M. de Montgaillard's calumnies against British policy; and of his "Display of the situation of Great Britain in the year 1811". 390p. *8°.* 1812.

20429 OBSERVATIONS upon commercial terms of peace with France, and our own resources. By a London merchant. 50p. *8°.* 1812. *With a manuscript note on the half-title, 'Major James for Mr. Taleyrand. By M. Walker'.*

20430 P., A. D., *Don.* Principios de la economía general, y de la estadística de España. 111p. *16°. Madrid,* 1812.

20431 PEACE with France! Ships, colonies, and commerce; bankruptcies considered; Sir Francis Burdett; some light thrown on the causes of the riots, April, 1810; bullion report; circulating medium; Peninsula; prophecies. 44p. *8°.* 1812.

20432 PEIGNOT, E. G. Répertoire bibliographique universel, contenant la notice raisonnée des bibliographies spéciales publiées jusqu'a ce jour... 514p. *8°. Paris,* 1812.

20433 PHILLIMORE, J. A letter addressed to a member of the House of Commons, on the subject of the notice given by Mr. Brougham, for a motion respecting the Orders in Council and the licence trade. 56p. *8°. London & Oxford,* 1812.

20434 The PICTURE of Newcastle upon Tyne, being a brief historical & descriptive guide to the principal buildings, streets...manufactures...within that town... an account of the Roman wall, and a detailed history of the coal trade... 306p. *12°. Newcastle upon Tyne & London,* 1812. *For another edition, see* 1807.

20435 ROCQUES DE MONTGAILLARD, J. G. M., *Comte de Montgaillard.* The situation of Great Britain, in the year 1811...Faithfully translated from the French. 225p. *8°.* 1812.

20436 ROTULI Hundredorum temp. Hen. III. et Edw. I. in Turr' Lond' et in curia receptæ Scaccarij Westm. asservati...Printed by command of...King

George III...[Edited by W. Illingworth.] 2 vols. *fol.* [*The Record Commission,*] 1812–18.

20437 *SMITH, ADAM. An inquiry into the nature and causes of the wealth of nations...A new edition, to which is prefixed, an account of the life of the author, and a view of his doctrine compared with that of the French economists...[By G. Garnier.] 3 vols. *8°.* 1812. *The copy that belonged to Augustus De Morgan. For other editions, see 1776.*

20438 —— The works of Adam Smith...With an account of his life and writings by Dugald Stewart... 5 vols. *8°.* 1812, 1811. *See also 1822, 1825.*

20439 UNITED STATES OF AMERICA. Congress. *House of Representatives.* Report, or manifesto of the causes and reasons of war with Great Britain, presented to the House of Representatives, by the Committee of Foreign Relations. June 3, 1812. Read, and ordered to lie on the table. 17p. *8°. Washington*, 1812.

20440 WAKEFIELD, EDWARD (1774–1854). An account of Ireland, statistical and political... 2 vols. *4°.* 1812.

20441 WEBB, DANIEL C. Observations and remarks, during four excursions, made to various parts of Great Britain, in...1810 and 1811... 384p. *8°.* 1812.

20442 WILLIAMS, SIR JOHN (1777–1846). The laws of trade and commerce, designed as a book of reference in mercantile transactions. 584p. *8°. London, Birmingham, &c.,* 1812.

20443 YOUNG, ARTHUR (1741–1820). An enquiry into the progressive value of money in England, as marked by the price of agricultural products; with observations upon Sir G. Shuckburgh's Table of appreciation; the whole deduced from a great variety of authorities not before collected. [An extract from vol. 46 of *Annals of Agriculture.*] p. 66–137. *8°.* 1812. *Young's own copy.*

AGRICULTURE

20444 BALD, R. A general view of the coal trade of Scotland, chiefly that of the River Forth and Mid-Lothian. To which is added, an inquiry into the condition of the women who carry coals under ground in Scotland, known by the name of bearers. With an appendix, in which a review of the trade is taken...since the treatise was first published in 1808; and a statement given of the steps lately taken by Government, with the view of placing the coal trade under an excise... 203p. *8°. Edinburgh, Glasgow, &c.,* 1812. *For another edition, see 1808.*

20445 BEAZLEY, S. A general view of the system of enclosing waste lands; with particular reference to the proposed enclosure at Epsom in Surrey. 51p. *8°.* 1812.

20446 BOARD OF AGRICULTURE. Premiums offered by the Board...1812. 7p. *8°.* [1812] *Addressed in manuscript to Lord Sheffield. See also 1804, 1808, 1809, 1810, 1816, 1818.*

20447 [BRICKWOOD, J.] Thoughts upon the immediate means of meeting the pressure of want. By a London merchant. 16p. *8°.* 1812.

20448 CHITTY, JOSEPH (1776–1841). A treatise on the game laws, and on fisheries; with an appendix, containing all the statutes and cases on the subject... 2 vols. *8°.* 1812. *Presentation copy from the author to Lord Ellenborough.*

20449 COVENTRY, A. Notes on the culture and cropping of arable land. [With 'Abstract & tables' and an appendix.] 46, 31, 8p. *8°. Edinburgh,* 1812. *Presentation copy, with inscription, from the author to 'James Gibson, Esqre'. For another edition, see 1811.*

20450 DUBOURDIEU, J. Statistical survey of the county of Antrim, with observations on the means of improvement; drawn up...by direction of the Dublin Society. 630, 112p. *8°. Dublin,* 1812.

20451 EDINBURGH AND LEITH WHALE-FISHING COMPANY. Contract of the Edinburgh and Leith Whale-Fishing Company. 13p. *8°.* [*Edinburgh,* 1812]

20452 ENGLAND. *Laws, etc.* [*Endorsed:*] An Act for draining, inclosing, and improving...Borough Fen Common, and the Four Hundred Acre Common, in the county of Northampton; and for forming the same into a parish, to be called Newborough; and for building and endowing a church... ⟨Royal Assent, 9 June 1812.⟩ 52 Geo. III. 1812. 65p. *fol. n.p.* [1812] *See note to no.* 25484.

20453 —— —— [*Endorsed:*] An Act for inclosing lands within the...parish of Burton-upon-Trent, in the counties of Stafford and Derby, and for selling part of the said lands, and applying the produce thereof in aid of the poor's rates of the said parish. Geo. III. 35p. *fol. n.p.* [1812]

20454 GRAHAM, P. General view of the agriculture of Stirlingshire; with observations on the means of its improvement. Drawn up for the consideration of the Board of Agriculture... 413p. *8°. Edinburgh, London, &c.,* 1812.

20455 HALL, WILLIAM (*fl.* 1812–1818). A sketch of local history, being a chain of incidents relating to the state of the Fens...With a life of the author...[Part 1.] 22, [2]p. *8°. Lynn,* 1812.

20456 HENDERSON, JOHN. General view of the agriculture of the county of Sutherland, with observations on the means of its improvement. Drawn up for the consideration of the Board of Agriculture...To which is annexed, a particular account of the more recent improvements... 238p. *8°. London, Edinburgh, &c.,* 1812. *See also* 1815.

20457 HUGHES, JOHN (*fl.* 1812). A statement of facts, recommended to the attentive perusal of the agriculturists of the British Empire. [An advertisement for Hughes's (formerly Pick's) cattle cordial, with a list of vendors.] 14p. *8°.* 1812.

20458 MERINO SOCIETY. The second report of the Merino Society... 161p. *8°.* 1812. *The Sheffield copy. See also* 1811, 1813.

20459 NICOL, W. The planter's kalendar; the nurseryman's & forester's guide, in the operations of the nursery, the forest, and the grove...Edited and completed by Edward Sang... 595p. *8°. Edinburgh, London, &c.,* 1812. *See also* 1820.

20460 PARMENTIER, A. A. Le maïs ou blé de Turquie, apprécié sous tous ses rapports; mémoire couronné, le 25 août 1784, par l'Académie Royale des

Sciences, Belles-Lettres et Arts de Bordeaux...Nouvelle édition, revue et corrigée... 303p. 8°. *Paris, 1812.*

20461 **QUAYLE**, T. General view of the agriculture of the Isle of Man. With observations on the means of its improvement. Drawn up for the consideration of the Board of Agriculture... 293[193]p. 8°. *1812.*

20462 **RICHARDSON**, WILLIAM (1740–1820). Memoir on the cultivation of fiorin grass...in a letter addressed to the Bath and West of England Agricultural Society. [With 'On the cultivation of dry heaths, downs, and generally of light sandy soils, with fiorin'.] 53p. 8°. *Bath, 1812.*

20463 **SCUDERI**, S. Dissertazioni agrarie riguardanti il Regno di Sicilia. 196p. 4°. *Catania, 1812.*

20464 **SINCLAIR**, SIR JOHN, *Bart.* An account of the systems of husbandry adopted in the more improved districts of Scotland; with some observations on the improvements of which they are susceptible. Drawn up for the...Board of Agriculture, with a view of explaining how far these systems are applicable to the less cultivated parts of England, and Scotland. 432, 152, 77p. 8°. *Edinburgh, London, &c., 1812. See also 1813, 1814.*

20465 —— Some particulars regarding the farm occupied by J. C. Curwen, Esq. of Workington Hall in Cumberland, (from information collected at the Workington meeting, in September 1812), with some remarks on the improvements of which Mr. Curwen's system is susceptible. 12p. 4°. *Edinburgh, [1812] The Sheffield copy.*

20466 **SINGER**, W. General view of the agriculture, state of property, and improvements, in the county of Dumfries: drawn up under the direction of the Board of Agriculture, and at the request of the landholders of the county. 696p. 8°. *Edinburgh & London, 1812.*

20467 **SOUTER**, D. General view of the agriculture of the county of Banff; with observations on the means of its improvement. Drawn up for the consideration of the Board of Agriculture... 339, 85p. 8°. *Edinburgh, [London,] &c., 1812.*

20468 **SPENCE**, W. Observations on the disease in turnips, termed in Holderness "fingers and toes;" in a letter to John Broadley...read to the Holderness Agricultural Society, December 23, 1811... 20p. 8°. *Hull, 1812.*

20469 **STRICKLAND**, H. E. A general view of the agriculture of the East-Riding of Yorkshire; published by order of the Board of Agriculture... 332p. 8°. *York & London, 1812.*

20470 The **SUBSTANCE** of the leases, granted on the Lovat Estate, 1811, with their clauses arranged under their respective heads. 35p. 8°. *Inverness, 1812.*

20471 **TRIMMER**, JOSHUA K. Further observations on the present state of agriculture, and condition of the lower classes of the people, in the southern parts of Ireland: with an estimate of the agricultural resources of that country; and a plan for carrying into effect a commutation for tithe, and a project for poor laws. 118p. 8°. *London, Dublin, &c., 1812. Another edition, with the title,* Observations on the state of agriculture...in the southern parts of Ireland, *was published in 1822 (q.v.).*

20472 **TUSSER**, T. Five hundred points of good husbandry...A new edition, with notes...by William Mavor. 36, xl, 338p. 4°. *1812. For other editions, see 1574.*

20473 **WALKER**, JOHN (1731–1803). An economical history of the Hebrides and Highlands of Scotland... 2 vols. 8°. *London & Edinburgh, 1812. The copy that belonged to George Chalmers, with his book-plate. For another edition, see 1808.*

20474 **WILSON**, JOHN, *of Thornly.* General view of the agriculture of Renfrewshire; with observations on the means of its improvement; and an account of its commerce and manufactures. Drawn up for the consideration of the Board of Agriculture... 370p. 8°. *Paisley, London, &c., 1812.*

POPULATION

20475 **CLERICUS**, *Dromorensis, pseud.* An essay on the comparative number of Protestants and Roman Catholics in the United Kingdom, in which the true grounds of Protestant ascendancy are stated. [Dated: Nov. 26, 1812.] 22p. 8°. *Dublin, 1812.*

TRADES & MANUFACTURES

20476 [*Begin.*] **BRETHREN,** this day the action, now depending between the operative weavers and manufacturers of Glasgow, came before the Quarter-Session of the Peace...[A case about prices charged for weaving. Dated: 12th May, 1812.] s.sh.4°. *[Glasgow, 1812] [Br. 479(1)]*

20477 **GLASGOW.** Table of the prices of weaving cotton goods, recommended to be adopted by a general meeting of the manufacturers of Glasgow, 10th February, 1812. [Signed: John Graham, preses. With, printed on the other half of the sheet 'Report of the Committee of the Muslin Manufacturers of the City of Glasgow, 10th February, 1812'.] 2l. 4°. *Glasgow, [1812] [Br. 476]*

20478 **HATELY**, J. A treatise on the manufacturing arts of pig metal and bar iron, with pit coal and cokes... with plans and sections of fineries, furnaces and cupels... 14p. 8°. *Dudley, 1812.*

20479 **HOPPUS**, E. Practical measuring made easy to the meanest capacity by a new set of tables...A new edition, revised by T. Crosby, head master of the York Charity Schools... 207p. *long 12°. York, 1812. For other editions, see 1759.*

20480 **LONDON.** Livery Companies. *Clockmakers.* [*Begin.*] It is generally acknowledged, indeed nothing can be more clear or demonstrable...that all those persons who have devoted a considerable portion of their lives... by apprenticeship, in the pursuit and attainment of knowledge and skill...[An address to freemen, adjuring them to confer the freedom of the Company on their sons and apprentices, in order that the Company may be strengthened to speak for the trade. Dated: September 25, 1812.] [4]p. *fol. Hoxton,* [1812] *See note to no.* 13563.

20481 —— [Another edition, abridged, dated: October 1st, 1812, and signed, George Atkins, clerk.] [2]p. *fol. Hoxton,* [1812] *See note to no.* 13563.

20482 —— —— *Goldsmiths.* Goldsmiths' Hall, London, December 22, 1812. [A notice warning watchmakers and case makers that component parts of gold or silver watch cases, and the pendants and bows to go with them, must all conform to the prescribed standards, 22 ct. or 18 ct. fine for gold and 11 oz. 2 dwt. fine for silver. All the pieces in a parcel will be defaced if one part of one piece is found to be defective. Signed: Thomas Lane, clerk.] *s.sh.fol.* [1812] *See note to no.* 13563. *See also* 1813.

20483 —— [Another edition.] *s.sh.4°. n.p.* [1812] *Enclosed in a printed circular letter, dated, 'Dec. 26, 1812' to be sent out by case makers to suppliers of pendants, on the price of cases, credit, etc. See note to no.* 13563.

20484 OBSERVATIONS on the art and trade of clock and watch-making; the causes and consequences of the numerous frauds and innovations resulting from the defect of the laws... 23p. *8°.* 1812.

20485 PERING, R. A brief enquiry into the causes of premature decay, in our wooden bulwarks, with an examination of the means, best calculated to prolong their duration. 78p. *8°. Plymouth-Dock & London,* 1812.

20486 April 1812. Second edition of **SKYRING'S** new and complete list of builders' prices, calculated to do justice to the proprietor, master builders, and their workmen. 66p. *8°.* 1812. *Compiled by Z. Skyring, who signed and numbered each copy in manuscript. A copy without the Abstract of the Building Act (14 Geo. III, cap. 78). See also 1818, 1819, 1827, 1831, 1838, 1845, 1846.*

20487 SMEATON, J. Reports of the late John Smeaton, F.R.S. made on various occasions, in the course of his employment as a civil engineer...[With 'The miscellaneous papers of John Smeaton...comprising his communications to the Royal Society...forming a fourth volume to his reports'.] 4 vols. *4°.* 1812–14.

20488 TABLE of prices, for weaving various fabrics of cotton cloth, constructed by the Committee of Operative Weavers, met at Paisley, for Renfrewshire. 28th Dec. 1812. *s.sh.fol. n.p.* [1812] [*Br.* 479(2)]

COMMERCE

20489 ASHE, T. A commercial view, and geographical sketch, of the Brasils in South America, and of the Island of Madeira; being a description of the Portuguese colonies ...together with their climate, soil, and produce; trade... &c. Serving as a guide to the commercial world, and pointing out to the manufacturing towns of Sheffield, Birmingham...Coventry...Painswick, &c. new sources of wealth and springs of industry, by directing their attention to the formation of such goods as are consumed in the New World...160p. *8°. London,* 1812.

20490 ATTWOOD, T. Speech of Thomas Attwood, Esq. High Bailiff of Birmingham, to a general meeting of the merchants, manufacturers and other inhabitants, held on the 4th of March, 1812, "to take into consideration the present state of the manufactures and commerce of the United Kingdom, and the propriety of petitioning... Parliament to discontinue such parts of the East India Charter as exclude British merchants from trading to the East". *s.sh.fol. Birmingham,* [1812] *In a volume of pamphlets and broadsides concerned with Birmingham between the years 1791 and 1841, collected by Benjamin Hadley, secretary of the Birmingham Political Union.*

20491 [BLANC DE LANAUTTE, A. M., *Comte d'Hauterive.*] Mémoire sur les principes et les lois de la neutralité maritime, accompagné de pièces officielles justificatives. 160p. *8°. Paris,* 1812.

20492 [BRICKWOOD, J.] Observations upon the supplies of provisions to the Metropolis, and upon the means of their continuance in case of invasion. By a London merchant. 44p. *8°.* 1812.

20493 CONSIDERATIONS on the policy of renewing the exclusive privileges of the East India Company. 42p. *8°.* 1812.

20494 COSSIM, *pseud.* Considerations on the danger and impolicy of laying open the trade with India and China; including an examination of the objections commonly urged against the East India Company's commer-

cial and financial management. [The substance of a series of letters which appeared in the Morning Post...under the signature of Cossim.] 218p. *8°.* 1812. *See also* 1813.

20495 CRUMP, T. V. A plan for the better protection of British commerce, with a decided method for totally destroying Bonaparte's infant navy; in a letter to the merchants and naval officers of Great Britain... 23p. *8°.* 1812.

20496 EAST INDIA COMPANY. Correspondence and proceedings in the negociation for a renewal of the East-India Company's charter. 92p. *8°.* 1812. *Two copies, one addressed to the Earl of Morton, the other to the Earl of Sheffield.*

20497 FREE TRADE; or, an inquiry into the pretensions of the Directors of the East India Company, to the exclusive trade of the Indian and China Seas. Addressed to the great body of the merchants and manufacturers of the United Kingdom. 71p. *8°.* 1812.

20498 FREE TRADE to India. Letters addressed to the merchants and inhabitants of the town of Liverpool, concerning a free trade to the East Indies. By a Member of Parliament. 32p. *8°. Liverpool,* 1812.

20499 HULL. East India trade. Report of the proceedings of the meeting at Kingston-upon-Hull, 6th April, 1812, on the subject of laying open the trade to the East-Indies. 22p. *12°. Hull,* 1812.

20500 —— A full report of the proceedings at two meetings, of the merchants, ship-owners, &c....at Kingston-upon-Hull, April 4, 1811, and February 11, 1812, respecting the granting of licences, to foreign ships; together with a copy of the memorial laid before the Board of Trade; and the petition presented to the House of Commons. 48p. *8°. Hull & London,* [1812]

20501 JACKSON, RANDLE. Substance of the speech of Randle Jackson, Esq. delivered at a General Court of Proprietors of East India stock...May 5, 1812, upon the subject of the negociation with His Majesty's ministers, for a prolongation of the term of the Company's exclusive charter... 62p. *8°.* 1812.

20502 LEE, THOMAS, *barrister.* The right of every British merchant to trade within the geographical limits defined by the charter of the East India Company, vindicated; with important...documents, peculiarly applicable to the question of a modified open trade to China... 73p. *8°.* 1812.

20503 A LETTER to Edward Parry and Charles Grant, Esqrs. Chairman and Deputy Chairman of the Court of Directors in 1809, on the commercial monopoly of the East India Company, and on the policy of the establishment of a new company. Second edition. 73p. *8°.* 1812.

20504 LETTERS on the East India monopoly, originally published in the Glasgow Chronicle, with additions and corrections. Second edition. 137p. *8°. Glasgow, Edinburgh, &c.,* 1812.

20505 MACPHERSON, DAVID. The history of the European commerce with India. To which is subjoined a review of the arguments for and against the trade with India, and the management of it by a chartered company. 440p. *4°.* 1812.

20506 To the NOBLEMEN, gentlemen, and adventurers, interested in the tin mines of Cornwall. [Concerning the purchase and exportation of Cornish tin by the East India Company.] *s.sh.4°.* 1812.

20507 PHILLIMORE, JOSEPH. Reflections on the nature and extent of the license trade...Third edition. 96p. *8°.* 1812. *For another edition, see 1811.*

20508 PRINCE'S LONDON PRICE CURRENT...No. 1865. Friday the 3d. of January [—No. 1916. Friday, the 25th of December,] 1812. 52 nos. *fol.* [1812] *See also* 1813, 1814, 1815, 1817, 1818, 1820.

20509 The QUESTION as to the renewal of the East India Company's monopoly examined. 117p. *8°. Edinburgh,* 1812.

20510 UNWIN, G. [*Begin.*] Kennington Cross, Lambeth, Surry, October 1, 1812. My Lords and gentlemen, Having had the honor of being nominated...[A collection of letters, reports and memorials, 1789–1812, on the export of Cornish tin to the Far East through the East India Company. Collected on behalf of the tin interests of Cornwall on the occasion of the renewal of the East India Company's charter, and issued, with a prefatory letter, by George Unwin.] 41p. *8°.* [*London,* 1812] *Two copies, one of which has manuscript additions to the table of tin exports, continuing it to 1815, and an additional table beginning 'The following statement will shew the progressive improvement in the export of copper...', signed: George Unwin, 1st May, 1813.*

20511 WAR without disguise; or, brief considerations on the political and commercial relations of Great Britain and Ireland, with the United States of America, at the close of the year 1811. 9p. *8°. Liverpool & London,* 1812.

COLONIES

20512 GRANT, CHARLES (1746–1823), *and others.* A letter signed by C. Grant Esq. [and others]...Directors of the East-India Company; containing a minute examination and full vindication of the measures adopted by Sir George Barlow, during the dissentions at the Presidency of Madras. Extracted from the papers laid before Parliament. 131p. *8°.* 1812.

20513 JACKSON, WILLIAM C. Memoir of the public conduct and services of William Collins Jackson, Esq., late senior merchant on the Company's Madras establishment. 85p. *8°.* 1812. *The copy that belonged to David Ricardo.*

20514 A LETTER to the chairman of the Court of Directors, containing observations on the regulations likely soon to take place relative to the India army, on the

expected renewal of the Company's charter. [Signed: A Bengal officer.] 52p. *8°. Newark & London,* 1812.

20515 MEREDITH, H. An account of the Gold Coast of Africa: with a brief history of the African Company. 264p. *8°.* 1812.

20516 REMARKS on the extension of territory which has taken place in India, subsequent to the Acts of Parliament, passed in 1784, and 1793; submitted to the consideration of Parliament, previous to the proposed renewal of the charter of the East India Company. 28p. *8°.* 1812.

20517 SAALFELD, J. C. F. Geschichte des holländischen Kolonialwesens in Ostindien... 2 vols. *8°. Göttingen,* 1812–13.

FINANCE

20518 ABNORMIS, RUSTICUS, *pseud.* A review of the Report of the Bullion Committee; of the pamphlets written upon it; of the debate and decision of the House of Commons upon that important subject: with some observations on the corn and distillery laws. 67p. *8°. Edinburgh,* 1812.

20519 An ABSTRACT of the several Acts of Parliament relating to the collection and application of county rates, including the Acts for providing relief for the families of militiamen, with the adjudged cases, and observations thereon; and a list of all the treasurers of counties, divisions, cities and boroughs, in England and Wales. 275p. *8°.* 1812.

20520 An APPEAL to common sense in the bullion-question. By a merchant. 69p. *8°.* 1812.

20521 [AUGET DE MONTYON, A. J. B. R., *Baron.*] Particularités et observations sur les ministres des finances de France les plus célèbres, depuis 1660 jusqu'en 1791. 362p. *8°. Londres,* 1812.

20522 [——] [Another edition.] 397p. *8°. Paris,* 1812.

20523 BANK OF ENGLAND. A list of the names of all such proprietors of the Bank of England, who are qualified to vote at the ensuing election...March 24th, 1812. 18p. *fol.* [1812] *See also* 1738, 1749, 1750, 1789, 1790, 1791, 1792, 1793, 1794, 1795, 1796, 1797, 1798, 1799, 1801, 1803, 1804, 1808, 1809, 1816, 1819, 1836, 1843.

20524 CHITTY, JOSEPH (d. 1838). A practical treatise on bills of exchange, checks on bankers, promissory notes, bankers' cash notes, and bank notes. Fourth edition, considerably enlarged and improved, with an appendix of precedents. 638p. 8°. 1812.

20525 [CLARKE, P.] A list of bankrupts, with their dividends, certificates, &c. from January 1, 1812, to July 1, 1812...transcribed from the London Gazettes, and arranged alphabetically; forming an index of commercial information... [122]p. 8°. 1812.

20526 CRUMP, T. V. A practicable plan for abolishing tithes in England and Ireland, advantageous to all persons connected with them, as well as the public at large... 52p. 8°. 1812.

20527 ENGLAND. *Assessors of Taxes.* No. III. Duty on property, &c. Assessors' warrant and instructions. 27p. 8°. [London,] 1812. *Addressed in manuscript to the Assessors for Studley in Warwickshire.*

20528 —— *Commissioners for the Reduction of the National Debt.* Tables of the rates of government life annuities. 11p. 4°. [1812]

20529 —— *Exchequer.* An account of the income and charge upon the Consolidated Fund; in the year ending the 5th day of January, 1812...[With 'An account of the Public Funded Debt of Great Britain, as it stood on the 1st February, 1812...'] s.sh.4°. [London,] 1812.

20530 GRANT, SIR JOHN P. Essays towards illustrating some elementary principles relating to wealth and currency. 170p. 8°. London & Edinburgh, 1812.

20531 GREEN, A. An essay, tending to shew the impolicy of the laws of usury. 20p. 8°. 1812. *With a manuscript note on the title-page: 'The arguments are drawn from Bentham's book, JBS'.*

20532 GRELLIER, J. J. The terms of all the loans which have been raised for the public service: with observations on the rate of interest...And an account of Navy and Exchequer Bills...The third edition, considerably enlarged and improved...With an appendix from the year 1805 to the present year: by R. W. Wade... 92, 12p. 8°. 1812. *For other editions, see 1799.*

20533 [HEYWOOD, BENJAMIN A.] Observations on the circulation of individual credit, and on the banking system of England. 97p. 8°. 1812. *The author's own copy, with manuscript notes by him. For the second part of this work, see 1820; an earlier version of this second part was printed with the title* Arguments, demonstrating from recent facts, the solid foundation of individual circulating credit, *in 1819 (q.v.).*

20534 HOLMES, WILLIAM A. An examination of Mr. Parnell's arguments and plan for a commutation of tithe in Ireland; as submitted to the House of Commons in...1812; in a letter to...Viscount Castlereagh. 43p. 8°. Belfast, 1812.

20535 The **LACK** of gold; or, an enquiry into the state of the paper currency of England, under the operation of Lord Stanhope's Act. 48p. 8°. 1812.

20536 LAURADOUX, F. Comptes faits, ou tableaux comparatifs des anciens poids et mesures qui étaient usités dans le département du Rhône avant le système métrique. A l'usage des hommes-de-loi...des négocians ...des ouvriers... 118p. 4°. Lyon, 1812.

20537 LIPS, A. Ueber die allein wahre und einzige Steuer die Einkommen-Taxe und ihre Ausführbarkeit...

Ein Seitenstück zu der Brochüre: Wie kann sich ein Staat der Last von Quieszenten auf eine gerechte Weise entledigen &c. 47p. 8°. Erlangen, 1812.

20538 MAITLAND, JAMES, *8th Earl of Lauderdale.* The depreciation of the paper currency of Great Britain proved. 196p. 8°. London & Edinburgh, 1812.

20539 MAJOR, W. Theory of money and exchanges; and the causes of its present depreciation indisputably pointed out; with some thoughts on the progress and termination of the Sinking Fund: illustrated in a series of familiar dialogues. Part I. 80p. 8°. 1812. *The preface is signed in manuscript by the author.*

20540 MONCK, J. B. A letter to the Right Hon. Spencer Percival, on the present state of our currency; with hints for its gradual improvement. 22p. 8°. Reading & London, [1812]

20541 PARIS. *Cour Impériale. Cour de Justice Criminelle et Spéciale.* Arrêt de la Cour Spéciale de Paris, qui condamne à la peine de mort Jean-François Firmin Ganneron...pour crime de faux-monnoyage. Du 12 août 1812. 4p. 4°. [Paris, 1812]

20542 PARNELL, H. B., *Baron Congleton.* Substance of a speech made by Henry Parnell, Esq. on the 9th of May, 1811, in the Committee of the Whole House of Commons, to which the Report of the Bullion Committee was referred. 60p. 8°. 1812.

20543 [——] Summary of the arguments and plan for a commutation of tithes in Ireland, submitted to the House of Commons in the session of 1812. [With 'List of the members who have voted...in favour of an inquiry into the tithe system of Ireland'.] 20p. 8°. 1812.

20544 PHILO-COLONUS, *pseud.* A letter to the Right Honourable Spencer Perceval on the expediency of imposing a duty on cotton wool of foreign growth, imported into Great Britain. 16p. 8°. 1812.

20545 *PRICE, RICHARD. Observations on reversionary payments; on schemes for providing annuities for widows, and for persons in old age...In two volumes. The whole new arranged, and enlarged...by William Morgan, F.R.S. Seventh edition. 2 vols. 8°. 1812. *The copy that belonged to Augustus De Morgan. For other editions, see 1771.*

20546 Look to your **PROPERTY**: addressed to the landlords, stock-holders, mortgagees, annuitants, and other money claimants of Great Britain. [On paper money.] 20p. 8°. 1812.

20547 PROSPECTUS of a plan for establishing in Scotland a general fund for securing provision to widows, sisters, &c. and insuring capital sums on lives. To be called the Scottish Widows' Fund, and Equitable Assurance Society. [With a list of officers.] 24, 22p. 12°. Edinburgh, 1812.

20548 RUTHERFORD, A. W. Depreciation caused by conflicting coins; or, a letter to the Earl of Lauderdale, in reply to The depreciation of the paper-currency of Great Britain proved. 75p. 8°. 1812.

20549 SMITH, THOMAS, *accountant, of London.* The bullion-question impartially discussed: an address to the editors of the Edinburgh Review. 95p. 8°. 1812.

20550 STEUART, SIR J., *Bart.* Principles of banks and banking of money, as coin and paper, with the consequences of any excessive issue on the national currency, course of exchange...and fixed incomes...Second edition. 314p. 8°. 1812. *For another edition, see 1810.*

20551 SUGDEN, E. B., *Baron St. Leonards*. A cursory inquiry into the expediency of repealing the Annuity Act and raising the legal rate of interest, in a series of letters. 60p. *8°*. 1812. *A manuscript copy, on eighty pages, of the printed original.*

20552 Brief **THOUGHTS** on the present state of the currency of this country. By a merchant. 48p. *8°*. *Edinburgh & London*, 1812. *Tentatively attributed by HSF, in a manuscript note, to Sir John Peter Grant.*

20553 TORRENS, R. An essay on money and paper currency. 301p. *8°*. 1812.

20554 WILSON, GLOCESTER. A further defence of abstract currencies. 111p. *8°*. 1812.

20555 [WILSON, ROBERT, *accountant*?] Remarks on the Earl of Lauderdale's pamphlet, entitled The depreciation of the paper currency of Great Britain proved. 40p. *8°*. *Edinburgh*, 1812.

20555A YOUNG, Arthur (1741–1820). An enquiry into the progressive value of money in England, as marked by the price of agricultural products... p. [65]–135. *8°*. 1812. *No. 270, vol. 46 (issued only in this form), of* Annals of Agriculture. *Young's own copy.*

TRANSPORT

20556 COURTIN,   , *Secrétaire général de la Direction générale des Ponts-et-Chaussées*. Travaux des ponts-et-chaussées, depuis 1800, ou tableau des constructions neuves faites sous le règne de Napoléon Ier., en routes, ponts, canaux, et des travaux entrepris pour la navigation fluviale, les desséchemens, les ports du commerce, etc. [With 'Observations' consisting of notes and corrections.] xi, 348, ivp. *8°*. *Paris*, 1812.

20557 DABBADIE, M. An impartial view of the Royal Canal Company's affairs, in reply to the report of their committee; with a full statement of the several sums appropriated, and due by the same Company, and some directors, to the Canal Fund; together with a computation of interest thereon. 112p. *8°*. *Dublin*, 1812.

20558 ENGLAND. *Laws, etc.* ⟨Royal assent, 9th June.⟩ An Act to explain, amend, and enlarge the powers of certain Acts passed for making and maintaining the Grand Junction Canal. 24p. *fol. n.p.*, 1812.

20559 —— Parliament. *House of Commons.* London and Cambridge Junction Canal. Minutes of the evidence taken before a Committee of the House of Commons, with an appendix. 451p. *12°*. 1812.

20560 KENNET AND AVON CANAL NAVIGATION. Report of the Committee of Management to the Company of Proprietors of the Kennet and Avon Canal. [Signed: C. Dundas, chairman, and dated, July 21, 1812.] 2p. *fol. n.p.* [1812] *See also* 1813, 1815, 1816, 1823, 1824, 1825, 1826, 1838.

20561 MEDHURST, G. Calculations and remarks, tending to prove the practicability, effects and advantages of a plan for the rapid conveyance of goods and passengers upon an iron road through a tube of 30 feet in area, by the power and velocity of air. 18p. *8°*. 1812.

SOCIAL CONDITIONS

20562 ADELPHI SCHOOL, *Philadelphia*. The following annual report of the Board of Managers... to the "Philadelphia Association of Friends for the Instruction of Poor Children" is published for the information of the patrons of that institution. [Signed: Roberts Vaux, secretary. Dated: Twelfth Month, 30th, 1812.] *s.sh.fol. n.p.* [1812] [*Br.* 478]

20563 BECHER, JOHN T. Observations on the punishment of offenders, and the preservation of the peace, occasioned by the trespasses, riots, and felonies, now prevalent in the county of Nottingham. 56p. *8°*. *Newark & London*, 1812.

20564 BENTHAM, J. Panopticon, or, the inspection-house; in which... any number of... persons, may at all times be inspected without change of place; and the establishment managed, upon a plan, applicable (with the requisite variations) to penitentiary and other prisons, work-houses, manufactories, mad-houses, lazarettos and schools. Printed anno 1791, with the ensuing title-page: and now first published... 3 vols. *8°*. [*London*,] 1812. *A reissue of the edition of 1791 (q.v.), with the addition of a new title-page in vol. I only. The 'Advertisement' on the verso of this title-page lists the establishments in which the central-inspection principle has been adopted since 1791.*

20565 —— Panopticon versus New South Wales: or, the panopticon penitentiary system, and the penal colonization system, compared. Containing, 1. Two letters to Lord Pelham... comparing the two systems on the ground of expediency. 2. Plea for the constitution: representing the illegalities involved in the penal colonization system... Anno 1803, printed: now first published. 80, 72, 68p. *8°*. [*London*,] 1812.

20566 —— Pauper management improved; particularly by means of an application of the panopticon principle of construction. Anno 1797, first published in Young's Annals of agriculture: now first published separately. 34, 288p. *8°*. [*London*,] 1812. *Presentation copy from the author to Henry Coulson. A new issue of* Situation and relief of the poor, *1797 (q.v.), and* Outline of a work entitled Pauper management improved, *1798 (q.v.).*

20567 BERNARD, SIR T., *Bart*. The Barrington School; being an illustration of the principles, practices, and effects, of the new system of instruction, in facilitating the religious and moral instruction of the poor. 207p. *8°*. *The Society for Bettering the Condition of the Poor*, 1812. *For another edition, see* 1809.

20568 COMMITTEE FOR ASSISTING THE MAGISTRATES AND BOROUGHREEVE AND CONSTABLES IN SUPPORTING THE PEACE, *Manchester*. To the inhabitants of Manchester and Salford. Printed by order of the Committee... [Ways to prevent a recurrence of the late unrest.] 8p. *8°*. [*Manchester*, 1812]

20569 DAY AND SUNDAY FREE SCHOOL, *Circus Street, Liverpool.* Ninth annual report of the Day and Sunday Free School...(From July 1, 1811 to July 1, 1812.) [With 'List of annual subscribers', etc.] 16p. *8⁰. Liverpool,* [1812]. *See also* 1811, 1813, 1814.

20570 —— [*Begin.*] Sunday next, the 21st instant, being the ninth anniversary of the establishment of Circus-Street Free School, a sermon in favour of the Institution, will be preached...by the Rev. Thos. Coles... [Dated: 19th June, 1812.] [4]p. *8⁰. n.p.* [1812] *Addressed in manuscript to 'Mr. John Lang, Drury Lane'.*

20571 EDINBURGH. *General Commissioners of Police.* Report of the committee appointed by the Commissioners of Police, to inquire into the practicability of suppressing the practice of common begging, and relieving the industrious and destitute poor. 19p. *8⁰. Edinburgh,* 1812.

20572 ENGLAND. *Laws, etc.* Abstract of an Act passed in the fifty-second year of the reign of...George III, entitled An Act for the more effectual preservation of the peace, within the county...and the town...of Nottingham. To which is added, an abstract of an Act passed in the same year, entitled An Act for the more exemplary punishment of persons destroying or injuring any stocking or lace frames, or other machines...used in the framework-knitting manufactory... 28p. *12⁰. Nottingham,* 1812.

20573 GLOUCESTER, *County of.* Laws, rules, orders, and regulations, for the government and controul of the several prisons in the county of Gloucester. 109p. *8⁰. Gloucester,* 1812.

20574 GODALMING SUBSCRIPTION SCHOOL. An address to the parents or friends of the children educated at the Godalming Subscription Schools, on the Royal British plan. *s.sh.fol.* [*London,* 1812 ?]

20575 GOODENOUGH, S., *Bishop of Carlisle.* A sermon preached before the incorporated Society for the Propagation of the Gospel in Foreign Parts; at their anniversary meeting...February 21, 1812. [With 'An abstract of the charter, and...proceedings of the Society ...1811, to...1812'.] 89p. *4⁰.* 1812.

20576 GREEN, WILLIAM (*fl.* 1788–1818). Plans of economy; or, the road to ease and independence, both in town and country: illustrated by estimates...A new edition, considerably improved. 126p. *12⁰. Bath & London,* 1812. *For other editions, see* 1804.

20577 HEADS of proposed Act for the registering and securing of charitable donations for the benefit of poor persons in England and Wales. 16p. *8⁰.* [*London,* 1812]

20578 HINTS towards the formation of a society, for promoting a spirit of independence among the poor [the Prudent Man's Friend Society]. Second edition. 29p. *12⁰. Bristol,* [1812]

20579 HITCHCOCK, D. The bond of friendship. Being an address, delivered before the Great-Barrington branch of the Washington Benevolent Society—April 21, 1812... 15p. *8⁰. Stockbridge* [*Mass.*], 1812.

20580 HOLLINGSWORTH, N. J. An address to the public in recommendation of the Madras system of education as invented and practised by the Rev. Dr. Bell ...with a comparison between his schools and those of Mr. Joseph Lancaster. To which is added, the third

edition of a sermon on the same subject preached in... Hartlepool...August 26, 1810. 44p. *8⁰.* 1812.

20581 JARVIS, W. C. An oration, delivered at Pittsfield, (Mass.) before the Washington Benevolent Society of the county of Berkshire, on the 4th July, 1812. [Second edition.] 24p. *8⁰. Stockbridge* [*Mass.*], 1812.

20582 JOURNEYMEN TIN-PLATE WORKERS. [*Begin.*] Gentlemen, several of us having read the Address of the Journeymen Tin-Plate Workers to their employers...[Reasons offered by the journeymen for their petition for an increase in wages.] [2]p. *fol.* [1812 ?] *See note to no.* 13563.

20583 KNIGHT, JOHN. A correct report of the proceedings on the trial of thirty-eight men, on a charge of administering an unlawful oath...at Lancaster on Thursday, 27th August, 1812...With an introductory narrative, &c. by John Knight, one of the defendants. 150p. *8⁰. Manchester,* 1812.

20584 MARTIN, MATTHEW. An appeal to public benevolence, for the relief of beggars; with a view to a plan for suppression of beggary...published by desire of the Committee for superintending the management of the subscription fund connected with the mendicity enquiry. 18p. *8⁰.* 1812.

20585 MINCHIN, W. R. Present state of the debtor and creditor law: being an essay on the effects of imprisonment...and an analysis of the Lords' Committee's report on imprisonment for civil debt. With an abstract of Lord Redesdale's Bill... 162p. *8⁰.* 1812.

20586 MONNEY, W. Considerations on prisons, with a plan for their better regulation, the treatment of criminal prisoners, and the prevention of crimes... 64p. *8⁰.* 1812.

20587 NEILD, J. State of the prisons in England, Scotland and Wales...not for the debtor only, but for felons also, and other less criminal offenders. Together with some useful documents, observations, and remarks, adapted to explain and improve the condition of prisoners in general. 643p. *4⁰.* 1812.

20588 PEARSON, RICHARD. An account of a particular preparation of salted fish, to be used with boiled rice, or boiled potatoes, for the purpose of lessening the consumption of wheaten bread. 16p. *8⁰. Reading & London,* [1812]

20589 PRUDENT MAN'S FRIEND SOCIETY. The rules, with a short explanation of the views of the Prudent Man's Friend, a society established in Bristol... on the 22d of December, 1812...Second edition. 24p. *12⁰.* [*Bristol,* 1812]

20590 RIGBY, E. Further facts relating to the care of the poor, and the management of the workhouse, in... Norwich, being a sequel to a former publication. [With an appendix.] 101, 15p. *8⁰. Norwich & London,* 1812. *A second copy, which lacks the appendix, was presented, with an inscription, by the author to Patrick Colquhoun; from the library of James Colquhoun. For the 'former publication' see the author's Reports of the special provision committee, appointed by the Court of Guardians, in the City of Norwich, published in 1788.*

20591 SOCIETY FOR THE SUPPRESSION OF VAGRANTS, *Bath.* Report of the Bath Society for the Suppression of Vagrants...With an account of the receipts and disbursements [and a list of subscribers] from Jan. 1, 1811, to Jan. 1, 1812... 24p. *12⁰. Bath,* 1812. *See also* 1810, 1811, 1813, 1816.

POLITICS

20592 BURDETT, Sir F., *Bart.* Eleventh edition. Sir Francis Burdett's address to the Prince Regent; as proposed in the House of Commons...on the 7th of Jan. 1812. To which is prefixed the speech upon that occasion; and to which is subjoined the speech of Lord Cochrane, who seconded the motion. 19p. *8°.* 1812.

20593 CARTWRIGHT, J. Six letters to the Marquis of Tavistock, on a reform of the Commons House of Parliament, discussing the best mode of uniting policy with principle. 44p. *8°.* 1812.

20594 EATON, D. I. Trial of Mr. Daniel Isaac Eaton, for publishing the third and last part of Paine's Age of reason; before Lord Ellenborough, in the Court of King's Bench, Guildhall, March 6, 1812; containing the whole of his defence, and Mr. Prince Smith's speech in mitigation of punishment. 80p. *8°.* 1812.

20595 GRENVILLE, W. W., *Baron Grenville.* A letter to the Earl of Fingal, on the claims of the Roman Catholics...A new edition, corrected. 18p. *8°.* 1812. *For another edition, see* 1810.

20596 Behold the MAN! [A handbill protesting at the trial and imprisonment of Daniel Isaac Eaton for publishing the third part of Paine's *Age of reason.*] *s.sh.8°.* D. I. Eaton, [*London*, 1812] [*Br.* 477]

20597 MARGAROT, M. Proposal for a grand national jubilee; restoring to every man his own, and thereby extinguishing both want and war. [With an appendix.] 51, 4p. *8°. Sheffield*, [1812?]

20598 —— Thoughts on revolutions. 42p. *8°. Harlow & London*, 1812.

20599 [MEADLEY, G. W.] A sketch of the various proposals for a constitutional reform in the representation of the people, introduced into the Parliament of Great Britain from 1770 to 1812. 16p. *8°.* 1812.

20600 A REFUTATION of the statement of the penal laws which aggrieve the Catholics of Ireland. Chapter I. Second edition. 87p. *8°. Dublin*, 1812.

20601 [Begin.**]** Relying on **SPEECHES** that never were spoken...[An acrostic on the name of Robert Peel.] *s.sh.8° Warwick*, [1812?] *See note to no.* 20490.

20602 UNION FOR PARLIAMENTARY RE-FORM ACCORDING TO THE CONSTITU-TION. An appeal to the nation by the Union for Parliamentary Reform... 75p. *8°.* 1812.

20603 —— Institution and early proceedings of the Union...[An account of the inaugural meeting, 10 June, 1812.] 7p. *8°.* 1812.

20604 WALKER, C. H. An independent address to the electors of Bristol, upon the state of the representation of the people, with free remarks upon the present candidates, Sir Samuel Romilly, Richard Hart Davis, Esq., Edw. Protheroe, Esq., Henry Hunt. To which is subjoined the...debate...on the motion of Mr. Madocks for an inquiry into the sale of seats by the Treasury. 33p. *8°. Bristol*, [1812]

20605 WELLESLEY, R. C., *Marquis Wellesley.* The substance of the speech of the Marquis Wellesley, on the 31st January, 1812...on the motion of Earl Fitzwilliam, respecting the present state of Ireland. 34p. *8°.* 1812.

SOCIALISM

20606 SPENCE, T. Spence's songs. 12, [8], [4]p. *8°.* [1812?] *For another edition, see* 1802.

MISCELLANEOUS

20607 ENSOR, G. Defects of the English laws and tribunals. 507p. *8°.* 1812.

20608 *LONDON. Livery Companies. *Salters.* A list of the Master, Wardens, Court of Assistants, and Livery, of the Worshipful Company of Salters. 14p. *8°.* 1812. *See also* 1784, 1787, 1790, 1792, 1794, 1797, 1799, 1801, 1803, 1806, 1809, 1815, 1818, 1821, 1824, 1827, 1830.

20609 MANDERSON, J. Twelve letters, addressed to the Right Honourable Spencer Perceval. Wherein a view is taken of the present magnitude of the British Navy ...Also, of the policy of the measures about to be adopted for the supplying of the evident defects in the present anchorages and royal dock-yards. 150p. *8°.* 1812.

20610 [ROMILLY, Sir S.] Objections to the project of creating a Vice Chancellor of England. 18p. *8°.* 1812.

20611 SEYER, S., *ed.* The charters and letters patent, granted by the kings and queens of England to the town and city of Bristol. Newly translated, and accompanied by the original Latin. 317p. *4°. Bristol & London*, 1812.

20612 WALKER, JOHN (1768–1833). An essay on the following prize-question, proposed by the Royal Irish Academy, "Whether and how far the cultivation of science and that of polite literature assist or obstruct each other?". 38p. *8°. Dublin*, 1812. *The Agar Ellis copy.*

20613 WYVILL, C. Papers on toleration...The fourth edition. 207p. *8°.* 1812.

1813

GENERAL

20614 The **BANKERS'** and merchants' almanack for 1814: to be continued annually. 243[280]p. *12°*. [1813]

20615 BOAZ, J. General report of Scotland. Chap. XVI. Sect. 4. on the manufactures, navigation, commerce, fisheries, and banking establishments of Scotland... Drawn up for the consideration of the Board of Agriculture and Internal Improvement. [With an appendix.] 286, 23p. *8°. Edinburgh*, 1813.

20616 BRAMWELL, G. An analytical table of the private statutes, passed between the 1st Geo. II. A.D.1727, and 52d Geo. III. A.D.1812 [and between the 53d Geo. III. A.D.1813, and 4th & 5th Will. IV. A.D.1834]... 2 vols. *8°.* 1813–35. *Presentation copy, with inscription, from the compiler to Wm. Tidd, Esq.*

20617 CAMPBELL, HECTOR. The impending ruin of the British Empire; its cause and remedy considered. 96p. *8°.* 1813.

20618 DAGEVILLE, G. J. De la propriété politique et civile. 420p. *8°. Paris*, 1813. [*Binding 62*] *The copy bound for C. F. Lebrun, Duc de Plaisance (1739–1824).*

20619 EDWARDS, GEORGE. Select general associations, and subassociations, proposed throughout the Kingdom... for introducing and co-operating with Government to carry into effect... the important discovery... of the original scheme and millenium of true policy. 2p. *s.sh.fol. B[arnar]d. Castle*, [1813 ?] [*Br.* 673(2)]

20620 EUSTAPHIEVE, A. The resources of Russia, in the event of a war with France; and an examination of the prevailing opinion relative to the political and military conduct of the Court of St. Petersburgh: with a short description of the Cozaks... Third edition. 52p. *8°.* 1813. *For another edition, see* 1812.

20621 GAMBLE, J. A view of society and manners, in the north of Ireland, in the summer and autumn of 1812. 399p. *8°. London, Edinburgh, &c.*, 1813.

20622 GRIMM, F. M. VON, *Freiherr.* Correspondance littéraire, philosophique et critique, adressée à un souverain d'Allemagne, depuis 1753 jusqu'en 1769 [–1790], par le Baron de Grimm et par Diderot... [With 'Supplément ...Contenant, 1°. les Opuscules de Grimm...3°. plusieurs morceaux de la Correspondance de Grimm, qui manquent aux 16 volumes; 4°. des Remarques sur les 16 volumes, par Ant.-Alex. Barbier...'.] 17 vols. *8°. Paris*, 1813, 1812–14. *The first part was edited by J. F. Michaud and F. Chéron, the second part, 1812 (of the second edition in this set) by J. B. Salgues and the third part by J. B. A. Suard.*

20623 HIGHLAND AND AGRICULTURAL SOCIETY OF SCOTLAND. Report on weights & measures. By a committee of the Highland Society of Scotland, and of gentlemen from the different counties of Scotland, and from the convention of Royal Burghs. 76p. *8°. Edinburgh*, 1813. *For another edition, see* 1812.

20624 HORSLEY, S., *Bishop of St. Asaph.* The speeches in Parliament of Samuel Horsley...[Edited by J. Horsley.] 544p. *8°. Dundee, London, &c.*, 1813.

20625 KINNEIR, J. M. A geographical memoir of the Persian Empire... 486p. *4°.* 1813.

20626 LETTER from —— —— to his friend in London, on the present state of public affairs, recommended to the serious consideration of every man of property in Great Britain and Ireland. [Recording a discussion with Patrick Miller of Dalswinton on fiorin grass and naval ordnance.] 45p. *8°. Dumfries*, 1813.

20627 [LOWELL, J.] Perpetual war, the policy of Mr. Madison. Being a candid examination of his late message to Congress, so far as respects the following topicks; viz. the pretended negotiations for peace; the important and interesting subject of a conscript militia...By a New-England farmer, author of..."Mr. Madison's war". 120p. *8°.* 1813.

20628 [——] The road to peace, commerce, wealth and happiness. By an old farmer. [On the war between the United States and Great Britain.] 18p. *8°. n.p.* [1813]

20629 MILBURN, W. Oriental commerce; containing a geographical description of the principal places in the East Indies, China, and Japan, with their produce, manufactures and trade...Also the rise and progress of the trade of the...European nations with the Eastern World, particularly that of the English East India Company... 2 vols. *4°.* 1813. *The copy bound for Eleanor Agnes, wife of the 4th Earl of Buckinghamshire (1777–1851), with her book-plate. See also* 1825.

For the **PAMPHLETEER,** *1813–28, see vol. III, Periodicals list.*

20630 PEARCE, THOMAS, *vestry clerk.* The history and directory of Walsall, containing its antiquities, and a modern survey of its improvements...and an enumeration of its local and commercial advantages... 234p. *8°. Birmingham & Walsall*, 1813.

20631 PLAYFAIR, W. Outlines of a plan for a new and solid balance of power in Europe...shewing the extent, population, forces... 64p. *8°.* [*London*,] 1813.

20632 The **POST-OFFICE** annual directory for 1813...By Critchett & Woods. The fourteenth edition. [With 'A new guide to stage coaches, waggons, carts, vessels, &c. for 1813. The eleventh edition. By Critchett & Woods'.] 417, 139p. *12°.* [1813] *See also* 1805, 1810, 1814, 1820 (Post Office London directory), 1823, 1825, 1830, 1832, 1834, 1836, 1841.

20633 On the past **RELATIONS** between Great Britain and the United States. [Extracted from No. 4 of the *New Quarterly Review and British Colonial Register.*] 59p. *8°.* 1813. *The caption reads: A review of the past relations...*

20634 [SCHLEGEL, A. W. VON.] Ueber das Continentalsystem und den Einfluss desselben auf Schweden. Von A. W. S. 109p. *8°. n.p.*, 1813.

20635 [——] Sur le système continental et sur ses rapports avec la Suède. 91p. *8°. Londres*, 1813.

20636 SCHWARTNER, M. VON. Statistique du royaume de Hongrie...Abrégée et traduite de l'allemand sur la seconde édition de Bude de 1809–1811 par N. Wacken... 3 vols. *8°. Francfort sur le Mein*, 1813–16.

20637 [SLACK, A.] The instructor, or young man's best companion; containing spelling...Also merchants' accompts...likewise receipts for dying, colouring...the practical gauger made easy...By George Fisher, accomptant. The thirty-first edition, corrected and improved throughout. 303p. *12°. 1813. For another edition, see* 1810.

For **STAATSBLAD DER VEREENIGDE NEDERLANDEN**, 1813–15, *continued as* Staatsblad van het Koningrijk der Nederlanden, 1816–44, *see* vol. III, *Periodicals list.*

AGRICULTURE

20638 **BAILEY,** JOHN. General view of the agriculture of the county of Durham; with observations on the means of its improvement. Drawn up for the consideration of the Board of Agriculture... 412p. *8°. London, Durham, &c.,* 1813. *A reissue of the edition of* 1810 (*q.v.*).

20639 —— and **CULLEY,** G. General view of the agriculture of the county of Northumberland; with observations on the means of its improvement. Drawn up for the consideration of the Board of Agriculture... The third edition. [With 'General view of the agriculture of the county of Cumberland' by the same authors, and 'General view of the agriculture of the County of Westmoreland...By Mr. A. Pringle'.] 361p. *8°.* 1813. *A reissue of the edition of* 1805 (*q.v.*). *For other editions, see* 1794.

20640 **BOYS,** J. General view of the agriculture of the county of Kent; with observations on the means of its improvement. Drawn up for the consideration of the Board of Agriculture...from the original report...with additional remarks of several respectable country gentlemen and farmers. To which is added a treatise on paring and burning...The second edition, with amendments and additions. 293p. *8°.* 1813. *A reissue of the edition of* 1805 (*q.v.*). *For other editions, see* 1794.

20641 **COOKE,** L. Tables adapted to the use of farmers and graziers; calculated to ascertain the quantity of land which may be worked with agricultural implements of various dimensions, in a given space of time...also, tables for reducing measures...to the standard of the Winchester bushel: together, with tables shewing...the net profitable weight of cattle... 103p. *8°.* 1813.

20642 **DAVIS,** THOMAS. General view of the agriculture of Wiltshire. Drawn up for the consideration of the Board of Agriculture...[Prepared for the press, and with an introduction by the author's son.] 268p. *8°. London & Winchester,* 1813. *For another edition, see* 1794.

20643 **DAVY,** SIR H., *Bart.* Elements of agricultural chemistry, in a course of lectures for the Board of Agriculture. [With 'Appendix. An account of the results of experiments on the produce and nutritive qualities of different grasses, and other plants, used as the food of animals. Instituted by John, Duke of Bedford'. By G. Sinclair. Edited by Sir H. Davy.] 323, lxiiip. *4°. London & Edinburgh,* 1813. *See also* 1814, 1819, 1821.

20644 **DICKSON,** R. W. The farmer's companion; being a complete system of modern husbandry...Second edition... 2 vols. *8°.* 1813. *An abridged edition of* Practical agriculture, *1805* (*q.v.*).

20645 **DUNCUMB,** J. General view of the agriculture of the county of Hereford. Drawn up for the consideration of the Board of Agriculture... 173p. *8°. London & Hereford,* 1813. *A reissue of the edition of* 1805 (*q.v.*).

20646 **ENGLAND.** *Laws, etc.* An Act for dividing and inclosing certain tracts or parcels of moor, common, or waste grounds within, and parcel of the manor of East Teignmouth, in the county of Devon. 53 Geo. III. 1812–13. 17p. *fol.* [1813]

20647 **GABIOU,** J. F. Quelques aperçus d'exploitation et d'économie rurale. 35p. *8°. Paris,* 1813.

20648 **GOOCH,** W. General view of the agriculture of the county of Cambridge. Drawn up for the consideration of the Board of Agriculture... 303p. *8°. London & Cambridge,* 1813.

20649 **GREG,** T. A system for managing heavy and wet lands without summer fallows; under which a considerable farm in Hertfordshire is kept perfectly clean, and made productive...Third edition. With an appendix, pointing out how the infant turnip may be protected from insects by a critical application of lime... 76p. *8°.* 1813.

20650 **HEADRICK,** J. General view of the agriculture of the county of Angus, or Forfarshire; with observations on the means of its improvement: drawn up for the consideration of the Board of Agriculture... 590, 120p. *8°. Edinburgh & London,* 1813.

20651 **KENT,** N. General view of the agriculture of the county of Norfolk; with observations on the means of its improvement. Drawn up for the consideration of the Board of Agriculture...with additional remarks of several respectable gentlemen and farmers. 236p. *8°.* 1813. *A reissue of the edition of* 1796 (*q.v.*). *For another edition, see* 1794.

20652 **KERR,** ROBERT. General view of the agriculture of the county of Berwick; with observations on the means of its improvement. Drawn up for the consideration of the Board of Agriculture...and brought down to the end of 1808. 504, 73p. *8°. London & Edinburgh,* 1813.

20653 **LESLIE,** W. General view of the agriculture of the counties of Nairn and Moray; with observations on the means of their improvement. Drawn up for the consideration of the Board of Agriculture... 536p. *8°. London, Edinburgh, &c.,* 1813. *A reissue of the edition of* 1811 (*q.v.*).

20654 **LOWE,** R. General view of the agriculture of the county of Nottingham; with observations on the means of its improvement. Drawn up for the consideration of the Board of Agriculture... 192p. *8°.* 1813. *A reissue of the edition of* 1798 (*q.v.*). *For another edition, see* 1794.

20655 **MacKENZIE,** SIR GEORGE S., *Bart.* General view of the agriculture of the counties of Ross and Cromarty. Drawn up for the consideration of the Board of Agriculture... 353p. *8°. London, Edinburgh, &c.,* 1813. *A reissue of the edition of* 1810 (*q.v.*).

20656 **MAVOR,** W. General view of the agriculture of Berkshire. Drawn up for the consideration of the Board of Agriculture... 548p. *8°. London, Abingdon, &c.,* 1813. *A reissue of the edition of* 1809 (*q.v.*).

20657 MERINO SOCIETY. The third report of the Merino Society... 146p. *8°. 1813. See also* 1811, 1812.

20658 MIDDLETON, JOHN. General view of the agriculture of Middlesex; with observations on the means of its improvement, and several essays on agriculture in general. Drawn up for the consideration of the Board of Agriculture...Accompanied with remarks of several respectable gentlemen and farmers. Second edition. [With 'Addition to the introductory address'.] 704p. *8°. 1813. The 'Addition to the introductory address' was originally intended to be part of the preliminary matter of the second edition, 1807, but was suppressed by the Board of Agriculture. The author had this half-sheet, paginated 11–14, printed for insertion in the appropriate place in copies of this edition. The present copy of the 'Addition' belonged to Lord Sheffield. For another edition of the whole work, see* 1798.

20659 PARKINSON, RICHARD (1748–1815). General view of the agriculture of the county of Huntingdon. Drawn up for the consideration of the Board of Agriculture... 351p. *8°. London, Huntingdon, &c.,* 1813. *A reissue of the edition of* 1811 *(q.v.).*

20660 [*Endorsed:*] June 1, 1813. **PARTICULARS** of Herstmonceux Estate, for sale, by private contract, with its hundred, manors, and residence. 3p. *fol. Lewes,* [1813] *The Sheffield copy.*

20661 [*Endorsed:*] **PARTICULARS** of the Herstmonceux estate, in...Sussex. Claridge and Iveson, Pallmall, London. [Details of Rockland Farm, Wartling.] *s.sh.fol. n.p.* [1813?] *Caption title: Rockland Farm, in the parish of Wartling. The Sheffield copy, addressed in manuscript to 'Col. H. Baillie, Bristol'.*

20662 PITT, WILLIAM (1749–1823). General view of the agriculture of the county of Stafford; with observations on the means of its improvement. Drawn up for the consideration of the Board of Agriculture...With the additional remarks of...gentlemen and farmers in the county. The second edition. 327p. *8°. London, Wolverhampton, &c.,* 1813. *A reissue of the edition of* 1808 *(q.v.). For other editions, see* 1794.

20663 PLYMLEY, J. General view of the agriculture of Shropshire; with observations on the means of its improvement. Drawn up for the consideration of the Board of Agriculture... 366p. *8°.* 1813. *A reissue of the edition of* 1803 *(q.v.).*

20664 PRIEST, ST. J. General view of the agriculture of Buckinghamshire. Drawn up for the consideration of the Board of Agriculture...With an appendix, containing extracts from a survey of the same county, delivered to the Board by Mr. Parkinson. 412p. *8°. London, Buckingham, &c.,* 1813. *A reissue of the edition of* 1810 *(q.v.).*

20665 PRINCE, J. H. Remarks on the best method of barring dower, and curtesy, with an appendix of select precedents of limitations to prevent dower, &c....Third edition, with great additions. 8, 31p. *8°.* 1813.

20666 RICHARDSON, WILLIAM (1740–1820). A new essay on fiorin grass, including the history of its discovery, and an account of its valuable qualities, and mode of culture...With an appendix, containing some recent experiments, and observations by the editor. 91p. *8°.* 1813. *The copy that belonged to Patrick Colquhoun.*

20667 ROBERTSON, JAMES. General view of the agriculture in the county of Perth: with observations on the means of its improvement...Drawn up for the consideration of the Board of Agriculture...Second edition... 566p. *8°. Perth & London,* 1813. *For other editions, see* 1794.

20668 RUDGE, T. General view of the agriculture of the county of Gloucester. Drawn up for the consideration of the Board of Agriculture... 408p. *8°. London, Gloucester, &c.,* 1813. *A reissue of the edition of* 1807 *(q.v.).*

20669 SCHULTES, H. A dissertation on the public fisheries of Great Britain; explaining the rise, progress, and art of the Dutch fishery; and shewing...that the establishment of a national fishery on similar principles will...augment the wealth of the nation... 101p. *8°.* 1813.

20670 SINCLAIR, GEORGE (1786–1834). An account of the results of experiments on the produce and nutritive qualities of different grasses, and other plants, used as the food of animals. Instituted by John Duke of Bedford. [Edited by Sir H. Davy.] 63p. *4°.* 1813. *The copy presented to the Earl of Sheffield by the Duke of Bedford, with an accompanying letter. For the letter, see* vol. III, A.L. 144. *See also* 1825 *(Hortus gramineus Woburnensis).*

20671 SINCLAIR, SIR JOHN, *Bart.* An account of the systems of husbandry adopted in the more improved districts of Scotland...Drawn up for the consideration of the Board of Agriculture...The second edition... 2 vols. *8°. Edinburgh, London, &c.,* 1813. *For other editions, see* 1812.

20672 —— Address to the Board of Agriculture, on... the 9th of March, 1813; detailing the advantages, of making extensive enquiries, the basis of condensed information. 14p. *4°.* [*London,* 1813] *The Sheffield copy.*

20673 —— Some particulars regarding the origin and progress of a work, entitled, An account of the husbandry of Scotland...With extracts from the letters of... correspondents, approving of that work...Together with an appendix, containing some communications and papers, regarding Sir John Sinclair's other publications. 28, 48p. *8°. Edinburgh,* 1813.

20674 STEVENSON, W. General view of the agriculture of the county of Surrey. Drawn up for the consideration of the Board of Agriculture... 616p. *8°. London, Guildford, &c.,* 1813.

20675 YOUNG, ARTHUR (1741–1820). General view of the agriculture of Hertfordshire, drawn up for the consideration of the Board of Agriculture...By the secretary of the Board. 236p. *8°.* 1813. *A reissue of the edition of* 1804 *(q.v.).*

20676 —— General view of the agriculture of Oxfordshire. Drawn up for the consideration of the Board of Agriculture...By the secretary of the Board. 362p. *8°. London, Oxford, &c.,* 1813. *A reissue of the edition of* 1809 *(q.v.).*

20677 YOUNG, ARTHUR (1769–1827). General view of the agriculture of the county of Sussex. Drawn up for the consideration of the Board of Agriculture... 471p. *8°. London, Brighton, &c.,* 1813. *A reissue of the edition of* 1808 *(q.v.). For other editions, see* 1793.

TRADES & MANUFACTURES

20678 ADDRESS, from the Committee of practical clock and watch makers, to all the practical artisans in every branch of the art. [Signed: Samuel Joyce, chairman. Enumerating the evils which have led to the decay of the trade: smuggling of cheap foreign wares and laxity in the enforcement of apprenticeship laws.] 3p. *fol.* [1813?] *See note to no.* 13563.

20679 CULVERHOUSE, C. An arrangement of the bread laws, relating to bakers out of the City of London, and beyond ten miles of the Royal-Exchange...with an historical introduction and some curious specimens of the ancient bread laws. 160p. *8°. Bath & London,* 1813. *See also* 1819.

20680 HUMPHREYS, T. The Irish builder's guide, exhibiting the valuation of buildings throughout Ireland; with reference to the rise and fall of materials and workmens' wages... 349p. *12°. Dublin,* 1813.

20681 LONDON. Livery Companies. *Goldsmiths.* Goldsmiths' Hall, London, January 5, 1813. [A notice warning watchmakers and case makers that component parts of gold or silver watch cases, and the pendants and bows to go with them, must all conform to the prescribed standards. Signed: Thomas Lane, Clerk to the Company.] *s.sh.fol.* [1813] *See note to no.* 13563.

20682 —— [Another edition.] Goldsmiths' Hall, London, January 16, 1813. *s.sh.fol.* [1813] *There is an alteration in the regulations governing the marking of pendants and bows in this edition. See note to no.* 13563. *For other editions, see* 1812.

20683 REES, J. F. The art and mystery of a cordwainer; or, an essay on the principles and practice of boot and shoe-making. With...copper-plates. 140p. *12°.* 1813.

20684 SVEDENSTIERNA, E. T. Några underrättelser om engelska jernhandteringen. 397p. *8°. Stockholm,* 1813.

COMMERCE

20685 AMERICAN COTTON WOOL. An appeal to the public, on the admission of cotton wool from the United States into Great Britain, by the joint committees of the shipping interest, and of the West India, East India, Brazil and Portugal trade. [Dated: 9th April 1813.] 3p. *fol.* [1813]

20686 The **ANTIQUITY,** honor and dignity of trade, particularly as connected with the City of London; written by a Peer of England...[From a manuscript belonging to the Sidney family, of Penshurst.] 65p. *8°. Westminster,* 1813.

20687 ATTWOOD, T. Speech of Thomas Attwood, Esq. at the town's meeting, against the renewal of the East India charter, held...in Birmingham, on...January 8, 1813... 12p. *4°. Birmingham,* [1813]

20688 —— [Another issue.] 12p. *4°. Birmingham,* [1813] *A corrected version of the final sentence, on a printed slip, has been pasted over the original text. See note to no.* 20490 *for both issues.*

20689 BATH SOCIETY FOR THE PROTECTION OF FAIR AND REGULAR TRADE. [A circular lithographed letter, signed: Thos. Harvey, secretary, and dated, 24th March, 1813, to accompany the petition against irregular auctions.] *s.sh.fol. Bath,* [1813] *For the petition, see no.* 20711. *See also note to no.* 13563.

20690 COMMON SENSE, *pseud.* Third edition. Free trade with India. An enquiry into the true state of the question at issue between His Majesty's ministers...the East India Company, and the public at large, on the justice and policy of a free trade to India. 23p. *8°.* 1813. *The copy that belonged to David Ricardo.*

20691 A short **CONVERSATION** on the present crisis of the important trade with the East Indies. 32p. *8°.* 1813.

20692 COSSIM, *pseud.* Considerations on the danger and impolicy of laying open the trade with India and China; including an examination of the objections commonly urged against the East India Company's commercial and financial management. [The substance of a series of letters which appeared in the Morning Chronicle ...under the signature of Cossim.] Second edition. 237p. *8°.* 1813. *The Sheffield copy.*

20693 —— Third edition. 237p. *8°.* 1813. *For another edition, see* 1812.

20694 DUNDAS, H., *Viscount Melville.* Letters from the Right Hon. Henry Dundas to the Chairman of the Court of Directors of the East-India Company, upon an open trade to India. 47p. *8°.* 1813.

20695 —— Opinions of the late Lord Melville and Marquis Wellesley upon an open trade to India. 18p. *8°.* 1813.

20696 EAST INDIA COMPANY. Debates held on the 19th, 22d, and 26th January, 1813, at the several adjoined courts of East-India proprietors with an appendix, &c. By an impartial reporter. [The 'Advertisement' is signed: J. R.] 354p. *8°.* 1813.

20697 —— East-India question. Substance of a report submitted to the Court of Proprietors by the Committee of Correspondence, containing observations on the petitions to Parliament from the outports against the East-India Company's exclusive privileges. 39p. *8°.* 1813. *The Sheffield copy.*

20698 —— Resolutions of the General Court of Proprietors of East-India stock, relative to an application to Parliament for a renewal of their exclusive privileges. 18p. *8°.* 1813. *The Sheffield copy.*

20699 EDINGTON, R. A treatise on the coal trade; with strictures on its abuses, and hints for amelioration. 261p. *8°.* 1813. *See also* 1817.

20700 FABIUS, *pseud.* A letter to the Right Honorable the Earl of Buckinghamshire...on the subject of an open trade to India. 91p. *8°.* 1813. *The Sheffield copy.*

20701 GLADSTONE, Sir J., *Bart.* Letters addressed to the Right Honourable the Earl of Clancarty...

on the inexpediency of permitting the importation of cotton wool from the United States, during the present war. 35p. 8°. 1813.

20702 GLASGOW COMMITTEE OF THE SUBSCRIBERS FOR THE OBJECT OF OBTAINING A FREE TRADE TO INDIA AND CHINA. Report of the Glasgow Committee...29th October, 1813. 27p. 8°. Glasgow, 1813.

20703 HOLROYD, J. B., Earl of Sheffield. On the trade in wool and woollens, including an exposition of the commercial situation of the British Empire. Extracted from the reports addressed to the Wool-Meetings at Lewes...1809, 1810, 1811, and 1812, by the President, John, Lord Sheffield. From the communications to the Board of Agriculture. 45p. 4°. 1813. The Sheffield copy.

20704 ——— [Another edition.] 87p. 8°. Dublin, 1813.

20705 LETTERS on the East India Company's monopoly. Second series. 104p. 8°. Glasgow, Edinburgh, &c., 1813.

20706 LEVANT COMPANY. By-laws of the Levant Company. 1812. 46p. 8°. 1813. 'The oath which is directed to be taken by every person who is admitted to the freedom of the Levant Company' is inserted.

20707 LYNE, C. A letter to the Right Honourable Lord Castlereagh...on the North American export-trade during the war, and during any time the import and use of our manufactures are interdicted in the United States. To which is added, the resolutions of the manufacturers, exporters of goods, and merchants, of the City of Glasgow. 46p. 8°. 1813.

20708 MACLEAN, C. A view of the consequences of laying open the trade to India, to private ships; with some remarks on the nature of the East India Company's rights to their territories, and the trade depending upon them; and on the conduct and issue of the late negociation for a renewal of their exclusive privileges...Second edition. 82p. 8°. 1813.

20709 MASSACHUSETTS. General Court. *House of Representatives.* Report of the Committee...on the subject of impressed seamen; with the evidence and documents accompanying it... 84p. 8°. Boston, 1813.

20710 MOUSLEY, J. To the market gardeners, landholders, and growers of fruits, flowers, roots and herbs, in...Middlesex, Essex, Kent & Surry. Report of the proceedings in Parliament upon the late opposition to the Bill for the regulation of Covent Garden Market... 123p. 8°. 1813.

20711 To the honourable the Commons of the United Kingdom...in Parliament assembled. The **PETITION** of the traders and shopkeepers of the City of Bath. [Praying for legislative measures to restrain speculators from conducting frequent auctions of articles irregularly acquired, to the detriment of honest and resident traders.] 2p. 4°. Bath, [1813?] *Addressed with a covering letter (see no. 20689) to Paul Barraud, a leading member of the Clockmakers' Company of London, by Rob[ert] Waithman. See note to no. 13563.*

20712 PRINCE'S LONDON PRICE CURRENT...No. 1917. Friday, the 1st of January, [—No. 1969. Friday, the 31st December,] 1813. 52 nos. *fol.* [1813] *See also* 1812, 1814, 1815, 1817, 1818, 1820.

20713 [PUGH, E.] The East-India question fairly elucidated, by considerations on the expediency and wisdom of allowing the out-ports to infringe upon the rights and privileges of the charter, purchased...by the East-India Company...By D. Hughson. 71p. 8°. 1813.

20714 STEEL'S original and correct list of the Royal Navy, and Hon. East India Company's shipping...June 1, 1813. 90p. *12°.* [1813]

20715 TYSON, JAMES. A brief historical view of the causes of the decline of the commerce of nations. 80p. 8°. 1813.

20716 VERAX, *pseud.* East-India question. Four letters respecting the claims of the East-India Company for a renewal of their exclusive privileges. 30p. 8°. 1813.

COLONIES

20717 BUCHANAN, C. Colonial ecclesiastical establishment: being a brief view of the state of the colonies of Great Britain, and of her Asiatic empire, in respect to religious instruction: prefaced by some considerations on the national duty of affording it. To which is added, a sketch of an ecclesiastical establishment for British India... 199p. 8°. 1813.

20718 CIVIS, *pseud.* Letters of Civis upon the India question. 49p. 8°. 1813.

20719 CONSIDERATIONS on colonial policy, with relation to the renewal of the East India Company's charter. By an impartial observer. 92p. 8°. 1813. *The Sheffield copy.*

20720 ——— Second edition. 92p. 8°. 1813.

20721 EAST INDIA COMPANY. East-India question. A debate at a General Court of Proprietors of East-India stock, on Wednesday the 24th of March, 1813, for taking into consideration the propositions submitted by Lord Castlereagh to the...House of Commons. By the editor of the former debates. With an appendix. 172p. 8°. 1813. *The Sheffield copy.*

20722 ——— East-India question. Debates at the General Court of Proprietors...on the 22nd and 26th June, 1813, on a Bill pending in Parliament for a renewal of the Company's charter. By the editor of the former debates ... 316p. 8°. 1813.

20723 ——— A list of the names of the members of the United Company of Merchants of England, trading to the East-Indies, who stood qualified as voters on the Company's books, 13th April 1813. [With 'A list of the names of the Directors...for...1813'.] 97, [3]p. 8°. [London, 1813.] *The Sheffield copy. See also* 1690 (COMMERCE), 1708, 1773 (COLONIES), 1795, 1809.

20724 ——— The preliminary debate at the East-India House...5th January, 1813, on the negociation with His Majesty's ministers relative to a renewal of the charter; with an appendix containing all the letters and documents referred to upon the subject. By an impartial reporter. 65p. 8°. 1813.

20725 EAST INDIA QUESTION. A short abstract of the argument in support of the East-India Company's petition to Parliament, for a renewal of their charter. 15p. 8°. 1813. *The Sheffield copy.*

20726 ENGLAND. Parliament. *House of Commons.* Nos. I. to IV. [to Nos. IX. and X.] East-India question. Abstract of the minutes of evidence taken in the Hon. House of Commons before a Committee of the whole House to consider the affairs of the East India Company. By the editor of the East India debates. 138p. *8⁰*. 1813.

20727 GRANT, SIR R. The expediency maintained of continuing the system by which the trade and government of India are now regulated. 404p. *8⁰*. 1813.

20728 —— A sketch of the history of the East-India Company, from its first formation to the passing of the regulating Act of 1773; with a summary view of the changes which have taken place since that period in the internal administration of British India. 397p. *8⁰*. 1813.

20729 GRENVILLE, W. W., *Baron Grenville.* Substance of the speech of Lord Grenville, on the motion made by the Marquis Wellesley, in the House of Lords, on…the 9th of April, 1813, for the production of certain papers on Indian affairs. 71p. *8⁰*. [1813]

20730 —— [Another edition.] The speech of Lord Grenville, on the Marquis Wellesley's motion in the House of Lords, on…the 9th of April, 1813… 72p. *8⁰*. [1813]

20731 HUME, JOSEPH. The substance of the speech of Joseph Hume, Esq. delivered at an adjourned General Court of the Proprietors of East India stock, held in the India House, on the 19th of January, 1813, for the purpose of taking into consideration the papers and correspondence between the Court of Directors and His Majesty's ministers, for the renewal of the Company's charter. With an appendix…Second edition. 196p. *8⁰*. 1813.

20732 LETTERS which seem to deserve and require the most serious attention of the members of both Houses of Parliament, in the present stage of the India question. 15p. *8⁰*. 1813. *The Sheffield copy.*

20733 MACLEAN, C. Abstract of the East India question, illustrating in a concise manner the controversy between the East India Company and His Majesty's ministers. 22p. *8⁰*. 1813.

20734 —— Remarks on the evidence delivered before both Houses of Parliament, on the East-India Company's affairs. 16p. *8⁰*. 1813.

20735 MALTHUS, T. R. A letter to the Rt. Hon. Lord Grenville, occasioned by some observations of his lordship on the East India Company's establishment for the education of their civil servants. 38p. *8⁰*. 1813.

20736 MARSH, C. Substance of the speech of Charles Marsh Esq. in a Committee of the House of Commons, July the 1st, 1813…on the clause in the East-India Bill, "enacting further facilities to persons to go out to India for religious purposes." 64p. *8⁰*. 1813. *The Sheffield copy.*

20737 MARSHMAN, J. Advantages of Christianity in promoting the establishment and prosperity of the British government in India; containing remarks occasioned by reading a memoir on the Vellore mutiny. [Extracted from the periodical accounts of the Baptist Mission, no. XVIII. Written 1807. With an appendix.] 10p. *8⁰*. [*London,*] 1813.

20738 OBSERVATIONS on the territorial rights and commercial privileges of the East India Company, with a view to the renewal of the Company's charter; in a letter to a Member of Parliament. 83p. *8⁰*. 1813.

20739 O'HARA, P. A letter to a friend in Ireland, on India affairs. 24p. *8⁰*. 1813.

20740 PLUMMER, T. W. A letter to the Right Honourable the Earl of Buckinghamshire…on the renewal of the East-India Company's charter. [With an appendix.] 220, lxp. *8⁰*. 1813.

20741 PROBUS, *pseud.* Letters of Probus, on the East-India question. 39p. *8⁰*. 1813.

20742 REMARKS on the charter of the East India Company. 60p. *8⁰*. *Cambridge,* 1813.

20743 REMARKS on the propositions submitted by His Majesty's Ministers to Parliament, on the renewal of the East-India Company's charter…By an impartial observer. 24, 29p. *8⁰*. 1813.

20744 RIVAZ, F. F. A proposal, by which two essential objects would be simultaneously attained: firstly, the complete security of the British territories in India… secondly, a new, extensive, and profitable, channel of commerce opened…by a simple modification in the East-India Company's charter. 40p. *8⁰*. 1813.

20745 [**T., J.**] Hints on the present state of the question between His Majesty's ministers and the Court of Directors relative to the renewal of the East-India Company's Charter. 23p. *8⁰*. 1813. *The second edition, published in The Pamphleteer, vol. 2, no. 3, was signed 'J. T'. The Sheffield copy.*

20746 TWINING, RICHARD (1772–1857). Observations relative to the renewal of the East India Company's charter. 36p. *8⁰*. 1813. *The Sheffield copy.*

20747 Last **WARNING!** A letter from ——, to ——, on the India question, as it stood on the 3d of May, 1813; and its probable issue. Recommended to the consideration of both Houses of Parliament. 15p. *8⁰*. 1813.

20748 WEYLAND, J. Letter to Sir Hugh Inglis, Bart. …on the state of religion in India, with suggestions for its improvement. 16p. *8⁰*. *Windsor, London, &c.,* 1813. *The Sheffield copy.*

FINANCE

20749 *BAILY, F. The doctrine of life-annuities and assurances, analytically investigated and practically explained. Together with…tables connected with the subject. To which is now added an appendix, containing a new method of calculating…such tables. In two volumes… 621, 68p. *8⁰*. 1813. *The pagination is continuous throughout the two volumes. The copy that belonged to Augustus De Morgan, with manuscript notes by him and by the author. See also 1836, 1850.*

20750 BRIQUET DE LAVAUX, F. Traité des faillites. 315p. *12⁰*. *Paris,* 1813.

20751 BRITISH LINEN COMPANY. Proceedings in an application at the Treasury for an increase of capital by the British Linen Company. 174p. *8°*. 1813.

20752 CORRIE, E. Letters on the subject of the duties on beer, malt, and spirits. 27p. *8°*. *Liverpool & London*, 1813.

20753 FRANCE. *Ministère du Trésor Impérial*. Compte du Trésor de l'Empire pour l'année 1811, presenté à S.M. l'Empereur et Roi par son Ministre du Trésor. 82p. *4°*. *Paris*, 1813. *See also* 1811.

20754 GALTON, S. T. A chart, exhibiting the relation between the amount of Bank of England notes in circulation, the rate of foreign exchanges, and the prices of gold and silver bullion and of wheat; accompanied with explanatory observations. 32p. *8°*. *London & Birmingham*, 1813.

20755 GOODCHILD, CALVERT & LANDER. Scale of exchanges; shewing at one view, the comparative exchanges of the following places on London with each other ... Malta ... Lisbon ... Cadiz ... Gibraltar ... Sicily ... Smyrna ... Equated by Goodchild, Calvert & Lander of Malta 1813. [22]p. *8°*. *n.p.* [1813]

20756 HAMILTON, ROBERT (1743–1829). An inquiry concerning the rise and progress, the redemption and present state, and the management of the National Debt of Great Britain. 212p. *8°*. *Edinburgh, Glasgow, &c.*, 1813. *See also* 1814, 1817, 1818.

20757 HAUTENVILLE, H. B. A digest of the duties of customs, and excise, payable upon all foreign articles imported into or exported from Ireland ... Together with extracts from various statutes, also useful notes and observations ... 153p. *8°*. *Dublin*, 1813. *The copy that belonged to Sir Robert Peel. For another edition, see* 1811.

20758 HUSKISSON, W. Substance of the speech of W. Huskisson, Esq. in the House of Commons ... upon the resolutions proposed by the Chancellor of the Exchequer respecting the state of the finances and the Sinking Fund of Great Britain, on ... the 25th of March, 1813. 80p. *8°*. 1813.

20759 LEEKEY, G. The Stamp-Office list of country bankers, containing all the banking companies in England and Wales, who issue promissory notes payable on demand ... 88p. *8°*. 1813.

20760 LUYANDO, J. Examen de las ventajas que producira el desestanco del tabaco y ensayo de unica contribucion. 76p. *8°*. *Cadiz*, 1813.

20761 McSIMPLE, SAWNEY, *pseud*. A letter to the Bullion Committee by their sincere and humble servant, Sawney McSimple. 15p. *12°*. *Glasgow*, 1813.

20762 MAITLAND, JAMES, *8th Earl of Lauderdale*. Further considerations on the state of the currency; in which the means of restoring our circulation to a salutary state are fully explained, and the injuries sustained by the public treasury ... from our present pecuniary system, are minutely detailed. [With an appendix of tables.] 69, 39p. *8°*. *Edinburgh & London*, 1813.

20763 NARRATIVE respecting the various bills which have been framed for regulating the law of bankruptcy in Scotland; with observations ... and a supplement, in which is considered the Bill now pending in Parliament ... Recommended to the attention of the public by the Chamber of Commerce and Manufactures of Edinburgh. [With an extract from the minutes of the meeting of the Chamber of Commerce of 15 May, 1813.] 58, 15p. *8°*. *Edinburgh*, 1813.

20764 OBSERVATIONS on the evidence relating to the duties on leather, taken before the Committee of the House of Commons: ordered to be printed, 5th April, 1813: shewing the chief causes which have induced the trade to petition Parliament for relief. 38p. *8°*. 1813.

20765 April 15. 1813. To the Right Honourable the Lords Commissioners of His Majesty's Treasury. The humble **PETITION** of the subscribers—private bankers, partners, or managers, or cashiers of private banking companies, carrying on the business of issuing and re-issuing promissory notes ... in ... Scotland. [Signed: James Brand, for the Banking Company in Aberdeen, and 19 other representatives of private banking companies in Scotland.] 8p. *4°*. *n.p.* [1813]

20766 PHILANTHROPIC ANNUITY INSTITUTION. Philanthropic Annuity Institution, 109, Pall Mall, London. [An account of the objects of the Institution, and its terms of investment and insurance.] 22p. *8°*. [*London*, 1813 ?]

20767 POPE, C. A practical abridgment of the laws of the customs, relative to the import, export, and coasting trade, of Great Britain and her dependencies: including a statement of the duties, drawbacks, and bounties ... The whole interspersed with Orders in Council, and brought down to the 10th September 1813. [With a supplement.] 610, 130p. *8°*. 1813. *See also* 1818.

20768 PROPOSALS for reducing the price of silver, and for raising the value and diminishing the amount of our paper currency. 76p. *8°*. 1813.

20769 QUESTION to the receiver of taxes. [A poem.] *s.sh.4°*. *Warwick*, [1813] *See note to no.* 20490.

20770 SILVER, F. Letters to the Most Noble Charles, Duke of Norfolk ... on revenue. 19p. *8°*. 1813.

20771 SMITH, JOHN PRINCE (1774?–1822). The elements of the science of money, founded on principles of the law of nature. 496p. *8°*. 1813.

20772 SOCIETY FOR EQUITABLE ASSURANCES. A short account of the Society for Equitable Assurances on Lives and Survivorships, established by deed, inrolled in His Majesty's Court of King's Bench, at Westminster. 18, [2]p. *8°*. 1813. *For other editions, see* 1762.

20773 [VANSITTART, N., *Baron Bexley*.] Outlines of a plan of finance: proposed to be submitted to Parliament. 1813. 36p. *8°*. [1813] *The copy that belonged to David Ricardo, with some pages of additional tables from a later edition.*

20774 [——] [Another edition.] 54p. *8°*. [1813]

20775 [——] [Another edition.] 42p. *8°*. *J. Hatchard*, [1813]

20776 VIEW of the effect of the existing laws, imposing a tax on income, as applicable to tenants and occupiers of land in Scotland: and suggestion of a mode of relief. [With an appendix.] 24, xip. *8°*. *Edinburgh & London*, 1813.

TRANSPORT

20777　COVE, A. The second edition...of The tocsin sounded, or a libel extraordinary!...Being "A case submitted to Sir Samuel Romilly", with his opinion thereupon ...proving the...crimes of swindling, perfidy...and... ingratitude, &c....have...been transacted upon the person and property of Augustus Cove, by..."The Grand Junction Canal Company"...Demonstrating that the laws relative to ejectment, are...nullified...No. 1.... [With 'The tocsin sounded a second time!...No. 11'.] 85p. *8°. [London,]* 1813.

20778　DUMBELL, J. A letter to the Worshipful the Mayor of Liverpool, relative to a bridge at Runcorn, &c.&c. 27p. *8°.* [1813] *Presentation copy from the author to the Earl of Cholmondeley.*

20779　EDGEWORTH, R. L. An essay on the construction of roads and carriages. [With 'Appendixes, containing No. 1. Extract from an essay of Dr. Hook's.

11. The reports of the Committee'.] 202, 194p. *8°.* 1813. *See also* 1817, 1827.

20780　KENNET AND AVON CANAL NAVIGATION. Report of the Committee of Management to the Company of Proprietors of the Kennet and Avon Canal. [Signed: C. Dundas, chairman, and dated, July 20, 1813.] 2p. *fol. Marlborough,* [1813]. *See also* 1812, 1815, 1816, 1823, 1824, 1825, 1826, 1838.

For a **NEW GUIDE TO STAGE COACHES, WAGGONS**...&c. for 1813, *see no.* 20632.

20781　[VAYSSE DE VILLIERS, R. J. F.] Description routière et géographique de l'Empire français, divisé en quatre régions. 1ère partie.—Région du sud. Section 1ère—Sud-est. Par R.V.★★★, inspecteur des postes-relais... 6 vols. *8°. Paris,* 1813.

SOCIAL CONDITIONS

20782　ADDRESS from the Committee of Manufactures, on the Statute of Apprenticeship. 25th November 1813. [Signed: Charles Alsager and 9 other members of the sub-committee. Appealing for support by means of petitions to Parliament, for Mr. Sergeant Onslow's Bill to repeal part of the Statute 5 Eliz. cap. 4.] 6p. *fol. [London,* 1813] *See note to no.* 13563.

20783　[Begin.] By the **ADVICE** of several gentlemen, Freemen and Liverymen of the City of London...[A circular addressed to masters and others throughout the country, soliciting support for the work of a Committee to oppose Mr. Sergeant Onslow's intended Bill. Signed: Josiah Clinton, secretary, and dated, November 29th. 1813.] 2p. *4°.* [1813] *See note to no.* 13563.

20784　—— [Another edition. Dated: December 23d. 1813.] Circular. 2p. *4°.* [1813] *See note to no.* 13563.

20785　ALTERATIONS & amendments proposed to be made in the Statute of 5th Elizabeth, cap. 4. 4p. *fol.* [1813] *See note to no.* 13563.

20786　ASSOCIATION FOR THE RELIEF OF THE MANUFACTURING AND LABOURING POOR. Report of the Association, formed in London on the 3d day of May, 1812... 37p. *8°.* 1813. *See also* 1815, 1825.

20787　[BEAUMONT, G.] The beggar's complaint, against rack-rent landlords, corn factors, great farmers, monopolizers, paper money makers and war...Also, some observations on the conduct of the Luddites, in reference to the destruction of machinery, &c.&c. By one who pities the oppressed. The second edition greatly enlarged. 130p. *12°. Sheffield,* 1812[1813]

20788　BERNARD, SIR T., *Bart.* An account of a supply of fish, for the manufacturing poor; with observations. 23p. *8°. The Society for Bettering the Condition of the Poor,* 1813.

20789　BRYDGES, SIR S. E., *Bart.* Letters on the poor laws, shewing the necessity of bringing them back nearer to the simplicity of their ancient provisions, especially with regard to settlements, as well for the relief

of the rates, as for the comfort and moral character of the poor themselves. 65p. *8°.* 1813.

20790　CHAVANNES, D. A. Rapport de Mr. D. A. Chavannes à ses commettans sur l'Institut d'Éducation des Pauvres à Hofwyl. Suivi de l'acte pour la création d'une commission perpétuelle chargée de surveiller cet institut, et des observations de M. C.Pictet, sur les moyens que l'agriculture fournit à l'éducation... 64p. *8°. Paris & Genève,* 1813. *The copy that belonged to William Whewell with his signature and the date '1821' on the title-page, and the book-stamp of the Herschel Library.*

For the **CHEAP MAGAZINE,** 1813–14, *see vol.* III, *Periodicals list.*

20791　(CIRCULAR.) [Addressed to individual masters by the Committee of journeymen mechanics, handicraftsmen and artificers, soliciting advice and assistance in amending part of the Statute of Apprentices. Signed: P. Cunningham, secretary.] *s.sh.4°.* [1813] *The name of the secretary has been altered in manuscript to 'J. Clinton'. See note to no.* 13563.

20792　COMMITTEE...TO MAKE ENQUIRY INTO THE PROCESS PRACTISED BY MESSRS. DELAHOYDE AND LUCETT. Report [on the treatment of insane patients]. 20p. *8°.* [1813]

20793　DAY AND SUNDAY FREE SCHOOL, *Circus Street, Liverpool.* A few moral and devotional selections, together with an address to the congregation [on the work of the school], recited by the children of Circus Street Free School...27th June, 1813, on occasion of the anniversary sermon, preached by the Rev. Thomas Roberts, of Bristol. 12p. *12°. Liverpool: Free School, Circus Street,* [1813]

20794　—— Tenth annual report of the Day and Sunday Free School...(From July 1, 1812, to July 1, 1813.) [With 'List of annual subscribers', etc.] 20p. *8°. Liverpool: Printed at the Free-School,* [1813] *See also* 1811, 1812, 1814.

20795　EATON, D. I. Extortions and abuses of Newgate; exhibited in a memorial and explanation, presented to the Lord Mayor, &c.&c.&c. February 15, 1813... 24p. *8°*. [1813]

20796 ENGLAND. *Laws, etc.* An Act (passed 3d June 1813) for the better relief and employment of the poor, and for the enlargement of the burial grounds in the parish of Saint Leonard Shoreditch... 143p. *8°*. 1813.

20797 FISH ASSOCIATION. The first report of the Committee of the Fish Association for the Benefit of the Community, respecting the measures to be adopted for the supply of the Metropolis and its neighbourhood. 20p. *8°*. 1813.

20798 FREEMAN, J. A method of teaching adult persons to read...and which is likewise adapted to the circumstances of those uninstructed children whose opportunities of learning to read are very precarious... To which is added a table of the elementary sounds of the English language... 48p. *8°*. 1813.

20799 [*Begin.*] GENTLEMEN, The masters and journeymen mechanics, handicraftsmen, and artificers in England, have for a series of years past, laboured under great oppressions...[A circular letter, setting out the reasons for the demand for amendments, which would enforce apprenticeship, to the Statute 5 Eliz. cap. 4. Signed: P. Cunningham, secretary, by order of the Committee, and dated, June 18th, 1813.] 3p. *4°*. [*London*, 1813] *See note to no.* 13563.

20800 [*Begin.*] GENTLEMEN, The subjoined is the form of a petition intended to be presented to the House of Commons in the ensuing session...from every town throughout the United Kingdom. [Signed: P. Cunningham, sec., by order of the Committee. A statement of subscriptions received and expenditure to 23 August 1813 is enclosed.] 3, [2]p. *fol.* [1813] *See note to no.* 13563.

20801 GODALMING SUBSCRIPTION SCHOOL. Godalming Subscription School, on the Royal British plan, (established Dec. 17th, 1812) for the education of the children of the poor of Godalming and its vicinity, under the following regulations; revised and altered at a general meeting, June 14th, 1813. 8p. *8°*. *Guildford*, 1813.

20802 HOPE, THOMAS C. and TELFORD, T. Reports on the means of improving the supply of water for the city of Edinburgh, and on the quality of the different springs in the neighbourhood. 76p. *4°*. *Edinburgh*, 1813. *Inscribed in manuscript 'To Mr. Playfair with Mr. Allan's compliments'.*

20803 IREMONGER, F. Suggestions to the promoters of Dr. Bell's system of tuition; with an account of the Hampshire Society for the education of the poor... a general list of schools and the number of children now receiving instruction... 292p. *8°*. *Winchester & London*, 1813.

20804 The LADIES' companion for visiting the poor: consisting of familiar addresses, adapted to particular occasions. By the author of "Lucy Franklin". 92p. *12°*. 1813.

20805 LETTERS on the subject of the Lancashire riots, in the year 1812. [Letters from Colonel Fletcher and Dr. Robert Taylor, with an account of the riots at Bolton-le-Moors and elsewhere in January 1812.] 15p. *8°*. *Bolton*, [1813]

20806 LONDON, April 8th, 1813. [*Begin.*] We humbly request leave to submit to your consideration the following statement of our proceedings, with the causes that led to them... [A circular letter to Members of Parliament, setting out the reasons for the petition to be presented in favour of amending the Statute 5 Eliz. cap. 4., and soliciting their support. Signed: P. Cunningham, sec., by order of the Committee of Trades.] 2p. *4°*. [1813] *See note to no.* 13563.

20807 M'KIMMIE, W., *and others.* The trial and sentence of William M'Kimmie, Charles Christie, James Johnston and James Granger, weavers, in the High Court of Justiciary, Edinburgh, on Friday the 12th March, 1813, for illegal combination to obtain a rise of wages. *s.sh.fol. Glasgow*, [1813] [*Br.* 481]

20808 MAIBEN, JOHN, & CO. A statement of the advantages to be derived from the introduction of coal gas into factories and dwelling houses, as a substitute for the lights now in use; together with observations on the method of making and using it. 41p. *8°*. *Perth*, 1813.

20809 MUSEUM Tavern, October 29, 1813. [*Begin.*] At a select meeting of master manufacturers...[An account of the inaugural meeting and appointment of a Committee in support of Mr. Sergeant Onslow's Bill to repeal part of the Statute, 5 Eliz. cap. 4, with an invitation to a meeting on 11 November 1813. Signed: Alexander Galloway and 7 other committee members.] *s.sh.4°. n.p.* [1813] *See note to no.* 13563.

20810 OBJECTIONS to the repeal of so much of the Statute of 5th Elizabeth, cap. 4, as subjects to penalties persons who carry on or follow any trades without having served an apprenticeship of seven years thereto. 3p. *fol. n.p.* [1813] *See note to no.* 13563.

20811 PARKER, T. N. Plans, specifications, estimates, and remarks on cottages, drawn up at the request of the Oswestry Society, for bettering the condition...of the poor...And published by their direction. 23p. *8°*. *Oswestry, Shrewsbury, &c.*, 1813.

20812 On the PETITION of the tradesmen & artificers, presented to Parliament, on the 28th of April, 1813, with the substance of the proposed clauses, to amend the Statute 5th of Elizabeth, cap. 4, and the reasons assigned for the same. [With the text of the petition.] 7p. *fol.* [1813] *See note to no.* 13563.

20813 To the honourable the Commons of the United Kingdom...in Parliament assembled; the humble PETITION of the several persons whose names are hereunto subscribed, being masters and journeymen mechanics, artificers, and handicraftsmen...[Against the Bill sponsored by Mr. Sergeant Onslow, to repeal part of the Act 5 Eliz. cap. 4.] 2l. *fol.* [1813 ?] *See note to no.* 13563.

20814 PRUDENT MAN'S FRIEND SOCIETY. First report...1813. 7p. *8°. n.p.* [1813] *See also* 1814, 1815, 1816.

20815 RIGBY, E. Report of the Norwich pauper vaccination, from August 10, 1812, to August 10, 1813, &c. 14p. *8°*. *Norwich*, [1813].

20816 ROYAL LANCASTERIAN INSTITUTION FOR THE EDUCATION OF THE POOR. Report of the Finance Committee and Trustees of the...Institution...for the year 1812. 54p. *8°*. 1813. *The copy that belonged to David Ricardo.*

20817 SINCLAIR, SIR JOHN, *Bart.* An account of the Highland Society of London, from its establishment in May 1778, to the commencement of the year 1813... Drawn up at the desire of the Society. [With a list of members.] 83p. *8°. London, Edinburgh, &c.,* 1813. *Presentation copy, with inscription, from the author to the Earl of Fife.*

20818 SOCIETY FOR BETTERING THE CONDITION OF THE POOR, *Liverpool.* The second report of the Society...[With 'Appendix no. II. Rules...of the Liverpool Female Friendly Society' and 'Appendix no. III. The mechanics, servants, and labourers' fund'.] [10], 17, 19, 4p. *8°.* [*Liverpool,*] 1813. *'Appendix no. II' has a separate title-page dated 1811. See also* 1811.

20819 SOCIETY FOR BETTERING THE CONDITION OF THE POOR, *London.* Printed for distribution by the Society...and to be had gratis at Hatchard's, 190, Piccadilly. Medical cautions recommended by the physicians...of the Bath Hospital, to those who have received benefit by the use of the Bath waters, in cases where the poison of lead is concerned... [Dated: April 18, 1813.] *s.sh.fol. n.p.* [1813] [*Br. 480*]

20820 SOCIETY FOR BETTERING THE CONDITION OF THE POOR, *Oswestry.* The following caution to ale-house keepers...having been approved of and signed by the magistrates, is now pasted up in all the publick houses, in the Hundred of Oswestry. 3p. *8°.* [*Oswestry,*] 1813.

20821 —— Zekiel Jobson; or, the dangers of drunkenness, set forth by a fearful example. 7p. *8°. Oswestry,* [1813]

For **SOCIETY FOR PROMOTING THE EDUCATION OF THE POOR OF IRELAND,** *Dublin,* 1st–6th Reports 1813–1818, *continued as* Reports of the Committee to the annual meeting, 1827, 1831, 1834, 1836–37, 1840, *see* vol. III, *Periodicals list,* Report...

20822 SOCIETY FOR THE SUPPRESSION OF VAGRANTS, *Bath.* Report of the Bath Society, No. 6, Pierrepont-Place...With an account of the receipts and disbursements [and a list of subscribers] from Jan. 1,

1812, to Jan. 1, 1813... 38[40]p. *16°. Bath,* 1813. *See also* 1810, 1811, 1812, 1816.

20823 TOONE, W. The magistrate's manual: or, a summary of the duties and powers of a justice of the peace ...with extracts from adjudged cases...To which is added a...collection of precedents of summonses, warrants, convictions, &c. 486p. *8°.* 1813.

20824 To **TRADESMEN** and manufacturers. [An address of the Sub-Committee of Manufacturers for obtaining the repeal of the restraints on trade, including 'Copy of the circular of the journeymen' in favour of the retention of the Statute 5 Eliz. cap. 4 in its entirety. Signed: Charles Alsager and 9 members of the sub-committee, and dated, 14th December, 1813.] [2]p. *fol.* [1813] *See note to no.* 13563.

20825 TUKE, S. Description of the Retreat, an institution near York, for insane persons of the Society of Friends. Containing an account of its origin and progress, the modes of treatment, and a statement of cases... 227p. *8°. York, Bristol, &c.,* 1813.

20826 WEST LONDON LANCASTERIAN ASSOCIATION. Schools for all. Report of the first public meeting of the West London Lancasterian Association. 18p. *8°. n.p.* [1813]

20827 WESTMINSTER FREE SCHOOL. First report of the Westminster Free School, designed for instructing one thousand children; united to...the National Society for Promoting the Education of the Poor in the Principles of the Established Church...[With a list of subscribers.] 39p. *8°.* [1813] *See also* 1814, 1816.

20828 YORK, *County of.* Report of proceedings under Commissions of Oyer & Terminer and Gaol Delivery, for the County of York...from the 2d to the 12th of January, 1813. [The trials of the Luddite rioters.]...To which are subjoined two proclamations issued in consequence of the result of those proceedings. 215p. *8°.* [1813]

20829 —— Second edition. 215p. *8°.* [1813]

SLAVERY

20830 SAMO, S., *and others.* The trials of the slave traders, Samuel Samo, Joseph Peters, and William Tufft, tried in April and June, 1812, before the Hon. Robert Thorpe...With two letters on the slave trade, from a gentlemen resident at Sierra Leone... 56p. *8°.* 1813.

POLITICS

20831 An **APPEAL** to Protestant charity and English justice. 16p. *8°.* 1813.

20832 An **APPEAL** to the Protestants of Great Britain and Ireland, on the subject of the Roman Catholic question: first published in the papers of the Protestant Union, in reply to a late address by Charles Butler, Esq. 92p. *8°.* 1813.

20833 AUSTRIA. *Laws, etc.* Austrian declaration against France. Aug. 1813. Manifesto of His Majesty the Emperor of Austria, King of Hungary and Bohemia. 16p. *8°. Broxbourne,* [1813]

20834 BUTLER, C. An address to the Protestants of

Great Britain and Ireland...Second edition, with additions. 23p. *8°.* 1813.

20835 [*Begin.*] Those who have read Mr. **BUTLER'S** Address...and conceived it to speak the sense of the general body of Roman Catholics will do well to peruse the following extract from the Kilkenny Chronicle of Feb. 23, 1813... 3p. *8°.* [1813]

20836 The **CASE** stated upon the claims of the opposition to public confidence: with some preliminary observations upon the state of the press and public opinion, in the commencement of the year 1813. 112p. *8°.* 1813.

20837 CHANCERY injunction! Letters to Her Royal Highness Caroline, Princess of Wales, comprising the only true history of the celebrated book; disclosing a full account of an extraordinary prosecution, commenced against the author...through having a copy thereof in his possession...By the gentleman who was the object of the prosecution...The second edition. 143p. 8°. 1813.

20838 CLARKE, MARY A. A letter addressed to the Right Honourable William Fitzgerald [upon his personal conduct and character]... 63p. 8°. 1813.

20839 DETECTOR, *pseud.* A refutation of the second part of the book, entitled, A statement of the penal laws which aggrieve the Catholics of Ireland, with commentaries; in which the several falsehoods...are set forth; and the insolence...of the whole exposed, by Detector. 148p. 8°. *Dublin*, 1813.

20840 DILLON, SIR JOHN J. Cursory suggestions for the consideration of an approaching meeting of the British Catholics, in a letter to E. Jerningham, Esq. 36p. 8°. *Glasgow*, 1813.

20841 ENSOR, G. An answer to the speeches of Mr. Abbot, Sir John Nicholl, Mr. Banks, &c.&c. on the Catholic question, debated in the House of Commons, 24th May, 1813; with additional observations. 116p. 8°. *Dublin*, 1813.

20842 EVANS, SIR WILLIAM D. Letters on the legal disabilities of Roman Catholics and dissenters; and on the dangers apprehended from their removal. [With an appendix.] 218, 35p. 8°. 1813.

20843 Plain **FACTS** for plain folks, addressed to the good sense and other feelings of Englishmen, upon the proposed scheme for new modeling the constitution, and bringing royalty into disrepute. 64p. 8°. 1813.

20844 LE MESURIER, T. A counter address to the Protestants of Great Britain and Ireland; in answer to the Address of Charles Butler, Esq. 24p. 8°. *London & Oxford*, 1813.

20845 A **LETTER** to a member of Parliament, upon the subject of the Roman Catholic claims, from a clergyman of the Established Church. 29p. 8°. *Dublin*, 1813.

20846 A **LETTER** to His Royal Highness the Duke of Sussex, on the dinner of the self-mis-named Friends of Civil & Religious Liberty. By an Orange Man. 27p. 8°. 1813.

20847 MacDONNELL, E. Plain facts, demonstrating the injustice and inconsistency of anti-Catholic hostility, fairly illustrated in a letter to the Rev. J. Coates... chairman of the meeting of clergy, gentry, and inhabitants of Huddersfield, and its vicinity, who have resolved to petition Parliament against the Roman Catholic claims. 24p. 8°. *London, Huddersfield, &c.*, 1813.

20848 MAGEE, J. The trial of Mr. John Magee, for a libel on the Duke of Richmond, which took place in the Court of King's-Bench, Dublin on...July 26th and 27th, 1813. 74p. 8°. [1813]

For **PROTESTANT UNION**, *see vol. III, Periodicals list.*

20849 [**SCHLEGEL**, A. W. VON.] Bemerkungen über einen Artikel der Leipziger Zeitung vom 5ten October 1813. [With the text of the article, attacking the Crown Prince of Sweden.] 32p. 8°. *n.p.*, 1813.

20850 [——] Betrachtungen über die Politik der dänischen Regierung. Von A.W.S. 46p. 8°. *n.p.*, 1813.

20851 SOMERS, JOHN, *Earl Somers.* Reply to the Protestant letter of the Right Reverend the Bishop of Gloucester [concerning the Catholic question]. 148p. 8°. *London, Worcester, &c.*, 1813.

20852 STEPHENS, ALEXANDER. Memoirs of John Horne Tooke, interspersed with original documents... 2 vols. 8°. 1813.

20853 THORP, W. Catholic emancipation. The substance of a speech, intended to have been spoken at a meeting convened at the Guildhall...Bristol, December 23, 1812, for the purpose of taking into consideration the expediency of presenting a petition to Parliament against the claims of the Roman Catholics. 15p. 8°. 1813.

SOCIALISM

20854 OWEN, ROBERT. A new view of society: or, essays on the principle of the formation of the human character, and the application of the principle to practice ... 23, 39, 93, 61p. 8°. 1813–14. *Each essay has a separate title-page and pagination and its own dedication. The title-pages of the third and fourth essays (dated 1814) bear the words: Not published.*

20855 —— [Another edition.] 23, 39, 124p. 8°. 1813. *The first and second essays have separate title-pages and pagination. The third and fourth essays each have a half-title,* *but their pagination is continuous. There are a number of textual alterations in this edition of the third and fourth essays, most of which were adopted for the 1816 edition.*

20856 *—— [A proof copy of the first two essays, with the words 'A proof copy' printed on the half-title of the second, and in which the signatures and pagination are continuous throughout the two essays.] 64p. 8°. 1813. See also 1816, 1817, 1818, 1825, 1826, 1834 (Essays on the formation of the human character), 1837.

MISCELLANEOUS

20857 ALCHORNE, S. Catalogue of a portion of the valuable library of the late Stanesby Alchorne, Esq. of the Mint. Containing various rare books and first editions printed in the fifteenth century...To which are added the valuable duplicates of a nobleman. The whole will be sold by auction, on...22nd of May, by R. H. Evans... 21p. 8°. [*London*,] 1813. *Annotated in manuscript with prices and names of buyers.*

20858 BRITISH MUSEUM. Synopsis of the contents of the British Museum. [With an introductory statement on the rise and progress of the British Museum and on its existing constitution.] Sixth edition. xxxv, 100p. 8°. 1813.

20859 A short **DESCRIPTION** of Badajoz, and the surrounding country; with extracts from the London

Gazette: explanatory of the picture exhibiting in the Panorama [of H. A. Barker], Leicester Square, representing the siege in 1812... 12p., 1 plate. *8°. [London,]* 1813.

20860 LINDSAY, James. A sermon preached at the Meeting-House, Salters Hall, Cannon-Street, on the 8th of August, 1813, on the death of the Rev. Hugh Worthing-ton...With explanatory notes. 32p. *8°.* 1813. *The copy that belonged to David Ricardo.*

20861 SOMERSET, E., *2nd Marquis of Worcester.* A century of the names and scantlings of such inventions as at present I can call to mind to have tried and perfected ... 46p. *16°.* 1813. *For other editions, see 1746.*

1814

GENERAL

20862 ACCURSIO DAS NEVES, J. Variedades, sobre objectos relativos a's artes, commercio, e manufacturas, consideradas segundo os principios da economia politica. 2 vols. *4°. Lisboa,* 1814–17.

20863 *BARLOW, S. The history of Ireland, from the earliest period to the present time; embracing also a statistical and geographical account of that kingdom; forming together a complete view of its past and present state, under its political, civil, literary, and commercial relations... 2 vols. *8°. London & Dublin,* 1814.

20864 BEAUJOUR, L. A. F. de, *Baron.* Aperçu des États-Unis, au commencement du xixe. siècle, depuis 1800 jusqu'en 1810, avec des tables statistiques. 274p. *8°. Paris,* 1814.

20865 BIGNON, L. P. E., *Baron.* Exposé comparatif de l'état financier, militaire, politique et moral de la France et des principales puissances de l'Europe. 504p. *8°. Paris,* 1814.

20866 BIRKBECK, M. Notes on a journey through France, from Dieppe through Paris and Lyons, to the Pyrennees, and back through Toulouse, in...1814, describing the habits of the people, and the agriculture of the country. 115p. *8°.* 1814. *See also 1815.*

20867 CHATEAUBRIAND, F. R. de, *Vicomte.* De Buonaparte et des Bourbons, et de la nécessité de se rallier à nos princes légitimes pour le bonheur de la France et celui de l'Europe...Seconde édition, revue et corrigée. 86p. *8°. Londres,* 1814.

20868 COLQUHOUN, P. British Empire. [A prospectus of Colquhoun's *A treatise on the wealth, power, and resources, of the British Empire.*] 16p. *8°.* [1814]

20869 —— A treatise on the wealth, power, and resources, of the British Empire, in every quarter of the world, including the East Indies: the rise and progress of the Funding System explained...[With an appendix.] 451, 91p. *4°.* 1814. *See also 1815.*

20870 CONSIDERATIONS on the importation of foreign corn; arising out of the proceedings, at a meeting of the Heritors of Fifeshire, proposing to petition the Legislature for further restriction...Comprising a review of the usual arguments adopted by agriculturists, in support of this measure; shewing, that the present high price of every thing has been caused by the excessive increase of the rent of land, and a circulating taxation... Also, exhibiting the true cause of the rise in the price of gold and silver in Britain; and thereby shewing, that it is independent of the circulation of bank-notes. 115p. *8°.* 1814.

20871 CRAIG, John (*fl.* 1814–1821). Elements of political science. 3 vols. *8°. Edinburgh & London,* 1814.

20872 DAWSON, William (*fl.* 1805–1814). An inquiry into the causes of the general poverty and dependence of mankind; including a full investigation of the corn laws. [With 'Appendix. Report of the Committee of the Privy Council, &c.'.] 255, 75p. *8°. Edinburgh & London,* 1814.

20873 DUMBELL, J. A letter to His Royal Highness the Prince of Wales...[On weights and measures.] 26p. *8°.* [1814]

20874 *The EAST-INDIA register and directory, for 1814; corrected to the 8th September, 1814; containing...lists of the Company's servants...Together with lists of...mariners, &c. not in the service of the...Company and merchant vessels employed in the country trade. Compiled...by John Mathison & Alexander Way Mason ...Second edition. 476p. *12°. London, Dublin, &c.,* [1814] *For other editions, see 1804.*

20875 EDWARDS, George. Effectual means of relieving the exigencies & grievances of the times, or of introducing the new and happy era of mankind, at the same time consummating the private, local, and primary interests of the kingdom at large...20p. *8°.* 1814.

20876 —— A final address on the original scheme and millennium of true policy, national and individual, now rendered practicable & complete... 156p. *8°.* 1814.

20877 ENGLAND. *Parliament.* Papers presented to Parliament in 1813. 830, xxip. *8°.* [1814]

20878 —— —— *House of Commons.* Report on weights and measures. [An extract from the Report from the Select Committee on weights and measures, reprinted for circulation to local officials of the counties and burghs of Scotland.] 4p. *fol. n.p.* [1814] *Addressed in manuscript to the Clerk of Supply, County of Renfrew.*

20879 ENSOR, G. Observations on the present state of Ireland. 123p. *8°. Dublin,* 1814.

20880 [FAUVEAU, .] Réflexions sur les finances et le commerce. Par M. F***. 42p. *8°. Paris,* 1814.

20881 FLETCHER, William. A charge delivered to the Grand Jury of...Wexford, at the Summer Assizes, 1814. 48p. *8°.* 1814.

20882 HESS, J. L. von. On the value and utility of the freedom of the Hanse-towns...Translated from the German manuscript, by B. Crusen. 159p. *8°.* 1814.

20883 HOARE, Peter R. Tracts on our present money system, and national bankruptcy: comprising strictures on the price and trade of corn; with tables of the prices of wheat and butcher's meat, and of the quantities of corn imported. 24, 83, 76, 28, 111p. *8°*. 1814. *A reissue, with a general title-page, preface and other preliminary matter, of four works published by the author in 1810, 1811 and 1812.*

20884 KAUFFMAN, C. H. The dictionary of merchandize, and nomenclature in all languages, for the use of counting-houses, &c. Containing the history, places of growth, culture, use, and marks of excellency, of such natural productions as form articles of commerce; with their names in all European languages... Third edition, considerably enlarged and improved. 396p. *8°*. 1814. *For another edition, see 1805.*

20885 LEET, A. A directory to the market towns, villages, gentlemen's seats and other noted places in Ireland... To which is added a general index of persons names... together with lists of the post towns and present rates of postage throughout the Empire. Second edition... 394p. *8°. Dublin*, 1814.

20886 LEVIS, P. M. G. DE, *Duc.* L'Angleterre au commencement du dix-neuvième siècle. [Vol. 1.] 420p. *8°. Paris*, 1814.

20887 MASON, W. S. A statistical account, or parochial survey of Ireland, drawn up from the communications of the clergy... 2 vols. *8°. Dublin, London, &c.*, 1814–16.

20888 PLAÑA, A. Manifesto del vecindario, producciones, y cargas de Aragon, ántes del año 1808, y en el de 1813: con motivo del cargamento de contribucion directa, decretado por las Córtes generales y extraordinarias á dicha Provincia. 28p. *4°. Zaragoza*, 1814.

20889 The **POST-OFFICE** annual directory for 1814 ...By Critchett & Woods. The fifteenth edition. [With 'A new guide to stage coaches, waggons, carts, vessels, &c. for 1814...The twelfth edition. By Critchett & Woods'.] 426, 144p. *12°*. [1814] *See also* 1805, 1810, 1813, 1820 (Post Office London directory), 1823, 1825, 1830, 1832, 1834, 1836, 1841.

20890 SAMPSON, G. V. A memoir, explanatory of the chart and survey of the county of London-Derry, Ireland. 359p. *4°*. 1814.

20891 SAY, J. B. Traité d'économie politique, ou simple exposition de la manière dont se forment, se distribuent et se consomment les richesses; seconde édition entièrement refondue et augmentée d'un épitome des principes fondamentaux de l'économie politique... 2 vols. *8°. Paris*, 1814. *For other editions, see 1803.*

20892 SERRES, P. T. M. DE. Voyage en Autriche, ou essai statistique et géographique sur cet Empire; avec une carte physique, des coupes de nivellement, et divers tableaux comparatifs sur l'étendue et la population de l'Autriche... 4 vols. *8°. Paris & London*, 1814.

20893 SHOBERL, F., *ed.* Narrative of the most remarkable events which occurred in and near Leipzig, immediately before, during and subsequent to the... engagements between the Allied Armies and the French, from the 14th to the 19th October, 1813...Compiled and translated from the German by Frederic Shoberl. Tenth edition. 104p. *8°*. 1814.

20894 [SIMPSON, THOMAS (*fl.* 1814–1816).] A defence of the land-owners and farmers of Great Britain; and an exposition of the heavy parliamentary and parochial taxation under which they labour; combined with a general view of the internal and external policy of the country: in familiar letters from an agricultural gentleman in Yorkshire to a friend in Parliament. 105p. *8°. London & Stockton-upon-Tees*, 1814.

20895 SMITH, ADAM. An inquiry into the nature and causes of the wealth of nations... In three volumes. With notes, and an additional volume, by David Buchanan... 4 vols. *8°. Edinburgh*, 1814. *For other editions, see 1776.*

20896 SOCIEDAD ECONOMICA DE MADRID. Informe de la Sociedad Ecónomica de Madrid al Real y Supremo Consejo de Castilla en el expediente de ley agraria, extendido per su individuo de numéro el Sr. D. Gaspar Melchor de Jovellanos... 192p. *4°. Palma*, 1814. *For other editions, see 1795.*

20897 THOM, WALTER. A synopsis of the science of political economy. 32p. *8°. Dublin*, 1814.

AGRICULTURE

20898 BOARD OF AGRICULTURE. Explanation of the principles on which the General report regarding the agricultural state and the political circumstances of Scotland, has been drawn up; with a statement of the particulars therein discussed. 4p. *8°*. [*Edinburgh*, 1814]

**20899 —— ** General report of the agricultural state, and political circumstances, of Scotland. Drawn up for the consideration of the Board...under the directions of... Sir John Sinclair... 3 vols. *8°. Edinburgh & London*, 1814.

**20900 —— ** Appendix to the General report... 2 vols. *8°. Edinburgh & London*, 1814.

20901 COPY of an award, made in pursuance of an Act, passed 46th George 3d, intituled "An Act for inclosing lands in the parish of Witchford, in the Isle of Ely, in the County of Cambridge". 83p. *8°. Ely*, 1814.

20902 DARD, H. J. B. Du rétablissement des rentes foncières, mélangées de féodalité, abolies sans indemnité par les lois des 6 juillet et 25 août 1792, et 17 juillet 1793, et de la jurisprudence de la Cour de Cassation et du Conseil-d'Etat sur ces lois. 198p. *8°. Paris*, 1814.

20903 DAVY, SIR H., *Bart.* Elements of agricultural chemistry, in a course of lectures for the Board of Agriculture. Second edition. [With 'Appendix. An account of the results of experiments on the produce and nutritive qualities of different grasses, and other plants, used as the food of animals'. By G. Sinclair, edited by Sir H. Davy.] 479p. *8°. London & Edinburgh*, 1814. *For other editions, see* 1813.

20904 ENGLAND. *Laws, etc.* An Act for inclosing lands in the manors of Great Chelworth and Little Chelworth in the parishes of Cricklade Saint Sampson, and Cricklade Saint Mary, in the county of Wilts. ⟨Royal Assent, 17 June 1814.⟩ 54 Geo. III. Sess. 1813–14. 22p. *fol.* [*London*, 1814]

20905 ESTEVES DE CARVALHO, V. A. Memoria sobre a origem, e progressos da emphyteuse e sua influencia sobre a agricultura em Portugal. 32p. *4°. Lisboa*, 1814.

20906 GRAHAM, P. A general view of the agriculture

of the counties of Kinross and Clackmannan, drawn up for the consideration of the Board of Agriculture. 435p. *8°. Edinburgh & London*, 1814.

20907 GRAY, A. Explanation of the engravings of the most important implements of husbandry used in Scotland. From drawings prepared for the Board of Agriculture, by Mr. Andrew Gray, engineer. 79p. *4°. Edinburgh & London*, 1814.

20908 GRIFFITH, SIR RICHARD J., Bart. Geological and mining report on the Leinster coal district. [Presented to the Dublin Society.] 135p. *8°. Dublin*, 1814.

20909 HORNBY, THOMAS, surgeon. Dissertation on lime, and its use and abuse in agriculture, embracing a view of its chemical effects... Second edition. 32p. *8°. York, London, &c.*, [1814]

20910 JACOB, W. Considerations on the protection required by British agriculture, and on the influence of the price of corn on exportable productions. 195p. *8°.* 1814. *For a supplement, see the author's* A letter to Samuel Whitbread, *1815.*

20911 RENNIE, JOHN (1761–1821). Reports as to the Wisbech Outfall, and the drainage of the North Level and South Holland...with a statement, &c. as to the drainage of the fens north of Boston, by Anthony Bower: printed dy [*sic*] the order of the Governor, bailiffs and conservators, of the Bedford Level Corporation. 33p. *4°.* 1814.

20912 SINCLAIR, SIR JOHN, Bart. An account of the systems of husbandry adopted in the more improved districts of Scotland...Drawn up for the consideration of the Board of Agriculture...The third edition... 2 vols. *8°. Edinburgh, London, &c.*, 1814. *For other editions, see* 1812.

CORN LAWS

20913 BARBÉ-MARBOIS, F. DE, Marquis de Marbois. Chambre des Pairs de France. Opinion de M. de Marbois, sur le projet de loi relatif à l'exportation des grains... 50p. *8°.* [*Paris*, 1814]

20914 BARRIN DE LA GALLISSONNIÈRE, A. F. E., Comte de la Gallissonnière. Chambre des Députés. Opinion de M. le Comte de la Gallissonière sur le projet de loi relatif à l'exportation des grains...Séance du 10 octobre 1814. 10p. *8°.* [*Paris*, 1814]

20915 BECQUEY, L. Chambre des Pairs de France. Séance du mardi 8 novembre 1814. Discourse de M. Becquey...en réponse au rapport de la Commission spéciale chargée de l'examen du projet de loi sur l'exportation des grains... 19p. *8°.* [*Paris*, 1814]

20916 —— Chambre des Pairs de France. Séance du samedi 12 novembre 1814. Discourse de M. Becquey... sur le projet de loi relatif à l'exportation des grains... 14p. *8°.* [*Paris*, 1814]

20917 BOISSY D'ANGLAS, F. A. DE, Comte. Chambre des Pairs de France. Séance du mardi 8 novembre 1814. Opinion de M. le Comte Boissy D'Anglas sur le projet de loi relatif à l'exportation des grains... 34p. *8°.* [*Paris*, 1814]

20918 BOOTH, GEORGE, merchant. Observations on lowering the rent of land, and on the corn laws. 33p. *8°. Liverpool & London*, [1814] *See also* 1815.

20919 BRAND, T., Baron Dacre. A letter from the Hon. Thomas Brand, M.P. to W. Wilshere, Esq. on the subject of the corn laws. 21p. *8°.* 1814.

20920 BRICKWOOD, J. Observations on the corn laws and the corn trade in 1813 & 1814. 48p. *8°.* [1814] *The Sheffield copy.*

20921 BROADHURST, J. Substance of a speech against the proposed alteration of the corn laws, intended to have been spoken in the House of Commons, on June 6, 1814. 58p. *8°.* 1814.

20922 CAMPBELL, JOHN, of Carbrook. A letter on the proposed alteration of the corn laws. Addressed to Sir Henry Parnell, Bart. 48p. *8°. Edinburgh, Glasgow, &c.*, 1814.

20923 CLÉMENT DE RIS, D., Comte. Chambre des Députés. Opinion de M. Clément...sur le projet de loi relatif à l'exportation et à l'importation des grains... Séance du 10 octobre 1814. 18p. *8°.* [*Paris*, 1814]

20924 CORNUDET DES CHOMETTES, J., Comte. Chambre des Pairs de France. Séance du mardi 8 novembre 1814. Opinion de M. le Comte Cornudet sur le projet de loi relatif à l'exportation des grains... 20p. *8°.* [*Paris*, 1814]

20925 CORRIE, E. Letters on the subject of the corn laws. 16p. *8°. Liverpool & London*, 1814. *The Sheffield copy.*

20926 COSSÉ, A. M. P. P. T., Duc de Brissac. Chambre des Pairs de France. Séance du jeudi 10 novembre 1814. Opinion de M. le Duc de Brissac sur le projet de loi relatif à l'exportation des grains... 31p. *8°.* [*Paris*, 1814]

20927 [CURWEN, J. C.] Cursory observations on the corn laws; submitted to the consideration of the members of the Workington Agricultural Society. 1814. By the President. 16p. *8°. Workington*, [1814] *See also* 1815.

20928 DEPÈRE, M., Comte. Chambre des Pairs de France. Séance du jeudi 10 novembre 1814. Opinion de le Comte Depère sur le projet de loi relatif à l'exportation des grains... 25p. *8°.* [*Paris*, 1814]

20929 ENGLAND. Parliament. *House of Commons.* Report from the Select Committee of the House of Commons on petitions relating to the corn laws... Together with the minutes of evidence, and an appendix of accounts. 260, xlvip. *8°.* 1814.

20930 —— Second edition. 260, xlvip. *8°.* 1814.

20931 —— —— *House of Lords.* First and second Reports from the Committees of the House of Lords, appointed to inquire into the state of the growth, commerce, and consumption of grain, and all laws relating thereto: to whom were referred the several petitions presented...1813–1814, respecting the corn laws. 343p. *8°.* 1814.

20932 FRANCE. *Chambre des Députés.* Motifs du projet de loi sur le mode et les conditions de l'exportation des grains. Séance du 13 septembre, 1814. 24p. *8°.* [*Paris*, 1814]

20933 HEPBURN, Sir G. B., *Bart.* The speech of the Hon. Mr. Baron Hepburn of Smeaton, on the subject of the corn laws; delivered in a...meeting of the county of East Lothian...3d of March, 1814... 76p. *8°. Edinburgh & London,* 1814.

20934 LAPLACE, P. S. de, *Marquis.* Chambre des Pairs de France. Opinion de M. le Comte Laplace, sur le projet de loi relatif à l'exportation des grains... 6p. *8°.* [*Paris,* 1814]

20935 LA ROCHEFOUCAULD-LIANCOURT, F. A. F. de, *Duc de La Rochefoucauld.* Chambre des Pairs de France. Séance du mardi 8 novembre 1814. Opinion de M. le Duc de La Rochefoucauld sur le projet de loi relatif à l'exportation des grains... 14p. *8°.* [*Paris,* 1814]

20936 LECOUTEULX DE CANTELEU, J. B., *Comte.* Chambre des Pairs de France. Séance du mardi 8 novembre 1814. Opinion de M. le Comte Lecouteulx de Canteleu, sur le projet de loi relatif à l'exportation des grains... 28p. *8°.* [*Paris,* 1814]

20937 A LETTER to the Earl of Liverpool, on the probable effect of a great reduction of corn prices, by importation; upon the relative condition of the state and its creditors, and of debtors and creditors in general. 108p. *8°.* 1814. *With a note by HSF: 'It seems to me like C. R. Prinsep's work'.*

20938 LETTER to the Hon. Mr Baron Hepburn, in answer to his speech, delivered at a meeting of the freeholders of the county of Haddington, March 3. 1814, on the corn-laws. [Signed: a Hammerman.] 16p. *8°. Edinburgh,* 1814.

20939 MAITLAND, James, *8th Earl of Lauderdale.* A letter on the corn laws. 89p. *8°. London & Edinburgh,* 1814. *The Sheffield copy.*

20940 MALTHUS, T. R. Observations on the effects of the corn laws, and of a rise or fall in the price of corn on the agriculture and general wealth of the country. 44p. *8°.* 1814. *The Sheffield copy.*

20941 —— Second edition. 44p. *8°.* 1814. *See also* 1815.

20942 MARTIN SAINT-JEAN, H. H. J. Chambre des Députés. Amendemens proposés par M. Martin Saint-Jean au projet de loi sur l'exportation des grains... Séance du 8 octobre 1814. 6p. *8°.* [*Paris,* 1814]

20943 MASON, James. A review of the principal arguments in favour of restricting the importation, and allowing the exportation, of corn. 68p. *8°.* 1814.

20944 MORISSET, R. J., *Baron.* Chambre des Députés. Opinion de M. le Baron Morisset, relative au projet de loi sur le mode et les conditions de l'exportation des grains...Séance du 10 octobre, 1814. 11p. *8°.* [*Paris,* 1814]

20945 PARNELL, H. B., *Baron Congleton.* The substance of the speeches of Sir H. Parnell, Bart. in the House of Commons, with additional observations, on the corn laws. 70p. *8°.* 1814.

20946 —— Second edition. 70p. *8°.* 1814.

20947 QUELEN DE STUER DE CAUSSADE DE LA VAUGUYON, P. F. de, *Duc de la Vauguyon.* Chambre des Pairs de France. Séance du jeudi 10 novembre 1814. Second rapport de M. le Duc de la Vauguyon sur le projet de loi relatif à l'exportation des grains... 21p. *8°.* [*Paris,* 1814]

20948 ROSE, G. The speech of the Right Hon. George Rose, in the House of Commons, on the 5th of May 1814, on the subject of the corn laws. 79p. *8°.* 1814. *The Sheffield copy, with a letter from the author to Lord Sheffield inserted. For the letter, see* vol. III, *A.L.* 277.

20949 SILANS, M. A. F. P. de. Chambre des Députés. Opinion de M. de Silans, sur le projet de loi relatif à l'exportation des grains...Séance du 10 octobre 1814. 41p. *8°.* [*Paris,* 1814]

20950 STRICKLAND, T. Observations on an intended proposition to the Legislature, in regard to a new arrangement, as to the limiting price of corn. 28p. *8°. Liverpool & London,* 1814.

20951 THOUGHTS on the question of an alteration of the corn laws. 17p. *8°.* 1814.

20952 VILLEMANZY, de, *Comte.* Chambre des Pairs de France. Séance du 8 novembre 1814. Opinion de M. le Comte de Villemanzy sur le projet de loi relatif à l'importation et à l'exportation des grains... 12p. *8°.* [*Paris,* 1814]

20953 WESTERN, C. C., *Baron Western.* Letter of Charles C. Western...to his constituents, on the subject of the foreign corn trade, August 5th, 1814. 32p. *8°.* 1814. *The Sheffield copy.*

20954 —— Substance of the speech of Charles C. Western, Esquire, in the House of Commons, May, 1814, with additional observations, on the subject of the corn laws. Second edition. 44p. *8°.* 1814. *The Sheffield copy.*

POPULATION

20955 CANDOLLE-BOISSIER, de. Observations sur la population de Genève. 22p. *8°. Genève & Paris,* 1814.

TRADES & MANUFACTURES

20956 ADOLPHUS, J. The substance of the speech of John Adolphus, Esq. before a Select Committee of the House of Commons, in summing up the case of the English ship-builders, on their petition respecting ships built in India, on Monday, May 23, and Tuesday, May 24, 1814... 46p. *8°.* 1814.

20957 BECKMANN, J. A history of inventions and discoveries...Translated from the German, by William Johnston. Second edition...enlarged by a fourth volume... 4 vols. *8°.* 1814. *For other editions, see* 1797.

20958 HARRISON, W. The substance of the speech of William Harrison, Esq. before the Select Committee of the House of Commons, on East India-built shipping, on Monday, April 18, 1814... 23p. *8°.* 1814.

20959 —— The substance of the reply of William Harrison, Esq. before the Select Committee of the House of Commons, on East India-built shipping, on Tuesday, June 28, 1814, in reply on the whole case. 56p. *8°. 1814.*

20960 KINGSBURY, B. A treatise on razors; in which the weight, shape, and temper of a razor, the means of keeping it in order, and the manner of using it, are particularly considered... Seventh edition. 47p. *8°. 1814.*

20961 LONDON. Livery Companies. *Clockmakers.* Office of the Company of Clock-makers, 35, Clements Lane, Lombard Street. [June] 1814. [A circular letter, signed: George Atkins, Clerk to the Company, calling upon the recipient to bring to the notice of the Company instances of foreign makers of clocks or watches engraving the names of English makers on their products so that they may be sold as of English manufacture.] *s.sh.4°. n.p.* [1814] *See note to no. 13563.*

20962 REMARKS on the calumnies published in the Quarterly Review, on the English ship-builders. 44p. *8°. 1814.*

20963 SOCIETY FOR PREVENTING ACCIDENTS IN COAL MINES, *Sunderland.* The first report of a Society for Preventing Accidents in Coal Mines, comprising a letter to Sir Ralph Milbanke, Bart., on the various modes employed in the ventilation of collieries... By John Buddle. 28p. *8°. Newcastle, 1814. The copy that belonged to Joseph Lawson of Walls End, with his signature on the title-page, and with another inscription recording its presentation to 'Mr. J. Sharp—October 1831'.*

20964 SOCIETY FOR THE ENCOURAGEMENT OF ARTS, MANUFACTURES AND COMMERCE. A catalogue of the machines, models, and other articles, in the repository of the Society... 24p. *8°. 1814.*

20965 STOWER, C. The printer's price-book, containing the master printer's charges to the trade for printing works of various descriptions... Also, a new, easy, and correct method of casting off manuscript and other copy, exemplified in specimen pages of different sizes and types... 446p. *8°. 1814.*

COMMERCE

20966 BARRIN DE LA GALLISSONNIÈRE, A. F. E., *Comte de la Gallissonnière.* Chambre des Députés. Développemens de la proposition concernant la libre exportation des productions du sol de la France, notamment des grains et des bestiaux, faite le 30 juillet 1814... Séance du 4 août, 1814. 10p. *8°. [Paris, 1814]*

20967 COMMITTEE OF LONDON MERCHANTS. Report of the Committee of London Merchants, appointed to confer with the Lords of the Treasury, on the subject of the warehousing system... With an appendix, containing their original resolutions, and their memorial to the Lords of the Treasury... [Signed: Charles Price, chairman.] 45, 20p. *8°. 1814.*

20968 DAY, , and **WILLIAMS,** . Leerboek der koophandelkunst. Opgedragen aan de maatschappij: tot nut van't algemeen. 135p. *8°. Zutphen, 1814.*

20969 DESROUSSEAUX, J. A. Chambre des Députés. Opinion de M. Desrousseaux, sur le projet de loi relatif à l'exploitation de quelques productions du sol français, prononcée en comité secret. Séance du 20 septembre, 1814. 18p. *8°. [Paris, 1814]*

20970 An ESSAY on the effects of the inequitable modes of pursuing trade: with analogous remedies: comprising a dissertation upon the diminution and remuneration of labor. By a Liveryman of London. 86p. *8°. 1813–14.*

20971 HILLS, R. The causes of the present high price of coals, in the Port of London, explained; in a letter to the editor of the Times. 34p. *8°. London & Newcastle, 1814.*

20972 POYFÉRÉ DE CÈRE, J. M., *Baron.* Discours sur l'exportation et l'importation des produits bruts, prononcé... à la séance de la Chambre des Députés, le 14 juillet. 12p. *8°. [Paris, 1814]*

20973 —— Chambre des Députés. Proposition relative à l'exportation de quelques productions du sol français... Séance du 4 août, 1814. 12p. *8°. [Paris, 1814]*

20974 PRINCE'S LONDON PRICE CURRENT... No. 1970. Friday, the 7th January, [—No. 2021. Friday, the 30th December] 1814. 51 nos. *fol.* [1814] *Wanting No. 1985 for 22 April. See also 1812, 1813, 1815, 1817, 1818, 1820.*

20975 RIGAUD DE L'ISLE, L. M. Chambre des Députés. Rapport fait en comité secret, au nom d'une commission centrale, sur la proposition de M. Poyféré de Cère, relativement à l'exportation de quelques productions du sol français... Du 6 septembre, 1814. 20p. *8°. [Paris, 1814]*

20976 Du TABAC, considéré sous le rapport du monopole et du commerce libre. 15p. *4°. [Paris, 1814?]*

20977 TABACS, Mémoire en faveur de l'agriculture, des concommateurs et des intérêts de l'état. [Signed: le chevalier Boussin, le chevalier Joly, le chevalier Lambert, entreposeurs délégués par leurs collégues. Addressed to the Chambre des Députés.] 20p. *4°. [Paris, 1814?]*

20978 THORNTON, Thomas. A compendium of the laws recently passed for regulating the trade with the East Indies; the duties of customs and excise on goods imported from thence... With a... description of the chief articles of import from those parts. To which are subjoined, schedules of rates charged by the East India Company... 118p. *8°. 1814. See also 1815.*

COLONIES

20979 ANDERSON, David, *merchant.* Canada: or, a view of the importance of the British American Colonies; shewing their extensive and improveable resources and pointing out the... advantages which have been allowed to the Americans over our own colonists; together with the great sacrifices which have been made by our late commercial regulations of the commerce and carrying-trade of Great Britain to the United States... 355p. *8°*. 1814.

20980 ENGLAND. Parliament. *House of Commons.* Interesting extracts from the minutes of evidence taken before the Committee of the whole House, to whom it was referred to consider of the affairs of the East India Company, in the sessions of 1813; illustrative of the improvements in the manufacture of iron, steel, brass... &c. by the natives of India. 41p. *8°*. 1814. *The Sheffield copy.*

20981 HUME, JOSEPH. The substance of the speech of Joseph Hume, Esq. at a General Court of proprietors at the East-India House, on the 9th of June, 1814; upon the motion for granting a pension of £2000 per annum, for ten years, to the present Lord Melville, in considera-tion of the eminent services of the late Lord Melville to the East-India Company. 60p. *8°*. [1814]

20982 —— The substance of the speech of Mr. Joseph

Hume, at the East-India House, on the 6th of October, 1813, upon the motion for an increase of the salaries to the Directors of the East-India Company, from the sum of £300 per annum to £1000, and of the Chairman and deputy from £500 to £1500. 47p. *8°*. 1814. *The copy that belonged to David Ricardo.*

20983 RAFFLES, SIR T. S. Substance of a minute recorded by the Honourable Thomas Stamford Raffles, Lieutenant-Governor of Java...on the 11th February 1814; on the introduction of an improved system of internal management and the establishment of a land rental on the island of Java: to which are added several of the most interesting documents therein referred to. 293p. *4°*. 1814.

20984 RICKARDS, R. The speeches of Robert Rickards, Esq, in the debate in Parliament on the renewal of the charter of the Hon. East India Company, the 2nd and 14th of June, 1813; with appendices, and an examina-tion of the Company's accounts laid before the Select Committee of the House of Commons. 96, 252p. *8°*. 1814.

FINANCE

20985 A........., *M.* Lettre de M. A........., à un de ses compatriotes, Membre de la Chambre des Députés des Départemens. [Dated: 10 août 1814.] 13p. *8°*. [*Paris*, 1814]

20986 ADAMS, R., *and others.* Report of the case of Adams and others v. Malkin and another. Being an issue out of chancery, to try if a London attorney-at-law was liable to the bankrupt laws as a money-scrivener. With a copious appendix relative to scriveners. By Philip Hurd... 146p. *8°*. 1814.

20987 The calumnious **ASPERSIONS** contained in the report of the sub-committee of the Stock-Exchange, exposed and refuted in so far as regards Lord Cochrane... the Hon. Cochrane Johnstone, M.P. and R. G. Butt, Esq. To which are added...copies of the purchases and sales of Omnium and Consols, referred to in the report of the sub-committee. Second edition. 62p. *8°*. [1814]

20988 —— Third edition. 62p. *8°*. [1814]

20989 BANK OF SCOTLAND. Regulations by the Court of Directors of the Bank of Scotland, for negotiation of bills received for the Bank. [Dated: 19th December 1814.] [4p.] *fol. n.p.* [1814]

20990 [BEAUMONT, JOHN T. B.] Life insurance. Important facts, shewing the successive reductions that have taken place in the terms for the insurance of lives, and the probability of ultimate failure in some recent schemes...By Philanthropos. 29p. *8°*. 1814.

20991 BENETT, J. An essay on the commutation of tithes; to which was adjudged the Bedfordean Gold Medal, by the Bath and West of England Society, for the En-couragement of Agriculture...December 13th, 1814. 15p. *8°*. *Bath & London*, 1814.

20992 BUESCH, J. G. Traité des banques, de leur différence réelle, et des effets qui en résultent dans leur usage et leur administration, traduit de l'Allemand...par Francois de L-C. [Las Casas]. 272p. *8°*. *Paris*, 1814.

20993 CAMPBELL, JAMES (*fl.* 1814). The memoirs of Lord Cochrane, son of the Earl of Dundonald, Captain

in the Navy, Knight of the Bath, and Member for West-minster... 30p. *8°*. 1814.

20994 CANDOLLE-BOISSIER, DE. Projet pour la création d'un établissement public dans le Canton de Genève, sous le nom de Caisse d'Epargne, pour recevoir à intérêt le fruit des économies de classes peu aisées de la société genèvoise; présenté au Conseil Représentatif...10 décembre 1814. 40p. *8°*. *Genève*, 1814.

20995 The **CASE** of Lord Cochrane considered, in a letter to the electors of Westminster, and a candidate recommended to their choice, on the next vacancy. By an old inhabitant. 63p. *8°*. 1814.

20996 CHRISTIAN, G. J. Des impositions et de leur influence sur l'industrie agricole, manufacturière et commerciale, et sur la prospérité publique. 192p. *8°*. *Paris*, 1814.

20997 [FOSTER, R.] Thoughts on peace, in the present situation of the country, with respect to its finances and circulating medium; with an appendix, concerning the theory of money. 194p. *8°*. 1814.

20998 FRANCE. *Administration Générale des Mon-naies.* Préfecture de Police. Avis. Tarif du change des monnaies. Valeur, en monnaies françaises, des pièces d'or, d'argent et de billon des Empires de Russie et d'Autriche, des Cercles d'Allemagne, du Royaume de Prusse et du Pays de Hollande. [Drawn up by the Administration Générale des Monnaies, signed: L. B. Guyton, Monges. Issued by the Préfecture, and signed by the Préfet: Pasquier.] 12p. *4°*. *Paris*, 1814. *The text is printed in French, Russian and German.*

20999 —— *Chambre des Députés.* Motifs du projet de loi sur les finances, présenté par M. le Baron Louis, Ministre des Finances. Séance du 22 juillet, 1814. [With 'Tableaux annexés au projet de loi sur les finances'.] 30, [12]p. *8°*. [*Paris*, 1814]

21000 —— —— Rapport fait au nom de la Commission Centrale, sur la loi relative aux budgets de 1814 et 1815, et à la liquidation des dettes arriérées, par M. Delhorme. Séance du 23 août 1814. 78p. *8°*. [*Paris*, 1814]

21001 GANILH, C. Réflexions sur le budget de 1814. 48p. *8°. Paris, 1814.*

21002 GRENFELL, J. Observations on the expediency and facility of a copper coinage of uniform weight and a standard value according with the mint prices of gold and silver bullion. 28p. *8°. 1814.*

21003 —— Second edition. 31p. *8°. 1814.*

21004 HAMILTON, ROBERT (1743–1829). An inquiry concerning the rise and progress, the redemption and present state, and the management, of the National Debt of Great Britain. The second edition, enlarged. 272p. *8°. Edinburgh, Glasgow, &c., 1814. For other editions, see 1813.*

21005 IRELAND. *Trustees of the Linen and Hempen Manufactures.* Minutes of the Trustees of the Linen and Hempen Manufactures of Ireland, respecting the proposed repeal of the transit-duties on foreign linens. 42p. *8°. n.p., 1814. The Sheffield copy.*

21006 L., S. F. B. Tarif des droits de douanes à percevoir à l'entrée et à la sortie du Royaume de France. Edition corrigée et considérablement augmentée... 106p. *16°. Lille, 1814.*

21007 MUELLER, C. A. J. Tafels dienende tot de berekeningen voortvloeijende uit de wet tot herstel der nationale schuld, gearresteerd...in dato 14 Mei 1814, n°.2. Vervaardigd...door C. A. J. Müller. 113p. *8°. Amsterdam & 's Gravenhage, 1814.*

21008 NOTES concernant la première partie de l'opinion d'un créancier de l'état sur le budget, et sur les observations et réflexions dont il à été l'objet, adressée aux créanciers de l'état. [Signed: l'Ami de la vérité.] 20p. *4°. [Paris, 1814]*

21009 OBSERVATIONS et éclaircissemens sur le paragraphe concernant les finances, dans l'Exposé sur la situation du royaume, présenté à la Chambre des Pairs et à celle des Députés. Seconde édition. 39p. *4°. Paris, 1814.*

21010 PARIS. *Cour Royale. Cour Spéciale du Département de la Seine.* Arrêt de la Cour Spéciale du Département de la Seine, séante à Paris, qui condamne à la peine de mort le nommé Louis-Jacques-François Mary, déclaré convaincu d'une tentative de fabrication de fausse monnoie. Du 23 mai 1814. 4p. *4°. [Paris, 1814]*

21011 PELICAN OFFICES FOR INSURANCE ON LIVES. Endowments for children, by the Pelican Life-Insurance Office, in Lombard-Street. [A prospectus, with a table of rates for the purchase of endowment policies.] 2l. *fol. [London, 1814?]*

21012 —— Pelican Offices, Lombard-Street, and Spring Gardens, London, for insurance on lives, granting annuities, and endowment of children. [With 'A list of the trustees and directors'.] 14, [2]p. *8°. 1814. See also 1820.*

21013 PENNSYLVANIA COMPANY FOR INSURANCES ON LIVES AND GRANTING ANNUITIES. An address from the President and directors of the...Company...to the inhabitants of the United States, upon the subject of the beneficial objects of that institution. 45p. *8°. Philadelphia, 1814.*

21014 RANDOM DE BÉRENGER, C., *Baron de Beaufain, and others.* The trial of Charles Random de Bérenger, Sir Thomas Cochrane, commonly called Lord Cochrane, the Hon. Andrew Cochrane Johnstone, Richard Gathorne Butt, Ralph Sandom, Alexander M'Rae, John Peter Holloway and Henry Lyte; for a conspiracy, in the Court of King's Bench, Guildhall, on...the 8th and...9th of June, 1814: with the subsequent proceedings in the Court of King's Bench... 604p. *8°. 1814. The copy that belonged to Charles Nairne, deputy-chairman of the sub-committee of the Stock Exchange which investigated the fraud, with his signature on the title-page.*

21015 Strong **REASONS** for the continuance of the property tax. To which is added, an estimate of the national income, recently made by Patrick Colquhoun, L.L.D....By a friend to his country. [With 'Appendix. Mr. Pitt's speech in 1798, on introducing the resolution relative to the income tax in the Committee of Supply'.] 109p. *8°. 1814.*

21016 RÉFLEXIONS sur le rapport du Ministre des Finances au Roi et aux deux Chambres. 24p. *8°. Paris, 1814.*

21017 [SAINT-SARDOS DE MONTAGU, J., *Marquis de Mondenard.]* Moyens de remédier aux inconvenients du budget proposé par le Ministre des Finances. Par l'auteur des Considérations sur l'organisation sociale, imprimées en 1802 chez Migneret. 15p. *8°. Paris, 1814.*

21018 SCOTTISH WIDOWS' FUND AND LIFE ASSURANCE SOCIETY. Deed of constitution, and articles and regulations of the Scottish Widows' Fund and Life Assurance Society. Registered in the books of Council and Session, 4th October, 1814. 77p. *8°. Edinburgh, 1814.*

21019 —— Exposition of the objects of the institution, formed under the denomination of the Scottish Widows' Fund...and of the principles upon which it is founded... 19p. *8°. Edinburgh, 1814.*

21020 SMITH, THOMAS, *accountant, of London.* A letter to the Earl of Lauderdale, in reply to his "Depreciation of paper-currency proved". 114p. *8°. 1814. Presentation copy, with inscription, from the author to Patrick Colquhoun.*

21021 STOCK EXCHANGE. Report of the Sub-Committee of the Stock-Exchange relative to the late fraud [of C. Random de Bérenger and others]. 22p. *8°. Printed for the use of Members of the Stock Exchange only, 1814. The copy, bound with other works on the same subject, that belonged to Charles Nairne, deputy-chairman of the sub-committee, with his signature on the title-page.*

21022 STOCK-EXCHANGE laid open. The cause of the rise and fall of the public funds explained; with observations on the mischievous tendency of time bargains, and the...necessity of abolishing the present Stock-Exchange, and establishing an open public market...By a gentlemen of the Exchange. 34p. *8°. 1814. See also 1816 (The art of stock-jobbing explained), 1819.*

21023 The **WATCH-LIGHT;** illustrative of many new and curious facts, relative to Lord Cochrane's commission of the fraud upon the Stock Exchange, and his connection with de Berenger. Also, a full consideration of that palladium of British justice, the Court of King's Bench...By a student of Lincoln's-Inn. 88p. *8°. 1814.*

TRANSPORT

21024 **BALD,** R. Report of a mineral survey along the track of the proposed north or level line of canal betwixt Edinburgh and Glasgow, as projected by John Rennie... 1798...May, 1814. [With 'Observations occasioned by the mineral survey and report of Mr. Robert Bald...in which a comparison is attempted...between the utility of that canal and of the proposed Union Navigation, by John Paterson' and 'Prospectus of revenue on the proposed level canal between Edinburgh and Glasgow'.] 25, 12p. *4°. Leith,* [1814] *The Rastrick copy.*

21025 **CORRESPONDENCE** between the committee of subscribers to the proposed Union Canal between Edinburgh and Glasgow, and...the Lord Provost and Magistrates of Edinburgh, relative to that undertaking. 15p. *8°. Edinburgh,* 1814.

21026 **EDINBURGH AND GLASGOW UNION CANAL.** Observations [on the proposed level line for a canal between Leith, Edinburgh and Glasgow, surveyed by John Rennie in 1798, in which a comparison is drawn between that canal and the proposed Union Canal. With minutes concerning the presentation of the Observations to the Lord Provost of Edinburgh.] 14p. *4°. n.p.* [1814] *The Rastrick copy.*

21027 **ÉTAT** général des postes du royaume de France, avec les routes qui conduisent aux principales villes de l'Europe, dressé par ordre du Conseil d'Administration, pour l'an 1814. 309p. *8°. Paris,* 1814. *See also* 1818, 1819, 1823, 1835 (*Livre de poste...*), 1838.

21028 **HEBERT,** L. and **DUPONT,** G. An actual survey and itinerary of the road from Calais to Paris, shewing the distance between each town and village... surveyed with a perambulator; also, the post-houses, with the number of posts, inns, rivers, woods... 96p. *8°.* 1814. *With the text in French and English in parallel columns.*

21029 **KENNET AND AVON CANAL NAVIGATION.** Kennet and Avon Canal. [*Begin.*] Sir, Inclosed we send you a copy of the reports of the Committee of Management, and the auditors...[Signed: Ward & Merriman, clerks, and dated, 22nd July 1814.] *s.sh.fol. Marlborough,* [1814]

For a **NEW GUIDE TO STAGE COACHES, WAGGONS...&c.** for 1814, *see no.* 20889.

21030 **PROCEEDINGS** of a committee of merchants, manufacturers, shipowners, and others, interested in the improvement of the harbour of Dundee; appointed by a general meeting...February 2, 1814. 44p. *8°. Dundee,* 1814.

21031 **PROSPECTUS** of a plan, and proposals for forming a joint stock company, to be entitled the Orford Harbour Company, under an Act of Parliament to be solicited...in the ensuing session for the improvement of Orford Haven or Harbour, in the River Ore, in the County of Suffolk. [Dated: 1st Nov. 1814.] 3p. *fol. n.p.* [1814]

SOCIAL CONDITIONS

21032 [**BEAUMONT,** John T. B.?] A private address to the magistrates acting in and about the Metropolis, on the evils produced by the present mode of licensing new public-houses, with hints for their remedy. By Humanitas. 13p. *8°.* 1814. *Attributed to Beaumont by HSF in his manuscript catalogue of the Goldsmiths' Library.*

21033 The **COMMITTEE** for conducting the bringing a Bill into Parliament, to alter and amend the Statute of the 5th of Eliz. cap. 4 respecting apprentices, artizans, &c. consider it necessary to lay the following circular before the public. [Signed: Josiah Clinton, and dated, August 8th, 1814.] 3p. *fol.* [1814] *See note to no.* 13563.

21034 **COMMITTEE FOR RELIEVING THE DISTRESS IN GERMANY.** Reports of the Committee formed in London in the year 1814, for the relief of the unparalleled distresses in Germany, and other parts of the Continent, occasioned by the war which terminated in the Treaty of Paris, 31st March, 1814. 27, 14, 18, 13, 15, 10p. *8°.* 1814. *Contents: 1st–2nd reports of the Committee for Relieving the Distress in Germany; 3rd report; 4th report; 5th report; 6th report; report of the Committee of the Westminster Association, 7th April 1814.*

21035 **COMMITTEE OF MANUFACTURERS OF LONDON AND ITS VICINITY.** The origin, object and operation of the apprentice laws; with their application to times past, present and to come. Addressed to the Committee of General Purposes of the City of London...Extracted from No. v. of The Pamphleteer [i.e. vol. III, no. VI.] 26p. *8°.* 1814. *The copy that belonged to Francis Place.*

21036 —— [Another edition.] 28p. *8°.* 1814. *Without the note on the title-page: 'Extracted from No. V of the Pamphleteer'.*

21037 **CORK INSTITUTION.** The annual report of the managers & auditors of the Cork Institution, previous to the general meeting at the Spring Assizes, 1814. 44p. *8°. Cork,* [1814].

21038 **CORRECTOR,** *pseud.* A few free remarks on Mr. Godfrey Higgins's publications respecting the York Lunatic Asylum. 14p. *8°. York,* 1814.

21039 **DAY AND SUNDAY FREE SCHOOL,** *Circus Street, Liverpool.* Eleventh annual report of the Day and Sunday Free School...(From July 1, 1813, to July 1, 1814.) [With 'List of annual subscribers' etc.] 19p. *8°. Liverpool: printed at the Sunday School Press,* [1814] *See also* 1811, 1812, 1813.

For **FEMALE SCHOOL OF INDUSTRY,** *Farnham.* 1st–9th annual reports, 1814–22, *see vol. III, Periodicals list,* Annual report of the Committee...

21040 **GROCER COMPANY OF EDINBURGH AND LEITH.** Proposed regulations of the Grocer Company...for providing annuities for their widows. 14p. *8°. Edinburgh,* 1814.

21041 HIGGINS, G. A letter to the Right Honourable Earl Fitzwilliam...respecting the investigation which has lately taken place, into the abuses at the York Lunatic Asylum...Together with various letters, reports, &c. and the new code of regulations for its future management [and 'Report of the Committee of Inquiry into the rules and management of the York Lunatic Asylum']. 29, 46, 52p. *8°. Doncaster, London, &c., 1814.*

21042 KERRISON, R. M. An inquiry into the present state of the medical profession in England, containing an abstract of all the Acts and charters granted to physicians, surgeons, and apothecaries, and a comparative view of the profession in Scotland, Ireland, and on the continent of Europe...and the merits of the Bill about to be presented to Parliament by the apothecaries and surgeon-apothecaries of England and Wales. xv, 96p. *8°. London, Edinburgh, &c., 1814.*

21043 LONDON SOCIETY FOR THE EN-COURAGEMENT OF FAITHFUL FEMALE SERVANTS. Report of the London Society...With the rules, list of subscribers, &c. Printed by order of the general meeting...April 29, 1814. 23p. *8°. 1814. For later reports, see vol. III, Periodicals list, Report of the London Society...*

21044 MANCHESTER AND SALFORD CO-OPERATING NATIONAL SOCIETY. The second report of the...Society, for promoting the education of the poor in the principles of the Established Church. With a list of the subscribers and benefactors. M.DCCC.XIII. 34p. *8°. Manchester, [1814]*

21045 MYERS, T. An essay on improving the condition of the poor: including an attempt to answer the important question, how men of landed property may... contribute towards the general improvement of the lower classes of society on their estates... 77p. *8°. 1814. The copy that belonged to William Allen.*

21046 A few substantial OBJECTIONS to the repeal of the Statute of Apprentices [5 Eliz. cap. 4]. 2p. *fol.* [1814?] *Endorsed: Objections to the repeal of the apprentice laws. See note to no. 13563.*

21047 Mr. Sergeant ONSLOW'S Act. [An address of the Sub-Committee of Manufacturers for obtaining the repeal of the restraints on trade, announcing the passing of the amending Act, and appending a copy of it. Signed: Charles Alsager and 9 members of the Sub-Committee, and dated, July 29th, 1814.] [4]p. *fol.* [1814] *See note to no. 13563.*

21048 PLAYFAIR, W. A letter to the Right Honourable and Honourable the Lords and Commons of Great Britain on the advantages of apprenticeships. 32p. *8°. 1814.*

21049 POLE, T. A history of the origin and progress of adult schools; with an account of some of the beneficial effects already produced on the moral character of the labouring poor...With an appendix containing rules for the government of adult school societies... 108p. *8°. Bristol & London, 1814. The copy that belonged to Joseph Priestley.*

21050 PRUDENT MAN'S FRIEND SOCIETY. State of the Prudent Man's Friend Society, for the year 1814. [With a list of subscribers.] 20p. *12°. Bristol, [1814]. See also 1813, 1815, 1816.*

21051 [*Endorsed:*] RESOLUTIONS of the master manufacturers and tradesmen of the Cities of London & Westminster, and the vicinity, on the Statute of 5 Eliz. cap. 4, for the regulation and protection of the arts, manufactures, and trades of this Kingdom. Freemason's Tavern, January 14th, 1814. 3p. *fol.* [London, 1814] *With manuscript comments originally made by Lord Ellenborough when the document was sent to him; these have been copied on to this copy from that in the possession of the chairman of the meeting, Peter Laurie. There is in the same volume a proof copy, entitled, 'Draft of Resolutions...' with extensive manuscript corrections, and a corrected issue, without the endorsed title, printed on finer paper. The circular invitation to the meeting, addressed to Isaac Rogers, is also included. See note to no. 13563.*

21052 SALIS, J. DE, *Comte.* A proposal for improving the system of friendly societies, or, of poor assurance offices; and, by increasing their funds, rendering...all parochial taxation for the relief of the poor unnecessary... 100p. *8°. London & Uxbridge, 1814.*

For SOCIETY FOR THE SUPPRESSION OF BEGGARS, *Edinburgh.* First [–fifteenth] Report, 1814–30, *see vol. III, Periodicals list, First report of the Society...*

21053 SPARKE, B. E., *Bishop of Ely.* A sermon preached before the incorporated Society for the Propagation of the Gospel in Foreign Parts; at their anniversary meeting...February 18, 1814. [With 'An abstract of the charter, and...proceedings of the Society...1813, to... 1814'.] 75p. *4°. 1814.*

21054 THOUGHTS on the late inquiry & report into the system of parochial government of the United Parishes of St. Margaret and St. John the Evangelist, Westminster; with remarks on the proposed Poor Bill. 29p. *8°. Chelsea, 1814.*

21055 WALTHEW, R. A moral and political essay on the English poor laws shewing their abuse and the injuries resulting therefrom...With a plan for correcting the same...With a law appendix from modern authorities... 142p. *8°. 1814.*

21056 WESTMINSTER ASSOCIATION FOR THE RELIEF OF DISTRESS IN GERMANY. Instructions to the continental committees, issued by the Westminster and London committees for the distribution of 100,000 l. granted by the imperial Parliament of Great Britain, and also of the private subscriptions for the relief of the sufferers by the late war in Germany. 11p. *8°.* [London, 1814] *See also no. 21034.*

21057 WESTMINSTER FREE SCHOOL. Second annual report...10th May 1814. [With a list of subscribers.] 37p. *8°.* [1814] *See also 1813, 1816.*

SLAVERY

21058 APPEL aux souverains réunis à Paris, pour en obtenir l'abolition de la traite des négres. 7p. *8°. Londres,* [1814?]

21059 [BLANCO Y CRESPO, J. M., afterwards BLANCO WHITE, J.] Bosquexo del comercio en esclavos: y reflexiones sobre este tráfico considerado moral, politica, y cristianamente. 144p. *8°. Londres*, 1814. *See also* 1821.

21060 CLARKSON, T. Essai sur les désavantages politiques de la traite des nègres...Traduit de l'anglais sur la dernière édition qui a paru à Londres en 1789. 144p. *8°. Paris*, 1814. *For other editions, see* 1788.

21061 CONSIDERATIONS importantes sur l'abolition générale de la traite des nègres, addressées aux négociateurs des puissances continentales qui doivent assister au Congrès de Vienne. Par un Portugais. 31p. *8°. Paris*, 1814.

21062 ENGLAND. Parliament. *House of Commons.* Abrégé des preuves données devant un comité de la Chambre des Communes de la Grande Bretagne, en 1790 et 1791, en faveur de l'abolition de la traite des nègres. Traduit de l'anglois par Jean de Carro. 186p. *8°. Vienne*, 1814. *For other editions, see* 1791.

21063 MONTGOMERY, JAMES (1771–1854). The abolition of the slave trade, a poem, in four parts... Embellished with engravings...from pictures...by R. Smirke. 53p. *4°.* 1814.

21064 ROMILLY, SIR S. The speech of Sir Samuel Romilly, in the House of Commons, on the twenty-eighth June, 1814, on that article in the treaty of peace which relates to the slave trade. 34p. *8°.* 1814.

21065 SIMONDE DE SISMONDI, J. C. L. De l'intérêt de la France à l'égard de la traite des nègres. 59p. *8°. Genève & Paris*, 1814. *Presentation copy, with inscription, from the author to Thomas Clarkson.*

21066 —— [Another edition.] 52p. *8°. Londres*, 1814.

21067 —— Troisième édition, contenant de nouvelles réflexions sur la traite des nègres. 100p. *8°. Genève, Paris, &c.*, 1814. *Presentation copy to the Marquis of Lansdowne.*

21068 STEELE, J. Mitigation of slavery...Part I: Letters and papers of...Joshua Steele...Part II: Letters to Thomas Clarkson...by William Dickson... 528p. *8°.* 1814.

21069 *WILBERFORCE, WILLIAM (1759–1833). A letter to...the Prince of Talleyrand Perigord...on... the slave trade. 83p. *8°.* 1814.

POLITICS

21070 ABOU ALI MOHAMMED, *Ben Ali, pseud.* Al Kalomeric, the son of Maugraby: an Arabian tale. Now first faithfully translated from the original MSS....Discovered since the taking of Paris by the Allied Powers of Europe, and replete with marvellous coincidences! [A satire on the history of Napoleon I.] 49p. *8°.* 1814.

21071 BERGASSE, N. Réflexions de M. Bergasse ...sur l'acte constitutionnel du Sénat. 16p. *8°. n.p.* [1814]

21072 EDWARDS, GEORGE. The means of introducing the happy order of things and parliamentary reform... 7p. *4°.* [*London*, 1814] *With manuscript additions by the author.*

21073 FRANCIS, SIR PHILIP (1740–1818). Letter from Sir Philip Francis...to Earl Grey [occasioned by the blockade of the ports of Norway by the English fleet]. 26p. *8°.* 1814.

SOCIALISM

21074 SAINT-SIMON, C. H. DE, *Comte,* and **THIERRY**, J. N. A. De la réorganisation de la société européenne, ou de la nécessité et des moyens de rassembler les peuples de l'Europe en un seul corps politique, en conservant à chacun son indépendance nationale. 112p. *8°. Paris*, 1814.

21075 —— Deuxième édition. 122[112]p. *8°. Paris*, 1814. *Imperfect; wanting p. xvii–32. Presentation copy from*

the author. *A manuscript note on the half-title explains the manuscript corrections in the text as follows: 'Cet ouvrage imprimé d'abord pendant le peu de temps ou la presse a été libre n'a pu être reimprimé sans être soumis à la censure. Les censeurs ont altéré des passages et ont ajouté d'autres de leur façon, on a rétabli à la main ce qu'ils avaient défiguré et supprimé ce qu'ils avaient ajouté'.*

MISCELLANEOUS

21076 DESCRIPTION of the view of the battle of Vittoria, and the great victory gained by the Marquis of Wellington over the French army...now exhibiting in Henry Aston Barker's Panorama, Leicester Square. 12p., 1 plate. *8°.* [*London,*] 1814.

21077 PROCLAMATION. [*Begin.*] Napoleon, late Emperor of the French...To all our late friends... throughout England...[A satire, signed: Napoleon, inviting those dissatisfied with peace and prosperity in England to follow him into exile.] *s.sh.4°. Birmingham*, [1814]

21078 ROBERTS, P. Animadversions on a pamphlet, entitled, "Authentic documents relative to the miraculous cure of Winefrid White, of Wolverhampton, at St.

Winefrid's Well, alias Holywell, in Flintshire, on the 28th of June, 1805." 107p. *8°.* 1814.

21079 ROYAL IRISH INSTITUTION FOR PROMOTING THE FINE ARTS. Royal Irish Institution, founded 24th June, 1813. The prospectus, rules and regulations, and a list of the subscribers... together with the report of the committee for the year ending 24th June, 1814. 29p. *8°. Dublin*, 1814.

21080 STARK, W. Report to the Right Honourable the Lord Provost, Magistrates, and Council of the City of Edinburgh, and the Governors of George Heriot's Hospital...on the plans for laying out the grounds for buildings between Edinburgh and Leith. 21p. *8°. Edinburgh*, 1814.

21081 [SWIFT, E. L. L.] The ecclesiastical supremacy of the crown proved to be the Common Law of England. With preliminary observations, and an appendix. By Basilicus. xiv, 82p. *8°.* 1814.

21082 TRAVERS, B. The sinfulness of war: illustrated and enforced in a discourse delivered before a society of Christians of the Unitarian denomination, at their chapel, in Southampton, on December the 18th, 1814. 26p. *8°. Southampton,* [1814] *The copy that belonged to David Ricardo.*

21083 WHEELER, E. The divine presence implored in God's earthly temple. A sermon, delivered at the dedication of the new meeting-house in Great-Barrington, December 30, 1813. 13p. *8°. Stockbridge* [*Mass.*], 1814.

1815

GENERAL

21084 ARBUTHNOT, JAMES (*fl.* 1815). An historical account of Peterhead, from the earliest period to the present time. Comprehending an account of its trade, shipping, commerce, and manufactures, mineral wells, baths, &c. With an appendix, containing a copy of the original charter of erection, together with all the bye-laws ...relative to the harbours, &c. Also, a natural history of the fishes found on the coasts of Buchan. 159p. *8°. Aberdeen & Peterhead,* 1815. *Presentation copy, with manuscript inscription, from the author 'to James Brodie Esqr. of Brodie'.*

21085 [AUBERT DE VITRY, F. J. P.] Recherches sur les vraies causes de la misère et de la félicité publiques, ou de la population et des subsistances. Par un ancien administrateur. 212p. *8°. Paris,* 1815.

21086 BIRKBECK, M. Notes on a journey through France, from Dieppe through Paris and Lyons, to the Pyrennees, and back through Toulouse, in...1814, describing the habits of the people, and the agriculture of the country...The fifth edition. With the appendix. 115, 23p. *8°.* 1815. *For another edition, see* 1814.

21087 BLACKNER, J. The history of Nottingham, embracing its antiquities, trade, and manufactures, from the earliest authentic records, to the present period... 459p. *4°. Nottingham & London,* 1815 [–1817?] *The Appendix contains letters dated 1816, and the inscription below the frontispiece portrait of the author states that he died on 22 Dec. 1816.*

21088 CAREY, M. The olive branch, or faults on both sides, federal and democratic. A serious appeal on the necessity of mutual forgiveness and harmony, to save our common country from ruin. Third edition, greatly enlarged and improved. 336p. *12°. Boston,* 1815.

21089 —— Sixth edition, enlarged. 454p. *8°. Philadelphia,* 1815.

21090 —— Seventh edition, enlarged. 486p. *8°. Philadelphia,* 1815. *See also* 1817.

21091 COBBETT, W. Letters on the late war between the United States and Great Britain: together with other miscellaneous writings, on the same subject. 407p. *8°. New-York,* 1815.

21092 COLQUHOUN, P. A treatise on the wealth, power, and resources, of the British Empire, in every quarter of the world, including the East Indies: the rise and progress of the Funding System explained...The second edition, with additions and corrections...[With an appendix.] 456, 93p. *4°.* 1815. *For another edition, see* 1814.

21093 [DALLAS, ALEXANDER J.] An exposition of the causes and character of the late war with Great Britain. Published by authority of the American Government. 101p. *8°.* 1815.

21094 *The EAST-INDIA register and directory, for 1815; corrected to the 17th November, 1814; containing...lists of the Company's servants...Together with lists of...mariners, &c. not in the service of the... Company; and merchant vessels employed in the country trade. Compiled...by J. Mathison, A. W. Mason, & J. S. Kingston... 489p. *12°. London, Dublin, &c.,* [1815]

21095 *—— Corrected to the 4th August, 1815...by A. W. Mason, J. S. Kingston, & Geo. Owen, (2d.)... Second edition. 483p. *12°. London, Dublin, &c.,* [1815] *For other editions, see* 1804.

21096 EDWARDS, GEORGE. A general appeal, addressed in particular to the Lords Spiritual and Temporal, and nobility...gentry...commercial, manufacturing, and corporate interests of the kingdom, explaining the practical plan or design of the new and happy era of mankind... 76p. *8°. York,* [1815]

21097 —— Three most important objects proposed; the original system of human economy...a specific plan for the removal of all our public or financial burdens...lastly, appropriate means for the immediate introduction of the system and plans by the Crown and Parliament... 60p. *8°. York,* 1815.

21098 A FALMOUTH guide: containing a concise account of the history, trade, port, and public establishments of Falmouth; directions to the public offices, lodging-houses, inns...Being a complete directory to strangers, going abroad in the packets. 96p. *8°. Falmouth, Truro, &c.,* 1815.

21099 [FOSTER, R.] An address to the nation, on the relative importance of agriculture, and manufactures... together with remarks on the doctrines lately advanced by Mr. Malthus, on the nature of rent...and a prefatory letter to C. M. Talleyrand Perigord...on his late exposé of the financial state of the French nation. By the author of "Observations on the National Debt"... 124p. *8°.* 1815.

21100 GANILH, C. La théorie de l'économie politique, fondée sur les faits résultans des statistiques de la France et de l'Angleterre; sur l'expérience de tous les peuples célèbres par leurs richesses; et sur les lumières de la raison... 2 vols. *8°. Paris,* 1815. *With a manuscript* *inscription on the half-title:* 'Pour Monsieur Lacretelle ainé, Membre de l'Institut'. *See also* 1822.

21101 GIOJA, M. Nuovo prospetto delle scienze economiche ossia somma totale delle idee teoriche e pratiche in ogni ramo d'amministrazione privata e pubblica ... 6 vols. *4°. Milano,* 1815–17.

21102 GRAY, S. The happiness of states: or, an inquiry concerning population, the modes of subsisting and employing it, and the effects of all on human happiness. 598p. *4°. London & Edinburgh,* 1815. *See also* 1819.

21103 [LEGRAND DE BOISLANDRY, F. L.] Examen des principes les plus favorables aux progrès de l'agriculture, des manufactures et du commerce en France. Par L^s.D.B. 2 vols. *8°. Paris,* 1815.

21104 [MICHAUD, J. F.] Histoire des quinze semaines, ou le dernier règne de Bonaparte. Douzième édition. 80p. *8°. Paris,* 1815.

21105 MORGAN, W. Memoirs of the life of the Rev. Richard Price, D.D. F.R.S. 189p. *8°.* 1815. *Presentation copy, with inscription, from the author to 'Rajah Ram Mohun Roye'.*

21106 NELKENBRECHER, J. C.   J. C. Nelkenbrechers Taschenbuch der neuesten Münz-, Maass- und Gewichtsverfassung aller Länder und Oerter...Zum bequemern Gebrauche, und schnellern Uebersicht für die österreichischen Staaten, nach wiener oder niederöstr. Münz, Maass und Gewicht bearbeitet. Von S. Gunz... Zweyte, durchgesehene und verbesserte Auflage. 498p. *8°. Prag,* 1815. *See also* 1830, 1832, 1844.

21107 OBSERVATIONS on rents and the price of grain, and on their relatives; property tax, tithes, poor rates, labour, window tax, horses, malt, weights, and measures: with hints to assist in the regulation of them. 60p. *8°.* 1815.

21108 SAY, J. B. Catéchisme d'économie politique, ou instruction familière qui montre de quelle façon les richesses sont produites, distribuées et consommées dans la société... 160p. *12°. Paris,* 1815. *See also* 1816, 1822, 1834.

21109 —— De l'Angleterre et des Anglais. 56p. *8°. Paris & Londres,* 1815. *See also* 1816.

21110 SCHULTES, H. Reflections upon the progressive decline of the British Empire, and the necessity of public reform. Addressed to...the Earl of Liverpool. Second edition. 28p. *8°.* 1815.

21111 [SIMOND, L.] Journal of a tour and residence in Great Britain, during the years 1810 and 1811, by a French traveller: with remarks on the country, its arts, literature, and politics, and on...its inhabitants. [With an appendix on Ireland.] 2 vols. *8°. Edinburgh & London,* 1815.

21112 SOCIEDAD ECONOMICA DE MADRID. Parere della Societa' Economica di Madrid sullo stabilimento di un codice di leggi agrarie, umiliato al Supremo Real Consiglio di Castiglia disposto da D. Gaspare Melchior de Jovellanos. Tradotto dall' originale spagnuolo dall' avv. Gio: Battista Nicolosi e dal medesimo corredato di note. 153, 70p. *4°. Palermo,* 1815. *For other editions, see* 1795.

21113 STORCH, H. F. VON. Cours d'économie politique, ou exposition des principes qui déterminent la prospérité des nations... 6 vols. *8°. St. Petersbourg,* 1815. *See also* 1823.

21114 A TOUR through some parts of Istria, Carniola, Styria, Austria, the Tyrol, Italy, and Sicily, in the spring of 1814. By a young English merchant. 268p. *8°.* 1815.

21115 *[TYTLER, P. F.] Travels in France, during the years 1814–15. Comprising a residence at Paris, during the stay of the allied armies, and at Aix, at the period of the landing of Bonaparte...[With a section by Sir Archibald Alison.] 2 vols. *12°. London, Edinburgh, &c.,* 1815. *The copy that belonged to George Grote.*

21116 UNITED STATES OF AMERICA. *Treaties, etc.* All the treaties between the United States and Great-Britain; from the definitive treaty of peace, signed at Paris, 1783; to the treaty of peace, signed at Ghent, 1814. Published by order of the House of Representatives of Massachusetts. 48p. *8°. Boston,* 1815.

AGRICULTURE

21117 An ABSTRACT of the several deeds and muniments [concerning the honor and manor of Hampton Court]. 76p. *8°. n.p.* [c. 1815]

21118 COOPER, WILLIAM (*fl.* 1815). The timely monitor; or, the cause of the agriculturist advocated... To which are added, observations on draining... 68p. *8°. Derby,* [c. 1815].

21119 DAVIES, WALTER. General view of the agriculture and domestic economy of South Wales; containing the counties of Brecon, Caermarthen, Cardigan, Glamorgan, Pembroke, Radnor. Drawn up for the consideration of the Board of Agriculture... 2 vols. *8°. London, Monmouth, &c.,* 1815.

21120 ENGLAND. *Commissioners for the Herring Fishery.* Additional instructions for an officer of the fishery, under the Acts 48 Geo. III. cap. 110, and 55 Geo. III, cap. 94. [With an appendix of forms.] 135p. *8°. Edinburgh,* 1815. *Issued to Hugh Sutherland, Officer of the Fishery for Northumberland &c., with his name supplied in manuscript.*

21121 An ENQUIRY into the causes that have impeded the increase and improvement of arable farms, and that have principally depressed the landed interest; with some suggestions for establishing a system of permanent relief. 44p. *8°. Bath & London,* 1815.

21122 FAREY, J. General view of the agriculture and minerals of Derbyshire; with observations on the means of their improvement. Drawn up for the consideration of the Board of Agriculture... 2 vols. *8°. London, Derby, &c.,* 1815.

21123 FRENCH, J. A statement and calculation of the various expenses incident to the entering upon a farm of 200 acres, of wet heavy land...To which is added, an estimate of the returns, at the expiration of the first year. 19p. *8°. Chelmsford,* 1815.

21124 HALL, G. W. Letters on the importance of encouraging the growth of corn and wool, in the United Kingdom of Great Britain & Ireland. 82p. *8°.* [1815]

21125 HENDERSON, John. General view of the agriculture of the county of Caithness; with observations on the means of its improvement. Drawn up for the consideration of the Board of Agriculture...With an appendix, including an account of the improvements carried on, by Sir John Sinclair, Bart....on his estates in Scotland. 222p. *8°. London, Edinburgh, &c., 1815. The copy that belonged to Robert Southey, with his signature and the date 'London 1830' at the foot of the title-page.*

21126 —— General view of the agriculture of the county of Sutherland; with observations on the means of its improvement. Drawn up for the consideration of the Board of Agriculture...To which is annexed, a particular account of the more recent improvements... 238p. *8°. London, Edinburgh, &c., 1815. A reissue of the edition of 1812 (q.v.).*

21127 JACOB, W. A letter to Samuel Whitbread... being a sequel to Considerations on the protection required by British agriculture; to which are added remarks on the publications of a Fellow of University College, Oxford; of Mr. Ricardo, and Mr. Torrens. 38p. *8°. 1815. Author's presentation copy that belonged to David Ricardo. For* Considerations on the protection required by British agriculture, *see 1814.*

21128 A LETTER on the game laws. By a country gentleman, a proprietor of game. 44p. *8°. 1815.*

21129 [MACONOCHIE, Allan, *Lord Meadowbank.*] Directions for preparing manure from peat. Instructions for foresters. 98p. *8°. Edinburgh & London, 1815. See also 1845.*

21130 MALTHUS, T. R. An inquiry into the nature and progress of rent, and the principles by which it is regulated. 61p. *8°. John Murray, 1815. The Sheffield copy.*

21131 —— [Another issue.] 61p. *8°. John Murray & J. Johnson, 1815.*

21132 MERLINI, L. Breve manuale teorico per uso dei periti stimatori di beni di suolo in Toscana, che può essere utile ai possidenti, ai compratori, ai venditori dei medesimi col corredo d'alcune annotazioni, e regole generali da sostituirsi a dei sistemi attuali per ottenere il resultato del loro giusto valore. 34p. *8°. Firenze, 1815.*

21133 MURRAY, ADAM. General view of the agriculture of the county of Warwick: with observations on the means of its improvement. Drawn up for the consideration of the Board of Agriculture... 187p. *8°. London, Birmingham, &c., 1815.*

21134 PETTMAN, W. A letter to Arthur Young... on the situation of the growers of corn in Great Britain. 46p. *8°. Canterbury & London, 1815.*

21135 PLAN for regulating the rents of land in Scotland, with equal safety both to landlord and tenant. With reasons to prove, that it will add to the stability & permanent benefit of agriculture. 31p. *8°. Cupar & Edinburgh, 1815. See also 1816, 1817, 1834.*

21136 RICHARDSON, WILLIAM (1740–1820). Directions for the cultivation of fiorin grass in the island of Newfoundland. 24p. *12°. Newry, [1815]*

21137 RIGBY, E. Suggestions for an improved and extended cultivation of mangel wurzel. 28p. *8°. Norwich & London, [1815].*

21138 ROUGIER, J. B., *Baron de la Bergerie.* Histoire de l'agriculture française, considérée dans ses rapports avec les lois, les cultes, les mœurs et le commerce; précédée d'une notice sur l'empire des Gaules et sur l'agriculture des anciens. 460p. *8°. Paris, 1815.*

21139 SINCLAIR, SIR JOHN, *Bart.* Account of some experiments to promote the improvement of fruit trees by peeling the bark; with a description of the instruments calculated for that purpose, and engravings of them. 16p. *8°. London & Edinburgh, [1815].*

21140 —— Hints regarding the agricultural state of the Netherlands, compared with that of Great Britain; and some observations on the means of diminishing the expence of growing corn...and the introduction of other improvements into British agriculture. [With an appendix and an addendum.] 65, xlivp. *8°. London & Edinburgh, 1815.*

21141 —— Thoughts on the agricultural and financial state of the country; and on the means of rescuing the landed and farming interests from their present depressed state. 14p. *8°. London & Edinburgh, [1815]*

21142 *SOCIEDAD ECONOMICA DE AMIGOS DEL PAIS DE MADRID. Descripcion y diseño del trillo presentado a la Real Sociedad Economica de Amigos del Pais de Madrid, anunciado de orden de S.M. en la Gaceta de 27 de junio de este año. 26p. *4°. Madrid, 1815.*

21143 THOMAS, WILLIAM. Hints for establishing an office in Newcastle, for collecting and recording authentic information relative to the state of the collieries ...and the progress that has been made towards ascertaining the nature...of the strata below those seams, to which the workings in this country have been confined... To which are added, Observations on the necessity of adopting legislative measures to diminish the...recurrence of fatal accidents in collieries, and to prolong the duration of the coal mines of the United Kingdoms. By William Chapman... 34p. *8°. Newcastle, Shields, &c., 1815.*

21144 TOWNSEND, H. A general and statistical survey of the county of Cork...Second edition... 2 vols. *8°. Cork, 1815. For another edition, see 1810.*

21145 [WEST, SIR EDWARD.] Essay on the application of capital to land, with observations shewing the impolicy of any great restriction of the importation of corn, and that the bounty of 1688 did not lower the price of it. By a Fellow of University College, Oxford. 69p. *8°. 1815.*

21146 WORGAN, G. B. General view of the agriculture of the county of Cornwall. Drawn up for the consideration of the Board of Agriculture...[Revised and corrected by R. Walker, J. Trist and C. V. Penrose.] 192p. *8°. 1815.*

21147 YOUNG, ARTHUR (1741–1820). The farmer's calendar: containing the business necessary to be performed on various kinds of farms during every month in the year...The tenth edition greatly enlarged and improved. 658p. *8°. 1815. For other editions, see 1771.*

CORN LAWS

21148 ANDERSON, E. Bad times among the farmers. [A poem.] *s.sh.fol. n.p.* [1815] [*Br.* 482(6)]

21149 [—— ?] On the times, corn bills, paper money, and trade. [A poem.] *s.sh.fol. Whitehaven,* [1815] [*Br.* 482(5)]

21150 BOOTH, GEORGE, *merchant.* Observations on lowering the rent of land, and on the corn laws, and their effects on the manufacturing interest. [With a postscript and a supplement.] 49, 7p. *8°. Liverpool & London,* [1815] *For another edition, see 1814.*

21151 BOSMAN'S balance for weighing a corn law. 20p. *8°.* 1815.

21152 —— [Another edition.] p.3–18. *8°.* 1815.

21153 BRICKWOOD, J. Facts relative to the corn-laws, with observations on them, as they affect the industrious classes, the manufacturers, and the public. 94p. *8°.* 1815.

21154 BROUGHTON, THOMAS (*fl.* 1815–1819). A letter to the Right Hon. Lord Sheffield, in reply to his observations on the corn laws; shewing the impolicy of the present Bill, and suggesting a measure...to promote the general interest. 27p. *8°.* 1815. *The Sheffield copy.*

21155 —— The question fairly stated relative to the revision of the corn laws, and a permanent measure suggested, to secure a moderate price to the manufacturer, without injury to the farmer...Second edition, with additions. 50p. *8°.* 1815.

21156 CHAPMAN, WILLIAM (1749–1832). Observations on the effects that would be produced by the proposed corn laws, on the agriculture, commerce, & population of the United Kingdom. 37p. *8°. London, Winchester, &c.,* 1815. *Two copies: one a presentation copy, with inscription, from the author to William Vaughan; the other the copy that belonged to David Ricardo.*

21157 CHRONICLES of the Isles. [An attack on the Corn Bill in the style of the Old Testament.] *s.sh.fol. Glasgow,* [1815] [*Br.* 482(1)]

21158 CIVIS, *pseud.* An address to the public on the impolicy of the new Corn-Bill, and on the alarming tendency of a late compromise. 20p. *8°.* 1815.

21159 [**CLISSOLD,** S.] The letters of Cincinnatus: one addressed to...Lord Grenville; and three to the woollen manufacturers of the County of Gloucester, on the resolutions entered into by that body, at a meeting held at Rodborough, March 8, 1815, on the subject of the Corn Bill. 38p. *8°. Gloucester,* 1815.

21160 CONSIDERATIONS upon the Corn Bill; suggested by a recent declaration from high authority, that it was calculated "to throw the burden from those upon whom it ought to rest, to those upon whom it ought not". 51p. *8°. Bath & London,* 1815.

21161 CORN Bill. [An excerpt from the *Evening Post,* followed by a poem 'Commerce in tears' signed: J. Parkerson, jun.] *s.sh.4°. Norwich,* [1815] [*Br.* 482(2)]

21162 CORN Bill shortly considered, in a dialogue, between a poor man and a clergyman of his parish, in London. 8p. *4°.* [*London,* 1815 ?] *The Sheffield copy.*

21163 CURRY, J. A brief sketch of the causes which first gave rise to the late high price of grain in Great Britain; and to the consequent apparent necessity for the Corn Bill: with some proposals for a more equitable taxation: in a letter addressed to the editor of the Times newspaper. 35p. *8°.* 1815.

21164 CURWEN, J. C. Cursory observations on the corn laws. 38p. *8°.* 1815. *For another edition, see 1814.*

21165 D., J. Observations on the justice and policy of regulating the trade in corn... 34p. *8°. Exeter, London, &c.,* 1815.

21166 DUPPA, R. Observations on the price of corn as connected with the commerce of the country and the public revenue. 62p. *8°.* 1815. *The copy that belonged to David Ricardo.*

21167 EDYE, J. A letter to William Wilberforce...on the consequences of the unrestrained importation of foreign corn. 24p. *8°. London...Chard, &c.,* 1815.

21168 [**FRENCH,** J.] A letter to the Right Hon. Samuel Birch, Lord Mayor of the City of London, on the subject of the corn laws. By an Essex farmer. 24p. *8°.* 1815.

21169 [——] A second letter to the Right Hon. Samuel Birch, Lord Mayor of the City of London, on the subject of the corn laws, and the price of bread. By an Essex farmer. 23p. *8°.* 1815.

21170 H., J. Lines on the Corn Bill. [Dated: Tynemouth, March 1815.] *s.sh.8°. Newcastle,* [1815] [*Br.* 482(4)] *The signature 'J.H.' at the end of the ballad, has been extended in manuscript to 'Jane Harvey'.*

21171 HOLROYD, J. B., *Earl of Sheffield.* A letter on the corn laws, and on the means of obviating the mischiefs and distress, which are rapidly increasing... 44p. *8°.* 1815.

21172 —— Second edition, corrected and considerably enlarged. 62p. *8°.* 1815. *Two copies: one from the Sheffield Collection; the other a presentation copy, with an inscription from the author to Thomas William Coke (1752–1842), Earl of Leicester.*

21173 HUME, JAMES D. Thoughts on the corn laws, as connected with agriculture, commerce, and finance. 80p. *8°.* 1815.

21174 The **IMPOLICY** of the C—— Bill. Or the unbiassed voice of the people, the voice of Heaven. *s.sh.fol. n.p.* [1815] [*Br.* 482(3)]

21175 The **INFLUENCE** of taxation on the price of corn, considered; with reference to the resolutions for restricting importation, proposed by the Deputy President of the Board of Trade. 16p. *8°. Windsor,* 1815.

21176 —— Second edition. [With 'Appendix. Resolutions on the corn laws, proposed by the Hon. Deputy President of the Board of Trade' and a 'Postscript'.] 20, [2]p. *8°. Windsor & London,* 1815.

21177 MALTHUS, T. R. The grounds of an opinion on the policy of restricting the importation of foreign corn; intended as an appendix to "Observations on the corn laws". 48p. *8°.* 1815. *The Sheffield copy.*

21178 —— Observations on the effects of the corn laws, and of a rise or fall in the price of corn on the agriculture and general wealth of the country...Third edition. 47p. 8°. *John Murray*, 1815. *The Sheffield copy.*

21179 —— [Another issue.] 47p. 8°. *John Murray & J. Johnson & Co.*, 1815. *For other editions, see 1814.*

21180 NEWNHAM, G. L. A review of the evidence before the Committees of the two Houses of Parliament, on the corn laws. 66p. 8°. 1815.

21181 The **OBJECTIONS** against the Corn Bill vindicated. 32p. 8°. 1815.

21182 **OBSERVATIONS** relative to the corn laws, and on the evidence given before both Houses of Parliament, on that important subject. By a friend to his country. 39p. 8°. 1815.

21183 [QUESNAY, F.] On the corn laws; being a digest of extracts from The œconomical table: an attempt towards ascertaining and exhibiting the source, progress, & employment of riches, with explanations, by the... Marquis de Mirabeau... 110p. 8°. 1815. *For an edition of* The œconomical table, *see* 1766 (GENERAL).

21184 RICARDO, D. An essay on the influence of a low price of corn on the profits of stock; shewing the inexpediency of restrictions on importation: with remarks on Mr. Malthus' two last publications: "An inquiry into the nature and progress of rent" and "The grounds of an opinion on the policy of restricting the importation of foreign corn". 50p. 8°. 1815. *The Sheffield copy.*

21185 —— Second edition. 50p. 8°. 1815. *The copy that belonged to S. J. Loyd, Baron Overstone, formerly among his papers, for which see* vol. III, *MS.* 804.

21186 SIMPSON, THOMAS (*fl.* 1814–1816). Letters to the Honourable and Right Reverend the Lord Bishop of Durham...Lord Dundas and...George Rose...together with other public letters and observations upon the subject of the corn laws. 113p. 8°. *London & Stockton-upon-Tees*, 1815.

21187 SMITH, JOHN PRINCE (1774?–1822). An argument and constitutional advice for the petitioners against the Corn Bill. 44p. 8°. 1815.

21188 SPENCE, W. The objections against the Corn Bill refuted; and the necessity of this measure to the vital interests of every class of the community, demonstrated. 46p. 8°. 1815.

21189 —— Second edition. 46p. 8°. 1815.

21190 —— Fourth edition. 46p. 8°. *London & Dublin*, 1815.

21191 TORRENS, R. An essay on the external corn trade; containing an inquiry into the general principles of that important branch of traffic; an examination of the exceptions to which these principles are liable, and a comparative statement of the effects which restrictions on importation and free intercourse, are calculated to produce upon subsistence, agriculture, commerce, and revenue. 348p. 8°. 1815. *See also* 1820, 1826, 1827, 1829.

21192 A plain **VIEW** of the corn question. Shewing that the price of corn naturally falls with the progress of cultivation: that restrictions upon importations are injurious... 36p. 8°. 1815. *Attributed in a manuscript note to J. Brandreth.*

TRADES & MANUFACTURES

21193 ACCUM, F. C. A. A practical treatise on gas-light; exhibiting a summary description of the apparatus and machinery best calculated for illuminating streets, houses, and manufactories, with carburetted hydrogen, or coal-gas; with remarks on the utility, safety, and general nature of this new branch of civil economy... 186p. 8°. 1815. *See also* 1818.

21194 *The **BOOK** of trades; or, library of the useful arts...The sixth edition. 3 vols. 12°. 1815. *For other editions, see* 1811.

21195 COBBETT, W. Five letters to Lord Sheffield, on his speech at Lewes Wool Fair, July 26, 1815. With an appendix, containing his Lordship's report at the Lewes Wool Fair, July 29, 1811. [Reprinted from *The Political Register*, 26 August, 1815.] 33p. 8°. 1815.

21196 ENGLAND. Parliament. *House of Commons.* Minutes of the evidence taken before the Committee appointed by the House of Commons, to inquire into the state of the existing laws which regulate the manufacture and sale of bread, in the Metropolis and its neighbourhood ... 239p. 8°. 1815.

21197 HUDDART, JOSEPH (*fl.* 1815). Observations in consequence of the debate on the Navy estimates. [Dated: 29th April 1815. On the improvements in the manufacture of cordage made by his father Joseph Huddart (1741–1816).] [4]p. 4°. *n.p.* [1815]

21198 The landed **INTEREST.** [On the scarcity of English oak timber and the importance of maintaining the ship-building industry in England.] 2p. *fol. n.p.* [*c.* 1815] *The Sheffield copy.*

21199 LONDON. Livery Companies. *Clockmakers.* Abstracts from Acts of Parliament, &c. orders, and bye-laws, of the Worshipful Company of Clock-makers, London: and regulations for the manufacture of clocks, watches, and mathematical instruments. 14p. 8°. *Hoxton*, [*c.* 1815]

21200 **REPORTS** on warm registered cordage, manufactured by Messrs. Huddart & Co. Limehouse. 22p. 8°. 1815. *With a page of manuscript notes on 'Experiments on preserving from decay and increasing the strength of timber, made by Capt. Layman before the Navy Board... 1812'.*

COMMERCE

21201 An **ADDRESS** to the inhabitants of St. Pancras, St. Mary-le-Bone, St. Giles and St. George, Bloomsbury, and St. George, Hanover Square, pointing out the means of obtaining a plentiful supply of fish; with a plan for raising, by small subscriptions, a considerable sum of money...in order to carry it into execution. 15p. *8°. 1815.*

21202 **ALLEN**, Edward. The corn traders' assistant; or, explanatory tables, of the Liverpool market, for all sorts of grain, flour, & malt... 57, 20p. *8°. Liverpool,* [1815 ?]

21203 **BREST**. Extrait des registres de délibérations de la mairie de Brest. [Regulations concerning second-hand dealers.] 4p. *4°. Brest,* [1815]

21204 **CANDOLLE-BOISSIER**, DE. Genève considérée sous le rapport de ses importations de grains, avec un projet d'établissement public pour cette denrée, et des notes sur les produits en pain de différens grains. 239p. *8°. Genève,* 1815.

21205 **HODGKINS**, E. A series of mercantile letters, with the weights, measures and monies, reduced into the English standard: and an explanation of foreign exchanges: intended to give a general knowledge of business to... young persons...Second edition...enlarged...by the editor of the Commercial dictionary... 296p. *12°.* 1815.

21206 **HOLROYD**, J. B., *Earl of Sheffield.* Report made to the wool meeting at Lewes, on the 26th of July, 1815, by the President. [On the wool trade.] 12p. *8°. Lewes,* 1815. *With manuscript additions and corrections by the author. See also 1811, 1816, 1819.*

21207 **PRINCE'S LONDON PRICE CURRENT**...No. 2022. Friday, the 6th January [–No. 2073. Friday, the 29th December,] 1815. 52 nos. *fol.* [1815] *See also 1812, 1813, 1814, 1817, 1818, 1820.*

21208 The complete **READY RECKONER,** in miniature; containing, tables accurately cast up, shewing at one view, the amount or value of any number or quantity of goods or merchandize...To which are prefixed, a list of commercial stamp duties, commencing September 1, 1815... 207p. *32°.* [1815 ?]

21209 **REMARKS** on the commercial policy of Great Britain, principally as it relates to the corn trade. 104p. *8°.* 1815.

21210 **TELLTRUTH**, T., *pseud.* A dark story; or, a brief developement of the nefarious conduct of the black-diamond mongers, with regard to the present system of the coal trade. Seriously recommended to the attention of the public, whose interest is so materially affected by the scandalous imposition of high prices and short measure... 32p. *8°.* 1815.

21211 **THORNTON**, Thomas. A compendium of the laws and regulations concerning the trade with the East Indies; the duties of customs and excise on goods imported from thence...With a concise historical account of the principal articles of import from those parts. To which are subjoined, schedules of rates charged by the East India Company...Second edition, corrected to the present period. 141p. *8°.* 1815. *For another edition, see* 1814.

21212 **YOUNG**, Arthur (1741–1820). An enquiry into the rise of prices in Europe, during the last twenty-five years, compared with that which has taken place in England; with observations on the effects of high and low prices. p.141–220. *8°.* 1815. *No. 271, vol. 46 (issued only in this form),* of Annals of Agriculture. *Two presentation copies, with inscriptions from the author, one to Lord Sheffield, the other to John Forbes Esq.*

COLONIES

21213 **ARNOLD**, Thomas (1795–1842). The effects of distant colonization on the parent state; a prize essay, recited in the theatre at Oxford, June 7, 1815. 36p. *8°.* [*Oxford,* 1815]

21214 **YORKSHIRE AND LANCASHIRE ASSISTANT BAPTIST MISSIONARY SOCIETY.** Baptist Mission in India. Account of the formation of the Yorkshire and Lancashire Assistant Baptist Missionary Society, on...the 1st...of November, 1815, in...Manchester...with an address to the friends of the Baptist Mission in India. [4]p. *fol. Rochdale,* [1815]

FINANCE

21215 **BECHER**, W. Observations on the malt duties. 8p. *8°.* [*c.* 1815]

21216 **BENETT**, J. Reply to the letter of the Revd. William Coxe...on the subject of commutation of tithes ...Also the prize essay, which gave rise to this correspondence. 71p. *8°. Salisbury & London,* [1815]

21217 **BOOTH**, George, *merchant.* Observations on paper currency, the Bank of England notes, and on the principles of coinage, and a metallic circulating medium. 41p. *8°. Liverpool & London,* 1815.

21218 **BOYD**, Walter. Reflections on the financial system of Great Britain, and articularly [*sic*] on the Sinking Fund... 46p. *8°.* 1815. *A second edition was published with the author's Observations on Lord Grenville's Essay on the Sinking Fund in 1828 (q.v.).*

21219 [**BRICOGNE**, A. J. B.] Observations et éclaircissemens, par un créancier de l'état, sur les différens systèmes de finances suivis en France depuis l'an VIII jusqu'au 8 juillet 1815, et notamment sur le paragraphe concernant les finances, dans l'Exposé de la situation de l'empire, sur le budget et le compte, et sur le projet de loi de finances présenté en juin 1815. Seconde édition. 94p. *4°. Paris,* 1815.

21220 —— Opinion et observations sur le budget de 1814, sur le budget de juin 1815, et sur les différens systèmes de finances suivis en France depuis l'an VIII jusqu'au 8 juillet 1815. Par un créancier de l'état. Troisième édition. 302p. *8°. Paris, 1815.*

21221 COBBETT, W. Paper against gold and glory against prosperity. Or, an account of the rise, progress, extent, and present state of the Funds and of the paper money of Great Britain… 2 vols. *8°. 1815. See also 1817, 1820, 1828, 1841.*

21222 COCHRANE, THOMAS, *10th Earl of Dundonald.* A letter to Lord Ellenborough from Lord Cochrane [on his trial. With an appendix]. 138, [38]p. *8°. 1815.*

21223 CONSIDERATIONS addressed to the people of Great Britain, on the expediency of continuing the property-tax a certain number of years. 75p. *8°. 1815.*

21224 COXE, W. Letter to John Benett…on his essay relative to the commutation of tithes, to which was adjudged the Bedfordean Gold Medal, by the Bath and West of England Society…at their annual meeting, December 13, 1814. Second edition. 32p. *8°. Salisbury & London, [1815]*

21225 —— Three additional letters to J. Benett, Esq. on the commutation of tithe; in answer to his Reply. 91p. *8°. Salisbury & London, [1815]*

21226 DUNCAN, H. An essay on the nature and advantages of parish banks: together with a corrected copy of the rules and regulations of the parent institution in Ruthwell: and directions for conducting the details of business, forms shewing the method of keeping the accounts, &c. 28p. *8°. Edinburgh, 1815. Presentation copy, with inscription, from the author to Patrick Colquhoun. See also 1816.*

21227 ETTRICK FOREST SAVINGS BANK. Plan of the Ettrick Forest Savings Bank, established, 7th April, 1815. [With a list of officers.] 22p. *8°. Hawick, 1815.*

21228 [**FORBES,** JOHN H., *Lord Medwyn.*] A short account of the Edinburgh Savings Bank, containing directions for establishing similar banks, with the mode of keeping the accounts and conducting the details of business. 14p. *8°. Edinburgh, 1815. The copy presented to Patrick Colquhoun by Sir William Forbes, Bart. See also 1816.*

21229 GANILH, C. Considérations générales sur la situation financière de la France, en 1816. 69p. *8°. Paris, 1815.*

21230 GOURLAY, R. F. The right to Church property secured, and commutation of tythes vindicated, in a letter to the Rev. William Coxe, Archdeacon of Wilts. 41p. *8°. 1815. This may be a facsimile reprint of the 1815 edition, made in 1831 for the author's collection entitled: Early publications, q.v.* (GENERAL).

21231 HIGHLAND AND AGRICULTURAL SOCIETY OF SCOTLAND. Report of the Committee appointed by the Highland Society of Scotland, to consider what is the best mode of forming institutions of the nature of savings banks, for receiving the deposits of labourers and others… 14p. *8°. Edinburgh & London, 1815. The copy presented to Patrick Colquhoun by Sir William Forbes, Bart*

21232 *HILBERS, H. G. The statement of H. G. Hilbers, partner of the late house of Hilbers, James, and Co. By himself. [Disproving the accusations of fraudulent

dealings brought against him at the time of the failure of his firm.] 134p. *8°. 1815.*

21233 ⟨From the Bath Chronicle of Aug. 24, 1815.⟩ Provident **INSTITUTIONS.** *s.sh.4°. Bath, [1815] The copy that belonged to Patrick Colquhoun.*

21234 LAURIE, D. A treatise on finance, under which, the general interests of the British Empire, are illustrated: comprising, a project for their improvement; together with a new scheme for liquidating the National Debt. 1220p. *8°. Glasgow, 1815.*

21235 LIST of subscribers to the tontine scheme in the city of Glasgow, instituted in…February, 1781. With the names of the nominees and present proprietors. 3p. *4°. n.p. [1815]*

21236 *MILNE, JOSHUA. A treatise on the valuation of annuities and assurances on lives and survivorships… and on the probabilities and expectations of life…2 vols. *8°. 1815. The copy that belonged to Augustus De Morgan.*

21237 The **NATURE** and principles of the property tax; being an appeal to the grave and sober sense of the people of England. 77p. *8°. 1815.*

21238 OBSERVATIONS on the new duty on wine. [With a postscript. signed: A wine merchant.] 18p. *8°. 1815.*

21239 To his Royal Highness the Prince Regent, the Lords Spiritual and Temporal, and the Commons of Great Britain and Ireland, in Parliament assembled, are humbly submitted the following **OBSERVATIONS** on behalf of the labourers, the farmers, the manufacturers, and people of England, by the farmer. [With 'Further observations addressed to Mr. Vansittart'.] 19, 12p. *8°. [London, 1815]*

21240 The **POOR** enriched! To the magistrates of the Borough of Berwick-upon-Tweed in particular; and to those, in general, in the northern counties of England, the following letter, on the utility of parish, or savings-banks, is humbly addressed. 29p. *8°. Berwick, 1815.*

21241 PROVIDENT INSTITUTION FOR SAVINGS, *Bath.* Provident Institution established at Bath, January 1815…Regulations. 2p. *s.sh. fol. Bath, [1815] The copy that belonged to Patrick Colquhoun.*

21242 —— [Another edition.] 3, [5]p. *obl.8°. Bath, [1815] The text of the Regulations is followed by a table showing the amount of 5% stock purchasable with £1 at quotations from 80 to 110, followed by 4 blank balance sheets, with some entries in manuscript. The copy presented to Patrick Colquhoun by 'J.H.', i.e. John Haygarth, M.D., one of the managers?*

21243 ROLLE, J., *Baron Rolle.* The pocket companion to the law of bills of exchange, promissory notes, drafts, checks, &c. With tables of the stamp duties… Corrected to the end of the last session of Parliament… Second edition. 130p. *24°. 1815.*

21244 ROSE, GEORGE. The speech of the Right Hon. George Rose, in the House of Commons, on the 20th of February, 1815, on the subject of the property tax. 23p. *8°. 1815.*

21245 STOCK EXCHANGE. Report of the Committee of the Stock-Exchange, appointed for the distribution of the money, stopped on account of the late fraud [of de Bérenger and others]. 15p. *8°. Printed for the* use of Members of the Stock Exchange only, 1815. The copy which belonged to the deputy-chairman of the sub-committee, Charles Nairne.

21246 —— Second Report of the Sub-Committee of the Stock-Exchange, relative to the late fraud [of C. Random de Bérenger and others]. 15p. 8°. Printed for the use of Members of the Stock Exchange only, 1815. Two copies, one bound with the first report (see note to no. 21021) which belonged to Charles Nairne, and the other, which belonged to David Ricardo.

21247 SYMONS, W. The practical gager; or, the young gager's assistant…Adapted for the use of collectors …of the Excise and Customs; as well as for maltsters, distillers…A new edition… 384p. 12°. 1815. For other editions, see 1782.

21248 UNITED STATES OF AMERICA. Laws, etc. Laws of the United States laying a direct tax, and laying duties on household furniture and on gold and silver watches. With an act to amend the same. 30p. 8°. Washington City, 1815.

21249 VIOLET, T. An humble declaration to the Right honourable the Lords and Commons…touching the transportation of gold and silver…presented the 12th day of April, 1643… 16p. 8°. 1643 [Hull, c. 1815] For another edition, see 1643.

21250 [WEYLAND, J. ?] A pat from the lion's paw, inflicted in the name of common sense, upon the railers against the property tax. By Leo Britannicus. 23p. 8°. 1815.

21251 WILSON, ROBERT, accountant. An enquiry into the causes of the high prices of corn and labour, the depressions on our foreign exchanges, and high prices of bullion during the late war; and consideration of the measures to be adopted for relieving our farming interest from the…difficulties to which they are now reduced… 87p. 8°. Edinburgh & London, 1815.

TRANSPORT

21252 *CARY, JOHN (d. 1835). Cary's new itinerary: or, an accurate delineation of the great roads…throughout England and Wales; with many of the principal roads in Scotland…Sixth edition, with improvements. [58]p., 124 col., [62]p., 874 col., p.875–946. 8°. 1815.

21253 COMPANY OF UNDERTAKERS OF THE GRAND CANAL, Dublin. Grand Canal. Defence of the Court of Directors; including a statement of the true situation of the Company's affairs; made by the Hon. Sir William Cusack Smith, Bart. at a general meeting of the Company, held…the 25th day of November, 1815, for the purpose of hearing…certain complaints preferred against the directors… 52p. 8°. Dublin, [1815]

21254 —— To the proprietors of Grand Canal stock, 1815. [A statement of the constitution of the Company.] 23p. 8°. Dublin, [1815]

21255 ENGLAND. Laws, etc. Anno quadragesimo secundo Georgii III. Regis. [Local & Personal.] Cap. 25. An Act to enable the Company of Proprietors of the Navigation from the Trent to the Mersey, to make railways, to alter the course of the railway from Froghall to Caldon, and…of the canal from Froghall to Uttoxeter; and to amend the Trent and Mersey Canal Acts. ⟨15th April 1802.⟩ p.357–370. fol. 1815.

21256 —— Anno quinquagesimo quinto Georgii III. Regis. Cap. lxv. An Act for making and maintaining a navigable canal from Sheffield to Tinsley, in the West Riding of the county of York. ⟨7th June 1815.⟩ p.1585–1655. fol. 1815.

21257 —— —— The new district, or Isleworth Turnpike Acts of Parliament, with a correct list of the trustees. Printed by order of the Board of Trustees of the 10th day of January, 1814. 106p. 8°. Brentford, 1815.

21258 KENNET AND AVON CANAL NAVIGATION. Report of the Committee of Management, to the Proprietors of the Kennet and Avon Canal Navigation. [Signed: Charles Dundas, chairman, and dated, 15th August 1815.] 2p. fol. Marlborough, [1815] See also 1812, 1813, 1816, 1823, 1824, 1825, 1826, 1838.

21259 North LEITH church lands, &c. [Documents, including an abstract of the Charter of Queen Mary, 1566, concerned with the glebe lands of the parish kirk of Leith, printed in connection with the building of new docks at Leith.] 8p. 4°. n.p. [1815] The Rastrick copy.

21260 MacCARTHY, J. J. A. Prospectus of a new pavement for the carriageways of the Metropolis. Second edition. 11p. 4°. [c. 1815]

21261 MAXWELL, JOHN I. Hints for protecting the public against the extortion and insolence of hackney-coachmen: a critical inquiry into the power vested in the commissioners… 49p. 8°. [London,] 1815.

SOCIAL CONDITIONS

21262 ASSOCIATED CATHOLIC CHARITIES. The Associated Catholic Charities, for educating, clothing & apprenticing the children of poor Catholics, and providing for destitute orphans. [With a list of officers, general rules, and regulations for the various departments.] 22, 23p. 12°. 1815. See also 1829, 1830.

21263 ASSOCIATION FOR THE RELIEF OF THE MANUFACTURING AND LABOURING POOR. Second report of the Association…relative chiefly to the general supply of fish in the Metropolis and the interior…[With a list of officers and subscribers.] 59p. 8°. 1815. See also 1813, 1825.

21264 BENEVOLENT INSTITUTION FOR THE RELIEF OF AGED WORKMEN…OF THE WATCH AND CLOCK TRADE. To all persons interested in the watch and clock trade. [Rules adopted at the inaugural meeting, 6 March 1815, members of the provisional committee, and list of subscriptions.] 3p. fol. [London, 1815] With a printed covering letter on a separate leaf. See note to no. 13563.

21265 BOWLES, J. A letter to Robert Wissett, Esq. in answer to four letters, addressed by Mr. Wissett to the author, on the subject of licensing and regulations for public-houses and liquor-shops. 126p. *8°*. 1815. *See also* 1816.

21266 BREST. Règlement sur la police du spectacle. [Extrait des registres des arrêtés du maire de la ville de Brest.] 10p. *4°*. *Brest*, 1815.

21267 CHARITY FOR THE RELIEF OF WIDOWS AND ORPHANS OF POOR CLERGYMEN *Lewes.* An account and state [for the year 1814] of the Charity for the relief of widows... within the Archdeaconry of Lewes... 12p. *12°*. *Lewes*, 1815. *See also* 1794.

21268 CHARITY SCHOOL, *St. Mary-le-Bone.* A concise account of the Charity School, for maintaining and educating one hundred and eight children of the industrious poor parishioners of...St. Mary-le-Bone... [With 'Abstract of receipts and disbursements...for the year 1814'.] 41p. *8°*. 1815. *See also* 1816.

21269 CLARKSON, W. An inquiry into the cause of the increase of pauperism and poor rates; with a remedy for the same and a proposition for equalizing the rates throughout England and Wales. 77p. *8°*. 1815. *See also* 1816.

21270 CONSIDERATIONS addressed to the journeymen calico printers, by one of their masters. 19p. *8°*. *Manchester*, 1815.

21271 [DUNCAN, JOHN S.] Collections relative to systematic relief of the poor, at different periods, and in different countries: with observations on charity... 220p. *8°*. *Bath & London*, 1815.

21272 EDDY, T. Hints for introducing an improved mode of treating the insane in the asylum; read before the governors of the New-York Hospital, on the 4th of Fourth-month, 1815. 18p. *8°*. *n.p.*, 1815.

21273 ENGLAND. Parliament. *House of Commons.* Minutes of the evidence taken before the Committee...to inquire into the state of mendicity and vagrancy in the Metropolis and its neighbourhood. Ordered to be printed, July 11, 1815. 152p. *8°*. 1815. *See also* 1816.

21274 ———— ———— Report, together with the minutes of evidence, and an appendix of papers, from the Committee appointed to consider of provision being made for the better regulation of madhouses in England. Ordered, by the House of Commons, to be printed, 11th July, 1815. Each subject of evidence arranged under its distinct head, by J. B. Sharpe, member of the Royal College of Surgeons. 399p. *8°*. 1815.

21275 General Post-Office. A candid **EXAMINATION** of the origin and management, of what is called the Inland Letter-Carrier's Superannuated Fund. In which the necessity of adopting a better system...will be made manifest, from the example of an unfortunate individual [William Wood]...By a friend to impartial justice. 48p. *8°*. 1815.

21276 EXTRAIT du second cahier des Feuilles d'économie rurale d'Hofwyl, publié en 1809. [On Fellenberg's industrial establishments.] 16p. *8°*. *n.p.* [1815]

21277 FREE-SCHOOL SOCIETY, *New York.* Tenth annual report of the trustees of the Free-School Society of New-York. [Signed: De Witt Clinton, president, Thomas Buckley, secretary; dated: Fifth Month (May) 1st, 1815.] [4]p. *fol. New-York*, [1815] [*Br.* 483]

21278 GOURLAY, R. F. Tyranny of poor laws,

exemplified. 15p. *8°*. *Bath, Devizes, &c.*, 1815. *Reissued by the author with other pamphlets in a volume entitled:* Early publications, *in 1831, q.v.* (GENERAL).

21279 GRAY, JONATHAN. A history of the York Lunatic Asylum: with an appendix, containing minutes of the evidence on the cases of abuse lately inquired into ...Addressed to William Wilberforce, Esquire, one of the contributors to Lupton's Fund. [With an appendix.] 99, 52p. *8°*. *York & London*, 1815.

21280 [IRVINE, A.] Reflections on the education of the poor, submitted particularly to the consideration of the landholders and principal manufacturers. 52p. *8°*. 1815.

21281 ———— The second edition, with additions. 72p. *8°*. 1815. *Presentation copy, with inscription, from the author to George Gunning, M.P.*

21282 LIVERPOOL RELIGIOUS TRACT SOCIETY. First report of the Liverpool Religious Tract Society, M.DCCC.XV, with extracts of correspondence, and a list of subscribers and benefactors [and 'Catalogue of the publications of the Society']. 44p. *8°*. *Liverpool*, [1815] *See also* 1816.

21283 LIVERPOOL SUNDAY SCHOOL UNION. [*Begin.*] At a public meeting held at the school-room of Great George Street Chapel, on the 18th August, 1815, for the purpose of forming a day and Sunday school union for Liverpool...Archibald Keightley, Esq. in the chair, it was...resolved...[The resolutions, preceded by a printed covering letter signed: James Walker, Samuel Hope, secretaries, and dated, Liverpool, 2d September, 1815.] [4]p. *8°*. *n.p.* [1815] *Addressed in manuscript to 'Mr. John Lang'.*

21284 LONDON FEMALE PENITENTIARY. The eighth annual report of the Committee of the London Female Penitentiary, with lists of its officers and subscribers. 31, 44p. *8°*. 1815.

21285 MINCHIN, WILLIAM. An essay to illustrate the rights of the poor, by law: being a commentary on the statute of King Henry the VII. chapter 12. With observations on the practice of suing and defending in forma' pauperis. And suggestions for extending the benefits of such practice...Together with a succinct account of all the public charities in and near London... 144p. *8°*. 1815.

21286 MORGAN, , *Miss.* The gaol of the City of Bristol compared with what a gaol ought to be. Intended to diffuse a more general knowledge of the requisites of a good prison. By a citizen. With an appendix, containing a brief account of the Panopticon, a prison upon a new plan, proposed to government by Jeremy Bentham, Esq. 95p. *8°*. *Bristol & London*, 1815.

21287 NEW YORK HOSPITAL. State of the New-York Hospital for the year 1814. [Dated: February 7, 1815.] [4]p. *fol. n.p.* [1815]

21288 NEWMAN, A., & CO. The newspapers versus the Echo offices; or, an appeal to the liberality of an enlightened and discerning public. [Containing allegations concerning the functioning of the Echo's situations department.] 7p. *8°*. 1815.

21289 OVINGTON, J. Conversations on matrimony. Intended as an accompaniment to the letters lately published on the duties, advantages, pleasures, and sorrows of the marriage state. 143p. *12°*. *London & Clapham Common*, [1815 ?]

21290 [OWEN, ROBERT.] Observations on the effect of the manufacturing system: with hints for the improvement of those parts of the system which are the most injurious. 16p. *8°.* [1815]

21291 —— [Another edition.] 18p. *8°.* 1815. *See also* 1818.

21292 PROVIDENT INSTITUTION, *Liverpool.* The Liverpool Provident Institution, established in 1815. 12p. *12°. Liverpool,* [1815]

21293 PRUDENT MAN'S FRIEND SOCIETY. State of the…Society, for the year 1815. [With a list subscribers.] 30p. *12°. Bristol,* [1815] *See also* 1813, 1814, 1816.

21294 RENGGER, A. Rapport sur l'Institut d'Education des Pauvres à Hofwyl. rédigé par Mr. A. Rengger, ci-devant Ministre de l'Intérieur de la République Helvétique, au nom de la Commission établie pour l'inspection de l'Etablissement. 115p. *8°. Paris & Genève,* 1815.

21295 RICE, THOMAS. An inquiry into the effects of the Irish grand jury laws, as affecting the industry, the improvement and the moral character, of the people of Ireland. 120p. *8°.* 1815.

21296 RIPLEY, J., *and others.* The trial of James Ripley, Richard Burton, Robert Herbert and Richard Matthews, for the murder of Jane Watson…the 8th of April, 1815… 100p. *8°.* 1815.

21297 RITSON, J. The office of constable: being an entirely new compendium of the law…Carefully compiled from the best authorities. With an introduction, containing some account of the origin and antiquity of the office…Second edition, corrected and enlarged. 88p. *8°.* 1815. *The first edition, published anonymously in 1791, is also in the Library, for which see* vol. III, *Addenda.*

21298 SOCIETY FOR THE ENCOURAGEMENT OF SERVANTS. Society for the encouragement of servants, &c.&c. [Regulations of a 'register office for good domestic servants'.] [2]p. *s.sh.8°. Liverpool,* [1815 ?]

21299 SOCIETY FOR THE SUPPORT OF GAELIC SCHOOLS. The fourth annual report of the Society…With an appendix respecting the present state of the highlands and islands of Scotland, the operations of the committee, &c. 58p. *8°. Edinburgh, London, &c.,* 1815.

21300 SOCIETY FOR THE SUPPRESSION OF BEGGARS, *Edinburgh.* Plan of an institution for the suppression of begging. Abstracted from the reports of the Society…for the Suppression of Beggars…and particularly recommended to the attention of the inhabitants of Greenock. 27p. *8°. Greenock,* 1815.

21301 SURREY. *Court of Quarter Sessions.* [*Begin.*] At a meeting of a committee of magistrates, at the Session House in Newington…on…the seventh day of November, one thousand eight hundred and fifteen, appointed… to consider the great increase in the number of shops for the sale of gin and other spirituous liquors in the Borough of Southwark…and the most efficient means of suppressing or regulating the same…Mr. Jackson laid before the Committee the following report and moved that it be adopted… 6p. *4°. n.p.* [1815]

21302 TOONE, W. A practical guide to the duty and authority of overseers of the poor; with full and plain directions to them in the execution of their office. Interspersed with numerous precedents…relating to the poors' law… 191p. *8°.* 1815.

21303 URQUHART, T. Substance of a letter to Lord Viscount Melville, written in May, 1815, with the outlines of a plan to raise British seamen…to do away with the evils of impressment, and man our ships effectually with mercantile seamen… 16p. *8°.* 1815.

21304 A **VIEW** of the New-York State prison in the City of New-York. By a member of the institution. [With an appendix of documents.] 89p. *8°. New-York,* 1815. *The copy that belonged to Patrick Colquhoun.*

21305 WEYLAND, J. The principle of the English poor laws illustrated from the evidence given by Scottish proprietors (before the Corn Committee) on the connexion observed in Scotland between the price of grain and the wages of labour. 78p. *8°.* 1815.

21306 WISSETT, R. Letters to John Bowles, Esq. on the subject of licensing & regulations for public houses and liquor shops. [With an appendix of documents.] 89, 68p. *8°.* 1815.

SLAVERY

21307 AFRICAN INSTITUTION. Reasons for establishing a registry of slaves in the British Colonies: being a report of a committee of the African Institution. Published by order of that society. 118p. *8°.* 1815.

21308 [GRÉGOIRE, H. B., *Comte.*] De la traite et de l'esclavage des noirs et des blancs; par un ami des hommes de toutes les couleurs. 84p. *8°. Paris,* 1815. *With a manuscript note on the verso of the half-title: 'A Son Altesse royale Monseigneur le Duc de Sussex De la part de l'auteur M. Grégoire évêque démissionnaire de Blois'.*

21309 MACAULAY, Z. A letter to…the Duke of Gloucester, President of the African Institution… Occasioned by a pamphlet lately published by Dr. Thorpe …entitled, "A letter to William Wilberforce, Esq." &c. &c. [With an appendix.] 46, 60p. *8°.* 1815. *The copy that belonged to Stephen Lushington, inscribed: 'From the author'.*

21310 —— Second edition, enlarged. 62, 60p. *8°.* 1815.

21311 A **REVIEW** of the reasons given for establishing a registry of slaves in the British colonies in a report of a committee of the African Institution, entitled "Reasons," &c.&c. 32p. *8°.* [*London,* 1815]

21312 THORPE, R. A letter to William Wilberforce …containing remarks on the reports of the Sierra Leone Company, and African Institution: with hints respecting the means by which an universal abolition of the slave trade might be carried into effect. 84p. *8°.* 1815.

21313 —— The third edition, with a preface. xxvi, 84p. *8°.* 1815. *The Sheffield copy.*

POLITICS

21314 [BINS DE SAINT VICTOR, J. M. B.] Des révolutionnaires et du ministère actuel. Par M.***. 84p. *8°. Paris, 1815.*

21315 BLANC, bleu, rouge. [A political dialogue.] 16p. *8°. Lyon, 1815.*

21316 [BOWDLER, T.] Liberty civil and religious. By a friend to both. 73p. *8°. 1815.*

21317 CARNOT, Lazare N. M., *Comte.* Mémoire adressé au Roi, en juillet 1814, par M. Carnot; précédé de la préface, et suivi de son discours prononcé au Tribunat...le 11 floréal, an XII, sur la motion relative au gouvernement héréditaire. Avec les notes. Neuvième édition, suivi de l'exposé de la situation de l'Empire, fait à la Chambre des Pairs et à celles des Représentans... 13 juin, 1815... 91p. *8°. Paris, 1815.*

21318 CARTWRIGHT, J. Letter, &c. [Dated 12th Dec. 1815; to Sir Francis Burdett, on parliamentary reform.] 14p. *8°. [1815]*

21319 CHABANNES, J. B. M. F. DE, *Marquis de Chabannes Courton et de la Palice.* Lettres de M. le Marquis de Chabannes, à S. Exc. M. le Cte. de Blacas, suivies de quelques éclaircissemens et extraits de mémoires relatifs aux événemens présens. 74p. *8°. Londres, 1815.*

21320 COBBETT, W. The pride of Britannia humbled; or, the queen of the ocean unqueen'd, "by the American cock boats"...Illustrated and demonstrated by four letters addressed to Lord Liverpool, on the late American war...To which is added, a glimpse of the American victories...A new edition. [Edited by T. Branagan.] 215p. *12°. Philadelphia, New York, &c., 1815.*

21321 *COMTE, F. C. L. De l'impossibilité d'établir une monarchie constitutionelle sous un chef militaire, et particulièrement sous Napoléon. Quatrième édition, revue corrigée et augmentée. [With 'Pièces justificatives'.] 72p. *8°. Paris, 1815. The copy that belonged to George Grote, inscribed: 'from the author' on the flyleaf of the volume.*

21322 DESAUGIERS, M. A. M. Le terme d'un règne, ou le règne d'un terme; relation véridique, écrite en forme de pot-pourri, sous la dictée de Cadet Buteux, par Désaugiers, son secrétaire intime. Seconde édition, corrigée et augmentée de Vive le Roi! chanson inédite du même auteur. 47p. *8°. Paris, 1815.*

21323 FLEURY, A. M. Réponse au mémoire de M. Carnot. 21p. *8°. Paris, 1815.*

21324 [GUILLIÉ, S.] Histoire du cabinet des Tuileries, depuis le 20 mars 1815, et de la conspiration qui a ramené Buonaparte en France. Seconde édition. 94p. *8°. Paris, 1815.*

21325 KERGORLAY, L. F. P. DE, *Comte.* Des lois existantes, et du décret du 9 mai 1815. 8p. *8°. Paris, 1815.*

21326 L***. Essai sur l'esprit public; par L***, ancien consul de France. 36p. *8°. Paris, 1815.*

21327 LA MARTELIÈRE, J. H. F. Conspiration de Buonaparte contre Louis XVIII, Roi de France et de Navarre, ou relation succincte de ce qui s'est passé depuis la capitulation de Paris, du 30 mars 1814, jusqu'au 22 juin 1815, époque de la seconde abdication de Buonaparte... Deuxième édition, corrigée et augmentée. 118p. *8°. Paris, 1815.*

21328 LE SAGE, . Peut-on être plus royaliste que le Roi? 39p. *8°. Paris, 1815.*

21329 MASSACRÉ, L. DE. Du ministère. [An attack on the appointment of Joseph Fouché.] 63p. *8°. Paris, 1815.*

21330 NAPOLÉON, Louis XVIII et Bonaparte. [An account of political events from the Battle of Leipzig to the entry of the Allies into Paris in 1815.] 56p. *8°. [Paris, 1815]*

21331 Le Maréchal NEY devant les maréchaux de France. 41p. *8°. Paris, 1815.*

21332 —— Second partie. 29p. *8°. Paris, 1815.*

21333 PLAYFAIR, W. A statement, which was made in October, to Earl Bathurst...and in November, 1814, to the Comte de la Châtre...of Buonaparte's plot to re-usurp the crown of France. 33p. *8°. 1815.*

21334 SAINT DIDIER, . Nuits de l'abdication de l'Empereur Napoléon. 44p. *8°. Paris, 1815.*

21335 SENANCOUR, E. P. DE. Quatorze juillet, 1815. [An extract from his journal for that date.] 8p. *8°. n.p. [1815 ?]*

21336 STEWART, John (1749–1822). Système nouveau de la philosophie physique, morale, politique et speculative...Adressé au Congrès des Princes Souverains Pacificateurs du Monde Civilisé, assemblés à Vienne. 260p. *12°. Londres, 1815. Presentation copy, with inscription, from the author to Baron Jacobi.*

21337 [TASCHEREAU DE FARGUES, P. A. J.] Clémence et justice. 52p. *8°. Paris, 1815.*

SOCIALISM

21338 MELISH, J. Account of a society at Harmony, (twenty-five miles from Pittsburg) Pennsylvania...Taken from "Travels in the United States of America, in the years 1806 and 1807, and 1809, 1810, and 1811. By John Melish." ⟨From the Philanthropist, No. xx.⟩ 12p. *8°. [1815]*

21339 SAINT-SIMON, C. H. DE, *Comte,* and THIERRY, J. N. A. Opinion sur les mesures à prendre contre la coalition de 1815. 47p. *8°. Paris, 1815. The copy that belonged to Victor Considérant.*

21340 SOCIETY OF SPENCEAN PHILANTHROPISTS. The address and regulations, of the Society...with an abstract of Spence's plan. 12p. *12°. 1815.*

MISCELLANEOUS

21341 [DELBARE, F. T.] Relation fidèle et détaillée de la dernière campagne de Buonaparte, terminée par la Bataille de Mont-Saint-Jean, dite de Waterloo ou de la Belle-Alliance. Par un témoin oculaire. 93p. *8°. Paris*, 1815.

21342 HAMILTON, RICHARD W. A sermon, preached at Leeds, April 16th, MDCCCXV. On occasion of the execution of Mr. Joseph Blackburn, attorney at law, for forgery; with details of conversations with him during his imprisonment...Third edition. 62p. *8°. London & Leeds*, 1815.

21343 LANCASHIRE AUXILIARY MISSIONARY SOCIETY. [*Begin.*] Dear Sir, I have pleasure to inform you...[A letter signed: P. S. Charrier, secretary, announcing the first anniversary meeting of the Society, in Liverpool, with the programme of events, August 1–3, 1815.] [4]p. *8°. n.p.* [1815]

21344 —— [Another edition of the programme.] *s.sh.8°. n.p.* [1815]

21345 *LONDON. Livery Companies. Salters.* A list of the Master, Wardens, Court of Assistants, and Livery, of the Worshipful Company of Salters. 14p. *8°.* 1815. *See also* 1784, 1787, 1790, 1792, 1794, 1797, 1799, 1801, 1803, 1806, 1809, 1812, 1818, 1821, 1824, 1827, 1830.

21346 LONDON SOCIETY FOR PROMOTING CHRISTIANITY AMONGST THE JEWS. The first report of the London Ladies' Auxiliary Society, in aid of the London Society for Promoting Christianity amongst the Jews... 15p. *8°.* 1815.

21347 A PLAN for the better maintenance and more general residence of the curates of the Established Church, upon their cures. By the stipendiary curate of Ash, in Surrey. 66p. *8°. London, Farnham, &c.*, [1815]

21348 Biographical SKETCH of the late William Murray, Esq. of Touchadam. 31p. *8°. n.p.* [1815?]

21349 TRUCHSESS VON WALDBURG, L. F. VON, *Graf.* Nouvelle relation de l'itinéraire de Napoléon, de Fontainebleau à l'Ile d'Elbe...Ouvrage traduit de l'allemand sous les yeux de l'auteur...Troisième édition. On a ajouté dans les notes...plusieurs anecdotes relatives à la bataille de Craonne et deux lettres de l'archiduchesse Marie Louise. 76p. *8°. Paris*, 1815.

21350 YEATS, G. D. A statement of the early symptoms which lead to the disease termed water in the brain; with observations on the necessity of a watchful attention to them, and on the fatal consequences of their neglect. In a letter to Martin Wall, Esq. M.D.... 114p. *8°.* 1815. *The copy that belonged to David Ricardo.*

1816

GENERAL

21351 ACCOUNT of the proceedings of the public meeting of the burgesses, householders and inhabitants of the Royal Burgh of Renfrew, held on the 23d November, 1816, respecting the distresses of the country. With a full report of the speeches... 28p. *12°. Glasgow*, 1816.

21352 AINSLIE, R. Practical observations for the landed and agricultural interest, on the question of corn and money, in a series of letters... being an answer to the late publication on that subject by Robert Wilson, Esq.... with a disquisition on the question of altering the laws regarding the rate of interest of money. 50p. *8°. Edinburgh, Glasgow, &c.*, 1816.

21353 ASTON, J. The picture of Manchester. 230p. *18°. Manchester & London*, [1816] *For another edition, see* 1804.

21354 [ATKINSON, WILLIAM (1758–1846).] Letters on the wool question: to which is annexed a second letter on tithes, addressed to Lords Holland and Rosslyn. By the Old Inquirer. 22p. *8°. Bradford & London*, 1816.

21355 [——] Useful hints to the agricultural faction, communicated in a letter to Lords Holland & Rosslyn. By the Old Inquirer. 21p. *8°. Bradford*, 1816.

21356 B., H. Thoughts upon the causes of the present distress of the country, and upon their remedy. By a baronet. 24p. *8°. Bath & London*, 1816.

21357 BENTHAM, J. Chrestomathia: being a collection of papers explanatory of the design of an institution proposed to be set on foot under the name of the Chrestomathic Day School...for the extension of the new system of instruction to the higher branches of learning, for the use of the middling and higher ranks in life. [With 'Chrestomathia Part II. Containing Appendix No. V. Being an essay on nomenclature and classification.'] 347, 24p. *8°.* 1816–17.

21358 BROUGHAM, H. P., *Baron Brougham and Vaux.* Speech of Henry Brougham, Esq., M.P. on...the 9th of April, 1816; in the Committee of the whole House, upon the state of the agricultural distresses. 61p. *8°.* 1816.

21359 CAMBRIENSIS, *pseud.* Observations on the present difficulties of the country, contained in strictures on two pamphlets, lately published by J. H. Moggridge, Esq. 31p. *8°. London & Swansea*, 1816.

21360 CAMERON, D. Thaumaturgus; or, the wonders of the magic lantern; exhibiting at one view the distresses of the country and some of the consequences of the late just and necessary war; in which some living characters are set off in a stile entirely new. [A series of three letters, the first signed: Donald Cameron.] 76, 36p. *12°. Edinburgh [Glasgow]*, 1816.

21361 CANDOLLE-BOISSIER, DE. Examen de quelques questions d'économie politique, sur les blés, la population, le crédit public, et les impositions. 67p. *8°. Genève & Paris*, 1816.

21362 CHALMERS, G. The state of the United-Kingdom at the peace of Paris, November 20, 1815; respecting the people; their domestic energies; their agriculture; their trade; their shipping; and their finances ...A new edition. 16p. 8°. 1816.

21363 CLELAND, J. Annals of Glasgow, comprising an account of the public buildings, charities, and the rise and progress of the city... 2 vols. 8°. Glasgow, 1816. For an abridged edition, see 1817.

21364 COBBETT, W. Ninth edition...The life of William Cobbett...Written by himself. 16p. 8°. 1816. For other editions, see 1798.

21365 COELLN, G. F. W. F. VON. Praktisches Handbuch für Staats- und Regierungsbeamte besonders in den preussischen Staaten, nach Anleitung Adam Smiths Untersuchung über die Natur des Nationalreichtums...Zweite Auflage des Buchs neue Staatsweisheit. 430p. 8°. Berlin, 1816.

21366 The **CRISIS;** or, a letter to the Right Honorable the Chancellor of the Exchequer: stating the true cause of the present alarming state of the country, with a remedy—at once safe, easy and efficacious. 80p. 8°. London, Oxford, &c., 1816.

21367 —— Second edition. 80p. 8°. London, Oxford, &c., 1816. The copy presented to Patrick Colquhoun by the anonymous author.

21368 National **DIFFICULTIES** practically explained. By a member of the Lowestoft Book-Club. 45p. 8°. London, Lowestoft, &c., 1816.

21369 DISTRESSES of the country. The hour of danger; or, public distress and public remedy. By a commoner, author of the "Extraordinary red book." 37p. 8°. [1816]

21370 DOMESDAY-BOOK, seu libri censualis, Willelmi primi Regis Angliæ, indices. Accessit dissertatio generalis de ratione hujusce libri. Printed by command of His Majesty King George III. in pursuance of an address of the House of Commons of Great Britain. [Edited by Sir Henry Ellis.] 579p. fol. 1816. The colophon is dated 1814.

21371 —— Additamenta ex codic. antiquiss. Exon' domesday. Inquisitio Eliensis. Liber Winton'. Boldon book. Printed by command of His Majesty King George III. in pursuance of an address of the House of Commons of Great Britain. [Edited by Sir Henry Ellis.] 635p. fol. 1816. For other editions of the whole, or part of Domesday Book, see 1783.

21372 DUFOUR DE PRADT, D., Archevêque de Malines. Récit historique sur la restauration de la royauté en France, le 31 mars 1814. 103p. 8°. 1816.

21373 *The **EAST-INDIA** register and directory, for 1816; corrected to the 21st November 1815; containing... lists of the Company's servants...Together with lists of the...mariners, &c. not in the service of the...Company; and merchant vessels employed in the country trade. Compiled...by A. W. Mason, J. S. Kingston, & Geo. Owen, (2d.)... 499p. 12°. London, Dublin, &c., [1816]

21374 *—— Corrected to the 15th August 1816... Second edition. 494p. 12°. London, Dublin, &c., [1816] For other editions, see 1804.

21375 [FRANKLIN, B.] The way to wealth. [Signed: B.F.] 8p. 8°. Newcastle, 1816. For other editions, see 1793.

21376 GREGOR, F. The works of Francis Gregor, of Trewarthennick, Esq. 307p. 8°. Exeter, 1816.

21377 HARRIS, WILLIAM (1776–1830). On the present distresses of the country, and suitable remedies. 121p. 8°. London, Wallingford, &c., 1816.

21378 HOLDSWORTH, A. H. A second letter to a friend in Devonshire, on the present situation of the country. [Dated: March 23, 1816.] 23p. 8°. 1816.

21379 HOYLAND, J. A historical survey of the customs, habits & present state of the Gypsies; designed to develope the origin of this singular people, and to promote the amelioration of their condition. 265p. 8°. York & London, 1816.

21380 JACOB, W. An inquiry into the causes of agricultural distress. 50p. 8°. 1816.

21381 KELLY, P. Metrology; or, an exposition of weights and measures, chiefly those of Great Britain and France...[With an appendix.] 117, 20p. 8°. 1816.

21382 Eighty fourth edition. **KENT'S** original London directory: 1816. Being an alphabetical list of more than 17,000 merchants & traders of London...[With 'Kent's original tradesman's assistant: 1816. Being a guide to all the stage coaches, carriers, coasting vessels, &c.&c....'.] 390, 144, 24p. 12°. [1816] See also 1740 (Kent's London directory), 1804, 1825, 1826, 1827.

21383 MADDEN, S. Reflections and resolutions proper for the gentlemen of Ireland, as to their conduct for the service of their country... 224p. 8°. Dublin, 1816. [Hanson 5136n] Edited by 'R.E.M.' and printed for free distribution at the expense of Thomas Pleasants. Originally published anonymously in 1738 (q.v.).

21384 [MARCET, J.] Conversations on political economy; in which the elements of that science are familiarly explained. By the author of "Conversations on chemistry." 464p. 12°. 1816. See also 1817, 1825, 1827, 1839.

21385 PALAISEAU, J. F. G. Métrologie universelle, ancienne et moderne, ou, rapport des poids et mesures des empires, royaumes...des quatre parties du monde... 472p. 4°. Bordeaux, 1816.

21386 PARKER, WILLIAM, of Cork. Observations on the intended amendment of the Irish grand jury laws ...To which is added, a plan for the general survey and valuation of Ireland, and for the commutation of tithes; with several important hints relative to the internal economy of Ireland, and the distressed state of the poor. 184p. 8°. Cork, 1816.

21387 PRESTON, R. Further observations on the state of the Nation. The means of employment of labor. The Sinking Fund... 44p. 8°. London, Edinburgh, &c., 1816.

21388 —— A review of the present ruined condition of the landed and agricultural interests...Printed in the Pamphleteer, no. XIII. 64p. 8°. 1816.

21389 PRYME, G. A syllabus of a course of lectures on the principles of political economy. 25p. 8°. Cambridge, 1816.

21390 RYMER, T., comp. Fœdera, conventiones, litteræ, et cujuscunque generis acta publica, inter Reges Angliæ et alios...ab ingressu Gulielmi I. in Angliam, A.D.1066. Ad nostra usque tempora habita aut tractata... Primum in lucem missa de mandato...Annæ Reginæ; cura...Thomæ Rymer...et Roberti Sanderson...Denuò aucta...jussu...Regis Georgii Tertii. Accurantibus Adamo Clarke...et Fred. Holbrooke... 4 vols. fol. Londini: [The Record Commission,] 1816–69.

21391 SARRAZIN, N. J. Le retour du siècle d'or, ou rêve véritable et surprenant, suivi des moyens de rendre infaillible son accomplissement. viii, 40, 24, 10, 105p. *8°. Metz*, 1816.

21392 —— De l'existence de Dieu, pour servir de suite au Retour du siècle d'or. Par le même auteur...[With 'Errata...en forme d'appendice au Siècle d'or'.] 16, [4]p. *8°. Metz*, [1816 ?]

21393 SAY, J. B. Catechism of political economy; or, familiar conversations on the manner in which wealth is produced, distributed and consumed in society... Translated from the French by John Richter. 131p. *8°.* 1816. *For other editions, see* 1815.

21394 —— De l'Angleterre et des Anglais...Seconde édition, revue et augmentée. 63p. *8°. Paris & Londres*, 1816.

21395 —— England, and the English people...Second edition, revised and enlarged. Translated by John Richter. 68p. *8°.* 1816. *For another edition, see* 1815.

21396 SELLAR, P. Report of the trial of Patrick Sellar, Esq. factor for the most noble the Marquis and Marchioness of Stafford, for the crimes of culpable homicide, real injury and oppression...23d April 1816... [in evicting tenants, burning pastures and pulling down crofts and barns]. 67p. *8°. Edinburgh, Aberdeen, &c.*, 1816.

21397 SILENT, PAUL, *pseud.* Three letters of Paul Silent to his country cousins. 82p. *8°.* 1816.

21398 SIMPSON, THOMAS (*fl.* 1814–1816). A brief exposition of the actual state of the land owners and of the farmers of Great Britain... 18p. *8°.* 1816.

21399 —— Letter to the Right Honorable Lord Castle-reagh upon the subject of the present state of Great Britain; describing the origin...and probable consequences of the distress in which the whole kingdom is involved...[With an appendix.] 234, 26p. *8°. Stokesley,* [*London,*] *&c.*, 1816.

21400 A **SKETCH** of a new universal division of time, accompanied with a few articles connected with it. To which is added, by way of an appendix, a brief sketch of a new universal system of measures, weights, and coins. 68p. *8°.* 1816.

21401 THOUGHTS on the causes and consequences of the present depressed state of agricultural produce. Addressed to the consideration of those who have property in the funds. 16p. *8°. London, Bath, &c.*, 1816.

21402 National **UTILITY**, in opposition to political controversy: addressed to the friends of American manufactures. [A letter from Benjamin Austin, dated 'Dec. 9, 1815' to Thomas Jefferson, with Jefferson's reply, dated 'Jan. 9th, 1816'.] *s.sh.fol. Boston,* [1816] [*Br.* 484]

21403 WESTERN, C. C., *Baron Western.* The speech of Chas. C. Western, Esq. M.P. on moving that the House should resolve itself into a Committee of the whole House to take into consideration the distressed state of the agriculture of the United Kingdom. March 7, 1816. 40p. *8°.* [1816] *Presentation copy from the author to Lord Sheffield.*

21404 WHEATLEY, J. A letter to Lord Grenville, on the distress of the country. 87p. *8°.* 1816.

21405 WHITE, JOSHUA E. Letters on England: comprising descriptive scenes; with remarks on the state of society, domestic economy, habits of the people, and condition of the manufacturing classes generally... 2 vols. *8°. Philadelphia*, 1816.

21406 [**YATES**, JOHN A.] A letter to His Royal Highness the Duke of Kent, upon the "revulsion of trade", and "our sudden transition from a system of extensive war to a state of peace." 168p. *8°. London, Liverpool, &c.*, [1816] *See also* 1817.

AGRICULTURE

21407 BESNARD, P. Observations on the promoting the cultivation of hemp and flax, and extending the linen and hempen manufactures in the south of Ireland. [With an appendix containing instructions for growing hemp and flax.] 26, 16p. *8°.* [*Cork,*] 1816.

21408 BOARD OF AGRICULTURE. The agricultural state of the Kingdom, in February, March and April, 1816; being the substance of the replies of many of the most opulent and intelligent landholders to a circular letter sent by the Board of Agriculture to every part of England, Wales and Scotland. 436p. *8°.* 1816.

21409 —— Premiums offered by the Board...for 1816–17. 6p. *8°.* [1816] *Addressed in manuscript to the Earl of Morton. See also* 1804, 1808, 1809, 1810, 1812, 1818.

21410 CROMBIE, A. Letters on the present state of the agricultural interest, addressed to Charles Forbes, Esq. M.P. 86p. *8°.* 1816. *Inscribed in manuscript: 'From Dr. Crombie by his friend Major Torrens to David Ricardo Esqr.'.*

21411 EDMEADS, W. National establishment, national security. Or thoughts on the consequences of commuting the tithes. 34p. *8°. Oxford & London*, 1816.

21412 —— Third edition. 33p. *8°. Oxford & London*, 1816.

21413 ENGLAND. *Laws, etc.* [*Endorsed:*] An Act for amending several Acts...for improving the drainage of the Middle and South Levels, part of...Bedford Level... and for improving the navigation of the River Ouze, in the county of Norfolk, and of the several rivers communicating therewith. Royal Assent, 31 May 1816. 56 Geo. III. sess. 1816. 19p. *fol.* [*London*, 1816]

21414 —— —— An Act for inclosing lands in the parishes of Newcastle-under-Lyme, Trentham, Woolstanton and Stoke-upon-Trent, in the county of Stafford. 56 Geo. III, sess. 1816. ⟨Royal Assent, 20 June 1816.⟩ 67p. *fol.* [*London*, 1816]

21415 HOLMES, J. H. H. A treatise on the coal mines of Durham and Northumberland; with information relative to the stratifications of the two counties: and containing accounts of the explosions from fire-damp, which have occurred therein for the last twenty years; their causes, and the means proposed for their remedy, and for the general improvements of the mining system, by new methods of ventilation... 259p. *8°.* 1816. *Presentation copy, with inscription, from the author to Frank Franck.*

21416 A **PLAN** for a general enclosure Bill, for commons of a limited extent, in which the practicability and advantages of such a Bill are...explained, and...improvements, connected with the agriculture of the country, are humbly submitted to the consideration of Parliament. By a country gentleman, formerly a member of the House of Commons. 45p. *8°*. 1816.

21417 PLAN for regulating the rents of lands in Scotland, with equal safety both to landlord and tenant. With reasons to prove, that it will add to the stability & permanent benefit of agriculture. To which is added an account of the mode of reduction adopted by the Earl of Galloway. Second edition. 48p. *8°*. *Cupar, Edinburgh, &c.*, 1816. *For other editions, see 1815.*

21418 REMARKS upon the state of agriculture, by a farmer. Addressed to the aristocracy of Great Britain. 64p. *8°*. [*London,* 1816 ?]

21419 RITSON, J. The jurisdiction of the court leet: exemplified in the articles which the jury or inquest for the King, in that court, is charged and sworn...to inquire of and present...The third edition, corrected. 166p. *8°*. 1816. *For another edition, see 1809.*

21420 SELLON, J. An inquiry into the extent of the present real depreciation of landed property, with its causes; and the best mode of managing estates under the present circumstances. 55p. *8°*. 1816.

21421 SMITHFIELD CLUB. Members of the Smithfield Club. 1816. [12]p. *24°*. *n.p.* [1816]

21422 TORRENS, R. A letter to the Right Honorable the Earl of Liverpool, on the state of the agriculture of the United Kingdom, and on the means of relieving the present distress of the farmer, and of securing him against the recurrence of similar embarrassment. 34p. *8°*. 1816.

21423 VANDERSTRAETEN, F. Analysis of the views contained in a work just published, entitled, Improved agriculture... 30p. *8°*. 1816.

21424 —— Improved agriculture, and the suppression of smuggling, property-tax, and poor's-rates; with the maintenance of rents, cheapness of living, the prosperity of the farmer, the advancement of commerce...the... employment of the poor: being a display of the augmentability of the resources of the British Empire, principally on the basis of an improved agriculture; including a sketch of the Flemish system... 296p. *8°*. 1816.

CORN LAWS

21425 BANNATYNE, D. Observations on the principles which enter into the commerce in grain, and into the measures for supplying food to the people; being the substance of an essay read to the Literary and Commercial Society of Glasgow. 32p. *8°*. *Glasgow, Edinburgh, &c.*, 1816.

21426 PARRY, CHARLES H. Hone's genuine edition ...The question of the necessity of the existing corn laws, considered, in their relation to the agricultural labourer, the tenantry, the landholder, and the country. 229p. *8°*. *Bath & London,* 1816.

POPULATION

21427 GRAHAME, JAMES, *advocate.* An inquiry into the principle of population: including an exposition of the causes and the advantages of a tendency to exuberance of numbers in society, a defence of poor-laws, and a critical and historical view of the doctrines and projects of the most celebrated legislators and writers, relative to population, the poor and charitable establishments. 332p. *8°*. *Edinburgh & London,* 1816.

21428 KEITH, G. S. Statement of facts respecting the increase of the population of Great Britain, as connected with the increase and decrease of the corn trade, and the rise or fall in the price of corn: together with some hints or remedies for relieving the present distress of the farmers. [Offprint from *The Farmer's Magazine,* no. LXVI.] 24p. *8°*. *Edinburgh & London,* 1816. *The copy given to HSF by William Cunningham (1849–1919).*

21429 WEYLAND, J. The principles of population and production, as they are affected by the progress of society; with a view to moral and political consequences. 493p. *8°*. *London, Oxford, &c.*, 1816.

TRADES & MANUFACTURES

21430 BOVILL, . Report of the trial of Bovill v. Moore & others, tried in the Court of Common Pleas, Guildhall, London...on...the first of March...1816... [arising from the complaint of Mr. Bovill that Messrs. Moore, Longmire, Noble and Company of Nottingham had used a piratical imitation of his patented lace-making machine]. 196p. *8°*. 1816.

21431 [BUNN, T.] Remarks on the buildings and improvements in London, and elsewhere. 155p. *8°*. *Bath & London,* 1816. *In a volume of the author's own pamphlets, with his manuscript notes.*

21432 COSTAZ, C. A. Mémoire sur les moyens qui ont amené le grand développement que l'industrie française à pris depuis vingt ans; suivi de la législation relative aux fabriques, aux ateliers, aux ouvriers, et aux découvertes dans les arts. 364p. *8°*. *Paris,* 1816.

21433 FISCHER, JOHANN C. Tagebuch einer im Jahr 1814 gemachten Reise über Paris nach London und einigen Fabrikstädten Englands vorzüglich in technologisher Hinsicht. 218p. *8°*. *Arau,* 1816.

21434 GREGSON, J. An essay on those defects of buildings dependant on the nature and properties of air: containing a report on the cause of the dry rot in the Royal Navy, and the means of prevention, as now adopted in His Majesty's dock yards... 63p. *8°*. 1816.

21435 LONDON. Livery Companies. *Goldsmiths.* Goldsmiths' Hall, London, October 10th, 1816. [A notice to tradesmen sending parcels of work to the Hall to be assayed that only one such parcel will in future be received from each tradesman on any one day. Signed: Thomas Lane, Clerk to the Company.] *s.sh.fol.* [1816] *See note to no. 13563.*

21436 MANBY, G. W. Considerations on destructive fires and the means of prevention in future. [An advertisement, dated July 1816, for the author's 'machine for the extinction of fires'.] 3p. *fol.* [1816]

21437 PACKER, T. The dyer's guide; being an introduction to the art of dying linen, cotton, silk, and wool, silk and muslin dresses, furniture &c.... 144p. *12°.* 1816.

21438 [PLUMPTRE, J.] The experienced butcher: shewing the respectability and usefulness of his calling ...the laws relating to it, and various profitable sugges-

tions for the rightly carrying it on: designed not only for the use of butchers, but also for...readers in general. [By J. Plumptre, assisted by T. Lantaffe, butcher.] 198p. *12°.* 1816.

21439 SOCIETY FOR THE ENCOURAGEMENT OF ARTS, MANUFACTURES AND COMMERCE. Premiums offered in the year 1816, by the Society... 31p. *8°.* [1816] *See also* 1759, 1760, 1771, 1778.

21440 —— Rules and orders of the Society... 42p. *8°.* 1815[1816]. *See also* 1760, 1763, 1772, 1795.

COMMERCE

21441 [ATKINSON, WILLIAM (1758–1846).] An appeal to every honest man in England, upon an attempt to repeal the Acts to prevent the exportation of wool. By the Old Inquirer. 8p. *8°. Bradford & London,* 1816.

21442 BURT, W. Review of the mercantile, trading, and manufacturing state, interests, and capabilities of the port of Plymouth, by William Burt, Secretary to the Chamber of Commerce in that port, with miscellaneous additions by other persons, and notes. 270p. *8°. Plymouth, London, &c.,* 1816.

21443 EAST INDIA COMPANY. Supplement to the Report of the Committee appointed to inspect the East-India Company's by-laws. 6th June 1816. [On the ineligibility of proprietors who hold offices under the Crown to become directors.] 4p. *4°.* 1816.

21444 ENGLAND. *Laws, etc.* An alphabetical abridgment of the laws for the prevention of smuggling. 1816. 152p. *8°.* 1816.

21445 [FRY, J. S.] Letters on the corn-trade. Containing considerations on the combinations of farmers, and the monopoly of corn. Also remarks on the trade...To which are added an inquiry into the origin of the corn-laws... With a postscript, occasioned by the late extraordinary fluctuations in the corn market. 37p. *8°. Bristol,* 1816.

21446 HOLDEN'S annual directory. Class first, combining the merchants, ship owners, bankers, &c. residing in London and 480 separate towns, in England, Ireland, Scotland and Wales, and the Isles of Guernsey, Jersey, Man...[Compiled by Thomas Underhill.] 230p. *8°.* [1816]

21447 HOLROYD, J. B., *Earl of Sheffield.* Report of the Earl of Sheffield to the meeting at Lewes Wool Fair, 26th July, 1816. [On the wool trade.] Enlarged and amended. 37p. *12°.* [1816] *Inscribed in manuscript: 'The Earl of Harrowby from the President'.*

21448 —— [Another edition.] Re-printed by order of the Farming Society of Ireland. 37p. *12°. Dublin,* [1816] *See also* 1811, 1815, 1819.

21449 MEMORIAL to the Lords of the Treasury, of the proprietors of collieries on the River Wear, and of the ship-owners of the port of Sunderland, in the county of Durham; for a reduction of the export duty on coals: with observations. 15p. *8°. n.p.* [1816?]

21450 The **MERCHANT** and ship-master's assistant:

or, an account of the monies, exchanges, weights and measures of the principal commercial places of Europe, America, East and West Indies, the weights and measures of each place accurately compared with those of Great Britain...A new edition, enlarged. 140, 154p. *8°. North Shields, London, &c.,* 1816.

21451 NERI, G. A. Introduzione alla pratica del commercio...Nuova edizione diligentemente corretta ed ampliata, giusta le variazioni di recente avvenute nel commercio... 343p. *4°. Livorno,* 1816.

21452 NIGHTINGALE, J. The bazaar, its origin, nature, and objects explained, and recommended as an important branch of political economy...To which is added a postscript, containing an account of every establishment, bearing this name, in the Metropolis. 70p. *8°.* 1816. *With a note by HSF: 'may have given Owen the idea of his Labour Exchange'.*

21453 OBSERVATIONS upon our present system of commercial intercourse with the continent of Europe; shewing the necessity of a change of our commercial policy during a state of peace. 22p. *8°.* 1816.

21454 S., J. B. Two letters to the Right Honourable the Earl of Sheffield; in which his lordship's Report to the meeting at Lewes Wool-Fair, and the proceedings at a recent meeting of wool-growers, at the Free Mason's Tavern, are examined...[On the export of wool.] 76p. *8°.* 1816. *The Sheffield copy.*

21455 SEUTTER, A. L. VON. Ueber die allgemeine Getreide-Theurung im Jahr 1816. Eine Staats- und National-ökonomische Abhandlung. 140p. *8°. Regensburg,* [1816]

21456 SOLLY, E., *ed.* Ueber den englischen Handel. Aus den Rheinischen Blättern abgedruckt... 30p. *8°. Berlin,* 1816.

21457 TORRES, M. An exposition of the commerce of Spanish America; with some observations upon its importance to the United States. To which are added, a correct analysis of the monies, weights, and measures of Spain, France, and the United States; and of the new weights and measures of England: with tables of their reciprocal reductions; and of the exchange between the United States, England, France...and between England, Spain, France, and the several states of the Union. 119p. *8°. Philadelphia,* 1816.

COLONIES

21458 BEATSON, A. Tracts relative to the island of St. Helena; written during a residence of five years... lxxxvii, 330p. *4°. 1816.*

21459 BRITISH JUSTICE in Africa; developed in official and other documents, concerning certain recent proceedings at the British forts on the coast of Guinea [in a dispute involving Anthony Calvert Hutton]: to which is prefixed, an introduction, by the English editor... xliv, 149[49]p. *8°. [1816]*

21460 —— [Another edition.] British justice in Africa: developed in official and other documents concerning certain recent proceedings at the British forts on the Gold Coast... xliv, 49p. *8°. [1816]*

21461 COLONIST, *pseud.* The Edinburgh Review and the West Indies; with observations on the pamphlets of Messrs. Stephen, Macaulay &c. and remarks on the Slave Registry Bill. 360p. *8°. Glasgow, Edinburgh, &c.,* 1816.

21462 DOUGLAS, T., *Earl of Selkirk.* A sketch of the British fur trade in North America; with observations relative to the North-West Company of Montreal. 130p. *8°. 1816.*

21463 JORDAN, G. W. Copies of a letter containing queries respecting the state of the silver and copper coins in Barbados, and of an answer describing the same, and recommending measures necessary to be adopted for furnishing a full and perfect supply to all the colonies. By the agent for Barbados. 30p. *8°. 1816.*

21464 MACCAULY, T. The Indian trader's complete guide; being a correct account of coins, weights, measures, &c.&c. at the different settlements of India, and adjacent native sovereignties of Asia... 116p. *8°. Calcutta,* 1816.

21465 The colonial **POLICY** of Great Britain, considered with relation to her North American provinces, and West India possessions; wherein the dangerous tendency of American competition is developed...with plans for the promotion of emigration, and strictures on the Treaty of Ghent. By a British traveller. 238p. *8°. London & Glasgow,* 1816.

21466 REVIEW of the administration, value and state of the colony of Java with its dependencies, as it was, — as it is, — and as it may be. 165p. *8°. 1816.*

FINANCE

21467 An **ADDRESS** to the Honourable House of Commons of Great Britain and Ireland, on the state of the nation. By a Yorkshire freeholder. [On the advantages of a paper currency.] 18p. *8°. 1816.*

21468 ADDRESS to the inhabitants of the parishes of Nantmel, &c. in the county of Radnor, on the subject of tithes; shortly refuting the...representation of their being the cause of the present distresses. Also containing some observations respecting those real grievances the poor's rates. By the impropriator. 27p. *8°. 1816.*

21469 The **ART** of stock-jobbing explained. Exposing the secret manœuvres, tricks and contrivances, delusion of the monied interest, and general speculation...To which is added, considerations on the security of funded property...By a practical jobber. Fourth edition. 95p. *8°.* [1816]

21470 —— Fifth edition. 95p. *8°.* [1816] *Originally published with the title:* Stock-Exchange laid open, *in 1814* (*q.v.*).

21471 [ATTWOOD, T.] Remedies proposed as certain, speedy, and effectual, for the relief of our present embarrassments. By an independent gentleman. 51p. *8°.* 1816. *Presentation copy from the author to Patrick Colquhoun.*

21472 [——] The remedy; or, thoughts on the present distresses. In a letter to a public editor, July 3d 1816. Second edition; with additions. 71p. *8°.* 1816. *Presentation copy from the author to Viscount Lowther (i.e. William, 2nd Earl of Lonsdale (1787–1872), with a footnote to the inscription: 'published in July 1816'.*

21473 BANK OF ENGLAND. A list of the names of all such proprietors of the Bank of England, who are qualified to vote at the ensuing election...March 26th, 1816. 18p. *fol.* [1816] *See also* 1738, 1749, 1750, 1789, 1790, 1791, 1792, 1793, 1794, 1795, 1796, 1797, 1798, 1799, 1801, 1803, 1804, 1808, 1809, 1812, 1819, 1836, 1843.

21474 BEAUMONT, JOHN T. B. An essay on provident or parish banks, for the security and improvement of the savings of tradesmen, artificers, servants, &c. until required for their future wants, or advancement in life...To which is added, a detailed account of the plan, regulations, and routine of management of the Provident Bank in the parish of St. Paul, Covent Garden. 69p. *8°.* 1816.

21475 BECHER, W. Propositions for relieving the present difficulties of the landed and agricultural interest; as submitted to the Right Hon. N. Vansittart. With further observations thereon. 11p. *8°.* [1816?]

21476 BENETT, J. Replies to the three additional letters of the Rev. William Coxe...on the subject of commutation of tithe. 117p. *8°. 1816.*

21477 BENTHAM, J. Defence of usury; shewing the impolicy of the present legal restraints on the terms of pecuniary bargains...To which is added, a letter to Adam Smith, Esq. LL.D. on the discouragements opposed by the above restraints to the progress of inventive industry. The third edition. And to which is also added, second edition, A protest against law taxes. 206, 70p. *12°.* 1816. *The copy that belonged to Francis Place, with his book-plate, an autograph letter to him from Henry Warburton, two pages of manuscript notes, and cuttings from various contemporary newspapers. For other editions, see 1787. A protest against law taxes was first published alone in 1793 (q.v.), and with Supply without burthen in 1795 (q.v.).*

21478 Extraordinary red **BOOK.** A list of all places, pensions, sinecures, &c. with the various salaries and emoluments arising therefrom, exhibiting also, a complete view of the National Debt...By a commoner. 213p. *12°*. 1816. *Attributed by HSF to R. J. Richardson. See also nos. 21480–81 (John Bull's mirror), and 1817, 1820 (The Englishman's mirror), 1821 (Extraordinary red book).*

21479 BRICOGNE, A. J. B. Examen impartial du budget proposé à la Chambre des Députés, le 23 décembre 1815, et projets d'amendements. Par l'auteur de l'Opinion et des observations d'un créancier de l'état. 120p. *8°. Paris,* 1816.

21480 John **BULL'S** mirror, or, corruption & taxation unmasked; containing a list of the Members of the House of Commons...Also shewing the manner in which the public money is expended in pensions, places, sinecures, &c.&c....[Extracted from *Extraordinary red book...by a commoner.*] 32p. *8°.* [1816]

21481 —— Second edition, corrected and enlarged. 32p. *8°.* [1816] *For editions of* Extraordinary red book, *see no.* 21478.

21482 CAESAR, J. S. Der geschwinde Intressen-Rechner, oder die Berechnung der Intressen von 1 schilling bis zu 1000 Pfunden, und von 25 Cents bis zu 1000 Thalern, zu 6 pro Cent, von einem Tage bis zum ganzen Jahr. [44]p. *8°. Reading (Penn.),* 1816.

21483 CAMPBELL, JOHN, *a proprietor of the Royal Bank of Scotland.* Letter to the proprietors; and to the Governor, Deputy-Governor, and Directors, ordinary and extraordinary, of the Royal Bank of Scotland, who were in office from March 1815 to March 1816. 11p. *4°. Edinburgh,* 1816.

21484 ——, *and others.* Remarks by certain Directors of the Royal Bank of Scotland, on a letter addressed by Messrs Ramsays, Bonars, and Co. to the proprietors. [Signed: John Campbell, James Dundas, Charles Skelkrig, Hugh Warrender, Alex. Duncan, Jas. Ferrier.] 15p. *4°. Edinburgh,* 1816. *The copy that belonged to Macvey Napier.*

21485 CHAMBRE DE COMMERCE, *Amiens.* Projet présenté par la Chambre de Commerce d'Amiens, pour le remplacement des droits actuels de circulation, d'entrée et de vente en détail, par un droit unique de consommation...[Concerning the taxes upon the wine, cider and beer trades.] 45p. *8°. Amiens,* 1816.

21486 CHRISTIAN, EDWARD (*d.* 1823). A plan for a county provident bank. With observations upon provident institutions already established. 78p. *8°.* 1816.

21487 [COLQUHOUN, P.] Epitome of a scheme of finance; whereby a considerable revenue may be obtained, without taxation...by lending money on mortgages... With observations on the means of improving and extending the general resources of the British Empire. 24p. *8°.* 1816. *The copy that belonged to James Colquhoun.*

21488 COMMITTEE OF LICENSED VICTU-ALLERS. [*Begin.*] Licensed property. The committee appointed to seek redress of the grievances of the licensed victuallers, have commenced a subscription to obtain the highest legal information...[A prospectus.] [4]p. *4°. n.p.* [1816?]

21489 COMMUTATION of tythe, by an acreable charge upon land, calculated to prevent the necessity of tythe proctors, &c.&c. by a beneficed clergyman of the Established Church. 39p. *8°. London,* 1816.

21490 CONSIDÉRATIONS sur les finances. Par M. *****. 43p. *8°. Paris,* 1816.

21491 CORRESPONDANCE législative, et financière, entre un Membre de la Chambre des Députés, et un Membre de Collége Électoral. Première partie. 60p. *8°. Paris,* 1816.

21492 CRAUFURD, G. The present state of Great Britain. 38p. *12°. Rotterdam,* 1816.

21493 DECIMAL, *pseud.* Decimal's letters to the editor of the Times. London, 25 July, 1816. 10p. *4°.* [*London,* 1816] *The copy that belonged to Nicholas Vansittart, Baron Bexley.*

21494 DUNCAN, H. An essay on the nature and advantages of parish banks, for the savings of the industrious. Second edition, greatly altered, and enlarged by an account of the rise and progress of the scheme; and remarks on the propriety of uniting these institutions with friendly societies. Together with an appendix, containing a copy of the rules of the Dumfries Parish Bank... 88p. *8°. Edinburgh, Dumfries, &c.,* 1816. *For another edition, see* 1815.

21495 FAIRMAN, WILLIAM. An account of the several public funds...Transferrable at the Bank of England; together with an account of the stock of the principal public companies in London...Also statements of the National Debt and of the Sinking Fund. The sixth edition. 210p. *8°.* 1816. *Originally published with the title:* The stocks examined and compared, *in 1795 (q.v.).*

21496 [FORBES, JOHN H., *Lord Medwyn.*] A short account of the Edinburgh Bank for Savings, containing directions for establishing similar banks, with the mode of keeping the accounts, and conducting the details of business. Fourth edition. 28p. *8°. Edinburgh, London, &c.,* 1816. *For another edition, see* 1815.

21497 FRANCE. *Chambre des Députés.* No. 219. Opinion. M. le Baron de Barante, Député du Département du Puy-de-Dôme...sur le budget de 1816. Prononcée dans la séance du 16 mars, 1816. Imprimé par ordre de la Chambre. 19p. *8°.* [*Paris,* 1816]

21498 GARNIER, G., *Marquis.* Rapport de M. le Comte Germain-Garnier...Ministre d'État...au nom de la Commission Spéciale de sept membres chargés, par la Chambre des Pairs, dans la séance du 20 avril 1816, de l'examen du projet de loi sur les finances. 54p. *8°. Paris,* 1816.

21499 [GOODWYN, H.] A plan for a new general system of weights, as a supplement to the plan for a new silver coinage, published 22d June, 1816; with additional suggestions respecting the currency of the kingdom, and an abstract of the new Coinage-Act, &c.&c.&c. 36p. *4°.* 1816. *The copy that belonged to Nicholas Vansittart, Baron Bexley.*

21500 [——] Short account of a plan for the new silver coinage, for improving the currency of the Kingdom, and for introducing the decimal principle into all money transactions. 15p. *4°.* 1816. *Two copies; one which belonged to Nicholas Vansittart, Baron Bexley, and the other to Rogers Ruding.*

21501 GRENFELL, P. The speech of Pascoe Grenfell, Esq. in the House of Commons, on Tuesday, the 13th of February, 1816, on certain transactions subsisting betwixt the public & the Bank of England. With an appendix. 120p. *8°.* 1816.

21502 H., W. A letter to the Right Hon. Nich. Vansittart...on the benefits which would result to the poor, and the advantages which would accrue to the agriculture, the fisheries, the manufactures and the commerce, of the United Kingdom, from a repeal of the duty on salt. 21p. *8°. Liverpool & London,* [1816]

21503 HENNET, A. J. U. Théorie du crédit public. 587p. *4°. Paris,* 1816.

21504 HILL, ROWLAND (1744–1833). Religious freedom in danger; or, the Toleration Act invaded, by parochial assessments on places of religious worship, shewing the dangerous and destructive consequences thereof, as tending to the ruin of the religious privileges, so long enjoyed under the Toleration Act. 55p. *8°.* 1816.

21505 A few **HINTS** suggested for the abolition of tithes, and the general good of the church establishment. 11p. *8°. Bath,* 1816. *The Sheffield copy.*

21506 [**HONE**, W.] The political catechism; dedicated ...to His Highness Omar, Bashaw, Dey and Governor of the warlike Kingdom of Algiers; the Earl of Liverpool, Lord Castlereagh and Co. By an Englishman. 8p. *8°. Manchester: Wardle & Pratt; reprinted by Sutton & Son, Nottingham; also, reprinted...by James Williams, 47, Queen Street, Portsea,* [1816]

21507 HUME, JOSEPH. An account of the Provident Institution for Savings, established in the western part of the Metropolis; with observations upon different publications relating to such establishments; and some suggestions for rendering them general by the assistance of Government. 64p. *8°.* 1816. *Presentation copy, with inscription, from the author to David Ricardo.*

21508 KEARNEY, R. A plan for the payment of the National Debt, and for the immediate reduction of taxation. 36p. *8°. Dublin,* 1816.

21509 LEFEBVRE, . Observations sur le mode de perception des impôts indirects, et particulièrement sur les effets de l'art. 370 de la Loi proposée le 23 décembre 1815. 24p. *8°. Paris,* 1816.

21510 LETTERS addressed to the proprietors of bank stock. By an old proprietor. [Reprinted from the *British Press* and the *Morning Chronicle.*] 28p. *8°.* 1816.

21511 LOWE, JOHN, *of Birmingham.* A treatise on profits, discounts, and interest: epxlaining how to compute the gross amount of any net sum to secure a certain net profit, after a discount has been allowed therefrom... [With 'A table of gross charge, from one penny to one shilling, and from one shilling to one pound...'] 159, 8p. *8°. Birmingham & London,* 1816.

21512 McCULLOCH, JOHN R. An essay on a reduction of the interest of the National Debt, proving, that this is the only possible means of relieving the distresses of the commercial and agricultural interests; and establishing the justice of that measure... 53p. *8°. London & Edinburgh,* 1816.

21513 —— An essay on the question of reducing the interest of the National Debt; in which the justice and expediency of that measure are fully established. 213p. *8°. Edinburgh & London,* 1816. *Presentation copy from the author to his friend Gibson Craig, with a note in McCulloch's hand on p. iii: 'This tract I have suppressed and disavowed long ago: J.R.M^cC., Edin^h. 1845'.*

21514 MASSON, V. A. Considérations sur la nature, les bases, et l'usage du crédit publique; particulièrement en ce qui concerne les finances de la France. 70p. *8°. Paris,* 1816.

21515 MODENA, *Duchy of.* Tariffa generale per l'esazione dei dazj, d'introduzione, uscita e transito nel territorio degli Stati Estensi sanzionata col decreto sovrano del i xv maggio MDCCCXVI. [Tables, preceded by the decree.] 76p. *8°. n.p.* [1816]

21516 MUELLER VON NITERSDORF, A. H. Versuche einer neuen Theorie des Geldes mit besonderer Rücksicht auf Grossbritannien. 308p. *8°. Leipzig & Altenburg,* 1816.

21517 NORWICH UNION LIFE INSURANCE SOCIETY. Outline of the plan of the Norwich Union Office, for insurance on lives, and granting or purchasing annuities, endowments, &c.&c. 24p. *8°. Norwich,* [1816]

21518 OBSERVATIONS on illicit distillation and smuggling; with some remarks on the reports of Woodbine Parish Esq., chairman of the Excise Board. 57p. *8°. Edinburgh & London,* 1816. *Attributed to 'Dr. Jamieson' in a contemporary manuscript note on the title-page.*

21519 OXFORD PROVIDENT BANK. Rules of the Oxford Provident Bank, opened April 22, 1816. [With a list of patrons, trustees and managers.] 6p. *8°. Oxford,* 1816.

21520 PAYNE, D. B. An address to the proprietors of bank stock on the management of the Governor and Directors of the Bank of England, and on the laws relating thereto. 66p. *8°.* 1816.

21521 PHILELEUTHEROS, *Overiensis, pseud.* Remarks on the property tax, as connected with a standing army in time of peace. 15p. *8°. Burnham, Norwich, &c.,* 1816.

21522 PRINSEP, C. R. A letter to the Earl of Liverpool, on the cause of the present distresses of the country, and the efficacy of reducing the standard of our silver currency towards their relief. 45p. *8°.* 1816.

21523 PROVIDENT INSTITUTION FOR SAVINGS, *Bath.* First year's report of the Provident Institution established at Bath, January 1815. 22p. *8°. Bath,* [1816]. *The copy that belonged to Patrick Colquhoun.*

21524 PROVIDENT INSTITUTION FOR SAVINGS, *London.* Depositor's book of the Provident Institution for Savings...[With the regulations.] 7p. *8°. n.p.* [1816]

21525 —— [Another edition.] 8p. *8°.* [*London,* 1816]

21526 —— The Provident Institution for Savings, established in the western part of the Metropolis, on the 3rd of January, 1816...[By-laws.] 8p. *8°.* 1816. *An advance copy, with spaces for lists of trustees and managers.*

21527 —— [Another edition.] By-laws of the Provident Institution for Savings, established...on the 3rd of April, 1816... 8p. *8°.* [1816?]

21528 —— The Provident Institution for Savings... No. 13, Panton Street, Haymarket, late of 28, Leicester Square. [List of officers, aims of the Institution, examples of possible savings and hours of opening.] *s.sh.fol. n.p.* [1816] *A poster, the text surrounded by a border in a Greek key pattern.*

21529 —— The Provident Institution for Savings... No. 11, Panton Street, Hay-Market. [Lists of officers, aims of the Institution, examples of possible savings, information for those desirous of founding similar institutions.] *s.sh.fol. n.p.* [1816?] *A poster, with a different text from that above (no. 21528), the text surrounded by a border in a Greek key pattern.*

21530 —— The Provident Institution for Savings... No. 13, Panton Street, Haymarket. (Late of 28, Leicester Square.) [Regulations.] 4p. *4⁰. n.p.* [1816]

21531 —— [Another edition.] 4p. *4⁰. n.p.* [1816?]

21532 RAMSAYS, BONARS & CO. Letter to the proprietors of the Royal Bank of Scotland. [With appendixes of documents illustrating the firm's relations with the Royal Bank of Scotland.] 11, 8p. *4⁰.* [*Edinburgh,* 1816]

21533 RANDOM DE BÉRENGER, C., *Baron de Beaufain.* The noble stock-jobber, or facts unveiled: irrefutably to disprove Lord Cochrane's affidavits...and most incontrovertibly proving that Lord Cochrane was previously acquainted with...the events that on the 21st of February, 1814, affected the Stock-Exchange...[Part I. With an appendix of documents.] 308, 93p. *8⁰.* 1816.

21534 READ, S. An inquiry concerning the nature and use of money; with a full developement of the operation and effects of the laws of restriction on the Bank of England from payment of its notes in specie... 233p. *8⁰. Edinburgh,* 1816.

21535 REASONS for the establishment of savings' banks, with a word of caution respecting their formation. 28p. *12⁰.* 1816.

21536 RENOUARD, A. A. L'impôt du timbre sur les catalogues de librairie, ruineux pour les libraires, et arithmétiquement onéreux au Trésor Public. 27p. *8⁰. Paris,* 1816.

21537 RICARDO, D. Proposals for an economical and secure currency; with observations on the profits of the Bank of England, as they regard the public and the proprietors of bank stock. 126p. *8⁰.* 1816.

21538 —— Second edition. 128p. *8⁰.* 1816. *See also* 1819.

21539 ROCK LIFE ASSURANCE COMPANY. No. 14, New Bridge Street, Blackfriars. [*Begin.*] Sir, I transmit to you the tables for ordinary assurances on lives...[Signed: William Frend. A prospectus, with tables of premiums.] 4p. *fol.* [*London,* 1816?] *For another edition, see* 1809.

21540 ROSE, GEORGE. Observations on banks for savings. 57p. *8⁰.* 1816. *Presentation copy from the author to Lord Sheffield.*

21541 —— [Second edition.] 57p. *8⁰.* 1816.

21542 —— Third edition. 57p. *8⁰.* 1816. *See also* 1817.

21543 ROUSE, W. An investigation of the errors of all writers on annuities, in their valuation of half-yearly and quarterly payments...With tables showing the correct values when payments are made in less periods than yearly, and a specimen of a set of tables on a new principle...for the valuation of leases, estates, annuities... 40p. *8⁰.* 1816.

21544 ROYAL BANK OF SCOTLAND. Warrants of the Charter erecting confirming, and granting new privileges to the Royal Bank of Scotland. p. 1–284, 311–336. *8⁰. Edinburgh,* 1816. *Wanting the text of the sixth Warrant; the text of the seventh Warrant is bound separately.*

21545 RUSSIA. *Laws, etc.* Tarif des droits de douane de l'Empire Russe. 164p. *8⁰. St. Pétersbourg,* 1816.

21546 Small **SAVINGS** make great gains; or, an easy and safe method of securing a friend in need. [Signed: A depositor in the Savings' Bank, Bishopsgate Church Yard.] 9p. *8⁰.* 1816.

21547 SINCLAIR, SIR JOHN, *Bart.* On the state of the country, in December 1816. 14p. *8⁰.* 1816.

21548 SMITH, THOMAS, *accountant, of London.* A letter to the Right Honourable the Earl of Liverpool, on the proposed new coinage. 41p. *8⁰.* 1816. *The copy that belonged to Patrick Colquhoun.*

21549 —— A reply to Mr. Ricardo's Proposals for an economical and secure currency. 44p. *8⁰.* 1816.

21550 —— A second letter to the Right Honourable the Earl of Liverpool, on the proposed new coinage. 26p. *8⁰.* 1816.

21551 SUGDEN, E. B., *Baron St. Leonards.* Considerations on the rate of interest, and on redeemable annuities...The second edition. 35p. *8⁰.* 1816.

21552 TATHAM, E. Observations on the scarcity of money; and its effects upon the public. 47p. *8⁰. Oxford & London,* 1816.

21553 —— Second edition. 32p. *8⁰. Oxford & London,* 1816.

21554 —— The third edition. 26p. *8⁰. Oxford & London,* 1816.

21555 TAYLOR, CHARLES, *provisional manager of the London Savings' Bank.* A summary account of the London Savings' Bank: including its formation, progress, and present state: the steps successively resorted to, and their applicability in various circumstances... 60p. *8⁰.* [*London,*] 1816.

21556 TWISS, H. A tract on saving banks; addressed to the editors of the principal newspapers, and other periodical publications: to which is added, a short and practical plan, consisting of twelve plain regulations, easily applicable to the circumstances of any district. 16p. *8⁰.* 1816.

21557 UNITED STATES OF AMERICA. *Laws, etc.* An Act to incorporate the subscribers to the Bank of the United States. 39p. *12⁰. Philadelphia,* 1816.

21558 VERMIGLIOLI, G. B., *ed.* Della zecca e delle monete Perugine, memorie e documenti inediti. [With 'Appendice de monumenti inediti'.] 171, 74p. *4⁰. Perugia,* 1816.

21559 A **VIEW** of the causes of our late prosperity, and of our present distress; and of the means which have been proposed for our relief. 72p. *8⁰. Exeter & London,* 1816.

TRANSPORT

21560 BUCHANAN, ROBERTSON. A practical treatise on propelling vessels by steam... 187p. *8⁰. Glasgow & London,* 1816. *With a manuscript list of steamboats plying on the Clyde in 1820.*

21561 COMPANY OF PROPRIETORS OF THE FORTH AND CLYDE NAVIGATION. Accounts relative to the Forth and Clyde navigation, for the year 1815. 5p. *fol.* [1816]

21562 —— [*Endorsed:*] Minutes of a general meeting of the Company of Proprietors of the Forth and Clyde Navigation. 20th...March, 1816. 5p. *fol.* [1816]

21563 CONVENERY OF THE TRADES OF LEITH. Resolution of the Convenery of the trades of Leith, respecting the proposed Union Canal. 14p. *8°. Leith,* [1816]

21564 CRICHTON, G. Hints for the improvement of the trade between London and Leith, by the establishment of a regular daily conveyance between these ports. 1816. 20p. *8°. Edinburgh,* 1816.

21565 EDGEWORTH, R. L. A letter to the Dublin Society, relative to experiments on wheel carriages. 22p. *8°. Dublin,* 1816.

21566 HOPKIRK, JAMES. Account of the Forth and Clyde Canal Navigation, from its origin, to the present time. 82p. *8°. Glasgow, Edinburgh, &c.,* 1816. *Presentation copy, with inscription, from the author to George Chalmers. With an autograph letter from W. Logan to James Buchanan bound in. For the letter, see vol. III, A.L. 246.*

21567 KENNET AND AVON CANAL NAVIGATION. Report of the Committee of management, to the proprietors of the Kennet and Avon Canal Navigation. [With 'Receipt and expenditure...to...29th May, 1816'.] 2p. *fol. Marlborough,* [1816] *Addressed in manuscript to James Colquhoun. See also* 1812, 1813, 1815, 1823, 1824, 1825, 1826, 1838.

21568 McADAM, JOHN L. Observations on the highways of the kingdom, in a report to the House of Commons. 23p. *8°. Worcester,* [1816?]

21569 —— Remarks on the present system of road making; with observations, deduced from practice and experience, with a view to a revision of the existing laws, and the introduction of improvement in the method of making, repairing, and preserving roads, and defending the road funds from misapplication. 32p. *8°. Bristol,* 1816. *See also* 1819, 1820, 1821, 1822, 1824.

21570 OBSERVATIONS on the prospectus of the proposed Union Canal. 8p. *8°.* [*Edinburgh,*] 1816.

21571 PROSPECTUS of a new shipping company, between Glasgow and London...under the firm of the Glasgow and London Shipping Company... *s.sh.4°.* [*Glasgow,* 1816?] *The copy that belonged to Patrick Colquhoun.*

21572 REMARKS on the advantages of a new shipping company, proposed to be established between Grangemouth and London, for passengers and goods. 3p. *8°. Glasgow,* [1816?] *The copy that belonged to Patrick Colquhoun.*

21573 REMARKS on the affairs of the Frome Turnpike Road Trust, and on the Trust [the Black Dog Trust] affairs of the road from Warminster and Frome towards Bath; with a justification of the conduct of the undersigned, with respect to both Trusts. 41, 50p. *8°.* 1816. *The identity of 'the undersigned' is not disclosed.*

21574 SUTCLIFFE, J. A treatise on canals and reservoirs, and the best mode of designing and executing them; with observations on the Rochdale, Leeds and Liverpool, and Huddersfield canals...Likewise observations on...cotton twist...Also instructions for...building a corn mill...directions on public drains. 413p. *8°. Rochdale, London, &c.,* 1816.

21575 [TARRANDS, .] A new system of practical economy, adapted to the peculiar circumstances of the present times...Illustrated by...plates of the structure and machinery of the improved hydrostatic ship. [A scheme for improving the food supply of London by improved methods of transport.] 34, 57p. *8°.* [1816]

SOCIAL CONDITIONS

21576 ACCOUNT of the proceedings of the public meeting at Westminster, on the distresses of the country, held on September 11, 1816. With the petition to the Prince Regent. 24p. *12°. Glasgow,* 1816.

21577 An authenticated **ACCOUNT** of the proceedings at the Mansion House, on...November 26, 1816, for the purpose of relieving the distressed manufacturers of Spitalfields and elsewhere. With some peculiar observations on the distress of the times; by a spectator. 16p. *8°.* 1816.

21578 An **ADDRESS** to the proprietors and occupiers of landed estates. [On methods of reducing the poor's rate.] 8p. *8°. Dorchester,* 1816

21579 BATH PENITENTIARY AND LOCK HOSPITAL. Bath Penitentiary and Lock Hospital. [An account of the inaugural meeting of June 12th 1816.] *s.sh.fol.* [*Bath,* 1816]

21580 —— Bath Penitentiary and Lock Hospital. [A prospectus, with rules and list of donations and subscriptions.] 35p. *8°. Bath,* 1816. *With an accompanying letter, dated '18 September 1816', from John Fisher, Bishop of Salisbury (1748–1825) to Patrick Colquhoun. For other editions of both these items, see Collective reports of the Bath Penitentiary and Lock Hospital, 1824.*

21581 [BEAUMONT, JOHN T. B.] Letters on public-house licensing; shewing the errors of the present system...Together with a proposal for their cure. By a magistrate for Middlesex. 31p. *8°.* 1816.

21582 BENEVOLENT OR STRANGERS' FRIEND SOCIETY. For the year 1816. Report of the Committee of the...Society, instituted for the purpose of visiting and relieving sick and distressed strangers, and other poor...in London and its vicinity: with an account of some of the cases visited in...1815, and a list of subscribers. 108p. *12°.* 1816. *The Sheffield copy. See also* 1817, 1844.

21583 BOWLES, J. A letter to Robert Wissett, Esq. in answer to four letters, addressed by Mr. Wissett to the author, "on the subject of licensing and regulations for public-houses and liquor-shops"...The second edition, with additions. 140p. *8°.* 1816. *The Sheffield copy. For another edition, see* 1815.

21584 [BUNN, T.] An appeal to those who possess the wealth and the power of Great Britain, on behalf of the loyal and industrious artificers, labourers...discharged soldiers, sailors, and servants, now unemployed, and in want: and a statement of some of the means which may be adopted, for their immediate employ and relief. 38p. *8°.* 1816. *In a volume of the author's own pamphlets, with his manuscript notes.*

21585 BUTLER, C. The inaugural oration spoken on the 4th day of November, 1815, at the ceremony of laying the first stone of the London Institution, for the Diffusion of Science and Literature. 42p. *8⁰. 1816. The copy that belonged to David Ricardo.*

21586 BUXTON, Sir Thomas F., *Bart.* The speech of Thomas Fowell Buxton, Esq. at the Egyptian Hall, on the 26th November, 1816, on the subject of the distress in Spitalfields. To which is added the report of the Spitalfields Association, read at the meeting. Published by order of the Committee then appointed, and for the benefit of its funds. 20p. *8⁰. 1816.*

21587 —— [Another edition.] The distresses of the people, the blessed effects of the Pitt system, described, in a speech at length, at a meeting for sufferings in the Egyptian Hall, Mansion House... With other speeches and proceedings... 8p. *8⁰. 1816.*

21588 CAMERON, Charles R. Friendly and familiar hints to colliers, miners and others, especially those in the neighbourhood of Snedshill, and parish of Wombridge. Pointing out some of the causes of our present distresses, and the means of removing them. 16p. *8⁰. Wellington, Salop & London, 1816.*

21589 CHARITY SCHOOL, *St. Mary-le-Bone.* A concise account of the Charity School, for maintaining and educating one hundred and eight children of the industrious poor parishioners of... St. Mary-le-Bone... [With 'Abstract of receipts and disbursements... for the year 1815'.] 42p. *8⁰. 1816. See also 1815.*

21590 CLARKSON, W. An inquiry into the cause of the increase of pauperism and poor rates; with a remedy for the same, and a proposition for equalizing the rates throughout England and Wales... Second edition. 77p. *8⁰. 1816. For another edition, see 1815.*

21591 COMMERCIAL TRAVELLERS' SO-CIETY. Articles and rules of a friendly society... called the Commercial Travellers' Society... [With lists of officers and members and of donations and subscriptions.] 44p. *8⁰. 1816.*

21592 COMMITTEE FOR INVESTIGATING THE CAUSES OF THE ALARMING IN-CREASE OF JUVENILE DELINQUENCY IN THE METROPOLIS. Report of the Committee... 32p. *8⁰. 1816.*

21593 COMMITTEE FOR THE RELIEF OF THE LABOURING CLASSES, *Edinburgh.* Report of the committee, to whom it was remitted to suggest a plan for affording relief to the labouring classes in the city and suburbs. Ordered to be printed at the general meeting, 10th December, 1816. 16p. *8⁰. Edinburgh, 1816.*

21594 COMMITTEE OF LICENSED VIC-TUALLERS. London, [*blank*] 1816. [*Begin.*] At a meeting of licensed victuallers... to take into considera-tion the grievances under which they labour by the present mode of licensing public houses... Mr. Richard Jackson in the chair. *s.sh.fol.* [*London,* 1816] [*Br.* 485]

21595 CURWEN, J. C. The speech of J. C. Curwen, Esq. M.P. in the House of Commons, on the 28th of May, 1816. On a motion for a committee for taking into con-sideration the state of the poor laws. Second edition. [From *The Pamphleteer,* vol. VIII, no. 15.] 32p. *8⁰. 1816.*

21596 D., W. Thoughts on the reduction of the poor rates, by the establishment of charitable loans, schools of industry, and provident banks. [A series of 4 letters, nos. I, II and IV signed: W.D.] 29p. *8⁰. Southampton, 1816.*

21597 DAVIDSON, R. A short exhibition of the poor laws of Scotland, drawn from authentic documents. To which is added, the answers to five queries, relative to the rights of the poor. 12p. *12⁰. Glasgow, 1816.*

21598 DAY AND SUNDAY FREE SCHOOL, *Circus Street, Liverpool.* Circus-Street Free-School. [Letter announcing a meeting to consider the plan of local printers and booksellers to assist the funds of the school. Signed: B. Baldwin, master... 3d June 1816.] [4]p. *16⁰. n.p.* [1816] *Addressed in manuscript to 'Mr. Simon Fraser, Castle Ditch'.*

21599 [DEFAUCONPRET, A. J. B.] Quinze jours à Londres, à la fin de 1815. Par M. ***. 214p. *8⁰. Paris, 1816.*

21600 DOWNS SOCIETY OF FISHER-MENS' FRIENDS. Report of the committee... 41[48]p. *8⁰. Deal,* [1816]

21601 ELY, *Isle of. Special Assizes.* A full and correct report of the trials for rioting, at Ely and Littleport, in May, 1816... at a special Assize, held at Ely, on... the 17th day of June and following days, with... a prefatory chapter on the state of the country... By a Member of the Inner Temple. 87p. *12⁰. London, Ely, &c., 1816.*

21602 ENGLAND. *Laws, etc.* Anno, quinquagesimo sexto Georgii III. Regis. cap. lxxxvii. An Act to alter and enlarge the powers of two Acts... for granting certain powers to the Gas Light and Coke Company. ⟨2d. July 1816.⟩ p. 1857–1864. *fol. 1816.*

21603 —— Parliament. *House of Commons.* Minutes of the evidence taken before the Committee... to inquire into the state of mendicity and vagrancy in the Metropolis and its neighbourhood. To which is added, the second Report, ordered to be printed, May 28th, 1816. 244p. *8⁰. 1816. For another edition of* Minutes of the evidence *see* 1815.

21604 —— —— —— First Report of the minutes of evidence taken before the Select Committee of the House of Commons appointed to inquire into the education of the lower orders of the Metropolis. Ordered by the House of Commons to be printed 7th June, 1816. 194[180]p. *8⁰. 1816.*

21605 —— —— —— Minutes of evidence taken before a Select Committee appointed by the House of Commons, to inquire into the state of the police of the Metropolis. With notes, observations and a preface, by a magistrate of the county of Middlesex. 518p. *8⁰. 1816.*

21606 —— —— —— Clement's official edition of the Police Report... Report from the Committee on the state of the police of the Metropolis: with the minutes of evidence... and an appendix, containing abstracts of the several Acts now in force for regulating public houses... Ordered by the House of Commons to be printed, July 1, 1816. 396, 32p. *8⁰. 1816.*

21607 GRAHAM, I. The power of faith: exemplified in the life and writings of the late Mrs Isabella Graham, of New-York. 474p. *8⁰. 1816. The life of Mrs Graham was written by her son-in-law Divie Bethune, and the selections from her writings were made by her daughter Joanna Bethune.*

21608 HACKNEY LITERARY INSTITUTION. A catalogue of books in the library of the... Institution. 8p. *8⁰. Hackney, 1816.*

21609 **HALE**, WILLIAM. A letter to Samuel Whitbread, Esq. M.P., containing observations on the distresses peculiar to the poor of Spitalfields, arising from their local situation... The third edition. Printed by order of the Spitalfields Association. 31p. *8°. 1816. For another edition, see 1806.*

21610 **HALLIDAY**, SIR A. A letter to the Right Honourable Lord Binning, M.P., containing some remarks on the state of lunatic asylums, and on the number and condition of the insane poor in Scotland. [With an appendix.] 24, 10p. *8°. Edinburgh & London,* 1816.

21611 **HIGGINS**, G. The evidence [of Godfrey Higgins, Bryan Cooke and Charles Best] taken before a Committee of the House of Commons respecting the Asylum at York; with observations and notes, and a letter to the Committee, &c.&c.&c. 59, 18p. *8°. Doncaster, London, &c.,* 1816.

21612 **KELLY**, P. Plan and terms of the Finsbury Square Academy. [4]p. *4°. n.p. [1816?]*

21613 **LANCASTERIAN SCHOOL OF INDUSTRY FOR GIRLS**, *Sheffield*. ⟨1816.⟩ Report and proceedings of the first annual meeting of the Sheffield Lancasterian School of Industry for Girls. [With a list of subscribers.] 15p. *8°. Sheffield, [1816]*

21614 **LIVERPOOL FEMALE TRACT ASSOCIATION.** The Liverpool Female Tract Association, in aid of the Liverpool Religious Tract Society, from its commencement in August 1815, to August 1816... [2]p. *s.sh.8°. [Liverpool, 1816]*

21615 **LIVERPOOL RELIGIOUS TRACT SOCIETY.** Second report of the Liverpool Religious Tract Society, M.DCCC.XVI, with extracts of correspondence, and a list of subscribers and benefactors [and 'Catalogue of the publications of the Society']. 40p. *8°. Liverpool, [1816] See also 1815.*

21616 **LONDON.** *Court of Aldermen.* Report from the Committee of Aldermen [Samuel Birch, John Perring, Matthew Wood, Samuel Goodbehere], appointed to visit several gaols in England. Printed by an order of the Court ...of the 26 September 1815. 217p. *4°. 1816.*

21617 **MAXWELL**, JOHN I. A brief narrative of the circumstances attending the suppressed pamphlet, entitled Wine vaults vindicated. Addressed to Richard Jackson, Esq. Chairman of the Committee of Licensed Victuallers ... 4p. *4°. [London, 1816]*

21618 [——] Wine-vaults vindicated: remarks upon the partial and arbitrary conduct of magistrates with respect to publicans licenses...With a refutation of the... aspersions cast upon the retailers of wines and spirits; remarks upon the evidence before the police committee... addressed to the Hon. H. G. Bennett, M.P. [Signed: Non unde sed quid.] 90p. *8°. 1816. The Sheffield copy. With 'suppressed' on the half-title, probably in Lord Sheffield's hand.*

21619 **MONTAGU**, B. Enquiries respecting the Insolvent Debtors' Bill, with the opinions of Dr. Paley, Mr. Burke, and Dr. Johnson, upon imprisonment for debt. Second edition. 38p. *8°. 1816. Presentation copy from the author to 'Ed. Wakefield Esqʳ.' (probably Edward Gibbon Wakefield).*

21620 **OVINGTON**, J. A certain remedy for existing distresses, or the labouring man's advocate: an appeal to the justice and humanity of the British public, respecting the wages of labour. 326p. *8°. London & Clapham, [1816?]*

21621 **PARKER**, WILLIAM, *of Cork*. General improvement of the state of the poor of Ireland...[A series of letters originally published in *The Cork Advertiser*.] 158p. *8°. Cork, 1816.*

21622 **PIMLICO BIBLE ASSOCIATION.** The first annual report of the Committee of the Pimlico Bible Association, presented at the general anniversary meeting ...on...July 8, 1816. 15p. *8°. 1816.*

21623 Dedicated to the British nation. A **PLAN**, for employing the poor, and for reducing the national expenditure four millions annually...By an advocate for the poor. 22p. *8°. Shrewsbury & London, [1816]*

21624 **PROPOSALS** for establishing in the Metropolis, a day school, in which an example may be set of the application of the methods of Dr. Bell, Mr. Lancaster, and others, to the higher branches of education. 16p. *8°. 1816. The copy that belonged to David Ricardo.*

21625 **PRUDENT MAN'S FRIEND SOCIETY.** State of the...Society, for the year 1816. [With a list of subscribers.] 24p. *12°. Bristol, [1816]. See also 1813, 1814, 1815.*

21626 **REPORT** of the meeting, held in the Relief Church, Paisley, on...the 5th October, 1816, to consider the present distresses of the country, their causes and probable remedies. 40p. *12°. Paisley, 1816.*

21627 **ST. LUKE**, Middlesex. [*Begin.*] At a meeting of the inhabitants of this parish...December 12, 1816... "to take into consideration the propriety of entering into an immediate subscription for the alleviation of the distresses of the poor resident therein"...[Signed: John Wilks, hon. secretary, and dated, December 13, 1816. With a list of subscriptions.] 2p. *fol. [London, 1816] See note to no. 13563.*

21628 —— [Another edition.] An address on behalf of the distressed poor, in the northern parts of the Metropolis, and especially of the watch and clock manufacturers, within the Parish of St. Luke, Middlesex. [Signed: John Wilks, hon. sec., and dated, Dec. 16.] [4]p. *fol. [London, 1816] The same text as the earlier edition, with the addition of the Address. See note to no. 13563.*

21629 **SOCIETY FOR BETTERING THE CONDITION OF THE POOR**, *London*. To the Committee of the Society...At a meeting of the Society, held...the 2d of February, 1816, the following annual report of the accounts of the Society for 1815, was read and ordered to be printed... 4p. *8°. London, [1816]*

21630 **SOCIETY FOR SUPERSEDING THE NECESSITY OF CLIMBING BOYS**, *London*. A short account of the proceedings of the Society...Published in consequence of the general meeting of the inhabitants of London and Westminster convened...on the 12th of June, 1816, for the purpose of promoting the use of the machine. 24p. *8°. 1816.*

21631 **SOCIETY FOR THE SUPPRESSION OF VAGRANTS**, *Bath*. Report of the Bath Society, No. 6, Pierrepont-Place...With an account of the receipts and disbursements [and a list of subscribers] from Jan. 1, 1815, to Jan. 1, 1816... 40p. *16°. Bath, 1816. See also 1810, 1811, 1812, 1813.*

21632 ***SOCIETY OF ANCIENT BRITONS.** A brief account of the rise, progress, and present state, of the...Society of Ancient Britons, for supporting the Charity School...Gray's Inn Lane, London; with a list of the President, Vice-Presidents... 59p. 8°. 1816. *The copy presented to the Charity Organisation Society (Family Welfare Association) by H.M. Queen Mary.*

21633 SOCIETY OF FRIENDS OF FOREIGN-ERS IN DISTRESS. Report and state of the Society...1816. 25p. 8°. [1816]

21634 THOUGHTS on the poor laws; and on the improvement of the condition and morals of the poor. By the author of "The History of the House of Romanof", &c.&c. 23p. 8°. *London & Edinburgh*, 1816.

21635 URQUHART, T. A letter to Wm. Wilberforce Esq. M.P. on the subject of impressment...Published for the benefit of the Maritime Society. 22p. 8°. 1816. *Also printed in no. 21636, below.*

21636 —— Letters on the evils of impressment, with the outline of a plan for doing them away, on which depend the wealth, prosperity and consequence of Great Britain ...Second edition. 100p. 8°. 1816.

21637 VIVIAN, RICHARD. A letter on friendly societies and savings banks, from the Rev. Richard Vivian ...occasioned by Mr. Rose's letter, [With 'Rules of the Bushey Benefit Society', and 'Rules of the Bushey Female Benefit Society'.] 35p. 8°. 1816.

21638 WESTMINSTER FREE SCHOOL. Fourth annual report...14th May 1816. [With a list of subscribers.] [40]p. 8°. [1816] *See also* 1813, 1814.

21639 WILLIAMS, THOMAS (1760–1844). Means of improving the condition of the poor in morals and happiness considered, in a lecture delivered at the Minor Institute, August 22, 1816: to which is prefixed, a short account of that institution... 64p. 8°. [1816]

SLAVERY

21640 ADAMS, R. The narrative of Robert Adams, a sailor, who was wrecked on the western coast of Africa, in ...1810, was detained three years in slavery by the Arabs of the Great Desert, and resided several months in the city of Tombuctoo...[Edited by S. Cock.] 231p. 4°. 1816.

21641 ANTIDOTE to West-Indian sketches, drawn from authentic sources. No. I [–VII]. 8, 8, 8, 11, 11, 16, [65]–79p. 8°. 1816–17. *Contents: I. Condition of the slaves in the British Colonies, from Pinckard's Notes on the West Indies. II. A short account of the African Institution, and refutation of the calumnies of the directors, by Sir James Leith. III. The actual condition of the negroes in the British West India Colonies; and a further exposure of the calumnies of the African Institution. IV. The calumnies of the African Institution further illustrated by Parliamentary Papers... V. An illustration of the principles of the African Institution ...and...account of the Berbice Commissioners. VI. Observations on the ameliorated condition of the negroes... VII. Observations on the necessary of a...change in the... management of the African Institution. For West-Indian sketches, see no. 21663.*

21642 *Entry cancelled.*

21643 BARBADOS. *House of Assembly.* The report from a Select Committee of the House of Assembly, appointed to inquire into the origin, causes, and progress, of the late insurrection. 63p. 8°. *Barbados*, [1816]

21644 CHALMERS, G., ed. Proofs and demonstrations how much the projected registry of colonial negroes is unfounded and uncalled for: comprehending, the reports and resolves of the Bahama Assembly, on the principle and detail of the proposed registry: with the examinations on oath, of the most respectable persons, as to the facts of the case... 55p. *fol.* 1816.

21645 CLARKSON, T. The history of the rise, progress and accomplishment of the abolition of the African slave-trade, by the British Parliament...Abridged by Evan Lewis. 348p. *12°. Wilmington*, 1816. *For another edition, see* 1808.

21646 The penal **ENACTMENTS** of the Slave Registry Bill examined, in a letter to Charles N. Pallmer, Esq. M.P. 56p. 8°. 1810.

21647 An **EXPOSURE** of some of the numerous mistatements and misrepresentations contained in a pamphlet commonly known by the name of Mr. Marry-att's pamphlet, entitled "Thoughts on the abolition of the slave trade..." 65p. 8°. 1816. *The Sheffield copy.*

21648 An **INQUIRY** into the right and duty of compelling Spain to relinquish her slave trade in northern Africa. 96p. 8°. 1816.

21649 The **INTERFERENCE** of the British Legislature, in the internal concerns of the West India Islands, respecting their slaves, deprecated. By a zealous advocate for the abolition of the slave trade. 58p. 8°. 1816.

21650 JAMAICA. *House of Assembly.* Further proceedings of the Honourable House of Assembly of Jamaica, relative to a Bill introduced into the House of Commons, for effectually preventing the unlawful importation of slaves, and holding free persons in slavery, in the British Colonies. To which are annexed, examinations, taken...before a Committee of that House, for the purpose of disproving the allegations of the said Bill. 100p. *fol.* 1816. *The copy that belonged to William Frend.*

21651 JORDAN, G. W. An examination of the principles of the Slave Registry Bill, and of the means of emancipation, proposed... 147p. 8°. 1816.

21652 A **LETTER** to the members of the Imperial Parliament, referring to the evidence contained in the proceedings of the House of Assembly of Jamaica, and shewing the injurious and unconstitutional tendency of the proposed Slave Registry Bill. By a colonist. 24p. 8°. 1816.

21653 [**MARRYAT,** J.] Thoughts on the abolition of the slave trade, and civilization of Africa; with remarks on the African Institution, and an examination of the report of their committee, recommending a general registry of slaves in the British West India Islands. 235p. 8°. 1816. *The Sheffield copy.*

21654 —— More thoughts, occasioned by two publications which the authors call "An exposure of some of the numerous misstatements and misrepresentations contained in a pamphlet, commonly known by the name of Mr. Marryat's pamphlet...and "A defence of the Bill for the registration of slaves." 143p. 8°. 1816.

21655 **MATHISON**, G. A short review of the reports of the African Institution, and of the controversy with Dr. Thorpe, with some reasons against the registry of slaves in the British Colonies. 78p. *8°*. 1816.

21656 **OBSERVATIONS** upon the oligarchy, or committee of soi-disant saints, in a letter to the Right Honorable Viscount Sidmouth, Secretary of State...By an hereditary planter. [An attack on the Slave Registry Bill.] 67p. *8°*. 1816.

21657 **PINCKARD**, G. Extract, from "Notes on the West Indies." Observations on the emancipation of the slaves. 10p. *8°*. [1816?] *For the original work, see* 1806 (COLONIES).

21658 Brief **REMARKS** on the Slave Registry Bill; and upon a special report of the African Institution, recommending that measure. 67p. *8°*. 1816.

21659 **REMARKS** on the insurrection in Barbadoes, and the Bill for the registration of slaves. 15p. *8°*. 1816.

21660 **STEPHEN**, J. A defence of the Bill for the registration of slaves...In letters to William Wilberforce Esq. M.P. Letter the first. 50p. *8°*. 1816.

21661 —— —— Letter the second. 218p. *8°*. 1816.

21662 **VAUX**, R. Memoirs of the lives of Benjamin Lay and Ralph Sandiford; two of the earliest public advocates for the emancipation of the enslaved Africans. 47p. *12°*. 1816.

21663 **WEST-INDIAN SKETCHES.** Drawn from authentic sources. No. I [–v, vII]. p. 1–51, 72–84. *8°*. 1816–17. *Contents: I. Punishment of the maroons of Demarara. From Pinckard's Notes...II. State of the slave population...in...Nevis. III. Legal condition of the slave exemplified. IV. The nature of West-Indian slavery...in... Tortolo. V. Anecdotes, tending to elucidate the nature of our colonial bondage. VII. Further remarks occasioned by the Antidote to West-Indian sketches (no. 21641).*

POLITICS

21664 **CHARACTERS** of the Court. A poem. With notes. 24p. *8°*. Oxford, 1816.

21665 **ENGLAND.** Parliament. *House of Lords.* 1816. Standing Orders of the House of Peers, relative to the bringing in and proceeding on private Bills. 20p. *4°*. 1816.

21666 **ENSOR**, G. On the state of Europe in January 1816. 133p. *8°*. 1816.

21667 **HONE**, W. The meeting in Spa-Fields. Hone's authentic and correct account, at length, of all the proceedings on Monday, December 2d; with the resolutions and petition of Nov. 15, 1816. 2p. *s.sh.fol.* [*London,* 1816]

21668 —— The riots in London. Hone's full and authentic account, containing...particulars of the events in the Metropolis, on Monday the 2d of December 1816 ... 2p. *s.sh.fol.* [*London,* 1816]

21669 —— Hone's Riots in London, Part II. With most important and full particulars...Elucidating the events of Monday, December 2, 1816. Including original memoirs and anecdotes of Preston, Dyall, the Watson family, Thomas Spence...and a variety of circumstances... shewing the real occasion and true character of the tumults. 2p. *s.sh.fol.* [*London,* 1816]

21670 **KINNAIRD**, C., *8th Baron Kinnaird.* A letter addressed to the Earl of Liverpool by Lord Kinnaird. [On his expulsion from France by the government of Louis XVIII.] Fourth edition. 37p. *8°*. 1816.

21671 **MASSACHUSETTS PEACE SO-CIETY.** A circular letter from the Massachusetts Peace Society, respectfully addressed to the various associations ...and meetings of the ministers of religion in the United States. [Describing the objects of the Society.] 16p. *8°*. Cambridge [*Mass.*], 1816.

21672 **OLDFIELD**, T. H. B. The representative history of Great Britain and Ireland: being a history of the House of Commons, and of the counties, cities, and boroughs, of the United Kingdom, from the earliest period ... 6 vols. *8°*. 1816.

21673 The **PEOPLE'S** mirror; or, corruption & taxation unmasked: containing a list of the members of the House of Commons, with the names of the counties and towns from whence returned—the number of voters in each—by whom influenced...Also showing the manner in which the public money is expended in pensions, places, sinecures, &c.&c....Second edition, with additions. To which is prefixed...Magna Charta, Bill of Rights, Habeas Corpus, Act of Settlement, &c. 34p. *8°*. 1816. *The Agar Ellis copy.*

21674 **PHILLIPS**, CHARLES. The eloquent speech on the dethronement of Napoleon, the state of Ireland, the dangers of England, and the necessity of immediate parliamentary reform...Sixth edition. 16p. *8°*. 1816.

SOCIALISM

21675 **EVANS**, T. Christian policy, the salvation of the Empire. Being a clear...examination into the causes that have produced the impending...national bankruptcy ... 48p. *8°*. 1816.

21676 —— Second edition. 48p. *8°*. 1816.

21677 **OWEN**, ROBERT. An address delivered to the inhabitants of New Lanark, on the first of January, 1816, at the opening of the institution established for the formation of character. 48p. *8°*. London, Edinburgh, &c., 1816. *Presentation copy, with inscription, from the author to James Colquhoun.*

21678 —— Second edition. 48p. *8°*. London, Edinburgh, &c., 1816. *See also* 1817, 1819, 1825, 1841.

21679 —— A new view of society...Second edition. 184p. *8°*. London, Edinburgh, &c., 1816. *Presentation copy from the author; from the library of Sir Robert Peel, with his book-plate. For other editions, see* 1813.

21680 **SPENCES** plan, for parochial partnerships in land...[Announcing the meetings of the Society of Spencean Philanthropists.] *s.sh.8°*. *n.p.* [1816?]

MISCELLANEOUS

21681 ENGLAND. *Admiralty.* [B.] No.[2]. Telegraphic signals for the use of His Majesty's Fleet. [202]p. *4°.* 1816. *The copy specially bound for William IV when Duke of Clarence, with a manuscript inscription on the title-page: For His Royal Highness the Admiral of the Fleet.*

21682 GOODWYN, H. The first centenary of a series of concise and useful tables of all the complete decimal quotients, which can arise from dividing a unit...by all integers from 1 to 1024. [The introduction, signed by the author, dated: March 5th 1816.] 18p. *4°.* n.p. [1816] *The copy that belonged to Nicholas Vansittart, Baron Bexley. See also 1818.*

21683 MacCULLOCH, JOHN. Marbles of Scotland. [Extracts from papers published in vol. 3 of the Transactions of the Geological Society. Apparently prepared for printing by Thomas Bunn.] 29p. *8°.* [1816 ?] *The copy that belonged to Thomas Bunn.*

21684 PAYNE, G. [*Begin.*] The Rev. G. Payne, Edinburgh, begs to call the attention of the friends of religion, to the following statement concerning the Church and congregation where he labours...[An appeal for contributions to the cost of a chapel in the New Town of Edinburgh.] [4]p. *8°.* n.p. [1816 ?] *Addressed in manuscript to 'Mr. John Lang, Printer No. 1 Water St'.*

21685 PEACE SOCIETY, *New York.* Observations on the kingdom of peace, under the benign reign of Messiah. 11p. *8°. New-York*, 1816. *With a note on the verso of the title-page '...read before the Peace Society in New-York, by one of the members, and...published by their request'.*

21686 PHILLIPS, CHARLES. Asperne's genuine edition...The speech of Mr. Phillips, as delivered by him in the Court of Common Pleas, Dublin, in the case of Guthrie versus Sterne, for adultery. With some introductory remarks. By W. G. H. [H. G. White]. 20p. *8°.* 1816.

21687 *[WORCESTER, N.] Friend of peace: containing a special interview between the President of the United States and Omar, an officer dismissed for duelling; six letters from Omar to the President; with a review of the power assumed by rulers over the laws of God and the lives of men, in making war...By Philo Pacificus, author of "A solemn review of the custom of war." 40p. *8°.* 1816.

21688 [——] A solemn review of the custom of war; showing that war is the effect of popular delusion, and proposing a remedy. By Philo Pacificus. Fifth edition. 32p. *8°. Cambridge & Boston*, 1816.

21689 [——] Tract of "The Society for the Promotion of Permanent and Universal Peace." The substance of a pamphlet, entitled A solemn review of the custom of war; showing that war is the effect of popular delusion, and proposing a remedy. 24p. *8°. Stockport*, 1816.

1817

GENERAL

21690 AIKIN, A. An address, delivered on the 27th of May, 1817, at the annual distribution...of the rewards adjudged by the Society for the Encouragement of Arts, Manufactures, and Commerce. [On the function and orgnaization of the Society.] 27p. *8°.* 1817.

21691 BARTON, J. Observations on the circumstances which influence the condition of the labouring classes of society. 80p. *8°.* 1817.

21692 BENTHAM, J. A table of the springs of action: shewing the several species of pleasures and pains, of which man's nature is susceptible: together with the several species of interests, desires and motives...corresponding to them...to which are added explanatory notes and observations... 32p. *8°.* 1817.

21693 BERNARD, SIR T., *Bart.* On the supply of employment and subsistence for the labouring classes, in fisheries, manufactures, and the cultivation of waste lands; with remarks on the operation of the salt duties and a proposal for their repeal... 72p. *8°.* 1817.

For the **BIRMINGHAM INSPECTOR** [edited by W. Hawkes Smith], *see vol.* III, *Periodicals list.*

21694 [BLANC DE LANAUTTE, A. M., *Comte d'Hauterive.*] Elémens d'économie politique, suivis de quelques vues sur l'application des principes de cette science aux règles administratives. 384p. *8°. Paris*, 1817.

21695 The BRITISH IMPERIAL CALENDAR for the year...1817...Being a general register of the United Kingdom...and its colonies...Compiled by R. Capper. [With 'The companion or key to the Imperial Calendar for 1817'.] 348, 71p. *12°.* [1817] *See also 1822, 1828, 1837, 1838, 1849.*

21696 BROUGHAM, H. P., *Baron Brougham and Vaux.* The speech of Henry Brougham, Esq. M.P. in the House of Commons, March 13, 1817, on the state of the nation. 82p. *8°.* 1817.

21697 —— Speech of Henry Brougham, Esq. M.P. delivered on the 13th instant, in the House of Commons, previous to moving a series of resolutions, pledging the House to an inquiry into the causes of the present distressed state of manufacturing and commercial interests. Second edition. 42p. *8°. Edinburgh*, 1817.

21698 BUTTERWORTH, J. An historical and descriptive account of the town and parochial chapelry of Oldham...including some biographical sketches...together with a directory, &c. 211p. *12°. Oldham, London, &c.*, 1817.

21699 The following CALCULATIONS of the reductions of English weights and measures, to those of France, and vice versa, have been made by an Officer of the Army of Occupation, for the convenience of the individuals composing it. Paris, 1st. January 1817. 27p. *8°*. [*Cambrai,*] 1817.

21700　CAREY, M. The olive branch: or, faults on both sides, federal and democratic. A serious appeal on the necessity of mutual forgiveness and harmony...Eighth edition, enlarged. [With an appendix.] 452, 56p. *8°*. *Philadelphia,* 1817. *The Sheffield copy. For other editions, see* 1815.

21701　CHALMERS, G. Comparative views of the state of Great Britain and Ireland; as it was, before the war; as it is, since the peace. 96p. *8°*. 1817.

21702　CHEETHAM, J. The life of Thomas Paine. 187p. *8°*. 1817.

21703　CLELAND, J. Abridgment of the Annals of Glasgow, comprising an account of the public buildings, charities, and the rise and progress of the city. 522p. *8°*. *Glasgow,* 1817. *For Annals of Glasgow, see* 1816.

21704　New COMPANION to the London and Royal Calendars; or court and city register, for...1817... 142p. *12°*. [1817]

21705　A CONVERSATION on the causes of our present distress, and on the remedies for it. By a Forfarshire justice of peace. 12p. *12°*. *Dundee,* 1817.

21706　[COPLESTON, E., *Bishop of Llandaff?*] Cursory hints on the application of public subscriptions in providing employment and relief for the labouring classes. In a letter [dated: Oriel College, Jan. 14, 1817] to the editor of "The Times." By a member of the University of Oxford. 22p. *8°*. 1817. *Conjecturally attributed to Bishop Copleston or to his brother W. J. Copleston by HSF. Both were members of Oriel College.*

21707　[CRAUFURD, C.] Observations on the state of the country since the Peace. 84p. *8°*. 1817.

21708　—— A supplementary section on the poor laws; and a list of errata and omissions in the pamphlet entitled "Observations on the state of the country since the Peace." 48p. *8°*. 1817.

21709　DESTUTT DE TRACY, A. L. C., *Comte*. A treatise on political economy; to which is prefixed a supplement to a preceding work on the understanding, or elements of ideology; with an analytical table, and an introduction on the faculty of the will...Translated from the unpublished French original. [Revised and corrected by Thomas Jefferson.] 90, 254p. *8°*. *Georgetown, D.C.,* 1817.

21710　The EAST-INDIA register and directory, for 1817; corrected to the 19th November 1816; containing ...lists of the Company's servants...Together with lists of...mariners, &c....and merchant vessels employed in the country trade. Compiled...by A. W. Mason, J. S. Kingston, & Geo. Owen, jun.... 495p. *12°*. *London, Dublin, &c.,* [1817].

21711　*—— Corrected to the 1st August 1817... [Second edition.] 512p. *12°*. *London, Dublin, &c.,* [1817] *For other editions, see* 1804.

21712　[EWING, J.] View of the history, constitution, & funds, of the Guildry, and Merchants' House of Glasgow. 112p. *8°*. *Glasgow,* 1817.

21713　FRANKLIN, B. The private correspondence of Benjamin Franklin...Comprising a series of letters on miscellaneous, literary and political subjects: written between...1753 and 1790; illustrating the memoirs of his...life...Published from the originals by his grandson William Temple Franklin...Second edition, with additions. 2 vols. *8°*. 1817. *Vols. 3 and 4 of Franklin's Memoirs in 6 vols.*

21714　[GRAY, S.] All classes productive of national wealth; or, the theories of M. Quesnai, Dr. Adam Smith and Mr. Gray, concerning the various classes of men, as to the production of wealth to the community, analysed and examined, by George Purves, LL.D. 320p. *8°*. 1817. *See also* 1840.

21715　[GREGORY, O. G.] A dissertation on weights and measures, and the best means of revising them: published originally in the British Review, No. XVIII. 1817. 35p. *8°*. *London & Edinburgh,* 1817.

21716　[HOLBACH, P. H. D. VON, *Freiherr*.] The system of nature; or, the laws of the moral and physical world. Done from the original French of M. de Mirabaud. The third edition, with additions... 2 vols. *8°*. 1817. *For other editions, see* 1770.

21717　HUTTON, W. The history of Derby...The second edition, with additions. 267p. *8°*. *London, Derby, &c.,* 1817. *For another edition, see* 1791.

21718　An INQUIRY into several questions of political economy, applicable to the present state of Great Britain. 94p. *8°*. 1817.

21719　IRELAND. *Trustees of the Linen and Hempen Manufactures*. Minutes of the Trustees of the Linen and Hempen Manufactures of Ireland, containing the report of a tour of inspection through the provinces of Leinster, Munster & Connaught, by Mr. Peter Besnard, Inspector General of those provinces, in...1817. [With an appendix, containing information on brown linen markets in the three provinces.] 83, 62p. *8°*. *Dublin,* 1817.

21720　—— Minutes of the Trustees of the Linen and Hempen Manufactures of Ireland, containing the reports of their secretary [James Corry], on a tour of inspection through the Province of Ulster, in October, November, and December, 1816. [With an appendix.] 121, 152p. *8°*. *Dublin,* 1817.

21721　JAMES, HENRY, *of Birmingham*. Observations on the state of the country; or, a concise statement of its present situation and resources, and what it was previous to the late long and expensive war with France; compared with the present situation of the neighbouring states on the continent. 15p. *8°*. 1817.

21722　KEITH, G. S. Different methods of establishing an uniformity of weights and measures stated and compared. 32p. *8°*. *London, Edinburgh, &c.,* 1817. *Presentation copy from the author to Robert D. H. Elphinstone of Logie Elphinstone.*

21723　KOCH, C. G. DE. Histoire abrégée des traités de paix, entre les puissances de l'Europe, depuis la Paix de Westphalie...Ouvrage entièrement refondu, augmenté et continué jusqu'au Congrès de Vienne et aux Traités de Paris de 1815; par F. Schoell... 15 vols. *8°*. *Paris,* 1817–18. *For another edition, see* 1796.

21724　LESUR, C. L. La France et les Français en 1817. Tableau moral et politique, précédé d'un coup d'œil sur la Révolution. 496p. *8°*. *Paris,* 1817.

21725　LETTERS from Scotland: by an English commercial traveller. Written during a journey to Scotland in the summer of 1815. 224p. *12°*. *London, Edinburgh, &c.,* 1817.

21726 [MARCET, J.] Conversations on political economy; in which the elements of that science are familiarly explained. By the author of "Conversations on chemistry." Second edition. 486p. *12°. 1817. For other editions, see 1816.*

21727 MAUBACH, J. Nouveau système d'économie politique ou sociale...Troisième édition, revue et augmentée. 137p. *8°. Bruxelles, 1817.*

21728 MORGAN, S., *Lady.* France...Second edition ...[With 'Four appendices on the state of law, finance, medicine, and political opinion, in France. By Sir T. Charles Morgan'.] 2 vols. *8°. 1817.*

For the **NORTHERN STAR,** or Yorkshire magazine, 1817–18, *see* vol. III, *Periodicals list.*

21729 OUTLINE of the revolution in Spanish America; or an account of the origin, progress and actual state of the war carried on between Spain and Spanish America; containing the principal facts which have marked the struggle. By a South-American. 219p. *12°. New-York, 1817.*

21730 PAINE, T. The political works of Thomas Paine... 2 vols. *8°. 1817. See also 1819, 1840.*

21731 PITKIN, T. A statistical view of the commerce of the United States of America: its connection with agriculture and manufactures: and an account of the public debt, revenues, and expenditures of the United States...Accompanied with tables, illustrative of the principles and objects of the work...Second edition, with additions and corrections. 445p. *8°. New-York, 1817. See also 1835.*

21732 PLEES, W. An account of the island of Jersey; containing...its...history...commerce, population, and produce...[With 'A descriptive tour round the island of Jersey...1813'.] 358p. *4°. Southampton, London, &c., 1817.*

21733 PLUMPTRE, A. Narrative of a residence in Ireland during the summer of 1814, and that of 1815... 398p. *4°. 1817.*

For the **REPUBLICAN,** 1817–22, *superseded by* Sherwin's political register, 1817–19, *then the Republican,* 1819–22, *see* vol. III, *Periodicals list.*

21734 RICARDO, D. On the principles of political economy, and taxation. 589p. *8°. 1817. See also 1819, 1821.*

21735 RIDER'S British Merlin: for...1817...With notes of husbandry, fairs, marts, and tables...Compiled by Cardanus Rider. 60p. *12°. [1817] For other editions, see 1693.*

21736 SAY, J. B. Petit volume contenant quelques aperçus [*sic*] des hommes et de la société. 176p. *12°. Paris, 1817.*

21737 —— Traité d'économie politique...Troisième édition, à laquelle se trouve joint un épitome des principes fondamentaux de l'économie politique... 2 vols. *8°. Paris, 1817. For other editions, see 1803.*

21738 SHAMROCK SOCIETY. Emigration to America. Hints to emigrants from Europe, who intend to make a permanent residence in the United States, on subjects economical and political, affecting their welfare: drawn up...in July last. By the Shamrock Society of New York. 29p. *8°. 1817. Reprinted in Melish, J.* Travels through the United States of America, *in 1818 (q.v.).*

For **SHERWIN'S POLITICAL REGISTER,** 1817–19, *see* vol. III, *Periodicals list.*

21739 SMITH, ADAM. An inquiry into the nature and causes of the wealth of nations...With notes, and an additional volume, by David Buchanan. Second edition. 4 vols. *8°. Edinburgh, 1817.*

21740 —— [Another edition.] With a life of the author. Also, a view of the doctrine of Smith, compared with that of the French economists; with a method of facilitating the study of his works; from the French of M. Garnier... 3 vols. *8°. Edinburgh, 1817. For other editions, see 1776.*

21741 [SMITH, THOMAS, *accountant, of London*?] An address to the merchants and manufacturers of Great Britain, on the present state of the country. [Signed: S.T.] 76p. *8°. 1817. Originally bound in a volume of tracts, most of which were undoubtedly written by Smith.*

21742 YATES, JOHN A. A letter on the distresses of the country; addressed to His Royal Highness the Duke of Kent...in which the supposed influence of our debt and taxes, upon our manufactures and foreign trade, is investigated...Second edition. 211, 17p. *8°. London & Liverpool, 1817. Presentation copy, with inscription, from the author to his brother, Richard V. Yates. For another edition, see 1816.*

AGRICULTURE

21743 BERNARD, SIR T., *Bart.* Case of the salt duties. With proofs and illustrations. 304p. *8°. 1817.*

21744 —— A postscript to a letter to the Right Hon. Nicholas Vansittart, in which some popular objections to the repeal of the salt duties are considered. 24p. *8°. 1817.*

21745 —— On the repeal of the salt duties, and its effects in relieving the present distresses of the poor, being a second postscript to a letter addressed to the Rt. Hon. Nicholas Vansittart. 14p. *8°. 1817.*

21746 Le BON JARDINIER, almanach pour l'année 1817, contenant des préceptes généraux de culture; l'indication, mois par mois, des travaux à faire dans les jardins...commencé par de Grace et Mordant de Lannay; et continué par MM. Féburier...Vilmorin...et Noisette ... 971p. *12°. Paris, 1817.*

21747 BROWNE, JOHN (*fl.* 1817). A treatise on irrigation, or the watering of land. With some observations on cattle, tillage, and planting. 88p. *8°. 1817.*

21748 [HUZARD, J. B.] Instruction sur les soins à donner aux chevaux, pour les conserver en santé sur les routes, dans les camps, aux relais, etc., etc., et remédier aux accidens qui pourroient leur survenir. Nouvelle édition, augmentée. 76p. *8°. Paris, 1817.*

21749 ONORATI, N. C. Dell' agricoltura pratica della pastorizia e di molte altre dottrine che riguardano la medicina veterinaria e l'economia domestica pei dodici mesi dell' anno...Seconda edizione. 314p. *8°. Milano, 1817.*

21750 PARKES, S. Thoughts on the laws relating to salt; with arguments for the repeal of those laws, collected from a variety of sources; and arranged under distinct heads. To which is prefixed, the author's evidence given to the...Board of Trade, on the 8th and 11th of April, 1817, on the same subject. 229p. *8°*. 1817.

21751 PHELPS, S. Observations on the importance of extending the British fisheries, and of forming an Iceland Fishing Society, connected with establishments and stations on the British and Irish coasts. Likewise, a short treatise on the quality of salt fit for the fisheries... Also an account of the first introduction of the British trade with Iceland, &c. 118p. *8°*. 1817.

21752 PLAN for regulating the rents of land in Scotland, with equal safety both to landlord and tenant... Third edition. In which the principles of the plan...are more fully considered...To which is added a proposal for the permanent regulation of tithes in England & Ireland. 88p. *8°*. *Cupar, Edinburgh, &c.,* 1817. *For other editions, see* 1815.

21753 RE, F., *Conte.* Saggio storico sullo stato e sulle vicende dell' agricoltura antica... 288p. *8°*. *Milano,* 1817.

21754 REMONSTRANCE presented to the Government, in or about 1653, on the inestimable riches of the British seas. 22p. *8°*. 1817.

21755 REPORT upon the claims of Mr. George Stephenson, relative to the invention of his safety lamp. By the committee appointed at a meeting holden in Newcastle, on the first of November, 1817. With an appendix, containing the evidence. 26p. *8°*. *Newcastle, London, &c.,* 1817.

21756 RICHARDSON, WILLIAM (1740–1820). Letter on the improvement of grassy mountains, detailing the measures by which they may be made to maintain through winter the whole stock that grazed upon them in summer. 19p. *12°*. *Newry,* 1817.

21757 RIGBY, E. Holkham, its agriculture, &c. 39p. *8°*. *Norwich & London,* 1817.

21758 —— The second edition, with corrections and considerable additions. 61p. *8°*. *Norwich & London,* 1817. *See also* 1818.

21759 RYAN, JAMES. The appeal of James Ryan, director of mines, to proprietors of collieries, and men of humanity. 36p. *12°*. *Birmingham,* 1817.

21760 SINCLAIR, SIR JOHN, *Bart.* The code of agriculture; including observations on gardens, orchards, woods, and plantations. [With an appendix.] 492, 96p. *8°*. *London, Edinburgh, &c.,* 1817. *Presentation copy, with inscription, from the author to Hudson Gurney. See also* 1821.

POPULATION

21761 MALTHUS, T. R. An essay on the principle of population...The fifth edition, with important additions. 3 vols. *8°*. 1817.

21762 —— Additions to the fourth and former editions of An essay on the principle of population, &c.&c. 327p. *8°*. 1817. *For other editions, see* 1798.

TRADES & MANUFACTURES

21763 An **ADDRESS** to the public, shewing the evils, and pointing out the remedies of the present injurious system of apprenticing boys to the watch trade. By a watch-maker. 12p. *12°*. *Coventry,* 1817.

21764 MacCULLOCH, JOHN. Remarks on the art of making wine, with suggestions for the application of its principles to the improvement of domestic wines. Second edition. 261p. *12°*. 1817.

21765 REQUÊTE au roi et mémoire sur la nécessité de rétablir les corps de marchands et les communauté des arts et métiers; présentés à sa majesté le 16 septembre 1817, par les marchands et artisans de la Ville de Paris, assistés de M. Levacher-Duplessis... 68p. *4°*. *Paris,* 1817.

21766 SHARP, JOSEPH B. Letters on the exportation of cotton-yarns, from a series, originally published in the Day and New Times newspaper, under the signature of S....Second edition. 64p. *8°*. 1817.

COMMERCE

21767 BLANE, SIR G., *Bart.* Inquiry into the causes and remedies of the late and present scarcity and high price of provisions, in a letter to the Right Hon. Earl Spencer...dated 8th November, 1800, with observations on the distresses of agriculture and commerce which have prevailed for the last three years...Second edition; with considerable alterations and additions. Printed exclusively in the Pamphleteer. 1817. No. XVII...vol. IX. p. [257]–312. *8°*. *n.p.* [1817] *For other editions, see* 1800.

21768 EDINGTON, R. A treatise on the abuses of the coal trade; commencing with the shipping of coals in the principal ports in the north, and proceeding with the carrying trade, delivery, &c. more especially in the Port of London; the impositions to which the dealers and consumers are...liable...Second edition. 132p. *8°*. 1817. *For another edition, see* 1813.

21769 LANARK, *County of. Commissioners of Supply for Lanarkshire.* Report of a committee of the Commissioners of Supply for Lanerkshire; appointed to inquire into the procedure by which the fiars of grain for that county were struck, for the year 1816; together with some investigation of its principles, and some suggestions for its improvement. 64p. *8°*. *Edinburgh,* 1817.

21770 LEUCHS, J. M. System des Handels... Zweyte sehr vermehrte Ausgabe. 3 vols. *8°*. *Nürnberg,* 1817–18.

21771 LEVANT COMPANY. By-laws of the Levant Company. 1817. [With 'The capitulations and articles of peace, between His Majesty the King of Great Britain and Ireland, and the Sultan of the Ottoman Empire, as...finally confirmed by the Treaty of Peace concluded at the Dardannelles in 1809', and 'Members of the Turkey Company'.] 61, 56, [70]p. *8°. 1817. The list of members of the Turkey Company has manuscript additions covering the year 1818.*

21772 LONG, CHARLES, *Baron Farnborough.* A temperate discussion of the causes which have led to the present high price of bread...Second edition. [From *The Pamphleteer*, vol. X, no. 19.] p. [33]–*48[52]. *8°. 1817. For other editions, see* 1800.

21773 LOWDEN, J. Report of the late important trial, in the Court of Common Pleas: in which John Lowden and Robert Prince, lessees of Covent Garden Market...were plaintiffs, and John Hierons, a market gardener, the defendant. Respecting tolls claimed in Covent Garden Market. Tried...December 6, 1817. 135p. *8°.* 1817.

21774 MEMOIR on the spirit and reason of the navigation acts; and on the policy of establishing a commercial entrepôt at the Isle of France. In a letter ...to the Right Honourable Earl Bathurst. 27p. *8°.* 1817.

21775 PRINCE'S London price current...No. 2126. Friday, the 3d January, [—No. 2177. Friday the 26th Dec.] 1817. 52 nos. *fol.* [1817] *See also* 1812, 1813, 1814, 1815, 1818, 1820.

21776 ROYAL EXCHANGE WINE COMPANY. Royal Exchange Wine Company, No. 20, Fenchurch-Street...established for the sole purpose of selling genuine wines from the Cape of Good Hope... The proprietors...beg leave to call your attention to the annexed price current of wines...[Addressed in manuscript to J. Colquhoun, together with an invoice.] [4]p. *4°. n.p.* [1817]

21777 TELFER, A. An illustration of the mistaken notions entertained with respect to the price of provisions, and the oppression of taxation...It is likewise demonstrated that if the late Corn Bill had not passed our state would have been much worse than it is at present. 59p. *8°. Glasgow & London,* 1817.

21778 THOUGHTS on the impolicy of altering the present rate of duty on foreign timber and deals. 14p. *8°.* 1817.

21779 TOENNIES, F. W. A peep behind the curtain: addressed to the merchants of Hamburg, all Germany, London, St. Petersburg, &c.&c. [An account of a lawsuit between Toennies and Schädtler.] 148p. *8°.* 1817.

COLONIES

21780 BERTOLACCI, A. A view of the agricultural, commercial, and financial interests of Ceylon. With an appendix; containing some of the principal laws and usages of the Candians... 577p. *8°.* 1817.

21781 DUFOUR DE PRADT, D., *Archbishop of Mechlin.* Des colonies, et de la révolution actuelle de l'Amérique. 2 vols. *8°. Paris,* 1817.

21782 —— The colonies, and the present American revolutions...Translated from the French. 501p. *8°.* 1817.

21783 HOGENDORP, G. K. VAN, *Grave.* Du système colonial de la France, sous les rapports de la politique et du commerce. Accompagnée d'un tableau donnant la nomenclature technologique de tous les établissemens coloniaux et de commerce des Européens dans les autres parties du monde. 207p. *8°. Paris,* 1817.

21784 MALTHUS, T. R. Statements respecting the East-India College, with an appeal to facts, in refutation of the charges lately brought against it, in the Court of Proprietors. 105p. *8°.* 1817.

21785 MARTINIQUE. Observations sur le système monétaire. [With 'Tarif des monnaies'.] 2, [4]p. *4°. n.p.* [1817] *At the foot of the title-page:* '8e *cahier'.*

21786 A **NARRATIVE** of occurrences in the Indian countries of North America, since the connexion of the Right Hon. the Earl of Selkirk with the Hudson's Bay Company, and his attempt to establish a colony on the Red River; with a detailed account of His Lordship's military expedition to, and subsequent proceedings at Fort William, in Upper Canada. [With a postscript and an appendix of documents.] 152, 87p. *8°. 1817. Variously attributed to Simon McGillivray, Edward Ellice the elder and Samuel Hall Wilcocke. The copy that belonged to David Ricardo.*

21787 RAFFLES, SIR THOMAS S. The history of Java... 2 vols. *4°.* 1817.

21788 WIMPFFEN, F. A. S. DE, *Baron.* A voyage to Saint Domingo, in the years 1788, 1789, and 1790... Translated from the original manuscript...by J. Wright. 371p. *8°.* 1817.

FINANCE

21789 A short **ACCOUNT** of Scotish money and coins, with tables of their value at different periods, and the price of commodities, &c.: together with tables of the revenues of the archbishoprics, bishoprics, abbeys, nunnerys, &c. at the Reformation... 16p. *8°. Edinburgh,* 1817.

21790 [ATKINSON, WILLIAM (1758–1846).] Arguments against tithes answered; in a third letter to Lords Holland and Rosslyn. By the Old Inquirer. p. 23–50. *8°. Bradford & London, 1817. Paginated in sequence with the author's* Letters on the wool question, *1816 (q.v.* GENERAL).

21791 ATTWOOD, T. A letter to the Right Honourable Nicholas Vansittart, on the creation of money, and on its action upon national prosperity. 111p. *8°. Birmingham & London,* 1817.

21792 [——] Prosperity restored; or, reflections on the cause of the public distresses, and on the only means of relieving them. By the author of The remedy... 222p. *8°. 1817. Presentation copy from the author to Viscount Lowther, with a footnote to the inscription, 'published in January 1817'. See also note to no.* 21472.

21793 BANK OF SCOTLAND. A list of proprietors in the stock of the Bank of Scotland. March 6th, 1817. [With 'List of the present directors'.] [4]p. *n.p.* [1817] *See also* 1704, 1737, 1753, 1754, 1756, 1765, 1767, 1774, 1775, 1776, 1777, 1778.

21794 BANK OF THE UNITED STATES. Report as amended and adopted by the Board of Directors of the Bank of the United States, July 18, 1817. [With the supplementary report of the same date.] 22p. *12°. n.p.* [1817]

21795 —— Rules and regulations for the government of the offices of discount and deposit, established by the Bank of the United States. 14p. *12°. Philadelphia*, 1817.

21796 BENTHAM, J. Defence of economy against the late Mr. Burke...Original. [From *The Pamphleteer*, vol. IX, no. 17. A criticism of the proposals in Burke's speech of 11 Feb. 1780.] 47p. *8°. n.p.*, 1817.

21797 The extraordinary red **BOOK**; containing a list of all places, pensions, and sinecures; the droits of the Crown and Admiralty; rents of Crown lands; the expenditure of the Civil List...with a complete view of the finance and debt of Great Britain...Second edition, with copious alterations and corrections...By a commoner. 184, 69p. *12°.* 1817. *Attributed by HSF to R. J. Richardson. For other editions, see* 1816.

21798 BOWLES, J. Reasons for the establishment of provident institutions, called savings' banks; with a word of caution respecting their formation: and an appendix, containing a model for the formation of savings' banks, according to the plan adopted by the Provident Institution established in...the Metropolis, and by that for the City of London...The third edition, with additions. 45p. *8°. London & Bath*, 1817.

21799 —— Reasons for the establishment, and suggestions for the formation and management, of banks for savings; agreeably to the Act of Parliament lately passed for the encouragement and protection of such institutions; with an appendix, containing a set of approved rules and regulations for the formation of banks for savings...The fourth edition, with additions. 70p. *8°. London & Bath*, 1817.

21800 BRUGIÈRE DE BARANTE, A. G. P., *Baron de Barante.* Discours prononcé à la Chambre des Députés, dans la séance du 7 février 1817...sur le budget de 1817; imprimé par ordre de la Chambre. 24p. *8°. Paris*, 1817.

21801 BURNABY, E. A. A letter to the Cabinet Ministers, suggesting a mode to relieve (in part) the distresses of the Empire, and to make its income and expenditure balance, being a supplement...to "England may be extricated from her difficulties, consistently with the strictest principles of policy...and justice." 35p. *8°.* 1817.

21802 A curious **CALCULATION** on the National Debt. *s.sh.fol.* [London, 1817?] [*Br.* 486] *In the text, the problems, numbered 1–9, are said to have been taken from Lettsom's Hints respecting the distresses of the poor, 1795* (*q.v.* SOCIAL CONDITIONS).

21803 COBBETT, W. Cobbett's paper against gold: containing the history and mystery of the Bank of England, the Funds, the Debt, the Sinking Fund, the Bank stoppage, the lowering and raising of the value of paper money ... 470 cols. *8°.* [*London*, 1817] *Issued in 15 parts. For other editions, see* 1815.

21804 COMBER, W. T. A view of the nature and operation of bank currency; as connected with the distresses of the country. 54p. *8°.* 1817.

21805 COMYN, R. B. A treatise on the law of usury. 292p. *8°.* 1817.

21806 CRAUFURD, SIR C. G. Reflections upon circulating medium; currency; prices; commerce; exchanges, &c. With immediate reference to the present state of the country. 225p. *8°.* 1817.

21807 CROMBIE, A. A letter to D. Ricardo, Esq. containing an analysis of his pamphlet on the depreciation of bank notes. 143p. *8°.* 1817.

21808 DEVON AND EXETER SAVINGS BANK. The first annual report of the Devon & Exeter Savings Bank, established at Exeter, January 1816. 3p. *4°. Exeter*, [1817] *See also* 1829.

21809 DUNCAN, H. A letter to John H. Forbes, Esq., Advocate; containing an answer to some remarks and statements in his "Observations on banks for savings" and his "Letter to the editor of the Quarterly Review;" to which are added, some cursory remarks relative to a proposed Act of Parliament for the protection and encouragement of banks for savings, in Scotland. 58p. *8°. Edinburgh, Dumfries, &c.*, 1817.

21810 EDYE, J. A letter to the Right Hon. Lord Rolle, on the present distresses of the country. 23p. *8°. London & Bristol*, 1817.

21811 ENGLAND. *Proclamations.* By His Royal Highness the Prince of Wales, Regent of the United Kingdom...A Proclamation. George R. [*Begin.*] Whereas by an Act passed in the fifty-sixth year of His Majesty's reign...[12 February 1817. From 13 February 1817 a limitation of forty shillings is placed on silver coin as legal tender.] *s.sh.fol.* 1817.

21812 FERRIER, F. L. A. Mémoire sur le crédit... Seconde édition. 72p. *8°. Lille*, [1817?]

21813 FORBES, JOHN H., *Lord Medwyn.* Observations on banks for savings; to which is prefixed a letter to the editor of the Quarterly Review. 87p. *8°. Edinburgh & London*, 1817.

21814 FRANCE. *Chambre des Députés.* No. 111. Opinion de M. de Bonald, Député de l'Aveyron, sur l'article 1er du Titre XI du projet de loi de finances. Imprimée par ordre de la Chambre. 45p. *8°.* [*Paris*, 1817]

21815 —— *Chambre des Pairs.* Impressions No. 79... Session de 1816. Séance du samedi 8 mars 1817. Projet de loi sur les finances, adopté par la Chambre des Députés le 6 mars, 1817; présenté à la Chambre des Pairs le 8 du même mois. Discours de M. le Duc de Richelieu... Ordonnance du Roi portant consentement...aux amendments proposés par la Chambre des Députés. Texte du projet de loi. Imprimés par ordre de la Chambre. 96p. *8°.* [*Paris*, 1817]

21816 —— *Louis XVIII, King.* Loi, sur les finances. A Paris, le 25 mars, 1817. No. 243. [With 'États annexés à la Loi sur les finances'.] 55p. *8°. Paris*, [1817]

21817 —— Suite des États annexés à la Loi sur les finances du 25 mars 1817, insérée dans le Bulletin des Lois, No. 145. No. 243 bis. 9p. *8°. Paris*, 1817.

21818 —— Loi relative aux douanes. A Paris, le 27 mars, 1817. No. 245. 16p. *8°. Paris*, [1817]

21819 —— *Ministère des Finances.* Rapport présenté à son excellence le Ministre secrétaire d'État des Finances, par le Commissaire Royal du Cadastre [A. J. U. Hennet]. 272p. *4°. n.p.* [1817]

21820 FREND, W. The National Debt in its true colours, with plans for its extinction by honest means. 36p. *8°.* 1817.

21821 GALERIE métallique des grands hommes français. [Prospectus for a series of medallions, engraved by Pierre Lévêque? Subscriptions to be taken in by the publisher A. A. Renouard, and others.] 4p. *8°. n.p.* [1817]

21822 GARNIER, G., *Marquis*. Mémoire sur la valeur des monnaies de compte chez les peuples de l'antiquité...Lu à l'Académie [Royale des Inscriptions et Belles-Lettres]...1817. 91p. *4°. Paris,* 1817.

21823 GAUDIN, M. M. C., *Duc de Gaëte*. Aperçu théorique sur les emprunts, suivi de quelques observations sur le chapitre 8 de l'ouvrage de M. Ganilh...concernant la législation, l'administration et la comptabilité des finances depuis la restauration. 39p. *8°. Paris,* 1817.

21824 GRAHAME, JAMES, *advocate*. Defence of usury laws against the arguments of Mr. Bentham and the Edinburgh Reviewers. 37p. *8°.* 1817.

21825 —— Defence of usury laws, and considerations on the probable consequences of their projected repeal... The second edition, enlarged and corrected. 52p. *8°. Edinburgh & London,* 1817.

21826 GRENFELL, P. Substance of a speech addressed to the House of Commons, on the 28th April, 1814 ...on the subject of applying the Sinking Fund towards any loans raised for the public service. 31p. *8°.* 1817.

21827 HAMILTON, ROBERT (1743–1829). Recherches sur l'origine, les progrès, le rachat, l'état actuel et la régie de la dette nationale de la Grande-Bretagne... Traduites de l'anglais sur la deuxième édition, par J. Henri La Salle. 302p. *8°. Paris,* 1817. *For other editions, see* 1813.

21828 HOMO, *pseud.* Homo's letters on a national currency, addressed to the people of the United States. 37p. *8°. Washington,* 1817.

21829 HUME, D. Insecurity of the British Funds. Essay on public credit: by David Hume, (reprinted from the edition of 1752). With observations on the sound and prophetic nature of its principles, shewing...that a perseverance in the Pitt and paper system must eventually produce a national bankruptcy...Addressed to the British people by Imlac. 357p. *8°. London, Manchester, &c.,* 1817.

21830 LAFFITTE, J. Opinion de M. Laffitte, Député de la Seine, sur le projet de loi relatif aux finances pour 1817. Prononcée à la séance du 10 février 1817. 37p. *8°. Paris,* 1817.

21831 LETRONNE, J. A. Considérations générales sur l'évaluation des monnaies grecques et romaines, et sur la valeur de l'or et de l'argent avant la découverte de l'Amérique...[With 'Quelques observations sur le second Mémoire de M. le Comte Germain Garnier'.] 144p. *4°. Paris,* 1817.

21832 [LUSHINGTON, STEPHEN R.] A letter, &c.&c.&c. [On the deficiency of the revenue in 1816.] 40p. *8°.* [1817] *Addressed in manuscript: 'To the Earl of Liverpool K.G., from S. R. Lushington Esqr.', and dated '18 Feby 1817'.*

21833 [MUELLER VON NITERSDORF, A. H., *ed.*] Die Forschritte der nationökonomischen Wissenschaft in England während des laufenden Jahrhunderts. Eine Sammlung deutscher Uebersetzungen der seit dem Jahr 1801 bis jetzt erschienenen bedeutendsten Parlamentarischen Reports, Flug- und Streitschriften, Recensionen, u.s.f., welche zur Förderung und Berichtigung der staatswirtschaftlichen Theorie beigetragen haben. [Vol. I.] 235p. *8°. Leipzig & Altenburg,* 1817. *No more published. The volume contains translations of five reviews which were published between 1802 and 1805 in the Edinburgh Review.*

21834 MURHARD, J. C. A. Theorie des Geldes und der Münze. 396p. *8°. Altenburg & Leipzig,* 1817.

21835 PAINE, T. The decline and fall of the English system of finance. 26p. *8°.* 1817. *For other editions, see* 1796.

21836 PERIER, C. Réflexions sur le projet d'emprunt. 23p. *8°.* [*Paris,* 1817]

21837 —— Dernières réflexions sur le projet d'emprunt; ou réponse à un article anonyme du Moniteur. [With the article, 'Note anonyme sur la brochure de M. Casimir Perier, insérée dans le Moniteur du 28 janvier 1817'.] 37p. *8°.* [*Paris,* 1817]

21838 *PETITION to the House of Commons for a reduction of the duty on wine. 25p. *8°.* 1817. *The copy that belonged to Augustus De Morgan.*

21839 REDUCCION completa y recíproca de las monedas de Castilla con las de Cataluña, Aragon, Valencia, Mallorca y Navarra: obrita útil á toda clase de personas. 281p. *8°. Barcelona,* 1817.

21840 ROCK BENEFIT SOCIETY. Rules, orders and regulations, of the Rock Benefit Society, now held at the White Horse, Fan-Street, Aldersgate-Street, in the city of London...Corrected and revised, November, 1816. 34p. *8°.* 1817.

21841 ROSE, GEORGE. Observations on banks for savings...The fourth edition, with alterations and additions, in consequence of the Act which was passed in the last session of Parliament to encourage those establishments. 66p. *8°.* 1817. *For other editions, see* 1816.

21842 RUSSIA. *Laws, etc.* Regulation of the Committee of the Sinking Fund. Approved by His Majesty the Emperor of all the Russias, St. Petersburgh, 16th April, 1817. [64]p. *8°.* 1817. *The French and English texts are printed on opposite pages. A summary of the text is printed in nos.* 21843–4, *below.*

21843 —— —— Ukase of His Imperial Majesty the Emperor of Russia [of 6 April 1817], on the promulgation of the new regulations published by the Committee created in 1810, at St. Petersburgh, for the discharge of the Public Debt. 1817. [16]p. *8°.* 1817. *The French and English texts are printed on opposite pages. The copy that belonged to James Colquhoun.*

21844 —— —— [Another edition, with a summary of the text of a Ukase of 10 May 1817.] 4p. *4°. Westminster,* [1817] *The copy that belonged to James Colquhoun.*

21845 SABATIER, J. J. Des banques, de leur influence pour faciliter la circulation des capitaux, faire baisser le trop haut prix de l'intérêt, et des mesures à adopter pour que l'agriculture, l'industrie, le commerce de la France et des divers états jouissent de l'avantage de tels établissemens. 95p. *8°. Paris,* 1817.

21846 *SEÑAN Y VELAZQUEZ, J. Guia o estado general de la real hacienda de España año de 1817. 305, 335p. *8°. Madrid,* [1817]

21847 SIMENCOURT, E. DE. Tableaux des monnoies de change et des monnoies réelles, des poids et mesures, des cours des changes et des usages commerciaux des principales villes de l'Europe. Ou répertoire du banquier... [11]p., 41 l. *4°. Paris, 1817.*

21848 SINCLAIR, SIR JOHN, *Bart.* On the means of arresting the progress of national calamity. 18p. *8°. London & Edinburgh, 1817.*

21849 STATEMENT of the distillers in Scotland, who make spirits for the consumption of England; containing an account of the hardships to which they are subjected in exporting their spirits to England from the unequal duties imposed on them by the existing laws. [Setting out the experiences of James Haig, distiller, and containing his petition to the Lords of the Treasury against a judgment in the Exchequer Court, and other documents.] 36, 25p. *8°. Edinburgh, 1817.*

21850 TIARKS, J. L. Tables for easily determining the arbitration of exchanges between London and the principal commercial towns in Europe. 130p. *8°. 1817. Copy 13, numbered and signed by the author.*

21851 VILLÈLE, J. B. G. M. S. J. DE, *Comte.* Chambre des Députés. Opinion de M. de Villèle, Député de la Haute-Garonne, sur le projet de loi relatif aux finances. Imprimé par ordre de la Chambre... 39p. *8°. Toulouse, [1817]*

21852 WESTON, S. Observations on the origin and antiquity, use and advantage of Cufic coins. Communicated to the Society of Antiquaries, in a letter...to the Earl of Aberdeen...Read before the Society, June 13, 1816. From the Archaeologia, Vol. XVIII. 4p. *4°. [London, 1817]*

TRANSPORT

21853 COLDEN, C. D. The life of Robert Fulton... Comprising some account of the invention, progress, and establishment of steam-boats; of improvements in the construction and navigation of canals, and other objects of public utility. With an appendix. 371p. *8°. New-York, 1817.*

21854 EDGEWORTH, R. L. An essay on the construction of roads and carriages...The second edition: with a report of experiments tried by order of the Dublin Society. 171p. *8°. 1817. The Rastrick copy. For other editions, see 1813.*

21855 ENGLAND. *Laws, etc.* Anno quinquagesimo septimo Georgii III. Regis. Cap. xxxvii. An Act for making and maintaining a railway or tram road from Bull's Head Lane, in the parish of Mansfield, in the county of Nottingham, to communicate with the Cromford Canal at Pinxton Basin in the parish of Pinxton, in the county of Derby. ⟨16th June 1817.⟩ p. 901–950. *fol. 1817.*

21856 STEVENSON, R. Report relative to a line of canal upon one level, between the cities of Edinburgh and Glasgow, to form a junction with the Forth and Clyde canal at lock No. 20, and also with the port of Leith, and the Broomielaw at Glasgow. [With 'Estimates of revenue and expence'.] 29, 7p. *4°. Edinburgh, 1817.*

21857 SUGDEN, J. The traveller's guide to France and the Netherlands; containing the various modes & expences of travelling...the comparative value of French, Dutch, Belgian & English money; the custom house duties, post regulations, sailing of packets...And exhibiting twelve routes to Paris, Amsterdam, Rotterdam...&c.... To which is added, the route from London to Geneva, Lausanne, and Neuchatel. 162p. *12°. 1817.*

SOCIAL CONDITIONS

21858 An **ACCOUNT** of the society, denominated the Associated Proprietors of the Gas Light and Coke Company: containing particulars of the rise, the progress, the principles, the object, and the usefulness of that society. By an associated proprietor. 39p. *8°. [1817]*

21859 ALEXANDER, A. Facts relative to the state of children who are employed by chimney sweepers, as climbing boys; with observations and outlines of a plan for the amelioration of their condition. 48p. *12°. York & London, 1817.*

21860 ALPHA, *pseud.* A letter addressed to C. C. Curwen, Esq. M.P. on the poor laws, containing a safe, easy and economical substitute for the present system. 32p. *8°. Warwick, London, &c., 1817.*

21861 ASHDOWNE, J. An essay on the existing poor-laws, and present state of the labouring poor, chiefly with a view to shew the means of bettering the condition of the poor, and alleviating the burdens on parishes, by a reduction of the poor's rate. 30p. *8°. 1817.*

21862 ASSOCIATION OF THE PARISH OF ST. JAMES. An account of the proceedings of the Association...formed December 9, 1816, for the relief and employment of the poor. [With a list of subscribers.] 24p. *12°. 1817.*

21863 BANFILL, S. A letter to Sir T. D. Acland, Bart. M.P. containing hints for improving the condition of the laboring classes of the community, and reducing parochial assessments, by adapting the poor laws to the present state of society. 17p. *8°. Exeter, 1817. See also 1828* (Third letter to Sir T. D. Acland...).

21864 BEAUMONT, JOHN T. B. A letter to the Right Honourable Lord Sidmouth...shewing the extreme injustice to individuals and injury to the public, of the present system of public-house licensing; and proposing a constitutional remedy for its numerous evils. 44p. *8°. 1817.*

21865 BENEVOLENT OR STRANGERS' FRIEND SOCIETY. [*Begin.*] At a meeting of the committee of the Benevolent or Strangers' Friend Society instituted for the purpose of visiting and relieving sick and distressed strangers and other poor...in London and its vicinity, held 24th January, 1817... 3p. *4°. [1817]*

21866 —— For the year 1817. Report of the committee of the...Society; instituted for the purpose of visiting and relieving sick and distressed strangers, and other poor... With an account of some of the cases visited in...1816, and a list of subscribers. 108p. *12°. 1817. See also 1816, 1844.*

21867 BICHENO, J. E. An inquiry into the nature of benevolences, chiefly with a view to elucidate the principles of the poor laws, and to show their immoral tendency. 145p. *8°*. 1817.

21868 BOWLES, J. The existing law respecting the right of retailing spirituous liquors stated and vindicated: with some brief remarks on the baneful effects, physical and moral, produced by ardent spirits... Extracted chiefly from Mr. Bowles's reply to a letter addressed to him by Robert Wissett... 29p. *8°*. 1817. *For editions of* A letter to Robert Wissett, Esq., *see* 1815.

21869 BRANDRETH, JEREMIAH, *and others.* The trials of Jeremiah Brandreth, William Turner, Isaac Ludlam, George Weightman, and others, for high treason, under a special commission at Derby on...16th...[to] 25th October, 1817. With the antecedent proceedings... 2 vols. *8°*. 1817.

21870 BROCK, I. A letter to the inhabitants of Spital-Fields, on the character and views of our modern reformers. By a member of the Spital-Fields Benevolent Society. 37p. *8°*. 1817.

21871 BRYDGES, SIR S. E., *Bart.* Arguments in favour of the practicability of relieving the able-bodied poor, by finding employment for them; and of the beneficial consequences of such employment...Addressed to the Committee on the Poor Laws. 39p. *8°*. 1817.

21872 [BURGOYNE, M.] A statistical account of the hundreds of Harlow, Ongar, and the half hundred of Waltham, with the particulars of the expenditure of the poor's rates in 42 parishes of these divisions. By a magistrate of the county of Essex. 11p. *8°*. 1817.

21873 CALEDONIAN ASYLUM. The Corporation of the Caledonian Asylum, for supporting and educating the children of soldiers, sailors and marines, natives of Scotland, and of indigent Scotch parents resident in London not entitled to parochial relief. Instituted and incorporated anno 1815. [With a list of subscribers.] 32, 10p. *8°*. 1817.

21874 CANDIDUS, *pseud.* Observations on gaslights: being an impartial inquiry concerning the injurious effects on the health of the community, from the use of coal-gas for lighting the Metropolis. 48p. *8°*. 1817.

21875 CHALMERS, T. The influence of Bible societies, on the temporal necessities of the poor...Third edition. 40p. *8°*. *Edinburgh, Glasgow, &c.*, 1817. *See also* 1818.

21876 CONSIDERATIONS on the poor laws, and the treatment of the poor; with suggestions for making the public annuitants contributory to their support. By one of His Majesty's justices of the peace [Samuel Parr ?]. 64p. *8°*. 1817. *The author was conjecturally identified by HSF as William Wilshere. The work has also been attributed to Samuel Parr.*

21877 COURTENAY, T. P. Copy of a letter to the Right Honorable William Sturges Bourne, Chairman of the Select Committee of the House of Commons appointed for the consideration of the poor laws. From a member of that Committee. 39p. *8°*. [1817]

21878 CUNNINGHAM, JOHN W. A few observations on friendly societies, and their influence on public morals. 31p. *8°*. 1817.

21879 CURWEN, J. C. Sketch of a plan by J. C. Curwen, Esq., M.P. for bettering the condition of the labouring classes of the community, and for equalizing, and reducing the amount of the present parochial assessments. Submitted to the Committee appointed by the House of Commons for taking the laws respecting the poor into consideration. 24p. *8°*. [1817]

21880 —— Speech of J. C. Curwen, Esq., in the House of Commons, on the 21st of February, 1817, on a motion for a Committee to take into consideration the poor laws. 23p. *8°*. 1817.

21881 DAVIS, WILLIAM. Friendly advice to industrious and frugal persons, recommending provident institutions, or savings banks...Fourth edition. Enlarged. 31p. *8°*. *London, Bath, &c.*, 1817.

21882 DAVISON, J. Considerations on the poor laws. 122p. *8°*. *Oxford & London*, 1817. *See also* 1818.

21883 DISTRESSES of the workmen in the watch and clock trade, resident in the Metropolis. [A printed form to be filled in by applicants for relief.] [2]p. *s.sh.fol. n.p.* [1817] *See note to no.* 13563.

21884 DORKING PROVIDENT INSTITUTION. The report of the committee of the Provident Institution established at Dorking, June the 4th, 1816, with a list of the labouring class subscribers and the regulations of the society for the present year... 20p. *8°*. *Dorking*, 1817.

21885 DUBOIS BERGERON, P. Des nouvelles écoles à la Lancaster, comparées avec l'enseignement des frères des écoles chrétiennes, légalement établis depuis plus d'un siècle...Troisième édition, revue, corrigée et augmentée... 46p. *8°*. *Paris*, 1817.

21886 EDMONDS, G. A letter to the inhabitants of Birmingham; being a vindication of the conduct of the writer, at the late meeting at the Shakespeare, February 11, 1817: with animadversions upon the proceedings of the locked up meeting, at the prison in Moor-Street, on the following day. 24p. *8°*. *Birmingham*, 1817.

21887 ENGLAND. *Laws, etc.* Anno quinquagesimo septimo Georgii III. Regis. Cap. xxiii. An Act for better lighting the streets and houses of the Metropolis with gas. [Incorporating the City of London Gas Light and Coke Company.] ⟨23d May 1817⟩. p. 453-474. *fol.* 1817.

21888 —— Parliament. *House of Commons.* Police report of May, 1817. Relative to public house licences. Report of the Committee on the state of the police of the Metropolis, with the minutes of evidence...and an appendix. 360[460]p. *8°*. 1817. *The copy that belonged to J. T. Barber Beaumont.*

21889 —— —— —— Report from the Committee of the honourable the House of Commons, on the employment of boys in sweeping of chimneys. Together with the minutes of the evidence taken before the Committee, and an appendix...Published under the direction of the Society for Superseding the Necessity of Climbing Boys. With notes and observations; a complete list of persons using the machine [for cleaning chimneys] and a descriptive engraving of it. [Edited by W. Tooke.] 142p. *8°*. 1817.

21890 —— —— —— Report from the Select Committee on the Poor Laws; with the minutes of evidence taken before the Committee. Ordered by the House of Commons to be printed, July 4, 1817. 240p. *8°*. [1817]

21891 —— [Another edition.] To which is added, the Report of the Lords Committees on the subject... 201p. *8°*. 1817. *See also* 1818.

21892 —— —— —— New police report for 1817. The second Report [ordered to be printed July 8, 1817] of the Select Committee on the state of the police of the Metropolis: to which are added, the minutes of evidence... p. 465–706[806]. *8°.* 1817. *Paginated in sequence with the first Report (no.* 21888).

21893 EVANS, Sir William D. Address...at the New Bayley Court-House, Salford, on discharging the prisoners who were apprehended, on account of an illegal assembly at Manchester, on the 10th of March, 1817. 7p. *8°. Manchester,* 1817.

21894 —— A charge to the grand jury, at the Quarter Sessions of the peace for the county of Lancaster, held by adjournment at Preston, on the 16th day of January, 1817. 21p. *8°. Manchester,* 1817.

21895 EXPOSITION of one principal cause of the national distress, particularly in manufacturing districts; with some suggestions for its removal. 41p. *8°.* 1817.

21896 [**GASCOIGNE,** H. B.] The antidote to distress; containing observations and suggestions calculated to promote the employment of the poor, the improvement of trade, the mutual interests of landlords and tenants and other public and private advantages. By Farmer Meanwell. 59p. *8°.* 1817. *With a manuscript note on the title-page: H. B. Gascoigne's Respects, 73 Cornhill.*

21897 —— Suggestions for the employment of the poor of the Metropolis, and the direction of their labours to the benefit of the inhabitants: with hints on mendicity... 32p. *8°.* 1817.

21898 GIOJA, M. Problema quali sono i mezzi più spediti, più efficaci, più economici per alleviare l'attuale miseria del popolo in Europa: discorso popolare dell'autore del Nuovo prospetto delle scienze economische. Seconda edizione accresciuta dall'autore. 167p. *8°. Milano,* 1817.

21899 GLOVER, G. Observations on the present state of pauperism in England, particularly as it affects the morals and character of the labouring poor; in a letter to T. W. Coke, Esq., M.P. one of the Committee on the Poor Laws. 42p. *8°.* 1817.

For the **GOOD OLD TIMES,** *see vol.* III, *Periodicals list.*

21900 GOURLAY, R. F. The village system, being a scheme for the gradual abolition of pauperism, and immediate employment and provisioning of the people. 40p. *8°. Bath, London, &c.,* 1817. *Published in two parts, headed 'Poor Laws. (No. 2.)' and 'Poor Laws. (No. 3.)' respectively. Reissued by the author with other pamphlets in a volume entitled:* Early publications, *in 1831 (q.v.* GENERAL).

21901 [**HAYTER,** Sir W. G. ?] Proposals for the redemption of the poor's rates by means of emigration. 27p. *8°.* 1817. *Attributed to Hayter by John Weyland, in his copy of the pamphlet.*

21902 HENDERSON, Robert, *attorney.* An inquiry into the nature and object of the several laws for restraining and regulating the retail sale of ale, beer, wines and spirits...and an appendix of cases...of individual calamity suffered under the existing mode of granting and withholding licenses...without the power of appeal. In a letter to the Hon. Henry Grey Bennett... 144p. *8°.* 1817. *The Sheffield copy.*

21903 HIBERNIAN SOCIETY, *London.* The eleventh annual report of the Hibernian Society, for establishing schools, and circulating the Holy Scriptures in Ireland: with interesting extracts of correspondence. 69p. *8°. London & Edinburgh,* 1817. *See also* 1818.

21904 HILL, S. A plan for reducing the poor's rate, by giving permanent employment to the labouring classes: with some observations on the cultivation of flax and hemp; and an account of a new process for dressing and preparing flax and hemp... 27p. *8°.* 1817.

21905 —— With the report of a Committee of the House of Commons on the merits of the invention. Second edition. 34p. *8°.* 1817.

21906 An **INQUIRY** into the causes of the increased amount of the poor's rates, with suggestions for reducing the expenditure and equalizing the assessments. By a gentleman of Norfolk. 33p. *8°. Norwich & London,* 1817. *Wanting the title-page.*

21907 JEE, T. Practical observations on the management of the poor, and the laws relating to them... ⟨Original.⟩ [From *The Pamphleteer,* vol. IX, no. 18.] p. 564–81. *8°.* 1817.

21908 LANGLEY, E. A statement of the proceedings of the Dorking Provident Institution...Illustrating and practically proving, the facility of engaging the poor in measures conducive to their own support: in a letter to William Joseph Denison, Esq. 43p. *8°. Dorking & London,* 1817.

21909 A **LETTER** addressed to the Right Honourable N. Vansittart, Chancellor of the Exchequer, &c. &c. on the revenue and public morals, as connected with restoring the wine, beer, and spirit trade to its proper channels. With remarks upon the gin-shop petition presented to Parliament; a defence of the licensing magistrates; hints for preventing frauds on the revenue, &c. &c. By a friend to justice. 43[44]p. *8°.* 1817.

21910 —— Second edition, with additions and improvements. 44p. *8°.* 1817.

21911 A **LETTER** to Lord Viscount Sidmouth... proposing an improvement in the mode of licensing and regulating public-houses, with some observations on a letter to His Lordship from J. T. Barber Beaumont, Esq. By a magistrate. 17p. *8°.* 1817.

21912 A **LETTER** to the Right Honorable Viscount Sidmouth, Secretary of State for the Home Department, on the subject of the present defective system of licensing public-houses and liquor-shops...and an appeal in behalf of the body of licensed victuallers...for the protection of trial by jury. By a licensed victualler. 74p. *8°.* 1817.

21913 M'LAREN, Alexander. The trial of Alexander M'Laren, and Thomas Baird, before the High Court of Justiciary, at Edinburgh, on the 5th and 7th March 1817, for sedition... 153p. *8°. Edinburgh, Glasgow, &c.,* 1817.

21914 NEW TOWN DISPENSARY, *Edinburgh.* Observations by the managers of the New Town Dispensary, on the report to the quarterly meeting of managers of the Purlic [*sic*] Dispensary, 7th August, 1817. 24p. *8°. Edinburgh,* 1817.

21915 PARKER, T. N. Objections to the proposed eleemosynary grant of exchequer bills; and another plan submitted for alleviating the present distress. 8p. *8°. Oswestry, Shrewsbury, &c.,* [1817]

21916 The **POOR LAWS** England's ruin. By a country overseer. 16p. *8°.* 1817.

21917 —— Second edition. 16p. *8°*. 1817.

21918 **RAYNES**, F. An appeal to the public: containing an account of services rendered during the disturbances in the north of England in...1812 [the Luddite riots]...Together with a correspondence with Government, and others, on the subject of a remuneration for these services. 184p. *8°*. *London & Gainsburgh*, 1817.

For the **REFORMISTS' REGISTER AND WEEKLY COMMENTARY**, by William Hone, *see* vol. III, *Periodicals list.*

21919 **REMARKS** on an article in the Edinburgh Review on the causes and cure of pauperism. 16p. *8°*. *Glasgow, Edinburgh, &c.*, 1817. *For* Additional remarks on an article..., *see* 1818.

21920 **ROSE**, W. A letter to the Right Honourable the Earl of Radnor, Recorder of Salisbury, on the state of the poor. 12p. *12°*. *Salisbury*, [1817?]

21921 [**SLANEY**, R. A.] Some facts, shewing the vast burthen of the poor's rate in a particular district; and a view of the very unequal mode in which different kinds of property contribute to the support of paupers; with a few observations on Mr. Clarkson's late pamphlet. By a member of the Shropshire county committee, for the employment of the poor destitute of work. 44p. *8°*. 1817.

21922 [**SMITH**, THOMAS, *accountant, of London*?] An address to the Guardian Society. [Contrasting its plan and its mode of action. Signed: S.T.] 56p. *8°*. 1817. *Originally bound in a volume of tracts, most of which were undoubtedly written by Smith.*

21923 **SOCIETY FOR BETTERING THE CONDITION OF THE POOR**, *Oswestry*. The family receipt book, or, the cottager's cook, doctor, and friend. 21p. *8°*. *Oswestry*, 1817.

21924 —— Reports of the Society for Bettering the Condition of the Poor, in the Hundred of Oswestry, and the parishes of Chirk, Llansilin, and Llanarmon. From the year 1812, to the year 1817, inclusive... 101p. *8°*. *Oswestry*, [1817] *See also* 1818, 1819.

21925 *****SOCIETY FOR SUPERSEDING THE NECESSITY OF CLIMBING BOYS**, *Southampton*. [*Begin.*] The friends of the proposed society are assured...[An appeal for funds for the purchase of Smart's machine for sweeping chimneys.] *s.sh.fol. n.p.* [1817?]

21926 **TOWLE**, J. Second edition. Reports of the trial of James Towle, at Leicester, August 10, 1816, for shooting at John Asher; of Daniel Diggle...at Nottingham, March 18th, 1817, for shooting at George Kerry; also of John Clarke, James Watson, Thomas Savidge, Wm. Withers, Joshua Mitchell, Wm. Towle, John Crowder & John Amos...at Leicester, March 31st, and April 1st, 1817, for firing at John Asher, in the attack on Messrs. Heathcoat and Boden's factory, at Loughbro'; including a variety of interesting particulars relative to Samuel Caldwell...and...the whole of the men concerned in that memorable outrage. Copied, with considerable additions, from the Nottingham Review of the 4th of April, 1817. 58p. *12°*. *Nottingham*, [1817]

21927 **TOWNSEND**, J. A dissertation on the poor laws... 108p. *8°*. 1817. *For another edition, see* 1786.

21928 **VIVIAN**, RICHARD. Thoughts on the causes and cure of excessive poor rates; and on the injustice of rating the funds in aid of the land. 32p. *8°*. 1817.

21929 **VOGHT**, C. VON, *Freiherr*. Account of the management of the poor in Hamburgh, between the years 1788 and 1794. In a letter to some friends of the poor in Great Britain...Published in 1796. Now re-published by permission of the author, and dedicated to the Rt. Hon. George Rose, M.P. [The dedication signed by R. Wigram and others.] 42p. *8°*. 1817. *The copy which belonged to Sir Robert Wigram, Bart., one of the committee responsible for reprinting the work, with his book-plate. For other editions, see* 1795.

21930 **WATERLOO** subscription. General account of the Waterloo Subscription to the 31st May, 1817. [Signed: John Wray, chairman, and dated, 18th June 1817.] *s.sh.fol. n.p.* [1817] [*Br.* 487]

21931 **WATSON**, JAMES (1766?–1838). The trial of James Watson for high treason, at the Bar of the Court of King's Bench, on...the 9th...10th...11th...12th... 13th...14th and...16th of June, 1817, with the antecedent proceedings... 2 vols. *8°*. 1817.

21932 **WILKINS**, W., *and others*. An appeal to the public, by the master chimney-sweepers residing in the city of Bristol, against the erroneous application to their practice and character, of..."Facts relative to the state of children employed as climbing-boys, &c." Published to recommend the exclusive use of machines. With a plate, descriptive of the various constructions of chimneys in which no machine can operate. 23p. *12°*. *Bristol*, 1817.

21933 **WISSETT**, R. A letter to the Right Honourable Visct. Sidmouth, Secretary of State for the Home Department, on the subject of licensing public houses and liquor shops. 57p. *8°*. *Westminster*, 1817.

21934 **WORCESTER INSTITUTION FOR THE RELIEF OF THE POOR**. An account of the Worcester Institution for the Relief of the Poor, in the year 1817, containing its rules and regulations, with a description of the steam apparatus used in making the soup...By a member of the Committee (G. Pumphrey). 33p. *8°*. *Worcester*, [1817]

SLAVERY

21935 **CECIL**, R. Memoirs of the Rev. John Newton ...with general remarks on his life, connections, and character...A new edition. 204p. *8°*. 1817.

21936 **HENRY**, JABEZ. Points in manumission, and cases of contested freedom. 164p. *8°*. 1817. *Presentation copy, with inscription, from the author to Stephen Lushington.*

21937 **MARRYAT**, J. An examination of the report of the Berbice Commissioners, and an answer to the letters of James Stephen, Esq. respecting the crown estates in the West Indies, published in the Courier, under the signature of "Truth." 122p. *8°*. 1817.

21938 **STEPHEN**, J. The speech of James Stephen, Esq. at the annual meeting of the African Institution... on the 26th March, 1817... 56p. *8°*. 1817.

21939 **VAUX**, R. Memoirs of the life of Anthony Benezet. 136p. *12°*. *Philadelphia*, 1817. *See also* 1824.

POLITICS

21940 An **ADDRESS** to the men of Hampshire, intended as a postscript to Cobbett's Weekly Political Register, of the 15th of March. [An anti-Cobbett tract.] 16p. *8°. Winchester & London,* [1817]

21941 An **ADDRESS** to the Right Honourable John Somers, Lord Somers, on the subject of his late pamphlet, entitled A defence of the constitution of Great Britain, and Ireland...With some remarks upon the suspension of the Habeas Corpus Act...By one of the multitude. 40p. *8°. Brecon, London, &c.,* 1817.

For **ANTI-COBBETT**, or, the weekly patriotic register, *see* vol. III, *Periodicals list.*

21942 [**ATKINSON**, WILLIAM (1758–1846).] A letter to the reforming gentlemen. By the Old Inquirer. 27p. *8°. Bradford & London,* 1817.

For the **BLACK DWARF**, 1817–21, *see* vol. III, *Periodicals list.*

21943 **CARTWRIGHT**, J. No. I. [–No. IV.] Letters to the Lord Mayor, with an appendix containing an analysis and new classification of the state of the representation, and the House of Commons. 102p. *8°.* [1817] *Published in parts.*

21944 **COCHRANE**, THOMAS, *10th Earl of Dundonald.* The answer of Lord Cochrane to the address of the electors of Westminster...at a general meeting on the 17th of December 1816...To which are prefixed the resolutions and address. 24p. *8°.* 1817.

21945 *****COMTE**, F. C. L. Du nouveau projet de loi sur la presse. 79p. *8°. Paris,* 1817. *The copy that belonged to George Grote, with a manuscript note, 'from the author' on the flyleaf of the volume.*

21946 **ENGLAND**. *Parliament.* The Bill of the late Duke of Richmond, for universal suffrage, and annual Parliaments, presented by him [3rd June, 1780] to the House of Lords; with his declaration of those rights of the commonalty of Great Britain without which they cannot be free. 16p. *8°.* 1817.

21947 [**ERSKINE**, T., *Baron Erskine.*] Armata: a fragment. 209p. *8°.* 1817.

21948 [——] Second edition. 210p. *8°.* 1817.

21949 [——] The second part of Armata. 209p. *8°.* 1817.

21950 [——] Second edition. 209p. *8°.* 1817.

21951 **EVANS**, ROBERT H. A letter on the expediency of a reform in Parliament, addressed to the Right Hon. Lord Erskine. 198p. *8°.* 1817.

21952 **FAWKES**, W. The Englishman's manual; or, a dialogue between a Tory and a reformer...Third edition. 86p. *8°. London, York, &c.,* 1817.

21953 [**FERRAND**, A. F. C., *Comte.*] Théorie des révolutions, rapprochée des principaux événemens qui en ont été l'origine, le développement ou la suite; avec une table générale et analytique; par l'auteur de l'esprit de l'histoire. 4 vols. *8°. Paris,* 1817.

21954 [**HONE**, W.] The bullet Te Deum; with the canticle of the stone. [Parodies.] 8p. *8°.* 1817.

21955 [——] A new form of prayer; or, the political Litany, diligently revised; to be said or sung, until the appointed change come, throughout the Dominion of England and Wales and the town of Berwick upon Tweed. By special command. [A parody.] 8p. *8°. London & Portsea,* 1817.

21956 [——] The sinecurist's creed, or belief; as the same can or may be sung or said throughout the Kingdom. By authority. From Hone's Weekly Commentary. No. 2. [A parody on the Athanasian Creed.] 7p. *8°. Wm. Hone,* 1817.

21957 [——] [Another edition.] 8p. *8°. R. Carlile,* [1817]

21958 [——] [Another edition.] 7p. *8°. Portsea,* [1817]

21959 **HORNE**, M. A word for my country; or, an address to the parishioners of Crosstone, and all whom it may concern. 16p. *8°.* 1817. *The copy that belonged to M. T. Sadler.*

21960 **LENNOX**, C., *3rd Duke of Richmond.* The right of the people to universal suffrage and annual Parliaments, clearly demonstrated [in a letter to Lieut. Col. Sharman dated 15 Aug., 1783.] 8p. *8°.* 1817.

21961 **PAINE**, T. A letter to the English people, on the invasion of England. [Dated: America, May, 1804.] 11p. *8°.* 1817.

21962 **PEACOCK**, D. M. Remarks on the essentials of a free government, and on the genuine constitution of the British House of Commons, in answer to the theories of modern reformers. 55p. *8°. Cambridge, London, &c.,* 1817. *The copy that belonged to M. T. Sadler.*

21963 Price two-pence. Full **REPORT** of the third Spa-Fields meeting, with the previous arrests. [14]p. *8°.* [1817]

21964 **SADLER**, M. T. A first letter to a reformer, in reply to a pamphlet lately published by Walter Fawkes, Esquire...entitled The Englishman's manual. 108p. *8°. London & Leeds,* 1817.

21965 —— Second edition. 108p. *8°. London & Leeds,* 1817. *Sadler's own copy.*

21966 **SAXO**, *pseud.* A hasty sketch of the origin, nature, and progress, of the British Constitution... 31p. *8°. York,* 1817. *The copy that belonged to M. T. Sadler.*

21967 **SOCIETY OF THE FRIENDS OF THE PEOPLE**. Plan of a reform in the election of the House of Commons, adopted by the Society of the Friends of the People in 1795: with a new introduction, and other documents. Republished by Sir Philip Francis. 30p. *8°.* 1817. *For another edition, see* 1795.

21968 **SOUTHEY**, R. A letter to William Smith, Esq. M.P....Second edition. [Answering an attack made upon him by Smith in the House of Commons, on the occasion of the unauthorized reprinting of Southey's *Wat Tyler.*] 45p. *8°.* 1817.

21969 [——] Parliamentary reform. [First published in the Quarterly Review, No. XXXI, here reprinted as a separate pamphlet by a society of gentlemen in Manchester.] 42p. *8°. Manchester,* [1817]

21970 —— Sherwin's edition.—Price three pence. Wat Tyler, a dramatic poem. [From no. 5 of *The Republican.*] 15p. *8°.* [1817]

21971 TRIUMPHS of justice over unjust judges. Exhibiting I. The names and crimes of four and forty judges, hanged in one year, in England...for their corrupt judgments. II. The case of Lord Chief Justice Tresilian...To which is added...VII. The case of William Penn, for a riot in Fenchurch Street. 36p. *8°*. [1817]

21972 WALLACE, *pseud.* A letter on burgh reform. 12p. *12°*. *Edinburgh & Musselburgh,* [1817]

21973 WOOLER, T. J. An appeal to the citizens of London against the alledged lawful mode of packing special juries. 32p. *8°*. 1817.

21974 —— A correct report of the trials of Thomas Jonathan Wooler, for two libels contained in the third and tenth numbers of the Black Dwarf...on...June 5th, 1817. 46p. *8°*. 1817.

21975 —— A verbatim report of the two trials of Mr. T. J. Wooler, editor of the Black Dwarf, for alledged libels...Revised by T. J. Wooler. 151[143]p. *8°*. 1817.

21976 —— [Another issue.] 143p. *8°*. 1817.

SOCIALISM

21977 BROWN, JOHN, *minister of the Associate Congregation, Biggar.* Remarks on the plans and publications of Robert Owen, Esq., of New Lanark. 60p. *8°*. *Edinburgh, Glasgow, &c.,* 1817.

21978 EVANS, T. The petition of Thomas Evans, Librarian to the Spencean Philanthropist Society...to the Honourable the House of Commons. [Against his imprisonment without trial on suspicion of treasonable activities.] February 28, 1817. 8p. *8°*. 1817.

For the **MIRROR OF TRUTH** [edited by R. Owen], *see* vol. III, *Periodicals list.*

21979 OWEN, ROBERT. An address delivered to the inhabitants of New Lanark...Third edition. 48p. *8°*. *London, Edinburgh, &c.,* 1817. **Another, the FWA copy, that belonged to William Pare, is bound with* A new view of society, *4th edition, 1818, with which it was probably issued, and this copy of which was presented by Robert Owen to Emma Smith. For other editions, see* 1816.

For —— [Letter on his plan for employment of the poor, extracted from *The Times* of Thursday, May 29, 1817] *see* vol. III, *Periodicals list,* Evening Mail.

21980 —— A new view of society...Third edition. 184p. *8°*. *London, Edinburgh, &c.,* 1817. *For other editions, see* 1813.

21981 —— [*Endorsed:*] No. 1. New view of society. Extracted from the London daily newspapers of the 30th of July and the 9th and 11th of August 1817. With reference to a public meeting held...on Thursday August 14, 1817. For the consideration of a plan...to reduce the poor's rate, and to gradually abolish pauperism... [4]p. *fol.* [1817]

21982 —— [*Endorsed:*] No. II. Mr. Owen's report to the committee of the Association for the Relief of the Manufacturing and Labouring Poor...Accompanied by his address...at a public meeting expressly convened to consider a plan to relieve the country, from its present distress...which was adjourned to...August 21, 1817... [4]p. *fol.* [1817]

21983 —— [*Endorsed:*] No. III. New state of society. Mr. Owen's second address, delivered at the City of London Tavern, on...August 21, 1817, at the adjourned public meeting, to consider a plan to relieve the country from its present distress...To which is added, a farther developement of the plan, as published in the London daily newspapers of Sept. 10, 1817; together with an address to the public... [4]p. *fol.* [1817] **Another, the FWA copy, belonged to William Pare. In both copies blank paper has been pasted over the text of the 'Address to the public'.*

21984 —— Peace on earth—good will towards men! Development of the plan for the relief of the poor, and the emancipation of mankind. 15p. *8°*. [1817]

21985 *—— Relief of the poor. (From the Courier of April 9) [The substance of Robert Owen's memorial to the Committee of the House of Commons, on the poor laws.] *s.sh.fol.* [*London,* 1817] *FWA copy that belonged to William Pare, with a manuscript note, 'The Scheme herein was adopted in 1822 by the B & For: Philanthropic Society'.*

For the **PEOPLE,** *see* vol. III, *Periodicals list.*

21986 SAINT-SIMON, C. H. DE, *Comte.* L'industrie, ou, discussions politiques, morales et philosophiques, dans l'intérêt de tous les hommes livrés à des travaux utiles et indépendans. Vols. 1–2, Vol. 4, cahier 1. *8°*. *Paris,* 1817–18. *Wanting Vol. 3 and p. 1–4 of cahier 2 of Vol. 4; no more was published. Vol. 4, cahier 1 is a presentation copy, with inscription from the author, and has a manuscript note in his hand, concerning the printing, at the end of the list of contents.*

21987 SOCIETY OF SPENCEAN PHILANTHROPISTS. Address of the Society of Spencean Philanthropists to all mankind, on the means of promoting liberty and happiness. 24p. *12°*. [1817 ?]

MISCELLANEOUS

21988 BENTHAM, J. "Swear not at all:" containing an exposure of the needlessness and mischievousness, as well as antichristianity of the ceremony of an oath...predetached from An introduction to the rationale of evidence. 97p. *8°*. 1817.

21989 BERNET, J., *Cardinal.* Panégyrique de Jeanne d'Arc, prononcé le 8 mai 1817, dans l'Église cathédrale d'Orléans. 52p. *8°*. *Orléans,* 1817.

21990 CLARKSON, T. Tract (No. 3.) of "The Society for the promotion of permanent and universal peace." An essay on the doctrines and practice of the early Christians, as they relate to war. Addressed to those who profess to have a regard for the Christian Name. 22p. *8°*. *Ipswich & London,* [1817]

21991 CLERKE, G., *and others.* (Copy.) To the Master, Wardens, and Court of Assistants, of the Worshipful Company of Clock-Makers, London. [A complaint by a group of freemen on the deficiencies in the method of governing the Company. Signed: George Clerke, Wm. Harris, James Rawlins, P. T. Lemaitre, E. Griffiths, Tho. Humphries, and dated, April 7, 1817.] [2]p. *s.sh.fol. Hoxton*, [1817] *See note to no.* 13563.

21992 —— [Another edition.] [2]p. *s.sh.fol.* [1817] *See note to no.* 13563.

21993 MASSACHUSETTS PEACE SOCIETY. Correspondence of the Massachusetts Peace Society, with the Emperor of Russia, and Prince Alexander Gallitzin. 4p. *8°. [London*, 1817]

21994 PHELAN, W. The Bible, not the Bible Society: being an attempt to point out that mode of disseminating the Scriptures, which would most effectually conduce to the security of the Established Church and the peace of the United Kingdom...Second edition. 183p. *8°. Dublin*, 1817. *The Agar Ellis copy.*

21995 PHILELEUTHERUS, *pseud.* An appeal to equity, showing the unreasonableness and injustice of obliging Dissenters to contribute towards the support of the Church of England: with some remarks on tythes. 56p. *8°. London & Exeter*, 1817.

21996 RICHARDSON, JOHN (*fl.* 1817). Octary arithmetic; or, the art of doubling and halving by the cypher: containing a perfect system of measure and weight, with speciments [*sic*] of the new logarithms. 13p. *8°.* 1817.

21997 RUSSIA. *Alexander I., Emperor.* Alexander of Russia. Ukase addressed to the Legislative Synod at Moscow...Oct. 27, 1817. [Forbidding the clergy to use 'unbecoming expressions of praise' when addressing him.] [4]p. *8°. Liverpool*, [1817 ?]

21998 SCOTT, JOHN (*d.* 1832). Tract No. 1. of the Society for the Promotion of Permanent and Universal Peace. War inconsistent with the doctrine and example of Jesus Christ. In a letter to a friend... 20p. *8°.* 1817.

21999 SILLIMAN, BENJAMIN (1779–1864). A sketch of the life and character of President Dwight, delivered as an eulogium...February 12th, 1817, before the academic body of Yale College... 47p. *8°. New-Haven*, 1817.

22000 SOCIETY FOR THE PROMOTION OF PERMANENT AND UNIVERSAL PEACE. Address of the Society...[Signed: Robert Marsden, chairman of the committee, and dated, January 9, 1817. With lists of the committee and of the Society's publications.] 2p. *8°.* [1817]

1818

GENERAL

22001 An **ADDRESS** to the electors of the United Kingdom, containing an inquiry into the real causes of the present distress; with observations on the corn laws, the income tax, the poor laws, a general inclosure bill and a reform in Parliament. By a Glocestershire freeholder. 58p. *8°. Stroud, Cheltenham, &c.*, 1818.

22002 ADOLPHUS, J. The political state of the British Empire; containing a general view of the domestic and foreign possessions of the Crown; the laws, commerce, revenues, offices, and other establishments, civil and military. 4 vols. *8°.* 1818.

22003 ATTWOOD, T. Observations on currency, population and pauperism, in two letters to Arthur Young, Esq. 254p. *8°. Birmingham & London*, 1818. *Two presentation copies, one from the author to the Duke of Sussex, with his book-plate, the other from the author to Viscount Lowther (see also note to no.* 21472).

22004 BIRKBECK, M. Letters from Illinois... 154p. *12°. Philadelphia*, 1818. *Inscribed in manuscript: 'George Morison to his Friend William Dillwyn Esqr. Walthamstow'.*

22005 *—— Third edition. 114p. *8°.* 1818. *The copy that belonged to George Grote.*

22006 —— Notes on a journey in America, from the coast of Virginia to the territory of Illinois. 144p. *8°.* 1818.

22007 [**BOSSE,** R. H. B.] Essai sur l'histoire de l'économie politique des peuples modernes, jusqu'au commencement de l'année 1817... 2 vols. *8°. Paris & Londres*, 1818.

22008 BRISTED, J. America and her resources; or, a view of the agricultural, commercial, manufacturing, financial, political, literary, moral and religious capacity and character of the American people. 504p. *8°.* 1818.

22009 COBBETT, W. A year's residence, in the United States of America. Treating of the face of the country...the mode of cultivating the land...the expenses of house-keeping...the manners and customs of the people; and of the institutions of the country...In three parts...617p. *8°.* 1818–19. *See also* 1822, 1828.

22010 COSTAZ, C. A. Essai sur l'administration de l'agriculture, du commerce, des manufactures et des subsistances. Suivi de l'historique des moyens qui ont amené le grand essor pris par les arts depuis 1793 jusqu'en 1815. 419p. *8°. Paris*, 1818.

22011 CURWEN, J. C. Observations on the state of Ireland, principally directed to its agriculture and rural population; in a series of letters, written on a tour through that country. 2 vols. *8°.* 1818.

22012 The commercial **DIRECTORY,** for 1818–19–20, containing the names, trades, and situations of the merchants, manufacturers, tradesmen, &c. in Ashton, Barnsley, Beverley...York. Together with a list of the London, country, & Irish bankers, tables of the current coins of twenty-eight countries... 510p. *8°. Manchester: J. Pigot*, 1818.

22013 *The **EAST-INDIA** register and directory, for 1818; corrected to the 2d December 1817; containing ...lists of the Company's servants...Together with lists of...mariners, &c. not in the service of the...Company; and merchant vessels employed in the country trade. Compiled...by A. W. Mason, J. S. Kingston, & Geo. Owen... 509p. *12°. London, Dublin, &c.*, [1818]

22014 *—— Corrected to the 15th September 1818...
Compiled...by A. W. Mason & Geo. Owen...[Second
edition.] 498p. *12°. London, Dublin, &c.,* [1818] *For other
editions, see* 1804.

22015 The **EDINBURGH REVIEW,** for the year
1755. The second edition, with a preface and explanatory
notes. 135p. *8°.* 1818. [*Higgs* 1105] *For the periodical,
originally published in 1755–6, see* vol. III, *Periodicals list.*

22016 FEARON, H. B. Sketches of America. A
narrative of a journey...through the eastern and western
states of America; contained in eight reports addressed to
the...English families by whom the author was deputed
in June 1817, to ascertain...what part of the United
States would be suitable for their residence. With remarks
on Mr. Birkbeck's "Notes" and "Letters."...Second
edition. 454p. *8°.* 1818.

22017 GALIANI, F. Correspondence inédite de
l'Abbé Ferdinand Galiani, Conseiller du Roi, pendant les
années 1765 à 1783...précédée d'une notice historique
sur l'Abbé Galiani, par B. Mercier de Saint-Léger...à
laquelle il a été ajouté diverses particularités inédites
concernant...l'auteur. Par M. C*** de St-M*****
[A. Sérieys]... 2 vols. *8°. Paris,* 1818.

22018 [**GELONE,** F. D.] Manuel-guide des voyageurs
aux États-Unis de l'Amérique du Nord...Adressé particulièrement aux commerçans, aux agriculteurs...Par M.
F.D.G***. 196p. *12°. Paris,* 1818.

22019 GORE, J. Gore's directory, of Liverpool and its
environs; containing an alphabetical list of the merchants,
traders, and principal inhabitants: also, lists of the mayor
and council...post office and pilots' rates and regulations,
bankers, trading vessels...coaches, carriers...[With an
appendix.] 316, 163p. *12°. Liverpool,* [1818] *See also* 1823,
1829, *and for a reprint of the edition of 1766,* 1840.

22020 HOLDITCH, R. The emigrant's guide to the
United States of America; containing the best advice and
directions... 123p. *8°.* 1818.

22021 HULL, H. Familiar conversations on the real
causes of England's distresses; showing the pernicious
tendency of overgrown wealth; the evils that result from
the monopolizing spirit of the age; as exemplified in the
destruction of small farms, and ruin of the inferior classes
of tradesmen...[Dialogues between Henry Hull and
John.] 100p. *8°.* 1818.

22022 KNIGHT, JOHN, *ed.* Important extracts from
original and recent letters, written by Englishmen, in the
United States of America, to their friends in England,
containing unquestionable information respecting...that
country, together with the price of land, labour and
provisions...Second series. 48p. *8°. Manchester, Leeds,
&c.,* 1818.

22023 LONDON. Livery Companies. *Drapers.* Two
reports of a deputation who in pursuance of the resolutions
of the Court of Assistants...of the 23rd January 1817,
and 3rd August 1818, visited the estates of the Company
in the county of Londonderry in Ireland, in those years;
and which were ordered by the Court to be printed...
90p. *8°.* 1818. *With the book-plate of Henry Petty-Fitz-
maurice, 3rd Marquis of Lansdowne. See also* 1829, 1833.

22024 MELISH, J. Travels through the United States
of America, in the years 1806 & 1807, and 1809, 1810, &
1811; including an account of passages betwixt America &
Britain, Ireland, and Canada. With corrections and
improvements till 1815...With an appendix, containing

a letter from Clements Burleigh, Esq. to Irish emigrants
removing to America, and hints by the Shamroc Society,
New York, to emigrants from Europe [and 'Of the cause
of yellow-fever...By Thomas Paine']. 648p. *8°. Belfast,*
1818.

22025 MILLAR, JAMES (*fl.* 1818–1824). Funding
system. Computed with a view to benefit the rising generation...With a mode of safety in cautionary engagements,
remedying the calamitous effects...resulting from the
present plan...Also a plan for forming reading societies.
[Second edition.] 64p. *8°. Stirling,* 1818. *See also* 1824.

22026 ORTLOFF, J. A. Das Recht der Handwerker
nach den allgemeinen in den deutschen Staaten geltenden
Gesetzen und Zunft- und Innungsverordnungen. Ein
nützliches Handbuch für den Rechtsbefliessenen wie für
jeden Handwerker...Zweite Ausgabe. 350p. *8°. Erlangen,*
1818.

22027 PALMER, JOHN (*fl.* 1818). Journal of travels
in the United States of North America, and in Lower
Canada, performed in...1817; containing particulars
relating to the prices of land and provisions, remarks on
the country and people...and an account of the commerce, trade... 456p. *8°.* 1818.

22028 PARSON, W. and **BRADSHAW,** T. Staffordshire general & commercial directory, for 1818, Part
first, containing the borough of Newcastle-under-Line,
the Potteries, and the town of Leek, &c. Presenting an
alphabetical list of the merchants, manufacturers, and
inhabitants in general. To which is prefixed a...history of
the county... c, 129p. *12°. Manchester, Liverpool, &c.,*
[1818]

22029 REYNIER, J. L. A. De l'économie publique et
rurale des Celtes, des Germains et des autres peuples du
nord et du centre de l'Europe. 551p. *8°. Genève & Paris,*
1818.

22030 SAY, L. Principales causes de la richesse ou de
la misère des peuples et des particuliers. 156p. *8°. Paris,*
1818.

22031 SEYBERT, A. Statistical annals: embracing
views of the population, commerce, navigation...
revenues...public debt and sinking fund, of the United
States of America: founded on official documents: commencing on the fourth of March seventeen hundred and
eighty-nine and ending on the twentieth of April eighteen
hundred and eighteen. 803p. *4°. Philadelphia,* 1818.

22032 SMITH, ADAM. An inquiry into the nature and
causes of the wealth of nations...From the eleventh
London edition: with notes and supplementary chapters,
by William Playfair. And an account of Dr. Smith's life,
by Dugald Stewart... 2 vols. *8°. Hartford,* 1818. *For
other editions, see* 1776.

22033 SMITHERS, H. Observations made during a
tour in 1816 and 1817, through that part of the Netherlands, which comprises Ostend, Bruges, Ghent, Brussels,
Malines & Antwerp; with remarks on...art...and enquiries into the present state of agriculture, political
oeconomy... 269p. *8°. Brussels,* [1818 ?]

22034 VERRI, P., *Conte.* Opere filosofiche e d'economia politica...Prima edizione compiuta. 4 vols. *16°. Milano,*
1818. *For another edition, see* 1784.

22035 WARBURTON, J. History of the city of
Dublin, from the earliest accounts to the present time;
containing its annals, antiquities...its present extent...

institutions, &c. To which are added, biographical notices of eminent men, and copious appendices of its population, revenue, commerce and literature. By...J. Warburton... J. Whitelaw...and...Robert Walsh... 2 vols. *4°*. 1818.

22036 [**YEATS**, G. D.] A biographical sketch of the life and writings of Patrick Colquhoun...By Ἰατρος. 64p. *8°*. 1818. *Two copies, one which belonged to P. Colquhoun the younger, the other the copy presented by James Colquhoun to Lord Sheffield.*

AGRICULTURE

22037 [**AGNEW**, J. V.] Some important questions in Scots entail law briefly considered. 36p. *8°*. *Edinburgh*, 1818.

22038 **BLAIKIE**, F. On the husbanding of farm-yard manure, and on other rural subjects...Second edition. 27p. *8°*. 1818. *See also* 1820.

22039 **BOARD OF AGRICULTURE.** Premiums offered by the Board...for 1818–1819. 9p. *8°*. [1818] *Addressed in manuscript to the Earl of Morton. See also* 1804, 1808, 1809, 1810, 1812, 1816.

22040 **DRURY**, C. Important hints and discoveries in agriculture; or, a new system of farming in general; whereby such essential advantage is gained over the general system in practice, as is judged nearly to equal the rent...The fourth edition...enlarged and improved. [With a supplement.] 304, [4]p. *8°*. 1818.

22041 **ÉTABLISSEMENT** du cens géneral. 15p. *4°*. *Rome*, 1818. *A description of the system of land tenure initiated in Poland by Prince Stanislas Poniatowski.*

22042 **FRANCIS**, WILLIAM (*fl.* 1806–1818). The gentleman's, farmer's, and husbandman's most useful assistant, in measuring, and expeditiously computing the amount of any quantity of land, at various given prices per acre...Second edition...To which is now added, a comprehensive treatise on timber and wood measuring. 118p. *8°*. 1818.

22043 **FRANÇOIS DE NEUFCHÂTEAU**, N. L., *Comte.* Rapport fait à la Société royale et centrale d'Agriculture...sur l'agriculture et la civilisation du Ban de la Roche; suivi de pièces justificatives. Séance publique du 29 mars 1818. [On the work of J. F. Oberlin.] 46p. *8°*. *Paris*, 1818.

22044 **FRASER**, R. A review of the domestic fisheries of Great Britain and Ireland. [With an appendix.] 161, 126p. *4°*. *Edinburgh, London, &c.*, 1818.

22045 **MARSHALL**, W. The review and abstract of the county reports to the Board of Agriculture; from the several agricultural departments of England... 5 vols. *8°*. *York, London, &c.*, 1818.

22046 **PHELPS**, S. A treatise on the importance of extending the British fisheries; containing a description of the Iceland fisheries, and of the Newfoundland fishery and colony; together with remarks and propositions for the better supply of the Metropolis and the interior, with cured and fresh fish... 232p. *8°*. 1818.

22047 **PICKERING**, T. Address to the Essex Agricultural Society. May 5, 1818. 27p. *8°*. *Salem*, 1818.

22048 **RICHARDSON**, WILLIAM (1740–1820). An essay on agriculture; containing an introduction, in which the science of agriculture is pointed out...also, the means of rendering barren soils...productive...and of beneficially employing the industrious and un-occupied poor. To which is added, a memoir...on the nature and nutritive qualities of fiorin grass... 173p. *8°*. 1818.

22049 **RIGBY**, E. Holkham, its agriculture, &c.... The third edition, considerably enlarged. 140p. *8°*. *Norwich & London*, 1818. *The copy that belonged to Thomas Graham, Baron Lynedoch. For other editions, see* 1817.

22050 **TAYLOR**, JOHN (1753–1824). Arator, being a series of agricultural essays, practical and political: in sixty-four numbers...Fifth edition, revised and enlarged. 239p. *12°*. *Petersburg* [*Va.*], 1818.

22051 **WORTHINGTON**, R. An invitation to the inhabitants of England, to the manufacture of wines, from the fruits of their own country; on a plan not hitherto practised...with remarks on the character and price of foreign wines, and suggestions for the establishment of vineyards...Third edition. 44p. *8°*. *Worcester & London*, 1818.

CORN LAWS

22052 **COLEBROOKE**, H. T. On import of colonial corn. 233p. *8°*. 1818.

POPULATION

22053 **BURROWS**, G. M. Strictures on the uses and defects of parish registers, and bills of mortality...to the probabilities of the expectancy of life; and to the ascertaining of the progress of populations: with suggestions for improving and extending the system of parochial registry. 72p. *8°*. 1818.

22054 **ENSOR**, G. An inquiry concerning the population of nations: containing a refutation of Mr. Malthus's Essay on population. 502p. *8°*. 1818.

22055 [**GRAY**, S.] Gray versus Malthus. The principles of population and production investigated: and the questions, does population regulate subsistence, or subsistence population...and should government encourage or check early marriage; discussed: by George Purves. 496p. *8°*. *London & Edinburgh*, 1818. *See also* 1840.

22056 SUMNER, J. B., *Archbishop of Canterbury.* A treatise on the records of the Creation...with particular reference to the Jewish history and to the consistency of the principle of population with the wisdom and goodness of the Deity...Second edition, corrected. 2 vols. *8°. 1818. See also 1825, 1850.*

TRADES & MANUFACTURES

22057 ACCUM, F. C. A. A practical treatise on gaslight: exhibiting a summary description of the apparatus and machinery best calculated for illuminating streets, houses, and manufactories, with carburetted hydrogen, or coal-gas...Fourth edition. 194p. *8°. 1818. For another edition, see 1815.*

22058 [HAMILTON, ROBERT, *of Edinburgh.*] A scale of prices for binding books. Edinburgh, 1818... 12p. *8°. Edinburgh, 1818. With a manuscript note on the title-page: Arranged for private Gent[n]. by Robert Hamilton.*

22059 KENNEDY, JOHN (1769–1855). Observations on the rise and progress of the cotton trade in Great Britain, particularly in Lancashire and the adjoining counties...From the Manchester Memoirs, Vol. III, second series. 25p. *8°. Manchester, 1818.*

22060 McWILLIAM, R. An essay on the origin and operation of dry rot, with a view to it's prevention or cure. To which are annexed, suggestions on the cultivation of forest trees, and an abstract of the several forest laws... 420p. *4°. 1818.*

22061 OBSERVATIONS, &c. [*Begin.*] A candid review of the history of the poor...[A description of the advantages of the decorticator, a new machine to extract fibre from flax.] 5p. *fol. n.p.* [1818?] *The Sheffield copy.*

22062 1818. Eighth edition. **SKYRING'S** correct list of builders' prices; calculated to do justice to the employer, master builder and their workmen. [With 'Abstract of the Building Act, 14th George III. c.78, and 'Alphabetical list of surveyors'.] 115p. *8°.* [1818] *Compiled by Z. Skyring, who signed and numbered each copy in manuscript. With the contemporary owner's name, 'Wm. Lee' stamped in gilt on the upper cover. See also 1812, 1819, 1827, 1831, 1838, 1845, 1846.*

COMMERCE

22063 BEAUMONT, JOHN T. B. Substance of a speech on the best means of counteracting the existing monopoly in the supplying of beer; exemplifying the evil, and tracing its source to the...arbitrary licensing of victualling houses: delivered at a public meeting...on January the 26th 1818...With the resolutions entered into at the meeting. 32p. *8°. 1818. Presentation copy from the author to the Earl of Lauderdale.*

22064 BREWERS' monopoly!!! Being an enquiry into the causes of the late advance on porter; with hints for reducing its price, remarks on the proceedings of the Anti-monopoly Committee, and the police report, relative to brewers' leases...Addressed to the Hon. H. G. Bennet. By an impartial observer. 35p. *8°. 1818.*

22065 [DICKINSON, W.] Universal commerce; or, the commerce of all the mercantile cities and towns of the world: containing...their weights, measures, monies; course and operation of exchange; imports and exports, &c....By the editor of Mortimer's commercial dictionary. 318p. *8°. 1818.*

22066 DUBOST, C. The elements of commerce; or, a treatise on different calculations, operations of exchange ...description and tables of monies, weights, and measures...Second edition, greatly improved, and corrected to the present time, by the editor of "Mortimer's commercial dictionary" [William Dickinson]. 544p. *8°. 1818. For another edition, see 1805.*

22067 ENGLAND. *Laws, etc.* An alphabetical abridgment of the laws for the prevention of smuggling, from 12 Car. II. to 58 Geo. III. inclusive. 196p. *8°. 1818.*

22068 FRANCE. *Chambre des Députés.* Chambre des Députés. Opinion de M. le Mis. de Villefranche, Député de l'Yonne, prononcée dans la séance du 16 février, pour le développement de sa proposition tendante à supplier Sa Majesté de faire présenter une loi qui puisse dégager le commerce des grains et farines des abus et des dangers qui l'accompagnent dans l'état actuel de la législation... [With 'Projet de loi'.] 27p. *8°.* [*Paris,*] 1818.

22069 GLASGOW, LEITH AND HAMBURGH SHIPPING COMPANY. Contract of copartnery of the Glasgow, Leith and Hamburgh Shipping Company. April, 1818. 38p. *8°. Edinburgh, 1818.*

22070 A LETTER on the true principles of advantageous exportation. In refutation of certain popular notions on that subject. [From *The Pamphleteer,* vol. XII, no. 23.] 11p. *8°. 1818.*

22071 MACONOCHIE, ALEXANDER. A summary view of the statistics and existing commerce of the principal shores of the Pacific Ocean. With a sketch of the advantages...which would result from the establishment of a central free port within its limits, and also of one in the southern Atlantic... 365p. *8°. London & Edinburgh, 1818.*

22072 MAITLAND, JOHN (1754?–1831). Observations on the impolicy of permitting the exportation of British wool, and of preventing the free importation of foreign wool. 60p. *8°. 1818.*

22073 —— [Another edition.] 60p. *8°. 1818. See also 1820.*

22074 MARTIR COLL Y ALSINA, P. Tratado elemental teorico y practico de comercio en que se presentan varias formulas de contratas de fletamentos, conocimientos...letras de cambio...contratas de compañia, cartas, &c. Que para gobierno de un hijo suyo joven comerciante compuso, y ha corregido y aumentado en esta edicion, D. Pedro Martir Coll, y Alsina. 254p. *4°. Barcelona, 1818.*

22075 PEREZ Y COMOTO, F. Representacion que a favor del libre comercio dirigieron al exelentisimo señor Don Juan Ruiz de Apodaca Virrey, Gobernador...de Nueva-España, doscientos veinte y nueve vecinos de la ciudad de Veracruz... 82p. *4°. Habana, 1818.*

22076 PRINCE'S LONDON PRICE CURRENT...No. 2178. Friday the 2nd Jan. [–No. 2229. Friday, the 25th Dec.] 1818. 52 nos. *fol.* [1818] *See also* 1812, 1813, 1814, 1815, 1817, 1820.

22077 REAL SOCIEDAD ECONOMICA DE LA HABANA. Suplemento à las Memorias de la real Sociedad...del mes de marzo de 1818. Estado demostrativo del comercio de importacion y exportacion que se ha hecho por el puerto de la Habana en...1816, con distincion de buques nacionales y extrangeros, efectos introducidos y extrahidos, sus valores por aforos y derechos reales y municipales que han adeudado. 22p. *fol. Habana*, [1818]

22078 RÖRDANSZ, C. W. European commerce; or, complete mercantile guide to the continent of Europe; comprising an account of the trade of all the principal cities of the continent...the local regulations of each place, their tariffs of duties, methods of buying and selling, tares, and other allowances...[Edited by H. E. Lloyd.] 691p. *8°.* 1818.

22079 ZUAZNAVAR Y FRANCIA, J. M. DE. Discurso sobre el comercio exterior de granos, del Reyno de Navarra. 121p. *4°. Pamplona*, 1818.

COLONIES

22080 [COLQUHOUN, P.] Considerations on the means of affording profitable employment to the redundant population of Great Britain and Ireland, through the medium of an improved and correct system of colonization in the British territories in Southern Africa. 40p. *8°.* 1818. *The copy that belonged to James Colquhoun.*

22081 EARNSHAW, W. A digest of the laws (from 12 Charles II. to 58 George III. inclusive) relating to shipping, navigation, commerce and revenue, in the British Colonies in America and the West Indies, including the laws abolishing the slave trade... 424p. *8°.* 1818.

22082 JAMAICA. *Assembly.* A Report of a Committee of the Honourable House of Assembly of Jamaica, presented...December 10, 1817, relative to the present state of the Island, with respect to its population, agriculture, and commerce... 55p. *8°.* 1818.

22083 LOVELL, L. A letter to a friend, relative to the present state of the Island of Dominica. 39p. *8°. Winchester*, 1818.

FINANCE

22084 ANDREWES, G. P., *ed.* Considerations of a national plan for relieving the landed interest, and ameliorating the condition of the labouring poor. Collected (by authority) from the manuscripts of a professional man of experience, now abroad. 57p. *8°.* 1818.

22085 ANTICIPATION the second; or, a statement of the finances of Great Britain for 1818. 22p. *8°.* [1818]

22086 ATTEMPT of the Duke of Marlborough to prove his father incompetent to the transacting of any business [in order to avoid payment of debt on a mortgage executed by his father]. 3p. *4°. n.p.* [1818]

22087 B., A. The Government and the Bank: being a statement of transactions subsisting betwixt the public and the Bank of England; contained in six letters which have appeared in the British Press & Globe newspapers. 36p. *8°.* [*London*,] 1818. *The copy that belonged to David Ricardo.*

22088 B***, M. J. B., *Mr.* Observations contre le système d'emprunter pour l'état, en vendant des rentes; et projet d'emprunt, en remplacement du crédit de seize millions demandé par le Budget de 1818. Par Mr. M.J.B. B*****. 56p. *8°. Paris*, 1818.

22089 BANK FOR SAVINGS, *Bloomsbury.* First annual report of the Bank for Savings, Southampton Row, Bloomsbury. Printed by order of the general meeting, 7th February, 1818. 4p. *8°.* [*London*, 1818]

22090 BANK OF ENGLAND. A copy of the charter of the Bank of England: and also the by-laws for the good government of the said Corporation. 27, 11p. *fol.* 1818.

22091 BARNES, R. Observations on a Bill, introduced into Parliament in the session of 1817, for the amendment of the law in respect of modus for tithes. 63p. *8°. Cambridge*, 1818.

22092 BEARBLOCK, J. A treatise upon tithes: containing an estimate of every titheable article in common cultivation; with the various modes of compounding for the same. Fifth edition, much enlarged, with an index... 229p. *8°. London, Cambridge, &c.*, 1818.

22093 BENTHAM, J. Defence of usury; shewing the impolicy of the present legal restraints on the terms of pecuniary bargains...To which is added, a letter to Adam Smith, Esq, LL.D. on the discouragements opposed by the above restraints to the progress of inventive industry. The fourth edition. And to which is also added, third edition, A protest against law-taxes. 206, 70p. *12°.* 1818. *For other editions of* Defence of usury *see* 1787; A protest against law taxes *was first published alone in 1793 (q.v.), with* Supply without burthen *in 1795 (q.v.) and with the third edition of the present work in 1816 (q.v.).*

22094 BIGNON, L. P. É., *Baron.* Discours sur la loi générale des finances, pour 1818, considérée dans son rapport avec la situation politique et la situation administrative de la France. Prononcé par M. Bignon, Député du Département de l'Eure. Séance du 4 avril. 65p. *8°. Paris*, 1818.

22095 BINGHAM, RICHARD. Facts and observations on tithes, tithe owners, tithe renters, and tithe payers, in a letter addressed to agriculturists and the members of agricultural societies. 23p. *8°. Leeds, London, &c.*, 1818.

22096 BROOKES, J. Forged bank notes. A full... report of the trial, Brookes against Warwick, inspector of the Bank of England, for false imprisonment...22nd of

June, 1818, wherein a verdict was given for the plaintiff... 34p. *8°*. 1818.

22097 [BURDETT, Sir F., *Bart.*] Annals of banks for savings. Containing an account of their rise and progress, reports and essays on their national importance, their constitution... 192p. *8°*. *London & Edinburgh, &c.*, 1818. *The copy that belonged to David Ricardo.*

22098 C., B. H. A letter to Jeremiah Barman, Esq. on the circulating medium of the Kingdom, and the means of diminishing the practice of forgery. 40p. *8°*. 1818.

22099 CARDONNEL, P. S. F. de. Chambre des Députés. Opinion de M. de Cardonnel, Député du Tarn, sur la proposition de M. Laisné de Villévêque, Député du Loiret, tendante à restituer aux émigrés leurs rentes sur l'état. Prononcée dans la séance du 25 février 1818. 16p. *8°*. [*Paris,*] 1818.

22100 CAREY, G. G. A complete system of theoretical and mercantile arithmetic. Comprehending a full view of the various rules necessary in calculation. With practical illustrations... Particularly, interest, stocks, annuities, marine insurance, exchange, &c.... Compiled for the use of the students at the Commercial Institution, Woodford. 574p. *8°*. 1818.

22101 CHATEAUDOUBLE, P. de. Opinion de M. Paul-Chateaudouble, Député du Var, sur la loi des finances de 1818. 16p. *8°*. [*Paris,*] 1818.

22102 CHAUVELIN, F. B. de, *Marquis.* Opinion de M. Chauvelin, Député de la Côte d'Or, sur la loi de finances de 1818. 57p. *8°*. [*Paris,* 1818]

22103 CHICHESTER, E. Oppression & cruelties of Irish Revenue officers [in putting down the practice of illicit distilling]. Being the substance of a letter to a British Member of Parliament. 128p. *8°*. 1818.

22104 *CLARK, J. Observations on the nature of annuities, life insurances, endowments for children, and investment of money for accumulation; with a general outline of the plan, laws, and regulations of the European Life Insurance and Annuity Company... 66p. *8°*. 1818. *The copy that belonged to Augustus De Morgan.*

22105 [COCKBURN,   .] Commercial œconomy: or, the evils of a metallic currency. By an old country gentleman. 28p. *8°*. 1818.

22106 COOKE, Edward (1792?–1862). Thoughts on the expediency of repealing the usury laws. 58p. *8°*. 1818.

22107 —— [Another edition.] [From *The Pamphleteer*, vol. XIII, no. 25.] 26p. *8°*. 1818.

22108 CORNET-DINCOURT, C. N. Chambre des Députés. Opinion de M. Cornet-Dincourt, Député de la Somme, sur la proposition tendant à restituer aux émigrés leurs rentes sur l'état. Prononcé en comité secret le 24 février 1818. 8p. *8°*. [*Paris,*] 1818.

22109 —— Opinion de M. Cornet-Dincourt, Député de la Somme, sur le projet de loi de finances de 1818... 22p. *8°*. [*Paris,* 1818]

22110 CRAVEN, A. A plan, calculated to reduce the expenditure of the nation, and to enable officers of all ranks, on half-pay... to realise the greatest part of the purchase-money of their commissions. 31p. *8°*. 1818.

22111 CRIGNON D'AUZOUER, A. Chambre des Députés. Opinion de M. Grignon-Auzouer [*sic*], Député du Loiret, sur les impositions indirectes, formant le développement de l'amendement qu'il a proposé à la séance du 17 avril, 1818. 16p. *8°*. [*Paris,* 1818]

22112 CRUTTWELL, R. English finance, with reference to the resumption of cash-payments at the Bank... [With 'Additional remarks, corroborative of the justice of the author's principles'.] 152p. *8°*. 1818.

22113 DENMARK. *Frederick VI, King.* Bekanntmachung der Octroy der Nationalbank in Kopenhagen, für die Herzogthümer Schleswig und Holstein. Bekjendtgjørelse af Octroyen for Nationalbanken i Kjøbenhavn, for Hertugdommene Slesvig og Holsten. Kopenhagen, den 21sten Julii 1818. 51p. *4°*. *Kopenhagen,* [1818] *The German and Danish texts are printed on opposite pages.*

22114 DEW, D. A digest of the duties of customs and excise, payable upon all foreign articles imported into and exported from Great Britain: duties outwards, and countervailing duties between Great Britain and Ireland. Customs and excise bounties... duties coastwise; quarantine laws; tonnage duties... regulations of the Commercial, East India, London, and West India Docks... together with a copious appendix. Brought up to 1st Dec. 1818... 526p. *8°*. 1818.

22115 [DICKINSON, W.] The American negociator; consisting of tables of exchange of the United States, calculated from one cent up to one thousand dollars... To which is annexed, the new tariff of duties... By the editor of Mortimer's Commercial dictionary... 88p. *12°*. 1818.

22116 DOR DE LASTOURS, M. J., *Marquis de Lastours.* Opinion de M. de Lastours, Député du Tarn, sur le projet de loi de finances de 1818... 51p. *8°*. [*Paris,* 1818]

22117 The ENGLISH SYSTEM of finance; or, the operation of the Sinking Fund, as it affects the value of funded property by the reduction of interest; also the total change of our financial system, by the innovations made on the stability of the Public Funds; shewing that the National Debt, from its own magnitude, will ultimately undermine & reduce itself, and that with the free will and consent of the holders of funded property. By the author of the Art of stock jobbing. 32p. *8°*. [1818?]

22118 FRAITER, R. A short system of practical arithmetic, chiefly designed for the use of schools... Second edition, corrected, improved, and greatly enlarged. [Including brokerage, insurance, and foreign exchange.] 209p. *12°*. 1818.

22119 FRANCE. *Chambre des Députés.* No. 72. Opinion de M. le Comte de la Bourdonnaye, Député de Maine-et-Loire, sur le projet de loi de finances de 1818... Imprimé par ordre de la Chambre. 32p. *8°*. [*Paris,* 1818]

22120 —— —— No. 79. Opinion de M. Piet, Député du Département de la Sarthe... sur le Budget. Imprimée par ordre de la Chambre. 51p. *8°*. [*Paris,* 1818]

22121 —— —— No. 89. Opinion de M. de Villèle, Député de la Haute-Garonne, sur le projet de loi de finances de 1818. Imprimée par ordre de la Chambre. 74p. *8°*. [*Paris,* 1818]

22122 —— —— No. 90. Opinion de M. de Bonald, Député de l'Aveyron, sur le projet de loi de finances de 1818. Imprimée par ordre de la Chambre. 30p. *8°*. [*Paris,* 1818]

22123 —— —— No. 96. Opinion de M. Cornet-Dincourt, Député de la Somme, sur l'article 4 du titre VI de la loi de finances. Imprimée par ordre de la Chambre. 13p. *8°*. [*Paris,* 1818]

22124 —— *Louis XVIII, King.* ⟨B.211. No. 4101.⟩ Loi sur les finances. A Paris, le 15 mai, 1818. 35p. *8°.* *Paris,* [1818]

22125 GARNIER, G., *Marquis.* Observations en réponse aux Considérations générales sur l'évaluation des monnaies grecques et romaines... 78p. *4°. Paris,* 1818.

22126 [GRAY, CHARLES, *of Carse.*] Extract from the second edition of Letters on Scotch entails, and English poor-rates, by a country gentleman. 3p. *8°. n.p.* [1818] *The Sheffield copy.*

22127 GURNEY, H. Substance of the speech of Hudson Gurney, Esq. in the House of Commons...the 18th of May, 1818, on the farther consideration of the report of the Bank Restriction Continuance Bill. 16p. *8°.* 1818.

22128 HAMILTON, ROBERT (1743–1829). An inquiry concerning the rise and progress, the redemption and present state, and the management, of the National Debt...The third edition, enlarged. 340p. *8°. Edinburgh, Glasgow, &c.,* 1818. *The copy that belonged to Sir Robert Peel. For other editions, see 1813.*

22129 [HARBORD, E., *Baron Suffield*?] A word to the wise, among the labouring classes, resident at Blandford and its vicinity. [With 'Rules, orders and regulations, for the management of a bank for savings established at Blandford Forum, January the 31st, 1818'.] 28p. *8°. Blandford,* 1818. *Attributed to 'Harbord' in a manuscript note on the title-page. The Hon. Edward Harbord is listed in the text as one of the trustees of the Blandford Savings Bank.*

22130 HOLDSWORTH, A. H. A letter to a friend in Devonshire, on the importance of country bankers. 19p. *8°.* 1818.

22131 HORNE, afterwards **HORNE TOOKE,** J. The causes and effects of the National Debt and paper money on real and natural property in the present state of civil society...To which is added, an appendix, containing a just and impartial review of the funds of England...By the late Dr. Price. 50p. *8°.* 1818.

22132 An INQUIRY into the state of the currency of the country, its defects and remedy. 56p. *8°.* 1818.

22133 JAMES, HENRY, *of Birmingham.* Considerations on the policy or impolicy of the further continuance of the Bank Restriction Act. 68p. *8°.* 1818.

22134 LABOURDONNAYE, F. R. DE, *Comte.* Chambre des Députés. Opinion de M. le Cte de la Bourdonnaye, Député de Maine et Loire, dans la discussion du Budget. Séance du 22 avril 1818. 8p. *8°.* [*Paris,* 1818]

22135 LAISNÉ DE VILLÉVÊQUE, G. J. Chambre des Députés. Discours de M. Laisné de Villévêque, Député du Département du Loiret, sur le projet de loi relatif au Budget, prononcé dans la séance du 31 mars 1818. (Extrait du Moniteur du 2 avril, 1818.) 8p. *8°.* [*Paris,* 1818]

22136 —— Chambre des Députés. Opinion de M. Laisné de Villévêque, Député du Loiret, sur les impôts perçus sur les boissons. Séance du mardi 31 mars 1818. 24p. *8°.* [*Paris,* 1818]

22137 —— Chambre des Députés. Opinion de M. Laisné de Villévêque, Député du Loiret, sur le Budget de la Marine. Prononcée dans la séance du 24 avril 1818. 11p. *8°.* [*Paris,* 1818]

22138 LANJUINAIS, J. D., *Comte.* Des dépenses et des recettes de l'état pour l'an 1818, et du crédit public. 48p. *8°. Paris,* 1818.

22139 —— An enquiry into the state of the French finances, and that of public credit; with observations on the budget of 1818...Translated from the French by George Hurdis. 27p. *8°.* [1818]

22140 LEEDS GROCERS' SOCIETY. Articles of agreement of the Leeds Grocers' Society for the insurance of goods, one with the other, by the respective owners thereof. 21p. *8°. Leeds,* 1818.

22141 LEREBOURS, P. R. De la répartition de l'impôt foncier et du cadastre. 110p. *8°. Paris,* 1818.

22142 A LETTER on the price of the Funds, as connected with the Bank Restriction Act. Addressed to ——, Esq. [Signed: ***, and dated, Oct. 24, 1818.] 23p. *8°.* 1818.

22143 MACDONALD, W. P. The moneiad: or, the power of money. [A poem in three cantos.] 180p. *12°. London, Edinburgh, &c.,* 1818.

22144 MIREHOUSE, J. A practical treatise on the law of tithes. 260p. *8°. London & Dublin,* 1818.

22145 MORRISON, JAMES (*fl.* 1812–1825). The elements of book keeping, by single & double entry. Comprising several sets of books. Arranged according to present practice...To which is annexed an introduction on merchant's accounts... 3d. edition. 232p. *8°.* 1818.

22146 OBSERVATIONS. Of the influence of savings banks on the habits and morals of society. March 31, 1818. [Signed: A friend to honest industry.] 3p. *fol.* [1818]

22147 OBSERVATIONS on Cobbett's tremendous and alarming scheme for the annihilation of the Bank of England paper system, by means of forged bank notes; with reflections on its fatal tendency. 8p. *8°.* [1818]

22148 OBSERVATIONS upon the Report from the Select Committee of the House of Commons, on the poor laws; with a demonstration of the injustice of the present laws of taxation, and the remedy suggested. 40p. *8°. Birmingham & London,* 1818. *The Sheffield copy.*

22149 PHILODICAEUS, *pseud.* A letter to the Rt. Hon. W. W. Pole, respecting the disappearance of the gold coin, and the resumption of cash payments. Original. [From *The Pamphleteer,* vol. XII, no. 23.] 30p. *8°.* 1818.

22150 POPE, C. A practical abridgment of the laws of customs and excise, relative to the import, export, and coasting trade...To which are now added the Russia & Levant dues; duties of scavage...Together with the American navigation laws and tariff. The Statutes...to September 1, 1818. Fourth edition. 18, [1170]p. *8°. London, Edinburgh, &c.,* 1818. *For another edition, see 1813.*

22151 PRINSEP, C. R. An essay on money. 154p. *8°.* 1818.

22152 PROPOSALS for the grant of ten annuities, of £.600 each, upon lives, between five, and twenty-one, years of age... 2p. *fol.* 1818. [*Br.* 488] [*Endorsed:*] *Proposals for raising £150,000 by grant of annuities, to increase by survivorship.*

22153 READ, S. The problem solved: in the explication of a plan, of a safe, steady and secure government paper currency, and legal tender. 16p. *8°. Edinburgh &*

London, 1818. Presentation copy, with inscription, from the author to 'Wm. Kerr Esqr.'

22154 REMARKS on the projected abolition of the usury laws, and the probable effects of the measure upon the commerce and general prosperity of the nation. 52p. *8°. Edinburgh, Glasgow, &c., 1818.*

22155 RUSSIA. *Imperial Bank of Commerce.* Regulations of the Imperial Bank of Commerce. Approved by His Majesty the Emperor, May 7th, 1817. [44]p. *8°. 1818. The French and English texts are printed on opposite pages. The copy that belonged to James Colquhoun.*

22156 The SAVINGS' BANK: a dialogue intended to illustrate the nature and advantages of these institutions. By a member of the provisional committee for the establishment of a Savings' Bank at Buckingham. 12p. *12°. 1818.*

22157 SCHMIDT-PHISELDEK, C. F. VON. Ueber den Begriff vom Gelde, und den Geldverkehr im State. 167p. *8°. Kopenhagen, 1818.*

22158 SCHOOL STREET SAVINGS BANK, *Dublin.* Some account of the establishment of the Savings Bank, School-Street, Dublin, with the rules and regulation for its management. [With a list of officers.] 32p. *8°. Dublin, 1818.*

22159 SÉGUIN, A. Des finances de la France, à partir de 1818. 59p. *obl.4°. Paris, 1818. With an accompanying letter from the author to an unidentified recipient.*

22160 —— Observations sur un ouvrage de M. le Duc de Gaëte, ayant pour titre, Aperçu théorique sur les emprunts. 20p. *8°. Paris, 1818.*

22161 SINCLAIR, SIR JOHN, *Bart.* On the approaching crisis; or, on the impracticability and injustice of resuming cash payments at the Bank, in July 1818; and on the means of elevating the internal prosperity of the British Empire...by a judicious application of the profits derived from a farther suspension of payments in cash. 33p. *8°. London & Edinburgh, 1818.*

22162 SLOCOCK, S. A sermon preached in the parish church of Newbury...on...January 18. 1818, in

recommendation of the bank for savings established in that place... 23p. *8°. London & Newbury, 1818.*

22163 SOMERSET. *General Quarter Sessions.* Somerset. Report of a committee of justices relative to the annual expenditure of the County, from Easter 1759, to Easter, 1818; together with the table accompanying the same. Ordered to be printed, by the Court of General Quarter Session, held at the Castle of Taunton, October 19th, 1818. [Signed: John Acland, Richard Thos. Combe, Francis Drake.] 12p. *4°. Taunton, [1818]*

22164 WESTON, A. Two letters, describing a method of increasing the quantity of circulating money: upon a new and solid principle...Printed for private circulation in the year 1799, and now published from the author's corrected copy. With a short preface by the editor [James Weston]. 56p. *8°. 1818. For another edition, see 1799.*

22165 WILLIAMS, CHARLES W. Considerations on the alarming increase of forgery on the Bank of England, and the neglect of remedial measures; with an essay on the remedy for the detection of forgeries and an account of the measures adopted by the Bank of Ireland... 190p. *8°. London & Dublin, 1818.*

22166 WOODROW, J. Remarks on banks for savings and friendly societies; with an original plan combining the principles of both institutions: a friendly loan fund, and other important advantages. 42[44]p. *8°. 1818. Two copies, one of which belonged to David Ricardo, and one which was presented to Patrick Colquhoun, with an accompanying letter inviting him to attend a meeting on 30 May 1818 to inaugurate an establishment based on the author's plan. See also 1821.*

22167 WORKSOP SAVINGS BANK. Worksop Savings Bank, established on the 29th of December, 1817. [List of officers, rules and blank pages for the entry of deposits.] 8, [8]p. *8°. Worksop, [1818].*

22168 WRAY, J. Dangers of an entire repeal of the Bank Restriction Act: and a plan suggested for obviating them. 24p. *8°. London & Ramsgate, [1818]. With a leaf inserted containing manuscript comments on the pamphlet. There are other notes in the margins in the same hand, and a note about the author on the title-page.*

TRANSPORT

22169 CHAPMAN, WILLIAM (1749–1832). Mr. Chapman's report on the proposed canal navigation between Carlisle and Solway Firth. Second edition. 48p. *8°. Carlisle, 1818.*

22170 COTTON, J. Memoir on the origin and incorporation of the Trinity House of Deptford Strond. 247p. *8°. 1818.*

22171 ENGLAND. *Laws, etc.* Anno quinquagesimo octavo Georgii III. Regis. [Local & Personal.] Cap. xvi. An Act to enable the Grand Junction Canal Company to vary the line of part of their canal in the county of Hertford, and for altering and enlarging the powers of several Acts relating to the said canal. ⟨17th March 1818.⟩ p.321–334. *fol. 1818.*

22172 —— —— Anno quinquagesimo octavo Georgii III. Regis. [Local & Personal.] Cap. xvii. An Act to enable the Gloucester and Berkeley Canal Company to vary and alter the line of their canal; and for altering and enlarging the powers of several Acts passed for making and main-

taining the said canal. ⟨17th March 1818.⟩ p.334–350. *fol. 1818.*

22173 —— —— Anno quinquagesimo octavo Georgii III. Regis. [Local & Personal.] Cap. xix. An Act for altering, explaining, and amending the several Acts of Parliament passed, relating to the Birmingham Canal Navigations; and for improving the said Canal Navigations. ⟨17th March 1818.⟩ p.361–370. *fol. 1818.*

22174 —— —— Anno quinquagesimo octavo Georgii III. Regis. [Local & Personal.] Cap. lxxv. An Act to explain and amend an Act of the fifty-second year of His Present Majesty, intituled An Act for the improvement of the Harbour of Kidwelly, and for making and maintaining a navigable canal or tramroads in Kidwelly and Llanelly... in the county of Carmarthen; and to alter and enlarge the powers thereof. ⟨18th May 1818.⟩ p.1721–1732. *fol. 1818.*

22175 ÉTAT général des postes du royaume de France, suivi de la carte géométrique des routes desservies en poste, avec désignation des relais et des distances. 192p. *8°.*

Paris, 1818. *See also* 1814, 1819, 1823, 1835 (Livre de poste...), 1838.

22176 FRISI, P. A treatise on rivers and torrents; with the method of regulating their course and channels ...To which is added, an essay on navigable canals... Translated by Major-General John Garstin... 184p. *4°*. 1818.

22177 McADAM, JOHN L. Memorial on the subject of turnpike roads. 12p. *8°. n.p.* [1818 ?]

22178 OBSERVATIONS on the importance of improving the navigation of the river Schuylkill, for the purpose of connecting it with the Susquehanna, and through that river extending our communication to the Genesee Lakes and the Ohio. 21p. *8°. n.p.* [1818]

22179 SAY, J. B. Des canaux de navigation dans l'état actuel de la France. 35p. *8°. Paris*, 1818.

SOCIAL CONDITIONS

22180 [*Endorsed:*] An **ADDRESS** to the honorable the members of both Houses of Parliament of the United Kingdom of Great Britain and Ireland. [Signed: A silk weaver of London. Advocating the extension of the provisions of the Spitalfields Act to silk weavers working outside London and Dublin.] 3p. *fol. n.p.* [1818]

22181 BALLANCHE, P. S. Essai sur les institutions sociales dans leur rapport avec les idées nouvelles. 420p. *8°. Paris*, 1818.

22182 BOOTH, H. The question of the poor laws considered, and the causes and character of pauperism, in connection with the laws and principle of population, briefly explained and illustrated. 48p. *8°. Liverpool & London*, 1818.

22183 BROUGHAM, H. P., *Baron Brougham and Vaux*. A letter to Sir Samuel Romilly, M.P., from Henry Brougham, Esq., M.P., F.R.S., upon the abuse of charities. 67p. *8°*. 1818.

22184 —— Third edition. 67p. *8°. London & Edinburgh*, 1818.

22185 —— Appendix to Mr. Brougham's Letter: containing minutes of evidence taken before the Education Committee, 104p. *8°. London & Edinburgh*, 1818.

22186 —— Eighth edition. [With the appendix.] 67, 104p. *8°. London & Edinburgh*, 1818. *The Sheffield copy.*

22187 BUXTON, SIR THOMAS F., *Bart*. An inquiry, whether crime and misery are produced or prevented, by our present system of prison discipline. Illustrated by descriptions of the Borough Compter...The jail at Bristol...The Philadelphia Prison. The Penitentiary, Millbank...Third edition. 146p. *12°*. 1818.

22188 —— Sixth edition. 184p. *12°*. 1818.

22189 CHALMERS, T. The influence of Bible societies, on the temporal necessities of the poor...Fourth edition. 44p. *8°. Edinburgh, Glasgow, &c.*, 1818. *The copy that belonged to Patrick Chalmers. For another edition, see* 1817.

22190 CLARKE, L. A letter to H. Brougham, Esq., M.P., F.R.S. In reply to the strictures on Winchester College, contained in his Letter to Sir Samuel Romilly, M.P. 73p. *8°. Winchester, Oxford, &c.*, 1818.

22191 COURTENAY, T. P. A treatise upon the poor laws. 168p. *8°*. 1818.

22192 DAVISON, J. Considerations on the poor laws ...Second edition. 128p. *8°. Oxford & London*, 1818. *For another edition, see* 1817.

22193 ENGLAND. *Laws, etc*. Anno quinquagesimo Georgii III. Regis. [Local & Personal.] Cap. 163. An Act for granting certain powers and authorities to a company to be incorporated by chapter, to be called, The Gas Light and Coke Company... ⟨9th June 1810.⟩ p.3741–3755. *fol*. 1818.

22194 —— —— [*Endorsed:*] An Act for lighting with gas the town...of Sheffield, in the county of York. [Incorporating the Sheffield Gas Light Company.] ⟨Royal Assent, 23 May 1818.⟩ 58 Geo. III. 1818. 38p. *fol*. [*London*, 1818]

22195 —— *Parliament*. [*Endorsed:*] An Act [a Bill] for lighting with gas, the town...of Nottingham. 58 Geo. III. sess. 1818. 32p. *fol*. [*London*, 1818]

22196 —— —— [*Endorsed:*] A Bill for lighting with gas the town of Brighthelmston, in the county of Sussex. 58 Geo. III. sess. 1818. 34p. *fol*. [*London*, 1818]

22197 —— —— *House of Commons*. Rapports présentés en 1817 et 1818, à la Chambre des Communes d'Angleterre, par le Comité chargé de l'examen des lois relatives aux pauvres, traduits de l'anglais. 164p. *8°. Paris*, 1818. *Translated by E. Laffon de Ladébat. The copy that belonged to King Louis XVIII of France, with his arms on the spine, and the library stamp 'Bibliothèque du Roi, Neuilly' on the title-page. For other editions, see* 1817.

22198 EVANSON, W. A. Suppression of mendicity! A sermon preached in Bethesda Chapel on Sunday, 11th October, 1818, in aid of the funds of the Association for Suppressing Mendicity in Dublin. 32p. *8°. Dublin*, 1818.

22199 EWING, J. Report for the directors of the Town's Hospital of Glasgow on the management of the city poor, the suppression of mendicity, and the principles of the plan for the new Hospital. 220p. *8°. Glasgow*, 1818.

22200 GASCOIGNE, H. B. Pauperism; its evils and burden reduced by calling into action the labours of the poor, and by the useful direction of charity: containing the substance of an essay on the means of employing the labouring poor... 80p. *8°*. 1818.

22201 [**GOULD**, NATHANIEL, *of Manchester, and others*.] Information concerning the state of children employed in cotton factories, printed for the use of the members of both Houses of Parliament. [Signed in manuscript: Nath¹· Gould, T. O. Gill, Nath¹· Shelmerdine.] 28p. *8°. J. Gleave: Manchester*, 1818. *The Oastler copy.*

22202 —— [Another edition.] 28p. *8°. J. Aston: Manchester*, 1818. *The authors' signatures at the end are printed. The copy that belonged to Joseph Brotherton, with his signature on the title-page.*

22203 HANNING, W. A letter to the members of the Select Committees of the two Houses of Parliament appointed to examine and report on the poor laws. 46p. *8°. Taunton*, 1818.

22204 HIBERNIAN SOCIETY, *London*. The twelfth annual report of the Hibernian Society...for establishing schools and circulating the Holy Scriptures in Ireland: with interesting extracts of correspondence. 116p. *8°. London & Edinburgh*, 1818. *See also* 1817.

22205 HINDLEY, W. A report of the proceedings in the case of William Hindley, charged with felony, and with falsely preferring an accusation against Rd. Hill and Thos. Lear. Second edition. 53p. *8°. Manchester*, [1818]

22206 HOLROYD, J. B., *Earl of Sheffield*. Observations on the impolicy, abuses and false interpretation of the poor laws; and on the Reports of the two Houses of Parliament. 60p. *8°*. 1818. *Presentation copy from the author to Patrick Colquhoun.*

22207 —— Second edition, considerably enlarged and amended. 78p. *8°*. 1818. *Presentation copy from the author to Patrick Colquhoun, with a manuscript note inserted.*

22208 —— Postscript to the second edition of Observations on the impolicy and ruinous consequences of the poor laws, and on the Bill now before Parliament to amend the laws for the relief of the poor. 8p. *8°*. 1818.

22209 An **INQUIRY** into the principle and tendency of the Bill now pending in Parliament, for imposing certain restrictions on cotton factories. 56p. *8°*. 1818.

22210 INSTITUTION FOR THE EDUCATION OF DEAF AND DUMB CHILDREN, *Edinburgh*. Report of the Institution...established... 1810...with specimens of composition, &c. May 1818. 72p. *8°. Edinburgh*, 1818.

22211 JERRAM, C. Considerations on the impolicy and pernicious tendency of the poor laws; with remarks on the Report of the Select Committee of the House of Commons upon them; and suggestions for improving the condition of the poor. 157p. *8°. London, Chertsey, &c.*, 1818.

22212 KIRKCALDY. Abstract of the receipts and expenditure of the poor's funds of the parish of Kirkcaldy, for the last ten years. [Prepared and submitted by John Martin, minister of the parish.] 27p. *8°. Kirkcaldy*, 1818.

22213 A **LETTER** addressed to the Right Honourable Lord Viscount Castlereagh, on the subject of the proposed alterations in the poor laws...To which is annexed, a letter to the writer from a Scotch farmer, who has had experience of the management of the poor in England and Scotland. 43p. *8°*. 1818.

22214 A **LETTER** to Henry Brougham, Esq. M.P. from a Master of Arts of Queen's College, Oxford, upon the best method of restoring decayed grammar schools. Original. [From *The Pamphleteer*, vol. XIII, no. 25.] 25p. *8°*. 1818.

22215 A **LETTER** to the Right Hon. Sir Wm. Scott, &c.&c. M.P. for the University of Oxford, in answer to Mr. Brougham's Letter to Sir Samuel Romilly upon the abuse of charities...To which is added, an appendix: containing an abstract of the principal Acts of Parliament relating to charities... 76p. *8°*. 1818.

22216 Two **LETTERS** on the contested origin, nature, and effects, of the poor laws. By a student at law. 56p. *8°. Andover*, 1818.

22217 LONDON. *Parish of Saint Pancras.* St. Pancras, Middlesex. Report of the committee appointed by a public vestry, held on the 30th day of July, 1817, to investigate the affairs of the Directors of the Poor of the parish of St. Pancras, as delivered in vestry, March 2, 1818. 17p. *8°*. [1818]

22218 LUSHINGTON, STEPHEN. The reply of Dr. Lushington, in support of the Bill for the better regulation of chimney-sweepers and their apprentices... before the Committee of the House of Lords...the 20th April, 1818. 32p. *8°*. 1818.

22219 —— The speech of Dr. Lushington, in support of the Bill for the better regulation of chimney-sweepers and their apprentices, and for preventing the employment of boys in climbing chimneys, before the Committee in the House of Lords...the 13th March, 1818. 23p. *8°*. 1818.

22220 M'KINLEY, A. The trial of Andrew M'Kinley, before the High Court of Justiciary at Edinburgh, on the 26th July, 1817, for administering unlawful oaths: with the antecedent proceedings against William Edgar, John Keith, and Andrew M'Kinley... 65, 48, 37, 97, 118, 72, 87, 9p. *8°. Edinburgh & London*, 1818.

22221 Distressed **MINERS.** Report of the proceedings at a public meeting held at the London Tavern...on the 24th of February, 1818, to take into consideration the best means of alleviating the condition of the distressed miners in different parts of the kingdom...Also is added, the affidavit of Mr. T. Buxton as to cases of great distress in Swaledale in Yorkshire. 72p. *8°. London, York, &c.*, 1818.

22222 MOGGRIDGE, J. H. Remarks on the Report of the Select Committee of the House of Commons on the poor-laws; in which the proposed alteration of the laws of settlement; and pauperism, its causes, consequences, and remedies are distinctly considered. By a Monmouthshire magistrate. 59p. *8°. Bristol & London*, 1818.

22223 MONTAGU, B. Some enquiries into the effects of fermented liquors. By a water drinker. Second edition. 365p. *8°*. 1818.

22224 NICOLL, S. W. A summary view of the Report and evidence, relative to the poor laws, published by order of the House of Commons, with observations & suggestions. 111p. *8°. York, London, &c.*, 1818.

22225 OWEN, ROBERT. Observations on the effect of the manufacturing system: with hints for the improvement of those parts of it which are most injurious to health and morals...The third edition. To which are added two letters on the employment of children in manufactories, and a letter on the union of churches and schools. 44p. *8°. London, Edinburgh, &c.*, 1818. *★Another, the FWA copy, that belonged to William Pare, is bound with* A new view of society, *4th edition (no. 22273) which was presented by Robert Owen to Emma Smith, and with which it was probably issued. For other editions, see* 1815.

22226 PARRY, F. C. An account of the charitable donations to places within the county of Berks. 216p. *4°*. 1818.

22227 PARSONS, JOHN, *Bishop of Peterborough*. A sermon preached before the incorporated Society for the Propagation of the Gospel in Foreign Parts; at their anniversary meeting...February 20, 1818. [With 'An abstract of the charter, and...proceedings of the Society ...1817, to...1818'.] 99p. *8°*. 1818.

22228 PHILANTHROPICUS, *pseud*. A letter addressed to the Right Honourable Nicholas Vansittart, Chancellor of the Exchequer, &c.&c.&c. on the subject of parochial schools. 30p. *8°*. 1818.

22229 Ten **POUNDS** reward, for apprehending a sheep stealer. [A handbill, describing Arthur Hancock, the wanted man, and dated: January 13th, 1818.] *s.sh.4⁰. Wiveliscombe, [1818] With, on the verso, a manuscript list of constables in Devon, Dorset and Somerset to whom the handbill was circulated.*

22230 **PRESTON**, R. The poor-rates gradually reduced and pauperism converted into profitable industry ...Original. [From *The Pamphleteer*, vol. XI, no. 22.] 18p. *8⁰.* 1818.

22231 Additional **REMARKS** on an article in the Edinburgh Review on the causes and cure of pauperism. 16p. *8⁰. Glasgow & Edinburgh, 1818. For* Remarks on an article..., *see 1817.*

22232 **REMARKS** on two articles in the Edinburgh Review, on the causes and cure of pauperism. By the author of "Letters from Scotland." 35p. *8⁰. Manchester, 1818. Attributed to Archibald Prentice in a manuscript note on the title-page.*

22233 **RICHARDS**, G. The immoral effects of the poor laws considered, in a sermon preached at the parish church of Bampton, Oxfordshire...1818, at the annual meeting of the friendly societies of that place. 52p. *8⁰.* 1818.

22234 **SCHOOL FOR THE INDIGENT BLIND**, *Liverpool*. School for the Blind. [*Begin.*] The committee for the management of the school...beg leave respectfully to submit to the public an arrangement of considerable importance...the erection of a chapel... [4]p. *4⁰. Liverpool: Circus-street Free-school Press, [1818] Addressed in manuscript to 'Mr. John Lang, Drury Lane'.*

22235 **SCOTS HOSPITAL OF KING CHARLES II.** Kinloch bequest, in trust to the Scottish Hospital, for specific purposes. 10p. *8⁰.* [1818]

22236 A brief **SKETCH** of various attempts which have been made to diffuse a knowledge of the Holy Scriptures, through the medium of the Irish language. [With an appendix.] 143, 16p. *8⁰. Dublin, 1818.*

22237 **SKETCHES** of the Merino Factory, descriptive of its origin and progress, and of its system of discipline and moral government. [Being 'Sketch of the origin and progress of the Merino Factory...presented to the Dublin Society, 19th December 1816' by Thomas Nowlan, 'A sketch of the present state of Ireland' signed 'an English traveller' and 'Observations on the influence of epidemic fever, and of the Merino Factory, on the lower orders', signed 'K.W.'.] 53p. *8⁰. Dublin, 1818.*

22238 **SMITH**, GEORGE C. A report detailing the extreme miseries of the off-islands of Scilly...Second edition. 61p. *8⁰.* 1818.

22239 **SOCIETY FOR BETTERING THE CONDITION OF THE POOR**, *Oswestry*. The sixth report of the Society... p.103–126. *8⁰. Oswestry, 1818. Paginated in sequence with the collection of the first five reports, 1817 (q.v.). See also 1819.*

22240 **SOCIETY FOR SUPERSEDING THE NECESSITY OF CLIMBING BOYS**, *Leeds*. An address, from the Society at Leeds, for Superseding the Necessity of Climbing Boys, employed by chimney sweepers; instituted October the 27th, 1817. 16p. *8⁰. Leeds, 1818.*

22241 **SOCIETY FOR SUPERSEDING THE NECESSITY OF CLIMBING BOYS**, *London*. Address from the Committee...with the report of the Committee of the House of Lords on the Chimney Sweepers' Regulation Bill. Published in pursuance of a resolution...at a general meeting...May 1, 1818. [With a list of subscribers.] 32p. *8⁰.* 1818. *The copy that belonged to James Colquhoun.*

22242 **SOCIETY FOR THE IMPROVEMENT OF PRISON DISCIPLINE**, *London*. Report of the Committee of the Society for the Improvement of Prison Discipline, and for the Reformation of Juvenile Offenders. 32p. *8⁰.* 1818. *See also 1824, 1827, 1832.*

22243 **SOCIETY FOR THE RELIEF OF AGED OR INFIRM BAPTIST MINISTERS.** Proceedings of the annual meeting at Bristol, June 10, 1818. [With 'Abstract of the second annual report'.] [2]p. *s.sh.8⁰. Bath, [1818]*

22244 **STEVEN**, R. An inquiry into the abuses of the chartered schools in Ireland. With remarks upon the education of the lower classes in that country. Second edition. 206p. *8⁰.* 1818.

22245 **TEALE**, G. A refutation of "A report of the proceedings in the case of William Hindley, charged with felony, and with falsely preferring an accusation against Richard Hill & Thomas Lear." 41p. *8⁰. Manchester, 1818.*

22246 **THACKERAY**, E. General report of the charter schools of Ireland. Visited in the summer and autumn of the year 1817. Presented to the Incorporated Society [for Promoting English Protestant Schools in Ireland], in...February 1818. 68p. *8⁰. Dublin, 1818.*

22247 **THORP**, C. Economy, a duty of natural and revealed religion, with thoughts on friendly societies and savings' banks. A sermon preached at the anniversary meeting of the Gateshead Friendly Society, January 5, 1818...To which is added an appendix, containing regulations for friendly societies and savings' banks... 58p. *8⁰. Newcastle, London, &c., 1818.*

22248 **THOUGHTS** on the employment of the poor, in dressing flax, with Messrs. Hill & Bundy's patent machines, with notes and observations made during the process at Clay Farm, Old Windsor, December 1817 & January 1818...[With 'Sketch of a plan of an adult orphan asylum for the daughters of clergymen and naval and military officers'.] 43p. *8⁰.* 1818.

22249 **WAKE**, H. A brief statement of facts, submitted to the candid and unprejudiced. 100p. *8⁰. Andover, 1818. The copy that belonged to Patrick Colquhoun.*

22250 **WARDLAW**, R. An essay on benevolent associations for the relief of the poor: of which the substance was read to the Literary and Commercial Society of Glasgow, April 1817. 67p. *8⁰. Glasgow, Edinburgh, &c., 1818.*

22251 **WOODROW**, J. Remarks on banks for savings and friendly societies; with an original plan combining the principles of both institutions; a friendly loan fund, and other important advantages. 42[44]p. *8⁰.* 1818. *The copy that belonged to David Ricardo.*

22252 —— [Another issue, with a supplement, added in 1821.] 50[52]p. *8⁰.* 1818[–21]. *The copy that belonged to David Ricardo.*

22253 **YEATMAN**, J. C. Remarks on the medical care of parochial poor, with a few observations on the improvement of poor-houses, and on the necessity of establishing small infirmaries in populous towns. 34p. *8⁰.* 1818.

SLAVERY

22254 ADRESSE à leurs Majestés impériales et royales et à leur représentans au Congrès d'Aix-la-Chapelle. [Against the slave trade.] 24p. *8º. n.p.* [1818]

22255 AMERICAN CONVENTION FOR PROMOTING THE ABOLITION OF SLAVERY. Minutes of the proceedings of a special meeting of the fifteenth American Convention for Promoting the Abolition of Slavery...at Philadelphia...December, 1818 ...[With 'Address of the free people of colour in Philadelphia'.] 68, ivp. *8º. Philadelphia, 1818. The copy that belonged to Stephen Lushington.*

22256 CASE in Nevis, 1817. [On the maltreatment of slaves. With an appendix of documents.] 22, 39p. *8º. [London, 1818]*

22257 L'EUROPE chatiée, et l'Afrique vengée, ou raisons pour regarder les calamités du siècle comme des punitions infligées par la Providence pour la traite des nègres. 124p. *8º. Londres, 1818. The 'Avertissement' reads: 'Cet ouvrage est la traduction d'une série de lettres*

insérées dans un journal de Londres, intitulé le New-Times, et adressées aux Souverains alliés assemblés en congrès à Aix-la-Chapelle, en septembre et octobre 1818'.

22258 MARRYAT, J. More thoughts still on the state of the West India Colonies, and the proceedings of the African Institution: with observations on the speech of James Stephen, Esq. at the annual meeting of that Society, held on the 26th of March, 1817. 147p. *8º. 1818.*

22259 *Entry cancelled.*

22260 THORPE, R. A view of the present increase of the slave trade, the cause of that increase, and suggesting a mode for effecting its total annihilation; with observations on the African Institution and Edinburgh Review, and on the speeches of Messrs. Wilberforce and Brougham ...7th July, 1817; also, a plan submitted for civilizing Africa, and introducing free labourers into our colonies in the West Indies. 128p. *8º. 1818. The copy that belonged to Stephen Lushington.*

POLITICS

22261 BENTHAM, J. Plan of parliamentary reform, in the form of a catechism, with reasons for each article. With an introduction shewing the necessity of radical, and the inadequacy of moderate, reform. 156p. *8º. 1818.*

22262 COCHRANE, T., *10th Earl of Dundonald.* Lord Cochrane's farewell address to the electors of Westminster. Second edition. 8p. *8º. [1818]*

22263 *COMTE, F. C. L. Lettre à M. le Garde des Sceaux, Ministre de la Justice; par M. Comte. [Concerning an attempt on the part of the police to arrest him.] 68p. *8º. Paris, [1818] The copy that belonged to George Grote, with a manuscript note, 'from the author' on the flyleaf of the volume.*

22264 FERRIER, R. E. Some remarks on the present state of the country, and on the only means of salvation and future prosperity. 28p. *8º. 1818.*

22265 HONE, W. The three trials of William Hone, for publishing three parodies; viz., the late John Wilkes's catechism, the Political litany, and the Sinecurist's creed; on three ex-officio informations...December 18, 19, & 20, 1817... 48, 45, 44p. *8º. 1818. A reissue of separate editions of each trial, with a general title-page. The first trial is of the tenth, the third trial of the third edition.*

22266 —— [Another edition, with a prefatory address by William Hone, dated January 23, 1818.] 48, 45, 44p. *8º. 1818. The first trial is of the seventeenth edition, the second of the fifteenth and the third of the fourteenth edition.*

22267 LAWSON, M. The substance of a speech delivered at the Boroughbridge election, previous to the poll; on...June the 20th, 1818...Second edition. 36p. *8º. Cambridge, York, &c., 1818. The Agar Ellis copy.*

22268 A LETTER to the Right Honourable George Canning, M.P. [Signed: Your countryman. An attack on his political conduct.] 33p. *8º. 1818.*

For **SHADGETT'S WEEKLY REVIEW,** of Cobbett, Wooler, Sherwin, and other democratical & infidel writers...[edited by W. H. Shadgett], 1818–19, *see vol. III, Periodicals list.*

22269 TRIAL by jury and liberty of the press. The proceedings at the public meeting, December 29, 1817, at the City of London Tavern, for the purpose of enabling William Hone to surmount the difficulties in which he has been placed by being selected by the Ministers of the Crown as the object of their persecution...Fifth edition. 28p. *8º. 1818.*

22270 WESTMINSTER ELECTION. A correct report of the proceedings of the meeting held at the Crown and Anchor, Strand...June 1, 1818, by that part of the electors of Westminster, who advocate annual Parliaments, universal suffrage, and vote by ballot; to take into consideration...the best means to secure the election of Henry Hunt, Esq....With the...speech...of Mr. Gale Jones. 24p. *8º. [1818]*

SOCIALISM

22271 [**ALLEN,** WILLIAM (1770–1843).] Reply on behalf of the London proprietors to the address of the inhabitants of New Lanark. [With the address.] 12p. *8º. 1818.*

22272 Price four pence. **CHRISTIAN POLICY** in full practice among the people of Harmony, a town in... Pennsylvania...as described in Melish's Travels through the United States, and Birkbeck's Notes on a journey in

America. To which are subjoined, a concise view of the Spencean system of agrarian fellowship...By a Spencean philanthropist [i.e. T. Evans?]. 16p. 8°. 1818.

For the **GORGON**, *1818–19, see vol. III, Periodicals list.*

22273 OWEN, ROBERT. A new view of society... Fourth edition. 176p. 8°. *London, Edinburgh, &c.,* 1818. *★Another, the FWA copy, was presented by the author, with a manuscript inscription, to Emma Smith, and later belonged to William Pare. For other editions, see 1813.*

22274 —— New view of society. Tracts relative to this subject; viz. Proposals for raising a colledge of industry of all useful trades and husbandry. By John Bellers. (Reprinted from the original, published in...1696). Report to the Committee of the Association for the Relief of the Manufacturing and Labouring Poor. A brief sketch of the religious society of people called Shakers [communicated ...by W. S. Warder]. With an account of the public proceedings connected with the subject, which took place in London in July and August 1817. Published by Robert

Owen. 43, 24, 16, 83p. 8°. *London, Edinburgh, &c.,* 1818. *★Another, the FWA copy that belonged to William Pare, is bound with A new view of society, (no. 22273, above), which was presented by Robert Owen to Emma Smith, and with which it was probably issued.*

22275 —— Two memorials on behalf of the working classes; the first presented to the governments of Europe and America, the second to the Allied Powers assembled in congress at Aix-la-Chapelle. 27p. 8°. *London, Edinburgh, &c.,* 1818. *★Another, the FWA copy, that belonged to William Pare, is bound with A new view of society, (no. 22273, which was presented by Robert Owen to Emma Smith, and with which it was probably issued.*

22276 SAINT-SIMON, C. H. DE, *Comte.* Lettre de Henry Saint-Simon, à messieurs les publicistes... Opinion qui sera émise dans le troisième volume de L'industrie. [3]p. 4°. *[Paris,* 1818?] *Addressed in the author's own hand to 'Messieurs les redacteurs des annales au bureau du journal'. See note to no.* 19751.

MISCELLANEOUS

22277 BAILY, F. Memoir relative to the annular eclipse of the sun, which will happen on September 7, 1820. 32p. 8°. 1818. *The copy that belonged to David Ricardo.*

22278 BENTHAM, J. Church-of-Englandism and its catechism examined: preceded by strictures on the exclusionary system, as pursued in the National Society's schools... 248, 456p. 8°. 1818.

22279 BRITISH MUSEUM. A catalogue of manuscripts, formerly in the possession of Francis Hargrave... now deposited in the British Museum. [Edited by Sir H. Ellis.] 188p. 4°. 1818.

22280 BUNYAN, J. The pilgrim's progress...A new edition...With the life of the author. To which are added, explanatory and practical notes... 433p. 8°. *Newark, N.J.,* 1818.

22281 GOODWYN, H. The first centenary of a series of concise and useful tables of all the complete decimal quotients which can arise from dividing a unit...by all integers from 1 to 1024. To which is now added a tabular series of complete decimal quotients for all the proper vulgar fractions... 18, 30p. 4°. 1818. *The copy that belonged to Nicholas Vansittart, Baron Bexley. For another edition, see 1816.*

22282 HEYWOOD, S. A dissertation upon the distinctions in society, and ranks of the people, under the Anglo-Saxon governments. 435p. 8°. 1818.

22283 KINNAIRD, C., *Baron Kinnaird.* A letter to the Duke of Wellington, on the arrest of M. Marinet. 40p. 8°. 1818.

22284 —— Pétition et mémoire, addressées [*sic*] à la

Chambre des Pairs de France. [Against the violation of Marinet's safe-conduct.] 38p. 8°. *Londres,* 1818.

22285 LAS CASES, M. J. E. A. D. DE, *Marquis de la Caussade.* Mémoires d'Emmanuel-Auguste-Dieudonné Comte de Las Casas, communiqués par lui-même, contenant: l'histoire de sa vie...ainsi qu'une lettre adressée à Lord Bathurst...Seconde édition, revue et corrigée. 116p. 8°. *Bruxelles,* 1818.

22286 ★LONDON. Livery Companies. *Salters.* A list of the Master, Wardens, Court of Assistants, and Livery, of the Worshipful Company of Salters. 15p. 8°. 1818. *See also* 1784, 1787, 1790, 1792, 1794, 1797, 1799, 1801, 1803, 1806, 1809, 1812, 1815, 1821, 1824, 1827, 1830.

22287 MONK, JAMES, H., *Bishop of Gloucester and Bristol.* A vindication of the University of Cambridge, from the reflections of Sir James Edward Smith, President of the Linnæan Society, contained in a pamphlet, entitled 'Considerations respecting Cambridge,' &c....Second edition. [On the teaching of botany in the University and the ineligibility of Sir James Smith for the professorship on the ground of dissent.] 95p. 8°. *London & Cambridge,* 1818.

22288 PLOWDEN, F. A disquisition concerning the law of alienage and naturalization, according to the Statutes in force between the 10th of June, 1818, and the 25th of March, 1819; offered to the consideration of the new Parliament...Illustrated in an...opinion of counsel, written upon the claim of Prince Giustiniani to the Earldom of Newburgh. 74p. 8°. *Paris,* 1818.

22289 SOCIETY FOR DIFFUSING SCRIPTURAL KNOWLEDGE BY THE DISTRIBUTION OF TRACTS. The Society for Diffusing Scriptural Knowledge...[The aims and rules of the Society. Dated: London, June, 1818.] 4p. 8°. *n.p.* [1818]

1819

GENERAL

22290 BACON, F., *Viscount St. Albans.* Essays, moral, economical, and political...A new edition...387p. *12°. London & York, 1819.*

22291 BRITISH MUSEUM. A catalogue of the Lansdowne manuscripts in the British Museum, with indexes of persons, places, and matters...[By Sir H. Ellis and F. Douce.] 303, [148]p. *fol. n.p., 1819.*

22292 BRYDGES, SIR S. E., *Bart.* The population and riches of nations, considered together, not only with regard to their positive and relative increase, but with regard to their tendency to morals, prosperity and happiness. [With a bibliography.] 248p. *8°. Paris...London, 1819.*

22293 CAREY, M. Vindiciæ Hibernicæ: or, Ireland vindicated: an attempt to develop and expose a few of the multifarious errors and falsehoods respecting Ireland, in the histories of May, Temple...Hume, and others: particularly in the legendary tales of the conspiracy and pretended massacre of 1641. 504p. *8°. Philadelphia, 1819.*

22294 CHAPTAL, J. A. C., *Comte de Chanteloup.* De l'industrie françoise... 2 vols. *8°. Paris, 1819.*

22295 CHRISTOPHORO D'AVALOS, F. A. DE. Essai sur le commerce et les intérêts de l'Espagne et de ses colonies. 160p. *8°. Paris, 1819.*

22296 COMPANION to the calendars, for...1819: being a list of all the changes in administration, from the commencement of the present century... 142p. *12°. 1819. See also 1830.*

22297 [CURTIUS, W. B. D.] Vrijmoedige gedachten over de tegenwoordige huishouding van staat der Nederlanden, ten gevolge der brieven over den tegenwoordigen toestand des koophandels in de Nederlanden. Briefwijze medegedeeld. [Two letters, each signed: Z.] 33, 44p. *8°. Amsterdam, 1819. See also 1822.*

22298 *The **EAST-INDIA** register and directory, for 1819; corrected to the 3d February 1819; containing ...lists of the Company's servants...Together with lists of...mariners, &c. not in the service of the...Company; and merchant vessels employed in the country trade. Compiled...by A. W. Mason & Geo. Owen... 504p. *12°. London, Dublin, &c., [1819]*

22299 *—— Corrected to the 25th September 1819... Second edition. 500p. *12°. London, Dublin, &c., [1819] For other editions, see 1804.*

For **EDMONDS'S WEEKLY REGISTER,** 1819–20, *see* vol. III, *Periodicals list.*

22300 EDWARDS, GEORGE. The forlorn hope of the United Kingdom...in three detached parts. I. An address to the landed, manufacturing, commercial, agricultural, and other constituent interests...II. A petition, containing specific propositions...III. A letter to Lord L——s, pointing out the...means we possess for effecting those specific propositions...Part I. With an appendix, containing a plan of finance competent to meet the present situation of the United Kingdom. 24p. *8°. 1819.*

22301 —— The plan and documents, whereby the new era of our predestined earthly happiness...not only can be formed...everywhere...but is now actually and actively set on foot...In three parts. Part I. 83p. *8°. 1819.*

22302 [FRY, J. S.] The history of John Bull and his three sons by Peter Bullcalf. [With 'Matters of fact. The quartern loaf at fifteen pence, cheaper than the quartern loaf at nine pence...'. Signed: John Bull.] 8p. *8°. 1819.*

22303 GIOJA, M. Sulle manifatture nazionali e tariffe daziarie, discorso popolare. 178, lvp. *8°. Milano, 1819.*

22304 GRAY, S. The happiness of states: or, an inquiry concerning population, the modes of subsisting and employing it, and the effects of all on human happiness: in which is developed the new or productive system of statistics...Republished with an additional book and a copious index. 672p. *4°. London & Edinburgh, 1819. For another edition, see 1815.*

22305 HIGGINS, G. A letter to the House of Commons on the causes of, and the proper remedies for, the present difficulties and discontents of the British Empire. 64p. *8°. 1819. See also 1820.*

22306 [LARKIN, .] Sketch of a tour in the Highlands of Scotland; through Perthshire, Argyleshire, and Inverness-shire, in September and October, 1818: with some account of the Caledonian Canal. 352p. *8°. 1819.*

22307 LAVOISIER, A. L. Résultats d'un ouvrage intitulé: De la richesse territoriale du royaume de France; par M. Lavoisier...imprimés par ordre de l'Assemblée nationale, en 1791. Suivis d'un essai d'arithmétique politique sur les premiers besoins de l'intérieur de la France, par M. de la Grange. [Extrait des *Annales de l'Agriculture française,* 2e série, tome VI.] 66p. *8°. Paris, 1819.*

22308 MAITLAND, JAMES, *8th Earl of Lauderdale.* An inquiry into the nature and origin of public wealth, and into the means and causes of its increase...Second edition, greatly enlarged. 465p. *8°. Edinburgh & London, 1819. For other editions, see 1804.*

22309 MAN, *Isle of.* The Lex scripta of the Isle of Man; comprehending the ancient ordinances and statute laws, from the earliest to the present date. A new edition. Published by authority. 539p. *8°. Douglas & London, 1819.*

22310 MATHEWS, JOSEPH, *ed.* Mathews's annual Bristol directory for the year 1819. The twenty-first edition... 207p. *12°. Bristol & Bath, [1819]*

22311 [MAXWELL, SIR JOHN, *Bart.]* A letter addressed to the honest reformers of Scotland; with remarks on the poor rates, corn law, religious establishment, right of property, equality of ranks and revolution. [The introduction signed: A Renfrewshire reformer.] 40p. *8°. Glasgow, Paisley, &c., 1819.*

For the **MEDUSA,** 1819–20, *see* vol. III, *Periodicals list.*

22312 MENGOTTI, F., *Conte.* Il Colbertismo. Dissertazione coronata dalla Reale Società Economica Fiorentina detta de Georgofili li 13 giugno 1792...Nuovo edizione con l'aggiunta di alcuni articoli di una memoria inedita interessante l'istoria dell'arte della seta in Toscania. 149p. *8°. Firenze, 1819. For another edition, see 1797.*

22313   PAINE, T. Agrarian justice, opposed to agrarian law, and to agrarian monopoly; being a plan for meliorating the condition of man, by creating...a national fund... 19p. *8°. 1819. For other editions, see 1797.*

22314 —— The political and miscellaneous works of Thomas Paine...[With a life of Paine, by Richard Carlile.] 2 vols. *8°. 1819. For other editions, see 1817.*

22315   PHILADELPHIA SOCIETY FOR THE PROMOTION OF NATIONAL INDUSTRY. Address of the Philadelphia Society for the Promotion of National Industry, to the citizens of the United States. [By Mathew Carey.] No. I [–Nos. VII–VIII]. *8°. n.p.* [1819]

22316 —— National interests & domestic manufactures. Address of the Philadelphia Society for the Promotion of Domestic Industry [*sic*], to the citizens of the United States. [A new edition of nos. 1–13, the first eleven by Mathew Carey, nos. 12–13 by Dr. Samuel Jackson.] 116p. *8°. Boston, 1819.*

22317   PICOT, J. Statistique de la Suisse, ou état de ce pays et des vingt-deux cantons dont il se compose, sous le rapport de leur situation...étendue...climat... population...de leurs produits...impôts...revenus, de leur industrie et...commerce... 574p. *12°. Genève & Paris, 1819. See also 1830.*

22318   PLAYFAIR, J. A geographical and statistical description of Scotland. Containing a general survey of that kingdom...A description of every county...and a statistical account of every parish... 2 vols. *8°. Edinburgh & London, 1819.*

22319   PRIOR, SIR J. Voyage along the eastern coast of Africa, to Mosambique, Johanna, and Quiloa; to St. Helena; to Rio de Janeiro, Bahia, and Pernambuco in Brazil, in the Nisus frigate. 114p. *8°. 1819.*

22320   RAFFLES, THOMAS. Letters, during a tour through some parts of France, Savoy, Switzerland, Germany, and the Netherlands, in the summer of 1817... Second edition. 336p. *12°. Liverpool, London, &c., 1819.*

For the **REPUBLICAN** [edited by R. Carlile], 1819–25, *see* vol. III, *Periodicals list.*

22321   REYNIER, J. L. A. De l'économie publique et rurale des Perses et des Phéniciens. 416p. *8°. Genève & Paris, 1819.*

22322   RICARDO, D. On the principles of political economy and taxation...Second edition. 550p. *8°. 1819. The copy that belonged to Sir Robert Peel (1788–1850), with his signature on the title-page.*

22323 —— First American edition. 448p. *8°. Georgetown, D.C., 1819.*

22324 —— Des principes de l'économie politique, et de l'impôt...Traduit de l'anglais par F. S. Constancio; avec des notes explicatives et critiques par M. Jean-Baptiste Say... 2 vols. *8°. Paris, 1819. For other editions, see 1817.*

22325   RICKMAN, T. C. The life of Thomas Paine ... 277p. *8°. 1819.*

22326   RIDER'S British Merlin: for...1819...With notes of husbandry, fairs, marts, and tables...Compiled ...by Cardanus Rider. 60p. *12°.* [1819] *For other editions, see 1693.*

22327   [ROSE, W. S.] Letters from the north of Italy. Addressed to Henry Hallam, Esq....[The introduction signed: W.S.R.] 2 vols. *8°. 1819.*

22328   The ROYAL KALENDAR: and court and city register, for...1819... 404p. *12°.* [1819] *For other editions, see 1779.*

22329   SAVAGE, W. Observations on emigration to the United States of America [referring particularly to Kentucky]... 66p. *8°. 1819.*

22330   SAY, J. B. Traité d'économie politique... Quatrième édition, corrigée et augmentée... 2 vols. *8°. Paris, 1819. For other editions, see 1803.*

22331   SEWELL, I. Hints to proprietors of real property; suggesting a plan to counteract the rapid increase of pauperism, by removing some defects in banks for savings, and preventing early and improvident marriages: also observations on the tendency of offhand farms, and the peculiar mode of charging tithes, to occasion an increase of poor rates. 90p. *8°.* [1819]

22332   SHERWIN, W. T. Memoirs of the life of Thomas Paine, with observations on his writings, critical and explanatory. To which is added, an appendix, containing several of Mr. Paine's unpublished pieces. 232, xlviiip. *8°. 1819.*

22333   SIMONDE DE SISMONDI, J. C. L. Nouveaux principes d'économie politique, ou de la richesse dans ses rapports avec la population... 2 vols. *8°. Paris, 1819. The copy that was sent to Napoleon at St. Helena by Lady Holland, with the name 'Napoléon' and her initials 'E.V.H.' on the title-page of volume 1 and the half-title of volume 2, in her hand.*

22334 —— Nuovi principj di economia politica o sia della ricchezza, posta in raffronto colla popolazione... Traduzione del professore Gaetano Barbieri. 3 vols. *12°. Milano, 1819. See also 1827.*

22335   SMITH, ADAM. An inquiry into the nature and causes of the wealth of nations...With a life of the author. Also, a view of the doctrine of Smith, compared with that of the French economists; with a method of facilitating the study of his works; from the French of M. Garnier... 3 vols. *8°. London & Edinburgh, 1819.*

22336   SONNENFELS, J. VON. Grundsätze der Polizey, Handlung und Finanz...Achte Auflage. 3 vols. *8°. Wien, 1819–22.*

22337   TATE, WILLIAM (1781?–1848). The elements of commercial calculations, and an introduction to the most important branches of the commerce & finances of this country. 2 vols. *8°. 1819.*

22338   TOURMACHON DE MONTVÉRAN, . Histoire critique et raisonné de la situation de l'Angleterre au 1er janvier 1816, sous les rapports de ses finances, de son agriculture, de ses manufactures, de son commerce et sa navigation, de sa constitution et ses lois, et de sa politique extérieure. Vols. 1–3. *8°. Paris, 1819.*

22339   VANDERSTRAETEN, C. De l'état actuel du Royaume des Pays-Bas, et des moyens de l'améliorer. 2 vols. *8°. Bruxelles, 1819–20.*

22340   VIEW of the history, constitution, and funds, of the Trades' House of Glasgow. 55p. *8°. Glasgow, 1819.*

22341   WALSH, ROBERT (1784–1859). An appeal from the judgments of Great Britain respecting the United States of America. Part first, containing an historical outline of their merits and wrongs as colonies; and strictures upon the calumnies of the British writers. 512p. 8°. *Philadelphia*, 1819.

22342 WARDEN, D. B. A statistical, political, and historical account of the United States of North America; from the period of their first colonization to the present day. 3 vols. 8°. *Edinburgh & London*, 1819.

AGRICULTURE

For the **AMERICAN FARMER**, 1819–29, *see* vol. III, *Periodicals list*.

22343 DAVY, Sir H., *Bart*. Elémens de chimie agricole, en un cours de leçons, pour le Comité d'Agriculture...Traduit de l'anglais, avec un traité sur l'art de faire le vin et de distiller les eaux-de-vie, par A. Bulos... [With 'Appendice. Tableau des résultats obtenus dans les expériences faites par ordre du duc de Bedford, pour déterminer le produit et les qualités nutritives de différentes herbes et autres plantes employées comme fourrages'. By George Sinclair. Edited by Sir H. Davy.] 2 vols. 8°. *Paris*, 1819. *For other editions, see* 1813.

22344 ENGLAND. *Laws, etc.* [*Endorsed:*] An Act to amend and enlarge the powers of an Act [of 1812]...for draining, inclosing and improving the lands called Borough Fen Common and the Four Hundred Acre Common, in the county of Northampton, and for forming the same into a parish, to be called Newborough... ⟨Royal Assent, 24 June 1819.⟩ 59 Geo. III. sess. 1819. 10p. 4°. *Peterborough*, [1819] *See note to no.* 25484.

22345 FOURNEL, J. F. Les lois rurales de la France, rangées dans leur ordre naturel... 2 vols. 8°. *Paris*, 1819.

22346 GRISENTHWAITE, W. A new theory of agriculture, in which the nature of soils, crops and manures is explained...and the application of bones, gypsum, lime, chalk &c. is determined on scientific principles. 139p. 8°. *Wells, Norwich, &c.*, 1819.

22347 [HALL, G. W.] The origin and proceedings of the agricultural associations in Great Britain, in which their claims for protection against foreign produce, duty-free, are fully and ably set forth. Printed for the use of the members of both Houses of Parliament... 39p. 8°. [1819] *See also* 1820.

22348 JACOB, Giles. The complete court-keeper; or, land-steward's assistant...The eighth edition, enlarged and corrected to the present time, by a barrister. 338p. 8°. 1819. *For another edition, see* 1715.

22349 A LETTER to Sir John Shelley, on the game laws. By a country gentleman. 24p. 8°. 1819.

22350 LOW, D. Report relative to the lordship and estate of Marchmont, the Barony of Hume, &c. with the various additions made to the original property by purchase, drawn up by order of Sir William Purves Hume Campbell, of Marchmont and Purves, Baronet. 203p. 4°. 1819.

22351 LULLIN DE CHATEAUVIEUX, J. F. Italy, its agriculture, &c. From the French of Mons. Chateauvieux, being letters written by him in Italy, in the years 1812 & 1813. Translated by Edward Rigby... 358p. 8°. *Norwich & London*, 1819.

22352 MACDOUGALL, A. A treatise on the Irish fisheries, and various other subjects, connected with the general improvement of Ireland. 220p. 8°. *Belfast*, 1819.

22353 M'PHAIL, J. The gardener's remembrancer ...containing practicable methods of gardening...To which is now added, the culture of the cucumber...the management of timber trees. The second edition, greatly improved and corrected. 428p. 12°. 1819.

22354 PARKES, S. A letter to the farmers and graziers of Great Britain, to explain the advantages of using salt in the various branches of agriculture, and in feeding all kinds of farming stock...Second edition. 88p. 8°. *London, Liverpool, &c.*, 1819.

22355 PICOT DE LA PEYROUSE, P. I., *Baron*. The agriculture of a district in the south of France [the canton of Montastruc]. Translated from the French... To which are added, notes, by a recent traveller in France. 105p. 8°. 1819. *With the book-plate (mutilated) of the* [*Agri*]*cultural and Gen*[*eral*] *Library Scarborough*.

22356 RADCLIFF, T. A report on the agriculture of eastern and western Flanders; drawn up at the desire of the Farming Society of Ireland... 329p. 8°. *London & Dublin*, 1819.

22357 REMARKS upon trade and commerce, as connected with agriculture; with suggestions for their relief. Or, the farmer's complaint, defence, and remedy. By an agriculturist. 64p. 8°. 1819.

22358 The RIGHTS of the farmer, or, a short view of the causes which oppress and degrade the cultivators of the soil of Great Britain, and a statement of the just claims of the farmers to legislative protection...including observations on the rise and progress of the Rounds' System...By a farmer. 80p. 8°. 1819.

22359 VILLENEUVE, L. DE, *Comte*. Essai d'un manuel d'agriculture, ou exposition du système de culture suivi pendant dix-neuf ans dans le domaine d'Hauterive, commune de Castres, département du Tarn. 399p. 8°. *Toulouse*, 1819. *A circular letter, signed: Carrère, Sre-E. de la Société Royale d'Agriculture de la Haute-Garonne, bringing this work to the attention of the mayors of the Département, is inserted in the volume*.

CORN LAWS

22360 [DECIUS, *pseud.*] Refutation of the arguments used on the subject of the agricultural petition. [Reprinted from *The Pamphleteer*, vol. XIV, no. 27, there signed 'Decius', with a preface, signed 'A.B.C.'] 15p. 8°. *Newbury*, [1819].

22361 [GAMBINI, F.] Delle leggi frumentarie in Italia. 152p. 8°. *n.p.*, 1819.

22362 A LETTER to the Right Honorable Frederick Robinson, President of the Board of Trade, &c.&c. on the policy and expediency of further protection to the corn trade of Great Britain: and on the necessity of revising and amending the last Corn Bill; particularly as regards the mode of making the returns and of striking the averages, &c.&c. By a corn factor. 36p. *8°*. 1819. *The copy that belonged to David Ricardo.*

22363 An important **STATEMENT**; proving that the corn laws, since 1793, have inflicted five times the amount of misery and oppression on this country that the interest of the National Debt has. By a Briton... 16p. *8°*. *Westminster*, [1819]

TRADES & MANUFACTURES

22364 **ACCUM**, F. C. A. Description of the process of manufacturing coal gas, for the lighting of streets, houses, and public buildings, with...plans of the most improved sorts of apparatus now employed at the gas works in London... 334p. *8°*. 1819. *See also* 1820.

22365 An **ADDRESS** to the nobility and gentry of Ireland, on the subject of distillation, as affecting the agriculture and revenue of that part of the United Kingdom. 34p. *8°*. *Dublin*, 1819.

22366 **ARTIFICIANA**; or, a key to the principal trades. Embellished with...wood-cuts, descriptive of each trade. 126p. *12°*. *Edinburgh*, [1819]

22367 **C***, *Mr. le Comte de*. Quelques réflexions sur l'industrie en général, à l'occasion de l'Exposition des produits de l'industrie française en 1819. 84p. *8°*. *Paris*, 1819.

22368 **CHAPMAN**, THOMAS, *manufacturer*. Interesting and most severe case of Mr. Thomas Chapman, who first discovered the means of making the fur of the seal available. [Signed in manuscript: Thos. Chapman. On his failure to cover his invention by patent.] 15p. *8°*. 1819.

22369 **CULVERHOUSE**, C. An arrangement of the bread laws, relating to bakers out of the City of London and beyond ten miles of the Royal Exchange...with an historical introduction, and some curious specimens of the ancient bread laws. Second edition. 160[168]p. *8°*. *Bath*, 1819. *For another edition, see* 1813.

22370 **EXPOSITION DES PRODUITS DE L'INDUSTRIE FRANÇAISE**, 1819. Rapport du jury central sur les produits de l'industrie française présenté à S.E.M. le Comte Decazes...Ministre Secrétaire d'État de l'Intérieur; rédigé par M. L. Costaz. [Including 'Ordonnances, rapports et circulaires qui ont préparé l'Exposition de 1819'.] 492p. *8°*. *Paris*, 1819.

22371 **GRAY**, A. A treatise on spinning machinery... With some preliminary observations...and a postscript, including an interesting account of the mode of spinning yarn in Ireland. 91p. *8°*. *Edinburgh & London*, 1819.

22372 **HOPPUS**, E. Practical measuring made easy to the meanest capacity, by a new set of tables...A new edition, revised by T. Crosby, head master of the York Charity Schools... 208p. *long 12°*. *York*, 1819. *For other editions, see* 1759.

22373 The **JOURNEYMEN** carpenters price book, for labour only. Published by order and for the use of the trade. 45p. *8°*. 1819.

22374 **PECKSTON**, T. S. The theory and practice of gas-lighting: in which is exhibited an historical sketch of the rise and progress of that science...with descriptions of the most approved apparatus for generating, collecting, and distributing, coal-gas for illuminating purposes... 438p. *8°*. *London, Edinburgh, &c.*, 1819.

22375 **POWELL**, JOHN, *statistical writer*. A letter addressed to Edward Ellice, Esq. M.P. on the general influence of large establishments of apprentices in producing unfair competition...parish burthens, insufficient workmen...and decay of trade. With remarks on the prevailing theories, on freedom of trade, and the justice and policy of regulation. [With particular reference to the watch-making trade in Coventry.] 32p. *8°*. 1819.

22376 March 1819. The ninth edition of **SKYRING'S** builders' prices, corrected from the prime cost of materials and labor to the present month...[With 'Abstract of the Building Act, 14th George III. c. 78' and 'Alphabetical list of surveyors'.] 115p. *8°*. [1819] *Compiled by Z. Skyring, who signed and numbered each copy in manuscript. See also* 1812, 1818, 1827, 1831, 1838, 1845, 1846.

22377 **STATEMENT**, for the information of the manufacturers of leather in Edinburgh and its vicinity, as to the appointment of inspectors of raw hides and skins. By a committee of the trade in Edinburgh. [Signed: John Swan, convener of the committee.] 20p. *8°*. *Edinburgh*, 1819.

COMMERCE

22378 **ASSEY**, C. On the trade to China, and the Indian Archipelago; with observations on the insecurity of the British interests in that quarter...Second edition. 72p. *8°*. 1819.

22379 **BORISSOW**, C. I. The commerce of St. Petersburg, with a brief description of the trade of the Russian Empire. To which is added an appendix, containing an account of the usual charges on imports and exports, custom-house duties, tares, &c. exemplified by invoices and account sales. 179p. *8°*. 1819.

22380 **CLAY**, J. A free trade essential to the welfare of Great Britain, or an inquiry into the cause of the present distressed state of the country...To which are added, some observations on two letters to the Right Hon. Robert Peel, M.P., by one of his constituents... 76p. *8°*. *London & Leeds*, 1819. *See also* 1820.

22381 **CRIGNON D'AUZOUER**, A. Opinion de M. Crignon d'Auzouer, Député du Loiret, sur la loi qui établit le transit par l'Alsace et un entrepôt de denrées coloniales à Strasbourg. 15p. *8°*. [*Paris*, 1819]

22382 **GLOYER**, J. N. Darstellung des Englisch-Ostindischen Compagnie- und Privathandels, in Bezug auf die Mittel, die Dänische Niederlassung in Ostindien, Trankebar, in Aufnahme zu bringen, und auf eine, den

Hanseestädten und den Amerikanern dahin zu eröffnende Handelsfreyheit. 170p. 8°. Altona, 1819.

22383 HOLROYD, J. B., *Earl of Sheffield*. Lord Sheffield's report at the Lewes Wool Fair, July 26, 1819. [On the wool trade.] 8p. 8°. [1819] *See also* 1811, 1815, 1816.

22384 KING, R. The speech of Rufus King, Esq. in the Senate on the navigation laws of the United States, which is at this time deserving of the serious attention of the British Legislature. 24p. 8°. 1819.

22385 The **LONDON TRADESMAN**; a familiar treatise on the rationale of trade and commerce, as carried on in the Metropolis of the British Empire...By several tradesmen. 368p. 8°. 1819. *See also* 1820.

22386 PHILADELPHIA SOCIETY FOR THE PROMOTION OF NATIONAL INDUSTRY. Address of the Philadelphia Society for the Promotion of National Industry, to the citizens of the United States.

New series. No. 1. [By Mathew Carey.] Second edition. 20p. 8°. n.p. [1819]

22387 RUSSELL, JOHN, *6th Duke of Bedford*. Report of the late important trial, in the Court of King's Bench, in which...John, Duke of Bedford was plaintiff, and Richard White, a potatoe dealer, the defendant. Respecting tolls claimed in Covent Garden Market. Tried...the 23rd of February, 1819. 156p. 8°. 1819.

22388 SOCIETY OF MERCHANTS, SHIP-OWNERS AND UNDERWRITERS. The register of shipping, for 1819. Instituted in 1798...[A rival list to the Register of shipping issued from Lloyd's. With a list of subscribers for 1818/19.] [736]p. 4°. 1819.

22389 ZIEGLER, J. F. Ueber Gewerbefreiheit und deren Folgen, mit besonderer Rücksicht auf den preussischen Staat, nach den bisher gemachten Erfahrungen. 112p. 8°. Berlin, 1819.

COLONIES

22390 BAPTIST MISSIONARY SOCIETY. Baptist mission. Brief review of the stations on the continent, as addressed by the senior missionaries to their brethren in India. 2p. s.sh.fol. n.p. [1819]

22391 —— Recent pleasing intelligence [concerning converts in India, Batavia, etc.]. s.sh.fol. n.p. [1819]

22392 DOUGLAS, T., *Earl of Selkirk*. A letter to the Earl of Liverpool from the Earl of Selkirk; accompanied by a correspondence with the Colonial Department (in the years 1817, 1818 and 1819), on the subject of the Red River Settlement, in North America [being letters by J. Halkett to Lord Bathurst with acknowledgements to them on behalf of Lord Bathurst by Henry Goulburn]. 224p. 8°. [1819] *The copy that belonged to David Ricardo.*

22393 EDWARDS, BRYAN. The history, civil and commercial, of the British West Indies...With a continuation to the present time. Fifth edition...[Edited by Sir W. Young.] 5 vols. 8°. London, Edinburgh, &c., 1819. *For other editions, see* 1793.

22394 M'DONELL, A. A narrative of transactions in the Red River country; from the commencement of the operations of the Earl of Selkirk, till the summer of the year 1816...With a map... 85p. 8°. 1819.

22395 PRITCHARD, J., *and others*. Narrative of John Pritchard, Pierre Chrysologue Pambrun, and Frederick Damien Heurter, respecting the aggressions of the North-West Company, against the Earl of Selkirk's settlement upon Red River. 91p. 8°. [1819] *The copy that belonged to David Ricardo.*

FINANCE

22396 The **ART** of stock jobbing explained; exposing the secret manœuvres, tricks, and contrivances, and the cause of the rise and fall of the funds...To which is added, some serious advice to fundholders on the operation of the Sinking Fund...By a practical jobber. Seventh edition. 136p. 8°. [1819] *Originally published with the title:* Stock-Exchange laid open, *in 1814 (q.v.).*

22397 [**ATKINSON**, JASPER.] Cursory observations on some parts of the evidence before the Committees of both Houses of Parliament, on the expediency of resuming cash-payments at the Bank of England, in a second letter to a friend. [With 49 appendixes.] 192p. 8°. 1819. *In a volume of his pamphlets collected and bound for presentation by the author, with a specially printed title 'Cash-Resumption, 1819' and a summary of the contents. The collection has a presentation inscription 'For Samuel Gardiner Esqr., Coombe Lodge, Oxon. From the author'. This copy of the work has a greatly extended appendix, which in other copies ends at p. 165. Here the tables include statistics up to August 1819. There is also a separately paged copy of the Appendix in the Goldsmiths' Library, paginated 1–35.*

22398 [——] A letter to a friend, upon the late rise in

the foreign exchanges, &c.&c. Not published. 23p. 8°. 1819. *See note to no. 22397 above.*

22399 [——] Observations on the Reports of the Committees of both Houses of Parliament, on the expediency of resuming cash-payments at the Bank of England, in a letter to a friend. 60p. 8°. London & Bath, 1819. *See note to no. 22397.*

22400 [——] Remarks on some occurrences since the Reports of the Committees of both Houses of Parliament, on the expediency of the resumption of cash-payments at the Bank of England. 40p. 8°. 1819. *See note to no. 22397.*

22401 ATTWOOD, T. A second letter to the Earl of Liverpool, on the Bank Reports, as occasioning the national dangers and distresses. 113p. 8°. Birmingham & London, 1819. *The copy that belonged to David Ricardo.*

22402 AURRAN-PIERREFEU, J. C., *Baron*. Chambre des Députés. Opinion de M. Aurran-Pierrefeu, Député du Var, dans la séance du 28 juin, sur la loi des voies et moyens. 16p. 8°. [Paris, 1819]

22403 BANK FOR SAVINGS, *East Grinstead*. Bank for savings, established at East Grinsted, for the parishes of East Grinsted, West Hoathly, Horsted Keynes, Worth, Horne, Burstow, Godstone, Longfield, and other places within ten miles. [Minutes of the inaugural meeting, January 1819, list of officers, and rules.] 4p. *fol. East Grinsted*, [1819]

22404 BANK OF ENGLAND. A list of the names of all such proprietors of the Bank of England, who are qualified to vote at the ensuing election...March 23d, 1819. 19p. *fol.* [1819] *See also* 1738, 1749, 1750, 1789, 1790, 1791, 1792, 1793, 1794, 1795, 1796, 1797, 1798, 1799, 1801, 1803, 1804, 1808, 1809, 1812, 1816, 1836, 1843.

22405 BEAUVOIR, J. Chambre des Députés. Opinion de M. Josse Beauvoir, Député de Loir-et-Cher, sur la création dans les départemens de grands-livres auxiliaires de la dette publique. 15p. *8°.* [*Paris*, 1819]

22406 BOLLMANN, E. A letter to Thomas Brand, Esq., M.P. for the County of Hertford; on the practicability and propriety of a resumption of specie payments. 98p. *8°.* 1819.

22407 —— A second letter to the Honourable Thomas Brand, M.P. for the County of Hertford; in which doubts are suggested on the practicability of the new system of bullion-payments; and on its efficacy to regulate and control the amount of bank notes in circulation, by their convertibility. 45p. *8°.* [*London,*] 1819. *Presentation copy, with inscription, from the author to the Earl of Lauderdale.*

22408 BONALD, L. G. A. DE, *Vicomte.* Opinion de M. de Bonald, Député de l'Aveyron, sur la fixation des dépenses de la guerre. 16p. *8°.* [*Paris*, 1819]

22409 BRICOGNE, A. J. B. Situation des finances au vrai, mise à la portée des contribuables, pour prouver qu'une réduction de cinquante millions sur la contribution foncière, dont cinq millions à la ville de Paris, doit être accordée dès 1819; suivie de 36 doutes et questions sur les comptes et les budgets. 128p. *8°. Paris*, 1819.

22410 —— Errata du Rapport de M. le Comte Beugnot, sur les voies et moyens de 1819, pour faire suite à la Situation des finances au vrai. 34p. *8°. Paris*, 1819.

22411 BRITISH LINEN COMPANY. [*Endorsed:*] 1st. March 1819. List of the proprietors of the British Linen Company. A General Court to be held...for election of Governor...for the year ensuing. *s.sh.fol. n.p.* [1819] [*Br.* 491] *See also* 1845, 1846.

22412 BROUGHTON, THOMAS (*fl.* 1815–1819). The cure for pauperism...with a plan of an effectual measure of finance. 67p. *8°.* 1819.

22413 BRUGIÈRE DE BARANTE, A. G. P., *Baron de Barante.* Discours prononcé à la Chambre des Députés, dans la séance du 7 avril 1819, par M. de Barante, l'un des Commissaires du Roi, pour la défense de la loi sur l'impôt des tabacs. 23p. *12°. Paris*, 1819.

22414 [**CALLAGHAN,** G.] A letter from a new member of the House of Commons, to the Right Hon. George Canning, on the probable safety in resuming cash payments. 50p. *8°.* 1819.

22415 CHAMBERS, A. H. Comments on some recent political discussions, with an exposure of the fallacy of the Sinking Fund. 52p. *8°.* 1819.

22416 —— Thoughts on the resumption of cash payments by the Bank; and on the Corn Bill, as connected with that measure: in a letter, addressed to the... Chancellor of the Exchequer. 38p. *8°.* 1819.

22417 CHATEAUDOUBLE, P. DE. Chambre des Députés. Opinion de M. Paul Chateaudouble, Député du Var, sur le projet de loi relatif à la continuation du monopole des tabacs, jusqu'au 1er janvier 1826. 11p. *12°.* [*Paris*, 1819]

22418 CHICHESTER, E. A second letter to a British Member of Parliament, relative to the oppressions & cruelties of Irish revenue officers [in putting down the practice of illicit distilling], wherein the observations [by A. Coffey] on a former letter are considered and refuted. 71p. *8°.* 1819.

22419 [——, *ed.*] Documents illustrative of the oppressions & cruelties of Irish revenue officers. 43p. *8°.* 1819.

22420 CONGREVE, SIR WILLIAM, *Bart.* Of the impracticability of the resumption of cash payments; of the sufficiency of a representative currency in this country, under due regulations; and of the danger of a reduction of the circulating medium, in the present state of things. 46p. *8°.* 1819.

22421 CONSIDERATIONS on the Sinking Fund. 136p. *8°.* 1819.

22422 COOKE, EDWARD (1792?–1862). An address to the public on the plan proposed by the Secret Committee of the House of Commons, for examining the affairs of the Bank. 29p. *8°.* 1819.

22423 [——] The real cause of the high price of gold bullion. Second edition, corrected, with an appendix. 51p. *8°.* 1819. *Presentation copy from the author to David Ricardo.*

22424 [**COPLESTON,** E., *Bishop of Llandaff.*] A letter to the Right Hon. Robert Peel, M.P. for the University of Oxford, on the pernicious effects of a variable standard of value, especially as it regards the condition of the lower orders and the poor laws. By one of his constituents. 102p. *8°. Oxford & London*, 1819.

22425 [——] Second edition. 104p. *8°. Oxford & London*, 1819.

22426 [——] Third edition. 104p. *8°. Oxford & London*, 1819.

22427 CORNET-DINCOURT, C. N. Chambre des Députés. Discours sur la contribution personnelle et mobilière, prononcé dans la séance du 1er mai 1819, par M. Cornet-Dincourt, Député de la Somme, à l'occasion de la pétition du Sieur Lortel, de Vitry-le-Français. 10p. *8°.* [*Paris*, 1819]

22428 —— Chambre des Députés. Opinion de M. Cornet-Dincourt, Député de la Somme, sur le projet de loi relatif au changement de l'année financière. (Séance publique du 13 février 1819.) 10p. *8°.* [*Paris*, 1819]

22429 —— Chambre des Députés. Opinion de M. Cornet-Dincourt, Député de la Somme, sur le projet de loi relatif aux dépenses de l'année 1819...Séance du 26 mai, 1819. 15p. *8°.* [*Paris*, 1819]

22430 COURTARVEL DE PÈZE, C. R. C., *Comte de Courtarvel.* Chambre des Députés. Opinion de M. de Courtarvel, Député d'Eure-et-Loir, sur le Budget de 1819 (des voies et moyens). 15p. *8°.* [*Paris*, 1819]

22431 CRIGNON D'AUZOUER, A. Chambre des Députés. Opinion de M. Crignon d'Auzouer, Député du Loiret, sur la prolongation du monopole du tabac. 16p. *8°.* [*Paris*, 1819]

22432 —— Chambre des Députés. Opinion de M. Crignon d'Auzouer, Député du Loiret, sur les contributions indirectes, servant de développement à trois amendemens, qu'il demande, à la loi du 28 avril 1816. 16p. *8°.* [*Paris*, 1819]

22433 The **DANGER** of forcing a return to cash payments by the Bank: and the expediency of some new arrangement of the currency. 4p. *fol.* [*London*, 1819]

22434 DENISON, N. J. Thoughts on the funding and paper system, and especially the Bank restriction and resumption of cash payments, as connected with the national distresses; with remarks on the observations of Mr. Preston and Sir John Sinclair. Addressed to the landed interest. 96p. *8°.* 1819.

22435 [**DICKINSON**, W.] Foreign exchanges; being a complete set of tables, calculated from the lowest exchange to the highest usual rates...By the editor of Mortimer's Commercial dictionary. Revised by Mr. W. Tate. 1179p. *8°.* 1819.

22436 DOR DE LASTOURS, M. J., *Marquis de Lastours.* Chambre des Députés. Opinion de M. de Lastours, Député du Tarn, sur le Budget de 1819 (voies et moyens). 22p. *8°.* [*Paris*, 1819]

22437 —— Chambre des Députés. Opinion de M. de Lastours, Député du Tarn, sur la fixation de l'année financière. (Sèance publique du 13 février 1819.) 11p. *12°.* [*Paris*, 1819]

22438 —— Opinion de M. de Lastours, Député du Département du Tarn, sur le cadastre; prononcée dans la séance du 11 juin 1819. (Extrait du Moniteur du 18 juin 1819.) 11p. *12°.* [*Paris*, 1819]

22439 DUNCAN, H. A letter to W. R. K. Douglas, Esq., M.P. on the expediency of the Bill brought by him into Parliament, for the protection and encouragement of banks for savings in Scotland, occasioned by a report of the Edinburgh Society for the Suppression of Beggars. 61p. *8°. Dumfries*, 1819.

22440 DUNN, WILLIAM (*fl.* 1819). The soul of Mr. Pitt; developing that eighteen millions of taxes may be taken off and the three per cent. consols be constantly above 100. Third edition. 16p. *8°.* 1819.

22441 DUTIES payable on goods, wares and merchandise, imported into the United States of America, from and after June 30, 1816, with the letter of instructions, from the Comptroller to the collectors, respecting the alterations and additions to the tariff, agreeably to Acts of...1818. To which are added rates of tonnage, drawbacks, tares, fees, &c....Orders and regulations for the port of New-York, rates of pilotage...and instructions to aliens...Second edition, improved and enlarged. 60p. *8°. New-York*, 1819.

22442 ENGLAND. *Commissioners of Customs.* Instructions to officers appointed to examine the masters of all ships and vessels arriving from foreign parts. 15, 6p. *4°.* 1819.

22443 —— Parliament. *House of Commons.* [Second] Report from the Secret Committee on the expediency of the Bank resuming cash payments, with the minutes of evidence of [*list of witnesses*]... 382p. *8°.* 1819.

22444 FRANCE. *Chambre des Députés.* No. 137. Opinion de M. le Marquis de Villefranche, Député de l'Yonne, sur le chapitre xv du Budget du Ministère des Finances. Imprimée par ordre de la Chambre. 20p. *8°.* [*Paris*, 1819]

22445 —— *Louis XVIII, King.* Loi relative au réglement définitif des Budgets de 1815, 1816 et 1817, et à la rectification proviisore de celui de 1818. A Paris, le 27 juin, 1819. No. 404. 15p. *8°. Paris,* [1819]

22446 —— —— Loi relative à la fixation du Budget des Dépenses de 1819. Au château de Saint-Cloud, le 14 juillet, 1819. No. 409. 7p. *8°. Paris,* [1819]

22447 —— —— Loi relative à la fixation du Budget des Recettes de 1819. Au château de Saint-Cloud, le 17 juillet, 1819. No. 412. 20p. *8°. Paris,* [1819]

22448 FREWIN, R. A digested abridgment of the laws of the Customs, imposing prohibitions and restrictions relative to the importation and exportation of goods, wares, and merchandize, into and from Great Britain... with tables of the duties and drawbacks...Compiled, by direction of the Lords Commissioners of His Majesty's Treasury, by R. Frewin, Esq. assisted by Nicholas Jickling. 629p. *8°.* 1819.

22449 [**FRY**, J. S.] A concise history of tithes, with an inquiry how far a forced maintenance for the ministers of religion is warranted by the examples and precepts of Jesus Christ and his Apostles. 32p. *8°. London & Bristol*, 1819. *See also* 1829.

22450 GARNIER, G., *Marquis.* Histoire de la monnaie, depuis les temps de la plus haute antiquité, jusqu'au règne de Charlemagne. [With 'Notice historique sur la vie et les ouvrages de M. le Marquis Garnier...Par M. Dacier'.] 2 vols. *8°. Paris*, 1819.

22451 GIDDY, afterwards **GILBERT**, D. A plain statement of the bullion question, in a letter to a friend... Second edition. [From *The Pamphleteer*, vol. xiv, no. 27.] 21p. *8°.* 1819. *For another edition, see* 1811.

22452 [**GOLDSMITH**, L. ?] A few observations on the Reports of the Committees to Parliament, on the resumption of cash-payments by the Bank. 8p. *8°.* 1819.

22453 [——] [Another edition, condensed.] 4p. *8°.* 1819.

22454 HALL, WALTER. A view of our late and of our future currency. 80p. *8°.* 1819.

22455 HEATHFIELD, R. Elements of a plan for the liquidation of the Public Debt of the United Kingdom; being the draught of a declaration, submitted to the attention of the landed, funded, and every other description of proprietory, of the United Kingdom. With an introductory discourse. 38p. *8°.* 1819.

22456 —— The second edition. 38p. *8°.* 1819.

22457 —— The fourth edition, with supplementary observations. 47p. *8°.* 1819. *See also* 1820.

22458 HEYWOOD, BENJAMIN A. Arguments demonstrating from recent facts, the solid foundation of individual circulating credit... 38p. *8°. Liverpool*, 1819. *This work was printed but not published; it was expanded and published as* Observations on the circulation of individual credit...Part II, *in 1820 (q.v.). Two copies, both of which belonged to the author. One is interleaved with his manuscript additions and corrections and has the title as published substituted in manuscript.*

22459 —— Facts, collected with a view to shew, that it is impossible, by the legislative enactments at present under consideration, to restore and retain the circulation of gold coin in this kingdom. 40p. *8°. Liverpool*, 1819.

22460 HUSKISSON, W. The question concerning the depreciation of our currency stated and examined... New edition. 152p. *8°. 1819. For other editions, see 1810.*

22461 IBBETSON, J. H. A specimen of a plan for protecting bank notes against forgery. [A broadside headed with a specimen of the author's engraved designs for banknotes. Dated: 29th April 1819.] *s.sh.fol. n.p.* [1819]

22462 —— [Another edition, printed on fine paper, and dated: 21st May 1819.] *s.sh.fol. n.p.* [1819]

22463 An **INQUIRY** into the conduct of Mr. Serjeant Praed, as chairman of the Audit Board... 74p. *8°. Paris, 1819. The imprint is in French.*

22464 JENKINSON, R. B., *2nd Earl of Liverpool.* Substance of the speech of the Right Hon. the Earl of Liverpool, on the Report of the Bank Committee. Printed also in The Pamphleteer, No. xxviii. 23p. *8°. 1819.*

22465 LA BOURDONNAYE, F. R. DE, *Comte.* Chambre des Députés. Opinion de M. le Comte de la Bourdonnaye, Député de Maine-et-Loire, sur le Budget des dépenses du Ministère de la Guerre. 16p. *8°. [Paris, 1819]*

22466 —— Chambre des Députés. Opinion de M. le Comte de la Bourdonnaye, Député de Maine-et-Loire, sur le projet de loi relatif à l'année financière. (Séance publique du...13 février 1819.) 20p. *8°. [Paris, 1819]*

22467 —— Chambre des Députés. Opinion de M. le Comte de la Bourdonnaye, Député de Maine-et-Loire, sur le projet de loi relatif aux livres auxiliaires du grand-livre de la dette publique. (Séance du 24 mars 1819.) 19p. *8°. [Paris, 1819]*

22468 LEMONTEY, P. E. Moyen sûr et agréable de s'enrichir, ou, les trois visites de M. Bruno. [A tale on the advantages of savings banks.] 26p. *8°. [Paris, 1819?] The copy which belonged to Maria Edgeworth, with her signature on the title-page.*

22469 Three **LETTERS** on the causes of the present state of the exchanges, and price of gold bullion, as printed in "The Times" under the signature of "An old merchant;" with an introductory address by the Earl of Lauderdale. 54p. *8°. 1819.*

22470 M., L. To the Governor and Directors of the Bank of England. [Dated: May 18, 1819.] *s.sh.4°. n.p.* [1819] [*Br.* 490]

22471 MAITLAND, JAMES, *8th Earl of Lauderdale.* Protest, entered in the Journals of the House of Lords, against the second reading of a Bill, entitled An Act to continue the restrictions contained in several Acts, on payments in cash by the Bank of England until the 1st day of May, one thousand eight hundred and twenty-three, and to provide for the gradual resumption of such payments, and to permit the exportation of gold and silver. 16p. *8°. 1819.*

22472 —— Protests entered on the Journals of the House of Lords, against the Act of the fifty-sixth of the King, altering the antient regulations of the Mint; and on the subject of the enactments of the Act for further restraining the Bank of England from payments in cash, passed 1818. With some notes and additions. 31p. *8°. 1819.*

22473 MARTIN, THOMAS, *of Allerton, Liverpool.* Observations on payments and receipts in Bank of England notes, reduced to their value in gold; and on consequences which would have resulted to the nation if this system of currency had been instituted at the passing of the Bank Restriction Act. Together with remarks... 70p. *8°. Liverpool, London, &c., 1819.*

22474 MARTIN DU TYRAC, L. M. A. DE, *Comte de Marcellus.* Chambre des Députés (Session de 1818). Discours prononcé par M. le Comte de Marcellus, Député de la Gironde, dans les séances publiques du 18 et 21 juin 1819. 4p. *8°. [Paris, 1819]*

22475 —— Opinion de M. le Comte de Marcellus, Député de la Gironde, prononcée dans la séance publique du 24 mars 1819, sur le projet de loi relatif à la création de titres auxiliaires du grand-livre dans les départemens. 16p. *8°. [Paris, 1819]*

22476 —— Opinion de M. le Comte de Marcellus, Député de la Gironde, sur le Budget du Ministère de la Guerre. 11p. *8°. [Paris, 1819]*

22477 MARYLAND. *General Assembly.* an act to incorporate the stockholders in the Union Bank of Maryland. Passed at Nov. session, 1804, chap. 48. Together with the several supplements, and the by-laws of said institution. 44p. *12°. Baltimore, 1819.*

22478 Safe **METHOD** of rendering income, arising from personal property, available for reducing the poor rates; improving the moral condition of the poor, and lessening their number in future. 28p. *8°. 1819.*

22479 MOORE, JOHN (1742–1821). Case respecting the maintenance of the London clergy further considered ...First printed in 1817. 46p. *8°. 1819.*

22480 NETHERLANDS. *Algemeene Commissie van Liquidatie.* Den [31 Maart 1819.] No. [161]. Orde van behandeling der zaken den achterstand, van Franckrijk betreffende, bij de Algemeene Commissie van Liquidatie in 's Gravenhage. 55p. *8°. n.p.* [1819] *The date and number are supplied in manuscript.*

22481 OBSERVATIONS on bank forgeries and the expediency of resuming cash payments by the Bank. 41p. *8°. 1819.*

22482 OBSERVATIONS on bullion payments, and on a free trade in gold. 15p. *8°. 1819.*

22483 PAGE, R. The letters of Daniel Hardcastle to the editor of "The Times" journal, on the subject of the Bank restriction, the regulations of the Mint, &c. With notes and additions. 209p. *8°. 1819. The copy that belonged to the Earl of Lauderdale.*

22484 PAGÈS, E. Dissertation sur le prêt à intérêt, où, après avoir déterminé...en quoi consiste le prêt usuraire, on expose les circonstances qui autorisent à percevoir en intérêt à l'occasion du prêt. 108[124]p. *8°. Paris, Lyon, &c., 1819.*

22485 PERIER, C. Chambre des Députés. Opinion de M. Casimir Périer, Député de la Seine, sur le projet de loi relatif à la création de livres auxiliaires du grand-livre de la dette publique dans les départemens. Séance du 26 mars 1819. 16p. *8°. [Paris, 1819]*

22486 A **PLEA** for pawnbrokers. Being an attempt to rescue them from the influence of prejudice and mis-representation. 73p. *12°. London & Leicester, 1819.*

22487 PONTET, P. B. D. DE. Chambre des Députés. Opinion de M. Pontet, Député de la Gironde, sur le projet de loi relatif à la création de titres auxiliaires du grand-livre dans les départemens. (Séance du 24 mars 1819.) 16p. *8°. [Paris, 1819]*

22488 PRICE, T. E. V. Thoughts on the system of credit. 32p. *8°. 1819.*

22489 Rotten **RAG MANUFACTORY!!!** The Threadneedle-Street catechism; or, Bank-bubble exposed ...to be read in all public and private houses...for the instruction of John Bull and family in the history and mystery of bank notes. Seventh edition, with additions. 8p. *8°.* [1819]

22490 On the **RELATION** of corn and currency. 4op. *8°.* 1819.

22491 Some **REMARKS** upon the measures recommended in the Reports of the Secret Committees on the state of the Bank of England, and a plan suggested in lieu thereof. p.1–10. *8°.* 1819.

22492 A **REPLY** to the author of A letter to the Right Hon. Robert Peel on the pernicious effects of a variable standard of value. 63p. *8°.* 1819.

22493 **RICARDO,** D. Proposals for an economical and secure currency: with observations on the profits of the Bank of England, as they regard the public, and the proprietors of bank stock...Third edition. 128p. *8°.* 1819. *The copy that belonged to S. J. Loyd, Baron Overstone, formerly among his papers, for which see* vol. III, *MS.* 804. *For other editions, see* 1816.

22494 [**RICHARDS,** JOHN(*fl.* 1819).] Consequences of returning to the old standard of the currency: with remarks on the evidence published by the Secret Committees of the two Houses of Parliament; including the substance of two letters, dated April 3d and 10th, to the Right Hon. the Chancellor of the Exchequer: and also of a paper, presented May 21st, to the Earl of Liverpool. By Philopatris Vigorniensis. 46p. *8°. London & Worcester,* 1819.

22495 [**ROOKE,** J.] Remarks on the nature and operation of money, with a view to elucidate the effects of the present circulating medium of Great Britain; intended to prove that the national distresses are attributable to our money system. By Cumbriensis. 75p. *8°.* 1819. *The copy that belonged to David Ricardo.*

22496 —— A supplement to the Remarks on the nature and operation of money, &c. By Cumbriensis. By the author. 103p. *8°.* 1819. *The copy that belonged to David Ricardo.*

22497 **ROYAL BANK OF SCOTLAND.** Rules, orders, and bye-laws, for the good government of the Corporation of the Royal Bank of Scotland. 16p. *8°. Edinburgh,* 1819.

22498 **RUDING,** R. Annals of the coinage of Britain and its dependencies, from the earliest period of authentick history...The second edition, corrected, enlarged and continued to the close of...1818. 6 vols. *8°. & 4°.* 1819. *See also* 1840.

22499 **SINCLAIR,** SIR JOHN, *Bart.* Observations respectfully submitted to the Select and Secret Committees of both Houses of Parliament, appointed to consider the propriety of resuming cash-payments, or continuing the Bank restriction. 31p. *8°.* 1819.

22500 **SMITH,** THOMAS, *accountant, of London.* An address to the Right Hon. Robert Peel, late chairman to the Committee on the currency. 39p. *8°.* 1819.

22501 [——?] A few remarks on the Reports of the Committees on the currency: addressed to the members of both Houses of Parliament. 16p. *8°.* 1819.

22502 [——?] Further remarks on the Reports of the

Committees on the currency. By the author of "A few remarks," &c.&c. 15p. *8°.* 1819.

22503 **SOCIETY FOR THE ENCOURAGEMENT OF ARTS, MANUFACTURES AND COMMERCE.** Report of the committee of the Society ...relative to the mode of preventing the forgery of bank notes. Printed by order of the Society. 72p. *8°.* 1819.

22504 **SOLON,** *pseud.* Aphorisms on currency, as connected with the distress of the country. 15p. *8°. Glasgow, Paisley, &c.,* 1819.

22505 National **SWINDLING.** The Bank-Restriction Catechism; or, the Threadneedle-Street jugglers exposed; wherein it is clearly proved, that the causes of the high price of bread and the low price of labour...have all been occasioned by the unconstitutional power with which the Governor and Company of the Bank of England are invested by...the Bank Restriction Act...By the author of the Rotten-rag manuafctory [*sic*]...Third edition. 8p. *8°.* [1819]

22506 Copious and correct **TABLES** for ascertaining the increase or decrease of gold and silver in bars: according to the Assay Master's report. 41p. *8°. Walworth,* 1819.

22507 **TABLES** and facts relative to the coal duties. [With a list of the members of the Committee for Equalizing the Duty on Coals, signed by the secretary, James McAdam.] 10p. *8°.* 1819.

22508 The **THEORY** of currency, demonstrating the means of establishing a paper currency, liable to fluctuate only with the value of gold; founded on the principles of Adam Smith. [With 'Appendix. Heads of a proposed Bill for regulating the currency of the United Kingdom'. Printed in parallel columns with the author's observations.] 27p. *8°. Barnstaple,* 1819.

22509 **THORNTON,** THOMAS. The duties of customs and excise on goods, wares, and merchandise imported; and the duties, drawbacks, bounties, and allowances on goods exported to foreign parts, or brought or carried coastwise. Corrected to July 17, 1819. p. 1–74. *8°.* 1819.

22510 **TORRENS,** R. A comparative estimate of the effects which a continuance and a removal of the restriction upon cash payments are respectively calculated to produce: with strictures on Mr. Ricardo's proposal for obtaining a secure and economical currency. 8op. *8°.* 1819.

22511 **TURNER,** SAMUEL, *F.R.S.* A letter addressed to the Right Hon. Robert Peel, &c.&c. late chairman of the Committee of Secrecy appointed to consider of the state of the Bank of England, with reference to the expediency of the resumption of cash payments, at the period fixed by law. 88p. *8°.* 1819.

22512 —— Second edition. 88p. *8°.* 1819.

22513 —— Third edition. 88p. *8°.* 1819.

22514 [**VALERIANI MOLINARI,** L.] Ricerche critiche ed economiche sull' agostaro di Federigo II, sul ducato detto del Senato, sul fiorin d'oro di Firenze, sul ragguaglio fra l'agostaro, e questi e con ciò sulle monete di conto in genere...[In two parts.] 192p. *4°. Bologna,* 1819. *For continuations of this work, see* 1821, 1822.

22515 [**VAN NESS,** W. P.] A letter to the Secretary of the Treasury on the commerce and currency of the United States. By Aristides. 39p. *8°. New-York,* 1819.

22516 **VILLÈLE,** J. B. G. M. S. J. DE, *Comte.* Chambre des Députés. Opinion de M. de Villèle, Député de la

Haute-Garonne, sur le projet de loi relatif au changement de l'année financière. (Suite de la Séance publique du 13 février 1819.) 23p. *8°.* [*Paris,* 1819]

22517 [WEYLAND, J. ?] A remonstrance addressed to the author of two letters to the Right Honourable Robert Peel, on the effects of a variable standard of value, and on the condition of the poor. By an English Gentleman. 70p. *8°.* 1819. *From Weyland's own library, where it was formerly bound up with a number of other pamphlets by him.*

22518 WHEATLEY, J. A report on the Reports of the Bank Committees. 51p. *8°.* *Shrewsbury & London,* 1819.

22519 WILLIAMS, CHARLES W. Exposure of the fallacies contained in the Letter to the Right Hon. Robert Peel. With remarks on the late auspicious change in the sentiments of the Earl of Lauderdale on paper currency. 68p. *8°.* 1819.

22520 Z., Y. Two supplementary letters (being the 5th and 6th of a series) on the circulating medium of the British Isles; addressed to the editor of the Royal Cornwall Gazette, and originally published in the numbers of that paper for 13th, 20th and 27th Feb. 1819; with a summary of the contents of each of the six letters prefixed … 40p. *8°.* *Truro, London, &c.,* [1819]

22521 [ZORNLIN, F. F.] Statement of a few facts, respecting the pars of exchange and trade in bullion. 38p. *8°.* 1819.

TRANSPORT

22522 BARTLETT, J. M. On propelling vessels by means of windmill sails…Original. [From *The Pamphleteer,* vol. XIV, no. 27.] 7p. *8°.* 1819.

22523 CORDIER, J. L. E., *ed.* Histoire de la navigation intérieure, et particulièrement de celle d'Angleterre, jusqu'en 1803, traduite de l'ouvrage anglais de Philipps… Tome premier. [With 'Histoire de la navigation intérieure, et particulièrement de celle des États-Unis d'Amérique, traduit de l'ouvrage de M. A. Gallatin…Tome second'.] 2 vols. *8°.* *Paris,* 1819–20. *For editions of Phillips,* A general history of inland navigation, *see* 1792.

22524 DUPIN, F. P. C., *Baron.* Two excursions to the ports of England, Scotland, and Ireland, in 1816, 1817, and 1818; with a description of the breakwater at Plymouth, and of the Caledonian Canal. Translated from the French…with notes, critical and explanatory, by the translator. 108p. *8°.* 1819.

22525 DUTENS, J. M. Mémoires sur les travaux publics de l'Angleterre, suivis d'un mémoire sur l'esprit d'association…et de quinze planches avec une carte générale de la navigation intérieure… 374p. *4°.* *Paris,* 1819. *The copy that belonged to the Société de Lecture de Genève, with their library stamp on the title-page.*

22526 EGERTON, F. H., *8th Earl of Bridgewater.* The first part of a letter, to the Parisians, and, the French nation, upon inland navigation, containing a defence of the public character of His Grace Francis Egerton, late Duke of Bridgewater…And, including some notices, and, anecdotes, concerning Mr. James Brindley. [With 'The second part of a letter to the Parisians'.] 99p. *8°.* [*Paris,* 1819–20]

22527 ENGLAND. *Laws, etc.* A collection of the several Acts relating to the canals of the late…Duke of Bridgewater. 404p. *8°.* [1819 ?]

22528 —— Parliament. *House of Commons.* An abstract of proceedings and evidence, relative to London Bridge; taken from the reports of a Select Committee of the House of Commons, made in…1799, 1800, and 1801; and from the journals of the Court of Common Council, and the Committee for letting the Bridge House estate. 140p. *fol.* 1819.

22529 —— —— —— Report from the Select Committee on the highways of the Kingdom: together with the minutes of evidence taken before them. 78p. *8°.* *Edinburgh,* 1819.

22530 ÉTAT général des postes du royaume de France, suivi de la carte géométrique des routes desservies en poste, avec désignation des relais et des distances, pour l'an 1819. 188p. *8°.* *Paris,* 1819. *See also* 1814, 1818, 1823, 1835 (Livre de poste…), 1838.

22531 KENNET AND AVON CANAL NAVIGATION. Observations on the proposed canal, from the Grand Junction Canal, near Cowley, to the Thames, near Maidenhead, with a branch to Windsor. [Issued from the offices of the Kennet and Avon Canal Navigation to the proprietors, with a covering letter, dated 19 October 1819, setting out the terms of a subscription of £130,000 to the proposed canal.] 2p. *fol.* *Marlbro',* [1819]

22532 KNARESBOROUGH RAIL-WAY COMMITTEE. Report of the Knaresborough Railway Committee. [Containing the results of a survey made by Thomas Telford for the purpose of linking Pately Bridge and Knaresborough with the River Ouse by means of a railway.] 36p. *8°.* *Leeds,* [1819]

22533 McADAM, JOHN L. Remarks on the present system of road making…Second edition, carefully revised, with considerable additions and an appendix. 47p. *8°.* *Bristol,* 1819. *For other editions, see* 1816.

22534 The PARISH SURVEYOR'S appointment and guide for the highways. 16p. *8°.* *Newport* [*Mon.*], 1819. *The commission of appointment of Summers Harford as surveyor for the Parish of Bedwelty for 1823–24, a printed document completed in manuscript, occupies p.3.*

22535 PATERSON, JAMES. A practical treatise on the making and upholding of public roads… 93p. *12°.* *Montrose, Dundee, &c.,* 1819.

22536 REID, W., *publisher.* Reid's Leith & London smack directory, containing a correct chart and table of the distances…with relative notices of the…places and objects observable on the journey from Leith to London, and also accounts of the rise and progress of the trade… the different companies now engaged in it… 22p. *8°.* *Leith, London, &c.,* 1819.

22537 SANDILANDS, M. Letter to the Right Honourable the Lord Provost, Magistrates, Town-Council, and inhabitants of Edinburgh, calling their attention to consider of the best means of reducing as low as possible the expence of the carriage of coals, from the Mid-Lothian collieries, to Edinburgh and Leith. 16p. *8°.* *Edinburgh,* 1819.

22538 STEVENSON, R. Report relative to various lines of railway, from the coal-field of Mid-lothian to the City of Edinburgh and Port of Leith; with plans and sections, showing the practicability of extending these lines of railway to Dalkeith, Musselburgh, Haddington and Dunbar, &c. 47p. *4°. Edinburgh, 1819.*

SOCIAL CONDITIONS

22539 A serious **ADDRESS** to the licensed victuallers, both in town and country, in consequence of a declaration made by the Honourable Mr. Bennet, in the Commons House of Parliament, to bring the licensing system before that honourable House. By a licensed victualler. 19p. *8°.* 1819.

22540 ANDREW, WILLIAM. A masterpiece on politics, &c.&c. [A series of letters addressed to G. Beaumont, author of The beggar's complaint; some are signed 'W.A.' and others 'William Andrew'.] 49p. *8°.* [*London*, 1819] *Wanting the title-page.*

22541 ANSWERS to certain objections made to Sir Robert Peel's Bill, for ameliorating the condition of children employed in cotton factories. [With the text of the Bill.] 74p. *8°. Manchester, 1819. The Oastler copy.*

22542 ANTI-WATER-MONOPOLY ASSOCIATION. Extract from the Times newspaper, Sept. 7, 1819. Water monopoly. [With a prospectus of the Association.] [4]p. *8°.* [*London*, 1819] *Bound with seven other pamphlets on London's water supply in a volume (numbered '63' at the head of the contents list) which belonged to Sir Francis Burdett.*

22543 An **APPEAL** to the governors & directors of the poor, of the parish of St. James's, Westminster; respecting the great injury of abolishing, and the benefit of continuing the School of Industry. By a parishioner. 14p. *8°.* 1819.

22544 ASSOCIATION FOR THE SUPPRESSION OF MENDICITY, *Dublin.* Report of the Association...for the year 1818. 41p. *8°. Dublin, 1819. See also 1821, 1825, 1831, 1837.*

22545 BAKER, JAMES. The life of Sir Thomas Bernard, Baronet. 190p. *8°.* 1819.

22546 BAYLEY, P. Observations on the plan of an institution for the promotion of industry and provident economy among the manufacturing and labouring classes, and for the consequent reduction of the number of those who are supported by the poor-rates. 19p. *8°.* 1819.

22547 BELL, ANDREW. The wrongs of children; or, a practical vindication of children from the injustice done them in early nurture and education...in a series of essays on education, to be published periodically... 16p. *8°. London, Edinburgh, &c.*, 1819.

22548 BICHENO, J. E. Observations on the philosophy of criminal jurisprudence, being an investigation of the principles necessary to be kept in view during the revision of the penal code, with remarks on penitentiary prisons. [With an appendix.] 254, xxxip. *8°.* 1819.

22549 BOWDLER, C. On the punishment of death, in the case of forgery; its injustice and impolicy demonstrated...Second edition. 59p. *8°.* 1819.

22550 BOWLES, WILLIAM L. Thoughts on the increase of crimes, the education of the poor and the National Schools; in a letter to Sir James Mackintosh... Second edition. [From *The Pamphleteer*, vol. xv, no. 29.] 33p. *8°.* 1819.

22551 [BUGG, G.] The curates' appeal to the equity and Christian principles of the British Legislature, the bishops, the clergy and the public, on the peculiar hardships of their situation; and on the dangers, resulting... from the arbitrary nature of the laws, as they are now frequently enforced against them. 177p. *8°.* 1819.

22552 BURGESS, H. On the establishment of an extra post, for the purpose of multiplying and improving the means of postage communications between the distant and important parts of the Kingdom. 23p. *8°.* 1819. *The copy that belonged to David Ricardo.*

22553 BURNS, R. Historical dissertations on the law and practice of Great Britain, and particularly of Scotland, with regard to the poor; on the modes of charity; and on the means of promoting the improvement of the people... Second edition, enlarged. 503p. *8°. Edinburgh, 1819.*

22554 [CANNING, R.] An account of the gifts and legacies that have been given and bequeathed to charitable uses, in the town of Ipswich; also abstracts of charters and Acts of Parliament relating to the improvement of the town, together with some account of the various public institutions, charity schools, benevolent societies, &c.&c. 300p. *8°. Ipswich, 1819.*

22555 CHAILEY FRIENDLY SOCIETY. Rules, orders, regulations, of the Chailey Friendly Society...for the purpose of raising a fund by subscription of the members, to be applied to their relief and maintenance in sickness, old age & infirmity... 15p. *8°. Lewes, 1819. The Sheffield copy.*

22556 CHALMERS, T. Considerations on the system of parochial schools in Scotland, and on the advantage of establishing them in large towns. 32p. *8°. Glasgow, 1819.*

22557 CHAMBERLIN, W. H. A plan for the employment of labourers, as adopted in Cropredy, and several other parishes. 10p. *8°. Banbury,* [1819]

22558 [COPLESTON, E., *Bishop of Llandaff.*] A second letter to the Right Hon. Robert Peel, M.P. for the University of Oxford, on the causes of the increase of pauperism and on the poor laws. By one of his constituents. 111p. *8°. Oxford & London, 1819.*

22559 [——] Second edition. 112p. *8°. Oxford & London,* 1819.

22560 DUTHY, J. Letters on the agricultural petition, and on the poor laws, addressed to the members for the county of Hants. 118p. *8°. Winchester, Gosport, &c., 1819.*

22561 ENGLAND. *Laws, etc.* Anno quinquagesimo quarto Georgii III. Regis. [Local & Personal.] Cap. 116. An Act for enlarging the powers of an Act...for granting certain powers and authorities to the Gas Light and Coke Company. ⟨17th June 1814.⟩ p.2161-2164. *fol.* 1819.

22562 —— *Parliament.* [*Endorsed:*] An Act [a Bill] for better supplying the town of Birmingham, in the county of Warwick, with gas. 59 Geo. III. sess. 1819. 29p. *fol.* [1819]

22563 —— —— [*Endorsed:*] A Bill for enabling the Governor and Guardians of the Poor of the City of

Gloucester to light the said city with gas, and to enter into the necessary contracts for that purpose. 59 Geo. III. sess. 1819. 19p. *fol.* [*London*, 1819]

22564 —— —— [*Endorsed:*] A Bill for lighting the city of Carlisle, and the suburbs thereof, with gas. 59 Geo. III. sess. 1819. 32p. *fol.* [*London*, 1819]

22565 —— —— [*Endorsed:*] A Bill for lighting with gas the city of Bristol, and certain parishes adjacent thereto. 59 Geo. III. 1819. 42p. *fol.* [*London*, 1819]

22566 —— —— [*Endorsed:*] A Bill for lighting with gas the town and parish of Cheltenham and precincts thereof, in the county of Gloucester. 59° Geo. III. sess. 1819. 35p. *fol.* [*London*, 1819]

22567 —— —— [*Endorsed:*] A Bill to alter and enlarge the powers of "The Gas Light and Coke Company," and to amend three Acts... relating to the said Company. 59° Geo. III. sess. 1819. 6p. *fol.* [*London*, 1819]

22568 —— —— [*Endorsed:*] A Bill to establish a company [the Newcastle-under-Lyme Gas Light Company] for lighting the borough of Newcastle-under-Lyme with gas. 59 Geo. III. sess. 1819. 44p. *fol.* [*London*, 1819]

22569 —— —— *House of Lords.* Abstract of the evidence given in the Committee of the House of Lords, appointed to enquire into the state and condition of the children employed in cotton factories. 121p. *8°.* 1819.

22570 *——* —— —— —— Copy of Mr. G. Davis's letter to the Surveyor General of the Board of Works. And also of opinion of surveyors, and petition of chimney sweepers in favour of the Chimney Sweeps' Regulation Bill. Committee of the House of Lords on the Bill, Monday 15th March 1819. 3p. *fol. Westminster*, [1819]

22571 **ENQUIRY** into the consequences of the present depreciated value of human labour, &c.&c. In letters to T. F. Buxton, Esq. M.P. author of "An inquiry into our present system of prison discipline." 116p. *8°.* 1819. *The copy presented to M. T. Sadler by J. Cort.*

22572 An **ESSAY** on the practicability of modifying the present system of the poor laws; which... introduces a plan for preventing a recurrence of that distress which is occasioned by our incapability of employing the superabundant population. 54p. *8°. Andover & London*, 1819.

22573 An **EXAMINATION** of the cotton factory question; with remarks upon two pamphlets, privately circulated, in support of Sir Robert Peel's Bill for the regulation of cotton factories. 157p. *8°. London & Manchester*, 1819.

22574 **GURNEY**, JOSEPH J. Notes on a visit made to some of the prisons in Scotland and the north of England, in company with Elizabeth Fry; with some general observations on the subject of prison discipline. 170p. *12°. London & Edinburgh*, 1819.

22575 —— Second edition. 170p. *12°. London & Edinburgh*, 1819.

22576 [**HALL**, ROBERT.] An appeal to the public on the subject of the framework knitters' fund. 18p. *8°. Leicester*, 1819. *See also* 1820.

22577 **HEREFORD**, *County of.* Proceedings at a meeting of the freeholders and householders of the County of Hereford... the 12th of November, 1819, to consider the necessity of an inquiry into the late unhappy events at Manchester: with copies of the... resolutions... Also the amended protest against it... 32p. *8°. Hereford*, 1819.

22578 **HOLROYD**, J. B., *Earl of Sheffield.* Remarks on the Bill of the last Parliament for the amendment of the poor laws; with observations on their impolicy, abuses, and ruinous consequences; together with some suggestions for their melioration, and for the better management of the poor. 106p. *8°.* 1819. *Presentation copy from the author to Patrick Colquhoun.*

22579 The theatrical **HOUSE** that Jack built [i.e. the Theatre Royal, Covent Garden: a satire]. With thirteen cuts. Second edition. 27p. *8°.* 1819.

22580 **HUNT**, H. Final examination and committal of Henry Hunt, Esq. together with Messrs. Johnson, Saxton, Moorhouse, and others... confined in the New Bailey Prison, Manchester, on a pretended charge of high treason. 15p. *8°.* [1819]

22581 —— Letter from Mr. Hunt to Mr. Giles. 4p. *8°.* [1819]

22582 An **INQUIRY** into the law relative to public assemblies of the people. By a friend to the constitution. 48p. *8°.* 1819.

22583 **INSTRUCTIONS** for the relief of the sick poor, in some diseases of frequent occurrence: addressed to a parochial clergyman, residing at a distance from professional aid. By a physician. 43p. *8°. Gloucester*, 1819.

22584 **JAMIESON**, J. The substance of an address, delivered at a meeting of the Edinburgh Society for Promoting the Education of the Poor in Ireland; April 22d, 1819. 15p. *8°. Edinburgh, Glasgow, &c.,* 1819.

22585 **JONES**, SIR WILLIAM. An inquiry into the legal mode of suppressing riots, with a constitutional plan of future defence. 18p. *8°.* [1819]

22586 *****KINDLINGER**, V. N. Geschichte der deutschen Hörigkeit insbesondere der sogenannten Leibeigenschaft... Mit Urkunden. 734p. *8°. Berlin*, 1819. *The copy that belonged to George Grote.*

22587 The oppressed **LABOURERS**, the means for their relief, as well as for the reduction of their number, and of the poor-rates, presented to public notice. Dedicated in the first instance to the agricultural societies of Great Britain. 40p. *8°.* 1819.

22588 [**LAVIGNE**, L.] Mémoires sur l'état des Israélites, dédiés et présentés à leurs Majestés Impériales et Royales, réunies au Congrès d'Aix-la-Chapelle. 78p. *8°. Paris*, 1819.

22589 **MACPHAIL**, J. Observations, exhibiting the propriety and advantageous tendency of the poor laws, their policy vindicated... the state of England compared with that of Scotland, Ireland, and France, where no poor rate is levied, and means proposed for improving the condition of the poor and lowering the poor rate. 58p. *8°.* 1819.

22590 The **MANCHESTER TRAGEDY.** The suppressed narrative of the Courier reporter, who, through the... manner in which he described the tragical events of the 16th of August, lost the confidence of his employers. 12p. *8°.* [1819]

22591 **MARRIOTT**, H. Essay on the Madras system of education; its powers... and its utility as an instrument to form the principles and habits of youth in the higher orders of society... 64p. *8°.* 1819.

22592 **MARTIN DU TYRAC**, L. M. A., *Comte de Marcellus.* Opinion de M. le Comte de Marcellus, Député de la Gironde, sur l'article du Budjet de 1819 qui concerne l'instruction publique. 8p. *8⁰*. [*Paris*, 1819]

22593 MERCERON, J. Merceron's trials for fraud and corruption. The trials at large of Joseph Merceron Esq. for fraud, as treasurer of the poor rate funds of St. Matthew, Bethnal Green, and also for corrupt conduct as a magistrate, in re-licensing disorderly public houses, his property...To which are added the proceedings...in the case of the King v. the Rev. W. F. Platt, and others, for conspiring with...Joseph Merceron, in defrauding the poor rate funds of...£925 1s. 3d.... 187, 156, 9p. *8⁰*. 1819.

22594 MONTE-PIO LITTERARIO. Compromisso de hun Monte-pio que em seu commnun beneficio, e de suas mulheres, filhos pais e irmans instituem os particulares liçenciadors na corte...Seu primeiro author J. A. de Lamos Seixas e Castel-Branco. Segunda edição... illustrada com notas á margem das resoluções da meza, e mais deliberações definitivas. 32p. *fol. Lisboa*, 1819. *With other pieces, and accounts of the years 1817–19.*

22595 An impartial **NARRATIVE** of the late melancholy occurrences in Manchester. 58p. *8⁰*. *Liverpool & London*, 1819.

For the **NEWS** [22 August 1819, largely concerned with accounts of Peterloo], *see* vol. III, *Periodicals list.*

22596 NICOLL, S. W. A view of the principles on which the well-being of the laboring class depends, together with observations on the direction of charity. 44p. *8⁰*. *York*, 1819.

22597 A few **OBSERVATIONS** on All Souls' College, Oxford, relative to the abuse of charities. 32p. *8⁰*. 1819.

22598 OBSERVATIONS, &c. as to the ages of persons employed in the cotton mills, in Manchester. With extracts of evidence against Sir Robert Peel's Bill taken before the Lord's [*sic*] Committees. 72p. *8⁰*. *Manchester*, 1819. *The Oastler copy.*

22599 OVINGTON, J. The sin & danger of oppressing the poor, selected from the Scriptures, for the benefit of all classes of society. 68p. *8⁰*. *London & Clapham*, [1819?]

22600 OWEN, ROBERT. An address to the master manufacturers of Great Britain, on the present existing evils in the manufacturing system. 8p. *8⁰*. *Bolton*, 1819.

22601 PHILADELPHIA SOCIETY FOR THE ESTABLISHMENT AND SUPPORT OF CHARITY SCHOOLS. Annual report of the Board of Managers of the Philadelphia Society...with the annual report of the treasurer... 15p. *8⁰*. *Philadelphia*, 1819.

22602 PHILIPS, F. An exposure of the calumnies circulated by the enemies of social order, and reiterated by their abettors, against the magistrates and the yeomanry cavalry of Manchester and Salford. xxvi, 59, xxixp. *8⁰*. *London & Manchester*, 1819.

22603 —— The second edition. xxvi, 64, xxixp. *8⁰*. *London & Manchester*, 1819. *Presentation copy, with inscription, from the author to the Rev. D. Smith.*

22604 PHILLPOTTS, H., *Bishop of Exeter.* A letter to the Right Honourable William Sturges Bourne, M.P. on a Bill introduced by him into Parliament "to amend the laws respecting the settlement of the poor"...Second edition. 24p. *8⁰*. *Durham & London*, 1819.

22605 REASONS in favour of Sir Robert Peel's Bill, for ameliorating the condition of children employed in cotton factories; comprehending a summary view of the evidence in support of the Bill, taken before the Lords' Committees in the present session of Parliament. 27p. *4⁰*. 1819.

22606 A full **REPORT** of the speeches and proceedings of the Westminster general meeting, held...September 2, 1819, to take into consideration the propriety of addressing the Prince Regent and the nation, on the subject of the late barbarous transactions at Manchester...By an eminent short-hand writer. 19p. *8⁰*. 1819.

22607 ROBERTS, S. A defence of the poor laws, with a plan for the suppression of mendicity, and for the establishment of universal parochial benefit societies. 52p. *8⁰*. *Sheffield & London*, 1819. *The Oastler copy.*

22608 ROGAN, F. Observations on the condition of the middle and lower classes in the North of Ireland, as it tends to promote the diffusion of contagious fever; with the history...of the late epidemic disorder...and a detail of the measures adopted to arrest its progress. 159p. *8⁰*. 1819.

22609 ROSCOE, W. Observations on penal jurisprudence, and the reformation of criminals. With an appendix; containing the latest reports of the state-prisons or penitentiaries of Philadelphia, New-York and Massachusetts; and other documents. 179, 144p. *8⁰*. 1819.

22610 ROYAL DUBLIN SOCIETY. Report of a committee of the Dublin Society respecting the Merino Factory, Co. Kilkenny; presented to the Society on the 9th December, 1819. [With 'Appendix to the report... containing the evidence adduced before the Committee'.] 36p. *8⁰*. *Dublin*, 1819.

22611 ROYAL LANCASTERIAN FREE SCHOOL, *Manchester.* Report of the committee of the Royal Lancasterian Free School, from January 31st, 1815, to January 25th, 1819. [With a list of subscribers.] 22p. *4⁰*. *Manchester*, 1819.

22612 SLANEY, R. A. An essay on the employment of the poor. 78p. *12⁰*. 1819. *See also* 1822.

22613 SMITH, HENRY L. Observations on the prevailing practice of supplying medical assistance to the poor, commonly called the farming of parishes; with suggestions for the establishment of parochial medicine chests; or, infirmaries in agricultural districts. 32p. *8⁰*. 1819.

22614 SOCIÉTÉ PHILANTHROPIQUE. Annuaire de la Société Philanthropique, contenant l'indication des meilleurs moyens qui existent à Paris, de soulager l'humanité souffrante et d'exercer utilement la bienfaisance. 180p. *8⁰*. [*Paris*,] 1819.

22615 SOCIETY FOR BETTERING THE CONDITION OF THE POOR, *Oswestry.* The seventh report of the Society... p.127–152. *8⁰*. *Oswestry*, 1819. *Paginated in sequence with the sixth report, 1818, (q.v.). See also* 1817.

22616 SOCIETY FOR THE PREVENTION OF PAUPERISM IN NEW-YORK. Documents relative to savings banks, intemperance, and lotteries. Published by order of the Society... 26p. *8⁰*. [*New-York*,] 1819.

22617 —— Report to the managers of the Society...by their committee on idleness and sources of employment.

Presented December 1, 1819... 13p. *8°. New-York, 1819.*
See also 1820.

22618 SOCIETY FOR THE SUPPRESSION OF MENDICITY, *London.* Society for the Suppression of Mendicity, established in London, March 25th, 1818: supported by voluntary contributions. [Signed: W. H. Bodkin, hon. sec., and dated, 6th Sept. 1819.] *s.sh.fol. n.p.* [1819] [*Br.* 489]

22619 —— The first report of the Society established in London for the Suppression of Mendicity. 61p. *8°.* 1819. *See also* 1820, 1822, 1825.

22620 STATEMENT of the bankrupt laws: including the substance of the last Act (49 Geo. III.) to alter and amend the laws relating to bankrupts, commonly called "Sir Samuel Romilly's Act." 44p. *8°.* [1819?] *The date on the front printed paper wrapper is '1810' but the advertisements on the back wrapper include books published in 1814–1816. It appears that the printed date may have been altered by hand.*

22621 STEPHENS, JOHN (1772–1841). The mutual relations, claims, and duties of the rich and the poor. A sermon adapted to the state of the times: preached on behalf of the Strangers' Friend Society, in...Manchester, on...September 12th, 1819... 42p. *8°. Manchester & London,* [1819]

22622 [**TAUNTON,** SIR WILLIAM E.] Hints towards an attempt to reduce the poor rate; or, at least, to prevent its further increase. 16p. *8°. Oxford & London,* 1819.

22623 [**TAYLOR,** JOHN E.?] Peterloo massacre, containing a faithful narrative of the events which preceded, accompanied and followed the fatal sixteenth of August 1819...including the proceedings which took place at the inquest at Oldham on the body of John Lees ...To which is added, an accurate alphabetical list of the names...of those who were killed, wounded and maimed ...Edited by an observer. 216p. *8°. Manchester & London,* 1819. *Published in 14 parts. Part 1 is of the second edition, Attributed to Taylor by F. A. Bruton in The story of Peterloo, 1919. Attributed to J. Harmer in a manuscript note on the title-page of the second edition, below.*

22624 [**——**] Second edition. 216p. *8°. Manchester & London,* 1819.

22625 A VIEW of the alterations that have occurred in the condition of industrious agricultural labourers; with a remedy derived from facts. By a member of the Society for Bettering the Condition of the Poor. 23p. *12°.* 1819.

22626 A VINDICATION of the enquiry into charitable abuses with an exposure of the misrepresentations contained in the Quarterly Review. 129p. *8°.* 1819.

22627 WEALE, JAMES. Water monopoly. Letters on the recent conduct of the Metropolitan Water Companies; (first printed in "The New Times" journal,) exposing the illegality of their proceedings...with additional letters and a preface... 50p. *8°.* 1819. *See note to no.* 22542.

22628 —— Water monopoly. Speech of James Weale, Esq. addressed to the Committee of Lords, to whom was referred the Bill intituled "An Act to regulate the supply of water by the Company of Proprietors of the West Middlesex Water Works and the Grand Junction Water Works Company..."... 32p. *8°.* 1819. *See note to no.* 22542.

22629 WHITWELL, C. V. Education. An address to mothers in the British Empire; in which a scheme of simplicity and economy is illustrated, and the establishment of a free school for the daughters of professional men who have lost their property, recommended... 71p. *8°.* 1819. *The copy that belonged to David Ricardo.*

22630 WILLIAMS, JAMES (*fl.* 1819). Thoughts on the prevalence of crime and misery: in a letter to Lord Viscount Sidmouth. 20p. *8°.* 1819.

SLAVERY

22631 DUMONT, P. J. Narrative of thirty-four years slavery and travels in Africa, by P. J. Dumont. Collected from the account delivered by himself, by J. S. Quesné. 42p. *8°.* 1819. *See also* 1820.

22632 JAMAICA. *Laws, etc.* An abstract of the laws of Jamaica relating to slaves. (From 33 Charles II. to 59 Geo. III. inclusive.) With the slave law at length. Also, an appendix, containing an abstract of the Acts of Parliament relating to the abolition of the slave trade. By John Lunan. 192p. *4°. Jamaica,* 1819. *Presentation copy, with accompanying letter, from the author to Sir Home Popham. For the letter, see vol. III, A.L. 253.*

22633 THORPE, R. A commentary on the treaties entered into between His Britannic Majesty, and His Most Faithful Majesty...the 28th of July, 1817; between His Britannic Majesty, and His Catholic Majesty...the 23rd of September, 1817; and between His Britannic Majesty, and His Majesty the King of the Netherlands...the 4th of May, 1818, for the purpose of preventing their subjects from engaging in any illicit traffic in slaves. 60p. *8°.* 1819. *The copy that belonged to Stephen Lushington.*

22634 [**WALSH,** ROBERT (1784–1859)?] Free remarks on the spirit of the federal constitution...and the obligations of the Union, respecting the exclusion of slavery from the territories and New States...By a Philadelphian. 118p. *8°. Philadelphia,* 1819. *Attributed in manuscript on the title-page to 'Walsh'.*

POLITICS

22635 ANTI-JUNIPER, *pseud.* Second edition. Anti-Juniper to his brother radicals. [A satire on radical reform.] 8p. *8°. Birmingham,* [1819]

22636 —— Second letter of Anti-Juniper to his brother radicals. 8p. *8°. Birmingham,* [1819]

22637 ATKINSON, WILLIAM (1758–1846). Free remarks, upon the conduct of the Whigs, and radical reformers, in Yorkshire: with some slight allusions to the Court party. 15p. *8°. Bradford,* 1819.

22638 BENTHAM, J. Bentham's radical reform Bill, with extracts from the reasons. 17, 85p. *8°.* 1819.

22639 BERGUER, L. T. A warning letter to His Royal Highness the Prince Regent, intended principally as a call upon the middle ranks, at this important crisis. 58p. *8°.* 1819.

22640 —— The fourth edition. 6op. *8°.* 1819.

22641 BIRMINGHAM. A correct report of the proceedings of a meeting, held at Newhall Hill, Birmingham, on Monday, July 12, 1819, for the purpose of obtaining the representation of the people of Birmingham, in Parliament. 8p. *4°. Birmingham,* [1819]

22642 BIRMINGHAM ASSOCIATION FOR THE REFUTATION AND SUPPRESSION OF BLASPHEMY AND SEDITION. An address to reformers. Published by the Birmingham Association ...[Signed: A Briton.] 8p. *8°. Birmingham,* [1819 ?]

22643 —— Politics for the People; by W. Cobbett. Published by the Birmingham Association...[A selection from Cobbett's writings designed to discredit him and the radical reform movement.] 8p. *8°. Birmingham,* [1819 ?]

22644 [BOWLES, WILLIAM L.] The sentiments of a true patriot and good man, (lately deceased) on the mischievous tendency of Tom Paine's "Rights of man", in the form of a protest against that publication, addressed to the members of a book society. 42p. *12°. Canterbury,* 1819.

22645 BRAYSHAW, J. Proceedings of the meeting held at Yeadon, on...28th June, 1819, containing the speech delivered on the occasion, the resolutions adopted ...an appeal to the nation, and a defence of the reformers ...To which is added, advice to the labouring classes... 23p. *8°. Dewsbury, Leeds, &c.,* [1819]

22646 BULL, JOHN, *pseud.* Third edition. An address from John Bull to his fellow-countrymen. In prose and verse. 8p. *8°. Birmingham,* [1819]

For the **CAP OF LIBERTY,** *see vol.* III, *Periodicals list.*

22647 CARLILE, R. The following publications may be had of R. Carlile, 183, Fleet Street...[With 'Address to the public [on Carlile's edition of Paine's Works]'.] 4p. *8°. n.p.* [*R. Carlile,* 1819]

22648 —— Vice versus reason. A copy of the bill of indictment, found at the Old Bailey Sessions, January 16, 1819, against Richard Carlile, for publishing Paine's Age of reason. 13p. *8°. R. Carlile,* 1819.

22649 CARTWRIGHT, J. Address to the electors of Westminster, by Major Cartwright. 19p. *8°.* [*London,* 1819]

22650 —— New preamble and explanatory table of contents, of a bill of rights and liberties; or, an act for a constitutional reform of Parliament. 16p. *8°.* 1819.

22651 CONCILIATOR, *pseud.* An appeal to the artisans of Birmingham. 8p. *8°.* [*Birmingham,* 1819]

22652 CROKER, J. W. Substance of the speech of John Wilson Croker, Esq. in the House of Commons, on Monday, 4th May, 1819; on the Roman Catholic question. 86p. *8°.* 1819.

22653 DECLARATION of the merchants, bankers, traders, and others of London. October, 1819. [A protest against the misleading policies of the radicals. With a list of signatories.] 136p. *8°.* 1819.

22654 A DIALOGUE on the approaching trial of Mr. Carlile, for publishing The age of reason. With the trial anticipated. Principal speakers: Cantwell, a member of the Society for the Suppressing of Vice, Officio, attorney general to the Holy League...From Wooler's British Gazette, Sunday, April 18, 1819. 16p. *8°.* 1819.

22655 DOLBY, T. A letter to the friends of liberty, on the correspondence between Mr. Cobbett, Mr. Tipper and Sir Francis Burdett... 8p. *8°.* [*London,* 1819]

22656 The **DORCHESTER** guide, or, a house that Jack built. [An anti-radical satire.] With thirteen cuts. Fourth edition. 35p. *8°.* [1819]

22657 The triumphal **ENTRY** of Henry Hunt, Esq. into London, on...September 13, 1819... 16p. *8°.* [1819]

For the **GHOST OF JUNIUS,** *see vol.* III, *Periodicals list.*

22658 GRACCHUS, *pseud.* A letter to Lord Sidmouth, on the recent disturbances at Manchester. 22p. *8°.* 1819.

22659 GROSVENOR, ROBERT, *1st Marquis of Westminster.* The dignified and truly patriotic speech of Lord Grosvenor [on reform]...delivered in the House of Peers, December 17, 1819... 8p. *8°.* [*London,* 1819]

22660 HINTS addressed to radical reformers. 27p. *8°. Glasgow, Edinburgh, &c.,* 1819.

22661 [HOBHOUSE, J. C., *Baron Broughton.*] A trifling mistake in Thomas Lord Erskine's recent Preface, shortly noticed and respectfully corrected, in a letter to His Lordship, by the author of the "Defence of the people". 56p. *8°.* 1819.

22662 [HONE, W.] The political house that Jack built. [With 'The clerical magistrate'.] With thirteen cuts [by G. Cruikshank]. Fourth edition. [24]p. *8°.* 1819.

22663 [——] Fifth edition. [24]p. *8°.* 1819.

22664 [——] Fifteenth edition. [24]p. *8°.* 1819. *See also* 1820, 1821.

22665 The financial **HOUSE** that Jack built. [A political satire.] Second edition, with additions. 1op. *8°.* 1819.

22666 The real or constitutional **HOUSE** that Jack built. [A political satire.] With twelve cuts. Ninth edition. [24]p. *8°.* 1819. *See also* 1820.

22667 HUNT, H. The green bag plot; being a detailed account of some of the transactions...which ultimately led to the suspension of the Habeas Corpus Act; including an extract from the green bag, purporting to be a memorandum relative to the origin of the conspiracy at Pentridge, in Derbyshire; which ended in a special commission, and the execution of Brandreth, Turner and Ludlam for high-treason... 16p. *8°.* [1819]

22668 —— Letter from Mr. Hunt to Mr. West. [A description of Hunt's trial at Manchester for conspiracy and sedition in connection with his part at the meeting in St. Peter's Fields.] 3p. *8°.* [1819]

22669 [JAMES, J. T. ?] What is a revolution? Original. [From *The Pamphleteer,* vol. XIV, no. 27.] 19p. *8°.* 1819.

22670 JONES, JOHN G. The speech of John Gale Jones, delivered at the British Forum, held at the Crown and Anchor Tavern...on the following question: "Ought the conduct of Mr. Carlile, the bookseller, in continuing to publish Paine's Age of reason...to be censured...or approved..." 13p. *8°. R. Carlile,* 1819.

22671 —— Substance of the speeches of John Gale Jones, delivered at the British Forum, March 11, 18 & 22, 1819, on the following question: "Ought the prosecution instituted against Mr. Carlile and others for the publication of Paine's Age of reason, to be approved...or censured..." 10p. *8°. R. Carlile*, 1819.

22672 [KENNEY, A. H.] A letter to Earl Fitzwilliam, demonstrating the real tendency of the proceedings of the late York meeting for taking into consideration the transactions at Manchester, on the 16th of August last; and of other meetings called for the same object...By a member of no party. 94p. *8°.* 1819.

22673 A LETTER to Edward Bootle Wilbraham, Esq. M.P. on his late charge to the grand jury, at the Quarter Session for the County of Lancaster; held in Liverpool on the 2nd of August, 1819, containing an exposition of the views of the radical reformers, as shewn by their public meetings...By an Englishman. 20p. *8°. Liverpool, Manchester, &c.,* 1819.

22674 A LETTER to his fellow-countrymen, by an Englishman. In prose and verse. 8p. *8°. Birmingham,* [1819]

22675 A LETTER to John Bull, Esq., showing the advantages of a division of land. By a friend. With hints for the guidance of every loyal subject. 8p. *8°. Birmingham,* [1819?]

22676 A LETTER to Sir Robert Gifford, His Majesty's Attorney General. By a radical reformer. [Signed: A radical.] 16p. *8°. Southwark,* 1819.

22677 A LETTER to William Cobbett. [An attack, signed: A Briton, on Cobbett's change of heart over Thomas Paine.] 8p. *8°.* [*Birmingham,* 1819?]

22678 LEWES. To the chief officers of the Borough of Lewes. [A demand for the holding of a town meeting 'to take into consideration the late proceedings at Manchester', followed by a notice convening the meeting for 4 October 1819, signed: W. Stuard, chief officer.] *s.sh.fol. Lewes,* [1819] [*Br.* 492]

22679 A LIST of the jurors nominated to try the two informations by the Attorney-General, and three indictments by the Society for the Suppression of Vice, against Mr. Carlile, for publishing Paine's Age of reason, Sherwin's Register, and Palmer's Principles of nature, in the Deist, a work now publishing in weekly numbers. 8p. *8°. R. Carlile,* 1819.

For the **LONDON ALFRED,** *see* vol. III, *Periodicals list.*

For the **LOYALIST,** *see* vol. III, *Periodicals list.*

22680 [METHUEN, P., *Baron Methuen, and others.*] The new Tory guide. [Lampoons, reprinted from *The Morning Chronicle.*] 216p. *8°.* 1819.

22681 [MONTAGU, B.] Some thoughts upon liberty and the rights of Englishmen. By a lover of order. 75p. *8°.* 1819.

22682 NOTT, J. Third edition. Letters from John Nott to his fellow townsmen. 24p. *8°. Birmingham,* [1819]

22683 PAINE, T. Dissertation on first principles of government. [With 'Speech of Thomas Paine, on the constitution; the translation of which was read by Citizen Lanthera, in the Convention, July 7th, 1795'.] 28p. *8°. R. Carlile,* 1819. *For other editions, see* 1795.

22684 PHILLIPS, CHARLES. Missionary Society. Phillips's speech. The speech, of C. Phillips, Esq. as delivered at the fourth anniversary of the Glocestershire Missionary Society. 4p. *8°.* 1819.

22685 —— Phillips's speeches. Speech delivered at the recent meeting of the Gloucestershire Missionary Society, held at Cheltenham. [With 'Mr. Phillips's speech delivered at the meeting of the British and Foreign Auxiliary Bible Society, held at the Mansion House...November 4, 1819'.] 8p. *8°. Birmingham,* [1819]

22686 PHILLPOTTS, H., *Bishop of Exeter.* A letter to the freeholders of the County of Durham on the proceedings of the County meeting [which censured the conduct of magistrates and military at St. Peter's Fields] ...21st October instant; and particularly on the speech of John George Lambton, Esq., M.P. 35p. *8°. Durham,* 1819.

22687 PLUNKET, W. C., *Baron Plunket.* The substance of the speech of the Right Honourable W. C. Plunket, in the House of Commons on...the 23rd of November, 1819. [On the suppression of the meeting in St. Peter's Fields.] 24p. *8°. Manchester & London,* 1819.

22688 —— Second edition. 24p. *8°. Manchester & London,* 1819.

22689 PROCEEDINGS at a meeting of Herefordshire freeholders, held...8th October, 1819, for the purpose of presenting a silver cup to Colonel Foley, of Newport...with a detail of the speeches delivered on the occasion. 32p. *8°. Hereford,* 1819.

22690 R., A. Reflections suggested by the propensity at present manifested by the disaffected to destroy the religion and laws of the British nation; in a letter from a gentleman at Bath to his friend in Ireland. 32p. *8°. Bath & London,* 1819.

22691 REFORM of Parliament. Westminster election, 1819. At a general...meeting of the electors of Westminster...on...the 9th...of February, 1819, to receive the report of the Committee appointed on the 17th day of November last...the following Report was ordered to be printed... 14p. *8°.* [1819] *The copy that belonged to David Ricardo.*

22692 REMARKS upon a Bill for altering the right of voting for members of Parliament, for the borough of Barnstaple. 24p. *8°.* 1819.

22693 A REPORT of the meeting held in Smithfield, on Wednesday, July 21, to consider of the best means of recovering our lost rights. W. Hunt, Esq. in the chair. 16p. *8°.* [*London,* 1819]

22694 [SCOTT, SIR WALTER, *Bart.*] The visionary, Nos. I, II, III [being political satires first published in the *Edinburgh Weekly Journal*, each signed Somnambulus]. 55p. *12°. Edinburgh & London,* 1819.

22695 SHREWD, JOE, *die sinker, pseud.* A few more words to my neighbours...together with a new ditty, called The Coventry garland; or, the orator's overthrow. 8p. *8°.* [*Birmingham,* 1819]

22696 [TEMPLE, H. J., *Viscount Palmerston, and others.*] The new Whig guide. [The Advertisement signed: E.] 240p. *8°.* 1819.

SOCIALISM

22697 CHRISTIANUS, *pseud.* Mr. Owen's proposed villages for the poor shown to be highly favourable to Christianity: in a letter to William Wilberforce Esq. M.P. 20p. *8°.* 1819.

22698 *COMMITTEE APPOINTED TO INVESTIGATE THE PLAN OF ROBERT OWEN, ESQ. OF NEW LANARK. [*Endorsed:*] Farther address of the Committee on Mr. Owen's plan for providing employment for the poor. 1. December, 1819. [Signed: James Millar, hon. sec.] 2p. *4°. n.p.* [1819] *Caption title: Mr. Owen's plan. FWA copy that belonged to William Pare, with his signature and a manuscript note, 'duplicate of this paper sent to R.O. 24 June 1857'.*

22699 MACNAB, H. G. The new views of Mr. Owen of Lanark impartially examined, as rational means of ultimately promoting the...improvement, and happiness of the labouring classes of society, and of the poor...Also observations on the New Lanark School, and on the systems of education of Mr. Owen, of the Rev. Dr. Bell... 234p. *8°.* 1819. *See also 1821.*

22700 [MORGAN, JOHN M.] Remarks on the practicability of Mr. Robert Owen's plan to improve the condition of the lower classes. [The dedication signed: Philanthropos.] 87p. *8°.* 1819. **Another, the FWA copy, belonged to William Pare.*

22701 OBSERVATIONS on the critique contained in the Edinburgh Review for October 1819, of Mr. Owen's plans, for relieving the national distress. By a lover of truth. 8p. *8°. Edinburgh,* 1819.

22702 OWEN, ROBERT. An address delivered to the inhabitants of New Lanark...Fourth edition. 48p. *8°. London, Edinburgh, &c.,* 1819. *With the signature 'Rowland Hill' on the title-page. For other editions, see 1816.*

22703 Mr. **OWEN'S** proposed arrangements for the distressed working classes, shown to be consistent with sound principles of political economy: in three letters addressed to David Ricardo... 102p. *8°.* 1819.

MISCELLANEOUS

22704 [ATKINSON, WILLIAM (1758-1846).] A peep at deans, chapters, and very wise archdeacons; in a letter to the Right Honourable the Lord Mayor and Corporation of the...City of York. By the Old Inquirer. 31p. *8°. London & Bradford,* 1819.

22705 BILLS of costs, and allowances, in the Court of King's Bench, according to the present scale of allowance; with a precedent for affidavits of increase. Fourth edition; corrected to Easter Term, 59 Geo. III. 1819. 55p. *8°.* 1819.

22706 CHANNING, E. T. Inaugural discourse, delivered in the chapel of the University of Cambridge, December 8, 1819. 31p. *8°. Cambridge,* 1819.

22707 COBBETT, W. A grammar of the English language, in a series of letters. Intended for the use of schools and of young persons in general; but more especially for the use of soldiers, sailors, apprentices and plough-boys. 186p. *12°.* 1819. *See also 1829, 1836, 1850.*

22708 COMBE, T. An account of some Anglo-Saxon pennies found at Dorking, in Surrey...Read 12th March, 1818. [From *The Archaeologia*, vol. 19.] p.109–119. *4°.* [*London*, 1819]

22709 FLETCHER, ARCHIBALD. A memoir concerning the origin and progress of the reform proposed in the internal government of the Royal Burghs of Scotland; which was first brought under public discussion in 1782. To which is added, the Bill for reforming the internal government of the Burghs...To which are farther added, the substance of the reports of specific grievances... 261, 138p. *8°. Edinburgh,* 1819.

22710 LONDON. *Court of Common Council.* Right of appeal. Debate in the Court of Common Council on a motion respecting the right of appeal. ⟨From the Champion.⟩...Feb. 25, 1819. 8p. *8°. n.p.* [1819] *The copy that belonged to David Ricardo.*

22711 NICHOLS, JOHN B. A brief account of the Guildhall of the City of London. 64p. *8°.* 1819.

22712 OBSERVATIONS on the automaton chess player, now exhibited in London, at 4, Spring Gardens. By an Oxford graduate. 32p. *8°.* 1819. *The copy that belonged to David Ricardo.*

22713 PAINE, T. The age of reason, part the first, being an investigation of true and fabulous theology. [With 'Part the second', 'Part the third; being an examination, of passages in the New Testament...called prophecies...To which is prefixed, an essay on dreams' and 'Part the fourth, containing A letter to the Hon. T. Erskine...A discourse delivered to the Society of Theophilanthropists...Letter to Camille Jordan. An essay on ...Free-masonry...'.] 4 vols. *8°. R. Carlile,* 1819. *See also 1826, 1831.*

22714 PHILLIPS, CHARLES. Fitzgerald versus Kerr. The genuine speech, at length, of C. Phillips, in the case of Charles Lionel Fitzgerald, Esq. plaintiff, and Charles Kerr, defendant, tried...on the 22nd day of March, 1819, for adultery. 12p. *8°.* 1819.

22715 —— The speech of Charles Phillips, Esq....to General d'Evereux, and the regiments under his command, previous to their embarkation at Dublin, to join the Spanish patriots in South America. 7p. *8°.* [1819]

22716 —— [Another edition.] Fairburn's edition of the speech of Chas. Phillips, Esq.... 7p. *8°.* [1819]

22717 [POLIDORI, G.] The vampyre; a tale. [Attributed in the introduction to Lord Byron. With 'Extract of a letter, containing an account of Lord Byron's residence in the Island of Mitylene' by John Mitford.] 84p. *8°.* 1819. *The Agar Ellis copy.*

22718 READ, S. Exposure of certain plagiarisms of J. R. Macculloch, Esq. author of two essays on reduction of the interest of the National Debt, committed in the last published of those essays, the Scotsman newspaper, and Edinburgh Review. 41p. *8°. Edinburgh,* 1819.

22719 RITCHIE, A. Address delivered to the Massachusetts Peace Society, at their third anniversary, December 25, 1818... 16p. *8⁰. Boston,* 1819.

22720 STOCKDALE, W. The present peerage of the United Kingdom, for...1819; with the arms of the peers... 178p., 72 plates. *12⁰.* [1819] *See also* 1830.

22721 THOUGHTS on suicide, in a letter to a friend. 56p. *8⁰.* 1819.

22722 TORRENS, R. A letter to the independent freemen of the City of Rochester, on the petition against Lord Binning's return being declared frivolous and vexatious; and of the right of the eldest son of a Scotch peer to represent an English county, city, or borough, without possessing a landed qualification in England... Second edition. [From *The Pamphleteer,* vol. XIV, no. 27.] 16p. *8⁰.* 1819.

22723 WATSON, RICHARD, *Bishop of Llandaff.* Reply of the Bishop of Llandaff to the second part of The age of reason, in a series of letters addressed to Thomas Paine; being an apology for the Bible. [With a preface by Richard Carlile.] 79p. *8⁰. R. Carlile,* 1819.

22724 WILLIAMS COLLEGE. [An account of a protest meeting, 6th October 1819, to oppose the removal of the College from Williamstown, followed by 'Address to the public' setting out arguments against removal, signed: Daniel Noble, Henry W. Dwight, William C. Jarvis.] 16p. *8⁰. n.p.* [1819]

22725 WINSLOW, M. A sermon delivered at the Old South Church, Boston, June 7, 1819, on the evening previous to the sailing of the Rev. Miron Winslow, Levi Spaulding and Henry Woodward & Dr. John Scudder, as missionaries to Ceylon. 22p. *8⁰. Andover* [*U.S.A.*], 1819.

1820

GENERAL

22726 ACCURSIO DAS NEVES, J. Memoria sobre os meios de melhorar a industria portugueza, considerada nos seus differentes ramos. 116p. *4⁰. Lisboa,* 1820.

22727 AITON, R. An inquiry into the causes of the present distresses; the effects of taxation; and of the Corn Bill; the probable consequences of paying off the National Debt; and of radical reform. 6op. *8⁰. Glasgow, Paisley, &c.,* 1820. *Presentation copy from the author to the Provost of Glasgow, with a manuscript letter of presentation on the verso of the Advertisement, dated: 'Janʸ 1820'.*

22728 An **APPEAL** to the mercantile interest of the United Kingdoms on behalf of Southern Columbia: shewing the importance of...contributing to secure the independence of that country, and the many advantages which await those who enter into commercial relations with the Republic. 45p. *8⁰.* 1820.

22729 ARCHER, W. S. Speech of Mr. Archer, of Virginia, on the tariff bill, delivered in the House of Representatives of the United States, April 26, 1820. 21p. *12⁰. n.p.* [1820]

22730 BARTON, J. An inquiry into the causes of the progressive depreciation of agricultural labour in modern times; with suggestions for it's remedy. 128p. *8⁰.* 1820.

22731 BLAND, T. The present state of Chili, from the report laid before Congress... 83p. *8⁰.* 1820.

22732 BOYES, J. An attempt to suggest some reflections on the present state of society and the country ...Second edition, greatly enlarged; also with remarks on the agricultural association, established at Henderson's Hotel, Westminster... 81p. *8⁰. York, London, &c.,* 1820.

22733 The **BRITISH METRE** and its derivatives; being a sketch of a proposed reformation in the British measures, weights and coins; founded on a system from which, as a universal basis, may emanate...the different systems of all civilised nations. Original. [From *The Pamphleteer,* vol. XVI, no. 31.] 12p. *8⁰.* 1820.

22734 BRODIE, J. Fair prices for ever! Live and let live; or, we are all friends. Extracted from The happiness of states, for the use and benefit of the working classes... 47p. *16⁰.* 1820. *Presentation copy, with inscription, from the author to Lady Castlereagh.*

22735 CAREY, M. The new olive branch: or, an attempt to establish an identity of interest between agriculture, manufactures and commerce; and to prove, that...the manufacturing industry of this nation has been sacrificed to commerce... 248p. *8⁰. Philadelphia,* 1820. *See also* 1821.

22736 On the **CAUSES** of the present discontents, with strictures on the politics of the last number of the Edinburgh Review. [Reprinted from *Blackwood's Magazine.*] 62p. *8⁰. Edinburgh & London,* 1820.

22737 CHALMERS, T. The application of Christianity to the commercial and ordinary affairs of life, in a series of discourses...Fourth edition. 278p. *8⁰. Glasgow, Edinburgh, &c.,* 1820.

22738 CLELAND, J. The rise and progress of the city of Glasgow, comprising an account of its public buildings, charities, and other concerns. 296p. *8⁰. Glasgow,* 1820. *Presentation copy, with inscription from the author to Robert McNair, dated: Glasgow, 21 December 1819.*

22739 [**CLISSOLD,** S.] Considerations on the trade, manufactures, and commerce, of the British Empire, addressed to the merchants of the Metropolis, on their late petition to Parliament. 7op. *8⁰.* 1820.

22740 The **COMMERCIAL DIRECTORY,** of Scotland, Ireland, and the four most northern counties of England [Northumberland, Durham, Cumberland and Westmorland] for 1820–21 & 22, containing a representation of the professional & mercantile inhabitants of the principal towns...Embellished with...maps...[With a leaf of additions to Scotland.] 337, 248p. *8⁰. Manchester: J. Pigot and Co.; London, &c.,* 1820.

22741 —— Second edition...for 1821–22 & 23, containing a representation of the professional & mercantile inhabitants of the principal towns...Embellished with...

maps of Ireland and Scotland. [With a leaf of additions to Scotland and 'Additional towns in Scotland, taken for the second edition'.] 248, 461p. *8°. Manchester: J. Pigot and Co.; London, &c.*, 1820.

22742 CRAWFURD, John (1783–1868). History of the Indian Archipelago. Containing an account of the manners, arts, languages, religions, institutions, and commerce of its inhabitants... 3 vols. *8°. Edinburgh & London*, 1820.

22743 D*** de P***, Paul, [and **REGNAULT-WARIN**, J. B. I. P.]. Dictionnaire de l'ancien régime et des abus féodaux, ou les hommes et les choses des neufs derniers siècles de la monarchie française... 479p. *8°. Paris*, 1820.

22744 DAUXION LAVAYSSE, J. F. A statistical, commercial, and political description of Venezuela, Trinidad, Margarita, and Tobago...from the French... with an introduction [signed: E. B., i.e. E. Blaquiere] and explanatory notes, by the editor. 479p. *8°.* 1820.

22745 A DESCRIPTION of York, containing some account of its antiquities, public buildings, &c., particularly the cathedral. Compiled from the most authentic records...Sixth edition revised... 118p. *12°. York*, 1820. *The Rastrick copy.*

22746 DETAILS of the combination to raise the price of bread; and arguments for allowing the exchange of English labour for foreign corn...By the author of a pamphlet entitled "Relief of the Poor." 137p. *8°.* 1820.

22747 *The EAST-INDIA register and directory, for 1820; corrected to the 25th March 1820; containing... lists of the Company's servants...Together with lists of ...mariners, &c. not in the service of the...Company; and merchant vessels employed in the country trade. Compiled...by A. W. Mason & Geo. Owen... 515p. *12°. London, Dublin, &c.*, [1820]

22748 *—— Corrected to the 26th September 1820... Second edition. 515p. *12°. London, Dublin, &c.*, [1820] *For other editions, see* 1804.

22749 EDWARDS, George. The five practical plans whereby we are able effectually to meet and remedy our present distressed and dangerous situation... 140p. *4°. Barnard-castle*, 1820.

22750 FILANGIERI, G. La scienza della legislazione e gli opuscoli scelti. 5 vols. *8°. Firenze*, 1820–21.

22751 FISHER, John (*fl.* 1820). The political plough that Jack built. A touch upon the times, by a farmer commenced author. With ten cuts. 22p. *8°.* 1820.

22752 GENOVESI, A. Lezioni di commercio o sia di economia civile...Cui vanno uniti opuscoli interessantissimi risguardanti l'economia politica e l'agricoltura. (*Biblioteca Scelta di Opere Italiane Antiche e Moderne*, 89–90.) 2 vols. *16°. Milano*, 1820. [*Higgs* 4572n] *For other editions, see* 1768.

22753 GRAY, S. Remarks on the production of wealth, and the influence, which the various classes of society have, in carrying on that process: in a letter to the Rev. T. R. Malthus, occasioned by his attempt to maintain the division of classes into productive and unproductive... Original. [From *The Pamphleteer*, vol. XVII, no. 34.] 32p. *8°.* 1820.

22754 GRENVILLE, W. W., *Baron Grenville*. Substance of the speech of the Right Hon. Lord Grenville in the House of Lords, November 30, 1819, on the Marquis of Lansdowne's motion, that a Select Committee be appointed to inquire into the state of the country, and more particularly into the distresses...in the manufacturing districts... 62p. *8°.* 1820. *The Agar Ellis copy.*

22755 —— Second edition. 62p. *8°.* 1820.

22756 —— Fourth edition. 62p. *8°.* 1820.

22757 HARFORD, J. S. Some account of the life, death, and principles of Thomas Paine, together with remarks on his writings, and on their intimate connection with the avowed objects of the revolutionists of 1793, and of the radicals in 1819...Third edition, corrected and considerably enlarged. 102p. *8°. Bristol, London, &c.*, 1820.

22758 HERTSLET, L. A complete collection of the treaties and conventions at present subsisting between Great Britain & foreign powers; so far as they relate to commerce and navigation; to the repression and abolition of the slave trade; and to the privileges and interests of the subjects of the high contracting parties...Compiled from authentic documents by Lewis Hertslet... 2 vols. *8°.* 1820. *The copy that belonged to Sir Charles Stuart (1779–1845), later Baron Stuart de Rothesay, with his arms on the binding.*

22759 HIGGINS, G. A letter to the House of Commons on the causes of, and the proper remedies for, the present difficulties and discontents of the British Empire...Second edition. 64p. *8°.* 1820. *For another edition, see* 1819.

22760 HODGSKIN, T. Travels in the north of Germany, describing the present state of the social and political institutions, the agriculture, manufactures, commerce...particularly in the Kingdom of Hannover. 2 vols. *8°. Edinburgh & London*, 1820. *The copy that belonged to Sir Robert Peel.*

22761 JACOB, W. A view of the agriculture, manufactures, statistics, and state of society of Germany, and parts of Holland and France. Taken during a journey through those countries in 1819. 454p. *4°.* 1820.

For **JOHN BULL**, 1820–33, *see vol.* III, *Periodicals list.*

22762 KINGDOM, W. America and the British colonies. An abstract of all the most useful, information relative to the United States of America, and the British colonies of Canada, the Cape of Good Hope, New South Wales, and Van Dieman's Island...Second edition. 359p. *8°.* 1820.

22763 LESTERIENSIS, *pseud.* Thoughts on the state of the nation. 52p. *8°.* 1820.

22764 A LETTER to the Right Honourable the Earl of Liverpool, First Lord of the Treasury, on the present distressed state of agriculture, and its influence on the manufactures, trade, and commerce, of the United Kingdom. 115p. *8°.* 1820.

22765 LIPS, A. Deutschlands Retorsions Princip in seiner siegenden Kraft als unfehlbares Heilmittel deutscher Industrie und deutschen Handels...mit besonderer Prüfung der in der Schrift: über das Retorsions Princip, Leipzig 1820, dagegen erhobenen Zweifel. 88p. *8°. Erlangen*, 1820.

22766 M'LANE, L. Speech of Mr. M'Lane, of Delaware, on the proposed tariff, in the House of Representatives of the United States, on the 26th April, 1820. 32p. *8°. n.p.* [1820]

22767 MALTHUS, T. R. Principles of political economy considered with a view to their practical application. 601p. *8°. 1820.*

22768 —— Principes d'économie politique, considérés sous le rapport de leur application pratique... Traduits de l'anglais par M. F. S. Constancio. 2 vols. *8°. Paris*, 1820. *See also* 1821, 1836.

22769 MANUEL d'économie rurale et domestique; ou recueil de plus de 700 recettes, ou instructions excellentes pour l'économie rurale et domestique, pour la santé et les agrémens de la vie... Traduit de l'anglais, par M***. 450p. *12°. Paris*, 1820.

22770 MOTIVES for an enquiry into the present distresses, addressed to members of both Houses of Parliament; showing, that the artificial high price of corn occasions a much greater pressure than the whole amount of the taxes. 31p. *8°. 1820.*

22771 PINSENT, J. Letters addressed to the Earl of Liverpool... on the distress of the mercantile, shipping, agricultural, and manufacturing interests, with the several remedies proposed... 56p. *8°. 1820.*

22772 The **POST OFFICE** London directory for 1820... By Critchett & Woods. The twenty-first edition. [With 'A new guide to stage-coaches, waggons, carts, vessels, &c. for 1820... The eighteenth edition. By Critchett & Woods'.] 395, lxix, 136p. *12°.* [1820] *See also* 1805 (Post-Office annual directory), 1810, 1813, 1814, 1823, 1825, 1830, 1832, 1834, 1836, 1841.

22773 PRIOR, Sir J. Narrative of a voyage in the Indian seas, in the Nisus frigate, to the Cape of Good Hope, Isles of Bourbon, France, and Scychelles [*sic*]; to Madras; and the isles of Java, St. Paul, and Amsterdam. During the years 1810 and 1811. 112p. *8°.* [1820]

22774 RAYMOND, D. Thoughts on political economy. In two parts. 470p. *8°. Baltimore*, 1820.

22775 REYNIER, J. L. A. De l'économie publique et rurale des Arabes et des Juifs. 543p. *8°. Genève & Paris*, 1820.

22776 ROBINSON, William D. Memoirs of the Mexican Revolution: including a narrative of the expedition of General Xavier Mina. With some observations of the practicability of opening a commerce between the Pacific and Atlantic Oceans, through the Mexican Isthmus in the Province of Oaxaca, and at the Lake of Nicaragua; and of the future importance of such commerce... especially to the United States. 396p. *8°. Philadelphia*, 1820.

22777 ROMILLY, Sir S. The speeches of Sir Samuel Romilly, in the House of Commons... [Edited, and with a memoir of the author, by William Peter.] 2 vols. *8°. 1820.*

22778 RUDGE, E. J. A short account of the history and antiquities of Evesham. 145p. *8°. Evesham*, 1820.

22779 SALISBURY, W. A treatise on the practical means of employing the poor in cultivating and manufacturing articles of British growth... as practised in the Royal School of Economy in London. Also, a plan for forming county asylums for the industrious as communicated to the author, by... Edward Duke of Kent and Stratherne. 46p. *8°. 1820.*

22780 SAY, J. B. Lettres à M. Malthus sur différens sujets d'économie politique, notamment sur les causes de la stagnation générale du commerce. 184p. *8°. Paris & Londres*, 1820. *See also* 1821.

22781 SCORESBY, W. An account of the Arctic regions, with a history and description of the northern whale-fishery... 2 vols. *8°. Edinburgh & London*, 1820.

22782 SEYBERT, A. Annales statistiques des États-Unis... Traduit de l'anglais par C. A. Scheffer. 455p. *8°. Paris*, 1820.

22783 SMYTHIES, J. R. Thoughts on the agricultural question, contained in a letter to the Right Honourable the Earl of Liverpool. 22p. *8°. 1820.*

22784 SOCIEDAD ECONOMICA DE MADRID. Informe de la Sociedad Economica de Madrid al Real y Supremo Consejo de Castilla en el expediente de ley agraria, extendido por su individuo de numero el Senor Don Gaspar Melchor de Jovellanos... nueva edicion. 239p. *4°. Madrid*, 1820.

22785 —— [Another edition.] Informe de D. Gaspar de Jovellanos en el expediente de ley agraria. Tratanse en este informe las questiones mas importantes de economía política, adaptadas al estado presente de la Espana. 384p. *12°. Burdeos*, 1820. *For other editions, see* 1795.

22786 TATHAM, E. A letter to the Right Honourable Viscount Sidmouth, Secretary of State for the Home Department, on the difficulty of the times. 15p. *8°. Oxford & London*, 1820.

22787 —— Second edition. 15p. *8°. Oxford & London*, 1820.

22788 TOMLINS, Sir T. E. The law-dictionary: explaining the rise, progress and present state of the British law; defining and interpreting the terms or words of art; and comprising also copious information on the subjects of trade and government... The third edition, with considerable additions... 2 vols. *4°. London & Dublin*, 1820. *Based on the works of Giles Jacob.*

22789 La **VOIX** de la nature et de son auteur, sur l'origine des sociétés, des inégalités, des droits, des propriétés, des autorités, des pouvoirs... des constitutions... Troisième édition. 374p. *8°. Paris*, 1820. *The copy that belonged to Prince de Talleyrand.*

22790 WILLIAMS, J. F. L. An historical account of inventions and discoveries in these arts and sciences, which are of utility or ornament to Man... 2 vols. *8°. 1820.*

AGRICULTURE

22791 ARTIGUES, D'. Mémoire sur la conservation des blés... Lu à la séance de la Société royale et centrale d'Agriculture, le 15 décembre 1819, et imprimé par ses ordres. 14p. *8°. Paris*, 1820.

22792 ATTWOOD, T. State of Ireland. ⟨The cause of the present disturbances in Ireland, as shewn by Mr. Attwood in his seventh letter on the subject of the currency, addressed to the editor of the Farmers' Journal,

and inserted in that paper on the 15th May, 1820. ⟩ 8p. *8°.*
[1820] *The copy that belonged to David Ricardo.*

22793 BAKEWELL, T. Remarks on a publication by
James Loch, Esq. entitled "An account of the improvements on the estates of the Marquis of Stafford." 148p.
8°. London, Birmingham, &c., 1820.

22794 BEATSON, A. A new system of cultivation,
without lime, or dung, or summer fallows, as practiced at
Knowle-Farm in...Sussex. 163p. *8°.* 1820. *For a supplement to this work, see* 1821.

22795 BEDFORD LEVEL CORPORATION.
The lot book of the Bedford Level Corporation, for the
Middle and South Levels. Printed and circulated as notice
to the parties who may be charged with an increase in the
quantity of the land, for which they have hitherto paid the
Adventurer's tax. [The preface signed: Robert Bevill,
register.] 48p. *8°. [London,]* 1820. *See also* 1841.

22796 BLAIKIE, F. On the management of farm-
yard manure, and on other rural subjects...Third edition
enlarged. With a plate and description of the inverted
horse-hoe. 40p. *12°.* 1820. *For another edition, see* 1818.

22797 —— A treatise on mildew, and the cultivation of
wheat, including hints on the application of lime, chalk,
marl, clay, gypsum, &c.&c....Second edition, enlarged.
36p. *12°.* 1820.

22798 BUDD, W. A reply to the "Land-owners" [*sic*]
facts & remarks," respecting the proposed inclosure in
Newbury. [Dated: Feb. 8th, 1820.] 7p. *fol. Newbury,*
[1820]

22799 BURROUGHS, E. Essays on practical
husbandry, and rural economy. 83p. *8°. London & Dublin,*
1820.

22800 EDMONDSTON, A. Observations on the
nature and extent of the cod fishery, carried on off the
coasts of the Zetland and Orkney Islands. 38p. *8°. Edinburgh & London,* 1820.

22801 ENGLAND. *Commissioners for the Herring
Fishery.* Instructions for an officer of the fishery, under
the Act 1 Geo. IV. cap. 103, granting bounties for the
encouragement of the cod and ling fishery, &c. 59p. *8°.
Edinburgh,* 1820. *The instructions issued to Hugh Sutherland,
Officer of the Fishery for Northumberland, with his name
inserted in manuscript.*

22802 ————— Regulations made by the Commissioners for the Herring Fishery, in virtue of the Act 1
Geo. IV. cap. 103, granting bounties for the encouragement
of the cod and ling fishery, &c. 25p. *8°. Edinburgh,* 1820.
With additions and corrections in manuscript.

22803 FRASER, R. Report on the advantages of the
establishment of a Board of Commissioners for Fisheries
in London, for encouraging the taking and bringing fish to
the cities of London and Westminster, and other cities and

towns of the United Kingdom. Drawn up for the consideration of the Board of Trade. 23p. *4°.* 1820.

22804 GAYME,   . Manuel du bon fermier, ou cours
théorique et pratique d'agriculture, renfermant tous les
principes généraux...propres à la Savoie et aux pays
voisins. 205p. *8°. Chambéry,* 1820.

22805 [HALL, G. W.] The origin and proceedings of
the agricultural associations in Great Britain, in which
their claims to protection against foreign produce, duty-
free, are fully and ably set forth. Printed for the use of the
members of both Houses of Parliament... 46p. *8°.* [1820]
*The copy that belonged to David Ricardo. For another
edition, see* 1819.

22806 LARDIER, J. S. Essai sur les moyens de
régénérer l'agriculture en France, et plus particulièrement
dans les départemens du Midi. [Vol. 1.] 154, 291p. *8°.
Marseille,* 1820.

22807 LOCH, J. An account of the improvements on
the estates of the Marquess of Stafford, in...Stafford and
Salop, and on the estate of Sutherland. With remarks.
236, 118p. *8°.* 1820.

22808 NICOL, W. The planter's kalendar; or the
nurseryman's & forester's guide, in the operations of the
nursery, the forest, and the grove...Edited and completed
by Edward Sang...Second edition, improved and enlarged. 589p. *8°. Edinburgh & London,* 1820. *For another
edition, see* 1812.

22809 PETERKIN, A. Rentals of the ancient earldom
and bishoprick of Orkney; with some other explanatory
and relative documents. 101, 155, 98, 32, 32, 67, 135p. *8°.
Edinburgh,* 1820.

22810 RADCLIFF, T. Reports on the fine-wooled
flocks of the Messrs. Nolan...in...Kilkenny; on the
merino factory of Messrs. Nolan & Shaw...and on the
fine-wooled flocks of Lord Viscount Lismore...in...
Tipperary. [With 'Appendix. On the culture and manufacture of woad'.] 40p. *8°. Dublin,* 1820.

22811 REMARKS on the waste lands of Ireland. 67p.
8°. Dublin, 1820.

22812 RIGBY, E. Framingham, its agriculture, &c.
including the economy of a small farm. 107p. *8°. Norwich
& London,* 1820.

22813 A VIEW of the British and Irish fisheries, with
recommendations for the establishment of an Irish National Fishing Company. By an old sailor. 104p. *8°.
Dublin,* 1820.

For **WORKINGTON AGRICULTURAL SO-
CIETY,** The President's report to the Workington
Agricultural Society, 1819, 1820, *see* vol. III, *Periodicals
list,* the Rules and the proceedings of the anniversary of
the Workington Agricultural Society.

CORN LAWS

22814 CHAILLOU DES BARRES, C. E., *Baron.*
Essai historique et critique sur la législation des grains
jusqu'à ce jour, ou mémoire sur cette question proposée
par la Société d'Agriculture...du département de la
Marne: quels sont les meilleurs moyens de prévenir...la

disette des blés et les trop grandes variations dans leurs
prix?... 180p. *8°. Paris,* 1820.

22815 HALL, G. W. Letter from Geo. Webb Hall,
Esq. chairman to the general committee of management

for the agricultural associations in Great Britain; to the Right Honorable Frederick John Robinson...on the impolicy of the present corn laws, as affecting the general industry of the United Kingdom. 27p. *8°.* [1820]

22816 TORRENS, R. An essay on the influence of the external corn trade upon the production and distribu-

tion of national wealth; containing...a comparative statement of the effects which restrictions on importation... are...calculated to produce upon subsistence, agriculture, commerce, and revenue...Second edition, with considerable additions. 442p. *London & Edinburgh,* 1820. *For other editions, see 1815.*

POPULATION

22817 CLELAND, J. Enumeration of the inhabitants of the City of Glasgow and its connected suburbs; together with population & statistical tables, relative to Scotland & England. 39p. *fol. Glasgow,* 1820.

22818 GODWIN, W. Of population. An enquiry concerning the power of increase in the numbers of mankind, being an answer to Mr. Malthus's essay on that subject. 626p. *8°.* 1820. *Presentation copy, with inscription, from the author to M. J. Godwin. See also 1821.*

TRADES & MANUFACTURES

22819 ACCUM, F. C. A. Description of the process of manufacturing coal gas, for the lighting of streets, houses, and public buildings, with...plans of the most improved sorts of apparatus now employed at the gasworks in London...The second edition. 330p. *8°.* 1820. *For another edition, see 1819.*

22820 —— A practical treatise on the use and application of chemical tests, with concise directions for analyzing metallic ores, earths, metals, soils, manures, and mineral waters...Third edition, with plates, enlarged. 527p. *12°.* 1820.

22821 —— A treatise on adulterations of food, and culinary poisons, exhibiting the fraudulent sophistications of bread, beer, wine...tea, coffee...and other articles employed in domestic economy. And methods of detecting them. 372p. *12°.* 1820.

22822 —— A treatise on the art of brewing, exhibiting the London practice of brewing porter, brown stout, ale, table beer... 268p. *12°.* 1820. *See also 1821.*

22823 APPENDIX to the Marquis de Chabannes' publication, On conducting air by forced ventilation, and equalizing the temperature of dwellings; published in 1818. Being a continuation of the description of the patent apparatus for warming and cooling air...and containing an account of the new water calorifere, and other apparatus: and also of the manner in which the following places have been warmed...this year: viz. the House of Commons, the Hospital, in the Marylebone Fields...Fort Clarence, Chatham; and the Olympic Theatre... [32]p. *8°.* [*London,* 1820 ?]

22824 BISCHOFF, J. Reasons for the immediate repeal of the tax on foreign wool...Third edition, with an appendix. 11, 47p. *8°.* 1820. *Presentation copy from the author to W. M. Maude, with an autograph letter from the latter to John Mitchell, M.P., accompanying the book, soliciting his support for the opposition in the Commons to the tax. Mitchell's reply is also bound in. For the letters, see* vol. III, *A.L.* 204.

22825 A COLLECTION of royal grants and other

documents, relative to the constitution and privileges of the Incorporation of Goldsmiths, 1483-1687. 44p. *8°. Edinburgh,* 1820.

22826 COLLEGIO DEGLI OREFICI ED ARGENTIERI DI ROMA. Nuovo statuto del nobil Collegio degli Orefici ed Argentieri... 40p. *4°. Roma,* 1820.

22827 COOK, A. G. The new builder's magazine, and complete architectural library, for architects...bricklayers, &c....Consisting of designs in architecture... together with the plans, sections, and elevations...in the construction of any building...Also...the laws for the regulation of buildings; the substance of the Builders' Act, &c.; and a list of the prices allowed by...surveyors in London... 2 vols. *4°.* 1820. *Based on* The builder's magazine, *1774 (q.v.).*

22828 DAWSON, R. [*Begin.*] R. Dawson, engineer to His Majesty & one of the new established mechanics, gives the simplest & greatest improved plans on machinery ...[Engraved advertisement.] *s.sh.4°. n.p.* [*c.* 1820]

22829 MARTIN, THOMAS, *civil engineer.* The circle of the mechanical arts; containing practical treatises on the various manual arts, trades, and manufactures...Second edition... 616p. *fol.* 1820.

22830 MORISOT, J. M. R. Tableaux détaillés des prix de tous les ouvrages de bâtiment, divisés suivant les différentes espèces de travaux...Deuxième édition, revue, corrigée et augmentée. Vols. 1-6. *8°. Paris,* 1820-36.

22831 RAUCOURT, A. A manual of lithography, or memoir on the lithographical experiments made in Paris at the Royal School of the Roads and Bridges; clearly explaining the whole art...Translated from the French by C. Hullmandel. 138p. *8°.* 1820.

22832 A STATEMENT of facts and circumstances relative to the gun trade, with the Board of Ordnance. [Signed: A gun-maker, and dated, March 1820.] 30p. *8°. n.p.,* 1820.

COMMERCE

22833 ANTHOINE, A. I., *Baron de Saint-Joseph*. Essai historique sur le commerce et la navigation de la Mer-Noire...Seconde édition. 394p. *8°. Paris, 1820. For another edition, see* 1805.

22834 BENOISTON DE CHATEAUNEUF, L. F. Recherches sur les consommations de tout genre de Ville de Paris en 1817, comparées à ce qu'elles étaient en 1789...(Mémoire lu à l'Académie des Sciences...11 janvier 1819.) 109p. *8°. Paris, 1820. See also* 1821.

22835 BREDERLOW, G. VON, *Freiherr*. Geschichte des Handels und der gewerblichen Kultur der Ostsee-Reiche im Mittelalter bis zum Schlusse des sechzehnten Jahrhunderts; mit besonderem Bezug auf Danzig als Quartierstadt des Hansebundes, und der sich in dieser Zeit entwickelnden innern Staats-Verhältnisse Preussens. 379p. *8°. Berlin, 1820.*

22836 CAREY, M. A view of the ruinous consequences of a dependence on foreign markets for the sale of the great staples of this nation, flour, cotton, and tobacco...Read before, and ordered to be printed by, the Board of Manufactures of the Pennsylvanian Society for the Promotion of American Manufactures. 42p. *8°. Philadelphia, 1820.*

22837 CLAY, J. A free trade essential to the welfare of Great Britain, or an inquiry into the cause of the present distressed state of the country...To which are added, some observations on two letters to the Right Hon. Robert Peel, M.P. by one of his constituents...[From *The Pamphleteer*, vol. XVII, no. 34.] 44p. *8°. 1820. For another edition, see* 1819.

22838 GARONNE,   . Mémoire sur la demande que fait la Ville de Paris d'un entrepôt de denrées coloniales. 24p. *8°. [Paris, 1820]*

22839 HAMILTON, ROBERT (1743–1829). An introduction to merchandise: containing the theory and practice of arithmetic; algebra, with the doctrine of annuities; and commerce including treatises on monies, weights, measures, exchanges and book-keeping...The whole, new-modelled, and adapted to the improved methods and information of the present time by Elias Johnston. 563p. *8°. Edinburgh, Aberdeen, &c., 1820.*

22840 HOLT, F. L. A system of the shipping and navigation laws of Great Britain: and of the laws relative to merchant ships and seamen; and maritime contracts.... To which is added, an appendix of Acts of Parliament, forms, &c.... 2 vols. *8°. London & Dublin, 1820.*

22841 JENKINSON, R. B., *2nd Earl of Liverpool*. The speech of the Right Hon. the Earl of Liverpool, in the House of Lords on...the 26th of May, 1820, on a motion of the Marquis of Lansdown, "That a select committee be appointed to inquire into the means of extending and securing the foreign trade of the country". With an appendix containing the official accounts referred to in the speech. 56p. *8°. 1820.*

22842 —— Second edition. 56p. *8°. 1820.*

22843 —— Third edition. 56p. *8°. 1820. The Agar Ellis copy.*

22844 —— Fourth edition. 56p. *8°. 1820.*

22845 A **LETTER** to the Marquis of Lansdown, President of the Bath and West of England Society, on the subject of the late tax on wool; with some observations on Lord Sheffield's report at Lewes Fair, July 20, 1820. By one of the Vice-Presidents. 22p. *8°. Bath, 1820.*

22846 LIVERPOOL EAST INDIA ASSOCIATION. Liverpool, 31st May 1820. [*Begin.*] Sir, I am directed by our East India Association to transmit for your consideration, a copy of a Memorial [signed: Robert Gladstone, chairman] which we have presented to the Lords of Trade [asking for a Bill to relax the restrictions on trade]... 3p. *fol. n.p.* [1820]

22847 LONDON GENUINE TEA COMPANY. The history of the tea plant; from the sowing of the seed, to its package for the European market...To which are added remarks on imitation tea, extent of the fraud, legal enactments against it and the best means of detection... 60p. *8°.* [1820?]

22848 The **LONDON TRADESMAN**; a familiar treatise on the rationale of trade and commerce, as carried on in the Metropolis of the British Empire...By several tradesmen. Second edition. 386[368]p. *8°. 1820. For another edition, see* 1819.

22849 MAITLAND, JOHN (1754?–1831). Observations on the impolicy of permitting the exportation of British wool, and of preventing the free importation of foreign wool...Third edition. 88p. *8°. 1820. For other editions, see* 1818.

22850 MARRYAT, J. Speech of Joseph Marryat, Esq. in the House of Commons, on...June 5, 1820, upon the petition of the ship owners of the Port of London against any alteration in the duties on timber. Published by the Committee of the Society of Ship Owners. 32p. *8°. 1820.*

22851 Algumas **OBSERVAÇÕES** sobre o commercio de Portugal. [The introduction signed: Hum Portuguez.] 64p. *4°. Lisboa, 1820.*

22852 OBSERVATIONS on the Reports of the Select Committees of both Houses of Parliament, on the subjects of the timber trade and commercial restrictions; in which are pointed out the real bearings of those questions on the shipping and manufacturing interests...and the great importance of the trade with the North American colonies as compared with that to Norway and Sweden. Also some remarks on Canada and the United States, and the trade between those countries and the West India colonies. 72p. *8°. 1820.*

22853 OWEN, W. Owen's New book of fairs, published by the King's authority. Being a complete and authentic account of all the fairs in England and Wales... Noting likewise the commodities which each fair is remarkable for furnishing; also the days on which markets are respectively held...A new edition...corrected, and with considerable additions. 148p. *12°. 1820. For other editions, see* 1756.

22854 PRINCE'S LONDON PRICE CURRENT...No. 2283. Friday, the 7th January, [–No. 2334, Friday the 29th Dec.] 1820. 52 nos. *fol.* [1820] *See also* 1812, 1813, 1814, 1815, 1817, 1818.

22855 REMARKS on the merchants' petitions and publications respecting restrictions on foreign commerce; on the depression of agriculture; and also on the petitions praying the repeal of the duty on foreign wool. Reprinted, amended and enlarged. 16p. *8°. 1820.*

22856 [ROBERTSON, ALEXANDER, M.P.] Reflexions on the present difficulties of the country; and on relieving them, by opening new markets to our commerce, and removing all injurious restrictions. By an old Asiatic merchant. 100p. *8°. 1820.*

22857 SAINT-CHAMANS, A. L. P. DE, *Vicomte.* Du système d'impôt fondé sur les principes de l'économie politique. 640p. *8°. Paris, 1820.*

22858 SHEPPARD, J. The British corn merchant's and farmer's manual; or, tables for facilitating the calculations of the corn merchant and farmer, throughout Great Britain and Ireland; being a complete and accurate arrangement and equalization of the measures peculiar to each place with the standard bushel; interspersed with a variety of tables... 145p. *8°. Derby, [1820]*

22859 SKETCH of the rise and fall of the manufacturing system of Great Britain. In which are shown the mischievous effects of our present restrictive laws; and the beneficial results that would accrue from a free trade. 31p. *8°. 1820.*

22860 TABLE of the prices of barley and oats, at Montrose and Arbroath. *s.sh.8°. Arbroath, [c. 1820]*

22861 TOLLENARE, L. F. DE. Essai sur les entraves que le commerce éprouve en Europe. 498p. *8°. Paris, 1820.*

COLONIES

22862 BAPTIST MISSIONARY SOCIETY. [*Endorsed:*] 1820. List of stations occupied by the Baptist Missionary Society. 4p. *fol. n.p. [1820]*

22863 EAST INDIA COMPANY. Selection of papers from the records at the East-India House, relating to the revenue, police, and civil and criminal justice, under the Company's governments in India. 4 vols. *fol. 1820–26.*

22864 MAITLAND, JAMES, *8th Earl of Lauderdale.* Substance of the Earl of Lauderdale's speech in the House of Lords, on moving for copies of despatches, &c. explanatory of Sir Thomas Maitland's conduct as Lord High Commissioner of the Ionian Islands. 43p. *8°. 1820.*

FINANCE

22865 BANK FOR SAVINGS, *New York.* First report of the Bank for Savings in the City of New-York. Made to the...Legislature of the State, and the...Mayor, Aldermen and commonalty of the City of New-York, pursuant to the Act of Incorporation. 13p. *8°. New-York, 1820.*

22866 BOYD, C. The British tariff, and commercial guide. [696]p. *8°. 1820.*

22867 BRICKWOOD, J. A plan for reducing the capital and the annual charge of the National Debt. Humbly suggested to the consideration of Members of Parliament. 43p. *8°. [London,] 1820. See also 1822, 1828.*

22868 C——, A——. Letters addressed to the Right Honourable the Earl of Liverpool, and the Right Hon. Nicholas Vansittart. [Against the resumption of cash payments by the Bank of England.] 33p. *8°. 1820. The copy that belonged to Thomas Spring Rice, Baron Monteagle. Both this and a second copy in the Library have extensive manuscript notes in the margins, and some textual corrections. Doubtfully attributed to Simon Gray by HSF in a note in the Kress copy.*

22869 CAISSE HYPOTHÉCAIRE. Caisse Hypothécaire. Statuts. Exposé sommaire. 24p. *8°. Paris, [1820?]*

22870 CLERK, SIR J., *Bart.* and SCROPE, J. Historical view of the forms and powers of the Court of Exchequer in Scotland; to which is added, an appendix, containing the rules of procedure, and certain minutes of Court relating thereto. 342p. *4°. Edinburgh, 1820.*

22871 COATPONT, C. Considérations politiques sur les monnaies, sur les variations qu'elles ont subies, et celles qu'elles peuvent subir encore, si le système politique de l'Europe d'éprouve aucun changement. 109p. *8°. Paris, Troyes, &c., 1820. A letter from the author is attached to the verso of the title-page, addressed to 'Monsieur Coudert, imprimeur libraire' at Bordeaux, sending him six copies of the work to sell.*

22872 COBBETT, W. Paper against gold: or, the history and mystery of the Bank, the Funds, the Debt... and the miseries of England...Ninth edition. 470p. *8°. [1820?] Made up from the sheets of the 1817 edition, published in parts. With a title-page and an 'Advertisement' by Cobbett. For other editions, see 1815.*

22873 CONGREVE, SIR WILLIAM, *Bart.* An analysis of the true principles of security against forgery; exemplified by an enquiry into the sufficiency of the American plan for a new bank note...by which it is proved that there is no adequate security to be achieved in one colour, in the present state of the arts, and that the true basis of security is in the due application of relief engraving, and printing in two or more colours. 36p. *8°. 1820.*

22874 [DRUMMOND, H.] Elementary propositions illustrative of the principles of currency. Second edition, corrected. To which are added outlines of political economy. 22p. *8°. 1820. See also 1826, 1848.*

22875 ENGLAND. *Commissioners of Customs.* Instructions for the boatmen in the service of His Majesty's Customs, at the out ports. 9p. *4°. 1820.*

22876 —— —— Instructions for the clerks to the collector in the service of His Majesty's Customs, at the out ports. 4p. *4°. 1820.*

22877 —— —— Instructions for the clerks to the comptrollers of His Majesty's Customs at the out ports. 6p. *4°. 1820.*

22878 —— —— Instructions for the coast waiters in His Majesty's Customs at the out ports. 12p. *4°. 1820.*

22879 —— —— Instructions for the comptrollers of the Customs at the out ports. 18p. *4°. 1820.*

22880 —— —— Instructions for the landing surveyors of His Majesty's Customs in the out ports; comprehending the duty of the surveyor of searchers and coastwaiters, and of the jerquer. 28p. *4⁰*. 1820.

22881 —— —— Instructions for the landing waiters of His Majesty's Customs at the out ports. 32p. *4⁰*. 1820.

22882 —— —— Instructions for the lockers in the service of His Majesty's Customs, at the out ports. 12p. *4⁰*. 1820.

22883 —— —— Instructions for the mensuration of masts, timber, plank, wainscot logs, and boards... 67p. *4⁰*. 1820. *For another edition, see* 1796.

22884 —— —— Instructions for the principal coast officers in the service of His Majesty's Customs, at creeks, where coast documents are allowed to be issued, but where duties are not permitted to be received, in the out ports. 9p. *4⁰*. 1820.

22885 —— —— Instructions for the principal surveyor of warehouses, and surveyor of the searchers, in the service of His Majesty's Customs, at the out ports. 18p. *4⁰*. 1820.

22886 —— —— Instructions for the searchers of His Majesty's Customs in the out ports. 16p. *4⁰*. 1820.

22887 —— —— Instructions for the sitter in the tide surveyor's boat, in the service of His Majesty's Customs, at the out ports. 9p. *4⁰*. 1820.

22888 —— —— Instructions for the surveyor or other officer appointed to inspect the coal meters, in the service of His Majesty's Customs, at the out ports. 5p. *4⁰*. 1820.

22889 —— —— Instructions for the tide surveyors of the Customs at the out ports. 52p. *4⁰*. 1820.

22890 —— —— Instructions for the tide waiters of the Customs at the out ports. 35p. *4⁰*. 1820.

22891 —— —— Instructions for the weigher, meter & measurer, of coals, culm & cinders, in the service of His Majesty's Customs, at the out ports. 11p. *4⁰*. 1820.

22892 —— —— Instructions for the weighing porters in the service of His Majesty's Customs, at the out ports. 10p. *4⁰*. 1820.

22893 The **ENGLISHMAN'S** mirror; or, corruption & taxation unmasked! Containing a list of the new Parliament...also shewing the manner in which the public money is expended in useless places, pensions, sinecures, &c.... [Extracted from *Extraordinary red book* ...*by a commoner*.] 32p. *8⁰*. 1820. *For editions of* Extraordinary red book, *see* 1816.

22894 An **ENQUIRY** into the causes of the present commercial embarrassments in the United States. With a plan of reform of the circulating medium. In two letters, addressed to the Secretary of the Treasury. By an anti-bullionist. 44p. *8⁰*. *n.p.* [1820?]

22895 **FLUEGEL**, G. T. Georg Thomas Flügel's erklärte Courszettel der vornehmsten Handelsplätze in Europa...Sechszehnte, durchaus umgearbeitete Auflage. 326p. *8⁰*. *St. Gallen*, 1820.

22896 **FRANCE.** *Chambre des Pairs.* Chambre des Pairs de France. Session de 1819, séance du...6 mars 1820. Rapport fait à la Chambre des Pairs, en exécution de l'article CXIV de la loi du 28 avril 1816, sur la direction morale et sur la situation matérielle de la Caisse d'amortissement, et de la Caisse des consignations et dépôt; par la Commission de Surveillance de ces établissements. Imprimé par ordre de la Chambre. 21p. *8⁰*. [*Paris*, 1820] *The copy that belonged to David Ricardo. See also* 1821.

22897 —— *Louis XVIII, King.* Lois sur les finances de 1820, contenant les divers supplémens de crédit sur le Budget de 1818, et son réglement définitif, la fixation du Budget des Dépenses et des Recettes de 1820, avec les tableaux de répartition des contributions directes, &c. 43p. *8⁰*. *Paris*, 1820.

22898 *****GOMPERTZ**, B. A sketch of an analysis and notation applicable to the value of life contingencies... From the Philosophical Transactions. 83p. *4⁰*. 1820. *The copy that belonged to George Grote.*

22899 **GOMPERTZ**, E. A theoretic discourse on the nature and property of money, canvassing, particularly, the notion respecting its dependency on the precious metals: in which its abstract quality is likewise considered according to its relation with foreign exchanges...and concluding with some observations on the connexion between the Bank of England and Government. 82p. *8⁰*. 1820.

22900 **GOUVÉA PINTO**, A. J. DE. Memoria em que se mostra a origem e progresso do estabelecimento do papel-moeda em o nosso reino, e apontão os meios de verificar a sua amortização... 35p. *4⁰*. *Lisboa*, 1820.

22901 A **GUIDE** to the electors of Great Britain, upon the accession of a new King, and the immediate prospect of a new Parliament. [Signed: Brother Elector.] Fourth edition, with corrections and additions. 48p. *8⁰*. 1820.

22902 **HEATHFIELD**, R. Elements of a plan for the liquidation of the Public Debt of the United Kingdom; being the draught of a declaration, submitted to the attention of the landed, funded, and every other description of proprietor...With an introductory address. [The seventh edition, with supplementary observations.] 47p. *8⁰*. 1820. *Presentation copy, with inscription, from the author to George Frere. For other editions, see* 1819.

22903 —— Further observations on the practicability and expediency of liquidating the Public Debt of the United Kingdom; with reference, particularly, to the landed proprietor; including some considerations on population and the poor. 123p. *8⁰*. *London & Edinburgh*, 1820. *Two copies; one presented, with inscription, by the author to David Ricardo, the other to George Frere, with a letter accompanying the book.*

22904 —— Addenda to Mr. Heathfield's second publication, on the liquidation of the Public Debt, entitled, "Further observations on the propriety and expediency of liquidating the Public Debt of the United Kingdom." 22p. *8⁰*. *London, Edinburgh, &c.*, 1820. *Presentation copy, with inscription, from the author to George Frere.*

22905 —— [Another edition. With the Addenda.] 143p. *8⁰*. *London & Edinburgh*, 1820.

22906 **HEYWOOD**, BENJAMIN A. Observations on the circulation of individual credit and on the banking system of England, and on the Lancashire means of circulation. Part II. 75p. *8⁰*. *Liverpool*, 1820. *For the first part of this work, see* 1812. *An earlier version of this part, with the title* Arguments demonstrating from recent facts, the solid foundation of individual circulating credit, *was issued in* 1819 (*q.v.*).

22907 [**HONE**, W.] The Bank restriction barometer; or, scale of effects on society of the bank note system, and payments in gold. By Abraham Franklin. *s.sh.fol.* [1820]

[*Br.* 493] *Sold with the 'Bank Restriction Note' signed 'J. Ketch', designed by George Cruikshank, a copy of which is in the Goldsmiths' Library.*

22908 HUBBERSTY, J. L. Brief observations on the necessity of a renewal of the property tax, under certain modifications. 48p. *8°*. 1820.

22909 IBBETSON, J. H. A practical view of an invention for the better protecting bank-notes against forgery. Illustrated by various specimens. [With a supplement, commenting on Sir William Congreve's *Analysis*.] 68p. *8°*. 1820. *See also* 1821.

22910 JAMES, HENRY, *of Birmingham*. Essay on the currency; or, the alterations in the value of money, the great cause of the distressed state of the country. With a comparison between the state of the currency in the reign of William III. and its present debased or depreciated state. Original. [From *The Pamphleteer*, vol. XVII, no. 34.] 22p. *8°*. 1820.

22911 —— Essays on money, exchanges and political economy, showing the cause of the fluctuation in prices and of the depreciation in the value of property of late years... 70, 216p. *8°*. *London & Bristol*, 1820.

22912 A LETTER to the King; shewing...the fundamental causes of our unexampled national distress; and containing a proposition whereby we may hope to obtain...permanent relief compatibly with the preservation of the established order of society: in contra-distinction to the...fallacious theories of Messrs. Baring, Ricardo, Heathfield, and the whole fraternity of paper money men without real capital. By a commoner. [Signed: British commoner.] 64p. *8°*. 1820.

22913 A LETTER to the Right Hon. Robert Peel, M.P. for the University of Oxford, on the comparative operation of the corn laws, and of public taxation, as causes of the depression of trade, and of the distressed state of the industrious classes. By a Briton. 69p. *8°*. 1820.

22914 A MANUAL of foreign exchanges, monies, weights, and measures...Intended as an assistant to the counting-house. 175p. *12°*. *Glasgow, Edinburgh, &c.*, 1820.

22915 MÉDAILLE pour la naissance de S. A. R. Mgr. le Duc de Bordeaux. [Engraved by A. A. Caqué. A prospectus.] *s.sh.4°*. *n.p.* [1820?]

22916 MILES, C. An essay on the National Debt. [In verse.] 32p. *8°*. 1820.

22917 NEBENIUS, C. F. E. Der öffentliche Credit dargestellt in der Geschichte und in den Folgen der Finanzoperationen der grossen europäischen Staaten seit Herstellung des allgemeinen Land- und Seefriedens... [With appendixes.] 448, 256p. *8°*. *Carlsruhe & Baden*, 1820. *See also* 1829.

22918 PELICAN OFFICES FOR INSURANCE ON LIVES. Pelican Offices, Lombard Street, and Spring Gardens, London, for Insurance on Lives and granting annuities. [Rules, rates, list of trustees and directors.] 13p. *8°*. 1820. *See also* 1814.

22919 PLAÑA, A. Agravios hechos en el repartimiento de la contribucion directa de Aragon en especial, y á toda la agricultura de España en general: vicios inseparables de la estadística; y metodo de repartir aquella contribucion mas facil y equitativamente. 61p. *4°*. *Zaragoza*, 1820.

22920 —— Discurso sobre la abolicion de diezmos y primicias, propuesta en las Cortes ordinarias. 57p. *4°*. [*Zaragoza*,] 1820.

22921 PRUSSIA. *Justiz Ministerium.* Instruction für die Ober- und Untergerichte zur Ausführung der königlichen Verordnung vom 16ten Juni d. J. wegen Einrichtung des Hypotheken-Wesens in dem mit den preussischen Staaten vereinigten Herzogthum Sachsen. [12ten August 1820.] 13p. *8°*. *Berlin*, 1820.

22922 —— Anhang zur Instruktion für die Gerichte wegen Bearbeitung des Hypothekenwesens in dem mit den Preussischen Staaten vereinigten Herzogthum Sachsen. De dato Berlin, den 12ten August 1820. 37p. *8°*. *Berlin*, 1820.

22923 RODRIGUES, B. O. and **MAAS,** . Théorie de la caisse hypothécaire, ou examen du sort des emprunteurs, des porteurs d'obligations et des actionnaires de cet établissement. 39p. *8°*. *Paris*, 1820.

22924 [SARRAZIN, N. J.] Traité de la vraie théorie de l'impôt. Extrait d'un ouvrage où l'on traite de l'impôt en général...comme aussi de la vraie...méthode d'acquitter les...dettes arriérées d'un état...[Signed: P. N. J. S. With 'Appendice à la théorie de l'impôt, par le même auteur', signed: N. J. S.] 51, 14p. *8°*. *Pont-à-Mousson*, [1820] *The appendix was printed at Metz.*

22925 The SAVING BANK: a dialogue, between Ralph Ragged & Will Wise. 12p. *12°*. *Saffron Walden & London*, [1820?]

22926 —— Part second. Ralph Ragged & Will Wise. 12p. *12°*. *Saffron Walden & London*, [1820?]

22927 SEVERN, KING AND CO. A report of the trial of the action, brought by Messrs. Severn, King and Co. against the Imperial Insurance Company: before Lord Chief Justice Dallas, and a special jury. In the Court of Common Pleas, at Guildhall, April, 1820. Taken in short-hand, by W. B. Gurney. [Concerning the loss by fire of the sugar refinery of Messrs. Severn, King and Co. in Whitechapel.] 248p. *8°*. 1820.

22928 [SMITH, SYDNEY (1771–1845).] [*Begin.*] We have taxes upon every article which enters into the mouth, or covers the back, or is placed under the foot... *s.sh.fol. n.p.* [1820] [*Br.* 494]

22929 TATHAM, E. A letter to the Right Honourable Lord Grenville, Chancellor of the University of Oxford, on the metallic standard. [An attack on the Bank Restriction Act of 1819.] 29p. *8°*. *Oxford & London*, 1820.

22930 TELONES, *pseud.* A letter to the Right Honourable Nicholas Vansittart, Chancellor of the Exchequer; on the subject of oaths and affirmations, connected with the exportation of exciseable goods on drawback...[Signed: Τελωνης.] 31p. *8°*. *Edinburgh, London, &c.*, 1820.

22931 TRENOR, K. A letter to the Right Hon. Robert Peel, M.P. for the University of Oxford: in answer to a letter on the comparative operation of the corn laws and public taxation as causes of the depression of trade... 77p. *8°*. 1820.

22932 UNITED STATES OF AMERICA. *Treasury Department.* Report of the Secretary of the Treasury [Wm. H. Crawford]...transmitting statements in relation to the condition of the Bank of the United States and its offices; also statements in relation to the situation of the different chartered banks in the different states, and the district of Columbia, &c. Now first printed in this country. [From *The Pamphleteer*, vol. XVII, no. 33.] 45p. *8°*. 1820.

22933 WILKINSON, H. The principles of an equitable and efficient system of finance; founded upon self-evident...principles, capable of diminishing taxes and poor-rates, proving the necessity of repealing all existing taxes...and adopting one... 95p. *8°.* 1820.

22934 X., D. L. Prospectus. Médaille relative à la naissance de S.A.R. Mgr. le Duc de Bordeaux. [To be engraved by R. Gayrard.] 4p. *8°.* [*Paris*, 1820 ?]

TRANSPORT

22935 CHAMBERS, A. H. Observations on the formation, state and condition of turnpike roads and other highways with suggestions for their permanent improvement...by means of the natural materials of which they are composed: to which is added, a practical system...for the construction of sound substantial roads and under-drains, by means of a patent substitute for hard road materials... 28p. *8°.* 1820. *The copy that belonged to David Ricardo.*

22936 FRY, J. S. An essay on the construction of wheel-carriages, as they affect both the roads and the horses; with suggestions relating to the principles on which tolls ought to be imposed, and a few remarks on the formation of roads. 137p. *8°. London & Bristol,* 1820. *Presentation copy, with inscription, from the author to George Haden.*

22937 HINTS to country road-surveyors, being in great measure the substance of an article [by Edward Berens ?] in the Quarterly Review for May, 1820. No. XLV. [Signed: A friend to the publick, and dated, Sept. 1820.] 23p. *12°. London & Oxford,* 1820.

22938 McADAM, JOHN L. Remarks on the present system of road making...Third edition, carefully revised with considerable additions, and an appendix. [With 'Report from the Select Committee on the highways of the Kingdom: together with the minutes of evidence taken before them'.] 196p. *8°.* 1820. *For other editions, see* 1816.

For a **NEW GUIDE TO STAGE-COACHES, WAGGONS**...&c. for 1820, *see no.* 22772.

SOCIAL CONDITIONS

22939 BAYLY, W. D. The state of the poor and working classes considered, with practical plans for improving their condition in society, and superseding the present system of compulsory assessment. 118p. *8°. London, Bristol, &c.,* 1820.

22940 CHRISTIAN, EDWARD (*d.* 1823). General observations on provident banks; with a plan of the Unlimited Provident Bank at Cambridge; and a scale of the price of debentures, without loss to the revenue... Original. [From *The Pamphleteer*, vol. XVII, no. 33.] 14p. *8°.* 1820.

22941 COTTU, C. De l'administration de la justice criminelle en Angleterre, et de l'esprit du gouvernement anglais. 317p. *8°. Paris,* 1820. *The copy that belonged to George Agar Ellis, Baron Dover, with his crest on the binding.*

22942 COURTAULD, G. Address to those who may be disposed to remove to the United States of America, on the advantages of equitable associations of capital and labour, in the formation of agricultural establishments in the interior country. Including remarks on Mr. Birkbeck's opinions upon this subject. 40p. *8°. Sudbury & London,* 1820.

22943 CULL, J. A letter addressed to the Right Honorable William Sturges Bourne, M.P. on the subject of the poor laws. 35p. *8°.* 1820.

22944 CUNNINGHAM, F. Notes recueillies en visitant les prisons de la Suisse, et remarques sur les moyens de les améliorer, avec quelques détails sur les prisons de Chambéry et de Turin...Suivies de la description des prisons améliorées de Gand, Philadelphie, Bury, Ilchester et Millbank, et d'un rapport sur le Comité des Dames à New-Gate. Par T. F. Buxton, Esq. Membre du Parlement. lxviii, 87p. *8°. Genève & Paris,* 1820.

22945 DOWLING, J. A., *ed.* The whole proceedings before the coroner's inquest at Oldham, &c. on the body of John Lees, who died of sabre wounds at Manchester, August 16, 1819; being the fullest and only authentic information concerning...that fatal day...Taken in short-hand and edited by Joseph Augustus Dowling, Esq. With an accurate plan of St. Peter's Field. 580, 37p. *8°.* 1820.

22946 ENGLAND. *Laws, etc.* Pancras Southampton paving Acts. 41st, 43d, 52d, and 55th George III. 186p. *8°.* [*c.* 1820]

22947 —— Parliament. *House of Commons.* Report of the Select Committee of the House of Commons [12th July 1819], appointed to inquire into the state and description of gaols, and other places of confinement, &c.&c. [From *The Pamphleteer*, vol. XV, no. 30.] 6p. *8°.* 1820.

22948 FACTS relative to the state of the poor, and the labouring classes, in the south of France, in the north of Italy, and Switzerland. Collected during the summer of 1820. 16p. *8°. Bath,* [1820]

22949 GASCOIGNE, H. B. The old views of society revived; with remarks on the present state and prospects of orphan and pauper children: and outlines of a plan for their future training in mutual habits of instruction, industry and self-dependence... 35p. *8°.* [1820]

22950 GERANDO, J. M. DE, *Baron.* Le visiteur du pauvre; mémoire qui a remporté le prix proposé par l'Académie de Lyon sur la question suivante: "Indiquer les moyens de reconnaître la véritable indigence, et de rendre l'aumône utile à ceux qui la donnent comme à ceux qui la reçoivent. [The preface signed: B. Degerando.] 158p. *8°. Paris,* 1820. *See also* 1833.

22951 GORDON, SIR ALEXANDER. An address to the inhabitants of the Stewartry of Kirkcudbright... particularly to the magistrates and to the kirk-sessions, respecting the laws relating to the poor. With an appendix, containing the Acts of Parliament and of the Privy Council of Scotland, and other important documents relative to the poor. 79, 189p. *8°. Edinburgh & Dumfries, 1820.*

22952 [**HALL**, ROBERT.] An appeal to the public, on the subject of the framework-knitters' fund. 19p. *8°. Leicester & London, 1820. For another edition, see 1819.*

22953 **HINTS** for improving the condition of [women] prisoners; derived from a plan which has been tried and found beneficial in Newgate, and which appears capable of being introduced, with advantage, into most prisons throughout the Empire. [With 'Rules' and 'Class list'.] [4]p. *fol. [London, c. 1820]*

22954 **HUNT**, H. To the radical reformers, male and female, of England, Ireland and Scotland. [A series of 44 of the 46 tracts written by Hunt during his imprisonment in Ilchester Jail.] 2 vols. *8°. [London, 1820–22]*

22955 —— The trial of Henry Hunt, Esq., Jno. Knight, Jos. Johnson, Jno. Thacker Saxton, Samuel Bamford, Jos. Healey, James Moorhouse, Robert Jones, Geo. Swift and Robert Wylde, for an alledged conspiracy to overturn the government, &c. by threats and force of arms. Before Mr. Justice Bayley and a special jury, at the York Lent Assizes, 1820. 309p. *8°. 1820. Published in 10 parts.*

22956 —— [Another edition.] p.3–130. *8°. [London, 1820] Published in parts. This copy contains parts 1–5 only.*

22957 —— [Another edition.] The trial of Mr. Hunt, Mr. Johnson, and others, for a conspiracy at the Manchester meeting, on the 16th August last; before Mr. Justice Bailey and a special jury at York; which commenced on Thursday, March 17th, 1820 and closed on Monday, March 27th, 1820. 120p. *8°. Leeds, 1820.*

22958 —— An impartial report of the proceedings in the cause of the King versus Henry Hunt [and others]...for a conspiracy, tried before Mr. Justice Bayley...at York Spring Assizes...March, 1820. [With 'Appendix. Proceedings in the Court of King's Bench, on Mr. Hunt's application for a new trial'.] 180p. *8°. Manchester, 1820.*

22959 **JOHNSON**, JAMES. An address to the inhabitants of Bristol, on the subject of the poor-rates, with a view to their reduction, and the ameliorating the present condition of our poor. 75p. *8°. Bristol, 1820.*

22960 **JUSTICE** to the poor; and justice to every other class of the people, as respects the situation of the poor, and the state of agriculture and commerce. 91p. *8°. Northampton, 1820.*

22961 **LABOURERS'** wages. Copy of the Act of Parliament, passed the 24th July, 1820; which enacts that the wages of labourers...shall not be paid directly nor indirectly otherwise than in money. The speeches of those gentlemen...who spoke on the Bill. Some observations tending to shew the...evils resulting from too low wages. 27p. *8°. 1820.*

22962 **LESSONS** of thrift, published for general benefit, by a member of the Save-all Club. 240[190]p. *8°. 1820.*

22963 A **LETTER** to the Right Honourable the Speaker of the House of Commons, on the subject of the poor laws; in which the evils of the present system, the origin of those evils, and their remedy, are considered. By a countryman. 35p. *8°. Salisbury & London, [c. 1820]*

22964 **MACLEAN**, C. Specimens of systematic misrule; or, immense sums annually expended in upholding a single imposture, discoveries of the highest import-ance to all mankind smothered, and injustice perpetrated for reasons of state. From official proceedings and correspondence of the ministers of the Crown, the Privy Council, the Board of Trade, the Levant Company... 122p. *8°. 1820.*

22965 On the **MEANS** of benefitting the poor. Original. [From *The Pamphleteer*, vol. XVI, no. 32.] 12p. *8°. 1820.*

22966 **METROPOLITAN AND CENTRAL COMMITTEE FOR THE RELIEF OF THE MANCHESTER SUFFERERS.** Report of the Metropolitan and Central Committee...With an appendix containing the names of the sufferers...Also, an account of the distribution of the funds and other documents. Published by order of the Committee. 70p. *8°. 1820. The copy that belonged to David Ricardo. *Another, the FWA copy, belonged to William Pare.*

22967 **OBSERVATIONS** on a letter by John Eardley Eardley-Wilmot, Esq. one of His Majesty's justices of the peace...to the magistrates of Warwickshire. 23p. *8°. London & Birmingham, 1820.*

22968 [**O'DRISCOL**, J. ?] Thoughts and suggestions on the education of the peasantry of Ireland. 58p. *8°. London & Edinburgh, 1820. Attributed to 'Mr. O'Driscol, Cork' in a manuscript note on the title-page. The Agar Ellis copy.*

22969 A **PLAN** to regulate the employment of the labouring poor, as acted upon in the parish of Oundle. [Second edition.] 6p. *8°. Oundle, 1820. See also 1823.*

22970 **PLAYFAIR**, W. The advantages of emigration to France, clearly shewn to be infinitely superior to all others. 16p. *8°. [1820 ?]*

22971 [*Endorsed:*] **PROPOSALS** for erecting in London, by voluntary donations, a building for the sole and exclusive purpose of the meetings of religious and charitable institutions. [4]p. *fol. Chelsea, [c. 1820]*

22972 **RADICAL**, ROGER, *Esq., pseud.* Why are we poor? An address to the industrious and laborious classes of the community; proving their distresses to arise from the combination of the rich and powerful... 24p. *8°. 1820.*

22973 **REPORTS** and other documents upon the patent, moveable, inodorous conveniences, by the Royal and Central Agricultural Society of France, with a supplement by the Comte François de Neufchâteau; the Royal Medical Society of Marseilles; the Society for the Encouragement of National Industry; the Medical Society of Lyons...&c. Translated from the French. [Second edition, issued by the Antimephitical Company.] 72p. *8°. 1820. The half-title reads: Moveable and inodorous conveniences. Antimephitical Company...Second edition.*

22974 **SERMONS** preached before friendly and charitable societies in the country: and written chiefly with the view of illustrating the principles delivered by Mr. Malthus, in his Essay on population...By a clergyman of the Established Church. 168p. *12°. 1820.*

For **SOCIETY FOR RELIEVING THE HOUSELESS POOR**, *London,* Reports 1820–47, *see* vol. III, *Periodicals list,* Report of a committee appointed to manage a subscription...

22975 **SOCIETY FOR THE IMPROVEMENT OF PRISON DISCIPLINE,** *London.* Rules proposed for the government of gaols, houses of correction and penitentiaries, compiled from various Acts of Parliament...and selected from rules in force at the best conducted gaols in Europe; to which are added, plans of prisons on improved principles and a description...of a corn mill and water mill adapted for the employment of prisoners... 65p. *8°.* 1820.

22976 SOCIETY FOR THE PREVENTION OF PAUPERISM IN NEW-YORK. The second annual report of the managers of the Society...Read and accepted, December 29, 1819. To which is added an appendix on the subject of pauperism. 91p. *8°. New-York,* 1820. *See also* 1819.

22977 SOCIETY FOR THE SUPPRESSION OF MENDICITY, *London.* [*Begin.*] At a meeting of the Board of Management...May 8th 1820...[Proceedings concerned with a gift to the Secretary, W. H. Bodkin.] [4]p. *8°. n.p.* [1820]

22978 ——— Rota of attendance of the Board of Management, to superintend the examination, relief, and disposal of cases at the office. [With resolutions, dated May 8, 1820, and signed: W. H. Bodkin's, Secretary.] *s.sh.fol. n.p.* [1820]

22979 ——— The second report of the Society...[With a list of subscribers.] 55, [35]p. *8°.* 1820. *See also* 1819, 1822, 1825.

22980 SOCIETY OF ASSOCIATED HOUSE-WRIGHTS, *Boston.* The constitution of the Society of Associated Housewrights, of the town of Boston, as revised in April, 1820...[With a list of members.] 16p. *8°. Botton* [sic], 1820. *For another edition, see* 1805.

22981 SPEEN. Comparative statement of the accounts of the Parish of Speen, Berks, for the years ending Easter 1819, and Easter, 1820. With some prefatory observations [and a folded table, dated 'Speen, April 8th 1820', beginning: 'The magistrates recommend to the overseers of the...parishes within the division of Newbury, to produce, annually...a statement of the accounts of the parish...in the following form...']. 12p. *4°. Newbury,* [1820] *A letter, dated 'Speen Farm, May 5, 1820', from Richard Basing to an unknown recipient is inserted, containing the table of subsistence allowances in the parish of Speen.*

22982 The **STATE** of the poor of Ireland briefly considered and agricultural education recommended, to remedy redundant population and to promote national improvement. [With an appendix containing a description of the Fellenberg school at Hofwyl.] 46p. *8°. Dublin,* 1820.

22983 STEPHENSON, ROWLAND. A plan for the

diminution of poor rates in country parishes, by classification and distribution of labour. 29p. *8°.* 1820.

22984 [SYMES,   .] The absentee; or, a brief examination into the habits and condition of the people of Ireland, and the causes of the discontent and the disorganized state of the lower classes. By an officer of the Customs of Ireland. 42p. *8°.* 1820.

22985 [TAYLOR, JOHN E.] Notes and observations, critical and explanatory, on the papers relative to the internal state of the country, recently presented to Parliament, to which is appended, a reply to Mr. Francis Philips's "Exposure of the calumnies circulated by the enemies of social order...". By a member of the Manchester Committee for relieving the Sufferers of the 16th August, 1819. 206p. *8°.* 1820.

22986 TOZER, T. The tricks of the bakers exposed; giving an account of the ingredients used by bakers in the making of the best London loaf, and the still worse practices of the cheap bakers...together with a full account of the mysteries of the bakehouse, in the exchanging of joints, pouring off the fat, or stealing the pudding or potatoes from the poor man's Sunday dinner. By a journeyman baker [signed: Titus Tozer]. 12p. *12°.* [c. 1820]

22987 VILLERMÉ, L. R. Des prisons telles qu'elles sont, et telles qu'elles devraient être; ouvrage dans lequel on les considère par rapport à l'hygiène, à la morale et à l'économie politique. 191p. *8°. Paris,* 1820.

22988 [WADE, JOHN.] Manchester massacre!! An authentic narrative of the magisterial and yeomanry massacre, at Manchester, with remarks on the illegal conduct of the magistrates in suppressing the meeting... By the editor of "The black book". 48p. *8°.* [1820?]

22989 WEALE, JAMES. Water monopoly. The case of the water companies stated and examined: or, the calm address dissected; with remarks thereon, calculated to settle opinions on the subject of the additional water rates. 114p. *8°.* 1820. *See note to no.* 22542.

22990 WILMOT, SIR J. E. E., *Bart.* A letter to the magistrates of Warwickshire, on the increase of crime in general, but more particularly in the county of Warwick; with a few observations on the causes and remedies of this increasing evil. 39p. *8°.* 1820.

22991 ——— A second letter to the magistrates of Warwickshire on the increase of crime in general, but more particularly of juvenile delinquency: with a few observations on the causes and remedies of this increasing evil. 14p. *8°.* 1820.

SLAVERY

22992 AFRICAN INSTITUTION. A review of the colonial slave registration acts, in a report of a committee of the Board of Directors...made on the 22d of February, 1820... 139p. *8°.* 1820. *The copy that belonged to David Ricardo.*

22993 BARBOUR, J. Speech of Mr. J. Barbour, of Virginia, on the restriction of slavery in Missouri. Delivered in the Senate of the United States, Jan. 31, 1820. 26p. *12°. n.p.* [1820]

22994 BARBOUR, P. P. Speech of Mr. P. P. Barbour, of Virginia, delivered in the House of Repre-

sentatives of the United States, February 10, 1820. [On the restriction of slavery in Missouri.] 28p. *12°. n.p.* [1820]

22995 CONSIDERATIONS on the impropriety and inexpediency of renewing the Missouri question. By a Pennsylvanian. 88p. *8°. Philadelphia,* 1820.

22996 DUMONT, P. J. Histoire de l'esclavage en Afrique (pendant trente-quatre ans) de P. J. Dumont... rédigée sur ses propres déclarations par J. S. Quesné... Troisième édition, revue, corrigée et augmentée... 157p. *8°. Paris,* 1820. *For another edition, see* 1819.

22997 HOARE, Prince. Memoirs of Granville Sharp...composed from his own manuscripts, and other authentic documents...of his family and of the African Institution...With observations on Mr. Sharp's biblical criticisms, by the...Bishop of St. David's. [With 'Catalogue by Mr. Sharp of the books written by him'.] 524, xxxiiip. *4°*. 1820. *See also* 1828.

22998 LOWNDES, William J. Speech of Mr. Lowndes, on the admission of Missouri. Delivered in the House of Representatives, Dec. 13, 1820. 23p. *12°*. *n.p.* [1820]

22999 M'LANE, L. Speech of Mr. M'Lane, of Delaware, on the admission of Missouri. Delivered in the House of Representatives, Dec. 12, 1820. 22p. *12°*. *n.p.* [1820]

23000 MEMORANDA respecting the French slave trade in 1820. Drawn up at the close of that year. 44p. *8°*. 1820. *The copy that belonged to Stephen Lushington.*

23001 PENNSYLVANIA SOCIETY FOR PROMOTING THE ABOLITION OF SLAVERY. Constitution and act of incorporation [1789] of the...Society. To which are added abstracts of the laws...respecting slavery and the slave trade. 31p. *8°*. *Philadelphia*, 1820.

23002 PLUMER, W. Speech of Mr. Plumer, of New-Hampshire, on the Missouri question, delivered in the House of Representatives of the United States, February 21, 1820. 42p. *12°*. *n.p.* [1820]

23003 SMYTH, Alexander. Speech of Mr. Smyth [of Virginia], on the restriction of slavery in Missouri. Delivered in the House of Representatives of the United States, January 28, 1820. 36p. *12°*. *n.p.* [1820]

23004 VAN DYKE, N. Speech of Mr. Van Dyke, on the amendment offered to a bill for the admission of Missouri into the Union, prescribing the restriction of slavery as an irrevocable principle of the State Constitution. Delivered in the Senate of the United States, January 28, 1820. 14p. *12°*. *n.p.* [1820]

POLITICS

23005 ADAMS, M. A parody on The political house that Jack built [by William Hone]: or the real house that Jack built...With fourteen cuts. [24]p. *8°*. 1820.

23006 An ADDRESS to the higher classes in the town of Manchester and the vicinity. By an inhabitant. [An attack on the newspapers catering for the lower orders and a refutation of attacks in the press on the Manchester Infirmary.] 68p. *8°*. *Manchester & London*, 1820.

23007 [ATKINSON, William (1758–1846).] The retort courteous; or, the descent of Mr. Baines, from the pinnacle to the pickle pot. By the Old Inquirer. 31p. *8°*. *Bradford*, 1820.

23008 BAKER, John, *of Sydenham*. The Christian house, built by truth on a rock. Or, an antidote to infidelity. Embellish'd with engravings. 20p. *8°*. 1820.

23009 BATHURST, Henry, *Archdeacon*. A sermon, intended to have been preached before...the Queen, on the occasion of her public thanksgiving at St. Paul's Cathedral...29th of November, 1820: with an introductory letter to the Lord Bishop of Llandaff. 23p. *8°*. 1820. *The Agar Ellis copy.*

23010 BENTHAM, J. The King against Edmonds, and others: set down for trial, at Warwick, on the 29th of March, 1820. Brief remarks, tending to show the untenability of this indictment. 25p. *8°*. 1820.

23011 —— The King against Sir Charles Wolseley, Baronet, and Joseph Harrison, schoolmaster: set down for trial, at Chester, on the 4th of April, 1820. Brief remarks, tending to shew the untenability of this indictment. p.[23]–39. *8°*. 1820. *Presumably paginated in sequence with the pamphlet on Rex v. Edmonds, to which it is closely allied.*

23012 BIRMINGHAM, 25th October, 1820. To the Bailiffs of Birmingham. [A poem.] *s.sh.8°*. *n.p.* [1820] *See note to no.* 20490.

23013 BRAYSHAW, J. Remarks upon the character and conduct of the men who met under the name of the British Parliament at the latter end of the year 1819, with an account of the manner in which they obtained their seats. To which is added, a letter to the Lord Advocate of Scotland, on the state of that country. 40p. *8°*. *Newcastle*, [1820]

23014 The BRITISH CONSTITUTION triumphant; or, a picture of the Radical conclave...[A satire.] Sixth edition. [20]p. *8°*. [1820 ?] *The half-title reads: The loyalist's house that Jack built.*

23015 —— Eighth edition. [20]p. *8°*. [1820 ?]

23016 BROOM, Harry, *pseud*. A king in a pickle! With a cabinet of curiosities, collected by Harry Broom. Second edition. 22p. *8°*. 1820.

23017 BURDETT, Sir F., *Bart*. The green bag! Sir Francis Burdett's celebrated green bag speech, delivered in the House of Commons, on...June 22d, 1820, in the debate on the charges against...Her Majesty Queen Caroline. 7p. *8°*. [*London*, 1820]

23018 —— The trial of Sir Francis Burdett, on a charge of publishing a seditious and malicious libel against His Majesty's Government, including the Baronet's very eloquent defence...Tried at Leicester, March 22, 1820... 32p. *8°*. 1820.

23019 CANNING, George (1770–1827). Speech of the Right Hon. George Canning to his constituents at Liverpool, on...March 18th, 1820, at the celebration of his fourth election. [On the principles of radical reform.] 43p. *8°*. 1820.

23020 —— [Another edition.] Speech of the Rt. Hon. George Canning, delivered at the Liverpool dinner, given in celebration of his re-election, March 18, 1820. 32p. *8°*. 1820. *The copy that belonged to Earl De Grey.*

23021 —— Second edition, revised and corrected. 32p. *8°*. 1820.

23022 —— [Another edition.] The principles and tendency of radical reform... 22p. *12°*. 1820.

23023 —— Substance of the speech of the Right Hon. George Canning, in the House of Commons, on... November 24, 1819, on the Address to the Throne upon the opening of the session... 54p. *8°*. 1820.

23024 The CENSOR; or, political investigator. April 1, 1820. 40p. *4°*. *n.p.* [1820]

23025 The first **CHAPTER** of a new book; or, the complaints & sufferings of a patient nation made manifest by the Goddess of Liberty... 4p. 8°. [1820?]

23026 The second **CHAPTER** of a new book... 4p. [1820?]

23027 **COBBETT**, W. The beauties of Cobbett: in three parts...[A selection from some of his works designed to discredit Cobbett.] 16, 16, 16p. 8°. [1820?]

23028 [——] The Queen's letter to the King. [Dated: August 7th, 1820; with reference to the Bill of Pains and Penalties then pending against her.] 8p. 8°. [London:] W. Smith, [1820]

23029 [——] [Another edition. With 'Sir Gerard Noel to the Earl of Liverpool'.] 8p. 8°. [London:] T. Dolby, [1820]

23030 [——] [Another edition.] The Queen's letter to the King; a corrected sketch of Lord John Russel's [sic] petition; Sir Gerard Noel's letter to the Earl of Liverpool; together with Mr. Brougham's and Dr. Denman's speeches, and Mr. Brougham's reply to the Attorney-General, in the House of Lords on...the 17th, 18th and 19th August, 1820, on the Bill of Pains and Penalties against Her Majesty. From the Kendal Chronicle. 40p. 12°. Kendal, [1820]

23031 [——] [Another edition.] Letter from the Queen to the King. 8p. 8°. [London:] W. Benbow, [1820]

23032 **COTTLE**, J. The Brunswick, or true blue. [The prospectus of a weekly newspaper.] 4p. 8°. [London, 1820]

23033 [**CRAVEN**, HON. K. R.] Sketch of the late revolution at Naples. By an eye-witness. 51p. 8°. 1820. *Attributed to Keppel Craven in a manuscript note on the title-page. The copy that belonged to George Agar Ellis, Baron Dover.*

23034 **DAVISON**, T. The trial of Thomas Davison, for publishing a blasphemous libel in the Deists' Magazine, in the Court of King's Bench...October 23d, 1820. With a prefatory letter [signed: Erasmus Perkins] to Mr. Justice Best. 58p. 8°. 1820.

23035 The political **DEATH** of Mr. William Cobbett. [An account of the case Wright v. Clement, with quotations from Wright's edition of the trial.] 39p. 8°. Edinburgh, 1820.

23036 A **DEFENCE** of the loyal inhabitants of Dudley. By a member of the Pitt Club. [A satire.] 22p. 8°. 1820.

23037 The **DEVIL** and the radicals. [A ballad.] s.sh.fol. Oxford, [1820] [Br. 677(1)]

23038 **DOLL** Tear-sheet, alias the Countess 'Je ne me rappelle pas', a match for "Non mi ricordo"...[A satire upon the evidence given by Louise Demont at the trial of Queen Caroline.] Second edition. [34]p. 8°. [1820]

23039 The r----l **FOWLS**; or, the old black cock's attempt to crow over his illustrious mate. A poem [against George IV]. By the author of the R——l brood. Sixth edition. 23p. 8°. 1820.

23040 A **GROAN** from the throne. [A satire on George IV.] 28p. 8°. 1820.

23041 [**HONE**, W.] The man in the moon, &c.&c.&c. [Satires on George IV and others.] With fifteen cuts [by George Cruikshank]. Tenth edition. [24]p. 8°. 1820. See also 1821.

23042 [——] The political house that Jack built. [With 'The clerical magistrate'.] With thirteen cuts [by G. Cruikshank]. Forty-third edition. [24]p. 8°. 1820. *For other editions, see 1819.*

23043 [——] The Queen's matrimonial ladder, a national toy, with fourteen step scenes; and illustrations in verse, with eighteen other cuts [by G. Cruikshank]. By the author of "The political house that Jack built". [A folding cardboard plate with accompanying text.] [22]p. 8°. 1820.

23044 [——] Eleventh edition. [22]p. 8°. 1820.

23045 [——] Thirty-seventh edition. [22]p. 8°. 1820.

23046 The real or constitutional **HOUSE** that Jack built. With twelve cuts. Twelfth edition. [24]p. 8°. 1820. *For another edition, see 1819.*

23047 The true political **HOUSE** that Jack built: being a parody on "The political house that Jack built [by William Hone]". With thirteen cuts. [24]p. 8°. 1820.

23048 **HUNT**, H. Memoirs of Henry Hunt...Written by himself, in...jail at Ilchester... 3 vols. 8°. 1820.

23049 **JENKINSON**, R. B., *2nd Earl of Liverpool.* The speech of the Right Hon. the Earl of Liverpool, in the House of Lords, on...3rd, &...4th November, 1820, on the second reading of the Bill of Pains and Penalties [against Caroline, consort of George IV]. Second edition. 80p. 8°. 1820.

23050 **LETTER** to Lord Castlereagh, found near his lordship's house, in St. James's Square. [Signed: A loyal pioneer.] 4p. 8°. [London, 1820]

23051 **LEWIS**, W. G. A peep at the Commons; or, an alphabetical list of all the counties, cities and boroughs which send members to Parliament...To which is added, an alphabetical list of the members of the present House of Commons, with the names of the places for which they sit. 28p. 8°. [1820]

23052 —— Second edition. 28p. 8°. [1820]

23053 [——?] Fourth edition. A peep at the Peers. Or, an alphabetical list of all the peers who sit in the House... including the Bishops...showing the offices, grants, church preferment...belonging...to the peers and their families. 24p. 8°. [London, 1820] *Variously attributed to W. G. Lewis, William Cobbett and William Benbow, the publisher of the work.*

23054 [**LULLIN DE CHATEAUVIEUX**, J. F.] Lettres de Saint-James. [On the political state of Great Britain and other countries of Europe.] 103, 142, 185p. 8°. Genève & Paris, 1820–22.

23055 **MACRAINBOW**, RIGHT HON. JOHN, *pseud.* A volley at the Peers both spiritual and temporal, or, a veto upon the votes of some of them: facts respecting Baron Bergami... 32p. 8°. [1820]

23056 **MAITLAND**, JAMES, *8th Earl of Lauderdale.* Substance of the Earl of Lauderdale's speech in the House of Lords, on...the 2d of November, 1820, on the second reading of the Bill, entitled, An Act to deprive Her Majesty, Caroline Amelia Elizabeth, of the titles... privileges, and exemptions of Queen Consort...and to dissolve the marriage between His Majesty and the said Caroline Amelia Elizabeth. 83p. 8°. Edinburgh & London, 1820.

23057 Third edition. The loyal **MAN** in the Moon. [A satire, in verse, upon the supporters of Queen Caroline.]

With thirteen cuts. By the author of the Constitutional house that Jack built. 28p. *8°*. 1820.

23058 MIDDLESEX. A full report of the Middlesex County Meeting, held at Hackney on...August 8, 1820 to take into consideration the propriety of presenting an address to the Queen, in which the eloquent and impressive speeches of Sir Francis Burdett, Bart., Messrs. Hobhouse, Wood, &c. &c. are given at full length. 16p. *8°*. [1820]

23059 NICOLL, S. W. A second letter to the members of the York Whig Club, including a general view of parliamentary reform...Second edition. 24p. *8°*. *York,* [*c.* 1820] *A London imprint has been added in manuscript below the York one.*

23060 Read! Marvellous and disinterested **PATRIOTISM** of certain learned Whigs, illustrated in prose and rhyme, for the use of "The inhabitants of Edinburgh". By Fair Play and Have at Them. Third edition. 32p. *8°*. *Edinburgh,* 1820.

23061 PEEL, SIR ROBERT, *1st Bart.* The substance of the speech of Sir Robert Peel, Bart. addressed to the freeholders at Warwick, on his nomination of Mr. Spooner as a representative in Parliament for that county, October 24, 1820. *s.sh.fol. Birmingham,* [1820] *See note to no.* 20490.

23062 A **PEEP** at the origin of some of the King's pretended friends, and the Queen's real enemies. With occasional political and biographical observations, &c.&c. &c. 16p. *8°*. 1820.

23063 PRESTON, THOMAS. A letter to Lord Viscount Castlereagh; being a full development of all the circumstances relative to the diabolical Cato Street plot. 12p. *8°*. [1820]

23064 The **QUEEN** that Jack found...[On the reception given to Queen Caroline, upon her return to England. Signed: an Irishman.] Tenth edition. [36]p. *8°*. 1820.

23065 The **RADICAL-HOUSE** which Jack would build. With ten caricature engravings. [A political satire.] 10f. *8°*. *Exeter & London,* [1820 ?]

23066 RUSSELL, JOHN, *Earl Russell.* A letter from Lord J. Russell to Mr. Wilberforce, on the proceedings against the Queen, with the petition to his Majesty, assigning powerful reasons for suspending all those proceedings. 8p. *8°*. [1820]

23067 SINECURE, SHANDY, *Esq., F.R.S., pseud.* Third edition. Fair play; or, who are the adulterers, slanderers and demoralizers? Being an answer to the editor of "The News", on his enquiry "How many of the Queen's judges have been convicted of adultery?"... 32p. *8°*. 1820.

23068 A radical **SONG,** to the tune of "Lilibulero". *s.sh.fol. Oxford,* [*c.* 1820] [*Br.* 677(2)]

23069 [**STODDART,** SIR J.] Slop's shave at a broken Hone. [Satires, in verse, on W. Hone, anticipating his *Slap at Slop.*] 42p. *8°*. 1820.

23070 THISTLEWOOD, A. The trial of Arthur Thistlewood, on a charge of high treason in attempting to depose the King and assassinate his ministers. Including the whole of the evidence, speeches of counsel, &c.&c. Tried at the Sessions House, Old Bailey...April 17, 1820. 62p. *8°*. [1820]

23071 [**WADE,** JOHN.] The black book; or, corruption unmasked! Being an account of places, pensions, and sinecures...To which is added...lists of both Houses of Parliament...The whole forming a complete exposition of the cost, influence, patronage, and corruption of the borough government. 2 vols. *8°*. 1820–23. *See also* 1831 (FINANCE), 1835 (POLITICS); *for* New Parliament. An appendix to The black book, *see* 1826 (POLITICS).

23072 [**WASBOROUGH,** .] A letter from the King to his people. [A fictitious letter defending the King's conduct towards Queen Caroline.] 54p. *8°*. [1820]

23073 WESTMINSTER. A full report of the speeches and proceedings at a public meeting of the inhabitant householders, of the city...of Westminster... July 4th, 1820...To consider of an address of congratulation to be presented to Her Majesty Queen Caroline, on her arrival in this country. 19p. *8°*. [1820]

SOCIALISM

23074 ELLIS, G. A. New Britain. A narrative of a journey, by Mr. Ellis, to a country so called by its inhabitants, discovered in the vast plain of the Missouri, in North America, and inhabited by a people of British origin, who live under an equitable system of society, productive of peculiar independence and happiness... 336p. *8°*. 1820.

23075 HALL, CHARLES (1745 ?–1825 ?). An enquiry into the cause of the present distress of the people... Second edition. 324p. *8°*. 1820. *For other editions, see* The effects of civilization, *1805.*

23076 LEGOUIX, , *maître.* Cour d'Assises de Paris. Audience du 20 mars 1820. Procès de l'Organisateur. Plaidoyer de Me. Legouix, pour M. Henry de Saint-Simon. 55p. *4°*. [*Paris,* 1820] *The copy that belonged to Victor Considérant.*

23077 SAINT-SIMON, C. H. DE, *Comte.* Considerations sur les mesures à prendre pour terminer la révolution, présentées au Roi, ainsi qu'à messieurs les agriculteurs, négocians, manufacturiers et autres industriels qui sont membres de la Chambre des Députés. 98p. *8°*. *Paris,* 1820. *Reprinted in* Du système industriel, *1821 (q.v.).*

23078 —— Lettres de Henri Saint-Simon à Messieurs les jurés qui doivent prononcer sur l'accusation intendée contre lui. 42p. *8°*. *Paris,* 1820.

23079 A **VINDICATION** of Mr. Owen's plan for the relief of the distressed working classes, in reply to the misconceptions of a writer in No. 64 of the Edinburgh Review. 67p. *8°*. 1820.

MISCELLANEOUS

23080 **ATTORNIES** not conveyancers. Observations occasioned by...a Bill, purporting to be "To prevent unskilful persons from practising as conveyancers;" including, a refutation of the proposition...that in establishing regulations to secure efficiency in the practisers of conveyancing, it is unnecessary to require any qualification from attornies and solicitors. By a conveyancer. 71p. *8°.* 1820. *The Agar Ellis copy.*

23081 **CARTWRIGHT,** J. A bill of free and sure defence, or an act for a constitutional revival of the county power, or proper militia of the realm... 31p. *8°.* 1820.

23082 A **DIALOGUE** between John Smith and Thomas Brown, two fellow-apprentices, with a particular character of each. [A religious tract.] 8p. *8°.* [*c.* 1820]

23083 The **LIFE** of David; or, the history of the man after God's own heart...Reprinted from the edition of 1766. 68p. *8°.* 1820. *Variously attributed to Archibald Campbell (1726?–1780), John Noorthouck, and Peter Annet.*

23084 **LYSONS,** S. An account of the remains of a Roman villa discovered at Bignor...in the year 1811 and four following years. 37p. *12°. London, Chichester, &c.,* 1820. *The copy that belonged to George Agar Ellis, Baron Dover.*

23085 Great moral **PICTURE,** The court of death, painted by Rembrandt Peale, of Baltimore. 4p. *8°. N. York,* [*c.* 1820]

23086 **T.,** Y. S. A letter to the Right Hon. Lord Holland. A plan for a reform of abuses in the Church, and applying its valuable patronage to the present exigencies of the State, without the slightest oppression on the clergy. 11p. *8°.* [1820 ?] *Presentation copy to David Ricardo.*

23087 **WEDDERBURN,** R. Cast-iron parsons, or, hints to the public and the Legislature, on political economy, clearly proving that the clergy can be entirely dispensed with without injury to the Christian religion or the Established Church, and to the great advantage of the State... 11p. *8°.* [1820]

23088 **WESLEYAN METHODIST MISSIONARY AUXILIARY SOCIETY FOR THE LIVERPOOL DISTRICT.** The third report of the Wesleyan Methodist Auxiliary Society...for 1819. [With a list of subscribers and benefactors.] viii, 22, [12]p. *8°. Liverpool,* [1820]

23089 **YORKSHIRE AND LANCASHIRE AUXILIARY BAPTIST MISSIONARY SOCIETY.** Corrected notice. Baptist Missionary Society. [*Begin.*] The annual meeting of the...Society is intended to be held...the 13th inst....[With the programme of sermons to be preached. Dated: Liverpool, July 11, 1820.] *s.sh.8°. n.p.* [1820]

1821

GENERAL

23090 [**ATKINSON,** WILLIAM (1758–1846).] A letter to Lord Liverpool, on political economy. By the Old Inquirer. 29p. *8°. Bradford,* 1821.

23091 [**BANNISTER,** JOHN W.] Sketch of a plan for settling in Upper Canada, a portion of the unemployed labourers of England. By a settler. 25p. *8°.* 1821.

23092 **BOYES,** J. Observations addressed to the Right Hon. Lord Stourton, occasioned by his two letters to the Earl of Liverpool. 45p. *8°. York, London, &c.,* 1821.

23093 **BRYDGES,** SIR S. E., *Bart.* What are riches ? Or an examination of the definitions of this subject given by modern economists. 40p. *8°. Geneva,* 1821. *See also* 1822.

23094 **BURROUGHS,** E. A view of the state of agriculture in Ireland, with some remarks on the impediments to its prosperity...This work appeared in letters originally in the Dublin Journal, under the signature of Agricola. 62p. *8°. Dublin,* 1821.

23095 [**CALVERT,** W. J.] Monopoly and taxation vindicated against the errors of the legislature. By a Nottinghamshire farmer. 62p. *8°. Newark & London,* 1821. *For the supplement to this work, see* 1822.

23096 **CAREY,** M. Address to the farmers of the United States, on the ruinous consequences to their vital interests, of the existing policy of this country. 84p. *8°. Philadelphia,* 1821.

23097 —— The new olive branch: or, an attempt to establish an identity of interest between agriculture, manufactures, and commerce and to prove, that...the manufacturing industry of this nation has been sacrificed to commerce...Second edition. 130p. *8°. Philadelphia,* 1821. *For another edition, see* 1820.

23098 **CONSIDERAÇÕES** importantes sobre o papel-moeda, divida publica, contrabandos, alfandegas, industria, e commercio nacional, etc. 80p. *4°. Lisboa,* 1821.

23099 **CRAIG,** JOHN (*fl.* 1814–1821). Remarks on some fundamental doctrines in political economy; illustrated by a brief inquiry into the commercial state of Britain, since the year 1815. 244p. *8°. Edinburgh & London,* 1821.

23100 *The **EAST-INDIA** register and directory, for 1821; corrected to the 28th February 1821; containing ...lists of the company's servants...Together with lists of...mariners, &c. not in the service of the...Company; and merchant vessels employed in the country trade. Compiled...by A. W. Mason & Geo. Owen... 518p. *12°. London, Dublin, &c.,* [1821]

23101 *—— Second edition, corrected to 28th August 1821. 491p. *12°.* [1821] *For other editions, see* 1804.

23102 [ELLIDGE, J. P.] An appeal to the farmers and land proprietors of Great Britain, on their present situation, the causes which have produced it and the political duties which it imposes on them; in remarks on the debates which took place in the House of Commons, respecting the repeal of the malt tax, and the agricultural horse tax: on the present system of taxation, and on the report of the agricultural committee. By a farmer's son. 62p. *8°. Hereford*, [1821] *Two presentation copies, with inscriptions from the author, one to the Hon. Henry Grey Bennet, the other to David Ricardo.*

23103 ENGLAND. Parliament. *House of Commons.* Report from the Select Committee, to whom the several petitions complaining of the depressed state of the agriculture of the United Kingdom were referred... 56p. *8°. 1821.*

23104 An ESSAY on the political economy of nations: or, a view of the intercourse of countries, as influencing their wealth. 288p. *8°. 1821.*

23105 FERRIER, F. L. A. Du gouvernement considéré dans ses rapports avec le commerce. Ou de l'administration commerciale opposée à l'economie politique... Seconde édition. 578p. *8°. Paris & Lille, 1821. The copy that belonged to the Société de Lecture de Genève. For other editions, see 1805.*

23106 FROST, J. A letter to Sir Charles Morgan, of Tredegar, Monmouthshire, Baronet, M.P. 44p. *8°. Cardiff, Newport printed, 1821.*

23107 GANILH, C. Des systèmes d'économie politique, de la valeur comparative de leurs doctrines, et de celle qui parait la plus favorable aux progrès de la richesse. Seconde édition, avec de nombreuses additions relatives aux controverses récentes de MM. Malthus, Buchanan, Ricardo, sur les points les plus importans de l'économie politique... 2 vols. *8°. Paris, Strasbourg, &c., 1821. For other editions, see 1809.*

23108 GELL, R. and BENNETT, R. Sheffield general and commercial directory, in which the names, occupations, &c. are... alphabetically arranged; also, a classification of all that are engaged in the various branches of the Sheffield manufacture, under their respective denominations... With a list of all the bankers in the kingdom... 176p. *12°. Sheffield, 1821.*

For GIORNALE DI AGRICOLTURA, ARTI E COMMERCIO, 1821–24, *see vol. III, Periodicals list.*

23109 HALL, G. W. Observations on the report from the Select Committee of the House of Commons, to whom the several petitions complaining of the depressed state of the agriculture of the United Kingdom, were referred in the session of 1821. 156p. *8°.* [1821]

23110 An INQUIRY into those principles, respecting the nature of demand and the necessity of consumption, lately advocated by Mr. Malthus, from which it is concluded, that taxation and the maintenance of unproductive consumers can be conducive to the progress of wealth. 128p. *8°. 1821.*

23111 [KANKRIN, E. F., *Graf.*] Weltreichthum, Nationalreichthum und Staatswirthschaft. Oder, Versuch neuer Ansichten der politischen Oekonomie. 247p. *8°. München, 1821.*

23112 LABORDE, A. L. J. DE, *Comte.* De l'esprit d'association dans tous les intérêts de la communauté, ou essai sur le complément du bien-être et de la richesse en France par le complément des institutions... Seconde édition, revue et augmentée. 2 vols. *8°. Paris, 1821. See also 1834.*

23113 LABOULINIÈRE, P. T. DE. De la disette et de la surabondance en France; des moyens de prévenir l'une, en mettant l'autre à profit, et d'empêcher les trop grandes variations dans le prix des grains... 2 vols. *8°. Paris, 1821.*

23114 LOTZ, J. F. E. Handbuch der Staatswirthschaftslehre. 3 vols. *8°. Erlangen, 1821–22.*

23115 M'QUEEN, J. A geographical and commercial view of northern central Africa: containing a particular account of the course and termination of the great River Niger in the Atlantic Ocean. 288p. *8°. Edinburgh, London, &c., 1821.*

23116 MAITLAND, JAMES, *8th Earl of Lauderdale.* Sketch of an address to His Majesty; submitted to the consideration of all who wish to call the attention of their Sovereign and of Parliament to the real grievance under which the nation is now suffering. 16p. *8°. n.p., 1821. The Agar Ellis copy.*

23117 MALTHUS, T. R. Principles of political economy considered with a view to their practical application. 472p. *8°. Boston, 1821. For other editions, see 1820.*

23118 MILL, JAMES. Elements of political economy. 235p. *8°. 1821. See also 1823, 1824, 1826, 1844.*

23119 MORELLET, A. Mémoires de l'abbé Morellet de l'académie française, sur le dix-huitième siècle et sur la Révolution; précédés de l'Eloge de l'abbé Morellet, par M. Lémontey. 2 vols. *8°. Paris, 1821. See also 1822.*

23120 MORGAN, S., *Lady.* Italy... [With 'Appendix. On the state of medicine in Italy, with brief notices of some of the universities and hospitals. (By Sir T. Charles Morgan.)'.] 2 vols. *4°. 1821.*

23121 NOTICE sur l'état actuel de la Turquie, considérée sous ses rapports commerciaux et politique avec l'Angleterre. 22p. *8°. Londres, 1821.*

23122 —— Remarks on the present state of Turkey, considered in its commercial and political relation with England. 20p. *8°. 1821.*

23123 NOTICES on political economy; or, an inquiry concerning the effects of debts and taxes, of the state of the currency and exchange, and of the balance of trade, as they operate on the community considered as a whole. 77p. *8°. 1821.*

23124 OBSERVATIONS on certain verbal disputes in political economy, particularly relating to value, and to demand and supply. 84p. *8°. 1821.*

23125 PARIS, JEAN J. Mémoire sur cette question: quelle est, dans l'état actuel de la France et dans ses rapports avec les nations étrangères, l'extension que l'industrie... doit donner aux différens genres d'inventions qui suppléent le travail des hommes par le travail des machines?... 122p. *8°. Paris, 1821.*

23126 PIGOT & Deans' New directory of Manchester, Salford, &c. for 1821–2... 335, 12p. *8°. Manchester,* [1821]

23127 PINSENT, J. Conversations on political economy; or, a series of dialogues... with remarks on our present distresses, their causes, and the remedies applicable to them. 108p. *8°. 1821. The copy that belonged to David Ricardo.*

23128 —— Letters to the Chairman of the Committee of the Honourable the House of Commons on the agricultural distresses, stating the causes of those distresses, and pointing out the remedies for them; and to David Ricardo ...in answer to his speech of the 7th of March, 1821... 36p. *8°.* 1821. *With a manuscript note by the author.*

23129 PLAYFAIR, W. A letter on our agricultural distresses, their causes and remedies; accompanied with tables and...charts, shewing and comparing the prices of wheat, bread, and labour, from 1565 to 1821... 72p. *8°.* 1821. *The copy that belonged to T. Spring Rice, Baron Monteagle. See also* 1822.

23130 RAVENSTONE, PIERCY, *pseud.?* A few doubts as to the correctness of some opinions generally entertained on the subjects of population and political economy. 474p. *8°.* 1821. *Two copies, one a presentation copy from the author to Henry Brougham, the other the copy that belonged to Sir Robert Peel.*

23131 RICARDO, D. On the principles of political economy and taxation...Third edition. 538p. *8°.* 1821. *For other editions, see* 1817.

23132 ROBERTSON, WILLIAM (1721–1793). An historical disquisition concerning the knowledge which the ancients had of India; and the progress of trade with that country...The eighth edition. 372p. *8°.* 1821. *The copy presented by T. C. Marsh to Thomas Westropp MacMahon (1813–1892), on his leaving Eton, in 1828. For other editions, see* 1791.

23133 ROUSSEAU, J. J. Contrato social, ou principios de direito politico...Por B. L. Vianna. 325p. *12°. Paris,* 1821. *For other editions, see* 1762.

23134 ROYAL INSTITUTION OF GREAT BRITAIN. A catalogue of the Library of the Royal Institution...including a complete list of all the Greek writers by the late Rev. Charles Burney...With an alphabetical index of authors by William Harris, keeper of the library. The second edition...enlarged and improved. 507p. *8°.* [*London,*] 1821. *Presentation copy from William Harris to T. Holt White.*

23135 SAY, J. B. Letters to Mr. Malthus, on several subjects of political economy, and on the cause of the stagnation of commerce. To which is added a catechism of political economy, or familiar conversations on the manner in which wealth is produced, distributed and consumed in society. Translated from the French...by John Richter. 82, 131p. *8°.* 1821. *With the library stamp of the National Political Union on the title-page.*

23136 —— [Another edition.] Letters to Mr. Malthus, on various subjects of political economy; particularly on the causes of the general stagnation of commerce... Translated for the Pamphleteer exclusively. [From *The Pamphleteer,* vol. XVII, no. 34.] 57p. *8°.* 1821. *For other editions, see* 1820 *and no.* 23139.

23137 —— A treatise on political economy; or, the production, distribution, and consumption of wealth... Translated from the fourth edition of the French, by C. R. Prinsep, M.A. With notes by the translator... 2 vols. *8°.* 1821.

23138 —— A treatise on political economy; or the production, distribution, and consumption of wealth... Translated from the fourth edition of the French by C. R. Prinsep, M.A. With notes by the translator. To which is added, a translation of the introduction, and additional notes, by Clement C. Biddle... 2 vols. *8°. Boston,* 1821.

23139 —— Tratado de economía política ó exposicion sencilla del modo con que se forman, se distribuyen y se consumen las riquezas. Cuarta edicion corregida y aumentada. A la cual se ha añadido un epitome de los principios fundamentales de la economía política... Nueva traduccion por D. Juan Sanchez Rivera...[With 'Cartas á M. Malthus sobre varios puntos de economía política'.] 2 vols. *4°. Madrid,* 1821. *For other editions, see* 1803.

23140 SEINE, *Département de la. Administration.* Recherches statistiques sur la ville de Paris et le Département de la Seine, recueil de tableaux dressés et réunis d'après les ordres de Monsieur le Comte de Chabrol... 113, [41]p., 63 tables. *8°. Paris,* 1821. *Published under the direction of J. B. J. Fourier, with some contributions by him. See also* 1823, 1826, 1829.

23141 SINCLAIR, SIR JOHN, *Bart.* A code of political economy, founded on the basis of statistical inquiries. Sketch of the introduction and Chapter I...A private communication, circulated for the purpose, of obtaining the assistance...to render the chapter...more complete. 69p. *8°. Edinburgh,* 1821. *For Chapter III, see* 1825.

23142 SMITH, THOMAS, *accountant, of London.* An attempt to define some of the first principles of political economy. 222p. *8°.* 1821. *Two presentation copies, with inscriptions from the author, one to Sir Robert Peel, the other to Nicholas Vansittart.*

23143 SOLLY, E. Considerations on political economy ...Translated from the German by Thomas Wilkinson. [With 'On the principles of national wealth...Berlin, 1816', and 'On the trade with England, reprinted from the Rhenish newspaper...Berlin, 1816'.] 102p. *8°.* 1821.

23144 STANHOPE, PHILIP H., *4th Earl Stanhope.* Proposed address to His Majesty on the present distress of the country. 49p. *8°.* 1821.

23145 STOKES, WHITLEY. Observations on the population and resources of Ireland. 95p. *8°. Dublin,* 1821.

23146 STOURTON, W., *Baron Stourton.* A third letter to the Right Honourable the Earl of Liverpool, in which the justice, policy, and necessity, of legislative relief to the agricultural distresses of the country are considered. 111p. *8°.* 1821.

23147 —— Two letters to the Right Honourable the Earl of Liverpool...on the distresses of agriculture, and their influence on the manufactures, trade, and commerce, of the United Kingdom: with observations on cash payments and a free trade. 175p. *8°.* 1821.

23148 —— Second edition, with additions. 188p. *8°.* 1821.

23149 SYME, J. The principles of political economy applied to the financial state of Great Britain...1821. 355p. *8°.* 1821.

23150 Loose **THOUGHTS** on agricultural distress and a national bankruptcy. By a Sussex freeholder. 38p. *8°.* 1821.

23151 TORRENS, R. An essay on the production of wealth; with an appendix, in which the principles of political economy are applied to the actual circumstances of this country. 430p. *8°.* 1821.

23152 TYDEMAN, H. W. Antwoord op de vrang, over de inrigtingen der gilden. (*Nieuwe Verhandelingen van het Zeeuwsch Genootschap der Wetenschappen,* 4, 1.) 123p. *8°. Middelburg,* 1821.

23153　W., W. A letter on the subjects of economical retrenchment, and Parliamentary reform, addressed to the middle ranks of the people of England. By a gentleman farmer. 6op. *8°. 1821.*

23154　WELBY, A. A visit to North America and the English settlements in Illinois, with a winter residence at Philadelphia; solely to ascertain the actual prospects of the emigrating agriculturist, mechanic and commercial speculator. 224p. *8°. London, Stamford, &c., 1821.*

23155　WILLIAMS, Peter B. The tourists' guide through the county of Caernarvon, containing a short sketch of its history, antiquities, &c. [With an appendix.] 189, xxiiip. *8°. Caernarvon, Chester, &c., 1821. The Rastrick copy.*

23156　[WRIGHT, F.] Views of society and manners in America; in a series of letters from that country to a friend in England, during...1818, 1819, and 1820. By an Englishwoman. 523p. *8°. 1821. See also 1822.*

AGRICULTURE

23157　BACON, Richard N. A report of the transactions at the Holkham sheep-shearing [organised by T. W. Coke], on...July 2, 3, 4 and 5, being the forty-third anniversary of that meeting. [With 'An attempt to explain the cause of the commercial...difficulties' by Robert Owen.] 124p. *8°. Norwich & London, [1821]*

23158　BEATSON, A. A supplement to A new system of cultivation, without lime, or dung, or summer fallows, as practised at Knowle Farm, in...Sussex, containing observations upon the construction and uses of a new agricultural implement... xxx, 59p. *8°. 1821. For* A new system of cultivation, *see 1820.*

23159　CHAPTAL, J. A. C., *Comte de Chanteloup.* Mémoire sur le sucre de betterave...Lu à l'Académie Royale des Sciences de l'Institut, le 23 octobre 1815. Troisième édition, corrigée et augmenté. 7op. *8°. Paris, 1821.*

23160　COBBETT, W. The American gardener; or, a treatise on the situation, soil, fencing and laying-out of gardens... [276]p. *12°. 1821.*

23161　—— Cottage economy: containing information relative to the brewing of beer, making of bread, keeping of cows, pigs...and relative to other matters deemed useful in the conducting of the affairs of a labourer's family. [Nos. 3–8.] p.[49]–207; iv, [48]p. *12°. [1821–23] First edition, in separate parts as issued. The title-page, dated 1822, list of contents and index were issued with no. 7, which was intended to be the last of the series. No. 8 was issued after the two collected editions of 1822. See also 1822, 1824, 1826, 1828, 1831, 1838.*

23162　COMMITTEE OF MANAGEMENT FOR THE AGRICULTURAL ASSOCIATIONS. Report of the Committee of Management for the Agricultural Associations throughout Great Britain; with observations on the report of the Select Committee of the House of Commons, to whom their petitions were referred in the session of Parliament 1821... 2op. *8°. [1821]*

23163　DAVY, Sir H., *Bart.* Elements of agricultural chemistry, in a course of lectures for the Board of Agriculture; delivered between 1802 and 1812...The third edition. 415p. *8°. London & Edinburgh, 1821. For other editions, see 1813.*

23164　ENGLAND. *Laws, etc.* An Act for dividing allotting and inclosing lands, in the parish and manor of Kenn, in the county of Devon. 2 Geo. IV. sess. 1821. 24p. *fol. n.p. [1821]*

23165　MUNRO, I. A guide to farm book-keeping, founded upon actual practice, and upon new and concise principles... 143p. *8°. Edinburgh, London, &c., 1821.*

23166　PLUMER, W. An address delivered before the Rockingham Agricultural Society, October 18th, 1821. 24p. *8°. Exeter [N.H.], 1821.*

23167　SINCLAIR, Sir John, *Bart.* The code of agriculture; including observations on gardens, orchards, woods, and plantations...Third edition... 593, 153p. *8°. London, Edinburgh, &c., 1821. For another edition, see 1817.*

CORN LAWS

23168　CONSIDERATIONS on the corn question &c.&c. ⟨Printed also in The Pamphleteer, No. xxxiv. for February, 1821.⟩ 32p. *8°. 1821.*

POPULATION

23169　GODWIN, W. Recherches sur la population, et sur la faculté d'accroissement de l'espèce humaine; contenant une réfutation des doctrines de M. Malthus sur cette matière...Traduit de l'anglais par F. S. Constancio ... 2 vols. *8°. Paris, 1821. For another edition, see 1820.*

23170　The QUESTION of population, particularly as it relates to the increase of numbers in the inhabitants of the United States, carefully examined...Being a detection of the gross blunders...of the article on Mr. Godwin's Enquiry concerning population, which appeared in the seventieth number of the Edinburgh Review. 52p. *8°. 1821.*

23171　READ, S. General statement of an argument on the subject of population, in answer to Mr. Malthus's theory. 44p. *8°. London & Edinburgh, 1821. Two presentation copies, with inscriptions from the author, one to William Godwin, the other to David Ricardo.*

23172　—— [Another issue.] 44p. *8°. Edinburgh & London, 1821. Presentation copy, with inscription, from the author to Alexander Macdonald.*

23173　REMARKS on Mr. Godwin's Enquiry concerning population. 98p. *8°. 1821.*

TRADES & MANUFACTURES

23174 ACCUM, F. C. A. A treatise on the art of brewing, exhibiting the London practice of brewing porter, brown stout, ale, table beer...Second edition. 252p. *12⁰*. 1821. *For another edition, see 1820.*

23175 The **BOOK** of English trades, and library of the useful arts...A new edition. 374p. *12⁰*. 1821. *For other editions, see 1811.*

23176 ÉTIENNE DE JOUY, V. J. État actuel de l'industrie française, ou coup d'œil sur l'exposition de ses produits, dans les salles du Louvre, en 1819. 221p. *8⁰*. *Paris,* 1821.

23177 KNOWLES, J. Letters which have passed between Messrs. Brunton, Middleton & Brunton...and John Knowles, Esq., of the Navy Office, respecting the invention and manufacture of chain cables. 30p. *12⁰*. 1821.

23178 SOCIÉTÉ D'ENCOURAGEMENT POUR L'INDUSTRIE NATIONALE. Extrait du Bulletin de la Société...no. CCVI. Rapport fait à la Société...au nom d'une commission spéciale, sur un appareil substitué à l'emploi de la forge dans plusieurs opérations de la fabrication des médailles, présenté à la Société par M. de Puymaurin fils...par M. Mérimée. 8p. *4⁰*. *Paris,* 1821.

COMMERCE

23179 BENOISTON DE CHATEAUNEUF, L. F. Recherches sur les consommations de tout genre de la ville de Paris en 1817; comparées à ce qu'elles étaient en 1789...Mémoire lu à l'Académie des Sciences...11 janvier 1819. Seconde édition, corrigée et augmentée. 157p. *8⁰*. *Paris,* 1821. *For another edition, see 1820.*

23179A —— Seconde partie. Consommation industrielle. 168p. *8⁰*. *Paris,* 1821.

23180 BENTHAM, J. Observations on the restrictive and prohibitory commercial system; especially with a reference to the decree of the Spanish Cortes of July 1820 ...From the MSS. of Jeremy Bentham, Esq. By John Bowring. 44p. *8⁰*. 1821.

23181 [**COCK,** S.] Observations on the report of the Select Committee of the House of Lords, relative to the timber trade. By a British merchant. 118p. *8⁰*. 1821.

23182 [——] Second edition. 118p. *8⁰*. 1821.

23183 HALL, Sir John. Observations upon the warehousing system and navigation laws, with a detailed account of many of the burthens to which the shipping and trade are subjected...To which is added, a corrected account of the substance of the speech delivered in the House of Commons, by the Right Honorable T. Wallace ...upon the introduction of the Bills for extending the warehousing system, and modifying the laws of navigation, copies of which are annexed. 133p. *8⁰*. [*London,* 1821]

23184 MORTON, G. An exposition of the privileges of the City of London, in regard to the claims of non-freemen to deal by wholesale within its jurisdiction. 72p. *8⁰*. 1821.

23185 REMARKS on the impolicy of restrictions on commerce; with a particular application to the present state of the timber trade. 33p. *8⁰*. 1821.

23186 A **REPLY** to the Observations of a British merchant on the Report of the Select Committee of the House of Lords, relative to the timber trade. By a merchant. 97p. *8⁰*. 1821.

COLONIES

23187 EMIGRATION to Canada. Narrative of a voyage to Quebec, and journey from thence to New Lanark, in Upper Canada...with an account of the country, as regards its climate, soil, and the actual condition of its inhabitants. By an emigrant from Glasgow. 30p. *12⁰*. *Glasgow,* 1821.

23188 HENRY, Jabez. Report on the criminal law at Demerara, and in the ceded Dutch colonies...With an appendix on the nature of the office of fiscal. 112p. *8⁰*. 1821.

23189 [**JAMESON,** Robert F.] Letters from the Havana, during the year 1820; containing an account of the present state of the island of Cuba, and observations on the slave trade. 135p. *8⁰*. 1821.

23190 MACQUARIE, L. A letter to the Right Honourable Viscount Sidmouth, in refutation of statements made by the Hon. Henry Grey Bennet, M.P. in a pamphlet "On the transportation laws, the state of the hulks, and of the colonies in New South Wales". 92p. *8⁰*. 1821. *The Agar Ellis copy.*

23191 SABATIER, W. A letter to the Right Honorable Frederick J. Robinson...on the subject of the proposed duties on colonial timber, and on some other colonial subjects; and on the relative situation of the British North American possessions, with the United States of America and Great Britain; pointing out the value and importance of the North British Colonies to the parent state, and the means of increasing their mutual prosperity. 75p. *8⁰*. 1821.

23192 THOUGHTS how to better the condition of Indo-Britons; by a practical reformer. 33p. *8⁰*. *Calcutta,* 1821.

FINANCE

23193 ATTWOOD, M. The speech of Matthias Attwood, Esq. M.P. in the House of Commons, April 9, 1821, on seconding Mr. Baring's amendment for the appointment of a Select Committee on the Bank Cash Payments Bill. 62p. *8°.* [1821]

23194 [BAILLEUL, J. C.] Principes sur lesquels doivent reposer les établissemens de prévoyance, tels que caisses d'épargnes, tontines, assurances sur la vie, etc. Suivis de l'Analyse comparée de la Caisse Lafarge, de la Tontine perpétuelle d'amortissement... 126p. *8°. Paris,* 1821.

23195 BELEUCHTUNG der in München erschienenen Schrift: Die Stock-Jobbery, und der Handel mit Staatspapieren nach dem jetzigen Zustande, politisch und juristisch betrachtet. 39p. *8°. Wien,* 1821.

23196 BIZET, L. C. Précis des diverses manières de spéculer sur les fonds publics en usage à la Bourse de Paris; avec des considérations sommaires sur les effets publics et les finances en général...Quatrième édition, revue, corrigée et...augmentée. 199p. *8°. Paris,* 1821.

23197 Fourth edition! The extraordinary red **BOOK:** an account of all places, pensions, sinecures, grants, &c. the expenditure of the Civil List, the finances and debt of Great Britain; with a variety of official documents... among which are Admiralty droits, land and other Crown revenues to February, 1821...By a commoner. 248, 57p. *12°.* 1821. *Attributed by HSF to R. J. Richardson. For other editions, see 1816.*

23198 BOOTH, D. The tradesman, merchant, and accountant's assistant; being tables for business in general, on a new plan of arrangement: shewing the value of 1. Any number of articles at any price, from 1 farthing to 20 shillings. 2. Dividends on bankrupt estates...3. Parts of an ounce of gold, or silver, at any price per ounce... 8, [334]p. *8°.* 1821.

23199 [CAMBRELENG, C. C.] An examination of the new tariff proposed by the Hon. Henry Baldwin...By one of the people. 268p. *8°. New-York,* 1821.

23200 COBBETT, W. Preliminary part of Paper against gold; the main object of which is to show the justice and necessity of reducing the interest of that which is called the National Debt...[Articles reprinted from *Cobbett's Political Register,* 1803–6.] 202 cols. *8°.* 1821.

23201 COMPAGNIE D'ASSURANCES GÉNÉRALES. Compagnie d'Assurances générales contre les risques maritimes et de navigation intérieure. Rapport fait à l'assemblée générale des actionnaires, par M. de Gourcuff, Directeur. 31p. *4°. n.p.* [1821] *See also* 1823, 1824, 1825, 1827.

23202 ENGLAND. *Commissioners of Customs.* Instructions for the controlling surveyor of warehouses, in the service of His Majesty's Customs at the out ports. 16p. *4°.* 1821.

23203 —— —— Instructions for the warehouse keepers of bonded goods, in the out ports. 19p. *4°.* 1821.

23204 On the **EXPEDIENCY** and necessity of striking off a part of the National Debt; with observations on its practicability, with the least possible injury... [From *The Pamphleteer,* vol. XVIII, no. 36.] 23p. *8°.* 1821.

23205 FRANCE. *Chambre des Députés.* No. 112. Opinion de M. le Vicomte Donnadieu, Député des Bouches-du-Rhône, sur le projet de loi relatif au Budget de 1821. (Dépenses.) Imprimée par ordre de la Chambre. 50p. *8°. [Paris,* 1821]

23206 —— —— No. 254. Opinion de M. le Vicomte de Castelbajac, Député de la Haute-Garonne, sur le Budget des Recettes de l'exercice 1821. Imprimée par ordre de la Chambre. 28p. *8°. [Paris,* 1821]

23207 —— —— No. 255. Opinion de M. le Cte. Humbert de Sesmaisons, Député de la Loire-Inférieure, sur le Budget des Recettes de l'exercice 1821. Imprimé par ordre de la Chambre. Séance du 10 juillet 1821. 7p. *8°.* [*Paris,*] 1821.

23208 —— *Chambre des Pairs.* Session de 1820. Séance du...24 février, 1821. Rapport fait à la Chambre ...et à celle des Députés par la Commission de Surveillance de la Caisse d'amortissement et de celle des dépôts et consignations, en exécution des articles 114 et 115 de la loi du 28 avril, 1816. Imprimé par ordre de la Chambre. 13p. *8°. n.p.* [1821] *The copy that belonged to David Ricardo. See also* 1820.

23209 IBBETSON, J. H. A practical view of an invention for the better protecting bank-notes against forgery. Illustrated by various specimens. [With a supplement, containing comments on Sir William Congreve's *Analysis.*] 68p. *8°.* 1821. *A reissue of the edition of 1820 (q.v.), with an engraved title-page, dated 1821, preceding the original printed title.*

23210 KEARNEY, R. A plan for the effectual and permanent relief of the agricultural and commercial distresses, of the United Kingdom of Great Britain and Ireland. 43p. *8°. Dublin,* 1821.

23211 KELLY, P. The universal cambist and commercial instructor; being a full and accurate treatise on the exchanges, monies, weights, and measures, of all trading nations and their colonies; with an account of their banks, public funds, and paper currencies...The second edition, including a revision of foreign weights and measures... 2 vols. *4°.* 1821. *For other editions, see* 1811.

23212 [LANCASTER, J. ?] The Bank – the Stock Exchange – the bankers – the bankers' clearing house – the Minister, and the public. An exposé touching their various mysteries, from the times of Boyd...to those of Bowles, Aslett, Lord Peterborough, Cochrane, &c.... With a plan for the indubitable advantage of the Minister by the daily purchases for the Sinking Fund being made openly...[First Part.] 108p. *8°.* 1821. *No more published.*

23213 [——] [Another issue.] An exposé, touching the various mysteries of the Bank – the Stock Exchange... 108p. *8°.* [1821 ?] *The title-page is a cancel. There is no indication that a second part was still planned.*

23214 A LETTER to the landlords & tenants, of Hampshire, on the subject of rents. [Signed: A Hampshire farmer.] 28p. *8°. Andover,* 1821.

23215 LUMBY, T. A copy of a letter, to the Right Honorable the Chancellor of the Exchequer, upon the illegal nature and pernicious tendency of a system in operation upon the public funds, under the appellation of stock jobbing. 14p. *8°*. [1821] *The copy that belonged to David Ricardo.*

23216 MORGAN, W. The principles and doctrine of assurances, annuities on lives, and contingent reversions, stated and explained. 326p. *8°*. 1821.

23217 MOYES, L. A letter to the Earl of Liverpool, on the necessity of amending the excise system, for the purpose of promoting the comforts and morals of the inhabitants of the northern districts of Scotland. 22p. *8°*. *Aberdeen*, 1821.

23218 MUSHET, R. A series of tables exhibiting the gain and loss to the fundholder, arising from the fluctuations in the value of the currency. From 1800 to 1821. [With 'Abstract of the foregoing tables'.] xi, [57]p. *8°*. 1821.

23219 —— Second edition, corrected. xii, [36]p. *8°*. 1821.

23220 [PLACE, F.] The mystery of the Sinking Fund explained. ⟨From "The Traveller" of Thursday, January 4.⟩ [Signed: F.P.] 8p. *8°*. [*London*, 1821]

23221 RATTON, D. Reflexões sobre o papel-moeda em circulação...em 11 de outubro de 1821. 6p. *fol. n.p.* [1821]

23222 A **REVIEW** of the banking system of Britain; with observations on the injurious effects of the Bank of England charter, and the general benefits of unrestricted banking companies. 248p. *8°*. *Edinburgh & London*, 1821.

23223 SPAIN. *Tesorería General de la Real Casa.* Estado general clasificado de lo ingresado y pagado por la Tesoreria General de la Real Casa, desde 1°. de mayo de 1814, á fin de enero de 1821. 14p. *4°*. *Madrid*, 1821.

23224 [TAYLOR, JOHN (1781–1864).] The restoration of national prosperity, shewn to be immediately practicable. By the author of "Junius identified". [Concerning the currency and the National Debt.] 93p. *8°*. 1821. *Presentation copy, with inscription, from the author to the Right Hon. Henry Grey Bennett.*

23225 [VALERIANI MOLINARI, L.] Contro la sentenza del celebre...Adam Smith che l'unità monetaria moneta di conto traggesi nella colta Europa dall' argento piuttosto per particolari consuetudini che per universali cagioni...Dissertazione...chiamata nella parte seconda delle Ricerche sull' agostaro... 207p. *4°*. *Bologna*, 1821. *For* Ricerche critiche ed economiche sull' agostaro di Federigo II, *see 1819, and for another continuation, see 1822.*

23226 A full **VIEW** of the British Commons, as constituted in the nineteenth century of the Christian era, when the debt of Great Britain had reached to 1,206,159,466 pounds sterling, under "the gigantic system of swindling," called paper currency; as denounced by William Pitt, in his best days. 35p. *8°*. 1821.

23227 A **VIEW** of the circulating medium of the Bank of England, from its incorporation to the present time; including, reflections on the nature of its liability to furnish gold for the King's Mint, account of the profits derived from the Bank Restriction Acts...and the necessity of obtaining a more enlarged and economical medium for circulating the Debt... 41p. *8°*. 1821. *With the signature 'Robt. Mayne' on the title-page, here tentatively identified as that of the author by HSF in a note in the volume.*

23228 VOX populi vox Dei: a complaynt of the commons against taxes. [A sixteenth-century metrical tract, printed from MS.Harl.367.] 37p. *4°*. 1821.

23229 WILKINSON, H. Property against industry: or, an exposition of the partiality, oppression, inequality & injustice, of the present system of finance: demontrating [sic] that property is the only just source of revenue; and that all taxes ought to be imposed on property, and not unjustly collected from daily labour... 60p. *8°*. 1821.

23230 WILKS, J. A practical scheme for the reduction of the public debt and taxation, without individual sacrifice. 41p. *8°*. *London, Edinburgh, &c.*, 1821.

23231 WOODROW, J. Remarks on banks for savings and friendly societies; with an original plan combining the principles of both institutions: a friendly loan fund, and other important advantages. 50[52]p. *8°*. 1818 [1821]. *A reissue of the pamphlet published in 1818 (q.v.) with an 8-page supplement, dated 'March 1821', at the end. The copy that belonged to David Ricardo.*

TRANSPORT

23232 BRUSCHETTI, S. Istoria dei progetti e delle opere per la navigazione-interna del Milanese. 291p. *4°*. *Milano*, 1821.

23233 ENGLAND, *Laws, etc.* An Act for making and maintaining a railway or tramroad from the River Tees at Stockton, to Witton Park Colliery, with several branches therefrom, all in the county of Durham. ⟨Royal Assent, 19 April 1821.⟩ 2 Geo. IV. sess. 1821. 67p. *fol.* [*London*, 1821]

23234 ENGLEFIELD, SIR H. C., *Bart.* Observations on the probable consequences of the demolition of London Bridge. 63p. *8°*. 1821.

23235 LONDON. *Court of Common Council.* Thorp, Mayor. A Common Council, holden...5th day of April, 1821. A brief statement of the produce of the Bridge-House estates...for the year ending 31st December, 1820 ... 15p. *fol.* [1821]

23236 —— —— Thorp, Mayor. A Common Council holden...2d day of June 1821. [*Begin.*] The committee for letting the Bridge-House estates did this day deliver...a report...[With 'London Bridge Minutes taken before the Select Committee of the House of Commons...1820, to enquire into the state of London Bridge'.] 149p. *fol.* [1821]

23237 McADAM, JOHN L. Remarks on the present system of road making...Fourth edition, carefully revised, with considerable additions, and an appendix. [With 'Report from the Select Committee on the highways of the Kingdom: together with the minutes of evidence taken before them'.] 196p. *8°*. 1821. *For other editions, see 1816.*

23238 [*Begin.*] At a numerous and respectable **MEETING** of merchants, traders and inhabitants...residing near the public highway, abutting upon the river Thames, westward of London Bridge...held...5th...of March,

1821: James Ebenezer Saunders, Esq. in the chair; re-solved...That the public highway along the waterside...is likely to be materially affected...by the operation of a Bill...for repealing so much of an Act of the 22nd year of King Charles II. as restrains the proprietors of wharfs...from erecting any buildings or inclosures thereon...[With 'Extracts from the proclamation and several Acts of Parliament passed in the reign of King Charles II. relating to the open wharf or key along the north bank of the river Thames, from London Bridge to the Temple'.] 5p. *fol.* [*London*, 1821]

23239 Interesting **PARTICULARS,** relative to that great national undertaking, the breakwater, now con-structing in Plymouth Sound, together with a copy of the Order in Council [and the reports of J. Rennie and J. Whidbey]... 34p. *8°. Plymouth Dock*, [1821]

23240 A further **REPORT,** of the intended rail or tram road, from Stockton, by Darlington, to the collieries, with a branch to Yarum. 22p. *8°. Darlington*, 1821. *The Rastrick copy.*

23241 STEVENSON, R. To His Grace the Duke of Roxburgh...and the other noblemen...of Mid-Lothian,

Roxburgh, Selkirk, and Berwick, the report of Robert Stevenson, civil engineer [on the proposed Roxburgh and Selkirk Railway. With 'Estimates of expence and revenue'.] 12p. *4°. n.p.* [1821] *The Rastrick copy.*

23242 WICKENS, W. The improvement of the public roads urged, during the existing dearth of employ-ment for the poor. Republished with alterations and addi-tions. 61[55]p. *8°*. 1821.

23243 WINGROVE, B. Remarks on a Bill now before Parliament, to amend the general laws for regulating turnpike-roads: in which are introduced, strictures on the opinions of Mr. M'Adam, on the subject of roads, and to which are added, suggestions...on various points essential to the perfection of the road system. 35p. *8°. Bath*, 1821.

23244 WORCESTER, *County of. Quarter Sessions.* The parish surveyor's appointment and guide, for the highways. 14p. *8°. Worcester*, 1821. *p.3 contains the form, completed in manuscript in October 1821, appointing Sir Thomas Phillipps, Bart. and Michael Russell surveyors for the parish of Broadway.*

SOCIAL CONDITIONS

23245 ALLEN, L. B. Brief considerations on the present state of the police of the Metropolis: with a few suggestions towards its improvement. 76p. *8°*. 1821.

23246 ASSOCIATION FOR THE SUPPRES-SION OF MENDICITY, *Dublin.* Report of the general committee of the Association...for the year 1820. 55p. *8°. Dublin*, 1821. *See also* 1819, 1825, 1831, 1837.

23247 BOSCH, J. VAN DEN, *Graaf.* De la colonie de Frederiks-Oord et des moyens de subvenir aux besoins de l'indigence par le défrichement des terres vagues et incultes. Traduction d'un manuscrit du Général-Major van den Bosch; par le Baron de Keverberg...Avec une préface du traducteur. [With 'Pièces à l'appui du Mémoire sur la colonie de Frederiks-Oord'.] 110p. *8°. Gand*, 1821. *The copy presented, with an inscription, by Baron de Kever-berg to Lady Strickland.*

23248 BUXTON, SIR THOMAS F., *Bart.* Severity of punishment. Speech of Thomas Fowell Buxton, Esq. in the House of Commons...May 23rd, 1821, on the Bill "for mitigating the severity of punishment in certain cases of forgery, and the crimes connected therewith". 70p. *8°*. 1821.

23249 CARLILE, R. An address to men of science; calling upon them to stand forward and vindicate the truth from...superstition...In which a sketch of a proper system for the education of youth is submitted to their judgment. 48p. *8°*. 1821.

23250 CHALMERS, T. The Christian and civic economy of large towns. 3 vols. *8°. Glasgow, Edinburgh, &c.*, 1821–26. *See also* 1840.

23251 DAVIS, WILLIAM. Hints to philanthropists; or, a collective view of practical means for improving the condition of the poor and labouring classes of society...160p. *8°. Bath & London*, 1821. *The copy that belonged to William Allen.*

23252 ENGLAND. *Laws, etc.* A collection of the Statutes relating to the Post Office in Scotland. 11, 413, 10p. *12°. Edinburgh*, 1821.

23253 —— *Parliament.* [*Endorsed:*] An Act [a Bill] for lighting with gas, the borough of Leicester...and the liberties precincts and suburbs thereof. 2 Geo. IV. sess. 1821. 39p. *fol.* [*London*, 1821]

23254 —— —— [*Endorsed:*] An Act [a Bill] for supply-ing the towns of Old and New Brentford, and the villages of Turnham Green, Hammersmith, and Kensington, in the county of Middlesex, with gas. 1821. 40p. *fol.* [*London*, 1821]

23255 —— —— [*Endorsed:*] A Bill for supplying the parish of All Saints, Poplar, in the county of Middlesex, with gas. 1821. 44p. *fol.* [*London*, 1821]

23256 FRIENDLY SOCIETY OF JOINERS, *Newcastle-upon-Tyne.* Rules and regulations to be observed by the Friendly Society of Joiners; instituted at Newcastle upon Tyne January 1, 1777, for the relief of each other in distress...These rules were altered and amended January 1, 1821. 28p. *8°. Newcastle*, 1821.

23257 GENEVA. Projet de code pénal pour la Répu-blique et Canton de Genève; présenté par le Comité préparatoire à la Commission, établie par un arrêté du Conseil d'Etat, le 28 mai, 1817. 89p. *8°. Genève*, 1821. *The copy that belonged to David Ricardo.*

23258 GREAT YARMOUTH. A copy of the rate and assessment made on the occupations, stocks in trade of the principal inhabitants of Great Yarmouth, towards the relief of the poor...ending Michaelmas, 1821, at the rate of 4s. on the pound. 30p. *fol. Yarmouth*, [1821]

23259 [HALL, ROBERT.] A reply to the principal objections advanced by Cobbett and others against the Framework-Knitters' Friendly Relief Society. By the author of "The appeal." 32p. *8°. Leicester & London*, 1821.

23260 HOLFORD, G. P. Thoughts on the criminal prisons of this country, occasioned by the Bill now in the House of Commons, for consolidating and amending the laws relating to prisons. 80p. *8°*. 1821.

23261 HUNT, H. A peep into a prison; or, the inside of Ilchester Bastile... 24p. *8°*. 1821.

23262 INVESTIGATION at Ilchester Gaol, in the county of Somerset, into the conduct of William Bridle, the gaoler, before the Commissioners appointed by the Crown. The evidence taken by H. B. Shillibear. Dedicated, with an address to his Majesty, King George the Fourth, by Henry Hunt, Esq. [With 'To the Sheriff, magistrates, freeholders, and county-rate-payers of the county of Somerset' by Henry Hunt.] 271, 8p. *8°.* 1821.

For the LABOURER'S FRIEND *and handicraft's chronicle, 1821–24, see vol. III, Periodicals list.*

23263 LA VIEUVILLE, DE, *Comte.* Des Instituts d'Hofwyl, considérés, plus particulièrement, sous les rapports qui doivent occuper la pensée des hommes d'état. [An account of the educational community established at Hofwyl by Philipp Emanuel von Fellenberg.] Par le Cte L. de V. 209p. *8°. Genève & Paris,* 1821.

23264 A LETTER addressed to the Honourable John Frederick Campbell, M.P. on the poor laws, and the practical effect to be produced by the Act of 59 Geo. III, c. 12. commonly called the Select Vestry Act. By a magistrate of the county of Pembroke. 60p. *8°.* 1821.

23265 A LETTER to a Member of Parliament, on the police of the Metropolis. By a barrister. 42p. *8°.* 1821.

23266 LETTER to the Right Honble. John, Earl of Eldon, Lord High Chancellor of England, on the subject of forgeries and bank prosecutions, and on the proposed amelioration of the criminal laws. 31p. *8°.* 1821. *A manuscript note on the verso of the half-title reads: Received by the 2d. post, on the envelope was written 'From John Hill Wagstaff...'.*

23267 LONDON. *Court of Common Council.* Report of the Committee for General Purposes: with minutes of evidence relative to the disturbance at Knightsbridge on ...the 26th day of August 1821. Ordered to be printed by Co.Co. 6th December 1821. 71p. *fol.* [1821]

23268 —— —— [*Begin.*] Thorp, Mayor. A Common-Council holden...18th day of October, 1821...[An order for better regulating the nightly watch and beadles within the City of London.] 10p. *fol.* [1821]

23269 MONTAGU, B. Thoughts upon the abolition of the punishment of death in cases of bankruptcy. [With the evidence before the Committee, its Report and the text of the Act 1 Geo. IV, c. 115.] 71p. *8°.* 1821. *The copy that belonged to David Ricardo.*

23270 MYNSHUL, G. Essayes and characters of a prison and prisoners. xviii, 91p. *8°. Edinburgh,* 1821. *A facsimile of the 1618 edition, with an introduction on the author.*

23271 OBSERVATIONS, chiefly in reply to remarks made in Parliament, during the last session, on the subject of government clerks. By a clerk. [Concerning a proposed reduction of their salaries.] 78p. *8°.* 1821.

23272 OBSERVATIONS on Mr. Brougham's Bill "for better providing the means of education for His Majesty's subjects;" shewing its inadequacy to the end proposed, and the dangers that will arise from it to the cause of religious liberty. Second edition. 34p. *8°.* 1821.

23273 PEMBROKE, *County of. Quarter Sessions.* Additional rules, orders, and regulations, to be strictly observed...in the infliction of punishment, by hard labour, and occasional solitary confinement, in the House of Correction, for the county of Pembroke, approved and adopted by the magistrates...on the eleventh day of July,

1821. [Signed: Saml. Heywood, J. Balguy.] 8p. *8°. n.p.* [1821 ?] *The copy bound, with other papers concerning the Gaol and House of Correction, for the Earl of Cawdor, with his name in gilt on the upper cover.*

23274 —— —— Letter from the Committee of magistrates of the County of Pembroke, to Samuel Hoare, Esq. chairman of the Society for Promoting Prison Discipline, Lombard Street, London. [Signed: H. Leach, chairman, and dated, 30th August, 1821.] 10p. *8°. Haverfordwest,* [1821 ?] *See note to no.* 23273 *above.*

23275 —— —— Report of the Committee of magistrates, appointed by the Quarter Sessions, to carry into execution, an unanimous vote of the justices...for improving and making additions to the Gaol and House of Correction of the said county. [Signed: H. Leach, chairman.] 19p. *8°.* [1821 ?] *See note to no.* 23273.

23276 The QUESTION &c. [Endorsing the views of Robert Hall in *An appeal to the public on the subject of the framework knitters' fund.*] 17p. *8°.* [*Nottingham,* 1821 ?] *Wanting the title-page. It seems likely that the full title of this pamphlet is* The question at issue (*see no.* 23277 *below*).

23277 The "QUESTION at issue" decided! Or remarks on the inefficacy and inexpediencey of funds and agreements to keep up the price of labour. With some strictures on an Appeal to the public [by Robert Hall]. 18p. *8°. Nottingham,* 1821.

23278 [ROBERTSON, JOSEPH C. and BYERLEY, T.] The Percy anecdotes, original and select. By Sholto and Reuben Percy... 178p. *12°.* 1821.

23279 SAUNDERS, WILLIAM H. An address to the Imperial Parliament, upon the practical means of gradually abolishing the poor-laws, and educating the poor systematically. Illustrated by an account of the colonies of Fredericks-Oord...and of the Common Mountain, in the south of Ireland... 125p. *8°.* 1821.

23280 SMITH, JOHN, *cooper, and others.* Report of the trial of an indictment, prosecuted at the instance of the West India Dock Company, versus John Smith, Walter Foreman, Samuel Hucks, and Daniel Hall for an alledged conspiracy...tried...the 13th of December, 1821... 250p. *8°.* [1821]

23281 SOCIETY FOR RELIEF OF THE DESTITUTE SICK. Report of the Society...December, 1821. [With a list of subscribers.] 28p. *8°. Edinburgh,* 1821.

23282 SOCIETY FOR SUPERSEDING THE NECESSITY OF CLIMBING BOYS, *London.* Society for superseding the necessity of climbing boys... [Tenth report of the Committee, read at the annual general meeting, 1st May 1821.] 32p. *8°.* 1821. *See also* 1834.

23283 SOCIETY FOR THE PREVENTION OF PAUPERISM, *New York.* Plain directions on domestic economy, showing particularly what are the cheapest and most nourishing articles of food and drink, and the best modes of preparation... 16p. *8°. New-York,* 1821.

23284 SOCIETY OF ANTIQUARIES. Extracts from the household book of the Lord North, in the time of Queen Elizabeth. Communicated to the Society of Antiquaries by William Stevenson...in a letter to Thomas Amyot...From the Archaeologia, vol. XIX. 19p. *4°.* 1821.

23285 SOCIETY OF INDUSTRY, *Caistor.* Reports of the several institutions of the Society of Industry established at Caistor, A.D. 1800, for the better relief and employment of the poor, and to save the parish money... [Edited by W. Dixon.] 3 vols. *8°. Caistor, London, &c.,* 1821.

23286 TALE of woe; or, an account of the distresses of the year 1820; also a view of the wonderful events which will take place in the present year, by a distressed prophet, to a run-away emigrant. *s.sh.fol.* [*Glasgow,* 1821] [*Br.* 495]

23287 TAYLOR, B., *and others.* A report of the proceedings on the conviction of Benjamin Taylor, John Ball, Wm. Rutherford, and James Snow, part of the Framework-knitters' Committee... at the Town Hall, in Nottingham, April 30, 1821. 12p. *8°.* [*Nottingham,* 1821]

23288 TAYLOR, J., *M.D.* A letter addressed to the Legislature on vaccination. 14p. *8°. Bath,* [1821]

23289 The TURN OUT; or, an inquiry into the present state of the hosiery business; with a particular reference to the distressed condition of the frame-work knitters, and the appeals made on their behalf to the public at large. By an observer. 16p. *8°. Derby, Nottingham, &c.,* 1821.

23290 WESTERN, C. C., *Baron Western.* Remarks upon prison discipline, &c. &c. In a letter addressed to the Lord Lieutenant and magistrates of the county of Essex. 117p. *8°.* 1821. *See also* 1825.

SLAVERY

23291 AFRICAN INSTITUTION. Foreign slave trade. Abstract of the information recently laid on the table of the House of Commons on the subject of the slave trade; being a report made by a committee specially appointed for the purpose, to the directors of the African Institution on the 8th of May, 1821, and by them ordered to be printed... 180p. *8°.* 1821.

23292 [BLANCO Y CRESPO, J. M., afterwards **BLANCO WHITE, J.]** Bosquéjo sobre o commercio em escravos, e reflexoes sobre este trafico considerado moral, politica, e cristamente. 98p. *8°. Londres,* 1821. *The copy that belonged to Stephen Lushington. For another edition, see* 1814.

23293 BOWRING, Sir J. Contestacion á las observaciones de D. Juan Bernardo O'Gavan, sobre la suerte de los negros de Africa, y reclamacion contra el tratado celebrado con los ingleses en 1817. 31p. *4°. Madrid,* 1821.

23294 Breve RESUMO sobre a natureza do commercio de escravatura e das atrocidades que d'elle resultam: seguido de huma relaçao historica dos debates que terminaram a final aboliçaõ. 112p. *8°. Londres,* 1821. *The copy that belonged to Stephen Lushington.*

23295 SEVERIANO MACIEL DA COSTA, J. Memoria sobre a necessidade de abolir a introdução dos escravos africanos no Brasil; sobre o modo e condiçõis com que esta abolição se deve fazer; e sobre os meios de remediar a falta de braços que ela pode ocasionar... Oferecida aos Brasileiros seus compatriotas. 90p. *4°. Coimbra,* 1821.

23296 UNITED STATES OF AMERICA. Congress. *House of Representatives.* [59] Report of the committee to which was referred so much of the President's message as relates to the slave trade. February 9, 1821. Read, and ordered to lie upon the table. [With 'Papers relating to the slave trade. Presented to both Houses of Parliament [of Great Britain], by command of the Prince Regent, February, 1819'.] 88p. *8°. n.p.* [1821]

POLITICS

23297 [ADAIR, Sir Robert.] The declaration of England against the acts and projects of the Holy Alliance. With an appendix containing official documents. 83p. *8°.* 1821. *Attributed to Sir Robert Adair in a manuscript note by George Agar Ellis, Baron Dover, on the title-page of this copy.*

23298 —— Two letters from Mr. Adair to the Bishop of Winchester, in answer to the charge of a high treasonable misdemeanour, brought by His Lordship against Mr. Fox and himself, in his Life of the Right Honourable William Pitt. 87p. *8°.* 1821. *The Agar Ellis copy.*

23299 [ATKINSON, William (1758–1846).] Letters to Lord Viscount Milton: to which is added, a sermon to electors and men in office. By the Old Inquirer. 35p. *8°. Bradford,* 1821.

23300 [——] Remarks on the strictures in the Leeds Mercury, upon the Rev. M. Jackson's coronation sermon, &c.&c.&c. By the Old Inquirer. 34p. *8°. Bradford,* 1821.

23301 [——] A speech intended to have been spoken at the meeting of the clergy, at Wakefield, upon the Popish question, March 20th, 1821. 9p. *8°. Bradford,* 1821.

23302 [BENTINCK, Lord William C. C.] A short statement of the past and present political state of the Sicilian nation... To which is added a summary of the constitution of 1812; and copies of the papers relative to Sicily, laid before Parliament, May 14th, 1821. 62p. *8°.* 1821. *Attributed to Lord William Bentinck in a manuscript note on the title-page of this copy by George Agar Ellis, Baron Dover.*

23303 BRUGIÈRE DE BARANTE, A. G. P., *Baron de Barante.* Des communes et de l'aristocratie. 256p. *8°. Paris,* 1821.

23304 CARLILE, Jane. Report of the trial of Mrs. Carlile, on the Attorney-General's ex-officio information for the protection of tyrants; with the information and defence at large... 24p. *8°.* 1821.

23305 CARLILE, M. A. Bridge-Street banditti, versus the press. Report of the trial of Mary-Anne Carlile, for publishing A New-Year's address to the reformers of Great Britain, written by Richard Carlile... With the... speech of Mr. Cooper in defence... 53p. *8°.* 1821.

23306 —— Suppressed defence. The defence of Mary-

Anne Carlile, to the Vice Society's indictment against the Appendix to the theological works of Thomas Paine; which defence was suppressed by Mr. Justice Best... 44p. *8°*. 1821.

23307 [CARLILE, R.] The character of a peer, by Philanthropos. 8p. *8°*. 1821.

23308 [——] The character of a priest; by Philanthropos. 8p. *8°*. 1821.

23309 [——] The character of a soldier; by Philanthropos. 8p. *8°*. 1821. *See also* 1822.

23310 —— An effort to set at rest some little disputes and misunderstandings between the reformers of Leeds, upon the subject of some late deputy meetings and a declaration of sentiments arising therefrom. 28p. *8°*. 1821.

23311 —— Price fourpence. A New Year's address to the reformers of Great Britain. [Jan. 1st.] 16p. *8°*. [*London:*] *R. Carlile*, [1821]

23312 —— [Another edition.] Price two pence... 16p. *8°*. [*London:*] *M. A. Carlile*, [1821]

23313 —— To the reformers of Great Britain. Dorchester Gaol, March 3... 15p. *8°*. 1821.

23314 —— Price two pence. To the reformers of Great Britain. Dorchester Gaol, April 23... 16p. *8°*. [1821]

23315 —— Price sixpence. To the reformers of Great Britain. Dorchester Gaol, June 24... 32p. *8°*. [1821]

23316 —— Price six pence. To the reformers of Great Britain...Dorchester Gaol, October 13th...[With 'Catalogue of R. Carlile's publications'.] 43, 5p. *8°*. [1821]

23317 CATO, *pseud*. Cato's letters; to the Earl of Harewood, and the Earl of Liverpool; with a letter to the Queen, by a widowed wife. 66p. *8°*. *Canterbury*, 1821.

23318 CROLY, G. The Coronation. Observations on the public life of the King. 56p. *8°*. *London & Edinburgh*, 1821.

23319 DEATH-BED confessions of the late Countess of Guernsey, to Lady Anne H*******; developing a series of mysterious transactions connected with the most illustrious personages in the Kingdom: to which are added, the Q——'s last letter to the K——, written a few days before Her M——'s death, and other authentic documents, never before published. 48p. *8°*. [1821]

23320 FOX, afterwards VASSALL, H. R., *3rd Baron Holland*. Speech of Lord Holland, in the House of Lords, February 19. 1821, on Earl Grey's motion for the production of papers on the subject of Naples. 18p. *8°*. *Edinburgh*, 1821.

23321 FUDGE, BOB, *pseud*. Radical Monday. A letter from Bob in Gotham to his cousin Bob in the country, containing an account of that glorious day!! With notes, illustrative, explanatory, and corrective, by the editor. [A poem, giving an account of a meeting, protesting at the Peterloo massacre, held on October 11th, 1819 at Newcastle]. 24p. *8°*. *Newcastle upon Tyne*, 1821.

23322 [GROTE, G.] Statement of the question of Parliamentary reform; with a reply to the objections of the Edinburgh Review, No. LXI. 139p. *8°*. 1821.

23323 HALL, ROBERT. An apology for the freedom of the press, and for general liberty: to which are prefixed, remarks on Bishop Horsley's sermon, preached on the 30th of January, 1793...The sixth edition with correc-

tions. 108p. *8°*. *London & Bristol*, 1821. *For other editions, see* 1793.

23324 HONE, W. Hone's select popular political tracts: consisting of The house that Jack built, The man in the moon, The political showman — at home, The Queen's ladder, and The form of prayer for Queen Caroline. A new edition. With numerous cuts, by Cruikshank, Williams, &c. [98]p. *8°*. [1821]

23325 [——] The man in the moon, &c.&c.&c. [Satires on George IV and others.] With fifteen cuts [by George Cruikshank]. Twenty-seventh edition. [24]p. *8°*. 1821. *For another edition, see* 1820.

23326 [——] The political house that Jack built. [With 'The clerical magistrate'.] With thirteen cuts. Fifty-second edition. [24]p. *8°*. 1821.

23327 [——] Fifty-third edition. [24]p. *8°*. 1821. *For other editions, see* 1819.

23328 [——] The political showman — at home! Exhibiting his cabinet of curiosities and creatures — all alive! By the author of the political house that Jack built... Twentieth edition. [32]p. *8°*. 1821.

23329 [KNOX, V.] The spirit of despotism. Dedicated to Lord Castlereagh. Edited by the author of "The political house that Jack built" [William Hone]...Second edition. 94p. *8°*. 1821.

23330 [——] Fifth edition. 94p. *8°*. 1821.

23331 [——] Sixth edition. 94p. *8°*. 1821.

23332 A LETTER to both sexes, on the case of Mrs. and Miss Carlile. 4p. *8°*. [*London*, 1821]

23333 A LETTER to the Lord Mayor and Common Council of the City of London. [Concerning their address to the Queen.] By a barister [*sic*]. 24p. *8°*. 1821.

23334 A LETTER to the Right Reverend the Lord Bishop of Winchester. [Signed: a Catholic, and dated, June 21, 1821.] 2p. *s.sh.fol. n.p.* [1821] *The Agar Ellis copy.*

23335 LINKS of the lower House. Or, an alphabetical list of the members of the House of Commons, showing the counties, cities, or boroughs for which they sit; and also...the offices, pensions, grants... 32p. *8°*. [*London*, 1821]

23336 [MILL, JAMES.] The article Government, reprinted from the supplement to the Encyclopædia Britannica. [Signed: F.F. Republished from the reprint of the article in the Traveller Evening Paper.] 32p. *8°*. *n.p.* 1821. *The copy that belonged to David Ricardo.*

23337 PEPE, G. A narrative of the political and military events, which took place at Naples, in 1820 and 1821; with observations explanatory of the national conduct in general, and of his own in particular, during that period...With an appendix of official documents... 130p. *8°*. 1821.

23338 PHILLPOTTS, H., *Bishop of Exeter*. A letter to the Right Hon. Earl Grey, on certain charges advanced by His Lordship in his speech at the late county meeting in Northumberland, against the clergy of the county of Durham...Second edition. 44p. *8°*. *London & Durham*, 1821.

23339 [SMITH, WILLIAM H.] A radical misrepresented and truly-represented or, a two-fold character of radicalism...To which is added a brief history of the rise and fall of the Island of Peterloo. [Signed: W.H.S.]

30p. *8°.* [*London, 1821 ?*] *The FWA copy that belonged to William Pare, who attributed the work to Hawkes Smith in a manuscript note below the printed signature.*

23340 A political **VIEW** of the times; or, a dispassionate inquiry into the measures and conduct of the Ministry and opposition. 174p. *8°.* 1821.

23341 [**WADE,** JOHN.] A political dictionary; or, pocket companion...being an illustration and commentary on all words...in the vocabulary of corruption... with biographical illustrations...By the editor of the "Black book". 140p. *12°.* 1821.

SOCIALISM

For the **ECONOMIST:** a periodical paper, explanatory of the new system of society projected by Robert Owen [edited by G. Mudie], 1821–22, *see* vol. III, *Periodicals list.*

23342 **EVANS,** T. A brief sketch of the life of Mr. Thomas Spence, author of the Spencean system of agrarian fellowship or partnership in land, with an illustration of his plan in the example of the village of Little Dalby, Leicestershire; accompanied with a selection of the songs... 24p. *12°.* Manchester, 1821.

23343 **HUNT,** ROBERT, *and others.* Report of the committee appointed at a meeting of journeymen, chiefly printers, to take into consideration certain propositions submitted to them by Mr. George Mudie, having for their object a system of social arrangement calculated to effect essential improvements in the condition of the working classes and of society at large. [Signed: Robert Hunt, James Shallard, John Jones, George Hinde, Robert Dean, Henry Hetherington.] 26p. *8°.* [1821]

23344 —— The second edition. 26p. *8°.* [1821]

23345 **MACNAB,** H. G. Examen impartial des nouvelles vues de M. Robert Owen, et de ses établissemens à New-Lanark en Écosse...Avec des observations sur l'application de ce système à l'économie politique de tous les gouvernemens...Traduit de l'anglais par Laffon de

Ladébat...On y a joint une préface... 76, 224, [28]p. *8°.* *Paris, Londres, &c., 1821. For another edition, see 1819.*

23346 **OWEN,** ROBERT. Report to the county of Lanark, of a plan for relieving public distress, and removing discontent, by giving permanent, productive employment, to the poor and working classes...[With 'Prospectus of a plan for establishing an institution on Mr. Owen's system in the middle ward of the county of Lanark' and a prospectus for the *Economist.*] 73, 3, 2p. *4°. Glasgow, Edinburgh, &c., 1821. Two copies; one with the inscription 'With Mr. Hamilton's Compts.'; the other, which lacks the prospectus for the Economist, inscribed 'With Mr. Owen's Compliments', belonged to George Agar Ellis, Baron Dover. *A third, interleaved, copy, the FWA copy, belonged to William Pare. See also 1832; and for a manuscript version of part of the text,* vol. III, *MS. 692.*

23347 **SAINT-SIMON,** C. H. DE, *Comte.* Adresse aux philanthropes...extraite de son ouvrage sur le système industriel. 46p. *8°.* [*Paris, 1821*]

23348 —— Du système industriel. 2 vols. *8°. Paris, 1821. Wanting p. 179–96 and 213–20 of Part 2. A second copy of Part 1 belonged to Victor Considérant.*

23349 The **SOURCE** and remedy of the national difficulties, deduced from principles of political economy, in a letter to Lord John Russell. 40p. *8°.* 1821.

MISCELLANEOUS

23350 **BENTHAM,** J. The elements of the art of packing, as applied to special juries, particularly in cases of libel law. 269p. *8°.* 1821.

23351 —— On the liberty of the press, and public discussion. 38p. *8°.* 1821.

23352 **BERKSHIRE BIBLE SOCIETY.** Fourth annual meeting of the Berkshire Bible Society, held at the Old Court-House in Lenox, May 29th, 1821. 16p. *8°. Pittsfield* [*Mass.*], 1821.

23353 **DUNCAN,** H. The young south country weaver; or, a journey to Glasgow: a tale for the radicals. And Maitland Smith, the murderer, a true narrative... Second edition. 239p. *12°. Edinburgh & London, 1821.*

23354 **FOX,** WILLIAM (*fl. 1801–1821*). The Grecian, Roman and Gothic architecture, considered as applicable to public and private buildings, in this country; to which are added, some remarks on ornamental landscape... 91p. *8°.* 1821. *Presentation copy from the author to David Ricardo.*

23355 **GREENLEAF,** J. Sketches of the ecclesiastical history of the state of Maine, from the earliest settlement

to the present time. [With an appendix.] 293, 77p. *12°. Portsmouth* [*N.H.*], 1821.

23356 **HOLBACH,** P. H. D. VON, *Freiherr.* La moral universal, ó los deberes del hombre fundados en su naturaleza...Traduccion: por D.M.D.M. 3 vols. *12°. Valladolid, 1821. For another edition, see 1796.*

23357 **LONDON.** *Court of Common Council.* A Bill to prevent vexatious actions in the Court of Mayor and Aldermen, against non-freemen. 8th February, 1821. 5p. *fol.* [1821]

23358 —— —— An Act to prevent vexatious actions in the Court of Mayor and Aldermen [against non-freemen] ...[10 May, 1821.] 7p. *fol.* [1821]

23359 *—— Livery Companies. Salters.* A list of the Master, Wardens, Court of Assistants, and Livery, of the Worshipful Company of Salters. 15p. *8°.* 1821. *See also* 1784, 1787, 1790, 1792, 1794, 1797, 1799, 1801, 1803, 1806, 1809, 1812, 1815, 1818, 1824, 1827, 1830.

23360 **WEBSTER,** D. A discourse, delivered at Plymouth, December 22, 1820, in commemoration of the first settlement of New-England. 104p. *8°. Boston, 1821.*

1822

GENERAL

23361 [ADAMS, WILLIAM B.] A political dialogue, relative to our farming and trading distress, between the Old Lady of Threadneedle Street and Junius Redivivus. 16p. *8°*. 1822.

23362 AGAZZINI, M. La science de l'économie politique, ou principes de la formation, du progrès, et de la décadence de la richesse; et application de ces principes à l'administration économique des nations. 389p. *8°. Paris & Londres*, 1822.

23363 An ANSWER to The state of the nation at the commencement of the year 1822, and the declarations and conduct of His Majesty's Ministers fairly considered. 102p. *8°*. 1822.

23364 —— [Another edition.] The state of the nation at the commencement of the year 1822, and the declarations and conduct of His Majesty's Ministers fairly considered. 102p. *8°*. 1822. *A reply to no.* 23452.

23365 ATTWOOD, M. Substance of the speech of Matthias Attwood, Esq. in the House of Commons, May the 7th 1822, on the Report of the Committee on agricultural distress. ⟨From Hansard's Parliamentary debates, new series, vol. VII....⟩ 13p. *8°*. [1822] *The Agar Ellis copy.*

23366 —— Substance of the speech of Matthias Attwood, Esq. in the House of Commons, May the 13th, 1822, on receiving the Report of the Committee...on agricultural distress. ⟨From Hansard's Parliamentary debates, new series, vol. VII....⟩ 7p. *8°*. [1822] *The Agar Ellis copy.*

23367 BAINES, EDWARD. History, directory & gazetteer, of the county of York; with select lists of the merchants & traders of London, and the principal commercial and manufacturing towns of England...By E. Baines. The directory department by W. Parsons... 2 vols. *12°. Leeds & London*, 1822–23.

23368 BALBI, A. Essai statistique sur le royaume de Portugal et d'Algarve, comparé aux autres états de l'Europe, et suivi d'un coup d'œil sur l'état actuel des sciences, des lettres et des beaux-arts parmi les Portugais des deux hemispheres... 2 vols. *8°. Paris*, 1822.

23369 BECCARIA BONESANA, C., *Marchese.* Elementi di economia pubblica con varii opuscoli di Cesare Beccaria. 485p. *4°. Milano*, 1822. *Reprinted from the text published by Custodi in 1804, with corrections furnished by the author's son, Marchese Giulio Beccaria.*

23370 BRAMSTON, T. G. A practical inquiry into the nature and extent of the present agricultural distress, and the means of relieving it. 53p. *8°*. 1822.

23371 —— Second edition. 53p. *8°*. 1822.

23372 The BRITISH IMPERIAL CALENDAR for the year...1822...Containing a general register of the United Kingdom...and its colonies...By John Debrett ... 398p. *12°*. [1822] *For other editions, see* 1817.

23373 BROWN, WILLIAM, *framework-knitter*. The spirit of the times; or, the leading political questions by which the public mind has of late been so much agitated temperately discussed, in a series of dialogues between two workmen. 116p. *8°. Nottingham*, 1822.

23374 BRYDGES, SIR S. E., *Bart.* What are riches? Or an examination of the definitions of this subject given by modern economists. 48p. *8°. Kent: printed at the private press of Lee Priory*, 1822. *For another edition, see* 1821.

23375 BUTTERWORTH, J. The antiquities of the town, and a complete history of the trade of Manchester; with a description of Manchester and Salford: to which is added an account of the late improvements in the town, &c. 302, xiip. *12°. Manchester*, 1822. *See also* 1823.

23376 CALVERT, W. J. The demand for labour is wealth. Supplement to Monopoly and taxation vindicated against the errors of the legislature. [With addenda.] 54, [6]p. *8°. Newark & London*, 1822. *For* Monopoly and taxation vindicated, *see* 1821.

23377 CAREY, M. Essays on political economy; or, the most certain means of promoting the wealth, power, resources, and happiness of nations: applied particularly to the United States. 546p. *8°. Philadelphia*, 1822. *Contents: Addresses of the Philadelphia Society...Sixth edition; The new olive branch...Second edition; Address to Congress...Second edition; Address to the farmers of the United States; The farmer's & planter's friend; Strictures on Mr Cambreleng's work, entitled, "An examination of the new tariff". Presentation copy, with inscription, from the author to Rev. W. V. Harold, D.D.*

23378 [——] Facts and observations, illustrative of the past and present situation, and future prospects of the United States: embracing a view of the causes of the late bankruptcies in Boston. To which is annexed, a sketch of the restrictive systems of the principal nations...By a Pennsylvanian. Third edition, improved. 54p. *8°. Philadelphia*, 1822.

23379 [——] Hamilton. —— No. IV. To the editors of the National Intelligencer. [Signed: Hamilton. October 12, 1822. On protection.] 4p. *8°. n.p.* [1822]

23380 [——] Hamilton. —— No. V. To the editors of the National Intelligencer. [Signed: Hamilton. Philadelphia, October 29, 1822. On protection.] 7p. *8°. n.p.* [1822]

23381 [——] Hamilton. —— New series, no. IV. Protection of commerce. [Signed: Hamilton. Philadelphia, Nov. 29, 1822.] 7p. *8°. n.p.* [1822]

23382 [——] Hamilton. —— New series, no. V. Protection of manufactures. [Signed: Hamilton. Philadelphia, Dec. 3, 1822.] 8p. *8°. n.p.* [1822]

23383 [——] Hamilton. —— New series. No. VI. [Signed: Hamilton. December 11, 1822. On protection to manufactures.] 8p. *8°. n.p.* [1822] *See also* 1823, 1824.

23384 [CAZENOVE, J.] Considerations on the accumulation of capital and its effects on profits and on exchangeable value. 64p. *8°*. 1822.

For the CHAMPION, *see vol.* III, *Periodicals list.*

23385 CHASTELLUX, F. J. DE, *Marquis.* De la

félicité publique, ou considerations sur le sort des hommes dans les différantes époques de l'histoire...Nouvelle édition. Augmentée de notes inédites de Voltaire... 2 vols. *8°. Paris, 1822. [Higgs 5631 n] For other editions, see 1772.*

23386 CLEGHORN, J. On the depressed state of agriculture...Being the essay for which the Highland Society of Scotland...voted a piece of plate...and published by order of the Society. 140p. *8°. Edinburgh & London, 1822.*

23387 COBBETT, W. Cobbett's collective commentaries: or, remarks on the proceedings in the collective wisdom of the nation, during the session...of...1822. To which are subjoined, a complete list of the Acts passed ... 320p. *8°. 1822.*

23388 —— Cobbett's gridiron: written to warn farmers of their danger; and to put landholders, mortgagers, lenders, borrowers, the labouring, and indeed all classes of the community on their guard. [Extracts from Cobbett's writings, selected to discredit him.] 32p. *8°. 1822.*

23389 —— [Another issue.] 32p. *8°. 1822. The first issued is priced at one shilling, the second, printed on poorer paper, at sixpence.*

23390 —— Cobbett's sermons...Stereotype edition. 295p. *12°. 1822. Originally published in twelve numbers, from March 1821 to March 1822, with the title: Cobbett's Monthly Religious Tracts. See also 1823 (Twelve sermons), 1828, 1834 (Thirteen sermons).*

23391 —— The farmer's friend. To the farmers of this kingdom. [On Mr. Webb Hall's errors as to the cause of the distress of the farmers.] ⟨From Cobbett's Weekly Register, Dec. 15, 1821.⟩ 32 col. *8°. [London, 1822]*

23392 —— A year's residence, in the United States of America. Treating of the face of the country...the mode of cultivating the land... 360p. *12°. 1822. For other editions, see 1818.*

23393 COLLIER, JOSHUA. A reply to the sixth edition of a pamphlet (supposed official) on the state of the nation at the commencement of the year 1822...With a third chapter on the subject of agricultural distress. 76p. *8°. 1822. The copy that belonged to David Ricardo.*

23394 COMBER, W. T. An inquiry into the state of national subsistence, as connected with the progress of wealth and population: to which is subjoined a digest of the corn laws...Second edition. 323, 59p. *8°. 1822. For another edition, see 1808.*

23395 [CROKER, JOHN W.] A sketch of the state of Ireland, past and present. A new edition. Revised by the author. 68p. *8°. 1822.*

23396 [——] Eighth edition. 65p. *8°. Dublin, 1822. For other editions, see 1808.*

23397 [CURTIUS, W. B. D.] Vrijmoedige gedachten over de tegenwoordige huishouding van staat in de Nederlanden, punten van verbetering en bezuiniging in de algemeene administratie: op het krijgswezen en de justitie, enz. enz. Briefsgewijze medegedeeld. [Two letters, signed: Z.] 94p. *8°. Amsterdam, 1822. [Knuttel 25096] For another edition, see 1819.*

23398 A DEFENCE of a letter to E. J. Littleton...By a mine adventurer, of Staffordshire. 20p. *8°. Birmingham, [1822] The copy that belonged to David Ricardo.*

23399 DUPIN, F. P. C., *Baron.* Discours d'inaugura-

tion de l'amphithéâtre du Conservatoire des Arts et Métiers, prononcé le 8 janvier 1821. 26p. *8°. Paris, 1822.*

23400 *The EAST-INDIA register and directory, for 1822; containing...lists of the Company's servants... mariners &c., not in the service of the...Company; private vessels...and merchant vessels employed in the country trade...compiled...by A. W. Mason, Geo. Owen, and G. H. Brown...Corrected to 19th December 1821. 529p. *12°. [1822]*

23401 *—— Second edition. Corrected to 14th August 1822. 530p. *12°. [1822] For other editions, see 1804.*

23402 ENSOR, G. An address to the people of Ireland, on the degradation and misery of their country, and the means which they (in themselves) possess, not only to save it from utter ruin, but to raise it to its proper rank and consequence amongst nations...Re-printed from the Dublin Morning Post. 27p. *8°. n.p., 1822.*

23403 [EVERETT, A. H.] Europe: or a general survey of the present situation of the principal powers; with conjectures on their future prospects. By a citizen of the United States. 451p. *8°. Boston, 1822.*

23404 An EXPOSITION of the real causes, and effective remedies of the agricultural distress. By an impartial looker-on. 42p. *8°. 1822.*

23405 FERRIER, F. L. A. Du gouvernement considéré dans ses rapports avec le commerce, ou de l'administration commerciale opposée aux economistes du 19e. siècle...Troisième edition. 587p. *8°. Paris & Lille, 1822. For other editions, see 1805.*

23406 [FOUNTAIN, J.] An address to the King, both Houses of Parliament, and...his Majesty's subjects... shewing the various causes of the late & present distresses of trade, manufactories and agriculture, with the only... cure...By J.F. a real friend to the people. 30p. *8°. Greenwich & London, 1822. The copy that belonged to David Ricardo.*

23407 FRASER, R. Review of the state of Ireland, with regard to the best means of employing the redundant population, in useful and productive labour... 30p. *4°. Dublin, 1822.*

23408 [FUOCO, F.] Saggio su i mezzi da moltiplicare prontamente le ricchezze della Sicilia. [Dedication signed: G^e de Welz, pseudonym of Fuoco.] 137p. *4°. Parigi, 1822.*

23409 G., J. H. Thoughts on the necessity of emigration; on the impolicy of leaving this country for the United States of America; and on the means of permanently providing for our surplus or unemployed population [by emigration to New Holland]. In a letter to...Earl Bathurst. 58p. *8°. 1822.*

23410 GANILH, C. La théorie de l'économie politique, fondée sur les faits recueillis en France et en Angleterre... Seconde édition, entièrement revue, corrigée et augmentée. 2 vols. *Paris, Strasbourg, &c., 1822. For another edition, see 1815.*

23411 GOODENOW, S. A brief topographical and statistical manual of the State of New-York...Second edition — enlarged and improved. Containing, also, an account of the grand canals... 72p. *8°. New-York, 1822.*

23412 H., E. Propositions for the prompt, certain, and durable relief of agricultural distress, humbly submitted to the consideration of His Majesty's ministers...By one who wishes well to his country. 30p. *8°. Bristol, 1822.*

23413 HALL, G. W. Observations on the report from the Select Committee of the House of Commons, appointed to inquire into the allegations of the several petitions presented to the House in the last and present sessions of Parliament, complaining of the depressed state of the agriculture of the United Kingdom, in the session of 1822. 38p. *8°.* [1822]

23414 HARCOURT, E. D', *Vicomte.* Réflexions sur l'état agricole et commercial des provinces centrales de la France. 163p. *8°. Paris,* 1822.

23415 HEATHFIELD, R. Observations on trade, considered in reference, particularly, to the public debt, and to the agriculture of the United Kingdom. 71p. *8°. London & Edinburgh,* 1822. *The copy that belonged to David Ricardo.*

For the **HERALD OF PEACE,** 1822, 1827–28, 1833–34, *see* vol. III, *Periodicals list.*

23416 HEYWOOD, BENJAMIN A. Address delivered to the meeting of the proprietors of the Liverpool Royal Institution on the 27th February, 1822. [A history of Liverpool.] 31p. *8°.* [*Liverpool,*] 1822. *The author's own copy, with some manuscript notes by him.*

23417 —— Report of the state of the Liverpool Royal Institution, made to the meeting of the proprietors on the 14th March, 1820. 19p. *8°.* [*Liverpool,*] 1822. *The author's own copy.*

23418 The **HISTORY** of Preston, in Lancashire; together with the Guild Merchant, and some account of the Duchy and County Palatine of Lancaster... 156p. *4°. London & Preston,* 1822.

23419 HOPKINS, T. Economical enquiries relative to the laws which regulate rent, profit, wages, and the value of money. 112p. *8°.* 1822.

For the **INQUIRER,** 1822–23, *see* vol. III, *Periodicals list.*

23420 INQUIRY into the capacity of government to administer relief (and into the best mode of administering relief) to agricultural distress. With an examination into the actual operation of Mr. Peel's Bill upon the existing prices. 80p. *8°.* 1822.

23421 JENKINSON, R. B., *2nd Earl of Liverpool.* The speech of the Earl of Liverpool, delivered in the House of Lords...26th day of February, 1822, on the subject of the agricultural distress of the country, and the financial measures proposed for its relief. With an appendix... 64, [8]p. *8°. London & Dublin,* 1822.

23422 A **LETTER** to E. J. Littleton, Esq. one of the representatives in Parliament of the County of Stafford, on the causes of the disturbances in the mining district of that county. [Signed: A mine adventurer.] 16p. *8°. Birmingham,* [1822] *Attributed in manuscript to 'Mr. Corrie'.*

23423 LOWE, JOSEPH. The present state of England in regard to agriculture, trade, and finance; with a comparison of the prospects of England and France. [With an appendix.] 352, 130p. *8°.* 1822. *See also* 1823.

23424 [**MEASON,** G. L. A letter to William Joseph Denison, Esq. M.P. on the agricultural distress. [With an appendix.] 22, 6p. *8°. Edinburgh,* 1822. *A second copy, which belonged to David Ricardo, lacks the last leaf. See also* 1823.

23425 MELISH, J. A statistical view of the United States, containing a geographical description of the United States, and of each state and territory; with topographical tables of the counties, towns, population, &c. 45p. *12°. Philadelphia,* 1822. *Bound in a pocket-book with Melish's* The traveller's directory, *1822 (no. 23596) with which it was issued, although also available separately.*

23426 MORELLET, A. Mémoires inédits de l'abbé Morellet, de l'académie française sur le dix-huitième siècle et sur la Révolution; précédés de l'Éloge de l'Abbé Morellet, par M. Lémontey...Deuxième édition, considérablement augmentée... 2 vols. *8°. Paris,* 1822. *For another edition, see* 1821.

23427 NICHOLLS, JOHN (1745?–1832). Recollections and reflections, personal and political, as connected with public affairs, during the reign of George III... Second edition. 2 vols. *8°.* 1822.

23428 OBSERVATIONS on the causes and cure of the present distressed state of agriculture, addressed to the gentry, clergy, farmers, and others, constituting what is commonly called the landed interest, containing a reply to the Edinburgh Review, No. LXX, on the subject of cash payments and foreign corn trade. By a landholder. 104p. *8°. Chester,* 1822.

23429 OBSERVATIONS on the present state of agriculture, tithes, poor's rates, and taxes in England. 38p. *8°. Yarmouth, London, &c.,* 1822.

23430 PLAYFAIR, W. A letter on our agricultural distresses, their causes and remedies; accompanied with tables and...charts, shewing...the prices of wheat, bread and labour, from 1565 to 1821...The second edition... 79p. *8°.* 1822.

23431 —— Third edition, with an additional chart. 84p. *8°.* 1822. *For another edition, see* 1821.

23432 PRACTICAL SOCIETY, *Edinburgh.* Second report of the Economical Committee of the Practical Society, 13th February, 1822. 15p. *8°. Edinburgh,* [1822].

23433 —— Third report...13th April, 1822. 16p. *8°. Edinburgh,* [1822]

23434 REIFFENBERG, F. A. F. T. DE, *Baron.* Mémoire couronné en réponse à cette question proposée par l'Académie Royale de Bruxelles: "Quel a été l'état de la population, des fabriques et manufactures, et du commerce dans les Provinces des Pays-Bas, pendant les XVme et XVIme siècles?" 286p. *4°. Bruxelles,* 1822.

23435 REMARKS upon the last session of Parliament. By a near observer. The second edition. 79p. *8°.* 1822.

23436 REPORT on the present state of the disturbed district, in the south of Ireland: with an enquiry into the causes of the distresses of the peasantry & farmers. 92p. *8°. Dublin,* 1822.

23437 REYNOLDS, JOHN S. Practical observations on Mr. Ricardo's Principles of political economy and taxation. 99p. *8°.* 1822.

23438 RICARDO, D. On protection to agriculture. 95p. *8°.* 1822.

23439 —— Second edition. 95p. *8°.* 1822.

23440 —— Fourth edition. 95p. *8°.* 1822. *The copy that belonged to S. J. Loyd, Baron Overstone, formerly among his papers, for which see* vol. III, *MS.* 804.

23441 RICHARDS, JAMES. A letter to the Earl of

Liverpool, on the agricultural distress of the country; its cause demonstrated in the unequal system of taxation; and a just system suggested...The second edition. 57p. *8°*. 1822. *See also* 1833, 1836.

23442 SAY, J. B. Cartilla de economía política ó instruccion familiar, que manifiesta cómo se producen, distribuyen y consumen las riquezas...Traducida...por Don Agustin Pascual. [Segunda edicion.] 200p. *8°*. *Madrid*, 1822. *For other editions, see* 1815.

23443 SAY, L. Considérations sur l'industrie et la législation, sous le rapport de leur influence sur la richesse des états, et examen critique des principaux ouvrages qui ont paru sur l'économie politique. 412p. *8°*. *Paris*, 1822.

23444 SINCLAIR, Sir John, *Bart.* Address to the owners and occupiers of land, in Great Britain and Ireland; pointing out effectual means, for remedying the agricultural distresses of the country; more especially, in so far as respects the importation of foreign corn. With an appendix...The second edition. 47p. *8°*. 1822.

23445 —— An answer to a tract recently published by David Ricardo, Esq. M.P. on protection to agriculture. 20p. *8°*. *Edinburgh, London, &c.*, 1822. *The copy that belonged to David Ricardo.*

23446 SLANEY, R. A. Two letters on the distress of the landed-interest, and its cure. 27p. *8°*. 1822.

23447 SMITH, Adam. An inquiry into the nature and causes of the wealth of nations...A new edition. 3 vols. *8°*. 1822.

23448 —— Recherches sur la nature et les causes de la richesse des nations...Seconde édition, avec des notes et observations nouvelles; par le Marquis Garnier... 6 vols. *8°*. *Paris*, 1822. *For other editions, see* 1776.

23449 —— The whole works of Adam Smith, LL.D., F.R.S., &c. in five volumes...A new edition, with a life of the author. 5 vols. *8°*. *London, Edinburgh, &c.*, 1822. *For other editions, see* 1812.

23450 [SOLLY, E.?] Letters on the new political economy, and the injurious influence of the theoretical opinions of some of the members of Administration, upon agriculture and commerce. 52p. *8°*. 1822. *Tentatively attributed to Solly by HSF. This copy has an inscription (cut into) on the title-page:* '...with Mʳ[?] Solly's Compᵗˢ'.

23451 SPENCE, W. Tracts on political economy. Viz. 1. Britain independent of commerce; 2. Agriculture the source of wealth; 3. The objections against the Corn Bill refuted; 4. Speech on the East India trade. With prefatory remarks on the causes and cure of our present distresses... 265p. *8°*. 1822. *Two presentation copies, one inscribed to Sir Robert Peel, the other, given to William Farr, with a manuscript note by the author, dated:* 'June 18, 1851'.

23452 The **STATE** of the nation at the commencement of the year 1822. Considered under the four departments of the finance – foreign relations – home department – colonies, Board of Trade, &c.&c.&c. 207p. *8°*. 1822. *Tentatively attributed to J. S. Copley, Baron Lyndhurst in the BM Catalogue, and by Barbier to the Marquis of Londonderry.*

23453 —— Second edition. 207p. *8°*. 1822. *The copy that belonged to James Bischoff (1776–1845), with his signature on the half-title.*

23454 —— Third edition. 207p. *8°*. 1822.

23455 —— Fourth edition. 203p. *8°*. 1822.

23456 —— Sixth edition. With an appendix. 220p. *8°*. 1822.

23457 STATEMENT and reports, relative to public works, collieries and improvements, &c....intended in the disturbed and distressed parts of Munster. 22, 16p. *8°*. *Dublin*, 1822. *Tentatively attributed by HSF to N. P. Leader.*

23458 STEVEN, R. Remarks on the present state of Ireland; with hints for ameliorating the condition...of the peasantry of that country. The result of a visit during the summer and autumn of 1821: with an appendix; containing an outline of the system of education pursued in the schools of the London Hibernian Society...The second edition, enlarged. 72p. *8°*. *London, Glasgow, &c.*, 1822. *The Agar Ellis copy.*

23459 STEWART, R., *2nd Marquis of Londonderry.* Substance of the speech of the Marquis of Londonderry, delivered in the House of Commons, on...the 15th day of February, 1822, on the subject of the agricultural distress of the country, and the financial measures proposed for its relief. With an appendix, containing the several accounts referred to. 89, [15]p. *8°*. *London & Dublin*, 1822.

23460 —— Second edition. 89, [15]p. *8°*. *London & Dublin*, 1822. *The copy that belonged to T. Spring Rice, Baron Monteagle.*

23461 —— Third edition. 89, [15]p. *8°*. *London & Dublin*, 1822.

23462 —— Substance of a second speech of the Marquis of Londonderry, delivered in the Committee of the House of Commons, on Monday, 29th April, 1822, on the subject of the agricultural distress of the country, and the financial and other measures proposed for its relief; also, the resolutions of the Committee, on the 3rd day of June, 1822. 78p. *8°*. 1822. *The copy that belonged to T. Spring Rice, Baron Monteagle.*

23463 STOURTON, W., *Baron Stourton.* Further considerations, addressed to the...Earl of Liverpool, on agricultural relief, and the extent of the national resources. 115p. *8°*. 1822.

23464 —— Three letters to the Right Honourable the Earl of Liverpool, on the distresses of agriculture in the United Kingdom: in which the influence of these distresses on our manufactures, trade, and commerce, is considered; as well as the justice, policy, and necessity, of legislative relief. With observations on cash payments and a free trade...A new edition, with additions. [With 'Postscript to the Right Hon. Lord Stourton's considerations on agricultural relief'.] 438p. *8°*. 1822.

23465 SYMMONS, J. The causes of the present distressful state of the country investigated; and the supposed easiest, speediest, and most effectual remedies submitted...to the members of both Houses of Parliament. 168p. *8°*. 1822.

23466 On our commercial **SYSTEM**; shewing the cause of the present fall of prices, &c.&c. 29p. *8°*. 1822.

23467 A free **TRADE** in beer, the most effectual remedy for agricultural distress. 15p. *8°*. 1822.

23468 TRENOR, K. An inquiry into the political economy of the Irish peasantry, as connected with the commissariat resources of Ireland. 52p. *8°*. 1822.

23469 TURNER, Samuel, *F.R.S.* Considerations upon the agriculture, commerce, and manufactures of the

British Empire; with observations on the practical effect of the Bill...for the resumption of cash payments by the Bank of England; and also upon the pamphlet lately published by David Ricardo, Esq. entitled "Protection to agriculture." 111p. *8°*. 1822.

23470 [WALKER, ALEXANDER (*fl.* 1822).] Colombia: being a geographical, statistical, agricultural, commercial and political account of that country, adapted for the general reader, the merchant and the colonist. 2 vols. *8°*. 1822.

23471 WALLACE, ROBERT (*d.* 1858). Observations on weights and measures; containing a plan for uniformity, founded on the weights and measures of Scotland, particularly those of Glasgow: being an essay read before the Glasgow Philosophical Society... 103p. *8°*. *Glasgow, Edinburgh, &c.*, 1822.

23472 WHITMORE, W. W. A letter on the present state and future prospects of agriculture. Addressed to the agriculturists of the county of Salop. 86p. *8°*. 1822. *See also* 1823.

23473 WOODLEY, G. A view of the present state of the Scilly Islands: exhibiting their vast importance to the British Empire; the improvements of which they are susceptible... 344p. *8°*. *London & Truro*, 1822.

23474 WRIGHT, F. Views of society and manners in America; in a series of letters from that country to a friend in England during...1818, 1819, and 1820... Second edition. 483p. *8°*. 1822. *For another edition, see* 1821.

AGRICULTURE

23475 CARTIER, F. État de l'agriculture dans l'arrondissement de Neufchâtel, au 1er janvier 1822. 28p. *8°*. *Neufchâtel*, 1822.

23476 COBBETT, W. Cottage economy...[Stereotype edition.] 207p. *12°*. 1822.

23477 —— Stereotype edition. 207p. *12°*. 1822. *For other editions, see* 1821.

23478 DAVIS, JONAS. Common sense on agricultural distress; its reality, its causes, and its remedies. 46p. *8°*. 1822.

23479 FRASER, R. Sketches and essays on the present state of Ireland, particularly regarding the bogs, waste lands and fisheries; with observations on the best means of employing the population in useful and productive labour. [With 'Report on the advantages of the establishment of a general board of commissioners for fisheries in London'.] 88p. *8°*. *Dublin & London*, 1822.

23480 HINTS on the duties and qualifications of land stewards & agents...with a plan for the management of neglected estates, beneficial to landlord & tenant: by a steward. 44p. *8°*. *Faversham & London*, [1822]

23481 LETTER to the noblemen, gentlemen, and farmers of the United Kingdom...and in particular to the members of the Committee appointed by Parliament to enquire into the causes of the agricultural distresses of the country. [Signed: A Scotch landholder. With 'Appendix. Schedule of the constitution of a joint land stock or assurance company, to be incorporated by royal charter'.] 26, 3p. *8°*. *Edinburgh*, 1822.

For the NEW ENGLAND FARMER...By T. G. Fessenden [and H. Colman], 1822–39, *see* vol. III, *Periodicals list.*

For NORTH WEST OF IRELAND SOCIETY. North West of Ireland Society magazine, 1822–25, *see* vol. III, *Periodicals list.*

23482 PHILLIPS, H. History of cultivated vegetables; comprising their botanical, medicinal, edible, and chemical qualities; natural history; and relation to art, science, and commerce...Second edition... 2 vols. *8°*. 1822.

23483 SALISBURY, W. The cottager's agricultural companion; comprising a complete system of cottage agriculture... 96p. *12°*. 1822.

23484 —— The cottager's companion, or, a complete system of cottage horticulture...Second edition. 76p. *12°*. 1822.

23485 TRIMMER, JOSHUA K. Observations on the state of agriculture, and conditions of the lower classes of the people, in the southern parts of Ireland, in...1812. To which are added further observations relating to the same subjects, in...1822. 118, 25p. *8°*. 1822. *First published as* Further observations on the present state of agriculture...in the southern parts of Ireland *in 1812* (*q.v.*).

23486 TULL, J. The horse-hoeing husbandry: or, a treatise on the principles of tillage and vegetation...To which is prefixed an introduction, explanatory of some circumstances connected with the history and division of the work; and containing an account of certain experiments of recent date. By William Cobbett. 332p. *8°*. 1822. *For other editions, see* 1731.

23487 VALLANCE, J. Observations on the preservation of hops; pointing out a remedy for the distress of the growers. 63p. *8°*. 1822. *The copy that belonged to David Ricardo.*

23488 [WIGGINS, J.] A letter to the absentee landlords of the south of Ireland; on the means of tranquillizing their tenantry, and improving their estates. 62p. *8°*. 1822. *The copy that belonged to David Ricardo.*

23489 YOUNG, ARTHUR (1741–1820). The farmer's calendar: containing the business necessary to be performed on various kinds of farms during every month in the year...The twelfth edition, corrected, and several new chapters added, by John Middleton, Esq. 696p. *12°*. *London, Dublin, &c.*, 1822. *For other editions, see* 1771.

CORN LAWS

23490 PLANS for affording to agriculture prompt, efficacious & permanent relief; and for an improved system of colonial and foreign corn trade; as well as in respect to currency. 32p. *8°. 1822.*

23491 THOUGHTS on the expediency of a relaxation of the corn laws, as the most effectual remedy for agricultural distress; with critical remarks on some prevalent opinions, relative to the influence of taxes and money on the prices of commodities. 59p. *8°. London & Newcastle, 1822.*

23492 TURCKHEIM, J. DE, *Baron*. Opinion de M. de Turckheim, Député du Bas-Rhin, sur les subsistances dans leurs rapports avec les intérêts commerciaux. 24p. *8°. [Paris,] 1822. The copy that belonged to David Ricardo.*

POPULATION

23493 PLACE, F. Illustrations and proofs of the principle of population: including an examination of the proposed remedies of Mr. Malthus, and a reply to the objections of Mr. Godwin and others. 280p. *8°. 1822. Presentation copy, with inscription, from the author to Henry Mitchel.*

TRADES & MANUFACTURES

23494 LILLIE, C. The British perfumer: being a collection of choice receipts...made during a practice of thirty years, by which any lady or gentleman may prepare their own articles...whether of perfumery, snuffs, or colours...Now first edited by Colin Mackenzie. Second edition. 372p. *12°. London & New-York, 1822.*

23495 LOWNDES, THOMAS, *of Blackheath*. Four letters on Lowndes's bay salt, published last year in the Morning Post...With extracts of letters on the same subject by his great uncle Thomas Lowndes, Esq., the inventor of that salt, from a printed pamphlet, published by him in 1748. 30p. *8°. Dover, 1822. The copy that belonged to David Ricardo.*

23496 PARTINGTON, C. F. An historical and descriptive account of the steam engine, comprising a general view of the various modes of employing elastic vapour as a prime mover in mechanics; with an appendix of patents and Parliamentary Papers connected with the subject... 187, 90p. *8°. 1822. The Rastrick copy. See also 1826, 1836.*

23497 SCHOOL OF ARTS, *Edinburgh*. First report of the Directors of the School...for the education of mechanics in such branches of physical science as are of practical application in their several trades. 50p. *8°. [Edinburgh,] 1822. See also 1827, 1845.*

23498 WARE, S. Tracts on vaults and bridges. Containing observations on the various forms of vaults; on the taking down and rebuilding London Bridge; and on the principles of arches...Also containing the principles of pendent bridges, with reference to the properties of the catenary, applied to the Menai Bridge... 73, 71, 176p. *8°. 1822.*

COMMERCE

23499 BORTHWICK, W. M. Proceedings against Wm. Murray Borthwick, at the instance of His Majesty's Advocate and of Robert Alexander, styling himself editor and proprietor of the Glasgow Sentinel newspaper. [Concerned with negotiations for a newspaper in Hamilton.] With an appendix of documents, and a preface by William Murray Borthwick. 57, 28p. *8°. Edinburgh, 1822. The copy that belonged to David Ricardo.*

23500 John **BULL'S** petition for cheap beer. Containing taproom topics, or advice to brewers. [A ballad.] *s.sh.fol. Newcastle, [1822] [Br. 496]*

23501 CIVITATIS MUNDI, *pseud*. Remarks, with an attempt to determine the first and universal principles of trade. 130p. *8°. 1822.*

23502 Sobre **COMMERCIO** e porto-franco. 22p. *4°. Lisboa, 1822.*

23503 COMMITTEE OF MERCHANTS, AGENTS & SHIP-OWNERS IN LONDON. Report of the Committee of Merchants, Agents, & Ship-owners, in London, connected with the trade of the East Indies. Presented to a general meeting of the Society... 45p. *8°. 1822.*

23504 DUPIN, F. P. C., *Baron*. Influence du commerce sur le savoir, sur la civilisation des peuples anciens, et sur leur force navale; discours prononcé le 24 avril M.DCCC.XXII, dans la séance générale de l'Institut de France. 54p. *8°. Paris, 1822.*

23505 GASTINE, C. DE. Pétition a messieurs les députés des départemens, sur la nécessité ou se trouve la France de faire un traité de commerce avec la république d'Haïti, et sur les avantages qu'en retireraient les deux nations. 16p. *8°. Paris, 1822.*

23506 HENDERSON, JAMES (1783?–1848). A series of observations submitted to the Right Honourable Thomas Wallace, M.P., Vice President of the Board of Trade, on the expediency of Great Britain entering into commercial regulations with the South American states, accompanied by brief commercial notices of the five republics. 24p. *8°. 1822.*

23507 HINTS suggested for consideration in drawing up a petition to Parliament for a repeal of the protecting duty on sugar imported from the East Indies. [4]p. *fol. n.p. [1822?] A lithographed manuscript facsimile. The text differs considerably from the work with a similar title (no. 23508 below) printed at much the same time.*

23508 HINTS suggested for consideration, in drawing up a petition to Parliament on the subject of the East India trade. *s.sh.fol. Liverpool,* [1822?] [*Br.* 497(2)] *Probably sponsored by the Liverpool East India Association; it has been tentatively attributed to Robert Benson, chairman of the Association.*

23509 A LETTER to the most noble the Marquess of Lansdowne...relative to the present depressed state of British shipping. More particularly as respects the carrying trade with France. By a ship owner. 16p. *8°.* 1822. *The copy that belonged to David Ricardo.*

23510 LIVERPOOL EAST INDIA ASSOCIATION. [*Begin.*] At a general meeting of the...Association held...the 10th of May, 1822, Robert Benson, Esq., chairman. [Minutes of a meeting and resolutions supporting the extension of the relaxation of the restrictions on trade to the West and to the East Indies. 3p. *fol.* [*Liverpool,* 1822]

23511 —— [*Begin.*] At a general meeting of the... Association, held the 13th of May 1822. [Resolutions deploring the restrictions imposed on British shipping in the East Indies. Signed: Robert Benson, chairman.] *s.sh.fol.* [*Liverpool,* 1822] [*Br.* 497(1)]

23512 —— Report of a committee of the...Association, appointed to take into consideration the restrictions on the East India Trade. Presented to the Association at a General Meeting, 9th May 1822...[With an appendix.] 57, 40p. *8°. Liverpool,* 1822.

23513 LULLIN DE CHATEAUVIEUX, J. F. Du commerce des Suisses avec la France. 15p. *8°. Genève & Paris,* 1822. *The copy that belonged to David Ricardo.*

23514 Practical OBSERVATIONS on the British West India sugar trade. 22p. *8°.* 1822.

23515 PLAN for indemnifying the West India proprietors, for the loss which they may possibly sustain from the introduction of East India sugar. 4p. *fol.* [*London,* 1822?]

23516 PREVOST, A. L. Lettre à Monsieur F. Lullin-de Chateauvieux, en réponse à son écrit sur le commerce des Suisses avec la France. 16p. *8°. Genève & Paris,* 1822. *The copy that belonged to David Ricardo.*

23517 To the PROPRIETORS of East India stock. [Signed: an East Indian. Calling on directors to support the Bill for the regulation of private trade, and to agree to the curtailing of the chartered rights of the Company.] 3p. *4°. n.p.* [1822?]

23518 ROBINSON, F. J., *Earl of Ripon.* Substance of the speech of the Right Hon. Frederick Robinson, on moving the resolution to bring in two Bills for regulating the intercourse between the West Indies, and other parts of the world. 24p. *8°.* 1822.

23519 UNITED STATES OF AMERICA. Congress. *Senate.* Letter from the Secretary of the Treasury, transmitting statements shewing the commerce and navigation of the United States, for the year ending the 30th September, 1821. January 24, 1822. Printed by order of the Senate of the United States. 165p. *8°. Washington,* 1822. *See also* 1826, 1830 (*House of Representatives*).

23520 WEST INDIA DOCK COMPANY. Substance of the memorial of the West India Dock Company, with explanatory notes and an appendix. [For the renewal of their monopoly.] 24, 13p. *8°.* 1822.

COLONIES

23521 [BEAUMONT BRIVAZAC, H. DE, *Comte de Beaumont.*] L'Europe et ses colonies. Par le Comte de B......Seconde édition. 2 vols. *8°. Paris,* 1822.

23522 CROPPER, J. Letters addressed to William Wilberforce, M.P. recommending the encouragement of the cultivation of sugar in our dominions in the East Indies, as the natural and certain means of effecting the total and general abolition of the slave-trade. 54p. *8°. Liverpool & London,* 1822.

23523 EAST INDIA COMPANY. East-India sugar. Papers respecting the culture and manufacture of sugar in British India: also notices of the cultivation of sugar in other parts of Asia. With miscellaneous information respecting sugar. [Being the report of the Committee of Buying and Warehouses on the culture and manufacture of sugar in the East Indies, with four appendices. Ordered to be printed 18 December 1822.] xv, 275, 54, 131, 78p. *fol.* 1822.

23524 FLETCHER, T. Letters in vindication of the

rights of the British West India colonies, originally addressed to the editors of the Liverpool Mercury, in answer to Mr. James Cropper's Letters to W. Wilberforce, Esq. M.P. 68p. *8°. Liverpool,* 1822. *The copy that belonged to David Ricardo.*

23525 *HUMBOLDT, F. H. A. VON, Freiherr.* Political essay on the Kingdom of New Spain. Containing researches relative to the geography of Mexico...the population, the state of agriculture and manufacturing and commercial industry; the canals projected...the crown revenues, the quantity of the precious metals which have flowed from Mexico into Europe and Asia...and the military defence of New Spain...Translated from the original French by John Black...Third edition. 4 vols. *8°.* 1822. *For another edition, see* 1811.

23526 [YOUNG, GAVIN.] An inquiry into the expediency of applying the principles of colonial policy to the government of India; and of effecting an essential change in its landed tenures, and...in the character of its inhabitants. 382p. *8°.* 1822. *For a continuation, see* 1828.

FINANCE

23527 ATTWOOD, M. Substance of the speech of Matthias Atwood, Esq. in the House of Commons, June the 12th, 1822, on Mr. Western's motion concerning the state of the currency. ⟨From Hansard's Parliamentary

debates, new series, Vol. VII....⟩ 24p. *8°.* [1822] *The Agar Ellis copy.*

23528 —— Speech of Matthias Attwood, Esq. in the

House of Commons, July the 10th, 1822, on Mr. Western's motion respecting the altered state of the currency. ⟨From Hansard's Parliamentary debates, new series, Vol. VII.... ⟩ 14p. 8°. [1822] *The Agar Ellis copy.*

23529 BRICKWOOD, J. A plan for reducing the capital and the annual charge of the National Debt; humbly suggested to the consideration of Members of Parliament. 82p. 8°. [*London, 1822*] *The copy that belonged to Thomas Spring Rice, Baron Monteagle. For other editions, see* 1820.

23530 CAMPBELL, AUGUSTUS. The rights of the English clergy asserted, and the probable amount of their incomes estimated, in a letter to the author of "Remarks on the consumption of public wealth, by the clergy of every Christian nation". 43p. 8°. *Liverpool & London*, 1822.

23531 CAREY, M. An appeal to common sense and common justice; or, irrefragable facts opposed to plausible theories: intended to prove the extreme injustice...of the existing tariff...Second edition improved. 112, [6]p. 8°. *Philadelphia*, 1822.

23532 [CLEYNMANN, .] Materialien für Münzgesetzgebung und dabei entstehende Erörterungen. Staatsmännern und Rechtsgelehrten zur Beherzigung. 494p. 8°. *Frankfurt a. M.*, 1822.

23533 [——] Ueber Münzgesetzgebung. Ein Beitrag zur Erörterung einiger wichtigen Momente und Grundsätze der Münzgeschichte und Münzlegislation. 44p. 8°. *Frankfurt a. M.*, 1822.

23534 COHEN, B. Compendium of finance: containing an account of the origin, progress, and present state, of the public debts, revenue, expenditure, national banks and currencies...Also an historical sketch of the National Debt of the British Empire. Authenticated by official documents. 264, 280p. 8°. 1822. *See also* 1828.

23535 COMBER, W. T. The claims of the agriculturists, considered, in reference to the recent developments of our money-system. 82p. 8°. 1822.

23536 CONSIDERATIONS sur la refonte des anciennes monnaies. 10p. 8°. [*Paris*, 1822?]

23537 DENISON, N. J. [A] letter to G. Webb Hall, Esq. on the currency question, &c.&c. 28p. 8°. 1822. *With manuscript notes by the author, and a letter from him to Sir Charles Colvile bound in at the end. The author has added the 'A' at the head of the title.*

23538 DUNLOP, A., and others. Memorial in behalf of the distillers making spirits for the home-consumption of Scotland. [Signed: Arch. Dunlop, Andrew Taylor, John Harvie, John Padon.] 32p. 8°. *Haddington*, [1822]. *Presentation copy, with inscription, from Archibald Dunlop.*

23539 ELLIS, HENRY (*fl.* 1822). A few words of money and taxation. 24p. 8°. 1822.

23540 [ELRINGTON, T., *Bishop of Ferns and Leighlin*.] An inquiry whether the disturbances in Ireland have originated in tithes, or can be suppressed by a commutation of them. By S.M. 48p. 8°. *Dublin*, 1822.

23541 ENGLAND. Parliament. *House of Commons*. Report of the Select Committee of the House of Commons, 5th June, 1822, on the local taxation of the City of Dublin; with extracts from the tenth report of the Commissioners for Auditing Public Accounts; also, the reports of said Commissioners (now first published) on the pipe-water and metal-main accounts for 1818 and 1819; together with other documents relative to said local taxation. 158p. 8°. *Dublin*, 1822.

23542 ERSTE OESTERREICHISCHE SPAR-CASSE. Statuten und Reglement der Ersten Oester-reichischen Spar-Casse. [Dated: 24. Januar 1822.] 16p. 8°. *n.p.* [1822]

23543 FINLAY, J. Letters addressed to the Irish Government, on local taxes, the Irish collieries, &c.&c. 89p. 8°. *Dublin*, 1822.

23544 GALERIE numismatique des généraux qui ont commandé en chef les armées françaises depuis 1792 jusqu'en 1815... [A prospectus for the series to be published by Pélissier, beginning with Latour-D'Auvergne, Dampierre and Oudinot.] 4, 8, 4p. 8°. *Paris*, 1822.

23545 GERVAISE, P. C. Traité des contributions directes en France. 2 vols. 8°. *Paris*, 1822.

23546 GIBSON, JAMES, *of Ingliston*. Report of the trial of the issues, in the action of damages for libel in the Beacon, James Gibson of Ingliston, Esq. clerk to the signet — pursuer, against Duncan Stevenson, printer in Edinburgh — defender...[Concerning prosecutions for forgery of banknotes, brought by Gibson.] 139, 2p. 8°. *Edinburgh & London*, 1822.

23547 HUME, JOSEPH. Speech of Joseph Hume, Esq. in the House of Commons...July 25, 1822, on the National Debt and the operation of the Sinking Fund. ⟨From Hansard's Parliamentary debates, new series, Vol. VII.... ⟩ 23p. 8°. [1822]

23548 [JOPLIN, T.] An essay on the general principles and present practice of banking in England and Scotland; with observations upon the justice and policy of an immediate alteration of the Charter of the Bank of England... 70p. 8°. *Newcastle upon Tyne, London, &c.*, 1822. *Presentation copy, with inscription, from the author to William M. Maude.*

23549 —— Second edition. 70p. 8°. *Newcastle upon Tyne, London, &c.*, 1822.

23550 —— Third edition. [With 'Supplementary observations to the third edition...'.] 70, 20p. 8°. *Newcastle upon Tyne, London, &c.*, 1822. *See also* 1826, 1827, 1838.

23551 A LETTER to the Right Honourable Lord Redesdale, touching the Bill now pending in the House of Lords, intituled, "A Bill to explain an Act...respecting the enrolment of memorials of grants of annuities". 25p. 8°. 1822.

23552 LETTER to the Right Honourable William Conyngham Plunket...by an Irish landlord, on the subject of tithes; and particularly the great vital question, whether they are to be regarded like any other private property. 45p. 8°. 1822.

23553 A short LETTER to the Earl of Liverpool, on an amelioration of the taxes. By a Whig of the old school. 16p. 8°. 1822.

23554 LIFE of the late Thomas Coutts, Esq. banker, in the Strand, with...anecdotes of his first wife, Betty Starky, and of the present Mrs Coutts. By a person of the first respectability. To which is added an account of the manner in which his immense property has been bequeathed. 17p. 8°. [1822]

23555 —— [A reissue, with a general title-page.]

Life of the late Thomas Coutts, Esq. banker, of the Strand, to which is added, a Biographical and historical addenda, containing some curious anecdotes, and an official copy...of his will and codicil... 17, 20p. 8°. [1822]

23556 LIVERPOOL. [*Begin.*] To the honourable Commons of the United Kingdom of Great Britain and Ireland...the humble petition of the undersigned merchants, agents, shipowners and others interested in the trade with the East Indies, and resident in Liverpool. [Against an intended Bill to increase the duty on East India sugar.] [2]p. *fol. n.p.* [1822 ?] [*Br.* 497(3)]

23557 McCAY, J. A general view of the history and objects of the Bank of England; with extracts from the Charter, Acts of Parliament, and bye-laws regulating that corporation... 99p. 8°. *London & Dublin*, 1822. *The Agar Ellis copy.*

23558 [MAITLAND, JAMES, *8th Earl of Lauderdale.*] Sinking Fund, or, the system which recommends the repeal of five millions of taxes, compared with the system which recommends levying five millions by taxation, for the redemption of the public debt. 16p. 8°. *n.p.*, 1822. *The copy that belonged to David Ricardo.*

23559 —— Sketch of a petition to the Commons House of Parliament, submitted to the consideration of all who feel for the welfare of the country, or for the distresses of the lower orders of the people. [For suspending the operation of the Sinking Fund, etc.] 11p. 8°. *Edinburgh*, 1822.

23560 [MEDLEY, W.] The crisis; being a letter to J. W. Denison, Esq. M.P. on the present calamitous situation of the country. By W.M. 18p. 8°. 1822. *Attributed to Medley in a manuscript note on the title-page. The copy that belonged to David Ricardo.*

23561 [MOLÉ, L. M., *Comte.*] Observations sur le dernier Budjet [*sic*], adressées par un pair aux deux Chambres, à l'ouverture de la session. 40p. 8°. *Paris*, 1822.

23562 MONTAGU, B. Some observations upon the Bill for the improvement of the bankrupt laws. 73p. 8°. 1822. *Presentation copy from the author, that belonged to E. B. Sugden, Baron St. Leonards.*

23563 MOORE, R. A plan for paying off the present National Debt, in forty-two years, with a Sinking Fund of only five millions. 18p. 8°. 1822.

23564 NORTH, HON. SIR D. Discourses upon trade. 23p. 4°. *Edinburgh*, 1822. *For other editions, see 1691.*

23565 PAGET, THOMAS. A letter addressed to David Ricardo, Esq. M.P. on the true principle of estimating the extent of the late depreciation in the currency; and on the effect of Mr. Peel's Bill for the resumption of cash payments by the Bank. [With 'The price of gold an imperfect index of the depreciation in the currency. A letter addressed to Sir Francis Burdett, Bart. upon the occasion of his presenting the petition of...Westminster to the House of Commons'.] 47p. 8°. 1822. *The Agar Ellis copy.*

23566 PEW, R. A letter to the Marquis of Londonderry, in which it is demonstrated beyond the possibility of refutation that two hundred millions of the National Debt, and one-fourth of all the taxes might be instantly annihilated...[With 'Hints for raising the supplies with the most equable pressure...1803' signed: Plus Ultra.] 60p. 8°. 1822. *The copy that belonged to David Ricardo.*

23567 REASONS why the Bank of England ought not to reduce the rate of discount to four per cent. New edition. To which are added, some observations on a recent publication [by David Ricardo], entitled "A protection to agriculture". By an impartial observer. 51p. 8°. 1822.

23568 REMARKS on the consumption of public wealth by the clergy of every Christian nation, and particularly by the Established Church in England and Wales, and in Ireland; with a plan for altering its revenues... 84p. 8°. 1822.

23569 —— Third edition. 86p. 8°. 1822. *The Agar Ellis copy.*

23570 —— The fourth edition. 86p. 8°. 1822.

23571 RICARDO, D. Mr. Ricardo's speech on Mr. Western's motion, for a Committee to consider of the effects produced by the presumption of cash payments, delivered the 12th of June, 1822. 14p. 8°. 1822. *Ricardo's own copy.*

23572 [ROBERTSON, ALEXANDER, *M.P.*] An address to the members of the House of Commons, upon the necessity of reforming our financial system, and establishing an efficient Sinking Fund for the reduction of the National Debt; with the outline of a plan for that purpose. By one of themselves. 75p. 8°. *London & Edinburgh*, 1822. *Attributed in manuscript on the title-page to 'Alexr. Robertson, M.P. for Grampound'. A refutation of this work An examination of the currency question, 1830 (q.v.), also refers to Robertson as the commonly accepted author.*

23573 ROBERTSON, JOHN, *of Hatton Garden.* A letter to the Right Hon. Robert Peel, M.P.... Secretary of State for the Home Department, upon the subject of bank-note forgery, clearly demonstrating, that a bank-note may be produced, which shall be more difficult to be imitated than even the metallic currency of the country... 16p. 8°. 1822.

23574 ROGERS, E. An essay on some general principles of political economy, on taxes upon raw produce, and on commutation of tithes. 72p. 8°. 1822.

23575 ROOKE, J. An essay on the National Debt, shewing the use and abuse of the funding system. 45p. 8°. 1822.

23576 SINCLAIR, SIR JOHN, *Bart.* Hints on circulation; and the means of re-establishing the prosperity of the country, by an improved system of currency; uniting the advantages of a metallic and of a paper circulation. With an account of the paper circulation of Scotland... 47, 15p. 8°. *Edinburgh, London, &c.*, 1822.

23577 SOLLY, E. To the Right Honourable Robert Peel, &c.&c.&c. [Two letters on currency, one dated May 18, 1822 and the other May 30.] [4]p. 4°. *n.p.* [1822] *Reissued in Remarks on the policy of repealing Mr. Peel's Bill, 1823 (q.v.).*

23578 THORNE FUNDING SOCIETY. Articles of a money society, called the Thorne Funding Society, now held at the house of Mr. George Kemp, sign of the Red Bear, Thorne. Commencing...2d July, 1822. 8p. 8°. *Doncaster*, 1822.

23579 [VALERIANI MOLINARI, L.] Seconda dissertazione chiamata nella Ricerche sull' agostaro del secondo Federigo...contente un'esposizione delle monete di conto portate nel famoso papiro ottantesimo fra quelli della raccolta di Monsignor Gaetano Marini... 182p. *4°.* *Bologna, 1822. For* Ricerche critiche ed economiche sull' agostaro di Federigo II, *see 1819, and for an earlier continuation, see 1821.*

23580 WESTERN, C. C., *Baron Western.* Address to the landowners of the united Empire. 47p. *8°. 1822.*

23581 —— Supplement to the address to the landowners of the united Empire...published in February, 1822. 11p. *8°. 1822.*

23582 —— Second edition, with a supplementary letter. 47, 11p. *8°. 1822.*

23583 —— Second address to the landowners of the united Empire. [With an appendix.] 59p. *8°. 1822.*

23584 —— [Another issue.] 60p. *8°. 1822. The pagination of the appendix has been altered to include a folded table (foliated), which was unnumbered in the earlier issue.*

23585 —— Second edition. 60p. *8°. 1822. The copy that belonged to David Ricardo.*

TRANSPORT

23586 BIRKINSHAW, J. [and **LONGRIDGE**, M.]. Specification of John Birkinshaw's patent, for an improvement in the construction of malleable iron rails, to be used in rail roads; with remarks on the comparative merits of cast metal and malleable iron rail-ways. 10p. *8°. Newcastle, 1822. The Rastrick copy. See also 1824, 1832.*

23587 CARY, JOHN (*d. 1835*). Cary's traveller's companion, or, a delineation of the turnpike roads of England and Wales... [22]p., 43 maps. *8°. 1822. For other editions, see 1806.*

23588 COMPARISON between the two proposed new lines of road between London and Edinburgh, the one by Jedburgh, and the other by Wooler. 32p. *8°. Edinburgh, 1822.*

23589 ENGLAND. *Laws, etc.* An Act (3° Geo. IV. cap. cxii.) for more effectually amending certain roads in the several parishes of Lambeth, Newington, St. George Southwark, Bermondsey, and Christchurch, in...Surrey, and for watching, lighting, and otherwise improving the said roads. ⟨Passed 29th July 1822.⟩ 162, 6p. *8°. 1822.*

23590 [*Endorsed:*] **ENGLISH AND BRISTOL CHANNELS JUNCTION CANAL.** 1822, December, 18th. Angel Inn, Chard, resolutions of a meeting this day held. [Signed: William Hanning.] 3p. *fol. Chard,* [1822]

23591 [**GRAY**, T.] Observations on a general iron rail-way: (with a geographical map of the plan,) showing its great superiority, by the general introduction of mechanic power, over all the present methods of conveyance by turnpike roads and canals...Third edition. Revised and...enlarged. 131p. *8°. 1822. See also 1823,* 1825.

23592 GREEN, JAMES. The report of James Green, civil engineer, on a proposed small canal, to open a communication between the English Channel at Beer, and the Bristol Channel near Bridgewater...[With 'Estimate of the probable expence'.] 13p. *fol. Chard, 1822.*

23593 HUERNE DE POMMEUSE, M. L. F. Des canaux navigables. Atlas de la navigation intérieure de l'Angleterre et de la France. 6p., 13 maps. *4°. [Paris, 1822]* Part of Des canaux navigables considérés d'une manière générale, *wanting vol. 2 of the text. Vol. 1 was never published.*

23594 ITINÉRAIRE général des postes et relais, à l'usage des personnes qui voyagent sur le continent européen...Suivi des routes principales de la Suisse. Pour l'an 1822. 312p. *8°. Bruxelles, 1822.*

23595 McADAM, JOHN L. Remarks on the present system of road making...Sixth edition, carefully revised, with considerable additions, and an appendix. [With 'Report from the Select Committee on the highways of the kingdom: together with the minutes of evidence taken before them'.] 196p. *8°. 1822. For other editions, see 1816.*

23596 MELISH, J. The traveller's directory through the United States; containing, a description of all the principal roads...with copious remarks on the rivers, and other objects. To which is added, an appendix, containing Post-Office regulations, land-offices, military posts, census of the United States, and a comparative...view of the population... 183p. *12°. Philadelphia, 1822. Bound in a pocket-book with the author's* A statistical view of the United States (*no. 23425), with which it was issued, although also available separately.*

23597 PATERSON, JAMES. A series of letters and communications, addressed to the Select Committee of the House of Commons, on the highways of the kingdom ... 87p. *12°. Montrose, London, &c., 1822. Presentation copy with inscription from the author to 'David Carnegie Esqr of Craigs'.*

23598 PLAN for expediting the mail from London to Edinburgh; so that it shall arrive at one o'clock on the second day, (and eventually earlier,) proceed immediately for the north of Scotland, and cross at the Queensferry all the year in day-light. 36p. *8°. Edinburgh, 1822.*

23599 WAKE, B. J. Observations and critical reflections upon the last Act of Parliament relating to the turnpike roads in England, intended to point out its imperfections and inconsistencies... 37p. *8°. London & Sheffield,* 1822.

SOCIAL CONDITIONS

23600 ALLEN, T. Hell upon earth; or, devils let loose: being a representation of an English wake. 30p. *12°. London & Birmingham, 1822.*

23601 AMICABLE SOCIETY, *Patrington.* Articles of the Amicable Society at Patrington. Established October 17th, 1792. Held at the house of John Escreet. 16p. *8°. Hedon, 1822.*

23602 An **APPEAL** to the inhabitants of Edinburgh, on the necessity of individual exertion to the reform of prison discipline. 16p. *8°. Edinburgh, 1822.*

23603 [BENNETT, H. G.] Considerations on the present state of the police of the Metropolis. 16p. *8°.* 1822. *Presentation copy from the author to David Ricardo. The author's name has been supplied in manuscript on the title-page.*

23604 BRIDLE, W. A narrative of the rise and progress of the improvements effected in His Majesty's Gaol at Ilchester...between July 1808 and November 1821, under the governance, suggestion, and superintendence of Wm. Bridle, Keeper: being the first part of his exposition of, and answer to, the charges lately brought against him by Henry Hunt, a prisoner confined in the said gaol. [With an appendix.] [154], 36p. *8°. Bath, Bristol, &c.,* 1822.

23605 BROOKES, S. Thoughts on the poor laws; with a plan for reducing the poors' rates, preparatory to their abolition. 43p. *8°.* 1822.

23606 The CASE of the clerks in public offices, whose salaries have been reduced by a recent arrangement made by the Lord's [sic] of the Treasury: most respectfully submitted for the considerations of the members of the House of Commons. 12p. *8°. n.p.,* 1822. *The copy that belonged to David Ricardo.*

23607 CHALMERS, T. A speech, delivered on the 24th of May, 1822, before the General Assembly of the Church of Scotland, explanatory of the measures which have been successfully pursued in St. John's parish, Glasgow, for the extinction of its compulsory pauperism. With an appendix. 97p. *8°. Glasgow, Edinburgh, &c.,* 1822. *Presentation copy, with inscription, from the author to George Forbes. Reissued in* Tracts on pauperism *in 1833 (q.v.).*

23608 COMMITTEE APPOINTED TO INVESTIGATE THE CLAIMS...OF THE NEW GRINDER'S HEALTH PRESERVATIVE. Observations on the grinder's asthma...an extract from a paper on the grinder's asthma, read before the Medical and Surgical Society of Sheffield, Sept. 1, 1819, by Arnold Knight, M.D.: and remarks delivered before the Committee...by Samuel Roberts. Together with the resolutions of the Committee. 16p. *8°. Sheffield,* 1822.

23609 COMMITTEE TO ENQUIRE INTO THE PRESENT STATE OF THE POOR AND WORKHOUSES IN...IPSWICH. Report of the Committee...with a view, by means of consolidation, to the employment & classification, the general comfort and moral improvement of the poor, and to the reduction of the poor's rate. 26p. *8°. Ipswich,* 1822.

23610 Practical ECONOMY; or, the application of modern discoveries to the purposes of domestic life. Second edition. 379p. *12°.* 1822.

23611 ENGLAND. *Home Office.* Summary statements of the number of criminal offenders committed to the several gaols in England and Wales, &c.&c.&c. 19p. *8°. n.p.,* 1822. *See also* 1824, 1831, 1833, 1834.

23612 ——— *Laws, etc.* Copy of an Act of Parliament for preventing clandestine marriages; together with an Act to prevent cruelty to animals...Also, an appendix containing Sir Christopher Robinson...and Dr. Phillimore's opinions on certain queries in the Marriage Act. 12p. *8°. Leeds,* 1822.

23613 FRIEDLANDER, M. Bibliographie méthodique des ouvrages publiés en Allemagne sur les pauvres; précédée d'un coup d'œil historique sur les pauvres, les prisons, les hôpitaux, et les institutions de bienfaisance de ce pays. [An extract from *La Revue Encyclopédique,* December, 1821.] 24, 44p. *8°. Paris,* 1822.

23614 FRIENDLY SOCIETY OF JOURNEY-MEN BOOKBINDERS, *London.* Friendly Society of Bookbinders. Abstract of the audit-account of the income and expenditure of the five lodges, from June, 1821, to May, 1822... 4p. *8°.* [*London,* 1822] *Bound in a volume with other publications of the Society, which belonged to John Shaw, a member of Lodge 1 and one of the auditors from 1830. See also vol. III, Periodicals list, Report of the Audit-Committee. For the Articles...finally agreed to... 1820, also in the volume, see vol. III, MS. 481.*

23615 HALE, WILLIAM. An appeal to the public, in defence of the Spitalfields Act: with remarks on the causes which have led to the miseries and moral deterioration of the poor. 46p. *8°.* 1822.

23616 ——— [Another edition.] 32p. *8°.* [1822]

23617 HAMILTON, ROBERT (1743–1829). An address to the inhabitants of Aberdeen, on the management of the poor; with statements of the income and expenditure of the United Fund, from 1813 to 1821, inclusive. 46p. *8°. Aberdeen,* 1822.

23618 HENDERSON, WILLIAM, *M.D.* Address to the inhabitants of Aberdeen, respecting the medical attendance of the poor, at their own houses. 44p. *8°. Aberdeen,* 1822.

23619 HIGHMORE, A. Philanthropia metropolitana; a view of the charitable institutions established in and near London, chiefly during the last twelve years. 647p. *12°.* 1822.

23620 [HILL, MATTHEW D.] Plans for the government and liberal instruction of boys, in large numbers; drawn from experience. [Revised by T. W. Hill and Arthur Hill.] 238p. *8°.* 1822. *Presentation copy, with inscription, 'To Richard Watson Esq. with the friendly respects of the authors'. See also* 1827.

23621 HOLFORD, G. P. A short vindication of the general penitentiary at Millbank, from the censures contained in "A letter addressed by C. C. Western, Esq., to the Lord Lieutenant and magistrates...of Essex;" to which are added a few remarks on the punishment of juvenile offenders. 35p. *8°.* 1822.

23622 JUSTUS, *pseud.* Letters on the subject of the pending measures for the reduction of the civil establishment: and more especially on the Superannuation Amendment Bill now in progress through the House of Commons. 64p. *8°.* 1822. *The copy that belonged to David Ricardo.*

23623 LE BRETON, T. Thoughts on the defective state of prisons, and suggestions for their improvement; together with hints for the discipline, police and labour of prisoners. With the plan of a gaol and house of correction for the accommodation and labour of 280 persons. 52p. *8°.* 1822. *Presentation copy, with inscription, from the author to David Ricardo.*

23624 LONDON. *Court of Common Council.* A Bill for repealing sundry clauses, in certain Acts of Common Council, touching the regulation of the Fellowship of Free Porters of the City of London, commonly called Billingsgate Porters, and for the further and better regulation of the said Fellowship. 18p. *fol.* [1822]

23625 ——— ——— The several acts of Common Council,

and orders of the Court of Lord Mayor and Aldermen of the City of London, for the regulation and government of the Fellowship of Free Porters of the City of London, commonly called Billingsgate Porters, otherwise Corn and Salt Porters. Together with the standing orders...of the said Fellowship. 86p. *8°*. 1822.

23626　NEW TOWN DISPENSARY, *Edinburgh.* Annual report of the New Town Dispensary, submitted to the general meeting of the governors and subscribers, by the managers and medical officers...on the 14th January, 1822. [With a list of subscribers.] 22, 38p. *8°*. *Edinburgh,* 1822.

23627　[NICHOLLS, Sir George.] Eight letters on the management of our poor, and the general administration of the poor laws; in which is shewn the system that has been adopted...in the two parishes of Southwell and Bingham, in the county of Nottingham...By an overseer. Prefixed is an address to James Scarlett, Esq., M.P. 70p. *8°*. *Newark, London, &c.,* 1822. *Presentation copy from the author to 'J. Birch, Esq.' with a manuscript note, initialled by the author, at the foot of the last page of text.*

23628　NOLAN, M. The speech of Michael Nolan, Esq. delivered in the House of Commons...July 10, 1822, on moving for leave to bring in a Bill to alter and amend the laws for the relief of the poor. 66p. *8°*. 1822.

23629　OBSERVATIONS on the poor laws, and pauperism, shewing the effects resulting from cumulative parish rates, levied to feed and clothe the able indolent, as well as the weak involuntary poor. 58p. *8°*. 1822.

23630　OBSERVATIONS on the ruinous tendency of the Spitalfields Act to the silk manufacture of London. [Dated: 2nd Jan. 1822.] 40p. *8°*. 1822.

23631　—— To which is added a Reply to Mr. Hale's Appeal to the public in defence of the Act. Third edition. 101p. *8°*. 1822. *The copy that belonged to David Ricardo.*

23632　OBSERVATIONS on the superannuation fund, proposed to be established in the several public departments by the Treasury Minute of the 10th August, 1821. 68p. *8°*. 1822.

23633　—— Supplement to Observations on the superannuation fund, proposed to be established...by the Treasury Minutes of the 10th August, 1821, and 8th January, 1822. 15p. *8°*. 1822. *Both the main work and the supplement to it belonged to David Ricardo.*

23634　PAGE, Frederick. The principle of the English poor laws illustrated and defended, by an historical view of indigence in civil society; with observations and suggestions relative to their improved administration. 108p. *8°*. *London & Bath,* 1822. *See also* 1829, 1830.

23635　PHILLIMORE, Joseph. Substance of the speech of Joseph Phillimore, LL.D. in the House of Commons...March 27, 1822, on moving for leave to bring in a Bill to amend the Marriage Act. 80p. *8°*. 1822. *The Agar Ellis copy.*

23636　REDFORD, T. In the King's Bench. Between Thomas Redford, plaintiff; and Hugh Hornby Birley, Alexander Oliver, Richard Withington and Edward Meagher, defendants. For an assault on the 16th of August, 1819. Report of the proceedings on the trial... at Lancaster...April 1822...and the judgment of the Court of King's Bench in Easter Term following, upon an action on the part of the plaintiff, for a rule to shew cause why a new trial should not be granted... 632p. *8°*. *Manchester, & London,* [1822]

23637　REMARKS upon Mr. Hale's Appeal to the public, in defence of the Spitalfields Act. 52p. *8°*. 1822. *The copy that belonged to David Ricardo.*

23638　** True and effectual **REMEDY for the disturbances in Ireland. 15p. *8°*. *n.p.* [1822] *The copy that belonged to David Ricardo.*

23639　A REPLY to Mr. Hale's Appeal to the public, in defence of the Spitalfields Act...By the author of "Observations on the ruinous tendency of the Spitalfields Act." Second edition. 63p. *8°*. 1822. *For the third edition, see no.* 23631.

23640　SLANEY, R. A. An essay on the employment of the poor...Second edition, with additions. To which is prefixed, a letter to the author, by James Scarlett, Esq. M.P.... 95p. *8°*. 1822. *For another edition, see* 1819.

23641　SOCIETY FOR THE IMPROVEMENT OF PRISON DISCIPLINE, *London.* Description of the tread mill invented by Mr. William Cubitt, of Ipswich, for the employment of prisoners, and recommended by the Society...Published by the committee. 10p. *8°*. 1822.

23642　—— Description d'un moulin de discipline, appelé tread mill, inventé en Angleterre, par M. Cubitt, d'Ipswich...pour servir d'occupation aux prisonniers, et recommandé...par la...Société ayant pour objet l'amélioration de la discipline intérieure des prisons...Traduit de l'anglais. 10p. *8°*. *Londres,* 1822.

23643　SOCIETY FOR THE SUPPRESSION OF MENDICITY, *London.* The fourth report of the Society...[With a list of subscribers.] 70, [40]p. *8°*. 1822. *See also* 1819, 1820, 1825.

23644　STUART, James, *younger, of Dunearn.* The trial of James Stuart...before the High Court of Justiciary, at Edinburgh, on Monday, June 10, 1822 [for the murder of Sir A. Boswell, Bart., in a duel]...With an appendix of documents. 186, 20p. *8°*. *Edinburgh & London,* 1822. *The copy that belonged to David Ricardo.*

23645　THOUGHTS on prison discipline, and the present state of the police of the Metropolis: with some notice of the article on Mr. Western's pamphlet in the Edinburgh Review. 61p. *8°*. 1822.

23646　TOWNSEND, E. A view of the injurious effects of the present bankrupt system, in regard to property and public morals; with hints at improvements. 20p. *8°*. 1822.

23647　—— Second edition...with remarks on the Lord Chancellor's late Bills... 24p. *8°*. 1822. *The copy that belonged to David Ricardo.*

23648　—— A view of the present operation of the bankrupt laws, in regard to property and public morals. 20p. *8°*. 1822. *The copy that belonged to David Ricardo.*

23649　UNUS POPULI, *pseud.* A letter to Mr. Scarlet on the poor laws... 87p. *8°*. 1822.

23650　VERAX, *pseud.* Review of the statements in Mr. Hale's Appeal to the public on the Spitalfields Act. 28p. *8°*. 1822. *The copy that belonged to David Ricardo.*

23651　WILCOCKSON, I. Authentic records of the Guild Merchant of Preston...in...1822; with an introduction, containing an historical dissertation on the origin of guilds... 128p. *8°*. *Preston, Lancaster, &c.,* [1822]

SLAVERY

23652 ASHMUN, J. Memoir of the life and character of the Rev. Samuel Bacon...late, an officer of Marines...and principal agent of the American Government for persons liberated from slave-ships, on the coast of Africa ...288p. *8°. Washington City, Richmond, &c.*, 1822.

23653 BROGLIE, A. L. V. C. DE, *Duc*. Discours prononcé...à la Chambre des Pairs le 28 mars 1822, sur la traite des nègres. 154p. *8°. [Paris, 1822]*

23654 CLARKSON, T. The cries of Africa, to the inhabitants of Europe, or, a survey of...the slave-trade. 50p. *8°.* 1822.

23655 —— Le cri des Africains...Traduit de l'anglais. 56p. *8°. Londres*, 1822.

23656 —— [Another edition.] 57p. *8°. Paris*, 1822.

23657 —— De kreet der Afrikanen...Uit het Engelsch vertaald. 62p. *8°. Amsterdam & 's Gravenhage*, 1822. *See also 1823.*

23658 COMMITTEE FOR PROMOTING AFRICAN INSTRUCTION. Report of the Committee managing a fund raised by some Friends, for the purpose of promoting African instruction; with an account of a visit to the Gambia and Sierra Leone [by William Singleton]. 71p. *8°.* 1822. *See also 1824.*

23659 ENGLAND. Parliament. *House of Commons.* Substance of the proceedings in the House of Commons on...July 25, 1822, on the occasion of two addresses to his Majesty: one moved by Mr. Wilberforce, for preventing the extension of slavery at the Cape of Good Hope; and the other by Mr. Wilmot, for sending commissioners of inquiry to certain British colonies. 46p. *8°.* 1822.

23660 FRIENDS, *Society of.* An address to the inhabitants of Europe on the iniquity of the slave trade; issued by the Religious Society of Friends, commonly called Quakers, in Great Britain and Ireland. 15p. *8°.* 1822.

23661 HARRIS, THADDEUS M. A discourse delivered before the African Society in Boston, 15th of July 1822, on the anniversary celebration of the abolition of the slave trade. 27p. *8°. Boston*, 1822.

23662 TORREY, J. American slave trade...with reflections on the project for forming a colony of American blacks in Africa, and certain documents respecting that project...With...plates. [With a preface by Cobbett.] 119p. *12°.* 1822.

23663 WILBERFORCE, WILLIAM (1759–1833). Lettre à l'Empereur Alexandre sur la traite des noirs. 83p. *8°. Londres*, 1822.

POLITICS

23664 [ATKINSON, WILLIAM (1758–1846).] A speech intended to have been spoken at a second meeting of the clergy upon the Popish question: to which is added, a sermon, on the subject of reform: together with a candid inquiry into the crudities...of the dissenters from the Church of England. By the Old Inquirer. 63p. *8°. Bradford*, 1822.

23665 BARKLEY, J. Report of the trial of John Barkley, (one of the shop-men of Richard Carlile,) prosecuted by the Constitutional Association for publishing a seditious and blasphemous libel. 20p. *8°.* 1822.

23666 BOYLE, HUMPHREY. Report of the trial of Humphrey Boyle, indicted at the instance of the Constitutional Association...for publishing an alledged blasphemous and seditious libel, as one of the shopmen of Mr. Carlile...on the 27th of May, 1822...To which is attached, the Trial of Joseph Rhodes, under the name of Wm. Holmes...for publishing a copy of the same pamphlet. 32p. *8°.* 1822.

23667 CANNING, GEORGE (1770–1827). Corrected report of the speech of the Right Honble. George Canning, in the House of Commons, 25th April, 1822, on Lord John Russell's motion for a reform of Parliament. 65p. *8°.* 1822. *The copy that belonged to M. T. Sadler.*

23668 [CARLILE, R.] The character of a soldier: by Philanthropos. Second edition. 8p. *8°.* 1822. *For another edition, see 1821.*

23669 —— The report of the proceedings of the Court of King's Bench...on the 12th, 13th, 14th, and 15th days of October [1821]; being the mock trials of Richard Carlile, for alledged blasphemous libels, in publishing Thomas Paine's theological works and Elihu Palmer's Principles of nature...203p. *8°.* 1822.

23670 CIVIS, *pseud.* The important discovery; or, a reply from Civis, to a letter addressed by Daniel O'Connel, Esq. to His Excellency the Marquis Wellesley...[With the text of O'Connell's letter.] 22p. *8°. Dublin*, 1822.

23671 [ESQUIRON DE SAINT-AGNAN, A. T. D'.] Des niveleurs. 350p. *8°. Paris*, 1822.

23672 EUPHILONOMUS, GERARDUS, *the Philadelphian, pseud.* Political considerations on Ireland. 44p. *8°.* 1822. *The copy that belonged to David Ricardo.*

23673 An **EXPOSITION** of the principles and views of the middling interest, in the City of Boston. 8p. *8°. Boston*, 1822.

23674 FOSTER, JOHN, *of Knaresborough.* A letter to Walter Fawkes, Esq. on his recent address to the County of York. 14p. *8°. Knaresborough*, 1822.

23675 FROST, J. Part the first. The trial between Thomas Prothero attorney at law, and John Frost, Newport. With remarks on the mode which T. Prothero has taken to clear his character. 44p. *8°. Newport [Mon.]*, 1822.

23676 —— Part the second... 44p. *8°. Newport [Mon.]*, 1822.

23677 HALL, ROBERT. An apology for the freedom of the press, and for general liberty: to which are prefixed, remarks on Bishop Horsley's sermon, preached January 30, 1793...The seventh edition, with corrections. 108p. *8°. London & Bristol*, 1822. *For other editions, see 1793.*

23678 —— A reply to a review in the Christian Guardian, Jan. 1822, of "An apology for the freedom of the press, and for general liberty, &c." In a letter addressed to the editor of the Leicester Journal...With the review, extracted from the Christian Guardian. 18p. *8°. London & Bristol*, 1822.

23679 [**HOOK**, T. W.] Holkham, a poem; dedicated, without permission, to Joseph Hume. 78p. *12°*. 1822.

23680 JOHNSON, JOSEPH, *of Northen*. A letter to Henry Hunt, Esq. [On the reasons for ending their friendship.] 36p. *8°. Manchester*, 1822.

23681 —— A second letter to Henry Hunt, Esq. 20p. *8°. Manchester*, 1822.

23682 MAITLAND, SIR T. Substance of Sir Thos. Maitland's address to the Legislative Assembly of the Ionian Islands, 4th March, 1822. 18p. *8°*. 1822. *The copy that belonged to David Ricardo, with an engraved inscription 'From the Earl of Lauderdale' on the title-page.*

23683 Historical **NOTICES** of the several rebellions, disturbances, and illegal associations in Ireland, from the earliest period to the year 1822; and a view of the actual state of the country…With suggestions…for promoting the national prosperity and happiness. 121p. *8°. Dublin*, 1822.

23684 The **PROCEEDINGS** in Herefordshire, connected with the visit of Joseph Hume, Esq., M.P. and a detail of the speeches delivered at a public dinner… on…December 7, 1821, for the purpose of presenting that gentleman with a silver tankard and a hogshead of cider…in approbation of his parliamentary conduct; with an appendix of documents referred to by Mr. Hume, and elucidatory of the important statements in his speech. 48p. *8°. Hereford & London*, 1822.

23685 SIÉYÈS, E. J. Qu'est-ce que le Tiers Etat? Précédé de l'Essai sur les priviléges…Nouvelle édition, augmentée de vingt-trois notes, par l'abbé Morellet. 224p. *8°. Paris*, 1822. *For other editions of both works, see 1789.*

23686 THOMAS, JOHN P. A legal and constitutional argument against the alleged judicial right of restraining the publication of reports of judicial proceedings, as assumed in the King v. Thistlewood and others, enforced against the proprietor of the Observer by a fine of £500, and afterwards confirmed by the Court of King's Bench. 147p. *8°*. 1822.

23687 A few **THOUGHTS** on the probable renewal of the Alien Bill [Act]. By a Member of Parliament. 37p. *8°*. 1822. *The Agar Ellis copy.*

23688 WESTMINSTER. Public distress. The true causes of the public distress and discontent set forth in the petition of the Electors of Westminster to the House of Commons, an example which ought to be followed by the whole of the people of the United Kingdom. *s.sh.fol.* [*London*, 1822] [*Br.* 498]

23689 WIX, S. Plain reasons why political power should not be granted to Papists. 16p. *8°*. 1822. *The copy that belonged to David Ricardo.*

23690 WRIGHT, SUSANNAH. Report of the trial of Mrs. Susannah Wright, for publishing, in his shop, the writings and correspondences of R. Carlile…in the Court of King's Bench…July 8, 1822. Indictment at the instance of the Society for the Suppression of Vice. 59p. *8°*. 1822.

SOCIALISM

23691 [**BLATCHLY**, C. C.] An essay on common wealths. Part I. The evils of exclusive and the benefits of inclusive wealth. Part II. Extracts from Robert Owen's New view of society. Part III. Melish's account of the Harmonists. 64p. *8°. New-York: The New-York Society for Promoting Communities*, 1822.

23692 BRITISH AND FOREIGN PHILANTHROPIC SOCIETY. Proceedings of the British and Foreign Philanthropic Society for the Permanent Relief of the Labouring Classes; held at the Freemasons' Hall…on…the 1st of June, 1822. 56p. *8°*. 1822. *★Another, the FWA copy, belonged to William Pare.*

23693 ★—— Summary of Mr. Owen's plan, for the permanent relief of the working classes. 10p. *12°*. 1822. *The FWA copy that belonged to William Pare.*

23694 FOURIER, F. C. M. Traité de l'association domestique-agricole. Vols. 1–2. *8°. Paris & Londres*, 1822. *Signed in manuscript by the author. The copy that belonged to Victor Considérant. See also 1823.*

23695 ★[**OWEN**, ROBERT.] Permanent relief for the British agricultural & manufacturing labourers, and the Irish peasantry. 9p. *fol.* [1822?] *The FWA copy, with William Pare's signature on the title-page and at the head of the first page.*

MISCELLANEOUS

23696 ALEN, L. Observations on the case of Col. Luke Alen, C.B. late 55th Regiment. Dublin, 2nd April 1822. 33p. *8°. Dublin*, 1822. *The copy that belonged to David Ricardo.*

23697 BECCARIA BONESANA, C., *Marchese*. Richerche intorno alla natura dello stile. Opera di Cesare Beccaria. [Parte prima.] 178p. *4°. Milano*, 1822. *Reprinted from the text published by Custodi in 1804.*

23698 BENTHAM, J. Codification proposal, addressed…to all nations professing liberal opinions; or idea of a proposed all-comprehensive body of law, with an accompaniment of reasons, applying all along to the several proposed arrangements… 78p. *8°*. 1822. *Presentation copy, with inscription, from the author to Sutton Sharpe.*

23699 BROUGHAM, H. P., *Baron Brougham and Vaux*. The speech of Henry Brougham, Esq. in the case of the King v. Williams, for a libel on the clergy; tried before Baron Wood and a special jury. 18p. *8°*. 1822.

23700 [**COCKBURN**, H., *Lord Cockburn*.] Observations on the mode of choosing juries in Scotland. [From Edinburgh Review, vol. XXXVI, no. 71.] 119p. *12°. Edinburgh*, 1822. *The Agar Ellis copy.*

23701 COLOGNA, A. DE. Discours prononcé à l'occasion de l'inauguration du nouveau temple israélite de Paris, célébrée le 12 adar 5582 (5 mars 1822). 18p. *8°. Paris*, 1822.

23702 GRIFFIN, E. D. An address delivered to the

class of graduates of Williams College, at the Commencement, Sep. 4, 1822... 12p. *8°. Pittsfield, 1822.*

23703 HARVEY, D. W. A letter to the burgesses of Colchester, containing a plain statement of the proceedings before the Benchers of the Inner Temple, upon his application to be called to the Bar, and upon his appeal to the judges. 68p. *8°. London, Colchester, &c., 1822. The copy that belonged to David Ricardo.*

23704 HÖENE WROŃSKI, J. M. Pétition au Parlement Britannique sur la spoliation d'un savant étranger [J. Höene Wroński] par le Bureau des Longitudes de Londres. Soumise par Höene Wroński. 59p. *8°. Londres, 1822. The copy that belonged to David Ricardo.*

23705 ——— Trois lettres à Sir Humphry Davy, Président de la Société Royale de Londres, sur l'imposture publique des savans à privilèges, ou des sociétés savantes. 72p. *8°. Londres, 1822. The copy that belonged to David Ricardo.*

23706 HORNOR, T. Prospectus of a view of London and its environs, taken from the summit of St. Paul's Cathedral, by Thomas Hornor. [With a lithographed letter referring to the same project.] [2], [2]p. *4°. [1822 ?] The Agar Ellis copy.*

23707 NOLAN, F. Deposition made, under oath, by an ecclesiastic to attest the spoliation of a learned foreigner (Hoëne Wronski), by the British Board of Longitude. 8p. *8°. 1822. The copy that belonged to David Ricardo.*

1823

GENERAL

23708 ALBERTI, L. Quadro del sistema di commercio e d'industria vigente nelle provincie venete. 232p. *8°. Venezia, 1823.*

23709 ATKINSON, A. Ireland exhibited to England, in a political and moral survey of her population, and in a statistical and scenographic tour of certain districts; comprehending specimens of her colonisation, natural history and antiquities, arts, sciences, and commerce... Violent inequalities in her political and social system, the true source of her disorders... 2 vols. *8°. 1823.*

23710 [BAILEY, S.] Questions in political economy, politics, morals, metaphysics, polite literature, and other branches of knowledge... By the author of Essays on the formation and publication of opinions. 400p. *8°. 1823.*

23711 BALL, C. J. Etat des juifs en France, en Espagne, et en Italie, depuis le commencement du cinquième siècle... jusqu'à la fin du seizième, sous les divers rapports du droit civil, du commerce et de la littérature... 203p. *8°. Paris, 1823.*

23712 BENTHAM, J. An introduction to the principles of morals and legislation... A new edition, corrected by the author. 2 vols. *8°. 1823. For another edition, see 1789.*

23713 [BUTTERWORTH, J.] A complete history of the cotton trade, including also, that of the silk, calico-printing, & hat manufactories; with remarks on their progress in Bolton, Bury, Stockport, Blackburn, and Wigan. To which is added, an account of the chief mart of these goods, the town of Manchester. By a person concerned in trade. 302, xiip. *12°. Manchester, 1823. A reissue of The antiquities of... Manchester, 1822 (q.v.).*

23714 CAREY, H. C. and **LEA,** J. The geography, history, and statistics, of America, and the West Indies; exhibiting a correct account of the discovery, settlement, and progress of the... western hemisphere to... 1822... With additions relative to the new states of South America, &c.&c.... 477p. *8°. 1823.*

23715 [CAREY, M.] The crisis: a solemn appeal to the President, the Senate and House of Representatives, and the citizens of the United States, on the destructive effects of the present policy of this country, on its agricul-

ture, manufactures, commerce and finances. With a comparison between the extraordinary prosperity of Great Britain, and the general depression in the United States. By a Pennsylvanian. Second edition. 79p. *8°. Philadelphia, 1823.*

23716 [———**]** Extracts from The crisis... Second edition. viii, 53–79p. *8°. Philadelphia, 1823.*

23717 [———**]** Hamilton ——— no. VII. (Second edition.) [Signed: Hamilton. Philadelphia, Jan. 1, 1823. On protection.] 8p. *8°. n.p. [1823] For earlier numbers see 1822 and for later 1824.*

23718 CLELAND, J. Statistical tables relative to the City of Glasgow, with other matters therewith connected ... Third edition, with additions. 208p. *8°. Glasgow, Edinburgh, &c., 1823.*

23719 CLOET, J. J. DE. Manuel de l'administrateur, du manufacturier et du négociant, ou tableau statistique de l'industrie des Pays-Bas. 108p. *8°. Bruxelles, 1823. See also 1826.*

23720 COBBETT, W. Twelve sermons... 295p. *12°. 1823. For other editions, see 1822.*

23721 COLOMBIA. Colombian state papers, translated and published from official copies; being the Act of Installation of the Houses of Senate and Representatives; the message of the Vice-President on the opening of Congress; a report on the diplomatic relations of Colombia, &c.&c. 48p. *8°. 1823.*

23722 COMMITTEE FOR THE RELIEF OF THE DISTRESSED DISTRICTS IN IRELAND. Report of the Committee... appointed at a general meeting held at the City of London Tavern, on the 7th of May, 1822... 346p. *8°. 1823.*

23723 [COPLEY, J. S., *Baron Lyndhurst.*] Administration of the affairs of Great Britain, Ireland, and their dependencies, at the commencement of the year 1823, stated and explained under the heads of finance, national resources, foreign relations, colonies, trade and domestic administration. 207p. *8°. 1823.*

23724 [———**]** Second edition. 207p. *8°. 1823. The copy that belonged to Earl De Grey.*

23725 [——] Third edition. 207p. *8°. 1823. The copy that belonged to David Ricardo.*

23726 [——] Fourth edition. 207p. *8°. 1823.*

23727 [——] Sixth edition. 207p. *8°. 1823.*

23728 [——] Seventh edition. 207p. *8°. 1823.*

23729 [——] État de l'Angleterre au commencement de 1823...Traduit sur la 4ᵉ édition anglaise; par MM. P.-A. Dufau et J. Guadet... 233p. *8°. Paris, 1823.*

23730 CRUICKSHANK, John. Observations on the Bill for establishing uniformity of weights and measures, and on the amendments proposed by John Wilson, Esq. of Thornly: submitted to a meeting of the Commissioners of Supply of the County of Aberdeen, in April 1823. 4p. *4°. Paisley, [1823]*

23731 DESTUTT DE TRACY, A. L. C., *Comte.* Traité d'économie politique. 356p. *12°. Paris, 1823.*

23732 Commercial **DIRECTORY;** containing, a topographical description, extent and productions of different sections of the Union, statistical information relative to manufactures, commercial and port regulations, a list of the principal commercial houses, tables of imports and exports...tariff of duties. 242, 41p. *4°. Philadelphia: John C. Kayser & Co., 1823.*

23733 DUBOIS AYMÉ, J. M. J. Examen de quelques questions d'économie politique, et notamment de l'ouvrage de M. Ferrier intitulé: Du gouvernement considéré dans ses rapports avec le commerce. 248p. *8°. Paris, 1823.*

23734 DUPIN, F. P. C., *Baron.* Du commerce et de ses travaux publics, en Angleterre et en France, discours prononcé le 2 juin 1823, dans la séance publique de l'Académie des Sciences. 40p. *8°. Paris, 1823. Presentation copy with inscription, from the author, 'To Mr. Isaac Solly Esqr.'.*

23735 —— Système de l'administration britannique en 1822, considéré sous les rapports des finances, de l'industrie, du commerce et de la navigation, d'après un exposé ministériel. 160p. *8°. Paris, 1823.*

23736 *The **EAST-INDIA** register and directory, for 1823; containing...lists of the Company's servants... mariners &c. not in the service of the...Company; private vessels...merchant vessels employed in the country trade ...Compiled...by A. W. Mason, Geo. Owen, and G. H. Brown...Corrected to 25th January 1823. 535p. *12°.* [1823]

23737 *—— Second edition. Corrected to 16th September 1823. 530p. *12°.* [1823] *For other editions, see 1804.*

23738 [EMERSON, J. S.] One year of the administration of His Excellency the Marquess of Wellesley in Ireland. 137p. *8°. London & Dublin, 1823.*

23739 ERSKINE, T., *Baron Erskine.* A letter to the proprietors and occupiers of land, on the causes of, and the remedies for, the declension of agricultural prosperity. 47p. *8°. 1823.*

23740 FAUX, W. Memorable days in America: being a journal of a tour to the United States, principally undertaken to ascertain...the condition and probable prospects of British emigrants: including accounts of Mr. Birkbeck's settlement in the Illinois... 488p. *8°. 1823.*

23741 GORE, J. Gore's Liverpool directory...containing an alphabetical list of the merchants, traders and principal inhabitants. The appendix contains lists of the mayor and council, officers of the customs and excise, dock duties... 276, 162p. *12°. Liverpool, Manchester, &c., 1823. See also 1818, 1829.*

23742 A new and easy **INTRODUCTION** to the principles of political economy. 48p. *8°. [1823]*

23743 JOPLIN, T. Outlines of a system of political economy; written with a view to prove to Government and the country, that the cause of the present agricultural distress is entirely artificial; and to suggest a plan for the management of the currency...Together with the fourth edition of an Essay on the principles of banking [with an appendix]. 300, 52, 92, 19p. *8°. 1823. Presentation copy from the author to Joseph Hume, M.P., with an accompanying letter, for which see vol. III, A.L. 64.*

23744 JUARROS, D. A statistical and commercial history of the Kingdom of Guatemala...With an account of its conquest by the Spaniards, and a narrative of the principal events down to the present time...Translated by J. Baily... 520p. *8°. 1823.*

23745 KEITH, G. S. On the embarrassments affecting the interests of agriculture. 42p. *8°. Aberdeen & Edinburgh, 1823. Presentation copy, with inscription, from the author to David Erskine of Cardross.*

23746 LESLIE, Sir John. Weights and Measures Bill. Letter...to John Wilson...[With 'Excerpts from a letter addressed to John Wilson by R. Hamilton...20th March 1824'.] *s.sh.4°. n.p.* [1823] *The second letter is printed on the verso of the first.*

23747 LOW, D. Observations on the present state of landed property, and on the prospects of the landholder and the farmer. 126p. *8°. Edinburgh & London, 1823.*

23748 LOWE, Joseph. The present state of England in regard to agriculture, trade, and finance; with a comparison of the prospects of England and France...Second edition, with...additions and emendations [and an appendix]. 418, 106p. *8°. London & Edinburgh, 1823. A manuscript note by the author, entitled 'Memorandum relative to the second edition', is inserted before the introduction. The copy that belonged to Sir Robert Peel. For another edition, see 1822.*

23749 [MacDONNELL, E.] Practical views and suggestions on the present condition and permanent improvement of Ireland. By Hibernicus. Author of the letters...under the same signature in the Courier... 173p. *8°. Dublin, 1823.*

23750 MALTHUS, T. R. The measure of value stated and illustrated, with an application of it to the alterations in the value of the English currency since 1790. 81p. *8°. 1823.*

23751 MANGLES, P. A letter to the freeholders of the county of Surrey, upon the causes and the remedies of the present agricultural distress. 52p. *8°. 1823.*

23752 MEASON, G. L. A letter to William Joseph Denison, Esq. M.P. on the agricultural distress and on the necessity of a silver standard. [With an appendix.] 47, 6p. *8°. 1823. For another edition, see 1822.*

23753 MENOT, A. J. Quelques réflexions sur la législation commerciale et les moyens de la mettre plus en harmonie avec la monarchie... 150p. *8°. Paris, 1823.*

23754 MILL, James. Elémens d'économie politique ...Traduits de l'anglais par J. T. Parisot. 318p. *8°. Paris, 1823. For other editions, see 1821.*

23755 [MITCHELL, W. A.] The letters of Tim. Tunbelly, Gent....on the Tyne, the Newcastle corporation, the freemen, the tolls, &c.&c. To which is prefixed, a memoir of his public and private life...Vol. I. 155p. *8°. Newcastle upon Tyne*, 1823. *No more published.*

23756 MORTIMER, THOMAS (1730–1810). A general commercial dictionary: comprehending trade, manufactures, and navigation; as also agriculture, so far as it is connected with commerce...compiled...by Thomas Mortimer...With considerable alterations and additions by William Dickinson, Esq. The third edition, corrected and revised. 1155p. *8°.* 1823.

23757 OPINIONS as to the real state of the nation, with strictures on a pamphlet intitled 'The administration of the affairs of Great Britain', &c.&c. By the ghost of the Marquess of Londonderry. 122p. *8°.* 1823.

23758 PETTMAN, W. An address to the Members of both Houses of Parliament, on the injury the landholders sustain for the want of a protecting duty on imported corn; and by the inequality of their present burthens for the support of his Majesty's Government and the poor. With a few hints on the expediency of equalizing the poor rates... 93p. *8°. Canterbury*, 1823.

23759 PIGOT and Co.'s London & provincial new commercial directory, for 1823-4... 372, 141, 525p. *8°. London & Manchester*, [1823]

23760 The POST OFFICE London directory for 1823...By Critchett & Woods. The twenty-fourth edition. [With 'A new guide to stage-coaches, waggons, carts, vessels, &c. for 1823...The twenty-first edition. By Critchett & Woods'.] 412, lxxi, 136p. *12°.* [1823] *See also* 1805 (Post Office annual directory), 1810, 1813, 1814, 1820 (Post Office London directory), 1825, 1830, 1832, 1834, 1836, 1841.

23761 PRYME, G. An introductory lecture and syllabus, to a course delivered in the University of Cambridge, on the principles of political economy. 36p. *8°. Cambridge & London*, 1823.

23762 REID, T. Travels in Ireland, in the year 1822, exhibiting brief sketches of the moral, physical, and political state of the country: with reflections on the best means of improving its condition. 375p. *8°. London, Dublin, &c.*, 1823.

23763 RENFREW, *County of. Commissioners of Supply.* Weights and Measures Bill. Renfrew 30th April, 1823. At a general meeting of the Commissioners of Supply of the County of Renfrew...Mr. Wilson of Thornly...laid before the meeting a number of important papers...on this subject.... *s.sh.4°. n.p.* [1823]

23764 REYNIER, J. L. A. De l'économie publique et rurale des Egyptiens et des Carthaginois, précédé de considérations sur les antiquités Éthiopiennes. 520p. *8°. Genève & Paris*, 1823.

23765 [SEELEY, R. B.] The case of the landed interests, and their just claims. 39p. *8°.* 1823.

23766 SEINE, *Département de la. Administration.* Recherches statistiques sur la ville de Paris et le Département de la Seine; recueil de tableaux dressés et réunis d'après les ordres de Monsieur le Comte de Chabrol... xxviii, [52], 30p., 104 tables. *4°. Paris*, 1823. *Published under the direction of J. B. J. Fourier, with some contributions by him. With the book-plate of the third Marquis of Lansdowne. See also* 1821, 1826, 1829.

23767 STORCH, H. F. VON. Cours d'économie politique, ou exposition des principes qui déterminent la prospérité des nations...Avec des notes explicatives et critiques par J.-B. Say... 5 vols. *8°. Paris*, 1823–24. *For another edition, see* 1815.

23768 The STRANGER in Liverpool; or, an historical and descriptive view of the town of Liverpool and its environs. The seventh edition, with corrections and additions. 315p. *12°. Liverpool*, 1823. *A different work from that by Stonehouse published in 1849 (q.v.).*

23769 TAYLOR, N. W. A sermon, addressed to the legislature of the state of Connecticut, at the annual election in Hartford, May 7, 1823...Second edition. 40p. *8°. New-Haven*, 1823.

23770 The UNIQUE. [A collection of portraits, with biographical notices, by G. Smeeton ?] 2 vols. *8°.* [1823–24]

23771 VERRI, P., *Conte.* Méditations sur l'économie politique...Traduit de l'italien par Frédérick Neale. 215p. *8°. Paris*, 1823. [*Higgs* 5167*n*] *For other editions, see* 1771.

23772 WHITMORE, W. W. A letter on the present state and future prospects of agriculture. Addressed to the agriculturists of the county of Salop...The second edition, with some additions. 111p. *8°.* 1823. *For another edition, see* 1822.

23773 WILSON, JOHN, *of Thornly.* Observations on the Bill for ascertaining and establishing uniformity of weights and measures, now in Parliament, submitted to the consideration of the Chamber of Commerce of the City of Glasgow. To which is added, the substance of this Bill, with the amendments proposed by the Chamber of Commerce. 11p. *4°. Glasgow*, 1823.

23774 —— Weights & Measures Bill. [A circular in engraved manuscript facsimile, signed by John Wilson, and dated 7, May 1823, advocating that the changes in corn measures suggested by the Glasgow Chamber of Commerce should be incorporated in the Bill.] [4]p. *4°. n.p.* [1823]

23775 [YOUNGS, B. S.] The testimony of Christ's second appearing; containing a general statement of all things pertaining to the faith and practice of the Church of God in this latter day. Published by order of the ministry, in union with the church...[Written by B. S. Youngs. The preface signed: David Darrow, John Meacham and Benjamin S. Youngs.] Third edition, corrected and improved. 573p. *8°. Union Village (Ohio)*, 1823.

AGRICULTURE

For **AGRICULTURAL AND HORTICULTURAL SOCIETY OF ST. HELENA**, Proceedings, 1823–[28], *see* vol. III, *Periodicals list*, Proceedings of the Agricultural and Horticultural Society of St. Helena.

23776 BAYLDON, J. S. The art of valuing rents and tillages; wherein is explained the manner of valuing the tenant's right on entering and quitting farms, in Yorkshire and the adjoining counties... 187p. *8°. London & Sheffield*, 1823. *See also* 1827, 1840, 1844.

23777 A simple, certain, and immediate **CURE,** for the agricultural distresses of the country, now in the power of the landed interest. By a farmer. 38p. *8°.* 1823. *The copy that belonged to David Ricardo.*

23778 ENGLAND. *Laws, etc.* An Act for inclosing lands in the parish of Abthorpe, in the county of Northampton. ⟨Royal Assent, 17 June 1823.⟩ 4 Geo. IV. sess. 1823. 23p. *fol.* [*London,* 1823]

23779 FARMING SOCIETY OF IRELAND. For the Farming Society of Ireland. The report of their secretary, respecting the agricultural school of Bannow, in the Barony of Bargie, and county of Wexford. As ordered by the Board. 16p. *8°. Dublin,* 1823.

23780 FISKE, O. Address delivered before the Worcester Agricultural Society, October 8, 1823, being their anniversary cattle show and exhibition of manufactures...Published by order of the Trustees. [With 'Reports of the several committees' and 'Officers... elected April 17, 1823'.] 36p. *8°. Worcester* [*Mass.*], [1823]

23781 HERBERT, HON. WILLIAM (1778–1847). A letter to the chairman of the Committee of the House of Commons, on the game laws. 16p. *8°.* 1823.

23782 PLAN for the relief of the agricultural poor, with a view to diminish the poor-rates, and give permanent employment to the labourer... 36p. *12°. Wycombe,* 1823. *The Agar Ellis copy.*

CORN LAWS

23783 NETHERLANDS. *Laws, etc.* Recueil de pièces, relatives à la liberté illimitée du commerce des grains. Publié par ordre du Roi. 307p. *8°. La Haye,* 1823.

POPULATION

23784 BOOTH, D. A letter to the Rev. T. R. Malthus ...being an answer to the criticism, on Mr. Godwin's work on population, which was inserted in the LXXth number of the Edinburgh Review: to which is added an examination of the censuses of Great Britain and Ireland. 124p. *8°.* 1823.

23785 CLELAND, J. By permission. Enumeration of the inhabitants of Scotland, taken from the Government abstracts of 1801, 1811, 1821; containing a particular account of every parish in Scotland, and many useful details respecting England, Wales and Ireland. 91p. *8°. Glasgow, Edinburgh, &c.,* 1823.

23786 EVERETT, A. H. New ideas on population: with remarks on the theories of Malthus and Godwin. 125p. *8°. Boston,* 1823.

23787 —— [Another edition.] 94p. *8°.* 1823. *See also* 1826.

23788 MALTHUS, T. R. Essai sur le principe de population...Trad. de l'anglois sur la 5e édit., par Pierre Prévost...et...Gme. Prévost...2de édition françoise... 4 vols. *8°. Genève & Paris,* 1823. *For other editions, see* 1798.

TRADES & MANUFACTURES

23789 ACADÉMIE DES SCIENCES. Institut Royale de France. Académie Royale des Sciences. Rapport sur les procédés chimiques et mécaniques employés par M. de Puymaurin fils, pour la fabrication des médailles de bronze montées et frappées, fait à l'Académie...le lundi 13 janvier 1823. [Signed: Chaptal, Mongez, Molard.] 27p. *4°. Paris,* 1823.

23790 BESNARD, P. Report of a tour of inspection through the province of Ulster, on the treatment of flax, as practised in the Netherlands. [With an appendix.] 31, 31p. *8°. Dublin,* 1823. *Presentation copy, with inscription, from the author to George Agar Ellis.*

23791 COMMITTEE OF MASTER CHAIR-MANUFACTURERS AND JOURNEYMEN. The London chair-makers' and carvers' book of prices for workmanship. As regulated and agreed to by a Committee of Master Chair-manufacturers and Journeymen. With the methods of computation adopted in the work... 108p. *4°.* 1823. *For other editions, see* 1802; *for the first and second supplements see* 1808 *and* 1811; *for the third supplement see* 1844.

23792 [DEURBROUCG, G. and **NICHOLS,** .] Observations on the vinous fermentation; with a description of a patent apparatus to improve the same [invented by the authors]. Also, a statement of the advantages to be derived from this system when applied to the process of brewing, as confirmed by the testimony of Messrs. Gray and Co., Brewers, of Westham, in the County of Essex. 30p. *8°.* 1823. *The copy that belonged to David Ricardo.*

23793 FORSYTH, J. S. The farmer, maltster, distiller, & brewer's practical memorandum book: containing a concise treatise on the different methods of making malt ...To which is added, an abstract of the new Beer Act. 132p. *12°.* [1823] *An interleaved copy with contemporary manuscript additions, which belonged to G. E. Fussell, with his signature.*

23794 GUEST, R. A compendious history of the cotton-manufacture; with a disproval of the claims of Sir Richard Arkwright to the invention of its ingenious machinery. 70p. *4°. Manchester & London,* 1823.

23795 HOPPUS, E. Hoppus's Tables for measuring, or, practical measuring made easy, by a new set of tables ...The eighteenth edition... 226p. *long 12°.* 1823. *For other editions of* Practical measuring made easy, *see* 1759.

23796 LESLIE, T. The Edinburgh builder's new price-book, for 1823; containing an account of the prices allowed to masons, wrights, sawers...shewing the price of materials, the price of work when materials are furnished, and the price of labour only. With an appendix, containing observations on roofing, and a table of the price of rough scantling. 65p. *12°. Edinburgh*, 1823.

23797 MARCASSUS DE PUYMAURIN, A. DE. Mémoire sur les procédés les plus convenables pour remplacer le cuivre par le bronze dans la fabrication des médailles...Précédé des rapports faits à l'Académie des Sciences, et à celles des Inscription et Belles-Lettres. 58p. *8°. Paris*, 1823.

For the **MECHANICS' MAGAZINE**, 1823–52, *see* vol. III, *Periodicals list*.

23798 [**NICHOLSON**, P.] The new practical builder,

and workman's companion...Illustrated...with... plates, from original drawings...by Michael Angelo Nicholson, R. Elsam, W. Inwood...[With 'The practical builder's perpetual price-book'.] 3 vols. *4°.* 1823–25. *A second title-page reads: Architectonick. The new practical builder...*

23799 OBSERVATIONS on such parts of a Report lately submitted to the House of Commons, on gas light establishments, as relate to the dangers of explosion. 24p. *8°.* 1823. *The copy that belonged to David Ricardo.*

23800 TAYLOR, I. Scenes of British wealth, in produce, manufactures, and commerce, for the amusement and instruction of little tarry at-home travellers. 301p. *12°.* 1823.

COMMERCE

23801 BREWER, N. A narrative of the life and sufferings of Nicholas Brewer, of the town of Cardiff... master mariner; and of the oppression he has suffered at the hands of certain custom house officers of...Cardiff; by their wrongfully seizing and detaining his vessel, under the...pretence of her bowsprit being longer than by law allowed...Written by the said Nicholas Brewer... 52p. *8°.* 1823. *The copy that belonged to David Ricardo.*

23802 BROWN, WILLIAM K. Letters to the late Marquis of Londonderry...to T. S. Gooch...and to others, relative to the British trade at Genoa; also on the general importation of foreign wool into, as compared with the exportation of woollens from Great Britain. 60p. *8°. Harleston*, 1823.

23803 EAST INDIA COMPANY. Debates at the General Court of proprietors of East-India stock, on the 19th and 21st March, 1823, on the East-India sugar trade. Extracted from the Asiatic Journal for April 1823. 48p. *8°.* [1823]

23804 ENGLAND. Parliament. *House of Commons.* Substance of a debate, in the House of Commons, on the 22nd of May, 1823, on the motion of Mr. W. W. Whitmore, "that a Select Committee be appointed, to inquire into the duties payable on East and West India sugar". 142p. *8°.* 1823. *With a newspaper account of the debate bound in.*

23805 [**EVERETT**, A. H.] A few notes on certain passages respecting the law of nations, contained in an article in the July no. of the North American Review, upon the work entitled "Europe, by a citizen of the United States". By the author of that work. [With a 'Postscript to the preceding pamphlet', dated Oct. 15, 1824.] 32, 6p. *8°. Boston*, 1823[–24].

23806 FRESHFIELD, J. W. Law relating to principal and factor. Address delivered...to the Select Committee of the House of Commons, to whom the petition of the merchants, bankers, and others, of London, was referred... 148p. *8°.* 1823.

23807 —— Second edition. 148p. *8°.* 1823. *Presentation copy, with inscription, from the author to James Gibson Craig.*

23808 GUTCH, J. M. Letters on the impediments which obstruct the trade & commerce of the city and port of Bristol; which appeared in Felix Farley's Bristol Journal, under the signature of Cosmo. [With an appendix.] 120, iip. *8°. Bristol*, 1823.

23809 HENDERSON, JAMES. Observations on the great commercial benefits that will result from the Warehousing-Bill, particularly as regards the free transit of foreign linens, silks, & woollens, respectfully addressed to the consideration of the members of the British Parliament. 47p. *8°.* 1823. *The copy that belonged to David Ricardo.*

23810 HILLARY, SIR W., *Bart.* An appeal to the British nation, on the humanity and policy of forming a national institution, for the preservation of lives and property from shipwreck. 25p. *8°.* 1823.

23811 [**LARPENT**, SIR G. G. DE H.] On protection to West-India sugar. 71p. *8°.* 1823. *The copy that belonged to David Ricardo.*

23812 [——] Second edition, corrected and enlarged, and containing an answer to a pamphlet written by Joseph Marryat...entitled "A reply", &c., &c. 159p. *8°.* 1823.

23813 [**MACAULAY**, Z.] East and West India sugar; or, a refutation of the claims of the West India colonists to a protecting duty on East India sugar. 128p. *8°.* 1823.

23814 [——] A letter to William W. Whitmore, Esq. M.P. pointing out some of the erroneous statements contained in a pamphlet by Joseph Marryat, Esq. M.P. entitled "A reply to the arguments contained in various publications, recommending an equalization of the duties on East and West India sugars." By the author of a pamphlet entitled "East and West India sugar." 38p. *8°.* 1823.

23815 MARRYAT, J. A reply to the arguments contained in various publications, recommending an equalization of the duties on East & West India sugar. 111p. *8°.* 1823.

23816 NEDHAM, W. T. Corn tables, shewing the cost of any number of quarters and bushels, from ten shillings to eighty shillings per quarter. 143p. *8°.* 1823.

23817 OBSERVATIONS on the claims of the West-India colonists to a protecting duty on East India sugar. 52p. *8°.* 1823.

23818 PHIPPS, JOHN. A guide to the commerce of Bengal, for the use of merchants, ship owners...and others, resorting to the East Indies, but particularly of those connected with the shipping and commerce of Calcutta. Containing a view of the shipping, and external commerce of Bengal... [With an appendix of regulations of major trading areas of Asia, Australia and South America, and addenda.] 325, 164, 20p. *4°. n.p.*, 1823.

23819 PRINSEP, JOHN. Suggestions on freedom of commerce and navigation, more especially in reference to the East-India trade. [With an appendix.] 68, [4]p. *8°.* 1823.

23820 RAINIER, J. S. A synopsis of the prices of wheat, and of circumstances affecting them; particularly of the Statutes which relate to it, from the commencement of the thirteenth century to the end of 1822...Together with statements which indicate the situation of the country as to its agriculture, commerce...population, public revenue, &c. 19l. *fol.* 1823.

23821 RAITHBY, J., *ed.* The Statutes relating to the Admiralty, Navy, shipping and navigation, of the United Kingdom, from 9 Hen. III to 3 Geo. IV inclusive. With notes...Collected and arranged, under the authority of the Lords Commissioners of the Admiralty. 1168p. *4°.* 1823.

23822 REMARKS on the "Reciprocity of duties Bill", now under the consideration of Parliament. By a member of the committee of the Ship-Owners' Society. 32p. *8°.* 1823.

23823 SEELY, J. B. A few hints to the West-Indians, on their present claims to exclusive favour and protection, at the expense of the East-India interests, with some observations and notes on India... 93p. *8°.* 1823.

23824 A STATEMENT of the claims of the West India colonies to a protecting duty against East India sugar. 120p. *8°.* 1823.

23825 TOOKE, T. Thoughts and details on the high and low prices of the last thirty years. [In four parts.] 2 vols. *8°.* 1823. *See also 1824.*

23826 WAGENER, J. D. Merkantilische Notizen über Spanien begleitet mit einer historisch-statischen Einleitung...Erste Lieferung. 176p. *8°. Königsberg*, 1823.

COLONIES

23827 Some CONSIDERATIONS on the present distressed state of the British West India Colonies, their claims on the Government for relief, and the advantages to the nation in supporting them, particularly against the competition of East India sugar. By a West Indian. 63p. *8°.* 1823. *Attributed, in a manuscript note on the title-page, to 'Sir Simon Clarke Bt.'.*

23828 CROPPER, J. Relief for West-Indian distress, shewing the inefficiency of protecting duties on East-India sugar, and pointing out other modes of certain relief. 36p. *8°. London & Liverpool*, 1823. *The copy that belonged to David Ricardo.*

23829 MARRYAT, J. The substance of a speech... in the House of Commons, on Thursday, July 25th, 1822, upon Mr. Hume's motion for appointing a commission of enquiry to report on the state of the Island of Trinidad. 115p. *8°.* 1823. *The copy that belonged to David Ricardo.*

23830 PRINSEP, G. A. Remarks on the external commerce and exchanges of Bengal, with appendix of accounts and estimates. 72, [44]p. *8°.* 1823. *With manuscript additions and corrections, presumably by the author, in the text, and manuscript appendixes, the first of which is dated: 31st March 1824. For the manuscript, see vol.* III, *MS. 694.*

23831 ROUGHLEY, T. The Jamaica planter's guide; or, a system for planting and managing a sugar estate, or other plantations in that island, and throughout the British West Indies in general. Illustrated with interesting anecdotes. 420p. *8°.* 1823.

23832 STEWART, JOHN (*fl.* 1808–1823). A view of the past and present state of the island of Jamaica; with remarks on the moral and physical condition of the slaves, and on the abolition of slavery in the colonies. 363p. *8°. Edinburgh & London*, 1823.

23833 WEST INDIA agricultural distress, and a remark, on Mr. Wilberforce's appeal. By a Member of the House of Commons. 56p. *8°.* 1823. *The copy that belonged to Stephen Lushington.*

23834 WHITE, WILLIAM, *Capt.* A letter addressed to the proprietors of India stock, demonstrating British justice in India. [With 'Appendix. Proceedings of a Court of Enquiry...1817'.] 128, xxivp. *8°.* 1823. *The copy that belonged to David Ricardo.*

23835 —— Third edition. 128, xxivp. *8°.* 1823. *The Agar Ellis copy.*

23836 —— Petition of Capt. William White, to the proprietors of East India stock. Also the petition of Mayput Sing, subedar, to the Marquis of Hastings, praying against injustice and oppression. 47p. *8°.* 1823. *The copy that belonged to David Ricardo.*

FINANCE

23837 An ADDRESS to the Members of both Houses of Parliament, on the inefficiency of the present Insolvent Acts, and offering to their consideration a few arguments ...in support of a petition...agreed to at a meeting of the merchants and traders of...Westminster, held on the 24th of April, 1823...By two gentlemen of the committee. 46p. *8°.* 1823. *The Agar Ellis copy.*

23838 [ATKINSON, WILLIAM (1758–1846).] A rapid sketch of some of the evils of returning to cash payments, and the only remedies for them: to which are added, the Leeds Mercury turned into a frog, the billy-goats in leading-strings, and the march of reason. By the Old Inquirer. 35p. *8°. Bradford*, 1823.

23839 BANK OF ENGLAND. The names and descriptions of the proprietors of unclaimed dividends on Bank stock, and on all Government funds and securities transferable at the Bank of England, which became due on and before the 5th January, 1820, and remained unpaid the 31st December, 1822...By order of the Court of Directors of the Bank of England. 586p. *8°.* 1823. *See also 1791, 1836.*

23840 BLAKE, W. Observations on the effects produced by the expenditure of Government during the restriction of cash payments. 121p. 8°. 1823.

23841 COMPAGNIE D'ASSURANCES GÉ-NÉRALES. Compagnie d'Assurances générales contre les risques maritimes et de navigation intérieure. Rapport de M. de Gourcuff, Directeur. 14p. 4°. [Paris, 1823] See also 1821, 1824, 1825, 1827.

23842 DUBLIN. *Committee of St. Mary's Parish.* Reports of the Committee...on local taxation. 104p. 8°. *Dublin*, 1823.

23843 EAST INDIA COMPANY. The names and descriptions of the proprietors of unclaimed dividends on East-India stock, to July 1820 inclusive; with the dates when the first dividends respectively became payable, and the number of dividends due. By order of the Court of Directors of the East-India Company. 28p. 8°. 1823.

23844 EDEN, R. H., *Baron Henley.* An analysis of the Bill now depending in Parliament, for the consolidation and amendment of the bankrupt law. 66p. 8°. 1823.

23845 ENGLAND. *Commissioners of Inquiry into the Collection and Management of the Revenue arising in Ireland, Scotland, &c.* Reports of the Commissioners of Enquiry ...[First–sixth report. With 'Schedules for the present and proposed establishments in the ports of Scotland'.] 185, [31]p. 8°. *Dublin*, 1823.

23846 —— Parliament. *House of Commons.* Report of the debate in the House of Commons, on the 11th and 12th of June, 1823, upon Mr. Western's motion for a Committee on the state of the currency. 66p. 8°. [1823]

23847 FARREN, G. Treatise on life assurance; in which the systems...of the leading life institutions are stated and explained, and the Statutes...affecting such institutions brought under review. With an appendix of cases, including arguments particularly relating to the formation of trading joint stock companies. 200p. 8°. 1823. *See also* 1824.

23848 FORDAL, J. A letter to the Right Honourable the Earl of Liverpool, on the present state of the nation. [On the currency.] 78p. 8°. 1823.

23849 FRANCE. *Chambre des Députés.* No. 155. Session de 1823. Développemens de l'amendement proposé par M. de Ricard, Député de la Haute-Garonne, sur la loi de finances pour l'exercise 1824, à l'article 4. chapitre III. Imprimés par ordre de la Chambre. 10p. 8°. [Paris, 1823]

23850 GILES, D. Observations on the letters of C. C. Western, Esq., M.P. 73p. 8°. *Doncaster & London*, 1823.

23851 HANNAY, R. Defence of the usury laws. With a proposal to lower the legal rate of interest to four per cent. 195p. 12°. *Edinburgh & London*, 1823.

23852 HIGGINS, JOHN (*fl.* 1823). A plan for the effectual relief of agricultural distress, by an immediate application of a portion of the Sinking Fund to the poors' rate throughout the kingdom. 19p. 8°. 1823. *The copy that belonged to David Ricardo.*

23853 [HINCKS, W.] The claims of the clergy to tithes and other Church revenues, so far as they are founded on the political expediency of supporting such a body; on divine right; on history; or on the notion of unalienable property, examined. 40p. 8°. *London, Liverpool, &c.,* 1823.

23854 HUSKISSON, W. Equitable adjustment. Speech of the Right Hon. W. Huskisson, in the House of Commons, Tuesday the 11th of June, 1822. On Mr. Western's motion concerning the resumption of cash payments. 51p. 8°. 1823.

23855 KLAPROTH, H. J. VON. Origin of paper-money. [Translated from the French.] 23p. 8°. *London, Paris printed,* 1823.

23856 LABORDE, A. L. J. DE, *Comte.* Aperçu de la situation financière de l'Espagne. 32p. 8°. *Paris,* 1823.

23857 —— Seconde édition, revue et augmentée. 47p. 8°. *Paris,* 1823.

23858 LA BOURDONNAYE, F. R. DE, *Comte.* Opinion de M. de la Bourdonnaie, Député de Maine-et-Loire, sur l'emprunt de cent millions. (Séance du 24 février, 1823.) 18p. 8°. *Paris,* 1823.

23859 [LAURENCE, R., *Archbishop of Cashel.*] Remarks upon certain objections published in the Dublin newspaper called The Warder, against the Tithe Composition Bill, now pending in Parliament. 15p. 8°. 1823. *The copy that belonged to David Ricardo.*

23860 LEPAGE, P. Des émigrés et de leurs créanciers, depuis la Restauration. 330p. 8°. *Paris,* 1823.

23861 A LETTER to Lord Archibald Hamilton, on alterations in the value of money; and containing an examination of some opinions recently published on that subject. 100p. 8°. 1823. *Originally attributed by HSF to Thomas Attwood, but later (tentatively) to Thomas Paget. See also* 1847.

23862 A LETTER to Mr. Canning, on agricultural distress. By a country gentleman. 32p. 8°. 1823. *Presentation copy from the anonymous author to David Ricardo.*

23863 LETTER to the Right Honourable the Chancellor of the Exchequer, on the repeal of the assessed taxes. [Signed: One of us.] 32p. 8°. 1823. *Presentation copy from the anonymous author to David Ricardo.*

23864 A LETTER to the Right Honourable the Earl of Liverpool on the origin, title, effects, and commutation of tithes. 156p. 8°. 1823.

23865 L'HORME, B. F. DE. Quelques réflexions sur l'Ordonnance du Roi du 12 novembre 1823, et sur la protection que le gouvernement doit aux Français créanciers de l'Espagne par suite des emprunts de 1820 et 1821. 23p. 8°. *Paris,* 1823.

23866 LOWNDES, THOMAS, *of Blackheath.* A letter to Messrs. Coke, Curwan, and Co. With a postscript and notes on their injustice, in expecting the reduction of national interest, to keep up war rents... 156p. 8°. *Dover,* 1823.

23867 [McCULLOCH, JOHN R.] Errors in our funding system, and the management of our money concerns, with the mode of retrieving them; as pointed out in the New Edinburgh Review for January, 1823 [in a review of John Brickwood's *A plan for reducing the capital and the annual charge of the National Debt*]. 19p. 8°. *Edinburgh & London,* 1823.

23868 MARSHALL, JAMES, *accountant.* Tables of interest at four per cent...with equalizing tables...to which are added, tables of compound interest, annuities, commission, and values of stocks: also, tables of exchanges ... viii, [389]p. 8°. *Edinburgh & London,* 1823.

23869 MARTIN, M. A compendium of the practice of stating averages, for the use of counting-houses...

ship-masters, and others; consisting of an enumeration of the items in general average statements...Containing also, some new analysises and occasional observations on Mr. Stevens' Essay on average, and other matters connected with marine insurance. 167p. *4°. Liverpool & London*, 1823.

23870 **MEYER**, JOHANN H. Allgemeine Anleitung zur Berechnung der Leibrenten und Anwartschaften... 2 vols. *8°. Kopenhagen*, 1823.

23871 **MOLARD**, C. P. Notice sur les diverses inventions de feu Jean-Pierre Droz, graveur-mécanicien; relatives à l'art du monnoyage, ainsi qu'à plusieurs autres branches d'économie industrielle. 35p. *4°. Versailles*, [1823] *With an inscription, 'Offert par Mme Veuve Droz', dated (in a different hand) '24 septemb^e. 1846'.*

23872 [**MUNDELL**, A.] The principles which govern the value of paper currency, with reference to banking establishments, as stated in the New Edinburgh Review for January, 1823; with some observations on joint stock companies. 18p. *8°. Edinburgh, London, &c.*, 1823. *Attributed to Mundell in a manuscript note on the title-page, which records that the volume is a presentation copy from the author.*

23873 **NATIONAL ASSURANCE COMPANY OF IRELAND.** Articles of agreement of the National Assurance Company of Ireland, dated ninth of January, 1823. [With a list of the 'Original subscribers to the... Company'.] 34p. *8°. Dublin*, 1823.

23874 **NETHERLANDS.** *Permanente Commissie uit het Amortisatie-Syndicaat.* De Permanente Commissie uit het Amortisatie-Syndicaat...brengt bij deze ter kennisse van allen en een iegelijk het navolgende berigt eener negotiatie tot de te geldmaking van tachtig duizend stuks of tachtig millionen guldens kapitaal, schuldbekentenissen van het Amortisatie-Syndicaat à 4½ pCt., uitgegeven ten gevolge van art. 35 der wet van 27 December 1822... 8p. *12°. n.p.* [1823]

23875 **NORFOLK.** *Quarter Sessions.* Report of the proceedings on hearing an appeal between the Hamlets of Norwich, and the Court of Guardians, at an adjourned Quarter Sessions...held the ninth and tenth of December, 1822...To which is prefixed a statement of the mode of assessing stock, in Norwich, since the passing of the Workhouse Act, and of the efforts of the Hamlets to obtain a fair assessment. 123p. *8°. Norwich*, 1823.

23876 [*Begin.*] Sir, We, **OWNERS** and occupiers of public houses, beg leave to submit the following observations to your consideration. [A circular letter from publicans in Chelmsford appealing against the proposed alteration of the laws respecting the sale of beer.] [4]p. *fol. Chelmsford*, [1823] *Sent by post to Sir W. C. Clinton, Bart., M.P., with the postmark '7 My 1823'.*

23877 **PAYNE**, D. B. A letter to the Marquess of Lansdowne, on the reputed excess and depreciation of bank notes, and on the consequences of the new metallic currency. 29p. *8°. 1823.*

23878 **PRIEUR DE LA COMBLE**, E. Des marchés à terme d'effets publics, considérés d'après les principes généraux des contrats, sous le rapport de la légalité du titre et de la validité de l'engagement. 69p. *8°. Paris*, 1823.

23879 **PROSPECTUS.** Médaille de M. Manuel. [By A. H. Veyrat.] [2]p. *s.sh.8°.* [*Paris*, 1823 ?]

23880 [*Endorsed:*] **REASONS** for the repeal of the leather tax, shewing the releif [*sic*] it would give to agriculture; also prices of raw hides, bark, and leather, before and since the repeal of the additional tax. February 17, 1823. 2p. *fol.* [*London*, 1823]

23881 **RICARD**, F. L. C. DE. Opinion de M. de Ricard, Député de la Haute-Garonne, inscrit pour parler sur la loi de finances pour 1824. 19p. *8°.* [*Paris*, 1823]

23882 —— Opinion de M. de Ricard, Député de la Haute-Garonne, inscrit pour parler sur la proposition d'exclure M. Manuel de la Chambre des Députés. 15p. *8°.* [*Paris*,] 1823.

23883 **ROBINSON**, F. J., *Earl of Ripon.* Speech of the Right Honble. F. J. Robinson, Chancellor of the Exchequer, delivered in the Committee of Ways and Means, on Friday, 21st of February, 1823, on the financial situation of the country. To which is added, an appendix, containing various accounts referred to. 38, [4]p. *8°. 1823. The copy that belonged to Henry Goulburn (1784–1856), with his signature on the half-title.*

23884 [**ROSSER**, A.] Credit pernicious. 43p. *8°. 1823. See also* 1834.

23885 **SCHMALZ**, T. A. H. Encyclopädie der Cameralwissenschaften...Zweite, vom Herrn...Thaer ...Hartig...Rosenstiel...Hermbstädt und vom Verfasser verbesserte und vermehrte Auflage. 388p. *8°. Leipzig*, 1823.

23886 **SOLLY**, E. Remarks on the policy of repealing Mr. Peel's Bill [for the resumption of cash payments]. [With 'Letters to the Right Honourable Robert Peel, &c.&c.&c.'.] 35p. *8°. 1823. There are four letters, two of which were printed in quarto in 1822 (q.v.).*

23887 **TITHES** 37th Henry VIII. Important argument at the Mansion House, on Saturday, 8th February, 1823, before...the Lord Mayor, upon the Rev. Dr. Owen's application for a warrant for tithes, at 2s. 9d. in the pound, upon rack-rental, under the statute of 37th Henry VIII. and the alleged decree in pursuance thereof, when his Lordship...refused to grant the warrant...With an appendix of documents... 122p. *8°.* [1823]

23888 **VAUX**, T. Relative taxation; or, observations on the impolicy of taxing malt, hops, beer, soap, candles, and leather...with reasons for substituting a tax on property; concluding with an inquiry into the effects arising from perpetuating the land tax. 232p. *8°. 1823.*

23889 **WARRE**, J. The past, present & probably the future state of the wine trade; proving that an increase of duty caused a decrease of revenue; and a decrease of duty, an increase of revenue... 102p. *8°. 1823. The copy that belonged to David Ricardo.*

23890 **WESTERN**, C. C., *Baron Western.* Observations on the speech of the Right Hon. W. Huskisson, in the House of Commons...the 11th of June, 1822, on Mr. Western's motion concerning the resumption of cash payments, published March 20th, 1823. 40p. *8°. 1823. The Agar Ellis copy.*

TRANSPORT

23891 BATEMAN, J., *ed.* The General Turnpike Road Act, 3 Geo. IV. cap. 126. With an appendix of forms, and the standing orders of both Houses of Parliament with respect to private road bills, &c. To which are added, an index and notes...Second edition. 189p. *12°. London & Birmingham*, 1823.

23892 —— A supplement to The General Turnpike Road Act, of 3 Geo. IV, cap. 126. Containing the three Acts of 4 Geo. IV with notes and additional forms and general rules for repairing roads. To which is prefixed, a digested index to the whole of the turnpike road Acts now in force. 126p. *12°. London & Birmingham*, 1823.

23893 ENGLAND. *Commissioners for the Improvement of the Holyhead Road.* General Rules for repairing roads recommended, by the Parliamentary Commissioners for the improvement of the mail coach road from London, by Coventry, to Holyhead, to the turnpike trustees between London and Shrewsbury...Fourth edition. 8p. *8°.* 1823. *See also* 1827.

23894 —— *Laws, etc.* Anno quadragesimo sexto Georgii III. Regis. Cap. 20. An Act for enabling the Company of Proprietors of the Rochdale Canal more effectually to provide for the discharge of their debts; and to amend the several Acts passed for making and maintaining the said canal. ⟨21st April 1806.⟩ p.329–343. *fol.* 1823.

23895 —— —— [*Endorsed:*] An Act to enable the Stockton and Darlington Railway Company to...alter the line of their railway...and to make an additional branch therefrom...⟨Royal Assent, 23 May 1823.⟩ 4 Geo. IV. sess. 1823. 21p. *fol.* [*London*, 1823]

23896 —— Parliament. *House of Commons.* Report of the Select Committee on Foreign Trade; with an abstract of the case of the West India Dock Company, as established in evidence. By N. Hibbert... 101p. *8°.* 1823. *For another edition of the* Abstract, *see no.* 23899.

23897 ÉTAT général des postes du Royaume de France, suivi de la carte géométrique des routes desservies en poste, avec désignation des relais et des distances : pour l'an 1823. 225p. *8°. Paris*, 1823. *See also* 1814, 1818, 1819, 1835 (*Livre de poste*...), 1838.

23898 [GRAY, T.] Observations on a general iron rail-way: (with plates and map illustrative of the plan,) showing its great superiority, by the general introduction of mechanic power, over all present methods of conveyance...Fourth edition. Considerably improved. 131p. *8°.* 1823. *For other editions, see* 1822.

23899 HIBBERT, N. An abstract of the case of the West India Dock Company, as established in evidence before the Committee on Foreign Trade. 69p. *8°.* 1823. *Presentation copy, with inscription, that belonged to David Ricardo. For another edition, see no.* 23896.

23900 [JAMES, WILLIAM (1771–1837).] Report, or essay, to illustrate the advantages of direct inland communication through Kent, Surrey, Sussex, and Hants, to connect the Metropolis with the ports of Shoreham, (Brighton) Rochester, (Chatham) and Portsmouth, by a line of engine rail-road, and to render the Grand Surrey Canal, Wandsworth and Merstram rail-road, Shoreham Harbour, and Waterloo Bridge shares, productive property : with suggestions for diminishing poors-rates, and relieving agriculture. 31p. *8°.* 1823. *The Rastrick copy.*

23901 KENNET AND AVON CANAL NAVIGATION. Report of the Committee of Management of the Kennet and Avon Canal Navigation. [Signed: C. Dundas, chairman, and dated, 29th July, 1823.] [3]p. *fol. Marlborough*, [1823]. *See also* 1812, 1813, 1815, 1816, 1824, 1825, 1826, 1838.

23902 MARRYAT, J. Observations on the application of the West India Dock Company for a renewal of their charter; with an analysis of the evidence given before the Committee of the House of Commons on foreign trade, to which their petition was referred : and a copy of the Report of the said Committee. 418p. *8°.* 1823.

For a NEW GUIDE TO STAGE-COACHES, WAGGONS...&c. for 1823, *see no.* 23760.

23903 PALMER, HENRY R. Description of a railway on a new principle; with observations on those hitherto constructed. And a table, shewing the comparative amount of resistance on several now in use. Also an illustration of a newly observed fact relating to the friction of axles, and a description of an improved dynamometer... 60p. *8°.* 1823. *See also* 1824.

23904 REPLY to the Observations of Joseph Marryat, Esq. M.P. on the West-India Dock charter. 107p. *8°.* 1823.

SOCIAL CONDITIONS

23905 A full ACCOUNT of the atrocious murder of the late Mr. W. Weare; containing the examinations before the magistrates, the proceedings of the coroner's inquest, with...the confessions of Hunt...To which is prefixed, an introduction, containing anecdotes of the deceased... 56p. *8°.* 1823.

23906 An APOLOGY for the poor; shewing, by an exhibition of the evils to which that class of society is exposed, how the debasement of its own character, and the existing serious public injuries are produced; with... suggestions for general improvement. 2d edition. 163p. *8°.* 1823.

23907 BRIGSTOCK INDEPENDENT CLUB. Brigstock Independent Club, established Dec. 4, 1823... [List of officers and members, rules, and account of the inaugural meeting.] 12p. *8°. Northampton*, 1823.

23908 [CARMALT, W. ?] A letter to the Right Honourable George Canning, on the principle and the administration of the English poor laws. By a select vestryman of the parish of Putney, under the 59 Geo. 3, cap. 12. 109p. *8°.* 1823. *The copy presented by the anonymous author to Sir Harry Verney. See also* 1831.

23909 CHALMERS, T. Statement in regard to the pauperism of Glasgow, from the experience of the last eight years. 78p. *8°. Glasgow, Edinburgh, &c.,* 1823. *Reissued in* Tracts on pauperism *in 1833 (q.v.).*

23910 COMMITTEE FOR THE RELIEF OF THE GREEKS. Address of the Committee appointed at a public meeting held in Boston, December 19, 1823, for the relief of the Greeks, to their fellow citizens. 18p. *8°. n.p.* [1823]

23911 COXE, P. The social day: a poem, in four cantos... 354p. *8°.* 1823.

23912 DAVENPORT, RICHARD. A practicable, easy and safe plan for checking the increase of pauperism, and the evils resulting from the poor laws. 38p. *8°. London, Battle, &c.,* 1823.

23913 DOYLE, SIR JOHN, *Bart.* Speech of Gen. Sir John Doyle...President of the first anniversary meeting of the Society for Improving the Condition and Increasing the Comforts of the Irish Peasantry... 18p. *8°.* 1823.

23914 ENSOR, G. The poor and their relief. 384p. *8°.* 1823.

23915 The **FARMERS:** or, tales for the times, addressed to the yeomanry of England. By the author. [On emigration.] 132p. *12°.* 1823.

23916 FRIENDLY INSTITUTION, *Southwell.* The Friendly Institution established at Southwell...[A report of the first three months of the Institution, with list of officers, and a description, 'On the nature and intent of the Institution' by J. T. Becher.] 13p. *8°.* [1823]

For **FRIENDLY SOCIETY OF JOURNEYMEN BOOKBINDERS,** *London,* Friendly Society of Bookbinders, Report of the Audit-Committee, 1822/3–1836/7, 1823–37, *see* vol. III, *Periodicals list,* Report of the Audit-Committee...

23917 GERANDO, J. M. DE, *Baron.* De la coopération des jeunes gens aux éstablissemens d'humanité. 22p. *8°. Paris,* 1823. *Presentation copy, with inscription, from the author to William Allen.*

23918 *GISBORNE, THOMAS (1758–1846). An enquiry into the duties of the female sex...The thirteenth edition. 288p. *12°. London & Edinburgh,* 1823.

23919 HAY, J. An appeal to the British public, by John Hay, late merchant in Leith; of injustice, oppression, cruelty and wrongous imprisonment, which he has suffered at the instance of Lord President Hope and others of the Court of Session of Scotland. 16p. *8°. Edinburgh,* [1823] *The copy that belonged to David Ricardo.*

23920 HEADLAM, J. A letter to the Right Honourable Robert Peel...on prison labour. 62p. *8°.* 1823.

23921 HIPPISLEY, SIR JOHN C., *Bart.* Prison labour, &c. Correspondence and communications addressed to His Majesty's Principal Secretary of State for the Home Department, concerning the introduction of tread-mills into prisons... 228p. *8°.* 1823.

23922 HUTCHINSON, B. Observations on prison discipline, exemplified by the tread-mill & dietary adopted in the Nottinghamshire House of Correction at Southwell. 55p. *8°. Newark & London,* [1823].

23923 HUTCHISON, A. C. A statement of the transactions on occasion of the extraordinary sickness which has lately occurred at the General Penitentiary at Milbank. 32p. *8°.* 1823. *The Agar Ellis copy.*

23924 The **IMPOLICY** of imprisonment for debt; considered in relation to the attempts at present made to procure a repeal of the Insolvent Debtors' Act. [Signed: A merchant.] 20p. *8°.* 1823.

23925 JOHNSON, RICHARD M. Speech of Col. Richard M. Johnson, of Kentucky, on a proposition to abolish imprisonment for debt, submitted...to the Senate of the United States, January 14, 1823. 23p. *8°. Boston,* 1823.

23926 A LETTER to the Chairman, deputy-chairman, and Court of Directors, of the East-India Company, on the subject of their college, at Haileybury. By a civilian. 27p. *8°.* 1823. *Attributed in a manuscript note on the title-page to Mr. [Benjamin Guy ?] Babington.*

23927 *LONDON MECHANICS' INSTITUTION. Rules and orders of the Mechanics' Institution for the Promotion of useful Knowledge among the Working Classes. Established November 11, 1823. 19p. *8°. n.p.* [1823] *The copy that belonged to George Grote.*

23928 —— [Another edition, enlarged, with a printed notice of the meeting of the Committee, dated November 22, 1823, at the head of the title-page.] 28p. *8°. n.p.* [1823] *With a manuscript note on the leaf preceding the title-page: 'This is to be returned to F.P. [Place ?]. You shall have the Laws of the "City Institution" – either tomorrow evening or on Sunday Morning'. See also 1841.*

23929 [MADEN, J. ?] Observations on the use of power looms. By a friend to the poor. 16p. *8°. Rochdale, Manchester, &c.,* 1823.

23930 MARTENS, A. E. Das hamburgische Criminal-Gefängniss gennant: das Spinnhaus und die übrigen Gefängnisse der Stadt Hamburg nach ihrer innern Beschaffenheit und Einrichtung beschrieben... 70p. *4°. Hamburg,* 1823.

23931 Legalized **MURDER;** or, killing no crime. [An attack on the game laws.] By a Yorkshireman. 16p. *8°. York,* [1823] *The Oastler copy.*

23932 NARRATIVE of the murder of Mr. Weare, at Gill's Hill, near Aldenham, Hertfordshire, on the evening of Friday, October 24. With original letters, never before published. Compiled from communications made by Mr. Heward...Mr. James Woods...and various...sources ... 56p. *8°.* [1823]

23933 PEMBROKE, *County of. Quarter Sessions.* Second report of the Committee, appointed to carry out the resolution of the justices...for improving and making additions to the Gaol and House of Correction of the said county. [Signed: H. Leach, chairman.] 6p. *8°. n.p.* [1823 ?] *See note to no.* 23273.

23934 Third edition, 1823. A **PLAN** to regulate the employment of the labouring poor, as acted upon in the parish of Oundle. Adapted to all parishes; and sanctioned by the magistrates of the County of Northampton. 6p. *8°. Oundle & London,* [1823] *For another edition, see* 1820.

23935 POLE, T. Observations relative to infant schools, designed to point out their usefulness to the children of the poor, to their parents and to society at large... 83p. *8°. Bristol & London,* 1823.

23936 RYDING, A. An account of the trial of Andrew Ryding, on a charge of attempting to commit murder on S. Horrocks, Esq. M.P. in Preston...27th July 1823. Before Mr. Justice Bayley, at Lancaster...August 18th, 1823. [An attempt to carry out a threat made in consequence of Horrocks's failure to raise weavers' wages.] 27p. *8°. Preston,* 1823.

23937 SKETCH of a simple, original, and practical plan, for suppressing mendicity, abolishing the present system of parochial taxation, and ameliorating the condition of the lower classes of society. 28p. *8°*. 1823.

23938 SMITH, George C. No. 1[–6]. Bristol fair, but no preaching!...Second edition. Containing remarks on fairs in general. — A correct view of Bristol Fair this year... 96p. *8°*. *Bristol,* 1823.

23939 SOCIETY FOR MAINTAINING AND EDUCATING POOR ORPHANS OF THE CLERGY. Supplement to the report of 1822, of the incorporated Society... 20p. *8°*. 1823.

23940 SOCIETY OF PATRONS OF THE ANNIVERSARY OF THE CHARITY SCHOOLS. List of the Patrons...MDCCCXXIII. [With the rules and accounts of the Society.] 44p. *8°*. 1823.

23941 SUGGESTIONS how the poor laws of England, with their attendant evils, may be gradually superseded; as pointed out in the New Edinburgh Review for April 1823. 34p. *8°*. *Edinburgh, London, &c.,* 1823.

23942 A new **SYSTEM** of practical domestic economy ...Third edition, revised and greatly enlarged. To which are now first added, estimates of household expenses... adapted to families of every description. 402, 76p. *12°*. 1823.

23943 [WHITE, George (*fl.* 1823–1825) and **HENSON,** G.] A few remarks on the state of the laws at present in existence for regulating masters and workpeople, intended as a guide for the consideration of the House, in their discussions on the Bill for repealing several Acts relating to combinations of workmen... 142p. *8°*. 1823. *Presentation copy to David Ricardo. The text of this work was incorporated in a larger work by George White, entitled:* A digest of all the laws at present in existence respecting masters and work people, *in 1824 (q.v.).*

23944 WITSON, G. P. A letter to the gentlemen of Great Britain and Ireland, on the rate of wages that they are now paying to their man-servants; with an account of the duties and annual wages of stewards, butlers, gardeners... 48p. *8°*. 1823.

SLAVERY

23945 BAHAMA ISLANDS. *Office of Correspondence.* An official letter from the Commissioners of Correspondence of the Bahama Islands, to George Chalmers ...concerning the proposed abolition of slavery in the West Indies. 78p. *8°*. 1823.

23946 BARHAM, J. F. Considerations on the abolition of negro slavery, and the means of practically effecting it. 85p. *8°*. 1823. *The copy that belonged to Stephen Lushington.*

23947 —— The second edition. 85p. *8°*. 1823.

23948 BARING, A., *Baron Ashburton.* Mr. Alexander Baring's speech in the House of Commons, on the 15th day of May, 1823, on Mr. Buxton's motion for a resolution declaratory of slavery in the British colonies being contrary to the English constitution and to Christianity. 17p. *8°*. 1823.

23949 BRIDGES, George W. A voice from Jamaica; in reply to William Wilberforce, Esq. M.P.... 50p. *8°*. 1823. *The copy that belonged to Stephen Lushington.*

23950 CASE of the Vigilante, a ship employed in the slave-trade; with some reflections on that traffic. 13p. *8°*. 1823.

23951 CHESTER. Proceedings at a public meeting, held at the town-hall, Chester, on...the first of May, 1823, for the purpose of taking into consideration the present state of slaves in our West India colonies, and the propriety of petitioning Parliament for their relief... 15p. *8°*. *Chester,* [1823]

23952 CLARKSON, T. Os gemidos dos Africanos... 52p. *8°*. *Londres,* 1823. *For other editions see* 1822.

23953 —— Thoughts on the necessity of improving the condition of the slaves in the British colonies, with a view to their ultimate emancipation; and on the practicability, the safety, and the advantages of the latter measure. 60p. *8°*. 1823. *The copy that belonged to Stephen Lushington.*

23954 —— Second edition corrected. 57p. *8°*. *Society for the Mitigation and Gradual Abolition of Slavery throughout the British Dominions,* 1823. *See also* 1824.

23955 CROPPER, J. A letter addressed to the Liverpool Society for promoting the Abolition of Slavery, on the injurious effects of high prices of produce, and the beneficial effects of low prices, on the condition of slaves. 32p. *8°*. *Liverpool & London,* 1823.

23956 ENGLAND. *Parliament. House of Commons.* Substance of the debate in the House of Commons, on the 15th May, 1823, on a motion for the mitigation and gradual abolition of slavery throughout the British Dominions. With a preface and appendixes...illustrative of colonial bondage. 248p. *8°*. *Society for the Mitigation and Gradual Abolition of Slavery throughout the British Dominions,* 1823.

23957 [HEDGE, M. A.] Samboe; or, the African boy. By the author of "Twilight hours improved," &c.... 175, [11]p. *12°*. 1823.

23958 HODGSON, A. A letter to M. Jean-Baptiste Say, on the comparative expense of free and slave labour. [With an appendix.] 55, 17p. *8°*. *Liverpool & London,* 1823. *Presentation copy, with inscription from the author.*

23959 —— The second edition. [With 'Letter from J. B. Say to the author'.] 58, [2]p. *8°*. *Liverpool & London,* 1823. *The copy that belonged to Stephen Lushington.*

23960 JAMAICA. *Assembly.* Proceedings of the Honourable House of Assembly of Jamaica, in relation to those which took place in the British House of Commons, on the 15th of May last, in consequence of Mr. Buxton's motion for the gradual abolition of slavery throughout these colonies... 22p. *8°*. *Jamaica,* 1823.

23961 KENNEDY, James (1798–1859). An address to the inhabitants of Hull and its neighbourhood, on the formation of the Hull and East-Riding Association for the Mitigation and Gradual Abolition of Slavery, being the substance of a speech, delivered at a meeting held for that purpose, November 6, 1823. 21p. *8°*. *Hull,* 1823.

23962 A **LETTER** to John Bull: to which is added the sketch of a plan for the safe, speedy, and effectual abolition of slavery. By a free-born Englishman. 32p. *8°*. 1823.

23963 LIVERPOOL SOCIETY FOR THE ABOLITION OF SLAVERY. Declaration of the objects of the...Society...25th March, 1823. 14p. *8°*. *Liverpool & London,* [1823]

23964 [MACAULAY, Z.] Negro slavery; or, a view of some of the more prominent features of that state of society, as it exists in the United States of America and in the colonies of the West Indies, especially in Jamaica. 118p. 8°. *London & Liverpool, 1823. Author's presentation copy, which belonged to Stephen Lushington. See also 1824.*

23965 MARTIN, Sir Henry W., *Bart.* A counter appeal, in answer to "An appeal" from William Wilberforce...designed to prove that the emancipation of the negroes in the West Indies, by a legislative enactment, without the consent of the planters, would be a flagrant breach of national honour, hostile to the principles of religion, justice, and humanity, and highly injurious to the planter and to the slave. 52p. 8°. 1823.

For NEGRO SLAVERY, 1823–30, *see* vol. III, *Periodicals list.*

23966 Brief REMARKS on scriptural notices, respecting bondmen, and a plan for the gradual manumission of slaves, without violation of public faith, or infringement of vested rights. [Signed: a British planter.] 9p. 8°. 1823.

23967 A REVIEW of some of the arguments which are commonly advanced against parliamentary interference in behalf of the negro slaves, with a statement of opinions which have been expressed on that subject by many of our most distinguished statesmen... 32p. 8°. 1823. *Three author's presentation copies, two of which belonged to Stephen Lushington. See also 1824.*

23968 ROSE, Sir George H. A letter [to James Laing] on the means and importance of converting the slaves in the West Indies to Christianity. 87p. 8°. 1823. *Author's presentation copy, which belonged to Stephen Lushington.*

23969 —— The second edition. 87p. 8°. 1823.

23970 STEPHEN, J. The slavery of the British West India colonies delineated, as it exists both in law and practice, and compared with the slavery of other countries, antient and modern. p.viii, 1–80. 8°. 1823. *A proof copy of part of the work published in 1824 (q.v.), presented, with an inscription, by the author to Stephen Lushington.*

23971 WILBERFORCE, William (1759–1833). An appeal to the religion, justice, and humanity of the inhabitants of the British Empire, in behalf of the negro slaves in the West Indies. 77p. 8°. 1823. *Author's presentation copy, which belonged to Stephen Lushington.*

23972 —— A new edition. 56p. 8°. 1823.

POLITICS

23973 [ATKINSON, William (1758–1846).] A critique on the last dying speech and confession of the Yorkshire Whigs: to which is added, the electric shock, and the Black Knight's case resumed. By the Old Inquirer. 36p. 8°. *Bradford, 1823.*

23974 BENTHAM, J. A fragment on government; or, a comment on the Commentaries: being an examination of what is delivered on the subject of government in general, in the introduction to Sir William Blackstone's Commentaries...Second edition, enlarged. 143p. 8°. 1823. *For other editions, see 1776.*

23975 BOWRING, Sir J. Details of the arrest, imprisonment and liberation, of an Englishman, by the Bourbon Government of France. 147p. 8°. 1823.

23976 CANNING, George (1770–1827). Substance of the speech of the Right Honourable George Canning, in the House of Commons on...the 30th of April, 1823, on Mr. Macdonald's motion respecting the negotiations, at Verona, Paris, and Madrid. With an appendix, containing papers presented to both Houses of Parliament. 91, cp. 8°. *[London,] 1823.*

23977 CHATEAUBRIAND, F. R. DE, *Vicomte.* Speech of Viscount de Chateaubriand...Secretary of State for Foreign Affairs, delivered in the Chamber of Deputies, on...25th of February, 1823. 35p. 8°. 1823.

23978 —— The speech of the Viscount de Chateaubriand, Minister of Foreign Affairs, delivered in the Chamber of Peers, on...30th April, 1823. 17p. 8°. 1823.

23979 The CRISIS of Spain...Second edition. 81p. 8°. 1823.

23980 [DUPIN, A. M. J. J.] Pièces judiciaires et historiques relatives au procès du Duc d'Enghien, avec le journal de ce prince depuis l'instant de son arrestation. Précédées de la discussion des actes de la commission militaire instituée en l'an XII, par le gouvernement consulaire, pour juger le Duc d'Enghien. Par l'auteur de l'opuscule intitulé De la libre défense des accusés. Troisième tirage. 40, xxxiip. 8°. *Paris, 1823.*

23981 ENGLAND. Parliament. *House of Commons.* The debate in the House of Commons, on...March 26, 1823; on Mr. Hume's presenting a petition from Mary Ann Carlile, a prisoner in Dorchester gaol. 24p. 8°. 1823.

23982 ERSKINE, T., *Baron Erskine.* A letter to the Earl of Liverpool, on the subject of the Greeks...Fourth edition: with a postscript addressed to the Central Greek Committee of London. 59p. 8°. 1823. *Presentation copy from the author to David Ricardo.*

23983 An EXPOSITION of the British House of Commons, as at present constituted; in which is exhibited the nature and extent of the suffrage in every county, city, and borough, returning members to Parliament in the United Kingdom... 47p. 8°. [1823]

23984 HULIN, P. A., *Comte.* Explications offertes aux hommes impartiaux par M. le Comte Hulin, au sujet de la commission militaire instituée en l'an XII pour juger le Duc d'Enghien. Deuxième édition. 15p. 8°. *Paris, 1823.*

23985 JACKSON, Robert. An outline of hints, for the political organization and moral training of the human race... 253p. 8°. *Stockton, London, &c., 1823. Presentation copy, with inscription, from the author to Thomas Chalmers.*

23986 JENKINSON, R. B., *2nd Earl of Liverpool.* The speech of the Earl of Liverpool, in the House of Lords, on...14th April, 1823, upon laying on the table of the House...certain papers relative to the negotiations at Verona, Paris, and Madrid, on the differences which had arisen between France and Spain. 55p. 8°. 1823.

23987 JONES, John G. A vindication of the press against the false and scurrilous aspersions of William Cobbett, including a retrospect of his political life, and opinions; with notes critical and explanatory. 28p. 8°. 1823. *The copy that belonged to David Ricardo.*

23988 —— Second edition, corrected and enlarged, with additional notes... 43p. *8°.* 1823.

For the **NORTHERN REFORMER'S MONTHLY MAGAZINE** and political register, *see* vol. III, *Periodicals list.*

23989 **PRICE,** S. G. The speech of Samuel Grove Price, Esq....at the Hertford county meeting, 8th February, 1823, upon a petition for parliamentary reform. 44p. *8°.* 1823.

23990 **SAVARY,** A. J. M. R., *Duc de Rovigo.* Extrait des mémoires de M. le Duc de Rovigo, concernant la catastrophe de M. le Duc d'Enghien. Troisième édition. 72p. *8°. Paris,* 1823.

23991 [**WALLACE,** THOMAS (*b.* 1766?).] The Orange system exposed; and the Orange societies proved to be unconstitutional, illegal and seditious, in a letter to the Marquess Wellesley [signed: a Protestant]. 91p. *8°. Dublin,* 1823. *The copy that belonged to David Ricardo.*

23992 **WHITE,** HENRY. A calm appeal to the friends of freedom and reform, on the double dealings of Mr. Cobbett, and the baneful tendency of his writings. With a vindication of the Whigs, and the patriots of Westminster and the borough of Southwark, against his scurrilous and malignant aspersions. 42p. *8°.* 1823.

SOCIALISM

23993 **BEATSON,** J. An examination of Mr. Owen's plans, for relieving distress, removing discontent, and "recreating the character of man:" showing that they are directly calculated to root out all the virtuous affections of the human mind; and to destroy all that is valuable in the institutions, the manners and the laws, of human society. 68p. *8°. Glasgow, Edinburgh, &c.,* 1823.

23994 **COMBE,** ABRAM. An address to the conductors of the periodical press, upon the causes of religious and political disputes, with remarks on the local and general definition of certain words and terms which have been often the subject of controversy. 48p. *8°. Edinburgh, Glasgow, &c.,* 1823.

23995 —— Metaphorical sketches of the old and new systems, with opinions on interesting subjects. 186p. *12°. Edinburgh, Glasgow, &c.,* 1823.

23996 —— Observations on the old and new views, and their effects on the conduct of individuals, as manifested in the proceedings of the Edinburgh Christian Instructor and Mr. Owen. 25p. *8°. Edinburgh & Glasgow,* 1823.

23997 **FOURIER,** F. C. M. Sommaire de la théorie d'association domestique-agricole... [A prospectus.] [2], viii, [10]p. *8°. n.p.* [1823] *The copy that belonged to Victor Considérant.*

23998 —— Sommaire du Traité de l'association domestique-agricole; ou attraction industrielle. 16, [1329]–1448p. *8°. Paris & Londres,* 1823. *The copy that belonged to Victor Considérant. For the original work, see 1822.*

23999 A **LETTER,** containing some observations on the delusive nature of the system proposed by Robert Owen, Esq. for the amelioration of the condition of the people of Ireland: as developed by him at the public meetings held for that purpose in Dublin...1823. 41p. *8°. Dublin & London,* 1823. **Another, the FWA copy, belonged to William Pare.*

24000 ***OWEN,** ROBERT. An explanation of the cause of the distress which pervades the civilized parts of the world, and of the means whereby it may be removed. 12p. *12°. British and Foreign Philanthropic Society,* 1823. *The FWA copy that belonged to William Pare.*

24001 —— Report of the proceedings at the several public meetings, held in Dublin, by Robert Owen, Esq. on the 18th March–12th April–19th April and 3d May; preceded by an introductory statement of his opinions and arrangements at New Lanark; extracted from his "Essays on the formation of human character." 161p. *8°. Dublin,* 1823. **Another, the FWA copy, belonged to William Pare.*

24002 No. 19. Robert **OWEN** Esq. The Unique: a series of portraits of eminent persons. With their memoirs. [6]p. *12°.* [1823] *For the collected edition of* The unique, *see no.* 23770.

24003 [**SAINT-SIMON,** C. H. DE, *Comte.*] Catéchisme des industriels. [With 'Système de politique positive, par Auguste Comte...élève de Henri Saint-Simon. Tome premier. Première partie'.] 186, 236p. *8°. [Paris,* 1823–24] *A second copy of part 1 (p. 1–66), and of part 3, 'Système de politique positive', belonged to Victor Considérant. See also* 1832.

MISCELLANEOUS

24004 **BERR,** M. Littérature hébraïque. Extrait du Journal Asiatique, (15e cahier, de la 2e année). 12p. *8°. Paris,* 1823.

24005 **PHILLPOTTS,** H., *Bishop of Exeter.* A letter to Francis Jeffrey, Esq., the reputed editor of the Edinburgh Review, on an article entitled "Durham case — clerical abuses". 39p. *8°. Durham, London, &c.,* 1823.

24006 —— Second edition. 39p. *8°. Durham, London, &c.,* 1823.

24007 **WOODBRIDGE,** J. An address delivered before the Society of the Alumni of Williams College, on the day of the Annual Commencement, September 3, 1823. 18p. *8°. Hartford,* 1823.

1824

GENERAL

24008 ANDERSON, John (1795–1845). Political and commercial considerations relative to the Malayan Peninsula, and the British settlements in the Straits of Malacca. [With an appendix.] 204, lxviiip. *4°. Prince of Wales Island,* 1824.

24009 The complete **ASSISTANT** for the landed proprietor, estate and house agent, land-steward... architect...builder...cabinet-maker, &c.... 476p. *8°.* 1824.

24010 BARBOUR, P. P. Speech of Mr. P. P. Barbour, of Vir. on the tariff bill. Delivered in the House of Representatives U.S. March 26, 1824. 38p. *12°. Washington,* 1824.

24011 BATE, R. B. The new set of standard weights and measures. *s.sh.fol.* [1824]

For the **BIRMINGHAM SPECTATOR,** *see* vol. III, *Periodicals list.*

24012 BLANQUI, J. A. Voyage d'un jeune Français en Angleterre et en Écosse, pendant l'automne de 1823... 396p. *8°. Paris,* 1824.

24013 BLIGH, John, *4th Earl of Darnley.* Speech of the Earl of Darnley in the House of Lords...8th of April, 1824, on moving for an inquiry into the state of Ireland. 47p. *8°. London & Dublin,* 1824. *The Agar Ellis copy.*

24014 BOWDLER, T. Memoir of the life of John Bowdler, Esq. 296p. *8°.* 1824.

24015 BRASBRIDGE, J. The fruits of experience; or, memoir of Joseph Brasbridge, written in his 80th year. 257p. *8°.* 1824.

24016 BUESCH, J. G. Johann Georg Büsch's... Sämmtliche Schriften über die Handlung. 8 vols. *8°. Hamburg,* 1824–27.

24017 [**CANDLER,** I.] A summary view of America: comprising a description of the face of the country, and of several of the principal cities; and remarks on the social, moral and political character of the people: being the result of observations and enquiries during a journey in the United States. By an Englishman. 503p. *8°. London & Edinburgh,* 1824.

24018 CAREY, M. Address delivered before the Philadelphia Society for Promoting Agriculture, at its meeting, on the twentieth of July, 1824... 80p. *8°. Philadelphia,* 1824.

24019 —— Second edition. 66p. *8°. Philadelphia,* 1824.

24020 —— Fourth edition, revised and corrected. 108p. *12°. Philadelphia,* 1824. *The copy given to HSF by Henry Carey Baird. See also* 1827.

24021 [——] Examination of a tract on the alteration of the tariff, written by Thomas Cooper, M.D. By a Pennsylvanian. Second edition. 36p. *8°. Philadelphia,* 1824.

24022 [——] Fifty-one substantial reasons against any modification whatever of the existing tariff: whereby the consistency and propriety of the opposition of the cotton planters, the tobacco planters, and the merchants to the "infernal bill," are fully justified. By a Pennsylvanian. 12p. *8°. Philadelphia,* 1824. *See also no.* 24025.

24023 [——] Hamilton, no. 1. To the honourable James Lloyd, Esq. one of the Senators of the United States, from...Massachusetts. [Signed: Hamilton. Philadelphia, March 31, 1824. On protection to manufactures.] 4p. *8°. n.p.* [1824]

24024 [——] Hamilton —— No. v. To the cotton planters of the United States. [Signed: Hamilton. Philadelphia, Nov. 10, 1824. On protection.] p.21–24. *8°. n.p.* [1824] *For earlier numbers, see* 1822, 1823.

For [—— *ed.*] The political economist. *Philadelphia, see* vol. III, *Periodicals list,* The political economist.

24025 [——] Twenty-one golden rules to depress agriculture, impede the progress of manufactures, paralize commerce, impair national resources, produce a constant fluctuation in the value of every species of property...In a word, to cripple a great nation...To which is annexed, a copious appendix, containing fifty-one substantial reasons against any alteration whatever, of the existing tariff. By a Pennsylvanian. 60p. *8°. Salem,* 1824.

24026 [——] A warning voice to the cotton and tobacco planters, farmers, and merchants of the United States, on the pernicious consequences to their respective interests of the existing policy of the country. By a Pennsylvanian. 76p. *8°. Philadelphia,* 1824. *Presentation copy, with inscription, from the author to Daniel Webster.*

24027 CLAY, H. Speech in support of an American system for the protection of American industry; delivered in the House of Representatives, on the 30th and 31st of March, 1824. 39p. *8°. Washington City,* 1824.

24028 COBBETT, James P. A ride of eight hundred miles in France; containing a sketch of the face of the country, of its rural economy...To which is added, a general view of the finances of the kingdom. 202, [10]p. *12°.* 1824.

24029 —— Second edition. [214]p. *12°.* 1824. *See also* 1827.

24030 COBBETT, W. A history of the Protestant "Reformation," in England and Ireland; showing how that event has impoverished and degraded the...people ...In a series of letters... 2 vols. *12°.* 1824–27. *See also* 1825, 1829.

24031 COLOMBIA. State of Colombia, or reports of the Secretaries of State of the Republic of Colombia, presented to the first Constitutional Congress in...1823 ...Translated from the official documents. 199p. *8°.* 1824.

24032 COUP D'ŒIL sur Paris, ou premiers moyens d'indemnité disponibles offrant plus de 20 millions de rente, à accorder de suite aux émigrés...tendant succursalement à l'embellissement du Palais du Roi et de la Capitale... 154p. *8°. Paris,* 1824.

24033 DONNADIEU, G., *Vicomte.* Chambre des Députés. Discours de M. le Général Donnadieu, Député des Bouches-du-Rhône, sur la réduction des rentes. 15p. *8°. [Paris,* 1824]

24034 DUFOUR DE PRADT, D., *Archbishop of Mechlin.* La France, l'émigration, et les colons. 2 vols. *8°. Paris, 1824. With the Holland House book-plate.*

24035 *★The **EAST-INDIA** register and directory for 1824; containing...lists of the Company's servants... mariners, &c. not in the service of the...Company; merchant vessels employed in the country trade...Compiled...by A. W. Mason, Geo. Owen, and G. H. Brown ...Corrected to 25th March 1824. 545p. *12°. [1824] For other editions, see 1804.*

24036 EASTON, J. A chronology of remarkable events relative to the city of New Sarum...from A.D.1227 to 1823...Including the prices of wheat and barley from an early æra: to which are added, their annual average prices for 28 years, being from 1796 to 1823. Fifth edition, improved. 25p. *12°. Salisbury, London, &c., 1824.*

For the **ECONOMIST** and general advertiser, 1824–5, *see* vol. III, *Periodicals list.*

24037 De l'**ÉMIGRATION** et des dédommagemens qu'il convient d'accorder aux émigrés: par un propriétaire. 35p. *8°. Paris, 1824.*

24038 ENCYCLOPAEDIA BRITANNICA. [Extracts from the Supplement to the fourth, fifth and sixth editions of the Encyclopædia Britannica. By James Mill, T. R. Malthus, J. R. McCulloch, and others.] *4°. Edinburgh, 1824. Contents: articles and plates on the following subjects of economic interest: annuities; banking; banks for savings; beggar; benefit societies; bills of mortality; brewing; coinage; colony; commerce; corn laws and trade; cottage system; credit; crimes and punishments; economists; education; exchange; funding system; government; interest; jurisprudence; liberty of the press; money; mortality; humans, law of; nations, law of; political economy; poor laws; population; prisons and prison discipline; taxation; weights and measures. See also 1842.*

24039 EVERETT, E. An oration [in the presence of La Fayette] pronounced at Cambridge [Massachusetts], before the Society of Phi Beta Kappa. August 27, 1824... 67p. *8°. Boston, 1824.*

24040 FRANKLIN, B. The works of Dr. Benjamin Franklin: consisting of essays, humorous, moral, and literary; with his life, written by himself. 109p. *8°. 1824. See also 1840.*

24041 GENOVESI, A. Opere scelte. [Lezioni di economia civile.] 2 vols. *8°. Milano, 1824–25. See also 1835.*

24042 HAMILTON, JAMES (1786–1857). Speech of Mr. Hamilton of S.C. on the tariff bill. Delivered in the House of Representatives U.S. April 6th, 1824. 41p. *12°. Washington, 1824.*

24043 HEEREN, A. H. L. Ideën over de staatkunde, onderlinge verkeering en den handel van de voornaamste volken der oudheid...Naar de vierde zeer verbeterde uitgaaf, met platte gronden en kaarten, vertaald en met eenige aanmerkingen en platen voorzien, door Mr. G. Dorn Seiffen. 6 vols. *8°. Rotterdam, 1824–27. See also 1838, 1845, 1846.*

24044 HODGSON, A. Letters from North America, written during a tour in the United States and Canada. 2 vols. *8°. London & Edinburgh, 1824.*

24045 LEE, F. Means of wealth to the nation, and every individual...an improved system of political economy, exemplified in one, and applicable to every district; for obtaining, at the least expense, the most

lucrative results. Submitted to the public, and particularly to the Right Honourable George Canning... 34p. *8°. London & Lancaster, 1824.*

24046 *★***MABERLY,** F. H. Speech of Captain Maberly, Member for Northampton, on the employment of the poor in Ireland, delivered in the House of Commons, on ...the 4th of May, 1824... 26p. *8°. 1824. The copy that belonged to George Grote.*

24047 McCULLOCH, JOHN R. Contributions to the Edinburgh Review...1818–1824[–1837]. 3 vols. *8°. [Edinburgh, 1824–37] A collection of excerpts from the Edinburgh Review, with a general title-page to each volume. In addition, each article has a separate title-page partly printed and partly in manuscript. The manuscript portions and other notes in the volumes are in the hand of H. G. Reid, McCulloch's secretary and author of 'Biographical notice of J. R. McCulloch'.*

24048 —— A discourse on the rise, progress, peculiar objects, and importance, of political economy: containing an outline of a course of lectures on the principles and doctrines of that science. 118p. *8°. Edinburgh, London, &c., 1824. See also 1825.*

24049 [——] Memoir of François Quesnay. [From the Supplement to the Encyclopædia Britannica, volume sixth.] 18p. *8°. n.p. [1824?] See also 1842.*

24050 [——] Political economy. ⟨From the Supplement to the Encyclopædia Britannica, vol. VI. part I.⟩ [Signed: S.S.] 64p. *4°. n.p. [1824]*

24051 MILL, JAMES. Elements of political economy ...Second edition, revised and corrected. 299p. *8°. 1824. For other editions, see 1821.*

24052 MILLAR, JAMES (*fl.* 1818–1824). The funding system; or, a plan for accumulating capital, and improving ...the circumstances of the working classes of society... The third edition. With an introduction...on benefit societies...Together with a descriptive account of the State of Ohio... 64p. *8°. Glasgow, 1824. For another edition, see 1818.*

24053 NICOLAS, SIR N. H. Notitia historica: containing tables, calendars, and miscellaneous information, for the use of historians, antiquaries, and the legal profession. 270p. *8°. 1824.*

For the **NORTHERN WHIG,** 1824–25, *see* vol. III, *Periodicals list.*

24054 [**O'SULLIVAN,** M.] Captain Rock detected: or, the origin and character of the recent disturbances, and the causes...of the present alarming condition of the South and West of Ireland, fully and fairly considered and exposed: by a Munster farmer. 450p. *12°. 1824.*

24055 [**PHILLIPS,** WILLIAM.] An appeal on the subject of the accumulation of wealth, addressed to the Society of Friends, usually called Quakers, individually and collectively. 40p. *8°. 1824.*

24056 PIGOT, JAMES, **& CO.** Pigot & Co.'s City of Dublin and Hibernian provincial directory, containing... the nobility, gentry, clergy, professional gentlemen, merchants, and manufacturers of Dublin and upwards of two hundred & twenty of the principal cities, seaports and towns of Ireland...To which is added a comprehensive directory of London...directories of the merchants, manufacturers, and wholesale traders in Birmingham, Bristol, Leeds, Liverpool, Manchester and Sheffield... The whole concluding with a complete Isle of Man directory and guide... 428, 372, 248p. *fol. London & Manchester*, 1824.

24057 POINSETT, J. R. Speech of Mr. Poinsett, of S.C....on the tariff bill. Delivered in the House of Representatives, U.S. April 8, 1824. 23p. *12°. Washington*, 1824.

24058 PURDY, J. The Colombian navigator; or, sailing-directory for the American coasts and the West-Indies. Volume the second. 204p. *8°*. 1824.

24059 QUADRI, A. Storia della statistica dalle sue origini sino alla fino del secolo XVIII per servire d'introduzione ad un Prospetto statistico delle Provincie Venete. 245, [67]p. *8°. Venezia*, 1824. *For* Prospetto statistico, *see* 1826.

24060 RANKIN, J. Speech of Mr. Rankin, of Mississippi, on the tariff bill. Delivered in the House of Representatives, U.S. April 1st and 2d, 1824. 31p. *12°. Washington*, 1824.

24061 ROOKE, J. An inquiry into the principles of national wealth, illustrated by the political economy of the British Empire. 476p. *8°. Edinburgh*, 1824.

24062 RYAN, R. Prize essay. An essay upon the following subject of inquiry, "What are the best means of rendering the national sources of wealth possessed by Ireland effectual for the employment of the population?" proposed by the Royal Irish Academy, 1822. 89p. *12°*. 1824.

24063 SAINT-CHAMANS, A. L. P. DE, *Vicomte.* Nouvel essai sur la richesse des nations. 422p. *8°. Paris*, 1824.

24064 SIMMONS, JOHN. A letter to...the Duke of Northumberland, on the very extraordinary transactions of the Society for the Encouragement of Arts, Manufactures, and Commerce, relative to...the Duke of Sussex, (their president,) and the author. 38p. *8°*. 1824.

24065 SINCLAIR, SIR JOHN, *Bart.* Prospectus of a work to be entitled, "Analysis of the Statistical account of Scotland..."... 59, 38p. *8°. Edinburgh, London, &c.*, 1824. *For* Analysis of the Statistical account of Scotland, *see* 1831.

24066 SLANEY, R. A. Essay on the beneficial direction of rural expenditure. 239p. *12°*. 1824.

24067 [STAUNTON, M., *comp.*] Tracts on Ireland, political and statistical. Containing No. I. Lists of absentees at different periods...No. II. Peculiar causes relating to Ireland which produce absenteeism...No. III. Sketches of the various insurrections...No. IV. History of the Treaty of Limerick...No. V. Famine of 1822...To which is added [No. VI.], Mr. Scully's celebrated statement of the penal laws: published first in 1812, by H. Fitzpatrick. 348p. *8°. Dublin*, 1824. *Published in parts, and dedicated to Daniel O'Connell by the compiler and publisher, Michael Staunton.*

24068 STERNDALE, M. Vignettes of Derbyshire. 135p. *8°*. 1824.

24069 STEVENSON, WILLIAM (1772–1829). Historical sketch of the progress of discovery, navigation and commerce, from the earliest records to the beginning of the nineteenth century. [With 'Catalogue of voyages and travels'.] 654p. *8°. Edinburgh & London*, 1824.

24070 STORCH, H. F. VON. Considérations sur la nature du revenu national. 198p. *8°. Paris*, 1824.

24071 SUMMARY of the Report of a Select Committee appointed to enquire into the causes which have led to the extensive depreciation or reduction in the remuneration for labour in Great Britain, and the extreme privation and calamitous distress consequent thereupon. 19p. *8°*. [*London*, 1824]

24072 [THOM, WALTER.] Plan for the improvement of the condition of the people of Ireland. By W—— T——. 33p. *8°. Dublin*, 1824.

24073 TOD, J. Speech of Mr. Tod, of Pennsylvania, on the tariff bill. Delivered in the House of Representatives U.S. April 7th, 1824. 24p. *12°. Washington*, 1824.

24074 WATT, ROBERT (1774–1819). Bibliotheca Britannica; or a general index to British and foreign literature...In two parts: – Authors and subjects. 4 vols. *4°. Edinburgh & London*, 1824.

24075 WEBSTER, D. Speech of Mr. Webster, upon the tariff; delivered in the House of Representatives of the United States, April, 1824. 47p. *8°. Boston*, 1824.

For the **WEEKLY DISPATCH,** 1824–25, *see vol.* III, *Periodicals list.*

24076 WHITE, JOHN, *U.S. Navy.* A voyage to Cochin China. 372p. *8°*. 1824.

AGRICULTURE

24077 CHAMBERS, SIR ROBERT (1737–1803). A treatise on estates and tenures...Edited by Sir Charles Harcourt Chambers. 311p. *8°. London & Dublin*, 1824.

24078 COBBETT, W. Cottage economy...to which are added, instructions relative to the selecting, the cutting and the bleaching of the plants of English grass and grain, for the purpose of making hats and bonnets...A new edition. [196]p. *12°*. 1824. *For other editions, see* 1821.

24079 CORNISH, JAMES, *of Devon.* A view of the present state of the salmon and channel-fisheries, and of the statute laws by which they are regulated; showing, that it is to the defects of the latter that the present scarcity of the fish is to be attributed...Together with the form of a new Act, designed to remedy the evils so generally complained of; and an abstract of the evidence before the Committee of the House of Commons...217p. *8°*. 1824.

24080 CORNWALL. *Stannaries.* The laws of the Stannaries of Cornwall; with marginal notes and references to authorities. To which are added the several Acts of Parliament...and a copious index. Second edition, corrected. 136p. *8°. Truro & London*, 1824. *For other editions, see* 1753.

24081 CURTIS, WILLIAM. Practical observations on the British grasses, especially such as are best adapted to the laying down or improving meadows and pastures... Sixth edition, with considerable additions, by John Lawrence. To which is subjoined, a short account of the causes of the diseases in corn, called by farmers the blight, the mildew, and the rust; by Sir Joseph Banks, Bart. 165p. *8°*. 1824.

24082 DUTTON, H. A statistical and agricultural survey of the county of Galway, with observations on the means of improvement; drawn up...by the direction of the Royal Dublin Society. [With an appendix.] 528, 112p. *8°. Dublin*, 1824.

24083 GYLLENBORG, G. A., *Grefve.* A natural and chymical treatise on agriculture, from the works of Count Gustavus Adolphus Gyllenborg, with practical remarks and additions. By W. Pilkington...Fourth edition... 258p. *8°. Bury St. Edmunds'*, 1824.

24084 [LAWRENCE, J.] A practical treatise on breeding, rearing, and fattening, all kinds of domestic poultry, pheasants, pigeons, and rabbits; including an... account of the Egyptian method of hatching eggs by artificial heat, and the author's experiments thereon. Also the management of swine, milch cows, and bees, and instructions for the private brewery; by Bonington Moubray, Esq. Fifth edition. 355p. *12°.* 1824.

24085 [LONG, CHARLES E.] Considerations on the game laws. 40p. *8°.* 1824.

24086 MONTEATH, H. The forester's guide and profitable planter: containing a practical treatise on planting moss, rocky, waste, and other lands; also a new...plan of transplanting large trees, and of valuing growing wood and trees of all descriptions. To which is added, the prevention and cure of dry rot...Second edition, with important additions and improvements... 395p. *8°. Edinburgh, London, &c.,* 1824.

24087 OBSERVATIONS regarding the salmon fishery of Scotland. Especially with reference to the stake-net mode of fishing; the regulation of the close-time; and the necessity of a legislative revisal of the antiquated Scots statutes at present applicable to these subjects. 60p. *8°. Edinburgh & London*, 1824.

24088 —— Second edition. 69p. *8°. Edinburgh & London*, 1824.

24089 PENNSYLVANIA AGRICULTURAL SOCIETY. Memoirs of the Pennsylvania Agricultural Society: with selections from the most approved authors, adapted to the use of the practical farmers of the United States. 1824. 322p. *8°. Philadelphia*, 1824.

24090 ROBINSON, S. Remarks on the culture and management of flax; proposed as a means to assist the Irish poor, by giving them employment, thus rendering their situations more comfortable and encreasing the national wealth. 12p. *8°. Dublin*, 1824. *See also* 1825.

24091 WIGGINS, J. South of Ireland. Hints to Irish landlords, on the best means of obtaining and increasing their rents; improving their estates; and bettering the condition of the people. By a land agent. With an appendix... 70p. *8°.* 1824.

CORN LAWS

24092 HAYS, J. Observations on the existing corn laws. 34p. *8°.* 1824.

TRADES & MANUFACTURES

24093 The **BOOK** of English trades, and library of the useful arts...A new edition enlarged, with 500 questions ...[The twelfth edition.] 454, 18p. *8°.* 1824. *For other editions, see* 1811.

24094 BRITISH DISTILLERY COMPANY. Contract of copartnery of the British Distillery Company. Instituted 1824. 33p. *8°. Edinburgh*, 1824.

24095 COMMITTEE OF MASTER CABINET MAKERS AND JOURNEYMEN. The London cabinet makers' union book of prices. By a committee of masters and journeymen. [Second edition. With 'Additions to the general observations in the London Cabinet Makers' Union price book'.] 474p. *4°.* 1824. *For supplements, see* 1831 *and* 1837; *for another edition, see* 1836.

24096 DUPIN, F. P. C., *Baron.* Avantages sociaux d'un enseignement public appliqué a l'industrie, en réponse aux observations de la commission du Budjet de 1825... 30p. *8°. Paris*, 1824.

24097 —— Progrès de l'industrie française depuis le commencement du XIXe. siècle. Discours prononcé, le 29 novembre 1823... 56p. *8°. Paris*, 1824.

24098 HAWNEY, W. The complete measurer... being a plain and comprehensive treatise on practical geometry and mensuration. Containing the substance of Hawney's Mensuration, newly arranged...and incorporated with a variety of original...matter...By Thomas Keith. A new edition, corrected. 276p. *12°. London & York*, 1824. *For another edition, see* 1743.

24099 The **LICENSED VICTUALLERS'** companion, and publicans' guide...With observations on porter, ale, wine, and spirits, method of making...British wines, cordials, &c. How to detect adulterations, &c....To which is added, lists of London...brewers, distillers... maltsters...merchants... 324p. *12°.* 1824.

For the **LONDON MECHANICS' REGISTER,** 1824–26, *see vol.* III, *Periodicals list.*

24100 LOWNDES, THOMAS, *of Blackheath.* A letter addressed to Joseph Hume, Esq. M.P. & Friend Buxton, M.P. on that black act, the slavery of the publicans, too long held in bondage by the tyrannical brewers... 24p. *8°.* 1824.

24101 MATON, J. Tricks of bakers unmasked. A letter addressed to the Right Honourable the Lord Mayor of London. 28p. *8°.* 1824.

24102 [MEIKLEHAM, R. S.] A descriptive history of the steam engine. By Robert Stuart, Esq. civil engineer ... 228p. *8°.* 1824. *A second (the Rastrick) copy, lacks the preface.*

24103 [——] Second edition. 228p. *8°.* 1824. *See also* 1825, 1831.

24104 MORTON, T. Infringement of a patent. Notes of a trial before the Jury Court of Edinburgh, 15th March, 1824. Thomas Morton, ship-builder...pursuer, versus John Barclay...carrying on business...under the firm of the Stobcross Shipwright Company; defenders. For an infringement of a patent...for an invention called a slip, by which ships are hauled out of the water... 24p. *8°*. *Leith*, 1824.

For **REGISTER OF THE ARTS AND SCIENCES,** *see* vol. III, *Periodicals list.*

24105 SMITH, JAMES, *publisher in Liverpool.* History and description of the steam engine. 20p. *8°*. [1824 ?]

COMMERCE

24106 ADAMS, JOHN Q., *President of the USA.* A letter to Mr. Harrison Gray Otis, a member of the Senate of Massachusetts, on the present state of our national affairs, with remarks upon Mr. T. Pickering's letter, to the Governor of the Commonwealth...With an appendix, written July, 1824. 29p. *12°*. *Baltimore*, 1824. *For another edition, see* 1808.

24107 CHAMBER OF COMMERCE AND MANUFACTURES, *Glasgow.* Report of the committee of the directors of the Chamber of Commerce... appointed to consider the Bill now before Parliament, for establishing uniformity of weights & measures. [On the commercial implications of the Bill. Signed: Kirkman Finlay and 4 others.] 4p. *fol. n.p.* [1824]

24108 FAUST, B. C. Kornvereine, Kornhäuser, Kornpapiere in jeder ansehnlichen Stadt des Deutschen Vaterlandes... 32p. *16° Bückeburg*, 1824.

24109 FRANCE. *Laws, etc.* Analyse raisonné du Code de Commerce. Cet ouvrage contient: 1° l'explication de la Loi par ses motifs; 2° sa mise en action par la jurisprudence et le rapprochement de toutes les lois et ordonnances; 3° l'examen de questions neuves...4° la discussion de principes du domaine de l'économie politique ...[With the text of the *Code de Commerce*.] Par M. Mongalvy et M. Germain. 2 vols. *4°*. *Paris*, 1824. *For other editions of the Code, see* 1807.

24110 [HALL, SIR JOHN.] Review of Mr. Longlands' pamphlet, entitled "A review of the warehousing system;" or, the advocate for exclusive privileges unmasked: with observations upon the necessity of additional wet dock accommodation in the Port of London. 54p. *8°*. 1824.

24111 [——] Second edition. 54p. *8°*. 1824.

24112 KENNEDY, JOHN (1769–1855). On the exportation of machinery. A letter addressed to the Hon. E. G. Stanley, M.P. 27p. *8°*. *London & Manchester*, 1824.

24113 LONDON DOCK COMPANY. London-Dock-Company. Copies of resolutions, declaration and papers, relating to the transfer of goods at the London-Docks; the right of stopping goods in transitu, and the responsibility of wharfingers: with the opinions of the judges of the Court of King's Bench, upon a motion for a new trial, in the cause of Hawes v. Watson. 32p. *8°*. 1824.

24114 LONGLANDS, H. A review of the warehousing system as connected with the port of London... 59p. *8°*. 1824. *With the half-title, title-page, and Preface to the second edition bound in.*

24115 [McCULLOCH, JOHN R.] Effects of the East India Company's monopoly on the price of tea. [A review of] Observations on the trade with China. London, 1822. [Reprinted from *The Edinburgh Review*, Jan. 1824.] 10p. *8°. n.p.* [1824]

24116 OWEN, W. Owen's new book of fairs, published by the King's authority. Being a complete and authentic account of all the fairs in England and Wales, as they have been settled to be held since the alteration of the style...A new edition, carefully corrected, and with considerable additions. 148p. *12°*. 1824. *For other editions, see* 1756.

24117 PALYART, H. Segunda memoria que sobre a instituição dos portos francos em Portugal tem a honra de offerecer aos negociantes Portuguezes. 24p. *12°*. *Lisboa*, 1824.

24118 A SKETCH drawn from the records of the British Factory at St. Petersburg, and designed to elucidate the history of that body. From 1716 to 1824. 40p. *8°*. 1824.

24119 TOOKE, T. Thoughts and details on the high and low prices of the thirty years, from 1793 to 1822. In four parts...Second edition. 392, 15, 4, 39, 79p. *8°*. 1824. *The copy that belonged to Joseph Hume. For another edition, see* 1823.

24120 VIENNOT DE VAUBLANC, V. M., *Comte de Vaublanc.* Du commerce de la France. Examen des états de M. le Directeur Général des Douanes. 240p. *8°*. *Paris*, 1824.

24121 WILLIAMS, F. Observations on the state of the wine trade, occasioned by the perusal of a pamphlet on the same subject, by Mr. Warre. Most respectfully submitted to His Majesty's ministers...Second edition. 23p. *8°*. 1824.

24122 The WINE QUESTION considered, or, observations on the pamphlets, of Mr. James Warre & Mr. Fleetwood Williams, respecting the General Company for the Agriculture of the Vineyards, on the upper Douro, known in England, under the name of the Royal Oporto Wine Company. By a Portuguese. [With an appendix.] 65, 15p. *8°*. 1824.

COLONIES

24123 An ADDRESS to the Right Hon. Earl Bathurst ...relative to the claims which the coloured population of Trinidad have to the same civil and political privileges with their white fellow-subjects. By a free mulatto of the Island. 298p. *8°*. 1824. *The copy that belonged to Stephen Lushington.*

For the **COLONIAL REGISTER,** and West India journal, *see* vol. III, *Periodicals list.*

24124 EAST INDIA COMPANY. Papers regarding the administration of the Marquis of Hastings in India. Printed in conformity to the resolution of the Court of Proprietors...of 3d March 1824. 8 vols. *fol.* [*London*,] 1824.

24125 —— The Marquis of Hastings' summary of the operations in India, with their results; from the 30th April 1814 to the 31st January 1823. Printed in conformity to the resolution of the Court of Proprietors...of the 23d June 1824. 41p. *fol.* [*London*,] 1824.

24126 —— Papers respecting a reform in the administration of the government of His Excellency the Nawaub Vizier [of Oudh], and the employment of British troops in his dominions, from the 1st January 1808 to the 31st December 1815. Also relating to the negotiation of the several loans contracted with the Vizier, between... October 1814 and May 1815. Printed in conformity with a resolution of the Court of Proprietors...of the 23rd June 1824. 1041p. *fol.* [*London*,] 1824.

24127 EAST INDIA SUGAR, or an inquiry respecting the means of improving the quality and reducing the cost of sugar raised by free labour in the East Indies. With an appendix containing proofs and illustrations. 41p. *8°.* 1824.

24128 HASTINGS, F. R., *Marquis of Hastings.* Summary of the administration of the Indian government, from October 1813, to January 1823. 130p. *8°. Malta,* 1824. *With an inscription on the title-page, 'Ellenborough from the Marchioness of Bute Nov. 22 1857'.*

24129 *HUMBOLDT, F. H. A. von, *Freiherr.* Selections from the works of the Baron de Humboldt, relating to the climate, inhabitants, productions, and mines of Mexico. With notes by John Taylor, Esq. treasurer to the Geological Society, etc. 310p. *8°.* 1824.

24130 PROCEEDINGS of an inquiry and investigation instituted by Major General Codd, His Majesty's Superintendent and Commander-in-Chief at Belize, Honduras...relative to Poyais, &c.&c.&c. 171p. *8°. Published...by order of the Magistrates of Honduras,* 1824. *The Agar Ellis copy.*

24131 An old **PROPRIETOR** begs to submit to his Brethren of the Court of Proprietors the following documents which throw a considerable light on the important question now before the General Court. [On the Hyderabad question.] 13p. *fol. n.p.* [1824]

24132 SAY, J. B. Historical essay on the rise, progress, and probable results of the British dominion in India. 36p. *8°.* 1824.

24133 SOCIETY FOR THE RELIEF OF DISTRESSED SETTLERS IN SOUTH AFRICA, *Cape Town.* Report of the committee of the Society... with the resolutions passed and speeches delivered at a general meeting, held at Cape Town, 17th Sept. 1823. To which is subjoined an appendix of letters and other documents, illustrative of the present condition of the settlers. 31p. *8°.* 1824.

24134 SOCIETY FOR THE RELIEF OF THE DISTRESSED SETTLERS AT THE CAPE OF GOOD HOPE, *London.* Report of the committee of the Society...with letters and other documents illustrative of their present condition [reprinted from the Report of the Society for the Relief of Distressed Settlers in South Africa]. 24p. *8°.* 1824. *The Agar Ellis copy.*

24135 SPIX, J. B. von, and **MARTIUS,** C. F. P. von. Travels in Brazil, in...1817–1820... 2 vols. *8°.* 1824. *Translated from the German by H. E. Lloyd.*

24136 TALBOT, E. A. Five years' residence in the Canadas: including a tour through part of the United States of America, in...1823... 2 vols. *8°.* 1824.

24137 WENTWORTH, W. C. A statistical account of the British settlements in Australasia; including the colonies of New South Wales and Van Diemen's Land... The third edition. With an appendix, containing the Acts of Parliament, and other documents relating to these settlements... 2 vols. *8°.* 1824.

FINANCE

24138 ALIQUIS, *pseud.* England her own enemy. A letter to the British Parliament, with remarks upon public brewers, publicans, pawnbrokers, and public companies. 23p. *8°.* 1824.

24139 An **APOLOGY** for the pawnbrokers, most respectfully addressed to the members of both Houses of Parliament, the judges of the land, and the justices of the peace throughout the kingdom. 38p. *8°.* 1824.

24140 [**AZAÏS,** L.] Opinion sur le prêt gratuit et sur prêt utile, par M. L....***. [The preface signed: A....] 326p. *8°. Castres,* 1824. *The author's name on the title-page is extended in a manuscript note: par M. Louis Azaïs frère de Monsieur Le président du tribunal de premiére instance a Castres.*

24141 BARNES, John H. A list of articles free of duty and tariff or rates of duties, from and after the 30th June, 1824, on all goods, wares and merchandise imported into the United States of America; established by Acts of Congress of 27th April, 1816, 20th April, 1818, 3d March, 1819, and 22d May, 1824, on importations by American vessels or vessels entitled to the benefits of the Convention with foreign powers. To which is added an appendix containing several important revenue laws... 84, lxxvip. *8°. Philadelphia,* 1824.

24142 BENECKE, W. A treatise on the principles of indemnity in marine insurance, bottomry and respondentia, and on their practical application in effecting those contracts, and in the adjustment of all claims arising out of them... 498p. *8°.* 1824.

24143 BOUYON, J. B. Réfutation des systèmes de M. l'Abbé Barronat et de Mgr. de la Luzerne, sur la question de l'usure. 463p. *8°. Clermont-Ferrand,* 1824.

24144 BRITISH ANNUITY COMPANY. British Annuity Company for the purchase of annuities secured on property in Great Britain & Ireland. Capital three millions... [A prospectus.] 14p. *8°.* [1824]

24145 CHUBB, W. P. Usury versus equity. The speeches of the pawnbrokers, at the Horns meeting, contrasted with their public habits and the secret resolutions, formed at, and delivered in, their private assemblies, in reference to the formation of an equitable loan institution. 16p. *8°.* [1824]

24146 COMPAGNIE D'ASSURANCES GÉNÉRALES. Compagnie d'Assurances générales contre les risques maritimes et de navigation intérieure. Rapport de M. de Gourcuff, Directeur. 20p. *4°. n.p.* [1824] *See also 1821, 1823, 1825, 1827.*

24147 Serious **CONSIDERATIONS** on the proposed Bill of Mr. Serjeant Onslow, to repeal the laws of

usury, and throw open the money-market. Addressed to
...the public at large. By a gentleman. 34p. *8°*. 1824.

24148 CORBAUX, F. A further inquiry into the
present state of our National Debt, and into the means
and the prospect of its redemption...With a plan of
finance for the redemption of the National Debt...and an
appendix on state lotteries, with new illustrations of the
doctrine of chances... 95p. *4°*. 1824.

24149 D****, M. *le Comte*. Encore un mot sur la
réduction de l'intérêt de la dette publique. 15p. *8°*. *Paris*,
1824.

24150 DEFENCE of the principles of the Equitable
Loan Bank, and Mont de Piété, against the attacks of the
meeting of pawnbrokers. 20p. *8°*. 1824.

24151 DEGRAND, P. P. F. Tariff of duties, on importations into the United States: and revenue laws and
custom-house regulations. Compiled by P. P. F. Degrand,
under the direction of General H. A. S. Dearborn...
Third edition... 106p. *12°*. [*Boston*,] 1824.

24152 DUFRESNE DE SAINT-LEON, L. C. A.
Étude du crédit public et des dettes publiques. 284p. *8°*.
Paris, 1824.

24153 EGAN, P. Pierce Egan's account of the trial of
Mr. Fauntleroy, for forgery, at the Session's-House, in the
Old Bailey, on Saturday, the 30th of October, 1824...
67p. *8°*. [1824]

24154 ENGLAND. *Laws, etc*. An Act to commute, for
a corn rent, certain tithes and dues payable to the vicar of
the parish of Lancaster, in the county of Lancaster. 5 Geo.
IV. sess. 1824. 31p. *fol*. [*London*, 1824]

24155 —— *Parliament*. [*Endorsed:*] An Act [i.e. a Bill]
for the establishment and regulation of "The Equitable
Loan Bank Company." 5 Geo. IV. sess. 1824. 57[67]p. *fol*.
[*London*, 1824]

24156 —— —— [*Endorsed:*] A Bill to commute for a
corn rent, certain tithes and dues payable to the vicar of
the parish of Lancaster, in the county of Lancaster. 5 Geo.
IV. sess. 1824. 22p. *fol*. [*London*, 1824] *For the Act, see no.*
24154.

24157 —— —— [*Endorsed:*] A Bill to commute for a
corn rent the tithes and dues payable to the vicar of the
parish...of Cockerham, in the county of Lancaster. 1824.
25p. *fol*. [*London*, 1824]

24158 —— —— *House of Commons*. Epitome of the
evidence on Grand Jury cess, taken before a Select Committee of the House of Commons, appointed to inquire
into the local taxation of Dublin, in the Session of 1823:
with notes and illustrations by the officers of the prisons.
180p. *8°*. *Dublin*, 1824.

**24159 EQUITABLE LOAN BANK COM-
PANY.** [*Endorsed:*] Equitable Loan Bank. Plan of the
Company. [Dated: April 5, 1824.] [4]p. *fol*. *n.p.* [1824]

**24160 EQUITABLE LOAN COMPANY OF
SCOTLAND.** Contract of copartnery of the Equitable
Loan Company of Scotland. Instituted 1824. 21p. *8°*.
Edinburgh, 1824.

24161 Oppressive EXACTION of tithes! Remarks on
the rapacity of the London clergy and lay impropriators;
with observations on their present salaries, surplice-fees,
&c....showing the injustice and illegality of the present
system of tithes and church-dues...32p. *8°*. [1824?]

24162 FAIRMAN, WILLIAM. An account of the
public funds transferrable at the Bank of England, and of
the stocks of some of the principal public companies in
London...Also, a history of the National Debt and
Sinking Fund...The seventh edition, enlarged...and
brought down to the year 1824. By Bernard Cohen. 287p.
8°. 1824. *For other editions, see* 1795.

24163 FARREN, G. A treatise on life assurance; in
which the systems and practice of the leading life institutions are stated...and the Statutes...affecting such
institutions brought under review. With an appendix,
including arguments...relating to...trading joint-stock
companies. 76p. *8°*. 1824. *For another edition, see* 1823.

24164 FAUNTLEROY, H. The trial of Mr. H.
Fauntleroy, for forgery, before Mr. Justice Parke, at the
Sessions House, Old Bailey...October 30, 1824. With his
...defence, and many particulars and facts relative to that
unfortunate gentleman... 26p. *8°*. [1824]

24165 FORTUNE, E. F. THOMAS. Fortune's
epitome of the stocks and public funds...Eleventh edition, with additions, revised and corrected to the present
time...By a member of the Stock Exchange. 119p. *12°*.
1824. *For other editions, see* 1796.

24166 FRANCE. *Chambre des Pairs*. Impressions No.
68. Session de 1824. Séance du...26 mai 1824. Opinion
de M. le Baron Pasquier, sur le projet de loi relatif au
remboursement ou à la réduction de l'intérêt des rentes
cinq pour cent. Imprimée par ordre de la Chambre. 88p.
8°. *n.p.* [1824] *Presentation copy, with inscription, from the
author to the Marquis de Chateaugiran.*

24167 FROUST, J. M. Nouveau mode pour le
remboursement effectif, en trente ans, du capital de cent
quarante millions de rentes de la dette publique...
Adressé à MM. les membres de la Chambre des Députés,
le 18 avril 1824. 23p. *8°*. *Paris*, 1824.

24168 [FUOCO, E.] La magia del credito svelata,
instituzione fondamentale di pubblica utilità da Giuseppe
de Welz... 2 vols. *4°*. *Napoli*, 1824.

24169 GANILH, C. De la réduction des rentes en
1824. 46p. *8°*. *Paris*, 1824.

24170 [GODARD, P.] Réflexions sur le projet de
remboursement de la dette publique. Par M. G** auteur
de l'ouvrage intitulé: Mémoire et propositions sur la
comptabilité générale des finances du royaume. 41p. *8°*.
Paris, 1824.

24171 GRAY, W. Petition in favor of the Equitable
Loan Bill. [To the Honourable the Commons of the
United Kingdom of Great Britain and Ireland in Parliament assembled. The humble petition of William Gray,
and other inmates of the Fleet Prison.] 37p. *8°*. [*London*,
1824]

24172 An INQUIRY, but not a parliamentary inquiry
into the past and present abuses of the Irish revenue, and
into the plunder of the Irish patronage. 94p. *8°*. *Dublin*,
1824.

24173 [JOPLIN, T.] Prospectus of a joint-stock
banking company, with £3,000,000 of capital, to be
established in London. 2p. *fol*. [*London*, 1824]

24174 LEGRAND DE BOISLANDRY, F. L.
Des impôts et des charges des peuples en France. xci,
391p. *8°*. *Paris*, 1824.

24175 A LETTER to the Right Hon. George Canning,

on the subject of the Spanish bonds of 1821. 13p. *8°. Bristol & London*, 1824.

24176 [**McCULLOCH**, JOHN R.] Interest. [From the Supplement to the Encyclopædia Britannica.] 11p. *4°. n.p.* [1824]

24177 —— Money. [From the Supplement to the Encyclopædia Britannica, Vol. v. Part II. Signed: S.S.] 46p. *4°. n.p.* [1824]

24178 —— Taxation. ⟨From the Supplement to the Encyclopædia Britannica, Vol. VI. Part II.⟩ [Signed: S.S.] 39p. *4°. n.p.* [1824]

24179 MALBOUCHE, F. Opinion sur le remboursement de la rente. 26p. *8°. Paris*, 1824.

24180 MARRYAT, J. The substance of a speech delivered in the House of Commons...February, 1810, upon a motion for a Select Committee to consider of... the means of effecting marine insurances: also Observations on the Report of the Committee...To which are added, the proceedings in the House of Commons in February, 1811, and at Lloyd's...June, 1810, and... April 1811. 40, 94, 21p. *8°.* 1824. *The copy presented to the Hon. George Agar Ellis by the Committee for Managing the Affairs of Lloyd's, with an engraved presentation slip. For other editions of the speech and of* Observations on the Report of the Committee, *see* 1810.

24181 MASSACHUSETTS. *General Court.* An Act to incorporate the President, Directors and Company of the Commonwealth Bank. Passed February 20, 1824. 24p. *12°. Boston*, 1824.

24182 MAUGHAM, R. A treatise on the principles of the usury laws; with disquisitions on the arguments adduced against them by Mr. Bentham and other writers, and a review of the authorities in their favor. 81p. *8°.* 1824.

24183 MOSBOURG, J. A. M. A. DE, *Comte.* Lettre à son Excellence M. le Comte de Villèle, Ministre des Finances...sur le projet de remboursement ou de réduction des rentes. 27p. *8°. Paris*, 1824.

24184 —— Seconde lettre à son Excellence M. le Comte de Villèle, Ministre des Finances...sur le projet de remboursement ou de réduction des rentes. 52p. *8°. Paris*, 1824.

24185 Un **MOT** sur quelques questions à l'ordre du jour. Par l'auteur de la Politique de M. de Villèle, et des Lettres au comte de ***, Pair de France, sur la septennalité et la réduction des rentes. 34p. *8°. Paris*, 1824.

24186 NETHERLANDS. *Departement van Financien.* Vrijmoedige en bescheidene aanmerkingen op de concept-wet, betrekkelijk de uitloting en den inkoop van kansbilletten en uitgestelde schuld, enz. Door...den Minister van Financien medegedeeld...den 22 October, 1824. 24p. *8°. Haarlem*, 1824.

24187 —— *Permanente Commissie uit het Amortisatie-Syndicaat.* De Permanente Commissie uit het Amortisatie-Syndicaat...brengt bij deze ter kennisse van allen en een iegelijk, het navolgende berigt van eene negotiatie van nationale effecten groot honderd millioenen guldens onder verband der domeinen welke krachtens de wet van den 27 december 1822... 12p. *12°. n.p.* [1824]

24188 [**PASQUIER**, ÉTIENNE D., *Duc.*] De la réduction des cinq pour cent, et de la facilité d'acquitter les dettes provenant des confiscations. 36p. *8°. Paris*, 1824.

Presentation copy, with inscription (in the same hand as in no. 24166), from the author to the Marquis de Chateaugiran.

24189 PÉRIER, C. Opinion de M. Casimir Périer, Député de la Seine, sur le projet de loi relatif au remboursement et à la réduction des rentes cinq pour cent; prononcé dans la séance du 28 avril 1824. 31p. *8°. [Paris*, 1824]

24190 PIERCY, R. Bubble and squeak; or, a sound from the frying-pan: being a letter addressed to "My uncle's" friends. [An attack on the Equitable Loan Bank.] 24p. *8°.* 1824.

24191 POHLMAN, J. G. Interest tables, at 3, 3½, 4, 4½, 5, and 6 per cent., upon a new, simple, and comprehensive plan; with separate tables for India bonds, and Exchequer bills [compiled by R. Pohlman]: to which are added, Smart's compound interest tables: also, tables of life annuities, reversionary payments... 296, [64]p. *8°.* 1824.

24192 The **PRACTICABILITY** and expediency of abolishing direct taxation, by repealing...the remaining moiety of the assessed taxes, considered, in a letter to the ...Chancellor of the Exchequer, and to the Members of the House of Commons. By a magistrate of the county of *****. 15p. *8°.* 1824.

24193 —— [Another edition.] 16p. *8°.* 1824.

24194 RAVENSTONE, PIERCY, *pseud.?* Thoughts on the funding system, and its effects. 80p. *8°.* 1824.

24195 RICARDO, D. Plan for the establishment of a national bank. 32p. *8°.* 1824. *The copy that belonged to S. J. Loyd, Baron Overstone, and was formerly among his papers. For these, see vol. III, MS. 804. There is a slightly imperfect copy among the collection of pamphlets, many of them Ricardo's own copies, made by his son, Osman.*

24196 ROBINSON, F. J., *Earl of Ripon.* Speech of the Right Hon. F. J. Robinson, Chancellor of the Exchequer, on the financial situation of the country, delivered in a Committee of the Whole House, on the Four Per Cent. Acts, on...the 23rd of February, 1824. To which is added, an appendix containing various accounts referred to. 59p. *8°.* 1824. *The copy that belonged to Earl De Grey.*

24197 SÉGUIN, A. Barème des contribuables, ou, de l'égale répartition de la contribution foncière entre les quatre-vingt-six départemens de la France. 32p. *8°. Paris*, 1824.

24198 —— Du projet de remboursement ou de réduction des rentes...Sixième édition. 231p. *8°. Paris*, 1824.

24199 Short **STATEMENT** relative to the Bishops' Court in Ireland, and the conduct of tithe proctors in the country. [Report of the committee of the parish of Blackrath, in the county of Kilkenny.] 16p. *8°.* 1824. *The Agar Ellis copy.*

24200 TUCKER, T. Report by Thomas Tucker upon the settlement of the revenues of excise and customs in Scotland. [Edited by J. A. Murray.] A.D.MDCLVI. 68p. *4°. Edinburgh: Bannatyne Club*, 1824.

24201 WATT, P. Comparative tables of the rates of life assurance demanded in Scotland; with an exposition of the doctrine of life assurance and annuity, shewing how the rates are calculated, and the present value ascertained, when claimed to be ranked on a bankrupt estate, or sold for their true value. 29, 35p. *8°. Edinburgh*, 1824.

24202 WAYS and means; or, every man his own financier. Explaining the various modes of raising money . . . with hints to monied men on the best mode of employing dormant capital. [A guide, recommending the services of Messrs. Smith & Co. 34, Golden Square.] 29p. *12°*. 1824.

24203 WEST OF SCOTLAND INSURANCE COMPANY. Abstract of the articles of copartnery of the West of Scotland Insurance Company. 13p. *8°. n.p.* [1824]

24204 WOOD, JOHN PHILIP. Memoirs of the life of John Law of Lauriston, including a detailed account of the rise, progress, and termination of the Missisippi [*sic*] system. 234p. *12°. Edinburgh & London,* 1824.

TRANSPORT

24205 BAIRD, H. Reports on the improvements of the river Leven and Loch Lomond . . . August 24, and October 20, 1824. 18p. *4°. n.p.* [1824] *The Rastrick copy.*

24206 BIRKINSHAW, J. [and **LONGRIDGE,** M.] Specification of John Birkinshaw's patent, for an improvement in the construction of malleable iron rails, to be used in rail roads; with remarks on the comparative merits of cast metal and malleable iron rail-ways. [With correspondence extracted from the Newcastle Courant, 23 Nov.–10 Dec., 1824.] 14, 8p. *8°. Newcastle,* 1824. *For other editions, see* 1822.

24207 BRUNEL, M. J. A new plan of tunnelling, calculated for opening a roadway under the Thames. 4p., 5 plates. *8°.* [1824] *Presentation copy, with inscription, from the author to Sir John Copley.*

24208 BURN, W. and **HAMILTON,** THOMAS (1784–1858). Report relative to the proposed approaches from the south and west to the Old Town of Edinburgh, &c.&c.&c. [With 'Appendix. No. I. Abstract of Mr. Jardine's report regarding the levels of the proposed new streets in Edinburgh' and 'No. II. Statement respecting the proposed street shown in the plan, as leading from Adam's Square to Brown's Square' by W. H. Playfair.] 10, 7p. *4°. n.p.* [1824] *The Rastrick copy.*

24209 C., T. A summary of the turnpike law of the county of Edinburgh: combining the General Turnpike Act of 4 Geo. IV., ch. 49; with the local Acts of the said county of Edinburgh. 92p. *8°. Edinburgh,* 1824.

24210 CHAPMAN, WILLIAM (1749–1832). Observations on the most advisable measures to be adopted in forming a communication for the transit of merchandise and the produce of land, to or from Newcastle and Carlisle, or the places intermediate, in a letter . . . to Sir James Graham, of Kirkstall, Bart. 10p. *8°. Newcastle,* 1824.

24211 —— A report on the cost and separate advantages of a ship canal and of a rail-way, from Newcastle to Carlisle, published by order of and addressed to the committee of enquiry. Second edition. 21p. *8°. Newcastle,* 1824.

24212 —— Report relative to the improvement of the harbour of Leith. Addressed to the Lord Provost, magistrates, and council, of the city of Edinburgh. 9p. *4°. n.p.* [1824] *The Rastrick copy.*

24213 CONSIDERATIONS on the expediency of incorporating by Act of Parliament, a joint stock company, for constructing wet docks at St. Catherine's. 15p. *8°.* [1824] *The Agar Ellis copy.*

24214 CUMMING, T. G. Description of the iron bridges of suspension now erecting over the Strait of Menaï, at Bangor, and over the river Conway, in North Wales . . . also some account of the different bridges of suspension in England and Scotland; particularly of Captain S. Brown's iron bar bridge over the river Tweed. With remarks on the proposed suspension bridge over the river Mercy [*sic*], at Runcorn Gap . . . 55p. *8°.* 1824. *The Rastrick copy.*

24215 —— Illustrations of the origin and progress of rail and tram roads, and steam carriages, or loco-motive engines . . . Particularly those . . . communications projected between Liverpool and Birmingham, and Liverpool and Manchester, with a view to the more general employment of steam carriages, or loco-motive engines, for the conveyance of passengers as well as merchandise. With remarks on the public advantages likely to accrue therefrom . . . 64p. *8°. Denbigh & London,* 1824.

24216 DONKIN, B. A paper, read before the Institution of Civil Engineers, on the construction of carriageway pavements. 13p. *8°.* 1824.

24217 DUPIN, F. P. C., *Baron.* Force commerciale de la Grande-Bretagne . . . Tome premier. Voies publiques, places, rues, routes, canaux, ponts et chaussées [–Tome II. Côtes et ports maritimes]. (*Voyages dans la Grande-Bretagne* . . . Troisième partie . . . Section des Travaux Publics et d'Association, 5–6.) 2 vols. *4°. Paris,* 1824. *Presentation copy, with inscription, from the author to William Huskisson, See also* 1825 *and, for the third edition, the author's* Voyages dans la Grande-Bretagne, 1826 (GENERAL).

24218 ENGLAND. *Laws, etc.* Anno quadragesimo septimo Georgii III. Regis. Sess. 2. [Local & Personal.] Cap. 81. An Act to alter, amend, explain, and enlarge the powers of the several Acts passed for making and maintaining the Rochdale Canal Navigation. p.1529–34. *fol.* 1824.

24219 —— —— Anno quadragesimo nono Georgii III. Regis. [Local & Personal.] Cap. 73. An Act to amend and enlarge the powers of the several Acts passed for making a navigable canal from the Trent to the Mersey, and other canals connected therewith. ⟨20th May 1809.⟩ p.1341–1346. *fol.* 1824.

24220 —— —— [*Endorsed:*] An Act to authorize the Company of Proprietors of the Stockton and Darlington Railway to relinquish one of their branch railways, and to enable them to make another branch railway in lieu thereof; and to enable the said Company to raise a further sum of money . . . ⟨Royal Assent, 17 May 1824.⟩ 5 Geo. IV. sess. 1824. 21p. *fol.* [*London,* 1824]

24221 ENGLISH AND BRISTOL CHANNELS SHIP CANAL COMPANY. English and Bristol Channels Ship Canal. Prospectus, and Mr. Telford's preliminary report, dated 2d August, 1824. 10, 8p. *8°.* 1824.

24222 FACTS plainly stated: in answer to a pamphlet entitled "Plain statement of facts, connected with the proposed St. Katharine's Dock." By a London-Dock proprietor. 31p. *8°*. 1824.

24223 [HALL, SIR JOHN.] Plain statement of facts connected with the proposed St. Katharine Dock, in the Port of London, to be established upon the principle of open and general competition. 29p. *8°*. 1824. *The Agar Ellis copy.*

24224 KENNET AND AVON CANAL NAVIGATION. Report of the Committee of Management... [Signed: C. Dundas, chairman, and dated, 20th July, 1824.] [3]p. *fol. n.p.* [1824] *See also* 1812, 1813, 1815, 1816, 1823, 1825, 1826, 1838.

24225 LIVERPOOL. *Dock Committee.* Report to the dock-rate payers of Liverpool, by the commissioners appointed to "inspect, audit, and adjust" the accounts of the Liverpool Dock Estate, for the year...ending the 24th June, 1824. [Largely concerned with irregularities in the accounts concerned with the supply of construction materials.] Published by order of the Annual Meeting of dock-rate payers...25th June, 1824. 48p. *8°*. *Liverpool,* 1824.

24226 The **LONDON** and Leith smack and steam yacht guide; comprehending a copious topographical description of the coast between London, Leith and Aberdeen; a correct table of distances...and an appendix ... 230p. *12°*. *Leith, Edinburgh, &c.,* 1824.

24227 McADAM, JOHN L. Remarks on the present system of road making...Eighth edition, carefully revised, with an appendix, and Report from the Select Committee of the House of Commons, June 1823, with extracts from the evidence. 236p. *8°*. 1824. *For other editions, see* 1816.

24228 PALMER, HENRY R. Description of a railway on a new principle; with observations on those hitherto constructed...Second edition, revised. 60p. *8°*. 1824. *For another edition, see* 1823.

24229 PENNSYLVANIA SOCIETY FOR THE PROMOTION OF INTERNAL IMPROVEMENTS IN THE COMMONWEALTH. Constitution of the...Society... 4p. *8°*. *n.p.* [1824]

24230 QUAIFE, J. The hackney coach directory.

Second edition. 396p. *12°*. 1824. *Signed in manuscript by the author. See also* vol. III. *Addenda.*

24231 REMARKS on the proposed measure of building a bridge over the River Thames at Hammersmith; and on the Bill for that purpose, now before the House of Commons. 21p. *8°*. 1824. *The Agar Ellis copy.*

24232 RENNIE, JOHN (1761–1821). Report by Mr. John Rennie, engineer, respecting the proposed railway from Kelso to Berwick. 14th November 1809. 16p. *4°*. *Edinburgh,* 1824.

24233 A **REPLY** to the authorized defence of the St. Katherine's Dock project... 36p. *8°*. 1824.

24234 SAINT KATHARINE'S DOCK. A letter from an inhabitant of St. Katharine's, addressed to Mr. John Hall...with observations on a pamphlet entitled "A plain statement of facts..." 24p. *8°*. [1824]

24235 SANDARS, J. A letter on the subject of the projected rail road, between Liverpool and Manchester, pointing out the necessity for its adoption and the manifest advantages it offers to the public, with an exposure of the exorbitant & unjust charges of the water carriers. 32p. *8°*. *Liverpool, Manchester, &c.,* [1824] *See also* 1825.

24236 STEVENSON, R. An account of the Bell Rock Light-house...To which is prefixed a historical view of the institution and progress of the northern lighthouses... 533p. *4°*. *Edinburgh & London,* 1824.

24237 TELFORD, T. Report respecting the mailroad between the City of Edinburgh and town of Morpeth, by the towns of Berwick & Alnwick... 15p. *fol.* 1824.

24238 —— Ship canal, for the junction of the English and Bristol Channels. Reports of Mr. Telford and Captain Nicholls; with plans annexed. 41p. *fol.* 1824.

24239 UNITED COMMITTEE FOR THE STOUR NAVIGATION AND SANDWICH HARBOUR. Stour Navigation and Sandwich Harbour. Prospectus; sketch of the plan; the report of the engineer [James Morgan], with the estimates; and a statement of the revenue, calculated on the trade carried on, in 1823. [Signed: Henry Cooper, chairman.] 7p. *fol. Canterbury,* 1824.

SOCIAL CONDITIONS

24240 ADOLPHUS, J. Observations on the Vagrant Act, and some other Statutes, and on the powers and duties of justices of the peace. 112p. *8°*. 1824.

24241 The **BALLS** in mourning, or the lamentation of the pawnbrokers, who are crying and roaring, and loudly deploring, for this Loan Institution will give them a flooring. [A dialogue between Mrs. Cush and Mrs. Logan on the imminent opening of the Equitable Loan Institution.] *s.sh.4°*. [*London,* 1824] [*Br.* 499]

24242 BARBÉ-MARBOIS, F. DE, *Marquis.* Rapport sur l'état actuel des prisons dans les départements du Calvados, de l'Eure, de la Manche et de la Seine-Inférieure, et sur la maison de correction de Gaillon. Octobre 1823... 34p. *4°*. [*Paris,*] 1824.

24243 BARDIN, C. A sermon, preached in St. Peter's Church, Dublin, on...January 4th, 1824...in aid of the Shelter for Females discharged from Prison. [With

'Second report of the Shelter for Females discharged from Prison, 31st December, 1823'.] 19, vip. *8°*. *Dublin,* 1824.

24244 BATH PENITENTIARY AND LOCK HOSPITAL. The collective reports of the Bath Penitentiary and Lock Hospital, from 1816 to 1824; when arrangements were entered into which constituted a new æra in this establishment. 208p. *8°*. *Bath,* 1824.

24245 BECCARIA BONESANA, C., *Marchese.* Opere di Cesare Beccaria. Volume unico. (*Classica biblioteca italiana antica e moderna.*) 317p. *8°*. *Milano,* 1824.

24246 BECHER, JOHN T. The constitution of friendly societies upon legal and scientific principles, exemplified by the rules...adopted...for...the Friendly Institution, at Southwell; together with observations of the rise & progress...of friendly societies...Second edition. 12, 70p. *8°*. 1824. *See also* 1828.

24247 BICHENO, J. E. An inquiry into the poor laws, chiefly with a view to examine them as a scheme of national benevolence, and to elucidate their political economy...Second edition. 162p. *8°*. 1824. *The copy presented by the author to the Athenæum Club.*

24248 BOSWORTH, J. The practical means of reducing the poor's rate, encouraging virtue, and increasing the comforts of the aged...poor; as well as of repressing able-bodied pauperism, by a proper application of the existing laws respecting select vestries and incorporated houses of industry. 48p. *8°*. 1824. *The copy that belonged to William Allen.*

24249 BREAD for all. A plan for doing away with the poor's rates; or, parochial, agricultural, and national, hints. By an English gentleman. 23p. *8°*. [1824] *Attributed to William Newnham Blane (Black 3443).*

24250 BRERETON, C. D. Observations on the administration of the poor laws in agricultural districts. 119p. *8°*. *Norwich & London,* [1824]

24251 —— Second edition. 119p. *8°*. *Norwich & London,* [1824] *The copy that belonged to William Allen.*

24252 —— Third edition. 119p. *8°*. *Norwich & London,* [1824]

24253 BRIDEWELL HOSPITAL. Bridewell Hospital. New rules and orders [in conformity with the new Prison Act]. 46p. *8°*. 1824. *The Agar Ellis copy.*

24254 BRISCOE, JOHN I. A letter on the nature and effects of the tread-wheel as an instrument of prison labour and punishment, addressed to the Right Hon. Robert Peel...With an appendix of notes and cases. By one of his constituents, and a magistrate of the county of Surrey. 174p. *8°*. 1824.

24255 COLLETT, A. A letter to Thomas Sherlock Gooch, Esq., M.P. upon the present ruinous system of relieving unemployed men with money instead of providing them with work; detailing a legislative plan for the employment of the poor...To which is added, a statement of the appeal A. Collett, clerk, v. parish officers of Kelsale, and report of the case, Rex v. A. Collett, clerk. Second edition, with...additions and alterations. 65p. *8°*. *Halesworth & London,* 1824.

24256 *COMBINATION & arbitration laws, artizans and machinery. Abstract of the Acts repealing the laws against combinations of workmen, and emigration of artizans; abstract of the Act for arbitrating differences between workmen and their employers; speech of Joseph Hume, Esq. M.P. in the House of Commons, on the 12th February 1824...Lists of the Committee of the House of Commons, of the witnesses examined; and an address to the working people, by George White, clerk to the... Committee. 32p. *8°*. [1824] *The FWA copy, that belonged to William Pare.*

24257 COPLAND, W. A letter to the Rev. C. D. Brereton, in reply to his "Observations on the administration of the poor laws in agricultural districts"; containing, also, some remarks on his attack upon the magistrates of the county, and tracing the great increase of pauperism to its proper source. 126p. *8°*. *Norwich & London,* 1824.

24258 DEYKES, W. Considerations on the defective state of the pavement of the Metropolis: with observations on its causes and consequences. Together with a plan for paving upon a new principle. 16p. *8°*. 1824.

24259 DRUMMOND, H. A letter to the justices of the peace for the county of Surrey, on the cases in the House of Correction at Guildford, presented by Mr.

Briscoe to them at their quarter sessions...January, 1824. 41p. *8°*. 1824.

24260 The fatal **EFFECTS** of gambling exemplified in the murder of Wm. Weare, and the trial and fate of John Thurtell, the murderer, and his accomplices...To which is added, the gambler's scourge; a complete exposé of the whole system of gambling in the Metropolis... 512p. *8°*. 1824.

24261 EGAN, P. Pierce Egan's account of the trial of John Thurtell and Joseph Hunt. With an appendix... portraits and...engravings. 105p. *8°*. 1824.

24262 —— Recollections of John Thurtell, who was executed at Hertford...the 9th of January, 1824; for murdering Mr. W. Weare...By Pierce Egan...Being an appendix to his account of the trial... 44p. *8°*. 1824.

24263 ENGLAND. *Home Office.* Comparative summary statements of the number of criminal offenders committed to the several gaols in England and Wales, during the two last seven years, &c.&c.&c. 35p. *8°*. *n.p.,* 1824. *See also* 1822, 1831, 1833, 1834.

24264 ERSKINE, T., *Baron Erskine.* Cruelty to animals. The speech of Lord Erskine in the House of Peers on 15th May, 1809 on the second reading of the Bill for preventing malicious and wanton cruelty to animals. 31p. *8°*. *The Society for the Prevention of Cruelty to Animals,* 1824. *The Agar Ellis copy.*

24265 FINLAY, J. The office and duty of churchwarden and parish officer in Ireland...Second edition. 204p. *8°*. *Dublin,* 1824.

24266 HALL, JOHN (*fl.* 1824). A plan for the abolition of the present poor rates; and for effecting a grand moral improvement in the lower classes of society; with a view to the ultimate annihilation of pauperism. 33p. *8°*. 1824. *The title on the printed paper wrapper reads: 'Ten minutes consideration for the executive government; the members of both Houses of Parliament; and the people of England: not altogether undeserving the attention of the stockholders, whose property it has been proposed to charge to the poor rates'. The copy that belonged to William Allen.*

24267 HASE, W. Description of the patent improved tread mill, for the employment of prisoners, also of the patent portable crank machine, for producing labour of any degree of severity, in solitary confinement...To which is added, the description of the gyrometer or calculator, by R. B. Bate...for registering the exact amount of labour performed by the prisoners. 24p. *8°*. *Norwich,* [1824]

24268 HEADLAM, J. A second letter to the Right Honourable Robert Peel...on prison labour; containing a vindication of the principles and practice of the magistrates of the North Riding of the county of York, with respect to their treatment of prisoners before trial. With a postscript in reply to the 2d article of the 78th number of the Edinburgh Review. 54p. *8°*. 1824.

24269 HIGHLAND AND AGRICULTURAL SOCIETY OF SCOTLAND. Report on friendly or benefit societies, exhibiting the law of sickness, as deduced from returns by friendly societies in...Scotland. To which are subjoined tables, shewing the rates of contribution necessary for the different allowances, according to the ages of the members at entry, &c.&c. Drawn up by a Committee of the...Society... 288p. *8°*. *Edinburgh & London,* 1824.

24270 KENT AND SUSSEX FRIENDLY BROTHERS' SOCIETY. Rules & regulations of the...Society, established at Hawkhurst, Kent, the fifth day of May, 1823. 63p. *16°. Cranbrook,* 1824.

24271 A LETTER to a Member of Parliament, on the impropriety of classing players with rogues and vagabonds in the Vagrant Act. By the author of "The Vagrant Act in relation to the liberty of the subject." 22p. *8°.* 1824.

24272 MONTGOMERY, JAMES (1771–1854). The chimney-sweeper's friend, and climbing-boy's album... Arranged by James Montgomery. With illustrative designs by Cruickshank. 428p. *12°.* 1824. *See also* 1825.

24273 MOREWOOD, S. An essay on the inventions and customs of both ancients and moderns in the use of inebriating liquors...With an historical view of...distillation... 375p. *8°.* 1824.

24274 OBSERVATIONS on a statement published in the Morning Chronicle newspaper, of the 22d. July 1824; purporting to be the evidence of Henry Drummond, Esq....before a Select Committee of the House of Commons, in the last session of Parliament "on laborers' wages." By some of the farmers, parish officers, and others, holding lands...within the hundreds of Blackheath, Godalming, and Woking in Surrey...[With the text of the evidence.] 27p. *8°. Guildford & London,* [1824]

24275 Nouveau **PROJET** sur le Calvaire du Mont Valérien. 30p. *8°. [Paris,* 1824 ?]

24276 PROJET d'élargissement de la rue du Bac. 8p. *8°. [Paris,* 1824 ?]

24277 RICHMOND, A. B. Narrative of the condition of the manufacturing population; and the proceedings of Government which led to the state trials in Scotland for administering unlawful oaths...in Glasgow and its neighbourhood. Also, a summary of similar proceedings, in other parts of the country, to the execution of Thistlewood and others...in 1820. 196p. *8°.* 1824.

24278 SINGLE, T. Hints to Parliament for a general Act to prevent parochial squabbles, for a reduction of one half of the poors' rate, and to better the condition of the poor. 50p. *8°.* 1824.

24279 SOCIETY FOR ENCOURAGEMENT OF INDUSTRY AND REDUCTION OF POOR RATES. Society for Encouragement of Industry... King's Head Tavern, Poultry, Aug. 1824. Public address. [An outline of the Society's functions, signed: Benj. Wills, Hon. Sec.] 12p. *8°. [London,* 1824]

24280 SOCIETY FOR THE IMPROVEMENT OF PRISON DISCIPLINE, *London.* The sixth report of the Committee of the Society for the Improvement of Prison Discipline and the Reformation of Juvenile

Offenders, 1824. With an appendix ['Extracts from the correspondence of the Committee']. 365p. *8°. London, Edinburgh, &c.,* [1824] *The copy that belonged to George Agar Ellis, Baron Dover, with his arms stamped in gilt on the binding. See also* 1818, 1827, 1832.

24281 SOCIETY FOR THE PREVENTION OF CRUELTY TO ANIMALS. A sermon on the unjustifiableness of cruelty to the brute creation, and the obligations we are under to treat it with lenity and compassion. By a clergyman of the Church of England. 24p. *12°.* 1824. *The Agar Ellis copy.*

24282 SOUTH SHIELDS GAS COMPANY. A copy of the deeds relating to the South Shields Gas Company. Established 1824. 46p. *4°. South Shields,* 1824.

24283 Some **SUGGESTIONS** for the improvement of benefit clubs, and assurances for the lower classes; founded on the reasoning of a petition, presented by the late D. Ricardo, Esq., to the House of Commons, for the author: also suggestions for a modification of the poor laws: with remarks on the comparative situation of the landholder and the fundholder... 30p. *8°.* 1824. *The copy that belonged to William Allen.*

24284 THOUGHTS on prison labour, &c.&c. By a student of the Inner Temple. [With an appendix of documents referring to the use of treadmills in prisons.] 126, cccviiip. *8°. London, Oxford, &c.,* 1824. *The copy that belonged to Sir Robert Peel.*

24285 —— [Another edition.] 144, cccxlviiip. *8°. London, Oxford, &c.,* 1824.

24286 The **VAGRANT ACT,** in relation to the liberty of the subject...By a barrister. Second edition. With a postscript. 89p. *8°.* 1824.

24287 WALKER, JAMES, *of Newcastle,* and **RICHARDSON,** M. A. The armorial bearings of the several incorporated companies of Newcastle upon Tyne, with a brief historical account of each company; together with notices of the Corpus Christi, or miracle plays, anciently performed by the trading societies of Newcastle upon Tyne... 64p. *8°. Newcastle,* 1824.

24288 WARDROP, J. Biographical sketch of the late Matthew Baillie, M.D....From the Edinburgh Medical and Surgical Journal, January 1824. 17p. *8°. [London,]* 1824.

24289 WHITE, GEORGE (*fl.* 1823–1825). A digest of all the laws at present in existence respecting masters and work people: with observations thereon. 159p. *8°.* 1824.

24290 —— A digest of the minutes of evidence taken before the Committee on Artizans and Machinery. 478p. *8°.* 1824.

SLAVERY

24291 ANTHROPOS, *pseud.* The rights of man, (not Paines,) but the rights of man, in the West Indies. 47p. *8°.* 1824. *Sometimes attributed to* —— *Matthews, of Histon, Cambridgeshire.*

24292 An **APPEAL** and caution to the British nation; with proposals for the immediate or gradual emancipation of the slaves. Indemnity must precede emancipation. By a member of the Dominica Legislature. 82p. *8°.* 1824.

24293 ARMSTRONG, JOHN, *B.A.* A candid examination of "The defence of the settlers of Honduras;" or, a fair inquiry into the truth and justice of their accusations against Colonel George Arthur... 67p. *8°.* 1824. *The copy that belonged to Stephen Lushington.*

24294 BAILEY, B. The house of bondage. A dissertation upon the nature of service or slavery under the Levitical law, among the Hebrews in the earliest ages, and in the Gentile world, until the coming of Christ...with reflections on the change, which Christianity has made, and continues to make, in the condition of that class of people who are servants. 74p. *8°*. 1824.

24295 BEVERLEY ANTI-SLAVERY ASSO-CIATION. Speeches delivered in the Town-Hall of Beverley, at a public meeting...for the purpose of petitioning Parliament to abolish slavery in the West Indies... February 26th, 1824. [Speeches by W. Beverley, J. Coltman and R. M. Beverley, with resolutions passed at the meeting of 3 March 1824, and lists of officers and subscribers to the Association.] 36p. *12°. Beverley,* [1824]

24296 BUXTON, SIR THOMAS F., *Bart.* Société de la Morale Chrétienne. Comité pour l'Abolition de la Traite des Noirs. Discours prononcé dans la Chambre des Communes d'Angleterre, à l'appui de la motion pour l'adoucissement et l'extinction graduelle de l'esclavage dans les colonies anglaises...traduit de l'Anglais, précédé d'une introduction sur l'état des esclaves dans ces colonies, par Charles Coquerel... 62p. *8°. Paris,* 1824.

24297 CANNING, GEORGE. The speech of the Rt. Hon. George Canning, in the House of Commons, on the 16th...of March, 1824, on laying before the House the "Papers in explanation of the measures adopted by His Majesty's Government, for the amelioration of the condition of the slave population...in the West Indies". 44p. *8°*. 1824.

24298 —— [Another edition.] Speech...on laying before the House of Commons the papers in explanation of the measures adopted by His Majesty's government with a view of ameliorating the condition of the negro slaves in the West Indies, on...the 17th [*sic*] of March, 1824. To which is added, an Order in Council, for improving the condition of the slaves in Trinidad... 78p. *8°*. 1824.

24299 CLARKSON, T. The argument, that the colonial slaves are better off than the British peasantry, answered from the Royal Jamaica Gazette of June 21, 1823. 17p. *8°. Whitby: The Whitby Anti-Slavery Society,* 1824.

24300 —— Thoughts on the necessity of improving the condition of the slaves in the British colonies, with a view to their ultimate emancipation...Fourth edition corrected. 57p. *8°. Society for the Mitigation and Gradual Abolition of Slavery throughout the British Dominions,* 1824. *For other editions, see* 1823.

24301 COMMITTEE FOR PROMOTING AFRICAN INSTRUCTION. Second report of the Committee managing a fund raised for the purpose of promoting African instruction. With an appendix. 48p. *8°*. 1824. *See also* 1822.

24302 CONSIDERATIONS on negro slavery; with a brief view of the proceedings relative to it, in the British Parliament. 24p. *8°. Edinburgh: The Edinburgh Society for Promoting the...Abolition of Negro Slavery,* 1824.

24303 COOPER, THOMAS (1791?-1880). Correspondence between George Hibbert, Esq., and the Rev. T. Cooper, relative to the condition of the negro slaves, in Jamaica, extracted from the Morning Chronicle: also, a libel on the character of Mr. and Mrs. Cooper, published, in 1823, in several of the Jamaica journals. With notes and remarks. 67p. *8°*. 1824. *The copy that belonged to Stephen Lushington.*

24304 —— Facts illustrative of the condition of the negro slaves in Jamaica: with notes and an appendix. 64p. *8°*. 1824. *The copy that belonged to Stephen Lushington.*

24305 —— A letter to Robert Hibbert...in reply to his pamphlet, entitled, "Facts verified upon oath, in contradiction of the report of...Thomas Cooper, concerning the...condition of the slaves in Jamaica,"...to which are added, a letter from Mrs. Cooper...and an appendix, containing an exposure of the falsehoods...of that gentleman's affidavit-men. 90p. *8°*. 1824. *The copy that belonged to Stephen Lushington.*

24306 CROPPER, J. The support of slavery investigated. 27p. *8°. Liverpool & London,* 1824. *The copy that belonged to Stephen Lushington.*

24307 EDINBURGH SOCIETY FOR PROMOTING THE...ABOLITION OF NEGRO SLAVERY. The first annual report of the Edinburgh Society for Promoting the Mitigation and Ultimate Abolition of Negro Slavery; with an appendix. 29p. *8°. Edinburgh,* 1824. *See also* 1825.

24308 The injurious **EFFECTS** of slave labour: an impartial appeal to the reason, and patriotism of the people of Illinois on the injurious effects of slave labour. 18p. *8°. The Society for the...Abolition of Slavery,* 1824. *The copy that belonged to Stephen Lushington.*

24309 EMANCIPATION of the negro slaves in the West India colonies considered, with reference to its impolicy and injustice; in answer to Mr. Wilberforce's Appeal. By the author of 'A statement of the claims of the West India colonies to a protecting duty against East India sugar.' No. I. 44p. *8°*. 1824. *The copy that belonged to Stephen Lushington.*

24310 ENGLAND. Parliament. *House of Commons.* Debate in the House of Commons, on the 16th day of March, 1824, on the measures adopted by his Majesty's Government, for the amelioration of the condition of the slave population...in the West Indies. 71p. *8°*. 1824.

24311 —— —— —— The missionary Smith. Substance of the debate in the House of Commons on...the 1st and...11th of June, 1824, on a motion of Henry Brougham...respecting the trial and condemnation to death by a court martial of the Rev. John Smith, late missionary in...Demerara. With a preface, containing some new facts... 255p. *8°*. 1824. *The copy that belonged to Stephen Lushington.*

24312 FOX, CHARLES J. The speech of the Rt. Hon. Chas. James Fox in the House of Commons, June 10th, 1806, on a motion preparatory to the introduction of a Bill for the abolition of the slave trade. 8p. *8°. Newcastle,* 1824.

24313 GLADSTONE, SIR J., *Bart.* The correspondence between John Gladstone, Esq. M.P., and James Cropper, Esq., on the present state of slavery in the British West Indies and in the United States of America; and on the importation of sugar from the British settlements in India. With an appendix; containing several papers on the subject of slavery. 122, xvii, xviii, xp. *8°. Liverpool: The West India Association & London,* 1824.

24314 GROSETT, J. R. Remarks on West India affairs. 114p. *8°*. 1824. *The copy that belonged to Stephen Lushington.*

24315 GURNEY, JOSEPH J. Substance of a speech, delivered at a public meeting of the inhabitants of...

Norwich, on the subject of British colonial slavery...
30p. *8°. Norwich*, [1824]

24316 —— [Another edition.] 16p. *8°.* [1824]

24317 [HEYRICK, E.] Immediate, not gradual
abolition; or, an inquiry into the shortest, safest, and most
effectual means of getting rid of West Indian slavery. 24p.
8°. 1824.

24318 [——] Third edition. With an appendix, containing Clarkson's comparison between the state of the
British peasantry and that of the slaves in the colonies,
&c. 32p. *8°.* 1824.

24319 [——] [Another edition.] 20p. *8°.* [1824]

For the **HUMMING BIRD**, 1824–25, *see* vol. III,
Periodicals list.

24320 **IMPOLICY** of slavery. [With 'Remarks on the
probable extension of British commerce'.] 3p. *fol. Liverpool*, [1824?]

24321 **INCOGNITUS**, *pseud.* Thoughts on the
abolition of slavery; humbly submitted in a letter to the
King. 22p. *8°. London* [*Penzance printed*], 1824.

24322 **JOANNA**, or the female slave. A West Indian
tale. Founded on Stedman's Narrative of an expedition
against the revolted negroes of Surinam. 176p. *12°.
London, Edinburgh, &c.*, 1824.

24323 **LEICESTER AUXILIARY ANTI-
SLAVERY SOCIETY.** An address on the state of
slavery in the West-India islands. 28p. *8°. London &
Leicester*, 1824.

24324 —— [Another edition.] An address to the public
on the state of slavery... 16p. *8°.* 1824.

24325 **LINDOE**, R. Observations upon slavery;
setting forth, that to hold the principle of slavery is to
deny Christ. 34p. *8°.* 1824.

24326 **LIVERPOOL SOCIETY FOR THE
ABOLITION OF SLAVERY.** An address from the
Liverpool Society...on the safest and most efficacious
means of promoting the gradual improvement of the negro
slaves in the British West India Islands, preparatory to
their becoming free labourers... 18p. *8°. Liverpool*, 1824.
The copy that belonged to Stephen Lushington.

24327 **LOSH**, J. The speech of James Losh, Esq., in
the Guildhall, Newcastle upon Tyne, on the 31st March,
1824, at a meeting of the inhabitants called...for the
purpose of petitioning Parliament for the improvement
and gradual emancipation of the slave population of the
British colonies. 12p. *8°. Newcastle*, 1824. *The copy sent
through the post to Stephen Lushington.*

24328 [MACAULAY, Z.] Negro slavery; or a view
of some of the more prominent features of that state of
society, as it exists in the United States of America and
in the colonies of the West Indies, especially in Jamaica.
Fourth edition. 92p. *8°. The Society for the Mitigation and
Gradual Abolition of Slavery throughout the British
Dominions*, 1824. *For another edition, see* 1823.

24329 **M'DONNELL**, A. Considerations on negro
slavery. With authentic reports, illustrative of the actual
condition of the negroes in Demerara. Also, an examination
into the propriety and efficacy of the regulations...now
in operation in Trinidad... 338p. *8°.* 1824. *See also* 1825.

24330 **M'QUEEN**, J. The West India colonies; the
calumnies and misrepresentations circulated against them

by the Edinburgh Review, Mr. Clarkson, Mr. Cropper,
&c....examined and refuted. 427p. *8°. London, Edinburgh,
&c.*, 1824.

24331 **NEGRO EMANCIPATION** morally and
practically considered: in which the justice, policy, and
expediency of the measure, are impartially stated and
candidly examined. With a critique on the petition of the
West-India planters, &c...to the King. To which is
added, a postscript. 50p. *8°.* 1824.

24332 **PITT**, WILLIAM (1759–1806). The speech of
the Right Hon. William Pitt, in the House of Commons, on
the 2d. of April, 1792, on the subject of the African slave
trade. 35p. *8°. Newcastle*, 1824. *For another edition, see*
1792.

24333 A **REVIEW** of some of the arguments which are
commonly advanced against parliamentary interference in
behalf of the negro slaves, with a statement of opinions
which have been expressed on that subject by many of our
most distinguished statesmen... 31p. *8°. Manchester*,
1824. *For another edition, see* 1823.

24334 **REVIEW** of the Quarterly Review; or, an
exposure of the erroneous opinions promulgated in that
work on the subject of colonial slavery: being the substance of a series of letters which appeared in the "New
Times" of September and October 1824... 104p. *8°.*
1824. *The copy that belonged to Stephen Lushington.*

24335 **SANDARS**, J. A letter, addressed to the
Liverpool Society for the Abolition of Slavery. By a
member of that society. 15p. *8°.* [1824] *The copy that
belonged to Stephen Lushington.*

24336 **SMITH**, JOHN, *missionary to Demerara.* The
London Missionary Society's report of the proceedings
against the late Rev. J. Smith...who was tried under
martial law, and condemned to death, on a charge of
aiding...in a rebellion of the negro slaves; from a...copy,
transmitted...by Mr. Smith's counsel, and including the
documentary evidence omitted in the Parliamentary copy;
with an appendix... 204p. *8°.* 1824. *The copy that
belonged to Stephen Lushington.*

24337 **SOCIETY FOR THE ABOLITION OF
SLAVERY THROUGHOUT THE BRITISH
DOMINIONS.** Report of the committee of the Society
for the Mitigation and Gradual Abolition of Slavery
throughout the British Dominions, read at the general
meeting of the Society, held on the 25th day of June, 1824,
together with an account of the proceedings... 112p. *8°.*
1824. *See also* 1825, 1826.

24338 **STEPHEN**, J. The slavery of the British West
India colonies delineated, as it exists both in law and
practice, and compared with the slavery of other countries,
antient and modern... 2 vols. *8°.* 1824–30. *See also* 1831,
and for a proof copy of part of vol. 1, 1823.

24339 Is the **SYSTEM** of slavery sanctioned or condemned by Scripture? To which is subjoined an appendix,
containing two essays upon the state of the Canaanite and
Philistine bondsmen, under the Jewish theocracy. 92p. *8°.*
1824.

24340 **TAYLOR**, JOHN (*d.* 1857). Negro emancipa-
tion and West Indian independence the true interest of
Great Britain...Second edition. 16p. *8°. Liverpool &
London*, 1824.

24341 —— De l'émancipation des noirs et de l'indépendance des Indes-Occidentales, considérées comme

étant dans l'interêt bien entendu de la Grande Bretagne... Extrait du second numéro du Philanthrope chrétien. 16p. *8°. Londres, 1824.*

24342 VAUX, R. Mémoires sur la vie d'Antoine Benezet...Abrégé de l'ouvrage original, traduit de l'anglais. 88p. *12°. Paris, 1824. For another edition, see 1817.*

24343 WATSON, RICHARD (1781–1833). The religious instruction of the slaves in the West India colonies advocated and defended. A sermon preached before the Wesleyan Methodist Missionary Society...April 28, 1824. 35p. *8°. 1824. The copy that belonged to Stephen Lushington.*

24344 —— Fourth edition. 35p. *8°.* [1824]

24345 WINN, T. S. Emancipation; or practical advice to British slave-holders: with suggestions for the general improvement of West India affairs. 111p. *8°. 1824. The copy that belonged to Stephen Lushington.*

24346 YATES, JOHN A. Colonial slavery. Letters to the Right Hon. William Huskisson, President of the Board of Trade, &c.&c. on the present condition of the slaves, and the means best adapted to promote the mitigation and final extinction of slavery in the British colonies. 86p. *8°. Liverpool & London, 1824.*

24347 YORK. Proceedings in the city of York, in reference to negro slavery in the West Indies. 18p. *8°. York, 1824. With a manuscript note on the title-page: Anti-Slavery Committee.*

POLITICS

24348 On the **ALIEN BILL**. By an alien. 44p. *8°.* 1824.

24349 ALISSAN DE CHAZET, A. R. P. Louis XVIII à son lit de mort, ou récit exact et authentique de ce qui s'est passé au Chateau des Tuileries les 13, 14, 15 et 16 septembre; 1824. 48p. *8°. Paris, 1824.*

24350 BENTHAM, J. The book of fallacies: from unfinished papers of Jeremy Bentham. By a friend. 411p. *8°.* 1824.

24351 CHATEAUBRIAND, F. R. DE, *Vicomte.* Le Roi est mort: vive le Roi. 37p. *8°. Paris, 1824.*

24352 DUMESNIL, A. Considérations sur les causes et les progrès de la corruption en France. 79p. *8°. Paris, 1824.*

24353 ENGLAND. Parliament. *House of Commons.* Debate in the House of Commons, on the 25th of June, 1823, upon Mr. Hume's motion, respecting the Vice Regal government of Ireland. ⟨From Hansard's Parliamentary Debates...⟩ 16p. *8°.* [*London,*] 1824.

SOCIALISM

24354 AITON, J. Mr. Owen's objections to Christianity, and New view of society and education, refuted, by a plain statement of facts. With a hint to Archibald Hamilton...Second edition. 92p. *8°. Edinburgh, Glasgow, &c.,* 1824.

24355 COMBE, ABRAM. The religious creed of the new system, with an explanatory catechism, and an appeal in favour of true religion, to the ministers of all other religious persuasions and denominations. 68p. *8°. Edinburgh,* 1824.

24356 [**FOURIER**, F. C. M.] Mnémonique géographique, ou méthode pour apprendre en peu de leçons la géographie, la statistique et la politique. 15p. *8°.* [*Paris,* 1824] *The copy that belonged to Victor Considérant.*

24357 A **LETTER** to the working classes of Edinburgh, on the formation of new societies, and an outline of regulations for their government, adapted to the spirit of the age. 10p. *8°. Edinburgh,* 1824.

24358 M'GAVIN, W. The fundamental principles of the New Lanark system exposed, in a series of letters to Robert Owen, Esq. 96p. *12°. Glasgow, 1824. Published in eight parts with the caption title: Letters on Mr. Owen's new system.*

24359 MUIRON, J. Sur les vices de nos procédés industriels, aperçus démontrant l'urgence d'introduire le procédé sociétaire. 176p. *8°. Paris, 1824. The copy that belonged to Victor Considérant. See also 1846.*

24360 OWEN, ROBERT D. An outline of the system of education at New Lanark. 103p. *8°. Glasgow, Edinburgh, &c., 1824. The copy that belonged to Sir Robert Peel.*

24361 THOMPSON, WILLIAM (1785?–1833). An inquiry into the principles of the distribution of wealth most conducive to human happiness; applied to the newly proposed system of voluntary equality of wealth. 600p. *8°.* 1824. *See also* 1850.

MISCELLANEOUS

24362 BULLOCK, W. Catalogue of the exhibition called Modern Mexico; containing a panoramic view of the city, with specimens of the natural history of New Spain...at the Egyptian Hall, Piccadilly. 28p. *8°.* 1824.

24363 —— A description of the unique exhibition, called Ancient Mexico; collected on the spot in 1823...and now open for public inspection at the Egyptian Hall, Piccadilly. 50p. *8°. London, 1824. The Agar Ellis copy.*

24364 —— A descriptive catalogue of the exhibition entitled Ancient and modern Mexico; containing a panoramic view of the present city, specimens of the natural history of New Spain...at the Egyptian Hall, Piccadilly. 32p. *8°.* [1824?]

24365 COBBETT, W. A French grammar, or, plain instructions for the learning of French. In a series of letters. [404]p. *12°.* 1824.

24366 HINTS relative to the Bill lately introduced into Parliament, intituled, "An Act for the better regulating of the forms of process in the courts of law in Scotland." 22p. *8°. Edinburgh,* 1824.

24367 HONE, W. Another article for the Quarterly Review. 32p. *8°.* 1824.

24368 —— Aspersions answered: an explanatory statement, addressed to the public at large, and to every reader of the Quarterly Review in particular. [Being a reply to an article on the 'Apocryphal New Testament', edited by Hone.] 68p. *8°.* 1824.

24369 *LONDON. Livery Companies. *Salters.* A list of the Master, Wardens, Court of Assistants, and Livery, of the Worshipful Company of Salters. 15p. *8°.* 1824. *See also* 1784, 1787, 1790, 1792, 1794, 1797, 1799, 1801, 1803, 1806, 1809, 1812, 1815, 1818, 1821, 1827, 1830.

24370 MACKENZIE, SIR ALEXANDER M., *Bart.* Letter to the landed proprietors of Scotland, on the Bill, entitled An Act for better regulating the forms of process in the courts of law in Scotland. 29p. *8°. Edinburgh,* 1824.

24371 MURRAY, JOHN (1778–1843). Notes on Captain Medwin's Conversations of Lord Byron. 15p. *8°. n.p.* [1824] *The Agar Ellis copy.*

24372 PFYFFER VON ALTISHOFEN, C. Récit de la conduite du régiment des Gardes Suisses à la journée du 10 août, 1792. 68p. *4°. Genève,* 1824.

24373 RICHARDS, G. A sermon preached at the parish church of Saint Martin in the Fields…22nd August, 1824… 28p. *8°.* [*London,*] 1824. *Presentation copy, with inscription, from the author to George Agar Ellis, Baron Dover.*

24374 [RYDER, D., *Earl of Harrowby.*] Letters on the proposed vote for building churches, which have appeared in the New Times and Courier. [Signed: A.B.] 27p. *8°.* 1824. *The Agar Ellis copy.*

24375 SMITH, GEORGE, *writing-master.* Principles of epistolary & mercantile writing: containing easy and infallible rules for facilitating the attainment of a free and expeditious hand…To which are added instructions for making pens. 22p. *8°. Edinburgh,* 1824.

24376 SMITH, SYDNEY (1771–1845). The judge that smites contrary to the law. A sermon preached in the Cathedral Church of St. Peter, York…March XXVIII, MD.CCC.XXIV. 16p. *8°. York,* [1824] *The Agar Ellis copy.*

24377 —— The lawyer that tempted Christ. A sermon preached in the Cathedral Church of St. Peter, York… August 1, M.DCCC.XXIV. 17p. *8°. York,* [1824] *Presentation copy from the author to George Agar Ellis, Baron Dover.*

24378 TOPHAM, J. A sermon in which is attempted to be shewn, how far the use of music is allowable or serviceable in religious exercises; preached in the parish church…Droitwich on…March 21st, 1824, in aid of a contribution for the benffit [sic] of the organist. 22p. *4°.* [1824] *The Agar Ellis copy.*

24379 WEBB, R. T. The phrenologist; a farce, in two acts: containing a popular summary of that pseudo, or real science. 38p. *12°.* 1824.

1825

GENERAL

24380 ALMANACH du commerce de Paris, des départemens de la France, et des principales villes du monde de J. de la Tynna; continué et mis dans un meilleur ordre par Séb. Bottin…1825. (XXVIIIe année de la publication)… cclxxxviii, 918p. *8°. Paris,* [1825]

24381 [BAILEY, S.] A critical dissertation on the nature, measures, and causes of value; chiefly in reference to the writings of Mr. Ricardo and his followers. By the author of Essays on the formation and publication of opinions, &c.&c. 255p. *8°.* 1825.

24382 BARATIER, P. and **CHARRIER,** L. L. Esprit de la loi de l'indemnité, tiré de la discussion de cette loi dans les deux Chambres… 168p. *8°. Paris,* 1825.

24383 Du BESOIN de nouvelles institutions en faveur du commerce et des manufactures, ou, réflexions d'un fabricant sur cette matière. 40p. *8°. Paris,* 1825.

24384 [BLANC DE LA NAUTTE, A. M., *Comte d'Hauterive.*] Notions élémentaires d'économie politique à l'usage des jeunes gens…Nouvelle édition augmentée d'une introduction contenant des considérations générales sur la théorie de l'impôt et des dettes; par le Comte d'H****. cl, 387p. *8°. Paris,* 1825.

24385 BLONDEL, J. J. M. Almanaque politico y de comercio de la ciudad de Buenos Ayres para el año de 1826. Contiene lo que es relativo al gobierno, a los ministerios, administraciones…los nombres y domicilios de los negociantes y mercaderes…los varios estados y profesiones…Año primero. 305p. *4°. Buenos Ayres,* 1825. *With additional indexes in French and English.*

24386 [BROWNE, JAMES (1793–1841).] A critical examination of Dr. Macculloch's work on the Highlands and Western Isles of Scotland. 302p. *8°. Edinburgh,* 1825.

24387 BUCHANAN, G. C. Ireland as she ought to be: or, a serious and impressive call to the nobility, gentry, agricultural and trading interests of Ireland… 36p. *8°. Dublin,* 1825.

24388 CARRION-NISAS, A. H. F. V. DE, *Marquis.* Principes d'économie politique. 287p. *12°. Paris,* 1825.

24389 CHARDON, J. Tableau historique et politique de Marseille ancienne et moderne, ou guide fidèle du voyageur et des négocians dans cette ville…Quatrième édition, revue, corrigée…et augmentée d'un précis historique de tous les événemens remarquables arrivés dans cette ville depuis 1789 jusqu'au 25 juin 1815. 204, 96p. *12°. Marseille,* 1825.

24390 COBBETT, JOHN M. Letters from France; containing observations made in that country during a journey…commencing in April, and ending in December, 1824. 288p. *12°.* 1825.

24391 COBBETT, W. Cobbett's book of the Roman-Catholic Church. In four parts. Being a familiar introduction to his "History of the Protestant reformation."...[A collection of extracts published to discredit Cobbett.] Parts 1–3. *8°. London & Dublin, 1825.*

24392 —— A history of the Protestant "Reformation," in England and Ireland; showing how that event has impoverished and degraded the...people...In a series of letters...[vol. 1]. *12°. 1825. For other editions, see 1824.*

24393 CORRY, JOHN. The history of Lancashire... 2 vols. *4°. 1825.*

24394 CRESSWELL, D. Remarks upon the principal Statutes concerning weights and measures: with tables of the dimensions proper for heaped measures; and instructions for examiners of weights, balances, and measures... 40p. *8°. 1825.*

24395 CROPPER, J. Present state of Ireland: with a plan for improving the condition of the people. 59p. *8°. Liverpool & London, 1825. The Agar Ellis copy.*

24396 D., F. L. Un coup-d'œil sur la situation de la France en 1825, et considérations sur le gouvernement, l'administration des finances, les manufactures, les arts, le commerce intérieur et extérieur, les colonies, la marine marchande et royale, suivies, d'un résumé. 35p. *8°. Nantes, 1825.*

24397 [DOYLE, JAMES W., *R.C. Bishop of Kildare and Leighlin.*] Letters on the state of Ireland; addressed by J.K.L. to a friend in England. 364p. *8°. Dublin & London, 1825.*

24398 DUNOYER, C. B. L'industrie et la morale considérées dans leurs rapports avec la liberté. 450p. *8°. Paris, 1825.*

24399 ENGLAND. *Parliament.* The evidence taken before the Select Committees of the Houses of Lords and Commons, appointed in the sessions of 1824 and 1825, to inquire into the state of Ireland. 580p. *8°. 1825. See also 1826.*

24400 —— —— *House of Commons.* Extracts from the minutes of evidence taken before the Select Committee of the House of Commons appointed to enquire into the state of Ireland. 1824–25. 201p. *8°. [1825] See also 1826.*

24401 ENSOR, G. A defence of the Irish, and the means of their redemption. [With an appendix.] 149, ixp. *8°. Dublin & London, 1825.*

24402 EVERETT, E. An oration [in commemoration of the Pilgrim Fathers] delivered at Plymouth December 22, 1824. 73p. *8°. Boston, 1825.*

24403 —— An oration [in commemoration of the Battle of Lexington] delivered at Concord, April the nineteenth, 1825. 56p. *8°. Boston, 1825.*

24404 FONTAINE, J. The philosophy of trade and manufactures: and its application to the relative situation of England and Ireland. 23p. *8°. 1825. *Another, the FWA copy, belonged to William Pare.*

24405 GORST, G. A narrative of an excursion to Ireland, by the Deputy Governor, two members of the Court, and the assistant secretary, of the Honorable Irish Society, of London. 1825...By the Deputy Governor. 103p. *4°. [1825] Presentation copy, with inscription, from the author to W. L. Newman.*

24406 H., R. T. One more specific for Ireland. Containing observations on the corn laws – tythes – taxes...

and proposed arrangement with respect to forfeited estates. 38p. *8°. 1825.*

24407 HALL, FRANCIS. Colombia: its present state, in respect of climate, soil, productions, population, government, commerce, revenue, manufactures, arts, literature, manners, education, and inducements to emigration. With itineraries, partly from Spanish surveys, partly from actual observation. 131p. *12°. Philadelphia, 1825. See also 1827.*

24408 HAMILTON, WALTER. A hand-book; or concise dictionary of terms used in the arts and sciences. 451p. *8°. 1825.*

24409 [HAZLITT, WILLIAM (1778–1830).] The spirit of the age: or contemporary portraits...Second edition. 408p. *12°. 1825.*

24410 HUSKISSON, W. Substance of two speeches, delivered in the House of Commons, on the 21st and 25th of March, 1825...respecting the colonial policy, and foreign commerce of the country. 88p. *8°. 1825.*

24411 JARDINE, J., *and others.* Report to Adam Duff, Esq., his Majesty's Sheriff-Depute of the County of Edinburgh, regarding the weights and measures heretofore in use...By James Jardine, engineer, Alexander Adie, optician and David Murray, accountant, all in Edinburgh. 7p. *4°. [Edinburgh,] 1825.*

24412 Ninety-third edition. **KENT'S** original London directory: 1825. Being an alphabetical list of 20,000 merchants, manufacturers, traders, &c. of London and the environs... 448p. *12°. [1825] See also 1740, 1804, 1816, 1826, 1827.*

24413 LANGFORD, R. An introduction to trade and business...A new edition. 120p. *12°. [1825]*

24414 McCULLOCH, JOHN R. A discourse on the rise, peculiar objects, and importance, of political economy: containing an outline of a course of lectures on the principles and doctrines of that science...Second edition, corrected...124p. *8°. Edinburgh & London, 1825. Bound with the copy of An essay on the question of reducing the interest of the National Debt, 1816, presented by the author to James Gibson Craig. For another edition, see 1824.*

24415 [——] Memoir of the life and writings of David Ricardo, Esq. M.P. 32p. *8°. 1825. The copy that belonged to S. J. Loyd, Baron Overstone, formerly among his papers. For these, see vol. III, MS. 804. Published as an introduction to The works of David Ricardo, in 1846 (q.v.).*

24416 —— Outlines of political economy: being a republication of the article upon that subject contained in the Edinburgh supplement to the Encyclopedia Britannica. Together with notes explanatory and critical, and a summary of the science. By Rev. John M'Vicar, A.M. 188p. *8°. New-York, 1825.*

24417 —— The principles of political economy: with a sketch of the rise and progress of the science. 423p. *8°. Edinburgh & London, 1825. Presentation copy, with an inscription, accompanying letter, and other manuscript material, from the author to Joseph Hume. See also 1829, 1830, 1831, 1843, 1849.*

24418 —— Syllabus of a course of lectures on political economy: to commence, in the City of London, on the 23d of March 1825. 20p. *8°. London & Edinburgh, 1825.*

24419 MACLEAN, J. H. Remarks on fiar prices and produce rents. 82p. *8°. Edinburgh, 1825.*

24420 [MARCET, J.] Entretiens sur l'économie politique, ou, éléments d'économie politique dégagée de ses abstractions; d'après Adam Smith, Say, Malthus, Mill, etc. 452p. *12°. Paris, 1825. Translated by Guillaume Prévost. For other editions, see 1816.*

24421 MILBURN, W. Oriental commerce; or the East India trader's complete guide; containing a geographical and nautical description of the maritime parts of India, China, Japan and neighbouring countries... With an account of their respective commerce, productions...and a description of the commodities imported... into Great Britain...[Edited] by Thomas Thornton. 586p. *8°.* 1825. *For another edition, see 1813.*

24422 *MILL, JAMES. Essays on I. Government, II. Jurisprudence, III. Liberty of the press, IV. Prisons and prison discipline, V. Colonies, VI. Law of nations, VII. Education...Reprinted...from the Supplement to the Encyclopædia Britannica. Not for sale. 32, 41, 34, 24, 33, 33, 46p. *8°.* [1825 ?] *The Goldsmiths' Library has the earlier printing of the* Article Government, *1821 (q.v.* POLITICS*), other copies of the 2nd, 3rd, 5th and 7th essays, and another issue of the 3rd. See also 1828.*

24423 MOLINA, G. I. Report of the soil and mineral productions of Chili, being an extract from the work of the Abbé Don. J. Ignatius Molina, originally published in Italian. 39p. *8°.* 1825.

24424 MORGAN, S., *Lady.* Absenteeism. 160p. *12°.* 1825.

24425 [MUDIE, R.] Babylon the Great: a dissection and demonstration of men and things in the British Capital. By the author of "The modern Athens"... 2 vols. *8°.* 1825.

24426 MUNDELL, A. The influence of interest and prejudice upon proceedings in Parliament stated and illustrated by what has been done in matters relative to education – religion – the poor – the corn laws – joint stock companies – the Bank of England and banking companies – and taxes. 210p. *8°.* 1825.

24427 NOTES of Mr. McCulloch's lecture on the wages of labour and the condition of the labouring people. 16p. *8°.* 1825. *Taken during a course of McCulloch's lectures on political economy, and published with his permission. *Another, the FWA copy, belonged to William Pare.*

24428 A few **OBSERVATIONS** on some topics in political economy. 39p. *8°.* 1825.

24429 PENNSYLVANIA SOCIETY FOR THE PROMOTION OF INTERNAL IMPROVEMENTS. [*Begin.*] Sir, We respectfully inform you that the delegates for the proposed Convention for Internal Improvements, have been appointed by the City and County of Philadelphia...[Signed: Mathew Carey and others, acting Committee, and Gerard Ralston, secretary. Dated: June 29, 1825.] *s.sh.4°. n.p.* [1825] [*Br.* 500]

24430 [PHILLIPS, SIR RICHARD ?] The hundred wonders of the world, and of the three kingdoms of nature, described according to the best and latest authorities, and illustrated by engravings. By the Rev. C. C. Clarke... Eighteenth edition. Enlarged and improved. 668p. *12°.* 1825.

24431 The **POST-OFFICE** London directory for 1825...By Critchett and Woods. The twenty-sixth edition. [With 'A new guide to stage-coaches, waggons, carts, vessels, &c. for 1825...The twenty-third edition...

By Critchett and Woods'.] 528, 135p. *12°.* [1825] *See also* 1805 (Post-Office annual directory), 1810, 1813, 1814, 1820 (Post Office London directory), 1823, 1830, 1832, 1834, 1836, 1841.

24432 [POWELL, JOHN, *statistical writer.*] Statistical illustrations of the territorial extent and population; commerce, taxation, consumption, insolvency, pauperism, and crime, of the British Empire. 88p. *8°.* 1825. *See also* 1827 *and, for an appendix to this edition,* 1826.

For le **PRODUCTEUR**, *1825–26, see vol.* III, *Periodicals list.*

24433 PYE, C. The stranger's guide to modern Birmingham, with an account of its public buildings and institutions, its show rooms and manufactories. With observations on the surrounding neighbourhood... 194p. *12°. Birmingham,* 1825. *See also* 1835.

24434 ROENTGEN, T. G. J. Recherches sur les sources de la prospérité publique. 48p. *8°. Paris,* 1825.

24435 ROOKE, J. Claim to the original publication of certain new principles in political economy, addressed in a letter to E. D. Davenport, Esq. 6p. *8°.* 1825. *Two copies, one inscribed 'From the author', the other the copy that belonged to Matthias Attwood.*

24436 [ROSS, J. C.] Principles of political economy, and of population: including an examination of Mr. Malthus's essay on those subjects. By John McIniscon, a fisherman... 2 vols. *8°.* 1825. *Re-issued, with the author's real name on the title-page, as An examination of opinions maintained in the "Essay on the principles of population", by Malthus; and in the "Elements of political economy", by Ricardo, in 1827 (q.v.).*

24437 The **ROYAL KALENDAR**, and court register, for England, Scotland, Ireland, and the colonies, for...1825, including a...list of the seventh Imperial Parliament, summoned to meet...in April, 1820. 116p. *12°. Jamaica,* [1825] *For other editions, see* 1779.

24438 SANDERS, C. K. A series of tables, in which the weights and measures of France are reduced to the English standard. 109p. *8°.* 1825.

24439 *SINCLAIR, SIR JOHN, *Bart.* ⟨Sketch for consideration.⟩ The code of political economy, founded on the basis of political researches...Chapter III. The fine arts. 25p. *8°. n.p.* [c. 1825] *With a manuscript note on the title-page, 'A private communication'. The FWA copy that belonged to William Pare, with his manuscript notes. For Chapter I, see* 1821.

24440 SMITH, ADAM. The works of Adam Smith, LL.D., F.R.S. With a life of the author [and 'A short view of the doctrine of Smith, compared with that of the French economists. Translated from the French of M. Garnier']... 5 vols. *12°.* 1825. *For other editions, see* 1812.

24441 SMITHERS, H. Liverpool, its commerce, statistics, and institutions; with a history of the cotton trade. 461p. *4°. Liverpool & London,* 1825.

24442 STATE of Ireland. Letters from Ireland, on the present political, religious, & moral state of that country. Republished from the "Courier" newspaper, with emendations & notes. 86p. *8°. London & Dublin,* 1825.

24443 VERRI, P., *Conte.* Scritti inediti. 244p. *8°. Londra,* 1825.

24444 WHILLIER, T. A general directory to all the counties, hundreds...cities...parishes...hamlets...in

England: with the population and areas of the several counties, alphabetically arranged... 347p. *8°*. 1825.

24445 WHITE, George (*fl.* 1823–1825). A digest of the evidence in the first [and second] Report from the Select Committee on the state of Ireland. 302p. *8°*. 1825.

24446 WILSON, Robert, *of Hawick.* A sketch of the history of Hawick: including some account of the manners and character of the inhabitants; with occasional observations. To which is subjoined a short essay, in reply to Doctor Chalmers on pauperism and the poor-laws. 355p. *12°*. *Hawick,* 1825. *See also* 1841.

AGRICULTURE

24447 ADAMS, afterwards **RAWSON,** Sir William (1783–1827). The actual state of the Mexican mines, and the reasonable expectations of the shareholders of the Anglo-Mexican Mine Association, being the substance of a letter addressed to the directors of that company; with a supplement, containing additional data, confirmed by recent intelligence from Mexico; and an appendix of original Mexican documents. 87p. *8°*. 1825.

24448 —— The present operations and future prospects of the Mexican mine associations analysed. By the evidence of official documents, English and Mexican. And the national advantages expected from joint stock companies, considered; in a letter to the Right Hon. George Canning. 88p. *8°*. 1825.

24449 BILLINGTON, W. A series of facts, hints, observations, and experiments on the different modes of raising young plantations of oaks... with remarks upon the fencing, draining, pruning, and training young trees ...With hints and experimental remarks upon fruit trees ... 330p. *8°*. *London & Newcastle upon Tyne,* 1825.

24450 BLACKBURN, James. Observations on the recovery of land from the sea, in connexion with the National Inclosure Company... Second edition, with additions. 43p. *8°*. 1825.

24451 BOSSON, A. Second mémoire en réponse à cette question: Quels sont les changemens que peut occasioner le déboisement de forêts considérables sur les contrées et communes adjacentes... ? Pour le concours de 1825, et qui a obtenu l'accessit et la médaille d'argent. 22p. *4°*. *Bruxelles,* 1825.

24452 COBBETT, W. The woodlands: or, a treatise on the preparing of ground for planting... Describing the usual growth and size and the uses of each sort of tree... [344]p. *8°*. 1825.

24453 DANDOLO, V., *Conte.* The art of rearing silkworms. Translated from the work of Count Dandolo. 365p. *12°*. 1825.

24454 [DISRAELI, B., *Earl of Beaconsfield.*] An inquiry into the plans, progress, and policy of the American mining companies. 88p. *8°*. 1825.

24455 [——] Second edition. 88p. *8°*. 1825. *The Agar Ellis copy.*

24456 [——] Lawyers and legislators: or, notes on the American mining companies. 99p. *8°*. 1825.

24457 ENGLAND. *Commissioners for the Herring Fishery.* Additional instructions for an officer of the fishery, under the Acts 48th Geo. III. cap. 110, 55th Geo. III. cap. 94, and 5th Geo. IV. cap. 64. 16p. *8°*. *Edinburgh,* 1825. *The instructions issued to Hugh Sutherland, Officer of the Fishery at Northsunderland [sic], with his name filled in in manuscript.*

24458 —— —— Regulations for the cod and ling fishery made by the Commissioners for the Herring Fishery, in virtue of the Acts 1 Geo. IV. cap. 103, and 5 Geo. IV. cap. 64. 21p. *8°*. *Edinburgh,* 1825.

24459 ENGLISH, H. A general guide to the companies formed for working foreign mines, with their prospectuses, amount of capital...And an appendix, showing their progress since their formation... 106p. *8°*. 1825. *For continuations of this work, see* 1826 *and* 1827 (FINANCE).

24460 An **ESSAY** on the rent of land. 54p. *8°*. *London & Edinburgh,* 1825.

24461 The practical **FARMER,** or every landlord his own steward; containing directions for the management of every variety of soil; the mode of preserving turnips from the fly and anberry, and wheat from smut...By a Norfolk farmer. 250p. *12°*. 1825. *From the library of William Wyndham Grenville, Baron Grenville, with his arms on the upper and lower covers.*

24462 HARBORD, E., *Baron Suffield.* Considerations on the game laws. 107p. *8°*. [*London &*] *Norwich,* [1825]

24463 —— Second edition. 105p. *8°*. [*London &*] *Norwich,* [1825]

24464 HAYES, W. A letter to the Right Hon. Robert Peel...on the law of real property, and the practice of conveyancing. 48p. *8°*. *London & Dublin,* 1825.

24465 LASTEYRIE DU SAILLANT, C. P. de, *Comte de Lasteyrie.* Des fosses à conserver les grains et de la manière de les construire. 32p. *8°*. [*Paris,* 1825 ?]

24466 LETTER to John Taylor, Esq. respecting the conduct of the Directors of the Real del Monte Company, relative to the mines of Tlalpuxahua. [Signed: A merchant. With a statement issued by the Association for working the Mines of Tlalpuxahua and others in Mexico, dated: January 20, 1825.] 20, 4p. *8°*. 1825.

24467 LOUDON, J. C. An encyclopædia of agriculture; comprising the theory and practice of the valuation, transfer...and management of landed property; and the cultivation...of the...productions of agriculture... 1226p. *8°*. 1825. *See also* 1831, 1835.

24468 MEXICAN MINING ASSOCIATION. United Mexican Mining Association. Report of the Court of Directors addressed to the shareholders. [Dated: 7th Sept. 1825. With an appendix.] 55, xivp. *8°*. 1825. *See also* 1826, 1827.

24469 MOREAU DE JONNÈS, A. Premier mémoire en réponse à la question proposée par l'Académie Royale de Bruxelles: Quels sont les changemens que peut occasioner le déboisement de forêts considérables sur les contrées et communes adjacentes... ? 207p. *4°*. *Bruxelles,* 1825.

24470 NORTH, Hon. Roger. A treatise on fish and fish-ponds... 92p. *4°*. [1825 ?]

24471 POWLES, J. D. A letter to Alexander Baring, Esq. M.P. on the subject of some observations reported to have been made by him in the House of Commons, on the 16th March, 1825, in relation to the foreign mining associations. 21p. *8°.* 1825.

24472 REDEMPTION of the Land Tax. [The official notice sent to owners or occupiers of estates.] 4p. *4°.* [*London, 1825 ?*]

24473 Sur le **RÉSULTAT** moral de l'entreprise du desséchement des marais de la Linth... 34p. *8°. Genève & Paris, 1825. Presentation copy from the anonymous author to William Allen.*

24474 ROBINSON, S. Remarks on the culture and management of flax; proposed as a means to assist the Irish poor, by giving them employment: with the memorial of a scutch miller, complaining of the present mode of preparing flax...which drew forth from Peter Besnard...strong animadversions and assertions, refuted by a variety of facts... 33p. *8°. Dublin, 1825. For another edition, see 1824.*

24475 SINCLAIR, GEORGE (1786–1834). Hortus gramineus Woburnensis: or, an account of the results of experiments on the produce and nutritive qualities of different grasses...used as the food of the more valuable domestic animals...Second edition. 438p. *8°.* 1825. *A much enlarged version of the work originally entitled* An account of the results of experiments on...different grasses, *1813 (q.v.).*

24476 SINCLAIR, SIR JOHN, *Bart.* Defence of the landed and farming interests, pointing out, the ruinous effects of any alteration in our present system of corn laws, and the important changes to which it would lead, in the frame of our government. 14p. *8°. Edinburgh & London, 1825. With an accompanying letter of presentation from the author to James Gibson Craig, for which see vol. III. A.L. 296.*

24477 SPAIN. *Laws, etc.* The ordinances of the mines of New Spain; translated from the original Spanish. With observations upon the mines and mining associations. By Charles Thomson. 76, 196p. *8°.* 1825. *The copy that belonged to James Colquhoun, with his book-plate. For other editions, see 1783.*

24478 TAYLOR, JOHN (1779–1863). Statements respecting the profits of mining in England considered in relation to the prospects of mining in Mexico. In a letter to Thomas Fowell Buxton... 56p. *8°.* 1825.

24479 A **TREATISE** on milk, as an article of the first necessity to the health and comfort of the community. A review of the different methods of production; and suggestions respecting the best means of improving its quality, reducing its price, and increasing its consumption. 122p. *8°.* 1825.

CORN LAWS

24480 BROWN, WILLIAM K. A letter to the Right Honourable George Canning...relative to a free trade in corn in Great Britain. 76p. *8°. Canterbury, 1825.*

24481 COMBER, W. T. [*Endorsed:*] Corn laws. Graduated scale of duties on consumption of foreign wheat, proposed by Mr. Comber. 7p. *fol.* [1825] *The title on p. 1 reads: Explanation of Mr. Comber's graduated scale of duties on consumption of foreign wheat.*

24482 [——?] An examination of the resolutions of a meeting of the merchants, bankers, ship-owners, manufacturers and traders of the City of London, held the 13th day of April, 1825...to consider the expediency of petitioning Parliament for a revision of the corn laws. 83p. *8°.* 1825. *Attributed to Comber in a pencil note on the half-title.*

24483 [**DAVENPORT,** E. D.] The corn question; in a letter addressed to the Right Hon. W. Huskisson. By one of the proscribed class. 33p. *8°.* 1825.

24484 *[**DRUMMOND,** H.] Cheap corn best for farmers, proved in a letter to George Holme Sumner, Esq. M.P. for the county of Surrey. By one of his constituents. 37p. *8°.* 1825. *The copy that belonged to George Grote. See also 1826.*

24485 [**GRAY,** CHARLES, *of Carse.*] Thoughts on the corn laws; by a farmer. 3p. *4°. Edinburgh,* [1825] *Two copies, each bound with four other works by the author, and presented, with inscriptions by him, one to 'Thos. Graham Henbury(?) Esq.', the other to 'the Hble W. Maude'.*

24486 LETTER to a Member of Parliament, on the contemplated changes in the corn laws. 20p. *8°. Edinburgh, 1825. Sometimes attributed to David Low.*

24487 WHITMORE, W. W. Substance of a speech delivered in the House of Commons on the 28th April, 1825...respecting the corn laws. 32p. *8°.* 1825.

POPULATION

24488 *DAVIES, G. Tables of life contingencies; containing the rate of mortality among the members of the Equitable Society, and the values of life annuities, reversions, &c. computed therefrom: together with a more extensive scale of premiums for life assurances, deduced from the Northampton rate of mortality, than any hitherto published... xl, [78]p. *8°.* 1825. *The copy that belonged to Augustus De Morgan.*

24489 SUMNER, J. B., *Archbishop of Canterbury.* A treatise on the records of the Creation...with particular reference to the Jewish history, and to the consistency of the principle of population with the wisdom and goodness of the Deity...Fourth edition, corrected. 2 vols. *8°.* 1825. *For other editions, see 1818.*

TRADES & MANUFACTURES

24490 BRUNTON, R. A compendium of mechanics; or, text book for engineers, mill-wrights, machine-makers, founders, smiths, &c. Containing practical rules and tables connected with the steam engine, water wheel, force pump, and mechanics in general...Second edition, improved and enlarged. 148p. *12°. Glasgow, London, &c.,* 1825. *See also* 1842.

24491 The CABINET of useful arts and manufactures, designed for the perusal of young persons. 180p. *18°. Dublin,* 1825.

24492 CLARK, N. G., *and others.* A scale of prices for job work, on old ships...compiled, by Nathaniel G. Clark, Richard W. Marks, James Mallett, John Purdy, Thomas J. Howes, Richard Tucker. For the shipwrights of the river Thames. 164p. *8°.* 1825.

24493 DEBRAINE-HELFENBERGER,   .
Manuel du distillateur et du liquoriste, ouvrage ou l'on trouvera les principes de l'art du distillateur fabricant d'eaux-de-vie...l'application de la distillation à l'agriculture et aux arts du parfumeur, du confiseur et du liquoriste... 428p. *24°. Paris,* 1825.

24494 EDINBURGH, GLASGOW, AND ALLOA GLASS COMPANY. Contract of copartnery of the Edinburgh, Glasgow, and Alloa Glass Company. Instituted 1825. 16p. *8°. Edinburgh,* 1825.

24495 ENGLAND. *Parliament.* Enquête faite par ordre du Parlement d'Angleterre, pour constater les progrès de l'industrie en France et dans les autres pays du Continent. Présenté à la Chambre du Commerce de Paris. 359p. *8°. Paris,* 1825. *Translated and presented by Raymond Balthazar Maiseau.*

24496 JULLIEN, A. The wine merchant's companion and butler's manual, containing the best information on the selection and management of French wines. From the French [by W. H. Hilton]. 107p. *12°.* 1825.

24497 LEWIS, JAMES H. The best method of pen-making, illustrated by practical observations on the art of writing. To which are added, directions for holding the pen properly... 32p. *8°. [London &] Manchester,* [1825]

24498 LINGARD, J. J. H. A comparative view of the beauty, durability, and economy of the invulnerable oil paint, prepared by John Lingard, Jun. Bedford Colour-Works, Southampton-Street...with his remarks on the destructive and baleful properties of tar, used as a preventive against the decomposition of wood, iron, and stone, exposed to the atmosphere. 16p. *8°.* 1825. *The Agar Ellis copy.*

24499 LIST of prices allowed for the making of tin-plate wares, as arranged by committees appointed from the Manufacturers & Journeymen Tin-Plate Workers of Glasgow, and agreed to at a meeting...held in the Trades' Hall, the 16th day of December [1824]... [66]p. *8°. Glasgow,* 1825.

24500 LONDON. Livery Companies. *Clockmakers.* Charter and bye laws of the Worshipful Company of Clock Makers, of the City of London, incorporated 1631; 7th Charles 1st. 104p. *8°. [London,]* 1825.

24501 MACKENZIE, COLIN. One thousand processes in manufactures and experiments in chemistry; collected from the best modern authorities, British and foreign...The fifth edition. 646p. *8°.* 1825.

24502 [MEIKLEHAM, R. S.] A descriptive history of the steam engine. By Robert Stuart, Esq. civil engineer ...The third edition. 228p. *8°.* 1825. *For other editions, see* 1824.

24503 NICHOLSON, JOHN (*fl.* 1825). The operative mechanic, and British machinist; being a practical display of the manufactories and mechanical arts of the United Kingdom. 795p. *8°. London & Dublin,* 1825.

24504 —— Second edition. 795p. *8°.* 1825. *See also* 1826 *A supplement was published by Charles Taylor in 1829 (q.v.).*

24505 NICHOLSON, P. An improved and enlarged edition of Nicholson's New carpenter's guide. Being a complete book of lines, for carpenters, joiners, and workmen in general, on methods entirely new, founded on geometrical principles...[Edited by John Bowen. With a memoir of the author.] 121p. *4°.* 1825. *For another edition, see* 1805, *and for a continuation,* 1826.

24506 RENOUARD, A. C. Traité des brevets d'invention, de perfectionnement et d'importation; suivi d'un appendice contenant le texte des lois et réglemens rendus en France; un précis de la législation anglaise; les lois des États-Unis de l'Amérique Septentrionale et des cortès d'Espagne. 501p. *8°. Paris,* 1825.

24507 ROSE, HENRY. Manual labour, versus brass and iron: reflections in defence of the body of cotton spinners, occasioned by a perusal of the description of Mr. Roberts's self-acting mule. 8p. *8°. [Manchester,* 1825]

24508 SUPPLEMENT to the cabinet-makers book of prices. [Drawn up by the Journeymen Cabinet-Makers, with an introduction dated 'July 8, 1825'.] 44p. *8°. n.p.* [1825] *For the original work, see* 1805 (Edinburgh book of prices).

For **TILLOCH**, A. The mechanic's oracle, *see* vol. III, *Periodicals list,* Mechanic's oracle.

COMMERCE

24509 BILLIET,   . Du commerce, des douanes, et du système des prohibitions; considéré dans ses rapports avec les intérêts respectifs des nations...Augmenté par M. Marie du Mesnil. 151p. *8°. Paris,* 1825.

24510 CLARKE, HENRY. Application for mandamus, and proceedings in the Court of King's Bench, H. Clarke, Esq. versus the Mayor and Town Clerk of the Borough of Boston, relative to the tolls, &c. [With 'Appendix. The correspondence referred to in the affidavits of the Mayor and Town Clerk' and 'Notes'.] 44, 14p. *8°. Stamford* [& *Boston,* 1825]

24511 Free **COMMERCE** with India. A letter addressed to the Right Honourable President of the Board of Trade, with reference to his late propositions in Parliament for the improvement of the colonial mercantile policy of Great Britain. By a Madras civil servant. 16p. *8°. 1825.*

24512 **FRANCE.** *Bureau de Commerce et des Colonies.* Documens relatifs au commerce des nouveaux états de l'Amérique, communiqués par le Bureau... aux principales chambres de commerce de France. (Publiés par le Journal du Commerce.) 100p. *12°. Paris, 1825.*

24513 **GEORGE,** JOHN. A view of the existing law, affecting unincorporated joint stock companies. 74p. *8°. 1825.*

24514 —— A new edition with additional matter on the repeal of the Bubble Act, and the new power conferred on the Crown, by Stat. 6 Geo. 4, c. 91, on granting charters of incorporation. 110p. *8°. 1825.*

24515 **GRANVILLE,** A. B. A letter to the Right Honble. W. Huskisson, M.P. President of the Board of Trade, on the Quarantine Bill. [Reprinted from *The Times.* On the injurious effects of relaxations in British quarantine laws on trade and shipping.] 16p. *8°. 1825. The Agar Ellis copy.*

24516 **KEELE,** G. Seventh edition. The excise trader's guide: containing an abstract of the new Act of Parliament [6 Geo. IV, c. 81]... relative to excise licences: with useful directions for new traders. 33p. *8°. London, Edinburgh, &c., 1825.*

24517 —— Eighth edition. The excise guide for dealers in spirits, innholders and publicans, containing explanations of the Acts of Parliament, and some useful observations relative to their business. 40p. *8°. 1825. This edition is completely reorganized and rewritten.*

24518 **KIRKCALDY AND LONDON SHIPPING COMPANY.** Contract of copartnery of the Kirkcaldy and London Shipping Company, instituted 21st March, 1825. 28p. *8°. Kirkcaldy, 1825.*

24519 A **LETTER** addressed to a Member of Parliament, in reply to one of inquiry, respecting the commercial relations of Great Britain with Russia. By a Russia-merchant. 27p. *8°. 1825.*

24520 **LEVANT COMPANY.** Proceedings of the Levant Company, respecting the surrender of their charters, 1825. 48[46]p. *8°. 1825. Inscribed in manuscript: The H^{ble} Mr Agar Ellis from Ld Grenville.*

24521 **LIPS,** A. Ueber den gegenwärtig tiefen Stand der Getraide-Preise in Deutschland, ihr nothwendig immer tieferes Sinken, die Ursachen dieser Erscheinung und die Mittel, sie zu heben. Ein Versuch... 72p. *8°. Nürnberg, 1825.*

24522 **MOREAU DE JONNÈS,** A. Le commerce au dix-neuvième siècle... 2 vols. *8°. Paris, 1825. The copy that belonged to the Société de Lecture de Genève.*

24523 **PASLEY,** SIR C. W. An inquiry into the system of general or commissariat contracts, for supplying His Majesty's forces in Great Britain with bread and meat, as compared with that of regimental purchases: with a recommendation, that the former shall be entirely abolished. 232p. *8°. Chatham, 1825.*

24524 **PINNOCK,** W. Pinnock's catechisms. A catechism of trade and commerce, intended to lay the basis of practical commercial knowledge in the youthful mind; by an easy explanation of its fundamental principles, and an accurate definition of the terms and customs applicable to business in general. Fifth edition. 72p. *12°. 1825. With a second, engraved title-page, dated 1823, which reads: Pinnock's Catechism of trade & commerce.*

24525 **RODET,** D. L. Du commerce extérieur et de la question d'un entrepôt à Paris. 199p. *8°. Paris, 1825.*

24526 **STARK,** JAMES. A treatise on the law of partnership. 369p. *8°. Edinburgh & London, 1825.*

24527 **TRADUCÇÃO** de hum requerimento dirigido ao governor de S.M.B. por alguns negociantes inglezes da cidade do Porto contra a Companhia Geral do Alto Douro; e observações de hum curioso sobre a materia. 39p. *8°. Porto, 1825. The English merchants' petition and the Portuguese translation are printed in parallel columns.*

24528 **UNITED STATES OF AMERICA.** Congress. *House of Representatives.* 18th Congress, 2d Session. ⟨50⟩ Letter from the Secretary of the Treasury, transmitting the annual statement of the district tonnage of the United States, to the 31st December, 1823. January 14, 1825... 6p. *8°. Washington, 1825.*

24529 **VERPLANCK,** G. C. An essay on the doctrine of contracts; being an inquiry how contracts are affected in law and morals, by concealment, error, or inadequate price. 234p. *8°. New-York, [1825]*

24530 [**WALSH,** ROBERT (1772–1852).] Account of the Levant Company; with some notices of the benefits conferred... by its officers, in promoting the cause of humanity, literature, and the fine arts; &c.&c. 64p. *8°. 1825.*

COLONIES

24531 [**BUXTON,** SIR THOMAS F., *Bart.*] Observations on the West-India Company Bill as printed and read a second time on Tuesday, March 29, 1825. 32p. *8°. 1825.*

24532 **CAPE OF GOOD HOPE.** Statement of the population and the quantity of lands, cattle, &ct. at the Cape of Good Hope from 1806 to 1824 inclusive. [With 'Summary' dated '30th May 1825'.] [28]p. *fol. n.p. [1825] Printed forms filled in in manuscript. The 'Summary' is entirely in manuscript, with manuscript additions for 1825 and 1826. Printed, without the additions, as Document V, no. 8 in* Documents referred to in the reports of the Commission of Inquiry upon the government and finances

of the Cape of Good Hope... ordered, by the House of Commons, to be printed, 30 May 1827.

24533 **DOYLE,** SIR JOHN, *Bart.* Substance of the speech of General Sir John Doyle, Bart. at the India House upon the Hyderabad papers, on... March 4, 1825. 77p. *8°. 1825. With a letter from the author, a presentation inscription to George Agar Ellis, Baron Dover, and manuscript notes in the author's hand.*

24534 **EAST INDIA COMPANY.** Correspondence of the Honourable Court of Directors of the East India Company, and of the Governor General in Council, respecting the permanent settlement of the land revenue. 38p. *8°*. 1825.

24535 —— Dissent from the resolution of the Court of Directors of the 20th July 1825; under which certain documents were added to the collection of Oude Papers... [Signed: Robert Campbell, H. Lindsay, John Morris.] Printed by order of the Court of Proprietors, of 28th September, 1825. 8p. *fol.* [*London,*] 1825.

24536 ENGLAND. Parliament. *House of Commons.* An authentic report of the debate in the House of Commons, June the 23d, 1825, on Mr. Buxton's motion relative to the demolition of the Methodist chapel and mission house in Barbadoes, and the expulsion of Mr. Shrewsbury, a Wesleyan missionary, from that island. 119p. *8°*. 1825. *The copy that belonged to Stephen Lushington.*

24537 GRANT, P. W. Considerations on the state of the colonial currency and foreign exchanges, at the Cape of Good Hope: comprehending also, some statements relative to the population, agriculture, commerce and statistics of the Colony. 190p. *8°*. *Cape Town,* 1825.

24538 HALLIBURTON, Sir B. Observations upon the importance of the North American Colonies to Great-Britain. By an old inhabitant of British America. 34p. *8°*. *Halifax* [*Nova Scotia*], [1825] *The copy that belonged to Sir Francis Freeling (1764–1836).*

24539 HASTINGS, F. R., *Marquis of Hastings.* Comments excited by the conduct of the chairman at a meeting of proprietors of the East India Company, on the 11th February 1825. 249p. *8°*. *Malta,* 1825. *With an inscription on the title-page, 'Ellenborough from the Marchioness of Bute Nov. 22 1857'.*

24540 HOWISON, J. Sketches of Upper Canada... to which are added practical details for the information of emigrants of every class; and some recollections of the United States of America...Third edition. 353p. *8°*. *Edinburgh & London,* 1825.

24541 The **JAMAICA ALMANACK** for the year 1825...[With 'Return of proprietors, properties, &c.&c. given in to the vestries, for the March quarter 1824'.] 124, 140p. *12°*. *Kingston, Jamaica,* [1825]

24542 M'QUEEN, J. The colonial controversy, containing a refutation of the calumnies of the anticolonists; the state of Hayti, Sierra Leone, India, China, Cochin China, Java, &c....the production of sugar, &c. and the state of the free and slave labourers in those countries; fully considered, in a series of letters, addressed to the Earl of Liverpool; with a supplementary letter to Mr. Macaulay. 223p. *8°*. *Glasgow,* 1825.

24543 MUSSON, J. P. A letter to ministers, suggesting improvements in the trade of the West Indies and the Canadas; in which are incidentally considered, the merits of the East and West India sugar question, reasons in favour of the independence of Spanish America, and a liberal and practical plan of forwarding slave-emancipation. 109p. *8°*. 1825.

24544 RUMBOLD, Sir W., *Bart.* A letter to the Court of Directors of the East-India Company; on the subject of the pecuniary transactions of Messrs. William Palmer and Co. with the Government of His Highness the Nizam [of Hyderabad]. 125p. *fol. n.p.* [1825]

24545 STROMBOM, I. A statement of the origin, fluctuation, and great depression in value of the government paper-currency at the Cape of Good Hope. Together with a letter, &c.&c. addressed to the Rt. Hon. the Earl of Bathurst... 40p. *8°*. [*London,*] 1825.

24546 TUCKER, H. St. G. A review of the financial situation of the East-India Company, in 1824. 244p. *8°*. 1825.

FINANCE

24547 ALLLEGATIONS [*sic*] of the necessity of an equitable loan bank, to correct the present oppressive system of lending money on pledge, by pawnbrokers & others. With proofs thereof, extracted from the evidence taken before a Committee of the House of Lords. By a friend to fair dealing. 57p. *12°*. [1825]

24548 The **BANK OF ENGLAND** case, under Marsh and Company's commission, briefly stated and discussed. By a solicitor. 36p. *8°*. 1825.

24549 The **BANK OF ENGLAND** claim, under Marsh and Company's commission, further discussed, in reply to Mr. Wilkinson's report upon the facts, and, to a letter, to the author, upon the law of the case. By the author of "The Bank of England case, under Marsh and Co.'s commission, briefly stated and discussed." 72p. *8°*. 1825.

24550 BANK OF MAURITIUS. Prospectus of the establishment of a bank at Port Louis, for the colonies of Mauritius, Bourbon, and dependencies; with the support and under the immediate patronage of government. [Published, with an introduction, by Sir Robert Townsend Farquhar, Governor of Mauritius.] 27p. *8°*. 1825.

24551 BECHER, John T. Tables, shewing the... contributions to be paid, the allowances to be granted, and the method of calculating...the value of the assurances, effected by members of friendly societies, together with a system of book-keeping, recommended for the use of such institutions. 18, [36], 24p. *8°*. *Newark & London,* 1825.

24552 BENTHAM, J. Indications respecting Lord Eldon, including history of the pending judges'-salary-raising measure. 85p. *8°*. 1825. *For the postscript, see 1826.*

24553 —— Observations on Mr. Secretary Peel's House of Commons speech, 21st March, 1825, introducing his Police Magistrates' Salary Raising Bill...Also on the announced Judges' Salary Raising Bill, and the pending County Courts Bill. 62p. *8°*. 1825.

24554 [BONNARDIN, .] Gardons nos cinq pour cent! Avis aux rentiers, par un de leurs compagnons d'infortune, qui ne veut pas croire que quatre francs soient préférables à cinq; contenant en outre la loi sur la conversion des rentes et l'Ordonnance du Roi y relative. 22p. *8°*. *Paris,* 1825.

24555 —— Oraison funèbre de l'infortuné Trois pour cent, mort à la fleur de son âge; prononcée par M. Bonnardin, rentier converti, faisant suite à la brochure intitulée Gardons nos cinq pour cent! Deuxième édition. 15p. *8°*. *Paris,* 1825.

24556 BRESSON, J. Des fonds publics français et étrangers, et des opérations de la Bourse de Paris... Cinquième édition, revue et augmentée... 247p. *12⁰. Paris*, 1825. *See also* 1843.

24557 CHESTER, E. Sketch of a Bill intended to be submitted to Parliament, in lieu of the Bill recently proposed by Lord Viscount Althorp, "for the more easy and speedy recovery of small debts;" with observations thereon. 23p. *8⁰*. 1825.

24558 COBBETT, W. Gold for ever! Real causes of the fall of the Funds: also wholesome advice to holders of Funds, scrip, shares, and all sorts of paper-money. 12p. *12⁰*. [1825]

24559 COLDWELL, T. Coldwell's tables, for reducing Irish money into British currency; arranged on a new plan and calculated according to the 2d, 5th and 13th sections of the Act for assimilating the currency, to commence on the 5th January, 1826. Second edition, with... additions and improvements. 60p. *24⁰. Cork*, 1825.

24560 COMPAGNIE D'ASSURANCES GÉ-NÉRALES. Compagnie d'Assurances générales contre les risques maritimes et de navigation intérieure. Rapport de M. de Gourcuff, Directeur. 24p. *4⁰. n.p.* [1825] *See also* 1821, 1823, 1824, 1827.

24561 *CORBAUX, F. The doctrine of compound interest, illustrated and applied to perpetual annuities, to those for terms of years certain, to life-annuities...with new and compendious tables...and other original tables, expressing...the probabilities and the expectations of life at each age... 140, 53p. *8⁰*. 1825. *The copy that belonged to Augustus De Morgan.*

24562 CRUTTWELL, R. A treatise on the state of the currency at the present time, 1824–5...showing the numberless evils...resulting from our present...money-standard; recommending also a plan for fixing the same in future upon a permanently reduced gold-scale of continental prices... 594p. *8⁰. London, Oxford, &c.*, 1825. *The copy that belonged to Sir Robert Peel.*

24563 DESMARAIS, C. Épitre au Trois pour cent [in verse]...Deuxième édition. 15p. *8⁰. Paris*, 1825.

24564 DUBOIS, T. K. Tariff, or rates of duties, payable on goods, wares, and merchandise, imported into the United States of America, after the 30th of June, 1824. Exhibiting, also, in an adjoining column, the former rates of duty. To which is added, forms, for the direction of merchants...And an appendix, containing several important laws of the United States, and State of New-York, relating to commerce... 96p. *12⁰. New-York*, 1825.

24565 ENGLAND. *Laws, etc.* Copy of Bubble Act, 6 Geo. I. c. 18. Notes relating to præmunire. Draft Bill proposed to be introduced by Mr. Peter Moore for the amendment of the Bubble Act, and for the prevention of frauds in the establishment of joint stock companies. 72p. *8⁰*. [*London,*] 1825.

24566 An ESSAY on the management and mis-management of the currency. By the author of "An essay on the rent of land". 42p. *8⁰. London & Edinburgh*, 1825.

24567 An EXAMINATION of the present modes of granting temporary loans on pledges, by pawnbrokers, and of those proposed by the London Equitable Loan Bank Company...With a few remarks on the objections which have been urged by pawnbrokers and others against the Equitable Loan Bank. By a retired pawnbroker. 92p. *8⁰*. 1825.

24568 [EXTER, J.] Causes of the present depression in our money market, with a suggestion for its relief. 22p. *8⁰*. [*London,*] 1825.

24569 —— [Another edition.] 22p. *8⁰*. 1825.

24570 GANILH, C. De la science des finances, et du ministère de M. le Comte de Villèle. 295p. *8⁰. Paris*, 1825.

24571 GRANT, ALEXANDRE. Observations sur le papier-monnoie de la Russie. 83p. *8⁰. Londres*, 1825.

24572 HANDLEIDING voor de houders van kans-billetten, ter berekening van hun belang tegen de vijfentwintigjarige loting. 30p. *8⁰. Haarlem*, 1825.

24573 [HÉLOT, .] Dissertation sur le système de Law; son identité avec le système actuel de l'Angleterre et avec celui que veut faire adopter le Ministère français. 44p. *8⁰. Paris*, 1825.

24574 An ILLUSTRATION of Mr. Joplin's views on currency, and plan for its improvement; together with observations applicable to the present state of the money-market; in a series of letters [signed: An economist, and addressed to the editor of The Courier during 1823]. 120p. *8⁰*. 1825.

24575 IRELAND. *Treasury.* Tables for converting Irish into British currency...prepared under the orders of the...Vice Treasurer by Mr. Thomas Haffield... 235p. *8⁰. Dublin*, 1825.

24576 *JUVIGNY, J.-B. Coup-d'œil sur les assurances sur la vie des hommes, suivi de la comparaison des deux modes d'assurances, mutuelles et à primes, contre l'incendie; terminé par une notice historique...sur la Caisse Lafarge. Quatrième édition; revue, corrigée et considérablement augmentée. 148p. *8⁰. Paris*, 1825. *The copy that belonged to Augustus De Morgan.*

24577 KING, EDWARD (*fl.* 1825–1845). An essay on the creation and advantages of a cultural and commercial triform stock, as a counter-fund to the National Debt, and for the unlimited investment of capital at £5. per cent. per annum... 112p. *8⁰*. 1825.

24578 LEBRUN, I. F. T. L'émigration indemnisée par l'ancien régime et depuis la restauration...Deuxième édition, corrigée et augmentée. 192p. *8⁰. Paris*, 1825.

24579 A LIST of joint-stock companies, the proposals for which are now, or have been lately, before the public. From "The Monthly Repository of theology and general literature," February, 1825. 8p. *8⁰*. 1825.

24580 LONDON. *Court of Common Council.* [*Endorsed:*] A report of the proceedings in the Court of Common Council...relative to the Equitable Loan Bank Company, March 11, 1825. 4p. *fol. n.p.* [1825]

24581 —— ——- A statement of the produce and expenditure of the City's estate, for the year ending the 31st of December, 1824. To which is subjoined the balance remaining in Mr. Chamberlain's hands...of all the several accounts kept in the Chamber of London. [With 'A statement of the produce and expenditure of the Bridge-House estates, for the year ending the 31st of December, 1824'. Ordered to be printed and circulated 26 May 1825.] 71, 15p. *fol.* 1825. *See also* 1828.

24582 [McKONOCHIE, J.] Thoughts on a poll-tax. 20p. *8⁰. Edinburgh*, 1825. *Presentation copy, with a letter from the author to an unnamed recipient.*

24583 MARSHALL, JAMES, *accountant*. Report to the Directors of the Provincial Bank of Ireland, suggesting a plan for commencing and conducting the business of said bank. 70p. *8°*. 1825.

24584 [MENDHAM, J.] Taxatio Papalis; being an account of the Tax-Books of the United Church and Court of modern Rome; or, of the Taxæ Cancellariæ Apostolicæ, and Taxæ Sacræ Pœnitentiariæ Apostolicæ. By Emancipatus. 63p. *8°*. 1825.

24585 MEXICO. *Congreso.* Report presented to the General Constituent Sovereign Congress of Mexico, by their Commissions upon the systems of finance and mines; on the inexpediency of augmenting the duties on the exportation of gold and silver. Translated from the Spanish. 19p. *8°*. 1825.

24586 —— —— *Senado.* Analysis of the Memorial presented by the Secretary of the Treasury, to the First Constitutional Congress of the United Mexican States: being the substance of a report of the Financial Committee of the Chamber of Senators... Translated from the official copy published in Mexico. 96p. *8°*. 1825.

24587 NATIONAL BANK OF SCOTLAND. Contract of copartnership of the National Bank of Scotland. [With a printed circular letter dated '23d September 1825', to shareholders, asking that the mandate on p. 2 should be completed and returned within 14 days.] 2p. *fol. n.p.* [1825] *Sent through the post to Dr. Benjamin Brown, 10 Nicholson Street, Edinburgh, and postmarked 'Sep. 24 1825'. With the mandate completed as requested.*

24588 [*Endorsed:*] **OBSERVATIONS** on the Bill for the regulation of banking partnerships in Ireland, as reprinted for the House of Commons...2nd May, 1825. 3p. *fol.* [*London,* 1825]

24589 O'CALLAGHAN, J. Usury or interest proved to be repugnant to the divine and ecclesiastical laws, and destructive to civil society. 176p. *12°*. 1825. *See also* 1828, 1834.

24590 The **PAWNBROKERS'** reply to the pretended fair and candid statement of the Equitable Loan Bank Company. April, 1825. 30p. *8°*. *Islington,* [1825]

24591 REASONS against the repeal of the usury laws. [Being an examination of Bentham's *Defence of usury*, and of the evidence laid before the Committee of the House of Commons, which reported in 1818.] 144p. *8°*. 1825.

24592 REMARKS on joint stock companies. By an old merchant. 100p. *8°*. 1825.

24593 ROBINSON, F. J., *Earl of Ripon*. Speech... on the financial situation of the country, on...the 28th of February, 1825. To which is added, an appendix, containing various accounts referred to. 59p. *8°*. 1825.

24594 ROMNEY, A. Three letters, on the speculative schemes of the present times, and the projected banks. Addressed to his cousin Richard in the country, by A. Romney. 50p. *8°*. *Edinburgh,* 1825.

24595 [RONALDSON, J.?] On paper money: its influence on national prosperity, and the happiness of the people. [The preface signed: A Bank stockholder.] 15p. *8°*. *Philadelphia,* 1825. *Attributed to Ronaldson on the authority of a contemporary manuscript note on the title-page. Also attributed to Laban Heath (Kress C1442).*

24596 SÉGUIN, A. De la nécessité de prescrire une règle positive pour l'emploi des sommes affectées à l'amortissement, dans le cas de l'adoption des projets ministériels sur la dette publique. 55p. *8°*. *Paris,* 1825.

24597 —— Memento, et barème de la perspective de notre avenir financier, en cas de naufrage au port. [With 'Plan extrait de l'ouvrage sur les finances, en 4 volumes in-8°'.] 28, 119p. *8°*. *Paris,* 1825.

24598 —— Moyen de parer aux principaux inconvéniens des projets ministériels sur les indemnités et sur la dette publique... 20p. *8°*. *Paris,* 1825.

24599 —— Observations sur la nouvelle conception financière présentée à la Chambre des Députés, par M. le Président du Conseil des Ministres, le 3 janvier 1825. 120p. *8°*. *Paris,* 1825.

24600 —— Observations sur le rapport fait au nom de la commission de la Chambre des Deputés chargée d'examiner le projet de loi sur la dette publique et l'amortissement. 38p. *8°*. *Paris,* 1825.

24601 —— Observations sur les discussions relatives aux indemnités et aux acquisitions de domaines nationaux. 15p. *8°*. *Paris,* 1825.

24602 —— Régulateur des rentes, ou guide et résultat des combinaisons et des speculations rentières qu'engendrera la loi sur la dette publique et l'amortissement; et considérations...sur les emprunts que pourroient nécessiter...les besoins...de la nouvelle ère financière de la France...Huitième édition. 24p. *8°*. *Paris,* 1825.

24603 [SEYERTZ, L.?] Des avantages d'une assurance générale contre l'incendie, étendue à tous les immeubles de la France sous le contrôle des chambres. [Signed: L.S.] 39p. *8°*. *Paris.* 1825. *Attributed, in a manuscript note on the title-page, to 'Louis Seyertz de Strasbourg'.*

24604 The **SOUTH SEA BUBBLE** and the numerous fraudulent projects to which it gave rise in 1720, historically detailed as a beacon to the unwary against modern schemes (enumerated in an appendix) equally visionary and nefarious. 143p. *12°*. 1825.

24605 SULLY, Colbert et Villèle. [A comparison between former and present financial policies.] 15p. *8°*. *Paris,* 1825.

24606 *THATCHER, G. A treatise on annuities for fixed periods, particularly Government long annuities. Shewing a defect in theory, with its remedy; and when annuities are dear or cheap. To which is added, a practical table for calculating long annuity. 182p. *8°*. 1825. *The copy that belonged to Augustus De Morgan.*

24607 UNITED STATES OF AMERICA. Congress. *House of Representatives*. 18th Congress, 2d Session. ⟨26⟩ Report from the Secretary of the Treasury, on the state of the finances [for the years 1823 and 1824]. January 3, 1825... 40p. *8°*. *Washington,* 1825.

24608 WILKINSON, ROBERT (*fl.* 1825). Report to the assignees of the late banking-house of Marsh, Stracey, Fauntleroy & Graham, on the state of the accounts of that firm. By Mr. Robert Wilkinson, the accountant. 36p. *8°*. 1825.

24609 WILLIAMS, F. Further observations on the wine trade, and on the reduction of duties, &c. in a letter addressed to the Right Honorable the Chancellor of the Exchequer. 10p. *8°*. 1825.

TRANSPORT

24610 An earnest **APPEAL** to the Lords and Commons in Parliament, at this time assembled, against the destruction of the ancient collegiate church of St. Katharine, by the Tower, by constructing wet docks in that precinct. By a clergyman. 8p. *8°*. 1825.

24611 BIRMINGHAM and Liverpool Railway. [Report from the committee of management of the intended Birmingham and Liverpool Railway Company to the subscribers, on the failure to obtain Parliamentary sanction for the Bill giving effect to their plans. Dated: September 23, 1825.] 2p. *fol. Birmingham*, [1825]

24612 CAREY, M. Second edition, enlarged. An appeal to the justice and humanity of the stockholders of the Chesapeake and Delaware Canal. 20p. *8°. n.p.* [1825]

24613 COCK, S. Case of the London Dock Company. 92[91]p. *8°*. 1825.

24614 —— Second edition. 94p. *8°*. 1825. *Presentation copy, with inscription, from the author to William Harrison, solicitor to the Company; bound with the first edition, in a volume with his book-plate.*

24615 COLLIER DOCK COMPANY. Collier Dock – Isle of Dogs. Directors...Report of the directors to the proprietors, at their first general meeting, 18th August, 1825. [With the resolutions of the proprietors.] 5p. *fol. n.p.* [1825]

24616 —— Collier Dock, Isle of Dogs, Middlesex. [*Begin.*] In the course of the discussions to which the... state and...increase of the trade and navigation of the Port of London have...given rise...[With a list of directors of the company and an appeal for subscriptions. Dated: 14th January, 1825.] 2p. *s.sh.fol.* [*London*, 1825]

24617 DUPIN, F. P. C., *Baron.* The commercial power of Great Britain; exhibiting a complete view of the public works of this country, under the several heads of streets, roads, canals, aqueducts, bridges, coasts, and maritime ports...Translated from the French [of volumes 5 and 6 of *Voyages dans la Grande-Bretagne*]. 2 vols. *8°*. 1825.

24618 —— Plans, elevations, sections, &c.&c. to Dupin's Commercial power of Great Britain. [10] plates. *4°. n.p.* [1825] *For other editions, see* 1824.

24619 ENGLAND. *Commissioners appointed for Improving and Completing the Navigation of the Rivers Thames and Isis.* Thames navigation. Observations upon the evidence adduced before the Committee of the House of Commons, upon the late application to Parliament for a Bill for making a navigable canal, from the river Kennet, at Midgham, to join the Basingstoke Canal; to be called the Hants and Berks canal. [The speech of Mr. Joy, summing up the case for the Commissioners opposing the Bill, with extracts from the evidence.] 116p. *8°. Maidenhead*, 1825.

24620 —— *Laws, etc.* An Act for making and maintaining a canal for ships and other vessels, to commence at or near Seaton Bay...and terminating in the Bristol Channel, at or near Stolford, or Bridgwater Bay...with several collateral branches to communicate therewith. ⟨Royal assent, 6th July, 1825.⟩ 146p. *fol. n.p.*, 1825.

24621 —— —— Collier Dock, Isle of Dogs, Middlesex. Act passed 6 George IV. sess. 1825. cap. cxix. With an index of matter, and alphabetical list of owners and occupiers... 108p. *fol.* 1825. *The index refers both to the pages in this private printing of the Act and to the sections in the official edition, which is bound in the same volume.*

24622 —— Parliament. *House of Commons.* Proceedings of the Committee of the House of Commons on the Liverpool and Manchester Railroad Bill. Sessions, 1825. 772p. *fol.* [1825]

24623 EXETER proposed rail road. [An account of a meeting held on 27 January 1825 to inaugurate a railway from the port to the city of Exeter. Signed: Geare and Mountford, and Terrell and Tucker, solicitors.] *s.sh.fol. Exeter*, [1825] *Sent through the post (postmark: 1 February 1825) to Messrs. Woolcombe & Jago, solicitors, at Plymouth, with a manuscript letter on the verso.*

24624 The **FINGERPOST**; or, direct road from John-o'-Groat's to the Land's End: being a discussion of the railway question. By ? ? ?. 48p. *8°*. [1825]

24625 —— [Third edition, with addenda.] 60p. *8°*. [1825]

24626 GEORGE, C. M. The national waggon-post; to travel at the rate of twenty miles per hour, carrying one thousand ton weight, all over the kingdom of England, with passengers, goods, and stock. Also a letter from the Chancellor of the Exchequer, and the author's reply. 47p. *8°. Paris*, 1825.

24627 GRAHAME, T. A letter, addressed to the proprietors and managers of canals and navigable rivers, on a new method for tracking and drawing vessels by a locomotive engine boat, with much greater speed and at less than one third of the present expense. 40p. *8°. London, Edinburgh, &c.*, 1825.

24628 GRAY, T. Observations on a general iron railway, or land steam-conveyance...showing its vast superiority...over all the present...methods of conveyance...Fifth edition. 233p. *8°*. 1825. *For other editions, see* 1822.

24629 HALL, B. Account of the ferry across the Tay at Dundee...(First printed in the Edinburgh Philosophical Journal.) With a letter from Messrs. J. and C. Carmichael...describing the machinery of the twin steamboats. To which are added the regulations for the ferry; the table of rates and duties...the regulations for porters, and the table of fares payable to them... 31, 24p. *8°. Dundee*, 1825.

24630 JAMES, WILLIAM (1771–1837). James's patent for improved rail or tram roads...⟨Sealed, 28th February, 1824.⟩ 8p. *8°. n.p.* [1825]

24631 KENNET AND AVON CANAL NAVIGATION. Report of the Committee of Management... [Signed: Charles Dundas, chairman, and dated, 19th July, 1825.] [3]p. *fol. n.p.* [1825] *See also* 1812, 1813, 1815, 1816, 1823, 1824, 1826, 1838.

24632 LANDALE, C. Report submitted to the subscribers for defraying the expense of a survey to ascertain whether it is practicable...to construct a railway between the Valley of Strathmore and Dundee. [With 'Observations upon the line of railroad projected by Mr. Landale, from Dundee to the Valley of Strathmore, by Matthias Dunn'.] 10, 5p. *4°. Dundee*, 1825.

24633 **LETTER** to James Caldwell, Esq. on canals and rail-roads. Second edition. 10p. *8°. 1825. The Rastrick copy.*

24634 1825, February. **LIST** of inhabitants of the precinct of St. Katharine, by the Tower, and that part of St. Botolph, Aldgate, who will be affected by the proposed new docks, many of whom will be deprived of the means of obtaining their livelihood... 21p. *8°.* [1825]

24635 **McADAM,** JOHN L. Observations on the management of trusts for the care of turnpike roads, as regards the repair of the road, the expenditure of the revenue, and the appointment and quality of executive officers. And upon the nature and effect of the present road law of this kingdom... 148p. *8°. 1825.*

24636 [**MACLAREN,** C.] Railways compared with canals & common roads, and their uses and advantages explained: being the substance of a series of papers published in The Scotsman, and now republished with additions and corrections. [Signed: C.M.] 66p. *12°. Edinburgh & London, 1825.*

24637 At a **MEETING** of landowners and others, holden at...Axminster...on...the 13th of January, 1825, for the purpose of taking into consideration the proposed ship canal, from the Bristol to the English Channel. [Resolutions against the canal. Signed: William Tucker.] 2p. *fol. Chard & Axminster,* [1825]

For a **NEW GUIDE TO STAGE-COACHES, WAGGONS**...&c. for 1825, *see no.* 24413.

24638 Cautionary **OBSERVATIONS** founded upon official documents: recommended to the serious consideration of those who contemplate an investment of property in new dock speculations. 39p. *8°. 1825.*

24639 **OBSERVATIONS** on the projected ship canal, [i.e. the English and Bristol Channels Ship Canal] from Stolford...Somerset, to Beer...Devon. Published by direction of several gentlemen opposed to the measure. 15p. *8°. Sherborne,* [1825]

24640 **OBSERVATIONS** upon the case of the London Dock Company. 59p. *8°. 1825. The copy that belonged to William Harrison, solicitor to the London Dock Company, with manuscript notes throughout. See also note to no.* 24614.

24641 [**PARKES,** J.] A statement of the claim of the subscribers to the Birmingham & Liverpool rail road to an Act of Parliament, in reply to the opposition of the canal companies. 67p. *8°. London, Birmingham, &c., 1825.*

24642 —— Second edition, with additions. 93p. *8°. London, Birmingham, &c., 1825.*

24643 **PITMAN,** R. B. A succinct view and analysis of authentic information...on the practicability of joining the Atlantic and Pacific Oceans, by a ship canal across the Isthmus of America. 229p. *8°. 1825.*

24644 A **REPLY** to an anonymous pamphlet, entitled A refutation of the mis-statements contained in an anonymous pamphlet, donatively circulated by the London Dock Company, entitled "Cautionary observations to those who contemplate an investment of property in new docks:" accompanied by some useful information to the subscribers to new wet docks. 75p. *8°. 1825.*

24645 **SANDARS,** J. A letter on the subject of the projected rail road, between Liverpool & Manchester, pointing out the necessity for its adoption and the manifest advantages it offers to the public...Third edition. 46p. *8°. Liverpool, Manchester, &c.,* [1825] *The Agar Ellis copy. For another edition, see* 1824.

24646 The **STEAM-BOAT** companion; and stranger's guide to the Western Islands and Highlands of Scotland...Second edition, greatly enlarged and improved. 212p. *long 12°. Glasgow, Edinburgh, &c., 1825.*

24647 **SYLVESTER,** C. Report on rail-roads and locomotive engines, addressed to the chairman of the committee of the Liverpool and Manchester projected rail-road. 39p. *8°. Liverpool & London, 1825. The Rastrick copy.*

24648 —— Second edition. 39p. *8°. Liverpool & London, 1825.*

24649 **THOMAS,** WILLIAM. Observations on canals and rail-ways, illustrative of the...advantages to be derived from an iron rail-way...between Newcastle, Hexham, and Carlisle...Also, second edition, report of Barrodall Robert Dodd...on a proposed navigable canal, between Newcastle and Hexham; with appendix, containing remarks on...a proposed junction canal, or railway, uniting Newcastle upon Tyne and Carlisle with Liverpool...Bristol, and London. 52p. *8°. Newcastle upon Tyne, London, &c., 1825.*

24650 **TREDGOLD,** T. A practical treatise on rail-roads and carriages, shewing the principles of estimating their strength, proportions, expense, and annual produce, and the conditions which render them effective, economical, and durable; with the theory, effect, and expence of steam carriages, stationary engines, and gas machines... 184p. *8°. 1825. The Rastrick copy. See also* 1831, 1835.

24651 —— Remarks on steam navigation, and its protection, regulation, and encouragement. In a letter to the Right Honourable William Huskisson... 31p. *8°. 1825.*

24652 **VALLANCE,** J. Considerations of the expedience of sinking capital in railways. 112p. *8°. 1825.*

24653 **WOOD,** N. A practical treatise on rail-roads, and interior communication in general; with original experiments, and tables on the comparative value of canals and rail-roads... 314p. *8°. London, Newcastle-upon-Tyne, &c., 1825. See also* 1831, 1832, 1838.

SOCIAL CONDITIONS

24654 **ASSOCIATION FOR THE RELIEF OF THE MANUFACTURING AND LABOURING POOR.** Substance of the first and second reports of the Association...relative chiefly to the general supply of fish in the Metropolis and the interior. Established in May 1812. Ceased to exist with the year 1815. 31p. *8°. 1825. The Agar Ellis copy. See also* 1813, 1815.

24655 **ASSOCIATION FOR THE SUPPRESSION OF MENDICITY,** *Dublin.* Seventh report of the general committee of the Association...for the year 1824. [With lists of subscribers, one of residents of Dublin listed street by street.] 118p. *8°. Dublin, 1825. See also* 1819, 1821, 1831, 1837.

24656 BENTHAM, J. The rationale of reward. [With additions by Etienne Dumont. Edited by Richard Smith.] 352p. *8°*. 1825. *Originally published as part of* Théorie des peines et des récompenses, *1811 (q.v.).*

24657 [BOWLES, M.] Some account of the utility, as practically exemplified, of small clubs, in country villages. By the wife of a clergyman. 19p. *8°*. *Bath,* 1825. *Presentation copy, inscribed on the title-page 'From Mrs. Bowles'.*

24658 BRERETON, C. D. An inquiry into the work-house system and the law of maintenance in agricultural districts. 124p. *8°*. *Norwich & London,* [1825] *The copy that belonged to William Allen. See also* 1826.

24659 BROUGHAM, H. P., *Baron Brougham and Vaux.* Practical observations upon the education of the people, addressed to the working classes and their employers. 33p. *8°*. 1825.

24660 —— Fifth edition. 33p. *8°*. 1825.

24661 —— Sixth edition. 33p. *8°*. 1825.

24662 —— Seventh edition. 33p. *8°*. 1825.

24663 —— Fourteenth edition. 33p. *8°*. 1825.

24664 —— Seventeenth edition. 33p. *8°*. 1825.

24665 —— Eighteenth edition. 33p. *8°*. 1825.

24666 CARNELL, P. P. A treatise on family wine-making...from the various fruits of this country...To which is subjoined, the description of part of a recent British vintage... 158p. *8°*. [*c.* 1825]

24667 DEPTFORD MECHANICS' INSTITUTION. Rules and orders of the Mechanics' Institution for Deptford and its vicinity...Established Michaelmas, 1825. 20p. *8°*. *Deptford,* [1825]

24668 DUNLOP, C. S. M. A treatise on the law of Scotland relative to the poor. 152p. *8°*. *Edinburgh & London,* 1825.

24669 EASTON, T. Statements relative to the pauperism of Kirriemuir, Forfarshire, from 1814 to 1825. With an appendix, giving an account of Eling and other parishes, Hampshire. 220p. *12°*. *Forfar, Edinburgh, &c.,* 1825.

24670 EDINBURGH AND LEITH WATER COMPANY. Address by the interim committee of the Edinburgh and Leith Water Company, to the inhabitants of Edinburgh and Leith. [In answer to the statement of the Edinburgh Joint Stock Water Company. With an appendix.] 37, [3]p. *8°*. *n.p.* [1825]

24671 EDINBURGH DRAWING INSTITUTION. Prospectus of a drawing academy in Edinburgh. Applications for shares may be lodged with Mr. Cameron, No. 12, Royal Exchange. [With 'Extracts [on drawing] from Macculloch's "Highlands and western isles of Scotland"'.] 17p. *8°*. *Edinburgh,* 1825.

24672 EDINBURGH JOINT STOCK WATER COMPANY. Statement by the directors of the Edinburgh Joint Stock Water Company. 41p. *8°*. *Edinburgh,* 1825.

24673 EDWARDS, T. A letter to the Lord Lieutenant of the county of Surrey, on the misconduct of licensing magistrates, and the consequent degradation of the magistracy. 135p. *8°*. 1825.

24674 EIGHT SEVEN, *pseud.* A simple and effectual mode of providing for the labouring classes; and, at the same time, of promoting the landed interest. 49p. *8°*. *Dublin,* 1825. *The copy that belonged to William Allen.*

24675 FOSTER, T. and **McWILLIAMS,** D. Observations on the state of the children in cotton mills. [A petition to be presented to Parliament consisting mainly of medical testimony on the health of children in factories (collected during 1816–1818), praying that the working day of children should be limited to 13 hours, with time allowed for meals.] 15p. *8°*. [1825] *★Another, the FWA copy, belonged to William Pare.*

24676 GREEN, C. J. Trials for high treason, in Scotland, under a Special Commission, held at Stirling, Glasgow, Dumbarton, Paisley, and Ayr, in the year 1820 ...Taken in short-hand by C. J. Green...3 vols. *8°*. *Edinburgh,* 1825.

24677 HACKNEY LITERARY AND MECHANIC INSTITUTION. Rules and orders of the... Institution, established August 2nd, 1825. 13p. *8°*. *Hackney,* [1825]

24678 HALL, WILLIAM, *cotton spinner.* William Hall's vindication of the Chorley spinners. [A letter, dated: 5th February 1825.] 32p. *8°*. *Manchester,* [1825] *The Oastler copy.*

24679 HAMPSHIRE FRIENDLY SOCIETY. Hampshire Friendly Society, established January 1st, 1825 ...The following explanatory tract...is printed for gratuitous circulation. By order of the trustees and directors... 15p. *8°*. *Romsey,* [1825]

24680 —— The Hampshire Friendly Society. [Rules and regulations.] 20p. *8°*. *Winchester,* [1825 ?]

24681 [HAWKSLEY, J. W.] A few short hints on the possible means of giving encouragement to the honesty and industry of day labourers in husbandry; intended to promote their domestic comforts and to effect a gradual reduction...of parish poor's-rates, in agricultural districts. Addressed in a familiar letter to John Lee, Esq.... by a clergyman. [Signed: J.W.H.]... 27p. *8°*. *Bedford,* [1825] *Presentation copy, with inscription, from the author to William Allen.*

24682 HEYWOOD, SIR B., *Bart.* An address to the mechanics, artisans, &c. Delivered at the opening of the Manchester Mechanics' Institution, on...30th March, 1825. 15p. *8°*. *Manchester,* 1825.

24683 [HUME, JOSEPH ?] The present system of education [being a review of the second edition of George Jardine's *Outlines of philosophical education*]. Taken, by permission, from the seventh number of the Westminster Review. p.147–76. *8°*. *n.p.* [1825] *Presentation copy, inscribed: With Mr. Humes Comᵖˡˢ.*

24684 JEFFREY, F., *Lord Jeffrey.* Combinations of workmen. Substance of the speech of Francis Jeffrey Esq. upon introducing the toast...at the public dinner given at Edinburgh to Joseph Hume Esq., M.P. on...the 18th of November 1825. 23p. *8°*. *Edinburgh, London, &c.,* 1825.

24685 LITERARY AND SCIENTIFIC MECHANICS' INSTITUTE, *Hull.* Rules for the management of the...Institute, established in Hull, June 1, 1825. 11p. *8°*. *Hull,* [1825]

24686 LITERARY, SCIENTIFIC AND MECHANICAL INSTITUTION, *Newcastle-upon-Tyne.* A catalogue of the library of the...Institution... To which are prefixed, the first annual report, a list of the members, and the rules of the Institution. 48p. *8°*. *Newcastle upon Tyne, 1825. See also 1826, 1827.*

24687 LIVERPOOL MECHANICS' SCHOOL OF ARTS. Address delivered by Thos. Stewart Traill ...and resolutions adopted at a general meeting of the inhabitants, held on the 8th of June, 1825; with an exposition of the objects and general regulations of the institution... xiii, 13p. *8°. Liverpool, 1825.*

24688 LONDON MECHANICS' INSTITUTION. The eloquent speeches of Dr. Birkbeck and Mr. Brougham, at the opening of the new lecture room, Southampton Buildings, on...the 8th of July, 1825. 16p. *8°. 1825.*

24689 M., P. Narrative of the late occurrences at the cotton mills in Glasgow: in answer to the statement of these occurrences, by the proprietors. 26p. *8°. Glasgow, 1825.*

24690 McCULLOCH, JOHN R. A discourse delivered at the opening of the City of London Literary and Scientific Institution, 30th May 1825. [With a prospectus of the Institution.] 30, 3p. *8°. 1825.*

24691 MECHANICS' INSTITUTION, *Darlington.* Rules and regulations of the Mechanics' Institution, of Darlington and its vicinity. Established the 13th day of May, 1825. 8p. *8°. Darlington, 1825.*

24692 MILLAR, JAMES (*fl. 1818–1824*). The friendly society guide; or, a series of letters, conferences, and essays on the formation and improvement of benefit or friendly societies... 88p. *8°. Dundee & Edinburgh, 1825. Published in 11 parts.*

24693 MONTGOMERY, JAMES (1771–1854). The chimney-sweeper's friend, and climbing-boy's album... Arranged by James Montgomery. With illustrative designs by Cruickshank. Second edition, with alterations and additions. 474p. *12°. London & York, 1825. For another edition, see 1824.*

24694 —— On the employment of children in sweeping chimneys. Chiefly extracted from "The chimney-sweeper's friend and climbing-boy's album..." 34p. *12°. 1825. For editions of the complete work, see 1824 and no. 24693 (above).*

24695 [MOOR, E.] Letters on the kind and economic management of the poor, chiefly as regarding incorporated poor houses; with copious tables of actual expenditure, &c.&c. [Reprinted from the Ipswich Journal.] 133p. *8°. 1825.*

24696 MUTUAL INSURANCE BENEFIT INSTITUTION. Authorized and enrolled by Act of Parliament. An abstract of the rules, orders, and regulations, of the Mutual Insurance Benefit Institution...to be observed by members who insure for weekly sums of money with medical attendance and medicines...Capital £20,000. 23p. *8°. 1825. See also 1833.*

24697 NOLAN, M. A treatise of the laws for the relief and settlement of the poor...The fourth edition, with considerable additions... 3 vols. *8°. 1825. For another edition, see 1805.*

24698 OBSERVATIONS addressed to all classes of the community on the establishment of mechanics' institutions. 11p. *8°. Derby & London, [1825]*

24699 [PLACE, F.] Observations on Mr. Huskisson's speech on the laws relating to combinations of workmen. [Signed: F.P.] 32p. *8°. [1825] *Another, the FWA copy, belonged to William Pare.*

24700 ROYAL NATIONAL INSTITUTION FOR THE PRESERVATION OF LIFE FROM SHIPWRECK. On the means of assistance in cases of shipwreck. [On lifeboats and Captain Manby's apparatus.] 40p. *8°. Norwich, 1825.*

24701 RULES, regulations, and tables of contributions and allowances recommended for the constitution of a friendly society [to be known as the Dorset Friendly Society], in the county of Dorset...on the plan of the Rev. John Thomas Becher, A.M. [With an introduction by E. B. Portman, Viscount Portman.] 51p. *8°. Blandford, 1825.*

24702 ST. GEORGE'S HOSPITAL. Report of the weekly board, respecting certain charges brought against St. George's Hospital. 40p. *8°. 1825. The Agar Ellis copy.*

24703 SHARP, T. A dissertation on the pageants or dramatic mysteries anciently performed at Coventry, by the trading companies of that city; chiefly with reference to the vehicle, characters, and dresses of the actors...To which are added, the pageant of the Shearmen & Taylors' Company, and other municipal entertainments... 226p. *4°. Coventry, London, &c., 1825.*

24704 SOCIETY FOR THE SUPPRESSION OF MENDICITY, *London.* The seventh report of the Society...[With a list of subscribers.] 53, [49]p. *8°. 1825. See also 1819, 1820, 1822.*

24705 STATEMENT by the proprietors of cotton works in Glasgow and the vicinity: case of the operative cotton-spinners in answer to that statement: reply by the proprietors, and an introduction and appendix. 78p. *8°. Glasgow, 1825.*

24706 *SUGGESTIONS for bettering the condition of society in general, and of the operatives in particular [by compulsory savings]. By one of the people. 16p. *8°. Liverpool, [c. 1825] The FWA copy that belonged to William Pare.*

24707 THOMPSON, WILLIAM (1785?–1833). Appeal of one half the human race, women, against the pretensions of the other half, men, to retain them in political, and thence in civil and domestic, slavery; in reply to a paragraph of Mr. Mill's..."Article on government." 221p. *8°. 1825.*

24708 TRADES' NEWSPAPER ASSOCIATION. Laws and regulations of the Trades' Newspaper Association. 12p. *12°. [1825] The copy that belonged to William Lovett.*

24709 VOELKER, C. Professor Voelker's Gymnasium, no. 6, North Bank, Park Road, Regent's Park. [A prospectus, with testimonials from Emanuel de Fellenberg and Robert Dale Owen.] 8p. *8°. [London, 1825?]*

24710 WESLEY, J. A letter to a friend concerning tea. (Printed verbatim from the first edition, published in 1748.) [On its medical and sociological effects.] 16p. *12°. 1825.*

24711 WESTERN, C. C., *Baron Western.* Remarks upon prison discipline, &c.&c. In a letter addressed to the Lord Lieutenant and magistrates of the county of Essex ...Second edition, with a prefatory letter and an appendix ...Also, a copy of a Bill, to render persons possessed of... property liable to serve on juries... 117, 20p. *8°. 1825. For another edition, see 1821.*

SLAVERY

24712 An **ACCOUNT** of the proceedings of a meeting on the subject of slavery, held at Birmingham, the 10th Nov. 1825. 12p. *12°. Bristol*, 1825.

24713 **ALFRED**, *pseud*. Account of a shooting excursion on the mountains near Dromilly Estate, in the parish of Trelawny, and island of Jamaica, in the month of October, 1824!!! 15p. *8°*. 1825.

24714 **BARCLAY**, D. An account of the emancipation of the slaves of Unity Valley Pen, in Jamaica. 20p. *8°. Dorking* [& *London*], 1825. *For other editions, see* 1801.

24715 **BICKELL**, R. The West Indies as they are; or, a real picture of slavery: but more particularly as it exists in the island of Jamaica... 256p. *8°*. 1825. *Presentation copy, with inscription, from the author to Stephen Lushington.*

24716 —— The West Indies as they are; or a real picture of slavery, but more particularly as it exists in... Jamaica. [From the Christian Observer, March, 1825. An abridgment.] 10p. *4°. Birmingham*, [1825]

24717 A **DIALOGUE** between a well-wisher and a friend to the slaves in the British colonies. By a lady. 12p. *8°*. [1825?]

24718 **EDINBURGH SOCIETY FOR PROMOTING THE...ABOLITION OF NEGRO SLAVERY.** The second annual report of the Edinburgh Society for Promoting the...Abolition of Negro Slavery. 43p. *8°. Edinburgh*, 1825. *See also* 1824.

24719 **ENGLAND.** Parliament. *House of Commons.* Report of the debate in the House of Commons, June the 16th, 1825. On Dr. Lushington's motion respecting the deportation of Messrs. L. C. Lecesne and J. Escoffery, two persons of colour, from Jamaica... 19p. *8°*. [1825] *Stephen Lushington's own copy.*

24720 [**FISHER**, Thomas (*fl.* 1825).] The negro's memorial, or abolitionist's catechism; by an abolitionist. 127p. *8°*. 1825.

24721 **JANSON**, E. The following considerations on the slave trade and slavery, are submitted to the public, under a conviction of the soundness of the principles on which they are founded, and which have long been advocated. 4p. *8°*. [*London*, 1825?]

24722 **M'DONNELL**, A. Considerations on negro slavery. With authentic reports, illustrative of the actual condition of the negroes in Demerara. Also, an examination into the propriety and efficacy of the regulations... now in operation in Trinidad...Second edition. 340p. *8°*. 1825. *For another edition, see* 1824.

24723 No. 2. The **NEGRO'S** remembrancer...What can we do for the poor slaves? 4p. *8°*. [*London, c.* 1825]

24724 **NEWCASTLE UPON TYNE SOCIETY FOR PROMOTING THE GRADUAL ABOLITION OF SLAVERY THROUGHOUT THE BRITISH DOMINIONS.** First report of the committee of the Newcastle upon Tyne Society...read at the general meeting held on...the 16th June, 1824; with an account of the proceedings... 28p. *8°. Newcastle on Tyne*, 1825.

24725 **REASONS** for preferring immediate to what is called gradual emancipation. 12p. *12°. n.p.* [1825?]

For **SOCIETY FOR THE ABOLITION OF SLAVERY THROUGHOUT THE BRITISH DOMINIONS.** Anti-slavery monthly reporter, 1825–33, *see* vol. III, *Periodicals list*, Anti-slavery reporter.

24726 —— Second report of the Committee of the Society...Read at the general meeting...held on the 30th day of April, 1825. 191p. *8°*. 1825. *See also* 1824, 1826.

24727 —— Extracts from the second report of the Committee of the Society... 36p. *8°. Manchester*, 1825.

24728 —— The slave colonies of Great Britain; or, a picture of Negro slavery drawn by the colonists themselves; being an abstract of the various papers recently laid before Parliament on that subject. 164p. *8°*. 1825. *See also* 1826.

24729 **SUFFOLK AUXILIARY SOCIETY FOR THE...GRADUAL ABOLITION OF SLAVERY.** First report of the...Society... 12p. *8°. Ipswich*, 1825.

24730 **WEST INDIA SLAVERY.** A review of "The slavery of the British West India colonies delineated ...By James Stephen, Esq. Vol. 1..." Extracted...from the Edinburgh Review – No. LXXXII. 24p. *12°. Aberdeen: The Aberdeen Anti-Slavery Society*, 1825. *Attributed to T. B. Macaulay and to Henry Brougham. The copy that belonged to Stephen Lushington.*

24731 —— Second edition. 26p. *12°. Aberdeen: The Aberdeen Anti-Slavery Society*, 1825.

24732 **WINN**, T. S. A speedy end to slavery in our West India colonies, by safe, effectual, and equitable means, for the benefit of all parties concerned. 123p. *8°*. 1825. *See also* 1827.

24733 **YOUNG**, Robert (1796–1865). A view of slavery in connection with Christianity: being the substance of a discourse delivered in...Jamaica, Sept. 19, 1824...With an appendix, containing the resolutions of the missionaries in that connection, at a general meeting held in Kingston, Sept. 6, 1824. 41p. *8°*. 1825.

POLITICS

24734 **ENGLAND.** *George IV.* A letter from the King to his Catholic subjects. 56p. *8°*. [*London*,] *Dublin, &c.*, 1825.

24735 Political **FALLACIES.** Reprinted from the fourth number of the Westminster Review. [Being a review of Bentham's *The book of fallacies*, and two other works.] p.410–442. *8°*. [*London*,] 1825. *Inscribed in manuscript: With Mr Humes comps.*

24736 De la **FRANCE** et de l'Espagne en 1825, par un officier supérieur qui a fait la guerre en Espagne avec l'ancienne Armée. 35p. *8°. Paris*, 1825.

24737 FREDERICK, *Duke of York and Albany.* Look at this and look at that. [Being the speech of the Duke of York to the House of Lords in support of a petition against Catholic emancipation, reprinted from the Morning Chronicle, and the speech of Mr. Hodgins, an operative cotton spinner, at Manchester, in favour of Catholic emancipation, from the Manchester Guardian's report of a meeting in Manchester, to consider a petition to Parliament in favour of the Catholic Emancipation Bill.] 4p. *8°.* [*London,* 1825] *The two speeches are printed in parallel columns. The Agar Ellis copy.*

24738 SALVANDY, N. A. DE, *Comte.* La verité sur les marchés Ouvrard. 330p. *8°. Paris,* 1825.

24739 SALVATOR, *pseud.* Emancipation and emancipators. An address to the people of England against Catholic emancipation, with a satirico-political poem. 27p. *8°.* [*London,* 1825]

24740 SIMONDE DE SISMONDI, J. C. L. Revue des efforts et des progrès des peuples dans les vingt-cinq dernières années. [Extrait de la Revue Encyclopédique...Janvier 1825.] 28p. *8°.* [*Paris,* 1825] *With a manuscript inscription which reads: To William Allen, London, from M. [illegible] Jullien, de Paris.*

24741 SMITH, SYDNEY (1771–1845). A sermon on religious charity. [On toleration.] 17p. *8°. York,* 1825. *Presentation copy, with inscription, to George Agar Ellis, Baron Dover, from the author, who added to the imprint: 'Published at the request of the Committee of the English Catholic Association'.*

SOCIALISM

24742 COMBE, ABRAM. The sphere for joint-stock companies: or, the way to increase the value of land, capital, and labour. With an account of the establishment at Orbiston in Lanarkshire. 69p. *8°. Edinburgh, Glasgow, &c.,* 1825.

24743 FIRST SOCIETY OF ADHERENTS TO DIVINE REVELATION, *Orbiston.* The new court. No. 1. – The first records of the new Court, established by the First Society of, &c. for the extinction of disputes. 22d March, 1825. [By Abram Combe?] 16p. *8°. n.p.* [1825]

For —— The register for the First Society...1825–27, *see* vol. III, *Periodicals list,* The Register for the First Society...

24744 GRAY, JOHN (1799–1883). A lecture on human happiness; being the first of a series of lectures on that subject, in which will be comprehended a general review of the causes of the existing evils of society...To which are added the articles of agreement drawn up...by the London Co-operative Society, for the formation of a community on principles of mutual co-operation, within fifty miles of London. 72, 16p. *8°.* 1825. *The copy that belonged to J. M. Ludlow.*

24745 HAMILTON, JAMES (1769–1829). Owenism rendered consistant [*sic*] with our civil and religious institutions, or a mode of forming societies for mutual benefit on rational and practical principles...[With a postscript.] 36, [2]p. *12°.* 1825. *Another, the FWA copy, with the signature 'John Powell Nov*ʳ*. 7 1825' on the wrapper, later belonged to William Pare.*

24746 HEBERT, W. A visit to the colony of Harmony, in Indiana...recently purchased by Mr. Owen for the establishment of a society of mutual co-operation and community of property...To which are added, some observations on that mode of society, and on political society at large: also, a sketch for the formation of a co-operative society. 35p. *8°.* 1825.

24747 [HODGSKIN, T.] Labour defended against the claims of capital; or, the unproductiveness of capital proved with reference to the present combinations amongst journeymen. By a labourer. 33p. *12°. London, Edinburgh, &c.,* 1825. *See also* 1831.

24748 LONDON CO-OPERATIVE SOCIETY. Articles of agreement for the formation of a community on principles of mutual co-operation, within fifty miles of London. Drawn up and recommended by the London Co-operative Society. 16p. *8°.* 1825. *See also no.* 24744, *and* 1826.

24749 —— Rules for the observance of the London Co-operative Society. 8p. *8°.* 1825.

For the **NEW-HARMONY GAZETTE,** 1825–26, *see* vol. III, *Periodicals list.*

24750 OPINIONS littéraires, philosophiques et industrielles. [By H. de Saint-Simon, L. Halévy, O. Rodrigues, J. B. Duvergier and — Bailly.] 392p. *8°. Paris,* 1825. *The copy that belonged to Victor Considérant.*

24751 *OWEN, ROBERT. An address delivered to the inhabitants of New Lanark, on the first of January, 1816, at the opening of the institution established for the formation of character...From the fourth London edition. [With extracts from the London daily papers of 1817, and 'Extracts from Mr. Owen's address; delivered at the City of London Tavern, August 14, 1817'.] 56p. *8°. Cincinnati,* 1825. *FWA copy that belonged to William Pare. Contained in a blue paper wrapper with* A new view of society (*no.* 24752 *below*), *with which it was probably issued. For other editions, see* 1816.

24752 *—— A new view of society: or, essays on the formation of the human character, preparatory to the development of a plan for gradually ameliorating the condition of mankind. To which are prefixed rules and regulations of a community...First American from the fourth London, edition. 88p. *8°. Cincinnati,* 1825. *The FWA copy that belonged to William Pare. Contained in a blue paper wrapper with* An address delivered to the inhabitants of New Lanark (*no.* 24751 *above*), *with which it was probably issued. For other editions, see* 1813.

24753 —— Owen's American discourses. Two discourses on a new system of society; as delivered in the Hall of Representatives at Washington...the first on the 25th of February, the second on the 7th of March, 1825. 36p. *8°.* 1825. *Another, the FWA copy, belonged to William Pare. For another edition of the first discourse, see* 1839.

For **PHOSPHOR,** morning star of liberty and equality, *see* vol. III, *Periodicals list.*

24754 [SAINT-SIMON, C. H. DE, *Comte.*] Nouveau Christianisme, dialogues entre un conservateur et un novateur. Premier dialogue. 91p. *8°. Paris,* 1825. *See also* 1832, 1834.

MISCELLANEOUS

24755 [CAREY, WILLIAM P.] The national obstacle to the national public style considered. Observations on the probable decline or extinction of British historical painting, from the effects of the Church exclusion of paintings... 151p. *8°.* 1825. *The Agar Ellis copy.*

24756 [CUST, HON. SIR E., *Bart.*] Considerations upon the expediency of building a metropolitan palace... By a Member of Parliament. 68p. *8°.* 1825. *Attributed to 'Honble. Edward Cust' in a manuscript note on the title-page by George Agar Ellis, Baron Dover, to whom this copy belonged.*

24757 A DESCRIPTION of the shield of Æneas [translated from the Aeneid, Book VIII], modelled by Mr. Wm. Pitts, for Mr. Joseph Widdowson, goldsmith, 100 Fleet Street, to be executed in gold...after the manner of Benvenuto Cellini. 15p. *8°.* [1825 ?] *The Agar Ellis copy.*

24758 *DIALOGUE between the Greek philosopher Epictetus and his son. 8p. *8°.* 1825. *The FWA copy that belonged to William Pare.*

24759 DUNNE, C. Mr. Dunne, Mr. Justice Best, and Serjeant Spankie, or the opinion of the Chief Justice of the Common Pleas on the subject's right of petitioning Parliament, and on the law of libel: – with animadversions on the counsellor's defence of slander and slanderers. 16p. *8°.* [*London,*] 1825.

24760 —— The Star Chamber, or a panorama of the moral assassins of the metropolis, together with reflections on the revival of this odious inquisition in Britain... [With 'Considerations on the true liberty of the press in Britain, and in France'.] 62, [2]p. *8°.* [*London,*] 1825.

24761 EGAN, A. The book of rates now used in the sin custom-house of the Church and Court of Rome... 1674...and now reprinted. 36p. *12°.* 1825. *For other editions, see* 1674.

24762 JONES, JOHN G. An oration on the late General Washington, including a retrospect of his life, character and conduct...Second edition, revised and corrected. 20p. *8°.* 1825. *With two letters from the author, probably to George Agar Ellis, to whom this copy belonged, and manuscript additions to the list of subscribers to the memorial to Washington for which Jones was making an appeal. For the letter, see vol.* III, *A.L.* 290.

24763 SOMERSET, E., *2nd Marquis of Worcester.* The century of inventions of the Marquis of Worcester. From the original MS., with historical and explanatory notes and a biographical memoir by C. F. Partington. lxxxiv, 138p. *8°.* 1825. *For other editions, see* 1746.

24764 VERITAS, *pseud.* On the proposed payment, by Government, of the Roman Catholic priesthood in Ireland. Extracted from the St. James's Chronicle of the 31st March, 1825. 13p. *8°. n.p.* [1825]

1826

GENERAL

24765 ANDERSON, ADAM (*d.* 1846) and FORBES, JOHN (*fl.* 1826). Report to Duncan Macneill Esq. Sheriff-Depute of the County of Perth, regarding the weights and measures heretofore in use in that county, and the relations which they bear to the new Imperial Standard. [With an appendix.] 18, 14p. *8°. n.p.* [1826] *For a second appendix to this report see* 1827.

24766 ANDERSON, JOHN (1795–1845). Mission to the east coast of Sumatra, in M.DCCC.XXIII...including historical and descriptive sketches of the country, an account of the commerce, population, and the manners and customs of the inhabitants, and a visit to the Batta cannibal states in the interior. 424p. *8°. Edinburgh & London,* 1826.

24767 ANDERSON, WILLIAM, *of London.* The London commercial dictionary, and sea-port gazetteer, exhibiting a clear and comprehensive view of the productions, manufactures, and commerce, of all nations...A new edition...[With an appendix.] 848, 40p. *8°. London, Bristol, &c.,* 1826.

24768 [BAILEY, S.] A letter to a political economist; occasioned by an article in the Westminster Review on the subject of value. By the author of the Critical dissertation on value therein reviewed. 101p. *8°.* 1826.

24769 [BULMER, J.] A letter addressed to farmers and manufacturers, in which the writer endeavours to shew the mischief likely to arise from too great a use of machinery, and from too great an importation of foreign corn. [Signed: A looker-on.] 15p. *8°. York,* [1826] *The copy that belonged to Oastler who attributed it to James Bulmer in the manuscript index to his pamphlet collection.*

24770 BURKE, E. The works of the Right Honourable Edmund Burke. [Edited by W. King and F. Laurence.] A new edition. 16 vols. *8°.* 1826–27.

24771 BURNET, RICHARD. A word to the members of the mechanics' institutes. [With engravings by G. Banks.] 145p. *8°. Devonport,* 1826.

24772 CAREY, M. Reflections on the subject of emigration from Europe, with a view to settlement in the United States: containing brief sketches of the moral and political character of this country...Third edition, corrected and enlarged. 28p. *8°. Philadelphia,* 1826. *Presentation copy from the author to the American Antiquarian Society.*

24773 CARTWRIGHT, F. D. The life and correspondence of Major Cartwright. Edited by his niece... 2 vols. *8°.* 1826.

24774 CAYLEY, EDWARD. Corn, trade, wages, and rent; or, observations on the leading circumstances of the present financial crisis... 47p. *8°.* 1826. *See also* 1827.

24775 CLOET, J. J. DE. Handboek voor staatsmannen, kooplieden, fabrijkanten, trafijkanten, en manufakturiers, of statistiek tafereel, der Nederlandsche nijverheid... Naar den tweeden druk, uit het Fransch vertaald, en met vele bijvoegsels vermeerderd door Paulus van Griethuizen. 270p. *8°. Utrecht, 1826. For another edition, see 1823.*

24776 COOPER, THOMAS (1759-1839). Lectures on the elements of political economy. 280p. *8°. Columbia [S.C.], 1826. See also 1830.*

24777 CRUDEN, R. P. Observations upon the municipal bodies in cities and towns, incorporated by royal charters, within England and Wales. 72p. *8°. 1826. The copy that belonged to T. Spring Rice, Baron Monteagle.*

24778 DUPIN, F. P. C., *Baron.* Voyages dans la Grande-Bretagne, entrepris relativement aux services publics de la guerre, de la marine, et des ponts et chaussées, au commerce et à l'industrie, depuis 1816... 6 vols. *8°. Bruxelles, 1826-27. Contents: vols 1-2. Force militaire ...Troisième édition, publiée par L. A. Paulmier et Jobard; vols. 3-4. Force navale...Troisième édition... vols. 5-6. Force commerciale...Troisième édition.*

24779 —— Voyages dans la Grande-Bretagne. Planches ... 3 vols. *obl. fol. n.p., 1826.*

24780 *The **EAST-INDIA** register and directory, for 1826; containing...lists of the Company's servants... mariners &c. not in the service of the Company, merchant vessels employed in the country trade...Compiled...by A. W. Mason, Geo. Owen, and G. H. Brown... 588p. *12°. [1826] For other editions, see 1804.*

24781 The **ELECTOR'S GUIDE**...Addressed to the freeholders of the county of York. Conducted by a committee of Yorkshire-men. (Jan. 1826-Feb. 18, 1826.) Nos. 1-3. *8°. York, Leeds, &c., 1826.*

24782 ENGLAND. *Parliament.* A digest of the evidence taken before Select Committees of the two Houses of Parliament appointed to inquire into the state of Ireland; 1824-1825: with notes historical and explanatory, and a copious index. By the Rev. William Phelan, and the Rev. Mortimer O'Sullivan. 2 vols. *8°. London, Dublin, &c., 1826. For another edition, see 1825.*

24783 *G., A. P. D. Sketches of Portuguese life, manners, costume, and character... 364p. *8°. 1826. The copy that belonged to George Grote.*

24784 GANILH, C. Dictionnaire analytique d'économie politique. 437p. *8°. Paris & Bruxelles, 1826.*

24785 GEORGE IV, *King.* The King's speech to both Houses of the new Parliament, on...the 21st Nov. 1826... *s.sh.fol. [Glasgow, 1826] [Br. 501]*

24786 GRÉGOIRE, H. B., *Comte.* Essay on the nobility of the skin. Or, the prejudice of white persons against the colour of Africans and their progeny, black and of mixed-blood: freely translated from the French... By Charlotte Nooth. 83[99]p. *8°. 1826. The copy that belonged to Stephen Lushington.*

24787 GRIFFITH, S. Y. Griffith's new historical description of Cheltenham and its vicinity... 289p. *4°. Cheltenham & London, 1826.*

24788 GRIMSHAW, WILLIAM. History of the United States, from their first settlement as colonies, to the cession of Florida, in eighteen hundred and twenty-one: comprising every important political event; with a progressive view of the...population...agriculture, and commerce...Revised edition. 308p. *8°. Philadelphia, 1826.*

24789 HARCOURT, E. D', *Vicomte.* Réflexions sur la richesse future de la France, et sur la direction qu'il convient de donner à la prospérité du royaume. 303p. *8°. Paris, 1826.*

24790 HEAD, SIR F. B., *Bart.* Rough notes taken during some rapid journeys across the Pampas and among the Andes. 309p. *8°. 1826. See also 1828.*

24791 JOPLIN, T. Views on the subject of corn and currency. 80p. *8°. 1826.*

24792 KENT'S original London directory: 1826. Being an alphabetical list of more than 20,000 merchants, manufacturers, traders, &c. of London and the environs ...Ninety-fourth annual edition. 439p. *12°. [1826] Interleaved and bound in two volumes. See also 1740, 1804, 1816, 1825, 1827.*

24793 LAMBARD, W. A perambulation of Kent, conteining the description, hystorie, and customes of the shire...First published in...1576, and now increased and altered from the author's own last copie. 538p. *8°. Chatham, 1826. For other editions, see 1576.*

24794 LANE, C. A classification of sciences and arts; or, a map of human knowledge. 20p. *8°. 1826.*

24795 LETTER to a noble lord in administration, on the present distressed state of the country. By a calm observer. 32p. *8°. 1826.*

24796 [**McCULLOCH,** JOHN R.] An essay on the circumstances which determine the rate of wages, and the condition of the labouring classes. [Introductory note signed: J.R.M'C.] p.111-222. *12°. Edinburgh & London, 1826.*

24797 M'DONNELL, A. Free trade: or an inquiry into the expediency of the present corn laws; the relations of our foreign and colonial trade...and the circumstances which occasion a derangement of the currency... 468p. *8°. 1826.*

24798 MIERS, J. Travels in Chile and La Plata, including accounts respecting the geography...statistics, government, finances, agriculture...and the mining operations in Chile. Collected during a residence of several years in these countries... 2 vols. *8°. 1826.*

24799 MILL, JAMES. Elements of political economy ...Third edition, revised and corrected. 304p. *8°. 1826. For other editions, see 1821.*

24800 PEBRER, A. P. Five questions on the actual mercantile distress. 34p. *8°. 1826.*

24801 PHILLIPS, SIR RICHARD. Golden rules of social philosophy; or, a new system of practical ethics. 376p. *8°. 1826.*

24802 PICTURE of England at the close of the year 1826; her colonies; her manufacturers; her Navy; her sailors; her crowded prisons; and her starving population. 9p. *8°. [1826]*

24803 [**POWELL,** JOHN, *statistical writer.*] Appendix to the first edition of the Statistical illustrations of the territorial extent...of the British Empire...with a preface and notes...illustrative of the nature and effects of the corn laws and currency. 56p. *8°. 1826. For editions of Statistical illustrations, see 1825.*

24804 PRIESTLEY, JOSEPH (1733–1804). Lectures on history and general policy; to which is prefixed, an essay on a course of liberal education for civil and active life...A new edition, with numerous enlargements: comprising a lecture on "The constitution of the United States", from the author's American edition; and additional notes, by J. T. Rutt [and Richard Taylor]. 598p. *8°*. 1826. *For another edition, see 1788.*

24805 QUADRI, A. Prospetto statistico delle provincie Venete. 276p. *8°*. *Venezia*, 1826. *For the author's introduction to this work, see Storia della statistica, 1824.*

24806 *SAY, J. B. Economie politique. [With 'Bibliographie de l'économie politique'.] [An offprint from *Encyclopédie progressive*, p.217–304.] 88p. *8°*. *n.p.* [1826] *Presentation copy from the author to Mrs. George Grote.*

24807 *—— Traité d'économie politique, ou simple exposition de la manière dont se forment, se distribuent et se consomment les richesses. Cinquième édition, augmentée d'un volume, et à laquelle se trouvent...un épitome des principes fondamentaux de l'économie politique... 3 vols. *8°*. *Paris*, 1826. *Presentation copy, with inscription, from the author to Mrs. George Grote. For other editions, see 1803.*

24808 SCHMALZ, T. A. H. Économie politique, ouvrage traduit de l'allemand de M. Schmalz...par H. Jouffroy. Revu et annoté sur la traduction, par M. Fritot ... 2 vols. *8°*. *Paris*, 1826. *For another edition, see vol. III, Addenda, (1818).*

24809 SEINE, *Département de la. Administration.* Recherches statistiques sur la ville de Paris et le Département de la Seine; recueil de tableaux dressés et réunis d'après les ordres de Monsieur le Comte de Chabrol... xxxi, [70], 49p., 132 tables. *4°*. *Paris*, 1826. *Published under the direction of J. B. J. Fourier, with some contributions by him. The copy presented to Sir George Stainton, with an inscription from 'Marcellus De Brun'[?]. See also 1821, 1823, 1829.*

24810 SMITH, ADAM. An inquiry into the nature and causes of the wealth of nations...Complete in one volume... 933p. *8°*. 1826. *For other editions, see 1776.*

24811 SOCIETY OF THE GOVERNOR AND ASSISTANTS IN LONDON, OF THE NEW PLANTATION IN ULSTER. A report of a deputation to Ireland in the year 1825. [Signed: G. Gorst, Dep. Govr. Jno. Drinkald. Edwd. Hamblet Noy.] Printed by order of the Court. [With 'Appendix. Londonderry School account for ten years'.] 24, xiiip. *8°*. 1826. *See also 1834 (AGRICULTURE), 1835, 1836, 1838, 1841.*

For the **SPIRIT OF THE TIMES;** or essence of the periodicals, *see* vol. III, *Periodicals list.*

24812 TABLEAU statistique historique d'Amsterdam, ou guide du voyageur en cette ville. Nouvelle édition. 300p. *12°*. *Amsterdam*, 1826.

24813 THOMPSON, THOMAS P. An exposition of fallacies on rent, tithes, &c. containing an examination of Mr. Ricardo's theory of rent and of the arguments brought against the conclusion that tithes and taxes on the land are paid by the landlords...With an inquiry into the comparative consequences of taxes on agricultural and manufactured produce. Being in the form of a review of the third edition of Mr. Mill's Elements of political economy. By a member of the University of Cambridge. 64p. *8°*. 1826.

24814 —— The true theory of rent, in opposition to Mr. Ricardo and others. Being 'An exposition of fallacies on rent, tithes, &c.'. In the form of a review of Mr. Mill's Elements of political economy. By a member of the University of Cambridge. Second edition. 64p. *8°*. 1826. *See also 1828, 1829, 1830, 1832.*

24815 VERAX, *pseud.* A few remarks upon the true origin of rent, gluts, a corn trade, and the new issue of gold. 15p. *8°*. 1826.

24816 WEST, SIR EDWARD. Price of corn and wages of labour, with observations upon Dr. Smith's, Mr. Ricardo's, and Mr. Malthus's doctrines upon those subjects; and an attempt at an exposition of the causes of the fluctuation of the price of corn during the last thirty years. 150p. *8°*. 1826.

24817 WILLIAMS, I. Avarice exposed; or, a treatise on the corn and game laws. 30p. *8°*. 1826.

24818 [WILSON, JOHN (1785–1854).] Some illustrations of Mr. M'Culloch's Principles of political economy. By Mordecai Mullion, private secretary to Christopher North. 74p. *8°*. *Edinburgh & London*, 1826.

AGRICULTURE

24819 BAILLEUL, J. C. Du projet de loi sur les successions et les substitutions, pour comparaison, quelques idées sur des institutions appropriées à l'ordre de choses qui nous régit, et qui en seraient les garanties et les appuis. 51p. *8°*. *Paris*, 1826.

24820 BALD, R. Report regarding the coal field in the district of Whitburn in the counties of Linlithgow and Lanark; with the detail of the operations which have been carried on by boring, and the result thereof. 8p. *4°*. *Edinburgh*, [1826] *The Rastrick copy.*

24821 BREHIER, J. J. Du partage égal et du droit d'aînesse, dans leurs rapports avec nos institutions et l'état de la société en France. 95p. *8°*. *Paris*, 1826.

24822 BROGLIE, A. L. V. C. DE, *Duc.* Chambre des Pairs. Séance du 4 avril 1826. Opinion de M. le Duc de Broglie, sur le projet de loi relatif aux successions et aux substitutions. 58p. *8°*. *n.p.* [1826]

24823 COBBETT, W. Cottage economy...to which are added, instructions relative to the selecting...of English grass...for the...making hats...and also instructions for erecting and using icehouses, after the Virginian manner...A new edition. [220]p. *12°*. 1826. *For other editions, see 1821.*

24824 COIMPY, DE, *Marquis.* Du droit d'aînesse et du pouvoir de substituer, considérés sous les rapports de l'intérêt des familles, ou nouveaux aperçus sur le projet de loi soumis en ce moment à l'examen de la Chambre des Pairs. 12p. *8°*. *Paris*, 1826.

24825 COMMERSON, J. J. Le droit d'aînesse, nouvelle imitée de Schiller; et suivie d'un hommage au Général Foy. 27p. *8°*. *Paris*, 1826.

24826 COTTU, C. Observations sur le principe du droit d'aînesse et sur son application aux familles électorales. 34p. *8°*. *Paris*, 1826.

24827 DECAZES, E., *Duc.* Opinion de M. le Duc Decazes sur le projet de loi relatif aux successions et aux substitutions. 63p. *8°. Paris, 1826.*

24828 DELAUNAY, V. Du droit d'aînesse, de son origine, et de ses rapports avec les institutions qui nous régissent. 32p. *8°. Paris, 1826.*

24829 Le **DESSERT** d'un féodal, dialogue sur le droit d'aînesse, par l'auteur du Salon de Mondor. 47p. *8°. Paris, 1826.*

24830 DILLON, Sir John J. Observations sur la loi des successions en Angleterre et en Irlande; et sur le droit de primogéniture. 15p. *8°. Paris, 1826.*

24831 DUGUÉ, F. Réflexions sur les donations faites par des mineurs, dans les contrats de mariage, soumises à MM. les notaires et jurisconsultes. 45p. *8°. Paris, 1826.*

24832 DUPIN, A. M. J. J. Du droit d'aînesse. 119p. *8°. Paris, 1826.*

24833 —— Seconde édition. 119p. *8°. Paris, 1826.*

24834 DUVERGIER DE HAURANNE, J. M. De l'égalité des partages, et du droit d'aînesse. 56p. *8°. Paris, 1826.*

24835 ENGLISH, H. A compendium of useful information relating to the companies formed for working British mines...With general observations on their progress...and a table of the payments made, fluctuations in price, &c., up to the present period. 124p. *8°. 1826. Compiled as a second part of the author's A general guide to the companies formed for working foreign mines, published in 1825 (q.v.).*

24836 EXAMEN du projet de loi sur le rétablissement du droit d'aînesse et des substitutions: par un magistrat. 32p. *8°. Paris, 1826.*

24837 G., B. Lettre à un journaliste, relative au projet de loi sur les successions et substitutions. 15p. *8°. [Paris, 1826]*

24838 GIBSON, John, *general agent.* Comparative view of the respective modes of auction-sale of land estates, as practised in Scotland and England. With observations on...obstructions which occur in the common mode of recovery of heritable or mortgage debts in Scotland; and on certain abuses which prevail in the present system of management of Scotch voluntary or extra-judicial trusts. 86p. *8°. Edinburgh, 1826.*

24839 GIRARDIN, L. S. C. X. de, *Comte.* Opinion de Stanislas Girardin, Député de la Seine-Inférieure, contre le projet de loi destiné à rétablir les substitutions. 54p. *8°. n.p. [1826]*

24840 GRENIER, H. Aperçu sur la division et le morcellement des héritages, et sur le choix des moyens pour y remédier. 46p. *8°. Montpellier, 1826.*

24841 GROSSIN DE BOUVILLE, L. A. H., *Comte de Bouville.* Opinion de Monsieur de Bouville, Député de la Seine-Inférieure, prononcée dans la séance du mercredi 10 mai 1826, contre la loi de substitution. 68p. *8°. Paris, 1826.*

24842 IVERNOIS, Sir F. d'. Matériaux pour aider à la recherche des effets passés, présens et futurs du morcellement de la propriété foncière en France. [With a supplement.] 136, 57p. *8°. Genève & Paris, 1826. Presentation copy from the author to the Société de Lecture de Genève.*

24843 LANJUINAIS, J. D., *Comte.* Discours contre le projet de rétablir et d'aggraver les priviléges d'aînesse, de masculinité, de substitution. 46p. *8°. Paris, 1826.*

24844 —— Nouvelle édition, corrigée, augmentée. On y a joint le Discours special du même orateur sur les substitutions, déjà imprimé par ordre de la Chambre des Pairs. 62p. *8°. Paris, 1826.*

24845 LETTRE adressée à un pair de France, relativement au droit d'aînesse et au pouvoir de substituer. 24p. *8°. Paris, 1826.*

24846 [MASSABIAU, J. A. F.] Quelques observations sur le projet de loi relatif aux successions, présenté à la Chambre des Pairs, dans la séance du 10 février 1826... 23p. *8°. Paris, 1826.*

24847 MEXICAN MINING ASSOCIATION. United Mexican Mining Association. [*Begin.*] At a special general meeting, held at the City of London Tavern, the 19th July 1826...[With the Report.] 40p. *8°. [London, 1826] See also 1825, 1827.*

24848 —— Circular of the Court of Directors... addressed to the proprietors. Dated London, 11th November, 1826. 15p. *8°. [London, 1826]*

24849 —— United Mexican Mining Association. Report of Don Lucas Alaman, addressed to the Directors; dated at Mexico, the 28th May, 1826; and a letter from Baron de Humboldt, addressed to the Secretary. 85p. *8°. 1826.*

24850 MOREAU DE BELLAING, M. J. L. J. Note sur la loi du droit d'aînesse. 7p. *4°. Paris, [1826]*

24851 MOREL VINDÉ, C. G. T. de, *Vicomte.* Considérations sur le morcellement de la propriété térritoriale en France; mémoire présenté à l'Académie des Sciences le 1er. mai 1826. 28p. *8°. Paris, 1826.*

24852 Un **PÈRE** de famille à Monsieur le Garde-des-Sceaux sur le projet de loi relatif au droit d'aînesse et aux substitutions, par lui présenté à la Chambre des Pairs, le 10 février 1826. 43p. *8°. Paris, 1826.*

24853 PERSIL, J. C. Dissertation sur le rétablissement du droit d'aînesse et des substitutions. 39p. *8°. Paris & Bruxelles, 1826.*

24854 PEYRONNET, P. D. de, *Comte.* Chambre des Pairs. Discours prononcé par Mgr le Garde des Sceaux, sur le projet de loi relatif aux successions et substitutions. Séance du 29 mars 1826. 37p. *8°. [Paris,] 1826.*

24855 POINTU, J. Oraison funèbre de l'infortuné droit d'aînesse, immolé avant sa naissance. 15p. *8°. Paris, 1826.*

24856 R..., Émile. Du droit d'aînesse, impolitique, antisocial, impossible dans un gouvernement représentatif, et contraire à la morale. 25p. *8°. Paris, 1826.*

24857 SIBUET, G. Observations à M. le Comte de Peyronnet, Ministre de la Justice, Garde-des-Sceaux; sur son projet de loi concernant les successions et le rétablissement d'un droit d'aînesse. 19p. *8°. Paris, 1826.*

24858 STEPHENS, George, *land-drainer.* Essay on the utility, formation & management of irrigated meadows; with an account of the success of irrigation in Scotland... 81p. *8°. Edinburgh, 1826. With a manuscript note from D. Campbell to J. Gibson Craig inserted. See also 1829, 1834.*

24859 TAILLARD, C. Le droit d'aînesse, élégie. [In acrostic form.] *s.sh.fol.* [Paris, 1826]

24860 THIEBAULT, D. A. P. F. C. H., *Baron.* Réponse à M. Dupin, avocat, sur le droit d'aînesse, suivie de quelques remarques suggérées par les écrits de M. Persil, avocat à la Cour royal de Paris, et de M. Duvergier de Hauranne. 86p. *8°. Paris,* 1826.

24861 WITHERS, W. A memoir, addressed to the Society for the Encouragement of Arts, Manufactures, and Commerce, on the planting and rearing of forest-trees. 42p. *8°. Holt & London,* 1826.

CORN LAWS

24862 [ANDERSON, WILLIAM (*fl.* 1797–1832).] The iniquity of the landholders, the mistakes of the farmers...in regard to the corn laws, clearly demonstrated ...By the author of "The iniquity of banking"... 48p. *8°.* 1826.

24863 An **APOLOGY** for the corn laws; or, high wages and cheap bread incompatible. By a country curate. 184p. *8°.* 1826.

24864 ARTOPHAGOS, *pseud.* A letter to James John Farquharson, Esq. on the subject of the late meeting at Blandford, Dorset, on the corn laws. 15p. *8°.* 1826.

24865 ATHERLEY, E. G. A letter to the Earl of Liverpool, on the present distresses of the country: shewing, that they do not proceed from taxation...but from the want of a sufficiency of food...and proving that a repeal of the corn laws...would not only be a complete remedy for the distress, but would...be attended with great advantages even to the land-owners themselves. 108p. *8°.* [*London,*] *Dublin, &c.,* 1826.

24866 —— A letter to the Earl of Liverpool, shewing, that a repeal of the corn laws will be attended with great injury and injustice to the land-owners and farmers, unless accompanied, either by a reduction of their taxes and other burthens, or by measures to keep up the prices of English-grown corn... 32p. *8°.* 1826. *Presentation copy from the author to George Pryme.*

24867 —— A letter to the Earl of Liverpool, shewing, that the objections which are made to the admission of foreign corn, are either totally unsound, or may be easily obviated. 24p. *8°. London, Dublin, &c.,* 1826.

24868 —— [Another issue.] A second letter to the Earl of Liverpool on the distresses of the country, and the remedy for them. 24p. *8°. London, Dublin, &c.,* 1826.

24869 A **COMPENDIUM** of the laws, passed...for regulating and restricting the importation, exportation, and consumption of foreign corn, from the year 1660. And a series of accounts...shewing the operation of the several Statutes, and the average prices of corn: presenting a complete view of the corn trade of Great Britain... 59p. *8°.* 1826. *A compilation sometimes attributed to Sir James Graham. See also* 1827, 1833.

24870 COOKE, L. Practical observations on the importation of foreign corn. 28p. *8°.* 1826. *See also* 1827.

24871 The **CORN LAWS;** a correspondence addressed to the farmers and manufacturers of the county of Warwick. [A reply to the Rev. James Roberts' letter on Chandos Leigh's Essay on free trade, both of which are printed in the introduction.] 43p. *8°.* 1826.

24872 The **CORN LAWS** considered, in their effect on the labourer, tenant, landlord, &c. 31p. *8°.* 1826.

24873 COURT, M. H. Illustration of theory and facts, giving a solution of the intricacies of the corn question, with respect to importation and restriction; in further proof of the necessity for the repeal of the tithe laws. 17p. *8°.* 1826.

24874 [DRUMMOND, H.] Cheap corn best for farmers, proved in a letter to George Holme Sumner, Esq., M.P. for the County of Surrey. By one of his constituents. Second edition. 37p. *8°.* 1826. *For another edition, see* 1825.

24875 ELLMAN, J. A letter on the corn laws, addressed to the Legislature shewing the amount of duty necessary for agricultural protection: containing also Mr. Huskisson's letter to his constituents at Chichester, in 1814. 36p. *8°.* [1826]

24876 The **GROUNDS** and danger of restrictions on the corn trade considered: together with a letter on the substance of rent. 134p. *8°.* 1826.

24877 HIGGINS, G. An address to the Houses of Lords and Commons in defence of the corn laws. 60p. *8°.* 1826.

24878 HOLDSWORTH, A. H. A letter to the members for the County of Devon, on the monopoly of the landed interest. 23p. *8°. Exeter & London,* [1826]

24879 HUSKISSON, W. A letter on the corn laws, by the Right Hon. W. Huskisson, to one of his constituents, in 1814. 16p. *8°.* 1826. *See also* 1827.

24880 MAITLAND, JAMES, *8th Earl of Lauderdale, and others.* Protest [signed: Lauderdale, Newcastle, Montfort, Rosslyn] on the subject of the measures now impending in Parliament in relation to the corn laws; entered against the second reading of a Bill "to empower His Majesty to admit foreign corn for home consumption under certain limitations." 16p. *8°.* 1826.

24881 PAPER CURRENCY and corn laws considered separately and conjointly. 56p. *8°.* [1826]

24882 SCOTT, SIR C. *Bart.* Some brief observations relative to the practical effect of the corn laws; being the substance of two letters addressed to a Member of the House of Commons. 16p. *8°.* 1826.

24883 SLOANE, V. Letter to the Right Honourable the Chancellor of the Exchequer, illustrative of the operation and effect of the corn restriction laws upon landed property, and the probable consequences of their abrogation to land-owners and the public. 43p. *8°. Edinburgh, London, &c.,* 1826.

24884 STANHOPE, PHILIP H., *4th Earl Stanhope.* A letter from Earl Stanhope, on the corn laws. 46p. *8°.* 1826.

24885 STRICKLAND, afterwards **CHOLMLEY,** SIR G., *Bart.* Observations upon the corn laws, addressed to the farmers and manufacturers of Yorkshire. 64p. *8°. Leeds & London,* 1826.

24886 TORRENS, R. An essay on the external corn trade... Third edition. 416p. *8°. 1826. For other editions, see* 1815.

24887 WHITMORE, W. W. A letter to the electors of Bridgenorth, upon the corn laws. 84p. *8°. Edinburgh & London,* 1826.

24888 —— Second edition. 84p. *8°. Edinburgh & London,* 1826.

24889 WILSON, ROBERT, *of Hawick.* A disquisition on the corn-laws, with a few observations on pauperism, as it appears among the higher orders as well as among the lower orders of society. 188p. *12°. Hawick, Edinburgh, &c.,* 1826.

24890 A few WORDS to the Agricultural Committee of either House, on the present crisis. 16p. *8°.* 1826.

POPULATION

24891 EVERETT, A. H. New ideas on population: with remarks on the theories of Malthus and Godwin. Second edition. To which is prefixed a new preface, containing a brief examination of the opinions of MM. Say and Sismondi on the same subject. 125p. *8°. Boston,* 1826.

24892 —— Nouvelles idées sur la population, avec des remarques sur les théories de Malthus et de Godwin...

Ouvrage traduit sur l'édition anglaise publiée à Boston, en 1823, avec une nouvelle préface de l'auteur; par C. J. Ferry. 127p. *8°. Paris,* 1826. *The copy that belonged to N. W. Senior. For other editions, see* 1823.

24893 MALTHUS, T. R. An essay on the principle of population... Sixth edition... 2 vols. *8°.* 1826. *For other editions, see* 1798.

TRADES & MANUFACTURES

24894 CORPORATION OF JOYNERS, CEILERS AND WAINSCOTTERS, *Dublin.* The charter, rules, regulations, oaths, &c. of the corporation... Presented... 1826. 23p. *4°. n.p.* [1826]

24895 HOLMES, T. An essay on the principles and application of the lever... Being the... prize essay and rewarded at the third anniversary meeting of the London Mechanics' Institution... 1826... 24p. *8°.* [1826]

24896 HOME, G. Suggestions for giving employment and permanent relief to the manufacturers now so distressed in the Liberty [Dublin]. 20p. *8°. Dublin,* 1826.

24897 INCORPORATION OF GOLD-SMITHS, *Edinburgh.* Laws of the Incorporation of Goldsmiths of Edinburgh. Revised by T. W. Baird, Esq. Advocate. Ratified by the Magistrates and Town-Council, 12th April 1826. 37p. *8°. Edinburgh,* 1826.

24898 IRELAND. *Trustees of the Linen and Hempen Manufactures.* Report from the associations in the provinces of Munster and Connaught, to whom aid has been granted by the Trustees... in answer to queries from Peter Besnard, Esq. Inspector General of these provinces. 56p. *8°. Cork,* 1826.

24899 JOHNSON, W. C. A few hints to iron masters, on the reduction of ores, and the manufacture of pig-iron; showing the proper fluxes and management of different ores of iron. 16p. *8°. Birmingham,* 1826.

24900 NICHOLSON, JOHN (*fl.* 1825). Le mécanicien anglais, ou description raisonnée de toutes les machines, mécaniques, découvertes nouvelles, inventions et perfectionnemens... Traduit de l'anglais sur la dernière édition,

et revu et corrigé par M***, ingénieur [P. Pierrugues]... 5 vols. *8°. Paris,* 1826. *For other editions, see* 1825.

24901 NICHOLSON, P. The carpenter and builder's complete measurer. Intended as a sequel to the "Carpenter's guide." A practical treatise on mensuration, for the use of carpenters, builders, and surveyors... 240p. *4°.* [*London*, 1826] *Signed in sequence with* An improved and enlarged edition of Nicholson's New carpenter's guide, *1825 (q.v.).*

24902 PARTINGTON, C. F. A course of lectures on the steam engine, delivered before the members of the London Mechanics' Institution... To which is subjoined, a copy of the rare and curious work on steam navigation, originally published by Jonathan Hulls in 1737... 92p. *12°.* 1826. *The Rastrick copy.*

24903 —— An historical and descriptive account of the steam engine... with an appendix of patents and parliamentary papers connected with the subject... Second edition, corrected and enlarged... 300p. *8°.* 1826. *For other editions, see* 1822.

24904 PENNSYLVANIA SOCIETY FOR THE PROMOTION OF MANUFACTURES. Constitution of the Pennsylvania Society... Debated and ratified, Dec. 14, 1826. *s.sh.8°. n.p.* [1826]

24905 SMITH, GEORGE. The cabinet-maker and upholsterer's guide... in which will be comprised treatises on geometry and perspective... To which is added, a complete series of new and original designs for household furniture, and interior decoration... 219p. *4°.* 1826.

24906 WYATT, W. H. A compendium of the law of patents for inventions. 52p. *8°.* 1826.

COMMERCE

24907 The ABOLITION of the General Company for the Cultivation of the Vines in the Upper Douro, shewn to be equally advantageous to the English as the con-

sumers, and to the Portuguese as the growers of the port wine. By a Portuguese. 139p. *8°.* 1826.

24908 [BOURGUIGNON D'HERBIGNY, P. F. X.] Paris port de mer; par l'auteur de la Revue politique de l'Europe en 1825. Deuxième édition. 83p. *8°. Paris,* 1826.

24909 BROWN, WILLIAM K. Three letters to the editor of the Maidstone Gazette, relative to a free trade in corn in Great Britain, with some prefatory remarks. Also an appendix, upon the state of the wool and woollen trades. 64p. *8°. Maidstone,* 1826.

24910 CANARD, N. F. Mémoire sur les causes qui produisent la stagnation et le décroissement du commerce en France, et qui tendent à anéantir l'industrie commerciale; moyen simple de les faire cesser. 48p. *8°. Paris,* 1826.

24911 [CAREY, M.] Cursory views of the liberal and restrictive systems of political economy; and of their effects in Great Britain, France, Russia, Prussia, Holland, and the United States. With an examination of Mr. Huskisson's system of duties on imports. By a citizen of Philadelphia. [Signed: Hamilton.] Second edition, greatly enlarged and improved. 26p. *8°. Philadelphia,* 1826.

24912 [——] Fourth edition, greatly enlarged and improved. 30p. *8°. Philadelphia,* 1826.

24913 [——] Essay on free trade: from Blackwood's Magazine, of May, 1825. To which are prefixed a preface [signed: Hamilton] and a few explanatory notes. By a citizen of Philadelphia. 27p. *8°. Philadelphia,* 1826.

24914 CASE of the British merchants, sufferers by the confiscations made in 1807 of the book debts due to them from the subjects of Denmark and Norway. [As in the case of Mr. James Shillito.] 19p. *8°.* 1826. *The Agar Ellis copy.*

24915 *COMMITTEE ON THE LAW RELATING TO PRINCIPAL AND FACTOR.* Law relating to principal and factor. The second report of the Committee for conducting the proceedings in Parliament, made on the 30th September, 1826. 24p. *8°.* 1826. *The copy that belonged to George Grote.*

24916 DOCUMENTOS relativos ao commercio dos novos estados da America, communicados pela Secretaria principal do Commercio de França as principaes Camaras do commercio do Reyno, vertidos em lingua vulgar. 48p. *4°. Lisboa,* 1826.

24917 DUCHATELLIER, A. R. M. Du commerce et de l'administration, ou coup d'œil sur le nouveau système commercial de l'Angleterre. Quels sont les intérêts de la France. 123p. *8°. Paris,* 1826.

24918 FRANCE. *Laws, etc.* The Code de commerce, translated from the French for the use of mercantile agents and ship-masters, as well as gentlemen of the law. 215p. *12°. London & Edinburgh,* 1826. *For other editions, see* 1807.

24919 [GRAY, CHARLES, *of Carse.*] Insanire docent certâ ratione modoque. [On corn importation. The text in English.] 3p. *4°. Edinburgh,* [1826] *In a collection of five of the author's works, presented by him, with an inscription, to 'Thos. Graham Henbury[?] Esq'.*

24920 [——] [Another edition.] 7p. *4°. Dundee,* [1826]

24921 HORSBURGH, J. India directory, or directions for sailing to and from the East Indies, China, New Holland, Cape of Good Hope, Brazil, and the interjacent ports: compiled chiefly from original journals at the East India House... Third edition. 2 vols. *4°.* 1826–27. [*Binding* 28] *The copy bound for King William IV, with his book-plate as Duke of Clarence.*

24922 HUSKISSON, W. Free trade. Speech of the Right Hon. W. Huskisson in the House of Commons, Thursday, the 23d of February, 1826, on Mr. Ellice's motion for a Select Committee, to inquire into...the statements contained in the various petitions from persons engaged in the silk manufacture. 59p. *8°.* 1826.

24923 —— Navigation laws. Speech of the Right Hon. W. Huskisson in the House of Commons, Friday, the 12th of May, 1826, on the present state of the shipping interest. With an appendix, containing the several accounts referred to. 70p. *8°.* 1826. *See also* 1827.

24924 JACOB, W. Report on the trade in foreign corn, and on the agriculture of the north of Europe... (Ordered to be printed by the House of Commons.) To which is added an appendix of official documents, averages of prices, shipments... 249p. *8°.* 1826.

24925 —— Second edition. 249p. *8°.* 1826.

24926 —— Third edition. 249p. *8°.* 1826.

24927 MOORE, JAMES C. Freedom of trade... Second edition, corrected and enlarged. 56p. *8°.* 1826.

24928 OBSERVATIONS addressed to the shipping, the agricultural and the commercial interests, on the impolicy of the free trade system pursued by His Majesty's ministers. [Reports of meetings of ship-owners of the port of Newcastle, under the chairmanship of William Richmond, to organize a petition against the relaxation of the navigation laws, together with reprints of two articles from *Blackwood's Magazine.*] 84p. *8°. Newcastle,* 1826.

24929 Some POINTS in the question of the silk trade stated: in a letter addressed to the Right Hon. George Canning, M.P....[Signed: One who is no enemy to free trade on just principles, and dated, 18th February, 1826.] 16p. *4°.* 1826.

24930 RAYNAL, G. T. F. Histoire philosophique et politique des établissemens et du commerce des Européens dans l'Afrique septentrionale; ouvrage posthume de G. T. Raynal, augmentée d'un aperçu de l'état actuel de ces établissemens et du commerce qu'y font les Européens, notamment avec les puissances barbaresques et la Grèce moderne; par M. Peuchet... 2 vols. *8°. Paris,* 1826. *For other editions, see* 1773.

24931 ROME, *Empire of.* An Edict of Diocletian, fixing a maximum of prices throughout the Roman Empire, A.D.303. [Published, with an introduction and a translation into English, by W. M. Leake.] 42p. *8°.* 1826.

24932 SHACKLETON, W. The wool-dealer's calculator; being a new and complete set of tables, so constructed that staplers buying or selling wool...may find the amount thereof immediately... lx, 251p. *12°. Bradford & London,* 1826.

24933 STEIMMIG, K. P. Missverhältnisse des brittischen Korngesetzes...Beleuchtung veranlasst durch Sir John Sinclair. 43p. *8°. Danzig,* 1826.

24934 SWEDEN. *Treaties, etc.* Convention de commerce & de navigation, entre Sa Majesté, le Roi de Suède & de Norvège, & Sa Majesté, le Roi du Royaume Uni de la Grande Bretagne & de l'Irlande, conclue à Londres, le 18 mars 1826. 10p. *4°. Stockholm,* 1826.

24935 UNITED STATES OF AMERICA. Congress. *House of Representatives.* 19th Congress, 2d session...Doc. no. 45. Statutes of the British Parliament, in relation to the colonial trade: to which are appended the

Acts of Congress on the same subject. December 19th, 1826... 106p. *8°. Washington*, 1826.

24936 —— —— *Senate*. 19th Congress... ⟨76⟩ Letter from the Secretary of the Treasury, transmitting statements of the commerce and navigation of the United States, for the year ending on the 30th September, 1825. March 31, 1826... 278p. *8°. Washington*, 1826. *See also* 1822, 1830 *(House of Representatives)*.

24937 WILLIAMS, Sir John (1777–1846), *and others*. Speeches in the House of Commons, on Friday, the 24th of February, 1826, of Mr. John Williams...of the Right Hon. Wm. Huskisson...and...of the Right Hon. George Canning...on the motion, that a Select Committee be appointed to consider of the petition presented from persons connected with the silk trade. 100p. *8°*. 1826.

24938 WYATT, J. Observations on the question of the corn laws and free trade...To which is added, a short account of Mr. Jacob's report on foreign corn and agriculture. 43p. *8°*. 1826.

COLONIES

24939 AUBER, P. An analysis of the constitution of the East-India Company, and of the laws passed by Parliament for the government of their affairs...To which is prefixed, a brief history of the Company... 804p. *8°*. 1826. *For a supplement, see* 1828.

24940 [COLERIDGE, H. N.] Six months in the West Indies, in 1825. 332p. *8°*. 1826. *See also* 1832, 1841.

24941 A DECLARATION of inhabitants of Barbados, respecting the demolition of the Methodist Chapel. With an appendix. 20p. *8°. Barbados*, 1826. *The copy that belonged to Stephen Lushington.*

24942 On the increasing **IMPORTANCE** of the British West-Indian possessions. 29p. *8°*. 1826.

24943 STEWART, M. Some considerations on the policy of the Government of India, more especially with reference to the invasion of Burmah. 136p. *8°. Edinburgh & London*, 1826.

24944 WILLIAMS, Cynric R. A tour through the island of Jamaica, from the western to the eastern end, in the year 1823. 352p. *8°*. 1826.

FINANCE

24945 BABBAGE, C. A comparative view of the various institutions for the assurance of lives. 170p. *8°*. 1826.

24946 Safe **BANKS**: a proposal to the landed interest. By a Member of Parliament. 19p. *8°*. 1826.

24947 BECHER, John T. Observations upon the Report from the Select Committee of the House of Commons, on the laws respecting friendly societies; exemplifying and vindicating the principles of life assurance, adopted in calculating the Southwell tables; together with the heads of a Bill for improving...such institutions. 123p. *8°. Newark & London*, 1826.

24948 BENTHAM, J. Postscript to Indications respecting Lord Eldon, &c.&c. 24p. *8°*. 1826. *For* Indications, *see* 1825.

24949 [BLANSHARD, R.] Thoughts on the present commercial distress, and on the means to prevent its recurrence. By a merchant. 23p. *8°*. 1826.

24950 BLAYNEY, F. A practical treatise on life-assurance, in which the statutes and judicial decisions affecting unincorporated joint stock companies...are fully considered and explained...together with...tables, &c.&c. 195p. *8°*. 1826.

24951 BRITANNICUS, *pseud*. A treatise on the currency, in which the principle of uniformity is advocated, and in which all the great bearings of the question are considered. 75p. *8°. Edinburgh & London*, 1826.

24952 BURGESS, H. A letter to the Right Hon. George Canning, to explain in what manner the industry of the people, and the productions of the country, are connected with, and influenced by, internal bills of exchange, country bank notes, and branch banks...With a postscript on the tendency of the wages of labour in England to become equal... 139p. *8°*. 1826.

24953 C., D. R. M. Cartas económicas escritas por un amigo a otro, ó sea tratado teórico-práctico elemental sobre la naturaleza de cada una de los rentas de la corona, y de su régimen administrativo...Por D.R.M.C.... 146, 80, 82p. *4°. Madrid*, 1826.

24954 True **CAUSE** of the late panic, and present distress, fairly stated. By an observer. 26p. *8°*. 1826.

24955 A COMMENT upon Thomas Tooke, Esq. By a member of the Russia and Levant Companies, and one of the Court of Assistants of the East-land Company. 12, 53p. *8°*. 1826.

24956 COMMERCE in consternation! Or, the banking bubble burst! Being a sketch of the rise, progress, and decline, of the late paper panic. 124p. *8°*. 1826.

24957 CORT, R. A letter to the shareholders of the British Iron Company, showing the past and present losses of the speculation; with suggestions to realize the future profit of the concern. [With an appendix, containing reports and accounts of the Company for the years 1825–26.] 35, livp. *8°*. 1826.

For the **COURIER**, *see* vol. III, *Periodicals list.*

24958 COURT, M. H. Theory and facts in proof, that the laws for the imposition of tithes are attended with the most calamitous consequences to the country, with plans for the redemption of tithes, and a comparison of the effects of a repeal of the tithe laws, with the proposed repeal of the corn laws. 42p. *8°*. 1826.

24959 [CROKER, John W.] Two letters on Scottish affairs, from Edward Bradwardine Waverley, Esq. to Malachi Malagrowther, Esq. 62p. *8°. London & Edinburgh*, 1826.

24960 [——] Second edition. 62p. *8°. London & Edinburgh*, 1826.

24961 DOUBLEDAY, T. Remarks on some points of the currency question, in a review of Mr. Tooke's "Considerations." 46p. *8°. London & Newcastle upon Tyne*, 1826.

24962 DRUMMOND, H. Elementary propositions on the currency. The third edition; with additions, showing their application to the present times. 69p. *8°.* 1826.

24963 —— The fourth edition. 69p. *8°.* 1826. *For other editions, see* 1820.

For the EDINBURGH WEEKLY JOURNAL, *see* vol. III, *Periodicals list.*

24964 An ENQUIRY into the origin and increase of the paper currency of the Kingdom, a subject deserving and requiring the serious consideration of the Legislature and of every man in England. 36p. *8°.* 1826.

24965 An ESSAY showing the erroneousness of the prevalent opinions with respect to the injurious effects of absenteeism [among landlords]. From the eighty-fifth number of the Edinburgh Review. 29p. *8°.* 1826.

24966 EUNOMIA. With brief hints to country gentlemen and others of tender capacity on the principles of the new sect of political economical philosophers termed Eunomians: which principles are applied to the grand question, "What is money, its office and effects in society?" ...With some strictures upon banks and the banking system, in answer to the Right Hon. Sir John Sinclair, Bart., Malachi Malagrowther, Sir Robert Peel, Bart.... 80p. *8°.* 1826.

24967 FAZY, J. J. Opuscules financiers sur l'effet des priviléges, des emprunts publics et des conversions sur le crédit de l'industrie en France. 295p. *8°. Paris & Genève*, 1826.

24968 FLOREZ ESTRADA, A. Reflections on the present mercantile distress experienced in Great Britain, and more or less affecting other nations on the continent of Europe, &c.&c. 36p. *8°.* 1826.

24969 FORTUNE, E. F. THOMAS. Fortune's epitome of the stocks & public funds...Twelfth edition, with additions...Revised and corrected to the present time, by J. J. Secretan. 108p. *12°.* 1826. *For other editions, see* 1796.

24970 GAUDIN, M. M. C., *Duc de Gaëte.* Mémoires, souvenirs, opinions et écrits du Duc de Gaëte...ancien ministre des finances...(*Collection des Mémoires relatifs à la Révolution française.*) 2 vols. *8°. Paris & Bruxelles*, 1826. *For a supplement, see* 1834.

24971 GOLDSMID, SIR I. L., *Bart.* Remarks on the Bank Restriction Act and the Sinking Fund. 24p. *8°.* 1826.

24972 GRAHAM, SIR JAMES R. G., *Bart.* Corn and currency; in an address to the land owners. 114p. *8°.* 1826. *See also* 1827, 1828.

24973 [GRAY, CHARLES, *of Carse.*] —— Quidquid novisti rectius istis Candidus imperti, ——. [On banking. Text in English.] 3p. *4°. Edinburgh*, [1826] *Two presentation copies from the author. See note to no.* 24485.

24974 [GROOM, R.] The Bank of England defended, or the principal cause of the high prices demonstrated, by an inquiry into the...present system of coinage, also by an examination of certain opinions in regard to a metallic currency, the foreign exchanges, and the effects of our paper currency; with suggestions for forming a more accurate monetary system. [The preface signed: Verax.] 74p. *8°.* 1826.

24975 [——] A defence of our laws against usury; by an inquiry into the causes and consequences of the several reductions in the rate of interest in England; proving... that even a further reduction in the rate of interest would be more beneficial for the kingdom...By the author of an inquiry into the effects of the debasement of our silver coins, intitled The Bank of England defended. 29p. *8°.* 1826.

24976 HANNING, W. Proposal of a plan for making country bank paper equally secure, with that of the Bank of England, and for keeping in circulation the requisite supply of coin and paper money, to support trade. In a letter to the Earl of Liverpool. 29p. *8°. Taunton*, [1826]

24977 JOPLIN, T. An essay on the general principles and present practice of banking, in England and Scotland: with supplementary observations on the steps proper to form a public bank, and the system on which its accounts ought to be kept...Fifth edition. xx, 130p. *8°.* 1826. *Presentation copy, with inscription, from the author to T. Spring Rice, Baron Monteagle. For other editions, see* 1822.

24978 —— [Another edition of the Preface.] xxivp. *8°. n.p.* [1826?] *This edition contains the text of the prospectus for a Provincial Bank of England.*

24979 JOYCE, T. A letter to the Right Hon. Robert Peel, proposing means, whereby the importation of foreign corn may be rendered conducive to the relief and interest of the British farmers. 15p. *8°.* 1826.

24980 KENSINGTON BANK. By-laws, rules and regulations of the Board of Directors of the Kensington Bank, with Acts of Assembly relative to the government of banks. 46p. *12°. Philadelphia*, 1826.

24981 A LETTER to the Earl of Liverpool, on the erroneous information that His Majesty's Ministers have adopted regarding country banks and the currency in the manufacturing districts; and suggesting means for correcting some of the existing evils in the circulation of country bank notes. By a manufacturer, in the north of England. 25p. *8°.* 1826.

24982 A LETTER to the Right Hon. Robert Peel, M.P. &c.&c. upon the necessity of adopting some parliamentary measure to control the issues of country bankers, and to prevent the recurrence of the late shock to public and private credit, with the heads of a Bill for that purpose. 75p. *8°.* 1826.

24983 —— Second edition. 75p. *8°.* 1826.

24984 The LIFE, adventures & serious remonstrances of a Scotch guinea note, containing a defence of the Scotch system of banking, and a reply to the late letters of E. Bradwardine Waverley. By the author of the "Letters of a plain man." 21p. *8°. Edinburgh, Glasgow, &c.*, 1826.

24985 LYNE, C. A letter to the Lord High Chancellor, on the nature and causes of the late and present distress in commercial, manufacturing, and banking concerns. With proposed partial remedies. 23p. *8°.* 1826.

24986 [McCULLOCH, JOHN R.] On fluctuations in the supply and value of money, and the banking system of England. ⟨From the Edinburgh Review, No. 86, about to appear.⟩ 33p. *8°.* [*Edinburgh*, 1826]

24987 MILFORD, J. Observations on the proceedings of country bankers during the last thirty years; and on their communications with government: together with a remedy proposed against the alarming consequences arising from the circulation of promissory notes; in a letter addressed to the Chancellor of the Exchequer. 46p. 8°. 1826.

24988 MITCHELL, JAMES (1786?–1844). A treatise on benefit or friendly societies: containing a statement of the laws of the land respecting these institutions; the probabilities of sickness, mortality, births... With practical instructions for the formation of rates, the investment of the funds, and general management... 40p. 8°. 1826.

24989 MOORE, R. The outline of a plan for bringing the Scotch and English currency to the same standard bullion value, and producing a sterling country bank note of exchangeable value, convertible in every place to gold coin... 76p. 8°. 1826. *See also* 1827.

24990 MUSHET, R. An attempt to explain from facts the effect of the issues of the Bank of England upon its own interests, public credit and country banks. 215p. 8°. 1826.

24991 NEALE, F. An essay on money-lending; containing a defence of legal restrictions on the rate of interest, and an answer to the objections of Mr. Bentham. 92p. 8°. 1826.

24992 NETHERLANDS. *Permanente Commissie uit het Amortisatie-Syndicaat.* De Permamente Commissie uit het Amortisatie-Syndicaat...brengt bij deze ter kennisse van allen en een iegeijk het navolgende berigt eener negotiatie, tot te geldemaking van een kapitaal van veertig millioenen domein-losrenten, voortgesproten uit de negotiatie van honderd millioenen, geopend bij berigt van den 19 Junij 1824... 11p. 12°. *n.p.* [1826]

24993 [—— —— *Begin.*] De...Commissie uit het Amortisatie-Syndicaat willende voldoen aan het verlangen aan haar kenbaar gemaakt door houders van Uitgeloten kansbiljetten en tot dat einde door den Koning gemagtigd, brengt bij dezen ter kennis van het publiek... 3p. 12°. *n.p.* [1826]

24994 [**PAGE,** R.] Letters to the editor of "The Times" journal, on the affairs and conduct of the Bank of England; the introduction of British silver money into the colonies; and generally, on the currency of the United Kingdom, both paper and metallic. With notes, and an appendix. By Daniel Hardcastle. 310p. 8°. 1826. *Presentation copy, with inscription, from the author to Henry Goulburn, then Chief Secretary for Ireland.*

24995 The **PANIC.** 24p. 8°. 1826.

24996 PECCHIO, G., *Conte.* Saggio storico sulla amministrazione finanziera dell' ex-regno d'Italia dal 1802 al 1804. Seconda edizione. 150p. 8°. *Londra,* 1826.

24997 [**PETIT,** P. F. V. A.?] Mémoire sur les engagemens de bourse, dits marchés à terme. 143p. 8°. *Paris,* 1826. *Attributed to Petit on the evidence of the binder's title.*

24998 PHILLIPS, SIR RICHARD. Golden rules for bankers; with a postscript on the present panic, and on the destruction of commercial credit. 79p. 8°. [1826]

24999 POLŒCONOMICUS. (Letter first.) Currency—banking in Scotland. From the Edinburgh Times, February 18. 1826. 6 col. 4°. *n.p.* [1826] *Letters I–VI tentatively attributed by HSF to Robert Bell.*

25000 —— (Letter second.) The currency. From the Edinburgh Times, February 25. 1826. 6 col. 4°. *n.p.* [1826]

25001 —— Currency. From the Edinburgh Times, March 4, 1826. [Letter third. Signed: P.O.] *s.sh.4°. n.p.* [1826]

25002 —— (Letter fourth.) Currency—Banking in Scotland. From the Edinburgh Times, March 11, 1826. [2]p. 4°. *n.p.* [1826]

25003 —— (Letter fifth.) The banking system of Britain. From the Edinburgh Times, April 8, 1826. [2]p. 4°. *n.p.* [1826]

25004 —— (Letter sixth.) The banking system of Britain. From the Edinburgh Times, April 15, 1826. [2]p. 4°. *n.p.* [1826]

25005 Some practical **REMARKS** on the effect of the usury laws on the landed interests, in a letter to John Calcraft, Esq. M.P. By a solicitor. 18p. 8°. 1826.

25006 ROBINSON, F. J., *Earl of Ripon.* Speech of the Right Hon. F. J. Robinson, Chancellor of the Exchequer, on the financial situation of the country, delivered in a Committee of Ways and Means...the 13th of March 1826. To which is added, an appendix, containing various accounts referred to. 55p. 8°. 1826.

25007 [**SCOTT,** SIR WALTER, *Bart.*] Thoughts on the proposed change of currency, and other late alterations, as they affect, or are intended to affect, the Kingdom of Scotland. [Signed: Malachi Malagrowther.] 60p. 8°. *Edinburgh,* 1826. *The copy that belonged to Henry Richard Vassall Fox, 3rd Baron Holland.*

25008 [——] A letter to the editor of the Edinburgh Weekly Journal, from Malachi Malagrowther, Esq. on the proposed change of currency, and other late alterations, as they affect, or are intended to affect, the Kingdom of Scotland. Second edition. 60p. 8°. *Edinburgh,* 1826.

25009 [——] Third edition. 60p. 8°. *Edinburgh & London,* 1826. *See also* 1844.

25010 [——] A second letter to the editor of the Edinburgh Weekly Journal, from Malachi Malagrowther, Esq. on the proposed change of currency, and other late alterations, as they affect, or are intended to affect, the Kingdom of Scotland. 84p. 8°. *Edinburgh,* 1826.

25011 [——] Second edition. 86p. 8°. *Edinburgh & London,* 1826.

25012 [——] Third edition. 86p. 8°. *Edinburgh & London,* 1826. *See also* 1844.

25013 [——] A third letter to the editor of the Edinburgh Weekly Journal, from Malachi Malagrowther, Esq. on the proposed change of currency, and other late alterations, as they affect, or are intended to affect the Kingdom of Scotland. 39p. 8°. *Edinburgh & London,* 1826.

25014 [——] Second edition. 39p. 8°. *Edinburgh & London,* 1826.

25015 [——] Third edition. 39p. 8°. *Edinburgh & London,* 1826. *See also* 1844.

25016 SCOTT, WILLIAM (*fl.* 1826). Mr. Scott's speech, and letters upon the currency, in answer to Malachi Malagrowther. 23p. 12°. *Edinburgh, London, &c.,* 1826.

25017 SEDGWICK, J. Twelve letters addressed to the Right Hon. Thomas Wallace, M.P., chairman of the

Commission of Revenue Inquiry. [Refuting charges of corruption made against him as chairman of the Board of Stamps.] 200p. *8°. London & Edinburgh,* 1826.

25018 SIBUET, G. Opinion prononcé à l'Assemblée Générale des 200 plus forts actionnaires de la Banque de France, le 26 janvier 1826; suivie de notes explicatives. 20p. *8°. [Paris,* 1826]

25019 SINCLAIR, SIR JOHN, *Bart.* The late prosperity, and the present adversity of the country, explained; the proper remedies considered, and the comparative merits of the English and Scottish systems of banking discussed, in a correspondence between Sir John Sinclair and Mr. Thomas Attwood. 134p. *8°.* 1826. *Another, the FWA copy, belonged to William Pare, with manuscript notes throughout in the hand of Thomas Attwood.*

25020 [SURR, T. S.] The present critical state of the country developed; or an exhibition of the true causes of the calamitous derangement of the banking and commercial system…shewing the essential distinction between the solidity of the national Bank of England and that of country banks. By an individual of thirty years' practical experience in banking and commercial affairs. 84p. *8°.* 1826. *See also* 1832.

25021 TAYLOR, JAMES (1788–1863). No trust, no trade! Or, remarks on the nature of money: in which the cause of the present national distress is pointed out, and a prompt and efficacious remedy is suggested. 50p. *8°.* 1826. *Presentation copy from the author to Thomas Bateman. See also* 1842.

25022 THIERS, L. A. Encyclopédie progressive… Law, et son système de finances. [An offprint of p.49–128.] 80p. *8°. n.p.* [1826]

25023 THOMSON, JOHN, *accountant.* Tables of interest, at 3, 4, 4½, and 5 per cent. From £1. to £10,000. And from one to three hundred and sixty-five days… Also tables, shewing the exchange on bills, or commission on goods, &c. from one-eighth to five per cent…To which are prefixed a table of discount on bills…The ninth edition, carefully corrected. 532p. *12°. London, Edinburgh, &c.,* 1826. *For another edition, see* 1794.

25024 TOOKE, T. Considerations on the state of the currency. 152p. *8°.* 1826.

25025 —— Second edition. [With a postscript.] 196p. *8°.* 1826. *Two copies, one that belonged to Francis Place, with his book-label, and a note in his hand on the flyleaf 'From Mr. Tooke Francis Place April 1 1826'; and a second copy, which lacks the half-title, that belonged to Sir Robert Peel.*

25026 [WADE, JOHN.] Digest of facts and principles, on banking and commerce, with a plan for preventing future re-actions. 118p. *12°.* 1826. *See also* 1836.

25027 WESTERN, C. C., *Baron Western.* A letter to the Earl of Liverpool on the cause of our present embarrassment and distress: and the measures necessary for our effectual relief. 43p. *8°.* 1826.

25028 —— [Another edition.] 51p. *8°.* 1826.

TRANSPORT

25029 ADAMSON, J. Sketches of our information as to rail-roads…Also, an account of the Stockton and Darlington rail-way, with observations on rail-ways, &c.&c. (Extracted from the Caledonian Mercury.) 60p. *8°. Newcastle,* 1826.

25030 *CARY, JOHN (*d.* 1835). Cary's new itinerary: or an accurate delineation of the great roads…throughout England and Wales; with many of the principal roads in Scotland…Tenth edition, with improvements. 41p., 124 col., [66]p., 968 col., p.969–1070. *8°.* 1826.

25031 ENGLAND. *Laws, etc.* Anno septimo Georgii IV. Regis. [Local & Personal.] cap. xlix. An Act for making and maintaining a railway or tramroad from the town of Liverpool to the town of Manchester, with certain branches therefrom, all in the county of Lancaster. ⟨5th May, 1826.⟩ p.1385–1494. *fol.* 1826. *See note to no.* 25927.

25032 —— Parliament. *House of Commons.* Abstract of the minutes of evidence, taken before the Committee of the House of Commons, during…1826, on the Bill for making a navigable communication for ships…between …Norwich and the sea at…Lowestoft… 56p. *8°. Norwich & London,* 1826.

25033 KENNET AND AVON CANAL NAVIGATION. Report of the Committee of Management… [Signed: Charles Dundas, chairman, and dated, 18th July, 1826.] [3]p. *fol. n.p.* [1826] *See also* 1812, 1813, 1815, 1816, 1823, 1824, 1825, 1838.

25034 LAMB, A. Suggestions for converting Portland Roads into a harbour. Printed for the information of… the members of both Houses of Parliament, and for the

consideration of His Majesty's ministers. 12p. *fol. n.p.* 1826.

25035 LIVERPOOL AND MANCHESTER RAIL-WAY. Specification for excavating the tunnel at Liverpool. *s.sh.fol. n.p.* [1826]

25036 MIDDLESEX. *Quarter Sessions.* Report of the Committee of magistrates appointed to make enquiry respecting the public bridges in the county of Middlesex. [Presented October, 1825.] 46op. *4°.* 1826.

25037 NIMMO, A. The report of Alexander Nimmo …on the proposed railway between Limerick and Waterford. 39p. *8°. Dublin,* 1826. *The Rastrick copy.*

25038 NORWICH AND LOWESTOFT NAVIGATION. Prospectus. 3p. *4°. n.p.* [1826]

25039 PENNSYLVANIA SOCIETY FOR THE PROMOTION OF INTERNAL IMPROVEMENTS IN THE COMMONWEALTH. The first annual report of the acting Committee of the Society …[being mainly an account of the mission of the Society's agent, William Strickland, to investigate transport and technological advances in Europe]. 45p. *8°. Philadelphia,* 1826. *For an edition of Strickland's report, see no.* 25042.

25040 SANDERSON, H. Considerations on the proposed communication by a navigable canal, between the town of Sheffield and the Peak Forest Canal; with remarks and calculations tending to prove the superiority of an edge-railway for passing over a mountainous district, and a comparative account of the several practicable lines … 91p. *8°. Sheffield,* 1826.

25041 SCHLICK, B. Rapport fait à l'Académie des Beaux Arts de l'Institut de France...sur le chemin souterrain dit: tunnel, qui s'exécute en ce moment sous la Tamise à Londres. Lu le 25 novembre. 12p. *4°. Paris, 1826. Presentation copy to Francis Whishaw, subsequently presented by him to the Institution of Civil Engineers.*

25042 STRICKLAND, W. Reports on canals, railways, roads, and other subjects made to "The Pennsylvania Society for the Promotion of Internal Improvement." 51p. *obl.fol. Philadelphia, 1826. See also no. 25039.*

SOCIAL CONDITIONS

25043 ASSOCIATION FOR THE SUPPRESSION OF MENDICITY, *Dublin.* General account of the numbers supported by the Association...for the week ending Saturday the [5th] of [August] 182[6]. *s.sh.fol. n.p.* [1826] *A printed form completed in manuscript.*

25044 BAINES, SIR EDWARD. An address to the unemployed workmen of Yorkshire and Lancashire, on the present distress, and on machinery...(From the Leeds Mercury of May 13, 1826.) 15p. *8°. London & Leeds,* 1826.

25045 BRERETON, C. D. An inquiry into the workhouse system, and the law of maintenance in agricultural districts...Second edition. 124p. *8°. Norwich & London,* [1826?] *The copy that belonged to William Allen. For another edition, see 1825.*

25046 —— A practical inquiry into the number, means of employment, and wages, of agricultural labourers... Third edition. 140p. *8°. Norwich & London,* [1826] *The copy that belonged to William Allen.*

25047 [BRUCE, W.] Poor rates the panacea for Ireland. 15p. *8°. London & Bristol,* [1826] *See also* 1828.

25048 BURFORD FRIENDLY INSTITUTION. Burford Friendly Institution...Rules and regulations. 29p. *8°. Burford,* 1826.

25049 [CARLILE, R.] Every woman's book; or, what is love? Fourth edition. 48p. *8°.* 1826. *See also* 1828.

25050 COBBETT, W. No. 1.[–v.] Cobbett's poor man's friend: or, useful information and advice for the working classes: in a series of letters addressed to the working classes of Preston. [120]p. *12°.* [1826–27] *Published in parts, nos. 1–4 from August to November 1826, no. 5 in October 1827. See also* 1829, 1830.

25051 *The CONSEQUENCES of a scientific education to the working classes of this country pointed out; and the theories of Mr. Brougham on that subject confuted; in a letter to the Marquess of Lansdown. By a country gentleman. 77p. *8°.* 1826.

25052 [DALLAS, ALEXANDER R. C.] Protestant sisters of charity; a letter addressed to the Lord Bishop of London, developing a plan for improving the arrangements...for administering medical advice, and visiting the sick poor. 38p. *8°.* 1826.

25053 Public **DISTRESS.** A full...account of the present awful distress of the manufacturing districts of England and Scotland and the means employed by public as well as private individuals to alleviate the same... *s.sh.fol. Gateshead,* [1826] [*Br.* 502(2)]

25054 ENGLAND. *Commissioners for Inquiring concerning Charities.* Reports of the Commissioners...in the hundreds of Banbury & Bloxham, also some places in the hundreds of Wootton, Ploughley, Chadlington, & Bullington, Oxon; and a few places in Northamptonshire: from the twelfth and thirteenth reports. 188p. *8°. Banbury,* 1826.

25055 EVERETT, E. Remarks of Mr. Everett on the bill for the relief of the revolutionary officers, in the House of Representatives, April 25, 1826. 18p. *8°. Cambridge,* 1826.

25056 An **EXAMINATION** of the policy and tendency of relieving distressed manufacturers by public subscription: with some remarks on Lord Liverpool's recommendation of those distressed persons in a mass to the poor's rates, and some inquiry as to what law there exists wherewith to support His Lordship's recommendation. 40p. *8°.* 1826.

25057 FRIENDLY INSTITUTION, *Worcester.* The rules, regulations and tables of contributions and allowances of the Friendly Institution, established at Worcester, for the county and city of Worcester... 43p. *8°. Worcester,* 1826.

25058 FRIENDLY SOCIETY OF JOURNEYMEN BOOKBINDERS, *London.* Friendly Society of Bookbinders. The fifth annual report of the receipts and expendidture [*sic*] of Lodge Four, from June 1825 to May 1826...Secretary, Henry Robinson. 4p. *8°.* 1826. *See note to no.* 23614.

25059 —— Report of the committee of investigation appointed by the Friendly Society...to examine the accounts of Lodge Three...from May 1823, to May 1825; and to inquire into the charges preferred by James Carss, of Lodge Three...against Joseph Wortham formerly secretary of the said Lodge... 32p. *8°.* 1826. *See note to no.* 23614.

25060 HACKNEY LITERARY AND MECHANIC INSTITUTION. The first year's report ...read August 3rd, 1826: To which are annexed, catalogues of the apparatus and books belonging to the Institution. 20p. *8°. Hackney,* 1826.

25061 HALCOMB, J. A practical measure of relief from the present system of the poor-laws... 32p. *8°.* 1826.

25062 HALE, WILLIAM. An address to the manufacturers of the United Kingdom, stating the causes which have led to the unparalleled calamities of our manufacturing poor; and the proposal of a remedy... 32p. *8°.* 1826.

25063 HILL, ROWLAND (1744–1833). Village dialogues, between Farmer Littleworth, Thomas Newman, Rev. Mr. Lovegood, and others...Twenty-fifth edition, with additional dialogues and enlargements. 2 vols. *12°.* 1826–28. *For other editions, see* 1803.

25064 HOUSE OF INDUSTRY, *Dublin.* Annual report of the House of Industry, Dublin, and the three general hospitals attached. 1st August, 1826. [4]p. *4°. n.p.* [1826]

25065 *HUELLMANN, C. D. Stædtewesen des Mittelalters... 4 vols. 8°. *Bonn*, 1826–29. *The copy that belonged to George Grote.*

25066 An **INQUIRY** into the nature and effects of flogging...and the alleged necessity for allowing seamen to be flogged at discretion, in the Royal Navy and the merchant service. To which is added, a seaman's appeal ...on the necessity of adopting such measures as would prevent a recurrence to the horrible system of impressment. 46p. 8°. 1826. *Presentation copy, inscribed: With Mr. Hume's Comps. There seems to be no reason to suppose that Hume was the author.*

25067 **JOHNSON,** JAMES. Transactions of the Corporation of the Poor, in the City of Bristol, during a period of 126 years, alphabetically arranged, with observations, and a prefatory address to the Guardians of 1826. 175p. 8°. *Bristol*, 1826.

25068 **LITERARY, SCIENTIFIC AND MECHANICAL INSTITUTION,** *Newcastle-upon-Tyne.* The second annual report of the...Institution... To which are added, a statement of the accounts of the Institution, a list of new members, and a supplement to the catalogue. 26p. 8°. *Newcastle upon Tyne*, 1826. *See also* 1825, 1827.

25069 **LITERARY, SCIENTIFIC, AND MECHANICAL INSTITUTION,** *South Shields.* A catalogue of the library of the...Institution...To which are added the first annual report, and a list of the members. 26p. 8°. *South Shields*,1826.

25070 **LUDLOW ASSOCIATION FOR THE PROSECUTION OF FELONS.** Articles of the Ludlow Association for the Discovery, Apprehension and Prosecution of Felons and other offenders. Dated Dec. 15, 1826. [With a list of subscribers, added to in manuscript, and with two manuscript additions, dated 1828 and 1829, to the articles of agreement.] 15p. 8°. *Ludlow*, [1826]

25071 The poor **MAN'S** friend; or, a plain statement, in which the causes of the alarming increase of pauperism are explained, and means for its prevention suggested. 44p. 8°. *London, Brighton, &c.*, 1826.

25072 **MARTIN,** HENRY (*fl.* 1826). Observations on the importance and advantages of the education of the people; in a letter to James Taylor, Esq. High Sheriff of Worcestershire. 20p. 8°. 1826.

25073 **MECHANICS' INSTITUTION,** *Darlington.* The first report of the Mechanics' Institution... 23p. 8°. *Darlington*, 1826.

25074 **PEEL,** SIR ROBERT, *2nd Bart.* Substance of the speech of the Right Honourable Robert Peel, in the House of Commons, on...March 9th, 1826, on moving for leave to bring in a Bill for the amendment of the cri-minal law, and a Bill for consolidating the laws relating to larceny. 51p. 8°. 1826.

25075 **RENWICK,** T. A letter to the Trustees of the Liverpool Infirmary. 20p. 8°. *Liverpool*, 1826.

25076 Serious **RIOT** at Blackburn, near Manchester... 28th April 1826. s.sh.fol. *Glasgow*, [1826] [*Br.* 502(1)]

25077 **SALISBURY,** W. Economic institution, to promote the knowledge, collection, manufacture and use of articles, the growth of this country; and other objects calculated to give employment to the poor in Great Britain and Ireland. Second edition. To which is added, an account of operative measures...now in progress at the site of the late botanic garden, Brompton. 20p. 8°. 1826.

25078 **SOCIETY FOR THE EDUCATION OF THE POOR IN THE HIGHLANDS.** Moral statistics of the Highlands and Islands of Scotland, compiled from returns received by the Inverness Society... To which is prefixed, a report on the past and present state of education in three districts. [With an appendix of letters.] 73, xlviiip. 8°. *Inverness, London, &c.*, 1826.

25079 The **SPINNING-MILL:** or, suggestions, for the moral improvement of such establishments. Illustrated in the History of George Melville. By the author of "the Infidel reclaimed", and "Early impressions." 107p. *12°.* [*Edinburgh*,] *Glasgow, &c.*, 1826.

25080 **STARK,** W. Considerations addressed to the heritors and kirk-sessions of Scotland, particularly of the border counties, on certain questions connected with the administration of the affairs of the poor. 213p. *12°.* *Edinburgh, Glasgow, &c.*, 1826.

25081 **WALKER,** THOMAS (1784–1836). Observations on the nature, extent, and effects of pauperism; and on the means of reducing it. 95p. 8°. 1826. *See also* 1831.

25082 **WIRE,** D. An address delivered the 6th day of December, 1825, on the formation of the Colchester Free Burgesses Literary and Scientific Institution. 19p. 8°. *Chelsea, London, &c.*, 1826.

25083 **WRIGHT,** G. Mischiefs exposed. A letter addressed to Henry Brougham, Esq., M.P. shewing the inutility, absurdity and impolicy of the scheme developed in his "Practical observations", for teaching mechanics and labourers the knowledge of chemistry, mathematics, party and general politics, &c. 24p. 8°. *York & London*, 1826.

25084 **Z.,** A. Observations on power-looms, and their effect on the hand-loom weaver, being part of a correspondence between a gentleman at Leeds and his friend at Paisley. 23p. 8°. *Glasgow*, 1826. *The Oastler copy.*

SLAVERY

25085 **ABERDEEN ANTI-SLAVERY SOCIETY.** The first annual report of the Aberdeen Anti-Slavery Society for promoting the mitigation and ultimate abolition of negro slavery, read at the general meeting, held on...the 16th January, 1826. With an account of the proceedings of the meeting, &c. 22p. 8°. *Aberdeen*, 1826.

25086 An **ADDRESS** to the members of the new Parliament, on the proceedings of the Colonial Department, in furtherance of the resolution of the House of Commons of the 15th May 1823, "for ameliorating the condition of the slave population in His Majesty's colonies;" and on the only course that ought now to be pursued by His Majesty's Government. 36p. 8°. 1826.

25087 —— Supplement to An address to the members ... 5p. 8°. n.p. [1826] *The copy that belonged to Stephen Lushington.*

25088 **ANTI-SLAVERY.** More exposures. By the author of the former specimen. 16p. 8°. *Aberdeen*, [1826]

25089 B., P. A general history of negro slavery, collected from the most respectable evidence and unquestionable authorities. By a late resident in the West Indies. [The author's introduction, 'An address to planters and slave proprietors' is signed: P.B.] 218p. *12º. Cambridge*, 1826.

25090 BEAUMONT, A. H. Compensation to slave owners fairly considered in an appeal to the common sense of the people of England...Fourth edition. 23p. *8º.* 1826. *The copy that belonged to Stephen Lushington.*

25091 [BELDAM, J.] Reflections on slavery: in reply to certain passages of a speech recently delivered by Mr. Canning. Addressed to the Right Hon. Lord Dacre. By a barrister. 25p. *8º.* 1826.

25092 BROUGHAM, H. P., *Baron Brougham and Vaux.* Opinions of Henry Brougham, Esq. on negro slavery: [being extracts from his *Inquiry into the colonial policy of the European powers*] with remarks. 47p. *8º.* 1826. *The copy that belonged to Stephen Lushington. See also* 1830, *and, for the original work,* 1803 (COLONIES).

25093 To the **CONSUMERS** of sugar. [Maintaining the speciousness of the arguments used to support a boycott of West India sugar, in favour of East India sugar.] 8p. *8º. n.p.* [1826?] *The copy that belonged to Stephen Lushington.*

25094 ENGLAND. Parliament. *House of Lords.* Slavery in the West Indies. The substance of the debate in the House of Lords, March 7, 1826, on Lord Bathurst's motion for adopting the resolutions of the House of Commons of the 15th May, 1823. 54p. *8º.* 1826.

25095 FEMALE SOCIETY FOR BIRMING-HAM, WEST-BROMWICH, WEDNESBURY, WALSALL...FOR THE RELIEF OF BRITISH NEGRO SLAVES. The first report of the Female Society...for the relief of British negro slaves. 32p. *8º. Birmingham,* 1826. *See also* 1830.

25096 GOULTY, J. N. A discourse on colonial slavery. 47p. *8º.* 1826. *Two copies, both with presentation inscriptions from the author, one to 'the Committee of the Anti-Slavery Society', the other to Stephen Lushington.*

25097 HAYTI. Extracts from the Code Rural of Hayti. 3p. *8º. n.p.* [1826] *For an edition of the complete Code, see* 1827 (SOCIAL CONDITIONS).

25098 [HORTON, SIR R. J. W., *Bart.*] The West India question practically considered. 121p. *8º.* 1826.

25099 LEICESTER, *County of.* A report of the speeches at a county meeting, held at the Castle of Leicester, on...January 20th, 1826, on the subject of colonial slavery. 52p. *8º. Leicester,* 1826.

25100 LETTER to Robert Wilmot Horton, Esq. M.P. ...containing strictures on a pamphlet entitled "The West-India question practically considered." 16p. *8º.* 1826.

25101 LETTERS on the necessity of a prompt extinction of British colonial slavery; chiefly addressed to the more influential classes. To which are added, thoughts on compensation. 219p. *8º. London & Leicester,* 1826. *The Agar Ellis copy.*

25102 —— Second edition. 100p. *8º. London & Leicester,* 1826.

25103 M'DONNELL, A. The West India legislatures vindicated from the charge of having resisted the call of the mother country for the amelioration of slavery. 104p. *8º.* 1826. *Presentation copy, with inscription, from the author to William Leake.*

25104 NEGRO SLAVERY. Observations, in answer to an "Address to the clergy of the Established Church, and to Christian ministers of every denomination." 16p. *8º.* 1826.

25105 —— [Another issue.] 16p. *8º.* 1826.

25106 The **NEGRO'S** friend, or, the Sheffield anti-slavery album. [In prose and verse, by various authors, including Samuel Roberts, and the editors, John Holland and James Montgomery.] 204p. *12º. Sheffield, Hartshead, &c.,* 1826.

25107 REFLECTIONS on recent occurrences at Lichfield; including an illustration of the opinions of Samuel Johnson, LL.D. on slavery, and the general distribution of the scriptures. Addressed to the Rev. Thomas Gisborne... 52p. *8º.* 1826.

25108 REMARKS on An address to the members of the new Parliament, on the proceedings of the Colonial Department, with respect to the West India question. By a member of the late Parliament. 78p. *8º.* 1826.

25109 SCOTT, JOHN, *Earl of Eldon.* Slavery in the West Indies. The substance of the speech of the Lord Chancellor, delivered in the House of Lords, March 7, 1826, on Lord Bathurst's motion for adopting the resolution of the House of Commons of the 15th May, 1823. 8p. *8º.* 1826. *The copy that belonged to Stephen Lushington.*

25110 SOCIETY FOR THE ABOLITION OF SLAVERY THROUGHOUT THE BRITISH DOMINIONS. The necessity of abolishing negro slavery demonstrated; being an abridgement of a pamphlet, entitled, "The slave colonies of Great Britain..." with an appendix, containing extracts from the record of the proceedings of the Fiscal of Berbice, in his capacity of guardian of the slaves. 39p. *8º. Edinburgh,* 1826.

25111 —— The progress of colonial reform; being a brief view of the real advance made since May 15th, 1823, in carrying into effect the recommendations of His Majesty, the unanimous resolutions of Parliament, and the universal prayer of the nation, with respect to negro slavery. Drawn from the papers printed for the House of Commons... 49p. *8º.* 1826. *Two copies, one a presentation copy from the author to William Leake, the other the copy that belonged to Stephen Lushington.*

25112 —— The slave colonies of Great Britain; or a picture of negro slavery drawn by the colonists themselves ...Second edition, corrected. 124p. *8º.* 1826. *The copy that belonged to Stephen Lushington. For another edition, see* 1825; *see also no.* 25110.

25113 —— Third report of the committee of the Society...Read at a special meeting of the members and friends of the Society, held (on the 21st of December 1825) for the purpose of petitioning Parliament on the subject of slavery. With notes and an appendix. 24p. *8º.* 1826.

25114 —— [Another edition.] 35p. *8º.* 1826. *See also* 1824, 1825.

25115 STEPHEN, J. England enslaved by her own slave colonies. An address to the electors and people of the United Kingdom. 91p. *8º.* 1826. *Presentation copy from the author to Stephen Lushington.*

25116 —— Second edition. 68p. *8º.* 1826. *Presentation copy, with inscription, from the author to William Leake.*

25117 SWANSEA AND NEATH AUXILIARY ANTI-SLAVERY ASSOCIATION. First annual report of the...Association; together with the resolutions passed at the general meeting. 12p. 8°. *Swansea*, 1826.

25118 TREW, J. M. An appeal to the Christian philanthropy of the people of Great Britain and Ireland, in behalf of the religious instruction and conversion of three hundred thousand negro slaves. 48p. 8°. 1826. *The Agar Ellis copy.*

25119 WARD, JOHN W., *Earl of Dudley*. Slavery in the West Indies. The substance of the speech of Lord Viscount Dudley, delivered in the House of Lords, March 7, 1826, on Lord Bathurst's motion for adopting the resolutions of the House of Commons of the 15th May, 1823. 12p. 8°. 1826. *The copy that belonged to Stephen Lushington.*

POLITICS

25120 BRASH, R. A general account of Cobbett's conspiracy against public confidence, to which may be attributed various causes of the late panic... 226p. *12°.* 1826. *Presentation copy from the author to Joseph Hume.*

25121 A COLLECTION of addresses, squibs, songs, &c. together with the Political mountebank, (shewing the changeable opinions of Mr. Cobbett,) published during the contested election for the borough of Preston, which commenced June 9th and ended June 26th, 1826...The candidates were Hon. E. G. Stanley, John Wood, Esquire, Captain Barrie, C. B., R.N., William Cobbett, Esquire. 127p. 8°. *Preston, Blackburn, &c.*, [1826].

25122 ENGLAND. *Foreign Office.* No. 14. Secret and confidential. Instructions given to the Duke of Wellington, on proceeding to St. Petersburgh, in February, 1826. 32p. *fol.* [*London,* 1826] *Addressed in manuscript to 'the Rt. Hon. C. W. Williams Wynn'.*

25123 ENSOR, G. Irish affairs, at the close of 1825. [With an appendix.] 77, [3]p. 8°. *Dublin & London*, 1826.

25124 EVERETT, E. An oration delivered at Cambridge on the fiftieth anniversary of the Declaration of the Independence of the United States of America. 51p. 8°. *Boston*, 1826.

25125 —— Speech of Mr. Everett on the proposition to amend the constitution of the United States. Delivered in the House of Representatives, March 9, 1826. 51p. 8°. *Washington*, 1826.

25126 The poor **MAN'S** friend; or companion for the working classes; giving them useful information and advice: being the system of moral and political philosophy laid down and exemplified by W. Cobbett. [An anti-Cobbett tract.] 32p. 8°. 1826.

25127 MILTONICS: a mock-heroic poem, dedicated to the freeholders of the county of York. [An attack on Viscount Milton.] 24p. 8°. *London & York*, 1826. *The copy that belonged to M. T. Sadler.*

25128 NAPOLEON I, *Emperor of the French.* Discours de Napoléon sur les vérités et les sentiments qu'il importe le plus d'inculquer aux hommes pour leur bonheur, ou ses idées sur le droit d'aînesse et le morcellement de la propriété, suivies de pièces sur son administra-

tion et ses projets en faveur des Grecs; publiées par le Général Gourgaud. 170p. 8°. *Paris*, 1826.

25129 PAINE, T. Rights of man, part the second, combining principle and practice. 118p. 8°. *R. Carlile*, 1826. *For other editions, see* 1792.

25130 The **PAPAL SUPREMACY**. With remarks on the Bill for restoring the intercourse between the See of Rome and the United Kingdom, passed by the Commons, and rejected by the Lords, in the year 1825. 103p. 8°. 1826.

25131 PECCHIO, G., *Conte*. Relazione degli avvenimenti della Grecia nella primavera del 1825. Prima edizione italiana tratta dal manoscritto originale. 150p. 8°. *Lugano*, 1826.

25132 A full, accurate, and authentic **REPORT** of the speeches delivered at a meeting of the Protestant gentlemen of...Armagh, on the 5th October, 1826, at a dinner given to Colonel Verner, candidate at the late general election... 43p. 8°. *Dublin*, [1826] *The copy that belonged to Earl De Grey.*

25133 REYNAUD, F. D. DE, *Comte de Montlosier.* Mémoire à consulter sur un système religieux et politique, tendant à renverser la religion, la société et le trône... Cinquième édition. 339p. 8°. *Paris*, 1826.

25134 A calm **STATEMENT** of the Catholic question. Respectfully addressed to all electors throughout the United Kingdom. By a clergyman of the Established Church. 35p. 8°. 1826.

25135 STORRS, H. R. Speech of Mr. Storrs, on the proposition to amend the constitution of the U. States, respecting the election of president & vice-president. Delivered in the House of Representatives, February 17, 1826. 28p. 8°. *Washington*, 1826.

25136 [**WADE**, JOHN.] New Parliament. An appendix to The black book; comprising a list and analysis of the new House of Commons, with strictures on their parliamentary conduct and principles: also, remarks on the reduction of the National Debt, and the best means of relieving public distress; with documents...of the "dead weight" and public expenditure. 44p. 8°. [1826] *For editions of* The black book, *see* 1820.

SOCIALISM

For the **CO-OPERATIVE MAGAZINE**, 1826–29, *continued as* the London co-operative magazine, 1830, *see* vol. III, *Periodicals list.*

25137 LONDON CO-OPERATIVE SOCIETY. Articles of agreement (drawn up and recommended by the London Co-operative Society,) for the formation of a community within fifty miles of London, on principles of

mutual co-operation. 12p. 8°. [*London,*] 1826. *For other editions, see* 1825.

25138 [**MORGAN**, JOHN M.] The revolt of the bees. 272p. 8°. 1826. *See also* 1839, 1849.

25139 OWEN, ROBERT. A new view of society... 96p. *12°. Edinburgh, Orbiston, &c.*, 1826. *For other editions, see* 1813.

MISCELLANEOUS

25140 CHALMERS, T. Speeches and tracts. 40, 32, 97, 22, 78, 16p. *8°. Glasgow, Edinburgh, &c.,* [1826?] *A reissue of six separately published works with a general title-page. Contents: The substance of a speech, delivered in the General Assembly...1809, respecting the merits of a Bill for the augmentations of stipends to the clergy of Scotland, 2nd edition, 1818; Considerations on the system of parochial schools in Scotland, 1819; A speech, delivered...May, 1822, before the General Assembly...explanatory of the measures ...in St. John's Parish, Glasgow, for the extinction of its compulsory pauperism, 1822; A speech delivered before the Synod of Glasgow and Ayr...October, 1823, in the case of Principal M'Farlane, on the subject of pluralities, 1823; Statement in regard to the pauperism of Glasgow, from the experience of the last eight years, 1823; A few thoughts on the abolition of colonial slavery, 1826.*

25141 CHAPMAN, EDWIN. The nature and use of language, popularly considered. A lecture, delivered before the members of the Deptford Mechanics' Institution on May 30, 1826. 32p. *8°. 1826.*

25142 [COURTELIN, .] Réfutation de l'écrit de M. le Comte de Montlosier, intitulé: Mémoire à consulter. Par M***. 48p. *8°. Paris, 1826.*

25143 ENGLAND. *Henry VIII, King.* Warwick Borough Charter. Copies of the fifth section of the patent of the thirty-seventh of King Henry the Eighth, granted to the burgesses of Warwick...1546; and of Warwick Charter, granted to the burgesses by Letters Patent...in the fifth year of William and Mary. 20p. *8°. Warwick, 1826. Copy in contemporary boards, bound with no. 26368, with which it was perhaps reissued.*

25144 —— Parliament. *House of Commons.* Standing Orders of the House of Commons relating to private Bills, and other matters, 1685–1822. With table of fees. [A new edition.] 43p. *4°. 1826.*

25145 EVERETT, E. An address delivered at Charlestown August 1, 1826, in commemoration of John Adams and Thomas Jefferson. 36p. *8°. Boston, 1826.*

25146 Sur les LIBERTÉS gallicanes: réponse à l'ouvrage de M. de la Mennais, intitulé: De la religion considérée dans ses rapports avec l'ordre civil et politique. Par un Catholique gallican. 52p. *8°. Paris, 1826.*

25147 MILES, WILLIAM AUGUSTUS (*fl.* 1826–1839). A description of the Deverel Barrow, opened A.D.1825. Also a minute account of the Kimmeridge coal money... 53p. *4°. London, Salisbury, &c.,* 1826.

25148 PAINE, T. The age of reason, part the first, being an investigation of true and fabulous theology. [With 'The age of reason, part the second', 'An examination, of the passages in the New Testament...called prophecies...To which is prefixed, an essay on dreams', 'A letter to the Hon. Thomas Erskine', 'A discourse delivered to the Society of Theophilanthropists', 'An essay on the origin of Free Masonry' and 'A letter to Camille Jordan'.] 52, 90, 59, 29, 10, 14, 10p. *8°. R. Carlile,* 1826. *For other editions, see* 1819.

25149 SMITH, SYDNEY (1771–1845). A letter to the electors, upon the Catholic question. 43p. *8°. York & London,* 1826.

25150 SOMEBODY, *pseud.* Eighteen hundred and twenty-six. Carmen seculare. 29p. *8°. 1826.*

25151 UNIACKE, C. A letter to Horace Twiss, Esq. M.P. being an answer to his "Inquiry into the means of consolidating and digesting the laws of England." 68p. *8°. 1826.*

1827

GENERAL

25152 ANDERSON, ADAM (*d.* 1846). Appendix to the Report on the weights and measures of Perthshire. 22p. *8°. Perth, 1827. For the Report, see* 1826.

25153 ANDERSON, JOHN (*fl.* 1825–1827). Prize essay on the state of society and knowledge in the Highlands of Scotland...at the period of the rebellion in 1745, and of their progress up to the establishment of the Northern Institution...1825. 176p. *8°. Edinburgh & London,* 1827.

25154 The BELFAST ALMANAC for the year 1828...containing a correct calendar and tide-table, calculated for the latitude and meridian of Belfast: together with...a list of stamp-duties, licenses...list of roads and post towns; rates of postage...with an alphabetical list of the fairs of Ireland, &c.&c.&c. 106p. *12°. Belfast,* [1827?]

25155 BENETT, J. The national interest considered; or, the relative importance of agricurture [*sic*] and foreign trade...Second edition. 58p. *8°. 1827.*

25156 BOYCE, E. The Belgian traveller, being a complete guide through Belgium and Holland, or Kingdom of the United Netherlands...To which is prefixed a brief sketch of the history, constitution, and religion of the Netherlands...and the manners and customs of the inhabitants...Fifth edition...enlarged... 410p. *12°. 1827.*

25157 CAREY, M. Address delivered before the Philadelphia Society for Promoting Agriculture, at its meeting on the twentieth of July, 1824...Fifth edition, revised and corrected. 71p. *8°. Philadelphia, 1827. For other editions, see* 1824.

25158 CASTELNAU, G. DE, *Marquis.* Essai sur l'histoire ancienne et moderne de la nouvelle Russie. Statistique des provinces qui la composent. Fondation d'Odessa...Voyage en Crimée, dans l'intérêt de l'agriculture et du commerce...Seconde édition. 3 vols. *8°. Paris, 1827.*

25159 CAYLEY, EDWARD. Corn, trade, wages, and

rent; or, observations on the leading circumstances of the present financial crisis...Second edition. 47p. *8°*. 1827. *For another edition, see* 1826.

25160 CHAMBERS, ROBERT (1802–1871). The picture of Scotland... 2 vols. *8°*. *Edinburgh*, 1827. *See also* 1840.

25161 COBBETT, JAMES P. A ride of eight hundred miles in France; containing a sketch of the face of the country, of its rural economy...To which is added, a general view of the finances of the kingdom...Third edition. [214]p. *12°*. 1827. *For other editions, see* 1824.

25162 DUPIN, F. P. C., *Baron*. Forces productives et commerciales de la France... 2 vols. *4°*. *Paris*, 1827.

25163 *The EAST-INDIA register and directory, for 1827; containing...lists of the Company's servants... mariners &c. not in the service of the...Company; merchant vessels employed in the country trade...Compiled...by A. W. Mason, Geo. Owen, and G. H. Brown ...Corrected to 24th April 1827. 595p. *12°*. [1827]

25164 *—— Second edition, corrected to 1st September 1827. 598p. *12°*. [1827] *For other editions, see* 1804.

25165 ELMES, J. Metropolitan improvements; or, London in the nineteenth century: displayed in a series of engravings of the new buildings...from original drawings ...by...Thos. H. Shepherd...With historical, topographical, and critical illustrations by James Elmes. 172p., 79 plates. *4°*. 1827.

25166 FROST, C. Notices relative to the early history of the town and Port of Hull; compiled from original records and unpublished manuscripts, and illustrated with engravings, etchings, and vignettes. 150, 58p. *4°*. *London, Hull, &c.*, 1827.

25167 GILES, W. B. Mr. Clay's speech upon the tariff [of 30–31 March 1824. With the text of the speech]: or the "American system," so called; or the Anglican system, in fact, introduced here and perverted...by the omission of a system of corn laws...Mr. Giles' speech upon the resolutions of inquiry in the House of Delegates of Virginia, in reply to Mr. Clay's speech: also his speech in reply to Gen. Taylor's...[Published as Part 1 of W. B. Giles' *Political miscellanies*, and as a justification of his political conduct and his opposition to Henry Clay.] 188p. *8°*. *Richmond* [*Va.*], 1827.

25168 [GRAY, CHARLES, *of Carse*.] An essay on the philoso-political economy of the modern Athens, with its southern ramifications. Dedicated to the Athenians. 7p. *4°*. *Dundee*, [1827] *Two presentation copies from the author. See note to no.* 24485.

25169 [——] Felix quem faciunt aliena pericula cautum. [On the importance of agriculture and the need to restore Government authority. Text in English.] 7p. *4°*. *Dundee*, [1827] *Two presentation copies from the author. See note to no.* 24485.

25170 GUITTET, F. M. Le grand indicateur du commerce de la France. Sur ses productions; sur son industrie, sur ses fabriques et sur ses manufactures; 1° avec les noms...et demeures des principaux négocians, banquiers, agens de change...2° avec un dictionnaire géographique de toutes les villes...la statistique de chacune d'elles...A cette seconde édition, l'auteur a joint un tableau des nouvelles mesures... 295p. *8°*. *Marseille*, 1827.

25171 HALL, FRANCIS. Colombia: its present state, in respect of climate, soil, productions, population, government, commerce, revenue, manufactures...and inducements to emigration...The second edition, with a tariff of the duties on exports and imports. 179p. *8°*. 1827. *For another edition, see* 1825.

25172 HODGSKIN, T. Popular political economy. Four lectures delivered at the London Mechanics' Institution. 268p. *12°*. *London & Edinburgh*, 1827. *The copy presented by the author to George Birkbeck.*

25173 I'TIṢĀM AL-DĪN, *Mīrzā*. Shigurf Nahma i Velaët, or excellent intelligence concerning Europe; being the travels of Mirza Itesa Modeen, in Great Britain and France. Translated from the original Persian manuscript into Hindoostanee, with an English version and notes, by James Edward Alexander... 221, 197p. *8°*. 1827.

25174 Second edition for the year. **KENT'S** original London directory: 1827. Being an alphabetical list of more than 20,000 merchants, manufacturers, traders, &c. of London and the environs...Ninety-fifth annual edition. [With 'Kent's original tradesman's assistant: 1827. Being a guide to all the stage coaches, carriers, coasting vessels, &c.&c....'] 435, 24p. *12°*. [1827] *See also* 1740, 1804, 1816, 1825, 1826.

25175 LANARK, *County of*. Report of the committee appointed by the honourable William Rose Robinson, sheriff depute of the county of Lanark, to examine and ascertain the capacity of the weights and measures in use in the county of Lanark, &c.&c. 1826. [With 'Extract – Verdict of the jury'.] 32p. *8°*. *Glasgow*, 1827.

25176 LA ROCHEFOUCAULD LIANCOURT, F. G. DE, *Marquis*. Vie du Duc de la Rochefoucauld Liancourt (François-Alexandre-Frédéric). 108p. *8°*. *Paris*, 1827.

25177 LONGSON, W. An appeal to masters, workmen & the public, shewing the cause of the distress of the labouring classes, and a measure which...will prevent the ...increase of that distress, give greater security to the profits of capital, render a gradual rise of wages practicable, and put an end to all combinations. 35p. *8°*. *Manchester*, 1827.

25178 [McCULLOCH, JOHN R.] A review of Definitions in political economy. By the Rev. T. R. Malthus. [Reprinted, with corrections, from the Scotsman of 10th March, 1827.] 10p. *8°*. *n.p.* [1827]

25179 MACKENZIE, E. A descriptive and historical account of the town and county of Newcastle upon Tyne, including the borough of Gateshead... 780p. *4°*. *Newcastle upon Tyne, London, &c.*, 1827.

25180 MALTHUS, T. R. Definitions in political economy, preceded by an inquiry into the rules which ought to guide political economists in the definition and use of their terms; with remarks on the deviation from these rules in their writings. 261p. *8°*. 1827.

25181 [MARCET, J.] Conversations on political economy; in which the elements of that science are familiarly explained. By the author of "Conversations on chemistry". Sixth edition, revised and enlarged. 494p. *12°*. 1827. *16 pages of publisher's advertisements, dated: May 1838, are inserted at the front of the volume. For other editions, see* 1816.

25182 MATERIALIEN zur Kritik der National-ökonomie und Staatswirthschaft. Erstes Heft. Was ist

Geld? [–Zweites Heft. Was ist Werth und Preis?] 61, 80p. *8°. Berlin, Posen, &c., 1827–29.*

25183 MEMOIRS of the public life and administration of the Right Honourable the Earl of Liverpool. 649p. *8°. 1827.*

25184 MÉRILHOU, J. Essai historique sur la vie et les ouvrages de Mirabeau. ccxixp. *8°. Paris, 1827. The introduction only to Œuvres de Mirabeau. Précédées d'une notice...par M. Mérilhou, Paris, 1826–27.*

25185 MONTAGU, B. Reform. 55p. *8°. 1827. Bound in a folio volume, interleaved, with numerous manuscript comments, corrections and additions in several hands, probably for a revised edition.*

25186 [NILES, J. M.] A view of South America and Mexico, comprising their history...agriculture, commerce, &c. of the republics of Mexico, Guatemala, Colombia, Peru, the United Provinces of South America and Chili...By a citizen of the United States...2 vols. in 1. *12°. New-York, 1827.*

25187 PECCHIO, G., *Conte.* L'anno mille ottocento ventisei dell' Inghilterra colle osservazioni di Giuseppe Pecchio. 196p. *8°. Lugano, 1827.*

25188 [POWELL, JOHN, *statistical writer.*] Statistical illustrations of the territorial extent and population, rental, taxation, finances, commerce, consumption, insolvency, pauperism, and crime, of the British Empire. Compiled for and published by order of the London Statistical Society. Third edition. xxviii, 170p. *8°. 1827. With the book stamp of the Harmony Hall library. For another edition, see 1825.*

25189 QUETELET, L. A. J. Recherches sur la population, les naissances, les décès, les prisons, les dépôts de mendicité, etc., dans le royaume des Pays-Bas. [With 'Notes par M. le Baron de Keverberg'.] 90p. *8°. Bruxelles, 1827. Presentation copy from the author to N. W. Senior.*

25190 On the frequent **RECURRENCE** of national distress, and the best mode of permanently relieving it... in a letter addressed to H.R.H. the Duke of Sussex. 16p. *8°. 1827.*

25191 REMARKS on certain modern theories respecting rents and prices. 100p. *8°. Edinburgh & London, 1827.*

25192 ROBERTS, O. W. Narrative of voyages and excursions on the east coast and in the interior of Central America; describing a journey up the River San Juan, and passage across the Lake of Nicaragua to the city of Leon ...With notes and observations by Edward Irving. 302p. *12°. Edinburgh & London, 1827.*

25193 ROSS, J. C. An examination of opinions maintained in the "Essay on the principles of population," by Malthus; and in the "Elements of political economy," by Ricardo; with some remarks in reply to Sir James Graham's "Address to the land-owners"... 2 vols. *8°. 1827. A reissue of Principles of political economy and of population, published under the pseudonym 'John McIniscon' in 1825 (q.v.).*

25194 SANTIAGO ROTALDE, N. DE. A short descriptive sketch of the country of Andalusia, and a general outline of the history of Spain. Dedicated to the benevolent Committee of Ladies for the Relief of the Spanish and Italian emigrants. 31p. *8°. 1827. The Agar Ellis copy.*

25195 *SAY, J. B. De l'objet et de l'utilité des statistiques. [Extrait de la Revue Encyclopédique (105e Cah. T. xxxv.) Neuvième année. – Seconde série. – Septembre 1827.] 27p. *8°. Paris, [1827] The copy that belonged to George Grote.*

25196 —— Traité d'économie politique...Septième édition, augmentée d'un volume... 3 vols. *12°. Bruxelles, Leipzig, &c., 1827. This is not the true 7th edition, which was published in 1861.*

25197 —— A treatise on political economy...Translated from the fourth edition of the French by C. R. Prinsep, M.A. With notes by the translator. Third American edition. Containing a translation of the introduction. and additional notes, by Clement C. Biddle... 455p. *8°. Philadelphia, 1827. For other editions, see 1803.*

25198 SAY, L. Traité élémentaire de la richesse individuelle et de la richesse publique, et éclaircissemens sur les principales questions d'économie politique. 327p. *8°. Paris, 1827. See also 1835.*

25199 SCOTT, ANDREW. Proposed measures for the removal of national distress and establishment of permanent prosperity... 41p. *8°. 1827.*

25200 SENIOR, N. W. An introductory lecture on political economy, delivered before the University of Oxford, on the 6th of December, 1826. 39p. *8°. 1827. See also 1831.*

25201 SIMONDE DE SISMONDI, J. C. L. Nouveaux principes d'économie politique, ou de la richesse dans ses rapports avec la population...Seconde édition... 2 vols. *8°. Paris, 1827. For other editions, see 1819.*

25202 SMITH, ADAM. An inquiry into the nature and causes of the wealth of nations...With a life of the author. Also, a view of the doctrine of Smith, compared with that of the French economists; with a method of facilitating the study of his works; from the French of M. Garnier. Complete in one volume. 404p. *8°. Edinburgh, 1827. For other editions, see 1776.*

25203 SMITH, R. Notes made during a tour in Denmark, Holstein...Prussia, Poland, Saxony...Holland, Brabant, the Rhine country, and France. Interspersed with some observations on the foreign corn trade. [With an appendix.] 504, xxivp. *8°. 1827.*

25204 THOMSON, THOMAS (1773–1852), *and others.* Report regarding the weights and measures of the County of Renfrew, to John C. Dunlop, Sheriff Depute, by Dr. Thomas Thomson, John Wilson of Thornly; and William Wilson, younger, of Thornly. 15p. *4°. n.p. [1827]*

25205 WATSON, WILLIAM, *F.A.S.* An historical account of the ancient town and port of Wisbech...and of the circumjacent towns and villages, the drainage of the great level of the Fens... 700p. *8°. Wisbech & London, 1827. The copy that belonged to George Pryme.*

25206 [WILLOUGHBY, SIR H., *Bart.*] The apology of an English landowner, addressed to the landed proprietors of the county of Oxford. By one of them. [On the importation of foreign corn, the corn laws, tithes and taxation.] 43p. *8°. Oxford & London, 1827. Presentation copy from the author to the Earl of Westmorland.*

AGRICULTURE

25207 ALLEN, WILLIAM (1770–1843). Colonies at home; or, the means for rendering the industrious labourer independent of parish relief; and for providing for the poor population of Ireland, by the cultivation of the soil. 27p. *8°. Lindfield: at the Schools of Industry; London, &c.,* [1827] *Presentation copy, with inscription, from the author to George Agar Ellis, Baron Dover.*

25208 *—— Second edition. 27p. *8°. Lindfield: at the Schools of Industry; London, &c.,* [1827] *The FWA copy that belonged to William Pare. See also 1828, 1832, 1833.*

25209 BARLOW, J. H. The art and method of hatching and rearing all kinds of domestic poultry and game birds by steam...Also is added, the method by which the Egyptians hatch ninety-six millions a-year... 20p. *8°.* 1827.

25210 BAYLDON, J. S. The art of valuing rents and tillages, and the tenant's right of entering and quitting farms, explained...Third edition, corrected. 192p. *8°.* 1827. *For other editions, see* 1823.

For **BOLANOS MINING COMPANY,** [Proceedings at annual and special General Courts of Proprietors, reports of directors and reports of the manager, 1827–38,] *see vol.* III, *Periodicals list,* Proceedings.

25211 CAVOLEAU, J. A. Oenologie française, ou statistique de tous les vignobles et de toutes les boissons vineuses et spiritueuses de la France, suivie de considérations générales sur la culture de la vigne... 436p. *8°. Paris,* 1827.

25212 COVENTRY, THOMAS (1797?–1869). Observations on the title to lands derived through inclosure acts. 167p. *8°.* 1827.

25213 ENGLAND. *Commissioners for the Herring Fishery.* Rules and regulations made by the Commissioners for the Herring Fishery, appointed pursuant to the Acts 48th Geo. III. cap. 110 and 55th Geo. III. cap. 94. Directing in what form and manner every journal, declaration or account required by the said Acts shall be kept... and what marks or characters shall be set on barrels of herrings at the Fishery, &c. 43p. *8°. Edinburgh,* 1827.

25214 HEAD, SIR F. B., *Bart.* Reports relating to the failure of the Rio Plata Mining Association, formed under an authority signed by his Excellency Don Bernardino Rivadavia. 228p. *8°.* 1827.

25215 HORNBY, THOMAS, *land surveyor.* A treatise on the new method of land surveying, with the improved plan of keeping the field book... 207p. *8°. London & Hull,* 1827.

25216 An INQUIRY into the present state and means of improving the salmon fisheries: including a digest of the evidence taken by a Select Committee of the House of Commons. 193p. *8°. London, Edinburgh, &c.,* 1827.

25217 MEXICAN MINING ASSOCIATION. United Mexican Mining Association. Extract of a letter from Don Lucas Alaman, addressed to the Secretary, dated at Mexico, 8th May, 1827. (Translated from the Spanish.) [4]p. *8°. n.p.* [1827]

25218 —— United Mexican Mining Association. Report of proceedings at a general meeting of proprietors, 25th July, 1827. 58p. *8°.* 1827. *See also* 1828.

25219 —— United Mexican Mining Association. Report of the Court of Directors, addressed to the proprietors at a general meeting on the 7th March, 1827. [With an appendix.] 19, xxxp. *8°.* 1827.

25220 —— United Mexican Mining Association. Report of the Court of Directors, dated 13th June, 1827. 12, cvp. *8°.* 1827. *See also* 1825, 1826.

25221 MONTEATH, R. Miscellaneous reports on woods and plantations, shewing a method to plant, rear, and recover all woods, plantations and timber trees on every soil and situation...with plans for employing the operatives, and improving the waste lands of Great Britain and Ireland. In a letter to the Right Hon. Robert Peel... 155p. *8°. Dundee, London, &c.,* 1827.

25222 TWIGG, J. A. Report on the iron works and collieries, at Arigna, Roscommon, Ireland; the property of the Arigna Iron and Coal Company: furnished to the committee of investigation. 55p. *8°.* 1827.

25223 WITHERS, W. A profit and loss view of planting one acre of land, on the system recommended by Mr. Withers, and that generally adopted by Scotch planters...[A table, dated: September 19th.] *s.sh.fol. Holt* [& *London*], 1827. [*Br.* 504]

CORN LAWS

25224 BRAMSTON, T. G. The principle of the corn laws vindicated. 93p. *8°.* 1827.

25225 BURTON, N. A petition, with seasonable advice, to the Members of the new Parliament, from Nathaniel Burton, of St. Mary-Axe, garrett-holder. [A satirical account of the benefits of free trade, with particular reference to the corn laws.] 61p. *8°.* 1827.

25226 CANNING, GEORGE (1770–1827). Corrected report of the speech delivered by the Right Hon. George Canning, in the House of Commons, March 1st, 1827, on the corn laws. 43p. *8°.* 1827.

25227 A COMPENDIUM of the laws, passed...for regulating and restricting the importation, exportation, and consumption of foreign corn, from the year 1660. And a series of accounts...shewing the operation of the several Statutes, and the average prices of corn: presenting a complete view of the corn trade of Great Britain... Second edition. 61p. *8°.* 1827. *A compilation sometimes attributed to Sir James Graham. For other editions, see* 1826.

25228 COOKE, L. Practical observations on the importation of foreign corn, under a graduated scale of duty...Second edition, with additions. 31p. *8°.* 1827. *For another edition, see* 1826.

25229 CORN LAWS. Reasonable protection defended; or, "Cheap corn best for farmers" refuted. Also, a letter by Mr. Huskisson to his constituents in 1814; with remarks. By a Cumberland farmer. 31p. *8°*. 1827.

25230 GENERAL AGRICULTURAL COMMITTEE. Twenty questions submitted by the General Agricultural Committee, sitting at Henderson's Hotel, Palace Yard: and the answers returned from various parts of the Kingdom. [With 'Appendix. Corn importation, &c. demonstrated. By the Rev. William Claye'.] 24[20]p. *4°*. 1827. *The Agar Ellis copy.*

25231 —— [Another issue.] 20p. *4°*. 1827.

25232 HINTS to landlords and tenants in the neighbourhood of Doncaster. By a farmer. [With an appendix containing Huskisson's 'Letter to a constituent at Chichester, 1814', and other papers.] 57p. *8°*. *Doncaster & London*, 1827.

25233 HUSKISSON, W. A letter on the corn laws, by the Right Hon. W. Huskisson, to one of his constituents, in 1814. 16p. *8°*. 1827. *For another edition, see* 1826.

25234 LETTER to the Right Honourable William Huskisson, on the corn laws. 28p. *8°*. *Devonport*, 1827.

25235 Two **LETTERS** on the corn laws: first, to the Right Honourable Lord Milton, shewing that the farmer is...doomed to ruin, in any sudden depression of prices, by a free trade in corn...Originally published in the Huntingdon Journal. With an introductory letter to T. W. Coke, Esq. M.P. for the County of Norfolk. To which are added, Notes on the paper currency & poor laws...By a plain farmer of Huntingdonshire. 28p. *8°*. *Oundle & London*, 1827.

25236 NOLAN, G. Remarks upon the alterations proposed to be made in the corn laws...Second edition. 26p. *8°*. 1827.

25237 REMARKS on the respective interests of land and trade, as mutually concerned in maintaining restrictions on the importation of foreign corn. 98p. *8°*. 1827. *Sometimes attributed to 'Lawrence'.*

25238 STANHOPE, PHILIP H., *4th Earl Stanhope*. A letter from Earl Stanhope, on the proposed alteration of the corn laws. 30p. *8°*. 1827.

25239 THOMPSON, THOMAS P. A catechism on the corn laws, with a list of fallacies and the answers. By a member of the University of Cambridge. Second edition ... 58p. *8°*. 1827. *See also* 1828, 1829, 1832, 1833, 1839, 1841.

25240 THOUGHTS on the policy of the proposed alteration of the corn laws. 61p. *8°*. 1827.

25241 TORRENS, R. An essay on the external corn trade...Fourth edition. 450p. *8°*. 1827. *For other editions, see* 1815.

25242 WIGGINS, J. The case of the landed interest fairly stated, in a letter to the Hon. George Winn, M.P. By a land agent. December 1826. 40p. *8°*. 1827.

POPULATION

25243 [**QUETELET**, L. A. J.] Statistique. A Monsieur Villermé, de l'Académie Royale de Médecine de Paris, etc. [Signed: A.Q.] 11p. *8°*. *Gand*, [1827]. *Presentation copy from the author to N. W. Senior.*

TRADES & MANUFACTURES

25244 ACCURSIO DAS NEVES, J. Noções historicas, economicas, e administrativas sobre a producção e manufactura das sedas em Portugal, e particularmente sobre e Real fabrica du suburbio do Rato e suas annexas. 405p. *8°*. *Lisboa*, 1827.

25245 CRISPIN anecdotes; comprising interesting notices of shoemakers, who have been distinguished for genius, enterprise, or eccentricity: also curious particulars relative to the origin, importance, & manufacture of shoes: with other matters illustrative of the history of the gentle craft. 214p. *12°*. *Sheffield & London*, 1827.

25246 FROME COMMITTEE. Plain and practical observations on the use and application of machinery, in a series of letters, drawn up at the request of the Frome Committee...To which is prefixed copies of a petition... praying for the restriction or abolition of certain parts of machinery...viz. gigs, shearing frames, and the... apparatus for dressing cloth, power, spring looms, and mules...which by abridging manual labour in the several branches...of the woollen trade, have thrown upwards of sixty thousand families out of employ... 39p. *8°*. *Bath*, 1827.

25247 HULLMANDEL, C. J. On some important improvements in lithographic printing. 8p. *8°*. *n.p.* [1827]

25248 [**McCULLOCH**, JOHN R.] An essay on the rise, progress, present state, and prospects, of the cotton manufacture. (From the Edinburgh Review, no. 91.) 39p. *8°*. *n.p.* [1827]

25249 MEMOIRS of the late Philip Rundell, Esq. goldsmith and jeweller...late of the Golden Salmon, Ludgate Hill...To which is added, his will. By a gentleman many years connected with the firm. 42p. *8°*. 1827.

25250 MURPHY, JOHN. A treatise on the art of weaving...With calculations and tables for...manufacturers ...Second edition, revised and enlarged. 518p. *8°*. *Glasgow & Edinburgh*, 1827. *See also* 1836.

25251 PARIS. *Préfecture de Police*. Recherches et considérations sur l'enlèvement et l'emploi des chevaux morts, et sur la nécessité d'établir...un clos central d'écarrissage...Travail demandé par M. Delavau... Préfet de Police, et exécuté par une commission speciale ...MM. Arcet...président; Huzard...Rohault...Damoiseau...Parton...et Parent-Duchâtelet... 124p. *4°*. *Paris*, 1827.

25252 REY, JEAN. Mémoire sur la nécessité de bâtir un édifice spécialement consacré aux expositions générales des produits de l'industrie. 36p. *8°*. *Paris*, 1827.

25253 SCHOOL OF ARTS, *Edinburgh.* Sixth report of the Directors of the School of Arts of Edinburgh. 59p. *8°.* [*Edinburgh,*] 1827. *See also 1822, 1845.*

25254 The seventeenth edition of **SKYRING'S** builders' prices, for 1827: corrected from the prime cost of materials and labour, calculated from the reduced price of bricks, slates, &c. to the present time...[With 'Abstract of the Building Act, 14th George III. c. 78' and 'Alpha-

betical list of surveyors'.] 114p. *8°.* [1827] *Compiled by Z. Skyring, who signed and numbered each copy in manuscript. See also 1812, 1818, 1819, 1831, 1838, 1845, 1846.*

25255 WATSON, RALPH. A brief explanatory statement of the principle and application of a life and ship preserver, invented, or contrived, by Ralph Watson. 16p. *8°.* 1827. *Presentation copy, with accompanying letter, from the author to George Agar Ellis, afterwards Baron Dover.*

COMMERCE

25256 ATKINSON, S. The effects of the new system of free trade upon our shipping, colonies & commerce, exposed, in a letter to the Right Hon. W. Huskisson... 63p. *8°.* 1827.

25257 —— A second letter to the Right Hon. W. Huskisson on the effects of free trade on our shipping, colonies and commerce. 51p. *8°.* 1827.

25258 CANTON. Two edicts from the Hoppo of Canton to the Hong merchants. Translated by John Francis Davis, Esq. M.R.A.S. (From the Transactions of the Royal Asiatic Society of Great Britain and Ireland, vol. I.) 6p. *4°.* 1827.

25259 [**CAREY,** M.] To the thinking few. [Signed: Hamilton, and dated, Nov. 20, 1827. On the failure of the campaign to secure protection to American manufactures.] *s.sh.fol. n.p.* [1827] [*Br. 503*] *A footnote by the author records that a few copies only have been printed and that not more than forty are to be distributed at present. This copy is numbered '20' in manuscript at the head of the text.*

25260 CINCINNATUS, *pseud.* Remarks on "A letter to the electors of Bridgenorth upon the corn laws. By W. W. Whitmore, M.P.". 45p. *8°. Dublin,* 1827.

25261 COMPANY OF SCOTLAND TRADING TO AFRICA AND THE INDIES. A perfect list of the several persons residenters in Scotland, who have subscribed as adventurers in the joynt-stock of the Company of Scotland trading to Africa and the Indies. Together with the respective sums which they have severally subscribed...1696. 32p. *8°. Glasgow,* 1827. *For another edition, see 1696.*

25262 CRUEGER, C. Protection to the agriculturist. A detail of facts and observations addressed to the members of the British Parliament and to the nation at large from the Continent... 16p. *8°. Hamburg,* 1827.

25263 DIROM, ALEXANDER (*d. 1830*). Remarks on free trade, and on the state of the British Empire. 72p. *8°. Edinburgh & London,* 1827.

25264 —— Supplement to Remarks on free trade, and on the state of the British Empire...16th March, 1827. 8p. *8°. Dumfries,* [1827]

25265 ÉMÉRIGON, B. M. Traité des assurances et des contrats à la grosse d'Emérigon, conféré et mis en rapport avec le nouveau Code de commerce et la jurisprudence; suivi d'un vocabulaire des termes de marine et des noms de chaque parte d'un navire, par P. S. Boulay-Paty...Nouvelle édition... 2 vols. *4°. Rennes & Paris,* 1827. *For another edition, see 1783.*

25266 FLETCHER, M. Reflexions on the causes

which influence the price of corn. [Parts I & II.] 2 vols. *8°.* 1827–28.

25267 HAAN, P. DE. De invoer van thee, ter overweging voorgesteld. 85p. *8°. Leyden,* 1827.

25268 HULL. Report of the proceedings at a general meeting of ship-owners and others, interested in the trade of the port, held at the Guild-Hall, Hull, on...the 28th June, 1827, to receive the report of the delegates to London &c.&c. [Including the text of the speech of Edmund Gibson, one of the delegates.] 54p. *8°. Hull,* [1827]

25269 HUSKISSON, W. De l'état actuel de la navigation de l'Angleterre; discours prononcé dans la Chambre de Communes, le 12 mai 1826...Accompagné de pièces justificatives, et suivi du discours de M. Huskisson, sur le commerce des colonies, dans la séance du 22 mars 1825. Traduit par M. Pichon avec des notes et des observations. 120p. *8°. Paris,* 1827. *For another edition of the first speech see 1826.*

25270 —— Shipping interest. Speech of the Right Hon. W. Huskisson in the House of Commons, Monday, the 7th of May, 1827, on General Gascoyne's motion, "That a Select Committee be appointed, to inquire into the present distressed state of the British commercial shipping interest". With an appendix, containing the several accounts referred to. 93p. *8°.* 1827.

25271 On the **IMPORTATION** of foreign corn. [Two letters to the editor of *The Scotsman,* reprinted from that journal.] 31p. *8°. n.p.* [1827]

25272 MERCATOR, *pseud.* Shipping interest. Two letters in reply to the speech of...W. Huskisson, in the House of Commons...May 7, 1827, on General Gascoyne's motion...To which are added, three letters previously published in the "Morning Post" on this same subject. With notes. 74p. *8°.* 1827.

25273 PENNSYLVANIA SOCIETY FOR THE PROMOTION OF MANUFACTURES AND THE MECHANIC ARTS. [*Begin.*] At a meeting of the Pennsylvania Society...held in Philadelphia on the 14th day of May, 1827...[An address on the depression in the American export trade and on measures to improve it.] 12p. *8°. n.p.* [1827]

25274 The high **PRICE** of bread shown to be the result of commercial prosperity, not the cause of national distress; and the dangers of a free trade in corn pointed out. By a warning voice. 201p. *8°.* 1827.

25275 RENFREW, *County of.* Inquisition regarding the weights and measures of the County of Renfrew, 1827. 15p. *4°. Paisley,* [1827]

25276 SHIPPING interest. Mr. Huskisson's speech,

from the Glasgow Courier of May 31st, &c., 1827. [A review of the speech.] 40p. 8°. *Glasgow*, 1827.

25277 WARIN, A. Influence du commerce sur la prospérité du Royaume des Pays-Bas, exposée à la Seconde Chambre des Etats-Généraux, le 21 mars 1826

...Avec des notes, dont une au sujet du Canal de Marken et de la fermeture de l'Y... 104p. 8°. *Bruxelles*, 1827.

25278 WYATT, H. An address to the owners and occupiers of land on the importance of an adequate protection to agriculture. 52p. 8°. 1827.

COLONIES

25279 CUNNINGHAM, P. Two years in New South Wales; comprising sketches of the actual state of society in that colony; of its peculiar advantages to emigrants; of its topography, natural history, &c.... Second edition, revised and enlarged. 2 vols. *12°*. 1827.

25280 DONKIN, Sir R. A letter on the government of the Cape of Good Hope, and on certain events which have occurred there of late years, under the administration of Lord Charles Somerset; addressed...to Earl Bathurst. 147p. 8°. 1827.

25281 DWARRIS, Sir F. W. L. Substance of the three reports of the Commissioner of Inquiry, into the administration of civil and criminal justice in the West Indies. Extracted from the Parliamentary Papers, with the general conclusions, and the Commissioner's scheme of improvement, complete and in full. 475p. 8°. 1827.

25282 ENGLAND. Parliament. *House of Commons.* The Report of the Select Committee on emigration in 1826, with a brief analysis of the evidence and appendix. 177p. 8°. 1827.

25283 HOWARD, John H., *comp.* The laws of the

British Colonies in the West Indies and other parts of America concerning real and personal property, and manumission of slaves; with a view of the constitution of each colony... 2 vols. 8°. 1827.

25284 KENNEDY, James (1798–1859). England and Venice compared. An argument on the policy of England towards her colonies. 47p. 8°. 1827.

25285 MACAULAY, K. The colony of Sierra Leone vindicated from the misrepresentations of Mr. Macqueen of Glasgow. 127p. 8°. 1827.

25286 STRACHAN, John, *Bishop of Toronto.* Remarks on emigration from the United Kingdom... addressed to Robert Wilmot Horton, Esq., M.P. Chairman of the Select Committee of emigration in the last Parliament. 96p. 8°. 1827.

25287 THOMPSON, George, *traveller in Africa.* Travels and adventures in southern Africa...Comprising a view of the present state of the Cape Colony. With observations on the progress and prospects of British emigrants. Second edition... 2 vols. 8°. 1827.

FINANCE

25288 BANK OF NORTH AMERICA. Act of incorporation of the Bank of North America, as rechartered on the 21st March, 1825, together with the by-laws. 36p. 8°. *Philadelphia*, 1827.

25289 Cheap **BREAD** injurious to the working classes, and gold unnecessary as a circulating medium. By no landowner. 22p. 8°. 1827.

25290 BURGESS, H. A memorial, addressed to the Right Honourable Lord Viscount Goderich, on the fitness of the Bank of England, – of the country banks, – and of the branch banks of England, – to the wants of the people: and on the ample means of protection, which private bankers and the public have, against the monopoly of the Bank of England...Second edition. 53p. 8°. 1827. *Presentation copy, with inscription, from the author to T. Spring Rice, Baron Monteagle.*

25291 —— Third edition. 55p. 8°. 1827.

25292 CAISSE HYPOTHÉCAIRE. Assemblée Générale Annuelle. Session de mars 1827. Compte rendu par le Conseil d'Administration de la Caisse Hypothécaire. 32p. 8°. *n.p.* [1827]

25293 CEDRIC, *pseud.* The distribution of the national wealth, considered in its bearings upon the several questions now before the public, more especially those of the corn laws, and restriction in general. 104p. 8°. 1827.

For the **CIRCULAR TO BANKERS,** 1827–50, *see* vol. III, *Periodicals list.*

25294 COMPAGNIE D'ASSURANCES GÉ-NÉRALES. Compte rendu le 30 janvier 1827, à l'assemblée générale des actionnaires...sur les opérations des trois sociétés pour les assurances contre les risques maritimes, l'incendie, et sur la vie des hommes. [Rapport de M. de Gourcuff, Directeur.] 25p. *4°. Paris,* [1827] *See also* 1821, 1823, 1824, 1825.

25295 CRUTTWELL, R. Petition to His Majesty the King, on the currency or standard of value... 49p. 8°. *Halesworth* [& *London,*] 1827.

25296 DIALOGUES on corn and currency, between Sir John Thickscull, M.P. and Mr. Wiseacre. 8p. 8°. 1827.

25297 ENGLISH, H. A complete view of the joint stock companies, formed during the years 1824 and 1825 ...shewing the amount of capital, number of shares... And an appendix, giving a list of companies formed, antecedent to that period... 42[43]p. 8°. 1827. *Published as the third and last part of* A general guide to the companies formed for working foreign mines, *first published in 1825 (q.v.* AGRICULTURE).

25298 FRANCE. *Charles X, King.* Ville de Caen. Département du Calvados. Octroi de Caen...le 8 avril 1827. Ordonnance du Roi. [With a tariff in accordance with the Octroi, issued by the Mayor of Caen on 5 May 1827.] 60p. *4°.* [*Caen,* 1827]

25299 GARDINER, H. Essays on currency and absenteeism, &c.&c. With strictures on Mr. Drummond's pamphlet, entitled "Elementary propositions on the currency." 188p. *8°. Liverpool & London,* [1827]

25300 GILBART, J. W. A practical treatise on banking, containing an account of the London and country banks... Also a view of joint stock banks, and the branch banks of the Bank of England... 80p. *8°. London, Dublin, &c.,* 1827. *See also* 1828, 1834, 1836, 1849.

25301 GILLESPIE, M. A report of the trial of Malcolm Gillespie and George Skene Edwards, for forgery... Together with the life and dying declaration of Malcolm Gillespie. Written by himself. 48, 107p. *12°. Aberdeen, Edinburgh, &c.,* 1827.

25302 GRAHAM, SIR JAMES R. G., *Bart.* Corn and currency; in an address to the land owners... Third edition, with additions. 119p. *8°.* 1827. *For other editions, see* 1826.

25303 HUDDERSFIELD BANKING COMPANY. Dated 1st June, 1827. Huddersfield Banking Company deed of settlement... 56p. *8°. Huddersfield,* 1827.

25304 [JERDAN, W.] National polity and finance; plan for establishing a sterling currency, and relieving the burdens of the people. Extracted from [ten weekly numbers, October–December 1826, of] the Literary Gazette, by the editor. [80]p. *8°.* 1827.

25305 JOPLIN, T. An essay on the general principles and present practice of banking, in England and Scotland: with supplementary observations on the steps proper to form a public bank, and the system on which its accounts ought to be kept... Sixth edition. 200p. *8°.* 1827. *For other editions, see* 1822.

25306 A LETTER to the Right Honourable the Earl of Liverpool, clearly and distinctly shewing that the burdens of the country may be lightened fifty-two millions annually... By a member of the Merchant Company of Edinburgh. 17p. *8°. Edinburgh & London,* 1827.

25307 McCULLOCH, JOHN R. Note on money. From Mr. M'Culloch's edition of the Wealth of nations. 118p. *8°. Edinburgh,* 1827.

25308 MOORE, R. The outline of a plan for bringing the Scotch and English currency to the same standard bullion value, and producing a sterling country bank note, of exchangeable value, convertible in every place to gold coin... The second edition, with additions. 38p. *8°.* 1827. *With manuscript additions, probably by the author. For another edition, see* 1826.

25309 OASTLER, R. Vicarial tithes, Halifax: a true statement of facts and incidents. 186p. *8°. Halifax,* 1827.

25310 OUVRARD, G. J. Mémoires de G.-J. Ouvrard, sur sa vie et ses diverses opérations financières ...Quatrième édition. 3 vols. *8°. Paris,* 1827. *Vol. 2 is of the third edition, vol. 3 is published for the first time.*

25311 PARNELL, H. B., *Baron Congleton.* Observations on paper money, banking, and overtrading; including those parts of the evidence taken before the Committee of the House of Commons, which explain the Scotch system of banking. 177p. *8°.* 1827. *See also* 1828, 1829, 1835.

25312 PENNINGTON, JAMES. Memorandum [on currency. Submitted to the Right Hon. W. Huskisson, with his reply]. 14p. *8°. Clapham,* [1827]

For **PERRY'S BANKRUPT AND INSOLVENT GAZETTE,** 1827–61, *continued as* Perry's bankrupt monthly gazette, 1862–83, *see vol.* III, *Periodicals list.*

25313 ROYAL NAVAL ANNUITANT SOCIETY. Rules and regulations of the... Society, established at Devonport, in the county of Devon, on the 9th day of April, 1823. 75p. *12°. Devonport,* 1827.

25314 SÉGUIN, A. De la création des trois pour cent et de l'annihilation des rachats de rentes, dans leurs rapports avec les rentiers, les indemnisés, les contribuables et l'état. 119p. *8°. Paris,* 1827.

25315 STEWART, DAVID. Observations on the distillery laws. [Being the report of a general meeting of the freeholders, justices of the peace and commissioners of supply of the Weem District in the County of Perth, convened to consider the laws of excise, on 10 December 1827, to which this paper is annexed, having been ordered to be printed by the meeting.] 29p. *8°. Perth,* [1827]

25316 STEWART, M. A brief statement of some views suggested by the financial circumstances of the country. 19p. *8°. [Edinburgh,* 1827]

25317 SYKES, G. Two letters from Godfrey Sykes, Esq., Solicitor of Stamps in England; from Charles Bremner, Esq.... assistant of the late Solicitor of Stamps in Scotland, addressed to James Sedgwick, Esq., late Chairman of the Board of Stamps [in reply to his *Twelve letters addressed to the Right Hon. Thomas Wallace*]. 79p. *8°.* 1827.

25318 YATES, JOHN A. Essays on currency and circulation, and on the influence of our paper system on the industry, trade, and revenue of Great Britain. 188p. *8°. Liverpool & London,* 1827.

TRANSPORT

25319 CUNDY, N. W. Reports on the Grand Ship Canal from London to Arundel Bay and Portsmouth, with an abstract of Messrs. Rennie and Giles's report thereon. Also an estimate of the probable expense and revenue, with plan and section of the approved line of canal, a memorial to... the Treasury, and an outline of the proposed Act... with the names of the Commissioners... 58p. *8°. London, Dorking, &c.,* 1827.

25320 EDGEWORTH, R. L. Essai sur la construction des routes et des voitures... traduit de l'anglais sur la deuxième édition, et augmenté d'une notice sur le système Mac-Adam... suivi de considérations sur les voies publiques de France... 477p. *8°. Paris,* 1827. *Translated by A. A. D. Ballyet, who contributed 'Considérations sur les voies publiques de France'. For other editions, see* 1813.

25321 ENGLAND. *Commissioners for the Improvement of the Holyhead Road.* General rules for repairing roads, published, by order of the Parliamentary Commissioners, for the improvement of the mail coach roads from London to Holyhead, and from London to Liverpool, for the use of the surveyors on these roads... A new edition, enlarged. 11p. *8°.* 1827. *For another edition, see* 1823.

25322 —— *Laws, etc.* Anno quadragesimo quinto Georgii III. Regis. [Local & Personal.] cap. 11. An Act for enabling the Company of Proprietors of the Canal Navigation from Manchester to or near Ashton-under-Lyne and Oldham more effectually to provide for the discharge of their debts, and to complete the said Canal... ⟨18th March 1805.⟩ p.185–194. *fol.* 1827.

25323 —— —— Anno quarto Georgii IV. Regis. cap. lxxxvii. An Act to enable the Company of Proprietors of the Navigation from the Trent to the Mersey to make an additional tunnel through Harecastle Hill in the county of Stafford, and an additional reservoir in Knypersley Valley in the said county... ⟨17th June 1823.⟩ p.1833–1852. *fol.* 1827.

25324 —— —— Anno septimo & octavo Georgii IV. Regis. Cap. xxi. An Act for amending and enlarging the powers and provisions of an Act relating to the Liverpool and Manchester Railway. ⟨12th April 1827.⟩ p.313–328. *fol.* 1827. *See note to no.* 25927.

25325 **HARVEY,** JOHN. Remarks on the subject of a breakwater, for Portland Roads, as projected. 24p. *12°. Weymouth & London,* 1827.

25326 **HILL,** THOMAS (*fl.* 1827–1829). A treatise, upon the utility of a rail-way from Leeds to Selby and Hull, with observations & estimates upon rail-ways generally as being pre-eminent to all other modes of conveyance for dispatch and economy. 32p. *8°. Leeds,* 1827. *For a supplement, see* 1829.

25327 **KITCHINER,** W. The traveller's oracle; or, maxims for locomotion...Part I. Comprising estimates of the expenses of travelling...With seven songs...composed by W. Kitchiner. [With 'Part II. Comprising the horse and carriage keeper's oracle...by John Jervis... The whole revised by William Kitchiner'.] Second edition. 2 vols. *8°.* 1827. *For another edition of Part 2, by John Jervis, see* 1828.

25328 **MEDHURST,** G. A new system of inland conveyance, for goods and passengers, capable of being... extended throughout the country; and of conveying all kinds of goods, cattle, and passengers, with the velocity of sixty miles in an hour...without the aid of horses or any animal power. [With 'A catalogue...of the various... patent scales, made...by...G. Medhurst'.] 38p. *8°.* 1827.

25329 **OBSERVATIONS** on the practicability and advantages of the continuation of the Stockton and Darlington railway, from Croft Bridge to the city of York, and by means of collateral branches, to effect a speedy, cheap, and direct communication between the counties of Northumberland and Durham...Yorkshire and Lancashire, &c. [A letter signed: A practical farmer, in answer to one published in the York Herald (here reprinted), signed: A constant reader.] 18p. *8°. Ripon, York, &c.,* 1827.

25330 The **ORIGIN,** progress, and present state of the Thames Tunnel; and the advantages likely to accrue from it, both to the proprietors and to the public. 26p. *8°.* 1827.

25331 —— Fifth edition. 28p. *8°.* 1827.

25332 **PEMBERTON,** J. An address to the county of York, respecting the formation of a railway company, and the making a railway from York to the Darlington Railway, with a branch to Ripon: and the rules of such company. 16p. *8°. York,* [1827]

25333 A **PROPOSAL** for steam navigation, from Europe to America, and the West Indies. 31p. *8°.* 1827. *The half-title and caption: American and colonial steam navigation.*

25334 **STEEDMAN,** J. To the subscribers to the survey of the proposed railway from the Forth and Clyde Canal to Stirling and Callander of Monteith, and to Alloa Ferry, near Kersie Nook, the report of John Steedman, engineer. [With 'Estimate of the expense and revenue'.] 18p. *4°. n.p.* [1827] *The Rastrick copy.*

25335 **THAMES TUNNEL COMPANY.** Thames Tunnel Company, incorporated June 24, 1824. Directors ...[With 'The Thames Tunnel. March, 1827'.] 8p. *4°.* [1827] *The Rastrick copy.*

25336 **TRENCH,** SIR FREDERICK W. A collection of papers relating to the Thames Quay, with hints for some further improvements in the Metropolis... 176p. *4°.* 1827.

SOCIAL CONDITIONS

25337 **AGED FEMALE SOCIETY.** Report of the Aged Female Society, 1827; established in the year 1811. Read...on...May 14, 1827. 15p. *8°. Sheffield,* 1827.

25338 **BADELEY,** I. C. Reply to Mr. Sleigh's letter to the governors of St. George's Hospital. 11p. *8°.* 1827.

25339 **BRITISH SOCIETY OF LADIES FOR PROMOTING THE REFORMATION OF FEMALE PRISONERS.** Sketch of the origin and results of ladies' prison associations, with hints for the formation of local associations. 66p. *12°.* 1827.

25340 [**CAREY,** M.] The infant school. [Description of an exhibition of work at the Infant School, Chester Street, Philadelphia. Signed: Howard.] 4p. *8°. n.p.* [1827]

25341 **CHALMERS,** T. On the use and abuse of literary and ecclesiastical endowments. 194p. *8°. Glasgow, Edinburgh, &c.,* 1827.

25342 **COMMITTEE FOR...RELIEF TO THE MANUFACTURERS AND OTHER OPERATIVES,** *Edinburgh.* Report of the Committee, appointed at a general meeting of the inhabitants of Edinburgh...Ordered to be printed...at the general meeting...4th June 1827. 18p. *8°. Edinburgh,* 1827.

25343 **COMMITTEE TO CONSIDER THE PAUPER SYSTEM OF THE CITY AND DISTRICTS,** *Philadelphia.* Report of the committee appointed at a town meeting of the citizens of the city and county of Philadelphia, on the 23d of July, 1827, to consider the subject of the pauper system of the city and districts, and to report remedies for its defects. [Signed: William Boyd and 21 other members of the Committee.] 28p. *8°. Philadelphia,* 1827.

25344 A **COPY** of a letter, from Mr. Hunter to the Common Council in London, describing the shocking death of a poor weaver and his wife, from starvation. And further particulars of the distresses of the starving manufacturers. Addressed to the independent electors for Northumberland...and all the candidates for seats in the next Parliament. 2p. *4°. Newcastle*, [1827 ?] [*Br.* 548] *The account of the death of the weaver was reprinted from the Warwickshire and Leamington Gazette, 13 May 1826.*

25345 COPY of the petition against the impress service, from the seamen of the port of Newcastle, to the Commons House of Parliament. 12p. *8°. South Shields*, 1827.

25346 DUCPÉTIAUX, E. De la justice de prévoyance, et particulièrement de l'influence de la misère et de l'aisance, de l'ignorance et de l'instruction sur le nombre des crimes. 36p. *8°. Bruxelles*, 1827.

25347 —— De la mission de la justice humaine et de l'injustice de la peine de mort. De la justice de répression, et particulièrement de l'inutilité et des effets pernicieux de la peine de mort. 105p. *8°. Bruxelles*, 1827. *Presentation copy from the author to the Athenæum Club.*

25348 ELMES, J. A practical treatise on architectural jurisprudence; in which the constitutions, canons, laws and customs relating to the art of building, are collected from the best authorities: for the use of architects, surveyors, landlords, tenants, incumbents, churchwardens and ecclesiastical persons in general. 279p. *8°. London, Edinburgh, &c.*, 1827.

25349 A general **FORM** of contract, between manufacturers and workmen: with notes. 12p. *8°. Wolverhampton*, [1827]

25350 FRY, E. Observations on the visiting, superintendence, and government, of female prisoners. 76p. *12°. London & Norwich*, 1827.

25351 —— Second edition. 79p. *12°. London & Norwich*, 1827. *Presentation copy from the author to Robert Southey, with an inscription to this effect in his hand on the title-page.*

25352 —— and **GURNEY**, J. J. Report addressed to the Marquess Wellesley, Lord Lieutenant of Ireland, by Elizabeth Fry and Joseph John Gurney, respecting their late visit to that country. 95p. *8°. London, York, &c.*, 1827.

25353 GASCOIGNE, H. B. Society for Promoting the Employment of the Poor; with brief remarks on the present state of society in England... 18p. *8°.* 1827.

25354 *GENERAL ASSOCIATION FOR THE PURPOSE OF BETTERING THE CONDITION OF MANUFACTURING AND AGRICULTURAL LABOURERS. A narrative and exposition of the origin, progress, principles...of the... Association... 72p. *8°.* 1827. *The FWA copy that belonged to William Pare. The Goldsmiths' Library copy is imperfect, wanting the title-page and chapter I.*

25355 HARVEY, A. Moral causes of the present commercial distress; a sermon, delivered in the Relief Church, Kilmarnock, 25th January, 1827...The profits to the fund for unemployed operatives. 25p. *8°. Kilmarnock, Glasgow, &c.*, 1827.

25356 HAYTI. The rural code of Haiti; in French and English. With a prefatory letter to the Right Hon. the Earl Bathurst, K.G. 100p. *8°.* 1827. *The Agar Ellis copy.*

25357 HENRY VIII, *King of England*. The privy purse expences of King Henry the Eighth, from November

MDXXIX, to December MDXXXII: with introductory remarks and illustrative notes, by Nicholas Harris Nicolas. 372p. *8°.* 1827.

25358 HEYWOOD, Sir B., *Bart*. An address delivered at the opening of the new building for the Manchester Mechanics' Institution, on Monday 14th May, 1827. 16p. *8°. Manchester*, 1827.

25359 *[HILL, Matthew D.] Public education. Plans for the government and liberal instruction of boys, in large numbers; as practised at Hazelwood School. Second edition. [Revised by T. W. Hill and Arthur Hill.] 390p. *8°.* 1827. *For another edition, see 1822.*

25360 HINTS to agriculturists and others residing in the neighbourhood of Colchester, upon the advantages which may be derived from benefit societies...To which are added directions, rules, &c. for the use of those who may wish to establish insurance societies for the poor... [With 'Rules, &c. for the government...of the Aldham and United Parishes Institution or Insurance Society'.] 119, [19]p. *8°. Colchester, London, &c.*, 1827.

25361 HULBERT, J. F. Farming the sick poor. Observations on the necessity of establishing a different system of affording medical relief to the sick poor: than by the practice of contracting with medical men, or the farming of parishes. 51p. *8°. Shrewsbury, London, &c.*, 1827. *Presentation copy, with accompanying letter, from the author to William Allen.*

25362 A **LETTER**, on the present state of the labouring classes in America; with an account of the wages given to weavers...spinners, masons...smiths...labourers... servants, prices of provisions, &c....By an intelligent emigrant at Philadelphia. 16p. *8°. Bury*, 1827.

25363 LITERARY, SCIENTIFIC AND MECHANICAL INSTITUTION, *Newcastle-upon-Tyne*. The third annual report of the...Institution...To which are added, a statement of the accounts of the Institution, a list of new members, and a supplement to the catalogue. 16p. *8°. Newcastle upon Tyne*, 1827. *See also 1825, 1826.*

25364 LIVINGSTON, E. Introductory report to the code of prison discipline...Being part of the system of penal law prepared for the state of Louisiana. 78p. *8°.* 1827.

25365 [MARTINEAU, H.] The rioters; or, a tale of bad times. 122p. *12°. Wellington*, 1827.

25366 MATTHEWS, W. An historical sketch of the origin, progress, & present state, of gas-lighting. 434p. *12°.* 1827. *See also 1832.*

25367 PERCY, H. A., *Earl of Northumberland*. The regulations and establishment of the household of Henry Algernon Percy, the fifth Earl of Northumberland, at his castles of Wresill and Lekinfield in Yorkshire. Begun Anno Domini M.D.XII. [Edited, with a preface, by Thomas Percy, Bishop of Dromore.] 464p. *8°.* 1827.

25368 PHIPPEN, T. and F. A letter to Thomas G. B. Estcourt, Esq., M.P. for the University of Oxford, upon the Bill now pending in Parliament, "To regulate the granting of licenses to keepers of inns, alehouses, and victualling houses in England." [On the administrative and social inconveniences of the licensing arrangements proposed in the Bill.] 37p. *8°.* 1827.

25369 [POWELL, H. T.] A memoir of the Warwick County Asylum, instituted in the year 1818...shewing that it has answered the purposes of reformation, and diminished the county expenditure. Published under the sanction of the Committee... 82p. *8°. London, Warwick, &c., 1827.*

For **PRISON DISCIPLINE SOCIETY,** *Boston,* 1st–19th annual report of the board of managers, 1826–44, 1827–44, *see* vol. III, *Periodicals list,* Annual report...

25370 PYE, H. J. Summary of the duties of a justice of the peace out of sessions: with some preliminary observations...Fourth edition, with considerable additions. 295p. *12°. 1827.*

25371 ROLPH, T. A letter to the Rev. Henry Butts Owen, D.D. Rector of St. Olave's, Hart Street, occasioned by his appeals against payment of the poor rates. 19p. *8°. 1827.*

25372 SLEIGH, W. W. A letter to the independent governors of St. George's Hospital. Proving a loss to the poor, by mismanagement, of (even in eight items,) ninety thousand pounds! 8p. *8°. [London,] 1827.*

25373 SOCIETY FOR THE IMPROVEMENT OF PRISON DISCIPLINE, *London.* The seventh report of the Committee of the Society...1827. With an appendix ['Extracts from the correspondence of the Committee']. 144, 411p. *8°. London, Edinburgh, &c.,*

[1827] *The copy that belonged to George Agar Ellis, Baron Dover, with his arms in gilt on the binding. See also 1818, 1824, 1832.*

25374 STRICKLAND, afterwards **CHOLMLEY,** SIR G., *Bart.* A discourse on the poor laws of England and Scotland, on the state of the poor of Ireland, and on emigration. 127p. *8°. London & York, 1827. See also 1830.*

25375 TAMLYN, J. A digest of the laws of friendly societies and savings banks, including all the Acts of Parliament...and the various decisions of the courts of law and equity. 137p. *12°. 1827.*

25376 WATKINS, H. G. Affectionate advice to apprentices, on their being bound at Weavers' Hall, presented by the Bailiffs, Wardens, and assistants, of the Worshipful Company of Weavers...Printed for the Company, by permission of the author. 56p. *12°. 1827. The copy presented in 1832 to the apprentice William Harvey.*

25377 WEST, G. A plan for bettering the condition of the working classes, by the establishment of friendly societies upon legal and scientific principles, exemplified by practical illustrations, in a letter to Henry Lawes Long, Esq.... 51p. *8°. Farnham & London,* [1827]

25378 YATES, JAMES. Thoughts on the advancement of academical education in England...Second edition. 184p. *8°. 1827.*

SLAVERY

For the **AFRICAN REPOSITORY,** 1827, 1830–34, 1836–37, 1848, 1884–86, *see* vol. III, *Periodicals list.*

25379 ANECDOTES of Africans. 88p. *12°. 1827.*

25380 BARCLAY, A. A practical view of the present state of slavery in the West Indies; or, an examination of Mr. Stephen's "Slavery of the British West India Colonies"...also, strictures on the Edinburgh Review, and on the pamphlets of Mr. Cooper and Mr. Bickell... Second edition. 462p. *8°. 1827. The copy, with inscription, presented to 'Willm. Thompson Esq M.P.,' by the publisher.*

25381 [BARRET, .] The genuine speech of Charles Nicholas Pallmer, Esq. in reply to Dr. Lushington's address to the House of Commons, on the 12th June, 1827, on presenting the petitions of the free people of colour of the West Indies, (first published in the Kingston Chronicle and Jamaica Journal). 18p. *8°. Kingston, Jamaica, 1827. A note on the authorship by the publishers is included in the second edition, 1828 (q.v.).*

25382 CONSIDERATIONS on certain remarks on the negro slavery and abolition questions, in Lord Stowell's judgment in the case of the slave "Grace". By a Briton. 18p. *8°. Newcastle, 1827. Two copies with presentation inscriptions from the anonymous author, one to the Anti-Slavery Society, London, the other to Stephen Lushington, M.P.*

25383 EPITOME of the West India question, in the form of a dialogue, between an abolitionist and a West Indian. 49p. *8°. 1827.*

25384 FERNANDEZ, JOHN. An address to His Majesty's ministers, recommending efficacious means for the most speedy termination of African slavery. 36p. *8°. 1827.*

25385 HAGGARD, J. The judgment of the Right

Hon. Lord Stowell, respecting the slavery of the mongrel woman, Grace, on an appeal from the Vice-Admiralty Court of Antigua. Michaelmas Term, 1827. 49p. *8°. 1827.*

25386 JAMAICA. The consolidated slave law, passed the 22d December, 1826, commencing on the 1st May, 1827. With a commentary, (shewing the difference between the new law and the repealed enactments,) marginal notes, and a copious index. Second edition, carefully compared with the original. 47p. *8°. [Jamaica,] 1827.*

25387 LADIES' ASSOCIATION FOR CALNE, MELKSHAM, DEVIZES...IN AID OF THE CAUSE OF NEGRO EMANCIPATION. The second report of the Ladies' Association... 28p. *8°. Calne, 1827.*

25388 M'DONNELL, A. Compulsory manumission; or an examination of the actual state of the West India question. 86p. *8°. 1827.*

25389 MANCHESTER ANTI-SLAVERY SOCIETY. Report of the committee of the Manchester Society, for the furtherance of the gradual abolition of slavery, and the amelioration of the condition of slaves in the British colonies. 11p. *8°. Manchester, 1827.*

25390 MATHISON, G. A critical view of a pamphlet, intitled "The West India question practically considered," with remarks on the Trinidad Order in Council: in a letter addressed to the Rt. Hon. Robert Wilmot Horton. 78p. *8°. 1827.*

25391 MORE, H. The feast of freedom, or the abolition of domestic slavery in Ceylon; [a play in verse,] the vocal parts adapted to music by Charles Wesley...To which are added, several unpublished little pieces. 39p. *8°. 1827.*

25392 A short **REVIEW** of the slave trade and slavery, with considerations on the benefit which would arise from cultivating tropical productions by free labour. 129p. *8°. Birmingham, 1827. A copy in the library of the Anti-Slavery Society for the Protection of Human Rights has a manuscript attribution to John Sturge.*

25393 RILAND, J., *ed.* Memoirs of a West-India planter. Published from an original ms. With a preface and additional details... 218p. *12°.* 1827.

25394 SHEFFIELD FEMALE ANTI-SLAVERY SOCIETY. Report of the Sheffield Female Anti-Slavery Society. Established midsummer, 1825. 15p. *8°. Sheffield, 1827. See also 1833.*

25395 SOCIETY FOR THE ABOLITION OF SLAVERY THROUGHOUT THE BRITISH DOMINIONS. Account of the receipts & disbursements of the...Society, for the years 1823, 1824, 1825, & 1826: with a list of the subscribers. 28p. *8°.* [*London*, 1827] *See also 1829, 1831, 1832.*

25396 —— The further progress of colonial reform; being an analysis of the communication made to Parliament by His Majesty, at the close of the last Session, respecting the measures taken for improving the condition of the slave population in the British colonies...⟨In continuation of..."The slave colonies of Great Britain," &c. and "The progress of colonial reform,"...⟩. 78p. *8°.* 1827. *The copy that belonged to Stephen Lushington.*

25397 —— The petition and memorial of the planters of Demarara and Berbice, on the subject of manumission, examined: being an exposure of the inaccuracy of the statements, and the fallacy of the views, on which they have proceeded in their recent application to His Majesty in Council. 6op. *8°.* 1827. *The copy that belonged to Stephen Lushington.*

25398 STROUD, G. M. A sketch of the laws relating to slavery in the several states of the United States of America. 18op. *8°. Philadelphia, 1827.*

25399 WEST INDIA sugar. 4p. *8°. Liverpool, 1827.*

25400 WINN, T. S. (Second edition enlarged.) A speedy end to slavery in our West India colonies, by safe, effectual and equitable means, for the benefit of all parties concerned. To which is added a supplement. 127, 32p. *8°.* 1827. *For another edition, see 1825.*

POLITICS

25401 DENNIS, JOHN (*b.* 1778). A speech delivered by the Revd. John Dennis, A.B....at a meeting held at Teignmouth on...May 24th 1827, for the purpose of petitioning both Houses of Parliament to grant no further concessions to the Roman Catholics. 14p. *8°. Teignmouth,* 1827.

25402 ENGLAND. *Treaties, etc.* No. 15. Secret and confidential. Abstracts of proceedings in the Greek question, to the conclusion of the Treaty between England, Russia, and France, of July 6th, 1827. 14, 6, 16p. *fol. n.p.,* 1827. *Addressed in manuscript to 'the Rt. Hon. C. W. Williams Wynn'.*

25403 —— —— [Papers relative to the Treaty of London for the pacification of Greece, consisting of the text of the Treaty with 7 protocols and their annexes, preceded by a list of the papers.] [84]p. *fol. n.p.* [1827] *Addressed in manuscript to 'the Rt. Hon. C. W. Williams Wynn'.*

25404 FOX, afterwards **VASSALL,** H. R., *Baron Holland.* Letter to the Rev. Dr. Shuttleworth, Warden of New College, Oxford. [On Catholic emancipation.] 33p. *8°.* 1827.

25405 *FRIENDS OF CIVIL AND RELIGIOUS LIBERTY. Account of the meeting of the Friends of Civil & Religious Liberty, at the Crown & Anchor Tavern in the Strand, on Monday, the 12th of Feb. 1827. 16p. *8°.* [1827] *The copy that belonged to George Grote.*

25406 [**GROSVENOR,** ROBERT, *Baron Ebury?*] A short consideration of the measures recently proposed in the House of Commons, for the relief of Ireland. Addressed to the citizens of Chester. By one of their representatives. 24p. *8°. Chester,* 1827. *It is possible that the author was Lord Robert Grosvenor's elder brother, Richard, Viscount Belgrave, who was the other M.P. for Chester at this time.*

25407 HONE, W. Facetiæ and miscellanies...With ...engravings drawn by George Cruikshank. Second edition. [380]p. *8°.* 1827. *A collection of Hone's separately published political satires, reissued with a general title.*

25408 HOWARD, HENRY. Historical references, in support of the remarks on the erroneous opinions entertained respecting the Catholic religion: and to prove that its principles are not adverse to civil liberty, and that religious liberty is a civil right. 94p. *8°. Carlisle,* 1827.

25409 MacDONNELL, E. Catholic question. Practical views of the principles and conduct of the Catholic clergy and laity of Ireland, respectfully submitted to the consideration of Members of Parliament. 18p. *8°.* 1827. *The Agar Ellis copy.*

25410 O'CONNELL, D. A full report of the speech of Daniel O'Connell, on the subject of church rates and parish cess, as delivered at a meeting of Catholics, on... the 10th of January, 1827. By James Sheridan. 65p. *8°. Dublin,* 1827.

25411 PHILLPOTTS, H., *Bishop of Exeter.* A letter to the Right Honourable George Canning, on the Bill of 1825, for removing the disqualifications of His Majesty's Roman Catholic subjects, and on his speech in support of the same. 167p. *8°.* 1827.

25412 —— Second edition. 167p. *8°.* 1827.

25413 —— Third edition. 167p. *8°.* 1827.

25414 —— Fourth edition. 167p. *8°.* 1827.

25415 —— Sixth edition. [From *The Pamphleteer,* vol. XXVII, no. 54.] 75p. *8°.* 1827.

25416 —— A short letter to the Right Honourable George Canning, &c.&c.&c. on the present position of the Roman Catholic question. 4op. *8°.* 1827.

25417 —— [Another edition. From *The Pamphleteer,* vol. XXVII, no. 54.] 17p. *8°.* 1827.

25418 SMITH, LEVESON. Remarks upon an Essay on government by James Mill, Esq., published in the supplement to the Encyclopædia Britannica. [With other papers by Leveson Smith, published after his death by his mother, Mrs. C. M. Smith.] 48p. *4⁰*. 1827. *The Agar Ellis copy.*

25419 STATEMENT of the case of the Protestant Dissenters under the Corporation & Test Acts, published

for the United Committee appointed to conduct their application for relief. 16p. *8⁰*. 1827.

25420 The grand **VIZIER** unmasked; or, remarks on the supposed claims of Mr. Canning to public confidence: in an appeal to the British Parliament and people. By a Protestant Tory. Second edition. 64p. *8⁰*. 1827.

SOCIALISM

25421 An **ADDRESS** to the members of trade societies, and to the working classes generally: being an exposition of the relative situation, condition, and future prospects of working people in the United States of America. Together with a suggestion and outlines of a plan, by which they may gradually...improve their condition. By a fellow labourer. Re-printed from the original edition published in Philadelphia. 36p. *12⁰*. 1827. *Another, the FWA copy, belonged to William Pare. See also 1833, 1839.*

25422 BROWN, P. Twelve months in New-Harmony; presenting a faithful account of the principal occurrences which have taken place there within that period... 128p.

8⁰. Cincinnati, 1827. *The copy that belonged to Stanley Jevons.*

25423 LONDON CO-OPERATIVE TRADING FUND ASSOCIATION. London Co-operative Trading Fund Association. At a meeting of the shareholders held at 36 Red Lion Square...11th Dec. 1827. [Report of meeting and regulations of the Society. Signed: George Green Ward, chairman.] [2]p. *8⁰*. *n.p.* [1827]

25424 [THOMPSON, WILLIAM (1875?–1833).] Labor rewarded. The claims of labor and capital conciliated: or, how to secure to labor the whole products of its exertions...By one of the idle classes. 127p. *8⁰*. 1827.

MISCELLANEOUS

25425 ADDRESS of the Catholics of Ireland to the people of England. [With 'Resolutions of the Archbishops and Bishops of Ireland...21st January 1826'.] 7p. *8⁰*. *Dublin*, [1827?]

25426 BARRY, JOHN M., *Baron Farnham*. The substance of a speech delivered by the Rt. Hon. Lord Farnham, at a meeting held in Cavan on...January 26, 1827, for the purpose of promoting the Reformation in Ireland. 32p. *8⁰*. *Dublin & London*, 1827.

25427 BENTHAM, J. Article eight of the Westminster Review, No. XII. for October, 1826, on Mr. Humphreys' Observations on the English law of real property, with the outline of a code, &c. 63p. *8⁰*. 1827.

25428 BURGESS, T., *Bishop of Salisbury*. A discourse [on the authenticity of the MS. 'De doctrina Christiana', attributed to John Milton] delivered at the anniversary meeting of the Royal Society of Literature, April 26, 1827 by the President. 27p. *4⁰*. 1827. *The Agar Ellis copy.*

25429 DEMANGEAT, G. Principes de la morale universelle, ou élémens de la physiologie de l'homme moral. 120p. *8⁰*. *Paris*, 1827.

25430 FREDERICK, *Duke of York and Albany*. The posthumous letter of His Royal Highness the Duke of York. 68p. *8⁰*. 1827.

25431 *LONDON. Livery Companies. *Salters.* A list of the Masters, Wardens, Court of Assistants, and Livery, of the Worshipful Company of Salters. 15p. *8⁰*. 1827. *See also* 1784, 1787, 1790, 1792, 1794, 1797, 1799, 1801, 1803, 1806, 1809, 1812, 1815, 1818, 1821, 1824, 1830.

25432 REMARKS on the improvements now in progress in St. James's Park. Humbly addressed to the Members of both Houses of Parliament. [Signed: An old inhabitant of Pall-Mall.] 8p. *8⁰*. *n.p.* [1827?]

25433 SPENCER, HON. G. A visitation sermon, preached at Northampton, on...July 16, 1827, before the ...Lord Bishop of Peterborough... 20p. *8⁰*. 1827.

25434 WELLESLEY, W. P. T. L., *4th Earl of Mornington*. Two letters to the Right Hon. Earl Eldon, Lord Chancellor, &c.&c.&c. With official and other documents. [On the dispute over his wife's will.] 130p. *8⁰*. 1827.

1828

GENERAL

25435 An **ANALYSIS** of the artificial wealth of England: in reply to Lord Grenville's Essay on the supposed advantages of the Sinking Fund. 50p. *8⁰*. 1828.

25436 BOECKH, A. The public economy of Athens

...to which is added, a dissertation on the silver-mines of Laurion. Translated from the German of Augustus Boeckh [by G. C. Lewis]... 2 vols. *8⁰*. 1828. *See also* 1842.

25437 Published under the superintendence of the

Society for the Diffusion of Useful Knowledge. The **BRITISH ALMANAC**, for...MDCCCXXVIII...[With 'The companion to the Almanac; or year-book of general information...The second edition'.] 60, 186p. *12°*. [1828] *See also the years 1829–1850 inclusive.*

25438 The **BRITISH IMPERIAL CALENDAR** for the year...1828...Containing a general register of the United Kingdom...and its colonies...Carefully corrected at the public offices and institutions...[With 'A companion to the British Imperial Calendar, for... 1828'.] 432, 113p. *12°*. [1828] *For other editions, see* 1817.

25439 **COBBETT**, W. Twelve sermons...A new edition. 240p. *12°*. 1828. *For other editions, see* 1822.

25440 —— A year's residence, in the United States of America...Third edition... 370p. *12°*. 1828. *A reprint of the third edition, 1822 (q.v.). For other editions, see* 1818.

25441 **COLLAMER**, J. Oration delivered before the Phi Sigma Nu Society, of the University of Vermont, Burlington, August 6, 1828. 19p. *8°*. *Royalton,* [1828]

25442 *The **EAST-INDIA** register and directory, for 1828; containing...lists of the Company's servants... mariners &c. not in the service of the...Company; merchant vessels employed in the country trade...Compiled...by A. W. Mason, Geo. Owen, and G. H. Brown ...Second edition, corrected to 13th May, 1828. 609p. *12°*. [1828] *For other editions, see* 1804.

25443 **ÉCOLE SPÉCIALE DE COMMERCE ET D'INDUSTRIE**. Discours prononcés [par MM. le Chevalier des Taillades, Poux-Franklin, Adolphe Blanqui] à la quatrième séance du Conseil de Perfectionnement de l'École Spéciale de Commerce et d'Industrie, sous la présidence de M. le Cte. Chaptal...le 12 août, 1828. 92p. *8°*. *Paris,* 1828.

25444 Political **ECONOMY** condensed; or, the natural cause and proper means of improving the human intellect, and civilizing mankind. By the author of The effects of property, &c. 42p. *8°*. [1828?]

25445 **EDMONDS**, T. R. Practical moral and political economy; or, the government, religion and institutions, most conducive to individual happiness and to national power. 304p. *8°*. 1828.

25446 **ELMORE**, J. R. Letters to the Right Hon. the Earl of Darnley, on the state of Ireland, in advocacy of free trade and other measures of practical improvement, more especially calculated to supersede the necessity of emigration. 136p. *8°*. 1828.

25447 **ENSOR**, G. Letters showing the inutility, and exhibiting the absurdity of what is rather fantastically termed "the new Reformation". 84p. *8°*. *Dublin,* 1828.

25448 **EXPERIENCE**, *pseud*. No emigration. The testimony of Experience, before a committee of agriculturists and manufacturers, on the report of the Emigration Committee of the House of Commons: Sir John English in the chair. 60p. *8°*. 1828.

25449 **FLOREZ ESTRADA**, A. Curso de economia politica... 2 vols. *8°*. *Londres,* 1828. *See also* 1833.

25450 **FRANKLIN**, *pseud*. [*Begin.*] Fellow Citizens of Pennsylvania! I intend to present to your consideration a few plain matters of fact...[An attack on the candidature of Jackson for President, in the light of his opposition to protection of American industry and expansion of road and canal building.] 12p. *12°*. *n.p.* [1828?] *Attributed by HSF to Mathew Carey.*

25451 **FRANKLIN**, JAMES. The present state of Hayti, (Saint Domingo,) with remarks on its agriculture, commerce, laws, religion, finances, and population, etc.... 411p. *8°*. 1828.

25452 **HEAD**, SIR F. B., *Bart*. Rough notes taken during some rapid journeys across the Pampas and among the Andes...Third edition. 321p. *8°*. 1828. *For another edition, see* 1826.

25453 **HOPKINS**, T. On rent of land, and its influence on subsistence and population: with observations on the operating causes of the condition of the labouring classes in various countries. 140p. *8°*. 1828.

25454 A **LETTER** to His Grace the Duke of Wellington, containing practical suggestions, founded on simple principles, for the regulating of the currency; the relieving of the country from pauperism and a redundant population, and for the preventing, detecting, and correcting of crime. By an Englishman. 66p. *8°*. 1828.

25455 A **LETTER** to the Right Hon. Mr. Lamb, containing a few practical hints for the improvement of Ireland. By a landowner. Third edition. [With 'First letter. To the Committee lately appointed on combination', signed: a workman and employer, and 'Second letter. To employers and employed', signed: a manufacturer.] 28p. *8°*. *Dublin,* 1828.

For the **LION**, *1828–29, see vol.* III, *Periodicals list.*

25456 **LYON**, G. F. Journal of a residence and tour in the Republic of Mexico in...1826. With some account of the mines of that country... 2 vols. *8°*. 1828.

25457 [**MACKINNON**, W. A.] On the rise, progress, and present state of public opinion, in Great Britain, and other parts of the world. 343p. *8°*. 1828. *Subsequently rewritten and published in 1846 as* History of civilisation.

25458 **MILL**, JAMES. Essays on government, jurisprudence, liberty of the press, and law of nations. Written for the Supplement to the Encyclopædia Britannica...Not for sale. 32, 41, 34, 33p. *8°*. [1828?] *For other editions, see* 1825.

25459 **MUNDELL**, A. Reasons for a revision of our fiscal code; arising from the continuing defalcation in the supply of gold and silver from the mines, and the consequent depression of money prices. Addressed to the Finance Committee...Second edition. 104p. *8°*. 1828. *For the supplementary tables to this work, see* 1829, 1830.

25460 *PALMER, HENRY. Remarks on the nature of value; for the consideration of the labouring classes... The second edition, with additions. 48p. *8°*. 1828. *The FWA copy, that belonged to William Pare. The Goldsmiths' Library copy lacks the half-title.*

25461 [**PETTMAN**, W. R. A.] An essay on political economy; shewing in what way fluctuations in the price of corn may be prevented, and the means by which all the advantages of a free trade in corn may be attained... Part I. 83p. *8°*. 1828.

25462 —— An essay on political economy; shewing the means by which the distresses of the labouring poor may be relieved...the resources of the country increased; and, a permanent value given to a paper currency...Part II. 123p. *8°*. 1828.

25463 **PHILLIPS**, WILLARD. A manual of political economy, with particular reference to the institutions, resources, and condition of the United States. 278p. *8°*. *Boston,* 1828.

25464 The **POST OFFICE** annual directory for 1828–29; containing an alphabetical list of the nobility, gentry, merchants, and others, in Edinburgh, Leith, and Newhaven. With an appendix, and a street directory. Twenty-third publication. 231, 79p. *long 12°. Edinburgh, 1828. See also 1835, 1841.*

25465 **PRACTICE** opposed to theory; or, an inquiry into the nature of our commercial distress, with a view to the developement of its true causes, and the suggestion of a suitable remedy. By a practical man. 207p. *8°.* 1818 [1828].

25466 **RIDER'S** British Merlin: for…1828…With notes of husbandry, fairs, marts, and tables…Compiled by Cardanus Rider. 60p. *12°.* [1828] *For other editions, see* 1693.

25467 **SADLER,** M. T. Ireland; its evils, and their remedies: being a refutation of the errors of the Emigration Committee and others, touching that country. To which is prefixed a synopsis of an original treatise…on the law of population… 414p. *8°.* 1828. *The copy that belonged to the Earl of Ranfurly. See also* 1829.

25468 **SAY,** J. B. Cours complet d'économie politique pratique; ouvrage destiné à mettre sous les yeux des hommes…l'économie des sociétés. [With 'Mélanges et correspondance d'économie politique'.] 7 vols. *8°. Paris, 1828–33. There are second copies of vols. 1–3, presented by the author to Francis Place; with an inscription in vol. 2 and a letter to Place from the author in vol. 3. For the first issue of Mélanges et correspondance d'économie politique, see 1833.*

25469 **SMITH,** ADAM. An inquiry into the nature and causes of the wealth of nations…With a life of the author, an introductory discourse, notes, and supplemental dissertations. By J. R. McCulloch. 4 vols. *8°. Edinburgh & London, 1828. For other editions, see 1776.*

25470 **SMYTH,** A. Outlines of a new theory of political economy. 48p. *8°. Cork & London, 1828. The copy that belonged to the Duke of Wellington.*

25471 **SOCIETY FOR THE IMPROVEMENT OF IRELAND.** Statement of the proceedings of the Society…for the year 1828. With an appendix, containing its rules and regulations, names of members… 116p. *8°. Dublin, 1828. See also 1829, 1846.*

25472 **TEELING,** C. H. Personal narrative of the "Irish Rebellion" of 1798. 285p. *8°.* 1828.

25473 **THOMPSON,** THOMAS P. The true theory of rent, in opposition to Mr. Ricardo and others. Being an exposition of fallacies on rent, tithes, &c. In the form of a review of Mr. Mill's Elements of political economy. By a member of the University of Cambridge. Third edition… 60p. *8°.* 1828. *For other editions, see* 1826.

25474 **VILLELA DA SILVA,** L. D. Observações criticas sobre alguns artigos do Ensaio estatistico do reino de Portugal e Algarves publicado em Paris por Adriano Balbi. 137p. *4°. Lisboa,* 1828.

25475 **WARD,** SIR H. G. Mexico im Jahre 1827. Nach dem Englischen des H. G. Ward. (*Neue Bibliothek der wichtigsten Reisebeschreibungen zur Erweiterung der Erd- und Völkerkunde,* 49.) 2 vols. *8°. Weimar, 1828–29. See also* 1829.

AGRICULTURE

25476 **ALLEN,** WILLIAM (1770–1843). Colonies at home; or, the means for rendering the industrious labourer independent of parish relief, and for providing for the poor population of Ireland by the cultivation of the soil…Printed for the Society for Improving the Condition of the Lower Order of Tenantry, and of the Labouring Population of Ireland. 52p. *8°. Lindfield: at the Schools of Industry; London, &c.,* 1828. *For other editions, see* 1827.

25477 **COBBETT,** W. Cottage economy…A new edition. [184]p. *12°.* 1828. *For other editions, see* 1821.

25478 —— A treatise on Cobbett's corn… [296]p. *12°.* 1828. *See also* 1831.

25479 **KENNEDY,** L. and **GRAINGER,** T. B. The present state of the tenancy of land in Great Britain: showing the principal customs and practices between incoming and outgoing tenants; and the most usual method under which land is now held in the several counties. Collected from a survey made in 1827 and 1828 … 384p. *8°.* 1828

25480 **M'INTOSH,** CHARLES (1794–1864). The practical gardener, and modern horticulturist; containing the latest and most approved methods for the management of the kitchen, fruit, and flower-garden, the green-house, hot-house, &c.&c. for every month in the year… 1122p. *8°.* 1828[–1829]

25481 **MEXICAN MINING ASSOCIATION.** Report on the affairs of the United Mexican Mining Association, made to the Court of Directors, by the Secretary [Richard Heathfield], on his return from Mexico. Dated 31st May, 1828. 58p. *8°.* 1828.

25482 —— Substance of information received by the Court of Directors of the United Mexican Mining Association, since the return of the Secretary from Mexico. Dated 14th June, 1828. 15p. *8°.* [*London,* 1828]

25483 —— United Mexican Mining Association. Report of proceedings at a general meeting of proprietors, 30th July, 1828. [With an appendix.] 21, lxviiip. *8°.* 1828. *See also* 1827.

25484 **NEWBOROUGH.** Book of reference to the lithographic map of the Parish of Newborough, in the county of Northampton. 28l. *8°.* [1828] *Bound with the map, dated 1823, which is in sections, and with Acts of 1812 and 1819 establishing the parish; for which see 1812 and 1819.*

For the **QUARTERLY JOURNAL OF AGRICULTURE,** 1828–43, *continued as* the Journal of agriculture, 1843–68, *see vol.* III, *Periodicals list,* Journal of agriculture.

25485 **SINCLAIR,** SIR JOHN, *Bart.* On the culture and uses of potatoes; accompanied by engravings, and practical directions, explanatory of the best modes of raising, preserving, and using that root…[With an appendix.] 63, 32p. *8°. Edinburgh, London, &c.,* 1828.

25486 **STEUART,** SIR H., *Bart.* The planter's guide; or, a practical essay on the best method of giving immediate effect to wood, by the removal of large trees and underwood...interspersed with observations on general planting...originally intended for the climate of Scotland ...Second edition. Greatly improved and enlarged. 527p. *8°. Edinburgh & London*, 1828.

25487 TRIMMER, Joshua K. Practical observations on the improvement of British fine wool, and the national advantages of the arable system of sheep husbandry. 80p. *8°.* 1828.

CORN LAWS

25488 AGRICULTOR, *pseud.* A letter to the Right Hon. Charles Grant, President of the Board of Trade, &c.&c. on the corn laws, wool laws, and rents in kind. 48p. *8°. Edinburgh, London, &c.,* 1828.

25489 FOSTER, John, *of Bedford.* Six letters on the corn question, under the following heads: on the corn question as affecting the general interests of the nation. On the subsistence of the people. On the corn laws, as affecting the owners...of land. On the corn laws, as affecting labourers...On the corn laws as affecting manufacturers. On the corn question, as it affects Ireland. 32p. *8°.* [1828]

25490 MAITLAND, James, *8th Earl of Lauderdale,* and **STANHOPE**, Philip H., *4th Earl Stanhope.* Protest against the decision of the House of Lords of [*sic*] the Corn Importation Bill. June 13, 1828. 16p. *8°.* [1828]

25491 NOLAN, G. Practical observations upon the projected alterations of the law for regulating the import of corn into the United Kingdom of Great Britain & Ireland: in a letter addressed to His Grace the Duke of Wellington. 29p. *8°.* 1828.

25492 OBSERVATIONS on the pernicious tendency of a free trade in corn. 31p. *8°. Edinburgh,* 1828.

25493 REMARKS upon the corn laws of the United Kingdom of Great Britain. 46p. *8°. Edinburgh,* [1828]

25494 THOMPSON, Thomas P. A catechism on the corn laws; with a list of fallacies and the answers. By a member of the University of Cambridge. Fourth edition ... 123p. *8°.* 1828. *For other editions, see 1827.*

POPULATION

25495 SENIOR, N. W. Two lectures on population, delivered before the University of Oxford in Easter Term, 1828...To which is added, a correspondence between the author and the Rev. T. R. Malthus. 90p. *8°.* 1828. *See also* 1829, 1831.

TRADES & MANUFACTURES

25496 ADCOCK, H. Improved pocket-book for engineers, architects, manufacturers, millwrights, and builders, for the year 1828. Containing...tables and rules connected with the subjects of practical science. 194p. *16°.* 1828. *The Rastrick copy, with manuscript notes.*

25497 CLAUGHTON, T. L., *Bishop of St. Albans.* Machinæ vi vaporis impulsæ: carmen latinum, in Theatro Sheldoniano recitatum MDCCCXXVIII. 15p. *8°. Oxonii,* 1828.

25498 GUEST, R. The British cotton manufactures, and a reply to an article on the spinning machinery, contained in a recent number of the Edinburgh Review. 230p. *8°. Manchester & London,* 1828.

25499 LARDNER, D. Popular lectures on the steam engine, in which its construction and operation are familiarly explained; with an historical sketch of its invention and progressive improvement... 164p. *12°.* 1828.

25500 RADCLIFFE, William (1760–1841). Origin of the new system of manufacture, commonly called "power-loom weaving," and the purposes for which this system was invented...fully explained in a narrative, containing William Radcliffe's struggles through life to remove the cause which has brought this country to its present crisis. Written by himself. 216p. *8°. Stockport, London, &c.,* 1828.

25501 A REVIEW of the present Malt Act; with a comparative sketch of the former malting laws: addressed to both Houses of Parliament. [Signed: A member of the Maltsters' Committee, and dated, March 4, 1828. A complaint against the multiplication of penalties to which maltsters are subject.] 24p. *8°.* 1828.

25502 VULLIAMY, B. L. Some considerations on the subject of public clocks, particularly church clocks: with hints for their improvement... 15p. *8°.* 1828.

25503 WHITE, John, *baker.* A treatise on the art of baking, with a preliminary introduction, shewing the various productions of the different quarters of the globe, observations on the present state of agriculture, the farmer and middleman, strictures on the corn bill, &c. With a number of...receipts...for the baker and domestic circle. 376p. *8°. Edinburgh,* 1828.

COMMERCE

25504 **BADNALL**, R. A view of the silk trade; with remarks on the recent measures of government in regard to that branch of manufacture. 108p. *8°.* 1828.

25505 **BOSTON**. Report of a committee of the citizens of Boston and vicinity, opposed to a further increase of duties on importations. [Drawn up by Henry Lee.] 196p. *8°. New-York*, 1828.

25506 **BROWN**, WILLIAM K. Remarks upon the alleged deterioration of British short clothing wool, in a letter to a Member of the House of Commons. 27p. *8°.* [1828]

25507 [**CAREY**, M.] Second edition – March 14, 1828. The Boston Report and mercantile memorials. No. 1. [Signed: Hamilton.] 3p. *8°. n.p.* [1828]

25508 —— Second edition – Feb. 29 [March 14], 1828. To Messrs. N. Goddard, Shaw, Winslow, W. Goddard [and others]...the Committee of the Boston merchants. No. 1.[–v.]. 16p. *8°. n.p.* [1828] *Published in parts. Part 5 is of the first edition.*

25509 **ENGLAND**. Parliament. *House of Lords.* Abstracts of the evidence taken before the Select Committee of the House of Lords, appointed to take into consideration the state of the British wool trade... 67p. *8°.* 1828.

25510 [**GRAHAM**, SIR JAMES R. G., *Bart.*] Free trade in corn the real interest of the landlord, and the true policy of the state. By a Cumberland landowner. 83p. *8°.* 1828. *Presentation copy from Sir James Graham to T. Spring Rice, Baron Monteagle.*

25511 **HUME**, JAMES D. The laws of the customs, compiled by direction of the Lords Commissioners of His Majesty's Treasury...With notes and indexes, and also with supplements for the years 1826, 1827, and 1828. [With a supplement for 1829.] 500, 62, 26, 77, 30p. *8°.* 1828. *See also* 1836.

25512 **JACOB**, W. Tracts relating to the corn trade and corn laws: including the second Report ordered to be printed by the two Houses of Parliament. [With 'Notes respecting the commerce of the Black Sea and of the Sea of Azoff; more especially as regards the trade in wheat' and 'Observations on the benefit arising from the cultivation of poor soils, by the application of pauper labour...'.] 293, 85, 41p. *8°.* 1828.

25513 **JOUSSE**, D. Commentaire sur l'ordonnance du commerce, du mois de mars 1673...avec des notes et explications coordonnant l'ordonnance, le commentaire et le Code de Commerce, par V. Bécane. Suivi du Traité du contrat de change, par Dupuy de la Serra. 536p. *8°. Paris*, 1828. *For a separate edition of Dupuis de la Serra, see* 1767 (FINANCE).

25514 **LINDO**, A. A. The injurious tendency of the modifying of our navigation laws, made manifest; and the consequent necessity for revising the concessions made in favor of the navigation of other nations, clearly proved... 216p. *8°.* 1828.

25515 **LIVERPOOL EAST INDIA ASSOCIATION**. Report of the committee of the Liverpool East India Association, on the subject of the trade with India. Presented to the Association at a general meeting, 21st March, 1828. [Including a statement on the American trade to China during 1825–26, compared with 1824–25 and 1823–24, from the records of the American consulate at Canton.] 40p. *8°. Liverpool & London*, 1828.

25516 **MITFORD**, J. F., *Baron Redesdale.* Observations upon the importation of foreign corn: with the resolutions moved by Lord Redesdale in the House of Lords, March 29, 1827; and his speech thereupon, May 15, 1827...And, also, remarks upon an Act permitting importation of corn, meal, and flour, until May 1, 1828. 137p. *8°.* 1828.

25517 **NANQUETTE-BILLUART**, . Charleville, le 10 juin 1828. [*Begin.*] J'ai l'honneur de vous informer qu'à dater du premier septembre prochain j'établirai, en cette ville, une maison de commission pour la réception et la réexpédition de toute espèce de marchandises pour la France et l'étranger. [A circular letter.] [4]p. *4°. n.p.* [1828]

25518 **REASONS** why the present system of auctions ought to be abolished. [With the minutes of a meeting held in New York in May 1828 to initiate a protest against the auction system.] 16p. *8°. New-York*, 1828.

25519 **REVIEW** of the Report of a committee of the citizens of Boston and vicinity, opposed to a further increase of duties on importations. 87p. *8°. Philadelphia*, 1828. *Attributed by Henry Carey Baird to Redwood Fisher.*

25520 **SENIOR**, N. W. Three lectures on the transmission of the precious metals from country to country and the mercantile theory of wealth, delivered before the University of Oxford in June 1827. 96p. *8°.* 1828. *See also* 1830.

25521 **STANHOPE**, PHILIP H., *4th Earl Stanhope.* A letter to the owners and occupiers of sheep farms from Earl Stanhope. [Containing a summary of part of the evidence taken before the Select Committee of the House of Lords on the state of the wool trade.] 35p. *8°.* 1828.

25522 **VIENNOT DE VAUBLANC**, V. M., *Comte de Vaublanc.* Du commerce maritime, considéré sous le rapport de la liberté entière du commerce, et sous le rapport des colonies. 232p. *8°. Paris*, 1828.

COLONIES

25523 An **APPEAL** to England against the new Indian Stamp Act; with some observations on the condition of British subjects in Calcutta, under the government of the East India Company. 141p. *8°.* 1828.

25524 **AUBER**, P. Supplement to An analysis of the constitution of the East-India Company, and of the laws passed by Parliament for the government of their affairs [containing laws passed 1826–28]...To which is prefixed, a brief history of the Company... 203p. *8°.* 1828. *For An analysis see* 1826.

25525 [CRAWFURD, JOHN (1783–1868).] A view of the present state and future prospects of the free trade and colonisation of India. 124p. *8°*. 1828. *See also* 1829.

25526 GRIFFIN, C. Society for the Propagation of the Gospel. A letter to the Right Hon. Earl Bathurst, Lord Goderich and the Right Rev. the Lord Bishop of London; in refutation of some of the gross misstatements ...in the...reports of their speeches in the House of Lords on the motion of the Right Honourable Lord King "For a committee to be appointed to inquire into the expenditure of the public money granted to the Society for the Propagation of the Gospel in foreign parts, in His Majesty's colonies of North America." 41p. *8°*. 1828.

25527 JAMAICA. *Assembly.* Addresses and memorials to His Majesty, from the House of Assembly at Jamaica. Voted in the years 1821 to 1826 inclusive: and which have been presented to His Majesty by the island agent. [On the decay of Jamaican industries and trade.] Printed by order of the House of Assembly of Jamaica. Second edition. 39p. *8°*. [1828]

25528 M'DONNELL, A. Colonial commerce; comprising an inquiry into the principles upon which discriminating duties should be levied on sugar, the growth respectively of the West India British possessions, of the East Indies, and of foreign countries. 302p. *8°*. 1828.

25529 SKETCHES and recollections of the West Indies. By a resident. 330p. *12°*. 1828.

25530 [YOUNG, GAVIN.] A further inquiry into the expediency of applying the principles of colonial policy to the government of India; and of effecting an essential change in its landed tenures...By the author of the original "Inquiry". 293p. *8°*. 1828. *For the original work, see* 1822.

FINANCE

25531 An ADDRESS to the proprietors of Bank stock, the London and country bankers, and the public in general, on the affairs of the Bank of England. 121p. *8°*. 1828.

25532 ALFRED, *pseud.* The Bank of England and the country bankers: three letters addressed to the editor of the Tyne Mercury, under the signature of Alfred, pointing out the danger to be apprehended from the provincial establishments of the Bank of England, and in particular the inexpediency of the establishment of a branch of the Bank of England in Newcastle upon Tyne. 36p. *8°*. *Newcastle & London*, 1828.

25533 ATTWOOD, T. An exposition of the cause and remedy of the agricultural distress. [The advertisement signed: W.K.] 16p. *8°*. *Hertford*, 1828.

25534 [——] The Scotch banker; containing articles under that signature on banking, currency, &c. republished from the Globe newspaper. With some additional articles. 175p. *8°*. 1828. *See also* 1832.

25535 The BANK of England, and the country bankers. By an Englishman. 23p. *8°*. 1828.

For the BANKER'S CIRCULAR, *continued as* the Circular to bankers, 1828–50, *see* vol. III, *Periodicals list*, Circular to bankers.

25536 BASTARD, A. Recueil de tarifs, contenant la réduction réciproque des monnaies de Suisse, de France, de Piémont, et du canton de Genève, suivant leurs rapports actuels entr'elles. Sixième édition, augmentée d'un tarif pour les écus de Brabant... 93p. *8°*. *Genève*, 1828.

25537 BAYLDON, J. S. A treatise on the valuation of property for the poor's rate; showing the method of rating lands, buildings, tithes, mines, woods, river and canal tolls, and personal property; with an abstract of the poor laws relating to rates and appeals. 227p. *8°*. 1828.

25538 BENTHAM, J. Défense de l'usure, ou lettres sur les inconvénients des lois, qui fixent le taux de l'intérêt de l'argent...Traduit de l'anglais sur la 4e édition; suivi d'un mémoire sur les prêts d'argent, par Turgot, et précédé d'une introduction contenant une dissertation sur le prêt à intérêt. 293p. *8°*. *Paris*, 1828. *The translation is conjecturally attributed to Saint Amand Bazard. For other editions, see* 1787.

25539 BLANC DE LANAUTTE, A. M., *Comte d'Hauterive.* Faits, calculs et observations sur la dépense d'une des grandes administrations de l'état à toutes les époques, depuis le règne de Louis XIV, et inclusivement jusqu'en 1825. Suivi d'un appendice sur la progression des dépenses...et de tableau du prix des principaux objets de consommation à la fin du XVIIe siècle. 157p. *8°*. *Paris*, 1828.

25540 BOYD, WALTER. Observations on Lord Grenville's Essay on the Sinking Fund. [With 'Reflections on the financial system of Great Britain, and particularly on the Sinking Fund. Written in France in the summer of 1812...Second edition'.] 16, 64p. *8°*. 1828. *For another edition of* Reflections on the financial system of Great Britain, *see* 1815.

25541 BRICKWOOD, J. A plan for reducing the capital, and the annual charge of the National Debt, humbly suggested to the consideration of His Majesty's government...Fourth edition. 64p. *8°*. 1828. *For other editions see* 1820.

25542 BROOKE, HENRY J. Observations on a pamphlet lately published by Mr. Morgan, entitled A view of the rise and progress of the Equitable Society, &c. 49p. *8°*. 1828.

25543 BROOKMAN, J. Stock jobbing extraordinary!!! Brookman v. Rothschild. "The man wot knows how to drive a bargain." 60p. *8°*. [1828]

25544 [BUNN, T.] Remarks on the necessity and the means of extinguishing a large portion of the National Debt. With notes, partly on miscellaneous topics. 95p. *8°*. *Bath*, 1828. *In a volume of the author's own pamphlets, with his manuscript notes.*

25545 CALVERT, A. A. Observations on select vestries, to shew that much unnecessary local taxation, is the consequence of undue authorities exercised by a self-appointed...and self-continuing vestry...occasioned by the imposition of a church-rate, now under collection in the parish of Walcot, Bath... 15p. *8°*. [*London*,] 1828.

25546 COBBETT, W. Noble nonsense! Or, Cobbett's exhibition of the stupid and insolent pamphlet of Lord Grenville. 16p. *8°*. [*London*, 1828]

25547 —— Paper against gold; or, the history and mystery of the Bank of England, of the Debt, of the stocks, of the Sinking Fund, and of all the other tricks and contrivances, carried on by the means of paper money. 332p. *12°*. 1828. *This edition contains only 29 letters instead of the 32 of the earlier editions, those written in 1815 being omitted. For other editions, see 1815.*

25548 COHEN, B. Compendium of finance: containing an account of the origin, progress, and present state, of the public debts, revenue, expenditure, national banks and currencies...Also, an historical sketch of the National Debt of the British Empire. Authenticated by official documents. Second edition. 264, 280p. *8°*. 1828. *For another edition, see 1822.*

25549 COSTAZ, C. A. De l'état actuel de la Banque de France, et de la nécessité d'en modifier le régime, et de diminuer son capital. 36p. *8°*. *Paris*, 1828.

25550 COURTENAY, T. P. A letter to Lord Grenville, on the Sinking Fund. 136p. *8°*. 1828.

25551 CRUTTWELL, R. The system of country-banking defended; with reference to corn, currency, panic, population, bankruptcy, crime, pauperism and so forth. A letter to Lord Goderich...Also remarks on two recent letters in the Globe newspaper, signed "A Scotch banker;" and on the reply of Kirkman Finlay, Esq. of Glasgow objecting to Sir John Sinclair's proposal for 'raising the standard-price of gold to £5 the ounce'... 30p. *8°*. 1828.

25552 CURRENCY & finance, 1828. A short examination of the calculations of the Chancellor of the Exchequer, respecting the small currency; with remarks on the finances and taxation of the country. 16p. *8°*. 1828.

25553 DILWORTH, T. The young book-keeper's assistant: shewing him, in the most plain and easy manner, the Italian way of stating debtor and creditor...A new edition. [156]p. *8°*. *York*, 1828. *For another edition, see 1761.*

25554 Breve **ENSAIO** para servir a'historia do Banco de Lisboa. 63p. *4°*. *Lisboa*, 1828.

25555 ESSAY on the warehousing system and government credits of the United States. [Reprinted from *The Aurora and Pennsylvania Gazette* in accordance with a resolution of the Philadelphia Chamber of Commerce.] 57p. *8°*. *Philadelphia*, 1828.

25556 FARREN, G. Letter to the Earl of Eldon, on the report of the Finance Committee. 9p. *8°*. 1828.

25557 FORWOOD, G. The equity and necessity of equalising parochial assessments, and of regulating parochial accounts, as recommended in the reports of several Committees of the House of Commons...exemplified in a letter to the Right Hon. Wm. Sturges Bourne, with an appendix, containing extracts from those reports and documents and complete forms for the accounts. 51p. *8°*. *Liverpool & London*, 1828.

25558 FREESE, J. H. The cambist's compendium; or, two familiar practical treatises on bills of exchange... on calculations of foreign exchanges...and on operations in coin and bullion...To which are added, tables...of foreign coins; of logarithms... 371, xxxviip. *8°*. 1828.

25559 GARDINER, H. On the reduction of the rate of discount by the Bank of England. 24p. *8°*. [1828]

25560 GILBART, J. W. A practical treatise on banking...Second edition. 115p. *8°*. 1828. *For other editions, see 1827.*

25561 GRAHAM, Sir James R. G., *Bart*. Corn and currency; in an address to the land owners...A new edition. 119p. *8°*. 1828. *For other editions, see 1826.*

25562 GRANT, A. W. Remarks on the influence attributed to the state of the currency on prices and credit, and on the suppression of small notes. 39p. *8°*. 1828.

25563 GRENVILLE, W. W., *Baron Grenville*. Essay on the supposed advantages of a Sinking Fund...Part the first. 82p. *8°*. 1828. *The copy that belonged to James Fenimore Cooper.*

25564 —— [Another edition.] 85p. *8°*. *London: J. Murray*, 1828.

25565 —— Second edition, corrected. 87p. *8°*. 1828.

25566 —— Third edition. 87p. *8°*. 1828.

25567 HINCHLIFFE, H. J. Thoughts on the repeal of the usury laws, enclosed in a letter to a friend. 35p. *8°*. 1828.

25568 *HULLEY, E. Tables showing the values of annuities and assurances upon lives of equal ages; in single and annual payments; according to the Northampton table of mortality, rate of interest three per cent... 160p. *8°*. 1828. *The copy that belonged to Augustus De Morgan.*

25569 JONES, Edward T. Metodo di tenere i libri di commercio in iscrittura semplice e doppia....Modificato da Onofrio Luigi Ferrari... 325p. *4°*. *Bologna*, 1828.

25570 JOPLIN, T. A plan for improving and extending the branch establishments of the Bank of England. A few copies printed for the use of the Directors. 30p. *8°*. *Newcastle*, [1828]

25571 —— Views on the Corn Bill of 1827, and other measures of government; together with a further exposition of certain principles on corn and currency before published. 248p. *8°*. 1828.

25572 —— [Another issue.] Views on the currency: in which the connexion between corn and currency is shown: the nature of our system of currency explained; and the merits of the Corn Bill, the branch banks, the extension of the Bank Charter and the Small Note Act examined. 248p. *8°*. 1828. *For an edition of p. 201–16 entitled:* The principle of the personal liability of the shareholders in public banks examined, *see 1830.*

25573 LAW, T. An address to the Columbian Institute, on a moneyed system. 95p. *8°*. *Washington*, 1828.

25574 LEGISLATION gone astray; or, a review of the banking controversy, and thoughts upon the inexpediency of putting down the one-pound-note circulation; to which is added a plan for the prevention of forgery of Bank of England notes. 72p. *8°*. 1828. *Sometimes attributed to Horace Herbert.*

25575 A LETTER [signed: A clerk] to the Right Hon. Robert Peel...on the recommendation of the finance committee, that the superannuation tax should be re-enacted, with remarks and statements shewing the extent to which reductions of salaries in the public offices, during the last seven years, have been already made. xxixp. *8°*. [1828]

25576 The **LETTERS** which have appeared in the Newcastle Chronicle on the petition of the Chamber of Commerce of Newcastle upon Tyne, for the continued circulation of local one pound notes; with a prefatory address to the country bankers, additional notes, appendix,

&c., by a member of the Chamber. 67p. *8°. Newcastle,* 1828.

25577 LONDON. *Court of Common Council.* A statement of the produce and expenditure of the City's estate, for the year ending the 31st day of December, 1827. To which is subjoined the balance remaining in Mr. Chamberlain's hands...of all the several accounts kept in the Chamber of London. [With 'A statement of the produce and expenditure of the Bridge-House estates, for the year ending the 31st of December, 1827'. Ordered to be printed and circulated 23 May 1828.] 71, 15p. *fol.* 1828. *See also* 1825.

25578 [**McCULLOCH**, JOHN R.] Progress of the National Debt – best method of funding. (From the Edinburgh Review, No. XCIII.) 28p. *8°.* [*Edinburgh,* 1828]

25579 *MORGAN, W. A view of the rise and progress of the Equitable Society, and of the causes which have contributed to its success. To which are added, remarks on some of the late misrepresentations respecting the rules and practice of the society. 65p. *8°.* 1828. *Presentation copy from the author to Augustus De Morgan.*

25580 NOTLEY, S. Tablas para la reduccion del oro y la plata, y para calcular la cantidad de oro que contiene una pieza de plata de ley, asi como el valor del oro a 135 pesos 6 reales el marco... 105p. *fol. Mexico,* 1828.

25581 OBSERVATIONS des directeurs de la fabrication des monnaies, sur la partie du rapport du budget des dépenses relative aux frais des monnaies. 8p. *4°. Paris,* [1828?]

25582 O'CALLAGHAN, J. Usury; or, lending at interest; also, the exaction and payment of certain church-fees...all proved to be repugnant to the divine and ecclesiastical law...To which is prefixed a narrative of the controversy between the author and Bishop Coppinger ...With a dedication to the "Society of Friends," by William Cobbett. 230p. *12°.* 1828. *For other editions, see* 1825.

25583 PARNELL, H. B., *Baron Congleton.* Observations on paper money, banking, and overtrading; including those parts of the evidence taken before the Committee of the House of Commons, which explain the Scotch system of banking...Second edition. 177p. *8°.* 1828. *For other editions, see* 1827.

25584 PRINCIPLES of coinage; intended as an answer to the reported speech of the Right Hon Robert Peel...delivered by him in reply to Sir James Graham, Bart. of Netherby, who moved...for a Select Committee to inquire into the circulation of promissory notes, under the value of five pounds, on the 3d June, 1828. 56p. *8°.* 1828.

25585 PRINCIPLES of coinage intended as a commentary on a letter to the King on the coins of this realm by the late Earl of Liverpool. The first, second, third, and fourth parts. 208p. *8°.* [*London,*] 1828. *Part 1 is the same work as no.* 25584 *above. See also* 1829.

25586 The **PROMISSORY NOTE** question, considered as a case between the great capitalist, and the daily labourer, or, the monied interest and the nation at large. 52p. *8°.* 1828.

25587 PUSEY, P. An historical view of the Sinking Fund. In a letter addressed to the Earl of Carnarvon. 83p. *8°.* 1828.

25588 —— A letter to the Earl of Carnarvon, on the Right Hon. the Home Secretary's financial statement of ...15th of February, 1828. 82p. *8°.* 1828.

25589 REPORT and observations, on the banks, and other incorporated institutions, in the State of New-York. With an appendix, and notes. 40p. *8°. New-York,* 1828. *Presentation copy, with inscription, from the anonymous author to T. Spring Rice, Baron Monteagle.*

25590 RIVES, W. C. Speech of Mr. Rives of Virginia, on retrenchment and reform; delivered in the House of Representatives of the United States, on the 5th February, 1828. 21p. *8°. Washington,* 1828.

25591 SPENCE, G. Letters to the Right Honourable the Earl of Liverpool, the Right Honourable George Canning, and His Grace the Duke of Wellington, clearly ...shewing that the burdens of the country may be lightened fifty-two millions annually, and neither landholder, placeholder nor fundholder be injured...By a member of the Merchant Company of Edinburgh. Third edition. 26p. *8°. Edinburgh & London,* 1828.

25592 *A plain **STATEMENT** of some particulars of the financial situation of the United Kingdom; with brief remarks on the inutility of the Sinking Fund in the present state of the revenue. With an appendix. 24p. *8°.* 1828. *The copy that belonged to George Grote.*

25593 A short **STATEMENT** of the case of the Baron de Bode, regarding which a petition was presented on May the 18th, 1826, to the House of Commons... with an appendix, containing his petition, &c. [Concerning his claim for indemnity for his property in France, confiscated during the Revolution.] 48p. *8°.* [1828] *The Agar Ellis copy.*

25594 A summary **STATEMENT** of the one pound note question. 23p. *8°.* 1828.

25595 TAYLOR, JAMES (1788–1863). A view of the money system of England, from the Conquest; with proposals for establishing a secure and equable credit currency. 194p. *8°.* 1828.

25596 UNITED STATES OF AMERICA. Congress. *House of Representatives.* Letter from the Secretary of the Treasury, transmitting the annual report on the state of the finances, for the year 1828. 43p. *8°. Washington,* 1828.

25597 YEATMAN, H. F. An inquiry into the present state of the existing county rate, addressed to the owners and occupiers of lands within the county of Dorset. 56p. *8°. Sherborne,* [1828]

TRANSPORT

25598 ALLEN, GEORGE (1798–1847). Plans and designs for the future approaches to the new London Bridge, with a memorial submitted to the Court of Common Council, and now under the consideration of the New Bridge Committee; comprising suggestions for the formation of a quay for the reception of steam vessels, the opening of new streets and avenues... 36p. *8°.* 1828. *With a letter, accompanying the pamphlet, from the author to the Hon. George Agar Ellis, then a member of the Committee of Public Works.*

25599 BALTIMORE AND OHIO RAILROAD COMPANY. First annual report of the Board of Engineers to the Board of Directors of the Baltimore and Ohio Rail Road Company. 43p. *8°. n.p.* [1828] *The Rastrick copy.*

25600 —— Second annual report, of the President and directors, to the stockholders of the Baltimore and Ohio Rail Road Company. 11p. *8°. Baltimore,* 1828. *The Rastrick copy.*

25601 [CAREY, M.] Pennsylvania canals. [Signed: Hamilton.] 3p. *8°. n.p.* [1828]

25602 CUNDY, N. W. Imperial Ship Canal from London to Portsmouth. Mr. Cundy's reply to anonymous and other authors of malignant abuse and misrepresentation, on his projected line, furnishing truth for libel... 21p. *8°.* 1828.

25603 ENGLAND. *Laws, etc.* Anno tricesimo tertio Georgii II. Regis. [Private Acts, c. ii.] An Act to enable... Francis Duke of Bridgewater to make a navigable cut or canal from... Worsley Mill, over the river Irwell, to... Manchester in the County Palatine of Lancaster, and to... Longford Bridge in the township of Stretford... 8p. *fol.* 1828. *For another edition, see* 1760.

25604 —— —— Anno secundo Georgii III. Regis. [Private Acts, c. xi.] An Act to enable... Francis Duke of Bridgewater to make a navigable cut or canal from Longford Bridge in the township of Stretford, in the County Palatine of Lancaster, to the River Mersey, at... the Hempstones in... Halton in the county of Chester. 15p. *fol.* 1828.

25605 —— —— [*Endorsed:*] An Act to enable the Company of Proprietors of the Stockton and Darlington Railway to make a branch therefrom in the counties of Durham and York... ⟨Royal Assent, 23 May 1828.⟩ 9 Geo. IV. sess. 1828. 25p. *fol.* [*London,* 1828]

25606 —— —— Bristol and Gloucestershire Railway. An Act for making and maintaining a railway or tramroad from or near the city of Bristol to Coalpit Heath, in the parish of Westerleigh, in the county of Gloucester. ⟨Royal Assent, 19 June 1828.⟩ 9 Geo. IV. 1828. 84p. *fol. n.p.* [1828]

25607 ENGLISH AND BRISTOL CHANNELS SHIP CANAL COMPANY. [*Endorsed:*] Prospectus of the newly proposed ship canal, for connecting the English and Bristol Channels. 3p. *fol.* [*London,* 1828]

25608 JERVIS, JOHN. The horse and carriage oracle: or, rules for purchasing and keeping, or jobbing horses and carriages: accurate estimates of every expense occasioned thereby, and an easy plan for ascertaining every

coach fare...The whole revised by William Kitchiner... Third edition. 316p. *8°.* 1828. *The half-title reads: The traveller's oracle. Part II; for an edition of this work by William Kitchiner, see* 1827.

25609 LACY, H. C. Improvements in carriages. Being a description of the "New apparatus on which to suspend carriage bodies." Invented by Henry Charles Lacy, patentee...With an illustration of its advantages over every mode now in use. 32p. *8°. Manchester,* 1828. *The Rastrick copy.*

25610 LONDON. Livery Companies. *Watermen and Lightermen of the River Thames.* The laws & constitutions of the Master, wardens, & commonalty of Watermen & Lightermen of the River Thames. [With 'Rules and bye-laws for the regulation of the Watermen and Lightermen', 'Rules or bye-laws of the Company' and 'A table of rates, prices, or fares, to be taken by watermen on the River Thames, between New Windsor, Berks, and Yantlet Creek, Kent'.] 85, 48, 26, 22p. *8°.* 1828. *See also* 1730 *and for additional rules and bye-laws,* 1836.

25611 MONMERQUÉ, L. J. N. Les carrosses à cinq sols, ou les omnibus du dix-septième siècle. 74p. *12°. Paris,* 1828.

25612 SAVILE, SIR G., *Bart.* Letter of Sir George Savile, on an attempt made to interfere with the Aire and Calder Navigation, in...1772. 16p. *8°.* 1828.

25613 SKETCHES and memoranda of the works for the tunnel under the Thames from Rotherhithe to Wapping. [31]p. *obl.8°.* [*London,*] 1828.

25614 A plain **STATEMENT** of facts, relative to the proposed alterations [by the Tees Navigation Company] in the River Tees. 3p. *fol. Darlington,* [1828 ?]

25615 STEELE, T. Practical suggestions on the general improvement of the navigation of the Shannon, between Limerick and the Atlantic; and more particularly of that part of it named by pilots, the Narrows... 151p. *8°.* 1828.

25616 STEVENS, JOHN L. Description of a new method of propelling steam vessels, canals boats, &c. A relation of recent experiments; and copies of letters received by Mr. John Lee Stevens, the patentee. 17p. *8°.* 1828. *The Agar Ellis copy.*

25617 THAMES TUNNEL COMPANY. The Thames Tunnel. Report of the Court of Directors and of M. J. Brunel, Esq., the engineer of the Thames Tunnel Company, upon the state of the works...and the plan for raising money...With the resolutions passed at a special general assembly on the 11th day of June, 1828. 15p. *8°.* [1828]

SOCIAL CONDITIONS

25618 [ARRIVABENE, G., *Conte.*] Di varie società e instituzioni di beneficenza in Londra. 290p. *12°. Lugano,* 1828.

25619 ASSER, C. Apologie de la peine de mort. Avec quelques observations critiques. 57p. *8°. Bruxelles,* 1828. *The copy presented by Ducpétiaux, the author of the 'Observations critiques', to the Athenæum Club.*

25620 B., T. Remarks on Observations on the necessity of a legal provision for the Irish poor, as the means of

improving the condition of the Irish people...by John Douglas, Esq. With an epitome of the poor-laws of England... 40p. *8°. Edinburgh & Glasgow,* 1828.

25621 BANFILL, S. Third letter to Sir T. D. Acland, Bart., M.P. (with the First & Second letters originally printed in 1817 & 1818,) on the means of improving the condition of the laboring classes, and reducing parochial assessments; by adapting the poor laws to the present state of society: exemplified in the report of an attempt made in 1818, to bring into action such of those measures as were applicable to the...Parish of St. Thomas [near Exeter]; and of the results... 60, 22p. *8°. Exeter*, 1828. *For another edition of* The first letter to Sir T. D. Acland, *see* 1817.

25622 BECHER, JOHN T. The antipauper system; exemplifying the positive...good...under the...lawful administration of the poor laws, prevailing at Southwell ...with plans of the Southwell workhouse, and of the Thurgarton Hundred workhouse; and with instructions for book-keeping. 58p. *8°.* 1828. *See also* 1834.

25623 —— The constitution of friendly societies, upon legal and scientific principles, exemplified by the rules and tables adopted for...the Southwell Friendly Institution ...The fourth edition, with an annual graduation of the tables. 77p. *8°.* 1828. *For another edition, see* 1824.

25624 BLOMFIELD, C. J., *Bishop of London.* The Christian's duty towards criminals: a sermon preached in St. Philip's Chapel, Regent Street, for the benefit of the Society for the Improvement of Prison Discipline and for the Reformation of Juvenile Offenders...June 22, 1828 ...[With an account of the objects of the Society.] 20, iiip. *4°.* 1828. *The Agar Ellis copy.*

25625 BRERETON, C. D. The subordinate magistracy and parish system considered, in their connexion with the causes and remedies of modern pauperism, with some observations on the relief of the poor in England, Scotland, and Ireland, and on parochial emigration. 215p. *8°. Norwich & London*, [1828?]

25626 BRUCE, W. Poor rates, the panacea for Ireland...Second edition. 19p. *8°. Bristol*, 1828. *For another edition, see* 1826.

25627 CAREY, M. Essays on the public charities of Philadelphia...[Signed: Hamilton. Second edition.] 20p. *8°. n.p.* [1828] *See also* 1830.

25628 [CARLILE, R.] Every woman's book; or, what is love? Containing most important instructions for the prudent regulation of the principle of love, and the number of a family. 48p. *8°.* 1828. *For another edition, see* 1826.

25629 CARLISLE, N. An historical account of the origin of the Commission, appointed to inquire concerning charities in England and Wales, and an illustration of several old customs and words which occur in the reports. 330p. *8°.* 1828.

25630 CARLYON, C. A short appeal to the cottagers of Cornwall, on the subject of typhus fever, and its close connection with want of cleanliness. With some additional remarks of a moral and religious nature. 24p. *12°. Truro & London*, 1828.

25631 [CATHCART, E.] An account of the poor-colonies, and agricultural workhouses, of the Benevolent Society of Holland. By a member of the Highland Society of Scotland. 195p. *12°. Edinburgh & London*, 1828.

25632 DAVIES, D. The case of labourers in husbandry stated and considered...Second edition, abridged. 39p. *8°.* 1828. *For other editions, see* 1795.

25633 A DESCRIPTION of the King's Bench, Fleet and Marshalsea Prisons; being a brief review of their constitutions; the rules thereof...the orders and regulations of the courts, and containing all such other matter as is material to be known to all persons in custody... 24p. *12°.* 1828.

25634 DOUGLAS, JOHN (*fl.* 1828–1846). Observations on the necessity of a legal provision for the Irish poor, as the means of improving the condition of the Irish people, and protecting the British landlord, farmer and labourer. 40p. *8°. London, Dublin, &c.,* 1828.

25635 D'OYLY, G. A sermon preached at Lambeth Church on...February 17th, 1828, for the benefit of the Lambeth Pension Society... 20p. *8°. Lambeth,* 1828.

25636 DUDLEY, T. B. W. The tocsin; or, a review of the London police establishments, with hints for their improvement, and for the prevention of calamitous fires, &c. 109p. *8°.* 1828.

25637 [ELLIS, D.] Considerations relative to nuisance in coal-gas works, with remarks on the principles of monopoly and competition as applicable to those establishments: addressed to the proprietors, feuars, and others, in the vicinity of the oil-gas works at Tanfield, by one of themselves. 71p. *8°. Edinburgh,* 1828.

25638 ENGLAND. *Commissioners for Inquiring concerning Charities.* An account of public charities in England and Wales, abridged from the Reports of His Majesty's Commissioners on Charitable Foundations, with notes and comments. By the editor of "The cabinet lawyer" [John Wade]. 760p. *8°.* 1828.

25639 FRIENDLY SOCIETY OF JOURNEY-MEN BOOKBINDERS, *London.* Articles of the Friendly Society of Journeymen Book-Binders...agreed upon at a general meeting of the Lodges, April 21st, 1828. 29p. *8°.* 1828. *See note to no.* 23614.

25640 HANKIN, R. B. An account of the public charities of...Bedford, with a...statement of the laws... of the Harpur Free Grammar and other schools... 104p. *8°. Bedford, London, &c.,* 1828.

25641 HEDLEY, J. Letter to the Right Hon. the Lord Mayor on the supply of gas to the City of London. Containing the official documents laid before the Commissioners of Sewers; an epitome of a statement submitted to the Secretary of State...and an account of the proceedings before a Committee of the House of Commons, on the application of the Chartered Gas-Light and Coke Company, for their act of incorporation. 43, lxxxiip. *8°.* 1828.

25642 HINTS on emigration, as the means of effecting the repeal of the poor laws. 56p. *8°.* 1828.

25643 HOLFORD, G. P. An account of the General Penitentiary at Millbank...To which is added an appendix on the form and construction of prisons, intended to shew the superiority of prisons which surround their court-yards with their buildings, over a prison constructed on the plan published by the Society for the Improvement of Prison Discipline, called..."the radiating plan." lxiv, 394p. *8°.* 1828.

25644 HOULSTON'S gleaner. A selection from the works of authors who have written for the benefit of their fellow-creatures, particularly intended to furnish the working-classes with hints for the advancement of their comfort and respectability. 288p. *12°. Wellington, Salop & London,* 1828.

25645 HUMPHREY, H. Parallel between intemperance and the slave trade. An address delivered at Amherst College, July 4, 1828... 40p. *8°. Amherst,* 1828.

25646 JACOB, W. Observations on the benefits arising from the cultivation of poor soils, by the application of proper [*sic*] labour; as exemplified in the colonies for the indigent and for orphans in Holland. 41p. *8°. n.p.* [1828] *Presentation copy from the author to William Allen. A manuscript alteration on the title-page in another hand, of 'proper' to 'pauper', and the addition of the imprint of the Lindfield edition (no. 25647 below), suggest that this was used as copy for that edition.*

25647 **—— [Another edition.] 39p. 8°. Printed for the Society for Improving the Condition of the Lower Order of Tenantry, and of the Labouring Population of Ireland, by C. Greene at the Schools of Industry, Lindfield, Sussex, 1828. The FWA copy that belonged to William Pare.*

25648 JOURNEYMEN BROAD SILK WEAVERS OF SPITALFIELDS. Report adopted at a general meeting of the Journeymen Broad Silk Weavers, held in Saint John Street Chapel...Spitalfields, on...the 20th of February, 1828, to take into their consideration the necessity of petitioning the legislature for a wages protection bill...To which is appended, the petition. 36, 8p. *8°.* 1828.

25649 —— [Another edition.] 36, 8p. *8°.* 1828.

25650 KERRISON, R. M. A letter to the Right Hon. Robert Peel, Secretary of State for the Home Department, on the supply of water to the metropolis, containing a justification of the complaints of the house-keepers, served ...from the works of the Grand-Junction Company; and a refutation of the mis-statements...of "An old housekeeper". 35p. *8°.* 1828. *Presentation copy from the author to George Agar Ellis, Baron Dover.*

25651 LAMBE, W. An investigation of the properties of the Thames water... 65p. *8°.* 1828. *Presentation copy, with inscription, from the author to Sir Francis Burdett (see also note to no. 22542).*

25652 LEEDS. *Vestry.* Leeds Vestry Meetings. [Held on 19th June, 1828 'for the purposes of determining the mode in which property shall...be rated in this township for the poor's assessment'; and on 20th June 1828 'to pass the churchwardens' accounts'.] 15p. *8°. Leeds,* [1828] *The copy that belonged to M. T. Sadler.*

25653 A LETTER to the magistrates of the south and west of England, on the expediency and facility of correcting certain abuses of the poor laws. By one of their number. 30p. *8°.* 1828.

25654 A LETTER to the Right Hon. Robert Peel, Secretary of State for the Home Department, on the supply of water to the Metropolis. [Signed: An old housekeeper of the City of Westminster.] 25p. *8°.* 1828.

25655 LEWIN, SIR G. A. A summary of the laws relating to the government & maintenance of the poor. 746p. *12°.* 1828.

25656 LIVERPOOL MECHANICS' SCHOOL OF ARTS. Report and proceedings of the Liverpool Mechanics' School of Arts, at the half yearly meeting of the members, held...March 11, 1828. Printed by order of the meeting. 24p. *8°. Liverpool,* 1828.

25657 MACAREL, L. A. Législation et jurisprudence des ateliers dangereux, insalubres et incommodes, ou manuel des manufacturiers, propriétaires, chefs d'ateliers, etc. 306p. *12°. Paris,* 1828.

25658 [MANGIN, E.] Parish settlements and pauperism. 59p. *8°.* 1828.

25659 MEASE, J. Observations on the penitentiary system, and penal code of Pennsylvania: with suggestions for their improvement. 95p. *8°. Philadelphia,* 1828.

25660 [MILL, JAMES.] The article Education, reprinted from the Supplement to the Encyclopædia Britannica. 46p. *8°.* [1828 ?]

25661 NUGENT, G. T. J., *Earl of Westmeath.* A sketch of Lord Westmeath's case. [A dispute between Lord and Lady Westmeath, arising out of a separation which the Earl considered illegal.] 48p. *8°. n.p.,* 1828.

For the **ODD FELLOWS' MAGAZINE,** 1828–41, *continued as* Odd Fellows' quarterly magazine, 1842–47, *then* the Quarterly magazine of the Independent Order of Odd-Fellows, 1858–83, *then* the Monthly magazine of the Independent Order of Oddfellows, 1884–95, *see* vol. III, *Periodicals list.*

25662 PARKES, J. The state of the Court of Requests and the Public Office of Birmingham, with considerations on the increase and prosecution of crime in the county of Warwick; the expediency of an extended...jurisdiction for the recovery of small debts, and the establishment of a local prison...for Birmingham and its environs... 24p. *8°. Birmingham,* 1828.

25663 POLE, J. A few observations on the present state of the poor and poor laws, and a remedy for the evils respecting them. 16p. *8°. Portsmouth,* [1828]

25664 PRICE, H. A letter to the carpet manufacturers of Kidderminster; showing...that the manufacturers themselves are mainly amenable to the country in general, and to the inhabitants of Worcestershire in particular for the present appalling state of one of its principal manufacturing towns. 16p. *8°.* 1828.

25665 Brief REMARKS on a pamphlet, gratuitously circulated in Putney and Roehampton, entitled, "Martyn's Charity, Putney, Surrey". 35p. *8°.* 1828.

25666 SAINT GILES LOCAL DISTRICT SOCIETY. A short account of the wretched state of the poor, in a populous district, in the parish of St. Giles in the Fields. Prepared under the direction of a district committee. 51p. *12°.* 1828.

25667 SOCIÉTÉ ANONYME DU PRET CHARITABLE ET GRATUIT. Précis des statuts de la Société...fondée par actes des 6 mars, 1827 et 4 juillet, 1828, et autorisée par Ordonnance du Roi du 27 août, 1828. 12p. *12°. Toulouse,* [1828]

25668 SOCIETY FOR SUPERSEDING THE NECESSITY OF CLIMBING BOYS, *London.* Observations on the cruelty of employing climbing-boys in sweeping chimneys: and on the practicability of effectually cleansing flues by mechanical means. With extracts from the evidence before the House of Commons, &c.&c. 18p. *8°.* 1828.

25669 —— Practical information presented to the public by the Society...With a description of Glass's improved machinery for cleansing chimneys, and a list of subscribers. 16p. *8°.* 1828.

25670 UNIVERSITY COLLEGE, *London.* University of London. Annual general meeting of proprietors ...27th of February, 1828. 16p. *8°.* [1828] *The Agar Ellis copy.*

25671 WALSINGHAM. *House of Correction.* Rules and regulations to be observed in the House of Correction, at Little Walsingham, in the country of Norfolk. *s.sh.fol. n.p.* [1828 ?]

25672 WILLIAMS, JOHN (*fl.* 1828). An historical account of sub-ways in the British Metropolis, for the flow of pure water and gas into the houses of the inhabitants... 472p. 8°. 1828. *Presentation copy, with inscription, from the author to his daughter.*

25673 WILMOT, SIR J. E. E., *Bart.* A letter to the magistrates of England on the increase of crime; and an efficient remedy suggested for their consideration... Second edition. 46p. 8°. 1828. *The Agar Ellis copy.*

25674 WRIGHT, J. The water question. Memoir, addressed to the Commissioners appointed by His Majesty...to inquire into the state of the supply of water to the Metropolis. 96p. 8°. 1828. *The Agar Ellis copy; a second, imperfect, copy belonged to Sir Francis Burdett (see note to no. 22542).*

SLAVERY

25675 [ALEXANDER, W.] Address to the public, on the present state of the question relative to negro slavery, in the British colonies. 16p. 8°. *York, London, &c.,* 1828.

25676 [——] [3rd edition.] 16p. 8°. *York, London, &c.,* 1828.

25677 BARRET, . A reply to the speech of Dr. Lushington...on the condition of the free-coloured people of Jamaica. 58p. 8°. 1828. *For another edition, see* 1827.

25678 BRITISH SLAVERY described. 36p. 8°. *Newcastle* [*under Lyme*], 1828.

25679 —— Second edition. 38p. 8°. *Newcastle* [*under Lyme*]: *sold for the benefit of the North Staffordshire Ladies Anti-Slavery Society,* 1828.

25680 The **CONSUMERS** of West India sugar, the supporters of West India slavery. 12p. *12°. Bristol,* [1828 ?]

25681 DWARRIS, SIR F. W. L. The West India question plainly stated; and the only practical remedy briefly considered: in a letter to...Henry Goulburn... 80p. 8°. 1828.

25682 E. Observations on the Demerara memorial, in a letter from a gentleman in the country, to his friend in London. 34p. 8°. 1828. *See also* 1829.

25683 HOARE, PRINCE. Memoirs of Granville Sharp, Esq. composed from his own manuscripts, and other...documents...of his family and of the African Institution...With observations on Mr. Sharp's biblical criticisms, by the...Bishop of Salisbury...Second edition ...[With 'Catalogue, by Mr. Sharp, of the books written by himself'.] 2 vols. 8°. 1828. *For another edition, see* 1820.

25684 HONESTY the best policy. [On the advantages of the abolition of negro slavery.] 4p. 8°. *Leicester,* [1828]

25685 KILHAM, H. Report of a recent visit to the colony of Sierra Leone. 24p. 8°. 1828.

25686 LADIES' anti-slavery associations. 7p. 8°. [1828]

25687 The young **LOGICIANS;** or school-boy conceptions of rights and wrongs. With a particular reference to "Six months in the West Indies." Part the second. 91p. *12°. Birmingham & London,* 1828.

25688 M. How do we procure sugar ? A question proposed for the consideration of the people of Great Britain. By a naval officer. 12p. 8°. *Liverpool,* 1828.

25689 MARLY; or, the life of a planter in Jamaica: comprehending characteristic sketches of the present state of society and manners in the British West Indies. And an impartial review of the leading questions relative to colonial policy. Second edition. 363p. 8°. *Glasgow, Liverpool, &c.,* 1828.

25690 MITCHEL, H. Two letters to the Colonial Secretary...in answer to the Yellow book. 40p. 8°. *n.p.* [1828]

25691 A **PICTURE** of colonial slavery, in the year 1828, addressed especially to the ladies of Great Britain. 6p. 8°. [1828]

25692 A **PLAN** for the abolition of slavery, consistently with the interests of all parties concerned. 32p. 8°. 1828.

25693 REMARKS on the demoralizing influence of slavery. By a resident at the Cape of Good Hope. 16p. 8°. 1828.

25694 RILAND, J. Two letters, severally addressed to the editor of the Christian Observer and the editor of the Christian Remembrancer, relative to the slave-cultured estates of the Society for the Propagation of the Gospel. 15p. 8°. 1828.

25695 SOCIETY FOR THE ABOLITION OF SLAVERY THROUGHOUT THE BRITISH DOMINIONS. The new slave laws of Jamaica and St. Christopher's examined; with an especial reference to the eulogies recently pronounced upon them in Parliament. 24p. 8°. 1828.

25696 "What does your **SUGAR** cost ?" A cottage conversation on...British negro slavery. 15p. 8°. *Birmingham: for the Birmingham, West-Bromwich, &c. Female Society for the Relief of British Negro Slaves,* 1828.

25697 WILSON, D., *Bishop of Calcutta.* Thoughts on British colonial slavery. [Extracted from *The amulet, or Christian and literary remembrancer,* for 1828.] 7p. 8°. *Bagster and Thoms,* [1828]

25698 —— [Another edition.] 7p. 8°. *S. Bagster, jun.,* [1828]

POLITICS

25699 BURTON, T. Diary of Thomas Burton, Esq. Member in the Parliaments of Oliver and Richard Cromwell, from 1656 to 1659: now first published from the original autograph manuscript. With an introduction, containing an account of the Parliament of 1654; from the journal of Guibon Goddard, Esq. M.P. also now first printed. Edited and illustrated with notes historical and biographical by John Towill Rutt... 4 vols. *8°*. 1828.

25700 CHANNING, William E. Analysis of the character of Napoleon Bonaparte, suggested by the publication of Scott's Life of Napoleon. 48p. *8°*. 1828.

25701 —— Second edition. 52p. *8°*. 1828.

25702 CLINTON, H. P., *4th Duke of Newcastle.* A letter to the Right Hon. Lord Kenyon from His Grace the Duke of Newcastle [on Catholic emancipation]. 14p. *8°*. 1828. *The Agar Ellis copy.*

25703 EIRIONNACH, *pseud., ed.* Official documents, with extracts from state letters, and from other authentic sources...relative to the rights claimed by Roman Catholics to seats in both Houses of Parliament, freedom of corporations, &c....With an introductory preface tending to shew how far the claimants enjoyed those privileges from...the Act of Supremacy...of Queen Elizabeth, down to the accession of King William III. 84p. *8°*. Dublin, 1828. *The Agar Ellis copy.*

25704 EVERETT, E. An oration delivered before the citizens of Charlestown on the fifty-second anniversary of the Declaration of the Independence of the United States of America. 43p. *8°*. *Charlestown & Boston,* 1828.

25705 A critical **EXAMINATION** of the preliminary view of the French Revolution, prefixed to Sir Walter Scott's Life of Bonaparte. With observations on the work itself. From the Westminster Review, No. XVIII. 63p. *8°*. [1828]

25706 IRELAND described by Irishmen. [A reprint of the 'Dublin Merchants' report', dated Feb. 22, 1828, against Catholic emancipation in Ireland.] 12p. *12°*. Dewsbury, [1828]

25707 KNIGHT, Henry G. Foreign and domestic view of the Catholic question. 78p. *8°*. 1828. *The Agar Ellis copy.*

25708 LONDON SOCIETY OF DEPUTIES OF THE THREE DENOMINATIONS OF DISSENTERS. Corporation & Test Acts. [A statement of the legal position of the Society. Signed: Robert Winter, secretary.] 8p. *8°*. [London, 1828 ?] *The copy that belonged to M. T. Sadler.*

25709 Good **NEWS!!!** People of England — now or never! [A dialogue on Catholic emancipation, between Farmer Trueman and Farmer Gibbs. With 'The address to His Majesty signed by the farmers'.] 3p. *8°*. [1828] *The copy that belonged to M. T. Sadler.*

25710 PORTUGAL. *Cortes.* Solemn declaration of the three Estates of Portugal, assembled to consider the claims of Dom Miguel I. to the Crown of Portugal. 48p. *8°*. [1828] *Wanting the title-page. The Agar Ellis copy.*

25711 STEWART, M. Remarks on the state and policy of the nation. 121p. *8°*. 1828.

25712 THOUGHTS on the Roman Catholic question. By a Peelite. 59p. *8°*. 1828. *Attributed by HSF to the Rev. Henry Palmer.*

SOCIALISM

25713 BIRMINGHAM CO-OPERATIVE SOCIETY. An address delivered at the opening of the... Society, November 17, 1828, by a member [W. Pare ?]. To which is added the laws of the Society. 34p. *8°*. Birmingham, [1828] *★Another, the FWA copy, belonged to William Pare.*

25714 BUONARROTI, P. Conspiration pour l'égalité dite de Babeuf, suivie du procès auquel elle donna lieu, et des pièces justificatives, etc.... 2 vols. *8°*. Bruxelles, 1828. *See also 1836.*

For the **CO-OPERATOR,** edited by W. King, M.D., 1828–30, *see* vol. III, *Periodicals list.*

25715 FOURIER, F. C. M. Political economy made easy. A sketch...exhibiting the various errors of our present political arrangements. Presented to the London Co-operative Society, by the translator. 14p. *8°*. London, Worthing, &c., 1828. *★Another, the FWA copy, belonged to William Pare.*

25715A —— [Another edition.] 16p. *8°*. London, Worthing, &c.,1828.

25716 A **LETTER** to Sir James Graham, Bart. M.P., alias "A Cumberland landowner;" in reply to certain positions contained in a pamphlet, entitled "Free trade in corn the real interest of the landlord and the true policy of the state; by a Cumberland landowner." [Mainly a defence of Robert Owen and of the community at Orbiston, Scotland.] 30p. *8°*. 1828. *★Another, the FWA copy, that belonged to William Pare, contains an extra leaf, advertising works by James Jennings, who may have been the author of this pamphlet also.*

25717 LONDON CO-OPERATIVE TRADING FUND ASSOCIATION. To the operative classes. [An appeal for support, with the announcement of the establishment of a store.] 4p. *8°*. n.p. [1828]

25718 The **NATURE** and reasons of co-operation, addressed to the working classes. 4p. *8°*. Brighton, [1828 ?]

25719 OWEN, Robert. Memorial of Robert Owen to the Mexican Republic, and to the Government of the state of Coahuila and Texas. 11p. *4°*. [1828] *Presentation copy, with an inscription from the author to 'the Emperor of the Brazils'.*

25720 REY, Joseph A. Lettres sur le système de la coopération mutuelle et de la communauté de tous les biens, d'après le plan de M. Owen. 170p. *12°*. Paris, 1828.

25721 A new **THEORY** of moral and social reform; founded on the principal and most general facts of human nature. Or, essays, to establish a universal criterion of moral truth, that shall be intelligible and practicable alike to every individual, and to found thereon a plan of voluntary association and order...By a friend of the utmost reform... [With 'Prospectus of a real society, regulated by one law...especially eligible to those of moderate property and expectations'.] 147, 9p. *12°*. 1823–28. *With the original printed paper label, which reads 'A new theory of moral and social reform, to which is added a Prospectus of a real society', which indicates that the two parts were issued together.*

MISCELLANEOUS

25722 BROUGHAM, H. P., *Baron Brougham and Vaux*. Present state of the law. The speech of Henry Brougham, Esq. M.P., in the House of Commons, on... February 7, 1828, on his motion, that an humble address be presented to His Majesty, praying that he will...issue a Commission for inquiring into the defects occasioned by time...in the laws of this realm... 125p. *8°. 1828. One of an edition of 30 large-paper copies; presented, with an inscription, by the author to Sir Alexander Johnston.*

25723 —— [Another edition.] 125p. *8°*. 1828.

25724 —— A speech on the present state of the law of the country...Second edition. 48p. *8°*. 1828. *A reprint of the second edition.*

25725 —— Third edition. 125p. *8°*. 1828.

25726 ENGLAND. *Laws, etc.* Abstract of the Corporation and Test Acts; more particularly as to such parts of them as relate to the imposition of the sacramental test: also of subsequent Acts...which affect the same, including the Annual Indemnity Act. Published for the United Committee appointed to conduct the application of Protestant dissenters for relief. 15p. *8°*. 1828. *The Agar Ellis copy.*

25727 EXPOSTULATOR, *pseud.* An expostulatory letter from Edinburgh, addressed to the...Archbishops and the...Bishops of England and Ireland [on the condition of the Scots Episcopal clergy]. 48p. *8°*. 1828

25728 FIELD, B. A vindication of the practice of not allowing the counsel for prisoners accused of felony to make speeches for them. 30p. *8°*. 1828.

25729 HAYTER, Sir G. Copy of a letter dated Rome, Decr. 24th, 1827, from Mr. Hayter to His Grace the Duke of Bedford, on the unfortunate event which took place in his family at Florence [i.e. the death by poison of his mistress, Louisa C——]. 10p. *4°. n.p.* [1828] *The Agar Ellis copy.*

25730 HOWARD, George W. F., *7th Earl of Carlisle*. The last of the Greeks; or, the fall of Constantinople: a tragedy [in verse]. 79p. *8°*. 1828. *The Agar Ellis copy.*

25731 LEBER, J. M. C. Histoire critique du pouvoir municipal, de la condition des cités, des villes et des bourgs, et de l'administration comparée des communes, en France, depuis l'origine de la monarchie jusqu'à nos jours. 630p. *8°. Paris,* 1828.

25732 A LETTER to Sir Thomas D. Acland, Bart. M.P. on the repeal of the Sacramental Test...34p. *8°*. 1828. *The Agar Ellis copy.*

25733 MARKLAND, J. H. A letter to the...Earl of Aberdeen, K.T. President of the Society of Antiquaries, on the expediency of attaching a museum of antiquities to that Institution. 19p. *8°*. 1828. *The Agar Ellis copy.*

25734 [MOORE, Thomas (1779–1852).] Odes upon cash, corn, Catholics, and other matters. Selected from the columns of the Times Journal. 183p. *8°*. 1828.

25735 To the **PROTESTANTS** of Great Britain and Ireland. [On the hostility said to be evinced by Roman Catholics to the circulation of the Bible in English.] 16p. *8°. Gloucester,* [1828]. *The Agar Ellis copy.*

25736 [SCOTT, Sir Walter, *Bart.*] Religious discourses. By a layman. [The preface signed: W.S.] 79p. *8°*. 1828. *The Agar Ellis copy.*

25737 SMITH, Sydney (1771–1845). A sermon on those rules of Christian charity, by which our opinions of other sects should be formed...Second edition. 24p. *8°. Bristol & London,* [1828] *The Agar Ellis copy.*

25738 SYDNEY, *pseud.* Sydney's letters to the editor of the Courier, on the reported exclusion of Lord Byron's monument from Westminster Abbey. 14p. *8°*. 1828. *The Agar Ellis copy.*

25739 USE of the dead to the living. [To change the law on dissection.] 54p. *8°*. 1828. *The Agar Ellis copy.*

25739A A few **WORDS** on the subject of the "Denominated" act of the Three Estates of the kingdom of Portugal, assembled in Cortes...11th of July, 1828. Translated from the Portuguese. 23p. *8°. Plymouth,* 1828.

1829

GENERAL

25740 An **ADDRESS** on the state of the cotton trade, to the master spinners and weavers of Lancashire. Reprinted from the Manchester Gazette, of January 24, 31, February 7 and 14, 1829. [The advertisement signed by the printer, James Whittle, and the final letter by the editor.] 40p. *8°. Manchester,* 1829. *The Oastler copy.*

25741 ATTWOOD, T. Causes of the present distress. Speech of Thomas Attwood, Esq. at the public meeting, held in Birmingham, on the 8th of May, 1829, for the purpose of considering the distressed state of the country. 24p. *8°. Birmingham & London,* 1829.

25742 —— [Another edition.] Distressed state of the country. The speech of Thomas Attwood, Esq. on this important subject, at the town's meeting in Birmingham, held on the 8th of May, 1829... 83p. *8°. Birmingham & London,* 1829.

25743 The **BRITISH ALMANAC** of the Society for the Diffusion of Useful Knowledge for...1829. [With 'The companion to the Almanac, or year-book of general information'.] 72, 246p. *12°*. [1829] *For other editions, see* 1828.

25744 BUCHANAN, George. Tables for converting the weights and measures hitherto in use in Great Britain into those of the imperial standards established by the recent Act of Parliament...Together with a general view of the new system of weights and measures, and easy rules of conversion... 428p. *12°. Edinburgh, London, &c.,* 1829.

25745 CAREY, M. Common sense addresses to the citizens of the Southern States...Third edition, enlarged and improved. By a citizen of Philadelphia. 42p. *8°. Philadelphia,* 1829.

25746 —— Philadelphia, September 8th, 1829. [*Begin.*] Sir, When a man has devoted his utmost energies...[A circular letter, complaining of want of support in his campaign, and including testimonials.] *s.sh.4°. n.p.* [1829] [*Br.* 505(2)]

25747 [——] The protecting system. No. 8. [Signed: Hamilton; dated: Dec. 18, 1829. On the structure of the Spanish economy.] 4p. *8°. n.p.* [1829]

25748 COBBETT, W. The emigrant's guide; in ten letters, addressed to the tax-payers of England...including several authentic...letters from English emigrants, now in America, to their relations in England. 153p. *12°.* 1829. *See also* 1830.

25749 —— A history of the Protestant Reformation in England and Ireland; showing how that event has impoverished the...people...In a series of letters... 2 vols. *8°.* 1829. *For other editions, see* 1824.

25750 DEW, T. R. Lectures on the restrictive system, delivered to the senior political class of William and Mary College. 195p. *8°. Richmond* [*Va.*], 1829.

25751 DROZ, J. F. X. Économie politique ou principes de la science des richesses. (*Œuvres de Joseph Droz* ...Tome troisième.) 391p. *8°. Paris,* 1829. *See also* 1837, 1846.

For the **ECONOMIST,** advocate of free trade to China and the East Indies, and temperance reporter, *Edinburgh,* [1829], *see* vol. III, *Periodicals list.*

25752 ELOGIO di Luigi Valeriani Molinari recitato in occasione de premj distribuiti agli alunni del Ginnasio di Bagnacavallo il giorno xxvii. settembre MDCCCXXIX, anniversario della morte di quel chiarissimo da Domenico Vaccolini...[With 'Agl' illustrissimi signori Gonfaloniere Anziani e Consiglieri di Bagnacavallo' dated: 20. ottobre 1829 and signed: 'Varj concittadini'.] 20p. *12°. Lugo,* 1829.

For the **FREE TRADE ADVOCATE,** and journal of political economy, *see* vol. III, *Periodicals list.*

25753 GLOVER, S. The history, gazetteer, and directory of the county of Derby...containing...geological, mineralogical, commercial, and statistical information...The materials and directory collected by the publisher, Stephen Glover. Edited by Thomas Noble, Esq. [Vol. I., part 1.] 450, 107p. *8°. Derby & London,* 1829. *Wanting vol. II, part 1, the only other part published. See also* 1831.

25754 GORE, J., **AND SON.** Gore's Directory of Liverpool and its environs for 1829. [With an appendix.] 356, 100p. *8°. Liverpool,* [1829] *See also* 1818, 1823.

25755 HENDERSON, ANDREW (*fl.* 1826–1829). Practical hints on the principles of surveying and valuing estates, also on the making, repairing and management of roads... 24p. *8°. Edinburgh,* 1829.

For **HIGHLAND AND AGRICULTURAL SOCIETY OF SCOTLAND,** Prize-essays and transactions, 1829–37, *continued as* Transactions, 1843–63,

1867–1939, *see* vol. III, *Periodicals list,* Transactions of the Highland and Agricultural Society.

25756 JEFFERSON, T., *President of the USA.* Notes on the state of Virginia. 280p. *12°. Boston,* 1829. *For another edition, see* 1794.

25757 KNIGHT, G. Observations on some of the chief difficulties & disadvantages of English society, with suggestions of their remedy. 218p. *8°.* 1829.

25758 LONDON. Livery Companies. *Drapers.* Reports of deputations, who in pursuance of resolutions of the Court of Assistants...of...1817...1818...1819... 1820, and...1827, visited the estates of the Company, in the county of Londonderry in Ireland, in those years, and which were ordered by the Court to be printed... 211p. *8°.* 1829. *See also,* 1818, 1833.

25759 McCULLOCH, JOHN R. Macculloch's Principles of political economy abridged for scholar usage at Dr. Silvela's Hispano-Lusitanian Institution. [With 'Remarks on Mr. Macculloch's Principles of political economy. By Mr. Malthus'.] 117p. *12°. Paris,* 1829. *For editions of* Principles of political economy, *see* 1825.

25760 MacDONNELL, E. Social and political principles of the Roman Catholic prelates of Ireland, fairly stated. [Being extracts from the texts of pastoral charges made by the Roman Catholic bishops of Ireland in 1822 and 1824.] 21p. *8°.* 1829.

25761 [**MUDIE,** R.] A second judgment of Babylon the Great: or more men and things in the British Capital. By the author of "Babylon the Great"... 2 vols. *8°.* 1829.

25762 MUNDELL, A. Tables showing the amount, according to official and declared value, of every article of home produce and manufacture exported in every year from 1814 to 1828. Also of leading articles of import. With observations. Forming a supplement to "Reasons for a revision of our fiscal code." 38p. *8°.* 1829. *See also* 1830. *For* Reasons for a revision of our fiscal code, *see* 1828.

25763 MURRAY, H. Historical account of discoveries and travels in North America; including the United States, Canada, the shores of the Polar sea, and the voyages in search of a North-West passage. With observations on emigration... 2 vols. *8°. London & Edinburgh,* 1829.

25764 PECCHIO, G., *Conte.* Storia della economia pubblica in Italia, ossia epilogo critico degli economisti italiani, preceduto da un'introduzione. 310p. *8°. Lugano,* 1829. *See also* 1830, 1849.

25765 The **POST OFFICE** annual directory for 1829–30: containing an alphabetical list of the merchants, traders, manufacturers and principal inhabitants: with a street directory and an appendix...Second publication. 311, 84p. *12°. Glasgow,* 1829. *See also* 1836, 1842.

25766 QUETELET, L. A. J. Recherches statistiques sur le royaume des Pays-Bas...Mémoire lu à la séance de l'Académie du 6 décembre 1828. 57p. *4°. Bruxelles,* 1829.

25767 —— [Another edition.] 70p. *8°. Bruxelles,* 1829. *Presentation copy from the author to N. W. Senior.*

25768 READ, S. Political economy. An inquiry into the natural grounds of right to vendible property, or wealth. 398p. *8°. Edinburgh & London,* 1829.

25769 ROBERT-GUYARD, J. A. De la richesse ou essais de ploutonomie. Ouvrage dans lequel on se propose de rechercher et d'exposer les principes de cette science. [Livres I–III.] 320p. *8°. Paris,* 1829.

25770 SADLER, M. T. Ireland; its evils, and their remedies: being a refutation of the errors of the Emigration Committee and others, touching that country. To which is prefixed, a synopsis of an original treatise about to be published on the law of population... Second edition. 464p. *8°.* 1829. *For another edition, see 1828.*

25771 —— The speech of Michael T. Sadler, Esq. M.P. on the state and prospects of the country, delivered...at Whitby, on...September 15...Extracted from the Hull Advertiser, and the Leeds Intelligencer. 35p. *8°.* 1829.

25772 SCHNITZLER, J. H. Statistique et itinéraire de la Russie, ou manuel complet du diplomate, du négociant et de tout voyageur en Russie...Première partie. Essai d'une statistique générale de l'Empire de Russie. 494p. *12°. Paris & Saint-Pétersbourg,* 1829.

25773 SEINE, *Département de la. Administration.* Recherches statistiques sur la ville de Paris et le Département de la Seine; recueil de tableaux dressés et réunis d'après les ordres de Monsieur le Comte de Chabrol... xlviii, [82], 86p., 145 tables. *4°. Paris,* 1829. *Published under the direction of J. B. J. Fourier, with some contributions by him. See also 1821, 1823, 1826.*

25774 SKARBEK, F. F., *Hrabia.* Théorie des richesses sociales...Suivie d'une bibliographie de l'économie politique. 2 vols. *8°. Paris,* 1829.

25775 SMITH, BENJAMIN, *ed.* Twenty-four letters from labourers in America to their friends in England. Second edition. 48p. *8°.* 1829. *The copy that belonged to Patrick Chalmers.*

25776 SOCIETY FOR THE IMPROVEMENT OF IRELAND. [*Begin.*] At a meeting of the Society for Improvement of Ireland, held...on...the 14th of July, 1829...the following proceedings took place... [With 'Report of the committee appointed to take into consideration the most efficient means for procuring a complete statistical account of Ireland'.] 8p. *8°. Dublin,* [1829] *See also 1828, 1846.*

25777 *STEVENSON, ANDREW. Speech of Mr. Stevenson, of Virginia, on the powers of the general [i.e. Federal] Government over internal improvement; delivered in the House of Representatives, February 2, 1829. 32p. *8°. Washington,* 1829. *Presentation copy from the author to George Grote.*

25778 TANNER, H. S. Memoir on the recent surveys, observations, and internal improvements, in the United States, with brief notices of the new counties, towns, villages, canals, and rail roads, never before delineated... 108p. *12°. Philadelphia,* 1829.

25779 [THOMPSON, THOMAS P.] The article on "Essays on the pursuit of truth" [by S. Bailey]. Republished from the Westminster Review, No. XXII; on the 2nd November, 1829. 15p. *8°.* [1829] *Bound in a volume, which belonged to Francis Place, of reprints of Thompson's articles in the Westminster Review. *Another, the FWA copy, belonged to William Pare.*

25780 [——] The "greatest happiness" principle in morals and government, explained and defended. In answer to the Edinburgh Review. Stereotype. Republished from the Westminster Review, No. XXI.[–XXIII.] 16, 12, 16p. *8°.* 1829–30.

25781 —— Second edition. Stereotype...[Part I.] 16p. *8°.* 1829. *See note to no. 25779.*

25782 *—— Fourth edition. Stereotype...[Part I.] 16p. *8°.* 1829. *The FWA copy, that belonged to William Pare.*

25783 —— Sixth edition. Stereotype. [Part I.] 16p. *8°.* 1829.

25784 —— The true theory of rent, in opposition to Mr. Ricardo and others. Being an exposition of fallacies on rent, tithes, &c. In the form of a review of Mr. Mill's Elements of political economy. By the author of the Catechism on the corn laws...Fourth edition... 32p. *8°.* 1829. *For other editions, see 1826.*

25785 THOUGHTS on the present distress. 68p. *8°.* 1829.

25786 VADILLO, J. M. DE. Discursos económico-politicos sobre si la moneda es comun medida de los generos comerciables y el examen del influjo de la legislacion y de los gobiernos en el valor de la moneda y del interes del dinero; y sobre los medios de fomentar la industria española y de contener o reprimir el contrabando. 394p. *8°. Paris,* 1829.

25787 WARD, SIR H. G. Mexico...Second edition enlarged, with an account of the mining companies, and of the political events in that republic, to the present day... 2 vols. *8°.* 1829. *For another edition, see 1828.*

25788 WHEWELL, W. Mathematical exposition of some doctrines of political economy. From the Transactions of the Cambridge Philosophical Society. 39p. *4°. Cambridge,* 1829. *Presentation copy, with inscription, from the author to George Pryme.*

25789 YSARN, F. J. DE. Sur la baisse du prix courant des produits agricoles en Russie. Mémoire de concours à la question d'économie politique publiée par l'Académie Impériale des Sciences le 29 décembre 1829... 42p. *8°. St.-Pétersbourg,* 1829.

AGRICULTURE

25790 COBBETT, W. The English gardener; or, a treatise on the situation, soil, enclosing and laying-out of kitchen gardens...and on the...cultivation of...kitchen-garden plants, and of fruit trees...And also on the formation of shrubberies and flower-gardens...concluding with a kalendar... [480]p. *12°.* 1829. *See also 1838, 1845.*

25791 COOTE, RICHARD H. A letter to His Majesty's Commissioners for an inquiry into the state of the laws of real property on the subject of the proposed general registry. 26p. *8°.* 1829.

25792 DENMAN, T., *Baron Denman.* The modern law of landlord & tenant, delineated at large...In which are introduced the most modern and approved forms of practical proceedings in levying a distress, and actions of replevin and ejectment, &c.... 246p. *8°.* 1829.

25793 DIX, T. A treatise on land-surveying, in seven parts...Fifth edition, revised, corrected and improved. 216p. *12°.* 1829.

25794 DONCASTER AGRICULTURAL ASSOCIATION. Bone manure. Report of the committee

...on the advantages of bones as a manure. Founded on returns received in answer to the queries issued by the committee. [With the text of the queries, and a list of those who replied.] 33p. *8°.* 1829.

25795 ENGLAND. Parliament. *House of Lords.* The evidence taken before the Select Committee of the House of Lords, appointed to take into consideration the state of the coal trade in the United Kingdom, together with the duties of all descriptions, and charges affecting the same ...To which is now first added a list of explosions & inundations which have occurred in the coal mines of Northumberland and Durham; with notes and remarks. [Edited by John Sykes.] 99p. *8°. Newcastle upon Tyne,* 1829.

25796 FAIRBANKS, E. A compilation of articles relating to the culture and manufacture of hemp in the United States; selected principally from newspapers and journals devoted to the interest of agriculture. 39p. *12°. St. Johnsbury,* 1829.

25797 FAISEAU-LAVANNE, T. Recherches statistiques sur les forêts de la France, tendant à signaler le danger qu'il y aurait pour elles d'ouvrir nos frontières aux fers étrangers...Publiées par les soins des Commissaires délégués par MM. les propriétaires de bois. 100p. *4°. Paris,* 1829. *The copy specially bound for presentation to the Duc de Bourbon*

25798 HARLEY, W. The Harleian dairy system; and an account of the various methods of dairy husbandry pursued by the Dutch. Also, a new and improved mode of ventilating stables. With an appendix, containing useful hints...for the management of hedge-row fences, fruit trees, &c.; and the means of rendering barren land fruitful. 288p. *8°. London, Edinburgh, &c.,* 1829.

25799 HODGKIN, J. Observations on the proposed establishment of a general register. 55p. *8°.* 1829.

25800 KENNEDY, L. and **GRAINGER,** T. B. The present state of the tenancy of land in the highland and grazing districts in Great Britain; showing the principal customs...under which sheep farms are now held and managed in the several counties; with a brief history of sheep, and facts relative to the state of the British wool growers. Collected from a survey made in 1828 and 1829... 324p. *8°.* 1829.

25801 KLEINSCHROD, C. T. VON. Ueber die Beförderungsmittel der Agrikultur und des Gewerbwesens in Frankreich... 133p. *8°. München,* 1829.

25802 LAMBERT, JOSEPH. Observations on the rural affairs of Ireland; or a practical treatise on farming, planting and gardening, adapted to the circumstances, resources, soil and climate of the country; including some remarks on the reclaiming of bogs... 327p. *12°. Dublin,* 1829.

25803 MACKENZIE, GEORGE, *lieut.* Manual of the weather for the year MDCCCXXX: including a brief account of the cycles of the winds and weather, and of the circle of the prices of wheat. 103p. *12°. Edinburgh & London,* 1829.

25804 [MILLER, H.] Letters [signed: M.] on the herring fishing in the Moray Frith. By the author of "Poems written in the leisure hours of a journeyman mason." 50p. *12°. Inverness,* 1829.

25805 MONTEATH, R. A new and easy system of draining and reclaiming the bogs and marshes of Ireland: with plans for improving waste lands in general. To which are added miscellaneous reports of recent surveys of woods and plantations... 239p. *8°. Edinburgh & London,* 1829.

25806 *OUTLINES of a plan for the establishment of an Agricultural Model School in the province of Munster, recommended by the London Irish Relief Committee of 1822...Approved by the committee appointed by the Trustees for the Encouragement of Industry in the county of Cork. [With 'Appendix. Report of the committee of the N.W. Society concerning an agricultural seminary' and 'Extracts from Travels in Switzerland by S. Simond, respecting Mr. Fellenberg's establishment at Hofwyl'.] 50p. *8°. Cork,* 1829. *The FWA copy that belonged to William Pare.*

25807 QUEENBOROUGH. Appeal on behalf of the distressed burgesses and inhabitants of Queenborough, Kent, January, 1829. [Against abuses depriving them of their right to the oyster beds belonging to the town.] 15p. *8°.* [1829]

25808 ROBERTSON, GEORGE (1750?–1832). Rural recollections; or, the progress of improvement in agriculture and rural affairs. 636p. *8°. Irvine, Edinburgh, &c.,* 1829.

25809 SALISBURY, W. Western Literary and Scientific Institution, 47, Leicester Square. Proposals for publishing a new system of rural economy, for the immediate improvement of Ireland, by giving effective employment to the poor of Great Britain... 3p. *fol.* [*London,* 1829?] *Endorsed: Prospectus of a system of rural economy.*

25810 STEPHENS, GEORGE, *land-drainer.* The practical irrigator; being an account of the utility...of irrigated meadows...to which is added, a practical treatise on straightening water-courses, protecting river banks, and embanking low lands...Second edition, greatly enlarged. 136p. *8°. Edinburgh & London,* 1829. *For other editions, see 1826.*

25811 TAYLOR, JOHN (1779–1863), *ed.* Records of mining...[Papers by John Taylor and John Henry Vivian.] Part I. 174p. *4°.* 1829.

25812 TULL, J. The horse-hoeing husbandry: or, a treatise on the principles of tillage and vegetation...To which is prefixed an introduction...by William Cobbett. 466p. *8°.* 1829. *For other editions, see 1731.*

25813 WALTERS, R. A letter to the Lord Chancellor ...on the administration of the laws of real property. 28p. *8°.* 1829.

25814 WITHERS, W. A letter to Sir Henry Steuart, Bart. on the improvement in the quality of timber, to be effected by the high cultivation and quick growth of forest-trees, in reply to certain passages in his "Planter's guide." 133p. *8°. Holt & London,* 1829.

25815 WOOD, WILLIAM P., *Baron Hatherley.* A letter to His Majesty's Commissioners for an inquiry into the state of the laws of real property; in answer to some objections which have been advanced against a general register. 39p. *8°.* 1829.

CORN LAWS

25816 A **REFUTATION** of A catechism on the corn laws. By a Cumberland farmer. 26p. *8°. London & Carlisle,* 1829.

25817 **THOMPSON,** THOMAS P. Catechism on the corn laws; with a list of fallacies and the answers. By a member of the University of Cambridge. Fifth edition... 64p. *8°.* 1829.

25818 —— Sixth edition... 64p. *8°.* 1829.

25819 —— Thirteenth edition. Revised and corrected ... 64p. *8°.* 1829.

25820 —— Fourteenth edition, revised and corrected ...To which is added the article on free trade, from the Westminster Review, No. XXIII. 64p. *8°.* 1829. *For other editions, see* 1827.

25821 **TORRENS,** R. An essay on the external corn trade...With an appendix on the means of improving the condition of the labouring classes. A new edition. 477p. *8°.* 1829. *For other editions, see* 1815.

POPULATION

25822 **SENIOR,** N. W. Two lectures on population, delivered before the University of Oxford in Easter Term, 1828...To which is added, a correspondence between the author and the Rev. T. R. Malthus. 90p. *8°.* 1829. *For other editions, see* 1828.

TRADES & MANUFACTURES

25823 The **BRASS FOUNDERS',** braziers', and coppersmiths' manual; containing a scientific description of brass founding in all its several branches; valuable recipes for lackering; the rules and regulations of the trade society...and a complete list of all the master founders, braziers and coppersmiths, in the Metropolis and its environs. 78p. *12°.* 1829.

25824 The **BRICKLAYERS',** plasterers' and slaters' manual, containing a concise description of those trades in all their various branches. Together with a list of surveyors, master builders and trades connected therewith in the Metropolis and its environs. 122p. *12°.* 1829.

25825 **DECROOS,** G. Traité sur les savons solides, ou manuel du savonnier et du parfumeur... 421p. *8°. Paris & Bruxelles,* 1829.

25826 **DRYDEN,** J. Observations on the construction of railways, and upon mechanics. 158p. *8°. London & Darlington,* 1829.

25827 The **HAT MAKERS'** manual; containing a full description of hat making in all its branches; also copious directions for dyeing, blocking, finishing, and water proofing; together with a list of hat manufacturers ...in the Metropolis... 46p. *12°.* 1829.

25828 *****HOENE WRONSKI,** J. M. Machines à vapeur; aperçu de leur état actuel, sous les points de vue de la mécanique et de l'industrie, pour conduire à la solution accomplie du problême que présentent ces machines; avec un supplément donnant la théorie mathématique rigoureuse des machines à vapeur, fondée sur la nouvelle théorie générale des fluides. 51p. *4°. Paris,* 1829.

25829 **HUTTON,** C. The compendious measurer, being a brief, yet comprehensive treatise on mensuration, and practical geometry...The tenth edition, corrected and enlarged by Olinthus Gregory... 348p. *12°. London & Edinburgh,* 1829. *For another edition, see* 1796.

25830 [**MEIKLEHAM,** R. S.] Historical and descriptive anecdotes of steam-engines, and of their inventors and improvers: by Robert Stuart, civil engineer... 2 vols. *12°.* 1829.

25831 **NATIONAL REPOSITORY.** National repository in the gallery of the Royal Mews, Charing Cross ...A short statement of the nature and objects of the institution, established for the purpose of annually exhibiting to the public the new...productions of the artisans and manufacturers of the United Kingdom. With some remarks on the present state of the trade and manufactures of the country... 44p. *8°.* 1829.

25832 **PROUT,** J. Practical view of the silk trade, embracing a faithful account of the result of the measures enacted in 1824, for the encouragement of that manufacture. 60p. *8°. Macclesfield, Congleton, &c.,* 1829.

25833 **TAYLOR,** CHARLES, *engineer.* A supplement to Nicholson's Operative mechanic, and British machinist; consisting of a series of descriptions, elucidated by engravings...of the most remarkable public works and national improvements of the British Empire. Translated and arranged from Baron Charles Dupin, "On the commercial power of Great Britain,"... p.785-902. *8°.* 1829. *For editions of Nicholson's* Operative mechanic, *see* 1825.

25834 **THOROLD,** W. Remarks on the present state of the law relative to patents for inventions, in a letter to Davies Gilbert, Esq. M.P. P.R.S.... 36p. *8°. London & Norwich,* [1829]

25835 **UDNY,** J. Specification of the patent of John Udny, Esq. for improvement on the steam engine. By M. Daniel Glashien, agent for brevet's d'invention...Translated from the French. 16p. *8°.* [1829] *The Agar Ellis copy.*

COMMERCE

25836 ANISSON-DUPERRON, A. J. L., *Comte.* De l'affranchissement du commerce et de l'industrie. 36p. *8°. Paris*, 1829.

25837 —— De l'enquête sur les fers ou application des principes généraux à la question de la taxe sur les fers étrangers. 57p. *8°. Paris*, 1829.

25838 —— Examen de l'enquête commerciale sur les sucres en 1829, précédé de l'examen de l'enquête sur les fers (2e édition). 127p. *8°. Paris*, 1829. *Presentation copy, with inscription, from the author to L. F. M. R. Wolowski.*

25839 BALLANCE, J. A brief reply to the second pamphlet of Mr. R. Badnall, Jun. on the silk trade; addressed to the Rt. Hon. W. Vesey Fitzgerald. 27p. *8°.* 1829.

25840 —— Remarks on some of the important errors contained in Mr. Badnall's pamphlet, entitled 'A view of the silk trade'. 40p. *8°.* 1829.

25841 BAUDE, J. J., *Baron.* De l'enquête sur les fers, et des conditions du bon marché permanent des fers en France. 89p. *8°. Paris*, 1829.

25842 BERRYER, P. N. Dissertation générale sur le commerce, son état actuel en France, et sa législation. Servant d'introduction au Traité complet du droit commercial, en souscription. 215p. *8°. Paris*, 1829.

25843 BILBAO. *Universidad y Casa de Contratacion.* Ordenanzas de la ilustre Universidad y Casa de Contratación de la...Villa de Bilbao, aprobadas y confirmadas por...D. Felipe V en 2 de diciembre de 1737, y...D. Fernando VII en 27 de junio de 1814... 332, ccxixp. *8°. Paris*, 1829. *For an edition of the 1737 Ordinances, see* 1760 (GENERAL).

25844 BYLES, SIR J. B. A discourse on the present state of the law of England, the proposed schemes of reform and the proper method of study...Being the first of a series of lectures on commercial law. 42p. *8°.* 1829.

25845 DECHALOTTE, J. F. Traité sur les subsistances et projet d'un approvisionnement de réserve en grains pour toute la France, sans qu'il en coute rien au Trésor. 90p. *8°. Paris*, 1829.

25846 FOWLER, CHARLES (1791–1867). Description of the plan for the revival of Hungerford Market, with some particulars of the buildings proposed to be erected...Not published. 23p. *8°.* 1829.

25847 FRANCE. *Ministère du Commerce, et des Manufactures.* Commission formée avec l'approbation du Roi, sous la présidence du Ministère du Commerce et des Manufactures, pour l'examen de certaines questions de législation commerciale. Enquête sur les sucres. 324p. *4°.* [*Paris*, 1829]

25848 De l'**IMPORTANCE** du commerce des sucres, ou examen des questions proposées par le Bureau de Commerce de Paris, 60p. *8°. Le Havre*, 1829.

25849 JACKSON, JOHN (*fl.* 1829). A treatise of the capability of our eastern possessions to produce those articles of consumption, and raw material for British manufacture, for which we chiefly depend on foreign nations; and the incalculable advantages of a free trade to and settlement in India... 37p. *8°. London, Liverpool, &c.,* 1829.

25850 MACONOCHIE, ALEXANDER. Thoughts on the present state and future commercial policy of the country; with the plan of a periodical work, to be confined exclusively to commercial subjects. 20p. *8°.* 1829.

25851 MARSHALL, JOHN (*fl.* 1829). A statement of the various proceedings prior and subsequent to the appointment of a committee, in 1824, to inquire into the mode of classing the mercantile marine at Lloyd's, and to report their opinions thereon...To which is appended, the evidence obtained by the committee, and their report. 195p. *8°.* 1829.

25852 MEXICO. *Congreso.* Balanza general del comercio maritimo por los puertos de la Republica Mexicana en el año de 1827. Formada por orden del gobierno, en cumplimiento de lo mandado por el Congreso general en la ley de ocho de mayo de mil ochocientos veinte y seis. [Compiled by Y. Maniau.] 189p. *4°. Mexico*, 1829.

25853 The humble **PETITION** of the hens of the United Kingdom of Great Britain and Ireland, to the Lords spiritual and temporal...and likewise to the Commons of the United Kingdom...[A complaint against the unrestricted importation of foreign eggs.] 4p. *fol. n.p.* [1829] *The Agar Ellis copy. Also printed in the first number of* Chanticleer, *for which see* vol. III, *Periodicals list.*

25854 SAINZ ANDINO, P. Proyecto de codigo de comercio, formado de orden del Rey N. Sr. 316p. *4°. Madrid*, 1829.

25855 SPAIN. *Laws, etc.* Codigo de comercio, decretado, sancionado y promulgado en 30 de Mayo de 1829. Edicion oficial. 330p. *4°. Madrid*, 1829.

25856 TAZEWELL, L. W. A review of the negociations between the United States of America and Great Britain, respecting the commerce of the two countries, and more especially concerning the trade of the former with the West Indies...Norfolk, in Virginia: printed with the signature "Senex" in the "Norfolk Herald". 130p. *8°.* 1829.

25857 VERITAS, *pseud.* The present degraded state of trade, its cause and effects considered; in a letter to the Right Hon. W. F. Vesey Fitzgerald, President of the Board of Trade... 23p. *8°.* 1829. *The copy that belonged to Oastler, who attributed it to 'Underwood' in the manuscript index to his pamphlet collection.*

25858 WINE and spirit adulterators unmasked. Third edition, to which is annexed, a brief exposition of the deleterious nature of British brandy, and of the gross frauds which are practised therewith. By one of the old school. 216p. *12°.* [1829]

COLONIES

25859 ADDRESS to the members of the British Legislature, on the subject of eighty millions of their fellow creatures dependent on their determinations. By an East-India proprietor, late of the Bengal Civil Service. 98p. *8°*. [1829?]

25860 *CONSIDERATIONS on the renewal of the East India Company's charter. 56p. *8°. Calcutta,* 1829. *The copy that belonged to George Grote.*

25861 [CRAWFURD, John (1783–1868).] A view of the present state and future prospects of the free trade & colonization of India. Second edition, enlarged. 106p. *8°. London & Liverpool,* 1829. *For another edition, see* 1828.

25862 DESCRIPTION of a view of the town of Sydney, New South Wales; the harbour of Port Jackson, and surrounding country; now exhibiting in the Panorama, Leicester-Square. Painted by the proprietor, Robert Burford. 12p. *8°.* 1829.

25863 ENGLAND. *Colonial Office.* Statement of the receipts and expenditure, charges incurred for military defence, value of imports and exports, shipping, tonnage and men employed in the trade, and the population of the colonial possessions of Great Britain. 47p. *8°. n.p.* [1829]

25864 EVANS, Sir George De L. On the practicability of an invasion of British India; and on the commercial and financial prospects and resources of the Empire. lviii, 147p. *8°.* 1829.

25865 HALIBURTON, T. C. An historical and statistical account of Nova-Scotia... 2 vols. *8°. Halifax, Nova-Scotia, London, &c.,* [1829]

25866 HISTORY of the origin, rise, and progress, of the Van Diemen's Land Company. [From the *Colonial Advocate.*] 69p. *8°.* 1829.

25867 MacTAGGART, J. Three years in Canada: an account of the actual state of the country in 1826–7–8. Comprehending its resources, productions, improvements, and capabilities; and including sketches of the state of society, advice to emigrants, &c.... 2 vols. *12°.* 1829.

25868 [MUDIE, R.] The picture of Australia: exhibiting New Holland, Van Diemen's Land, and all the settlements, from the first at Sydney to the last at the Swan River. 370p. *12°.* 1829.

25869 OBSERVATIONS on the insolvent law of the Colony of the Cape of Good Hope; with an appendix of forms, applicable to the colonial ordinance, No. 64 [and the text of the ordinance]. 163, xcliip. *8°. Cape Town,* 1829.

25870 OBSERVATIONS on the progress of the episcopal establishment in the West Indies. 35p. *8°.* 1829.

25871 PEGGS, J. A voice from India. An appeal to Britain recommending the abolition of the practice of burning Hindoo widows, chiefly extracted from "The Suttees' cry to Britain", by the Rev. J. Peggs...Published by the Coventry Society for the Abolition of Human Sacrifices in India. 16p. *8°. London & Coventry,* 1829.

25872 [WAKEFIELD, Edward G.] A letter from Sydney, the principal town of Australasia. Edited by Robert Gouger. Together with the outline of a system of colonization. 222, xxivp. *12°.* 1829. *Presentation copy from the editor to the Society for the Encouragement of Arts, Manufactures, and Commerce.*

FINANCE

25873 BANK OF MANCHESTER. Deed of settlement of the Bank of Manchester, established December 1, 1828, under the authority of an Act of Parliament passed in the 7th year of George IV. To which is appended an abstract of the said Act, and a list of the shareholders. Capital two millions. 88p. *8°. Manchester,* 1829.

25874 BANK OF SCOTLAND. Rates of interest allowed by the Bank of Scotland on money deposited at Edinburgh. [Oct. 1810–1 Sept. 1829.] 3p. *fol. n.p.* [1829] *With manuscript additions to each table, of the rates at 1 Dec. 1836.*

25875 BECHER, John T. A compendium and practical system of book-keeping, for savings banks, together with tables for computing the interest on deposits at the several rates of 3l. 8s. 5¼d. and 3l. 6s. 8d. per cent, or upon the principal invested at the rate of 3l. 16s. 0½d. per cent. Exemplified with specimens of the account-books, in use at the Southwell Savings Bank and illustrated by explanatory remarks... 55p. *8°.* 1829.

25876 BEUGNOT, A. A., *Comte.* Des banques publiques de prêt sur gage et de leurs inconvéniens... Mémoire couronné en 1829 par l'Académie du Gard. 82p. *8°. Paris,* 1829.

25877 BRESSON, J. Histoire financière de la France, depuis l'origine de la monarchie jusqu'à l'année 1828, précédée d'une introduction sur le mode d'impôts en usage avant la Révolution, suivie de considérations sur la marche du crédit public... 2 vols. *8°. Paris,* 1829. *The copy that belonged to the Société de Lecture de Genève. See also* 1840, 1843.

25878 BRITISH LINEN COMPANY. Contract betwixt the officers, agents & others, employed in the business of the British Linen Company, instituted in 1808; with statement and remarks respecting the progress of the fund [for the benefit of the wives and children of employees], submitted to the committee of management, by Mr. Henderson, the treasurer, on first April, 1829. 61p. *fol. Edinburgh,* 1829.

25879 The **BRITISH TARIFF** for 1829–30...By Robert Ellis... 184p. *12°.* 1829. *See also* 1832, 1834, 1846, 1848.

25880 BURGESS, H. A petition to the honourable the Commons House of Parliament, to render manifest the errors, the injustice, and the dangers, of the measures of Parliament respecting currency and bankers... 152p. *8°.* 1829.

25881 CAPMAS, , *Curé de Saint-Jacques de Montauban.* L'intérêt de l'argent, dans le prêt ou l'usure, condamnée comme contraire au droit naturel, divin et politique, par toute l'antiquité comme depuis le XIIIe siècle; et réfutation d'un écrit intitulé Théorie de l'intérêt de l'argent contre l'abus de l'imputation d'usure et de plusieurs autres écrits, aussi en faveur de l'usure... 226p. *12°. Paris, 1829. For another edition, see 1782.*

25882 [CARBUTT, E.] The letters of Verax on the currency. Reprinted from the Manchester Gazette, and the Manchester Courier; with an epistle dedicatory to the Right Hon. Robert Peel, not before published. 40p. *8°. Manchester, 1829.*

25883 CAZENOVE, J. Questions respecting the National Debt and taxation stated and answered. 44p. *8°.* 1829.

25884 COBBETT, W. Mr. Cobbett's first lecture, on the present prospects of merchants, traders, and farmers, and on the state of the country in general, delivered in the theatre of the London Mechanics Institution, on Thursday, 26th November, 1829. 8p. *8°.* 1829.

25885 —— Mr. Cobbett's second lecture. Delivered 10th December, 1829. 8p. *8°. [London, 1829]*

25886 —— Mr. Cobbett's third lecture. Delivered 17th December, 1829. Second edition. 8p. *8°. n.p. [1829]*

25887 DANIEL, E. Two letters addressed to the Right Hon. Robert Peel...and a third addressed to the noble Duke of Wellington...wherein the expediency of the immediate abolition of the excise laws is considered... and of the assessed tax assessment: and of imposing...an equal tax upon all real, funded, and productive personal property...With the answers received from those gentlemen. 52p. *8°. Gloucester, London, &c., 1829. See also 1830.*

25888 DEVON AND EXETER SAVINGS BANK. The thirteenth annual report of the Devon and Exeter Savings Bank, established at Exeter, December 4, 1815...[With rules and regulations.] 18, [16]p. *8°. Exeter, 1829. See also 1817.*

25889 DUBLIN. The report on the taxation of Dublin, and the petition to Parliament, adopted at a general meeting of the inhabitants...on the 24 March, 1829...to which are added a preface, appendices, and tables, proving...the several allegations and complaints therein contained. The whole revised, and now published by the Committee of Inhabitants... 60p. *12°. Dublin, 1829.*

25890 An ESSAY on currency; being a serious research into the various bearings and morbid views of the subject. By an old practitioner. 44p. *8°. 1829. Tentatively attributed by HSF to Ephraim Gompertz.*

25891 FRY, J. S. A concise history of tithes, with an inquiry how far a forced maintenance for the ministers of religion is warranted by the example and precepts of Jesus Christ and his Apostles...Fifth edition. 24p. *12°. London & Bristol, 1828[1829] The printed paper wrapper bears the date 1829 and the name of an additional bookseller, in York. For another edition, see 1819.*

25892 HEATHFIELD, R. Thoughts on the liquidation of the public debt, and on the relief of the country from the distress incident to a population exceeding the demand for labour. 35p. *8°. [1829]*

25893 HINTS and observations respecting the parks and palaces...[An attack on the expense of Nash's alterations to Buckingham House. Signed: A householder of Queen Square, Westminster.] 19p. *8°. 1829.*

25894 A LETTER to the Earl of Mountcashel, on a change in the laws of property [i.e. tithes]. 48p. *8°. 1829.*

25895 LORD, E. Principles of currency and banking. 131p. *12°. New York, 1829.*

25896 [McVICKAR, J.] Considerations upon the expediency of abolishing damages on protested bills of exchange, and the effect of establishing a reciprocal exchange with Europe: to which are annexed, the report made to the House of Representatives of the United States, March 22, 1826, and an examination into the nature and operation of bills of exchange. 67p. *8°. New-York, 1829.*

25897 MADISON, J., *President of the USA.* Letters on the constitutionality of the power in Congress to impose a tariff for the protection of manufactures... Prefixed by a brief sketch of the life of the author, and the part he took in the formation of the constitution of the U.S. 24p. *12°. Washington City, 1829.*

25898 MAITLAND, JAMES, *8th Earl of Lauderdale.* Three letters to the Duke of Wellington, on the fourth Report of the Select Committee of the House of Commons, appointed in 1828 to enquire into the public income and expenditure of the United Kingdom; in which the nature and tendency of a Sinking Fund is investigated... 138p. *8°. 1829.*

25899 [MILLER, T. ?] Principles of life annuities and assurances, practically illustrated; showing the method of calculating the values of annuities...policies, &c. With... useful tables; comprising the values of annuities deduced from the Carlisle and Northampton tables of mortality... By an accountant. 114p. *8°. Edinburgh & London, 1829.*

25900 [MOOR, E.] The gentle sponge: being a safe, easy, certain, and just mode of reducing, to any desirable extent the National Debt of England. In a letter to...the Duke of Wellington. (With notes.) By an old soldier. 44p. *8°.* 1829.

25901 NEBENIUS, C. F. E. Ueber die Natur und die Ursachen des öffentlichen Credits, Staatsanlehen, die Tilgung der öffentlichen Schulden, den Handel mit Staatspapieren und die Wechselwirkung zwischen den Creditoperationen der Staaten und dem ökonomischen und politischen Zustande der Länder. 714p. *8°. Karlsruhe & Baden, 1829. A much enlarged version of the general conclusions of the author's Der offentliche Credit, 1820 (q.v.).*

25902 OBSERVATIONS on the moral and political effects of the tithe system in England, with a plan for a commutation of tithes, and for the more effectually providing for the clergy of our church establishment...By a clergyman of the diocese of Exeter. Printed 1801. – Reprinted...1829. [With a preface by James Rodd.] 52p. *8°. Exeter, [1829]*

25903 OBSERVATIONS on the state of the currency, with suggestions for equalising its value, and reducing to uniformity the banking system in the United States. 24p. *8°. n.p., 1829.*

25904 [OSIANDER, H. F.] Geschichtliche Darstellung der niederländischen Finanzen seit der wiedererlangten Selbstständigkeit des Staates in 1813. Vom Verfasser der Beleuchtung der Kampfes über Handelsfreiheit und Verbotsystem in den Niederlanden, etc. 149p. *8°. Amsterdam & Leipzig, 1829. Bound with a manuscript abridgment in Dutch on 58 leaves, entitled: 'Korte inhoud'.*

25905 [——] Exposé historique des finances du Royaume des Pays-Bas, depuis 1813. Par l'auteur de l'examen de la question sur la liberté du commerce et sur le système de prohibition dans les Pays-Bas, etc. Traduit de l'allemand par ******. 161p. *8°. Bruxelles, 1829. See also* 1830.

25906 PARNELL, H. B., *Baron Congleton.* Observations on paper money, banking, and overtrading; including those parts of the evidence taken before the Committee of the House of Commons, which explains the Scotch system of banking... Second edition. 177p. *8°.* 1829. *A reissue of the second edition, published in 1828 (q.v.). For other editions, see* 1827.

25907 PRINCIPLES of coinage; intended as a commentary on a letter to the King on the coins of this realm, by the late Earl of Liverpool. The first, second, third, and fourth parts. 208p. *8°.* [*London,*] 1829. *For another edition, see* 1828.

25908 REDFERN, W. A letter to Thomas Attwood, Esq. in reply to his speech, at the public meeting, held in Birmingham, May 8, 1829, for the purpose of considering the distressed state of the country. 30p. *8°. Birmingham,* 1829.

25909 *—— Second edition, with numerous important additions, and further statistical illustrations. 55p. *8°.* 1829. *The FWA copy, that belonged to William Pare.*

25910 Proposed **REMEDY** for the distresses of the country. 20p. *8°.* 1829.

25911 —— [Another edition.] To which is added, a letter to the editor of the Courier, on the present situation of the country bankers [Signed: A country banker]. 35p. *8°.* 1829.

25912 —— [Another edition.] 37p. *8°.* 1829.

25913 SINCLAIR, Sir John, *Bart.* Thoughts on currency and the means of promoting national prosperity

by the adoption of "an improved circulation," founded on the security of solid property, and adapted to the wants and necessities of the country. With an appendix "on the doctrines of free trade"... 136p. *8°.* 1829.

25914 SOCIETY OF WRITERS TO THE SIGNET. Report on the widows' scheme of the Society of Writers to the Signet. [By James Scott, accountant.] 3rd November 1829. 79p. *4°. Edinburgh,* 1829.

25915 TOOKE, T. A letter to Lord Grenville, on the effects ascribed to the resumption of cash payments on the value of the currency. 132p. *8°.* 1829.

25916 —— On the currency in connexion with the corn trade; and on the corn laws. To which is added a postscript on the present commercial stagnation. 119p. *8°.* 1829.

25917 —— Second edition. 119p. *8°.* 1829. *The half-titles of both editions read: A second letter to Lord Grenville.*

25918 A TREATISE on the law of bills of exchange, inland-bills, promissory-notes, &c., with an appendix, and a synopsis of the history of banking, explanatory of the mode in which banking is conducted in different countries of Europe. 342p. *12°. Edinburgh, Glasgow, &c.,* 1829.

25919 WEST OF ENGLAND FIRE AND LIFE INSURANCE COMPANY. Proposals and rates of the West of England Fire and Life Insurance Company, established in Exeter, 1807. Empowered by Act of Parliament, 1813. Capital, £600,000. Office for the Metropolis, No. 20, New Bridge-Street, Blackfriars. 24p. *8°. Exeter,* 1829.

25920 WESTERN, C. C., *Baron Western.* A letter on the present distress of the country, addressed to his constituents by Charles Callis Western, Esq. M.P. for the County of Essex. 15p. *8°. Chelmsford,* 1829.

TRANSPORT

25921 BRADSHAW, G. Appendix to G. Bradshaw's map of the canals... p.[5]–20. *8°.* 1829. *The Rastrick copy. Bound by Rastrick with his copies of Bradshaw's* Lengths and levels *to accompany the southern and northern maps, and continuously paged by him in manuscript, with manuscript notes in his hand throughout.*

25922 [CAREY, M.] Internal improvement. [On the canals of Pennsylvania. Signed: Hamilton.] 4p. *8°. n.p.* [1829]

25923 CLELAND, J. Report relative to the proposed road to connect the Inchbelly Bridge road with the Garscube road, on the east near the Monkland coal basin and the termination of the Garnkirk Railway, and on the west opposite to Sauchiehall Street. 6p. *4°. Glasgow,* 1829. *The Rastrick copy.*

25924 CUBITT, Sir W. A report and estimate, on the River Waveney, between Beccles Bridge and Oulton Dyke, towards making Beccles a port. Accompanied with a map of the navigation from Beccles to the intended new harbour at Lowestoft. 12p. *8°. Beccles,* 1829.

25925 ENGLAND. *Laws, etc.* Tricesimo secundo Georgii II. Regis. [Private Acts.] Cap. 2. An Act to enable ...Francis Duke of Bridgewater to make a navigable cut or canal from a certain place in the township of Salford to ...Worsley Mill and Middlewood in the manor of Worsley, and to or near...Hollin Ferry, in the County

Palatine of Lancaster. 23p. *fol.* 1829. *For another edition, see* 1759.

25926 —— —— Anno nono Georgii IV. Regis. Cap. vii. An Act to enable the Company of Proprietors of the Liverpool and Manchester Railway to alter the line of the said railway, and for amending...the powers...of the several Acts relating thereto. ⟨26th March 1828.⟩ p.89–98. *fol.* 1829. *See note to no.* 25927, *below.*

25927 —— —— Anno decimo Georgii IV. Regis. Cap. xxxv. An Act for enabling the Liverpool and Manchester Railway Company to make an alteration in the line of the said railway, and for amending...the powers...of the several Acts relating thereto. ⟨14th May 1829.⟩ p.601–624. *fol.* 1829. *The Act is followed by an 8-page index to the four Acts in the volume (the others being 7 Geo. IV. c.xlix, 7 & 8 Geo. IV. c.xxi, 9 Geo. IV. c.vii). The sections of all the Acts are numbered in manuscript in a single sequence to correspond with the references in the index.*

25928 —— 10 Geo. IV. – Sess. 1829. [Local & Personal, c.lxxviii.] An Act for more effectually repairing the road from James Deeping Stone Bridge to Peter's Gate in Stamford, in the county of Lincoln, and from thence to the south end of the town of Morcott, in the county of Rutland. ⟨Royal Assent, 22 May 1829.⟩ 8p. *fol. n.p.* [1829] *Endorsed: Deeping and Morcott Road. An Act...*

25929 —— Parliament. *House of Commons.* Copy of the

evidence, taken before a Committee of the House of Commons, on the Newcastle & Carlisle Railway Bill... Taken from the short hand notes of Mr. Gurney. To which is added the report of Mr. Leather, on the projected line of railway. 229p. *8°. Newcastle upon Tyne, 1829.*

25930 GIBBS, F. F. Remarks on the importance of the free navigation of the Rhine, as connected with the commerce of this country. And on the advantages which may be derived from employing steam power, as a medium of intercourse between London and Cologne. Addressed to merchants and capitalists. 27p. *8°. 1829.*

25931 GRAINGER, T. and **MILLER,** JOHN, *engineer.* Report of a survey undertaken for the purpose of ascertaining the line by which the best road from the city of Glasgow to Ayrshire...is to be obtained: with an appendix, containing the names of the owners and occupiers of the ground along which it is intended to carry the trunk line and branches... 35p. *4°. Edinburgh, Glasgow, &c., 1829. The Rastrick copy.*

25932 HILL, THOMAS (*fl.* 1827–1829). A supplement to the short treatise on rail-roads generally; explaining particularly the Liverpool and Manchester: also, the Leeds, Selby, and Hull rail-roads; the consequent great change that will be effected by them on property, with respect to innkeepers, coach proprietors...and which will shew that horse-power is...preferable, and more expeditious than locomotive engines...upon these lines of road... 16p. *8°. Leeds, 1829. For the author's* Treatise, *see* 1827.

25933 IMPERIAL SHIP CANAL COMPANY. Prospectus of the Imperial Ship Canal Company. [4]p. *fol. [London, 1829?]*

25934 JACKSON, WILLIAM (1783–1855). A lecture on rail roads, delivered January 12, 1829, before the Massachusetts Charitable Mechanic Association...Second edition. 36p. *12°. Boston, 1829.*

25935 MACQUISTEN, P. To the trustees and others interested in the proposed new approach from the two great north roads to the city of Glasgow. 6p. *4°. [Glasgow, 1829] The Rastrick copy.*

25936 PATERSON, D. Paterson's roads; being an entirely original and accurate description of all the direct and principal cross roads in England and Wales, with part of the roads of Scotland. The eighteenth edition...The whole, remodelled, augmented, and improved...By Edward Mogg. [With an appendix.] 82, 715, 44p. *8°. [1829] For other editions, see* 1771.

25937 RASTRICK, JOHN U. (1780–1858). Liverpool and Manchester Railway. Report to the Directors on the comparative merits of loco-motive & fixed engines, as a moving power...Second edition, corrected. 46p. *8°. Birmingham & London, 1829. The Rastrick copy. For another edition, see no.* 25941.

25938 STATEMENT by the committee appointed upon the line of road between Caitha, in the county of Roxburgh, by Jedburgh, and the Carter Fell, to Newcastle...[With 'Report by Mr. M'Adam to the subscribers', 'Forms of subscription papers' and minutes of meetings on the subject of the road held between 13 Jan. and 2 Feb., 1829.] 19p. *4°. n.p. [1829] The Rastrick copy.*

25939 STATEMENT respecting a northern approach to the city of Glasgow, along the line of Stirling's road. [With a report from Thomas Grainger and John Miller.] 4p. *4°. [Glasgow, 1829] The Rastrick copy.*

25940 TELFORD, T. Liverpool and Manchester Rail-way. Mr. Telford's report to the Commissioners for the Loan of Exchequer Bills. With observations in reply, by the Directors of the said rail-way. 16p. *8°. Liverpool, 1829. The Rastrick copy.*

25941 WALKER, JAMES (1781–1861). Liverpool and Manchester Railway. Report to the Directors on the comparative merits of locomotive & fixed engines, as a moving power. By Jas. Walker and J. U. Rastrick, Esqrs. civil engineers. 80p. *8°. Liverpool, 1829. For another edition of Rastrick's report, see no.* 25937.

25942 WOOLRYCH, H. W. A treatise on the law of ways, including highways, turnpike roads and tolls, private rights of way, bridges, and ferries. 395p. *8°. 1829.*

SOCIAL CONDITIONS

25943 An **ACCOUNT** of memorials presented to Congress during its last session, by numerous friends of their country and its institutions; praying that mails may not be transported, nor post-offices kept open, on the sabbath. 32p. *8°. Boston, 1829.*

25944 AMERICAN TEMPERANCE SOCIETY. Second annual report of the Executive Committee of the American Society for the Promotion of Temperance. Presented Jan. 28, 1829. 64p. *8°. Andover [Mass.], 1829. For editions of the 4th–9th annual reports see* 1835 *(Permanent temperance documents...).*

25945 ASSOCIATED CATHOLIC CHARITIES. Annual report presented...June 1st, 1829. 24p. *12°. n.p., 1829. See also* 1815, 1830.

25946 BOSWORTH, J. The necessity of the anti-pauper system, shewn by an example of the oppression and misery produced by the allowance system, which paralizes the beneficial operation of friendly societies, savings banks...and every other means of ameliorating

the condition of the poor... 50p. *8°. 1829. The copy that belonged to William Allen. An abstract of this work, entitled* Misery in the midst of plenty *was published in 1833 (q.v.).*

25947 *BURGOYNE, M. An address to the governors and directors of the public charity schools, pointing out some defects, and suggesting remedies. 42p. *8°. London & Brighton, 1829. See also* 1831.

25948 [CAREY, M.] Infant schools. [A description of the infant schools of Philadelphia. Signed: Hamilton.] 3p. *8°. n.p. [1829]*

25949 [——] Wages of female labour. [2]p. *s.sh.4°. n.p. [1829] [Br.* 505(1)]

25950 COBBETT, W. Advice to young men and (incidentally) to young women, in the middle and higher ranks of life. In a series of letters... [388]p. *12°. 1829. See also* 1837.

25951 —— The poor man's friend; or, essays on the

rights and duties of the poor. [Nos. I–v.] [120]p. *12⁰*. 1829. *For other editions, see* 1826.

25952 COMMITTEE APPOINTED FOR CONSIDERING THE BEST MEANS TO AFFORD RELIEF TO THE WORKING MANUFACTURERS. Report of the Committee appointed ...the 2nd of May, 1826, for considering the best means to afford relief to the "working manufacturers" suffering distress through want of employment. With an appendix. 118p. *8⁰*. 1829. *The copy presented to William Allen by the secretary to the committee, W. H. Hyett.*

25953 COOKE, EDWARD (1792?–1862). An inquiry into the state of the law of debtor and creditor in England: with reference to the expediency of allowing arrest for debt, as well upon mesne process, as in execution; and of discharging insolvents from actual custody. To which are added, suggestions for altering and improving some of the practical details of the existing system. 76p. *8⁰*. 1829.

25954 DALY, R., *Bishop of Cashel*. A letter to the editor of the Christian Examiner, on the subject of a legal provision for the poor of Ireland. 20p. *8⁰*. Dublin, 1829.

25955 DAVENPORT, RUFUS. Memorial of [*blank*] (added to the petition) for the free-debt-rules, addressed to the Legislature of the State of [*blank*], one of the United States of America. [Signed: Rufus Davenport, and dated 1828, Dec. 1st.] [4]p. *8⁰*. *n.p.* [1829]

25956 —— Memorial of [*blank*] (added to the petition) for the free-debt-rules, addressed United States of America, A.D.1829 to the Hon. the Senate and House of Representatives in Congress assembled. [Signed: Rufus Davenport.] [4]p. *8⁰*. *n.p.* [1829]

25957 DETROSIER, R. An address delivered at the new Mechanic's Institution, Pool-Street, Manchester, on ...December 30, 1829. 20p. *8⁰*. Manchester, [1829]

25958 DUCHÂTEL, C. M. T., *Comte*. De la charité, dans ses rapports avec l'état moral et le bien-être des classes inférieures de la société. 431p. *8⁰*. Paris, 1829.

25959 ENGLAND. *Commissioners for Inquiring concerning Charities*. The endowed charities of the City of London; reprinted at large from seventeen Reports of the Commissioners for Inquiring concerning Charities. With a copious index. 687p. *8⁰*. 1829.

25960 —— *Parliament*. [*Endorsed:*] Lambeth improvement. An Act [a Bill] for watching, lighting, cleansing and otherwise improving the roads, streets, and other public passages and places within the district left as belonging to the original parish church of Saint Mary Lambeth, in the county of Surrey, and the ecclesiastical district called the Waterloo district in the same parish. 10 Geo. IV. sess. 1829. 80p. *fol.* [*London*, 1829]

25961 FITZ-JOHN, W. 1829, or the present times; a poem, illustrative of the unexampled distresses in the manufacturing districts. 12p. *8⁰*. Huddersfield, [1829] *The Oastler copy.*

25962 FRIENDLY BREAD ASSOCIATION. [*Endorsed:*] Regulations of the...Association, adopted at their first annual meeting, held at Glasgow, the 8th day of March, 1825. [With 'Appendix. Additional regulations passed since the date of the formation of the Association'. Five regulations, the last one dated: '1829 – 11th August'.] *s.sh.fol. n.p.* [1829]

25963 HACKNEY FRIENDLY INSTITUTION. Rules and tables of the...Institution. Enrolled ...1829. 34p. *8⁰*. Hackney, [1829]

25964 HAWORTH, B. A dissertation on the English poor, stating the advantages of education; with a plan for the gradual abolition of the poor laws. 104p. *8⁰*. 1829.

For **HIBBERT,** J., Advice to labourers, *see* vol. III, *Periodicals list*, Advice to labourers.

25965 JOHNSTON, D. A general, medical, and statistical history of the present condition of public charity in France; comprising a detailed account of all establishments destined for the sick, the aged, and the infirm, for children and for lunatics, with a view of the extent of pauperism and mendicity... 605p. *8⁰*. Edinburgh & London, 1829.

25966 KENNEDY, L. On the cultivation of the waste lands in the United Kingdom, for the purpose of finding employment for the able poor...and on the expediency of making some provision for the aged and disabled paupers of Ireland. 66p. *8⁰*. 1829. *Presentation copy from the author to John Dundas, Esq.*

25967 KINAHAN, D. An outline of a plan for relieving the poor of Ireland, by an assessment on property. 32p. *8⁰*. Dublin, 1829.

25968 McKEON, H. An inquiry into the rights of the poor, of the parish of Lavenham, in Suffolk, with historical notes & observations...To which are added biographical sketches of some of the...natives of Lavenham ...134p. *8⁰*. London, Woodbridge, &c., 1829.

25969 MARSH, J. Putnam and the wolf; or, the monster destroyed. An address delivered at Pomfret, Con., October 28, 1829, before the Windham Co. Temperance Society. 24p. *12⁰*. Hartford, 1829.

25970 MELLOR, J. A letter to Lord Milton and Richard Otway Cave, Esq., Members of Parliament; on the present distress of the country, and on scarcity of work and the present low rate of wages. 4p. *8⁰*. *n.p.* [1829] *The Oastler copy.*

25971 MINCHINHAMPTON FRIENDLY INSTITUTION. The rules and regulations, and the tables of payments and allowances, of the Friendly Institution established at Minchinhampton...enrolled on the 20th day of October, 1829... 59p. *8⁰*. 1829.

25972 OBSERVATOR, *pseud*. The Tommy, or truck system, exposed, in three letters to the editor of the Birmingham Journal. [The first and third signed: Observator, the second, a reply to the first, signed: Fair Dealing.] 15p. *8⁰*. Dudley, [1829] *The copy that belonged to M. T. Sadler.*

25973 P., T. From the United States Gazette, Feb. 25, 1829. Solitary confinement. 2p. *8⁰*. *n.p.* [1829]

25974 PAGE, FREDERICK. The principle of the English poor laws illustrated and defended, by an historical view of indigence in civil society...Second edition, with additions. 130p. *8⁰*. London & Dublin, 1829. *For other editions, see* 1822.

25975 PEMBROKE OLD UNION SOCIETY. Rules, to be observed by a society of tradesmen and inhabitants called the Pembroke Old Union Society... begun at the King's-Arms...Nov. 6th, 1770. 14p. *8⁰*. Pembroke, [1829]

25976 New POLICE ACT. Full particulars of Mr. Peel's new Police Act...exemplified in a conversation between three persons...two of them watchmen, and the third I discovered was one of those gentlemen who keep

an oyster shop and converts it into other purposes...
s.sh.fol. [*London:*] *J. Catnach*, [1829] [*Br.* 506]

25977 PRICE, H. A verbatim report of the trial of the Rev. Humphrey Price...upon a criminal information... by the Kidderminster carpet manufacturers, for alleged inflammatory publications during the "turn-out" of the weavers in 1828... 88p. *8°.* 1829.

25978 A REPORT of the proceedings of a delegate meeting, of the operative spinners of England, Ireland and Scotland, assembled at Ramsey, Isle of Man, on Saturday, December 5, 1829, and three following days. [Signed: John Doherty, secretary.] 56p. *8°. Manchester*, [1829] *The copy that belonged to Francis Place.*

25979 SHAWS WATER JOINT STOCK COMPANY. A brief account of the Shaws Water scheme, and present state of the works: with copies of the feu charter...and...a letter from Mr. Thom, to Sir M. Shaw Stewart, on the principles of filtration... 88p. *8°. Greenock,* 1829.

25980 SOCIETY FOR BETTERING THE CONDITION OF THE POOR, *Clapham.* Rules and regulations of the Society...Instituted February 11, 1799. To which is prefixed an account of the origin and designs of the Society. 32p. *12°. Clapham,* 1829. *See also* 1805.

25981 THOMAS, JOHN P. Reports of two speeches against the establishment of mechanics' institutions at Rotherhithe and Southwark. 24p. *8°. n.p.,* 1829.

25982 TUNNARD, C. K. Employment of the poor. An address to the Grand Jury of the hundreds of Kirton and Skirbeck, in the parts of Holland...at the General Quarter Sessions of the Peace, held at Boston, October 20th, 1829... 15p. *8°. Boston* [*Lincs.*] *& London,* 1829.

25983 The WATER QUESTION. Animadversions on the reports, evidence, and documents relative to the supply of water to the Metropolis, published by order of the...House of Commons. By a water drinker. 94p. *8°.* 1829. *Presentation copy, from the anonymous author, to Sir Francis Burdett (see also note to no.* 22542).

25984 WHITE, JOHN M. Some remarks on the statute law affecting parish apprentices, with regulations applicable to local districts and parishes, for allotting and placing out poor children, in conformity to the 43 Eliz., c. 2, and subsequent statutes. 104p. *8°. Halesworth & London,* 1829. *The copy that belonged to Richard Whately, Archbishop of Dublin.*

25985 WILLIAMS, CADOGAN. Some suggestions for the improvement of benefit clubs, and assurances for the lower classes, founded on the reasoning of a petition presented by the late D. Ricardo, Esq. to the House of Commons, for the author...Also suggestions for a modification of the poor laws. With remarks on the comparative situation of the landholder and the fundholder... 31p. *8°.* 1829.

25986 WILSON, HARRY B. A second letter to the parishioners of St. Thomas the Apostle, in the City of London. To which is prefixed the report of His Majesty's Commissioners for Inquiring Concerning Charities, so far as relates to charitable devises, &c. in the parish of St. Thomas the Apostle. 23p. *4°.* 1829. *With an accompanying letter from the author to Hon. George Agar Ellis, afterwards Baron Dover.*

25987 WRIGHT, JAMES. A treatise on the internal regulations of friendly societies...also a code of rules: with forms, for the use of magistrates in questions relative to such societies...To which is added, an appeal to the Right Hon. Lord J. Russell, M.P. on the present state of the law...with practical suggestions of improvement: with a copious index. And the substance of the new Bill now before Parliament. 290p. *12°.* [1829]

SLAVERY

25988 *Entry cancelled.*

25989 CLARKSON, T. and **GREENE**, B. Slavery, as it now exists in the British West Indian colonies, discussed in a series of letters between Thomas Clarkson... and Benjamin Greene... 151p. *8°.* 1829.

25990 COMMON SENSE, *pseud.* Common Sense to John Bull; a friendly remonstrance. [In verse, signed: Common Sense.] 23p. *12°. Leicester,* [*London,*] *&c.,* 1829.

25991 The DEATH WARRANT of negro slavery throughout the British Dominions. [Reprints of articles from the *Edinburgh Review* and the *Westminster Review.*] 38p. *8°.* 1829. *The Agar Ellis copy.*

25992 E. Observations on the Demerara memorial, and on the false assumption, that enslaved British subjects are legal chattels. In a letter from a gentleman in the country, to his friend in London. [Second edition.] 73p. *8°.* 1829. *For another edition, see* 1828.

25993 Plain **FACTS.** By the author of "Honesty the best policy." 8p. *8°. Leicester,* [1829]

25994 INQUIRIES relating to negro emancipation. 99p. *8°.* 1829.

25995 KINGSLEY, Z. A treatise on the patriarchal, or co-operative system of society as it exists in some governments...in America, and in the United States, under the name of slavery, with its necessity and advantages. By an inhabitant of Florida. Second edition. 16p. *8°. n.p.,* 1829. *See also* 1834.

25996 LETTER to the Duke of Wellington, on the subject of West India slavery, by a Jamaica proprietor. 23p. *8°.* 1829.

25997 The wonderful **LIFE** and adventures of Three-fingered Jack, the terror of Jamaica! Giving an account of his...courage...in revenging the cause of his injured parents... 28p. *12°.* 1829.

25998 OBSERVATIONS upon the state of negro slavery, in the island of Santa Cruz, the principal of the Danish West India colonies; with miscellaneous remarks upon subjects relating to the West India question, and a notice of Santa Cruz. 113p. *8°.* 1829.

25999 An **ORATION,** pronounced on the 29th of July, 1829, after the funeral dirge of Doctor John Baptista

Philip, who died on the 16th of June, 1829, in Trinidad. Dedicated to his family by a friend. 30p. 8°. [1829]

26000 PENNOCK, . Reasons for using our utmost exertions to procure the abolition of slavery. An extract from the speech of the Rev. Mr. Pennock...Taken from the Newcastle Courant, of May 2, 1829. 4p. 8°. [1829]

26001 [POWNALL, H.] A word from the Bible, Common Prayer Book, and laws of England, on behalf of enslaved British subjects; with suggestions for securing the liberty of future children; and proofs of the beneficial effects of emancipation. In a letter to a friend [signed: H.P.]. 57p. 8°. 1829.

26002 RILAND, J. Letter addressed to a clerical advocate of the British & Foreign Bible, Church Missionary, and Hibernian Societies, on the intimate connexion of those and similar institutions with the abolition of colonial slavery. 12p. 8°. 1829.

26003 SAINTSBURY, G. East India slavery. 40p.

8°. 1829. *Presentation copy, with inscription, from the author to the editor of the Morning Post.*

26004 A SKETCH of the African slave trade, and the slavery of the negroes under their Christian masters, in the European colonies. Compiled from various authors of undoubted authority. 4p. 8°. [1829 ?]

26005 SOCIETY FOR THE ABOLITION OF SLAVERY THROUGHOUT THE BRITISH DOMINIONS. Account of the receipts & disbursements of the Anti-Slavery Society, for the years 1827 & 1828: with a list of the subscribers. 16p. 8°. [1829] *See also* 1827, 1831, 1832.

26006 THOMSON, ANDREW. Slavery not sanctioned, but condemned, by Christianity: a sermon. 24p. 8°. [1829]

26007 WEST INDIAN SLAVERY traced to its actual source; with remarks, illustrative of the present state of colonial affairs. And an appeal for sympathy and consideration. Second edition. 24p. *12°.* 1829.

POLITICS

For the **CHANTICLEER**, *see vol.* III, *Periodicals list.*

26008 DELAVAU, and **FRANCHET,** . Le livre noir de Messieurs Delavau et Franchet, ou répertoire alphabétique de la police politique sous le ministère déplorable; ouvrage imprimé d'après les registres de l'administration; précédé d'une introduction, par M. Année. Deuxième édition. 4 vols. 8°. *Paris,* 1829.

26009 ENGLAND. *Parliament.* The new Magna Charta, or historical record of the debates and proceedings in both Houses of Parliament, on the settlement of the Catholic claims in 1829. To which is added an appendix of valuable documents...Second edition... 32p. *fol.* [*London,*] 1829.

26010 FABER, G. S. The Rev. G. S. Faber's four letters to the editor of the "St. James's Chronicle," on Catholic emancipation. [8]p. 8°. [*London,* 1829]

26011 HOBHOUSE, J. C., *Baron Broughton.* The speech of John Cam Hobhouse, Esq. M.P. for Westminster, in answer to Cobbett, at the purity of election dinner, Crown and Anchor Tavern, 25 May, 1829. 8p. 8°. 1829. *The copy that belonged to M. T. Sadler.*

26012 [HONE, W.] Poor Humphrey's calendar... Prophecies concerning the signs of the times...in 1829... The second edition. [A fictitious almanack.] 51p. 8°. [1829]

26013 KNIGHT, HENRY G. A letter addressed to the Earl of Aberdeen, Secretary of State for Foreign Affairs... Second edition. 43p. 8°. 1829. *The Agar Ellis copy.*

26014 LEFROY, T. L. Report of the speech delivered by Mr. Sergeant Lefroy, at the second general meeting of the Brunswick Constitutional Club of Ireland...19th February, 1829. [Against Catholic emancipation.] 15p. 8°. *Dublin,* 1829.

26015 MONCREIFF, SIR J. W., *Bart., Lord Moncreiff, and others.* Report (taken from the Caledonian Mercury) of the speeches of Sir James W. Moncrieff... Dr. Chalmers and other distinguished individuals, at a meeting held in the Assembly Rooms on...the 14th

March, 1829, in order to petition Parliament for the removal of the disabilities affecting the Roman Catholics. 24p. 8°. *n.p.* [1829]

26016 NEWARK. A report of the proceedings at Newark, on...July 24, 1829, when the electors of the borough gave a dinner in compliment to their members, H. Willoughby, Esq. and M. T. Sadler, Esq.... 8p. 8°. *Newark,* [1829] *The copy that belonged to M. T. Sadler.*

26017 O'CONNELL, D. A letter to the members of the House of Commons of the United Kingdom...[stating his intention to take his seat in Parliament]. 29p. 8°. 1829.

26018 —— A letter to the members of the House of Commons...on the legal right of Roman Catholics to sit in Parliament; to which is added a reply to Edward Burtenshaw Sugden. 37p. 8°. 1829.

26019 PAGET, H. W., *Marquess of Anglesey.* Speech of the Marquess of Anglesey, K.G. in the House of Lords on...the 4th of May, 1829, on moving for papers relative to his recall from the government of Ireland. 75p. 8°. 1829.

26020 PEEL, SIR ROBERT, *2nd Bart.* By permission. The speech of the Right Honourable Mr. Secretary Peel, on...5th of March, 1829, on moving the appointment of a committee to enquire into the disabilities affecting His Majesty's Roman Catholic subjects. 86p. 8°. 1829.

26021 SADLER, M. T. The speech of Michael Thomas Sadler, Esq., M.P. in the House of Commons; on the second reading of the Roman Catholic Relief Bill, March 17, 1829. Fourth edition. 19p. 8°. [1829]

26022 SHANNON, R. Q. An address to the clergy of the United Church of England and Ireland, on behalf of the Roman Catholic claims; exposing the culpability and danger of resisting those claims and suggesting a plan for their immediate settlement. 80p. 8°. *London & Edinburgh,* 1829.

26023 STANLEY, EDWARD, *Bishop of Norwich.* A few words in favour of our Roman Catholic brethren: an address to his parishioners...Second edition. 16p. 8°. *London & Macclesfield,* [1829]

26024 TEMPLE, H. J., *Viscount Palmerston.* Speech of Viscount Palmerston, in the House of Commons on… the first of June, 1829, upon the motion of Sir James Macintosh [*sic*], respecting the relations of England with Portugal. 45p. *8°.* [1829]

26025 TENNYSON, afterwards **D'EYNCOURT,** C. Speech of Charles Tennyson Esq., in the House of Commons, May 19, 1828, on Mr. Nicholson Calvert's motion to substitute the Hundred of Bassetlaw for the town of Birmingham in the Bill for disfranchising the borough of East Retford. Third edition. 41p. *8°.* 1829.

26026 [THOMPSON, THOMAS P.] Catholic state waggon. ⟨From the Westminster Review, no. XIX, published Jan. 31, 1829.⟩ 16p. *8°.* 1829.

26027 [——] [Another edition.] 16p. *8°.* 1829. *See note to no.* 25779.

26028 THOMSON, R. An historical essay on the Magna Charta of King John: to which are added, the Great Charter in Latin and English; the charters of liberties and confirmations, granted by Henry III. and Edward I.; the original Charter of the Forests… 612p. *8°.* 1829.

26029 UNIVERSITY OF OXFORD. An authentic copy of the poll for a member to serve in the present Parliament for the University of Oxford…taken on… 26th…27th and…28th of February, MDCCCXXIX. Candidates. The Right Hon. Robert Peel, D.C.L. of Ch. Ch. Sir Robert Harry Inglis, Bart. D.C.L. of Ch. Ch. By authority of the Vice-Chancellor. 41p. *8°.* Oxford, 1829.

26030 WICKENS, W. An argument for more of the division of labour in civil life in this country. Part I. In which the argument is applied to Parliament. 182p. *8°.* 1829.

SOCIALISM

For the **ASSOCIATE,** *continued as* the Associate and co-operative mirror, 1829–30, *see* vol. III, *Periodicals list.*

For the **BIRMINGHAM CO-OPERATIVE HERALD,** 1829–30, *see* vol. III, *Periodicals list.*

26031 BRITISH ASSOCIATION FOR PROMOTING CO-OPERATIVE KNOWLEDGE. Report of the proceedings at the second quarterly meeting of the Society for the Promotion of Co-operative Knowledge, October 8th, 1829. ⟨Reprinted from the Weekly Free Press.⟩ 20p. *12°.* [1829] *See also* 1830.

26032 CAMPBELL, ALEXANDER (1788–1866), *ed.* Debate on the evidences of Christianity; containing an examination of the "social system," and of all the systems of scepticism of ancient and modern times. Held in… Cincinnati, Ohio, from the 13th to the 21st of April, 1829; between Robert Owen, and Alexander Campbell… Reported by Charles H. Sims…With an appendix, written by the parties. [With 'Proposals, by Alexander Campbell, for publishing by subscription, a monthly paper, to be denominated The Millennial harbinger'.] 2 vols. *12°.* Bethany, Va., 1829. *See also* 1839.

26033 CO-OPERATIVE SOCIETIES. To the working classes. [Dated: Carlisle, 18th August, 1829.] *s.sh.fol. n.p.* [1829] *Bound in a volume of newspaper cuttings relating to Owenite co-operation, the majority from The Weekly Free Press, which was compiled by William Pare.*

26034 FOURIER, F. C. M. Le nouveau monde industriel et sociétaire…Prospectus. 8p. *8°.* Besançon, [1829] *The copy that belonged to Victor Considérant.*

26035 —— Le nouveau monde industriel et sociétaire, ou invention du procédé d'industrie attrayante et naturelle distribuée en séries passionées. 576p. *8°.* Paris, 1829. *The copy that belonged to Victor Considérant. See also* 1830.

For the **FREE INQUIRER,** 1829–31, *see* vol. III, *Periodicals list.*

26036 A LETTER to the Rev. W. L. Pope, Tunbridge Wells, in reply to two sermons preached by him on the subject of co-operation. [Signed: A friend to co-operation, and dated, December 1829.] 4p. *8°.* Tunbridge Wells, [1829]

26037 OWEN, ROBERT. Robert Owen's opening speech, and his reply to the Rev. Alex. Campbell, in the recent public discussion in Cincinnati; to prove that the principles of all religions are erroneous…Also Mr. Owen's Memorial to the Republic of Mexico, and a narrative of the proceedings thereon… 226p. *8°.* Cincinnati, 1829. *For another edition of the* Memorial, *see* 1828.

26038 *PARE, W. An address to the working classes of Liverpool…on the formation of co-operative societies, or working unions… 12p. *12°.* Liverpool, [1829] *The FWA copy that belonged to the author.*

26039 SKIDMORE, T. The rights of man to property! Being a proposition to make it equal among the adults of the present generation: and to provide for its equal transmission to every individual of each succeeding generation, on arriving at the age of maturity… 405p. *12°.* New-York, 1829.

26040 WRIGHT, F. Course of popular lectures… With three addresses, on various public occasions. And a reply to the charges against the French reformers of 1789. Second edition. 239p. *8°.* New-York, 1829. *See also* 1835, 1836.

26041 —— A lecture on existing evils and their remedy: as delivered in the Arch Street Theatre, to the citizens of Philadelphia, June 2, 1829. 16p. *8°.* New York, 1829. *Also printed in the collected edition, no.* 26040, *above.*

MISCELLANEOUS

26042 CLARK, CHARLES (*fl.* 1829). Exposure of abuses and malpractices at that institution, called the Royal Veterinary College, stating the injurious effects of its corrupt influence on the veterinary profession and the public at large, with a letter addressed to the King as patron. 56p. *8°.* 1829.

26043 COBBETT, W. A grammar of the English language, in a series of letters. Intended for the use of schools and of young persons in general; but more especially for the use of soldiers, sailors, apprentices, and plough-boys... To which are added, six lessons, intended to prevent statesman from using false grammar... [240]p. *12°. 1829. For other editions, see 1819.*

26044 COOPER, B. B. Report of the trial, Cooper versus Wakley, for libel [following comments in the *Lancet* reflecting on the plaintiff's competence as a surgeon at Guy's Hospital]... With remarks on the evidence, by Bransby B. Cooper. 182p. *8°. London, Edinburgh, &c.,* 1829.

26045 DALE, T. University of London. An introductory lecture upon the study of theology and of the Greek Testament, delivered at the opening of the Theological Institution, Saturday, Nov. 21st, 1829. 38p. *8°.* 1829.

26046 FELTON, S. Gleanings on gardens, chiefly respecting those of the ancient style in England. 72p. *8°.* 1829.

26047 The FREEHOLDER. Part 1. Containing twelve letters, written originally for the Lichfield Mercury, from March 13 to May 29, 1829. [Letters I, V–VIII, XII only.] 7, 8, 7, 7, 7, 8p. *8°. Lichfield,* 1829. *Published in parts.*

26048 FRENCH, D. French versus Cobbett. Cobbett on the gridiron!! (grilled to a cinder!). Being an answer to Cobbett's Register of October 3, 1829. 24p. *8°. [London,* 1829]

26049 GRENVILLE, W. W., *Baron Grenville.* Oxford and Locke. [A vindication of the University from the charge of having expelled Locke.] 87p. *8°.* 1829. *Presentation copy from the author to the 7th Baron King.*

26050 HAYDON, B. R. Some enquiry into the causes which have obstructed the advance of historical painting for the last seventy years in England. 36p. *8°.* 1829. *Presentation copy, with an autograph letter from the author, to George Agar Ellis, afterwards Baron Dover.*

26051 HEATH, JOHN B., *Baron Heath.* Some account of the Worshipful Company of Grocers, of the City of London. 358p. *8°.* 1829.

26052 MIDOSI, P. Who is the legitimate King of Portugal? A Portuguese question submitted to impartial men. 91p. *8°. Plymouth,* 1829.

26053 A few REMARKS on the expediency and justice of emancipating the Jews, addressed to His Grace the Duke of Wellington... 82p. *8°.* 1829.

26054 ROYAL ASIATIC SOCIETY. Committee of Correspondence of the Royal Asiatic Society of Great Britain and Ireland. [Consisting of a prospectus, and a discourse by H. T. Colebrooke, the director.] 14p. *8°.* 1829.

26055 STEELE, T. An analytical exposition of the absurdity and iniquity of the oaths, when taken by Protestants, or any other sects of Christians, that the sacrifice of the Mass and the invocation of saints are superstitious, idolatrous and damnable. 79p. *8°.* 1829.

26056 *Entry cancelled.*

26057 ZOOLOGICAL SOCIETY. Report of the Council of the Zoological Society of London, read at the anniversary meeting, April 29, 1829. 21p. *8°.* 1829. *The Agar Ellis copy.*

1830

GENERAL

26058 ASSER, J. Communications to T. G. Bramston, Esq. M.P. and members of both Houses, for preventing frauds to the manufacturers and growers of wheat. 8p. *8°.* 1830.

26059 BADNALL, R. Letter to the Lords and Commons, on the present commercial and agricultural condition of Great Britain. 191p. *8°. London & Liverpool,* 1830.

26060 BAINES, SIR EDWARD. On the moral influence of free trade, and its effects on the prosperity of nations: a paper read before the Leeds Philosophical and Literary Society, on the 19th February, 1830. 56p. *8°. London & Leeds,* 1830.

26061 *BEAUMONT, JOHN T. B. Thoughts on the causes and cure of the present distresses; with a plan of parliamentary reform. 74p. *8°.* 1830. *The copy that belonged to George Grote, with a manuscript comment on the title-page: 'with many gross absurdities, frequently before published'.*

26062 BEDDOME, J. The British Empire on the brink of ruin. Second edition, enlarged. 8p. *4°. Manchester,*

[1830] *The Oastler copy, with manuscript notes in the margins, signed: R.O.*

26063 BENTHAM, J. Official aptitude maximized; expense minimized: as shewn in the several papers comprised in this volume. xxix, 22, 68, 27, 160, 62, 85, 24, 10, 13p. *8°.* 1830.

26064 BICHENO, J. E. Ireland and its economy; being the result of observations made in a tour through the country in... 1829. 308p. *8°.* 1830.

26065 BRAZIL. *Ministerio d'Estado dos Negocios Estrangeiros.* Relatorio do Ministro, e Secretario d'Estado dos negocias da Fazenda. Na sessão de 15 de Maio de 1830. [1012]p. *4°. Rio de Janeiro,* 1830.

26066 The BRITISH ALMANAC, of the Society for the Diffusion of Useful Knowledge, for... 1830. [With 'The companion to the Almanac; or year-book of general information'.] 72, 264p. *12°.* [1830] *For other editions, see 1828.*

26067 [CAREY, M.] Maxims for the promotion of the wealth of nations: being a manual of political economy, extracted from the writings of Franklin, Jefferson, Madison, Hamilton, Calhoun, Judge Cooper, Adam Smith, J. Baptiste Say, Anderson, &c.&c. [The preface is signed: Hamilton.] 32p. *12°. Philadelphia*, 1830.

26068 —— Miscellaneous essays: containing, among a variety of other articles, History of the yellow fever...in Philadelphia in...1793...Review of the evidence of the pretended general conspiracy of the Roman Catholics of Ireland...1641. Reflections on...emigration from Europe ...Essays on the public charities of Philadelphia... 472p. *8°. Philadelphia*, 1830. *Presentation copy from the author to Mrs. Juliana Miller.*

26069 [——] Prospects on and beyond the Rubicon. No. 1[–2]. [Signed: Hamilton.] 8p. *8°. n.p.* [1830] *For part 2 of this series, see 1832, and for the second series, see 1833.*

26070 [——] Thirteen essays on the policy of manufacturing in this country. From the New York Morning Herald. [Signed: Publicola.] 30p. *8°. Philadelphia*, 1830.

26071 CAYLEY, Edward S. On commercial economy, in six essays; viz. machinery, accumulation of capital, production, consumption, currency, and free trade. 260p. *8°.* 1830.

26072 COBBETT, James P. Journal of a tour in Italy, and also in part of France and Switzerland...from October 1828 to September, 1829... 329p. *12°.* 1830.

26073 COBBETT, W. The emigrant's guide; in ten letters, addressed to the tax-payers of England...including several authentic...letters from English emigrants, now in America, to their relations in England; and an account of the prices of house and land, recently obtained from America...A new edition. 168p. *12°.* 1830. *The second of two editions published in 1830. For another edition, see 1829.*

26074 —— Rural rides...With economical and political observations... 124, 45–668p. *12°.* 1830.

26075 COLLINS, S. H. The emigrant's guide to and description of the United States of America, including... letters from English emigrants now in America, to their friends in England...Fourth edition. 180p. *12°. Hull & London*, [1830?]

26076 COMPANION to the calendars, for...1830; being a list of all the changes in administration, from the commencement of the present century... 155p. *12°.* 1830. *For another edition, see 1819.*

26077 COMTE, I. A. M. F. X. Cours de philosophie positive. 6 vols. *8°. Paris*, 1830–42.

26078 COOKE, George A. A topographical and statistical description of the County of Wilts...To which is prefixed, a copious travelling guide...Also, a list of the markets and fairs...A new edition. 212p. *12°.* [*c.* 1830]

26079 COOPER, Thomas (1759–1839). Lectures on the elements of political economy...Second edition, with additions. [With 'The right of free discussion' and a list of the author's works.] 366, 17p. *8°. Columbia, S.C.*, 1829 [1830] *From internal evidence, it is clear that this edition was not published until 1830, and it is listed with this date in the bibliography of the author's writings at the end of the work. Presentation copy, with inscription, from the author to Jeremy Bentham, with a list of page references in Bentham's hand on a flyleaf. For another edition, see 1826.*

26080 CRAWFURD, John (1783–1868). Journal of an embassy from the Governor-General of India to the courts of Siam and Cochin-China; exhibiting a view of the actual state of those kingdoms...Second edition. 2 vols. *8°.* 1830.

26081 The **CRISIS** of Britain, in industry and finance; by one of the people. 132p. *8°.* 1830.

26082 DUNOYER, C. B. Nouveau traité d'économie sociale, ou simple exposition des causes sous l'influence desquelles les hommes parviennent à user de leurs forces avec le plus de liberté, c'est-à-dire avec le plus de facilité et de puissance. 2 vols. *8°. Paris*, 1830. *Presentation copy from the author, with an accompanying note on the circumstances of its publication, dated: 6 7bre 1840. The recipient's name was cut off when the volumes were bound.*

26083 EIGHT SEVEN, *pseud.* An antidote to revolution; or, a practical comment on the creation of privilege for quadrating the principles of consumption with production, and thereby creating stimulus for the unlimited production of national wealth, neutralizing the motives for political discontent, and establishing a solid base for the promotion of morality. 16p. *8°. Dublin*, 1830. *Presentation copy from the author to T. Spring Rice, Baron Monteagle.*

26084 —— Practicability of a legislative measure for harmonizing the conflicting interests of agriculture and manufactures, and by this means enabling Great Britain to obtain great additional benefits from her great resources. 16p. *8°. n.p.* [1830?]

26085 ESSAYS on the protecting system...I. Three of the addresses of the Philadelphia Society for the Promotion of National Industry...II. Essay on the maxims of free trade, promulgated by Adam Smith – From the London Quarterly Review. III. Essay on free trade – From Blackwood's Magazine...IV. Extract from a message of Governor Wolcott...[Edited by M. Carey?] p.1–14, 19–60. *8°. Philadelphia*, 1830. *Wanting part of the second and third, and all of the fourth Essay.*

26086 FAZY, J. J. Principes d'organisation industrielle pour le développement des richesses en France. Explication du malaise des classes productives et des moyens d'y porter remède. 294p. *8°. Paris*, 1830.

26087 GORDON, Adam J. Emigration and its evils; contrasted with the great and incalculable benefits which would arise from the cultivation of the waste lands of our colonies, and the importation of the corn and other produce into the mother country. Addressed to the National-Emigration Society. 16p. *8°.* [*London*, 1830] *The Agar Ellis copy.*

26088 [**GORE**, M.] A few brief hints on the causes of the present distress. 15p. *8°.* 1830.

26089 HAMILTON, Robert (1743–1829). The progress of society. 411p. *8°.* 1830.

For **HERALD TO THE TRADES' ADVOCATE**, 1830–31, *see vol.* III, *Periodicals list.*

26090 [**HICKEY**, W.] Hints addressed to the small holders and peasantry of Ireland, on road-making and on ventilation...By Martin Doyle... 88p. *12°. Dublin, London, &c.*, 1830. *See also no.* 26150.

26091 HOGENDORP, G. K. van, *Graaf.* Lettres sur la prosperité publique, adressées à un Belge dans les années 1828, 1829, 1830... 2 vols. *8°. Amsterdam*, 1830.

26092 HUGILL, J. An address to the inhabitants of Whitby and its vicinity: shewing the present declining state of the town...with a...plan for forming a company to ascertain...whether there is a bed of coal under our alum rock...and...observations on extending our commerce, by constructing a railway to Pickering and Malton. 70p. *8°. Whitby*, 1830.

26093 HUSKISSON, W. State of the country. Speech of the Right Hon. W. Huskisson in the House of Commons...18th of March, 1830; on Mr. E. D. Davenport's motion "That the petitions complaining of the distress of various classes of the community be referred to a Committee of the whole House...". 44p. *8°*. 1830. *The Agar Ellis copy.*

26094 ——— Speech...in the House of Commons, on...the 20th of May, 1830, on presenting the Liverpool petition, respecting our political and commercial relations with Mexico. 18p. *8°*. [1830]

26095 KING, PETER, *7th Baron King*. The life of John Locke, with extracts from his correspondence, journals, and common-place books...New edition. With considerable additions...[With 'Notes of domestic and foreign affairs' by P. King, 1st Baron King.] 2 vols. *8°*. 1830. *For another issue of* Notes of domestic and foreign affairs, *see no.* 26548.

26096 LUCAS, H. A letter to His present Majesty, (when Duke of Clarence,) during the illness of the late King; recommending...on the commencement of the new reign, a complete change of system, reduction of taxation, economy in the public expenditure; and submitting to His Royal Highness's consideration, a proclamation, for admitting Manchester, Birmingham...and all other large towns to be represented in Parliament, and for disfranchising all rotten boroughs. 15p. *8°. Liverpool*, 1830.

26097 McCULLOCH, JOHN R. The principles of political economy...Second edition, corrected and greatly enlarged. 563p. *8°. London, Edinburgh, &c.*, 1830. *For other editions, see* 1825.

26098 *MACHINERY versus manual labour. A letter to the Right Hon. Lord Grey, wherein is shown the justice and the expediency of taxing the produce of machinery in an equal proportion with the productive classes of the empire. [Dated: Nov. 30, 1830.] By a manufacturer. 7p. *8°. Loughborough & London*, [1830] *The FWA copy that belonged to William Pare.*

26099 M'KONOCHIE, J. Thoughts on the present crisis. 20p. *8°*. 1830.

26100 McVICKAR, J. Introductory lecture to a course of political economy; recently delivered at Columbia College, New York. 34p. *8°*. 1830. *The copy that belonged to T. Spring Rice, Baron Monteagle.*

For the **MORNING HERALD**, *see vol.* III, *Periodicals list.*

26101 MORRIS, W. A demonstration, that Great Britain and Ireland have resources to enrich the subjects of the state by manufacturing labor, through the medium of a free trade: which will necessarily supersede the collection of poor's rates...80p. *8°. London & Dublin*, 1830.

26102 MUNDELL, A. Tables, showing the amount, according to official and declared value, of every article of home produce and manufacture exported in every year, from 1814 to 1828. Also of leading articles of import. With observations. Forming a supplement to "Reasons for a revision of our fiscal code"...Second edition. 39p. *8°.*

1830. *For another edition, see* 1829, *and for the author's* Reasons for a revision of our fiscal code, *see* 1828.

26103 MUNTZ, G. F. Three letters to the Duke of Wellington, in 1829 and 1830, upon the distressed state of the country. 23p. *8°. Birmingham*, 1830.

26104 NATIONAL COLONIZATION SOCIETY. A statement of the principles and objects of a proposed national society, for the cure and prevention of pauperism, by means of systematic colonization. [With a prospectus of the Society and minutes of inaugural meetings, signed by Robert Gouger, the secretary.] 73p. *8°. Published for the Provisional Committee*, 1830. *The Agar Ellis copy.*

26105 NELKENBRECHER, J. C. Manuel universel à l'usage des negocians, banquiers, industriels, administrateurs, etc. ou traité des monnaies, poids et mesures et cours des changes, des principales villes de commerce...Traduit de l'allemand d'après la quatorzième et dernière édition; augmentée d'une instruction sur les effets publics et de notices géographiques et statistiques sur les places de commerce les plus importants. 334p. *8°. Bruxelles*, 1830. *For other editions, see* 1815.

26106 PARSON, W. and **WHITE**, WILLIAM (*fl.* 1826–1870). Directory of the borough of Leeds, the city of York, and the clothing district of Yorkshire...comprehending statements of all the public officers – clergy, and public institutions – with lists of merchants, manufacturers, traders, and inhabitants generally, a corrected list of London and provincial bankers, coaches, carriers, &c.&c. 529, xxivp. *12°. Leeds*, 1830.

26107 PECCHIO, G., *Conte*. Histoire de l'économie politique en Italie, ou abrégé critique des économistes italiens: précédée d'une introduction...Traduite de l'italien par M. Léonard Gallois. 424p. *8°. Paris*, 1830. *For other editions, see* 1829.

26108 PEREIRE, JACOB E. A Messieurs les membres de la Commission nommée par le gouvernement, pour rechercher les causes de la détresses de l'insutrie et du commerce, et proposer les moyens d'y porter remède. 3p. *8°. [Paris*, 1830]

26109 PETTMAN, W. R. A. Resources of the United Kingdom; or, the present distresses considered; their causes and remedies pointed out; and an outline of a plan for the establishment of a national currency, that would have a fixed money value, proposed. 291p. *8°*. 1830.

26110 PHILADELPHIA in 1830–1: or, a brief account of the various institutions and public objects in this metropolis. Forming a complete guide for strangers, and a useful compendium for the inhabitants. 288p. *12°. Philadelphia*, 1830.

26111 PICKERING, JOSEPH. Emigration, or no emigration; being the narrative of the author, (an English farmer) from the year 1824 to 1830; during which time he traversed the United States of America, and the British province of Canada, with a view to settle as an emigrant...132p. *12°*. 1830. *See also* 1832.

26112 PICOT, J. Statistique de la Suisse, seconde édition, revue, corrigée et augmentée. 609p. *12°. Genève & Paris*, 1830. *For another edition, see* 1819.

26113 The **POST-OFFICE** London directory for 1830...By B. Critchett. The thirty-first edition. [With 'A new guide to stage coaches, waggons, carts, vessels, &c. for 1830...The twenty-eighth edition. By B. Critchett'.]

550, 148p. *12°*. [1830] *See also* 1805 (Post-Office annual directory), 1810, 1813, 1814, 1820 (Post Office London directory), 1823, 1825, 1832, 1834, 1836, 1841.

For the **PROMPTER**, 1830–31, *see* vol. III, *Periodicals list.*

26114 Abstract **PROPOSITIONS** touching certain points in political economy; bearing chiefly upon questions relating to banking; to credit and capital; to the present prevailing distress; to wages; and to corn laws. 24p. *8°*. *Edinburgh*, 1830.

26115 **PUTT**, C. Essay on civil policy, or the science of legislation; comprising the origin and nature of government, religion, laws, population, wealth, and happiness. With a review of the practice of the English law and hints for its improvement. 468p. *8°*. 1830.

26116 The **REPEAL** of the legislative Union of Great Britain and Ireland, considered. 22p. *8°*. 1830.

26117 **RHODES**, J. B. La paix universelle, ou le mariage philosophique du commerce avec l'agriculture et sa famille entière... 95p. *8°*. *Tarbes*, 1830.

26118 —— Succint [*sic*] extrait de quelques fragmens de la Théocosmorhodie, ou nouveau système de la nature, de Jean-Baptiste Rhodes, de Plaisance, par l'auteur même. 19p. *8°*. *Tarbes*, 1830.

26119 **RIDER'S** British Merlin: for...1830...With notes of husbandry, gardening, fairs, marts, and tables... Compiled...by Cardanus Rider. 60p. *12°*. [1830] *For other editions, see* 1693.

26120 [**ROBERTSON**, GEORGE, *political economist.*] Essays on political economy: in which are illustrated the principal causes of the present national distress; with appropriate remedies. 463p. *8°*. 1830.

26121 **ROBINSON**, THOMAS. A treatise on the injurious effects of the free trade system, and the exportation of machinery; accompanied by illustrative facts and observations made in various parts of Europe. 24p. *8°*. *Leeds*, 1830.

26122 **ROYAL KALENDAR:** and court and city register, for England, Scotland, Ireland, and the colonies, for...1830... 405p. *12°*. [1830] *For other editions, see* 1779.

26123 —— An appendix to the Royal kalendar...for... 1830. Being an index... [60]p. *12°*. [1830]

26124 **SAY**, J. B. A treatise on political economy... Translated from the fourth edition of the French, by C. R. Prinsep, M.A. With notes by the translator. Fourth American edition. Containing a translation of the introduction, and additional notes, by Clement C. Biddle... 455p. *8°*. *Philadelphia*, 1830. *For other editions, see* 1803.

26125 **SENIOR**, N. W. Three lectures on the rate of wages, delivered before the University of Oxford, in Easter Term, 1830. With a preface on the causes and remedies of the present disturbances. 62p. *8°*. 1830. *Another, the FWA copy, belonged to William Pare.*

26126 —— Second edition. 62p. *8°*. 1830.

26127 **SOLLY**, E. On free trade, in relation to the present distress. 16p. *8°*. 1830.

26128 George-John **SPENCER**, Earl Spencer, K.G. [A memoir.] 8p. *8°*. [*London*, 1830] *The running-title reads: National portraits.*

26129 Alarming **STATE** of the nation considered; the evil traced to its source, and remedies pointed out. By a country gentleman. 99p. *8°*. 1830.

26130 On the distressed **STATE** of the country. By a merchant. 62p. *8°*. 1830.

26131 **SUGGESTIONS** on the best means of obtaining funds to enable Government to give beneficial employment to the labouring classes, thrown out of work by the introduction of machinery, or by any other cause. [Dated: 17th December, 1830.] 4p. *8°*. *Bristol*, [1830] *The Agar Ellis copy.*

26132 **THICK**, J. A review of the policy of the Government of England, the state of its trade, commerce, National Debt, and currency; with a plan of finance, submitted to the Government in 1827, 1828, & 1829. 171p. *8°*. 1830.

26133 [**THOMPSON**, THOMAS P.] The article on the distress of the country; from the Westminster Review, No. XXV. Republished on the 1st Aug. 1830... 8p. *8°*. 1830. *See note to no.* 25779.

26134 —— The true theory of rent, in opposition to Mr. Ricardo and others. Being an exposition of fallacies on rent, tithes, &c. In the form of a review of Mr. Mill's Elements of political economy. By the author of the Catechism on the corn laws...Seventh edition... 32p. *8°*. 1830. *For other editions, see* 1826.

26135 **WALSH**, J. B., *Baron Ormathwaite*. Poor laws in Ireland, considered in their probable effects upon the capital, the prosperity & the progressive improvement of that country. 124p. *8°*. 1830. *The copy that belonged to M. T. Sadler.*

26136 —— Second edition. 124p. *8°*. 1830. *See also* 1831.

26137 **WESTERN**, C. C., *Baron Western*. A second letter on the present distress of the country, addressed to his constituents by Charles Callis Western, Esq., M.P. for the County of Essex. 8p. *8°*. *Chelmsford*, 1830.

26138 —— A third letter on the present distress of the country, addressed to his constituents by Charles Callis Western, Esq., M.P. for the County of Essex. 15p. *8°*. *Chelmsford*, 1830.

AGRICULTURE

26139 *****AELBROECK**, J. L. VAN. L'agriculture pratique de la Flandre. 346p. *8°*. *Paris*, 1830. *The copy that belonged to George Grote. For a supplement, see* 1835.

26140 An **APPENDIX** to the dissertation on the nature of soils, and the properties of manure, &c....1828 ...A synopsis of the science of agriculture practically delineated; pointing out the necessary things to be taken into consideration in the management of a farm. 35p. *8°*. *London & Edinburgh*, 1830.

26141 **BEDFORD LEVEL CORPORATION.** The report of the special committee of finance, appointed at the April meeting of the Board in 1829. Ordered to be printed June, 1829; and to be re-printed April...1830. Also, the report of the committee for examining the books, furniture, papers, &c. and for considering the Register's remuneration, and the Fen Office establishment. 42p. *8°. Cambridge*, 1830. *The Rastrick copy.*

26142 BERRY, H. Improved short-horns, and their pretensions stated; being an account of this celebrated breed of cattle, derived from authentic sources. To which is added, an enquiry as to their value for general purposes placed in competition with the improved Herefords... Second edition. 81p. *8°.* 1830.

26143 BILLINGTON, W. Facts, observations, &c. being an exposure of the misrepresentations of the author's treatise on planting, contained in Mr. Wither's letters to Sir Walter Scott, Baronet, and to Sir Henry Steuart, Baronet; with remarks on Sir Walter Scott's essay on planting, and on certain parts of Sir Henry Steuart's Planter's guide; also, observations on the mode adopted in the royal forests of raising timber for future navies... 76p. *8°. Shrewsbury & London, &c.,* 1830.

26144 [BURT, J.] Real cases in Chancery. [A statement of the misconduct of Andrew Burt in reference to the trusteeship of estates belonging to the Hon. Thomas Bowes.] 32p. *8°.* 1830. *Attributed to John Burt, one of the trustees of the estate, in the manuscript index to the volume in which it is bound, which belonged to George Agar Ellis, Baron Dover.*

26145 The **CUSTOM** of the lead mines, within the Manor and Liberty of Crich, is as followeth...[Dated: 1830.] *s.sh.fol. Ashover,* [1830]

26146 DENSON, J. A peasant's voice to landowners, on the best means of benefiting agricultural labourers, and of reducing poor's rates. [Ten letters, most of them addressed to the Society for the Encouragement of Industry, republished from various newspapers.] 76p. *8°. Cambridge & London,* 1830.

26147 GAMBOA, F. X. DE. Commentaries on the mining ordinances of Spain...Translated from the original Spanish, by Richard Heathfield... 2 vols. *8°.* 1830.

26148 [GRIFFIN, R., *Baron Braybrooke.*] Report of the committee appointed to carry into effect a plan for ameliorating the condition of the poor at Saffron Walden ...and some account of the cottage allotments in the adjoining parish of Littlebury. 15p. *8°.* 1830. *See also* 1832.

26149 [HICKEY, W.] Hints to small holders on planting and on cattle, &c.&c. By Martin Doyle. 88p. *8°. Dublin, London, &c.,* 1830. *See also no.* 26150, *below;* 1832.

26150 [——] The works of Martin Doyle, containing 1. Hints to small farmers on land, fences...potatoes... manures, &c. 2. Hints on road-work, ventilation... education. 3. Hints on planting, cattle...agricultural implements, flax, &c. 4. Irish cottagers. 123, 88, 88, 137p. *12°. Dublin,* 1830.

26151 [HORNE, THOMAS H.] The complete grazier; or farmer's and cattle breeder's and dealer's assistant... By a Lincolnshire grazier...Fifth edition, revised, corrected, enlarged, and greatly improved... 655p. *8°. London, Edinburgh, &c.,* 1830. *For other editions, see* 1805.

26152 HUMPHRY, W. W. Contributory remarks on a general registry: with an appendix containing the questions and plan of the Real Property Commissioners. 105p. *8°. London & Sudbury,* 1830.

26153 KER, C. H. B. The question of registry or no registry considered, with reference to the interests of landowners & commercial credit, in a letter to the Right Honorable Robert Peel...To which is added, the plan of a register proposed by the Commissioners for Inquiring into the Laws of Real Property. 111p. *8°.* 1830.

26154 *LOUDON, J. C., and others.* A manual of cottage gardening, husbandry, and architecture...Extracted from the Gardener's Magazine. 72p. *8°.* 1830. *The FWA copy that belonged to William Pare.*

26155 MARSHAM, R. Indications of spring, observed by Robert Marsham, Esq. F.R.S. at Stratton, in Norfolk, Lat. 52, 45. Read before the Royal Society, April 2, 1789, [8]p. *32°. Norwich,* [1830?]

26156 MEWBURN, F. Observations on the second report of the Commissioners appointed to Enquire into the Law of Real Property, respectfully addressed to the serious consideration of the gentry, freeholders, and merchants of the county of Durham. 40p. *8°. Durham,* [1830]

26157 *[NEATE, C.]** Remarks on the suggested alterations in the game laws: with a new proposal for their amendment. By a student of Lincoln's Inn. 35p. *8°.* 1830. *The copy that belonged to Augustus De Morgan.*

26158 NOTICE sur les procédés du Parlement d'Angleterre, de 1814 à 1828, relativement à l'état de l'agriculture et à la législation du commerce des grains. 76p. *8°. Paris,* 1830.

26159 The **OUTLINE** of a plan for bettering the condition of the peasantry, reducing the poor rates, and adding to the stability of the state. [A scheme for the creation of an agricultural labour force with minimum wages, which every landowner shall be compelled to employ in proportion to the size of his estate.] 20p. *8°.* 1830.

For the **QUARTERLY MINING REVIEW,** 1830–32, *continued as the Mining review,* 1835–37, *see* vol. III, *Periodicals list,* Mining review.

26160 *RAU, K. D. H. Ueber die Landswirthschaft der Rheinpfalz und insbesondere in der Heidelberger Gegend... 102p. *8°. Heidelberg,* 1830. *The copy that belonged to George Grote.*

26161 STRICTURES on Sir Henry Steuart's "Planter's guide". By a planter, of some experience. 40p. *8°. Edinburgh & London,* 1830.

26162 WELLS, S. The history of the drainage of the Great Level of the Fens, called Bedford Level; with the constitution and laws of the Bedford Level Corporation. 2 vols. *8°.* 1830, 1828. *Vol. 2, published in 1828, is entitled: A collection of the laws which form the constitution of the Bedford Level Corporation.*

26163 WHALE-FISHING TRADE, &c. [A 'statement concerning the whale-fishing trade at Dundee, in reference to its proposed introduction into Burntisland'.] 8p. *8°. n.p.* [1830]

26164 *WHITLAW, C. On the management of dairies, as now conducted in London. [With 'On the management of dairies in Holland'.] 4p. *4°. n.p.* [1830?]

26165 WOOLRYCH, H. W. A treatise on the law of waters, and of sewers; including the law relating to rights in the sea, and rights in rivers, canals...&c. 501p. *8°.* 1830.

CORN LAWS

26166 CREWDSON, T. An inquiry into the effect of the corn laws on the prosperity of Great Britain and Ireland. 25p. *8⁰. London & Manchester, 1830.*

26167 [ELLIOTT, E.] Corn law rhymes. The ranter, written and published by order of the Sheffield Mechanics' Anti-Bread Tax Society. 12p. *12⁰. Sheffield, 1830. Included in the collected edition of his* Corn law rhymes *in 1831 (q.v.).*

26168 FORWOOD, G. An examination of the corn returns for the years 1826, 1827, 1828, & 1829, showing that the defective principle upon which they have been obtained has produced fallacious averages, exemplified by full statements, including the extraordinary returns which at one time produced a sudden increase, and at another a rapid decrease in the duty payable on foreign corn, materially affecting the agricultural produce of the United Kingdom. 80p. *8⁰. London & Liverpool, 1830.*

26169 SWANWICK, E. The doings of the corn law; being an exposition of its operation, past, present and prospective, illustrated by tables of averages, duties, imports, &c. 20p. *8⁰. 1830.*

POPULATION

26170 BARTON, J. A statement of the consequences likely to ensue from our growing excess of population, if not remedied by colonization. 48p. *8⁰. 1830.*

26171 MALTHUS, T. R. A summary view of the principle of population. [Extracted from an article in the supplement to *The Encyclopædia Britannica.*] 77p. *12⁰. 1830.*

26172 SADLER, M. T. The law of population: a treatise, in six books; in disproof of the superfecundity of human beings, and developing the real principle of their increase. 2 vols. *8⁰. 1830. Books 1–4 only. No more published. A manuscript note at the beginning contains a theory advanced by Thomas Doubleday, in a letter to Lord Brougham, 1 Jan., 1837, that when a nation is amply supplied with solid food, its tendency is upon the whole not to increase.*

26173 —— A refutation; of an article [by T. B. Macaulay] in the Edinburgh Review, (no. CII.) entitled 'Sadler's law of population, and disproof of human superfecundity.' Containing also, additional proofs of the principle enunciated in that treatise, founded on the censuses of different countries recently published. 103p. *8⁰. 1830.*

TRADES & MANUFACTURES

26174 Deadly **ADULTERATION** and slow poisoning; or, disease and death in the pot and the bottle...With tests or methods for ascertaining and detecting the fraudulent and deleterious adulterations and the good and bad qualities of those articles...By an enemy of fraud and villany. 187p. *12⁰.* [1830?] *The Turner copy.*

26175 The **BOOK** of English trades, and library of the useful arts...A new edition enlarged, with 500 questions ...[The twelfth edition.] 454, 18p. *8⁰. Sir Richard Phillips,* [c. 1830?] *A reissue of the twelfth edition, which was published in 1824, but containing advertising material dated 1831. For other editions, see 1811.*

26176 CABINET MAKERS' SOCIETY, *London.* Rules & orders of the...Society, established in the year 1815...for the benefit of industrious and ingenious mechanics...With a general list of prices. 60p. *8⁰.* [*London, 1830?*]

26177 ESPOSICION PUBLICA DE LOS PRODUCTOS DE LA INDUSTRIA ESPAÑ-OLA, 1828. Memoria de la Junta de Calificacion de los productos de la industria española remitidos á la Esposicion pública de 1828, presentada al Rey...por mano de su Secretario de Estado... 100p. *8⁰. Madrid, 1830.*

26178 GALLOWAY, E. History and progress of the steam engine...To which is added an extensive appendix ...by Luke Hebert... 863p. *8⁰. 1830.*

26179 HOLROYD, E. A practical treatise of the law of patents for inventions. 236p. *8⁰. 1830.*

26180 KENNEDY, JOHN (1769–1855). A brief memoir of Samuel Crompton; with a description of his machine called the mule, and of the subsequent improvement of the machine...From the memoirs of the Literary and Philosophical Society of Manchester. 38p. *8⁰. Manchester, 1830.*

26181 LONDON. Livery Companies. *Clockmakers.* A catalogue of books in the library of the Company of Clockmakers of the City of London. 27p. *8⁰. 1830.*

26182 MANN, WILLIAM, *of Brixton.* A description of a new method of propelling locomotive machines, and of communicating power and motion to all other kinds of machinery. 56p. *8⁰. 1830.*

26183 NEW YORK, *State of.* An act, to incorporate the Chemical Manufacturing Company, passed February 24, 1823. [With 'An act, entitled an act to amend an act to incorporate the New-York Chemical Manufacturing Company, passed April 1, 1824'.] 22p. *12⁰. New-York, 1830.*

26184 PERROT, A. M. Manuel du graveur, ou traité complet de l'art de la gravure en tous genres... 255p. *12⁰. Paris, 1830.*

26185 ROBERTS, R. Outlines of a proposed law of patents for mechanical inventions. 23p. *8⁰. Manchester, 1830.*

26186 SMITH, SETH. Description of the patent metallic lining and damper for the chimneys of dwelling and other houses and buildings invented by Mr. Seth Smith, of Wilton Crescent, Belgrave Square... 16p. *8°.* [1830]

26187 WILSON, Edward J. The artist's and mechanic's encyclopædia; or, a complete exposition of the arts and sciences, as applicable to practical purposes... By Edward James Wilson, A.M. and assistants... 2 vols. *4°. Newcastle upon Tyne,* [*c.* 1830]

COMMERCE

26188 BROOKE, S. An appeal to the Legislature, on the subject of the office of King's Printer, in England; lately renewed for thirty years; shewing that a large portion of the emoluments of the office belong to the public; with remarks on the injurious effects of contracts for terms of years, the Stationery Office system, &c. 72p. *8°.* 1830.

26189 [CRAWFURD, John (1783–1868).] An inquiry into some of the principal monopolies of the East India Company. 78p. *8°.* 1830.

26190 DEPPING, G. B. Histoire du commerce entre le Levant et l'Europe, depuis les Croisades, jusqu'à la fondation des colonies d'Amérique. 2 vols. *8°. Paris,* 1830.

26191 An EXPOSITION of the real state of the coal trade. [From the *Durham Chronicle.*] 26p. *8°. Durham,* [1830]

26192 FACTS and arguments addressed to manufacturers, on the present ruinous system of shipping goods abroad, under advances from merchants. 20p. *8°. Altrincham,* [1830]

26193 HEYWOOD, T. An enquiry into the impediments to a free trade with the peninsula of India. 44p. *8°.* 1830.

26194 LLOYD, W. F. Prices of corn in Oxford in the beginning of the fourteenth century; also from the year 1583 to the present time. To which are added some miscellaneous notions of prices in other places. Collected from manuscripts at Oxford. With a full account of the authorities on which the several prices are stated. 100p. *8°. Oxford,* 1830.

26195 LONDON. *Court of Common Council.* Charges upon coals. Report to the Court of Common Council, from the especial committee in relation to the charges upon coals. Presented 3d September, 1830. [With 'Report of the Select Committee of the House of Commons on the state of the coal trade, presented 13th July, 1830', and 'Report of the Select Committee of the House of Lords...presented 19th July, 1830'.] 39p. *fol.* [1830]

26196 [McCULLOCH, John R.] Rise, progress, and decline of commerce in Holland. [Extracted from the *Edinburgh Review,* vol. 51, 1830.] 27p. *8°. n.p.* [1830?]

26197 OBSERVATIONS on a Bill to permit the general sale of beer, by retail in England: most respectfully submitted to the members of the House of Commons. By a country brewer. 16p. *8°.* 1830. *The Agar Ellis copy.*

26198 SAINZ ANDINO, P. Proyecto de ley de enjuiciamiento sobre los negocios y causas de comercio, formado de orden del Rey N.S. 155p. *4°. Madrid,* 1830.

26199 SENIOR, N. W. Three lectures on the transmission of the precious metals from country to country, and the mercantile theory of wealth, delivered before the University of Oxford in June, 1827... The second edition. 96p. *8°.* 1830. *Presentation copy, with inscription, from the author to Harriet Martineau. For another edition, see 1828.*

26200 SPAIN. *Laws, etc.* Ley de enjuiciamiento sobre los negocios y causas de comercio, decretada...en 24 de Julio de 1830. Edicion oficial. 158p. *4°. Madrid,* 1830.

26201 TAYLOR, Isaac (1759–1829). Scenes of commerce, by land and sea; or, "where does it come from?" answered... 387p. *12°.* [1830]

26202 [THOMPSON, Thomas P.] The article on free trade, from the Westminster Review, No. XXIII. For January, 1830. To which is added a collection of objections and the answers. p.65–80. *8°.* 1830. A catechism of the corn laws, *p.1–64, was prefixed to some copies of this work.* *Another, the FWA copy, belonged to William Pare. See also 1832.*

26203 UNITED STATES OF AMERICA. Congress. *House of Representatives.* 21st Congress... ⟨Doc. no. 49.⟩ Ho. of Reps. Treas. Dept. Commerce and navigation of the United States. Letter from the Secretary of the Treasury...February 5, 1830. Read... 304p. *8°. n.p.* [1830] *See also 1822 (Senate),* 1826.

26204 —— —— —— *Committee on Commerce.* Report of the Committee on Commerce and Navigation. Read... in the House of Representatives of the United States, February 8, 1830. [Submitted by C. C. Cambreleng.] 63p. *8°.* [*New York,* 1830]

26205 —— [Another edition.] 72p. *8°.* 1830.

26206 WALKER, Alexander, *of Dover.* Plan of a protective system for the extinction of smuggling, and the consequent security of the revenue and encouragement of national industry, &c. 37p. *4°. Dover,* 1830. *The copy presented to the Duke of Wellington.*

COLONIES

26207 ACCURSIO DAS NEVES, J. Considerações politicas, e commerciaes sobre os descobrimentos, e possessões dos Portuguezes na Africa, e na Asia. 420p. *16°. Lisboa,* 1830.

26208 BANNISTER, S. Humane policy; or, justice to the aborigines of new settlements essential to a due expenditure of British money...With suggestions how to civilise the natives by an improved administration of existing means. [With appendixes.] 248, cclxxxiip. *8°.* 1830.

26209 BARCLAY, A. Effects of the late colonial policy of Great Britain described, in a letter to the Right Hon. Sir George Murray...shewing the effects produced in the West India Colonies by the recent measures of government...Second edition. 56p. *8°.* 1830.

26210 **BENTHAM**, J. Emancipate your colonies! Addressed to the National Convention of France, A° 1793, shewing the uselessness and mischievousness of distant dependencies to an European state...Now first published for sale. 48, 2p. *8°*. 1830. *The first publication of the sheets printed in 1793 (q.v.), with the addition of a title-page and a postscript, dated: 24 June, 1829.*

26211 **BUCKINGHAM**, J. S. Explanatory report on the plan and object of Mr. Buckingham's lectures on the oriental world, preceded by a sketch of his life, travels, and writings, and of the proceedings on the East India monopoly, during the past year. 40p. *8°*. 1830.

26212 —— Mr. Buckingham's alleged retainer from the East India Company. [With 'Sketch of Mr. Buckingham's life, travels, and lectures on the oriental world'.] 23p. *8°*. *n.p.* [1830]

26213 —— [Another edition.] 79p. *8°*. *n.p.* [1830]

26214 Some **CONSIDERATIONS** on the present state of our West India colonies, and on the regulations which influence their industry and trade. By a West Indian proprietor. 29p. *8°*. 1830.

26215 [**CRAIK**, G. L.] The New Zealanders. 424p. *12°*. *London, Edinburgh, &c.*, 1830.

26216 [——] [Another edition.] The New Zealanders, containing a narrative of the first discovery of the Island... 424p. *12°*. [1830?]

26217 **CREIGHTON**, O. A general view of the Welland Canal, in the province of Upper Canada... Published for the information of the stockholders in England, by... the Company. 23p. *8°*. 1830.

26218 **EAST INDIA COMPANY.** Memoir on the affairs of the East India Company. [A justification for the renewal of its charter.] 221p. *4°*. 1830.

26219 The **HOBART** Town almanack for the year 1830... 272p. *8°*. *Hobart Town*, [1830]

26220 **HOGENDORP**, C. S. W. van, *Graaf*. Coup d'oeil sur l'île de Java et les autres possessions néerlandaises dans l'archipel des Indes. 422p. *8°*. *Bruxelles*, 1830.

26221 **M'DONNELL**, A. An address to the Members of both Houses of Parliament on the West India question ...Second edition. 110p. *8°*. 1830.

26222 **MacDONNELL**, E. Speech...on the East India question. Delivered at a puplic meeting of the inhabitants of London and Westminster...May 8th, 1830, in reply to several statements and resolutions submitted to that meeting. 40p. *8°*. 1830. *The Agar Ellis copy.*

26223 **MOORSOM**, W. S. Letters from Nova Scotia; comprising sketches of a young country. 371p. *12°*. 1830.

26224 **O'BRIEN**, W. S. Considerations relative to the renewal of the East-India Company's charter. 75p. *8°*. 1830. *Presentation copy from the author to Earl Jermyn.*

26225 **PAUPERISM** on a great scale, or the case of the West India planters. 6p. *8°*. [1830?] *The Agar Ellis copy.*

26226 **PEGGS**, J. India's cries to British humanity, relative to the suttee, infanticide, British connexion with idolatry, Ghaut murders, and slavery in India; to which is added, human hints for the melioration of the state of society in British India...Second edition, revised and enlarged... 518p. *8°*. *London, Edinburgh, &c.*, 1830. *See also 1832.*

26227 —— Pilgrim tax in India. Facts and observations relative to the practice of taxing pilgrims in some parts of India, and paying a premium to those who collect them for the worship of Juggernaut at the great temple in Orissa...Second edition, enlarged. 76p. *8°*. [1830?]

26228 **PRINSEP**, G. A. An account of steam vessels and of proceedings connected with steam navigation in British India. [With appendixes.] 104, xxxviip. *4°*. *Calcutta*, 1830.

26229 **RAFFLES**, S. Memoir of the life and public services of Sir Thomas Stamford Raffles...particularly in the government of Java, 1811–1816, and of Bencoolen and its dependencies, 1817–1824; with details of the commerce and resources of the Eastern Archipelago, and selections from his correspondence. By his widow. [With an appendix.] 723, 100p. *4°*. 1830. *See also 1835.*

26230 **TENNANT**, C. A letter to the Right Hon. Sir George Murray...on systematic colonization. [With 'Appendix, containing the written controversy between the Right Hon. Robert Wilmot Horton and Col. Torrens, and the other members of the Committee of the National Colonization Society'.] 53p. *8°*. 1830. *[phc] From the LSE copy.*

26231 [**THOMPSON**, Thomas P.] The article on the colonization and commerce of British India. From the Westminster Review, No. XXII, for October, 1829. Republished on the 3rd Feb. 1830... 32p. *8°*. [1830] *See note to no. 25779.*

26232 **WILSON**, Horace H. A review of the external commerce of Bengal from 1813–14 to 1827–28. 98, 71p. *8°*. *Calcutta*, 1830.

FINANCE

26233 Some **ACCOUNT** of the Savings Bank for the town of Shaftesbury, and its vicinity, including the late proceedings relating to the rate of interest paid to depositors, and the advance of the salary paid to the actuary. By a manager of twelve years standing. 24p. *8°*. *Shaftesbury*, 1830.

26234 [**AINSLIE**, G. R.] Illustrations of the Anglo-French coinage... 168p. *4°*. 1830.

26235 **ATTWOOD**, M. Substance of the speech of Matthias Attwood, Esq., M.P., in the House of Commons, on...the 8th of June, 1830, in the debate on the state of the currency... 23p. *8°*. [1830]

26236 **BANQUE DE FRANCE.** Législation relative à la Banque de France, et réglements intérieurs. 79, 43p. *4°*. *Paris*, 1830.

26237 **BARNES**, R. A letter to a member of the House of Commons, on the Tithe Composition Bill. 73p. *8°*. *Exeter*, 1830. *Presentation copy from the author to the Solicitor General.*

26238 **BRICKWOOD**, J. Further remarks on the superiority of the new five per cent. stock. 15p. *8°*. 1830.

26239 —— A plan for redeeming the new four per cents. humbly suggested to the consideration of His Majesty's government. 48p. *8°*. 1830.

26240 —— Second edition. 48p. *8°*. 1830.

26241 **BULL**, JOHN, *pseud.* A letter from John Bull to His Grace the Duke of Wellington on the state of the country; with John's remedy for the distress... 8p. *8°*. 1830.

26242 **CAUSES** and cure of the present distress. [On the return to a metallic currency and the pressure of the public taxes.] 30p. *8°*. 1830. *With the signature of Richard Monckton Milnes, Baron Houghton, on the half-title.*

26243 **CIVIS**, *pseud.* A letter to His Grace the Duke of Richmond [on taxes], &c.... 16p. *8°*. 1830.

26244 **CLEGHORN**, J. (Final) Report on the proposed widows' scheme of the Faculty of Advocates. 84p. *4°*. *Edinburgh*, 1830.

26245 **CONSIDERATIONS** on some of the more popular mistakes and misrepresentations on the nature, extent, and circumstances of church property in a letter to a friend. By the incumbent of a country parish. 35p. *8°*. *London & Canterbury*, 1830.

26246 **CORN SPIRITS.** Remarks on a Letter addressed by John Innes, Esq. to the Right Honourable the Chancellor of the Exchequer, dated 12th of April, 1830. [Issued by Nettleshipp, Bicknell & Boulton, for the English Distillers, A. & R. Mundell, for the Scotch Distillers, P. Mahony, for the Irish Distillers.] 4p. *fol. n.p.* [1830]

26247 **CULLEN**, C. S. Reform of the Bankrupt Court; with a letter to John Smith, Esq., M.P. and an appendix... Second edition. 79p. *8°*. 1830.

26248 **DANIEL**, E. Letter to His Majesty recommending the immediate abolition of all imposts upon the produce of our soil...and the abolition of the assessed taxes, for the relief of the middle classes...[With an appendix of letters and a petition to the King, all dated 1830.] 44p. *8°*. *Gloucester*, [1830] *Presentation copy from the author to 'Mr. Serjt. Russell'.*

26249 —— Two letters addressed to the Right Hon. Robert Peel...and a third to the noble Duke of Wellington ...wherein the expediency of the immediate abolition of the excise laws is considered...and of the assessed tax assessment: and of imposing...an equal tax upon all real, funded, and productive personal property...With the answers received from those gentlemen. 87p. *8°*. *Gloucester, London, &c.*, 1829 [1830] *A greatly extended version of the work published in 1829 (q.v.) with four additional letters and appendixes added in 1830. Presentation copy from the author to 'Mr. Serjt. Russell', with manuscript alterations on the title-page.*

26250 [**DEAN**, R. B.] Remarks upon the revenue of customs; with a few observations upon a late work of Sir H. Parnell on financial reform, as far as relates to that revenue; in a letter to the Right Hon. Henry Goulburn, Chancellor of the Exchequer... 47p. *8°*. 1830.

26251 [——] Second edition. 47p. *8°*. 1830.

26252 **DE BODE**, C. J. P. P., *Baron.* No. I. French claims. An address to the Right Hon. the Lords Spiritual and Temporal, and the honourable the Members of the House of Commons, relative to a Bill...regarding the French claims. [With particular reference to his own claim against the French Government.] 23p. *8°* 1830. *The Agar Ellis copy.*

26253 —— No. II. French claims. A few words by the Baron de Bode, in relation to the funds paid by the French to the British Government under the Treaties and Conventions of 1814, 1815, and 1818: showing the respective rights of the governments, and of the parties claiming... 19p. *8°*. 1830. *The Agar Ellis copy.*

26254 **DRAUGHT** of a Bill, for an Act to enable the faculty of Advocates, of Scotland, to raise a fund, for making provision, by way of annuities, for their widows. 43p. *4°*. *n.p.* [1830]

26255 **DUNDEE UNION BANK.** Contract of copartnery of the Dundee Union Bank. 32p. *8°*. [*Dundee*, 1830]

26256 **ELIZABETH**, *of York, Queen Consort.* Privy purse expenses of Elizabeth of York: wardrobe accounts of Edward the Fourth. With a memoir of Elizabeth of York, and notes. By N. H. Nicolas, Esq. civ, 265p. *8°*. 1830.

26257 **ENGLAND.** *Commissioners of Excise.* A statement of the mode of charging and collecting the duties of excise; and of the regulations under which persons subject to these duties are required to carry on their business. 165p. *8°*. 1830. *The copy, presented with an accompanying letter from the officer for whom the work was compiled [F. H. Doyle?], to T. Spring Rice, Baron Monteagle.*

26258 An **ENQUIRY** as to the practicability and policy of reducing the duties on malt and beer, and encreasing those on British spirits. With suggestions for an equitable adjustment of the land tax. 47p. *8°*. 1830. *Presentation copy from the anonymous author to the editor of the Observer.*

26259 An **EXAMINATION** of the currency question, and of the project for altering the standard of value. [Originally published in the *Quarterly Review*, April 1822.] 63p. *8°*. 1830.

26260 **FACULTY OF ADVOCATES**, *Edinburgh.* Report of the committee of the Faculty of Advocates, appointed 8th July, 1829, in order to prepare a widows' scheme and a relative Bill. 4p. *4°*. [*Edinburgh*, 1830]

26261 **FAIRFAX**, *pseud.* Wrongs of man: in a series of observations on taxes, tithes, and Trinity, National Debt, church rates, poor rates, and poor laws; with other miscellanies. 69p. *8°*. *Windsor*, 1830.

26262 **FRANCE.** *Louis Philippe, King.* Extrait du Moniteur du 20 août 1830. Ordonnance du Roi. [17 August 1830. On the design of the new gold and silver coins.] [2]p. *s.sh.4°*. [*Paris*, 1830]

26263 —— [Another edition.] Extrait du Moniteur du 20 août, 1830. Orconnance [*sic*] du Roi, concernant les monnaies d'or et d'argent. [With 'Projet de loi, présenté à la Chambre des députés', concerning pensions, money for public works, and 'Discours du General Lafayette', on the abolition of the death penalty.] [2]p. *s.sh.4°*. [*Paris*, 1830]

26264 —— *Ministère des Finances.* Rapport au Roi sur l'administration des finances. [With appendixes.] 204, 74, 180p. *4°*. *Paris*, 1830.

26265 **GLASGOW UNION BANKING COMPANY.** Contract of co-partnership of the Glasgow Union Banking Company, instituted in terms of the Act, 7 Geo. IV. cap. 67. 1830. [With 'Abstract of the articles of the contract of co-partnership of the Glasgow Union Banking Company'.] 41, 4p. *8°*. *Edinburgh*, 1830. *Interleaved and bound in a volume with manuscript pieces concerning the Company. For these, see vol. III, MS. 579.*

26266 **HARRIS,** JAMES E., *2nd Earl of Malmesbury*. Debate on the distillery laws; in the House of Lords, on Thursday, the 29th of April, 1830: including the speeches of the Earl of Malmesbury, and Lord Viscount Goderich. 11p. *8°*. 1830.

26267 A concise **HISTORY** of tithes. 12p. *8°*. *Halifax*, [*c. 1830*] *The Oastler copy.*

26268 **INNES,** JOHN (*fl. 1830–1849*). A letter to the Rt. Hon. Henry Goulburn, M.P. Chancellor of the Exchequer...On the claims of the West India distiller to an equalization of the duties on rum and British spirits. 28p. *8°*. 1830. *Another edition, with the title:* Equalization of duty on rum and British spirits, *was published in 1846* (*q.v.*).

26269 **JOPLIN,** T. An examination of the principles of an improved system of banking, and the means of carrying it into effect. 32p. *8°*. 1830. *A proof copy, presented by the author to T. Spring Rice, Baron Monteagle. For the published edition, see 1831.*

26270 —— The principle of the personal liability of the shareholders in public banks examined. 15p. *8°*. 1830. *An edition of p. 201–216 of the author's* Views on the Corn Bill of 1827, *1828* (*q.v.*).

26271 **KENTISH,** W. A. A plan for the redemption of the public debt; and for the ultimate removal of all remaining taxation... 16p. *8°*. [*1830*]

26272 A **LETTER** to the Earl of Wilton, on the commutation of existing taxes for a graduated property and income tax; connecting therewith, a plan of parliamentary reform. By an Englishman. Second edition. 32p. *8°*. 1830.

26273 A **LETTER** to the Rt. Hon. Lord Althorp, Chancellor of the Exchequer...on the subject of the duty on printed cottons. By a calico printer. 48p. *8°*. *London & Manchester*, [*1830*]

26274 —— Second edition. 48p. *8°*. *London & Manchester*, [*1830*]

26275 De la **LOI** économique. [On taxation.] 39p. *8°*. *Paris*, 1830. *A printed note on the verso of the title-page reads: Cet écrit, est le résumé...de plusieurs brochures distribuées aux membres des deux chambres. There follows a list of 9 works of 1829 and 1830.*

26276 [**McCULLOCH,** JOHN R.] Observations on the duty on sea-borne coal; and on the peculiar duties and charges on coal, in the Port of London... 51p. *8°*. 1830. *See also 1831.*

26277 [——] Remarks on the coal trade, and on the various duties and charges on coal, in the Port of London, &c. Reprinted, with additions and corrections...from the Edinburgh Review, No. 101. 32p. *8°*. 1830.

26278 **M'DONNELL,** A. Rum and British spirit duties. A statement of the arguments for and against an equalization of the duties on British spirits, and West India rum. 52p. *8°*. 1830.

26279 **M'DUFFIE,** G. Speech...against the prohibitory system [of taxation]; in the House of Representatives, April, 1830. 68p. *8°*. *Columbia*, 1830.

26280 **MALCHUS,** C. A. VON, *Freiherr*. Handbuch der Finanzwissenschaft und Finanzverwaltung... 2 vols. *8°*. *Stuttgart & Tübingen*, 1830.

26281 **MÉDAILLE** pour perpétuer le souvenir de la conquête d'Alger, dont le produit sera consacré à offrir une épée d'honneur à Monsieur le Maréchal de Bourmont. [A prospectus.] 2p. *s.sh.8°*. *Paris*, [*1830 ?*]

26282 **METROPOLITAN COUNTY BANK OF ENGLAND.** A statement of proceedings which have been taken to promote the formation of a County Bank of England. 37p. *8°*. 1830.

26283 **MILLER,** SAMUEL, *cordwainer*. Small debts. Three letters addressed to, and published in, "The Times" newspaper, during the years 1827 and 1829, shewing the manifold advantages of enlarging the powers of the Court of Requests... 16p. *8°*. 1830.

26284 **MOSELEY,** J. The causes and remedies for general distress, and the principles of an equitable adjustment, impartially discussed in a letter to Sir W. Parker, Bart. of Melford Hall, dated March 3, 1830. 32p. *8°*. *Bury* [*St. Edmunds*], 1830.

26285 **MUNDELL,** A. The principle and operation of gold and silver in coin; of paper in currency; and of gold and silver in buying and selling... 15p. *8°*. 1830.

26286 **OBSERVATIONS** on a letter of John Innes, Esq. to the Right Honourable the Chancellor of the Exchequer, dated the 12th April, 1830. 3p. *fol. n.p.* [*1830*]

26287 [**OSIANDER,** H. F.] Exposé historique des finances des Pays-Bas, depuis la restauration en 1813 jusqu'à nos jours. Par l'auteur de La lutte entre la liberté du commerce et le système prohibitif dans les Pays-Bas, etc., etc. Traduit de l'allemand. 170p. *8°*. *Amsterdam*, 1830. *For other editions, see 1829.*

26288 **PARNELL,** H. B., *Baron Congleton*. On financial reform. [With an appendix.] 310, xliip. *8°*. 1830.

26289 —— Second edition. 294, xliip. *8°*. 1830. *See also* 1831.

26290 [**PENSAM,** J.] Address to the members of the Corporation of the Amicable Society for a Perpetual Assurance Office. By the Registrar. 22p. *8°*. 1830.

26291 **PRATT,** J. T. The history of savings banks in England, Wales, and Ireland. With the period of the establishment of each institution...The days and hours when open...classed according to the latest official returns... 336p. *12°*. 1830. *See also 1842.*

26292 **PREVOST,** A. L. Réflexions sur la loi relative au bureau de garantie et à la surveillance du titre des ouvrages d'or ou d'argent. 43p. *8°*. *Genève*, 1830.

26293 **PROPERTY** the only just ground of taxation. 15p. *8°*. 1830.

26294 *****RANKIN,** R. A familiar treatise on life assurances and annuities, comprising a historical sketch... of life assurance offices, with observations on the duration of human life...To which are appended original tables of the probabilities and expectations of life in the City of Bristol, etc. 99p. *8°*. *London & Bristol*, 1830. *Presentation copy from the author to William Frend; it afterwards belonged to Augustus De Morgan.*

26295 **REMARKS** on a recent publication, by a "manager of twelve years' standing" relative to the Savings Bank for the town of Shaftesbury, and its vicinity. 16p. *8°*. *Salisbury*, 1830.

26296 **REMARKS** on the question of again permitting the issue of one pound notes by the Bank of England, and also by country banks. 64p. *8°*. 1830.

26297 **REVIEW** of the case of Lord Cochrane, as one

of the defendants at the trial on the 8th and 9th of June, 1814, for an alleged conspiracy to raise the prices of the public funds on the 21st of February, 1814. 110p. 8°. 1830.

26298 **SCHENCK,** P. H. Frauds on the revenue, addressed to the people of the United States, and to their representatives in Congress. 13p. 8°. *New-York*, 1830.

26299 **SCOTTISH WIDOWS' FUND AND LIFE ASSURANCE SOCIETY.** Address by the manager of the Scottish Widows' Fund [John M'Kean] ...containing an account of the origin, constitution and progress of the Society. Read at 15th general anniversary meeting of the Society, held...January, 1829. Second edition. 43p. 8°. *Edinburgh*, 1830.

26300 —— Postscript to Address by the manager of the Scottish Widows' Fund...Read at 16th general anniversary meeting of the Society, held...January, 1830. With list of office-bearers, tables of rates, &c. annexed. 23p. 8°. *Edinburgh*, 1830.

26301 [**SCROPE,** G. P.] The currency question freed from mystery, in a letter to Mr. Peel, showing how the distress may be relieved without altering the standard. 50p. 8°. 1830.

26302 —— On credit-currency, and its superiority to coin, in support of a petition for the establishment of a cheap, safe, and sufficient circulating medium. 84p. 8°. 1830.

26303 [**SEELEY,** R. B.?] The present operation of the Act of Parliament of July, 1819, commonly called Mr. Peel's Bill. 52p. 8°. 1830.

26304 **SENIOR,** N. W. Three lectures on the cost of obtaining money, and on some effects of private and government paper money; delivered before the University of Oxford, in Trinity Term, 1829. 103p. 8°. 1830.

26305 **SMITH,** JOHN, *writer on finance*. Plan of finance for the reduction of the National Debt and relief of prevailing distress, in a letter to the Duke of Wellington, with an appendix addressed to the British public... Second edition. 60p. 8°. 1830. *The copy that belonged to T. Spring Rice, Baron Monteagle.*

26306 **SMYTH,** WILLIAM C. An appeal to the King's most excellent Majesty, and to the British nation by William Carmichael Smyth, Esq., thirteen years one of the Paymasters of Exchequer-Bills, from which office he was removed...1824... 160, 24p. 8°. 1830. *The Agar Ellis copy.*

26307 **SOLLY,** E. The present distress, in relation to the theory of money. 16p. 8°. 1830.

26308 **SZÉCHÉNYI,** I., *Gróf.* Ueber den Credit... Aus dem Ungarischen. 280p. 8°. *Leipzig*, 1830. *Translated by J. Vojdisek.*

26309 **TAYLOR,** JAMES (1788–1863). A letter to His Grace the Duke of Wellington, on the currency. [Dated: Dec. 26, 1829, with a postscript, dated, 13 Jan. 1830.] 112p. 8°. 1830. *Another edition, entitled*, Remarks on Mr. Tooke's letters to Lord Grenville on the currency, *was published in 1847 (q.v.).*

26310 —— To the Honorable the Commons of the United Kingdom of Great Britain and Ireland: the petition of James Taylor, of Bakewell in the county of Derby [for the continuance of cash payments by the Bank of England]. 8p. 8°. [1830]

26311 [**TAYLOR,** JOHN (1781–1864).] An essay on money. 111p. 8°. 1830. *See also* 1844, 1845 (Currency investigated).

26312 **TAYLOR,** JOHN, *memorialist, and others.* Additional memorial presented to the Board of Trade, April 29th, 1830, praying an increase of the protecting duties on lead. [Signed: John Taylor, Richard Fuller, Walter Hall.] 18p. 8°. *n.p.* [1830]

26313 **THOMPSON,** THOMAS P. The article on the instrument of exchange. Republished from the Westminster Review, No. I. With additions appropriate to the period of republication. By the author of the Catechism on the corn laws. 27p. 8°. 1830. *See note to no.* 25779.

26314 **THOMSON,** CHARLES E. P., *Baron Sydenham.* Speech...in the House of Commons, on the 26th of March, 1830, on moving the appointment of a Select Committee to inquire into the state of taxation of the United Kingdom. 77p. 8°. 1830.

26315 **UNITED STATES OF AMERICA.** Congress. *House of Representatives.* 21st Congress, 1st Session. ⟨Rep. No. 358.⟩...Bank of the United States. April 13th, 1830. Read, and laid upon the table. Mr. McDuffie, from the Committee of Ways and Means... made the following report... 32p. 8°. *n.p.* [1830]

26316 —— [Another edition.] Bank of the United States. Congress. House of Representatives, April 13, 1830... 31p. 8°. *n.p.* [1830]

26317 —— —— *Senate.* In the Senate of the United States, March 29, 1830. Read and ordered to be printed. Mr. Smith, of Maryland, made the following report: the Committee on Finance, to which was referred a resolution ...directing the Committee to inquire into the expediency of establishing an uniform national currency for the United States...report. 7p. 8°. *n.p.* [1830]

26318 **WOOD,** JOSEPH. Proposals for the immediate reduction of eight millions and a half of taxes, and the gradual liquidation of the National Debt, in a letter, addressed to the Right Honorable Henry Goulburn, Chancellor of the Exchequer. 42p. 8°. *London, & Wakefield*, 1830. *See also* 1832.

TRANSPORT

26319 **BARNET.** List of coaches from London. [With 'List of coaches to London'. Two timetables, showing destination, name of coach and the time of arrival at Barnet.] 2l. 4°. *Barnet: J. J. Cowing*, [c. 1830]

26320 **BOOTH,** H. An account of the Liverpool and Manchester Railway, comprising a history of the Parliamentary proceedings preparatory to the passing of the Act, a description of the railway...Also, an abstract of the expenditure... 104p. 8°. *Liverpool, Manchester, &c.*, [1830] *See also* 1831.

26321 [**CAREY,** M.] Essay on railroads. [Signed: Hamilton, and dated, Philadelphia, January 14th, 1830.] 26p. 8°. *n.p.* [1830]

26322 DICK, M. Description of the suspension railway invented by Maxwell Dick... 17p. *8°. Irvine,* 1830.

26323 ENGLAND. *Laws, etc.* Anno decimo Georgii II. Regis. Cap. IX. An Act for making navigable the river or brook called Worsley Brook, from Worsley Mill...in the County Palatine of Lancaster, to the River Irwell in the said county. 16p. *fol.* 1830.

26324 —— —— Anno sexto Georgii III. Regis. [Private Acts c.xvii.] An Act to enable...Francis Duke of Bridgewater to extend a branch of his navigable cut or canal, upon Sale Moor in the county of Chester, to the market town of Stockport... 11p. *fol.* 1830.

26325 —— —— Anno undecimo Georgii IV. Regis. Cap. l. An Act to consolidate and amend the Acts relating to the Sankey Brook Navigation in the county of Lancaster, and to make a navigable canal from the said Navigation at Fidler's Ferry to...the River Mersey at Widness Wharf ...⟨29th May 1830.⟩ p.1212–1294. *fol.* 1830.

26326 FORTUNE, F. London and Brighton junction rail road, as suggested to Government by F. Fortune in 1825. [With 'Prospectus of the Metropolitan Marine Bath Company. – 1824', 'Sea-water baths, under the patronage of the Prince Regent. – 1811' and 'London and Edinburgh grand trunk railway. Summary of the national advantages to be derived from railways, viewed in comparison with the three-fold system of conveyance by turnpike roads, canals and coasting vessels. To the editor of the Nottingham Review', signed: Thomas Gray.] 16p. *8°.* [London, 1830]

26327 —— [*Begin.*] Report agreed to, and referred to the committee appointed on the 23d. day of May, 1828, to enquire into all the charges on coals imported into the Port of London, to do therein as they deem most expedient ...[With 'Observations on the foregoing', signed: Francis Fortune. Advocating a general junction railway to transport coals to London.] 6p. *8°. n.p.* [1830]

26328 HARDAKER, J. The aeropteron; or, steam-carriage. A poem. [Second edition.] 24p. *8°. Keighley,* 1830.

26329 INVESTIGATOR, *pseud.* Remarks on the proposed railway between Birmingham & London, proving by facts and arguments that that work would cost seven millions and a half...and would never pay... 116p. *8°. London, Birmingham, &c.,* 1830. *See also* 1831.

26330 LEEDS AND LIVERPOOL CANAL. An account of the incomes and outgoings of the Leeds and Liverpool Canal and Douglas Navigation, from 1st January, 1829, to 1st January, 1830. [Signed: Robert Nicholson, and dated, March 10th, 1830.] *s.sh.fol. n.p.* [1830]

26331 [*Endorsed:*] **LIVERPOOL AND LEEDS RAILWAY.** Statement [on the advantages of the route, and announcing the application to Parliament for permission to build the line from Liverpool to Rochdale]. [4]p. *fol.* [London, 1830.]

26332 LIVERPOOL AND MANCHESTER RAILWAY COMPANY. Liverpool and Manchester Rail Road. [Report of the general annual meeting. With 'Fortune's general junction rail road, through England, as laid before Government in 1825...also, the Exchequer loan and fishery bills, supplying 111,694 fishermen. — Impressment no longer required with such a nursery for seamen'.] 16p. *8°. n.p.* [1830]

26333 MATHER, JAMES. An account of the ship life-boat. Second edition. 46p. *8°. Edinburgh,* 1830.

For a **NEW GUIDE TO STAGE COACHES, WAGGONS**...&c. for 1830, *see no.* 26113.

26334 STEPHENSON, G. Observations on the comparative merits of locomotive & fixed engines, as applied to railways; being a reply to the report of Mr. James Walker, to the directors of the Liverpool and Manchester Railway, compiled from the reports of Mr. George Stephenson. With an account of the competition of locomotive engines at Rainhill, in October, 1829, and of the subsequent experiments. By Robert Stephenson and Joseph Locke, civil engineers. 83p. *8°. Liverpool, London, &c.,* [1830]

26335 STRACHAN, JOHN, *civil engineer.* Prospectus of a railway between Edinburgh and the port of Leith. As projected by Mr. John Strachan. 12p. *8°. Edinburgh & Leith,* [1830 ?] *The Rastrick copy.*

26336 WALKER, JAMES S. An accurate description of the Liverpool and Manchester Rail-way, the tunnel, the bridges, and other works throughout the line; with a sketch of the objects which it presents interesting to the traveller or tourist. 46p. *8°. Liverpool, London, &c.,* [1830] *The Rastrick copy. See also* 1831, 1832.

SOCIAL CONDITIONS

26337 An **ADDRESS** to the men of Hawkhurst, (equally applicable to the men of other parishes) on their riotous acts and purposes. Second edition. 12p. *12°.* 1830.

26338 An earnest **ADDRESS** to the labouring classes occasioned by the late disturbances. By a clergyman. 8p. *8°.* 1830.

26339 AMICABLE SOCIETY, *Kinnersley.* Articles to be observed and kept by the members of the Amicable Society, who have agreed to meet at the house of Richard Williams, Kinnersley. 16p. *8°. Wellington* [*c.* 1830]

26340 ANTI-DRACO or, reasons for abolishing the punishment of death, in cases of forgery. By a barrister of the Middle Temple. 49p. *8°.* 1830. *The Agar Ellis copy.*

26341 ASSOCIATED CATHOLIC CHARITIES. Annual report presented...June 3, 1830. 24p. *12°. n.p.* 1830. *See also* 1815, 1829.

26342 BAKER, A. O. Considerations on the present state of the peasantry of England, with suggestions for the improvement of their condition. 17p. *8°. Winchester & London,* [1830]

26343 BEDDOME, J. If you ask me, what a manufacturer by power is ? I answer, a manufacturer of poverty. 7p. *4°. Manchester,* [1830] *The Oastler copy, with manuscript notes in the margins signed: R.O.*

26344 BENTHAM, J. The rationale of punishment. [With additions by Etienne Dumont. Edited by Richard Smith.] 441p. *8°.* 1830. *Originally published as part of*

Théorie des peines et des récompenses, 1811 edited and with additions by Dumont (q.v.).

26345 BOOKBINDERS' PENSION SOCIETY, *London.* Report and rules of the Bookbinders' Pension Society, as agreed to at a general meeting held...April 20, 1830, at the Mechanics' Institution... 8p. *8°. 1830.*

26346 —— Resolutions of the Bookbinders' Pension Society. Held at the Bell, Poppin's Court, Fleet Street... 8p. *8°. 1830.*

26347 BRADFORD. We the undersigned worsted spinners being desirous of promoting a legislative enactment, to diminish and limit the hours of labour in worsted mills...request the attendance of the trade generally, at the Talbot Inn, in Bradford, on Monday, the 22nd day of Nov. 1830...[A poster. Signed: Matthew Thompson, John Rand & Sons, and 21 other spinning firms in Bradford.] *s.sh.fol. Bradford, [1830] [Br. 508(1)] Sent by post to Richard Oastler, by John Wood (1793–1871) one of the signatories, with a letter written by him on the verso. For the letter, see vol. III, A.L. 473.*

26348 BRENTON, E. P. Address to the select vestry and guardians of the poor, in the parish of St. Mary-le-Bone, on the subject of agricultural labour for the poor, the more profitable application of the parish funds, and the reduction of the rates. 38p. *8°. 1830.*

26349 —— A letter to the committee of management of the Society for the Suppression of Mendicity, in Red Lion Square. 48p. *8°. 1830.*

26350 *[BROWN, HENRY.] The mechanic's Saturday night, a poem in the "vulgar tongue;" humbly addressed to the Rt. Hon. Sir Robert Peel. By a mechanic. [On the evils of drink.] 19p. *12°. 1830. The FWA copy, that belonged to William Pare.*

26351 BROWN, WILLIAM, *Rev., M.D.* Memoir relative to itinerating libraries. 16p. *8°. Edinburgh, [1830?] The Agar Ellis copy.*

26352 BRUCE, T., *Earl of Elgin and of Kincardine.* View of the present state of pauperism in Scotland. [With an appendix of documents.] 78p. *8°. 1830.*

26353 BURGES, G. An address to the misguided poor of the disturbed districts throughout the kingdom. 40p. *12°. London, Norwich, &c., 1830.*

26354 CAREY, M. Essays on the public charities of Philadelphia, intended to vindicate benevolent societies from the charge of encouraging idleness, and to place in strong relief...the sufferings and oppression under which the greater part of the females labour, who depend on their industry for a support for themselves and children. Fifth edition... 51p. *8°. Philadelphia, 1830. For another edition, see 1828.*

26355 CASES of distress and oppression, in the Staffordshire Potteries; by labourers wages being paid in truck. 12p. *12°. Burslem, 1830. The Agar Ellis copy.*

26356 CATHOLIC FRIENDLY SOCIETY, *Leeds.* Rules of the Catholic Friendly Society, established May 3rd, 1830, at the house of Mr. William Hauxworth, the Ship Inn, Briggate, Leeds. 60p. *8°. Leeds, 1830.*

26357 CHILDREN'S FRIEND SOCIETY. Statement of the views of the Society for the Suppression of Juvenile Vagrancy, upon the plan that has proved so successful in Holland, by providing agricultural and horticultural employment for the destitute children of the metropolis. 15p. *8°. 1830.*

26358 —— [Another edition.] Statement of the views and reports of the Society... 28p. *8°. 1830.*

26359 CLISSOLD, H. Prospectus of a central national institution of home colonies, designed to instruct and employ distressed unoccupied poor on waste lands in spade husbandry. 12p. *8°. 1830. The Agar Ellis copy.*

26360 COBBETT, W. Cobbett's poor man's friend; or a defence of the rights of those who do the work and fight the battles. 72p. *12°. [1830] The Oastler copy. This edition consists of letters II–IV only, renumbered I–III. For other editions, see 1826.*

26361 COLLINS, W. No. 10. Speech of Mr. William Collins at the first public meeting of the Edinburgh Association for the Suppression of Intemperance. 16p. *8°. Villafield, [1830?]*

26362 CONOLLY, J., *and others.* A letter [signed: John Conolly, Augustus De Morgan, Dionysius Lardner, George Long, J. R. McCulloch] to the shareholders and Council of the University of London, on the present state of that institution. 28p. *8°. 1830. The Agar Ellis copy.*

26363 —— Statements respecting the University of London, prepared at the desire of the Council, by nine of the professors [John Conolly, David D. Davis, Augustus De Morgan, Anthony A. Galiano, Dionysius Lardner, George Long, J. R. McCulloch, L. von Mühlenfels, Granville S. Pattison]. 46p. *8°. 1830. The Agar Ellis copy.*

26364 The **COTTAGER'S** friendly guide in domestic economy, compiled for the use of the industrious poor. By an economist. 48p. *12°. [c. 1830]*

26365 CULLEN, C. S. A letter on the arbitrary license system, addressed to the Right Hon. John Calcraft, M.P. chairman of the sale of beer committee. 26p. *8°. 1830. The copy sent by Joseph Hume to Thomas Attwood.*

26366 A **DIALOGUE** on rick-burning, rioting, &c. between Squire Wilson, Hughes, his steward, Thomas, the bailiff, and Harry Brown, a labourer. 23p. *12°. 1830. See also 1831.*

26367 DONOVAN, M. Domestic economy. (*The Cabinet Cyclopædia.*) 2 vols. *8°. 1830–37.*

26368 ENGLAND. *Commissioners for Enquiring concerning Charities.* Charities of the Borough of Warwick. Report of His Majesty's Commissioners...for inquiring into the public charities of the Borough of Warwick, August 1826. 192p. *8°. Warwick & London, 1830.*

26369 —— *Laws, etc.* Laws for the regulation of cotton mills and factories. *s.sh.fol. Stockport, [1830] [Br. 508(2)] The Oastler copy, sent by post from Manchester to John Wood (1793–1871).*

26370 —— *Parliament. House of Commons.* Debate upon Sir James Mackintosh's motion for abolishing the punishment of death in certain cases of forgery, in the House of Commons...7th of June, 1830. ⟨Extracted from the Mirror of Parliament, Part LX.⟩ 55p. *8°. 1830. The Agar Ellis copy.*

26371 EVELYN, JOHN (*fl.* 1830). Co-operation. An address to the labouring classes, on the plans to be pursued and the errors to be avoided in conducting trading unions. 28p. *8°. 1830.*

26372 FACTS for the consideration of the Christian and the philanthropist. [Concerning intoxicating drinks.] *s.sh.8°. Birmingham, [c. 1830]*

26373 [FANSHAWE, C. M.] Provision for a family. [A poem.] 2p. *s.sh.8⁰*. [*London, c.* 1830] [*Br.* 674]

26374 FEILD, E., *Bishop of Newfoundland*. An address on the state of the country, read to the inhabitants of Kidlington...Nov. 28, 1830...Second edition. 22p. *12⁰*. *Oxford & London*, 1830.

26375 [FENNELL, ?] M. Fellenberg, his schools and plans. To the editor of the Christian Observer. [The article is signed: F. and the introductory letter, Z.] 34p. *8⁰*. [1830 ?] *An inscription on the fly-leaf reads: The Honble. Agar Ellis, M.P., with Mr. Fennell's respects.*

26376 FINCH, JOHN (1783–1857). Friendly societies. The following letter was read at a general meeting of the officers of the Liverpool Friendly Societies Union, on... August 26, 1830, and now published at their request. To the officers and members of trade unions and benefit societies in Liverpool and other places. [Dated: Mill-street, Liverpool, Aug. 25, 1830.] *s.sh.fol. n.p.* [1830] *See note to no.* 26033.

26377 GOLDSMID, SIR F. H., *Bart.* Remarks on the civil disabilities of British Jews. 72p. *8⁰*. 1830. *The Agar Ellis copy.*

26378 [GOLDSMID, SIR I. L. ?] Two letters [the first signed: G. (i.e. Isaac Lyon Goldsmid ?), the second F.H.G. (i.e. Francis Henry Goldsmid)], in answer to the objections urged against Mr. Grant's Bill for the relief of the Jews: with an appendix. 20p. *8⁰*. 1830. *The copy that belonged to George Agar Ellis, Baron Dover, with a presentation inscription on the title-page: With Mr. I. L. Goldsmid's compliments.*

26379 GREEVES, J. W. A reply to Mr. Geary's appeal to the weavers of Norwich. [Dated: Feb. 10th, 1830.] 23p. *12⁰*. *Norwich*, [1830] *The Oastler copy.*

26380 GREGSON, H. Suggestions for improving the condition of the industrious classes, by establishing friendly societies and savings' banks, in co-operation with each other; accompanied by a set of rules and regulations for each; and also by abstracts from the two last Acts of Parliament... 184p. *8⁰*. 1830.

26381 GRIERSON, G. A. The circumstances of Ireland considered with reference to the question of poor laws. 64p. *8⁰*. *London & Dublin*, 1830.

26382 HANWAY, J. Domestic happiness promoted; in a series of discourses from a father to his daughter, on occasion of her going into service. Calculated to render servants in general virtuous and happy...Abridged from "Virtue in humble life"...New edition. 168p. *12⁰*. 1830. *For other editions, see* 1774.

26383 HARBORD, E., *Baron Suffield*. A charge delivered at the Quarter Sessions for the county of Norfolk, held by adjournment, March 10, 1830. With notes and appendix. 113p. *8⁰*. [*London &*] *Norwich*, 1830.

26384 *HILL, F. The national distress, with its remedies, real and imaginary, examined in three letters, to the mechanics and artisans of Birmingham. 80p. *8⁰*. *London & Birmingham*, [1830 ?] *Letter II paginated 1–12 instead of 13–24. The FWA copy, that belonged to William Pare.*

26385 Practical **HINTS** for improving the condition of the labouring classes. 16p. *8⁰*. [1830 ?]

26386 The **HISTORY** of all the charities, donations, gifts, &c.&c. belonging to the parish of St. Giles without

Cripplegate. Carefully extracted from the reports of His Majesty's Commissioners appointed to Enquire concerning Charities. 160p. *8⁰*. 1830.

26387 HODGSON, JOHN (1795–1871 ?). Proposed improvements in friendly societies, upon the Southwell system or any other similar to it, by the introduction into them of an 'early pay plan', as adopted by a society called "the Upper Division of the Lath of Scray Friendly Society", established at Sittingbourne, in and for the county of Kent. [Second edition.] 56p. *8⁰*. [1830]

26388 HOLFORD, G. P. Letter to the editor of the Quarterly Review, on a misstatement contained in the 42d volume of that work, page 155, relative to the supposed ill-success of the General Penitentiary at Millbank. 56p. *8⁰*. 1830.

26389 HOPPUS, J. An essay on the nature and objects of the course of study, in the class of the philosophy of the human mind and logic, in the University of London. 34p. *8⁰*. 1830. *Presentation copy, with inscription, from the author to George Agar Ellis, Baron Dover.*

26390 HORNER, L. Letter to the Council of the University of London...1st June, 1830. Not published. 49p. *8⁰*. 1830. *The Agar Ellis copy.*

26391 HORTON, SIR R. J. W., *Bart.* The causes and remedies of pauperism in the United Kingdom considered: introductory series. Being a defence of the principles and conduct of the Emigration Committee against the charges of Mr. Sadler. 150p. *8⁰*. 1830.

26392 —— An inquiry into the causes and remedies of pauperism. First series. Containing correspondence with C. Paulett Thomson, Esq., M.P. upon the conditions under which colonization would be justifiable as a national measure. 38p. *8⁰*. 1830. *See also* 1831.

26393 —— Causes and remedies of pauperism. Second series. Containing correspondence with M. Duchâtel, author of an essay on charity, with an explanatory preface. 46p. *8⁰*. 1830. *See also* 1831.

26394 —— Third series: containing letters to Sir Francis Burdett, Bt., M.P. upon pauperism in Ireland. 86p. *8⁰*. 1830. *See also* 1831.

26395 —— Causes and remedies of pauperism. Fourth series. Explanation of Mr. Wilmot Horton's Bill, in a letter and queries addressed to N. W. Senior, Esq. Professor of Political Economy in the University of Oxford. With his answers...[With appendixes.] 112, xxivp. *8⁰*. 1830.

26396 —— Correspondence between the Right Hon. R. Wilmot Horton and a select class of the members of the London Mechanics' Institution, formed for investigating the most efficient remedies for the present distress among the labouring classes in the United Kingdom...also a letter from the Right Hon. R. Wilmot Horton to Dr. Birkbeck, President of the Institution, and his answer... 21p. *8⁰*. 1830. *For another edition, appended to Horton's Lectures on statistics, see* 1832 (GENERAL).

26397 H——S, W——M. To rioters and incendiaries. A letter [dated: Dec. 4, 1830] containing the last advice of a rioter to two of his former associates. To which is added, a list of the penalties to which rioters and others expose themselves, together with a copy of the King's Proclamation... 32p. *8⁰*. 1830. *The copy that belonged to the Duke of Wellington, with his book-plate.*

26398 HULBERT, C. A letter to R. Jenkins, Esq.

M.P. offering a few brief hints on the distresses of the poor and middling classes, the increase of machinery, the local currency, &c. By a Burgess of Shrewsbury. 12p. *8°*. *Shrewsbury & London, 1830.*

26399 JAMAICA. *Assembly.* [*Begin.*] The following Bill passed the House of Assembly on the 17th of February last...Jew Bill... 3p. *8°*. *n.p.* [1830] *The Agar Ellis copy.*

26400 KITTREDGE, J. No. 2. Speech of Mr. J. Kittredge at the second anniversary of the American Temperance Society. 8p. *8°*. *Bradford Temperance Society,* [1830?]

26401 The **LABOURERS'** friend; or, a few words of advice to the rural peasantry. 16p. *8°*. 1830.

26402 —— Third edition. 16p. *8°*. 1830.

26403 LANCASHIRE lads! Stop and read! What the weavers of Perth say...A copy of a letter, addressed to His Grace the Duke of Athol, by the working weavers belonging to Perth. [Thanks for help at a time of distress. Signed: George Penny and others. With a supplementary paragraph addressed to the Lancashire weavers.] *s.sh.fol.* *Manchester,* [*c.* 1830]

26404 LAW, G. H., *Bishop of Bath and Wells.* Remarks on the present distresses of the poor. 26p. *8°*. *Wells, London, &c.,* 1830.

26405 LAW, JAMES T. The poor man's garden or, a few brief rules for regulating allotments of land to the poor, for potatoe gardens. With remarks, addressed to Mr. Malthus, Mr. Sadler, and the political economists, and a reference to the opinions of Dr. Adam Smith, in his "Wealth of nations"...Third edition. 23p. *8°*. 1830.

26406 LIGHT, A. W. A plan for the amelioration of the condition of the poor of the United Kingdom (more particularly Ireland); and for their permanent establishment, by means at once simple and economical... 186 [214]p. *8°*. 1830. *Presentation copy, with inscription and manuscript notes, from the author to an unnamed recipient.*

26407 —— [Another issue.] 186[212]p. *8°*. 1830.

26408 LITTLETON, EDWARD J., *Baron Hatherton.* The truck system. The speech of E. J. Littleton, Esq., M.P., (for Staffordshire,) in the House...March 17, on moving for leave to bring in a Bill "to render more effectual the laws requiring payment of wages in money." Taken from the "Mirror of Parliament," and published by the Dudley Anti-Truck Committee. 21p. *8°*. *London & Dudley,* 1830.

26409 M'CORMAC, H. An appeal in behalf of the poor; submitted to the consideration of those who take an interest in bettering their condition. 27p. *8°*. *Belfast,* 1830. *The copy that belonged to T. Spring Rice, Baron Monteagle.* **Another, the FWA copy, belonged to William Pare. The date in the imprint has been altered in manuscript to '1831' in Pare's copy.*

26410 —— On the best means of improving the moral and physical condition of the working classes; being an address, delivered on the opening of the first monthly scientific meetings, of the Belfast Mechanics' Institute. 24p. *8°*. 1830. *The copy that belonged to William Lovett.* **Another, the FWA copy, belonged to William Pare.*

26411 —— A plan for the relief of the unemployed poor. 32p. *8°*. *Belfast,* 1830. **Another, the FWA copy, belonged to William Pare.*

26412 MACHINE-BREAKING and the changes occasioned by it in the village of Turvey Down. A tale of the times, November, 1830. 37p. *12°*. *Oxford & London* 1830.

26413 [**M'LAREN,** C.] The Scotsman's advice to the labouring classes, on the best means of raising their wages, and securing themselves and their families against want. ⟨Reprinted from the Scotsman of Nov. 10. and 13. 1830.⟩ 16p. *8°*. *Edinburgh,* 1830.

26414 MACQUEEN, T. P. Thoughts and suggestions on the present condition of the country. 50p. *8°*. 1830.

For the **MAGAZINE OF USEFUL KNOWLEDGE** and co-operative miscellany, *see* vol. III, *Periodicals list.*

26415 MARRIAGE, J. Letters on the distressed state of the agricultural labourers, and suggesting a remedy, addressed to the nobility of England... 16p. *8°*. *Chelmsford & London,* 1830. *The Agar Ellis copy. See also* 1831, 1832.

26416 MATTHEWS, W. A letter to one of the proprietors of the Grand Junction Water Company, on... Mr. Peel's letter to the water companies of the Metropolis. 15p. *8°*. 1830. *Presentation copy, with inscription, from the author to Sir Francis Burdett (see also note to no. 22542).*

26417 —— A sketch of the principal means which have been employed to ameliorate the intellectual and moral condition of the working classes at Birmingham. 34p. *12°*. 1830.

26418 [**MOLESWORTH,** J. E. N.] The rick-burners: a tale for the present times. 16p. *8°*. *Canterbury,* 1830.

26419 [——] Third edition. 16p. *8°*. *Canterbury & London,* 1830.

26420 MOOR, J. F. The duty of submission to civil authority. A sermon, preached in the parish church of Bradfield, Berks, on...November 28, 1830, on occasion of the late disturbances in that neighbourhood. 27p. *12°*. *London & Reading,* 1830.

26421 NATIONAL ASSOCIATION FOR THE PROTECTION OF LABOUR. Address of the National Association...to the workmen of the United Kingdom. 4p. *12°*. *Manchester,* [1830] *Attributed by HSF to John Doherty, the secretary.*

26422 NEWMAN, ALAN. Criminal executions in England: with remarks on the penal code, prison discipline and abuses...To which are added, strictures on the character of "The Times" newspaper, and a demonstration of the innocence of James Butler, lately executed for...firing the floor-cloth manufactory of Messrs. Downing, at Chelsea. 222p. *8°*. 1830.

26423 O., B. V. Emancipation of the Jews. Copy of a letter, taken from the Times of February 3rd instant. [Dated: 12, Devonshire Square, January 30, 1830.] 8p. *8°*. [1830] *The Agar Ellis copy.*

26424 OASTLER, R. A letter on the horrors of white slavery...taken from the Leeds Mercury of October 16th, 1830: also a copy of verses written twelve years ago, on the same subject [signed: J.S., 1818]. *s.sh.fol. Leeds,* [1830] [*Br.* 513] *Oastler's own copy.*

26425 O'BRIEN, W. S. Plan for the relief of the poor in Ireland, with observations on the English and Scotch poor laws: addressed to the landed proprietors of Ireland. 59p. *8°*. 1830. *Presentation copy, with inscription, from the author to M. T. Sadler.*

26426 A few **OBSERVATIONS,** additional to those addressed to labourers under the authority of the Society for the Diffusion of Useful Knowledge. 4p. *8°.* [*London,* 1830 ?]

26427 **OKEDEN,** D. O. P. A letter, to the Members in Parliament, for Dorsetshire, on the subject of poor-relief and labourers' wages. 19p. *8°. Blandford, Dorchester, &c.,* 1830.

26428 **PAGE,** FREDERICK. The principle of the English poor laws illustrated and defended, by an historical view of indigence in civil society... To which are added observations on the state of the indigent poor in Ireland, and the existing institutions for their relief... Third edition, with additions. 130, 72p. *8°. London & Dublin,* 1830. *For other editions, see* 1822.

26429 **PATTISON,** G. S. Testimonials transmitted to the Council of the University of London by Granville S. Pattison, surgeon. 28p. *8°.* 1830. *The Agar Ellis copy.*

26430 ——, *and others.* Observations [by Granville S. Pattison, Dionysius Lardner, Augustus De Morgan, John Conolly, George Long and J. R. McCulloch] on a letter addressed by Leonard Horner, Esq. to the Council of the University, dated June 1, 1830. [With 'Statement of Dr. Mühlenfels'.] 35p. *8°.* 1830. *The Agar Ellis copy.*

26431 **PINNEY,** J. An exposure of the causes of the present deteriorated condition of health, and diminished duration of human life, compared with that which is attainable by nature; being an attempt to deduce... such rules of living as may greatly tend to correct the evil, and restore the health of mankind... forming a code of health and long life, founded on principles fixed and indisputable. 323p. *8°.* 1830.

26432 Random **RAMBLES.** [Anecdotes of London life, fashions, the book-trade, etc.] 4p. *8°.* [1830]

26433 **RANKEN,** A. A letter addressed to the Rev. Dr. Chalmers, occasioned by his frequent allusions to the "impregnable minds of certain convenors and councilmen" on the subject of pauperism in the city of Glasgow; accompanied with official documents. 32p. *8°. Glasgow,* 1830.

26434 *RECUEIL de documens relatifs à la Prison pénitentiaire de Genève.* 194p. *8°. Genève & Paris,* 1830[–34] *p.179–194 contain supplementary pieces published after the date on the title-page of the collection. The copy that belonged to George Grote.*

26435 **REFLECTIONS** on the injustice and impolicy of the truck system. By a Staffordshire moorlander. 25p. *8°. London, Hanley, &c.,* [1830]

26436 **RELIGIOUS TRACT SOCIETY.** No. 1614. The stone-breaker. 8p. *8°.* [*c.* 1830]

26437 **REMARKS** on the injurious effects of the truck system; with an appendix consisting of affidavits, &c. 20p. *8°. Dudley,* [1830] *The Agar Ellis copy.*

26438 —— Third edition, revised. 20p. *8°. Dudley,* 1830.

26439 A **REPORT** of the proceedings of the anti-truck meeting for the Staffordshire Potteries, held on the Pottery Race Ground, on... October 18, 1830, William Ridgway, Esq. chief bailiff of Hanley and Shelton, in the chair... 17p. *8°. Hanley,* [1830] *The Agar Ellis copy.*

26440 **RICHARDSON,** JOHN, *of Heydon.* A proposal for a change in the poor laws, and the reduction of the poor's rate by the beneficial employment of the labourers; in a letter... to the Right Hon. Edward, Lord Suffield. 47p. *8°. London & Norwich,* [1830] *See also* 1831.

26441 **S.,** G. W. A view and description of the Eastern Penitentiary of Pennsylvania. 8p. *8°. Philadelphia,* 1830.

26442 **SADLER,** M. T. The speech of Michael Thomas Sadler, M.P. for Newark, in the House of Commons, on... the third of June, on proposing poor laws for Ireland, preparatory to a general measure in behalf of the labouring classes of England. 51p. *8°.* 1830.

26443 **SCOTTISH TEMPERANCE SOCIETY.** First annual report of the Glasgow & West of Scotland Temperance Society... 48p. *8°. Glasgow,* 1830. *The copy that belonged to John C. Colquhoun (1803–1870), with his book-plate. See also* 1831.

26444 **SCROPE,** G. P. The common cause of the landlord, tenant, and labourer, and the common cure of their complaint. In a letter to the agriculturists of the south of England. 15p. *8°.* 1830. *Reissued in* On the poor laws and their abuse, *1832 (q.v.).*

26445 [——] A letter to the agriculturists of England, on the expediency of extending the poor law to Ireland. By a landowner. 22p. *8°.* 1830. *Reissued in* On the poor laws and their abuse, *1832 (q.v.).*

26446 **SEINE,** *Département de la.* Préfecture. *Bureau de Charité de Paris.* Manuel des commissaires et dames de charité. 80p. *8°. Paris,* 1830.

26447 **SENTENCES** of the prisoners tried before the Special Commission at Winchester, December, 1830. 2l. *s.sh.fol. Southampton,* [1830] [*Br.* 517]

26448 **SOCIETY FOR THE DIFFUSION OF USEFUL KNOWLEDGE.** An address to the labourers on the subject of destroying machinery. 8p. *8°.* 1830.

26449 **STEVENS,** JAMES, *accountant.* Remarks compiled for the use of benefit societies; with the recent Acts of Parliament applicable to friendly societies and savings' banks, and comments thereon. 73p. *8°. Plymouth & Devonport,* 1830.

26450 **STRICKLAND,** *afterwards* **CHOLMLEY,** SIR G., *Bart.* Discourse on the poor laws of England and Scotland, on the state of the poor of Ireland, and on emigration... Second edition, enlarged. 139p. *8°.* 1830. *For another edition, see* 1827.

26451 **SUGGESTIONS** respecting the object and management of mechanics' institutions. 10p. *12°. Manchester,* 1830. *Tentatively attributed to William Rathbone (1787–1868). The Agar Ellis copy.*

26452 **SWING,** FRANCIS, *pseud.* The life and history of Swing, the Kent rick-burner. Written by himself. 24p. *12°. R. Carlile,* 1830.

26453 —— [Another edition.] The life & history of Swing, the Kent rick burner, written by himself. 8p. *8°. W. P. Chubb,* [1830 ?]

26454 —— Swing and O'Connell. A letter from Swing, the rick-burner, to Daniel O'Connell, M.P. on the late proclamations. 8p. *8°.* [1830 ?]

For the **TEMPERANCE SOCIETY RECORD,** 1830–31, *see vol.* III, *Periodicals list.*

26455 **THOMSON,** ANTHONY T. Syllabus of lectures on medical jurisprudence in the University of London by Anthony Todd Thomson... Professor of Materia

Medica and Therapeutics; and Andrew Amos...Professor of Law. 15p. *8°.* 1830. *The Agar Ellis copy.*

26456 A dispassionate and succinct **VIEW** of the truck system, as it affects the labourer, the capitalist, the landlord, and the state; with an attempt to answer the query, "Is it a subject for legislative interference?"... 26p. *8°. Birmingham,* 1830.

26457 WATKINS, H. G. A letter to the heads of families, parishioners of St. Swithin and St. Mary Bothaw, London. By the Rector. [On the conduct of a Christian household.] 12p. *8°. [London,]* 1830.

26458 WEYLAND, J. Thoughts submitted to the employers of labour, in the county of Norfolk, with a few words to the employed. 14p. *8°. Norwich & London,* 1830.

26459 [WHATELY, R., *Archbishop of Dublin.*] A letter to his parishioners on the disturbances which have lately occurred. By a country pastor. 12p. *12°.* 1830.

26460 WHATELY, THOMAS (*d.* 1864). [*Begin.*] My Christian friends...[An address, dated November 27, 1830, against fire raising and other outrages.] 8p. *8°. Maidenhead,* [1830]

26461 WILLIS, THOMAS H. Hints on the poor rate and settlement law; equalization of rate, and diminution of poor houses; and of pauperism, how to be effected, so as to reduce the rate to the present rate payer upwards of three-fourths, without affecting the poor fund. 16p. *8°.* [1830] *The Agar Ellis copy.*

26462 —— [Another edition, with 'Proofs in support of my propositions'.] 23p. *8°.* 1830.

26463 WINTON, J. and **KYLE,** W. Report...to the proprietors of the estate of Milton; of the ground occupied by the Phoenix Foundry; and of the estate of Blythswood, relative to the proposed improvements on the burn or watercourse, traversing the lands belonging to them respectively. 11p. *4°. Glasgow,* 1830. *The Rastrick copy.*

26464 X. To the people. Friends and fellow countrymen, read, and attend to your true interests. [Against machine breaking and incendiarism. Signed: Your friend, X., and dated, December 7, 1830.] *s.sh.fol. Tunbridge Wells,* [1830] [*Br. 511*]

26465 To the **YEOMANRY** and farmers of the county of Devon. [A discussion of the causes and remedies of agricultural unrest. Signed: The country gentleman.] 16p. *8°. Exeter & London,* [1830]

SLAVERY

26466 An **ABSTRACT** of the British West Indian statutes, for the protection and government of slaves. 43p. *8°.* 1830.

26467 ALEXANDER, R. Fate of the colonies. A letter to the proprietors and planters of the West Indies, resident in the colonies. 31p. *8°.* 1830.

26468 B. Copy of a letter to the editor of the Wakefield and Halifax Journal, on the immediate abolition of slavery, published the 5th of November, 1830. *s.sh.fol. n.p.* [1830 ?] [*Br. 512*] *The Oastler copy.*

26469 BARRY, JOHN. Letter addressed to the Right Hon. Sir George Murray...occasioned by certain remarks contained in a pamphlet, by A. Barclay, Esq., of Jamaica, entitled, "Effects of the late colonial policy of Great Britain," &c. involving the characters of the missionaries in that island. 30p. *8°.* 1830.

26470 BRITISH COLONIAL SLAVERY, compared with that of pagan antiquity. 65p. *8°.* 1830.

26471 BROUGHAM, H. P., *Baron Brougham and Vaux.* Corrected report of the speech of Mr. Brougham in the House of Commons, Tuesday, May 13th, 1830, on colonial slavery. 12p. *8°. Leeds,* [1830]

26472 —— Opinions...on negro slavery. [Being extracts from his *Inquiry into the colonial policy of the European powers.*] 23p. *8°.* 1830. *For another edition, see* 1826, *and, for the original work,* 1803 (COLONIES).

26473 CAMPBELL, JOHN, *of Carbrook.* A letter to Sir Robert Peel, Bart. on the subject of British colonial slavery. 64p. *8°. Edinburgh,* 1830.

26474 CANDIDUS, *pseud.* A letter, addressed to Edward Bacon, Esq. upon his sentiments respecting slavery in the West Indies...at the corporation dinner, September 29th, 1830. Second edition. 12p. *12°. Ipswich,* [1830]

26475 DUNCAN, H. Presbyter's letters on the West India question; addressed to...Sir George Murray, G.C.B., M.P., Colonial Secretary, &c. &c. 139p. *8°.* 1830.

26476 DYMOND, J. Dymond on slavery. [Part of *Essays on the principles of morality.*] 8p. *8°. Plymouth,* [1830?] *The Agar Ellis copy. For an edition of the whole work, see* 1842 (GENERAL).

26477 FEMALE SOCIETY FOR BIRMINGHAM, WEST BROMWICH, WEDNESBURY, WALSALL...FOR THE RELIEF OF BRITISH NEGRO SLAVES. The fifth report of the Female Society for Birmingham...established in 1825. 68p. *8°. Birmingham,* 1830. *See also* 1826.

26478 GLADSTONE, SIR J., *Bart.* Facts, relating to slavery in the West Indies and America, contained in a letter addressed to...Sir Robert Peel...Second edition. 30p. *8°. London, Liverpool, &c.,* 1830. *The Agar Ellis copy.*

26479 GODWIN, B. The substance of a course of lectures on British colonial slavery, delivered at Bradford, York, and Scarborough. 171p. *8°.* 1830.

26480 GRANGER, T. C. Speech...at a meeting of the inhabitants of the city of Durham, on the 26th of October, 1830, for the purpose of petitioning Parliament for the abolition of colonial slavery. 7p. *8°. Durham,* [1830]

26481 HORTON, SIR R. J. W., *Bart.* First letter to the freeholders of the county of York, on negro slavery: being an inquiry into the claims of the West Indians for equitable compensation. [With 'Appendix. An order of the King in Council for consolidating the...laws...for improving the condition of the slaves in...Trinidad, Berbice, Demerara, St. Lucia, the Cape of Good Hope, and Mauritius'.] 112p. *8°.* 1830. *The Agar Ellis copy.*

26482 —— Second letter to the freeholders of the county of York, on negro slavery: being an inquiry into the claims of the West Indians for equitable compensation. [With 'Appendix. Speech of...R. Wilmot Horton in the House of Commons, on the 6th of March 1828, on moving for the production of the evidence...upon an appeal against the compulsory manumission of slaves in Demerara and Berbice'.] 74p. *8°*. 1830. *The Agar Ellis copy.*

26483 IGNOTUS, *pseud.* Nine letters to His Grace the Duke of Wellington on colonial slavery. 57p. *8°*. *London & Dublin*, 1830.

26484 KILHAM, H. The claims of West Africa to Christian instruction, through the native languages. 28p. *8°*. 1830.

26485 A LETTER to the most Honorable the Marquis of Chandos [on the injury inflicted on the planters by the abolition of slavery]. By a West India planter. 90p. *8°*. 1830.

26486 [LONG, CHARLES E.] Negro emancipation no philanthropy: a letter to the Duke of Wellington. By a Jamaica proprietor. 53p. *8°*. 1830. *Presentation copy, with inscription, from the author to E. W. Ridly Colborne.*

26487 MURRAY, JOHN (1778-1843). Report of the trial of Mr. John Murray, in the Court of King's Bench, at Westminster-Hall, the 19th December, 1829, on an indictment for a libel on Messrs. Lecesne and Escoffery, of Jamaica. 46p. *8°*. 1830.

26488 PHILAFRIS, *pseud.* A letter to Henry Brougham, Esq. M.P. upon the fall of Algiers, and the civilization of Africa. Not published. 8p. *8°*. 1830.

26489 PLANS of emancipation. 19p. *8°*. [1830] *Inscribed in manuscript 'Private & for consideration'.*

26490 REPRESENTATION of the state of government slaves and apprentices in the Mauritius; with observations. By a resident, who has never possessed either land or slaves in the colony. 78p. *8°*. 1830. *Presentation copy, with inscription, from the anonymous author to 'T. P. Platt Esq.'.*

26491 REVIEW of the Right Hon. R. Wilmot Horton's First letter to the freeholders of Yorkshire, on the claims of the West Indians for equitable compensation. ⟨Extracted from the Edinburgh Christian Instructor, for December 1830.⟩ 34p. *8°*. *n.p.* [1830]

26492 RICHMOND, L. The negro servant; an authentic and interesting narrative, in three parts. (*The Religious Tract Society*, 119.) 24p. *12°*. [1830?]

26493 RILAND, J. On the Codrington estates. A letter to...William, Lord Archbishop of Canterbury, President of the Society for the Propagation of the Gospel in Foreign Parts, on the connection of that institution with Codrington College, in the Island of Barbadoes. 12p. *8°*. 1830.

26494 A SCENE from real life. Enter J***** H***, Esq. candidate for the county of M******** [i.e. Joseph Hume, elected Member of Parliament for Middlesex in 1830. An anti-slavery leaflet in the form of a dialogue]. 2p. *s.sh.8°*. [1830]

26495 SHEFFIELD ANTI-SLAVERY ASSOCIATION. A word for the slave, by the ladies of the Sheffield Anti-slavery Association: and A cry from Africa, by James Montgomery. 16p. *8°*. *Sheffield: for the benefit of the Rotherham Anti-Slavery Bazaar*, 1830.

26496 SIMPSON, R. The duty of British Christians in reference to colonial slavery. A sermon, preached in the Parish Church of St. Peter, Derby, on...October 10th, 1830. 23p. *8°*. *Derby*, [1830]

26497 On SLAVERY; and the duty of the religious public with reference to the question of immediate or gradual abolition. [Signed: A friend to the negroes.] 14p. *8°*. *Pontefract*, 1830.

26498 SOCIETY FOR THE ABOLITION OF SLAVERY THROUGHOUT THE BRITISH DOMINIONS. Address to the electors and people of the United Kingdom. 2p. *s.sh.8°*. [1830]

26499 —— A brief view of the nature and effects of negro slavery, as it exists in the colonies of Great Britain. 4p. *8°*. [1830]

26500 STATE of the question of negro slavery, in January, 1830. Respectfully submitted to His Majesty's Government. 32p. *8°*. [1830] *Inscribed in manuscript: 'Confidential'.*

26501 [STUART, C.] On prospective emancipation of slaves' unborn children. 4p. *8°*. *Dublin: the Hibernian Negro's Friend Society*, [1830?]

26502 [——] Petitions respecting negro slavery. 4p. *8°*. *Bristol*, [1830?]

26503 TELFAIR, C. Some account of the state of slavery at Mauritius, since the British occupation, in 1810; in refutation of anonymous charges promulgated against government and the colony [in the *Anti-Slavery Monthly Reporter*]. 262p. *4°*. *Port-Louis*, 1830. *Presentation copy, with inscription, from the author to Earl Bathurst.*

26504 [THOMPSON, THOMAS P.] Slavery in the West Indies. Re-published from the Westminster Review, No. XXII, on the 1st Jan. 1830... 8p. *8°*. 1830. *See note to no. 25779.*

26505 THOMSON, ANDREW. Substance of the speech delivered at the meeting of the Edinburgh Society for the Abolition of Slavery, on October 19, 1830. 42p. *8°*. *Edinburgh*, 1830.

26506 A concise VIEW of colonial slavery. 20p. *8°*. *Newcastle: Newcastle Ladies' Anti-Slavery Association*, 1830.

26507 A summary VIEW of the progress of reform in the slave colonies of Great Britain, since the 15th of May, 1823. 7p. *8°*. *n.p.* [1830?]

26508 WALSH, ROBERT (1772-1852). Degradation and civilization, or landing at Rio Janeiro. [Extracted from *Notices of Brazil in 1828 and 1829*.] 8p. *8°*. *Bristol*, 1830.

26509 WEST INDIAN SLAVERY. Report of a public meeting held at the Assembly Rooms, Cheltenham, on Thursday, October 7, 1830, to consider the propriety of petitioning Parliament on the subject of the immediate amelioration and gradual abolition of slavery in the West Indies. [20]p. *12°*. *Cheltenham*, [1830]

26510 WEST, F. A. The duty of Britain Christians in reference to colonial slavery: a discourse delivered in... Newcastle-upon-Tyne, October 17th, 1830. 34p. *8°*. *Newcastle & London*, 1830.

26511 WILKS, S. C. The duty of prompt and complete abolition of colonial slavery: a sermon, preached at Bentinck Chapel, St. Mary-le-Bone...September 26, 1830, with a letter to...the Archbishop of Canterbury, and an appendix of episcopal testimonies. 51p. *8°*. 1830.

26512 —— [The second edition.] 53p. *8°*. 1830.

26513 WILSON, D., *Bishop of Calcutta.* The guilt of forbearing to deliver our British colonial slaves. A sermon preached at...Cheltenham...at...Islington...and at... Bedford Row, London... 22p. *8°*. 1830.

POLITICS

26514 The **ANTI-REVOLUTIONIST;** or, an address to the loyal and supine...Second edition. 24p. *8°*. 1830.

26515 BENTHAM, J. Jeremy Bentham to his fellow-citizens of France, on houses of peers and senates. 45p. *8°*. 1830.

26516 BEVERLEY election, 1830. A collection of all the placards, squibs, &c. issued during the above election. 50p. *12°*. *Beverley*, [1830]

26517 BIRMINGHAM. Copy of the petition from the inhabitants of Birmingham, as agreed to at the Town's Meeting held on the 25th January, 1830. [Dated: Feb. 23rd, 1830; presented to the House of Lords in April and to the House of Commons on 17th May.] *s.sh.fol. Birmingham*, 1830. *See note to no.* 26519.

26518 —— Report of the proceedings at the town's meeting...on Monday the 13th December, 1830, in support of parliamentary reform...[With 'Copy of the Petition of Rights passed at the public meeting of the inhabitants of Birmingham, on Monday, the 13th December, 1830'.] 10p. *4°*. *Birmingham*, [1830]. *See note to no.* 26519, *below.*

26519 BIRMINGHAM POLITICAL UNION. Report of the proceedings at the meeting of the inhabitants of Birmingham...the 25th of January, 1830...for the establishment of a General Political Union, with the view of obtaining a redress of public wrongs and grievances. 16p. *4°*. *Birmingham*, 1830. *In a volume of the publications of the Birmingham Political Union which belonged to Thomas Attwood, with notes in his hand throughout.*

26520 —— Authorized copy of the resolutions passed at the meeting at Birmingham, held on the 25th January, 1830, together with the declaration, rules and regulations, of the Political Union for the protection of public rights. 22p. *8°*. *Birmingham*, 1830.

26521 —— Corrected report of the proceedings of the first meeting of the Birmingham Political Union, held... on Monday, May 17, 1830. 15p. *4°*. *Birmingham*, 1830. *See note to no.* 26519.

26522 —— Report of the proceedings of the first annual meeting...held...on Monday, July 26, 1830. 15p. *4°*. *Birmingham*, 1830. *See note to no.* 26519. *See also* 1831, 1832, 1833.

26523 —— Report of the proceedings at the dinner of the Political Union, held...on Monday, October 11, 1830, to commemorate the French Revolution of July 1830. 8p. *4°*. *Birmingham*, 1830. *See note to no.* 26519.

26524 [**BROUGHAM,** H. P., *Baron Brougham and Vaux.*] The country without a government; or plain questions upon the unhappy state of the present administration. Second edition. 21p. *8°*. 1830. *The Agar Ellis copy.*

26525 [——] Third edition. 22p. *8°*. 1830.

26526 [—— ?] The result of the general election; or, what has the Duke of Wellington gained by the dissolution? 38p. *8°*. 1830.

26527 [——] Second edition. 38p. *8°*. 1830.

26528 [——] Fourth edition. 38p. *8°*. 1830.

26529 [**CANNING,** J., *Viscountess Canning.*] An authentic account of Mr. Canning's policy with respect to the constitutional charter of Portugal, in reply to "Observations on the papers laid before Parliament". [Revised by Charles Greville.] 50p. *8°*. 1830. *The Agar Ellis copy.*

For **CARLILE'S JOURNAL FOR 1830,** *see* vol. III, *Periodicals list.*

For **CARPENTER,** WILLIAM (1797–1874), Political letters and pamphlets, 1830–31, *see* vol. III, *Periodicals list, Political letters and pamphlets.*

26530 An Utilitarian **CATECHISM.** 64p. *8°*. 1830.

26531 CHANNING, WILLIAM E. Remarks on the disposition which now prevails to form associations, and to accomplish all objects by organized masses. 36p. *8°*. 1830.

26532 CHURCH, SIR R. Observations on an eligible line of frontier for Greece as an independent state...With a preface by the Rt. Hon. R. Wilmot Horton, M.P. 22p. *8°*. 1830. *The Agar Ellis copy.*

26533 CIVIS, *pseud.* General hints for a revision of the parliamentary representation in the House of Commons; in letters addressed to the editor of the Glasgow Courier by C.V., now changed to Civis. 14p. *8°*. *Edinburgh*, 1830. *The copy that belonged to M. T. Sadler.*

26534 COBBETT, W. Eleven lectures on the French and Belgian revolutions, and English boroughmongering: delivered in the Theatre of the Rotunda, Blackfriars Bridge... 11 parts. *8°*. 1830.

26535 —— History of the regency and reign of King George the Fourth. 2 vols. *12°*. 1830–34.

26536 —— A letter to the King. [An adaptation from Cobbett's *Petition to the King*, in favour of parliamentary reform and against the sinecure system. Edited by W. P. Chubb?] 8p. *8°*. [1830]

For **COMMON SENSE,** vox populi, *see* vol. III, *Periodicals list.*

26537 A **COPY** of the intended petition to Parliament. At a meeting...on Friday, the 12th of November 1830... signed by 28,344 old women, over eighty-six years of age. Betty Nobottom, in the chair...[A satire.] *s.sh.fol.* [*London*, 1830] [*Br.* 507(1)]

26538 No. 1. Saturday, Aug. 28, 1830. Price 3d. The **CRISIS,** or star to the Great Northern Union, containing an address to the people of England...on the plan to be adopted to effect an immediate reform of the House of Commons; and on the conduct of Mr. Prentice and the base faction of the Manchester Times newspaper, to Mr. Hunt, their guest. 16p. *8°*. *Manchester*, [1830]

26539 The present **CRISIS** in France considered in reference to England. 41p. *8°*. 1830. *Attributed in a pencil note on the title-page to 'the Reverend H. Raikes'.*

26540 Aux **ÉLECTEURS** du département de l'Isère. [An address, signed: Un électeur, in support of the candidature of M. Dubois-Aymé at the election of June 1830.] 8p. *8°*. *Grenoble*, [1830]

26541 ENGLISHMEN read!!! From the Morning Advertiser, Thursday, August 26, 1830. Nice pickings. [A list of the incomes of certain peers and bishops.] *s.sh.fol.* [*London*, 1830] [*Br.* 515]

26542 EQUALITY. [A poem, beginning 'Far through

the gloom, the philosophic eye...'.] p.3–14. *12°*. *n.p.* [*c.* 1830 ?]

26543 The moral and political **EVILS** of the taxes on knowledge; expounded in 1. The speeches delivered at the City of London Literary and Scientific Institution, on...a petition to Parliament against the stamps on newspapers ...2. The petition...3. A letter of the editor of "The Scotsman" to the Chancellor of the Exchequer: to which is appended an abstract of the parliamentary returns of the amount of stamps purchased, and of the advertisement duty paid by the leading metropolitan journals. 16p. *8°*. 1830. *With an inscription on the title-page, 'With Mr Humes Compts to Mr [illegible] Wilde'. *Another, the FWA copy, that belonged to William Pare, was given to him by Frederick Hill, and has the book-stamp of the Birmingham Co-operative Society.*

26544 A brief **EXPOSITION** of the foreign policy of Mr. Canning, as contrasted with that of the existing Administration. 50p. *8°*. 1830. *The Agar Ellis copy.*

26545 FRANCE. The French charters, the first granted by Louis XVIII, June 14 [or rather June 4], 1814; the second, remodelled by the Chamber of Deputies, and sworn to by Louis Philip d'Orleans, August 7th [or rather August 14], 1830. 14p. *8°*. *Birmingham,* [1830]

26546 FRENCH REVOLUTION. An address to the people of Paris agreed to at the London Tavern, Bishopgate Street, at a dinner of radical reformers, August 16, 1830. William Cobbett, Esq. in the chair. *s.sh.4°.* *Birmingham,* [1830]. [*Br.* 507(2)] *The copy that belonged to Francis Place.*

26547 HUNT, H. Mr. Hunt's letter to the King, upon the intended civic feast. [Dated: Oct. 21, 1830.] *s.sh.4°.* *Southwark,* [1830]. [*Br.* 509] *The copy that belonged to Francis Place.*

26548 KING, PETER, *1st Baron King.* Notes of domestic and foreign affairs, during the last years of the reign of George I. and the early part of the reign of George II. pp.1–132, 141–4. *8°*. [1830 ?] *A separate issue of part of vol. 2 of the 7th Baron King's* The life of John Locke, *1830* (*no.* 26095). *With the book-plate of P. J. Locke King.*

26549 [**KOZLOVSKY,** P. B., *Prince.*] Lettres au Duc de Broglie, sur les prisonniers de Vincennes. 24p. *8°*. *Londres,* 1830.

26550 M. To the people of England. [A letter: dated October 1, 1830, and signed M. Printed and circulated in defiance of the Stamp Act.] 4p. *8°*. [1830]

26551 METROPOLITAN POLITICAL UNION. An appeal to the people of England, by the Council of the Metropolitan Political Union. Reprinted from a monitory letter to Sir Robert Peel. [Signed: H. Hunt, chairman.] 12p. *12°*. 1830.

26552 [**MUNDELL,** A.] The result of the pamphlets; or, what the Duke of Wellington has to look to. 35p. *8°*. 1830.

26553 [**NICOLAS,** SIR N. H.] A letter to the Duke of Wellington, on the propriety and legality of creating peers for life: with precedents. Second edition. 56p. *8°*. 1830.

26554 NOTES on the pretended rights of the Princess of Grand Para to the Portugueze throne. 15p. *8°*. 1830. *The Agar Ellis copy.*

26555 OBSERVATIONS on the state of the

country, and on the proper policy of Administration. 32p. *8°*. 1830. *The Agar Ellis copy.*

26556 OBSERVATIONS on two pamphlets (lately published) attributed to Mr. Brougham. 80p. *8°*. 1830.

26557 —— [Another edition. With a postscript.] 95p. *8°*. 1830.

26558 PARTIES and factions in England, at the accession of William IV. 57p. *8°*. [1830]

For the **PENNY PAPERS FOR THE PEOPLE,** published by the Poor Man's Guardian, *see* vol. III, *Periodicals list.*

26559 *PHILO-JUNIUS, pseud.* Reform, in two parts. Part the first contains an introductory letter addressed to John George Lamberton [*sic*] Esq. M.P. with a from [*sic*] of a proposed Bill for a general reform in the Commons House of Parliament. Part the second, or the touchstone, contains some prefatory observations on the present system of elections, a proposed petition, and form of a Bill for the reform of a borough, with general remarks. [From *The Pamphleteer,* vol. XXIII, no. 46.] Sixteenth edition. 33p. *8°*. *London & Stroud, Gloucestershire,* 1830. *The FWA copy that belonged to William Pare, with manuscript notes throughout.*

26560 "Nice **PICKINGS.**" A countryman's remarks on Cobbett's "Letter to the King." 11p. *8°*. 1830.

26561 On the formal **RECOGNITION** of Chile and Peru. 8p. *8°*. 1830. *The Agar Ellis copy.*

26562 REFLECTIONS on the nullity of the elective franchise. By a freeholder. 24p. *8°*. 1830.

26563 REPLY to a pamphlet entitled "What has the Duke of Wellington gained by the dissolution?" By a graduate of the University of Oxford. 39p. *8°*. 1830.

26564 ROEDERER, P. L., *Comte.* De la propriété considérée dans ses rapports avec les droits politiques... Troisième édition. 47p. *8°*. *Paris,* 1830.

26565 S., G. The Duke of Wellington the champion of reform. 16p. *8°*. 1830. *The Agar Ellis copy.*

26566 SCARLETT, J., *Baron Abinger.* Speech of Sir James Scarlett, at a meeting of the electors of Malton, at the late general election, 1830. 34p. *8°*. 1830. *The Agar Ellis copy.*

26567 A **SCRAP** for the New Year; or the cause of national distress briefly considered. 24p. *12°*. *York, London, &c.,* 1830. *The Agar Ellis copy.*

26568 SINCLAIR, SIR JOHN, *Bart.* Thoughts on the means of preventing the public mischiefs which necessarily arise, from the great load of public and private business with which the House of Commons is at present overwhelmed. Addressed to the Right Hon. Sir Robert Peel... 19p. *8°*. 1830.

26569 SMITHSON, J. The substance of a speech delivered...in the Leeds Court-House...September 23rd, 1830, to consider the propriety of addressing the French people on the subject of their recent "Glorious" Revolution...Second edition. 12p. *8°*. *Leeds,* 1830. *The Oastler copy.*

26570 TEMPLE, H. J., *Viscount Palmerston.* Speech of Viscount Palmerston, in the House of Commons, on... the tenth of March, 1830, on moving for papers respecting the relations of England with Portugal. 50p. *8°*. [1830] *The Agar Ellis copy.*

26571 [**THOMPSON,** THOMAS P.] The article on

Belgium. (Originally entitled "On the change of ministry in France".) From the Westminster Review, No. XXII. First published in October 1829. With a postscript of the 30th of August 1830... 16p. *8°.* 1830. *See note to no.* 25779.

26572 [——] The article on Great Britain and France. From the Westminster Review, No. XXV. For July 1, 1830. With a postscript of July 28...with reference to the actual proceedings which have been recommended to the French Government on the subject of the right of election. Republished on the 29th July, 1830... 20p. *8°.* 1830.

26573 [——] The article on radical reform. From the Westminster Review, No. XXIII. For January 1830. Republished on the 1st Jan. 1830... 12p. *8°.* 1830. *See note to no.* 25779. *Another, the FWA copy, belonged to William Pare.*

26574 [——] The article on the Six Acts, especially taxes on literature: reprinted (by permission) from the Westminster Review, No. XXIV. For April 1830. 15p. *8°.* [*London,* 1830] *See note to no.* 25779.

26575 [——?] On the ballot; from the Westminster Review, for July, 1830. Third edition. With corrections and additions. 28p. *8°.* 1830. *Also attributed to James Mill. Attributed to Thompson by Francis Place, in whose collected volume of articles from the Westminster Review this is bound (see note to no. 25779). *Another, the FWA copy, belonged to William Pare, who also owned a second copy, with the stamp of the Birmingham Co-operative Society at the head of the title-page.*

26576 —— An abridgment of the article on the ballot, which appeared in the Westminster Review, No. XXV... (*National Political Union Pledges from Candidates,* 4.) 8p. *8°.* 1830.

26577 [——] On the revolution of 1830. From the Westminster Review, No. XXVI. For October 1, 1830. With a postscript. 16p. *8°.* [1830] *See note to no.* 25779.

26578 [——] The three days in Paris. From the Westminster Review, No. XXVI. For October 1, 1830... 16p. *8°.* 1830. *See note to no.* 25779.

26579 THOUGHTS on parliamentary reform, with a plan for the restoration of the constitution. 19p. *8°.* 1830.

SOCIALISM

26580 The **ADDRESS** of the working classes of Devonshire to their fellow labourers throughout Great Britain and Ireland. [Advocating the collection of funds for the formation of co-operative communities.] *s.sh.fol. Exeter,* [1830?]

26581 ARMAGH CO-OPERATIVE SOCIE-TY. Words of wisdom, addressed to the working classes; containing simple directions by which they may secure... an abundant supply of all the comforts and conveniences, with many of the luxuries...of life. To which are subjoined, the laws of the First Armagh Co-operative Society. 20, ivp. *8°. Armagh,* 1830. *The dedication to Robert Owen is signed in manuscript: J. Burns.*

26582 BAKER, F. The first lecture on co-operation; delivered...April 19, 1830 at the Sessions Room, Bolton. (Reprinted from "The Bolton Chronicle".) (*The Universal Pamphleteer,* 46.) 7p. *8°.* [*London,* 1830]

26583 —— The second lecture on co-operation; delivered...May 3, 1830, at the Sessions Room, Bolton. (Reprinted from "The Bolton Chronicle".) (*The Universal Pamphleteer,* 47.) 8p. *8°.* [*London,* 1830]

26584 [**BARRAULT,** E.] Aux artistes. Du passé et de l'avenir des beaux-arts. (Doctrine de Saint-Simon.) 84p. *8°. Paris,* 1830. *The copy that belonged to Victor Considérant.*

26585 BAZARD, SAINT-AMAND. Religion Saint Simonienne. Lettre à M. le Président de la Chambre des Députés. [Signed: Bazard-Enfantin.] 8p. *8°.* [*Paris,* 1830] *The copy that belonged to Victor Considérant.*

26586 BRITISH ASSOCIATION FOR PRO-MOTING CO-OPERATIVE KNOWLEDGE. Report of the proceedings at the third quarterly meeting of the...Association...January 7, 1830. 36p. *12°.* [1830]

26587 —— Report of the committee, and proceedings at the fourth quarterly meeting, of the...Association... April 8, 1830. 16p. *8°.* [1830] *See also* 1829.

For the **BRITISH CO-OPERATOR,** *see* vol. III, *Periodicals list.*

26588 [**CARNOT,** LAZARE H. and **BAZARD,** SAINT-AMAND, *eds.*] Doctrine de Saint-Simon. Exposition. 2me année. 1829–1830. 172p. *8°. Paris,* 1830. *The copy that belonged to Victor Considérant. For Doctrine Saint-Simonienne. Résumé général de l'exposition faite en 1829 et 1830, see* 1831.

26589 Second edition...**CO-OPERATION.** Dialogue between a shoe-maker and a tailor, on the subject of co-operation. By a member of the Metropolitan Co-operative Trading Association. 4p. *8°.* [*London,* 1830]

26590 The **CO-OPERATOR'S** song. [A ballad.] *s.sh.8°. Carlisle,* [1830?] *See note to no.* 26033.

26591 [**ENFANTIN,** B. P., *and others.*] Doctrine de Saint-Simon. Exposition. Première année. 1829. [By B. P. Enfantin, L. H. Carnot, H. Fournel and C. Duveyrier.] Seconde édition. 431p. *8°. Paris,* 1830. *The copy that belonged to Victor Considérant. See also* 1831.

26592 FOURIER, F. C. M. Le nouveau monde industriel, ou invention du procédé d'industrie attrayante et combinée, distribuée en séries passionnées...Livret d'annonce. p.[577]–664. *8°. Paris,* 1830. *Paginated in sequence with* Le nouveau monde industriel et sociétaire, *1829 (q.v.).*

26593 KING, WILLIAM, *M.D., of Brighton.* An important address to trade unions. [From the Co-operator, published at Brighton...in the year 1829.] 8p. *8°. Manchester,* [1830?] *The Oastler copy.*

For the **LONDON CO-OPERATIVE MAGA-ZINE,** *see* vol. III, *Periodicals list,* Co-operative magazine.

26594 MORGAN, JOHN M. Letter to the Bishop of London. [With 'Address...at the...Mechanics' Institution'.] 58p. *8°.* 1830.

26595 —— Second edition. [With 'Mr. Owen's reply to a letter signed: 'Amicus,' that appeared in the Weekly Free Press, July 17, 1830'.] 66p. *8°.* 1830.

26596 [——] The reproof of Brutus. [In verse.] 229p. *8°.* 1830.

For l'**ORGANISATEUR,** journal de la doctrine Saint-Simonienne, 1830–31, *see* vol. III, *Periodicals list.*

26597 *****OWEN,** ROBERT. Address to the operative manufacturers and agricultural labourers in Great Britain and Ireland. [Dated: January, 1830.] *s.sh.fol. n.p.* [1830] *A proof copy. The FWA copy, that belonged to William Pare.*

26598 —— The addresses of Robert Owen, (as published in the London journals), preparatory to the development of a practical plan for the relief of all classes... 49p. *8°.* 1830.

26599 —— Lectures on an entire new state of society; comprehending an analysis of British society, relative to the production and distribution of wealth; the formation of character; and government, domestic and foreign. 220p. *8°.* [1830] *Presentation copy, with inscription, from the author to Rowland Hill.* *****Another, the FWA copy, belonged to William Pare.

26600 —— The new religion; or, religion founded on the immutable laws of the universe, contrasted with all religions founded on human testimony, as developed in a public lecture, delivered by Mr. Owen...October 20, 1830. 11p. *8°.* [1830]

26601 —— Second lecture on the new religion... delivered by Mr. Owen...Dec. 15, 1830. 8p. *8°.* [1830]

26602 ***——** To the Imperial Parliament of Great Britain. *s.sh.fol. n.p.* [1830] *A proof copy. The FWA copy, that belonged to William Pare.*

26603 **OWEN,** ROBERT D., *ed.* Popular tracts. No. 1[–14]... *12°.* New-York, 1830. Contents: *1. Containing a tale of old England by Robert Dale Owen; 2. Truth and error.* ⟨*From the New Harmony Gazette...*⟩; *3. Containing an address to the industrious classes...by Frances Wright; and an address to the conductors of the New-York periodical press, by R. D. Owen; 4. Prossimo's experience.* ⟨*Extracted from the Free Enquirer.*⟩; *5. Cause of the people. By R. D. Owen.* ⟨*Extracted from the Free Enquirer.*⟩; *6. Containing a sermon on loyalty* [*by R. D. Owen*]; *a*

remonstrance to God [*by Antoine Vieira*]; *and a sermon on free enquiry* [*by R. D. Owen*]; *7. Containing effects of missionary labours; by R. D. Owen. And Religious revivals, by John Neale; 8. Fables. By F. Wright.* ⟨*Extracted from the Free Enquirer*⟩; *9. The French Revolution.* ⟨*Extracted from the Free Enquirer*⟩; *10. Containing Situations, by R. D. Owen; 11. Wealth and misery. By R. D. Owen.* ⟨*Extracted from the New-Harmony Gazette.*⟩; *12. Galileo and the Inquisition. By R. D. Owen.* ⟨*Extracted from the Free Enquirer.*⟩; *13. A tract and a warning. By R. D. Owen.* ⟨*Extracted from the Free Enquirer.*⟩; *14. The new book of chronicles.*

26604 Mr. **OWEN'S** Sunday morning lectures. [A handbill.] *s.sh.8°.* [1830] [*Br.* 514]

26605 [Robert **OWEN'S** creed.] [*Begin.*] I believe that to worship, by mere words... 3p. *8°. n.p.* [*c.* 1830] *The title is taken from a reprint in* The Prompter, *vol.* I, *p.* 233.

26606 **THOMPSON,** WILLIAM (1785 ?–1833). Practical directions for the speedy and economical establishment of communities, on the principles of mutual co-operation, united possessions and equality of exertions and of the means of enjoyments. 265p. *8°.* [1830] *With a presentation inscription on the title-page: 'Bermingham Esq., from the author, through Will. Pare'.*

26607 [**TRANSON,** A. L. E.] De la religion St.-Simonienne. Aux élèves de l'École Polytechnique. 70p. *8°.* Paris, 1830. *The copy that belonged to Victor Considérant.*

26608 **WHITWELL,** S. Description of an architectural model from a design by Stedman Whitwell, Esq. for a community upon a principle of united interests, as advocated by Robert Owen, Esq. 28p. *8°.* 1830. *****Another, the FWA copy, belonged to William Pare.*

26609 **WRIGHT,** F. An address to young mechanics. As delivered in the Hall of Science, June 13, 1830. 13p. *8°.* New-York, 1830.

MISCELLANEOUS

26610 **ALDINI,** G. A short account of experiments made in Italy and recently repeated in Geneva and Paris, for preserving human life and objects of value from destruction by fire... 24p. *8°.* London, Edinburgh, *&c.,* 1830. *The Agar Ellis copy.*

26611 [*Begin.*] **ATTENTION** is earnestly requested to the application...being made to Parliament by His Majesty's Commissioners for Building New Churches... [On the erection of proprietary chapels and the attachment of districts to them.] 2p. *8°.* [1830] *The Agar Ellis copy.*

26612 **BENTHAM,** J. Equity dispatch court proposal: containing a plan for the speedy and unexpensive termination of the suits now depending in equity courts. With the form of a petition, and some account of a proposed Bill for that purpose. 60p. *8°.* 1830.

26613 **BLOMFIELD,** C. J., *Bishop of London.* A letter on the present neglect of the Lord's Day, addressed to the inhabitants of London and Westminster...Fourth edition. 38p. *8°.* 1830. *The Agar Ellis copy.*

26614 **BUELOW,** G. P. VON. Reply supplementary to the author's legal opinion on the time of the coming of age of the reigning dukes of Brunswick-Lüneburg, with an appendix concerning Privy-Counsellor De Schmidt-

Phiseldeck's passing over from the service of the Duke of Brunswick into that of the Hannoverian Government, excited by the pamphlet Hints on the time of the coming of age of the Dukes of Brunswick-Lüneburg...by D. D. Keane...1828; translated by Professor Fr. de Vultejus. 40p. *8°.* Brunswick, 1830. *The Agar Ellis copy.*

26615 **BYRON,** A. I. N., *Baroness Wentworth.* Remarks occasioned by Mr. Moore's notices of Lord Byron's life. 15p. *8°.* [1830] *The Agar Ellis copy.*

26616 **COHEN,** S. J. Extracts from a work entitled Elements of faith, for the use of Jewish youth...Published in 1815. 3p. *8°.* 1830. *The Agar Ellis copy.*

26617 A **COPY** of a petition lately presented to the Hon. the House of Commons, praying for relief in the matter of oaths. With notes, by one of the petitioners... 36p. *8°.* 1830. *The Agar Ellis copy.*

26618 **DAWSON,** F. A sermon preached before the Honourable House of Commons, at the church of St. Margaret, Westminster, on...29th May, 1830 (being the day appointed to be observed as the day of the restoration of King Charles II.). 20p. *4°.* 1830.

26619 **GWYDIR** Chapel, Llanrwst. [A descriptive account.] *s.sh.fol.* Llanrwst, [1830?] *The Agar Ellis copy.*

26620 HORTICULTURAL SOCIETY. The report of the committee appointed on the 2nd of February, 1830, to enquire into the income and expenditure, the debts and assets, and the past and present management of the Horticultural Society... 24p. *4°.* 1830. *The Agar Ellis copy.*

26621 INTERMENT Bill. [A ballad interspersed with dialogue.] *s.sh.fol.* [*London,* 1830] [*Br.* 510]

26622 *LONDON. Livery Companies. *Salters.* A list of the Master, Wardens, Court of Assistants, and Livery, of the Worshipful Company of Salters. 15p. *8°.* 1830. *See also* 1784, 1787, 1790, 1792, 1794, 1797, 1799, 1801, 1803, 1806, 1809, 1812, 1815, 1818, 1821, 1824, 1827.

26623 PHILLPOTTS, H., *Bishop of Exeter.* Dr. Phillpotts' statement respecting the rectory of Stanhope, as given in the House of Commons, on the 22nd Nov., 1830, with the reply in refutation, by C. Rippon, Esq.... 8p. *8°. Newcastle-upon-Tyne,* [1830?]

26624 POCOCK, G. An accompaniment to Mr. G. Pocock's patent terrestrial globe. 25p. *8°. Bristol,* 1830. *The Agar Ellis copy.*

26625 PUTNEYENSIS, *pseud.* Election of churchwardens. A letter to the churchwardens of Putney, in answer to an anonymous pamphlet, entitled A plain statement of facts, &c.&c.&c. 31p. *8°.* 1830. *The Agar Ellis copy.*

26626 REMARKS on that part of the Lord Advocate's Bill for altering the judicial institutions of Scotland which relates to the Commissary or Consistorial Court. By a barrister. 36p. *8°. Edinburgh,* 1830. *The Agar Ellis copy.*

26627 SADLER, M. T. A dissertation upon the balance of food and numbers of animated nature; being the substance of two lectures... before the Philosophical and Literary Society of Leeds. 74p. *8°.* 1830. *The Oastler copy.*

26628 STOCKDALE, W. Stockdale's baronetage of the United Kingdom, for... 1830; with the arms of the baronets. 144p., 38 plates. *12°.* 1830.

26629 —— Stockdale's peerage of the United Kingdom, for... 1830; with the arms of the peers... 175p., 72 plates. *12°.* 1830. *For another edition, see* 1819.

26630 WESTMINSTER Review. [A leaflet outlining the progress of the periodical during the preceding year, with a list of articles reprinted in cheap editions. Dated: Jan. 31, 1830.] 2p. *s.sh.8°.* [1830] [*Br.* 516]

26631 WILLIAMS, THEODORE. To the inhabitants of Hendon. [A letter on the building of a chapel at Mill Hill by William Wilberforce.] 32p. *8°.* [1830] *The Agar Ellis copy.*

1831

GENERAL

26632 BANNATYNE CLUB. Compotum magistri fabrice pontis Dunkeldensis, M.D.XIII.–M.D.XVI. p.82–141. *4°. Edinburgh,* 1831. *Edited by Thomas Thomson (1768–1852). Printed as an appendix to the second edition of* Vitae Dunkeldensis ecclesiae episcorum, *by Alexander Myln.*

26633 BLANE, SIR G., *Bart.* Reflections on the present crisis of publick affairs, with an enquiry into the causes and remedies of the existing clamours, and alleged grievances, of the country, as connected with population, subsistence, wages of labourers, education, &c.... 74p. *8°.* 1831. *The Agar Ellis copy.*

26634 BOUCHER DE CRÈVECOEUR DE PERTHES, J. Opinion de M. Cristophe, sur les prohibitions et la liberté du commerce... Première partie. Deuxième édition. [–Quatrième partie.] 4 vols. *12°. Paris,* 1831–34. *Part 1 only is of the second edition.*

26635 The **BRITISH ALMANAC** of the Society for the Diffusion of Useful Knowledge, for... 1831. [With 'The companion to the Almanac; or year-book of general information'.] 72, 240p. *12°.* [1831] *For other editions, see* 1828.

26636 [**BROWN,** WILLIAM K.] A reform in national institutions essential to the stability and extension of national industry. [With 'Extracts from an essay from the French, on the advantages to be derived from new colonies, in the existing circumstances. Translated, 1814'.] 59p. *8°.* 1831. *Presentation copy, with inscription identifying himself as the author, from William Keer Brown to T. Spring Rice, Baron Monteagle.*

26637 BRYAN, J. B. A practical view of Ireland, from the period of the Union; with plans for the permanent relief of her poor and the improvement of her municipal organization. To which is annexed, a comparative survey of the laws... of foreign states for the maintenance, education, and protection of the working classes. 448p. *12°. Dublin & London,* 1831.

26638 BURGOYNE, M. A letter to the Right Honorable the Lord Duncannon and the Lords Commissioners of His Majesty's Woods and Forests; shewing the necessity of the removal of the deer from the forests of Waltham and Hainault, and also of an enclosure of parts of these forests, in order to... preserve the timber belonging to the Crown, and the crops of the farmers; to find employment and provision for the labouring poor, and... to suppress the vice and immorality which are encouraged and sheltered by the present state of these forests. 78p. *8°.* 1831.

26639 CAREY, M. The new olive branch: addressed to the citizens of South Carolina... [Second edition. No. XIII[–XXV].] p.1–56. *8°. Philadelphia,* 1831.

26640 —— Third edition... No. XV[–XVIII]. p.20–27. *8°. n.p.,* 1831.

26641 [**——**] To the citizens of the United States. Review of the address of the Free Trade Convention.– No. II. Free trade. [Signed: Hamilton, and dated: Oct. 17, 1831.] p.9–15. *8°. n.p.* [1831] *Presumably paginated in sequence with no. I.*

26642 CORN versus currency; or, the forgotten addresses presented to Parliament at the close of the session: being a supplement to a pamphlet lately published, entitled

"Considerations on the necessity and equity of a national banking and annuity system," &c. [Including the texts of a memorial to Parliament by the Staffordshire iron trade, on the state of the currency, and a petition from London and Westminster on the evils of the corn laws.] 24p. *8°. London, Edinburgh, &c.*, 1831.

26643 **COTTERILL**, C. F. An examination of the doctrines of value, as set forth by Adam Smith, Ricardo, M'Culloch, Mill...Torrens, Malthus, Say, &c., &c. Being a reply to those distinguished authors. 128p. *8°.* 1831.

26644 **DUPIN**, F. P. C., *Baron*. Mesure de la richesse française. p.29–46. *4°.* [*Paris*, 1831] *Part of* Institut de France. Séance publique annuelle...30 avril 1831.

26645 *The **EAST-INDIA** register and directory, for 1831; containing...lists of the Company's servants... mariners, &c. not in the service of the...Company; compiled...by G. H. Brown, and F. Clark... 261, 162, 138p. *12°.* [1831]

26646 —— Second edition, corrected to the 25th May, 1831... 496[272], 168, 141p. *12°. London & Edinburgh*, [1831] *For other editions, see* 1804.

26647 The **EFFECTS** of roads on population. 15p. *8°.* 1831.

26648 **ELMES**, J. A topographical dictionary of London and its environs... 418p. *8°.* 1831.

26649 **ENSOR**, G. Anti-union. Ireland as she ought to be. 166p. *8°. Newry & Dublin*, 1831.

26650 **EVERETT**, E. Speech of Mr. Everett, of Massachusetts, in the House of Representatives, on the 14th and 21st of February, 1831, on the execution of the laws and treaties in favor of the Indian tribes. 23p. *8°. n.p.* [1831]

26651 **FAURE**, R. Souvenirs du Midi, ou l'Espagne telle qu'elle est sous ses pouvoirs religieux et monarchique. 387p. *8°. Paris*, 1831.

26652 **FOWLER**, JOHN (*fl.* 1831). Journal of a tour in the state of New York, in the year 1830; with remarks on agriculture in those parts most eligible for settlers: and return to England by the Western Islands, in consequence of shipwreck in the Robert Fulton. 333p. *12°.* 1831.

26653 **FREE TRADE CONVENTION.** The journal of the Free Trade Convention, held in Philadelphia, from September 30 to October 7, 1831; and their address to the people of the United States: to which is added a sketch of the debates... 75p. *8°. Philadelphia*, 1831.

26654 **GLOVER**, S. The history and gazetteer of the county of Derby: drawn up from actual observation and from the best authorities...The materials collected by the publisher, Stephen Glover. Edited by Thomas Noble... Volume I. [part 1 and vol. II, part 1.] 2 vols. *4°. Derby & London*, 1831–33. *No more published. For another edition, see* 1829.

26655 **GODWIN**, W. Thoughts on man, his nature, productions, and discoveries. Interspersed with some particulars respecting the author. 471p. *8°.* 1831.

26656 **GOODFELLOW**, ROBIN, *pseud*. A letter to the working classes; containing remarks on the French and Belgic revolutions, the National Debt, reform, tithes, taxes, &c., with strictures on Cobbett, Carlile, O'Connell,

the "Devil's chaplain" & co. (*Horne's Political Tracts*, 2.) 15p. *8°.* [1831] *The Agar Ellis copy.*

26657 **GOURLAY**, R. F. Early publications. 5 parts. *8°.* [*Leith?* 1831] *A collection of the author's works, reissued or reprinted with a general title and list of contents. Only five out of the eight publications listed is present in this volume, with one not included in the list. Contents: 1. Letter to the Earl of Kellie, 1808; 3. An apology for Scotch farmers in England [with an appendix], 1813; 4. Liberty of the press asserted...and a letter on the corn laws [1815]; 7. Miscellaneous publications, in order of their dates [1814–16, reprinted 1831]; [unnumbered] To farmers of the hill country of Wilts, Hants and Dorset [1814, reprinted 1831]; 8. Poor laws, nos. 1, 2, 3 & 4 [A reissue of Tyranny of poor laws exemplified, 1815, To the labouring poor of Wily Parish [1816], The village system, 1817, and The petition for the benefit of the labouring poor, presented and not presented by Sir Francis Burdett, 1817].*

26658 **HAMILTON**, ROBERT (1743–1829). Essays. [Containing 'On peace and war', 'On the management of the poor' and 'On government'.] 217p. *8°. Aberdeen*, 1831.

26659 [**HICKEY**, W.] An address to the landlords of Ireland, on subjects connected with the melioration of the lower classes. By Mr. Martin Doyle. 164p. *12°. Dublin, London, &c.*, 1831.

26660 [**HICKSON**, WILLIAM E.] The rights of industry. [A galley proof of an article, signed 'W.E.H.', criticizing Charles Knight's work with this title.] 4l. *8°. n.p.* [1831] *Presentation copy from the author to Francis Place, with an accompanying letter stating that the article was written for Carpenter's Political Magazine. For the letter, see vol. III, A.L. 152.*

26661 **HOLLEYMAN**, J. A practical remedy for national distress; or, the only means of political salvation; the whole demonstrated upon divine and scientific principles. Including an original publication, entitled, Suggestions as to the best means for promoting and securing the permanent prosperity of the country... 45p. *8°.* 1831.

26662 *HOPKINS, T. Wages; or, masters and workmen. 32p. *8°. Manchester*, 1831. *Published in two parts. The FWA copy, that belonged to William Pare.*

26663 **HORTON**, SIR R. J. W., *Bart*. Lecture I[–IV] delivered at the London Mechanics' Institution... December 1830 [–January, 1831]: being...a series of lectures on statistics and political economy, as affecting the condition of the operative and labouring classes. With notes. 32, 32, 32, 32p. *8°.* 1831. *See also* 1832.

26664 **HUSKISSON**, W. The speeches of the Right Honourable William Huskisson, with a biographical memoir [by John Wright], supplied to the editor from authentic sources... 3 vols. *8°.* 1831.

26665 Has **IRELAND** gained or lost by the Union with Great Britain? 24p. *8°.* 1831.

26666 **JONES**, RICHARD (1790–1855). An essay on the distribution of wealth, and on the sources of taxation. [Part I. – Rent. With an appendix.] 329, 49p. *8°.* 1831. *See also* 1844.

26667 [**KNIGHT**, C.] Rights of industry. No. 1. ⟨Published monthly.⟩... 16p. *fol.* [1831]

26668 [——] [Another edition.] Under the superintendence of the Society for the Diffusion of Useful Knowledge. The working-man's companion. The rights of industry: addressed to the working-men of the United Kingdom. By the author of "The results of machinery". §1. Capital and labour. 213p. *18°. London, Birmingham, &c., 1831.*

26669 [——] The second edition. 213p. *18°. London, Birmingham, &c., 1831. A new version, with the title* Capital and labour, *was published in 1845 (q.v.).*

26670 [——] Under the superintendence of the Society for the Diffusion of Useful Knowledge. The working man's companion. The results of machinery, namely, cheap production and increased employment, exhibited: being an address to the working-men of the United Kingdom. 216p. *18°. London, Birmingham, &c., 1831.*

26671 [——] Third edition. 216p. *18°. London, Birmingham, &c., 1831.*

26672 [——] Fourth edition. 216p. *18°. London, Birmingham, &c., 1831. A new version was included in the work entitled* Capital and labour, *in 1845 (q.v.).*

26673 [LASCELLES, R.] The ultimate remedy for Ireland. 75p. *8°. 1831.*

26674 McCULLOCH, JOHN R. Grundsätze der politischen Oekonomie nebst kurzer Darstellung des Ursprungs und Fortschrittes dieser Wissenschaft...Aus dem Englischen übersetzt und mit einer Vorrede versehen von Georg Michael v. Weber. 399p. *8°. Stuttgart, 1831. For other editions, see 1825.*

26675 MACQUEEN, T. P. The state of the nation, at the close of 1830. 38p. *8°. 1831.*

26676 MOLLOY, P. On popular discontent in Ireland. 123p. *8°. Dublin & London, 1831. The copy that belonged to M. T. Sadler.*

26677 MULLINS, B. Observations upon the Irish grand jury system, by Bernard Mullins, of the late firm of Henry, Mullins, and MacMahon, architects and civil engineers. 35p. *8°. Dublin, 1831. Presentation copy, with inscription, from the author to M. T. Sadler.*

26678 N., H. An address to the people of Ireland on the repeal of the Legislative Union between Great Britain and Ireland... 117p. *8°. Dublin, 1831. The copy that belonged to M. T. Sadler.*

26679 OKEY, C. H. A concise digest of the law, usage and custom affecting the commercial and civil intercourse of the subjects of Great Britain and France. Third edition, with considerable additions. 260p. *8°. Paris & London, 1831.*

26680 PASLEY, SIR C. W. Observations on the propriety and practicability of simplifying the weights, measures & money used in this country without materially altering the present standards. 87p. *8°. Chatham, 1831. One of 24 copies, lithographed for private use. See also 1834.*

26681 PECCHIO, G., *Conte.* Osservazioni semi-serie di un esule sull' Inghilterra. 363p. *12°. Lugano, 1831. The Holland House copy, with book-plate.*

26682 To the Right Honorable...the Knights, Citizens, and Burgesses of the United Kingdom of Great Britain and Ireland, in Parliament assembled. The **PETITION** of the undersigned Operative Coach Makers of the City of Dublin [praying for a dissolution of the Union as the only means of maintaining the connection with the British Crown and restoring the prosperity of Ireland]. *s.sh.fol.* n.p. [1831] *Bound in a volume of pieces, mostly newspaper cuttings, relating to Irish affairs, 1822–1845.*

26683 [RENNY, J. H.?] Hints on wages, the corn laws, high and low prices, paper-money, and banking: arising from a consideration of three lectures on the cost of obtaining money...delivered before the University of Oxford, by Nassau William Senior...By a British merchant. [The prefatory note is signed: A merchant.] 332p. *8°. 1831. Attributed in a manuscript note on the verso of the half-title to 'J.H. Renny, Neal House, Chelsea'.*

26684 RIDDELL, R. A. The causes of the distress of the agricultural and manufacturing population considered and demonstrated. 16p. *8°. Barnstaple, 1831.*

26685 A new **SALVE** for the State, &c. [Claiming that lack of employment, not the want of currency, is the cause of distress in the country.] 16p. *8°. [London, 1831] The copy that belonged to the Duke of Wellington, with his book-plate.*

26686 SENIOR, N. W. An introductory lecture on political economy, delivered before the University of Oxford, on the 6th of December, 1826...The third edition. 33p. *8°. 1831. For another edition, see 1827.*

26687 SINCLAIR, SIR JOHN, *Bart.* Analysis of the Statistical account of Scotland; with a general view of the history of that country, and discussions on some important branches of political economy...In two parts; now first published together. 359, 83, 226, 59p. *8°. Edinburgh, Glasgow, &c., 1831.*

26688 —— The correspondence of...Sir John Sinclair ...With reminiscences of...distinguished characters... 2 vols. *8°. 1831.*

26689 SISSON, J. Letter to the Right Hon. Earl Grey, proposing the appointment of a Board of Trade for Ireland. 81[18]p. *8°. Dublin, 1831.*

26690 SMITH, SIR WILLIAM CUSACK, *2nd Bart.* Tracts upon the union. 234p. *8°. Dublin & London, 1831. Contents: The substance of Mr. William Smith's speech... January 24, 1799; and now reduced to the form of an address to the people of Ireland, seventh edition; Review of...the speech of the Right Honourable John Foster...fourth edition; Letter to Henry Grattan, Esq. M.P....Fourth edition; Animadversions on the published speeches of Mr. Saurin and Mr. Bushe. For another edition, see 1800.*

26691 SOUTHEY, R. Sir Thomas More; or, colloquies on the progress and prospects of society...The second edition... 2 vols. *8°. 1831.*

26692 TOURNON, P. C. C. M. DE, *Comte.* Études statistiques sur Rome et la partie occidentale des états romains; contenant une description topographique et des recherches sur la population, l'agriculture, les manufactures...et une notice sur les travaux exécutés par l'administration française. 2 vols. *8°. Paris, 1831.*

26693 WALRAS, A. De la nature de la richesse, et de l'origine de la valeur... 334p. *8°. Evreux [& Paris], 1831.*

26694 WALSH, J. B., *Baron Ormathwaite.* Poor laws in Ireland, considered in their probable effects upon the capital, the prosperity, & the progressive improvement of that country...Third edition. 124p. *8°. 1831. For other editions, see 1830.*

26695 WALTON, WILLIAM (1784–1857). A letter, addressed to the Right Honourable Earl Grey...on the state of our political & commercial relations with Portugal. 174p. *8°. 1831. The Agar Ellis copy.*

26696 WHATELY, R., *Archbishop of Dublin.* Introductory lectures on political economy, being part of a course delivered in Easter term, MDCCCXXXI. 238p. *8°.* 1831. *See also 1832, 1847.*

26697 WHEWELL, W. Mathematical exposition of some of the leading doctrines in Mr. Ricardo's "Principles of political economy and taxation." From the Transactions of the Cambridge Philosophical Society. 44p. *4°. Cambridge,* 1831. *Presentation copy, with inscription, from the author to George Pryme.*

26698 WILLIAMS, CHARLES W. Observations on an important feature in the state of Ireland, and the want of employment of its population; with a description of the navigation of the River Shannon... 59p. *8°. Westminster,* 1831. *The Agar Ellis copy. See also 1833.*

26699 [WRIGHT, JOHN (1770?–1844).] A biographical memoir of the Right Honourable William Huskisson ... 275p. *8°.* 1831. *With the book-plate of the Dukes of Sutherland.*

AGRICULTURE

26700 An earnest **APPEAL** to every lover of his country, on the necessity of forming associations in every town and village in England, for encouraging industrious labourers and mechanics by providing allotments of land which they may rent and cultivate for their own advantage. By the Secretary of the Wantage Society for Providing the Poor with Land. [With 'Friendly hints to labourers and mechanics in reference to the cultivation of portions of land for their own benefit. By a friend'.] 28p. *8°.* 1831.

26701 B., A. A letter to a Member of Parliament, on the proposed Register Bill: being a reply to A circular letter printed at Northallerton. 37p. *8°.* 1831. *The Agar Ellis copy.*

26702 [BURGOYNE, M.] A letter from a friend of enclosures and allotments of land, provided for the labouring poor in preference to emigration, addressed to the Secretary of the Labourers' Friend Society. [Signed: M.B.] 4p. *8°. n.p.* [1831]

26703 COBBETT, W. Cottage economy...A new edition. [200]p. *12°.* 1831. *For other editions, see 1821.*

26704 —— A treatise on Cobbett's corn...With...a statement of the result of experience up to the harvest of 1831. [348]p. *12°.* 1831. *For another edition, see 1828.*

26705 [COSENS, T.] A new treatise on agriculture and grazing; clearly pointing out to landowners and farmers the most profitable plans. To which are added remarks on the poor rates, the employment of the poor, &c. By an experienced farmer. 49p. *8°. Lymington,* 1831. *Presentation copy from the author to George Agar Ellis, Baron Dover, with an accompanying letter, soliciting 'a small preasant towards relieving your obg^d ...s^t'.*

26706 DEMAINBRAY, S. G. F. T. The poor man's best friend; or, land to cultivate for his own benefit: being the results of twenty-four years' experience. In a letter to the Marquess of Salisbury, as given in evidence before the House of Lords' Committee on the poor laws... Second edition. 38p. *8°. London, Oxford, &c.,* 1831.

26707 GORE, M. Allotments of land. A letter to landed proprietors, on the advantages of giving the poor allotments of land. 14p. *8°.* 1831.

26708 Friendly **HINTS** to the labourers and mechanics of Wantage, occasioned by the establishment of a society for providing the poor with land. By a friend. 8p. *8°.* 1831. *See also no. 26700.*

26709 LAWRENCE, C. Practical directions for the cultivation and general management of cottage gardens, with plans for laying them out for five years: also, hints on keeping pigs in service, &c. 32p. *8°. Cirencester,* 1831.

26710 A **LETTER** to the editor of the St. James's Chronicle, on the price of agricultural labour, by a magistrate, of the county of Devon. 24p. *8°. Dartmouth,* 1831.

26711 LOUDON, J. C. An encyclopædia of agriculture: comprising the theory and practice of the valuation, transfer...and management of landed property; and the cultivation...of the...productions of agriculture... Second edition... 1282p. *8°.* 1831. *For other editions, see* 1825.

26712 OLIVER, T. Notes on agricultural topics. 16, 31, 16, 20p. *8°. Edinburgh,* [1831]

26713 POOR COLONIES at home! Shewing how the whole of our pauper population may be profitably employed in England. By a magistrate, and a clergyman of Chichester. Second edition. 28p. *8°.* 1831.

26714 SINCLAIR, SIR JOHN, *Bart.* On the means of improving the condition of the industrious labourers in husbandry, and effectually relieving their distresses. 8p. *8°. n.p.* [1831] *Presentation copy, with inscription, from the author to M. T. Sadler.*

26715 SPADE CULTIVATION tried for ten years on an estate in Wiltshire; in a letter to the Right Hon. W. Sturges Bourne. By a magistrate for the counties of Hants and Wilts. Second edition. 16p. *8°.* 1831.

26716 WILKINSON, WILLIAM I. Registration considered; with a view to prevent the adoption of the plan for a metropolitan registry, proposed by His Majesty's Commissioners, appointed to enquire into the laws of real property. 32p. *8°. Newcastle,* 1831.

CORN LAWS

26717 [ELLIOTT, E.] Corn law rhymes. Third edition. 115p. *12°. London & Sheffield,* 1831. *For another edition of the first poem, The ranter, see 1830.*

26718 HUNT, H. The corn laws. Speech of the late Henry Hunt, Esq., in the House of Commons on... September 15, 1831. (Reprinted from the "Mirror of Parliament".) 12p. *12°. Manchester,* [1831]

26719 A **LETTER** to the Right Hon. Earl Grey, First Lord of the Treasury, on his speech in favour of the corn laws. By an old farmer. 22p. *8°.* 1831.

26720 MUNDELL, A. The necessary operation of the corn laws: in driving capital from the cultivation of the soil: diminishing the means of employing agricultural labour; rendering Great Britain dependent upon foreign countries for a supply of grain, and endangering her manufacturing superiority. With a remedy for those evils. 52p. 8°. 1831.

26721 TORRENS, R. Address to the farmers of the United Kingdom, on the low rates of profit in agriculture and in trade. [The reasons why a revision of the corn laws will benefit the agriculturists.] 16p. 8°. 1831.

POPULATION

26722 MARSHALL, JOHN (1783-1841). An account of the population in each of six thousand of the principal towns and parishes in England and Wales, as returned to Parliament at each of the three periods 1801, 1811, & 1821 ...Shewing also the estimated annual value of the real property in each town and parish as assessed to the Property Tax in 1815... 131p. 4°. 1831. *The label on the front cover reads: Marshall's Statistics of the British*

Empire. Part I. Population. Reissued with a new title-page as Part I of A digest of all the accounts, *in 1833 (q.v.* GENERAL).

26723 SENIOR, N. W. Two lectures on population, delivered before the University of Oxford, in Easter Term, 1828...To which is added, a correspondence between the author and the Rev. T. R. Malthus. 90p. 8°. 1831. *For other editions, see 1828.*

TRADES & MANUFACTURES

26724 ANDERSON, JOHN W. The barilla question discussed, in a letter to the Right Honourable Lord Althorpe, Chancellor of the Exchequer, shewing the effect of the late Order in Council, reducing the duty on foreign barilla, on the manufacture of kelp and other British alkalies; with observations relative to the manufactures of soap and window glass. 55p. 8°. *Edinburgh, Glasgow, &c.,* 1831.

26725 BLANKET TRADE. Weaver's statement, March 18th, 1831. [Details of prices paid for various kinds of work in the industry.] *s.sh.4°. Dewsbury,* [1831] [*Br.* 518] *The Oastler copy.*

26726 COMMITTEE OF MASTER CABINET MAKERS AND JOURNEYMEN. The London cabinet makers book of prices; for work not provided in the Union book. By a committee. 53p. 4°. 1831. *For other editions of the original work, see 1824; for another supplement, see 1837.*

26727 The GLASGOW MECHANICS' MAGAZINE; and annals of philosophy...[1824-26] New edition, corrected. 5 vols. 8°. *Glasgow,* 1831, 1830. *Stereotyped, but with some numbers of the original edition.*

26728 HENSON, G. The civil, political and mechanical history of the framework-knitters, in Europe and America... Vol. 1. 425p. 8°. *Nottingham,* 1831.

26729 [HOLLAND, JOHN (1794-1872).] A treatise on the progressive improvement and present state of the manufactures in metal. (*The Cabinet Cyclopædia.*) 3 vols. 8°. 1831-34.

26730 [MEIKLEHAM, R. S.] Stuart's descriptive history of the steam engine. A new edition, with a supplement, continuing the subject to...1829. 249p. 8°. 1831. *For other editions, see 1824.*

26731 [NEEDHAM, M.] Manufacture of iron. (*Library of Useful Knowledge.*) 32p. 8°. 1831. *Caption title: On the manufacture of iron.*

26732 O'SHAUGHNESSY, SIR W. B. Poisoned confectionary. Detection of gamboge, lead, copper, mercury and chromate of lead, in various articles of sugar confectionary...(From The Lancet, No. 402.) 8p. 8°. [*London,* 1831] *The Agar Ellis copy.*

26733 [PORTER, G. R.] A treatise on the origin, progressive improvement, and present state of the silk manufacture. (*The Cabinet Cyclopædia.*) 339p. 8°. 1831.

26734 An historical **REVIEW** of the rise, progress, present state, and prospects, of the silk culture, manufacture, and trade, in Europe & America. Being an article [in the form of a review of *Essays on American silk,* 1830, by J. D'Homergue and P. S. Duponceau] extracted from the American Quarterly Review for December, 1831. 34p. 8°. *Philadelphia,* 1831. *With an accompanying letter from Duponceau to J. Vaughan, for which see vol. III, A.L. 47.*

26735 SADLER, J. H. The new invention of double and quadruple, or British national looms: being so named by "A practical master weaver" of Manchester... including a few remarks upon the bad policy of permitting the exportation of yarns...Published as an explanatory statement, by John Harvey Sadler, inventor and sole patentee. 56p. 8°. [*London,*] 1831. *The Oastler copy.*

26736 Corrected to 1831: **SKYRING'S** builders' prices, calculated from the prime cost of materials and labour...with a list of district surveyors. Abstracts of the Building and Paving Acts, &c. Twenty-first edition. 114p. 8°. [1831] *Compiled by William Henry Skyring, who signed and numbered each copy in manuscript. See also 1812, 1818, 1819, 1827, 1838, 1845, 1846.*

COMMERCE

26737 ALETHES, *pseud.* The Edinburgh reviewer refuted: being an exposure of gross misstatements in the leading article of No. CIV., entitled "The East-India Company — China question". [Second edition.] 58p. 8°. [1831]

26738 —— [Another issue.] 58p. 8°. 1831. *The Agar Ellis copy.*

26739 BLISS, H. On the timber trade. 117p. 8°. 1831.

26740 A **CAUTION** to bankers, merchants, and

manufacturers, against a series of commercial frauds prevalent throughout Great Britain and Ireland. By friends of commerce. [With an appendix.] 148, 24p. *8°. Edinburgh, 1831.*

26741 COVENT GARDEN MARKET. Rules, orders, and bye-laws. [A poster.] *s.sh.fol. [London, 1831]*

26742 FRIENDS OF DOMESTIC INDUSTRY. Address of the Friends of Domestic Industry, assembled in convention, at New-York, October 26, 1831, to the people of the United States. Published by order of the Convention. [Signed: William Wilkins, of Pennsylvania, president, and other officers. With a list of the delegates.] 44p. *8°. Baltimore, 1831.*

26743 GEORGE, James. Three letters on the important subject of the timber duties. Quebec, Sept. 1831. 7p. *4°. [Quebec, 1831] With a manuscript note on the title-page: '2nd Edition'.*

26744 LAMPREDI, G. M. Del commercio dei popoli neutrali in tempo di guerra... 408p. *8°. Milano, 1831.*

26745 [McCULLOCH, John R.] Observations on the influence of the East India Company's monopoly on the price and supply of tea; and on the commerce with India, China, etc. Reprinted...with corrections and amendments, from the Edinburgh Review, No. CIV. 41p. *8°. 1831.*

26746 M'DONNELL, A. An examination into the expediency of permitting foreign sugar to be refined in this country for exportation. [Indicating the adverse effect of this policy on efforts to stamp out the slave trade.] 22p. *8°. 1831.*

26747 MURHARD, J. C. A. Theorie und Politik des Handels. Ein Handbuch für Staatsgelehrte und Geschäftsmänner. 2 vols. *8°. Göttingen, 1831.*

26748 *REVANS, J. Observations on the proposed alteration of the timber-duties, with remarks on the pamphlet of Sir Howard Douglas. 34p. *8°. 1831. The copy that belonged to George Grote.*

26749 [THOMPSON, Thomas P.] The article on East-India and China trade, republished from the Westminster Review, No. XXVII, for January 1831. 11p. *8°. 1831. See note to no. 25779.*

26750 [TRUEMAN & COOK.] The state of the commerce of Great Britain with reference to colonial and other produce, for the year 1830. 31p. *8°. 1831. See also 1832, 1833, 1834.*

COLONIES

26751 DAWSON, Robert. The present state of Australia; a description of the country, its advantages and prospects, with reference to emigration: and a particular account of the manners, customs, and condition of its aboriginal inhabitants...Second edition. 464p. *8°. 1831.*

26752 DOUGLAS, Sir H., *Bart.* Considerations on the value and importance of the British North American Provinces, and the circumstances on which depend their further prosperity and colonial connection with Great Britain...Second edition. 42p. *8°. 1831.*

26753 *EAST INDIA COMPANY. Report on the military expenditure of the Honourable East India Company. Addressed to Major-General the Honourable Sir John Malcolm, G.C.B. K.L.S., Governor. By Lieut.-Colonel Edward Frederick. 138p. *fol. 1831. The copy that belonged to Lord William Cavendish Bentinck, and afterwards to George Grote.*

26754 GRANT, Sir R., *and others.* The East India question fairly stated. Comprising the views and opinions of some eminent and enlightened members [Robert Grant, Henry Ellis and Charles Grant, President of the Board of Commissioners for the Affairs of India] of the present Board of Control. 52p. *8°. 1831.*

26755 JOHNSTON, James H. Précis of reports, opinions, and observations on the navigation of the rivers of India, by steam vessels. 29p. *8°. 1831.*

26756 ONTARIO. *Legislative Assembly.* First report on the state of the representation of the people of Upper Canada in the Legislature of that province. First edition, of one thousand copies, printed for gratuitous distribution among the freeholders. March 1831. 23p. *8°. York [Toronto], 1831. The copy that belonged to M. T. Sadler.*

26757 PORET, B. E., *Marquis de Blosseville.* Histoire des colonies pénales de l'Angleterre dans d'Australie. 596p. *8°. Paris, 1831. With a bibliography.*

FINANCE

26758 A., C. The farmers and the clergy. Six letters to the farmers of England, on tithes and church property. Second edition, revised and corrected. 79p. *8°. 1831.*

26759 An ANSWER to the speech of the late Right Hon. W. Huskisson, delivered on Thursday, March 18, 1830, on the state of the country. 92p. *8°. 1831.*

26760 The BANK of the United States, an article reprinted from the North American Review, for April, 1831. 44p. *8°. Boston, 1831.*

26761 BANK OF LIVERPOOL. Deed of settlement (dated 15th August, 1831) of the Bank of Liverpool, established under the authority of an Act of Parliament, passed in the seventh year of the reign of George the Fourth...Capital – two millions and a half sterling. 69p. *8°. Liverpool, 1831.*

26762 BEDENKINGEN over het ontwerp van wet, tot daarstelling van middelen ter dekking van de buitengewone staatsbehoeften, over 1832. [With an appendix incorporating a correction to the work.] 29, 4p. *8°. Leyden, [1831]*

26763 BENTON, T. H. Speech delivered in the U.S. Senate, Feb. 2, 1831, introducing a resolution against the renewal of the charter of the Bank of the United States. 22p. *8°. Geneva, N.Y., 1831.*

26764 [BJORNSTERNE, M. F. F., *Grefve.*] The Public Debt, its influence and its management considered in a different point of view from Sir Henry Parnell, in his work on financial reform. By M.B. 60p. *8°. 1831. Translated from the Swedish. See also 1834.*

26765 BRIGGS, W. A letter to John Wood, Esq. M.P. on the principle of taxation, as connected with the liberty of the subject. 46p. *8°. 1831.*

26766 BRITAIN regenerated: or, the National Debt shewn capable of immediate redemption. With some remarks on the electioneering system. 62p. *8°. Bridgnorth & London*, 1831. *The copy that belonged to T. Spring Rice, Baron Monteagle.*

26767 BRUEFL, L. A. Materialen für die zu erwartende Reform des deutschen Münzwesens...Zweite verbesserte Auflage. 60p. *8°. Hannover*, 1831.

26768 BUCKINGHAM, J. S. Outlines of a new budget, for raising eighty millions, by means of a justly graduated property tax. With suggestions on the representative system, the National Debt...Prepared for the consideration of the reformed Parliament of England. 60p. *8°. 1831.*

26769 The BUDGET exchequered: the song of scaccaria. [A ballad on Lord Althorp's Budget of 1831.] *s.sh.fol. Hoxton*, [1831] *See note to no. 26994.*

26770 CAEN. Réglement de l'octroi de la Commune de Caen. [Preceded by the authorizing Ordonnance of King Louis Philippe of 21 December, 1831.] 71p. *12°. Caen*, [1831]

26771 CONSIDERATIONS addressed to the clergy and laity, shewing the advantages of leases on corn rents, as compositions for tythes, and their preferableness to a commutation of tythes for land or money payments. 8p. *8°. 1831.*

26772 CONTÉ, . Mémoire sur la nécessité de modifier le système monétaire actuel en lui donnant un contre-poids. Adressé au Roi dans son conseil... p.1–48. *8°. Paris*, 1831.

26773 COURT, M. H. Tithes. Commutation versus composition: the rights of the laity, and the rights of the Church, illustrated and proved not to be the same; in a letter to the Lord Chancellor Brougham. [With 'To the ...Lords Spiritual and Temporal...The petition of the undersigned, being principal owners...of lands, in the parish of Wargrave...' and 'Remarks in support of the Wargrave petition'.] 42p. *8°. 1831. Presentation copy from the author to the Rev. James Hitchings.*

26774 CRUTTWELL, R. Letter to the Right Honorable Lord Althorp, &c.&c.&c. on Mr. Attwood's motion for enquiry, touching the state of the currency, the cause and key-stone of the late awful disturbances throughout the country. 32p. *8°. Halesworth & London*, 1831. *With manuscript notes and additions, probably by the author.*

26775 DANIEL, J. D. Miscellaneous information [concerning the practice of the Bank of England], &c.&c. 40p. *8°.* [*London*, 1831]

26776 DUBOIS AYMÉ, J. M. J. Chambre des Députés. Session de 1831. Discours de M. Dubois-Aymé ...dans la discussion relative au budget, des dépenses et des recettes de 1831; prononcé dans la séance du 26 septembre 1831. (Extrait du Moniteur du 27 septembre 1831.) 7p. *8°.* [*Paris*, 1831]

26777 —— Discours prononcé à la Chambre des Députés...dans la séance du 12 février 1831, à l'occasion du projet de loi tendant à autoriser la ville de Paris à contracter un emprunt de 15 millions. 8p. *8°.* [*Paris*, 1831]

26778 DUCHESNE, A. L. H. Essai sur les finances, sur les économies de cent millions, au moins, à faire aux divers budgets des dépenses; sur les changemens à introduire dans la division et la répartition des differentes branches de nos impôts directs ou indirects. 540p. *8°. Paris*, 1831.

26779 EAGLE, W. A legal argument shewing that tithes are the property of the public, and of the poor... The third edition. 20p. *8°. 1831. See also 1832.*

26780 ENGLAND. *William IV.* Warrant for the charter of the Commercial Bank of Scotland. 15p. *8°. Edinburgh*, 1831.

26781 ESSAY on tithes: Nos. 17 & 18 of the "Library of Ecclesiastical Knowledge". Second edition. p.239–336. *12°. 1831.*

26782 EVILS of taxation, with outlines of a practical plan for the speedy and satisfactory liquidation of the National Debt and revision of the corn laws. By a capitalist. 34p. *8°. 1831.*

26783 The EXPEDIENCY of a property tax considered in relation to the objections of Earl Grey and Lord Brougham. 25p. *8°. 1831.*

26784 GALLATIN, A. Considerations on the currency and banking system of the United States. 106p. *8°. Philadelphia*, 1831.

26785 GODDARD, THOMAS H. A general history of the most prominent banks in Europe: particularly the banks of England and France; the rise and progress of the Bank of North America; a full history of the late and present Bank of the United States: to which is added, a statistical...view of the moneyed institutions of New York and...other principal cities of the United States... 254p. *8°. New York*, 1831.

26786 HALIFAX JOINT STOCK BANKING COMPANY. Deed of settlement of the Halifax Joint Stock Banking Company, established under the authority of Act 7th George IV.... 58p. *8°. Halifax*, 1831.

26787 HODGSON, JOHN, *director of the Amicable Society.* A letter to the members of the Amicable Society, comprising the substance of a speech delivered at the special general court on December 18, 1830 with additional observations. 54p. *8°. 1831.*

26788 JACOB, W. An historical inquiry into the production and consumption of the precious metals... 2 vols. *8°. 1831.*

26789 JOPLIN, T. An examination of the principles of an improved system of banking, and the means of carrying it into effect. 38p. *8°. 1831. For a proof copy, see 1830.*

26790 [—— ?] The plan of a national establishment for country banking, and the principles by which it is recommended; also, the prospectus of the committee which has been formed to carry such an establishment into effect. 64p. *8°. 1831. With a manuscript note on the title-page: 'for correction please'.*

26791 KELLY, P. The universal cambist and commercial instructor: being a full and accurate treatise on the exchanges, coins, weights and measures, of all trading nations and their colonies; with an account of their banks ...The second edition, containing the results of the universal comparison of foreign weights and measures... to which are added...supplementary articles. 2 vols. *4°.* 1831. *For other editions, see* 1811.

26792 LAWLESS, V. B., *Baron Cloncurry.* Suggestions on the necessity, and on the best mode of levying assessments for local purposes, in Ireland. 20p. *8°. Dublin,* 1831.

26793 LETTERS to the Duke of Wellington, from 1828 to 1830, on currency. By a citizen of London. 30p. *8°.* 1831.

26794 [McCULLOCH, JOHN R.] Historical sketch of the Bank of England: with an examination of the question as to the prolongation of the exclusive privileges of that establishment. 77p. *8°.* 1831. *The Agar Ellis copy.*

26795 [——] Observations on the duty on sea-borne coal; and on the peculiar duties and charges on coal. In the Port of London... 23p. *8°.* 1831. *For another edition, see* 1830.

26796 [MACLEAN, A. W.?] An essay on the necessity and equity of a national parish bank and annuity system, adapted for the lower classes; showing its... advantages as a source of independent pecuniary relief... to the community; and of immense voluntary revenue to the state. 32p. *8°. Edinburgh: A. W. Maclean,* 1831.

26797 [——] Second edition. Considerations, addressed to all classes, on the necessity & equity of a national banking & annuity system...containing also some hints on the means of improving the condition of the Irish peasantry. 71p. *8°. London, Edinburgh, &c.,* 1831. *For a supplement, see* Additional considerations...on the necessity...of a national system of deposit banking, *1835.*

26798 MANCHESTER AND LIVERPOOL DISTRICT BANKING COMPANY. Deed of settlement of the Manchester and Liverpool District Banking Company, established 30th of April, 1829, under the authority of an Act of Parliament passed in the seventh year of Geo. IV. Capital, five millions. 35p. *8°. Stockport,* 1831.

26799 [*Begin.***]** At a **MEETING** of the Staffordshire iron trade, held at Dudley, the 4th of October, 1831. Michael Grazebrook, Esq. in the chair. [With the text of a memorial on the depressed prices in the iron trade, here attributed to an antiquated currency system, presented to Earl Grey by a deputation.] [4]p. *fol. n.p.* [1831] *With manuscript alterations and additions, added after the presentation of the memorial on 8 August 1832.*

26800 MILLAR, R. Address to the citizens of Edinburgh on the subject of annuity and impost taxes, submitted to their consideration previous to a general meeting. By a member of the inhabitants' committee... [With an account of the public protest meeting held on 8 April 1831, with the resolutions carried.] 8p. *8°. n.p.* [1831] *The copy sent through the post to James Gibson Craig, and postmarked 16 April 1831.*

26801 [MORGAN, A.?] Remarks on the National Debt; the principal cause of the present distress; and statement of a plan for effectual relief from its pernicious effects. 27p. *8°.* 1831.

26802 The **NATIONAL DEBT,** its evils, and their remedy. By a land and fund holder. 46p. *8°.* 1831. *The Agar Ellis copy.*

26803 *Entry cancelled.*

26804 Brief **OBSERVATIONS** on the policy of relieving the labour & industry of the Empire from taxation, by means of a direct tax on property. Addressed to the Right Honorable Lord Goderich by a plain enquirer. [Dated: Feb. 1831.] 14p. *8°. Stroud & London,* [1831]

26805 OBSERVATIONS on a letter lately addressed by a "calico printer," to the Right Honorable Lord Viscount Althorp, Chancellor of the Exchequer. [On the taxation of particular commodities, notably calico.] 22p. *8°.* [1831]

26806 OBSERVATIONS on the present financial embarrassments. 22p. *8°.* 1831.

26807 O'NEILL, P. C. A brief review of the Irish Post-Office from 1784 to 1831 when Sir Edward Lees was removed from that establishment, in a letter to the Right Honourable Lord Melbourne. [An attack on financial and other abuses in the department.] 98p. *8°. n.p.* [1831]

26808 PARLIAMENTARY REFORM, combined with an enlargement of credit and a virtual diminution of the National Debt. 21p. *8°.* 1831.

26809 PARNELL, H. B., *Baron Congleton.* On financial reform...Third edition. 383p. *16°.* 1831. *For other editions, see* 1830.

26810 *PEREIRE, JACOB E. Examen du Budget de 1832. Réformes financières; examen théorique et pratique de l'amortissemet [*sic*]; reconstitution des rentes viagères; moyen de supprimer immédiatement la totalité des impôts du sel, des boissons, du tabac et de la loterie. 55p. *8°. Paris,* 1831. *The copy that belonged to George Grote.*

26811 PITT, CHARLES. 1831. The Privy Purse of His Majesty. Considerably above 20 years has probably elapsed since what was called the Privy Purse, was given up to the people, and a stipulated sum by Act of Parliament to the King... 20p. *12°.* 1831. *The Agar Ellis copy.*

26812 PRATT, J. T. The savings banks in England, Wales, and Ireland, arranged according to counties; with the period of the establishment of each institution, and the increase or decrease of each class of depositors; &c. since November 1829...Not published for sale. 74p. *obl. fol.* 1831. *Presentation copy from the author to Stephen Lushington. See also* 1834.

26813 REFORM of the Church establishment, the remedy for the distresses of the poor. A letter addressed to the Right Honorable the Lord Chancellor. [On the financial burdens of the poor rates and pluralism.] 28p. *8°.* 1831.

26814 ROBERTS, O. O. Church revenues revealed; or, the true origin of tithes. In reply to a pamphlet published by the Rev. J. W. Trevor. Addressed to rate payers. 22p. *12°. London & Carnarvon,* 1831.

26815 [SAYER, B.] First part. On the advantages of substituting an income tax for the present taxes. Second part. On the objections to the plan of the late property tax and on modifications of it, and on the different plans of an income or property tax. Third part. On the superior means afforded by an income or property tax of reducing the National Debt...[With an appendix.] 317, 63p. 8°. 1831. *Presentation copy, with an accompanying letter from the author to J. W. Croker, M.P., for which see* vol. III, *A.L. 281. See also 1833.*

26816 SKETCH of the Ryotwar system of revenue administration. 94p. 8°. 1831.

26817 STATE of the country. Essay on the currency question. Re-printed...from the Leeds Intelligencer of Feb. 3, 1831. 16p. 8°. *Leeds*, 1831.

26818 A fair STATEMENT of the case of the Bank of Bengal versus the Hon'ble East India Company: with a summary of the arguments and decisions affecting the principal question involved in that action. By a looker-on. 53, 18p. 8°. *Calcutta*, 1831.

26819 STROMBOM, I. Remarks and suggestions on the actual commercial and financial state of Great Britain, with observations on the currency... 51p. 8°. 1831. *Presentation copy, with accompanying letter, from the author to Sir Charles Forbes (1774–1849).*

26820 STUCKEY'S BANKING COMPANY. Deed of settlement. 31p. 8°. 1831.

26821 SUGGESTIONS for combining an improved system of taxation with a wide diffusion of the elective franchise. 16p. 8°. 1831. *The Agar Ellis copy.*

26822 [THORN, W.] The history of tithes, patriarchal, levitical, Catholic and Protestant; with reflections on the extent and evils of the English tithe system; and suggestions for abolishing tithes and supporting the clergy. By Biblicus. Second edition, enlarged. 64p. 8°. 1831.

26823 *Entry cancelled.*

26824 VEITCH, H. Means for paying off half of the National Debt, and relieving the country from fourteen millions of its present annual taxation. 55p. 8°. 1831.

26825 [WADE, John.] The extraordinary black book: an exposition of the united Church of England and Ireland; Civil List and Crown revenues; incomes, privileges, and power, of the aristocracy...The whole corrected from the latest official returns, and presenting a complete view of the expenditure, patronage, influence, and abuses of the government, in church, state, law, and representation. By the original editor. 576p. 8°. 1831. *For other editions, see* 1820 (POLITICS).

26826 YORK CITY AND COUNTY BANKING COMPANY. Deed of settlement...under the authority of an Act of Parliament passed in the 7th year of George IV. To which is appended an abstract of the said Act. Capital £500,000. 46p. 8°. *York*, 1831.

TRANSPORT

26827 BOOTH, H. An account of the Liverpool and Manchester Railway, comprising a history of the Parliamentary proceedings, preparatory to the passing of the Act...Second edition. 104p. 8°. *Liverpool, Manchester, &c.*, 1831. *For another edition, see* 1830.

26828 BOSWALL, J. D. Letter to the proprietors of steam vessels connected with the Firth of Forth, and others interested in the trade carried on by steam navigation... With an appendix: ['Report by William Matheson...upon the practicability of erecting a low water pier, and other works, for the accomodation of steam vessels, at Wardie']. 12p. 4°. *Edinburgh*, 1831. *The Rastrick copy.*

26829 COMMITTEE OF THE PROPOSED LINE OF RAILWAY FROM PERRANPORTH BY PERRAN ALMS-HOUSE TO TRURO. An answer to remarks on the proposed railway, from Perran Porth to Truro. [With a letter from Richard Thomas to the Committee.] 15p. 8°. *Truro*, [1831]

26830 [CRUDEN, R. P.] An account of the origin of steam-boats, in Spain, Great Britain, and America, and of their introduction and employment upon the River Thames, between London and Gravesend, to the present time. 75p. 8°. 1831.

26831 FAIRBAIRN, Sir W., *Bart.* Remarks on canal navigation, illustrative of the advantages of the use of steam, as a moving power on canals. With an appendix, containing a series of experiments, tables, &c....Also, plans and descriptions of certain classes of steam-boats, intended for the navigation of canals... 93p. 8°. *London, Edinburgh, &c.*, 1831.

26832 GRAHAME, T. A letter addressed to Nicholas Wood, Esq. on that portion of Chapter IX. of his Treatise on railroads, entitled, "Comparative performances of motive power on canals and railroads." 40p. 8°. *Glasgow, Edinburgh, &c.*, 1831. *Author's presentation copy, from the Rastrick Collection.*

26833 GRAINGER, T. and MILLER, John, *engineer.* Report to the trustees for the Roxburghshire turnpikes, relative to the proposed alterations of the road from Hundalee Smithy, near Jedburgh, by Ferniehurst, and Edgerston Rig, to Whitelee Toll-bar...With observations [on the proposed tunnel]...by William Oliver... 19p. 4°. *Jedburgh*, 1831. *The Rastrick copy.*

26834 INVESTIGATOR, *pseud.* Beware the bubbles!!! Remarks on proposed railways, more particularly on that between Birmingham and London...Second edition... 116p. 8°. 1831. *The Rastrick copy. For another edition, see* 1830.

26835 KIRWAN, J. A descriptive and historical account of the Liverpool and Manchester Railway, from its first projection to the present time: containing all the facts and information that have yet appeared on the subject, with...original details, estimates of expenses... Second edition. 32p. 8°. *Glasgow & London*, 1831.

26836 LAURIE, D. The case of Gorbals, in regard to the bridges over the Clyde, its dependence on Glasgow, and plea for direct parliamentary representation; submitted to Parliament, and the parties interested. 24p. 12°. *n.p.* [1831]

26837 At a MEETING of proprietors and occupiers

of houses and lands, and other persons interested... between Paddington and Leighton...likely to be destroyed or deteriorated by the projected rail road from London to Birmingham, holden at the Essex Arms, Watford, on...the 28th of January, 1831...for the purpose of adopting such means of opposing the same as may be deemed expedient. 2p. *s.sh.fol. Hemel Hempsted*, [1831]

26838 At a **MEETING** of the proprietors and occupiers of lands in the County of Northampton, through which the projected London and Birmingham Railway is intended to pass, holden at the White Horse Inn at Towcester, on the 30th day of December 1830...for the purpose of...adopting such measures as may be expedient on the occasion. Sir William Wake, Bart. in the chair. [3]p. *fol. n.p.* [1831] *A lithographed manuscript facsimile.*

26839 MOREAU, P. Description raisonnée et vues pittoresques du chemin de fer de Liverpool à Manchester; publiées par P. Moreau, constructeur, d'après son examen sur les lieux, les renseignemens fournis par M. Stephenson, ingénieur, et les documens tirés des ouvrages de ce dernier, de M. Wood, etc....et mis en ordre par Auguste Notré. 98p. *4°. Paris*, 1831.

26840 OBSERVATIONS on railways particularly on the proposed London and Birmingham Railway. 20p. *8°. London & Birmingham*, 1831. *The Rastrick copy.*

26841 PRIESTLEY, JOSEPH, *of the Aire and Calder Navigation Office.* Historical account of the navigable rivers, canals, and railways, throughout Great Britain, as a reference to Nichols, Priestley & Walker's new map of inland navigation, derived from original and Parliamentary documents... 776p. *4°. London & Wakefield*, 1831.

26842 —— [Another edition.] 702p. *8°. London & Wakefield*, 1831.

26843 SADLER, M. T. Mr. Sadler's reply to the calumnies and misrepresentations of the Leeds Mercury.

Letter from Michael Thomas Sadler, Esq. M.P. to a friend resident in Leeds. [Dated: 26th Sept. 1831. A statement on his conduct in presenting petitions in Parliament against two railway bills in which Leeds was concerned.] *s.sh.fol. Leeds*, [1831] [*Br.* 524(2)] *The Oastler copy.*

26844 SHEFFIELD, ASHTON-UNDER-LYNE, AND MANCHESTER RAILWAY. Appendix to the report of the provisional committee of the Sheffield & Manchester Railway to the company of proprietors, at their first general assembly...October 20, 1831, at...Manchester...[With 'Report upon the practicability of making the line, and the mode and cost of working it. By Geo. Stephenson'.] 52p. *8°. Liverpool*, [1831]

26845 A professional **SURVEY** of the old and new London Bridges, and their approaches, including historical memorials of both structures; with remarks on the probable effects of the changes in progress on the navigation of the Thames... 46p. *8°.* 1831.

26846 TREDGOLD, T. Caminos de hierro. Tratado practico...sobre los caminos de carriles de hierro, y los carruages, maquinas de vapor y de gas...Puesto en castellano por D. Gregorio Gonzalez Azaola. 126p. *4°. Madrid*, 1831. *For other editions, see* 1825.

26847 WALKER, JAMES S. An accurate description of the Liverpool and Manchester Rail-way, the tunnel, bridges, and other works throughout the line; with an account of the opening of the rail-way, and the melancholy accident which occurred; a short memoir of the late... William Huskisson...Third edition. 52p. *8°. Liverpool, London, &c.*, 1831. *For other editions, see* 1830.

26848 WOOD, N. A practical treatise on rail-roads, and interior communication in general. Containing an account of the performances of the different locomotive engines at and subsequent to the Liverpool contest... 530p. *8°.* 1831. *For other editions, see* 1825.

SOCIAL CONDITIONS

26849 ADAMS, S. A letter to the Right Hon. Lord Suffield, on the degraded condition of the labouring poor, occasioned by the modern administration of the poor laws; and...recommending the adoption of an equitable labour-rate; together with the heads of a proposed Bill for that purpose. 44p. *8°. Norwich, Yarmouth, &c.*, 1831.

26850 Under the superintendence of the Society for the Diffusion of Useful Knowledge. A short **ADDRESS** to workmen, on combinations to raise wages. 12p. *8°.* 1831. **Another*, the FWA copy, belonged to William Pare. The Library also possesses a copy of the final revise, with manuscript corrections, without the date on the title-page or the list of errata on p. 12.*

26851 ADVICE to the labouring poor, with especial reference to tumultuous assemblages, and the breaking of machinery. 8p. *8°.* 1831.

26852 [**ALSOP**, .] On machinery. To all. [Signed: S.P.] 2p. *s.sh.4°.* [*London*, 1831 ?] *Two copies in a volume of tracts collected by Francis Place, who supplied the author's name in his manuscript index to the volume.*

26853 ASSOCIATION FOR THE SUPPRESSION OF MENDICITY, *Dublin.* Thirteenth report of the managing committee of the Association...for the

year 1830. [With lists of subscribers, one of residents of Dublin arranged street-by-street.] 69, cvip. *8°. Dublin*, 1831. *The copy that belonged to M. T. Sadler. See also* 1819, 1821, 1825, 1837.

26854 BARNES, R. A letter to Henry Gervis, Esqr., portreeve of Ashburton, on agricultural labour & wages, 1831. 16p. *8°. Exeter*, 1831.

26855 BAXTER, S. S. The poor laws, stated and considered; the evils of the present system exposed, and a plan suggested, founded on the true principles of political economy, for placing such laws on a firm and equitable basis. 44p. *8°. London & Atherstone*, 1831.

26856 BENTHAM, J. Jeremy Bentham to his fellow citizens of France, on death punishment. 13p. *8°.* 1831.

26857 BLAKISTON, P. Hints for the improvement of the condition of the labouring classes...With an appendix containing practical plans for the reduction of poor rates and for restoring the comforts and independence of the peasantry, by their own means. 64p. *8°. London & Lymington*, 1831.

26858 BURGOYNE, M. An address to the governors and directors of the public charity schools, pointing out some defects and suggesting remedies. Third edition, with an additional preface, and a particular account of the school of industry at Potton, in the county of Bedford... In the appendix of this edition...a copy of a petition to both Houses of Parliament for the inclosure of Epping Forest... 32p. *8°. London & Brighton, 1831. For another edition, see 1829.*

26859 CALVERT, F. Suggestions for a change in the administration of the poor laws. 53p. *8°. 1831.*

26860 [CARMALT, W.?] A defence of the English poor laws, with remarks on the applicability of the system to Ireland: and practical instructions for relieving and employing paupers: being the substance of a letter on those subjects, addressed to Mr. Canning, in 1823. By a select vestryman of the Parish of Putney. 102p. *8°. 1831. The copy that belonged to M. T. Sadler. For another edition, see 1823.*

26861 [COLERIDGE, H. N.] The genuine life of Mr. Francis Swing. 23p. *12°. 1831.*

26862 COLTMAN, J. To the inhabitants of the parish of St. Martin. [An address on the objects of the Church of England Visiting Society.] 8p. *8°. Beverley, [1831]*

26863 On COMBINATIONS of trades. [With an appendix of documents connected with the National Association for the Protection of Labour.] 94p. *8°. 1831. The Agar Ellis copy.*

26864 COMMON SENSE, addressed to the peasantry and labourers of the county of Wilts, &c.&c. on their situation and conduct, by a friend... 8p. *8°. Sherborne, [1831?]*

26865 *DAVIES, JOHN, Vice-President of the Mechanics' Institution.* An appeal to the public, in behalf of the Manchester Mechanics' Institution, Cooper Street. 8p. *8°. Manchester, 1831.*

26866 DAY, C. An address to those whom it may concern, but principally the poor; containing an account of the late trials and executions which have taken place, with a brief statement of the causes that...occasioned those acts of insubordination...Second edition. 48p. *8°. Ipswich, 1831.*

26867 DETROSIER, R. An address, delivered to the members of the New Mechanics' Institution, Manchester, on...March 25, 1831, on the necessity of an extension of moral and political instruction among the working classes. [With a note on the author by John Kay.] 16p. *8°. Manchester [London], [1831]. With a manuscript note on the title-page: With Mr. Hume's comps.*

26868 *—— [Another edition.] 16p. *8°. Manchester [London], [1831] The FWA copy that belonged to William Pare. See also 1832, 1835.*

26869 —— An address on the advantages of the intended Mechanics' Hall of Science, delivered at the Manchester New Mechanics' Institution, on...December 31st, 1831 ... 8p. *8°. Manchester, [1831]*

26870 A DIALOGUE on rick-burning, rioting, &c. between Squire Wilson, Hughes, his steward, Thomas, the bailiff, and Harry Brown, a labourer. 23p. *8°. 1831. For another edition, see 1830.*

26871 A second DIALOGUE on rick-burning, rioting, tithes, &c. between Squire Wilson, Hughes, his steward, Thomas, the bailiff, and Harry Brown, a labourer. 24p. *12°. 1831.*

26872 [DICKENSON,   ?] Hymns for factory children, original and paraphrased; to which are added, three songs and a short heroic. 23p. *12°. Leeds, 1831. The copy that belonged to Oastler, who attributed it to 'Dickenson' in the manuscript index to his pamphlet collection.*

26873 DOHERTY, J. A letter to the members of the National Association for the Protection of Labour. 24p. *12°. Manchester, [1831] The Oastler copy.*

26874 DOYLE, JAMES W., *Bishop of Kildare and Leighlin.* Letter to Thomas Spring Rice, Esq. M.P. &c.&c. on the establishment of a legal provision for the Irish poor, and on the nature and destination of Church property. 133p. *8°. Dublin & London, 1831.*

26875 The DRONES and bees; a fable [in verse. On the condition of the people]. 38p. *8°. Edinburgh, 1831.*

26876 DUCPÉTIAUX, E. Des caisses d'épargnes, et de leur influence sur la condition des classes laborieuses. 24p. *8°. Bruxelles, 1831. Presentation copy from the author to N. W. Senior.*

26877 DUPPA, B. F. The causes of the present condition of the labouring classes in the South of England. With a few hints as to the manner of permanently bettering it... 110p. *8°. London & Maidstone, 1831. Presentation copy, with inscription, from the author to James Yates.*

26878 EDGAR, J. A complete view of the principles and objects of temperance societies...Fourth edition. 44p. *12°. Bradford, 1831. The Turner copy.*

26879 The EFFECTS of machinery on manual labour, and on the distribution of the produce of industry. Reprinted...from Carpenter's Political Magazine. 8p. *8°. [1831?] The copy that belonged to Francis Place. *Another, the FWA copy, belonged to William Pare.*

26880 ENGLAND. *Commissioners for Inquiring concerning Charities.* The Bristol charities, being the report of the Commissioners...so far as relates to the charitable institutions in Bristol...Edited by Thomas John Manchee ... 2 vols. *4°. Bristol, 1831.*

26881 —— *Home Office.* Summary statements of the number of criminal offenders committed to the several gaols of England and Wales, during the last seven years, &c.&c.&c. [22]p. *8°. n.p., 1831. See also 1822, 1824, 1833, 1834.*

26882 —— *Laws, etc.* [Endorsed:] Bristol poor. An Act to alter, amend and enlarge the powers of an Act passed in the third year of the reign of His late Majesty King George the Fourth, for regulating the poor of the City of Bristol, and for other purposes connected therewith. ⟨Royal Assent, 11 March 1831.⟩ 1 Will. IV. sess. 1830–31. 17p. *fol. [Bristol, 1831]*

26883 ENGLAND in 1830; being a letter to Earl Grey, laying before him the condition of the people as described by themselves in their petitions to Parliament. [With extracts from the petitions.] 30, 122p. *8°. 1831. See also 1847.*

26884 EPISCOPAL CHURCH, *Amsterdam.* The English poor. [An appeal for help for the English poor in Amsterdam, with details of work done by the Ladies' Committee. Dated: 15th Oct. 1831.] [4]p. *8°. n.p. [1831] Addressed in pencil at the head of the first page of text to 'William Allen Esqr.'.*

26885 [FACTORY BILL.] [Begin.] 1. Resolved, – that the safety, strength and dignity of the country are best secured by a healthy, moral, and contented people... [Six resolutions in support of Sadler's Factory Bill, including a resolution to petition Parliament.] 2l. *fol. n.p.* [1831 ?] *The Oastler copy.*

26886 GOLDSMID, Sir F. H., *Bart.* The arguments advanced against the enfranchisement of the Jews, considered in a series of letters. 37p. *8°.* 1831. *The Agar Ellis copy.*

26887 GORE, M. More words of advice to householders. [On the desirability of volunteer corps to defend property and keep the peace.] 8p. *8°.* 1831.

26888 [GREG, W. R.] An enquiry into the state of the manufacturing population, and the causes and cures of the evils therein existing. 40p. *8°.* 1831. *Two copies, one which belonged to Victor Considérant, the other the Oastler copy. *A third, the FWA copy, belonged to William Pare.*

26889 *GREGG, F. Suggestions for some alteration of the present state of the bankrupt law. 43p. *8°.* 1831. *The copy that belonged to George Grote.*

26890 [HANSON, John, *socialist.*] Humanity against tyranny, being an exposé of a petition, presented to the House of Commons, by Lord Morpeth...from ten factory-mongers, resident in Huddersfield...against Sir J. C. Hobhouse's Factories Bill...ordered to be printed ...July 18th, 1831. 41p. *12°.* Leeds, [1831] *The copy that belonged to Oastler, who attributed it to Hanson in the manuscript index to his pamphlet collection.*

26891 HORTON, Sir R. J. W., *Bart.* An inquiry into the causes and remedies of pauperism. First series. Containing correspondence with C. Poulett Thomson, Esq., M.P. upon the conditions under which colonization would be justified as a national measure...Second edition. 38p. *8°.* 1831. *For another edition, see 1830.*

**26892 —— Causes and remedies of pauperism. Second series. Containing correspondence with M. Duchâtel, author of an essay on charity; with an explanatory preface ...Second edition. 46p. *8°.* 1831. *For another edition, see 1830.*

**26893 —— Third series. Containing letters to Sir Francis Burdett, Bart., M.P. upon pauperism in Ireland ...Second edition. 86p. *8°.* 1831. *For another edition, see 1830.*

26894 HUDDERSFIELD SHORT-TIME COMMITTEE. Address to the friendly societies and unions of all descriptions. [Signed, by order of the Short-Time-Bill Committee of Operatives: John Leech, and dated, October 8th, 1831. An appeal that only those candidates pledged to the support of measures to reduce the hours of children in factories should be supported at the General Election.] *s.sh.4°.* Huddersfield, [1831] [*Br.* 526(1)] *The Oastler copy.*

26895 IRISH DISTRESS COMMITTEE. Report of the committee appointed at a public meeting... 24th March, 1831, for the purpose of adopting measures for the temporary relief of the distress...in the west of Ireland. Together with an appendix. 36p. *8°.* 1831. *The Agar Ellis copy.*

26896 KING'S COLLEGE, London. Preliminary statement of the arrangements for conducting the various departments of King's College, London, July, 1831. 15p. *8°.* [1831] *The Agar Ellis copy.*

26897 To the **LABOURERS** of the southern counties of England. [Signed: A magistrate, and dated, January 14th, 1831. On damaging church property and machine breaking.] 8p. *8°.* [Tunbridge Wells, 1831] *Attributed to*

R. W. Blencowe in a manuscript note on the first page of the text.

For **LABOURERS' FRIEND SOCIETY,** *London,* Facts and illustrations, 1831–34, *continued as* the Labourers' friend magazine, 1834–44, *then* the Labourer's friend, 1844–55, *see* vol. III, *Periodicals list,* Labourer's friend.

26898 LAVELEYE, A. de, and **AJASSON DE GRANDSAGNE,** J. B. F. E., *Vicomte.* Nécessité et moyen d'occuper les ouvriers qui manquent d'ouvrage en France. Mémoire présenté au Roi et au Chambres. 78p. *8°. Paris,* 1831.

26899 A **LETTER** to the Right Honorable the Earl of Darnley, on the introduction of a labour rate, for the employment of the poor in Ireland. 79p. *8°. Dublin,* 1831. *The copy that belonged to M. T. Sadler.*

26900 Two **LETTERS** on the state of the agricultural interest, and the condition of the labouring poor. 25p. *8°.* 1831. *Attributed in a manuscript note on the title-page to 'John Grey [or Greg], Esq.'.*

26901 LIVINGSTONE, J. L. Mr. Livingstone's letters to the King and to Lord Brougham and Vaux, on the subject of a plan for the formation of a society for the abolition of poor's rate in England, and the prevention of it in Ireland...Mr. Livingstone's petition to the House of Commons on the same subject, and his observations on a Bill for the relief of the aged...and infirm poor of Ireland ... 16p. *8°.* 1831.

For the **LOYAL REFORMERS' GAZETTE,** 1831–32, *continued as* the Reformers' gazette, 1832–33, *see* vol. III, *Periodicals list,* Reformers' gazette.

26902 MARRIAGE, J. Letters on the distressed state of the agricultural labourers, and suggesting a remedy...Second edition. 16p. *8°. Chelmsford & London,* 1831. *For other editions, see 1830.*

26903 MARSH, William. The cholera, its symptoms, preventives and cure, with certain alleviations and support under its most alarming forms. 24p. *12°. Birmingham, London, &c.,* 1831.

26904 MARY I, *Queen of England.* Privy purse expenses of the Princess Mary, daughter of King Henry the Eighth, afterwards Queen Mary. With a memoir of the Princess, and notes. By Frederick Madden. ccv, 285p. *8°.* 1831.

26905 *METROPOLITAN MODEL SCHOOL OF INDUSTRY. Metropolitan Model School of Industry, for the purpose of protecting and providing for destitute youth. 16p. *8°.* [London, 1831] *The copy that belonged to George Grote.*

26906 MILLER, Samuel, *cordwainer.* Pauper police. Letters addressed, through "The Times", to the churchwardens, overseers and parishioners of the several parishes in the City of London, showing the necessity and advantages of a pauper police. Containing also Mr. Colquhoun's observations on the state of the poor... 16p. *8°.* 1831.

For the **MORAL REFORMER**...By J. Livesey, 1831–33, *continued as* Livesey's moral reformer, 1838–39, *see* vol. III, *Periodicals list.*

26907 MUSSELBURGH AND PORTOBELLO GAS-LIGHT COMPANY. Contract of copartnery of the Musselburgh Gas-Light Company. January 1831. 21p. *8°. Edinburgh,* 1831.

**26908 —— Deed of accession and contract by the

Musselburgh and Portobello Gas-Light Company. September 16. 1831. 18p. *8°. Edinburgh*, 1831.

26909 NEWCASTLE UPON TYNE SUBSCRIPTION GAS LIGHT COMPANY. Deed of settlement of the Newcastle upon Tyne Subscription Gas Light Company. 71p. *8°. Newcastle upon Tyne*, 1831.

26910 [NICHOLS, JOHN G.] London pageants. I. Accounts of fifty-five royal processions and entertainments in the City of London...II. A bibliographical list of Lord Mayors' pageants. 121p. *8°*. 1831.

26911 [NICHOLSON, JOHN (1790–1843).] The factory-child, a poem. 54p. *12°*. 1831. *The Oastler copy. See also 1832.*

26912 Interesting original and selected **NOTICES** of the cholera morbus, amongst which are the orders and regulations of the Privy Council [dated: 20 October 1831], editorial article from the London Medical Gazette..., letters and papers...by J. Johnson, M.D. and Silas Blandford... To which are added, interesting notices respecting the Great Plague in London in 1665. 60p. *8°. Liverpool*, 1831.

26913 OASTLER, R. Exposition of the factory system. Mr. Oastler versus the Leeds Mercury. [A correspondence.] 4p. *fol. Leeds*, [1831] *Oastler's own copy.*

26914 [OSBORNE, R. B.] Plan, or proposed system, by which above fifty thousand poor in Ireland may not only be supported, but...made useful members of society...without any additional taxation. [By housing labourers employed in the making and upkeep of public roads.] By an Irish magistrate and landed proprietor. [Dedication signed: R.B.O.] xii, 9p. *8°. Wexford*, 1831.

26915 OUTLINE of the proceedings of a meeting of the operatives in Leeds, on the subject of the Factory Bill, held on the 10th December, 1831. *s.sh.fol. Leeds*, [1831] [*Br.* 519] *The Oastler copy.*

26916 OWEN, ROBERT D. Moral physiology; or, a brief and plain treatise on the population question... Second edition. 72p. *12°. New-York*, 1831. *See also 1835, 1842, 1844.*

26917 PATTISON, G. S. University of London. Professor Pattison's statement of the facts of his connexion with the University of London. 43p. *8°*. 1831. *The Agar Ellis copy.*

26918 PETITION to Parliament for a restriction of the hours of labour, for children in factories, to ten hours per day...The humble petition of the undersigned inhabitants of the town and neighbourhood of Huddersfield, in the County of York... *s.sh.fol. Leeds*, [1831 ?] [*Br.* 581(2)] *The Oastler copy.*

26919 PHILANTHROPOS, *pseud.* The two subjects which remain in dispute between the coal-owners and the pitmen candidly considered, in a letter addressed to the pitmen of the Tyne and Wear; to which the attention of the coal-owners is also invited. 12p. *12°. Newcastle*, 1831.

26920 [PLACE, F.] An essay on the state of the country, in respect to the condition and conduct of the husbandry labourers, and to the consequences likely to result therefrom. Not for sale. 16p. *8°*. [1831] *Place's own copy, in a volume of tracts collected by him.*

26921 A **PLAN** for the amelioration of the condition of the poor, with observations on the evil tendency of the laws affecting them. 39p. *8°*. 1831.

For the **POLITICAL MAGAZINE**, 1831–32, *see* vol. III, *Periodicals list.*

26922 POSTANS, T. Letter to Sir Thomas Baring ...on the causes which have produced the present state of the agricultural labouring poor; to which are added practical hints for bettering their condition. With a drawing and plan for a double cottage. 29p. *8°*. 1831.

26923 PROPOSAL for the establishment of village schools of industry, submitted to the consideration of land-owners and clergymen. 15p. *8°*. 1831.

26924 REASONS for contentment, addressed to the labouring part of the British public. Together with the fable of the bee hive. Second edition. 24p. *12°*. [1831] *See note to no.* 26994.

26925 The **REPLY** of the journeymen bookbinders, to remarks on a memorial addressed to their employers, on the effects of a machine, introduced to supersede manual labour, as appeared in a work published by the Society for the Diffusion of Useful Knowledge, with observations on the influence of machinery on the working classes in general. 30p. *8°*. 1831.

26926 REPORT of the proceedings of the Huddersfield and Bradford meetings, held on the 26th and 27th of December, 1831, to petition Parliament in favour of Mr. Sadler's Ten-Hour-Bill for the regulation of the employment of children in factories. 8p. *fol. Leeds*, [1831] *The Oastler copy.*

26927 [RICHARDSON, C. ?] An address to the working classes of Leeds, and the West-Riding of Yorkshire. By a sincere friend to them. [Signing himself 'A lover of the poor'.] 10p. *12°. Leeds*, [1831] *The copy that belonged to Oastler, who attributed it to Cavie Richardson in the manuscript index to his pamphlet collection.*

26928 [——] The factory system; or, Frank Hawthorn's visit to his cousin, Jemmy Cropper, of Leeds. 12p. *12°. Leeds*, 1831.

26929 [——] [Another edition.] 12p. *12°. Leeds*, 1831. *Both editions belonged to Oastler, who attributed the work to Richardson in the manuscript index to his pamphlet collection.*

26930 RICHARDSON, JOHN, *of Heydon.* A letter to the Right Hon. Henry Lord Brougham and Vaux, Lord High Chancellor of Great Britain, on an alteration in the poor laws, the employment of the people, and a reduction of the poor rate...Second edition, with large additions. 90p. *8°. London & Norwich*, 1831. *The copy that belonged to William Allen. For another edition, see 1830.*

26931 SADLER, M. T. The cause of the poor. The speech of M. T. Sadler, Esq. M.P. in the House of Commons, on...the 29th of August, on bringing forward his Resolution for the permanent relief of the Irish poor. *s.sh.fol. Leeds*, [1831] [*Br.* 524(1)] *The Oastler copy.*

26932 —— Condition of the labouring poor. Speech of Michael Thomas Sadler, Esq. in the House of Commons, on...October 11, 1831, on obtaining leave to bring in a Bill for bettering the condition of the labouring poor of England. *s.sh.fol. Leeds*, [1831] [*Br.* 526(2)] *The Oastler copy.*

26933 —— The distress of the agricultural labourers, illustrated by the speech of M. T. Sadler, Esq. M.P. upon a motion for leave to bring in a Bill for their relief, on October eleventh, 1831. 55p. *8°. Leeds*, [1831] *The Oastler copy. See also 1833.*

26934 SANDERSON, W. A proposal for union chambers of wages, to regulate the price of labour in the manufacturing districts, by which it is submitted turn outs may be prevented amongst the working classes of the community. 12p. *12°. Lancaster, 1831.*

26935 SCOTTISH TEMPERANCE SOCIETY. Second annual report of the Scottish Temperance Society ... 99p. *8°. Glasgow, 1831. The copy that belonged to John C. Colquhoun, with his book-plate. See also 1830.*

26936 SCROPE, G. P. A letter to the magistrates of the South of England, on the urgent necessity of putting a stop to the illegal practice of making up wages out of rates, to which alone is owing the misery and revolt of the agricultural peasantry. 24p. *8°. 1831. Reissued in* On the poor laws, and their abuse, *1832 (q.v.).*

26937 —— A second letter to the magistrates of the South of England, on the propriety of discontinuing the allowance system, the means for employing or disposing of the excess of labour, and for diminishing the unequal pressure of the poor rate. 51p. *8°. 1831. See note to no. 26936, above.*

26938 S——E, G. W. A short account of the life & death of Swing, the rick-burner, written by one well acquainted with him. Together with the confession of Thomas Goodman, now under sentence of death, in Horsham Jail, for rick-burning. 26p. *12°. [1831]*

26939 —— A true account of the life & death of Swing, the rick-burner...The nineteenth edition. 26p. *12°. [1831]*

26940 —— A new edition. 26p. *12°. [1831]*

26941 SENIOR, N. W. A letter to Lord Howick, on a legal provision for the Irish poor; commutation of tithes, and a provision for the Irish Roman Catholic clergy. 104p. *8°. 1831.*

26942 —— Second edition. 104p. *8°. 1831. Both editions belonged to M. T. Sadler. See also 1832.*

26943 [——] Remarks on emigration, with a draft of a Bill. 40[46]p. *8°. 1831.*

26944 Plain **SENSE** and reason. Letters to the present generation on the unrestrained use of modern machinery, particularly addressed to my countrymen, and fellow citizens. 30p. *8°. Norwich & London, [1831] *Another, the FWA copy, belonged to William Pare.*

26945 SHAFTESBURY MENDICITY SOCIETY. Shaftesbury Mendicity Society. [An account of its work.] 4p. *8°. Shaftesbury, [1831]*

26946 *[SMITH, Henry L.] Self-supporting charitable and parochial dispensaries. [Issued by the Society for Promoting the Objects of the Self-Supporting Dispensaries.] 23p. *8°. n.p. [1831] The FWA copy, that belonged to William Pare.*

26947 [——] [Another issue.] 23p. *8°. London, Coventry, &c., 1831. Presentation copy from the author to 'Dr. Kerr'.*

26948 SOCIÉTÉ D'INSTRUCTION ÉLÉMENTAIRE. Des machines, de leur influence sur la prospérité de la nation et le bien-être des ouvriers. [By E. Celnart. With 'Dialogue entre plusieurs ouvriers sur les avantages des machines', by ——Turck; 'De l'influence des mécaniques sur le prix des salaires et le bien-être du peuple', by —— Beranger; and 'Rapport de M. Francœur au nom de la commission chargée d'examiner les mémoires envoyés au concours ouvert par la Société, le 18 août 1830'.] 67, 32, 76p. *12°. Paris, 1831.*

26949 SOCIETY FOR THE DIFFUSION OF

INFORMATION ON THE SUBJECT OF CAPITAL PUNISHMENTS. Prospectus of the Society...[Signed: Thomas Clarkson. Distributed with nos. 1 and 3 of the Society's publications 'Punishment of death'.] [8]p. *8°. n.p., [1831]*

26950 —— Punishment of death...No. 1. Speech of the Right Hon. Sir William Meredith, Bart. In the House of Commons, May 13, 1777, in Committee on a Bill creating a new capital felony. Second edition. p.1–8. *8°. London, Edinburgh, &c., 1831. See also 1832.*

26951 —— Punishment of death...The substance of the speeches of S. Lushington, LL.D. and J. Sydney Taylor, M.A....at a public meeting...May 30, 1831, on the resolution relative to the punishment of death. No. 3. p.21–35. *8°. [1831] The Agar Ellis copy.*

26952 —— Second edition. p.21–35. *8°. [1831]*

26953 —— Punishment of death...A comparative view of the punishments annexed to crime in the United States of America and in England. By J. Sydney Taylor, A.M.... No. 4. p.37–59. *8°. 1831.*

26954 SOCIETY FOR THE IMPROVEMENT OF THE WORKING POPULATION IN THE COUNTY OF GLAMORGAN. [Tracts published by the Society.] 12 parts. *12°. Cardiff, Swansea, &c., [1831] Contents: 1. On the principle of compensation, as between the different conditions of human life; 2. On the principle of compensation, as respecting the condition of the working classes at different periods; 3. On the principle of compensation, as respecting the condition of the working classes in Wales and England; 4. On the institution of property; 5. On the advantages of friendly societies; 6. On the advantages of savings' banks; 7. To the labourers of Glamorganshire; 8–11. [Marcet, J. Five stories, entitled 'The rich and the poor: a fairy tale', 'Wages: another fairy tale', 'Population: or Patty's marriage', 'The poor's rate: or the treacherous friend' and 'Foreign trade: or the wedding gown';] 12. Summary of the objects attained or projected by the Society, in the course of its first year [signed: B. H. Malkin, chairman]. The volume is lettered: Cowbridge Tracts.*

26955 SOCIETY FOR THE PERMANENT SUPPORT OF ORPHAN & DESTITUTE CHILDREN. Society for the Permanent Support of Orphan & Destitute Children by means of apprenticeship in the colonies. [Objects of the Society, with special reference to emigration to South Australia.] 8p. *8°. 1831.*

26956 SOMERTON, W. H. A narrative of the Bristol riots, on the 29th, 30th and 31st of October, 1831...With ...a preface, introductory remarks and concluding observations...Fourth edition. 40p. *8°. Bristol, [1831]*

26957 A plain **STATEMENT** of the case of the labourer; for the consideration of the yeomen and gentlemen of the southern districts of England. Second edition. 24p. *8°. London & Winchester, 1831. The copy that belonged to William Allen.*

26958 A plain **STATEMENT** with respect to wages, addressed chiefly to agricultural labourers. 23p. *12°. [1831] See note to no. 26994.*

26959 —— Third edition. 23p. *12°. [1831]*

26960 STEVENS, James (1809–1843). The poor laws an interference with the divine laws by which the interests and welfare of society are maintained; with a plan for their gradual abolition... 92p. *8°. 1831.*

26961 SUSSEX ASSOCIATION FOR IMPROVING THE CONDITION OF THE LABOURING CLASSES. Quarterly report of the Sussex Association...No. 1. 47p. *8°. Lindfield, London, &c., 1831. The copy that belonged to William Allen. See also 1832.*

26962 TALBOT, J., *Earl of Shrewsbury.* Suggestions for the improvement of the condition of the labouring poor. Addressed to every member of the Legislature. 28p. *8°. 1831. The Agar Ellis copy.*

26963 The **TAX** list, being an authentic statement of the exorbitant taxes levied on the poor, by which twenty-two millions are starving!!! *s.sh.fol. [London, 1831 ?]* [*Br. 525*]

26964 TAYLOR, ROBERT (1784–1844). Swing: or, who are the incendiaries ? A tragedy, founded on late circumstances, and as performed at the Rotunda. 48p. *8°. 1831.*

26965 The **TEN-HOUR-BILL.** Report of the proceedings of the great Leeds meeting to petition Parliament in favour of Mr. Sadler's Bill for the regulation of the hours of children's labour in factories, held on Monday, January 9, 1831... 36p. *12°. Leeds, [1831] The Oastler copy.*

26966 THACKRAH, C. T. The effects of the principal arts, trades and professions, and of civic states and habits of living, on health and longevity: with a particular reference to the trades and manufactures of Leeds: and suggestions for the removal of many of the agents, which produce disease and shorten the duration of life. 126p. *8°. London & Leeds, 1831. See also 1832.*

26967 [THOMPSON, THOMAS P.] The article on machine-breaking. (In answer to 'Swing'.) Republished from the Westminster Review, No. XXVII. For January, 1831... 22p. *8°. 1831. See note to no. 25779.*

26968 [TRENCH, FRANCIS.] Hints for the establishment of charitable loan funds. By F.T. 32p. *8°. Dublin, 1831. *Another, the FWA copy, that belonged to William Pare, has manuscript notes. See also 1833.*

26969 TURNER, E. Two letters to the proprietors of the University of London, in reply to some remarks in Mr. Pattison's statement. By Edward Turner...Professor of Chemistry...and Anthony Todd Thomson...Professor of Materia Medica and Therapeutics... 16p. *8°. 1831. The Agar Ellis copy.*

26970 UNIVERSITY OF VERMONT. An exposition of the system of instruction and discipline pursued in the University of Vermont. By the faculty. Second edition. 32p. *8°. Burlington, 1831.*

26971 WAKEFIELD, EDWARD G. Householders in danger from the populace. 16p. *8°. [London, 1831 ?] The Agar Ellis copy.*

26972 —— Swing unmasked; or, the causes of rural incendiarism. 46p. *8°. [1831]*

26973 WALKER, J. K. On the late population returns of the manufacturing districts... ⟨Extracted from the fourteenth number of the Midland Reporter.⟩ [On conditions in factories, mortality rates, education, etc.] 16p. *8°. n.p. [1831]*

26974 WALKER, THOMAS (1784–1836). Observations on the nature, extent, and effects of pauperism, and of the means of reducing it. Second edition, revised. 89p. *8°. 1831. Presentation copy from the author to T. Spring Rice, Baron Monteagle.*

26975 —— Abridged from the second edition. 73p. *8°. 1831. Presentation copy from the author to 'C. Butterfield Esq.'. For another edition, see 1826.*

26976 WEST RIDING CENTRAL COMMITTEE. [*Begin.*] As the rich opponents of the Factory Bill have succeeded in referring it to a Select Committee of the House of Commons, the poor operatives are compelled of necessity to make out their children's case...[An appeal for funds.] [4]p. *4°. n.p. [1831] The Oastler copy. A lithographed manuscript facsimile letter; printed with the title The Factories Bill! An address to the inhabitants of Bradford, in 1832 (q.v.).*

26977 A few **WORDS** to the working classes, and others, on past & present times. 8p. *12°. Guildford, 1831.*

SLAVERY

26978 ENGLAND. Parliament. *House of Commons.* Report of the debate in the House of Commons, on...the 15th of April, 1831; on Mr. Fowell Buxton's motion to consider...the best means for effecting the abolition of colonial slavery. Extracted from the Mirror of Parliament. – Part LXXXIII. 112p. *8°. 1831.*

26979 April 10, 1831. **EXPOSURE** of an attempt recently made by certain West-Indian agents to mislead Parliament on the subject of colonial slavery. 24p. *8°. [1831]*

26980 JEREMIE, SIR J. Four essays on colonial slavery. 123p. *8°. 1831. See also 1832.*

26981 A **LETTER** to the Marquis of Chandos. [Signed: A proprietor of West-India property by inheritance, and dated, 1st July, 1831. On slavery in the West Indian colonies.] 16p. *8°. [London,] 1831. The Agar Ellis copy.*

26982 ORPEN, C. E. H. The principles, and objects, of "The Hibernian Negro's Friend Society," contrasted with those of the previously existing "Anti-slavery societies"; being a circular, addressed to all the friends of the negro, and advocates for the abolition and extinction of slavery; in the form of a letter, to Thomas Pringle, Esq. Secretary of "The London Anti-Slavery Society." 16p. *8°. n.p. [1831]*

26983 PENNSYLVANIA COLONIZATION SOCIETY. Reports of the Board of Managers of the Pennsylvania Colonization Society, with an introduction and appendix. 48p. *8°. 1831. Presentation copy, with inscription: 'Wm. Sheepshanks Esq – Leeds with the grateful remembrance of his obliged friend Elliott Cresson [representative of the American Colonization Society]'.*

26984 PHILANDER, *pseud.* Legalized prostitution; or, the Codrington brothel: addressed to the Society for the Propagation of the Gospel in Foreign Parts. 15p. *8°. Sheffield, 1831.*

26985 [PRICE, SIR ROSE, *Bart.* ?] Slavery. [A letter, signed: Z, addressed 'To the editor of the English

Chronicle and Whitehall Evening Post', headed 'To the West India planters and abolitionists. – Negro slavery'.] 6p. *8°. Penzance*, [1831 ?] *Inscribed: 'For Mr. Taylor, with Sir Rose Price's Compliments. May 12th, 1831'.*

26986 PRINCE, M. The history of Mary Prince, a West Indian slave. Related by herself. With a supplement by the editor [T. Pringle]. To which is added, the narrative of Asa-Asa, a captured African. 44p. *8°. London & Edinburgh*, 1831.

26987 —— Third edition. 44p. *8°. London & Edinburgh*, 1831.

26988 REPORT, containing an abstract of the new Order in Council, for the government and protection of slaves, with observations on some of its provisions, October 15, 1831. This paper to be considered as strictly private, and not to be published or circulated without permission. 24p. *8°.* [1831]

26989 SOCIETY FOR THE ABOLITION OF SLAVERY THROUGHOUT THE BRITISH DOMINIONS. Account of the receipts & disbursements of the Anti-Slavery Society, for the years 1829 & 1830: with a list of the subscribers. 16p. *8°.* [1831] *See also* 1827, 1829, 1832.

26990 —— Address to the people of Great Britain and Ireland, unanimously adopted at a general meeting of the London Anti-Slavery Society, held, April 23, 1831. 3p. *8°.* [1831]

26991 STEPHEN, J. Extracts from a West India plantation journal, kept by the manager: showing the treatment of the slaves and its fatal consequences. (Reprinted from the second volume of Mr. Stephen's work, entitled, "The slavery of the British West India colonies delineated, as it exists both in law and practice.") 8p. *8°.* [1831 ?] *For an edition of* The slavery of the British West India colonies delineated, *see* 1824.

26992 THOMSON, ANDREW. Review of Dr. H. Duncan's letters on the West India question. ⟨Extracted from the Christian Instructor for January and September 1831.⟩ 49p. *8°. Edinburgh*, 1831.

26993 WARNER, A. Negro slavery described by a negro: being the narrative of Ashton Warner...With an appendix, containing the testimony of four Christian ministers, recently returned from the colonies, on the system of slavery...By S. Strickland. 144p. *12°.* 1831.

POLITICS

For an **ADDRESS FROM HENRY HUNT TO THE RADICAL REFORMERS,** *see* vol. III, *Periodicals list.*

26994 An **ADDRESS** to the supporters of Lord Grey and the friends of reform. 12p. *12°.* 1831. *One of a collection of pamphlets on the Reform Bill and allied subjects which belonged to Anthony Ashley Cooper, seventh Earl of Shaftesbury, with his signature: 'Ashley', on the upper cover.*

26995 Valedictory **ADDRESS** to the readers of the late "Herald to the Trades' Advocate." 16p. *8°. Glasgow*, [1831] *Published in continuation of the suppressed Herald to the Trades Advocate, for which see* vol. III, *Periodicals list.*

26996 The **ADVANTAGES** of reform, as proposed by the present ministers. Seventh edition. 33p. *12°.* [1831]

26997 —— Eighth edition. 33p. *12°.* [1831] *See note to no.* 26994.

26998 ÆSOP in Downing Street. Part I. Published under the superintendence of a Society for the Diffusion of Useful Knowledge. [In verse.] 23p. *12°.* 1831. *See note to no.* 26994.

26999 ALLEN, JOHN (1771–1843). A short history of the House of Commons, with reference to reform. 30p. *8°.* 1831. *The Agar Ellis copy.*

27000 ANGLICUS, *pseud.* A letter to the Right Hon. Lord John Russell...containing suggestions towards the improvement of the English Reform Bill. 43p. *8°.* 1831. *The Agar Ellis copy.*

27001 ANTI-RADICAL, *pseud.* Letters of Anti-Radical [against the Reform Bill]. 23p. *8°.* 1831.

27002 An **APPEAL** to the electors of England. [Against the Reform Bill.] 12p. *12°.* 1831. *See note to no.* 26994.

27003 * [**BAILEY,** S.] A discussion of parliamentary reform...By a Yorkshire freeholder. 55p. *8°.* 1831. *The*

FWA copy, that belonged to William Pare, who added the author's name to the dedication.

27004 The **BALANCE** of power; demonstrating that the "Reform Bill" of Earl Grey is false and unjust in principle... 118p. *8°.* [1831] *The copy that belonged to M. T. Sadler.*

27005 BALTHAZAR, *pseud.* Reasons against the ballot, candidly addressed to all reformers. 16p. *8°. Newcastle upon Tyne*, 1831. *The copy that belonged to M. T. Sadler.*

27006 BENNETT, S. An address to the men of England, on the prospect of a revolution. 12p. *12°.* [*Bath*, 1831]

27007 —— A second letter to the Mayor and Corporation of the City of Bath, on their situation and prospects, in consequence of the downfall of the rotten borough system. 12p. *12°.* [*Bath*, 1831]

27008 [**BENTHAM,** J.] Parliamentary candidate's proposed declaration of principles: or say, a test proposed for parliamentary candidates. [Being Chap. 7 of the author's *Constitutional code* reprinted.] 18p. *8°.* 1831.

For **BERTHOLD'S POLITICAL HANDKERCHIEF,** *see* vol. III, *Periodicals list.*

27009 BIRMINGHAM POLITICAL UNION. Declaration of the Council of the Birmingham Political Union. [Signed by T. Attwood, chairman, and the other members of the Council, and dated, 20th December, 1831. In support of the Reform Bill.] *s.sh.fol. Birmingham*, [1831] *See note to no.* 20490.

27010 *—— Proposed plan for the organization of the Birmingham Political Union. Reprinted from the Midland Representative. [Signed: Charles Jones, secretary of the committee, and dated, Nov. 9, 1831.] 8p. *16°. Birmingham*, 1831. *The FWA copy, that belonged to William Pare.*

27011 —— Prorogation of Parliament. Second address of the Council of the Birmingham Political Union to all their fellow countrymen...Birmingham, October 21, 1831. [Signed: T. Attwood, chairman.] *s.sh.fol. Birmingham,* [1831] *See note to no.* 20490.

27012 —— Report of the proceedings at a meeting of the inhabitants of Birmingham held on Newhall Hill, October 3, 1831; convened by the Council of the Political Union, for the purpose of petitioning the House of Lords to pass the Reform Bill. 9p. *4°. Birmingham,* 1831. *See note to no.* 26519.

27013 —— Report of the proceedings at a town's meeting convened by the Birmingham Political Union, in support of His Majesty's Ministers' measure of parliamentary reform, held...on Monday, March 7, 1831. 8p. *4°. Birmingham,* 1831. *See note to no.* 26519.

27014 —— Report of the proceedings at a town's meeting, convened by the Council of the Political Union, for the purpose of expressing their approbation and admiration of His Majesty's conduct in dissolving the late Parliament. Held...on Monday, May 2, 1831. 8p. *4°. Birmingham,* [1831] *See note to no.* 26519.

27015 —— Report of the proceedings of the second annual meeting...held...on Monday, July 4, 1831. 8p. *4°. Birmingham,* 1831. *See note to no.* 26519. *See also* 1830, 1832, 1833.

For the **BRISTOL JOB NOTT,** 1831–33, *see vol.* III, *Periodicals list.*

27016 **BRITONS!** Support your patriot King and his enlightened ministers, against an unwise faction, whose measures would lead to revolution. 13p. *8°.* 1831. *The Agar Ellis copy.*

27017 [**BROUGHAM,** H. P., *Baron Brougham and Vaux.*] Friendly advice, most respectfully submitted to the Lords, on the Reform Bill. 31p. *8°.* 1831.

27018 [——] Second edition. 31p. *8°.* 1831.

27019 —— Speech of the Right Honourable Lord Brougham...on the second reading of the Reform Bill, delivered in the House of Lords on...7th of October, 1831. [With 'List of the majority and minority in the division...in the House of Lords'.] 15p. *4°.* 1831.

27020 *——* Genuine verbatim edition. The speech of Lord Brougham, Lord High Chancellor of England, delivered in the House of Lords, Oct. 7, 1831, on the second reading of the English Reform Bill; with Earl Grey's reply to the Opposition; and a list of the majority and minority. Fifth edition, corrected and revised by W. Harding. 40p. *8°.* [1831] *The FWA copy, that belonged to William Pare.*

27021 —— Ninth edition, corrected and revised by W. Harding. 40p. *8°.* [1831]

27022 **BULL,** JOHN, *pseud.* Gratitude to our late honest Premier, the Duke of Wellington, for reducing the beer tax three millions a year. [Signed: John Bull, but not a mad bull.] 4p. *8°. Dover,* [1831] *The copy that belonged to M. T. Sadler.*

27023 **BURKE,** E. A letter from the Right Honourable Edmund Burke, to a noble lord, on the attacks made upon him and his pension, in the House of Lords...A new edition. [Edited by T. H. Burke.] 59p. *8°.* 1831. *The copy presented by the editor to M. T. Sadler. For other editions, see* 1796.

27024 —— Opinions on reform, by the late Right Honourable Edmund Burke. [Selections, edited by T. H.

Burke.] 48p. *8°.* 1831. *The copy presented by the editor to M. T. Sadler.*

27025 —— Speech of the late Right Honble. Edmund Burke, on reform, delivered in the House of Commons, 1782. To which are added some extracts from the speech of the late Right Honble. William Windham on Mr. Curwen's Reform Bill, 1809. [Edited by T. H. Burke.] 32p. *8°.* 1831. *The copy presented by the editor to M. T. Sadler.*

27026 **CARPENTER,** WILLIAM (1797–1874). An address to the working classes, on the Reform Bill. 16p. *8°.* [1831]

27027 —— The people's book; comprising their chartered rights and practical wrongs. 427p. *8°.* 1831.

27028 *[——] Political and historical essays...[Being a reissue, with a general title-page, of *Political tracts*.] Nos. 1–9. *12°.* 1831. *The FWA copy, that belonged to William Pare. The Goldsmiths' Library copy wants the general title-page and no.* 9.

27029 The **CHARACTER** and tendency of the proposed reform. 36p. *12°.* [1831]

27030 —— Second edition. 36p. *12°.* [1831]

27031 —— Twenty-sixth edition. 36p. *12°.* [1831] *See note to no.* 26994.

27032 The new **CHARTER.** Humbly addressed to the King and both Houses of Parliament; proposed as the basis of a constitution for the government of Great Britain and Ireland, and as a substitute for the Reform Bill rejected by the Lords. 16p. *8°.* 1831. *The Agar Ellis copy.*

27033 [**CHEVALIER,** M.] La presse. 28p. *8°.* [*Paris,* 1831] *Three articles reprinted from Le Globe.*

27034 **COBBETT,** W. A full and accurate report of the trial [for libel] of William Cobbett, Esq. (before Lord Tenterden and a special jury,) on...July 7, 1831, in the Court of King's Bench, Guildhall. 45p. *8°.* 1831.

27035 —— Second edition. 47p. *8°.* 1831.

For **COBBETT'S PENNY TRASH,** [in imitation of Cobbett's Two-penny trash, and consisting of excerpts from his works designed to discredit him], *see vol.* III, *Periodicals list.*

For **COBBETT'S TWO-PENNY TRASH;** or politics for the poor, 1831–32, *see vol.* III, *Periodicals list.*

27036 [**COLERIDGE,** SIR J. T.] Notes on the Reform Bill. By a barrister. 63p. *8°.* 1831. *The Agar Ellis copy.*

27037 [**COLQUHOUN,** J. C.] The constitutional principles of parliamentary reform. By a freeholder and landholder of Scotland. 68p. *8°. Edinburgh, Glasgow, &c.,* 1831.

27038 —— Reform: the Lords against the Commons, and public opinion over all. 48p. *8°. Glasgow, Edinburgh, &c.,* 1831. *The Agar Ellis copy.*

27039 The **COMPLAINT** of the bull: and other poems [on reform]. 24p. *12°.* 1831.

27040 **CONSIDERATIONS** on the Reform Bill, by a Westminster elector. May 1831... 16p. *8°.* [1831]

27041 The new **CONSTITUTION.** "The Bill, the whole Bill and nothing but the Bill." Eighth edition. 32p. *12°.* [1831]

27042 —— Ninth edition. 32p. *12°*. [1831] *See note to no. 26994.*

27043 —— Tenth edition. 32p. *12°*. [1831]

27044 Our glorious **CONSTITUTION!** A new song. *s.sh.fol. Hoxton*, [1831?] *See note to no. 26994.*

27045 The **CRISIS**; or, a warning voice to the Lords. 13p. *8°*. 1831.

27046 The present political **CRISIS**, and its causes. By the author of "Spain in 1830". 26p. *8°*. 1831.

27047 **D., R. K.** Letter to Lord Viscount Althorp, on the proposed reduction in the newspaper stamp and advertisement duties. 16p. *8°*. 1831. *The Agar Ellis copy.*

27048 A **DIALOGUE** on parliamentary reform. 23p. *12°*. 1831. *See note to no. 26994.*

27049 —— Third edition. 23p. *12°*. 1831.

27050 **DOUBLEDAY**, T. The question of the vote by ballot plainly stated, and objections fully examined and refuted, in a letter to John Hodgson, Esq., M.P. 17p. *8°*. *London & Newcastle upon Tyne*, 1831.

27051 [**DRUMMOND**, H.] Reformers versus borough-mongers, and constitution-mongers. 65p. *8°*. *Chelsea*, [1831] *The Agar Ellis copy.*

27052 **EFFECTS** of reform. Extracts from the newspaper called "The Times," of Wednesday, the 18th of May, 1831. 11p. *12°*. [1831] *See note to no. 26994.*

27053 **ENGLAND.** *Parliament.* Bill for parliamentary reform, as proposed by the Marquess of Blandford in the House of Commons, Feb. 18, 1830, with the declaration of the Birmingham Political Council thereon. 69p. *8°*. 1831. *Presentation copy from the Marquess of Blandford to George Agar Ellis.*

27054 —— —— Official edition of Lord John Russell's Bill [12 December 1831], to reform the representation of the people in England and Wales; with the amended schedules, as intended to be proposed in the Committee. 39p. *8°*. 1831.

27055 —— —— Official edition of Lord John Russell's Bill, to amend the representation of the people in England and Wales; as read a second time in the House of Commons, December 16, 1831. 72p. *8°*. 1831.

27056 —— —— New Reform Bill. A Bill to amend the representation of the people in England and Wales; read a second time...December 18, 1831. 36p. *8°*. 1831.

27057 —— —— *House of Commons.* The whole debate on the first and second reading of Lord John Russell's Reform Bill; and on General Gascoyne's motion: with a verbatim report of the extraordinary proceedings...on the day of the prorogation of Parliament, April 22, 1831; and His Majesty's...speech. 225p. *8°*. 1831.

27058 **ESCOTT**, B. S. A letter to the farmers of the United Kingdom...Second edition, with additions. 20p. *8°*. *Taunton, London, &c.*, 1831. *The copy that belonged to M. T. Sadler.*

27059 [**EVERETT**, E.] The prospect of reform in Europe. From the North American Review, published at Boston, N.A., July 1, 1831. Second edition. 55p. *8°*. 1831.

27060 The **EVILS** political & moral arising out of the unnatural union of Church & State. A letter to the Right Hon. Lord Brougham and Vaux, Lord High Chancellor of Great Britain. 42p. *8°*. 1831.

27061 **FITZGERALD**, J. R. To the electors of Preston, London, October 6th, 1831. [Containing Henry Hunt's speech in the House of Commons, 15 Sept., 1831, on a motion for a total repeal of the existing corn-laws.] 8p. *4° Southwark*, [1831] *This work is also a prospectus for the periodical* An address of Henry Hunt to the radical reformers, *with the first 7 numbers of which Fitzgerald was associated as printer or publisher.*

27062 **GORDON**, H. Considerations on the war in Poland, and on the neutrality of the European powers at the present crisis. 59p. *8°*. 1831. *The Agar Ellis copy.*

27063 **GORE**, M. Further observations on the Reform Bill; or, what are the advantages of close boroughs? 31p. *8°*. 1831.

27064 —— Second edition. 36p. *8°*. 1831.

27065 —— Observations on the Reform Bill, and on the dangers of the present crisis. 31p. *8°*. 1831.

27066 [——] What will be the practical effects of the Reform Bill? 25p. *8°*. 1831. *Presentation copy from the author to George Agar Ellis. The author's name is added in manuscript on the title-page.*

27067 **GREAT BRITAIN** in 1841. Or, the results of the Reform Bill. 25p. *12°*. 1831.

27068 **GREY**, CHARLES, *2nd Earl Grey.* Corrected verbatim edition. The speech of Earl Grey, delivered in the House of Lords, October 3, 1831, on the second reading of the English Reform Bill. New edition, corrected and revised by W. Harding... 16p. *8°*. [1831]

27069 Lord **GREY'S** pledge considered, in relation to the ten-pound franchise. Addressed to all members of political unions. By a member of the National Political Union. 15p. *8°*. 1831.

27070 **GROTE**, G. Essentials of parliamentary reform. 75p. *8°*. 1831.

27071 ***HILL**, MATTHEW D. The speech of M. D. Hill, Esq., at a public dinner, given to him by the electors of Newark, on...March 10, 1831. [On reform.] 28p. *8°*. 1831. *The FWA copy, that belonged to William Pare.*

27072 **HINTS** for reform; or, taxation the true test of the right to vote for representatives in Parliament. A letter addressed to the Right Hon. Lord John Russell, Paymaster of the Forces. By a north countryman. 20p. *8°*. *Newcastle upon Tyne*, 1831. *The Agar Ellis copy.*

27073 **HINTS** to electors; or, answers to a few plain questions on the new constitution. Second edition. 23p. *12°*. 1831. *See note to no. 26994.*

27074 The **HOUSE** of Lords and the Reform Bill. 16p. *8°*. *Glasgow*, [1831] *Published in continuation of the suppressed* Herald to the Trades' Advocate *for which see* vol. III, *Periodicals list.*

27075 **HUNTER**, R., *of Lunna.* For the Members of the House of Commons. A collection of the principal memorials and petitions respecting the Zetland case and interests in the Scotch Reform Bills. [Each signed by Robert Hunter on behalf of the proprietors, leaseholders and inhabitants of Zetland.] 6, 13, 4, 4p. *8°*. [*London,*] 1831. *The copy that belonged to M. T. Sadler.*

27076 **I., C.** Reform, accompanied by the repeal of five millions of taxes, and the redemption of one hundred and seventeen millions of the National Debt. Addressed "to Philip, when sober." 40p. *8°*. 1831.

27077 IMPOSTURE unmasked; in a letter to the labourers & working people of England, on the schemes of the Church robbers & revolutionists with regard to the Church. By a true Englishman. [An attack on Cobbett.] Third edition. 23p. *12°*. [1831] *See note to no.* 26994.

27078 INGLIS, Sir Robert H., *Bart.* Reform. Substance of the speech delivered in the House of Commons, 1 March, 1831, on the motion of Lord John Russell for a reform in the representation. 68p. *8°. London & Oxford*, 1831. *The copy that belonged to M. T. Sadler.*

27079 JONES, Sir William (1746–1794). The principles of government; in a dialogue between a scholar and a peasant. 8p. *8°. R. Carlile*, 1831. **Another, the FWA copy, belonged to William Pare. For other editions, see* 1782.

27080 [KER, H. B.] The patriot King to his people. Addressed to every elector of Great Britain. 16p. *8°*. 1831. *Attributed to Ker by George Agar Ellis in the manuscript index to the volume in which the work is bound.*

27081 [——] Plain reading for plain people! Being an account of the English constitution; and the King's Reform Bill. 31p. *8°*. 1831. *Attributed to Ker by George Agar Ellis in the manuscript index to the volume in which the work is bound.*

27082 [——] [Another issue.] 31p. *8°*. 1831.

27083 [——] The result of the late elections and some of the consequences of reform considered. 51p. *8°*. 1831. *Two copies of which one, lacking p. 51, is a presentation copy from the author to George Agar Ellis, Baron Dover, who attributed the work to him.*

27084 [——] To the anti-reformers. 16p. *8°*. 1831. *Attributed to Ker by George Agar Ellis in the manuscript index to the volume in which the work is bound.*

27085 A **LEAF** from the future history of England, on the subject of reform in Parliament. Third edition. 12p. *12°*. [1831] *See note to no.* 26994.

27086 —— Fourth edition. 12p. *12°*. [1831]

27087 The splendid national **LEGACY** of Lord Castlereagh. 16p. *8°. Glasgow*, [1831] *Published in continuation of the suppressed Herald to the Trades' Advocate, for which see vol. III, Periodicals list.*

27088 A **LETTER** to Earl Grey on the subject of the adjustment of the House of Peers. 15p. *8°*. 1831.

27089 LETTER to the Lords [on reform]. By a Member of the House of Commons. Sept. 22, 1831. 10p. *8°*. 1831.

27090 Black **LIST!** Being the annual amount of pickings of the peers and their families, who voted against the Reform Bill, in the House of Lords, on Saturday, Oct. 8, 1831. *s.sh.fol.* [London: *W.P. Chubb*, 1831] [*Br.* 523]

27091 LIST of all the members composing the House of Peers, on Saturday morning, October 8, 1831; shewing the manner in which they voted on the Reform Bill, as well as those who were absent from the division; together with other lists, illustrative of that proceeding...26p. *8°*. 1831. *The Agar Ellis copy.*

27092 The **LORDS** have resolved to do their duty: a constitutional reply to "What will the Lords do?". By an Englishman. 68p. *8°*. 1831. *The copy that belonged to M. T. Sadler.*

27093 What have the **LORDS** done? and what will they do next? 37p. *8°*. 1831.

27094 What will be done with the **LORDS?** 32p. *8°*. 1831.

27095 LOSH, J. Observations on parliamentary reform...To which is added, the petition from the Society of the Friends of the People, presented to Parliament by Charles Grey, Esq. in the year 1793. 33p. *8°. London & Newcastle upon Tyne*, 1831. *For an edition of the petition, see* 1793.

27096 MACKENZIE, P. The life of Thomas Muir, Esq., advocate...who was tried for sedition before the High Court of Justiciary in Scotland, and sentenced to transportation for fourteen years. With a full report of his trial. 160p. *8°. Glasgow & London*, 1831. *See also* 1837.

27097 [MAHONY, P.] Letter to —— —— &c.&c. on a Bill, now before Parliament, for regulating the appointments of Lieutenants & Deputy Lieutenants for counties in Ireland. 46p. *8°*. 1831. *Attributed to Pierce Mahony by George Agar Ellis, in the manuscript index to the volume in which the work is bound.*

27098 [——] Letters to a friend, by a liberal supporter of Roman Catholic emancipation and Parliamentary reform, on the Irish Reform Bill. 42p. *8°. n.p.*, 1831. *Presentation copy from the anonymous author to George Agar Ellis, who attributed it to Mahony in the manuscript index to the volume in which it is bound.*

27099 MALCOLM, Sir John. Letter on the state of public affairs...to a friend in India. 31p. *8°*. 1831. *The copy that belonged to Earl De Grey.*

27100 MARTIN, John C. Reform considered; or, a comparison between the ancient and the reformed constitutions: more especially with reference to their own stability, and to the protection which they respectively afford to the rights and liberties of the people... 104p. *8°. Dublin & London*, 1831. *The Agar Ellis copy.*

27101 MURRAY, David W., *3rd Earl of Mansfield.* Substance of a speech of the Earl of Mansfield, upon the motion that the Reform Bill be now read a second time, on the 3rd of October, 1831. 39p. *8°*. 1831. *The copy that belonged to M. T. Sadler.*

27102 NATIONAL POLITICAL UNION. [*Begin.*] National Political Union...The Committee... invite the public generally to form district unions throughout the country... [With a notice of a general meeting on 9 November 1831.] 2p. *8°. Southwark*, 1831.

27103 —— 1. National Political Union. List of the Council. [With minutes of a Council meeting on 16 November 1831.] 4p. *8°. Southwark*, [1831].

27104 —— 5. Political unions not contrary to law. The King's Proclamation examined, in an address by the National Political Union. [With the text of the Proclamation.] 15p. *8°*. [London,] 1831. *Attributed to Francis Place in a manuscript note on the title-page.*

27105 —— Authorised copy. 6. Objects and rules of the National Political Union, instituted October 31st, 1831, with an address [by William Johnson Fox] to the people of England... 10p. *8°*. [London,] 1831.

27106 OBSERVATIONS on a pamphlet falsely attributed to a great person; entitled 'Friendly advice to the Lords on the Reform Bill.' 79p. *8°*. 1831. *The Agar Ellis copy.*

27107 OBSERVATIONS on the measure of reform, introduced by Lord John Russell, in the House of Commons, on the first of March, 1831. [Signed: A reformer, but no revolutionist.] 16p. *8⁰*. *Truro*, [1831] *The Agar Ellis copy.*

27108 King **OMEGA'S** vision; or, a midsummer night's dream in 1831. [Strictures on the Reform Bill, in verse.] 11p. *12⁰*. 1831. *See note to no. 26994.*

27109 **P.** On the laws and liberties of Englishmen. 15p. *8⁰*. 1831. *The copy that belonged to M. T. Sadler.*

27110 —— Fourth edition. 21p. *12⁰*. 1831. *See note to no. 26994.*

27111 ——Sixth edition. 21p. *12⁰*. 1831.

27112 **PALGRAVE,** SIR F. Conciliatory reform. A letter, addressed to the Right Hon. Thomas Spring Rice, M.P....on the means of reconciling parliamentary reform to the interests and opinions of the different orders of the community: together with the draft of a Bill, founded on the ministerial Bill, but adapted more closely to the principles...of the constitution. 48p. *8⁰*. [1831] *The Agar Ellis copy.*

27113 **PARLIAMENTARY CANDIDATE SOCIETY.** Parliamentary Candidate Society, instituted to support reform by promoting the return of fit and proper members to Parliament. 8p. *8⁰*. 1831.

27114 —— Proceedings of the Parliamentary Candidate Society... 15p. *8⁰*. 1831. *The Agar Ellis copy.*

27115 **PEEL,** SIR ROBERT, *2nd Bart.* An important question!!! How will the agriculturists be benefited by the Reform Bill? As shown in a speech delivered by Sir Robert Peel, Bart. in the House of Commons, July 27, 1831. 23p. *12⁰*. 1831. *See note to no. 26994.*

27116 The **PEOPLE'S** manual; or notices respecting the majority of 199 peers, who...8th of October, 1831, rejected the Reform Bill. 32p. *8⁰*. 1831. *The Agar Ellis copy.*

27117 [**PETER, W.**] Questions on the ballot, for the calm consideration and deliberate judgment of the people of England. 7p. *8⁰*. *Plymouth*, [1831] *The Agar Ellis copy. See also 1833.*

27118 **PHILALETHES,** *pseud.* A word in season! Addressed to persons desirous of change. Second edition. 12p. *12⁰*. 1831. *See note to no. 26994.*

27119 [**PLACE, F.**] A letter to a minister of state, respecting taxes on knowledge. Not for sale. 16p. *8⁰*. [1831] *Another, the FWA copy that belonged to William Pare, was given by Joseph Hume to the Birmingham Co-operative Society and has their book-stamp.*

27120 [——] Second edition, with a postscript and appendices. Not for sale. 16p. *8⁰*. [1831]

27121 **POLAND.** Constitutional Charter of the Kingdom of Poland, in the year 1815, with some remarks on the manner in which the Charter, and the stipulations in the treaties relating to Poland, have been observed. Sold for the benefit of the military hospitals in Poland. 63p. *8⁰*. 1831. *The Agar Ellis copy.*

For the **POLITICAL ANECDOTIST AND POPULAR INSTRUCTOR,** see vol. III, *Periodicals list.*

For the **POOR MAN'S GUARDIAN,** 1831–35, *see* vol. III, *Periodicals list.*

27122 **POTTER,** RICHARD. To the independent inhabitants of Wigan. [On the right of the borough to be represented by two members in Parliament. Dated: February 22, 1831.] *s.sh.fol.* 1831.

27123 A **PROTESTANT FREEMAN'S** appeal to the Protestant electors of Great Britain and Ireland. 12p. *12⁰*. 1831. *See note to no. 26994.*

27124 **PUSEY,** P. The new constitution: remarks by Philip Pusey, Esq., M.P. 52p. *8⁰*. 1831. *The copy that belonged to M. T. Sadler.*

27125 The **QUESTION** of reform considered; with hints for a plan. 142p. *8⁰*. 1831.

27126 **REFORM.** A letter to Lord Russell on reform in Parliament. 46p. *8⁰*. 1831. *The Agar Ellis copy.*

27127 **REFORM,** revolution, republicanism. [Containing extracts from the works of Charles Leslie and the Marquis de Pastoret.] 12p. *8⁰*. [*Winchester*, 1831?] *The copy that belonged to M. T. Sadler.*

27128 The **REFORM BILL** for England and Wales examined. 60p. *8⁰*. 1831. *The copy that belonged to M. T. Sadler.*

27129 **REMARKS** on the suppression of the late "Herald to the Trades' Advocate," by the Solicitor of Stamps, with letter of Joseph Hume... p. 1–10, [xi]–xvi. *8⁰*. *Glasgow*, [1831] *Published in continuation of the suppressed* Herald to the Trades' Advocate (*see* vol. III, *Periodicals list); p.[xi]–xvi contain an index to the periodical.*

27130 **REMARKS** on the word reform. 8p. *8⁰*. *Bristol*, [1831?] *The copy that belonged to M. T. Sadler.*

27131 **REPLY** to a pamphlet, entitled Speech of the Right Hon. Lord Brougham...delivered in the House of Lords on Friday, Oct. 7, 1831. [Second edition.] 100p. *8⁰*. 1831.

27132 **REPRESENTATION** of the case of Gorbals, in reference to the elective franchise, on the principle of Lord John Russell's Bill: respectfully submitted to His Majesty's Minister. [A memorial of the proprietors and householders of the Burgh of Gorbals.] 15p. *8⁰*. *Glasgow*, [1831]

For the **REPUBLICAN; OR, VOICE OF THE PEOPLE,** 1831–32, *see* vol. III, *Periodicals list.*

27133 **REVELL,** H. Speech of Henry Revell, Esq. delivered at the Clerkenwell Political Union...November 23, 1831. Published by order of the Council of the... Union. [With the resolutions of the meeting.] 14p. *8⁰*. 1831.

27134 [**RICH,** SIR H., *Bart.*] What will the Lords do? 33p. *8⁰*. 1831. *Presentation copy, with inscription, from the author to George Agar Ellis.*

27135 [——] Second part of What will the Lords do? Second edition. 44p. *8⁰*. 1831. *The Agar Ellis copy.*

27136 **ROSCOE,** W. A letter to Henry Brougham, Esq., M.P. now Lord Brougham and Vaux, Lord High Chancellor, &c. on the subject of reform in the representation of the people in Parliament. 16p. *8⁰*. *London & Liverpool*, 1831.

27137 **RUSSELL,** J., *Earl Russell.* Lord John Russell's speech on reform; delivered in the House of Commons, March 1, 1831. 20p. *8⁰*. 1831.

27138 —— Corrected report of the speech of Lord John Russell, in the House of Commons, on...the 1st of March, 1831, on introducing a Bill for a reform of the Commons House of Parliament. 19p. *8⁰*. [1831]

27139 SADLER, M. T. The speech of Michael Thomas Sadler, M.P. on the ministerial plan of reform, delivered in the House of Commons, on seconding General Gascoyne's motion for retaining the present number of members for England and Wales. 47p. *8°.* 1831. *Sadler's own copy.*

27140 SAINT-JUST, L. A. DE. Fragmens sur les institutions républicaines, ouvrage posthume de Saint-Just, précédé d'une notice, par Ch. Nodier. 79p. *8°.* Paris, 1831. *The copy that belonged to Victor Considérant.*

27141 SCARLETT, J., *Baron Abinger.* Substance of the speech of Sir James Scarlett, on the motion for the second reading of the Bill for reform, in the House of Commons, with a letter to Lord Viscount Milton. 32p. *8°.* 1831. *The Agar Ellis copy.*

27142 SCROPE, G. P. Speech of G. Poulett Scrope, Esq…at the Wiltshire meeting held at Devizes, on… September 30, 1831. 15p. *8°.* 1831. *The Agar Ellis copy.*

27143 SEBRIGHT, SIR J. S., *Bart.* County reform. Opinion of Sir J. S. Sebright, in reply to a letter from a freeholder at Nutford…on the subject of votes being given to, or withheld from, farmers being tenants at will, or under a lease, for a less term than 21 years… 11p. *12°.* 1831. *See note to no. 26994.*

27144 A **SERIES** of dissertations on political economy, designed for gratuitous distribution among such members of the Legislature as may deem them worthy their perusal and acceptance. No. 1. On parliamentary reform. By a Member of the Royal College of Physicians. 11p. *8°.* 1831. *The Agar Ellis copy.*

27145 [**SMITH**, SYDNEY (1771–1845).] Mr. Dyson's speech to the freeholders, on reform. 27p. *8°.* 1831. *The Agar Ellis copy.*

27146 [——] Thirty-fifth edition. 27p. *8°.* 1831.

27147 [——] [Another edition.] 16p. *8°.* [1831]

27148 Aristocratic **SPIRIT** of the British people. 14p. *8°.* Glasgow, [1831] *Published in continuation of the suppressed* Herald to the Trades' Advocate, *for which see* vol. III, *Periodicals list.*

27149 The **STATE** of the times, and the necessity of reform. 59p. *8°.* 1831.

27150 SUGGESTIONS respecting the political education of the lower orders… 32p. *8°.* London & Liverpool, 1831. *By the same author as no. 26451, who has been tentatively identified as William Rathbone (1787–1868). The copy that belonged to William Allen.*

27151 SUGGESTIONS supposed calculated to reconcile party differences in the measure of parliamentary reform. [Reprinted from the *Glasgow Courier*.] 8p. *8°.* n.p. [1831] *The copy that belonged to M. T. Sadler.*

27152 [**THOMPSON**, THOMAS P.] The article on parliamentary reform, republished from the Westminster Review, No. XXVIII. For April 1830… 16p. *8°.* 1831. *See note to no. 25779.*

27153 [——] The article on the European Revolution. Republished from the Westminster Review, No. XXVII, for January, 1831. 8p. *8°.* 1831. *See note to no. 25779.*

27154 [——] The article on the prospects from Tory reaction. From the Westminster Review, No. XXX. For October 1831… 15p. *8°.* 1831. *See note to no. 25779.*

27155 [——] Belgium and the Holy Alliance. From the Westminster Review, No. XXIX. For July 1, 1831. 8p. *8°.* [1831] *See note to no. 25779.*

27156 [——] On the taxes on knowledge. From the Westminster Review, No. XXIX. For July 1, 1831. 32p. *8°.* [1831] *See note to no. 25779. *Another, the FWA copy, that belonged to William Pare, has a manuscript inscription, 'With Mr. Hume's Complts'.*

27157 THOUGHTS on the present aspect of foreign affairs. By an Englishman. 118p. *8°.* 1831. *The Agar Ellis copy.*

27158 TREVOR, A. H., *Viscount Dungannon.* A letter to His Grace the Duke of Rutland, K.G. on the present crisis. 16p. *8°.* 1831. *The copy that belonged to M. T. Sadler.*

27159 The last **TRUMPET** of the boroughmongers. By a radical reformer. 22p. *8°.* Glasgow, 1831. *The Agar Ellis copy.*

27160 The **TRUTH** respecting the revolution which broke out in Paris, in the month of July, 1830; its causes and its consequences. Translated from the French. 64p. *8°.* 1831. *The Agar Ellis copy.*

For **UNION**, 1831–32, *see vol.* III, *Periodicals list.*

27161 A **VIEW** of the representation of England, Feb. 28, 1831. 16p. *8°.* [1831]

27162 VYVYAN, SIR R. R., *Bart.* Cornwall election: speech of Sir R. R. Vyvyan, Bart. 11p. *12°.* [London, 1831] *See note to no. 26994.*

27163 W., L. Two letters, addressed to Earl Grey, upon the substance and tendency of the Reform Bill, as introduced into the House of Commons by Lord John Russell. 35p. *12°.* 1831. *See note to no. 26994.*

27164 W., S., *Esq., Member of the Honourable Society of the Inner Temple.* A word in season; addressed to the opposers of the present Reform Bill; proving the projected reform not only not revolutionary, but the only means of preventing revolution. 16p. *8°.* [1831] *The Agar Ellis copy.*

27165 WALL, C. B. A few words to the electors of Guildford, on reform. 34p. *8°.* 1831. *The Agar Ellis copy.*

27166 WALSH, J. B., *Baron Ormathwaite.* Observations on the ministerial plan of reform. 83p. *8°.* 1831. *Presentation copy from the author to Lord Henry Cholmondeley.*

27167 —— Fourth edition. 83p. *8°.* 1831.

27168 —— Popular opinions on parliamentary reform, considered. 99p. *8°.* 1831.

27169 —— Second edition. 99p. *8°.* 1831.

27170 —— Fifth edition, with additions, and a postscript to the ballot. 114p. *8°.* 1831.

27171 —— Sixth edition, with additions, and a postscript to the ballot. 114p. *8°.* 1831.

27172 Rev. R. **WATSON**, Mr. Macaulay, & Mr. Sadler. [Signed: a Methodist, and dated, Sept. 20, 1831. An attack on Sadler.] s.sh.fol. Leeds, [1831] [*Br. 521*] *The Oastler copy.*

27173 WILSON, JOHN, *of Thornly.* The political state of Scotland: with notices concerning the population and representatives of counties and burghs: arranged from public records. [4]p. *8°.* 1831. *The copy that belonged to M. T. Sadler.*

27174 **WOOD,** Joseph. A letter by Captain Wood, of Sandal, near Wakefield, to the members of the Huddersfield Union of the Working Classes. [Dated: December 5th, 1831.] *s.sh.fol. Halifax,* [1831] [*Br.* 527] *The Oastler copy.*

27175 A few **WORDS** to the Lords and the people about reform. Second edition. 36p. *12°.* [1831] *See note to no.* 26994.

SOCIALISM

27176 *****ASSOCIATION FOR REMOVING IGNORANCE AND POVERTY BY EDUCATION AND EMPLOYMENT.** The resolutions intended to be proposed at the public meeting to be held on the 12th instant, at the Royal London Bazaar [to establish 'an association to remove the causes of ignorance and poverty', under the direction of Robert Owen]. *s.sh.fol. n.p.* [1831] *The FWA copy that belonged to William Pare.*

27177 **BERANGER,** C. Pétition d'un prolétaire à la Chambre des Députés. 16p. *8°. Paris,* 1831. *Reprinted from Le Globe.*

27178 *****CAMPBELL,** Alexander (1796–1870). An address on the progress of the co-operative system. [Report of an address delivered by Mr. Campbell at a meeting of the Cambuslang Co-operative Society on 7 March.] 12p. *12°.* [*Glasgow,* 1831] *The FWA copy that belonged to William Pare.*

27179 [**CARNOT,** Lazare H.] Doctrine Saint-Simonienne. Résumé général de l'exposition faite en 1829 et 1830. Extrait de la Revue Encyclopédique. Deuxième édition. 45p. *8°. Paris,* 1831.

27180 [——] Troisième édition. 45p. *8°. Paris,* 1831. *Two copies that belonged to Victor Considérant.* For Doctrine de Saint-Simon. Exposition...1829–30, *see* 1830.

27181 [**CHEVALIER,** M.] Religion Saint-Simonienne. Politique européenne. Articles extraits du Globe. 127p. *8°. Paris,* 1831.

27182 **CO-OPERATIVE CONGRESS, May, 1831.** Address. [*Begin.*] The Co-operative delegates in Congress assembled, to the numerous societies throughout the United Kingdom, – greeting...[Signed: By order of the delegates. Elijah Dixon, Joseph Marriott, chairmen.] *s.sh.fol. Birmingham,* [1831]

27183 —— Co-operative Congress. The following is a list of delegates, who attended... *s.sh.fol. n.p.* [1831]

27184 —— Resolutions, &c. passed at the first meeting of the Co-operative Congress, held in Manchester...May 26 and 27, 1831...[With 'Laws for the government of the "North West of England United Co-operative Company"'.] *s.sh.fol. n.p.* [1831]

27185 —— Statistical table of co-operative societies represented in Congress. *s.sh.fol. n.p.* [1831]

27186 —— To the [Owenian] Co-operative Society. [*Begin.*] Brother Co-operators...[A letter calling a meeting of delegates, signed: Joseph Smith, president, Wm. Carson, Elijah Dixon, E. T. Craig, &c....] [2]p. *s.sh.8°.* [*Salford?* 1831]

27187 **CO-OPERATIVE CONGRESS, October, 1831.** Co-operative Congress. A list of the co-operative societies represented by delegates or letters...with answers to the questions in the circular. *s.sh.fol. n.p.* [1831]

27188 —— Proceedings of the second Co-operative Congress, held in Birmingham, October 4, 5, and 6, 1831 ...Reported by order of the Congress. By John and James Powell. 24p. *12°. Birmingham,* [1831]

27189 **DECOURDEMANCHE,** A. Aux industriels. Lettres sur la législation dans ses rapports avec l'industrie et la propriété, dans lesquelles on fait connaître les causes de la crise actuelle, et les moyens de la faire cesser...(Extrait du Globe.) 2 vols. *8°. Paris,* 1831. *The copy that belonged to Victor Considérant.*

27190 **EICHTHAL,** G. d', *and others.* Religion Saint-Simonienne. Rapports adressés aux Pères Suprêmes sur la situation et les travaux de la Famille. [By Gustave d'Eichthal, Stéphane Flachat and Henri Fournel.] 33p. *8°.* [*Paris,* 1831] *The copy that belonged to Victor Considérant.*

27191 [**ENFANTIN,** B. P.] Religion Saint-Simonienne. Économie politique et politique. Articles extraits du Globe. 176p. *8°. Paris,* 1831. *The copy that belonged to Victor Considérant. See also* 1832.

27192 —— Religion Saint-Simonienne. Lettre du Père Enfantin à Charles Duveyrier. Lettre du Père Enfantin à François et à Peiffer, chefs de l'Église de Lyon. Le prêtre – L'Homme et la femme. (Extrait du Globe du 18 juin 1831.) 22p. *8°. Paris,* 1831. *The copy that belonged to Victor Considérant.*

27193 [——] Religion Saint-Simonienne. Réunion générale de la Famille. Séances des 19 et 21 novembre. Note sur le mariage et le divorce...par le Père Rodrigues. 64p. *8°. Paris,* 1831. *The copy that belonged to Victor Considérant. See also* 1832.

27194 [——], *and others.* Doctrine de Saint-Simon. Exposition. Première année. 1828–1829. [By B. P. Enfantin, L. H. Carnot, H. Fournel and C. Duveyrier.] Troisième edition. Revue et augmentée. 432p. *8°. Paris,* 1831. *For another edition, see* 1830.

27195 **FINCH,** John (1783–1857). Important meeting of the working classes, delegates from fifty co-operative societies. To the editor of the Liverpool Chronicle. [A letter, dated: Liverpool, June 8, 1831, on the proceedings at the first Cooperative Congress, in Manchester.] *s.sh.8°. n.p.* [1831]

27196 **FOURIER,** F. C. M. Piéges et charlatanisme des deux sectes Saint-Simon et Owen, qui promettent l'association et le progrès. Moyen d'organiser en deux mois le progrès réel, la vraie association, ou combinaison des travaux agricoles et domestiques... 72p. *8°. Paris,* 1831. *The copy that belonged to Victor Considérant.*

27197 **GRAY,** John (1799–1883). The social system: a treatise on the principles of exchange. 374p. *8°. Edinburgh, London, &c.,* 1831. *Presentation copy, with inscription, from the author to James Mill.*

27198 [**HASPOTT,** E.] Religion Saint-Simonienne. Aux ouvriers, par un ouvrier. 12p. *8°.* [*Paris,* 1831]

27199 [**HODGSKIN,** T.] Labour defended against the claims of capital; or, the unproductiveness of capital

proved. By a labourer. Second edition. 33p. *12°.* 1831.
For another edition, see 1825.

27200 [KING, WILLIAM, *of Charlotte St., London.*]
Dedicated with permission to the useful part of the
community, viz. the real wealth creators... The workings
of money and its results on what the political economists
call – the profitable investment of capital as represented
by money. Facts for consideration. [Signed: K.] 2p.
s.sh.8°. [*London*, 1831] [*Br.* 542(3)] *Two copies, one that
belonged to William Lovett, the other to Francis Place.*

27201 [——] Dedicated to the useful part of the community – viz., the wealth creators. The workings of capital,
at present represented by money. Part the second.
[Signed: K.] 2p. *s.sh.8°.* [*London*, 1831] *The copy that
belonged to William Lovett.*

27202 [——] [Another edition.] Dedicated to the useful
part of the community... The workings of capital. Part
the second. [Signed: K.] 2p. *s.sh.8°.* [*London*, 1831]
[*Br.* 542 (6)] *The copy that belonged to Francis Place.*

27203 [——] Published by a few friends of truth and
common sense. To the useful working population.
[Signed: K.] 2p. *s.sh.8°.* [*London*, 1831] [*Br.* 542(9)] *The
copy that belonged to Francis Place.*

27204 [——] Published by a few friends of truth and
common sense. To the well disposed of all classes. The
source of wealth. [Signed: K.] 2p. *s.sh.8°.* [*London*, 1831]
[*Br.* 542(2)] *The copy that belonged to Francis Place.*

27205 [——] To the makers of wealth, the useful work-
ing population. [Signed: K.] 2p. *s.sh.8°.* [*London*, 1831]
[*Br.* 542(8)] *Two copies, one that belonged to William
Lovett, the other to Francis Place.*

27206 [——] To the useful classes. Second edition.
[Signed: K.] 2p. *s.sh.8°.* [*London*, 1831] [*Br.* 542(10)]
*Two copies, one that belonged to William Lovett, the other
to Francis Place.*

27207 [——] The workings of money capital. [Signed:
K.] *s.sh.8°.* [*London*, 1831] [*Br.* 542(4)] *Two copies, one
that belonged to William Lovett, the other to Francis Place.*

27208 [——] [Another edition.] The workings of capital.
s.sh.8°. [*London:*] *Common Sense Society*, [1831] [*Br.*
542(5)] *The copy that belonged to Francis Place.*

For the **LANCASHIRE CO-OPERATOR,** *continued as* the Lancashire and Yorkshire co-operator,
1831–32, *see* vol. III, *Periodicals list,* Lancashire and
Yorkshire co-operator.

27209 LAURENT, P. M. Religion Saint-Simonienne.
Prédication du 9 octobre. 16p. *8°.* [*Paris*, 1831] *The copy
that belonged to Victor Considérant.*

27210 LECHEVALIER SAINT ANDRÉ, L. J.
Aux Saint-Simoniens. Lettre sur la division survenue dans
l'association Saint-Simonienne. 56p. *8°. Paris*, 1831. *The
copy that belonged to Victor Considérant.*

27211 —— Religion Saint-Simonienne. Enseignement
central. (Extrait de l'Organisateur.) [L'introduction et la
première leçon...prononcées à la Sorbonne par M.
Léchevalier.] 64p. *8°. Paris*, 1831. *The copy that belonged
to Victor Considérant.*

27212 M. From my Uncle Toby's portfolio. "Gen-
tility". [An Owenite leaflet.] *s.sh.8°.* [*London*, 1831]
[*Br.* 542(13)] *Two copies, one that belonged to William
Lovett, the other to Francis Place.*

27213 MACLURE, W. Opinions on various subjects,
dedicated to the industrious producers. Vols. 1–2. *8°.
New-Harmony, Indiana*, 1831.

27214 OWEN, ROBERT. Outline of the rational
system of society, founded on demonstrable facts developing the constitution and laws of human nature; being the
only effectual remedy for the evils experienced by the
population of the world... [4]p. *4°.* [*London*, 1831]
*Another, the FWA copy, belonged to William Pare. See
also 1837, 1839, 1840.*

27215 [PEREIRE, J. E.] Religion Saint-Simonienne.
Moyens de supprimer immédiatement tous les impôts des
boissons, l'impôt sur le sel, et la loterie. Examen pratique
de la question de l'amortissement. Extrait du Globe du
25 octobre 1831. 15p. *8°. Paris*, 1831. *See also no.* 27222.

27216 RELIGION Saint-Simonienne. Cérémonie du
27 novembre. 24p. *8°. Paris*, 1831. *The copy that belonged
to Victor Considérant.*

27217 RELIGION Saint-Simonienne. Communion
générale de la Famille Saint-Simonienne. Extrait de
l'Organisateur. 40p. *8°. Paris*, 1831.

27218 RELIGION Saint-Simonienne. Correspondance. Articles extraits du Globe. 56p. *8°. Paris*, 1831.

27219 RELIGION Saint-Simonienne. Enseignement
des ouvriers. Séance du dimanche 18 décembre 1831. 23p.
8°. Paris, 1831.

27220 RELIGION Saint-Simonienne. Evénemens de
Lyon. 16p. *8°.* [*Paris*, 1831]

27221 RELIGION Saint-Simonienne. Missions Saint-
Simoniennes. (Extrait de l'Organisateur)...Mission du
Midi. [Discours de Jean Reynaud.] 23p. *8°.* [*Paris*, 1831]
The copy that belonged to Victor Considérant.

27222 RELIGION Saint-Simonienne. Projet de discours de la couronne pour l'année 1831. Moyens de
supprimer immédiatement tous les impôts des boissons,
du sel, et la loterie. Examen pratique de l'amortissement.
La Vendée. Extraits du Globe. 35p. *8°. Paris*, 1831. *The
first and the third parts were by Michel Chevalier, the second,
also published separately, was by Emile Pereire (see no.*
27215).

27223 RODRIGUES, B. O. Religion Saint-Simonienne. Appel. [With 'Association financière des Saint-
Simoniens'.] 15p. *8°. Paris*, 1831.

27224 RODRIGUES, E. Lettres sur la religion et la
politique, 1829; suivies de l'éducation du genre humain,
traduit de l'allemand, de Lessing. 180p. *8°. Paris*, 1831.
*The copy that belonged to Victor Considérant. Another
edition was published with Saint Simon's* Nouveau Christianisme *in 1832 (q.v.).*

27225 ROSSER, C. Thoughts on the new era of
society. A lecture at Mr. Owen's institution, Burton Street,
Burton Crescent...November 13th, 1831... 16p. *8°.*
[*London*, 1831]

27226 —— Second edition. 16p. *8°.* [*London*, 1831]

27227 [ROUX, P. C.] Science nouvelle. Lettre d'un
disciple de la science nouvelle aux religionnaires prétendus
Saint-Simoniens, de l'Organisateur et du Globe. Par
P.C.R.....x. 124p. *8°. Paris*, 1831.

27228 T. Dedicated to the useful part of the com-
munity – viz. the wealth-creators. A riddle. 2p. *s.sh.8°.*
[*London*, 1831] [*Br.* 542(14)] *The copy that belonged to
Francis Place.*

27229 [——] [Another edition, without the signature.] 2p. *s.sh.8°*. [*London*, 1831] *The copy that belonged to William Lovett.*

27230 **WHITCOMB**, S. An address before the Working-Men's Society of Dedham, delivered on... September 7, 1831...Published by request of the Society. 24p. *8°. Dedham, Mass.*, 1831.

MISCELLANEOUS

27231 **BENTHAM**, J. The book of Church reform: containing the most essential part of Mr. Bentham's "Church of Englandism examined," &c. Edited by one of his disciples. 27p. *8°*. 1831.

27232 **BEVERLEY**, ROBERT M. A letter to His Grace the Archbishop of York, on the present corrupt state of the Church of England. 41p. *8°. Beverley*, 1831. *With a manuscript note on the half-title: With Mr. Hume's Compts.*

27233 —— Sixth edition. 41p. *8°. Beverley*, 1831.

27234 **BROUGHAM**, H. P., *Baron Brougham and Vaux*. Lord Brougham's speech on reform in Chancery; delivered in the House of Lords, February 22, 1831. 24p. *8°*. 1831.

27235 **BULL**, G. S. [*Begin*.] Christian friends, neighbours, and countrymen. [An exhortation, followed by 'A form of prayer, on account of the troubled state of certain parts of the United Kingdom'.] [3]p. *n.p.* [1831]

27236 [**CONOLLY**, J.] Under the superintendence of the Society for the Diffusion of Useful Knowledge. The working man's companion. Cottage evenings. 215p. *18°. London, Birmingham, &c.*, 1831.

27237 **HAWKINS**, E. Remarks on the coins of the kings of Mercia. From the Archaeologia, Vol. XXIII. 3p. *4°*. [*London*, 1831.]

27238 **ILLINGWORTH**, W. Observations on the public records of the four courts at Westminster, and on the measures recommended by the Committee of the House of Commons in 1800; for rendering them more accessible to the public. Drawn up by the desire of His Majesty's Commissioners on the Public Records. 67p. *8°. n.p.* [1831] *One of the 50 copies printed for the use of the Commissioners.*

27239 **LE NORMAND**, M. A. A. Le petit homme rouge au Château des Tuileries. La verité à Holy-Rood. Prédictions, etc. 106p. *8°. Paris*, 1831.

27240 **MASSIAS**, N., *Baron*. Réponse à une brochure intitulée Questions sur le droit d'hérédité specialement considéré dans la monarchie et dans la pairie, par M. le Baron Massias. [With 'L'oisif antique et l'oisif moderne'.] 30p. *8°*. [*Paris*, 1831] *The copy that belonged to Victor Considérant.*

27241 **NICOLAS**, SIR N. H. Refutation of Mr. Palgrave's remarks in reply to "Observations on the state of historical literature." With additional facts relative to the Record Commission, and record offices...[With an appendix.] 198, xxivp. *8°*. 1831. *The Agar Ellis copy.*

27242 **OUSELEY**, SIR WILLIAM. Catalogue of several hundred manuscript works in various oriental languages, collected by Sir William Ouseley, LL.D., &c. 24p. *4°*. 1831. *Presentation copy, with an inscription signed 'W.O.', from the author to George Agar Ellis, Baron Dover.*

27243 **PAINE**, T. The age of reason. 159p. *8°. New-York*, 1831. *For other editions, see* 1819.

27244 **PALGRAVE**, SIR F. Remarks, submitted to the Right Hon. Viscount Melbourne, Secretary of State for the Home Department, in reply to a pamphlet addressed to him by Nicholas Harris Nicolas, Esq., and entitled "Observations on the state of historical literature," &c. 62p. *8°*. 1831. *The Agar Ellis copy.*

27245 **ROYAL SOCIETY**. A statement of circumstances connected with the late election for the Presidency of the Royal Society. 47p. *8°*. [*London*,] 1831. *The Agar Ellis copy.*

27246 **SOCIETY OF DILETTANTI**. [A lithographed copy, which was circulated among the members of the Society, of a letter from Sir William Gell to William Sotheby, on the discovery of Etruscan antiquities.] [4]p. *4°. n.p.* [1831] *The Agar Ellis copy.*

27247 [**THOMAS**, V.] The legality of the present academical system of the University of Oxford asserted against the new calumnies of the Edinburgh Review [i.e. Sir William Hamilton's article on the state of the English universities]. By a member of Convocation. 147p. *8°. Oxford, London, &c.*, 1831.

27248 **THRUSH**, T. A letter to Lord Viscount Morpeth, M.P. and to Members of Parliament generally, on the subject of a petition relating to religious reform, presented to Parliament by His Lordship, on the behalf of Thomas Thrush, late a captain in the Royal Navy. With a copy of the petition. 39p. *8°. Liverpool & London*, [1831] *The Agar Ellis copy.*

27249 *[**WHEATLEY**, G.] Remarks upon the rights and duties of jurymen, in trials for libel, in a letter addressed to Jeremy Bentham, Esq. Not for sale. 24p. *12°*. 1831. *The FWA copy that belonged to William Pare.*

27250 **ZOOLOGICAL SOCIETY**. Reports of the auditors of the accounts of the Zoological Society for the year 1830, and of the Council, read at the anniversary meeting, April 29th, 1831. 27p. *8°*. 1831. *The Agar Ellis copy.*

1832

GENERAL

For **ACADÉMIE ROYALE DES SCIENCES, DES LETTRES ET DES BEAUX ARTS DE BELGIQUE,** Bulletin, *see* vol. III, *Periodicals list,* Bulletin de l'Académie...

27251 [ADAMS, WILLIAM B.] The rights of morality; an essay on the present state of society...in England: with the best means of providing for the poor and...operatives who may be suddenly thrown out of their regular employments by the substitution of new inventions. By Junius Redivivus. Addressed to the productive classes of the community. 153, [9]p. *12°.* 1832. *Another edition, entitled* The producing man's companion, *was published in 1833 (q.v.).*

27252 [ARNOLD, THOMAS (1795–1842).] Thirteen letters on our social condition, addressed to the editor of the Sheffield Courant. 37p. *8°. Sheffield,* 1832.

27253 ARRIVABENE, G., *Conte.* Considérations sur les principaux moyens d'améliorer le sort des classes ouvrières. 70p. *8°. Bruxelles,* 1832. *Presentation copy from the author to J. R. McCulloch.*

27254 BAIRD, A. A New Year's gift for Dr. Cleland; or, a detection of the errors and blunders in his late book, called "Enumeration of the inhabitants of Glasgow and county of Lanark". 8p. *8°. Glasgow,* 1832.

27255 BRIDGES, M. An address to the electors of England: more especially those of the middle and operative classes. 45p. *8°.* 1832.

27256 The **BRITISH ALMANAC** of the Society for the Diffusion of Useful Knowledge, for...1832. [With 'The companion to the Almanac; or year-book of general information'.] 72, 240p. *12°.* [1832] *For other editions, see 1828.*

27257 [CAREY, M.] Philadelphia, Feb. 22, 1832. [*Begin.*] Should the nullifiers succeed in their views of separation, and the Union be in consequence dissolved, as is highly probable, the following will be an appropriate epitaph... 4p. *8°. n.p.* [1832]

27258 [——] Prospects on the Rubicon. Part II. Letters on the prevailing excitement in South Carolina. On the means employed to produce it. On the causes that led to the depreciation of the great staple of the state. And on the misconception of the effects of the tariff. Addressed to the Hon. H. Clay...By the author of The olive branch. [Signed: M.C.] Third edition. 52p. *8°. Philadelphia,* 1832. *For part I of this series, see 1830.*

27259 [CAZENOVE, J.] Outlines of political economy; being a plain and short view of the laws relating to the production, distribution, and consumption of wealth; to which is added, a brief explanation of the nature and effects of taxation... 161p. *12°.* 1832.

27260 CHALMERS, T. On political economy, in connexion with the moral state and moral prospects of society. 566p. *8°. Glasgow, Edinburgh, &c.,* 1832.

27261 —— Second edition. 566p. *8°. Glasgow, Edinburgh, &c.,* 1832.

27262 —— The supreme importance of a right moral to a right economical state of the community: with observations on a recent criticism in the Edinburgh Review. 102p. *8°. Glasgow, Edinburgh, &c.,* 1832.

27263 CLAY, H. Speech of Henry Clay, in defence of the American system, against the British colonial system: with an appendix of documents referred to in the speech. Delivered in the Senate of the United States, February 2d, 3d, and 6th, 1832. 43p. *8°. Washington,* 1832.

27264 COBBETT, W. Cobbett's Manchester lectures, in support of his fourteen reform propositions... delivered...on the last six days of the year 1831. To which is subjoined a letter to Mr. O'Connell, on his speech... against the proposition for establishing poor laws in Ireland. 179p. *12°. London, Manchester, &c.,* 1832.

27265 —— A geographical dictionary of England and Wales... 546p. *8°.* 1832.

27266 COLTON, C. Manual for emigrants to America. 203p. *12°.* 1832.

For the **COSMOPOLITE,** *see* vol. III, *Periodicals list.*

27267 CROMBIE, A. A letter to Lieut. Col. Torrens, M.P., in answer to his address to the farmers of the United Kingdom. 23p. *8°.* 1832.

27268 D'ALTON, J. The history of tithes, church lands, and other ecclesiastical benefices; with a plan for the abolition of the former, and the better distribution of the latter... 138p. *12°. Dublin,* 1832.

27269 *The **EAST-INDIA** register and directory, for 1832; containing...lists of the Company's servants... mariners, &c. not in the service of the...Company, compiled...by G. H. Brown, and F. Clark... 281, 170, 141p. *12°. London & Edinburgh,* [1832] *For other editions, see 1804.*

27270 EDEN, R. H., *Baron Henley.* A plan of church reform...Third edition. [Concerned with land, leases, ecclesiastical finances and administrative reorganization.] 65, 17p. *8°.* 1832.

27271 **FREE TRADE CONVENTION.** An exposition of evidence in support of the Memorial to Congress "setting forth the evils of the existing tariff of duties..." prepared in pursuance of instructions from the Permanent Committee appointed by the Free Trade Convention assembled at Philadelphia to prepare the memorial to Congress. By Henry Lee of Massachusetts, one of the Committee. [Nos. 4–11.] 14, 32, 37, 17, 19, 22, 6, 42p. *8°. Boston,* 1832.

27272 —— An exposition of the unequal, unjust and oppressive operation of the present tariff system, in relation to iron, wool, hemp, paper, and the manufactures thereof. Compiled in obedience to instructions from the Select Committee appointed by the Free Trade Convention to prepare a memorial to Congress, from documentary and other evidence furnished...by intelligent, practical men engaged in these various branches of business. 68p. *8°. Philadelphia,* 1832.

27273 —— Memorial of the Committee appointed by the "Free Trade Convention," held at Philadelphia, in

September and October 1831, to prepare...a memorial to Congress remonstrating against the existing tariff of duties...[Signed: Albert Gallatin, chairman.] 87p. *8°. New York,* 1832.

27274 GOLDSMITH, L. Statistics of France. 336p. *8°.* 1832.

27275 GORTON, J. G. Population of Great Britain, according to the returns made to Parliament in 1831; together with the annual value of real property as assessed in 1815...[With 'Analysis of the Reform and Boundary Bills'.] 109, 45, 88p. *8°.* 1832. *See also* 1833.

27276 HERMANN, F. B. W. VON. Staatswirthschaftliche Untersuchungen über Vermögen, Wirthschaft, Productivität der Arbeiten, Kapital, Preis, Gewinn, Einkommen und Verbrauch. 374p. *8°. München,* 1832.

27277 HORTON, SIR R. J. W., *Bart.* Lectures on statistics and political economy, as affecting the condition of the operative and labouring classes. Delivered at the London Mechanics' Institution, in 1830 and 1831. With notes...To which are prefixed correspondence and resolutions, published in 1830 by a select class of members of the London Mechanics' Institution. 11 parts. *8°.* 1832. *For another edition of Lectures I–IV, see* 1831; *for another edition of the Correspondence, see* 1830 (SOCIAL CONDITIONS).

27278 [HOWELLS, H. C., *ed.*] Advice to emigrants, who intend to settle in the United States of America. Second edition, greatly enlarged and improved. 24p. *12°. Bristol,* [1832]

27279 LAWRENCE, WILLIAM B. Two lectures on political economy, delivered at Clinton Hall, before the Mercantile Library Association of the City of New-York, on the 23d and 30th of December, 1831. 72p. *8°. New-York,* 1832.

27280 [LEIGH, C., *Baron Leigh.*] Tracts written in the years [1821–]1823 & 1828. By C.L., Esq. Privately printed. 247p. *8°. Warwick,* 1832.

For the **LITERARY TEST,** *see vol.* III, *Periodicals list.*

27281 McCULLOCH, JOHN R. A dictionary, practical, theoretical, and historical, of commerce and commercial navigation: illustrated with maps. 1143p. *8°.* 1832. *See also* 1834, 1840, 1844, *and, for a supplement,* 1846.

27282 M'DUFFIE, G. Defence of a liberal construction of the powers of Congress, as regards internal improvement, etc....To which are prefixed, an encomiastic advertisement of the work by Major (now Governor) Hamilton, and a preface by the Philadelphia editor [M. Carey]. Second Philadelphia edition. 24p. *8°. Philadelphia,* 1832.

27283 MARTIN, J. Trial extraordinary, in the new court of common sense, Conscience Hall, in the county of Mechanics, Bull v. Steam and Free-trade. Second edition. 8p. *8°.* 1832.

27284 MUNDELL, A. A comparative view of the industrial situation of Great Britain, from the year 1775 to the present time. With an examination of the causes of her distress. 133p. *8°.* 1832.

27285 NELKENBRECHER, J. C. J. C. Nelkenbrecher's allgemeines Taschenbuch der Münz-, Mass- und Gewichtskunde für Banquiers und Kaufleute. Herausgegeben und mit allen bekannten Handelsplätzen, so wie mit den Usancen der Staatspapiere vermehrt von

J. H. D. Bock...und mit neuen Münz-Tabellen versehen von H. C. Kandelhardt...Fünfzehnte Auflage. 637p. *8°. Berlin,* 1832. *For other editions, see* 1815.

27286 OBSERVATIONS on the state of Ireland. Addressed to impartial inquirers. 36p. *8°.* 1832.

27287 OUSELEY, SIR WILLIAM G. Remarks on the statistics and political institutions of the United States ...To which are added statistical tables, &c. 208p. *8°.* 1832.

27288 —— [Another edition.] 225p. *8°. Philadelphia,* 1832.

27289 [PARNELL, H. B., *Baron Congleton.*] Coup-d'œil sur les avantages des relations commerciales entre la France et l'Angleterre, basées sur les vrais principes de l'économie politique; par un membre du Parlement d'Angleterre. Traduit de l'anglais. 46p. *8°. Paris,* 1832. *The copy that belonged to N. W. Senior, with his signature on the title-page.*

27290 PECCHIO, G., *Conte.* Sino a qual punto le produzioni scientifiche e litterarie seguano le leggi economiche della produzione in generale. Dissertazione. 199p. *12°. Lugano,* 1832.

27291 PICKERING, JOSEPH. Inquiries of an emigrant: being the narrative of an English farmer from the year 1824 to 1830; with...additions, to March, 1832; during which period he traversed the United States and Canada, with a view to settle as an emigrant...Fourth edition; including the information published by His Majesty's Commissioners for Emigration. 207p. *8°.* 1832. *For another edition, see* 1830.

27292 The **PICTURE** of Liverpool, or stranger's guide: containing a history of the...town, with a description of its public works...scientific, and charitable institutions, and an account of its population and commerce; with...a description of the railway...228p. *12°. Liverpool,* 1832. *Not the same work as that with a similar title published in 1805 (q.v.)*

27293 The **POST-OFFICE** London directory for 1832...By B. Critchett. The thirty-third edition. [With 'A new guide to stage coaches, waggons, carts, vessels, &c. for 1832...The thirtieth edition. By B. Critchett'.] 528, 156p. *12°.* [1832] *See also* 1805 (Post-Office annual directory), 1810, 1813, 1814, 1820 (Post Office London directory), 1823, 1825, 1830, 1834, 1836, 1841.

27294 QUETELET, L. A. J. Sur la possibilité de mesurer l'influence des causes qui modifient les élémens sociaux. Lettre à M. Villermé...28p. *8°. Bruxelles,* 1832. *Presentation copy from the author to N. W. Senior.*

For the **REGENERATOR,** *or guide to happiness, see* vol. III, *Periodicals list.*

27295 SCROPE, G. P. Extracts of letters from poor persons who emigrated last year [from Corsley, Wilts.] to Canada and the United States...Second edition, with additions. 35p. *8°.* 1832.

27296 —— A plain statement of the causes of, and remedies for, the prevailing distress. For the consideration of a reformed Parliament, and of those who will have to elect its members. 29p. *8°.* 1832.

27297 Open **SESAME!** or, the way to get money. By a rich man who was once poor. Third edition. (*Economical Library,* 4.) 35p. *12°.* 1832.

27298 SIMPSON, S. Biography of Stephen Girard,

with his will affixed...together with a detailed history of his banking and financial operations for the last twenty years...Second edition. 281, 35p. *12°. Philadelphia, 1832.*

27299 **SISSON,** J. Second letter to the Right Hon. Earl Grey on the necessity of the appointment of a Board, or Council at Dublin, for the internal interests of Ireland, similar in principle to that formed under the Duke of Ormonde's Viceroyalty, 1664... 80p. *8°. London & Dublin, 1832.*

27300 **SMETHURST,** J. The political multum in parvo; causes of distress and remedy for the causes... containing remarks on the use of machinery, and on foreign and domestic commerce; with observations upon the present system of taxation... 16p. *8°. 1832. The copy that belonged to Francis Place.*

27301 **SOUTHEY,** R. Essays, moral and political... Now first collected... 2 vols. *8°. 1832.*

27302 **STOVEL,** C. A letter to the Right Honourable Lord Henley, containing remarks on his plan of church reform...Second edition. 96p. *8°. 1832.*

27303 [**TAYLOR,** JOHN (1781–1864).] An essay on the standard and measure of value. By the author of an "Essay on money." Second edition, revised and corrected. 83p. *8°. 1832. In a volume of the author's pamphlets presented to Sir Robert Peel. See also 1844, and the collection of the author's pamphlets entitled* Currency investigated, *1845* (FINANCE).

27304 **THOMPSON,** THOMAS P. The true theory of rent, in opposition to Mr. Ricardo and others. Being an exposition of fallacies on rent, tithes, &c. In the form of a review of Mr. Mill's Elements of political economy... Ninth edition, with alterations and corrections. To which is added a postscript containing a translation of chap. XX of vol. IV of the 'Cours complet d'économie politique pratique' of M. Jean-Baptiste Say... 34p. *8°. 1832. See note to no. 25779. For other editions, see 1826.*

27305 **TRAVELS** in England and Wales. Compiled from the most authentic and recent authorities. 172p. *12°. Dublin, 1832.*

27306 **UNITED STATES OF AMERICA.**

Congress. *House of Representatives.* 22d. Congress, 1st Session ⟨Doc. No. 299.⟩...Comparison of weights and measures of length and capacity, reported to the Senate of the United States by the Treasury Department in 1832, and made by Ferd. Rod. Hassler. 122p. *8°. Washington, 1832.*

27307 *——— ——— ———* 22d Congress, 2d Session. ⟨Doc. No. 2.⟩...Message from the President [A. Jackson]... to the two Houses...at the commencement of the second session...December 4, 1832. Read, and committed to a committee of the whole House on the state of the Union. 240p. *8°. Washington, 1832. The copy that belonged to George Grote.*

27308 **WEIDEMANN,** F., *ed.* Rapports et différences entre les principes de la doctrine du docteur Quesnay et de celle d'Adam Smith. Tirés des oeuvres posthumes d'un célèbre savant et publiés par Fr. Weidemann, Dr. en Dr. 84p. *8°. Mersebourg, 1832.*

27309 **WHATELY,** R., *Archbishop of Dublin.* Introductory lectures on political economy, delivered in Easter Term M DCC XXXI...Second edition, including lecture IX. and other additions. 279p. *8°. 1832. For other editions, see 1831.*

27310 **WOOD,** JOSEPH. Right of labour to legislative protection demonstrated: with remarks on the practicability of taking off ten millions of annual taxation, and the reduction of the public debt, in a letter addressed to the electors and inhabitants of Huddersfield. 26p. *8°. 1832. The copy sent to Francis Place by Mr. Pitkethley, one of those concerned in organizing Joseph Wood's election campaign in Huddersfield, soliciting his influence in bringing it to public notice. With Place's copy of his letter in reply written on the same sheet. For the letters, see vol. III, A.L. 252. *Another, the FWA copy, belonged to William Pare.*

For the **WORKING MAN'S FRIEND;** and political magazine, 1832–33, see vol. III, *Periodicals list.*

For the **YORKSHIRE MISCELLANY,** see vol. III, *Periodicals list.*

27311 **YOUNG,** GAVIN. An essay on the mercantile theory of wealth. 92p. *12°. Calcutta, 1832.*

AGRICULTURE

27312 **ALLEN,** WILLIAM (1770–1843). Colonies at home...A new edition with additions. [With 'Appendix to the sixth edition'.] 52, 8p. *8°. Lindfield: at the Schools of Industry; London, &c., 1832. For other editions, see 1827.*

For the **BRITISH YEOMAN,** see vol. III, *Periodicals list.*

27313 **CONNER,** W. The speech of William Conner, Esq. against rack-rents, &c. Delivered at a meeting at Inch ...convened for the purpose of taking into consideration the condition of the farming and labouring classes, and of petitioning Parliament for a Bill for the applotment or valuation of land by a sworn jury. 32p. *8°. Dublin, 1832. One of a collection of the author's pamphlets on the Irish land question, made by John Stuart Mill. See also 1835.*

27314 **GRIFFIN,** R., *Baron Braybrooke.* Two reports from the committee appointed to enquire into the condition of the poor at Saffron Walden...and some account of the cottage allotments in the adjoining parishes of Little-

bury and Wenden. 15p. *8°. London, Cambridge, &c., 1832. For another edition of the first report, see 1830.*

27315 [**HICKEY,** W.] Hints to small holders on planting, cattle, poultry, agricultural implements, flax, &c. By Martin Doyle. Second edition, carefully revised by the author. 88p. *12°. Dublin, London, &c., 1832. For another edition, see 1830.*

27316 **JONES,** E. Review of facts and observations... on the properties and productions of the sugar maple tree; the process of extracting its sap, converting it into sugar, &c.&c. 72p. *8°. 1832.*

27317 **LANCE,** E. J. The cottage garden; or, farmer's friend. Pointing out the means of making the earth serviceable to the rich and poor, by giving employment to capital and labour on all sorts of land. 32p. *8°. 1832. *Another, the FWA copy, belonged to William Pare.*

27318 **POLE,** J. A short statement, showing that if the allotment system were adopted, there would be no excess of population; no necessity for emigration, nor cultivating waste lands; nor for the importation of food. 27p. *8°. 1832. Presentation copy from the author to M. T. Sadler.*

27319 [POTTER, P.] Land owners and their cottagers. A letter on the present state of farm labourers, with a few hints for bettering their future condition, respectfully addressed to M. T. Sadler, Esq. M.P. By a friend to the industrious poor. 18p. *8°. Walsall,* [1832] *Presentation copy to M. T. Sadler from the author, with his signature at the end of the text. A printed note on the verso of the title-page records that whereas in published copies blanks represent the name of the landowner (the Earl of Bradford), in this copy the author has added this and other names in manuscript.*

27320 PROVIS, J. Tables, useful in several branches of the copper trade, in four parts. A new edition, with considerable additions and improvements. 376p. *8°. Redruth, 1832. For another edition, see 1801.*

27321 SCOBELL, G. T. An essay on field gardens for the labouring poor. Read before the Bath and West of England Agricultural Society, at their annual meeting, Dec. 13, 1832. 12p. *12°. Bath, 1832.*

27322 SINCLAIR, SIR JOHN, *Bart.* To the friends of agriculture. [Advocating the formation of a General Association to resist the abolition of the corn laws.] 2p. *s.sh.8° n.p.* [1832] [*Br. 545*]

27323 WELD, I. Statistical survey of the county of Roscommon, drawn up under the directions of the Royal Dublin Society. 710, lxxiip. *8°. Dublin, 1832.*

27324 WITHER, L. B. Cottage allotments in some parishes of north Hampshire. [With 'To the cottagers and others, who rent land in the parishes of Wootton, Worting, and Monk Sherborne'.] 20p. *8°. 1832.*

27325 —— A letter to the farmers of some parishes in north Hampshire, on the means of reducing the poor rates: to which is added an address to the cottagers who rent land. 44p. *8°. 1832.*

For **ZEITSCHRIFT FÜR DIE LANDWIRTH-SCHAFTLICHEN VEREINE DES GROSS-HERZOGTHUMS HESSEN,** 1832–37, *see* vol. III, *Periodicals list.*

CORN LAWS

27326 DURHAM, J. Questions on that great curse of our land the tax on bread, commonly called the corn laws. Extracted from the Times newspaper, of December 28, 1831. 10p. *12°. Birmingham, 1832. *Another, the FWA copy, belonged to William Pare.*

27327 FITZWILLIAM, C. W. W., *Earl Fitzwilliam.* Address to the landowners of England, on the corn laws ...Second edition. 46p. *8°. 1832.*

27328 *——* Third edition. 46p. *8°. 1832. The copy that belonged to George Grote.*

27329 —— Fourth edition. 46p. *8°. 1832.*

27330 —— Fifth edition. 46p. *8°. 1832. With extensive manuscript notes.*

27331 —— A new edition, with notes, and additions. 44p. *12°. 1832. See also 1839.*

27332 HALL, G. W. Letter to the Right Hon. Viscount Milton; being a review of the various sources of national wealth, and a reply to the recent publication of His Lordship against the corn laws. 56p. *8°. 1832.*

27333 PIGOTT, G. A letter on the nature of the protection afforded by the present corn laws, and on the probable results of a free trade in corn, addressed to the land-owners, farmers, and electors of Buckinghamshire. 67p. *8°. London & Aylesbury, 1832.*

27334 RUSSELL, JOSEPH. Observations on the growth of British corn; in which the impolicy of the present corn laws is clearly pointed out; the principles of free trade investigated, their fallacy exposed, and their ruinous effects upon the country exhibited... 73p. *8°. Kenilworth & London, 1832.*

27335 THOMPSON, THOMAS P. Catechism on the corn laws; with a list of fallacies and the answers. Sixteenth edition. Stereotype...To which is added the article on free trade, from the Westminster Review, No. XXIII, with the article on the silk and glove trade, from No. XXXII, and the supplements from No. XXXIII and XXXIV... 88p. *8°. 1832. For other editions, see 1827.*

POPULATION

27336 BENOISTON DE CHATEAUNEUF, L. F. Essai sur la mortalité dans l'infanterie française. [Extrait des Annales d'Hygiène Publique, (Tome x, 2e partie).] 80p. *8°.* [Paris, 1832]

27337 CLELAND, J. Enumeration of the inhabitants of the city of Glasgow and county of Lanark, for the... census of M.DCCC.XXXI. With population and statistical tables relative to England and Scotland. Classified and arranged [with a biographical and historical appendix] by James Cleland...Second edition. 318p. *fol. Glasgow, Edinburgh, &c., 1832. Presentation copy, with inscription, from the author to 'Charles Wood Esquire, Secretary to the Treasury'.*

27338 [EDMONDS, T. R.] An enquiry into the principles of population, exhibiting a system of regulations for the poor; designed immediately to lessen, and finally to remove, the evils which have hitherto pressed upon the labouring classes of society. 336p. *8°. 1832.*

27339 *——* Life tables founded upon the discovery of a numerical law, regulating the existence of every human being. Illustrated by a new theory of the causes producing health and longevity. xlii, 38p. *8°. 1832. The copy that belonged to Augustus De Morgan, with excerpts from journals, manuscript notes, etc. concerned with the controversy as to whether the author borrowed an essential part of his theory from the work of Benjamin Gompertz without proper acknowledgment.*

27340 ENGLAND. *General Register Office.* As printed

for the House of Commons. The population returns of 1831, with a statement of progress in the enquiry regarding the occupation of families and persons, and the duration of life [by J. Rickman]...and a summary of the population of Great Britain, in 1801, 1811, 1821, 1831. To which is added, an appendix, containing a...description of the effects of the cholera morbus in England, in the fourteenth century. Extracted from the History of Edward III, by Joshua Barnes... 100p. *8°*. 1832.

27341 MARSHALL, JOHN (1783–1841). Mortality of the Metropolis. A statistical view of the number of persons reported to have died, of each of more than 100 kinds of disease, and casualties within the Bills of Mortality...1629–1831...Accompanied with a variety of statistical accounts, illustrative of the progress and extent of the amount expended for the maintenance of the poor ... 82p. *4°*. 1832.

27342 PHILO-MALTHUS, *pseud.* A conversation in political economy; being an attempt to explain...the true causes of the evil operation of any general system of poor laws...[With notes, and a 'Sketch of an Act of Parliament, for the gradual abolition of the poor laws, upon a plan originally proposed by the author of "An essay upon the principle of population."'] 72p. *8°*. 1832.

27343 QUETELET, L. A. J. and **SMITS,** E. Recherches sur la reproduction et la mortalité de l'homme aux différens ages, et sur la population de la Belgique. 150p. *8°*. *Bruxelles,* 1832.

27344 UNITED STATES OF AMERICA. Congress. *House of Representatives.* 22d Congress, 1st session. ⟨Doc. No. 263.⟩...Abstract of the returns of the Fifth Census, showing the number of free people, the number of slaves, the federal or representative number; and the aggregate of each county of each state of the United States... 51p. *8°*. *Washington,* 1832. *The copy that belonged to T. Spring Rice, Baron Monteagle.*

27345 [YOUNG, GAVIN.] Observations on the law of population; being an attempt to trace its effects from the conflicting theories of Malthus and Sadler. By the author of "Reflections on the present state of British India." 79p. *8°*. 1832. *For a manuscript version, containing text not included in the published work, see vol.* III, *MS.* 170.

TRADES & MANUFACTURES

27346 BABBAGE, C. On the economy of machinery and manufactures. 320p. *8°*. 1832. *A large-paper copy, presented by the author to Sarah Nicolas. See also* 1833, 1834, 1835, 1846.

27347 BIRLEY, J. Sadler's Bill. Cotton branch. [Concerned with the organization and profits of the cotton industry.] 8p. *8°*. *Manchester,* 1832. *The Oastler copy.*

27348 HAYNES, M. P. A letter to Earl Grey on the distress which exists in Birmingham. (From the Birmingham Journal of July 28, 1832.) [2]p. *4°*. *Birmingham,* [1832] *See note to no.* 20490.

27349 HULL, W. A reply to the speech of the Right Hon. P. Thompson on the motion of Col. Davies, for "a Committee of the House of Commons, to enquire into the present distressed state of the glove trade." With some remarks on the free trade system. 16p. *8°*. 1832.

27350 [MONTGOMERY, JAMES (1792–1880).] The carding and spinning master's assistant; or, the theory and practice of cotton spinning...[The preface signed: J.M.] 282p. *8°*. *Glasgow, London, &c.,* 1832. *See also* 1833.

27351 PERKINS, J. Steam navigation. Improvements, by Jacob Perkins. Part I. The boiler. [A description of Perkins' patent steam generator.] 21p. *8°*. 1832.

27352 [PORTER, G. R.] A treatise on the origin, progressive improvement and present state of the manufacture of porcelain and glass. (*The Cabinet Cyclopædia.*) 334p. *8°*. 1832.

27353 SMITH, JAMES (*fl.* 1832). The panorama of science and art; embracing the principal sciences and arts; the methods of working in wood and metal; and a miscellaneous selection of...processes and experiments... Thirteenth edition. 2 vols. *8°*. 1832.

COMMERCE

27354 BROOKE, S. A second appeal to the Legislature, shewing the large sums of money diverted from the public service, in consequence of the erroneous...terms and conditions attached to the grant of the office of King's Printer, in England. With a copy of the grant itself, which expired in 1829, and remarks on its renewal in 1830, &c.&c. 28p. *8°*. 1832.

27355 [CAREY, M.] The olive branch. No. IV. [Signed: Hamilton. On protection.] 4p. *8°*. *n.p.* [1832]

27356 CHAPMAN, H. S. A statistical sketch of the corn trade of Canada, &c.... Extracted from the British Farmer's (Quarterly) Magazine, No. 23, for May 1832. 47p. *8°*. 1832. *Presentation copy from the author to Harriet Martineau.*

27357 The third edition of the **CORN DEALER'S** assistant, shewing exactly the price of any quantity of corn, from one quarter to five hundred, from 20s. to 100s. per qr.... [319]p. *long 8°*. 1832.

27358 COVE, L. H. The coal merchant's and coal factor's assistant. Consisting of a series of tables accurately calculated for the convenience of all persons concerned in the coal trade; to which are added correct tables for readily ascertaining the discount, scorage, &c. 48p. *4°*. 1832.

27359 DOUGLAS, K. To merchants, manufacturers, tradesmen, and others, interested in the preservation of our national prosperity. [An extract from The Mirror of Parliament, part CLXVII, containing the speech of Mr. Keith Douglas on the effects on commerce of the abolition of compulsory labour, of 2nd July, 1832.] 8p. *8°*. [1832]

27360 GEDACHTEN over den handel, onder anderen, met betrekking tot den geoprojecteerden ijzerenspoorweg naar Keulen. Door den schrijver van de Bedenkingen over het crediet. 159p. *8°*. *Amsterdam,* 1832.

27361 GUILD OF MERCHANTS, *Dublin.* A translation of the charters of the Corporation of Merchants, or, Guild of the Holy Trinity, Dublin. Addressed to the Right Hon. Thomas S. Rice, M.P....By Stephen Fox Dickson. 26p. *8°. Dublin*, 1832.

27362 [**MARTIN**, ROBERT M.] British relations with the Chinese Empire in 1832. Comparative statement of the English and American trade with India and Canton. 148p. *8°.* 1832.

27363 —— The past and present state of the tea trade of England, and of the continents of Europe and America; and a comparison between the consumption, price of, and revenue derived from, tea, coffee, sugar, wine, tobacco, spirits, &c. 222p. *8°.* 1832.

27364 *****MIERS**, J. [*Begin.*] To the Right Hon. Lord Viscount Palmerston, &c.&c. Rio de Janeyro, 4th Dec. 1832. [A petition that the British Government should intervene in his dispute with the Brazilian Government over their failure to pay him for providing machinery for the Brazilian Mint. With relevant documents annexed.] 16p. *8°.* [*London*, 1832 ?] *The copy that belonged to George Grote.*

27365 **ROBINSON**, GEORGE R. Speech...in the House of Commons, May 22, 1832, on the trade, commerce & navigation, of the British Empire. Second edition.

[With the text of a petition against free trade from the inhabitants of Worcester.] 73p. *8°.* 1832.

27366 **SAN SEBASTIAN.** Memoria justificativa de lo que tiene espuesto y pedido la ciudad de San Sebastian para el fomento de la industria, y comercio de Guipuzcoa. Publicada por acuerdo del Ayuntamiento general de vecinos concejantes y Junta de Comercio de la misma ciudad. [With an appendix.] 192, 75p. *4°. San Sebastian,* 1832.

27367 **SPRAGUE**, P. Speech of Mr. Sprague, of Maine, upon the arrangement of the colonial trade with Great Britain. Delivered in the Senate of the United States, on the 3d day of April, 1832. 23p. *8°. Washington,* 1832.

27368 [**THOMPSON**, THOMAS P.] Les singes économistes ou qu'est-ce que la liberté du commerce? Extrait de la Revue de Westminster; traduit de l'anglais par Benjamin Laroche. 47p. *8°. Paris,* 1832. *A translation of* The article on free trade, from the Westminster Review, No. XXIII, *1830 (q.v.).*

27369 **TRUEMAN & COOK.** The state of the commerce of Great Britain with reference to colonial and other produce, for the year 1831. 30p. *8°. n.p.* [1832] *See also* 1831, 1833, 1834.

COLONIES

27370 **ADDRESS** to manufacturers, traders, and others, on the importance of preserving the colonies. [Concerned with the alleged rights of West Indian property owners in their slaves, and the effects of abolition. Dated: June 1832.] 21p. *8°.* [*London*, 1832]

27371 **BISCHOFF**, J. Sketch of the history of Van Diemen's Land...and an account of the Van Diemen's Land Company. 260p. *8°.* 1832.

27372 **BOUCHETTE**, J. The British dominions in North America; or, a topographical and statistical description of the provinces of Lower and Upper Canada, New Brunswick, Nova Scotia, the islands of Newfoundland, Prince Edward, and Cape Breton. Including considerations on land-granting and emigration. To which are annexed, statistical tables and tables of distances, &c.... 2 vols. *4°.* 1832.

27373 —— A topographical dictionary of the province of Lower Canada. [372]p. *4°.* 1832.

27374 **CHISHOLME**, D. Observations on the rights of the British colonies to representation in the Imperial Parliament. 301p. *18°. Three-Rivers,* 1832. *Presentation copy, with inscription, from the author to 'Captain Robertson'.*

27375 **COLERIDGE**, H. N. Six months in the West Indies, in 1825...Third edition, with additions. 311p. *8°.* 1832. *For other editions, see* 1826.

27376 **DYKE**, T. Advice to emigrants; or an impartial guide to the Canadas...the United States, New South Wales...with the latest government instructions. 87p. *12°.* 1832.

27377 **ENGLAND.** *Colonial Office.* Information published by His Majesty's Commissioners for Emigration, respecting the British colonies in North America. [Dated: 9th February, 1832.] 18p. *8°.* [1832]

27378 **GOUGER**, ROBERT, **& CO.** An address to magistrates, landowners and rate-payers. [A prospectus of the General Colonial Agency Office.] 8p. *8°.* 1832.

27379 [**HALHED**, N. J.] A memoir on the land tenure and principles of taxation, obtaining in the provinces attached to the Bengal Presidency, under the ancient Hindoo system pending the duration of the Mohummedan rule, and under the British Government...By a civilian in the East India Company's service. For private circulation among his friends. [With an appendix.] 160, xip. *8°. Calcutta,* 1832. *Presentation copy, with inscription, 'from NJH the author to his old friend and contemporary William Fairlie Clark Esq.ʳ '.*

27380 [**HICKEY**, W.] Hints on emigration to Upper Canada; especially addressed to the middle and lower classes in Great Britain and Ireland. By Martin Doyle... Second edition enlarged. 92p. *12°. Dublin, London, &c.,* 1832. *See also* 1834.

27381 **LETTERS** from poor persons, who have very recently emigrated to Canada from the parish of Frome, in the county of Somerset...Third edition. 24p. *8°. Frome, Bristol, &c.,* 1832.

27382 [**MARTIN**, ROBERT M.] The political, commercial & financial condition of the Anglo-Eastern Empire, in 1832; an analysis of its home and foreign governments, and a practical examination of the doctrines of free trade and colonization, with reference to the renewal...of the hon. East-India Company's charter. By the author of "The past and present state of the tea trade of England...". 403p. *8°.* 1832.

27383 **MUDIE**, R. The emigrant's pocket companion; containing what emigration is, who should be emigrants, where emigrants should go; a description of British North America, especially the Canadas; and full instructions to intending emigrants. 276p. *12°.* 1832.

27384 PEGGS, J. India's cries to British humanity, relative to infanticide, British connection with idolatry, Ghaut murders, suttee, slavery, and colonization in India; to which are added, humane hints for the melioration of the state of society in British India... Third edition, revised and enlarged with a book on colonization in India. 500p. *8⁰. London, Edinburgh, &c.*, 1832. *For another edition, see* 1830.

27385 PICKEN, A. The Canadas, as they at present commend themselves to the enterprize of emigrants, colonists, and capitalists, comprehending a variety of topographical reports...and the fullest general information. Compiled and condensed from original documents furnished by John Galt...and other authentic sources, by A. Picken. [With an appendix.] 349, lxxxviip. *8⁰.* 1832. *See also* 1836.

27386 RĀMAMOHANA RĀYA. Exposition of the practical operation of the judicial and revenue systems of India, and of the general character and condition of its native inhabitants, as submitted in evidence [before a Select Committee of the House of Commons on the renewal of the East India Company's charter] to the authorities in England. With notes and illustrations. Also a brief preliminary sketch of the ancient and modern boundaries, and of the history of that country... 130p. *8⁰.* 1832.

27387 A short **REVIEW** of leading and operating causes of the distress of the British West India colonies, particularly as they bear upon the justice and policy of the experimental Foreign Sugar Refinery Bill. With remedies suggested for relieving that distress. 39p. *8⁰.* 1832.

FINANCE

27388 An **ADDRESS** to dissenters on the subject of tithes: by a dissenter. Second edition, with a notice of a criticism in the Eclectic Review, &c. [Dated: Lyme Regis, July 1832.] 24p. *8⁰.* [1832]

27389 The **AGE** of gold not a golden age. Paper and gold compared. Also, plan for a national bank, to which is added, a plan for a new system of taxation. 30p. *8⁰.* 1832. *For an edition of the Plan, with more detailed information, see no.* 27438.

27390 ANDERSON, WILLIAM (*fl.* 1797–1832). A letter to the Right Honourable Lord Althorp, in consequence of his proposal of enquiring into the expediency of renewing the Bank charter; in which a plan is submitted for introducing...a safe, fixed...paper currency; calculated to meet...every possible exigency, and at the same time to yield a considerable revenue to the state. 20p. *8⁰. Worcester,* 1832. *The copy that belonged to T. Spring Rice, Baron Monteagle.*

27391 ATTWOOD, T. The currency. From the Birmingham Journal of January 14th, 1832. [Being 'Letter from Mr. Attwood to Sir John Sinclair, on the future operation of the metallic standard, and on the two modes of carrying it into full effect', dated: January 4 1826.] *s.sh.fol. Birmingham,* [1832] *See note to no.* 26519.

27392 —— The Scotch banker; containing articles under that signature on banking, currency, &c. Second edition. 175p. *8⁰.* 1832. *A reissue of the sheets of the 1828 edition (q.v.) with a cancel title-page bearing the author's name.*

27393 BAIN, D. Tithes, their origin, and now proper use. 31p. *8⁰. Edinburgh, London, &c.*, 1832.

27394 *BANK CHARTER. Letters to Lord Althorp, in May and June, 1832. By a citizen of London. 16p. *8⁰.* 1832. *The copy presented to George Grote by George Bartley, possibly the author.*

27395 Ellis's **BRITISH TARIFF** for 1832–33...By Robert Ellis... 282p. *12⁰.* 1832. *See also* 1829, 1834, 1846, 1848.

27396 BROWNE, WILLIAM (*fl.* 1832). Banking. Reasons in support of a Bill for rendering country bankers' circulation invariable, and convertible into a metallic currency, and for granting licences to chartered banks...To which are added tables... 12p. *4⁰.* 1832. *Presentation copy from the author to the Earl of Ripon.*

27397 BURGESS, H. The evidence of Henry Burgess, Esq. relative to joint stock banks, as delivered before the Committee on the Bank of England charter. 34p. *8⁰. Newcastle,* 1832.

27398 CARDWELL, E. Lectures on the coinage of the Greeks and Romans; delivered in the University of Oxford. 238p. *8⁰. Oxford & London,* 1832.

27399 [**CAZENOVE,** J.] The evidence that would have been given by Mr. ——, late a continental merchant, before the Committee of Secrecy appointed to inquire into the expediency of renewing the Bank charter. 22p. *8⁰.* 1832.

27400 CHAPMAN, H. S. Thoughts on the money and exchanges of Lower Canada. 64p. *8⁰. Montreal,* 1832. *Presentation copy from the author to Harriet Martineau.*

27401 CHATFIELD, F. Review illustrative of various bearings peculiar to interests and discounts, and demonstrative of two systems in commercial transactions ...simple interest and discount interest...With some useful hints on discounts off bills and discounts off list prices in business... 16p. *8⁰.* 1832.

27402 CLARKE, MATTHEW ST. C. and **HALL,** D. A. Legislative and documentary history of the Bank of the United States: including the original Bank of North America. 832p. *8⁰. Washington,* 1832.

27403 COLLIER, JOHN A. Speech of Mr. Collier, of New-York, upon Mr. Clayton's resolution, that a committee be appointed to examine into the affairs of the United States Bank. Delivered in the House of Representatives, U.S. 13th March, 1832. 16p. *8⁰. Binghampton,* 1832.

27404 What has the **CURRENCY** to do with the present discontents? 24p. *8⁰.* 1832.

27405 *No. III. On the **CURRENCY FRAUD.** 4p. *4⁰* [*London,* 1832] *The FWA copy that belonged to William Pare.*

27406 EAGLE, W. A legal argument shewing that tithes are the property of the public and of the poor... The seventh edition. 20p. *8⁰.* 1832. *The Oastler copy. For another edition, see* 1831.

27407 EDMONDS, J. W. Bank of the United States. Speech of the Hon. John W. Edmonds, in the Senate of New-York, Jan. 28, 1832, in favor of the resolution offered by Mr. Deitz, "That it is the sentiment of this Legislature, that the charter of the Bank of the United States ought not to be renewed..." 8p. *8°*. *n.p.* [1832]

27408 ENGLAND'S curse. Being the rise, progress, and curious calculation of the English National Debt. *s.sh.fol.* [*London*, 1832] [*Br.* 539]

27409 Awkward **FACTS** respecting the Church of England and her revenues, from Parliamentary documents. *s.sh.fol. Cambridge*, [1832] [*Br.* 679]

27410 FIELDEN, J. The mischiefs and iniquity of paper-money, and of the present system of banking and funding. In three letters, showing how manufacturers have been brought to ruin, and their working people brought to want and misery by the joint operation of the taxes and the paper money. [With a preface by William Cobbett.] 55p. *8°*. 1832.

27411 *GENEVA, *Canton of. Caisse d'Épargnes et de Prévoyance.* 16me rapport des Administrateurs de la Caisse d'Épargnes...Au 31 décembre 1832. 11p. *8°*. [*Genève*,] 1832. *The copy that belonged to George Grote.*

27412 GRAULHIÉ, G. An outline of a plan for a new circulating medium; in three letters addressed to the Chancellor of the Exchequer. 31p. *8°*. 1832.

27413 HINCKS, E. What is to be done with the tithes in Ireland? The question answered by Edward Hincks, D.D., Rector of Killyleagh. 56p. *8°*. *London & Belfast*, 1832.

27414 [HOFFMANN, JOHANN G.] Drei Aufsätze über das Münzwesen. Abgedruckt aus der Allgemeinen Preussischen Staatszeitung mit Rücksicht auf beabsichtete Münzvereine. 109p. *8°*. *Berlin*, 1832.

27415 HUDSON, THOMAS. Some observations on the currency, its defects and remedies. In a letter to a friend. 14p. *8°*. 1832.

27416 JONES, CHARLES. A plan for realizing the perfection of money; in which it is demonstrated that "paper is capable of being made, a much more... unvarying standard of value, than...either gold or silver can be." Addressed to the Right Hon. Earl Grey. 19p. *8°*. *London & Birmingham*, 1832. *The copy that belonged to Thomas Attwood. See also 1837.*

27417 JOPLIN, T. An analysis and history of the currency question; together with an account of the origin and growth of joint stock banking in England. Comprised in a brief memoir of the writer's connexion with these subjects. 339p. *8°*. 1832. *Presentation copy, with accompanying letter, from the author to Joseph Hume. For this and 2 other letters, see vol.* III, *A.L.* 66.

27418 —— To the honourable the Commons of the United Kingdom of Great Britain and Ireland, in Parliament assembled; the petition of Thomas Joplin humbly sheweth...[An offer to give evidence before the Committee on the renewal of the Bank of England's charter.] 2p. *fol. n.p.* [1832] [*Br.* 537(1)]

27419 —— [Another edition, enlarged.] 2p. *fol. n.p.* [1832] [*Br.* 537(2)]

27420 [KING, WILLIAM, *M.D. of Brighton?*] The circulating medium, and the present mode of exchange, the cause of increasing distress amongst the productive classes. And an effectual measure for their immediate and permanent relief, pointed out in the universal establishment of labour banks, in which all the business of life may be transacted without money. By a co-operator. 8p. *8°*. [*London*,] 1832. *Attributed to King by HSF.*

27421 KLABER, H. Anweisung zur leichten Berechnung der zusammengesetzten Interessen, Jahrrenten, Leib- oder Lebensrenten, Tontinen, mit erläuternden Beispielen und den nöthigen Erklärungen... 42p. *8°*. *Prag*, 1832.

27422 LAMBERT, H. A letter on the currency, to the Right Hon. the Viscount Althorp, Chancellor of the Exchequer, &c.&c.&c. 52p. *8°*. 1832.

27423 LE MONNIER, V. Des banques en général et de la Banque de France en particulier. 71p. *8°*. *Paris*, 1832.

27424 LETTER to the Right Hon. Lord Viscount Althorp, suggesting a more equitable taxation on wines. [Dated: 22nd March, 1832.] 19p. *8°*. [*London*,] 1832.

27425 LUBÉ, D. G. An argument against the gold standard, with an examination of the principles of the modern economists. Theory of rent. Corn laws, &c. Addressed to the landlords of England. 192p. *8°*. 1832.

27426 [MACARDY, J.] Considerations, especially addressed to the electors of the United Kingdom; or, the Bank monopoly, a deficient currency, and excessive taxation, the ruin of England. Second edition. 30p. *8°*. 1832.

27427 —— A tabular view of the Bank of England, and important considerations on the Bank monopoly – a deficient currency – and excessive taxation...Third edition. 30p. *8°*. *Manchester & London*, 1832.

27428 MASTROFINI, M. Le usure libri tre. Discussione dell' abate M. Mastrofini. (*Biblioteca Scelta di Opere Italiane Antiche e Moderne*, 294.) 478p. *8°*. *Milano*, 1832. *See also 1834.*

27429 [MILNE, DAVID.] On circulating credit: with hints for improving the banking system of Britain; and preliminary observations on some of the modern doctrines of political economy. By a Scottish banker. [With an appendix.] 210p. *8°*. *Edinburgh, London, &c.*, 1832. *Presentation copy, with (anonymous) inscription from the author, to R. Montgomery Martin.*

27430 MITCHELL, W. A treatise on the law of bills of exchange, inland-bills, promissory-notes, &c.; with an appendix, and a synopsis of the history of banking... Third edition. 342p. *12°*. *Edinburgh, Glasgow, &c.*, 1832.

27431 MOORE, R. A treatise on paper and gold money, shewing the necessity for instituting an imperial, paper, standard, mint note, to be made co valuable and co current, with our gold standard money...The second edition, with additions. 169p. *8°*. 1832.

27432 MUNDELL, A. An examination of the evidence taken before the Committee of Secrecy on the Bank of England charter. 75p. *8°*. 1832.

27433 —— Supplement to An examination of the evidence... 24p. *8°*. 1832.

27434 N., D. Six letters on the Bank of England, branch banks and the currency. 40p. *8°*. *Manchester*, 1832. *Presentation copy from the author to Sir Benjamin Heywood.*

27435 The **NATIONAL DEBT** of Great Britain. December 1832. 22p. *8°*. *n.p.* [1832] *Tentatively attributed by HSF to T. Hagart of Edinburgh. With considerable manuscript additions, probably by the author.*

27436 PAINE, T. The decline and fall of the English system of finance. [With 'Results of the funding system.

From a tract issued by "The Chard Political Union"'.]
24p. 8°. 1832. *For other editions, see* 1796.

27437 [**PARNELL**, H. B., *Baron Congleton*.] A plain statement of the power of the Bank of England, and of the use it has made of it; with a refutation of the objections made to the Scotch system of banking; and a reply to the "Historical sketch of the Bank of England" [by J. R. McCulloch]. 98p. 8°. 1832.

27438 **PLAN** for a national bank and a new system of taxation, by a poundage on expenditure. 12p. 8°. [*London*, 1832 ?] *For another edition, see no.* 27389.

27439 A practical **PLAN** for the immediate annihilation of taxes, and equitable liquidation of the National Debt. By a capitalist. Second edition with additions. 36p. 8°. 1832.

27440 **PRENTICE**, D. Policy of a free trade in corn, accompanied by a measure for preventing any consequent change in the value of the currency. 8p. 8°. *Glasgow*, [1832]

27441 A **PROPERTY TAX** the only effectual remedy for the present embarrassment of the country. 8p. 8°. *Birmingham & London*, 1832.

27442 —— [Another issue, with an introductory note on the verso of the title-page, and a postscript, dated: October 8, 1832.] 8p. 8°. *Birmingham & London*, 1832. **Another, the FWA copy, belonged to William Pare.*

27443 —— Second edition. [With a postscript dated: October 20th, 1832.] 8p. *Birmingham & London*, 1832.

27444 —— Third edition. [With a postscript dated: October 30th, 1832.] 8p. 8°. *Birmingham & London*, 1832.

27445 [**REID**, WILLIAM, *political economist*.] The life and adventures of the Old Lady of Threadneedle Street; containing an account of her numerous intrigues with various eminent statesmen, of the past and present times. Written by herself. 62p. 8°. 1832.

27446 A few plain **REMARKS** on the currency question, with reference to trade, taxation, and reform; containing also, strictures on the plan of the Council, for restoring the prosperity of the country. By a Birmingham manufacturer. 30p. 8°. *Birmingham*, 1832.

27447 **REPORT** of the important discussion, held... in Birmingham, August 28 and 29, 1832, between Messrs. T. Attwood and C. Jones and Mr. Cobbett, on the question "Whether it is best for the safety...of the nation to attempt to relieve the existing distress by an action on currency, or by...adjustment of the taxes...which now strangle the industry of the country?"... 12p. 4°. *Birmingham*, [1832] *See note to no.* 26519.

27448 —— [Another edition.] Mansell and Co.'s report of the important discussion held in Birmingham, August the 28th and 29th, 1832, between William Cobbett, Thomas Attwood and Charles Jones, Esqrs. on the question whether it is best for the safety and welfare of the nation to attempt to relieve the existing distress "by an action on the currency" or by an "equitable adjustment" of the taxes, rents, debts, contracts and obligations, which now strangle the industry of the country? 28p. 8°. *Birmingham, London, &c.*, [1832]

27449 **REVIEW** of the Veto. Containing an examination of the principles of the President's message [i.e. Andrew Jackson's first annual message to Congress], and his objections to the Bill to modify and continue the act rechartering the Bank of the United States. 66p. 8°. *Philadelphia*, 1832.

27450 **RICHARDSON**, JAMES (*fl.* 1832–1833). Unequal taxation, the chief cause of the misery now suffered by the industrious and middle classes of society; and its remedy, a graduated tax upon property. Second edition. 12p. 8°. 1832.

27451 **SANDYMOUNT LOAN FUND**. First report and statement of accounts of the Sandymount Loan-Fund Committee. January, 1832. [With 'Rules and regulations of the Sandymount Loan Fund, embracing the entire parish of Saint Mary's, Donnybrook'.] 8, [6]p. 8°. *Dublin*, 1832.

27452 **SMITH**, FREDERICK G. Practical remarks on the present state of fire insurance business: the evils of competition pointed out; with hints for improvement. 123p. 8°. *Edinburgh*, 1832.

27453 **SMITH**, SAMUEL (1752–1839). Speech of the Hon. Samuel Smith; in the Senate of the United States, on the renewal of the charter of the Bank of the United States. 6p. 8°. *Washington*, 1832.

27454 **SMITH**, THOMAS, *accountant, of London*. An essay on currency and banking. Being an attempt to show their true nature, and to explain the difficulties that have occurred in discussing them. With an application to the currency of this country. 76p. 8°. *Philadelphia*, 1832.

27455 [**SURR**, T. S.] Facts relative to the Bank of England, explaining the nature and influence of the Bank charter; with a view of the cause and consequences of the suspension and restoration of the use of standard coin. 84p. 8°. [1832] *A new issue of* The present critical state of the country developed, *1826 (q.v.), in which the first four leaves have been cancelled and eight leaves substituted, to incorporate further material on pp. 1–4. Presentation copy, with inscription, from the author to Thomas Attwood; with a manuscript note, attributing the work to Surr, in Attwood's hand.*

27456 **TALLMADGE**, N. P. Albany Argus, Extra. Speech of the Hon. N. P. Tallmadge delivered in the Senate of the State of New-York, February, 1832, on the resolution against renewing the charter of the Bank of the United States. 37p. 8°. *Albany*, 1832.

27457 [**TAYLOR**, JAMES (1788–1863).] What is money?... 29p. 8°. [1832 ?]

27458 [**TAYLOR**, JOHN (1781–1864).] An attempt at an analysis of the subjects of currency, and the merits of the Bank of England. 32p. 8°. 1832. *Attributed by HSF to Ephraim Gompertz.*

27459 [**THOMPSON**, THOMAS P.] The article on the renewal of the Bank charter. From the Westminster Review, No. XXXIII. For July 1832. 23p. 8°. 1832. *See note to no.* 25779.

27460 **UNITED STATES OF AMERICA**. Congress. *House of Representatives.* 22d Congress, 1st Session. ⟨Rep. no. 460.⟩...Bank of the United States. April 30, 1832. [The report of the Committee appointed to inspect the books and examine into the proceedings of the Bank of the United States.] 572p. 8°. *n.p.* [1832]

27461 —— —— —— 22d Congress, 2d Session. ⟨Doc. no. 9.⟩...Letter from the Secretary of the Treasury, transmitting the correspondence with the Bank of the United States upon...the postponement of the payment of the three per cent. stock...13p. 8°. *n.p.* [1832]

27461A —— *Treasury Department.* Report on the finances of the United States... Submitted to Congress [by Louis McLane], December 7th, 1831. 33p. *8°. Washington & London,* 1832. *The copy that belonged to George Grote.*

27462 **VERE,** CHARLES. The Mediterranean cambist, containing the monies, weights, and measures of the various ports in the Mediterranean and Levant; with their equivalents in English and Malta weights and measures... including...tables of exchange... 168p. *8°. Malta,* 1832.

27463 A **VIEW** of the banking question, resulting from practice and experience. 159p. *8°.* 1832.

27464 **WARNER,** JOHN (*fl.* 1832). Brief remarks on the present depression of agriculture and trade, and its consequent effects upon the labouring population of the country. Printed for John Warner. 26p. *8°.* 1832.

27465 **WEBSTER,** D. Speech of the Hon. Daniel Webster, in the Senate of the United States, on the President's veto of the Bank Bill, July 11, 1832. 32p. *8°. Boston,* 1832.

27466 **WELLS,** S. Continuance of the Bank charter, a legal statement of the real position of the Government with relation to the Bank of England... Second edition, with additions. 58p. *8°.* 1832.

27467 **WHATELY,** R., *Archbishop of Dublin.* The evidence of his Grace the Archbishop of Dublin, as taken before the Select Committee... appointed to inquire into the collection and payment of tithes in Ireland...98p. *8°.* 1832. *With a note by HSF: The Archbishop's own copy.*

27468 **WHITE,** HUGH L. Speeches of Mr. White of Tennessee delivered in the Senate of the U.S. June, 1832, on the Bill to re-charter the Bank of the United States. 22p. *8°. n.p.* [1832]

27469 **WINTER,** J. P. An address to the proprietors of bank stock, on the subject of the charter, the exclusive privilege of banking, the production of accounts, and an increase of dividend. 42p. *8°.* 1832. *Presentation copy from the author to Edward Ellice (1781–1863); it afterwards belonged to Lord Monteagle.*

27470 ⋆**WOOD,** JOSEPH. Proposals for the immediate reduction of eight millions and a half of taxes, and the gradual liquidation of the National Debt, in a letter, addressed to the Right Honorable Henry Goulburn, Chancellor of the Exchequer... Second edition, by desire of the electors of Huddersfield, with a preface by Major General Johnson. 32p. *8°. Huddersfield,* 1832. *The FWA copy, that belonged to William Pare. For another edition, see* 1830.

27471 **WOODWARD,** H. A letter to the Right Hon. E. G. Stanley, on tithes in Ireland. 11p. *8°. Dublin,* 1832.

27472 [**YOUNG,** S.] Considerations on the Bank of the United States; in which its repugnance to the Constitution, its hostility to the rights of the states and the liberties of the citizen, are briefly discussed. [Reprinted from the *Saratoga Sentinel,* originally printed 1831–32.] 30p. *8°. Albany,* 1832.

TRANSPORT

27473 [**BIRKINSHAW,** J. and **LONGRIDGE,** M.] Remarks on the comparative merits of cast metal and malleable iron rail-ways; and an account of the Stockton and Darlington Rail-way, and the Liverpool and Manchester Rail-way, &c.&c. 26, 39, 38p. *8°. Newcastle,* 1832. *For other editions, see* 1822.

27474 **BOSTON AND PROVIDENCE RAIL ROAD CORPORATION.** Report of the Board of Directors to the stockholders of the... Company, submitting the report of their engineer [William Gibbs McNeill]... and estimates of the cost of a rail-road from Boston to Providence. To which are annexed the Acts of Incorporation. [With 'Geological memoir of the country between Massachusetts and Narragansett Bays' by H. E. Rogers.] 87p. *8°. Boston,* 1832. *The Rastrick copy. See also* 1833, 1834, 1849.

27475 **BRADSHAW,** G. Lengths and levels to Bradshaw's maps of canals, navigable rivers, and railways. From actual survey [in the southern counties]. Taken from a datum of six feet ten inches under the sill of the old dock gates at Liverpool... 15p. *8°.* 1832. *The Rastrick copy. See note to no.* 25921.

27476 **ENGLAND.** *Laws, etc.* Anno undecimo Georgii IV. Regis. [Local & Personal.] Cap. lxi. An Act for making a railway from the Cowley Hill Colliery in the parish of Prescot to Runcorn Gap...(with several branches therefrom), all in the County Palatine of Lancaster; and for constructing a wet dock at the termination of the said railway at Runcorn Gap... ⟨29th May 1830.⟩ p. 1853–1939. *fol.* 1832.

27477 —— —— [*Endorsed:*] Hartlepool Docks and Railway. An Act for making and maintaining wet docks in the port of Hartlepool, and a railway from the said docks into the township of Moorsley...in the county of Durham. ⟨Royal Assent, 1 June 1832.⟩. 2 Will. IV. sess. 1831–2. 87p. *fol.* [*London,* 1832]

27478 —— *Parliament.* [*Endorsed:*] London and Birmingham Railway. A Bill for making a railway from London to Birmingham. Session 1831–2. 130p. *fol.* [*London,* 1832]

27479 —— [Another edition.] [*Endorsed:*] ⟨As amended by the Committee⟩. 154p. *fol.* [*London,* 1832]

27480 —— [Another edition.] [*Endorsed:*] An Act [a Bill] for making a railway from London to Birmingham. Session 1831–2. 154p. *fol.* [*London,* 1832]

27481 —— —— [*Endorsed:*] In Parliament. London & Birmingham Railway. Copy preamble [of the Bill], with numerical statement of assents, &c. and observations and petition in support of the measure, 2nd July, 1832. 3p. *fol.* [*London,* 1832]

27482 —— —— [*Endorsed:*] London & Birmingham Railway Bill. Copy preamble, &c. Committee meet Thursday, 5th April, 1832, one o'clock. [Text of the preamble, with the advantages of the railway, and a petition in its favour from the inhabitants of London and Westminster.] 3p. *fol.* [*London,* 1832]

27483 —— —— [*Endorsed:*] London & Birmingham Railway. Preamble [of the Bill], numerical list of assents, &c. and summary of evidence to May 14th, 1832. 6p. *fol. n.p.* [1832]

27484 —— —— *House of Lords.* Extracts from the minutes of evidence given before the Committee of the Lords on the London and Birmingham Railway Bill. 73p. *8°.* 1832. *The Rastrick copy.*

27485 —— [Another edition.] 65p. *8°.* 1832. *Two copies,* *one the Rastrick copy, the other the copy that belonged to Isaac Solly, chairman of the London directors.*

27486 GORDON, ALEXANDER (1802–1868). An historical and practical treatise upon elemental locomotion, by means of steam carriages on common roads: showing the commercial, political, and moral advantages ...and embodying the Report of, and almost the whole evidence before, the Select Committee of the House of Commons. With an appendix. 192p. *8°. London & Edinburgh,* 1832. *The Rastrick copy. See also* 1834, 1836.

27487 A **HISTORY** and description of the Liverpool & Manchester Railway. 71p. *12°. Liverpool,* 1832. *The Rastrick copy.*

27488 LECOUNT, P. Mr. Lecount's "General results of the traffic returns, &c. between London and Birmingham, for one year; also the expenses of travelling and carriage by the present means and by the Railway." 6p. *fol. [London,* 1832]

27489 A **LETTER** to the proprietors of the Thames Tunnel. 12p. *8°. [London,* 1832] *The Rastrick copy.*

27490 LIVERPOOL. Liverpool docks. The report of the Committee appointed at a meeting of rate-payers on the 21st September, 1832, to take preliminary measures for a public meeting, to...adopt proceedings for procuring a more...effectual representation of the rate-payers in the management of the estate. 15p. *8°. Liverpool,* [1832]

27491 LIVERPOOL AND MANCHESTER RAILWAY. Liverpool and Manchester Railway. Answer of the Directors to an article in the Edinburgh Review, for October, 1832 [criticising the management of the Liverpool and Manchester Railway. With 'Letter from Mr. Earle to Dr. Lardner'.] 32p. *8°. Liverpool,* 1832. *The Rastrick copy.*

27492 [*Endorsed:*] 1832. In Parliament. **LONDON** & Birmingham Railway. List of Committee on this Bill. [A lithographed list.] [4]p. *fol. [London,* 1832] *With manuscript interpolations and a list of those who voted for and against the Preamble, 1 June 1832.*

27493 [*Endorsed:*] In Parliament. **LONDON** and Birmingham Rail Road. [A series of objections, dated: February 27, 1832.] 2p. *fol. [London,* 1832]

27494 [*Endorsed:*] In Parliament. **LONDON** and Birmingham Railway. Measurement of property on the line. [A table issued by the opposition to demonstrate that property holders on the line were overwhelmingly against the railway.] [4]p. *fol. [London,* 1832]

27495 [*Endorsed:*] In Parliament. **LONDON** and Birmingham Railway. Statement of the case of the petitioners for a Committee of Appeal, respecting the variation of the surface of the railway from the red line on the section. Session 1832. 2p. *fol. [London,* 1832]

27496 [*Endorsed:*] **LONDON** and Birmingham Railway. Advantages of this mode of conveyance, the Bill for effecting which stands for second reading this day, Tuesday, 28th February, 1832. [A handbill.] *s.sh.fol. n.p.* [1832]

27497 [*Endorsed:*] **LONDON** & Birmingham Railway. Copy. Petition [to the House of Commons] of subscribers to the measure against the Bill. 3p. *fol. Hemel Hempsted,* [1832?]. *Dated in manuscript: 'May 1832'.*

27498 [*Endorsed:*] **LONDON** and Birmingham Railway. (Copy.) Further petition of subscribers to the measure against the Bill... 3p. *fol. Westminster,* [1832]

27499 [*Endorsed:*] **LONDON** and Birmingham Rail-

way. Extract from the Courier and Morning Post, of the 21st June 1832. [4]p. *fol. [London,* 1832]

27500 LONDON AND BIRMINGHAM RAILWAY COMPANY. At a meeting of the General Board of Management of the Company for making a railway between London and Birmingham...held at no. 69, Cornhill, on 31st January 1832, Isaac Solly, Esq., in the chair, it was ordered that the following circular be published. [4]p. *fol. n.p.* [1832]

27501 —— London and Birmingham Railway. MDCCXXXII. Board of management. Directors. [A prospectus.] *s.sh.fol. n.p.* [1832]

27502 LONDON AND SOUTHAMPTON RAILWAY. Southampton and London Railway. Minute of documents and details submitted to the Committee of Investigation, and to the meeting of the 23rd January, 1832. [2]p. *fol. n.p.* [1832]

27503 MACGREGOR, JOHN, *surgeon.* Observations on the River Tyne, with a view to the improvement of its navigation; addressed to the coal owners of the district, the merchants and ship owners of Newcastle, and of North and South Shields. 118p. *8°. Newcastle,* 1832.

27504 MULLINS, B. Thoughts on inland navigation ...and observations upon propositions for lowering the waters of the Shannon, and of Lough Neagh, addressed to the Right Hon. E. G. Stanley, Chief Secretary for Ireland. 54p. *8°. Dublin,* 1832. *Presentation copy from the author to Charles Vignoles.*

For a **NEW GUIDE TO STAGE COACHES, WAGGONS**...&c. *for* 1832, *see no.* 27293.

27505 [**PAGE,** F. ?] A letter to a friend, containing observations on the comparative merits of canals and railways, occasioned by the reports of the committee of the Liverpool and Manchester Railway. [Signed: F.P. With 'Liverpool and Manchester Railway. Report for the six months ending 30th June, 1831'.] 32, 5p. *8°. [London,]* 1832. *Inscribed in manuscript on the title-page: 'Col: Page to Mr Priestley'.*

27506 [——] Second edition, with additions, arising from the evidence on the London and Birmingham Railway. 42p. *8°.* 1832.

27507 PROSPECTUS of a proposed rail road between London and Dover, with a steam boat ferry across the River Thames, forming a communication between the counties of Kent and Essex, and a steam boat dock, connected by rail road with the Metropolis. 8p. *4°.* 1832.

27508 WALKER, JAMES S. An accurate description of the Liverpool and Manchester Railway and branch railways...with an account of the opening of the railway, and of the...accident which occurred to the late Rt. Hon. Wm. Huskisson...The third edition. 53p. *8°. Liverpool,* 1832. *For other editions, see* 1830.

27509 WHITBY AND PICKERING RAILWAY COMPANY. Whitby and Pickering Railway, in the North Riding of the county of York. Capital £80,000... Prospectus. 3p. *fol. Whitby,* [1832]

27510 WOOD, N. A practical treatise on rail-roads, and interior communication in general. Containing an account of the performances of the different locomotive engines at and subsequent to the Liverpool contest... Second edition [second issue]. 530p. *8°.* 1832. *For other editions, see* 1825.

SOCIAL CONDITIONS

27511 On **ABRIDGING** the time of labour in factories. In a letter from the cotton spinners of Glasgow, to M. T. Sadler, Esq. M.P. [Followed by an 'Address to the cotton spinners of the United Kingdom' signed by John Nibblock and six other spinners.] *s.sh.fol. n.p.* [1832] [*Br. 547(7)*] *The Oastler copy.*

27512 An **ADDRESS** to the inhabitants of Chorlton-upon-Medlock. [An appeal for support for the ten-hour movement, signed: Eli Higginbottom, chairman, and Samuel Moore, secretary.] *s.sh.fol. Manchester,* [1832] [*Br. 547(1)*] *The Oastler copy. The text is the same as that of no.* 27513 *below.*

27513 An **ADDRESS** to the inhabitants of the Borough of Salford. [An appeal for support for the ten-hour movement, signed John Smith, chairman, Thomas Blakey, secretary.] *s.sh.4°. n.p.* [1832] [*Br. 547(2)*] *The Oastler copy. See note to no.* 27512 *above.*

27514 **ADMINISTRATION** of the poor laws. ⟨Not published.⟩ [Contrasting the operation of the English and Scottish systems.] 40p. *8°.* 1832.

27515 **ATKINSON, J.,** *printer.* The British Labourer's Protector, and factory child's friend. [A prospectus.] *s.sh.8°. n.p.* [1832?] *The Oastler copy.*

27516 **ATKINSON, WILLIAM** (*fl.* 1832–1833). Lecture upon home colonization...To which is subjoined a copy of a memorial which was presented to Earl Grey, by Thomas Attwood, Esq. praying for its early application. 44p. *12°. Leeds,* 1832. *The Oastler copy.*

27517 **BICKERSTETH,** E. The national fast of 1832. A help for duly observing it...Seventy-sixth edition, corrected. 12p. *12°.* 1832.

27518 **BIGSBY,** J. J. A brief exposition of those benevolent institutions, often denominated self-supporting dispensaries; with a view to recommend them to the... support of the public, as tending to raise the moral character and improve the condition of the laboring classes. 67p. *8°. Newark, Grantham, &c.,* 1832.

27519 **BLUE COAT CHARITY SCHOOL,** *Birmingham.* A short account of the Blue Coat Charity School, in St. Philip's church yard, Birmingham, from its institution in 1724, to 1830. 88p. *8°. Birmingham,* 1832.

27520 No. 1. The **BOGGART!!** Saturday, December 1, 1832. [An attack on mill owners in Bradford who work their mills from 6 to 8 or 9 o'clock.] *s.sh.fol. Bradford,* [1832] [*Br. 530*] *The Oastler copy.*

27521 **BOOKBINDERS' PENSION SOCIETY,** *London.* The second annual report of the Bookbinders' Pension Society...To which are added, the rules and a list of the members. 32p. *8°.* 1832.

For the **BRITISH AND FOREIGN TEMPERANCE HERALD,** 1832–35, *see vol.* III, *Periodicals list.*

For the **BRITISH LABOURER'S PROTECTOR AND FACTORY CHILD'S FRIEND,** 1832–33, *see vol.* III, *Periodicals list.*

27522 **BROWN,** JOHN (*d.* 1829). A memoir of Robert Blincoe, an orphan boy; sent from the workhouse of St. Pancras, London, at seven years of age, to endure the horrors of a cotton-mill... 64p. *8°. Manchester,* 1832.

*Two copies, one of which belonged to Richard Oastler, and the other to J. M. Cobbett. *A third, the FWA copy, belonged to William Pare.*

27523 *——* [Another edition.] 56p. *8°.* R. Carlile, [1832] *The copy that belonged to George Grote.*

27524 **BULL,** G. S. The factory system. [An appeal for subscriptions in aid of the expenses incurred in the campaign for the Ten Hours Bill.] 2p. *4°. n.p.* [1832] *The Oastler copy.*

27525 *——* Reply to the Leeds Mercury's remarks on the letter of the Rev. G. S. Bull to T. B. Macaulay, Esq. 4p. *8°. Leeds,* [1832] *The Oastler copy.*

27526 *——* A respectful and faithful appeal to the inhabitants of the parish of Bradford, on the behalf of the factory children. 34p. *12°. Bradford,* 1832. *The Oastler copy.*

27527 *——* The evils of the factory system, illustrated in a respectful and faithful appeal to the inhabitants of the parish of Bradford, on the behalf of the factory children. [Second edition.] 34p. *12°. Bradford,* 1832. *The Oastler copy.*

27528 *——* To the candidates for the Borough of Bradford. [A letter dated, December 11th, 1832, appealing for support for the Ten Hours Bill.] 4p. *8°. Bradford,* [1832] [*phc*] *From the Oastler copy, in the collection of his pamphlets at Columbia University (Seligman Collection).*

27529 *——* To the inhabitants of the agricultural districts, of the United Kingdom. [An appeal for support and funds, dated, July 10th, 1832.] *s.sh.fol. Ipswich,* [1832] [*Br. 531*] *The Oastler copy.*

27530 *——* To the inhabitants of the neighbourhood of Byerley Chapel. 4p. *8°. Bradford,* [1832] *The Oastler copy.*

27531 *——* To Thos. B. Macaulay, Esq. a candidate for the representation of the Borough of Leeds. [Dated: December 7th, 1833[1832].] *s.sh.fol. Leeds,* [1832] [*Br. 557(11)*] *The Oastler copy.*

27532 **BURROWS,** G. C. A word to electors. Letters to the present generation on the unrestrained use of modern machinery...[Second issue.] 30p. *8°. Norwich & London,* [1832] *The Oastler copy.*

27533 **CAREY,** M. A plea for the poor. No. III. [Signed: Hanway, and dated: Philadelphia, January 24, 1832.] 4p. *8°. n.p.* [1832] *The author's name is in the text.*

27534 **CLARKE,** WILLIAM (*d.* 1832). The petition of William Clarke, convicted...at Bristol of demolishing the gaol and Bridewell prisons of that city, and executed ...the 27th January, 1832; copies of fifteen exculpatory affidavits, with prefatory observations...and a report of his trials. By C. H. Walker, of Bristol, his solicitor. 28p. *8°. London, Bristol, &c.,* 1832.

27535 [**CONOLLY,** J.] Under the superintendence of the Society for the Diffusion of Useful Knowledge. The working-man's companion. The physician. I. The cholera. 209p. *12°. London, Birmingham, &c.,* 1832.

27536 **COUNTY** meeting. Order of the procession. [Details for the contingents from Huddersfield and the vicinity, Halifax, Keighley, Bradford, Dewsbury and Batley, to assemble for the march to York.] *s.sh.4°. Leeds,* [1832] [*Br. 547(10)*] *The Oastler copy.*

27537 CRABB, J. The Gipsies' advocate; or observations on the origin, character, manners, and habits, of the English Gipsies... Third edition, with additions... 199p. *12°. London, Edinburgh, &c., 1832.*

27538 DAY, WILLIAM, *Asst. Poor Law Commissioner.* An inquiry into the poor laws and surplus labour and their mutual re-action. 58p. *8°. [Lewes &] London, 1832. See also 1833.*

27539 DETROSIER, R. An address, on the necessity of an extension of moral and political instruction among the working classes... (With a brief memoir of the author [by John Kay].) 24p. *12°. [1832] *Another, the FWA copy, belonged to William Pare. For other editions, see 1831.*

27540 DEWSBURY. Dewsbury meeting on the Factory Bill, held in the Parish Church Sunday school room, Monday, February 6, 1832. 4p. *fol. Leeds, [1832] The Oastler copy.*

27541 A DIALOUGE [*sic*] between owd carder Joan oth Mumps, an Tim o lung Harrys i Owdham. [On the Ten Hours Bill and the Factory Commission.] *s.sh.fol. Huddersfihd* [*sic*], *[1832] [Br. 547(4)] The Oastler copy.*

27542 DRUMMOND, H. Substance of the speech of Henry Drummond Esq. at the meeting of magistrates of the county of Surrey, January 3, 1832. [On poor relief.] With notes and an appendix. 30p. *8°. 1832.*

27543 DUCPÉTIAUX, E. De l'état des aliénés en Belgique, et des moyens d'améliorer leur sort; extrait d'un rapport adressé au Ministre de l'Intérieur, suivi d'un projet de loi relatif au traitement et à la séquestration des aliénés. 50p. *8°. Bruxelles, 1832. Presentation copy from the author to the Athenæum Club.*

27544 —— Des moyens de soulager et de prévenir l'indigence, et d'éteindre la mendicité, extrait d'un rapport adressé au Ministre de l'Intérieur, suivi d'un projet de loi pour l'extinction de la mendicité, et de renseignemens statistiques sur l'état des établissemens de bienfaisance, en Belgique. 89, [31]p. *8°. Bruxelles, 1832. Two copies, one which belonged to Nassau Senior and the other the author's presentation copy to the Athenæum Club.*

27545 [EAGLES, J.] The Bristol riots, their causes, progress and consequences. By a citizen. 403p. *8°. Bristol, London, &c., 1832.*

27546 EDWARDS, BENJAMIN. The trial, conduct and execution of Benj. Edwards and James Strowger, who suffered at Ipswich, on Saturday, August 18, 1832... for feloniously setting fire to an out-house, stable, barn, and other buildings, in the occupation of Mr. Adolphus Stanford, at Westleton, Suffolk, on the night of the 30th of April last. *s.sh.fol. Ipswich, [1832] [Br. 536]*

27547 ELD, G. Remarks on certain statements and charges contained in a pamphlet, entitled a Report of the committee appointed to investigate the accounts of the parish of Foleshill. 34p. *8°. Coventry, [1832]*

27548 To the worthy, free, and independent **ELECTORS** of the Borough of Leeds. [An address by the operative spinners in Bolton-le-Moors supporting the parliamentary candidature of Sadler. Dated: October 8th, 1832.] *s.sh.fol. Bolton, [1832] [Br. 544] The Oastler copy.*

27549 ENGLAND. *Commissioners for Inquiring into the Administration and Practical Operation of the Poor Laws.* Instructions from the Central Board of Poor Law Commissioners to assistant commissioners. 62p. *8°. n.p. [1832] Reprinted as an appendix to* Extracts from the information received... as to the administration and operation of the poor laws, *in 1833 and 1837 (qq.v.).*

27550 —— Laws, etc. [*Endorsed:*] Bristol Damages Compensation. An Act for more easily providing compensation for the damage and injury committed within the City of Bristol... during the late riots and disturbances therein. ⟨Royal Assent, 23 June 1832.⟩ 2 Will. IV. sess. 1831-2. 23p. *fol. [Bristol, 1832]*

27551 —— Parliament. [*Endorsed:*] Bristol, St. James, &c. Without, improvement. An Act [a Bill] for repairing, lighting and watching the district of the united parishes of Saint James and Saint Paul, in the County of Gloucester, and for the care of the poor thereof. 2 Will. IV. sess. 1831-2. 71p. *fol. [Bristol, 1832]*

27552 EXETER. *Corporation of the Poor.* A list of persons relieved by the Corporation of the Poor... from 1st May, 1831, to 30th April, 1832, during the treasurership of Samuel Langston, Esq. [14]p. *4°. Exeter, [1832] See also 1833.*

27553 EXPOSITION of the factory question. 19p. *8°. Manchester, 1832. The Oastler copy.*

27554 The FACTORY SYSTEM. Opinion of Mr. Thackrah, surgeon, given at the Leeds meeting. Opinion of Mr. S. Smith, surgeon, given also at the Leeds meeting. *s.sh.fol. n.p. [1832 ?] [Br. 571(2)] The Oastler copy.*

27555 On the FACTORY SYSTEM. 9p. *8°. n.p. [1832 ?] The Oastler copy.*

27556 The FAMILY temperance meeting. 166p. *12°. Glasgow, 1832. The Turner copy.*

27557 FERRERS, J. B. Observations on the present administration of the poor laws: addressed to all persons of landed property... and respectfully submitted to the consideration of both Houses of Parliament. 15p. *8°. 1832.*

27558 GURNEY, SIR JOHN. The charge of Mr. Baron Gurney, to the Grand Jury of the county of Gloucester, and the Grand Jury of the county of the city of Gloucester, at the Summer Assizes, 1832... 12p. *8°. Gloucester, 1832.*

27559 H., J. S. Narrative of conversations held with Christopher Davis and Wm. Clarke, who were executed January 27th, 1832, for the part they took in the Bristol riots: to which is added a letter by W. Clarke, finished on the day of his execution, on the evils of Sabbath-breaking and drunken-ness. By a layman. 31p. *12°. Bristol & London, 1832.*

27560 HARRIS, S. Abstinence from all intoxicating liquors the only remedy for drunkenness. 12p. *12°. [London, 1832 ?]*

27561 HILL, SIR ROWLAND (1795-1879). Home colonies. Sketch of a plan for the gradual extinction of pauperism, and for the diminution of crime. 52p. *8°. 1832. Presentation copy from the author to William Allen. *Another, the FWA copy, belonged to William Pare.*

27562 The HISTORY of Richard Mac Ready, the farmer lad. [Reprinted for the Sussex Association for Improving the Condition of the Agricultural Classes.] 177p. *16°. Lindfield, 1832.*

27563 HOLMFIRTH SHORT-TIME COMMITTEE. The Short Time Bill. An address to the inhabitants of Holmfirth & its vicinity. [Signed: J. Brook, chairman, and dated, March 22, 1832.] *s.sh.fol. Huddersfield, [1832] [Br. 547(12)] The Oastler copy. The text is the same as that of no. 27566.*

27564 HOOLE, H. A letter to the Right Honourable Lord Viscount Althorp, M.P., Chancellor of the Exchequer; in defence of the cotton factories of Lancashire. 16p. *8°. Manchester, 1832. The Oastler copy, with extensive marginal notes.*

27565 HUDDERSFIELD SHORT-TIME COMMITTEE. County meeting on the Ten Hours Bill. [Arrangements for the procession from Huddersfield to York. Signed: J. Brook, secretary.] *s.sh.fol. Huddersfield,* [1832] [*Br.* 547(3)] *The Oastler copy.*

27566 —— The Ten Hour Bill. An address to the inhabitants of Huddersfield and its vicinity. [Signed: John Leech, chairman, and dated, March 24, 1832.] *s.sh.fol. Huddersfield,* [1832] [*Br.* 547(13)] *The Oastler copy. The text is the same as that of no.* 27563.

27567 HUERNE DE POMMEUSE, M. L. F. Des colonies agricoles et de leurs avantages pour assurer des secours à l'honnête indigence, extirper la mendicité... avec des recherches comparatives sur les divers modes de secours publics... 940p. *8°. Paris, 1832.*

27568 HULL, J. On popular education. Plans for the establishment of day schools, on the British system; and of agricultural schools. 12p. *12°.* [1832]

27569 HUMANITAS, *pseud.* A letter to the judges, under His Majesty's Special Commission appointed to deliver His Majesty's gaol, for the City of Bristol, upon the impropriety of punishing the rioters with death. 8p. *12°. Bristol,* [1832]

27570 To the **INHABITANTS** of Holbeck. [Signed: A clothier, and dated, September 3, 1832. An attack on John Marshall and T. B. Macaulay, Parliamentary candidates for Leeds.] *s.sh.4°. Leeds,* [1832] [*Br.* 547(16)] *The Oastler copy.*

27571 JUNIUS, *pseud.* The anti-reformers' address from amid the ruins of Bristol. 4p. *8°. Bristol,* [1832]

27572 JUSTICE and humanity!! "Let everyman do his duty." Men of Sheffield, sign the petition for the regulation of the hours of labour for children employed in mills and factories...[A poster, printed on yellow paper, signed 'on behalf of the Committee' by Abraham Wildman, and dated, May 7, 1832.] *s.sh.fol.* [*Sheffield,* 1832] [*Br.* 534(1)] *The Oastler copy.*

27573 KAY, afterwards **KAY-SHUTTLE-WORTH,** SIR JAMES P., *Bart.* The moral and physical condition of the working classes employed in the cotton manufacture in Manchester. 72p. *8°.* 1832. *Two copies, one the Oastler copy (imperfect), the other a presentation copy from the author to 'Thos. Fordington Esq.', from the library of E. B. Sugden, Baron St. Leonards (1781–1875). ★A third, the FWA copy, belonged to William Pare.*

27574 —— Second edition, enlarged: and containing an introductory letter to the Rev. Thomas Chalmers, D.D.... 120p. *8°.* 1832. *The copy that belonged to Victor Considérant.*

27575 KEIGHLEY SHORT-TIME COMMITTEE. To the inhabitants of Keighley. [A warning against the promoters of a twelve-hour Bill. Dated: February 7th, 1832.] *s.sh.fol. Keighley,* [1832] [*Br.* 547(17)] *The Oastler copy.*

27576 LABOURERS' FRIEND SOCIETY, *London.* Labourers' Friend Society...[List of officers, prospectus and list of contributors to December 1831.] 15p. *8°. n.p.* [1832]

27577 LANCASHIRE CENTRAL SHORT-TIME COMMITTEE. Report of the Committee for the support of Mr. Sadler's Ten Hours' Bill, and to lay all the restriction on the moving power. [Signed: Peter Berry, Philip Grant, auditors, Thomas Daniel, secretary.] *s.sh.fol. Manchester,* [1832] [*Br.* 547(11)] *The Oastler copy.*

27578 LEEDS GENERAL COMMITTEE FOR PROMOTING THE BILL FOR RESTRICTING THE HOURS OF JUVENILE LABOUR IN THE FACTORIES. The Leeds General Committee...[A circular letter from the secretaries, William Osburn and Ralph Taylor, asking for support.] 3p. *4°. n.p.* [1832] *The Oastler copy.*

27579 —— [*Begin.*] Sir, I have the honor, under the directions of the Central Committee for supporting the Factories Bill, to inform you...[An announcement of preliminary meetings to make arrangements for a county meeting in Yorkshire on April 24th, 1832. A lithographed letter, signed in manuscript: Wm. Osburn, Jun[r].] *s.sh.4°. n.p.* [1832] *The Oastler copy.*

27580 LEEDS SHORT-TIME COMMITTEE. To the public...Addressed to the editors of the Leeds Intelligencer and Patriot. [A refutation, signed by Ralph Taylor and John Hannam on behalf of the Committee, of charges made in the Leeds Mercury that the Committee is misapplying money raised. Dated: July 24, 1832.] *s.sh.fol. Leeds,* [1832] [*Br.* 538] *The Oastler copy.*

27581 A **LETTER** to Sir John Cam Hobhouse, Bart M.P. on "the Factories Bill". By a manufacturer. 52p. *8°. London, Leeds, &c.,* 1832. *The Oastler copy.*

27582 LETTER to the requisitionists of the meeting for petitioning against the plan of public education of poor Protestants and Catholics [in Ireland]. By a lay Presbyterian. With report of the proceedings of the subsequent public meeting. 24p. *8°. London, Glasgow, &c.,* 1832.

27583 ★MACAULEY, E. W. Lecture addressed to the inhabitants of Surrey and Southwark, delivered at the New Surrey & Southwark Institution, (late Rotunda, Blackfriar's Road,) by Miss Macauley, proprietress of the Institution, on...July 29th, 1832. 12p. *12°.* 1832. *The FWA copy, that belonged to William Pare.*

27584 [MACKENZIE, P.] An exposure of the spy system pursued in Glasgow, during the years 1816–17–18–19 and 20. With copies of the original letters...of Andrew Hardie, who was executed for treason at Stirling, in...1820. The whole edited...by a Ten-Pounder. 242p. *8°. Glasgow & Paisley,* 1832. *Published in 15 parts.*

27585 [——] The trial of James Wilson for high treason, with an account of his execution at Glasgow, September, 1820...Now respectfully submitted to the consideration of the reformers of Glasgow, by...the exposer of the spy system &c.&c. 48p. *8°. Glasgow & Paisley,* 1832. *Published in 2 parts.*

27586 The **MAGISTRATES** of Bristol brought to the bar of public opinion; being a consideration of the charges to which the Mayor and Corporation of this city are liable, as regards their conduct in connexion with the late riots. Chiefly grounded on their own statement. [Signed: an impartial citizen.] 12p. *12°. Bristol,* [1832]

27587 MANCHEE, T. J. The origin of the riots of Bristol, and the causes of the subsequent outrages... Second edition. 40p. *8°. Bristol & London,* [1832 ?]

27588 MARRIAGE, J. Letters on the distressed state of the agricultural labourers, and suggesting a remedy...Third edition. 22p. *8°. Chelmsford & London,* 1832.

27589 —— Fourth edition. 22p. *8°. Chelmsford & London,* 1832. *For other editions, see* 1830.

27590 MARSHALL & Macaulay. A conversation between them and an elector of Leeds. [On the condition of factory children and support for Sadler's Ten Hours Bill.] *s.sh.fol. Leeds,* [1832] [*Br.* 565(7)] *The Oastler copy.*

27591 MATTHEWS, W. An historical sketch of the origin and progress of gas-lighting...Second edition. 440p. *12°.* 1832. *For another edition, see* 1827.

27592 MECHANICS' Institution. (From the Birmingham Journal of June 30, 1832.) [An account of a meeting of the Birmingham Mechanics' Institution.] *s.sh.fol.* [*Birmingham,* 1832] [*Br.* 529(1)]

27593 MECHANICS' Institution. [A reprint from the Birmingham Journal, of reports of two meetings of the Institution, 4 and 5 July, 1832.] *s.sh.fol. Birmingham,* [1832] [*Br.* 529(2)] *The copy presented to Egerton Smith, 'with Mr. W. Hawkes Smith's respects'.*

27594 MECHANICS' Institution. (From the Birmingham Journal of July 28, 1832.) [A report of the meeting of the Birmingham Mechanics' Institution on July 20th 1832.] *s.sh.fol. Birmingham,* [1832] [*Br.* 529(3)]

27595 MEN of Bradford, and the neighbourhood. [An election address, asking all operatives to support the movement by obtaining pledges from candidates to support the Ten Hours Bill.] *s.sh.4°. Bradford,* [1832] [*Br.* 565(8)] *The Oastler copy.*

27596 NEWTON, JAMES. To the electors of the Borough of Stockport. [An election address, pledging support for, among other things, the emancipation of slaves and the Ten Hours movement. Dated: July 5th, 1832.] *s.sh.fol. Stockport,* [1832] [*Br.* 540] *The Oastler copy.*

27597 [**NICHOLSON,** JOHN (1790–1843).] The factory child, a poem; with considerable alterations and additions. By an operative. Second edition. 64p. *12°.* 1832. *The copy that belonged to Oastler, who attributed it to Nicholson in the manuscript index to his pamphlet collection. It is suggested by James Ross, in his introduction to* The factory child's father's reply to the factory child's mother (*no.* 27624) *that Nicholson only wrote part of this poem, which presumably means that the 'operative' of the title-page is someone else, and explains the unflattering footnote about Nicholson, on p. 40. For another edition, see* 1831.

27598 —— The factory child's mother; the voice of true humanity; a poem. 23p. *8°. Leeds, Bradford, &c.,* 1832. *The Oastler copy.*

27599 OASTLER, R. The factory system. To the chairman of the meeting of the working classes...held at the Mechanics' Institution, Manchester...March 14, 1832. *s.sh.fol. Bolton,* [1832] [*Br.* 541(1)] *Oastler's own copy.*

27600 —— A letter to Mr. Holland Hoole, in reply to his letter to the Right Hon. Lord Viscount Althorp, M.P., Chancellor of the Exchequer, in defence of the cotton factories of Lancashire. 31p. *8°. Manchester,* [1832] *Oastler's own copy.*

27601 —— Mr. Oastler's speech at Huddersfield, on his return from London. (From the Leeds Intelligencer of July 12, 1832.) 8p. *8°. Leeds,* [1832] *Oastler's own copy.*

27602 —— Operatives of Leeds! [A letter calling for support in the election campaign against John Marshall and T. B. Macaulay, candidates for Leeds. Dated: Aug. 29, 1832.] *s.sh.fol. Leeds,* [1832] [*Br.* 541(2)] *Oastler's own copy.*

27603 —— Slavery in Yorkshire! Yorkshiremen! The requisitors have done their duty!!...On Tuesday next, in the Castle yard, at York, you will do yours!! [A poster, dated: April 17th 1832.] *s.sh.fol. Leeds,* [1832] [*Br.* 534(3)] *Oastler's own copy.*

27604 —— To the editor of the [Leeds] Intelligencer. [A letter, challenging his opponents the Baines's, to discuss their differences at any meeting-place they chose. Dated: December 22nd, 1832.] *s.sh.fol. n.p.* [1832] [*Br.* 541(3)] *Oastler's own copy.*

27605 The **OPERATIVES** of Bradford and its vicinity, who can spare time from their long hours of toil, to attend Mr. Thompson's lectures on negro slavery on Wednesday, Aug. 15. would be glad to learn a few particulars from the worthy lecturer on the occasion. [An attack on those who support emancipation of slaves, but remain unmoved by the plight of children in factories.] *s.sh.fol. Leeds,* [1832] [*Br.* 547(8)]

27606 —— [Another edition.] *s.sh.fol. Bradford,* [1832] [*Br.* 547(9)] *Both editions belonged to Oastler.*

27607 Preserve **ORDER** forsooth!! Disgraceful outrage by the friends of order!!! [Dated: December 10, 1832.] *s.sh.4°. Leeds,* [1832] [*Br.* 534(2)] *The Oastler copy.*

27608 [**OSBURN,** W. ?] "Mr. Macaulay's claims." A letter to an elector of Leeds. [Signed: Common Sense.] 12p. *12°. Leeds,* [1832] *The copy that belonged to Oastler, who attributed it to Osburn in the manuscript index to his pamphlet collection.*

27609 PALMER, JAMES. A treatise on the modern system of governing gaols, penitentiaries, and houses of correction...also, a detail of the duties of each department of a prison, together with some observations on the state of prison discipline...and on the management of lunatic asylums. 99p. *8°. Dublin,* 1832.

27610 PEMBROKE, *County of. Quarter Sessions.* Third report of the Committee, appointed to carry into execution the resolution of the justices...for improving and making additions to the Gaol and House of Correction ...and adopting a system of prison discipline. [Signed: H. Leach, chairman. With an appendix of accounts covering the years 1823–32.] 16p. *8°. Haverfordwest,* [1832 ?] *See note to no.* 23273.

27611 The **PETITION** to the King on behalf of the prisoners convicted under the late special commissions at Bristol and Nottingham. 28p. *8°.* 1832. *Presentation copy from the anonymous author to M. T. Sadler.*

27612 —— [Another edition.] True causes of riot and rebellion. Petition to the King on behalf of the prisoners convicted under the late special commissions at Bristol and Nottingham. 16p. *8°. n.p.* [1832]

27613 To the honourable the Commons of the United Kingdom of Great Britain and Ireland...the **PETITION** of the undersigned operative spinners, and others employed in the spinning of cotton wool into yarn, in Ashton-under-Lyne and its neighbourhood. [Praying that there shall be legislative limitation of the hours during which machinery may be run, and that these may be not more than 12 hours per weekday and 8 on Saturdays.] *s.sh.fol. Ashton-under-Lyne,* [1832 ?] [*Br.* 565(19)] *The*

Oastler copy. The final paragraph has been corrected in manuscript to read 'Your petitioners therefore humbly pray your honourable house to pass a law [altered to] Mr. Sadder's [sic] Bill into a law with such additional clauses as will prohibit the working of any steam engines and water wheels ...'.

27614 [**POLE**, E. S. C.] Reasons for a revision of the rate raised upon the county of Derby. 23p. *8°.* 1832. *With manuscript notes signed by the author.*

For the **POOR MAN'S ADVOCATE AND PEOPLE'S LIBRARY,** 1832–33, *see* vol. III, *Periodicals list.*

27615 **PUBLIC HOUSES;** or, the miseries of intemperance; being a few thoughts concerning the hopeless state of those who frequent and encourage these dens of vice and depravity. 48p. *12°. Dumfries,* 1832.

27616 **R.,** V. Mr. Sadler, M.P., his factory time Bill, and his party, examined. 36p. *8°.* 1832.

For the **REFORMERS' GAZETTE,** 1832–33, *see* vol. III, *Periodicals list.*

27617 General **REMARKS** on the state of the poor, and poor laws, and the circumstances affecting their condition, viz. game laws, currency, free trade... 55p. *8°.* 1832.

27618 A full **REPORT** of the trials of the Bristol rioters before the Special Commission appointed to deliver the Gaol of this city in January 1832, with the sentences & executions consequent thereon; also, a report of the proceedings of the court martial appointed to investigate the conduct of Lieut-Colonel Brereton... To which is subjoined a full report of the court martial on Captain Warrington. 124, 22p. *8°. Bristol,* [1832] *Published in 16 parts.*

27619 **REPORT** &c. [An allegorical account of a meeting on the factory question.] 4p. *8°. Bradford,* [1832 ?]

27620 **REPORT** of the trials of the pitmen and others, concerned in the late riots, murders, &c., in the Hetton and other collieries, at the Durham Summer Assizes, 1832, including a full report of Mr. Justice Parke's charge to the Grand Jury. 40p. *12°. Durham,* 1832.

27621 [**RICHARDSON**, C.] The day-dream, or, a letter to King Richard [i.e. R. Oastler], containing a vision of the trial of Mr. Factory Longhours, at York Castle. 12p. *12°. Leeds,* 1832. *The copy that belonged to Oastler, who attributed it to Richardson in the manuscript index to his pamphlet collection. *Another, the FWA copy, belonged to William Pare.*

27622 —— Factory slavery. Reply to a letter in the Nottingham Review, headed "Mr. Sadler and his Bill." 12p. *12°. Nottingham,* 1832. *The Oastler copy.*

27623 —— A short description of the factory system. 7p. *8°. Bawtry,* [1832] *The Oastler copy.*

27624 **ROSS,** JAMES. The factory child's father's reply to The factory child's mother. A poem... To which are subjoined poems by two ladies [including 'Song of the factory children. (Contributed by a mother [Mary Oastler])']. 42p. *12°. Leeds, Bradford, &c.,* [1832] *The Oastler copy.*

27625 **SADLER,** M. T. Mr. Sadler's speech on moving the second reading of the Factories' Regulation Bill. Ordered to be printed by the cotton spinners of

Glasgow, as a mark of gratitude for his exertions in their cause. 24p. *8°. Glasgow,* 1832.

27626 —— Speech of Michael Thomas Sadler, Esq. in the House of Commons...March 16, 1832, on moving the second reading of the Factories' Regulation Bill. Third edition. 46p. *8°.* 1832. *The Oastler copy.*

27627 Mr. **SADLER** and the Ten-Hour Bill. (From the Leeds Intelligencer of August 30, 1832.) 36p. *12°. Leeds,* [1832] *The Oastler copy.*

27628 Mr. **SADLER'S** Factory Bill. Report of the proceedings of a public meeting, held in...Halifax, on... March 6th, 1832, for the purpose of petitioning Parliament in favour of the Ten-Hour Factory Bill. 24p. *12°. Leeds,* [1832] *The Oastler copy.*

27629 **SANDFORD,** SIR D. K. Speech of Sir Daniel K. Sandford, at a meeting of the Protestant inhabitants of Glasgow, held on Tuesday, May the first, 1832, to consider the subject of the government plan of education for Ireland. 19p. *8°. Glasgow, Edinburgh, &c.,* 1832.

27630 **SAWBRIDGE,** H. B. A letter addressed to Michael Thomas Sadler, Esq. M.P. on the subject of emigration. 49p. *8°.* 1832.

27631 **SCROPE,** G. P. On the poor laws, and their abuse. 44, 15, 24, 51, 22p. *8°.* 1832. *A reissue, with a general title-page, of works on the poor laws published by the author from 1829 to 1831. The copy presented by him to the Athenæum Club.*

27632 **SENIOR,** N. W. A letter to Lord Howick, on a legal provision for the Irish poor; commutation of tithes, and a provision for the Irish Roman Catholic clergy... Third edition. With a preface, containing suggestions as to the measures to be adopted in the present emergency. xvii, 104p. *8°.* 1832. *For other editions, see 1831.*

27633 **SHAW,** JOHN, *bookbinder.* Society of Bookbinders. [A leaflet, soliciting support for his candidature for the office of Secretary to Lodge 1 of the Friendly Society of Journeymen Bookbinders. Dated: Jan. 10, 1832.] *s.sh.8°. n.p.* [1832] *See note to no. 23614.*

27634 **SMITH,** HUGH (*fl.* 1832). The poetical miscellany of morals and religion. 203p. *12°. Irvine,* 1832. *The Turner copy.*

27635 **SOCIETY FOR THE DIFFUSION OF INFORMATION ON THE SUBJECT OF CAPITAL PUNISHMENTS.** Punishment of death ...No. 1. Speech of the Right Hon. Sir William Meredith, Bart. In the House of Commons...1777, in committee on a Bill creating a new capital felony. Fifth edition. 8p. *London, Edinburgh, &c.,* 1832. *Another, the FWA copy, belonged to William Pare. For another edition, see 1831.*

27636 **SOCIETY FOR THE IMPROVEMENT OF PRISON DISCIPLINE,** *London.* The eighth report of the Committee of the Society...1832. With an appendix ['Extracts from the correspondence of the Committee']. 98, 320p. *8°. London, Edinburgh, &c.,* [1832] *The copy that belonged to George Agar Ellis, Baron Dover, with his arms stamped in gilt on the binding. See also 1818, 1824, 1827.*

27637 The **SPIRIT** of Toryism exemplified in the brutal conduct exhibited towards Alexander Sommerville of the Scots Greys. No. I. 8p. *8°. Glasgow,* 1832.

27638 A **SUMMARY** of the most material points contained in the evidence on the subject of the Cotton Factory Bill. [A series of contradictory statements on temperature and ventilation, health, accidents, proportion of children, hours of labour, etc.] 8p. *4°. Manchester,* [1832] *The Oastler copy.*

27639 **SUSSEX ASSOCIATION FOR IM- PROVING THE CONDITION OF THE LABOURING CLASSES.** Second quarterly report ...No. 2. 30p. *8°. Lindfield, London, &c.,* 1832. *The copy that belonged to William Allen. See also* 1831.

27640 **TABLE** of medical opinion & testimony before the Select Committee on the Ten Hour Bill. *s.sh.fol. Bradford,* [1832] [*Br.* 547(14)] *The Oastler copy.*

27641 **TAYLOR,** RALPH. To the editors of the Leeds Mercury [on the Ten Hours' Bill]. 7p. *8°. n.p.* [1832] *The Oastler copy.*

27642 The **TEN-HOUR FACTORY BILL.** Keighley meeting, Monday, January 30, 1832. 4p. *fol. Leeds,* [1832] *The Oastler copy.*

27643 The **TEN HOURS BILL.** M. T. Sadler, Esq. M.P. [Arrangements for a procession and address of thanks to Sadler on his return to Leeds, 3rd September 1832. Dated: Sept. 1st, 1832.] *s.sh.fol. Leeds,* [1832] [*Br.* 547(15)] *The Oastler copy.*

27644 **THACKRAH,** C. T. The effects of arts, trades, and professions, and of civic states and habits of living, on health and longevity: with suggestions for the removal of many of the agents which produce disease, and shorten the duration of life...Second edition, greatly enlarged. 238p. *8°. London & Leeds,* 1832. *For another edition, see* 1831.

27645 **THWAITES,** J. S. A letter addressed to the president and members of the Limerick Board of Health, on the treatment of spasmodic cholera. 32p. *8°. Limerick,* 1832.

27646 **WAKEFIELD,** EDWARD G. Facts relating to the punishment of death in the Metropolis...Second edition; with an appendix, concerning murder for the sale of the dead body. 213p. *8°.* 1832.

27647 **WALKER,** WILLIAM, *of Bradford.* Poetical strictures on the factory system and other matters. 34p. *12°. Leeds, Bradford, &c.,* 1832. *The Oastler copy.*

27648 **WARREN,** Z. S. Scriptural education, the foundation of national morality: a sermon preached at... Hull on...October 7th, 1832...in aid of the Incorporated Society for Promoting National Education in the Principles of the Established Church. 34p. *8°. Beverley,* 1832.

27649 The late **WEST RIDING** meeting. *s.sh.fol. Leeds,* [1832] [*Br.* 547(6)] *The Oastler copy.*

27650 **WEST RIDING CENTRAL COMMIT- TEE.** 'The Factories Bill'. An address to the inhabitants of Bradford and its vicinity. [Dated: April 2d, 1832.] *s.sh.fol.* [*Bradford,* 1832] [*Br.* 547(5)] *The Oastler copy. Originally issued as a lithographed manuscript facsimile letter in* 1831 *(q.v.).*

27651 —— Memorandum. [A circular issued to local committees particularizing the kind of evidence needed from 'overlookers, operatives and others who work, or have worked in factories of various descriptions affected by the [Factory] Bill'.] 3p. *fol. n.p.* [1832] *The Oastler copy.*

27652 **WHATELY,** R., *Archbishop of Dublin.* Educa- tion in Ireland. Replies of the Archbishop of Dublin, to the memorial and addresses of the clergy of his diocese and others. 29p. *8°. Edinburgh,* 1832.

27653 —— Thoughts on secondary punishments, in a letter to Earl Grey...To which are appended, two articles on transportation to New South Wales, and on secondary punishments; and some observations on colonization. 204p. *8°.* 1832.

27654 **WHIELDON,** G. A letter to the Rev. Richard Rawlins, curate of the parish of Foleshill, in answer to a calumnious attack publicly made by him, upon one of the principal rate-payers of the parish, and an address to the rate-payers of Foleshill, on the subject of the resolutions of the minister and officers of the parish. 22p. *8°. Coventry,* [1832]

27655 A **WORD,** addressed to the wool-sorters, comb- ers, and others connected with mills and factories, on the subject of the Ten Hours' Bill. 4p. *8°. Halifax,* [1832] *The Oastler copy.*

27656 Important to the **WORKING CLASSES** of Nottingham and the country. A statistical and comparative statement of the rate of wages for the manufacture of hosiery &c.&c.; price of the necessaries of life; the year 1792, contrasted with that of 1832; with observations on the twist net manufacture...Copies of letters from Joseph Hume, Esq. M.P. and...Lord Auckland...to J. Clayton, Nottingham... 12p. *12°. Nottingham,* [1832] *The Oastler copy.*

SLAVERY

27657 **AGENCY ANTI-SLAVERY SOCIETY.** Report of the agency committee of the Anti-slavery Society, established in June, 1831, for the purpose of disseminating information by lectures on colonial slavery ... 22p. *8°.* 1832.

For the **ANTI-SLAVERY RECORD,** 1832–33, *see* vol. III, *Periodicals list.*

27658 **CAREY,** M. Letters on the Colonization Society; with a view of its probable results, under the following heads: the origin of the Society; increase of the coloured population; manumission of slaves in this country...Second edition, enlarged and improved. 32p. *8°. Philadelphia,* 1832.

27659 —— Third edition, enlarged and improved. 32p. *8°. Philadelphia,* 1832.

27660 —— Fourth edition, greatly enlarged and im- proved. 32p. *8°. Philadelphia,* 1832.

27661 —— Sixth edition. 32p. *8°. Philadelphia,* 1832. *See also* 1833, 1834.

27662 **CROPPER,** J. A letter to Thomas Clarkson, by James Cropper. And Prejudice vincible; or, the practicability of conquering prejudice by better means than by slavery and exile; in relation to the American Colonization Society. By C. Stuart. 24p. *8°. Liverpool,* 1832.

27663 *DEW, T. R. Review of the debate in the Virginia Legislature of 1831 and 1832. 133p. 8°. *Richmond*, 1832. *The copy that belonged to George Grote.*

27664 GARRISON, W. L. Thoughts on African colonization; or an impartial exhibition of the doctrines, principles and purposes of the American Colonization Society. Together with the resolutions, addresses and remonstrances of the free people of color. 160, 76p. 8°. *Boston*, 1832.

27665 IVIMEY, J. The utter extinction of slavery an object of Scripture prophecy: a lecture the substance of which was delivered at the annual meeting of the Chelmsford Ladies' Anti-slavery Association in the Friend's meeting-house on...the 17th of April 1832... 74p. 8°. 1832.

27666 JACKSON, T. An appeal to the freeholders of the county of Cambridge, and Isle of Ely, on the subject of colonial slavery. 26p. 8°. *Cambridge, Wisbech, &c.*, 1832.

27667 —— Britain's burden; or, the intolerable evils of colonial slavery exposed. 38p. 8°. *Cambridge, Wisbech, &c.*, 1832.

27668 JEREMIE, SIR J. Four essays on colonial slavery...Second edition. 125p. 8°. 1832. *For another edition, see* 1831.

27669 KILHAM, H. Present state of the colony of Sierra Leone, being extracts of recent letters...Second edition, with considerable additions. 26p. 8°. *Lindfield: Printed at the Schools of Industry, by C. Greene, & London*, 1832.

27670 PAPERS regarding the progressive abolition of slavery, on the island of St. Helena. August 1818. 42p. 8°. [1832] *The copy that belonged to Earl De Grey.*

27671 PAUL, N. Reply to Mr. Joseph Phillips' enquiry, respecting "the light in which the operations of the American Colonization Society are viewed by the free people of colour in the United States." 8p. 8°. [*London*, 1832]

27672 [PRICE, SIR ROSE, *Bart.*?] Pledges on colonial slavery, to candidates for seats in Parliament, rightly considered. [A letter to the editor of the English Chronicle, dated October 6th, 1832, and signed: Z. With 'Negro provisions in Jamaica' and 'Addenda', dated December 7th, 1832.] 32p. 8°. *Penzance*, [1832]

27673 —— To the editor of the West Briton, Truro. [A letter signed: Rose Price, and dated, 12th December, 1832, on "Cart whip and driver's whip of Jamaica".] 4p. 8°. *Penzance*, [1832]

27674 SOCIETY FOR THE ABOLITION OF SLAVERY THROUGHOUT THE BRITISH DOMINIONS. Account of the receipts and disbursements of the Anti-Slavery Society, for the year 1831: with a list of the subscribers. 9p. 8°. [1832] *See also* 1827, 1829, 1831.

27675 STUART, C. The West India question. Immediate emancipation would be safe for the masters; – profitable for the masters...right in the Government... An outline for immediate emancipation and remarks on compensation...Reprinted from the Quarterly Magazine and Review, of April, 1832. 44p. 8°. 1832. *Another, the FWA copy, belonged to William Pare.*

POLITICS

27676 An ACCOUNT of the public entry given by the inhabitants of Birmingham to Thomas Attwood, Esq., and the London deputation, on Monday, the 28th day of May, 1832. 7p. 4°. *Birmingham*, 1832. *See note to no.* 26519.

27677 [ADAMS, WILLIAM B.] What the people ought to do, in choosing their representatives at the general election, after the passing of the Reform Bill. A letter, addressed to the electors of Great Britain. By Junius Redivivus. 47p. 8°. 1832.

27678 An ADDRESS from one of the 3730 electors of Preston to his fellow-countrymen. [Signed: A radical reformer.] 8p. 4°. *Preston, London, &c.*, 1832. *The copy that belonged to Francis Place.*

27679 AYTOUN, J. Speech addressed to the electors of the southern districts of Edinburgh, on...the 11th July 1832. [On reform.] 8p. 8°. *n.p.* [1832] *The Oastler copy.*

27680 BECKETT, W. Speech of William Beckett, Esq. in seconding the nomination of Michael Thomas Sadler, Esq. as a candidate for the representation of the Borough of Leeds, at the election holden in the Mixed Cloth Hall, on Monday the tenth of Dec. 1832. *s.sh.fol. Leeds*, [1832] [*Br.* 528] *The Oastler copy.*

27681 Two BILLS: the outline of a reform founded on the ancient model of the constitution. 29p. 8°. 1832. *The copy that belonged to M. T. Sadler.*

27682 BIRMINGHAM POLITICAL UNION. Address of the council of the Birmingham Political Union to all their fellow-countrymen in the United Kingdom. [Signed: Thomas Attwood, chairman, and dated, June 12, 1832.] *s.sh.fol. Birmingham*, [1832] *See note to no.* 20490.

27683 —— [*Begin.*] At a meeting of the council of the Birmingham Political Union, held...this 15th day of May, 1832, Thomas Attwood, Esq: in the chair...[A resolution to send out the Solemn Declaration in support of the Reform Bill for signatures.] *s.sh.4°.* [*Birmingham*, 1832] *See note to no.* 20490.

27684 —— [Circular, dated May 15, 1832, containing the Solemn Declaration. Signed: Benjamin Hadley, hon. sec.] [4]p. 4°. *Birmingham*, [1832] *See note to no.* 20490.

27685 —— Grand meeting on New Hall Hill, in support of reform, on...May 7, 1832. Order of the meeting. [Signed: Thomas Attwood.] *s.sh.fol. Birmingham*, [1832] *See note to no.* 20490.

27686 —— Report of the proceedings of the great meeting of the inhabitants of the Midland districts, held ...May 7, 1832; convened by the Council of the Political Union, for the purpose of petitioning the House of Lords to pass the Reform Bill. 11p. 4°. *Birmingham*, 1832. *Two copies, in which the setting of the final note differs slightly, one the copy that belonged to Thomas Attwood (see note to no.* 26519), *the other Benjamin Hadley's copy (see note to no.* 20490).

27687 —— Report of the proceedings of the public meeting of the inhabitants of Birmingham held...May 10,

1832; convened by the Council of the Political Union, for the purpose of determining what measures were necessary to be taken on the resignation of ministers. 7p. *4°. Birmingham*, 1832. *See note to no.* 26519.

27688 —— Report of the proceedings of the public meeting of the inhabitants of Birmingham held...May 16, 1832; convened by the Council of the Political Union, for the purpose of presenting an address to Earl Grey, on his re-instatement to the office of Premier. 8p. *4°. Birmingham*, 1832. *See note to no.* 26519.

27689 —— Report of the proceedings of the public meeting of the inhabitants of Birmingham, held...on... June 25, 1832; convened by the Council of the Political Union, for the purpose of expressing their opinion on the Irish Reform Bill... 7p. *4°. Birmingham*, 1832. *See note to no.* 26519.

27690 —— Report of the proceedings of the third annual general meeting...held...on Monday, July 30, 1832, to elect the Council...to consider the extreme distress of the times, and the wretched condition of Poland... 11p. *4°. Birmingham*, 1832. *See note to no.* 26519. *See also* 1830, 1831, 1833.

27691 *—— The substance of the extraordinary proceedings at the Birmingham Political Council, on...July 3, on the subject of pledges, intended to be taken from the candidates for Birmingham, Mr. Attwood's condemnation of the person proposing the same. The resolutions & petition resolved on at Dudley, on Monday last, for a just reform bill for Ireland. 8p. *8°.* [*Birmingham*, 1832] *The FWA copy that belonged to William Pare.*

27692 BOYTON, C. Speech delivered by the Rev. C. Boyton, F.T.C.D., at a meeting of the Protestant Conservative Society on...the 10th July, 1832. 23p. *8°. Dublin*, [1832] *Presentation copy from the author to M. T. Sadler.*

27693 The great **CHARTER** of 1832; comprised in the three Reform Bills. Introductory history of the progress of constitutional reform...(as published in the double Atlas newspaper of August 19th, 1832, and the following number). [With the text of the Bills.] 24p. *fol.* [*London*, 1832]

27694 CLINTON, H. P., *4th Duke of Newcastle.* An address to all classes and conditions of Englishmen. 70p. *8°.* 1832. *The copy that belonged to M. T. Sadler.*

27695 —— Third edition. 29p. *8°.* 1832.

27696 [**CONDY**, G.] Letter from the editor of the Manchester & Salford Advertiser, to Ebenezer Elliott, author of "Rhymes on the corn laws". [Attacking his political opinions.] *s.sh.fol. Manchester*, [1832] [*Br.* 532] *The Oastler copy.*

27697 Northern Division of **DERBYSHIRE.** [An account of an election meeting of Sir George Sitwell, Bart. at Chesterfield, 4 August, 1832.] *s.sh.fol. Chesterfield*, [1832] [*Br.* 546] *Sent through the post to Oastler from Chesterfield.*

27698 DETROSIER, R. Lecture on the utility of political unions, for the diffusion of sound moral & political information amongst the people...Delivered to the members of the National Political Union...March 26th, 1832. 24p. *8°.* 1832. *Presentation copy, with inscription, from the author to Peter Francis Clark.*

27699 The **DEVIL'S** menagerie of state paupers pensioners placemen sinecurists bishops &c.&c.&c.&c. No. 1. 8p. *8°. n.p.* [1832?]

27700 EDINBURGH. Report of the proceedings at the public meeting of the electors of Edinburgh, on Thursday, 2d August, 1832, and the Right Honourable James Abercromby's address on that occasion. Extracted from the New North Briton newspaper, 4th August, 1832. 16p. *8°. Edinburgh*, 1832.

27701 To the **ELECTORS** of the Borough of Leeds. [An attack on T. B. Macaulay in the form of a satirical election address signed: 'T. B. Mac All Hay'.] *s.sh.fol. Leeds*, [1832] [*Br.* 562(2)] *The Oastler copy.*

27702 To the **ELECTORS** of the Borough of Leeds. [Signed: A hater of indecency and cant. An attack on the election campaign waged by Edward Baines, in his paper the *Leeds Mercury.*] *s.sh.fol. Leeds*, [1832] [*Br.* 562(3)] *The Oastler copy.*

27703 [*Begin.*] To the **ELECTORS** of the City of Edinburgh. Requisitions...having been forwarded to... the Lord Advocate [Francis Jeffrey] and the Right Honourable James Abercromby, requesting they would permit themselves to be put in nomination for the representation of the City, the following answers have been received. [Letters of acceptance from both.] 7p. *8°.* [*Edinburgh*, 1832]

27704 (Private and confidential.) To the worthy liberal and philanthropic **ELECTORS** of Leeds. [A satirical election address, signed 'Thomas Babbington Hyena' [i.e. Macaulay.] *s.sh.fol. Leeds*, [1832] [*Br.* 562(5)] *The Oastler copy.*

27705 *Part I. **FACTS** & suggestions for the consideration of voters at the approaching election; or directions to the people for administering "Russell's purge" to the aristocracy. 8p. *8°. Birmingham & Wolverhampton*, 1832. *The FWA copy, that belonged to William Pare.*

27706 GORE, M. Reply to Sir John Walsh's pamphlet, entitled, "The present balance of parties". 76p. *8°.* 1832.

27707 —— Second edition. 76p. *8°.* 1832.

27708 HARDY, THOMAS (1752–1832). Memoir of Thomas Hardy, founder of, and secretary to, the London Corresponding Society...from its establishment, in Jan. 1792, until his arrest...May, 1794. Written by himself. [The Advertisement signed: D. Macpherson.] 127p. *8°.* 1832.

27709 *[**HOLWORTHY**, W.] What will reform do? Or a brief statement of the practical benefits of a reform in Parliament; addressed more especially to the operative classes. By Caleb Croxall, member of the University of Cambridge. 24p. *12°. Birmingham & London*, 1832. *The FWA copy, presented to William Pare by the author.*

27710 The new **HOUSE** of reform that Jack built. *s.sh.fol.* [*London*, 1832] [*Br.* 543(2)]

27711 HUDDERSFIELD election. Public entry of Joseph Wood, Esq. into Huddersfield. [An account of the adoption meeting.] ⟨From the Wakefield Journal.⟩ *s.sh.fol. Wakefield*, [1832] [*Br.* 535] *The Oastler copy.*

27712 HUNT, H. Lecture on the conduct of the Whigs, to the working classes, delivered at Lawrence Street Chapel, Birmingham, on Wednesday, October 31st, 1832. 7p. *4°. London, Birmingham, &c.*, [1832]

27713 —— Second edition. 8p. *4°. London, Birmingham, &c.*, 1832.

27714 To the **INHABITANTS** of Leeds. [An anti-Macaulay election poster.] *s.sh.fol. Leeds*, [1832] [*Br.* 562(4)] *The Oastler copy.*

For the **ISIS**...Edited by the lady of the Rotunda [E. Sharples], *see* vol. III, *Periodicals list.*

For the **LAUGHING PHILOSOPHER,** *see* vol. III, *Periodicals list.*

27715 LEEDS. Representation of Leeds. Reform celebration and electioneering movements at Leeds. (From the Leeds Intelligencer, June 21, 1832.) 8p. *4°. Leeds,* [1832] *The Oastler copy.*

27716 LEMAISTRE, J. G. How will it work? Or, conjectures as to the probable effects of "An Act of Parliament to amend the representation of the people"... passed June 7, 1832. 40p. *8°. Cheltenham & London,* 1832.

27717 LEMONTEY, P. É. Histoire de la régence et de la minorité de Louis xv, jusqu'au ministère du Cardinal de Fleury. 2 vols. *8°. Paris,* 1832.

27717A Two **LETTERS** to the Right Honourable Lord John Russell, on the classification of boroughs. 28p. *8°.* 1832.

27718 LONDON. *Court of Common Council.* A correct report of the proceedings before the Lord Mayor and Court of Common Council, in the City of London, on presenting an address from the reformers of Birmingham to the Corporation of London, also of the presentation of the freedom of the City to T. Attwood, Esq.... *s.sh.fol. Birmingham,* [1832] *See note to no.* 20490.

27719 LOYD, S. J., *Baron Overstone.* To the electors of the borough of Manchester. [Election address, July 4th, 1832. With 'Representation of Manchester' and 'Mr Loyd's address to the electors on the exchange'.] 16p. *8°.* [*Manchester,* 1832] *Loyd's own copy, formerly among his papers, for which see vol. III, MS.* 804.

27720 —— To the electors of the borough of Manchester. [Extract from his electoral address, and speech on 10 October.] 18p. *12°. n.p.* [1832] *Two copies, one the Oastler copy, the other the author's own copy, formerly among his papers, for which see vol. III, MS.* 804.

27721 John **MARSHALL'S** address to the electors of Holbeck. [A satire in verse on Marshall as a supporter of emigration schemes.] *s.sh.4°. Leeds,* [1832] [*Br.* 533] *The Oastler copy.*

27722 MAURIZE, A. Dangers de la situation actuelle de la France. Aux hommes sincères de tous les partis. 255p. *8°. Paris,* 1832. *The copy that belonged to Victor Considérant.*

27723 NATIONAL POLITICAL UNION. No. 13...Taxes on knowledge. Debate in the House of Commons, on the 15th June, 1832, on Mr. Edward Lytton Bulwer's motion "For a select committee to consider the propriety of establishing a cheap postage on newspapers and other publications." With a comment...and the article from the "Examiner" newspaper, of Sunday, 17th June, 1832. 48p. *8°. Southwark,* 1832. *The copy that belonged to M. T. Sadler.* *Another, the FWA copy, belonged to William Pare.*

27724 —— [Another issue.] 48p. *8°. Southwark* [& *London*], 1832.

27725 —— No. 15...On pledges, to be given by candidates. To the electors of the United Kingdom. [Signed: Rowland Detrosier, secretary, and dated, July 11, 1832.] 8p. *8°.* [*London,* 1832]

27726 *——* A test for candidates; or the address of the National Political Union to the electors of Great Britain and Ireland, on the choice of their representatives in the reformed Parliament. 8p. *8°.* [*London,* 1832?] *The FWA copy, that belonged to William Pare.*

27727 Mr. **OASTLER,** of Fixby-Hall, will address the electors opposite the platform after Lord Morpeth and Mr. Strickland. [A poster.] *s.sh.fol. Keighley,* [1832] [*Br.* 563(1)] *Oastler's own copy.*

27728 O'CONNELL, D. Mr. O'Connell's letter to the members of the National Political Union. 4p. *8°.* [*Manchester,* 1832] *The Oastler copy.*

27729 ORANGE ASSOCIATION. *Prince Ernest's Lodge.* Orange Institution. Report of the proceedings at Birmingham, of Prince Ernest's Lodge, 253, on the fifth of November, 1832... 36p. *8°. Birmingham & London,* [1832] *The copy that belonged to M. T. Sadler.*

27730 PAINE, T. Dissertation on first principles of government... 24p. *8°.* 1832. *For other editions, see* 1795.

27731 —— Rights of Man: being an answer to Mr. Burke's attack on the French Revolution. [With 'Rights of Man. Part II'.] 160p. *8°.* 1832. *For other editions of Part I, see* 1791; *of Part II, see* 1792.

27732 PALGRAVE, SIR F. Not published. Observations on the principles to be adopted in the establishment of new municipal corporations, together with the heads of a Bill for their future regulation and government. 71, xlvip. *8°.* 1832. *Presentation copy, with inscription, from the author to the Lord Advocate.*

27733 [**PARKES,** W.] Letter, to the rate payers of the metropolitan districts, on their adoption of the new Vestries Act; and on the passing of the English Reform Bill. By a rate payer of St. Pancras. 25p. *8°.* 1832.

For the **POLITICAL UNION REGISTER,** *see* vol. III, *Periodicals list.*

For the **POLITICAL UNIONIST,** *see* vol. III, *Periodicals list.*

27734 The **PROGRESS** of the revolutions of 1640 and 1830. 69p. *8°.* 1832.

27735 RAPIER, G. C. The constitutionalists' scheme for amending the Bill. 34p. *8°. Newcastle,* 1832. *The copy that belonged to M. T. Sadler.*

For the **REPUBLICAN AND RADICAL RE-FORMER,** *see* vol. III, *Periodicals list.*

27736 The **RIGHTS** of nations: a treatise on representative government, despotism, and reform; in which, political institutions are deduced from philosophical principles, and systematized...By the author of "The reformer's catechism," & "The people's charter." 454p. *8°.* 1832.

27737 ROPER, afterwards **ROPER-CURZON,** H. F., *Baron Teynham.* How it must work: in an address to the freeholders and electors of the United Empire. 43p. *8°.* 1832. *The copy that belonged to M. T. Sadler.*

27738 S., T. W. A treatise on government and general politics. 33p. *12°.* [1832]

27739 An excellent new **SONG,** called "Rascals ripe!" In which some account is given of a very noted character [William Cobbett]. *s.sh.fol.* [1832?] *See note to no.* 26994.

27740 STEPHEN, T. The book of the constitution, with the Reform Bills abridged. 422p. *12°. Edinburgh & London,* 1832.

27741 **T.,** F. G. A map of Society Island. Situate in the Ocean of Injustice. By F.G.T. geographer to their Majesties, the Rabble, from observations taken on the spot, with particulars descriptive of the country laid down. *s.sh.fol.* [*London*, 1832] [*Br.* 543(1)]

27742 The **TABLES** turned; a reply to a non-elector signing himself "Common-Sense", on the respective claims of the candidates for the representation of Leeds. By an elector. [Signed: Common Honesty.] 16p. *8°. Leeds*, [1832] *The Oastler copy.*

27743 [**THOMPSON,** THOMAS P.] The article on the adjustment of the House of Peers. From the Westminster Review, No. XXXI. For January, 1832. 8p. *8°.* [1832] *See note to no. 25779.*

27744 [——] The article on the prospects of reform, from the Westminster Review, No. XXXIII. For July, 1832. 15p. *8°.* 1832. *See note to no. 25779.*

27745 **TWISS,** H. Conservative reform, being outlines of a counterplan, enclosed in a letter to Lord Lyndhurst. 36p. *8°.* 1832. *Presentation copy from the author to M. T. Sadler.*

27746 **WALSH,** J. B., *Baron Ormathwaite.* On the present balance of parties in the state. 131p. *8°.* 1832. *Presentation copy from the author to Lord Henry Cholmondeley.*

27747 —— Third edition. 131p. *8°.* 1832.

27748 **WHIG GOVERNMENT,** or, two years retrospect. 39p. *8°.* 1832.

27749 **WILLIAMS,** THOMAS W. Parliamentary reform. A full and correct abstract of the Act (2 Will. IV, chap. 45) to amend the representation of the people in England and Wales. (Passed 7th June 1832)...The third edition. 48p. *8°.* 1832.

27750 **WOOD,** JOSEPH. Report of the speech of Capt. Wood, to the electors of Huddersfield, in the Court-House, on Friday evening, November thirtieth, 1832: enlarged from the report in the Halifax and Huddersfield Express of Saturday, Dec. 1st. *s.sh.fol. Halifax*, [1832] [*Br.* 549]

SOCIALISM

27751 **ASSOCIATIONFORREMOVINGTHE CAUSES OF IGNORANCE AND POVERTY BY EDUCATION AND EMPLOYMENT.** Address to all classes in the state from the Governor, Directors and Committee of the Association. [By R. Owen.] 8p. *4°. n.p.* [1832] **Another, the FWA copy, belonged to William Pare, and has his signature on the title-page.*

27752 [**BARRAULT,** P. A. C. E.] Barrière d'Italie, 15 décembre 1832. A Paris! 7p. *8°.* [*Paris*, 1832]

27753 **BAZARD,** SAINT AMAND. Religion Saint-Simonienne. Discussions morales, politiques et religieuses qui ont amené la séparation...dans le sein de la société Saint-Simonienne...Première partie... 30p. *8°. Paris*, 1832. *The copy that belonged to Victor Considérant.*

27754 **BENBOW,** W. Grand national holiday, and congress of the productive classes, &c. 15p. *8°.* [1832]

27755 ——, *and others.* Middlesex Sessions, May 16th, 1832. A correct report of the trial of Messrs. Benbow, Lovett, & Watson, as the leaders of the farce day procession. 40p. *8°.* [1832]

27756 —— The trial of William Benbow, and others [i.e. William Lovett and James Watson], at the Middlesex Sessions, May 16th, 1832, for leading the procession on the fast day, March 21st. 8p. *4°.* [*London*, 1832]

27757 **CABET,** E. Révolution de 1830, et situation présente (septembre 1832) expliquées et éclairées par les révolutions de 1789, 1792, 1799 et 1804, et par la Restauration. 389p. *8°. Paris*, 1832. *See also 1833.*

27758 [**CHEVALIER,** M.] Ménilmontant, le 23 novembre 1832. A Lyon! 8p. *8°.* [*Paris*, 1832]

27759 [——] Ménilmontant, 12 décembre 1832. [*Begin.*] Au nom de Dieu, qui veut aujourd'hui l'égalité de l'homme et de la femme...[An appeal to sympathisers to attend a meeting at the cemetery of Père-Lachaise on December 14th. Signed: Michel.] *s.sh.4°. n.p.* [1832]

27760 —— Religion Saint-Simonienne. Politique industrielle. Système de la Méditerranée...articles extrait du Globe. 56p. *8°. Paris*, 1832. *See also no.* 27761, *below.*

27761 ——, *and others.* Religion Saint-Simonienne. Politique industrielle et Système de la Méditerranée. [By M. Chevalier, S. Plechat, C. Duveyrier and H. Fournel.] 150p. *8°. Paris*, 1832.

27762 On **CO-OPERATION.** This article appeared in the Monthly Repository, July, 1832, as a review of the Report of the third Co-operative Congress, held in London, April, 1832; and other works. 8p. *8°.* [1832]

27763 **CO-OPERATIVE CONGRESS,** April 1832. Proceedings of the third Co-operative Congress; held in London...April 1832...Reported and edited, by order of the Congress, by William Carpenter. 129p. *12°.* 1832.

For **CO-OPERATIVE CONGRESS,** October 1832. Proceedings of the fourth Congress *see* vol. III, *Periodicals list*, the Lancashire & Yorkshire Co-operator, and useful classes' advocate, new series, [no. 10], 1832.

27764 **CO-OPERATIVE SONGS.** Hail the great, the glorious plan. Each for all. *s.sh.8°. Salford, Manchester*, [1832?]

27765 **CRAIG,** E. T. The co-operators' song...Tune "Hearts of oak". [*Begin.*] Fair hope's lucid beams brightly dawn on our day... *s.sh.8°. n.p.* [1832?]

For the **CRISIS,** or the change from error and misery to truth and happiness, 1832–33, *continued as* the Crisis and National Co-operative Trades Union and Equitable Labour Exchange gazette, 1833–34, *see* vol. III, *Periodicals list.*

27766 **DECOURDEMANCHE,** A. Est-ce légalement que le gouvernement a fait suspendre l'exercice du culte Saint-Simonien? Questions à poser au jury. 18p. *8°. Paris*, [1832] *The copy that belonged to Victor Considérant.*

27767 **EMPRUNT** Saint-Simonien. 16p. *8°.* [*Paris* 1832] *Reprinted from Le Globe.*

27768 [ENFANTIN, B. P.] L'attente. [A prayer.] 6p. 8°. *Angers*, [1832]

27769 [———] Le Père à Fournel, apôtre. [With 'Au Père, Fournel, apôtre'.] 4p. 8°. [*Paris*, 1832] *The copy that belonged to Victor Considérant.*

27770 [———] Religion Saint-Simonienne. Économie politique et politique. Articles extraits du Globe. Deuxième édition. 181p. 8°. *Paris*, 1832. *For another edition, see* 1831.

27771 ——— Religion Saint-Simonienne. Procès en police correctionnelle le 19 octobre, 1832. Avec le portrait du Père...et celui de H. Fournel...[With 'Parole de Henri Fournel. Parole de M. Duvergier. Note de Barthélemy Enfantin sur la condamnation de son fils. Pièces justificatives'.] 105p. 8°. *Paris*, 1832. *The copy that belonged to Victor Considérant.*

27772 ——— Religion Saint-Simonienne. La prophétie. Articles extraits du Globe. Du 19 février au 20 avril, 1832. Ménilmontant, le 1er juin, 1832. [With 'A tous. 20 avril, 1832'. Articles by Prosper Enfantin, Charles Duveyrier, Gustave d'Eichthal, Michel Chevalier and Emile Barrault.] 114p. 8°. *Paris*, [1832]

27773 [———] Religion Saint-Simonienne. Réunion générale de la famille. Séances des 19 et 21 novembre 1831. Enseignemens faits par le Père Suprême...[With 'Note sur le mariage et le divorce...par le Père Rodrigues'.] 154p. 8°. *Paris*, 1832. *The copy that belonged to Victor Considérant.*

27774 [———] [Another edition.] Religion Saint-Simonienne, morale, réunion générale...Enseignemens du Père Suprême. Les trois familles. [By Emile Barrault.] [With 'Note sur le mariage et le divorce...par le Père Rodrigues'.] 207p. 8°. *Paris*, 1832. *The copy that belonged to Victor Considérant. For another edition, see* 1831.

27775 [———] Retraite de Ménilmontant. 6 juin, 1832. 12p. 8°. [*Paris*, 1832] *The copy that belonged to Victor Considérant.*

27776 ——— and others. Religion Saint-Simonienne. A tous. 33p. 8°. *Paris*, 1832. *Articles extracted from Le Globe, signed by Prosper Enfantin, Michel Chevalier, Emile Barrault and Charles Duveyrier.*

27777 ——— Religion Saint-Simonienne. Procès en la Cour d'assises de la Seine, les 27 et 28 août, 1832. [With 'Pièces justificatives'. Defendants: Prosper Enfantin, Michel Chevalier, Emile Barrault, Charles Duveyrier, Olinde Rodrigues.] 405p. 8°. *Paris*, 1832. *The copy that belonged to Victor Considérant.*

27778 EQUITABLE LABOUR EXCHANGE. Rules and regulations of the Equitable Labour Exchange, Gray's Inn Road, London. For the purpose of relieving the productive classes from poverty, by their own industry, and for the mutual exchange of labour for equal value of labour. Established 1832. 12p. *12°*. 1832.

27779 Published by a few friends of truth and common sense. To the members of co-operative societies and others. **EXCHANGE** of labour. Objections, &c. [An Owenite tract.] 2p. *s.sh.8°*. [*London*, 1832 ?] [*Br*. 542(7)] *The copy that belonged to Francis Place.*

For la **FEMME LIBRE,** *see vol.* III, *Periodicals list.*

27780 [FEUILLES populaires.] 79 leaflets. 8°. [*Paris*, 1832.] *A collection of Saint-Simonian leaflets, generally called Feuilles populaires, although the name does not appear on any of them. The leaflets were issued between* March and June 1832. *The set that belonged to Victor Considérant.*

27781 H. Published by a few friends of truth and common sense. A fable for the times. Addressed to the working classes. [An Owenite tract, with a footnote signed: K., i.e. William King, of Charlotte Street, London.] 2p. *s.sh.8°*. [*London*, 1832] [*Br*. 542(11)] *The copy that belonged to Francis Place.*

27782 Angers, 19 août 1832...[*Begin*.] Mon cher **HAWKE**...[A letter in defence of Saint-Simonism.] 4p. 8°. *Angers*, [1832]

27783 [HODGSKIN, T.] The natural and artificial right of property contrasted. A series of letters [signed: a labourer], addressed...to H. Brougham, Esq. M.P....by the author of "Labour defended against the claims of capital." 188p. 8°. 1832. *With a manuscript inscription: Dr. Birkbeck with the authors respects.*

27784 LECHEVALIER SAINT ANDRÉ, L. J. Extrait de la Revue de Paris. Résumé du système social de M. Charles Fourier. 20p. 8°. [*Paris*, 1832 ?]

27785 ——— Leçons sur l'art d'associer les individus et les masses...en travaux d'industrie, – science et beaux-arts. Exposition du système social de Charles Fourier, de Besançon...Ces leçons s'adressent spécialement aux personnes qui sont occupées, du saint-simonisme. 362p. 8°. *Paris*, 1832. *The copy that belonged to Victor Considérant.*

27786 LEE, R. E. Victimization, or, Benbowism unmasked. Addressed to the National Union of the Working Classes. 8p. 8°. [*London*, 1832]

27787 LEMONNIER, C. Les Saint-Simoniens!!! 4p. *4°*. [*Paris*, 1832]

27788 ——— [Another edition.] 6p. 8°. [*Paris*, 1832] *The copy that belonged to Victor Considérant.*

27789 M. Irresponsibility, a New-Year's gift for 1832. [An Owenite leaflet.] *s.sh.8°*. [*London*, 1832] [*Br*. 542(12)] *Two copies that belonged to Francis Place.*

27790 *MACCONNELL, T. The signs of the times. A lecture on the signs of the times: delivered in...Robert Owen's Institution...on...November 18, 1832. Printed ...from the recollections of Thomas Macconnell, Esq. lecturer. 14p. 8°. [*London*,] 1832. *The FWA copy that belonged to William Pare.*

27791 MÉNILMONTANT. Mort de Talabot, apôtre. 24p. 8°. [*Paris*, 1832] *The copy that belonged to Victor Considérant.*

27792 [MUIRON, J.] Les nouvelles transactions sociales, religieuses et scientifiques de Virtomnius. Tome 1. 208p. 8°. *Paris*, 1832. *The copy that belonged to Victor Considérant.*

27793 OWEN, ROBERT. Report to the county of Lanark, of a plan for relieving public distress and removing discontent, by giving permanent, productive employment to the poor & working classes... 75p. 8°. 1832. **Another, the FWA copy, belonged to William Pare. For another edition, see* 1821.

27794 ——— Robert Owen's reply to the question "What would you do, if you were Prime Minister of England?" ...Second edition. 12p. *12°*. *Stockport*, [1832 ?]

27795 PEREIRE, JULES. Religion Saint-Simonienne. Leçons sur l'industrie et les finances, prononcées à la salle de L'Athénée...suivies d'un projet de banque. 105p. *8⁰*. *8⁰. Paris, 1832. The 'Projet de banque' was by Jules and Emile Pereire. The copy that belonged to Victor Considérant.*

For le **PHALANSTÈRE,** *1832, continued as* la réforme industrielle, *1832–34, continued as* la Phalange, *1836–40, 1845–49, see vol.* III, *Periodicals list,* la Phalange.

27796 *****PRODUCTION** the cause of demand, being a brief analysis of a work entitled "The social system : – a treatise on the principle of exchange," – by John Gray... With a short illustration of the principles of equitable labour exchange. 8p. *8⁰. Birmingham, 1832. The FWA copy that belonged to William Pare.*

For the **RATIONAL REFORMER,** *see vol.* III, *Periodicals list.*

27797 **RELIGION** Saint-Simonienne. Enseignement des ouvriers. Séance du dimanche 25 décembre, 1831. 26p. *8⁰. Paris, 1832. The copy that belonged to Victor Considérant.*

27798 **RELIGION** Saint-Simonienne. Poursuites dirigées contre notre Père Suprême Enfantin, et contre notre Père Olinde Rodrigues. 40p. *8⁰. [Paris, 1832]*

27799 **RELIGION** Saint-Simonienne. Recueil de prédications. 2 vols. *8⁰. Paris, 1832. By E. Barrault, P. M. Laurent, A. Transon, M. Retournet, J. Reynaud, E. Charton, O. Rodrigues. Edited by E. Barrault.*

27800 **REMARKS** on the rational system, as developed by Robert Owen, Esq., and on the prospects of society, in reference to its introduction into practice...By a co-operator. 12p. *12⁰. 1832.*

27801 **REPORT** of the Committee appointed by a public meeting, held on the 24th September, 1832, at the Equitable Labour Exchange, Gray's-Inn Road; for the purpose of taking into consideration the increasing distress of the non-productive and industrious classes, and to devise efficient means for their permanent relief. 7p. *8⁰. 1832.*

27802 **RETRAITE** de Ménilmontant. [An account of the return of Prosper Enfantin to the Famille Saint-Simonienne at Ménilmontant.] 18p. *8⁰. [Paris, 1832] The copy that belonged to Victor Considérant.*

27803 **RETRAITE** de Ménilmontant. Cérémonie du dimanche 1er juillet, et récit de ce qui s'est passé les jours suivans. Ouverture des travaux du temple. 27p. *8⁰. [Paris, 1832] The copy that belonged to Victor Considérant.*

27804 **ROSSER,** C. Thoughts on the progress and prospects of man, and on the new era of society...(Third edition.) First lecture. 8p. *8⁰. [London, 1832 ?]*

27805 **ROUSSEAU,** A. Ménilmontant. Le peuple. Chanson religieuse. *s.sh.4⁰. n.p. [1832]*

27806 **SAINT-SIMON,** C. H. DE, *Comte.* Catéchisme politique des industriels. 1824. Vues sur la propriété et la législation. 1818. Seconde livraison. 364p. *8⁰. Paris, 1832. For another edition of the* Catéchisme, *see* 1823.

27807 —— Saint-Simon. Son premier écrit; Lettres d'un habitant de Genève à ses contemporains, 1802; sa Parabole politique, 1819; Le nouveau Christianisme, 1825; précédés de fragmens de l'Histoire de sa vie écrite par lui-même; publiés par Olinde Rodrigues... xxxviii, 201p. *8⁰. Paris, 1832. Another copy, wanting p. 81–201,* Le Nouveau christianisme, *belonged to Victor Considérant.*

27808 —— Nouveau Christianisme. Lettres d'Eugène Rodrigues sur la religion et la politique. L'éducation du genre humain, de Lessing, traduit, pour la première fois, de l'allemand par Eugène Rodrigues. 346p. *8⁰. Paris, 1832. The copy that belonged to Victor Considérant. For other editions of Saint-Simon, see 1825. For another edition of Rodrigues and Lessing, see 1831.*

27809 *****SARGEANT,** E. L. Co-operation, a poem. 27p. *8⁰. 1832. The FWA copy that belonged to William Pare.*

27810 **TABLE TALK** on the state of society, – competition and co-operation, – labour and capital, – morals and religion. 16p. *8⁰. Birmingham, 1832.*

27811 **THIMBLEBY,** J. Monadelphia; or, the formation of a new system of society, without the intervention of a circulating medium. 76p. *12⁰. Barnet & London, 1832.*

27812 **TRANSON,** A. L. E. Religion Saint-Simonienne. Affranchissement des femmes. Prédication du 1er janvier, 1832. 10p. *8⁰. Paris, 1832. The copy that belonged to Victor Considérant.*

27813 —— Simple écrit d'Abel Transon aux Saint-Simoniens. 32p. *8⁰. Paris, 1832. The copy that belonged to Victor Considérant.*

27814 —— Théorie sociétaire de Charles Fourier, ou art d'établir en tout pays des associations domestiques-agricoles de quatre à cinq cents familles. Exposition succincte par Abel Transon. 60p. *8⁰. Paris, 1832. Reprinted from La Revue Encyclopédique. The copy that belonged to Victor Considérant. See also 1841.*

27815 **WARDEN,** B. Rewards of industry. The labour exchange the only true way to wealth for the working classes. 4p. *8⁰. [London, 1832 ?]*

27816 **WAYLAND,** T. National advancement and happiness considered in reference to the equalization of property, and the formation of communities. 48p. *8⁰. 1832.*

MISCELLANEOUS

27817 **BENTHAM,** J. Lord Brougham displayed: including I. Boa constrictor, alias Helluo curiarum; II. Observations on the Bankruptcy Court Bill...III. Extracts from proposed constitutional code. [With 'Boa constrictor alias Helluo curiarum. Speech of Lord Chancellor Brougham as printed in the Morning Chronicle...Sept. 2nd, 1831'.] 24, 24, 4p. *s.sh. 1l., fol. & 8⁰. 1832.*

27818 **GRENVILLE,** G. N. T., *Baron Nugent.* A letter to John Murray, Esq....touching an article [by

R. Southey] in the last Quarterly Review, on a book called "Some memorials of Hampden, his party and his times." 6[16]p. *8⁰. 1832.*

27819 **MACERONI,** F. Reply to a pretended review, in the United Services Journal for May, 1832, on Colonel Macerone's work entitled "Defensive instructions for the people"... 16p. *8⁰. 1832.*

27820 **MORTIMER,** THOMAS (*fl.* 1832). The

unpaid; being a brief exposition of the abuses arising from the employment of an unpaid magistracy, together with an effectual and economical remedy; a letter to Lord John Russell. 15p. *8°*. [1832]

27821 *[PLACE, F.] Anatomy. Proceedings at the National Political Union, respecting legislative interference in the study of anatomy, and the supply of bodies for anatomical research. [A discussion of Mr. Warburton's

Bill.] Not for sale. 24p. *8°*. [*London,*] 1832. *The FWA copy, that belonged to William Pare.*

27822 [WARD, JOHN (1781–1837).] The first part, price one penny, of the most important discovery ever made known to mankind. By an imprisoned reformer. Wherein it is clearly shewn that all people are entirely freed from every charge of sin whatever... 8p. *8°*. *Birmingham,* [1832 ?]

1833

GENERAL

27823 [ADAMS, WILLIAM B.] The producing man's companion; an essay on the present state of society...in England: with the best means of providing for the poor and...operatives who may be suddenly thrown out of their regular employments by the substitution of new inventions. By Junius Redivivus...Second edition, with additions. 238p. *12°*. 1833. *For another edition, see* The rights of morality, 1832.

27824 ATKINSON, WILLIAM (*fl.* 1832–1833). To the Honourable the Commons of the United Kingdom of Great Britain and Ireland in Parliament assembled. The humble petition of William Atkinson, of Leeds...mill owner...[In favour of home colonization as a remedy for agricultural distress and the economic difficulties of the nation.] [4]p. *fol. n.p.* [1833] *The Oastler copy.*

27825 BARCLAY, C., *ed.* Letters from the Dorking emigrants, who went to Upper Canada, in the spring of 1832. 44p. *8°*. *London & Dorking,* 1833.

27826 BOSWELL, E. The civil division of the county of Dorset, methodically digested and arranged, comprizing lists of the civil ministerial officers, magistrates ...with a complete nomina villarum...a list of bridges; together with the annual value of real property...the land-tax...poor's rate...population...Also, an appendix, containing abstracts of returns of charitable donations ...The second edition... 192, 98p. *8°*. *Dorchester,* 1833.

27827 BOWES, J. The right use of money, scripturally stated, or an answer to the question, "Ought Christians to save money?" A sermon preached in...Dundee ...17th February, 1833. 28p. *12°*. *Dundee, London, &c.,* 1833. *Bound in a volume with other separately published pamphlets, bearing a printed label, 'J. Bowes's Works. Vol. IV. Price 2s. 6d.'. One of the other pamphlets has a printed note: 'John Bowes, Works, 4 vols., cloth, price 10s. 6d., may be had from Houlston & Stoneman, London'.*

27828 The BRITISH ALMANAC of the Society for the Diffusion of Useful Knowledge, for...1833. [With 'The companion to the Almanac; or year-book of general information'.] 72, 256p. *12°*. [1833] *For other editions, see* 1828.

27829 BULL, JOHN, *pseud.* A scheme for a general taxation on property, income, and trade [in two letters to Lord Althorp]...To which is added, a proposal...on the subject of the abolition of negro slavery; with a plan for carrying that object into effect... 21p. *8°*. [1833] *The copy that belonged to Earl De Grey.*

27830 [CAREY, M.] Second edition corrected, March

7, 1833. Prospects beyond the Rubicon. Second series. No. I[–II. Signed: Hamilton.] 6p. *8°*. *n.p.* [1833] *For the first series see* 1830.

27831 [——] Supplement to the Gazette of the United States. Prospects beyond the Rubicon. [Nos. VI–VIII. Signed: Hamilton.] 8p. *8°*. *n.p.* [1833]

27832 COBBETT, W. Cobbett's tour in Scotland; and in the four northern counties of England in the autumn of the year 1832. 264p. *12°*. 1833.

27833 [COLTON, C.] The Americans. By an American in London. 389p. *12°*. 1833.

For the **COMPANION TO THE NEWSPAPER,** 1833–37, *see* vol. III, *Periodicals list.*

27834 CROSS, M., *ed.* Selections from the Edinburgh Review; comprising the best articles in that journal...to the present time...Vol. IV. [Containing articles on political economy, politics, etc.] 679p. *8°*. 1833.

27835 DICKSON, WILLIAM (1799–1875). Northumberland. The wards, divisions, parishes, and townships of Northumberland, according to the ancient and modern divisions, shewing the annual value and population of each parish and township, maintaining its own poor, from the returns of 1831; also the places for which surveyors of highways and constables are appointed... 104p. *4°*. *Alnwick,* 1833.

27836 Public ECONOMY concentrated; or, a connected view of currency, agriculture, and manufactures. By an enquirer into first principles. 95p. *8°*. *Carlisle, London, &c.,* 1833.

27837 ELLIOTT, E. The splendid village, corn law rhymes and other poems. [Being volume I of a collected edition of the poems of Ebenezer Elliott. With 'The village patriarch, Love and other poems' and 'Kerhonah, The vernal walk, The Win Hill and other poems'.] 3 vols. *12°*. 1833–35. *See also* 1840.

27838 ELLIS, SIR HENRY (1771–1869). A general introduction to Domesday Book; accompanied by indexes of the tenants in chief, and under tenants, at the time of the survey: as well as of the holders of lands mentioned in Domesday anterior to the formation of that record; with an abstract of the formation of that record; with an abstract of the population of England at the close of the reign of William the Conqueror... 2 vols. *8°*. *Record Commission,* 1833. *For editions of Domesday Book, see* 1783.

27839 ENGLAND. *Commissioners appointed to Report ...upon the Boundaries...of certain Boroughs and Cor-*

porate Towns in England and Wales. Investigation, by His Majesty's Commissioners, into the state of the Borough of Gateshead, the 8th and 9th Nov, 1833; also the memorial of the inhabitants for a new charter, and the statement of the grievances sustained by Gateshead from the corporate power of Newcastle, as presented to the Secretary of State and Commissioners of Inquiry. 28p. *8°. Gateshead, 1833.*

27840 —— —— Report of the inquiry by the Government Commissioners, into the existing state of the Corporation of York...22nd, 23rd, and 25th...of November, 1833. Extracted from the York Herald. With an index. Also an appendix, containing a brief notice of the Merchants' Company, and the Merchant Tailors' Company. Together with a list of the charters of the Corporation. 83p. *12°. York,* [1833]

27841 **EVANS,** EYRE. The evils which afflict Ireland referred to primogeniture, the laws of entail, and the legislative Union of that country with England. 40p. *8°. Liverpool & London,* 1833.

For the **EXAMINER,** *and journal of political economy, 1833–35, see vol.* III, *Periodicals list.*

27842 [**FANSHAWE,** C. M.] Speech of the member for Odium. [A satire in verse on William Cobbett.] 3p. *8°.* [*London,* 1833] *The Sheffield copy.*

27843 **FIDLER,** I. Observations on professions, literature, manners, and emigration, in the United States and Canada, made during a residence there in 1832. 434p. *12°.* 1833.

For **FIGARO IN LONDON,** *see vol.* III, *Periodicals list.*

27844 **FLOREZ ESTRADA,** A. Cours éclectique d'économie politique, écrit en espagnol...et traduit sur les manuscrits originaux...par L. Galibert...3 vols. *8°. Paris & Londres,* 1833. *For another edition, see* 1828.

27845 **FLURY,** L. N. De la richesse. Sa définition, et sa génération, ou notion primordiale de l'économie politique. 275p. *8°. Paris & Versailles,* 1833.

27846 **GLADSTONE,** SIR J., *Bart.* Mercator's reply to Mr. Booth's pamphlet on free trade, as published in the Liverpool Standard [in a series of letters during February 1833]. To which are added, two letters on the currency question, and one on taxation. 52p. *8°. Liverpool & London,* 1833. *Presentation copy, with inscription, from the author to T. Spring Rice, Baron Monteagle.*

27847 **GORTON,** J. G. Population of Great Britain, according to the returns made to Parliament in 1831; together with the annual value of real property as assessed in 1815...Second edition, with an analysis and statistic tables... 109, 88p. *8°.* 1833. *For another edition, see* 1832.

27848 *****HIGGINS,** G. Address to the electors and others of the West-Riding of the county of York: second edition, with notes: and an appendix on the fund and corn laws. 36p. *8°. Doncaster & London,* 1833. *The FWA copy that belonged to William Pare. The Goldsmiths' Library copy lacks the title-page.*

27849 *—— Second letter...to the manufacturers and farmers of the [West] Riding, and particularly to the political unions of Leeds, Halifax, Huddersfield... 7p. *8°. Hackney,* [1833] *The FWA copy that belonged to William Pare.*

27850 An **INVESTIGATION** into the causes of the present distress; as arising from taxation, free trade, or currency. 31p. *8°.* 1833.

27851 **JONES,** RICHARD (1790–1855). An introductory lecture on political economy, delivered at King's College, London, 27th February, 1833. To which is added a syllabus of a course of lectures on the wages of labor, to be delivered at King's College...in...April, 1833. 64p. *8°.* 1833.

27852 —— Syllabus of a course of lectures on the wages of labor, proposed to be delivered at King's College, London. 24p. *8°.* 1833.

27853 **JORDAO,** J. L. Elementos de riqueza publica ...Segunda ediçao. 343p. *8°. Lisboa,* 1833.

27854 **JULLIEN,** M. A. Lettre à la nation anglaise, sur l'union des peuples et la civilisation comparée; sur l'instrument économique du tems, appelé biomètre, ou montre morale; suivie de quelques poésies... 50p. *8°. Londres,* 1833.

27855 A **LETTER** of appeal to the members of the first reformed House of Commons, on behalf of the working classes of the United Kingdom. By one of their own order. [On remedies for unemployment and general distress.] 22p. *8°.* 1833.

27856 **LLWYD,** A. A history of the island of Mona, or Anglesey; including an account of its natural productions, druidical antiquities, lives of eminent men, the customs of the court of the antient Welsh princes, &c. Being the prize essay...at the Royal Beaumaris Eisteddfod, held in the month of August, 1832. [With 'A brief sketch of the Royal Eisteddfod...Selected from the Bangor and Chester papers'.] 413, 61p. *4°. Ruthin, London, &c.,* 1833.

27857 **LONDON.** Livery Companies. *Drapers.* Report of the deputation, who in pursuance of a resolution of the Court of Assistants...of the 12th July, 1832, visited the estates of the Company, in the county of Londonderry... Ordered...to be printed... 38p. *4°.* 1833. *See also,* 1818, 1829.

27858 **MacDONNELL,** E. Repeal of the Union. Letter of Eneas MacDonnell, Esq. to the editor of the "Mayo Telegraph," in opposition to that measure; illustrating its impracticability, and the injurious results and tendency of its agitation in Ireland... 15p. *8°. Chelsea,* 1833.

27859 [**MARCET,** J.] John Hopkins's notions on political economy. By the author of "Conversations on Chemistry, Political Economy," &c.&c. 188p. *8°.* 1833.

27860 —— Second edition. 168p. *12°.* 1833. *See also* 1834.

27861 **MARSHALL,** JOHN (1783–1841). A digest of all the accounts diffused through more than 600 volumes of journals, reports, and papers, presented to Parliament since 1799. In four parts... 192, 208, 258p. *4°.* 1833–[35]. *Part IV was reissued with additions in 1838 (q.v.* POPULATION).

27862 —— A digest of all the accounts relating to the population, productions, revenues, financial operations, manufactures, shipping, colonies, commerce...of the United Kingdom of Great Britain and Ireland, diffused through more than 600 volumes of journals, reports, and papers, presented to Parliament during the last thirty-five years. In two parts... 92, 238p. *4°.* 1833. *The copy given to Richard Cobden by James Smith, with an inscription.*

27863 MARTIN, ROBERT M. Ireland, as it was, – is, – and ought to be; with a comparative statistical chart ...of each county. 174p. 8°. 1833.

27864 MATSON, J. The catechism to be learned by a Member of Parliament, in order that he may introduce proper measures on taxation, tithe, poor laws, free trade, emigration, machinery and currency. 42p. 8°. 1833.

27865 MURAT, N. A., *Prince.* A moral and political sketch of the United States of North America...With a note on negro slavery by Junius Redivivus [William Bridges Adams]. 402p. *12°. London, Dublin, &c.,* 1833.

27866 [OGILVIE, H.] Suggestions for the improvement of the domestic policy of the British Government. 119p. 8°. 1833.

27867 PEBRER, A. P. Taxation, revenue, expenditure, power, statistics and debt of the whole British Empire; their origin, progress and present state. With an estimate of the capital and resources of the Empire, and a practical plan for applying them to the liquidation of the National Debt... 547p. 8°. 1833. *See also* 1834.

27868 REFLECTIONS on the domestic and foreign policy of Great Britain since the war. By a British merchant long resident abroad. [Dated: Edinburgh, January 1833.] 236p. 8°. 1833.

27869 REID, WILLIAM, *political economist.* An inquiry into the causes of the present distress: with an attempt to explain the theory of national wealth. 34p. *8°. Edinburgh & London,* 1833.

27870 A few **REMARKS** on the present state of Ireland, sufficient to set others thinking. 16p. 8°. 1833.

For le **RÉPUBLICAIN,** journal d'observation des sciences sociales et revue politique, *see* vol. III, *Periodicals list.*

27871 [RICHARDS, JAMES.] A letter addressed to the late Earl of Liverpool, in the year 1822, shewing that unjust taxation is the cause of the evils complained of; with a just system then suggested. To which is now added, preliminary observations. 69p. 8°. 1833. *The copy that belonged to Earl De Grey. For other editions, see* 1822.

27872 ROBERT, A. Atlas historique et statistique de la Révolution Française, contenant la série chronologique des événemens politiques, militaires, et scientifiques depuis la première Assemblée des Notables jusqu'à l'an 1833... [10]p., 15 tables. *fol. Paris,* 1833.

27873 ROBSON, W. Robson's London directory, street key, and conveyance list...also a list of coaches, waggons, vans...coasting vessels, steam packets and inland navigation...for 1834. The fourteenth edition. 576p. 8°. [1833]

27874 RUBICHON, M. Du mécanisme de la société en France et en Angleterre. 451p. *8°. Paris,* 1833.

27875 SAY, J. B. Mélanges et correspondence d'économie politique, ouvrage posthume de J.-B. Say; publié par Charles Comte, son gendre. 472p. *8°. Paris,* 1833. *A second copy, with an error in pagination corrected, has HSF's note in the volume recording that the wrapper was dated 1844. The same sheets were issued in 1833 as a supplementary volume to the author's* Cours complet d'économie politique pratique, *for which see* 1828.

27876 SCOTT, JOHN (1777–1834). The character, principles, and public services of the late William Wilberforce: including notices of his early life. A discourse delivered in the church of...Holy Trinity, Hull, on... August 7, 1833. 40p. 8°. 1833.

27877 SCROPE, G. P. Principles of political economy, deduced from the natural laws of social welfare, and applied to the present state of Britain. 457p. 8°. 1833.

27878 SKIRVING, J. A comparative view of the situation of Great Britain, from the conclusion of the American war in 1783, to the year 1832, with a glance at its future prospects. 170[136]p. *12°. Elgin,* 1833.

27879 STATE RIGHTS AND FREE TRADE ASSOCIATION. The state rights and free trade almanac for the year of our Lord 1833, containing the usual astronomical calculations, and local information; together with moral and political maxims and extracts... [72]p. *12°. Charleston,* 1833.

27880 The **STRANGERS'** guide to the islands of Guernsey and Jersey; embracing a brief history of their situation, extent, population, laws, customs...Together with a complete commercial directory of both islands; coins, weights, measures, &c. 145, 130p. *12°. Guernsey,* 1833.

27881 *STUART, JAMES, *younger, of Dunearn.* Three years in North America. 2 vols. *12°. Edinburgh & London,* 1833. *The copy that belonged to George Grote.*

27882 URBAIN, C. N. N. Introduction à l'étude de l'économie politique. 259[258]p. *8°. Paris, Leipzig, &c.,* 1833.

27883 URQUHART, D. Turkey and its resources: its municipal organization and free trade; the state and prospects of English commerce in the east, the new administration of Greece, its revenue and national possessions. 328p. 8°. 1833.

27884 A practical **VIEW** of the amendments needful in the existing weights and measures of the United Kingdom. (Being an article from No. 31 of the Westminster Review.) 30p. *8°. Glasgow & Edinburgh,* 1833.

27885 VINTON, S. F. Speech of Mr. Vinton, of Ohio, on the Tariff Bill. Delivered in the House of Representatives, on the 24th of January, 1833. 16p. *8°. Washington,* 1833.

27886 VIVIAN, RICHARD H., *Baron Vivian.* Opinions on tithes, and on the state of Ireland, expressed, at different times, in the House of Commons, by Sir Hussey Vivian. 53p. 8°. 1833.

27887 VOLCKMAN, J. The house tax defended, and the cause of the working classes advocated; with general observations on taxation & political economy... 28p. 8°. 1833.

27888 —— Second edition; with much additional matter relative to machinery... 24p. 8°. 1833.

27889 VOLNEY, C. F. DE, *Comte.* The law of nature, or principles of morality, deduced from the physical constitution of mankind and the universe. Translated from the French... 40p. 12°. 1833.

27890 [WAKEFIELD, EDWARD G.] England and America. A comparison of the social and political state of both nations... 2 vols. 8°. 1833. *See also* 1834.

27891 WILLIAMS, CHARLES W. Observations on

the inland navigation of Ireland and the want of employ- ment for its population, with a description of the River Shannon...Second edition, comprising an examination of the application of money grants in aid of public works. 108p. 8°. *London, Dublin, &c.*, 1833. *For another edition, see 1831.*

AGRICULTURE

27892 ABBOTT, G. An essay on the mines of England; their importance as a source of national wealth, and as a channel for the advantageous employment of private capital. 227p. 8°. 1833.

27893 ALLEN, WILLIAM (1770–1843). Ueber Ackerbau-Kolonien...Nach der handschriftlichen Mit- theilung des Verfassers aus dem Englischen übersetzt und als Manuscript gedruckt. 62p. 8°. *München*, 1833. *A translation, with an introduction by the translator, C. T. Kleinschrod, of* Colonies at home, *first published in 1827. The copy presented to the author by the translator, with an inscription in English, dated: 15 Mai 1835. For other editions, see 1827.*

27894 —— A plan for diminishing the poor's rates in agricultural districts. Being a brief account of the objects and plans pursued upon "Gravely Estate" in the parish of Lindfield, in Sussex, by John Smith, M.P. and Wm. Allen, for bettering the condition of the agricultural poor ...[With 'Appendix: Hints to a cottager for the manage- ment of his garden, from "Richard Macready, the farmer lad"'.] 28p. 8°. 1833.

27895 ARRIVABENE, G., *Conte.* Lettre sur les colonies agricoles de la Belgique. 8p. *n.p.* [1833]

27896 BALD, R. Treatise on the mining of coal and the conducting of collieries. [An extract, being the article 'Mine', from the Encyclopædia Britannica, 6th edition, 1833.] p.314–378. 4°. [*London*, 1833] *Preceded by a manuscript title-page, incorporating a presentation inscrip- tion from the author to Robert Dundas of Arniston.*

27897 The **CASE** of the lessees of the Kennington property, held under the constitution of the Duchy of Cornwall. [For the renewal of their leases. With Mr. Sydney Taylor's opinion on the case, dated: December 3rd 1833.] 12p. 8°. *n.p.* [1833]

27898 H., J. W. Brief remarks on small farms, and cottagers' spade husbandry; addressed to landlords, and to the whole of the agricultural community. To which are added, by way of appendix, two letters [signed: J.W.H.] connected with the same subject, and written by the same author... 31p. 8°. *Bedford*, 1833. *The copy that belonged to William Allen.*

27899 [**HICKEY**, W.] Hints originally intended for the small farmers of the County of Wexford; but suited to the circumstances of most parts of Ireland. By Martin Doyle. Published at the...desire of the North and South Wexford Agricultural Associations. New edition. 118p. *12°. Dublin, London, &c.*, 1833. *For another edition, see no.* 26150.

27900 HINCHLIFFE, H. J. Proposal of a method for abridging conveyances, and of an Act for registering titles to real property. 104p. 8°. 1833.

27901 [**HORNE**, THOMAS H.] The complete grazier; or farmer's and cattle breeder's and dealer's assistant... By a Lincolnshire grazier...Sixth edition, revised, cor- rected, and greatly improved. 622p. 8°. *London, Dublin, &c.*, 1833. *For other editions, see 1805.*

27902 JACKSON, JAMES. Essays on various agricul- tural subjects, and an account of the Parish of Penicuik, for which the Highland Society of Scotland awarded premiums, in 1823–25–26–27–29–30. 354p. 8°. *Edinburgh*, 1833.

27903 OBSERVATIONS on the proposed measure for the commutation of tithes. 10p. 8°. *Royston*, 1833.

27904 PORTER, G. R. The tropical agriculturist: a practical treatise on the cultivation and management of various productions suited to tropical climates. 429p. 8°. 1833.

27905 SCOBELL, G. T. The progress and effects of field gardens to the labouring poor. Read before the Bath and West of England Agricultural Society...Dec. 10, 1833. 8p. 8°. *Bath*, 1833.

27906 SHAW, J. H. Local registry of deeds. A speech delivered at a meeting of solicitors held at Wakefield, on ...May 31, 1833. 34p. 8°. 1833.

27907 SOPWITH, T. An account of the mining districts of Alston Moor, Weardale, and Teesdale, in Cumberland and Durham; comprising descriptive sketches of the scenery, antiquities, geology, and mining operations, in the upper dales of the rivers Tyne, Wear, and Tees. 183p. *12°. Alnwick*, 1833.

27908 SPAIN. *Laws, etc.* Reales ordenanzas para la direccion, rejimen y gobierno del importante Cuerpo de la Minería de Nueva-España, y de su real Tribunal Jeneral. De orden de su majestad. Impresa...1783. [With 'Real orden de 8 de diciembre de 1785...'.] 108, 36, xxxiiip. *fol. Santiago*, 1833. *Edited by M. Carvallo. For other editions, see 1783.*

27909 *STRICKLAND, afterwards CHOLM- LEY*, SIR G., *Bart.* An alarm on the rights of the poor, and the property of the rich, in danger, from a supposed law reform [referring to four Bills before the House of Commons for the limitation of actions relating to real property, for altering the law of inheritance, of the curtesy of England, and of dower]...Second edition. 32p. 8°. 1833. *The copy that belonged to George Grote.*

27910 —— Third edition. 32p. 8°. 1833.

27911 —— Fourth edition. 32p. 8°. 1833.

For **TIDSKRIFT FÖR HÄSTVÄNNER OCH LANDTMÄN**, utgifven af Alexis Noring, 1833–34, *see* vol. III, *Periodicals list.*

CORN LAWS

27912 BARTON, J. An inquiry into the expediency of the existing restrictions on the importation of foreign corn: with observations on the present social and political prospects of Great Britain. 128p. *8°. 1833.*

27913 *COGHLAN, F. A letter to the farmers of England on the tendency of the corn laws. [With an appendix.] 12, [4]p. *8°. 1833. The FWA copy that belonged to William Pare.*

27914 A COMPENDIUM of the laws, passed...for regulating and restricting the importation, exportation, and consumption of foreign corn, from the year 1660. And a series of accounts...showing the operation of the several Statutes, the average prices of corn, &c.&c. Presenting a complete view of the corn trade of Great Britain... brought down to the present time. 71p. *8°. 1833. A compilation sometimes attributed to Sir James Graham. For other editions, see 1826.*

27915 A FORM of a petition to the Upper House, against any alterations of the corn law, recommended to the general adoption of the country at large, but more especially to agriculturists, farmers, labourers... 24p. *8°. 1833. See also 1834.*

27916 MONCK, C. A. An address to the agricultural classes of Great Britain, on the evils which are the consequence of restricting the importation of foreign corn. 60p. *8°. 1833.*

27917 MUNDELL, A. The operation of the corn laws during the last sixty years, stated in the shape of substantive propositions. 19p. *8°. 1833.*

27918 OSWALD, R. A. Remarks on the corn laws, and some of those institutions which affect the interests of society, and particularly of the working classes, in their consideration. 24p. *8°. 1833.*

27919 PARKER, George. Letter to Viscount Milton, containing remarks on his lordship's Address to the landowners of England on the corn laws. 39p. *8°. Doncaster, 1833.*

27920 SHEPPARD, J. Hints to the landlord and tenant; being a review of the present averages & showing their fallacy, with a plan for an alteration in the mode of taking the graduated scale of duties, and remarks upon Lord Milton's letter...Second edition. 31p. *8°. Doncaster, 1833.*

27921 THOMPSON, Thomas P. Catechism on the corn laws; with a list of fallacies and the answers. Seventeenth edition. Stereotype...To which is added the article on free trade, from the Westminster Review, no. XXIII. with the article on the silk and glove trades, from no. XXXII...By a member of the University of Cambridge. 92p. *8°. 1833. For other editions, see 1827.*

27922 WESTLAKE, W. C. Practical remarks on the corn laws as viewed in connexion with the corn trade; and suggestions for their improvement. By a merchant. 30p. *8°. London & Southampton, 1833.*

POPULATION

27923 CORBAUX, F. On the natural and mathematical laws concerning population, vitality, and mortality...with tables of mortality applicable to five classes of each sex; and other tables, expressing the relations between capital and income, under the operation of compound-interest. 208, 53p. *8°. 1833. One of an edition limited to 250 copies.*

27924 *IVERNOIS, Sir F. d'. Sur la mortalité proportionnelle des peuples, considérée comme mesure de leur aisance et de leur civilisation. (Érreurs concernant les populations.)...Tiré de la Bibliothèque Universelle... 1833. 93p. *8°. Genève, 1833. The copy that belonged to George Grote. The fourth of the author's essays on this subject.*

27925 LLOYD, W. F. Two lectures on the checks to population, delivered before the University of Oxford, in Michaelmas Term 1832. 75p. *8°. Oxford & London, 1833. The copy that belonged to Francis Place. Reissued in Lectures on population, value, poor-laws and rent in 1837, q.v. (GENERAL).*

TRADES & MANUFACTURES

27926 BABBAGE, C. On the economy of machinery and manufactures...Third edition enlarged. 392p. *8°. 1832[1833] The preface is dated: February 11, 1833.*

27927 —— Traité sur l'économie des machines et des manufactures...Traduit de l'anglais sur la troisième édition, par Éd. Biot. 515p. *8°. Paris, 1833.*

27928 —— On currency, on a new system of manufacturing, and on the effect of machinery on human labour. Being three chapters extracted from the third edition of "The economy of machinery and manufactures." 31p. *8°. 1833. For other editions, see 1832.*

27929 BENNETT, John (*fl.* 1833–1837). The artificer's complete lexicon, for terms and prices adapted for gentlemen, engineers, architects, builders, mechanists, millwrights, manufacturers, tradesmen, etc.... 476p. *8°. 1833. See also 1837.*

27930 BLACHETTE, L. I. and **ZOEGA,** F. Manuel du fabricant et du raffineur de sucre...Seconde édition, considérablement augmentée et enrichie de planches par J. de Fontenelle. 442p. *12°. Paris, 1833.*

27931 LONDON, SURREY AND KENT SAFETY BRICK COMPANY. Description of the safety bricks, and various other improved building materials, manufactured by the...Company, and sold at their premises, the Patent Chimney Works, (established in 1825,) Stangate Wharf, Westminster Bridge... 16p. 8°. [*London*, 1833]

27932 —— A descriptive catalogue of models, examples, and specimens, prepared for the inspection of architects and builders, and also for the instruction of workmen; illustrating the various improvements in brick-work, &c. submitted...by the...Company. 16p. 8°. 1833.

27933 MONTGOMERY, JAMES (1792–1880). The theory and practice of cotton spinning; or, the carding and spinning master's assistant...Second edition. 332p. 8°. *Glasgow, London, &c.*, 1833. *For another edition, see* 1832.

27934 RUDKIN, H. Remarks humbly submitted to the Right Hon. Lord Althorp, Chancellor of the Ex-chequer, and the Right Hon. Sir Henry Parnell, M.P. &c., on the insufficiency of the system now in use for determining and securing the spirit revenue, arising from the licensed distilleries of the United Kingdom; with a proposed plan for superseding the saccharometer, and all other fallacious implements...illustrated by experiments lately prosecuted by command of the...Lords Commissioners of His Majesty's Treasury... 35p. 8°. 1833.

27935 TEMPLETON, W. The millwright & engineer's pocket companion...Second edition, carefully revised and considerably enlarged; to which is added an appendix... 202p. 12°. *London, Liverpool, &c.*, 1833.

27936 The Library of Entertaining Knowledge. **VEGETABLE SUBSTANCES**: materials of manufactures. 456p. 12°. *London, Edinburgh, &c.*, 1833.

COMMERCE

27937 ATKINSON, WILLIAM (*fl.* 1833–1858). The reason for protecting home trade; or, the principle of free trade refuted. 36p. 8°. 1833.

27938 BOOTH, H. Free trade, as it affects the people, addressed to a reformed Parliament. 40p. 8°. *Liverpool, Manchester, &c.*, 1833. *The copy that belonged to Francis Place.*

27939 —— Substance of Mr. Henry Booth's pamphlet on Free trade, as it affects the people. Addressed to a reformed Parliament. Published by a few friends to free trade and to sound principles, for circulation and for sale. 16p. 8°. [1833]

27940 CHAMBER OF COMMERCE AND MANUFACTURES, *Glasgow*. Origin, rules and constitution of the Chamber of Commerce and Manufactures of the city of Glasgow. Published...for the use of the members. [With a list of members at its foundation in 1783.] 25p. 8°. *Glasgow*, 1833.

27941 DUBOIS AYMÉ, J. M. J. Lettre de Mr. du Boisaymé à Mr. Odilon-Barrot, insérée dans le Journal du Commerce du 13 juillet 1833. 10p. 8°. *Grenoble*, [1833]

27942 FOERE, L. DE. Mémoire présenté à l'appui du projet de loi, tendant à restreindre l'exportation des lins indigènes et l'importation des toiles étrangères. 66[64]p. 8°. *Bruges*, [1833?].

27943 GREY, *Messrs*, Practical arithmetic; or, concise calculator, adapted to the commerce of Great Britain and Ireland. By Messrs Grey. Thirteenth edition, enlarged and improved. 60p. 12°. 1833.

27944 INQUIRY into the navigation laws, and the effects of their alteration; with tables of shipping and trade compiled from official documents. 107p. 8°. 1833.

27945 A LETTER to Lord Althorp, on the China trade. Occasioned by an article in the "Edinburgh Review," No. CIV. 46p. 8°. 1833.

27946 MACARDY, J. The commercial cyclopædia; or dictionary of practical commerce... [570]p. 8°. *Manchester*, 1833.

27947 McCULLOCH, JOHN R. Library of Useful Knowledge. On commerce... 128p. 8°. 1833.

27948 MARJORIBANKS, C. Letter to the Right Hon. Charles Grant, President of the Board of Controul, on the present state of British intercourse with China. 66p. 8°. 1833.

27949 MOORSOM, R. Thoughts on the changes which have taken place in the navigation laws of England, and their effects on the shipping interest: together, with observations on a trade of export, and the benefits to be derived by British ships from the termination of the East India Company's charter. 76p. 8°. 1833.

27950 NOTES on the British and Indian trade with China. No. I. The Chinese regulations and the British Acts of Parliament; and the manner in which they affect the trade. 15p. 8°. 1833. *With a manuscript list of errata on the verso of the last page.*

27951 PEEL, SIR ROBERT, *2nd Bart.* Speech of the Right Honourable Sir Robert Peel, Bart., M.P. for Tamworth, respecting the Dutch embargo, in the House of Commons, on...February 15th, 1833. Extracted from the Mirror of Parliament. – Part CLXXXVI. 20p. 8°. 1833. *The copy that belonged to Lord Ellenborough, with his signature on the title-page.*

27952 PITA PIZARRO, P. Lecciones generales de comercio, seguidas de una nocion ó rapida ojeada sobre la historia universal del mismo. 435p. 8°. *Madrid*, 1833.

27953 Cui bono? Or, the **PROSPECTS** of a free trade in tea. A dialogue between an antimonopolist and a proprietor of East India stock. 38p. 8°. 1833.

27954 A few **REMARKS** on the tea trade. By a dealer. 23p. 8°. 1833.

27955 REMARKS on the averages of Hamburg and on the commercial policy of Great Britain towards Prussia and other northern states. 74p. 8°. *London, Liverpool, &c.* [*Hamburg printed*], 1833.

27956 REMARKS on the importance of preserving the existing scale of duties on North American & foreign wood; with an appendix, containing evidence taken before a Select Committee of the House of Commons, on manufactures, commerce, and shipping. 141p. 8°. *Glasgow:* [*British American, West Indian, and General Shipping Association,*] 1833. *With a second title-page, printed before the Appendix was added, on which the name of the Association appears. See also* 1834.

27957 REUSS, W. F. Calculations and statements relative to the trade between Great Britain and the United

States of America...of the statistics of the commerce, navigation, produce and manufactures of the United States. 287p. *8°*. 1833.

27958 RICHMOND, W. A series of maritime and mercantile tables, illustrative of the shipping as connected with the trade and commerce of Great Britain...from authentic parliamentary documents, and accompanied by lengthened and explanatory notes. [64]p. *fol. Newcastle upon Tyne,* 1833.

27959 STAUNTON, Sir G. T., *Bart.* Corrected report of the speeches of Sir George Staunton, on the China trade, in the House of Commons, June 4, and June 13, 1833... 55p. *8°*. 1833.

27960 *SWITZERLAND. *Eidgenössische Experten-Commission in Handelssachen.* Bericht über die schweizerischen Handelsverhältnisse zu den verschiedenen Staaten

des Auslandes, erstattet an den eidgenössischen Vorort von der in Angelegenheiten des schweizerischen Handels im Christmonat 1833 einberufenen Eidgenössischen Expertenkommission. 24p. *8°*. *n.p.* [1833] *The copy that belonged to George Grote.*

27961 The TIN DUTIES. 16p. *8°*. 1833.

27962 TORRENS, R. Letters on commercial policy [first printed in the Bolton Chronicle]. 80p. *8°*. 1833. *The copy that belonged to Francis Place, with his manuscript note on the title-page: 'N.B. The argument is founded on a Gross Fallacy – which having been exposed – the whole of the edition was sent to Bolton and none were sold in London. F.P.' There seems to be little evidence for this assertion.*

26963 TRUEMAN & COOK. The state of the commerce of Great Britain with reference to colonial and other produce, for the year 1832. 32p. *8°*. *n.p.* [1833] *See also 1831, 1832, 1834.*

COLONIES

27964 BLISS, H. The colonial system. Statistics of the trade, industry and resources of Canada, and other plantations in British America...Second edition. 170p. *8°*. 1833.

27965 BROWN, William, *of Bristol.* To the public. Emigration shown to be the only effectual method to relieve the people, from the heavy burthen of the poors' rates...[With 'Rates of passage and provisions to Australia' issued by the Australian Emigration Office, Bristol.] 22p. *8°*. *Bristol,* 1833.

27966 CRAWFURD, John (1783–1868). Notes on the settlement or colonization of British subjects in India: with an appendix of proofs and illustration. 52p. *8°*. 1833.

27967 CROPPER, J. A vindication of a loan of £15,000,000 to the West India planters, shewing that it may not only be lent with perfect safety, but with immense advantage both to the West Indians and to the people of England. 16p. *8°*. 1833.

27968 EVANS, F. A. The emigrant's directory and guide to obtain lands and effect a settlement in the Canadas. 180p. *12°*. *Dublin, London, &c.,* 1833.

27969 [FAIRPLAY, F.] The Canadas as they now are. Comprehending a view of their climate, rivers, lakes, canals, government, laws, taxes, towns, trade, &c. with a description of the soil and advantages...of every township in each province...compiled...by a late resident. [With an appendix.] 87, 102p. *12°*. 1833.

27970 GILCHRIST, J. B. A bold epistolary rhapsody, addressed to the Proprietors of East-India stock in particular, and to every individual of the Welch, Irish, Scottish and English nations in general... 33p. *8°*. 1833.

27971 *HOPKIRK, J. G., *ed.* An account of the insurrection in St. Domingo, begun in August 1791, taken from authentic sources. 59p. *8°*. *Edinburgh & London,* 1833. *A new edition with an introduction by Hopkirk of the con-*

temporary work A particular account of the insurrection of the negroes of St. Domingo, *first published in 1791 (q.v.).*

27972 INNES, W. Liberia; or the early history & signal preservation of the American colony of free negroes on the coast of Africa...Second edition, with a copious appendix from materials furnished by E. Cresson, Esq. 234p. *12°*. *Edinburgh,* 1833.

27973 KENNET, C. The Madras commercial ready assistant, containing correct tables, of the exchange of money, current...in the East Indies...Second edition, revised, improved and greatly enlarged... 228p. *fol. Madras,* 1833.

27974 *LARPENT, Sir G. G. de H., *Bart.* Some remarks on the late negotiations between the Board of Control and the East-India Company. [On the effects of the new arrangements for the renewal of the Company's charter.] 62p. *8°*. 1833. *Presentation copy from the author to George Grote.*

27975 LEBRUN, I. F. T. Tableau statistique et politique des deux Canadas. 538p. *8°*. *Paris,* 1833.

27976 A LETTER to the proprietors of East-India stock [signed: a proprietor], and Observations on the projected opening of the China trade. 67p. *8°*. [*London,*] 1833.

27977 NAPIER, Sir Charles J. The colonies: treating of their value generally – of the Ionian Islands in particular; the importance of the latter in war and commerce...strictures on the administration of Sir Frederick Adam. 608p. *8°*. 1833.

27978 NEWNHAM, H. East India question. Facts and observations intended to convey the opinions of the native population of the territory of Bengal respecting the past and the future...Second edition, revised and enlarged. 149p. *8°*. 1833.

FINANCE

27979 ARMY reform. A practical method of reducing the Army Estimates a million, without diminution of its numerical force: exhibiting the sinecures and pluralities

held by general officers, abolition of flogging...By a cidevant cavalry officer. 104p. *8°*. 1833.

27980 BAIN, D. Letter to the Right Honourable Lord Althorp, Chancellor of the Exchequer, &c.&c.&c., on the settlement of the charter of the Bank of England, and regarding the establishment of banks generally. 20p. *8°. London & Edinburgh,* [1833]

27981 The **BANK** of England and its charter, considered in a letter to the Right Hon. Lord Althorp, &c.&c.&c. 59p. *8°.* 1833.

27982 BANK OF ENGLAND. A copy of the correspondence between the Chancellor of the Exchequer and the Bank of England relative to the renewal of the charter. 30p. *8°. n.p.* 1833.

27983 —— A copy of the correspondence between the Chancellor of the Exchequer, and the Bank of England, relative to the renewal of the charter, which has taken place since the 5th of June last, as reported to a General Court of Proprietors on the 13th August, 1833. 21p. *8°. n.p.,* 1833.

27984 —— Opinions of Sir James Scarlett, Sir Edward B. Sugden, and Mr. Richards, on the privilege of the Bank of England. Read at a General Court of Proprietors, 16th August, 1833. 18p. *8°. n.p.* 1833. *With a newspaper cutting giving the opinion of the Law Officers of the Crown.*

27985 BANK OF MANCHESTER. Evidence given by the deputation from the Bank of Manchester before the Committee of Enquiry on the Bank of England charter in July, 1832. Extracted from the minutes of evidence printed by order of the House of Commons... 97p. *8°. Manchester,* 1833.

27986 BANK OF THE UNITED STATES [1816–1836]. Report of a Committee of Directors of the Bank of the United States. 52p. *8°. n.p.* [1833]

27987 —— Report of the Bank of the United States, to the Committee of Ways and Means of the House of Representatives, January 28, 1833. 48p. *8°. n.p.* [1833]

27988 [**BREED,** .] An impartial inquiry into the bank question; with observations on banking and currency. By a merchant. 88p. *8°.* 1833.

27989 BULL, JOHN, *pseud.* Dialogue between Mr. John Bull, a merchant of London, and Mr. George Farren, respecting his "Hints by way of warning"...[on the difficulties of joint stock banks]. 32p. *8°.* 1833. *Attributed to John Duncan in a manuscript note on the title-page.*

27990 A **CALL** to women of all ranks in the British Empire, on the subject of the National Debt. [With a postscript, dated February 2, 1833, and signed: A sailor's daughter.] 62, 16p. *8°.* 1830[–33]. *The postscript of 1833 states: 'the foregoing pamphlet was printed, and published, above two years ago; but...was suppressed...till now'.*

27991 CAREY, M. Collectanea: displaying the rise and progress of the tariff system of the United States: the various efforts made from the year 1819, to establish the protecting system; its final triumph in the tariff of 1824; and its prospective abandonment by the tariff of 1833... 18p. *8°. Philadelphia,* 1833.

27992 —— Second edition, improved. [With an appendix.] 25p. *8°. Philadelphia,* 1833.

27993 CIVIS, *pseud.* A few facts and reasons in favour of joint stock banks; in reply to the pamphlet of G. Farren Esq....on the alleged "legal, practical, and commercial difficulties attending the foundation and management" of those establishments. 22p. *8°.* 1833.

27994 COBBETT, W. The flash in the pan; or, Peel in a passion. Containing the resolution moved by Mr. Cobbett in the House of Commons, on the 16. of April [May], for an address to the King to dismiss...Sir Robert Peel from...[the] Privy Council, together with Mr. Cobbett's speech on making, and Mr. John Fielden's speech on seconding, the motion; also, Sir Robert Peel's speech in answer, and Mr. Cobbett's reply... 32p. *8°.* [1833]

27995 [**COLLIER,** JOSHUA.] Graduated scale for a property tax. By the author of "The reply to 'the State of the nation'." Anno 1822. 19p. *8°.* 1833. *See also* 1842.

27996 COMMITTEE OF COUNTRY BANKERS. [*Begin.*] At a meeting of the Committee...held at the London Hotel, New Bridge-Street, Blackfriars, on Saturday, the 8th of June, 1833...[Resolutions declaring opposition to Bank of England notes becoming legal tender. Signed: Henry Hobhouse, chairman.] [2]p. *s.sh.4°. n.p.* [1833] [*Br.* 550]

27997 COMMUTATION of taxes. From the Monthly Magazine for August, 1833. 8p. *8°. Sherborne,* [1833]

27998 COMPTON, C. A treatise on tontine: in which the evils of the old system are exhibited, and an equitable plan suggested for rendering the valuable principle of tontine more beneficially applicable to life annuities. With an account of the successful operation of the General Annuity Endowment Association... 36p. *8°.* 1833.

27999 CONSIDERATIONS on joint-stock banking, chiefly with reference to the situation and liabilities of shareholders. 16p. *8°.* 1833.

28000 COSMOPOLITE, *pseud.* A concise treatise on the wealth, power, and resources of Great Britain, showing the means by which the country may be restored to its former vigor and prosperity; respectfully submitted to...His Majesty's Privy Council... 173p. *8°.* 1833.

28001 DANIEL, E. An appeal to the landed, manufacturing, trading, and professional interests of Great Britain, exhorting them to insist upon the immediate redemption of the Public Debt, by a contribution from all real and productive personal property...and the repeal of the excise, assessed, stamp, and license duties to the amount of the dividend payable on that Debt... 23p. *8°.* 1833.

28002 DE BODE, C. J. P. P., *Baron.* French claims. An address to...the House of Commons...With a copy of the petition to be presented on the 18th of April, 1833, to the House of Commons, concerning his claims for indemnification, under the treaties and conventions made between Great Britain and France in 1814, 1815 and 1818 ... 56p. *8°.* 1833.

28003 ENGLAND. *Commissioners of Excise.* A detailed statement of the mode in which the revenue under the management of the Commissioners of Excise, is, after its final collection remitted and paid into the Exchequer... 66p. *8°.* 1833.

28004 —— Parliament. *House of Commons.* A digest of the evidence on the Bank charter taken before the Committee of 1832, arranged together with the tables under proper heads; to which are prefixed strictures and illustrative remarks. Also copious indexes, &c.&c. xxii, 296p. *8°.* 1833. *The copy that belonged to Patrick Chalmers, with his signature on the title-page. The compilation is sometimes attributed to Thomas Joplin.*

28005 FACTS (founded upon Parliamentary returns,) illustrative of the great inequality of the taxes on houses and windows, shewing how unjustly and oppressively they bear upon the middle and industrious classes. 36p. *8⁰.* [1833]

28006 FARREN, G. Hints, by way of warning, on the legal, practical, and mercantile difficulties, attending the foundation and management of joint stock banks. 33p. *8⁰.* 1833.

28007 ―― Second edition. 33p. *8⁰.* 1833.

28008 ―― Third edition. 33p. *8⁰.* 1833. *Presentation copy from the author to T. Spring Rice, Baron Monteagle.*

28009 FINLAISON, J. Tables for providing relief in sickness and old age, for payments at death, and endowments for children. Computed by John Finlaison, Esq. actuary of the National Debt; and published for the use of benefit societies, &c....by John Tidd Pratt. 8p. *8⁰.* 1833.

28010 FORTUNE, E. F. THOMAS. Fortune's epitome of the stocks and public funds...Thirteenth edition, revised and considerably improved...By J. J. Secretan. 152p. *8⁰.* 1833. *For other editions, see* 1796.

28011 ★GENEVA, *Canton of. Conseil d'Etat.* Rapport du Conseil d'État fait au Conseil Représentatif, sur les comptes du Canton et de la Ville de Genève, de l'année 1832. Par M. le Syndic Lullin. 59p. *8⁰. Genève,* 1833. *The copy that belonged to George Grote.*

28012 [GILBART, J. W.?] (From the London Encyclopædia.) History of the rise, progress, and present state of banking, in all parts of the world; in which is developed an entirely new principle of circulating medium, for the United Kingdom of Great Britain and Ireland. And to which are appended all the accounts annexed to the evidence and report of the Committee of Parliament on the Bank of England charter... p.[463]–480, 459★–474★, iv. *8⁰.* [*London,* 1833] *Conjecturally attributed to Gilbart by HSF.*

28013 GOUGE, W. M. A short history of paper money and banking in the United States, including an account of provincial and continental paper money. To which is prefixed an inquiry into the principles of the system... 140, 240p. *12⁰. Philadelphia,* 1833. *See also* 1835.

28014 ―― [Another edition of Part 2.] The curse of paper-money and banking; or a short history of banking in the United States of America...To which is prefixed an introduction. By William Cobbett. 200p. *12⁰.* 1833.

28015 [GRENFELL, G.] Coinage restrictions. 8p. *8⁰. Penzance,* [1833] *With an accompanying letter from the author to Col. C. R. Fox, M.P. (1796–1873).*

28016 HAMILTON, WILLIAM (1780–1835). The importance of savings banks: a lecture delivered in the Mechanics' Institution, Glasgow, February 4, 1833. 23p. *12⁰. Glasgow,* 1833.

28017 HEATHFIELD, R. Observations occasioned by the motion in the House of Commons, on the 26th of March, 1833, by Geo. R. Robinson, Esquire, for a Select Committee "To consider and revise our existing taxation...". Addressed to the landed proprietors of the United Kingdom... 20p. *8⁰.* 1833. *Two presentation copies from the author, one to Lord Grantham (De Grey copy) and the other to T. Spring Rice, Baron Monteagle.*

28018 House of Commons. **HOUSE** & window taxes, &c. The following letter [signed: a Liberal] appeared in the Bath Journal of February 25, 1833. The correctness of the principles therein contained are made manifest by the late proceedings in Parliament. 8p. *8⁰. Bath,* 1833.

28019 An **INQUIRY** into the principles of the American banking system. 42p. *8⁰. n.p.* [1833]

28020 JACKSON, GEORGE. Jackson's complete system of practical book-keeping, by single and double entry...To which are added, observations on exchange and the relative value of monies of different countries. With tables of exchange...A new edition, adapted to the present improved practice of merchants. For the use of schools. 244p. *8⁰. Belfast,* 1833.

28021 JAGO, R. H. General and equitable commutation of tithes. A plan for the general commutation of lay and ecclesiastical tithes into corn rents: being a self-adjusting mode of payment in exact ratio to the half yearly average price of agricultural produce; proposed and exemplified in three letters... The second edition. 41p. *8⁰.* 1833. *Presentation copy from the author, with 4 pages of additional text in manuscript by him.*

28022 JONES, EDWARD (*fl.* 1833). Reflections on a graduated property and income tax, to raise the sum of £17,822,000, so as to repeal all the duties now received from malt, hops, tea, coffee, sugar...windows, inhabited houses, receipt stamps, and percentage on compositions, and relieve the people from an oppressive and unjust system of taxation... 60p. *8⁰.* 1833.

28023 JONES, RICHARD (1790–1855). A few remarks on the proposed commutation of tithe, with suggestions of some additional facilities. 19p. *8⁰.* 1833.

28024 JOPLIN, T. The advantages of the proposed National Bank of England, both to the public and its proprietory, briefly explained. [With 'Prospectus of a national metropolitan establishment for banking in the country'.] 36p. *8⁰.* 1833.

28025 ―― [Another issue.] 30p. *8⁰.* 1833. *In this issue, the Prospectus (p.29–36) has been replaced by a 2-page account of the establishment of the National Provincial Bank of England, with a list of directors.*

28026 LEEDS BANKING COMPANY. Deed of settlement (dated 19th November, 1832) of the Leeds Banking Company, established under the authority of an Act of Parliament, passed in the seventh year of the reign of King George IV., cap. 46. To which is appended, an abstract of the said Act. Capital – one million pounds sterling. 52p. *8⁰. Leeds,* 1833.

28027 [LLOYD, F.?] A letter to the Right Hon. the Viscount Althorp, Chancellor of the Exchequer...on his proposed interference with the present system of country banking. By a country banker. 72p. *8⁰.* 1833. *★Another, the FWA copy, that belonged to William Pare, is a presentation copy with inscription, 'T. C. Salt, Esq with the authors respects'.*

28028 LOUISIANA. *House of Representatives.* An act to incorporate the Commercial Bank of New-Orleans. 32p. *8⁰. New Orleans,* 1833.

28029 [McCULLOCH, JOHN R.] Commutation of taxes. [From the *Edinburgh Review,* April, 1833.] 26p. *8⁰.* [*Edinburgh,* 1833] *The running title reads: Commutation of taxes – Proposed tax on property and income. Presentation copy, with inscription, from the author to T. Spring Rice, Baron Monteagle.*

28030 MASSACHUSETTS. General Court. *House of Representatives.* House. . . . . .No. 12. Report of the special committee, to whom was referred so much of the Governor's address as relates to assignment of property by debtors, and to imprisonment for debt. 95p. *8°. Boston*, 1833.

28031 —— —— —— House. . . . . .No. 29. Amendments proposed by Mr. Bliss. . .to the Bill for the relief of insolvent debtors. 3p. *8. n.p.* [1833]

28032 —— —— *Senate.* Senate. . . . . .No. 49. Amendment proposed by Mr. Barton, to the Bill concerning arrests and imprisonment in civil cases. 5p. *8°. n.p.* [1833]

28033 MOORE, R. Important notices of that which concerns the pecuniary credit of a state, and in particular that of England. 52p. *8°. Kingston & London,* [1833]

28034 MUNDELL, A. The reviewer of publications on the Bank charter, in the last number of the Edinburgh Review, reviewed. 15p. *8°.* 1833.

28035 NEBENIUS, C. F. E. Denkschrift für den Beitritt Badens zu dem zwischen Preussen, Bayern, Würtemberg, den beiden Hessen und mehren andern deutschen Staaten abgeschlossenen Zollverein. [With an appendix.] 62, 32p. *8°. Karlsruhe,* 1833.

28036 OBSERVATIONS for the consideration of a reformed Parliament, on the alterations proposed for the Exchequer, and also on a mode, submitted to the Lords Commissioners of His Majesty's Treasury, for abolishing the Exchequer. . .Second edition. 8p. *8°.* [*London,*] 1833.

28037 OUTLINE of a plan for amending the system of taxation. 8p. *8°. Birmingham,* 1833.

28038 [**OWEN,** ROBERT D.] No. 20. . .British taxes dissected, being a plain letter addressed to the working men of Great Britain and Ireland. . .By one of the Council of the National Political Union. 16p. *8°. National Political Union,* 1833. **Another, the FWA copy, belonged to William Pare.*

28039 [——] Second edition. 16p. *8°. National Political Union,* 1833.

28040 PENNY, J. Practical retrenchment the legitimate object of reform. 56p. *8°. London, Sherborne, &c.,* [1833]

28041 A **PLAN** for procuring the residence of ministers of the Established Church, without interfering with vested interests; contained in a letter to Lords Brougham and Althorp, and respectfully submitted to the consideration of both Houses of Parliament. By the son of a lawyer. 14p. *8°.* 1833.

28042 QUIN, M. J. The trade of banking in England: embracing the substance of the evidence taken before the Secret Committee of the House of Commons, digested and arranged under appropriate heads. Together with a summary of the law applicable to the Bank of England, to private banks of issue, and joint-stock banking companies. To which are added an appendix and index. 385, lxviiip. *12°.* 1833.

28043 R., W. A letter to the editor of the Times on the question of the Bank charter, shewing the inconsistency of some of the accounts lately furnished by the Bank to the Committee of the House of Commons. 15p. *8°. Camberwell,* 1833.

28044 RAILWAY TAXATION considered in a letter to the Right Hon. Lord Althorp. . .[Signed: A coach proprietor.] 15p. *8°.* 1833.

28045 The **REAL DEL MONTE** mining concerns unmasked, and a few facts on stock jobbing schemes, with a view to prevent the public from becoming the dupes of self-interested speculators and adventurers. 16p. *8°.* 1833.

28046 REMARKS on the objections to joint stock banks. 24p. *8°.* 1833.

28047 Dedicated to the Right Honourable Thomas Spring Rice, Secretary of the Treasury, &c.&c.&c. **REPLY** to the charge of fallacy brought against the exposition of the state of the stamp laws, contained in the Law and Commercial Remembrancer for 1833. [With a preface by the editor.] 20p. *8°.* [1833]

28048 RICE, T. S., *Baron Monteagle.* Repeal of taxes and reduction of expenditure. Speech of the Right Honourable Thomas Spring Rice, joint Secretary to the Treasury. . .in the House of Commons, on. . .July 16, 1833. Extracted from the Mirror of Parliament. Part CCXXXV. 20p. *8°.* 1833. *The copy that belonged to Earl De Grey.*

28049 —— [Another edition.] 21p. *8°. Edinburgh,* 1833.

28050 —— Speech. . .in the House of Commons on . . . April 30, 1833; in the debate on the house and window tax. ⟨Extracted from the Mirror of Parliament, Part CCVIII.⟩ 14p. *8°.* 1833.

28051 —— Speech. . .in the House of Commons on. . . May 3, 1833; in the debate on the stamp duties. ⟨Extracted from the Mirror of Parliament, Part CCIX.⟩ 22p. *8°.* 1833.

28052 RICHARDSON, JAMES. A paper currency; or, notes, (issued with security,) the best circulating medium. 12p. *12°.* 1833.

28053 —— Second edition, enlarged and improved. 12p. *12°.* 1833.

28054 RIVES, W. C. Speech of Mr. Rives, of Virginia, on the bill further to provide of the collection of duties on imports. Delivered in Senate, February 14, 1833. 32p. *8°. City of Washington,* 1833.

28055 *ROYAL NAVAL ANNUITANT SOCIETY. Documents and reports of the. . .Society, ordered to be printed, at a special general meeting of the members, held at the Society's building in Ker-Street, Devonport, on the 15th of November, 1833. 76p. *8°. Devonport,* [1833] *The copy that belonged to Augustus De Morgan.*

28056 SADDLEWORTH BANKING COMPANY. Deed of settlement, (dated 9th September, 1833,) of the Saddleworth Banking Company, established pursuant to Statute 7th George 4th, chap. 46. Capital, three hundred thousand pounds. 64p. *8°. Lees,* 1833.

28057 The **SAFETY** and advantages of joint-stock banking. By an accountant. Second edition. 16p. *8°.* 1833.

28058 SAINZ ANDINO, P. Alegacion por el derecho de la real hacienda en los autos pendientes ante el Supremo Consejo de ella entre su Fiscal mas antiguo el ilustrisimo Sr. D. Pedro Sainz de Andino, ministro honorario de la Real Camara, y el excelentisimo Señor Duque del Infantado. . .consejero de estado, sobre reivindicacion por parte de la misma real hacienda de las alcabalas de las villas del Prado, Arenas y Alamin, y demas pueblos y despoblados de su territorio. 172p. *4°. Madrid,* 1833.

28059 [**SAYER,** B.] An attempt to shew the justice

and expediency of substituting an income or property tax for the present taxes, or a part of them, as affording the most equitable...mode of taxation, also the most... effectual plans of reducing the National Debt. [With a supplement and an appendix.] 356, 72p. *8°*. 1833. *For another edition,* On the advantages of substituting an income tax for the present taxes, *see* 1831.

28060 SCROPE, G. P. An examination of the Bank charter question, with an inquiry into the nature of a just standard of value, and suggestions for the improvement of our monetary system. 77p. *8°*. 1833.

28061 SOCIETY FOR EQUITABLE ASSURANCES. The deed of settlement of the Society for Equitable Assurances on Lives and Survivorships...With the bye-laws and orders. To which are appended reports ...by the Court of Directors, and nine addresses by William Morgan...late actuary of the society. 316p. *8°*. 1833. **Another copy, that belonged to Augustus De Morgan, has an extra section, p. 317–331, which was printed after the main part of the work. For another edition, see* 1801.

28062 —— A short account of the Society for Equitable Assurances on Lives and Survivorships, established by deed, inrolled in His Majesty's Court of King's Bench, at Westminster. 22, [2]p. *8°*. 1833. *For other editions, see* 1762.

28063 STALEY, J. Taxation not the cause of distress, by a tradesman, shewing the practicability of paying off the National Debt, and proving that the same beneficial effects would result from paying the Debt: as arose from its contraction. 16p. *8°*. 1833. **Another, the FWA copy, belonged to William Pare.*

28064 STANDARD LIFE ASSURANCE COMPANY. Proposals and rates of the Standard Life Assurance Company, established in 1825...for assurance on lives and survivorships...and for the purchase of reversions and annuities. 16p. *8°*. *Edinburgh,* [1833]

28065 [TAYLOR, JOHN (1781–1864).] Currency fallacies refuted, and paper money vindicated. By the author of "An essay on money"... 108p. *8°*. 1833. *See also* 1844, 1845 (Currency investigated).

28066 [THOMPSON, THOMAS P.] The article on

equitable adjustment, from the Westminster Review, No. XXXVI. For April, 1833. 18p. *8°*. [1833] *See note to no.* 25779.

28067 *TYLER, J. *President of the USA.* Speech of Mr. Tyler, of Virginia, on the bill to provide further for the collection of duties on imports, delivered in the Senate of the United States...February 6, 1833. 21p. *8°*. *Washington,* 1833. *The copy that belonged to George Grote.*

28068 UNITED STATES OF AMERICA. *Laws, etc.* An act to alter and amend the several acts imposing duties on imports. Passed July, 1832. [4]p. *4°*. *n.p.* [1833]

28069 VIRGO, W. A plan for immediately reducing the National Debt and taxation; by an alteration in the value of the currency, and the adoption of a secure banking system. Addressed to His Majesty's Ministers by an experienced broker of the Royal Exchange. 16p. *8°*. 1833. *Presentation copy from the author to T. Spring Rice, Baron Monteagle.*

28070 WATT, H. The practice of banking in Scotland and in England; with observations and suggestions on the renewal of the Bank of England charter, on the principles and regulation of joint stock banks, and on the one pound note circulation. 84p. *8°*. *London, Edinburgh, &c.,* 1833.

28071 WHYMPER, W. Reasons why landlords should pay the rates, for tenements of £10. rent, and under. 13p. *8°*. *Woodbridge,* 1833. *With corrections and a note in the text, and a folio sheet bound at the end, entitled, 'A Statement of poor rates collected for 1 year' written by the author. For this, see vol. III, MS. 521.*

28072 WORTLEY, J. S., afterwards **MACKENZIE,** J. S. W., *Baron Wharncliffe.* A brief inquiry into the true award of an "equitable adjustment" between the nation and its creditors. With tables. 39p. *8°*. 1833.

28073 YORK UNION BANKING COMPANY. Deed of settlement (dated 1st May, 1833,) of the York Union Banking Company, established under the authority of an Act of Parliament, passed in the seventh year of the reign of George the Fourth: to which is appended an abstract of the Act. Capital – six hundred thousand pounds. 75p. *8°*. *York,* 1833.

TRANSPORT

28074 BADNALL, R. A treatise on railway improvements, explanatory of the chief difficulties and inconveniences which at present attend the general adoption of railways, and the means by which these objections may be overcome...To which are added, various remarks on... locomotive power. 142p. *8°*. 1833. *The Rastrick copy.*

28075 BOSTON AND PROVIDENCE RAIL ROAD CORPORATION. Annual report of the Directors...with that of the agent and engineer [William Gibbs McNeill]. January 2, 1833. 32p. *8°*. *Boston,* 1833. *The Rastrick copy. See also* 1832, 1834, 1849.

28076 BOWIE, R. A brief narrative, proving the right of the late William Symington, civil engineer, to be considered the inventor of steam land carriage locomotion; and also the inventor and introducer of steam navigation ... 30p. *8°*. *London & Croydon,* 1833. *A lithographed appeal for contributions in aid of Symington's widow is mounted on the verso of the last leaf.*

28077 BRADSHAW, G. Lengths and levels to

Bradshaw's maps of the canals, navigable rivers, and railways, in the principal part of England [the northern map]. 15p. *8°*. 1833. *The Rastrick copy. See note to no.* 25921.

28078 ENGLAND. *Parliament. House of Lords.* Extracts from the minutes of evidence, given before the Committee of the Lords on the London and Birmingham Railway Bill, in June, 1832; shewing the great advantage to landowners and the public, of this mode of communication in general. [With 'Great Western Railway, between Bristol and London. Shares £100 each...', a prospectus.] 24, [2]p. *8°*. *Bristol,* 1833. *A selection from the pamphlet with the same title issued by the directors of the London and Birmingham Railway in 1832 (q.v.).*

28079 FOURNEL, H. Communication des deux mers. Henri Founrel à A..... 3 septembre 1833. [A discussion of the importance of a communication between the Mediterranean and the Indian Ocean through Suez.] 8p. *8°*. *Paris,* [1833] *The original imprint 'Marseille' has been cancelled by a printed slip.*

28080 GRAND WESTERN CANAL COMPANY. Grand Wesern [*sic*] Canal. Report of the Committee to the General Assembly. [Dated: July 15th 1833. Report and statements of accounts for the year 27 June 1832 to 26 June 1833.] 3p. *fol. Collumpton*, [1833] *Addressed and sent through the post to one of the proprietors, W. E. Elliot, Gedlington, near Nottingham.*

28081 HAWKINS, JOHN I. [*Endorsed:*] Prospectus of the experimental railway, Park Street, Camden Town, near Gloucester Gate, Regent's Park, to prove Mr. Saxton's locomotive differential pulley, Oct. 17, 1833. [4]p. *fol. n.p.* [1833]

28082 LONDON AND SOUTHAMPTON RAILWAY COMPANY. London and Southampton Railway. [Prospectus, dated: 21st Sept. 1833.] [4]p. *fol. n.p.* [1833]

28083 —— [Another edition. Dated: 5th December, 1833.] [4]p. *fol. n.p.* [1833]

28084 MacNEILL, SIR J. B. Canal navigation. On the resistance of water to the passage of boats upon canals, and other bodies of water, being the results of experiments. 55p. *4°. London, Bath, &c.,* 1833.

28085 OBSERVER, *pseud.* Thoughts on railways, and projected railways, by Observer. 15p. *8°. Liverpool,* 1833. *The Rastrick copy.*

28086 PARNELL, H. B., *Baron Congleton.* A treatise on roads; wherein the principles on which roads should be made are explained and illustrated, by the plans, specifications, and contracts made use of by Thomas Telford, Esq. on the Holyhead Road. [With appendixes.] 438p. *8°.* 1833. *See also* 1838.

28087 SCHUYLKILL NAVIGATION COMPANY. Opinion of counsel, on the right of the Schuylkill Navigation Company to make another lock and canal for the use of the navigation at the Fair Mount dam. 34p. *8°. Philadelphia,* 1833.

28088 SOCIETY FOR THE DIFFUSION OF USEFUL KNOWLEDGE. Monthly Supplement of the Penny Magazine of the Society for the Diffusion of Useful Knowledge. 69. March 31 to April 30, 1833. The Manchester and Liverpool Rail-road. p.161–168. *8°.* 1833.

28089 WHITBY AND PICKERING RAILWAY COMPANY. [*Endorsed:*] Whitby and Pickering Railway. Observations in favour of the undertaking, with a list of subscriptions. 2p. *fol. Whitby,* [1833]

28090 WILSON, JOHN H. On steam communication between Bombay and Suez, with an account of the Hugh Lindsay's four voyages. [Dated: June 19th, 1833. With 'Supplementary observations' dated August 1st.] 69, 20p. *8°. Bombay,* 1833.

SOCIAL CONDITIONS

28091 ADAMS, GEORGE (*fl.* 1833). Causes of the wretched condition of the Irish peasantry, with a sketch of a plan for restoring them to habits of industry and good order, in lieu of a poor rate. In a letter addressed to Sir Robert Price, Bart. M.P. 56p. *8°.* [1833] *The copy presented to the Marquis of Ormonde by L. Hanbury, 'late Secretary to the London Irish Relief & antislavery Committee'.*

28092 The **ADDRESS** of the operatives of England and Scotland, to all ranks and classes of the land. [An appeal for support for Lord Ashley, who is introducing the Ten Hours Bill in Parliament. Signed: Geo. Higginbottom, chairman, and dated, April 25, 1833.] *s.sh.fol. Manchester,* [1833] [*Br.* 565(1)] *The Oastler copy.*

28093 ADDRESS to the friends of justice and humanity, in the West Riding of York, from the meeting of delegates of the short time committees, established to promote the legislative adoption of the Ten Hour Factory Bill, assembled at the Yew Tree Inn, Birstall, October 28th, 1833. 24p. *8°. Bradford,* [1833] *The Oastler copy.*

28094 An **ADDRESS** to the members of the trades union. [On the evils of the apprenticeship system. Signed: A friend of the labouring class, and dated, August 7th, 1833.] 4p. *8°. Huddersfield,* [1833] *The Oastler copy.*

28095 ADDRESS. To the nobility, clergy, gentry, master-manufacturers, agriculturists, tradesmen, and operatives of the United Kingdom. [Signed: William Halliwell, chairman, G. S. Bull, secretary to the Committee of Delegates of the Short-Time Committees of the manufacturing districts of the United Kingdom, and dated, January 14th, 1833. A plea for the Ten Hours Bill.] *s.sh.fol. Bradford,* [1833] [*Br.* 565(2)] *The Oastler copy.*

For the **ADVOCATE;** or, artizans' and labourers' friend, *see* vol. III, *Periodicals list.*

28096 *ALLIN, T. Mechanics' institutions defended on Christian principles. A lecture delivered on the opening of the Sheffield Mechanics' Institution, on the 14th January, 1833. 24p. *8°. Sheffield,* 1833. *The FWA copy, that belonged to William Pare.*

28097 [**ANDERSON,** ARTHUR, *defendant.*] Important to every person who rents a house! A caution to tenants against the injustice and legal chicanery to which they are exposed, under the existing state of the law of landlord and tenant...Intended to point out the necessity for a reform in the law... 40p. *8°.* 1833.

28098 [**ANDRÉ,** , *Madame?*] Instruction élémentaire pour la formation et la tenue des salles d'asyle de l'enfance. 44p. *8°. Paris,* 1833. *Attributed to Madame André in a manuscript note on the title-page. The copy that belonged to Victor Considérant.*

28099 An **APPEAL** to the public, by the "factory masters" in Cragg Valley, against the misrepresentations and lies of the Rev. T. Crowther, R. Oastler, and G. Crabtree. [Dated: July 9th, 1833.] *s.sh.fol. Todmorden,* [1833] *The Oastler copy. For a reply see no.* 28114.

28100 The **ARTICLE** on the condition of the working classes, and the Factory Bill. From the Westminster Review, No. XXXV, for April, 1833. 24p. *8°.* 1833. *The Oastler copy.*

28101 [**ASHWORTH,** H.] Letter to the Right Hon. Lord Ashley, on the cotton factory question, and the Ten Hours' Factory Bill; with an appendix, containing an abstract of the Bill. By a Lancashire cotton spinner. Manchester, 30th March, 1833. 40p. *8°. Manchester,* 1833.

28102 B., J. The abolition of the poor laws, the safety of the state. Considerations on the calamitous results of the present system of pauperism...With an appendix; containing an account of the Labourers' Friend Society, with extracts from its publications. 40p. *8°.* 1833.

28103 BARNETT, A. The poor laws, and their administration; being an enquiry into the causes of English pauperism and the failure of measures intended for its relief... 81p. *8°. 1833. The Oastler copy.*

28104 BAXTER, J. Thoughts on the condition of agricultural labourers, with hints for their improvement. Extracted (by permission) from the second edition of... Baxter's Library of agricultural and horticultural knowledge... 7p. *8°. Lewes & London, 1833.*

28105 BENEVOLENT SOCIETY, *Torrington.* The regulations of a Benevolent Society, at the Malt Scoop Inn, Great Torrington. 12p. *12°. Torrington, 1833.* [*phc*]

28106 BENNET, W. Excise Widows' Fund. Appeal to the Legislature and the public, on the preservation of the same. [With a list of contributors to the Fund.] 73p. *8°. Glasgow, 1833.*

28107 BOSWORTH, J. Misery in the midst of plenty! or, the perversion of the poor laws: being an abstract from a larger pamphlet published in 1829, under the title "The necessity of the antipauper system," but now brought down to 1833. 33p. *8°. 1833. For the original work, see 1829.*

28108 [BOWLES, CAROLINE.] Tales of the factories: respectfully inscribed to Mr. Sadler. [In verse.] By the authoress of "Ellen Fitzarthur"... 85p. *8°. Edinburgh & London, 1833.*

28109 BRADFORD. The proceedings of a public meeting of the people of Bradford, Yorkshire, (held...on ...July 25, 1833, to deliberate upon the position of the Ten-Hour Bill,) with the address of the Rev. G. S. Bull... 23p. *8°. Bradford, 1833. The Oastler copy.*

28110 BRADFORD, July 1st, 1833. [*Begin.*] Sir, I hope you will favour our cause by the insertion of the following paragraph. – [A circular letter, unsigned, to be sent to newspaper editors, containing an account of the meeting in support of the Ten Hour Bill on Wibsey Low Moor.] [4]p. *fol. n.p.* [1833] *The Oastler copy.*

28111 BRADFORD SHORT-TIME COMMITTEE. Memorial to his Grace the Archbishop of York. [On the sufferings of factory children.] *s.sh.fol. n.p.* [1833] [*Br.* 557(4)] *The Oastler copy.*

28112 —— The Ten Hour Bill is not lost. [Announcing a public meeting on July 25th 1833. Signed: Joseph Woodhall, chairman, John Hall, secretary.] *s.sh.fol. Bradford,* [1833] [*Br.* 565(15)] *The Oastler copy.*

28113 —— To the Commissioners for collecting further evidence on the condition of the children employed in factories. [Setting out the views on the Factory Commission of the Bradford Committee and those of the surrounding districts.] *s.sh.fol. Bradford,* [1833] [*Br.* 558(15)] *The Oastler copy.*

28114 —— To the nameless factory masters in Cragg-Valley. [Signed: Joseph Woodhall, chairman, and dated, 2d August, 1833.] *s.sh.fol. Bradford,* [1833] [*Br.* 557(10)] *A reply to no. 28099. Sent through the post to Oastler, with a letter written on the verso signed: John Hall sen., asking for his help in getting copies displayed in Cragg Valley.*

28115 BULL, G. S. Factory children. [A speech.] At a public meeting of the Borough of Bradford, held on... February 19th, 1833, to consider of the propriety of petitioning Parliament respecting the Factories Regulation Bill... 12p. *12°. [London,* 1833] *The Oastler copy.*

28116 —— The Factory Commission. [A letter to the *Leeds Mercury* reprinted. Dated: May 18th, 1833.] *s.sh.fol. Leeds,* [1833] [*Br.* 558(4)] *The Oastler copy.*

28117 —— Friends of humanity! [An appeal to Yorkshiremen to continue to give their support to the Ten Hours Bill, which has been given its second reading. Dated: June 19, 1833.] *s.sh.fol. Bradford,* [1833] [*Br.* 565(4)] *The Oastler copy.*

28118 —— A last lift for the Ten Hour Bill. [A circular letter, dated June 20, 1833, announcing a West Riding meeting for July 1st 1833.] *s.sh.fol. n.p.* [1833] [*Br.* 565(6)] *The Oastler copy.*

28119 [——] The march of freedom and knowledge, 1833. 4p. *8°. Bradford,* [1833] *The copy that belonged to Oastler, who attributed it to Bull in the manuscript index to his pamphlet collection.*

28120 —— [*Begin.*] On Tuesday evening, June 11th, 1833, in consequence of many misrepresentations... respecting the advice given to the factory children about the Ten Hour Bill, by the Rev. G. S. Bull, a large meeting of the children took place...Mr. Bull addressed the children as follows... *s.sh.fol. n.p.* [1833] [*Br.* 557(6)] *On the verso a printed letter asking recipients to furnish numbers of copies required for distribution among factory hands. Dated: Bradford, June 13th, 1833. The Oastler copy.*

28121 —— [Another edition.] 8p. *16°. Bradford,* [1833] *The Oastler copy.*

28122 —— Protest of the Rev. G. S. Bull, addressed to the Commissioners for Factory Enquiry. [Dated: June 4th, 1833.] *s.sh.fol. Bradford,* [1833] [*Br.* 558(13)] *The Oastler copy.*

28123 BULLOCK, R. On mending the times: addressed to the author's friends and acquaintances, engaged in manufacture; briefly shewing the true cause of low wages; with a natural, easy, and effectual mode on improving our system. 16p. *8°. Macclesfield, 1833. The Oastler copy.*

28124 CAREY, M. Appeal to the wealthy of the land, ladies as well as gentlemen, on the character, conduct, situation, and prospects of those whose sole dependence for subsistence is on the labour of their hands...Second edition, improved. 36p. *8°. Philadelphia, 1833.*

28125 —— Third edition, improved. 36p. *8°. Philadelphia, 1833.*

28126 —— To the humane and charitable. [On the distress of the working classes, notably women workers, and the need to alleviate it. Dated: Sept. 6, 1833.] 2p. *s.sh.4°. n.p.* [1833] [*Br.* 553]

28127 CHALMERS, T. Tracts on pauperism. 97, 78, 34p. *8°. Glasgow, London, &c.,* 1833. *A reissue of three earlier publications with a general title-page and a preface.*

28128 CHILD murder no crime!! [A poster, announcing a meeting to draw up a petition. Dated: April 12th, 1833.] *s.sh.4°. Huddersfield,* [1833] [*Br.* 557(2)] *The Oastler copy.*

28129 COBBETT, W. Rights of industry. (Extracted from "Cobbett's Register" of December 14, 1833.) To John Fielden, Member of Parliament for Oldham. [With 'Mr. Fielden's letter to Mr. Cobbett'.] 8p. *8°. [London,* 1833] *The Oastler copy.*

28130 The **COMMISSION** for perpetuating factory infanticide. Extracted from Fraser's Magazine for June

1833. [A criticism of the way the Factory Commission conducted its inquiries.] 11p. *8°*. [*London*, 1833] *The Oastler copy.*

28131 The **COMMISSIONERS** came in last night, under the cover of darkness, which they love, they are at the Talbot. [Summoning the local factory children to deliver a protest against the Factory Commission. Dated: June 5th, 1833.] *s.sh.4°*. *Bradford*, [1833] [*Br.* 558(1)] *The Oastler copy.*

28132 The **COMMISSIONER'S** vade mecum, whilst engaged in collecting evidence for the factory masters. [A satire on the work of the Factory Commissioners.] 8p. *8°*. *Leeds*, 1833. *The Oastler copy.*

28133 COMMITTEE OF SUPERINTENDENCE FOR THE RELIEF OF SUFFERERS BY THE CONFLAGRATION AT CUMBERLAND. Cumberland sufferers. [An appeal for contributions. Signed by Mathew Carey and 11 other members of the Committee, and dated, Philadelphia, April 29th, 1833.] *s.sh.8°*. [1833] [*Br.* 555]

28134 The **CONDITION** of the West India slave contrasted with that of the infant slave in our English factories. With fifteen illustrations from the graver of Robert Cruikshank. 37p. *12°*. [1833?]

28135 CONDY, G. An argument for placing factory children within the pale of the law. 60p. *8°*. *London & Manchester*, 1833. *Two copies, one the Oastler copy, the other a presentation copy, with a printed notice inserted after the title-page, to 'Colonel Fox', i.e. Charles Richard Fox (1796–1873).*

28136 CONNERY, J. The reformer, or, an infallible remedy to prevent pauperism & periodical returns of famine, with other salutary measures...and establishing the futility of the plan of William Smith O'Brien, Esq., (late Member of Parliament for Ennis,)...Fifth edition... 61p. *12°*. *Limerick*, 1833. *See also* 1836.

28137 CONVERSATION among factory children about the Commission. *s.sh.fol.* [1833] [*Br.* 558(2)] *The Oastler copy.*

28138 *****CORBET,** D. An address delivered to the members of the Worcester Literary and Scientific Institution, on...March 27th, 1833. 26p. *8°*. *Worcester*, [1833] *The FWA copy, that belonged to William Pare.*

28139 CRABTREE, GEOFFREY. Factory Commission: the legality of its appointment questioned, and the illegality of its proceedings proved. Addressed to Lord Althorpe. 20p. *8°*. 1833. *Presentation copy, with inscription, from the author to the Rev. G. S. Bull. It afterwards belonged to Oastler.*

28140 CRABTREE, GEORGE. A brief description of a tour through Calder Dale, being a letter to Richard Oastler... 26p. *8°*. *Huddersfield & Manchester*, 1833. *The Oastler copy. *Another, the FWA copy, belonged to William Pare.*

28141 DAY, WILLIAM, *Asst. Poor Law Commissioner.* An inquiry into the poor laws and surplus labour, and their mutual reaction: with a postscript containing observations on the commutation of tithes, and remarks on Lord Milton's address on the corn-laws...Second edition, enlarged. 112p. *8°*. 1833. *Another, the FWA copy, belonged to William Pare. For another edition, see* 1832.

28142 DOHERTY, J. and **TURNER,** JAMES. To the Central Board of the Factory Commission. [Declining,

on behalf of those whom they are representing in London, to take part in the proceedings of the Commission. Dated: May 24, 1833.] *s.sh.fol. n.p.* [1833] [*Br.* 558(14)] *The Oastler copy.*

28143 A capital **DOZEN.** [*Begin.*] A reward is hereby offered to any one who is able and willing to declare the name of a certain worsted spinner, resident somewhere between Bradford and Skipton...[A fraud has been perpetrated on his workmen by the factory owner.] *s.sh.fol. Bradford*, [1833?] [*Br.* 551(1)] *The Oastler copy.*

28144 DRINKWATER, J. E. Letter to Michael Thos. Sadler, F.R.S. 14p. *8°*. *Leeds*, 1833. *The Oastler copy.*

28145 —— Replies to Mr. M. T. Sadler's protest against the Factory Commission. By John Elliot Drinkwater, Esq. and Alfred Power, Esq. 12p. *8°*. *Leeds*, 1833. *The Oastler copy.*

28146 ENGLAND. *Commissioners for Inquiring into the Administration and Practical Operation of the Poor Laws.* Extracts from the information received by His Majesty's Commissioners, as to the administration and operation of the poor-laws. [With 'Appendix. Instructions from the Central Board of Poor-Law Commissioners to assistant commissioners', originally issued in 1832.] 432p. *8°*. 1833. *See also* 1837.

28147 —— *Factory Commission.* Instructions from the Central Board of Factory Commissioners to district civil and medical commissioners. 43p. *8°*. *n.p.* [1833] *The Oastler copy.*

28148 —— *Home Office.* Summary statements of the number of criminal offenders committed to the several gaols in England and Wales, &c.&c.&c. 31p. *8°*. *n.p.* 1833. *See also* 1822, 1824, 1831, 1834.

28149 —— *Laws, etc.* An Act for collecting the poor's rates, &c. of the parish of Saint Luke, Chelsea [1 & 2 Geo. IV, c.lxvii]; to which is added, the by laws, made by the Committee-men. 43, 53p. *8°*. *Chelsea*, 1833.

28150 —— *Parliament. House of Commons.* Factories regulation. Debate in the House of Commons, on...July 18, 1833, in committee on the Factories Regulation Bill. Extracted from the Mirror of Parliament, Part CCXXXVII. 84p. *8°*. 1833.

28151 ENGLISHMEN! And men of Huddersfield ...[A poster appealing for further effort for the Ten Hours' Bill.] *s.sh.fol. Huddersfield*, [1833] [*Br.* 565(3)] *The Oastler copy.*

28152 *****EVANS,** GEORGE, *M.P.* Remarks on the expediency of introducing poor rates into Ireland. 75p. *8°*. 1833. *The copy that belonged to George Grote.*

28153 EXETER. *Corporation of the Poor.* A list of persons relieved by the Corporation of the Poor...from 1st May 1832, to 30th April, 1833, during the Treasurership of Michael Franklin, Esq. [14]p. *4°*. *Exeter*, [1833] *See also* 1832.

28154 Just published, price four-pence, an **EXPOSURE** of the ruinous, impracticable, and most unjust measure of Lord Althorpe, 'The Factories' Regulation Act'... *s.sh.fol. Bradford*, [1833] [*Br.* 565(5)] *Printed on yellow paper. The Oastler copy.*

28155 EXTRACT from the London Times, of Monday June 3d, 1833 [on the instructions issued by the Central Board to the Subordinate Factory Commissioners]. *s.sh.8°. n.p.* [1833] *The Oastler copy.*

28156 EXTRACTS from a letter addressed to Montague Gore, Esq. M.P. containing observations on the present state of the poor. Potterne, Feb. 9th, 1833. 16p. *8°. Devizes,* [1833] *The copy presented to an unidentified recipient 'with Major Oliver's Co[mpliments]'; Major Oliver was possibly the author.*

28157 EXTRACTS from the medical evidence of the Factory Commission. Delivered to the House of Commons, this evening, July 17, 1833. [From the evidence of Dr. Hawkins and Dr. Loudon.] 3p. *4°. n.p.* [1833] *The Oastler copy.*

28158 The **FACTORY BILL.** Lord Ashley's Ten-Hour Bill and the scheme of the Factory Commissioners compared. 15p. *8°.* [1833] *The Oastler copy.*

28159 FACTORY COMMISSION. Correspondence between Mr. Wilson, Secretary to the Central Board of Factory Commissioners, and Mr. Stuart, one of the Commissioners. 16p. *8°.* [*London,* 1833] *The Oastler copy.*

28160 The **FACTORY COMMISSIONERS** at Leeds. [Signed: an eye witness, and dated, May 20th, 1833.] *s.sh.4°. Bradford,* [1833] [*Br.* 558(6)] *The Oastler copy.*

28161 FACTORY COMMISSIONERS' report. Medical opinions, &c.&c.&c. 12p. *8°.* [*London,* 1833] *The Oastler copy.*

28162 The **FACTORY QUESTION.** 8p. *8°. Glasgow,* [1833] *The Oastler copy.*

28163 FACTORY SYSTEM. [Selections from evidence in support of the Ten Hours Bill.] 3p. *fol.* [1833] *The Oastler copy.*

28164 The **FACTORY SYSTEM** and the Ten Hours Bill. Extracted from Fraser's Magazine, April, 1833. Article, "National Economy, no. v." 16p. *8°.* [*London,* 1833] *The Oastler copy.*

28165 FEMALE MODEL SCHOOL, *Dublin.* A concise account of the mode of instructing in needle-work, as practised in the Female Model School, Kildare Place, Dublin. [With the rules of the school.] 39p. *8°.* [*Dublin,*] 1833.

28166 FINLAY, K. Letter to the Right Hon. Lord Ashley, on the cotton factory system and the Ten Hours' Factory Bill. 19p. *8°. Glasgow,* 1st March 1833. *The Oastler copy.*

28167 —— [Another issue.] 19p. *8°. Glasgow, Edinburgh, &c.,* 1833. *Presentation copy, with inscription, from the author to T. Spring Rice, Baron Monteagle.*

28168 FONNEREAU, W. C. Remarks and suggestions relative to the management of the poor in Ipswich. 86p. *8°. Ipswich,* 1833.

28169 GAGERN, H. C. E., *Freiherr von.* England rebuked by Germany; or, the speech of Baron von Gagern...Darmstadt, June 4, 1833, on the British factory system. *s.sh.8°. n.p.* [1833] *The Oastler copy.*

28170 GASKELL, P. The manufacturing population of England, its moral, social, and physical conditions, and the changes which have arisen from the use of steam machinery; with an examination of infant labour. 361p. *8°.* 1833.

28171 GENERAL UNION OF THE BUILDING TRADES, *Manchester.* Brief history of the proceedings of the operative builders' trades unions in Manchester, and the consequent turn-out of the journeymen masons, bricklayers, joiners, slaters, & other trades, with copies of letters, placards, union rules and other particulars. 16p. *8°. Manchester,* 1833.

28172 *GENEVA.* Dispositions réglementaires concernant les détenus dans la prison pénitentiaire de Genève. 28p. *8°. Genève,* 1833. *The copy that belonged to George Grote.*

28173 GERANDO, J. M. DE, *Baron.* The visitor of the poor, designed to aid in the formation and working of provident and other kindred societies. Translated from the French...With an introduction by the Rev. J. Tuckerman [and a preface signed: J.R.B., i.e. J. R. Beard]. xxxviii, 191p. *12°.* 1833. *For another edition, see* 1820.

28174 "GET away!! Get away!!!" said "King Richard." [An announcement that the members of the Royal Commission have left for London. Dated: June 15th, 1833.] *s.sh.fol. Bradford,* [1833] [*Br.* 558(7)] *The Oastler copy.*

28175 GOUGER, R. Emigration for the relief of parishes practically considered. [With prospectuses issued by Robert Gouger & Co. to would-be emigrants.] 14p. *8°.* 1833.

28176 —— Second edition. 14p. *8°.* 1833.

28177 [GREEN, ?] A few arguments in favour of Mr. Sadler's Bill, for shortening the hours of labour in factories: and against oppression in general. By a member of the Huddersfield Political Union. 16p. *8°. Huddersfield,* 1833. *The copy that belonged to Oastler, who attributed it to 'Green' in the manuscript index to his pamphlet collection.*

28178 GUERRY, A. M. Essai sur la statistique morale de la France, précédé d'un rapport à l'Académie des Sciences, par MM. Lacroix, Silvestre et Girard. 70p. *4°. Paris,* 1833.

28179 GWYNN, W. J. Reasons for withholding an official approval of spirit licenses; addressed to the spirit dealers of the parish of Antrim. [Third edition. A temperance tract.] 16p. *8°.* [1833]

28180 HACKNEY PAROCHIAL ASSOCIATION. Address to the inhabitants of the parish of Hackney: together with the rules of Hackney Parochial Association, for the Correction and Prevention of Abuses. 8p. *8°. Hackney,* 1833.

28181 HARDY'S ticket withdrawn as well as Oastler's! [A satirical reference, presumably to the dinner of 26 December 1833.] *s.sh.4°. Huddersfield,* [1833] [*Br.* 559(2)] *The Oastler copy.*

28182 HILL, ROWLAND (1744–1833). Village dialogues, between Farmer Littleworth, Thomas Newman, Rev. Mr. Lovegood and others...Thirty-third edition, with additional dialogues and enlargements... 2 vols. *12°.* 1833, 1829. *Vol. II is of the 29th edition. For other editions, see* 1803.

28183 HOLDER, R. Lines on the factory system. [In verse.] *s.sh.fol. n.p.* [1833 ?] [*Br.* 557(3)] *The Oastler copy.*

28184 HUMANITY and justice!! Ten Hour Bill. [An appeal to supporters of the Ten Hours Bill in Dewsbury to attend a meeting of the Short-Time Committee there.] [2]p. *8°. n.p.* [1833] *The Oastler copy.*

28185 Disgusting unfeeling **IMPUDENCE!!!** To the "swinish multitude." [An attack on the Factory

Commission.] *s.sh.fol. n.p.* [1833] [*Br.* 558(3)] *The Oastler copy.*

28186 INSTRUCTIONS to the Short Time Committee of England and Scotland, with reference to the [Factory] Commission. [With 'Minutes of a meeting of delegates representing the Short Time Committees of England and Scotland, held at Manchester... April, 1833...' Signed: Geo. Higginbottom, chairman, G. S. Bull, secretary.] [4]p. *fol. n.p.* [1833] *The Oastler copy.*

For JAHRBUECHER DER STRAF- UND BESSERUNGS-ANSTALTEN, *see* vol. III, *Periodicals list.*

28187 The JUSTICE, humanity, and policy, of restricting the hours of children & young persons in the mills & factories of the United Kingdom, illustrated in the letters, speeches, &c., of persons... many of them resident in... those districts where the evils exist, which it is sought to mitigate by Mr. Sadler's Ten Hour Bill. 136p. *8°. Leeds,* 1833. *The Oastler copy.*

28188 KENWORTHY, R. [*Begin.*] To the Right Hon. Lord Brougham, and the rest of His Majesty's Ministers. [Calling on the Government to promote 'an equitable adjustment of all kinds of labour'. Dated: February 1833.] *s.sh.4°. Lees,* [1833] [*Br.* 567(2)] *The Oastler copy.*

28189 LA BONNINIÈRE DE BEAUMONT, G. A. DE, and CLÉREL DE TOCQUEVILLE, C. A. H. M., *Comte de Tocqueville.* Origin and outline of the penitentiary system in the United States of North America, translated and abridged from the French official report of Messrs. G. de Beaumont & A. de Tocqueville. By William B. Sarsfield Taylor. 36p. *8°. London, Edinburgh, &c.,* 1833. *The copy that belonged to William Allen.*

28190 LABOURERS' FRIEND SOCIETY, *London.* The second general report of the committee of the... Society, read at the public meeting... on... the 17th of May, 1833: together with resolutions adopted, and a list of the subscribers and benefactors... 42p. *8°.* 1833.

28191 LA FAYETTE COLLEGE. The second annual report of the Board of Trustees of La Fayette College. Read at the public exhibition, October 7th, 1833. 16p. *8°. Easton, Pa.,* [1833]

28192 LANCASHIRE CENTRAL SHORT-TIME COMMITTEE. Ten Hours' Bill. The public set right. [Signed: George Higginbottom, chairman, and dated, April 5th, 1833.] *s.sh.fol.* [*Manchester,* 1833] [*Br.* 565(18)] *The Oastler copy. A reply to no.* 28277.

28193 LEEDS GENERAL COMMITTEE FOR PROMOTING THE BILL FOR RESTRICTING THE HOURS OF JUVENILE LABOUR IN THE FACTORIES. To the operatives of Leeds and the West Riding of Yorkshire. [An exhortation to support renewed pressure for the Ten Hours Bill, and extracts from newspaper comment on the Report of the Select Committee. Signed: John Hannam, president, R. Taylor, secretary.] *s.sh.fol. Leeds,* [1833 ?] [*Br.* 547(18)]

28194 LEEDS SHORT-TIME COMMITTEE. More lies of the Mercury. [Refuting the allegation in the *Leeds Mercury* that members of the Short-Time Committee had accompanied the Factory Commissioners on their visits of inspection. Signed: Wm. Rider, secretary, and dated, May 27th, 1833.] *s.sh.fol. Leeds,* [1833]. [*Br.* 558(9)] *The Oastler copy.*

28195 —— [*Begin.*] The Ten Hour Bill passed the second reading in the House of Commons on Monday night... [A warning against the Government's intention to bring in an Eight Hour Bill and to allow relays of children to work in the mills. Signed: John Stubbs, chairman, Wm. Rider, secretary, and dated, June 18, 1833.] *s.sh.fol. Leeds,* [1833] [*Br.* 565(16)] *The Oastler copy.*

28196 LETTER to the Right Hon. Lord Althorp, on the Factory Bill. [Signed: a Scotch mill-spinner.] 12p. *8°. Montrose,* [1833] *The Oastler copy.*

28197 LUTHER, S. An address to the working men of New England, on the state of education, and on the condition of the producing classes in Europe and America. With particular reference to the effect of manufacturing (as now conducted) on the health and happiness of the poor... Second edition, corrected by the author. *8°. New York,* 1833.

28198 MACERONI, F. Hints to paviors... with an introductory review by J. C. Robertson, Esq. editor of the Mechanics' Magazine, of the various plans proposed for the improvement of carriage pavements; also, a paper on the increasing of day-light in London, &c. Second edition. 36p. *8°.* 1833.

28199 M'GILL, J. A letter to ministers of the Gospel, upon the subject of temperance societies. 39p. *8°. Dumfries, Edinburgh, &c.,* 1833. *The Turner copy.*

28200 MACKENZIE, P. Reply to the letter of Kirkman Finlay, Esq. on the spy system. [Second edition.] 16p. *8°. Glasgow,* 1833.

28201 MANCHESTER. The Factory Commission arrived. Memorial of the factory children presented. [Dated: May 8th, 1833.] *s.sh.fol. Mancheester* [*sic*], [1833] [*Br.* 558(8)] *The Oastler copy.*

28202 MANCHESTER SHORT-TIME COMMITTEE. Protest against the Parliamentary Commission, to collect further evidence on the factory system. [Signed: George Higginbottom, chairman.] *s.sh.fol. Manchester,* [1833] [*Br.* 558(12)] *The Oastler copy.*

28203 MARTIN, ROBERT M. Poor laws for Ireland, a measure of justice to England; of humanity to the people of both islands; and of self-preservation for the Empire. With a practical development of an improved system of settlement, assessment, and relief. 49p. *8°.* 1833. *A proof copy, with manuscript corrections in the text.*

28204 MARTINEAU, H. Illustrations of political economy. No. III. Brooke and Brooke Farm. A tale... Third edition. 319p. *12°.* 1833. *For an edition of the complete series, see* 1834 (GENERAL).

28205 —— Under the superintendence of the Society for the Diffusion of Useful Knowledge. Poor laws and paupers illustrated. [Tales.] 4 vols. *12°.* 1833–34.

28206 MASSACHUSETTS. General Court. *House of Representatives.* House. No. 6. Report of the Commissioners appointed by an order of the House of Representatives, Feb. 29, 1832, on the subject of the pauper system of the Commonwealth of Massachusetts. 97p. *8°. Boston,* 1833.

28207 Great MEETING in Leeds, on... the 16th of May, 1833 of the factory children, to present their protest to the Commissioners appointed through Mr. Wilson Patten's motion for further enquiry, &c.&c. 7p. *8°. Leeds,* 1833. *The Oastler copy.*

28208 Great MEETING of the West-Riding in

support of the Ten-Hour Bill. (From the Leeds Intelligencer of July 6, 1833.) 16p. *8°. Leeds,* [1833] *The Oastler copy.*

28209 Public **MEETING** and dinner, to John Fielden, Esq. M.P....on Thursday December 26th, 1833...will be holden in the White Hart Inn yard. [An announcement and invitation to the dinner, dated 10th December 1833, signed in manuscript: Wm. Williams, secretary.] *s.sh.fol. Huddersfield,* [1833] [*Br.* 559(1)] *Addressed in manuscript to 'Richd Oastler Esq.'.*

28210 Public **MEETING** in Halifax, on the Ten Hour Bill, held on...July 13th, 1833. 18p. *12°. Halifax,* [1833] *The Oastler copy.*

28211 Public **MEETING.** To Mr. W. Barcroft, Constable of the Township of Wadsworth...[A request for a meeting to plan the strategy of the movement to secure the Ten Hours Bill, signed by Robert Sutcliffe and 9 others, with the Constable's notice calling the meeting for August 24th, 1833.] *s.sh.fol. Todmooden* [*sic*], [1833] [*Br.* 565(10)] *Printed on yellow paper. The Oastler copy.*

28212 MINUTES and resolutions of a meeting of delegates from the Short Time Committees of the West Riding of Yorkshire, established to promote the legislative adoption of the Ten Hour Factory Bill, assembled at the Yew Tree Inn, Birstall, October 28th, 1833. [Condemning Lord Althorp's Factories Regulation Act, and making arrangements to continue the agitation for a Ten Hours Bill. Signed: James Bedford, chairman, S. Glendenning, secretary.] *s.sh.fol. Bradford,* [1833] [*Br.* 565(9)] *The Oastler copy.*

28213 MINUTES, resolutions, &c.&c. A meeting of delegates from the committee of the manufacturing districts, established for the furtherance and support of Mr. Sadler's Factories Regulation Bill, was held...at Bradford, Yorkshire, on...the 11th day of January 1833... [Signed: William Halliwell, chairman, G. S. Bull, secretary. Dated: January 14th, 1833.] 3p. *fol. Bradford,* [1833] *The Oastler copy.*

28214 [**MORGAN,**   ?] A brief review of the British Labourer's Protector, and factory child's friend. 8p. *8°.* [*Leeds, Bradford, &c.,* 1833?] *The copy that belonged to Oastler, who attributed it to 'Morgan' in the manuscript index to his pamphlet collection.*

28215 MUTUAL INSURANCE BENEFIT INSTITUTION. Rules of the Mutual Insurance Benefit Institution... 32p. *8°.* 1833. *See also* 1825.

28216 NEW YORK, *State of.* The act of incorporation of the Manhattan Company [for supplying the city of New-York with pure and wholesome water], passed April 2, 1799. [With a supplementary act of 1808.] 12p. *8°. New-York,* 1833.

28217 OASTLER, R. [*Begin.*] Dear Sir, You will receive herewith [*blank*] copies of The delegates' address for sale... *s.sh.8°. n.p.* [1833] *Oastler's own copy.*

28218 —— The "factory masters" in Cragg Dale, who have "challenged" Richard Oastler without publishing their names. [Dated: July 15, 1833.] *s.sh.fol. Huddersfield,* [1833] [*Br.* 563(4)] *Oastler's own copy.*

28219 —— Facts and plain words on every-day subjects, comprised in two speeches delivered at Wakefield on the day of the first election for the West-Riding of Yorkshire, December 20, 1832... 60p. *8°. Leeds,* 1833. *Two copies, one Oastler's own, the other that belonged to M. T. Sadler.*

28220 —— Infant slavery. Report of a speech, delivered in favour of the Ten Hours' Bill by Richard Oastler, Esq. at Preston, on the 22nd of March, 1833. With extracts from his speech at Bolton. 16p. *8°. Preston,* 1833. *Oastler's own copy.*

28221 —— Slavery in Yorkshire. To the editor of the Intelligencer. [Dated: July 29, 1833.] *s.sh.fol. Leeds,* [1833] [*Br.* 565(12)] *Oastler's own copy.*

28222 —— Speech delivered at a public meeting held ...in...Huddersfield, on...June 18, 1833, to petition the House of Commons against the report of the Factory Commissioners being received...With an address to the Queen. 16p. *8°. Leeds,* 1833. *Oastler's own copy.*

28223 —— A speech delivered by Richard Oastler at a meeting held in...Manchester, on...April 27th, 1833, to consider of the propriety of petitioning the Legislature to pass the Ten Hours Factories' Regulation Bill, without waiting for the report of that 'mockery of inquiry', the mill-owners commission. 16p. *8°. Huddersfield & Manchester,* 1833. *Oastler's own copy.*

28224 OASTLER and the factory children's rights for ever!! [A ballad.] *s.sh.4°. Halifax,* [1833] [*Br.* 557(5)] *The Oastler copy.*

28225 April 2, 1833. **OBSERVATIONS** on a Bill now pending in the House of Commons for the better observance of the Lord's-day. 14p. *8°.* [1833]

28226 OKEDEN, D. O. P. A letter to the Rev. Harry Farr Yeatman, on his inquiry, &c.&c. 10p. *8°. Salisbury,* 1833.

28227 PEEL, SIR ROBERT, *2nd Bart.* Speech of the Right Honourable Sir Robert Peel, Bart. in the House of Commons, on...March 1st, 1833, on the Bill for suppressing disturbances in Ireland. 56p. *8°.* 1833. *The copy that belonged to Lord Ellenborough, with his signature on the half-title.*

28228 —— Second edition. 56p. *8°.* 1833.

28229 PEMBERTON, B. An address of the bricklayers & plasterers, to the tradesmen of the City of Dublin, on the necessity of ... co-opperating [*sic*] for the attainment of their corporate rights and privilege, their report to the Trades' Political Union on the state of their respective trades...also, the petition of Mr. Benjamin Pemberton, against the undue return of a late measurer and metal sash maker, as two...proper persons to represent their guild in the Common Council...together with his appeal... 36p. *12°. Dublin,* 1833.

28230 PENDLETON AND NEW WINDSOR TEMPERANCE ASSOCIATION. First annual report of the Committee of the...Association. 4p. *12°. n.p.* [1833] *The Turner copy.*

28231 Unrivalled **PERFORMANCES!** That great mountebank, R. Oastler, will exhibit to the public, at Hebden-Bridge, on Saturday afternoon next. [An attack on Oastler and the Rev. G. S. Bull for their views on the corn laws and landlords. Dated: August 22nd, 1833.] *s.sh.fol. n.p.* [1833] [*Br.* 565(20)] *Printed on yellow paper. The Oastler copy.*

28232 To the King's most excellent Majesty the **PETITION** of your dutiful and loyal subjects inhabitants of Halifax. [Against the projected Commission to reopen the factory question.] *s.sh.fol. n.p.* [1833] [*Br.* 557(9)] *The Oastler copy.*

28233 Nice **PICKINGS!!** Commissioning is no bad

job. [An account of the money to be spent on the Factory Commission.] *s.sh.fol. Bradford,* [1833] [*Br.* 558(10)] *The Oastler copy.*

28234 PINNEY, C. Trial of Charles Pinney, Esq. in the Court of King's Bench, on an information...charging him with neglect of duty, in his office as Mayor of Bristol, during the riots... 432p. *8°. Bristol, London, &c.,* 1833.

28235 POOR LAW INQUIRY. Labour vote. [The reply of the Commissioners for Inquiring into the Administration of the Poor Laws to a question put by Lord Althorp, whether the Bill to continue the practice of supplementing the poors-rate by parochial levy will increase the existing evils of the poor laws.] 4p. *8°.* [*London,* 1833] *The copy that belonged to Francis Place.*

28236 POWER, SIR A. Letter to Michael Thos. Sadler, Esq., F.R.S. 12p. *8°. Leeds,* 1833. *The Oastler copy.*

28237 PRESTON SHORT-TIME COMMITTEE. [*Begin.*] Reverend Sir, the Short Time Committee of Preston...[An invitation, dated August 19th 1833, to clergymen to attend a meeting to be held on August 22nd, 1833, concerning children in factories.] *s.sh.8°. Preston,* [1833] *Addressed in manuscript to the Rev. W. Dixon. The Oastler copy.*

28238 PROCEEDINGS of a public meeting held at Hebden-Bridge...Halifax, Yorkshire, on...August 24th, 1833...for the purpose of promoting the Ten Hour Factory Bill... 25p. *8°. Huddersfield,* [1833] *The Oastler copy.*

28239 Public **PROTEST** against the Factory Commission. Meeting in the Free Market, Leeds, May 20, 1833. 8p. *8°. Leeds,* [1833] *The Oastler copy.*

28240 Don **QUIXOTE** [Edward Baines] and his esquires [John Elliot Drinkwater and Alfred Power]. [Quotations from statements by Drinkwater and Power, and a report of the meeting of the Short-Time Committee on 18 June 1833, signed by John Stubbs, chairman, and William Rider, secretary, at which the two Factory Commissioners were declared to be unfit to present any report.] 8p. *8°. Leeds,* 1833 *The Oastler copy.*

28241 REMARKS on the propriety and necessity of making the Factory Bill of more general application. 10p. *8°. London, Manchester, &c.,* 1833.

28242 REPLY to R. Oastler. [Dated: Cragg-Valley, July 22nd, 1833.] *s.sh fol. Todmorden,* [1833] [*Br.* 563(2)] *Sent through the post to Oastler, with a Huddersfield postmark, dated 'Jy. 26 1833'.*

28243 On the **REPORT** of the Factory Commission. The great West Riding meeting on the present state of the factory question, on Monday, July 1st. (From the Leeds Times, of July 4.) *s.sh.fol. Leeds,* [1833] [*Br.* 558(11)] *The Oastler copy.*

28244 REPORT of a most important meeting of the operatives of Glasgow, upon the Ten Hour Bill, on... August 1st, 1833, in the Lyceum...(From the Glasgow "Liberator.") 8p. *8°. Bradford,* 1833. *The Oastler copy.* *Another, the FWA copy, belonged to William Pare.*

28245 REPORT of a public meeting to consider of a petition to Parliament, in support of Lord Ashley's Factory Bill, held...on...April 8th, 1833, at the Old Assembly Room, Halifax, Yorkshire. 12p. *8°. Halifax* [1833] *The Oastler copy.*

28246 RESOLUTIONS of the Committee of Master Cotton-Spinners, assembled at the Union Hotel, London, 18th June, 1833. [The terms upon which a Bill to limit the hours of factory labour will be acceptable to them. Signed by Holland Hoole, chairman, R. Hyde Gregg and 13 other representatives.] *s.sh.fol.* [*London,* 1833] [*Br.* 565(11)] *The Oastler copy.*

28247 RICHARDS, JOHN (*fl.* 1832–1837). Speech in the House of Commons, May 2, 1833, on a motion for the introduction of poor laws into Ireland, with historical notes, &c. 35p. *8°.* 1833.

28248 [**RICHARDSON,** C.] [*Begin.*] Gentlemen, I am deputed to attend the childien [*sic*] of the poor and helpless to protest against your making enquiry...[Text of a speech read by Cavie Richardson to the members of the Factory Commission when they received a deputation of children at Leeds, May 1833.] *s.sh.fol. n.p.* [1833] [*Br.* 580] *The Oastler copy, endorsed in his hand: Cavie Richardsons speech to the Factory Com^{rs} at Leeds.*

28249 —— Speech delivered April 19, 1833, before the Short-Time Committee, and...delegates assembled for the purpose of considering the best methods of dealing with the Special Commission on the Factories' Regulation Bill. 8p. *8°. Leeds,* 1833. *The Oastler copy.*

28250 —— The Ten Hours' Bill will increase wages. A speech delivered at Bradford, at a meeting to promote Mr. Sadler's Bill; held...Jan. 14th, 1833... 11p. *12°. Leeds,* [1833] *The Oastler copy.*

28251 RIDER, W. Observations on a pamphlet by Messrs. Drinkwater and Power, the Factory Commissioners, purporting to be "Replies" to Mr. Sadler's protest against the said Commission...Published at the request of the Short Time Committee. 10p. *8°. Leeds,* 1833 *The Oastler copy.*

28252 The **RIGHTS** of the poor, and the poor laws. 64p. *8°. Leeds,* 1833.

28253 ROBERTS, S. An address to the members of the two Wilberforce-Committees, London and York. [On a suitable memorial to the late William Wilberforce.] 3p. *4°. Sheffield,* [1833] *Presentation copy from the author to George Thompson, with the postmark 'Oct. 28 1833', and a manuscript letter at the end of the printed text. For this, see vol.* III, *A.L.* 207.

28254 ROYLE, V. The factory system defended, in reply to some parts of the speech of G. Condy, Esq., barrister-at-law, at a public meeting held in Manchester, on the 14th of February 1833. 44p. *8°. Manchester,* 1833. *The Oastler copy.*

28255 SADLER, M. T. The distress of the agricultural labourers, illustrated by the speech of M. T. Sadler, Esq. M.P. upon a motion for leave to bring in a Bill for their relief, on October eleventh, 1831. 32p. *8°. Bradford,* 1833. *The Oastler copy. For another edition, see* 1831.

28256 —— Protest against the secret proceedings of the Factory Commission, in Leeds. Published at the request of the Short Time Committee. 16p. *8°. Leeds,* 1833. *The Oastler copy.*

28257 —— Reply to the two letters of John Elliot Drinkwater, Esquire, and Alfred Power, Esquire, Factory Commissioners, &c.&c. 23p. *8°. Leeds,* 1833. *The Oastler copy.* *Another, the FWA copy, belonged to William Pare.*

28258 SARDINIA AND PIEDMONT. *Ministero degli Affari dell'Interno.* Lettera circolare del primo Segretario di Stato per gli affari dell'interno [Antonio

Tonduti, Conte della Escarena] sul modo di provvedere al sollievo, ed alla assistenza dei poveri. 46p. *8°. Torino*, 1833.

28259 SCROPE, G. P. Plan of a poor-law for Ireland, with a review of the arguments for and against it. 88p. *8°*. 1833. *See also 1834.*

28260 SEDGWICK, J. A letter to the rate-payers of Great Britain, on the repeal of the poor-laws; to which is subjoined the outline of a plan for the abolition of the poor-rates at the end of three years. 167p. *8°. London & Brighton*, 1833.

28261 SHILLITOE, T. The speech of Thomas Shillitoe, at the second anniversary of the British and Foreign Temperance Society, held at Exeter Hall, London, 21st May, 1833. 4p. *12°. Ipswich*, [1833] *The Turner copy.*

28262 SKETCH of an association for gathering and diffusing information on the condition of the poor. 14p. *8°. London, Dublin, &c.*, 1833. *The copy presented, with an inscription on the title-page, to Robert Southey by J. W. Blakesley (1808–1885).*

28263 SOCIÉTÉ DES AMIS DU PEUPLE. Procès du droit d'association, soutenu et gagné en décembre 1832, par la Société des Amis du Peuple. 60p. *8°. Paris*, 1833.

28264 SOCIETY FOR PROMOTING MANUAL LABOR IN LITERARY INSTITUTIONS. First annual report of the Society... including the report of their general agent Theodore D. Weld. January 28, 1833. 120p. *8°. New-York*, 1833. *The copy that belonged to William Lovett, with his signature on the title-page.*

28265 SOCIETY FOR PROMOTING NATIONAL REGENERATION. Catechism of the Society... whose object is to remove as far as possible, the social and commercial evils now existing... 8p. *8°. Bradford*, 1833. *The Oastler copy.*

28266 —— [Another edition.] 8p. *8°. Hanley*, [1833]

28267 —— Rights of industry. [An account of the inaugural meeting of the Society on 25th November 1833. Signed: Joshua Milne, chairman.] [With 'Catechism of the Society'.] 3p. *4°. Manchester*, [1833] *The Oastler copy.*

28268 * —— [Another edition.] Rights of industry. Catechism of the Society... 12p. *12°. Manchester*, [1833] *The FWA copy that belonged to William Pare.*

28269 SOCIETY FOR THE IMPROVEMENT OF THE CONDITION OF FACTORY CHILDREN. [A statement of the objects of the Society and an appeal for support and for funds. Signed: Thomas Hodgkin, chairman, *pro tem.*] *s.sh.fol. n.p.* [1833] [*Br.* 557(7)] *The Oastler copy.*

28270 —— [Report of the meeting of 23 February, 1833, with speeches by G. S. Bull, Daniel O'Connell, and others.] 24p. *12°.* [*London*, 1833] *The Oastler copy.*

28271 An impartial **STATEMENT** of the proceedings of the members of the trades union societies, and of the steps taken in consequence by the master tradesmen of Liverpool, with correspondence between the parties. 24p. *8°. Liverpool*, 1833.

28272 STEPHEN, Sir G. A letter to the proprietors and occupiers of land in the parish of Bledlow, in Buckinghamshire, on their system of giving bread-money in aid of wages. 32p. *8°.* 1833.

28273 To Wm. **STOCKS**, Jun. Esq. Constable of Huddersfield. [A request, signed by James Brook, John Hanson, Richard Oastler and 21 others, that a meeting be called to petition the King against sending the commissioners to the factory districts; with the Constable's notice, calling the meeting for 13 April 1833.] *s.sh.fol. Huddersfield*, [1833] [*Br.* 558(16)] *The Oastler copy.*

28274 Long **STRINGS!!** And the payment of wages in goods!!! [Calling upon the operatives of Yorkshire to petition the House of Lords against Lord Morpeth's Bill to repeal an Act of 13 Geo. I. Signed: John Pawlett, secretary, for the Trades' Union Committee, and dated, June 27th, 1833.] *s.sh.fol. Leeds*, [1833] [*Br.* 567(1)] *Addressed in manuscript on the verso to the Rev. G. S. Bull. The Oastler copy.*

For **TAYLER**, C. B., Social evils and their remedy, *see* vol. III, *Periodicals list*, Social evils...

28275 The **TEN-HOUR BILL** in Parliament again! A letter from London, Tuesday, March 5th. *s.sh.fol. Otley*, [1833] [*Br.* 565(13)] *The Oastler copy.*

28276 The **TEN HOUR BILL** is lost! [Signed: An old friend.] *s.sh.fol. Leeds*, [1833] [*Br.* 565(14)] *The Oastler copy, sent through the post, and postmarked 'Jy 20, 1833'.*

28277 TEN HOURS' BILL. [An address, signed: A manufacturer, on the danger to the textile industries of American competition, and the adverse effect that shorter working hours may have. Dated: March 22, 1833.] *s.sh.fol. Manchester*, [1833] [*Br.* 565(17)] *The Oastler copy.*

28278 Medical **TESTIMONY** and opinion, before the Select Committee, on the Ten Hour Bill. [Extracts.] 4p. *8°. Bradford*, [1833] *The Oastler copy.*

28279 THORNE'S Towers of Warsaw, Market-Place, Bradford... [*Begin.*] Mr. Thorne respectfully takes the liberty of announcing... This present Saturday evening, June 15th, 1833... The factory child; or the Ten Hour Bill. [A playbill.] *s.sh.fol. Bradford*, [1833] [*Br.* 557(8)] *The Oastler copy.*

28280 THOUGHTS on the mixed character of government institutions in Ireland, with particular reference to the new system of education. By a Protestant. Extracted from the Belfast News Letter of June 18 and 21, 1833. 47p. *8°.* 1833. *The copy that belonged to Earl De Grey.*

28281 TRENCH, Francis. Remarks on the advantages of loan funds for the benefit of the poor and industrious, with directions for their establishment. 43p. *8°. London & Dublin*, 1833.

28282 —— Second edition. 43p. *8°. London & Dublin*, 1833. *For another edition, see 1831.*

28283 TYRANNY'S last shift!! [A poster announcing a meeting at Huddersfield on 13 April to hear George Condy and Richard Oastler on measures to be taken to frustrate the objects of the Factory Commission.] *s.sh.4°. Huddersfield*, [1833] [*Br.* 558(17)] *The Oastler copy.*

28284 VERDICT of the London press. Factory Commissioners' Report. [A series of excerpts from the newspapers published between 1 and 15 July.] *s.sh.fol.* [1833] [*Br.* 558(18)] *The Oastler copy. Sent through the post to 'John Wood, Jun.' and postmarked '5 Sept. 1834'.*

28285 WADE, John. History of the middle and working classes; with a popular exposition of the economic and political principles which have influenced the past and present condition of the industrious orders. Also an appendix of prices, rates of wages, population, poor-rates ... 604p. *8°*. 1833. *See also* 1834, 1842.

28286 WAKEFIELD, EDWARD G. The hangman and the judge or, a letter from Jack Ketch to Mr. Justice Alderson; revised by the Ordinary of Newgate and edited by E. G. Wakefield. [On the proposed reduction in the number of crimes punishable by death.] 16p. *8°*. [*London*, 1833] *The copy that belonged to Rowland Hill (1744–1833), with his signature at the head of the first page of text.*

28287 —— The terrorstruck town [Dunkirk. A pamphlet illustrating the evil results of capital punishment]. (*The Monthly Tract Book.* No. 1, October, 1833.) 16p. *8°*. [1833]. *The copy that belonged to Rowland Hill (1744–1833), with his signature on the title-page.*

28288 WEST RIDING meeting. Freinds of humanitty [*sic*], be at your post! [A poster advertising a meeting at Wibsey Low Moor to support the Ten Hours' Bill. Dated: June 27th, 1833.] *s.sh.fol. Huddersfield*, [1833] [*Br.* 565(21)] *The Oastler copy.*

28289 WEST RIDING meeting, on Wibsey Low-Moor, on Monday, July 1st...Address of the Delegates of the Short Time Committees of the West-Riding of York, to the friends of justice, humanity, and industry. [Signed: Charles Etherington, chairman, William Rider, secretary, and dated, June 24th, 1833.] *s.sh.fol. Bradford*, [1833] [*Br.* 565(22)] *The Oastler copy.*

28290 WEST RIDING meeting, on Wibsey Low Moor, on Monday, July 1st, 1833, at ten o'clock. Order of the meeting. [Signed: John Hall, on behalf of the committee of management, and dated, June 25, 1833.] [4]p. *4°. Bradford*, [1833] [*Br.* 565(23)] *The Oastler copy.*

28291 WETHERELL, C. The present state of the poor-law question; in letters to the Marquess of Salisbury. [With an appendix of documents.] 116, xxxiip. *8°*. 1833.

28292 WHATELY, THOMAS (*d.* 1864). The evidence of the Rev. Thomas Whately, Vicar of Cookham, Berks, before the Committee of the House of Lords, on the state of the poor, in the years 1830, 1831: with introductory remarks on poor laws in Ireland, and on an article in the XCVII. No. of the Quarterly Review. 56p. *8°*. 1833.

28293 The WHIGS in a stew!! *s.sh.4°. Huddersfield*, [1833] [*Br.* 559(3)] *The Oastler copy.*

28294 WHITE SLAVERY. To the honorable the Commons of the United Kingdom of Great Britain and Ireland, in Parliament assembled, the humble petition of ...the undersigned inhabitants of the City of Norwich. [Dated: February 18th, 1833.] *s.sh.fol. Norwich*, [1833] [*Br.* 557(12)] *The Oastler copy.*

28295 WHITE, FRANCIS, *M.R.C.S.* Report and observations on the state of the poor of Dublin. 32p. *8°*. *Dublin*, 1833.

28296 WHITECHAPEL FREE SCHOOL. Reports of the Free-School, Gower's Walk, Whitechapel, London: for training up children in the principles of the Christian religion, and in habits of useful industry. In union with the National Society. [1st–20th reports, for the years 1809–1827, with a single report for the years 1828–1831.] 219p. *8°*. [*London*,] 1833.

28297 WHITEHEAD, A. A. Whitehead to his friend. [A vindication of his evidence before the Factory Commission on the condition of children in factories. Dated: January 25th, 1833.] *s.sh.fol. Huddersfield*, [1833] [*Br.* 557(13)] *The Oastler copy.*

28298 WILLIAMS, GEORGE. Copy of a letter received by the chairman of Col. William's Committee, Ashton under Lyne. [2]p. *8°*. *Lees*, [1833] *The copy sent, with a covering note, by George Downs to Richard Oastler.*

28299 [WONTNER, T.] Old Bailey experience. Criminal jurisprudence and the actual working of our penal code of laws. Also, an essay on prison discipline... By the author of "The schoolmaster's experience in Newgate." 447p. *8°*. 1833.

28300 [WOOD, JOHN (1793–1871)?] [*Begin.*] In presuming to address [*blank*] regarding Lord Ashley's proposed Bill...[A circular letter asking for support for a Bill to limit the hours of children and young persons under eighteen to the normal hours of the working day.] 4p. *fol. n.p.* [1833] *The Oastler copy.*

28301 A WORD from Wm. Rider to Edward Baines, on being told that he not only praised...those individuals who voted that the bodies of the poor of Leeds should go for dissection, but that he also expressed his willingness to bequeath his own body...for the same purpose...[A satirical ballad.] *s.sh.fol. Leeds*, [1833 ?] [*Br.* 564] *The Oastler copy.*

28302 A few WORDS to the working classes of Great Britain, particularly applicable to the present state of their affairs, and shewing the only means of bettering their condition. By a labouring man. 21p. *8°*. *Nottingham*, [1833?]

28303 WORKSOP PROVIDENT SOCIETY. Rules, orders and regulations, of the Worksop Provident Society, established July the tenth, 1833... 14p. *8°*. *Worksop*, [1833]

28304 WRIGHT, JAMES. A summary of objections to Act 10 Geo. IV, c. 56, and of the grievances thence resulting to benefit societies; with propositions for a new Act, and for a national set of tables, also a letter addressed to John Wilkes, Esq. M.P. 16p. *8°*. 1833.

28305 *WRIGHTSON, T. On the punishment of death. 44p. *8°*. 1833. *The copy that belonged to George Grote. See also* 1837.

28306 YEATMAN, H. F. A letter to D. O. P. Okeden, Esq. together with an inquiry into the merits of his poor law report, as assistant commissioner. 63p. *8°*. *Sherborne*, 1833.

28307 —— A letter to D. O. P. Okeden, Esq. on the merits of his poor law report. 25p. *8°*. *Sherborne*, 1833. *A reply to no.* 28226.

SLAVERY

28308 **BARRET,** . The speeches of Mr. Barrett, and of Mr. Burge, at a general meeting of planters...and others, interested in the West-India colonies...on the 18th May, 1833. 114p. *8°.* 1833.

28309 [**BUNN,** T.] An essay on the abolition of slavery throughout the British Dominions, without injury to the master or his property, with the least possible injury to the slave, without revolution, and without loss to the revenue. 97p. *8°. Frome,* 1833.

28310 **BURNLEY,** W. H. Opinions on slavery & emancipation in 1823; referred to in a recent debate in the House of Commons, by Thomas Fowell Buxton...with additional observations, applicable to...E. G. Stanley's plan for the extinction of slavery. lv, 44p. *8°.* 1833.

28311 **CAREY,** M. Letters on the Colonization Society...Seventh edition. 32p. *8°. Philadelphia,* 1833. *For other editions, see* 1832.

28312 **CLARK,** George D. Proposals for the formation of a West India free labour company, for effecting the abolition of slavery, and affording equitable protection to the holders of colonial property, without imposing a burthen upon the nation. 55p. *8°.* 1833. *The copy that belonged to Earl De Grey.*

28313 **CLERICUS,** *pseud.* Facts designed to exhibit the real character and tendency of the American Colonization Society. 19p. *8°. Liverpool & London,* 1833.

28314 *[——] A review of the Report of the Select Committee of the House of Commons, on the state of the West India colonies, ordered to be printed, 13th April, 1832; or, the interests of the country and the prosperity of the West India planters mutually secured by the immediate abolition of slavery. 30p. *8°. Liverpool & London,* 1833. *The copy that belonged to George Grote.*

28315 **CONDER,** J. Wages or the whip. An essay on the comparative cost and productiveness of free and slave labour. 91p. *8°.* 1833.

28316 **CROPPER,** J. The extinction of the American Colonization Society the first step to the abolition of American slavery. 24p. *8°.* 1833.

28317 **DANFORTH,** J. N. Twelve reasons why all the people of New England should engage heart and hand in supporting the Colonization Society; with notices of some popular objections. 4p. *8°. n.p.* [1833]

28318 **ENGLAND.** *Parliament.* The condition of the slave, not preferable to that of the British peasant, from the evidence before the Parliamentary committees on colonial slavery. 16p. *8°. The Agency Anti-Slavery Committee,* 1833.

28319 —— —— *House of Commons.* Analysis of the Report of a Committee of the House of Commons on the extinction of slavery. With notes by the editor. 213p. *8°. The Society for the Abolition of Slavery Throughout the British Dominions,* 1833.

28320 —— —— *House of Lords.* Abstract of the Report of the Lords Committees on the condition and treatment of the colonial slaves, and the evidence taken by them on that subject; with notes by the editor. 122p. *8°. The Society for the Abolition of Slavery Throughout the British Dominions,* 1833.

28321 **FRIENDS,** *Society of.* Some reflections on the subject of slavery, respectfully submitted on behalf of the Religious Society of Friends, to the Christian public in the British Dominions. 3p. *4°. n.p.* [1833]

28322 **HALLEY,** R. The sinfulness of colonial slavery. A lecture, delivered at the monthly meeting of congregational ministers and churches...on February 7th, 1833. 28p. *8°.* 1833.

28323 —— Second edition. 28p. *8°.* 1833.

28324 **HODGKIN,** T. An inquiry into the merits of the American Colonization Society: and a reply to the charges brought against it. With an account of the British African Colonization Society. 62p. *8°.* 1833.

28325 —— On negro emancipation and American colonization. 24p. *8°.* [*London,* 1833 ?]

28326 **IRVING,** E. A statement of the cause which affects the decrease or increase of the slave population in the British colonies. 44p. *8°.* 1833. *The copy that belonged to Earl De Grey.*

28327 **LEGION,** *pseud.* A letter from Legion to...the Duke of Richmond, &c....chairman of the Slavery Committee of the House of Lords: containing an exposure of the character of the evidence on the colonial side produced before the Committee. [With 'Summary of the colonial evidence'.] 196p. *8°.* [1833] *'Summary of the colonial evidence' is on a separate folded folio sheet.*

28328 —— A second letter from Legion to...the Duke of Richmond...containing an analysis of the anti-slavery evidence produced before the Committee. 151p. *8°.* 1833.

28329 **LEONARD,** P. Records of a voyage to the western coast of Africa, in His Majesty's ship Dryad, and of the service on that station for the suppression of the slave trade, in the years 1830, 1831, and 1832. [With 'List of vessels...captured'.] 267, [5]p. *8°. Edinburgh, London, &c.,* 1833.

28330 A **LETTER** to the Lord Chancellor on the abolition of slavery. By a West Indian. 16p. *8°.* 1833. *The copy that belonged to Earl De Grey.*

28331 **M'DONNELL,** A. A letter to Thos. Fowell Buxton...in refutation of his allegations respecting the decrease of the slaves in the British West India colonies. 80p. *8°.* 1833. *The copy that belonged to Earl De Grey.*

28332 **MASSACHUSETTS ANTI-SLAVERY SOCIETY.** Credentials of William Lloyd Garrison, Esq. from the managers of the New England Anti-Slavery Society, and the free people of colour. 16p. *8°.* [*London,* 1833]

28333 *MORTIMER, G. F. W. The immediate abolition of slavery, compatible with the safety and prosperity of the colonies. In a letter to the representatives of the southern division of Northumberland and of the town and county of Newcastle on Tyne. 24p. *8°. Newcastle upon Tyne,* 1833. *The copy that belonged to George Grote.*

28334 **PHILLIPS,** Joseph. West India question. The outline of a plan for the total, immediate, and safe abolition of slavery throughout the British colonies. 14p. *8°.* 1833.

28335 **PLAN** for the safe and profitable conversion of the colonial slaves into free labourers. 24p. *8°*. [1833 ?] *The copy that belonged to Earl De Grey.*

28336 SHEFFIELD FEMALE ANTI-SLA-VERY SOCIETY. Concluding report of the... Society. 12p. *12°*. *Sheffield*, 1833. *See also* 1827.

28337 STRICTURES on Dr. Hodgkin's pamphlet on negro emancipation and American colonization. ⟨From "the Imperial Magazine" for July, 1833.⟩ 8p. *8°*. 1833. *There is a manuscript note on the title-page: 'Joseph Cooper', which is possibly an attribution of authorship.*

28338 STUART, C. Liberia; or, the American colonization scheme examined and exposed. A full and authentic report of a lecture delivered...at a public meeting in...Glasgow, 15th April, 1833. 24p. *12°*. *Glasgow*, 1833.

28339 WHITELEY, H. Three months in Jamaica, in 1832: comprising a residence of seven weeks on a sugar plantation. 24p. *8°*. 1833.

28340 —— Verbatim reprint of a pamphlet...entitled Three months in Jamaica, in 1832; comprising a residence of seven weeks on a sugar plantation. 24p. *12°*. [*London*, 1833] *The Oastler copy.*

28341 WILKINSON, J. W. Thoughts on negro slavery. 16p. *8°*. 1833.

POLITICS

For the **AGITATOR,** [*Glasgow*,] *see* vol. III, *Periodicals list.*

For the **AGITATOR, AND POLITICAL ANAT-OMIST,** [*London*,] *see* vol. III, *Periodicals list.*

28342 BAYNTUN, S. A. Yorkshire Spring Assizes, 1833. Report of the cause Bayntun versus Cattle, tried before Mr. Justice Alderson and a Special Jury on... March 11, 1833. [Concerning the misuse of money for expenses in the election of 1830.] 30p. *12°*. *York*, [1833]

28343 BIRMINGHAM POLITICAL UNION. Report of the proceedings of the fourth annual meeting... held...on Monday, September 16, 1833. 8p. *4°*. *Birmingham*, 1833. *See note to no.* 26519; *see also* 1830, 1831, 1832.

28344 —— Report of the proceedings of the great public meeting of the inhabitants of Birmingham...held...on Monday, May 20, 1833, convened by the Council...for the purpose of petitioning His Majesty to dismiss his ministers, &c.... 11p. *4°*. *Birmingham*, 1833. *See note to no.* 26519.

For le **BONNET ROUGE, THE REPUBLICAN MAGAZINE,** *see* vol. III, *Periodicals list.*

28345 CALVERT, F. Letter to the members of the Bucks Agricultural Association, upon their assuming a political character. 34p. *8°*. *London, Aylesbury, &c.*, 1833. *Presentation copy from the author to the Earl of Ripon.*

28346 "His first **CAMPAIGN:**" a letter, addressed to the electors of the Borough of Wolverhampton. By one of themselves. [An attack on Richard Fryer, one of the Members of Parliament for Wolverhampton.] 19p. *8°*. *London & Wolverhampton*, 1833.

28347 CARPENTER, WILLIAM (1797–1874). The political text book; comprising a view of the origin and objects of government, and an examination of the principal social and political institutions of England. Compiled from the best authorities. 248p. *8°*. 1833. *Published in 16 parts.*

For the **CHRONICLER OF THE TIMES,** *see* vol. III, *Periodicals list.*

28348 COBBETT, W. The adjourned debate on the address! The speeches of W. Cobbett, M.P. for Oldham. Delivered...February 7, [and 11 February] 1833. [With 'Stamp and auction duties!!! The speech of W. Cobbett, M.P. for Oldham. Delivered February 18, 1833'. With an account of a meeting of the National Union of the Working Classes, at which O'Connell was the chief speaker, 23 February.] 16p. *4°*. [1833] *Published in two parts, in a format uniform with The Working Man's Friend.*

28349 —— Popay the police spy; or, a report on the evidence laid before the House of Commons by the Select Committee appointed to inquire into the truth of the allegations of a petition, presented by Mr. Cobbett, from members of the National Union of the Working Classes (resident in Camberwell and Walworth), in which they complained that policemen were employed as government spies. 24p. *8°*. 1833. *With the signature of the publisher, John Cleave, on the title-page.*

28350 CONDY, G. The speech of George Condy, Esq., at the public meeting, held in the Manor Court Room, Manchester, on...May 13, 1833, for the repeal of the malt, hop, and soap duties, and the assessed taxes... *s.sh.fol. n.p.* [1833] [*Br.* 554] *The Oastler copy.*

For the **"DESTRUCTIVE"** and poor man's conservative, 1833–34, *continued as* the People's conservative and trades' union gazette, 1834, *see* vol. III, *Periodicals list.*

28351 EMMET, R. The speech of Robert Emmet, Esq. as delivered at the Sessions House, Dublin, before Lord Norbury...on being found guilty of high treason, as leader of the insurrection of 1803...[Reprinted from the *Poor Man's Guardian*, No. 34.] 8p. *8°*. 1833. **Another, the FWA copy, belonged to William Pare. See also* 1839.

For the **GAUNTLET,** 1833–34, *see* vol. III, *Periodicals list.*

28352 GROTE, G. Speech of George Grote, Esq. M.P. delivered April 25th, 1833, in the House of Commons, on moving for the introduction of the vote by ballot at elections. 40p. *8°*. 1833.

28353 [LE MARCHANT, SIR D., *Bart.*, *ed.*] The reform Ministry, and the reformed Parliament. [With contributions by Lord Althorp, Lord Stanley and Sir James Graham.] Fourth edition. 108p. *8°*. 1833.

28354 [——] [Another edition.] Cheap edition...Reprinted from the sixth fine edition. 68p. *8°*. 1833. *See also* 1834.

28355 LETHEM, J. Copy of a petition [to the House of Commons] by the people called "Separatists," and other nonjuring Christians resident in Edinburgh and Leith [praying to be relieved of the legal penalties for refusal to take oaths]. To which is subjoined a letter to the Right Hon. Lord John Russell. By James Lethem, tobacco manufacturer, Leith. 8p. *8°*. *Leith*, 1833.

28356 MARAT, J. P. Les chaînes de l'esclavage, ouvrage destiné à développer les noirs attentats des princes contre les peuples...Précédées d'un discours préliminaire, et accompagnées de nouvelles notes, par M. A. Havard. 330p. *8°. Paris*, 1833.

For the **NEW ANTI-JACOBIN,** *see* vol. III, *Periodicals list.*

28357 OASTLER, R. Representation of Huddersfield. Mr. Oastler's speech. [23 December, 1833.] *s.sh.fol. Leeds*, [1833] [*Br.* 563(3)] *Oastler's own copy.*

28358 PARDON asked. The Devil's ass caught, whipped, and set at liberty a short time longer!! [An attack on Edward Baines 'the great liar of the north'.] *s.sh.fol. Bradford*, [1833 ?] [*Br.* 551(2)] *The Oastler copy.*

28359 [PETER, W.] Questions on the ballot, for the calm consideration and deliberate judgment of the people of England. Fourth edition. 13p. *8°.* 1833. *For another edition, see* 1831.

28360 —— A speech delivered in the House of Commons, in the debate of Thursday, April 25, 1833, on Mr. Grote's motion relative to the ballot... ⟨Extracted from the Mirror of Parliament. Part CCV. ⟩ 11p. *8°.* 1833.

For the **REFORMER,** a daily evening newspaper, *see* vol. III, *Periodicals list.*

28361 REPORT of speeches delivered at the public dinner given to the Hon. Admiral Fleming, in Lennoxtown, Stirlingshire...January, 1833. 43p. *12°. Edinburgh*, 1833.

28362 SOMERS, JOHN, *Earl Somers.* Political lucubrations of John Somers, Earl Somers, His Majesty's Lieutenant of the County of Hereford. 67p. *8°.* 1833.

28363 UNITED STATES OF AMERICA. Proclamation by the President [Jackson], dated Washington, Dec. 10th, 1832 [declaring an ordinance of the State Convention of South Carolina affirming that the state is not bound by the revenue laws of the United States, to be a violation of the constitution of the Union]. 25p. *8°.* 1833.

For the **VOICE OF THE WEST-RIDING,** *see* vol. III, *Periodicals list.*

28364 The **WOODITES'** "forget me not!" being a sketch of a new political farce, called the Whig tomfoolery election, and first acted in Huddersfield on the 10th, 12th and 13th days of December last...when Captain Fenton, the nominee of Byrom House, was returned...in opposition to Captain Wood, the man of the people: with other incidents connected with the proceedings: by an observer. 16p. *8°. Huddersfield*, 1833. *The Oastler copy.*

28365 YEATS, J. A letter to the poor men who have lost their elective franchise; showing that it was unnecessary taxation which occasioned their loss. What, under present circumstances, they ought to do, and why they ought to do it. 16p. *8°. Boston* [*Lincs.*] & *London*, 1833.

SOCIALISM

28366 An **ADDRESS** to the members of trade unions ...being an exposition of the relative situation, condition, and future prospects of working people in England, Scotland and Ireland...By a journeyman bootmaker. 48p. *8°.* 1833. *For other editions, see* 1827.

28367 BARRAULT, P. A. C. E. Compagnonage de la Femme. Chant. Paroles de É. Barrault, musique de F. David. 3p. *8°. Lyon*, [1833]

28368 —— 1833, ou l'année de la Mère. [Janvier.] 47p. *8°. Lyon*, [1833]

28369 —— 1833, ou l'année de la Mère. [Février.] 45p. *8°. Lyon*, [1833]

28370 BERBRUGGER, L. A. Conférences sur la théorie sociétaire de Charles Fourier, faites...à Lyon, en septembre, 1833. 105p. *8°. Lyon*, 1833.

For the **BIRMINGHAM LABOUR EXCHANGE GAZETTE,** *see* vol. III, *Periodicals list.*

28371 BONNIN, C. J. B. Doctrine sociale, textuellement formée des Déclarations de droits françaises et américaines...Quatrième édition. 181p. *18°. Paris*, 1833.

28372 CABET, E. Révolution de 1830 et situation présente (novembre 1833) expliquées et éclairées par les révolutions de 1789, 1792, 1799 et 1804 et par la Restauration... 3e. édition. 2 vols. *12°. Paris*, 1833. *For another edition, see* 1832.

28373 DAVID, F. Lyon, le 22 février. 1833. [*Begin.*] Je pars pour l'Orient...[A farewell address, with a prospectus of his songs.] *s.sh.4°. Lyon*, [1833]

28374 DUGUET, C. Adieux à l'ancien monde. 4p. *8°.* [*Paris*, 1833]

28375 —— [*Begin.*] Il y a dix-huit siècles que le Fils de l'Homme...est mort sur une croix... 4p. *8°.* [*Paris*, 1833]

28376 —— [Another edition.] Salut au nouveau monde 4p. *8°.* [*Paris*, 1833]

For **ESSAYS** and articles on subjects connected with popular political economy, illustrative of the condition and prospects of the working classes...[being nos. 1–5 of the *Birmingham Labour Exchange Gazette*, reissued with a general title-page.], *see* vol. III, *Periodicals list*, Birmingham Labour Exchange Gazette.

28377 FOURNEL, H. Bibliographie Saint-Simonienne...De 1802 au 31 décembre 1832. 130p. *8°. Paris*, 1833. *Presentation copy, with inscription from the author 'pour mon bon ami Lambert'.*

28378 INSTITUTION OF THE INTELLIGENT AND WELL-DISPOSED OF THE INDUSTRIOUS CLASSES. Institution of the Intelligent and Well-Disposed of the Industrious Classes, founded by the Association to Remove Ignorance and Poverty by Education and Employment. Prospectus of the system of education to be pursued in the schools attached to the Institution. 3p. *4°. n.p.* [1833 ?] *Inscribed: 'Charlotte Street Prospectus written by R. Owen'.*

28379 [KING, WILLIAM, *of Charlotte Street, London.*] Gothic Hall Labour Bank. [Signed: W.K.] 4p. *8°.* [*London*, 1833 ?] *Bound in a volume with four other separately published pieces by William King. In a manuscript note HSF says: 'they seem to have been collected, and issued in a brown wrapper in 1845'.*

28380 LECHEVALIER SAINT ANDRÉ, L. J. Question sociale. De la réforme industrielle, considérée comme problême fondamental de la politique positive. 76p. *8°. Paris*, 1833. *The copy that belonged to Victor Considérant.*

28381 LEMOYNE, N. R. D. Association par phalange agricole-industrielle. Notions élémentaires et pratiques sur la système sociétaire de M. Charles Fourier... 114p. 8°. [Paris,] 1833. *The copy that belonged to Victor Considérant.*

28382 —— Association par phalange agricole-industrielle. Sommaire et annonce d'un écrit consacré à des notions élémentaires et pratiques sur le système sociétaire de M. Charles Fourier. 16p. 8°. *Paris*, 1833. *For the work described in this prospectus, see* 1834.

28383 MANDLEY, G. Lines on the death of W. Thompson, Esqr. of Cork, author of "An enquiry into the distribution of wealth,"...intended to be sung by the members of the Social Brotherhood...upon the occasion of an oration...in the Salford Co-operative Institution... April 21, 1833. *s.sh.8°. Salford*, [1833]

28384 *MANIFESTO of the productive classes of Great Britain and Ireland, to the governments and people of the continents of Europe, and of North and South America. (Passed unanimously at the great public meeting held at the National Equitable Labour Exchange, Charlotte-Street, Fitzroy-Square, London, on the 13th May, 1833.) *s.sh.fol.* [*London:*] *United Trades' Association for Employing the Unemployed, and Educating the Children of the Working Classes, through the Medium of Equitable Labour Exchange,* [1833] *The FWA copy that belonged to William Pare.*

28385 OWEN, ROBERT. Lecture I.[–VI.] delivered by Robert Owen, at the Institution of New Lanark, upon the 13th Chapter of the 1st Epistle to the Corinthians. 47p. 8°. [*London*, 1833.] *See also* 1834 (Six lectures on charity).

28386 *[—— ?] To the leaders of all the various parties, agricultural, commercial, political, scientific, and religious, in Birmingham and its neighbourhood. *s.sh.fol. n.p.* [1833 ?] *A proof ? Printed in one column. The FWA copy that belonged to William Pare.*

For the **PIONEER**, 1833–34, *see vol.* III, *Periodicals list.*

28387 SALFORD CO-OPERATIVE SCHOOL. To the friends of education...[An appeal for assistance with funds, equipment, gifts of books, to be forwarded 'care of Mr. George Mandley'.] *s.sh.8°. Salford,* [1833 ?]

28388 SMITH, JAMES E. The Antichrist, or, Christianity reformed. In which is demonstrated from the Scriptures, in opposition to the prevailing opinion of the whole religious world, that evil and good are from one source; devil and God one spirit; and that the one is merely manifested to make perfect the other. [Sixteen lectures, given between 23 Sept., 1832 and 17 March, 1833.] 252p. 8°. [1833]

28389 —— Lecture on a Christian community; delivered...at the Surry Institution. 20p. 8°. 1833.

28390 VINÇARD, P. Aux Compagnons de la Femme. Chant. Paroles de Vinçard. 3p. 8°. *Lyon*, [1833]

MISCELLANEOUS

28391 BABBAGE, C. A word to the wise. [Advocating life peerages.] 16p. 8°. [1833]

28392 BATHURST, HENRY, *Archdeacon*. A letter to the Archbishop of Canterbury, proposing a satisfactory adjustment...of the Irish Church Bill... 15p. 8°. 1833. *The copy that belonged to Earl De Grey.*

28393 COOPER, THOMAS (1805–1892). The Wesleyan chiefs; and other poems. 95p. 8°. *London*, [*Sheffield printed,*] 1833.

28394 Second edition. The **DINNER** to Mr. Coke, at St. Andrew's Hall [Norwich], Friday, April 12, 1833. *s.sh.fol. n.p.* [1833] *Reprinted from the Norwich Mercury.*

28395 HOWARD, L. The climate of London, deduced from meteorological observations made in the Metropolis, and at various places around it...A second, much enlarged and improved edition, in which the observations are continued to the year MDCCCXXX... 3 vols. 8°. 1833.

28396 HYMNS to be sung at the Anniversary of the Byerley and Bowling Sunday-School, 1833. 8p. 8°. *Bradford*, [1833] *The Oastler copy.*

28397 MILLER, JAMES. Notes on the Irish Church Reform Bill. 19p. 8°. *Durham*, [1833] *The copy that belonged to Earl De Grey.*

28398 OWEN, ROBERT D. An address on the influence of the clerical profession. As delivered in the Hall of Science, New York. 20p. 8°. 1833. *See also* 1840.

1834

GENERAL

28399 AGAZZINI, M. Sconvenevolezza delle teoriche del valore insegnate da Smith, dai professori Malthus e Say, e dagli scrittori più celebri di pubblica economia, e sunto della nuova teorica de' valori contenuta nel libro La scienza dell' economia politica. 431p. 8°. *Milano*, 1834. *Presentation copy, with inscription, from the author to N. W. Senior.*

28400 BATTERSBY, W. J. The fall and rise of Ireland; or the repealer's manual...Second edition, with additions. 394p. 12°. *Dublin & London*, 1834.

28401 BIGOT DE MOROGUES, P. M. S., *Baron*. Recherche des causes de la richesse et de la misère des peuples civilisés: application des principes de l'économie politique et des calculs de la statistique au gouvernement de l'état... 649p. 4°. *Paris*, [1834 ?]

28402 The **BRITISH ALMANAC** of the Society for the Diffusion of Useful Knowledge, for...1834. [With 'The companion to the Almanac; or year-book of general information'.] 72, 250p. 12°. [1834] *For other editions, see* 1828.

28403 BROWNING, G. The domestic and financial condition of Great Britain; preceded by a brief sketch of her foreign policy; and of the statistics and politics of France, Russia, Austria, and Prussia. 632p. *8°.* 1834.

28404 BULWER, W. H. L. E., *Baron Dalling and Bulwer.* France, social, literary, political. [First series. With 'The monarchy of the middle classes. France, social literary, political. Second series'.] 4 vols. *12°.* 1834–36.

28405 —— La France sociale, politique et littéraire... Traduit par l'un des traducteurs des Voyages de Basil Hall. 4 vols. *8°. Paris,* 1834–36.

28406 Le **CITATEUR** républicain, recueil de principes, de liberté, ou choix principaux de traités de démocratie extraits de divers écrits de philosophie, ancienne et nouvelle. Nouveaux corps d'ouvrage... 324p. *8°. Paris,* 1834. *Edited by M. G. F. Rouanet.*

28407 COBBETT, W. Life of Andrew Jackson, President of the United States of America. Abridged and compiled by William Cobbett...[Partly taken from *The life of Andrew Jackson* by J. H. Eaton.] 142p. *12°.* 1834.

28408 —— Thirteen sermons...To which is added, an address to the working people on the new Dead Body Bill. 288p. *12°. New York,* 1834. *For other editions, see* 1822.

28409 [COLEBROOKE, Sir W. M. G.] A plan for the improvement of Ireland, by the union of English and Irish capital, and the co-operation of the people in both countries; with a map and appendix, containing extracts from parliamentary reports and other publications. 88p. *8°.* 1834.

28410 COMTE, F. C. L. Traité de la propriété... 2 vols. *8°. Paris,* 1834.

28411 COUNSEL for emigrants, and interesting information from numerous sources; with original letters from Canada and the United States. 140p. *12°. Aberdeen,* 1834.

28412 ENGLAND. *Commissioners appointed to Report ...upon the Boundaries...of certain Boroughs and Corporate Towns in England and Wales.* Great Yarmouth Corporation. A report of the investigation before His Majesty's Municipal Commissioners, J. G. Hogg, and J. Buckle, Esqrs....appointed to examine into, and report on the corporate affairs of this Borough. Compiled [with an introduction and conclusion] by Henry Barrett. 352p. *8°. London, Norwich, &c.,* 1834. *Published in 22 parts.*

28413 —— —— Report of the proceedings during the inquiry into the state of the Corporation of Kingston-upon-Hull; to which is appended a copy of the governing charter, with a report of the inquiry into the affairs of the Trinity-House. [With a preface by the editor of the *Hull Advertiser,* dated: December 31st, 1833.] 288p. *12°. Hull,* [1834]

28414 —— [Another edition.] A report of an inquiry into the existing state of the Corporation of Hull, taken at the Guild-Hall, before F. Dwarris and S. A. Rumball, Esqrs....Also, the proceedings relative to the Trinity House. With an appendix, containing many...authentic documents. By William Gawtress. 419p. *8°. Hull,* 1834.

28415 —— *Commissioners for Inquiring concerning Charities.* A report of the proceedings of a court of inquiry into the existing state of the Corporation of Liverpool, held... before Geo. Hutton Wilkinson and Thos. Jefferson Hogg,

Esqrs. two of His Majesty's Commissioners...in...1833. [With an appendix.] 554, cxxviiip. *fol. Liverpool,* [1834?]

28416 —— Parliament. *House of Commons.* Repeal of the Union. Report of the debate in the House of Commons, on Mr. O'Connell's motion, and the proceedings in the House of Lords on Earl Grey's motion for concurring in the address in the Commons. April, 1834. 200p. *8°.* 1834.

28417 An **ESSAY** in answer to the question, whether does the principle of competition, with separate individual interests; or the principle of united exertions, with combined and equal interests; form the most secure basis for the formation of society? [A prize essay in answer to a question set by John Minter Morgan, by an apprentice mathematical instrument maker, a member of the London Mechanics' Institution.] 68p. *8°.* 1834.

28418 [EVERETT, J.] Panorama of Manchester, and railway companion. [The publisher's preface signed: J.E.] *12°. Manchester & London,* 1834.

28419 FRANKLIN INSTITUTE. Report of the managers of the Franklin Institute, of the State of Pennsylvania, for the promotion of the mechanic arts, in relation to weights and measures. Presented in compliance with a resolution of the House of Representatives...82p. *8°. Philadelphia,* 1834.

28420 *GENEVA, *Canton of. Conseil d'Etat.* Compte rendu de l'administration du Conseil d'État, pendant l'année 1833, par M. Rigaud, premier Syndic; lu au Conseil représentatif le 25 décembre 1833. 65p. *8°. Genève,* 1834. *The copy that belonged to George Grote.*

28421 HEEREN, A. H. L. A manual of the history of the political system of Europe and its colonies, from its formation at the close of the fifteenth century, to its re-establishment upon the fall of Napoleon...Translated from the fifth German edition [by D. A. Talboys]. 2 vols. *8°. Oxford,* 1834. *See also* 1840.

28422 HINTS to all parties, by a man of no party. 98p. *8°.* 1834. *The copy that belonged to Earl De Grey.*

28423 HOLBACH, P. H. D. von, *Freiherr.* Nature and her laws: as applicable to the happiness of man, living in society...From the French of M. de Mirabaud... [With a life of the author, here identified as d'Holbach, and bibliography of his writings by J. Hibbert.] 2 vols. *8°.* 1834. *For other editions, see* 1770.

28424 HOPKINS, T. Great Britain, for the last forty years; being an historical and analytical account of its finances, economy, general condition, during that period. 340p. *8°.* 1834.

28425 *—— Second edition. 340p. *8°.* 1834.

28426 [HUME, James D.] Letters on the corn laws, and on the rights of the working classes, originally inserted in the Morning Chronicle, shewing the injustice...of empowering those...who have obtained the proprietary possession of the lands...to increase, artificially, the money value of their exclusive estates, by means of arbitrary charges made on the rest of the people...By H.B.T. 49p. *8°.* 1834. *See also* 1835, 1841.

28427 [JOBARD, J. B. A. M.] Un coup-d'oeil en arrière sur l'état de l'industrie avant la Révolution Française. 7p. *8°. n.p.* [1834?]

28428 LABORDE, A. L. J. de, *Comte.* De l'esprit d'association dans tous les intérêts de la communauté...

Troisième édition. 496p. *8°. Paris*, 1834. *For another edition, see 1821.*

28429 LERMINIER, J. L. E. De l'influence de la philosophie du xviiie siècle sur la législation et la sociabilité du xixe. 442p. *12°. Bruxelles*, 1834.

28430 LILLINGSTON, C. The causes of the present agricultural distress clearly proved...and the only practicable remedies fully explained. Also a general view of the state and prospects of the different interests in the Kingdom...[Part 1.] 40p. *8°. Warwick, Birmingham, &c.*, 1834. *No more published. With a second (abbreviated) title with a London imprint.*

28431 LINNING, M. Memoranda publica. 67p. *8°. Edinburgh*, 1834.

28432 LLOYD, W. F. A lecture on the notion of value, as distinguishable not only from utility, but also from value in exchange. Delivered before the University of Oxford, in Michaelmas term 1833. 40p. *8°. London, Oxford, &c.*, 1834. *Reissued in* Lectures on population, value, poor-laws and rent *in 1837 (q.v.).*

28433 LOCH, J. Memoir of George Granville, late Duke of Sutherland, K.G. [With 'Appendix. Funeral of the Duke of Sutherland, July 31st, 1833' and 'Subscribers to the monuments in the counties of Stafford, Salop, and Sutherland'.] 83p. *4°.* 1834.

28434 LONGFIELD, M. Lectures on political economy, delivered in Trinity and Michaelmas terms, 1833. 267p. *8°. Dublin*, 1834.

28435 LOWNDES, WILLIAM T. The bibliographer's manual of English literature containing an account of rare ...books, published in, or relating to, Great Britain and Ireland... 4 vols. *8°.* 1834.

28436 McCULLOCH, JOHN R. A dictionary, practical, theoretical, and historical, of commerce and commercial navigation...Second edition, corrected throughout and...enlarged. [With a supplement supplying the deficiencies and bringing the information contained in the work to October, 1835.] 2 vols. *8°.* 1834–35. *For other editions, see 1832.*

28437 MACKENZIE, E. and **ROSS**, M. An historical, topographical, and descriptive view of the county Palatine of Durham...by E. Mackenzie and [continued by] M. Ross. 2 vols. *4°. Newcastle upon Tyne*, 1834.

28438 [MARCET, J.] John Hopkins's notions on political economy...Third edition. 189p. *8°.* 1834. *For other editions, see 1833.*

28439 MARTINEAU, H. Illustrations of political economy...In nine volumes... 25 parts. *12°.* 1834. *The dates of the separately issued parts range from 1832 to 1834. In this copy the first part 'Life in the wilds' is of the second edition.*

28440 MONE, F. J. Théorie de la statistique, traduite de l'allemand et du latin...et augmentée d'additions, de notes et d'une bibliographie par Émile Tandel. 145p. *8°. Louvain*, 1834.

28441 MONFALCON, J. B. Histoire des insurrections de Lyon, en 1831 et en 1834, d'après des documents authentiques; précédée d'un essai sur les ouvriers en soie et sur l'organisation de la fabrique. 334p. *8°. Lyon & Paris*, 1834.

28442 MOREAU DE JONNÈS, A. Statistique de l'Espagne, territoire, population, agriculture, industrie, commerce, navigation, colonies, finances. 318p. *8°.* [*Paris*,] 1834.

28443 MOULTON, R. K. The constitutional guide; comprising the constitution of the United States; with notes and commentaries from the writings of Judge Story, Chancellor Kent, James Madison and other...American citizens. 147p. *12°. New-York*, 1834.

28444 MUNDELL, A. The philosophy of legislation, an essay. 208p. *8°.* 1834.

28445 PARSONS, E. The civil, ecclesiastical, literary, commercial and miscellaneous history of Leeds, Halifax, Huddersfield, Bradford, Wakefield, Dewsbury, Otley and the manufacturing district of Yorkshire. 2 vols. *8°. Leeds*, 1834.

28446 PASLEY, SIR C. W. Observations on the expediency and practicability of simplifying and improving the measures, weights and money, used in this country, without materially altering the present standards. 176p. *8°.* 1834. *For the original edition, lithographed for private use, see 1831. A prospectus for a continuation was published in 1835 (q.v.).*

28447 PEBRER, A. P. Histoire financière, et statistique générale de l'Empire Britannique, avec un exposé du système actuel de l'impôt...Traduit de l'anglais, par J. M. Jacobi... 2 vols. *8°. Paris, Londres, &c.*, 1834. *For another edition, see 1833.*

28448 PIGOT, JAMES, & CO. Pigot and Co.'s national commercial directory, comprising a directory and classification of the merchants, bankers...manufacturers and traders, together with lists of the nobility, gentry & clergy, resident...in the counties of Chester, Cumberland, Durham, Lancaster, Northumberland, Westmoreland and York... 1024p. *8°. London & Manchester*, 1834.

28449 The **POST-OFFICE** London directory for 1834...By B. Critchett. The thirty-fifth edition. [With 'A new guide to stagecoaches, waggons, carts, vessels, &c. for 1834...The thirty-second edition. By B. Critchley'.] 612, 156p. *12°.* [1834] *See also* 1805 (Post Office annual directory), 1810, 1813, 1814, 1820 (Post Office London directory), 1823, 1825, 1830, 1832, 1836, 1841.

28450 RAE, J. Statement of some new principles on the subject of political economy, exposing the fallacies of the system of free trade, and of some other doctrines maintained in the "Wealth of nations." 414p. *8°. Boston*, 1834.

28451 RIQUETTI, H. G., *Comte de Mirabeau*. Œuvres de Mirabeau, précédées d'une notice sur sa vie et ses ouvrages, par M. Mérilhou... 8 vols. *8°. Paris*, 1834–35. *For another edition of the introduction by Mérilhou, see 1827.*

28452 ★SAY, J. B. Catéchisme d'économie politique, ou instruction familière qui montre de quelle façon les richesse sont produites, distribuées et consommées dans la société...Quatrième édition, revue et augmentée de notes et d'une préface, par M. Charles Comte. 348p. *12°. Paris*, 1834. *The copy that belonged to George Grote, with his book-plate. For other editions, see 1815.*

**28453 —— ** A treatise on political economy...Translated from the fourth edition of the French, by C. R. Prinsep, M.A. With notes by the translator. Sixth American edition, containing a translation of the introduction, and additional notes, by Clement C. Biddle... 493p. *8°. Philadelphia*, 1834. *For other editions, see 1803.*

28454 SOCIEDAD ECONOMICA DE MADRID. Informe de la Sociedad Economica de Madrid al Real y Supremo Consejo de Castilla en el espediente de ley agraria, estendido por su individuo de numero el Sr. D. Gaspar Melchor de Jovellanos... 250p. 4°. *Madrid*, 1834. *For other editions, see 1795.*

For **SOCIETY FOR THE ENCOURAGEMENT OF DOMESTIC INDUSTRY,** The agricultural and industrial magazine, *see* vol. III, *Periodicals list*, Agricultural and industrial magazine. *See also* 1836.

28455 THOUGHTS on the reformed Parliament, and the reformed ministry; or, a view of the present state and future prospects of the country. 48p. 8°. *Edinburgh*, 1834.

28456 UNITED STATES OF AMERICA. *Congress.* ⟨Doc. No. 2.⟩ Documents accompanying the President's message at the opening of the second session of the twenty-third Congress. 390p. 8°. *n.p.* [1834] *Imperfect; wanting all before p. 33.*

28457 VILLENEUVE-BARGEMONT, J. P. A. DE, *Vicomte.* Économie politique chrétienne, ou, recherches sur la nature et les causes du paupérisme, en France et en Europe, et sur les moyens de le soulager et de le prévenir. 3 vols. 8°. *Paris, Marseille, &c.*, 1834.

28458 [**WADE,** JOHN.] The book of penalties; or, summary of the pecuniary penalties inflicted by the laws of England, on the commercial, manufacturing, trading, and professional classes, in their several occupations and businesses. With an abstract of the local acts and customs of London, relative to commerce, trade and residence. By the author of "The cabinet lawyer," &c. 552p. 8°. *London, Edinburgh, &c.*, 1834.

28459 [**WAKEFIELD,** EDWARD G.] England and America. A comparison of the social and political state of both nations. 376p. 8°. *New-York*, 1834. *For another edition, see 1833.*

28460 WHITE, WILLIAM (*fl.* 1826–1870). History, gazetteer, and directory, of Staffordshire, and the city... of Lichfield... 772p. 12°. *Sheffield*, 1834.

28461 A WOMAN'S thoughts on public affairs, including the Church, pauperism, and the game laws. By the wife of a country gentleman. 28p. 8°. *Norwich*, [1834]

28462 WYATT, H. Considerations on the present state of the different classes of the landed interest; on the causes of the distress which exists among the farmers and labourers...also, on the effects which a general free trade in corn...would produce on...the landed interest... 119p. 8°. 1834.

AGRICULTURE

28463 ADAM, WILLIAM (1751–1839). Remarks on the Blair-Adam estate. With an introduction, and appendix. [With 'Observations on the woods and plantations of Blair-Adam. Woods of succession and selection...', 'Observations on the woods and plantations of Blair-Adam. Woods of ornament and policy...', 'Observations on the grass parks; farms in lease; houses and buildings, &c. population, and the coal', and 'Blair-Adam garden, with a plan and views'.] 116, 109, 126, 26, 67, 12, 35p. 8°. *n.p.*, 1834. *The half-title reads: Blair-Adam, from MDCCXXXIII to MDCCCXXXIV.*

28464 AGRICOLA, *pseud.* Brief remarks on the rise and progress of agriculture; with a refutation of Lord Milton's theories on the corn question, &c. 19p. 8°. *Aberdeen*, [1834]

28465 BAXTER, J., *ed.* The library of agricultural and horticultural knowledge; with a memoir of Mr. Ellman, late of Glynde [by F. P. Walesby]: and an appendix, containing a farmer's and a gardener's calendar; and a collection of useful tables. Third edition, greatly enlarged. lxiv, 695p. 8°. *Lewes & London*, 1834.

28466 [**BIRCH,** S.] Agricultural distress. An address to the nobility and landed proprietors of Great Britain and Ireland, by a London merchant; on the distressed state of the agricultural population and the baneful effects of absenteeism. In which the benefits arising from small allotments of land...are displayed, as exhibited on the estates of Sir Gerard Noel Noel...under the...superintendence of Richard Westbrook Baker, Esq., of Cottesmore. To which is added, an appendix, showing the progress made in the small allotment system... 106p. 8°. 1834.

28467 BLACKER, W. An essay on the improvement to be made in the cultivation of small farms by the introduction of green crops and housefeeding the stock thereon

...Tenants' edition. 96p. 12°. *Dublin*, [1834] *See also* 1837.

28468 —— Prize essay, addressed to the agricultural committee of the Royal Dublin Society. On the management of landed property in Ireland; the consolidation of small farms, employment of the poor, etc. etc.... 41p. 8°. *Dublin, Belfast, &c.*, 1834.

28469 BUELAU, F. Der Staat und der Landbau. Beiträge zur Agriculturpolitik. 210p. 8°. *Leipzig*, 1834.

28470 BURGOYNE, M. An answer to Juvenis, or a recommendation of the allotment system, in providing a small portion of land to every poor labourer, to be cultivated by him for his own benefit. 43p. 8°. 1834.

28471 [**BURKE,** J. F.] British husbandry; exhibiting the farming practice in various parts of the United Kingdom...(*Library of Useful Knowledge.*) 2 vols. 8°. 1834–37.

28472 A CLUE to the cause of dear bread and fallen rents: submitted to the consideration of members of Parliament. By a landed proprietor. [Recommending the use of spade husbandry to provide employment and reduce the poor rate. A letter from Archibald Scott of Haddington is included.] 8p. 8°. [*London*,] 1834.

28473 CROPPER, J. Outline of a plan for an agricultural school, and for the employment of agricultural labourers by spade cultivation at Fearnhead, near Warrington. 12p. 8°. *Liverpool*, 1834.

28474 [**HAINES,** J.] Case between Sir William Clayton, Bart. and the Duchy of Cornwall. [Concerning a dispute over the lease of an estate in Kennington. Signed: J.H.] [131], 34p. 8°. 1834.

28475 —— The history of the constitution of the Duchy of Cornwall, and its tenants, as established...by an Act of Parliament...A.D.1622...And containing a refutation of all the arguments of the Lord Chancellor, which he was pleased to make use of in his judgment of the Clayton case... 148, 9p. *8°*. 1834.

28476 HUTTON, J. Letter to the farmers of Great Britain, on the means of rendering their crops more productive, and of superseding the necessity for the importation of foreign corn. 28p. *8°*. 1834.

28477 JOHNSTONE, JOHN (*fl.* 1797–1834). A systematic treatise on the theory and practice of draining land, &c.... With an appendix, containing hints and directions for the culture... of bog, moss, moor, and other unproductive ground, after being drained... Third edition, revised and enlarged. 250p. *4°*. *Edinburgh,* 1834. *Originally published with the title* An account of the most improved mode of draining land *in 1797 (q.v.).*

28478 LE PLAY, P. G. F. Observations sur l'histoire naturelle, et sur la richesse minérale de l'Espagne. 243p. *8°*. *Paris,* 1834.

28479 LOW, D. Elements of practical agriculture; comprehending the cultivation of plants, the husbandry of the domestic animals, and the economy of the farm. 695p. *8°*. *Edinburgh & London,* 1834. *See also* 1847.

28480 PLAN for regulating the rent of land in Scotland, with equal safety to landlord and tenant; containing safe principles for a lease of any length of endurance, &c.&c. Third edition, revised. 88p. *8°*. *Edinburgh,* 1834. *A reissue of the third edition, 1817 (q.v)., with new preliminary leaves. For other editions, see* 1815.

28481 PROSPECTUS of a joint stock company, for the improvement of Ireland [to be known as the Irish Land Company]. 8p. *8°*. 1834. *The copy that belonged to T. Spring Rice, Baron Monteagle.*

28482 A few **REMARKS** on the proposed Tithe Bill. Addressed to the clergy of the county of Dorset. By a country clergyman. 15p. *8°*. *London, Dorchester, &c.,* 1834.

For **ROYAL CORNWALL POLYTECHNIC SOCIETY,** 1st–72nd annual reports, 1833–1904, 1834–1905, *see* vol. III, *Periodicals list,* Report....

28483 SOCIETY OF THE GOVERNOR AND ASSISTANTS IN LONDON, OF THE NEW PLANTATION IN ULSTER. Report of a visit [by W. Tite] to the estates of the honorable the Irish Society, in Londonderry and Coleraine in the year 1834. 48p. *8°*. 1834. *See also* 1826 (GENERAL), 1835 (AGRICULTURE), 1836, 1838, 1841.

28484 STEPHENS, GEORGE, *land-drainer.* The practical irrigator and drainer. [Third edition. With 'Report to the Royal Agricultural Society at Örebro' on Elkington's system of draining land.] 195p. *8°*. *Edinburgh & London,* 1834. *For other editions, see* 1826.

28485 SUGDEN, E. B., *Baron St. Leonards.* Cursory observations on a general register [of land]. 23p. *8°*. 1834.

28486 VIEW of the present state of the salmon fishery of Scotland, with observations on the nature, habits, and instincts, of the salmon race; and on Scotch law and Scotch justice. By a salmon fisher. 198p. *8°*. [1834 ?]

28487 YORKSHIRE CENTRAL AGRICULTURAL ASSOCIATION. From The Yorkshireman of Saturday, November 15th, 1834. [Speeches by the chairman, E. S. Cayley, and others.] *s.sh.fol.* York, [1834] [*Br.* 584] *The Oastler copy.*

CORN LAWS

28488 The **ABOLITION** of corn laws ruinous to England. Addressed to all classes of persons. By a Yorkshireman. 40p. *8°*. *London & York,* 1834.

28489 A **FORM** of a petition to the Upper House, against any alterations of the corn laws, recommended to the adoption of the country at large, but more especially to agriculturists, farmers, labourers... Second edition. 16p. *8°*. 1834. *For another edition, see* 1833.

28490 PICKERING, . Remarks on the impolicy of corn laws. By Pickering. 16p. *8°*. *Liverpool,* 1834. *The author was possibly William Pickering.*

28491 VERE, SIR CHARLES B. The danger of opening the ports to foreign corn at a fixed duty, considered. 15p. *8°*. *Ipswich, London, &c.,* 1834.

POPULATION

28492 CLELAND, J. Statistics relative to Glasgow. 7p. *8°*. *Glasgow,* [1834]

28493 IVERNOIS, SIR F. D'. Sur la mortalité proportionnelle des peuples, considérée comme mesure de leur aisance et de leur civilisation. Analyse des quinze registres de l'état civil en France... 1817–1831... Tiré de la Bibliothèque Universelle, 1834. 82[84]p. *8°*. *Genève & Paris,* 1834. *The copy that belonged to N. W. Senior (HSF note). The fifth of the author's essays on this subject.*

28494 *SOCIETY FOR EQUITABLE ASSURANCES. Tables showing the total numbers of persons assured in the Equitable Society from its commencement in September 1762, to January 1, 1829, distinguishing their ages at the time of admission... and exhibiting the number of years during which they have continued members... the periods of life at which their assurances have terminated; and the ages which the surviving members had attained on the 1st of January 1829. To which are added tables of the probabilities and expectations of the duration of human life deduced from these documents... and a supplement showing the mortality of the Society for the years 1829, 1830, 1831 and 1832. [Compiled by Arthur Morgan.] 29p. *fol.* 1834. *The copy that belonged to Augustus De Morgan.*

28495 VILLERMÉ, L. R. Sur la population de la Grande-Bretagne, considérée principalement et comparativement dans les districts agricoles, dans les districts manufacturiers et dans les grandes villes. [Extrait des Annales d'Hygiène publique. (Tome XII, 2e partie.)] 57p. *8°*. [*Paris,* 1834] *Presentation copy from the author to N. W. Senior.*

TRADES & MANUFACTURES

28496 ALDERSON, M. A. An essay on the nature and application of steam, with an historical notice of the rise and progressive improvement of the steam-engine... Being the prize essay on this subject at the London Mechanics' Institution in the year 1833. 124p. *8°. 1834.*

28497 BABBAGE, C. Science économique des manufactures, traduit de l'anglais de Ch. Babbage, sur la troisième édition, par M. Isoard. 392p. *8°. Paris, 1834.* *A translation of chapters 13–34 of* On the economy of machinery and manufactures. *For editions of the complete work, see 1832.*

28498 BOOTH, D. The art of wine-making, in all its branches... To which is added an appendix, concerning cider and perry. 123p. *8°. 1834.*

28499 HALL, SAMUEL. Samuel Hall's improvements on steam engines; consisting of an improved method of condensing the steam and supplying water to the boilers ...An improved method of lubricating engine pistons, piston rods and valves or cocks: and an improved piston and valve... 16p. *8°. Nottingham, 1834.*

28500 HULL, W. The history of the glove trade, with the customs connected with the glove: to which are annexed some observations on the policy of the trade between England and France, and its operation on the agricultural and manufacturing interests. 144p. *8°. 1834.*

28501 JAMES, HENRY, *defendant.* British Iron Company. Small and others v. Attwood and others. Particulars of the sale of the Corngreaves estates, mines, and works, to Messrs. R. Small, J. H. Shears, and John Taylor. An account of the legal proceedings, the judgment of Lord Lyndhurst, and comments...thereon...with an appendix, containing letters...&c. relating to the above affair. By Henry James, one of the defendants in the cause. 192, 464p. *8°. London & Birmingham, 1834.*

28502 JOBARD, J. B. A. M. Coup-d'œil sur la propriété de la pensée...Opinion émise par le Liberal du 15 août 1834. 8p. *8°. [Bruxelles, 1834]*

28503 —— Développemens. [A series of questions and answers on patents.] 16p. *8°. [Bruxelles, 1834?]*

28504 LEUTNER, P. Mémoire aux deux Chambres sur la question d'admission des cotons filés anglais. 16p. *8°. [Paris, 1834.]*

28505 ROYAL SOCIETY. Proceedings of the Excise Committee, with documents relating thereto. [Concerning technical methods of assessing the excise duty payable on spirits. The meetings of the committee extended from December 1832 to November 1834.] 20p. *8°. [London, 1834] See also 1836.*

COMMERCE

28506 BAINEN, W. Tables for reducing Russian money into British sterling, from 9 pence to a shilling per rubel. [With 'London proportionate rates of freight from the Baltic and Archangel' and 'A table of the freight of stowage goods and grain in proportion to clean hemp'.] 196p. *fol. & 8°. Cronstadt, 1834.*

28507 BOULAY-PATY, P. S. Cours de droit commercial maritime, d'après les principes et suivant l'ordre du Code de commerce... 4 vols. *8°. Paris, 1834.*

28508 *COMMISSION COMMERCIALE DU HAVRE.* Adresse de la Commission...aux Chambres Législatives. [Dated: 10 mars 1834.] 27p. *4°. Havre, 1834.* *The copy that belonged to George Grote.*

28509 Proposed **FRENCH CUSTOMS LAW.** Case of the British merchants and of the British ship-owners trading with France, submitted to Lord Strangford. By the Paris correspondent of the Standard. [Reprinted from the *Standard* of 18, 20, 24 and 25 Feb. 1834. With a postscript of 3 March 1834.] 45p. *8°. Paris, 1834.*

28510 HENTIG, J. W. The Baltic merchant's guide, containing calculations of the prices of all Russian articles of export...tables of the proportionate weight of grain, list of rates, &c.&c....Adapted for the use of merchants, brokers and others. 89p. *8°. London, Liverpool, &c., 1834.*

28511 [KINGTON, J. B.] Thirty letters on the trade of Bristol, the causes of its decline and means of its revival; by a Burgess. With notes...additional information relative to its commercial and municipal history, tables... 346p. *12°. Bristol, 1834.*

28512 KRAUSE, G. F. Der grosse Preussisch-Deutsche Zollverein in besonderer Beziehung auf den Thüringischen Zollverband... 144p. *8°. Ilmenau, 1834.*

28513 LINDSAY, H. H. Report of proceedings on a voyage to the northern ports of China, in the ship Lord Amherst. [By H. H. Lindsay and C. F. A. Gutzlaff.] Extracted from papers, printed by order of the House of Commons, relating to the trade with China. Second edition. 296p. *8°. 1834.*

28514 MARTIN, ROBERT M. ⟨From the Asiatic Journal.⟩ Facts relative to the East and West-India sugar trade, addressed to the editors of the public press, with supplementary observations. 8p. *8°. [1834?]*

28515 REMARKS on the importance of preserving the existing scale of duties on North American and foreign timber. Published under the direction of the British American, West Indian, and General Shipping Association of Glasgow. 26p. *8°. Sunderland, 1834. This edition does not contain the appendix, published in the Glasgow edition of 1833 (q.v.).*

28516 REMARKS on the sugar trade. 36p. *8°. 1834.*

28517 RIGAUDIER, J. B. B. M. Prototype commercial ou pratique élémentaire sur la forme, les règles et l'usage des lettres de change... 123[223]p. *4°. Lyon, 1834. With the book stamp of the Société de Lecture de Genève.*

28518 The **TEA TRADE.** A full and accurate report of the extraordinary proceedings at the East India House, on the commencement of the March sale. Containing also copies of the correspondence between the East India Company and the Committee of the Tea Trade: together with the correspondence of the Committee of Wholesale

Tea Dealers with Government and the East India Company, relative to the repeal of the new scale of tea duties... 40p. *8º*. [1834]

28519 TRAVERS, J. A letter to the author of remarks, contained in a leading article of the Courier newspaper of the 22d August, including a copy of that article, with some notices of the evidence taken before the Select Committee of the House of Commons, upon the subject of the tea duties. 42p. *8º*. 1834.

28520 —— A letter to the editor of the Courier newspaper in reply to an article inserted in that journal... Together with a list of that Committee, and the copy of a letter from Sir George T. Staunton...Second edition, with additions. 59p. *8º*. 1834.

28521 [TRUEMAN & COOK.] The state of the commerce of Great Britain with reference to colonial and other produce, for the year 1833. 34p. *8º*. *n.p.* [1834] *See also* 1831, 1832, 1833.

28522 URMSTON, Sir J. B. Observations on the China trade, and on the importance and advantages of removing it from Canton, to some other part of the coast of that Empire. 149p. *8º*. 1834.

28523 YOUNG, George F. Shipping interest. Speech...in the House of Commons, on...June the 5th, 1834, on moving for the repeal of the 4 Geo. 4, c. 77, commonly called the Reciprocity of Duties' Act. Printed ...by the General Ship-Owners' Society. 73p. *8º*. 1834.

COLONIES

28524 *BRETON, W. H. Excursions in New South Wales, Western Australia, and Van Dieman's Land, during the years 1830, 1831, 1832, and 1833...Second edition revised, with additions. 420p. *8º*. 1834.

28525 BRITISH AMERICAN LAND COMPANY. Report of the Court of Directors of the British American Land Company, to the proprietors, 19th June, 1834. [With an appendix and 'Letters from the eastern townships of Lower Canada, containing information... which will be useful to emigrants'.] 14p. *8º*. 1834.

28526 BRYDONE, J. M. Narrative of a voyage, with a party of emigrants, sent out from Sussex, in 1834, by the Petworth Emigration Committee, to Montreal, thence up the River Ottawa and through the Rideau Canal, to Toronto...To which is added a comparison of the route to Upper Canada by Quebec, with that by New York; and observations on the proper mode of fitting out emigrant ships. 65p. *8º*. *Petworth & London*, 1834.

28527 CARMICHAEL, Mrs. A. C. Domestic manners and social condition of the white, coloured, and negro population of the West Indies...Second edition... 2 vols. *12º*. 1834.

28528 CARMICHAEL, H. Hints relating to emigrants and emigration; embracing observations and facts intended to display the real advantages of New South Wales as a sphere for the successful exercise of industry... To which are added tables of population; revenue; imports and exports; prices current at Sydney; returns of emigrants, etc. 48p. *12º*. 1834.

28529 On the **CAUSES** of the progressive depreciation of the price of grain prior to the late scarcity; with observations on the Madras ryotwar system. 37p. *8º*. *Madras*, 1834.

28530 DAVIS, William. A proposal for cultivating silk in the British colonies. By a member of the Society of Friends. Re-printed from the Wesleyan-Methodist Magazine for May. 8p. *8º*. 1834.

28531 ENGLAND. Parliament. *House of Commons.* Debate on the motion of T. Fowell Buxton, Esq., M.P., for protecting the civil rights and imparting civilization and the Christian religion to the native inhabitants of the British colonies; in the House of Commons...July 1, 1834. Extracted from the "Mirror of Parliament." 11p. *8º*. 1834.

28532 [HICKEY, W.] Hints on emigration to Upper Canada; especially addressed to the middle and lower classes in Great Britain and Ireland. By Martin Doyle... Third edition, corrected. 92p. *12º*. *Dublin, London, &c.*, 1834. *For another edition, see* 1832.

28533 HOWISON, J. European colonies, in various parts of the world, viewed in their social, moral, and physical condition. 2 vols. *8º*. 1834.

28534 LANG, John D. An historical and statistical account of New South Wales, both as a penal settlement and as a British colony. 2 vols. *12º*. 1834. *See also* 1840.

28535 MARTIN, Robert M. History of the British colonies. 5 vols. *8º*. 1834–35. *For another edition, entitled* The British colonial library, *see* 1836.

28536 PARKER, Henry W. Van Diemen's Land; its rise, progress, and present state, with advice to emigrants. Second edition, containing a supplement, shewing the state of the colony in May, 1834. [With appendixes.] 244, xiv, 22, xviiip. *12º*. *London, Edinburgh, &c.*, 1834. *Presentation copy from the author to E. Forster.*

28537 PRINSEP, James. Useful tables, forming an appendix to the Journal of the Asiatic Society. Part the first. Coins, weights, and measures of British India. 92p. *8º*. *Calcutta*, 1834. *The author's name is on a printed paper label on the wrapper. See also* 1835.

28538 STURT, C. N. Two expeditions into the interior of southern Australia, during the years 1828, 1829, 1830, and 1831 : with observations on the soil, climate, and general resources of the colony of New South Wales... Second edition. 2 vols. *8º*. 1834.

28539 [WAKEFIELD, Edward G.] The new British province of South Australia; or a description of the country, illustrated by charts and views, with an account of the principles, objects, plan, and prospects of the colony. [With appendixes and a bibliography.] 220p. *8º*. 1834.

28540 YOUNG, George R. The British North American Colonies. Letters to the Right Hon. E. G. S. Stanley, M.P. upon the existing treaties with France and America, as regards their "rights of fishery" upon the coasts of Nova Scotia, Labrador, and Newfoundland; the violations of these treaties by the subjects of both powers, and their effect upon the commerce...of the mother country and the colonies... 193p. *8º*. 1834.

FINANCE

28541 ADAMS, John Q., *President of the USA.* Speech ⟨suppressed by the previous question⟩ of Mr. John Quincy Adams, of Massachusetts, on the removal of the public deposites, and its reasons. 43p. *8°. Washington,* 1834.

28542 [BALLINGALL, J.] The pernicious effects of sea insurance. 22p. *8°. Kirkcaldy & London,* 1834.

28543 Albany Argus. Extra. — April 29, 1834. The **BANK** riots in New-York. A full and authentic account of the late riotous attack upon the State Arsenal in the city of New-York, and the seizure of the public property, by the Bank party. ⟨In Assembly, April 22, 1834.⟩ 8p. *8°. n.p.* [1834]

28544 BELL, D. A letter to Lord Althorp, on the subjects of a repeal of the corn laws, the malt tax, and the assessed taxes; including some observations connected with other branches of the revenue and taxation: respectfully submitted to the members of both Houses of Parliament. 18p. *8°. London, Glasgow, &c.,* 1834.

28545 BENTON, T. H. Albany Argus. Extra. — June 3, 1834. Mr. Benton's speech, on Mr. Clay's resolutions directing the restoration of the government deposites to the U.S. Bank, &c. United States Senate, May 28. 3p. *8°. n.p.* [1834]

28546 —— Albany Argus. Extra. — June 3, 1834. Mr. Benton's speech, on the subject of the President's delay to nominate Mr. Taney – the sources of "distress" – condition of the country, &c. 7p. *8°. n.p.* [1834]

28547 —— Speech of Mr. Benton, of Missouri, on the resolutions offered by Mr. Clay, on 26th December, relative to the removal of the public deposites from the Bank of the United States. Delivered in the Senate, January...1834. 44p. *8°. Boston,* 1834.

28548 [BJÖRNSTERNE, M. F. F., *Grefve.]* Influence of the Public Debt, over the prosperity of the country. By M.B. 58p. *8°. [London,]* 1834. *For another edition, see* 1831.

28549 BLANQUI, J. A. Des banques. [Extrait du tome II du Dictionnaire de l'industrie manufacturière commerciale et agricole.] 29p. *8°. [Paris,* 1834]

28550 BRANCH, J. The crisis of England; her danger and remedy. A statement of financial economy; also remarks on the currency, with a plan of equitable adjustment, for reducing the National Debt from eight hundred millions to five hundred millions. 31p. *8°. Eye, London, &c.,* 1834.

28551 BRANFILL, C. E. The right of the titheholder to his present exemption from the burthens of national taxation considered, in a reply to certain strictures upon a proposition contained in a letter to the Rt. Hon. Lord Althorp. 68p. *8°. Romford, London, &c.,* 1834.

28552 [BREED, .] Local issues. Joint stock banks and Bank of England notes, &c. contrasted. By a merchant. 16p. *8°.* 1834.

28553 Ellis's **BRITISH TARIFF** for 1834–35... By Robert Ellis... 288p. *12°.* 1834. *See also* 1829, 1832, 1846, 1848.

28554 CALHOUN, J. C. Remarks of the Hon. John C. Calhoun delivered in the Senate of the U. States, on the subject of the removal of the deposites from the Bank of the U. States, January 13, 1834. 14p. *8°. [Washington,]* 1834.

28555 —— Remarks of the Hon. John C. Calhoun, delivered in the Senate of the United States, March 21, 1834, on the motion of Mr. Webster, for leave to introduce a bill to continue the charter of the Bank of the United States for six years... 12p. *8°. n.p.* [1834]

28556 —— [Another edition.] 15p. *8°. Washington,* 1834.

28557 CAMPBELL, James, *deputy collector of the port of New York.* Tariff, or rates of duties payable on goods...imported into the United States of America, after the first day of January, 1834, until December 31, 1835. With the rates of duty of the tariff of 1828. To which are added forms...and an appendix containing several important laws of the United States and State of New-York relating to commerce. Revised and corrected by James Campbell. [With 'New tariff law, 1833'.] 156, 105–112p. *8°. New-York,* [1834] *See also* 1837.

28558 [CAREY, M.] To whom it may concern. [A leaflet adjuring his countrymen to support the Senate in the financial crisis. Dated: June 16.] *s.sh.8°. n.p.* [1834]

28559 CASE of the London and Westminster Bank. [Against the opposition of the Bank of England to its establishment.] 11p. *8°. [London,* 1834]

28560 CLAY, H. Speech of the Hon. Henry Clay, on the subject of the removal of the deposites; delivered in the Senate of the United States, December 26, 30, 1833. 31p. *8°. Washington: D. Green,* 1834.

28561 —— [Another edition.] 48p. *8°. Washington: Gales & Seaton,* 1834.

28562 COBBETT, W. Four letters to the Hon. John Stuart Wortley; in answer to his "Brief inquiry into the true award of an equitable adjustment between the nation and its creditors." [Reprinted from the *Political Register* of 31 August, 7, 28 September and 19 October, 1833.] 86p. *8°.* 1834.

28563 CORCELLE, F. T. DE. Extrait de la Revue des Deux Mondes. Livraison du 1er mars, 1834. Impôts des États-Unis. 24p. *8°. [Paris,* 1834]

28564 DELAUNAY, J.-B. Lettre à Mr. Tanneguy-Duchâtel, Ministre du Commerce. [On customs duties.] 40p. *8°. Le Havre,* 1834. *Presentation copy, with inscription, from the author to C. Poulett Thomson, Baron Sydenham.*

28565 DUDLEY AND WEST BROMWICH BANKING COMPANY. Deed of establishment of the Dudley and West Bromwich Banking Company, established under the authority of an Act of Parliament, passed in the seventh year of his late Majesty George the Fourth, to which is appended an abstract of the Act. Capital £400,000... 80p. *8°. Dudley,* 1834.

28566 DUJARDIN-SAILLY, . Tarif des douanes de Belgique au 15 mai 1834, exposant, dans l'ordre de la consommation et de la production, les denrées et les marchandises frappées de droits ou de prohibitions... suivi: 1° du tarif du droit de tonnage; 2° du tarif des droits d'accises; 3° du tarif des frais d'entrepôt... 111p. *8°. Bruxelles,* 1834.

28567 ENGLAND. Parliament. *House of Commons.* Debate on the third reading of the London and Westminster Bank Bill, in the House of Commons, on...May 26, 1834. Extracted from the Mirror of Parliament. 38p. 8°. 1834.

28568 FORRESTER, JAMES. A letter to the Right Honorable E. J. Littleton, M.P. Secretary of State for Ireland. Containing some account of the office of the Court for Relief of Insolvent Debtors in Ireland. And a report of an investigation into abuses alleged to exist in that office. Held by Serjeant O'Loghlin, in...1833. 35p. 8°. *n.p.*, 1834.

28569 GASPARIN, AGÉNOR E., *Comte*, and REBOUL, J. J. A. De l'amortissement. 106p. 8°. *Paris*, 1834.

28570 GAUDIN, M. M. C., *Duc de Gaëte.* Supplément aux Mémoires et souvenirs... 317p. 8°. *Paris*, 1834. *For the Memoirs, see 1826.*

28571 *GENEVA. Projet de budget de la Ville de Genève, pour l'année 1834. Avec les modifications proposées par la Commission. 7p. 4°. *Genève*, 1834. *The copy that belonged to George Grote.*

28572 *GENEVA, Canton of. Projet de budget du Canton de Genève, pour l'année 1834. Avec les modifications proposées par la Commission. 23p. 4°. *Genève*, 1834. *The copy that belonged to George Grote.*

28573 GESELLSCHAFT FÜR NATUR- UND HEILKUNDE IN DRESDEN. Auszüge aus den Protokollen der Gesellschaft...Jahr 1833. 204p. 8°. *Dresden*, 1834. *Containing a paper entitled 'Geschichte des Goldes' by W. H. C. R. A. von Ungern-Sternberg, published separately in 1835 (q.v.).*

28574 GILBART, J. W. The history and principles of banking. 220p. 8°. 1834. *See also 1837.*

28575 —— A practical treatise on banking...Third edition. 126p. 8°. 1834. *For other editions, see 1827.*

28576 GRUNDY, F. Speech of Mr. Grundy, of Tennessee, on the report of the Secretary of the Treasury, and the resolutions of Mr. Clay, relative to the removal of the public deposites, from the Bank of the United States. Delivered in the Senate...January, 1834. 24p. 8°. *Washington*, 1834.

28577 HALL, H. Remarks of the Hon. Hiland Hall, made in the House of Representatives, May 5, 1834, on presenting a memorial from Windham County, Vermont, on the subject of the removal of the public deposites. 7p. 8°. *Washington*, 1834.

28578 HARE, R. Proofs that credit as money, in a truly free country, is to a great extent preferable to coin... Abstracted from a pamphlet published in 1810, and revised, by the author. 12p. 8°. *Philadelphia*, 1834.

28579 LEE, JOHN. A letter to the Right Honourable the Lord Provost, relating to the annuity tax, and the ecclesiastical arrangements now proposed for the city of Edinburgh. 58p. 8°. *Edinburgh*, 1834.

28580 LETTER to the Rt. Hon. C. P. Thomson, M.P., President of the Board of Trade, &c. in explanation and defence of the principles and practices of joint stock banking. [Signed: A free trader in banking.] 23p. 8°. *Manchester & London*, 1834.

28581 A LETTER to the Right Honourable Sir Charles Manners Sutton, K.G.C.B. Speaker of the first House of Commons elected under the Reform Bills of 1832, on the measures required for the immediate relief and permanent benefit of the United Kingdom. 88p. 8°. 1834.

28582 LINDEN, J. Abhandlungen über Cameral- und fiscalämtliche Gegenstände...nebst einer besondern Abhandlung über Adelsanmassungen. xviii, 408p. 8°. *Wien*, 1834.

28583 The LONDON and Westminster Bank. Hints by way of encouraging the formation of a joint-stock banking company in London, with some account of the present state of private banking in the Metropolis, and of the amount of current cash balances in the hands of the London bankers. 64p. 8°. 1834. *Conjecturally attributed to J. W. Gilbart.*

28584 —— Second edition. 64p. 8°. 1834.

28585 LONDON PROVIDENT INSTITUTION. London Provident-Institution, or Bank for Savings, Blomfield Street, Moorfields; established at Bishopsgate Church Yard...1816. 40p. 8°. [*London*,] 1834. *The copy that belonged to William Allen.*

28586 LORD, E. On credit, currency and banking... Second edition. 130p. 12°. *New-York*, 1834.

28587 MACARDY, J. A practical essay on banking: in which the operations of the Bank of England – the vicissitudes of private banks – and the character and security of unchartered joint-stock banks, are considered. Illustrated with a sketch of the district-plan, operations, and policy of the Commercial Bank of England. 40p. 8°. 1834.

28588 —— Stability of the English joint-stock banks. Also a retrospective glance at the metallic currency of England; with an address to English banking companies. 20p. 8°. 1834.

28589 *MAHONY, P. Observations by Mr. Mahony on the Tithe Bill (Ireland), for the Right Hon. E. J. Littleton, M.P. &c.&c.&c. 12p. 8°. 1834. *The copy that belonged to Augustus De Morgan. With a manuscript note at the head of the title-page: For private circulation only.*

28590 *—— Tithe Bill — Ireland. Letter from Mr. Mahony to the Right Hon. E. J. Littleton, M.P. Chief Secretary for Ireland, on the Irish Tithe Bill. 31p. 8°. 1834. *The copy that belonged to Augustus De Morgan.*

28591 —— Tithe Bill — Ireland. Letters from Mr. Mahony to the Right Hon. E. J. Littleton, M.P., and Chief Secretary for Ireland, on the Irish Tithe or Land-Tax Bill of 1834...Third edition. 89p. 8°. 1834. *The copy that belonged to Earl De Grey.*

28592 MARTINEAU, H. Illustrations of taxation... 140, 144, 122, 136, 134p. 12°. 1834. *There is no general title-page in this copy.*

28593 MASTROFINI, M. Discussion sur l'usure... Ouvrage où l'on démontre que l'usure modérée n'est contraire ni à l'Écriture Sainte ni au droit naturel ni aux décisions de l'Église. Traduit de l'italien, sur la 4me édition, par M. C***...suivi du recueil des décisions du Saint Siége qui ont paru dans ces derniers temps... 523p. 8°. *Lyon*, 1834. *For another edition, see 1832.*

28594 MEDLEY, W. An address to the agriculturists of the county of Bucks. [With 'Extract from the preface of the celebrated work of Pablo Pebrer, lately published'.] 9p. 8°. [1834]

28595 MOLLOT, F. E. Bourses de commerce, agens de change et courtiers; ou, législation, principes et jurisprudence qui les organisent, et qui les régissent... 171p. *8°. Bruxelles*, 1834.

28596 MOORE, R. Observations on the necessity for instituting an auxiliary standard in the shape of a mint paper coin, to be granted the use of on deposits made with the Crown, to secure its sterling value. 112p. *8°. Kingston & London, 1834. Presentation copy from the author to Earl De Grey, then Lord Lieutenant of the County of Bedford.*

28597 MORGAN, H. D. The beneficial operation of banks for savings, affirmed in an address to...the Bank for Savings for the Hundred of Hinckford, in the county of Essex...Annexed is a brief memoir of the late Lewis Majendie, Esq. of Hedingham Castle. 69p. *8°.* 1834.

28598 MOULTON, R. K. Legislative and documentary history of the banks of the United States, from the time of establishing the Bank of North America, 1781, to October, 1834. With notes and comments. 227p. *12°. New-York*, 1834.

28599 MURHARD, J. K. A. Theorie und Politik der Besteuerung. Ein Handbuch für Staatsgelehrte, Volks-Vertreter und Geschäftsmänner. 683p. *8°. Göttingen*, 1834.

28600 NOTTINGHAM AND NOTTINGHAM-SHIRE BANKING COMPANY. Deed of settlement of the...Company, established under the authority of an Act of Parliament passed in the seventh year of the reign of King George the fourth. Capital, £500,000 in 10,000 shares of £50 each. 53p. *8°. Nottingham*, 1834.

28601 OASTLER, R. A letter to the editor of the 'Argus and Demagogue' on the validity of Sir John Ramsden's title to the sums of money he claims for canal dues, and on other subjects. 36p. *12°. Huddersfield, 1834. Oastler's own copy.*

28602 OBSERVATIONS on the receipt tax, and some other stamp duties, by which labour is wasted: with suggestions for commuting them. By a Conservative. 16p. *8°.* 1834.

28603 OBSERVATIONS on the Trading Companies' Bill. [With the text of the Bill.] 18p. *8°. 1834. Presentation copy to C. Poulett Thomson, Baron Sydenham.*

28604 O'CALLAGHAN, J. Usury, funds, and banks; also forestalling traffick & monopoly; likewise pew rent, and grave tax...are all repugnant to the divine and ecclesiastical laws...To which is prefixed a narrative of the author's controversy with Bishop Coppinger... 380p. *12°. Burlington [Vt.], 1834. For other editions, see 1825.*

28605 OSSIANDER, H. F.GeschichtlicheDarstellung der niederländischen Finanzen vom Anfange des Jahres 1830 bis Ende des Jahres 1835. Mit einigen Betrachtungen über das niederländische Grundgesetz. 256p. *8°. Stuttgart & Amsterdam*, 1834.

28606 PEBRER, A. P. Mémoire sur la situation financière de l'Espagne. Des ressources intérieures et extérieures applicables à la liquidation de sa dette, et de la mesure proposée d'une banqueroute nationale et étrangère pour consolider le crédit de cet état. Présenté à S.M. la Reine et Régente...Traduit de l'espagnol par le Marquis de Sainte-Croix. 71p. *8°. Paris*, 1834.

28607 PHILO JUSTICIÆ, *pseud.* The repeal of the assessed taxes and malt duty, and the imposition of a property tax. In a letter to the Right Hon. the Earl Grey. 18p. *8°. Glasgow, Edinburgh, &c.*, 1834.

28608 PRATT, J. T. The savings banks in England, Wales, and Ireland, arranged according to counties, and the increase or decrease of each class of depositors, &c. since November 1831...With an appendix, containing all the returns relating to savings banks, printed by order of the House of Commons, since November 1830. 63p. *12°. 1834. For another edition, see 1831.*

28609 Ten REASONS why I will not pay church rates. 4p. *8°. London & Manchester,* [1834]

28610 Quelques RÉFLEXIONS sur le projet de supprimer en 1835, les douze hôtels de monnaie dans les départemens, et de ne conserver que celui de Paris. 15p. *8°. Lyon,* [1834 ?]

28611 RIVES, W. C. Remarks of William C. Rives, of Virginia, on resigning his seat in the Senate of the United States [owing to his inability to vote as instructed by the Legislature of Virginia, on the bank question]. 4p. *8°. n.p.* [1834]

28612 —— Speech of the Hon. William C. Rives, on the subject of the removal of the deposites; delivered in the Senate of the United States, January 17, 1834. 32p. *8°. City of Washington*, 1834.

28613 ROSSER, A. Credit pernicious...Second edition. 85p. *8°. 1834. Two presentation copies, both with inscriptions from the author, one to Charles Williams Allen, the other to Harriet Martineau. For another edition, see 1823.*

28614 *ROYAL NAVAL ANNUITANT SOCIETY.* Final report of the Committee of Investigation of the...Society, ordered to be printed. 19p. *8°. Devonport, [1834] The copy that belonged to Augustus De Morgan.*

28615 SCOTTISH WIDOWS' FUND AND LIFE ASSURANCE SOCIETY. Deed of constitution of the...Society as...recorded in the Books of Council and Session 4th October, 1814; to which are added bye-laws, forms, &c.; also reports and addresses read to the general courts; giving a complete view of the Society's...progress...down to 15th January, 1834... With tables of rates, &c. 131p. *8°. Edinburgh, 1834–[35] Two leaves, paginated ★113–★116, are inserted following p. 116, containing an account of the 21st annual general court, 15 January, 1835.*

28616 —— Report of the proceedings at the twentieth annual general court...held...on...15th January, 1834. [With tables of rates.] 43p. *8°. Edinburgh,* [1834]

28617 SETTLEMENT of the tithe question and plan of church reform in Ireland. August 24th, 1834. 18p. *8°. n.p. [1834] The copy that belonged to Earl De Grey.*

28618 —— [Another edition.] Settlement of the tithe question in Ireland. August 24th, 1834. 18p. *8°. n.p.* [1834] *The editions differ in detail, notably in sums of money quoted. The copy that belonged to Earl De Grey.*

28619 SHARP, T. A catalogue of provincial copper coins, tokens, tickets, and medalets, issued in Great Britain, Ireland, and the colonies, during the eighteenth and nineteenth centuries...Described from the originals in the collection of Sir George Chetwynd, Baronet, of Grendon Hall...Warwick. 280p. *4°. 1834. With engravings of some of the coins inserted.*

28620 SKRIMSHIRE, F. Letters on the consumption of malt, addressed respectively to the farmer, labourer, and labourer's friend. [On the supposed advantages of the repeal of the malt tax.] 31p. *8°.* 1834.

28621 SPENCER, J. C., *3rd Earl Spencer*. Financial statement of the Right Honourable the Chancellor of the Exchequer, in the House of Commons, on...14th February, 1834. Extracted from the Mirror of Parliament – Part CCLVIII. 11p. *12°*. 1834.

28622 STUCKEY, V. Thoughts on the improvement of the system of country banking. In a letter to Lord Viscount Althorp...⟨Not published.⟩ 35p. *8°*. 1834. *See also* 1836.

28623 TALLMADGE, N. P. Speech of the Hon. Nathaniel P. Tallmadge, of New York, on the subject of the removal of the deposites from the Bank of the United States; delivered in the Senate of the United States, March, 1834. 34p. *8°*. *City of Washington*, 1834.

28624 TATE, WILLIAM (1781?–1848). The modern cambist; forming a manual of foreign exchanges, in the direct, indirect, and cross operations of bills of exchange, and bullion; including an extensive investigation of the arbitrations of exchange...With numerous formulae and tables of the weights and measures...Second edition. 224p. *8°*. *London...Paris*, 1834. *See also* 1842, 1849.

28625 THONNELIER,   . Exposition des Produits de l'Industrie française, année 1834. Notice historique sur le balancier et sur la presse monétaire. Dédiée au Roi des Français. 8p. *4°*. *Paris*, 1834.

28626 UNION COMMITTEE, *New York*. Report of the "Union Committee" appointed by the meeting of the signers of the memorial to Congress, held on the 11th day of February, 1834, at the Merchants' Exchange, in the City of New-York. 34p. *8°*. *New-York*, 1834.

28627 UNITED STATES OF AMERICA. Congress. *House of Representatives*. Report on gold and silver coins, by a Select Committee of House of Representatives of the United States, February 19, 1834. 119p. *8°*. *Washington*, 1834. *The copy that belonged to James Pennington.*

28628 —— —— —— 23d Congress, 1st Session. ⟨Rep. No. 481.⟩ United States Bank. May 22, 1834. 93p. *8°*. [*Washington*, 1834]

28629 —— —— —— Albany Argus. Extra. — May 30, 1834. Bank of the United States. Resistance of the Bank to an investigation by the representatives of the people. Report of the Committee of Investigation. 8p. *8°*. *n.p.* [1834]

28630 VAN SOMMER, J. Tables, exhibiting the various fluctuations in three per cent. consols, in every month during each year from 1789 to 1833 inclusive; to which are annexed the amounts, and rate of interest of all the loans contracted since 1788; and the amount of Navy, victualling, and Exchequer bills funded. [With an appendix.] [46]l., 12p. *4°*. 1834. *See also* 1848.

28631 WAKEFIELD, DANIEL (1798–1858). Public expenditure apart from taxation; or, remarks on the inadequate and excessive pay of public servants. 281p. *8°*. 1834.

28632 WEBSTER, D. Remarks of Mr. Webster on the removal of the deposites, and on the subject of a national bank: delivered in the Senate of the United States, January 1834. 23p. *8°*. *Washington*, 1834.

28633 —— Speech of Mr. Webster, on moving for leave to introduce a bill to continue the Bank of the United States for six years. Delivered in the Senate of the United States, March 18, 1834. 18p. *8°*. *Washington*, 1834.

28634 WELLS, S. The revenue and the expenditure of the United Kingdom. 491p. *8°*. 1834.

28635 Three WORDS on the pension list. 10p. *8°*. 1834.

28636 WRIGHT, SILAS. Albany Argus — Extra. Remarks of Mr. Wright, in the U.S. Senate, on submitting the resolutions of the State of New-York against the restoration of the deposites, and against the recharter of the U.S. Bank. 7p. *8°*. *n.p.* [1834]

28637 —— Albany Argus....Extra — May 20, 1834. Speech of Mr. Wright, on the President's protest. Speech ...in the Senate of the U.S., May 5, 1834, on the resolutions of Mr. Poindexter, with the amendment offered by Mr. Bibb, declaring the refusal of the Senate to receive the protest of the President, and pronouncing the President guilty of a violation of the constitution and law. 12p. *8°*. *n.p.* [1834]

28638 —— Albany memorials. Mr. Wright's speech. The memorial from the citizens of Albany, in favor of a recharter of the Bank of the United States, and of the restoration of the public deposites to that institution, being under consideration. 8p. *8°*. *n.p.* [1834 ?]

28639 Das neueste ZOLL-GESETZ und die Zoll-Ordnung des deutschen Zoll- und Handels-Vereins nebst den Grundverträgen desselben. Eine besondere Ausgabe aus der Schönbrodt'schen Sammlung... 222p. *8°*. *Potsdam*, 1834.

TRANSPORT

28640 ACKERLEY, C. H. A plan for the better security of vessels navigating the River Thames. With appendices on nautical subjects resulting therefrom. [Second edition, with addenda.] vii, 17, xxix, xip. *8°*. *London, La Haye, &c.*, 1834.

28641 The ADVANTAGES and profits of the Southampton Railway analysed. 58p. *8°*. 1834. *The Rastrick copy.*

28642 BASING AND BATH RAILWAY COMPANY. Bath and Basing Railway. Meeting at Frome, on...17th December 1834 [for the inhabitants of Frome and its neighbourhood to hear a statement from a deputation from the Basing and Bath Railway Company on the objects and advantages of the railway which would link up with the London and Southampton Railway at Basing]. 3p. *4°*. [*London*, 1834]

28643 —— Railway from Basing, in the county of Hants, to Bath [being an extension of the London and Southampton Railway. Prospectus, incorporating the report of Francis Giles and William Brunton, engineers, dated: 8th July 1834]. 2p. *fol*. [*London*, 1834] *See also* 1835.

28644 BERMINGHAM, T. Additional statements on the subject of the River Shannon to the reports published in 1831. 40p. *8°*. 1834.

28645 BOSTON AND PROVIDENCE RAIL

ROAD CORPORATION. Third annual report of the Directors...with that of the agent and engineer [William Gibbs McNeill], and other documents. June 4, 1834. 79p. *8°. Boston, 1834. The Rastrick copy. See also 1832, 1833, 1849.*

28646 BROUN, SIR RICHARD, *Bart.* Appeal to our rulers and ruled, in behalf of a consolidation of the Post Office, roads, and mechanical conveyance, for the service of the State. 41p. *8°.* 1834.

28647 Descriptive **CATALOGUE** of the padorama; of the Manchester and Liverpool Rail-road...now exhibiting at Baker Street, Portman Square. Illustrated with...views, taken on the spot... 16p. *8°.* 1834.

28648 COMPANY OF PROPRIETORS FOR THE FORMATION OF AN ASYLUM HARBOUR AT REDCAR. To be incorporated by Act of Parliament. The Company of proprietors for the formation of an asylum harbour at Redcar...to be called Port William...Prospectus [with the report of W. A. Brooks, engineer]. 18p. *8°. [London, 1834]*

28649 CORT, R. Rail-road impositions detected; or, facts and arguments, being an exposé of the estimates for the Grand Northern Railway, submitted to public meetings at Norwich, Bury, Cambridge, &c. with disclosures ...important to the canal interests of Great Britain. [With a single sheet entitled 'Proofs that the two best railways in the world are...bubble speculations'.] 40p. *8°.* 1834.

28650 —— Rail-road impositions detected: or, facts and arguments to prove that the Manchester and Liverpool Railway has not paid one per cent. nett profit; and that the Birmingham, Bristol, Southampton, Windsor, and other railways, are...only bubble speculations...Second edition. 195p. *8°.* 1834.

28651 CUBITT, SIR W. A report on the financial state of the Birmingham & Liverpool Junction Canal... With an appendix of correspondence and calculations relating thereto. March, 1834. 37p. *8°.* 1834.

28652 CUNDY, N. W. Inland transit. The practicability, utility, and benefit of railroads; the comparative attraction and speed of steam engines, on a railroad, navigation, and turnpike road; report of a Select Committee of the House of Commons on steam carriages, with an abstract of the evidence...on the Birmingham Railroad Bill...also, the plans...of the projected grand southern and northern railroads...Second edition. 161p. *8°.* 1834.

28653 EAST INDIA DOCK COMPANY. Report of the Court of Directors of the East-India Dock Company, read at an extraordinary general meeting of proprietors, held at their house in St. Helen's Place, on...the 8th of August 1834. 16p. *8°.* 1834.

28654 ENGLAND. *Laws, etc.* Anno tertio Gulielmi IV. Regis. Cap. xxxvi. An Act for making a railway from London to Birmingham. ⟨6th May 1833.⟩ p.737–874. *fol.* 1834.

28655 —— —— [*Endorsed:*] Hartlepool Railway, Durham branch. An Act to enable the Hartlepool Dock and Railway Company to make a new branch of railway to the City of Durham, and for amending an Act of the second year to his present Majesty, relative to the Hartlepool Railway. ⟨Royal Assent, 16 June 1834.⟩ 4 Will. IV. sess. 1834. 19p. *fol. [London,]* 1834.

28656 —— Parliament. *House of Commons.* Extracts from the minutes of evidence given before the Committee of the House of Commons on the Great Western Railway Bill. 51p. *8°. Bristol, 1834. The Rastrick copy. For another issue, see no. 28661.*

28657 —— —— *House of Lords.* Extracts from the evidence given on the London and Southampton Railway Bill; as printed by order of the House of Lords. 68p. *8°. n.p. [1834] The Rastrick copy.*

28658 FLYNN, H. E. A glance at the question of a ship canal connecting the asylum harbour at Kingstown with the River Anna Liffey at Dublin, &c.&c.&c. 82p. *8°. Dublin, 1834.*

28659 GORDON, ALEXANDER (1802–1868). A treatise upon elemental locomotion, and interior communication, wherein are explained and illustrated, the history, practice, and prospects of steam carriages; and the comparative value of turnpike roads, railways, and canals. Second edition, improved and enlarged, with an appendix ... 326p. *8°. London, Glasgow, &c., 1834. For other editions, see 1832.*

28660 GRAHAME, T. A treatise on internal intercourse and communication in civilised states, and particularly in Great Britain. [Part 1.] 160p. *8°.* 1834.

28661 GREAT WESTERN RAILWAY COMPANY. An account of the proceedings of the Great Western Railway Company, with Extracts from the evidence given in support of the Bill, before the Committee of the House of Commons, in the session of 1834. 68, 51p. *8°. London [& Bristol], 1834. For another issue of the Extracts, see no. 28656.*

28662 LONDON AND SOUTHAMPTON RAILWAY COMPANY. London and Southampton Railway. Capital, one million – Shares £50 each. [Prospectus, incorporating a map showing the connection with the Basing and Bath Railway.] 2p. *fol. n.p. [1834]*

28663 MACERONI, F. A few facts concerning elementary locomotion...Second edition. [With 'Appendix. Macerone versus Mechanics' Magazine'.] 131p. *8°.* 1834.

28664 MINARD, C. J. Leçons faites sur les chemins de fer à l'École des Ponts et Chaussées en 1833–1834. 84p. *4°. Paris, 1834. With the signature of George Rennie on the half-title.*

For a **NEW GUIDE TO STAGECOACHES, WAGGONS**...&c. *for 1834, see no.* 28449.

28665 PENFOLD, C. A proposed amendment in the highway laws of England, addressed to the members of both Houses of Parliament; with some observations upon the best mode of repairing roads. 18p. *8°. Croydon, 1834.*

28666 PHILIPS, F. Analysis of the defective state of turnpike roads and turnpike securities, with suggestions for their improvement. 67p. *8°. London, Manchester, &c., 1834. Presentation copy from the author to T. Spring Rice, Baron Monteagle.*

28667 [*Endorsed:*] **PROSPECTUS** of the Great Northern Railway, from London to York, Cambridge, Lincoln, Selby, and Norwich, &c.&c. [An abortive scheme.] 3p. *4°. n.p. [1834]*

28668 Short **REASONS,** shewing why the Southampton Railway can never answer. *s.sh.fol. n.p. [1834]*

28669 STEVENSON, ROBERT, **& SON.** To His Grace the Duke of Buccleuch and Queensbery, &c.&c.&c.

the report of Robert Stevenson and Son, civil-engineers. [On the practicability of establishing a deep-water harbour at Granton, near Leith. Dated: May 22, 1834.] 7p. *fol. n.p.* [1834]

28670 Thirteen **VIEWS** on the Dublin and Kingstown railway. [16]p. *8°. Dublin,* 1834.

28671 WARD, JOHN (*fl.* 1834). Manual labour superior to steam, used upon railways. A new discovery whereby manual labour, can be most advantageously substituted for steam power upon railways...being an exposition of the...patent improvements in railways and carriages... 19p. *8°.* 1834.

SOCIAL CONDITIONS

28672 A faithful **ACCOUNT** of the great meeting [21 April 1834] and procession of the trades' union, to present a petition to the King, on behalf of the Dorchester labourers. *s.sh.fol.* [*London,* 1834]

28673 ACTS of the Houses that Jack built, (i.e. King John,) on whose Magna Charta was built the H—— of L—— & of C——. [A poem on the poor laws.] Humbly dedicated to the Poor Law Commissioners. *s.sh.fol. n.p.* [*c.* 1834] *The copy that belonged to N. W. Senior.*

28674 ADDRESS of the united delegates, from the factory districts throughout the kingdom, assembled at Manchester, to their operative friends. [Signed: John Doherty, chairman.] 8p. *8°. Manchester,* [1834?] *The Oastler copy.*

28675 AMATOR PATRIAE, *pseud.* A proposal for improving the condition of the working classes, giving a spur to trades, and alleviating the general distress of the country. 8p. *8°.* 1834.

28676 The most blessed **AMENDMENT** of the poor laws, by the dear Whigs. 4p. *8°. Leeds,* [1834] *The Oastler copy.*

28677 ANALYSIS of the evidence taken before the Factory Commissioners, as far as it relates to the population of Manchester and the vicinity, engaged in the cotton trade. Read before the Statistical Society of Manchester, March, 1834. 33p. *8°. Manchester,* 1834. *The copy that belonged to N. W. Senior, with his signature on the half-title.*

28678 BECHER, JOHN T. The antipauper system; exemplifying the positive...good...under the...lawful administration of the poor laws, prevailing at Southwell ...with plans of the Southwell workhouse, and of the Thurgarton Hundred workhouse; with statistical tables; and with instructions for book-keeping. To which is now prefixed an introduction, exhibiting the rise...of the antipauper system...Second edition, continued to the present time. 79p. *8°.* 1834. *For another edition, see* 1828.

28679 BIGOT DE MOROGUES, P. M. S., *Baron de Morogues.* Du paupérisme, de la mendicité, et des moyens d'en prévenir les funestes effets. 675p. *8°. Paris,* 1834.

28680 BLIGH, R. Bellum agrarium. A foreview of the winter of 1835; suggested by the poor law project: with observations on the Report and the Bill. 37p. *8°.* 1834.

28681 BLOMFIELD, C. J., *Bishop of London.* Speech of the Right Reverend the Lord Bishop of London, in the House of Lords, on Friday, August 8, 1834; on the third reading of the Poor Laws Amendment Bill. Extracted from the Mirror of Parliament, part CCCXIV. 11p. *8°.* 1834.

28682 BRENTON, E. P. Observations on the training and education of children in Great Britain: a letter to Sir James Graham on impressment: and a translation from the French of M. Ducpétiaux's work on mendicity. With an appendix. 119p. *8°.* 1834. *For another edition of Ducpétiaux's work, see* 1832.

For the **BRITISH AND FOREIGN TEMPER-ANCE ADVOCATE,** 1834-35, *see* vol. III, *Periodicals list.*

28683 BROUGHAM, H. P., *Baron Brougham and Vaux.* Corrected report of the speech of the Lord Chancellor in the House of Lords, on July 21, 1834, on moving the second reading of the Bill to amend the poor laws. 65p. *8°.* 1834. *The copy that belonged to William Allen.*

28684 —— Second edition. 65p. *8°.* 1834.

28685 —— Third edition. 65p. *8°.* 1834.

28686 BUCHANAN, JAMES, *British Consul at New York.* Facts and observations in relation to the extension of state prisons in England: also bearing on poverty and crime. 84p. *8°. New York,* 1834.

28687 BULL, G. S. Another "Reverend friend," for the poor curate of Byerley...Second edition, enlarged. [A reprint of a letter to the *Leeds Mercury,* dated September 12th, 1834.] *s.sh.fol. Bradford,* [1834] [*Br.* 569(1)] *The Oastler copy.*

28688 —— The duty of the ministers of the Gospel, to plead the cause of the industrious & injured labourers of their country. [A speech at Manchester, April 1833.] 4p. *8°. Huddersfield,* [1834] *The Oastler copy.*

28689 [——] The entire demolition of trades' unions, by the recent discharge of an old rusty parchment blunderbuss. Printed for the special gratification of the Whigs, by order of John Poulett. 16p. *32°. n.p.* [1834] *The Oastler copy.*

28690 —— Examples of prayer for Sunday School children... 12p. *24°. Bradford,* 1834. *The Oastler copy.*

28691 —— Late meeting at Bradford on national regeneration. Bradford politeness and consistency! [A reprint of a letter to the *Leeds Times,* dated March 13, 1834.] *s.sh.fol. n.p.* [1834] [*Br.* 569(2)] *The Oastler copy.*

28692 —— Letter from the Rev. G. S. Bull to R. Rickards, Esq. (From the Manchester and Salford Advertiser of Nov. 29, 1234 [*sic*].) [On the first report of the factory inspectors.] *s.sh.fol. n.p.* [1834] [*Br.* 569(3)] *The Oastler copy.*

28693 —— [Another edition.] Remarks upon the character of the working classes; and some partial and unfair statements exposed; in a letter from the Rev. G. S. Bull to R. Rickards, Esq....(From the Manchester and Salford Advertiser of Nov. 29th, 1834.) 4p. *8°. Bradford,* [1834] *The Oastler copy.*

28694 —— Mr. Bull and the Regeneration Society. [A letter from G. S. Bull to 'the Friends of the National Regeneration Society' transmitted for publication, with an accompanying letter to the editor of the *Leeds Times* by Peter Bussey, chairman of the Society.] 4p. *8°. n.p.* [1834] *The Oastler copy.*

28695 —— The Poor Law Act. To the inhabitants of Bradford and the neighbourhood. 4p. 8°. *Bradford*, [1834] *The Oastler copy.*

28696 —— The sins of the poor, and of the great men, exposed and reproved; and the necessity of curtailing the present term of labour...of the industrious classes of society insisted upon; in a sermon...December 8th, 1833 ...24p. 8°. *Huddersfield*, 1834. *The Oastler copy.*

28697 —— The substance of a lecture upon the new Poor-Law Act, falsely called "the amendment," delivered ...at...Great-Horton, near Bradford, on...December 29th, 1834. 12p. 8°. *Bradford*, [1834]

28698 —— To the editor of the Leeds Times. [A letter, dated: March 20, 1834.] *s.sh.fol. n.p.* [1834] [*Br.* 569(6)] *The Oastler copy.*

28699 —— To the people of Bradford, including the unrepresented. [A defence of his conduct at a political meeting on the Poor Law and emigration.] 4p. 8°. [*Bradford*, 1834]

28700 —— To the public. [A notice, dated Sept. 23, 1834, challenging the Rev. Winterbotham to prove his charges at a public meeting.] *s.sh.4°. Bradford*, [1834] [*Br.* 569(7)] *The Oastler copy.*

28701 BUNN, T. A letter relative to the affairs of the poor of the parish of Frome Selwood in Somersetshire; written for the information of His Majesty's Commissioners, with notes and observations on the extinction of pauperism in Great Britain... 158p. 8°. *Frome*, 1834. *In a volume of the author's pamphlets, with his manuscript notes.*

28702 BURGES, G. Unrestrained machinery must ere long be the ruin of the country. (Extracts from the evidence of George Burges, Esquire, M.A. before the Hand-Loom Weavers' Committee: 1834.) [2]p. *s.sh.fol. Bradford*, [1834] [*Br.* 576] *The Oastler copy.*

28703 CAMERON, CHARLES H. and WROTTESLEY, J. Two reports addressed to His Majesty's Commissioners appointed to inquire into the administration and operation of the poor laws, by C. H. Cameron, John Wrottesley and J. W. Cowell, Esquires [the first report by C. H. Cameron and J. Wrottesley, the second by J. W. Cowell] and a letter from Count Arrivabene, on the management of the poor in Belgium. 224p. 8°. 1834. *The copy that belonged to Sir Harry Verney (1801–1894), with his signature on the title-page.*

28704 CAPPER, D. Practical results of the workhouse system, as adopted in the parish of Great Missenden, Bucks, during the year, 1833–4; with remarks on the principal details of the system, and the benefits arising to the poor from the limitation of charitable efforts to the encouragement of industrious and provident habits. 79p. 8°. 1834.

28705 —— Second edition, enlarged. 95p. 8°. 1834. *The copy that belonged to Sir Harry Verney.*

28706 [**CAREY, M.**] Annals of liberality, generosity, public spirit, &c. Third series, No. v. [Signed: M.C.] 4p. 8°. *n.p.* [1834] *With manuscript corrections, probably by the author.*

28707 CARLTON EQUITABLE FRIENDLY SOCIETY. The constitution and rules of the Carlton Equitable Friendly Society for Carlton in Lindrick... Nottingham...With tables and calculations of the various assurances... 13, 21p. 8°. 1834.

28708 A CHRISTMAS hymn. [To be sung on the occasion of a visit of the children of John Wood's mill to his home, on Christmas morning 1834, to deliver an address of thanks for his kindness to them. Dated: Dec. 22, 1834.] *s.sh.fol. Bradford*, [1834] [*Br.* 583] *Printed on pink paper. The Oastler copy.*

28709 COBBETT, W. To the Earl of Radnor, on his reported speech, in the House of Lords, on the 21. July, on the poor-law scheme. [Letter I.–Letter V. reprinted from the *Political Register*.] 5 vols. 8°. [*London*, 1834]

28710 COMMITTEE OF MANUFACTURERS AND WEAVERS, *Bolton.* A letter addressed to the members of both Houses of Parliament, on the distresses of the hand loom weavers, as a remedy for which the expediency...of a Board of Trade for the equalization of wages is proposed... 15p. 8°. *Bolton*, 1834. *The Oastler copy.*

28711 The present **CONDITION** of British workmen. [A ballad on the evils of machinery and the new Poor Law.] *s.sh.fol. n.p.* [1834?] [*Br.* 579(2)]

28712 A CONVERSATION between George Hadfield & Charles Comber. [On machinery, emigration and free trade.] *s.sh.fol. Bradford*, [1834?] [*Br.* 560] *The Oastler copy.*

28713 COOTE, R. E. P. A letter to the Right Honorable Lord Althorp, Chancellor of the Exchequer, on the means of employing the labouring classes, and reducing the amount of poor's rates. [With a letter to the editor of *Felix Farley's Bristol Journal*, written in 1827, and signed: R.E.P.C., recommending the abolition of the tax on servants, and 'Suggestions on the best means of obtaining funds to enable Government to give beneficial employment to the labouring classes', signed in manuscript: R. E. Purdon Coote, and dated, 7th December 1830.] 11, [7]p. 8°. [*Bristol*, 1834]

28714 COWELL, J. W. A letter to the Rev. John T. Becher, of Southwell, in reply to certain charges and assertions made in the introduction to a second edition of his Anti-pauper system, recently published. [With an appendix, comprising extracts from Becher's introduction which relate to J. W. Cowell.] 62p. 8°. 1834.

28715 DUCPÉTIAUX, E. Statistique des tribunaux et des prisons de la Belgique. Comparaison entre la criminalité et la moralité des provinces flamandes et des provinces wallonnes. 25p. 8°. *Gand*, 1834. *Presentation copy from the author to the Athenæum Club.*

28716 EMIGRATION recommended, by George Hadfield, Esq. &c.&c.&c. [A satirical poem.] *s.sh.fol. Bradford*, [1834?] [*Br.* 556] *Printed on yellow paper. The Oastler copy.*

28717 EMMERSON, W. [*Begin.*] Friends and fellow-workmen...[Inviting delegates to a meeting at Birstall to discuss the case of the Dorchester labourers.] *s.sh.8°. n.p.* [1834] *The Oastler copy.*

28718 ENGLAND. *Commissioners for Inquiring into the Administration and Practical Operation of the Poor Laws.* Report from His Majesty's Commissioners... [With a supplement containing extracts from the evidence, and from the replies to questions asked by assistant commissioners.] 362, 128p. 8°. 1834. *The copy that belonged to Sir Harry Verney.*

28719 —— —— The poor laws: their present operation, and their proposed amendment. Chiefly drawn from the evidence and reports of the Poor-Law Commissioners.

Section I[–II. Part I. Present operation of poor laws, concluded. Part II. Proposed remedial measures]. 95p. *8⁰*. 1834.

28720 —— *Home Office.* Summary statements of the number of criminal offenders committed to the several gaols in England and Wales, &c.&c.&c. 31p. *8⁰. n.p.*, 1834. *See also* 1822, 1824, 1831, 1833.

28721 —— *Laws, etc.* The Act for the amendment and better administration of the laws relating to the poor, in England and Wales. With explanatory notes and a copious index. By John Tidd Pratt... 140p. *12⁰*. [1834]

28722 —— Second edition, with a preface [by N. W. Senior], containing a popular outline of the Act. xxviii, 140p. *12⁰*. [1834] *The preface was also published separately as* Outline of the Poor Law Amendment Act, *1834 (no.* 28787). *The copy presented by Senior to Dr. Hawtrey, with an inscription on the title-page in his hand. See also* 1835.

28723 —— Parliament. *House of Commons.* Evidence on drunkenness, presented to the House of Commons, by the Select Committee appointed... to inquire into this subject ...J. S. Buckingham, Esq., M.P., in the chair. 591p. *8⁰*. [1834] *The Turner copy.*

28724 —— —— —— In Parliament. Session, 1834. Leeds New Gas Company. Committee on the Bill: Copy of evidence given by the promoters and opponents of the Bill. As taken down by Mr. Gurney, short-hand writer to the House of Commons. 72p. *8⁰. Leeds*, 1834.

28725 EXTRACT from records of Clapperton's last expedition to Africa, by R. Lander, Vol. II, page 114. [Followed by a satirical account of the visit of an African chieftain to Leeds.] *s.sh.fol. Bradford*, [1834] [*Br.* 571(1)] *The Oastler copy.*

28726 FITTON, W., *and others.* National regeneration. 1. Letter from Mr. Fitton to Mr. Fielden. 2. Letter from Mr. Fielden to Mr. Fitton. 3. Letter from Mr. Holt to Mr. Fielden. Which letters contain a development of all the principles... connected with this important contemplated change in the manufacturing affairs of the country. 39p. *8⁰*. 1834. *The Oastler copy. ⋆A second, the FWA copy, belonged to William Pare.*

28727 **FRIENDLY SOCIETY OF OPERATIVE METAL WORKERS.** The laws of the... Society... 16p. *8⁰*. 1834.

28728 **FRIENDLY SOCIETY OF OPERATIVE TIN-PLATE WORKERS.** Bye laws of the Friendly Society of Operative Tin-plate Workers, held at the Pewter Platter, St. John Street, Clerkenwell. 11p. *12⁰*. 1834.

28729 **GASPARIN**, AUGUSTE DE. Considérations sur les machines...Lues à la Société d'Agriculture, Histoire naturelle et Arts utiles de Lyon, en 1833, et imprimées par ordre de cette Société. 56p. *8⁰. Lyon*, 1834.

28730 **GOODFELLOW**, J. Plan for the reduction of the poor rates in the city of New Sarum, and Close, and the parishes of Fisherton and Milford...[Able-bodied youths to be employed on the carriage of coals.] 44p. *8⁰. Devizes, Salisbury, &c.*, [1834]

28731 [**GOULD**, NATHANIEL.] Emigration. Practical advice to emigrants on all points connected with their comfort and economy, from making choice of a ship to settling on and cropping a farm. 120p. *8⁰*. 1834.

28732 [——] Second edition. 120p. *8⁰*. 1834.

28733 **GUNN**, W. Remedial measures suggested in alleviation of agricultural distress; with an historical survey of the rise and progress of pauperism in this country. 33p. *8⁰*. 1834.

28734 **HINCHY**, J. A plan for a modified system of poor laws, and employment for the people of Ireland. In a letter to His Excellency the Most Noble Marquis... Wellesley... 8p. *8⁰. Dublin*, 1834.

28735 **HINTON CHARTERHOUSE.** Hinton National School. Established in May 1828 by the Rev. T. Spencer, Minister of the parish, and supported by voluntary contributions. [With 'Hinton Clothing Club' and 'Hinton allotments of land'.] [4]p. *4⁰. Bradford* [*on Avon*, 1834]

28736 **HINTON CHARTERHOUSE** Parochial Circulating Library, instituted June, 1834 by the Rev. T. Spencer...[Accounts, rules and a catalogue of books.] 3p. *4⁰. n.p.* [1834]

28737 **HINTS** on the mal-administration of the poor laws: with a plan for bringing the collection and appropriation of the poor rates under the immediate superintendence and control of His Majesty's Government. 26p. *8⁰*. 1834.

28738 **⋆HÔPITAL DE GENÈVE.** Rapport sur l'administration de l'Hôpital...pendant l'année 1833. 12p. *4⁰. n.p.* [1834] *The copy that belonged to George Grote.*

28739 **HORNER**, L. The Factories Regulation Act explained, with some remarks on its origin, nature, and tendency. 27p. *12⁰. Glasgow, Edinburgh, &c.*, 1834.

28740 **HUDDERSFIELD SHORT-TIME COMMITTEE.** Notice to the factory children, their parents and friends. [A poster announcing a presentation ceremony to the Rev. G. S. Bull. Signed: Jas. Brook, secretary, and dated, Oct. 13th, 1834.] *s.sh.fol. Huddersfield*, [1834] [*Br.* 569(5)] *The Oastler copy.*

28741 —— A token of respect to the Rev. G. S. Bull. [A poster announcing a presentation, signed: Jas. Brook, secretary, and dated, Sep. 20th 1834.] *s.sh.fol. Huddersfield*, [1834] [*Br.* 569(8)] *The Oastler copy.*

28742 **⋆HUNZIKER**, C. Die Land-Spitäler, ihre Bedeutung und Beziehung zum Armenwesen des Landes. Ein Beitrag zur richtigen Würdigung der wahren Interessen seiner Revision. 63p. *8⁰. Burgdorf*, 1834. *The copy that belonged to George Grote.*

28743 **JACK**, W. Plan of a fund for the aged, as an antidote to pauperism and substitute for poor rates. 41p. *8⁰*. 1834.

28744 **KERR**, G. Kerr's exposition of legislative tyranny, and defence of the trades' union... 22p. *12⁰. Belfast*, 1834.

28745 Royal Oak Inn, **LEDBURY**, 14th April, 1834. [*Begin.*] To the public. A meeting of master tradesmen of Ledbury, recently took place, at which resolutions condemnatory of the principles and effects of "trades' unions," were passed... *s.sh.fol. Ledbury*, [1834]

28746 **⋆LESLIE**, JOHN, *Commissioner of Sewers.* Remarks on the present state of the poor law question, with illustrations of the advantages arising to the poor by means of the workhouse system of relief. 26p. *8⁰*. 1834. *The copy that belonged to George Grote.*

28747 —— Second edition. 30p. *8⁰*. 1834.

28748 A **LETTER** to the Right Honourable Lord Althorp, on the Bill for amending the poor laws. By a chairman of Quarter Sessions. 15p. *8°*. 1834.

28749 **LONGFIELD**, M. Four lectures on poor laws, delivered in Trinity Term, 1834. 100p. *8°*. *Dublin* & *London*, 1834.

28750 *****LUCKCOCK**, J. Hints for practical economy, in the management of household affairs, with tables, shewing different scales of expences, from £50 to £400 per annum... 27p. *12°*. *Birmingham* & *London*, 1834. *The FWA copy, that belonged to William Pare.*

28751 *****LUETTWITZ**, H. E. VON. Ueber Verarmung, Armen-Gesetze, Armen-Anstalten, und ins besondere über Armen-Colonieen, mit vorzüglicher Rücksicht auf Preussen. 98p. *8°*. *Breslau*, 1834. *The copy that belonged to George Grote.*

28752 **MACNISH**, R. The anatomy of drunkenness ...Fifth edition. 270p. *12°*. *Glasgow*, 1834. *The Turner copy. See also 1836, 1840.*

28753 **MARTIN**, WILLIAM (1772–1851). The flash of forked lightning from the dark thunder cloud! Murder will not hide! Wm. Martin, the natural philosopher's improvement of Newcastle and Gateshead, and the River Tyne. 8p. *8°*. *Newcastle*, 1834.

28754 **MARTINEAU**, H. The tendency of strikes and sticks to produce low wages, and of union between masters and men to ensure good wages. 29p. *12°*. *Durham*, [*London*,] *&c.*, 1834.

28755 **MAXWELL**, SIR JOHN, *Bart.* Manual labour, versus machinery, exemplified in a speech, on moving for a committee of parliamentary enquiry into the condition of half-a-million hand-loom weavers, in reference to the establishment of local guilds of trade; with an appendix, containing affidavits of general distress, rates of wages and prices...By the Member for Lanarkshire. 47p. *8°*. 1834.

28756 Important public **MEETING**. [A poster announcing a meeting to protest against the sentence on the Dorchester labourers, and to discuss means to rescue them. Signed: John Powlett, Phineas Ditchfield, secretaries, and dated, March 31st, 1834.] *s.sh.fol. Huddersfield*, [1834] [*Br.* 574(2)] *The Oastler copy.*

28757 *****MILLAR**, JAMES (*fl.* 1834). Letter to Randle Jackson, Esq. on the necessity of promoting education among the industrious classes in the parish of Lambeth, by the establishment of infant and other schools. 31p. *8°*. 1834.

28758 **MONYPENNY**, D. Remarks on the poor laws, and on the method of providing for the poor in Scotland. 250p. *8°*. *Edinburgh*, 1834.

28759 **OASTLER**, R. A few words to the friends and enemies of trades' unions. 8p. *8°*. *Huddersfield*, 1834. *Oastler's own copy.*

28760 —— Mr. Bull and Mr. Winterbotham. [Letter to the *Leeds Intelligencer*, dated October 24, 1834, desiring it to print the writer's letter to the *Bradford Observer* on the controversy between Mr. Bull and Mr. Winterbotham, and his letter to Mr. Winterbotham.] *s.sh.fol. n.p.* [1834] [*Br.* 569(4)] *Oastler's own copy.*

28761 —— A serious address to the millowners, manufacturers, and cloth-dressers of Leeds, who have organized themselves into a 'trades' union' to compel their workmen to abandon a right, which the laws of Britain grant, to

every subject. 8p. *8°*. *Huddersfield*, 1834. *Oastler's own copy.*

28762 —— To the editor of the Argus. [A reprint of a letter, dated August 8th, 1834, attacking the new Poor Law Act as being totally destructive of the rights and liberties of English men and women.] *s.sh.fol. n.p.* [1834] [*Br.* 578(1)] *Oastler's own copy.*

28763 —— To the editor of the Intelligencer. [A reprint of a letter dated Oct. 31st, 1834. Calling for a new ten hours' Bill in place of Althorp's Factory Act, which is impossible to enforce.] *s.sh.fol. n.p.* [1834] [*Br.* 581(3)] *Oastler's own copy.*

28764 —— A well seasoned Christmas-pie for "The Great Liar of the North" [Edward Baines], prepared, cooked, baked and presented by Richard Oastler. 36p. *8°*. *Bradford*, 1834.

28765 **OBSERVATIONS** on retail spirit licences, and excessive dram-drinking; with hints for the improvement of poor-laws and suppression of vagrancy, in a letter to Lord Melbourne, February, 1834. [Signed: Philanthropist.] 15p. *8°*. [1834]

28766 **OBSERVATIONS** on the poor laws, as they are generally administered; on the effects which they have produced; and on some of the systems which have been proposed to amend the condition of the poor, and to decrease the poor rates. By a county magistrate. 48p. *8°*. 1834.

28767 **OBSERVATIONS** on the present state of the poor laws. 28p. *8°*. 1834.

28768 **PAINE**, J. M. Strictures on the "Reply" of the Poor-Law Commissioners, to the inquiry of the Right Honourable Lord Viscount Althorp, Chancellor of the Exchequer, &c.&c. on the subject of labour-rates, in a letter addressed to His Lordship. 17p. *8°*. *Farnham*, [1834]

28769 **PETITION** to the "swell mob," from the tribe of "blacklegs, prigs, & pickpockets;" requesting to enjoy the same privileges as their "brethren" the "millocrats". *s.sh.fol. Huddersfield*, [1834?] [*Br.* 572] *The Oastler copy.*

28770 **PHILANTHROPIC LOAN SOCIETY**, *London*. Prospectus of the...Society, to be enrolled agreeably to Act of Parliament...[With 'Extracts from a work on loan funds... By Francis Trench...1833'.] *12°*. 1834. *For Trench's work, see 1833.*

28771 **PHILLIPPS**, E. T. M. A plain sermon on drunkenness. Addressed to the inhabitants of Hathern, Nov. 2nd, 1834. 23p. *12°*. *Loughborough* & *London*, [1834] *The Turner copy.*

28772 **PLACE**, F. Improvement of the working people. Drunkenness – education. 22p. *12°*. 1834. *The Oastler copy.*

28773 **POLISH SOCIETY OF MUTUAL INSTRUCTION**. Polish Society of Mutual Instruction. [Aims and statutes of the Society.] 15p. *8°*. [*London*, 1834]

28774 **POOR LAW BILL!** An interesting, diverting and entertaining dialogue...[A satire, partly in verse.] *s.sh.fol. Cambridge*, [1834] [*Br.* 579(1)]

28775 **PRESTON SHORT-TIME COMMITTEE**. Address of the operatives of Preston, Lancashire, to their brother workmen and fellow-sufferers in the manufacturing districts. [Dated: Dec. 19, 1834. On the distresses of the manufacturing districts and the need for further effort for a ten hours Bill]. *s.sh.fol. Preston*, [1834] [*Br.* 581(1)] *The Oastler copy.*

For the **PRESTON TEMPERANCE ADVO-CATE,** 1834–37, *see* vol. III, *Periodicals list.*

28776 The **PRINCIPLES** of delegated, central & special authority, applied to the Poor-Laws Amendment Bill. 16p. *8°.* 1834. *Attributed to Daniel Wakefield (1798–1858) in a note by George Grote in his copy.*

28777 **REES,** T. A sketch of the history of the Regium Donum, and Parliamentary grant, to poor dissenting ministers of England and Wales; with a vindication of the distributors and recipients from the charge of political subserviency... To which is added an appendix, containing a brief statement of the Regium Donum... by the Trustees. 104p. *8°.* 1834.

28778 **REMARKS** on the Report of the Poor Law Commissioners. [Signed: An observer in an agricultural district. With extracts from the *Sherborne Journal* of March–April 1834.] 16p. *8°.* [1834]

28779 Some **REMARKS** on the Poor Law Amendment Bill; suggested by the article on this subject in the Quarterly Review, of August, 1834. By a friend to the measure. 26p. *8°. Shrewsbury*, 1834.

28780 Legislative **REPORTS** on the poor laws, from the years 1817, to 1833, inclusive, with remedial measures proposed. [Being quotations from Reports of Select Committees of the House of Commons in 1817, 1819 and 1824, and of the House of Lords in 1819 and 1830, with discussions of particular points in the light of the evidence before the Poor Law Commission of 1834.] 56p. *8°.* 1834.

28781 **RICHMOND,** L. Annals of the poor... A new edition, enlarged and illustrated, with an introductory sketch of the author, by the Rev. John Ayre. 276p. *16°.* 1834.

28782 **ROBERTS,** S. Inscribed to her Majesty, the Queen. An address to British females of every rank and station, on the employment of climbing boys in sweeping chimnies. 22p. *12°. Sheffield*, 1834.

28783 **RODWELL,** W. An analytical index to the Act for the amendment of the poor laws, with preliminary observations. 35p. *8°. Ipswich*, 1834.

For the **SATURDAY MAGAZINE,** [containing an account of Fellenberg's school at Hofwyl,] *see* vol. III, *Periodicals list.*

28784 **SCROPE,** G. P. Friendly advice to the peasantry of Ireland. 8p. *8°. Dublin*, 1834.

28785 —— Plan of a poor-law for Ireland, with a review of the arguments for and against it... Second edition. 24p. *8°.* 1834. *The Oastler copy.*

28786 —— [Another issue.] 24p. *8°.* 1834. *For another edition, see* 1833.

28787 [**SENIOR,** N. W.] Outline of the Poor Law Amendment Act. 24p. *8°.* 1834. *Presentation copy, with inscription, from Senior to T. Spring Rice, Baron Monteagle. For another edition, see no.* 28722.

28788 **SHEAHAN,** T. Irish destitution in 1834; or, the working classes of Cork... Being a collection of facts submitted (for the greater part) in evidence... the 23rd of March 1834, to... the Assistant Commissioners of Irish Poor Enquiry. [With 'To the absentees of the City and County of Cork' signed: An eye-witness.] 32p. *8°. Cork,* [1834]

28789 The **SIGHING** of the prisoner; a letter from George Loveless to his affectionate wife, with a reply [by William Rider of Leeds. Dated: May 17th 1834]. *s.sh.fol. Leeds,* [1834] [*Br.* 574(1)] *The Oastler copy.*

28790 **SIMPSON,** C. A peep into the Poor Laws' Report, and the parish boarding school. 22p. *8°.* 1834.

28791 **SINERIZ,** J. F. Nuevo plan de gobierno económico doméstico, en el cual se dan lecciones para vivir sin empeñarse... 2a edicion corregida y aumentada con un suplemento. 376p. *8°. Madrid,* 1834.

28792 **SMITH,** GEORGE, *architect, of Edinburgh.* Essay on the construction of cottages suited for the dwellings of the labouring classes, for which the premium was voted by the Highland Society of Scotland... 38p. *8°. Glasgow, Edinburgh, &c.,* [1834]

28793 **SOCIETY FOR SUPERSEDING THE NECESSITY OF CLIMBING BOYS,** *London.* Society for Superseding the Necessity of Climbing Boys, by encouraging a new method of sweeping chimneys, and for improving the condition of children and others employed by chimney sweepers... [The nineteenth report.] 31p. *8°.* 1834. *See also* 1821.

28794 **SOCIETY FOR THE PREVENTION OF CRUELTY TO ANIMALS,** *Liverpool.* Report of the Society... established in Liverpool, Sept. 1833. [With 'On the duty of humanity to animals'.] 8, 4p. *8°. Liverpool,* [1834]

28795 **SOCKETT,** T. Emigration. A letter to a Member of Parliament, containing a statement of the method pursued by the Petworth Committee, in sending out emigrants to Upper Canada, in... 1832 and 1833, and a plan upon which the sums required for defraying the expence of emigration may be raised. Second edition. 17p. *8°. Petworth & London,* 1834.

28796 *STACE,* W. Provision for all without poor laws. 22p. *8°. Lewes & London,* 1834. *The FWA copy, that belonged to William Pare.*

28797 **STATEMENT** of the master builders of the Metropolis, in explanation of the differences between them and the workmen, respecting the trades' unions. 20p. *8°.* 1834.

28798 The **STRIKE;** or, a dialogue between Andrew Plowman and John Treadle. 23p. *8°.* 1834.

28799 **SWABEY,** W. Brief remarks on Lord Althorpe's Bill for the amendment of the poor laws, and hints for its improvement. By a country magistrate. 15p. *8°.* 1834.

28800 **THIERS,** L. A. Chambre des Députés, session de 1834. Discours prononcé par M. Thiers, Ministre du commerce et des travaux publics, dans le discussion du projet de loi sur les associations. (Séance du 17 mars, 1834.) [Extrait du Moniteur du 19 mars 1834.] 31p. *12°.* [*Paris,* 1834]

28801 **TORRENS,** R. On wages and combination. 133p. *8°.* 1834. *Presentation copy, with inscription, from the author to Daniel Wakefield. See also* 1838.

28802 **TOTTENHAM.** *Select Vestry.* Report of a Committee of the Select Vestry of the Parish of Tottenham, appointed to enquire into the state of the surplus labouring, and pauper poor of the parish... 25p. *8°. Tottenham,* 1834.

28803 **TRADES' UNIONS** and strikes. 99p. *12°.* 1834.

28804 [TUFNELL, E. C.] Character, object and effects of trades' unions; with some remarks on the law concerning them. 140p. *8°*. 1834.

28805 VESTRIAN, *pseud*. Poor Law Report. Illegitimates; their case considered in reference to the abolition of poor laws, by which they now receive some protection ...a letter to the Right Reverend the Lords Bishops of London and Chester. 24p. *8°*. *London & Liverpool*, 1834.

28806 WADE, JOHN. History of the middle and working classes; with a popular exposition of the economical and political principles which have influenced the past and present condition of the industrious orders. Also, an appendix of prices, rates of wages...Second edition. 604p. *8°*. 1834. *For other editions, see 1833.*

28807 WALTER, J. A letter to the electors of Berkshire, on the new system for the management of the poor, proposed by the Government. 74p. *8°*. 1834. *The Oastler copy. See also 1839.*

28808 *WATT, J. A. Ueber die dringende Nothwendigkeit einer Finanz-Reform im Kanton Bern, deren Nutzen und Folgen, hauptsächlich in Beziehung auf das Strassen-, Schul-, Armen- und Tellwesen. 40p. *8°*. [*Bern*,] 1834. *The copy that belonged to George Grote.*

28809 WHATELY, R., *Archbishop of Dublin*. Remarks on transportation, and on a recent defence of the system; in a second letter to Earl Grey. 172p. *8°*. 1834.

28810 WHITE, JOHN M. Remarks on the Poor Law Amendment Act, as it affects unions, or parishes, under the government of guardians, or select vestries. 52p. *8°*. 1834.

28811 A WORD in season, to the labourers in agriculture. [Warning against itinerant agitators advocating the formation of trades' unions to raise wages. Signed: Your friend and well-wisher, and dated, February 1834.] 4p. *8°*. *Dorchester*, [1834]

SLAVERY

28812 BIRNEY, J. G. Letter on colonization, addressed to the Rev. Thornton J. Mills, corresponding secretary of the Kentucky Colonization Society. 46p. *12°*. *Boston*, 1834.

28813 CAREY, M. Letters on the Colonization Society...Ninth edition. To which is prefixed the important information collected by Joseph Jones, a coloured man, lately sent to Liberia, by the Kentucky Colonization Society [entitled The Liberian colony. From the Kentucky Commonwealth]... 4, 32p. *8°*. *Philadelphia*, 1834. *For other editions, see 1832.*

28814 ENGLAND. *Parliament*. The debates in Parliament – session 1833 – on the resolutions and Bill for the abolition of slavery in the British colonies. With a copy of the Act... 964p. *8°*. 1834. *The copy that belonged to Joseph Hume.*

28815 GROSVENOR, C. P. Address before the Anti-Slavery Society of Salem and the vicinity... February 24, 1834. 48p. *8°*. *Salem*, 1834.

28816 [KINGSLEY, Z.] A treatise on the patriarchal system of society, as it exists in...America, and in the United States, under the name of slavery, with its necessity and advantages. By an inhabitant of Florida. Fourth edition, with an appendix. 24p. *8°*. *n.p.*, 1834. *For another edition, see 1829.*

28817 THOMAS, E. A concise view of the slavery of the people of colour in the United States; exhibiting some ...cases of cruel and barbarous treatment of the slaves by their...masters...and also showing the absolute necessity for the most speedy abolition of slavery...To which is added, a short address to the free people of colour... 178p. *12°*. *Philadelphia*, 1834.

28818 WARDLAW, R. The jubilee: a sermon preached in...Glasgow, on...August 1st, 1834, the memorable day of negro emancipation in the British colonies. 37p. *8°*. *Glasgow, Edinburgh, &c.*, 1834.

POLITICS

28819 BETHAM, SIR W. The origin and history of the constitution of England, and of the early parliaments of Ireland. 386p. *8°*. *Dublin*, 1834.

28820 BIRMINGHAM. Full report of the proceedings of the meeting of the electors of Birmingham, held... on Friday, the 28th of November, 1834, with introductory remarks by the editor of the Birmingham Journal, extracts from the Examiner and Mr. Bulwer's pamphlet, and the ...speech of O'Connell in Dublin on the recent change of ministers... 12p. *4°*. *Birmingham*, [1834] *See note to no. 26519.*

28821 BISH, THOMAS. A plea for Ireland; submitting the outline of a proposition for holding the Court and Parliament, at occasional intervals, in Dublin...The second edition. 48p. *8°*. *London & Dublin*, [1834]

28822 [BROUGHAM, H. P., *Baron Brougham and Vaux*.] Four years of a liberal government. [A summary of the achievements of the Whigs, written for the election of 1834.] 40p. *8°*. 1834.

28823 [——] [Another edition.] 16p. *8°*. 1834. **Another*, the FWA copy, belonged to William Pare.*

28824 —— Taxes on knowledge. Stamps on newspapers. Extracts from the evidence of the Right Honourable Baron Brougham and Vaux, Lord High Chancellor of England, before the Select Committee of the House of Commons, on libel law, in June 1834... 8p. *8°*. [1834] **Another*, the FWA copy, belonged to William Pare.*

28825 BULWER, afterwards BULWER LYTTON, E. G. E. L., *Baron Lytton*. A letter to a late Cabinet Minister on the present crisis...Sixth edition. 88p. *8°*. 1834.

28826 —— The present crisis. A letter to a late Cabinet Minister...Twelfth edition. 25p. *8°*. 1834.

28827 *—— Fifteenth edition. 25p. *8°*. 1834. *The FWA copy, that belonged to William Pare.*

28828 —— Seventeenth edition. 25p. *8°*. 1834.

28829 —— Twentieth edition. 25p. *8°*. 1834.

28830 CARPENTER, WILLIAM (1797–1874). Can the Tories become reformers? 32p. *8°.* 1834. **Another, the FWA copy, belonged to William Pare.*

28831 COBBETT, W. Cobbett's legacy to labourers; or, what is the right which the lords, baronets, and 'squires, have to the lands of England? In six letters, addressed to the working people of England... 141p. *8°.* 1834.

For the **DEMAGOGUE,** *see vol.* III, *Periodicals list.*

28832 To the ELECTORS of Leeds. [Two addresses against the election of Edward Baines to Parliament, one from Richard Oastler, dated, Jan. 27, 1834, and the other from G. S. Bull, dated January 30, 1834.] *s.sh.fol. n.p.* [1834] [*Br.* 578(2)] *Oastler's own copy.*

28833 FRAGMENTS from the history of John Bull. How John desired his servants to walk about their business, as they could not agree, and took his old steward back again. [An account of the resignation of Lord Melbourne.] *s.sh.fol. Bradford,* [1834] [*Br.* 568(2)] *The Oastler copy.*

28834 [GATLIFF,   ?] Report of the sayings & doings at the grand yellow dinner, in a wool warehouse, Market-Street, Huddersfield, April 4th, 1834. By an absent Tory from notes taken by a present Whig. 16p. *8°. Huddersfield,* 1834. *The copy that belonged to Oastler, who attributed it to 'Gatliff' in the manuscript index to his pamphlet collection.*

28835 GISBORNE, THOMAS (1794–1852). On the present crisis! Mr. Gisborne's address to the electors of North Derbyshire. [Dated: December 30, 1834.] 7p. *8°.* [1834?]

28836 INCONSISTENCY!! In October, Mr. Peter Bussey, wrote a letter...condemning...the new poor laws, and now, after all, he is a great stickler for Hadfield, who declares his approbation of that oppressive Act! *s.sh.fol. Bradford,* [1834?] [*Br.* 552] *The Oastler copy.*

28837 LAMBTON, J. G., *Earl of Durham.* Speech of the Earl of Durham at the Newcastle dinner, Wednesday, Nov. 19, 1834. 8p. *8°.* [*London,* 1834]

28838 LEEDS Borough races. [A skit on the candidates in the Leeds by-election of 1834.] *s.sh.fol. Leeds,* [1834] [*Br.* 562(1)] *The Oastler copy.*

28839 [LE MARCHANT, SIR D., *Bart., ed.*] The reform ministry, and the reformed Parliament. [With contributions by Lord Althorp, Lord Stanley and Sir James Graham.] Ninth edition. 116p. *8°.* 1834.

28840 [——] Eleventh edition. 116p. *8°.* 1834. *For other editions, see* 1833.

28841 MANCHESTER. Great meeting at Manchester. Dissolution of the Melbourne Ministry. Manchester, Nov. 28, 1834. [Anti-Whig meeting, addressed by John Fielden, Cobbett, and others.] *s.sh.fol. Bradford,* [1834] [*Br.* 577] *The Oastler copy.*

28842 MATHER, JAMES, *comp.* The constitutions of Great Britain, France, and the United States of America... Magna Charta, Bill of Rights, and Coronation Oath; French Declaration of Rights, Charter of Louis XVIII, and Constitution of 1830; American Declaration of Independence... 76p. *8°. London, Edinburgh, &c.,* 1834.

28843 MAW-RISON, *pseud.* Address of the great slaughter-house M.P., to his constituents, soon after the change of ministry, 1834. Second edition. [A satirical address giving the reasons why James Morrison is not standing again for Ipswich.] *s.sh.fol. Bradford,* [1834] [*Br.* 568(1)] *The Oastler copy.*

28844 OPERATIVES of Huddersfield! Understand your own position, and that of the class to which you belong! [An attack on local Whig politicians and the attempts to discredit trades unions. Signed: A looker on.] *s.sh.fol. Huddersfield,* [1834] [*Br.* 566] *The Oastler copy.*

28845 To the OPERATIVES of the Borough of Leeds. [Signed: An operative, and dated, February 1st. 1834. Opposing the election of Edward Baines, whose 'darling friend' is Macaulay, the former Member for Leeds.] *s.sh.fol. Leeds,* [1834] [*Br.* 575] *The Oastler copy, addressed to him in manuscript on the verso. With a manuscript note by Oastler in the margin: 'Put out by Rider [i.e. William Rider] on Saturday'.*

28846 PAINE, T. Common sense, addressed to the inhabitants of America...To which is added, an appendix; together with an address to the people called Quakers. [With an introduction, written for this edition.] 48p. *8°.* [1834] *The note concerning the new introduction is printed only on the paper wrappers. For other editions, see* 1776 (COLONIES).

28847 PARKER, JOHN. To the electors of the borough of Sheffield, by John Parker, M.P. one of their representatives in Parliament. [On the work of the first reformed Parliament.] 26p. *8°. Sheffield,* 1834.

28848 PEEL, SIR ROBERT, *2nd Bart.* An address to the electors of the borough of Tamworth. 15p. *8°.* 1834.

28849 *The PEERS; or, the people. A word of advice to the electors of the British Empire. [Signed: A reformer.] 8p. *8°.* 1834. *The FWA copy that belonged to William Pare.*

28850 "POKING" extraordinary! [A satire on the fall of Lord Melbourne's Government expressed in terms of a woollen mill.] *s.sh.4°. Bradford,* [1834] [*Br.* 571(3)] *The Oastler copy.*

28851 POZZO, F. DAL, *Conte.* Programme d'un prix d'une médaille en or de la valeur de mille francs, fondé par le Comte Ferdinand dal Pozzo, pour le meilleur écrit qui aura pour objet de réfuter son ouvrage intitulé: Della felicità che gl' Italiani possono e debbono dal Governo austriaco procacciarsi, ou de confirmer les opinions qui y sont exprimées... 27p. *8°. Paris,* 1834.

28852 A PROTEST against the Reform Ministry and the reformed Parliament. By an opposition member. 67p. *8°.* 1834.

28853 REFORM at home!! [An election poster, signed: a hater of cant and humbug, and dated, Nov. 22, 1834.] *s.sh.fol. Bradford,* [1834] [*Br.* 568(3)] *The Oastler copy.*

28854 A full and accurate REPORT of the proceedings at the grand public dinner given to Thomas Attwood, Esq. and Joshua Scholefield, Esq., members for the Borough of Birmingham...on Monday, Sept. 15, 1834. 8p. *4°. Birmingham,* [1834] *See note to no.* 26519.

28855 REPORT of the dinner given to T. Attwood and J. Scholefield, Esqrs., the members for the Borough of Birmingham...on Monday, the 15th September, 1834. 7p. *4°. Birmingham,* [1834] *See note to no.* 26519.

28856 TENNYSON, C., afterwards **D'EYN-COURT,** C. T. Mr. Tennyson's address to the electors of the metropolitan borough of Lambeth. Eighth edition. 8p. *8°. London & Lambeth, 1834.*

28857 —— Repeal of the Septennial Act. Speech of the Right Honourable Charles Tennyson in the House of Commons, on moving for a Bill to shorten the duration of Parliaments, 23rd July, 1833. ⟨Extracted from the Mirror of Parliament.⟩ Third edition. 28p. *8°. 1834. The copy that belonged to Earl De Grey.*

28858 'WHA wants me?' Men of Bradford. [An election poster attacking George Hadfield.] *s.sh.fol. Bradford, [1834] [Br. 568(4)] The Oastler copy.*

28859 The WHIGS and the press. Report of the trial of the proprietors [Patrick Grant, John Bell] and printer [John Ager] of the True Sun, for recommending non-payment of the assessed taxes...Before Mr. Justice Patteson and a special jury. 14p. *8°. 1834.*

28860 The WHIGS. (From The True Sun.) [A list of eighteen reasons put forward by a radical elector for not voting again for the Whigs.] *s.sh.fol. Huddersfield, [1834] [Br. 582] The Oastler copy.*

28861 Was Mr. WOOD the "whipper-in?" [An address to the electors of Halifax, signed The "Stranger", on Joseph Wood's record as a reformer.] *s.sh.fol. Huddersfield, [1834] [Br. 573] The Oastler copy.*

SOCIALISM

28862 BAUDET-DULARY, A. F. Crise sociale. 1834. 48p. *8°. Paris, 1834. The copy that belonged to Victor Considérant.*

28863 From the BIRMINGHAM ADVERTISER, July 31, 1824[1834]. The errors of the social system; being an essay on wasted, unproductive, and redundant labour. By W. Hawkes Smith...[A review.] 4p. *8°. [Birmingham, 1834]*

28864 *The CHARTER of the Rights of Humanity, passed at a great public meeting of the producers of wealth and knowledge, held in the metropolis on... February 12, 1834. *s.sh.fol.* [London: Social Missionary Union, 1834] The FWA copy that belonged to William Pare.*

28865 CONSIDÉRANT, V. P. Considérations sociales sur l'architectonique. xlix, 84p. *8°. Paris, 1834. Considérant's own copy.*

28866 —— Destinée sociale. Vols. 1–2, 3, pt. i. *8°. Paris, 1834–38. Considérant's own copy. Vol. 2 has an 'Avertissement' explaining that this volume having become too long, Considérant decided that part of it (by inference already in print in 1838) should form a third volume. In this copy this part, from p. 353 onwards, is present, without title-page or other preliminary pages, and lacking chapter 8. The third volume, made up from the sheets printed in 1838, with 8 pages of prelims printed later, was published in 1844 (q.v.). See also 1837, 1847, 1848.*

28867 FONTANA,   , and PRATI,   . St. Simonism in London. On the pretended community of goods, or the organization of industry. On the pretended community of women, or matrimony and divorce... Second edition. 28p. *8°. 1834.*

28868 GRAND NATIONAL CONSOLIDATED TRADES' UNION OF GREAT BRITAIN AND IRELAND. Rules and regulations of the Grand National Consolidated Trades' Union... instituted for the purpose of the more effectually enabling the working classes to secure...the rights of industry. 23p. *12°. [London,] 1834. The Oastler copy.*

28869 —— [Another issue.] 23p. *12°. 1834. The copy that belonged to William Lovett, with his signature on the verso of the title-page.*

For the HERALD OF THE RIGHTS OF INDUSTRY, *see vol. III, Periodicals list.*

28870 LECHEVALIER SAINT ANDRÉ, L. J. Études sur la science sociale...Année 1832. Théorie de Charles Fourier. 462p. *8°. Paris, 1834. The copy that belonged to Victor Considérant.*

28871 LEMOYNE, N. R. D. Association par phalange agricole-industrielle. Ensemble du système. 56p. *8°. Metz, [1834]*

28872 [MORGAN, JOHN M.] The critics criticised: with remarks on a passage in Dr. Chalmers's Bridgewater treatise. By the author of "Hampden in the nineteenth century." 56p. *8°. 1834.*

28873 [——] Hampden in the nineteenth century; or, colloquies on the errors and improvement of society. 2 vols. *8°. 1834. For a supplement, see 1837 (Colloquies on religion and religious education).*

For the NEW MORAL WORLD...conducted by Robert Owen and his disciples, 1834–45, *see vol. III, Periodicals list.*

For *the OFFICIAL GAZETTE OF THE TRADES' UNIONS, *see vol. III, Periodicals list.*

28874 *OWEN, ROBERT. Essays on the formation of human character. 36p. *4°. 1834. An edition of A new view of society, published in 9 weekly parts. The FWA copy that belonged to William Pare. For other editions, see 1813.*

28875 —— Six lectures on charity, delivered at the Institution of New Lanark, upon the thirteenth chapter of the First Epistle to the Corinthians. 47p. *8°. [1834] For another edition, see 1833.*

28876 [PUYCOUSIN, É. DE, ed.] 1833 ou l'année de la Mère. Juillet. Mission de l'Est, rédigée par Collin, Rogé, Maréchal, Charpin, Lamy. 63p. *8°. Toulon, 1834. The copy that belonged to Victor Considérant.*

28877 RICHER, É. Extraits de l'ouvrage intitulé: De la nouvelle Jérusalem, par Édouard Richer...contenant l'avant-propos de l'éditeur [L. F. de Tollenare]. Exposé analytique de la doctrine de la Nouvelle-Jérusalem. lxi, 121p. *8°. Paris & Nantes, 1834. The copy that belonged to Victor Considérant.*

28878 ROBERT DE LA MENNAIS, H. F. Paroles d'un croyant...1833. 216p. *12°. Bruxelles, 1834.*

28879 *—— Cinquième édition. 92p. *8°. Genève, 1834. The copy that belonged to George Grote.*

28880 S., F. K. Trades' triumphant, or, unions' jubilee!! A plan for the consoildation [sic] of popular power and restoring to the people their long lost rights. 15p. *8°. n.p. [1834?] The Oastler copy.*

28881 SAINT-SIMON, C. H. DE, *Comte.* New Christianity...Translated from the original French, by the Rev. J. E. Smith, A.M. [With 'Life of St. Simon, by a St. Simonian'.] 52p. *12°.* 1834. *For other editions, see* 1825.

For the **SHEPHERD,** 1834–38, *see* vol. III, *Periodicals list.*

28882 SMITH, WILLIAM H. The errors of the social system; being an essay on wasted, unproductive, and redundant labour. 42p. *12°. Birmingham & London,* 1834.

28883 TERSON, . Un St.-Simonien au peuple de Lyon, à l'occasion des événemens d'avril, 1834. 15p. *8°. Lyon,* 1834. *The copy that belonged to Victor Considérant.*

28884 THOMSON, WILLIAM (*fl.* 1834). The age of harmony; or, a new system of social economy, eminently calculated to improve the circumstances of the oppressed ...portion of the people of Great Britain and Ireland... Second edition. 36p. *12°. Glasgow,* 1834. *The Oastler copy.*

28885 VIGOUREUX, C. Parole de providence. 214p. *8°. Paris,* 1834. *The copy that belonged to Victor Considérant.*

MISCELLANEOUS

28886 BULL, G. S. The Church her own enemy. To the editor of the Intelligencer...June 24, 1834. [A letter on pluralities and Church reform.] 4p. *8°. Wakefield,* [1834] [*phc*] *From the Oastler copy, in the collection of his pamphlets at Columbia University (Seligman Collection).*

28887 —— A letter to the Rev. T. R. Taylor, and Mr. Henry Forbes, of Bradford, Yorkshire. 8p. *8°. Bradford,* 1834. [*phc*] *From the Oastler copy, in the collection of his pamphlets at Columbia University (Seligman Collection).*

28888 CARLILE, R. A respectful address to the inhabitants of Newcastle upon Tyne and its vicinity. [On Christianity.] 16p. *8°. Newcastle upon Tyne,* 1834.

28889 F., W. Hints on the unlimited diffusion of useful knowledge, at no expense to the reader, through the medium of the mercantile and trading classes. Practically illustrated by a history of printing, specimen of types and guide to authors in correcting the press. [An advertisement for Neill and Co., printers of Edinburgh.] 19p. *8°. Edinburgh,* 1834.

28890 GLOVER, W. Lord Brougham's law reforms, and courts of local jurisdiction: with practical reflections on the justice...of establishing new local courts in Eng-

land, and a general vindication of the Lord Chancellor... Third edition, with a postscript. 116p. *8°.* 1834.

28891 JOHNS, W. Third edition. An appeal, on behalf of the Committee of United Dissenters of Manchester, to the people of England. 8p. *8°. Manchester,* 1834.

28892 LONDON. Livery Companies. *Goldsmiths.* A list of the wardens, assistants and livery of the Worshipful Company of Goldsmiths, London. 35p. *8°.* [*London,* 1834]

28893 PLACE, F. A brief examination of the dramatic patents...Extracted from "the Monthly Magazine" for March, 1834. 12p. *8°.* 1834.

28894 [**STOWELL,** H.] I am a churchman. Intended particularly for the younger and unlearned members of the Church of England. Part second. By Ithuriel. [A satirical attack on the established Church.] 4p. *8°. Manchester,* 1834.

28895 [**WARREN,** S.] Lords Lyndhurst, Brougham, and local courts. Reprinted from Blackwood's Magazine, with corrections and additions. 52p. *8°.* 1834.

28896 —— Second edition. 52p. *8°.* 1834.

1835

GENERAL

28897 AGAZZINI, M. Illustrazione del principio della nuova teorica de' valori por servire di riposta all'invito fatto dal Sig. Professore Giandomenico Romagnosi a Michele Agazzini negli Annali universali di statistica...di confutare...le idee che il Sig. Romagnosi si è fatte intorno al valore, qualora queste idee ad Agazzini non aggradano. 54p. *8°. Milano,* 1835. *Probably presented by the author to N. W. Senior, with his earlier work,* Sconvenevolezza delle teoriche del valore, *1834 (q.v.), with which it is bound.*

28898 BERMINGHAM, T. The social state of Great Britain and Ireland considered, with regard to the labouring population, &c.... 216p. *8°.* 1835.

28899 The **BRITISH ALMANAC** of the Society for the Diffusion of Useful Knowledge, for...1835. [With 'The companion to the Almanac; or year-book of general information'.] 96, 263p. *12°.* [1835] *For other editions, see* 1828.

28900 C., S. No. 1. The rationalist, or an inquiry into the nature, progress, and prospects of Man. 8p. *8°.* [*c.* 1835] *The author has been tentatively identified with the publisher, S. Cornish.*

28901 CAREY, H. C. Essay on the rate of wages: with an examination of the causes of the differences in the condition of the labouring population throughout the world. 255p. *12°. Philadelphia,* 1835

28902 *CLÉREL DE TOCQUEVILLE, C. A. H. M., *Comte de Tocqueville.* De la democratie en Amérique...Orné d'une carte d'Amérique... 2 vols. *8°. Paris,* 1835. *The copy that belonged to George Grote.*

28903 —— Seconde édition... 4 vols. *8°. Paris,* 1835–40. *Vols. 1–2 only are in the Goldsmiths' Library, *vols. 3–4 belonged to George Grote.*

28904 *—— Democracy in America [Vols. 1–2]...

Translated by Henry Reeve, Esq.... 2 vols. *8°. 1835. The copy that belonged to George Grote. See also* 1838.

28905 COBBETT, W. Cobbett's legacy to labourers; or, what is the right which the lords, baronets, and squires, have to the lands of England? In six letters to the working people of England, with a dedication to Sir Robert Peel, Bart. 141p. *8°.* 1835.

28906 —— Third edition. 141p. *8°.* 1835. *See also no.* 29124.

28907 —— Cobbett's legacy to parsons; or, have the clergy of the Established Church an equitable right to the tithes, or to any other thing called Church property, greater than the Dissenters have to the same? And ought there, or ought there not, to be a separation of the Church from the State? In six letters, addressed to the Church-parsons...With a dedication to Blomfield, Bishop of London. 192p. *8°.* 1835.

28908 —— Second edition. 190p. *8°.* 1835.

28909 —— Sixth edition. 190p. *16°.* 1835.

28910 —— The life of W. Cobbett, Esq., M.P. for Oldham. Written by himself. 32p. *8°. W. Strange & A. Wakelin,* [1835]

28911 —— [Another issue.] 32p. *8°. W. Strange,* [1835]

28912 —— Selections from Cobbett's political works: being a complete abridgment of the 100 volumes which comprise the writings of "Porcupine" and the "Weekly political register." With notes, historical and explanatory. By John M. Cobbett and James P. Cobbett... 6 vols. *8°. London, Edinburgh, &c.,* [1835–37] *Published in weekly parts.*

28913 [**COBDEN,** R.] England, Ireland, and America. By a Manchester manufacturer. 160p. *8°.* 1835.

28914 [——] Second edition. 160p. *8°.* 1835. *See also* 1836.

28915 DAVIES, R. O. An essay upon the sole causes of the distress existing in Great Britain, which have never come under the observation of Parliament or any political meeting in the Kingdom... 27p. *8°. Ludlow,* 1835.

28916 The **DIRECTORY** of Birmingham; including an alphabetical list of the inhabitants of the town; a classification of its merchants, manufacturers &c.&c.; a new arrangement of mails, coaches, and carriers, a list of the civil officers of the town; together with an alphabetical street directory, &c.&c. [200]p. *8°. Birmingham,* 1835. *The title stamped in gilt on the upper cover reads: Wrightson & Webb's Directory of Birmingham. See also* 1839.

28917 DUTENS, J. M. Philosophie de l'économie politique, ou nouvelle exposition des principes de cette science... 2 vols. *8°. Paris,* 1835.

28918 EFFECT on England of the Prussian Commercial League. Extracted from "The British and Foreign Review; or, European Quarterly Journal," No. II. 63p. *8°.* 1835.

28919 The **ELEMENTS** of political economy, intended for the use of young persons. 89p. *18°. London & Nottingham,* 1835.

28920 ENGLAND. *Commissioners appointed to Report ...upon the Boundaries...of certain Boroughs and Corporate Towns in England and Wales.* The report of the Municipal Commissioners on the City and County of Coventry. 96p. *8°. Coventry,* 1835.

28921 —— *Laws, etc.* The Act for the regulation of municipal corporations in England and Wales...With a complete index and notes...By H. S. Chapman. Also the Order in Council, issued September 11, 1835, for delaying certain proceedings directed by the Act to be done, and reasons given in the conferences between the Houses of Parliament for several of the provisions of the Act. 168p. *12°.* 1835.

28922 —— [Abridged edition.] The Municipal Corporation Reform Act. An abstract of the Act. v. & vi. Will. IV. cap. 76...passed 9th September, 1835, to which is appended, all the schedules referred to by the Act...with the Order in Council, for carrying it into immediate effect ... 30p. *8°.* [1835].

28923 FOX, WILLIAM J. Finsbury lectures. Reports of lectures delivered at the Chapel in South Place, Finsbury...No. I[–VI]. 32, 36, 36, 35, 32, 36p. *8°.* 1835. *Contents: 1. The morality of poverty; 2. Aristocratical & political morality; 3. Morality of the mercantile and middle classes; 4. Military morality; 5. Legal morality; 6. The morality of the press. For other lectures in this series, see* 1836, 1837, 1838, 1839 (CORN LAWS).

28924 FRANCE. *Ministère de Commerce.* Documents statistiques sur la France, publiés par le Ministre du Commerce. 205p. *4°. Paris,* 1835. *See also* 1837 (*Ministère des Travaux Publics*), 1847 (*Ministère de l'Agriculture et du Commerce*).

28925 GANILH, C. Principes d'économie politique et de finance, appliqués, dans l'intérêt de la science, aux fausses mesures des gouvernemens, aux fausses spéculations du commerce, et aux fausses entreprises des particuliers. 10, 490p. *8°. Paris & Strasbourg,* 1835.

28926 GENOVESI, A. Della diceosina o sia della filosofia del giusto e dell' onesto. 578p. *8°. Milano,* 1835.

28927 —— Logica e metafisica. 760p. *8°. Milano,* 1835. *Both works were published as supplements to* Opere scelte *1824–25* (q.v.) *in the series* Classici italiani del Secolo XVIII.

28928 GREG, W. R. Social statistics of the Netherlands...Read before the British Association for the Advancement of Science, August, 1835. 29, [15]p. *8°.* [1835]

28929 GUÉPIN, A. and **BONAMY,** C. E. Nantes au XIXe. siècle; statistique topographique, industrielle et morale, faisant suite à l'Histoire des progrès de Nantes. 650p. *8°. Nantes,* 1835.

28930 HAZLITT, WILLIAM (1778–1830). The character of W. Cobbett, M.P....To which is added, several interesting particulars of Mr. Cobbett's life and writings. 16p. *8°.* 1835.

28931 HUGO, J. A., *Comte.* France pittoresque; ou, description pittoresque, topographique et statistique des départements et colonies de la France...Avec des notes sur les langues, idiomes et patois, sur l'instruction publique et la bibliographie locale, sur les hommes célèbres, etc.; et des renseignements statistiques...accompagnée de la statistique générale de la France... 3 vols. *4°. Paris,* 1835.

28932 [**HUME,** JAMES D.] Letters on the corn laws, and on the rights of the working classes; originally inserted in the Morning Chronicle; shewing the injustice...of empowering those...who have obtained the proprietary possession of the lands...to increase, artificially, the money value of their exclusive estates, by means of arbitrary charges, made on the rest of the people...by H.B.T. 48p. *8°*. 1835. *For other editions, see* 1834.

28933 HUTTON, W. The history of Birmingham... With considerable additions...also an appendix containing a life of the author. [Edited by J. Guest.] Sixth edition. 2 vols. *8°. Birmingham*, [1835] *For other editions, see* 1781.

28934 INGLIS, H. D. Ireland in 1834. A journey throughout Ireland, during the spring, summer, and autumn of 1834...Second edition... 2 vols. *12°*. 1835. *The copy that belonged to Robert Hyde Greg, with his book-plate.*

28935 JERVIS, T. B. Records of ancient science, exemplified and authenticated in the primitive universal standard of weights and measures. Communicated in an essay transmitted to Capt. Henry Kater, Vice-President of the Royal Society. 97p. *8°. Calcutta*, 1835.

28936 KENNEDY, JOHN P. Instruct; employ, don't hang them: or, Ireland tranquilized without soldiers, and enriched without English capital. Containing observations on a few of the chief errors of Irish government and Irish land proprietors, with the means of their correction... 166p. *8°*. 1835.

28937 LEIGH, S. Leigh's new pocket road-book of Ireland, containing an account of all the direct and cross roads; together with a description of every remarkable place...[Edited by C. C. Hamilton.] Third edition considerably enlarged and improved. 528p. *12°*. 1835.

28938 L'HERBETTE, A. J. De la liberté commerciale, et de la réforme de nos lois de douanes. 130p. *8°. Paris*, 1835.

28939 The **LIFE** of William Cobbett. 422p. *8°*. 1835.

28940 —— Second edition. 422p. *8°*. 1835.

28941 The **LIFE** of William Cobbett, Esq. late M.P. for Oldham... 216p. *12°. Manchester*, 1835. *This is a different work from nos.* 28939–40, *above.*

For the **LINDFIELD REPORTER**, 1835–42, *see* vol. III, *Periodicals list*, Philanthropist.

28942 LONDON INSTITUTION. A catalogue of the Library of the London Institution: systematically classed. Preceded by an historical and bibliographical account of the establishment. [By W. Upcott, R. Thomson and E. W. Brayley.] 4 vols. *8°*. 1835–52.

28943 LONGFIELD, M. Three lectures on commerce, and one on absenteeism, delivered in Michaelmas Term, 1834, before the University of Dublin. 111p. *8°. Dublin & London*, 1835.

28944 MARTIN, WILLIAM (1801–1867). The parlour-book: or familiar conversations, on science and the arts. For the use of schools and families. 274p. *16°*. [1835?]

28945 MEMOIRS of Wm. Cobbett, Esq. M.P. for Oldham; and the celebrated author of the "Political Register." 184p. *12°. Leeds*, 1835. *Published in parts.*

28946 MEREWETHER, H. A. and **STEPHENS**, ARCHIBALD J. The history of the boroughs and municipal corporations of the United Kingdom, from the earliest to the present time... 3 vols. *8°. London, Dublin, &c.*, 1835.

28947 MURRAY, THOMAS (1792–1872). A catechism of political economy, in which the principles of the science are explained in a popular form. 72p. *12°. Edinburgh & London*, 1835.

28948 NEBENIUS, C. F. E. Der deutsche Zollverein, sein System und seine Zukunft. 474p. *8°. Carlsruhe*, 1835.

28949 NEWMAN, S. P. Elements of political economy. 324p. *12°. Andover [Mass.] & New York*, 1835.

28950 OASTLER, R. Eight letters to the Duke of Wellington: a petition to the House of Commons: and a letter to the editor of the Agricultural and Industrial Magazine. 174p. *8°. London & Huddersfield*, 1835. *Oastler's own copy.*

28951 PASLEY, SIR C. W. Chatham, the 10th of February, 1835. The following remarks on the present state of the law of this country relating to weights and measures, are extracted from, and will appear in, the second part or continuation of Colonel Pasley's treatise on measures, weights and money, which is now preparing for publication. Extract, &c. [4]p. *8°. n.p.* [1835] *For editions of the work* Observation on the...practicability of simplifying and improving the measures, weights and money used in this country, *see* 1831.

28952 PEEL, SIR ROBERT, *2nd Bart.* Speech of the Right Hon. Sir Robert Peel, Bart. in the House of Commons, on...2d of April, 1835, on the motion "That this House do resolve itself into a Committee, in order to consider the present state of the Church establishment in Ireland, with a view of applying any surplus of its revenues ...to the general education of all classes of the people..." 61p. *8°*. 1835.

28953 A **PETITION** to Parliament against the new Poor Law Act, the present working of machinery, and for the extension of the present elective qualification. [Drawn up by G. S. Bull.] 4p. *8°. Bradford*, [1835] *The Oastler copy.*

28954 PITKIN, T. A statistical view of the commerce of the United States of America: including also an account of banks, manufactures and internal trade and improvements: together with that of the revenues and expenditures of the general government... 600p. *8°. New Haven*, 1835. *For another edition, see* 1817.

28955 Under the patronage of Sir Edward S. Lees, Secretary to the General Post-Office for Scotland. The **POST-OFFICE** annual directory [for Edinburgh and Leith], and calendar, for 1835–6. Thirtieth publication. 259, lxxiip. *8°. Edinburgh*, 1835. *See also* 1828, 1841.

28956 PRIESTLEY, JOSEPH (1733–1804). An essay on the first principles of government, and on the nature of political and civil liberty...New edition. 27p. *8°*. 1835.

28957 [**PYE**, C.] The stranger's guide to modern Birmingham, with an account of its public buildings and institutions, its show rooms and manufactories. With observations on the surrounding neighbourhood... 194p. *12°. Birmingham*, [1835?] *For another edition, see* 1825.

28958 QUETELET, L. A. J. Sur l'homme et le développement de ses facultés, ou, essai de physique sociale... 2 vols. *8°. Paris*, 1835. *See also* 1836, 1842.

28959 QUIN, M. J. A steam voyage down the Danube. With sketches of Hungary, Wallachia, Servia, and Turkey, &c....Second edition, revised and corrected. 2 vols. *8°*. 1835.

28960 RAGUET, C. The principles of free trade, illustrated in a series of short and familiar essays. Originally published in the Banner of the Constitution. 432p. *8°. Philadelphia*, 1835. *See also* 1840.

28961 REFLEXOENS sobre o estado actual de Portugal, e suggestoens sobre as medidas que se devem tomar para promover a industria nacional, e igualar a receita á despeza. Offerecidas...a...consideracaó dos dignos pares do reino...por hum seu compatriota... negoceante Portuguez. Septembro de 1835. 16p. *8°. n.p.* [1835]

28962 ROEBUCK, JOHN A. The Dorchester labourers. By J. A. Roebuck, M.P. On the qualification clause of the Corporation Bill. [By T. Falconer.] Edited by J. A. Roebuck, M.P. 16p. *8°.* [1835]

For ——, *ed.* Pamphlets for the people, *see* vol. III, *Periodicals list,* Pamphlets for the people.

28963 ROOKE, J. Free and safe government, traced from the origin and principles of the British constitution. By a Cumberland landowner... 319p. *8°.* 1835.

28964 SAY, L. An elementary treatise on individual and public wealth. In which the principal questions of political economy are explained and elucidated. 320p. *8°.* 1835. *For another edition, see* 1827.

28965 [SENIOR, N. W.] On national property, and on the prospects of the present administration and of their successors. Third edition. 132p. *8°.* 1835.

28966 SHIRREFF, P. A tour through North America; together with a comprehensive view of the Canadas and United States. As adapted for agricultural emigration. 473p. *8°. Edinburgh, London, &c.,* 1835.

28967 SKENE, G. R. On the condition of land-capitalists and agriculturists...[Four letters, dated, from December 1834 to January 1835.] Reprinted from the Leamington Press. 31p. *8°. [Leamington,]* 1834[1835]

28968 STENGEL, . Von dem ausländischen Handel und der Seemacht deutscher Städte im Mittelalter, und von den finanziellen Verhältnissen des jetzigen deutchen Zollvereins...(Aus Schönbrodt's Sammlung abgedruckt.) 99p. *8°. Potsdam,* 1835.

For **WALKER,** THOMAS (1784–1836), The original, *see* vol. III, *Periodicals list,* the Original. *See also* 1836.

28969 WETHERELL, SIR C. Speech of Sir Charles Wetherell, at the Bar of the House of Lords, against the iniquitous Corporation Bill, on...30th and...31st July, 1835. 32p. *8°.* 1835.

28970 [WHATELY, R., *Archbishop of Dublin.*] Ꞃeꞃoh-ⱡeⱡꞡhin aiꞃ ꞡhnoꞇhúibh ceaꞃba, ꞇꞃachꞇaiⱡ, ꞇuaꞃaꞃoaⱡ, ꞃeic ꞡ ceannach... Ꞇaiꞃꞇeanꞡꞇa anoiꞃ maiⱡⱡe ꞃe biꞃeac ⱡe Ꞇaohꞡ O Coinniaⱡⱡain. [With 'Easy lessons on money matters, commerce, trade, wages, etc. etc. for the use of young people...Further enlarged by Thaddeus Connellan.'] 83, 1–168, xiip. *12°.* Cⱡoꞎbuaiⱡꞇe an Aꞇ-cⱡiaꞇa, 1835. *See also* 1836.

28971 [WILMOT, R.] Disinherited, or principle and expediency; explained as affecting public welfare and private happiness. In answer to "Poor laws and paupers," by Miss Martineau; also a proposal for a new code of laws ...Vol. I. [With 'National debt, demonstrated as capable of being paid without taxes, or principle and expediency ...Vol. II'.] 2 vols. *12°. Exeter,* 1835.

28972 WILSON, JOHN, *of Thornly.* Second edition. Address to the justices of peace in the cities, burghs and counties of Scotland, relating to weights and measures. [4]p. *fol. n.p.* [1835]

28973 YEATMAN, H. F. Minutes of evidence before a Select Committee of the House of Lords, appointed to inquire into the charges on county rates in England and Wales. 72p. *8°. Dorchester, Lyme, &c.,* 1835.

AGRICULTURE

28974 A brief **ADDRESS** on mining in Cornwall, demonstrating some of the advantages resulting to commerce, and the profit to capitalists, by investment in these national undertakings, by the Secretary to the Kelewerris and West Tresavean mining companies, 55, Old Broad Street. 24p. *8°.* 1835.

28975 *AELBROECK, J. L. VAN. L'agriculture pratique de la Flandre...Supplément contenant le mémoire sur les prairies aigres, du même auteur. 48p. *8°. Paris,* 1835. *The copy that belonged to George Grote. For the original work, see* 1830.

28976 ANGLESEY HORTICULTURAL SOCIETY. Rules of the Anglesey Horticultural Society. Established January 1, 1835. 23p. *12°. Carnarvon,* 1835.

28977 —— Schedule and particulars of prizes for 1835. *s.sh.fol. Bangor,* [1835]

28978 BURROUGHS, E. Observations on the cultivation of hemp, as connected with the interests of the united Empire. 24p. *12°. Dublin,* [*c.* 1835]

28979 CAUGHY, J. An essay on the cultivation and management of the potato, together with the various purposes to which it may be applied. 12p. *12°. Belfast,* [*c.* 1835]

28980 CHADWICK, W. A letter to the tenant farmers of Thorne & Doncaster. 12p. *12°. Leeds,* 1835.

28981 CONNER, W. The true political economy of Ireland: or rack-rent the one great cause of all her evils: with its remedy. Being a speech delivered...at Inch, in the Queen's County. 58p. *8°. Dublin,* 1835. *Presentation copy from the author to John Stuart Mill. For another edition, see* 1832.

28982 DRUMMOND, WILLIAM, & SONS. The third report of Drummonds' Agricultural Museum, at Stirling, being from March, 1833, till November, 1834. With original communications on the advantages of agricultural museums... 159p. *8°. Stirling, Edinburgh, &c.,* 1835.

28983 ENGLAND. *Laws, etc.* Tavistock Inclosure. An Act for inclosing lands in the parishes of Tavistock, Milton-Abbot, Brentor and Lamerton in the county of Devon, called Heathfield. ⟨Royal Assent 3 July 1835.⟩ 5 & 6 Will. IV. sess. 1835. 24p. *fol. [London,* 1835]

28984 EVERETT, JAMES. The Wall's End miner; or a brief memoir of the life of William Crister; including an account of the catastrophe of June 18th, 1835. 168p. *12°. London, Newcastle upon Tyne, &c.,* 1835.

28985 FINLAY, J. A treatise on the law of landlord and tenant in Ireland. Second edition. 736p. *8°. Dublin,* 1835.

28986 GASPARIN, AUGUSTE DE. Du plan incliné,

comme grande machine agricole; mémoire lu à la Société Royale et Centrale de l'Agriculture...7 et 28 janvier 1835. [Considérations sur les machines. (Suite.) Première machine.] 60p. *8°. Paris, 1835.*

28987 GLOAG, W. Rentall of the county of Perth, by act of the Estates of Parliament of Scotland, 4th August, 1649; contrasted with the valuation of the same county, 1st January, 1835. 109p. *4°. Perth, 1835.*

28988 HARRISON, Sir George (*d.* 1841). Substance of a report on the laws and jurisdiction of the Stannaries in Cornwall...1829. 178p. *8°. 1835.*

28989 [*Begin.*] HINTON CHARTERHOUSE allotments. (Extracted from the Bath Herald, April 4, 1835.) [Account of the annual dinner.] *s.sh.8°. Bath, 1835.*

28990 [HOLLAND, John (1794–1872)]. The history and description of fossil fuel, the collieries, and coal trade of Great Britain. By the author of the "Treatise on manufactures in metal"...in Lardner's Cabinet cyclopædia. 485p. *8°. London & Sheffield, 1835. See also 1841.*

28991 HOWARD, C. Library of Useful Knowledge. A general view of the agriculture of the East Riding of Yorkshire, contained in detailed reports of individual farms in the three great natural divisions of the Riding, viz. Scoreby on the westward plain. Wauldby on the Wolds. Ridgemont in Holderness... 1–28, 97–156p. *8°. London, York, &c., 1835. It appears from the introduction that the sections of the work on Wauldby and Ridgemont may be a reissue of the sheets of another publication.*

28992 LABOURERS' FRIEND SOCIETY, *London.* The labourers' friend: a selection from the publications of the Labourers' Friend Society, showing the utility and national advantage of allotting land for cottage husbandry. 299p. *8°. 1835. The copy specially bound for presentation to the Duke of Sussex, accompanied by a letter from the secretary of the Society, John Wood, soliciting the Duke's patronage.*

28993 ——— [Another edition.] Cottage husbandry; the utility and national advantage of allotting land for that purpose; being a selection from the publications of the Labourers' Friend Society, and reissued under their direction. 299p. *8°. 1835.*

28994 LOUDON, J. C. An encyclopædia of agriculture: comprising the theory and practice of the valuation, transfer...laying out...and management of landed property; and the cultivation...of the animal and vegetable productions of agriculture...Third edition... 1378p. *8°. 1835. For other editions, see 1825.*

28995 [MARTIN, William, *of Montrose.*] Remarks upon a proposed Bill, entitled, A Bill (as amended by the Committee,) to amend an Act of the ninth year of his late Majesty King George the Fourth, for the preservation of the salmon fisheries in Scotland. 15p. *8°. Aberdeen, 1835. Presentation copy, with an inscription implying that William Martin was the author, to Patrick Chalmers, M.P. for Montrose. Sent through the post from Montrose, 9 December, 1835.*

For the **MINING REVIEW,** 1835–37, *see* vol. III, *Periodicals list.*

28996 ROYAL DUBLIN SOCIETY. Prize essays on the potato [by W. G. Andrews and N. Niven], and the causes of the late partial failures, which obtained the gold and silver medals of the Royal Dublin Society, 1835. 72p. *8°. Dublin, 1835.*

28997 SALMON fisheries (Scotland) Bill. Case of the petitioners against the Bill. *s.sh.fol. n.p.* [1835]

28998 [SENIOR, N. W.] On national property, and on the prospects of the present Administration and of their successors...Third edition. 132p. *8°. 1835.*

28999 SOCIETY OF THE GOVERNOR AND ASSISTANTS IN LONDON, OF THE NEW PLANTATION IN ULSTER. Report of a deputation [W. A. Peacock, J. Evans, E. Tickner, J. E. Davies] to Ireland in the year 1835. [With an appendix and 'Report of Mr. Secretary Davies upon the Fishery Cause'.] 56, 47p. *8°. 1835. See also 1826 (GENERAL), 1834 (AGRICULTURE), 1836, 1838, 1841.*

29000 *THIERY, P. J. Mémoire sur l'amélioration des chevaux dans les deux Départemens du Rhin; traitant; 1º De l'origine des chevaux de sang et de leur utilité; 2º De l'avantage de l'éducation domestique, de divers abus et des moyens de les prévenir, ou d'y remédier...5º De l'arrosement des prairies; 6º Du dessèchement des marais. 53p. *8°. Strasbourg, 1835. The text is in French and German, printed on opposite pages. The copy that belonged to George Grote.*

29001 WESTERN, T. G. The juridical argument... against the decree of the...late Lord High Chancellor of England, upon the case of the late Sir William Clayton, Bart. and the Duchy of Cornwall...[With 'Further observations by Mr. Haines'.] 73, 9p. *8°. 1835.*

CORN LAWS

29002 FAWCETT, S. The corn laws. [A ballad reprinted from the Leeds Times.] *s.sh.fol.* [*c.* 1835] [*Br.* 671]

29003 The **REFORM** and the farmers. [A song.] *s.sh.fol. Hoxton,* [1835?] *See note to no.* 26994.

29004 THOMPSON, Henry. An appeal to the people of England on free corn; together with strictures on the currency as relates to agriculture. Third edition, greatly improved. 50p. *8°. London & York, 1835.*

POPULATION

29005 COBBETT, W. Surplus population and Poor-Law Bill. A comedy, in three acts. 24p. *8°.* [1835]

29006 LOMBARD, H. C. De l'influence des professions sur la durée de la vie. Recherches statistiques. [Extrait du tome VII des Mémoires de la Société de Physique et d'Histoire naturelle de Genève.] 44p. *4°. Genève, 1835.*

TRADES & MANUFACTURES

29007 BABBAGE, C. On the economy of machinery and manufactures...Fourth edition enlarged. 408p. *8°.* 1835. *For other editions, see* 1832.

29008 BAINES, SIR EDWARD. History of the cotton manufacture in Great Britain: with a notice of its early history in the East...a description of the great mechanical inventions, which have caused its unexampled extension in Britain; and a view of the present state of the manufacture... 544p. *8°.* [1835]

29009 The BOOK of trades; or, circle of the useful arts... 356p. *16°. Glasgow, London, &c.,* 1835. *See also* 1837.

29010 COOPER, WILLIAM, *glass cutter.* The crown glass cutter and glazier's manual... 125p. *8°. Edinburgh & London,* 1835.

29011 LONDON UNION OF COMPOSITORS. The London scale of prices for compositors'

work: agreed upon, April 16th, 1810, with explanatory notes, and the scales of Leeds, York, Dublin, Belfast and Edinburgh. Second edition. [With a list of London printers.] 106p. *8°.* [1835 ?]

29012 PLATTNER, C. F. Die Probirkunst mit dem Löthrohre, oder Anleitung, Mineralien, Erze, Hüttenproducte und verschiedene Metallverbindungen vor dem Löthrohre... 358p. *8°. Leipzig,* 1835.

29013 URE, A. The philosophy of manufactures or, an exposition of the scientific, moral, and commercial economy of the factory system of Great Britain. 480p. *12°.* 1835. *The copy that belonged to Sir Edward Baines.*

29014 WILDS, W. Elementary and practical instructions on the art of building cottages and houses for the humbler classes...To which are added practical treatises on the manufacture of bricks and lime...for the use of emigrants... 143p. *8°.* 1835.

COMMERCE

29015 ABOLITION of arrest not detrimental to trade. A letter addressed to Sir John Campbell, M.P. by a barrister of the Middle Temple. 15p. *8°.* 1835.

29016 BAINEN, W. Mercantile tables shewing the average stowage of ships, and the proportionate stowage of goods to each other; deduced from upwards of 1000 cargoes of goods, shipped from St. Petersburg. 8p. *obl.fol. Cronstadt,* 1835.

29017 BETTONI, N. Mémoires biographiques d'un typographe italien. 120p. *8°. Paris,* 1835. *The volume also contains 6 prospectuses for other works to be published by Bettoni: Panorama monumental de Paris; Cours d'études pour la jeunesse française; Panthéon des nations; Iconographie et biographie des Français illustres.*

29018 *COMMISSION COMMERCIALE DU HAVRE. Rapport de la Commission...à ses commettans. 62p. *4°. n.p.* [1835] *The copy that belonged to George Grote.*

29019 Breves CONSIDERAÇÕES sobre o commercio e navegação de Portugal para a Asia. Por hum Portuguez. 12 de Junho de 1835. 20p. *8°. Lisboa,* [1835]

29020 EDINBURGH. *Town Council.* Report to the Lord Provost, Magistrates and Council of the City of

Edinburgh, relative to the eligibility of that city for manufacturing establishments, by the committee appointed by the Town Council. Approved of by the Magistrates and Council, 31st March 1835. 24p. *8°. n.p.* [1835]

29021 HAGEMEISTER, J. VON. Mémoire sur le commerce des ports de la Nouvelle-Roussie, de la Moldavie et de la Valachie. 199p. *12°. Odessa & Simphéropol,* 1835.

29022 MUTINELLI, F. Del commercio dei Veneziani. 184p. *8°. Venezia,* 1835.

29023 PHIPPS, JOHN. A practical treatise on the China and eastern trade: comprising the commerce of Great Britain and India, particularly Bengal and Singapore, with China and the eastern islands...[With an appendix.] 338, lxvip. *8°. Calcutta,* 1835. *See also* 1836.

29024 THOMPSON, JOSEPH. Considerations respecting the trade with China. 177p. *8°.* 1835.

29025 The WAREHOUSING SYSTEM. Extracts from various publications and documents relating to the warehousing of goods in the Port of London, and the outports; with observations upon the impolicy...of extending the privilege to in-land towns or up-town warehouses. 73p. *8°.* 1835.

COLONIES

29026 EAST INDIA COMPANY. Treaty with the Nawaub Vizier Saadut Alee. 10th Nov. 1801. [With 'Final arrangement with the Nawaub Vizier Saadut Alee. 1802'.] 16p. *8°.* [*c.* 1835 ?]

29027 JEREMIE, SIR J. Recent events at Mauritius. By John Jeremie, Esq. Attested also by John Reddie, Esq. 153p. *8°.* 1835.

29028 JERVIS, T. B. Indian weights and measures. The following compendious summary of the exact

quantities of the principal weights and measures of Bengal, Madras, Bombay, and Ceylon – extracted from Captain T. B. Jervis's essay on the primitive standard, will be found very useful for immediate reference. *s.sh.fol. n.p.* [1835] [*Br.* 588] *For the complete work, see no.* 28935.

29029 LLOYD, S. H. Sketches of Bermuda. 258p. *8°.* 1835.

29030 NAPIER, SIR CHARLES J. Colonization;

particularly in southern Australia: with some remarks on small farms and over population. 268p. *8°.* 1835.

29031 PRINSEP, JAMES. Useful tables, forming an appendix to the Journal of the Asiatic Society... 2 vols. *8°. Calcutta, 1834[1835]–36. The copy that belonged to the Library of the East India Company, with its bookstamp on the title-page of part 1, which is a reissue, with a new half-title, of the edition of 1834 (q.v.).*

29032 RAFFLES, S. Memoir of the life and public services of Sir Thomas Stamford Raffles...particularly in the government of Java, 1811–1816, Bencoolen and its dependencies, 1817–1824; with details of the commerce ...of the Eastern Archipelago...A new edition... 2 vols. *8°.* 1835. *For another edition, see 1830.*

29033 THORNTON, EDWARD (1799–1875). India, its state and prospects. 354p. *8°.* 1835. *Presentation copy from the author to T. F. Ellis.*

29034 TORRENS, R. Colonization of South Aus-tralia. [With appendixes.] 303, xxiip. *8°.* 1835. *Presentation copy from the author to Charles Babbage.*

29035 TREVELYAN, SIR C. E., *Bart.* A report upon the inland customs and town duties of the Bengal Presidency...Second edition. [With 'Selected papers of the appendix to the custom duty report', 'Town-duty report', and 'Selected paper of the appendix to the town-duty report'.] 180, 28p. *8°. Calcutta,* 1835.

29036 WILSON, THOMAS B. Narrative of a voyage round the world; comprehending an account of the wreck of the ship "Governor Ready," in Torres Straits; a description of the British settlements on the coasts of New Holland...with an appendix, containing remarks on transportation...and advice to persons intending to emigrate to the Australian colonies. 349p. *8°.* 1835.

29037 YATE, W. An account of New Zealand; and of the formation and progress of the Church Missionary Society's mission in the northern island. 310p. *8°.* 1835.

FINANCE

29038 *ANSELL, C. A treatise of friendly societies, in which the doctrine of interest of money, and the doctrine of probability, are practically applied to the affairs of such societies: with...tables; and an appendix, containing the Acts of Parliament relating to friendly societies ... 198p. *8°.* 1835. *The copy that belonged to Augustus De Morgan.*

29039 ASSOCIATED MERCHANTS OF LIVERPOOL. Report of the proceedings of the Associated Merchants of Liverpool, who have recently resisted the payment of the town's dues. To which is added, an appendix, containing the bill of exceptions filed in the cause, the Corporation of Liverpool v. Bolton and others. 67, xcixp. *8°.* 1835.

29040 BOLGENI, G. V. Dissertazione undecima fra le morali sopra l'impiego del danaro e l'usura. 349p. *8°. Lugano,* 1835.

29041 Edinburgh Annuity Bill, No. 1. **CASE** of the promoters of a Bill for "Regulating the annuity leviable for payment of the stipends to the ministers of the City of Edinburgh..."... 3p. *fol.* [*London,* 1835] *Endorsed: Case of the promoters of the Edinburgh Annuity Tax Bill, No. 1.*

29042 CAYLEY, EDWARD S. Agricultural distress – silver standard. Speech of Edward Stillingfleet Cayley... in the House of Commons, on...June 1, 1835, on moving "That a Select Committee be appointed to inquire if there be not effectual means...to afford substantial relief to the agriculture of the United Kingdom, and especially to recommend...a silver, or a conjoined standard of silver and gold." Extracted from the "Mirror of Parliament." 50p. *8°.* 1835.

29043 COMMITTEE OF LONDON SOAP MANUFACTURERS. A circular addressed by the soap manufacturers in the country. [On the trade and the duty on soap. The authorisation signed: Charles Williams, sec., and dated, Nov. 7, 1835.] 22p. *8°.* 1835.

29044 COWAN, C. Letter to Messrs. Dickinson, Phipps & Magnay, paper-manufacturers, regarding certain statements contained in their evidence before the Com-missioners of Excise Revenue Inquiry. 20p. *8°. Edinburgh,* 1835.

29045 DICKINSON, G. A new system; or, taxation no longer a burthen. 63p. *8°. London & Dover,* [1835]

29046 EDINBURGH. *Town Council.* Report of the Treasurer's Committee, to the Town Council, respecting the ecclesiastical revenues of the City of Edinburgh. (Approved of by the Magistrates and Council, 17th February, 1835.) 20p. *8°. Edinburgh,* [1835]

29047 FRANCE. *Chambre des Députés.* (No. 89.) Chambre des Députés. Session 1835. Rapport fait au nom de la commission chargée de l'examen de la proposition relative aux caisses d'épargne, de MM. B. Delessert et C. Dupin, par M. Charles Dupin...[With 'Rapport fait dans la session de 1834, au nom de la commission chargée de l'examen de la première proposition de M. Le Baron Benjamin Delessert'.] 54p. *8°.* [*Paris,*] 1835. *Presentation copy, with inscription from the author, 'To my friend Mr. Isaac Solly, Esq.'.*

29048 —— —— (No. 121.) Chambre des Députés. Session 1835. Second rapport sur la proposition relative aux caisses d'épargne de MM. Benjamin Delessert et Charles Dupin, par M. Charles Dupin... 10p. *8°.* [*Paris,*] 1835. *Presentation copy, with inscription from the author.*

29049 GOUGE, W. M. A short history of paper-money and banking in the United States. Including an account of provincial and continental paper-money. To which is prefixed an inquiry into the principles of the system...Second edition. 64p. *8°. New-York,* 1835. *For another edition, see 1833.*

29050 HUME, JOSEPH. Speech of Mr. Hume, in the debate on the motion of the Marquis of Chandos, on the 10th of March, 1835, for the total repeal of the malt tax. From the Mirror of Parliament, revised, with notes explanatory. 17p. *8°.* 1835.

29051 [JAMES, HENRY, *of Birmingham.*] State of the nation. Causes and effects of the rise and fall in value of property and commodities, from...1790 to the present time: with tables, of taxation, loans, exchequer bills, bank issues, bullion, imports, exports, prices, &c.&c. 191p. *8°.* 1835.

29052 JOPLIN, T. Case for parliamentary inquiry, into the circumstances of the panic: in a letter to Thomas Gisborne, Esq., M.P. 47p. *8°.* [1835 ?] *Afterwards included in the author's* An examination of the Report of the Joint Stock Bank Committee, *1836 (q.v.).*

29053 KELLY, J. B. A summary of the history and law of usury, with an examination of the policy of the existing system, and suggestions for its amendment, together with an analysis of the parliamentary proceedings relative to the subject...and a collection of statutes. 275p. *8°.* 1835.

29054 *KELLY, P. The universal cambist and commercial instructor: being a full and accurate treatise on the exchanges, coins, weights, and measures, of all trading nations and their colonies... The second edition, corrected ...and kept correct during subsequent alterations by a series of supplements, comprising the new laws for establishing the Imperial system of British weights and measures. 2 vols. *4°.* 1835. *The copy that belonged to Augustus De Morgan. For other editions, see* 1811.

29055 The LAW of stock jobbing, as contained in Sir John Barnard's Act, and the cases decided thereon. Also, an answer to the question, Are time-bargains in the foreign funds illegal ? By a solicitor. 30p. *8°.* 1835. *The copy that belonged to T. Spring Rice, Baron Monteagle.*

29056 A LETTER to the landowners of Great Britain and Ireland, on the advantages that would result from taking off the tax on malt. [Signed: A landowner.] Second edition. 16p. *8°.* 1835.

29057 LIVERPOOL UNION BANK. The deed of settlement of the Liverpool Union Bank, established 1st May, 1835, under the authority of an Act of Parliament, passed in the seventh year of the reign of his late Majesty King George the Fourth. With an abstract of the Act. 78p. *8°. Liverpool,* 1835.

29058 To the LORDS COMMISSIONERS of His Majesty's Treasury. [A petition, to be signed by manufacturers of soap, on the injury sustained by the trade through the operation of the excise laws and the duty on soap.] 3p. *fol. n.p.* [1835 ?]

29059 [MACLEAN, A. W. ?] Additional considerations, addressed to all classes, on the necessity and equity of a national system of deposit-banking and paper currency. 64p. *8°. Edinburgh,* 1835. *For the original work, see the author's* An essay on the necessity and equity of a national parish bank, *1831.*

29060 MILLS, JAMES. Letters addressed to Earl Grey in the early part of his administration, on the absolute necessity for the extinction of the tythe of agricultural produce as a clerical revenue... 23p. *8°.* 1835.

29061 MUTUAL LIFE ASSURANCE SOCIETY. A short account of the Mutual Life Assurance Society, instituted for assurances on lives and survivorships. Established in the year, 1834... 19p. *8°.* [1835 ?]

29062 OBSERVATIONS on the new Bankruptcy Court Act [1 & 2 Will. IV, c. 56], particularly as regards official assignees. Shewing the great additional expense to the public...and proposing means to render their service effective...[Signed: A lover of justice.] 20p. *8°.* 1835.

29063 The ORIGIN and principles of the Agricultural and Commercial Bank of Ireland. 68p. *12°. Dublin,* 1835.

29064 PARNELL, H. B., *Baron Congleton.* Observations on paper money, banking, and overtrading; including

those parts of the evidence taken before the Committee of the House of Commons, which explain the Scotch system of banking...New edition. 177p. *8°.* 1835. *For other editions, see* 1827.

29065 PEEL, SIR ROBERT, *2nd Bart.* Speech of the Right Honorable Sir Robert Peel, Bart., Chancellor of the Exchequer...in the House of Commons, March 10, 1835, on the motion of the Marquis of Chandos relating to the repeal of the malt-tax. 44p. *8°.* 1835.

29066 To the honourable the Commons House of Parliament, assembled. The humble PETITION of the undersigned soap manufacturers of London...[Pointing out the burden of the excise duties and the failure to prevent smuggling of soap.] *s.sh.fol.* [*London,* 1835 ?]

29067 The PRINCIPLE of the Corporation Reform Bill applied to counties, in a letter to the Chancellor of the Exchequer. [Concerned with the control of the county rate.] 15p. *8°.* 1835.

29068 RICE, THOMAS S., *Baron Monteagle.* The Budget. Speech of the Right Honourable Thomas Spring Rice, Chancellor of the Exchequer...in the House of Commons, on...August 14, 1835. Extracted from the "Mirror of Parliament." 31p. *8°.* 1835.

29069 —— Speech of the Right Honourable Thomas Spring Rice, Chancellor of the Exchequer...respecting the West India loan, in the House of Commons, on... September 4, 1835. Extracted from the "Mirror of Parliament." 13p. *8°.* 1835.

29070 ROY, J. The currency and banking system of England and the sister kingdom. 32p. *8°. Edinburgh,* 1835.

29071 *ROYAL NAVAL ANNUITANT SOCIETY. Reports and correspondence of the...Society, ordered to be printed at a meeting of the committee of management, held at the Society's building, Ker-Street, Devonport, on the 28th of February, 1835. 66p. *8°. Devonport,* [1835] *The copy that belonged to Augustus De Morgan.*

29072 SAINT-FERRÉOL, . Exposition du système des douanes en France, depuis 1791 jusqu'à 1834, précédée de quelques réflexions sur les causes qui ont amené l'enquête commerciale actuelle, et suivie d'autres réflexions sur les modifications à apporter au tarif actuel des douanes. 222p. *8°. Marseille,* 1835.

29073 SVAIGER, E. A. Monographia fisci regii. 103p. *8°. Weszprimii,* 1835.

29074 TAYLOR, JOHN (1781–1864). A catechism of the currency. 112p. *8°.* 1835.

29075 —— A catechism of foreign exchanges, and the effects of an abasement of bullion. [With an appendix.] 136p. *8°.* 1835. *A continuation of no. 29074 above. Both works were republished together as* Catechisms of the currency and exchanges, *in 1836 (q.v.). See also* 1850.

29076 THONNELIER, . Mémoire au Roi. [Concerning the author's 'presse monétaire'.] 19p. *4°.* [*Paris,* 1835 ?]

29077 THOUGHTS on the means of preventing abuses in life assurance offices. Second edition. 16p. *8°. Norwich & London,* 1835.

29078 UNGERN-STERNBERG, W. H. C. R. A. VON. Geschichte des Goldes. 86p. *8°. Dresden,* 1835.

29079 WESTERN, C. C., *Baron Western.* A letter to the President and members of the Chelmsford Agricultural Society, upon the causes of the distressed state of the agricultural classes of the United Kingdom of Great Britain and Ireland. 16p. *8°. London & Brighton,* [1835]

29080 —— Lord Western's second letter to the President and members of the Chelmsford and Essex Agricultural Society. 16p. *8°. Bath & London,* [1835]

29081 WOODWARD, HENRY, *Rector.* A letter on tithe; addressed to the editor of the Christian Examiner, in December 1834; to which is prefixed, one on the same subject addressed in 1832, to the Right Hon. E. G. Stanley (now Lord Stanley). 48p. *8°.* 1835.

TRANSPORT

29082 BABINGTON, M. A letter, in reply to Observations on the subject of the Midland Counties' Railway, by N. W. Cundy, civil engineer. 14p. *8°. Leicester & London,* [1835]

29083 BARLOW, P. Experiments on the transverse strength and other properties of malleable iron, with reference to its uses for railway bars; and a report founded on the same, addressed to the directors of the London and Birmingham Railway Company. 97p. *8°.* 1835.

29084 —— Second report addressed to the directors and proprietors of the London and Birmingham Railway Company, founded on an inspection of, and experiment made on the Liverpool and Manchester Railway. 1–67, 82–116p. *8°.* 1835. *See also* 1837.

29085 BASING AND BATH RAILWAY COMPANY. Railway from Basing, in the county of Hants, to Bath [being an extension of the London and Southampton Railway. A revised prospectus, dated: 1st January 1835]. 2p. *fol. n.p.* [1835] *For the original version, see* 1834.

29086 COGHLAN, F. The steam-packet and coast companion, or general guide to Gravesend – Herne Bay – Canterbury – Margate – Broadstairs – Ramsgate – Dovor [sic] – Hastings – Brighton – Worthing – Bagnor [sic] – Southampton – and the Isle of Wight. For the present season... 250p. *12°.* [1835 ?]

29087 CORT, R. The anti-rail-road journal; or, rail-road impositions detected, contains an answer to the Edinburgh Review and Mechanic's Magazine, &c. 122p. *8°.* 1835.

29088 [*Endorsed:*] **EASTERN COUNTIES RAILWAY.** Resolutions of meetings [on the need for railway communication between London and the counties of Essex, Suffolk and Norfolk] at Ipswich, Harleston, Beccles, Chelmsford, Colchester. 3p. *fol. n.p.* [1835]

29089 ENGLAND. *Laws, etc.* [*Endorsed:*] An Act for making a railway from Bristol to join the London and Birmingham Railway near London, to be called "The Great Western Railway," with branches therefrom to the towns of Bradford and Trowbridge, in the county of Wilts. ⟨Royal Assent, 31 August 1835.⟩ 5 Will. IV. sess. 1835. 202p. *fol.* [*London,* 1835 ?]

29090 —— The General Highway Act of the 5 & 6 Will. IV. c. 50. With notes explaining the alterations in the law of highways; also new forms and general rules for making and repairing roads. By Leonard Shelford. 214p. *12°.* 1835.

29091 FINDLATER, J. R. Report relative to the formation of a railway between...Dundee and Perth, passing through the districts of the Carse of Gowrie... And supplementary report by George Buchanan... 24p. *8°. Dundee,* 1835.

29092 GIBBS, JOSEPH. Report of Mr. Gibbs...upon the several proposed lines for a Brighton Railway. Second edition. 91p. *8°.* [1835] *The Rastrick copy.*

29093 GRAHAME, T. Essays and letters on subjects conducive to the improvements and extension of inland communication and transport. 61p. *4°. Westminster,* 1835.

29094 GREAT NORTH OF ENGLAND RAILWAY COMPANY. [*Endorsed:*] The Great North of England Railway, completing the connexion between London, Leeds, York, and Newcastle-upon-Tyne. Prospectus 1835. 2p. *fol. Darlington,* [1835] *The copy sent through the post by Mewburn & Coates, solicitors to the Railway, to 'Capt. Moorsom, R.N., Railway Office, Birmingham'.*

29095 To the **INHABITANTS** of Beccles. [Signed: A looker on. A discussion of the local politics of shipping and the port of Beccles, with reference to the Lowestoft Shipping Company.] *s.sh.dol. n.p.* [*c.* 1835]

29096 LIVRE de poste, ou état général des postes aux chevaux du Royaume de France, des relais des routes desservies en poste...précédée d'un extrait de la nouvelle instruction sur le service des postes, et suivi de la carte géométrique des routes desservies en poste, avec désignation des relais et des distances: pour l'an 1835. 322p. *8°. Paris,* 1835. *See also* 1814 (État général des postes...), 1818, 1819, 1823, 1838 (Livre de poste...).

29097 LONDON AND SOUTHAMPTON RAILWAY COMPANY. At the second general half-yearly meeting of the proprietors...held...on...the 31st of August, 1835...Report. 3p. *fol.* [*London,* 1835]

29098 LONDON GRAND JUNCTION RAILWAY. Report of the directors...[Dated: 20th November, 1835. Not incorporated.] [4]p. *fol. n.p.* [1835]

29099 MACERONI, F. Expositions and illustrations, interesting to all those concerned in steam power, whether as applied to rail-roads, common roads, or to sea and inland navigation. 126p. *8°.* 1835. *Presentation copy from the author to William Boulnois.*

29100 NEWCASTLE AND CARLISLE RAILWAY COMPANY. The Managing Committee's report to the Directors...March 17th, 1835. [Signed: Benjamin Thompson, George Johnson, Nicholas Wood.] 7p. *8°. Newcastle,* [1835] *Addressed in manuscript to 'George Silvertop Esq?'. See also* 1837, 1838, 1839.

29101 —— Report of the Directors...read to the shareholders at their annual meeting, March 18, 1835. 12p. *8°. Newcastle-upon-Tyne,* 1835. *See also* 1837, 1838, 1843, 1845.

29102 PARSONS, E. The tourist's companion; or, the history of the scenes and places on the route by the rail-road and steam-packet from Leeds and Selby to Hull. 243p. *8°.* 1835. *The engraved title reads: The tourist's companion from Leeds thro' Selby to Hull...*

For the **RAILWAY MAGAZINE**, 1835–87, *see* vol. III, *Periodicals list.*

29103 1835. **REPORT** of the committee appointed at Lincoln, to examine the proposals for a northern railway. 16p. *8°. Lincoln*, [1835]

29104 **SPEECH** on the improvement of the Shannon, being in continuation of the debate in the House of Commons, 12th May, 1835, giving a comparative view of the navigation of the Rideau Canal, in Canada, and the River Shannon, in Ireland; with observations on the value of a connection by steam packets, with British America. 60p. *8°.* 1835.

29105 **TREDGOLD**, T. A practical treatise on railroads and carriages, shewing the principles of estimating their strength, proportions, expense, and annual produce, and the conditions which render them effective, economical, and durable...The second edition. 184p. *8°.* 1835. *The Rastrick copy. For other editions, see* 1825.

29106 **VIGNOLES**, C. B. Two reports, addressed to the Liverpool & Manchester Railway Company, on the projected north line of railway from Liverpool to the Manchester, Bolton, and Bury Canal...By Charles Vignoles...and Joseph Locke. 32p. *8°. Liverpool*, 1835. *The Rastrick copy.*

SOCIAL CONDITIONS

29107 **AMERICAN TEMPERANCE SOCIETY.** Permanent temperance documents of the... Society. [Being the 4th–9th annual reports, 1831–36.] Vol. 1. 568p. *12°. Boston, New York, &c.*, 1835[–36] *Each report has two sets of pagination, its own, and that of the volume. Copies of this work usually contain the 4th–8th reports only. The ninth report, for 1836, was apparently printed in the same format as the earlier reports, paginated p. [515]–568, for addition to the volume. The Turner copy. See also* 1841, *and, for an earlier report,* 1829.

For the **ANIMALS' FRIEND**, *see* vol. III, *Periodicals list.*

29108 **BEECHER**, L. The remedy of intemperance. Extracted from a sermon...with a few alterations. (*British Tee-total Temperance Society,* 15.) 8p. *8°.* [1835?] *The Turner copy.*

29109 **BIRD**, C. Copy of the petition of Charles Bird, Esq. barrister-at-law, as presented to the Honourable the House of Commons by D. W. Harvey, Esq. M.P. on the 25th June, 1835, relative to the trial of the Dorchester labourers, and the danger to be apprehended from a dependent Bar. With the notices of the same by the London journals. 12p. *12°. Exeter*, 1835.

29110 **BOOKBINDERS' CONSOLIDATED UNION**, *Manchester.* Rules and regulations of the Bookbinders' Consolidated Relief Fund, agreed upon at the meeting of delegates...1835. Established January 1st, 1836. Second edition. 12p. *12°. Ashton-under-Lyne*, [1835]

29111 **BOWEN**, J. A letter to the King in refutation of some of the charges preferred against the poor: with copious statistical illustrations demonstrative of the injustice with which that body has been assailed. 111p. *8°.* 1835. *See also* 1837.

29112 **BOWRING**, SIR J. Copy of correspondence, between Dr. Bowring and the Associated Weavers' Committee, Kilmarnock; together with an extract from the evidence; also, an extract from the report of the Parliamentary Committee on hand-loom weavers. 24p. *12°. Kilmarnock*, 1835. *The Oastler copy.*

29113 —— Hand-loom weavers. Speech of Dr. Bowring, M.P. in the House of Commons, on Tuesday, July 28, 1835. Extracted from the "Mirror of Parliament". 14p. *8°.* 1835. *The copy that belonged to Victor Considérant.*

29114 **BRADFORD SHORT-TIME COMMITTEE.** Insolent stupidity corrected, by common sense. [Signed: Charles Simons, chairman.] 4p. *8°. Bradford*, [1835] *The Oastler copy.*

29115 —— Protest of the Bradford Short-Time Committee against the proceedings of Mr. Rickards, the factory inspector, and of the mill owners of this neighbourhood. [Signed: Charles Simons, chairman.] 4p. *8°. Bradford*, [1835] *The Oastler copy.*

29116 **BRISTOL.** *Commissioners appointed under the Bristol Damages Compensation Act. Bristol riots,* 1831. Report of the Commissioners...and statement of actions for damages, and proceedings had therein...with their general results. 5, [9]p. *fol. Bristol*, 1835.

29117 **BRITISH AND FOREIGN TEMPERANCE SOCIETY.** Tracts and handbills sanctioned by the Committee of the...Society, and regularly kept for sale. Nos. 1–57. *12°.* [1835?] *The Turner copy.*

29118 **BROUGHAM**, H. P., *Baron Brougham and Vaux.* A full report of the speeches delivered by Lord Brougham & Vaux, at Liverpool on...July 20th, 1835; on laying the first stone of the new Mechanics' Institution, and at the dinner given to His Lordship at the Amphitheatre... 16p. *8°. Liverpool*, 1835.

29119 **BULL**, G. S. The cause of industry. A letter to the Hon. John Stuart Wortley, candidate for the West-Riding. 4p. *8°. Bradford*, [1835] *The Oastler copy.*

29120 The Rev. Jabez **BUNTING**; or, begging. With other humorous poems. 12p. *12°. Bradford*, [c. 1835].

29121 **BUXTON**, SIR THOMAS F., *Bart.* Speech of Thomas Foxwell Buxton, Esq., M.P., in the House of Commons, on...April 2, 1835, on the motion...to consider the present state of the church establishment in Ireland, with a view of applying any surplus of its revenue ...to the general education of all classes of the people... Extracted from the "Mirror of Parliament." 9p. *8°.* 1835.

29122 **CAREY**, M. Letters on the condition of the poor: addressed to Alexander Henry, Esq. containing a vindication of poor laws and benevolent societies: proofs of the injustice of the general censure of the poor... instances of intense suffering in Philadelphia...examples of the gross inconsistency of the Edinburgh Review, on the subject of poor laws; with a view of the system and operations of the Union Benevolent Association. By a citizen of Philadelphia. Second edition, improved. 20p. *8°. Philadelphia*, 1835. *See also* 1836.

29123 **CLÉREL DE TOCQUEVILLE**, C. A. H. M., *Comte de Tocqueville.* Mémoire sur le paupérisme. [From the *Mémoires de la Société Académique de Cherbourg,* 1835.] p.293–344. *8°. n.p.* [1835]

29124 COBBETT, W. Mr. Cobbett and the new Poor Law Act. A letter to Sir Robert Peel... ⟨From "Cobbett's legacy to labourers."⟩ 24p. *12°.* [1835?]

29125 COTES, P. The new Poor Law a benefit to the poor; being the substance of two sermons preached in Litchfield Church. 50p. *8°.* 1835.

29126 [CRABTREE, GEOFFREY?] A dialogue betwixt Tummus and Mary. 8p. *8°. Rochdale,* [1835] *The copy that belonged to Oastler, who attributed it to Crabtree in the manuscript index to his pamphlet collection.*

29127 The **DENS** of London exposed. 106p. *8°.* 1835.

29128 DETROSIER, R. An address on the necessity of an extension of moral and political instruction among the working classes... With a memoir of the author [by John Kay]. 23p. *12°.* [1835] *For other editions, see 1831.*

29129 EDMONDS, G. George Edmonds' appeal to the labourers of England, an exposure of aristocrat spies, and the infernal machinery of the Poor Law Murder Bill ... 12p. *12°.* [1835]

29130 ENGLAND. *Barrister appointed to Certify the Rules of Friendly Societies.* Instructions for the establishment of friendly societies, with a form of rules and tables applicable thereto. 32p. *8°.* 1835.

29131 —— *Commissioners for Inquiring into the Administration and Practical Operation of the Poor Laws.* Extrait du Rapport des Commissaires de S.M. Britannique qui ont exécuté une enquête générale sur l'administration des fonds provenants de la taxe des pauvres en Angleterre. 81p. *8°. Turin,* 1835. *The copy that belonged to T. Spring Rice, Baron Monteagle.*

29132 —— *Commissioners for Inquiring into the Condition of the Poorer Classes in Ireland.* Selection of parochial examinations relative to the destitute classes in Ireland, from the evidence received by His Majesty's Commissioners... By authority. 430p. *8°. Dublin & London,* 1835. *Copy specially bound for presentation to Leopold I, King of the Belgians, with inscription from Sir John Caradoc, British ambassador to Belgium.*

29133 —— *Laws, etc.* The Act for the Amendment of the Poor Laws, with a practical introduction, notes and forms. Third edition. With many valuable additions... and an appendix... By J. F. Archbold... 267p. *12°.* 1835. *For the editions of the Act with notes by J. Tidd Pratt, see 1834.*

29134 —— —— A collection of the Statutes in force respecting the relief and regulation of the poor, with notes and references, by John Tidd Pratt, Esq. 452p. *8°.* 1835.

For —— *Poor Law Commission* [*1834–1847*], First[–fourteenth] annual report of the Poor Law Commissioners for England and Wales, 1835–48, *see vol. III, Periodicals list,* Annual report... *See also* 1836.

29135 —— —— Orders and regulations issued by the Poor Law Commissioners for England and Wales, for the guidance and government of the Board of Guardians of the Wangford Union. 35p. *8°. Bungay,* 1835.

29136 FARISH, H. Drunkenness. A sermon preached at St. Mary's Church, Sheffield, on... March 22, 1835. 12p. *12°. Sheffield,* [1835]

For the **FARTHING CANDLE,** *see vol. III, Periodicals list.*

29137 FORSS, C. Practical remarks upon the educa-

tion of the working classes; with an account of the plan pursued under the superintendence of the Children's Friend Society at the Brenton Asylum, Hackney Wick. 58p. *8°.* 1835.

29138 GARNIER, T. Plain remarks upon the new Poor Law Amendment Act, more particularly addressed to the labouring classes. 35p. *12°. Winchester & London,* 1835.

29139 GASKELL, P. Prospects of industry; being a brief exposition of the past and present conditions of the labouring classes. With remarks on the operation of the Poor-Law Bill, workhouses, &c.... 44p. *8°.* 1835.

29140 GASKELL, W. P. An address to the operative classes, being the substance of a lecture explanatory and in defence of the nature and objects of the Cheltenham Mechanics' Institution... delivered May 8, 1835... 16p. *8°. Cheltenham & Stroud,* [1835]

29141 H., J. Some remarks on the government of workhouses; in a letter addressed to Sir Culling Eardley Smith, Bart., of Bedwell Park, Herts. 38p. *8°. Hull & London,* 1835.

29142 HAMMOND, W. O. An address to the churchwardens, guardians, overseers of the poor, and rate payers, of Wingham division of Saint Augustine, on the resolution adopted at a meeting, held at Wingham, on... twenty-second of January, before Sir Francis Head, assistant commissioner of the Poor Laws. 24p. *8°. Canterbury,* 1835.

29143 HAND IN HAND PHILANTHROPIC SOCIETY OF OPERATIVE PAINTERS. The rules and regulations of the Hand in Hand Philanthropic Society... held at the Shepherd & Flock, High Street, Marylebone. Enrolled pursuant to Act of Parliament... 24p. *8°.* 1835.

29144 HAND-LOOM WORSTED WEAVERS' CENTRAL COMMITTEE. The report and resolutions of a meeting of deputies from the hand loom worsted weavers, residing in and near Bradford, Leeds, Halifax, &c. in Yorkshire. [With an account of the inaugural meeting of 21 March 1835. On the low wages of weavers and the threat to their standard of living posed by the power loom.] 12p. *12°. Bradford,* [1835] *The Oastler copy.*

29145 [HEAD, SIR F. B.] English charity. [From the Quarterly Review, vol. 53. An elucidation of the Poor Law Amendment Act.] 106p. *12°.* 1835. *The Oastler copy.*

29146 HINTON CHARTERHOUSE. Account of payments from September 29th, 1834 to March 25th, 1835. James White, overseer. 3p. *4°. Bradford [on Avon,* 1835]

29147 The whole **HISTORY** and mystery of the new Poor Law. 12p. *12°. Bishops Stortford,* 1835.

29148 HULL, J. The philanthropic repertory of plans and suggestions for improving the condition of the labouring poor... Fifth edition. 84p. *12°.* 1835. *See also* 1841.

29149 JONES, H. Lecture on the combinative principle as applicable to modes of collegiate life. Addressed to the settlers of Sarnia, and the adjoining townships, in the western district of Upper Canada. 12p. *8°. Maxwell, Upper Canada,* 1835.

29150 KING, T. I. Buckingham Poor Law Union. Report by Mr. T. I. King of his mission to the manufacturing districts, in company with Edward Quainton, of Steeple Claydon, and Benjamin Stevens, of Adstock. 12p. *8°. Buckingham,* [1835] *The Oastler copy.*

29151 KIRK, E. N. "Thou shalt not kill"...A sermon [On temperance.]...(From the American Intelligencer.) 8p. *4°. Preston*, [1835] *The Turner copy.*

For **LABOURERS' FRIEND SOCIETY,** *London,* Useful hints for the labourer, [1835–43] *see* vol. III, *Periodicals list*, Useful hints for the labourer.

29152 LABOURERS' FRIEND SOCIETY, *Wallington.* The Labourers' Friend Society, for bettering the condition of the labouring classes, particularly in allotting to them small portions of land. Established at Wallington in Surrey, in...1835. [Objects, rules, regulations and premiums.] 25p. *4°. 1835.*

29153 LESLIE, JOHN, *Commissioner of Sewers.* A letter to the industrious classes, on the operation of the poor laws as affecting their independence and comfort... Fifth edition. 12p. *8°. 1835.*

29154 —— A practical illustration of the principles upon which the Poor Law Amendment Act is founded, as exhibited in the administration of the poor rates in the parish of St. George, Hanover Square, for the year ending Lady-Day, 1835. 30p. *8°. 1835. The copy that belonged to Sir Harry Verney.*

29155 —— Eighth edition. 36p. *8°. 1835.*

29156 —— Ninth edition. 36p. *8°. 1835.*

29157 —— Eleventh edition. 36p. *8°. 1835.*

29158 —— Thirteenth edition. 36p. *8°. 1835.*

29159 —— Fourteenth edition. 36p. *8°. 1835.*

29160 —— Fifteenth edition. 36p. *8°. 1835.*

29161 —— Sixteenth edition. 36p. *8°. 1835.*

29162 LLOYD, W. F. Four lectures on poor-laws, delivered before the University of Oxford, in Michaelmas term, 1834. 128p. *8°. London & Oxford, 1835. Reissued in* Lectures on population, value, poor-laws and rent *in 1837, q.v.* (GENERAL).

29163 MACKENZIE, P., *ed.* Letters of the Tory Orange conspirators in Glasgow [L. W. Craigie and others], to Colonel Fairman: extracted from the Report of the Select Committee of the House of Commons by P. Mackenzie. 16p. *8°. Glasgow, 1835.*

29164 MAHON, J. N. The poor laws, as they were, and as they are: or, the recent alterations in the poor laws, by the Statute 4 & 5 William IV. cap. 76. With the reasons for those alterations, plainly stated... 189p. *12°. 1835.*

29165 MANCHESTER STATISTICAL SOCIETY. Report of a committee of the Manchester Statistical Society on the state of education in the Borough of Manchester in 1834. 45p. *8°. London & Manchester, 1835. See also 1837.*

29166 MARSTERS, T. Reform and workhouses! or considerations suggested by what is called the Poor-Law Amendment Bill. 26p. *8°. Lynn, 1835.*

29167 MARTIN, C. W. An address to the labourers of Egerton in Kent, and the adjoining parishes. 12p. *12°. 1835.*

29168 MARTIN, ROBERT M. [*Begin.*] I have the honour to inform you, that a society has been formed for the Encouragement of Domestic Industry...[A circular letter, signed in manuscript, appealing for contributions towards the publication of the *Agricultural and Industrial Magazine.*] [4]p. *4°. n.p.* [1835] *The Oastler copy.*

29169 MATTHEWS, W. Hydraulia: an historical and descriptive account of the water works of London, and the contrivances for supplying other great cities, in different ages and countries. 454p. *8°. 1835.*

29170 MIDDLESEX. *Quarter Sessions.* The thirty-first report of the visiting justices appointed to superintend the building, erection, and management of the County Lunatic Asylum. 14p. *8°.* [1835]

29171 MINUTES of meetings of Members of Parliament & others, to take into consideration the best means of employing and instructing the unemployed & uninstructed; and the report of a sub-committee, appointed to devise the best means of carrying the object of the meeting into execution. 20p. *8°. The Association of All Classes of All Nations,* 1835.

29172 MUSSEY, R. D. The physiological influence of alcohol, from the temperance prize essays, by Drs. Mussey and Lindsly. An American publication. 8p. *4°. Preston,* [1835 ?] *The Turner copy.*

29173 NOEL, HON. B. W. The state of the Metropolis considered, in a letter to the Right Honorable and Right Reverend the Lord Bishop of London...Third edition, enlarged. 72p. *12°. 1835.*

29174 OASTLER, R. The Huddersfield Dissenters in a fury. And why? Because the mask is falling! A third letter addressed to Edward Baines, Esq., M.P. 12p. *8°. Leeds,* [1835] *Oastler's own copy.*

29175 —— The Huddersfield Dissenters stark staring mad!!! because the mask has fallen!!!! The fourth letter to Edward Baines, Esq. M.P. 8p. *8°. Leeds,* [1835] *Oastler's own copy.*

29176 —— Richard Oastler on the new Poor-Law Act. A letter to the editor of the Argus and Demagogue, August 8th, 1834. [With a letter to the men of Bradford dated February 19th, 1835.] 4p. *8°. Bradford,* [1835] *Oastler's own copy.*

29177 —— Slavery in Yorkshire. Monstrous barbarity!!! To Edward Baines, Esq., M.P. [A letter.] 8p. *8°. Bradford,* [1835] *Oastler's own copy.*

29178 —— Yorkshire slavery. The "Devil-to-do" amongst the Dissenters in Huddersfield. A letter addressed to Edw. Baines, Esq., M.P. 8p. *8°. Leeds,* 1835. *Oastler's own copy.*

29179 OBSERVATIONS and documents respecting the petitions presented to Parliament from the parish of Stoke Poges, in the county of Bucks. [Against its incorporation with the Eton Poor Law Union.] 39p. *8°. 1835.*

29180 [OSBORNE, LORD S. G.] A familiar explanation of that part of the new Poor Law which relates to the maintenance of illegitimate children. Addressed especially to the mothers of, and mistresses over, young females. By a beneficed clergyman of the county of Bucks, author of "A word or two on the new Poor Law." 16p. *8°.* [1835 ?]

29181 [——] The prospects and present condition of the labouring classes, considered with respect to the probable operation of the new Poor Law. Together with some practical observations on loan funds, savings banks, etc., etc. By a beneficed clergyman of the county of Bucks, author of "A word or two about the new Poor Law." 16p. *8°.* [1835 ?]

29182 OWEN, ROBERT D. Moral physiology; or, a brief and plain treatise on the population question. 48p.

8°. London, Manchester, &c., 1835. For other editions, see 1831.

29183 Able-bodied **PAUPERISM.** By an observer. [Reprinted from no. XXVIII of the Law Magazine. With an extract from the report of one of the assistant poor law commissioners.] 37p. *8°. 1835.*

29184 PHILLIPS, M. Substance of the evidence, observations and printed documents, illustrative of the best means of employing and benefitting the working classes and the poor, without encroaching on the rights, properties, or privileges of the rich. 4l. *obl.fol. n.p. [c. 1835]*

29185 POLISH SOCIETY OF MUTUAL INSTRUCTION. Rules of the Polish Association of Mutual Instruction, for the regulation of pupils attending their gratuitous lectures. [May 19th 1835.] [2]p. *8°. [London, 1835]*

29186 The old and new **POOR LAW:** who gains? and who loses? explained by conversations on facts of daily occurrence. 63p. *16°. 1835. *Another, the FWA copy, belonged to William Pare, and has an inscription on the wrappers, 'John Walter Esq., M.P. with J. Scholefield's respects'.*

29187 POOR LAW Starvation Bill. A dialogue between a poor law commissioner and the paupers, &c. *s.sh.fol. Norwich, [1835 ?]*

29188 Liberal **PRINCIPLES!!!** [A petition to the House of Commons on the factory question. Signed: J. C. Boddington, J. S. Smith, G. S. Bull, and dated, March 26th 1835.] *s.sh.8°. n.p., 1835. The Oastler copy.*

29189 PRISON DISCIPLINE, with hints on other preventive and remedial measures required to diminish crime. A letter to His Grace the Duke of Richmond, K.G. chairman of the Committee of the House of Lords, appointed to inquire into the state of the prisons...by a county magistrate. 58p. *8°. 1835.*

29190 A **REPORT** of the proceedings and speeches of a public meeting, held in...Oldham on...March 14th, 1835, to petition the House of Commons, to limit the period of working in cotton and other mills to ten hours per day, and eight on Saturdays; including a...report of the address of Richard Oastler, Esq.... 20p. *8°. Oldham, 1835. The Oastler copy.*

29191 *REVANS, J. Evils of the state of Ireland: their causes, and their remedy – a poor law. 152p. *8°. [1835] Presentation copy, with inscription, from the author to George Grote. See also 1837.*

29192 SAINT ANN'S SOCIETY. Prospectus of Saint Ann's Society schools, Brixton Hill, Surrey, and Aldersgate, London, for the educating, clothing, and wholly providing for the legitimate children of necessitous persons... 17p. *8°. [London,] 1835.*

29193 ST. EWE FRIENDLY SOCIETY. Rules to be observed by a Friendly Society, begun the 2nd day of July, 1787, in the parish of St. Ewe, in the county of Cornwall. 17p. *8°. St. Austell, [1835 ?]*

29194 SCROPE, G. P. Political economy versus the hand loom weavers. The letter of George Poulett Scrope, Esq., M.P. to the Chairman of the Central Committee of the Hand Loom Worsted Weavers of the West Riding of York. With their answer to the same [corrected by G. S. Bull]. 16p. *8°. Bradford, [1835] The Oastler copy.*

29195 —— Political economy, versus the hand-loom weavers. Two letters of George Poulett Scrope, Esq., M.P. to the chairman of the Central Committee of the Hand-Loom Worsted Weavers, of the West-Riding of York, with their answers to the same [the first corrected by G. S. Bull, the second written by Richard Oastler]. 38p. *8°. Bradford, 1835. The Oastler copy.*

29196 SENIOR, N. W. Statement of the provision for the poor, and of the condition of the labouring classes, in a considerable portion of America and Europe...Being the preface to the foreign communications contained in the appendix to the Poor Law Report. 238p. *8°. 1835.*

29197 SMITH, SIR CULLING EARDLEY, *Bart.* Suggestions addressed, (by permission of the Board,) to the Secretary of the Poor Law Commissioners. 44p. *8°. 1835.*

29198 SOCIETY FOR THE EDUCATION OF THE POOR IN THE HIGHLANDS. Report of the committee of the Society...Read at the general meeting, at Inverness, 11th November, 1834. 46p. *8°. Inverness, 1835.*

29199 SPENCER, T. Observations on the state of the poor and the practical tendencies of the new Poor Law; addressed to the clergy, rate-payers, boards of guardians ... 56p. *8°. 1835.*

For the **STAR OF TEMPERANCE,** *1835–36, see* vol. III, *Periodicals list.*

29200 SWABEY, M. A practical explanation of the duties of parish officers in electing guardians for unions of parishes and places under the Poor Law Amendment Act, and of the duties of guardians when elected. 22p. *8°. 1835. The copy that belonged to Sir Harry Verney.*

29201 TEMPERANCE picture gallery! [8]p. *4°. Preston, [1835 ?] The Turner copy.*

29202 TEMPERANCE poetry. 8p. *4°. Preston, [1835 ?] The Turner copy.*

29203 TINMOUTH, W. Unparalleled injustice! As developed in the case of Mr. William Tinmouth, who has been imprisoned fourteen years and upwards...for an alleged debt of twenty pounds! An authentic narrative of the proceedings...at Durham, Tinmouth v. Taylor, afterwards Tinmouth v. Hutton...[With letters and a petition to the King from William Tinmouth.] 31p. *8°. [1835]*

29204 Short time **TRACTS.** No. 1[–No. 6]. Nov., 1835. *8°. Bradford, 1835. The Oastler copies. Contents: 1. Sharp, W., The judgment of the late William Sharp, Esq. of Bradford, consulting surgeon to the Bradford Infirmary [on the effects of long hours in factories]...2. Hawkins, F. B., The sentence of Dr. Bissett Hawkins, who was sent by the King to enquire into the truth of the evidence laid before the Select Committee...on the factory system, June 1833. 3. Idem, Intemperance & vice, the effect of long hours and a bad system. From the report of Dr. Bissett Hawkins, one of the medical officers of the Factory Commission, 1833. 4. Anon., The piecener's complaint. [In verse.] (New edition.) 5. Piecenwell, P, pseud., Intemperance and long hours, inseparable evils. A letter from Patty Piecenwell, to the members of Bradford Temperance Society. [With extracts from An inquiry into the state of the manufacturing population, 1831, by W. R. Greg.] 6. Kay, afterwards Kay-Shuttleworth, Sir James P., Bart., The system of long hours proved to be unhealthy, anti-social and immoral. [Extracts from The moral and physical condition of the working classes, 1832.]*

29205 The **TRIAL** of alcohol, charged with robbery, murder, &c. (From the American Temperance Recorder.) 8p. *4°. Preston*, [1835 ?] *The Turner copy.*

29206 UNITED STATES OF AMERICA. *Congress.* Noble reply of the Congress of the United States to the Agnews of America, being a death blow to cant, priestcraft and intolerance. [On Sunday observance.] 8p. *8°. 1835.*

29207 WALKER, J. K. Some observations on the peculiarity of diseases of infants and children... ⟨Extracted from the Transactions of the Provincial Medical and Surgical Association.⟩ 90p. *8°. Worcester, 1835.*

29208 WATTS, I. No. 228. Against drunkenness and lewdness. Extracted from Dr. Watts's Miscellaneous thoughts, nos. 35 and 36 with a few reflections subjoined. 4p. *8°. The Religious Tract Society,* [*c.* 1835 ?]

29209 WHITE, John M. Parochial settlements an obstruction to poor law reform. 30p. *8°. 1835.*

29210 The **WINE** question. 8p. *4°. Preston*, [1835 ?] *The Turner copy.*

29211 [**WONTNER,** T.] Abolition of pauperism. A discovery in internal national polity. Independence for every man, woman, and child in the country; developed in the heads of a plan recently submitted to Lord Brougham ...To cause the abrogation of the poor laws, and to concentrate the benefits of all charities, while it removes the degradation inflicted on the recipients. By the author of "Old Bailey experience", &c.&c.&c. 24p. *8°. 1835.*

For the **WORKING MAN'S ADVOCATE,** *see* vol. III, *Periodicals list.*

SLAVERY

29212 BOURNE, G. Picture of slavery in the United States of America; being a practical illustration of voluntaryism and republicanism. 188p. *12°. Glasgow,* 1835.

29213 GURLEY, R. R. Life of Jehudi Ashmun, late colonial agent in Liberia. With an appendix, containing extracts from his journal and other writings; with a brief sketch of the life of the Rev. Lott Cary. 396, 160p. *8°. Washington, 1835.*

29214 INNES, John (*fl.* 1838–1849). Letter to Lord Glenelg, Secretary of State for the Colonies; containing a report from personal observation, on the working of the new system in the British West India colonies. 119p. *8°. 1835. See also 1836.*

29215 LA BONNINIÈRE DE BEAUMONT, G. A. DE. Marie ou l'esclavage aux Etats-Unis, tableau de mœurs américaines... 2 vols. *8°. Paris, 1835.*

29216 LETTER to a member of the Congress of the United States of America, from an English clergyman; including a republication, with considerable additions, of the tract entitled, 'Every man his own property.' 30p. *8°. London & Birmingham, 1835.*

29217 MACAULAY, Z., *and others.* Faits et renseignemens, prouvant les avantages du travail libre sur le travail forcé, et indiquant les moyens les plus propres à hâter l'abolition de l'esclavage dans les colonies européennes. 128p. *8°. Paris, 1835. This work consists of two pieces by Macaulay, with extracts from works by Flinter, Fleming and Sismondi, collected and published with an introduction by Macaulay.*

29218 MADDEN, R. R. A twelvemonth's residence in the West Indies, during the transition from slavery to apprenticeship; with incidental notices of the state of society, prospects, and natural resources of Jamaica and other islands... 2 vols. *12°. 1835.*

29219 MASSACHUSETTS ANTI-SLAVERY SOCIETY. Third annual report of the Board of Managers of the New-England Anti-Slavery Society, presented Jan. 21, 1835. 23p. *8°. Boston, 1835.*

29220 To the Right Honourable Charles, Baron Glenelg ...Secretary of State for the Colonial Department. The **MEMORIAL** of the anti-slavery and abolition societies of the United Kingdom [appealing against the apprenticeship system in Jamaica. [Signed: Henry Waymouth, chairman. With 'Appendix, (consisting of extracts from... documents in possession of the metropolitan anti-slavery committees,) showing the condition of the apprenticed labourers']. 36p. *8°.* [1835]

29221 MONTROL, M. F. DE. Société Française pour l'Abolition de l'Esclavage. Analyse de la discussion de la Chambre des Députés et de la Chambre des Pairs relative à l'émancipation des esclaves...Troisième publication. 35p. *8°. Paris, 1835.*

29222 —— Société Française pour l'Abolition de l'Esclavage. Des colonies anglaises depuis l'émancipation des esclaves, et de l'influence de cette émancipation sur les colonies françaises...Seconde publication. 18p. *8°. Paris,* 1835.

29223 NEWTON, John (1725–1807). Memoirs of the Rev. John Newton...With selections from his correspondence. 323p. *8°. 1835.*

29224 REESE, D. M. Letters to the Hon. William Jay, being a reply to his "Inquiry into the American Colonization and American Anti-Slavery Societies." 120p. *12°. New-York & Boston, 1835.*

29225 Second edition. A full and corrected **REPORT** of the proceedings at the public meeting held in Hope Street Baptist Chapel, to present the Emancipation Society's address to Daniel O'Connell, Esq, M.P. 23d September, 1835. 11p. *8°. Glasgow,* [1835]

29226 ROSE, R. A full report of the speech of Mr. Robert Rose, a West Indian, delivered at the public dinner given to the Right Honourable Henry Lord Brougham & Vaux, July 20, 1835, at the Amphitheatre, Liverpool, in reply to the sentiment "civil and religious liberty all over the world."...Fourth edition. 15p. *8°. Liverpool & London, 1835.*

29227 The commemorative **WREATH:** [poems] in celebration of the extinction of negro slavery in the British dominions. 112p. *12°. 1835.*

POLITICS

29228 AMES, F. The influence of democracy on liberty, property, and the happiness of society, considered. By an American...To which is prefixed, an introduction [and life of the author] by Henry Ewbank, Esq. 199p. 8°. 1835.

29229 An **APPEAL** to the English nation, against the revival of Toryism; by a late commoner. 72p. 8°. 1835. *The phrase 'by a late commoner' has been amended in manuscript to read 'by a late fellow commoner, Cambridge'.*

29230 BACON, RICHARD M. The aristocracy of England. A reply to Isaac Tomkins, Gent. 39p. 8°. *London & Norwich,* 1835.

29231 Borough of **BECCLES.** The names of the following gentlemen are respectfully submitted to the consideration of the burgesses of Beccles, as persons from among whom a proper and efficient council may be selected. [Signed in manuscript: J. Chinery, and dated, 21st Dec. 1835.] *s.sh.fol. n.p.* [1835]

29232 BIRMINGHAM. Re-establishment of the Political Union. A report of the proceedings at the great town's meeting...in Birmingham, on...the 4th of September, 1835. 7p. 4°. *Birmingham,* [1835] *See note to no. 26519.* *★Another, the FWA copy, belonged to William Pare.*

29233 BROCKETT, W. H. An exposure of the attempt of fifty-four individuals, to hoodwink the House of Lords and deprive the people of Gateshead of that corporate property, the control of which is given to them by the Municipal Reform Bill. 26p. 8°. *Gateshead,* 1835.

29234 [BROUGHAM, H. P., *Baron Brougham and Vaux.*] A letter to Isaac Tomkins, Gent. author of the Thoughts upon the aristocracy, from Mr. Peter Jenkins. 11p. 8°. 1835.

29235 [——] Ninth edition, with a postscript. 16p. 8°. 1835.

29236 [——] Thoughts on the ladies of the aristocracy. By Lydia Tomkins. 58p. 8°. 1835.

29237 [——] Second edition. 58p. 8°. 1835.

29238 [——] Thoughts upon the aristocracy of England. By Isaac Tomkins, Gent. 23p. 8°. 1835.

29239 [——] Eighth edition 23p. 8°. 1835.

29240 ★[——] [Another edition.] Strongly recommended for perusal. A sketch of the aristocracy of England, in the year 1835, by Isaac Tomkins, Gent. and a letter to that gentleman, on the same subject, by Mr. Peter Jenkins. 16p. 8°. 1835. *The FWA copy that belonged to William Pare.*

29241 [——] "We can't afford it!" Being Thoughts upon the aristocracy of England. Part the second. By Isaac Tomkins, Gent. 19p. 8°. 1835.

29242 [——] Third edition. 19p. 8°. 1835.

29243 BULL, G. S. "Morpeth, the friend of the oppressed!!" [An attack on Lord Morpeth's conduct during the election.] 3p. 8°. *Leeds,* [1835] *The Oastler copy.*

29244 [——] A remonstrance [against profanity in a recent election at Bradford]. 4p. 8°. *Bradford,* 1835. *The copy that belonged to Oastler, who attributed it to Bull in the manuscript index to his pamphlet collection.*

29245 CAMPBELL, ALEXANDER (1796–1870). Trial and self-defence of Alexander Campbell, operative, before the Exchequer Court, Edinburgh, for printing and publishing "The Tradesman," contrary to the infamous gagging Act. 30p. 8°. *Glasgow,* 1835.

29246 COBBETT, JOHN M. To the electors of Oldham. [An election address, dated: 26th June, 1835.] *s.sh.fol.* [*London,* 1835] [*Br.* 586]

29247 CRITO, *pseud.* Crito's first letter to the burgesses and freedmen of Beverley. [Dated: 24th September 1835.] 8p. 8°. *Beverley,* 1835.

29248 —— Crito's second letter to the burgesses and freedmen of Beverley. [Dated: December 1835.] 12p. 8°. *Beverley,* 1835.

29249 [DAVIS, CHARLES A.] Letters of Jack Downing, Major, Downingville Militia, second Brigade, to his old friend Mr. Dwight, of the New-York Daily Advertiser. From the latest New-York edition. 215p. 12°. 1835.

29250 DOUBLEDAY, T. A letter to the radical reformers of Newcastle upon Tyne, on the late election and its attendant circumstances. 10p. 8°. *Newcastle,* 1835.

29251 The **DUTY** of a Conservative at the present juncture. ⟨Reprinted from Fraser's Magazine for June, 1835.⟩ 12p. 8°. [1835]

29252 ENGLAND. Parliament. *House of Commons.* Hull Election. Proceedings before the Committee of the House of Commons, in the matter of the petition against the return of Col. Thomas Perronet Thompson, on... July 22nd, 23rd, 24th, 25th, 27th & 28th... 26p. 8°. *Hull,* [1835]

29253 FIRE away! [An election poster affirming the sobriety of the supporters of Hardy, one of the candidates for Bradford. Signed: No drunkard, and dated, January 7th, 1835.] *s.sh.fol. Bradford,* [1835] [*Br.* 585(1)] *The Oastler copy.*

29254 FOLLETT, SIR W. W. The speech of Sir William Follett [to his constituents], delivered at Exeter, October 21st, 1835. [With an introductory note signed: Eboracensis.] 16p. 8°. *Beverley,* 1835.

29255 FRANC-COES, OMERO, *pseud.* Peerage, primogeniture, and aristocracy of England; or a plan to dispose of these subjects so as to serve government, people and aristocracy in a manner much more safe, expeditious and beneficial than that imagined by Messrs. Tomkins, Jenkins, and Winterbottom. In a series of letters... 48p. 12°. 1835.

29256 FRANCE. *Chambre des Députés.* Session 1835. Procès-verbaux des séances relatives à l'affaire du journal Le Reformateur. 58p. 8°. *Paris,* 1835.

29257 HARDY the brave and Bradford the fair. [An election ballad.] *s.sh.fol. n.p.* [1835 ?] [*Br.* 561] *The Oastler copy.*

29258 HYPOCRISY unmasked, or an answer to Crito's first letter to the burgesses of Beverley. [Signed: A brother Burgess.] 8p. 8°. *Beverley,* 1835.

29259 KNIGHT, JAMES L., afterwards **BRUCE, SIR** J. L. K. Speech of Jas. Lewis Knight, Esq., K.C. against the iniquitous Corporation Bill...31st July and...1st August, 1835. 32p. *16°*. [1835]

29260 The **LIFE** of Daniel O'Connell, Esq., M.P. for Dublin. 32p. *8°*. [1835]

29261 To E. C. **LISTER,** one of our candidates. [Accusing him of being either a Whig or a Tory because he insinuates that working men are too ignorant to be trusted with the franchise. Signed: A real radical, and dated, January 9th, 1835.] *s.sh.fol. Bradford,* [1835] [*Br.* 585(2)] *The Oastler copy.*

29262 What should the **LORDS** do with the Corporation Reform Bill? With tables; showing the extent of its proposed constituency in comparison with the Parliamentary franchise. 63p. *8°*. 1835.

29263 M., T. W. Liberalism versus Toryism, or a review of the causes which have led to the present demoralized state of England, with hints as to a mode of restoring it to a moral state, by the reformation of its government and the adoption of a constitution, popular, economical and impartial. 47p. *8°*. 1835.

29264 M'GHEE, R. J. A letter to the Protestants of the United Kingdom, exhibiting the real principles of the Roman Catholic bishops and priests in Ireland, as contained in their standard of theology adopted in 1808...39p. *8°*. 1835.

29265 The **MAGISTRACY** of England, its abuses, and their remedy in popular election. By a barrister. 30p. *8°*. 1835.

29266 MANCHESTER OPERATIVE CONSERVATIVE ASSOCIATION. Proceedings of the first anniversary meeting...August 24th, 1835. (From the Manchester Courier.) 12p. *12°*. *Manchester,* [1835]

29267 Great **MEETING,** in support of corporation reform, held...on Tuesday, the 18th of August, 1835. 8p. *4°*. *Birmingham,* [1835] *See note to no.* 26519.

29268 MERCATOR, *pseud.* Address to the burgesses of Saint Mary's, and the Minster Ward, within the Borough of Beverley. 8p. *8°*. *Beverley,* 1835. *Attributed in a manuscript note on the title-page and at the end of the text to 'Mr. Tigar, Grovehill'.*

29269 MIDDLESEX REFORM CLUB. Address of the...Club. 23d. April, 1835. [Signed: Jos. Davies, secretary.] 12p. *12°*. [1835]

For the **NEW POLITICAL REGISTER,** *see* vol. III, *Periodicals list.*

29270 Have you heard the **NEWS?** An address to the freemen of all corporations of Great Britain, upon the proposed destruction of their rights by the Whig ministry. By a Freeman. 12p. *8°*. 1835.

29271 O'CONNELL, D. A letter from Daniel O'Connell, Esq. M.P., to His Grace the Duke of Wellington. 8p. *8°*. 1835.

29272 —— Limbird's edition. The speech of Daniel O'Connell, Esq. M.P. at a public dinner at Manchester...September 10th, 1835. 8p. *8°*. 1835.

29273 —— Limbird's edition. The speech of Daniel O'Connell, Esq. M.P. at a public dinner at Newcastle-on-Tyne...September 14, 1835. 8p. *8°*. 1835.

29274 —— Limbird's edition. The speech of Daniel

O'Connell, Esq. M.P. at a public dinner in Edinburgh...September 17th, 1835. 8p. *8°*. 1835.

29275 —— Limbird's edition. The speech of Daniel O'Connell, Esq. M.P. in answer to an address presented to him from the trades' societies, on his arrival in Edinburgh on...September 17th, 1835. 8p. *8°*. 1835.

29276 PEEL, SIR ROBERT, *2nd Bart.* Speech of the Right Honourable Sir Robert Peel, Bart., Chancellor of the Exchequer...in the House of Commons, February 24, 1835, on the motion of an address of thanks to His Majesty in answer to His most gracious speech. 20p. *8°*. *Edinburgh,* 1835.

29277 —— Speech of the Right Hon. Sir Robert Peel, Bart, M.P. delivered at the dinner given to him by the merchants, bankers and traders of the City of London, at Merchant Tailors' Hall, on...11th May, 1835. Published for the City of London Conservative Association. 23p. *8°*. [1835]

29278 —— Published by authority...Eighth edition. 12p. *8°*. 1835.

29279 —— Published by authority. The corrected speech of Sir Robert Peel, Bart. on the Irish Church Bill, 21st July, 1835. Second edition. 32p. *8°*. 1835.

29280 The **PEOPLE** or the peerage? With an introductory letter to Edward Lytton Bulwer, Esq. [signed: One of the people]. Second edition. 18p. *8°*. 1835.

29281 PILGRIMAGE and pedigree of liberty. Illustrated by nine characteristic engravings. By a true Radical. 24p. *8°*. *London, Manchester, &c.,* [1835?]

29282 PLACE, F. The peers and the people: municipal reform: corn laws: taxes on knowledge. By Francis Place. Wholesale obstructiveness of the Lords. By H. S. Chapman. Votes of Mr. George Frederick Young, by H.S.C. Edited by J. A. Roebuck, M.P. 16p. *8°*. [*London,* 1835]

29283 PORTUGAL. *Commission for the Expeditions in favour of Donna Maria.* Reports, transmitted to the Portuguese Government, of the proceedings of the Commission...in the years 1831, 1832 and 1833; and of the operations of the financial agent to the Portuguese Government [J. Alvarez y Mendizabal], from August 1833 to August 1834. 110p. *8°*. 1835. *The copy presented by M. Alvarez y Mendizabal to Viscount Melbourne, with an inscription on the flyleaf.*

29284 PUCK, *pseud.* A letter to the commonalty and newly created burgesses of Beverley. [A reply to 'Crito's first letter to the burgesses'.] 8p. *8°*. *Hull,* 1835.

29285 To the real old well-tried radical **REFORMERS** of Bradford. [An election poster. Signed: A real Radical, and dated, January 7th, 1835. Asking why the West Riding candidates, Viscount Morpeth and Sir George Strickland, have not been questioned about the radical reform programme.] *s.sh.fol. Bradford,* [1835] [*Br.* 585(3)] *The Oastler copy.*

29286 RICHARDS, JOHN, *(fl. 1832–1837).* A letter to Lord Brougham, in reply to Isaac Tomkins, Gent. and Mr. Peter Jenkins. 29p. *8°*. 1835.

29287 SEINE, *Département de la. Cour d'Assises.* Procès du Réformateur. Cour d'Assises de la Seine. Audience du 27 octobre, 1835. 32p. *8°*. *Versailles,* [1835] *Edited by A. Dupoty, editor of the Réformateur.*

29288 ★The **"SPECTATOR'S"** complete lists of

the new House of Commons, and the numbers at the close of the polls throughout the kingdom...To which is added, a list of the late and present Ministry and the salary attached to each office. 16p. *8°*. [*London*, 1835] *The FWA copy, that belonged to William Pare.*

29289 STANLEY, E. G. G. S., *14th Earl of Derby.* Opinion of Lord Stanley on the unanswerable nature of the facts and arguments contained in Sir R. Peel's eloquent speech [of July 21, 1835, on the Irish Church Bill]. 2p. *8°*. *n.p.* [1835]

29290 Journal Office...January 10, 1835. **TRIUMPH** of reform! Great and overwhelming majority in favour of Attwood and Scholefield. Full reports of the election...in Birmingham...including the final close of the poll, with the speeches on that occasion. 15p. *4°*. *Birmingham*, 1835. *See note to no.* 26519.

29291 —— [Another edition.] Journal Office, Monday evening, January 12, 1835...including the official announcement of the poll, and the speeches of the members, &c., at the Town-hall this day. 15p. *4°*. *Birmingham*, 1835. *See note to no.* 26519.

29292 Free **VOTES** or faggot votes: or the way to repeal the Chandos clause and to check-mate the aristoc-racy. With suggestions for the formation of free vote clubs. 8p. *12°*. *Manchester*, [1835 ?]

29293 [**WADE**, JOHN.] The black book: an exposition of abuses in Church and State, courts of law, municipal corporations, and public companies; with a précis of the House of Commons, past, present, and to come. A new edition, greatly enlarged and corrected. By the original editor. With an appendix. 683p. *8°*. 1835. *For other editions, see* 1820.

29294 —— Appendix to The black book: an exposition of the principles and practices of the Reform Ministry and Parliament...and prospects of Tory mis-rule...By the original editor. Sixth edition, with the 'Crisis' and a characteristic list of the Anti-Reform Government. 132p. *8°*. 1835. *This is not the same appendix as that published with the title*, New Parliament. An appendix to The black book, *in 1826 (q.v.).*

29295 WINTERBOTTOM, TIMOTHY, *pseud.* A letter to Isaac Tomkins and Peter Jenkins on primogeniture. 30p. *8°*. 1835.

29296 A **YARN** spun for the use of the son of the cotton-spinner. By an operative. [A criticism, addressed to Sir Robert Peel, of his speech at Merchant Taylors' Hall, 11 May, 1835.] 20p. *8°*. 1835.

SOCIALISM

29297 ASSOCIATION OF ALL CLASSES OF ALL NATIONS. Social Bible. Laws & regulations of the Association...Social hymns for the use of friends of the rational system of society. lxii, 70p. *12°*. *Manchester*, 1835. *For another edition, issued by the Rational Society, see* 1840.

29298 FOURIER, F. C. M. La fausse industrie morcelée, répugnante, mensongère, et l'antidote, l'industrie naturelle, combinée, attrayante, véridique, donnant quadruple produit. 2 vols. *12°*. *Paris*, 1835–36. *The copy that belonged to Victor Considérant.*

29299 LOUDON, M. Philanthropic economy; or, the philosophy of happiness, practically applied to the social, political, and commercial relations of Great Britain. 312p. *8°*. 1835. *For selections from this work, see* 1842 (CORN LAWS).

29300 *Great public **MEETING** to be held on the 1st day of May, 1835, at the Institution, 14, Charlotte Street, Fitzroy Square...[to form the 'Association of All Classes of All Nations']. [Extracted from The New Moral World.] *s.sh.fol.* [*London*, 1835] *The FWA copy, that belonged to William Pare.*

29301 The **POWER** of the people, or, the way to wealth, prosperity & peace: a social pamphlet: shewing how the working classes may become possessed of immence [*sic*] landed estates... 12p. *12°*. *Leeds*, [1835 ?].

29302 WRIGHT, F. Course of popular lectures; with three addresses...[With 'Supplement course of lectures'.] 220p. *8°*. [1835 ?] *The Supplement is dated 1834.*

29303 —— Supplement course of lectures, containing the last four lectures delivered in the United States. 21, 20, 13, 22p. *12°*. *New York*, 1835. *For other editions of the Course of lectures and the Supplement, see* 1829.

MISCELLANEOUS

29304 BLOMFIELD, C. J., *Bishop of London.* The speech of Charles James, Lord Bishop of London, in the House of Lords August 24th 1835, on the Irish Church Bill. 30p. *8°*. 1835. *The copy that belonged to Earl De Grey, with his signature on the title-page.*

29305 ESTABLISHED CHURCH SOCIETY. The argument for national church-establishments stated, with some remarks upon the value of the English Church establishment. Fourth edition...No. II. 36p. *8°*. 1835.

29306 FRIENDS OF CIVIL AND RELIGIOUS LIBERTY. [*Begin.*] At a meeting of the Friends of Civil and Religious Liberty, held at the house of Mr. Joseph Morris...on...May 18, 1835, it was unanimously resolved, that a committee should be immediately formed for...watching the...proceedings in connection with the imprisonment of Mr. John Childs [for his refusal, as a matter of conscience, to pay church rates. Signed: C. J. Thomas, secretary]. *s.sh.fol. Bungay*, [1835]

29307 GREY, H. G., *3rd Earl Grey.* Speech of the Right Honourable Lord Viscount Howick, in the House of Commons on...July 22, 1835, respecting the Church establishment (Ireland). Extracted from the "Mirror of Parliament." 22p. *8°*. 1835.

29308 HUTCHISON, G. A treatise on the causes and principles of meteorological phenomena. Also, two essays; the one on marsh fevers; the other on the system of equality, proposed by Mr. Owen of New Lanark, for ameliorating the condition of mankind. 646p. *8°. Glasgow, Edinburgh, &c.*, 1835.

29309 JORDAN, T. The Goldsmiths jubile: or, Londons triumphs. Containing, a description of the several pageants...with the speeches spoken on each pageant. Performed Octob. 29, 1674, for the entertainment of...Sir Robert Vyner, Kt & Bart, Lord Mayor of the City of London: at the proper costs and charges of the Worshipful Company of Goldsmiths... 12p. *8°.* 1674 [1835]

29310 OASTLER, R. The Huddersfield Dissenters stark staring mad!!! because the mask has fallen!!!! The fourth letter to Edward Baines, Esq. M.P. 8p. *8°. Leeds*, [1835] *Oastler's own copy.*

29311 O'CONNELL, D. O'Connell's defence of the Catholics...To Mr. Buchan, of Kelloe. 8p. *8°. [London,* 1835]

29312 PUYCOUSIN, E. DE. Bibliothèque Méridionale. Proscenium. [The outline of a scheme for publishing books by authors from the Midi.] 96p. *8°. Paris & London*, 1835.

29313 REFORM ASSOCIATION. The Irish Church. The Reform Association to the reformers of England, Scotland and Wales. 39p. *8°.* [1835]

29314 RIDGWAY, JAMES, & SONS. 169 Piccadilly, November 1835. Prospectus of the British and Foreign Review; or, European Quarterly Journal. With a catalogue of splendidly illustrated works on botany, gardening, agriculture, geology, &c.&c.&c. [16], 3p. *8°. [London,* 1835 ?]

29315 The **SIGNS** of the times; in which the evils and dangers of the present system of tithes and regium donum are exposed, and some late improvements in Church and State pointed out by the Eastern Presbytery of the Reformed Presbyterian Church in Ireland. Second edition. 40p. *12°. Belfast*, 1835.

29316 WATKINS, H. G. Fifth edition. The established religion a national blessing. [A sermon.] With... notes. 24p. *8°.* 1835.

1836

GENERAL

29317 ALLART, H. T. S. S. A. La femme et la démocratie de nos temps. 24p. *8°. Paris*, 1836.

29318 BLACKER, W. The claims of the landed interests to legislative protection considered; with reference to the manner in which the manufacturing, commercial and agricultural classes contribute to national wealth and prosperity; and suitable remedies for relieving the distress of the latter suggested... 294p. *8°. London & Dublin*, 1836.

29319 BLANQUI, J. A. Histoire de l'économie politique, cours fait au Conservatoire des Arts et Métiers. 59p. *8°. Paris*, [1836 ?]

29320 The **BRITISH ALMANAC** of the Society for the Diffusion of Useful Knowledge, for...1836. [With 'The companion to the Almanac; or year-book of general information'.] 96, 250p. *12°.* [1836] *For other editions, see* 1828.

29321 [BROUGHAM, H. P., *Baron Brougham and Vaux* ?] Lectures on political economy, read in manuscript at the Mechanics' Institution, Glasgow, in the summer of MDCCCXXXV. (Private.) 103p. *8°. Glasgow*, 1836. *An introductory note states that the Lectures are usually ascribed to, and certainly revised by, Lord Brougham.*

29322 COBBETT, W. The beauties of Cobbett. Selected from his various works. [Edited by Jesse Oldfield.] No. I[-V]. p.[1]-142. *8°.* [1836]

29323 —— Cobbett's legacy to Peel; or, an inquiry with respect to what the Right Honourable Baronet will now do with the House of Commons, with Ireland, with the English Church and the Dissenters, with the swarms of pensioners, &c., with the Crown lands, and the Army, with the currency and the debt. In six letters. 192p. *16°.* 1836.

29324 [COBDEN, R.] England, Ireland, and America ...Fourth edition. 40p. *8°. Edinburgh, London, &c.*, 1836.

29325 *[——]* Fifth edition. 40p. *8°. Edinburgh, London, &c.*, 1836. *The FWA copy, that belonged to William Pare. For other editions, see* 1835.

29326 [——] Russia. By a Manchester manufacturer; author of "England, Ireland, and America"... 52p. *8°. Edinburgh, London, &c.*, 1836.

29327 FOX, WILLIAM J. Finsbury lectures. Reports of lectures delivered at the Chapel in South Place, Finsbury...No. VII. Clerical morality... 32p. *8°.* 1836. *For other lectures in this series, see* 1835.

29328 [GROSSE, E.] Dictionnaire statistique du département de la Meurthe, contenant une introduction historique sur le pays, avec une notice sur chacune de ses villes, bourgs, villages, hameaux, censes, rivières, ruisseaux, étangs et montagnes; par M. E.G★★★. Tome premier. cxiii, 190p. *8°. Lunéville*, 1836.

29329 HEAD, SIR G. A home tour through the manufacturing districts of England, in the summer of 1835. 434p. *8°.* 1836. *See also* 1840.

29330 HEEREN, A. H. L. Historical treatises: The political consequences of the Reformation. The rise, progress, and practical influence of political theories. The rise and growth of the continental interests of Great Britain. Translated from the German. 441p. *8°. Oxford*, 1836.

29331 HOUGH, W. Simplification of His Majesty's and hon'ble E.I. Company's Mutiny Acts & Articles of War, proposed military police and legislative enactments for courts of inquiry, inquest & ct. of requests, to render crying down credit a bar to the cognizance of soldier's debts. Precedents confirmed by authority... 291p. *8°. Calcutta*, 1836.

29332 HUISH, R. Memoirs of the late William Cobbett...Embracing all the interesting events of his memorable life, obtained from private and confidential sources; also a critical analysis of his...writings... 2 vols. 8°. 1836.

29333 HUSSEY, R. An essay on the ancient weights and money, and the Roman and Greek liquid measures, with an appendix on the Roman and Greek foot. 254p. 8°. *Oxford & London, 1836. Presentation copy from the author to Cornelius Walford.*

29334 KIDD, W. Kidd's London directory, on a novel plan. The book of books; or, London as it is, and as it ought to be: a hand-book showing...how to enjoy London, and containing hints invaluable, on the frauds, – deceptions, – and iniquities, – practised in the Metropolis ...Illustrated...by G. & R. Cruikshank, Seymour & Bonner. 4 vols. *12°*. [1836?]

29335 *LAING, SAMUEL (1780–1868). Journal of a residence in Norway, during the years 1834, 1835, and 1836; made with a view to inquire into the moral and political economy of that country, and the condition of its inhabitants. 482p. 8°. 1836. *The copy that belonged to George Grote. See also 1837.*

29336 LEIGH, S. Leigh's new pocket road-book of Scotland, containing an account of all the direct and cross roads; together with a description of every remarkable place...New edition, considerably enlarged and improved. 494p. *12°*. 1836.

29337 LEWIS, SIR GEORGE C., *Bart.* On local disturbances in Ireland; and on the Irish Church question. 458p. 8°. 1836.

29338 MACKENZIE, JAMES. The general grievances and oppression of the isles of Orkney and Shetland. 112p. 8°. *Edinburgh & London, 1836.* [*Hanson 6386n*] *A reprint, edited with memoir and notes by A. G. Groat and H. Cheyne, of the edition issued anonymously in 1750.*

29339 M'QUEEN, J. General statistics of the British Empire. 224p. 8°. 1836.

29340 MALTHUS, T. R. Principles of political economy considered with a view to their practical application...Second edition with considerable additions from the author's own manuscript and an original memoir [by W. Otter]. liv, 446p. 8°. 1836. *For other editions, see 1820.*

29341 MOCKETT, J. Mockett's journal. A collection of interesting matters, relating to remarkable personages, ancient buildings, manners and customs...from the year 50. Also, particulars of various churches...with observations on agriculture...and the price of corn, cattle, and labour... 328p. 8°. *Canterbury, 1836.*

29342 MORETON, HON. A. H. Civilization or a brief analysis of the natural laws that regulate the numbers and condition of mankind. 216p. 8°. 1836.

29343 MULLINS, E. A treatise on the magistracy of England, and the origin and expenditure of county rates; illustrating the present defective management of county financial affairs...To which is subjoined a full abstract of Mr. Hume's Bill, to authorize the rate-payers in every county in England and Wales to elect a council and auditors of accounts...Second edition. 119p. 8°. 1836.

29344 NOBLE, J. The professional practice of architects, and that of measuring surveyors, and reference to builders...from the time of the...Earl of Burlington. 216p. 8°. 1836.

29345 OASTLER, R. Mr. Oastler's three letters to Mr. Hetherington. [On the state of the country, December 1835–January 1836.] 12p. *12°*. [*London,* 1836] *Oastler's own copy.*

29346 PORTER, G. R. The progress of the nation, in its various social and economical relations, from the beginning of the nineteenth century to the present time... 3 vols. 8°. 1836–43. *See also 1837.*

29347 The **POST-OFFICE** annual directory for 1836–37: containing an alphabetical list of the merchants, traders, manufacturers, and principal inhabitants: and a second list of the names...in Glasgow and suburbs... arranged under each...trade or profession: with a street directory: and an appendix...Ninth publication. 341, 121p. *12°*. *Glasgow, 1836. See also 1829, 1842.*

29348 The **POST-OFFICE** London directory for 1836...By B. Critchett. The thirty-seventh edition. [With 'A new guide to stagecoaches, waggons, carts, vessels, &c. for 1836...The thirty-fourth edition. By B. Critchett'.] 727, 168p. *12°*. [1836] *See also* 1805 (Post-Office annual directory), 1810, 1813, 1814, 1820 (Post Office London directory), 1823, 1825, 1830, 1832, 1834, 1841.

29349 QUETELET, L. A. J. Sur l'homme et le développement de ses facultés, ou essai de physique sociale... 2 vols. *12°*. *Bruxelles, 1836. For other editions, see 1835.*

29350 RAMSAY, SIR G., *Bart.* An essay on the distribution of wealth. 506p. 8°. *Edinburgh & London, 1836.*

29351 RAUMER, F. L. G. VON. England in 1835: being a series of letters written to friends in Germany, during a residence in London and excursions into the provinces...Translated from the German by Sarah Austin [and H. E. Lloyd]. 3 vols. 8°. 1836. *The copy that belonged to the Brighton Book Society, with its rules and circulation list at the front of vol. 1.*

29352 REASONS and plans for the encouragement of agriculture, 1836. No. I[–III]. [With special reference to the price of tallow and the manufacture of soap.] 59p. 8°. 1836.

29353 RICE, THOMAS S., *Baron Monteagle.* The Budget. Speech of the Right Honourable T. S. Rice, (Chancellor of the Exchequer,) in the House of Commons; Friday, May 6, 1836. 36p. 8°. 1836.

29354 *[RICHARDS, JAMES.] A letter addressed to the late Earl of Liverpool, in the year 1822, shewing that unjust taxation is the cause of the evils complained of, with a just system then suggested. After which was added, preliminary observations, and now a form of petition for the consideration of the people generally of the United Kingdom. 75p. 8°. *Birmingham* [*& London*], 1836. *The FWA copy, that belonged to William Pare. For other editions, see 1822.*

29355 ROBERTS, S. The Gypsies: their origin, continuance, and destination. The fourth edition, greatly enlarged. 259p. 8°. 1836.

29356 SAY, J. B. A treatise on political economy; or the production, distribution, and consumption of wealth ...Translated from the fourth edition of the French, by C. R. Prinsep, M.A. with notes by the translator. New American edition. Containing a translation of the introduction, and additional notes, by Clement C. Biddle... 488p. 8°. *Philadelphia, 1836. For other editions, see 1803.*

29357 SAY, L. Études sur la richesse des nations, et réfutation des principales erreurs en économie politique. 172p. 8°. *Paris, 1836.*

29358 SEDGWICK, T. Public and private economy ...Part first [–second]. Vols. 1–2. *12°. New-York, 1836–38.*

29359 SENIOR, N. W. An outline of the science of political economy. [The following pages form the article Political economy in the Encyclopædia Metropolitana.] p.129–224. *4°.* 1836. *Two copies: one a presentation copy, with accompanying letter from the author to William Tinney; the other is interleaved, with manuscript notes by Archbishop Whately. See also* 1850. *For the letter, see* vol. III, *A.L.* 300.

29360 —— Principes fondamentaux de l'économie politique, tirés de leçons édites et inédites de Mr. N.-W. Senior, Professeur émérite d'économie politique à l'Université d'Oxford, par le Cte Jean Arrivabene. 403p. *8°. Paris,* 1836.

29361 SIMONDE DE SISMONDI, J. C. L. Études sur les sciences sociales. 3 vols. *8°. Paris & Strasbourg,* 1836–38. *Presentation copy, with a letter in vol.* 1, *from the author to J. W. Bruce. Contents: 1. Études sur les constitutions des peuples libres. 2–3. Études sur l'économie politique.*

29362 SOCIETY FOR THE ENCOURAGEMENT OF DOMESTIC INDUSTRY. The agricultural and industrial magazine of the Society... Vol. 1 [Nos. 1–20, October 1834–? August 1835.] *8°.* 1836. *A reissue of the sheets of the periodical, for which see* vol. III, *Periodicals list,* Agricultural and industrial magazine.

29363 SPENCE, W. On agricultural distress as connected with depreciation of the currency. A letter addressed to the editor of the Agricultural & Industrial Magazine...(From the Hull Rockingham of Jan. 23, 1836). 8p. *8°. Hull,* [1836]

29364 STATISTICAL SOCIETY OF LONDON. First series of questions circulated by the Statistical Society of London. [32]p. *8°.* 1836.

29365 —— Second annual report of the Council of the Statistical Society of London, with the regulations of the Society, and a list of the fellows, &c. March, 1836. 39p. *8°.* 1836. *See also* 1837.

29366 THOUGHTS on the elements of civil government, tending to prove as a fundamental principle...that the lower orders of society, the populace, cannot, consistently with the stability of good government, be suffered to exercise any share of political power or controlling influence over the constituted government. By a British jurist. 161p. *8°. London & Dublin,* 1836.

29367 VAGINA EMARESE, F. Dei primi elementi dell' economia politica seconde i progressi della scienza. Libri quattro di Filiberto d'Emarese Intendente della Provincia del' Ciablese con aggiunta d'una memoria sui vantaggi risultanti dalla coltura dei pubblici pascoli. 283p. *8°. Torino,* 1836.

29368 WAGNER, JOHANN J. System der Privatökonomie. Das Ganze des Familienhaushaltes für das gebildete Publikum dargestellt. 264p. *8°. Anarau,* 1836.

29369 WALKER, THOMAS (1784–1836). The original...Second edition. [Consisting of Vol. 1 (nos. 1–27), and Vol. 2 (nos. 28 and 29).] 444p. *8°.* 1836. *Originally published as a periodical in 1835, for which see* vol. III, *Periodicals list,* Original.

29370 [WHATELY, R., *Archbishop of Dublin.*] Easy lessons on money matters; for the use of young people. Published under the direction of the Committee of General Literature and Education, appointed by the Society for Promoting Christian Knowledge. The third edition. 86p. *16°.* 1836. *For another edition, see* 1835.

29371 WHEELER, JAMES. Manchester: its political, social and commercial history, ancient and modern. 538p. *12°. London & Manchester,* 1836. *Presentation copy from the author to Jane Lerescher.*

29372 Ueber den deutschen **ZOLLVEREIN.** 71p. *8°. Berlin,* 1836.

AGRICULTURE

29373 The **AGRICULTURAL AND HORTICULTURAL ANNUAL** for 1836, or annual register of the most important discoveries and improvements in farming, gardening, & floriculture... 322p. *12°. London & Lewes: Baxter & Son,* 1836.

29374 CAUGHY, J. The farmer's friend, No. I. An explanation of the failures in the growth of the potato... By an original observer. 24p. *12°. Belfast,* 1836.

29375 —— No. III. On the origin, formation, constituents, and use of turf bog...By a critical observer. 16p. *12°. Belfast,* 1836.

29376 CAYLEY, EDWARD S. Agricultural Committee of 1836. A letter to H. Handley, Esq., M.P., (a member of the late Committee on agricultural distress in the House of Commons,) on the proceedings of that Committee, and in answer to Mr. Shaw Lefevre's pamphlet. 22p. *8°. York & London,* 1836.

29377 *FAUCHER, L. État et tendence de la propriété en France. [Extrait de la Revue des Deux Mondes, livraison du 1er novembre 1836.] 28p. *8°. Paris,* 1836. *Presentation copy from the author to George Grote.*

29378 HIGHLAND AND AGRICULTURAL SOCIETY OF SCOTLAND. An itinerating agricultural book club has been founded in south Britain, for disseminating the valuable practical information conveyed in the quarterly journals, prize essays and transactions of the Agricultural Society of Scotland...[A prospectus. With a list of the members of the Highland and Agricultural Society of Scotland, 1835.] 16p. *8°. Brighton,* 1836.

29379 HILLYARD, C. A summary of practical farming; with observations on the breeding & feeding of sheep & cattle; on rents and tithes; and on the present state of agriculture. 52p. *12°. Northampton, London, &c.,* [1836] *See also* 1840, 1844.

29380 HOWE, . Howe, upon assessment; containing observations & improvements, which he has been making for many years. 18p. *8°. Hastings, London, &c.,* [1836?]

29381 KELLY, WILLIAM, *steward.* An essay on the general management of villa farms, the manures attainable, and applicable to such farms; also, a mode of cultivating two acres of ground, whereby eight cows can be fed throughout the year... 80p. *12°. Dublin,* 1836.

29382 LAWSON, PETER, **& SON.** Agriculturist's manual; being a familiar description of the agricultural plants cultivated in Europe, including practical observations respecting those suited to...Great Britain; and forming a report of Lawson's Agricultural Museum in Edinburgh. 430p. *8°. Edinburgh, London, &c.*, 1836.

29383 LE COUTEUR, SIR J. On the varieties, properties, and classification, of wheat. 122p. *8°. Jersey & London*, [1836] *Presentation copy from the author to Professor Graham. See also 1837.*

29384 LEFEVRE, C. S., *Viscount Eversley.* Remarks on the present state of agriculture. In a letter addressed to his constituents...Session 1836. 39p. *8°.* 1836.

29385 LEWIS, GEORGE, *tenant.* Observations on the present state and future prospects of agriculture, illustrative of the advantages of an experimental farm, being a fuller development of the author's views, first made public in a communication addressed to the Highland Society of Scotland. 123p. *8°. Cupar, Edinburgh, &c.*, 1836.

29386 LONDON. Livery Companies. *Skinners.* The Skinners' Company versus the Honourable the Irish Society and others. Proceedings upon the motion for a receiver, at the suit of the Skinners' Company, commencing November 23, 1835, in His Majesty's High Court of Chancery...[A dispute about the estates near Londonderry belonging to the Skinners' Company.] 608p. *8°.* 1836.

29387 MEMORANDUM respecting a cheap means of procuring a great increase of manure. July, 1836. 8p. *8°. Maybole*, 1836.

29388 MURRAY, HON. JAMES. Agricultural distress.

Hints to landlords & tenants upon the subject of the present agricultural distress. 117p. *8°.* 1836.

29389 PARKINSON, RICHARD (*fl.* 1836). The abolition of the malt-tax advocated; and the question enlarged upon as affecting agriculture and the public. 33p. *8°.* 1836. *Presentation copy from the author to Paul Bright.*

29390 REMARKS on the proposed changes in the laws regulating the salmon fishery of Scotland. 55p. *8°.* 1836.

29391 ROYAL ASIATIC SOCIETY. Minutes of a committee appointed to report to the council on the practicability and expediency of carrying into effect the recommendation of the Committee of Correspondence for the formation of a committee of trade and agriculture. May 7, 1836. [With 'Proceedings of a general meeting... held...19th of March, 1836'.] 30, 3p. *8°.* 1836.

29392 SMITH, THOMAS, *mine and land agent.* The miner's guide, being a description and illustration of a chart of sections of the principal mines of coal and ironstone in the counties of Stafford, Salop, Warwick, and Durham... 207p. *12°. London & Birmingham*, 1836.

29393 SOCIETY OF THE GOVERNOR AND ASSISTANTS IN LONDON, OF THE NEW PLANTATION IN ULSTER. Report of the deputation [E. Tickner, J. Harmer, J. K. Hooper, J. E. Davies] appointed by the honourable the Irish Society to visit the City of London's plantation in Ireland in the year 1836. 139p. *8°.* 1836. *See also* 1826 (GENERAL), 1834 (AGRICULTURE), 1835, 1838, 1841.

POPULATION

29394 ANGEVILLE, A. D'., *Comte.* Essai sur la statistique de la population française, considérée sous quelques-uns de ses rapports physiques et moraux. [With appendix of June 1837.] 356, xxxvp. *4°. Bourg*, 1836[–37]

29395 CLELAND, J. A historical account of bills of mortality, and the probability of human life, in Glasgow and other large towns. 16p. *8°. Glasgow*, 1836.

29396 IVERNOIS, SIR F. D'. De la fécondité et de la mortalité proportionnelles des peuples, considérées comme mesures de leur aisance et de leur civilisation. Tiré de la Bibliothèque Universelle, septembre 1835. 49p. *8°. Genève*, 1836. *Presentation copy, with inscription, from the author to N. W. Senior. The author's sixth (final) essay on the subject.*

29397 LOUDON, C. The equilibrium of population and sustenance demonstrated; showing, on physiological and statistical grounds, the means of obviating the fears

of the late Mr. Malthus and his followers. 15p. *8°. Leamington-Spa & London*, 1836. *Presentation copy, with inscription, from the author to N. W. Senior.* *Another, the FWA copy, belonged to William Pare.*

29398 REMARKS on the establishment in Ireland, of a general register of births, marriages & deaths, in a letter to Thomas Drummond, Esq. Under Secretary of Ireland. 11p. *8°. Dublin*, 1836.

29399 YATES, JAMES. Observations on Lord John Russell's Bill for registering births, deaths, and marriages in England, with the outlines of a plan for registering births, deaths, and marriages in Great Britain and Ireland. 48p. *8°.* 1836.

29400 —— Postscript to Observations on Lord John Russell's Bill...in reply to the Rev. W. H. Hale's remarks on the same subject. p.[49]–64. *8°.* 1836. *Paginated in sequence with the original work.*

TRADES & MANUFACTURES

29401 BARLOW, P. A treatise on the manufactures and machinery of Great Britain...To which is prefixed, an introductory view of the principles of manufactures, by Charles Babbage...Forming a portion of the Encyclopædia Metropolitana [Vol. VII]. 834p., 87 plates. *4°. London, Oxford, &c.*, 1836.

29402 COMMITTEE OF MASTER CABINET MAKERS AND JOURNEYMEN. The London cabinet makers' union book of prices. By a committee of

masters and journeymen. 474p. *4°.* 1836. *For another edition, see* 1824; *for supplements, see* 1831 *and* 1837.

29403 DUFRÉNOY, O. P. A. P. On the use of hot air in the iron works of England and Scotland. Translated from a report, made to the Director General of Mines in France, by M. Dufrénoy, in 1834. 103p. *8°.* 1836.

29404 DUPIN, F. P. C., *Baron.* Rapport du jury

central sur les produits de l'industrie française exposées en 1834... 3 vols. *8°. Paris*, 1836.

29405 FAIRBAIRN, Sir W., *Bart.* Reservoirs on the river Bann, in the county of Down, Ireland, for more effectually supplying the mills with water. 23p. *8°. Manchester*, 1836.

29406 GRAHAM, A. The impolicy of the tax on cotton wool, as aggravated by the progress and capabilities of foreign countries in cotton manufactures...[With an appendix.] 59, 49p. *8°. Glasgow: The Associated Cotton Spinners*, 1836.

29407 —— Second edition. 59, 49p. *8°. Glasgow: The Associated Cotton Spinners*, 1836. *Presentation copy to Sir Harry Verney.*

29408 HEBERT, Luke. The engineer's and mechanic's encyclopædia, comprehending practical illustrations of the machinery and processes employed in every description of manufacture of the British Empire... 2 vols. *8°*. 1836.

29409 LARDNER, D. The steam engine familiarly explained and illustrated; with an historical sketch of its invention and progressive improvement; its applications to navigation and railways; with plain maxims for railway speculators...Fifth edition, considerably enlarged. 379p. *12°*. 1836. *The Rastrick copy. See also* 1840.

29410 MURPHY, John. A treatise on the art of weaving, with calculations and tables for the use of manufacturers...Fifth edition, revised and enlarged. 518p. *8°. Glasgow & Edinburgh*, 1836. *For another edition, see* 1827.

29411 PARTINGTON, C. F. A popular and descriptive account of the steam engine...and on steam navigation; with an appendix of patents and Parliamentary Papers...Third edition, corrected and enlarged... 330p. *8°*. 1836. *For other editions, see* 1822.

29412 PATENT MARINE KITCHEN & PURIFYING SEA WATER COMPANY. Purification of sea water. [Proceedings and resolutions at a general meeting, 20 April, 1836, concerning the formation of a new company.] *s.sh.8°. n.p.* [1836]

29413 —— [*Endorsed:*] Patent Marine Kitchen and Purifying Sea Water Company...[A prospectus, dated: 30 April, 1836.] 3p. *fol.* [*London*, 1836]

29414 ROYAL SOCIETY. Proceedings of the Excise Committee, with documents relating thereto. [Concerning technical methods of assessing the excise duty payable on spirits. The meetings took place between November 1834 and March 1836.] 37p. *8°. n.p.* [1836] *See also* 1834.

29415 UNITED KINGDOM BEET ROOT SUGAR ASSOCIATION. Prospectus... [4]p. *fol. Southwark*, [1836 ?]

29416 URE, A. The cotton manufacture of Great Britain systematically investigated...with an introductory view of its comparative state in foreign countries... 2 vols. *12°*. 1836.

29417 WHITE, George S. Memoir of Samuel Slater, the father of American manufactures. Connected with a history of the rise and progress of the cotton manufacture in England and America. With remarks on the moral influence of manufactories in the United States...Second edition. 448p. *8°. Philadelphia*, 1836.

29418 WILDEY, W. Captain Wildey's substitute for horse-hair, straw, flock, cotton, wool, tow, alva marina and other substances now in general use for mattresses, pillows... 4p. *fol.* [*London*, 1836] *With an accompanying letter from Capt. Wildey to Sir John Phillipart soliciting his support, for which see* vol. III, *A.L.* 231/2.

COMMERCE

29419 ADDRESS to the people of Great Britain, explanatory of our commercial relations with the Empire of China, and of the course of policy by which it may be rendered an almost unbounded field for British commerce. By a visitor to China. 127p. *8°*. 1836.

29420 FAIRBAIRN, H. A letter to the Governor of the Bank of England, on the present state of trade, and influence of the banking institutions of the country. [With special reference to the cotton and iron trades.] 15p. *8°*. 1836.

29421 FRANCE. *Administration des Douanes.* Tableau général du commerce de la France avec ses colonies et les puissances étrangères, pendant l'année 1835. 422p. *4°. Paris*, 1836. *The copy that belonged to Michel Chevalier, with his book-plate.*

29422 —— *Laws, etc.* Code de commerce expliqué par ses motifs, par des exemples et par la jurisprudence... Suivi d'un formulaire des actes de commerce...Cinquième édition, augmentée du texte des arrêts-principes. Par J. A. Rogron. 712p. *12°. Paris*, 1836. *For other editions, see* 1807.

29423 HUME, James D. The laws of the customs, compiled by direction of the Lords Commissioners of His Majesty's Treasury...with notes, and a general index, and supplements for the years 1834, 1835, and 1836. 672, 32, 94p. *8°*. 1836. *For another edition, see* 1828.

29424 MATHESON, Sir J., *Bart.* The present position and prospects of the British trade with China; together with an outline of some leading occurrences in its past history. 135p. *8°*. 1836.

29425 NOTICE sur le commerce de la côte occidentale de l'Amérique du Sud, et sur le commerce avec Manille. Janvier 1836. 143p. *8°. Bruxelles*, [1836]

29426 PERKINS, E. E. A treatise on haberdashery and hosiery; including the Manchester, Scotch, silk, linen and woollen departments...With...remarks on the general retail trade...Fourth edition, carefully revised and corrected...including particulars of the Institution formed for the benefit of drapers and mercers [the Linen Drapers', Silk Mercers', Lacemen's, Haberdashers', and Hosiers' Institution]... 237p. *12°*. 1836.

29427 PHIPPS, John. A practical treatise on the China and eastern trade: comprising the commerce of Great Britain and India, particularly Bengal and Singapore, with China and the eastern islands...[With an appendix.] 338, lxviip. *8°. London & Calcutta*, 1836. *For another edition, see* 1835.

29428 REDDING, C. A history and description of modern wines...Second edition, with considerable additions, and a new preface developing the system of the port wine trade. xlviii, 423p. *8°*. 1836.

29429 REFUTAÇÃO a resposta analytica ao opusculo

intitulado Breves considerações sobre o commercio, e navegação de Portugal para a Asia. Por hum Portuguez não hypocritica. 26 de Janeiro de 1836. 19p. *8°. Lisboa*, 1836.

29430 UNITED STATES OF AMERICA. *Treasury Department.* Letter from the Secretary of the Treasury [Levi Woodbury], transmitting tables and notes on the cultivation, manufacture, and foreign trade of cotton. April 5, 1836. Ordered that...this document be printed for the use of the Senate. 120p. *8°. Washington*, 1836.

29431 ——— [Another edition.] Woodbury's Tables and notes on the cultivation, manufacture and foreign trade of cotton. 78p. *8°. Washington*, 1836. *Made up from the sheets of the edition printed for the House of Representatives.*

COLONIES

29432 An **ADDRESS** to the honorable the Commons of the United Kingdom...on the sugar duties. By a West Indian. 16p. *8°. Woolwich*, 1836.

For **AGRICULTURAL AND HORTICULTURAL SOCIETY OF INDIA,** Transactions, *see* vol. III, *Periodicals list*, Transactions...

29433 B. Observations relative to the establishment of the West India Agricultural Company. 40p. *8°.* 1836.

29434 BENNETT, J. W. Letter to the Earl of Ripon, K.G. setting forth a plain statement, including abstracts of correspondence and despatches, demonstrating the facts of a case of unprecedented injustice towards a colonial officer...upon frivolous and groundless pretexts... 108p. *8°.* 1836. *The copy that belonged to Earl De Grey.*

29435 EAST INDIA COMPANY. Debate at the East-India House [July 11. On the Bill to equalize the duties on East and West India sugars]. ⟨Extracted from the Asiatic Journal for August 1836.⟩ 19p. *8°. n.p.* [1836]

29436 ——— Reports and documents connected with the proceedings of the East-India Company in regard to the culture and manufacture of cotton-wool, raw-silk, and indigo in India. xxvii, 431, xliii, 222, viii, 96p. *8°.* 1836.

29437 FISHER, JAMES H. A sketch of three colonial Acts, suggested for adoption in the new province of South Australia, with a view to ensure the most perfect security of title to property, to simplify and facilitate the mode and moderate the expense of its transfer. With proposed forms of deeds. 63p. *8°.* 1836.

29438 LA PILORGERIE, J. DE. Histoire de Botany-Bay, état present des colonies pénales de l'Angleterre dans l'Australie; ou, examen des effets de la déportation, considérée comme peine et comme moyen de colonisation. 394p. *8°. Paris*, 1836.

29439 MARTIN, ROBERT M. The British colonial library. 10 vols. *8°.* 1836–37. *A revised version of the work entitled* History of the British colonies, *which began publication in 1834 (q.v.).*

29440 OBSERVATIONS on the advantages of emigration to New South Wales. Comprising valuable extracts from the minutes of evidence taken before a committee of the council at Sydney, also, the report of the Chief Justice...in 1835...Second edition. 84p. *12°.* 1836.

29441 ONTARIO. *Legislative Assembly.* Report of the Select Committee to which was referred the answer of His Excellency, the Lieut. Governor, to an address of the House of Assembly, relative to a responsible Executive Council...[With an appendix.] 103, 77p. *8°. Toronto*, 1836.

29442 PICKEN, A. The Canadas: comprehending topographical information concerning the quality of the land, in different districts; and the fullest general information: for the use of emigrants and capitalists. Compiled from original documents furnished by John Galt, Esq.... Second edition. 349, lxxxviip. *8°.* 1836. *For another edition, see 1832.*

29443 REMARKS on the salt monopoly of Bengal, and the report from the Board of Customs (Salt and Opium) of 1832. 68p. *8°.* 1836.

29444 ROEBUCK, JOHN A. Existing difficulties in the government of the Canadas. 68p. *8°.* 1836.

29445 ROLPH, T. A brief account, together with observations, made during a visit in the West Indies, and a tour through the United States of America in parts of the years 1832–3; together with a statistical account of Upper Canada. [With an appendix and 'Supplementary account'.] 272, [16]p. *8°. Dundas, U.C.*, 1836. *See also* A descriptive and statistical account of Canada, *1841.*

FINANCE

29446 AMERICAN LIFE INSURANCE AND TRUST COMPANY. Proposals and plan of the American Life Insurance and Trust Company. Offices... Baltimore...New York...London. Capital $2,000,000 ... 19p. *8°.* 1836.

29447 ANGLESEY SAVINGS BANK. Rules and regulations of the Anglesey Savings Bank, made conformable to the provisions of the several Acts relating thereto. 28p. *8°. Beaumaris*, 1836.

29448 BAILEY, C. An honest mode of commuting the tithes of England and Wales. 27p. *8°.* 1836.

29449 *BAILY, F. Théorie des annuités viagères et des assurances sur la vie, suivie d'une collection de tables ...Traduit de l'anglais par Alfred de Courcy, et publié par la Compagnie d'Assurances générales sur la Vie... 2 vols. *8°. Paris*, 1836. *The copy that belonged to Augustus De Morgan. For other editions, see 1813.*

29450 BANK IN ZÜRICH. Statuten der Bank in Zürich. [With a supplement describing the objects of the proposed Bank.] 20, 30p. *8°. Zürich*, 1836.

29451 BANK OF ENGLAND. A list of the names of all such proprietors of the Bank of England, who are qualified to vote at the ensuing election...April 2nd, 1836. 20p. *fol.* [1836] *See also* 1738, 1749, 1750, 1789, 1790,

1791, 1792, 1793, 1794, 1795, 1796, 1797, 1798, 1799, 1801, 1803, 1804, 1808, 1809, 1812, 1816, 1819, 1843.

29452 —— The names and descriptions of the proprietors of all government funds and securities, transferrable at the Bank of England, whose stock and dividends have been transferred to the Commissioners for the Reduction of the National Debt…as unclaimed for ten years and upwards, since the date of the last publication in 1823, to 5th January 1836, inclusive, with the dates when the first dividends respectively became payable thereon… 56p. *8°*. 1836. *See also 1791, 1823.*

29453 —— Report of the proceedings of the Governor and Company of the Bank of England, versus the London and Westminster Bank in the Court of Common Pleas. 165p. *8°*. 1836. *The copy that belonged to Hyde Clarke.*

29454 BANK OF THE UNITED STATES [1836–41]. Rules and regulations for conducting the business of the Bank of the United States. 17p. *12°*. n.p. [1836?]

29455 BARNES, R. Remarks on the Tithe Commutation Act. Addressed to the clergy of the diocese of Exeter …Second edition, with an appendix. 36p. *8°*. *London & Exeter,* 1836.

29456 BARROW, RICHARD and JOHN, *and others.* Copy of correspondence with the Boards of Trade, Treasury, and the Customs, relative to the overcharge of duty on tea, ex "Catherine" & "Post Boy." 26p. *8°*. 1836.

29457 BIRMINGHAM TOWN AND DISTRICT BANKING COMPANY. Deed of settlement (dated 30th June, 1836) of the Birmingham Town and District Banking Company, established under the authority of an Act of Parliament…To which is annexed an abstract of the Act (7th Geo. IV., c. 46). 89p. *8°*. *Birmingham,* 1836.

29458 BRITISH LINEN COMPANY. Report, tables, and statements by William Henderson, Esq. treasurer to the British Linen Company's Widows Fund, 1835 & 1836. 51p. *fol. Leith,* 1836.

29459 BURGON, T. An inquiry into the motive which influenced the ancients in their choice of the various representations which we find stamped on their money. Originally published in the Numismatic Journal, No. II. September, M.DCCC.XXXVI. 35p. *8°*. 1836. *Presentation copy, with a note from the author on the flyleaf, to Edward Hawkins.*

29460 BUXTON, SIR THOMAS F., *Bart.* Speech of Thomas Fowell Buxton, Esq. M.P. on the Irish Tithe Bill, delivered in the House of Commons, on…June 2, 1836. 27p. *8°*. 1836.

29461 CAIGNART DE SAULCY, L. F. J. Essai de classification des suites monétaires byzantines. [With 'Planches gravées par A. Dembour'.] 2 vols. *8°*. & *fol. Metz,* 1836.

29462 [CASSELS, W. G.] Remarks on the formation and working of banks called joint stock. With observations on the policy and conduct of the Bank of England towards these establishments. 32p. *8°*. 1836.

29463 [CHADWICK, SIR E.] An essay on the means of insurance against the casualties of sickness, decrepitude, and mortality: comprising an article reprinted from the Westminster Review (No. XVIII.) for April 1828, with additional notes and corrections. 63p. *8°*. 1836.

29464 CHRISTIAN, G. O. An essay upon tithes in Ireland, addressed to the Commons House of Parliament; accompanied by a few words of advice to the members… 47p. *8°*. 1836.

29465 CLAY, SIR W., *Bart.* Speech of William Clay, Esq., M.P. on moving for the appointment of a committee to inquire into the operation of the Act permitting the establishment of joint-stock banks. To which are added, reflections on limited liability, paid-up capital, and publicity of accounts…With some remarks on an article …in the last number of the Edinburgh Review. 144p. *8°*. 1836. *See also 1837.*

29466 COBBETT, W. Doom of the tithes. By the late Wm. Cobbett, M.P. for Oldham. 114p. *12°*. 1836. *A translation, edited by Cobbett and originally printed in the Political Register, of* Historia y orígen de las rentas de la Iglesia de Espana, *first published in Spain in 1793.*

29467 CONNERY, J. An essay on charitable economy, upon the loan bank system, called on the continent "mont de piété," that is, the mount, or rather the heap, for the distribution of charity; being an antidote to counteract the baneful effects of pawnbroking, and other rapacious systems of money lending…Second edition. 83p. *12°*. *Dublin,* 1836.

29468 COUNTY OF GLOUCESTER BANK. Deed of settlement of the County of Gloucester Banking Company. 120p. *8°*. *Gloucester,* [1836]

29469 CRAWFURD, JOHN (1783–1868). Taxes on knowledge. A financial and historical view of the taxes which impede the education of the people. 63p. *8°*. 1836. **Another, the FWA copy, belonged to William Pare.*

29470 CRUTTWELL, R. Currency! No. 1. The unequal distribution of national wealth… 20p. *8°*. *Halesworth,* 1836.

29471 —— Currency! No. II. The unequal distribution of national wealth… 36p. *8°*. *Halesworth & London,* 1836.

29472 DEVON, F., *ed.* Issues of the Exchequer; being payments made out of His Majesty's revenue during the reign of King James I. Extracted from the original records belonging to the ancient Pell Office… 448p. *8°*. 1836.

29473 DONALDSON, J. S. The first[–sixth] of a series of letters, addressed to the agriculturists of North Northumberland…[attributing the agricultural distress to the state of the currency]. 8, 7, 8, 11, 11, 15p. *8°*. *Berwick,* 1836. *Presentation copy from the author to Matthew Forster.*

29474 EDINBURGH YOUNG MEN'S VOLUNTARY CHURCH ASSOCIATION. Report of the speeches delivered at the soiree given as a public testimony in favour of Councillor Russell and Mr. Chapman. For their uncompromising conduct in reference to the annuity tax…11th May, 1836… 40p. *12°*. *Edinburgh,* 1836.

29475 To the **EDITOR** of the "Manchester Guardian". [A letter, signed: A manufacturer, and dated, February 9, 1836, commenting upon an article in the newspaper entitled 'Proposition for raising the duty on foreign tallow'.] 3p. *fol.* n.p. [1836]

29476 ENGLAND. *Commissioners appointed to Consider the State of the Established Church, with reference to Ecclesiastical Duties and Revenues.* The first and second Reports from His Majesty's Commissioners…[17 March, 1835 and 4 March, 1836.] 88p. *8°*. 1836.

29477 —— *Commissioners of Inquiry into the Excise Establishment.* Extract from the fifteenth Report of the honourable the Commissioners of Excise Inquiry, relative to the grievances of the exporting brewers. [Including the text of the memorial presented to the Treasury by Messrs. John and Robert Tennent, brewers in Glasgow, on the heavy burdens upon their trade.] 13p. *8°. Glasgow,* 1836.

29478 An **EXPOSITION** of the principles of joint stock banking, in reference to the district system of the Northamptonshire Banking Company. 15p. *8°. Northampton,* 1836.

29479 *****FANE**, R. G. C. A letter addressed to the Lord Viscount Melbourne [on a fine imposed for contempt in the Court of Bankruptcy]. 60p. *8°.* 1836. *Presentation copy from the author, that belonged to George Grote.*

29480 On the **FLUCTUATIONS** in the money market, with a suggestion of a remedy. By a money dealer. 27p. *8°.* 1836.

29481 **GAUDIN**, M. M. C., *Duc de Gaëte.* Observations sur le rapport fait, en 1836 à la Chambre des Députés, d'une proposition concernant le remboursement ou la réduction de la rente... 73p. *8°. Paris,* 1836.

29482 **GILBART**, J. W. The history of banking in Ireland. 148p. *8°.* 1836.

29483 —— A practical treatise on banking...Fourth edition. 178p. *8°.* 1836. *For other editions, see* 1827.

29484 **GORDON**, JOHN. Enquiry into the expediency and practicability of reducing the interest on the National Debt; and a plan for effectuating that measure, with the concurrence of the fundholders. 32p. *8°. Edinburgh,* 1836.

29485 [**HALL**, JOHN, *Liverpool merchant.*] Letters on the Bank of England; with a prospectus of a new joint-stock banking-company. By a Liverpool merchant. 32p. *8°.* 1836. *The copy that belonged to T. Spring Rice, Baron Monteagle.*

29486 [**HANNAY**, .] Letter to William Clay, Esq., M.P. containing strictures on his late pamphlet on the subject of joint stock banks, with remarks on his favourite theories. By Vindex. 36p. *8°.* 1836.

29487 **HAWKES**, H. W. The National Debt: an original poem...referring to the tricks of the stock jobbers...To which is added, John Bull's Prayer for protection from the effects of the Debt, revolution, riot, &c., and for a blessing on his native country. 36p. *12°. Coventry,* 1836. *Bound with four other works by the author, and apparently sold in this form.*

29488 **HAYTIEN BANKING COMPANY.** [*Endorsed:*] Haytien Banking Company. Prospectus. 2p. *fol.* [1836] *With an accompanying letter to Sir John Phillipart offering him a directorship. For the letter, see vol.* III, *A.L.* 231/1.

29489 [**HEATH**, JOSEPH.] The currency and its connection with national distress. By 'HΘ. 135p. *8°.* 1836. *The copy that belonged to Thomas Attwood.*

29490 **HEREFORDSHIRE BANKING COMPANY.** The deed of settlement of the Herefordshire Banking Company, established MDCCCXXXVI, under...an Act of Parliament...With an abstract of the Act. Central Bank, Hereford. Capital, £300,000. 105p. *8°. Hereford,* 1836.

29491 **HODGSON**, C. Practical directions and suggestions concerning the voluntary commutation of tithes: with the Act of Parliament [6 & 7 Will. IV, c. 71]. 51p. *8°.* 1836.

29492 **HUMFREY**, C. A letter to the Rt. Hon. Lord Viscount Melbourne, First Lord of the Treasury, &c. and his right honourable colleagues, containing facts and practical observations relating to the currency, and other matters connected with it. 61p. *8°. Cambridge & London,* 1836.

29493 The **IMPOSITION** of an additional duty on foreign tallow and the repeal of the soap duty beneficial to agriculture. No. 2. Mr. Handley's motion for the imposition of an increased duty on Russian tallow and the repeal of the soap duty stands for the 15th of March. 3p. *fol.* [*London,* 1836 ?]

29494 **JONES**, RICHARD (1790–1855). Remarks on the Government Bill for the commutation of tithe. 58p. *8°.* 1836.

29495 —— Second edition. 32p. *8°.* 1836. *See also* 1837.

29496 **JOPLIN**, T. An examination of the report of the Joint Stock Bank Committee, &c.&c. 112p. *8°.* 1836. *The copy that belonged to T. Spring Rice, Baron Monteagle.*

29497 —— Second edition. 112p. *8°.* 1836. *See also* 1837.

29498 **LIVERPOOL COMMERCIAL BANK.** Deed of settlement of the Liverpool Commercial Bank, established 1st January 1833, under the authority of an Act of Parliament...To which is appended an abstract of the Act. Capital – Five hundred thousand pounds. 86p. *8°.* 1836.

29499 **LIVINGSTONE**, J. L. A letter to the most noble the Marquis of Clanricarde on Irish Church property; the usurpation of the rights of lay patrons by the Irish bishops; and the recent attempt made by Government to extinguish those rights for the purpose of creating a surplus fund. 31p. *8°.* 1836. *The copy that belonged to Earl De Grey.*

29500 [**McCULLOCH**, JOHN R.] Observations, illustrative of the practical operation and real effect of the duties on paper, showing the expediency of their reduction or repeal. 38p. *8°.* 1836.

29501 [——] Reasons for the establishment of a new bank in India; with answers to the objections against it. 44p. *8°.* 1836.

29502 **MACLAREN**, D. History of the resistance to the annuity tax under each of the four church establishments for which it has been levied; with a statement of its annual produce since 1690. From authentic documents. 96p. *12°. Edinburgh,* 1836.

29503 Let the poor **MAN** make his own malt. [A discussion of the evils of the malt tax.] A letter to the Right Hon. T. Spring Rice, Chancellor of the Exchequer. [Signed: A country rector.] 14p. *8°.* 1836. *Presentation copy to T. Spring Rice, Baron Monteagle, from the anonymous author.*

29504 **MANCHESTER AND SALFORD BANK.** Deed of settlement of the Manchester and Salford Bank, established fifteenth of August, 1836, under the authority of an Act of Parliament...With an abstract of the Act. Capital – One million sterling. 66p. *8°. Manchester,* 1836.

29505 **MOORE**, R. Strictures on the present mode of creating the state's standard money, shewing the necessity for its enlargement, upon an assayed public deposit, and its public mortgage, on a mint paper coin, thus made of gold standard value, with the outline of a plan for instituting the same. 68p. *8°. Kingston* [& *London*], 1836.

29506 NATIONAL SECURITY SAVINGS BANK. ⟨Proposed⟩ Rules of the National Security Savings Bank of Edinburgh, duly agreed to and sanctioned... 25p. *8°. Edinburgh*, 1836.

29507 —— [Another edition.] Rules of the National Security Savings Bank... 25p. *8°. Edinburgh*, 1836. *See also* 1844.

29508 NETHERLANDS. *Departement van Financien.* Berigt eener negotiatie, tot te geldemaking van een kapitaal van f14,000,000 aan obligatien, rentende 4 ten honderd in het jaar, ten laste van 'sRijks overzeesche bezittingen, waarvan de renten door het Rijk bij de wetten van 24 April 1836...zijn gewaarborgd. 6p. *8°. n.p.* [1836]

29509 NEWCASTLE, SHIELDS, AND SUNDERLAND UNION JOINT STOCK BANKING COMPANY. Deed of settlement of the Newcastle, Shields, and Sunderland Union Joint Stock Banking Company. Established July 1st, 1836. 81p. *8°. Newcastle*, 1836.

29510 NORTHUMBERLAND AND DURHAM DISTRICT BANKING COMPANY. The deed of settlement of the Northumberland and Durham District Banking Company, established under the Act VII. Geo. IV. Dated 1st July, 1836. Capital, 50,000 shares of £10. each. 74p. *8°. Newcastle upon Tyne*, 1836.

29511 A few **OBSERVATIONS** on joint stock banks; on private banks; and on the Bank of England, as the sole bank of issue in the Metropolis. 16p. *8°.* 1836.

29512 PALMER, JOHN H. Reasons against the proposed Indian joint-stock bank, in a letter to G.G. de H. Larpent, Esq. 29p. *8°.* 1836.

29513 PAYNE, J. To the freeholders of England and Wales. Reasons for opposing the compulsory commutation of tythes for money; and on the impolicy of the freeholders of England and Wales suffering their estates to be mortgaged for ever by a money annual payment. 16p. *8°. London & Nottingham*, 1836.

29514 PENNSYLVANIA. *General Assembly.* An act to incorporate the stockholders of the Bank of the United States, by the State of Pennsylvania. 20p. *12°. Philadelphia*, 1836. *See also* 1838 (Bank of the United States).

29515 To the Honorable the Commons of the United Kingdom of Great Britain & Ireland...The humble **PETITION** of the undersigned inhabitant housekeepers, engaged in husbandry, trade and manufacture, within the parishes of Tottenham, Edmonton, Enfield, Hadley, Mims and Barnet, in...Middlesex [against a surcharge for duties of assessed taxes upon business carts, horses, &c.]. 8p. *8°. Tottenham*, [1836]

29516 PICKERING, JOHN. An outline of the Tithes Act, in a popular form. 16p. *8°. Kingston & London*, 1836.

29517 [**POCOCK,** L.] A chronological list of books and single papers, relating to the subjects of the rate of mortality, annuities, and life-assurance. With the titles of the several parliamentary reports and tables connected with friendly societies: and of the publications, prospectus-papers, and proposals, concerning, and issued by, the various metropolitan life-assurance offices. 32p. *8°.* 1836.

One of a privately printed edition limited to 100 copies. See also 1842.

29518 PROGRESS of the consumption of soap from 1830 to 1835, both inclusive; extracted from the seventeenh [*sic*] Report of the Commissioners of Excise Inquiry. [Attributing its static condition to the heavy duty payable on soap.] *s.sh.fol. n.p.* [1836]

29519 REMARKS on the proposed "Bank of India;" its principles and practical working. By an India merchant. Printed for private circulation. 19p. *8°. Glasgow*, 1836.

29520 REPORT from the Select Committee on the timber duties. (Not ordered by the House of Commons to be printed.) [A satire.] 60p. *8°.* 1836.

29521 REVIEW of a pamphlet entitled "Reasons for the establishment" of a new bank in India. By an India merchant. 20p. *8°. Glasgow*, 1836.

29522 [**ROBINSON,** , *of the House of Representatives in Massachusetts.*] The evils of paper money: showing how it deteriorates the working man's condition. (From the New York Evening Post, April 11, 1836.) 8p. *8°.* [*London*, 1836]

29523 SHROPSHIRE BANKING COMPANY. The Shropshire Banking Company, 1836. [Deed of settlement.] Capital: £300,000 in 15,000 shares of £20 each... 72p. *12°.* [1836]

29524 SIMPSON, WILLIAM P. Tithe commutation. Tables, shewing at one view, the value, in corn rent, of the rent charge payable in lieu of tithe, and its relative value under every variation in the price of corn. With a practical digest of the Tithe Commutation Act. 40p. *8°. London & Norwich*, [1836]

29525 STRICTURES on the report of the Secret Committee [of the House of Commons], on joint stock banks, with an appendix, containing some valuable tables, compiled from the evidence. [With 'Appendix. ⟨Extract from the report⟩'.] 24p. *8°.* 1836.

29526 STUCKEY, V. Thoughts on the improvement of the system of country banking. In a letter to Lord Viscount Althorp...Second edition. 41p. *8°.* 1836. *For another edition, see* 1834.

29527 The new monetary **SYSTEM.** By a citizen of the world. 23p. *8°.* 1836. *Sometimes attributed to —— Sullivan.*

29528 TAYLOR, JOHN (1781–1864). Catechisms of the currency and exchanges. A new edition, enlarged. To which is prefixed the case of the industrious classes briefly stated. 21, 122, 160p. *8°.* 1836. *Editions of* A catechism of the currency *and* A catechism of foreign exchanges *were published separately in* 1835 (*q.v.*). *Here, the former is of the third, and the latter of the second edition.*

29529 TRAITTE des finances de France, de l'institution d'icelles, de leurs sortes et especes, de ce à quoy elles sont destinees, des moiens d'en faire fonds, de les bien emploier, et d'en faire reserue au besoing...M.D.LXXX. (*Archives curieuses de l'histoire de France depuis Louis XI jusqu'à Louis XVIII*...Par M. L. Cimber et F. Danjou, 1ère série, 9.) p.343–399. *8°.* [*Paris*, 1836]

29530 UNION BANK OF MANCHESTER. The deed of settlement of the Union Bank of Manchester, established 1836, under authority of an Act of Parliament ... 104p. *8°. Manchester*, 1836.

29531 VAN BUREN, M., *President of the USA.* A

letter from the Hon. Martin Van Buren, Vice-President of the United States, relative to the Bank of the United States, with an explanatory introduction. 36p. *8°.* 1836.

29532 VERE, CHARLES. Tables of monies of the principal cities in all parts of the world, with their value in sterling and in francs; likewise a table of Belgian, Swiss, and Saxon currency, reduced into francs; with tables of British currency, reduced into francs at various rates of exchange...Fourth edition. 36, [22]p. *12°. London & Paris,* 1836.

29533 VIRGINIA. *Laws, etc.* An act, for incorporating the Bank of Virginia, passed the 30th January, 1804, and an act, extending the charter of the Bank of Virginia, passed January 24th, 1814; with the rules and regulations for the government of the Bank. 44p. *12°. Richmond,* 1836.

29534 [WADE, JOHN.] Principles of banking and commerce, as elucidated by the great crisis of 1825–6; and applicable to the existing state of commercial activity and joint-stock speculations. 118p. *12°.* 1836. *A reissue of*

Digest of facts and principles on banking and commerce, *1826 (q.v.).*

29535 WALSALL. *Corporation.* A full statement of accounts of the late Corporation of the Borough and Foreign of Walsall; from 1802 to 1835...Taken verbatim from their own books. 243p. *8°. Walsall & Birmingham,* [1836]

29536 WALTON, WILLIAM *(fl.* 1836). Calculator's sure guide, or, the most comprehensive reckoner ever published; applicable to all business transactions. 596p. *8°.* 1836.

29537 WATT, P. The theory and practice of joint-stock banking: shewing the advantages which will arise... from the institution of joint-stock banks of issue, discount and deposit. 78p. *8°. Edinburgh & London,* 1836.

29538 A few **WORDS** on joint-stock banking in London. 20p. *8°.* 1836. *Sometimes attributed to J. W. Gilbart.*

TRANSPORT

29539 ARMSTRONG, W. Observations on the improvement of the navigation of the Tyne. 15p. *8°. Newcastle upon Tyne,* 1836.

29540 —— An appendix to Observations on the improvement of the navigation of the Tyne, in which the question of enclosing Jarrow Slake is more particularly considered. 8p. *8°. Newcastle upon Tyne,* 1836.

29541 BELCHER, H. Illustrations of the scenery on the line of the Whitby and Pickering Railway, in... Yorkshire. From drawings by G. Dodgson. With a short description of the district and undertaking. 115p. *8°.* 1836.

29542 Allgemeine **BELEHRUNGEN** über Eisenbahnen und Schienenwege in populär-fasslicher Darstellung von einem Techniker. 110p. *8°. Mainz,* 1836.

29543 BLACKMORE, J. Views on the Newcastle and Carlisle railway, from original drawings by J. W. Carmichael, with details by John Blackmore, engineer to the Company. [25]l., [23] plates. *4°. Newcastle, Carlisle, &c.,* 1836[–38]

29544 BOOTH, H. A letter to His Majesty's Commissioners on Railways in Ireland, in reply to a communication from H. D. Jones, Esq. secretary to the Commissioners...⟨Not published.⟩ 12p. *8°. Liverpool,* 1836.

29545 [BRUNEL, SIR M. I.] An explanation of the works of the tunnel under the Thames from Rotherhithe to Wapping. 32p. *obl.8°.* 1836. *Presentation copy from the author to Joseph Hume.*

29546 CONVENTION FOR...TAKING PRELIMINARY MEASURES FOR A RAIL ROAD ...TO THE ST. LAWRENCE. Proceedings of the convention, holden at Windsor, Vt., January 20, 1836: for the purpose of taking preliminary measures for a rail road through the valleys of the Connecticut and Passumpsic rivers to the St. Lawrence... 24p. *12°. Windsor, Vt.,* [1836] *The Rastrick copy.*

29547 DUBLIN, DROGHEDA AND NAVAN INLAND RAILWAY. [*Endorsed:*] Prospectus... 3p. *fol.* [*London,* 1836]

29548 EASTERN COUNTIES RAILWAY COMPANY. Proceedings of the first general meeting of the Eastern Counties Railway Company, incorporated ...1836. Held at the London Tavern...26th September, 1836. 43p. *8°.* [1836]

29549 ENGLAND. *Laws, etc.* [*Endorsed:*] An Act for making a railway from Aylesbury to join the London and Birmingham Railway, near the village of Cheddington, in the county of Birmingham. ⟨Royal Assent 19th May, 1836.⟩ ⟨6th Wm. 4th, session, 1836.⟩ 110p. *fol.* [*London,* 1836]

29550 —— —— [*Endorsed:*] Bristol and Exeter Railway. An Act for making a railway from Bristol to Exeter, with branches to the towns of Bridgwater in the county of Somerset, and Tiverton in the county of Devon. ⟨Royal Assent, 19 May, 1836.⟩ 6 Will. IV. sess. 1836. 178p. *fol.* [*London,* 1836]

29551 —— —— [*Endorsed:*] Great Western Railway. An Act to alter the line of the Great Western Railway, and to amend the Act relating thereto. ⟨Royal Assent, 19 May 1836.⟩ 6 Will. IV, sess. 1836. 14, [10]p. *fol.* [*London,* 1836]

29552 —— —— Anno sexto Gulielmi IV. Regis. [Local & Personal.] Cap. lxxx. An Act for making a railway from Kingston-upon-Hull to Selby. ⟨21st June 1836.⟩ p.3089–3196. *fol. n.p.* [1836]

29553 —— —— An Act for making a railway from the London and Croydon Railway to Dover, to be called the "South-Eastern Railway." Royal Assent, 21 June, 1836. [6 Will. IV. sess. 1836.] 166p. *fol.* [*London,*] 1836.

29554 —— —— [*Endorsed:*] An Act for making a railway from London to Norwich and Yarmouth, by Romford, Chelmsford, Colchester, and Ipswich, to be called "The Eastern Counties Railway." Royal Assent, 4th July, 1836. 6 Will. 4th. sess. 1836. 205p. *fol.* [*London,* 1836]

29555 —— —— [*Endorsed:*] Manchester and Leeds Railway. An Act for making a railway from Manchester to Leeds. ⟨Royal Assent, 4th July, 1836.⟩ 6 William IV. sess. 1836. 259p. *fol.* [*London,* 1836]

29556 —— The law relating to highways, comprising the Statute 5 & 6 Will. IV. cap. 50. (Passed 31st August 1835,) with table of contents, explanatory notes, forms, references, and a copious index. By John Tidd Pratt. xx, 200p. *8°*. 1836.

29557 —— Parliament. *House of Commons.* In the House of Commons. Minutes of evidence taken before the Committee on the London and Brighton Railway Bill; (Stephenson's Line.)...Copy from Mr. Gurney's short-hand notes. [Proceedings of the Committee from 16 March–12 April 1836.] 9 parts. *fol.* 1836.

29558 —— —— —— In the House of Commons. Minutes of evidence taken before the Committee on the London and Brighton Railway Bill; (Sir John Rennie's Line.)...Copy from Mr. Gurney's short-hand notes. [Proceedings of the Committee from 14 April–4 May 1836.] 15 parts. *fol.* 1836.

29559 —— —— —— In the House of Commons. Minutes of evidence taken before the Committee on the London and Brighton Railway Bill; (Gibbs' Line.)... Copy from Mr. Gurney's short-hand notes. [Proceedings of the Committee from 6–9 May 1836.] 2 parts. *fol.* 1836.

29560 —— —— —— In the House of Commons. Minutes of evidence taken before the Committee on the London and Brighton Railway Bill; (Cundy's Line.)... Copy from Mr. Gurney's short-hand notes. [Proceedings of the Committee from 10–12 May 1836.] 3 parts. *fol.* 1836.

29561 The **EXAMINATION** [of George Walter] examined; or, testimony on oath proving a failure in the Peers to support the London and Greenwich Railway. 32p. *8°*. 1836.

29562 FAIRBAIRN, H. A treatise on the political economy of railroads; in which the new mode of locomotion is considered in its influence upon the affairs of nations. 248p. *8°*. 1836.

29563 GIBBS, JOSEPH. Some observations relative to the introduction of railway bills into Parliament, respectfully addressed to the consideration of the Members of both Houses. 14p. *8°*. [1836] *The copy that belonged to I. Solly, with his signature on the title-page.*

29564 GORDON, ALEXANDER (1802–1868). A treatise upon elemental locomotion, and interior communication, wherein are explained and illustrated, the history, practice, and prospects of steam carriages, and the comparative value of turnpike roads, railways, and canals. With...an appendix. Third edition, containing a supplement wherein are given rules and tables, and the description of an improved road-surveying instrument for determining the comparative values of different roads. 344p. *8°*. London, Glasgow, &c., 1836. *For other editions, see* 1832.

29565 GRAHAME, T. A letter, on the present system of legislation which regulates internal intercourse in Great Britain; with strictures on the new principles rapidly being introduced in this department of British policy...Addressed to W. D. Gillon, Esq. M.P. 20p. *8°*. *Westminster,* 1836.

29566 GRAINGER, RICHARD. A proposal for concentrating the termini of the Newcastle and Carlisle, the Great North of England, and proposed Edinburgh Railways; and for providing...depôts...from these several railways to the town of Newcastle, submitted to the consideration of the respective companies, and to the proprietors of property interested in the same. 8p. *8°*. *Newcastle,* 1836.

29567 GREAT LEINSTER AND MUNSTER RAILWAY. Prospectus of the Great Leinster and Munster railway: first extension, from the city of Dublin to the city of Kilkenny, with estimated annual revenue, engineers' report, &c.... 26p. *8°*. 1836. *The copy that belonged to I. Solly, with his signature on the title-page.*

29568 [*Endorsed:*] In Parliament, — Session 1836. The **GREAT NORTH OF ENGLAND RAILWAY.** Case of the promoters of the Bill [to authorize the building of a line between Newcastle and the River Tees]. [4]p. *fol. n.p.* [1836]

29569 GUYONNEAU DE PAMBOUR, F. M., *Comte.* A practical treatise on locomotive engines upon railways...with practical tables, giving at once the results of the formulæ; founded upon...new experiments...To which is added, an appendix showing the expense of conveying goods, by locomotive engines, on railroads... 365p. *8°*. 1836. *The Rastrick copy. See also* 1840.

29570 HOLBORN LEVEL. Prospectus of a company, to be incorporated by Act of Parliament, for the formation of a new line of level street, to be erected upon a viaduct, extending from Hatton Garden to Snow Hill, Skinner Street, and parallel with Holborn Hill. Capital £350,000, in fourteen thousand shares of £25 each... 4p. *fol.* [*London,* 1836]

29571 HULL AND SELBY RAILWAY COMPANY. Hull and Selby Railway, connecting Liverpool with Hull, through Manchester and Leeds...Report of the Directors...Laid before the proprietors at their first general meeting, on...the 31st of August, 1836... 30p. *8°. Hull,* 1836. *See also* 1839.

29572 HUMBER UNION STEAM COMPANY. Deed of settlement of the Humber Union Steam Company. 65p. *8°. Hull,* 1836.

29573 HUNGERFORD and Lambeth suspension foot bridge over the Thames. [A prospectus.] 5p. *8°*. [*London,* 1836]

29574 [*Endorsed:*] (Private.) Prospectus. **INTERNATIONAL RAILWAY COMPANY,** connecting Great Britain with Paris and Brussels [in association with the South-Eastern Railway]. 5th July, 1836. 2p. *fol.* [1836]

29575 LAMB, A. Reasons by Alexander Lamb for converting Portland Roads into a harbour. Shewing that it will facilitate and lessen both the risk and outlay of commerce, benefit agriculture, reduce the expenditure of the country, and add to its security. 34p. *fol.* [*London,*] 1836.

29576 LECOUNT, P. An examination of Professor Barlow's reports on iron rails. 192p. *8°. London & Birmingham,* [1836] *Two copies, both of which belonged to Rastrick.*

29577 —— Remarks on the cheapest distance for railway blocks...To which is prefixed an explanation of the word "personal," intended for the managing editor of the Philosophical Magazine. 93p. *8°. London & Birmingham,* [1836]. *The Rastrick copy.*

29578 LONDON. Livery Companies. *Watermen and Lightermen of the River Thames.* Additional rules and bye-laws for the regulation of the Watermen and Lightermen of the River Thames. By the Court of Mayor and Aldermen of the City of London. 12p. *8°. Printed for the Company,* 1836. *For editions of the laws and constitution of the Company and its rules and bye-laws, see* 1730, 1828.

29579 LONDON AND BRIGHTON RAILWAY

COMPANY. The direct London and Brighton Railway, with a branch to Shoreham. Capital £800,000, in 16,000 shares of £50 each...[Prospectus, dated: February 1st, 1836.] 2p. *fol.* [1836] *See also* 1837.

29580 MANCHESTER AND CHESHIRE JUNCTION RAILWAY COMPANY. [Report of a public meeting on the 17th August 1836 to promote this railway, which was never incorporated.] *s.sh.fol. Manchester,* [1836]

29581 MARYPORT AND CARLISLE RAILWAY COMPANY. [*Endorsed:*] Maryport and Carlisle Railway. Capital £200,000. in 4000 shares at £50 each... [Prospectus. With a report on the line by George Stephenson, dated: 3rd May, 1836.] [4]p. *fol. Maryport,* [1836]

29582 —— [Another edition, with a map in place of Stephenson's report.] [4]p. *fol. Maryport,* [1836]

29583 MORRISON, JAMES (1790–1857). Rail roads. Speech of James Morrison, Esq. M.P. in the House of Commons, 17th May, 1836, on moving a resolution relative to the periodical revision of tolls and charges levied on rail roads and other public works. 23p. *8°.* 1836.

29584 NAVIER, C. L. M. H. On the means of comparing the respective advantages of different lines of railway; and on the use of locomotive engines. Translated from the French...By John MacNeill, civil engineer... 97p. *8°.* 1836.

For a **NEW GUIDE TO STAGECOACHES, WAGGONS**...&c. for 1836, *see no.* 29348.

29585 NORTHERN AND EASTERN RAILWAY COMPANY. [*Endorsed:*] Prospectus of the Northern & Eastern Railway. Continuation line from Cambridge to York. [Dated: November 1, 1836.] *fol.* [*London,* 1836]

29586 What will **PARLIAMENT** do with the railways? 16p. *8°.* 1836.

29587 —— Second edition. 16p. *8°.* 1836.

29588 RAILROADS. Statements and reflections thereon: particularly with reference to the proposed railroad without a tunnel, and the competition for the line between London and Brighton. By a shareholder...[With 'Addenda. London, Shoreham, and Brighton Railway, without a tunnel'.] 59, 10p. *8°.* 1836. *The Rastrick copy.*

29589 REMARKS on the regulation of railway travelling on Sundays, addressed to the directors and proprietors of the London and Birmingham Railway. By a railway director. 25p. *8°. London & Birmingham,* 1836. *Attributed, in the copy belonging to the Institution of Civil Engineers, to John Sturge of Birmingham.*

29590 SHEFFIELD, ASHTON-UNDER-LYNE, AND MANCHESTER RAILWAY. Sheffield, Ashton-under-Lyne, and Manchester Railway. Proposed capital, £1,000,000; in 10,000 shares of £100 each... Report of the directing committee to the subscribers to the above undertaking. 3p. *fol. Sheffield,* [1836] *The copy that belonged to Benjamin Skidmore, secretary of the Company.*

29591 A brief **SKETCH** of a proposed new line of communication between Dublin and London, via Portdynllaen...Worcester, and Oxford...To which are added the report of T. Rogers...engineer...and other documents published in 1807...Together with the resolutions of two public meetings...Second edition. 40p. *8°. Dublin, London, &c.,* 1836.

29592 SMITH, HORACE. Conjectures on the future effects of locomotion by steam. Read at the conversazione of the Brighton Scientific and Literary Institution. 32p. *8°. Brighton,* 1836.

29593 SOUTH EASTERN RAILWAY COMPANY. [*Endorsed:*] Prospectus. South-Eastern-Brighton, Lewes and Newhaven Railway. [4]p. *fol.* [1836]

29594 —— South-Eastern Railway. London to Dover, by Croydon, Oxted, Tunbridge and Ashford. With a branch to Tunbridge Wells. [Prospectus.] 2p. *fol.* [1836]

29595 SOUTH MIDLAND COUNTIES RAILWAY COMPANY. South Midland Counties Railway. Capital £1,200,000, in shares of £50 each. [Prospectus.] 4p. *fol.* [*London,* 1836?]

29596 STATEMENT of the public proceedings which have occurred in Brighton relative to a railway. Printed for the committee appointed at a town meeting held 18th February, 1836, to promote the line projected by Sir John Rennie. 8p. *8°. Brighton,* [1836]

29597 STOREY, T. Report on the Great North of England Railway, connecting Leeds and York, with Newcastle-upon-Tyne...1836. 25p. *8°. Darlington,* 1836.

29598 STRAKER, G. Practical hints and observations on the state and improvement of the Tyne. 19p. *8°. Newcastle upon Tyne,* 1836.

29599 WHITEHAVEN HARBOUR TRUSTEES. Plans suggested at different periods for the improvement of Whitehaven Harbour, with reports and memorials connected therewith [written between 1768 and 1836 by John Smeaton and others]. Printed by order of the Trustees. [38]p., 19 plates. *fol. Whitehaven,* 1836.

29600 WOOD, WILLIAM P., *Baron Hatherley.* Session 1836. Stephenson's London and Brighton Railway. Speech of W. P. Wood, Esq. on summing up the engineering evidence given in support of the Bill for Stephenson's line of railway, before the Right Hon. Committee of the House of Lords. 22d July, 1836. 31p. *8°. Westminster,* 1836. *The Rastrick copy.*

SOCIAL CONDITIONS

29601 ADDRESS to the clergy of Ireland, from the clergy of the united dioceses of Derry and Raphoe, on the subject of national education. 60p. *8°. Dublin,* 1836. *The copy that belonged to Earl De Grey.*

For **AGENCY AMONG THE SCOTTISH WORKING AND POORER CLASSES RESIDENT IN LIVERPOOL,** [First] report – seventh annual report, 1836–42, *see vol.* III, *Periodicals list,* Report of the agent...

29602 AMERICAN TEMPERANCE SOCIETY. Eighth report of the...Society. 8p. *4°. Preston,* [1836]. *The Turner copy. For another edition, see* 1835 (Permanent temperance documents of the...Society).

For —— Ninth report, 1836, *see* 1835 (Permanent temperance documents of the...Society).

29603 BARRINGTON, Sir M., *Bart.* An address to the inhabitants of Limerick, on the opening of the mont de piété, or charitable pawn office, for the support of Barrington's Hospital, in that city... 28p. *8°. Dublin,* 1836.

29604 BEAUMONT, John T. B. The consequences of the abolition of imprisonment for debt considered. 32p. *8°.* 1836.

29605 BÈRES, E. Les classes ouvrières. Moyens d'améliorer leur sort sous le rapport du bien-être matériel et du perfectionnement moral...Deuxième édition. 348p. *8°. Paris,* 1836.

29606 BIGSBY, J. J. A lecture on mendicity; its ancient and modern history, and the policy of nations and individuals in regard to it. As delivered before the Worksop Mechanics' Institute... April, 1836. 44p. *8°. Worksop, Retford, &c.,* 1836.

29607 BLACKBURN, T. A defence of the system [of religious education] adopted in the corporation schools of Liverpool. 46p. *8°. Liverpool,* [1836]

29608 BOWRING, Sir J. Speech of Dr. Bowring, M.P., on the Factories Regulation Act, in the House of Commons, Monday May 9th, 1836. 4p. *8°.* 1836.

29609 BRAY, C. The education of the body, an address to the working classes. 26p. *8°. Coventry,* 1836. *The copy that belonged to William Lovett, with his initials in his hand on the title-page. See also* 1847.

29610 [CAREY, M.] Letters on the condition of the poor: addressed to Alexander Henry, Esq. containing a vindication of poor laws and benevolent societies...With examples of the gross inconsistency of the Edinburgh Review, on the subject of poor laws. By a citizen of Philadelphia. Third edition, improved. 20p. *8°. Philadelphia,* 1836. *For another edition, see* 1835.

29611 CLIVE, A. A few words to the poor and to overseers, on the new Poor Law. 8p. *8°. Birmingham,* [1836] *See also* 1837.

29612 COBBETT, James P. Mr. J. P. Cobbett's petition to the House of Commons against the poor-law separation of man from wife and of parent from child. Presented by Mr. John Fielden, March 22, 1836. 16p. *8°.* [*London* &] *Manchester,* [1836] *The Oastler copy.*

29613 CONNERY, J. The reformer, or, an infallible remedy to prevent pauperism and periodical returns of famine, with other salutary measures...and establishing the futility of the plan of William Smith O'Brien, Esq., (formerly Member of Parliament for Ennis, and now for Co. Limerick.)...Sixth edition... 72p. *12°. London & Dublin,* 1836. *For another edition, see* 1833.

29614 CRUICKSHANK, W. To Christians of all persuasions. [A letter on intemperance.] 4p. *8°. n.p.* [1836] *The Turner copy.*

29615 *DESLOGES, L. C. A. Des enfans trouvés, des femmes publiques et des moyens à employer pour en diminuer le nombre. 47p. *8°. Paris,* 1836. *The copy that belonged to George Grote.*

29616 Self-supporting **DISPENSARIES.** To the industrious mechanics and working classes of the Borough of Southwark and its vicinity. [An account of the rise and progress of dispensaries, and the benefits available.] *s.sh.fol.* [*Southwark,* 1836?]

29617 DUNLOP, John. Artificial drinking usages of North Britain...Fourth edition, with large additions. 122p. *8°. Greenock, Glasgow, &c.,* 1836. *The Turner copy.*

29618 ENGLAND. *Barrister appointed to Certify the Rules of Friendly Societies.* Instructions for the establishment of loan societies with a form of rules, &c. applicable thereto. 15p. *8°.* 1836. *See also* 1837.

29619 —— —— An Act [57 Geo. 3. cap. xxix] for better paving, improving and regulating the streets of the Metropolis, and removing and regulating nuisances and obstructions therein. ⟨Passed 16th June 1817.⟩ 208, [20]p. *8°.* 1835[1836].

29620 —— *Laws, etc.* [*Endorsed:*] Bristol damages compensation. An Act to enable the Mayor, Aldermen and burgesses of...Bristol to raise...money towards discharging the monies borrowed under...an Act passed in the second year of the reign of His present Majesty. ⟨Royal Assent, 21 June 1836.⟩ 6 Will. IV. sess. 1836. 5p. *fol.* [*Bristol,* 1836]

29621 —— *Poor Law Commission* [*1834–1847*]. First annual report of the Poor Law Commissioners for England and Wales. With the appendices. (*Reports of Commissioners,* 1.) Second edition. 406p. *8°.* 1836.

29622 —— [Another edition.] 57p. *8°. n.p.* [1836] *For the series, see* vol. III, *Periodicals list,* First annual report...

29623 ESSAYS on the principles of charitable institutions: being an attempt to ascertain what are the plans best adapted to improve the physical and moral condition of the lower orders in England. 371p. *8°.* 1836.

29624 On the **FACTORY QUESTION.** [A statement of the situation and an appeal for support and funds, issued jointly by the Ashton and Dukinfield and the Stalybridge Short-Time Committees. Dated: 27th June, 1836.] 12p. *12°. Ashton,* [1836] *The Oastler copy.*

29625 FIELDEN, J. The curse of the factory system; or, a short account of the origin of factory cruelties; of the attempts to protect the children by law... 74p. *8°.* [1836] *Two copies, one the Oastler copy and the other the copy that belonged to J. M. Cobbett.*

29626 FINCH, John (1783–1857). Teetotalism: containing a portraiture and the ancient and modern history of teetotalism; together with some account of the botheration moderation temperance societies, and a letter to the Liverpool Anti-Temperance Society. (From the Liverpool Albion of July and August, 1836.) (*John Finch's Temperance Tracts,* 4.) 8p. *8°. Liverpool,* [1836]

29627 FOOTE, S. The tailors (or "quadrupeds",) a tragedy for warm weather in three acts...(*Thomas's Burlesque Dramas.*) 69p. *12°.* 1836. *The authorship is doubtful.*

29628 GASKELL, P. Artisans and machinery: the moral and physical condition of the manufacturing population considered with reference to mechanical substitutes for human labour. 399p. *8°.* 1836.

29629 GODFERY, J. A continuation of The poor man's friend, printed at the request of several individuals; being a few plain words from a poor man... 51p. *8°. Lynn,* 1836.

29630 GURNEY, John H. The new Poor Law the poor man's friend. A plain address to the labouring classes among his parishioners...Third edition. 54p. *12°. Leicester,* 1836.

29631 HALE, William H. Remarks on the two Bills

now before Parliament, entitled, a Bill for registering births, deaths and marriages in England; and a Bill for marriages in England. 40p. *8°*. 1836.

29632 HAWES, SIR B. The abolition of arrest and imprisonment for debt considered in six letters addressed to a constituent. 75p. *8°*. 1836.

29633 HINDLEY, C. Factory question. Speech of Charles Hindley, M.P. for Ashton-under-Lyne, and manufacturer...in the House of Commons, May 9, 1836, on the debate upon the second reading of Mr. P. Thomson's Bill proposing to enact that children of twelve years of age should work twelve hours a day, exclusive of the time allowed for meals... 23p. *8°*. 1836. *The Oastler copy.*

29634 HINTS on district visiting societies; a plan for their formation, and suggestions to visitors... 60p. *12°*. 1836.

29635 HUGHES, E. Compendium of the operations of the Poor Law Amendment Act, with some practical observations on its present results, and future apparent usefulness. 127p. *8°*. *London, Maidstone, &c.*, 1836.

29636 IRELAND. *Commissioners of National Education.* Reports of the Commissioners...for the years 1834, 1835 and 1836. 142p. *8°*. *Dublin*, 1836. *See also* 1849.

29637 JENKINSON, CHARLES C. C., *3rd Earl of Liverpool.* An account of the operation of the poor law amendment in the Uckfield Union, in the County of Sussex, during the year ending Lady-Day, 1836. 43p. *8°*. 1836.

29638 —— Second edition. 43p. *8°*. 1836.

29639 [KNIGHT, C.] The newspaper stamp, and the duty on paper, viewed in relation to their effects upon the diffusion of knowledge. By the author of The results of machinery. 64p. *8°*. 1836.

29640 LESLIE, JOHN, *Commissioner of Sewers.* Further illustrations of the principles upon which a metropolitan poor rate is administered in the parish of St. George, Hanover Square; with a few desultory observations on the principle upon which poor laws are founded; and on the proposed extension of that system to Ireland. 30p. *8°*. 1836.

29641 LEWIS, SIR GEORGE C., *Bart.* Poor inquiry. – (Ireland.) Appendix G. Report on the state of the Irish poor in Great Britain. 104p. *12°*. 1836.

29642 LIVESEY, J. A temperance lecture based on the tee-total principle; including an exposure of the great delusion as to the properties of malt liquor... 35p. *8°*. *Preston, London, &c.*, 1836. *The Turner copy. See also* 1837.

29643 LLOYD, W. F. Two lectures on poor-laws, delivered before the University of Oxford, in Hilary term, 1836. 71p. *8°*. *London & Oxford*, 1836. *Reissued in* Lectures on population, value, poor-laws and rent *in 1837, q.v.* (GENERAL).

For the **LONDON TEMPERANCE INTELLIGENCER,** 1836, *continued as* the Weekly London temperance intelligencer, 1837, *then the* British and foreign temperance intelligencer, 1838, *then the* New British and foreign temperance intelligencer, *see* vol. III, *Periodicals list*, New British and foreign temperance intelligencer.

29644 MABERLY, F. H. To the poor and their friends. The substance of speeches by the Rev. F. H. Maberly, M.A. of Bourn...Cambridgeshire...exhibiting

the oppressive nature of the new Poor Law Amendment Act: delivered at public meetings...in the counties of Cambridge, Herts, Huntingdon & Essex, to petition against this abominable measure...Between June and September 1836. 48p. *12°*. 1836. *The Oastler copy.*

29645 MACNISH, R. The anatomy of drunkenness ...Sixth edition. 270p. *12°*. *Glasgow & London*, 1836. *The Turner copy. For other editions, see* 1834.

For the **MANCHESTER AND SALFORD TEMPERANCE JOURNAL,** *see* vol. III, *Periodicals list.*

29646 MANCHESTER STATISTICAL SOCIETY. Report of a committee of the Manchester Statistical Society, on the state of education in the borough of Liverpool in 1835–1836... 74p. *8°*. *London & Manchester*, 1836.

29647 —— Report of a committee of the Manchester Statistical Society, on the state of education in the borough of Salford, in 1835. 42p. *8°*. *London & Manchester*, 1836.

29648 MANIFESTO of the Chancellor of the Exchequer, against the moral interests of the productive classes. From the Monthly Repository for April, 1836. [On the desirability of the removal of the stamp duty on newspapers.] 8p. *8°*. [*London*,] 1836.

29649 NAVILLE, F. M. L. De la charité légale, de ses effets, de ses causes et spécialement des maisons de travail, et de la proscription de la mendicité...[With 'Index des sources'.] 2 vols. *8°*. *Paris & Saint-Pétersbourg*, 1836.

29650 NEWNHAM, W. H. Operations of the Poor Law Amendment Act, in the county of Sussex. Report of the auditor of the Uckfield Union, for the quarter ending December 25, 1835. 11p. *8°*. 1836.

29651 NIHIL, *pseud.* To the inhabitants of Newtown, particularly the members of benefit societies. [On schools for the children of members of benefit societies.] 8p. *8°*. *Newtown* [*Montgomeryshire*], [1836]

29652 *NOIRET, C. Mémoires d'un ouvrier rouennais. 100p. *12°*. *Rouen*, 1836. *The copy that belonged to George Grote.*

29653 NORRIS, W. A letter to the inhabitants of the parish of Warblington, Hants, on the new Poor Law, its origin, and intended effect...Third edition. 36p. *8°*. *London & Chichester*, 1836.

29654 NORTH WEST LONDON SELF-SUPPORTING DISPENSARY. Second annual report of the...Dispensary, No. 40, Manchester Street. 4p. *fol.* [*London*, 1836]

29655 [NORTON, C. E. S.] A voice from the factories. In serious verse. Dedicated to the Right Honourable Lord Ashley. 40p. *8°*. 1836.

29656 OASTLER, R. The factory question and the factory agitation, calmly considered, in a letter to those mill-owners who are the friends of the factory children, and...endeavouring...to obey the present Factories' Regulation Act. p.1–8. *8°*. *London & Manchester*, 1836. *Oastler's own copy.*

29657 —— The factory question. The law or the needle. 40p. *8°*. *London & Huddersfield*, [1836] *Oastler's own copy.*

29658 —— A letter to the Arch-bishop of York. [On the

Church of England and the factory question.] 28p. *8⁰*. *Huddersfield*, 1836. *Oastler's own copy.*

29659 —— A letter to those millowners who continue to oppose the Ten Hours Bill, and who...break the present Factories Act. 16p. *8⁰*. *Manchester*, 1836. *Oastler's own copy.*

29660 —— The rejected letter, with a dedication to the man wot would not have it read [J. Holdsworth]. A letter to the owners & occupiers of mills, in...Halifax, assembled ...on...3 August, 1836. 16p. *8⁰*. *Leeds*, 1836. *Oastler's own copy.*

29661 —— The unjust judge, or the 'Sign of the judge's skin'. A letter to George Goodman, Esq. Mayor of Leeds, on his...recent refusal to imprison a criminal under the Factories' Regulation Act... 15p. *8⁰*. *Leeds*, 1836. *Oastler's own copy.*

29662 O'CONNELL, D. Factory question. The sayings and doings of Daniel O'Connell, Esq. The former exemplified in his speeches on the protection of children... the latter, in his recent vote. [A compilation designed to discredit O'Connell.] 4p. *8⁰*. [1836] *The copy that belonged to Oastler, who attributed its compilation to 'Jowett' in the manuscript index to his pamphlet collection.*

29663 OPERATIVE conservative associations. Reprinted, for distribution, from Fraser's Magazine, for March...Third edition. 16p. *8⁰*. 1836.

29664 [**OSBORNE**, LORD S. G.] A word or two about the new Poor Law; addressed to his parishioners, by a beneficed clergyman in Buckinghamshire...S.G.O. Ninth edition. 14p. *8⁰*. [1836?] *The Oastler copy.*

29665 —— Eleventh edition. 14p. *8⁰*. [1836?]

29666 PARENT DU CHÂTELET, A. J. B. De la prostitution dans la ville de Paris, considérée sous le rapport de l'hygiène publique, de la morale et de l'administration: ouvrage appuyé de documens statistiques... Précédé d'une notice historique sur la vie et les ouvrages de l'auteur, par Fr. Leuret. 664p. *8⁰*. *Bruxelles*, 1836. *See also* 1837.

29667 PETTIGREW, T. J. The pauper farming system. A letter to the Right Hon. Lord John Russell... Secretary of State for the Home Department, on the condition of the pauper children of St. James, Westminster, as demonstrating the necessity of abolishing the farming system. 43p. *8⁰*. 1836.

29668 PHILO DEMOS, *pseud.* Appeal to Members of Parliament, and to the working classes, respecting the Ten Hours' Factory Bill, with sketches of its chief promoters. Dedicated to the Right Honbl. Lord Ashley. By M.R.C.S. [Consisting largely of an attack on Charles Hindley, M.P.] 59p. *8⁰*. *Stalybridge*, 1836.

29669 (Second edition.) The **POOR** robbed and the aristocracy receivers of the stolen property; being an address to all the true men of England. By an Englishman. 26p. *8⁰*. 1836.

29670 PROVINCIAL MEDICAL AND SURGICAL ASSOCIATION. The report of a Committee, on the new Poor Law Act, appointed by the Provincial Medical and Surgical Association, at its anniversary meeting...at Oxford, and read at the anniversary meeting...at Manchester, July 21st, 1836. 38p. *8⁰*. *Worcester*, 1836.

29671 The **PUNISHMENT** of death. A selection of articles from the Morning Herald, with notes. 2 vols. *12⁰*. 1836-37.

29672 A **REPORT** of the important proceedings of a public meeting, held in...Oldham on...the 11th...of November, 1836: on the subject of shortening the time of labour in the cotton, woollen, silk and other factories in Great Britain and Ireland. Chief speakers, John Fielden Esq. M.P., Charles Hindley, Esq. M.P., Richard Oastler, Esq. and the Rev. J. R. Stephens. 50p. *12⁰*. *Oldham*, 1836.

29673 ROBERTS, S. England's glory; or, the good old poor laws, addressed to the working classes of Sheffield. 56p. *12⁰*. *London & Sheffield*, 1836.

29674 ROBINSON, T. D. Ancient poor laws: an inquiry as to the provisions for the poor of Judea, Athens, and Rome; with a sketch of the English poor laws. xxviii, 68p. *8⁰*. 1836.

29675 SADLER, M. T. Factory statistics. The official tables appended to the report of the Select Committee on the Ten Hour Factory Bill vindicated in a series of letters addressed to John Elliot Drinkwater, Esq., one of the Factory Commissioners. 80p. *8⁰*. 1836. *The Oastler copy.*

29676 SCLATER, W. L. A letter to the Poor Law Commissioners for England and Wales, on the working of the new system. By the chairman of a Board of Guardians. 16p. *8⁰*. *Basingstoke & London*, [1836]

29677 SMITH, GERRIT. Two American villages. Peterboro' [signed: Gerrit Smith] and Auburn [signed: Abel Brown, jun.], the one reformed, and the other unreformed. The result of a careful visitation. 8p. *4⁰*. *Preston*, [1836] *The Turner copy.*

29678 SPENCER, T. The successful application of the new Poor Law to the parish of Hinton Charterhouse ... 60p. *8⁰*. 1836.

29679 A **STATEMENT** from the master cotton spinners; in support of the Factories' Act Amendment Bill. 7p. *8⁰*. *n.p.*, 1836.

29680 STEPHEN, SIR G. A letter to the Rt. Hon. Lord John Russell, &c.&c.&c. on the probable increase of rural crime, in consequence of the introduction of the new poor-law and railroad systems. 51p. *8⁰*. [1836]

29681 TAYLOR, THOMAS (*fl.* 1833-1839). Memoirs of John Howard, Esq., F.R.S., the Christian philanthropist: with a detail of his...labours in the cause of benevolence; and a brief account of the prisons, hospitals, schools ...and other public institutions he visited. 439p. *8⁰*. 1836.

29682 The **TEMPERANCE** doctor: ⟨principally from American authorities.⟩ 8p. *4⁰*. *Preston*, [1836] *The Turner copy.*

For **TEMPERANCE RECORDER**, *see* vol. III, *Periodicals list.*

29683 The **TRAFFIC!** Principally extracted from the American temperance publications. 8p. *4⁰*. *Preston*, [1836] *The Turner copy.*

29684 URE, A. Foreign competition and the Ten Hours' Bill. The letter of Dr. Andrew Ure to Charles Hindley, Esq., M.P. with a reply to the same [by G. S. Bull]. 4p. *8⁰*. *Bradford*, [1836] *The Oastler copy.*

29685 VICTORIA BENEVOLENT OR SELF-SUPPORTING MEDICAL INSTITUTION. Victoria Benevolent...Institution, for Cricklade and the neighbouring villages. [Rules.] 11p. *12⁰*. *Cirencester*, [1836]

29686 A **VIEW** of the state of pauperism in Ireland; its evils and its remedies. 79p. *8°. 1836.*

29687 **WARE,** J. An account of the several charities and estates, held in trust, for the use of the poor of the parish of Saint Leonard, Shoreditch, Middlesex; and of the benefactions to the same, compiled in the years 1833, 1834, 1835... 175p. *8°. London & Hoxton, 1836.*

29688 *****YATES,** JAMES. Observations on Lord John Russell's Bill for registering births, deaths, and marriages in England, with the outlines of a plan for registering births, deaths and marriages in Great Britain and Ireland. 48p. *8°. 1836. The FWA copy, that belonged to William Pare.*

29689 *——— Postscript to Observations on Lord John Russell's Bill for registering births, deaths and marriages in England, in reply to the Rev. W. H. Hale's Remarks on the same subject. p.[49]–64. *8°. 1836. Paginated in sequence with the original work. The FWA copy, that belonged to William Pare.*

SLAVERY

29690 **BALL,** CHARLES, *negro slave.* Slavery in the United States: a narrative of the life and adventures of Charles Ball, a black man... 400p. *12°. Lewistown, Pa., 1836.*

29691 **BOSTON FEMALE ANTI-SLAVERY SOCIETY.** Report of the Boston Female Anti-Slavery Society; with a concise statement of events, previous and subsequent to the annual meeting of 1835. 108p. *12°. Boston, Mass., 1836. The half-title reads: Right and wrong in Boston. See also 1842.*

29692 **BURLEIGH,** CHARLES C., *ed.* Reception of George Thompson in Great Britain. ⟨Compiled from various British publications.⟩ [With an introduction by C. C. Burleigh.] 238p. *12°. Boston, 1836.*

29693 **CHANNING,** WILLIAM E. Slavery...Reprinted from the Boston (U.S.) edition. 99p. *8°. Birmingham, 1836.*

29694 ——— Second edition. Revised. 183p. *8°. Boston, 1836.*

29695 **DAIN,** C. De l'abolition de l'esclavage...Suivi d'un article de M. Fourier. (Extrait de la Phalange, Journal de l'École Sociétaire.) 54p. *8°. Paris, 1836.*

29696 **DICK,** D. All modern slavery indefensible; intended for all places where slavery does exist, and for all legislative powers by whom it is allowed... 323p. *12°. Montrose, Dundee, &c., 1836.*

29697 **GRIMKÉ,** A. E. Appeal to the Christian women of the south [on slavery]. 36p. *8°. [New York:] The American Anti-Slavery Society, [1836]*

29698 **INNES,** JOHN (*fl.* 1830–1849). Rapport d'un témoin oculaire sur la marche du système d'émancipation des nègres dans les Antilles anglaises; ou lettre à Lord Glenelg...Traduit de l'anglais. 151p. *8°. Paris, 1836. For another edition, see 1835.*

29699 **MACAULAY,** Z., *ed.* Détails sur l'émancipation des esclaves dans les colonies anglaises, pendant les années 1834 et 1835, tirés des documens officiels présentés au Parlement anglais et imprimé par son ordre, avec des observations et des notes par Z. Macaulay. Traduit de l'anglais. 128p. *8°. Paris, 1836.*

29700 Twenty **MILLIONS** thrown away, and slavery perpetuated. Reprinted from the Radical...[Signed: An ex-member of the Jamaica Assembly.] 21p. *12°. [1836]*

29701 **PAULDING,** J. K. Slavery in the United States. 312p. *12°. New-York, 1836.*

29702 **RANKIN,** J. Letters on American slavery, addressed to Mr. Thomas Rankin, merchant...Second edition. 118p. *18°. Newburyport, 1836. For another edition, see vol. III, Addenda.*

29703 A full and corrected **REPORT** of the proceedings at the anti-slavery meeting, held in Mount-Zion Chapel, Birmingham, for the purpose of considering the propriety of petitioning the House of Commons, on the defeat of the Act for the abolition of colonial slavery, on Monday, February 1, 1836. 28p. *12°. Birmingham, 1836.*

29704 **ROBERTS,** T. The cruel nature and injurious effects of the foreign slave trade, represented in a letter, addressed to the Right Hon. Lord Brougham and Vaux. 40p. *8°. Bristol, 1836.*

29705 A full **STATEMENT** of the reasons which were in part offered to the Committee of the Legislature of Massachusetts...showing why there should be no penal laws enacted, and no condemnatory resolutions passed by the Legislature, respecting abolitionits [*sic*] and anti-slavery societies. 48p. *8°. Boston, 1836.*

29706 **STUART,** C. A memoir of Granville Sharp, to which is added Sharp's "Law of passive obedience," and an extract from his "Law of retribution." 156p. *12°. New-York: The American Anti-Slavery Society, 1836.*

29707 **THOMPSON,** GEORGE (1804–1878). Lectures of George Thompson, with a full report of the discussion between Mr. Thompson and Mr. Borthwick, the pro-slavery agent, held at...Liverpool...Also, a brief history of his connection with the anti-slavery cause in England, by Wm. Lloyd Garrison. 190p. *12°. Boston, 1836.*

POLITICS

29708 **APPEAL** to the electors of England, on the approaching dissolution. Extracted from a recent number of the Metropolitan Conservative Journal. 12p. *8°. [1836?]*

29709 **BIRMINGHAM.** Justice for Ireland! Report of the town's meeting held on...June 13, 1836 [to protest against the Lords' amendments to the Irish Municipal Bill]. 6p. *fol. Birmingham, [1836] See note to no. 20490.*

29710 **BIRMINGHAM POLITICAL UNION.** Proceedings of the important town's meeting convened by the Political Union, and held in the Birmingham Town

Hall, on...Jan. 18, 1836. 12p. *4°. Birmingham*, 1836. *See note to no. 26519.*

For the **BRAZEN HEAD,** *continued as the Reformer, see vol. III, Periodicals list, the Reformer.*

29711　BULWER, W. H. L. E., *Baron Dalling and Bulwer.* The Lords, the Government, and the country. A letter to a constituent on the present state of affairs... Third edition. 118p. *8°.* 1836.

29712　[CONSIDÉRANT, V. P.] Débacle de la politique en France. [With 'Mémoire justificatif présenté à la Cour des Pairs par l'accusé Rivière cadet'.] 152p. *8°. Paris,* 1836. *Considérant's own copy.*

29713　COPLEY, J. S., *Baron Lyndhurst.* Summary of the session. Speech of the Right Hon. Lord Lyndhurst, delivered in the House of Lords, on Thursday, August 18, 1836. To which is added, the substance of the speech of His Grace the Duke of Wellington, upon the same occasion. Twenty-second edition. 23p. *8°.* [1836]

29714　EMMET, R. The life, trial and conversations of Robert Emmet...leader of the Irish insurrection of 1803; also, the celebrated speech made by him on that occasion. 100p. *8°. Manchester, London, &c.,* 1836.

29715　HUISH, R. The history of the private and political life of...Henry Hunt...Exhibiting the rise and progress of those...events which led to the passing of the Reform Act... 2 vols. *8°.* 1836. *The engraved title-page is dated '1835'.*

29716　—— The memoirs, private and political, of Daniel O'Connell, Esq. from the year 1776 to the close of the proceedings in Parliament for the repeal of the Union. Compiled from official documents. 716p. *8°.* 1836.

29717　MacDONNELL, E. Vindication of the House of Lords, &c.&c.&c. In a series of letters addressed "To the editor of the Times." 39p. *8°.* [1836?] *Presentation copy from the author to Earl De Grey.*

29718　The NEWSPAPER STAMP and advertisement duties. A form of a petition to Parliament, accurately setting forth...the merits of much of the present newspaper press; and suggesting with respect to the above duties, an entirely novel mode of proceeding. 10p. *8°.* 1836.

29719　*NEWSPAPER STAMPS. Deputation to Lord Viscount Melbourne, to procure the total repeal of the stamp duty on newspapers. From Cleave's Gazette, of the 20th of Feb., 1836. 16p. *16°.* [1836] *The FWA copy that belonged to William Pare.*

29720　OASTLER, R. More work for the Leeds new thief-catchers. A letter to George Goodman, Esq., Mayor of Leeds, &c.&c. 8p. *8°. Huddersfield,* [1836] *Oastler's own copy.*

29721　PAINE, T. Dissertation on first principles of government. 16p. *8°. J. Watson,* 1835[1836] *The date '1836' is printed on the wrapper. For other editions, see 1795.*

29722　—— Rights of Man: being an answer to Mr. Burke's attack on the French Revolution. [With 'Rights of Man, part the second: combining principle and practice'.] 160p. *8°.* 1836. *The two parts were formerly published separately. For other editions of part 1, see 1791, and of part 2, 1792.*

29723　[PLACE, F.] The stamp duty on newspapers. From the Radical of Saturday, March 19, 1836. [Signed: F.P.] 14p. *8°.* [1836]

For **POLITICS FOR THE POOR AND RICH,** *see vol. III, Periodicals list.*

29724　*PRICE, H. Reasons in support of an extension of the elective franchise to the working classes; submitted to the serious consideration of the King and his ministers. In a letter from the Reverend H. Price to Joseph Hume, Esq. M.P. ⟨From 'Tait's Magazine'.⟩ 16p. *8°.* [1836] *The copy presented by Joseph Hume to Mrs. Grote.*

29725　—— Second edition. 16p. *8°.* [1836] *Another, the FWA copy, belonged to William Pare.*

For the **REFORMER,** [*Liverpool,*] *see vol. III, Periodicals list.*

29726　REPORT of the proceedings at the Grand Dinner of the non-electors to the Borough Members, T. Attwood, Esq. and J. Scholefield, Esq., on...February 1, 1836. 15p. *4°. Birmingham,* 1836. *See note to no. 26519.*

29727　TAXES on knowledge. Reduction or abolition of the newspaper stamp-duty? From the London Review for January, 1836. 20p. *8°.* [*London,* 1836]

29728　*—— [Another edition.] 16p. *8°.* [*London,* 1836] *The FWA copy, that belonged to William Pare.*

29729　THOMPSON, THOMAS P. Letters of a representative to his constituents, during the session of 1836. To which is added a running commentary on anti-commercial fallacies, reprinted from the Spectator of 1834. With additions and corrections. 208p. *8°.* 1836.

29730　WEST, M. J. A letter to the Right Hon. Viscount Melbourne, on the present mode of legislation in respect of public bills. 32p. *8°.* 1836.

29731　WESTMACOTT, C. M. The stamp duties. Serious considerations on the proposed alteration of the stamp duty on newspapers... 15p. *8°.* 1836.

29732　WORKING MEN'S ASSOCIATION. The rotten House of Commons, being an exposition of the present state of the franchise, and an appeal to the nation on the course to be pursued in the approaching crisis. Addressed to the working men of the United Kingdom. 20p. *8°.* [1836]

29733　*—— Second edition... 20p. *8°.* [1836?] *The FWA copy, that belonged to William Pare.*

SOCIALISM

29734　ASSOCIATION OF ALL CLASSES OF ALL NATIONS. Manual of the Association... Founded May 1, 1835. No. 2. 63p. *12°.* 1836.

29735　BUONARROTI, P. Buonarroti's History of Babeuf's conspiracy for equality; with the author's reflections on the causes & character of the French Revolution...Also, his views of democratic government, community of property, and political and social equality.

Translated from the French...and illustrated by original notes, etc. by Bronterre [i.e. J. B. O'Brien]... 454p. *12°.* 1836. *For another edition, see 1828.*

29736　COMMON SENSE, *pseud.* Common sense to the working classes, on the division of labour and profits. Letter I. Reprinted from the Radical, weekly stamped newspaper. 8p. *8°.* [1836] *Another, the FWA copy, belonged to William Pare.*

29737 —— Common sense to the working classes, on the causes of their existing slavery, and the means of redeeming themselves. From the Radical of Sunday, April 10, 1836. [Letter II.] 16p. *8°*. [1836] *Another, the FWA copy, belonged to William Pare.*

29738 —— Common sense to the working classes, on the means of attaining equality. Letter III. Reprinted from the Radical, weekly stamped newspaper. 12p. *8°*. [1836]

29739 COMMUNITY FRIENDLY SOCIETY. Rules to be observed for the government and management of the Community Friendly Society, established for the mutual relief and maintenance of the members, and for the purpose of promoting the well being of themselves and families upon the principles of co-operation... 34p. *8°*. 1836.

29740 DAIN, C., *and others.* Trois discours prononcé à l'Hôtel-de-Ville par MM. Dain, Considérant et d'Izalguier; faisant complément à la publication du Congrès Historique. 184p. *8°*. *Paris*, 1836. *Two copies, one that belonged to Charles Dain, the other to Victor Considérant.*

29741 DAVENPORT, A. The life, writings, and principles of Thomas Spence, author of the Spencean system, or agrarian equality. With a portrait of the author. 24p. *12°*. [1836]

29742 ETZLER, J. A. The paradise within the reach of all men, without labour, by powers of nature and machinery... 216p. *12°*. 1836. *See also* 1842.

29743 OWEN, ROBERT. The book of the new moral world, containing the rational system of society, founded on demonstrable facts, developing the constitution and laws of human nature and society. [Parts 1–7.] *8°*. 1836–44. *Another, the FWA copy of the first part, was presented by Owen, with an inscription, to 'Mr & Mrs Pare'. See also* 1837, 1847.

29744 OWEN, ROBERT D. Address on free inquiry... To which is added aphorisms on free inquiry by Thomas Jefferson, one of the Presidents of the United States. 16p. *8°*. [1836 ?] *See also* 1840.

29745 —— Address on the hopes and destinies of the human species. 18p. *12°*. 1836. *See also* 1840.

29746 VILLEGARDELLE, F. Accord des intérêts et des partis, ou l'industrie sociétaire. 34p. *8°*. *Paris*, 1836. *The copy that belonged to Victor Considérant.*

29747 WRIGHT, F. Course of popular lectures... With...addresses on various public occasions...Sixth edition. 239p. *12°*. *New York*, 1836. *For other editions, see* 1829.

MISCELLANEOUS

29748 CHURCH BUILDING SOCIETY. Incorporated Society for Promoting the Enlargement, Building and Repairing of Churches & Chapels. Annual report, May 18, 1836, &c. 82p. *8°*. 1836.

29749 COBBETT, W. A grammar of the English language, in a series of letters. Intended for the use of schools and of young persons in general; but more especially for the use of soldiers, sailors, apprentices, and plough-boys...To which are added, six lessons, intended to prevent statesmen from using false grammar... [240]p. *12°*. 1836. *For other editions, see* 1819.

29750 COBBETT'S questions in the "Legacy to parsons" answered by a parson. 21p. *12°*. *Newcastle & London*, 1836.

29751 COLQUHOUN, J. C. ⟨No. VI.⟩ Published under the superintendence of the Glasgow Protestant Association. Ireland: the policy of reducing the Established Church and paying the Roman Catholic priests. 68p. *8°*. *Glasgow*, 1836. *The copy that belonged to Earl De Grey.*

29752 COMBE, ANDREW. The physiology of digestion considered with relation to the principles of dietetics ...Second edition, revised and enlarged. 350p. *8°*. *Edinburgh & London*, 1836.

29753 ENSOR, G. Natural theology: the arguments of Paley, Brougham, and the Bridgewater Treatises on this subject examined: also the doctrines of Brougham and the immaterialists respecting the soul... 60p. *12°*. 1836.

29754 EWBANK, W. W. Sacrament Sunday: a dialogue. By the Rev. W. Withers Ewbank...Addressed to his parishioners. 20p. *8°*. 1836.

29755 [FOX, afterwards **VASSALL,** H. R., *3rd Baron Holland.*] Parliamentary talk, or, the objections to the late Irish Church Bill considered in a letter to a friend

abroad. By a disciple of Selden. Second edition. 52p. *8°*. 1836.

29756 [IRWIN, A.] Roman Catholic morality, as inculcated in the theological class-books used in Maynooth College. 25p. *8°*. *Dublin & London*, 1836.

29757 A LETTER to those ministers and members of the Church of Scotland, who have lent themselves to the Dens' theology humbug, showing...that John Knox and our Protestant reformers, together with assemblies of the Kirk...have all sanctioned the intolerant principles ascribed to Peter Dens...By a member of the General Synod of Ulster. 39p. *8°*. *Edinburgh*, 1836. *Attributed to James McKnight in a manuscript note on the title-page.*

29758 PERSECUTION sanctioned by the Westminster Confession: a letter, addressed to...the Synod of Ulster; shewing from...the public records of the Church of Scotland, the doctrines of intolerance to which the late vote of unqualified subscription has committed the General Synod of Ulster...By a member of the Synod of Ulster. 72p. *8°*. *Belfast*, 1836. *Attributed to James McKnight in a manuscript note on the title-page.*

29759 PHILLPOTTS, H., *Bishop of Exeter.* Charge delivered to the clergy of the diocese of Exeter, by the Right Reverend Henry Lord Bishop of Exeter, at his triennial visitation in the months of August, September, and October, 1836. Second edition. 48p. *8°*. 1836.

29760 RENDER, J. A lecture on persecution, delivered in the Catholic Chapel, Hull; April 7th, 1836. 32p. *12°*. *Hull*, [1836]

29761 SMITH, THOMAS, *of Marylebone.* Historical recollections of Hyde Park, compiled and arranged from numerous authentic works, public records, private documents, &c. 99p. *12°*. 1836. *The copy that belonged to John Burns (1858–1943), with his signature on the flyleaf.*

1837

GENERAL

29762 *AARGAU, *Canton of.* Kommissionalbericht über den Gesetzes-Vorschlag betreffend das Gewerbs-Polizei-Gesetz für den Kanton Aargau. Dem Grossen Rathe erstattet am 2. Juni 1837. [Signed: C. Bertschinger.] 15p. *8°. Aarau,* [1837] *The copy that belonged to George Grote.*

29763 **BINNS,** JONATHAN. The miseries and beauties of Ireland. 2 vols. *8°.* 1837.

29764 **BLANQUI,** J. A. Conservatoire des Arts et Métiers. Cours d'économie industrielle, 1836–37. Leçons sur les banques, les routes...les fers et fontes, la houille ...la laine...l'industrie parisienne, sur le commerce des ports: Marseille et Bordeaux...Recueillies par Ad. Blaise et Joseph Garnier. 537p. *8°. Paris,* 1837.

29765 —— Histoire de l'économie politique en Europe, depuis les anciens jusqu'à nos jours, suivie d'une bibliographie raisonnée des principaux ouvrages d'économie politique. 2 vols. *8°. Paris,* 1837. *See also* 1842, 1845.

29766 The **BRITISH ALMANAC** of the Society for the Diffusion of Useful Knowledge, for...1837. [With 'The companion to the Almanac; or year-book of general information'.] 96, 258p. *12°.* [1837] *For other editions, see* 1828.

29767 The **BRITISH IMPERIAL CALENDAR** for...1837...or general register of the United Kingdom ...and its colonies...[With 'A companion to the British Imperial Calendar, for...1837'.] 464, 114p. *12°.* [1837] *For other editions, see* 1817.

29768 **CAREY,** H. C. Principles of political economy ... 3 vols. *8°. Philadelphia & London,* 1837–40.

29769 **CHEVALIER,** M. Lettres sur l'Amérique du nord...Troisième édition, revue, corrigée et augmentée de plusieurs chapitres. 2 vols. *8°. Paris,* 1837. *Described in the signatures of vol. 1 and on the title-page of vol. 2 as 'Edition spéciale'.*

29770 **COOK,** G. A manual of political economy. Being a synopsis of a course of lectures on that science delivered in the University of St. Andrews. 143p. *8°. Edinburgh,* 1837.

29771 *DIXON, T. Who pays the taxes, and who ought to pay them? A controversy between the man who has money and the man who has none, as well as between the owner of the soil and the eater of its produce. 16p. *8°. Dublin,* [1837] *The copy that belonged to George Grote.*

29772 **DROZ,** J. F. X. Économie politique ou principes de la science des richesses. 271p. *12°. Bruxelles,* 1837. *For other editions, see* 1829.

29773 **DUVERGIER DE HAURANNE,** P. Chambre des Députes. Session de 1837. Discours de M. Duvergier de Hauranne, Député de Cher, dans la discussion du projet d'adresse en réponse au discours du trône. (Séance du 12 janvier 1837.) 26p. *8°.* [*Paris,* 1837]

29774 *The **EAST-INDIA** register and directory, for 1837; containing...lists of the Company's servants... mariners, &c. not in the service of the...Company; com-piled...by F. Clark... 273, 166, 173p. *12°. London & Edinburgh,* [1837] *For other editions, see* 1804.

29775 *FAUCHER, L. Extrait de la Revue des deux Mondes, livraison du 1er mars 1837. L'union du Midi. Association commerciale de la France avec la Belgique, l'Espagne et la Suisse. 48p. *8°.* [*Paris,* 1837] *The copy that belonged to George Grote. A greatly enlarged version was published in 1842 (q.v.).*

29776 **FOX,** WILLIAM J. Finsbury lectures. Reports of lectures delivered at the Chapel in South Place, Finsbury...No. VIII. The church-rate imposition. A lecture in aid of the subscription for defending the right of Mr. Burder, and the parishioners of Braintree, to refuse payment of a church-rate... 27p. *8°.* 1837. *For other lectures in this series, see* 1835.

29777 **FRANCE.** *Chambre des Députés.* (No. 312.)... Enquête sur les tabacs. 645p. *4°.* [*Paris,* 1837]

29778 —— *Ministère des Travaux Publics.* Archives statistiques du Ministère des Travaux Publics, de l'Agriculture et du Commerce... 306p. *4°. Paris,* 1837. *The copy specially bound for presentation to T. Spring Rice, as Chancellor of the Exchequer, from the Minister.*

29779 —— —— Statistique de la France, publiée par le Ministre des Travaux Publics, de l'Agriculture et du Commerce. [Territoire, population.] 511p. *4°. Paris,* 1837. *See also* 1835 (*Ministère du Commerce*), 1847 (*Ministère de l'Agriculture et du Commerce*).

29780 **GLASGOW AND CLYDESDALE STATISTICAL SOCIETY.** Constitution and regulations of the Glasgow and Clydesdale Statistical Society. Instituted April, MDCCCXXXVI. [With 'Transactions...I. An account of the former and present state of Glasgow... By James Cleland'.] 15, 98, [6]p. *4°. n.p.* [1837]

29781 **GRILLE DE BEUZELIN,** E. L. H. T. Statistique monumentale. (Specimen.) Rapport à M. le Ministre de l'Instruction publique sur les monuments historiques des arrondissements de Nancy et de Toul (Département de la Meurthe)... 159p. *4°. Paris,* 1837.

29782 **GUTIERREZ,** M. M. Impugnacion a las cinco proposiciones de Pebrer sobre los grandes males que causa la ley de aranceles a la nacion en general, a la Cataluna en particular, y a las mismas fabricas catalanas. 293p. *8°. Madrid,* 1837.

29783 *HERZOG, C. Staatshandbuch der schweizerischen Eidgenossenschaft für das Jahr 1837. 417p. *8°. Bern,* 1837. *The copy that belonged to George Grote.*

29784 **IBBOTSON,** W. Agricultural distress, its cause and remedy, introduced by some remarks on the duties which devolve on mankind...especially Christians, in reference to...political economy. 200p. *8°. London & Sheffield,* 1837.

29785 **LAING,** SAMUEL (1780–1868). Journal of a residence in Norway during the years 1834, 1835, & 1836; made with a view to enquire into the moral and political economy of that country, and the conditions of its inhabitants...Second edition. 482p. *8°.* 1837. *For another edition, see* 1836.

29786 LECOINTE, A. Annuaire statistique et administratif du département de l'Aisne, pour l'année 1837...27e année. 324p. 8°. *Laon,* [1837]

29787 LEIGH AND SON. Leigh's new pocket road-book of England and Wales: containing an account of all the direct and cross-roads; together with a description of every remarkable place; its curiosities, manufactures, commerce, population, and principal inns. To which are added, pleasure tours...Sixth edition, carefully revised. 511p. *12°.* 1837.

29788 LLOYD, W. F. Lectures on population, value, poor-laws, and rent, delivered in the University of Oxford, during the years 1832, 1833, 1834, 1835, and 1836. 75, 40, 128, 71, 106p. 8°. *London & Oxford,* 1837. *A collection of previously published works, reissued with a general title-page and list of contents.*

For —— Two lectures on the justice of poor-laws and one lecture on rent, delivered in the University of Oxford... 1836, *London & Oxford, see no. 29788 above.*

29789 *McCULLOCH, JOHN R. A statistical account of the British Empire: exhibiting its extent, physical capacities, population, industry, and civil and religious institutions... 2 vols. 8°. 1837. *The copy that belonged to George Grote. See also 1839, 1847.*

29790 MACNAGHTEN, SIR F. W., *Bart.* Some observations upon the present state of Ireland. 79p. 8°. 1837.

29791 [MARKLAND, J. H.] A sketch of the life and character of George Hibbert... 21p. 8°. 1837. *Presentation copy, with inscription, from the author to J. B. Philips.*

29792 *MARTINEAU, H. Society in America... 3 vols. *12°.* 1837.

29793 *—— [Another edition.] 2 vols. 8°. *Paris,* 1837.

29794 MERIVALE, H. An introductory lecture on the study of political economy. Delivered June 1. 1837. 38p. 8°. 1837.

For the **MIRROR OF LITERATURE, AMUSEMENT, AND INSTRUCTION,** *see* vol. III, *Periodicals list.*

29795 MOREAU DE JONNÈS, A. Statistique de la Grande-Bretagne et de l'Irlande. 2 vols. 8°. *Paris,* 1837–38.

29796 NEWCASTLE-UPON-TYNE. *Town Council.* The proceedings and reports of the Town Council ...for 1836, being their first year, after the passing of the Municipal Reform Act... [184]p. 8°. *Newcastle,* 1837. *See also,* 1838, 1839, 1840.

29797 NOEL, HON. B. W. Notes of a short tour through the midland counties of Ireland, in the summer of 1836, with observations on the condition of the peasantry. 389p. *12°.* 1837.

29798 PORTER, G. R. Progrès de la Grande Bretagne sous le rapport de la population et de la production. Traduit de l'anglais...et accompagné de notes et tableaux présentant les progrès analogues pour la France, par Ph. Chemin-Dupontès; précédé d'une préface par M. Michel Chevalier. lvii, 387p. 8°. *Paris,* 1837. *A translation of the first volume of* The progress of the nation, *1836 (q.v.).*

29799 RUSSIA. In answer to a Manchester manufacturer [Cobden]...Second edition. 33p. 8°. *London & Edinburgh,* 1837.

29800 SINCLAIR, JOHN (1797–1875). Memoirs of the life and works of...Sir John Sinclair, Bart.... 2 vols. 8°. *Edinburgh & London,* 1837.

29801 SLEEMAN, SIR W. H. Analysis and review of the peculiar doctrines of the Ricardo, or new school of political economy. 72p. 8°. *Serampore,* 1837. *Presentation copy, with inscription, from the author to F. C. Smith, Esq.*

29802 SMITH, JOHN R. Bibliotheca Cantiana: a bibliographical account of what has been published on the history, topography, antiquities, customs, and family history, of the county of Kent. 360p. 8°. 1837.

29803 SMITH, SYDNEY (1771–1845). The new reign. The duties of Queen Victoria: a sermon preached at the Cathedral Church of St. Paul's...Second edition. 24p. 8°. 1837.

For the **STATISTICAL JOURNAL AND RECORD OF USEFUL KNOWLEDGE,** 1837– 38, *see vol.* III, *Periodicals list.*

29804 STATISTICAL SOCIETY OF LONDON. Third annual report of the Council of the Statistical Society of London, with the regulations of the Society, and a list of the fellows, &c. March 1837. 40p. 8°. 1837. *See also* 1836.

29805 —— Transactions of the...Society...Vol. I. – Part I. 148p. 4°. 1837.

29806 STURZ, J. J. A review, financial, statistical, & commercial, of the Empire of Brazil and its resources: together with a suggestion of the expediency and mode of admitting Brazilian and other foreign sugars into Great Britain for refining and exportation. 151p. 8°. 1837.

29807 SYKES, W. H. On the increase of wealth and expenditure in the various classes of society in the United Kingdom, as indicated by the returns made to the tax office, exports and imports, savings' banks, &c.&c.... From the transactions of the Statistical Society of London, Vol. I. – Part I. 16p. 4°. 1837. *Presentation copy, with inscription, from the author to the Duke of Somerset.*

29808 TAITBOUT DE MARIGNY, E. Three voyages in the Black Sea to the coast of Circassia: including descriptions of the ports, and the importance of their trade, with sketches of the manners, customs, religion, &c.&c., of the Circassians. 303p. 8°. 1837.

29809 TEMPLE, J. What is property? Observations on property, addressed to the King, the Lords and the Commons... 8p. *12°. Wakelin,* [1837?]

29810 —— [Another edition.] 8p. *12°. J. Cleave,* [1837?] *Another, the FWA copy, belonged to William Pare.*

29811 TUCKER, G. The laws of wages, profits, and rent, investigated. 189p. 8°. *Philadelphia,* 1837.

29812 *WARD, SIR H. G. The first step [emigration] to a poor law for Ireland. [With 'Appendix...Report from the Select Committee on the disposal of waste lands in the British Colonies'.] 48p. 8°. 1837. *The copy that belonged to George Grote.*

29813 WATSON'S or the gentleman's and citizen's almanack, (as compiled by the late John Watson Stewart,) for the year...1837...Containing, the days of the year... the sovereigns of Europe; the names of the Lord Lieutenant...Privy Council [of Ireland], the peers of Ireland, and the Irish members of the House of Commons...also the judges...the fairs; and the post-towns...238p. 8°. *Dublin,* [1837] *See also* 1798, 1838.

29814 WAYLAND, F. The elements of political economy. 472p. *8°. New York,* 1837. *See also* 1838.

29815 WORKING MEN'S ASSOCIATION. Address and rules of the Working Men's Association, for benefiting politically, socially, and morally, the useful classes. 8p. *8°.* [1837?]

29816 *ZÜRICH im Jahre 1837. Nach den natürlichen und geselligen Verhältnissen geschildert für Einheimische und Fremde. 66p. *8°. Zürich,* 1837. *The copy that belonged to George Grote.*

AGRICULTURE

29817 *BLACKER, W. Fifth edition. An essay on the improvement to be made in the cultivation of small farms by the introduction of green crops, and house-feeding the stock thereon...With a preface, addressed to landlords... 114p. *8°. Dublin, London, &c.,* 1837. *The copy that belonged to George Grote.*

29818 —— [Another edition.] Fifth edition... p.1–80. *12°. Dublin, London, &c.,* 1837. *For another edition, see* 1834.

29819 —— Review of Charles Shaw Lefevre, Esq.'s letter to his constituents, as chairman of the Select Committee appointed to inquire into the present state of agriculture. 79p. *8°. London, Dublin, &c.,* 1837.

29820 BROUN, Sir Richard, *Bart.* Mr. Broun's letter to the Central Agricultural Society of Great Britain and Ireland, and its sixty-six corresponding local agricultural associations. 120p. *8°.* 1837. *A second (imperfect) copy belonged to Patrick Chalmers.*

29821 CAMBRIDGESHIRE AND ISLE OF ELY FARMERS' ASSOCIATION. Report of the committee of the...Association, upon the state of agriculture: deduced from the evidence laid before the two Houses of Parliament, during the session of 1836. 131p. *8°. Cambridge, Royston, &c.,* 1837.

29822 CAMPKIN, H. Remarks on the evils of primogeniture. 46p. *12°.* 1837.

29823 CORNWALL. *Stannaries.* The laws of the Stannaries together with the Stannaries' Courts' Act [6 & 7 Will. 4, cap. 106], passed on the 20th August, 1836 and the...rules and orders made to define...the practice and pleadings of the same courts. Also the tables of costs, court fees, &c. Also the times and places when and where the tin coinages are held in Cornwall and Devon. 17–48, 24, 9–120, 127–136p. *8°. Truro,* [1837] *The sheets containing the Laws are those of the 1824 edition (q.v.), without pp. 121–126, containing a schedule no longer applicable, and with a reprinted index. For other editions, see* 1753.

29824 DRUMMOND, William, **& SONS.** A general list, or compendium of seeds, plants, implements, &c. sold by W. Drummond & Sons, Stirling, seedsmen and nurserymen... 15p. *8°. Stirling,* 1837. *Issued with James Smith: Remarks on thorough draining and ploughing (no. 29834), with which it is bound. See also* 1838.

29825 ENGLAND. *Laws, etc.* Anno septimo Gulielmi IV. Regis. Cap. 4. An Act for inclosing lands in the parishes of Winfrith Newburgh and Wool in the county of Dorset. ⟨22d March 1837.⟩ p.114–44. *fol.* 1837.

29826 *GEGUF, J. C. Mittheilungen über die Nothwendigkeit und erweisliche Möglichkeit, die schweizerische Schafzucht zu vermehren und zu veredeln. Zur Beachtung aller hohen Stände, besonders Uri, Schwytz, Unterwalden, Glarus, Graubündten, Wallis, Tessin und Freyburg als höchst wichtiges National-Bedürfnis. 20p. *8°. Luzern,* 1837. *The copy that belonged to George Grote.*

29827 *HUMBERT, J. Sur le désastreux système du défrichement des forêts en France. 44p. *8°. Paris & Nancy,* 1837. *The copy that belonged to George Grote.*

29828 HUTT, Sir W. State and prospects of British agriculture; being a compendium of the evidence given before a Committee of the House of Commons appointed in 1836 to enquire into agricultural distress. With a few introductory observations...Second edition. 225p. *8°.* 1837.

29829 JOHNSON, C. W. On liquid manures. 39p. *8°.* 1837.

29830 KINDER, T. Mexican justice and British diplomacy. The case of Thomas Kinder as regards the Parras estates, purchased by him in joint account with Messrs. Baring, Brothers, and Co. [An appeal to the British Government to intervene to secure the author's possession of estates (including mines) purchased in Mexico.] 59p. *8°.* 1837.

29831 LE COUTEUR, Sir J. On the varieties, properties, and classification, of wheat. 122p. *8°. Jersey & London,* 1837. *For another issue, see* 1836.

29832 POOLER, R. The Irish farmer's manual: being a practical compendium of the most improved systems of husbandry; comprehending...manures, draining...the culture of clover, turnips...and the other crops cultivated in Ireland... 262p. *12°. Dublin,* 1837.

29833 RAINPRECHTER, K. Freimüthige, auf Selbsterfahrung gegründete, Ansichten über den Verfall des Ackerbau's in verschiedenen Gegenden unseres Vaterlandes, und über die geeignetsten Mittel, demselben kräftig vorzubeugen. Sendschreiben an alle rationelle Gross- und Klein-Gutsbesitzer in Bayern. 118p. *8°. Bamberg,* 1837.

29834 SMITH, James (1789–1850). Remarks on thorough draining and deep ploughing...Extracted from the third report of Drummonds' Agricultural Museum. 25p. *8°. Stirling,* 1837. *See also* 1838, 1844.

29835 SOCIEDAD ECONOMICA. Memorias sobre los perjuicios que causa la excesiva cantidad de trigo y cebada que nuestros labradores arrojan generalmente á la tierra en la sementera...Presentadas á la obtencion del premio ofrecido por la Sociedad Económica Matritense para el año de 1836, y que esta coronó con el premió [compuesta por la Señorita Doña Maria de la Concepcion de Arias y Ariñon] y el accessit [su autor Don José Echegaray]...[With 'Nota de la Sociedad Económica Matritense'.] 44p. *4°. Madrid,* 1837.

29836 TOWNSHEND, W. R. Directions on practical agriculture, for the working farmers of Ireland, originally published in the Cork Southern Reporter, under the signature of "Agricola." 64p. *12°. Cork,* 1837.

POPULATION

29837 IVERNOIS, Sir F. d'. Enquête sur les causes patentes ou occultes de la faible proportion des naissances à Montreux...Tiré de la Bibliothèque Universelle de Genève (mai 1837). 44p. *8°. Genève, 1837.*

29838 *[RICHERAND, B. A., *Baron.*] De la population dans ses rapports avec la nature des gouvernemens. 349p. *8°. Paris, 1837. The copy that belonged to George Grote.*

29839 —— [Another issue, with a cancel title-page bearing the author's name.] 349p. *8°. Paris, 1837.*

TRADES & MANUFACTURES

29840 BARLOW, P. A treatise on the strength of timber, cast iron, malleable iron, and other materials; with rules for application in architecture, construction of suspension bridges, railways, etc. With an appendix, on the power of locomotive engines... 492p. *8°. 1837.*

29841 BENNETT, John(*fl.* 1833–37). The artificer's lexicon, for terms and prices, adapted for gentlemen, engineers, architects, builders, mechanists, millwrights, manufacturers, tradesmen, etc....Including labour prices for builders' work, etc., with a concise and practical method of measuring...Second edition. 476, 84p. *8°. 1837. For another edition, see 1833.*

29842 BIRKBECK, G. A lecture on the preservation of timber by Kyan's patent for preventing dry rot; delivered by Dr. Birkbeck, at the Society of Arts... December 9, 1834. With an appendix, &c. 47p. *8°. [1837 ?] With a printed advertisement for the Anti Dry-Rot Company, who use Kyan's patent method, on the verso of the final page.*

29843 The **BOOK** of trades; or circle of the useful arts...Third edition. 388p. *16°. Glasgow & London, 1837. For another edition, see 1835.*

29844 BRIAVOINNE, N. Sur les inventions et perfectionnemens dans l'industrie, depuis le fin du XVIIIe siècle jusqu'à nos jours. [*Mémoires couronnés par l'Académie Royale,* 13.] 190p. *4°. [Bruxelles, 1837]*

29845 COMMITTEE OF MASTER CABINET MAKERS AND JOURNEYMEN. The London cabinit [*sic*] makers, book of prices for the most improved extensible dining tables...By a committee... 27p. *4°. 1837. For editions of the original work, see 1824; for another supplement, see 1831.*

29846 DEPPING, G. B., *ed.* Réglemens sur les arts et métiers de Paris, rédigés au XIIIe siècle, et connus sous le nom du Livre des métiers d'Étienne Boileau; publiés... d'après les manuscrits de la Bibliothèque du Roi et des Archives du Royaume, avec des notes et une introduction ...(*Collection de documents inédits sur l'Histoire de France.* Première série, 31.) lxxxvi, 474p. *4°. Paris, 1837.*

29847 DYCE, W. and **WILSON,** C. H. Letter to Lord Meadowbank, and the Committee of the Honourable Board of Trustees for the Encouragement of Arts and Manufactures, on the best means of ameliorating the arts and manufactures of Scotland in point of taste. 54p. *8°. Edinburgh, 1837.*

29848 ENGLAND. Parliament. *House of Commons.* Copy of the Report from the Committee appointed by the Lords Commissioners of the Admiralty to investigate Mr. Kyan's patent for the prevention of dry rot in timber, &c. With extracts from the minutes of evidence. Ordered... to be printed 9 July, 1835. 46p. *8°. 1837.*

29849 FARADAY, M. On the practical prevention of dry rot in timber; being the substance of a lecture delivered...at the Royal Institution, February 22, 1833. With observations, &c. [With 'Copies of documents submitted in proof of the efficacy of the process secured by patent to Mr. J. Kyan'.] 30p. *8°. 1837.*

29850 GRIER, W. The mechanic's pocket dictionary, being a note book of technical terms, rules, and tables, in mathematics and mechanics... 547p. *12°. Glasgow, Edinburgh, &c., 1837.*

29851 HALL, Samuel. Samuel Hall's address to the British Association, explanatory of the injustice done to his improvements on steam engines by Dr. Lardner. 10p. *4°. London & Nottingham, 1837.*

29852 —— [Another edition.] 10p. *4°. London & Liverpool, 1837.*

29853 —— Samuel Hall's patent improvements on steam engines. [Testimonials.] 20p. *4°. [1837]*

29854 HULL FLAX AND COTTON MILL COMPANY. The deed of settlement, of the... Company. Established in the year 1836. 59p. *8°. Hull, 1837.*

COMMERCE

29855 GARELLO, F. Trattato generale di commercio ... 400p. *8°. Genova, 1837.*

29856 *[GEGUF, J. C.] Beleuchtungen über die Handels- und Zoll-Verhältnisse der schweizerischen Eidgenossenschaft mit dem Auslande. Zur ernsthaften Berücksichtigung aller Miteidgenossen. [Signed: J.C.G.V.] 52p. *8°. Luzern, 1837. The copy that belonged to George Grote.*

29857 LAY, G. T. Trade with China. A letter addressed to the British public on some of the advantages that would result from an occupation of the Bonin Islands. 17p. *8°. 1837.*

29858 TERRISTORI, , *Conte.* A geographical, statistical and commercial account of the Russian ports of the Black Sea, the Sea of Asoph and the Danube: also an official report of the European commerce of Russia in 1835. From the German... 48p. *8°.* 1837. *Terristori's work, published in French, in 1832, is supplemented here by information from Taitbout de Marigny,* Portulan de la Mer Noire et de la Mer d'Azow, *1830.*

COLONIES

29859 BANNISTER, S. On abolishing transportation; and on reforming the Colonial Office: in a letter to Lord John Russell. 88p. *8°.* 1837.

29860 ENGLAND. Parliament. *House of Commons.* Report of the Parliamentary Select Committee on aboriginal tribes, (British settlements.) Reprinted, with comments, by the "Aborigines Protection Society." 140p. *8°.* 1837.

29861 GRINDLAY, R. M. A view of the present state of the question as to steam communication with India. With a map, and an appendix, containing the petitions to Parliament, and other documents. 99p. *8°. London, Liverpool, &c.,* 1837.

29862 —— Third edition. 99p. *8°. London, Liverpool, &c.,* 1837. *Presentation copy from the author to Robert Napier.*

29863 HILL, S. S. The emigrant's introduction to an acquaintance with the British American colonies, and the present condition and prospects of the colonists. 324p. *12°.* 1837.

29864 KAY, S. A succinct statement of the Kaffer's case; comprising facts, illustrative of the causes of the late war, and of the influence of Christian missions: in a letter to T. Fowell Buxton, Esq. M.P.... 92p. *8°. London & Nottingham,* 1837.

29865 LANG, JOHN D. Transportation and colonization; or, the causes of the comparative failure of the transportation system in the Australian colonies: with suggestions for ensuring its future efficiency in subserviency to extensive colonization. 244p. *12°. London & Edinburgh,* 1837.

29866 *MARTIN, ROBERT M. Colonial policy of the British Empire. Part I. – Government. 100p. *8°.* 1837. *The copy that belonged to George Grote.*

29867 MANSIE, A. Dedicated by permission to His Excellency the Governor. The apprenticed labourer's manual: or an essay on the apprenticeship system, and the duties of the apprenticed labourers...[A prize essay. With 'A catechism of certain moral, social, and civil duties; adapted to existing circumstances. By the Wesleyan missionaries of Antigua. Originally published by order of the Legislature of that Colony'.] 215, 13p. *8°. British Guiana* [*Demerary: The Society for the Instruction of the Labouring Classes*], 1837.

29868 SIMONDE DE SISMONDI, J. C. L. Les colonies des anciens comparées à celles des modernes, sous le rapport de leur influence sur le bonheur du genre humain. 51p. *8°. Genève,* 1837.

29869 SKETCH of the commercial resources and monetary and mercantile system of British India, with suggestions for their improvement, by means of banking establishments. 109p. *8°.* 1837. *Attributed to 'John Crawford, Esq.' in a manuscript note on the title-page.*

29870 [WAKEFIELD, EDWARD G. and **WARD,** JOHN (1805–1890).] The British colonization of New Zealand; being an account of the principles, objects, and plans of the New Zealand Association; together with particulars concerning the position, extent, soil and climate, natural productions, and native inhabitants of New Zealand... 423p. *8°.* 1837.

FINANCE

29871 AGRICULTURAL AND COMMERCIAL BANK OF IRELAND. Report of the Board of Directors...to the shareholders, on the present position of the...Bank; together with a balance sheet of the assets, as also the liabilities outstanding. 44p. *8°. Dublin,* 1837.

29872 ALIENUS, *pseud.* New light on the Irish Tithe Bill; or, the appropriation clause recommended by the heads of the Irish Church. In a series of letters. 62p. *8°.* 1837. *Presentation copy, with inscription, from the pseudonymous author to the Rev. William D. Sadleir, F.T.C.D.*

29873 ARNOLD, THOMAS J. The law upon church rates, as laid down by the Attorney General, vindicated... Second edition, with additions. 67p. *8°.* 1837.

29874 ATTWOOD, T. Letter of Mr. Thomas Attwood to the Right Hon. Sir Robert Peel, Bart. 8p. *8°.* [*London,* 1837]

29875 [BAILEY, S.] Money and its vicissitudes in value; as they affect national industry and pecuniary contracts: with a postscript on joint-stock banks. By the author of The rationale of political representation, A critical dissertation on value, &c. 224p. *8°.* 1837.

29876 BAILLY, A. Exposé de l'administration générale et locale des finances du Royaume Uni de la Grande-Bretagne et d'Irlande... 2 vols. *8°. Paris,* 1837.

29877 BANK OF BENGAL. Papers printed for the use of the proprietors of the Bank of Bengal, agreeably to a resolution at their special general meeting held the 25th February, 1837. With a preface, and copy of letter from Government with a draft Act of proposed new bank charter. 119p. *8°. Calcutta,* 1837.

29878 BARNES, R. A letter on church rates. 34p. *8°. London & Exeter,* 1837.

29879 BENNISON, W. The cause of the present money crisis explained, in answer to the pamphlet of Mr. J. Horsley Palmer; and a remedy pointed out. 28p. *8°.* 1837.

29880 —— Second edition. 28p. *8°.* 1837.

29881 —— Third edition. 28p. *8°.* 1837.

29882 BIDDLE, N. Two letters addressed to the Hon. J. Quincy Adams; embracing a history of the re-charter of the Bank of the United States; and a view of the present condition of the currency. 20p. *8°. 1837. The copy that belonged to T. Spring Rice, Baron Monteagle.*

29883 [BLECKLY, J.?] A letter to the Hon. the Secret Committee of the House of Commons upon joint-stock banks. The second edition, with observations in reply to Col. Torrens, Mr. Jones Loyd, Mr. Horsley Palmer, and Mr. Samuel Clay. By Alfred. 32p. *8°.* 1837.

29884 BOWRING, Sir J. Public revenues and accounts. Speech of Doctor Bowring, 15th June, 1837, on proposing resolutions for the greater safety of the public revenues, and the greater accuracy of the public accounts. 15p. *8°.* 1837.

29885 BURY BANKING COMPANY. Deed of settlement of the Bury Banking Company, dated May 13th, 1837. Established under the authority of an Act of Parliament...Capital two hundred thousand pounds. 73p. *8°. Bury,* 1837.

29886 —— [Another issue.] Deed of settlement... dated May 13, 1836... 73p. *8°. Bury, 1837. The date of the deed has been corrected to '1836'.*

29887 CAMPBELL, James, *deputy collector of the port of New York.* Tariff, or rates of duties payable on goods...imported...after the first day of January, 1838, until December 31st, 1839...Revised and corrected by James Campbell... 180p. *8°. New-York,* [1837] *For another edition, see 1834.*

29888 CAMPBELL, John, *Baron Campbell.* Letter to the Right Hon. Lord Stanley, M.P. for North Lancashire, on the law of church rates. 39p. *8°.* 1837.

29889 —— Second edition. 39p. *8°.* 1837.

29890 —— Third edition. 39p. *8°.* 1837.

29891 —— Fourth edition. 39p. *8°.* 1837.

29892 —— [Another edition.] 22p. *12°. Edinburgh,* 1837.

29893 [CAPPS, E.] The currency question in a nutshell. 16p. *8°. 1837. See also* 1838, 1844, 1848 (Currency tracts for the industrious).

29894 CASES, with the opinions of the Attorney-General of England, Edward Pennefather, K.C., R. B. Warren, K.C., and D. R. Pigot, K.C., shewing the defective state of the law regulating joint stock banks...and the total want of protection afforded to shareholders against the mismanagement or misconduct of directors, as exemplified by the facts stated in respect to the Agricultural and Commercial Bank of Ireland. 110p. *8°.* 1837.

29895 The **CAUSES** of the present crisis. Shown by an examiner. Originally published in the daily newspapers. [With 'Prospectus of the Financial Register of the United States'.] 23p. *12°. Philadelphia,* 1837.

29896 CHAPMAN, H. S. (Not yet published.) The safety-principle of joint-stock banks and other companies, exhibited in a modification of the law of partnership. 54p. *8°.* 1837.

29897 —— [Another edition.] 54p. *8°.* 1837.

29898 [CHAYTOR, J. M.] Monetary system. The injury, insufficiency, and inconvenience of a gold standard and circulating medium, fairly stated, with a proposed substitute. By J.M.C. 31p. *8°. London & Dublin,* 1837.

29899 Will you have your **CHURCH** repaired? For this is the object of a Bill recently proposed, and which is entitled A Bill for the abolition of church rates, and for the improvement of the land revenue of the Church of England. 34p. *12°.* 1837.

29900 —— A corrected edition. 36p. *8°.* 1837.

29901 CITY BANK OF NEW HAVEN. Answer of the Board of Directors of the City Bank by their agents, to the report of the Committee of Investigation made to the General Assembly, May session, 1837. 22p. *8°. Hartford,* 1837.

29902 CLAY, H. Speech of Henry Clay, of Kentucky, on the bill imposing additional duties, as depositaries, in certain cases, on public officers. In Senate of the United States, September 25, 1837. 19p. *8°. Washington,* 1837.

29903 CLAY, Sir W., *Bart.* Speech of William Clay, Esq., M.P. on moving for the appointment of a committee to inquire into the operation of the Act permitting the establishment of joint-stock banks. To which are added, reflections on limited liability, paid-up capital, and publicity of accounts...Second edition. 144p. *8°. 1837. For another edition, see* 1836.

29904 CLIBBORN, E. American prosperity. An outline of the American debit or banking system; to which is added, a justification of the veto of the late President: also an explanation of the true principles of banking, with a paper currency in the United Kingdom. [Read at the evening meeting of the Royal Dublin Society, 30 May, 1837.] 44p. *8°. London & Dublin, 1837. An offprint of the text of the paper, published as 'Remarks on banking' as Appendix VIII to the Minutes of the Society, is also in the Goldsmiths' Library.*

29905 The secret **COMMITTEE** and the joint stock banks. A letter to the Right Honorable T. Spring Rice, Chancellor of the Exchequer. By a Manchester banker. 29p. *8°.* 1837.

29906 CONNECTICUT. *General Assembly.* Report of the Committee appointed by the Legislature to visit and examine the banks in Connecticut, made at May session, 1837. 23p. *8°. Hartford,* 1837.

29907 COOK, John, *Esq.* Considerations on banking and joint stock banks in connection with trade. 31p. *8°.* [1837]

29908 *CORBAUX, F. A letter to the Family Endowment Society; exhibiting the errors and vices of their system... 12p. *12°. [London, 1837] Presentation copy from the author to Augustus De Morgan.*

29909 CORWIN, T. Speech of Mr. Corwin, of Ohio, on the bill from the Committee of Ways and Means, to reduce the revenue of the United States to the wants of the government. Delivered in the House of Representatives of the United States, January 12, 1837. 15p. *8°. Washington,* 1837.

29910 [CRAWFORD, John, *of Paisley.*] The philosophy of wealth: with an examination of the cause of the present distress. Second edition. 71p. *12°. Paisley, Glasgow, &c.,* 1837. *See also* 1846, 1847.

29911 CROSS, W. Monetary reform. A project for rendering paper money independent of the precious metals and invariable in its value. In three letters reprinted from "The Aberdeen Herald" of May 27, June 10, and June 24. 23p. *8°. Edinburgh & Aberdeen, 1837. Presentation copy from the author to T. Spring Rice, Baron Monteagle.*

29912 DE BODE, C. J. P. P., *Baron.* French claims. In the case of the Baron de Bode. [Dated: November 6th, 1837.] 30p. *8°.* [1837]

29913 EDINBURGH. *Town Council.* Report by the Lord Provost's Committee on remit by the Town Council of Edinburgh, regarding the probable future value of the revenues of the city clergy. With an appendix of relative documents. Approved in Council 4th January, 1837. 17, 20p. *8°. Edinburgh,* 1837.

29914 *ELLIOT, GILBERT, *Dean of Bristol.* A letter to a yeoman in favour of abolition of church rates. 26p. *8°.* 1837. *The copy that belonged to George Grote.*

29915 [ENDERBY, C.] The metallic currency the cause of the present crisis in England and America. By the author of "Money, the representative of value." 33p. *8°.* 1837. *See also* 1839.

29916 [——] Money the representative of value. With considerations on the bank question, railway companies, savings banks, and the National Debt. 79p. *8°.* 1837. *With a note in the volume, by HSF, recording another copy presented by the author, Charles Enderby.*

29917 ENGLAND. *Ecclesiastical Commissioners.* The correspondence between the Ecclesiastical Commissioners and the Bishop of Ely. [On the finances of the Bishopric.] 42p. *8°.* 1837.

29918 ESSAY on money; or, an inquiry into the nature of the circulating medium. 40p. *8°. Glasgow,* 1837.

29919 Important EXCISE trial. Revenue Exchequer, sittings at nisi prius, before the Chief Baron and a special jury, Dec. 12, 1836. Attorney-General v. Clotworthy Walkinshaw. 24p. *8°. Belfast,* 1837.

For the **FINANCIAL REGISTER OF THE UNITED STATES,** 1837–38, *see* vol. III, *Periodicals list.*

29920 FOULQUES, L. Essai historique sur l'art monétaire et sur l'origine des hôtels des monnaies de Lyon, Mâcon et Vienne, depuis les premiers temps de la monarchie française... 86p. *8°. Lyon,* 1837. *Presentation copy, with accompanying letter, from the author to an unidentified recipient.*

29921 FOX, CHARLES, *of Bristol.* A letter to the Rt. Hon. Viscount Melbourne, and the Rt. Hon. T. S. Spring Rice, on the abolition of the malt tax, and other excise duties. 12p. *8°. London & Taunton,* 1837.

29922 GILBART, J. W. The history and principles of banking...Third edition. 300p. *8°.* 1837. *For another edition, see* 1834.

29923 —— The history of banking in America: with an inquiry how far the banking institutions of America are adapted to this country; and a review of the causes of the recent pressure on the money market. 207p. *8°.* 1837. *Presentation copy, with accompanying letter, and inscription on the title-page, from the author to Joseph Hume.*

29924 GOUGE, W. M. An inquiry into the expediency of dispensing with bank agency and bank paper in the fiscal concerns of the United States. 56p. *8°. Philadelphia,* 1837.

29925 HALL, JOHN, *Liverpool merchant.* A letter to the Right Hon. Thos. Spring Rice, Chancellor of Her Majesty's Exchequer, &c.&c. containing a new principle of currency and plan for a national system of banking. By a Liverpool merchant. 28p. *8°. London & Liverpool,* 1837.

29926 HAWKES, H. W. A treatise on the National Debt: containing its history from the earliest period to the present day...To which is added, to teach the people the blessings of fortitude and patience, a poem, on the great storm, which happened in England on Tuesday, November 29, 1836. 24p. *12°. n.p.,* 1837. *See note to no.* 29487.

29927 [HILDRETH, R.] The history of banks: to which is added, a demonstration of the advantages and necessity of free competition in the business of banking. 142p. *12°. Boston,* 1837.

29928 [——] [Another edition.] 151p. *8°.* 1837.

29929 HILLS, W. The law of church rates, and the ministerial plan for their abolition, considered in a letter to Sir William W. Follett, M.P....Being a reply to Sir John Campbell's pamphlet...Second edition. 38p. *8°.* 1837.

29930 IMPERIAL BANK OF ENGLAND. Deed of settlement of the Imperial Bank of England, (dated the fourth September, 1837,) established under the authority of an Act of Parliament passed in the 7th year of the reign of his late Majesty King George the Fourth. Capital one million sterling. 60p. *8°. Manchester,* 1837.

29931 The national IMPOLICY of the present high duty on tobacco, extracted...from the evidence given before the Commissioners of Revenue Enquiry; the Select Committee on the growth and cultivation of tobacco; and the Commissioners of Excise Enquiry. 27p. *8°. Westminster,* 1837.

29932 INSTRUCTIONS for the establishment of savings' banks, with rules and forms applicable thereto. [With 'On the calculation of interest for savings' banks. By the Rev. John Thomas Becher, M.A.'.] 30p. *8°.* 1837.

29933 JOHNES, A. J. Correspondence on the subject of the Church in Wales with reference to "A letter" from A. J. Johnes, Esq. to Lord John Russell. [On the incomes of dignitaries of the Church.] 31p. *8°. London & Chester,* 1837.

29934 JOHNSON, WILLIAM C. Speech of William Cost Johnson, of Md., on the Sub-treasury Bill, entitled A bill imposing additional duties as depositaries, in certain cases, on public officers, delivered in the House of Representatives October 12, 1837. 22p. *8°. Washington,* [1837]

29935 JONES, CHARLES. A plan for realizing the perfection of money; in which it is demonstrated, that "paper is capable of being made, a much more... unvarying standard of value, than...either gold or silver can be."...Reprinted and addressed to the Right Hon. Viscount Melbourne... 19p. *8°.* [1837] *The copy that belonged to T. Spring Rice, Baron Monteagle. For another edition, see* 1832.

29936 JONES, RICHARD (1790–1855). Remarks on the government Bill for the commutation of tithe...Third edition. 32p. *8°.* 1837. *For other editions, see* 1836.

29937 *JOPLIN, T. An examination of the report of the Joint Stock Bank Committee, &c.&c. Second edition. To which is added an account of the late pressure in the money market, and embarrassment of the Northern and Central Bank of England. 122p. *8°.* 1837. *The copy that belonged to George Grote. A different printing, with the addition, from the 1836 second edition.*

29938 —— Third edition... 122p. *8°.* 1837.

29939 —— Fourth edition... 122p. *8°.* 1837. *For other editions, see* 1836.

29940 [**KEMBLE**, JOHN M.] A few historical remarks upon the supposed antiquity of church rates and the three-fold division of tithes. By a lay member of the Church of England. New edition. 30p. *12°.* 1837.

29941 **KING**, . Speech of a dissenter [Mr. King, surgeon] on church-rates [delivered at Chelmsford on 18 January, 1837]. 12p. *8°.* 1837.

29942 **KNOWLES**, SIR FRANCIS C., *Bart.* "The monetary crisis considered;" being incidentally a reply to Mr. Horsley Palmer's pamphlet "On the action of the Bank of England, &c." and a defence of the joint-stock banks against his accusations. 90p. *8°.* 1837. *Presentation copy from the author to C. R. Fox (1796–1873).*

29943 The **LAND TAX**, its origin, progress, and inequality, stated in a letter to the Chancellor of the Exchequer, with a view to its equalization. By a citizen of Westminster. 21p. *8°.* 1837.

29944 —— Third edition. 21p. *8°.* 1837.

29945 —— Fourth edition. 21p. *8°.* 1837.

29946 **LONDON AND COUNTY BANKING COMPANY.** The deed of settlement of the Surrey, Kent and Sussex Joint Stock Banking Company. 90p. *8°.* n.p., 1837. *The copy that belonged to Hyde Clarke.*

29947 [**LOYD**, S. J., *Baron Overstone.*] Further reflections on the state of the currency and the action of the Bank of England. 46p. *8°.* 1837. *With manuscript corrections possibly intended for incorporation in another edition. Some parts of the text have been cut out.*

29948 —— [Another edition.] 52p. *8°.* 1837. *The author's own copy, formerly among his papers, for which see* vol. III, *MS.* 804.

29949 —— Reflections suggested by a perusal of Mr. J. Horsley Palmer's pamphlet on the causes and consequences of the pressure on the money market. 56p. *8°.* 1837. *The author's own copy, formerly among his papers, for which see* vol. III, *MS.* 804.

29950 **MAHONY**, P. The Committee on Joint Stock Banks. A confidential letter to the Right Hon. (Thomas Spring Rice) the Chancellor of the Exchequer... 36p. *8°.* n.p., 1837.

29951 **MOORE**, R. The analysis. [On the currency.] [With 'Appendix. The writer's outline for instituting a mint paper coin, of gold standard value'.] 60p. *8°.* Kingston [& London], 1837.

29952 **MORRISON**, W. H. Observations on the system of metallic currency adopted in this country. 74p. *8°.* 1837.

29953 —— Second edition, with explanatory notes. 87p. *8°.* 1837. *The copy that belonged to T. Spring Rice, Baron Monteagle. See also* 1847.

29954 **MUNTZ**, G. F. The true cause of the late sudden change in the commercial affairs of the country... March 13, 1837. 12p. *8°.* Birmingham & London, 1837. *See also* 1843.

29955 **NATIONAL BANK OF IRELAND.** The deed of settlement of the National Bank of Ireland, established A.D. 1835. Capital – one million sterling. 153p. *8°.* 1837. *Interleaved, with amendments to the Deed from 1836 to 1869, printed in red, inserted facing the clauses to which they refer.*

29956 **NEBENIUS**, C. F. E. Ueber die Herabsetzung der Zinsen der öffentlichen Schulden, mit Rücksicht auf die Zeitverhältnisse und insbesondere auf die öffentlichen Verhandlungen über die Reduction der französischen Schuld. 141p. *8°.* Stuttgart & Tübingen, 1837.

29957 **NECKAR**, *pseud.* Seventeen numbers [from the Courier and Enquirer], under the signature of Neckar, upon the causes of the present distress of the country, with a proposed remedy. By a citizen of New-York. New-York, August, 1837. 68p. *8°.* New-York, 1837. *The copy that belonged to T. Spring Rice, Baron Monteagle.*

29958 **NEW YORK**, *State of.* Bank Commissioners. Bank Commissioners' report; made to the Legislature of New York, January 27, 1837. Also, extracts from the report of the Secretary of the Treasury of the United States. 20p. *8°.* Edinburgh, 1837.

29959 **OBSERVATIONS** on the crisis 1836–37, with suggestions for a remedy against commercial pressures. By a merchant. 23p. *8°.* 1837.

29960 **PAINE**, T. The decline and fall of the English system of finance. 22p. *8°.* 1837. *For other editions, see* 1796.

29961 **PALMER**, JOHN H. The causes and consequences of the pressure upon the money-market; with a statement of the action of the Bank of England from 1st October, 1833, to the 27th December, 1836. 65p. *8°.* 1837.

29962 —— Reply to the reflections, etc. etc. of Mr. Samuel Jones Loyd, on the pamphlet entitled "Causes and consequences of the pressure upon the money-market." 24p. *8°.* 1837.

29963 **PARRY**, JOHN. A plan for the equitable and just liquidation of the National Debt...instantly relieving the United Kingdom...from paying thirty millions, in taxes, annually and for ever. The original copy of this paper was sent to the Right Honorable Earl Grey in July or August, 1831. 17p. *8°.* Haverhill, Suffolk, 1837.

29964 **POWELL**, H. T. Tithe commutation in 1969: or, the working of the Tithe Act illustrated by an example of commutation in 1705. 33p. *8°.* 1837.

29965 A new financial **PROJECT**; together with some remarks upon the currency and credit system of the United States. 29p. *8°.* New-York, 1837.

29966 **PYNE**, H. Tithe commutation. Table, shewing the amount of the corn rent chargeable in lieu of tithes, to be inserted in apportionments made under the Act for the commutation of tithes in England and Wales. Framed and computed by Henry Pyne, of the Tithe Commission Office; and re-computed and certified to be correct by John Finlaison, Esq., actuary of the National Debt... 23p. *8°.* 1837.

29967 **RAFINESQUE SCHMALTZ**, C. S. Safe banking, including the principles of wealth; being an enquiry into the principles and practice of safe and unsafe banks, or monied institutions in North America, the defects of the American banking system and legislation, &c. 136p. *8°.* Philadelphia, 1837.

29968 **RICARDO**, S. Observations on the recent pamphlet of J. Horsley Palmer, Esq. on the causes and consequences of the pressure on the money market, &c. 43p. *8°.* 1837.

29969 **RICE**, THOMAS S., *Baron Monteagle.* Church rates. Substance of a speech delivered in the House of

Commons, on the 3d of March, 1837, by the Right Hon. T. Spring Rice, Chancellor of the Exchequer...Extracted from "The Mirror of Parliament"... 46p. *8°*. 1837.

29970 —— The speech of the Right Honourable Thomas Spring Rice, Chancellor of the Exchequer, on introducing his motion relative to pensions on the Civil List, on... December 8, 1837. From Hansard's Parliamentary Debates, Vol. XXXIX. Third series. 32p. *8°*. [*London*, 1837]

29971 RIVES, W. C. Speech of Mr. Rives, of Virginia, in support of the bill introduced by him designating the funds receivable in payment of the public revenue, and in opposition to the Sub-Treasury scheme. Delivered in the Senate of the U.S. September 19, 1837. 32p. *8°*. *Washington*, 1837.

29972 —— Speech of Mr. Rives, of Virginia, on the currency of the United States, and the collection of the public revenue. Delivered in the Senate U.S. January 10, 1837. 20p. *8°*. *Washington*, 1837.

29973 ROBINSON, GEORGE (*fl.* 1837). A letter to His (late) Majesty's Commissioners for "inquiring into the revenues and patronage of the Established Church", respecting the Wolverhampton Church estates. 16p. *8°*. *Wolverhampton*, 1837.

29974 SALOMONS, SIR D., *Bart.* A defence of the joint-stock banks, an examination of the causes of the present monetary difficulties, and hints for the future management of the circulation. 46p. *8°*. 1837.

29975 —— Second edition. 46p. *8°*. 1837.

29976 —— The monetary difficulties of America, and their probable effects on British commerce, considered. 45p. *8°*. 1837.

29977 [**SANKEY,** W. S. V.] Thoughts on the currency, as affecting production; suggested by the late commercial crisis, &c. In a letter addressed to the Honourable the Secretary of the American Treasury. By Κλεις. 20p. *8°*. *Edinburgh*, 1837.

29978 *****SAY,** H. Avant-propos à la discussion d'une nouvelle loi sur les faillites. 57p. *8°*. *Paris*, 1837. *The copy that belonged to George Grote.*

29979 SCOTT, D. G. History of the rise and progress of joint stock banks in England, with a statement of the law relating to them, also an analysis of the evidence before the Select Committee appointed to inquire into their affairs, and suggestions for legislative enactments... 108p. *8°*. 1837.

29980 STAPLETON, A. G. Observations on the report of the Bullion Committee in 1810. In a letter addressed to the members of the London Political Economy Club. 24p. *8°*. 1837.

29981 STATEMENT of facts showing the necessity of instituting an inquiry into the management and the appropriation of the funds of the Norwich Union Life Insurance Society. 16p. *8°*. 1837. *The copy that belonged to T. Spring Rice, Baron Monteagle, presented by 'Mr Withe[rs?]' who may have been the author.*

29982 SUGGESTIONS tending to afford protection to the proprietors of the Bank of England, to release private and joint stock banks of issue from their present dangerous state of dependence, and to prevent, in future, those fluctuations in the currency...which have proved so ruinous... 14p. *8°*. *London, Manchester, &c.*, 1837.

29983 A new **SYSTEM** of paper money. By a citizen of Boston. 20p. *8°*. *Boston*, 1837.

29984 TAYLOR, GEORGE T. The spirit of the general letters and orders issued by the Honourable Board of Excise, from 1828 to 1836, inclusive. Chronologically arranged, with marginal notes and...index... 264p. *8°*. *For the Excise Establishment*, 1837.

29985 Free **THOUGHTS** on the proposed Bank of India, in a letter to the provisional Board of Directors. By a friend. 50p. *8°*. *Liverpool*, 1837.

29986 THOUGHTS upon the principles of banks, and the wisdom of legislative interference. 77p. *8°*. 1837.

29987 TILL, W. An essay on the Roman denarius and English silver penny...To which is appended a list of English and Scotch pennies...an account of the farthings of Queen Anne, a list of books necessary to the collectors of medals, transactions of the Numismatic Society, with a list of its members, as well as that of collectors of medals ...likewise of medal engravers... 230p. *12°*. 1837. *See also* 1838.

29988 TORRENS, R. A letter to the Right Honourable Lord Viscount Melbourne on the causes of the recent derangement in the money market, and on bank reform. 66p. *8°*. 1837.

29989 —— Second edition, with additions. 82p. *8°*. 1837.

29990 —— Supplement to A letter...on the derangement in the money market and on bank reform. [With 'Appendix. Speech delivered by Colonel Torrens, in the House of Commons, 28th of June, 1833, on moving that the consideration of the question of renewing the charter of the Bank of England be postponed'.] 42, 8p. *8°*. 1837.

29991 WATT, P. Progress and present state of the science of life insurance, with thermometrical tables. Also, observations on health insurance, &c. 80p. *8°*. *Edinburgh & London*, 1837.

29992 *****WILLIAMS,** CADOGAN. A statement, corroborated by the letters of public men, of the conduct of ...Lord Althorp, to Mr. Cadogan Williams, in reference to the government scheme founded on the Act of Parliament entitled "An Act to enable depositors in the savings' banks and others to purchase government annuities," and to show there is unsoundness in the scheme, and that it must be re-constructed. 15p. *8°*. 1837. *The copy that belonged to George Grote.*

29993 WILLICH, C. M. Tithe commutation tables, for ascertaining, at sight, the amount of corn-rent in bushels, (as directed by the Act of 6 and 7 William IV. cap. 71), equivalent to the tithe-rent...also shewing the amount of tithe rent-charge payable for the year 1837 according to the average prices of wheat, barley, and oats, for the seven...years, to Christmas 1836... 12p. *8°*. 1837. *For an annual supplement, see* 1838.

29994 A **WORD** upon the bank and paper system of England. 31p. *8°*. 1837.

29995 YEADELL, T. A letter addressed to the Right Hon. Thomas Spring Rice, Chancellor of the Exchequer, etc. pointing out the contradictions...injustice, and impolicy of the law of auctions...and suggestions for alterations and improvements therein. 16p. *8°*. 1837.

TRANSPORT

29996 ADAMS, William B. English pleasure carriages; their origin...construction, defects...and capabilities: with an analysis of the construction of common roads and railroads, and the public vehicles used on them; together with descriptions of new inventions. Illustrated by numerous designs. For the use of carriage purchasers and constructors. 315p. *8°. 1837.*

29997 BARLOW, P. Report on the weight of rails, the description of chairs and fastenings, the distance of the supports, and the size of the blocks, of the Liverpool and Manchester Railway...Second edition. 1–67, 82–116p. *8°. 1837. The Rastrick copy. For another edition, see 1835.*

29998 BIOT, E. C. L'architetto delle strade ferrate ovvero saggio sui principi generali dell'arte di formare le strade a ruotaje di ferro...Recato in italiano con note ed aggiunte dall'ingegnere Luigi Tatti, unitavi una memoria di Davide Hansemann...(*Scelta Biblioteca dell' Ingegnere civile,* 16.) 371p. *4°. Milano, 1837.*

29999 BREES, S. C. Railway practice. A collection of working plans and practical details of construction in the public works of the most celebrated engineers on the several railways...A series of original designs for every description of railway works, in various styles of architecture, completes the volume. 108p. *4°. 1837. The copy that belonged to W. S. Moorsom. See also 1838, 1847, and for an appendix, 1839; for the second series, see 1840, and for the fourth, 1847.*

30000 [BURKE, St. G.] Remarks on the standing orders and resolutions of the last session of Parliament relating to railways, with practical instructions for their observance, and some suggestions for their amendment, by a Parliamentary agent. 168p. *8°. [London,] 1837.*

30001 [*Endorsed:*] **CASE** of the opponents of the lines of railway from Stone to Rugby [i.e. the London and Birmingham, the Grand Junction, and the Midland Counties Railways. With a map]. 4p. *fol. n.p.* [1837 ?]

30002 CAUTUS, *pseud.* Some words on railway legislation, in a letter addressed to Sir Robert Peel, Bart. 16p. *8°. 1837.*

30003 —— A second letter to Sir Robert Peel, Bart., M.P. on railway legislation. 23p. *8°. 1837.*

30004 CORNISH, James, *bookseller of Birmingham.* Second edition enlarged & improved. Cornish's Grand Junction, and the Liverpool and Manchester Railway companion... 172p. *18°. Birmingham & London, 1837.*

30005 CURTIUS, D. D. Iets over het nut der ijzeren wegen voor Nederland. 31p. *8°. s'Gravenhage, 1837.*

30006 DRAKE, James, *publisher.* Drake's road book of the Grand Junction Railway, from Birmingham to Liverpool & Manchester. Containing...the rules, regulations, fares, times of outset and arrival... 184p. *8°. Birmingham, Liverpool, &c.,* [1837] *p. 109–184 contain advertisements.*

30007 ENGLAND. *Laws, etc.* An Act for making a railway from Sheffield in the West Riding of the county of York to Manchester in the county of Lancaster. ⟨Royal Assent, 5th May 1837.⟩ 197p. *fol. Manchester,* 1837.

30008 —— —— Acts relating to the London and Birmingham Railway: viz. 3 Gulielmi IV. cap. xxxvi. 5 & 6 Gulielmi IV. cap. lvi. and 1 Victoriæ, cap. lxiv. With a general index. 440p. *8°.* 1837.

30009 —— —— Anno primo Victoriæ Reginæ, cap. cxix. An Act for making a railway from the London and Croydon Railway to Brighton, with branches to Shoreham, Newhaven, and Lewes. [Incorporating the London and Brighton Railway.] ⟨15th July 1837.⟩ [With an index.] p.4741–4931, 44p. *fol.* 1837. *The Rastrick copy.*

30010 —— —— [*Endorsed:*] Bishop Auckland and Weardale Railway. An Act for incorporating certain persons for the making and maintaining a railway from near the Black Boy branch of the Stockton and Darlington Railway...to or near to Witton Park Colliery, with a branch therefrom...to be called "The Bishop Auckland and Weardale Railway." ⟨Royal Assent, 15 July 1837.⟩ 1 Vict. sess. 1837. 92p. *fol.* [*London,* 1837]

30011 —— *Parliament.* [*Endorsed:*] Sheffield, Ashton-under-Lyne, and Manchester Railway. A Bill for making a railway from Sheffield in the West Riding of the County of York to Manchester in the County of Lancaster. ⟨5.⟩ 168p. *fol.* [*London,* 1837]

30012 —— —— *House of Commons.* Manchester and Tamworth Railway. Report of the debate in the House of Commons, (Friday, 24th February, 1837,) on the second reading of the Bill. 19p. *8°.* 1837.

30013 —— —— —— Railway subscription contracts ...deposited in the Private Bill Office of the House of Commons. Ordered, by the House of Commons, to be printed, 7 March 1837. Sheffield, Ashton-under-Lyne and Manchester Railway...List of subscribers. vip. *fol. n.p.,* 1837.

30014 —— —— —— In the House of Commons. Minutes of evidence taken before the Committee on the London and Brighton Railway Bills. (Stephenson's Line.) ...Copy from Mr. Gurney's short-hand notes. [Proceedings of the Committee from 3–13 March 1837.] 6 parts. *fol.* 1837.

30015 —— —— —— In the House of Commons. Minutes of evidence taken before the Committee on the Bill for the direct London and Brighton Railway, as proposed by Sir J. Rennie and J. U. Rastrick, Esq.... [Proceedings of the Committee from 13 March–7 April 1837.] 10 parts. *fol.* 1837.

30016 —— —— —— In the House of Commons. Minutes of evidence taken before the Committee on the Brighton Railway Bills; (South-Eastern Line.)...[Proceedings of the Committee from 10–17 April 1837.] 6 parts. *fol.* 1837.

30017 —— —— —— In the House of Commons. Minutes of evidence taken before the Committee on the London and Brighton Railway Bills; (Gibbs' Line.)... [Proceedings of the Committee from 18–21 April 1837.] 4 parts. *fol.* 1837.

30018 —— —— —— In the House of Commons. Minutes of evidence taken before the Committee on the Commercial (Blackwall) Railway Bill...[Proceedings of the Committee from 9–30 May, 1837.] 4 parts. *fol.* 1837.

30019 FRANCE. Ministère des Travaux Publics, de l'Agriculture et du Commerce. *Direction Générale des*

Ponts et Chaussées. Exposé général des études faites pour le tracé des chemins de fer de Paris en Belgique et en Angleterre, et d'Angleterre en Belgique, desservant, au nord de la France, Boulogne, Calais, Dunkerque, Lille et Valenciennes. Presenté par L.-L. Vallée. 223p. *4°. Paris,* 1837.

30020 —— —— —— Mémoire sur le projet d'un chemin de fer de Lyon à Marseille par M. F. Kermaingant. 172p. *4°. Paris,* 1837.

30021 FREELING, A. The Grand Junction Railway companion to Liverpool, Manchester, and Birmingham; and Liverpool, Manchester, and Birmingham guide... 192, viii, [193]–228p. *12°. Liverpool, Manchester, &c.,* 1837. *p.[193]–228 contain advertisements. See also* 1838.

30022 GALE, P. A letter to the Commissioners of Railway Inquiry in Ireland, on the advantages to the Empire, from increased facilities of international communication, also, observations on the proper position for a main trunk, to the south and west of Ireland... Second edition, corrected. 35p. *8°. Dublin & London,* 1837.

30023 GODWIN, G. An appeal to the public, on the subject of railways. 45p. *8°. London, Liverpool, &c.,* 1837.

30024 GORDON, Alexander, *civil engineer.* Observations addressed to those interested in either rail-ways or turnpike-roads; showing the comparative expedition, safety, convenience, and public and private economy of these two kinds of road for internal communication. 31p. *8°.* 1837.

30025 [*Endorsed:*] In Parliament, – session 1837. The **GREAT NORTH OF ENGLAND RAILWAY.** Case of the promoters of the Bill [to authorize the extension of the line to York]. *fol. n.p.* [1837]

30026 GUYONNEAU DE PAMBOUR, F. M., *Comte.* Traité théorique et pratique des machines locomotives... 407p. *8°. Bruxelles,* 1837. *See also* 1839.

30027 To the **INHABITANTS** of Birmingham. [A protest against diverting London to Lancashire railway traffic from Birmingham by means of the South Union Railway and the Tamworth and Rugby branch of the Birmingham and Derby Railway, and a plan to bring railway traffic to the town by the Grand Junction and the Manchester, Cheshire, and Staffordshire Railways. Signed: An inhabitant, and dated, Jan. 17, 1837.] [4]p. *fol. n.p.* [1837]

30028 JOHNSON, C. W. The advantages of railways to agriculture. By Cuthbert W. Johnson...Observations on the general importance of railways, by George W. Johnson...Second edition. 16p. *8°.* 1837.

30029 KREEFT, C. First Russian railroad from St. Petersburg to Zarscoe-selo and Pawlowsk, established by Imperial Decree of 21st March, 1836, and carried into execution by a company of shareholders in Russia, England and Germany. Translated from the German... 44p. *8°.* [1837]

30030 LARDNER, D. Steam communication with India by the Red Sea; advocated in a letter to the Right Honourable Lord Viscount Melbourne, illustrated by plans of the route, and charts of the principal stations. 123p. *8°.* 1837.

30031 LIVERPOOL AND MANCHESTER RAILWAY COMPANY. Reports of the Liverpool and Manchester Railway, as published by order of the proprietors at their general meetings. 100p. *8°.* 1837.

30032 LONDON AND BRIGHTON RAILWAY COMPANY. The Direct London and Brighton Railway, with branches to Shoreham, Lewes, Newhaven, and Reigate. Capital £1,200,000 divided into 16,000 shares of £75 each. [Prospectus, dated: January 9th, 1837.] [4]p. *fol.* [1837] *See also* 1836.

30033 MARTIN, William (1772–1851). The thunder storm of dreadful forked lightning: God's judgement against all false teachers, that cause the people to err, and those that are led by them are destroyed, according to God's word. Including an account of the railway phenomenon, the wonder of the world! 40p. *8°. Newcastle upon Tyne,* 1837.

30034 MUDGE, R. Z. Observations on railways, with reference to utility, profit, and the obvious necessity for a national system. 73p. *8°.* 1837.

30035 NEWCASTLE AND CARLISLE RAILWAY COMPANY. The Managing Committee's report to the Directors...March 27, 1837. [Signed: Benjamin Thompson, George Johnson, Nicholas Wood.] 6p. *8°. Newcastle,* [1837] *See also* 1835, 1838, 1839.

30036 —— Report of the Directors...read to the shareholders at their annual meeting, March 28th, 1837. 11p. *8°. Newcastle upon Tyne,* 1837. *See also* 1835, 1838, 1843, 1845.

30037 PILLET-WILL, M. F., *Comte.* De la dépense et du produit des canaux et des chemins de fer. De l'influence des voies de communication sur la prosperité industrielle de la France. 2 vols. *4°. Paris & Saint-Pétersbourg,* 1837.

30038 SCOTT, STEPHEN & GALE. An examination of Mr. G. Stephenson's report, on the two lines of railway projected between Glasgow and Ayrshire... also, an exposure of the misstatements contained in his report, as well as those...published by Messrs. Grainger and Miller; with a general view of the whole question involved. By Scott, Stephen, and Gale, engineers and architects. [With the text of Stephenson's report.] 40p. *8°. Glasgow & Edinburgh,* 1837.

30039 SCOTT, Hudson. Scott's railway companion, describing all the scenery on and contiguous to the Newcastle and Carlisle Railway, with a short sketch of Carlisle and Newcastle... 105p. *8°. Carlisle & Newcastle,* 1837. *The Rastrick copy.*

30040 SHEFFIELD, ASHTON-UNDER-LYNE, AND MANCHESTER RAILWAY. Report of the present traffic on the different lines of road between Sheffield and Manchester, and an estimate of the increased and additional traffic which may be expected to pass upon the railway between those towns...presented...by B. Skidmore, commercial agent, Sheffield. [4]p. *fol. n.p.* [1837]

30041 —— Report of the provisional committee to the shareholders in the above undertaking, submitted to a general meeting of the proprietors at the Cutlers' Hall in Sheffield, on the 23rd Oct., 1837. The Right Hon. Lord Wharncliffe in the chair. 3p. *fol. n.p.* [1837]

30042 —— Sheffield and Manchester Railway. (Extracted from the Sheffield Mercury of Oct. 28, 1837.) [Report of the first general meeting.] 3p. *fol. Sheffield,* [1837]

30043 SOUTH EASTERN RAILWAY COMPANY. South Eastern Railway. First half-yearly meeting of proprietors...held...on...the 18th day of May, 1837. 2p. *fol.* [1837]

30044 STOCKTON AND DARLINGTON RAILWAY. Coach between Darlington and Croft, three times a day each way. [Announcement of the service, to begin on 17 April 1837, with timetable.] *s.sh.fol. Darlington,* [1837]

30045 —— Information to travellers in South Durham. Stockton & Darlington Railway arrangements. Summer, 1837. [A timetable, with information about coaches connecting with the railway service.] *s.sh.fol. n.p.* [1837] *See also* 1839.

30046 —— Stockton and Darlington Railway coaches. Winter of 1837–38. [A timetable.] *s.sh.8°. Darlington,* [1837] *Printed in red. See also* 1839, 1842.

30047 WALKER, JOHN, *civil engineer.* Two letters to Matthew Barrington, Esq. on proposed southern railroads in Ireland, with an introductory letter to the Right Hon. Thomas Spring Rice, M.P.... 16p. *8°. Limerick,* 1837.

30048 WHISHAW, F. Analysis of railways: consisting of a series of reports on the twelve hundred miles of projected railways in England and Wales, now before Parliament... 296p. *8°.* 1837. *See also* 1838.

SOCIAL CONDITIONS

30049 ASSOCIATION FOR THE SUPPRESSION OF MENDICITY, *Dublin.* Nineteenth annual report of the managing committee of the Association... for the year 1836: with resolutions upon the subject of poor laws. 32p. *8°. Dublin,* 1837. *See also* 1819, 1821, 1825, 1831.

30050 AUBANEL, C. Mémoire sur le système pénitentiaire, adressé, en janvier 1837, à M. le Ministre de l'Intérieur de France...accompagné de plans et de devis de prisons d'après le système panoptique, par M. Vaucher-Crémieux, architecte; et suivi d'une notice sur l'oeuvre du patronage des détenus libérés de la Prison Pénitentiaire de Genève, par un membre du Comité de patronage. 102p. *8°. Genève,* 1837. *Presentation copy, with inscription, from the author to William Allen.*

30051 AYRE, J. A letter, addressed to the Right Honourable Lord John Russell, M.P....on the evil policy of those measures of quarantine, and restrictive police, which are employed for arresting the progress of the Asiatic cholera; with an enquiry into the nature of, and means of obviating, those circumstances in the physical condition of the labouring poor, by which they are especially predisposed to the disease... 39p. *8°. London & Hull,* 1837.

30052 BARNARD, M. Reasons of a clergyman for acting as a guardian of the poor. 49p. *8°. London & Ware,* 1837.

30053 BARRETTÉ, A. G. A few plain facts, in answer to a pamphlet entitled "The working of the new Poor Law in the Bath Union; or, a peep into the board room at Walcot;" with a statement of the case which lately called forth the interference of the city magistrates. 31p. *8°. Bath,* 1837.

30054 BLAKEY, R. Cottage politics; or letters on the new Poor-Law Bill. 184p. *12°. London, Manchester, &c.,* [1837]

30055 —— An exposure of the cruelty and inhumanity of the new Poor Law Bill, as exhibited in the treatment of the helpless poor by the Board of Guardians of the Morpeth Union. In a letter addressed to the mechanics and labouring men of the north of England. 16p. *8°. Newcastle,* 1837. *The Oastler copy.*

30056 —— A second letter to the mechanics and labouring-men of the north of England, being an exposure of the cruel inhumanities of the Board of Guardians of the Morpeth Union. 8p. *8°. Newcastle upon Tyne,* 1837. *The Oastler copy.*

30057 BOUDIER, J. Remarks on some of the more prominent features and the general tendency of the new Poor Law Bill, addressed to those who are disposed to think it a harsh and oppressive Act. 46p. *8°. Warwick,* [1837]

30058 BOWEN, J. Second edition (of a letter to his late Majesty; containing) A refutation of some of the charges preferred against the poor: with some account of the working of the new Poor Law, in the Bridgwater Union. 111p. *8°. London, Bridgwater, &c.,* 1837. *The Oastler copy. For another edition, see* 1835.

30059 *BUCKLE, J. Prison discipline. The charge of the Recorder to the grand jury of the city of Worcester, at the late Epiphany sessions. 68p. *8°.* 1837. *The copy that belonged to George Grote.*

30060 BULL, G. S. Horrors of the Whig poor laws! The Somerset House poor-starvers [the Poor Law Commissioners], versus a clergyman of the Church of England. [A correspondence.] 8p. *8°.* [*London,* 1837]

30061 —— Laying of the first stone of a new schoolroom near Bowling Toll-Bar. [An address.] 4p. *8°. Bradford,* [1837] *The Oastler copy.*

30062 BURY SHORT-TIME COMMITTEE. Address of the Bury Short-Time Committee to the ministers of the Gospel, and religious communities of every denomination. [An appeal for support to secure the passage of 'Mr. Hindley's Bill' through Parliament in the new session.] *s.sh.fol. Bury,* [1837] [*Br.* 590] *The Oastler copy.*

30063 [CAREY, M.] Reflections on the system of the Union Benevolent Association, stating its beneficient effects on the manners, and comforts of the poor; but the utter inadequacy of its means...and the necessity of raising funds...With suggestions for alterations...in order to carry into full operation the benevolent views of its founders. Second edition – considerably improved. By a citizen of Philadelphia. 13p. *8°. Philadelphia,* 1837.

30064 *CENTRAL SOCIETY OF EDUCATION, *London.* Schools for the industrious classes: or, the present state of education among the working people of England. Published under the superintendence of the ...Society... 58p. *8°.* 1837. *Reprinted in* Papers by George Long, Esq. [and others] *in 1838 (q.v.). The copy that belonged to Augustus De Morgan.*

30065 [CHADWICK, SIR E.] An article on the principles and progress of the Poor Law Amendment Act; and also on the nature of the central control and improved local administration introduced by that statute. Re-printed, by permission from the "Edinburgh Review." With notes and additions. 75p. 8°. 1837.

30066 —— Extracts from the evidence relating to the administration of the old poor-laws: and also as to an amended system of administering a compulsory tax for the legal relief of the destitute, and as to the administration of voluntary charities: collected by Edwin Chadwick Esq.... 139p. 8°. [London,] 1837.

30067 *CHANNING, WILLIAM E. An address on temperance...Delivered by request of the Council of the Massachusetts Temperance Society... 38p. 8°. 1837. *The copy that belonged to George Grote. See also 1838.*

30068 CITY OF WESTMINSTER LITERARY SCIENTIFIC AND MECHANICS' INSTITU-TION. Rules and orders of the...Institution, founded April 19, 1837. [With list of officers.] 15p. 8°. *Westminster,* [1837]

30069 CLARKE, WILLIAM (*fl.* 1837). A reply to 'An appeal to Members of Parliament, and the working classes, on the Ten Hours' Factory Bill;' or "the doctor dissected." 38p. 8°. *Ashton-under-Lyne,* [1837] *The Oastler copy.*

30070 CLIVE, A. A few words to the poor and to overseers, on the new Poor Law. 8p. 8°. 1837. *For another edition, see 1836.*

30071 COBBETT, W. Advice to young men, and (incidentally) to young women, in the middle and higher ranks of life. In a series of letters... 334p. 12°. 1837. *For another edition, see 1829.*

30072 [CORRIE, J.] Remarks on the Poor Law for Ireland. By Phil Hibernus. 24p. 8°. 1837.

30073 [——] Remarks on the Bill for the more effectual relief of the destitute poor in Ireland. By Philo-Hibernus. Second edition, revised and enlarged. [With a postscript.] 45p. 8°. 1837.

30074 [CRAIK, G. L.] Sketches of popular tumults; illustrative of the evils of social ignorance. (*Contributions to Political Knowledge.*) 318p. 12°. 1837. *See also 1847.*

30075 DAVIES, JOHN, *Rector.* The substance of a lecture delivered at the Guildhall, Worcester, on... November 7, 1836...on the state of religion and morals among that class of His Majesty's subjects who gain their subsistence by working upon our rivers and canals... 34p. 8°. 1837.

30076 DENISON, WILLIAM, *ed.* Abstract of evidence taken before the Committee appointed by the House of Commons, the 27th February, 1837, to inquire into the operation and effect of the Poor Law Amendment Act. With introductory remarks, etc. 118p. 8°. 1837. *The Oastler copy.*

30077 DONKIN, S. Observations upon the nature of parochial relief, and the principles upon which the Poor-Law Amendment Act is founded. 49p. 12°. *Newcastle,* 1837.

30078 ENGLAND. *Barrister appointed to Certify the Rules of Friendly Societies.* Instructions for the establish-ment of loan societies with a form of rules, &c. applicable thereto. 16p. 8°. 1837. *For another edition, see 1836.*

30079 —— —— Instructions for the establishment of parochial societies for granting government annuities, immediate or deferred...pursuant to Stat. Wm. IV. cap. 14. 44p. 8°. 1837.

30080 —— *Commissioners for Inquiring into the Adminis-tration and Practical Operation of the Poor Laws.* Extracts from the information received by His Majesty's Commis-sioners, as to the administration and operation of the poor-laws. [With 'Appendix XIX. Instructions from the Central Board of Poor-Law Commissioners to assistant commissioners', originally issued in 1832.] 432p. 8°. 1837. *For another edition, see 1833.*

30081 —— *Commissioners for Inquiring into the Condition of the Poorer Classes in Ireland.* Abstract of the Final Report of the Commissioners of Irish Poor Inquiry; with remarks thereon, and upon measures now before Parlia-ment for the relief of the destitute in Ireland. 36p. 8°. 1837.

30082 —— Second edition. [With 'Abstract of the letter from N. W. Senior, Esq., to Lord John Russell'.] 61p. 8°. 1837.

30083 —— *Home Office.* Extracts from the second Report of the Inspectors of Prisons for the Home District; addressed to...the Secretary of State for the Home Department. By authority. 197p. 8°. 1837.

30084 —— —— Extracts from the second Report of the Inspector of Prisons for the Northern District. Wakefield House of Correction for the West Riding of Yorkshire. 11p. 8°. [1837 ?]

30085 —— —— Poor laws – Ireland. Report of George Nicholls, Esq., to His Majesty's Principal Secretary of State for the Home Department. 67p. 8°. 1837. *The copy that belonged to T. Spring Rice, Baron Monteagle. See also no. 30579.*

30086 —— *Laws, etc.* An Act for better paving, cleans-ing, & lighting the parish of St. Martin in the Fields, within the Liberty of Westminster...and for removing and preventing nuisances & annoyances therein. With notes, etc. 93p. 8°. 1837.

30087 *—— —— The Act for suspending the operation of two Acts passed in the last session for registering births, deaths, and marriages in England, and for marriages in England. And the Act for explaining and amending the said two Acts. 31p. 8°. 1837. *The FWA copy that belonged to William Pare.*

30088 —— —— An Act for the better regulating, pav-ing, improving, and managing the town of Brighthelmston, in the county of Sussex, and the poor thereof. 134p. 8°. *Brighton,* 1837.

30089 *—— —— The Acts for marriages and registra-tion, 6 & 7 Will. IV, c. 85 & 86. With explanatory notes and index by William Eagle. xxviii, 180p. 8°. 1837. *The copy that belonged to Augustus De Morgan, with his manuscript note on the title-page: 'This act leaves all the law as to ordinary marriages wholly unaltered'.*

30090 —— *Parliament.* 7 William IV. – Session 1837. A Bill to regulate the labour of children and other persons, in the mills and factories of the United Kingdom. Ordered, by a meeting of delegates to be printed, 25th January, 1837. 8p. 8°. *Manchester,* [1837] *The Oastler copy.*

30091 —— —— *House of Commons.* The parish and the union; or, the poor and the poor laws under the old system and the new: being an analysis of the evidence contained in the twenty-two reports of the Select Com-mittee...to Inquire into the Administration of the Relief of the Poor...To which are added the report of the Committee and a summary of petitions and addresses. 246p. 8°. 1837.

30092 EXTRACTS from letters transmitted by clergymen, magistrates, and others, relative to the present destitution in the Highlands and Islands of Scotland. 8p. *8°.* [1837]

30093 FANE, R. G. C. A letter addressed to His Majesty's Attorney General [on the projected abolition of imprisonment for debt]... Second edition. 36p. *8°.* 1837. *The copy that belonged to C. Poulett Thomson, Baron Sydenham.*

30094 —— [*Endorsed:*] Letter from Mr. Fane to the members of the House of Commons, relating to the Bill for the abolition of imprisonment for debt... [On the abolition of remuneration for the Commissioners of the Court of Bankruptcy. Dated: 1st July 1837.] *s.sh.fol.* [*London,* 1837] [*Br.* 589]

30095 FELKIN, W. Remarks upon the importance of an inquiry into the amount and appropriation of wages by the working classes, addressed to the Statistical Section of the British Association, at its meeting in Liverpool, 13th September 1837... With some additional observations. 16p. *8°. London & Nottingham,* [1837] *Two copies, one a presentation copy from the author to 'Mr. Cockle', the other that belonged to Victor Considérant.*

30096 FIELDEN, J. Speech of John Fielden, Esq., M.P. in the House of Commons, Feb. 24., 1837, on seconding Mr. Walter's motion for an inquiry into the working of the Poor-law Act. (From The Champion newspaper.) 8p. *8°.* [*London,* 1837] *The Oastler copy.*

30097 FRIENDLY SOCIETY OF OPERA-TIVE HOUSE CARPENTERS AND JOINERS OF GREAT BRITAIN AND IRELAND. Minutes and resolutions adopted at the annual government delegate meeting... August 8, 1837 and four following days. 12p. *8°.* [*London,* 1837]

30098 GENT, H. Capital arraigned against labour; or, the hand-loom weaver contending for his right, the names of the witnesses and their respective evidences, being a correct... report of the dispute, Gent versus Broome, relative to the payment of wages... heard and settled at the County Police Office, Macclesfield... by the Rev. J. R. Browne... To which is added, some practical remarks and observations in exposition of... the "Arbitration Act"... 16p. *8°. Macclesfield,* 1837. *The Oastler copy.*

30099 "GIVE it a fair trial." [A satire on the new Poor Law.] 8p. *16°. Huddersfield,* [1837?] *The Oastler copy.*

30100 GOWER, S. What are poor laws for? Containing curse-ory remarks on some features of the Poor-Law Amendment Bill. 24p. *8°. London & York,* 1837. *The Oastler copy.*

30101 —— A word or two to Mr. George Tinker, of Scholes, in reply to his no-arguments in favour of the new poor law system... 10p. *8°. Holmfirth,* [1837] *The Oastler copy.*

30102 GREG, R. H. The factory question, considered in relation to its effects on the health and morals of those employed in factories. And the "Ten Hours Bill," in relation to its effects upon the manufactures of England, and those of foreign countries. 151p. *8°.* 1837.

30103 [**HANSON,** JOHN, *socialist.*] View extraordinary of Sir John's Huddersfield menagerie of political houhynims, ourang outangs... and hyænas. With a variety of other sectarian oddities of dissent, cantwells, mawworms... and hypocrites, in the Broughamic order of democracy. By Jay Aitch, "C. & F." 11p. *8°. Leeds,* 1837.

The copy that belonged to Oastler, who identified 'Jay Aitch' as John Hanson in the manuscript index to his pamphlet collection.

30104 [**HICKSON,** WILLIAM E.] Fallacies on poorlaws. From the 'London and Westminster Review' for January, 1837. 23p. *8°. n.p.* [1837]

30105 HILL, SIR ROWLAND (1795–1879). Private and confidential. Post Office reform; its importance and practicability. 73p. *8°.* [*London,*] 1837.

30106 —— [Another edition, with appendixes.] 104p. *8°.* 1837.

30107 HODGSON, WILLIAM B. Lecture on education; delivered in the Freemasons' Hall, at the opening of the second session of the Edinburgh Association of the Working Classes, for their social, intellectual and moral improvement... 16th October, 1837... 48p. *12°. Edinburgh,* 1837. *Presentation copy from the author to the London Working Men's Association.*

30108 HOGG, JOHN. London as it is; being a series of observations on the health, habits, and amusements of the people. 389p. *12°.* 1837.

30109 [**HOWORTH,** W.] The cry of the poor: a poem. [The prefatory sonnet signed: W.H.] 68p. *12°.* 1837. *The copy that belonged to Oastler, who attributed it to 'Ormrod' in the manuscript index to his pamphlet collection.*

30110 HUNTER, T., *and others.* The rights of labour defended: or the trial of the Glasgow cotton spinners [Thomas Hunter, Peter Hacket, Richard M'Neil, James Gibb, William M'Lean], for the alleged crime of conspiracy, &c.&c. to maintain or raise the wages of labour, before the High Court of Justiciary, at Edinburgh, on the 10th and 27th November [and from the 3rd–11th January, 1838. With a foreword to the first part by Hugh Alexander, chairman of the Glasgow Committee of Trades' Delegates]. 285p. *8°.* [*Glasgow,*] 1837. *Published in 18 parts. For other editions, entitled:* The trial of... the Glasgow cotton-spinners, *see* 1838.

30111 IRISH POOR. A word for Mr. Nicholls. By a looker on. 24p. *8°.* 1837.

For **ISLE OF MAN TEMPERANCE GUARD-IAN AND RECHABITE JOURNAL,** 1837–38, *see* vol. III, *Periodicals list.*

30112 JEE, T. Sermons on some of the doctrines and duties of the Christian religion, addressed particularly to political economists and guardians of the poor. 76p. *8°. London & Chelmsford,* 1837.

30113 KENNEDY, JOHN P. Analysis of projects proposed for the relief of the poor of Ireland; more especially that of Mr. George Nicholls, embodied in a Bill now before Parliament; that of the Commissioners for Inquiring into the Condition of the Poorer Classes in Ireland and that which has been brought into partial operation by the author. 54p. *8°. London & Dublin,* 1837.

30114 To the farming **LABOURERS** of Great Britain and Ireland. [A letter signed: A Freeman of Exeter, urging them to petition Parliament on their condition.] 8p. *8°.* 1837. *The Oastler copy.*

For the **LEEDS TEMPERANCE HERALD,** *see* vol. III, *Periodicals list.*

30115 LEGALITY or illegality of imprisonment for

debt? Section I. The case of prisoners stated. 34p. *8°*. [*London*, 1837?]

30116 —— Section II. The case of prisoners reconsidered. 40p. *8°*. [*London*, 1837?]

30117 A **LETTER** addressed to the Right Honourable John Frederick Earl of Cawdor, on the poor laws, and the practical effect to be produced by the Act of 4 & 5 Will. IV. c. 76. Together with an address to the members of benefit societies. By a magistrate of the counties of Pembroke and Glamorgan. 66p. *8°*. 1837.

30118 A **LETTER** [signed: A labourer] to Mr. George Stephen, in reply to his letter to Lord John Russell [on public order and the labouring classes]. 8p. *8°*. 1837.

30119 A **LETTER** to the electors of Cambridge, touching Mr. Knight, Mr. Sutton, and the poor-laws. By a member of the University. 13p. *8°*. *Cambridge*, 1837. *Conjecturally attributed by HSF to George Pryme.*

30120 A **LETTER** to the Rev. G. A. Evors, on poor laws, by a rate-payer. 16p. *8°*. *Newtown*, [1837]

30121 **LIVESEY**, J. A temperance lecture based on the tee-total principle; including an exposure of the great delusion as to the properties of malt liquor... 15p. *4°*. *Preston, London, &c.*, [1837] *The Turner copy. For another edition, see* 1836.

30122 **LONDON.** *Strand Union.* Strand Union. Report of the Board of Guardians, April 1837. With an appendix. 31p. *8°*. 1837.

30123 **LONDON HIBERNIAN SOCIETY.** A brief view of the London Hibernian Society for Establishing Schools and Circulating the Holy Scriptures in Ireland. 16p. *8°*. 1837. *The copy that belonged to Earl De Grey.*

30124 **LONDON UNION OF COMPOSITORS.** Annual report of the Trade Council to the members of the London Union of Compositors...Feb. 6, 1837. Mr. W. Edwards in the chair. To which are added, the rules & regulations of the Union, as amended to February 1837. [With 'Extract from the address of the Operative Letter-Press Printers of Glasgow', signed by W. Skirving, of the Glasgow Typographical Society.] 47p. *12°*. [*London*, 1837]

30125 *****LOVELESS**, G. The victims of Whiggery; being a statement of the persecutions experienced by the Dorchester labourers; their trial, banishment, &c.&c. Also reflections upon the present system of transportation; with an account of Van Dieman's Land... 32p. *8°*. *The Central Dorchester Committee*, [1837] *The FWA copy that belonged to William Pare.*

30126 —— Second edition. 32p. *8°*. *The Central Dorchester Committee*, [1837]

30127 —— Third edition. 32p. *8°*. *The Central Dorchester Committee*, [1837] *The Oastler copy. See also* 1838.

30128 **LOW**, J. Statement, relative to the reduction in the poor rates, resulting from the cessation of litigations, and diminution of suits of law: also letters to the Right Honorable the President of the Board of Trade, on the circulating mediums, &c. 25p. *8°*. *Hammersmith*, 1837.

30129 **MANCHESTER STATISTICAL SOCIETY.** Report of a committee of the Manchester Statistical Society on the state of education in the borough of Manchester, in 1834. Second edition, revised. 42p. *8°*. *London & Manchester*, 1837. *For another edition, see* 1835.

30130 —— Report of a committee of the Manchester Statistical Society on the state of education in the city of York. In 1836–1837. Read at the Statistical Section of the British Association...Liverpool, Sept. 12th, 1837. 16, xivp. *8°*. *London & Manchester*, 1837.

30131 Great **MEETING** at the Crown and Anchor [Strand, London] on the inhuman Poor-Law Act. ⟨Report, taken from the Champion newspaper, of the 5th of March.⟩ [With a report of the speech of Earl Stanhope.] 16p. *8°*. [*London*, 1837] *The Oastler copy. For other editions of Earl Stanhope's speech, see nos.* 30163–4.

30132 **MIGRATION** of agricultural labourers. Being a report of certain cases published in The Times, with the report of Mr. R. M. Muggeridge, P.L.C. Migration Agent, on those cases, and the reply of Mr. Fletcher, surgeon of Bury, Lancashire. [With an introduction by Fletcher.] 24p. *12°*. *Bury*, [1837] *The Oastler copy.*

30133 **MILES**, WILLIAM AUGUSTUS (*fl.* 1826–1839). A letter to Lord John Russell, concerning juvenile delinquency, together with suggestions concerning a reformatory establishment. 16p. *8°*. *Shrewsbury*, 1837. *With a manuscript note on the title-page: For private circulation.*

30134 **MILMAN**, H. H. Address delivered at the opening of the City of Westminster Literary, Scientific, and Mechanics' Institute...Printed at the request of the Society. 31p. *8°*. 1837. *Presentation copy, with inscription, from the author to the Rev. George Holme (?).*

30135 **MORRIS**, EVAN. Abolition of arrest not just, as between debtor and creditor. A letter, with various suggestions to benefit creditors, by extending the process of the courts, and to charge income. Addressed to Sir John Campbell, on the 20th February, 1837. 24p. *8°*. [*London*, 1837] *Presentation copy, with inscription, from the author to C. Poulett Thomson, Baron Sydenham.*

30136 **NEW YORK STATE TEMPERANCE SOCIETY.** Report and speeches delivered at the eighth annual meeting of the...Society. 8p. *4°*. *Preston*, [1837] *The Turner copy.*

30137 **NICHOLLS**, R. H. Practical remarks on the severities of the new Poor Law, shown in a letter addressed to the Right Hon. Earl Stanhope. 31p. *8°*. 1837. *The Oastler copy.*

30138 **OASTLER**, R. Damnation! Eternal damnation to the fiend-begotten, "coarser food" new Poor Law. A speech. 24p. *8°*. 1837. *Oastler's own copy.*

30139 —— West-Riding nomination riot. A letter to Viscount Morpeth, M.P. for the West-Riding of Yorkshire, Irish Secretary, &c. 32p. *12°*. 1837. *Oastler's own copy.*

30140 **OBSERVATIONS** on the causes and remedies of destitution in the Highlands of Scotland. 25p. *8°*. *Glasgow, London, &c.*, 1837.

30141 **O'MALLEY**, T. Poor laws – Ireland. An idea of a poor law for Ireland...Second edition. 82p. *8°*. 1837.

30142 **PARENT DU CHÂTELET**, A. J. B. De la prostitution dans la ville de Paris, considérée sous le rapport de l'hygiène publique, de la morale et de l'administration...Deuxième édition revue et corrigée... 2 vols. *8°*. *Paris & Londres*, 1837. *For another edition, see* 1836.

30143 *Entry cancelled.*

30144 **PICOT**, A. Visite dans quelques prisons de France en mai & juin 1836...et réflexions sur quelques points tendant à la réforme et à l'amélioration des prisons en général. 52p. *8°. Paris*, 1837.

30145 The POOR LAW ACT. Public meeting at Bradford, Yorkshire. Monday, March 6, 1837. Second edition, enlarged. [With the text of a petition adopted at the meeting.] 16p. *8°. Bradford*, [1837] *The Oastler copy.*

30146 The POOR LAW ACT. To the people of the 20 townships, which the Poor Law Commissioners propose to form into the Bradford Union. [A manifesto by a committee established to oppose the Act.] 4p. *8°. Bradford*, [1837] *The Oastler copy.*

30147 The POOR LAW BILL exposed. Is it a Whig measure? It cannot be introduced into these districts. By a friend to the manufacturers. [An election manifesto.] 8p. *8°. Huddersfield*, 1837. *The Oastler copy.*

30148 REMARKS on the new Poor Law in a letter to John Walter, Esq., M.P. with a few observations on the evidence taken before the Committee of the House of Commons. By a guardian of the Epsom Union. 28p. *8°.* 1837.

30149 A REPORT of the proceedings of a public meeting, on the factory question, held in...Leeds, on... the 9th day of November, 1837, and called by half-a-dozen Leeds mill-overlookers, (who dubbed themselves for the occasion, the 'Leeds Short Time Committee,') at the instance of the Government, Mr. Baker, Mr. Baines, and a portion of the mill-owners, to "settle the question"... 16p. *8°. Leeds*, 1837. *The Oastler copy.*

30150 REVANS, J. Evils of the state of Ireland: their causes and their remedy – a poor law...Second edition, revised and corrected. 161p. *8°.* [1837] *For another edition, see* 1835.

30151 RITCHIE, L. A bystander's view of the Irish poor law question. 55p. *8°.* 1837.

30152 ROBERTS, S. A cry from the chimneys; or an integral part of the total abolition of slavery throughout the world. [A plea for the abolition of the employment of climbing boys.] 44p. *8°.* 1837.

30153 —— A solemn appeal to ministers of every denomination, on the subject of the poor laws. 24p. *8°. Sheffield*, 1837. *The Oastler copy.*

30154 [ROZIER, P. M.] Des femmes, considérées sous le point de vue social, et de la recherche de la paternité, à l'occasion des enfans trouvés; par un sous-chef à l'Administration générale des Hospices. 32p. *8°. Paris*, 1837. *With a pencilled note on the title-page: 'Tiré à 25 exemplaires'.*

30155 SENIOR, N. W. Letters on the Factory Act, as it affects the cotton manufacture, addressed to the Right Honourable the President of the Board of Trade. 12p. *8°.* 1837.

30156 —— [Another edition.] To which are appended, a letter to Mr. Senior from Leonard Horner, Esq., and minutes of a conversation between Mr. Edmund Ashworth, Mr. Thomson and Mr. Senior. 52p. *8°.* 1837. *Two copies, one a presentation copy, with inscription, from the author to John Stuart Mill, the other that belonged to Victor Considérant. See also* 1844.

30157 SHERMAN, J. The advantages of abstinence from intoxicating liquor. A sermon preached to young persons, at Surrey Chapel, May 28, 1837...Fourth edition. 23p. *12°.* 1837. *The Turner copy.*

30158 SIMPLE, PETER, *Esq., R.N., pseud.* The horrible cruelty of the new Poor Law; or, a scene in the Bath Union bastile. [A satire.] 15p. *8°. Bath*, [1837]

30159 SLANEY, R. A. Speech of R. A. Slaney, Esq. M.P. in the House of Commons on...Nov. 30. 1837, on the state of education of the poorer classes in large towns. 24p. *12°.* 1837.

30160 SMITH, HENRY L. Alfred societies; or, a plan for very small sick clubs; recommended to the governors and free members of self-supporting, charitable, and parochial dispensaries...[With 'Appendix. Rules of Harbury Sick Club', with observations by the author.] 32p. *8°. Southam & London*, 1837.

30161 *SOCIÉTÉ VAUDOISE D'INDUS-TRIE.* De l'amélioration morale des classes industrielles dans le Canton de Vaud. Rapport présenté à la Société... par une commission composée de Messieurs André Gindroz...président, Victor Greux, George Noir, Théod. Rivier, préfet, et J. J. Mercier. 95p. *8°. Lausanne*, 1837. *The copy that belonged to George Grote.*

For the **SPITALFIELDS WEAVERS' JOURNAL,** *see vol. III, Periodicals list.*

30162 STANHOPE, PHILIP H., *Earl Stanhope.* New Poor Law. Letter from Earl Stanhope to Mr. Richard Oastler. 13p. *8°.* [1837] *The Oastler copy.*

30163 —— New Poor Law. Substance of the speech of Earl Stanhope, on February 27, 1837, at the Crown and Anchor Tavern. 15p. *8°.* [1837] *The Oastler copy.*

30164 —— [Another edition.] Earl Stanhope's speech, on the new Poor Law, at a meeting held at the Crown and Anchor Tavern, London, on...Feb. 27th, 1837...⟨Published by order of a meeting of delegates, representing the several townships in the Huddersfield "Union", to concert means to rid the Statute Book of the accursed Act.⟩ 8p. *8°. Leeds*, 1837. *The Oastler copy.*

30165 STANLEY, A. P. The Gipsies: a prize poem, recited in the Theatre, Oxford; June 7, 1837. 19p. *8°. Oxford*, 1837.

30166 STANLEY, W. Remarks on the government measure for establishing a poor-law in Ireland; chiefly with reference to the existing amount of pauperism, as stated in the report of the Irish Poor Inquiry Commissioners: and the necessary extent and character of the means for its relief...Second edition. 41p. *8°.* 1837.

30167 STONE, W., *and others.* Evidence of the Rev. William Stone, Rector of Spitalfields, and other witnesses, as to the operation of voluntary charities. Also evidence as to the principle of administering relief to the destitute, during a period of manufacturing distress. Extracted from a report by Edwin Chadwick, Esq.... 72p. *8°. n.p.*, 1837.

30168 SUSSEX PROVIDENT SOCIETY. Sussex Provident Society, established September 28th, 1836. [List of honorary members, with explanations of six plans for saving, with observations.] 16p. *8°. Lewes*, 1837.

30169 The new TEMPERANCE DOCTOR. ⟨Principally from American authorities.⟩ 8p. *4°. Preston*, [1837] *The Turner copy.*

30170 *A few plain THOUGHTS upon the subject of imprisonment for debt, with a view...to extend...the powers of the commissioners of the Court for the Relief of Insolvent Debtors...also some remarks upon the measure of last session...By a gentleman connected with the superior courts of law. 16p. *8°.* [*London,* 1837] *The copy that belonged to George Grote. See also* 1838.

30171 THOUGHTS on prison discipline. By a looker-on. 80p. *8°.* 1837.

30172 THOUGHTS on the new Poor-Law Bill. By an ex-officio guardian. Not published. 46p. *8°.* 1837.

30173 TORRENS, R. A letter to the Right Honourable Lord John Russell, on the ministerial measure for establishing poor laws in Ireland, and on the auxiliary means which it will be necessary to employ... 149p. *8°.* 1837. *See also* 1838.

30174 TYLDEN, Sir J. M. Address of Sir J. M. Tylden, the chairman of the Milton Union, to the Board of Guardians, on the close of their duties for the year ending March 25th, 1837. 24p. *8°. Sittingbourne,* [1837]

30175 UNITED BENEVOLENT CLUB. Rules of the United Benevolent Club, at Hampstead-Norris, established, January 2nd, 1837. 7p. *8°. Speenhamland,* 1837.

30176 A VOICE from the north of England on the new poor laws. Ought we to have them or ought we not? 92p. *8°. London & Manchester,* 1837. *The Oastler copy.*

For the WEEKLY LONDON TEMPERANCE INTELLIGENCER, *see* vol. III, *Periodicals list,* New British and foreign temperance intelligencer.

30177 WING, C. Evils of the factory system demonstrated by parliamentary evidence. clxxxvi, 498p. *8°.* 1837.

30178 The WORKING of the new Poor Law in the Bath Union; or a peep into the board room at Walcot. 16p. *8°. n.p.* [1837]

30179 WRIGHTSON, T. On the punishment of death... Third edition, greatly augmented. 113p. *8°.* 1837. *For another edition, see* 1833.

30180 YELLOLY, J. Observations on the arrangements connected with the relief of the sick poor; addressed in a letter to the Right Honourable Lord John Russell, Secretary of State for the Home Department. 36p. *8°.* 1837.

SLAVERY

30181 ASSOCIATION FOR THE UNIVERSAL ABOLITION OF SLAVERY, *Sheffield.* An appeal to the Christian women of Sheffield, from the Association... 18p. *8°. Sheffield,* 1837.

30182 BEECHER, C. E. An essay on slavery and abolitionism, with reference to the duty of American females... Second edition. 151p. *12°. Philadelphia & Boston,* 1837.

30183 BIRT, J. Official responsibility affirmed and enforced, in a letter to Sir George Grey, Bart., M.P., Under Secretary of State for the Colonies, on the administration of the Act for the abolition of British colonial slavery. 16p. *8°.* 1837. *The copy that belonged to Earl De Grey.*

30184 DUBLIN LADIES' ASSOCIATION. Second appeal from the Dublin Ladies' Association auxiliary to the Hibernian Anti-Slavery Society...to the females of Ireland. [Signed: Catharine Elizabeth Alma, corresponding secretary, and dated, October 26th, 1837.] *s.sh.4°. Cork,* [1837]

30185 IRENOPHILOS, *pseud.* A cursory examination of the respective pretensions of the colonizationists and abolitionists. 12p. *8°. New-York,* 1837.

30186 Colonial LAWS as examined by a committee of the House of Commons in...1836. Exhibiting some of the principal discrepancies between those laws, and the imperial Act of abolition. 22p. *8°.* 1837.

30187 LINCOLN, L. Speech of Mr. Lincoln, of Massachusetts: delivered in the House of Representatives of the United States, Feb. 7, 1837, on the resolution to censure the Hon. John Q. Adams, for inquiring of the Speaker, whether a paper, purporting to come from slaves,

came within the resolution laying on the table all petitions relating to slavery. ⟨Reported by the editor of the Boston Daily Advocate.⟩ 9p. *8°. Washington,* 1837.

30188 The MAURITIUS. An exemplification of colonial policy. Addressed to the electors of Cambridge and Devonport. 14p. *8°. Birmingham,* 1837.

30189 NEGRO APPRENTICESHIP in the colonies. A review of the report of the Select Committee of the House of Commons, appointed to inquire into "the working of the apprenticeship system in the colonies...". 44p. *8°.* 1837.

30190 The foreign SLAVE TRADE, a brief account of its state, of the treaties which have been entered into, and of the laws, enacted for its suppression, from the date of the English Abolition Act to the present time. 62p. *8°.* 1837.

30191 A STATEMENT of facts, illustrating the administration of the abolition law, and the sufferings of the negro apprentices, in the island of Jamaica. 36p. *12°.* 1837.

30192 STERNE, H. A statement of facts, submitted to the Right Hon. Lord Glenelg...preparatory to an appeal about to be made by the author, to the Commons of Great Britain, seeking redress for grievances of a most serious tendency, committed upon him, under the administration of...the Marquis of Sligo, the late governor, and Sir Joshua Rowe...with an exposure of the present system of Jamaica apprenticeship. 282p. *8°.* 1837.

30193 WILLIAMS, James (*fl.* 1837). A narrative of events, since the first of August, 1834, by James Williams, an apprenticed labourer in Jamaica. [Dated at the end of the text: June 1st, 1837.] 26p. *8°.* [1837] *See also* 1838.

POLITICS

30194 ABERDEEN WORKING MEN'S AS-SOCIATION. Address to the working classes, by the Aberdeen Working Men's Association; together with the objects and rules of the Association. [Signed: John Fraser, secretary.] 8p. *12⁰. Aberdeen*, [1837]

30195 —— Second edition. 8p. *12⁰. Aberdeen*, [1837]

30196 ADAM, JAMES (*fl.* 1837). The knowledge qualification. A plan for the reciprocal extension of education and the franchise. 23p. *8⁰. Edinburgh & Aberdeen*, 1837.

30197 [BEAUMONT, A. H.] Whig nullities: or, a review of a pamphlet attributed to the Right Hon. John Cam Hobhouse...entitled, "Domestic policy of the country under the new Parliament." By the late radical candidate for Newcastle-upon-Tyne. Reprinted from the London Dispatch. [Signed: A.H.B.] 12p. *4⁰.* 1837. *The copy that belonged to Francis Place, who inserted the author's name in manuscript on the title-page.*

30198 BIRMINGHAM POLITICAL UNION. Protest against the Political Union. List of merchants, traders and others who have protested against the right of the men of Birmingham...to associate themselves for the vindication of their constitutional privileges. Published by the Council of the Political Union... 12p. *8⁰. Birmingham*, 1837. *See note to no.* 20490.

For **BRONTERRE'S NATIONAL REFORMER,** *see vol.* III, *Periodicals list.*

30199 BULLER, C. (No. 2.) Speech of C. Buller, Esq. M.P. in the House of Commons, on the 21st of February, 1837, in support of the Bill for granting municipal corporations to Ireland. Published under the sanction of the Society for the Diffusion of Moral and Political Knowledge. From the Morning Chronicle of the 22nd of February, 1837. 8p. *8⁰.* [*London*, 1837]

30200 BURDETT, SIR F., *Bart.* Speeches and letters of Sir Francis Burdett...or on his behalf, during the late contest for the representation of the City of Westminster in Parliament. 1837. 71p. *8⁰.* 1837.

30201 CHANNING, WILLIAM E. Thoughts on the evils of a spirit of conquest, and on slavery. A letter on the annexation of Texas to the United States. 48p. *8⁰.* 1837.

30202 CRAUFURD, H. W. The Russian fleet in the Baltic in 1836. With some remarks intended to draw attention to the danger of leaving our Navy in its present extremely reduced state...Second edition. 19p. *8⁰.* 1837.

30203 CROMBIE, A. A letter to Henry William Tancred, Esq. M.P., on the ballot. 51p. *8⁰.* 1837.

30204 A DIALOGUE on politics, between Tommy Philpot, the publican, a radical; and Jack Spratt, the sailor, a conservative. On the House of Lords...universal suffrage...annual Parliaments. 36p. *12⁰.* 1837.

30205 ENGLAND. Parliament. *House of Commons.* An abridgement of the evidence given before the Select Committee, appointed in 1835, to consider the most effectual means of preventing bribery, corruption and intimidation, in the election of members to serve in Parliament. With remarks [by M.]. Printed for "The Reform Association"... 147p. *8⁰.* 1837. '*M*' *was Thomas Martin.*

30206 EWART, W. The reform of the Reform Bill, and its anticipated results. A letter to a cabinet minister. 32p. *8⁰.* 1837.

30207 FIALIN DE PERSIGNY, J. G. V., *Duc.* Relation de l'entreprise du prince Napoléon-Louis et motifs qui l'y ont déterminé. 55p. *8⁰.* 1837.

30208 GRENVILLE, GEORGE N. T., *Baron Nugent.* The ballot discussed, in a letter to the Earl of Durham. 63p. *8⁰.* 1837.

30209 *HINDLEY, C. To the electors of the borough of Ashton-under-Lyne. [An account of his Parliamentary career 1835–37, upon his seeking re-adoption as candidate at the General Election.] 17p. *8⁰.* [*London*, 1837] *The copy that belonged to George Grote.*

30210 KNOWLES, FRANCIS. A letter to the coerced electors of the United Kingdom. 12p. *12⁰. London, Manchester, &c.,* 1837.

30211 LAMBTON, J. G., *Earl of Durham.* Speech of the Earl of Durham, delivered at the first meeting of the North Durham Reform Society, on...October 17, 1837. 24p. *8⁰.* 1837.

30212 A LETTER to the Rev. George Bugg, A.B. Curate of Desborough, Northamptonshire. Containing a summary of the principles, objects and means of radicalism. By a member of the Kettering Radical Association. 10p. *12⁰. Kettering,* 1837. *The copy that belonged to William Lovett, with his signature on the title-page.*

30213 LEWIN, T. On the duties of voters, and on the vote by ballot. 16p. *8⁰.* 1837.

30214 LEWIS, J. H. A real Reform Bill; such as the people want. Printed for J. H. Lewis, Esq. With notes. 8p. *8⁰.* [*London*, 1837]

30215 MACKENZIE, P. The life of Thomas Muir, Esq., advocate...one of the celebrated reformers of 1792–93, who was tried for sedition before the High Court of Justiciary in Scotland, and sentenced to transportation for fourteen years. With a full report of his trial. [With reports of the trials of Margarot and Palmer.] xliv, 64p. *8⁰. Glasgow & Edinburgh,* 1837. *Published in parts. For another edition, see* 1831.

30216 OBJECTIONS to the ballot, answered from the writings and speeches of Mill, Grote, &c. 100p. *12⁰.* 1837.

30217 *—— [Another edition.] ⟨Copies printed for general distribution.⟩ 20p. *8⁰.* 1837. *The copy that belonged to George Grote.*

30218 O'CONNOR, F. A series of letters from Feargus O'Connor, Esq., barrister at law; to Daniel O'Connell, Esq. M.P. containing a review of Mr. O'Connell's conduct during the agitation of the question of Catholic emancipation; together with an analysis of his... actions, since he became a Member of Parliament. Second edition, containing the confirmation of T. Attwood, Esq. M.P. for Birmingham, of the principal charge brought by Mr. O'Connor against Mr. O'Connell. 94p. *8⁰.* 1837. *The Oastler copy.*

30219 PEEL, SIR ROBERT, *2nd Bart.* A correct report of the speeches delivered by the Right Honourable Sir Robert Peel, Bart., M.P., on his inauguration into the office of Lord Rector of the University of Glasgow, January 11, 1837; and at the public dinner at Glasgow, January 13, 1837. 48p. *8°*. 1837.

30220 —— Second edition. Speech of Sir Robert Peel, M.P. at Tamworth on...August 7, 1837, including the O'Connell and Ruthven correspondence on the Kildare County election. 15p. *8°*. [1837]

30221 PEMBERTON, afterwards **PEMBERTON LEIGH,** THOMAS, *Baron Kingsdown.* A letter to Lord Langdale on the recent proceedings in the House of Commons on the subject of privilege. 99p. *8°*. 1837.

30222 Domestic **PROSPECTS** of the country under the new Parliament. 47p. *8°*. 1837.

30223 REMARKS on the first Report of the Select Committee on fictitious votes in Scotland; with extracts from the evidence. 44p. *8°*. *Edinburgh*, 1837.

30224 [**RICH,** SIR H.] What next? or the Peers and the third time of asking. [A review of politics before the third session of Parliament.] 82p. *8°*. 1837.

30225 [——] Third edition. 82p. *8°*. 1837.

30226 [——] Sixth edition. 82p. *8°*. 1837.

30227 [——] New edition, corrected and altered from the seventh in octavo. 59p. *12°*. 1837. **Another, the FWA copy, belonged to William Pare.*

30228 ROGERS, G. A letter to Thos. Wakley, Esq. M.P....Being an answer to calumny, and a statement of reasons for not having supported Mr. Wakley at the recent Finsbury election. 23p. *8°*. [1837]

30229 SMYTH, J. The following case is submitted to the Queen, Lords, & Commons...to the honest...Rads; to the...brutal Whigs; to the...bloody Tories; to the British People...[Being letters addressed to Lord Melbourne.] 32p. *8°*. 1837. *The copy that belonged to Earl De Grey.*

30230 [**SOUTHERN,** H. and **VILLIERS,** GEORGE W. F., *4th Earl of Clarendon* ?] The policy of England towards Spain considered chiefly with reference to "A review of the social and political state of the Basque

provinces, and a few remarks on recent events in Spain, &c. by an English nobleman [H. J. G. Herbert, Earl of Carnarvon]." 151p. *8°*. 1837.

30231 [—— ?] Second edition. 151p. *8°*. 1837.

30232 [—— ?] Sequel of The policy of England towards Spain, in answer to the Earl of Carnarvon's work, entitled, "Portugal and Galacia," to which is prefixed an answer to an article in the Quarterly Review, no. CXV. 205p. *8°*. 1837.

30233 August 29, 1837. The **SPECTATOR'S** complete lists of Lord Melbourne's House of Commons. With the polls of 1837 and 1835...⟨Copied, with corrections, from the Spectator Newspaper of 19th August 1837.⟩ 20p. *8°*. *London, Edinburgh, &c.*, [1837]

30234 SYMONS, JELINGER C. A voice from Stroud. Addressed to the Right Hon. Lord John Russell, M.P. In reply to His Lordship's speeches in Parliament on Nov. the 20th and 21st, 1837. [On the ballot.] 31p. *8°*. 1837.

30235 TALK with electors. No. I. Toryism in 1834, and Toryism in 1837. [An anti-Tory tract.] 8p. *8°*. 1837.

30236 —— No. II. The Cumberland Tory proclamation [i.e. the Proclamation of the Duke of Cumberland as King of Hanover. An anti-Tory tract, with the text of the proclamation.] 8p. *8°*. 1837.

30237 TOWARZYSTWO DEMOKRATY-OZNE POLSKIE. Manifesto of the Polish Democratical Society. [Issued at Poitiers, December 4, 1836. Signed by the Central Committee, Lucien Joseph Zaczrynski and 7 others.] 16p. *8°*. [1837]

30238 TURNER, W. M. To the liberal electors of the borough of Dudley. No. I. [A letter to his supporters by the unsuccessful Parliamentary candidate. Dated: September 12, 1837.] 6p. *8°*. *Dudley*, [1837]

30239 WAGHORN, T. Egypt as it is in 1837. 29p. *8°*. 1837.

30240 *WORKING MEN'S ASSOCIATION. Address of the Working Men's Association to the radical reformers of Great Britain on the forthcoming elections. [Signed: Wm. Lovett, secretary.] 8p. *8°*. [1837] *The FWA copy that belonged to William Pare.*

SOCIALISM

30241 ASSOCIATION FOR THE INTERNAL COLONISATION OF ARTISANS AND THE POOR. To artisans and workmen. Rules and regulations of the Association for the Internal Colonisation of Artisans and the Poor by means of a new system of mutual labour. With a plan of the organization and colonisation of the settlements [drawn up by John Miller]... 16p. *8°*. 1837.

30242 ASSOCIATION OF ALL CLASSES OF ALL NATIONS. To the working classes. Competitive versus co-operative labour; or, labour as it is, and labour as it ought to be. Re-printed from the New Moral World. 12p. *12°*. *Salford, Manchester, &c.*, [1837]

30243 BERTRAND, HENRI, **ANDRÉ** , ET **COMPAGNIE.** Le socialisme. Société Henri Bertrand, André et Compagnie, créée en nom collectif et en commandite par acte passé devant Me. Lambert de Sainte-Croix, notaire...le 9 juin 1837. Publié conformément à la loi. 7p. *8°*. [*Paris*, 1837]

30244 [**BOURGEOIS,** C. F.] Aux Saint-Simoniens, et aux Saint-Simoniennes. Sur la nécessité et la possibilité de rallier la doctrine de Saint-Simon à la foi chrétienne et au Christianisme temporel annoncé dans les écritures. [The preface signed: Marie-Félix.] xxiii, 33p. *8°*. *Paris*, 1837.

30245 CONSIDÉRANT, V. P. Destinée sociale... 2 vols. *8°*. *Paris*, 1837–38. *Vol. 1 is a reissue of the sheets of the 1834 edition, with new prelims, vol. 2 was published in 1838 for the first time. For other editions, see 1834.*

30246 FINCH, JOHN (1783–1857). The Millennium. The wisdom of Jesus and the foolery of sectarianism, in twelve letters. 24p. *8°*. *Liverpool*, 1837. *Two copies, one a presentation copy with an inscription from the author to Lloyd Jones; the other the copy that belonged to J. M. Ludlow.*

30247 FLEMING, G. A. A vindication of the principles of the rational system of society, as proposed by

Robert Owen. A lecture delivered in...Manchester. 20p. *12°. Manchester & London*, [1837?] *Another, the FWA copy, belonged to William Pare.*

30248 FOURIER, F. C. M. Lettre confidentielle [des membres de la réunion du 31 juillet, en réponse à une brochure intitulée: Aux Phalanstériens, la Commission préparatoire de l'institut sociétaire]. 24p. *8°. Paris*, [1837] *The copy that belonged to Victor Considérant.*

30249 HANCOCK, E. Robert Owen's community system, &c. and the horrid doings of the St. Simonians in Beaumont Square, Mile End, a new sect from France. Letter third. p.33–44. *12°*. [*London*, 1837] *Presumably paginated in sequence with the first and second letters.*

30250 *HASLAM, C. J. A defence of the social principles, delivered in the Social Institution, Salford... being an answer to a lecture delivered by the Rev. J. R. Beard, Unitarian minister...April the 30th, 1837. 11p. *12°. Manchester*, [1837] *The FWA copy, that belonged to William Pare.*

30251 *—— The necessity of a change, or an exposure of the errors and evils of the present arrangement of society; with a partial development of a new arrangement. 16p. *8°. Manchester & London*, [1837?] *The FWA copy that belonged to William Pare.*

30252 —— Second edition. 16p. *8°. Manchester & London*, [1837?]

30253 JONES, LLOYD. A reply to Mr. R. Carlile's objections to the five fundamental facts as laid down by Mr. Owen. An answer to a lecture delivered in his chapel, November 27th, 1837. 15p. *8°. Manchester* [& *London*], 1837. *Another, the FWA copy, belonged to William Pare.*

30254 [MORGAN, JOHN M.] Colloquies on religion and religious education. Being a supplement to "Hampden in the nineteenth century." 219p. *8°*. 1837. *For* Hampden in the nineteenth century, *see* 1834.

30255 OWEN, ROBERT. The book of the new moral world, containing the rational system of society, founded on demonstrable facts, developing the constitution and laws of human nature and of society. [Part 1.] 75p. *12°. Glasgow*, 1837. *For the complete edition, see* 1836.

30256 —— Essays on the formation of the human character. 78p. *16°. Manchester*, 1837. *An edition of* A new view of society. *For other editions, see* 1813.

30257 —— Propositions fondamentales du système social, de la communauté des biens, fondé sur les lois de la nature humaine...Traduit de l'anglais, par Jules Gay. 16p. *8°. Paris*, 1837. *For other editions, see* 1831.

30258 —— Public discussion, between Robert Owen... and the Rev. J. H. Roebuck...Revised and authorized by the speakers... 168p. *12°. Manchester & London*, 1837.

30259 POMPÉRY, É. DE. Le docteur de Tombouctou. Nouveaux essais de science sociale et de philosophie. 390p. *8°. Paris*, 1837.

30260 SOCIÉTÉ PHALANSTÉRIENNE DE BORDEAUX. L'avenir. Aperçu du système d'association domestique, agricole et industriel, d'après la théorie de Charles Fourier; extrait des ouvrages de l'École Sociétaire par les membres de la Société Phalanstérienne de Bordeaux. [With 'Publications de l'École Sociétaire'.] 23p. *8°. Bordeaux*, 1837.

MISCELLANEOUS

30261 HAMILTON, JOSEPH. The love of country, home and kind: from The school for patriots and universal benevolists. 40p. *12°*. 1837.

30262 HERBERT, WILLIAM (1771–1851). The history of the twelve great livery companies of London; principally compiled from their grants and records. With an historical essay, and accounts of each company...with attested copies and translations of the companies' charters. 2 vols. *8°. Published by the author*, 1837, 1836.

30263 —— History of the Worshipful Company of Goldsmiths of London, principally compiled from their own records. p.121–298. *8°. J. and C. Adlard*, 1837. *A reissue of part of the author's* History of the twelve great livery companies, *with a separate title-page.*

30264 LONDON. The oath of every freeman of the City of London. *s.sh.8°*. [1837?]

30265 MOLESWORTH, J. E. H. ⟨Fifth edition.⟩ Resistance to church-rates: a letter to the people of England. 16p. *8°*. [1837]

30266 —— Church-rates: a second letter to the people of England exposing the fallacies by which the abolitionists have attempted to weaken the force of his first letter. 16p. *8°*. [1837]

30267 [PICKERING, P. A. ?] Remarks on a report from a Select Committee of the late House of Commons, on the publication of printed papers. 135p. *8°*. 1837. *Attributed in a manuscript note on the title-page to 'P. Pickering Esq. M.A. Fellow of St: John's Coll: Cam: & of the Inner Temple'.*

30268 SMITH, SYDNEY (1771–1845). A letter to Archdeacon Singleton, on the Ecclesiastical Commission. 50p. *8°*. 1837.

30269 —— Third edition. 55p. *8°*. 1837. *See also* 1839.

30270 THIERRY, J. N. A. Rapport sur les travaux de la Collection des monuments inédits de l'histoire du Tiers État adressé à M. Guizot, Ministre de l'Instruction Publique, le 10 mars 1837. 19p. *4°. Paris*, 1837. *Inscribed in manuscript on the wrapper, 'To Sir Frederick Madden'.*

30271 TOULMIN, G. H. The eternity of the universe. 61p. *12°*. 1837.

1838

GENERAL

30272 ATKINSON, WILLIAM (*fl.* 1833–1858). The state of the science of political economy investigated; wherein is shewn the defective character of the arguments which have hitherto been advanced for elucidating the laws of the formation of wealth. 73p. *8°.* 1838.

30273 BACON, RICHARD M. A memoir of the life of Edward, third Baron Suffield... 513p. *4°. Norwich,* 1838.

30274 The **BRITISH ALMANAC** of the Society for the Diffusion of Useful Knowledge, for...1838. [With 'The companion to the Almanac; or year-book of general information'.] 96, 248p. *12°.* [1838] *For other editions, see* 1828.

30275 The **BRITISH IMPERIAL CALENDAR** for...1838...or general register of the United Kingdom and its colonies...[With 'A companion to the British Imperial Calendar, for...1838'.] 464, 114p. *12°.* [1838] *For other editions, see* 1817.

30276 BUTT, I. Rent, profits, and labour. A lecture delivered before the University of Dublin in Michaelmas term, 1837. 32p. *8°. Dublin & London,* 1838.

30277 CARMICHAEL, JAMES, *of Stirlingshire.* Corn laws. Review of the evidence taken before the Select Committee of the House of Commons on agricultural distress, 1836. 133p. *8°. Edinburgh & London,* 1838.

30278 CLARKSON, T. Strictures on a life of William Wilberforce, by the Rev. W. [i.e. R. I.] Wilberforce and the Rev. S. Wilberforce...With a correspondence between Lord Brougham and Mr. Clarkson; also a supplement, containing remarks on the Edinburgh review of Mr. Wilberforce's Life, etc. 136p. *8°.* 1838. *Presentation copy, with inscription, from the editor, H. C. Robinson, to George Pryme.*

30279 CLÉREL DE TOCQUEVILLE, C. A. H. M., *Comte de Tocqueville.* Democracy in America...Translated by Henry Reeve, Esq. With an original preface and notes by John C. Spencer. 464p. *8°. New York,* 1838. *For other editions, see* 1835.

30280 [CONSIDÉRANT, V. P.] Le conversion [des rentes] c'est l'impôt. A MM. les membres de la Chambre élective; par un ancien député. 57p. *8°. Paris,* 1838. *Considérant's own copy.*

30281 COURNOT, A. A. Recherches sur les principes mathématiques de la théorie des richesses. 198p. *8°. Paris,* 1838. *Presentation copy from the author to 'M. Lacroix'.*

30282 CRAIK, G. L., *ed.* The pictorial history of England: being a history of the people, as well as a history of the kingdom [to the accession of George III]...[By C. Macfarlane and others.] 4 vols. *8°.* 1838–41. *The additional title-page in vol. 1 is dated 1837. For a continuation, see* 1841.

30283 DAVENPORT, B. A pocket gazetteer, or traveller's guide through North America and the West Indies; containing a description of all the states...To which is added...statistical information, relating to the population, revenue, debt, and various institutions of the United States... 468p. *12°. Baltimore,* 1838.

30284 DEWEY, O. Moral views of commerce, society, and politics, in twelve discourses. 300p. *12°.* 1838.

30285 The **DUBLIN ALMANAC,** and general register of Ireland, for...1838...Fifth annual impression. 376p. *8°. Dublin: Pettigrew & Oulton,* [1838] *See also* 1842.

30286 DUMORTIER, B. C. Belgium and the twenty-four articles: [translated, with an introduction] by Charles White, Esq....From the French of M. B. C. Dumortier... xxxvi, 85p. *12°. Brussels,* 1838.

30287 *DYOTT, W. H. A vindication of the tradesmen of Dublin, from the late calumnious charges of Daniel O'Connell... 16p. *8°. Dublin,* 1838. *The copy that belonged to George Grote.*

For the **FLY,** *1838–39, see vol.* III, *Periodicals list.*

30288 FOX, WILLIAM J. Reports of lectures delivered at the Chapel in South Place, Finsbury...No. XII. On right and expediency. 23p. *8°.* 1838. *For other lectures in this series, see* 1835.

30289 FRANCE. *Ministère de la Marine.* Catalogue général des livres composant les bibliothèques du Département de la Marine et des Colonies. 5 vols. *8°. Paris,* 1838–43.

30290 FRANKLIN, B. People's edition. The life of Benjamin Franklin, comprising the account of the early part of his life, written by himself; and a new and greatly extended narrative in continuation till his death. The whole illustrated with literary and biographical notes. Also, the miscellaneous writings of Franklin. 86p. *8°. Edinburgh, London, &c.,* 1838. *For another edition of the Life, see* 1809.

30291 FULLARTON, A. and **BAIRD,** C. R. Remarks on the evils at present affecting the Highlands & islands of Scotland; with some suggestions as to their remedies. 131p. *8°. Glasgow, Edinburgh, &c.,* 1838. *Presentation copy, with inscription, from the authors to the Rev. Robert Wallace.*

30292 GRANIER DE CASSAGNAC, A. Introduction à l'histoire universelle. première Partie. Histoire des classes ouvrières et des classes bourgeoises. xxxii, 574p. *8°. Paris,* 1838.

30293 —— [Another edition.] 439p. *12°. Bruxelles,* 1838. *See also* 1839.

30294 HADDAN, T. H. The tests of national prosperity considered. A prize essay read in the Sheldonian Theatre, Oxford, June 27, 1838. 49p. *8°. Oxford,* 1838.

30295 *HAWKINS, F. B. Germany; the spirit of her history, literature, social condition, and national economy; illustrated by reference to her physical, moral, and political statistics... 475p. *8°.* 1838. *The copy that belonged to George Grote. See also* 1839.

30296 HEEREN, A. H. L. Historical researches into the politics, intercourse, and trade of the Carthaginians,

Ethiopians, and Egyptians...Translated from the German [by D. A. Talboys]. The second edition, corrected throughout, and to which is now first added...a life of the author... 2 vols. *8°. Oxford*, 1838. *For other editions, see* 1824.

30297 National **INTERESTS** [in relation to Ireland]. By a member of the Labourer's Friend Society. Part I[–IV]. p.1–16. *8°. [Dublin*, 1838]

30298 MANNING, WILLIAM (*fl.* 1838). The wrongs of Man exemplified; or, an enquiry into the origin, the cause, and the effect, of superstition, conquest and exaction...With an appendix, in which the false doctrine attempted to be established by Malthus, in his Essay on population, is refuted... 334p. *8°.* 1838.

30299 MARTINEAU, H. Retrospect of western travel. 3 vols. *8°.* 1838.

30300 MENDEZ DE VIGO, P. Apuntes sobre las mejoras de que es susceptible nuestro sistema económico y gubernativo; y sobre las sociedades secretas. 19p. *4°. Sevilla*, 1838.

30301 MONBRION, . Dictionnaire universel du commerce, de la banque et des manufactures...Par une société de négocians et de manufacturiers, sous la direction de M. Monbrion... 2 vols. *fol. Paris*, 1838–41.

30302 NEWCASTLE-UPON-TYNE. *Town Council.* The proceedings and reports of the Town Council...for 1837... [202]p. *8°. Newcastle*, 1838. *See also* 1837, 1839, 1840.

30303 OLIVEIRA MARRECA, A. D'. Noçoens elementares de economia politica...opusculo que ha de servir de compendio as pessoas que frequentarem o curso d'economia politica, fundado pela Associação Mercantil de Lisboa, e dirigido pelo author. 122p. *8°. Lisboa*, 1838.

30304 POPE, C., *ed.* The yearly journal of trade, 1837–8...Seventeenth edition. [With 'The yearly journal of trade advertiser, 1837–8'.] 440, 54p. *8°.* [1838] *See also* 1840, 1842, 1843, 1844, 1845, 1846.

30305 PORTLOCK, J. E. An address, explanatory of the objects and advantages of statistical enquiries, delivered at the second general meeting of the Statistical Society of Ulster, on the 18th of May, 1838. 27p. *8°. Belfast*, 1838.

30306 PRICE, H. A glance at the present times, chiefly with reference to the working men. 16p. *8°.* [1838 ?]

30307 RAMSAY, SIR G., *Bart.* Political discourses, 383p. *8°. Edinburgh & London*, 1838.

30308 RIEDEL, A. F. Nationalökonomie oder Volkswirthschaft...[With 'Bibliothek des Volkswirtschaftslehre'.] 3 vols. *8°. Berlin*, 1838–42.

30309 SMITH, ADAM. An inquiry into the nature and causes of the wealth of nations...With a life of the author, an introductory discourse, notes, and supplemental dissertations. By J. R. McCulloch. A new edition, corrected throughout and greatly enlarged. 648p. *8°. Edinburgh & London*, 1838. *For other editions, see* 1776.

30310 TOOKE, T. A history of prices, and of the state of the circulation, from 1793 to 1837; preceded by a brief sketch of the state of the corn trade in the last two centuries... 2 vols. *8°.* 1838. *For continuations of this work, see* 1840, 1848.

30311 TOZER, J. Mathematical investigation of the effect of machinery on the wealth of a community in which it is employed, and on the fund for the payment of wages. From the Transactions of the Cambridge Philosophical Society, vol. VI. Part III. 16p. *4°. Cambridge*, 1838.

30312 VETHAKE, H. The principles of political economy. 415p. *8°. Philadelphia*, 1838. *Presentation copy, with inscription, from the author to the Rev. Thomas Chalmers.*

30313 A **VOICE** to the people of England [on the condition of the country]. [Signed: An Englishman.] 16p. *8°. Manchester*, 1838.

30314 [**WALLIS,** J., *ed.*] The Bodmin register [vol. 1]; containing collections relative to the past and present state of the parish of Bodmin: and also, a statistical view of the twenty-eight parishes within...eight miles round Bodmin church, together with many particulars...concerning... Cornwall; with an appendix on the Diocese of Exeter... Published in [24] numbers from 1827 to 1838. 411, 16p. *8°. Bodmin*, [1838]

30315 WATSON'S or the gentleman's and citizen's almanack, (as compiled by the late John Watson Stewart,) for the year...1838...Containing, the days of the year... the sovereigns of Europe; the names of the Lord Lieutenant...Privy Council [of Ireland], the peers of Ireland, and the Irish members of the House of Commons...also the judges...the fairs; and the post-towns... 239p. *8°. Dublin*, [1838] *See also* 1798, 1837.

30316 WAYLAND, F. The elements of political economy. Abridged, for the use of students, from the author's larger work. 192p. *8°.* 1838. *For the complete work, see* 1837.

30317 WILBERFORCE, R. L. and S., *Bishop of Winchester.* The life of William Wilberforce. By his sons ... 5 vols. *8°.* 1838.

AGRICULTURE

30318 ANGLESEY HORTICULTURAL SOCIETY. Gwobrwyon i fythynwyr. (Cottagers.) [Particulars of prizes, 1838.] *s.sh.fol. Bangor*, [1838]

30319 BLACKLOCK, A. A treatise on sheep; with the best means for their improvement, general management, and the treatment of their diseases. With a chapter on wool, and history of the wool trade. 228p. *12°. Glasgow, London, &c.*, 1838.

30320 CAMBRENSIS, *pseud.* A letter to the Right Honourable the Chancellor of the Exchequer, on the abuses stated in the petition of landowners, and others connected with the Principality of Wales. [Disputing the legality of the claims of the Crown to rights of overlordship in Wales.] 51p. *8°.* 1838.

30321 COBBETT, W. Cottage economy...Fifteenth edition. 199p. *12°.* 1838. *For other editions, see* 1821.

30322 —— The English gardener; or, a treatise on the ...kitchen gardens...Concluding with a kalendar... 338p. *8°.* 1838. *For other editions, see* 1829.

30323 DRUMMOND, WILLIAM, **& SONS.** A general list, or compendium, of seeds, plants, implements, &c. sold by W. Drummond & Sons, Stirling, seedsmen and nurserymen... 14p. *8°. Stirling, 1838. Issued with James Smith, Remarks on thorough draining and ploughing, 4th edition (no. 30341), with which it is bound. For another edition, see 1837.*

30324 ENGLAND. *Laws, etc.* [*Endorsed:*] Bratton Fleming (Devon) Inclosure. An Act for inclosing lands in the parish of Bratton Fleming in the county of Devon. ⟨Royal Assent, 9th May 1838.⟩ 40p. *fol.* [*London,* 1838]

30325 The practical **FARMER'S** manual: a popular treatise on agriculture: designed to show the tenantry, especially of the Highlands, how they may best increase their profits, and thereby improve their condition in life. By a country clergyman. [With 'Appendix. Of soils'. By 'Frank Sylvan', i.e. Ambrose Blacklock.] 144p. *12°. Glasgow, London, &c.,* 1838.

30326 FARMERS' CENTRAL AGRICULTURAL SOCIETY. The Farmers' Central Agricultural Society...Proposed address, with introductory circular, and resolutions of the meeting by which the Society was instituted on the 9th May, 1838. By the Committee of Management. [Signed: R. Cort, secretary.] 24p. *8°.* 1838. *The Oastler copy.*

30327 HANDLEY, H. A letter to Earl Spencer, (President of the Smithfield Club,) on the formation of a national agricultural institution. 36p. *8°.* 1838.

30328 HOLLIDAY, T. A complete treatise on practical land-surveying, &c.; or, the whole art of land-surveying...railway surveying, artificers' work, conic sections, gauging...levelling, and mensuration... 320p. *8°. London & York,* 1838.

30329 JOHNSTON, JAMES F. W. The economy of a coal-field: an exposition of the objects of the Geological and Polytechnic Society of the West Riding of Yorkshire, and of the best means of attaining them. [Lecture delivered at the second quarterly meeting of the Society.] 78p. *8°. Durham,* 1838.

30330 KREYSSIG, W. A. Der Fruchtwechsel im Feldbau mit seinen wesentlichen und unwesentlichen Forderungen, seinen grössern und geringern Schwierigkeiten, und den geeignetsten, praktisch anwendbarsten Mitteln zu Vermeidung und Umgehung der letztern. 190p. *8°. Königsberg,* 1838.

30331 —— Schutz- Spar- und Nothmittel gegen Verminderung des Rein-Ertrages der Landwirthschaft, welche durch zu geringe Produktenpreise, nachtheilige Witterung und andere Unfälle entstehen kann. 234p. *8°. Königsberg,* 1838.

30332 LANCE, E. J. The hop farmer; or, a complete account of hop culture, embracing its history, laws, & uses; a theoretical and practical inquiry into an improved method of culture, founded on scientific principles. To which are added, several useful tables & calculations... 212p. *12°. London, Southwark, &c.,* 1838.

30333 LEITHART, J. Practical observations on the mechanical structure, mode of formation, the repletion or filling up, and the intersection and relative age of mineral veins; with the application of several new theoretical principles to the art of mining... 83p. *8°. London & Newcastle,* 1838.

30334 M'INTOSH, CHARLES (1794–1864). The flower garden, with selected lists of annual, biennial and perennial flowering plants. 515p. *8°.* 1838.

30335 —— The greenhouse, hot house, and stove: including selected lists of the most beautiful species of exotic flowering plants, and directions for their cultivation. 415p. *8°.* 1838.

30336 MAISON rustique du XIXe siècle. Encyclopédie d'agriculture pratique, contenant les meilleures méthodes de culture usitées particulièrement en France, en Angleterre, en Allemagne et en Flandre...Cours élémentaire... d'économie rurale...Rédigé...par une réunion d'agronomes et de practiciens appartenant aux sociétés agricoles de France, sous la direction de M. C. Bailly [M. A. Bixio, M. Malepeyre]... 4 vols. *fol. Paris,* 1838, 1837–39.

30337 On the **MALTHUSIAN DOCTRINES.** [Noting the effects of agricultural improvement in counteracting the danger of overpopulation.] 3p. *8°. n.p.* [1838?]

30338 OBSERVATIONS on foreign mining in Mexico. By a resident. 48p. *8°.* 1838.

30339 RAINY, A. A brief exposition of some existing abuses, regarding the transfer of real property by public auction and private contract; with the outline of a proposed remedy. 15p. *8°.* [1838]

30340 SIMPSON, W. W., *land-agent.* Observations in reference to the present mode of effecting sales of landed estates and other property; with some remarks on a recent publication by Mr. Rainy, entitled "A brief exposition regarding the transfer of real property". 7p. *8°.* 1838.

30341 SMITH, JAMES (1789–1850). Remarks on thorough draining and deep ploughing...Extracted from the third report of Drummonds' Agricultural Museum. Fourth edition with notes. 31p. *8°. Stirling,* 1838. *For other editions, see* 1837.

30342 SMYTH, GEORGE L. Aids to the Irish poor law in the reclamation of Irish waste lands. A letter to the Right Hon. Lord John Russell, M.P., Secretary of State, &c.&c. on the propriety of reclaiming the waste lands of Ireland, under the authority of a commission from the Crown. 24p. *8°.* 1838.

30343 SOCIETY OF THE GOVERNOR AND ASSISTANTS IN LONDON, OF THE NEW PLANTATION IN ULSTER. Report of the deputation [D. Allan, J. Humphery, J. Southby Bridge, J. E. Davies] appointed by the honourable the Irish Society to visit the City of London's plantation in Ireland, in the year 1838. [With an appendix.] 46, 49p. *8°.* 1838. *See also* 1826 (GENERAL), 1834 (AGRICULTURE), 1835, 1836, 1841.

30344 WAGNER, JOHANN P. Ueber die fortschreitende Kultur und Verbreitung der Merinos-Schaafzucht mit statistischen Beiträgen und Uebersichten. Nebst einer Untersuchung der Ursachen des Fallens der Wollpreise im Jahr 1837. Als Anhang: einige Ansichten über den möglichen Einfluss der Eisenbahnen auf den Woll-Verkehr. 142p. *8°. Königsberg,* 1838.

30345 WESTERN, C. C., *Baron Western.* Letter from Lord Western to Earl Spencer. [On the breeding of sheep.] 12p. *8°. Kelvedon,* [1838]

30346 —— [Another edition, with a short postscript.] 13p. *8°. Chelmsford,* [1838?].

30347 —— Lord Western's practical remarks on the improvement of grass land, by means of irrigation, winter-flooding, and drainage, originally published by him in... 1824, in a letter to the owners and occupiers of land, in the county of Essex. 24p. *8°*. 1838.

30348 YELLOLY, J. Some account of the employment of spade husbandry on an extensive scale in the county of Norfolk; with...observations on the importance of cottage gardens: being a communication made to the Statistical Section of the British Association, at Liverpool ...1837. 16p. *8°*. 1838. *Presentation copy from the author to the Rev. James Yates.*

CORN LAWS

30349 BAKER, JOHN, *of Leeds*. On the corn laws. Addressed to the mercantile community of Great Britain. 20p. *8°*. *London, Leeds, &c.,* 1838.

30350 CLAYTON, J. Observations on the effects of the corn laws; with a statistical account of the average price of wheat, &c. &c. from the reign of William the Conquerer [*sic*], 1050, to the reign of Queen Victoria, 1837... 16p. *8°*. *Nottingham,* 1838.

30351 The **INJURY** inflicted upon the people by the corn laws and the prosperity that would result from their repeal, explained in a series of conversations between Thomas Tomkins and William Wilkins. 22p. *8°*. *New Brentford,* 1838.

30352 [WELFORD, R. G.?] The landlords' monopoly. Being two articles on the detestable bread tax, which appeared in the Weekly True Sun of August the 26th and September the 2d, 1838... 12p. *12°*. [*London,* 1838]

POPULATION

30353 MARCUS, *pseud.* On the possibility of limiting populousness. [With 'An essay on populousness. Printed for private circulation'.] 46, 27p. *8°*. 1838. *A note at the end of the first part reads: The reader is requested to consider the following piece as being the fourth chapter of the foregoing tract'. See also 1839.*

30354 MARSHALL, JOHN (1783–1841). Statistics of the British Empire, part V. (conclusion of supplement to part IV.) Digest of the analysis and compendium of all the returns made to Parliament, (since the commencement of the nineteenth century,) relating to the increase of population in the United Kingdom...the church establishment of England and Wales; and the amount...of parochial assessments... 258, 92p. *4°*. 1838. *A reissue of*

Part IV of A digest of all the accounts, 1833–[35] *q.v.* 1833 (GENERAL), *with a further digest to 1838.*

30355 *QUETELET, L. A. J. De l'influence des saisons sur la mortalité aux différens âges dans la Belgique. 42p. *4°*. *Bruxelles,* 1838. *Reprinted from the Mémoires of the Académie des Sciences, des Lettres et des Beaux-Arts de Belgique, vol. 11. The copy that belonged to Augustus De Morgan.*

30356 SCOTCH CHURCH YOUNG MEN'S SOCIETY, *Manchester.* Statistical report of the Scottish population of Manchester. Taken in 1837. 28p. *8°*. *Manchester, Liverpool, &c.,* 1838.

TRADES & MANUFACTURES

30357 [CARTER, THOMAS (1792–1867?).] The guide to trade. The plumber, painter, and glazier. 84p. *12°*. 1838. *For another part, see 1840.*

30358 Gründliche **DARSTELLUNG** der Künste und Gewerbe. Ein technologisches Lehrbuch für gewerb-, landwirtschaftliche und polytechnische Schuler...6te vermehrte und verbesserte Auflage. 158p. *8°*. *Erlangen,* 1838.

30359 DEVLIN, J. D. The boot and shoe trade of France, as it affects the interests of the British manufacturer in the same business: with instructions towards the French system of blocking. 47p. *8°*. 1838.

30360 DICKSON, ROBERT. A lecture on the dry rot, and on the most effectual means of preventing it; delivered before the Institute of British Architects, April 3, 1837. [An exposition of Mr. Kyan's plan to prevent dry rot.] 50p. *8°*. 1838. *Presentation copy, with inscription, from the author to John Britton.*

30361 [DUVAL, H. L. N., *and others*.] Nouveau manuel du limonadier, du glacier, du chocolatier et du confiseur...par MM. Cardelli [pseudonym of H. L. N. Duval], Lionnet-Clémandot, et Julia de Fontenelle...

Nouvelle édition...(*Manuels-Roret.*) 464p. *12°*. *Paris,* 1838.

30362 FOURNEL, H. A messieurs les membres des deux Chambres législatives. Mémoire présenté par les fabricants et marchands d'ouvrages d'or et d'argent de Paris, et rédigé par Henri Fournel. 187p. *4°*. *Paris,* 1838.

30363 HALL, SAMUEL. Address to the Rt. Hon. Lord William Bentinck, M.P., Chairman of the Select Committee of the House of Commons, on steam communication with India...on that part of the evidence relating to Samuel Hall's patent improvements on steam engines. 22p. *4°*. *London & Nottingham,* 1838.

30364 MACKINNON, W. A. Speech of William Alex. Mackinnon, Esq. M.P. in the House of Commons on...Feb. 14, 1837, on motion for leave to bring in a Bill to amend the practice relating to Letters Patent for inventions, and for the better encouragement of the arts and manufactures. Also, a copy of the Bill, proposed... by Mr. Mackinnon...Feb. 15, 1837. [With an appendix.] 44, xlvp. *8°*. 1838.

30365 MARTIN, WILLIAM (1772–1851). The defeat of the eighth scientific meeting of the British Association of Asses...[With 'On Unitarianism'.] 16p. *8°. Newcastle,* [1838]

30366 —— Light and truth. Martin's invention for destroying all foul air and fire damps in coal pits...[With 'Wm. Martin proving the Scriptures to be right'.] 8p. *8°. Newcastle,* [1838]

30367 MUSPRATT, J. A full report of the trial of the important indictment preferred by the Corporation of Liverpool, against James Muspratt, Esq., manufacturer of alkali, at the Liverpool Spring Assizes, 1838... 97p. *8°. Liverpool,* [1838]

30368 Corrected to 1838. **SKYRING'S** builders' prices, calculated to form a complete guide to employers, master builders, & workmen. To which has been added a daily or weekly journal...List of district surveyors; abstract of the Building and Paving Acts...Twenty-

eighth edition. [Compiled by W. H. Skyring.] 183p. *8°.* 1838. *See also* 1812, 1818, 1819, 1827, 1831, 1845, 1846.

30369 TERRY, CHARLES and PARKER, WILLIAM, *patentees.* On the advantages of a patent process for increasing the product of sugar from cane juice. 99p. *8°.* 1838. *Presentation copy from the authors to Sir Denis Le Marchant (1795–1874).*

30370 TREDGOLD, T. The steam engine; its invention and progressive improvement, and investigation of its principles, and its application to navigation, manufactures, and railways...A new edition, enlarged...and extended to the science of steam naval architecture. Revised and edited by W. S. B. Woolhouse...[With 'Illustrations of steam machinery and steam naval architecture'.] 2 vols. *4°. & fol.* 1838–40. *See also* 1850 (TRANSPORT).

COMMERCE

30371 ANSWERS to a few of the fallacies which are reported to have been spoken in the debate on the second reading of the Bill to amend the law of copyright in the House of Commons, on the 25th April 1838. 4p. *8°. n.p.* [1838 ?]

30372 BEAULIEU, C. Histoire du commerce, de l'industrie et des fabriques de Lyon, depuis leur origine jusqu'à nos jours. 310p. *8°. Lyon,* 1838.

30373 BISHOP, JAMES, *secretary of the Metropolitan Protection Society.* A defence of the new beer trade. 24p. *8°.* 1838.

30374 FOREIGN POLICY and commerce. Speeches delivered at a dinner given by the commercial community of Glasgow to David Urquhart, Esq., on the 23d of May, 1838... 51p. *8°.* 1838.

30375 FRANCE. *Administration des Douanes.* Tableau décennal du commerce de la France avec ses colonies et les puissances étrangères...1827 à 1836. 884p. *4°. Paris,* 1838. *See also* 1848.

30376 HAGEMEISTER, J. VON. Der europäische Handel in der Türkei und in Persien. 92p. *8°. Riga & Leipzig,* 1838.

30377 HAMER, J. A letter to Her Majesty's Ministers on the operation and beneficial results of the new Beer Act, and the evils of the licensing system: being a reply to a...scurrilous attack upon the beer sellers by a public brewer of Manchester. 23p. *8°. Manchester,* [1838]

30378 [INGLIS, ROBERT.] The Chinese security merchants in Canton and their debts. 33p. *8°. Canton,* 1838. *Attributed to Robert Inglis in a manuscript note on the printed paper wrapper.*

30379 [——] [Another edition.] 48p. *8°.* 1838.

30380 LEO, *pseud.* The commercial career of Sewell and Cross; with an account of the premature death of Thomas, and the subsequent extraordinary proceedings of John Kirby...Edited by Leo. 46p. *8°.* 1838. *The Oastler copy.*

30381 A **LETTER** to Her Majesty's Ministers, on the

operation and repeal of the new Beer Act, by an inhabitant of Manchester. 16p. *8°. Manchester,* 1838.

For **LONDON.** *Court of Common Council.* An account of coal, culm, and cinders, imported into the port of London, during the year 1837[–44], published by authority of the coal and corn committee, 1838–45, *see* vol. III, *Periodicals list,* Account of coal, culm, and cinders, imported...

For —— —— Coal market, monthly importation of coal, culm, & cinders...Published by authority of the coal and corn committee, 1838–44, *see* vol. III, *Periodicals list,* Coal market, monthly importation of coal...

30382 MINUTES of the proceedings of a convention of merchants and others, held in Augusta, Georgia, October 16, 1837; with an address to the people of the south and south-western states relative to the establishment of a direct export and import trade with foreign countries. 30p. *8°. Augusta,* 1838.

30383 PAGE, JAMES. The fractional calculator; or new ready reckoner: shewing at one view the value of any quantity of goods...with discount tables...being particularly adapted for merchants, lace manufacturers, cotton and commission agents, drapers, &c....Second edition, revised and corrected. 250p. *12°. London & Nottingham,* 1838.

30384 Official **PAPERS** respecting the suspension of trade at Canton, occasioned by the smuggling of opium; with notices of riot, &c. Republished from the Chinese Repository for December, 1838. 24p. *8°. Canton, China,* 1838.

30385 SAGOT, ED., & CE. Ed. Sagot et Cᵉ à Boulogne-sur-Mer et Calais. [A circular letter, dated in manuscript: 1er décembre 1838, announcing a regular freight service between Boulogne, Calais and London.] *s.sh.4°. n.p.* [1838]

30386 WHEELWRIGHT, W. Statements and documents relative to the establishment of steam navigation in the Pacific; with copies of the decrees of the governments of Peru, Bolivia, and Chile, granting exclusive privileges to the undertaking [i.e. the Pacific Steam Navigation Company]. 42p. *8°.* 1838.

COLONIES

30387 A. Lord Durham and the Canadians. A reprint from the January number of the London and Westminster Review. 32p. *8°. Montreal, 1838. With a manuscript note on the final page of text giving an account of proceedings taken against the printer.*

30388 Recommended for perusal by every reformer. A correct **ACCOUNT** of the rise and progress of the recent popular movements in Lower Canada. From the Patriot, Extra, (United States newspaper), Dec. 15th 1837. 12p. *8°. Bungay,* [1838]

30389 BEECHAM, J. Colonization: being remarks on colonization in general, with an examination of the proposals of the association which has been formed for colonizing New Zealand...Fourth edition. 72p. *8°.* 1838.

30390 —— Remarks upon the latest official documents relating to New Zealand: (ordered...to be printed, February 7, 1838:) with a notice of a pamphlet by Samuel Hinds...one of the committee of the New Zealand Association. In a letter to a friend...Second edition. 75p. *8°.* 1838.

30391 BENTHAM, J. Canada. Emancipate your colonies! An unpublished argument. [With a dedicatory letter to Viscount Melbourne, signed: Philo-Bentham.] 18p. *8°.* 1838. *For other editions, see* 1793.

30392 [BLAND, W.] New South Wales. Examination of Mr. James Macarthur's work, "New South Wales, its present state and future prospects." p.1–80. *8°. Sydney,* 1838. *No more of this edition was published.*

30393 BRITISH AND FOREIGN ABOR-IGINES' PROTECTION SOCIETY. The first annual report of the Aborigines Protection Society, presented at the meeting in Exeter Hall, May 16th, 1838, with list of officers, subscribers, and benefactors... 31p. *8°.* 1838.

30394 BROUGHAM, H. P., *Baron Brougham and Vaux.* Lord Brougham's speech in the House of Lords... January 18, 1838. Upon Canada. 61p. *8°.* 1838.

30395 —— Lord Brougham's speech in the House of Lords on...2nd February, 1838, on the maltreatment of the North American colonies. 37p. *8°.* 1838.

30396 BRUCE, C. A. An account of the manufacture of the black tea, as now practised at Suddeya in Upper Assam, by the Chinamen sent thither for that purpose. With some orservations [*sic*] on the culture of the plant in China, and its growth in Assam. 18p. *8°. Calcutta,* 1838.

30397 BUCHANAN, JAMES, *British Consul at New York.* A letter to the Right Honorable the Earl of Durham...Governor of Her Majesty's North American Possessions, &c....calling His Lordship's attention to the advantages to be derived by allowing a free transit of merchandise through Canada to the State of Michigan and Wisconsin Territory; as a means of preserving our friendly relations with the United States. With observations as to the River St. Lawrence, for extending the commerce of the Empire and enriching the Canadas. 25p. *8°. n.p.,* 1838. *Presentation copy, with inscription, from the author to E. M. Turton, Esq.*

30398 The **CANADIAN CONTROVERSY;** its origin, nature, and merits. 84p. *8°.* 1838.

For the **CANADIAN PORTFOLIO,** *see* vol. III, *Periodicals list.*

30399 CAPPER, H. South Australia. Containing hints to emigrants; proceedings of the South Australian Company; a variety of...information; a map of the eastern coast of Gulf St. Vincent, and a plan of Adelaide ...Second edition, considerably augmented. 118p. *12°. London & Edinburgh,* 1838.

30400 The **FRENCH** in Africa. 48p. *8°.* 1838.

30401 GORE, M. Observations on the disturbances in Canada. 38p. *8°.* 1838.

30402 HOWITT, W. Colonization and Christianity: a popular history of the treatment of the natives by the Europeans in all their colonies. 508p. *12°.* 1838.

30403 INDIA. *Committee for Investigating the Coal and Mineral Resources of India.* Reports of a Committee for investigating the coal and mineral resources of India. [Drawn up by J. McClelland.] 96, 14p. *8°. Calcutta,* 1838.

30404 INDIA, Great Britain, and Russia. 48p. *8°.* 1838.

30405 JAMES, T. H. Six months in South Australia; with some account of Port Philip and Portland Bay, in Australia, with advice to emigrants; to which is added a monthly calendar of gardening and agriculture, adapted to the climate and seasons. 295p. *8°.* 1838.

30406 M'QUEEN, J. A letter to the Right Honourable Lord Glenelg, on the West Indian currency, commerce, African slave trade, &c.&c. 52p. *8°.* 1838.

30407 MARTIN, ROBERT M. The history, antiquities, topography, and statistics of Eastern India... Surveyed under the orders of the...Government, and collated from the original documents at the E.I. House... 3 vols. *8°.* 1838.

30408 MOLESWORTH, SIR W., *Bart.* Sir William Molesworth's speech, in the House of Commons, March 6, 1838, on the state of the colonies. 59p. *8°.* 1838.

30409 [NEATE, C.] Plain statement of the quarrel with Canada; in which is considered who first infringed the constitution of the colony. 20p. *8°.* 1838.

30410 O., M. N. The Canadian crisis, and Lord Durham's mission to the North American colonies: with remarks, the result of personal observation in the colonies and the United States, on the remedial measures to be adopted in the North American provinces. 56p. *8°.* 1838.

30411 PARLBY, S. Hints to emigrants, in which the climate, capabilities, and geographical position of the British colony of the Cape of Good Hope are submitted for examination and consideration. 23p. *8°.* 1838.

30412 TURTON, T. E. M. Remarks on the petition to Parliament of the inhabitants of Bengal and Madras against the Act No. XI. of 1836. Passed by the Legislative Council of India. [With an appendix, containing the text of the petition and the repealed clauses of 53 Geo. III, c. 155.] 28, xxp. *8°.* 1838.

30413 WESTMACOTT, G. E. Indian commerce, and Russian intrigue. The present and future prospects of our Indian Empire. 84p. *8°*. [*London*,] 1838.

30414 WHITE, WILLIAM, *Capt.* Mirzas Kaiwan Jah, or the dethroned King of Oude, in chains!!! Being a letter to Lord Viscount Melbourne. 123p. *8°*. 1838.

FINANCE

30415 ALLEN, WILLIAM (1803–1879). Speech of Mr. Allen, of Ohio, on the bill to separate the government from the banks. Delivered in the Senate of the United States, February 20, 1838. 16p. *8°*. *Washington*, 1838.

30416 AMERICAN EXCHANGE BANK. The articles of association of the American Exchange Bank. An act of the Legislature of the State of New York to establish the business of banking. An address to the public and the proceedings of the commissioners for organizing the Bank. 25p. *8°*. *New York*, 1838.

30417 ANGERSTEIN, J. J. W. Memorandum of facts relating to the Mildenhall Savings Bank. 24p. *8°*. 1838.

30418 ARKANSAS. *General Assembly.* Charter. Sec. 1. [*Begin.*] Be it enacted by the General Assembly of the State of Arkansas, that there shall be established in this state, a bank under the name and title of "The Real Estate Bank of the State of Arkansas"...[With 'An act to increase the rate of interest of the bonds of the State, issued to the Real Estate Bank of the State of Arkansas'.] 26p. *8°*. *n.p.* [1838]

30419 ASSOCIATION OF SOAP MANUFAC-TURERS. Report and resolutions adopted at the annual meeting of the Association...January 25th, 1838. [To consider means to secure the repeal of the soap duty.] 15p. *8°*. [1838]

30420 The **BANK** of Ireland charter. Remarks on the proposed renewal of the charter of the Bank of Ireland. 26p. *8°*. 1838.

30421 BANK OF THE UNITED STATES [1836–1841]. An act to incorporate the stockholders of the Bank of the United States, by the State of Pennsylvania. [With 'Proceedings of a meeting of the stockholders of the Bank of the United States'.] 44p. *12°*. *Philadelphia*, 1838. *For another edition, see 1836 (Pennsylvania).*

30422 BECHER, S. Das österreichische Münzwesen vom Jahre 1524 bis 1838 in historischer, statistischer und legislativer Hinsicht... 2 vols. *8°*. *Wien*, 1838.

30423 BELL, ROBERT, *of Edinburgh.* Letter to James William Gilbart, Esquire, manager of the London and Westminster Bank, on the relative merits of the English and Scotch banking systems; with practical suggestions for the consolidation of the English joint stock banking interest. 24p. *8°*. *Edinburgh & London*, 1838.

30424 BENTON, T. H. Speech of Mr. Benton, of Missouri, on the bill to separate the government from the banks. Delivered in the Senate of the United States, March 14, 1838. 31p. *8°*. *Washington*, 1838.

30425 BLACKER, W. An inconvertible national paper currency, best adapted to increase the commerce, manufactures and revenues of the British Empire. An essay. 69p. *8°*. *Dublin*, 1838. *Other editions were published in London with the title:* The evils inseparable from a mixed currency, *in 1839 and 1844 (qq.v.).*

30426 CAISSE D'ÉPARGNE, *Paris.* Caisse d'Épargne et de Prévoyance de Paris, fondée en novembre 1818. Rapports et comptes rendus des opérations... pendant l'année 1837...Résumé des opérations des caisses d'épargne départementales, au 31 décembre 1837. 33p. *4°*. *Paris*, 1838. *The copy that belonged to Thomas Chalmers.*

30427 [**CAPPS,** E.] The currency question in a nutshell. Second edition. 16p. *8°*. 1838. *For other editions, see 1837.*

30428 CAREY, H. C. The credit system in France, Great Britain, and the United States. 130p. *8°*. *Philadelphia*, 1838.

30429 —— [Another edition.] 136p. *8°*. *London & Philadelphia*, 1838.

30430 CARLISLE CITY AND DISTRICT BANKING COMPANY. Deed of settlement of the Carlisle City and District Banking Company, established A.D. 1837...Capital – two hundred and fifty thousand pounds. 58p. *8°*. *Carlisle*, 1838.

30431 CASSELS, W. G. Narrative of the circumstances which have occasioned a dispute between the directors of the Northern and Central Bank of England and Walter Gibson Cassels, manager at Manchester, and afterwards agent for the Bank in London, with extracts from his letters written previously to the application to the Bank of England for assistance. 37, 38p. *8°*. *Boulogne*, [1838] *The copy that belonged to T. Spring Rice, Baron Monteagle.*

30432 CHAMBERS, G. Speech of George Chambers on the currency and banks. Delivered in the Convention of Pennsylvania, on the 22d & 26th December, 1837. 24p. *8°*. *Philadelphia*, 1838.

30433 CLAY, H. Speech of the Hon. Henry Clay, of Kentucky, establishing a deliberate design, on the part of the late and present Executive...to break down the whole banking system of the United States...and in reply to the speech of the Hon. J. C. Calhoun...Delivered in the Senate of the United States, February 19, 1838. 32p. *8°*. *Washington*, 1838.

30434 CLYDESDALE BANKING COMPANY. Contract of copartnery of the Clydesdale Banking Company. 70p. *8°*. *Glasgow*, 1838.

30435 COOKE, L. To Charles Shaw Lefevre, Esq., M.P. [A letter on parochial assessment for rates. Dated: 25th July, 1838.] 3p. *4°*. *n.p.* [1838]

30436 DELABORDE, L. J. H., *Comte.* Traité des avaries particulières sur marchandises, dans leurs rapports avec le contrat d'assurance maritime...Deuxième édition. 407p. *8°*. *Paris*, 1838. *With bibliographies.*

30437 DE MORGAN, A. An essay on probabilities, and on their application to life contingencies and insurance offices. 306, xlp. *8°*. 1838. *See also 1841.*

30438 DE MOUNTENEY, T. J. B. The case of a détenu. [A plea for indemnity for his detention in France as a prisoner of war from 1803 to 1814.] 20p. *8°*. 1838.

30439 EASTERN BANK OF SCOTLAND.

Contract of copartnery of the Eastern Bank of Scotland. 55p. *8°. Edinburgh*, 1838.

30440 ENGLAND. *Laws, etc.* The Tithe Act and the Tithe Amendment Act with notes...Together with the report of the Tithe Commissioners...with explanatory notes. By G. H. Whalley, Esq. of the Tithe Commission Office. 387p. *8°.* 1838.

30441 —— Parliament. *House of Commons.* Report by the Select Committee on pawnbroking in Ireland; together with minutes of evidence, an appendix and index. Ordered ...to be printed, 3rd August, 1838. 232p. *8°. Dublin*, 1838.

30442 —— *Privy Council.* Minutes of evidence taken before the committee of Her Majesty's most Honourable Privy Council, upon the subject of the coinage, at the Board of Trade...July 2, 1836. [With an appendix.] 85p. *fol. n.p.* [1838]

30443 ESTERNO, F. C. P. D', *Comte.* Des banques départementales en France, de leur influence sur les progrès de l'industrie, des obstacles qui s'opposent à leur établissement; et des mesures à prendre pour en favoriser la propagation. 242p. *8°. Paris*, 1838.

30444 *FANE, R. G. C. Bankruptcy reform: in a series of letters addressed to Sir Robert Peel, Bart.... Letters I. II. III. 35p. *8°.* 1838. *The copy that belonged to George Grote.*

30445 FORTUNE, E. F. THOMAS. Fortune's epitome of the stocks & public funds...Fourteenth edition. By John Field, jun. 304p. *8°.* 1838. *For other editions, see 1796.*

30446 FOSTER, B. F. The merchant's manual, comprising the principles of trade, commerce and banking; with merchants' accounts; inland and foreign bills; par of exchange; equation of payments, &c. 252p. *12°. Boston & Philadelphia*, 1838.

30447 *FRAMPTON, A. An account of the Mutual Life Assurance Society: with remarks on the subject of life assurance generally. 31p. *8°.* 1838. *The copy that belonged to Augustus De Morgan.*

30448 FRENCH CLAIMS. An exposé in relation to the application and misapplication of the funds paid by France to the British Government, for the indemnification of British subjects under the Treaty of Peace of 1814, and the conventions of 1815 and 1818. [With a preface and postscript by the Baron De Bode.] 39p. *8°.* 1838.

30449 FRICHOT, A. P. De la nécessité de refondre les sous, de supprimer le billon, et des améliorations à faire dans la fabrication des monnaies. Développemens pour faire suite au projet proposé à M. le Ministre des Finances, le 7 décembre 1835. 35p. *8°. Paris*, 1838.

30450 HALDANE, R. The duty of paying tribute enforced; in letters to the Rev. Dr. John Brown, occasioned by his resisting the payment of the annuity tax. 95p. *8°. Edinburgh, London, &c.*, 1838.

30451 HARPER, A. Speech of Mr. Harper, of Ohio, on the bill to authorize the reissuing of treasury notes. Delivered in the House of Representatives, May 12 and 14, 1838. 16p. *8°. Washington*, 1838.

30452 HAWKINS, E. An account of some Saxon pennies, and other articles, found at Sevington, North Wilts. Communicated to the Society of Antiquaries...in a letter to Sir Henry Ellis. [From The Archaeologia, Vol. XXVII.] 7p. *4°.* 1838.

30453 HOFFMANN, JOHANN G. Die Lehre vom Gelde als Anleitung zu gründlichen Urtheilen über das Geldwesen mit besonderer Beziehung auf den preussischen Staat. 199p. *8°. Berlin*, 1838. *For a supplement to this work, See 1841.*

30454 *Entry cancelled.*

30455 *INVESTIGATOR, *pseud.* Caution! Observations on the National Loan Fund Life Assurance and Deferred Annuity Society: with a few remarks on the subject of life assurance, generally. 30p. *8°. London & Nottingham*, 1838. *The copy that belonged to Augustus De Morgan.*

30456 JONES, RICHARD (1790–1855). Remarks on the manner in which tithe should be assessed to the poor's rate, under the existing law, with a protest against the change which will be produced in that law, by a Bill introduced into the House of Commons by Mr. Shaw Lefevre. 64p. *8°.* 1838.

30457 JOPLIN, T. Articles on banking and currency. From "The Economist" newspaper. 108p. *8°.* 1838.

30458 —— An essay on the general principles and present practice of banking, in England and Scotland, to which is added an explanation of bankers' book-keeping, and an essay on the prevention of forgery...Seventh edition. 136p. *8°.* 1838. *Presentation copy, with inscription, from the author to 'W. Harris Esq.'. For other editions, see 1822.*

30459 *LUPTON, JAMES. Church rates. The disadvantages under which the leasehold property of the Church labours, the possibility of giving to it an increased value, and the propriety of applying part of the surplus revenue thence arising as a substitute for church rates. 43p. *8°.* 1838. *Presentation copy from the author to George Grote.*

30460 [**MACLEAN,** A. W. ?] Eureka! or, the fundamental principles of monetary circulation. Shewing the advantages derived from a connection with joint-stock banks, and the impossibility of successful competition... without such connection, in the absence of a national deposit bank of issue. [With 'Unto...the Lords Commissioners of Her Majesty's Treasury, the Memorial of Alex. Walker Maclean' dated: 1st November 1837.] 40p. *8°. Edinburgh*, 1838. *It is not clear, from the text, that Alexander Walker Maclean wrote the work itself.*

For the **MANCHESTER MAGAZINE,** *see vol.* III, *Periodicals list.*

30461 MARSHALL, G. A view of the silver coin and coinage of Great Britain from the year 1662 to 1837; containing an account of every denomination of coin... also an account of the silver coins struck in Scotland, from the year 1662 to the Union...1707... 160p. *8°. London & Birmingham*, 1838.

30462 NATIONAL SECURITY SAVINGS BANK. Report on the affairs of the National Security Savings Bank of Edinburgh, presented to the annual general meeting of the trustees and managers, held on 13th February 1838. With the minutes of that meeting. 8p. *8°. Edinburgh*, 1838. *See also* 1840, 1841, 1845.

30463 NETHERLANDS. *Departement van Financien.* Berigt eener negotiatie, tot te geldemaking van losrenten, rentende 5 ten honderd in het jaar, ten laste van 's Rijks overzeesche bezittingen, waarvan de renten door het Rijk, bij de wet van 27 maart 1838...onvoorwaardelijk zijn gewaarborgd. 5p. *8°. n.p.* [1838]

30464 NEW YORK, *State of. Assembly.* Report [by S. B. Ruggles, Chairman of the Committee of Ways and Means] upon the finances and internal improvements of the State of New-York. 1838. [With an appendix.] 65, 6p. *8°. New-York,* [1838]

30465 *—— —— State of New-York. No. 242. In Assembly, March 12, 1838. Report of the Committee of Ways and Means [S. B. Ruggles, V. Birdseye, T. B. Cooke, A. Lewis] on the United States deposite fund, and on the recommendation of the Comptroller to levy a direct tax. 37p. *8°. n.p.* [1838] *The copy that belonged to George Grote.*

30466 [NOLHAC, J. B. M.] Histoire de la marche des idées sur l'emploi de l'argent, depuis Aristote jusqu'à nous. Par Mr. I.B.M.N.... 149p. *8°. Paris & Lyon,* 1838.

30467 NORMAN, G. W. Remarks upon some prevalent errors, with respect to currency and banking, and suggestions to the Legislature and the public as to the improvement of the monetary system. 109p. *8°.* 1838.

30468 NORTH AMERICAN TRUST AND BANKING COMPANY. Articles of association and bye-laws of the North American Trust and Banking Company: also, the general banking law, passed by the Legislature of the State of New-York... 40p. *8°. New-York,* 1838.

30469 NORVELL, J. Speech of Mr. Norvell, of Michigan, on the bill imposing additional duties as depositaries in certain cases, on public officers, &c. Delivered in the Senate of the United States, March 6, 1838. 14p. *8°. Washington,* 1838.

30470 OSBORNE, LORD S. G. The savings bank. Some particulars of the life and death of "Old Rainy Day," a lover of funerals...with a few observations added, in the hope of persuading others to do as he did, viz. save against "a rainy day"...Third edition. 20p. *8°.* [1838]

30471 —— Fourth edition. 20p. *8°.* [1838]

30472 OUTLINE of a plan for the future management of the circulation. 26p. *8°.* 1838.

30473 PHILLPOTTS, J. A letter to the Right Hon. Lord J. Russell, in answer to the pamphlet of the Rev. R. Jones...on the manner in which tithe should be assessed to the poor rate. 29p. *8°.* 1838.

30474 POTHERAT DE THOU, B. Recherches sur l'origine de l'impôt en France. 363p. *8°. Paris & Strasbourg,* 1838.

30475 PRO PATRIA, *pseud.* Thoughts on the National Debt. 30p. *8°.* 1838.

30476 The **REMEDY,** in a national bank of the people, versus a treasury bank, and a national bank of a party: an appeal to the people of the United States; with a plan: by an American citizen. 14p. *8°. New-York,* 1838.

30477 REVANS, S. Advantages of counter exchange with the United States of America. 24p. *8°.* 1838.

30478 RHETT, R. B. Speech of Mr. Rhett, of South Carolina, on the treasury note bill, delivered in the House of Representatives on the thirteenth of May, 1838. 16p. *8°. Washington,* 1838.

30479 RICARDO, S. A national bank the remedy for the evils attendant upon our present system of paper currency. [With 'Appendix. Plan for a national bank, by (the late) David Ricardo, Esq., M.P.'.] 65p. *8°.* 1838.

30480 *SAY, H. De la nécessité de réformer la loi relative à la surveillance du titre et à la perception des droits de garantie des matières et ouvrages d'or et d'argent. 16p. *8°. n.p.* [1838] *The copy that belonged to George Grote.*

30481 STRANGE, R. Speech of Mr. Strange, of North Carolina, on the bill imposing additional duties as depositaries in certain cases, on public officers, &c. Delivered in the Senate of the United States, March 6, 1838. 21p. *8°. Washington,* 1838.

30482 TILL, W. An essay on the Roman denarius and English silver penny...To which is appended a list of English and Scotch pennies, from the Conquest...Second edition. 230p. *12°.* 1838. *For another edition, see* 1837.

30483 UNITED STATES OF AMERICA. *Congress.* History of the extra session of Congress, convened...on the fourth of September, and terminated on the fourth of October, 1837. Embracing a faithful abstract of the important currency debates...on the proposed measures of financial legislation, and an accurate table of the yeas and nays... 105p. *8°. New York, Boston, &c.,* 1838.

30484 —— —— *House of Representatives.* Report of the minority of the Committee of Ways and Means on the state of the Treasury. March 23, 1838. 19p. *8°. Washington,* 1838.

30485 WEBSTER, D. Speech of the hon. Daniel Webster, on the Sub-Treasury Bill. Delivered in the Senate of the United States, January 31, 1838. 16p. *8°. Washington,* 1838.

30486 *—— Mr. Webster's second speech on the Sub-Treasury Bill. Delivered March 12, 1838. 60p. *8°. Washington,* 1838. *The copy that belonged to George Grote.*

30487 —— [Another edition.] Mr. Webster's speech on the bill imposing additional duties as depositaries, in certain cases, on public officers...commonly called the Sub-Treasury Bill; delivered in the Senate of the United States on March 12, 1838: and his speech of the 22d March, in answer to Mr. Calhoun. 111p. *8°. Washington,* 1838. *Presentation copy from the author to the 5th Earl Stanhope.*

30488 WESTPHAL, G. Grundsätze des Bankwesens und Bemerkungen über den Entwurf der Statuten der Leipziger Bank. 24p. *8°. Chemnitz,* 1838.

30489 WILLICH, C. M. Annual supplement to the Tithe commutation tables, for ascertaining, at sight, the tithe-rent charge...for the year 1838, according to the average prices of wheat, barley, and oats, for the seven... years, to Christmas 1837... [4]p. *8°.* 1838. *For* Tithe commutation tables, *see* 1837.

30490 YOUNG, GEORGE R. Upon the history, principles, and prospects of the Bank of British North America, and of the Colonial Bank; with an enquiry into colonial exchanges, and the expediency of introducing "British sterling and British coin"...as the money of account and currency of the North American colonies. 66p. *8°.* 1838.

TRANSPORT

30491 BREES, S. C. Railway practice. A collection of working plans and practical details of construction in the public works of the most celebrated engineers...on the several railways...throughout the kingdom...A series of original designs for every description of railway works, in various styles of architecture...Second edition, corrected and improved. 106p. *4°.* 1838. *For another edition, see* 1837, *and for an appendix,* 1839.

30492 CHEVALIER, M. Des intérêts matériels en France. Travaux publics. Routes. Canaux. Chemins de fer... 440p. *8°. Paris,* 1838.

30493 —— Deuxième édition. 440p. *8°. Paris,* 1838.

30494 COGHLAN, F. The iron road book and railway companion from London to Birmingham, Manchester, and Liverpool... 180p. *12°.* 1838.

30495 COMMERCIAL RAILWAY, afterwards **LONDON AND BLACKWALL RAILWAY.** London & Blackwall Commercial Railway. Report of Messrs. Geo. Stephenson, and G. P. Bidder. 22p. *8°.* [*London,* 1838]

30496 CONSIDÉRANT, V. P. Déraison et dangers de l'engouement pour les chemins de fer. Avis à l'opinion et aux capitaux. 90p. *8°. Paris,* 1838. *Considérant's own copy.*

30497 ELMES, J. A scientific, historical and commercial survey of the harbour and port of London, containing accounts of its history, privileges, functions and government...accompanied by plans and details... 70p., 22 plates. *fol.* 1838. *Another edition was published as Part IV of Simms'* Public works of Great Britain, *(q.v. no.* 30521).

30498 ENGLAND. *Commissioners appointed to Inquire into the Manner in which Railway Communications can be most advantageously promoted in Ireland.* Second report of the Commissioners...Abridged edition. 213p. *8°. Dublin,* 1838.

30499 —— *Laws, etc.* Anno quarto & quinto Gulielmi IV. Regis. Cap. lxxxviii. An Act for making a railway from London to Southampton. ⟨25th July 1834.⟩ p.2517–2636. *fol.* 1838. *The copy that belonged to William King-Noel, 1st Earl of Lovelace, with his monogram stamped at the head of the text.*

30500 —— —— [*Endorsed:*] Eastern Counties Railway. An Act to amend and enlarge the powers and provisions of the Act relating to the Eastern Counties Railway. 46, ivp. *fol.* [*London,* 1838]

30501 FREELING, A. Freeling's Grand Junction Railway companion to Liverpool, Manchester, and Birmingham; and Liverpool, Manchester & Birmingham guide... 192p. *12°. London, Liverpool, &c.,* 1838. *For another edition, see* 1837.

30502 —— The railway companion, from London to Birmingham, Liverpool, and Manchester... 204p. *12°. London, Liverpool, &c.,* [1838] *See also* 1841.

30503 GATESHEAD. Parish meeting. Proposed railway from Gateshead, to the Green Court, Newcastle...The surveyors of the highways of the parish of Gateshead hereby convene a parish meeting of the rate payers...on Monday, the 15th day of January...4th January, 1838. [Signed: Thomas Revely, James Hymers, John Edward, surveyors. A poster.] *s.sh.4°. Gateshead,* [1838]

30504 GREAT WESTERN, *Steam Ship.* The logs of the first voyage, made with the unceasing aid of steam, between England and America, by the Great Western, of Bristol, Lieut. James Hosken, R.N., Commander; also an appendix and remarks, by Christopher Claxton. 76p. *8°. Bristol,* [1838]

30505 GREAT WESTERN RAILWAY COMPANY. [Reports made to the Directors of the Great Western Railway, by Sir J. Hawkshaw, I. K. Brunel and N. Wood, with an introductory letter by the last.] 17, 31, 34, 82, 22p. *8°.* [*London & Newcastle-upon-Tyne,* 1838]

30506 HANCOCK, WALTER. Narrative of twelve years' experiments, (1824–1836,) demonstrative of the practicability and advantage of employing steam-carriages on common roads: with engravings and descriptions of the different steam-carriages constructed by the author, his patent boiler, wedge-wheels, and other inventions. 104p. *8°.* 1838.

30507 KENNET AND AVON CANAL NAVIGATION. Report of the Committee of Management... [Signed: J. W. D. Dundas, chairman, and dated, 17th July, 1838.] [3]p. *fol. Marlborough,* [1838] *See also* 1812, 1813, 1815, 1816, 1823, 1824, 1825, 1826.

30508 LIST, F. Das deutsche National-Transport-System in volks- und staatswirthschaftlicher Beziehung... 129p. *8°. Altona & Leipzig,* 1838.

30509 LIVRE de poste indiquant, 1. Les postes aux chevaux du Royaume de France; 2. Les relais des routes desservies en poste, conduisant des frontières de France aux principales capitales de l'Europe; 3. L'organisation du service des paquebots de la Méditerranée. Pour l'an 1838. 273[373]p. *8°. Paris,* 1838. *See also* 1814 (État général des postes...), 1818, 1819, 1823, 1835 (Livre de poste...)

30510 The LONDON, Birmingham, Liverpool & Manchester railway guide, giving a description of the entire route from London to Birmingham, with the fares & rates, and time of starting... 9, [5]p. *8°. G. Mansell,* [1838]

30511 NEWCASTLE AND CARLISLE RAILWAY COMPANY. The Managing Committee's report to the Directors...March 14th, 1838. [Signed: Benjamin Thompson, George Johnson, Nicholas Wood.] 7p. *8°. Newcastle,* [1838] *See also* 1835, 1837, 1839.

30512 —— Report of the Directors...read to the shareholders at their annual meeting, March 15, 1838. 13p. *8°. Newcastle-upon-Tyne,* 1838. *See also* 1835, 1837, 1843, 1845.

30513 A few general **OBSERVATIONS** on the principal railways executed, in progress, & projected, in the midland counties & north of England, with the author's opinion upon them as investments... 64p. *8°. London & Liverpool,* 1838.

30514 OLIVER, J. Stockton and Middlesbrough. General merchandize, ship goods, furniture, &c., carefully conveyed. [Announcement of a carrier service in association with the Stockton and Darlington Railway, to begin on 22 October, 1838. Dated: October 12th, 1838.] *s.sh.4°. Darlington,* [1838]

30515 OSBORNE, E. C. and W. Osborne's guide to

the Grand Junction, or Birmingham, Liverpool, and Manchester Railway, with...complete guides to the towns of Birmingham, Liverpool, and Manchester... 378p. *12°*. *Birmingham & London*, 1838.

30516 —— Second edition. 347p. *12°*. *Birmingham & London*, 1838.

30517 **PARNELL**, H. B., *Baron Congleton*. A treatise on roads; wherein the principles on which roads should be made are explained and illustrated, by the plans, specifications, and contracts made use of by Thomas Telford, Esq. on the Holyhead Road. Second edition. 465p. *8°*. 1838. *For another edition, see* 1833.

30518 The **PROJECTOR'S GAZETTE**. April 2, 1838. The monstrous delusion of the Eastern Counties Railway. 32p. *8°*. [*London*, 1838]

30519 **RAILROADIANA**. A new history of England, or picturesque, biographical, historical, legendary and antiquarian sketches. Descriptive of the vicinity of the railroads, first series...London and Birmingham Railway. 216p. *12°*. 1838.

For the **RAILWAY TIMES**, 1838–39, 1841–55, 1881–1904, *see vol.* III, *Periodicals list*.

30520 **RASTRICK**, JOHN U. West Cumberland, Furness, and Morecambe Bay railway. Reports of J. W. [*sic*] Rastrick, Esq., and John Hague, Esq. 23p. *8°*. [1838] *Rastrick's own copy*.

30521 **SIMMS**, F. W., *ed.* Public works of Great Britain. [Division I. Railways, locomotive engines, and carriages. Division II. Canals, wharf walls, bridges, and the docks and port of Liverpool. Division III. Turnpike roads, iron, steel, and gas works. Division IV. The port and docks of London. By J. Elmes.] 72, 32, 24, 70p., 153 plates. *fol*. 1838.

30522 **STATEMENT** of proceedings in India relative to the Calcutta and Saugur Railway and Harbour. 38p. *8°*. 1838.

30523 **STEAM** to India, via the Red Sea, and via the Cape of Good Hope. The respective routes, and the facilities for establishing a comprehensive plan, by way of Egypt, compared and considered... 82p. *8°*. 1838.

30524 **STEPHENSON**, ROBERT, **& CO.** Description of the patent locomotive steam engine of Messrs. Robert Stephenson and Co., Newcastle-upon-Tyne... [Written by W. P. Marshall under the direction of Robert Stephenson.] 67p. *4°*. 1838.

30525 **STEVENSON**, DAVID. Sketch of the civil engineering of North America; comprising remarks on the harbours, river and lake navigation, lighthouses, steam-navigation, water-works, canals, roads, railways, bridges, and other works in that country. 320p. *8°*. 1838. *The Rastrick copy, presented by the author to George Rennie*.

30526 STOCKTON AND DARLINGTON RAILWAY. Notice is hereby given, that all walking on the main line and branches of this Railway continues to be strictly forbidden...[With information about coaches and reduction of outside fares on the second-class train between Stockton and Yarm. Dated: Sept. 17th, 1838.] *s.sh.4°*. *Darlington*, [1838]

30527 —— Stockton & Darlington Railway coaches. [A notice of extra trains during the week beginning 27 August, 1838. Dated: August 24th, 1838.] *s.sh.fol*. *Darlington*, [1838]

30528 **TELFORD**, T. Life of Thomas Telford, civil engineer, written by himself; containing a descriptive narrative of his professional labours: with a folio atlas of copper plates. Edited by John Rickman...with a preface, supplement, annotations, and index. 2 vols. *4°*. & *fol*. 1838.

30529 **TOWN**, I. Atlantic steam-ships. Some ideas and statements, the result of considerable reflection on the subject of navigating the Atlantic Ocean with steam-ships of large tonnage: ⟨made known in 1830, and published in one of the city journals in 1832.⟩...Also, the arrival, description, and departure of the two first British steam-ships, Sirius and Great Western... 76p. *12°*. *New-York*, 1838.

30530 [**TOWNSEND**, R. E. A.] Visions of the western railways. Dedicated to Sir Charles Lemon, Bart. ...[In verse.] 49, 36p. *8°*. 1838. *Presentation copy, with unsigned inscription, from the author to 'Mrs. Middleton'*.

30531 **W.**, J. W. The London and Birmingham Railway guide, and Birmingham and London Railway companion: containing a minute description of the railroad... 179p. *12°*. *James Wyld*, 1838. *Binding title: Wyld's London and Birmingham Railroad guide*.

30532 —— Second edition. 179p. *12°*. *James Wyld*, 1838. *Bound with* Wyld's guide to the Grand Junction and Liverpool and Manchester Railways, *q.v. no*. 30536.

30533 **WHISHAW**, F. Analysis of railways: consisting of a series of reports on the railways projected in England and Wales, in the year M.DCCC.XXXVII...Second edition, with additions and corrections. 298p. *8°*. 1838. *For another edition, see* 1837.

30534 **WOOD**, N. A practical treatise on rail-roads, and interior communication in general...Third edition, with additions... 760p. *8°*. 1838. *For other editions, see* 1825.

30535 **WORTHINGTON**, B. Proposed plan for improving Dover Harbour, by an extension of the south pier head, &c. Also, copious extracts from various authors in support of the plan, and shewing the importance of Dover Harbour from the time of its first construction. Together with practical observations & illustrations. 174p. *8°*. *Dover*, 1838.

30536 **WYLD**, J. Wyld's guide to the Grand Junction and Liverpool and Manchester Railways...To which is added, a guide to Dublin. 36p. *12°*. [1838] *Binding title: Wyld's London and Birmingham Manchester & Liverpool Railway guide*.

SOCIAL CONDITIONS

30537 Second edition. An **ACCOUNT** of the desperate affray which took place in Blean Wood, near Boughton, on...the 31st of May, 1838, between a party of agricultural labourers headed by the self-styled Sir William Courtenay, and a detachment of the 45th. Regiment of Foot... 31p. *12°*. *Faversham*, [1838]

30538 An **ADDRESS** to the Glasgow Cotton-Spinners, on the moral bearing of their Association, as brought out on the recent trial of their Committee. By one of their own order. [Signed: A fellow-workman.] 12p. *12°. Glasgow*, 1838.

30539 AGRICULTURAL SEMINARY, *Temple-moyle*. Report of the Agricultural Seminary...for the year 1838. 15p. *8°. Londonderry*, 1838.

30540 ASHURST, W. H. Facts and reasons in support of Mr. Rowland Hill's plan for a universal penny postage...Second edition. 133p. *8°*. 1838.

30541 —— Observations on the law of bankruptcy and insolvency. 34p. *8°*. 1838.

30542 ASHWORTH, H. An inquiry into the origin, progress, and results of the strike of the operative cotton spinners of Preston, from October, 1836, to February, 1837. Read at Liverpool before the Statistical Section of the British Association, Sept. 14, 1837. 13p. *8°. Manchester*, 1838.

30543 BAKER, WILLIAM R. The curse of Britain: an essay on the evils, causes and cure of intemperance. 280p. *12°*. 1838. *The Turner copy.*

30544 [**BARNARD,** SIR J.] A present for an apprentice. To which is added, Franklin's Way to wealth. [Signed: Richard Saunders, i.e. Benjamin Franklin.] By a citizen of London... 400p. *16°. London: T. Tegg... Sydney*, 1838. *For other editions of Sir John Barnard's work, of which this is a much enlarged version, see* 1741, *and for other editions of Franklin's* Way to wealth, *see* 1793 (GENERAL).

30545 BENTHAM, J. Observations on the Poor Bill, introduced by the Right Honourable William Pitt. Written February, 1797...⟨Not for publication.⟩ 48p. *8°*. [1838]

30546 BORRETT, W. P. Three letters upon a poor law and public medical relief for Ireland, to Daniel O'Connell, Esq. M.P. 24p. *8°. London & Dublin*, 1838.

30547 BOSWORTH, J. The contrast; or, the operation of the old poor laws contrasted with the recent Poor Law Amendment Act, and the necessity of a legal provision for the poor generally, but especially for Ireland. 42p. *8°*. 1838.

30548 [**BOWEN,** J.] Letters to the editor of The Times, on the Reform Poor Law. [Signed: J.B.] 55p. *8°. n.p.* [1838]

30549 BOWRING, SIR J. Observations on the Oriental plague [cholera] and on quarantines, as a means of arresting its progress, addressed to the British Association of Science, assembled at Newcastle, in August, 1838. 45p. *8°. Edinburgh*, 1838.

For the **BRITISH AND FOREIGN TEMPERANCE INTELLIGENCER,** *see vol.* III, *Periodicals list*, New British and foreign temperance intelligencer.

30550 BROUGHAM, H. P., *Baron Brougham and Vaux*. Speech of Lord Brougham in the House of Lords, on...March 20th, 1838, on the new Poor Law. 29p. *8°*. 1838. *The Oastler copy.*

30551 BULL, G. S. The new Poor Law shewn to be unconstitutional...opposed to the Common Law...in a petition to the House of Lords from the Rev. George S. Bull...dated May 30, 1838. 16p. *8°*. 1838. *The Oastler copy.*

30552 BUTLER, WILLIAM J. New Poor Law. A friendly letter addressed to Richard Oastler, Esquire, on his speech...at Huddersfield, December 27, 1837. 16p. *8°. London, Nottingham, &c.*, 1838. *The Oastler copy.*

30553 CARLILE, JAMES (1784–1854). Defence of the national system of education in Ireland. In reply to the letters of J. C. Colquhoun, Esq., of Killermont, M.P. 75p. *8°. Dublin, Edinburgh, &c.*, 1838.

30554 CENTRAL SOCIETY OF EDUCATION, *London*. Central Society of Education. Second publication. Papers by George Long, Esq. [and others]. Also, the results of the statistical inquiries of the Society. 414p. *12°*. 1838.

30555 CHANNING, WILLIAM E. An address on temperance. 36p. *12°. Glasgow, Edinburgh, &c.*, 1838. *For another edition, see* 1837.

30556 —— Self-culture. An address introductory to the Franklin lectures, delivered at Boston, United States. 24p. *8°. London & Manchester*, [1838 ?] *See also* 1839.

30557 CHILDREN'S FRIEND SOCIETY. A statement of facts showing the claims of the Children's Friend Society, to public support. *s.sh.fol. Hackney Wick*, [1838]

30558 CLEMENTS, R. B., *Viscount Clements*. The present poverty of Ireland convertible into the means of her improvement, under a well administered poor law. With a preliminary view of the state of agriculture in Ireland. 178p. *8°*. 1838.

30559 CLOTHING SOCIETY FOR THE BENEFIT OF POOR PIOUS CLERGYMEN OF THE ESTABLISHED CHURCH. Clothing Society, for...clergymen of the Established Church and their families. [An account of the Society, with testimonials, accounts and lists of subscribers for 1837.] 37p. *12°. Birmingham*, 1838.

30560 COMITÉ DE PATRONAGE POUR LES PRÉVENUS ACQUITTÉS. Comité de patronage pour les prévenus acquittés. [Annual report for 1836–1837.] 4p. *8°*. [*Paris*, 1838] *The copy that belonged to Victor Considérant.*

30561 CONNECTICUT. *Board of Commissioners of Common Schools*. Address to the people of Connecticut by the Board of Commissioners...[Signed by William W. Ellsworth and others. With 'An act to provide for the better supervision of common schools' and 'Second report of the Joint Select Committee on Common Schools', signed: John A. Rockwell, chairman.] 24p. *8°. n.p.* [1838]

30562 COOKE, WILLIAM (1806–1884). The principles of total abstinence exhibited and defended; with a refutation of the Rev. Dr. Edgar's charges and objections against them, in a lecture...delivered and published by the request of the Committee of the Belfast Total Abstinence Society. 44p. *8°. Belfast*, 1838. *The Turner copy.*

30563 COPEMAN, E. Remarks on the Poor Law Amendment Act, with reference to pauper medical attendance and...clubs. 18p. *8°. Norwich & London*, 1838.

30564 COUSIN, V. On the state of education in Holland, as regards schools for the working classes and for the poor...Translated, with preliminary observations, on the necessity of legislative measures, to extend...education among the working classes...in Great Britain...by Leonard Horner. [With appendixes of documents.] lxxii, 294p. *8°*. 1838. *The copy presented to Lord John Russell by Leonard Horner.*

30565 COX, F. A. Our young men: their importance and claims. A prize essay... Fifth edition. 254p. *12°.* 1838.

30566 [CRABTREE, GEOFFREY?] A conversation between Peter Pickingpeg, Jack Shuttle, and Harry Emptybobbin. Carefully reported by Sally Bobbinwinder. 28p. *8°. Barnsley*, 1838. *The copy that belonged to Oastler, who attributed it to 'Crabtree' in the manuscript index to his pamphlet collection.*

30567 CUSHING, L. S., *ed.* An act for the relief of insolvent debtors and for the more equal distribution of their effects; passed by the Legislature of Massachusetts, April 23, 1838. With an outline of the system thereby introduced, and forms of proceeding under the same. 93p. *12°. Boston*, 1838.

30568 DAY, JOHN. A few practical observations on the new Poor Law, showing the demoralizing and enslaving effects of this anti-Christian enactment, containing various facts illustrating the working of the new law. Addressed to the ratepayers & labourers of England. 32p. *8°.* 1838.

30569 DEFENCE of the working classes, in reply to an article in 'Chambers's Edinburgh Journal,' entitled "Strikes – their statistics." To which are added a few remarks on trades' unions. 8p. *8°.* [1838]

30570 DUPPA, B. F. Industrial schools for the peasantry...Reprinted from the first publication of the Central Society of Education, for the use of visiting committees of union workhouses. 46p. *12°.* 1838.

30571 ELLIOTT, J. H. A remonstrance addressed to the Right Hon. Lord Brougham, on the injustice and impolicy of the proposed Bill for the abolition of imprisonment for debt. 24p. *8°.* 1838.

30572 ELMES, S. H. Knowledge and emancipation for and by the working classes. A lecture, delivered on April 2nd, 1838, before the Brentford Literary and Political Union for the Diffusion of Useful Knowledge... On the present state of the working classes; and detailing a plan [the provision of an agricultural school on a co-operative basis]...by which they will be enabled to provide such an efficient...system of national education, as cannot fail to work out a...speedy deliverance from the bondage they at present endure. 20p. *12°.* [1838]

30573 ENGLAND. *Commissioners for Inquiring into the Condition of the Unemployed Hand-Loom Weavers in the United Kingdom.* Instructions from the Central Board of the Hand-Loom Weavers' Inquiry Commission to their assistant commissioners. [Signed: Nassau W. Senior, Samuel Jones Loyd, William Edward Hickson, John Leslie.] 34p. *8°. n.p.* [1838] *The copy that belonged to Victor Considérant.*

30574 ★—— *General Register Office.* Regulations for the duties of registrars of births and deaths, and deputy registrars, made and approved in pursuance of the Act for registering births, deaths and marriages in England (6 & 7 Wm. IV, c. 86). January 1838. 68p. *8°.* [London,] 1838. *The FWA copy, that belonged to William Pare.*

30575 ★—— —— Regulations for the duties of registrars of marriages; made and approved in pursuance of the Act for registering births, deaths and marriages in England (6 & 7 Wm. IV, c. 86). January 1838. 18p. *8°.* [London,] 1838. *★The FWA copy that belonged to William Pare, with corrections and notes in his hand.*

30576 ★—— —— Regulations for the duties of Superintendent Registrars: made and approved in pursuance of the Act for registering births, deaths and marriages in England (6 & 7 Wm. IV, c. 86). January 1838. [With an appendix.] 82p. *8°.* [London,] 1838. *The FWA copy that belonged to William Pare.*

30577 —— *Home Office.* Extracts from the third Report of the Inspectors of Prisons for the Home District; addressed to...the Secretary of State for the Home Department. By authority. 248p. *8°.* 1838.

30578 —— —— Poor laws – Ireland. Second report of George Nicholls, Esq., to Her Majesty's Principal Secretary of State for the Home Department. [With an appendix.] 91p. *8°.* 1838. *The copy that belonged to T. Spring Rice, Baron Monteagle. See also no. 30579, below.*

30579 —— —— Poor laws – Ireland. Three reports by George Nicholls, Esq., to Her Majesty's Principal Secretary of State for the Home Department. 170p. *8°.* 1838.

30580 —— *Laws, etc.* An Act for the abolition of imprisonment for debt. Containing all the clauses, forms, schedules, &c.&c. Passed August 16th, 1838. 12p. *12°. n.p.* [1838] *The clauses are summarized.*

30581 —— —— 1 & 2 Victoriæ I. chap. 56. An Act for the more effectual relief of the destitute poor in Ireland, with prefatory remarks and a copious index. By John Kidd. xxxviii, 143p. *12°. Dublin*, 1838.

30582 —— —— [Another edition.] ⟨From the Monthly Law Magazine and Political Review for November 1838, no. x.⟩ 24p. *8°.* [1838] *See also 1839.*

30583 —— *Parliament.* De l'état actuel et de la réforme des prisons de la Grande-Bretagne. Extraits des rapports officiels publiés par ordre du Parlement, traduits par L.-M. Moreau-Christophe, Inspecteur général des prisons de France... 340p. *8°. Paris*, 1838.

30584 —— —— *House of Commons.* Debate on the factory question, House of Commons, June 22, 1838. [A report.] 8p. *8°. Manchester*, [1838] *The Oastler copy.*

30585 —— —— The evils of the factory system illustrated: being a debate in the House of Commons, July 20, on Lord Ashley's proposition...With an editorial article on the conduct of Mr. George William Wood. To which is affixed, a speech...February 23, 1833, by Daniel O'Connell, Esq....which will be the best answer to the "good-natured nonsense" delivered by Daniel O'Connell Esq....in 1838; and a list of the division. 24p. *12°. Manchester*, 1838. *The Oastler copy.*

30586 —— —— —— Report from the Select Committee of the House of Commons on transportation; together with a letter from the Archbishop of Dublin [Richard Whately] on the same subject: and notes by Sir William Molesworth, Bart., chairman of the Committee. 54p. *8°.* 1838.

30587 —— —— —— Twenty-first and twenty-second reports of the Select Committee of the House of Commons on the Poor Law Amendment Act, Parliamentary Papers, Nos. 258, 262. [Evidence of the Rev. G. S. Bull.] 52p. *8°.* 1838. *The Oastler copy.*

30588 —— *Poor Law Commission [1834–1847].* Report from the Poor Law Commissioners...relative to certain statements concerning the internal management of the workhouse at Eye, in the Hartismere Union, Suffolk. [With 'Enclosure in the foregoing. Report from Charles Mott, Esq., Assistant Poor Law Commissioner...2nd June 1838'.] 38p. *8°.* 1838.

30589 The EVIDENCE of witnesses examined upon

an investigation before W. J. Voules, Esq. Assistant Poor Law Commissioner, at Kirkby Lonsdale, upon an enquiry into a charge of wanton cruelty against the guardians of the Kendal Union, made by the Rev. W. Carus Wilson; and the correspondence connected therewith. 37p. *8°. Kendal*, 1838.

30590 To the **FACTORY OPERATIVES**, of England, Ireland & Scotland. [Extract of an account in the *London Standard*, May 31, 1838, by a private correspondent, of the proceedings in the French Chamber of Deputies on infant labour in factories.] 4p. *8°. Manchester*, [1838] *The Oastler copy.*

30591 FANE, R. G. C. Observations on the proposed abolition of imprisonment for debt on mesne process; shewing its probable effects in disabling creditors from forcing their debtors into bankruptcy, trust-deeds, or compositions, in a letter to Sir Robert Peel, Bart. 35p. *8°.* 1838.

30592 *FAUCHER, L. De la réforme des prisons... Se vend au profit des jeunes libérés. 290p. *8°. Paris*, 1838. *The copy that belonged to George Grote.*

30593 GOURLY, J. On the great evils of impressment, and its mischievous effects in the Royal Navy and the merchant ships, with the great benefits to the seamen, bestowed by the Registration Act, of the 30th July, 1835. 78p. *8°. Southampton & London*, 1838.

30594 GREEN, J. W. Address to the members of the New British and Foreign Temperance Society on the duties which they owe to themselves; to their fellow-members; and to the community at large. 12p. *8°. London, Birmingham, &c.*, 1838. *The Turner copy.*

30595 *HAMMOND, W. A letter to Sir R. Peel, Bart....on the practical operation of the Poor Law Amendment Act. By a guardian. 19p. *8°. London & New Brentford*, 1838. *The copy that belonged to George Grote.*

30596 [**HOBSON,** S.] The justice and equity of assessing the net profits of the land for the relief of the poor, maintained in a letter to the Poor Law Commissioners: with some remarks on the celebrated case of Rex v. Jodrell. By a Norfolk clergyman. 36p. *8°.* [1838]

30597 HOLLAND, P. H. Self-providence v. dependence upon charity. An essay on dispensaries...Shewing that at a much smaller cost a much greater amount of good might be effected; and that a very large proportion of the income of these institutions is not merely needlessly, but injuriously expended. 23p. *8°. Manchester & London*, 1838.

30598 HUNTER, T., *and others.* The trial of Thomas Hunter, Peter Hacket, Richard M'Niel, James Gibb, and William M'Lean, the Glasgow cotton-spinners, before the High Court of Judiciary, at Edinburgh, on charges of murder...and committing...violence to persons and property. Reported by James Marshall...To which is annexed statistics connected with the spinning trade, &c. of Glasgow, by Peter M'Kenzie, editor of "The Reformers' Gazette." With portraits of the prisoners. 141p. *8°. Edinburgh, Glasgow, &c.*, 1838.

30599 —— Cheap edition, revised and enlarged... Trial of the Glasgow cotton spinners for murder, conspiracies...With faithful portraits of the prisoners. 56p. *fol. Edinburgh, Glasgow, &c.*, 1838.

30600 —— [Another edition.] The trial of the Glasgow cotton spinners...from the 3rd to the 11th January, 1838, carefully condensed from the able reports published in the Edinburgh Scotsman and the Caledonian Mercury. Embellished with...authentic portraits of the prisoners. 24p. *12°. Liverpool*, [1838]

30601 —— [Another edition.] Report of the trial of Thomas Hunter, Peter Hacket, Richard M'Neil, James Gibb and William M'Lean, operative cotton-spinners in Glasgow...on...January 3, 1838, and seven following days, for the crimes of illegal conspiracy and murder; with an appendix of documents and relative proceedings. By Archibald Swinton, Esq. advocate. 382, xlvip. *8°. Edinburgh*, 1838. *For another edition, entitled:* The rights of labour defended, *which included the report of the trial in 1837, see* 1837.

30602 IRISH LANDLORDS as they are, and the Poor Law Bill accompanied as it ought to be; respectfully addressed to the Right Honourable...the Members of the Imperial Parliament; with a few words on landowners and slaveowners, waste lands and weighty debts. 44p. *8°. Dublin*, 1838.

30603 LAURIE, S I R P. A narrative of the proceedings at the laying of the first stone of the new buildings at Bethlem Hospital, on...the 26th...July, M.DCCC.XXX.VIII. With historical notes and illustrations, and official documents. 62p. *8°.* 1838.

30604 LIHOU, J. Suggestions for the establishment of a Royal Naval nursery for sailors to man Her Majesty's Fleet. 15p. *8°.* 1838.

30605 LIVERPOOL WORKING MEN'S ASSOCIATION. Address, with the objects and rules of the Liverpool Working Men's Association, established, January, 1838. 8p. *8°. Liverpool*, 1838.

For **LIVESEY'S MORAL REFORMER,** 1838–39, *see vol.* III, *Periodicals list*, Moral reformer.

30606 LONDON TRADES' COMMITTEE. An address from the London Trades' Committee, appointed to watch the Parliamentary inquiry into combinations, to the working classes. [Signed: W. Lovett, Sec. and dated, March 19, 1838.] 8p. *12°.* 1838.

30607 LOVELESS, G. The victims of Whiggery. A statement of the persecutions experienced by the Dorchester labourers; with a report of their trial; also a description of Van Dieman's Land, and reflections upon the system of transportation...Eighth edition. 32p. *8°. The Central Dorchester Committee*, [1838] *For other editions, see* 1837.

30608 LOVELESS, J. A narrative of the sufferings of Jas. Loveless, Jas. Brine, and Thomas and John Standfield, four of the Dorchester labourers; displaying the horrors of transportation, written by themselves. With a brief description of New South Wales, by George Loveless. Any profit on this work will go to the Dorchester tribute. 16p. *8°.* 1838.

30609 LUPTON, J O N. [*Endorsed:*] Observations on the poor laws. [4]p. *4°.* [1838] [*Br.* 593]

30610 LYNCH, A. H. An address to the electors of Galway, on the Poor-Law Bill for Ireland. With an appendix, containing extracts from the evidence taken before the Commissioners of Poor Inquiry, Ireland. 142p. *8°.* 1838.

30611 M., J. F. The doctrine of total abstinence justified. 76p. *12°. Cork*, 1838. *The Turner copy.*

30612 MACCONNELL, T. The prize essay on "the present conditions of the people of this country, and the best means of improving it"... 60p. *8°*. 1838. **Another, the FWA copy, belonged to William Pare.*

30613 [MACKENZIE, Sir F.] Hints for the use of Highland tenants and cottagers. By a proprietor. 273p. *8°*. *Inverness*, 1838. *The English and Gaelic texts are printed on opposite pages.*

30614 MACNAGHTEN, Sir F. W. Poor laws – Ireland. Observations upon the report of George Nicholls, Esq. 58p. *8°*. *London, Dublin, &c.*, 1838.

30615 MANCHESTER STATISTICAL SOCIETY. Report of a committee of the Manchester Statistical Society, on the condition of the working classes, in an extensive manufacturing district, in 1834, 1835, and 1836. Read at the Statistical Section of the British Association for the Advancement of Science, Liverpool, Sept. 13th, 1837. 15, xvp. *8°*. *London & Manchester*, 1838.

30616 Ten MINUTES' advice to labourers. Fourth edition, with additions. 71p. *18°*. *London, Manchester, &c.*, 1838.

30617 MITTRÉ, M. H. C. Des domestiques en France dans leurs rapports avec l'économie sociale, le bonheur domestique, les lois civiles, criminelles et de police...Le mémoire qui a servi de base à cet ouvrage a été couronné par la société des sciences morales, etc., de Seine-et-Oise, en mars 1837. 256p. *8°*. *Paris & Versailles*, 1838.

30618 MOLLET, J. E. Notice historique sur l'établissement et les progrès de la Société établie dans les Pays-Bas : pour l'amélioration morale des prisonniers ; suivie du réglement de la ditte [*sic*] société. 120p. *8°*. *Amsterdam*, 1838. *The copy that belonged to William Allen.*

30619 MOREWOOD, S. A philosophical and statistical history of the inventions and customs of ancient and modern nations in the manufacture and use of inebriating liquors ; with the present practice of distillation in all its varieties : together with an extensive illustration of the consumption and effects of opium, and other stimulants used in the East, as substitutes for wine and spirits. [Second edition.] 745p. *8°*. *Dublin, London, &c.*, 1838. *The Turner copy.*

30620 MORGAN, John M. A brief account of the Stockport Sunday School, with thoughts on the extension ...of Sunday schools in general, and more especially in the rural districts. 36p. *8°*. *London & Manchester*, 1838.

30621 MOSES, *ben Maimon.* The laws of the Hebrews, relating to the poor and the stranger. Written in Hebrew, in the 12th century, by the celebrated Rabbi M. Maimonides. 71p. *8°*. 1838. *Translated by J. W. Peppercorne. See also* 1840. *For an edition of the introduction, see* 1839 (The rights of necessity).

30622 [MYERS, Sir F.] Hints to the Legislature... on the provisions, character, and defects, of the Imprisonment for Debt Bill, as sent down from the House of Lords to the House of Commons, June 12, 1838. 85p. *8°*. 1838.

30623 NEVILE, C. The new Poor Law justified : with suggestions for the establishment of insurance offices for the poor. 30p. *8°*. 1838.

For the NEW BRITISH AND FOREIGN TEMPERANCE INTELLIGENCER, *see* vol. III, *Periodicals list.*

30624 NORTHAMPTONSHIRE SOCIETY FOR THE EDUCATION OF THE POOR IN

THE PRINCIPLES OF THE ESTABLISHED CHURCH. Report of the state of the...Society... from January 1, 1837 to January 1, 1838. 16p. *8°*. *Northampton*, 1838.

30625 NOTTINGHAM WORKING-MEN'S ASSOCIATION. Address of the...Association to the people of England, on the new poor laws. [Signed by John Barratt, chairman, and others.] 18p. *12°*. *London & Nottingham*, [1838] *The Oastler copy.*

30626 OASTLER, R. A letter to the Bishop of Exeter. [On the state of the poor law question in Yorkshire.] 23p. *12°*. *Manchester*, 1838. *Oastler's own copy.*

30627 —— The right of the poor, to liberty and life. A speech delivered at a public meeting of the inhabitants of Huddersfield...December 27th, 1837. 53p. *8°*. *London, Liverpool, &c.*, 1838. *Oastler's own copy.*

30628 A few cursory OBSERVATIONS on the proposed Bill for establishing poor laws in Ireland. By an Irish M.P. for a western county. 20p. *8°*. 1838.

30629 OSBORNE, Lord S. G. Hints to the charitable, being practical observations on the proper regulation of private charity. Intended principally for the use of those who take an active interest in village economy... 85p. *12°*. 1838.

30630 PERCEVAL, John T. A letter to Mr. John Bowen. [On the new Poor Law.] 4p. *8°*. *n.p.* [1838] *The Oastler copy.*

30631 [——] A letter [signed: Fidget] to the Lord Mayor, and citizens of London, respecting the introduction of the new police. 13p. *8°*. [1838] *Presentation copy from the author to Richard Oastler, who identified him in the manuscript index to his pamphlet collection.*

30632 —— Observations on the new Poor Law, its injustice and evil tendencies ; addressed to the Government, the gentry, and the rate-payers. 36p. *8°*. [1838] *Presentation copy from the author to Richard Oastler.*

30633 PERRY, Samuel. The powers under the new Poor Law of the vestry meetings, the boards of guardians, justices of the peace, and the Poor Law Commissioners, considered in a letter to Lord John Russell, Secretary of State for the Home Department. 20p. *8°*. *London & Brentwood*, 1838. *The copy sent to The Times for review, with accompanying letter from the author. See also* 1839.

30634 PIERS, O. An affectionate warning to the agricultural labourers in the parish of Preston-cum-Sutton, in the county of Dorset. [Against political agitators.] 8p. *8°*. *Weymouth & Dorchester*, 1838.

30635 —— A few hints respectfully addressed to landowners and farmers throughout the Kingdom : more particularly to those in the county of Dorset. 8p. *8°*. *London, Weymouth, &c.*, 1838.

30636 [PIRON, M. A.] Du service des postes et de la taxation des lettres au moyen d'un timbre. 145p. *8°*. *Paris*, 1838.

30637 POOLE, W. G. Regulations of the parish of St. Giles Camberwell, Surrey, with a statement of the duties of the several officers of the parish, and the local Acts of Parliament. 339p. *8°*. *London, Camberwell, &c.*, 1838.

30638 PORTER, G. R. Statistical inquiries into the social condition of the working classes, and into the means provided for the education of their children...Reprinted from the second publication of the Central Society of Education. [With a prospectus of the Society.] 23p. *12°*. 1838. *For the complete work, see no. 30554.*

30639 The **PRINCIPLE** of total abstinence from all inebriating liquors vindicated from the charge of "ultra and pharisaical morality," as preferred by the reviewer of the Rev. W. R. Baker's "Intemperance the curse of Britain," in the Evangelical Magazine for October, 1838. 11p. *8°. London, Manchester, &c.,* 1838. *The Turner copy.*

30640 *****PROVINCIAL MEDICAL AND SURGICAL ASSOCIATION.** Report of the Council of the...Association, on the poor law question; containing suggestions for an amended system of parochial medical relief: a list of the officers and council for 1838; and the additional laws, approved and confirmed at the general meeting...19th March, 1838. 8p. *8°.* 1838. *The copy that belonged to George Grote.*

30641 On the **RATEABILITY** of rent-charges for the support of the poor. ⟨From the Monthly Law Magazine and Political Review for September 1838, no. VIII.⟩ 20p. *8°.* [1838]

30642 **RAWSON,** J., *and others.* Minutes of the evidence of James Rawson, Esq., Mr. John Swain, and Richard Hall, Esq. before a Select Committee of the House of Commons, on the Poor Law Amendment Act, June 26th, 1838. 65p. *8°. Leicester,* [1838] *The Oastler copy.*

30643 **REMACLE,** B. B. Des hospices d'enfans trouvés, en Europe, et principalement en France, depuis leur origine jusqu'à nos jours...Ouvrage couronné par... la Société des Etablissemens charitables de Paris. [With 'Enfans trouvés. Tableaux statistiques officiels'.] 2 vols. *8°. & 4°. Paris & Strasbourg,* 1838.

30644 Brief **REMARKS** on the justification of the new Poor Law by the Rev. Christopher Nevile, an ex-officio guardian of the Lincoln Union. Wherein is given the opinion of J. M'Culloch, Esq., on the principles of the same law. By one of the Thompson family. 20p. *8°. Newcastle & London,* 1838.

30645 **ROBERTS,** S. A letter to the working classes, and H. G. Ward, Esq. Addressed to Richard Oastler, Esq. By a Sheffielder. 16p. *8°. Sheffield,* 1838. *The Oastler copy.*

30646 —— Lord Brougham and the new Poor Laws. 72p. *8°. London, Sheffield, &c.,* 1838. *The Oastler copy.*

30647 [——] The Peers, the people and the poor. By a retired tradesman. 82p. *8°. London, Sheffield, &c.,* 1838. *The copy that belonged to Oastler, who attributed it to 'Roberts' in the manuscript index to his pamphlet collection.*

30648 **S——.** Two letters to Daniel O'Connell, Esq. M.P. in reply to his letters to his constituents on the Irish Poor Law Bill. Reprinted from "The Courier," with notes. 20p. *8°.* 1838.

30649 **SANDIFORD,** P. S. V. G. The Oddfellow's companion; containing a collection of songs arranged to familiar airs, to which are added toasts and sentiments congenial to the views of Oddfellowship... 71p. *12°. Over,* 1838.

30650 **SANKEY,** W. S. V. A voice for the operatives ...Second edition. 11p. *8°. Edinburgh,* 1838.

30651 **SIBLY,** J. A letter on the superior advantages of separate confinement over the system of prison discipline, at present adopted in gaols and houses of correc-

tion, addressed to Benjamin Hawes, Esq., M.P.... 110p. *8°.* 1838.

30652 **SMITH,** HERBERT. A letter to the people of England in behalf of the deserving poor. 6p. *8°. London & Southampton,* [1838]

30653 **SOCIÉTÉ PATERNELLE POUR L'ÉDUCATION MORALE, AGRICOLE ET PROFESSIONNELLE DES JEUNES DÉTENUS.** Projet d'une société de patronage pour les jeunes filles libérées. [Signed: D., i.e. F. A. Demetz.] 16p. *8°.* [*Paris,* 1838] *The copy that belonged to Victor Considérant.*

30654 **SOCIETY FOR PROMOTING PRACTICAL DESIGN...AMONG THE PEOPLE.** Account of the inaugural meeting of the Society...held at Exeter Hall, January 11th, 1838. 32p. *8°.* 1838.

30655 **STANLEY,** EDWARD, *Bishop of Norwich.* Speech of the Lord Bishop of Norwich, delivered in the House of Lords, May 21st, 1838, on the national system of Irish education; with an appendix of letters on the causes of the opposition made to the system in Ireland. 45p. *8°.* 1838.

30656 **STATISTICAL SOCIETY OF LONDON.** First report of a committee of the...Society... on the state of education in Westminster, 1837. 77p. *8°.* 1838.

30657 [**STEPHENS,** JOSEPH R.] Sketch of the life and opinions of Richard Oastler. 20p. *8°. Leeds & London,* 1838.

For the **TEMPERANCE ADVOCATE AND HERALD,** *see vol.* III, *Periodicals list.*

30658 A few plain **THOUGHTS** upon the subject of imprisonment for debt, with a view to effect a gradual abolition, by extending and rendering more effectual the powers of the Commissioners of the Court for the Relief of Insolvent Debtors...By a gentleman connected with the superior courts of law. 16p. *8°.* [*London,* 1838] *For another edition, see* 1837.

30659 **TORRENS,** R. A letter to the Right Honourable Lord John Russell, on the ministerial measure for establishing poor laws in Ireland, and on the auxiliary means which it will be necessary to employ in carrying that measure into effect. 97p. *8°.* 1838. *For another edition, see* 1837.

30660 —— On wages and combination. Second edition. 133p. *8°.* 1838. *The copy that belonged to Patrick Chalmers. For another edition, see* 1834.

30661 **TURNBULL,** GEORGE, *W.S.* Report on the progress and present state of pauperism in Berwickshire; with suggestions as to the means of reducing its amount. 52p. *8°. Edinburgh,* 1838.

30662 Queen **VICTORIA** and the uniform penny postage; a scene at Windsor Castle. [2]p. *s.sh.8°.* [1838] [*Br.* 592]

30663 A **VINDICATION** of the principles, objects, & tendencies of trades unions, or associations of the working classes. By a unionist. 32p. *8°.* 1838.

30664 **WERDINSKY,** A. DE, *Count.* A letter to the proprietary of grammar schools in England, on the imperative necessity of a reform in the system of educating their youth. 23p. *8°.* 1838.

30665 **WILSON,** WILLIAM C. Remarks on certain

operations of the new Poor Laws. Respectfully submitted to the...consideration of the British Legislature. 31p. *8°*. *Kirkby Lonsdale, 1838. The Oastler copy.*

30666 WORKING MEN'S ASSOCIATION. An address from the Working Men's Association, to the working classes, on the subject of national education. 8p. *8°*. [1838 ?]

SLAVERY

30667 An **ADDRESS** to Her Majesty's ministers, the West India proprietors, dissenters, and abolitionists, on the premature termination of the negro apprenticeship; and to the proprietors and labourers. By a West India proprietor. 20p. *8°*. 1838.

30668 AMERICAN ANTI-SLAVERY SOCIETY. The constitution of the American Anti-slavery Society: with the declaration of the National Anti-slavery Convention at Philadelphia, December, 1833, and the address to the public, issued by the executive committee of the Society, in September, 1835. 12p. *12°*. *New-York, 1838.*

30669 ANTI-SLAVERY crisis. Policy of ministers. Reprinted from the Eclectic Review, for April, 1838. With a postscript on the debate and division in the House of Commons, on the 29th and 30th of March. 30p. *8°*. *London, Edinburgh, &c., 1838.*

30670 BEVAN, W. A letter to the Right Honorable Lord Brougham, on the alleged breach of the colonial apprenticeship contract. 15p. *8°*. *Liverpool & London, 1838.*

30671 ★—— The operation of the apprenticeship system in the British colonies. A statement, the substance of which was...adopted at the meeting of the Liverpool Anti-Slavery Society, December 19th, 1837; with references to official documents, authentic narratives, and additional subsequent information. 61p. *8°*. *Liverpool & London, 1838. The copy that belonged to George Grote.*

30672 [BEVERLEY, ROBERT M.] The evidence of the real merits of the negro apprenticeship in the British colonies, examined. By Justus, author of "The wrongs of the Caffre nation." 16p. *8°*. 1838.

30673 BROUGHAM, H. P., *Baron Brougham and Vaux.* Lord Brougham's speech in the House of Lords, Monday, January 29, 1838, upon the slave trade, with an abstract of the discussion which ensued. Printed for the London Anti-Slavery Society. 15p. *8°*. *Lindfield: printed at the Schools of Industry, 1838.*

30674 —— Lord Brougham's speech in the House of Lords, on Tuesday, the 20th of February, 1838, for the immediate emancipation of the negro apprentices. 50p. *8°*. 1838.

30675 —— [Another edition.] Immediate emancipation ... 24p. *12°*. *The Central Emancipation Committee, [1838]*

30676 —— One of twenty copies in quarto. Lord Brougham's speech in the House of Lords, Tuesday, March 6, 1838, upon the eastern slave trade. 65p. *4°*. 1838. *The copy that belonged to the Duke of Cambridge.*

30677 —— [Another edition.] 65p. *8°*. 1838.

30678 [BROWNE, H. P., *2nd Marquess of Sligo.*] Jamaica under the apprenticeship system. By a proprietor. [With an appendix.] 147p. *8°*. 1838.

30679 FAIR, R. A letter to the Hon. W. T. H. Fox Strangways...on the present state of the slave trade in the West Indies, and on the means of more effectually

counteracting it. 47p. *8°*. 1838. *The copy that belonged to Earl De Grey.*

30680 GASPARIN, AGÉNOR E. DE, *Comte.* Esclavage et traite. 261p. *8°*. *Paris, 1838.*

30681 GLADSTONE, W. E. Speech delivered in the House of Commons on the motion of Sir George Strickland, for the abolition of the negro apprenticeship, Friday, March 30, 1838. With an appendix. 64p. *8°*. 1838.

30682 HINTS on a cheap mode of purchasing the liberty of a slave population. 21p. *12°*. *New York, 1838. With manuscript note in German on the wrapper, signed: Chr. G. Eikel, presenting the pamphlet to Dr. Lorenz Dieffenbach.*

30683 ★INNES, JOHN (*fl.* 1830–1849). Letter to the Lord Glenelg...on negro apprenticeship. 29p. *8°*. *[London,] 1838. The copy that belonged to George Grote.*

30684 JAY, W. Inquiry into the character and tendency of the American Colonization, and American Anti-Slavery societies...Sixth edition. 206p. *12°*. *New York: The American Anti-Slavery Society, 1838.*

30685 The permanent **LAWS** of the emancipated colonies. 44p. *8°*. *London Anti-Slavery Society, 1838. A copy in the library of the Anti-Slavery Society has a manuscript attribution to Joseph Beldam.*

30686 MASSACHUSETTS ANTI-SLAVERY SOCIETY. An address to the abolitionists of Massachusetts, on the subject of political action. By the Board of Managers of the Mass. A. S. Society. 20p. *12°*. *n.p.* [1838]

30687 OBSERVATIONS upon Lord Glenelg's speech [on the protection of the apprenticed labourers in the West Indian colonies], delivered 20th February, 1838. 32p. *8°*. 1838. *The copy that belonged to Earl De Grey.*

30688 SCOBLE, J. British Guiana. Speech delivered at the anti-slavery meeting...on...4th of April, 1838... 35p. *8°*. *Central Negro Emancipation Committee, 1838.*

30689 SHARPE, H. E. On the abolition of the negro apprenticeship; in a letter to the Right Hon. the Lord Brougham. 27p. *8°*. 1838.

30690 SOCIETY FOR THE ABOLITION OF SLAVERY THROUGHOUT THE BRITISH DOMINIONS. Negro apprenticeship in the British colonies. 32p. *8°*. 1838. *The copy that belonged to Earl De Grey.*

30691 ★—— Food and other maintenance and allowances, under the apprenticeship system; extracted from the appendix to a report recently published by the committee of the London Anti-Slavery Society on negro apprenticeship in the British colonies. 34p. *8°*. 1838. *The copy that belonged to George Grote.*

30692 —— Punishments inflicted under the apprenticeship system; extracted from the appendix to a report recently published by the committee of the London Anti-

Slavery Society on negro apprenticeship in the British colonies. 16p. *8°*. 1838. *The copy that belonged to Earl De Grey.*

30693 STURGE, JOSEPH and **HARVEY**, T. The West Indies in 1837; being the journal of a visit to Antigua, Montserrat, Dominica, St. Lucia, Barbados and Jamaica; undertaken for the purpose of ascertaining the actual condition of the negro population of those islands. [With an appendix.] 380, xcivp. *12°*. 1838. *Presentation copy with inscription from Joseph Sturge to 'Geo. Thompson', dated '12 month 5th, 1837'.*

30694 THOME, J. A. and **KIMBALL**, J. H. Emancipation in the West Indies. A six months' tour in Antigua, Barbadoes, and Jamaica, in the year 1837. 489p.

12°. New York: American Anti-Slavery Society, 1838. *See also* 1839.

30695 [**WELD**, T. D.] The anti-slavery examiner. No. 5. The Bible against slavery. An inquiry into the patriarchal and Mosaic systems on the subject of human rights. Third edition – revised. 74p. *8°. New-York: American Anti-Slavery Society,* 1838.

30696 WILLIAMS, JAMES (*fl.* 1837). A narrative of events, since the first of August, 1834, by James Williams, an apprenticed labourer in Jamaica. [Dated at the end of the text: June 20, 1837. With a preface by T. Price and 'Official confirmation of this narrative' dated: Dec. 27, 1837.] 24p. *12°.* [1838 ?] *For another edition, see* 1837.

POLITICS

30697 *[**BOYD**, SIR WILLIAM.] A patriot's second letter to the British people on the present state of the country, &c.&c. With a letter to the operatives, and another to the Queen. À Gulielmo B★★★. 21p. *8°*. 1838. *Presentation copy from the author to George Grote.*

30698 [——] A patriot's third letter to the British people, on the state of the country, &c., with a second letter to the operatives, and a second letter to the Queen, correspondence of the court, &c. à Gulielmo B★★★. Third edition. 32p. *8°*. 1838. *Presentation copy, with inscription, from the author to T. Spring Rice, Baron Monteagle.*

30699 BRISTOL. Radical purity!!! A report of certain cases [at Bedminster and Clifton of bribery of voters, by paying their rates for them], as taken before the ...Mayor, and the assessors, at the Bristol Municipal Revision...October, 1838. 40p. *8°. Bristol,* 1838.

30700 BRITISH DIPLOMACY and Turkish independence. With a view of the continental policy required by British interests. 65p. *8°*. 1838.

30701 [**BROUGHAM**, H. P., *Baron Brougham and Vaux.*] Letter to the Queen on the state of the monarchy. By a friend of the people. 46p. *8°*. 1838.

30702 [——] Second edition. 46p. *8°*. 1838. *The copy that belonged to Earl De Grey.*

30703 [——] Fourth edition. 46p. *8°*. 1838.

30704 [——] Fifth edition. 46p. *8°*. 1838.

30705 —— [Another edition.] Lord Brougham! Letter to the Queen... 16p. *8°. n.p.* [1838 ?]

30706 DENISON, S. C. Is the ballot a mistake ? 116p. *8°*. 1838.

30707 —— Second edition corrected throughout, with remarks on the late debate, and an authentic account of an election at New-York. 139p. *8°*. 1838.

For the **EDINBURGH MONTHLY DEMO-CRAT, AND TOTAL ABSTINENCE ADVO-CATE**, *see* vol. III, *Periodicals list.*

30708 FAULKNER, SIR A. B. Sir Arthur Brooke Faulkner, to the radical reformers of Great Britain. 8p. *8°. Cheltenham,* [1838]

30709 GROTE, G. Vote by ballot. Speech of George Grote, Esq. M.P. in the House of Commons, on the 15th of February, 1838, on bringing forward his motion for leave to bring in a Bill for taking the votes of Parliamentary

electors by way of ballot. From the Morning Chronicle of the 16th of February, 1838. 16p. *8°*. [*London,* 1838]

30710 GUIZOT, F. P. G. Democracy in modern communities. Translated from the French of M. Guizot. [Originally published in the *Revue Française*.] 50p. *8°*. 1838.

30711 HOLROYD, A. T. Egypt and Mahomed Ali Pacha, in 1837; a letter, containing remarks upon "Egypt as it is in 1837". Addressed to the Right Hon. Viscount Palmerston, Secretary of State for Foreign Affairs, &c.&c. 37p. *8°*. 1838.

30712 A LETTER to Lord John Russell on registration, and the trial of controverted elections. By a Member of the three last Parliaments. 50p. *8°*. 1838.

30713 MANCHESTER POLITICAL UNION. Manchester Political Union, 1838. Regulations, &c. Published by order of the Union, 1838. 8p. *12°. Manchester,* [1838]

30714 MARTIN, WILLIAM (1772–1851). The second edition of a tract on parliamentary reform, with the method of supporting the poor members. The man by himself, neither Whig nor Tory, but a friend to all mankind and the Christian Church. 8p. *8°. Newcastle,* [1838]

For the **MONTHLY LIBERATOR**, *see* vol. III, *Periodicals list.*

30715 MURPHY, T. A letter to the radicals of the United Kingdoms describing the position of the radicals in the borough of Marylebone, and justifying their proceedings at the late election... 24p. *8°*. 1838.

30716 PAUL, WILLIAM, *secretary to the Leeds Operative Conservative Society.* A history of the origin and progress of operative conservative societies. 32p. *8°. Leeds,* [1838] *See also* 1839.

30717 The **PEOPLE'S CHARTER**; being the outline of an Act for the just representation of the people of Great Britain in the Commons' House of Parliament: embracing the principles of universal suffrage, no property qualification, annual parliaments, equal representation, payment of members, and vote by ballot. Prepared by a committee of twelve persons, six members of Parliament and six members of the London Working Men's Association, and addressed to the people of the United Kingdom. 36p. *12°. For the Working Men's Association,* [1838] *Drawn up by William Lovett and revised by Francis Place. See also* 1842, 1843, 1845, 1848.

30718 The **PROSPECTS** of the people. 32p. *8°*. 1838.

30719 **REMARKS** in refutation of an article in the 118th number of the Quarterly Review, on Lord John Russell's speech, at Stroud. 79p. *8°*. 1838.

30720 **SANDWITH**, T., *and others*. Speeches delivered at the first dinner of the Reform Association of Beverley, 10th January, 1838, by Thomas Sandwith, Esq. the Mayor, chairman, George Rennie, Esq. and James Clay, Esq.... 26p. *8°*. 1838.

30721 **SANKEY**, W. S. V. Popular control over hasty legislation. To which is subjoined, a letter to a Member of Parliament, on the English Bill for registration of births, marriages and deaths. 15p. *8°*. *Edinburgh*, 1838.

30722 **TOMKINS**, T., *pseud*. Rich and poor; a conversation between Thomas Tomkins and William Wilkins, shewing that the splendour of the aristocracy is the cause of the misery of the poor...that the income of the nation is entirely produced by the labourer; that the labourers do not obtain a fair portion of what they produce...and that the remedy for their sufferings is to be found in the extension of the franchise, the vote by ballot, and the shortening of the duration of Parliament... 8p. *8°*. *New Brentford*, 1838.

30723 **WORKING MEN'S ASSOCIATION.** The Working Men's Association, to the working classes of Europe, and especially to the Polish people. 8p. *8°*. [1838 ?]

SOCIALISM

30724 An **ANALYSIS** of human nature: a lecture delivered to the members and friends of the Association of All Classes of All Nations. By one of the honorary missionaries to that institution... 24p. *12°*. *Leeds*, 1838.

30725 **ASSOCIATION OF ALL CLASSES OF ALL NATIONS.** Proceedings of the third congress of the Association...and the first of the National Community Friendly Society...held in Manchester, in May, 1838... 64p. *12°*. *Birmingham, London, &c.*, 1838. *See also* 1839 (Rational Society).

30726 **BAINES**, EDWARD, *and others*. Mr. Owen's establishment, at New Lanark, a failure!! as proved by Edward Baines...and other gentlemen [Robert Oastler and John Cawood], deputed with him by the parishioners of Leeds, to visit and inspect that establishment and report thereon... 12p. *12°*. *Leeds: Leeds District Board of the Association of All Classes of All Nations*, 1838. *Another, the FWA copy, belonged to William Pare*.

30727 **BOWER**, S. The peopling of Utopia; or, the sufficiency of socialism for human happiness: being a comparison of the social and radical schemes... 15p. *8°*. *Bradford, London, &c.*, 1838. *Another, the FWA copy, belonged to William Pare*.

30728 —— A sequel to The peopling of Utopia... 20p. *8°*. *Bradford*, 1838. *Another, the FWA copy, belonged to William Pare*.

30729 **CAMPBELL**, ALEXANDER (1796–1870). Authentic report of the discussion at the Guildhall, Bath, on...the 13th, 14th, and 15th of September, 1838, between Mr. Alexander Campbell...and Mr. W. P. Roberts, on the principles of Mr. Robert Owen... 40p. *8°*. *Bath*, 1838.

30730 **CARLET**, H. Fourier et son système. [A criticism, reprinted from the *Journal de l'Aube*, of Madame Gatti de Gamond's *Fourier et son système*.] 16p. *8°*. [*Paris*, 1838] *Inserted in the copy of Gatti de Gamond (no. 30738) which belonged to Victor Considérant*.

For **CHRONIQUE DU MOUVEMENT SOCIAL**, *see* vol. III, *Periodicals list*.

30731 **CLARKE**, J. G. The Christian's looking-glass or a reply to the animadversions of the Rev. Dr. Redford ...and the clergy of all denominations, who attempt to oppose the religion of charity as propounded by Robert Owen, being a lecture, delivered in the Social Institution, Manchester... 16p. *8°*. *Manchester & Hulme*, 1838.

30732 Première **COMMEMORATION** du jour de naissance de Charles Fourier. 20p. *8°*. [*Paris*, 1838]

30733 **COOPER**, ROBERT. A contrast between the new moral world and the old immoral world; a lecture delivered in the Social Institution, Salford... 16p. *8°*. [*Manchester &*] *Hulme*, 1838.

30734 —— A lecture on original sin, delivered in the Social Institution...Salford...Second edition. 16p. *8°*. *Manchester...Hulme, &c.*, 1838.

30735 **CROWTHER**, R. A letter to the socialists, on the doctrine of irresponsibility, &c. 12p. *12°*. *Manchester*, 1838. *Another, the FWA copy, belonged to William Pare*.

30736 **DALTON**, T. Socialism examined. Report of a public discussion which took place at Huddersfield, on... December 13th, 14th, and 15th, 1837, between the Rev. T. Dalton...and Mr. Lloyd Jones...upon "the five fundamental facts, and the twenty laws of human nature, as found in The book of the new moral world, written by R. Owen, Esq."... 68p. *8°*. *Manchester*, 1838.

30737 *The **DAYS** of Queen Victoria, or a sketch of the times, by a citizen. Submitted to the consideration of the Working Men's Association, members of temperance and all other societies, having for their object the improvement of the present condition of the poorer classes. [On the progress of co-operation.] 12p. *12°*. *Bath*, 1838. *The FWA copy, that belonged to William Pare*.

30738 **GAMOND**, afterwards **GATTI DE GAMOND**, Z. DE. Fourier et son système. 426p. *8°*. *Paris*, 1838. *The copy that belonged to Victor Considérant*. *See also* 1841, 1842.

30739 **GARWOOD**, JOHN. The force of circumstance: a poem. 21p. *12°*. *Birmingham: The Association of All Classes of All Nations, London, &c.*, 1838. *Another, the FWA copy, belonged to William Pare*.

30740 **GILES**, J. E. Socialism, as a religious theory, irrational and absurd. The first of three lectures on socialism, (as propounded by Robert Owen and others,) delivered in...Leeds, September 23, 1838. 48p. *8°*. *London & Leeds*, 1838. *Another, the FWA copy, belonged to William Pare*. *See also* 1839.

30741 *GREEN, JOHN, *social missionary*. The emigrants; a lecture, delivered in the Social Institution, Tarlton-Street, Liverpool, in the month of August, 1838.

33p. *12°. Manchester & London, [1838] The FWA copy that belonged to William Pare.*

30742 HANSON, JOHN, *socialist.* The dissection of Owenism dissected: or a socialist's answer to Mr. Frederic R. Lees's pamphlet, entitled "A calm examination of the fundamental principles of Robert Owen's misnamed rational system." 34p. *12°. Leeds,* 1838.

30743 [HEATH, W.] Paul Pry's ramble through the "New Moral World," with "first impressions." [With 'Paul Pry's second ramble through the "New Moral World;" with rhymes and reflections on "the rights of woman"' and 'Paul Pry's third ramble through the "New Moral World," with "gatherings by the way"'.] 28, 28, 28p. *12°. Doncaster,* 1838–40. *With the original printed paper label, with the general title: Paul Pry's rambles...*

30744 HOBSON, J. Socialism as it is! Lectures in reply to the fallacies and misrepresentations of the Rev. John Eustace Giles... 144p. *12°. Leeds,* 1838.

30745 HORTON, H. H. Community the only salvation for man. A lecture delivered in the Social Institution, Salford...Sept. 16th, 1838. 22p. *12°. Manchester... Hulme, &c.,* 1838. *★Another, the FWA copy, belonged to William Pare.*

30746 KNIGHT, HENRY L. A lecture on irresponsibility, moral and natural, including animadversions on the objections of the author of the Electrical theory [T. S. Mackintosh]. Delivered in the Social Institution, Oldham. 16p. *8°. [Manchester &] Hulme,* 1838.

30747 LEES, F. R. Owenism dissected. A calm examination of the fundamental principles of Robert Owen's misnamed "Rational system." 36p. *12°. Leeds, London, &c.,* 1838.

30748 —— The Owenite anatomized. An analysis of the blunders and fallacies put forth by one John Hanson, in his mis-styled answer to "Owenism dissected." 36p. *12°. Leeds, London, &c.,* 1838.

30749 MARRIOTT, JOSEPH. Community. A drama. 64p. *16°. Manchester & London,* [1838]

30750 MORRISON, F. The influence of the present marriage system upon the character and interests of females contrasted with that proposed by Robert Owen, Esq. A lecture delivered in the Social Institution, Shudehill, Manchester, on...Sept. 2nd, 1838... 16p. *8°. Manchester, London, &c.,* [1838]

30751 NATIONAL COMMUNITY FRIENDLY SOCIETY. Social tracts. (No. 1[–6].) *8°. [London,* 1838] *Contents: 1. Observations upon political & social reform; 2. A calculation of the result of the industry of 500 persons of the working class; 3. The pull all together; 4. Man the creature of circumstances; 5. Human nature; or, the moral science of man; 6. The religion of the new moral world. ★Another, the FWA set, belonged to William Pare. For no. 7, see 1839 (Owen, Robert).*

30752 OWEN, ROBERT. The catechism of the new moral world...Second edition. 12p. *12°. Leeds,* 1838.

30753 —— A development of the origin and effects of moral evil, and of the principles and practices of moral good... 12p. *12°. Manchester, London, &c.,* 1838.

30754 —— A dialogue, in three parts, between the founder of "the Association of all Classes of all Nations", and a stranger desirous of being accurately informed respecting its origin and objects. 24p. *12°. Manchester, London, &c.,* 1838.

30755 —— Exposition of Mr. Owen's views on the marriage question. [Extract from Mr. Owen's address delivered at the Charlotte-st. Institution.] *s.sh.8°. Coventry,* [1838] [*Br.* 591]

30756 —— The marriage system of the new moral world; with a faint outline of the present very irrational system; as developed in a course of ten lectures. 96p. *12°. Leeds, Manchester, &c.,* 1838. *See also* 1840 (Lectures on the marriages of the priesthood...).

30757 PAGET, A. F. Introduction à l'étude de la science sociale contenant un abrégé de la théorie sociétaire, précédé d'un coup d'œil général sur l'état de la science sociale, et sur les systèmes de Fourier, d'Owen et de l'école Saint-Simonienne. 236p. *12°. Paris,* 1838. *The copy that belonged to Victor Considérant, with manuscript corrections. See also* 1841.

30758 RELIGION as now practised opposed to the laws of God, or remarks on the necessity of immediately reviving primitive Christianity, and community of goods. By a Christian socialist. 24p. *12°. Manchester, London, &c.,* 1838. *The copy that belonged to William Lovett.*

30759 ROBERT DE LA MENNAIS, H. F. Le livre du peuple. 211p. *16°. Paris,* 1838.

30760 —— Troisième édition. 191p. *16°. Paris,* 1838.

30761 The SCHOOLMASTER abroad...First lesson. 2p. *8°. n.p.* [1838 ?]

30762 —— The schoolmaster abroad. Second lesson. 2p. *8°. n.p.* [1838 ?] *These two Owenite statements of doctrine were presented to Oastler by Robert Owen, and are addressed in his hand to 'Richard Oastler Esq., Fixby Hall'.*

30763 SMITH, WILLIAM H. Letters on the state and prospects of society. [From the Philanthropist newspaper.] 58p. *12°. Birmingham,* 1838. *Presentation copy, with inscription, from the author to W. H. Ashurst.*

30764 ★WINKS, J. F. Christianity, and not Owenism, the regenerator of the world: being the substance of an address, (with some additions,) delivered in the New Hall, Leicester...August 22, 1838, in reply to four lectures delivered by Mr. Robert Owen in the same place: with an appendix... 23p. *8°. London & Leicester,* [1838] *The FWA copy that belonged to William Pare, with his manuscript notes.*

MISCELLANEOUS

30765 [BRAY, C.] The education of the feelings. 195p. *8°. London & Edinburgh,* 1838.

30766 CRUICKSHANK, W. A refutation of Dr. Hook's sermon "Hear the Church", preached before the Queen, June 17th, 1838, in four letters. 30p. *8°. Leeds & London,* 1838.

30767 HAWKES, H. W. A brief history of the Earl of Mercia, Lady Godiva, and Peeping Tom of Coventry, from the earliest period to the present day: accompanied with an original poem on the lady riding through the town: likewise a correct description of the grand cavalcade, as it proceeded through the city on Monday, June 6, 1836... Seventh edition... 12p. *12°*. *Coventry*, [1838 ?] *See note to no.* 29487.

30768 ——— A sermon on the immortality of the soul and the resurrection of the body... 24p. *12°*. *Coventry*, 1838. *See note to no.* 29487.

30769 ——— A treatise on original sin. 24p. *12°*. *Coventry*, [1838] *See note to no.* 29487.

30770 HERBERT, WILLIAM (1771–1851). History of the Worshipful Company of Skinners of London, principally compiled from their own records. p.299–382. *8°*. *J. and C. Adlard*, 1837[1838] *A reissue of part of the author's* History of the twelve great livery companies, *1837 (q.v.). The date on the printed paper label on the upper cover is 1838.*

30771 HUNTER, J. Three catalogues; describing the contents of the Red Book of the Exchequer, of the Dodsworth manuscripts in the Bodleian Library, and of the manuscripts in the library of the Honourable Society of Lincoln's Inn. 413p. *8°*. 1838.

30772 The **LAND** of contradictions [New South Wales. A poem, dated: Bath, October, 1838.] *s.sh.8°*. *n.p.* [1838]

30773 OBSERVATIONS on the necessity of betrothment, or the internal, mental, marriage, previous to wedlock, or the external, animal marriage. Illustrated by arguments and diagrams drawn from the science of phrenology. 16p. *8°*. 1838.

30774 PARKER, A. A sublime poem on banking, written at the request of a gentleman. 8p. *8°*. *Cheltenham & London*, 1838.

30775 PHILLPOTTS, H., *Bishop of Exeter*. Address of the Lord Bishop of Exeter to the clergy of his diocese, on the conduct of the Rev. Henry E. Head, Rector of Feniton; delivered...on...Oct. 9, 1838; with correspondence, &c.&c. 16p. *8°*. [1838]

30776 REFUTATION of the mistatements and calumnies contained in Mr. Lockhart's Life of Sir Walter Scott, Bart. respecting the Messrs. Ballantyne. By the trustees and son of the late Mr. James Ballantyne. 88p. *8°*. *London & Edinburgh*, 1838.

30777 SMITH, SYDNEY (1771–1845). A letter to Lord John Russell...on the Church Bills [the Residence and Plurality Bill, and the Dean and Chapter Bill]. 23p. *12°*. 1838.

30778 ——— Second letter to Archdeacon Singleton, being the third of the cathedral letters. [On the suggested abolition of prebends.] 43p. *8°*. 1838.

30779 TILL, W. Observations on the coronation medals of George the Fourth and William the Fourth. [4]p. *4°*. *n.p.* [1838 ?]

1839

GENERAL

30780 ALCOTT, W. A. Tea and coffee. [A history of their use, a discussion of their properties and statistics of their import into the United States.] 174p. *12°*. *Boston & New York*, 1839.

30781 BETHUNE, A. and JOHN. Practical economy, explained and enforced in a series of lectures. 278p. *8°*. *Edinburgh & London*, 1839.

30782 BLANQUI, J. A. Cours d'économie industrielle ...Recueilli et annoté par Ad. Blaise (d.V.). 1838–39. 507p. *8°*. *Paris*, [1839]

30783 BRIAVOINNE, N. De l'industrie en Belgique. Causes de décadence et de prospérité. Sa situation actuelle ... 2 vols. *8°*. *Bruxelles*, 1839.

30784 The **BRITISH ALMANAC** of the Society for the Diffusion of Useful Knowledge, for...1839. [With 'The companion to the Almanac; or year-book of general information'.] 96, 252p. *12°*. [1839] *For other editions, see* 1828.

30785 BROUGHAM, H. P., *Baron Brougham and Vaux*. Lord Brougham's speeches [6 August 1839] on the administration of justice in Ireland... 32p. *8°*. 1839.

30786 BUREAUD-RIOFFREY, A. M. Londres ancien et moderne, ou recherches sur l'état physique et social de cette métropole. 138p. *8°*. *Paris & Londres*, 1839. *Presentation copy from the author to 'Ad. von Zwehl'.*

30787 BURGON, J. W. The life and times of Sir Thomas Gresham; compiled chiefly from his correspondence...including notices of many of his contemporaries ... 2 vols. *8°*. 1839.

30788 CIBRARIO, G. A. L., *Conte*. Della economia politica del medio evo libri III che trattano della sua condizione politica morale economica. 614p. *8°*. *Torino*, 1839.

30789 COBBETT CLUB. A political tract. By the Cobbett Club of London. No. 1. Addressed to the people of the United Kingdom. To be repeated occasionally. 55p. *8°*. 1839.

30790 [**COLTON**, C.] A voice from America to England. By an American gentleman. 321p. *8°*. 1839.

30791 The **CRISIS** in France, by a recent visitor to Paris. 63p. *8°*. 1839.

30792 The late commercial **CRISIS**; being a retrospect of the years 1836 to 1838: with tables representing a safe, speedy, and equitable plan for the abolition of the corn laws. By a Glasgow manufacturer... 113p. *8°*. *Glasgow, Edinburgh, &c.*, 1839.

30793 DECORDE, J. F. Mémoire couronné par l'Athénée des Arts de Paris...1838, sur cette question: Quelle serait l'organisation du travail la plus propre à augmenter le bien-être des classes laborieuses ? [Preceded by 'Observations préliminaires'.] 45, 111p. *8°*. *Paris*, 1839.

30794 The **DIRECTORY** of Birmingham; including

an alphabetical list of the inhabitants of the town; a classification of its merchants, manufacturers, &c.; a new arrangement of mails, coaches, and carriers; together with an alphabetical street directory, &c. 227p. *8°. Birmingham*, 1839. *For another edition, see* 1835.

30795 EISDELL, J. S. A treatise on the industry of nations; or, the principles of national economy, and taxation... 2 vols. *8°.* 1839.

30796 ELLET, C. An essay on the laws of trade, in reference to the works of internal improvement in the United States. 284p. *12°. Richmond* [*Va.*], 1839.

30797 GRANIER DE CASSAGNAC, A. Geschichte der arbeitenden und der bürgerlichen Classen... Nach dem Französischen und mit einem Vorwort begleitet von H.H. 332p. *8°. Braunschweig*, 1839. *For another edition, see* 1838.

30798 GUILLAUMIN, G. U., ed. Encyclopédie du commerçant. Dictionnaire du commerce et des marchandises, contenant tout ce qui concerne le commerce de terre et de mer... 2 vols. *fol. Paris*, 1839.

30799 —— [Another issue.] 2 vols. *fol. Paris*, 1839–41.

30800 HAGEMEISTER, J. VON. Essai sur les ressources territoriales et commerciales de l'Asie occidentale, le caractère des habitans, leur industrie et leur organisation municipale. (*Beiträge zur Kenntniss des russischen Reichs*, 3.) 296p. *8°. St. Pétersbourg*, 1839.

30801 HAWKINS, F. B. Germany; the spirit of her history, literature, social condition, and national economy; illustrated by reference to her physical, moral and political statistics... Second edition, augmented and carefully revised. 713p. *18°. Frankfort o. M.*, 1839. *For another edition, see* 1838.

30802 HAXTHAUSEN, A. VON, *Freiherr*. Die ländliche Verfassung in den einzelnen Provinzen der preussischen Monarchie... Erster Band. 270p. *8°. Königsberg*, 1839.

30803 HOBBES, T. The English works of Thomas Hobbes of Malmesbury; now first collected and edited by Sir William Molesworth, Bart. 11 vols. *8°.* 1839–45.

30804 —— Thomæ Hobbes Malmesburiensis Opera philosophica quæ latine scripsit, omnia in unum corpus nunc primus collecta studio et labore Gulielmi Molesworth. 5 vols. *8°. Londini*, 1839–45.

30805 *LA BONNINIÈRE DE BEAUMONT, G. A. DE. L'Irlande sociale, politique et religieuse... 2 vols. *8°. Paris, Londres, &c.*, 1839. *Presentation copy from the author to George Grote.*

30806 —— Ireland: social, political and religious... Edited by W. C. Taylor, LL.D. of Trinity College, Dublin... 2 vols. *8°.* 1839.

30807 LAING, SAMUEL (1780–1868). A tour in Sweden in 1838; comprising observations on the moral, political, and economical state of the Swedish nation. 431p. *8°.* 1839.

30808 *LEFEBVRE LABOULAYE, E. R. Histoire du droit de propriété foncière en occident... 532p. *8°. Paris*, 1839. *The copy that belonged to George Grote.*

30809 LIEBER, F. Manual of political ethics. [Part I.] 413p. *8°.* 1839.

30810 [LOVE, B.] Manchester as it is; or, notices of the institutions, manufactures, commerce, railways, etc. of the metropolis of manufactures; interspersed with much valuable information useful for the resident and stranger ... 244p. *12°. Manchester & London*, 1839. *See also* 1842.

30811 LYNCH, A. H. Measures to be adopted for the employment of the labouring classes in Ireland; detailed in an address to the electors of Galway; with an appendix, containing abstracts of the reports of some of the provincial assemblies in Belgium. 252p. *8°.* 1839.

30812 McCULLOCH, JOHN R. Under the superintendence of the Society for the Diffusion of Useful Knowledge. A statistical account of the British Empire: exhibiting its extent, physical capacities, population, industry, and civil and religious institutions... Second edition, corrected throughout and enlarged. 2 vols. *8°.* 1839. *For other editions, see* 1837.

30813 MARCET, J. Conversations on political economy; in which the elements of that science are familiarly explained... Seventh edition, revised and enlarged. 416p. *8°.* 1839. *For other editions, see* 1816.

30814 MURRAY, H. An historical and descriptive account of British America; comprehending Canada... Nova Scotia, New Brunswick, Newfoundland, Prince Edward Island, the Bermudas and the fur countries... To which is added a full detail of the principles and best modes of emigration... With illustrations of the natural history, by James Wilson, R. K. Greville and Professor Traill... Second edition. 3 vols. *8°. Edinburgh & London*, 1839.

30815 NEWCASTLE-UPON-TYNE. *Town Council*. The proceedings and reports of the Town Council ...for 1838... [220]p. *8°. Newcastle*, 1839. *See also* 1837, 1838, 1840.

30816 PARISH, SIR W. Buenos Ayres, and the provinces of the Rio de La Plata: their present state, trade, and debt; with some account... of the progress of geographical discovery in those parts... during the last sixty years. 415p. *8°.* 1839.

30817 PARK, M. Travels in the interior districts of Africa: performed in the years 1795, 1796 and 1797. With an account of a subsequent mission to that country in 1805 ...To which is added an account of the life of Mr. Park. 330p. *8°.* 1839.

30818 PECQUEUR, C. N. S. Économie sociale. Des intérêts du commerce, de l'industrie et de l'agriculture, et de la civilisation en général, sous l'influence des applications de la vapeur... 2 vols. *8°. Paris*, 1839.

30819 —— Deuxième édition. 2 vols. *8°. Paris*, 1839.

30820 PEEL, SIR ROBERT, *2nd Bart*. Speech of Sir Robert Peel in the House of Commons, on...Feb. 19, 1839, on the corn laws. Letter of James M'Queen, Esq. to the Right Hon. Lord Melbourne, on the statistics, &c. of agriculture and manufactures. 34p. *4°. Chelmsford & London*, 1839.

30821 PHILO HIBERNICUS, *pseud*. Ireland's malady and its remedy. 15p. *8°. n.p.* [1839] *The copy that belonged to Earl De Grey.*

30822 RAU, K. D. H. Traité d'économie nationale... traduit de l'allemand sur la troisième et dernière édition, par Fréd. de Kemmeter. Première partie. Théorie de l'économie politique. 414p. *8°. Bruxelles*, 1839.

30823 RUSSELL, ARCHIBALD. Principles of statistical inquiry; as illustrated in proposals for uniting an examination into the resources of the United States, with the census to be taken in 1840. 263p. *8°. New-York*, 1839. *Presentation copy, with inscription, from the author to Thomas Chalmers.*

30824 SAY, H. Histoire des relations commerciales entre la France et le Brésil, et considérations générales sur les monnaies, les changes, les banques et le commerce extérieur. 333p. *8°. Paris*, 1839.

30825 SLADE, J. Narrative of the late proceedings and events in China. [With an appendix, 'Documents relating to opium, &c.'] 183, 75p. *8°. China: Canton Register Press*, 1839.

For **STATISTICAL SOCIETY OF LONDON.** Journal, 1839 —→, *see* vol. III, *Periodicals list*, Journal...

For —— Proceedings, *see* vol. III, *Periodicals list*, Proceedings...

30826 STEPHENS, George, *political writer.* Pol-

itical prophecy fulfilled; or, "Ireland," with a new preface ...Sixth edition. 16p. *8°.* 1839.

30827 SYMONS, Jelinger C. Arts and artisans at home and abroad: with sketches of the progress of foreign manufactures. 270p. *12°. Edinburgh, London, &c.*, 1839.

30828 THOUGHTS on Jeremy Bentham; or, the principle of utility, considered in connexion with ethical philosophy and criminal jurisprudence. By a member of the Manchester Athenæum. 40p. *8°. London & Edinburgh*, 1839.

30829 VERITY, R. Changes produced in the nervous system by civilization, considered according to the evidence of physiology and the philosophy of history... Second edition, enlarged. 143p. *8°. London & Paris*, 1839.

30830 VILLENEUVE-BARGEMONT, J. P. A. de, *Vicomte.* Histoire de l'économie politique. 682p. *8°. Bruxelles*, 1839. *See also* 1841.

AGRICULTURE

30831 COLMAN, H. Second report on the agriculture of Massachusetts...County of Berkshire, 1838. 194p. *8°. Boston*, 1839.

30832 CRAWFORD, William S. A defence of the small farmers of Ireland. [Against the dispossession of the small farmer in the interests of increased productivity.] 131p. *12°. Dublin*, 1839.

30833 DAVIS, H. The effects of the importation of wheat upon the profits of farming. Addressed to agriculturists...Second edition. 15p. *8°.* 1839.

30834 DIXON, William, *the younger.* Facts, established by authentic documents, bearing upon agriculture, as influenced by incautious legislation; particularly applicable to seasons of actual or apprehended scarcity. 59p. *8°. London, Cheltenham, &c.*, 1839. *Presentation copy from the author to the editor of the Free Press.*

30835 DUPPA, B. F. Agricultural colleges, or schools for the sons of farmers. 40p. *12°.* 1839.

30836 FALCONER, Thomas (1805–1882). Objections to proposed leases of part of the estates of the City of Bath. [Originally published as letters to the *Bath Guardian*.] 22p. *12°. Bath*, 1839.

30837 HAIR, T. H. Sketches of the coal mines in Northumberland & Durham. [Part 1.] 4p., 6 plates. *fol.* 1839.

30838 [HICKEY, W.] A cyclopædia of practical husbandry and rural affairs in general. By Martin Doyle ... 507p. *12°. Dublin*, 1839.

30839 HILL, Marcus L. French claims. Statement of Mr. Marcus Lewis Hill's claim [to be heir-at-law to one moiety of an estate in France called La Roche Talbot]. 17p. *8°. n.p.* [1839]

30840 HOMERGUE, J. D'. The silk culturist's manual: or, a popular treatise on the planting and cultivation of mulberry trees, the rearing and propagating of silk worms, and the preparation of the raw material for exportation...[With an appendix.] 406p. *12°. Philadelphia*, 1839.

30841 LONDON. *Corporation of the City of London.* Rules, orders, and ordinances for the fisheries in Thames and Medway [October 1785]. 36p. *8°.* 1839.

30842 —— Livery Companies. *Skinners.* The Skinners' Company against the Honourable the Irish Society, the Corporation of London, and others. Proceedings in Her Majesty's High Court of Chancery...in the Rolls Court, before the...Master of the Rolls, commencing February 9, 1838. [To ascertain the relationship of the Irish Society towards the Companies of the City of London holding property in or near Londonderry allotted to them at the time of the Plantation of Ulster.] 1249p. *8°.* 1839.

30843 NAPIER, Sir Charles J. An essay on the present state of Ireland, showing the chief causes of, and the remedy for, the existing distresses of that country... 70p. *8°.* 1839.

30844 OAKWOOD COAL AND IRON COMPANY. Reports, valuation, and estimates on, of, and relative to the property belonging to the Oakwood Coal and Iron Company, Port Talbot, Glamorganshire. By Messrs Brough & Son...Neath; John Buddle...Newcastle; T. E. Harrison...South Shields; David Mushet, Esq. Coleford; William Brunton...Neath. With explanatory accounts of the works... 56p. *8°.* 1839.

30845 OSAGE MINING AND SMELTING COMPANY. Private and confidential. Osage Mining and Smelting Company, State of Missouri, United States of America. Incorporated by an act of the Legislature, February 3, 1837. Capital one million of dollars. Statement of the objects, prospects, and advantages of the Company; and of the mineral and agricultural resources of the state of Missouri. 53p. *8°.* 1839.

30846 POYNTER, T. The cottage gardener: being a sketch on useful gardening, designed for the use of the labouring cottagers of England. [Second edition.] 104p. *12°. Manchester & London*, 1839. *The copy that belonged to J. M. Cobbett, with his signature on the title-page.*

30847 REBER, P. Handbuch der praktischen Landwirtschaft für Gutsbesitzer, Oekonomen und Landwirthe mit besonderer Rücksicht auf den landwirthschaftlichen Betrieb in Bayern... 570p. *8°. Nürnberg & Wien*, 1839.

30848 ROYAL ASIATIC SOCIETY. Royal Asiatic Society. Proceedings of the Committee of Agriculture and Commerce. April 8, 1837[–May 9, 1839]. 135p. *8°.* [1839]

30849 RYAN, C. An essay on Scottish husbandry, adapted to the use of the farmers of Ireland. 140p. *12⁰*. *Dublin, 1839. Presentation copy, with inscription, from the author to 'the Honble. & Revd. Jas. Agar'.*

30850 A **SECRET** worth knowing having been solved by the Labourers' Friends' Society, is respectfully addressed to Her Most Gracious Majesty, the Queen, patroness. 15p. *8⁰*. 1839. *Sometimes attributed to M. A. Gilbert.*

30851 —— [Another edition.] An important problem having been solved by the Labourers' Friends' Society, is respectfully addressed to...the Queen; patroness. 15p.

8⁰. 1839. With manuscript alterations, possibly for a revised edition.

30852 SILLIMAN, B. Extracts from a report made to the Maryland and New York Coal & Iron Company, on the estate of said Company, in the County of Alleghany, State of Maryland, by Benjamin Silliman, aided by Benjamin Silliman, Jr. To which are added, reports &c. by W. Young; David Mushet; Andrew Ure; Prof. Daniell; H. T. Weld; and J. Renwick. 80p. *8⁰*. 1839.

30853 WHITLAW, C. A short review of the causes and effects of the present distress, and its dreadful consequences on the labouring, manufacturing, and commercial classes. 43p. *8⁰*. [1839]

CORN LAWS

30854 Can the **ANTI-CORN LAW DELEGATES** prove their case? 23p. *8⁰*. [1839]

30855 ARTISANS, farmers and labourers. [An attack on the corn laws.] 38p. *8⁰*. 1839.

30856 ASHPITEL, A. The factor, the miller, and the baker get more than the farmer, and ten times more than the landlord out of the loaf. A few facts on the corn laws, defending the agricultural interest. 27p. *8⁰*. 1839. *See also* 1841.

30857 B., E. H. On the corn laws. The graduated scale of duties applied to quantity in relation to consumption, instead of to average market price, to produce steady prices. 15p. *8⁰*. 1839.

30858 BELL, JOHN, *protectionist writer.* Dedicated... to...the Duke of Newcastle, K.G....A vindication of the rights of British landowners, farmers, and labourers, against the claims of the cotton capitalists to a free trade in corn. 48p. *8⁰*. 1839.

30859 BROADHURST, J. Reasons for not repealing the corn laws. 47p. *8⁰*. 1839.

30860 BROUGHAM, H. P., *Baron Brougham and Vaux.* Lord Brougham's speech in the House of Lords, on...February 19, 1839, on moving for a Committee of the Whole House on the corn laws. 65p. *8⁰*. 1839.

30861 C., J. D. An address to the people of the United Kingdom on the corn laws. 28p. *8⁰*. 1839.

30862 CAYLEY, EDWARD S. Corn laws: speech of E. S. Cayley, Esq. M.P. on the motion of Mr. Villiers for "A Committee of the Whole House to consider Act 9 Geo. IV. c. 60, relating to foreign corn." March 12. 1839. 63p. *8⁰*. 1839.

30863 CHAMBER OF COMMERCE, *Manchester.* The corn laws. An authentic report of the...discussions in the Manchester Chamber of Commerce, on the destructive effects of the corn laws upon the trade and manufactures of the country. With notes and prefatory remarks... 112p. *8⁰*. 1839.

30864 COMMON-SENSE, *pseud.* The corn laws considered by "Common-Sense." 16p. *8⁰*. 1839.

30865 EDINBURGH ANTI-CORN-LAW ASSOCIATION. Corn laws. The nature & effect of these oppressive statutes...[Signed: George M. Sinclair, secretary, and dated, 19th December, 1839.] 8p. *8⁰*. [*Edinburgh,* 1839] *See also* 1840.

30866 FACTS for farmers. [On the corn laws.] 4p. *8⁰*. *Edinburgh,* [1839] *See also* 1842.

30867 FIFE. Report of the proceedings of the great public meeting [of the County of Fife], held in Cupar, on 7th March, in support of protection to agriculture by means of the corn laws. ⟨From the Fifeshire Journal of 14th March, 1839.⟩ 40p. *12⁰*. *Cupar-Fife, Kirkaldy, &c.,* 1839.

30868 FITZWILLIAM, C. W. W., *Earl Fitzwilliam.* First, second, and third addresses to the landowners of England on the corn laws...New edition. 60p. *12⁰*. 1839.

30869 —— Third address to the landowners of England, on the corn laws. 21p. *8⁰*. 1839.

30870 —— [Second edition.] 21p. *8⁰*. 1839.

30871 *FOX, WILLIAM J. Reports of lectures delivered at the chapel in South Place, Finsbury...No. XXI. The corn-law question considered in its moral bearings. 20p. *8⁰*. 1839. *The copy that belonged to George Grote. For other lectures in this series, see* 1835 (GENERAL).

30872 GLADSTONE, SIR J., *Bart.* The repeal of the corn laws with its probable consequences, briefly examined and considered. 20p. *8⁰*. 1839.

30873 —— Second edition. 20p. *8⁰*. 1839.

30874 GREY, H. G., *3rd Earl Grey.* Substance of the speech of Viscount Howick on the corn laws, March 13th, 1839. 63p. *8⁰*. 1839.

30875 HORTON, SIR R. J. W., *Bart.* A letter from the Right Honourable Sir Robert Wilmot Horton, Bart. Vice President, to Dr. Birkbeck, the President, and the members of the London Mechanics' Institution, on the subject of the corn laws. Accompanied by an illustrative tabular statement. [With appendixes.] 24, 12p. *8⁰*. *Richmond* [*Surrey*], 1839. *The table is entitled: Analysis of Pigot & Co.'s classified Directory, for the year 1838, on the professions and trades of London, and limited to London properly so called. See also* 1840.

30876 HUNTER, D. The corn law question shortly investigated; addressed principally to the agriculturists of Scotland. 22p. *8⁰*. *Edinburgh,* 1839.

30877 JUSTICE to corn-growers and to corn-eaters. 28p. *8⁰*. 1839.

30878 KENNEDY, L. On the necessity of protection to the agriculturists of the United Kingdom. xx, 64p. *8⁰*. 1839. *The preface, entitled: 'On the probable operation and*

*effect of the repeal of the duties on foreign corn to the manu-
facturing classes, the agricultural labourers...of the United
Kingdom', was reprinted separately in 1840 (q.v.).*

30879 LENNARD, T. B. An address to the members
of the Chelmsford and Essex Agricultural Society, on the
corn laws. 15p. *8°.* 1839.

30880 LETTER to the Duke of Buckingham, on the
corn laws. By a practical farmer. 40p. *8°. London &
Edinburgh,* 1839.

30881 MANUFACTURERS and corn-growers. A
letter to the public. 33p. *8°.* 1839.

30882 MORETON, HON. A. H. Thoughts on the
corn laws, addressed to the working classes of the county
of Gloucester. 24p. *8°.* 1839.

30883 MOSELEY, J. An inquiry into the probable
results consequent to a repeal of the corn law. 20p. *8°.
Woodbridge,* 1839. *See also* 1840.

30884 PEEL, SIR ROBERT, *2nd Bart.* The speech of
the Right Honourable Sir R. Peel, Bart. in the House of
Commons [15 March, 1839], on Mr. Villiers' motion on
the corn laws. 64p. *8°.* 1839.

30885 PLENTY versus starvation; or, who would gain
by the repeal of the corn laws? By a corn consumer. [A
conversation between Farmer Bull, Mr. Turnbull, cotton
spinner, John, farmer's man and James, mechanic.] 12p.
12°. London & Manchester, 1839.

30886 PORTER, G. R. The effect of restrictions on
the importation of corn, considered with reference to
landowners, farmers and labourers. 43p. *8°.* 1839. *Presentation copy from the author to T. Spring Rice, Baron
Monteagle.*

30887 QUIN, H. The corn laws. Substance of the
proceedings at a meeting, held with reference to the
attempted anti-agricultural agitation, at the Reading-
Room of the Hull Operative Conservative Society, on...
the 11th of February, 1839. Embracing the lecture
delivered on that occasion by Mr. Henry Quin, editor of
the Hull and East-Riding Times... 16p. *8°. Hull, Barton,
&c.,* 1839.

30888 REMARKS upon a few of the anti-corn law
fallacies. By a barrister. 15p. *8°.* 1839.

30889 SALOMONS, SIR D., *Bart.* Reflections on
the operation of the present scale of duty for regulating the
importation of foreign corn, addressed to the Borders of
Kent and Sussex Agricultural Association. 79p. *8°.* 1839.
See also 1840.

30890 SENIOR'S letters on the corn laws. A new
edition. By a member of the Temple. 47p. *8°.* 1839.

30891 SUTTIE, SIR G. G., *Bart.* Letter to the Right
Honourable Lord Viscount Melbourne, on the cause of
the higher average price of grain in Britain than on the
Continent. 14p. *8°. Edinburgh,* 1839.

30892 THOMPSON, HENRY. Free corn ruinous to
England. Fourth edition. 27p. *8°. London & York,* 1839.

30893 THOMPSON, THOMAS P. An abridgment

of the catechism on the corn laws, &c. 16p. *8°. Manchester
Anti-Corn-Law Association,* [1839?]

30894 —— Catechism on the corn laws; with a list of
fallacies and the answers. Twentieth edition. Stereotype
...To which is added the article on free trade, from the
Westminster Review, No. XXIII... 82p. *8°.* 1839. *For
other editions, see* 1827.

30895 —— Corn-law fallacies, with the answers.
(Reprinted from The Sun newspaper.) With a dedication
to the Manchester Chamber of Commerce. By the author
of the Catechism on the corn laws. Second edition. 80p.
8°. 1839.

30896 —— Third edition. 80p. *8°.* 1839.

30897 THOMSON, CHARLES E. P., *Baron Sydenham.*
Speech of the Right Hon. C. Poulett Thomson on the corn
laws, March 7, 1834. 32p. *8°.* 1839.

30898 —— The substance of a speech delivered by the
Right Hon. C. Poulett Thomson, on Mr. Villiers' motion
for going into a Committee of the Whole House on the
corn laws. 15p. *8°. Manchester: Anti-Corn-Law Association,* 1839. *With a manuscript note at the head of the title-
page: £3.0.0. per 1000.*

30899 TORRENS, R. Three letters to the Marquis
of Chandos, on the effects of the corn laws. 46p. *8°.* 1839.

30900 VILLIERS, C. P. Mr. Villiers' speech on the
corn laws, March 12, 1839. 23p. *8°. Manchester,* [1839]

30901 WESTERN, C. C., *Baron Western.* The maintenance of the corn laws essential to the general prosperity
of the Empire. 34p. *8°.* 1839.

30902 WESTHEAD, J. P. B. A letter to the Right
Honourable Sir Robert Peel, Bart. on the corn laws. 20p.
8°. London & Manchester, 1839.

30903 WHITMORE, W. W. A letter on the corn
laws, to the Manchester Chamber of Commerce. 22p. *8°.
London & Manchester,* 1839.

30904 —— A second letter on the corn laws, to the
Manchester Chamber of Commerce. 36p. *8°.* 1839.

30905 WICKHAM, H. L. A letter to Charles Shaw
Lefevre, Esq., on the subject of the corn laws. 12p. *8°.*
1839.

30906 WILSON, JAMES (1805–1850). Influences of
the corn laws, as affecting all classes of the community,
and particularly the landed interests. 135p. *8°.* 1839. *See
also* 1840.

30907 A few **WORDS** proving that high-priced bread
and high wages are no evil to the working classes. By one
who wishes them well. [Against the repeal of the corn
laws.] 10p. *8°. Wolverhampton,* 1839.

30908 WORKMAN, JOHN, *pseud.?* Remarks on the
late speeches in Parliament in support of corn laws,
addressed to James Emerson Tennent, Esq. M.P. 13p. *8°.
Belfast,* [1839] *The title has been altered in manuscript to:
The late speeches in Parliament in support of corn laws,
exposed.*

POPULATION

30909 ENGLAND. *General Register Office.* First annual report of the Registrar-General of births, deaths, and marriages in England. 168p. *8°.* 1839. *The University Library has a complete set of the annual reports to 1922.*

30910 MARCUS, *pseud.* Child murder!!! A reprint ...of the infamous production by Marcus advocating the murder of the children of the poor. On the possibility of limiting populousness; an essay on populousness; the theory of painless extinction. 32p. *8°. London & Manchester,* [1839] *The Oastler copy.*

30911 —— Second edition (with an additional preface) of The book of murder! Vade-mecum for the Commissioners and Guardians of the new Poor Law...being an exact reprint of the infamous essay on the possibility of limiting populousness, by Marcus, one of the three. With a refutation of the Malthusian doctrine. 48p. *8°.* [*London,* 1839] *The Oastler copy. For another edition, see* 1838.

TRADES & MANUFACTURES

30912 ARAGO, D. F. J. Historical eloge of James Watt...Translated from the French with additional notes and an appendix by James Patrick Muirhead... 261p. *8°. London & Edinburgh,* 1839.

30913 ARMSTRONG, R. An essay on the boilers of steam engines: their calculation, construction, and management, with a view to the saving of fuel...A new edition, considerably enlarged and improved. 264p. *8°.* 1839. *The Rastrick copy.*

30914 BRITISH ASSOCIATION FOR THE ADVANCEMENT OF SCIENCE. Catalogue of the illustrations of manufactures, inventions and models, philosophical instruments, etc., contained in the second exhibition of the British Association...held at Birmingham, August, 1839. 24p. *8°.* [*Birmingham,* 1839] *With the signature 'John Gray' on the title-page.*

30915 DAVY, C. The architect, engineer, and operative builder's constructive manual; or, a practical... treatise on the construction of artificial foundations for buildings, railways, &c....To which is added, an analysis of the principal...enactments affecting the operations of the practical builder...Second edition. 180p. *8°.* 1839.

30916 Theoretical and practical **ESSAY** on bitumen, setting forth its uses in remote ages and revival in modern times, and demonstrating its applicability to various purposes. 52p. *8°.* 1839.

For the **INVENTORS' ADVOCATE** *and patentees' recorder, see vol.* III, *Periodicals list,* Inventors' advocate and journal of industry.

30917 JOHNSON, JOSEPH, *of Liverpool.* On the state and prospects of the iron trade in Scotland and South Wales, in May, 1839... ⟨Extracted from the Mining Review, No. XVIII, (new series), June, 1839.⟩ 22p. *8°.* [1839] *Presentation copy, with inscription, from the author to 'Mr. D{d} Maxwell'.*

30918 —— Report of the iron trade in Scotland and South Wales, in May, 1839. [Taken from the article in the Mining Review, with 'Extract from a report by Mr. Daubrée, published in the Annales des Mines, Vol. 14' on the process used in the smelting of iron by George Crane of the Yniscedwyn Iron Works, and presented to both Houses of Congress by J. M. Sanderson.] 18p. *8°. Philadelphia,* 1839.

30919 MARTIN, WILLIAM (1772–1851). A proved imposition upon the public; exemplified in the suppression of the London report of the late scientific meeting [of the British Association]. [With 'Proving that Dr. Harvey did not discover the cause of the circulation of the blood' and 'The most effectual method that has ever been devised for taking the whale'.] 4p. *8°. Newcastle,* [1839]

30920 —— Remarks on the proposed new bridge across the Tyne; containing an exposure of an uncharitable prejudice, and an unmanly, unchristian-like feeling towards the philosopher... 4p. *8°. Newcastle,* [1839]

30921 TIMPERLEY, C. H. A dictionary of printers and printing, with the progress of literature...bibliographical illustrations, etc.... 996p. *8°. London, Edinburgh, &c.,* 1839.

30922 URE, A. A dictionary of arts, manufactures, and mines: containing a clear exposition of their principles and practice... 1334p. *8°.* 1839. *See also* 1843, *and, for a supplement,* 1846.

COMMERCE

30923 ANDERSON, R. A brief exposition of the present state of the coal trade, between the shipping ports in the north of England and London. 20p. *8°. Newcastle-upon-Tyne,* 1839.

30924 BANSA & SOHN. Preis nota der von den besten Lagen selbst bezogenen vollkommen rein gehaltenen Weinen welche nebst vielen anderen vorzüglichen Sorten abgegeben werden bey Bansa & Sohn in Frankfurt a. M. *s.sh.8°. n.p.* [1839 ?] *An engraved list, with manuscript additions, and subscribed:* 'presented by J. C. Dalwig at Manchester'.

30925 *BISHOP, JAMES, *secretary of the Metropolitan Protection Society.* A brief statement of facts in illustration of the operation of the new beer laws. Respectfully addressed to the Legislature, the agricultural interest, and the public. 7p. *8°.* 1839. *The copy that belonged to George Grote.*

30926 *BONNE-MAES, . Coup d'œil sur la situation respective des deux industries linières, suivi d'un rapport sur le projet de questions à soumettre au Ministre de l'Intérieure et des Affaires Étrangères, concernant la recherche de nouveaux débouchés pour nos toiles...

Deuxième édition. 22p. *8°. Gand*, 1839. *The copy that belonged to George Grote.*

30927 CHAMBER OF COMMERCE, *Newcastle-upon-Tyne.* Foreign policy and commerce. Speeches delivered at a meeting of the Chamber of Commerce of Newcastle-upon-Tyne, and at a public dinner given by that body, to David Urquhart, Esq. on the 15th and 20th November, 1838... 50p. *8°. Newcastle-upon-Tyne*, 1839.

30928 CRISIS in the opium traffic: being an account of the proceedings of the Chinese Government to suppress that trade, with the notices, edicts, &c., relating thereto. 107p. *8°. China: Office of the Chinese Repository*, 1839.

30929 DALWIG, J. C. On commerce: a letter to the merchants and manufacturers of Manchester. 10p. *8°. Manchester*, 1839.

30930 [KING, C. W.] Opium crisis. A letter addressed to Charles Elliot, Esq., chief superintendent of the British trade with China. By an American merchant, resident at Canton. 82p. *8°*. 1839.

30931 MILLER, H. Memoir of William Forsyth, Esq. a Scotch merchant of the eighteenth century. 133p. *8°*. 1839.

30932 PAPPAFFY, . Memorandum respecting the corn duties of England, and it's grain trade with the Mediterranean...Malta, December, 1838. 15p. *8°*. 1839.

30933 RATTENBURY, J. Memoirs of a smuggler, compiled from his diary and journal: containing the principal events in the life of John Rattenbury, of Beer, Devonshire; commonly called "the Rob Roy of the West"... 108p. *12°. Sidmouth & London*, 1837[1839] *The imprint on the printed paper wrapper is 'London & Sidmouth, 1839'.*

30934 [REDDING, C.] Every man his own butler. By the author of the "History and description of modern wines." 200p. *12°*. 1839.

30935 THELWALL, A. S. The iniquities of the opium trade with China; being a development of the main causes which exclude the merchants of Great Britain from the advantages of an unrestricted commercial intercourse with that vast empire...Drawn up at the request of several gentlemen connected with the East-India trade. 178p. *8°*. 1839.

COLONIES

30936 A short **ACCOUNT** of Prince Edward Island, designed chiefly for the information of agriculturist and other emigrants of small capital, by the author of The emigrant's introduction to an acquaintance with the British American colonies, &c. 90p. *12°*. 1839.

30937 ASSAM: sketch of its history, soil, and productions; with the discovery of the tea plant, and of the countries adjoining Assam. 57p. *8°*. 1839.

30938 BOILEAU, JOHN T. Report drawn up by Captain J. T. Boileau, Bengal Engineers, on the practicability and expense of a plan proposed for constructing docks at Diamond Harbour, on the river Hoogly, in Bengal; and for uniting them with the Presidency of Calcutta by a railroad, together with an estimate of the same. 35p. *8°*. 1839.

30939 BRITISH AND FOREIGN ABORIGINES' PROTECTION SOCIETY. Extracts from the papers and proceedings of the Aborigines Protection Society. No. 1. May, 1839. 32p. *8°*. 1839.

30940 —— Report on the Indians of Upper Canada. The Sub-Committee...present...the first part of their general report. 52p. *8°*. [1839?]

30941 —— The second annual report of the Aborigines Protection Society, presented at the...meeting in Exeter Hall, May 21st, 1839. With list of officers, subscribers, benefactors, and honorary members... 32p. *8°*. 1839.

30942 BRITISH INDIA. The duty and interest of Great Britain, to consider the condition and claims of her possessions in the East. Addresses, delivered before the members of the Society of Friends [by T. Frankland, G. Thompson, F. C. Brown, J. Bowring, J. Crawford, Major General Briggs, J. Pease] at their yearly meeting... on the 1st of June, 1839. [With 'Prospectus of the Provisional Committee (organized March 27, 1839,) for forming a British India Society', with an account of the inaugural meeting and a list of officers.] 64p. *8°*. 1839.

30943 BROWNE, H. P., *2nd Marquess of Sligo.* A letter to the Marquess of Normanby relative to the present state of Jamaica, and the measures which are rendered necessary by the refusal of the House of Assembly to transact business. 50p. *8°*. 1839.

30944 *BRUCE, C. A. Report on the manufacture of tea, and on the extent and produce of the tea plantations in Assam. [From the Journal of the Asiatic Society.] 36p. *8°. Calcutta*, 1839. *See also* 1840.

30945 BUTLER, SAMUEL (*fl.* 1839). The hand-book for Australian emigrants; being a descriptive history of Australia, and containing an account of the climate, soil, and natural productions of New South Wales, South Australia and Swan River Settlement... Third thousand 240p. *12°. Glasgow, London, &c.*, 1839.

30946 CRAWFURD, JOHN (1783–1868). An appeal from the inhabitants of British India to the justice of the people of England: a popular inquiry into the operation of the system of taxation in British India. [With an appendix.] 54, 35p. *8°*. 1839.

30947 DIXON, JOHN, *of Van Diemen's Land.* The condition and capabilities of Van Diemen's Land, as a place of emigration. Being the practical experience of nearly ten years' residence in the colony. 96p. *12°*. 1839. *p. 89–96 contain Smith, Elder's catalogue of works on emigration.*

30948 DODWELL, E. and **MILES,** J. S. Alphabetical list of the Honourable East India Company's Bengal civil servants, from...1780, to...1838...To which is attached a list of the Governors-General of India, from...1773, to...1838...Also a list of the East India Directors... 607p. *8°. London & Calcutta*, 1839.

30949 EASTERN COAST OF CENTRAL AMERICA COMMERCIAL AND AGRICULTURAL COMPANY. Brief statement, supported by original documents, of the important grants conceded to the Eastern Coast of Central America Commercial and Agricultural Company by the State of Guatemala. With a map of the territory of Vera Paz, and another of the Port of San Tomas. 137p. *8°*. 1839.

30950 *ENGLAND. Parliament. *House of Commons.* The debate upon Mr. Ward's resolutions, on colonization, in the House of Commons, June 27, 1839, containing the speeches of H. G. Ward, Esq. M.P. Sir W. Molesworth, Bart. M.P. Right Hon. H. Labouchère, M.P. W. Warburton, Esq. M.P. and Right Hon. Viscount Howick, M.P. Corrected by the several speakers. 84p. *8°.* 1839. *The copy that belonged to George Grote.*

30951 FACTS versus Lord Durham. Remarks upon that portion of the Earl of Durham's report, relating to Prince Edward Island, shewing the fallacy of the statements contained therein. To which is added, a tabular view of the British provinces in North America...By a proprietor. 21p. *8°.* 1839.

30952 GUILBERT, A. De la colonisation du nord de l'Afrique; nécessité d'une association nationale pour l'exploitation agricole et industrielle de l'Algérie. [With 'Extraits, opinions...sur d'Algérie, puisés dans les voyages...qui ont été publiés depuis le XVIIe siècle' and 'Liste bibliographique des auteurs qui ont écrit sur l'Afrique septentrionale, depuis la conquête...par les Arabes'.] 556p. *8°. Paris,* 1839.

30953 [HALIBURTON, T. C.] The bubbles of Canada. By the author of "The clockmaker." [The dedication is signed: S.S.] 332p. *8°.* 1839.

30954 HALLIDAY, SIR A. A letter to the Right Honble. the Secretary at War, on sickness and mortality in the West Indies; being a review of Captain Tulloch's statistical report. 63p. *8°.* 1839.

30955 HEAD, SIR F. B., *Bart.* A narrative. By Sir Francis B. Head, Bart....Second edition. [With 'Appendix A. Memorandum on the Aborigines of North America. Appendix B. Addresses to Sir Francis Head, Bart. from the legislatures of the British North American colonies, &c.&c.&c. on his resignation of the government of Upper Canada'.] 488, 38p. *8°.* 1839.

30956 HUNT, THORNTON L. Canada and South Australia. A commentary on that part of the Earl of Durham's Report which relates to the disposal of waste lands and emigration. In three papers, delivered at the South Australian rooms, No. 5 Adam Street, Strand. 95p. *8°.* 1839.

30957 LAMBTON, J. G., *Earl of Durham.* The report and despatches of the Earl of Durham, Her Majesty's High Commissioner and Governor-General of British North America. 423p. *8°.* 1839.

30958 LETTER to Viscount Melbourne on the ordinance of the Earl of Durham. By a commoner. 32p. *8°.* 1839.

30959 LONDON HIGHLAND DESTITUTION RELIEF COMMITTEE. Representation to Her Majesty's Government from the London Highland Destitution Relief Committee, urging the necessity of the immediate adoption of a systematic plan of emigration by whole families, for the relief of the destitute population of the Highlands and islands of Scotland...Submitted by a deputation from the London Committee to the...Government. June 26th, 1839. 10p. *8°.* 1839.

30960 LONG, CHARLES E. Letter to the Viscount St. Vincent, on the Jamaica House of Assembly's abandonment of the legislative functions. 32p. *8°.* 1839.

30961 MARTIN, ROBERT M. Statistics of the colonies of the British Empire...comprising the area, agriculture, commerce, manufactures...government, finances...rates of wages...&c. of each colony; with the charters and the engraved seals. From the official records of the Colonial Office. [With an appendix of official documents.] 602, 304p. *8°.* 1839.

30962 MATTHEW, P. Emigration fields. North America, the Cape, Australia, and New Zealand, describing these countries and giving a comparative view of the advantages they present to British settlers. 137p. *8°. Edinburgh & London,* 1839.

30963 MEREWETHER, H. A. Jamaica. The speech of Mr. Serjeant Merewether, at the Bar of the House of Commons, against the Bill intituled "An Act to make temporary provision for the government of Jamaica"...23d April 1839. 45p. *8°.* 1839.

30964 MERIVALE, H. Introduction to a course of lectures on colonization and colonies. Begun in March 1839. 40p. *8°.* 1839.

30965 *MOLESWORTH, SIR W., *Bart.* Speech...on seconding Mr. Ward's resolutions respecting the colonial lands, in the House of Commons, June 27, 1839. 23p. *8°.* 1839. *Bound in a volume which belonged to George Grote, and which was presented to Mrs. Grote by the author in 1840.*

30966 NEWBOLD, T. J. Political and statistical account of the British settlements in the Straits of Malacca, viz. Pinang, Malacca, and Singapore; with a history of the Malayan States on the peninsula of Malacca. 2 vols. *8°.* 1839.

30967 OGLE, N. The colony of Western Australia: manual for emigrants to that settlement or its dependencies: comprising its discovery, settlement, aborigines, land-regulations...statistical, financial and agricultural reports; also instructions and hints to settlers...With an appendix... 298p. *8°.* 1839.

30968 PRINGLE, J. W. Remarks on the state and prospects of the West Indian colonies. 20p. *8°.* 1839.

30969 ROLPH, T. Canada v. Australia; their relative merits considered in an answer to a pamphlet, by Thornton Leigh Hunt, Esq., entitled "Canada and Australia." 48p. *8°.* 1839.

30970 STEPHENS, JOHN (1806–1850). The history of the rise and progress of the new British province of South Australia; including particulars descriptive of its soil, climate, natural productions, &c....embracing also a full account of the South Australian Company, with hints to various classes of emigrants...Second edition. 224p. *8°.* 1839.

30971 STUHR, P. F. Die Geschichte der See- und Kolonialmacht des grossen Kurfürsten Friedrich Wilhelm von Brandenburg, in der Ostsee, auf der Küste von Guinea und auf den Inseln Arguin und St. Thomas, aus archivalischen Quellen dargestellt. 174p. *8°. Berlin,* 1839.

30972 WHITE, JOSEPH M., *ed.* A new collection of laws, charters and local ordinances of the governments of Great Britain, France and Spain, relating to the concessions of land in their respective colonies; together with the laws of Mexico and Texas on the same subject. To which is prefixed Judge Johnson's translation of Azo and Manuel's Institutes of the civil law of Spain... 2 vols. *8°. Philadelphia,* 1839.

30973 YOUNG, GILBERT A. The Canadian question. 83p. *8°.* 1839.

FINANCE

30974 *An **ACCOUNT** of the various societies or companies established in London, for the purpose of granting assurances on lives, with an investigation of the principles upon which they are severally grounded, and the rates of premium which they charge. 33p. *8°.* 1839. *The copy that belonged to Augustus De Morgan.*

30975 *ARABIN**, H. A plan for extending the paper currency on the security of the nation. 16p. *8°.* 1839. *The copy that belonged to George Grote.*

30976 **ARGUMENT** for the general relief of the country from taxation, and eventually from the corn laws, by an assessment on property. 16p. *8°.* 1839.

30977 **ATTWOOD**, T. Exportation of gold. Mr. T. Attwood's speech, in the House of Commons, on May 30, 1839. 8p. *8°.* *Birmingham,* [1839] *See note to no.* 20490.

30978 **AUDIFFRET**, C. L. G. D', *Marquis.* Examen des revenus publics. 135p. *8°. Paris,* 1839.

30979 **BAILLY**, A. Histoire financière de la France, depuis l'origine de la monarchie jusqu'à la fin de 1786, avec un tableau général des anciennes impositions et un état des recettes et des dépenses du Trésor royal à la même époque. 2 vols. *8°. Paris,* 1839.

30980 Our **BANKRUPT LAWS**. A letter to Robert Wallace of Kelly, Esq. M.P. By a merchant of the west. 29p. *8°. Glasgow,* 1839.

30981 **BLACKER**, W. The evils inseparable from a mixed currency, and the advantages to be secured by introducing an inconvertible national paper circulation, throughout the British Empire and its dependencies, under proper regulations. An essay. 69p. *8°. London, Dublin, &c.,* 1839. *For other editions, see* 1838 (An inconvertible national paper currency).

30982 **BLAKE**, W. Observations in reply to a pamphlet by the Rev. Richard Jones, one of the Tithe Commissioners...on the assessment of tithes to the poor's rate. 63p. *8°.* 1839.

30983 **BROUGH**, A. Conservative conversation on the corn laws, and the importance and necessity of encouraging British agriculture, between John Smith, trader, – and George Brown, farmer. 42p. *8°.* 1839.

30984 **CIESZKOWSKI**, A. D., *Hrabia.* Du crédit et de la circulation. 314p. *8°. Paris,* 1839. *The copy that belonged to Victor Considérant.*

30985 **COOK**, JOHN, *Esq.* An address to the proprietors of Bank stock, on the reduction of the dividend at the late meeting, the 14th March last. 15p. *8°.* 1839.

30986 **CORY**, I. P. A practical treatise on accounts... exhibiting a view of the discrepancies between the system of the law and of merchants, with a plan for the amendment of the law of partnership, by which such discrepancies may be reconciled and partnership disputes and accounts adjusted...Second edition. 370p. *8°.* 1839. *An adaptation of this work to official accounting, entitled:* A practical treatise on accounts, mercantile, private and official, *was published in 1840 (q.v.).*

30987 **CROWN LIFE ASSURANCE COMPANY**. Report delivered by the actuary to the Court of Proprietors of the Crown Life Assurance Company, at their second septennial meeting, held on the 24th of May,

1839...[Signed: J. M. Rainbow. With 'Tables of bonuses declared in 1832 & 1839'.] 12, [4]p. *8°.* [1839]

30988 **CRUTTWELL**, R. Reform, without revolution! in a strict union between the mercantile, trading, manufacturing, monied, agricultural, and labouring classes; on the principle of a really sound...standard capable of always adjusting itself to the wants of the people in regard both to price and taxation...By one of no party, a friend to the 'Chartists' but not to the Charter. 274p. *8°. Halesworth & London,* 1839.

30989 On the public **DEBT**, with a plan for its final extinction. 31p. *8°.* 1839. *HSF's note in the volume records an attribution to 'Abbott'. Another copy belonged to Earl De Grey.*

30990 *On the present **DERANGEMENT** of the currency of the United States, with suggestions for its better regulation. 25p. *8°.* 1839. *The copy that belonged to George Grote.*

30991 **DRUMMOND**, H. Causes which lead to a Bank Restriction Bill. 23p. *8°.* 1839.

30992 **EINERT**, C. Das Wechselrecht nach dem Bedürfniss des Wechselgeschäfts im neunzehnten Jahrhundert. 653p. *8°. Leipzig,* 1839.

30993 [**ENDERBY**, C.] Metallic currency the cause of the money crisis in England and America. Second edition. With a postscript. 43p. *8°.* 1839. *For another edition, see* 1837.

30994 **EQUITABLE SOCIETY**. Address delivered by the actuary [Mr. Morgan] to the General Court of the Equitable Society, on...the 5th December 1839. 18p. *8°.* [*London,* 1839]

30995 **FELT**, J. B. An historical account of Massachusetts currency. 259p. *8°. Boston,* 1839. *Presentation copy from the author to the Rev. William Tyler.*

30996 **FLETCHER**, ROBERT. Report of Mr. Robert Fletcher, presented to the Council of the City of Bristol, at a meeting held on the 25th day of February, 1839... To which is appended the report of Mr. Joshua Jones, referred to by Mr. Fletcher, and in the proceedings of the Charity Trustees of the 2nd October, 1837. [On the accounts relating to the Hospital of Queen Elizabeth.] 86p. *8°. Bristol,* 1839.

30997 **GAUTIER**, JEAN E. Encyclopédie du droit; ou, répertoire raisonné de législation et de jurisprudence. (Extrait du 2e volume.) Des banques et des institutions de crédit en Amérique et en Europe. 97p. *8°. Paris,* 1839. *Presentation copy from the author to 'Mr. Roullet premier président de la cour royale de Bordx'.*

30998 **GOODE**, W. Church rates. A reply to the answer of the Edinburgh Review to the two following publications; I. – A brief history of church rates...II. – A reply to the article on church rates in the Edinburgh Review, No. 134. In two letters to the Editor...Letter I. 39p. *8°.* 1839.

30999 —— Church rates, colonial Church, and national education. A reply to the answer of the Edinburgh Review, No. 134. In two letters to the editor...Letter II. 39p. *8°.* 1839.

31000 **HARLEY**, J. The currency; its influence on

the internal trade of the country: in a letter addressed to the drapers of Scotland...With a section from..."A history of prices", by Thos. Tooke, Esq. 43, 66p. *8°. Glasgow, Edinburgh, &c., 1839.*

31001 HINTS from Hamburg respecting the Stade duty. A pamphlet advocating the interest of British trade to Germany. 22p. *8°. n.p.,* 1839.

31002 Plain **HINTS** to rate payers, respecting the imposition of church-rates. Fifth edition. 8p. *8°. Church-Rate Abolition Society,* 1839.

31003 HUME, JOSEPH. On the Bank of England; and state of the currency. The speech of Joseph Hume, Esq. M.P. in the House of Commons, on the 8th of July, 1839, on a motion for "enquiry into the pecuniary transactions of the Bank of England, since the resumption of cash payments in 1821." 20p. *8°. n.p.,* 1839.

31004 HUTT, SIR W. The Stade duties considered. 74p. *8°.* 1839.

31005 *A proposed **JOINT STOCK BANK LAW,** with observations thereon. 40p. *8°. Berwick,* 1839. *The copy that belonged to George Grote.*

31006 JOPLIN, T. On our monetary system, &c.&c. with an explanation of the causes by which the pressures in the money market are produced, and a plan for their remedy... 67p. *8°.* 1839. *Presentation copy from the author to Hyde Clarke.*

31007 *KELLY,** P. The elements of book-keeping: comprising a system of merchants' accounts, founded on real business, and adapted to modern practice: with an appendix on exchanges, banking, and other commercial subjects...The eleventh edition. 240p. *8°.* 1839. *The copy that belonged to Augustus De Morgan. See also 1847.*

31008 LINDSAY, JOHN. A view of the coinage of Ireland, from the invasion of the Danes to the reign of George IV.... 143p. *4°. Cork, Dublin, &c.,* 1839.

31009 LOGAN, WILLIAM H. The Scotish [sic] banker; or, a popular exposition of the practice of banking in Scotland. 134p. *12°. Edinburgh, London, &c.,* 1839. *See also 1844.*

31010 MAILLARD, N. A proposed national guarantee for the interest of foreign loans raised and made payable in the United Kingdom. 15p. *8°.* 1839.

31011 MERCANTILE COMMITTEE ON POSTAGE, London. [*Endorsed:*] Reduction of postage. Report of the Mercantile Committee...[With a printed covering letter on p.1, dated 'April 1839' signed in manuscript by W. H. Ashurst.] 3p. *fol.* [1839] *The copy that belonged to S. J. Loyd, Baron Overstone, and was formerly among his papers, for which see vol. III, MS. 804.*

31012 METCALFE, W. The principle and law of assessing property to the poor's rate, under the 43rd of Elizabeth, cap. 2, stated and illustrated by numerous adjudged cases, and the method of assessment practised in Glasgow and Paisley, with remarks on the "Parochial Assessment Act," Mr. Shaw Lefevre's Declaratory Bill, and the means for obtaining an equitable settlement of the rating question. In a letter, addressed...to...the Earl of Hardwicke. 45p. *8°. Royston, London, &c.,* 1839.

31013 MILLER, C. The principles of Mr. Shaw Lefevre's Parochial Assessments Bill, and the Tithe Commutation Act, compared. In a letter to the Rev. Richard Jones, M.A., one of the Tithe Commissioners... 51p. *8°.* 1839.

31014 MILLER, SAMUEL, *barrister.* Suggestions for a general equalization of the land tax: with a view to provide the means of reducing or abolishing the malt duties: and a statement of the legal rights and remedies of persons unequally assessed to land tax in particular districts... 61p. *8°.* 1839. *See also* 1843.

31015 NOEL, HON. B. W. A letter to the Right Honourable Lord Viscount Melbourne, on church extension...Printed for the Christian Influence Society. [A plea for a government grant for building new churches.] 30p. *12°.* 1839.

31016 NORWICH UNION LIFE INSURANCE SOCIETY. Report of the London committee appointed by the policy holders of the Norwich Union Life Insurance Society, at a meeting...on 27th November...With an appendix, containing the first report of the examiners and the last-rendered accounts of the Society. 34[38]p. *8°.* 1839.

31017 NOTICE sur la réclamation adressée par les habitans de Verdun, au Gouvernement anglais, pour une somme de trois millions cinq mille francs. (Cent quarante mille livres sterling.) 27p. *8°.* 1839.

31018 PAGE, R. A critical examination of the twelve resolutions of Mr. Joseph Hume, respecting the loan of fifteen millions for slave compensation: also, a review of the financial operations of the British Government since 1794... 278p. *8°.* 1839.

31019 [PEDIE, J.] The causes of the distress of the country and of the sufferings of the people laid open, in an exposition of the derangement of the currency, and of the free trade system of modern economists. 42p. *8°. Edinburgh,* 1839. *Another edition, revised and re-written, The derangement of the currency the cause of the distress of the country, was published in 1840 (q.v.).*

31020 PESTALOZZI, L. Die Münzwirren der westlichen Schweiz nebst dem Versuche ihrer Lösung. 55p. *8°. Zürich,* 1839.

31021 PYM, JOHN (*fl.* 1839–1858). A remedy for the evils of banking. Dedicated by permission to the Right Hon. T. Spring Rice, Chancellor of the Exchequer. 32p. *8°.* 1839.

31022 RAGUET, C. A treatise on currency and banking, addressed to John W. Cowell, Esq. agent of the Bank of England in the United States. 262p. *8°.* 1839. *See also* 1840.

31023 REMARKS on the currency and the National Debt. [The foreword is signed: Friend to his country.] 35p. *8°. London & Taunton,* 1839. *A copy in the Kress Library (C 4980) has a contemporary(?) manuscript note on the title-page, attributing the work to 'Rev. Codrington of Bridgewater'.*

31024 RICE, THOMAS S., *Baron Monteagle.* The speech of the Right Honourable the Chancellor of the Exchequer, on the Budget, and postage duties, in the House of Commons, on...July 5th, 1839. From Hansard's 1839–1856 Parliamentary debates, session 1839. 46p. *12°.* [*London,*] 1839. *In a volume of his own speeches extracted from Hansard and bound up for Lord Monteagle at a later date, with a manuscript contents list.*

31025 SAULNIER, A. Recherches historiques sur le droit de douane depuis les temps les plus reculés jusqu'à la Révolution de 1789...Ouvrage présenté à M. le Conseiller d'État, Directeur de l'Administration des Douanes. 200p. *8°. Paris,* 1839.

For **SCOTTISH PROVIDENT INSTITUTION.** Proceedings at the first[–twelfth] annual general meeting of contributors, 1839–51, *see* vol. III, *Periodicals list,* Proceedings...

31026 SMITH, JOHN F. Proposed alterations in the system of joint stock banking; with a defence of the small note currency of Scotland. In a letter to the Right Honourable the Chancellor of the Exchequer. 47p. *8°. Edinburgh, Glasgow, &c.,* 1839.

31027 TROTTER, A. Observations on the financial position and credit of such of the states of the North American Union as have contracted public debts: comprising an account of the manner in which the sums raised by each state have been applied, and a consideration of the probable effects of such application... 455p. *8°.* 1839. *Presentation copy, with inscription, from the author to Sir Henry Lindesay Bethune.*

31028 TUCKER, G. The theory of money and banks investigated. 412p. *8°. Boston,* 1839.

31029 UNITED STATES OF AMERICA. *Congress.* The Sub-Treasury Bill...A bill more effectually to secure the public money in the hands of officers and agents of the government, and to punish public defaulters. [Ordered to be printed by the House of Representatives of the State of Vermont, Oct. 15, 1839.] 16p. *8°. n.p.* [1839]

31030 VOSTER, E. Arithmetic, in whole and broken numbers, digested...and chiefly adapted to the trade of Ireland. To which are added, instructions for bookkeeping; with the Dignity of trade in Great Britain and Ireland, extracted from the Mercantile library; or, complete English tradesman...Revised by Daniel Voster. A new edition, corrected, revised, and improved, by William Gutteridge...To which is now annexed, the butter trade of Cork... 240p. *12°. Cork,* 1839.

31031 WILSON, HORACE H. The Graeco-Bactrian coins. From the proceedings of the Numismatic Society of London, 1837–38. 32p. *8°.* [1839]

TRANSPORT

31032 BELGIUM. *Ministère des Travaux Publics.* Travaux publics en Belgique. Chemins de fer et routes ordinaires. 1830–1839. Rapport présenté aux Chambres législatives le 12 novembre 1839, par M. le Ministre des Travaux publics. 151p. *fol. Bruxelles,* [1839] *Presentation copy, with inscription, from the Belgian Minister, M. Nothomb, to Thomas Drummond (1797–1840), Undersecretary of State for Ireland. See also* 1845.

31033 BERMINGHAM, T. Irish railways. A full and interesting report of the public proceedings on this... question, with extracts from...journals...on foreign (especially those in Belgium) and English railways...Also observations on the advantageous prospects on forming railways in Ireland... 24, 50, 8p. *8°. London & Dublin,* 1839.

31034 BOURNE, JOHN C. Drawings of the London and Birmingham Railway, by John C. Bourne, with an historical and descriptive account by John Britton... xxxvii plates, 26p. *fol.* 1839.

31035 BRADSHAW, G. Tables of the gradients to Bradshaw's map of the railways, of Great Britain, containing particulars of the lengths, levels, and gradients, of all the principal railways in the kingdom... 26p. *8°. Manchester & London,* 1839.

31036 —— [Another edition. With the map.] 30p. *8°. Manchester & London,* 1839.

31037 BREES, S. C. Appendix to Railway practice, containing a copious abstract of the whole...of the evidence given upon the London and Birmingham, and Great Western Railway Bills...To which is added, a glossary of technical terms...and details of Hawthorne's celebrated locomotive engine, for the Paris and Versailles Railway. 373p. *4°.* 1839. *For editions of* Railway practice, *see* 1837.

31038 CLEGG, SAMUEL (1781–1861). Clegg's patent atmospheric railway. 20p. *8°.* 1839.

31039 DAY, JAMES. A practical treatise on the construction and formation of railways...Second edition. 210p. *8°.* 1839.

31040 DRAKE, JAMES *publisher.* Dedicated, by permission, to the chairman and directors of both companies. Drake's road book of the London and Birmingham and Grand Junction Railways...to which is appended, The visitor's guide to Birmingham, Liverpool, and Manchester. 112, 147p. *8°. London, Birmingham, &c.,* [1839]

31041 ENGLAND. *Laws, etc.* Anno primo Victoriæ Reginæ. Cap. cxxxiii. An Act to amend the Act relating to the Commercial Railway Company ⟨17th July 1837.⟩ p.5693–5695. *fol.* 1839.

31042 —— —— Anno secundo & tertio Victoriæ Reginæ. Cap. xcv. An Act for extending the line of the railway between London and Blackwall called "The Commercial Railway;" and for amending the Acts relating thereto. ⟨17th August 1839.⟩ p.2569–2608. *fol.* 1839.

31043 —— *Parliament. House of Commons.* In the House of Commons. Minutes of evidence taken before the Committee on the Commercial Railway Bill...⟨Copy from Mr. Gurney's short-hand notes.⟩ [Proceedings of the Committee from 18 April–7 May 1839.] 10 parts. *fol.* 1839. *The Rastrick copy.*

31044 FREELING, A. The London and Southampton Railway companion, containing a complete description of every thing worthy of attention on the line...with guides to Southampton and the Isle Wight; and a map... 191p. *12°. London, Liverpool, &c.,* 1839.

31045 GUYONNEAU DE PAMBOUR, F. M., *Comte.* The theory of the steam engine... 350p. *8°.* 1839. *For another edition, see* 1837.

31046 A HANDBOOK for travellers along the London and Birmingham Railway; with the fare and time tables, &c. corrected to the present day; and portions extracted...from Roscoe's larger work...147p. *12°. London & Birmingham,* [1839] *The timetable is undated.*

31047 —— [Another issue.] 147p. *12°. London & Birmingham,* [1839] *The time table is dated: Oct. 1839.*

31048 HULL AND SELBY RAILWAY COMPANY. Hull and Selby Railway, connecting Liverpool with Hull, through Manchester and Leeds...Report of the Directors...laid before the proprietors, at their third general meeting...February 1, 1839. 24p. *8°. Hull*, 1839. *See also* 1836.

31049 KOLLMANN, G. A. Railway papers. – No. 1. Some observations on the imperfections of the present system of constructing railways; with an account of the new method of construction invented by Mr. Kollmann. 16p. *8°*. 1839.

31050 LECOUNT, P. The history of the railway connecting London and Birmingham: containing its progress from the commencement. To which are added, a popular description of the locomotive engine: and a sketch of the geological features of the line. [With lists of the directors and the engineers.] 118, [2]p. *8°. London & Birmingham*, [1839] *The Rastrick copy.*

31051 —— A practical treatise on railways, explaining their construction and management...being the article "Railways" in the seventh edition of the Encyclopædia Britannica, with additional details. 422p. *12°. Edinburgh*, 1839. *The Rastrick copy.*

31052 LIVERPOOL AND MANCHESTER RAILWAY COMPANY. Liverpool & Manchester Railway. The Treasurer's report to the Directors on the comparative disbursements of the London and Birmingham and Liverpool and Manchester Railways. 21p. *8°. Liverpool*, 1839.

31053 LONDON AND BIRMINGHAM RAILWAY COMPANY. London and Birmingham Railway. Tables of fares and rates, distances and regulations, including hackney-coach fares in London and Birmingham ...New edition, with the latest alterations. 32p. *12°. London & Birmingham*, 1839.

31054 MACKAIN, D. Report relative to the discussions concerning the weir across the Clyde at Jamaica-Street, between the Clyde Trustees and the Bridge Trustees on the one part, and the Glasgow Water Company on the other; in connexion with the report of Mr. Bald. 20p. *8°. Glasgow*, 1839.

31055 MANCHESTER AND BIRMINGHAM RAILWAY COMPANY. Correspondence between the Manchester and Birmingham and the Grand Junction Railway Companies, with a prefatory letter [by Thomas Ashton] to the shareholders of the former company. 58p. *8°. Manchester*, [1839] *The Rastrick copy.*

31056 MARTIN, WILLIAM (1772–1851). The follies of the day, or the effects of a gold chain; with observations on the unnecessary expenses of the North Shields Railway ... 8p. *8°. Newcastle*, [1839]

31057 —— The philosopher's method of making a railway from the Red Sea to the Levant, through the sandy desert of Suez, which will save 12,000 miles of sailing. [With 'A philosophical poem'.] 8p. *8°. Newcastle*, [1839]

31058 MINIMUS, *pseud.* A plan for the improvement of the Port of London in the year 1840... 68p. *12°.* [1839]

31059 NEILL, P. An examination of the "Reply for the directors" of the Edinburgh, Leith, & Newhaven Railway Company. March 1839. 16p. *8°. Edinburgh, Liverpool, &c.*, 1839. *The Rastrick copy.*

31060 NEWCASTLE AND CARLISLE RAILWAY COMPANY. Report of the Managing Committee to the Directors...March 18th, 1839. [Signed: Benj. Thompson, Geo. Johnson, Nichs. Wood.] 7p. *8°. Newcastle-upon-Tyne*, [1839] *See also* 1835, 1837, 1838.

31061 NICHOLSON, P. The guide to railway masonry; comprising a complete treatise on the oblique arch. In three parts... 10, vl[lvi], 50p. *8°. London & Newcastle*, 1839. *The Rastrick copy. See also* 1846.

31062 The **NOTTINGHAM** and Derby Railway companion... 47p. *8°. London, Nottingham: R. Allen, &c.,* [1839 ?] *The Rastrick copy.*

31063 River **OUZE** outfall improvement. At a general meeting of parties interested in drainage and navigation through the River Ouze and the Lynn Deeps, held...1st day of July, 1839. [With the report, signed by John Rennie.] 13p. *4°. London*, [1839]

31064 PIM, JAMES. Irish railways. A letter to the Right Hon. Frederick Shaw... 16p. *8°.* 1839.

31065 QUIN, M. J. A letter to the House of Commons, on railways in Ireland. 40p. *8°.* 1839.

31066 RAWSON, SIR R. W. On railways in Belgium ...Extracted from the Journal of the Statistical Society of London, February, 1839. 16p. *8°. n.p.* [1839]

31067 A **REPORT** of the proceedings at two public meetings, held at the Thatched House Tavern, on the 13th and 20th of April, 1839, for the purpose of taking into consideration the necessity of forming railways throughout Ireland. Called by Thomas Bermingham Esq. ...chairman of the General Irish Rail-road Committee. 48p. *8°.* 1839.

31068 The **ROADS** and railroads, vehicles, and modes of travelling, of ancient and modern countries; with accounts of bridges, tunnels, and canals, in various parts of the world. 340p. *12°.* 1839. *The Rastrick copy.*

31069 ROSCOE, T. The London and Birmingham Railway; with the home and country scenes on each side of the line; including sketches of Kenilworth, Leamington ...&c. By Thomas Roscoe...assisted in the historical details by Peter Lecount... 192p. *8°. London & Birmingham*, [1839]

31070 SÉGUIN, M. De l'influence des chemins de fer et de l'art de les tracer et de les construire. 501p. *8°. Paris & Londres*, 1839.

31071 SMYTH, GEORGE L. Railways and public works in Ireland. Observations upon the Report of the Irish Railway Commissioners, with a review of the failures which have already occurred under the different government boards and commissions connected with public works in Ireland... 86p. *8°.* 1839. *Presentation copy, with inscription, from the author.*

31072 STEPHENSON, G. Report of George Stephenson, Esquire, [to the Directors of the Chester & Crewe Railway Company] on the comparative merits of the railway from Chester to Holyhead, and of that from Wolverhampton to Porthdynllaen. 8p. *8°. Chester*, 1839.

31073 STOCKTON AND DARLINGTON RAILWAY. Stockton & Darlington Railway coaches, commencing March [*blank*] 1839. [A poster, with time-tables of trains.] *s.sh.fol. Darlington*, [1839]

31074 STOCKTON AND DARLINGTON RAILWAY. Stockton and Darlington Railway coaches. Summer of 1839...[A poster, advertising connections of coaches with trains.] *s.sh.fol. Darlington*, [1839] *See also* 1837, 1842.

31075 TEISSERENC, E. Les travaux publics en Belgique et les chemins de fer en France. Rapport adressé à M. le Ministre des Travaux Publics. 672p. *8°. Paris*, 1839.

31076 VAUGHAN, William (1752–1850). Memoir of William Vaughan, Esq. F.R.S. with miscellaneous pieces relative to docks, commerce... 134p. *8°.* 1839.

31077 —— Tracts on docks and commerce, printed between the years 1793 & 1800, and now first collected; with an introduction, memoir, and miscellaneous pieces. 134, 27, 24, 23, 8p. *8°.* 1839. *Some of the pieces in this collection were first issued together with the title* A collection of tracts on wet docks for the Port of London, *in 1797 (q.v.).*

31078 WAREHOUSES upon the dock quays, as necessary to the promotion of the trade and prosperity of Liverpool, and of the neighbouring towns and counties in mercantile connexion therewith. 24p. *8°. Liverpool*, [1839]

31079 WYLD, J. The London and Southampton Railway guide...with a guide to the environs of Southampton, the Isles of Wight, Jersey, and Guernsey, and the opposite coast of France. 197p. *12°.* 1839. *Binding title: Wyld's South Western London and Southampton Railway guide. See also 1842.*

SOCIAL CONDITIONS

31080 An **ACCOUNT** of the deaths by destitution & starvation of the four children of Thomas Hardy, weaver, of Baguley, in the Altrincham Union...with the depositions of his neighbours and others. 12p. *12°. Manchester*, [1839] *The Oastler copy.*

31081 A friendly **APPEAL**, or word of advice, to the middle and working classes of Great Britain: (but more especially as relates to the latter class:) with an earnest exhortation to them...to wage war against the taxes... with some general remarks, and an exposition of the impolicy of the government system of taxation. 16p. *8°.* 1839.

31082 BISHOPS STORTFORD FRIENDLY SOCIETY. Rules of the Bishops Stortford Friendly Society. [Signed: Frederick Chaplin, Joseph Fairman, William Taylor, John Johnstone, hon. sec.] 14p. *8°. Bishops Stortford*, 1839.

31083 [**BOADE**, W.] Observations on the present system of education; with some hints for its improvement. Sixth edition. 24p. *8°.* 1839.

31084 BOWEN, J. New Poor Law. The Bridgewater case. Is killing in an union workhouse criminal, if sanctioned by the Poor Law Commissioners? A question raised on certain facts deposed to on oath before a late Committee of the House of Lords and...submitted to the ...consideration of both Lords and Commons. 89p. *8°.* 1839. *The Oastler copy.*

31085 BROUGHAM, H. P., *Baron Brougham and Vaux.* A letter on national education, to the Duke of Bedford, K.G. from Lord Brougham. 48p. *8°. Edinburgh & London*, 1839.

31086 BUCK, J. A letter on prison discipline, addressed to the Mayor and magistrates of Liverpool. By the Rev. J. Buck...chaplain of the Liverpool Borough Gaol. 24p. *8°. London & Liverpool*, 1839.

31087 BULL, G. S. The oppressors of the poor, and the poor their own oppressors. A sermon preached at... Bradford, Yorkshire, on...August 11th, 1839. 20p. *8°. Bradford & London*, [1839] *The Oastler copy.*

31088 CHANNING, William E. Self-culture. An address introductory to the Franklin Lectures, delivered at Boston, United States, September 1838. 28p. *8°. London & Manchester*, 1839. *HSF notes that this copy belonged to Lloyd Jones.*

31089 *—— [Another edition.] 56p. *8°.* 1839. *The copy that belonged to George Grote. For another edition, see 1838.*

31090 CHILDREN'S FRIEND SOCIETY. Report of the general committee of management of the...

Society, presented at their ninth annual meeting, held on May 16, 1839... 61p. *8°.* 1839. *The copy that belonged to William Allen.*

31091 CLOSE, F. Pauperism traced to its true sources by the aid of Holy Scripture and experience. A sermon in two parts. Second edition. 24p. *12°. London...Cheltenham*, 1839. *The Oastler copy.*

31092 CONNECTICUT. *Board of Commissioners of Common Schools.* First annual report of the Board of Commissioners...together with the first annual report of the Secretary of the Board [Henry Barnard, 2d.], May, 1839. 64p. *8°. Hartford*, 1839.

31093 COW CLUB, *Whitwell.* Articles of a Cow Club, held at the house of Mrs. Sarah Webster, the sign of the Boot and Shoe, in Whitwell. Meetings to be held on the first Monday in April, and on the first Monday in October. 8p. *8°. Worksop*, 1839.

31094 DE BARY, R. B. A charm against Chartism; in which the title of the operative is set forth, and his estate ascertained: comprising thoughts on education, and the expediency of instituting public games. 19p. *8°.* 1839.

31095 DEMOCRITUS, *pseud.* A medical, moral, and Christian dissection of tee-totalism. Fifth edition. 12p. *12°. Newcastle*, [1839]

31096 DUNDEE. Report on the pauperism of Dundee by a Committee appointed at a meeting of the Magistrates, Heritors, and General Session, on 5th February 1839, to consider the present mode of providing for the poor...and whether...it would be expedient to erect a poorhouse. Presented at an adjourned parish meeting, 7th May, 1839. [Signed: P. H. Thoms, convenor.] 33p. *8°. Dundee*, 1839. *The copy presented to Robert Chambers (1802–1871).*

31097 DUNMOW Union Workhouse. [Letters on the alleged insanitary character of the site.] 30p. *8°.* [*London*, 1839?] *Without a title-page.*

For the **EDUCATIONAL MAGAZINE**, *see vol.* III, *Periodicals list.*

31098 EDWARDS, F. Brief treatise on the law of gaming, horse-racing & wagers; with a collection of the Statutes in force in reference to those subjects... 141p. *12°.* 1839.

31099 ENGLAND. *Commissioners appointed to Inquire as to the Best Means of Establishing an Efficient Constabulary Force in...England and Wales.* First report of the Commissioners...[Signed: Charles Shaw Lefevre, Charles Rowan, Edwin Chadwick.] 416p. *8°.* 1839.

31100 —— *Commissioners for Inquiring concerning Chari-*

ties. An account of all the charity & trust estates, belonging to the parish of Hinckley...Taken from...the 32nd Report of the "Commissioners for Enquiring concerning Charities in England and Wales." By William Grant, Esquire, one of the Commissioners... 36p. *8°*. *Hinckley*, 1839.

31101 —— —— The charities in the county of Somerset. Selected from the voluminous reports of the Commissioners... 2 vols. *fol.* 1839. *The words 'County of Somerset' and the volume numbers are supplied in manuscript on the title-pages.*

31102 —— *Laws, etc.* An Act for better paving, improving, and regulating the streets of the Metropolis, and removing and preventing nuisances and obstructions therein. ⟨Passed 16th June 1817.⟩ [With an index.] 208, [20]p. *8°*. 1839.

31103 —— —— An Act for establishing a permanent fund for the relief...of skippers and keelmen employed on the River Tyne...and also for the relief of the widows and children of such skippers and keelmen. With the bye-laws of the Society [of Keelmen on the River Tyne] established by the said Act. Also, an Act for altering and amending an Act of his late Majesty. 1 George IV. – sess. 1820. 20p. *8°*. *Newcastle*, 1839.

31104 —— —— An Act (1° & 2° Victoriæ, c. 56.) for the more effectual relief of the destitute poor in Ireland; with notes, forms, and an index. 203, [40]p. *8°*. 1839. *For another edition, see 1838.*

31105 —— —— An Act [2 & 3 Vic. cap. 47] for further improving the police in and near the Metropolis. 16p. *8°*. [*London*, 1839]

31106 —— —— Berger's edition of the Penny Postage Act. The new Act (2 & 3 Victoria, cap. 52.) for establishing a uniform penny postage. Passed 17th August, 1839. With notes by R. Thompson, Esq. 8p. *8°*. *G. Berger*, [1839]

31107 —— Parliament. *House of Commons.* Report from Select Committee [appointed 1838] on Metropolis police offices. 55p. *8°*. 1839.

31108 —— —— *House of Lords.* Extracts from the Report of the Select Committee of the House of Lords respecting the operation of the Poor Law Amendment Act. 70p. *8°*. 1839. *The Oastler copy.*

31109 —— *Poor Law Commission [1834–1847].* Reports on the sanatory state of the labouring classes, as affected chiefly by the situation and construction of their dwellings, in and about the Metropolis. Extracted from the fourth and fifth annual reports of the Poor Law Commissioners. 56p. *8°*. 1839.

31110 The **FACTORY** lad; or, the life of Simon Smike; exemplifying the horrors of white slavery. 188p. *8°*. [1839] *Published in 24 parts. The Oastler copy.*

31111 *FAUQUET, J. Considérations sur le régime des prisons, adressées au Conseil Général de la Seine-Inférieure, dans sa session de 1839. 45p. *8°*. *Rouen*, 1839. *The copy that belonged to George Grote.*

31112 GERANDO, J. M. DE, *Baron.* De la bienfaisance publique... 4 vols. *8°*. *Paris*, 1839.

31113 —— Nouvelle édition... 2 vols. *8°*. *Bruxelles*, 1839.

31114 GRINDROD, R. B. Bacchus: an essay on the nature, causes, effects, and cure of intemperance...Third thousand. 535p. *8°*. 1839. *The Turner copy. See also 1843.*

31115 HART, J. The cause of the widow and the fatherless defended by the God of the Bible; being the substance of a sermon delivered...at Charlestown, in Ashton-under-Lyne, on...April 31st, 1839...dedicated to the congregation of the Rev. Joseph Rayner Stephens ... 24p. *12°*. *Manchester*, [1839] *The Oastler copy.*

31116 HIGGINBOTTOM, J. Alcohol as a medicine. 2p. *8°*. [*London*, 1839] *The Turner copy.*

31117 HILL, SIR ROWLAND (1795–1879). A report on the French Post-Office, in a letter addressed to the Rt. Hon. the Chancellor of the Exchequer. 14p. *fol. n.p.* [1839]

31118 [HOLLAND, GEORGE C.] An inquiry into the moral, social, and intellectual condition of the industrious classes of Sheffield. Part I. The abuses and evils of charity, especially of medical charitable institutions. 132p. *8°*. 1839.

31119 HOPE, C. D. Thoughts on national education, connected with other subjects. 12p. *12°*. *Manchester*, 1839.

31120 HOWARD, RICHARD B. An inquiry into the morbid effects of deficiency of food, chiefly with reference to their occurrence amongst the destitute poor... 77p. *8°*. *London & Manchester*, 1839.

For the **HULL TEMPERANCE PIONEER**, *see* vol. III, *Periodicals list.*

31121 [JERROLD, D. W.] The hand-book of swindling. By the late Captain Barabbas Whitefeather... Edited by John Jackdaw. With illustrations by Phiz. 87p. *8°*. 1839.

31122 *[KAY, afterwards **KAY-SHUTTLE-WORTH**, SIR JAMES P., *Bart.*] Recent measures for the promotion of education in England. Third edition. 92p. *8°*. 1839.

31123 [——] Seventh edition. 92p. *8°*. 1839.

31124 [——] Ninth edition. 92p. *8°*. 1839.

31125 [——] Tenth edition. 92p. *8°*. 1839. *See also* 1840.

31126 KINGSLEY, J. Preparations for the session of 1839. On the criminal returns of Ireland...For private circulation. 76p. *8°*. *Dublin*, 1839.

31127 LEVISON, J. L. Lecture on the hereditary tendency of drunkenness...108p. *12°*. [1839] *The Turner copy.*

31128 LOCK HOSPITAL, *London.* An account of the Lock Hospital; to which is added an account of the Lock Asylum. 2 vols. *8°*. *Pimlico*, 1839. *See also* 1796.

31129 LOGAN, WILLIAM (1813–1879). The principles of tee-totalism maintained and illustrated; or the nature, causes, evils, and remedy of intemperance. A lecture...Second edition. 24p. *12°*. *Shaw*, 1839. *The Turner copy.*

31130 LONDON JOURNEYMEN'S TRADES HALL. Laws for the constitution and government of the London Journeymen's Trades Hall, 1839. Enrolled according to Act of Parliament. 24p. *8°*. [1839] *The copy issued to William Lovett when he became a shareholder, with a certificate on the verso of the title-page, completed in manuscript.*

31131 MACMILLAN, A. Teetotalism triumphant: a tragi-comic dramatic tale, in five acts. 59p. *12°*. *Annan*, 1839. *The Turner copy.*

31132 MANCHESTER NIGHT ASYLUM FOR THE DESTITUTE POOR. The first annual report of the Manchester Night Asylum for the Destitute and Houseless Poor, for the year 1838, with an account of the proceedings at the annual meeting held in the Town Hall, Manchester, February 11th, 1839. Established 3rd February, 1838. 33p. *8°. Manchester*, 1839.

31133 MARTIN, WILLIAM (1772–1851). The philosopher's letter to the Queen and the British government on the new national education Bill. 4p. *8°. Newcastle,* [1839]

31134 —— The spiritual thunder-storm of divine truth upon infidels and mock Christians...shewing that the play-house is more esteemed than God's divine place of worship. 4p. *8°. Newcastle,* [1839]

31135 METROPOLITAN POLICE. Case of the City considered. By a citizen of the Metropolis. 38p. *8°.* 1839.

31136 MILES, WILLIAM AUGUSTUS (*fl.* 1826–1839). Poverty, mendicity and crime; or, the facts, examinations, &c. upon which the Report was founded, presented to the House of Lords by W. A. Miles, Esq. To which is added a dictionary of the flash or cant language, known to every thief and beggar. Edited by H. Brandon Esq. 168p. *8°.* 1839.

For **NEW BRITISH AND FOREIGN TEMPERANCE SOCIETY,** The journal, 1839–40, *see* vol. III, *Periodicals list,* Journal of the New British and Foreign Temperance Society.

For —— [Tracts] Nos. 1–142 [1839?–40], *see* vol. III, *Periodicals list.*

31137 NIHILL, D. Prison discipline in its relations to society and individuals as deterring from crime, and as conducive to personal reformation. 92p. *8°.* 1839.

31138 NORTHAMPTON GENERAL LUNATIC ASYLUM. The first annual report of the... Asylum, opened August 1, 1838. [With the Medical Superintendent's first annual report.] 24, 7p. *8°. Northampton,* 1839. *See also* 1842.

31139 OASTLER, R. Richard Oastler's letter to the nobility, clergy, farmers and shopkeepers, of the County of Nottingham. 8p. *8°. n.p.* [1839] *Oastler's own copy.*

31140 ONION, E. J. W. M. Elkins, of No. 4, Cook's Court, Carey Street, Lincoln's Inn Fields. [Begin.] Whereas, I, Edmund John Onion, of 16a, Lower Eaton Street, Pimlico, did employ the above individual to compel one Frederick James...late a lodger of mine, to pay his rent...[A complaint of Elkins' conduct in a case of debt. Dated: Aug. 5, 1839.] *s.sh.fol.* [*London,* 1839]

31141 OPERATIVE TIN-PLATE WORKERS' SOCIETY, London. Rules and regulations of the... Society, held at the Ben Jonson, 27, Great Bath Street, Cold Bath Square, Clerkenwell...C. Johnson, secretary, 1, Wood Street, King Square, Goswell Road. 12p. *12°.* 1839.

31142 *The unemployed **OPERATIVES**...[Report of a public meeting on the best means of relieving the distresses of the unemployed poor of Leeds, and notice of a further meeting to hear Robert Owen. Dated: Leeds, December 26th, 1839.] *s.sh.4°. n.p.* [1839] *The FWA copy that belonged to William Pare.*

31143 OSBORNE, LORD S. G. Hints for the ameli-oration of the moral condition of a village population... 92p. *12°. London, Eton, &c.,* [1839]

31144 PEGGS, J. Capital punishment: the importance of its abolition. A prize essay. 117p. *12°.* [1839]

31145 PERRY, SAMUEL. Third edition. The powers under the new Poor Law, of vestry meetings, boards of guardians, overseers and churchwardens, justices of the peace, and the Poor Law Commissioners; considered in a letter to Lord John Russell...To which is annexed, the petition of the author to the Queen in Council. 38p. *8°. London & Brentwood,* 1839. *For another edition, see* 1838.

31146 PHILLIPS, WILLIAM S. Considerations on the increase and progress of crime, accompanied by documentary evidence as to the...necessity of a revision ...of the existing penal statutes. With a view to the abolition of corporeal punishment; and more particularly the awful penalty of death. 83p. *8°. Liverpool,* 1839.

31147 PHIPPS, CONSTANTINE H., *Marquess of Normanby.* State of Ireland. Speech of the Marquess of Normanby, in the House of Lords, March 21, 1839, on Lord Roden's motion, for a committee to inquire into the state of crime in Ireland since MDCCCXXXV. 65p. *8°.* 1839.

31148 The **POOR** and the poor laws; the beer and the beer laws; corn laws and machinery; emigration and waste land. A concise view of the present state of society in this country, and the partiality of the present working of the laws, as regards the moral and religious character of its inhabitants; especially as to the state of the lower orders. By a poor man's friend. 48p. *8°.* 1839.

For the **POPULAR LECTURER,** *see* vol. III, *Periodicals list.*

For the **REGENERATOR AND ADVOCATE FOR THE UNREPRESENTED,** *see* vol. III, *Periodicals list.*

31149 *A **REPORT** of a scene at Windsor Castle respecting the uniform penny postage. 8p. *8°.* [*London,*] 1839. *The copy that belonged to George Grote.*

31150 The **RIGHTS** of necessity, and the treatment of the necessitous by various nations. [An introduction to 'The laws of the Hebrews, relating to the poor and the stranger, from the "Mischna-Hathora" of the Rabbi Maimonides: now first translated into English, by James W. Peppercorne' the second part entitled 'The Judaic law as opposed to English military-law, gaol-for-debt-law, the pauper-law, and factory-slave-law'.] 55, 2–31p. *8°.* 1839. *The copy presented by J. P. Cobbett to Oastler, who attributed it to Cobbett in the manuscript index to his pamphlet collection. For editions of Moses ben Maimon's work, see* 1838.

31151 ROBERTS, S. Mary Wilden, a victim to the new Poor Law, or the Malthusian and Marcusian system exposed; in a letter to His Grace the Duke of Portland. 50p. *12°.* 1839.

31152 —— The Rev. Dr. Pye Smith and the new Poor Law. 70p. *8°. London & Sheffield,* 1839.

31153 —— The wickedness of the new Poor Law, addressed to serious Christians of all denominations, with an appeal to the clergy. 8p. *8°. Sheffield,* 1839.

31154 SAINT MARTIN IN THE FIELDS, *Parish of.* St. Martin in the Fields. Report on the subject of casual poor admitted by relief tickets into the workhouse of the parish of St. Martin in the Fields. 8p. *8°.* 1839.

31155 SAINT MARTIN'S SUBSCRIPTION LIBRARY. First report of the St. Martin's Subscription Library, in connexion with that founded by Archbishop Tenison. 15p. *8⁰*. [1839]

31156 SHERMAN, J. The duty of Christians towards the intemperate. A sermon preached at Surrey Chapel, on ...November 19th, 1839. 19p. *8⁰*. [1839] *The Turner copy.*

31157 SHULDHAM, W. L. Remarks on the small loan-fund system, addressed to the Duke of Wellington. 35p. *8⁰*. 1839.

31158 [SLEIGH, .] Published by request. A visit to the Corporation Schools in Liverpool (April 1839.) By the late editor of the (resuscitated) Liverpool Standard. 15p. *8⁰. Liverpool,* 1839.

31159 SMITH, HERBERT. An account of a union chaplaincy, containing extracts from the chaplain's book; with some additional remarks on the treatment of the poor in connexion with the new Poor-Law, and a list of the inmates of the New Forest Union workhouse... 57p. *8⁰*. [1839]

31160 —— The poor man's advocate: or, a few words for and to the poor. In six letters. With an addenda. Parts I. & II. 6, 6, 8, 12, 8, 12, 12, 8p. *8⁰*. [1839] *A collection of 8 separately published pamphlets, reissued with a general title-page. Contents: A letter to the people of England in behalf of the deserving poor; A second letter...in behalf of the deserving poor; A letter to the bishops and parochial clergy in behalf of the deserving poor; A second letter to the bishops...in behalf of the deserving poor; A letter to the labouring classes in their own behalf; A second letter to the labouring classes in their own behalf...; An account of the situation and treatment of the women with illegitimate children in the New Forest Union Workhouse; An account (continued) of the situation...of the women with illegitimate children in the New Forest Union Workhouse. For a reissue of all the pamphlets in this collection, with others, see 1842 (The Church, God's appointed guardian of the poor).*

31161 SOCIÉTÉ PATERNELLE POUR L'ÉDUCATION MORALE, AGRICOLE ET PROFESSIONELLE DES JEUNES DÉTENUS. Fondation d'une colonie agricole de jeunes détenus à Mettray (département d'Indre-et-Loire). [With 'Statuts constitutifs de la Société Paternelle', and 'Règlement de la Colonie agricole de Mettray'.] 112p. *8⁰. Paris,* 1839. *The copy that belonged to Victor Considérant.*

31162 SOCIETY OF ANCIENT BRITONS. A brief account of the rise, progress, and present state of the most honourable and loyal Society of Ancient Britons for supporting the charity school erected at the north end of Gray's Inn Road, London... 80p. *8⁰*. 1839. *See also* 1788, 1796, 1816.

31163 —— The hundred and twenty-fifth anniversary festival of the honourable and loyal Society of Ancient Britons, celebrated in the Freemasons' Hall...March 1st, 1839. [Programme.] [4]p. *4⁰*. [*London,* 1839] *Endorsed: 1839. Anniversary festival. Welsh Charity School.*

31164 —— On Friday, March 1, 1839, will be celebrated, the hundred and twenty-fifth anniversary festival of the most honourable and loyal Society of Ancient Britons... [4]p. *4⁰*. [*London,* 1839] *Endorsed: 1839. Anniversary festival. Welsh Charity School.*

31165 STEPHENS, JOSEPH R. The political preacher: an appeal from the pulpit on behalf of the poor, an address delivered at Ashton-under-Lyne, January 6th, 1839. 40p. *8⁰. London, Manchester, &c.,* 1839. *The Oastler copy.*

31166 —— The political pulpit! A collection of sermons preached by the Rev. J. R. Stephens, in the present year ...in London, and various other places, principally in the open air; to which is added, the trial of the Rev. gentleman for uttering seditious language...at the assizes held at Chester, August 15, 1839. 120p. *8⁰*. 1839. *Published in 14 parts.*

31167 —— The Rev. J. R. Stephens in London. Three sermons preached in Shepherd and Shepherdess Fields, on Primrose Hill, and on Kennington Common, London, on...May 12, 1839. 27p. *8⁰. n.p.* [1839] *The Oastler copy.*

31168 STONE, W. Loan funds, as a means of benefiting the industrious classes. A lecture...delivered at the lecture room of the Mathematical Society, Spitalfields, November 19, 1838...with a view to the introduction of the system into the east of London. [16]p. *8⁰*. 1839.

31169 [TAYLOR, JAMES (1788–1863).] The new Poor Laws. [A reprint of an article in a newspaper.] 4p. *8⁰*. [1839 ?]

31170 THOUGHTS few and brief, touching the Government plan of education, and the Parliamentary debates thereon. By a clergyman. 48p. *8⁰*. [1839] *Author's presentation copy to the editor of the London and Westminster Review.*

31171 TRAILL, JAMES C. A letter to the Right Hon. Lord Brougham and Vaux, on the police Reports and the police Bills. 63p. *8⁰*. 1839. *Presentation copy from the author to T. Spring Rice, Baron Monteagle.*

31172 TUCKERMAN, J. Christian service to the poor in cities, unconnected with any religious denomination: a series of extracts from "The principles and results of the ministry at large" in Boston, U.S. [Edited by L. Carpenter.] 48p. *12⁰. Bristol & London,* 1839.

31173 [VINCENT, G. G.] An address to the English nation, against the new Poor Law. By the author of "The government of the mind," and "A letter to John Bowen, Esq., on the unprincipled nature of the new Poor Law, etc." 22p. *8⁰*. 1839. *The Oastler copy.*

31174 WALTER, J. A letter addressed in 1834 to the electors of Berkshire, on the new system for the management of the poor...together with speeches on the subjects connected therewith, delivered...in the House of Commons, in the two last Parliaments. 121p. *8⁰*. 1839. *For another edition, see* 1834.

31175 WHYTEHEAD, R. The claims of Christian philanthropy; or, the duty of a Christian government with respect to moral and religious education, and the manner in which its beneficial effects are counteracted by inordinate competition in trade, leading to inhumanity and intemperance. [A prize essay sponsored by the Philanthropic Society.] 258p. *8⁰*. 1839.

31176 WORKSOP POLICE AND WATCH ASSOCIATION. At the annual meeting of the subscribers held at the Red Lion Inn, in Worksop, on...the 6th day of June, 1839. Edward Woollett Wilmot Esq., in the chair. The following report was presented... 8p. *8⁰. Worksop,* [1839]

SLAVERY

31177 AMERICAN SLAVERY as it is: testimony of a thousand witnesses. 224p. *8°. New York: American Anti-Slavery Society*, 1839.

31178 BRAZILIAN SLAVE TRADE, 1838. [Return of vessels under the Portuguese flag engaged in the slave trade to the coast of Brazil, arriving at Rio de Janeiro in 1838. Reprinted from the Parliamentary Paper *Correspondence with foreign powers relating to the slave trade,* 1838.] 3p. *fol. Norwich,* [1839]

31179 BRITISH AND FOREIGN ANTI-SLAVERY SOCIETY. [*Begin.*] More than half a century has elapsed since the horrors...of the African slave trade awakened the sympathies of Britons... [Announcement of a general conference to be held in London, June, 1840. Signed: John H. Tredgold, secretary.] [2]p. *s.sh.fol.* [*London,* 1839]

31180 —— Address. 2p. *fol.* [1839]

31181 BUXTON, Sir Thomas F., *Bart.* The African slave trade. 240p. *8°.* 1839. *Presentation copy, with inscription, from the author to H. Warburton. See also* 1840.

31182 CHANNING, William E. Remarks on the slavery question, in a letter to Jonathan Phillips, Esq. 68p. *12°. London & Bristol,* 1839.

31183 COPLEY, E. A history of slavery, and its abolition...Second edition... 648p. *12°.* 1839.

31184 [DENMAN, Hon. J.] Practical remarks on the slave trade of the west coast of Africa, with notes on the Portuguese Treaty. 22p. *8°.* 1839.

31185 —— Practical remarks on the slave trade, and on the existing treaties with Portugal... (Second edition enlarged.) 39p. *8°.* 1839.

31186 GARRISON, W. L. An address delivered before the Old Colony Anti-Slavery Society, at South Scituate, Mass. July 4, 1839. 40p. *12°. Boston,* 1839.

31187 GURLEY, R. R. Address at the annual meeting of the Pennsylvania Colonization Society, November 11, 1839... 40p. *8°. Philadelphia,* 1839.

31188 An INQUIRY into the condition and prospects of the African race in the United States: and the means of bettering its fortunes...By an American. 214p. *12°. Philadelphia,* 1839.

31189 JAY, W. A view of the action of the Federal Government, in behalf of slavery. 217p. *12°. New-York,* 1839.

31190 MASSACHUSETTS ABOLITION SOCIETY. Formation of the Massachusetts Abolition Society. 36p. *12°. n.p.* [1839]

31191 PORTUGAL. *Camera dos Senadores.* Documentos officiaes relativos á negociação do tractado entre Portugal e a Gram Bretanha para a suppressão do trafico da escravatura. Mandados imprimir por ordem da Camera dos Senadores. 144, 82p. *fol. Lisboa,* 1839.

31192 TAYLOR, Thomas (*fl.* 1833–1839). A biographical sketch of Thomas Clarkson...with...brief strictures on the misrepresentations of him contained in The life of William Wilberforce; and a concise historical outline of the abolition of slavery. 152p. *8°.* 1839.

31193 THOME, J. A. and **KIMBALL,** J. H. Emancipation in the West Indies. A six months' tour in Antigua, Barbados, and Jamaica, in the year 1837... Second edition. 412p. *12°. New York: American Anti-Slavery Society,* 1839. *For another edition, see* 1838.

POLITICS

31194 An ADDRESS to the Chartists. 18p. *8°. Hinckley,* [1839 ?].

31195 [AIKEN, P. F.] The People's Charter; and old England for ever...Sixteenth thousand. 12p. *8°. London & Bristol,* 1839.

31196 BIGGS, W. A plan for the further extension and better distribution of the suffrage, in a letter to Joseph Hume, Esq. M.P. for Kilkenny. 11p. *8°. Leicester, Hinckley, &c.,* [1839]

31197 BLAKE, Sir Francis, *3rd Bart.* The House of Lords, the People's Charter and the corn laws. 24p. *8°.* 1839.

31198 [BLAKEY, R.] The political pilgrim's progress. From the Northern Liberator. 72p. *12°. Newcastle-upon-Tyne,* 1839.

31199 BROOKE, James W. The democrats of Marylebone. 192p. *8°.* 1839. *Presentation copy, with inscription, from the author to 'Freeman Smith Esqre'.*

31200 BROUGHAM, H. P., *Baron Brougham and Vaux.* Lord Brougham's reply to Lord John Russell's Letter to the electors of Stroud, on the principles of the Reform Act. 35p. *8°.* 1839.

31201 [BULWER, afterwards **BULWER LYTTON,** E. G. E. L., *Baron Lytton.*] The Tory Ex-Chancellor's review of the last session exposed; or, a defence of Lord Melbourne's Government and the Whigs. [Reprinted from the *Edinburgh Review.*] 36p. *12°. Edinburgh & London,* 1839.

31202 To the independent BURGESSES of Duddeston & Nechells. [Signed: A well-wisher of the Ward. Advising the burgesses to vote for residents of their own parish as town councillors of the newly incorporated borough of Birmingham, and not for those who have only Birmingham interests at heart.] *s.sh.fol. Birmingham,* [1839]

31203 CARLILE, R. An address to that portion of the people of Great Britain and Ireland, calling themselves reformers, on the political excitement of the present time. 16p. *8°. Manchester & London,* 1839.

31204 CAUTION. To the burgesses of the Ward of Duddeston and Nechells in the Borough of Birmingham. [Signed: A burgess. Warning voters of the penalties involved in offering or taking bribes to influence elections.] *s.sh.fol. Birmingham,* [1839 ?]

For the **CHARTIST CIRCULAR,** 1839–42, *see* vol. III, *Periodicals list.*

31205 A **CHARTIST'S** reply to "A few words to the Chartists", "by," one styling himself, "a friend." 8p. *8°. 1839.*

31206 **CHRISTIE**, W. D. An argument in favour of the ballot. 72p. *8°. 1839.*

31207 **CLOSE**, F. The Chartists' visit to the parish church. A sermon, addressed to the female Chartists of Cheltenham, Sunday, August 25th, 1839, on the occasion of their attending the parish church in a body. 24p. *12°.* 1839.

31208 [**COLLIER**, JOSHUA.] ⟨Second edition...⟩ Common sense, under a government "pro tempore," addressed to a body of gentlemen, deputed from certain large districts for national purposes [the Chartists]...By an octogenarian, author of "A reply to the State of the nation...1822"... 8p. *8°.* [1839]

31209 [——] Third edition of Votes for manhood, or common sense. By an octogenarian. [With 'Supplementary address', dated: August, 1839.] 8, [2]p. *8°.* [1839] *A reissue of the second edition with a new title-page and the Supplementary address.*

31210 **COMMITTEE ACTING ON BEHALF OF THE BRITISH CIVIL AND MILITARY CLAIMANTS ON PORTUGAL.** Narrative of the plans...of a Committee acting on behalf of the British civil & military claimants on Portugal. [With 'Propositions transmitted to Lord Palmerston by the Committee' and an appendix.] Second edition. 59p. *8°. 1839.*

31211 **COPLEY**, J. S., *Baron Lyndhurst.* Labours of the session. ⟨Painter's tenth edition.⟩ Lord Lyndhurst's speech in the House of Lords...August 23. 16p. *8°.* [*London*, 1839]

31212 **EMMET**, R. The speech of Robert Emmett, as delivered in the Sessions House, Dublin, on being found guilty of high treason, as leader of the insurrection of 1803... 10p. *12°.* [1839?] *For another edition, see* 1833.

31213 **GENERAL CONVENTION OF THE INDUSTRIOUS CLASSES.** Rules and regulations ... 12p. *12°.* [*London*, 1839?]

31214 **GISBORNE**, THOMAS (1794–1852). An address to the electors of Derbyshire on the recent ministerial crisis. 32p. *8°. 1839.*

31215 **GORE**, M. Letter to the middle classes on the present disturbed state of the country, especially with reference to the Chartist meetings. 14p. *8°. 1839.*

31216 —— Third edition. 14p. *8°. 1839.*

31217 **HALE**, MATTHEW B., *Bishop of Perth, Western Australia.* Second edition. First letter shewing the wicked and rebellious intentions of the Chartists, addressed to the inhabitants of all places in the west of England, where their destructive principles are upheld. 7p. *8°. Wotton-Underedge,* [1839]

31218 **HORTON**, SIR R. J. W., *Bart.* Letters on parliamentary reform, signed X.L. Published originally in 1831 [in *The Globe* newspaper], and now reprinted in 1839. 101p. *8°. 1839.*

31219 A **LETTER** to Sir Robert Peel on his present prospects. By an old school-fellow. 19p. *8°. 1839. The copy that belonged to Earl De Grey.*

31220 A **LETTER** to the Marquis of Lansdown, stating some legal objections to the late proceedings in the House of Lords, with reference to the Marquis of Normanby's government in Ireland. By a member of the Irish Bar. 23p. *8°. Dublin,* 1839.

31221 **LOVETT**, W. The eloquent and patriotic defence of William Lovett...as delivered by him during his trial at Warwick, on the 6th of August, 1839, for alleged libel and sedition...Second edition. 8p. *8°. Birmingham,* [1839]

31222 —— The trial of W. Lovett, journeyman cabinet-maker, for a seditious libel, before Mr. Justice Littledale, at the assizes at Warwick, on Tuesday, the 6th of August, 1839. ⟨Second edition.⟩ 20p. *8°.* [1839]

31223 **MARVELL**, *Redivivus, pseud.* A letter to the Earl of Durham on reform in Parliament, by paying the elected. 46p. *8°. 1839.*

31224 **MATTHEW**, P. Two addresses to the men of Perthshire and Fifeshire, containing propositions of a plan of national education, and other social improvements and reforms. [With 'Copy of the great national petition'.] 26p. *12°. Edinburgh,* 1839.

For the **NATIONAL**: a library for the people, *see* vol. III, *Periodicals list.*

31225 **PAUL**, WILLIAM, *secretary to the Leeds Operative Conservative Society.* A history of the origin and progress of operative conservative societies...Second edition. 32p. *8°. Leeds,* [1839] *For another edition, see* 1838.

31226 **PEEL**, SIR ROBERT, *2nd Bart.* The government of Ireland. The substance of a speech delivered in the House of Commons...April 15, 1839. 44p. *8°. 1839.*

31227 National **PETITION** unto the honourable the Commons of the United Kingdom of Great Britain and Ireland in Parliament assembled, the petition of the undersigned, their suffering countrymen. *s.sh.fol.* [*London,* 1839] [*Br.* 594] *The copy that belonged to William Lovett, with his signature on the verso.*

31228 **RICHARDSON**, J. R. From the report of the Champion and Weekly Herald...The right of Englishmen to have arms: as shown in a speech delivered in the National Convention, on Tuesday, 9th April, 1839. 11p. *12°. London, Manchester, &c.,* 1839.

31229 **RIOTS** in South Wales. An address to the working classes of Wales, on the late occurrences at Newport, by "One of the people." 20p. *8°. Swansea,* [1839?]

31230 **ROBERTS**, S. Chartism! Its cause and cure. Addressed to the clergy and others of Sheffield and Eccleshall. 12p. *8°. Sheffield,* 1839.

31231 **ROMAND**, G. DU B. DE, *Baron.* De l'état des partis en France...Dédié à la Chambre des Pairs. 59p. *8°. Paris,* 1839.

31232 **RUSSELL**, JOHN, *Earl Russell.* The government of Ireland. The substance of a speech delivered in the House of Commons on Monday, April 15th 1839. 46p. *8°. 1839.*

31233 —— Letter to the electors of Stroud, on the principles of the Reform Act. 44p. *8°. 1839.*

31234 —— Seventh edition. 44p. *8°. 1839.*

31235 **SMITH**, SYDNEY (1771–1845). Ballot. 46p. *8°.* 1839.

31236 —— Third edition. 48p. *8°. 1839.*

31237 SOMERVILLE, ALEXANDER. Dissuasive warnings to the people on street warfare. Letter II. 8p. *8°.* [1839]

31238 —— Public and personal affairs. Being an enquiry into the physical strength of the people, in which the value of their pikes and rifles is compared with that of the grape-shot, shells, and rockets of the Woolwich artillery. Also an exposure of treacherous patriots and drunken lawyers...connected with Alderman Harmer and the Weekly Dispatch... 90p. *8°.* [1839]

31239 STATE of the question between the people, the middle classes and the aristocracy. By a Member of the Northern Political Union. 24p. *12°. Newcastle-upon-Tyne,* 1839.

31240 TAYLOR, JOHN, *Dr.* Chartist prayer, delivered by Dr. John Taylor, at Dalston, on Sunday, the 8th of December, 1839. *s.sh.fol. Carlisle,* [1839]

31241 A **TEST** for the ballot, drawn from the principles of democratic government. In a letter to a Liberal Member of Parliament. 28p. *8°.* 1839.

31242 TOWNLEY, W. G. A sermon, occasioned by the late Chartist movements, preached at Upwell, St. Peter, in...Norfolk...the 17th of November, 1839. 14p. *8°.* 1839.

31243 WADE, EDWARD (*fl.* 1839). The ballot essential to the attainment of freedom of election, and the progress of real reform...Second edition. 18p. *8°. Cambridge, Huntingdon, &c.,* 1839.

31244 The **WAY** to universal suffrage. By a Tyne Chartist. 24p. *8°. Newcastle-upon-Tyne,* 1839.

31245 WILBERFORCE, WILLIAM (*b.* 1798). The law and practice of election committees, in a letter to the electors of Hull. [On corruption.] 65p. *8°.* 1839.

31246 WRIGHT, THOMAS (1810–1877), *ed.* The political songs of England, from the reign of John to that of Edward II. Edited and translated by Thomas Wright, Esq....(*Camden Society, Old Series,* 6.) xviii, 408p. *4°.* 1839. *Presentation copy from the editor to E. L. Charlton.*

31247 YMDDIDDAN rhwng Mr. Bowen, deiliad ffyddlon i'r Frenhines a William Thomas, siartist, ar ol y terfysg yn y Casnewydd, Tachwedd 4, 1839. 12p. *12°. Llanymddyfri,* 1839.

SOCIALISM

31248 An **ADDRESS** to the socialists, radicals, trades unions, and the working classes generally...By a working man. 48p. *8°. London & Manchester,* 1839. **Another, the FWA copy, belonged to William Pare. For other editions, see* 1827.

31249 BARKER, JOSEPH. The abominations of socialism exposed, in reply to the Gateshead Observer. 12p. *12°. Newcastle,* [1839]

31250 —— The Gospel triumphant: or, a defence of Christianity against the attacks of the socialists; and an exposure of the infidel character and mischievous tendency of the social system of R. Owen... 448p. *12°. Newcastle,* 1839. *See also* 1841.

31251 BEARD, J. R. The religion of Jesus Christ defended from the assaults of Owenism. In nine lectures. 240p. *12°. London & Manchester,* 1839. *See also* 1842.

31252 BIRCH, E. Remarks on socialism, designed to show the true character and licentious tendency of that system of infidelity... 20p. *12°.* [1839?]

31253 BOWER, S. Competition in peril; or, the present position of the Owenites, or Rationalists, considered; together with Miss Martineau's account of communities in America. 12p. *8°. London, Manchester, &c.,* [1839]

31254 [**BRAY**, C.] Socialism. A commentary on the public discussion on the subjects of necessity and responsibility, between Mr. A. Campbell...and the Rev. J. T. Bannister...in which it is clearly demonstrated that neither of the above gentlemen understood what they were talking about. By Jonathan Jonathan... 42p. *8°. Coventry,* 1839.

31255 BRAY, J. F. Labour's wrongs and labour's remedy; or, the age of might and the age of right. 216p. *12°. Leeds, Birmingham, &c.,* 1839. *See also* 1842.

31256 CAMPBELL, ALEXANDER (1788–1866), *ed.* Debate on the evidences of Christianity; containing an examination of the social system...held in...Cincinnati ...between Robert Owen...and Alexander Campbell... 545p. *8°. London, Nottingham, &c.,* 1839. *For another edition, see* 1829.

31257 CAMPBELL, ALEXANDER (1796–1870). Socialism. Public discussion between Mr. Alexander Campbell, socialist missionary, and the Rev. J. T. Bannister, of Coventry, held...on...January 14, 15, & 16, 1839. Carefully revised and corrected. [With 'Outline of the rational system of society. By Robert Owen' and 'Mr. Bannister's address to the readers of the discussion'.] 119p. *8°. Coventry,* 1839. *Entitled, on the upper cover: Owenism. Public Discussion...*

31258 An **EXPOSURE** of Joseph Mather's pamphlet, entitled "Socialism exposed, or The book of the new moral world examined, and brought to the test of fact and experience." By a lover of practical Christianity. In which it is clearly demonstrated that Joseph Mather did not understand his subject. 38p. *12°. Bilston, Birmingham, &c.,* [1839?]

31259 The "fundamental **FACTS**" of socialism, examined. 9p. *12°.* 1839.

31260 *[**FLEMING**, G. A.] A day at New Lanark, and a sketch of its present condition. By the editor of the "New Moral World." Reprinted from no. 25...new series. 12p. *12°. Birmingham,* 1839. *The FWA copy that belonged to William Pare.*

31261 *—— The infidelity of professed Christianity; or, the Church and competitive society tried by the Bible and convicted. A lecture, delivered at the Social Institution, Salford. 16p. *8°. Manchester & London,* [1839?] *The FWA copy that belonged to William Pare.*

31262 —— The right application of science: an address delivered at the opening of the Huddersfield Hall of Science, on Sunday, November 3rd, 1839. 24p. *12°. Leeds,* 1839. **Another, the FWA copy, belonged to William Pare.*

31263 GILES, J. E. Socialism, in its moral tendencies, compared with Christianity. The second of three lectures on socialism, (as propounded by Robert Owen and others,) delivered in...Leeds, September 30, 1838. p.[49]–95. *8°. 1839. Paginated in sequence with the first lecture, published in 1838 (q.v.).*

31264 HALL, T. The Gordian knot untied: or the moral impossibility of the Bible being true, being an answer to a work entitled The Gordian Knot of infidelity ...by the Rev. W. J. Kidd. [Containing a defence of Robert Owen, and the principles of socialism.] 48p. *12°. Manchester, [1839?]*

31265 HANSON, JOHN, *socialist*. The Owenite's escape from the charnel-house, and blow-up of the ostmachia; being a reply to Mr. F. R. Lees' pamphlet entitled 'The Owenite anatomized.' 24p. *12°. Manchester & London, [1839] *Another, the FWA copy, belonged to William Pare.*

31266 HAREL, C. Ménage sociétaire ou moyen d'augmenter son bien-être en diminuant sa dépense, avec indication de quelques nouvelles combinaisons pour améliorer et assurer son avenir. 212p. *8°. Paris, 1839. Presentation copy, with inscription, from the author, 'A Monsieur Haguette medecin'.*

31267 HUDSON, T. H. Christian socialism, explained and enforced, and compared with infidel fellowship, especially, as propounded by Robert Owen, Esq.... 319p. *12°. London, Hull, &c., 1839.*

31268 LA FARELLE, F. F. DE. Du progrès social au profit des classes populaires non indigentes, ou études philosophiques et économiques sur l'amélioration matérielle et morale du plus grand nombre... 2 vols. *8°. Paris, 1839. Presentation copy, with the inscription, 'A Monsieur le Victe. Alban de Villeneuve de la part de son disciple en économie politique. F. de Lafarelle'. See also 1847.*

31269 MARTIN, WILLIAM (1772–1851). An exposure of a new system of irreligion, which is in opposition to the Holy Scriptures, and is called "The new moral world," promulgated by Robert Owen, Esq.... 8p. *8°. Newcastle-upon-Tyne, [1839]*

31270 [MORGAN, JOHN M.] The revolt of the bees ...Third edition. 272p. *8°. 1839. For other editions, see 1826.*

31271 OWEN, ROBERT. The first discourse on a new system of society; as delivered in the Hall of Representatives at Washington...on the 25th of February, 1825. 16p. *16°. Manchester & London, [1839?] For another edition, see 1825.*

31272 —— Outline of the rational system of society, founded on demonstrable facts, developing the constitution and laws of human nature; being the only effectual remedy for the evils experienced by the population of the world... 16p. *16°. Birmingham: The Association of All Classes of All Nations, 1839. For other editions, see 1831.*

31273 —— Report of the discussion between Robert Owen, Esq., and the Rev. Wm. Legg, B.A., which took place in the Town Hall, Reading, March 5 & 6, 1839, on Mr. Owen's new views of society. 36p. *8°. London [Birmingham printed], 1839.*

31274 —— Robert Owen on marriage, religion, & private property and on the necessity of immediately carrying into practice the "Rational system of society," to prevent the evils of a physical revolution. [Dated: April 29, 1839.] *s.sh.fol. [1839] [Br. 595]*

31275 —— Six lectures delivered in Manchester previously to the discussion between Mr. Robert Owen and the Rev. J. H. Roebuck. And an address delivered at the annual congress of the "Association of All Classes of All Nations,"... 112p. *16°. Manchester & London, 1839. Entitled on the wrapper: Six lectures delivered in Manchester to the Wesleyan Associationists. *Another, the FWA copy, belonged to William Pare.*

31276 —— Social tracts. No. 7. Outline of the rational system of society, founded on demonstrable facts, developing the constitution and laws of human nature... 7p. *8°. Universal Community Society of Rational Religionists, [1839?] *Another, the FWA copy, belonged to William Pare. For other editions, see 1831 (Outline of the rational system). For Social tracts, nos. 1–6, see 1838 (National Community Friendly Society).*

31277 *—— To the Right Hon. the Earl of Eglinton, Eglinton Castle, Ayrshire. [With 'Robert Owen's challenge to the most learned and experienced in all countries'. Dated: London, 24th August, 1839.] *s.sh.fol. n.p. [1839] A proof, printed in one column, with manuscript corrections. The FWA copy that belonged to William Pare.*

31278 R. OWEN at New Lanark; with a variety of interesting anecdotes: being a brief and authentic narrative of the character and conduct of Mr. Owen while proprietor of New Lanark; with a complete refutation of a variety of false...statements...relative to the proceedings of that gentleman...By one formerly a teacher at New Lanark. 16p. *8°. Manchester, 1839. *Another, the FWA copy, belonged to William Pare.*

31279 OWEN, ROBERT D. Situations: lawyers – clergy – physicians – men and women. 15p. *8°. [1839?] See also 1830 (Popular tracts).*

31280 —— Tracts on republican government and national education. Addressed to the inhabitants of the United States of America. By R. D. Owen and Frances Wright [and G. Ticknor]. 24p. *12°. [1839]*

31281 —— Wealth and misery. 16p. *8°. [1839?] See also 1830 (Popular tracts), 1846.*

31282 PEARSON, G. The progress and tendencies of socialism. A sermon... 44p. *8°. Cambridge & London, 1839.*

31283 PELLARIN, C. Notice biographique sur Charles Fourier, suivie d'une exposition de la théorie sociétaire. 171p. *12°. Paris, 1839. See also 1843, 1848, 1849.*

31284 RATIONAL SOCIETY. The constitution and laws of the Universal Community Society of Rational Religionists, as revised by the congress, held in Birmingham, May 1839...[With 'Supplement' and index, 1840, 'Second supplement', 1840, and 'Third and fourth supplements', 1841.] 47p., 12, [1], 6f. *8°. London, Birmingham, &c., 1839[–41] *Another, the FWA copy (without the supplements), belonged to William Pare.*

31285 *—— Lectures against socialism. Correspondence between the London District Board of the Universal Community Society of Rational Religionists and the Committee of the London City Mission [on the subject of the lectures to be delivered under the direction of the latter in the Social Institution. Edited by 'W.N.', i.e. Walter Newall.] 12p. *12°. Leeds, 1839. The FWA copy, that belonged to William Pare.*

31286 —— Proceedings of the fourth congress of the Association of all Classes of all Nations, and the second of the National Community Friendly Society...now united and called the Universal Community Society of Rational

Religionists, held in Birmingham, in May, 1839... 161p. *12°. Leeds, Birmingham, &c., 1839. See also 1838 (Association of All Classes of All Nations).*

31287 *——— [Begin.]* To her Most Gracious Majesty Victoria. From the Congress of the Universal Community Society of Rational Religionists...[An address. Signed: Robert Owen, president, and dated, May twenty-six, 1839.] *s.sh.fol. n.p.* [1839] *Probably a galley proof. The FWA copy that belonged to William Pare.*

31288 SMITH, WILLIAM H. Letters on social science. [Reprinted from the *Birmingham Journal*. With 'Address of the congress of the "Association of All Classes of All Nations," and of the "National Community Friendly Society," to intending emigrants...'.] 70, vip. *12°. Birmingham, 1839.*

For the **SOCIAL PIONEER:** or, record of the progress of socialism, *see vol.* III, *Periodicals list.*

31289 SOCIALISM. 24p. *12°. 1839. Caption and running-title: What is socialism? See also 1840.*

31290 The **SOCIALIST:** a tale of philosophical religion. 60p. *12°. Leeds, 1839.*

31291 SPIER, W. The causes and cure of social unhappiness: a lecture, delivered in the Hall of Science, Glasgow...and published at the request of the Glasgow Branch, of Rational Religionists. 20p. *12°. Glasgow,* [1839]

31292 TEMPLE of free enquiry. A report of the proceedings consequent on laying the foundation stone, of the Manchester Hall of Science, with an address by Robert Owen. (Reprinted from no. 43, new series, of the New Moral World.) 32p. *12°. Leeds, 1839.*

31293 TROUP, G. Report of the discussion betwixt Mr. Troup...on the part of the Philalethean Society, and Mr. Lloyd Jones...on the part of the socialists, in... Dundee, on the...17th and 18th September 1839, on the propositions, I. That socialism is atheistical; and II. That atheism is incredible and absurd... 48p. *8°. Dundee, Edinburgh, &c., 1839.*

For the **WORKING BEE** and herald of the Hodsonian Community Society, 1839–41, *see vol.* III, *Periodicals list.*

MISCELLANEOUS

31294 ABERCROMBY, J., *Baron Dunfermline.* Correspondence between the Right Hon. the Speaker of the House of Commons [J. Abercromby] and Sir F. W. Trench, M.P. on the lighting of the House. 32p. *8°.* 1839.

31295 The Holy **BIBLE.** Being a collection of texts and references, especially recommended to the serious consideration of the religious world, and to the teachers of youth in the United Kingdom. 23p. *8°. London, Manchester, &c., 1839. The Oastler copy.*

31296 BRIGHAM, A. Remarks on the influence of mental cultivation and mental excitement upon health. [Second edition.] 48p. *8°. London & Manchester, 1839. The copy presented to William Lovett by the London publisher, John Cleave, with inscription.*

31297 ——— [Another issue.] 48p. *8°. London & Manchester, 1839. In this issue G. Berger and Henry Hetherington are associated with John Cleave as London publishers.*

31298 The **CHURCH OF SCOTLAND ALMANAC** for 1840; containing a brief sketch of the constitution of the Church, and of her General Assembly's five schemes for the promotion of the Gospel at home and abroad. Also the dates of about three hundred facts connected with the Church since the Reformation in 1560; with notes...By a layman. 23p. *12°. Belfast, 1839.*

31299 LUNN, E. A lecture on prayer, its folly, inutility, and irrationality demonstrated. Delivered in the Social Institution...Huddersfield. March 31st., 1839. 24p. *8°. Manchester & London,* [1839]

31300 A **NARRATIVE** of the dreadful disasters occasioned by the hurricane, which visited Liverpool and various parts of the kingdom, on the nights of Sunday and Monday, January 6th and 7th, 1839. [From the Liverpool Mercury of...Jan. 11.] 108p. *12°. Liverpool, 1839.*

31301 The **NAVY.** Observations upon "A letter addressed to the Earl of Minto, First Lord of the Admiralty, by one of the people." By a naval officer. 16p. *8°.* 1839.

31302 Our **NAVY** is not neglected!!! The Navy against Lord Minto and Sir John Barrow. 30p. *8°.* 1839.

31303 [PHILLIPPS, SIR T., *Bart.*] Index to cartularies now or formerly existing, since the dissolution of monasteries: by T.P. 46p. *12°. Typis Medio-Montanis, impressit C. Gilmour, 1839.*

31304 ROBERTS, S. Vital Christianity opposed to the Reformation Society. [Letters to the editors of the Sheffield Iris, signed: A Protestant.] 28p. *12°. Sheffield, 1839.*

31305 SMITH, SYDNEY (1771–1845). First letter to Archdeacon Singleton, on the Ecclesiastical Commission ...Eighth edition. 72p. *8°. 1839. For other editions, see 1837.*

31306 ——— Third letter to Archdeacon Singleton... Second edition. 40p. *8°.* 1839.

31307 SPENCE, G. An address to the public, and more especially to the members of the House of Commons, on the present unsatisfactory state of the Court of Chancery; and suggestions for an immediate remedy. 40p. *8°.* 1839.

31308 ——— First address to the public...Second edition, revised. 40p. *8°. 1839. Presentation copy from the author to George Pryme.*

31309 ——— Second address to the public, and more especially to the members of the House of Commons, on the present unsatisfactory state of the Court of Chancery; and suggestions for an immediate remedy. 24p. *8°. 1839. For the third address and a supplement, see 1840.*

31310 STATISTICS of popery in Great Britain and the colonies. Illustrated with a map, shewing the situation of each Roman Catholic chapel, college and seminary, throughout England, Scotland, and Wales. Reprinted from "Fraser's Magazine" for March and April, 1839. Second edition. 38p. *8°. The Reformation Society, 1839.*

31311 TAYLOR, RICHARD (1781–1858). The

Treasury and the Royal Exchange. A letter to Sir Robert Harry Inglis...on the conduct of the Lords of the Treasury with regard to the Gresham Trusts, and the rebuilding of the Royal Exchange. 19p. 8°. 1839.

31312 Good **WAGES,** good work, and a good Master, for labouring men. [A religious tract.] 16p. 8°. 1839.

31313 ⟨Painter's fifth edition.⟩ The **WELLINGTON**

banquet at Dover, on...August 30, 1839. 16p. 8°. [1839]

31314 **WOOD,** CHARLES, *Viscount Halifax.* State of the Navy. Corrected report of the speech of Charles Wood, Esq. M.P. Secretary of the Admiralty, on moving the Navy Estimates in Committee of Supply, March the 4th, 1839. 69p. 8°. 1839.

1840

GENERAL

31315 **AIRY,** SIR G. B. Extracts of papers printed and manuscript, laid before the Commission appointed to consider the steps to be taken for restoration of the standards of weight and measure...Arranged by G. B. Airy...Printed by order of the Lords Commissioners of the Treasury. [150]p. 4°. 1840.

31316 Political **ALMANAC** for 1840; and the annual Black book: showing the salaries, pensions, sinecures... and powers, of the Army, Navy, Church, Law Courts, Civil List, Courts of Commission, and others feeding on the taxes: compiled from Parliamentary papers, and dedicated to the tax payers of the United Kingdom. By R. J. Richardson. Second twentieth thousand. 64p. 16°. *Salford, London, &c.,* [1840] *The title on the original yellow printed paper wrappers is:* 'Read! mark! learn and inwardly digest, the annual Black book!!! or touchstone of political humbug, chicanery and fraud: compiled for the use of taxpayers'.

31317 **ATKINSON,** WILLIAM (*fl.* 1833–1858). Principles of political economy; or, the laws of the formation of national wealth: developed by means of the Christian law of government; being the substance of a case delivered to the Hand-Loom Weavers' Commission. 247p. 8°. 1840. *Presentation copy, with inscription dated 'May 1841', from the author to Richard Oastler. See also* 1843.

31318 **BIVORT,** J.-B., *ed.* Constitution belge expliquée et interprétée par les discussions du pouvoir législatif, les arrêts des cours supérieures de Belgique... précédée de notions sur les lois...par J.-B. Bivort... 160p. 8°. *Bruxelles,* 1840.

31319 **BRADFORD,** A. History of the federal government, for fifty years: from March 1789, to March, 1839. 480p. 8°. *Boston,* 1840.

31320 **BRIAUNE,** . Des crises commerciales, de leurs causes et de leurs remèdes. 55p. 8°. *Paris,* 1840.

31321 **BRIAVOINNE,** N. Mémoire sur l'état de la population, des fabriques, des manufactures et du commerce, dans les provinces des Pays-Bas, depuis Albert et Isabelle jusqu'à la fin du siècle dernier...Mémoire couronné le 7 mai 1840. [Mémoires couronnés par l'Académie Royale des Sciences et Belles-Lettres, Bruxelles, 14.] 217p. 4°. *n.p.* [1840]

31322 The **BRITISH ALMANAC** of the Society for the Diffusion of Useful Knowledge, for...1840. [With 'The companion to the Almanac; or year-book of general information'.] 96, 263p. 12°. [1840] *For other editions, see* 1828.

31323 The **BRITISH MECHANIC'S** and labourer's hand book, and true guide to the United States; with ample notices respecting various trades and professions. 288p. 12°. 1840. *Sometimes attributed to Charles Knight, whose initials were printed at the end of the preface (missing from this copy). See also* 1843.

31324 Sir John Yarde **BULLER'S** motion. A letter addressed to John Temple Leader, Esq., M.P. by a Whig county member. [A review of the achievements of the Whigs; signed: A Whig.] 26p. 8°. 1840.

31325 **CAZENOVE,** J. An elementary treatise on political economy; or a short exposition of its first and fundamental principles. 150p. 8°. 1840. *Presentation copy, with inscription, from the author to G. A. Muskett.*

31326 **CHAMBERS,** ROBERT (1802–1871). The picture of Scotland...Fourth edition. 599p. 12°. *Edinburgh,* 1840. *For another edition, see* 1827.

31327 **CHIDLAW,** B. W. Yr American, yr hwn sydd yn cynnwys nodau ar daith o ddyffryn Ohio i Gymru, golwg ar dalaeth Ohio; hanes sefydliadau Cymreig yn America; cyfarwyddiadau y ymofynwyr cyn y daith, ar y daith, ac yn y wlad. [An account of Welsh settlements in the valley of the Ohio.] 48p. 12°. *Llanrwst,* 1840.

For the **COLONIAL MAGAZINE** and commercial-maritime journal, 1840–42, *continued as* Fisher's colonial magazine, 1843–44, *see vol.* III, *Periodicals list,* Fisher's colonial magazine.

31328 **CRASTER,** T. A view of manufactures, money, and corn laws, adverse to every theory of the economists. With observations upon the national worth of machinery. 31p. 8°. 1840.

31329 **DETROSIER,** R. The benefits of general knowledge; more especially, the sciences of mineralogy, geology, botany, and entomology, being an address delivered at the opening of the Banksian Society, Manchester. On...January 5th, 1829. By the late Rowland Detrosier. 15p. 8°. [1840?]

31330 A **DIGEST** of the despatches on China (including those received on the 27th of March): with a connecting narrative and comments. 240p. 8°. 1840.

31331 **DOURSTHER,** H. Dictionnaire universel des poids et mesures anciens et modernes, contenant des tables des monnaies de tous les pays. 603p. 4°. *Bruxelles,* 1840.

31332 **DUNLOP,** JOHN. The universal tendency to association in mankind analyzed and illustrated. With practical and historical notices of the bonds of society, as regards individuals and communities... 243p. 8°. 1840. *p.229–243 contain extracts from reviews of the author's other works.*

31333 DUREAU DE LA MALLE, A. J. C. A. Économie politique des Romains. 2 vols. 8°. *Paris*, 1840.

31334 ELLIOTT, E. The poetical works of Ebenezer Elliott, the corn-law rhymer. 179p. 8°. *Edinburgh, London, &c.,* 1840. *With a manuscript note on the title-page, 'Mr. H. Colquhoun from his Brother 1840'. For another collection of Elliott's poems, see 1833.*

31335 ENGLAND. *Laws, etc.* Ancient laws and institutes of England...also, monumenta ecclesiastica anglicana...[Edited by B. Thorpe.] 548, [80]p. *fol.* [*The Record Commission,*] 1840.

31336 ENGLAND, her colonies and her enemies: how she may make the former protect her against the latter; and how make them sources of boundless wealth and power. 51p. 8°. 1840. *Reissued with the title* Corn-colonies, *in 1841 (q.v.). The Kress copy (C5433) of the 1841 edition has a manuscript attribution on the title-page to 'Mr. Atherley'.*

31337 EXTRACTS from the Britannia conservative weekly newspaper. 16p. 8°. [1840]

31338 FRANKLIN, B. The works of Benjamin Franklin; containing several political and historical tracts not included in any former edition, and many letters official and private not hitherto published; with notes and a life of the author [being a continuation of the Autobiography]. By Jared Sparks [the editor]... 10 vols. 8°. *Boston,* 1840, 1836–39. *For another edition, see 1824.*

31339 GORE, J. The Liverpool directory, for the year 1766: containing an alphabetical list of the merchants, tradesmen and principal inhabitants...[With Appendix. A reprint.] 28, [2]p. *12°. Liverpool,* 1766[1840?] [*Higgs 3894*] *See also* 1818, 1823, 1829.

31340 GRAY, S. All classes productive of national wealth; or the theories of M. Quesnay, Dr. Adam Smith, and Mr. Gray, concerning the various classes of men as to the production of wealth to the community, analysed and examined. To which are added, four letters to the celebrated French economist, Mr. Say, on his "De l'Angleterre et des Anglais". 320p. 8°. 1840. *For another edition, see* 1817.

31341 GRÜN, A. Manuel de législation commerciale et industrielle de la France. Contenant les textes du Code civil et du Code de commerce; des extraits du Code de procédure, du Code pénal, des lois et règlements sur les brevets d'invention, les patentes, les bourses de commerce, les livrets d'ouvriers, les manufactures, fabriques et ateliers, la contrainte par corps, et les vices redhibitoires. 462p. *18°. Paris,* 1840.

31342 HEAD, SIR G. A home tour through the manufacturing districts and other parts of England, Scotland, and Ireland, including the Channel Islands and the Isle of Man...New edition. 2 vols. *12°.* 1840. *For another edition, see* 1836.

31343 HEEREN, A. H. L. A manual of ancient history, particularly with regard to the constitutions, the commerce, and the colonies, of the states of antiquity... Translated from the German [by D. A. Talboys]. The third edition, corrected and improved. xxiii, 480p. 8°. *Oxford,* 1840. *For another edition, see* 1834.

31344 IRISH MANUFACTURE, by an Irishman, who has found out that 2 and 2 are equal to 4, and that 0 taken from 0 leaves nothing! 18p. *12°. Cork,* [1840?]

31345 JEVONS, T. The prosperity of the landholders not dependent on the corn laws. 68p. 8°. *London & Liverpool,* 1840.

31346 KNAPP, J. F. Vierzehn Abhandlungen über Gegenstände der Nationalökonomie und Staatswirthschaft. 221p. 8°. *Darmstadt,* 1840.

31347 LINDSAY, H. H. Is the war with China a just one?...Second edition. 40p. 8°. 1840.

31348 McCULLOCH, JOHN R. A dictionary, practical, theoretical, and historical, of commerce and commercial navigation...A new edition, corrected and improved, with an enlarged supplement. 2 vols. 8°. *London & Manchester,* [1840–42] *For other editions, see* 1832.

31349 MAELEN, P. M. G. VAN DER, and **MEISSER,** F. J. Epistémonie, ou tables générales d'indications des connaissances humaines...Prospectus et specimen. [With 'Sciences technologiques. Chemins de fer', a bibliography.] 8, [8]p. 8°. *Bruxelles,* 1840. *With a printed covering letter inserted. The work of which this is the prospectus was never published.*

31350 MALLINSON, J. A letter to merchants, manufacturers, and operatives, suggested by the enquiries ...what is the cause of our present distress? and what will become of our commerce, our manufactures, and our workpeople? 11p. *12°. Leeds,* 1840. *Presentation copy from the author to George Pryme.*

For the **MERCHANTS' MAGAZINE AND COMMERCIAL REVIEW,** 1840–70, [1850–60 *as* Hunt's merchants' magazine], *see* vol. III, *Periodicals list.*

31351 The Book of **MORMON.** Translated by Joseph Smith, Jr. Third edition, carefully revised by the translator. 571p. *12°. Nauvoo, Ill. & Cincinnati,* 1840. *See also* 1841.

31352 MUDIE, R. China and its resources, and peculiarities, physical, political, social, and commercial, with a view of the opium question, and a notice of Assam. 198p. 8°. 1840.

31353 NEWCASTLE-UPON-TYNE. *Town Council.* The proceedings and reports of the Town Council ...for 1839... [206]p. 8°. *Newcastle,* 1840. *See also* 1837, 1838, 1839.

31354 PAINE, T. The working man's political companion: containing the rights of Man. Common sense. Dissertation on first principles of government. Agrarian justice. Decline and fall of the English system of finance. 160, 48, 16, 16, 22p. 8°. [1840?] *Each part has a separate title-page, that of the* Dissertation *being dated 1835. Agrarian justice is of the second edition. For other editions of Paine's collected works, see* 1817.

31355 The **PARLIAMENTARY GAZETTEER** of England and Wales, adapted to the new poor-law, franchise, municipal, and ecclesiastical arrangements, and compiled [in 1840–42] with a special reference to the lines of railroad and canal communication, as existing at the close of the year 1839... 4 vols. 8°. *Glasgow, Edinburgh, &c.,* 1840–43. *Published in 12 parts.*

31356 PINHEIRO FERREIRA, S. Précis d'un cours d'économie politique...Suivi d'une bibliographie choisie de l'économie politique, par M. de Hoffmanns. 252p. *12°. Paris,* 1840.

31357 A **PLEA** for Ireland. By a member of the Royal Irish Academy. 96p. *8°*. 1840. *The author has been identified as John Brown.*

31358 **POPE,** C., *ed.* The yearly journal of trade, 1840 ...Nineteenth edition. 521p. *8°*. *London, Bristol, &c.,* [1840] *See also* 1838, 1842, 1843, 1844, 1845, 1846.

31359 **POTTER,** A., *Bishop.* Political economy: its objects, uses, and principles: considered with reference to the American people. With a summary for the use of students. 318p. *12°*. *New-York*, 1840.

31360 **R.,** C. Corn and cotton: with a postscript on distress. By one of the people. 78p. *8°*. *London & Edinburgh*, [1840]

31361 **RAGUET,** C. The principles of free trade, illustrated in a series of short and familiar essays originally published in the Banner of the Constitution...Second edition. 439p. *8°*. *Philadelphia*, 1840. *For another edition, see* 1835.

31362 **SAGRA,** R. DE LA. Lecciones de economia social, dadas en al Ateneo cientifico y literario de Madrid. [La primera parte.] 334p. *8°*. *Madrid*, 1840.

31363 **SARRANS,** B. De la décadence de l'Angleterre et des intérêts fédératifs de la France. 311p. *8°*. *Paris*, 1840.

31364 **SCIALOJA,** A. I principi della economia sociale, esposti in ordine ideologico. 379p. *8°*. *Napoli*, 1840. *Presentation copy, with inscription, from the author to J. R. McCulloch.*

31365 **SIMONDE DE SISMONDI,** J. C. L. Due saggi degli studi sulla economia politica...tradotti dal francese dal dottor L. Orioli. 132p. *8°*. *Ravenna*, 1840.

31366 **SMITH,** ADAM. An inquiry into the nature and causes of the wealth of nations...With a life of the author. Also, a view of the doctrine of Smith, compared with that of the French economists; with a method of facilitating the study of his works; from the French of M. Garnier. Complete in one volume. 404, 25p. *8°*. *Edinburgh*, 1840. *For other editions, see* 1776.

31367 **SMITH,** SYDNEY (1771–1845). The works of the Rev. Sydney Smith. Second edition... 3 vols. *8°*. 1840.

31368 **SPRINGER,** J. Statistik des österreichischen Kaiserstaates... 2 vols. *8°*. *Wien*, 1840.

For **STEPHENS' MONTHLY MAGAZINE OF USEFUL INFORMATION FOR THE PEOPLE,** *see* vol. III, *Periodicals list.*

31369 **TAYLOR,** WILLIAM C. The natural history of society in the barbarous and civilized state: an essay towards discovering the origin and course of human improvement. 2 vols. *12°*. 1840.

31370 **TOOKE,** T. A history of prices, and of the state of the circulation, in 1838 and 1839, with remarks on the corn laws, and on some of the alterations proposed in our banking system...Being a continuation of the History of prices, from 1793 to 1837. 298p. *8°*. 1840. *For the original work, see* 1838, *and for another supplement*, 1848.

31371 **TROUVÉ,** C. J., *Baron.* Jacques Cœur, commerçant, maître des monnaies, argentier du Roi Charles VII et négociateur. xve siècle. 472p. *8°*. *Paris*, 1840.

31372 **URQUHART,** D. Diplomacy and commerce. No. v. Rupture of alliance with France. [With an appendix.] 17, 10p. *8°*. *Glasgow, Edinburgh, &c.*, 1840. *For other numbers of this series, see nos.* 31459, 31797.

31373 **VARDON,** T. Index to the local and personal and private Acts; 1798–1839. 38 Geo. 3 – 2 & 3 Vict. 485p. *8°*. 1840.

31374 A **VIEW** of all religions in the world, in alphabetical order...and also the religious population of the globe, together with the state of education contrasted with the state of crime in England. 36p. *12°*. *Manchester*, [c. 1840]

31375 **WHITE,** WILLIAM (*fl.* 1826–1870). History, gazetteer, and directory, of the East and North Ridings of Yorkshire, comprising...a general survey of the Ridings, and of the Sees of York and Ripon; with separate historical, statistical and topographical descriptions of all the boroughs, towns, parishes... 804p. *12°*. *Sheffield & Leeds*, 1840.

31376 **WILBERFORCE,** WILLIAM (1759–1833). The correspondence of William Wilberforce. Edited by his sons, Robert Isaac Wilberforce...and Samuel Wilberforce... 2 vols. *8°*. 1840.

AGRICULTURE

31377 **ANGLESEY AGRICULTURAL SOCIETY.** Report of the Anglesey Agricultural Society. For the years, 1839 & 1840. 16p. *8°*. *Beaumaris*, 1840.

31378 **BAYLDON,** J. S. Bayldon's art of valuing rents and tillages, and the tenant's right on entering and quitting farms, explained...Fifth edition, re-written and enlarged by John Donaldson. 328p. *8°*. 1840. *For other editions, see* 1823.

31379 *CARRER, L., ed.* Tre trattati riguardanti l'agricoltura...['Lodi e coltivazione degli ulivi' by Pietro Vettori, 'Trattato della coltivazione delle viti' by Giovanvettorio Soderini, and 'Coltivazione toscana delle viti e d'alcuni arbori' by Bernardo Davanzati.] 310p. *12°*. *Venezia*, 1840. *The copy that belonged to George Grote.*

31380 Valuable and extensive **COAL MINES.** [A prospectus of properties in the parish of Pembrey to be leased as collieries.] 3p. *4°*. [1840 ?]

31381 **COLMAN,** H. Senate. No. 36. Third report of the agriculture of Massachusetts, on wheat and silk. 252p. *8°*. *Boston*, 1840.

For the **FARMER'S MAGAZINE,** 1840–43, *see* vol. III, *Periodicals list.*

31382 **GONSALEZ ALONSO,** D. La nueva ley agraria. 295p. *8°*. *Madrid*, 1840.

31383 **HAMILTON,** WILLIAM, *M.B.* Memoir on the cultivation of wheat within the tropics. 83p. *8°*. *Plymouth & London*, 1840.

31384 **HILLYARD,** C. Practical farming and grazing; with observations on the breeding and feeding of sheep and cattle; and tables to compute by measurement the weight of cattle...Third edition. 168p. *8°*. *Northampton, London, &c.*, 1840. *Originally published, with the title* A summary of practical farming, *in 1836 (q.v.).*

31385 JACKSON, James. A treatise on agriculture and dairy husbandry. 116p. *8°. Edinburgh,* 1840.

31386 JOHNSON, C. W. On saltpetre and nitrate of soda as fertilizers. 51p. *8°.* 1840.

31387 LOUDON, J. C. Library of Useful Knowledge. Farmer's series. The cottager's manual of husbandry, architecture, domestic economy, and gardening; originally published in the Gardener's Magazine... 56p. *8°.* 1840.

For **ROYAL AGRICULTURAL SOCIETY,** Journal, 1840——›, *see* vol. III, *Periodicals list,* Journal...

31388 RUSSELL, Joseph, *of Kenilworth.* An improved system of agriculture; wherein the defects of the old practice of fallowing are distinctly pointed out...To which are added, the management of the dairy...with observations on the horse, cattle, and sheep... 749p. *8°. Kenilworth, London, &c.,* 1840.

31389 —— A treatise on practical and chemical agriculture, compiled, principally, from the scientific works of Sir H. Davy...with a dissertation on the cultivation of the soil...an essay on red clover; likewise some useful observations on selecting, breeding, rearing and feeding of stock...The second edition. 424p. *8°. Kenilworth, London, &c.,* [1840]

31390 SOUTHEY, T. A treatise on sheep, addressed to the flock-masters of Australia, Tasmania, and Southern Africa, showing the means by which the wool of these colonies may be improved, and suggesting ideas for the introduction of other lanigerous animals... 118p. *8°.* 1840. *Presentation copy from the author to William Horsfall.*

31391 TAYLOR, Richard C. Two reports: on the coal lands, mines and improvements of the Dauphin and Susquehanna Coal Company, and of the geological examinations...and prospects of the Stony Creek Coal estate, in the townships of Jackson, Rush, and Middle Paxtang, in the county of Dauphin, and of East Hanover township in the county of Lebanon, Pennsylvania. With an appendix... 113, 74p. *8°. Philadelphia,* 1840.

31392 VAUX, T. Outlines of a new plan for tilling & fertilizing land. 214p. *8°.* 1840.

CORN LAWS

31393 ATKINSON, William (*fl.* 1833-1858). Mr. Huskisson, free trade and the corn laws; shewing that the Minister discerned the injurious nature of his policy; renounced the free trade principle; and supported the corn laws. 24p. *8°.* 1840.

31394 BAKER, John, *of Leeds.* An address to the landed interest in general, of Great Britain and Ireland, on their escape from a repeal or the destruction of the present corn laws. 7p. *8°. London & Leeds,* 1840.

31395 BALLANTYNE, T. The corn law repealer's hand-book; a complete manual for the use of those who wish to make themselves familiar with the statistics of the corn law question. 34p. *12°. London, Manchester, &c.,* [1840]

31396 CARPENTER, J. D., *Earl of Tyrconnel.* An address to the people of the United Kingdom, on the corn laws. 18p. *8°. Richmond* [*Yorks.*], 1840.

31397 —— [Another edition.] 32p. *8°.* 1840. *The copy that belonged to Earl De Grey.*

31398 CHILDERS, J. W. Remarks on the corn laws. 16p. *8°.* 1840.

31399 Ought the **CORN LAWS** to be repealed? A series of articles (with additions) from the Edinburgh Evening Post and Scottish Standard. Addressed to the common sense of the people. 24p. *12°. Edinburgh,* [1840?]

31400 DUTHIE, J. The effect of the corn laws on the price of human food and manufactures considered; shewing that their repeal would be equally injurious to the landowner and manufacturer. 16p. *8°.* 1840.

31401 EDINBURGH ANTI-CORN-LAW ASSOCIATION. Corn-laws. The nature and effect of these oppressive statutes...[Signed: T.M., and dated, 2d March 1840.] 8p. *8°. Edinburgh,* [1840] *An enlarged version of the edition of 1839 (q.v.).*

31402 —— Corn-laws. Tract No. II....February 1840. [Extracts from speeches at the Manchester anti-corn law meetings, 13 and 14 Jan., 1840.] 8p. *8°. Edinburgh,* [1840]

31403 FARR, T. A remedy for the distresses of the nation; showing a saving of fifty millions a year sterling, by an equitable adjustment of the corn laws, an increase of revenue of five millions, and a short plan for taking off half the assessed taxes, custom and excise duties. 90p. *8°.* 1840. *Two presentation copies, one from the author to the Chancellor of the Exchequer, the other to the Earl of Ripon.*

31404 GORE, M. Thoughts on the corn laws... Second edition. 32p. *8°.* 1840. *The copy that belonged to Earl De Grey. See also 1841.*

31405 HIND, T. A plan for the equitable adjustment of the corn laws proposed; in a letter addressed to the Earl of Lincoln... 16p. *8°. London & Nottingham,* 1840.

31406 HOLLAND, George C. An exposition of corn-law repealing fallacies and inconsistencies. 204p. *8°.* 1840. *The copy that belonged to Sir Robert Peel, with his book-plate.*

31407 —— Lecture on the corn laws, delivered in the Theatre Royal, Doncaster on...March 10th, 1840. 24p. *8°. Doncaster,* [1840]

31408 HORTON, Sir R. J. W., *Bart.* Letter on the corn laws, addressed to Dr. Birkbeck, the President, and the members of the London Mechanics' Institution... With an illustrative tabular statement. Second edition. [With appendixes.] 26, 12p. *8°. London & Richmond, Surrey,* 1840. *This edition has the same table as that of 1839 (q.v.).*

31409 KELL, E. The injurious effects of the corn laws, on all classes of the community, including the farmer and the landowner. A lecture. 45p. *8°. London & Huddersfield,* 1840.

31410 KELLY, R. N. A review of the corn law question. Addressed to the agriculturists, merchants, tradesmen, and working classes of Great Britain. 91p. *8°. Edinburgh & London,* 1840.

31411 KENNEDY, L. On the probable operation and effect of the repeal of the duties on foreign corn to the manufacturing operatives, the agricultural labourers, farmers and landlords of the United Kingdom. 16p. *8°.*

1840. *A separate edition of the preface to* On the necessity of protection to the agriculturists of the United Kingdom, *1839 (q.v.).*

31412 LUPTON, Jonn. On the corn laws: shewing their impolicy having caused taxation to be destructive of manufactures and of all the best interests of society. 22p. *8°.* 1840.

31413 MOORSOM, R. A letter to Edward Stilling-fleet Cayley, Esq. M.P. on the corn laws, and on the evil consequences of an irregular supply of foreign grain. 24p. *12°.* 1840.

31414 MOSELEY, J. An inquiry into the probable results consequent to a repeal of the corn law, with observations on the inconsistent statements made by manufacturers, and with arithmetical illustrations of the injury to tenants and labourers by annulling that law... Second edition, 1840. 44p. *8°.* [1840] *For another edition, see 1839.*

31415 P., F. Observations on a pamphlet relating to the corn laws, under the title of, "A remedy for the distresses of the nation, &c. By the Rev. Thomas Farr". 8p. *8°.* [1840]

31416 PEEL, Sir Robert, *2nd Bart.* Conservative speeches. – Painter's editions. The corn laws. Sir R. Peel's speech on Mr. Villiers' motion in the House of Commons, April 3, 1840. 16p. *8°.* [1840] *For another edition, see no.* 31964.

31417 PRYME, G. Corn laws. Speech of G. Pryme, Esq., M.P., in the House of Commons...April 2. 1840. 14p. *8°.* 1840.

31418 PUTT, C. Observations on the corn laws, or bread for thirty millions of inhabitants; without the importation of a single grain of corn: without loss to the farmer, the landlord, or the fundholder. 32p. *8°. London &* *Boston [Lincs.],* [1840]

31419 RUDALL, E. The complaints of the manufacturers against the corn laws, considered and answered in a

lecture, read to the Launceston Farmers' Association... Second edition. 32p. *8°. Launceston & London,* 1840.

31420 SALOMONS, Sir D., *Bart.* Reflections on the operation of the present scale of duty for regulating the importation of foreign corn, addressed to the Borders of Kent and Sussex Agricultural Association...Second edition, with a supplement. 95p. *8°.* 1840. *Presentation copy from the author to the Earl of Ripon. For another edition, see 1839.*

31421 SPENCER, T. The Prayer Book opposed to the corn laws; or, who are the Nonconformists? Also, a supplement to a speech delivered by the Rev. R. McGhee, at the anniversary of the Bath Protestant Association... Third thousand. 12p. *12°.* 1840.

31422 —— Seventh thousand. 12p. *12°.* 1840.

31423 THORNEYCROFT, G. B. The corn laws. The substance of two speeches...With an appendix, containing supplementary facts and remarks, addressed to the members of the Wolverhampton Operative Conservative Association. 44p. *8°. Wolverhampton & London,* 1840.

31424 VILLIERS, C. P. On the corn-laws. The speech of Hon. C. P. Villiers, M.P., in the House of Commons, on...1st of April, 1840. Extracted from Hansard's Parliamentary Debates. 55p. *8°.* [*London,*] 1840.

31425 —— Corn laws. Speech of C. P. Villiers, Esq., M.P., in the House of Commons...May 26. 1840. 32p. *8°.* 1840.

31426 WILSON, James (1805–1860). Fluctuations of currency, commerce, and manufactures; referable to the corn laws. 148p. *8°.* 1840.

31427 ✶—— Influences of the corn laws, as affecting all classes of the community, and particularly the landed interests...Second edition. 142p. *8°.* 1840. *The copy that belonged to George Grote.*

31428 —— Third edition. 142p. *8°.* 1840. *For another edition, see 1839.*

POPULATION

31439 ALISON, Sir A., *Bart.* The principles of population, and their connection with human happiness ... 2 vols. *8°. Edinburgh & London,* 1840.

31430 GRAY, S. Gray versus Malthus; or, the principles of population and production investigated, and the result found to be that population regulates subsistence, not

subsistence population... 496p. *8°.* 1840. *For another edition, see 1818.*

31431 ROBERTON, J. Thoughts on the excess of adult females in the population of Great Britain, with reference to its causes and consequences...(From the Edinburgh Medical and Surgical Journal, No. 145.) 17p. *8°. Edinburgh,* [1840]

TRADES & MANUFACTURES

31432 AJASSON DE GRANDSAGNE, J. B. F. E., *Vicomte,* and **PARISOT,** V. Notions générales sur l'industrie...première partie. 288p. *12°. Paris & La Rochelle,* 1840.

31433 On the general **APPLICATION** of low steam power to all vessels, instead of sails. [An offprint, dated: October 1840.] 28p. *8°. n.p.* [1840]

31434 [CARTER, Thomas (1792–1867?).] The guide to trade. The tailor. 96p. *12°.* 1840. *For another part, see 1838.*

31435 CATALOGUE of the exhibition of arts, manufactures, and practical science at Newcastle upon Tyne, 1840...(Tenth thousand.) [With addenda and 'Advertising sheet'.] 84, 2, [10]p. *8°. Newcastle,* 1840. *See also 1848.*

31436 CRAPELET, G. A. De la profession d'imprimeur, des maîtres imprimeurs, et de la nécessité actuelle de donner à l'imprimerie les règlemens promis par les lois. [With 'Liste générale des imprimeurs de Paris, depuis 1469 jusqu'en 1789'.] 130p. *8°. Paris,* 1840.

31437 —— Des brevets d'imprimeur, des certificats de capacité, et de la nécessité actuelle de donner à l'imprimerie les règlemens promis par les lois; suivi du tableau général des imprimeries de toute la France en 1704, 1739, 1810, 1830 et 1840. 92p. *8°. Paris*, 1840.

31438 CURTIS, W. J. Curtis's inventions, for railways, steam-vessels, &c. 78p. *8°.* 1840.

31439 EVANS, RICHARD. A report upon the strength and other properties of anthracite pig iron, conducted at Messrs. Whitworth & Co.'s, on account of the Ystalyfera Anthracite Iron Company. 22p. *8°. Manchester*, 1840.

31440 LARDNER, D. The steam engine explained and illustrated; with an account of its invention and progressive improvement, and its application to navigation and railways; including also a memoir of Watt... Seventh edition... 535p. *8°.* 1840. *For another edition, see* 1836.

31441 MARTIN, WILLIAM (1772–1851). The Christian philosopher's circular to the Houses of Lords & Commons. [On his invention of a safety lamp.] 2p. *8°. Newcastle*, [1840]

31442 —— Fraud detected and genius triumphant. The philosopher's just remarks on the polytechnic exhibition in the model room. 8p. *8°. Newcastle*, [1840]

31443 —— The philosopher's remarks on the blind leading the blind. [Including an account of the piracy of his swan-foot paddle by the Marquis de Jouffroy in France.] 4p. *8°. Newcastle*, [1840]

31444 MONTGOMERY, JAMES (1792–1880). A practical detail of the cotton manufacture of the United States of America; and the state of the cotton manufacture of that country contrasted and compared with that of Great Britain; with comparative estimates of the cost of manufacturing in both countries... 21p. *8°. Glasgow... New York*, 1840.

31445 PARTINGTON, C. F. Account of steam engines, and other models of machinery, illustrative of the latest improvements in railways, steam navigation, and the arts & manufactures; with an historical and descriptive account of the steam engine. 32p. *12°.* [1840?] *The Rastrick copy.*

31446 The **POLICY** of piracy: as a branch of national industry, and a source of commercial wealth...expounded and enforced in the evidence before the Select Committee of the House of Commons appointed to inquire into the expediency of extending the copyright of designs, of Daniel Lee, Esq. magistrate of the borough of Manchester, etc.etc. 36p. *8°. London & Manchester*, 1840.

31447 STATISTICS of Lowell manufactures. January 1, 1840. Compiled from authentic sources. [A table.] *s.sh.fol. Lowell*, [1840] [*Br. 597*] *See also* 1848.

31448 THOMSON, JAMES, *F.R.S.* A letter to the Vice-President of the Board of Trade on protection to original designs and patterns, printed upon woven fabrics ... 25p., 15 plates. *8°. Clitheroe*, [1840]

31449 WHITWORTH, SIR J., *Bart.* On plane metallic surfaces, and the proper mode of preparing them; read at the meeting of the British Association, at Glasgow ...1840. 16p. *8°.* 1840. *Presentation copy from the author to 'Ed^d Woods Esqre'.*

COMMERCE

31450 AMICUS CURIÆ, *pseud.* A word to the manufacturers of Great Britain on the prospects of the cotton trade. 25p. *8°.* 1840.

31451 BRITISH OPIUM TRADE with China. (From the Leeds Mercury, of September 7th, 1839[–February 8th, 1840].) 28p. *8°. Birmingham*, [1840]

31452 BULLOCK, T. H. The Chinese vindicated, or another view of the opium question; being in reply to a pamphlet, by Samuel Warren... 120p. *8°.* 1840.

31453 CARGILL, W. Address of William Cargill, Esq. to the South Shields Chamber of Commerce, May 4, 1840, on the foreign policy of England. [From the reports of the "Port of Tyne Pilot" and "Newcastle Journal," of 9th May, 1840.] 31p. *8°.* 1840.

31454 —— An examination of the origin, progress, and tendency of the commercial and political confederation against England and France called the "Prussian League." 50p. *8°. Newcastle*, 1840. *The copy that belonged to William Lovett.*

31455 —— Examen de l'origine, des progrès et de la tendance de la confédération commerciale et politique contre l'Angleterre et la France, nommée la Ligue Prussienne... Traduit de l'anglais. 68p. *8°. Paris*, 1840.

31456 CHINA. Portfolio Chinensis: or a collection of authentic Chinese state papers illustrative of the history of the present position of affairs in China. With a translation, notes and introduction, by J. Lewis Shuck. 191p. *8°.* *Macao, China*, 1840. *The text in Chinese has the translation printed below it.*

31457 CHINESE COMMERCE and disputes, from 1640 to 1840. Addressed to tea-dealers and consumers. By a looker-on. 32p. *8°.* 1840.

31458 CLEMENTS, G. Clements' customs guide [for 1840 & 1841], containing copious extracts of the laws, with tables of the duties payable upon goods imported and exported...to which is added a list of the warehousing ports...together with an appendix, containing an alphabetical arrangement of the different articles of merchandize...also, the London waterside practice... [Sixth annual edition.] 344p. *12°.* [1840] *See also* 1845.

31459 COOK, JAMES. Remarks on the law of principal and factor, with suggestions for remedying its defects. [With 'Appendix. An abstract of an Act to alter and amend an Act for the better protection of the property of merchants and others' and 'Evidence of James Manning, before the Committee of the House of Commons'.] 48p. *8°.* 1840.

31460 DIPLOMACY and commerce. No. II. I. Memorial of the operatives of Glasgow for the dismissal of Ministers. [With 'Conversation respecting the foregoing memorial, Star Hotel March 22d, 1840. Present, Mr. Urquhart [and others]'.] II. The sulphur monopoly. [With 'Conversation at the Star Hotel, March 31st, 1840. Present, Mr. Urquhart, Mr. Cargill, and merchants of the City of Glasgow'.] 36p. *8°. Glasgow, Edinburgh, &c.*, 1840. *For other numbers of this series, see nos.* 31372, 31797.

31461 ENGLAND. *Laws, etc.* [*Endorsed:*] Edinburgh market and petty customs. An Act for abolishing certain petty and market customs in the City of Edinburgh, and granting other duties in lieu thereof. ⟨Royal Assent, 3d April 1840.⟩ 3 Victoriæ, sess. 1840. 22p. *fol. Westminster,* [1840]

31462 FRY, W. S. Facts and evidence relating to the opium trade with China. [Dated: March 23d, 1840.] 64p. *8°.* 1840.

31463 —— Second thousand. [With a postscript, dated: April 14th, 1840.] 64, [2]p. *8°.* 1840.

31464 GRAHAM, Sir James R. G., *Bart.* Parliamentary speeches – Painter's edition. The war in China. Sir J. Graham's speech in the House of Commons... April 7, 1840. 15p. *8°.* [*London,* 1840]

31465 HUTT, Sir W. Published by the authority of the Chamber of Commerce of Kingston-on-Hull. Speech, delivered in the House of Commons, on...March 19, 1840...on the oppressive and illegal nature of the Stade duties. 23p. *8°.* 1840.

31466 MALES que tem resultado a Portugal dos tratados de commercio celebbados [*sic*] com a Inglaterra necessidade de promover a nossa industria fabril, e meios de tirar vantagem da navegação e commercio com as nossas possessões ultramarinas a despeito das tramas do governo daquelle paiz. Por um Portuguez verdadeiro amigo da sua patria. 24p. *8°. Lisboa,* 1840.

31467 NAVILLE, E. Du droit maritime et des relations commerciales des peuples considérés dans leur rapport avec les affaires d'Orient. 90p. *8°. Paris,* 1840.

31468 [PALMER, R., *Earl of Selborne.*] Statement of claims of the British subjects interested in opium surrendered to Captain Elliot at Canton for the public service. 209p. *8°.* 1840.

31469 REVIEW of the Neapolitan sulphur question. By a British merchant. 42p. *8°. n.p.,* 1840.

31470 SOETBEER, A. Ueber Hamburgs Handel. 304p. *8°. Hamburg,* 1840. *For continuations of this work, see* 1842 *and* 1846.

31471 STAUNTON, Sir G. T., *Bart.* Corrected report of the speech of Sir George Staunton, on Sir James Graham's motion on the China trade, in the House of Commons, April 7, 1840. With an appendix, containing resolutions on the China trade, moved [by Sir George Staunton] in the House of Commons, June 13, 1833. 20, ivp. *8°.* 1840.

31472 URQUHART, D. The sulphur monopoly... (From the "Newcastle Journal," of June 20, 1840.) 8p. *8°.* [1840]

31473 WARREN, S. The opium question. [With 'Addition. 14th January, 1840'.] 130p. *8°.* 1840.

31474 [——] The opium question, as between nation and nation. By a barrister at law. 52p. *8°.* 1840.

COLONIES

For **AGRICULTURAL AND HORTICULTURAL SOCIETY OF INDIA,** Proceedings, 1840–42, *see* vol. III, *Periodicals list,* Proceedings...

31475 ANDERSON, John (1795–1845). Acheen, and the ports on the north and east coasts of Sumatra; with incidental notices of the trade in the eastern seas, and the aggressions of the Dutch. 240p. *8°.* 1840.

31476 BARCLAY, A. Remarks on emigration to Jamaica: addressed to the coloured class of the United States. 16p. *8°. New-York,* 1840.

31477 BRIGGS, John. The cotton trade of India. Part I. Its past and present condition; Part II. Its future prospects... 88p. *8°.* 1840.

31478 BRUCE, C. A. Report on the manufacture of tea, and on the extent and produce of the tea plantations in Assam... 36p. *8°. Edinburgh & London,* 1840. *For another edition, see* 1839.

31479 BURN, D. Vindication of Van Diemen's Land; in a cursory glance at her colonists as they are, not as they have been represented to be. 79p. *8°.* 1840.

31480 CHAPMAN, Edward, *and others.* Outlines of a plan submitted to...Government for...establishing an authorized committee to regulate and carry on the introduction of Indian laborers at Mauritius [signed: Edward Chapman, Henry Barlow, C. C. Brownrigg, John P. Rowlandson, Robert Bullen, J. Edward Arbuthnot, and dated from Mauritius, 17th December 1839]...to which are added some observations on the causes which have led to the deficiency of laborers at Mauritius...together with reasons for having recourse to India for the laborers who

are required. The observations by Charles Anderson, Esq. Judge of the Court of Peace and Police... 23p. *8°.* 1840.

31481 DUTOT, S. De l'expatriation, considérée sous ses rapports économiques, politiques et moraux...suivi d'un mémoire de M. le Prince de Talleyrand de Périgord ['Essai sur les avantages à retirer des colonies nouvelles... lu à séance publique du 15 messidor an v']. 355p. *8°. Paris,* 1840.

31482 EMIGRATION its necessity and advantages. [With particular reference to Australia.] 15p. *8°. Exeter & London,* 1840. *The final page contains an advertisement of sailings during 1840 to Port Philip and Sydney, issued by John Marshall, Australian emigration agent.*

31483 Responsible GOVERNMENT for colonies. [Reprinted from a series of articles in the *Colonial Gazette* December 1839–February 1840.] Second edition. 107p. *12°.* 1840.

31484 GURNEY, Joseph J. A winter in the West Indies, described in familiar letters to Henry Clay, of Kentucky...Second edition. 282p. *8°. London & Norwich,* 1840.

31485 *HANCOCK, J. Observations on the climate, soil, and productions of British Guiana, and on the advantages of emigration to, and colonizing the interior of, that country. Together with incidental remarks on the diseases, their treatment and prevention...Second edition. 92p. *8°.* 1840. *The copy that belonged to George Grote.*

31486 HEAD, Sir F. B., *Bart.* An address to the House of Lords, against the Bill before Parliament for the union of the Canadas; and disclosing the improper means by which the consent of the Legislature of the Upper Province has been obtained to the measure. 52p. *8⁰*. 1840.

31487 JAMIESON, R. An appeal to the government and people of Great Britain, against the proposed Niger expedition: a letter, addressed to the Right Hon. Lord John Russell, Principal Secretary of State for the Colonies, &c.&c.&c. 27p. *8⁰*. 1840.

31488 LANG, JOHN D. An historical and statistical account of New South Wales, both as a penal settlement and as a British colony... Third edition. 2 vols. *12⁰*. 1840. *For another edition, see* 1834.

31489 NEW SOUTH WALES. *Colonial Secretary's Office.* Regulations for the introduction of emigrants into the colony of New South Wales, by private individuals, dated 3rd March, 1840. [Signed: E. Deas Thomson.] 10p. *12⁰*. *Sydney,* [1840]

**31490 —— ** *Legislative Council.* Debate in the Legislative Council of New South Wales, and other documents on the subject of immigration to the colony. October, 1840. Published under the direction of the Australian Immigration Association. 51p. *8⁰*. *Sydney,* [1840]

**31491 —— —— ** (No. 2.) Report of the debate in the Legislative Council of New South Wales... 10th December, 1840, upon a motion for an address to Her Majesty upon the subject of a proposed division of the territory; and the introduction of a new system for the disposal of crown lands... [With an appendix.] 41, 9p. *8⁰*. *Sydney,* [1840 ?]

31492 NOTICES of New Zealand. [Regulations of the New Zealand, Manakou and Waitemata Company. Terms of purchase of land. New Zealand Emigration Society, Manakou and Waitemata Company, dated 1st September 1840.] 43p. *8⁰*. *Edinburgh,* [1840]

31493 PRESTON, T. R. Three years' residence in Canada, from 1837 to 1839. With notes of a winter voyage to New York, and journey thence to the British possessions: to which is added, a review of the condition of the Canadian people. 2 vols. *12⁰*. 1840.

31494 Preliminary **PROSPECTUS** of the South African Company; with practical notes, containing a general description and some information on the natural

circumstances of the colony at the Cape of Good Hope. 38p. *8⁰*. 1840.

31495 ROBINSON, SIR JOHN B., *Bart.* Canada and the Canada Bill; being an examination of the proposed measure for the future government of Canada; with an introductory chapter, containing some general views respecting the British provinces in North America. [With the text of the Bill as an appendix.] 223p. *8⁰*. 1840.

**31496 —— ** [Another edition, without the appendix.] 198p. *8⁰*. *London,* [*Toronto reprinted,*] 1840.

31497 *SCHOMBURGK, SIR R. H. A description of British Guiana, geographical and statistical: exhibiting its resources and capabilities... 155p. *8⁰*. 1840. *The copy that belonged to George Grote.*

31498 STEPHEN, SIR G. A letter to the Rt. Hon. Lord John Russell, &c.&c.&c. in reply to Mr. Jamieson, on the Niger expedition. 36p. *8⁰*. [1840]

31499 [TRAILL, C. P.] The backwoods of Canada: being letters from the wife of an emigrant officer, illustrative of the domestic economy of British America. Fifth edition. 351p. *12⁰*. 1840.

31500 TUCKETT, H. The Indian revenue system as it is. A letter addressed to... the Manchester Chamber of Commerce and Manufactures... For the East India Cotton Company. 172p. *8⁰*. 1840.

31501 A **VIEW** of the evidence given before a Select Committee of the House of Commons, on a petition from the East India Company, praying for relief to India in reference to unequal duties and other grievances; with notes, containing portions of the evidence given on the same subjects before a Select Committee of the House of Lords. 102p. *8⁰*. 1840.

31502 WARD, JOHN (1805–1890). Information relative to New Zealand, compiled for the use of colonists... Second edition, corrected and enlarged. 168p. *12⁰*. 1840. *See also* 1841.

31503 A few **WORDS** on the promoting and encouraging of free emigration to the West India colonies. Addressed to the Right Honourable Lord John Russell, Secretary of State for the Colonial Department. 26p. *8⁰*. *Liverpool,* 1840.

FINANCE

31504 AKERMAN, J. Y. A numismatic manual. 420p. *8⁰*. 1840.

31505 AUDIFFRET, C. L. G. D', *Marquis.* Système financier de la France... 2 vols. *8⁰*. *Paris,* 1840.

31506 [BAILEY, S.] A defence of joint-stock banks and country issues. By the author of Money and its vicissitudes in value, Essays on the formation of opinions, &c.&c. 100p. *8⁰*. 1840.

31507 BANK OF MANCHESTER. [*Begin.*] Caution. The letters addressed to the Bank of Manchester having on... the 19th instant, been delivered at the Post-Office to some person not authorised to receive them, the public are informed that the following bills of exchange and Bank of England post bill were contained in the letters so fraudulently obtained... [A notice, dated: 23rd December 1840.] *s.sh.fol. n.p.* [1840]

31508 BATEMAN, J. The excise officer's manual,

and improved practical gauger; being a compendious introduction to the business of charging and collecting the duties of excise. 368p. *12⁰*. *London & Dublin,* 1840.

31509 BELL, GAVIN M. The philosophy of joint stock banking. 105p. *8⁰*. 1840.

31510 BELL, JOHN (1797–1869). Speech of Mr. Bell, of Tennessee, on the Sub-Treasury Bill, delivered in the House of Representatives, June 16 and 17, 1840. 43p. *8⁰*. *Washington,* 1840.

31511 BELL, ROBERT, *of Edinburgh.* A letter to James William Gilbart, Esq. general manager of the London and Westminster Bank, on the regulation of the currency by the foreign exchanges. And on the appointment of the Bank of England to be the sole bank of issue throughout Great Britain. 32p. *8⁰*. 1840. *Presentation copy from the author to John Thomson.*

31512 BLACK, DONALD. Observations on Henry

Drummond, Esq.'s pamphlet, entitled "Causes which lead to a bank restriction Bill;" with an argument as to what is gold and what is paper? Together with a plan for establishing a certain and fixed national currency. 25p. *8°.* 1840.

31513 BOND, Sir Edward A., *ed.* Extracts from the Liberate Rolls, relative to loans supplied by Italian merchants to the Kings of England, in the thirteenth and fourteenth centuries: with an introductory memoir... Communicated to the Society of Antiquaries by Charles George Young. [From The Archaeologia, vol. xxviii.] 120p. *4°.* 1840.

31514 BOUCHERETT, A. A few observations on corn, currency, &c., with a plan for promoting the interests of agriculture and manufactures. 24p. *8°.* 1840.

31515 *—— [Another edition.] 20p. *8°.* 1840. *Presentation copy from the author to George Grote.*

31516 BRESSON, J. Histoire financière de la France, depuis l'origine de la monarchie jusqu'à l'année 1828, précédée d'une introduction sur le mode d'impôts en usage avant la Révolution, suivie de considérations sur la marche du crédit public... Deuxième édition. 2 vols. *8°. Paris,* 1840. *For other editions, see* 1829.

31517 BRODIE, William B. Letter to the Rt. Hon. Sir Robert Peel, Bart., M.P. containing an answer to Mr. Samuel Jones Loyd's proposition for the suppression of the country banks of issue, and for the establishment of "one general bank of issue." 20p. *8°.* 1840.

31518 —— Third edition, with notes appended. 24p. *8°.* 1840.

31519 BUCHANAN, James, *President of the USA.* Remarks of Mr. Buchanan, of Pennsylvania, in reply to Mr. Davis, of Massachusetts, against the Independent Treasury Bill. Senate, U.S., March 3, 1840. 8p. *8°. Washington,* 1840.

31520 [CAPPS, E.] The nation in a dilemma; or, which shall we alter? the currency? or the mode of taxation? By the author of "The currency question in a nutshell." 39p. *8°.* 1840. *See also* 1843.

31521 CHAMBER OF COMMERCE, *Manchester.* Under the sanction of the Directors. Report of the Directors to a special general meeting of the Chamber of Commerce and Manufactures at Manchester, on the effects of the administration of the Bank of England upon the commercial and manufacturing interests of the country. 12th December 1839. [Compiled by Richard Cobden.] Third edition. 26p. *8°. London & Manchester,* 1840.

31522 —— Fourth edition. 26p. *8°. London & Manchester,* 1840.

31523 CHRISTIE, R. Annuity societies. An exposure of the unsoundness of the Western Annuity Society, established at Exeter for providing annuities to wives on the decease of their husbands, to children...and of certain kindred societies established in England and Ireland for the same purpose. 41p. *8°. Edinburgh, London, &c.,* 1840. *Presentation copy, in a volume with later pamphlets and inscription, dated 1856, from the author to John Whiteford McKenzie.*

31524 [COLTON, C.] The crisis of the country. By Junius...The credit system and the no credit system. 16p. *8°. New York & Boston,* [1840]

31525 CORVAJA, G., *Barone.* La bancocrazia o il

gran libro sociale novello sistema finanziario che mira a basare i governi su tutti gl'interessi positivi dei governati ...Espositore Michele Parma. 2 vols. *8°. Milano,* 1840–41.

31526 —— Die Bancocratie oder die den Staaten selbst angehörenden Bankanstalten, nach ihrem wahren Princip dargestellt als die einzige ächte Grundlage der materiellen Interessen und einer soliden socialen Ordnung... Ins Deutsche mit einigen Modificationen frei übersetzt und noch mit einer Einleitung und einigen Anmerkungen vermehrt herausgegeben von Ulrich von Mohr. [With 'Entwurf der organischen Statuten für eine National-bankanstalt nach unsern neuen Systeme'.] 94p. *8°. Heidelberg,* 1840.

31527 CORY, I. P. A practical treatise on accounts, mercantile, private, and official: exhibiting the manner in which the method of double entry may be applied to the accounts of Government; with proposals for the introduction of a uniform and centralized system of accounts in all the public offices. [With an appendix.] 184, 65p. *8°.* 1840. *For the author's earlier work, here adapted for official accounts, see* 1839.

31528 Monetary **CURRENCY:** or, the operation of money shown to be a perfect science, and that the unlimited amount and uncertain issue of paper, or other fictitious money, is the sole and immediate cause of all the commercial evils that now afflict the trading world. 30p. *8°.* 1840.

31529 DALY, T. The Cash-payment Bill of 1819, and the Bank of England. 116p. *8°.* 1840.

31530 DAVIS, John (1787–1854). Reply of John Davis, of Massachusetts, to Mr. Buchanan, of Pennsylvania on the reduction of wages and of the value of property. Delivered in the Senate...January 23, 1840. Together with extracts from the speeches of Messrs. Buchanan, Walker, Benton, and Calhoun. [With 'Reply ...to the charge of misrepresenting Mr. Buchanan's argument'.] 30p. *8°. Washington,* 1840.

31531 —— Speech of Mr. Davis of Massachusetts on the Sub-Treasury Bill, in the Senate...January 23, 1840. 16p. *8°. Brattleboro,* [1840]

31532 ELIOT, W. A letter to the Right Honourable the Chancellor of the Exchequer, on the question concerning the country banks of issue of England and Wales; with remarks on the projected establishment of "one general bank of issue." 22p. *8°. London & Weymouth,* 1840.

31533 FARREN, G. Joint stock banks. Legal decisions affecting the security of, and the remedies against, such associations. 28p. *8°.* [1840]

31534 FENN, C. A compendium of the English and foreign funds, and the principal joint stock companies; forming an epitome of the various objects of investment negotiable in London, with...tables for calculating the value of the different stocks, &c....The third edition, with addenda, brought down to the present time. 190, 22p. *12°.* 1840.

31535 FERGUSON, W. Tables of interest, for the use of bankers and others, at thirteen different rates, from a quarter to six per cent. To which is added, a table of commission or brokerage, at the same rates, from one shilling to twenty thousand pounds. 191p. *8°. Glasgow, Edinburgh, &c.,* 1840.

31536 FRANCE. *Administration des Douanes.* Tarif commercial des douanes françaises, suivi des tarifs de tous les droits accessoires, d'un tableau général des tares, des marchandises jouissant de la prime, et d'une grande quantité de notes explicatives. Par plusieurs employés des douanes... 153p. *4°. Havre,* 1840[–41 ?]. *Interleaved, with printed insertions in conformity with laws enacted in 1841. HSF's manuscript note records that the following was printed on a label on the contemporary boards: 'Par A. Réville, Verificateur des Douanes. 2e édition, revue et augmentée d'une grande quantité de notes et de renseignements communiqué par un employé supérieur de la Douane du Havre'.*

31537 GILBART, J. W. An inquiry into the causes of the pressure on the money market during the year 1839. 63p. *8°.* 1840.

31538 GONON, P. M. Médaille commémorative de l'établissement du système métrique et de son usage exclusif, publiée à Lyon par P. M. Gonon, dessinée et gravée par Marius Penin. 8p. *8°. Lyon,* 1840.

31539 [GREGG, St. G.] The currency; its laws, evils, and remedies. Panics prevented and high rates of interest removed. 28p. *8°.* 1840.

31540 —— St. George's vision of St. Patrick's ideas on currency and coin; with further observations on "The currency, its evils, and their remedies." 19p. *8°.* 1840.

31541 HABERSHAM, R. W. Speech of Mr. Habersham, of Georgia, on the Treasury Note Bill, delivered in the House of Representatives, March 24, 1840. 8p. *8°. Washington,* 1840.

31542 HAGGARD, W. D. Observations on the standard of value and the circulating medium of this country. 35p. *8°.* 1840. *See also* 1847.

31543 [HAZARD, T. R.] Facts for the laboring man. By a laboring man. [A series of articles signed: Narragansett, from the Newport, R.I., *Herald of the Times.*] 102p. *8°. Newport, R.I.,* 1840.

31544 HERRIES, J. C. Financial state of the country. Defeat of the Whig ministry. – No. II. Speeches of Mr. Herries and Mr. Goulburn, in the House of Commons, Feb. 13, 1840... 16p. *8°.* [*London,* 1840]

31545 HILDRETH, R. Banks, banking, and paper currencies; in three parts. I. History of banking and paper money. II. Argument for open competition in banking. III. Apology for one-dollar notes. 209p. *12°. Boston,* 1840.

31546 HOFFMANN, C. H. L. Das Finanzwesen von Württemberg zu Anfang des sechzehnten Jahrhunderts. Ein Beitrag zur württembergischen Finanzgeschichte. 92p. *8°. Tübingen,* 1840.

31547 HOFFMANN, Johann G. Die Lehre von den Steuern als Anleitung zu gründlichen Urtheilen über das Steuerwesen, mit besonderer Beziehung auf den preussischen Staat. 459p. *8°. Berlin,* 1840.

31548 HOWLEY, W., *Archbishop of Canterbury, and others.* Ecclesiastical Duties' and Revenues' Bill. Speeches of the Archbishop of Canterbury, Bishops of Winchester, Gloucester, Salisbury, Lincoln, Rochester, Exeter, and London. In the House of Lords, July 27th and 30th, 1840. 32p. *8°.* [*London,* 1840]

31549 HUME, Joseph, *and others.* Provision for Prince Albert. Defeat of Her Majesty's Ministers. – No. I. Speeches of Mr. Hume, Mr. Liddell, Sir R. Inglis, Mr. Goulburn, Col. Sibthorp, Sir James Graham, and Sir Robert Peel, in the House of Commons, January 28, 1840. 16p. *8°.* [*London,* 1840]

31550 JAKOB, L. H. von. Science des finances, exposée théoriquement et pratiquement, et expliquée par des exemples tirés de l'histoire financière moderne des états de l'Europe. Ouvrage traduit de l'allemand...par Henri Jouffroy... 2 vols. *8°. Leipsic & Paris,* 1840–41.

31551 JONES, Richard (1790–1855). A letter to the Right Honourable Sir Robert Peel Bart. on the Bill introduced into Parliament by the Attorney-General to exempt all persons from being assessed as inhabitants to parochial rates. 14p. *8°.* 1840.

31552 JOPLIN, T. A letter to the shareholders of the London & County Banking Company, on the propriety of making a change in the direction, at the annual general meeting on...February 6, 1840, and other improvements. 42p. *8°.* 1840. *The copy that belonged to Hyde Clark.*

31553 —— Prospectus of an association to promote the establishment of a uniform currency under one general head. 15p. *8°. London & Manchester,* 1840.

31554 LEATHAM, W. Letters on the currency, addressed to Charles Wood, Esq. M.P. chairman of the Committee of the House of Commons, now sitting; and ascertaining...the amount of inland and foreign bills of exchange in circulation for several consecutive years... 68p. *8°.* 1840.

31555 —— Second edition, with corrections and additions. Also, defending country bankers from the charge made against them in the work of S. Jones Loyd, Esq.... 70p. *8°.* 1840.

31556 A LETTER to the Right Honourable Lord Viscount Melbourne, upon the state of banking in England during the last fifty years; particularly with reference to the...proceedings of the Bank of England, and their effects on the trade, manufactures, and agriculture of the country, and on the condition of the working classes. By a merchant. 117p. *8°.* 1840.

31557 LIFE-ASSURANCE. (Extracted from an article in Chambers' Journal for March 1839.) 2p. *8°. n.p.* [1840 ?]

31558 LOWNDES, M. D. Review of the Joint Stock Bank Acts, and of the law as to joint stock companies generally; with the practical suggestions of a solicitor for their amendment; in a letter to the Right Honourable the Chancellor of the Exchequer. 45p. *8°.* 1840.

31559 LOYD, S. J., *Baron Overstone.* A letter to J. B. Smith, Esq. President of the Manchester Chamber of Commerce. [On the management of the Bank of England.] 28p. *8°.* 1840.

31560 —— Effects of the administration of the Bank of England. A second letter to J. B. Smith, Esq. President of the Manchester Chamber of Commerce. 58p. *8°.* 1840.

31561 —— Remarks on the management of the circulation; and on the condition and conduct of the Bank of England and of the country issuers, during the year 1839. 135p. *8°.* 1840. *The author's own copy, formerly among his papers, for which see vol.* III, *MS.* 804.

31562 —— Thoughts on the separation of the departments in the Bank of England. 44p. *8°.* 1840. *The author's own copy, formerly among his papers, for which see vol.* III, *MS.* 804. *See also* 1844.

31563 [LUBBOCK, Sir J. W., *Bart.*] On currency. [With an appendix.] 43, xxip. *8°.* 1840.

31564 MACARDY, J. Outlines of banks, banking and currency. 234p. *8°. Manchester,* 1840. *See also* 1842.

31565 MALET, W. W. On Church extension; or, an enquiry, what should the state do? Or, what can the Church do, unless her rights are restored and her efficiency upheld? 94p. *8°.* 1840.

31566 NATIONAL LOAN FUND LIFE AS-SURANCE, AND DEFERRED ANNUITY SOCIETY. First report of the Directors at the annual general meeting of proprietors, held on the 13th day of May, 1840... 23p. *8°.* [1840]

31567 NATIONAL SECURITY SAVINGS BANK. Report on the affairs of the National Security Savings Bank of Edinburgh, for the year to 20th November 1839...presented to the annual general meeting...14th February, 1840. Together with excerpts from the minutes of that meeting. 8p. *8°. Edinburgh,* 1840. *See also* 1838, 1841, 1845.

31568 NIMMO, T. Remarks on currency & banking; with suggestions for their improvement. 30p. *8°.* 1840.

31569 A few short **OBSERVATIONS** on the currency. By an old merchant. 16p. *8°.* 1840. *Attributed by HSF, in the Kress copy (C 5169), to 'Mr. Gibbs of the London and Westminster Bank', i.e. Charles Gibbes.*

31570 [OGDEN, JAMES DE P.] Remarks on the currency of the United States and present state and future prospects of the country. By Publius. 59p. *8°. New York,* 1840.

31571 PEDIE, J. The derangement of the currency the cause of the distress of the country and sufferings of the people, and the nature of that derangement; to which is added, a short dissertation on free trade as applicable to Great Britain. 72p. *8°.* 1840. *A revised and re-written edition of* The causes of the distress of the country, *1839* (q.v.).

31572 PELL, G. H. Outline of a plan of a national currency, not liable to fluctuations in value. 29p. *8°.* 1840.

31573 PENNINGTON, JAMES. A letter to Kirkman Finlay, Esq., on the importation of foreign corn, and the value of the precious metals in different countries. To which are added observations on money, and the foreign exchange. 114p. *8°.* 1840.

31574 PENZANCE. Tariff for all goods, wares, and merchandize imported at, or exported from, and for all ships, vessels, yachts, fishing boats, etc., etc., entering into the pier, quay, dock, or harbour, of Penzance... 24p. *fol. Penzance,* 1840.

31575 A **PLAN** for regulating the circulation on the principle of Sir Robert Peel's celebrated Currency Bill of 1819. By a man of business. 30p. *8°.* 1840. *Attributed to 'a Mr. W. Williams' in a manuscript note on the title-page. Manuscript copies of two letters from the author to the editor of the Morning Post, explaining the text, have been bound at the end of the volume.*

31576 RAGUET, C. A treatise on currency and banking...Second edition. 328p. *12°. Philadelphia,* 1840. *Presentation copy, with inscription, from the author to Edward Copleston, Bishop of Llandaff.*

31577 —— Traité des banques et de la circulation... Traduit par L. Lemaitre. xxviii, 371p. *8°. Paris,* 1840. *For another edition, see* 1839.

31578 REFLECTIONS on the proposed diminution of customs' duty on foreign brandy, and rumoured augmentation of excise duty on British spirit. 31p. *8°.* 1840.

31579 REINAGLE, R. R. An inquiry into the general system of banking...Also, a view of the practical means of converting the National Debt into one of the most powerful agents for national prosperity... 108p. *8°.* 1840.

31580 Practical **REMARKS** on currency and banking, particularly in reference to the system of Scotland: in a letter addressed to Samuel Jones Loyd, Esq....By a Scotch banker. 37p. *8°. Glasgow, Edinburgh, &c.,* 1840. *See also* 1841.

31581 REMARKS suggested by the present state of trade and credit. 32p. *8°.* 1840.

31582 ROYAL BANK OF AUSTRALIA. Deed of settlement of the Royal Bank of Australia. 67p. *4°. Edinburgh,* [1840]

31583 RUDING, R. Annals of the coinage of Great Britain and its dependencies; from the earliest period of authentic history to the reign of Victoria...Third edition ... 3 vols. *4°.* 1840. *For another edition, see* 1819.

31584 *[SAINT-CLAIR, W.] Popular view of life assurance...To which are added a condensed view of the principles of all the English and Scottish life offices of note...[With 'Appendix containing advertisements of the undermentioned [13] assurance offices'.] 78, [44]p. *8°. London & Edinburgh,* 1840. *The copy that belonged to Augustus De Morgan.*

31585 SALOMONS, SIR D., *Bart.* Reflections on the recent pressure on the money-market, and the means suggested to prevent future monetary difficulties. 82p. *8°.* 1840.

31586 SCOTTISH PROVIDENT INSTITU-TION. Summary of the principles and proceedings of the Scottish Provident Institution for Assurances and Annuities. With comparative tables of the annual premium required by each of the Scottish offices for the assurance of £100...[Containing excerpts from the proceedings of the first and second annual general meetings of contributors, 1839 and 1840.] 24p. *8°. Edinburgh,* 1840.

31587 SENIOR, N. W. ⟨Unpublished.⟩ Three lectures on the value of money, delivered before the University of Oxford, in 1829. 84p. *8°.* 1840.

31588 SMITH, JOHN B. Effects of the administration of the Bank of England. Reply to the letter of Samuel Jones Loyd, Esq. 22p. *8°. London & Manchester,* 1840.

31589 SMITH, THOMAS, *accountant, of Liverpool.* Commercial hints, and companion to the counting-house, &c. Single entry book-keeping on a new and important system. Double entry book-keeping practically explained and simplified. [Second edition of all three works.] 30, 58, 61p. *8°. Birmingham & London,* 1840. *Wanting two leaves, probably the general title and the title-page of the first work.*

31590 Ueber den **STAATSKREDIT.** Von einem russischen Staatsmanne. 176p. *8°. Leipzig,* 1840. *HSF note: From Professor Roscher's library.*

31591 TAYLOR, F. Works on banking and currency. Tables of contents of the Financial Register and Quinn's Trade of banking, for sale by Frank Taylor, bookseller, Washington City. 12p. *12°. Washington,* 1840.

31592 TORRENS, R. A letter to Thomas Tooke, Esq. in reply to his objections against the separation of the business of the Bank into a department of issue, and a department of deposit and discount: with a plan of bank reform. 48p. *8°. 1840. Presentation copy from the author to T. Spring Rice, Baron Monteagle.*

31593 UNDERWOOD, J. R. Speech of Mr. Underwood, of Kentucky, on the Sub-Treasury Bill, delivered in the House of Representatives, June 8, 1840. 36p. *8°. Washington, 1840.*

31594 VANDERPOEL, A. Speech of Mr. Vanderpoel, of New York, on the bill to authorize the issue of Treasury notes; delivered in Committee of the Whole. In the House of Representatives, March 19, 1840. 14p. *8°. Washington, 1840.*

31595 WARD, W. On monetary derangements, in a

letter addressed to the proprietors of bank stock. 40p. *8°.* 1840.

31596 [WILLIAMS, Henry.] Remarks on banks and banking; and the skeleton of a project for a national bank. By a citizen of Boston. 62p. *8°. Boston, 1840.*

31597 [WOOD, William R]. The management of the circulation in connection with the fluctuations of prices. 24p. *8°. Manchester, 1840.*

31598 WYLLIE, R. C. A letter to G. R. Robinson, Esq. chairman of the Committee of Spanish American Bondholders, on the present state and prospects of the Spanish American loans. 32p. *8°.* [1840]

TRANSPORT

31599 ANDERSON, Arthur (1792–1868). Steam communication with India. A letter to the directors of the projected East Indian Steam Navigation Company, containing a practical exposition of the prospects of that proposed undertaking, and of the real state of the question of steam communication with India. [With a prospectus of the Peninsular & Oriental Steam Navigation Company, printed on the final leaf.] 22p. *8°.* 1840.

31600 The earnest **APPEAL** of a Greenwich shareholder [of the Greenwich Railway Company] to the justice and consideration of Parliament. 16p. *8°.* 1840.

31601 BINEAU, J. M. Chemins de fer d'Angleterre. Leur état actuel; législation qui les régit; conditions d'art de leur tracé...Application à la France des résultats de l'éxperience de l'Angleterre et de la Belgique. 456p. *8°. Paris,* 1840.

31602 BOYMAN, B. Steam navigation, its rise and progress. With authentic tables of the extent of the steam marine of all parts of the globe, contrasted with the steam power of the British Empire; imperfections of the present system of steam navigation, and Symington's inventions ... 173p. *8°.* 1840.

31603 BREES, S. C. Second series of Railway practice: a collection of working plans and practical details of construction in the public works of the most celebrated engineers: comprising roads, tramroads, and railroads; bridges...canals...harbors, docks...drainage of marshes ...water-works... 124p. *4°. 1840. For editions of the first series, see 1837, and for the fourth 1847.*

31604 En **CHARGE** à Rouen. Pour Danzig, prenant le Kœnigsberg, le navire goelette, l'Auguste, capitaine N.-A. Persil...Pour Saint-Pétersbourg, le navire brick, les Deux Adèles, capitaine B. Damiens...[A handbill, with days of departure and costs of freight, dated: 26 février 1840.] *s.sh.8°. Rouen,* [1840]

31605 FAIRBAIRN, H. A letter to the shareholders of the Southampton Railway; on the practicability and expediency of carrying merchandise by horse power, without impeding the present arrangements of the steam locomotive passenger trains. 28p. *8°. 1840. The Rastrick copy.*

31606 *FRANCE. *Chambre des Députés.* (No. 168.) Session 1840. Rapport fait au nom de la Commission chargée d'examiner le projet de loi relatif aux chemins de fer. Par M. de Beaumont. Séance du 30 mai 1840. 88p. *8°.* [*Paris,*] 1840. *The copy that belonged to George Grote.*

31607 A **GUIDE** or companion to the Midland

Counties Railway, containing its parliamentary history, engineering facts...Also fare and time tables; with a plan, and section of the gradients, and numerous pictorial illustrations. 110p. *12°. Leicester: R. Tebbutt, London, &c., 1840. With an 84-page advertiser of Leicester, Nottingham and Derby.*

31608 GUYONNEAU DE PAMBOUR, F. M., *Comte.* A practical treatise on locomotive engines...A second edition, increased by a great many new experiments ... 583p. *8°. 1840. For another edition, see 1836.*

31609 A practical **INQUIRY** into the laws of excavation and embankment upon railways; being an attempt to develope the natural causes which affect the progress of such works, and to point out the means by which the greatest expedition and economy in execution may be obtained...By a resident assistant engineer. 173p. *8°.* 1840. *The Rastrick copy.*

31610 The **MIDLAND COUNTIES'** Railway companion, with topographical descriptions of the country through which the line passes; and time, fare, and distance tables, corrected to the 24th August. Also, complete guides to the London and Birmingham, and Birmingham and Derby Junction Railways. 135p. *12°. Nottingham: R. Allen, Leicester: E. Allen, &c., 1840. A 166-page advertiser of Leicester and other Midland towns, with a classified index, is bound at the end of the volume.*

31611 —— [Another issue, without the timetables.] 135p. *12°. Nottingham: R. Allen, Leicester: E. Allen, &c., 1840.*

31612 MOGG, E. Mogg's handbook for railway travellers; or, real iron-road book: being an entirely original and accurate description of all the travellable railways hitherto completed; pointing out the stations... on all the various lines. To which are added, topographical sketches of the several cities...Second edition... 235, 13p. *12°. 1840. The Rastrick copy.*

31613 —— An appendix to Mogg's hand book for railway travellers; being a description of the rail roads, at present in operation for the conveyance of passengers in various parts of the kingdom. 101, 34p. *12°. 1840. The Rastrick copy.*

31614 NAVIRE en charge à Rouen pour Elseneur, Dantzig et Kœnigsberg. [A handbill.] *s.sh.8°. Rouen,* [1840 ?] *Concerning the Dutch smack Vrouw-Alida, captain P. T. Swiers.*

31615 The **NORTH KENT RAILWAY,** from London to Ramsgate, passing through or near the towns

of Deptford, Greenwich, Woolwich, Dartford, Gravesend
...Rochester, Chatham...Canterbury & Margate, with a
branch from Rochester to Maidstone. [An early prospectus.] [4]p. *fol.* [*London*, 1840?]

31616 OSBORNE, E. C. and W. Osborne's London
& Birmingham railway guide... 270p. *12°. Birmingham* &
London, [1840]

31617 PALMER, HENRY R. Report on the improvement of the rivers Mersey and Irwell, between Liverpool
and Manchester, describing the means of adapting them
for the navigation of sea-going vessels. 44p. *8°.* 1840.

31618 SAINT-HILAIRE, DE. Dunkerque, 20
février 1840. [Circular letter, announcing a regular steam-boat service between Dunkirk, Rotterdam and Hamburg,
beginning 7 March 1840.] *s.sh.8°. n.p.* [1840]

31619 SMYTH, WILLIAM H. Nautical observations
on the port and maritime vicinity of Cardiff, with occasional strictures on the ninth report of the Taff Vale
Railway Directors; and some general remarks on the
commerce of Glamorganshire. [With 'Appendix. Rules
and regulations of the Bute Docks, at Cardiff'.] viii, 100,
12p. *8°. Cardiff*, 1840.

31620 An authentic **STATEMENT** of the affairs of
the Edinburgh, Leith and Newhaven Railway Company,
from the period of its projection in 1835, to the close of
the year 1840. By an original proprietor. 28p. *8°. Bristol*,
1840.

31621 STATEMENTS illustrative of the position
and prospects of steam navigation, in 1840. 52p. *8°.* 1840.

**31622 [STOCKTON AND DARLINGTON
RAILWAY.]** Cheap and rapid travelling between
Stockton and Sunderland. [A poster for an omnibus

service, beginning on 10 February 1840, linking Stockton
and Castle Eden, whence passengers may go by rail to
Sunderland. Dated: Feb. 4th 1849.] *s.sh.fol. Sunderland*,
[1840]

**31623 STOCKTON AND DARLINGTON
RAILWAY.** Excursion to the Tees Bay and Seaton.
Life boats & exhibition of rockets. Notice. [Dated:
August 22nd, 1840.] *s.sh.4°. Darlington*, [1840]

**31624 STOCKTON AND HARTLEPOOL
RAILWAY COMPANY.** To plate layers on railways.
Wanted immediately, a number of plate layers on the
Stockton and Hartlepool Railway...29th July, 1840. [A
poster.] *s.sh.4°. Hartlepool*, [1840]

31625 TANNER, H. S. A description of the canals
and rail roads of the United States, comprehending notices
of all the works of internal improvement throughout the
several states. 272p. *8°. New York*, 1840.

31626 —— [Another edition.] 272p. *8°. New York*,
London, &*c.*, 1840.

31627 WHISHAW, F. The railways of Great Britain
and Ireland practically described and illustrated. [With an
appendix.] xxvi, 500, lxivp. *4°.* 1840.

31628 WHITE, JOHN (*d.* 1850). An essay on the
formation of harbours of refuge, and the improvement of
the navigation of rivers and sea ports, by the adoption of
moored floating constructions as breakwaters... 59p. *8°.*
1840.

31629 YATES, JOSEPH B. Memoir on the...changes
which have taken place at the entrance to the River
Mersey, and the means now adopted for establishing an
easy and direct access for vessels resorting thereto...Read
before the Literary and Philosophical Society of Liverpool. 14p. *8°. Liverpool*, 1840.

SOCIAL CONDITIONS

31630 ALISON, W. P. Illustrations of the practical
operation of the Scottish system of management of the
poor...Read before the Statistical Section of the British
Association on 18th September 1840. [An offprint from
the *Journal of the Statistical Society of London*, vol. 3.]
47p. *8°. n.p.* [1840]

31631 —— Observations on the management of the poor
in Scotland, and its effects on the health of the great towns.
198p. *8°. Edinburgh* & *London*, 1840.

31632 —— [Second edition.] 123p. *8°. Edinburgh* &
London, 1840. *See also no.* 31635.

31633 —— Reply to the pamphlet entitled "Proposed
alteration of the Scottish Poor Law considered and commented on, by David Monypenny, Esq. of Pitmilly." 75p.
8°. Edinburgh & *London*, 1840.

31634 ASHWORTH, H., *and others.* Evidence as to
the administration of relief in periods of manufacturing
distress...[By] Henry Ashworth...John Ashworth...
William Miller...[With] extracts from Sixth annual
report of the Poor Law Commissioners. 15p. *8°.* 1840.

**31635 ASSOCIATION FOR OBTAINING AN
OFFICIAL INQUIRY INTO THE PAUPERISM OF SCOTLAND.** Association for Obtaining an
Official Inquiry into the Pauperism of Scotland. [An
account of the first and second meetings. With 'Abstract

of Dr. Alison's pamphlet "On the management of the poor
in Scotland"'.] 40p. *8°.* [*Edinburgh*, 1840]

31636 BAKER, WILLIAM R. Intemperance the
idolatry of Britain...Second edition, revised and enlarged.
155p. *12°.* 1840. *The Turner copy.*

31637 BATTIE, J. Joe Bradley, the runaway workhouse boy! [A ballad.] *s.sh.4°.* [*c.* 1840]

31638 BEARDSALL, F. Trial of John Barleycorn,
alias Strong Drink...Stereotyped edition. 31p. *12°.*
Manchester, London, &*c.*, [1840?] *The Turner copy.*

31639 BIRKETT, T. Extracts from a lecture delivered
in Manchester, by Mr. Thomas Birkett. (*Total Abstinence
Tracts*, 28.) 4p. *8°. Manchester*, [1840?] *The Turner copy.*

**31640 BIRMINGHAM TEMPERANCE SO-
CIETY.** American temperance poetry. No. 3. 4p. *8°.*
Birmingham, [1840?] *The Turner copy.*

31641 BIRMINGHAM, J. A memoir of the Very
Rev. Theobald Mathew, with an account of the rise and
progress of temperance in Ireland...Second edition. 83p.
8°. Dublin & *London*, 1840. *The Turner copy.*

For the **BORDER HERALD OF TEMPER-
ANCE**, 1840–41, *see* vol. III, *Periodicals list.*

31642 BOYD, SIR W. A patriot's fourth letter to the
British people; more particularly addressed to the opera-

tives of the United Kingdom, on the advantages and importance of a system of co-operative residence... Second edition. 16p. *8°.* 1840.

For **BRISTOL TEMPERANCE HERALD,** *see* vol. III, *Periodicals list.*

For the **BRITISH TEMPERANCE ADVOCATE AND JOURNAL,** 1840–41, *continued as* the National temperance advocate, 1842–49, *then the* British temperance advocate, 1850–61, *see* vol. III, *Periodicals list.*

31643 BROMLEY, J. *and* **LEES,** F. R. Report of the public discussion at Rotherham, on the 25th of August, 1840, on the question of teetotalism, between the Rev. James Bromley...and Frederic R. Lees... 43p. *8°. Sunderland,* 1840. *The Turner copy.*

31644 —— Second edition. 48p. *12°. Leeds, London, &c.,* 1840. *The Turner copy. See also* 1841.

31645 BROOKER, C. An appeal to the British Nation as to a petition for presentation to Parliament for the repeal of the Poor Law Amendment Act; with an introduction; together with a poor law case, as prefixed to the petition. 31p. *8°. Brighton, Lewes, &c.,* 1840.

31646 BULL, G. S. St. James's Church [Bradford]. Meeting of the congregation to present a valedictory address to their minister, the Rev. George S. Bull. [With Mr. Bull's reply.] 12p. *12°. n.p.* [1840] *The Oastler copy.*

31647 BURET, A. E. De la misère des classes laborieuses en Angleterre et en France. 2 vols. *8°. Paris,* 1840.

31648 CHALMERS, T. The Christian and civic economy of large towns...Three volumes in one. 358, 365, 408p. *8°. Glasgow, Edinburgh, &c.,* [c. 1840] *A re-issue of the original edition, 1821–26 (q.v.), with a new title-page.*

31649 CHANNING, WILLIAM E. Lectures on the elevation of the labouring portion of the community. 48p. *12°. Bristol & London,* [1840]

31650 —— Fifth edition. 59p. *12°.* [1840]

31651 —— [Another edition.] 87p. *12°. Glasgow, Edinburgh, &c.,* 1840.

31652 CHORLTON, Union. *Board of Guardians.* Annual Report of the Board of Guardians, for the year ending December 1839. [Signed: John Latham, jun., clerk to the Guardians.] 10p. *8°. n.p.* [1840] *The Oastler copy.*

31653 COOPER, A. A., *7th Earl of Shaftesbury.* Speech of Lord Ashley, in the House of Commons, on... August 4, 1840; on moving an humble address to Her Majesty, to appoint a commission of enquiry into the employment of children in mines, collieries, and other occupations not regulated by the Factory Acts. 26p. *12°.* 1840. *The Oastler copy. See also* 1841.

31654 COURTNEY, A. The moderate use of intoxicating drinks; being the substance of a lecture delivered at a meeting of the Isle of Thanet Temperance Society. 36p. *12°.* [1840] *The Turner copy.*

31655 CRUIKSHANK, W. God glorified by tee-totalism: a sermon, delivered in Wellington Road Chapel, Stockport. 18p. *8°. Stockport, London, &c.,* [1840?] *The Turner copy.*

31656 DEARDEN, J. A brief history of ancient and modern tee-totalism; with a short account of drunkenness,

and the various means used for its suppression. 39p. *8°. Preston,* [1840] *The Turner copy.*

31657 —— [Another edition.] A brief history of the commencement and success of tee-totalism... 39p. *8°. Preston,* [1840] *The Turner copy.*

31658 A DRINKING EDUCATION illustrated; or, the progress of intemperance. 8l. *8°.* [1840?] *The Turner copy.*

31659 EDINBURGH. *Town Council.* Report of the Lord Provost's Committee, on the best mode of conducting an enquiry into the condition of the poor in Scotland. Approved of by the magistrates and Council of Edinburgh, on 10th October 1840. [4]p. *4°. n.p.* [1840]

31660 EDWARDS' COLLEGE. A short account of the Edwards' College, built at South Cerney, for the reception of the widows & orphans of distressed clergymen, of the diocese of Gloucester. 48p. *12°. Cirencester,* 1840.

31661 ENGLAND. *Commissioners for Inquiring into the Employment and Condition of Children in Mines and Manufactories.* Instructions from the Central Board of the Children's Employment Commission to the sub-commissioners. 31p. *8°.* [1840] *The copy that belonged to Victor Considérant.*

31662 —— *Commissioners for Inquiring into the Laws relating to Bankruptcy and Insolvency.* Minutes of evidence taken before the Commissioners...[With appendixes to the Commissioners' first Report.] 2 vols. *fol. n.p.* [1840]

31663 —— *Home Office.* Regulations for prisons in England and Wales. 110p. *8°.* 1840.

31664 —— *Laws, etc.* An Act for better paving, cleansing, and lighting the parish of Saint Clement Danes, in the county of Middlesex, and certain places adjoining thereto; and for removing and preventing nuisances and annoyances therein. 23rd Geo. III, ch. 89. 88p. *8°.* 1840.

31665 —— *Poor Law Commission [1834–1847].* ⟨Private: not for public circulation.⟩ Appendix. – Education. Evidence of employers of labourers on the influence of training and education on the value of workmen, and on the comparative eligibility of educated and uneducated workmen for employment... 13p. *8°.* 1840. *A private printing, probably for the use of the Commission, of Appendix I of the* Report...*of the Poor Law Commissioners on the training of pauper children, published in 1841 (q.v.).*

For —— —— Official circulars, 1840–52, *see* vol. III, *Periodicals list,* Official circular of public documents...

31666 —— —— Report of the Poor Law Commissioners...on the continuance of the Poor Law Commission, and on some further amendments of the laws relating to the relief of the poor. With appendices. 306p. *8°.* 1840.

31667 —— *Privy Council. Committee on Education.* Minutes of the Committee on Education; with appendices and plans of school-houses. 1839–40. 172p. *8°.* 1840.

31668 EXTRACTS on the advantage of Mr. Wilderspin's training system. [Accounts of lectures and demonstrations by Samuel Wilderspin, reprinted from *The Scotsman* and an unidentified Edinburgh periodical.] 8p. *8°.* [1840]

31669 FACTS, relating to intoxicating drinks. Particularly addressed to philanthropists. 2p. *8°.* [*London,* 1840?] *The Turner copy.*

31670 FINCH, Hon. Daniel. Observations on grammar schools, and the means of improving their condition and extending their utility. Addressed to Sir Robert Harry Inglis, Bart. M.P. for the University of Oxford. 77p. *8°.* 1840.

31671 FOTHERGILL, J. The early Friends and the temperance cause; or the accordance of the principle of total abstinence from strong drink with the views of Penn and Woolman, shewn by copious extracts from their writings. 23p. *12°.* 1840. *The Turner copy.*

31672 FOUCHER, , *membre du Conseil général des Hospices de Paris.* Notice sur les principaux établissemens charitables de l'Italie. 124p. *8°. Paris,* 1840.

31673 FRÉGIER, H. A. Des classes dangereuses de la population dans les grandes villes et des moyens de les rendre meilleures... 632p. *8°. Bruxelles,* 1840.

31674 GEIJER, E. G. The poor-laws and their bearing on society. A series of political and historical essays. 184p. *8°. Stockholm,* 1840. *With a manuscript note by the translator, E. B. Hale Lewin. The copy that belonged to William Cunningham (1849–1919). See also 1842.*

31675 GREG, S. Two letters to Leonard Horner, Esq. on the capabilities of the factory system. Printed for private circulation only. 27p. *8°.* 1840.

For the HALFPENNY MAGAZINE OF ENTERTAINMENT AND KNOWLEDGE, 1840–41, *see* vol. III, *Periodicals list.*

31676 [HALL, John V.] No. 463. The sinner's friend. 32p. *8°. The Religious Tract Society,* [c. 1840?]

31677 HASSAN, J. Tee-totalism calmly investigated, and proved to be contrary to Scripture, religion, and reason. 24p. *12°. Manchester,* 1840. *The Turner copy.*

31678 HEAD, Sir E. W., *Bart.* Report on the law of bastardy; with a supplementary report on a cheap civil remedy for seduction. 31p. *8°.* 1840.

31679 HEATHFIELD, R. Poor laws and colonization. First published in the year 1820, in an essay on the practicability...of liquidating the public debt of the United Kingdom...Published also in The Pamphleteer ... 8p. *8°.* [*London,* 1840] *The Oastler copy. For editions of the essay,* Elements of a plan for the liquidation of the Public Debt, *see* 1819 (FINANCE).

31680 HONORÉ V, *Prince of Monaco.* Du paupérisme en France et des moyens de la détruire...Exposé théorique. – Application pratique. 260p. *8°. Paris,* 1839 et 1840.

31681 HORNER, L. On the employment of children in factories and other works in the United Kingdom, and in some foreign countries. 135p. *8°. London, Manchester, &c.,* 1840. *Three copies, one a presentation copy that belonged to Victor Considérant, one the Oastler copy, and the third that belonged to J. M. Cobbett.*

31682 "HOW to back out;" or, magisterial reasons for absence from duty. [A poem, referring to Chartist riots in Birmingham.] *s.sh.8°. Birmingham,* [c. 1840] *See note to no.* 20490.

31683 HOWITT, W. The rural life of England... Second edition, corrected and revised. With illustrations on wood by Bewick and S. Williams. 615p. *8°.* 1840.

31684 "INFANT SLAVERY," or the children of the mines and factories. [A poem, the dedication signed: A Templar.] 32p. *8°.* 1840.

31685 JONES, Richard, *secretary of the Ribbon Society.* Report of the trial had at the Court-House, Green-Street, on the 23rd, 24th, 25th, and 29th days of June, 1840, of Richard Jones, who was charged with being a member of an illegal society [the United Irish Sons of Freedom and Sons of the Shamrock, commonly known as the Ribbon Society]... 177p. *8°. Dublin,* 1840.

31686 JUNIUS, *pseud.* An essay on the nature and properties of porter: wherein is shewn, the delusion of the popular fallacy, that malt liquor is a necessary article of consumption for the working classes. 44p. *8°. London, Preston, &c.,* [1840?] *The Turner copy.*

31687 [KAY, afterwards KAY-SHUTTLE-WORTH, Sir James P., *Bart.*] Recent measures for the promotion of education in England. Seventeenth edition. 112p. *8°.* 1840. *For other editions, see* 1839.

31688 LIVERPOOL FARMERS' LIBRARY. Rules for the regulation and management of the... Library...together with a list of the subscribers' names and a catalogue of the books. 24p. *8°. Liverpool,* 1840.

31689 LIVERPOOL FRIENDLY SOCIETY. Rules of the...Society... 25p. *8°. Liverpool,* 1840.

31690 LONDON. Livery Companies. *Clothworkers.* Selections from the rules and orders of the court of the Clothworkers Company; together with the ordinances or bye laws, sanctioned by the judges in the year 1639. Prepared by W. B. Towse, under the superintendence of the Committee of Record and Trusts. 176p. *8°.* 1840.

31691 MACNISH, R. The anatomy of drunkenness ...With a sketch of the author's life. Ninth thousand. lii, 342p. *8°. Glasgow,* 1840. *The Turner copy. For other editions, see* 1834.

31692 MAGUIRE, Henry C. Distress, the consequence of capital: with some suggestions for the establishment of a refuge from the extremity of destitution for the working classes. 31p. *8°.* [1840?]

31693 MIREHOUSE, J. Crime and its causes: with observations on Sir Eardley Wilmot's Bill, authorizing the summary conviction of juvenile offenders in certain cases of larceny and misdemeanour. 32p. *8°.* 1840.

31694 *MOLESWORTH, Sir W., *Bart.* Speech... on transportation. Delivered in the House of Commons on the 5th May, 1840. 76p. *8°.* 1840. *See note to no.* 30965.

31695 MOLLET, J. E. Rapport fait au Comité de Direction de la Société Neêrlandaise, pour l'amélioration morale des prisonniers, au sujet de la visite qu'ont faite dans ce pays William Allen de Stoke Newington, Elisabeth Fry et Samuel Gurney, d'Upton...membres honoraires ... 32p. *8°. Amsterdam,* 1840. *The copy that belonged to William Allen.*

31696 MONYPENNY, D. Proposed alteration of the Scottish poor laws, and of the administration thereof, as stated by Dr. Alison, in his "Observations on the management of the poor in Scotland," considered and commented on. 119p. *8°. Edinburgh,* 1840.

31697 MORGAN, John M. Religion and crime; or, the distresses of the people, and the remedies...Second edition, enlarged. 79p. *8°.* 1840.

31698 —— Third edition, enlarged. [With 'Explanation of the design for a self-supporting institution'.] 8, 78p. *8°.* 1840.

31699 MOSES, *ben Maimon.* The laws of the Hebrews, relating to the poor and the stranger, from the

"Mischna-Hathora" of the Rabbi Maimonides: now first translated into English by James W. Peppercorne. With an introduction upon the "Rights of necessity;" an account of...Maimonides...and...notes. 54, xxxviii, 71, clxvip. *8°. 1840. For another edition, see 1838.*

31700 *[NAPIER, CATHERINE.] Woman's rights and duties considered with relation to their influence on society and on her own condition. By a woman... 2 vols. *8°. 1840. The copy that belonged to George Grote, with the attribution to Mrs. Richard Napier on the title-page in Mrs. Grote's hand.*

31701 **NEALE,** W. B. Juvenile delinquency in Manchester: its causes and history, its consequences, and some suggestions concerning its cure. 80p. *8°. Manchester, 1840.*

31702 **NEW YORK.** *Board of Aldermen.* The important and interesting debate, on the claim of the Catholics to a portion of the Common School Fund; with the arguments of counsel, before the Board of Aldermen of the City of New-York...the 29th and 30th of October, 1840. Specially reported by R. Sutton... 57p. *4°. New-York, 1840.*

31703 Uncoloured **OUTLINES:** exhibiting some practical workings of the new Poor Law system in an agricultural district: with a few consequent hints. Respectfully submitted to His Grace the Duke of Richmond, by an ex-guardian of a Sussex Union. 23p. *8°. Brighton, 1840.*

31704 **P.,** F. S. Supply of water to the Metropolis. A brief description of the various plans that have been proposed for supplying the Metropolis with pure water. Also, a short account of the different water companies that now supply London... 88p. *8°. 1840.*

31705 **PAISLEY,** *Presbytery of.* Paisley, Nov. 24, 1840. *[Begin.]* Sir, The Presbytery of Paisley having appointed a committee of enquiry into the existing state of destitution among the working classes...[A 4-page questionnaire, to be completed by 1st March 1841, and signed in manuscript: 'Rob. Burns, convener'.] [4]p. *fol. n.p.* [1840]

31706 **PATON,** T. S. Remarks on the Scottish and English poor-laws. Suggested by the recent movement on the subject of the Scottish Poor-Law. 28p. *8°. Edinburgh, 1840.*

31707 **PAUPERISM** and alms-giving. From the British Critic, and Quarterly Theological Review, No. LV. [A review of five works on the poor.] 65p. *8°.* [1840]

31708 **PENEY,** J. L. The test of Christian conduct applied to the use of intoxicating liquors, in a letter to Christians residing in the district of the South Midland Temperance Association. 16p. *8°. London & Market Harborough, 1840. The Turner copy.*

31709 Short **PERSUASIVES** to total abstinence. 2p. *8°. [London, 1840] The Turner copy.*

31710 On a **PROPOSAL** to withhold out-door relief from widows with families, contained in the last annual report of the Poor Law Commissioners for England and Wales. ⟨Read at a meeting of the Manchester Statistical Society, December 8th, 1840.⟩ 16p. *8°. [Manchester, 1840] HSF's note records that another copy contained an attribution to 'Mr. Roberton, surgeon'. i.e. John Roberton (1797–1876).*

31711 **RAWLINGS,** J. An address to the professing ministers of the gospel of Christ. [On their duty to remedy the social evils which afflict the labouring classes.] 24p. *12°. Bath & Trowbridge,* [1840]

For the **RECHABITE MAGAZINE AND TEMPERANCE RECORDER,** 1840–95, *see* vol. III, *Periodicals list.*

31712 **RÉMUSAT,** C. F. M. DE, *Comte.* Du paupérisme et de la charité légale: lettre adressée à MM. les préfets du royaume par M. Ch. de Rémusat, Ministre de l'Intérieur. Suivie d'observations de M. A.-P. de Candolle sur un traité De la bienfaisance publique. [With 'Note sur un ouvrage récemment publié par M. le docteur Villermé ...ayant pour titre Tableau de l'état des ouvriers employés dans les manufactures de coton, de la laine et de soie'.] 106p. *12°. Paris,* [1840]

31713 **RICHARDSON,** R. J. The rights of Woman! Exhibiting her natural, civil, and political claims to share in the legislative and executive power of the state. 23p. *12°. Edinburgh, London, &c., 1840.*

31714 **ROYAL STANDARD SAVINGS' FUND, AND BENEFIT BUILDING SOCIETY.** Rules of the Royal Standard Savings' Fund and Benefit Building Society. Established according to Act of Parliament, 6th and 7th Wm. 4, c. 32. 28p. *8°. Liverpool, 1840.*

31715 Some **RULES** for the conduct of life: to which are added a few cautions, for the use of such Freemen of London as take apprentices. 23p. *12°. 1840. For another edition, see 1800.*

31716 **RUSSOM,** J. An essay on Odd Fellowship; being an explanation and vindication of its principles, etc. 20p. *12°. London & Chester, 1840.*

31717 **SALFORD,** *Union. Board of Guardians.* Report on the operation of the new Poor Law in the Salford Union. By the Board of Guardians for 1838–1839. [Signed: Holland Hoole, chairman.] 8p. *8°. Manchester, 1840. The Oastler copy.*

31718 The **SANATORIUM:** a self-supporting establishment for the lodging, nursing, and cure of sick persons of the middle classes, of both sexes. 19p. *8°. 1840.*

31719 **SINCLAIR,** SIR GEORGE, *Bart.* Speech of Sir George Sinclair, Bart., M.P. on the condition and feelings of the working classes, delivered in the House of Commons, on...May 22, 1840. Second edition. 31p. *8°. 1840.*

31720 **SLANEY,** R. A. State of the poorer classes in great towns. Substance of a speech in the House of Commons, Feb. 4, 1840, on moving for a Committee to consider the causes of discontent. With notes and references. 66p. *12°. 1840.*

31721 **SLEIGH,** A. W. Nautical re-organisation and increase of the trading marine; also a practical plan for manning the Royal Navy without impressment, and proposals to ameliorate the present condition of the mariners of Great Britain, by a more equitable code of laws... 169p. *8°. 1840.*

31722 **SMITH,** THOMAS, *vice-chairman of the Thirsk Board of Guardians.* The old Poor Law and the new Poor Law contrasted. 34p. *8°. London & Thirsk, 1840.*

For **SOCIÉTÉ PATERNELLE POUR L'EDUCATION MORALE ET PROFESSIONNELLE DES JEUNES DÉTENUS,** Colonie agricole de Mettray, assemblée générale...[Annual reports to the Society, 1840–50], *see* vol. III, *Periodicals list,* Colonie agricole et pénitentiaire de Mettray...

31723 **SOCIETY FOR THE SUPPRESSION OF MENDICITY,** *Newbury.* The second report of the Society for the Suppression of Mendicity and Relief of Distressed Travellers, in the borough...of Newbury, Berks; supported by voluntary contributions. Established April, 1839. [With list of officers, rules, and subscribers for 1840.] 26p. *8°. Newbury, 1840.*

31724 SPENCER, T. Remarks on national education ...Fourth thousand. No. 5. 16p. *8°. London & Bath,* 1840.

31725 A general **STATEMENT** of the several charities in the borough of Reading in the county Berks, denominated general, Church, and Kendrick charities. 12, 13, 28p. *8°. Reading, 1840. Three separate pamphlets issued with a general title printed on the wrapper.*

31726 STEVEN, R. The trade of chimney-sweeping exhibited in its true light, together with the state of public feeling on this important subject, as shown by evidence before the House of Commons, &c. 24p. *4°.* [1840]

31727 STOWELL, H. The duty of England in regard to the traffic in intoxicating drinks...⟨Extracted from a lecture to the Manchester Mechanics' Institution.⟩ 4p. *8°. Leeds,* [1840] *The Turner copy.*

31728 The **SUNDAY-OPENING** of the lyceums and public gardens defended; being an answer to a letter by "J.H." to T. H. Williams, Esq., condemning the opening of lyceums and public gardens on the Sunday. By a member of a lyceum. [Signed: A working man.] 16p. *8°. Manchester,* 1840.

31729 The **TEETOTALER'S** text book, or statistics of intemperance, and striking facts. ⟨Second edition.⟩ 12p. *12°. Mossley,* [1840?] *The work has been attributed to 'Mr. Newton' of Todmorden, who distributed it. The Turner copy.*

For the **TEMPERANCE MESSENGER AND TRACT MAGAZINE,** 1840–41, *see* vol. III,*Periodicals list.*

For **TEMPERANCE TRACT DEPOSITORY,** [Tracts, 1840–50], *see* vol. III, *Periodicals list.* Tracts...

31730 TROLLOPE, F. The life and adventures of Michael Armstrong, the factory boy. 387p. *8°. London, Edinburgh, &c.,* 1840. *Issued in 12 monthly parts, from March 1839.*

31731 VILLERMÉ, L. R. Tableau de l'état physique et moral des ouvriers employés dans les manufactures de coton, de laine et de soie... 2 vols. *8°. Paris,* 1840.

31732 VINCENT, H., *and others.* No. 2. An address to the working men of England, Scotland, and Wales [on the evils of drink. Signed by Henry Vincent and 7 others. With 'Tobacco' from 'Mr. Errington Ridley's anti-tobacco lecture']. 4p. *8°.* [*London,* 1840?] *The second of a series later called 'Five a penny tracts for the people'.*

31733 WAGES in Poland and England. (No. 7.) *s.sh.fol. Manchester,* [1840?]

31734 WHATELY, R., *Archbishop of Dublin.* Substance of a speech on transportation, delivered in the House of Lords, on the 19th of May, 1840. 119p. *8°.* 1840.

31735 WHITECROSS, J. Temperance anecdotes and facts; with a selection of some of the principal arguments in support of temperance principles. 166p. *12°. Edinburgh, Glasgow, &c.,* 1840. *The Turner copy.*

31736 WORKING MEN of England. (*Total Abstinence Tracts,* 27.) 4p. *8°. Manchester,* [1840?]. *The Turner copy.*

31737 WRIGHT, HENRY G. and **WRIGHT**,   , *Miss.* Retrospective sketch of an educative attempt, at Alcott House, Ham Common, near Richmond, Surrey, by Mr. & Miss Wright. 7p. *8°.* 1840.

SLAVERY

31738 ADAM, WILLIAM (*fl.* 1840). The law and custom of slavery in British India, in a series of letters to Thomas Fowell Buxton, Esq. 279p. *12°.* 1840.

31739 —— Paper presented to the General Anti-Slavery Convention...Slavery in India. 12p. *8°.* [*London,* 1840]

31740 AMERICAN ANTI-SLAVERY SOCIETY. The anti-slavery examiner. No. 14. Address to the friends of constitutional liberty, on the violation by the United States House of Representatives of the right of petition. By the executive committee of the American Anti-Slavery Society. 12p. *8°. New York,* 1840.

31741 ARCHER, E. C. Free labour versus slave labour. A letter to...S. Lushington, M.P. and the opponents of free labour, shewing that in their opposition to emigration from India to the British Colonies they are virtually encouraging the slave trade. 23p. *8°.* 1840.

31742 BOTELHO, S. X. Escravatura, beneficios que podem provir ás nossas possessões d'Africa da prohibição daquelle trafico...obra posthuma de Sebastião Xavier Botelho offerecida ao Corpo do Commercio Portugues. 41p. *8°. Lisboa,* 1840.

31743 BUXTON, SIR THOMAS F., *Bart.* The African slave trade and its remedy. [Second edition of Part I.] 582p. *8°.* 1840. *For another edition of the first part, see* 1839.

31744 —— Abridgement of Sir T. Fowell Buxton's work entitled "The African slave trade and its remedy." With an explanatory preface [by Joseph Beldam?] and an appendix. Published under the sanction of the "Society for the Extinction of the Slave Trade and for the Civilization of Africa." Second edition. 71p. *8°.* 1840.

31745 —— De la traite des esclaves en Afrique, et des moyens d'y remédier...Traduit de l'anglais sur la seconde édition, par J. J. Pacaud. 650p. *8°. Paris,* 1840. *With a printed presentation leaf from 'La Société instituée à Londres pour l'Extinction de la Traite des Esclaves' inscribed in manuscript 'A Monsieur de Saint-Antoine' and signed 'D'Avezac'.*

31746 CLARKSON, T. [*Endorsed:*] Speech of Thomas Clarkson, Esq., as originally prepared by him in writing, and intended to have been delivered at the opening of the General Anti-Slavery Convention. 3p. *4°.* [*London,* 1840?]

31747 *DAWES, W. and **KEEP**, J. [*Endorsed:*] An appeal on behalf of the Oberlin Institute in aid of the abolition of slavery, in the United States of America 3p. *fol. n.p.* [1840] *The FWA copy that belonged to William Pare.*

31748 FRANCE. Ministère de la Marine et des Colonies. *Direction des Colonies.* Précis de l'abolition de l'esclavage dans les colonies anglaises. Imprimé par l'ordre de M. l'Amiral Baron Duperré... 2 vols. *8°. Paris, 1840–41. By F. V. C. Chassériau.*

31749 ★GREG, W. R. Past and present efforts for the extinction of the African slave trade. 99p. *8°.* [1840] *The copy that belonged to George Grote.*

31750 [HANCOCK, T.] Are the West India colonies to be preserved? A few plain facts; showing the necessity of immigration into British Guiana and the West Indies, and the utter futility of all efforts towards the abolition of slavery and the slave trade which do not include this... [Signed: T.H.] 16p. *8°.* 1840.

31751 HAUGHTON, J. To the Irish people. [A letter 'urging the propriety of giving up the use of all articles which are produced by slave labour'.] *s.sh.4°. n.p.* [1840]

31752 HILDRETH, R. Despotism in America; or an inquiry into the nature and results of the slave-holding system in the United States. By the author of "Archy Moore." 186p. *12°. Boston,* 1840.

31753 INGLATERRA e Portugal ou a questão do bill para a supressão do trafico portuguez de escravos. Observações sobre as ultimas negociações entaboladas entre os governos inglez e portuguez sobre a questão da escravatura. 24p. *8°. Lisboa,* 1840. *Translated from the Morning Chronicle of 5 March, 1840.*

31754 MADDEN, R. R. Address on slavery in Cuba, presented to the General Anti-Slavery Convention. 31p. *8°.* [1840]

31755 [MANZANO, J. F.] Poems by a slave in the Island of Cuba, recently liberated; translated from the Spanish, [into English verse] by R. R. Madden, M.D. With the history of the early life of the negro poet, written by himself; to which are prefixed two pieces descriptive of Cuban slavery and the slave-traffic, by R.R.M. 188p. *8°.* 1840.

31756 [MARTINEAU, H.] The martyr age of the United States of America [a review, signed: H.M.], with an appeal on behalf of the Oberlin Institute in aid of the abolition of slavery. Re-published from the London and Westminster Review [December 1838], by the Newcastle upon Tyne Emancipation and Aborigines Protection Society. 44p. *8°. Newcastle-upon-Tyne, London, &c.,* 1840. *★Another, the FWA copy, belonged to William Pare.*

31757 MASSACHUSETTS ANTI-SLAVERY SOCIETY. Catalogue of publications for sale at the depository of the Massachusetts Anti-Slavery Society, No. 25, Cornhill, Boston. [4]p. *8°. Boston,* 1840.

31758 ROBINSON, ROBERT (1735–1790). Slavery inconsistent with the spirit of Christianity. A sermon, preached at Cambridge...1788...Re-printed, 1840, at the request of W. Mortlock, Esq., for gratuitous distribution. 54p. *8°. Cambridge,* [1840] *For another edition, see 1788.*

31759 SA DA BANDEIRA,   DE, *Visconde.* The slave trade, and Lord Palmerston's Bill... 68p. *8°. n.p.,* 1840. *Translated from the Portuguese.*

31760 SCHŒLCHER, V. Abolition de l'esclavage; examen critique du préjugé contre la couleur des Africains et des sang-mêlés. 187p. *8°. Paris,* 1840.

31761 SCOBLE, J. British Guiana. Facts! Facts!! Facts!!! [An address on the coolie slave trade.] 3p. *fol.* [1840]

31762 SOCIETY FOR THE EXTINCTION OF THE SLAVE TRADE AND FOR THE CIVILIZATION OF AFRICA. [Appeal and subscription form.] [4]p. *4°. n.p.* [1840]

31763 —— Proceedings at the first public meeting of the Society...1st June, 1840... 73p. *8°.* 1840.

31764 —— Prospectus of the Society...instituted June 1839. 14p. *8°. n.p.* [1840]

31765 STURGE, JOHN. Report on free labour, presented to the General Anti-Slavery Convention. 31p. *8°.* [*London,* 1840]

31766 TURNBULL, D. Travels in the West. Cuba; with notices of Porto Rico, and the slave trade. 574p. *8°.* 1840.

POLITICS

31767 ALLETZ, E. Maximes politiques à l'usage de la démocratie nouvelle. 145p. *12°. Paris,* 1840.

31768 ANDERSON, JAMES S. M. Speech of the Rev. J. S. M. Anderson, at the dinner of the Brighton Conservative Association, on...13th January 1840. Third thousand. 16p. *8°. Brighton,* [1840]

31769 BOLWELL, C. A report of the trial of Charles Bolwell, at the Bath Spring Sessions, 1840, on a charge of conspiracy. 12p. *12°. Bath,* [1840]

31770 CARLYLE, T. Chartism. 113p. *12°.* 1840.

31771 —— Second edition. 113p. *12°.* 1840. *See also* 1842.

31772 COMMITTEE ACTING ON BEHALF OF THE BRITISH CIVIL AND MILITARY CLAIMANTS ON PORTUGAL. The case of the British naval and military claimants on Portugal, being the report made by the Committee to the general meeting, held at the King's Arms Hotel, Palace Yard...12th February, 1840. With the necessary documents, in proof, subjoined. 48p. *8°. Westminster,* 1840.

31773 DEFOE, D. An appeal to honour and justice, though it be of his worst enemies...being a true account of his conduct in public affairs...1715. 16p. *8°.* 1840. *For another edition, see* 1715.

31774 EMMET, R. The noble speech of Robert Emmet, Esq., leader of the Irish insurrection, 1803, delivered...at the close of his trial, for high treason. 8p. *12°. Manchester,* [1840?] *The Turner copy.*

31775 FINSBURY TRACT SOCIETY. No. 1. The question "What is a Chartist?" answered. (By the Finsbury Tract Society.) 4p. *8°.* [*London,* 1840] *The first of a series later called 'Five a penny tracts for the people'.*

31776 —— [Another edition. With 'Ode, by Sir William Jones'.] 4p. *8°. Manchester,* [1840?]

31777 [——] [Another edition. With 'Poverty versus royalty'.] 4p. *8°. Bath,* [1840?]

31778 [——] [Another edition.] 4p. *8°. Birmingham,* [1840?]

31779 FROST, J. The trial of John Frost, for high

treason. Under a special commission, held at Monmouth, in December 1839, and January 1840. Taken in short-hand by Joseph and Thomas Gurney. 778p. *8°.* 1840.

31780 —— [Another edition.] Trial of John Frost for high treason. Revised by a barrister. 160p. *8°.* [1840]

31781 GHAISNE, L. P. C. DE, *Comte de Bourmont.* Appel à tous les Français contre les calomnies par lesquelles on a cherché à flétrir la conduite du Comte de Bourmont [Maréchal de France] en 1815. 40p. *8°. Paris,* 1840.

31782 JENKINS, E. Chartism unmasked...Nineteenth edition. 35p. *12°. Merthyr Tydvil,* 1840.

31783 KETTLE, J. Lord Melbourne, and the House of Lords. [A dramatic dialogue attacking both, between John and Jonathan.] 19p. *8°.* [1840?]

31784 LADD, W. An essay on a congress of nations, for the adjustment of international disputes without resort to arms...Third thousand. [One of six prize essays originally published by the American Peace Society.] 32p. *8°.* 1840. *A circular letter, dated: March 29th, 1841, accompanying the pamphlet, from the Foreign Secretary of the Peace Society, N. M. Harry, is included in the volume.*

31785 LOVETT, W. and **COLLINS,** JOHN, *chartist.* Chartism; a new organization of the people, embracing a plan for the education and improvement of the people, politically and socially... 124p. *12°.* 1840. *With a manuscript inscription, 'From John Collins To Mrs Gray as a Small Token of Respect'. *Another, the FWA copy, belonged to William Pare. See also 1841.*

31786 PEEL, SIR ROBERT, *2nd Bart.* Conservative speeches – Painter's editions. The war in China. Sir R. Peel's speech in the House of Commons, April 10, 1840. 16p. *8°.* [*London,* 1840]

31787 —— Fourth edition...Want of confidence in Her Majesty's Ministers. Sir R. Peel's speech in the House of Commons, January 31, 1840. 24p. *8°.* [*London,* 1840]

31788 REPORT of the Committee, appointed at a public meeting held in Dublin...March 19, 1840, to consider the effect of Lord Stanley's Irish Registration Bill. [Signed: Daniel O'Connell, chairman.] 16p. *8°. n.p.* [1840]

31789 The **RISE** and fall of chartism in Monmouthshire. 90p. *8°.* 1840.

31790 SAUNDERS, J. Saunders' portraits and memoirs of eminent living political reformers. The portraits by George Hayter...And the memoirs by a distinguished literary character. To which is annexed a copious historical sketch of the progress of parliamentary reform, from...1734 to...1832. By William Howitt. 259p. *8°.* 1840.

31791 SPENCER, T. Religion and politics; or, ought religious men to be political?...Fifth thousand. 16p. *8°.* 1840.

31792 —— Sixth thousand. 16p. *8°.* 1840.

31793 —— [Another edition.] 12p. *12°.* 1840.

31794 STANLEY, EDWARD G. G. S., *14th Earl of Derby.* Conservative speeches – Painter's edition. Want of confidence in Her Majesty's Ministers. Lord Stanley's speech in the House of Commons, January 30, 1840. 15p. *8°.* [1840]

31795 TEMPLE, H. J., *Viscount Palmerston.* Letter from Lord Palmerston to M. Thiers, dated Foreign Office, August 31, 1840. Reply of M. Thiers to Lord Palmerston, dated Paris, October 3, 1840: with the additional memorandum. 43p. *8°.* 1840.

31796 THOUGHTS on reform, in a letter to Her Majesty the Queen. By an exile. 48p. *8°.* 1840.

31797 URQUHART, D. The crisis. France in face of the Four Powers...Translated from the French, Paris, 30 September, 1840. 58p. *8°. Paris, Glasgow, &c.,* 1840. *No. 6 of the series 'Diplomacy and Commerce'. For nos. 2 and 5, see nos. 31459, 31372.*

31798 WAGHORN, T. Truths concerning Mahomet Ali, Egypt, Arabia, and Syria; addressed to the Five Powers, or to their representatives in the contemplated congress. 23p. *8°.* 1840.

31799 WEMYSS, R. Victoria. A political poem. 40p. *12°.* 1840.

31800 [**WILKINSON,** SIR JOHN G.] Three letters on the policy of England towards the Porte and Mohammed Ali. 63p. *8°.* 1840.

31801 *[**WILLIAMS,** JOHN, *journalist.*] The letters of Publicola. From the Weekly Dispatch. With notes and emendations by Publicola. p.1–160. *8°.* 1840. *An edition, published in parts, of letters printed in the Weekly Dispatch during 1832 and 1833. This copy, containing 5 parts only, belonged to William Pare, who attributed the work to 'Harmer', i.e. Alderman James Harmer (1777–1853).*

31802 ZOEPFL, H. Historical essay upon the Spanish succession...Translated from the French version, of M. le Baron de Billing, by C.T.O'G. [With 'Appendix. Refutation of the pamphlet published by S. Schmerber on the question of the Spanish succession'.] 128p. *8°.* 1840.

SOCIALISM

31803 ADDRESS to the working classes on the system of exclusive dealing; and the formation of joint stock companies; shewing how the people may free themselves from oppression. By a member of the Nottingham Cooperative Store. [With 'Rules of the Nottingham Cooperative Society'.] 8p. *8°. Nottingham,* 1840.

31804 ALMANACH social pour l'année 1840. [With 'Biographie de Charles Fourier. – Résumé de sa théorie. – Étude sur Dieu, l'homme et l'univers', etc.] 192p. *16°.* [*Paris,*] 1840.

For **BAILEY,** JAMES N., The monthly messenger, *see* vol. III, *Periodicals list,* Monthly messenger.

31805 —— Preliminary discourse on the objects, pleasures, and advantages of the science of society. 32p. *8°. Leeds, Manchester, &c.,* 1840. *Reissued in the author's The social reformer's cabinet library, 1841 (q.v.).*

31806 BIARD, G., *and others.* Le carnet du théogyno-démophile. [Introduction signed: G. Biard, R. Bonheur, E. Iavary.] 16p. *8°.* [*Paris,* 1840?]

31807 BOWES, J. Third thousand. The "social beasts;" or, an exposure of the principles of Robert Owen, Esq. and the socialists. 16p. *8°. London...Liverpool, &c.,* [1840] *See note to no.* 27827.

31808 —— Socialism. Report of a public discussion, between John Bowes...and Lloyd Jones...in...Liverpool, May 5th, 6th, 7th, and 27th, 1840; "on the five facts, and constitution and laws of human nature, as propounded by Robert Owen;"... 108p. *12°. London & Liverpool,* 1840. *See note to no.* 27827. *★Another, the FWA copy, belonged to William Pare.*

31809 BRINDLEY, JOHN. Tract I. A refutation of Robert Owen's fundamental principles of socialism; proving the free agency of Man. 12p. *12°. Birmingham,* [1840]

31810 BRISBANE, A. Social destiny of Man: or, association and reorganization of industry. 480p. *8°. Philadelphia,* 1840. *Two copies, one with an inscription, 'A Madame Gatti de Gamond offert par Piero Maroncelli New-York 16 7ᵇʳᵉ 1840'; the other inscribed 'From Mr. Harney, Sepr. 1857[?] J.S.P.[?]'.*

31811 BROWN, D. A complete refutation of the principles of socialism or Owenism; by containing the proofs that man forms his own character, and possesses a freewill, the necessity of the application of rewards and punishments: also an investigation of The book of the new moral world. 92p. *8°. Glasgow,* 1840.

31812 BROWNSON, O. A. The laboring classes... an article from the Boston Quarterly Review...Second edition. 24p. *8°. Boston,* 1840.

31813 —— Fourth edition. 24p. *8°. Boston,* 1840. *See also* 1842.

31814 BUCHANAN, ROBERT. An exposure of the falsehoods, calumnies, and misrepresentations of a pamphlet entitled "The abominations of socialism exposed;" being a refutation of the charges and statements of the Rev. Joseph Barker, and all others who have adopted a similar mode of opposing socialism. 48p. *12°. Manchester, London, &c.,* [1840?] *★Another, the FWA copy, belonged to William Pare.*

31815 —— Socialism vindicated: in reply to a sermon entitled "Socialism denounced as an outrage upon the laws of God and Man," preached by the Rev. W. J. Kidd, in...Manchester, on...July 12th, 1840. 8p. *8°. Manchester, London, &c.,* [1840]

31816 A **BUDGET** for the socialists: containing The female socialist; or, the wise wench of Whitechapel; a doggrel, worthy of its burthen. Also, the Lord's Prayer of the Owenites; a lively ditty, well worthy of its psalmodists. And lastly, but not least of all, the Gospel according to Saint Owen; a revelation, worthy of Diabolus, the Saint's first cousin. 52p. *8°.* 1840.

31817 CABET, É. Comment je suis communiste. 16p. *8°. n.p.,* 1840.

31818 [——] Voyage et aventures de Lord Villiam Carisdall en Icarie, traduits de l'anglais de Francis Adams par Th. Dufruit... 2 vols. *8°. Paris,* 1840. *See also* 1848.

31819 CARTER, JOHN H. The voice of the past; written in defence of Christianity and the constitution of England, with suggestions on the probable progress of society, and observations on the resurrection of the body, phrenology and the immortality of the soul; being a reply to the manifesto of Mr. Robert Owen...Second edition. 28p. *8°. Portsea, Portsmouth, &c.,* 1840.

31820 CHERBULIEZ, A. E. Riche ou pauvre. Exposition succincte des causes et des effets de la distribution actuelle des richesses sociales. 296p. *8°. Paris & Genève,* 1840.

31821 [**CONSIDÉRANT,** V. P.] Contre M. Arago, réclamation adressée à la Chambre des Députés par les rédacteurs du feuilleton de la Phalange. Suivi de La théorie du droit de propriété. [With 'Critique des réformes électorales'.] 80p. *8°. Paris,* 1840. *Considérant's own copy.*

31822 [——] Principes de l'École sociétaire. [With 'Exposition élémentaire de l'économie sociale de Fourier'.] 80p. *8°. n.p.* [1840] *Considérant's own copy.*

31823 *★*Complete **DEFEAT** of Robert Owen and socialism, in the Staffordshire Potteries. [Public meetings reported in the *Staffordshire Mercury,* June 1840.] *s.sh.fol. Birmingham,* [1840] *The FWA copy, that belonged to William Pare.*

31824 The **ELEMENTS** of socialism. Compiled by the author of "An essay towards a science of consciousness." 28p. *12°. Birmingham, London, &c.,* 1840. *HSF quoted a note from a volume of tracts which attributed the work to 'Murphy'.*

31825 ENGLAND. Parliament. *House of Lords.* Reprint of the debate in the Lords on socialism, from the "Times" of February 5th, 1840. [Containing a report of the speech of the Bishop of Exeter on the progress of socialism.] For the especial use of the members of the "Universal Community Society of Rational Religionists." [8]p. *fol. Leeds,* [1840]

31826 ETHNICUS, *pseud.* Why am I a socialist? or, a defence of social principles; in a letter to a Christian friend. 16p. *8°. Glasgow, London, &c.,* 1840.

31827 *★*An **EXAMINATION** of Mr. Robert Owen's doctrines of human responsibility, and the influence of circumstances in the formation of character. [Reprinted from the *Weekly Free Press,* and *Co-operative Journal.*] 16p. *8°.* [1840?] *The FWA copy that belonged to William Pare.*

31828 A full and complete **EXPOSURE** of the atrocious and horrible doctrines of the Owenites; with a drawing from the bust, and a memoir of the author of this abominable system. [A pro-socialist satire.] 8p. *8°.* [1840] *Another edition, entitled* Socialism exposed, *in which the author used the pseudonym 'Publicola', was published in 1844 (q.v.).*

31829 EYRE, C. S. A few words on socialism. 16p. *16°. Coventry,* [1840?]

31830 *★***FAIRPLAY,** JOHN, *pseud.* Remarks on a sermon, &c. entitled "The use of the church service on a late occasion defended, and socialist crimes exposed, by the Rev. John Craig, M.A., Vicar of Leamington-Priors." [In which the suicide of two women was blamed upon their belief in Owenite doctrines.] 8p. *8°. Coventry,* 1840. *The FWA copy, that belonged to William Pare.*

31831 FESTEAU, L. Fourier. [A poem.] 3p. *8°.* [*Paris,* 1840?] *The copy that belonged to Victor Considérant.*

31832 FINCH, JOHN (1783–1857). Moral code of the new moral world, or rational state of society; containing the laws of human nature, upon which are based Man's duty to himself, to society, and to God...Corrected, revised, and approved by Robt. Owen. 8p. *8°. Liverpool, Manchester, &c.,* 1840. *★Another, the FWA copy, belonged to William Pare.*

31833 FOREST, P. Organisation du travail, d'après les principes de la théorie de Ch. Fourier. 105p. *8°. Paris,* 1840.

31834 FOURIER, F. C. M. Paroles de Fourier. Le monde phalanstérien. 16p. *8°. Genève,* 1840. *Extracts from Fourier's works.*

31835 GAMOND, afterwards **GATTI DE GAMOND,** Z. DE. Réalisation d'une commune sociétaire, d'après la théorie de Charles Fourier. 409p. *8°. Paris,* 1840. *Presentation copy, with inscription, from the author to 'Monsieur Cellier'. See also 1842.*

31836 GREEN, JOHN, *social missionary.* Caspar Hauser, or the power of external circumstances exhibited in forming the human character, with remarks. 36p. *12°. Manchester & London,* [1840?] *★Another, the FWA copy, belonged to William Pare.*

31837 ★HALE, G. A reasonable and just invitation or challenge to the founder of socialism. By a Christian... 8p. *8°.* [1840?] *The FWA copy that belonged to William Pare.*

31838 HASLAM, C. J. Who are the infidels, those who call themselves socialists, or followers of Robert Owen; or those who call themselves Christians, or followers of Jesus Christ?... Third edition. 12p. *12°. Manchester, London, &c.,* [1840?]

31839 HETHERINGTON, H. A full report of the trial of Henry Hetherington, on an indictment for blasphemy... at the Court of Queen's Bench... December 8, 1840; for selling Haslam's Letters to the clergy of all denominations: with the whole of the authorities cited in the defence, at full length. 32p. *8°.* 1840.

31840 HUGHES, H. What am I? The fourth of a series of lectures against socialism, delivered in the Mechanics' Institution, Southampton Buildings, under the direction of the London City Mission. 31p. *8°.* 1840. *★Another, the FWA copy, belonged to William Pare. Reissued in* Lectures against socialism, *no.* 31847.

31841 HUNT, THOMAS (*fl.* 1840–1853). Chartism, trades-unionism and socialism; or, which is the best calculated to produce permanent relief to the working classes? A dialogue. 20p. *8°.* 1840.

31842 JONES, L. Report of the discussion on marriage, as advocated by Robert Owen, between L. Jones and J. Bowes, in the Queen's Theatre, Christian-Street, Liverpool, on Wednesday, May 27, 1840. Re-printed from the Liverpool Journal. 16p. *16°. Liverpool, Manchester, &c.,* 1840.

31843 JUNIUS, *pseud.* Six letters on the theory and practice of socialism. Addressed to all classes of the population of Great Britain. 15p. *8°. London, Birmingham, &c.,* [1840]

31844 [KING, WILLIAM, *of Charlotte Street, London.*] Currency; or, the money juggle. To the producing classes. [Signed: W.K.] *s.sh.fol. n.p.* [*c.* 1840] *The copy that belonged to Francis Place.*

31845 —— Four letters on the workings of money capital; showing its present inefficient and limited agency for commercial and social purposes. With a proposed remedy for the evils resulting therefrom. 24p. *12°.* [1840] *The copy that belonged to Francis Place. See also* 1843.

31846 A LETTER to the Right Honourable Lord Viscount Melbourne, on the presentation of Mr. Robert Owen, at court. By a member of the Church of England. 31p. *8°.* 1840. *★Another, the FWA copy, belonged to William Pare.*

31847 LONDON CITY MISSION. Lectures against socialism. Delivered under the direction of the Committee of the London City Mission. 50, 47, 55, 31, 72, 62, 100, 52, 64p. *8°.* 1840. *A collection of nine pamphlets all separately published in 1840, reissued with a general title-page. Contents: R. Ainslie, Is there a God?; J. Garwood, Is the Bible of divine authority? 2nd edition; B. W. Noel, What is Christianity?; H. Hughes, What am I?; I. Taylor, Man responsible... Second thousand; G. Cubitt, The power of circumstances; J. Hoppus, The province of reason; R. Matthews, Is marriage worth perpetuating?; R. Ainslie, An examination of socialism. ★Other (FWA) copies of Hughes and Taylor belonged to William Pare.*

For the **LONDON SOCIAL REFORMER,** *see* vol. III, *Periodicals list.*

31848 LUNN, E. Divine revelation examined; a lecture on the nature & attributes of the deity, as revealed to us in the scriptures, or the truth of the first article of the creed of the new moral world demonstrated, as far as that article concerns the Bible. Delivered in the Social Institution... Huddersfield. 22p. *8°. Manchester, London, &c.,* [1840?]

31849 MACKINTOSH, T. S. An inquiry into the nature of responsibility, as deduced from savage justice, civil justice, and social justice; with some remarks upon the doctrine of irresponsibility, as taught by Jesus Christ and Robert Owen... 123p. *12°. Birmingham, London, &c.,* [1840?]

31850 MARRIOTT, JOSEPH. A catechism on circumstances; or, the foundation stone of a community. 12p. *12°. Salford: Association of All Classes of All Nations ...London, &c.,* [1840]

31851 MATHER, JOSEPH. Socialism exposed. [An examination of Owen's *The book of the new moral world.*] 24p. *12°.* [1840?] *An abridgment of an edition published in 1839.*

31852 Lord **MELBOURNE'S** chain unlinked with which he intended through Robert Owen, to fetter the people for ever. [With 'Substance of a discourse delivered by Zion [i.e. John Ward], at... Ashton-under-Line... 3rd of January, the 12th year'.] 12p. *12°. Nottingham,* 1840.

For ★the **MORNING STAR** *or Phalansterian gazette,* 1840–41, *see* vol. III, *Periodicals list.*

31853 OWEN, ROBERT. Lectures on the marriages of the priesthood of the old immoral world... Fourth edition. With an appendix, containing the marriage system of the new moral world... 92p. *12°. Leeds, Manchester, &c.,* 1840. *★Another, the FWA copy, belonged to William Pare. For another edition, see* 1838 (The marriage system of the new moral world).

31854 —— Manifesto of Robert Owen, the discoverer ...of the rational system of society... To which is added, a preface and an appendix, containing Mr. Owen's petitions to Parliament... Fifth edition... 59p. *8°.* [1840] *With manuscript corrections throughout in Owen's hand.*

31855 —— Sixth edition... 63p. *8°.* 1840. *With a cutting from the Star of 9 July 1831, containing a letter by Owen. See also* 1841.

31856 —— Outline of the rational system of society, founded on demonstrable facts, developing the constitution and laws of human nature; being the only effectual remedy for the evils experienced by the population of the world...Authorized edition. Sixth edition; revised and amended. 24p. *12°. Leeds*, 1840.

31857 —— [Another edition.] 12p. *12°. Manchester & London*, [1840] *The title on the printed paper wrapper: Social Bible; or, an outline... For other editions, see 1831.*

31858 OWEN, ROBERT D. Address on free inquiry. On fear as a motive of action. 16p. *8°*. 1840. *For another edition, see 1836. Also reprinted as no. 5 of The rational library, for which see no. 31861.*

31859 —— Address on the hopes and destinies of the human species: as delivered in London and New York. 16p. *8°*. [*London*, 1840] *Another, the FWA copy, belonged to William Pare. For another edition, see 1836. Also printed as no. 1 of The rational library, for which see no. 31861.*

31860 —— A lecture on consistency, as delivered in New York, Boston, and London. 16p. *8°*. [1840 ?] *Reprinted in nos. 3 and 4 of The rational library (no. 31861 below).*

31861 —— The rational library. [Nos. 1–6.] 16, 80p. *8°*. [1840 ?] *Nos. 2–6 are continuously paginated. Contents: Address on the hopes and destinies of the human species; Address on the influence of the clerical profession; A lecture on consistency; Effects of missionary labours; Address on free enquiry; Darby and Susan, a tale of old England.*

31862 PELLARIN, C. Sur le droit de propriété. Réponse à quelques attaques. 36p. *12°. Besançon*, [1840 ?]

31863 PHILIP, R. The royal marriage; an antidote to socialism and Oxfordism: a sermon preached...February 12, 1840. 35p. *8°*. 1840.

31864 PHILLPOTTS, H., *Bishop of Exeter*. Progress of socialism. The Bishop of Exeter's speech in the House of Lords...January 24, 1840. 16p. *8°*. [*London*, 1840]

31865 —— ⟨Painter's second edition.⟩ 16p. *8°*. [*London*, 1840]

31866 —— Conservative speeches – Painter's editions. Socialism. Second speech of the Bishop of Exeter, in the House of Lords, February 4, 1840. On moving an address to Her Majesty; with the Queen's gracious answer. 16p. *8°*. [*London*, 1840]

31867 POWELL, T. Socialism in its own colours. A plain tract on socialism for working men. 31p. *16°*. [1840 ?]

31868 RATIONAL SOCIETY. Address to all classes, sects and parties, containing an official declaration of principles, adapted for practice by the Congress of the Universal Community Society of Rational Religionists, held in Leeds, May, 1840. To which is added the proclamation of the Congress... [Signed: Robert Owen, president.] 8p. *8°*. 1840. *Another, one of several FWA copies that belonged to William Pare, has extensive manuscript corrections and additions, probably by Robert Owen, but not in his hand.*

31869 —— Social hymns, for the use of the friends of the rational system of society. Authorised version. Second

edition. vi, [174]p. *12°. Leeds*, 1840. *For another edition, see 1835 (Association of all Classes of all Nations).*

31870 —— Statement [signed: W.N., i.e. Walter Newall, general secretary] submitted to the most noble the Marquis of Normanby...relative to the principles and objects of the Universal Community Society of Rational Religionists. By the Branch A1 of that Society. 16p. *8°*. [1840]

31871 ROEBUCK, JOHN H. Rev. J. H. Roebuck's lectures. No. 1 [entitled 'Anti-Owenism']. 48p. *12°. Glasgow & London*, [1840] *Catalogued from the wrapper. This pamphlet is identical with p. 1–48 of the volume of Roebuck's lectures published in 1842 (q.v.), after his death. An inserted slip reads:'It is the intention of the author...to publish the whole course of his lectures, which may form, when completed, a volume of about 300 pages...The second lecture may be expected in a short time', etc. The notes are incomplete, the remainder being published at the beginning of lecture 2.*

31872 SAYINGS and doings about the new moral world. 8p. *8°. Leeds*, [1840]

31873 SHEPHEARD, A. Christianity and socialism examined, compared, and contrasted, as means for promoting human improvement and happiness. 44p. *12°*. 1840.

31874 SMITH, JAMES E. The little book; or, momentous crisis of 1840; in which the Bishop of Exeter and Robert Owen, are weighed in the two scales of one balance, and a new revelation of demonstrated truth is announced to the world. 36p. *12°*. [1840] *Another, the FWA copy, belonged to William Pare.*

31875 SMITH, WILLIAM H. *Birmingham*, 1840. [*Begin.*] Sir, Having observed your name connected with a reprobation of the principles of socialism... [A circular letter defending the principles of Robert Owen.] [4]p. *4°. n.p.* [1840] [*Br.* 598] *With a manuscript endorsement: Circular of William Hawkes Smith, notary public Birmingham Feby. 1840.*

31876 SOCIALISM. 24p. *12°. Society for Promoting Christian Knowledge*, 1840. *Caption and running-title: What is socialism? For another edition, see 1839.*

31877 SOUTHWELL, C. Socialism made easy; or, a plain exposition of Mr. Owen's views. 16p. *8°*. 1840.

31878 STURMER, F. Socialism, its immoral tendency; or, a plain appeal to common sense. 24p. *12°. London, Richmond* [*Surrey*], *&c.*, 1840.

31879 TAUNTON, W. A record of facts; being an exposure of the wilful falsehoods and mean hypocrisy of the Rev. John Sibree, of Coventry. Also, an account of the cowardly conduct of the Rev. T. Milner, of Northampton. 16p. *8°. Coventry & Northampton*, 1840. *Another, the FWA copy, was presented to William Pare by the author.*

31880 WRIGHT, HENRY G. Marriage and its sanctions. Second thousand. 8p. *8°. Cheltenham*, 1840. *Inscribed in manuscript on the title-page, 'Anti-Enclosure Association, from Goodwyn Barmby'.*

MISCELLANEOUS

31881 BACHELER, O. Discussion on the authenticity of the Bible, between Origen Bacheler and Robert Dale Owen. 235p. *8°*. 1840.

31882 —— Discussion of the existence of God, between Origen Bacheler, and Robert Dale Owen. 126p. *8°*. 1840.

31883 BROUN, SIR RICHARD, *Bart*. An address delivered before Her Majesty's Attorney and Solicitor Generals, in consequence of a reference from the Crown as to the right of the eldest sons of the baronets of Scotland & Nova Scotia...to claim and receive the dignity of knighthood. 24p. *8°*. 1840.

31884 BUCHANAN, ROBERT. A concise history of modern priestcraft, from the time of Henry VIII. until the present period. 172p. *12°*. *Manchester*, 1840.

31885 BUTT, I. Irish Corporation Bill. A speech delivered at the Bar of the House of Lords, on...the 15th of May, 1840, in defence of the city of Dublin; on the order for going into committee on the Irish Corporation Bill. 95p. *8°*. 1840. *The copy that belonged to Earl De Grey.*

31886 CLELAND, H. W. On the history and properties chemical and medical of tobacco, a probationary essay presented to the Faculty of Physicians & Surgeons, Glasgow... 68p. *4°*. *Glasgow*, 1840.

31887 COOPER, ROBERT. The "Holy Scriptures" analysed; or, extracts from the Bible, shewing its contradictions, absurdities and immoralities...Second edition. To which is added, a vindication of the work. 44p. *8°*. *Manchester & Hulme*, 1840.

31888 CORNISH, T. H. The juridical University of London. [An account of the history and customs of Gray's Inn.] *s.sh.fol. n.p.* [1840]

31889 DENMAN, T., *Baron Denman*. Parliamentary speeches – Painter's editions. Imprisonment of the Sheriffs. Lord Denman's speech in the House of Lord's, April 6, 1840. [On the privileges of the House of Commons.] 14p. *8°. n.p.* [1840]

31890 [ELLIOT, C.] A proposal in behalf of the seamen of the Kingdom, and for their better encouragement to seek service in the Royal Navy. 15p. *8°. n.p.* [1840?] *Presentation copy, with inscription, from the author to N. W. Senior.*

31891 FIELD, E. W. Observations of a solicitor on defects in the offices, practice, and system of costs of the equity courts. 96p. *8°*. 1840.

31892 [GEM, H.] Westminster Hall courts. Facts for the consideration of Parliament, before the final adoption of a plan perpetuating the courts of law on a site injurious and costly to the suitor. 44p. *8°*. 1840.

31893 —— Second edition. 48p. *8°*. 1840.

31894 GREGG, ST. G. Ambition, a poem...Second edition. 20p. *8°*. 1840. *Presentation copy, with inscription, from the author to W. D. Haggard.*

31895 HUME, D. An essay on miracles. [No. 10 of the Philosophical essays concerning human understanding.] 22p. *12°*. [*c.* 1840]

31896 HUTTON, W. The Court of Requests...With a memoir [of the author]. 62p. *8°*. *Edinburgh*, 1840.

31897 MATHEWS, G. Reasons for the abolition of manor courts, and for the improvement of petty session courts in Ireland. 36p. *8°*. *Dublin*, 1840.

31898 [NICHOLSON, WILLIAM, 1753–1815 ?] The doubts of infidels; or, queries relative to scriptural inconsistencies and contradictions, submitted for elucidation to the bench of Bishops...By a weak but sincere Christian [i.e. William Nicholson ?]...Second edition. 23p. *8°*. [1840]

31899 OWEN, ROBERT D. An address on the influence of the clerical profession. As delivered in the Hall of Science, New York...To which is added, A tract and a warning. 24p. *8°*. [*c.* 1840] *For other editions, see 1833, and no. 31861.*

31900 *PALMER, E. A letter to those who think. 18p. *12°*. *Worcester*, 1840. *The FWA copy, that belonged to William Pare.*

31901 SENIOR, N. W. Reviews of the Waverley novels, from Rob Roy to the Chronicles of the Canongate inclusive, with some miscellaneous articles [on agriculture, the corn trade, etc.]...Extracted from nos. L. LI. LII. LIII. and LIV. of the Quarterly Review, and no. I of the London Review. [194]p. *8°. n.p.* [*c.* 1840] *A collection of the original reviews, bound up with a special title-page, and presented, with an inscription from the author, to the Rev. E. C. Hawtrey, D.D.*

31902 SMYTH, J. The case of conspiracy contained in the annexed pamphlet is submitted to the grave and serious consideration of every reflecting mind and to the public generally. Do the laws sanction forgery, perjury, fraud, felony, swindling and murder?... 24p. *8°. n.p.*, 1840.

31903 SPENCE, G. Third address to the public, and more especially to the members of the House of Commons, on the present unsatisfactory state of the Court of Chancery; including observations on some of the propositions contained in the last number of the Quarterly Review. 33p. *8°*. 1840.

31904 —— Supplement to the first, second, and third addresses to the public, on the unsatisfactory state of the Court of Chancery; containing illustrations taken from Mr. Field's late pamphlet on the defects in the offices, and practice of the court, and other sources. 27p. *8°*. 1840. *For the first and second addresses, see 1839.*

31905 SPENCER, T. Clerical conformity and Church property, containing, with alterations, the substance of a pamphlet published...in...1830, entitled "The Church of England; or safe, liberal, and Christian principles of reform...by a clergyman."...Sixth thousand. 16p. *8°*. *London & Bath*, 1840.

31906 —— Practical suggestions on Church reform... Fourth thousand. 12p. *12°*. 1840.

31907 THORP, R. Reasons for the freedom of the sheriff deduced from the laws of England. 20p. *8°*. [1840]

1841

GENERAL

31908 **ANNUAIRE** général du commerce et de l'industrie, de la magistrature et de l'administration, ou almanach des 500,000 adresses, publié par Firmin Didot Frères...Le rapport du jury sur l'exposition faite en 1839 des produits de l'industrie française y est inséré en entier ...Avec une carte routière de France...1841. 4e année de la publication. lxxvi, 1711p. *8°. Paris*, [1841]

31909 **B.,** R. N. Corn and wages, or a few propositions and remarks on the variations in the price of corn and rate of wages. 35p. *12°.* 1841.

31910 **BEARD,** J. R. Diffusion, not restriction, the order of Providence: a discourse. 23p. *12°. London & Manchester*, 1841.

31911 Will cheap **BREAD** produce low wages? An inquiry for working men. 8p. *8°.* [1841]

31912 [**BREWER,** W. A.] Strictures on Montgomery on the cotton manufactures of Great Britain and America. Also, a practical comparison of the cost of steam and water power in America. By the author. [Signed: Justitia.] 75p. *8°. Newburyport*, 1841.

31913 The **BRITISH ALMANAC** of the Society for the Diffusion of Useful Knowledge, for...1841. [With 'The companion to the Almanac; or year-book of general information'.] 96, 256p. *12°.* [1841] *For other editions, see 1828.*

31914 **BUCKINGHAM,** J. S. America, historical, statistic, and descriptive. 3 vols. *8°. London & Paris*, [1841]

31915 —— Evils and remedies of the present system of popular elections...To which is added an address on the proposed reforms in the commerce and finance of the country. 315p. *12°.* 1841.

31916 **CAPPELLETTI,** G. L'Armenia... 3 vols. *8°. Firenze*, 1841.

31917 **CARLYLE,** T. On heroes, hero-worship, & the heroic in history. Six lectures. Reported, with emendations and additions. 393p. *12°.* 1841.

31918 **CHALMERS,** G. Catalogue of the...library of the late George Chalmers, Esq., F.R.S. F.S.A....which will be sold by auction by Messrs. Evans, No. 93, Pall Mall: on...September 27, and eight following days... 141p. *8°.* [*London*,] 1841. *With manuscript annotations (prices and names of buyers) and a note by HSF recording his acquisition (at the Crossley Sale in 1888) of many of the economic items, some of which had previously belonged to Stanesby Alchorne. For the second and third parts, see 1842.*

31919 —— The life of Daniel De Foe...To which are added, a list of De Foe's works, arranged chronologically. An appeal to honour and justice. A seasonable warning and caution. Reasons against the succession of the House of Hanover. What if the Pretender should come. An answer to a question which nobody thinks of, what if the Queen should die? The true-born Englishman... 7 parts. *8°. Oxford & London*, 1841. *This volume is vol. 20 of* The novels and miscellaneous works of Daniel De Foe, *1840–41.*

31920 **CIBRARIO,** G. A. L., *Conte.* Opusculi del

Cavaliere Luigi Cibrario...Delle giostre alla Corte di Savoia...MDCCCXXXV; Dell'Ordine dell'Annunziata; Del commercio degli schiavi a Genova; Esempio di' giustizia feudale; Necrologie; Dell'imputabilità nelle alienazioni di mente; Della pace pubblica interna; Delle finanze di Savoia ne' secoli XIII e XIV; Cronologia de' principi di Savoia rettificata. 375p. *12°. Torino*, 1841.

31921 **COBDEN,** R. To the manufacturers, mill-owners, and other capitalists, of every shade of political opinion, engaged in the various branches of the cotton trade, in the district of which Manchester is the centre. [On the necessity of free trade for future prosperity.] 8p. *8°. Manchester*, [1841]

31922 **COCKBURN,** SIR W. S. R., *Bart.* An address to the citizens of Bath...in reference to a mistake in the "Bath Journal" of 20th June, 1841; and upon the present crisis: cheap bread, poor laws, Chartists, &c.&c.&c. 36p. *8°. Bath*, 1841.

31923 Local **COLLECTIONS;** or records of remarkable events, connected with the borough of Gateshead. 1840[–1844]. 2 vols. *4°. Gateshead-on-Tyne*, 1841–45.

31924 **COMBE,** G. Notes on the United States of North America, during a phrenological visit in 1838–9–40 ... 3 vols. *8°. Edinburgh & London*, 1841.

31925 **COMMERZ-BIBLIOTHEK.** Katalog der Commerz-Bibliothek in Hamburg. 1841. 618 cols. *4°. Hamburg*, [1841]

31926 **CORBET,** T. An inquiry into the causes and modes of the wealth of individuals; or the principles of trade and speculation explained. In two parts. 256p. *12°.* 1841.

31927 **"CORN-COLONIES,"** an effectual remedy for the distress of the working classes, and for the embarrassments of commerce, manufactures and trade. 51p. *8°.* 1841. *A reissue of* England, her colonies and her enemies, *published in 1840 (q.v.). The Kress copy (C 5433) has a manuscript attribution on the title-page to 'Mr. Atherley'.*

31928 A **COUNTER-PLEA** for the poor, showing that the cause of their distress is not attributable to the corn laws. By the poor man's friend. In reply to a pamphlet by...the Hon. and Rev. W. Baptist Noel. 20p. *8°.* 1841. *For another issue, see no. 31964. See also 1843.*

31929 **CRAIK,** G. L., *ed.* The pictorial history of England during the reign of George the Third: being a history of the people as well as a history of the kingdom... By George L. Craik and Charles Macfarlane, assisted by other contributors... 4 vols. *8°.* 1841–44. *Published in parts. A continuation of the work covering an earlier period, published in 1838 (q.v.).*

31930 The present **CRISIS,** and its remedy: being a system for the equalisation of British and foreign prices... taking into account the National Debt, the revenue, and the public expenditure of the Government. 84p. *8°.* 1841. *Presentation copy from the anonymous author to the editor of the Edinburgh Review.*

31931 CRUCHLEY, G. F. Cruchley's picture of London, comprising the history, rise and progress of the Metropolis...To which is annexed, a new...map, with references to the principal streets, railway stations, etc. The sixth edition. 281p. *12⁰*. 1841.

31932 DAVENPORT, RICHARD A. Lives of individuals who raised themselves from poverty to eminence or fortune. 438p. *16⁰*. 1841.

31933 The EAST-INDIA register and directory, for 1841; containing...lists of the Company's servants... Second edition, corrected to the 12th May, 1841. Compiled...by F. Clark... 256, 165, 132p. *12⁰*. *London & Edinburgh*, 1841. *For other editions, see* 1804.

31934 EMERSON, R. W. Man the reformer. ⟨A lecture read before the Mechanics' Apprentices' Library Association, at the Masonic Temple, Boston, 25th January, 1841, and now published at their request⟩... 7p. *8⁰*. [*London*, 1841] *Another, the FWA copy, belonged to William Pare. It had been sent through the post in September 1841, addressed to 'Mr. Rigby, Queenwood, Tytherly'.*

31935 An ESSAY on civilization. Reprinted from the original, published thirty years ago. 15p. *8⁰*. 1841.

For FACTS AND FIGURES, 1841–42, *see vol.* III, *Periodicals list.*

31936 To the FARMERS of England. Foreign corn. Remarks on the cost price of producing wheat in foreign countries, and matters therewith connected. By a merchant, formerly a farmer of sixty thousand acres on the continent. 20p. *8⁰*. [1841]

31937 FARR, T. The principal difficulties of the sliding scale removed; with a plan for equalizing the expenditure and income of the United Kingdom. 16p. *8⁰*. 1841.

31938 FIELDEN, J. Important speech of John Fielden, Esq. M.P. for Oldham, on the sugar duties, May 19, 1841. [A description of the condition of N.W. England as a result of heavy taxation and declining industries.] 16p. *8⁰*. [1841]

31939 GALE, R. National granaries versus "union workhouses." 8p. *8⁰*. 1841.

31940 GLADSTONE, SIR J., *Bart.* Four letters addressed to the editor of the Morning Post on the objects of the Ministerial Budget, with additions...To which is added a letter written in October, 1839, on the then contemplated, and since adopted, changes in the rates of postage. 35p. *8⁰*. *London & Edinburgh*, 1841. *Presentation copy from the author to the Earl of Ripon.*

31941 GRAHAM, SIR JAMES R. G., *Bart.* Want of confidence. Sir James Graham's speech in the House of Commons, May 29, 1841. 16p. *8⁰*. *J. Ollivier*, [1841] *For another issue, see no.* 31964.

31942 —— [Another edition.] 16p. *8⁰*. *W. E. Painter*, [1841]

31943 HEUSCHLING, P. F. X. T. Essai statistique générale de la Belgique, composé sur les documents publics et particuliers par Xavier Heuschling, chef du Bureau de statistique générale au Ministère de l'Intérieur ...et publié par Ph. Vandermaelen. Deuxième édition, revue et mise au courant des documents nouveaux... 444p. *4⁰*. *Bruxelles*, 1841.

31944 HEYWORTH, L. To the working classes... On the national law of wages...Printed for the National Anti-Corn-Law League. 11p. *8⁰*. *Manchester*, 1841.

31945 HOLLAND, GEORGE C. The millocrat. No. I[–VII]. [A series of letters to J. G. Marshall, on the state of the manufacturing classes.] 19, 31, 32, 24, 24, 27, 29p. *8⁰*. 1841. *No. II is of the second edition.*

31496 —— [Another edition.] 8, 12, 12, 12, 11, 12, 12p. *12⁰*. 1841.

31947 HUME, D. Letters of David Hume, and extracts from letters referring to him. Edited by Thomas Murray. 80p. *8⁰*. *Edinburgh*, 1841. *The copy presented by the editor to 'James MacKnight, Esq. W.S.'.*

31948 [HUME, JAMES D.] Letters and extracts from letters on the corn laws, and on the rights of the working classes; shewing the injustice...of empowering those... who have obtained...possession of the lands...to increase ...the monetary value of their...estates, by means of arbitrary charges, made on the rest of the people...By H.B.T. 16p. *8⁰*. 1841. *For other editions, see* 1834.

31949 IRELAND: her Church and her people. By a Tory. 32p. *8⁰*. 1841.

31950 "What will the IRISH LORDS do?" A letter to the Earl of Listowel...By "A joint of the tail." [Signed: 'One of the tail!' Arguments for the repeal of the Union.] 37p. *8⁰*. 1841.

For the JOURNAL OF CIVILIZATION, *see vol.* III, *Periodicals list.*

31951 KNOX, C. H. Remarks on a war with America, and its probable consequences to that country...Second edition. 24p. *8⁰*. 1841.

31952 LABOUCHERE, H., *Baron Taunton.* Speech of the Right Hon. Henry Labouchere, in the House of Commons, on...May 10, 1841. Ways and means. Sugar duties, &c.&c.&c. 12p. *12⁰*. [1841]

31953 LAY, G. T. The Chinese as they are: their moral, social, and literary character; a new analysis of the language; with succinct views of their principal arts and sciences. 342p. *8⁰*. 1841.

31954 LEEDS. *Town Council.* Abstract of the report of the Statistical Committee (for 1838, 39, 40,)... 36p. *4⁰*. *Leeds*, 1841.

31955 LESTER, C. E. The glory and shame of England... 2 vols. *8⁰*. 1841.

31956 LIST, F. Das deutsche Eisenbahnsystem als Mittel zu Vervollkommnung der deutschen Industrie, des deutschen Zollvereins und des deutschen Nationalverbandes überhaupt. (Mit besonderer Rücksicht auf württembergische Eisenbahnen.) 37p. *8⁰*. *Stuttgart & Tübingen*, 1841. *The copy that belonged to Wilhelm Roscher.*

31957 —— Das nationale System der politischen Oekonomie...Erster Band. Der internationale Handel, die Handelspolitik und der deutsche Zollverein. 589p. *8⁰*. *Stuttgart & Tübingen*, 1841. *See also* 1844.

31958 McCULLOCH, JOHN R. A dictionary, geographical, statistical, and historical, of the various countries, places, and principal natural objects in the world... 2 vols. *8⁰*. 1841–42.

31959 MacDONNELL, E. "Repealers" and "sympathizers." Letter to Edward Everett, Envoy extraordinary and Minister plenipotentiary of the United States of America. 55p. *8⁰*. *London & Dublin*, 1841. *The copy that belonged to Earl De Grey.*

31960 The Book of MORMON...Translated by

Joseph Smith, Jun. First European, from the second American edition. 643p. *18°*. *Liverpool, 1841. For another edition, see 1840.*

31961 NEW YORK HISTORICAL SOCIETY. Collections of the New-York Historical Society. Second series. Vol. I. [Edited by G. Folsom.] 486p. *8°*. *New-York, 1841.*

31962 NOBLE, A. Narrative of the shipwreck of the "Kite," and of the imprisonment and sufferings of the crew and passengers; in a letter from Mrs. Anne Noble, to a friend. Macao, China; March 1841. 14p. *8°*. [*Canton, 1841*]

31963 [PAGE, R.] Action of the corn laws, and of the other provision laws, considered on the principles of a sound political economy and of common sense. By the author of Letters in the Times... more than twenty years since... 36p. *8°*. 1841.

31964 Conservative PAMPHLETS and speeches, principally upon the corn laws. 18 parts. *8°*. *1841. A collection of works, most already issued by the publisher, John Ollivier, in 1840 and 1841, reissued with a general title-page and list of contents. Contents: Anon. A counter-plea for the poor; G. C. Holland, An analysis of the address of F. H. Fawkes, Esq., to the landowners of England, 2nd edition; Idem, Letter to J. R. McCulloch, Esq. in answer to his statements on the corn laws, 2nd edition; Sir J. C. Dalbiac, A few words on the corn laws; Anon. Thoughts on the corn laws, 3rd edition; The saying of Sir Robert Peel, "My chief difficulty is Ireland," considered... in a letter to the... Baronet, by a clergyman of the Archdiocese of Canterbury; W. Skirrow, A letter to a noble lord on the causes which have produced the present reaction, 2nd edition; Remarks on a paper by Rowland Hill, Esq. on the results of the new postage arrangements... By one who has examined the statistics; Anon. Address to the electors of the manufacturing districts; S. Isaacson, The duty of electors at the present crisis; Corn laws. Appeal to tradesmen in town and country. By one of themselves; J. Robinson, The whole scheme of the corn-law abolitionists unmasked; Sir R. Peel, Address to the Queen... speech in the House of Commons... August 27, 1841; Sir R. Peel, Tamworth election. Speech... June 28, 1841; Sir R. Peel, Want of confidence in ministers. 4th edition... speech in the House of Commons... May 27, 1841; Sir R. Peel, No confidence in ministers. 3rd edition. Sir Robert Peel's reply in the House of Commons... June 4, 1841; Sir J. Graham, Want of confidence... speech in the House of Commons, May 29, 1841; Sir R. Peel, The corn laws... speech on Mr. Villiers' motion in the House of Commons, 1840.*

31965 PEEL, SIR ROBERT, *2nd Bart.* No confidence in ministers. Third edition. Sir Robert Peel's reply in the House of Commons... June 4, 1841. 14p. *8°*. [*London, 1841*] *For another issue, see no.* 31964.

31966 —— [Another edition.] Third edition... 14p. *8°*. *W. E. Painter,* [1841]

31967 —— Tamworth election. Speech of Sir Robert Peel, June 28, 1841. 24p. *8°*. *1841. For another issue, see no.* 31964.

31968 —— [Another edition.] Tamworth election. Sir R. Peel's speech at the nomination... 19p. *8°*. [1841]

31969 —— Third edition. Sir Robert Peel on the crisis... 15p. *8°*. [1841]

31970 *——* Fifth edition... 15p. *8°*. [1841] *The FWA copy that belonged to William Pare.*

31971 [PORTER, G. R.] The many sacrificed to the few; proved by the effects of the food monopoly. 16p. *8°*. [1841]

31972 [——] [Another edition.] 18p. *8°*. 1841.

31973 [——] The many sacrificed to the few; proved by the effects of the sugar monopoly. 24p. *8°*. [1841]

31974 [——] [Another edition.] 24p. *8°*. 1841.

31975 The POST-OFFICE annual directory [for Edinburgh, etc.], and calendar, for 1841–42. Thirty-sixth publication. 290p. *8°*. *Edinburgh, 1841. See also* 1828, 1835.

31976 The POST OFFICE London directory, 1841. Comprising, commercial directory; court directory; Post Office directory; conveyance directory; banking directory; &c.&c.&c. p.291–614, 929–998, 1204–1447. *8°*. *1841. The missing pages contain parts of the directory not listed on the title-page; these are recorded also in print on single leaves or pages at the appropriate points in the volume. See also 1805 (Post-Office annual directory), 1810, 1813, 1814, 1820 (Post Office London directory), 1823, 1825, 1830, 1832, 1834, 1836.*

31977 The present and future PROSPECTS of the country considered; and the Hon. and Rev. Baptist Noel's "Plea for the poor" dissected: with remarks on currency and banking, in a letter to Samuel Jones Loyd, Esq. By a citizen. [Signed: An honest citizen.] 44p. *8°*. 1841.

31978 *RAU, K. D. H. Grundsätze der Volkswirthschaftslehre...(Lehrbuch der politischen Oekonomie, 1–2.) Vierte vermehrte und verbesserte Ausgabe. 2 vols. *8°*. *Heidelberg, 1841, 1839. Vol. 2 is of The second edition. The copy that belonged to George Grote.*

31979 RHETT, R. B. Speech of Mr. Rhett, of South Carolina, on the protective or prohibitory policy... House of Representatives, December 22, 1841. 16p. *8°*. *n.p.* [1841]

31980 RUSSELL, JOHN, *Earl Russell.* The speech of Lord John Russell, in the House of Commons, on... the 7th of May, 1841. Ways and means – sugar duties. 40p. *8°*. 1841.

31981 —— [Another edition.] 24p. *12°*. *Manchester & London, 1841.*

31982 —— [Another edition.] 15p. *8°*. [1841]

31983 —— Speech of Lord John Russell, at a meeting of the electors of the City of London, held at the London Tavern, on... June 15, 1841. 11p. *8°*. [*London, 1841*]

31984 RUSSIA. *Commission pour fixer les Mesures et les Poids de l'Empire de Russie. Travaux de la Commission... Rédigés par A. Th. Kupffer...*[With a volume of plates.] 3 vols. *4°. & fol. St. Pétersbourg, 1841.*

31985 The SAYING of Sir R. Peel, "My chief difficulty is Ireland," considered, and a few remedial measures for that country suggested. In a letter to the Right Honourable Baronet, by a clergyman of the Archdiocese of Canterbury. 32p. *8°*. *1841. For another issue, see no.* 31964.

31986 [SENIOR, N. W.] Grounds and objects of the budget. Reprinted from No. 148 of the Edinburgh Review. 59p. *8°*. 1841.

31987 SHARP, G. An account of the constitutional English policy of congregational courts, and more particularly of the great annual court of the people called the View of Frankpledge... With two tracts on colonization... With a short memoir of the author by J. I. Burn... 124p. *12°*. 1841.

31988 SKIRROW, W. A letter to a noble Lord on the causes which have produced the present reaction; with remarks on Lord John Russell's Letter to the electors of the city of London...Second edition, revised and corrected. 25p. *8°.* 1841. *For another issue, see no.* 31964.

31989 STANSFELD, H. Monopoly and machinery: which is the real enemy of the working classes? A lecture, delivered before the Leeds Parliamentary Reform Association, on...November 8, 1841. 12p. *12°. Manchester,* [1841]

31990 SYPNIEWSKI, D. O. A discourse on the historical and political events of Poland; with a view of the present state of the Polish exiles. Second thousand. 33p. *8°. Brighton,* 1841.

31991 TALBOT, J., *Earl of Shrewsbury.* A second letter to Ambrose Lisle Phillipps, Esq. from the Earl of Shrewsbury. On the present posture of affairs [in Ireland]. 58p. *8°.* 1841.

31992 TENNANT, Sir J. E. Belgium... 2 vols. *12°.* 1841.

31993 TERNAUX-COMPANS, H. Bibliothèque asiatique et africaine ou catalogue des ouvrages relatifs à l'Asie et à l'Afrique qui ont paru depuis la découverte de l'imprimerie jusqu'en 1700. 347p. *8°. Paris,* 1841.

31994 [TORRENS, R.] The Budget. A series of letters on financial, commercial, and colonial policy. By a member of the Political Economy Club. No. I[–No. III.] p.1–78. *8°.* 1841. *The copies that belonged to Earl De Grey. Contents: Letter I. To the Lord John Russell, on the proposed alteration in the import duties upon corn and sugar; Letter II. To the Lord John Russell, on the manner in which the adoption of the Whig Budget would have altered the value of money; Letter III. To the Right Hon. Sir R. Peel, Bart., M.P. on commercial reform. Each letter was issued separately; it is possible that these copies belong to a reissue as a collection because they do not have the individual titles to each letter. See also* 1844.

31995 TOZER, J. On the effect of the non-residence of landlords on the wealth of a community. From the Transactions of the Cambridge Philosophical Society. Vol. VII. Part II. 8p. *4°. Cambridge,* 1841. *Presentation copy, with inscription, from the author to George Pryme.*

For **UNDERWOOD,** J. S., The philanthropist's magazine, *see* vol. III, *Periodicals list,* Philanthropist's magazine.

31996 UNITED STATES OF AMERICA. Congress. *House of Representatives.* 27th Congress, 2d Session. Doc. No. 2...Message from the President of the United States [John Tyler], to the two Houses of Congress, at the commencement of the second session of the twenty-seventh Congress. December 7, 1841. 16p. *8°. Washington,* 1841.

31997 [URQUHART, D.] The Syrian question. [A review signed X, reprinted from the *Westminster Review,* Vol. xxxv. With a postscript, signed W.] 38, [6]p. *8°. n.p.* [1841] *The copy that belonged to the 3rd Earl Radnor.*

31998 —— [*Endorsed:***]** Tabular view of the relations of Great Britain and Russia. [Extracted from "Exposition of transactions in Central Asia; through which the barriers to the British Possessions in India have been sacrificed to Russia, by Viscount Palmerston...By David Urquhart, Esq."] *s.sh.fol.* [1841]

31999 VIARDOT, L. De la crise anglaise. Eclaircissements sur la question de la réforme des tarifs. 61p. *16°. Paris,* 1841.

32000 VILLENEUVE-BARGEMONT, J. P. A. DE, *Vicomte.* Histoire de l'économie politique, ou études historiques, philosophiques et religieuses sur l'économie politique des peuples anciens et modernes. 2 vols. *8°. Paris,* 1841. *For another edition, see* 1839.

32001 WADE, JOHN. Reform government and its claims to the confidence of the electors of the United Kingdom. Abstracted, with additions, and by permission, from Mr. Wade's "Glances at the times," 5th edition. Fifteenth edition. 24p. *12°.* 1841.

32002 —— Sixteenth edition. 24p. *12°.* 1841.

32003 WESTHEAD, J. P. B. A letter to a Wesleyan elector of the borough of Manchester...No. 3. [On the prospects if the Tories win the election.] 20p. *8°. Manchester,* 1841.

32004 WILSON, ROBERT, *of Hawick.* The history of Hawick: including some account of the inhabitants...To which is appended a short memoir of the author. Second edition, corrected and considerably enlarged. 400p. *12°. Hawick & Edinburgh,* 1841. *For another edition, see* 1825.

32005 YATES, JOHN A. A letter on the present depression of trade and manufactures. Addressed to the landowners and farmers of the county of Carlow. 24p. *12°. Liverpool,* 1841.

32006 YOUNG, ANDREW W. Introduction to the science of government, and compend of the constitutional and civil jurisprudence of the United States; with a brief treatise on political economy. Designed for the use of families and schools...Fifth edition. 336p. *12°. Albany,* 1841

AGRICULTURE

32007 BAINBRIDGE, W. A practical treatise on the law of mines and minerals. [With an appendix.] 606p. *8°.* 1841.

32008 BEDFORD LEVEL CORPORATION. The lot book of the Bedford Level Corporation; with the orders as to the tax and arrear rolls, etc. etc. corrected to November, 1840, by Samuel Wells, Esq. 112p. *8°.* 1841. *See also* 1820.

32009 BOCCIUS, G. A treatise on the management of fresh-water fish, with a view to making them a source of profit to landed proprietors. 38p. *8°.* 1841.

32010 CONNER, W. The axe laid to the root of Irish oppression; and a sure and speedy remedy for the evils of Ireland. 23p. *8°. Dublin,* 1841. *See note to no.* 27313.

32011 DAUBENY, C. G. B. Three lectures on agriculture; delivered at Oxford on July 22nd, and Nov. 25th, 1840; and on Jan. 26th, 1841, in which the chemical operation of manures is particularly considered... 106p. *8°. Oxford & London,* 1841.

32012 DENTON, J. B. Outline of a method of model mapping; with a view to append, by an application of the art of levelling to that of area surveying, the advantage of a section of elevations and depressions to the uses of a map of superficial contents; with...remarks addressed to agriculturists, landed proprietors, and persons interested in the effectual drainage of towns...Second edition, with notes and appendix... 54p. *8°*. 1841.

32013 ENGLAND. *Laws, etc.* Anno quarto Victoriæ. Cap. 6. An Act for inclosing lands in the parish of Gamlingay in the county of Cambridge. ⟨18th May 1841.⟩ p.157–192. *fol.* 1841.

32014 ——— ——— [*Endorsed:*] Uplyme Inclosure. An Act for inclosing lands in the parish of Uplyme, in the county of Devon. ⟨Royal Assent, 18th May 1841.⟩ 36p. *fol.* [*London*, 1841]

32015 ——— Parliament. [*Endorsed:*] Blackburn Town's Moor. An Act [a Bill] for vesting in the overseers of the poor of...Blackburn, in the County Palatine of Lancaster, parts of the Town's Moor for sale, or other disposal thereof. 4 Victoria. Sess. 1841. 15p. *fol.* [*London*, 1841]

32016 ENSLIN, T. C. F. Bibliotheca economica oder Verzeichniss der in älterer und neurer Zeit bis zur Mitte des Jahres 1840 in Deutschland und den angränzenden Länden erschienenen Bücher über die Haus- und Landwirtschaft...Von neuem gänzlich umgearbeitete zweite Auflage von W. Engelmann... 438p. *8°*. *Leipzig*, 1841.

32017 The **FARM** and the garden: an account of every vegetable production cultivated for the table, by the plough and the spade. 60p. *8°*. 1841.

32018 GREY, J. A view of the past and present state of agriculture in Northumberland. [From the Journal of the Royal Agricultural Society of England, 1841, Vol. II, part II.] 42p. *8°*. 1841. *Presentation copy from the author to 'Mrs Loraine'.*

32019 HALL, G. W. The connexion between landlord and tenant, and tenant and labourer, in the cultivation of the British soil; their rights, their duties, and their interests...Second edition. 54p. *8°*. *London & Bristol*, 1841.

32020 [**HOLLAND**, JOHN (1794–1872).] The history and description of fossil fuel, the collieries, and coal trade of Great Britain. By the author of the "Treatise on manufactures in metal"...in the Cabinet cyclopædia. Second edition. xvi, 485p. *8°*. *London & Sheffield*, 1841. *For another edition, see 1835.*

32021 JOHNSON, C. W. On increasing the demand for agricultural labour. [With appendix containing an account of the self-supporting school at Willingdon, by its founder, George Cruttenden.] 64p. *8°*. 1841.

32022 LIEBIG, J. VON, *Freiherr*. Chimie organique appliquée à la physiologie végétale et à l'agriculture suivie d'un essai de toxicologie...Traduction faite sur les manuscrits de l'auteur par M. Charles Gerhardt. 392p. *8°*. *Paris*, 1841. *See also 1842, 1847.*

32023 [**NICHOLLS**, SIR GEORGE.] The farmer's guide, compiled for the use of the small farmers and cotter tenantry of Ireland. 183p. *12°*. *Dublin*, 1841. *With engraved presentation inscription from the author, dated: 10th December, 1841.*

32024 O'CONNOR, F. The labourers' library, nos. 2 & 3. The remedy for national poverty and impending national ruin: or the only safe way of repealing the corn laws by enabling each working family to produce a "big loaf" and a "cheap loaf" for themselves, at home. 24p. *12°*. *Leeds, Manchester, &c.*, 1841.

32025 ——— The labourers' library, nos. 2 & 3. "The land" the only remedy for national poverty...Second edition. 24p. *12°*. *Leeds, Manchester, &c.*, 1841.

32026 SMITH, ROBERT, *rat-catcher*. The universal directory, for taking alive and destroying rats, and all other kinds of four-footed and winged vermin, in a method hitherto unattempted; calculated for the use of the gentleman, the farmer, and the warrener...A new edition, carefully revised. 150p. *12°*. [1841]

32027 SOCIETY OF THE GOVERNOR AND ASSISTANTS IN LONDON, OF THE NEW PLANTATION IN ULSTER. Report of the deputation [W. Green, J. T. Norris, H. Patten, W. H. Pilcher, J. E. Davies] appointed by the honourable the Irish Society, to visit the City of London's plantation in Ireland, in the year 1840. 103p. *8°*. 1841. *See also 1826 (GENERAL), 1834 (AGRICULTURE), 1835, 1836, 1838.*

32028 SOPWITH, T. The award of the Dean Forest Mining Commissioners, under the Act of 1 and 2 Victoria, cap. 43, as to the coal and iron mines in Her Majesty's Forest of Dean; and the rules and regulations for working the same: with preliminary observations, and an explanation of a series of...engraved plans of the Dean Forest mines... 209p. *8°*. 1841.

32029 WALTON, WILLIAM (1784–1857). A memoir addressed to proprietors of mountain and other waste lands, and agriculturists of the United Kingdom, on the naturalization of the alpaca...(Enlarged from a paper in the Polytechnic Journal for April, 1841.) 44p. *8°*. *London, Liverpool, &c.: The Natural History Society of Liverpool*, 1841.

CORN LAWS

32030 ADDRESS to the electors of the manufacturing districts. [Against the repeal of the corn laws.] 32p. *8°*. 1841. *For another issue, see no. 31964.*

32031 ALLEN, J. H. A letter to the agriculturists of the county of Pembroke, on the influence of the corn laws ...October 28th, 1841. 20p. *12°*. *Pembroke*, [1841]

32032 An **ANALYSIS** of the population of Great Britain, their occupation and wheat consumption; also of its area and produce, in reference to a duty on corn. 6p. *8°*. 1841.

32033 The **ANTI-CORN-LAW ALMANACK**, for the year...1841, being...the twenty-sixth year of the bread tax; containing...duties on corn; imports and exports; wages in Warsaw...members of the House of Commons who voted for and against the bread tax... 48p. *12°*. *Manchester & London*, [1841] *See also* The Anti-Bread-Tax Almanack, 1842.

32034 An **APPEAL** to the tradesmen of Great Britain on cheap food and brisk trade [signed: An elector]; in answer to 'An appeal to the tradesmen of the Metropolis.' 8p. *8°*. [1841]

32035 ASHPITEL, A. The factor, the miller, and the baker get more than the farmer, and ten times more than the landlord out of the loaf. A few facts on the corn laws, defending the agricultural interest...Second edition, with a postscript. 32p. *8°*. 1841. *For another edition, see* 1839.

32036 BLAIN, H. A letter to Sir Robert Peel, exhibiting the defects of the present corn law, and submitting suggestions for its amendment. 27p. *8°*. 1841. *Two copies, one with a letter on his plan from the author to 'Jos. T. Pooley' inserted in the volume, the other the copy that belonged to Earl De Grey. For the letter, see* vol. III, *A.L.* 445.

32037 Cheap **BREAD** and its consequence. [Signed: A British farmer and landowner. Against modification of the corn law.] 15p. *8°*. 1841.

32038 Is cheap or dear **BREAD** best for the poor man? 16p. *8°*. 1841.

32039 BYRNE, J. F. Four letters on the corn laws, addressed to the Right Hon. Sir Robert Peel, Bart. 19p. *8°*. *London & Ringwood*, [1841]

32040 [**C.,** F. ?] The corn question. Mr. M'Culloch's pamphlet on the corn laws critically analysed; with a postscriptum on the latest fallacies of radicalism. By the author of "The cost price of growing foreign corn," and "An essay on free trade." 20p. *8°*. 1841.

32041 —— An essay on free-trade: its absolute value in theory, its relative value in practice, error and consequences of its application to the corn-laws. By F.C. [Dated: April 30th, 1841, with 'Postscriptum', dated May 1st.] 155p. *8°*. 1841. *The copy that belonged to Earl De Grey, with manuscript notes throughout.*

32042 CONFERENCE OF MINISTERS OF ALL DENOMINATIONS ON THE CORN LAWS. Report of the Conference...held in Manchester, August 17th, 18th, 19th, and 20th, 1841. With a digest of the documents contributed during the conference. Published under the auspices of the Committee. Third thousand. 264p. *12°*. *Manchester & London*, 1841.

32043 CORN LAW HYMN. Tune – Old 100th. [From the *Morning Chronicle*.] *s.sh.8°*. [*London:*] *Bethnal Green Anti-Corn Law Association*, [1841]

32044 CORN LAWS. An appeal to the tradesmen of the Metropolis. By one of themselves. [Signed: A London tradesman. Reprinted from *The Times* of May 28th, 1841.] 8p. *8°*. 1841.

32045 —— [Another issue.] Corn laws. Appeal to tradesmen in town and country. By one of themselves. 8p. *8°*. 1841. *For another issue, see no.* 31964.

32046 The **CORN LAWS,** considered in their origin, progress, and results. Extracted, by permission, from the British and Foreign Review, No. XXIV. 55p. *8°*. 1841.

32047 CORN LAWS. The farmer's case, shown from the evidence [given before the Select Committee of the House of Commons on the state of agriculture, 1836] of the following agriculturists: Mr. Ellis, a Leicestershire farmer...Mr. Bell, a Scotch farmer; Mr. Robertson, an English farmer [and others]. 16p. *8°*. 1841.

32048 CORN LAWS. The sliding scale. Facts for the farmers. 8p. *8°*. *Manchester*, [1841]

32049 —— [Another edition.] 8p. *8°*. [*London*, 1841]

32050 COURT, M. H. An analysis of the natural price of corn; with observations on the speech of Sir Robert Peel, Bart., M.P. to his constituents at Tamworth, in

illustration of the impolicy of existing corn laws by inducing the evil effects of artificial prices of corn. 52p. *8°*. 1841.

32051 CURTIS, JOHN, *of Ohio*. America and the corn laws; or, facts and evidence, showing the extensive supply of food which may be brought from America, and the effects of the restrictive system on the British and American trade...Printed for the National Anti-Corn-Law League. 35p. *8°*. *Manchester*, 1841.

32052 DALBIAC, SIR J. C. A few words on the corn laws, wherein are brought under consideration certain of the statements which are to be found in the third edition of Mr. McCulloch's pamphlet upon the same subject. 53p. *8°*. 1841. *For another issue, see no.* 31964.

32053 DIOGENES, *pseud.* The letters of Diogenes, to Sir Robert Peel, Bart. [On the corn laws.] 110p. *8°*. 1841.

32054 DRUMMOND, H. On the corn laws. 30p. *8°*. 1841.

32055 ELLIOT, HON. JOHN E. Letter to the Teviotside farmer. [Reply to a letter in the *Kelso Mail*, of 27th May, from 'a Teviotside farmer'. On the proposed new duties on corn.] 8p. *8°*. [1841]

32056 An historical **EXAMINATION** of the corn laws. 29p. *8°*. *Dublin & London*, 1841.

32057 GORE, M. Thoughts on the corn laws; with a few prefatory remarks addressed to the middle and labouring classes...Third edition. 38p. *8°*. 1841. *For another edition, see* 1840.

32058 GRÆME, O. A few thoughts on the proposed repeal of the corn laws. 16p. *8°*. *Edinburgh*, 1841.

32059 GREG, R. H. A letter to the Right Hon. Henry Labouchère, on the pressure of the corn laws and sliding scale, more especially upon the manufacturing interests and productive classes. 31p. *8°*. 1841. *The copy that belonged to T. Spring Rice, Baron Monteagle. See also* 1842.

32060 HEARN, W. Seventh thousand. Oppression: or the effects of monopoly on family expenditure. A tract for the times. 12p. *12°*. [1841]

32061 —— Thirteenth thousand... 12p. *12°*. [1841]

32062 HINDLEY, C. Speech of Charles Hindley, Esq., M.P. for Ashton-under-Lyne, in the House of Commons...June 15, 1841. 12p. *12°*. 1841.

32063 HOLLAND, GEORGE C. An analysis of the address of F. H. Fawkes, Esq., to the landowners of England...Second edition, greatly enlarged and revised. 44p. *8°*. 1841. *For another issue, see no.* 31964.

32064 —— Letter to J. R. M'Culloch, Esq. in answer to his statements on the corn laws. 27p. *8°*. *London & Sheffield*, 1841. *The copy presented to the editor of The Times.*

32065 —— Second edition. 27p. *8°*. *London & Sheffield*, 1841. *For another issue, see no.* 31964.

32066 —— Suggestions towards improving the present system of corn-laws. Inscribed, by permission, to the Right Hon. Sir R. Peel, Bart. 39p. *8°*. 1841.

32067 JAMES, G. P R. Some remarks on the corn laws, with suggestions for an alteration in the sliding scale, in a letter to Col. Charles Wyndham, M.P. 18p. *8°*. 1841.

32068 KENDAL ANTI-CORN-LAW ASSO-CIATION. An address to the inhabitants of Kendal, on the present state of trade in their borough, in connection with the corn-laws. Second edition, with additional notes. 24p. *12°. Kendal & London,* 1841.

32069 How fares the agricultural **LABOURER** under the present corn law? 4p. *8°.* [1841]

32070 LETTER to His Grace, the Duke of Wellington, on the corn laws. By a Forfarshire merchant. 16p. *8°. Edinburgh & Arbroath,* 1841.

32071 [LHOTSKY, J.] Daily bread; or, taxation without representation resisted: being a plan for the abolition of the bread tax. By one of the millions. 32p. *8°. London, Manchester, &c.,* [1841]

32072 A cheap **LOAF,** but no money to buy it, or the question of the corn laws plainly considered by a plain man in plain language, addressed to the working classes. Ninth edition. 24p. *12°. Sudbury & London,* 1841.

32073 [McCULLOCH, JOHN R.] Statements illustrative of the policy and probable consequences of the proposed repeal of the existing corn laws, and the imposition in their stead of a moderate duty on foreign corn when entered for consumption. 38p. *8°.* 1841.

32074 —— Second edition. With a postscript. 38[44]p. *8°.* 1841. *4 leaves, signed *B8, containing additional tables and text, have replaced leaf B8 of the original edition.*

32075 —— Third edition. With a postscript. 47p. *8°.* 1841.

32076 —— Sixth edition. With a postscript. 47p. *8°.* 1841. *The copy that belonged to T. Spring Rice, Baron Monteagle, with his signature on the title-page.*

32077 —— [Another issue.] Sixth edition. With a postscript. 47p. *8°.* 1841.

32078 —— [Another edition.] 24p. *8°. Edinburgh,* 1841. *The text of this edition is that of the second and later London editions.*

32079 MANCHESTER ANTI-CORN-LAW ASSOCIATION. Anti-bread-tax tracts for the people. Nos. 2–3. *s.sh.8°. & fol.* [*Manchester,* 1841]

32080 MARTIN, WILLIAM (1772–1851). The Christian philosopher on the corn laws, and other important subjects. 4p. *8°. Newcastle,* [1841]

32081 METROPOLITAN ANTI-CORN LAW ASSOCIATION. Address of the Metropolitan Anti-Corn Law Association, to the public. [Signed: Francis Place, chairman.] 8p. *8°.* [*London,* 1841]

32082 —— Agricultural prosperity under the corn laws. [A leaflet, dated: July 1st, 1841.] *s.sh.8°.* [*London,* 1841]

32083 —— Second report of the Business Committee …1st March, 1841. 8p. *8°.* 1841.

32084 MORRIS, A. J. The moral and religious bearings of the corn law. A lecture delivered in New Windsor Chapel, Salford, August 22, 1841… 24p. *12°. Manchester & London,* 1841.

32085 NAPIER, SIR W. F. P. Observations on the corn law…Addressed to Lord Ashley… 16p. *8°.* 1841.

32086 —— Second edition. 16p. *8°.* 1841.

32087 NEVILE, C. The sliding scale, or a fixed duty [on corn]. 34p. *8°.* 1841.

32088 NOEL, HON. B. W. A plea for the poor, showing how the proposed repeal of the existing corn laws will affect the interests of the working classes…Thirty-third thousand. 24p. *12°.* 1841.

32089 —— Fortieth thousand. 24p. *12°.* 1841.

32090 *—— [Another edition.] For general circulation! …Sold by the Bethnal Green Anti-Corn-Law Association … 24p. *12°.* 1841. *The FWA copy that belonged to William Pare, with extensive manuscript notes. See also* 1842.

32091 P., W. The incubus of the nation [the import duty on corn], and effects of its removal… 8p. *8°.* 1841. *A former owner of the pamphlet identified the author as 'Petrie' in a manuscript note.*

32092 PEOPLE of Great Britain…[An anti-corn-law tract. Signed: A Briton.] 4p. *8°.* [*London,* 1841]

32093 A **PLEA** for the total and immediate repeal of the corn laws: proving that the land rental has increased about twenty-fold; that the present income is greater than the value of the freehold before the protective system commenced in 1660…with a table of the land-rental of 100 parishes of Scotland, in 1791–96, and in 1832–41. (*Anti-Corn Law Tract,* 1.) 32p. *12°.* 1841.

32094 —— A plea for the total and immediate repeal of the corn laws: with a table of the land-rental of 100 parishes of Scotland, in 1791–96, and in 1832–41; and the official rental of 72 parishes in 1650. (*Anti-Corn Law Tract,* 1.) Third edition, enlarged. 55p. *12°.* 1841. *See also* 1842.

32095 The poor **PLEA** of the Queen's new chaplain. Being a letter to the Hon. and Rev. Baptist Noel, from a Rutlandshire freeholder. Second edition. 15p. *8°.* 1841.

32096 PLINT, T. Speech of Mr. Thomas Plint, delivered at the West-Riding meeting of anti corn law deputies, held in the Music Hall, Leeds, December 13th, 1841… 16p. *8°. Leeds,* [1841]

32097 PRAYER for food. [An attack on Sir Robert Peel for his failure to repeal the corn laws.] 3p. *12°. London,* [1841]

32098 Second thousand, with a postscript. Fifty searching **QUESTIONS** addressed to the Hon. & Rev. Baptist W. Noel, and all other corn law repealers, intended as an antidote to his recent dangerous and exciting pamphlet and showing how the repeal or non-repeal of the existing corn law really affect the interests of the working classes. To which is added a postscript, in reply to a letter of Mr. Noel's to the author…by a clergyman of the United Church of England and Ireland. 26p. *8°. London, Oxford, &c.,* 1841.

32099 QUESTIONS for the consideration of farmers. [No. I.] Exorbitant rents the true cause of agricultural distress. 8p. *8°.* 1841.

32100 —— No. II. The farmer uninjured by foreign competition. 8p. *8°.* 1841.

32101 —— No. III. Ruinous prices periodically produced by the sliding scale. 8p. *8°.* 1841.

32102 RAMSDEN, D. J. The people and the corn laws, with a reply to the Chartist's objections against their repeal. 24p. *12°. Mossley, Manchester, &c.,* [1841]

32103 RAUMER, F. L. G. VON. The corn laws of England…Copyright edition, translated from the German. 31p. *8°. London & Liverpool,* [1841]

32104 RENNY, J. H. Reflections upon the corn laws, and upon their effects on the trade, manufactures, and agriculture of the country, and on the condition of the working classes. 107p. *8°.* 1841. *The copy that belonged to Earl De Grey.*

For **ROBINSON,** JOHN, *M.B.,* The whole scheme of the corn-law abolitionists unmasked; addressed to my fellow-countrymen, *see no.* 31964.

32105 SALOMONS, SIR D., *Bart.* The corn laws. Their effects on the trade of the country considered, with suggestions for a compromise. 88p. *8°.* 1841. *Presentation copy from the author to the Earl of Ripon.*

32106 SPENCER, T. The corn laws and the National Debt; or, the parson's dream and the Queen's speech. By a Somersetshire clergyman. Eighth thousand. No. 7. 16p. *8°. London & Bath,* 1841.

32107 —— The parson's dream and the Queen's speech; or, the corn laws and the National Debt...Tenth thousand. No. 7. 16p. *8°. London & Bath,* 1841. *See also* 1843.

32108 SULLEY, R. The fallacies of the protective system exposed, and the effects of the corn laws especially considered. Addressed to the landowners of Great Britain ... 40p. *12°. Manchester,* 1841.

32109 SUPPLEMENT to the "Plea for the poor;" consisting of facts and opinions, gathered from speeches and examinations at the great Anti-Corn Law Conference, held in Manchester, on...August 17, 1841, and following days. 36p. *12°.* [1841]

32110 Second edition. The **THEORY** and practice of the sliding scale, familiarly explained and illustrated. Addressed to thinking men of all parties and classes. By one of the corn trade. 16p. *8°.* 1841.

32111 THOMPSON, THOMAS P. Catechism on the corn laws; with a list of fallacies and the answers. Edition 21. Stereotype...To which is added the article on free trade, from the Westminster Review, No. XXIII... 82p. *8°.* 1841. *For other editions, see* 1827.

32112 THORNTON, HENRY, *of the Custom House, London.* Historical summary of the corn laws, containing the substance of the Statutes passed from the year 1660, for regulating the importation and consumption of foreign, and the exportation of British, corn. With notes and an appendix of statements illustrative of the operation of the several Statutes. 56p. *8°.* 1841.

32113 THORNTON, W. T. The true consequences of the repeal of the corn-laws. [A reply to McCulloch.] 27p. *8°.* [1841]

For **THOUGHTS** on the corn laws, third edition, *see no.* 31964.

32114 WEST HACKNEY & STOKE NEW- INGTON ANTI-CORN-LAW ASSOCIA- TION. [*Begin.*] The following admirable and important letter of Dr. John Pye Smith [to Richard Cobden, against the corn laws]... 4p. *8°.* [*London,* 1841]

32115 WESTERN, C. C., *Baron Western.* Letter from Lord Western to Lord John Russell, on his proposed alteration of the corn laws, and on the causes of commercial distress. [With a postscript.] 49, iiip. *8°.* 1841. *With some manuscript corrections in the text on p. 18 and p. 19. These have been incorporated in the second edition, no.* 32116, *below.*

32116 —— Second edition. 43p. *8°.* 1841. *The copy that belonged to Earl De Grey.*

32117 —— Third edition. 45p. *8°.* 1841.

32118 —— A supplement to Lord Western's letter to Lord J. Russell, upon corn laws and commercial distress, with a brief review of the reports of the Manchester Chamber of Commerce, of December 1839, and March 1841. 12p. *8°.* 1841.

32119 —— [Another edition.] Together with an extract from a letter of R. Cobden, Esq., M.P., of the 12th of Sept., and Lord Western's reply. 16p. *8°.* 1841.

32120 WHITMORE, W. W. A letter to the agricul- turists of the county of Salop...June 5, 1841. [On the corn laws.] Second edition. 24p. *12°.* [1841]

32121 —— Third edition. 24p. *12°.* [1841]

32122 —— A second letter to the agriculturists of the county of Salop...August 5, 1841. 67p. *12°.* [1841]

32123 YEATMAN, H. F. The report of a speech on the policy of the existing corn laws, in opposition to the ministerial plan of a fixed duty on corn; delivered...at Dorchester, on the 15th of May, 1841. 106p. *8°. Sherborne,* 1841.

32124 YOUNG, J., *of Andover.* The corn laws, unjust and injurious: an address to the people of Great Britain... Second thousand. 16p. *8°.* [1841]

POPULATION

32125 ANTI-MARCUS, *pseud.* Notes on the population question. 44p. *8°.* 1841.

32126 *GALLOWAY, T. Tables of mortality de- duced from the experience of the Amicable Society for a Perpetual Assurance Office, during a period of 33 years, ending April 5, 1841. To which are added, comparisons of the mean duration and probabilities of life...Printed for the use of the members of the Society... xii, [24]p. *4°.* [1841] *The copy that belonged to Augustus De Morgan.*

32127 GLASGOW. The Glasgow Mortality Bill, for the year ending 31st December, 1840. Drawn up...under the authority of the Lord Provost, magistrates, and Town Council. Containing tables of the registered births and baptisms, marriages, burials...with the City and suburban districts of Gorbals and Barony parishes. By Alexander Watt...[With an appendix.] 36, [2]p. *4°. Glasgow,* 1841.

32128 WATT, A. Report of the local census of Lanark- shire, with other statistical information connected there- with. 26p. *8°. Glasgow,* 1841.

TRADES & MANUFACTURES

32129 AIKIN, A. Illustrations of arts and manufactures. Being a selection from a series of papers read before the Society for the Encouragement of Arts, Manufactures and Commerce. 376p. *8°*. 1841.

32130 BELGIUM. *Ministère de l'Intérieur.* Dispositions relatives à l'Exposition publique des produits de l'industrie nationale de 1841. 22p. *12°*. *Bruxelles*, 1841.

32131 —— *Direction de l'Industrie.* Ministère de l'Intérieur. Direction de l'Industrie. Enquête sur l'industrie linière. Interrogatoires. [With 'Rapport de la Commission. Explorations à l'étranger'.] 2 vols. *fol. Bruxelles*, 1841.

32132 BOYMAN, B. Pilbrow's condensing cylinder steam engine. 103p. *8°*. 1841.

32133 CLARK, THOMAS (1801–1867). A new process for purifying the waters supplied to the Metropolis by the existing water companies: rendering each water much softer, preventing a fur on boiling...and withdrawing from solution large quantities of solid matter not separable by mere filtration...Second edition. 15p. *8°*. 1841.

32134 The **CYCLOPÆDIA** of practical receipts in all the useful and domestic arts: being a compendious book of reference for the manufacturer, tradesman, and amateur. By a practical chemist. 281p. *12°*. 1841.

32135 DEVLIN, J. D. The guide to trade. The shoemaker. Part II: being the duties of the shop. 160p. *12°*. 1841.

32136 *GLIDDON, G. R. No. 1. A memoir on the cotton of Egypt. 64p. *8°*. 1841.

32137 MARTIN, WILLIAM (1772–1851). I begin the subject on one of the town council, a quayside old wife. [An attack, in verse, on, among others, John Buddle and Nicholas Wood.] *s.sh.8°*. *Newcastle*, [1841]

32138 —— The philosopher on the explosions of coal mines, and how to remedy those dreadful disasters that so often take place in the coal mining districts. [An attack on the Davy safety lamp and on John Buddle.] 4p. *8°*. *Newcastle*, [1841]

32139 —— The philosopher on the wreck of the Royal George, and other subjects. 4p. *8°*. *Newcastle*, [1841]

32140 —— The philosopher's remarks upon a preacher of Christ's gospel, for ignorantly saying the Martinian system is contrary to Christianity...[Including an attack on George Stephenson for having stolen the author's inventions.] 4p. *8°*. *Newcastle*, [1841 ?]

32141 ROSS, WILLIAM. Copyright in designs printed upon woven fabrics. The impolicy and peril of extending the existing copyright. [With an appendix] 52, 3p. *8°*. *Manchester*, 1841.

32142 STEVENSON, DAVID. On the building materials of the United States of North America...(From the Edinburgh New Philosophical Journal for July, 1841.) 18p. *8°*. *n.p.* [1841]

32143 STOKES, J. The complete cabinet-maker, and upholsterer's guide; containing the rudiments and principles of cabinet-making and upholstery, with familiar instructions, illustrated by examples, for attaining a proficiency in the art of drawing, as applicable to cabinet-work...and a number of receipts...Fourth edition. 167p. *12°*. [1841]

32144 TENNENT, SIR J. E. A treatise on the copyright of designs for printed fabrics; with considerations on the necessity of its extension: and copious notices of the state of calico printing in Belgium, Germany, and the states of the Prussian Commercial League. 283p. *12°*. 1841.

32145 THOMSON, JAMES, *F.R.S.* Notes on the present state of calico printing in Belgium: with prefatory observations on the competition and tariff of different countries...Second edition. 72p. *12°*. 1841.

32146 WHITWORTH, SIR J., *Bart.* On an uniform system of screw threads; communicated to the Institution of Civil Engineers...1841. 16p. *8°*. 1841.

32147 WICKSTEED, T. An experimental inquiry concerning the relative power of, and useful effect produced by, the Cornish and Boulton and Watt pumping engines, and cylindrical and waggon-head boilers. 34p. *4°*. 1841. *Presentation copy from the author to D. McKain.*

32148 WILLIAMS, CHARLES W. The combustion of coal and the prevention of smoke chemically and practically considered...Part the first. Second edition... [With appendixes.] 158, xxvip. *8°*. *London, Liverpool, &c.*, 1841.

COMMERCE

32149 CHAMBER OF COMMERCE, *Manchester.* Under the sanction of the Directors. Report of the Directors to a special general meeting of the Chamber of Commerce and Manufactures...on the injurious effects of restrictions on trade, and the necessity of immediate changes in our commercial policy; arising out of the Report and evidence of the Select Committee of the House of Commons on import duties, during the last session of Parliament. 11th March, 1841. [Signed: J. B. Smith, president.] 24p. *8°*. *London & Manchester*, 1841. *The copy that belonged to Victor Considérant.*

32150 —— Fifth thousand. 24p. *8°*. *London & Manchester*, 1841.

32151 CLARK, CHARLES (*fl.* 1841). The Russia trader's assistant, containing practical information concerning Russian monies, weights and measures; the course of exchange; bills of exchange; the commercial guilds; the trade of foreigners settled in or travelling to Russia... adapted for the use of merchants, shipowners, and brokers concerned in the Russia trade... 2 vols. *obl.8°*. *London & Hull*, 1841.

32152 ENGLAND. *Parliament. House of Commons.* A digest of the evidence given before the Committee of the House of Commons [of 1840] on the import duties. Second edition. 47p. *8°*. 1841.

32153 GALE, R. An extension of the home demand can alone save the Empire: the 'cheap bread' of the free-traders, a delusion. Second edition. 16p. *8°*. 1841.

32154 HUTT, SIR W. Sound dues, considered. 60p. *8°*. 1841.

32155 LONDON. Livery Companies. *Clockmakers*. A statement of the various proceedings and transactions that have taken place between the Court of Assistants of the Clockmakers' Company...and His Majesty's Government, in relation to the importation of foreign clocks and watches into these realms, from 1787 to 1834. Ordered, by the Court of Assistants...to be printed for the use of the members...the 8th of July, 1833: and the addenda, ordered...to be printed, the 22d November, 1841. 73, 59p. *8°*. 1841. *The phrase 'from 1787 to 1834' is printed on a slip, masking the original wording, which was 'subsequent to the 15th of March 1832'.*

32156 [MACGREGOR, JOHN (1797–1857).] The common sense view of the sugar question. Addressed to all classes and parties. By M.B.T. Second edition. 16p. *8°*. 1841.

32157 [MANGLES, R. D.] Wrongs and claims of Indian commerce. From the Edinburgh Review, No. CXLVI. 44p. *8°*. *Edinburgh*, 1841.

32158 MEMORIAL to Sir Robert Peel. To the Right Honourable Sir Robert Peel...The memorial of the undersigned merchants, manufacturers, and others, directly or indirectly interested in the trade with China... [Signed by 236 firms engaged in the textile manufacture and trade from the south-western and northern counties of England and from Scotland. On the resumption of trade with China and the desirability of the prohibition of the opium trade.] 8p. *8°*. [*London*, 1841 ?]

32159 MOTTE, W. R. S. A letter to the shareholders, relative to the present state and future prospects of the British Iron Company. 54p. *8°*. [1841]

32160 A few **REMARKS** on the corn, sugar & timber duties, with a glance at the conformation of our legislative bodies, together with observations on the necessity of agitation, in the present crisis; as an address to the electors of the borough of Preston Lancashire. By one of the "Broad cloth." 34p. *8°*. *London, Manchester, &c.*, [1841]

32161 RIES, J. Das merkantilische Gleichgewicht. 15p. *8°*. *Berlin*, 1841.

32162 ROBERTS, G. The terms and language of trade and commerce, and of the business of every-day life, alphabetically arranged, and fully explained. 62p. *12°*. 1841.

32163 SCRIVENOR, H. A comprehensive history of the iron trade throughout the world, from the earliest records to the present period. With an appendix containing official tables, and other public documents. 453p. *8°*. 1841.

32164 Commercial & financial **SITUATION** of the country considered with reference to the present crisis. 16p. *8°*. 1841.

32165 SOUTH SEA COMPANY. A list of the names of all such proprietors of the capital stock...who are qualified to vote at the ensuing election...January 1st, 1841. 8, [4]p. *fol*. 1841. *With manuscript additions and corrections. See also* 1712, 1747, 1790, 1793, 1796, 1799.

32166 SOUTHAMPTON and its commercial prospects. 15p. *8°*. 1841.

32167 [URQUHART, D., *ed*.] Documents and statements [by David Urquhart, William Cargill and others] respecting the sulphur monopoly, constituting grounds for Parliamentary inquiry into the conduct of the foreign secretary [Viscount Palmerston]. 77p. *8°*. 1841.

32168 WAR with China. [An account of the commercial relations between Great Britain and China, and the evils of the opium trade.] 19p. *8°*. 1841.

COLONIES

32169 BRIGHT, JOHN, *surgeon*. Hand-book for emigrants, and others, being a history of New Zealand, its state and prospects...also remarks on the climate and colonies of the Australian continent. 212p. *12°*. 1841.

32170 CANADA COMPANY. A statement of the satisfactory results which have attended emigration to Upper Canada, from the establishment of the Canada Company, until the present period...Compiled for the guidance of emigrants. 60p. *8°*. 1841. *See also* 1842.

32171 COLERIDGE, H. N. Six months in the West Indies...Fourth edition, with additions. 311p. *8°*. 1841. *For other editions, see* 1826.

32172 ELPHINSTONE, HON. M. The history of India. 2 vols. *8°*. 1841. *The copy that belonged to the East India College, Haileybury.*

32173 *ESSAY on the cultivation and manufacture of tea, in Java; taken from a periodical published at Batavia, under the title of "Tydschrift voor Neerlands Indie," third year, no. 1. Translated from the Dutch, by Thomas Horsfield, Esq., M.D., F.R.S. 48p. *8°*. 1841.

32174 Private circulation. **GREAT BRITAIN** and New South Wales: an appeal on behalf of that colony; against the oppressive charges for police and gaols, to which, since 1835, it has been subjected. [Dated: March 1841.] 47p. *8°*. 1841.

32175 GREY, SIR G. Journals of two expeditions of discovery in North-West and Western Australia, during the years 1837, 38, and 39...With observations on the moral and physical condition of the aboriginal inhabitants, &c.&c. 2 vols. *8°*. 1841.

32176 GURLEY, R. R. Letter to the Hon. Henry Clay, President of the American Colonization Society, and Sir Thomas Fowell Buxton, Chairman of the General Committee of the African Civilization Society, on the colonization and civilization of Africa. With other documents on the same subject. 66p. *8°*. 1841.

32177 HOWLEY, W., *Archbishop of Canterbury, and others*. Colonial bishoprics. Speeches of the Archbishop of Canterbury, Bishop of London, Mr. Justice Coleridge, Mr. Labouchere, and Mr. W. E. Gladstone. At Willis's Rooms, on...April 27, 1841. 15p. *8°*. [*London*, 1841]

32178 JAMIESON, R. A further appeal to the Government and people of Great Britain, against the proposed Niger expedition: a letter addressed to the Right Hon. Lord John Russell, Principal Secretary of State for the Colonies, &c. 30p. *8°*. 1841.

32179 **LEWIS,** SIR G. C., *Bart.* An essay on the government of dependencies. 382p. *8°*. 1841.

32180 **MORSON,** H. The present condition of the British West Indies; their wants, and the remedy for these: with some practical hints, shewing the policy of a new system, as a means to their future regeneration. 63p. *8°*. 1841.

32181 **NEW SOUTH WALES.** *Legislative Council.* Resolutions and debate in the Legislative Council of New South Wales, upon immigration and its results in that colony. 24p. *8°*. *Cambridge,* [1841]

32182 **PETRE,** HON. H. W. An account of the settlements of the New Zealand Company, from personal observation during a residence there. 87p. *8°*. 1841. *See also* 1842.

32183 **PRINCE EDWARD ISLAND.** *House of Assembly.* Public documents [covering the years 1829–1841] on various subjects connected with the interests of Prince Edward Island: ordered by the House of Assembly to be printed, April 23d, 1841. 104p. *8°*. *Charlottetown,* 1841.

32184 **QUESTEL,** P. J. An appeal on behalf of the British West Indies, as affected by the late proposed reduction of duty on foreign sugar. 39p. *8°*. 1841.

32185 **ROLPH,** T. A descriptive and statistical account of Canada: shewing its great adaptation for British emigration. Preceded by an account of a tour through portions of the West Indies and the United States [With an appendix and 'Supplementary account'.]... Second edition. 272, [16]p. *8°*. 1841. *An earlier edition, entitled* A brief account... made during a visit in the West Indies, *was published in 1836 (q.v.).*

32186 *****SPRY,** H. H. Suggestions received by the Agricultural & Horticultural Society of India for extending the cultivation and introduction of useful and ornamental plants, with a view to the improvement of the agricultural and commercial resources of India... 208p. *8°*. *Calcutta,* 1841.

32187 **STRACHAN,** JAMES M. A letter to the Right Honourable Sir John Cam Hobhouse, Bt., M.P., President of the Board of Controul... occasioned by his speech in the House of Commons, on July 27, 1840, on the question of the connexion of the East India Company, with the idolatry of that country. 37p. *8°*. 1841.

32188 *****SUTHERLAND,** J. Report on the Khalsa villages of Ajmere. 60p. *8°*. *Agra,* 1841.

32189 **TORRENS,** R. Printed for private circulation. Paper intended to have been given to the Committee on the affairs of South Australia, as part of his evidence, by Colonel Torrens... 30th of March, 1841. 42p. *8°*. 1841.

32190 **WARD,** JOHN (1805–1890). Information relative to New Zealand, compiled for the use of colonists... The fourth edition. 168p. *12°*. 1841. *For another edition, see* 1840.

FINANCE

32191 **AMICUS POPULI,** *pseud.* The currency question. The dream of a somnambulist. 11p. *12°*. 1841.

32192 **APPEAL** to the men of Yorkshire, on the great measures of Government for reducing the bread tax and the duties on timber and sugar. ⟨From the Leeds Mercury.⟩ 16p. *8°*. [1841]

32193 **APPLETON,** N. Remarks on currency and banking; having reference to the present derangement of the circulating medium in the United States. 73p. *8°*. *Boston,* 1841.

32194 **AUSTRALASIAN COLONIAL AND GENERAL LIFE ASSURANCE AND ANNUITY COMPANY.** The Australasian Colonial & General Life Assurance and Annuity Company, 126, Bishopsgate Street, corner of Cornhill. Capital £200,000 in 2,000 shares. [A prospectus.] 2p. *fol.* [1841]

32195 **BANK OF MANCHESTER.** Bank of Manchester. Report of the directors to the twelfth annual general meeting of proprietors, held at the York Hotel, King-Street, 13th October, 1841. [With a list of proprietors.] 16p. *8°*. *Manchester,* [1841] *See also* 1842.

32196 **BANK OF THE UNITED STATES** [1836–41]. Report of the Committee of Investigation appointed at the meeting of the stock-holders of the Bank of the United States, held January 4, 1841, made to an adjourned meeting, held April 5, 1841: also, a report of the Board of Directors. 79p. *8°*. *Philadelphia,* 1841.

32197 What **BANKS** are constitutional? 18p. *8°*. *n.p.* [1841 ?]

32198 **BARING,** F. T., *Baron Northbrook.* Speech of the Rt. Hon. Francis Baring, Chancellor of the Exchequer, on... May 17th, 1841, in the House of Commons. Ways and means, corn laws, sugar duties, &c. 23p. *12°*. 1841.

32199 **BARNARD,** D. D. Speech of Mr. Barnard, of New York, in opening the debate on the bankrupt bill in the House of Representatives. Also, his speech in reply on the same subject. Delivered in the House of Representatives, August 10 and 17, 1841. 20p. *8°*. *Washington,* 1841.

32200 **BAYERISCHE HYPOTHEKEN- UND WECHSELBANK.** Statuten der Bayerischen Hypotheken- und Wechselbank vom 17. Juni 1835, mit den durch das Gesetz vom 15. April 1840, und die allerhöchsten Entschliessungen vom 3. Februar 1839... und 4. Februar 1841... genehmigten Abänderungen und Zusätzen. 31p. *8°*. *München,* 1841.

32201 **BELASTING** op de rente van de nationale schuld. Belasting op de inkomsten. 23p. *8°*. *Amsterdam,* 1841.

32202 **BELL,** GAVIN M. The currency question; an examination of the evidence on banks of issue given before a Select Committee of the House of Commons in 1840. 75p. *8°*. 1841.

32203 **BIRDSEYE,** V. Remarks of Mr. Birdseye of New York, on the bankrupt bill. Delivered in the House of Representatives, in Committee of the Whole, August 13, 1841. 14p. *8°*. *Washington,* 1841.

32204 [**BLAIR,** A.] Some observations upon the present state of banking. To which is added, a letter addressed to a member of the Committee of the House of Commons on Banks of Issue. 2 vols. *8°*. *Edinburgh,* 1841.

32205 **BOULT,** S. The law and practice relating to the constitution and management of assurance, banking, and other joint stock companies. 66p. *8°*. *London & Liverpool*, 1841.

32206 BRACKENRIDGE, H. M. Speech of H. M. Brackenridge, of Pennsylvania, on the Treasury note bill. Delivered in the House of Representatives. February 3, 1841. 16p. *8°*. *Washington*, 1841.

32207 BUCHANAN, JAMES, *President of the USA.* Speech of Mr. Buchanan of Pennsylvania, in defence of the administration of Mr. Van Buren against the charge of extravagance in expending the public money. Delivered in the Senate...January 22, 1841. 14p. *8°*. *Washington*, 1840 [1841]

32208 COBBETT, W. Paper against gold; containing the history of the Bank of England, the Funds, the Debt, the Sinking Fund, and the Bank stoppage...Condensed by Margaret Chappellsmith. 171p. *12°*. *Manchester*, 1841. *An edition of letters 1–29 only, with an introduction by Margaret Chappellsmith, dated 1839. For other editions, see 1815.*

32209 COMMITTEE OF THE HOLDERS OF SPANISH BONDS. Spain in 1841, under the regency of His Highness General Espartero...Financial system of His Excellency Senor Surra y Rull...value of the national properties, sold up to 1st June, 1841, and unsold, estimates...for 1841, with remarks upon the ability of Spain to resume the regular payment of her dividends... after 31st December, 1842. Correspondence of Richard Thornton, Esq., with Lord Palmerston...and others, with valuable data for the consideration of the holders of Spanish bonds...by the Committee of the holders. The whole...published by authority of that Committee... 67p. *8°*. 1841.

32210 COOK, JOHN, *Esq.* Letter to the Lord High Chancellor of Great Britain, on the right of holders of bank stock to compensation. 8p. *8°*. 1841.

32211 —— Second letter to the First Lord of Her Majesty's Treasury, Sir Robert Peel, Bart., the Chancellor of the Exchequer, Lord High Chancellor, and the members of both Houses of Parliament, on the right of holders of bank stock to compensation, or their exclusive privileges as confirmed by law. 16p. *8°*. 1841.

32212 CROSBIE, G. Remarks on the Scotch system of banking, and the evidence of the Select Committee on Banks of Issue. December, 1840. 8p. *8°*. *Edinburgh*, 1841.

32213 DE MORGAN, A. An essay on probabilities and on their application to life contingencies and insurance offices...A new edition. (*The Cabinet Cyclopædia conducted by the Rev. Dionysius Lardner...Natural Philosophy.*) 306p. *12°*. 1841. *For another edition, see 1838.*

32214 DRUCKER, L. Nog eenige dringende woorden tot redding van de bedreigde eer en welvaart van Nederland: brief van den Heer Louis Drucker aan een lid van de Eerste Kamer der Staten-Generaal. [Dated: Amsterdam, 19 Sept. 1841, incorporating a memorial dated 17 September.] 15p. *8°*. *n.p.* [1841]

32215 DUNCAN, JONATHAN. A letter to George Grote, Esq., M.P. on fiscal reform. 46p. *8°*. *London & Manchester*, 1841.

32216 DUNCOMBE, C. Duncombe's free banking: an essay on banking, currency, finance, exchanges and political economy. [With 'Memorial to Congress upon the subject of republican free banking'.] 356p. *12°*. *Cleveland*, 1841.

32217 ENDERBY, C. National store and dock banks. [With 'Letter to the Members of both Houses of Parliament'. Signed: Robert Peel.] 23p. *8°*. 1841. *Presentation copy from the author to George Pryme.*

32218 ENGLAND. *Parliament. House of Commons.* Evidence of the witnesses connected with the chartered and joint-stock banks of Scotland, as reported by the Parliamentary Committee on Banks of Issue, 1841. 117p. *8°*. *Edinburgh* [1841]

32219 The EXCHEQUER Bills fraud [and the trial of E. B. Smith]. 16p. *8°*. 1841.

32220 FARR, T. A short statement of facts connected with the proposed changes in our commercial tarif, and the system of ad valorem duties. 16p. *8°*. 1841.

32221 GALE, R. The currency question analysed. 9[11]p. *8°*. 1841.

32222 GAMBLE, R. L. Speech of Mr. Gamble, of Georgia, on the bill to incorporate...a fiscal bank of the United States. Delivered in the House of Representatives, August 4, 1841. 15p. *8°*. *Washington*, 1841.

32223 GILBART, J. W. Currency and banking. A review of some of the principles and plans that have recently engaged public attention, with reference to the administration of the currency. 60p. *8°*. 1841.

For **GOUGE,** W. M., The journal of banking, 1841–42, *see* vol. III, *Periodicals list*, Journal of banking.

32224 HAWKINS, E. The silver coins of England arranged and described with remarks on British money previous to Saxon dynasties. 308p., 47 plates. *8°*. 1841.

32225 HEATH, JOSEPH. Currency and import duties; or the natural history of the principles and relations of the monetary system and the protective system: addressed to Charles Wood, Esq., M.P., chairman of the Committee on Banks of Issue. 80p. *8°*. 1841.

32226 —— A letter to Matthew Marshall, Esq., on the principles of the management of the currency, particularly in reference to ... the Bank of England. Not published. [With 'Summary of principles'.] 22p. *8°*. *Aylesbury*, 1841.

32227 HEATHFIELD, R. Outline of the expected operation of a tax or charge upon all property within the United Kingdom, at the rate of twenty per cent.... [Dated: 4th May 1841.] *s.sh.fol. n.p.* [1841] *Endorsed: Operation of a property tax.*

32228 *HICKSON, WILLIAM. Currency: the wrong and the remedy. 14p. *8°*. 1841. *The copy that belonged to George Grote.*

32228A HOFFMANN, JOHANN G. Die Zeichen der Zeit im deutschen Münzwesen, als Zugabe zu der Lehre vom Gelde und mit besonderer Rücksicht auf den preussischen Staat. 162p. *8°*. *Berlin*, 1841. *For the original work, see 1838.*

32229 HUBARD, E. W. Speech...on the United States Fiscal Bank Bill...in the House of Representatives, August 4, 1841. 37p. *8°*. *Washington*, 1841.

32230 HUGHES, THOMAS B. The advantages of friendly loan societies contrasted with the ruinous effects of pawning; and remarks on the benefits likely to arise... by the establishment of joint stock loan and discount companies under the recent Acts...82p. *12°*. 1841.

32231 HUMBERSTONE, M. The absurdity and

injustice of the window tax, considered with especial reference to the new survey...Fourth thousand. 23p. *12º*. *London & Bristol*, 1841.

32232 HUME, Joseph. Debate on sugar duties. Speech of Joseph Hume, Esq., M.P., in the House of Commons, on the 13th May, 1841...Ways and means, corn laws, sugar duties, &c. [Extracted from Hansard's Parliamentary Debates.] 22p. *8º. n.p.* [1841]

32233 IRVIN, J. Speech of Mr. Irvin, of Pennsylvania, on the revenue bill. Delivered in the House of Representatives, July, 1841. 11p. *8º. n.p.* [1841]

32234 IRWIN, W. W. Remarks of William W. Irwin, of Pennsylvania, on the resolution offered in the House of Representatives, by Mr. Fillmore, of New York, to refer that part of the President's Message relative to the tariff to the Committee on Manufactures. 7p. *8º. Washington,* 1841.

32235 JACKSON, George. A new check journal, upon the principle of double entry, combining the advantages of the day-book, journal, & cash-book...[With 'Appendix. On the most effectual means of preventing and detecting forgery, fraud, error, and embezzlement...'.] The sixth edition. 152p. *8º.* 1841.

32236 JOHNES, A. J. Statistical illustrations of the claims of the Welsh dioceses to augmentation out of the funds at the disposal of the Ecclesiastical Commissioners. In a letter to Lord John Russell. 43p. *8º.* 1841. *Presentation copy from the author to J. M. Herbert, Esq.*

32237 JOHNSTON, W. Letters on the nature and operations of the currency to Charles Wood, Esq., M.P., chairman of the Committee of the House of Commons on Banks of Issue. 18p. *8º. Edinburgh,* 1841. *The copy that belonged to T. Spring Rice, Baron Monteagle.*

32238 JONES, Charles. Currency. [A letter to the *Globe* newspaper.] 4p. *4º. n.p.* [1841] *Presentation copy from the author to Thomas Attwood.*

32239 —— Letter to Charles Wood, Esq. M.P. chairman of the Committee of the House of Commons on Banks of Issue, in reply to the doctrine of George Warde Norman, Esq. "On money, and the means of economizing the use of it." 67p. *8º.* 1841. *Presentation copy, with accompanying letter, from the author to Thomas Attwood. For the letter see* vol. III, *A.L.* 260.

32240 JOPLIN, T. The cause and cure of our commercial embarrassments. 77p. *8º.* 1841. *Presentation copy from the author to William Paul, Esq.*

32241 LA NOURAIS, P. A. DE, and **BÉRES,** E. L'association des douanes allemandes, son passé, son avenir; ouvrage augmenté du tableau des tarifs comparés de l'association allemande et de ceux de douanes françaises; et de trois cartes indiquant l'état de l'Allemagne avant et après l'association et celui de l'Europe sous le système des unions douanières. 211p. *8º. Paris,* 1841.

32242 LEATHAM, W. Second series. Letters to William Rayner Wood...containing remarks on the evidence of the members of the Manchester Chamber of Commerce, and others, given before the Committee of the House of Commons, on the currency...Also...statements of the amounts of bills of exchange, to illustrate their practical effects on the currency. 39p. *8º.* 1841.

32243 LEBER, J. M. C. Mémoires sur l'appréciation de la fortune privée au moyen âge, relativement aux variations des valeurs monétaires et du pouvoir commer-

cial de l'argent...Lus à l'Académie des Inscriptions et Belles-lettres, séances du 3 et du 10 septembre 1841. [Offprint from *Mémoires présentés par divers savants.*] p.330–338. *4º. n.p.* [1841] *For the greatly enlarged published work,* Essai sur l'appréciation de la fortune privée au moyen âge, *see* 1847.

32244 LECKIE, W. Review of the proceedings of the Committee of the House of Commons on Banks of Issue, 1840, and an inquiry into the effects of the bank restriction and the changes in the value of money; with an examination of the leading principles in the work on political economy of the late David Ricardo. 299p. *8º.* 1841.

32245 A LETTER to "A Scotch banker," in reply to certain remarks in his "Intimation, 14th April, 1841." By a bank depositor. 14p. *8º. Glasgow,* 1841.

32246 LEY, J. P. Letters addressed to the people on the currency. 60p. *8º.* 1841.

32247 LOMBARD, A. Notice sur la position financière actuelle des États de l'Amérique du Nord, accompagnée de quelques détails sur les dettes des principaux états européens. 67p. *8º. Genève,* 1841.

32248 MACGREGOR, John (1797–1857). The commercial and financial legislation of Europe and America, with a pro-forma revision of the taxation and the customs tariff of the United Kingdom. 320p. *8º.* 1841. *The copy that belonged to W. E. Gladstone, with his bookplate. There are numerous manuscript additions, presumably inserted by the author, and the publisher's name on the title-page has been scored through.*

32249 [——] The preference interests, or the miscalled protective duties, shown to be public oppression. Addressed to all classes and parties. By M.B.T. Second edition. 32p. *8º.* 1841.

32250 [——] Third edition. 32p. *8º.* 1841.

32251 MACKENZIE, Holt. Notes addressed to Mr. Pennington, on his pamphlet on the importation of foreign corn. 40p. *8º. London & Clapham,* 1841.

32252 MASON, S. Speech of Mr. S. Mason, of Ohio, on the objections of the President to the bill to establish a fiscal corporation. Delivered in the House of Representatives, September 10, 1841. 16p. *8º. Washington,* 1841.

32253 MONITOR, Abel, *pseud.* Facts and fallacies in the evidence taken by the "Committee on Banks of Issue;" exhibiting aggressions in the Bank of England... To which are added extraordinary suggestions of currency remedies for town and country bankers; in a letter to the Chancellor of the Exchequer. 102p. *8º.* 1841.

32254 —— Corn laws. Second letter. Facts and fallacies exhibiting aggressions in the Bank of England which makes its trade in bullion a source of oppressions on the people. Addressed to the Right Honourable the Chancellor of the Exchequer. 48p. *8º.* 1841.

32255 MORRIS, Jeffrey. Tables compiled for the use of valuators, guardians, rate payers, collectors, &c.&c. under the Irish Poor Relief Act. 54p. *12º. Dublin,* 1841. *Presentation copy from the author to the Duke of Wellington.*

32256 MUNTZ, G. F. Letter upon corn and currency, written during the recess of 1840. 23p. *8º. Birmingham,* 1841.

32257 NATIONAL SECURITY SAVINGS BANK. Report on the affairs of the National Security Savings Bank of Edinburgh, for the year to 20th November

1840. Prepared by the committee of accounts...and presented to the annual general meeting of the trustees and managers, held on the 21st January, 1841. 12p. *8⁰*. *Edinburgh*, 1841. *See also* 1838, 1840, 1845.

32258 NETHERLANDS. Kingdom of the Netherlands. *Departement van Financien.* Algemeen overzigt van den vermoedelijken toestand van's Rijks Schatkist op den 1sten januarij 1841, met inbegrip der baten en lasten van het Amortisatie-Syndicaat op hetzelfde tijdstip. [Dated: den 6den october 1840.] [16]p. *8⁰*. *Arnhem*, 1841.

32259 NORMAN, G. W. Letter to Charles Wood, Esq., M.P. on money, and the means of economizing the use of it. 106p. *8⁰*. 1841.

32260 PEDIE, J. A philosophical enquiry into the nature of a sound currency, in reference both to foreign and domestic commerce; and into the basis on which the standard of such a currency ought to rest. 87p. *8⁰*. *Edinburgh, Birmingham, &c.*, 1841. *Presentation copy from the author to D. Buchanan.*

32261 PEEL, SIR ROBERT, *2nd Bart.* The ministerial Budget. The sugar duties. Sir R. Peel's speech in the House of Commons, May 18, 1841, on Lord Sandon's amendment, "That...this House is not prepared...to adopt the measure proposed by Her Majesty's Government for the reduction of the duty on foreign sugar." Second edition. 30p. *8⁰*. [1841]

32262 —— Third edition. 30p. *8⁰*. [1841]

32263 —— Fourth edition. 30p. *8⁰*. [1841]

32264 PIESSE, C. A. J. Sketch of the loan fund system in Ireland, and instruction for the formation of a new society; with the Loan Fund Acts, and an index thereto. 82, 34p. *12⁰*. *Dublin*, 1841.

32265 A **PLAN** of a national bank of issue, on the principle of gradually replacing the circulation of the country bankers, making them interested parties therein. By a Lancashire banker. 32p. *8⁰*. *London & Manchester*, 1841.

32266 READ, compare, and judge! [An election leaflet on the financial record of Whig governments from 1831 to 1840.] 2p. *s.sh.4⁰*. *n.p.* [1841] [*Br.* 600]

32267 REID, JOHN. Manual of the Scottish stocks and British funds, with a list of the joint stock companies in Scotland, arranged in a tabular form...Third edition. 178p. *12⁰*. *Edinburgh*, [1841] *See also* 1842.

32268 Practical **REMARKS** on currency and banking, particularly in reference to the system of Scotland: in a letter addressed to Samuel Jones Loyd, Esq., by a Scotch banker. Second edition, with additions to April 14th, 1841. 36p. *8⁰*. *Glasgow, Edinburgh, &c.*, 1841. *For another edition, see* 1840.

32269 REMARKS upon Mr. Appleton's Remarks on currency and banking. By a disinterested witness. 64p. *8⁰*. *Boston*, 1841.

32270 REPORT of the deputation from the bankers of Scotland appointed to proceed to London pending the enquiry on banks of issue before a Select Committee of the House of Commons, session 1841. 15p. *8⁰*. 1841.

32271 REYNOLDS, JOHN S. The evidence of a witness not examined by the Committee of the House of Commons on Banks of Issue. 15p. *8⁰*. 1841.

32272 RICHARDSON, R. J. Exposure of the banking and funding systems. 32p. *12⁰*. 1841.

32273 *RITCHIE, L. The saddle on the right horse; or, how to save the country. An address to the electors and the people. [Advocating a property tax, as outlined by Richard Heathfield.] 8p. *8⁰*. [1841] *The FWA copy that belonged to William Pare.*

32274 SCHOLEFIELD, J. Speech of Joshua Scholefield, Esquire, on moving a Resolution in the House of Commons, on the 23rd. March, 1841, for the substitution of a property tax for the taxes of excise and customs; and an enquiry into the effects of a transfer of taxation to property, occasioned by the objections of the Right Honourable Henry Goulburn, M.P., to that measure, by Richard Heathfield, Esq. 16p. *8⁰*. 1841. *With an accompanying letter from H. Jones, secretary of the Property Tax Association, to Colonel Fox, candidate for the Tower Hamlets. For the letter, see* vol. III, *A.L.* 287.

32275 SCOTTISH PROVIDENT INSTITUTION. The Scottish Provident Institution...[A pamphlet explaining life-assurance and reprinting abridgments of articles on the subject from *Chambers' Journal* for March 1839 and October 1841; with extracts from the report of the Directors to the third annual meeting of the Institution, February 1841. Dated: October 1841.] 14p. *8⁰*. *Edinburgh*, [1841]

32276 SLADE, W. Speech of Mr. Slade, of Vermont, in favor of a protecting tariff, delivered in the House of Representatives, December 20, 1841. 24p. *8⁰*. *n.p.* [1841]

32277 SMITH, THOMAS, *editor of the London Mercantile Journal.* Import duties considered in reference to the present state of the trade of Great Britain, and her possessions, with the tables prepared by order of the Select Committee thereon. 54p. *8⁰*. 1841. *The copy that belonged to Joseph Hume.*

32278 SPURRELL, S. The deposit enigma unravelled. With detached remarks on the evidence of Messrs. Page, Tooke, Norman and Loyd, before the Banking Committee; concluding with a brief notice of Mr. Joseph Hume's interrogatories. 21p. *8⁰*. 1841.

32279 STANLEY, EDWARD G. G. S., *14th Earl of Derby.* Speech of the Right Honourable Lord Stanley, in the House of Commons...May 12, 1841, on the Ministerial financial Budget. 36p. *8⁰*. 1841.

32280 The present **STATE** of banking in England considered, in a letter addressed to the Right Hon. Earl Fitzwilliam, by a Scotch banker. 43p. *8⁰*. 1841.

32281 TATE, WILLIAM (1781?–1848). The system of the London bankers' clearances, and their effect upon the currency. Explained and exemplified by formulae of the clearing-house accounts. 32p. *8⁰*. 1841.

32282 TAYLOR, JOHN (1781–1864). Who pays the taxes? 44p. *8⁰*. 1841. *In a volume of the author's pamphlets presented to Sir Robert Peel. See also* 1844, 1845 (Currency investigated).

32283 UNITED STATES OF AMERICA. *Laws, etc.* The bankrupt law of the United States, passed August 19, 1841. With a commentary containing a full explanation of the law of bankruptcy, and ample references to English and American authorites [*sic*], prepared for popular and professional use. By a member of the Bar. 48p. *8⁰*. *Philadelphia, New York, &c.*, 1841.

32284 —— [Another edition.] United States bankrupt law, and the rules and forms in bankruptcy, in the District Court of the United States, for the district of Massachusetts. 11, 23p. *8⁰*. *n.p.* [1841]

32285 **VIVIAN**, RICHARD H., *Baron Vivian*. Speech of Sir Hussey Vivian, M.P. in the House of Commons, on ...May 14th, 1841. Ways and means. Corn laws, sugar duties, &c. 11p. *12°.* [1841]

32286 **WALLACE**, P. M. S. The trials of Patrick Maxwell Stewart Wallace, and Michael Shaw Stewart Wallace, for wilfully destroying the brig Dryad, off Cuba, with intent to defraud the marine assurance companies and underwriters. 294p. *8°.* 1841.

32287 **WILSON**, JAMES (1805–1860). The revenue; or, what should the Chancellor do ? 27p. *8°.* 1841.

32288 A few **WORDS** on corn, gold, and taxation. [Dated: July 30th, 1841. Containing a reprint of a letter on currency problems, signed: W.C.] 7p. *8°.* [1841]

32289 **WRIGHT**, H. J. The fluctuations of trade: or, the secret of foreseeing when prices are going to rise or fall: with an exposition of the power and workings of the Bank of England in reference to those important subjects. 33p. *8°.* 1841.

32290 **WRIGHT**, I. C. Thoughts on the currency. 55p. *8°.* 1841.

TRANSPORT

32291 **BERMINGHAM**, T. Statistical evidence in favor of state railways, in Ireland, with the speech of Thomas Bermingham, Esq....also an appendix containing over twenty statistical tables...with a map of Ireland...shewing...the lines of the Irish Railway Commissioners, with additions recommended by the author. 22, xcivp. *8°. Dublin*, 1841.

32292 **BOOTH**, H. The carrying question stated, in reference to railways and canals; also, considerations on the mode of levying the passenger tax on railways. 32p. *8°. Liverpool*, 1841.

32293 **BRADSHAW**, G. Bradshaw's railway companion, containing the times of departure, fares, &c. of the railways in England, and also hackney coach fares... [70]p. *32°. Manchester & London*, 1841. *See also* 1843, 1847.

32294 **BROOKS**, W. A. Treatise on the improvement of the navigation of rivers: with a new theory on the cause of the existence of bars. 154p. *8°.* 1841.

32295 **BRUNEL**, SIR M. I. and **DANIELL**, JOHN F. [*Begin.*] As the electric telegraph has recently attracted a considerable share of public attention...[A statement on the claims of Wm. F. Cooke and C. Wheatstone to have invented the electric telegraph. Dated: 27th April, 1841.] *s.sh.fol.* [1841] *The Rastrick copy.*

32296 The **CARRIERS'** case considered in reference to railways. 36p. *12°.* 1841. *The Rastrick copy.*

32297 **CURTIS**, C. B. Particulars of a method or methods, by self-acting apparatus to be used on railways, for obviating collisions between successive trains. For which a patent has been obtained by the inventor Charles Berwick Curtis, Esq. 12p. *8°.* [1841]

32298 **FANSHAWE**, F. Viæ per Angliam ferro stratæ carmen latinum in Theatro Sheldoniano recitatum die Junii XV MDCCCXLI. [12]p. *12°. Oxonii*, 1841.

32299 **FREELING**, A. New edition, with latest corrections. Freeling's railway companion, from London to Birmingham, Liverpool, and Manchester... 36, 204p. *12°. London & Liverpool*, [1841] *For another edition, see* 1838.

32300 **GORDON**, ALEXANDER (1802–1868). Observations on railway monopolies, and remedial measures. 57p. *8°.* 1841. *With manuscript notes by the author.*

32301 **GREAT NORTH OF ENGLAND RAILWAY**. Time table for passenger trains, – April, 1841. *s.sh.4°. Darlington*, [1841]

32302 **GREGORY**, C. H. Practical rules for the management of a locomotive engine; in the station, on the road, and in cases of accident. 48p. *16°.* 1841. *The copy that belonged to Richard Roberts (1789–1864), and afterwards to Henry Rastrick.*

32303 **GROVES**, J. R. Observations on the utility of floating breakwaters as a protection for shipping. 13p. *8°. Tiverton*, 1841. *See also* 1842.

32304 **HARTFORD AND SPRINGFIELD RAIL ROAD CORPORATION**. Report of the engineer [James N. Palmer] upon the several definite locations for the Hartford and Springfield Rail Road: with the acts of incorporation in Connecticut and Massachusetts. 32p. *8°. Hartford*, 1841.

32305 The **LONDON** and Brighton Railway guide, containing a correct description of the railway – historical and topographical notices of the places contiguous to the various stations – and the official map and section of the line; to which is added, a complete list of hackney coach and cab fares, with the distances to all parts of London and Brighton. Second edition. 54p. *12°. London: J. R. Jobbins, & Brighton*, [1841]

32306 **MARTIN**, WILLIAM (1772–1851). To the engineers and directors of railways. A revolution in colleges & mechanics, produced by the philosopher's discovery of the perpetual motion in 1807...I invented metallic railways in 1796...[With 'The Martinian bridge triumphant...likewise an improvement in the shape of locomotive engines'.] 4p. *8°. Newcastle*, [1841]

32307 **MINARD**, C. J. Cours de construction des ouvrages qui établissent la navigation des rivières et des canaux, professé à l'École des Ponts et Chaussées de 1832 à 1841. [With a volume of plates.] 2 vols. *4°. Paris*, 1841.

32308 **PIM**, JAMES. The atmospheric railway. A letter to the Right Hon. the Earl of Ripon, President of the Board of Trade. 26p. *8°.* 1841. *The copy presented by Charles Vignoles to Peter Barlow, with inscription. See also* 1842.

32309 **RAILWAYS** for Ireland. From the "Railroad Monthly Journal," for June, 1841. 15p. *8°.* [1841]

32310 **SERVICE** régulier de paquebots à vapeur entre Le Havre et St.-Pétersbourg touchant à Copenhague et Cronstadt. [A handbill.] *s.sh.8°. Havre*, 1841.

32311 **SKETCH** of a railway [Philadelphia and Pottsville Railway] judiciously constructed between desirable points. Exemplified by a map and an appendix of facts [about other American railways]. 125p. *8°. New-York*, 1841.

32312 TEMPLETON, W. The locomotive engine popularly explained...to which are added, rules and tables for ascertaining its amount of useful effect, resist-ance &c. Also, interesting statistical particulars connected with railways, for general information. 100p. *12°. London, Liverpool, &c.,* 1841.

SOCIAL CONDITIONS

32313 ABERDEEN. *Town Council.* Report by a committee of the Town Council...for inquiring into the mode of assessing and managing the poor's funds in burgal parishes in Scotland... 22p. *8°. Aberdeen,* 1841.

32314 ALISON, W. P. Further illustrations of the practical operation of the Scotch system of management of the poor. ⟨Read before the Statistical Society of London, 15th November, 1841.⟩ 32p. *8°. n.p.* [1841]

32315 AMERICAN TEMPERANCE SOCI-ETY. Permanent temperance documents of the American Temperance Society. [Containing the 4th–9th annual reports, 1831–36.] Vol. 1. 568, [4]p. *8°.* 1841. *The Turner copy. For another edition, see* 1835; *see also* 1829.

32316 ANALYSIS of the discussion, held in Cavendish Chapel, Ramsgate, February 4th, 1841, between J. Mortlock Daniell...and Frederic R. Lees...on the accordance of teetotalism with science and Scripture: also an outline of the public lecture...delivered by Mr. Lees the following night in further correction of Mr. Daniell's errors; and an exposure of the fallacies of Mr. Daniell's published lecture, entitled "Teetotalism." 44p. *12°. Leeds & London,* 1841.

32317 ANTONIN. Que les bons ménages ne s'alarment pas! Le divorce est la sauve-garde des bonnes mœurs. Rétablissement de la loi du divorce, d'après les principes de la Charte de 1830, qui a consacré les principes de 1789 et réprouvé ceux de la Charte de 1814... 16p. *8°. Paris,* 1841.

32318 BARNES, W. The rights of the necessitous, considered in connection with reason, law, and Scripture; in reply to the assault made by property on poverty in the new Poor Law...An original poem. 31p. *8°.* 1841.

32319 BARON, F. The mirror of the poor laws. From experience of them in England, in which is exhibited the impending ruin of Ireland, unless relieved by auxiliary measures, which are here glanced at. 19p. *8°. Enniskillen,* 1841. *Presentation copy, with inscription, from the author to Daniel O'Connell.*

32320 BAXTER, G. R. W. The book of the bastiles; or, the history of the working of the new Poor-Law. 609p. *8°.* 1841.

32321 BOLTON SOCIETY FOR THE PRO-TECTION OF THE POOR AND DISTRICT PROVIDENT SOCIETY. Report of the Bolton Society for the Protection of the Poor... 23p. *12°. Bolton,* 1841.

32322 BOSANQUET, S. R. The rights of the poor and Christian almsgiving vindicated; or, the state and character of the poor, and the conduct and duties of the rich, exhibited and illustrated. 416p. *12°.* 1841.

32323 BOWRING, SIR J. Distress at Bolton. The speech of Dr. Bowring, M.P. House of Commons... September 30, 1841. [Extracted from Hansard's Parliamentary Debates.] 23p. *12°. n.p.* [1841]

32324 BOYER, ADOLPHE. De l'état des ouvriers et de son amélioration par l'organisation du travail. 165p. *16°. Paris,* 1841.

32325 BROMLEY, J. and **LEES,** F. R. Authentic report of the public discussion at Rotherham, on the consistency of teetotalism with Scripture, between James Bromley...and Frederic R. Lees...Fourth edition. 48p. *12°.* 1841. *The Turner copy. For other editions, see* 1840.

32326 BURN, JOHN I. Familiar letters on population, emigration, &c. With introductory letters now added on labour and the advantages of the allotment system...The second edition. liv, 265p. *12°.* 1841.

32327 BURNS, R. A plea for the poor of Scotland, and for an enquiry into their condition: being the substance of two lectures, read before the Philosophical Institution of Paisley, February, 1841. 36p. *8°. Paisley,* 1841.

32328 CHALMERS, T. On the sufficiency of the parochial system, without a poor rate, for the right management of the poor. 336p. *12°. Glasgow, Edinburgh, &c.,* 1841.

32329 CHEVALIER, M. De l'industrie manufacturière en France...suivi d'une note de M. A.-P. de Candolle, sur le Tableau de l'état physique et moral des ouvriers employés dans les manufactures de coton, de laine et de soie. 68p. *12°. Paris,* 1841.

32330 CHURCH OF SCOTLAND. *General Assembly.* Report on the proposed inquiry into the state of the poor in Scotland. Presented to the General Assembly, 1841. [Signed: A. Dunlop, convener.] 19p. *8°. Edinburgh,* 1841.

32331 CLEGG, SAMUEL (1814–1856). A practical treatise on the manufacture and distribution of coal-gas; its introduction and progressive improvement...with general estimates. 208p. *4°.* 1841.

32332 CLERICUS, *pseud.* Pour et contre. A few humble observations upon the new Poor Law: with a short notice of a remedial measure for the labourer in sickness: a letter to the Right Hon. Lord John Russell, Secretary of State. 23p. *8°.* 1841.

32333 COOK, JOHN, *minister.* A brief view of the Scottish system for the relief of the poor; and of some proposed changes on it. 79p. *8°. Edinburgh,* 1841.

32334 COOPER, A. A., *7th Earl of Shaftesbury.* Speech of Lord Ashley in the House of Commons, on... August 4, 1840 on moving an humble address...to appoint a commission of inquiry into the employment of children in mines...and other occupations not regulated by the Factory Acts. 23p. *8°.* 1841. *Three copies, one a presentation copy, with inscription, from Lord Ashley to 'M. M. Villermé'; one that belonged to Victor Considérant, and another to J. M. Cobbett. For another edition, see* 1840.

32335 CURRIE, R., *ed.* Extracts from the Report of the Commissioners appointed to Inquire into the Condition of the Hand-Loom Weavers. Reprinted for the use of the working men of Northampton. 32p. *8°.* 1841.

32336 DODD, WILLIAM (b. 1804). A narrative of the experience and sufferings of William Dodd, a factory cripple. Written by himself... Second edition. 45p. 8°. 1841.

32337 DUNCOMBE, E. Gilbertise the new Poor-Law. "A fresh plan" in a letter to Sir Robert Peel: being an answer to his "I desire to know what system is to be adopted." (Speech, Feb. 8, 1841.) 258p. 8°. York, 1841.

32338 EAST ASHFORD, Union. Board of Guardians. East Ashford Union, extract from the quarterly abstract, shewing the number of paupers relieved, the amount of money expended and the balances due to and from the several parishes, for the quarter ending 25th of March, 1841. [A table. Signed: F. Underdown, clerk.] s.sh.fol. n.p. [1841] [Br. 599]

32339 ENGLAND. Laws, etc. The local Act of the united parishes of Saint Andrew, Holborn, and Saint George the Martyr, Middlesex, for the purposes of the poor and nightly watch thereof. [With an index and with 'Standing orders of the Governors and Directors of the Poor, for the united parishes of Saint Andrew, Holborn, above the bars, and Saint George the Martyr, Middlesex'.] 51, 22p. 8°. 1841.

32340 —— Parliament. House of Commons. Reports of the House of Commons on the education (1838), and on the health (1840) of the poorer classes in large towns: with some suggestions for improvement, by Robert A. Slaney, M.P., chairman of both Committees. 64p. 16°. [1841]

32341 —— Poor Law Commission [1834–1847]. General prohibitory order and instructional letter issued by the Poor Law Commissioners on the subject of out-relief. (Dated 2d August, 1841.) 32p. 8°. 1841.

32342 —— —— Report to the Secretary of State for the Home Department from the Poor Law Commissioners, on the training of pauper children; with appendices [by E. Chadwick, J. Kay, E. C. Tufnell, E. Twistleton, Sir E. Head, A. Power, E. Senior and Sir J. Walsham]. 421p. 8°. 1841.

32343 FERRAND, W. B. New Poor Law. The speech of W. Busfeild Ferrand, Esq. in the House of Commons ...September 28th, 1841, on seconding the instruction of W. S. Crawford, Esq., "That it shall not be lawful for the Commissioners...to declare the formation of any new unions in districts which are not already placed under the operation of the Act 4th and 5th of William the Fourth, c. 76." 15p. 8°. 1841.

32344 FIRTH, R. An essay on sacramental wine, in which is shewn the sinfulness of using intoxicating wine in the Holy Eucharist. 66p. 8°. London, Glasgow, &c., 1841. The Turner copy.

32345 GILLY, W. S. The peasantry of the Border: an appeal in their behalf...Give them good cottages and help them to educate their children. [With statistical tables of the parish of Norham, Northumberland, and an appendix.] 48, 5p. 8°. Berwick-upon-Tweed, [1841]

32346 GURNEY, JOHN H. The new Poor Law explained and vindicated. A plain address to the labouring classes among his parishioners...Fourth edition; with a prefatory letter and appendix. xxx, 102p. 8°. London & Leicester, 1841.

32347 HALL, B. The late Captain Hewett, of Her Majesty's Ship "Fairy." To the editor of the Hampshire Telegraph. [A reprint of a letter dated: 8th Jan. 1841,

soliciting aid for Captain Hewett's widow, and outlining his services to his country as a marine surveyor.] s.sh.fol. Portsmouth, 1841.

32348 [**HICKSON,** WILLIAM E.] Hints to employers. 'The elevation of the labouring class,' from the Westminster Review, No. LXVII [being a review of Lectures on the elevation of the labouring portion of the community, by W. E. Channing. Signed: W.E.H.]. Including Two Letters to Leonard Horner Esq. on the capabilities of the factory system. 24p. 8°. 1841. The copy that belonged to Victor Considérant.

32349 HILL, SIR ROWLAND (1795–1879). Results of the new postage arrangements...⟨Read before the Statistical Society of London, May 17th, 1841.⟩ [Published, with a prefatory address to the members of the London Mercantile Committee on postage, by W. H. Ashurst, parliamentary agent.] 16p. 8°. 1841.

32350 HINTS on poor law legislation; or, practical measures for diminishing pauperism. 23p. 8°. [1841]

32351 HOLLAND, GEORGE C. The mortality, sufferings and diseases of grinders [in Sheffield]. Part I. Fork-grinders. 34p. 8°. 1841.

32352 —— Second edition. 32p. 8°. 1841.

32353 HULL, J. The philanthropic repertory of plans and suggestions for improving the condition of the labouring poor...Sixth edition. 88p. 12°. 1841. For another edition, see 1835.

32354 LABOURERS' FRIEND SOCIETY, London. Useful hints for labourers; from the publications of the Labourers' Friend Society and republished under their direction. First series. Sixth thousand. [With a list of officers of the Society.] 143p. 8°. 1841.

32355 LATEY, J. L. Letters to working people on the new Poor Law. By a working man. 108p. 12°. 1841.

32356 A LETTER to the Queen, in behalf of her suffering people. To which is added, a plain and earnest appeal to the fears of the land-owners. By the Poor Man's Friend. 39p. 8°. 1841.

32357 L. ——H. Metropolitan improvements. (From the 'Westminster Review,' no. LXXI,) for October, 1841. With...plans of the new streets, and two maps of the Royal Victoria Park for the Tower Hamlets. 32p. 8°. 1841.

32358 LIVERPOOL. Proceedings of the public meeting on behalf of the shopkeepers' assistants, convened by the Mayor, and held in the Sessions House, on...the 22nd April, 1841, for the purpose of enquiring into the complaints of the assistants...in the employment of retail traders, and...to consider...any recommendation...for a curtailment of the hours of labour. (From the Liverpool Standard of April 23, 1841.) 23p. 12°. Liverpool, 1841.

32359 LONDON MECHANICS' INSTITUTION. Rules and orders of the...Institution, established ...1823, for the promotion of useful knowledge, among the working classes...Southampton Buildings, Chancery Lane. 24p. 8°. 1841. See also 1823.

32360 MACDONALD, G. B. An apology for the disuse of alcoholic drinks, in a letter to a friend...Seventh thousand. 36p. 12°. London, &c., 1841. The Turner copy.

32361 M'LEOD, D. History of the destitution in Sutherlandshire. Being a series of letters published in the Edinburgh Weekly Chronicle, in the years 1840 & 1841; with an appendix, containing some additional information. 84p. 8°. Edinburgh, 1841.

32362 MARSHALL, T. The life of Thomas Marshall, the Tweedside temperance advocate. Written by himself. Second edition, with additions and improvements. 144p. *12°. Berwick, 1841. The Turner copy.*

32363 MOORE, ELY. Trades' unions. An address to the members of the General Trades' Union of New York, as delivered by Ely Moore, President of that body, and one of the representatives to Congress for the state of New York. 16p. *8°.* [1841]

32364 NAISBY, W., *ed.* Evidence of witnesses in the cases of William Pearce and James Bristol, who died at Bolton from want of food; also on the general distress in that town; with remarks on that subject and on the assistant poor-law commissioner's report. 8p. *8°. Bolton,* 1841.

32365 [NEWMAN, J. H., *Cardinal.*] The Tamworth reading room. Letters on an address delivered by Sir Robert Peel, Bart. M.P. on the establishment of a reading room at Tamworth. By Catholicus. Originally published in The Times, and since revised and corrected by the author. 42p. *8°.* 1841.

For OASTLER, R., The Fleet papers, 1841–44, *see* vol. III, *Periodicals list,* Fleet papers.

32366 ONESIMUS, *pseud.* The shaver; being a dispassionate review of tee-totalism. Wherein the unscriptural and unWesleyan opposition to the temperance reformation by Messrs. Stanley, Bromley, and Osborn, is noticed and censured. 31p. *8°. Cranbrook & London,* 1841. *The Turner copy.*

32367 PAINE, D. G. Temperance lays and poems. 136p. *12°.* 1841. *The Turner copy.*

32368 PARKINSON, RICHARD (1797–1858). On the present condition of the labouring poor in Manchester; with hints for improving it. 23p. *8°. London & Manchester,* 1841.

32369 PARSONS, B. Anti-Bacchus: an essay on the crimes diseases and other evils connected with the use of intoxicating drinks...Ninth thousand. 136p. *8°.* 1841. *The Turner copy.*

32370 —— Tenth thousand. 136p. *8°.* 1841. *The Turner copy. See also* 1845, 1850.

32371 [PEACE, J.] A descant on the penny postage. [Signed: X.A.P.] [24]p. *8°.* 1841.

32372 [——] Second edition. [39]p. *8°.* 1841.

For the PEOPLE'S MAGAZINE, *see* vol. III, *Periodicals list.*

32373 PHILLIPS, SIR RICHARD. The four letters of Sir Richard Phillips to Lord Viscount Melbourne and to the editor of the Weekly Dispatch, on the new Poor Law Amendment Act; addressed to the understandings of the just and humane, by John Bull. 36p. *12°. Southampton & London,* [1841]

32374 PHIPPS, CONSTANTINE H., *Marquess of Normanby.* Speech of the Marquis of Normanby in the House of Lords, on Friday, the 12th of February, 1841. On moving the second reading of the Drainage of Buildings Bill. To which are subjoined the addresses of the Bishop of London and Lord Ellenborough on the same occasion. [With an abstract of the Bill.] 35p. *12°.* 1841. *The copy that belonged to William Lovett.*

32375 POWELL, G. ⟨Second thousand.⟩ The "calm considerations" of the Rev. Jacob Stanley, calmly considered, by an old Methodist local preacher, in a familiar letter to a friend in Bristol. 12p. *8°. Bristol,* [1841] *The Turner copy.*

32376 [*Begin.*] QUERY? Is there any reason why the Poor Law Commissioners should be voted for ten years longer before the public is informed of the amount of rates for the year ending Ladytide last? [Signed: A member of the English Agricultural Society.] 11p. *8°. n.p.* [1841?] *Imperfect; wanting the title-page.*

32377 Les RELAIS: ou, la mère de famille et le fileur; fiction d'une triste réalité, 1840 et 1841. Deuxième édition. 11p. *8°. Paris & Strasbourg,* 1841.

32378 REMARKS on a paper by Rowland Hill, Esq. on the results of the new postal arrangements, read before the Statistical Society of London, May 17, 1841. By one who has examined the statistics. 33p. *8°.* 1841. *The copy that belonged to Mark Pattison. For another issue, see no.* 31964.

32379 REMARKS on "the old principle" of assessment to the poor rate, as it affected the tithe-owner and the occupier of land, and as compared with the present state of the law of rating. By a by-stander. 67p. *8°.* 1841.

32380 ROBERTS, S. The pauper's advocate; a cry from the brink of the grave against the new Poor Law. 112p. *8°. London & Sheffield,* 1841.

32381 SAINT MARY-LE-BONE FEMALE PENITENTIARY SOCIETY. The third report of the Saint Mary-le-bone Female Penitentiary Society, 1840–41. 30p. *8°.* 1841.

32382 SCOTT, C. Remarks on the circumstances and claims of the indigent poor, and the inadequacy of the present system of parochial relief in Scotland, with reference especially to the town and parish of Peterhead and places similarly situated. 44p. *8°. Aberdeen, Edinburgh, &c.,* 1841.

32383 [SENIOR, N. W.] Remarks on the opposition to the Poor Law Amendment Bill. By a guardian. 115p. *8°.* 1841.

32384 SMITH, JAMES L. A poetical address to the patrons, members, and friends of the Braintree and Bocking Mutual Instruction Society, at their anniversary, 1841... 8p. *8°. Braintree,* 1841.

32385 SPENCER, T. The new Poor Law; its evils and their remedies...No. 9. 16p. *8°. London & Bath,* 1841.

32386 —— Second thousand. 16p. *8°. London & Bath,* 1841.

32387 —— Objections to the new Poor Law answered. Part I. No. 11. 16p. *8°. London & Bath,* 1841.

32388 —— Part IV. No. 14. 16p. *8°. London & Bath,* 1841.

32389 —— The outcry against the new Poor Law; or, who is the poor man's friend?...No. 8. 16p. *8°. London & Bath,* 1841.

32390 —— Second thousand. 16p. *8°. London & Bath,* 1841.

32391 —— Seventh thousand. 16p. *8°. London & Bath,* 1841.

32392 —— Ninth thousand. 16p. *8°. London & Bath,* 1841.

32393 —— The want of fidelity in ministers of religion

respecting the new Poor Law. No. 10. 16p. *8°. London & Bath*, 1841.

32394 STEVEN, R. The nature of chimney-sweeping, the attempts made to alter its character and the final accomplishment of this object, by the 3d and 4th Victoria, cap. 85, 1840. [With the text of the Act.] 30p. *4°.* [1841]

32395 STOPPAGE of the mails on Sunday. From the Scotsman of...April 14, 1841. 3p. *8°. n.p.* [1841]

32396 [STUBBIN, J.] Tirosh lo yayin; or the wine question considered in an entirely novel point of view; with a scheme of Hebrew wines, and illustrations (philosophical and critical) of the principal passages of the Bible connected with the subject. 162p. *8°. London, Leeds, &c.,* 1841. *The Turner copy.*

32397 SUGGESTIONS for the amendment of the Poor Law. By a guardian. 18p. *8°. Plymouth,* 1841.

For **SYDER,** M., Mingaye Syder's temperance lancet and penny trumpet, 1841, *continued as* the Temperance lancet and journal of useful intelligence, 1841–42, *see* vol. III, *Periodicals list,* Temperance lancet...

32398 TARBÉ, P. Travail et salaire. 491p. *8°. Paris & Reims,* [1841]

32399 TEETOTALISM in Barnard-Castle, with strictures on the recently published lecture by F. R. Lees, Esquire, in reply to the Rev. W. L. Prattman's objections to teetotalism. In a letter to a friend. 23p. *8°. Staindrop,* [1841] *The Turner copy.*

32400 The TEETOTALLERS, Wesleyan Conference and the Sacrament. A letter to the ministers and members of the Methodist societies, on the resolutions of last Conference. By a Wesleyan. Second edition. 12p. *12°. Leeds,* 1841. *The Turner copy.*

For the **TEMPERANCE LANCET AND JOURNAL OF USEFUL INTELLIGENCE,** 1841–42, *see* vol. III, *Periodicals list.*

32401 VAUD. *Conseil d'Etat.* Enquête sur le paupérisme dans le canton de Vaud, et rapport au Conseil d'État à ce sujet. 208, 231[331], xiip. *8°. Lausanne,* 1841.

32402 WALKER, GEORGE A. The grave yards of London; being an exposition of the physical and moral consequences inseparably connected with our...pestiential custom of depositing the dead in the midst of the living; with the examinations of the author...before a Select Committee of the House of Commons. 32, xivp. *8°.* 1841.

32403 WALKER, WILLIAM, *of Bradford,* and **RAND,** W. A letter addressed to the Right Honourable Sir James Graham, Bart. M.P....Secretary of State for the Home Department &c.&c., on the ten hours factory question. 15p. *8°. Bradford,* [1841] *Sent through the post addressed to Sir Edward Sugden.*

32404 WOODS, J., *of Lewes.* Notes on some of the schools for the labouring classes in Ireland. 51p. *12°. Lewes, London, &c.,* 1841.

SLAVERY

32405 BELDAM, J. A review of the late proposed measure for the reduction of the duties on sugar, so far as it relates to slavery and the slave trade, addressed to Sir T. F. Buxton, Bart. 79p. *8°.* 1841.

32406 CLARKSON, T. A letter to the clergy of various denominations, and to the slave-holding planters, in the southern parts of the United States of America. 64p. *8°.* 1841. *With the author's signature on the title-page.*

For the **FRIEND OF AFRICA,** 1841–42, *see* vol. III, *Periodicals list.*

32407 GENERAL ANTI-SLAVERY CONVENTION. Proceedings of the General Anti-Slavery Convention, called by the Committee of the British and Foreign Anti-Slavery Society, and held in London... 1840. 597p. *8°. London: British and Foreign Anti-Slavery Society, Birmingham, &c.,* 1841.

32408 —— Slavery and the internal slave trade in the United States of North America; being replies to questions transmitted by the committee of the British and Foreign Anti-Slavery Society...Presented to the General Anti-Slavery Convention, held in London, June 1840. By the executive committee of the American Anti-Slavery Society. 280p. *8°.* 1841.

32409 GURLEY, R. R. Mission to England, in behalf of the American Colonization Society. 264p. *12°. Washington,* 1841.

For the **LIBERATOR,** *see* vol. III, *Periodicals list.*

32410 MASSACHUSETTS ABOLITION SOCIETY. The second annual report of the Massachusetts Abolition Society: together with the proceedings of the second annual meeting, held at Tremont Chapel, May 25, 1841. 58p. *12°. Boston,* 1841.

32411 MASSACHUSETTS ANTI-SLAVERY SOCIETY. Ninth annual report of the Board of Managers...Presented January 27, 1841. With an appendix. 64, xvip. *8°. Boston,* 1841.

32412 SLAVERY and the slave trade in British India; with notices of the existence of these evils in the islands of Ceylon, Malacca, and Penang, drawn from official documents. 72p. *8°.* 1841.

32413 STURGE, JOHN. Remarks on the Society for the Extinction of the Slave-trade, and the Civilization of Africa; and on "The slave-trade, and its remedy." 16p. *8°.* 1841.

32414 TEMPLE, H. J., *Viscount Palmerston.* Speech of the Rt. Hon. Viscount Palmerston, in the House of Commons, on...May 19, 1841, on Lord Sandon's resolution, "That...this House is not prepared...to adopt the measure proposed by Her Majesty's Government for the reduction of the duties on foreign sugar." 38p. *8°.* 1841.

32415 —— [Another edition.] 23p. *12°.* [1841]

POLITICS

32416 ANAXAGORAS, *pseud.* A letter to the Queen on the Maynooth grant. 24p. *8°.* 1841.

32417 ARDEN, W., *Baron Alvanley.* The state of Ireland considered, and methods proposed for restoring tranquillity to that country. 35p. *8°.* 1841. *Presentation copy from the author to Earl De Grey.*

32418 —— Second edition. 36p. *8°.* 1841.

32419 ATKINSON, WILLIAM (*fl.* 1833–1858). The spirit of Magna Charta; or, universal representation the genius of the British Constitution. 78p. *8°.* 1841.

32420 ATTWOOD, T. Borough election, June 30th, 1841. Mr. Thomas Attwood's speech, on the nomination of Joshua Scholefield, Esq. as candidate for Birmingham. *s.sh.fol.* [*Birmingham,* 1841] *See note to no.* 20490.

32421 The **BOOK** of the poor man's church. [An attack on the Established Church.] 50p. *12°.* [1841 ?]

32422 BOWRING, SIR J. Syria. The speech of Dr. Bowring, M.P.... September 20, 1841. [Extracted from Hansard's Parliamentary Debates.] 12p. *12°. n.p.* [1841]

32423 The **CABINET** council: or, the rehearsal. A new play. Enacted by Her Majesty's servants, May, 1841. [A satire upon the Government.] 15p. *16°.* [1841]

32424 CARGILL, W. The Austrian treaty analyzed; and its baneful tendency exposed. [With an appendix. Reprinted from the *London Journal of Commerce,* May and July, 1840.] 48p. *8°.* 1841.

32425 CHARTISM v. Whigism. A letter to the Rev. R. S. Bayley, F.S.A. in reply to his charges against the Chartists. [Signed: An independent.] 12p. *12°.* [*Sheffield,* 1841] *Presumably William Lovett's copy, with the following manuscript note: 'The writer of this letter called on Mr Lovett about the first week in May, when some conversation took place respecting the prospects of the Chartists in Sheffield'.*

32426 CLEMENTS, E. Report on the two Bills brought into Parliament by Lord Morpeth and Lord Stanley, read at a meeting of the Loyal National Repeal Association, at Dublin, on...22nd February, 1841. 28p. *12°. n.p.* [1841]

32427 COBBETT, W. The labourer's library. – No. 1. The right of the poor to the suffrage of the People's Charter: or the honesty and justice...of universal suffrage, established and maintained...Together with Mr. Cobbett's Address to the farmers and tradesmen of England ...Reprinted from Cobbett's "Twopenny trash." Second edition. 12p. *12°. Leeds, Manchester, &c.,* 1841.

32428 The true **CURE** of monopoly upon radical principles, suggested in an address to the master spinners, merchants, and manufacturers of Lancashire, &c. By a son of commerce. 15p. *8°. Manchester,* 1841.

32429 DIXON, WILLIAM, *candidate for Wigan.* The speech delivered by Mr. William Dixon, the people's candidate, at the nomination of members, in the Moot Hall, Wigan, 1841. 12p. *12°. Wigan,* [1841]

For the **ENGLISH CHARTIST CIRCULAR: AND TEMPERANCE RECORD FOR ENGLAND AND WALES,** 1841–44, *see* vol. III, *Periodicals list.*

32430 FITZWILLIAM, C. W. W., *Earl Fitzwilliam.* Aristocracy and democracy. [Correspondence between Earl Fitzwilliam and James G. Marshall, Esq. of Leeds, for and against a further radical reform in the representation of the people in the House of Commons. Printed as a circular.] 4p. *8°.* [*London,* 1841]

32431 No. 3 Five a penny tracts for the people. A few **HINTS** about the army. [With '"Attention!" lads – "Will you enlist?"', an extract from Voltaire's *Candide.*] 4p. *8°.* [*London,* 1841]

32432 ISAACSON, S. The duty of electors at the present crisis. 16p. *8°.* 1841. *For another issue, see no.* 31964.

32433 JOCELYN, R., *Earl of Roden.* Observations on Lord Alvanley's pamphlet on the state of Ireland, and proposed measures for restoring tranquillity to that country. 34p. *8°.* 1841. *The copy that belonged to Earl De Grey.*

32434 JONES, WILLIAM, *of Liverpool.* Chartism. Authentic report of the speech of Mr. William Jones; upon responding to the toast of "the People's Charter, and may it soon become the law of the land"; at a soiree, held in... Liverpool, on...27th September, 1841; in celebration of the release of James Bronterre O'Brien, and Feargus O'Connor... 16p. *8°. Liverpool, Manchester, &c.,* [1841]

32435 A **LETTER** to Mr. William Lovett...[Signed: A non-voter.] 31p. *8°.* 1841.

32436 Six **LETTERS** to Sir Robert Peel, Bart., on the re-action in favour of a Tory Government, and on the vast improvement in the condition of the manufacturers, which may be expected to result from a sliding scale Ministry, and a monopolist majority...By a friend to the Monarchy. 30p. *8°.* 1841.

32437 LOVETT, W. and **COLLINS**, JOHN, *chartist.* Chartism; a new organization of the people...Second edition. 132p. *12°.* 1841. *William Lovett's own copy, with his signature on the title-page. For another edition, see* 1840.

32438 LOYD, S. J. *Baron Overstone.* Speeches of Samuel Jones Loyd, Esq., and Lord John Russell, at the London Tavern, on Tuesday, June 15th, 1841 [at an election meeting]. 16p. *8°.* 1841. *Loyd's own copy, formerly among his papers, for which see vol. III, MS. 804.*

For **MC.DOUALL'S CHARTIST AND REPUBLICAN JOURNAL,** *see* vol. III, *Periodicals list.*

32439 MARSHALL, JAMES G. The people still in want of good government; a letter from J. G. Marshall, Esq., chairman of the Leeds Parliamentary Reform Association, to the Earl Fitzwilliam. ⟨Extracted from the Leeds Times, of...Feb. 6.⟩ 8p. *12°. Leeds,* 1841. *Another edition was printed with Earl Fitzwilliam's letter, to which this is a reply, for which see no.* 32430.

32440 MARTIN, WILLIAM (1772–1851). The Martinean new mode of sending ingenious and wise men up to Parliament without voters. [Signed: William Martin, and dated, July 14, 1841.] 4p. *8°. Newcastle,* [1841]

32441 —— The philosopher's address to the British Queen and Government, on the meeting of the new Parliament for the good of the people; with remarks on Sir Robert Peel's speech at Tamworth. 4p. *8°. Newcastle,* [1841]

32442 MONTAGU, B. To the electors of Finsbury. [An address.] *s.sh.fol. n.p.* [1841 ?]

32443 MORRISON, R. T. Class legislation exposed; or, practical atheism identified with the advocates of property qualification for legislative enfranchisement. 12p. *12⁰.* London, Manchester, &c., 1841.

32444 NATIONAL ASSOCIATION FOR PROMOTING THE POLITICAL AND SOCIAL IMPROVEMENT OF THE PEOPLE. Plan, rules, and regulations of the... Association... 23p. *8⁰.* [1841]

32445 PAINE, T. Common sense, addressed to the inhabitants of America...To which is added, an appendix: together with an address to the people called Quakers. [With 'Introduction. Written for this edition, by a friend'.] 48p. *8⁰.* 1841. *The introduction is the same as that in the edition of 1834 (q.v.). For other editions, see 1776* (COLONIES).

32446 PEEL, SIR ROBERT, *2nd Bart.* Address to the Queen. Sir Robert Peel's speech in the House of Commons...August 27, 1841. 16p. *8⁰. W. E. Painter,* [1841] *For another issue, see no.* 31964.

32447 —— Want of confidence in Ministers. Sir R. Peel's speech in the House of Commons...May 27, 1841. 15p. *8⁰. W. E. Painter,* [1841]

32448 —— Fourth edition. 15p. *8⁰. J. Ollivier,* [1841] *For another issue, see no.* 31964.

32449 PEOPLE of Great Britain...[An attack on Sir Robert Peel for his failure to relieve national distress.] 4p. *8⁰.* [London, 1841]

32450 Past **PERFORMANCES** and present promises of the Liberal and Tory parties [before the General Election of 1841]. 8p. *8⁰.* [London, 1841]

32451 RECONCILIATION between the middle and labouring classes. [With a preface by Joseph Sturge.] 32p. *8⁰. Birmingham,* 1841. *See also* 1842.

32452 The radical **REFORMERS** of England, Scotland, & Wales, to the Irish people. [Signed: Your brother radicals. Followed by a list of the secretaries or chairmen of 134 radical and working mens' associations in Great Britain, headed by William Lovett.] 8p. *8⁰.* [1841 ?]

32453 National **REMONSTRANCE.** [From the National Association Gazette...N.A. tracts. No. 2.] 4p. *8⁰.* [London, 1841] *With the signature of William Lovett.*

32454 To the people of Great Britain and Ireland. **REPEAL** of the union between the monopoly and the bastile. By the author of "Thoughts on national education," "The doctrine of a triune God," &c.&c.&c. 8p. *8⁰.* 1841.

32455 *Entry cancelled.*

32456 RUSSELL, JOHN, *Earl Russell.* A corrected report of the speeches of the Rt. Hon. Lord John Russell, on the 27th and 30th of August, 1841, on the Address, and on the resignation of ministers. 46p. *8⁰.* 1841.

32457 SCOTT, ALEXANDER J. The social systems of the present day, compared with Christianity. In five lectures...delivered at Chadwell Street Chapel, Pentonville...October and November, 1841. Selected from the Pulpit [nos. 1022-26]. p. 305-376. *8⁰.* [1841]

32458 STANLEY, EDWARD G. G. S., *14th Earl of Derby.* North Lancashire election. Lord Stanley's speech at the Lancashire nomination...July 6, 1841. 15p. *8⁰.* [London, 1841]

32459 —— Want of confidence in Ministers. Lord Stanley's speech in the House of Commons Friday, June 4, 1841. 16p. *8⁰.* [1841]

SOCIALISM

32460 AINSLIE, R. An examination of socialism: the last of a series of lectures against socialism, delivered in the Mechanics Institution, Southampton Buildings... February 27, 1840, under the direction of the committee of the London City Mission...With a...letter to the Marquis of Normanby, and an appendix. 47p. *12⁰.* 1841. *Earlier printed in* Lectures against socialism, *1840 (no.* 31847).

For the **ANTI-SOCIALIST GAZETTE, AND CHRISTIAN ADVOCATE,** 1841-42, *continued as* the Antidote, 1842, *see vol.* III, *Periodicals list,* Antidote.

32461 ANTOINE, F. V. Prospectus du perfectibilisme ...Solution des problèmes d'économie politique...2me êditïon [*sic*], éditèe [*sic*] par l'autrur [*sic*]... 113p. *12⁰.* Paris, 1841.

32462 BAILEY, JAMES N. The social reformers' cabinet library of short treatises on important subjects. 31, 64, 32, 64, 64p. *8⁰. Leeds, Manchester, &c.,* 1841. *A collection of separately published pamphlets, reissued with a general title, taken from the wrapper. Contents: Lycurgus and the Spartans...Illustrating the power of circumstances in forming the human character, 1840; Sketches of Indian character...Illustrating the aphorism of the socialists, that "Man is the creature of circumstances", 1841; Preliminary discourse on...the science of society, 1840; The pleasures and advantages of literature and philosophy, 1841; Gehenna; its*

monarch and its inhabitants, 1841; Sophistry unmasked! A refutation of...a pamphlet...by John Brindley, entitled "A reply to the infidelity and atheism of socialism", 1841. See also 1848.

32463 —— Sophistry unmasked! A refutation of the arguments contained in a pamphlet, written and published by John Brindley, entitled "A reply to the infidelity and atheism of socialism,"... 64p. *8⁰. Leeds, Manchester,* 1841. *Reissued in* The social reformers' cabinet library, *no.* 32462 *above.*

32464 BARKER, JOSEPH. Christianity triumphant; or, an enlarged view of the character and tendency of the religion of Christ, shewing that it is...calculated to remedy the evils of a disordered and miserable world... Together with an appendix, containing the substance of various public discussions between the author and the socialists. 448p. *12⁰.* 1841. *The author's name is only on the spine of the volume. A reissue, with a new title-page, of the work published at Newcastle in 1839 (q.v.).*

32465 BRAY, C. The philosophy of necessity; or, the law of consequences; as applicable to mental, moral, and social science... [With an appendix by M. Hennell.] 2 vols. *8⁰.* 1841. *Presentation copy, with an autograph letter from the author to 'Dr. [Henry] Travis'. The appendix was separately published in 1844 (q.v.).*

32466 BRINDLEY, JOHN. A reply to the infidelity and atheism of socialism... 68p. *12°. Birmingham,* [1841]

32467 BUCHANAN, ROBERT. The past, the present, and the future. A poem. 72p. *12°. Manchester,* [1841]

32468 CANTAGREL, F. J. F. Publication de l'École sociétaire. Le fou du Palais-Royal. 504p. *8°. Paris,* 1841. *The copy that belonged to Victor Considérant, to whom the work is dedicated.*

32469 [CONSIDÉRANT, V. P.] Bases de la politique positive. Manifeste de l'École sociétaire, fondée par Fourier. 119p. *8°. Paris,* 1841. *See also 1842, 1847.*

32470 DOHERTY, H. False association and its remedy; or, a critical introduction to the late Charles Fourier's theory of attractive industry, and the moral harmony of the passions. To which is prefixed, a memoir of Fourier. 167p. *8°.* 1841. *Another copy, inscribed 'To Richard Oastler Esq with the author's kind regards' has, in error, the title-page of* Charles Fourier's theory of attractive industry... Translated from the French of Abel Transon *(no.* 32499*), which has an identical memoir. This was probably a fairly general error on the part of the publishers. The Kress copy (C5448) has Transon's text with the title* False association.

32471 ÉCOLE SOCIETAIRE. Acte de société pour la propagation et la réalisation de la théorie sociétaire. xxip. *8°. n.p.* [1841 ?] *Without title-page or imprint, this is possibly the introduction to a larger work. The copy that belonged to Victor Considérant.*

For the EDUCATIONAL CIRCULAR AND COMMUNIST APOSTLE, 1841–42, *see* vol. III, *Periodicals list.*

32472 ETZLER, J. A. The new world, or mechanical system, to perform the labours of man and beast by inanimate powers... for producing and preparing the substances of life... 75p. *8°. Philadelphia,* 1841.

32473 FOURIER, F. C. M. Œuvres complètes de Ch. Fourier... Deuxième édition, publiée par la Société pour la propagation et pour la réalisation de la théorie de Fourier. 6 vols. *12°. Paris,* 1841–48. *Vol. 6 is of the 3rd edition, 1848. In a second set, vols. 1 and 6 are of the 3rd edition, 1846–48.*

32474 FOURIER, ó sea explanacion del sistema societario. 410[310]p. *8°. Barcelona,* 1841.

32475 GAMOND, afterwards GATTI DE GAMOND, Z. DE. Fourier et son système... Cinquième édition. 384p. *12°. Paris,* 1841–42. *For other editions, see* 1838.

32476 —— The phalanstery; or, attractive industry and moral harmony. Translated from the French... by an English lady. 176p. *8°.* 1841.

32477 —— No. 1... The position of woman in harmony... Extracted... from "The phalanstery..."... 16p. *8°.* 1841.

32478 *HOME COLONIZATION SOCIETY. [Begin.]* I beg to call your attention to a work just published by the Society... [A circular letter, signed A. C. Cuddon, secretary, and dated: April, 1841, setting out the objects of the Society.] *s.sh.4°. n.p.* [1841] *The FWA copy that belonged to William Pare.*

For the LONDON PHALANX, 1841–43, *see* vol. III, *Periodicals list.*

For the NORTHERN STAR AND NATIONAL

TRADES' JOURNAL, 1841–43, 1848–50, *see* vol. III, *Periodicals list.*

32479 *OWEN, ROBERT. Address on opening the institution for the formation of character, at New Lanark, delivered on the 1st of January, 1816: being the first public announcement of the discovery of the infant school system. 32p. *8°. Home Colonization Society,* 1841. *The FWA copy that belonged to William Pare. For other editions, see* 1816.

32480 —— An address to the socialists on the present position of the rational system of society; and the measures required to direct most successfully the operations of the Universal Community Society of Rational Religionists: being the substance of two lectures, delivered in London, previous to the meeting of Congress, in May 1841. 14, [2]p. *8°. Home Colonization Society,* 1841.

32481 —— A development of the principles and plans on which to establish self-supporting home colonies... [With 'Appendix' and 'The signs of the times; or, the approach of the Millenium'.] 79, 47, 12p. *4°. Home Colonization Society,* 1841. *Two presentation copies from the author, one to Henry Travis, the other to Sibley Whittem?*

32482 —— Lectures on the rational system of society, derived solely from nature and experience, as propounded by Robert Owen, versus socialism, derived from misrepresentation, as explained by the Lord Bishop of Exeter... and versus the present system of society, derived from the... crude notions of our ancestors, as it now exists in all the opposing, artificial, and most injurious divisions in all civilized nations, but more especially in the British Empire and in the United States of North America... Delivered... in February, March, and April, 1841. 188p. *8°. Home Colonization Society,* 1841. *Published in parts. *Another copy of the final number, the FWA copy, containing p. i–iv, 177–188, in the original printed paper wrappers, belonged to William Pare.*

32483 *—— Manifesto of Robert Owen, the discoverer... of the rational system of society... Eighth edition. With an appendix... 63p. *8°. Home Colonization Society,* 1841. *The FWA copy that belonged to William Pare. For other editions, see* 1840.

32484 —— The signs of the times; or, the approach of the Millenium. An address to the Tories, Whigs, Radicals, and Chartists; churchmen... producers of wealth, and non-producers... [With 'To the electors of Great Britain and Ireland'.] Second edition. 15, [3]p. *8°. Home Colonization Society,* 1841.

32485 *—— To the electors of Great Britain and Ireland... [A recommendation to elect to Parliament only those candidates who would urge certain changes in the present social system. Signed: Robert Owen, and dated, 28th June, 1841. A prospectus and information about the activities of the House Colonization Society are printed on 3 of the 4 pages.] [4]p. *8°.* [*London,* 1841] *The FWA copy that belonged to William Pare.*

32486 —— What is Socialism? and what would be its practical effects upon society? A correct report of the public discussion between Robert Owen & Mr. John Brindley... in Bristol... January, 1841... With the preliminary correspondence... and an appendix... 68, [2]p. *8°. London: Home Colonization Society, Manchester, &c.,* 1841. **Another, the FWA copy, belonged to William Pare.*

32487 PAGET, A. F. Introduction à l'étude de la science sociale contenant un abrégé de la théorie sociétaire, précédé d'un coup d'œil général sur l'état de la science sociale, et sur les systèmes de Fourier, d'Owen et de Saint-Simon...Deuxième édition. 244p. *12°. Paris*, 1841. *For another edition, see* 1838.

32488 POMPÉRY, É. DE. Théorie de l'association et de l'unité universelle de C. Fourier; introduction religieuse et philosophique. 384p. *8°. Paris*, 1841.

32489 A PROSPECTUS for the establishment of a concordium; or an industry harmony college. 8p. *8°.* 1841.

32490 PROSPECTUS of the London Phalanx... 15p. *8°.* [*London*, 1841] *The copy that belonged to William Lovett.*

32491 PROUDHON, P. J. Avertissement aux propriétaires, ou lettre à M. Considérant rédacteur de La Phalange, sur une défense de la propriété. 115p. *12°. Paris & Besançon*, 1841. *Signed and dated, 'Besançon, 1er janvier 1842'. See also* 1848.

32492 —— Lettre à M. Blanqui professeur d'économie politique au Conservatoire des Arts et Métiers, sur le propriété...Deuxième mémoire. 188p. *12°. Paris*, 1841. *Presentation copy, with inscription, from the author to François Villegardelle. Another edition was published as the second part of* Qu'est-ce que la propriété? *in 1848 (q.v.).*

32493 —— Qu'est-ce que la propriété? Ou recherches sur le principe du droit et du gouvernement...Premier mémoire. 314p. *12°. Paris*, 1841. *See also* 1848.

32494 A REVIEW of the Social destiny of Man; or, general association. By Albert Brisbane. (From the United States Magazine and Democratic Review, of November and December, 1840. – Washington.)... 52p. *12°.* [1841]

32495 REYBAUD, M. R. L. Études sur les réformateurs contemporains, ou socialistes modernes...2ᵉ édition. 2 vols. *8°. Paris*, 1841–43. *Vol. 1 only is of the second edition. See also* 1844, 1849.

32496 ROBERT DE LA MENNAIS, H. F. Du passé et de l'avenir du peuple. 184p. *16°. Paris*, 1841.

32497 SAINT-SIMON, C. H. DE, Comte. Œuvres de Saint-Simon contenant: 1° Catéchisme politique des industriels. 2° Vues sur la propriété et la législation. 3° Lettres d'un habitant de Genève à ses contemporains. 4° Parabole politique. 5° Nouveau Christianisme. Précédés de fragmens de l'histoire de sa vie écrite par lui-même, publiés en 1832, par Olinde Rodrigues. 364, 201p. *8°. Paris*, 1841.

32498 [TAMISIER, A.] Congrès Scientifique de France. Théorie générale de Fourier. Mémoire de M.***. Lu dans la 5e section du Congrès, le 5 septembre, 1841, par M. Victor Considérant, pour répondre à cette question du programme: "Exposer et discuter la valeur des principes de l'École sociétaire fondée par Fourier." 16p. *8°. Lyon*, 1841. *Catalogued from the wrapper. A second copy, without the wrappers, belonged to Victor Considérant. See also* 1846 (Coup d'œil sur la théorie des fonctions).

32499 TRANSON, A. L. E. Charles Fourier's theory of attractive industry and the moral harmony of the passions. Translated from the French of Abel Transon... To which is prefixed, a memoir of Fourier by Hugh Doherty. 120p. *8°.* 1841. *For Transon's* Théorie sociétaire de Charles Fourier, *see* 1832.

MISCELLANEOUS

32500 BOWES, J. Second [–seventh] report of the means employed by the Christian church assembling in Hill-Street Room, Toxteth Park, and in the Preaching room, Gt. Crosshall-Street, for leading sinners to Christ; and a narrative of the travels, trial before the magistrate of Dundee, and extracts from the Journal of John Bowes, while engaged in promoting the unity of the church of God. 1841 [–1846]. 6 vols. *12°. Liverpool,* [*Aberdeen,*] &c., [1841–46] *See note to no.* 27827.

32501 CANDLISH, R. S. Third thousand. A letter to the Marquis of Normanby, &c.&c.&c. [Concerning the Church of Scotland.] 11p. *8°. Edinburgh & London*, [1841]

32502 CHANNING, WILLIAM E. The present age: an address delivered before the Mercantile Library Company of Philadelphia, May 11, 1841. 12p. *8°. Manchester*, 1841. *The Turner copy.*

32503 DIDEROT, D. Thoughts on religion. 8p. *8°.* 1841.

32504 FELLOWES, R. A lecture delivered on opening the chapel of the Philosophical Institution in Beaumont Square. 24p. *12°.* 1841.

32505 KENNEDY, C. R. A letter to the Lord Chancellor. On the subject of the revising barristers. 16p. *8°.* [1841]

32506 MILDMAY, SIR W., Bart. The method and rule of proceeding upon all elections, polls and scrutinies, at common halls and wardmotes, within the City of London...With additional notes on wardmote elections; an historical review of the City electoral franchises; and of the incorporated mysteries with their liverymen, electors of London. By Henry Kent S. Causton. ccclxxxviii, 309p. *12°.* 1841.

32507 OWEN, ROBERT D. Galileo and the inquisition. Effects of missionary labours. 16p. *8°.* 1841. *Also published as no.* 12 *of* Popular tracts, 1830, *q.v.* (SOCIALISM).

32508 —— Prossimo's experience. On the study of theology. "Safest to believe," or the balance struck. 16p. *8°.* [1841] *Also published as no.* 4 *of* Popular tracts, 1830, *q.v.*) SOCIALISM).

32509 RODRIGUES, B. O. Poésies sociales des ouvriers réunies et publiées par Olinde Rodrigues. 372p. *8°. Paris*, 1841.

32510 *SHARPE, JAMES B. An inquiry into the origin of the office and title of the justice of the peace, with an appendix, on some of the defects of our ancient Statute Book. 208p. *12°.* 1841. *The copy that belonged to George Grote.*

32511 STERLING, J. Sterling's letters to Coningham. Edited by William Coningham, Esq., M.P. Third edition. 27p. *8°. London & Brighton*, [1841]

32512 [WHATELY, R., Archbishop of Dublin.] Historic doubts relative to Napoleon Buonaparte. [A satire in refutation of certain propositions in Hume's Essay on miracles.] Seventh edition. 56p. *8°.* 1841.

1842

GENERAL

32513 ACKERSDIJCK, J. Redevoering over Adam Smith. Naar het Latijn...Overgedrukt uit het Tijdschrift voor Staathuishoudkunde en Statistiek, tweede deel, tweede stuk. 17p. *8°. n.p.* [1842 ?]

32514 ALLARDICE, R. B. Agricultural tour in the United States and Upper Canada, with miscellaneous notices. 181p. *8°. Edinburgh & London*, 1842.

32515 AMERICA & England contrasted: or, the emigrant's hand-book and guide to the United States. Comprising information respecting their constitution, best fields for agricultural and manufacturing employment, wages, climate, shipping, letters from emigrants, etc. Second edition. 52p. *12°.* [1842]

For the **AMERICAN LABORER**, 1842–43, *see vol.* III, *Periodicals list.*

32516 ARISTARCHUS, *pseud.* Internal free trade, & capitalists' trades' unions. The only conservative system of joint stock commercial and industrial association. Abridged from a familiar letter to a friend. 16p. *8°.* [*London*, 1842]

32517 [ASHWORTH, H.] Statistical illustrations of the past and present state of Lancashire. 15p. *8°. n.p.* [1842] *Signed in manuscript by the author.*

32518 —— Statistical illustrations of the past and present state of Lancashire, more particularly relating to the hundred of Salford. Read before the Statistical Section of the British Association...on the 27th June, 1841... 24p. *8°. London & Manchester*, 1842.

32519 ★B., J. I. A safe and efficient remedy for existing distress among the labouring classes. Addressed to the editor of the "Labourers' Friend Magazine." 16p. *8°.* 1842. *The FWA copy that belonged to William Pare.*

32520 BLANQUI, J. A. Histoire de l'économie politique en Europe, depuis les anciens jusqu'à nos jours, suivie d'une bibliographie raisonnée des principaux ouvrages d'économie politique...Deuxième édition. 2 vols. *8°. Paris*, 1842. *For other editions, see* 1837.

32521 BOECKH, A. The public economy of Athens; to which is added, a dissertation on the silver mines of Laurion...Translated by George Cornewall Lewis... Second edition, revised. 688p. *8°.* 1842. *For another edition, see* 1828.

32522 The **BRITISH ALMANAC** of the Society for the Diffusion of Useful Knowledge, for...1842. [With 'The companion to the Almanac; or year-book of general information'.] 96, 244p. *12°.* [1842] *For other editions, see* 1828.

32523 BROADHURST, J. Political economy. 297p. *8°.* 1842.

32524 BUCKINGHAM, J. S. The eastern and western states of America. 3 vols. *8°. London & Paris*, [1842]

32525 —— The slave states of America... 2 vols. *8°. London & Paris*, [1842]

32526 CADIZ. Representacion elevada al Sermo. Señor Regente del Reino por la diputacion provincial, ayuntamiento, junta de comercio, sociedad económica y proprietarios de Cádiz, demostrando los males que ocasiona la tardanza de la ley de algodones, y haciendo ver las ventajas de un tratado de comercio con la Inglaterra, y de la reforma de los aranceles y derogacion del sistema prohibitivo. 42p. *8°. Cadiz*, 1842.

32527 CAMPBELL, JOHN (*d.* 1845). Speech of Hon. John Campbell, of So. Carolina, on the general appropriation bill, and in defence of the 21st rule. Delivered in the House of Representatives of the U.S., April 15, 1842. 20p. *8°. Washington*, 1842.

32528 CHALMERS, G. Catalogue of the...library of the late George Chalmers, Esq., F.R.S. F.S.A....[Part the second.] 105p. *8°.* [*London*,] 1842.

32529 —— [Part the third.] 137p. *8°.* [*London*,] 1842. *For the first part, see* 1841.

32530 CHAMBERS, W. and ROBERT (1802–1871), *eds.* Chambers's information for the people. New and improved edition. 2 vols. *8°. Edinburgh*, 1842. *Published in 99 parts. See also* 1848.

32531 CHAMPAGNAC, J. B. J. Travail et industrie ou le pouvoir de la volonté. Histoires d'artisans, d'artistes et de négociants devenus célèbres...(*Bibliothèque Speciale de la Jeunesse.*) 287p. *12°. Paris*, [1842]

32532 CHEVALIER, M. Cours d'économie politique fait au Collège de France, par M. Michel Chevalier. Rédigé par M. A. Broët, et publié avec l'autorisation de M. Michel Chevalier. Année 1841–42. [With 'Deuxième année 1842–43' and 'Troisième volume. La monnaie'.] 3 vols. *8°. Paris*, 1842–50.

For **CHRISTIAN MISSIONARY CIVILIZATION**, *see vol.* III, *Periodicals list*, Journal of civilization.

32533 COBDEN, R. Alarming distress. Speech of Richd. Cobden, Esq. in the House of Commons on...July 8, 1842. 8p. *8°. Manchester*, [1842]

32534 CONSTANT, J. F. Du régime protecteur en économie politique, de son application à la Belgique, et des avantages que son agriculture, sa fabrication et son commerce pourraient en recueillir... 2 vols. *12°. Bruxelles*, 1842.

32535 CORY, I. P. Competition: its abuse one of the chief causes of the present distress among the trading, manufacturing, and commercial classes; with suggestions for remedying it. 28p. *8°.* 1842.

32536 COTTON TWIST, *pseud.* The Free Trader. Plenty to do, high profits, good wages, & cheap bread: letters [dated from May 1841 to January 1842] to the Right Honourable Sir R. Peel, Bart. 184p. *8°. n.p.*, 1842. *Note on the verso of the title-page: 25 re-printed from The Weekly Chronicle.*

32537 DEFOE, D. The works of De Foe. Remarks on the Bill to prevent frauds committed by bankrupts. An essay upon loans. An essay upon public credit. An essay on the South Sea trade. An essay on the treaty of commerce with France. Some further observations on the treaty of navigation and commerce between Great Britain and France. (*The Pulteney Library. Edited by William Hazlitt*, 27.) [64]p. *8°. 1842.*

32538 DIALOGUE between John and Thomas, on the corn laws, the Charter, teetotalism, and the probable remedy for the present disstresses [*sic*]. 8p. *8°. Paisley*, 1842.

32539 DOBELL, P. Sept années en Chine. Nouvelles observations sur cet empire, l'archipel Indo-Chinois, les Philippines et les Iles Sandwich...Traduit du Russe par le Prince Emmanuel Galitzin. Nouvelle édition. 358p. *8°. Paris*, 1842.

32540 The **DUBLIN** almanac, and general register of Ireland, for...1843...Tenth annual impression. 832p. *8°. Dublin: Pettigrew & Oulton*, [1842] *See also* 1838.

For the **DUBLIN JOURNAL OF TEMPER-ANCE, SCIENCE AND LITERATURE,** *see* vol. III, *Periodicals list.*

32541 DUTENS, J. M. Essai comparatif sur la formation et la distribution du revenu de la France en 1815 et 1835. 178p. *8°. Paris*, 1842.

32542 DYMOND, J. Essays on the principles of morality, and on the private and political rights and obligations of mankind...Fourth edition. 198p. *8°. London, Carlisle, &c.,* 1842.

32543 ENCYCLOPAEDIA BRITANNICA. [Extracts from the seventh edition of the *Encyclopaedia Britannica*.] *4°.* [*Edinburgh*, 1842] *Contents: articles and plates on the following subjects of economic interest: assaying; average; coinage; commerce; corn laws and trade; cotton manufacture; economists; emigration; gas light; insurance; interest; iron-making; Malthus; money; mortality, human; navigation, inland; paper-money; banks; political economy; poor-laws; population; railways; Ricardo; statistics; steam; steam engine; steam engine boilers; steam navigation; taxation. For an earlier edition of some of the articles, see* 1824.

32544 EXTRACTS from the Britannia Conservative weekly newspaper. A comprehensive journal of news, politics, literature and fine arts... 15p. *8°.* [1842]

32545 *FAUCHER, L. L'union du Midi. Association de douanes entre la France, la Belgique, la Suisse et l'Espagne, avec une introduction sur l'union commerciale de la France et de la Belgique. clxxxix, 166p. *8°. Paris*, 1842. *The copy that belonged to George Grote. For a shorter version of this work, see* 1837.

32546 FINCH, JOHN, *the younger, comp.* Statistics of Vauxhall Ward, Liverpool, shewing the actual condition of more than five thousand families, being the result of an inquiry recently instituted at the request of the Liverpool Anti-Monopoly Association, with observations, and explanatory letters. 55p. *8°. Liverpool & London*, 1842. **Another, the FWA copy, belonged to William Pare.*

32547 FROUDE, J. A. The influence of the science of political economy on the moral and social welfare of a nation. A prize essay read in the Sheldonian Theatre, Oxford; June 8, 1842. 44p. *8°. Oxford*, 1842.

32548 GALE, R. Address to the Queen on behalf of the manufacturing poor. [In verse.] 32p. *8°.* 1842.

32549 GIBSON, T. M. The shopkeepers' question. Speech of T. M. Gibson, Esq., M.P. in the House of Commons, on...July 22nd, in moving for inquiry into the distress of the country. 12p. *12°. Manchester*, [1842]

32550 GIDDINGS, J. R. Speech of Mr. Giddings, of Ohio, upon the proposition of Mr. Johnson, of Tennessee, to reduce the army to the basis of 1821. Delivered in the House of Representatives of the U. States, June 3, 1842. 19p. *8°. Washington*, 1842.

32551 GILMER, T. W. Speech of Mr. Gilmer, of Virginia, on the army bill. Delivered in the House of Representatives, in Committee of the Whole, May 26 and 30, 1842. 15p. *8°. n.p.* [1842]

32552 GODWIN, WILLIAM (1756–1836). An essay on trades & professions...containing a forcible exposure of the demoralizing tendencies of competition. [An extract from the *Enquirer*.] 24p. *12°. Manchester, London, &c.,* 1842. *For editions of* The enquirer, *see* 1797.

32553 GREG, W. R. Not over-production, but deficient consumption, the source of our sufferings...January 1842. [Illustrated from the state of the cotton manufacture.] 28p. *8°.* [1842]

32554 —— Second edition. 28p. *8°.* 1842.

32555 The **HACKNEY** almanack and directory, for 1843. 162p. *12°. Hackney,* [1842]

32556 [**HELPS,** SIR A.] Essays written in the intervals of business. [Second edition.] 144p. *8°.* 1842.

For **JOURNAL DES ÉCONOMISTES,** *Paris,* 1842–1940, [*Bruxelles*, 1844–52.] *see* vol. III, *Periodicals list.*

32557 KUX, J. P. Organismus und vollständige Statistik des preussischen Staats aus zuverlässigen Quellen ...Zweite nach den neuesten Verhältnissen berichtigte Auflage. 312p. *8°. Leipzig*, 1842.

32558 LAING, SAMUEL (1780–1868). Notes of a traveller, on the social and political state of France, Prussia, Switzerland, Italy, and other parts of Europe, during the present century. 496p. *8°.* 1842.

32559 LIEBER, F. Essays on property and labour as connected with natural law and the constitution of society. 225p. *12°. New-York*, 1842.

32560 LIST, F. Die Ackerverfassung die Zwergwirthschaft und die Auswanderung...(Aus der Deutschen Vierteljahrsschrift, 1842, Heft IV. Nr. xx, besonders abgedruckt.) 86p. *8°. Stuttgart & Tübingen*, 1842. *The copy that belonged to Wilhelm Roscher.*

32561 LIVERPOOL ANTI-MONOPOLY ASSOCIATION. Speeches delivered at the first meeting of the Liverpool Anti-Monopoly Association, Thos. Thornely, Esq. M.P. president, in the chair; together with a report on the present condition of the town. 31p. *12°. Liverpool,* [1842]

For **LIVESEY,** J., The struggle, 1842–46, *see* vol. III, *Periodicals list,* The struggle...

32562 LOVE, B. The hand-book of Manchester; containing statistical and general information on the trade, social condition, and institutions, of the metropolis of manufactures: being a second and enlarged edition of "Manchester as it is." 296p. *8°. Manchester & London*, 1842. *For another edition, see* 1839.

32563 [**McCULLOCH,** JOHN R.] Notice of Francis Quesnay, M.D., founder of the sect of the economists. [Reprinted from the seventh edition of the Encyclopædia Britannica.] 10p. *8°. n.p.* [1842 ?] *For another edition, see* 1824.

32564 MACGREGOR, JOHN (1797–1857). The Germanic Union of Customs. The commercial treaties and tariffs; the agriculture, manufactures, commerce, and the navigation of Prussia and other states of Germany, including the Hanse towns, Holstein, Hanover, Mecklenburg, and Oldenburg. 317p. *8°. 1842. Reissued with the title: Germany: her resources, government, union of customs, and power, in 1848 (q.v.).*

32565 M'LAWS, C. S. Statement explanatory of the independent system of emigration...read to the meeting in Eglinton Street Church, on...April 12, 1842...Sixth thousand. 20p. *8°. Glasgow, 1842.*

32566 *—— Seventh thousand. 20p. *8°. Glasgow, 1842. The FWA copy that belonged to William Pare.*

32567 MARLIANI, M. DE. De la influencia del sistema prohibitivo en la agricultura, industria, comercio y rentas publicas. 390p. *8°. Madrid, 1842.*

For the **MIDLAND COUNTIES STANDARD,** *see vol. III, Periodicals list.*

32568 MILES, *pseud.* A letter to Sir Robert Peel, Bart., on the causes of the success of the non-productive classes: by "Miles," author of "A letter to Lord John Russell...by Civis." 60p. *8°. 1842.*

32569 OSIANDER, H. F. Enttäuschung des Publikums über die Interessen des Handels, der Industrie und der Landwirthschaft, oder Beleuchtung der Manufacturkraft-Philosophie des Dr List, nebst einem Gebet aus Utopien. 228p. *8°. Tübingen, 1842.*

32570 PALETHORPE, J. An equalisation of every item of Scripture money, weight, and measure, whether of liquids, dry goods, or of distance, with the British... 143p. *4°. 1842.*

32571 A political **PAMPHLET.** By a radical of the olden day... 103p. *8°. 1842. The copy that belonged to Earl De Grey.*

32572 PLOUGH, PATRICK, *pseud.* Letters on the rudiments of a science, called formerly, improperly, political economy, recently, more pertinently, catallactics. From Patrick Plough, a yeoman in the country to his sons, young men in town. 349p. *8°. 1842.*

32573 POPE, C., *ed.* The yearly journal of trade, 1842 ...Twentieth edition. 590p. *8°. [1842] See also 1838, 1840, 1843, 1844, 1845, 1846.*

32574 The **POST-OFFICE** Glasgow annual directory for 1842–43: containing an alphabetical list of the merchants, traders, manufacturers, and principal inhabitants, with a second list of...names...arranged under ...trade or profession; also a street directory and an appendix. Fifteenth publication. 392, 168p. *12°. Glasgow, 1842. See also 1829, 1836.*

32575 QUETELET, L. A. J. A treatise on Man and the development of his faculties...Now first translated into English [under the superintendence of Dr. R. Knox, edited by Thomas Smibert. With a new preface by the author written for this edition]. 126p. *8°. Edinburgh, 1842. For other editions, see 1835.*

32576 RAUMER, F. L. G. VON. England in 1841: being a series of letters written to friends in Germany, during a residence in London and excursions into the provinces...Translated from the German by H. Evans Lloyd... 2 vols. *12°. 1842.*

32577 [REDDING, C.] An illustrated itinerary of the county of Lancaster. [The hundreds of Salford and Blackburn by J. R. Beard, Manchester and the cotton trade by W. Cooke Taylor.] 238p. *8°. 1842.*

32578 SANDERSON, RICHARD B. The stagnation of trade a subject of prophecy both in the Old and New Testament: also the law of leprosy as it relates to the present state of the establishment in these kingdoms. 24p. *8°. 1842.*

32579 [SEELEY, R. B.] Memoirs of the life and writings of Michael Thomas Sadler... 664p. *8°. 1842.*

32580 SMITH, J. GRAY. A brief historical, statistical and descriptive review of east Tennessee, United States of America: developing its immense agricultural, mining, and manufacturing advantages, with remarks to emigrants... 71p. *8°. 1842.*

32581 SMITH, THOMAS S. On the economy of nations. 130p. *8°. 1842.*

32582 SMYLES, J. Emigration to the United States. A letter addressed to Mr. Pitkethly, of Huddersfield, Yorkshire...With the writer's observations on the people ...etc. Also, remarks on the fitness of the territory of Wisconsin as a residence for English emigrants. [Advocating purchase of land in Wisconsin for co-operative settlement by emigrants.] 7p. *8°. 1842.*

32583 SOCIETY OF THE GOVERNOR AND ASSISTANTS IN LONDON, OF THE NEW PLANTATION IN ULSTER. A concise view of the origin, constitution and proceedings of the honorable Society of the Governor & Assistants of London, of the New Plantation in Ulster...commonly called the Irish Society. Compiled, principally from their records. [With an appendix of documents.] 189, ccxlvip. *8°. 1842.*

32584 SOLLY, H. What says Christianity to the present distress? [Advocating the union of corn law repealers and Chartists, middle and working classes.] 90p. *12°. 1842.*

32585 SOMERVILLE, ANDREW. Free trade in corn and other commodities the duty and the interest of nations. A lecture delivered in...Glasgow...22nd November. Under the auspices of the Glasgow Young Men's Free Trade Association... 16p. *8°. Glasgow, 1842.*

32586 SPACKMAN, W. F. Statistical tables of the agriculture, shipping, colonies, manufactures, commerce, and population of the United Kingdom of Great Britain and its Dependencies, brought down to...1842. 111p. *12°. [1842?]*

32587 STANSFELD, H. Compensation not emigration the one thing needful; justice, and not charity, what we want: being a series of lectures intended to explain to the working classes...the causes of their present unfortunate condition. [Delivered before the Leeds Parliamentary Reform Association, January...1842.] 40p. *12°. Leeds, 1842.*

32588 The **STATE** and prospects of the nation, with remarks on the present contest between labour and machinery, in a letter to the citizens of London. By a Conservative elector. 34p. *8°. 1842.*

32589 TAYLOR, WILLIAM C. Notes of a tour in the manufacturing districts of Lancashire; in a series of letters to his Grace the Archbishop of Dublin. 299p. *8°. 1842.*

32590 —— Second edition; with two additional letters on the recent disturbances. 331p. *8°. 1842.*

32591 THOMPSON, THOMAS P. Exercises, political and others...Consisting of the matter previously published with and without the author's name, and of some not published before... 6 vols. *8°. 1842.*

32592 THUENEN, J. H. VON. Der isolirte Staat in Beziehung auf Landwirthschaft und Nationalökonomie, oder Untersuchungen über den Einfluss, den die Getreidepreise, der Reichthum des Bodens und die Abgaben auf den Ackerbau ausüben...Erster Theil. Zweite vermehrte und verbesserte Auflage. 391p. *8°. Rostock, 1842. For the second part of this work,* Der naturgemässe Arbeitslohn und dessen Verhältniss zum Zinsfuss und zur Landrente, *see 1850.*

32593 [TORRENS, R.] The Budget. A series of letters on financial, commercial, and colonial policy. By a member of the Political Economy Club. No. IV. [Letter IV. To the Right Hon. Lord Stanley, on colonisation, considered as a means of removing the causes of national distress.] p.[79]-102. *8°. 1842. The copy that belonged to Earl De Grey. Each letter was issued separately, although continuously signed and paginated. For the collected edition, see 1844.*

32594 VALLE, E. M. DEL. Curso de economia politica. 495p. *8°. Madrid, 1842.*

32595 VYVYAN, SIR R. R., *Bart.* A letter from Sir Richard Vyvyan, Bart. M.P. to his constituents, upon the commercial and financial policy of Sir Robert Peel's administration. [With special reference to protection of the Cornish mining industry.] 55p. *8°. 1842.*

AGRICULTURE

32596 CONNER, W. The prosecuted speech; delivered at Mountmellick in proposing a petition to Parliament in favor of a valuation and perpetuity of his farm to the tenant. With an introductory address on... Toryism. xxx, 27p. *8°. Dublin, 1842. See note to no. 27313.*

32597 DAVIS, H. Observations on a recent pamphlet, by R. H. Greg, Esq. entitled "Scotch farming in the Lothians." 20p. *8°. 1842.*

32598 DENTON, J. B. General drainage and distribution of water. The question, what can be done for British agriculture? answered in a letter to Philip Pusey, Esq., M.P. President of the Royal Agricultural Society of England for the past year; advocating a general and uniform system of drainage, with a profitable distribution of the surface and drainage waters, and the refuse of towns. 43p. *8°. 1842.*

32599 DUSSARD, H. Des défrichements des forêts, de leurs effets physiques immédiats, et de leur influence sur le régime économique des contrées où ils ont lieu. [Extrait du Journal des Économistes.] 20p. *8°. Batignolles, [1842]*

32600 ENGLAND. *Laws, etc.* Kilmington Inclosure. 5 Victoriæ. – Sess. 1842. An Act for inclosing lands in the parish of Kilmington, in the county of Devon. ⟨Royal Assent, 22 June 1842.⟩ 33p. *fol. Westminster, [1842]*

32601 EWING, W. Observations on the practice of draining and succession of crops, with a few hints on the breeding of cattle and the composition of manures. 24p. *8°. Glasgow, [1842?]*

32602 GREG, R. H. Scotch farming in the Lothians. A letter addressed to the editor of the Manchester Guardian. 33p. *8°. 1842.*

32603 —— Second edition. 16p. *8°. 1842.*

32604 —— Third edition. 16p. *8°. 1842.*

32605 —— Scotch farming in England. A second letter addressed to the editor of the Manchester Guardian. 31p. *8°. 1842.*

32606 HOWARD, L. A cycle of eighteen years in the seasons of Britain; deduced from meteorological observations made at Ackworth, in the West Riding of Yorkshire, from 1824 to 1841; compared with others before made for a like period (ending with 1823) in the vicinity of London ... 22p. *8°. London, Leeds, &c., 1842. Presentation copy from the author to 'Colonel Sabine'.*

32607 JOHNSON, C. W. The cottage farmer's assistant in the cultivation of his land, and book of the household. 85p. *12°. 1842.*

32608 —— The farmer's encyclopædia, and dictionary of rural affairs; embracing all the most recent discoveries in agricultural chemistry. Adapted to the comprehension of unscientific readers... 1319p. *8°. 1842.*

32609 JOHNSTON, JAMES F. W. Elements of agricultural chemistry and geology. 237p. *8°. Edinburgh & London, 1842.*

32610 —— What can be done for English agriculture? A letter to the most noble the Marquis of Northampton, President of the Royal Society. 39p. *8°. Edinburgh, London, &c., 1842.*

32611 The **KITCHEN GARDENER'S** manual; containing practical instructions for the cultivation and management of culinary vegetables and herbs, adapted either to large or small gardens. A new edition. 60p. *8°. 1842.*

32612 LEMON, SIR C., *Bart.* On the proposed tariff as it affects tin, copper, and timber, used in mines. 20p. *8°. Truro, 1842.*

32613 LIEBIG, J. VON, *Freiherr.* Chemistry in its application to agriculture and physiology...Edited from the manuscript of the author by Lyon Playfair. Second edition, with very numerous additions. 409p. *12°. 1842. For other editions, see 1841.*

32614 MORTON, JOHN (1781-1864). The nature and property of soils...to which is added an account of the proceedings at Whitfield example-farm...a letter to Mr Pusey's tenants; and the mode of cultivation adopted on Stinchcombe farm. Third edition enlarged. 374p. *8°. 1842.*

32615 NEVILE, C. The new tariff. [A discussion of its effect on agriculture.] 36p. *8°. 1842.*

32616 O'CONNOR, F. First lecture. The land & its capabilities. A lecture...at the Hall of Science...Manchester...March 7, 1842...[With 'Second lecture. Repeal of the Union'.] 48p. *12°. Manchester, London, &c., [1842]*

32617 ROYAL SOCIETY FOR THE PRO-MOTION AND IMPROVEMENT OF THE GROWTH OF FLAX IN IRELAND. Proceedings of the second annual general meeting of the Society... with an appendix, a list of subscribers' names, and treasurer's statement of accounts. 52p. *8°. Belfast*, 1842.

32618 ROYLE, J. F. On the production of isinglass along the coasts of India, with a notice of its fisheries. 494p. *8°.* 1842.

32619 SIMPSON, WILLIAM W. A letter to His Excellency the Earl De Grey, Lord Lieutenant of Ireland, on the ameliorated condition of that country, more par- ticularly as regards the agricultural classes; with sugges- tions for their further improvement: to which is subjoined an appendix, containing original...papers. 123p. *8°. London, Dublin, &c.,* 1842.

32620 WELLWOOD, S. A letter to Feargus O'Connor, Esq., against his plan of dividing the land, and in favour of the association of property, skill, and labour. 15p. *8°.* [1842]

32621 WESTERN, C. C., *Baron Western.* A letter from Lord Western, on the management of his flock of merino sheep, addressed to James Bischoff, Esq. 16p. *8°.* 1842.

CORN LAWS

32622 An **ADDRESS** to farmers, on the way in which their families are to be provided for. [Signed: A farmer's son.] 4p. *8°. Manchester: National Anti-Corn-Law League,* [1842 ?]

32623 A friendly **ADDRESS** to the operatives of the manufacturing districts. [On the anti-corn law agitation.] 29p. *8°.* 1842.

32624 The **ANTI-BREAD-TAX ALMANACK,** for the year...1842, being...leap year...and the twenty- seventh year of the bread tax; containing...the land tax; the bread tax unveiled; mitred bread taxers; America and the British corn law...exports and imports... 48p. *12°. Manchester & London,* [1842] *See also* The Anti-Corn-Law Almanack, 1841.

32625 ANTI-CORN LAW CONFERENCE. The report of the statistical committee appointed by the Anti-Corn Law Conference, held in London...March, 1842. 49p. *8°.* [1842]

32626 An **ARGUMENT** for dishonesty, conducted in the manner of the corn-law advocates. Published from the papers of an executed convict [said to be George Mostyns. A satire]. 12p. *12°. Manchester,* 1842.

32627 BAIN, D. Letter to the Right Honourable Sir Robert Peel, Baronet, First Lord of her Majesty's Treasury, &c. &c. &c. on the principles of the corn laws. 16p. *8°. Edinburgh, London, &c.,* 1842. *The copy that belonged to Earl De Grey.*

32628 BEAUCLERK, G. R. The operation of monopolies on the production of food, as illustrated by the corn laws: for which the only adequate remedies are moral government and free trade. 88p. *8°.* 1842.

32629 BONNER, W. H. The unrighteousness of monopoly. Speech of the Rev. W. H. Bonner, of Bilston, to the members of the National Anti-Corn-Law League on...November 3, 1842. 8p. *12°. Manchester,* [1842]

32630 BOUVERIE, W. P., *Earl of Radnor.* Speech of the Earl of Radnor on the corn laws, in the House of Lords, August 4, 1842, on moving the second reading of a Bill to repeal the Corn Importation Act. Also a protest against the rejection of the Bill. With an appendix, con- taining a protest against the income-tax, &c. &c. 23p. *12°.* 1842.

32631 —— [Another edition.] ⟨Printed for the Metro- politan Anti-Corn-Law Association.⟩ [With 'The Anti- Corn-Law League. (From the Examiner)'.] 12p. *12°. n.p.* [1842]

32632 **C.** Nine letters on the corn laws. Originally pub- lished in the 'Morning Chronicle,' the 'Sun,' the 'Man- chester Guardian,' and the 'Manchester Times.' [Signed: C., a lover of justice, or C., a friend of the poor.] Corrected and revised by the author. 67p. *8°.* 1842.

32633 CAMPBELL, JOHN, *Chartist.* An examina- tion of the corn and provision laws, from their first enactment to the present period...Second edition. 72p. *12°. Manchester,* [1842]

32634 CARMICHAEL, JAMES, *of Stirlingshire.* Corn-laws. Remarks on Mr. M'Culloch's "Statement" illustrative of the policy of a fixed duty on foreign corn. 42p. *8°. Edinburgh & London,* 1842. *The copy that belonged to Earl De Grey.*

32635 The **CHURCH** and the [National Anti-Corn- Law] League. Re-printed from 'The vicar's lantern.' 8p. *12°. Manchester,* [1842]

32636 COBDEN, R. Twenty-second thousand – re- vised. Speech of R. Cobden Esq., M.P. in the House of Commons on...February 24, 1842. With his reply to Mr. Ferrand. 12p. *12°. Manchester,* [1842]

32637 —— The corn laws. Speech of R. Cobden... Second edition – revised. 12p. *12°. Manchester & London,* [1842]

32638 —— Speech of R. Cobden, Esq., M.P. on... October 6, 1842, at a meeting of members of the Anti- Corn-Law League held in the large room, Newall's Buildings; showing the true causes for the passing of the American tariff, and proving that Sir R. Peel's tariff is not the cause of the present low prices of food in England. 12p. *12°. London & Manchester,* 1842.

32639 —— Speech of R. Cobden, Esq., M.P., at Sheffield, November 23, 1842, showing the true character of the opponents of the League. 8p. *12°. Manchester,* [1842]

32640 CONFERENCE OF MINISTERS AND MEMBERS OF DISSENTING CHURCHES. Address to the people of Scotland on the principle and operations of the corn and provision laws, by the Ministers and Members of Dissenting Churches assembled in conference at Edinburgh...January, 1842. 8p. *8°. Edinburgh,* [1842]

32641 —— Circular from the Edinburgh Conference committee. [With 'Minutes of the Conference of 801 Ministers and Members of Dissenting Churches, from various parts of Scotland, held in Edinburgh...January 1842'.] 7p. *8°. n.p.* [1842]

32642 COOKE, L. Observations upon the construction and operation of duties on the importation of foreign corn, and suggestions for lessening fluctuations in the price of wheat... 34p. *8°.* 1842. *The copy that belonged to Earl De Grey.*

32643 The **CORN BILL.** [A ballad.] *s.sh.fol. Printed for Peter Putright, Snooks Alley,* [1842] [*Br.* 601]

32644 CORN-LAW OPPOSITION detected and exposed, and its real nature laid bare. A few words addressed to people of common sense. By a plain man. 30p. *8°.* 1842. *With a manuscript inscription:* 'For the editor of the Morning Herald'.

32645 DUNDEE ANTI-CORN LAW ASSOCIATION. Report of the great anti-corn law meeting held at Dundee, on...6th January, 1842. Second thousand. 51p. *8°. London, Manchester, &c.,* 1842.

32646 EDINBURGH CHARTIST ASSOCIATION. To the members of the Corn-Law Convention, to be held in Edinburgh...January 1842. [Disassociating the Association from the corn-law agitation. Signed: Thomas Blackie, secretary, and dated, January 10, 1842.] 4p. *8°. Edinburgh,* [1842]

32647 EDWARDS, H. "Union!" the patriot's watchword at the present crisis; or, cordial reconciliation and active co-operation urged on the serious consideration of the people as the only safe and sure path to a speedy victory. 24p. *12°. Manchester & London,* 1842.

32648 FACTS for farmers. 4p. *8°. Manchester: National Anti-Corn-Law League, printed by W. Irwin,* [1842]

32649 —— [Another edition.] 4p. *8°. Manchester: National Anti-Corn-Law League, printed by J. Gadsby,* [1842] *For another edition, see* 1839.

32650 FERRAND, W. B. The corn laws. The speech of W. Busfeild Ferrand, Esq. M.P. in the House of Commons, on...Feb. 14, 1842. On Lord J. Russell's amendment. Fourteenth edition. 16p. *8°.* [1842]

32651 —— [Another edition.] Price one penny. The speech of Mr. Ferrand on the corn laws. Delivered in the House of Commons on February 14th. 1842. *8°. Rochester,* [1842]

32652 —— The second speech. Corn laws. The speech of W. Busfeild Ferrand, Esq. M.P. in the House of Commons, on...February 24, 1842, on the amendment of Mr. Villiers, "that all duties payable on the importation of corn do now cease and determine." Twelfth edition. 8p. *8°.* 1842.

32653 FIELD, W. A lecture on the provision laws, chiefly considered as a moral and religious question, delivered in the High Street Chapel, Warwick, on... March 13. 1842. 40p. *12°.* [*Leamington* &] *London,* [1842]

32654 GILES, J. E. The corn laws. Speech of the Rev. J. E. Giles, of Leeds, to the National Anti-Corn-Law League, Dec. 1, 1842. 8p. *12°. Manchester,* [1842]

32655 GISBORNE, THOMAS (1794–1852). Letter to the Council of the Anti-Corn-Law League. 16p. *12°. Manchester & London,* 1842.

32656 —— A second letter to the Council of the Anti-Corn-Law League. 12p. *12°. Manchester,* [1842]

32657 GREG, R. H. A letter to the Right Hon. Henry Labouchere, on the pressure of the corn laws and sliding scale, more especially upon the manufacturing interests and productive classes...Second edition. 32p. *8°.* 1842. *The copy that belonged to T. Spring Rice, Baron Monteagle. For another edition, see* 1841.

32658 GRENVILLE, GEORGE N. T., *Baron Nugent.* A letter to the chairman of the committee of the Anti-Corn Law League of England. 33p. *8°.* 1842.

32659 GRIFFITH, C. D. Corn laws. Protection but not monopoly. 14p. *8°.* 1842.

32660 HEYWORTH, L. To the British public. How does cheap bread produce high wages and promote general prosperity ? 4p. *8°. Manchester,* [1842]

32661 HUBBARD, J. G., *Baron Addington.* Vindication of a fixed duty on corn: to which are added remarks suggested by the speech of R. A. Christopher, Esq. M.P. at Lincoln. 48p. *8°. London & Liverpool,* 1842. *The copy that belonged to Earl De Grey.*

32662 HUME, JAMES D. Corn laws. The evidence of James Deacon Hume, Esq., late Secretary to the Board of Trade, upon the corn law, before the Committee of the House of Commons on the import duties, in 1839. [With 'Extracts from a series of letters by Mr Deacon Hume, which appeared originally in the "Morning Chronicle," under the signature of H.B.T.'.] 16p. *8°. Manchester: National Anti-Corn-Law League, J. Gadsby, printer,* [1842]

32663 —— [Another edition.] 16p. *8°. Manchester: National Anti-Corn-Law League, A. Burgess & Co.,* [1842 ?]

32664 JENKYN, T. W. Corn laws & clergy: a letter to the Right Hon. Henry Lord Brougham. 8p. *8°. Manchester: National Anti-Corn-Law League,* [1842]

32665 A **LETTER,** addressed to the Lord Bishop of Chester, on the corn laws. By a layman. 32p. *8°.* 1842.

32666 A **LETTER** to his Grace the Duke of Buckingham. By a practical farmer and corn merchant. [Signed: A Lincolnshire farmer, and dated, February 21st, 1842. On the corn laws.] 18p. *8°. n.p.,* 1842.

32667 LOUDON, M. Corn laws. Selections from Mrs. Loudon's Philanthropic economy. 4p. *8°. Manchester: National Anti-Corn-Law League, printed by Simpson & Gillett,* [1842]

32668 —— [Another edition.] 4p. *8°. Manchester: National Anti-Corn-Law League, printed by J. Gadsby,* [1842] *For an edition of the complete work, see* 1835 (SOCIALISM).

32669 M'CULLAGH, W. T. The corn laws. Speech of W. Torrens M'Cullagh, Esq....To the National Anti-Corn-Law League, December 1, 1842. 8p. *12°. Manchester,* [1842]

32670 MASSIE, JAMES W. The arrogance of Sir Robert Peel exposed, and his sliding scale committed to the fire. Rev. J. W. Massie's speech, March 22nd, 1842. With the protest of the Manchester Anti-Corn-Law Associations against the new Corn Bill, and God's judgment on a Bishop. 12p. *12°. Manchester,* [1842]

32671 MURRAY, JOHN (*fl.* 1842). A letter to the President and members of the Birmingham Anti-Corn-Law Association on the corn and provision laws. 20p. *12°. Manchester,* 1842.

32672 NATIONAL ANTI-CORN-LAW LEAGUE. Authorities against the corn laws. [With 'The Anti-Corn-Law League and the Duke of Wellington', signed: P. A. Taylor, chairman, and dated, Aug., 1, 1842.] 4p. *8°. Manchester, printed by J. Gadsby*, [1842]

32673 —— [Another edition.] 4p. *8°. Manchester: printed by J. Gadsby*, [1842]

32674 —— [Another edition.] 4p. *8°. Manchester: printed at the Advertiser Office*, [1842]

32675 —— [Another edition.] 8p. *8°. Manchester: Haycraft, printer*, [1842 ?]

32676 —— The bazaar gazette, in connexion with the National Anti-Corn-Law Bazaar, held in the Theatre Royal, Manchester, during the week commencing January 31st, 1842. To be published on the mornings of the six Bazaar days. Monday [–Saturday]. 48p. *8°. Manchester*, 1842. *See also 1845.*

32677 —— The three prize essays on agriculture and the corn law. [By George Hope, Arthur Morse and William Rathbone Greg.] Published by the National Anti-Corn-Law League. 16, 16, 18p. *8°. Manchester & London*, 1842.

32678 —— [Another edition.] 16, 16, 18p. *8°. Manchester & London*, 1842.

32679 *—— [Another edition.] 16, 18, 16p. *8°. Manchester & London*, 1842. *The FWA copy that belonged to William Pare. See also 1843.*

32680 NEATE, C. Summary of debates and proceedings in Parliament relating to the corn laws, from the year 1812 to the year 1840. 56p. *8°.* 1842. *The copy that belonged to T. Spring Rice, Baron Monteagle.*

32681 NOEL, HON. B. W. Corn laws. Selections from A plea for the poor. 8p. *8°. Manchester: National Anti-Corn-Law League, printed by R. Wood*, [1842]

32682 —— [Another edition.] Corn laws: selections... 8p. *8°. Manchester: National Anti-Corn-Law League, printed by J. Gadsby*, [1842]

32683 —— [Another edition.] Corn laws. Selections... 8p. *8°. Manchester: National Anti-Corn-Law League, printed by J. Gadsby*, [1842] *For editions of the complete work, see 1841.*

32684 O'CONNELL, D. Observations on corn laws, on political pravity and ingratitude, and on clerical and personal slander, in the shape of a meek and modest reply to the second letter of the Earl of Shrewsbury, Waterford and Wexford, to Ambrose Lisle Phillipps. 182p. *8°. Dublin*, 1842.

32685 PEEL, SIR ROBERT, *2nd Bart.* Speech of Sir R. Peel on the proposed modification of the corn laws. Delivered in the House of Commons...February 8[9] 1842. 16p. *8°.* [1842]

32686 —— [Another edition.] No. I. – Speeches in Parliament – 1842. Speech of Sir Robert Peel on the corn laws, in the House of Commons...Feb. 9, 1842. 30p. *8°.* [1842]

32687 [**PERRY,** STEPHEN.] Dialogue on the corn laws, between a gentleman and a farmer. 16p. *8°.* 1842.

32688 [——] [Another edition.] 8p. *8°. Manchester: National Anti-Corn-Law League*, [1842 ?]

32689 PLATT, J. C. History of the corn-laws. 68p. *12°.* 1842.

32690 A **PLEA** for the English farmer and the English peasantry, in an appeal to the reason of the British public, on the corn laws. By a friend to the plough, the loom and the sail. [Dated: Middle Temple, Dec. 1841.] 32p. *8°.* 1842.

32691 A **PLEA** for the total and immediate repeal of the corn laws: with remarks on the land-tax fraud, and a table of the official "valued rental" of 100 parishes of Scotland in 1650–67; with the rental of the same in 1791–6, and at the present time, 1832–41, &c. &c. (*Anti-Corn Law Tract*, 1.) Fourth edition enlarged. 47p. *12°.* 1842. *For other editions, see 1841.*

32692 RUSSELL, JOHN, *Earl Russell.* Speech of Lord John Russell on the corn laws. Delivered in the House of Commons, February 14, 1842. 16p. *8°.* [1842]

32693 Som moar tauk [**TALK**] o beawt corn laws 'o fore breykfast' between Joan o'th Wams ud Ratton Barroks, near Littlebruff, un Bob o' Sawnis, ud Windy Harbur, e Rossendall. 8p. *12°. Manchester: J. Gadsby, Anti-corn-law Depot*, [1842 ?]

32694 [**TAYLOR,** WILLIAM C.] The Quarterly Reviewer reviewed; or, notices of an article entitled "Anti-corn-law agitation," which has appeared in the number just published of that quarterly organ of monopoly. By Censor. 8p. *8°. Manchester & London*, 1842.

32695 TEMPLE, H. J., *Viscount Palmerston.* Speech of the Right Honourable Viscount Palmerston, in the House of Commons on...the 16th of February, 1842, on Lord John Russell's motion against a sliding scale of duties on the importation of foreign corn. 20p. *8°.* 1842. *The copy that belonged to T. Spring Rice, Baron Monteagle, with his signature on the title-page.*

32696 —— Second edition. 20p. *8°.* 1842.

32697 THOMPSON, GEORGE (1804–1878). Farewell address of George Thompson, Esq., to the National Anti-Corn-Law League...Oct. 27, 1842, previous to his leaving England for India. 12p. *12°. Manchester*, [1842]

32698 —— Lecture on the corn laws. 18p. *12°. Carlisle*, [1842]

32699 —— Paradise regained by Sir James Graham, Bart. [An anti-corn-law lecture, at Longtown.] 24p. *12°. Carlisle*, [1842]

32700 —— Price one half-penny. Speech of Geo. Thompson, Esq. at the great Anti-Corn-Law Conference, held in London, on...the 6th July, 1842. (From the Morning Chronicle of July 7th.) 4p. *8°. Manchester*, [1842]

32701 THOMPSON, THOMAS P. Corn laws. Extracts from the works of Col. T. Perronet Thompson, author of the "Catechism on the corn laws." Selected and classified by R. Cobden, Esq., M.P., and published with the consent of the author. 16p. *8°. Manchester: National Anti-Corn-Law League, printed by J. Gadsby*, [1842]

32702 VERSES written expressly for the Rochdale table at the National Anti-Corn-Law Bazaar, held at Manchester, January 31st, 1842. 8p. *8°. Rochdale*, [1842] *Printed on yellow paper.*

32703 W——., E. To the landed proprietors...A dialogue between two farmers [Mr. Williams and Mr. Jones], on the present prospects of agriculture, the tendency of cheap bread, and the ruin that must inevitably fall upon old England under existing legislative measures ...Birkenhead, December, 1842. 24p. *12°. Birmingham*, [1842]

POPULATION

32704 LOUDON, C. Solution du problème de la population et de la subsistance, soumise à un médecin dans une série de lettres. 336p. *8°. Paris, Londres, &c.,* 1842. *Presentation copy from the author to Sir William Cubitt.*

TRADES & MANUFACTURES

32705 BISCHOFF, J. A comprehensive history of the woollen and worsted manufactures, and the natural and commercial history of sheep, from the earliest records to the present period. 2 vols. *8°. London & Leeds,* 1842.

32706 BRUNTON, R. A compendium of mechanics; or text book for engineers, mill-wrights, machine-makers, founders, smiths, &c.... Seventh edition, carefully revised and enlarged. 226p. *12°. Glasgow, London, &c.,* 1842. *For another edition, see* 1825.

32707 EWBANK, T. A descriptive and historical account of hydraulic and other machines for raising water, ancient and modern; including the progressive development of the steam engine... 582p. *8°.* 1842.

32708 FOWLER, CHARLES, *civil engineer.* Fowler's universal compendium of manufactories. Shewing, by a comparative statement, the rise, progress, and the present state of the cotton, flax, woollen, worsted, and silk mills... in... Great Britain and Ireland... with those of foreign states... and the British colonies. An analysis of the professions and trades of the West, and part of the East and North Ridings of Yorkshire... 19p. *12°. Leeds,* [1842]

32709 FRANCIS, G. W. The dictionary of the arts, sciences, and manufactures, illustrated with... engravings. [464]p. *8°.* 1842.

32710 GIGAULT DE LA BÉDOLLIÈRE, E. Les industriels, mètiers et professions en France... Avec cent dessins par Henry Monnier. 231p. *8°. Paris,* 1842.

32711 GRANTHAM, J. Iron, as a material for ship-building; being a communication to the Polytechnic Society of Liverpool. 96p. *8°. London, Liverpool, &c.,* 1842.

32712 MARTIN, WILLIAM (1772-1851). [*Begin.*] Martin's Swan-foot paddle oar for propelling water craft, whether boats or ships, or worked by hand or steam. (From the Great Northern Advertiser, Newcastle-upon-Tyne, Aug. 18, 1842.) *s.sh.12°. n.p.,* [1842]

32713 —— The philosopher's invention for purifying water; also, the blind ignorance of all medical men cleared away, the exposure of the twelfth scientific meeting at Manchester, and other subjects. 4p. *8°. Newcastle,* [1842]

32714 ROBERTSON, J. C., & CO. The Act (5 & 6 Vic., Cap. C.) to consolidate and amend the laws relating to copyright of designs for ornamenting articles of manufacture. With explanatory notes... 23p. *8°.* 1842.

32715 WHITTOCK, N., *and others.* The complete book of trades, or, the parents' guide and youths' instructor; forming a popular encyclopædia of trades, manufactures, and commerce... in England... including a copious table of every trade, profession... and calling... Together with the apprentice fee usually given with each, and an estimate of the sums required for commencing business. By several hands, viz. Mr. N. Whittock, Mr. J. Bennett, Mr. J. Badcock, Mr. C. Newton, and others... 495p. *12°.* 1842.

COMMERCE

32716 ALLEN, ELISHA H. Speech of Mr. Allen, of Maine, on the Bill "To provide revenue from imports, and to change and modify existing laws imposing duties on imports, and for other purposes." Delivered in the House of Representatives U.S. July 11, 1842. 20p. *8°. Washington,* 1842.

For **BEILAGE ZUR ALLGEMEINEN ZEITUNG** [nos. 221-243, containing 'Die englische Speculation auf Erhaltung der Hansestädte als Freihäfen im Zollverein' by M. Mohl], *see* vol. III, *Periodicals list.*

32717 COBDEN, R. Speech of R. Cobden, Esq., M.P. in reply to Sir Robert Peel, in the House of Commons, on... July 11, 1842. 4p. *12°. Manchester,* [1842]

32718 DUPIN, F. C. P., *Baron.* Sur l'importation des céréales dans la Grande-Bretagne. Extrait de la Revue Britannique, numéro de janvier 1842. 11p. *8°. Paris,* [1842] *Presentation copy, with inscription, from the author to the President of the Board of Trade (the Earl of Ripon).*

32719 FIFE, *County of.* Fife fiars from 1619 to 1841 inclusive, reckoned in Scots money from 1619 to 1787, and in sterling money from 1787 to 1841. To which is prefixed the Act of Sederunt, dated December 21, 1723, for regulating the proceedings. 69p. *12°. Cupar,* 1842. *Spaces for the years 1842-52 have been left blank, and are completed in manuscript. Inserted in the volume are forms for single-yearly fiars from the 1850 crop to that of 1884 (1876, 1878-9 supplied in manuscript). See also* 1846.

32720 HOFKEN, G. Der deutsche Zollverein in seiner Fortbildung. 596p. *8°. Stuttgart & Tübingen,* 1842.

32721 LAW of principal and factor. Statement of its defects and the remedy, read at a meeting of deputations from the commercial associations of Liverpool, appointed to consider the state of the law, on the 26th January, 1842, and ordered to be printed. 23p. *8°. Liverpool,* 1842. *Addressed and sent through the post to Col. Charles Richard Fox (1796-1873), M.P.*

32722 McCULLOCH, JOHN R. Memorandum on the proposed importation of foreign beef and live stock, addressed to Alexander Murray, Esq. M.P. 10p. *8°.* 1842.

32723 NOBACK, C. A. Der Handel in Compagnie, in

merkantilischer und rechtlicher Hinsicht theoretisch und praktisch erläutert...Zweite Auflage. 256p. *8°*. *Weimar*, 1842.

32724 NORTH AMERICAN COLONIAL ASSOCIATION. Memoir on the colonial timber trade, presented to the Right Honourable Sir Robert Peel, Bart. by the committee of the...Association. 27p. *8°*. 1842.

32725 NOTES on the commerce of France in 1840, considered principally with regard to the trade with England and the United States, and also the general trade in cotton and silk. Taken from official documents published by the French Government. 8, 50p. *8°*. *Manchester*, 1842.

32726 OSIANDER, H. F. Ueber den Handelsverkehr der Völker...Zweite Auflage. 2 vols. *8°*. *Stuttgart*, 1842.

32727 PETIT DE BARONCOURT, . Atteinte à la liberté des mers. Du droit de visite maritime accordé à l'Angleterre par les puissances du continent. [A discussion of the economic consequences to France and the rest of Europe.] 26p. *8°*. *Paris*, 1842.

32728 RIBEIRO SARAIVA, A. Do tratado de commercio entre Portugal e a Gram-Bretanha. 215p. *12°*. *Londres*, 1842.

32729 SCHAUER DE MARCKOLSHEIM, L. Encore le droit de visite. Revue administrative de la marine française. 120p. *8°*. *Paris*, 1842.

32730 SOETBEER, A. Statistik des hamburgischen Handels. 1839. 1840. 1841. (*Ueber Hamburgs Handel*, erste Fortsetzung.) 420p. *8°*. *Hamburg*, 1842. *For the original work*, Ueber Hamburgs Handel, *see* 1840; *for a later continuation*, 1846.

COLONIES

For **AGRICULTURAL AND HORTICULTURAL SOCIETY OF INDIA,** Journal, 1842–72, *see* vol. III, *Periodicals list*, Journal...

32731 BELL, Sir F. D. and **YOUNG,** F. Reasons for promoting the cultivation of the New Zealand flax. 34p. *8°*. 1842.

32732 BONNYCASTLE, Sir R. H. The Canadas in 1841. 2 vols. *12°*. 1842, 1841.

32733 BROOKE, Sir James, *Rajah of Sarawak*. A letter from Borneo; with notices of the country and its inhabitants. Addressed to James Gardner, Esq. [Edited by John C. Templer.] 40p. *8°*. 1842.

32734 CANADA. *Legislative Assembly*. Report of a special committee of the Legislative Assembly of Canada, on the subject of a free trade with Great Britain, in the agricultural productions of British North America. And of a protection to those productions from the competition of foreigners in the colonial and home markets. Ordered... to be printed, 10th October, 1842. 40p. *8°*. *Kingston* [*Ontario*], [1842]

32735 CANADA COMPANY. A statement of the satisfactory results which have attended emigration to Upper Canada, from the establishment of the Canada Company, until the present period...Compiled for the guidance of emigrants. Fourth edition. With additional information to the present time. 114p. *8°*. 1842. *For another edition, see* 1841.

32736 CRAWFORD, John, *Esq.* Employment for the million; or, emigration & colonization on a national or extended scale, the remedy for national distress; in a letter addressed to Her Majesty's Ministers. 12p. *8°*. 1842.

32737 *EDMONSTONE, G. F. Report on the settlement of the District of Mynpooree, completed... 16th November, 1840... 85p. *8°*. *Agra*, 1842.

32738 FOX, Sir William. Colonization and New Zealand. 24p. *12°*. 1842.

32739 [GORE, M.] Letter to His Grace the Duke of Wellington, &c. &c. &c. on the present state of affairs in India. 32p. *8°*. 1842.

32740 HEALE, T. New Zealand and the New Zealand Company: being a consideration of how far their interests are similar. In answer to a pamphlet entitled How to colonize: the interest of the country, and the duty of Government. 63p. *8°*. 1842.

32741 JAMESON, R. G. New Zealand, South Australia, and New South Wales: a record of recent travels in these colonies, with especial reference to emigration and the advantageous employment of labour and capital. 372p. *12°*. 1842.

32742 A LETTER to the Right Hon. Lord Stanley, M.P. Principal Secretary of State for the Colonies, on the sugar question, with some account of the anomalous position of Barbados, with reference to the other possessions of the Crown in the Western Archipelago. By a late member of the House of Assembly. 60p. *8°*. 1842. *The copy that belonged to Mark Pattison.*

32743 *MANSEL, C. G. Report on the settlement of the District of Agra, completed...30th April, 1841... 76p. *8°*. *Agra*, 1842.

32744 NEW ZEALAND COMPANY. Latest information from the settlement of New Plymouth, on the coast of Taranake, New Zealand. Comprising letters from settlers there...Published under the direction of the West of England Board of the New Zealand Company. 57p. *12°*. 1842.

32745 PETRE, Hon. H. W. An account of the settlements of the New Zealand Company, from personal observation during a residence there...The fifth edition. 48p. *12°*. 1842. *For another edition, see* 1841.

32746 *ROSE, Hugh. Report on the settlement of the District of Cawnpore, completed...15th February, 1841... 43p. *8°*. *Agra*, 1842.

32747 ROSS, H. J. Thoughts on the objectionable system of labour for wages in the West India colonies; and on the necessity of substituting a system of tenancy and allotment of the staple cultivation. 114p. *8°*. 1842. *The copy that belonged to G. R. Porter, with his signature on the half-title.*

32748 SPRYE, R. S. M. [*Begin.*] To George Lyall, Esquire...and the directors of the East India Company: the humble memorial of Richard S. M. Sprye...[Founded on the trials under martial law of Coormarauze Narraindra Row, Bahaudar, Rajah of Polcondah; Stree Pedda Juggiah, Mahadury, Ranee of Polcondah, Barsoor Nursimha

Patroodo, Deewan of the Rajah of Polcondah, and others. With appendixes.] 128, viiip. *8°. n.p.* [1842 ?]

32749 TERRY, CHARLES, *F.R.S.* New Zealand, its advantages and prospects, as a British colony; with a full account of the land claims, sales of Crown lands, aborigines, etc. etc. 366p. *8°.* 1842.

32750 *THORNTON, EDWARD (1799–1875). Report on the settlement of the District of Moozuffurnuggur, completed…14th. August, 1841… 36p. *8°. Agra,* 1842.

32751 TORRENS, R. A letter and a memorial addressed to the Right Honourable Lord John Russell [on the removal of Torrens from the Board of Commissioners for South Australia]. 31p. *8°.* 1842.

32752 *VIBART, J. Report submitted to Government …Dated 24th February, 1842. Containing a general account of measures adopted, or contemplated, for the improvement of the revenue administration, in the Bombay Presidency, from December 1838, to February 1840. 19p. *8°. n.p.* [1842 ?]

32753 The **WEST INDIA MANUAL;** containing general information respecting the British and foreign colonies, with the routes of the steam packets, &c. 157p. *12°.* 1842.

FINANCE

32754 APPLETON, N. Speech of Mr. Appleton, of Mass., on the tariff and compromise act, delivered in the House of Representatives, July 5, 1842. 10p. *8°. Washington,* 1842.

32755 ARISTIDES, *pseud.* A letter to the shareholders in the Bank of Western India…Reprinted from a copy received from Bombay by the last mail. 48p. *8°.* 1842.

32756 ATTWOOD, M. The speech of M. Attwood, Esq. M.P. on the income tax, Committee of Ways and Means, in the House of Commons, on…March 23rd, 1842. Extracted from Hansard's Parliamentary Debates. 16p. *8°.* [*London,* 1842]

32757 BANK OF ENGLAND. The names and descriptions of the proprietors of all government funds and securities, transferrable at the Bank of England, whose stock and dividends have been transferred to the Commissioners for the Reduction of the National Debt…With the dates when the first dividends respectively become payable thereon… 18p. *8°. Printed at the Bank of England,* 1842.

32758 BANK OF MANCHESTER. 7th October, 1842. [*Begin.*] Sir, I beg to inform you…[A circular letter, signed by William Smith, managing director, informing customers that the directors are about to recommend winding up the affairs of the Bank, and recommending them to transfer their accounts to the Manchester and District Banking Company.] *s.sh.4°. n.p.* [1842]

32759 —— 7th October, 1842. [*Begin.*] Sir, I do hereby give you notice…[Letter to shareholders, informing them of a call of £2 per share, on 12 December, 1842. Signed: William Smith, managing director.] *s.sh.4°. n.p.* [1842]

32760 —— 14th October, 1842. [*Begin.*] Notice is hereby given…[A circular convening a special general meeting for 7 December 1842, arising out of the financial difficulties of the Company. Signed, on behalf of the Board of Directors, by William Smith, managing director.] *s.sh.4°. n.p.* [1842]

32761 —— Report of the directors to the thirteenth annual general meeting of proprietors, held at Hayward's Hotel, Bridge-Street, 14th October, 1842. [Recommending the dissolution of the Company. With a list of proprietors.] 18p. *8°. Manchester,* [1842] *See also* 1841.

32762 BANKRUPTCY LAW amendment. At a meeting of members of the grocery, oil and wine & spirit trades, held…8th Sept. 1842, Ralph Price, Esq. in the chair. The following report of the committee appointed at a…meeting of the grocery, oil, and wine and spirit trades, held…on the 3rd day of May last, to improve the Bill for the amendment of the bankrupt law…was read. 3p. *fol. n.p.* [1842] *In a volume of papers relating to the reform of the bankruptcy laws, which belonged to Sir Benjamin Hawes, M.P.*

32763 BARNARD, D. D. Speech of Mr. Barnard, of New York, on the veto of the provisional tariff bill, delivered in the House of Representatives, July 1, 1842. 12p. *8°. Washington,* 1842.

32764 —— Speech of Mr. Barnard, of New York, on the policy of a protective tariff. Delivered in the House of Representatives U.S. July 6, 1842. 14p. *8°. Washington,* 1842.

32765 BARNES & CARROLL, *Ship and Insurance Brokers, comps.* Tariff, or rates of duties from…the 30th day of August, 1842, on all goods, wares and merchandise imported into the United States of America as established by Act of Congress. With an appendix, containing rules and regulations as adopted by the Chamber of Commerce …together with port wardens' regulations…useful to importers, ship owners and masters of vessels… 135p. *12°. Philadelphia,* 1842.

32766 BEAUMONT, JOHN A. Thoughts and details on life insurance offices, in a letter to the shareholders and insured in the Provident Life Office. [With an appendix containing an account of the Provident Life Office and a report of the annual general meeting of February 1842.] 46p. *8°.* 1842.

32767 BELL, GAVIN M. The country banks and the currency; an examination of the evidence on banks of issue, given before a Select Committee of the House of Commons in 1841. 150p. *8°.* 1842.

32768 BENDA, D. A. Robert Peel's Finanz-System oder ueber die Vorzüge der Einkommensteuer im Gegensatze zu Staats-Anleihen und Zinsreductionen. 139p. *8°. Berlin,* 1842.

32769 BERRY, C. The natural laws of money and commerce. 19p. *8°.* 1842.

32770 BIDLACK, B. A. Speech of Mr. Bidlack, of Pennsylvania, on the revenue bill: delivered in the House of Representatives, July 5, 1842. 16p. *8°. Washington,* 1842.

32771 BOSANQUET, J. W. Metallic, paper, and credit currency, and the means of regulating their quantity and value. 155p. *8°.* 1842.

32772 BOTTS, J. M. Speech of Mr. Botts, of Virginia,

on the tariff bill. Delivered in the House of Representatives, July 12, 1842. 15p. *8°. Washington,* 1842.

32773 *[BRIDGES, W.] The **hand-book** for life assurers. Being a popular guide to the knowledge of the system of life assurance; with an exposition of its advantage...together with an explanation of the various modes of doing business; also a general directory of insurance companies, in Great Britain and Ireland... 143p. *8°. London & Edinburgh,* 1842. *The copy that belonged to Augustus De Morgan.*

32774 **BRIERLY,** T. Thoughts on currency, banking, and the funds, home and foreign. A letter to the Right Hon. Henry Goulburn, Chancellor of Her Majesty's Exchequer, etc. 18p. *8°. Dublin,* 1842. *Presentation copy from the author to the Duke of Wellington.*

32775 **BROCKWAY,** J. H. Speech of Mr. Brockway, of Connecticut, upon the tariff bills reported by the Committee of Ways and Means and the Committee on Manufactures: delivered in the House of Representatives, June 20, 1842. 20p. *8°. Washington,* 1842.

32776 **BROUGHAM,** H. P., *Baron Brougham and Vaux.* Lord Brougham's speech on the income tax. In the House of Lords, March 17, 1842. 29p. *8°.* 1842.

32777 **BROWN,** M. Speech of Hon. Milton Brown, of Tenn., on the general tariff bill. Delivered in the House of Representatives of the U.S. July 7, 1842. 23p. *8°. Washington,* 1842.

32778 **CARUTHERS,** R. L. Speech of Mr. Caruthers, of Tennessee, on the veto of the temporary tariff bill. Delivered in the House of Representatives U.S. July 1, 1842. 28p. *8°. Washington,* 1842.

32779 The **CASE** of the bonâ fide holders of the repudiated Exchequer Bills, briefly stated. 14p. *8°.* 1842.

32780 **CHOATE,** R. Speech of Mr. Choate, of Massachusetts, on the power and duty of Congress to continue the policy of protecting American labor: delivered in the Senate of the United States March 14, 1842. [On the right of Congress to protect home industry by tariffs.] 36p. *8°. Washington,* 1842.

32781 **CIVIS,** *pseud.* A letter to Lord John Russell, on the cause of the distress of the manufacturing classes of England, with a proposed remedy. 39p. *8°.* 1842.

32782 **CLAY,** H. Speech of Mr. Clay, of Kentucky, upon his resolutions concerning the tariff, and other great objects of public polity. Delivered in the Senate of the United States, March 1, 1842. 23p. *8°. Washington,* 1842.

32783 **COBDEN,** R. The land-tax fraud. Speech of R. Cobden, Esq., M.P. in the House of Commons on... March 14th, 1842. 7p. *12°. Manchester & London,* [1842]

32784 —— The tariff, &c. Mr. Cobden's speech, April 18th, 1842. 4p. *12°. Manchester,* [1842]

32785 [COCKBURN, R.] Remarks on prevailing errors respecting currency and banking. 84p. *8°.* 1842. *See also* 1844.

32786 [COLLIER, JOSHUA.] Second edition... Graduated scale for a property tax. By the author of "The reply to the state of the nation," anno 1822. 20p. *8°.* 1842. *For another edition, see* 1833.

32787 **COMMITTEE OF MERCHANTS IN THE WINE AND SPIRIT TRADE.** Report of the Committee, appointed at a general meeting of the wine trade, held...26 July, 1842, to take into consideration the measures to be adopted in consequence of the reduction in the duties upon wine, expected to take place, on the conclusion of the commercial treaty with Portugal: George Barnes, Esq., in the chair. 40p. *8°.* 1842.

32788 **COMPANY OF MERCHANTS OF EDINBURGH.** Act of Parliament relative to the general and widows' scheme funds of the Company of Merchants...being 7° & 8° Geo IV. cap. 40. With the rules and bye-laws of the Company; and reports in reference to the above-mentioned funds, by Mr. Patrick Cockburn and Mr. Donald Lindsay, accountants, and index... 136p. *8°. Edinburgh,* 1842.

32789 **COOPER,** JAMES. Remarks of the Hon. J. Cooper, of Pennsylvania, on the Treasury note bill, in the House of Representatives of the United States, January 10, 1842. 8p. *8°. n.p.* [1842]

32790 **COPIES** of petitions presented to the Right Honourable Sir Robert Peel, Bart. M.P. On the timber duties. 45p. *8°.* 1842.

32791 **COWEN,** B. S. Speech of Hon. B. S. Cowen, of Ohio, in favor of a protective tariff. Delivered in the House of Representatives of the United States June 21, 1842. 16p. *8°. n.p.,* [1842]

32792 **CUNEO,** C. Memorie sopra l'antico Debito Pubblico, Mutui, Compere e Banca di S. Giorgio in Genova. 324p. *8°. Genova,* [1842]

32793 **CUSHING,** C. Tariff vs. distribution. [Speech of Mr. Cushing on his amendment to the tariff bill.] 8p. *8°. n.p.* [1842]

32794 **DALY,** T. The expediency of a national bank, with suggestions for the reform of our monetary system. 30p. *8°.* 1842.

32795 **DOUGLAS,** R. K. Brief considerations on the income tax and tariff reform, in connection with the present state of the currency. 32p. *8°. Birmingham,* 1842.

32796 **DRUCKER,** L. Public funds considered in regard to investment of money. 55p. *8°. Amsterdam,* 1842.

32797 —— [Another issue.] 55p. *8°. Amsterdam,* 1842.

32798 **DURIEU,** E. Formulaire de la comptabilité des percepteurs et des receveurs des communes, des hospices et des bureaux de bienfaisance, contenant les modèles de l'instruction générale du Ministère des Finances, en date du 17 juin 1840... 472p. *8°. Paris,* 1842.

32799 **EAST INDIA BANK.** Private and confidential – for consideration. The East India Bank. Capital £250,000... [A prospectus. Signed: R. Montgomery Martin.] 16p. *8°.* [1842]

32800 Mercantile **EMBARRASSMENTS,** and the present state of the banking system. [Two letters signed: A statist.] 47p. *8°. Edinburgh,* 1842.

32801 **ENDERBY,** C. Currency: inquiry solicited; but general declamation, without reasoning, disregarded. [With 'Court of Queen's Bench. The East India Company versus Lord Stenlee'. An imaginary trial.] 43p. *8°.* 1842.

32802 —— Second edition. 44p. *8°.* 1842.

32803 **EVANS,** GEORGE (1797–1867). Speech of Mr. Evans, of Maine, upon the resolutions of Mr. Clay, relating to the revenues and expenditures of the government, and the necessity of augmented duties upon imports. Delivered in the Senate of the United States, March 17 and 18, 1842. 44p. *8°. Washington,* 1842.

32804 FELKIN, W. Observations in favour of a property tax, made in the Town Council of Nottingham, August 12, 1841, and the petition ordered thereon. [With 'Property, not labour, the proper subject of taxation'.] 16p. *8°. Norwich, London, &c., 1842. With inscription on the title-page: With Mr. Wm. Felkin's respects.*

32805 FESSENDEN, W. P. Speech of Mr. Fessenden, of Maine, upon the army appropriation bill. Delivered in the House of Representatives of the United States, May 31, 1842. 16p. *8°. Washington, 1842.*

32806 FILLMORE, M., *President of the USA.* Speech of Mr. Fillmore, of New York, on the tariff bill. Delivered in the Committee of the Whole, House of Representatives, June 9, 1842. 24p. *8°. Washington, 1842.*

32807 GAMBLE, R. L. Speech of R. L. Gamble, of Georgia, in reply to Mr. M. A. Cooper, of Georgia, and on the subject of the tariff, both for revenue and protection. Delivered in the House of Representatives, July 7, 1842. 23p. *8°. Washington, 1842.*

32808 GENTRY, M. P. Speech of Mr. Gentry, of Tennessee, on an amendment submitted by him to the tariff bill, providing for the payment of certain debts of the States. Delivered in the House of Representatives, July 11, 1842. 16p. *8°. Washington, 1842.*

32809 —— Speech of Mr. Gentry, of Tennessee, on the loan bill, in reply to Messrs. Wise and Profitt. Delivered in the House of Representatives, March 28, 1842. 24p. *8°. Washington, 1842.*

32810 GILMER, T. W. Remarks of Mr. Gilmer, of Virginia, in Committee of the Whole, March 9, 1842, on the motion to strike out the contingent appropriations from the bill making appropriations for the civil and diplomatic expenses of government... 8p. *8°. n.p. [1842]*

32811 GOGGIN, W. L. Speech of Mr. Goggin, of Virginia, on the public lands; the policy of distributing the proceeds thereof among the States, and on the proper means of raising revenue. Delivered in the House of Representatives, United States, June 10, 1842. 21p. *8°. Washington, 1842.*

32812 The GOVERNMENT currency pamphlets. No. 1[–2]. 55p. *8°. [1842–43]*

32813 GRAHAM, JAMES (1793–1851). Speech of Mr. James Graham, of North Carolina, on the proposition to abolish the branch mints: delivered in the House of Representatives, April 4, 1842. 8p. *8°. Washington, 1842.*

32814 GRAHAM, W. A. Speech of Hon. William A. Graham, of North Carolina, on the loan bill. Delivered in the Senate of the United States, April 13, 1842. 13p. *8°. Washington, 1842.*

32815 [GREG, J. R.] Observations on the proposed duties on the exportation of coals; with tables and statements, from parliamentary returns and other authentic sources. April 1842. 41p. *8°. [1842]*

32816 HALL, H. Speeches of Mr. H. Hall, of Vermont, on the Virginia bounty land claims. Delivered in the House of Representatives of the U.S., June 16 and 25, 1842. 23p. *8°. Washington, 1842.*

32817 HASTINGS, J. Remarks of Mr. John Hastings, of Ohio, on the tariff bill. Delivered in the House of Representatives, July 9, 1842. 13p. *8°. Washington, 1842.*

32818 [HILDITCH, R.] Aristocratic taxation: its present state, origin, and progress, with proposals for reform. 52p. *8°. London & Manchester, 1842.*

32819 The HISTORY and mystery of the exchequer bills forgery examined: a letter to the Rt. Hon. Henry Goulburn, Chancellor of Her Majesty's Exchequer. 56p. *8°. 1842. The copy that belonged to T. Spring Rice, Baron Monteagle.*

32820 HODGES, SIR W. The law relating to the assessment of railways to the relief of the poor, with a report of the case and judgment in the Queen v. the London and South Western Railway Company. Decided in the Court of Queen's Bench, June 4th, 1842. 31p. *8°. 1842.*

32821 HUDSON, C. Speech of Mr. Hudson, of Massachusetts, on the subject of discriminating duties. Delivered in the House of Representatives, December 27 & 28, 1841. 16p. *8°. Washington, 1842.*

32822 —— Speech of Mr. Hudson, of Massachusetts, on the tariff bills. Delivered in the Committee of the Whole H.R. July 8, 1842. 20p. *8°. n.p., [1842]*

32823 HUNT, W. Speech of Mr. Hunt, of New York, on the tariff bills reported by the Committee of Ways and Means and the Committee on Manufactures. Delivered in Committee of the Whole, House of Representatives, June 20, 1842. 14p. *8°. Washington, 1842.*

32824 HUNTINGTON, J. W. Speech of Mr. Huntington, of Connecticut, upon the resolutions of Mr. Clay [on the tariff and free trade], delivered in the Senate of the United States, March 21, 1842. 18p. *8°. Washington, 1842.*

32825 HURD, J. R. A national bank, or no bank; an appeal to the common sense of the people of the United States; especially of the laboring classes. 104p. *8°. New York, 1842.*

32826 IRVIN, J. Speech of Mr. James Irvin, of Penn., in favor of the tariff bill reported by the Committee of Ways and Means. Delivered in the House of Representatives U.S. July 11, 1842. 27p. *8°. Washington, 1842.*

32827 IRWIN, W. W. Speech of Mr. William W. Irwin, of Pennsylvania, on the duty of Congress in the present crisis [i.e. the President's rejection of the tariff bill]; made in Committee of the Whole on the State of the Union, August 12, 1842. 8p. *8°. Washington, 1842.*

32828 JOLY, A. Mémoire au Roi sur la refonte des monnaies de billon... Nouveau système monétaire historique. 23p. *4°. Paris, 1842. Presentation copy, with inscription, from the author to the Duc d'Orléans.*

32829 JONES, ISAAC D. Remarks of Mr. I. D. Jones, of Maryland, on the apportionment bill. Delivered in the House of Representatives U.S. June 16, 1842. 8p. *8°. Washington, 1842.*

32830 [LA HAYE, L. M. DE, *Vicomte de Cormenin.*] Avis aux contribuables, par Timon. 3e édition. [With 'Pièces justificatives et curieuses'.] 62p. *16°. Paris, 1842.*

32831 [——] Deuxième avis aux contribuables, ou réponse au Ministre des Finances, par Timon. (2e édition.) [With 'Pièce justificative et curieuse'.] 40p. *16°. Paris, 1842.*

32832 LAMBERT, ALPHONSE, *Baron.* Deuxième lettre à un député sur la refonte des monnaies. 28p. *8°. Paris, 1842.*

32833 LANE, H. S. Remarks of Mr. Lane, of Indiana, on the loan bill. Delivered in Committee of the Whole House, March 28, 1842. 11p. *8°. Washington, 1842.*

32834 LANE, S. A rare row about the income tax; or,

the cat let out of the bag. [A ballad.] *s.sh.fol. n.p.* [1842]
[*Br.* 602(2)]

32835 LANG, G. H. Letter to the Right Hon. Henry Goulburn, M.P. Chancellor of the Exchequer, on the unequal pressure of the railway passenger tax. 16p. *8°. Glasgow*, 1842.

32836 LAWRENCE, ABBOTT. Remarks of Mr. Lawrence, of Boston, on the duty of Congress to continue by discriminating and specific duties, the protection of American labor, at the Convention of the shoe and leather dealers, held in Boston, March 2, 1842. 8p. *8°. Boston*, 1842.

32837 LINDSAY, JOHN. A view of the coinage of the Heptarchy; to which is added a list of unpublished mints and moneyers of the chief or sole monarchs from Egbert to Harold II.... 135p. *4°. Cork, Dublin, &c.*, 1842.

32838 LOANS by private individuals to foreign states entitled to government protection, by the fundamental laws, as a branch of trade; by parliamentary recognition; by the express declarations of Vattel; by the opinion of an eminent living jurist [William Burge], and by the official notes of the late Cabinet. 105p. *8°.* 1842.

32839 —— Second edition. 105p. *8°.* 1842. *For a continuation, see* 1843 (A sequel to loans by private individuals).

32840 LUEDERS, W. Meklenburgs Zoll-, Steuer- und Gewerbe-Verhältnisse. Beleuchtet von W. Lüders. 170p. *12°. Hamburg*, 1842.

32841 MACARDY, J. Outlines of banks, banking, and currency. 238p. *8°.* 1842. *For another edition, see* 1840.

32842 MAINE. *Laws, etc.* Twenty-second Legislature. No. 25. Senate. An act additional to an act relating to the Washington County Bank. 6p. *8°. n.p.* [1842]

32843 —— —— Twenty-second Legislature. No. 33. House. An act in relation to banks and banking. 14p. *8°. n.p.* [1842]

32844 —— —— Twenty-second Legislature. No. 36. Senate. An act in relation to institutions for savings. 7p. *8°. n.p.* [1842]

32845 —— *Secretary of State.* List of stockholders (with amount of stock held by each,) in the banks of Maine... 87p. *8°. Augusta*, 1842.

32846 On the financial MANAGEMENT of Ireland. (Reprinted from the Dublin Monthly Magazine.) [A discussion of the speech in the House of Commons, 21 July, 1842, of John O'Connell, M.P.] 20p. *8°. Dublin*, 1842.

32847 MARTIN, ROBERT M. Public proceedings and official correspondence relative to the "Bank of Asia;" collated for the information of the shareholders and supporters of that institution. 22, lxxvp. *8°.* 1842.

32848 MAYALL, T. First edition, for 1842-43. Tables of the customs and excise duties, drawbacks and bounties, to be paid...on all British and foreign goods... imported, exported, or carried coastwise, in the United Kingdom, carefully revised and brought down to the 20th day of July, 1842... 104p. *12°.* 1842.

32849 MEMORIAL of the paper manufacturers. 1842. [Signed: E. P. Tileston and 5 others, Committee in behalf of the Paper-manufacturers of the U.S., and dated, January 31, 1842. An appeal to Congress for the continuance of protection.] 14p. *8°. n.p.* [1842]

32850 MERIWETHER, J. A. Speech of J. A. Meri-wether, of Georgia, delivered in the House of Representatives, December 29 & 30, upon the motion to refer so much of the President's message as relates to discriminating duties and domestic manufactures to the Committee on Manufactures. 47p. *8°. Washington*, 1842.

32851 MILLER, JACOB W. Speech of Mr. Miller, of New Jersey, upon the resolutions of Mr. Clay: delivered in the Senate of the United States, March 15, 1842. 16p. *8°. Washington*, 1842.

32852 NATIONAL ANTI-CORN-LAW LEAGUE. The constitutional right to a revision of the land-tax. Being the argument on a case submitted to counsel on behalf of the...League. [With a prefatory note signed: George Wilson, chairman of the Council of the National Anti-Corn-Law League, and dated, March 1, 1842.] 55p. *8°. London & Manchester*, [1842]

32853 NICHOLSON, WILLIAM, *clerk to the Commissioners of the Leeds District.* The Income Tax Act, epitomized and simplified...Twenty-third thousand. 24p. *8°. London & Edinburgh*, 1842.

32854 —— Fifth edition. 24p. *8°. London & Edinburgh*, 1842.

32855 De l'ORGANISATION monétaire en France et de la refonte des monnaies de cuivre. Par un ancien fonctionnaire des monnaies. 44p. *8°. Paris*, 1842.

32856 [PAGE, R.] Banks and bankers. By Daniel Hardcastle, jun. 411p. *12°.* 1842. *See also* 1843.

32857 PAGET, J. The Income Tax Act, 5 & 6 Vict. c. 35, with a practical and explanatory introduction and index...Second edition. 178p. *12°.* 1842.

32858 PEEL, SIR ROBERT, *2nd Bart.* No. II. - Speeches in Parliament – 1842. Financial statement of Sir Robert Peel in the House of Commons...March 11, 1842. 32p. *8°.* [1842]

32859 —— Second edition. 32p. *8°.* [1842]

32860 —— Third edition. 32p. *8°.* [1842]

32861 —— [Another edition.] New scheme of taxation. A speech delivered by Sir Robert Peel in the House of Commons...March 11, 1842. 16p. *8°.* [1842]

32862 —— [Another edition.] Speech of Sir Robert Peel, on the financial condition of the country, on... March 11, 1842; with the schedules containing the new customs duties, and the tax upon property and income. Carefully revised. 52p. *8°.* 1842.

32863 —— [Another edition.] Sir Robert Peel's financial statement, as delivered by him in the House of Commons, on...March 11, 1842; with an appendix of documents, and a summary of the principal articles enumerated in the proposed new tariff. 22p. *8°. Edinburgh & London*, 1842.

32864 PEEL'S income tax, or, a miss at popularity!! [A ballad.]...No. 28. *s.sh.fol. n.p.* [1842] [*Br.* 602(1)]

32865 Sir Robert PEEL'S "Burdens on land." (*Anti-Corn Law Tract*, 2.) 36p. *12°.* 1842.

32866 PENNSYLVANIA. *General Assembly.* Majority and minority reports of the Joint Committee of the Senate and House of Representatives relative to an investigation into any corrupt means...employed by the banks, or their agents, for the purpose of influencing the action of the Legislature...in regard to any legislation for their benefit: accompanied with testimony. Read in the House of Representatives, July 12, 1842. 360p. *8°. Harrisburg*, 1842.

32867 POCOCK, L. A chronological list of books and pamphlets, relating to the doctrine of chances and the rate of mortality, annuities, reversions, marine and fire insurances, and life-assurance; with the titles of the several parliamentary reports connected with friendly societies, and of publications relating to particular life-assurance offices...The second edition. 47p. 8°. 1842. *One of a privately printed edition, limited to 100 copies. For another edition, see 1836.*

32868 —— A familiar explanation of the nature, advantages, and importance of assurances upon lives...including also a particular account of the routine required for effecting a policy...To which are added, the principles, terms, and tables, of seventy London assurance offices, and an extensive bibliographical catalogue of works on the subject. 228p. 8°. 1842.

32869 PRATT, J. T. The history of savings banks in England, Wales, Ireland, and Scotland; with the period of the establishment of each institution...and the number of depositors...with an appendix, containing all the parliamentary returns...and an account of the several savings banks in France... 79, [121]p. 8°. 1842. *A revised and enlarged version of a work published in 1830 (q.v.).*

32870 PRESTON, W. C. Speech of Mr. Preston, of South Carolina, on the loan bill. Delivered in the Senate of the United States, April, 1842. 16p. 8°. *Washington*, 1842.

32871 PRICE, D. Observations on banks of issue and the currency; addressed to Mark Philips, Esquire, M.P. London, 28th June, 1842. 6p. 8°. [1842]

32872 PYNE, H. Permanent tables, showing the value of tithe rent-charges under every variation in the price of corn...Third edition, to which is now added a particular table for each year since the passing of the Tithe Commutation Act. 162p. 8°. 1842.

32873 [*Endorsed:*] **RAILWAY-PASSENGER TAX.** Case. [A petition, with explanatory statistics, for the tax to be calculated on an ad valorem instead of a per capita basis. Signed: Archibald Grahame, Moncrieff, & Weems, Parliamentary Agents, and dated, 13th April 1842.] [4]p. *fol. n.p.* [1842]

32874 RANDOLPH, J. F. Speech of Mr. Randolph, of New Jersey, on the tariff bill, delivered in the House of Representatives, U.S., June 20, 1842. 24p. 8°. *Washington*, 1842.

32875 RAYNER, K. Speech of Mr. Rayner, of North Carolina, on the bill proposing to amend the loan bill of the last session. Delivered in Committee of the Whole, H.R., March 28, 1842. 15p. 8°. *n.p.* [1842]

32876 READ, J. M. Speech of Mr. Read, of Pennsylvania, on the bill to revise the tariff. Delivered in the House of Representatives, July 9, 1842. 7p. 8°. *n.p.* [1842]

32877 REID, JOHN. Manual of the Scottish stocks and British funds, with the anatomy of the joint stock companies in Scotland...Fourth edition. 177, 52, 74p. 12°. *Edinburgh, Glasgow, &c.,* [1842] *For another edition, see 1841.*

32878 REMARKS on trade and credit. Originally published in January, 1840; now reprinted with corrections and additions. 44p. 8°. 1842.

32879 RUSSELL, R. W. Financial reform. A digest of the reasons for and against a tax upon permanent property, in lieu of some of the present taxes, especially those on commodities. 40p. 8°. 1842.

32880 RUSSELL, WILLIAM (1782–1845). Speech of Mr. Russell, of Ohio, on the tariff bill. Delivered in the House of Representatives of the United States, July, 1842. 7p. 8°. *Washington*, 1842.

32881 SALTONSTALL, L. Speech of Mr. Saltonstall, of Massachusetts, upon the tariff bills reported by the Committee of Ways and Means and the Committee on Manufactures: delivered in the House of Representatives, June 17, 1842. 16p. 8°. *Washington*, 1842.

32882 SIMMONS, JAMES F. Speech of Mr. Simmons, of Rhode Island, on the resolutions of Mr. Clay, and in reply to Messrs. Wright, Woodbury and Calhoun. Delivered in the Senate of the United States...March 11, 1842. 20p. 8°. *Washington*, 1842.

32883 SLADE, W. Speech of Mr. Slade, of Vermont, on the tariff bill, delivered in Committee of the Whole on the State of the Union July 11 & 12, 1842. 16p. 8°. *n.p.* [1842]

32884 SMITH, OLIVER H. Speech of Hon. Oliver H. Smith, of Indiana, on the resolution of Mr. Clay and in reply to Mr. Wright, of New York. Delivered in the Senate of the United States, March 3, 1842. 28p. 8°. *Washington*, 1842.

32885 SOLLERS, A. R. Speech of A. R. Sollers, of Maryland, on the resolution offered by Mr. Fillmore, of New York, to refer that part of the President's message relative to the tariff to the Committee on Manufactures. Delivered in the House of Representatives, Dec. 21, 1841. 13p. 8°. *Washington*, 1842.

32886 STATEMENT by the distillers of the west of Scotland, respecting the distillery laws. [With an appendix of petitions, etc.] 61p. 8°. *Glasgow*, 1842.

32887 STUART, ALEXANDER H. H. Remarks of Mr. A. H. H. Stuart, of Virginia, on the veto message of the President, returning, with his objections the bill extending the laws for laying and collecting the duties on imports. Delivered in the House of Representatives, June 30, 1842. 11p. 8°. *Washington*, 1842.

32888 —— Speech of Mr. Stuart, of Virginia, on the tariff bill. Delivered in the House of Representatives, on the 8th of July, 1842. 24p. 8°. *n.p.* [1842]

32889 STUART, JOHN T. Remarks (in part) of Mr. Stuart, of Illinois, in reply to the remarks of Mr. Gwin, in relation to state banks, &c. Delivered in Committee of the Whole, House of Representatives, June, 1842. 11p. 8°. *Washington*, 1842.

32890 —— Speech of Mr. J. T. Stuart, of Illinois, on the tariff bill. Delivered in the House of Representatives of the U.S. July 9, 1842. 13p. 8°. *Washington*, 1842.

32891 TASKER, J. The case and claims, of the holders of Treasury Bonds, or exchequer bills of Spain, plainly stated in letters to the Minister of Finance, Senor Surra y Rull, the Earl of Aberdeen, and the Spanish Ambassador, General Sancho, &c. &c. with a few notes. 60p. 8°. 1842.

32892 TATE, WILLIAM (1781?–1848). The modern cambist: forming a manual of foreign exchanges, in the different occupations [*sic*] of bills of exchange and bullion; with various formulæ, and tables of foreign weights and measures...Fourth edition, with extensive alterations and additions. xviii, 212p. 8°. 1842. *For other editions, see 1834.*

32893 TAUNTON, E. The mystery of England's present misery unravelled! Or, the remedy twenty times worse than the disease; being an examination of the cause, effects and evil policy of our standard of gold being fixed at £3. 17s. 10½d. per oz. [2]p. *s.sh.fol. Birmingham*, [1842] [*Br.* 603(1)]

32894 —— Taking the bull by the horns; or, a remedy for some of old England's woes. [Signed: A traveller of 1805, E.T., and dated, August 17, 1842.] *s.sh.fol. Birmingham*, [1842] [*Br.* 603(2)]

32895 On the **TAXATION** of the United Kingdom, comprising remarks on the tax upon income, proposed to the House of Commons in 1842, and on a less objectionable direct tax. 62p. *8°*. 1842.

32896 **TAYLOR**, JAMES (1788–1863). Money should be the servant of the people not their master. A letter to William Leatham Esq. banker, Wakefield. 56p. *8°*. 1842.

32897 [——] No trust, no trade. The cause of national distress pointed out, and a prompt and effectual remedy suggested. 14p. *8°*. *G. Mann*, 1842.

32898 [——] [Another edition.] 14p. *8°*. *S. Clarke*, 1842. *For another edition, see* 1826.

32899 **THOMPSON**, RICHARD W. Speech of Mr. R. W. Thompson, of Indiana, on the tariff bills reported by the Committee of Ways and Means and the Committee on Manufactures. Delivered in the House of Representatives, June 20, 1842. 35p. *8°*. *Washington*, 1842.

32900 **THOUGHTS** on the currency. 62p. *8°*. 1842.

32901 **TILLINGHAST**, J. L. Speech of the Hon. Joseph L. Tillinghast, of Rhode Island, on the message of the President, returning the provisional tariff bill with his objections. Delivered in the House of Representatives, June 30, 1842. 20p. *8°*. *Washington*, 1842.

32902 **TORY** taxes. 19p. *8°*. 1842. *The copy presented to T. Spring Rice, Baron Monteagle.*

32903 **TRIPLETT**, P. Speech of Mr. Triplett, of Kentucky, on the tariff bill. Delivered in the Committee of the Whole, House of Representatives, July 6, 1842. 16p. *8°*. *Washington*, 1842.

32904 **VILLIERS**, C. P. Price one penny. The income tax. Mr. Villiers' speech, April 18th, 1842. 10p. *12°*. *Manchester*, [1842]

32905 **WADE**, JOHN. Principles of money: with their application to the reform of the currency and of banking, and to the relief of financial difficulties. 80p. *8°*. 1842.

32906 **WALLACE**, D. Speech of Mr. David Wallace, of Indiana, on the tariff bill reported by the Committee of Ways and Means. Delivered in the House of Representatives U.S., July 9, 1842. 14p. *8°*. *Washington*, 1842.

32907 **WARREN**, L. Speech of Mr. Lott Warren, of Georgia, on the tariff bill, and in reply to Messrs. Black and Cooper of Ga. Delivered in the House of Representatives, July, 1842. 12p. *8°*. *Washington*, 1842.

32908 **WELLS**, S. The true state of the national finances, with remedial suggestions. 340p. *12°*. 1842.

32909 **WHITE**, JOSEPH L. Remarks of Mr. White, of Indiana, on the bill to extend for a limited period the present laws for laying and collecting duties on imports. Delivered in the House of Representatives, in Committee of the Whole, June 15, 1842. 8p. *8°*. *Washington*, 1842.

32910 —— Speech of Mr. White, of Indiana, on the message of the President returning with his objections the bill "to extend for a limited period the present laws for collecting duties on imports." Delivered in the House of Representatives, U.S., July 1, 1842. 15p. *8°*. *Washington*, 1842.

32911 **WHYTOCK**, R. An inquiry into the cause of the present depression of trade, and a remedy proposed, in a measure calculated at the same time to obviate the necessity of an income-tax. 63p. *8°*. *Edinburgh, London, &c.*, 1842.

32912 **WILLICH**, C. M. Income tax tables, showing at sight the amount of duty at 7d. and 3½d. in the pound; accompanied by a variety of statistical information, extracted from parliamentary documents. [18]p. *8°*. 1842. *See also* 1843.

32913 **WINTHROP**, R. C. Speech of R. C. Winthrop, of Massachusetts, on the resolution offered by Mr. Fillmore, of New York, to refer that part of the President's message relative to the tariff to the Committee on Manufactures. Delivered in the House of Representatives, Dec. 30, 1841. 24p. *8°*. *Washington*, 1842.

32914 **WOOD**, CHARLES, *Viscount Halifax*. Speech of Charles Wood, Esq. on moving the reduction of the duty on sheep and lambs' wool, in the Committees on the Customs Acts, June 8, 1842. 36p. *8°*. 1842.

TRANSPORT

32915 **CHAMBRE DE COMMERCE**, *Boulogne*. Notice sur le port de Boulogne (Pas-de-Calais)...comparé, au point de vue du Chemin de fer de la Manche, au port de Calais... 54p. *8°*. *Boulogne*, 1842.

32916 **COOKE**, SIR WILLIAM F. Telegraphic railways; or, the single way recommended by safety, economy, and efficiency, under the safeguard and control of the electric telegraph: with particular reference to railway communication with Scotland, and to Irish railways. 39p. *8°*. 1842. *The Rastrick copy.*

32917 **GROVES**, J. R. Observations on the utility of floating breakwaters (manufactured in iron) as applied to the formation of harbours of refuge...Third edition. 29p. *8°*. 1842. *For another edition, see* 1841.

32918 **INSTITUTION OF CIVIL ENGIN-** EERS. Minutes of conversation of Institution of Civil Engineers. ⟨Excerpt from minutes of proceedings of the Institution of Civil Engineers.⟩ March 1, 1842. ['Description of the permanent way of the South-Eastern Railway', by John Pope. With discussion on it, by C. May, W. Cubitt and others.] 8p. *8°*. [1842]

32919 **LARDNER**, D. Reports on the determination of the mean value of railway constants. By Dionysius Lardner and Edward Woods, Esq. ⟨From the Report of the British Association for the Advancement of Science for 1841.⟩ p.205–306. *8°*. 1842.

32920 **LIVIUS**, B. A letter addressed to canal proprietors on the practicability of employing steam power on canals. 24p. *8°*. 1842.

32921 **LONDON**. *Court of Common Council*. Thames

embankment. Report to the Court of Common Council, from the Thames Navigation Committee. Presented 20th January, 1842. 41p. *fol. n.p.* [1842]

32922 MARTIN, William (1772–1851). Invention of metallic railways, being a refutation of a paragraph on the subject, which appeared in the newspapers. [With 'The Davy lamp condemned by the London press'.] 4p. *8°. Newcastle,* [1842]

32923 —— On railway gates, &c., &c. [With 'The philosopher's plan for clearing off the national debt'.] 4p. *8°. Newcastle,* [1842]

32924 [PEACE, J.] A descant upon railroads. By X.A.P. 41p. *8°.* 1842.

32925 PENNSYLVANIA. *Senate.* Report of the Canal Commissioners of Pennsylvania. Printed by order of the Senate, January 17, 1842. 87p. *8°. Harrisburg,* 1842.

32926 PIM, James. The atmospheric railway. A letter to the Right Hon. the Earl of Ripon, President of the Board of Trade...Second edition. 26p. *8°.* 1842. *For another edition, see* 1841.

32927 SOPWITH, T. On the preservation of railway sections, and of accounts of borings, sinkings, &c. in elucidation of the measures recently taken by the British Association. A paper read before the Geological and Polytechnic Society of the West-Riding of Yorkshire, Sept. 23rd, 1841. 16p. *8°. Leeds,* 1842. *The Rastrick copy.*

32928 STOCKTON AND DARLINGTON RAILWAY. Stockton and Darlington Railway coaches. Corrected to March 1st, 1842. [A timetable.] *s.sh.fol. Darlington,* [1842] *See also* 1837, 1839.

32929 WYLD, J. The South Western, or London, Southampton, and Portsmouth Railway guide...with a guide to the environs of Southampton, the Isles of Wight, Jersey and Guernsey, and the opposite coast of France. 200p. *12°.* [1842] *The Rastrick copy. For another edition, see* 1839.

SOCIAL CONDITIONS

32930 ADSHEAD, J. Distress in Manchester. Evidence (tabular and otherwise) of the state of the labouring classes in 1840–42. 56p. *8°.* 1842. *The copy that belonged to Victor Considérant.*

32931 [AITON, J.] Clerical economics; or, hints, rural and household, to ministers and others of limited income. By a clergyman of the old school. 260p. *8°. Edinburgh & London,* 1842.

32932 On the **APPLICATION** of mutual insurance to education. 15p. *8°.* 1842. *Attributed in the contents list to a volume of Augustus De Morgan's pamphlets to 'Coates'.*

32933 ASHWORTH, H. Statistics of the present depression of trade at Bolton; showing the mode in which it affects the different classes of a manufacturing population. 8p. *8°. n.p.* [1842]

32934 BABINGTON, T. H. Remarks on the medical charities of Ireland, and on the measures proposed for the government and support of these institutions. 17p. *8°. Coleraine,* 1842.

32935 BAUGH, F. Almsgiving; or, the duties of the rich. A sermon, preached at the visitation of...the Lord Bishop of London, at the parish church of Woodford, October 15, 1842. 32p. *8°.* 1842.

32936 BERRIEN, J. M. Speech of Mr. Berrien, of Georgia, on the Bill to repeal the bankrupt law. Delivered in the Senate of the United States, January [25 and] 26, 1842. 27p. *8°. Washington,* 1842.

32937 BOWEN, J. The union work-house and board of guardians system as worked under the control of Poor-Law Commissioners; exemplified by official documents and plan: with an address to Sir Robert Peel. 63p. *8°.* 1842.

32938 BOWRING, Sir J. The speech of Dr. Bowring, M.P. on the distress at Bolton. In the House of Commons...February 10th, 1842. Extracted from Hansard's Parliamentary Debates. 24p. *12°. n.p.,* 1842.

32939 BRENTON, Sir J., *Bart.* Memoir of Captain Edward Pelham Brenton...With sketches of his personal life, and exertions in the cause of humanity, as connected with the "Children's Friend Society," &c.... 359p. *8°. London, Edinburgh, &c.,* 1842.

32940 BROTHERS, T. The rights and the wrongs of the poor in a series of letters: addressed to the working classes of all denominations. To which, on the same subject, are appended six letters to the noblemen of England. 137p. *8°. London & Leamington,* 1842.

32941 BROWNING, C. A. England's exiles; or, a view of a system of instruction and discipline, as carried into effect during the voyage to the penal colonies of Australia. 238p. *8°.* 1842.

32942 CANTAGREL, F. J. F. Mettray et Ostwald. Étude sur ces deux colonies agricoles...Dédié à MM. les fondateurs et souscripteurs de la Société paternelle et à MM. les membres du Conseil municipal de Strasbourg. 65p. *8°. Paris,* 1842. *The copy that belonged to Victor Considérant.*

32943 CHAMBORANT, C. G. de. Du paupérisme, ce qu'il était dans d'antiquité, ce qu'il est de nos jours... suivi d'une analyse de la législation ancienne et moderne sur ce sujet... 496p. *8°. Paris,* 1842.

32944 COLERIDGE, D. A letter on the National Society's training-college for schoolmasters, Stanley Grove, Chelsea. Addressed to the Rev. John Sinclair, M.A., secretary of the Society. 46p. *8°.* 1842.

32945 COOPER, A. A., *7th Earl of Shaftesbury.* Speech of Lord Ashley, in the House of Commons, on Tuesday, 7th May [i.e. June], 1842, on moving for leave to bring in a Bill to make regulations respecting the age and sex of children and young persons employed in the mines and collieries of the United Kingdom. 58p. *8°.* 1842. *Presentation copy from the author, with the date 'May' on the title-page altered to 'June'.*

32946 COTTAGE IMPROVEMENT SOCIETY FOR NORTH NORTHUMBERLAND. Report of the committee of the...Society...for 1842. 55p. *8°. London & Alnwick,* [1842] *See also* 1843.

32947 D., M. Important suggestions in relation to the Irish Poor Law, designed to ameliorate the condition of the labouring class, obviate dearth from the land, and provide fuel to the poor. With selections from the best authorities on agriculture, husbandry, and planting. By a gentleman of Lincoln's Inn. 532p. *8°. Dublin*, [1842]

32948 DICKENSON, W. R. Rustic figures. [A collection of lithographic drawings, portraying national costume.] 2l., 23 plates. *fol.* [*London*, 1842]

32949 DODD, WILLIAM (*b.* 1804). The factory system illustrated; in a series of letters to the Right Hon. Lord Ashley. 264p. *8°.* 1842.

32950 DRUMMOND, H., *ed.* The condition of the agricultural classes of Great Britain and Ireland. With extracts from the parliamentary Reports and evidence, from 1833 to 1840. And remarks by the French editor, published at Vienna... 2 vols. *8°.* 1842.

32951 EAGLE, F. K. Observations upon the expediency of establishing a board for the superintendence of public endowed charities, and the easier and better application of...their funds...for the promotion of a general system of national education... 31p. *8°.* 1842.

32952 ENGLAND. *Commissioners for Inquiring into the Employment and Condition of Children in Mines and Manufactories.* The condition and treatment of the children employed in the mines and collieries of the United Kingdom. Carefully compiled from the appendix to the First Report of the Commissioners...With copious extracts from the evidence...[Edited, with a preface, by W.C.] 90p. *8°.* 1842. *'W.C.' has sometimes been identified as William Carpenter. The copy that belonged to Victor Considérant.*

32953 —— *Laws, etc.* An Act to continue the Poor Law Commission, &c.&c.&c. ⟨Passed 30th July, 1842.⟩ and an Act to explain and amend the Acts regulating the sale of parish property, and to make further provision for the discharge of debts, &c., incurred by parishes. ⟨Passed 13th May, 1842.⟩ With an analytical index. [16], 40p. *8°.* 1842.

32954 —— *Poor Law Commission [1834–1847].* General medical regulations and instructional letter, March 1842. 30p. *8°.* 1842.

32955 —— —— Instructional letter accompanying the general workhouse order. [Signed: Edwin Chadwick.] 22p. *fol.* [*London*, 1842]

32956 —— —— Report to Her Majesty's Principal Secretary of State for the Home Department, from the Poor Law Commissioners, on an inquiry into the sanitary condition of the labouring population of Great Britain [compiled by E. Chadwick]; with appendices. Presented to both Houses of Parliament...July 1842. 457p. *8°.* 1842. *For a supplementary Report by Edwin Chadwick, see* 1843.

32957 —— —— Sanitary inquiry:– England. Local reports on the sanitary condition of the labouring population of England [and Wales], in consequence of an inquiry directed to be made by the Poor Law Commissioners. Presented to both Houses of Parliament...July 1842. 444p. *8°.* 1842.

32958 —— —— Sanitary inquiry:– Scotland. Reports on the sanitary condition of the labouring population of Scotland, in consequence of an inquiry directed to be made by the Poor Law Commissioners. Presented to both Houses of Parliament...July 1842. 334p. *8°.* 1842.

32959 —— —— Workhouse rules. To the guardians of the poor...[With 'Schedule containing the names of the unions, and of the parishes under a board of guardians, to which the present order applies'.] [Signed: G. C. Lewis, Edmund W. Head.] 15p. *fol. n.p.* [1842]

32960 EXAMEN critique des bureaux administratifs. Mémoire présenté par les Commissionnaires, en réponse au projet de M. le Directeur du Mont-de-Piété de Paris. [With 'Annexes'.] 117p. *4°. Paris*, 1842.

32961 An **EXPOSURE** of the various impositions daily practised, by vagrants of every description. 39p. *12°. Birmingham*, [1842 ?]

32962 —— [Another edition.] 36p. *12°. Manchester*, [1842 ?]

32963 FLEMING, G. A., *and others.* The ten hours' factory question. A report addressed to the Short Time Committees of the West Riding of Yorkshire. [Verbatim reports of conferences with Sir Robert Peel and some of his colleagues. Signed: George A. Fleming, Joshua Hobson, John Leech, Mark Crabtree, Titus S. Brooke.] 35p. *8°.* 1842. *The copy that belonged to Mark Pattison.*

32964 GASPEY, W. Poor law melodies, and other poems. 78p. *8°. London, Blackburn, &c.*, 1842.

32965 GEIJER, E. G. The poor laws and their bearing on society. A series of political and historical essays... Translated from the Swedish, by E. B. Hale Lewin. 184p. *8°. Stockholm & London*, 1842. *For another edition, see* 1840.

For the **HEALTHIAN,** 1842–43, *see vol.* III, *Periodicals list.*

32966 HIGGIN, W. Lectures for the members of the Independent Order of Rechabites. 60p. *8°. Chester*, 1842. *The Turner copy.*

32967 A brief **HISTORY** of the proceedings respecting the Thames coal-whippers [including an account of the formation of the Coal-Whippers' Emancipation Society]. Price-threepence-or, what you please, for the benefit of distressed coal-whippers and their families. 16p. *8°.* 1842.

32968 HOARE, E. N. A letter to Lord Stanley, M.P. on the present state of the question of national education in Ireland. 30p. *8°. Dublin & London*, 1842. *The copy that belonged to Earl De Grey.*

32969 HUDSON, J. S. Home slavery or, an earnest appeal to the common sense of the nation, on the oppressive effects of the food laws. 20p. *8°. London & Manchester*, 1842.

32970 KENWORTHY, W. Inventions and hours of labour. A letter to master cotton spinners, manufacturers, and mill-owners in general...Second edition. 16p. *8°. Blackburn*, 1842. *Reprinted in John Fielden's* A selection of facts and arguments in favour of the Ten Hours Bill, *1845* (*q.v.*).

32971 KING, B. A poor man's mite towards the relief of the distressed classes, addressed to Members of Parliament. July, 1842. [Advocating improvements in husbandry, as practised at the self-supporting school at Willingdon by George Crittenden, and the termination of property qualifications for Boards of Guardians.] 16p. *8°.* 1842.

32972 LECTURES on the social and physical condition of the people, especially in large towns. By various ministers of Glasgow. 192p. *12°. Glasgow & London*, [1842]

32973 LEES, F. R. Prize essays to reconcile Deuteronomy XIV. 25, 26, with the principle of total abstinence from all intoxicating drinks. By F. R. Lees and the Rev. C. J. Kennedy. 48p. *12°. Aberdeen*, 1842. *The Turner copy.*

32974 A **LETTER** from a citizen of London to the Right Hon. Sir Robert Peel, Bart. . . . on the necessity of restricting and defining the power of magistrates, and protecting places of public entertainment from persecution. 24p. *8°*. 1842.

32975 A **LETTER** relating to climbing boys in flues, addressed to Members of Parliament in general, the metropolitan Members in particular. By a Briton. April 1842. 8p. *8°*. 1842.

32976 **LONDON.** Livery Companies. *Clothworkers.* Register of the trusts, charities & estates, administered by and belonging to the Clothworkers' Company. Abridged from the written register, for the use of the members of the Court, 1842. [Edited by T. M. Alsager.] 111p. *8°*. [*London*, 1842]

32977 The **MANUFACTURERS,** their system, and their operatives. A letter to W. Busfeild Ferrand, Esq. M.P. confirming the statements he made in his recent speeches in the House of Commons. By a factory operative of twenty-five years experience. 16p. *8°*. 1842.

32978 **MARSHALL,** H. J. On the tendency of the new Poor Law seriously to impair the morals and condition of the working classes. . . 47p. *8°*. 1842.

32979 **MILLER,** C. The offertory and the duty of the Legislature in the present relation between the poor and the state, briefly considered in a letter to George Palmer, Esq. M.P. [With an appendix 'Three sermons, or homilies, to move compassion towards the poor and needy, set forth by authority, A.D. 1596. New edition' and 'Prospectus of a publication entitled A catalogue of authorities, ecclesiastical and civil. . . bearing uniform witness to the system of tithes'.] 20, 55, ixp. *8°*. *London & Oxford*, 1842.

For the **NATIONAL TEMPERANCE ADVOCATE,** 1842–49, *see* vol. III, *Periodicals list*, British temperance advocate and journal.

32980 **NEWMARCH,** W. Appendix to fifth annual report of the Yorkshire Union of Mechanics' Institutes. Observations and statistics, relative to the experience and operations of the Mechanics' Institute at York. [An offprint.] p.41–45. *8°*. *Leeds*, [1842] *With a note by HSF to the effect that this copy of an early work by Newmarch was probably given him by Mrs. Newmarch when Foxwell was preparing the inaugural Newmarch Lecture in 1884.*

32981 **NORTHAMPTON GENERAL LUNATIC ASYLUM.** The fourth annual report of the. . . Asylum. . . from July 1, 1841, to June 30, 1842. [With the Physician Superintendent's fourth annual report.] 95p. *8°*. *Northampton*, 1842. *See also* 1839.

32982 **NUNNS,** T. A letter to the Right Hon. Lord Ashley, on the condition of the working classes in Birmingham, considered in reference to improvement in the condition of the same classes in manufacturing districts, and large towns. 62p. *8°*. *Birmingham & London*, 1842.

For **ODD FELLOWS' QUARTERLY MAGAZINE,** 1842–47, *see* vol. III, *Periodicals list*, Odd Fellows' Magazine.

33983 **OSCAR I,** *King of Sweden.* On punishments and prisons. . . Translated from the second Swedish edition, by A. May. 162p. *8°*. *London & Stockholm*, 1842.

32984 **OWEN,** ROBERT D. Moral physiology; or, a. . . treatise on the population question. 48p. *8°*. 1842. *For another edition, see* 1831.

32985 **PEMBROKE,** *County of.* Rules, orders & regulations, for the government of the Gaol and House of Correction, of the county of Pembroke, at Haverfordwest Castle. 84p. *8°*. *Haverfordwest*, 1842. *See note to no.* 23273.

32986 **PROVIDENT & FRIENDLY SOCIETY FOR STOKE NEWINGTON.** The rules and tables for the Provident & Friendly Society for Stoke Newington & its vicinity. Established MDCCCXL. . . Place of meeting, the School-Room of Abney Chapel. 32p. *8°*. 1842. *The names of the officers have not been filled in. With manuscript comments, probably by a lawyer to whom the work was submitted before publication. The copy that belonged to William Allen.*

32987 —— [Another edition.] The rules and tables of the Provident & Friendly Society for Stoke Newington, West Hackney, and their vicinities. Established MDCCCXLII . . . Office, High Street, Stoke Newington. . . 32p. *8°*. 1842. *A revised version, with a list of trustees, directors and other officers on the verso of the title-page. In this edition, the tables are printed in a separate section at the end, instead of throughout the text. The copy that belonged to William Allen.*

32988 **PROVINCIAL MEDICAL AND SURGICAL ASSOCIATION.** The administration of medical relief to the poor, under the Poor-Law Amendment Act. . . considered in the reports of the Poor-Law Committee of the. . . Association. To which are appended certain clauses suggested for. . . the contemplated Bill for the further amendment of the poor-laws. 136p. *8°*. 1842.

32989 **ROBBERS** detected; or, a consideration of the cause, and probable consequences, of the passing of the 4th and 5th William IV., Cap. 76. commonly called the Poor Law Amendment Act. By one of the Cobbett-Club. 74p. *12°*. 1842.

32990 **ROBERTS,** S. The voice of an octogenarian denouncing wickedness in high places. Addressed to Sir Robert Peel. 112p. *8°*. *London & Sheffield*, 1842.

32991 **ROYAL FREE HOSPITAL,** *London.* Instituted 1828. Royal Free Hospital, Gray's Inn Road. . . [Rules. – History. – Fourteenth annual report. – Governors and subscribers.] 65p. *8°*. [1842]

32992 [**RUSHTON,** E.] Juvenile delinquency. Reprinted from the Christian Teacher for July, 1842. 32p. *8°*. *London & Liverpool*, 1842.

32993 **SINCLAIR,** JOHN (1792–1875), *ed.* Correspondence on the subject of the late disturbances in the manufacturing and mining districts. . . 33p. *8°*. 1842.

32994 **SMITH,** HERBERT. The Church, God's appointed guardian of the poor; or the poor man's advocate. 14 parts. *8°*. 1842. *A collection, reissued with a general title-page, of 14 separately published pamphlets, eight of which were issued together with the title:* The poor man's advocate, *in 1839 (q.v.). The works new to the collection are as follows: A letter to the Poor Law Commissioners in behalf of the deserving poor [with 'First report of the Shirley Asylum for Virtuous Aged and Infirm Poor. . . 1841']; Letters to the Right Hon. Sir James Graham. . . and the Rev. Thomas Chalmers. . . on the poor law question; A letter defending the new Poor Law, in reply to a letter to the Rev. Herbert Smith, by a layman; Correspondence with the Poor Law Commissioners on the principle and working of the new Poor Law, in reference to cases that have been brought before them, parts 1 and 2; An account of a union chaplaincy. . . with some additional remarks. . . in connexion with the new Poor Law, and a list of the inmates of the New Forest Union Workhouse; An account of the situation and treatment of the* *women with illegitimate children in the New Forest Union Workhouse; An account (continued) of the situation...of the women with illegitimate children in the New Forest Union Workhouse.*

32995 SPENCER, T. Observations on the school return for the Diocese of Bath and Wells, showing the uncharitable nature and Puseyite tendency of some of the questions contained therein... Second thousand. No. 18. 16p. *8°. London & Bath, 1842.*

32996 STEWART, afterwards **VANE,** CHARLES W.,

3rd Marquis of Londonderry. A letter to Lord Ashley, M.P. on the Mines and Collieries' Bill. 164p. *8°. 1842.*

32997 WADE, JOHN. History and political philosophy of the middle and working classes...Fourth edition, considerably enlarged. 174p. *8°. Edinburgh, 1842. For other editions, see 1833.*

32998 WARE, H. The moral principle of the temperance movement. A sermon preached in the Chapel of Harvard College, October 17, 1841. 12p. *8°. 1842. The Turner copy. See also 1843.*

SLAVERY

32999 ALEXANDER, GEORGE W. Letters on the slave-trade, slavery, and emancipation; with a reply to objections made to the liberation of the slaves in the Spanish colonies; addressed to friends...during a visit to Spain and Portugal. 176p. *8°. 1842.*

33000 —— Observacões sobre a escravatura e commercio de escravos dirigidas a's Cortes e a' nação portugueza. 27p. *16°. Lisboa, 1842.*

33001 BANDINEL, J. Some account of the trade in slaves from Africa as connected with Europe and America; from the introduction of the trade into modern Europe, down to the present time... 323p. *8°. 1842.*

33002 BOSTON FEMALE ANTI-SLAVERY SOCIETY. Ninth annual report of the...Society. Presented October 12, 1842. 46p. *8°. Boston, 1842. The binding title and half-title read: Ten years of experience. Presentation copy with inscription from Maria Weston Chapman, the foreign corresponding secretary, to 'Mrs. Anderson'. See also 1836.*

33003 BRITISH AND FOREIGN ANTI-SLAVERY SOCIETY. The export of coolies from India to Mauritius. 14p. *8°. 1842.*

33004 BURNLEY, W. H. Observations on the present condition of the Island of Trinidad, and the actual state of the experiment on negro emancipation. [With 'Minutes of evidence taken by the sub-committee of the Agricultural and Immigration Society [March–July 1841]' and appendixes.] 177p. *8°. 1842.*

33005 CHANNING, WILLIAM E. An address delivered at Lenox, on the first of August, 1842, the anniversary of emancipation in the British West Indies. 38p. *8°. Lenox, Mass., 1842.*

33006 —— [Another edition.] Dr. Channing's last address. 24p. *12°. Boston, 1842.*

33007 —— The duty of the free states, or remarks suggested by the case of the creole. 54p. *12°. Boston, 1842. Presentation copy, with inscription, to the 'Hon. Wm. Slade from the Author'.*

33008 CLARKSON, T. Not a labourer wanted for Jamaica: to which is added, an account of the newly erected villages by the peasantry there, and their beneficial

results; and of the consequences of re-opening a new slave trade, as it relates to Africa, and the honour of the British Government in breaking her treaties with foreign powers: in a letter addressed to a Member of Parliament, appointed to sit on the West India Committee. 15p. *8°. 1842.*

33009 FRIENDS, *Society of, New England.* An appeal to the professors of Christianity, in the Southern States and elsewhere, on the subject of slavery: by the representatives of the Yearly Meeting of Friends for New England. [Signed: Samuel Boyd Tobey, clerk.] 24p. *8°. Providence, 1842.*

33010 GRAHAME, JAMES (1790–1842). Who is to blame? or, cursory review of "American apology for American accession to negro slavery." 112p. *8°. 1842. A reply to A letter to Lord Brougham on the subject of American slavery, by an American, i.e. Robert Baird.*

33011 JAY, J. The progress and results of emancipation in the English West Indies. A lecture delivered before the Philomathian Society of the city of New-York... 39p. *8°. New-York, 1842.*

33012 MOREAU DE JONNÈS, A. Recherches statistiques sur l'esclavage colonial et sur les moyens de le supprimer. 275p. *8°. Paris, 1842.*

33013 [OUSELEY, SIR WILLIAM G.] Reply to an "American's examination" of the "Right of search:" with observations on some of the questions at issue between Great Britain and the United States, and on certain positions assumed by the North American government. By an Englishman. [With an appendix.] 110, lxiip. *8°. 1842.*

33014 SOCIETY FOR THE EXTINCTION OF THE SLAVE TRADE AND FOR THE CIVILIZATION OF AFRICA. Report of the committee of the African Civilization Society to the public meeting of the Society, held...21st of June, 1842. With an appendix. 99, cxxxivp. *8°. 1842.*

33015 STURGE, JOHN. A visit to the United States in 1841. [A review of the progress of the anti-slavery movement.] 192, cxxiip. *8°. London & Birmingham, 1842. Presentation copy, with inscription, from the author to Joseph Lamb.*

POLITICS

33016 ALLEN, ELISHA H. Speech of Mr. Allen, of Maine, in reply to remarks of Mr. Holmes and other gentlemen on...(July 25,) during the discussion of the

Army bill, in allusion to the reported agreement between the Ministers of the United States and Great Britain for a settlement of the northeastern boundary. 8p. *8°. n.p.* [1842]

33017 ARCHER, W. S. Speech of Mr. Archer, of Virginia, on the resolution of Mr. Clay, proposing so to amend the constitution of the United States as to restrict the veto power. Delivered in the Senate of the United States, February 9, 1842. 14p. *8°. Washington, 1842.*

33018 BARNARD, D. D. Speech of Mr. Barnard, of New York, in favor of a uniform system of electing representatives by districts throughout the United States. Delivered in the House of Representatives of the U.S., April 28, 1842. 15p. *8°. Washington, 1842.*

33019 BATHURST, HENRY, *Archdeacon.* An Easter offering for the Whigs...being a supplement to the memoirs of the late Bishop of Norwich; consisting of letters hitherto suppressed, from and to the leading members of the late Whig Governments...and other matters omitted before, illustrative of personal and public conduct in the above individuals. 115p. *8°. London & Norwich, 1842. The copy that belonged to Earl De Grey.*

33020 BEGGS, T. History of the election for the borough of Nottingham. 1842. Candidates John Walter, Esquire. Joseph Sturge, Esquire. Revised from the published accounts of the period. By Thomas Beggs, secretary of the Complete Suffrage Association. 60p. *12°. Nottingham,* [1842]

33021 BERRIEN, J. M. Speech of Mr. Berrien, of Georgia, on the resolutions of Mr. Clay. Delivered in the Senate of the United States, on the 4th of March, 1842. 16p. *8°. n.p.* [1842]

33022 [BOURGUIGNON D'HERBIGNY, P. F. X.] Du déclin de la France et de l'égarement de sa politique. 195p. *8°. Paris, 1842.*

33023 BRIGGS, G. N. Speech of George N. Briggs, of Massachusetts, on the President's veto of the provisional tariff bill. Delivered in the House of Representatives, U.S., June 30, 1842. 12p. *8°. Washington, 1841* [1842]

33024 CARLYLE, T. Chartism...Second edition. 113p. *12°. 1842. A reissue of the second edition 1840, with a new title-page. For other editions, see 1840.*

33025 COMPLETE SUFFRAGE CONFERENCE. Minutes of the proceedings at the Conference of representatives of the middle and working classes of Great Britain, held...at...Birmingham, April 5th, 1842, and three following days. 42p. *8°. Birmingham, 1842.*

33026 —— Report of the proceedings at the Conference of delegates, of the middle and working classes, held at Birmingham, April 5, 1842...[Leading to the establishment of the National Complete Suffrage Union.] 78p. *12°.* 1842.

33027 [CONSIDÉRANT, V. P.] De la souveraineté et de la régence. 54p. *8°. n.p.* [1842] *Considérant's own copy.*

33028 EPITOME of Statutes affecting political societies [with particular reference to the National Complete Suffrage Union], with practical suggestions for avoiding their infringement. 3p. *8°. Birmingham,* [1842 ?]

33029 EVANS, SIR GEORGE DE L. Espartero. Sir De Lacy Evans' reply to Mr. O'Connell's attacks on the Regent, &c. of Spain. 15p. *8°.* [*London,*] 1842.

33030 GARDNER, R. An address to the middle and working classes engaged in trade and manufactures, throughout the Empire, on the necessity of union at the present crisis. 8p. *8°. Manchester, 1842.*

33031 GODWIN, WILLIAM (1756–1836). Enquiry concerning political justice...The fourth edition... 2 vols. *8°. 1842. For another edition, see 1793.*

33032 GRAHAM, W. A. Speech of Mr. Graham, of North Carolina, on the districting clause of the apportionment bill. Delivered in the Senate of the United States, June 3, 1842. 15p. *8°. Washington, 1842.*

33033 HALSTED, W. Speech of Mr. Halsted, of New Jersey, on the amendment offered to the apportionment bill, providing for the election of representatives by districts. Delivered in the House of Representatives of the U.S. May 2, 1842. 13p. *8°. Washington, 1842.*

33034 HODGSKIN, T. "Peace, law, and order," a lecture delivered in the hall of the National Association, on September 29, 1842. 24p. *12°.* [1842]

33035 HUNDESHAGEN, C. B. Ueber den Einflusz des Calvinismus auf die Ideen vom Staat und staatsbürgerlicher Freiheit. Rede zur Feier des Jahrstages der Eröffnung der Hochschule in Bern, gehalten am 15. November 1841. 55p. *8°. Bern, 1842.*

33036 HUNTINGTON, J. W. Speech of Mr. Huntington, of Connecticut, in favor of electing representatives by districts throughout the U. States. Delivered in the Senate of the United States, May 31, 1842. 8p. *4°. Washington, 1842.*

33037 LINN, A. L. Speech of Mr. Linn, of New York, upon the mission to Mexico, and annexation of Texas. Delivered in the House of Representatives of the U.S., April 13, 1842. 26p. *8°. Washington, 1842.*

33038 MARTIN, WILLIAM (1772–1851). The philosopher on politics, for the good of the British Nation. [With 'The philosopher's address to Her Majesty, the House of Lords, the Bishops, and the Commons, exhibiting the corruption of all colleges'.] 4p. *8°. Newcastle,* [1842]

33039 MASON, J. A letter to Mr. Macaulay, M.P., in reply to the charges made by that gentleman against the Chartists, in a speech...in the House of Commons, May the 3rd, on the motion of Mr. T. Duncombe, to hear the deputies from the working men...in support of the claims ...in the...national petition. 12p. *12°. Birmingham & London, 1842.*

33040 METROPOLITAN PARLIAMENTARY REFORM ASSOCIATION. No. 1. Prospectus of the Metropolitan Parliamentary Reform Association. [Signed: P. A. Taylor, chairman, J. Roberts Black, secretary.] 8p. *8°.* [1842]

33041 —— No. 2. The Metropolitan Parliamentary Reform Association. To the people of Great Britain. 4p. *8°. n.p.* [1842 ?]

33042 —— No. 3. The Metropolitan Parliamentary Reform Association. [Objects, list of officers and rules of the Association.] 4p. *8°.* [*London,* 1842 ?]

For the **NATIONAL ASSOCIATION GAZETTE,** *see vol. III, Periodicals list.*

33043 NATIONAL COMPLETE SUFFRAGE UNION. The Council of the National Complete Suffrage Union, to political reformers of all shades of opinion. [Signed: Joseph Sturge, president.] 4p. *8°. Birmingham,* [1842] *The copy that belonged to William Lovett, with a manuscript note in his hand at the head of the first page: 'Written by Wm. Lovett'.*

33044 —— To Victoria, Queen of Great Britain and Ireland, and the dependencies thereunto belonging. [A manifesto, signed: Joseph Sturge, president.] 4p. *8°. Birmingham*, [1842]

33045 [**NEWMARCH**, W.] Two letters, to Joseph Sturge, Esq., on "complete suffrage." (Reprinted from "The Yorkshireman" newspaper.) [Signed: Peter Principle.] 31p. *12°. London & New York*, 1842. *The copy presented to HSF by Mrs. Newmarch.*

33046 **O'BRIEN**, J. B. Mr. O'Brien's vindication of his conduct at the late Birmingham Conference; containing his "blackguard letter" to…the "Star"… 24p. *12°. Birmingham*, 1842.

33047 *★PEOPLE'S CHARTER.* 12p. *12°. London: H. Hetherington & Birmingham: Taylor*, [1842?] *The FWA copy, that belonged to William Pare. For other editions, see 1838.*

33048 **PHILP**, R. K. Robert Kemp Philp's vindication of his political conduct and an exposition of the misrepresentations of the Northern Star. Together with a few words of advice to Chartists. 28p. *12°. Bath*, [1842]

33049 **PRENTICE**, A. The Pitt–Peel income tax, and the necessity of complete suffrage. [A lecture to the Young Men's Anti-Monopoly Association.] 12p. *12°. Manchester & London*, [1842]

33050 **PRESTON**, W. C. Speech of the Hon. W. C. Preston, of So. Carolina, on the veto power, and in reply to Mr. Clay, of Kentucky, delivered in the Senate of the U.S., April, 1842. 15p. *8°. Washington*, 1842.

33051 **RECONCILIATION** between the middle and labouring classes. [With a preface by Joseph Sturge.] Re-printed from the Nonconformist. 32p. *8°*. 1842.

33052 —— [Another edition.] 32p. *8°. Birmingham & London*, 1842. *For another edition, see 1841.*

33053 **ROSS**, D. The state of the country, as the effect of class legislation; and the Charter as the remedy. A lecture delivered in…Manchester, April 10th, 1842… Reported by William Griffin. 12p. *12°. Manchester*, [1842]

33054 Brief **SKETCHES** of the Birmingham Conference [i.e. the Complete Suffrage Conference]. By a member. Comprising the following delegates: Joseph Sturge, William Lovett…Rev. H. Solly, etc. etc. 23p. *12°*. 1842.

33055 **SMILES**, S. The diffusion of political knowledge among the working classes. An address delivered before…the Bradford United Reform Club, February 14, 1842. 19p. *12°. Leeds*, 1842.

33056 **SPENCER**, T. The people's rights: and how to get them…Seventh thousand. No. 17. 20p. *8°. London & Bath*, 1842.

33057 Our representative **SYSTEM**, its tendency and effects. With practical suggestions for its formation on a new basis. 16p. *8°*. 1842.

33058 **THOMPSON**, JOHN B. Speech of Mr. J. B. Thompson, of Kentucky, on the apportionment bill. (In favor of reducing the number of reps.) Delivered in the House of Representatives of the United States June 21, 1842. 8p. *8°. n.p.* [1842]

33059 **THOUGHTS** on purity of election. By a Member of Parliament. 32p. *8°*. 1842.

33060 **UNDERWOOD**, J. R. Speech of Mr. J. R. Underwood, upon the resolution proposing to censure John Quincy Adams for presenting to the House of Representatives a petition praying for the dissolution of the Union. Delivered in the House of Representatives, on the 27th of January, 1842. 15p. *8°. Washington*, 1842.

SOCIALISM

For the **ANTIDOTE**, *see vol.* III, *Periodicals list.*

33061 **BEARD**, J. R. The religion of Jesus Christ defended from the assaults of English Chartism. In nine lectures. 240p. *12°*. [1842?] *A reissue, with a new title-page, of* The religion of Jesus Christ defended from the assaults of Owenism, *1839 (q.v.).*

33062 **BRAY**, J. F. The labourer's library, No. 4. Government and society considered in relation to first principles…Reprinted from "Labour's wrongs and labour's remedy." 12p. *12°. Leeds, Manchester, &c.*, 1842.

33063 **BROWNSON**, O. A. The laboring classes, an article from the Boston Quarterly Review…Fifth edition. 31p. *8°. Boston*, 1842. *The copy that belonged to William Lovett.* ★*Another, the FWA copy, belonged to William Pare. For other editions, see 1840.*

33064 [**CONSIDÉRANT**, V. P.] Bases de la politique positive; manifeste de l'École sociétaire, fondée par Fourier. Deuxième édition. [With 'Catalogue raisonné des publications de l'École sociétaire'.] 218, 47p. *12°. Paris*, 1842. *For other editions, see 1841.*

33065 The human **ECCALEOBĪON**: or, the new moral warren: being a concise but faithful exposition of socialism, instituted by Robert Owen, Esq. [In verse. With 'Extracts from "The new moral world," the "Out-

line of the rational system of society," and the "Declaration of principles," &c. &c.'.] 48p. *8°*. 1842.

33066 **ETZLER**, J. A. The paradise within the reach of all men, without labor, by powers of nature and machinery…Second English edition. 54, 40p. *8°*. 1842. *For another edition, see 1836.*

33067 **GAMOND**, afterwards **GATTI DE GAMOND**, Z. DE. Fourier and his system…Translated from the fourth French edition by C. T. Wood…With a short biographical sketch [by Hugh Doherty] extracted from "The London Phalanx". 104p. *8°*. 1842. *For other editions, see 1838.*

33068 —— Réalisation d'une commune sociétaire, d'après la théorie de Charles Fourier. 409p. *8°. Paris*, 1841–42. *A reissue, with a new title-page, of the sheets of the edition of 1840 (q.v.).*

33069 **GRAY**, JOHN (1799–1883). An efficient remedy for the distress of nations. 224p. *8°. Edinburgh, London, &c.*, 1842.

33070 *★HOME COLONIZATION COMPANY.* Home Colonization Company. Capital, one million, in shares of £50 each. A joint stock company to establish colonies in Great Britain and Ireland…Prospectus. [Signed: William Galpin, secretary, and dated, January

1842.] 3p. *fol. n.p.* [1842] *The FWA copy that belonged to William Pare.*

33071 LAFARELLE, F. F. DE. Plan d'une réorganisation disciplinaire des classes industrielles en France, précédé et suivi d'études historiques sur les formes anciennes et modernes du travail humain; ouvrage couronné par la Société Royale d'Émulation, d'Agriculture ...de l'Ain. 246p. *12°. Paris, 1842. Presentation copy, with inscription on the wrapper, from the author to 'Mons. de Salvandy'.*

33072 No. 3...**MAN'S** appeal to woman...[Signed: Man.] 30p. *8°.* 1842.

For **MAZEL**, B., Introduction familière à la pratique du système social de Charles Fourrier [*sic*], 1842, *see the author's* Code social, 1843.

33073 PECQUEUR, C. N. S. Théorie nouvelle d'économie sociale et politique, ou études sur l'organisation des sociétés. 898p. *8°. Paris, 1842.*

33074 RATIONAL SOCIETY. Address of the congress of the Rational Society, held in Harmony Hall... May, 1842, to the Chartists of Great Britain and Ireland. [With 'Address...to the trades' unions of Great Britain and Ireland'. Signed: Robert Owen, president.] 8p. *8°. n.p.* [1842]

33075 RENAUD, H. Solidarité. Vue synthétique sur la doctrine de Ch. Fourier. 291p. *8°. Paris, 1842. The copy that belonged to Victor Considérant. See also 1845.*

33076 RODBERTUS-JAGETZOW, J. C. Zur Erkenntniss unsrer staatswirthschaftlichen Zustände... Erstes Heft: fünf Theoreme. 175p. *8°. Neubrandenburg & Friedland, 1842.*

33077 ROEBUCK, JOHN H. Lectures [on 'Anti-Owenism'] and sermons of the Rev. J. H. Roebuck...with a sketch of his life. 235p. *12°. London, Leeds, &c., 1842.*

33078 The **SCHEME** of universal brotherhood; or the Christian system of mutual assistance. Proposing a system of society, natural in its construction...interfering with no sect in religion, or party in politics, and insuring the happiness and innocence of all mankind. Compiled from the works of celebrated authors. 134p. *8°.* [1842?] *HSF quoted a manuscript note from another copy, 'Compiled by Mr. Mullins, surgeon'.*

33079 *[**SOMERVILLE**, ALEXANDER.] A journey to Harmony Hall, in Hampshire, with some particulars of the socialist community, to which the attention of the nobility, gentry, and clergy, is earnestly solicited. By One who has whistled at the plough. ⟨Reprinted from the Morning Chronicle of Tuesday, Dec. 13th, 1842.⟩ 8p. *8°. London, Manchester, &c.,* [1842] *Catalogued from the wrapper. Caption title: Notes from the farming districts. No. XVII. The FWA copy that belonged to William Pare. The Goldsmiths' Library copy lacks the wrappers.*

33080 [——] [Another edition.] 8p. *8°.* [1842]

33081 *[——] [Another edition. With an extract from a subsequent letter to the same paper on the same subject.] 8p. *8°.* [1842?] *The FWA copy that belonged to William Pare.*

33082 STEIN, L. VON. Der Socialismus und Communismus des heutigen Frankreichs. Ein Beitrag zur Zeitsgeschichte. 475p. *8°. Leipzig, 1842.*

33083 Le **SYSTÈME** de Fourier étudié dans ses propres écrits. 84p. *12°. Paris, 1842.*

For the **UNION**, 1842–43, *see vol. III, Periodicals list.*

33084 WATTS, J. The facts and fictions of political economists: being a review of the principles of the science, separating the true from the false. 60p. *12°. Manchester & London, 1842.* *Another, the FWA copy, was presented by the author to Robert Owen, and later belonged to William Pare.*

MISCELLANEOUS

33085 BAILEY, JAMES N. Essays on miscellaneous subjects: historical, moral, and political. 212p. *12°. Leeds, Manchester, &c., 1842.*

33086 *The **BOOK** of the inspired British prophet of the seventeenth century, containing the religion of the Millenium, new law of righteousness and...prophesies, now fulfilling...First...published in the year 1649, and now reprinted from an original and genuine copy. Part the first. 28p. *12°. Liverpool, 1842. The FWA copy that belonged to William Pare.*

33087 CHANNING, WILLIAM H. A letter from the Rev. William H. Channing, to the Unitarian Society of Cincinnati [explaining his withdrawal from the office of pastor to the Society]. 23p. *8°. Cincinnati, 1842.*

33088 CHOATE, R. Speech of Mr. Choate, of Massachusetts, on the bill to provide further remedial justice in the courts of the U. States. Delivered in the Senate of the United States, May, 1842. 28p. *8°. Washington, 1842.*

33089 CLARIDGE, R. T. Abstract of hydropathy; or, the cold water cure, as practised by Vincent Priessnitz, at Graefenberg, Silesia, Austria. 72p. *12°.* 1842.

33090 The **DRESS** of the clergy. By a clergyman. 24p. *12°.* 1842.

33091 ENGLEDUE, W. C. Cerebral physiology and materialism, with the result of the application of animal magnetism to the cerebral organs. An address, delivered to the Phrenological Association...June 20th, 1842... With a letter from Dr. Elliotson, on mesmeric phrenology and materialism. 38p. *8°. H. Baillière, 1842.*

33092 —— [Another edition.] 32p. *16°. J. Watson, 1842.*

33093 HOLYOAKE, G. J. The spirit of Bonner in the disciples of Jesus, or the cruelty and intolerance of Christianity displayed, in the prosecution, for blasphemy, of Charles Southwell, editor of the Oracle of reason. 16p. *8°. London, Birmingham, &c.,* [1842]

33094 —— The trial of George Jacob Holyoake, on an indictment for blasphemy...August the 15th, 1842. From notes specially taken by Mr. Hunt... 68p. *8°. For the Anti-Persecution Union, 1842.*

33095 HUNTINGTON, J. W. Speech of Mr. Huntington, of Connecticut, on the bill to provide further remedial justice in the courts of the United States. Delivered in the Senate of the United States May 11, 1842. 26p. *8°. Washington, 1842.*

33096 LAWRENCE, SIR WILLIAM, *Bart.* Facts versus fiction! An essay on the functions of the brain. Second edition. [Selected from *Lectures on physiology,* *zoology and the natural history of Man,* by William Lawrence, F.R.S.] 16p. *8°.* 1842.

33097 OWEN, ROBERT D. Neurology. An account of some experiments in cerebral physiology by Dr. Buchanan, of Louisville. Communicated to an American newspaper, at Dr. Buchanan's request. By R. D. Owen. [With 'New Harmony'.] 16p. *12°.* 1842.

33098 PRESTON. *Guild Merchant.* A full and detailed account of the Guild Merchant of Preston, in the County Palatine of Lancaster, as celebrated in the year 1842. 52p. *8°. Preston,* [1842]

33099 A few **REMARKS** on some points contained in Mr. Sibthorp's letter to a friend, by a clergyman of the Archdiocese of Canterbury. Author of A letter to Sir R. Peel on the supposed difficulty which Ireland should present to his Government. 23p. *8°.* 1842.

33100 The **REVOLUTION SETTLEMENT** of the Church of Scotland vindicated; being the review of a lecture by the Rev. John Graham of Wishawtown...By a licentiate of the Established Church. 58p. *12°. Glasgow, Edinburgh, &c.,* 1842.

33101 WATTS, J. Metaphysical parallels; or, arguments in juxta-position for and against the existence of God; the immateriality and immortality of the soul, &c. 23p. *12°.* [1842]

33102 WHATELY, R., *Archbishop of Dublin.* Printed for private circulation. Letter from the Archbishop of Dublin to His Excellency the Lord Lieutenant of Ireland, relative to the re-establishment of the Bishoprick of Kildare, in union with that of Leighlin. 15p. *8°.* [1842]

1843

GENERAL

33103 ATKINSON, WILLIAM (*fl.* 1833–1858). Principles of political economy; or, the laws of the formation of national wealth, developed by means of the Christian law of government...With an introduction by Horace Greeley; treating of the present state of the science of political economy, and the adaptation of its principles to the condition of our own country. (*Useful Works for the People,* No. v.) 83p. *8°. New-York, New-Orleans, &c.,* 1843. *For another edition, see* 1840.

33104 BAMFORD, S. Passages in the life of a radical ...Fourth edition. 2 vols. *8°.* [1843 ?–]44.

33105 BENTHAM, J. The works of Jeremy Bentham, published under the superintendence of his executor, John Bowring. 11 vols. *8°. Edinburgh & London,* 1843.

33106 BISCHOFF, J. Foreign tariffs; their injurious effect on British manufactures, especially the woollen manufacture; with proposed remedies. Being chiefly a series of articles inserted in the Leeds Mercury, from October 1842 to February 1843. 69p. *8°. London & Leeds,* 1843.

33107 BLYTH, G. K. The Norwich guide and directory: being an historical and topographical description of the city and its hamlets; with an account of the public charities, and correct lists of the various professions, trades, public institutions... 315p. *12°. Norwich,* 1843.

33108 [BRIDGE, J.] Observations addressed to Lord John Russell, and a few modest questions put to his Lordship, suggesting reminiscences of the course of conduct most worthy of a great statesman. By Civis. 16p. *8°. Manchester,* 1843.

33109 [——] Two letters on the great distress that now prevails in the country: one addressed to the merchants, manufacturers, master spinners, &c. &c. of this manufacturing district, the other to the ladies and gentlemen of the Anti-Corn League, residents of Rochdale...[The letters signed: A townsman.] 8p. *8°. Manchester,* [1843]

33110 The **BRITISH ALMANAC** of the Society for the Diffusion of Useful Knowledge, for...1843.

[With 'The companion to the Almanac; or year-book of general information'.] 96, 260p. *12°.* [1843] *For other editions, see* 1828.

33111 —— A complete index to The companion to the Almanac, from its commencement, in 1828, to 1843, inclusive. 561p. *12°.* 1843.

33112 The **BRITISH MECHANIC'S** and labourer's hand book, and true guide to the United States; with ample notices respecting various trades and professions. A new and improved edition. 288p. *12°.* 1843. *Sometimes attributed to Charles Knight, whose initials were printed at the end of the preface (missing from this copy). For another edition, see* 1840.

33113 BUFFALO. Revised charter of the city of Buffalo: passed April 17, 1843, published by order of the Commons Council. To which are added the laws and ordinances. 2 vols. *8°. Buffalo,* 1843.

33114 [BULLEN, W.] A memoir of the Union, and the agitations for its repeal; in which...its causes and its consequences, are historically and politically reviewed; and its indissolubility demonstrated from many great authorities, and particularly by that of Daniel O'Connell, Esq., M.P. By an Irish Catholic. 133p. *8°. Dublin & London,* 1843. *The copy that belonged to Earl De Grey.*

33115 C., A. B. Observations relative to the situation of the country, at the commencement of the year 1820, in regard to its finances, morals, and religion, with a plan for their gradual improvement. By A.B.C. Second edition. 44p. *8°. Salisbury & London,* 1843.

33116 [CAPPS, E.] Not over-production, but imperfect distribution the cause of the distress. [Signed: C.] (*Emancipation of Industry,* 3–4.) 2 vols. *12°.* [1843]

33117 CARLYLE, T. Past and present. 399p. *12°.* 1843.

33118 CASWALL, H. The prophet of the nineteenth century [Joseph Smith]; or, the rise, progress, and present state of the Mormons, or Latterday Saints: to which is appended an analysis of the Book of Mormon. 277p. *12⁰.* 1843.

33119 CHEVALIER, M. Essais de politique industrielle. Souvenirs de voyage, France, République d'Andorre, Belgique, Allemagne. 451p. *8⁰. Paris,* 1843.

33120 COBDEN, R. The new emigration scheme. Speech of R. Cobden, Esq., M.P., in the Theatre Royal, Drury Lane, London, March 29, 1843. 8p. *12⁰. Manchester,* [1843]

33121 [COLLECTION des principaux économistes.] Vols. 1–7, 9–15. *8⁰. Paris,* 1843, 1840–48. *Contents: 1. Économistes financiers du XVIIIe siècle...Précédés de notices historiques...et accompagnés de commentaires...par M. Eugène Daire, 1843; 2. Physiocrates...Avec une introduction sur la doctrine des physiocrates, des commentaires et des notices historiques par M. Eugène Daire, 1846; 3–4. A. R. J. Turgot, Baron de l'Aulne, Œuvres...Nouvelle édition...et précédée d'une notice sur la vie et les ouvrages... par M. Eugène Daire, 1844; 5–6. Adam Smith, Recherches sur la nature et les causes de la richesse des nations... traduction du Comte Germain Garnier...précédée d'une notice biographique par M. Blanqui...Augmentée de notes inédits de Jean-Baptiste Say et d'éclaircissements historiques par M. Blanqui, 1843; 7. T. Malthus, Essai sur le principe de population...Précédé d'une introduction par M. Rossi... Avec les notes des traducteurs et de nouvelles notes par M. Joseph Garnier, 1845; 9. J. B. Say, Traité d'économie politique...Sixième édition...publiée...par Horace Say, 1841; 10–11. J. B. Say, Cours complet d'économie politique pratique...Seconde édition entièrement revue par l'auteur, publiée...par Horace Say, 1840; *12. J. B. Say, Œuvres diverses...Avec des notes par Ch. Comte, E. Daire et Horace Say, 1848; 13. D. Ricardo, Œuvres complètes... Traduites en français par MM. Constancio et Alc. Fonteyraud, 1847; 14–15. Mélanges d'économie politique. [Notes by MM. Eugène Daire and G. de Molinari], 1847–48. Vol. 12 belonged to George Grote and has his book-plate.*

33122 COSTAZ, C. A. Histoire de l'administration, en France, de l'agriculture, des arts utiles, du commerce ...Troisième édition revue, corrigée et considérablement augmentée. 3 vols. *8⁰. Paris,* 1843.

33123 A COUNTER-PLEA for the poor: a refutation of the assertions of the Anti-Corn Law League, and the Hon. and Rev. Baptist W. Noel. By the poor man's friend. Fifth edition. – With additions. 35p. *8⁰.* 1843. *The copy that belonged to the 3rd Earl of Radnor. For another edition, see* 1841.

33124 COURNOT, A. A. Exposition de la théorie des chances et des probabilités. 448p. *8⁰. Paris,* 1843.

33125 [COWARD, W. C.] Victoriaism; or, a reorganization of the people: moral, social, economical, and political, suggested as a remedy for the present distress... [A series of 4 letters, each signed: W.C.C.] 28p. *8⁰.* 1843.

33126 CRUTTWELL, R. The touchstone of England; oversight no crime!...Substance of two lectures given at Leeds, now twenty-two years ago; with some additional notes and remarks, bringing the subject down to the present time – 1843. 84p. *12⁰. Halesworth,* [1843]

33127 DEPPING, G. B. Histoire des expéditions maritimes des Normands, et de leur établissement en France au dixième siècle...Nouvelle édition entièrement refondue. 551p. *8⁰. Paris,* 1843.

33128 DESCRIPTION of improved farms in the state of Tennessee...describing the numbers of acres of arable, meadow, pasture, orchard, and woodland, the mansion and dwelling-houses, farm-buildings, mills, and water-power; with the manufacturing and other advantages of each locality. 58p. *8⁰.* [1843 ?]

33129 DUCLERC, E., *ed.* Dictionnaire politique. Encyclopédie de langage et de la science politiques, rédigé par une réunion de députés, de publicistes et de journalistes, avec une introduction par Garnier-Pagès. Publié par E. Duclerc et Pagnerre. Deuxième édition. 944p. *fol. Paris,* 1843.

For the **ECONOMIST,** or the political, commercial, agricultural and free-trade journal, 1843 ——→, *see* vol. III, *Periodicals list.*

33130 FANE, HON. H. The distress and the remedy. 20p. *8⁰.* 1843.

33131 FERRAND, W. B. The distress of the country: the speech of W. Busfeild Ferrand, Esq., M.P. in the House of Commons. On...Feb. 13, 1843. On Lord Howick's motion upon the distress of the country. Fourth edition. 24p. *8⁰.* [1843]

33132 FERRARI, G. Essai sur le principe et les limites de la philosophie de l'histoire. 551p. *8⁰. Paris,* 1843.

For **FISHER'S COLONIAL MAGAZINE,** 1843–44, *see* vol. III, *Periodicals list.*

33133 FLETCHER, WALTER. Letter on free trade, addressed to the Right Hon. Lord John Russell, M.P.... Third edition, enlarged. 24p. *8⁰. Liverpool,* 1843. *See also* 1844.

33134 GALE, R. Protection of labour and land, closely allied with Britain's destiny. 42p. *8⁰.* 1843.

33135 [GODLEY, J. R.?] Letter to an English Member of Parliament upon the subject of the present state of Ireland, by an Irish country gentleman. 26p. *8⁰. Dublin & London,* 1843. *Attributed to Godley in a manuscript note on the titlepage. The copy that belonged to Earl De Grey.*

33136 GOLOVIN, I. Esprit de l'économie politique. 369p. *8⁰. Paris,* 1843.

For **HIGHLAND AND AGRICULTURAL SOCIETY OF SCOTLAND,** Transactions, 1843–63, 1867–1939, *see* vol. III, *Periodicals list,* Transactions of the Highland and Agricultural Society.

33137 HOFFMANN, JOHANN G. Sammlung kleiner Schriften staatswirthschaftlichen Inhalts. 595p. *8⁰. Berlin,* 1843.

33138 HOLLAND, GEORGE C. The vital statistics of Sheffield. 263p. *8⁰. London & Sheffield,* 1843.

33139 HORNER, F. Memoirs and correspondence of Francis Horner...Edited by...Leonard Horner... 2 vols. *8⁰.* 1843.

33140 McCULLOCH, JOHN R. The principles of political economy...A new edition, enlarged and corrected throughout. [Third edition.] 574p. *8⁰. Edinburgh & London,* 1843. *For other editions, see* 1825.

33141 MARTIN, ROBERT M. Ireland before and after the Union with Great Britain. 424p. *8⁰.* 1843. *A second copy of Part I (p. 1–36) was presented by the author to Earl De Grey, See also* 1848.

33142 [MILLER, H.] Sutherland as it was and is; or, how a country may be ruined. 39p. *8⁰. Edinburgh & London,* 1843.

For the **MODEL REPUBLIC,** *see* vol. III, *Periodicals list.*

For the **MOVEMENT,** anti-persecution gazette and register of progress, 1843–45, *see* vol. III, *Periodicals list.*

33143 **O'BRIEN,** W. S. Speech of William Smith O'Brien, Esq. M.P. on the causes of discontent in Ireland, delivered in the House of Commons, on the 4th July, 1843. 51p. *8°. Dublin,* 1843.

33144 —— [Another edition.] 51p. *8°. Dublin: The Loyal Repeal Association of Ireland,* 1843. *The copy that belonged to Earl De Grey.*

33145 **O'CONNELL,** J. The "commercial injustices." Extract from appendix of a report to the Repeal Association, on the general case of Ireland for a repeal of the legislative Union...[With 'Addenda'.] 98p. *8°. Dublin,* 1843. *The copy that belonged to Earl De Grey.*

33146 **PEEL,** Sir Robert, 2nd Bart. The opinions of Sir Robert Peel, expressed in Parliament and in public. By W. T. Haly, Esq. of the Parliamentary galleries. 480p. *12°.* 1843.

33147 **PLUNKETT,** E., *Baron Dunsany.* Address to the landowners of Ireland upon the present agitation for a repeal of the Union. 20p. *8°.* 1843.

33148 **POPE,** C., *ed.* The yearly journal of trade, 1843 ...Twenty-first edition. [With 'The yearly journal of trade advertiser. 1843'.] 784p. *8°.* [1843] *See also* 1838, 1840, 1842, 1844, 1845, 1846.

For the **PORTFOLIO,** *see* vol. III, *Periodicals list.*

33149 **RAU,** K. D. H. Zur Kritik über F. List's Nationales System der politischen Oekonomie...Besonders abgedruckt aus Rau's Archiv der politischen Oekonomie, v. Band, Heft 2 und 3. 112p. *8°. Heidelberg,* 1843. *The copy that belonged to N. W. Senior.*

33150 **ROSSI,** P. L. O., *Conte.* Cours d'économie politique...Deuxième édition, revue et corrigée. 3 vols. *8°. Paris,* 1843–51.

33151 The **ROYAL COURT GUIDE** and fashionable directory, 1843... 65p. *4°.* 1843.

33152 **SAINT-HUBERT THÉROULDE,** . Voyage dans l'Inde, notes recueillies en 1838, 39 et 40. 250p. *8°. Paris,* 1843.

33153 **SCHLOSSER,** F. C. History of the eighteenth century and of the nineteenth till the overthrow of the French Empire. With particular reference to mental cultivation and progress...Translated, with a preface and notes, by D. Davison. 8 vols. *8°.* 1843–52.

33154 **SIMPSON,** Thomas (1808–1840). Narrative of the discoveries on the north coast of America; effected by the officers of the Hudson's Bay Company during the years 1836–39. [With 'Memoir of Thomas Simpson by his brother, Alexr. Simpson' and 'List of the plants collected during the Arctic journey of Messrs. Simpson and Dease. By Sir W. J. Hooker'.] 419p. *8°.* 1843.

33155 Biographical **SKETCHES.** George Thompson, Esq. (With portrait.) [From the *India Review.*] 20p. *8°. n.p.* [1843 ?]

33156 **SMITH,** Adam. An inquiry into the nature and causes of the wealth of nations...With notes from Ricardo, M'Culloch, Chalmers, and other political economists. Edited by Edward Gibbon Wakefield, Esq. With a life of the author, by Dugald Stewart. A new edition... 4 vols. *12°.* 1843. *For other editions, see* 1776.

33157 **SUGGESTIONS** for checking the repeal agitation. Addressed to the landlords of Ireland by one of themselves. 55p. *8°. Dublin & London,* 1843. *The copy that belonged to Earl De Grey.*

33158 [**TAYLOR,** John (1781–1864).] The case of the industrious classes briefly stated. (Second edition.) [Signed: T.] (*Emancipation of Industry,* 2). 12p. *12°.* [1843]

33159 [——] i. Propositions concerning the cause and remedy of the present distress. [With 'ii. Principles of a society for the emancipation of industry' and 'iii. Remarks on Sir Robert Peel's letter to the Chamber of Commerce, Birmingham, dated December 12, 1842', signed: T.] (*Emancipation of Industry,* 1). 12p. *12°.* [1843]

33160 **TORRENS,** R. A letter to Nassau William Senior, Esq. in reply to the article, "Free trade and retaliation" in the Edinburgh Review, no. CLVII. [With 'Letter to the independent electors of the borough of Sheffield' and letters to Cobden, Welford and Morse.] 99p. *8°.* 1843. *On the verso of the title-page a list of parts I–IX of* The Budget.

33161 —— [Another issue.] (*The Budget. A series of letters on financial, commercial, and colonial policy*...No. X.) p.331–427. *8°.* 1843. *For the collected edition of* The Budget, *see* 1844.

33162 —— A letter to the Right Honourable Sir Robert Peel, Bart., M.P., &c. &c. &c. on the condition of England, and on the means of removing the causes of distress. 95p. *8°.* 1843. *Also issued, with an appendix, as Letter IX of* The Budget, *for a collected edition of which see* 1844.

33163 —— Postscript to A letter to the Right Honourable Sir Robert Peel, Bart., M.P., &c., &c., &c., on the condition of England, and on the means of removing the causes of distress. [With notes.] 50p. *8°.* 1843. *On the verso of the title-page a list of parts I–IX of* The Budget, *here entitled:* 'Recent publications by Colonel Torrens'. *Also issued, following Letter IX, in* The Budget, *1844 (q.v.).*

33164 No. II. A free **TRADE** in corn, the currency question, and Scotch banking system, and the non-intrusion question, as debated between John and James, citizens of Edinburgh. Being the second and last debate. 11p. *8°. Edinburgh,* 1843.

33165 **TUCKER,** G. Progress of the United States in population and wealth in fifty years, as exhibited by the decennial census. 211p. *12°. New York, Philadelphia, &c.,* 1843.

33166 **WATERSTON,** W. A cyclopædia of commerce, mercantile law, finance, and commercial geography ...The law articles contributed by J. H. Burton. 684p. *8°. Edinburgh & London,* 1843. *See also* 1846.

33167 **WEBSTER,** N. A collection of papers on political, literary and moral subjects. 373p. *8°. New York, Boston, &c.,* 1843.

AGRICULTURE

33168 ACLAND, JAMES. The law-craft of land-craft, with legislative illustrations. 8p. *8°*. [*London*, 1843 ?]

33169 [**ANDERSON,** JAMES, *F.R.S.S.A.*] Timely hints, addressed to the landlords and tenantry of England, Scotland & Ireland; showing in a few words, the only obvious means by which they can...derive and pay fair rents from the soil...under the present certain... depreciation in value of British rural productive industry ...With the Premier's avowal, &c. &c. By their "country cousins." 45p. *8°*. 1843. *Presentation copy from the author to Henry James Baillie.*

33170 BANFIELD, T. C. Six letters to the Right Hon. Sir Robert Peel, Bart. Being an attempt to expose the dangerous tendency of the theory of rent advocated by Mr. Ricardo, and by the writers of his school. By a political economist. 59p. *8°*. 1843.

33171 BELLAMY, J. C. The housekeeper's guide to the fish-market for each month of the year; and an account of the fishes and fisheries of Devon and Cornwall, in respect of commerce, economy, natural history and statistics. 144p. *12°*. *London & Plymouth*, 1843.

33172 BOWKETT, T. E. Freehold property for mechanics. Notes of lectures delivered...at the Poplar Literary Institution in...1843; containing instructions for the formation of societies, by means of which every mechanic...may become a freeholder. 22p. *8°*. 1843.

33173 BRENTON, SIR J., *Bart.* Remarks on the importance of our coast fisheries, as the means of increasing the amount of food and employment for the labouring classes, and of maintaining a nursery for seamen. 45p. *8°*. 1843.

33174 CONNER, W. A letter to the Right Honourable Earl of Devon, Chairman of the Land Commission, on the rackrent system of Ireland: showing its cause, its evils and its remedy. 19p. *8°*. *Dublin*, 1843. *See note to no. 27313.*

33175 A **CRY** from Ireland; or, landlord and tenant exemplified. A narrative of the proceedings of Richard Shee, Esq., of Blackwell Lodge, county of Kilkenny, against his tenantry at Bennet's Bridge; to which are added several other cases and singular documents relative to the intimidation of witnesses in lawsuits. 48p. *8°*. [1843]

33176 EDWARDS, DANSON & CO. An account of the manure guano, and of authentic experiments made with it in Great Britain and in France; together with instructions for using it. 15p. *8°*. *Liverpool*, 1843.

33177 ENGLAND. *Laws, etc.* Anno sexto Victoriæ Reginæ. Cap. 6. An Act for inclosing lands in the township of Cliffe-cum-Lund in the parish of Hemingbrough in the East Riding of the County of York. ⟨31st May 1843.⟩ p. 137–71. *fol.* 1843.

33178 FALKNER, F. The muck manual: a practical treatise on the nature and value of manures...With a brief scientific account of agricultural chemistry. For the use of farmers. [With an appendix.] 351p. *8°*. 1843.

33179 —— [Another edition.] The farmer's manual; a practical treatise on the nature and value of manures... 153p. *12°*. *New-York & Philadelphia*, 1843. *This edition is without the extract in the appendix from the work of Dr. Dana on manures.*

33180 FERRAND, W. B. Allotment of waste lands. The speech of W. B. Ferrand, Esq., M.P., in the House of Commons, on...March 30, 1843; on moving for leave to bring in a Bill for the allotment of waste lands. 28p. *8°*. 1843.

33181 GOURCY, C. DE, *Comte.* Narrative of an agricultural tour in England and Scotland, in the year 1840...Translated from the French, for the "Farmer's Magazine." September, 1842. 71p. *8°*. [1843 ?]

33182 HENSLOW, J. S. Letters to the farmers of Suffolk, with a glossary of terms used, and the address delivered at the last anniversary meeting of the Hadleigh Farmers' Club. 114p. *8°*. *London & Hadleigh*, [1843]

33183 HUBENY, J. Entwurf einer Waldpolizei- und Waldstrafordnung für Ungarn und die Nebenländer... 119p. *8°*. *Pesth*, 1843.

33184 JOHNSON, C. W. On guano as a fertilizer. 44p. *8°*. 1843.

33185 KREYSSIG, W. A. Experimental-Oekonomie für die Gegenstände des Feldbaues und der Viehzucht, oder Ermittelung der Regeln und Wege zu Anstellung ökonomisch-praktischer Versuche in denselben. 508p. *8°*. *Braunschweig*, 1843.

33186 NAPER, J. L. W. Observations on the elective franchise and fixity of tenure as connected with agricultural improvement. Addressed to the landlords, landholders, and tenantry of Ireland. 29p. *8°*. *Dublin & London*, 1843.

33187 NESBIT, A. A complete treatise on practical land-surveying, in seven parts: designed chiefly for the use of schools and private students. The eighth edition, greatly enlarged by numerous additions and improvements ... 392p. *8°*. 1843.

33188 PARTOUNAU DU PUYNODE, M. G. Études d'économie politique sur la propriété territoriale. 213p. *8°*. *Paris*, 1843.

33189 ROYER, C. E. Notes économiques sur l'administration des richesses et la statistique agricole de la France. 471p. *8°*. *Paris*, 1843.

33190 SAINT-CLAIR DUPORT, . De la production des métaux précieux au Mexique, considerée dans ses rapports avec la géologie, la métallurgie et l'économie politique. 429p. *8°*. *Paris*, 1843.

33191 *Entry cancelled.*

33192 SMITH, JOSEPH A. Productive farming; or, a familiar digest of the recent discoveries of Liebeg [*sic*], Davy, and other celebrated writers on vegetable chemistry; showing how the results of English tillage might be greatly augmented...Second edition. 179p. *8°*. *Edinburgh, London, &c.*, 1843.

33193 *SOLLY,** E. Rural chemistry: an elementary introduction to the study of the science in its relation to agriculture. 169p. *8°*. 1843. *The copy that belonged to George Grote.*

33194 [SOMERVILLE, ALEXANDER.] A letter to the farmers of England, on the relationship of manufactures and agriculture. By One who has whistled at the plough. 16p. *8°. 1843.*

33195 TRIMMER, JOSHUA. Science with practice; or, guano, the farmers' friend. 30p. *8°.* [1843]

33196 VICE, W. The case of Vice against Thomas, determined on appeal before the Lord Warden of the Stannaries of Cornwall. With an appendix of records and documents illustrating the early history of the tin mines in Cornwall, and explanatory notes, by E. Smirke. 52, 132p. *8°. 1843.*

33197 WATSON, JOSEPH Y. A compendium of British mining, with statistical notices of the principal mines in Cornwall; to which is added, the history and uses of metals, and a glossary of the terms and usages of mining... 82p. *8°. 1843.*

33198 WELFORD, R. G. How will free trade in corn affect the farmer? Being an examination of the effects of corn laws upon British agriculture. 202p. *8°. 1843. Presentation copy, with accompanying letter, from the author to the 3rd Earl of Radnor. For the letter, see vol. III, A.L. 460.*

CORN LAWS

33199 ALMACK, J. Character, motives, and proceedings of the Anti-Corn Law Leaguers, with a few general remarks on the consequences that would result from a free trade in corn. Dedicated to W. R. Greg, Esq. 98p. *8°. 1843. The copy that belonged to the 3rd Earl of Radnor.*

33200 ANTI-CORN-LAW ASSOCIATION, *Glasgow.* [*Begin.*] Sir, The Anti-Corn-Law League of Manchester having resolved to send to every elector in Great Britain and Ireland, printed essays and pamphlets ...[A circular, appealing for funds, signed: Alex Johnston, president, J.P. Reid, treasurer, and dated, 25 January 1843.] [4]p. *4°. n.p.* [1843] *Accompanied by an envelope containing pamphlets published by the National Anti-Corn-Law League, addressed in manuscript to 'James Baynes Esq.'*

33201 ANTI-CORN LAW SOIRÉE in Leith. (From the Caledonian Mercury of Monday, 16th January 1843.) 32p. *12°. Edinburgh,* [1843]

33202 BAIN, D. The egregious and dangerous fallacies of the Anti-Corn Law League; or, the protection of agriculture not a question with landlords, but for the whole Kingdom. 62p. *8°. Edinburgh, 1843.*

33203 BAINES, SIR EDWARD. Reasons in favour of free trade in corn, and against a fixed duty. In three letters to the Right Honourable Lord John Russell. 24p. *12°. Leeds,* [1843]

33204 [BRIDGE, J.] A letter intended for the Manchester Guardian, now respectfully recommended to the earnest perusal of the ladies of the Anti-Corn Law League. By a fellow-townsman. 8p. *8°. Manchester,* [1843]

33205 CAMBRIDGESHIRE AND ISLE OF ELY FARMERS' ASSOCIATION. Things as they are and things as they ought to be; being a report of the committee of the...Association. 16p. *8°. 1843. The copy that belonged to the 3rd Earl of Radnor.*

33206 COBDEN, R. Distress of the country. Speech of R. Cobden, Esq., M.P., in the House of Commons, February 17, 1843. 12p. *12°. Manchester,* [1843]

33207 —— Speech of R. Cobden, Esq., M.P., to the Anti-Corn-Law League, in reference to the disturbances in the manufacturing districts. 8p. *8°. Manchester,* [1843?].

33208 DAY, G. G. Defeat of the Anti-Corn-Law League in Huntingdonshire. The speech of Mr George Game Day on that occasion at Huntingdon, June 17, 1843, (published by request) with notes and additions. 39p. *8°. 1843.*

33209 —— Fifth edition. 39p. *8°. 1843. See also 1844.*

33210 EASBY, J. Repeal! or sketches of the League, its leaders, its members, and its foes! 23p. *8°. London & Manchester, 1843.*

33211 EDWARDS, H. Address to agriculturists and others, in one of the rural districts, on the nature and effects of the present corn laws, as bearing on their interests. 62p. *8°. London & Manchester, 1843.*

33212 Old ENGLAND'S commerce: a story, illustrative of the connexion between the corn law and the home and foreign trade. 24p. *12°. 1843. The copy that belonged to the 3rd Earl of Radnor.*

33213 HARWOOD, P. Six lectures on the corn-law monopoly and free trade: delivered at the London Mechanics' Institution, Southampton Buildings, Chancery Lane. 123p. *8°. 1843.*

33214 HEYWORTH, L. On the corn laws, and other legislative restrictions...Sixth edition, containing new matter, in refutation of...fallacies on the monetary system, and additional evidences, that the tendency of a corn law is, to bring ruin on the agriculture and the revenue, as well as on the commerce of England. 11p. *8°. Manchester, 1843.*

33215 HILL, JAMES. The defeater defeated: being a refutation of Mr Day's pamphlet, entitled "Defeat of the Anti-Corn-Law League in Huntingdonshire"...Sixth edition. 60p. *8°. 1843.*

33216 HODGSKIN, T. A lecture on free trade, in connexion with the corn laws; delivered at the White Conduit House, on January 31, 1843. 23p. *12°. 1843.*

33217 HUBBACK, J. A letter on the corn laws: to which are appended miscellaneous remarks in favour of the protective system. 29p. *8°. Liverpool, London, &c., 1843. The copy that belonged to Earl De Grey.*

33218 —— Second edition. 29p. *8°. Liverpool, London, &c., 1843.*

33219 LACON, J. E. A letter to the inhabitants of the borough of Great Yarmouth, upon free trade in corn and its probable consequences...Second edition. 20p. *8°. Yarmouth, 1843.*

33220 Do as we bid you! or, LEAGUE freedom of discussion. 4p. *8°. n.p.* [1843]

33221 The LEAGUE and the aristocracy. 7p. *8°. n.p.* [1843]

33222 LEAGUE hypocrisy! or, the "friends of the poor" unmasked. 3p. *8°. n.p.* [1843]

For the **LEAGUE**...the organ of the National Anti-Corn-Law League, 1843–46, *see* vol. III, *Periodicals list.*

33223 Three **LETTERS** on corn, currency, and labour; intended to prove the ruinous effects of free trade in corn, as advocated by Mr Cobden, M.P. and the Anti-Corn-Law League. By a Suffolk farmer. 24p. *12°. London, Norwich, &c.,* [1843]

33224 NATIONAL   ANTI-CORN-LAW LEAGUE. The three prize essays on agriculture and the corn law. [By George Hope, Arthur Morse and William Rathbone Greg.] Published by the National Anti-Corn-Law League. 16, 15, 18p. *8°. Manchester & London,* 1843. *For other editions, see* 1842.

33225 Take care of your **POCKETS!** "We want £50,000." – League circular. [A letter.] 4p. *8°. n.p.* [1843]

32226 *Entry cancelled.*

33227 RICE, THOMAS S., *Baron Monteagle.* Corn laws. The consequences of the sliding scale examined and exposed, being the substance of a speech delivered in the House of Lords on...14th March, 1843. 83p. *8°.* 1843. *The author's own copy.*

33228 [**SOMERVILLE,** ALEXANDER.] A chapter on the men of the League [the Anti-Corn-Law League, Manchester]; being a note from the factory districts, which must not be overlooked by those interested in agriculture. [Signed: One who has whistled at the plough.] 2p. *s.sh.fol. Glasgow,* [1843] [*Br.* 604]

33229 SPENCER, T. The parson's dream and the Queen's speech; or, the corn laws and the National Debt ...Twelfth thousand. No. 7. 16p. *8°. London & Bath,* 1843. *Originally published as* The corn laws and the National Debt, *in 1841 (q.v.).*

33230 STRICTURES on the speech of Lord Ducie, on the corn laws, delivered at the meeting held at the Hall of Commerce in the City of London...May 29, 1843: in the form of a letter addressed to the editor of the Mark Lane Express. [Signed: One for Protection.] 22p. *8°.* 1843. *The copy that belonged to the 3rd Earl of Radnor.*

33231 SUUM CUIQUE, *pseud.* ⟨Reprinted from "The New Farmers' Journal", of Aug. 28, 1843.⟩ Moore League lies!!! [A letter refuting the attack by Robert R. R. Moore on George Game Day, quoting testimonials to the accuracy of Day's statements during his speech at Huntingdon.] 4p. *8°. n.p.* [1843]

33232 THOMAS, J. H. Practical consequences likely to result from a repeal of the corn laws...Exhibited in a speech delivered...at a meeting held in Devonport, in reply to Mr. Bright...to which is appended an enquiry into some of the causes of the present distress... 29p. *8°. Devonport & London,* 1843.

33233 TREACHERY of the League...Letter from a convict on board the – hulk to his friends at Stockport. 4p. *8°. n.p.* [1843]

33234 VILLIERS, C. P. Speech of the Hon. C. P. Villiers, M.P., to the members of the Anti-Corn-Law League, January 5, 1843. 14p. *12°. Manchester,* [1843]

33235 WARD, SIR H. G. Speech of H. G. Ward, Esq., M.P. for Sheffield, in the House of Commons, the 10th day of May, 1843, on Mr Villiers's motion for total repeal of the corn laws. 15p. *8°.* [1843]

For the **WEST KENT ANTI-CORN-LAW MAGAZINE,** *see* vol. III, *Periodicals list.*

33236 WHITE, JOHN, *A.M.* England and her interests: the "Times" and the Government and the Anti-Corn Law League, considered. 48p. *8°.* 1843.

33237 WILLIAMS, A. The law or the League? Which? A letter to Robert Palmer, Esq., M.P. 39p. *8°.* 1843. *The copy that belonged to the 3rd Earl of Radnor. Reissued in* Facts for philosophers, *1849, q.v.* (GENERAL).

33238 WRIGHTSON, W. B. Corn laws. Substance of a speech in the House of Commons, May 11, 1843. 20p. *8°.* 1843.

POPULATION

33239 CHADWICK, SIR E. On the best modes of representing accurately, by statistical returns, the duration of life, and the pressure and progress of the causes of mortality amongst different classes of the community, and amongst the population of different districts and countries ...⟨Read before the Statistical Society of London, December 18th, 1843.⟩ 44p. *8°. n.p.* [1843]

33240 DOUBLEDAY, T. The true law of population shewn to be connected with the food of the people. Second edition, with a postscript. 278p. *8°.* 1843. *See also* 1846.

33241 ENGLAND. *General Register Office.* Registration of the causes of death. Regulations; and a statistical nosology: comprising the causes of death, classified and alphabetically arranged, with notes and observations, for the use of those who return the causes of death under 6 & 7 Will. IV, c. 86...March, 1843. [Compiled by W. Farr.] 47p. *8°.* 1843.

33242 *TABLES exhibiting the law of mortality, deduced from the combined experience of seventeen life assurance offices, embracing 83,905 policies; of which 40,616 are distinguished by denoting the sex of the lives assured, and by classing them into town, country, and Irish assurances. [The introduction signed: Chas. Ansell, Griffith Davies, James J. Downes, Benjn. Gompertz, Geo. Kirkpatrick, Joshua Milne, J. M. Rainbow, W. S. B. Woolhouse, being members of the Committee of Actuaries who carried out the project.] 47p. *4°.* 1843. *The copy that belonged to Augustus De Morgan.*

TRADES & MANUFACTURES

33243 BOQUILLON, N. Dictionnaire des inventions et découvertes, depuis le commencement du monde jusqu'à nos jours. 392p. *12°. Paris*, 1843.

33244 DODD, G. Days at the factories; or, the manufacturing industry of Great Britain described, and illustrated by...engravings of machines and processes. Series I. – London. 548p. *12°.* 1843.

33245 HALL, SAMUEL. Description of the operation of Samuel Hall's patent condensers and testimonials respecting them, received subsequently to those contained in the accompanying pamphlet on his improvements on steam engines...Also a description of his patent smoke consuming apparatus and reefing paddle wheels. [With 'Samuel Hall's patent improvements on steam engines'.] 23, 8, 20p. *4°.* 1843. *The copy presented by the author to the London Institution.*

33246 MACKELCAN, F. P. Suggestions to iron-masters on increasing the demand for iron; also, to the iron-masters of Staffordshire, on competing with those of Scotland and Wales. 36p. *8°. London & Birmingham*, 1843. *Presentation copy from the author to 'Mr. Gray'.*

33247 MARTIN, WILLIAM (1772–1851). The destroying angel amongst the coal viewers, mock engineers, false philosophers, babbling astronomers, weathercock preachers, and Puseyite priests. [On the use of the Davy lamp; accusing John Buddle of pirating the author's invention of a fan-ventilator for mines.] 2p. *8°. Newcastle,* [1843]

33248 —— Important suggestions respecting the whale fishery, the war with China, and the proposed bridge across the Tyne, and other subjects. By the Christian philosopher. 4p. *8°. Newcastle,* [1843]

33249 —— The philosopher cutting up the Newcastle Town-Council, concerning the high-level bridge. 2p. *8°. Newcastle upon Tyne,* [1843]

33250 PORTER & COMPANY. Porter's patent anchor. 32p. *8°.* [1843 ?]

33251 PORTER, G. R. The nature and properties of the sugar cane; with practical directions for the improvement of its culture, and the manufacture of its products. Second edition, with an additional chapter on the manufacture of sugar from beet-root. 240p. *8°.* 1843.

33252 SIMMS, F. W. A treatise on the principles and practice of levelling, showing its application to purposes of civil engineering, particularly in the construction of roads, with Mr. Telford's rules for the same...Second edition... 115p. *8°.* 1843.

33253 STEINMAN, G. S. A letter to the Honble. Sidney Herbert, M.P., Chief Secretary of the Admiralty, &c., &c., &c. on submarine steam propelling: with remarks upon the late government trials in H.M. steamer "Bee." 16p. *8°.* 1843.

33254 [STRICKLAND, M.] A memoir of the life, writings, and mechanical inventions, of Edmund Cartwright...inventor of the power loom, etc....[Preface signed: M.S.] 372p. *12°.* 1843.

33255 TAYLOR, WILLIAM C. The hand book of silk, cotton, and woollen manufactures. 211p. *8°. London, Edinburgh, &c.,* 1843.

33256 URE, A. A dictionary of arts, manufactures, and mines: containing a clear exposition of their principles and practice...Third edition, corrected. 1334p. *8°.* 1843. *For another edition, see 1839, and, for a supplement, 1846.*

COMMERCE

33257 ANTI-MONOPOLIST, *pseud.* Remarks on the present state of the coal trade, with a retrospective glance at its history: addressed to the Marquis of Londonderry, K.C.B., Lord Lieutenant of the County of Durham... 52p. *8°. London & Newcastle on Tyne,* 1843.

33258 [BIERSACK, H. L.] Ueber Schutzzölle und andere, gegen das Ausland gerichtete, Schutzmassregeln zur Förderung der inländischen Industrie, so wie über Consumtionssteuern von ausländischen Waaren. Nebst der Handelsbilanz des Deutschen Zollvereins von den Jahren 1837–1841. [Signed: B.] 123p. *8°. Darmstadt,* 1843. *The copy that belonged to N. W. Senior.*

33259 BRIGHT, JOHN (1811–1889). Import duties. Speech of Mr. Bright in the House of Commons, August 7, 1843. 4p. *12°. Manchester,* [1843]

33260 BURNS, R. Restrictive laws on food and trade tried by the test of Christianity: a lecture delivered in John Street Chapel, Glasgow, on...December 6, 1842, under the auspices of the Glasgow Young Men's Free Trade Association. 16p. *8°. Glasgow,* 1843.

33261 CLAPHAM, D. H. The great cause of the present distress, and the remedy...Third edition. [An attack on the tariff of 1842.] 16p. *8°. Chelmsford, Colchester, &c.,* 1843.

33262 COMMERCIO entre Gram-Bretanha e Portugal. [A collection of tables.] [Segunda edição.] 62p. *obl.4°. Lisboa,* 1842[1843] *The number of the edition and the date '1843' are printed on the wrappers.*

33263 CROKER, JOHN D. A letter to the farmers of the counties of Cork, Kerry and Limerick, on the present state of the butter trade, and the abuses of the Cork Weigh-house, with hints on the management of the dairy, and directions for preparing butter for the English markets. 36p. *12°. Cork,* 1843.

33264 FERNLEY, J. D. An appeal to manufacturers on the removal of the restrictions from the exportation of machinery. 12p. *8°. Manchester,* 1843.

33265 FOUQUE, , of Arles. Histoire raisonnée du commerce de Marseille, appliquée aux développements des prospérités modernes. 2 vols. *8°. Paris & Toulon,* 1843.

33266 LIVERPOOL ANTI-MONOPOLY ASSOCIATION. First annual report of the Council of the Liverpool Anti-Monopoly Association for the year 1843...The treasurer's account and a list of members. 40p. *8°. Liverpool,* 1843.

33267 LYCURGUS, *pseud.* To the British Legislature. The repeal of the colonial produce duties, the only effectual measure for the removal of the present commercial distress in Great Britain and her colonies. 23p. *8⁰*. 1843.

33268 OWEN, ELI. Jonathan's visit to his grandmother; or, the free trade bubble exploded. 48p. *8⁰*. 1843.

33269 REFLEXÕES sobre o tratado de commercio entre Portugal e a Grã-Bretanha, e analyse do opusculo do Sr. Antonio Ribeiro Saraiva relativo ao mesmo assumpto. 103p. *8⁰*. *Lisboa*, 1843.

33270 RICARDO, J. L. Mr. Ricardo's speech on the subject of commercial treaties, in the House of Commons, on the 25th April, 1843. 23p. *8⁰*. 1843.

33271 *Entry cancelled.*

33272 SANCHEZ SILVA, M. Manifesto de Manuel Sanchez Silva a la provincia de Cadiz, e historia del

tratado de comercio entre la Inglaterra y España. 31p. *8⁰*. *Madrid*, 1843.

33273 SLEIGH, W. W. Free trade and its consequences...Second edition. 32p. *8⁰*. 1843.

33274 STAUNTON, SIR G. T., *Bart.* Corrected report of the speech of Sir George Staunton, on Lord Ashley's motion, on the opium trade, in the House of Commons, April 4, 1843. With introductory remarks and an appendix. 36p. *8⁰*. 1843.

33275 WILSON, JAMES (1805–1860). The cause of the present commercial distress, and its bearings on the interests of ship-owners; a speech delivered by James Wilson, Esq., of London, at the Free Trade banquet... Liverpool, on...31st January, 1843. 11p. *8⁰*. *Liverpool*, 1843. *The copy that belonged to the 3rd Earl of Radnor.*

COLONIES

For **AGRICULTURAL AND HORTICULTURAL SOCIETY OF WESTERN AUSTRALIA,** Journal, *see* vol. III, *Periodicals list*, Journal...

33276 ATKINSON, CHRISTOPHER W. A guide to New Brunswick, British North America, &c....Second edition. 220p. *8⁰*. *Edinburgh*, 1843. *The third edition, entitled,* A historical and statistical account of New Brunswick, *was published in 1844 (q.v.).*

33277 BACKHOUSE, J. A narrative of a visit to the Australian colonies... 560, cxlivp. *8⁰*. *London & York*, 1843.

33278 *BATTEN, J. H. Report on the settlement of the District of Gurhwal, in the Province of Kumaon. Completed...15th August, 1842. 50p. *8⁰*. *Agra*, 1843.

33279 BUCKINGHAM, J. S. Canada, Nova Scotia, New Brunswick, and the other British provinces in North America, with a plan of national colonization. 540p. *8⁰*. *London & Paris*, [1843]

33280 CHASE, J. C. The Cape of Good Hope and the eastern province of Algoa Bay, &c. &c. with statistics of the colony...Edited by Joseph S. Christophers. [With an appendix containing a directory of Grahamstown and other information for would-be settlers.] 338p. *12⁰*. *London, Cape Town, &c.*, 1843.

33281 *Entry cancelled.*

33282 ENFANTIN, B. P. Colonisation de l'Algérie. 542p. *8⁰*. *Paris*, 1843. *Presentation copy, with inscription, from the author to 'Monsieur de Beaumont, membre de l'institut et de la Commission académique de l'Algérie'.*

33283 JAMIESON, R. Sequel to appeals made to the Government and people of Great Britain, against the Niger expedition before its departure from England. With a letter, addressed to the Right Hon. Lord Stanley, Principal Secretary of State for the Colonies, &c. &c. &c. 32p. *8⁰*. 1843.

33284 JENNINGS, J. New Zealand colonization; details of the system of the New Zealand Company, and of the proceedings of the local government; with objections stated, and remedies proposed in a plan for the next settlement; suggested with the view of preserving all the advantages of colonization to the colonists themselves. 60p. *8⁰*. 1843.

33285 LETTERS from settlers & labouring emigrants, in the New Zealand Company's settlements of Wellington, Nelson, & New Plymouth. From February, 1842, to January, 1843. 211p. *12⁰*. 1843.

33286 MOREHEAD, R. A. A. Some words for and to the capitalists and shareholders in banks and other moneyed companies, connected with the colony of New South Wales. 15p. *8⁰*. *Sydney*, 1843.

33287 NEW BRUNSWICK AND NOVIA SCOTIA LAND COMPANY. Her Majesty's Province of New Brunswick, British North America. Practical information respecting New Brunswick, including details relative to its soil, climate, productions, and agriculture, published for the use of persons intending to settle upon the lands of the New Brunswick and Novia Scotia Land Company... 46p. *8⁰*. *London, Manchester, &c.*, 1843.

33288 PHILLIPPO, J. M. Jamaica: its past and present state...Third thousand. 487p. *8⁰*. 1843.

33289 POSTANS, T. A few observations on the increase of commerce by means of the River Indus. 31p. *8⁰*. 1843.

33290 *WIGHT, ROBERT. Extract notes on American cotton agriculture, as practised on the Government cotton farms in Coimbatore, by Dr. Wight, the superintendent. Dated 1st Feby. 1843. 38p. *8⁰*. *n.p.* [1843?] *A lithographed manuscript facsimile.*

FINANCE

33291 AKERMAN, J. Y. The forgeries of public money; being the substance of a lecture delivered before the Numismatic Society, April 23, 1843. 26p. *8°.* 1843.

33292 [ALLEN, JOHN, *of Liskeard.*] The cause of the heavy burdens of Great Britain, and of her National Debt; comprising a rapid survey of some of the great events especially connected with the finances of British history, during the last hundred and fifty years. Second edition, revised. 12p. *12°.* 1843.

33293 ATTWOOD, T. The currency. (From Aris's Birmingham Gazette, January 30.) 2p. *s.sh.fol. n.p.* [1843]

33294 BANK OF ENGLAND. A list of the names of all proprietors of stock... qualified to vote at the... election... of Governor and Deputy-Governor, on ... April 4, and of directors, on... April 5, 1843. Together with an abstract of the by-laws concerning elections. 92p. *8°.* 1843. *See also* 1738, 1749, 1750, 1789, 1790, 1791, 1792, 1793, 1794, 1795, 1796, 1797, 1798, 1799, 1801, 1803, 1804, 1808, 1809, 1812, 1816, 1819, 1836.

33295 BARNARD, D. D. Speech... on the President's exchequer plan; delivered in the House of Representatives, January 25, 1843. 12p. *8°. Washington,* 1843.

33296 BATEMAN, J., *ed.* The laws of excise; being a collection of all the existing statutes relating to the revenue of excise; with practical notes and forms, and an appendix of select cases. 983p. *8°. London & Dublin,* 1843.

33297 BIRMINGHAM CHAMBER OF COM-MERCE. The currency question. the memorials addressed by the Birmingham Chamber of Commerce to Sir Robert Peel, with his replies; from July 30, to December 12, 1842. 23p. *8°. Birmingham & London,* 1843. *Two copies, one that belonged to F. T. Baring, Baron Northbrook (1796–1866), and the other that belonged to Lord Worsley and afterwards to H. H. Gibbs, first Baron Aldenham.*

33298 BONNEVILLE, A. Nouveau système de réforme monétaire pour la refonte des monnaies d'argent, de billon, de cuivre et de bronze, présenté pendant la session de 1843. 126p. *8°. Paris,* 1843.

33299 BRESSON, J. Des fonds publics français et étrangers et des opérations de la Bourse de Paris... Huitième édition, entièrement refondue et beaucoup augmentée. 279p. *12°. Paris,* 1843. *For another edition, see* 1825.

33300 —— Histoire financière de la France depuis l'origine de la monarchie jusqu'à l'année 1828, précédée d'une introduction sur le mode d'impôts en usage avant la Révolution, suivie de considérations sur la marche du crédit public... Deuxième édition. 2 vols. *8°. Paris,* 1843. *For other editions, see* 1829.

33301 BURGE, W. Case. Her Majesty's Government not yet having proceeded by demand against Portugal for the debt owing to those subjects of this country who hold the public bonds of that state, – your further opinion... is requested, as to the course to be pursued by the creditors of that state. [Opinion dated: 24th May, 1843.] 4p. *n.p.* [1843] *Reprinted in* A sequel to Loans by private individuals to foreign states, entitled to government protection, *see no.* 33347.

33302 BYLES, SIR J. B. A practical treatise of the law of bills of exchange, promissory notes, bank-notes, bankers' cash-notes & checks. With an appendix of statutes and forms of pleading... Fourth edition, enlarged. 536p. *12°.* 1843.

33303 [CAPPS, E.] The nation in a dilemma; or, which shall we alter? the currency or the mode of taxation? By the author of "The currency question in a nutshell." 48p. *12°.* 1843. *For another edition, see* 1840.

33304 COCKBURN, SIR G. A dissertation on the state of the British finances, the debt, currency, and banking; with a plan for raising thirty millions or more, without loan or increased taxation. Also, some observations on Ireland. 94p. *8°. London & Dublin,* 1843. *Presentation copy from the author to Lord Fitzroy Somerset.*

33305 [COLTON, C.] The currency. By Junius. 16p. *8°. New York & Philadelphia,* 1843.

33306 COOKE, EDWARD (1792?–1862). Suggestions submitted to the Legislature for putting an end to all private trusts, and for establishing a general court of trusts for the due administration of trust property. 27p. *8°.* 1843.

33307 COWELL, JOHN W. Letters to the Right Honourable Francis Thornhill Baring on the institution of a safe and profitable paper currency. 127p. *8°.* 1843.

33308 CRAIG, JOHN, *of the Bank of Ireland.* Interest tables, at the rate of £3.6s.8d. per cent per annum, calculated to the hundredth part of a penny, and consisting of a distinct table for every week in half-a-year... computed expressly for the use of the Cork Savings' Bank. 93p. *4°. Cork,* 1843.

33309 CRUZ-LIMA, J. D. DA. Reflexões sobre o estado actual das finanças do Brasil e proposta de alguns melhoramentos e medi das que lhe podem ser applicadas. 75p. *8°. Rio de Janeiro,* 1843. *Presentation copy from the author to 'Dr. Demersay'.*

33310 CUNNINGHAM, SIR A. The ancient coinage of Kashmir. With chronological and historical notes, from the commencement of the Christian era to the conquest of the country by the Moguls... (Read before the Numismatic Society, January 26, 1843.) 38p. *8°.* [1843]

33311 D., J. S. The guide to service. The banker's clerk; comprising the principles and practice of banking. 215p. *12°.* 1843.

33312 DICKINSON, R. W. Vexata quæstio; being two addresses on the depreciation of the currency, delivered before the North Devon Agricultural Association, at Barnstaple... 3rd day of February and... 3rd day of March, 1843. 48p. *8°.* 1843.

33313 ENDERBY, C. The distress of the nation, its causes and remedies. 98p. *8°.* 1843. *See also* 1844.

33314 —— To the Right Honourable Sir Robert Peel, Bart. [A letter on the currency dated: 20th February, 1843.] 7p. *8°.* [*London,* 1843]

33315 —— To the Right Honourable W. E. Gladstone, M.P. [A letter on the currency dated: 30th May, 1843.] 8p. *8°.* [*London,* 1843]

33316 FAUCHER, L. Recherches sur l'or et sur l'argent considérés comme étalons de la valeur. (Mémoire lu à l'Académie des Sciences morales dans les séances du 16 et du 23 avril 1843). 107p. 8°. *Paris*, 1843.

33317 FRANCE. *Chambre des Députés.* (No. 33.) Chambre des Députés. Session 1843. Projet de loi relatif à la refonte des monnaies de cuivre, précédé de l'exposé des motifs présenté par M. le Ministre Secrétaire d'État au Département des Finances [Laplagne]. Séance du 4 mars 1843. 24p. 8°. [*Paris*,] 1843.

33318 —— —— (No 130.) Chambre des Députés. Session 1843. Rapport fait au nom de la commission chargée d'examiner le projet de loi relatif à la démonétisation des espèces de billon et de cuivre, à leur remplacement par une monnaie de bronze, et à la centralisation de la fabrication des monnaies, par M. Pouillet... Séance du 29 avril 1843. 42p. 8°. [*Paris*,] 1843.

33319 FRICHOT, A. P. Nouvelles observations sur la refonte des monnaies à l'occasion du rapport de M. Pouillet. 27p. 8°. *Paris*, 1843.

33320 —— Refonte des monnaies. Nouveaux développements du projet de A.-P. Frichot, manufacturier. Proposition de frapper après la refonte des médailles historiques à bon marché pour servir à l'instruction du peuple. 32p. 8°. *Paris*, 1843.

33321 Fourth edition. Penny edition for the millions of the **GOVERNMENT** currency plan. No. 1. *s.sh.fol.* [1843] [*Br.* 605(1)]

33322 Penny edition for the millions of the **GOVERNMENT** currency plan. No. 2. [Dated: March 29, 1843.] *s.sh.fol.* [1843] [*Br.* 605(2)]

33323 *GRAY, P. A commutation table for calculating the values of benefits depending upon a single male life. With explanatory remarks and illustrations. 8p. 8°. 1843. *The copy that belonged to Augustus De Morgan.*

33324 HELFERICH, J. A. R. Von den periodischen Schwankungen im Werth der edeln Metalle von der Entdeckung Amerika bis zum Jahr 1830. Eine historisch-ökonomische Monographie. 268p. 8°. *Nürnberg*, 1843.

33325 HEROS, M. DE LOS. Memoria que acerca de la administracion de la Real Casa y patrimonio de S.M. en el año de 1842. Presenta al Excmo. Sr. Tutor de S.M., D. Agustin Argüelles, el Intendente general en Comision de la misma Real Casa... 156p. 8°. *Madrid*, 1843.

33326 HINDLE, R. An account of the expenditure of the County Palatine of Lancaster, for a period of 23 years, commencing 1819, and ending 1842, with remarks. 317p. 8°. *London, Preston, &c.*, 1843.

33327 HUBBARD, J. G., *Baron Addington.* The currency and the country. 112p. 8°. 1843.

33328 *JONES, DAVID, *actuary.* On the value of annuities and reversionary payments, with numerous tables... 2 vols. 8°. 1843. *The copy that belonged to Augustus De Morgan.*

33329 *JONES, JENKIN. A series of tables of annuities and assurances calculated from a new rate of mortality among assured lives: with examples... [With 'Legal decisions on life assurance: a digest of all the reported cases, chronologically arranged'.] xxx, 55, [64], 10p. 8°. *London & Edinburgh*, 1843. *The copy that belonged to Augustus De Morgan.*

33330 [**JOPLIN,** T.] An essay on the condition of the National Provincial Bank of England, with a view to its improvement: in a letter to the shareholders, by the founder of the establishment. 71p. 8°. 1843.

33331 *LAWRANCE, F. A short treatise on life assurance: with the rates of all the offices in London, mutual, mixed, and proprietary, alphabetically arranged. 64p. 8°. 1843. *The copy that belonged to Augustus De Morgan.*

33332 LOMBARD, J. E. Du système monétaire à Genève et en Suisse. Mémoire lu à la Société d'Utilité Publique, dans sa séance du 3 février 1843. Par E. Ld. 34p. 8°. *Genève*, 1843.

33333 LOWNDES, , *pseud.* Plan of a currency agent, intended to obviate the honest objections of all parties, and to meet the views of moderate men of both parties. 8p. 8°. *n.p.* [1843] *The author has sometimes been identified as W. M. Gouge.*

33334 MARINER, W. Exchequer bills forgery. A statement. 85p. 8°. 1843.

33335 —— Second edition. 85p. 8°. 1843.

33336 MILLER, SAMUEL, *barrister.* Suggestions for a general equalization of the land tax; with a view to provide the means of the reducing the malt duties: and a statement of the legal rights and remedies of persons unequally assessed to land tax in particular districts... The third edition. 58p. 8°. 1843. *For another edition, see* 1839.

33337 MILNE, JAMES. Essay on the causes of, and the remedy for, the present distress of the country. 40p. 8°. *Newcastle*, 1843.

33338 MUNTZ, G. F. The true cause of the late sudden change in the commercial affairs of the country... March 13, 1837. Second edition with additions March 21, 1843. 17p. 8°. *Birmingham & London*, 1843. *For another edition, see* 1837.

33339 NEWMARCH, W. Legacy duty and annuity tables... With a practical introduction and a selection of useful official forms. 99p. 12°. *London & York*, 1843.

33340 O'CONNELL, J. The "taxation injustice." Extract from appendix of a report to the Repeal Association, on the general case of Ireland for a repeal of the legislative Union... 56p. 8°. *Dublin*, 1843. *The copy that belonged to Earl De Grey.*

33341 OGIE, N. Direct or indirect taxation? or, should the corn laws, customs and excise duties be abolished, how is the revenue now obtained from them to be replaced? 22p. 8°. 1843. *The copy that belonged to the 3rd Earl of Radnor.*

33342 [**PAGE,** R.] Banks and bankers. By Daniel Hardcastle, jun. Second edition, with an appendix, comprising a review of the failures amongst private and joint-stock banks. 460p. 12°. 1843. *For another edition, see* 1842.

33343 RECHTEREN, J. H. VAN, *Graaf.* Beschouwingen over eene vereenvoudigde huishouding van staat, en de daardoor mogelijke vermindering der uitgaven, in verband met de door de regering ontworpene staatsbegrooting over 1844 en 1845 voor het Koningrijk de Nederlanden... Tweede druk. 65p. 8°. *Zwolle*, 1843.

33344 SALOMONS, SIR D., *Bart.* Reflections on the connexion between our gold standard and the recent monetary vicissitudes; with suggestions for the addition of silver as a measure of value. 99p. 8°. 1843.

33345 SAUNDERSON, C. Suretiship. The dangers and defects of private security and their remedies. 30p. 8°. 1843. *See also* 1844, 1845.

33346 SCOTTISH PROVIDENT INSTITU-TION. Scottish Provident Institution...[*Begin.*] The Directors request the attention of agriculturists...to the peculiarly favourable provisions of this Institution. 4p. *8⁰. Edinburgh*, [1843]

33347 A SEQUEL to Loans by private individuals to foreign states, entitled to government protection... 42p. *8⁰*. 1843. *For the original work, see* 1842.

33348 SMITH, SYDNEY (1771–1845). Letters on American debts...First printed in the "Morning Chronicle." 24p. *8⁰*. 1843. *See also* 1844.

33349 [TAYLOR, JOHN (1781–1864).] Currency explained; in refutation of the last fallacy of "The Times," 8 Nov. 1843. By Verus. 30p. *8⁰*. 1843. *In a volume of the author's pamphlets presented to Sir Robert Peel. See also* 1845 (Currency investigated).

33350 [———] The Minister mistaken: or, the question of depreciation erroneously stated by Mr. Huskisson. 40p. *8⁰*. 1843. *In a volume of the author's pamphlets presented to Sir Robert Peel. See also* 1845 (Currency investigated).

33351 [———] The monetary policy of England and America. 44p. *8⁰*. 1843. *In a volume of the author's pamphlets presented to Sir Robert Peel. See also* 1845 (Currency investigated).

33352 TEGOBORSKI, L. Des finances et du crédit public de l'Autriche, de sa dette, de ses ressources financières et de son système d'imposition; avec quelques rapprochemens entre ce pays, la Prusse et la France... 2 vols. *8⁰. Paris*, 1843.

33353 TWISS, SIR T. On money and currency. A lecture delivered before the University of Oxford, in Lent Term, 1843...With an appendix on the paper money of the Chinese. 40p. *8⁰. Oxford & London*, 1843.

33354 URE, A. The revenue in jeopardy from spurious chemistry, demonstrated in researches upon wood-spirit and vinous-spirit. 35p. *8⁰*. 1843.

33355 WESTERN, C. C., *Baron Western*. A letter from Lord Western, to the chairman of the meeting of the Birmingham Chamber of Commerce, assembled at the Waterloo Rooms, on the 16th August. 10p. *8⁰*. 1843.

33356 WILLICH, C. M. Income tax tables, showing at sight the amount of duty at 7d. and 3½d. in the pound ...Second edition. [18]p. *8⁰*. 1843.

33357 ——— Fourth edition. [24]p. *8⁰*. 1843. *For another edition, see* 1842.

TRANSPORT

33358 [*Endorsed:*] **ARMAGH BRANCH CANAL.** 1843. Prospectus. [With a map.] 2p. *fol. Armagh*, [1843] *Addressed in manuscript 'To Thomas Townshend Esq. with T. Casebourne's respects'.*

33359 BRADSHAW, G. Bradshaw's railway companion, containing the times of departure, fares, &c. of the railways in Great Britain and Ireland, and also hackney coach fares... [38]p. *32⁰*. 1st mo. (January,) 1843. *Very imperfect, wanting most of the tables.*

33360 ——— Bradshaw's railway companion... 70[108]p. *32⁰*. 2nd mo. (February,) 1843. *See also* 1841, 1847.

33361 BRADSHAW'S monthly general railway and steam navigation guide, for Great Britain and Ireland, containing a correct account of the hours of departure of the trains...with a map...and list of shares... [March, 1843.] 36p. *4⁰*. [1843] *See also* 1846.

33362 BUSH, JOHN (*fl.* 1843). Memoir on the Canal of the Pyrenees, and its advantages as an investment for a limited amount of British capital...Second edition. With appendix and report of W. Gravatt, Esq. C.E. 35p. *8⁰*. 1843.

33363 CLARKSON, E. The Suez navigable canal, for accelerated communications with India. ⟨From the Foreign and Colonial Quarterly Review.⟩ 14p. *8⁰*. 1843.

33364 DARU, N., *Comte*. Des chemins de fer, et de l'application de la loi du 11 juin 1842. 400p. *8⁰. Paris*, 1843.

33365 DOBSON, E., *comp.* An historical, statistical, and scientific account of the railways of Belgium from 1834 to 1842. Translated and compiled from official documents by Edward Dobson... 101p. *8⁰*. 1843. *For another edition, see no.* 33379.

33366 EDDY, C. Historical sketch of the Middlesex Canal [Massachusetts], with remarks for the consideration of the proprietors. By the agent of the corporation. 53p. *8⁰. Boston*, 1843.

33367 ENGLAND. *Laws, etc.* The General Highways Act, 5 & 6 Will. IV. c. 50, and the statutes and cases relating thereto; with an introduction, notes, and index. By Alfred A. Fry. 134p. *8⁰*. 1843.

33368 [GALT, W.] Railway reform; its expediency and practicability considered. With a copious appendix, containing a description of all the railways in Great Britain and Ireland; fluctuations in the prices of shares; statistical and parliamentary returns, etc. 108p. *8⁰*. 1843.

33369 ——— Second edition, revised and considerably enlarged. 116p. *8⁰*. 1843. *See also* 1844.

33370 The **HIGHWAY** surveyor's guide. 50p. *12⁰*. 1843.

33371 JENNINGS, E. Hints on sea-risks, containing some practical suggestions for diminishing maritime losses both of life and property; addressed to merchants, shipowners, and mariners. 102p. *8⁰*. 1843. *Reissued, with the title* Practical hints addressed to seamen, *in 1844 (q.v.).*

33372 MARTIN, WILLIAM (1772–1851). The philosopher, with the eye of a hawk, exposing traitors, for imposing upon poor ingenious men. [On the pirating of his invention of a gate for the Brandling Junction Railway Company.] 2p. *8⁰*. [*Newcastle-upon-Tyne*, 1843]

33373 NEWCASTLE AND CARLISLE RAILWAY COMPANY. Report of the Directors...read to the shareholders at their annual meeting, March 28, 1843. 15p. *8⁰. Newcastle-upon-Tyne*, 1843. *See also* 1835, 1837, 1838, 1845.

33374 PALMER, W. The law of wreck, considered with a view to its amendment. 54p. *8⁰*. 1843.

33375 REMARKS on the proceedings in the Committee on the Northampton and Peterborough Railway Bill. 39p. *8⁰*. 1843.

33376 TAVARD, E. Le chemin de fer de Paris à Orléans. Itinéraire descriptif, historique et pittoresque, précédé d'un résumé des travaux de la Compagnie, d'une notice sur l'histoire et les progrès de la machine à vapeur ...Deuxième édition, augmentée du nouveau service pour la saison d'été. 216p. *12⁰*. *Paris*, 1843.

33377 VETCH, J. Inquiry into the means of establishing a ship navigation between the Mediterranean and Red seas...Illustrated by a map. 32p. *8⁰*. 1843.

33378 —— Second edition. [With 'Note. 1847'.] 34p. *8⁰*. 1843[–47]

33379 WEALE, JOHN. Ensamples of railway making; which, although not of English practice, are submitted, with practical illustrations, to the civil engineer, and the British and Irish public. [With 'Mechanical works on the Utica and Syracuse railroad', by R. F. Isherwood [i.e. B. F. Isherwood], and 'The railways of Belgium in 1842 ...By E. Dobson'.] xliii, 64, 101p. *8⁰*. 1843.

33380 WYDROFF, V. DE. Exposé d'un nouveau système de construction de chemins de fer. 22p. *4⁰*. *Londres & Paris*, 1843. *The Rastrick copy.*

SOCIAL CONDITIONS

33381 ALEXANDER, JOHN, *and others.* A letter addressed to a Member of Parliament, on the educational clauses in Sir James Graham's altered Factory Bill. [Signed: John Alexander, William Brock, Andrew Reed.] 8p. *8⁰*. *London & Norwich*, 1843.

For the **ANTI-SMOKER AND PROGRESSIVE TEMPERANCE REFORMER**, *see* vol. III, *Periodicals list.*

33382 BAINES, SIR EDWARD. The social, educational, and religious state of the manufacturing districts; with statistical returns of the means of education and religious instruction in...Yorkshire, Lancashire and Cheshire; in two letters to the Right Hon. Sir Robt. Peel, Bart. With an appendix containing a letter to...Lord Wharncliffe on Sir Jas. Graham's Factory Education Bill; also the objections to the amended Bill. 76p. *8⁰*. *London & Leeds*, 1843.

33383 —— Third edition. 76p. *8⁰*. 1843.

33384 BALY, W. On the prevention of scurvy, in prisons, pauper lunatic asylums, &c....From the London Medical Gazette, Feb. 10, 1843. 7p. *8⁰*. [1843]

33385 BATH. Rules & regulations for the government of the gaol for the City and Borough of Bath 1843. 63p. *8⁰*. *Bath*, [1843]

33386 CHADWICK, SIR E. Report on the sanitary condition of the labouring population of Great Britain. A supplementary Report on the results of a spiecal [*sic*] inquiry into the practice of interment in towns. Made at the request of Her Majesty's Principal Secretary of State for the Home Department...Presented to both Houses of Parliament. 279p. *8⁰*. 1843. *For the* Report...*on an inquiry into the sanitary condition of the labouring population, by the Poor Law Commission, see* 1842.

33387 CHANNING, WALTER. An address on the prevention of pauperism. 84p. *12⁰*. *Boston*, 1843.

33388 CHURCH EDUCATION considered. [An attack on the Factory Education Bill.] 24p. *8⁰*. [1843]

33389 CLEMENTS, W. S., *Earl of Leitrim.* Speech of Viscount Clements, M.P. calling attention to the charitable loan societies (Ireland), in the House of Commons...August 14th, 1843. Extracted from Hansard's Parliamentary Debates. 35p. *12⁰*. [*London,*] 1843.

33390 COMMITTEE OF INHABITANTS OF EDINBURGH AND LEITH. Evidence before the Parliamentary Committees on the Water Company's Bill, taken in short-hand by Mr. Gurney, with numerous notes and documents, including the principal clauses of the new Act. Edited for the Inhabitants' Committee by Duncan M'Laren. 110p. *8⁰*. *Edinburgh*, 1843. *The copy presented to the Lord Provost of Edinburgh.*

33391 COOPER, A. A., *7th Earl of Shaftesbury.* Moral and religious education of the working classes. The speech of Lord Ashley, M.P., in the House of Commons, on...February 28, 1843, on moving "That an humble address be presented...praying that Her Majesty will be graciously pleased to take into her...serious consideration, the best means of diffusing the benefits...of a moral and religious education amongst the working classes of her people." 38p. *8⁰*. 1843.

33392 COTTAGE IMPROVEMENT SOCIETY FOR NORTH NORTHUMBERLAND. Second annual report of the committee of the...Society...(1843.) 43p. *8⁰*. *London & Alnwick*, [1843] *See also* 1842.

33393 CREWE, SIR G., *Bart.* A word for the poor, and against the present Poor Law, both as to its principle and practice. 36p. *8⁰*. *Derby & London*, 1843.

33394 CROWTHER, R. An essay on the cause of bad trade, with a plan of legal protection for wages, proposed as a remedy. 15p. *8⁰*. *Manchester*, 1843.

33395 DAVIES, THOMAS, (*fl.* 1843). Prize essay on the evils which are produced by late hours of business, and on the benefits which would attend their abridgement. With a preface by the Hon. and Rev. Baptist W. Noel, M.A. 39p. *8⁰*. 1843. *See also* 1844.

33396 An analytical **DIGEST** of the education clauses of the Factories' Bill now before Parliament, with observations and objections; to which are added, practical suggestions to the opponents of the Bill. 43p. *8⁰*. 1843.

33397 DUNCOMBE, T. S. Conduct of Lord Abinger! A speech delivered in the House of Commons ...on...Feb. 21, 1843. 24p. *12⁰*. *n.p.* [1843]

33398 DUNN, H. The Bill or the alternative. A letter to the Right Honourable Sir James Graham, Bart., M.P., &c., &c. 31p. *8⁰*. 1843.

33399 EDUCATION and the voluntary principle. 16p. *8⁰*. *London & Bristol*, [1843]

33400 ENGLAND. *Commissioners for Inquiring into the Employment and Condition of Children in Mines and Manufactories.* The physical and moral condition of the children and young persons employed in mines and manufactures. Illustrated by extracts from the Reports of the Commissioners... 267p. *8⁰*. 1843. *With a manuscript note by HSF:* 'one of a few copies issued by Lord Ashley with specially prepared map & plates'.

33401 —— *Poor Law Commission* [*1834–1847*]. Reports of special Assistant Poor Law Commissioners on the employment of women and children in agriculture. 378p. *8°*. 1843.

33402 An **ESSAY** on the superiority of moral force over physical force, for the purpose of establishing and maintaining principles based upon truth and justice. Addressed to the people of Ireland. [Signed: An apprentice mechanic. With an introduction by James Haughton.] 16p. *8°*. *n.p.* [1843] *The Turner copy.*

33403 **EVANS,** James C. Letter to Sir James Graham, Bart., on the education clauses of the Factory Bill; with an appendix, containing Lord John Russell's resolutions, with remarks thereon...Sixth thousand. 12p. *8°*. 1843.

33404 **FACTS** and observations relating to the administration of medical relief to the sick poor, in England and Wales. Addressed to the members of the Commons House of Parliament. 32p. *8°*. 1843.

33405 **FARADAY,** M. Lecture on light and ventilation: delivered at the Royal Institution, April 7, 1843. [With 'Specification of the patent granted to Robert Faraday...gas fitter, for improvements in ventilating gas burners...1843'.] 23p. *12°*. [1843]

33406 **FLOWER,** E. Hours of business. A glance at the present system of business among shopkeepers, and the effect of that system upon the young men engaged in retail trades, as well as upon society at large. 46p. *8°*. *London, Liverpool, &c.,* 1843.

33407 **FOX,** William J. On the educational clauses in the Bill now before the House of Commons, "for regulating the employment of children and young persons in factories, and for the better education of children in factory districts." 30p. *8°*. 1843.

33408 —— Second edition. 30p. *8°*. 1843.

33409 **FRIENDS,** *Society of. London Committee for the Relief of the Distress in the Manufacturing Districts.* Report of the Friends' London Committee...[Signed: Samuel Fox.] 41p. *8°*. 1843.

33410 **GREY,** H. G., *3rd Earl Grey.* The speech of the Right Hon. Viscount Howick, in the House of Commons, on...Feb. 13, 1843, on moving for a Committee of the whole House to consider so much of Her Majesty's speech as refers to "that depression of the manufacturing interests of the country which has so long prevailed, and which Her Majesty has so deeply lamented." 26p. *8°*. 1843.

33411 **GRINDROD,** R. B. Bacchus: an essay on the nature, causes, effects, and cure of intemperance... Second edition. 379p. *8°*. 1843. *The Turner copy. For another edition, see* 1839.

33412 —— The wrongs of our youth; an essay on the evils of the late-hour system. 76p. *8°*. *London & Manchester,* 1843.

33413 —— ⟨Second thousand.⟩ 76p. *8°*. *London & Manchester,* 1843.

33414 "**HEALTH** of towns:" an examination of the report and evidence of the Select Committee; of Mr. Mackinnon's Bill; and of the Acts for establishing cemeteries around the Metropolis. 131p. *8°*. 1843.

33415 **HILL,** Sir Rowland (1795–1879). Proof – strictly confidential. Mr. Rowland Hill's correspondence with the Treasury, with reference to his appointment and removal, and to the introduction of the remaining parts of his plan of Post-Office improvement: including those letters which have been withheld as well as those which are given in the official copy. 32p. *8°*. 1843.

33416 —— Requisites to the completion of Mr. Rowland Hill's plan of Post-Office improvement. No. 1. [Being his letter of 24 April 1843 to the London Mercantile Committee on Postage, with his petition for inquiring into the state of the Post-Office, and the Committee's petition that his reforms be completed.] Third thousand. 16p. *8°*. 1843.

33417 **HINTON,** J. H. A plea for liberty of conscience: a letter to the Right Hon. Sir James Graham, Bart., on the educational clauses of the Factories' Bill. 16p. *8°*. 1843.

33418 —— Seventh thousand. Why not? Or, seven objections to the educational clauses of the Factories Regulation Bill. 8p. *8°*. [*London*, 1843]

33419 **HODGES,** T. L. A letter to the Poor Law Commissioners [pointing out errors in the statistics quoted for the parish of Benenden, Kent, in their eighth annual report]. 8p. *8°*. *Cranbrook*, [1843]

33420 **HOLY GILD OF ST. JOSEPH,** *Edinburgh.* A report [of the first annual festival of the Holy Gild of St. Joseph], &c., with an account of the speeches delivered, and of the gild premiums awarded for the cleanest and tidiest kept houses. Edinburgh, 21st October, 1842. And an appendix, containing...papers on the present condition of the working classes of the community, and its possible improvement. Edited by the Right Reverend Bishop Gillis. 64, cxxvp. *8°*. *Edinburgh*, 1843.

33421 **HONIBORNE,** T. A word for early closing: embracing a view of the evils connected with the late hour system of business; and showing the advantages resulting from an abridgment of the same, to the employer, the employed and the public. 31p. *8°*. [1843?]

33422 **KING,** A. J. The system of late hours in business: its evils, its causes, and its cure. 30p. *8°*. *London, Edinburgh, &c.,* 1843.

33423 **LEES,** F. R. The physiological question. The medical discussion, held at Framlingham, Suffolk, March 29th, 1843, between Frederick Richard Lees and William Jeaffreson, on the nature and uses of alcohol. 36p. *12°*. 1843. *The Turner copy.*

33424 —— The sacred writings rescued from the impious perversions of moderate-poison-drinkers: being the substance of an address delivered in the Music Hall, Worksop, June 22nd, 1843, (in review of certain statements made in public discussion...). 22p. *12°*. [*Worksop*, 1843] *The Turner copy.*

33425 —— The "strong drink" question. Teetotalism harmonized with the Scriptures generally and with Deut. XIV. 26, in particular...With introductory remarks in reply to Professor Maclean, by the author of Anti-Bacchus. Second edition. 72p. *8°*. 1843. *With manuscript notes and deletions. The Turner copy.*

33426 —— [Another issue.] 72p. *8°*. 1843. *The Turner copy.*

33427 ——, *ed.* Standard temperance library. 84p. *8°*. 1843. *The running title reads: British permanent temperance documents. The Turner copy.*

33428 **LEFEBVRE LABOULAYE,** E. R. Recherches sur la condition civile et politique des femmes, depuis les Romains jusqu'à nos jours... 528p. *8°*. *Paris & Leipsig,* 1843.

33429 **LEFEVRE,** Sir G. W. Thermal comfort; or, popular hints for preservation against colds, coughs, and consumption...Reprinted from the Lancet of November 5, 1842. 31p. *8°*. 1843.

33430 [LHOTSKY, J.] Hunger and revolution. By the author of "Daily bread." 38p. 8°. [1843]

33431 LLOYD, CHARLES, *barrister*. A calm inquiry into all the objections made to the educational provisions of the Factory Bill, exhibiting the nature, tendency, and object of the new principles by which the dissenting bodies stand opposed thereto. 25p. 8°. 1843.

33432 LOGAN, WILLIAM (1813–1879). An exposure, from personal observation, of female prostitution in London, Leeds, and Rochdale, and especially in... Glasgow. With remarks on the cause, extent, results, and remedy of the evil...Third edition. 48p. 12°. *Glasgow, Edinburgh, &c.*, 1843.

33433 MACHINERY: its tendency; viewed particularly in reference to the working classes. By an artizan. 31p. 8°. 1843.

33434 MAHOMED, H. The bath: a concise history of bathing, as practised by nations of the ancient and modern world. Including a brief exposition of the medical efficacy and salubrity of the warm, medicated, vapour, shampooing shower, and douche bath. With remarks on the moral and sanative influence of bathing. 80p. 12°. 1843.

33435 MARTIN, WILLIAM (1771–1851). The downfall of the devil's servants; or, babbling lecturers and weathercock preachers in an uproar, concerning the National Education Bill... 2p. 8°. *Newcastle*, [1843]

33436 —— The philosopher on the distress of the country, its causes and remedy. 4p. 8°. *Newcastle*, [1843]

33437 —— The philosopher's letter to the Queen & British Government, on the national education, a spiritual work of the mighty God of the universe... 2p. 8°. *Newcastle-on-Tyne*, [1843]

33438 MASLEN, T. J. Suggestions for the improvement of our towns and houses. 249p. 8°. 1843. *The author's own copy, bound in a volume with other pamphlets, offprints and plans of metropolitan improvements.*

33439 MATHEW, T. The proceedings of Father Mathew in administering the pledge, together with his sermon...at St. Patrick's Church. 12p. 12°. *Manchester*, 1843. *The Turner copy.*

33440 MURCH, S. Ten objections against the Factories' Education Bill, with an address to the people of England...In rhyme. 12p. 12°. 1843.

33441 NOBLE, D. Facts and observations relative to the influence of manufactures upon health and life. 81p. 8°. *London, Manchester, &c.*, 1843. *The copy that belonged to Victor Considérant.*

33442 PAGET, F. E. The pageant; or, pleasure and its price. A tale for the upper ranks of society. 208p. 12°. *London, Oxford, &c.*, 1843.

For the **POTTERS' EXAMINER AND WORKMAN'S ADVOCATE,** 1843–45, *see* vol. III, *Periodicals list.*

For **REVUE PÉNITENTIAIRE,** 1843–45, *see* vol. III, *Periodicals list.*

33443 ROBERTS, S. A dry crust of the Ecclesall Bierlow pauper bread for the Building Committee of the Sheffield Guardians of the Poor. 38p. 8°. *Sheffield*, 1843.

33444 ST. GEORGE'S SOCIETY. Constitution of the St. George's Society, established in the City of New-York, in 1786, for the purpose of relieving their brethren in distress. With a list of its officers and members. 39p. 12°. *New-York*, 1843.

33445 SANDYS, G. W. A letter to the Right Honourable Sir James R.G. Graham, Bart. M.P. Secretary of State for the Home Department, occasioned by a recent debate in the House of Commons, on the subject of national education. 19p. 8°. 1843.

33446 [SEELEY, R. B.] The perils of the nation. An appeal to the Legislature, the clergy and the higher and middle classes. [On the social evils afflicting the working classes.] 399p. 12°. 1843.

33447 SHAW, SIR C. Manufacturing districts. Replies of Sir Charles Shaw to Lord Ashley, M.P. regarding the education, and moral and physical condition of the labouring classes. 47p. 8°. 1843.

33448 STAPLETON, A. G. The real monster evil of Ireland [the poverty of the peasantry]. 38p. 8°. 1843.

33449 —— Sequel to The real monster evil of Ireland. 46p. 8°. 1843. *The copy presented by the author to Earl De Grey.*

33450 STEANE, E. The rights of conscience. An argument occasioned by the educational clauses of the Factories' Bill. 16p. 8°. 1843.

33451 SURREY. *Commissioners of Sewers for Surrey and Kent.* Sewers, Surrey and Kent. Reports relating to the sewage, with reference to the observations of the Poor Law Commissioners, on their inquiry into the sanitary condition of the labouring population of Great Britain. [The reports signed by William Nottidge, Joseph Gwilt, Edward Anson and John Newman.] Printed by order of the Court. 86p. 8°. 1843.

33452 SWAINE, E. Equity without compromise: or, hints for the construction of a just system of national education. 35p. 8°. 1843. *See also 1846.*

33453 SYMONS, JELINGER C. Light and life for the people. An appeal to the Lord Ashley, M.P. against the educational clauses of the new Factory Bill; with a substitute. 32p. 8°. 1843.

33454 The UNEMPLOYED, and the proposed new poor-law. A letter from a Renfrewshire heritor, to the holders of real property in that county, and other manufacturing districts of Scotland. 52p. 8°. *Glasgow, Edinburgh, &c.*, 1843.

33455 WARE, H. The moral principle of the temperance movement. A sermon preached in the chapel of Harvard College, United States, October 17, 1841... eleventh thousand. 11p. 8°. *Manchester & London*, 1843. *The Turner copy. For another impression, see 1842.*

33456 WILLIAMSON, JACOB. Report of the colliery cause Williamson v. Taylor and others. Tried at the Northumberland Assizes, August 4, 1843...involving the question whether the legal construction of the agreement, commonly called the pit bond, entered into between the owners of West Holywell Colliery, near Earsdon, and their workmen, enables the men to claim reasonable wages when the pit is laid off work... 28p. *Newcastle-upon-Tyne*, 1843.

SLAVERY

33457 BRITISH AND FOREIGN ANTI-SLAVERY SOCIETY. The fourth annual report of the...Society...presented to the general meeting held in Exeter Hall, on...June 21st 1843...With an appendix, list of contributions, &c. &c. &c. 188p. *8°.* 1843.

33458 GENERAL ANTI-SLAVERY CONVENTION. Proceedings of the General Anti-Slavery Convention, called by the committee of the British and Foreign Anti-Slavery Society, and held in London from ...June 13th to...June 20th 1843. [Edited] by J. F. Johnson, short-hand writer. 360p. *8°.* [1843]

POLITICS

33459 BREWSTER, P. The seven Chartist and military discourses libelled by the Marquis of Abercorn... To which are added, four other discourses... 424p. *12°. Paisley, Edinburgh, &c.,* 1843.

33460 BROUGHAM, H. P., *Baron Brougham and Vaux.* One of six copies in quarto. Lord Brougham's speech upon the Ashburton Treaty, delivered in the House of Lords on...7th April, 1843. 70p. *4°.* 1843.

33461 FINNELLY, W. Suggestions for improving the Bill for the registration of voters. 23p. *8°.* 1843.

33462 HERWEGH, G., *ed.* Einundzwanzig Bogen aus der Schweiz...Erster Theil. 336p. *8°. Zürich & Winterthur,* 1843.

33463 LOVETT, W. Letter from Mr. Lovett to Messrs. Donaldson and Mason. Containing his reasons for refusing to be nominated secretary of the National Charter Association. 4p. *8°.* [*London,* 1843]

33464 —— A letter to Daniel O'Connell, Esq., M.P. in reply to the calumnies he put forth in the Corn Exchange, August 8th, in answer to the address of the National Association to the people of Ireland. 8p. *8°.* [1843]

33465 MACINTYRE, J. J. The influence of aristocracies on the revolutions of nations; considered in relation to the present circumstances of the British Empire. 16, 448p. *8°. London & Paris,* 1843.

33466 MARTIN, WILLIAM (1772–1851). The philosopher on the expectation of an Irish rebellion. [An attack on Daniel O'Connell. In verse.] *s.sh. 8°.* [*Newcastle-upon-Tyne,* 1843]

33467 NATIONAL ASSOCIATION FOR PROMOTING THE POLITICAL AND SOCIAL IMPROVEMENT OF THE PEOPLE. Address of the National Association, London, to the people of Ireland. [Signed: W. Lovett, secretary.] 8p. *8°. London, Manchester, &c.,* [1843].

33468 —— Anniversary festival, in commemoration of the opening of the National Association, Tuesday, July 26th, 1843. W. J. Fox, Esq. in the chair. Programme of the music... 12p. *12°. Islington,* [1843]

33469 —— First annual report of the National Association... 7p. *8°.* [1843]

33470 O'CONNOR, F. A letter from Feargus O'Connor, Esq. to the Reverend William Hill, (late editor of the Northern Star,) in answer to several charges contained in recent documents published by that gentleman. 31p. *8°. London, Manchester, &c.,* [1843]

33471 —— North Lancashire Spring Assizes. Trial of Feargus O'Connor, Esquire, and 58 other Chartists, on a charge of seditious conspiracy...[Edited by O'Connor.] 446p. *8°.* [1843] *Issued in parts without a title-page. The title is taken from the caption of the first part.*

33472 PARRY, JOHN H. A letter to Feargus O'Connor, Esq., farmer and barrister...on the plan of organization issued by the Birmingham Conference, September, 1843. 12p. *12°.* 1843.

33473 The **PEOPLE'S CHARTER;** being an Act to provide for the just representation of the people of Great Britain and Ireland, in the Commons' House of Parliament. With a dedication to Feargus O'Connor, Esq. 16p. *8°. Manchester: A. Heywood, & London: J. Cleave, &c.,* [1843 ?] *For other editions, see* 1838.

33474 PETITION to the House of Lords, and Commons, of British claimants on Portugal; and a series of letters, from 1841 to 1843, of John Quail, M.D.... With correspondence of Her Majesty's Secretary of State for Foreign Affairs, the Right Hon. the Earl of Aberdeen, from Oct. 1841, to June 1843. 46p. *8°.* 1843.

For the **POOR MAN'S GUARDIAN, AND REPEALER'S FRIEND,** *see* vol. III, *Periodicals list.*

33475 SIDEBOTTOM, S. A walk into the franchise; or, the general and local government reformer: setting forth in a clear and concise manner, the only speedy, legitimate & effectual means, to enlarge the franchise, repeal all restrictive & obnoxious laws; and give permanent liberty, prosperity & happiness to the nation. 12p. *12°. Hyde,* [1843]

33476 SPENCER, H. The proper sphere of government: a reprint of a series of letters originally published in "The Nonconformist." 40p. *8°.* 1843.

33477 WELLESLEY, A., *Duke of Wellington.* Extracts from the Duke of Wellington's despatches, and other official documents, relating to the claims and services of the late Colonel Grant. 12p. *12°.* [1843?]

33478 WHITE, GEORGE, *Chartist.* An answer to John Humffreys of the Middle Temple...and an exposure of the self-styled liberals and free traders. 16p. *8°.* 1843.

SOCIALISM

For **ALLGEMEINE LITERATUR-ZEITUNG,** 1843–44, *see* vol. III, *Periodicals list.*

33479 BARMBY, J. G. ⟨No. 1[–5]. Vol. I.⟩...New tracts for the times: or, warmth, light, and food for the masses. 51p. *8°.* [1843] *Nos. 1–4 are in a printed wrapper and called* The communist miscellany. A collection of tracts, religious, political, and domestic. Edited by Goodwyn Barmby, and the Communist Church. *Contents: 1. Bible proofs from Isaiah against Jesus Christ's being the Messiah; 2. Twelve proofs of the existence of a present hell upon earth; 3. The demand for the emancipation of women, politically and socially. By Catherine Barmby; 4. The best and only true way of gaining the People's Charter; 5. The exposition of the "Lord's Prayer," according to the doctrines of the Communist Church.*

33480 —— The truth on baptism by water, according to the doctrine of the Communist Church. 4p. *8°. Ham Common: Concordium Press,* [1843] *Probably intended as no. 6 of* New tracts for the times, *with which it is bound.*

33481 —— The truth on the Sabbath, according to the doctrine of the Communist Church. 4p. *8°. Ham Common: Concordium Press,* [1843] *Probably intended as no. 7 of* New tracts for the times, *with which it is bound.*

33482 —— New tracts for the times, no. 8. The truth on the communion table, or the sacrament of the Lord's supper, according to the doctrine of the Communist Church. 4p. *8°. Ham Common: Concordium Press,* [1843]

33483 —— ⟨No. 9. Vol. 1.⟩ New tracts for the times: a brief statement of the views of Goodwyn Barmby on some important subjects, being an answer to a blasphemous pamphlet entitled "A voice of warning," which opposes the introduction of his scriptures into Ireland. 8p. *8°.* [1843]

33484 —— The Communist Church, the true and only catholic apostolic Christian church... 3p. *8°. n.p.* [1843 ?] *Probably printed at the Concordium Press, Ham Common, and intended as no. 10 of* New tracts for the times, *with which it is bound.*

33485 —— Unjust charge against Goodwyn Barmby the communist. [2]p. *s.sh.8°. n.p.* [1843 ?]

33486 CHANNING, WILLIAM H. A statement of the principles of the Christian Union. [Prepared by W. H. Channing.] 12p. *8°. New-York,* 1843.

33487 CONSIDÉRANT, V. P. De la politique nouvelle, convenant aux intérêts actuels de la société; et de ses conditions de développement par la publicité. 16p. *8°.* [*Paris,* 1843] *Considérant's own copy.*

33488 —— 2e édition. 36p. *12°. Paris,* 1843. *Considérant's own copy.*

33489 ETZLER, J. A. Dialogue on Etzler's paradise: between Messrs. Clear, Flat, Dunce, and Grudge. By the author of "Paradise within the reach of all men, without labor, by powers of nature and machinery"... 23p. *8°.* 1843.

33490 FIRST CONCORDIUM. A brief account of the First Concordium, or Harmonious Industrial College, a home for the affectionate, skilful, and industrious, uncontaminated by false sympathy, avaricious cunning, or excessive labour. 8p. *8°. Ham Common: Concordium Press,* [1843]

33491 —— Rejected address from the Concordists Society at Ham Common, to the London Peace Society, presented at their Convention, June 24, 1843, at the Freemason's Tavern. [Signed: W. Oldham, Pater.] And Temper and diet. [By C. Lane.] (Extracted from the New Age, July 1, 1843.) 8p. *8°. Ham Common & London: Concordium Press,* [1843]

33492 GREAVES, J. P. Letters and extracts from the MS. writings of James Pierrepont Greaves. [Edited by Alexander Campbell.] Vol. I. *8°. Ham Common: The Concordium,* 1843. *See also* 1845.

33493 HUGO, MINOR, *pseud.* Hints and reflections for railway travellers and others: or, a journey to the phalanx. By Minor Hugo... 3 vols. *12°.* 1843. *Conjecturally attributed to Luke Hansard.*

33494 HUNT, THOMAS (*fl.* 1840–1853). Report to a meeting of intending emigrants, comprehending a practical plan for founding co-operative colonies of united interests, in the north-western territories of the United States. 32p. *8°.* 1843.

33495 KING, WILLIAM, *of Charlotte Street, London.* Four letters on the workings of money capital; showing its present inefficient and limited agency for commercial and social purposes... 56p. *12°.* [1843] *This issue consists of the same sheets as that of 1840 (q.v.), with 'Chapter II', pages 25–56, added.*

33496 MAZEL, B. Code social. [With 'Introduction familière à la pratique du système social de Charles Fourrier [sic]'.] 139, 72p. *8°. Marseille,* 1843. *The* Introduction familière *has a separate title-page, dated 1842, but was presumably reissued with the* Code social *in 1843, as it is included in the contents to the latter as an appendix, and the list of errata includes corrections to be made in it.*

For the **NEW AGE,** and Concordium gazette and temperance advocate, 1843–44, *see* vol. III, *Periodicals list.*

33497 *Daniel **O'CONNELL** & socialism in Ireland. [Reprinted from the New Moral World... Feb. 11, 1843.] 4p. *8°.* [*London,* 1843] *The FWA copy that belonged to William Pare.*

33498 *OWEN,** ROBERT. No. 3.⟩ Preliminary charter of the rational system, by the founder of the system... Kilmarnock, Ayrshire, Jan. 25th, 1843. *s.sh.fol.* [*London:*] *Published by the Council of Branch 16, of the Rational Society,* [1843] *The FWA copy that belonged to William Pare.*

33499 PELLARIN, C. Charles Fourier sa vie et sa théorie...Deuxième édition. 556p. *8°. Paris,* 1843. *Presentation copy, with inscription, from the author to Émile Barrault. For other editions, see* 1839.

33500 PÉRUSSON, E. Union et bonheur pour tous, ou le Phalanstère mis à la portée de tout le monde, exposé succinct de la doctrine de l'harmonie universelle et de l'association agricole domestique de Charles Fourier. Avec un plan du Phalanstère. 160p. *12°. Chalon-sur-Saône,* 1843.

For the **PRESENT,** 1843–44, *see* vol. III, *Periodicals list.*

33501 PROJET financier pour la transformation de la

Phalange en journal quotidien. 16p. *8°*. [*Paris,* 1843] *The copy that belonged to Victor Considérant.*

33502 —— 2e édition. 35p. *12°*. *Paris,* 1843. *The copy that belonged to Victor Considérant.*

33503 RATIONAL SOCIETY. The constitution and laws of the Rational Society, as agreed at the annual congress...at Harmony Hall...May 10, 1843... 24p. *12°*. 1843.

33504 [——] Prospectus for raising an additional capital of £25,000, in five thousand preference shares, in aid of the educational and industrial college, at Harmony, Hants. [Issued by the Central Board of the Rational Society.] 3p. *4°*. *n.p.* [1843]

33505 —— Reports of the proceedings of the eighth annual congress of the Rational Society...held in Harmony Hall, Hants, May, 1843...Republished from the New Moral World... 259p. *12°*. 1843.

33506 RATIONAL TRACT SOCIETY. What is Man? [No. 2.] 4p. *8°*. [1843?] *Another, the FWA copy, belonged to William Pare.*

33507 *—— Marriage and divorce...No. 6. 4p. *8°*. [1843?] *The FWA copy that belonged to William Pare.*

33508 —— Third series. – No. 1[–6]. National evils and national remedies. *12°*. [*London,* 1843?] *Contents:* 1. Foreign trade versus home colonization; 2. Are Great Britain

and Ireland incapable of raising food for their population?; 3. Can our manufacturing system be extended beneficially for the Nation?; 4. Would an extension of foreign trade increase work and wages?; 5. On the organization of home colonies; 6. What good would home colonization do?

33509 REID, R. J. Exposure of socialism. A refutation of the letter on Harmony Hall, by "One who has whistled at the plough," which appeared in the Morning Chronicle of the 13th December last; with an appendix of facts regarding socialism and the conduct of the leading men among socialists, as exhibited at Queenwood, Hants. 40p. *8°*. [1843]

33510 Sacred **SOCIALISM!** A tract for the times... [A discussion, in the form of a dialogue, of a lecture by Alexander Campbell.] [2]p. *s.sh.8°*. *Leeds,* [1843?]

33511 STATUTS de la société pour la transformation de La Phalange en journal quotidien. Considérant et Compie. 23p. *8°*. *Paris,* [1843] *The copy that belonged to Victor Considérant, with the date '10 juin 1843' in his hand on the title-page.*

33512 ZÜRICH. Die Kommunisten in der Schweiz, nach den bei Weitling vorgefundenen Papieren. Wörtlicher Abdruck des Kommissionalberichtes an die H. Regierung des Standes Zürich. [Signed: Dr. Bluntschli.] 130p. *8°*. *Zürich,* 1843.

MISCELLANEOUS

33513 BROUGHAM, H. P., *Baron Brougham and Vaux.* Letters on law reform, to the Right Hon. Sir J. R. G. Graham, Bart. M.P. Secretary of State for the Home Department. 87p. *8°*. *London & Edinburgh,* 1843.

33514 BURNET, J. The sense in the House and the sense out of the House...A speech relating to the propositions made by the Government with respect to the Church Establishment in Ireland. Delivered at a meeting of the Evangelical Voluntary Church Association held in Craven Chapel, London. 8p. *8°*. 1843.

33515 ENGLAND. Parliament. *House of Commons.* The Law Courts and new Houses of Parliament. Extracts from the evidence taken before the Select Committee of the House of Commons in 1841 and 1842, proving the necessity of removing the Courts of Law to the neighbourhood of the Inns of Court. 24p. *8°*. 1843.

33516 FLETCHER, R., *of Manchester.* An English minister's account of the great secession from the Scottish Established Church; embracing a brief historical sketch of the working of those principles in that Establishment which have ultimately led to the formation of the Free Church of Scotland. Being a lecture delivered to his congregation, July 16th, 1843. 24p. *12°*. *London & Manchester,* 1843.

33517 FOSTER, S. S. The brotherhood of thieves; or, a true picture of the American Church and clergy: a letter to Nathaniel Barney, of Nantucket. 72p. *12°*. *Boston,* [1843]

33518 FREE CHURCH of Scotland. [An exposition of the principles in defence of which the Church has suffered, and a plea for money in aid of the building fund.] 8p. *8°*. [*London,* 1843]

33519 GRAY, Joshua T. Immortality: its real and

alleged evidences: being an endeavour to ascertain how far the future of the human soul is discoverable by reason. 32p. *8°*. 1843. *The Turner copy.*

33520 [**HAMILTON,** James (1814–1867).] Farewell to Egypt: or, the departure of the Free Church of Scotland out of the Erastian Establishment. 12p. *12°*. 1843.

33521 [**HICKSON,** William E.] The Corporation of London and municipal reform. From the Westminster Review for May, 1843 – no. 77. 92p. *8°*. [*London,* 1843]

33522 HOLYOAKE, G. J. Paley refuted in his own words. 39p. *12°*. [1843]

33523 —— A short and easy method with the saints. 28p. *12°*. [1843]

33524 HOOK-EM, Loyola, *Dr., pseud.* No. 94. A tract for the times. The Bill factory, with patent machinery for making Puseyites. A rhyming epistle, from Dr. Loyola Hook-em, inventor, to Sir J. Grasp-em, patron. 8p. *8°*. 1843.

33525 A **LETTER** to Lord John Manners, M.P., on his late plea for national holy-days, by a Minister of the Holy Catholic Church. 41p. *8°*. 1843.

33526 [**LINDLEY,** J.] The study of botany, facilitated by a familiar introduction to the natural system...comprising structural botany; or, a description of the component parts of plants, descriptive botany, and systematic botany... 60p. *8°*. 1843.

33527 LINWOOD, W. Great men: their characteristics, influence and destiny. A lecture occasioned by the death of the Rev. E. W. Channing [i.e. W. E. Channing] delivered in Stockwell Gate Chapel, Mansfield...Nov. 20, 1842. 41p. *12°*. *London, Nottingham, &c.,* 1843.

33528 MANNERS, J. J. R., *Duke of Rutland*. A plea for national holy-days. 34p. *8°. London, Oxford, &c.*, 1843.

33529 —— Second edition. 40p. *8°. London, Oxford, &c.*, 1843.

33530 METCALFE, J. J. Temporal prosperity ensured to mankind by the practice of Christianity; and proposals for establishing a society, for the purpose of bringing Christian principles into effective operation, to be entitled the Practical Christian Union. 50p. *8°.* 1843. *For a supplement, see 1844.*

33531 R., R. The Christian religion: an account of every sect, its origin, progress, tenets of belief and rites and ceremonies, carefully compiled from the latest and best authorities. A new edition. 60p. *8°.* 1843.

33532 REPORT of the proceedings and resolutions of the general meeting of artists, held at the Freemasons' Tavern, December 17, 1842 [in support of the Art-Union of London]. 36p. *12°.* 1843.

33533 ROSSER, C. Intellect; its nature, rights and duties. Being the substance of a lecture delivered to a scientific institution. 20p. *8°. London & Gloucester*, 1843. *Presentation copy from the author to James Jones.*

33534 ROYAL DUBLIN SOCIETY. Report of the first public distribution of premiums awarded to the successful pupils in the drawing and modelling schools,

at the annual competition. December 8th, 1842. 30p. *8°. Dublin*, 1843. *The copy that belonged to Earl De Grey.*

33535 SHREWSBURY, W. J. Christian thoughts on free trade, in a letter to Thomas, David, & Peter Whitehead, Esquires... 56p. *12°. Bacup, London, &c.*, 1843.

33536 The **SPIRIT** of the nation. By the writers of the Nation newspaper. [A collection of verses.] Second edition, revised. 76p. *12°. Dublin*, 1843.

33537 TESTIMONIES of the Free Church of Scotland. 8p. *12°.* [1843]

33538 WHATELY, R., *Archbishop of Dublin*. A charge to the clergy of Dublin and Glandelagh, delivered in St. Patrick's Cathedral, June 1843...To which is appended a petition to the House of Lords, praying for a church government; together with the report of the debate on its presentation and some additional remarks. 48p. *8°. London & Dublin*, 1843.

33539 [**WOOD,** James J.] Free Church of Scotland: demission of Rev. James Julius Wood. [The text of his statement of 6 August, 1843.] 4p. *12°.* [1843]

33540 WRIGHT, Thomas (1810–1877), *ed.* Three chapters of letters relating to the suppression of monasteries. Edited from the originals in the British Museum by Thomas Wright. (*Camden Society, Old Series*, 6.) 304p. *4°.* 1843.

1844

GENERAL

33541 *ANNUAIRE de l'économie politique pour 1844 par les rédacteurs du Journal des Économistes. 1re année. Agriculture...commerce...voies de communication...monnaies, etc.etc. 260p. *18°. Paris*, 1844. *Articles by Michel Chevalier, Eugène Daire, Joseph Garnier, Wolowski, and others. The copy that belonged to George Grote.*

33542 The **BEGINNING** of the end. [On the state of Ireland.] By a member of the Carlton Club. 76p. *8°.* 1844. *Sometimes attributed to B.-T. Ord.*

33543 BELGIUM. *Laws, etc.* Discussion de la loi des droits differentiels du 21 juillet 1844, d'après le Moniteur Belge, accompagnée des notes statistiques et d'éclaircissements historiques; précédée d'un aperçu de la politique commerciale de la Belgique depuis 1830, du texte des dispositions relatives à la construction des chemins de fer ...aux réductions des péages des canaux, aux services réguliers de navigation transatlantique...du texte de la convention du 16 juillet 1842 avec la France, et de tous les traités de navigation et de commerce conclus par la Belgique...des documents principaux émanés de la commission d'enquête...et suivie des actes d'exécution de la loi... cclvi, 1113p. *8°. Bruxelles*, 1844.

33544 BENTHAM, J. Benthamiana: or, select extracts from the works of Jeremy Bentham. With an outline of his opinions on the principal subjects discussed in his works. Edited by John Hill Burton. 446p. *8°. Philadelphia*, 1844.

33545 BLANC, J. J. L. The history of ten years, 1830–1840. 2 vols. *8°.* 1844–45.

33546 BORREGO, A. Principios de economía política con aplicacion à la reforma de aranceles de aduana, à la situacion de la industria fabril de Cataluña, y al mayor y mas rapido incremento de la riquenza nacional. 386p. *8°. Madrid*, 1844.

33547 The **BRITISH ALMANAC** of the Society for the Diffusion of Useful Knowledge, for...1844... [With 'The companion to the Almanac; or year-book of general information'.] 96, 252p. *12°.* [1844] *For other editions, see 1828.*

33548 BUREAUD-RIOFREY, A. M. Londres et les Anglais des temps modernes. 430p. *8°. Londres*, 1844. *Presentation copy from the author to 'Ad. von Zwehl'.*

33549 The **CALCUTTA** star almanac and strangers' guide in Calcutta, including commercial & trade list for MDCCCXLV. 160p. *8°. Calcutta*, [1844]

33550 CARY, T. G. Letter to a lady in France on the supposed failure of a national bank, the supposed delinquency of the national government, the debts of the several states, and repudiation; with answers to enquiries concerning the books of Capt. Marryat and Mr. Dickens... Third edition. 60p. *8°. Boston*, 1844.

33551 —— [Another edition.] The Americans defended. By an American. Being a letter to one of his countrymen in Europe in answer to inquiries concerning the late imputations of dishonour upon the United States. 37p. *8°.* 1844.

33552 CATINEAU LA ROCHE, P. M. S. La France et l'Angleterre comparées sous le rapport des industries agricole, manufacturière et commerciale, et conséquences que l'on doit tirer de cette comparaison. 298p. *8°. Paris*, 1844.

33553 CHOATE, R. Speech...upon the subject of protecting American labor, by duties on imports. Delivered in the Senate of the United States, on the 12th and 15th of April, 1844. 52p. *8°. Washington*, 1844.

For [**COLTON,** C.] The Junius tracts, *see* vol. III, *Periodicals list*, Junius tracts.

33554 The **CORN LAWS,** free trade, and colonization considered: in a letter to Richard Cobden, Esq., M.P., &c.,&c.,&c. By a Manchester man. 64p. *8°. London & Manchester*, 1844.

33555 D., T. D. A letter to Wm. Sharman Crawford, Esq., M.P. on the condition of Ireland. With an appendix containing extracts from letters on the state of Ireland, written between the years, 1829 & 1843. 30p. *8°. Cheltenham*, 1844.

33556 DAIRE, L. F. E. Notice historique sur la vie et les ouvrages de Turgot...Tirée de la nouvelle édition des Œuvres de Turgot... 114p. *8°. Paris*, 1844. *For the edition of Turgot's works from which this is taken, see 1843 (Collection des principaux economistes).*

33557 DEPPING, G. B. Les Juifs dans le moyen âge, essai historique sur leur état civil, commercial et littéraire ... 324p. *8°. Bruxelles*, 1844.

33558 DE QUINCEY, T. The logic of political economy. 260p. *8°. Edinburgh*, 1844.

33559 The **EAST-INDIA** register and directory, for 1844; containing complete lists of the Company's servants ...Compiled...by F. Clark... 271, 136p. *12°. London & Edinburgh*, 1844. *For other editions, see 1804.*

For **ÉCONOMIE POLITIQUE,** 1844-52, *see* vol. III, *Periodicals list*, Journal des économistes.

33560 EVANS, EDWARD J. Wages. Observations on the connexion between corn-law repeal and the price of labour: with a reply to some remarks contained in a pamphlet, signed "Britannicus." 24p. *8°*. 1844. *The copy that belonged to the 3rd Earl of Radnor.*

33561 FAUCHER, L. Manchester in 1844; its present condition and future prospects...Translated from the French, with copious notes appended, by a member of the Manchester Athenæum. 152p. *12°. London & Manchester*, 1844.

33562 FEATHERSTONHAUGH, G. W. Excursion through the slave states, from Washington on the Potomac to the frontier of Mexico; with sketches of popular manners and geological notices. 2 vols. *8°*. 1844.

33563 FINCH, JOHN (*fl.* 1833-1844). The natural boundaries of empires; and a new view of colonization. 279p. *12°*. 1844. *The copy which belonged to Mark Pattison, with his book-stamp on the title-page.*

33564 FINDEN, E. F. The ports, harbours, wateringplaces, and coast scenery of Great Britain. Illustrated by views taken on the spot by W. H. Bartlett; with descriptions by William Beattie. 2 vols. *4°*. 1844.

33565 FLETCHER, WALTER. Letter on free trade, addressed to the Right Hon. Lord John Russell, M.P.... Fourth edition. 31p. *8°. Liverpool*, 1844. *For another edition, see 1843.*

33566 FRANCIS, G. W. The dictionary of trade, commerce, and navigation: explanatory of...the general affairs of business, corrected up to the latest period... [384]p. *8°*. 1844.

33567 *GAUPP, E. T. Die Germanischen Ansiedlungen und Landtheilungen in den Provinzen des römischen Westreiches... 612p. *8°. Breslau*, 1844. *The copy that belonged to George Grote.*

33568 GISBORNE, THOMAS (1758-1846). A letter to the Right Honourable Sir Robert Peel, Bart. &c.&c.&c. respecting means of removing certain difficulties in the relative position of England and Ireland. 30p. *8°*. 1844.

33569 GRUEN, K. Bausteine. Zusammengetragen und mit einem Sendschreiben an seine Osnabrücker Freunde begleitet. xxxii, 366p. *8°. Darmstadt*, 1844.

33570 HAGEN, C. H. System of political economy... Translated from the German by John Prince Smith. 88p. *8°*. 1844.

33571 HELLER, A., *ed.* Preussen, der Beamtenstaat, in seiner politischen Entwickelung und seinen socialökonomischen Zuständen. Dargestellt durch Benjamin Constant und Samuel Laing. [I. Der Sieg der Constitution in Preussen, von J. F. Benzenberg. II. Betrachtungen eines britischen Reisenden über Preussen in Jahre 1842, von Samuel Laing.] xvi, 165p. *8°. Mannheim*, 1844.

33572 HERMES, K. H. Die Entdeckung von America durch die Isländer im zehnten und eilften Jahrhunderte... 134p. *8°. Braunschweig*, 1844.

33573 IRELAND under Lord De Grey. 55p. *8°. Dublin*, 1844. *Presentation copy from the anonymous author to the Earl of Ripon.*

33574 JAMESON, D. D. Practical measures. 23p. *8°*. 1844.

33575 JAMIESON, R. Is Central Africa to remain sealed against intercourse with the civilised world? or, can means be devised by which an intercourse may be opened up? A few remarks addressed to those who desire the amelioration of Africa: with an outline of a plan by which it is believed commercial intercourse with Central Africa may be established. 14p. *8°. Liverpool*, 1844.

33576 JONES, RICHARD (1790-1855). An essay on the distribution of wealth, and on the sources of taxation. Part I. – Rent. 355p. *8°*. 1844. *For another edition, see 1831.*

33577 KANE, SIR R. J. The industrial resources of Ireland. 417p. *8°. Dublin*, 1844. *See also 1845.*

33578 KEMP, G. B. A treatise on the science of trade, as applied to legislation. 232p. *12°*. 1844.

33579 KING, PETER, *7th Baron King.* A selection from the speeches and writings of the late Lord King. With a short introductory memoir, by Earl Fortescue. 471p. *8°*. 1844.

33580 [**KING-NOEL,** W., *Earl of Lovelace.*] Quetelet: Du système social. [An offprint of a review in the *Christian Teacher*, no. 43.] p.16–35. *8°. n.p.* [1844?]

33581 LAING, SAMUEL (1812-1897). Atlas prize essay. National distress: its cause and remedies. 169p. *8°*. 1844.

33582 LATIMER, H., *Bishop of Worcester.* Sermons by [and remains of] Hugh Latimer...martyr, 1555. Edited for the Parker Society, by...George Elwes Corrie. 2 vols. *8°. Cambridge*, 1844-45. *For another edition of Latimer's sermons, see 1584.*

33583 **LAWSON**, J. A. Five lectures on political economy; delivered before the University of Dublin, in Michaelmas term, 1843. 147p. *8°. London & Dublin: A. Milliken*, 1844.

33584 —— [Another issue.] 147p. *8°. London & Dublin: W. Curry, jun.*, 1844.

33585 **LETTERS** from the United States of America, exhibiting the working of democracy in that country for the last twenty years, both politically and morally. By an Anglo-American, of several years' residence. [Dated: April 10th, 1844.] 58p. *8°.* 1844.

33586 **LIST**, F. Das nationale System der politischen Oekonomie...Erster Band. Der internationale Handel, die Handelspolitik und der deutsche Zollverein. Neue unveränderte Auflage. 589p. *8°. Stuttgart & Tübingen*, 1844. *For another edition, see* 1841.

33587 [**LUMSDEN**, J.] American memoranda, by a mercantile man, during a short tour in the summer of 1843. For private circulation. [The preface is signed: J.L.] 60p. *8°. Glasgow*, 1844. *The copy that belonged to the Earl of Eglinton.*

33588 **McCULLOCH**, JOHN R. A dictionary, practical, theoretical, and historical, of commerce and commercial navigation...A new edition, corrected throughout, enlarged, and improved. 1378p. *8°.* 1844. *For other editions, see* 1832. *For a supplement to this edition, see* 1846.

33589 **MERYWEATHER**, W. S. An address to the landowners, & manufacturers, of England, on the corn laws, and on the state of the poor and working classes, with suggestions for their employment, and an amendment of the poor laws. 56p. *8°. London & Marlow*, 1844.

33590 **MILL**, JAMES. Elements of political economy ...Third edition, revised and corrected. 304p. *8°.* 1844. *A reissue of the original third edition of 1826 (q.v.). For other editions, see* 1821.

33591 **MILL**, JOHN S. Essays on some unsettled questions of political economy. 164p. *8°.* 1844.

33592 *****MUEHLENPFORDT**, E. Versuch einer getreuen Schilderung der Republik Mejico, besonders in Beziehung auf Geographie, Ethnographie und Statistik... Zweiter Band. Beschreibung der einzelnen Landestheile. 552p. *8°. Hannover*, 1844.

33593 **MURRAY**, H. The United States of America; their history from the earliest period; their industry, commerce, banking...institutions and character, political, social and literary; with a survey of the territory, and remarks on the prospects and plans of emigrants...With illustrations of the natural history by James Nicol... 3 vols. *8°. Edinburgh & London*, 1844.

33594 **NELKENBRECHER**, J. C. Nouveau manuel des monnaies, poids, mesures, cours des changes, fonds public, etc., à l'usage des banquiers, négociants et industriels...Traduit de l'allemand et augmenté par Jean-Marie Deschamps. 541p. *8°. Paris*, 1844. *For other editions, see* 1815.

For the **ODD-FELLOWS' CHRONICLE**, *see* vol. III, *Periodicals list.*

33595 [**PERCEVAL**, HON. A. P.] The amelioration of Ireland contemplated, in a series of papers. I. On the use of the Irish language in religious worship and instruction. Second edition. 24p. *8°.* 1844.

33596 —— II. The question of repeal and federation considered. 12p. *8°.* 1844. *For the third paper in the series, see* 1845.

33597 **POPE**, C., *ed*. The yearly journal of trade, 1844 ...Twenty-second edition. [With 'The yearly journal of trade advertiser. 1844'.] 624p. *8°.* [1844] *See also* 1838, 1840, 1842, 1843, 1845, 1846.

33598 **PORTER**, J. G. V. Ireland. The Union of 1801, 41 Geo. III., Cap. 47...does and always will draw away from Ireland her men of skill, genius, capital, and rank...A federal (the only fair) Union between Great Britain and Ireland inevitable, and the most desirable for both islands. Lord John Russell and the Whigs, better conservatives than Sir Robert Peel and the Tories... Third edition. 71p. *8°. London & Dublin*, [1844?]

33599 **PULLING**, A. A practical treatise on the laws, customs, usages and regulations of the City and Port of London, with notes of the various charters, by-laws, statutes, and judicial decisions by which they are established...Second edition, with considerable additions. 580p. *8°.* 1844.

33600 **RAMSAY**, R. Scotland interested in the question of federal or local parliaments. By a Scotchman. 15p. *8°. Glasgow*, 1844.

33601 **RAU**, K. D. H. Grundsätze der Volkswirthschaftspolitik mit anhaltender Rücksicht auf bestehende Staatseinrichtungen...Dritte Ausgabe. 683p. *8°. Heidelberg*, 1844.

33602 **REMARKS** by a junior to his senior, on an article in the Edinburgh Review of January, 1844, on the state of Ireland, and the measures for its improvement. 83p. *8°.* 1844.

33603 A **REPLY** to Mr. Montgomery Martin's "Ireland before and after the Union with Great Britain;" being a series of articles taken from the Dublin Weekly Register, edited by M. Staunton, Esq.... 56p. *8°. Dublin*, 1844.

33604 **ROLPH**, T. Emigration and colonization; embodying the results of a mission to Great Britain and Ireland, during the years 1839, 1840, 1841 and 1842; including a correspondence with many...gentlemen... descriptive accounts of various parts of the British American provinces; with observations, statistical, political, etc. 376p. *8°.* 1844.

33605 **RYAN**, JOHN. Protestant union. A letter to the Protestants of Ireland. 24p. *8°. Dublin*, 1844. *The copy that belonged to Earl De Grey.*

33606 *****S...**, D..., *Prince*. Aperçu sur la condition des classes ouvrières, et critique de l'ouvrage de M. Buret, sur la misère des classes laborieuses, &c. 107p. *8°. Paris*, 1844. *The copy that belonged to George Grote.*

33607 **SCIALOJA**, A. Les principes de l'économie sociale exposés selon l'ordre logique des idées...Ouvrage considérablement augmenté et entièrement fondu par l'auteur. Traduit et annoté par Hipte. Devillers. 459p. *8°. Paris*, 1844.

33608 **SCOTLAND**. *Laws, etc.* The Acts of the Parliaments of Scotland....A.D.M.C.XXIV[–A.D M.DCC.VII. Edited by Thomas Thomson and Cosmo Innes. With 'General index to the Acts of the Parliaments of Scotland, to which is prefixed a supplement to the Acts'. By Cosmo Innes, continued by Archibald Anderson.] 12 vols. *fol. n.p., Record Commission*, 1844, 1814–75. *Vols. 5 and 6 are of the revised edition.*

33609 SLATER, I. Pigot and Co.'s Royal national and commercial directory and topography...of Berkshire, Buckinghamshire, Cornwall, Devonshire, Dorsetshire, Gloucestershire, Hampshire, Herefordshire, Monmouthshire, Oxfordshire, Somersetshire, Wiltshire and... Wales. Comprising classified lists of all persons in trade, and of the nobility, gentry and clergy...An account of every mode of transit for passengers and merchandise: including...railway tables and lists of the bankers of the United Kingdom... 14 parts. *8°. London & Manchester,* 1844.

33610 *SLEEMAN, Sir W. H. Rambles and recollections of an Indian official... 2 vols. *8°.* 1844. *The copy that belonged to George Grote.*

33611 SMITH, Thomas S. On the source and on the relief of publick distress in Great Britain. 69p. *8°.* 1844.

33612 SMYTH, George L. Ireland, historical and statistical. 3 vols. *8°.* 1844–49.

33613 SOCIETY FOR THE EMANCIPATION OF INDUSTRY. An appeal to farmers and landowners. (*Emancipation of Industry,* 5.) 12p. *12°.* [1844]

33614 SOCIETY FOR THE PROTECTION OF AGRICULTURE AND BRITISH INDUSTRY. Agricultural Protection Society for Great Britain and Ireland. Address of the Publications Committee to the members of the country societies. 7p. *8°.* [1844]

**33615 —— ** Tracts issued by the Agricultural Protection Society up to August, 1844. 17 parts. *8°.* [*London,* 1844] *A collection of pamphlets originally separately published by other publishers, reissued with a general title-page. Contents: E. S. Cayley, Reasons for the formation of the Agricultural Protection Society; Sir A. Alison, Free trade and protection; G. G. Day, Defeat of the Anti-Corn-Law League in Huntingdonshire. The speech...June 17, 1843; Idem, The farmers and the League. The speech...January 27, 1844; A. S. O'Brien, History of the League. The speech...June 26, 1844; J. B. Sharp, The Anti-Corn-Law League and the cotton trade; Anon., Protection of British agriculture; Humanitas, Free trade; Anon., American notions of free trade; J. Almack, Cheap bread and low wages; Anon., To artisans and labourers; Anon., Corn laws; Anon., A letter from a crow to Mr. Cobden; G. Townsend and J. Tyson, The substance of two speeches...Feb. 20, 1844; J. Haddon, The substance of a speech...15th day of March, 1844; J. Barton,*

The influence of the price of corn on the rate of mortality; R. Baker, An answer...to Earl Ducie. See also 1846.

33616 [STONEHOUSE, James.] Pictorial Liverpool: its annals; commerce; shipping; institutions; public buildings; sights; excursions, &c., &c. A new and complete hand-book for resident, visitor, and tourist... 282p. *12°.* [*Liverpool,* 1844] *See also* 1849.

33617 [TAYLOR, John (1781–1864).] [*Begin.*] The following letter, addressed to the editor of The Times, on the 9th of January, 1844, was not inserted in that journal ...[Signed: M.M.] (*Emancipation of Industry,* 6.) 8p. *12°.* [1844]

33618 [——] The standard and measure of value. By the author of an "Essay on money." Third edition, revised and corrected. 62p. *8°.* 1844. *For another edition, see 1832 and for a reissue of this edition, see the collection of the author's pamphlets entitled* Currency investigated, *1845* (FINANCE).

For **TEGG'S MAGAZINE OF KNOWLEDGE AND AMUSEMENT,** *see* vol. III, *Periodicals list.*

33619 *THORNTON, Edward (1799–1875). A gazetteer of the countries adjacent to India on the northwest; including Sinde, Afghanistan, Beloochistan, the Punjab, and the neighbouring states. Compiled by the authority of the Hon. Court of Directors of the East-India Company... 2 vols. *8°.* 1844. *The copy that belonged to George Grote.*

33620 TORRENS, R. The Budget. On commercial and colonial policy. [Containing Letters I–XI, and letters to Richard Cobden and Arthur Morse, and to R. G. Welford.] With an introduction, in which the deductive method, as presented in Mr. Mill's System of logic, is applied to the solution of some controverted questions in political economy. lii, [456]p. *8°.* 1844. *A new edition of letters published separately between 1841 and 1843 (qq.v.).*

33621 TWISS, Sir T. Two lectures on machinery, delivered before the University of Oxford, in Lent term, 1844. 72p. *8°. Oxford, & London,* 1844.

33622 WHAT is to be done? or, past, present, and future. Second edition. 123p. *8°.* 1844.

For **ZEITSCHRIFT FÜR DIE GESAMTE STAATSWISSENSCHAFT,** 1844 ——→, *see* vol. III, *Periodicals list.*

AGRICULTURE

For the **ANNUAL REGISTER OF AGRICULTURAL IMPLEMENTS,** *see* vol. III, *Periodicals list.*

33623 The **ARISTOCRACY** of Britain and the laws of entail and primogeniture judged by recent French writers: being selections from the works of Passy, Beaumont, O'Connor, Sismondi, Buret, Guizot, Constant, Dupin, Say, Blanqui and Mignet: showing the advantage of the law of equal succession. With explanatory and statistical notes. 232p. *12°. London, Edinburgh, &c.,* 1844.

33624 BACON, Richard N. The report on the agriculture of Norfolk, to which the prize was awarded by the Royal Agricultural Society of England. 412p. *4°.* 1844. *See also* 1849.

33625 BAYLDON, J. S. Bayldon's art of valuing

rents and tillages, and the tenant's right on entering and quitting farms, explained...Sixth edition, corrected and revised by John Donaldson. 336p. *8°.* 1844. *For other editions, see 1823.*

33626 BERNAYS, A. J. A lecture on the theory of agriculture, delivered at Siddington, to the tenants of Mr. Davenport's estate, on the 4th of January, 1844. [With 'A lecture on the practices of farming adopted in Cheshire, based on the analysis of soils, with advice as to improvement, delivered at Siddington School, on the 25th of January, 1844, to Mr. E. D. Davenport's tenants'.] 22, 24p. *8°. Manchester,* [1844]

33627 CANTAGREL, F. J. F. A gagner quinze millions sur les bords de la Cisse, dans les cantons d'Amboise et de Vouvray. Mémoire présenté à la Société d'Agriculture d'Indre-et-Loire. 22p. *8⁰. Tours & Paris, 1844. The copy that belonged to Victor Considérant.*

33628 COOKE, L. The value of landed property demonstrated, by practical deductions...tending...to facilitate the valuation of estates, as applicable to the purposes of agriculture. 104, [108]p. *8⁰.* 1844.

33629 DAUBENY, CHARLES G. B. A lecture, on institutions for the better education of the farming classes, especially with reference to the proposed agricultural college near Cirencester, with some remarks on experimental farms...delivered at the Botanic Garden, Oxford, on...May 14, 1844. 32p. *8⁰. Oxford & London,* 1844. *Presentation copy, from the author to J. B. Estcourt, M.P.*

33630 DAVIS, H. The resources farmers possess for meeting the reduced prices of their produce. 46p. *8⁰.* 1844.

33631 DUNN, M. An historical, geological, and descriptive view of the coal trade of the north of England; comprehending its rise, progress, present state, and future prospects. To which are appended a concise notice of the peculiarities of certain coal fields in Great Britain and Ireland; and also a general description of the coal mines of Belgium, drawn up from actual inspection. 248p. *8⁰. Newcastle upon Tyne,* 1844.

33632 ENSOR, G. Of property, and of its equal distribution, as promoting virtue, population, abundance. 188p. *8⁰.* 1844.

33633 The **FRUIT-GARDENER'S** manual, and greenhouse companion; containing practical instructions for the cultivation and management of fruit trees and fruit-bearing shrubs, with directions for the conservatory and hothouse, adapted to small or large gardens. New edition. 60p. *8⁰.* 1844.

33634 GIBBS, ANTONY, **& SONS** and **MYERS, WILLIAM JOSEPH, & CO.** Peruvian and Bolivian guano: its nature, properties, and results. 95p. *8⁰.* 1844.

33635 HANNAM, J. Written for the Yorkshire Agricultural Society...The economy of waste manures, a treatise on the nature and use of neglected fertilizers. 114p. *8⁰.* 1844.

33636 HILLYARD, C. Dedicated, by special permission, to His Royal Highness, Prince Albert. Practical farming and grazing: with observations on the breeding & feeding of sheep & cattle...remarks on the probable effects of railroads and steam navigation upon agriculture; the amended poor laws...alteration of the tariff; the corn laws...Fourth edition. 352p. *8⁰. London & Northampton,* 1844. *The copy specially bound for presentation by Sir John Kennaway to Mr. John Pratt. Originally published, with the title* A summary of practical farming, *in 1836 (q.v.).*

33637 HOG, J. M. Correspondence [with Charles Waterton] regarding the injury supposed to be done to the farmer by the rook. 8p. *8⁰. n.p.* [1844]

33638 JOUBERT, P. C. Nouveau manuel complet du fabricant et de l'amateur de tabac, contenant l'histoire, la culture et la fabrication du tabac...Par une société de cultivateurs et de fabricants, sous la direction de P.Ch. Joubert. (*Manuels-Roret.*) 264p. *12⁰. Paris,* 1844.

33639 KENT, JAMES H. Remarks on the injuriousness of the consolidation of small farms, and the benefit of small occupations and allotments; with some observations on the past and present state of the agricultural labourers: in two letters...to His Grace the Duke of Grafton. 88p. *8⁰. Bury St. Edmund's & London,* [1844]

33640 LAMB, J. Corn-rents and money-rents. By the Master of Corpus Christi College. 16p. *8⁰. Cambridge,* 1844.

33641 LORD, J. First letter. A letter to the Right Hon. Henry Goulburn, M.P., Chancellor of the Exchequer, on the field, garden, or cottage allotment system, as a means for alleviating the distresses of the poor, diminishing poor rates and county rates...15p. *8⁰.* 1844.

33642 LOW, D. On landed property, and the economy of estates: comprehending the relation of landlord and tenant, and the principles...of leases... 680p. *8⁰.* 1844.

33643 LOYAL NATIONAL REPEAL ASSOCIATION. Report of the Sub-Committee of the... Association on the Irish fisheries. 33p. *8⁰.* [*Dublin,* 1844] *The copy that belonged to Earl De Grey.*

33644 MacKENZIE, SIR GEORGE S., *Bart.* Brief remarks on some subjects connected with the choice of wheat for seed, interesting to farmers, corn-factors, and bakers. 30p. *8⁰. Edinburgh & London,* 1844. *Presentation copy, with inscription, from the author to Robert Graeme.*

33645 MAIN, JAMES (1775 ?–1846). Cottage gardening. [From the Journal of the Royal Agricultural Society of England, 1841, vol. II., part III.] 24p. *8⁰.* 1844.

33646 NOWELL, J. An essay on cottage allotment, or field garden cultivation. From a paper read before the West-Riding Geological...Society... [Second edition.] 24p. *12⁰. Huddersfield, London, &c.,* 1844.

33647 The constitutional **RIGHTS** of landlords; the evils springing from the abuse of them in Ireland; and the origin and effects of banks, of funds, and of corn laws, considered. 44p. *8⁰. Dublin, Belfast, &c.,* 1844.

33648 SIMPSON, WILLIAM W. A defence of the landlords of Ireland, with remarks on the relation between landlord and tenant. 29p. *8⁰. London & Dublin,* 1844. *Presentation copy from the author to A. Shafto Adair, Esq.*

33648A SMITH, EDMUND J. Identity of interest between landlord, tenant-farmer and farm-labourer, as deduced from "Morton on soils." 14p. *8⁰.* 1844. *The copy that belonged to the 3rd Earl of Radnor.*

33649 *SMITH, JAMES (1789–1850). Remarks on thorough draining and deep ploughing...Extracted from the third report of Drummonds' Agricultural Museum. Seventh edition. 31p. *8⁰. Stirling,* 1844. *The copy that belonged to George Grote. For other editions, see* 1837.

33650 SOPWITH, T. The national importance of preserving mining records. 59p. *8⁰. London & Newcastle-on-Tyne,* 1844.

33651 SOUTH HETTON COLLIERY. Orders respecting the Davy lamps in use at South Hetton Colliery. [Signed: Edw. Potter, viewer. Dated: October, 1844.] *s.sh.fol. Newcastle-upon-Tyne,* [1844]

33652 SPOONER, W. C. The history, structure, economy, and diseases of the sheep... 466p. *12⁰.* 1844.

33653 SPROULE, J. Elements of practical agriculture, comprehending the nature, properties, and improvement of soils; the structure...of plants; and the husbandry of the domestic animals... Third edition, with corrections... 710p. *8⁰. London, Dublin, &c.,* 1844.

33654 STEPHENS, HENRY (1795–1874). The book of the farm, detailing the labours of the farmer, farm-steward, ploughman, shepherd...and dairy-maid... 3 vols. *8°. Edinburgh & London,* 1844.

33655 *TAYLOR, SAMUEL. Farming in the olden time: a review of Tusser's 500 points of good husbandry; compared and contrasted with the system of the present day...Reprinted from No. 29, New Series, of the British Farmer's Magazine. 31p. *8°. London & Liverpool,* 1844. *The copy that belonged to George Grote.*

33656 THAËR, A. D. The principles of agriculture... Translated by William Shaw, Esq., and Cuthbert W. Johnson, Esq....[With a memoir of Thaër and a bibliography of his writings.] 2 vols. *8°.* 1844.

33657 *TRATADO de las plantas tintoreas, de la barrilla y otras plantas que dan sosa, y del tabaco. Escrito segun los adelantos del dia y conforme a la practica de los mas celebres agricultores. 90p. *8°. Madrid,* 1844.

33658 WARNES, J. Extracts from ancient and modern writers on the flax crop, selected and arranged by John Warnes, jun., Esq....Published for the members of the National Flax and Agricultural Improvement Association. 59p. *8°. London & Norwich,* 1844.

33659 WEST, EDWARD (*fl.* 1844). Second letter to the farmers of Dorsetshire on the cause of depression in the prices of agricultural produce. 30p. *8°.* 1844.

33660 WIGGINS, J. The "monster" misery of Ireland; a practical treatise on the relation of landlord and tenant, with suggestions for legislative measures, and the management of landed property... 304p. *12°.* 1844.

33661 [WILSON, ROBERT, *solicitor.*] Suggestions towards the formation of a new method of transferring real property. 38p. *8°.* 1844.

33662 —— [Another edition.] Outlines of a plan for adapting the machinery of the public funds to the transfer of real property... 68p. *8°.* 1844.

CORN LAWS

33663 ALMACK, J. Reply to the speech of R. Cobden, Esq., M.P. delivered in the Town Hall, Hull on the 26th January, 1844. 64p. *8°. Hull,* 1844.

33664 BAINES, SIR EDWARD. Five letters to the Right Honourable the Earl of Harewood, president of the Yorkshire society for keeping up the price of bread and the rent of land [the Yorkshire Protective Committee for the Defence of British Industry]... 48p. *12°. London & Leeds,* 1844.

33665 CAYLEY, EDWARD S. Reasons for the formation of the Agricultural Protection Society, addressed to the industrious classes of the United Kingdom. 24p. *8°.* 1844.

33666 —— Thirteenth thousand. 24p. *8°.* 1844.

33667 —— Twenty-sixth thousand. 24p. *8°.* 1844. *One of a collection of pamphlets contained in a volume issued by the Society for the Protection of Agriculture and British Industry, for which see no.* 33615.

33668 Momentous **CONSIDERATIONS** on the corn law. 23p. *12°. Dulwich,* 1844.

33669 DAY, G. G. Defeat of the Anti-Corn-Law League in Huntingdonshire. The speech of Mr. George Game Day on that occasion, June 17, 1843, (published by request) with notes and additions. Twelfth edition. 40p. *8°.* 1844.

33670 —— Twenty-first edition. ⟨The people's edition.⟩ 24p. *8°.* 1844. *The copy that belonged to the 3rd Earl of Radnor.*

33671 —— Forty-ninth edition. ⟨The people's edition.⟩ 24p. *8°.* 1844. *One of a collection of pamphlets contained in a volume issued by the Society for the Protection of Agriculture and British Industry, for which see no.* 33615. *For other editions, see* 1843.

33672 —— A letter to Richard Cobden, Esq., M.P., in reply to remarks contained in his speech, delivered at Covent-garden theatre, on...March 20, 1844. 8p. *8°.* 1844.

33673 —— ⟨Mr. Day's second speech.⟩ The farmers and the League. The speech of Mr. George Game Day, of St. Ives, at Huntingdon, January 27, 1844, on the occasion of forming an Anti-League Association for the county of Huntingdon. With notes. Reported by his brother, William Day...Second edition. 28p. *8°.* 1844.

33674 —— Fifth edition. 28p. *8°.* 1844.

33675 —— Tenth edition. 28p. *8°.* 1844.

33676 —— Thirty-first edition. ⟨The people's edition.⟩ 23p. *8°.* 1844. *One of a collection of pamphlets contained in a volume issued by the Society for the Protection of Agriculture and British Industry, for which see no.* 33615.

33677 DAY, WILLIAM, *protectionist.* Incendiarism!!! Who are the instigators? First thousand. 16p. *8°.* 1844.

33678 GREY, H. G., *3rd Earl Grey.* The speech of the Right Hon. Viscount Howick, in the House of Commons on...June 25, 1844, on the motion of the Hon. C. P. Villiers, for the repeal of the corn laws. 25p. *8°.* 1844.

33679 HALEY, W. T. Lies of the League refuted and denounced, in a series of corn-law essays. 36p. *8°.* 1844.

33680 HERTFORDSHIRE AGRICULTURAL PROTECTION SOCIETY. Protection to agriculture. Speeches delivered at a meeting of landowners and tenant farmers held at the Town Hall, St. Alban's... February 2nd, 1844, to establish the Herts. Agricultural Protection Society...[With 'Declaration and rules of the ...Society'.] 38p. *8°. Hertford,* 1844.

33681 The **LEAGUE** and the beleaguered. A free discussion of the points at issue. 52p. *8°.* 1844.

33682 M'LAREN, D. To the members of the Edinburgh Anti-Corn Law Association. Substance of a speech delivered at the meeting of the Edinburgh Anti-Corn Law Association...9th May, 1844, in reference to the letter of the Right Honourable T. B. Macaulay, M.P. for the City, dated 1st May 1844, and addressed to the secretary... 15p. *8°. Edinburgh,* [1844]

33683 —— No. II. – To the members of the Edinburgh Anti-Corn-Law Association. Who has "perverted" and "distorted" Mr. Macaulay's letter? A letter to the editor of The Scotsman. 15p. *8°. Edinburgh,* [1844]

33684 PRINSEP, H. T. Notions on corn-laws and customs' duties. 56p. *8°.* 1844.

33684A REASONS for supporting the Government and opposing the League... By a commercial man. 60p. *12⁰. Hull, 1844. The copy that belonged to the 3rd Earl of Radnor.*

33685 SLEIGH, W. W. The speech... delivered on his nomination for the representation of the Borough of Hastings... March 28th, 1844, exposing the sophisticated arguments of the Anti-Corn Law League. Published by desire of the friends of Musgrave Brisco Esq., M.P. who was returned... 36p. *8⁰.* 1844.

33686 VERNEY, Sir H., *Bart.* A letter to the farmers of Buckinghamshire. [On the corn laws.] 16p. *8⁰.* [1844]

33687 A VIEW of the corn laws with reference to wheat, from the earliest times to the present. (*Emancipation of Industry*, 7.) 12p. *12⁰.* [1844]

33688 WILLIAMS, A. Great facts concerning free trade and free trade essays. 30p. *8⁰.* 1844. *The copy that belonged to the 3rd Earl of Radnor. Reissued in* Facts for philosophers, *1849, q.v.* (GENERAL).

POPULATION

33689 FARREN, E. J. Historical essay on the rise... of the doctrine of life-contingencies in England, leading to the establishment of the first life-assurance society in which ages were distinguished. 94p. *8⁰.* 1844.

33690 Two **LECTURES** on population, as affecting the welfare and happiness of nations, on the laws which regulate its increase, the effects to be anticipated, and the remedies.... Delivered in the Mechanics' Institute in Chester, in... 1842 and 1843. 76p. *8⁰. Chester*, 1844.

33691 VERHULST, P. F. Récherches mathématiques sur la loi d'accroisement de la population... [From *Mémoires de l'Académie Royale de Bruxelles*, vol. 18.] 38p. *4⁰. n.p.* [1844]

TRADES & MANUFACTURES

33692 BRONGNIART, A. Traité des arts céramiques ou des poteries considérées dans leur histoire, leur pratique et leur théorie... [With a volume of plates.] 3 vols. *8⁰. & obl.8⁰. Paris*, 1844.

33693 COMMITTEE OF JOURNEYMEN UPHOLSTERERS. An address of a Committee of Journeymen Upholsterers, appointed to consider the best plan of organizing an institute for the diffusion of information, and to promote the study of design among the members of the trade. 8p. *8⁰.* 1844.

33694 DODD, G. The textile manufactures of Great Britain. [British manufactures: Chemical. Metals. Series 4–6.] 6 vols. *12⁰.* 1844–46.

33695 ETZLER, J. A. Description of the naval automaton, invented by J. A. Etzler... 12p. *12⁰.* [1844]

33696 HIRST, W. History of the woollen trade, for the last sixty years; shewing the advantages which the west of England manufacturers had over those of Yorkshire up to 1813 – how these were gradually overcome until 1818... With a memoir of the author... 47, 48, 16, 32p. *12⁰. Leeds*, 1844.

33697 —— [Another edition.] [With 'Additional remarks relating to Mr. Abraham Naylor' and 'Summary of facts brought before a meeting of gentlemen held at Scarbrough's Hotel on... October 24, 1844, respecting matters in dispute between Mr. Wm. Hirst and Mr. Abraham Naylor'.] 47, 48, 60, 12, 12p. *12⁰. Leeds*, 1844.

33698 JOBARD, J. B. A. M. Nouvelle économie sociale, ou monautopole industriel, artistique, commercial et littéraire : fondé sur le pérennité des brevets d'invention, dessins, modèles et marques de fabriques. 475p. *12⁰. Paris & Bruxelles*, 1844.

33699 MARTIN, William (1772–1851). The Martinian fan-ventilators the best security for pitmen. 2p. *8⁰. Newcastle-upon-Tyne*, [1844]

33700 —— The Martinian new system of building ships mechanically, so that they may sail around the globe without taking in a pail of water, and cannot spring a leak, except from striking against a rock... 4p. *8⁰. Newcastle*, [1844]

33701 —— On manslaughter. The philosopher begging the attention of Her Most Gracious Majesty and British Government, as a great destruction has been wilfully made by pride amongst the poor pitmen, when it might have been prevented these 39 years [by the adoption of the fan-ventilators the author claims to have invented in 1806]. 2p. *8⁰. Newcastle*, [1844]

33702 —— The philosopher on the wonderful improvements for both Newcastle and Gateshead; making both the same town, and will make them places of renown. 2p. *8⁰. Newcastle*, [1844]

33703 —— The philosopher's improvement upon ropes, which engineers seem to take no notice of. 2p. *8⁰. Newcastle*, [1844]

33704 —— The philosopher's notice upon the ignorance of coal-viewers and the British Association at York, 1844. *s.sh.fol. Newcastle-upon-Tyne*, [1844]

33705 POLE, W. A treatise on the Cornish pumping engine; in two parts. Part I. Historical notice of the application of the steam engine to the purpose of draining the mines... Part II. Description of the Cornish pumping engine... contrasted with the ordinary Boulton and Watt single-acting engine... 164p. *4⁰.* 1844. *The half-title reads: Appendix G. to the new edition of Tredgold on the steam engine and on steam navigation.*

33706 REID, D. B. Illustrations of the theory and practice of ventilation, with remarks on warming, exclusive lighting, and the communication of sound. 451p. *8⁰.* 1844.

33707 SOCIETY OF CHAIR-MAKERS AND CARVERS, *London.* Third supplement to the London chair-makers' book of prices for workmanship. As regulated and agreed to by a committee. With the methods of computation adopted in the work. 175p. *4⁰.* 1844. *For editions of the original work, see* 1802 (COMMITTEE OF MASTER CHAIR-MANUFACTURERS AND JOURNEYMEN); *for the first and second supplements, see* 1808 *and* 1811.

COMMERCE

For an **ACCOUNT OF COALS AT LONDON MARKET,** *Newcastle, 1844–46, see* vol. III, *Periodicals list,* Prices of coals at the London market.

33708 [**ACKROYD**, E.] Reciprocity. By a manufacturer. 73p. *8°. Leeds & London,* [1844] *Presentation copy from the author to Henry Ashworth.*

33709 **ALISON**, SIR A., *Bart.* Free trade and protection. 75p. *8°. Edinburgh & London,* 1844.

33710 —— [Another edition.] 79p. *8°. Edinburgh & London,* 1844. *One of a collection of pamphlets contained in a volume issued by the Society for the Protection of Agriculture and British Industry, for which see no. 33615.*

33711 **AMERICAN INSTITUTE,** *New York.* Report on the commercial intercourse of the United States and Great Britain. January 1844. 12p. *8°. New-York,* 1844.

33712 **ANALYSE** ao tratado de commercio e navegação de 3 de Julho de 1842 entre Portugal e a Gram Bretanha: negociações sobre a reducção de direitos em virtude do artigo 7.°; e males que ella devia causar a Portugal se fosse levada a effeito. Por um ex-deputado ás Côrtes, amigo da industria do seu paiz. 124p. *8°. Lisboa,* 1844.

33713 **BARBEY**, T. Agence générale de rail-way. [Circular letter dated: 10 mai 1844. With 'Prix des transports de Paris au Havre pour les vins de Champagne, avec ou sans la mise à bord'.] [4]p. *fol.* [*Paris,* 1844]

33714 —— Théodore Barbey, commissionaire-expéditeur, Havre. Maison à Paris. [Circular letter, dated: 1er septembre 1844, announcing freight rates for wine in bottle.] [4]p. *fol. n.p.* [1844]

33715 *****BARTH**, H. Corinthiorum commercii et mercaturae historiae particula. Dissertatio inauguralis quam... in... Universitate Friderica Guilelma ad summos in philosophia honores rite obtinendos... publice defendet Henricus Barth. 55p. *8°. Berolini,* [1844] *The copy that belonged to George Grote.*

33716 **BATES**, I. C. Speech of Mr. I. C. Bates of Massachusetts, in the Senate of the United States, in defence of the protective system: delivered February 21, 1844. 18p. *8°. Washington,* 1844.

33717 **BOGAERDE VAN TER BRUGGE,** A. J. L. VAN DEN, *Baron.* Essai sur l'importance du commerce, de la navigation, et de l'industrie, dans les provinces formant le Royaume des Pays-Bas, depuis les temps les plus reculés jusqu'en 1830. 3 vols. *8°. La Haye & Bruxelles,* 1844–45.

33718 The **CORN LAWS.** "Facts are stubborn things." [An attack on the Anti-Corn Law League for the inaccuracy of its statistics on commerce.] 2p. *8°.* [1844]

33719 **CRAIK**, G. L. The history of British commerce from the earliest times. Reprinted from the Pictorial history of England; with corrections, additions, and a continuation to the present day. 3 vols. *12°.* 1844.

33720 **DEDE**, J. Der Handel des russischen Reichs. 330p. *8°. Mitau & Leipzig,* 1844.

33721 **DELVAUX DE FENFFE,** A. De la situation de l'industrie du fer en Prusse (Haute-Silésie), ou Mémoire sur les usines à fer de ce pays et sur la crise actuelle, suivi de quelques détails sur l'union douanière allemande, et sur la production et l'importation du fer de la fonte dans les états qui la composent. 128p. *8°. Liége, Bonn, &c.,* 1844.

33722 **ENGLAND.** *Laws, etc.* [*Endorsed:*] Edinburgh Cattle Market. An Act to amend an Act passed in the third year of... Her present Majesty for abolishing certain petty and market customs in the City of Edinburgh and granting other duties in lieu thereof. ⟨Royal Assent, 10th May 1844.⟩ 7 Victoriæ, sess. 1844. 7p. *fol. Westminster,* [1844]

33723 **FORBES**, R. B. Remarks on China and the China trade. 80p. *8°. Boston,* 1844.

33724 **GREELEY**, H. Protection and free trade. The question stated and considered. 16p. *8°. New York,* [1844]

33725 **HECHT**, M. Prix de transport de Maurice Hecht à Strasbourg. Commission & frais de place compris, par 100 kilo. *s.sh.4°. Strasbourg,* 1844. *A lithographed table.*

33726 **LOYAL NATIONAL REPEAL ASSOCIATION.** First report of the Sub-Committee of the ... Association on the papers in course of presentation to Parliament, entitled "Commercial tariffs and regulations of the several states of Europe and America." Read at a meeting of the Association... on the 20th day of May, 1844. 34p. *8°. n.p.* [1844] *The copy that belonged to Earl De Grey.*

33727 **MORRISON**, HON. JOHN R. A Chinese commercial guide, consisting of a collection of details and regulations respecting foreign trade with China... Second edition, revised throughout, and made applicable to the trade as at present conducted. 280p. *8°. Macao,* 1844.

33728 **NOUGUIER,** L. Des tribunaux de commerce, des commerçants et des actes de commerce... 3 vols. *8°. Paris,* 1844.

33728A **RICE**, THOMAS S., *Baron Monteagle.* The speech of... Lord Monteagle, on moving for... a Select Committee on the import duties... June 13th 1844. Extracted from Hansard's Parliamentary Debates. 91p. *12°. n.p.,* 1844. *The copy that belonged to the 3rd Earl of Radnor.*

33729 **SHARP**, JOSEPH B. The Anti-Corn-Law League, and the cotton trade. A letter to a noble lord. 22p. *8°.* 1844. *One of a collection of pamphlets contained in a volume issued by the Society for the Protection of Agriculture and British Industry, for which see no. 33615.*

33730 **SMITH**, THEOPHILUS I. Remarks on Mr. MacGregor's fourteenth report to Her Majesty's Privy Council for Trade, touching the customs' tariff, commercial regulations, and trade of Portugal. 25p. *8°. Oporto,* 1844.

33731 —— Reprinted by order of the Commercial Association of Oporto. Third edition. 30p. *8°.* 1844.

COLONIES

33732 ATKINSON, CHRISTOPHER W. A historical and statistical account of New-Brunswick, B.N.A. with advice to emigrants...Third edition, greatly improved and corrected. 284p. *8°. Edinburgh, 1844. For another edition, see* 1843 (A guide to New Brunswick).

33733 [BANISTER, T.] Britain and her colonial dependencies; and their right to be represented in Parliament. 24p. *8°.* 1844.

33734 COATES, D. The New Zealanders and their lands. The report of the Select Committee of the House of Commons on New Zealand, considered in a letter to Lord Stanley...Second edition, with additions, and an appendix. 72p. *8°.* 1844.

33735 COMPAGNIE BELGE DE COLONIS-ATION. Amérique centrale. Colonisation du district de Santo-Thomas de Guatemala par la Communauté de l'Union, fondée par la Compagnie Belge de la Colonisation. Collection de renseignements publiés ou recueillis par la Compagnie. 64, 169, 70, 64p. *8°. Paris,* 1844.

33736 FALCONER, T., *ed.* I. On the nomination of agents formerly appointed to act in England for the colonies of North America. [Letters by J. A. Roebuck, G. Bancroft and J. Sparks.] II. A brief statement of the dispute between Sir C. Metcalf and the House of Assembly of the Province of Canada [by T. Falconer]. 21p. *8°.* 1844.

33737 *GUBBINS, M. R. Reports on the settlement of Zillah Etawah. 105p. *8°. Agra,* 1844.

33738 *KING, EDWARD (*fl.* 1825–1845). On the advantages of a triform system of colonization in South Africa... 44p. *8°.* [London &] Bicester, 1844. Presentation copy with inscription from the author to Robert Owen. The FWA copy that belonged to William Pare.*

33739 LAVERDANT, D. G. Colonisation de Madagascar. 197p. *8°. Paris,* 1844. *With a 2-page list of books and articles about Madagascar. Presentation copy from the author, with an inscription on the half-title: 'A mon bon ami Bourdon'. The copy that afterwards belonged to Victor Considérant.*

33740 NEW ZEALAND COMPANY. The twelfth report of the directors of the New Zealand Company, presented to an adjourned special court of proprietors, held on the 26th April, 1844. 38p. *8°.* 1844.

33741 —— Documents appended to the twelfth report ... [1223]p. *8°.* 1844.

33742 —— Fourteenth report...presented to an adjourned special Court of Proprietors, held on the 31st July, 1844. 216p. *8°.* 1844. *See also* 1847.

33743 *NORTH WESTERN PROVINCES. Directions for settlement officers, promulgated under the authority of the Honorable the Lieutenant Governor of the North Western Provinces, September 1844. [With appendixes.] 56, xlviiip. *8°. Agra,* 1844.*

FINANCE

33744 The ARTICLE on the debts of the States. From the Democratic Review, for January, 1844. 19p. *8°. Boston,* 1844.

33745 BANK OF ENGLAND. A copy of the correspondence [of April and May, 1844] between the Chancellor of the Exchequer and the Bank of England relative to the renewal of the charter. 28p. *8°.* [London,] 1844. *In 1858 supplementary letters of 1857–58 (paginated 29–41) printed at the Bank of England, were added. The volume also contains a reprint and the original edition of* A copy of the correspondence...since 5th June last, *1833 (q.v.) and a copy of the original edition of* Opinions of Sir James Scarlett, *1833 (q.v.).*

For the BANKERS' MAGAZINE, 1844——→, *see* vol. III, *Periodicals list.*

33746 BLACKER, W. The evils inseparable from a mixed currency, and the advantages to be secured by introducing an inconvertible national paper circulation, throughout the British Empire and its dependencies, under proper regulations. An essay...Second edition. 132p. *8°.* 1844. *For other editions, see* 1838 (An inconvertible national paper currency).

33747 BLYDENBURGH, J. W. A treatise on the law of usury; to which is added, the statutes of the several states relating to interest now in force: together with a digest of all the decisions, and an index to the reported adjudications from the Statutes of Henry VIII. to the present time. xxv, 322p. *8°. New-York,* 1844.

33748 BOUCHERETT, A. Fallacy of Sir Robert Peel's speech on the renewal of the Bank charter. 7p. *8°.*

n.p. [1844] *The copy that belonged to T. Spring Rice, Baron Monteagle.*

33749 BOWKETT, T. E. Alchemy, or, the art of converting the baser metals into gold, familiarly explained. Containing also, among such important information, a highly valuable receipt for the manufacture of an accumulating fund, investment, provident, building, equitable association. 15p. *8°.* 1844.

33750 BUCHANAN, D. Inquiry into the taxation and commercial policy of Great Britain; with observations on the principles of currency, and of exchangeable value. 340p. *8°. Edinburgh, London, &c.,* 1844. *Presentation copy from the author to Sir Robert Peel.*

33751 [CAPPS, E.] Published under the superintendence of the Society for the Emancipation of Industry. The currency question in a nutshell. Third edition, with an additional dialogue. 24p. *12°.* [1844] *For other editions, see* 1837.

33752 —— Sir Robert Peel's currency plan. A lecture delivered at the British Coffee-House, in Cockspur-Street, on...the 13th of June, 1844, on the currency plan of Sir Robert Peel; showing its tendency and probable effects. 44p. *8°.* 1844.

33753 CLAY, SIR W., *Bart.* Remarks on the expediency of restricting the issue of promissory notes to a single issuing body. 91p. *8°.* 1844.

33754 COCKBURN, R. Remarks on prevailing errors respecting currency and banking...A new edition.

84p. *8°.* 1844. *Presentation copy from the author to Sir Henry Jardine. For another edition, see* 1842.

33755 COMPANY OF MERCHANTS, *Edinburgh.* [*Begin.*] At a general meeting of the Company of Merchants of the City of Edinburgh...22d day of November, 1844...the Company on hearing a report... in regard to the proposed abolition of the small-note currency...unanimously adopted the following resolutions... [2]p. *fol. n.p.* [1844]

33756 [**COWELL,** JOHN W.] ⟨Not for publication.⟩ [*Begin.*] I am about to offer a few remarks concerning my letters to Mr. Baring on the subject of the currency... 16p. *8°. Bristol,* [1844]

33757 A metallic **CURRENCY** a barrier to the progress of civilization and primary cause of restrictions on international commerce; with suggestions for placing the currency of Great Britain on a new basis. 20p. *8°.* 1844.

33758 [**CURTIS,** B. R.] An article on the debts of the States. From the North American Review, for January, 1844. 36p. *8°. Boston,* 1844.

33759 DELUSIONS and fallacies in the Bill brought into the House of Commons for the renewal of the charter of the Bank, and in the statements and arguments in support of it. By the author of "An attempt to give a popular explanation of the theory of money." 59p. *8°.* 1844.

33760 DUNEDIN BANK OF SCOTLAND. Prospectus of the Dunedin Bank of Scotland. 14p. *8°. Edinburgh,* 1844.

33761 DUPIN, F. P. C., *Baron.* Constitution, histoire et avenir des caisses d'épargne de France. 344p. *18°. Paris,* 1844. *Presentation copy, with inscription, from the author to* 'M. Vaulin-Varis'.

33762 DU VERGIER DE LA ROCHE-JAQUELEIN, H. A. G., *Marquis.* Considérations sur l'impôt du sel. 56p. *8°. Paris,* 1844.

33763 EDINBURGH AND GLASGOW BANK. Contract of copartnership of the Edinburgh and Glasgow Bank [uniting the Edinburgh and Leith Bank and the Glasgow Joint Stock Banking Company]. 76p. *8°. Edinburgh,* 1844.

33764 ENDERBY, C. The distress of the nation, its causes and remedies. 98p. *8°.* 1844. *For another edition, see* 1843.

33765 ENGLAND. *Court of Requests.* Courts of Requests. Returns of the number of causes, and executions against the bodies of debtors from the principal courts in ...1843. [4]p. *fol. n.p.* [1844?] *In manuscript on the endorsement:* 'No. 1'. *See note to no.* 32762.

33766 —— —— Courts of Requests. Return of the number of causes for six months after the abolition of imprisonment for debt under £20. and for the corresponding six months in...1843. [4]p. *fol. n.p.* [1844?] *In manuscript on the endorsement:* 'No. 2'. *See note to no.* 32762.

33767 —— *Laws, etc.* The Acts of Parliament now in force, relating to bankruptcy, the various rules and orders, and a complete list of all the commissioners...and other officers of the London and District Courts of Bankruptcy. To which is added, the Act for the relief of insolvent debtors... 255p. *8°.* 1844. *The copy that belonged to R. G. C. Fane.*

33768 EVANS, GEORGE (1797–1867). The tariff of 1842 vindicated. Speech of George Evans, of Maine, in reply to the Hon. Mr. McDuffie, of South Carolina, on the tariff. Delivered in the Senate of the United States, January 22 and 23, 1844. 40p. *8°. Washington,* 1844.

33769 FANE, R. G. C. [*Endorsed:*] Outline of a plan for improving the law of debtor and creditor, without abolishing imprisonment for debt. Submitted to...the Society for Promoting the Amendment of the Law. 2p. *fol.* [1844] *See note to no.* 32762.

33770 FULLARTON, J. On the regulation of currencies; being an examination of the principles on which it is proposed to restrict, within certain fixed limits, the future issues on credit of the Bank of England, and of the other banking establishments throughout the country. 227p. *8°.* 1844. *See also* 1845.

33771 [**GIBBON,** A.] The theory of money: being an attempt to give a popular explanation of it. With an epitome of the history of the Bank of England, shewing that corporation, with its charter and exclusive privileges, to be an unjust...monopoly. 231p. *8°.* 1844. *Presentation copy from the author to Sir Robert Peel. The inscription is in the same hand as those in later works by Alexander Gibbon, in which his name is printed on the title-pages.*

33772 GREELEY, H. The tariff as it is compared with the substitute proposed by its adversaries... 16p. *8°. New-York,* [1844]

33773 HAMMOND, JOHN W. A tabular view of the financial affairs of Pennsylvania, from the commencement of her public works to the present time; in which are included the cost, revenue and expenditures of the several lines of canals and rail-roads, &c. The whole prepared from the official records. 60p. *8°. Philadelphia,* 1844.

33774 HAWES, SIR B. Speech of Benj. Hawes, Jun., Esq. in opposition to the second reading of the Bank of England Charter Bill, Thursday 13th June, 1844. 47p. *8°.* 1844.

33775 HUEBLER, G. Handbuch der Nachtrags- und Ergänzungs-Vorschriften zur Zoll- und Staats-Monopols-Ordnung. Gesammelt und herausgegeben von Gottfried Hübler. 310p. *8°. Wien,* 1844.

33776 JOPLIN, T. Currency reform: improvement not depreciation. 87p. *8°.* 1844. *Presentation copy, with accompanying letter, from the author to Sir Edward Knatchbull. For the letter, see vol.* III, *A.L.* 68.

33777 —— An examination of Sir Robert Peel's currency Bill of 1844, in a letter to the bankers of the United Kingdom, proposing arrangements for their adoption, to prevent the evils in which it will otherwise involve the country. 95p. *8°.* 1844.

33778 [**KELLOGG,** E.] Currency: the evil and the remedy. By Godek Gardwell. Fourth edition, improved. 43p. *8°. n.p.* [1844?]

33779 [**KNOTT,** J. M.] The national currency. Reprinted...from the "Metropolitan Magazine," of November 1, 1844. 8p. *8°.* [*London,* 1844] *One of a collection of his own pamphlets, with a manuscript title-page in his hand, bound in a single volume for the author.*

33780 LANE, B. ⟨From Felix Farley's Bristol Journal, March 30, 1844.⟩ The Bank charter. To the editor of the Bristol Journal. *s.sh.fol. n.p.* [1844]

33781 LETTER on Sir Robert Peel's Currency Bill.

[Signed: A Liverpool broker.] From the Liverpool Albion, of Monday, July 8th, 1844. *s.sh.fol. n.p.* [1844]

33782 Two **LETTERS** to the Right Hon. Sir R. Peel, Bart. M.P. &c.&c.&c. on his proposed banking measures. By an ex-M.P. 34p. *8°.* 1844.

33783 **LOGAN,** WILLIAM H. The Scotish [*sic*] banker; or, a popular exposition of the practice of banking in Scotland...Second edition. 218p. *12°. Edinburgh, London, &c.,* 1844. *For another edition, see* 1839.

33784 **LOYAL NATIONAL REPEAL ASSO-CIATION.** First report of the Committee of the... Association on the glass duties. 15p. *8°. Dublin,* [1844] *The copy that belonged to Earl De Grey.*

33785 —— First report of the Sub-Committee of the... Association, on the Estimates for 1844–5. 41p. *8°. Dublin,* [1844] *The copy that belonged to Earl De Grey.*

33786 —— Report of the Committee of the...Association, appointed to inquire into the state of "joint-stock banking in Ireland," particularly as regards the effects of the Bank of Ireland monopoly, upon the general prosperity of Ireland. 43p. *8°. Dublin,* [1844]

33787 —— Report of the Committee of the...Association on the Commissariat Estimates for 1844–5, and on the Commissariat accounts. 7p. *8°. Dublin,* [1844] *The copy that belonged to Earl De Grey.*

33788 —— Report of the Parliamentary Committee of the...Association, on the Army Estimates for 1844–5. 67p. *8°. Dublin,* [1844] *The copy that belonged to Earl De Grey.*

33789 —— Report of the Parliamentary Committee of the...Association on the Militia Estimates for 1844–5. 7p. *8°. Dublin,* [1844] *The copy that belonged to Earl De Grey.*

33790 —— Report of the Parliamentary Committee of the...Association, on the Navy Estimates for 1844–5. 19p. *8°. Dublin,* [1844] *The copy that belonged to Earl De Grey.*

33791 —— Report of the Parliamentary Committee of the...Association, on the Ordnance Estimates for 1844–5. 23p. *8°. Dublin,* [1844] *The copy that belonged to Earl De Grey.*

33792 **LOYD,** S. J., *Baron Overstone.* Thoughts on the separation of the departments of the Bank of England. 56p. *8°.* 1844. *Presentation copy from the author to T. Spring Rice, Baron Monteagle. For another edition, see* 1840.

33793 **METROPOLITAN LIFE ASSURANCE SOCIETY.** [*Begin.*] Metropolitan Life Assurance Society...This Society was established...with a view to giving the greatest advantage to its members that life assurance is capable of affording...A prospectus. [With 'Rules and regulations'.] 16p. *8°.* [*London,* 1844]

33794 **MILES,** *pseud.* A letter to His Grace the Duke of Richmond, and the Agricultural Protection Society, on the question "What shall we do to be saved," submitted to their consideration before the passing of the new banking and currency Bill... 15p. *8°.* 1844.

33795 —— A letter to the Lords and Commons, in Parliament assembled, on the "condition of England question," as affected by the currency question. 15p. *8°.* 1844.

33796 **MILLER,** H. Words of warning to the people of Scotland, on Sir R. Peel's Scotch currency scheme. By the editor of the "Witness." 8op. *8°. Edinburgh, Glasgow, &c.,* 1844.

33797 The **MINISTRY** and the sugar duties. 5op. *8°.* 1844.

33798 **NATIONAL SECURITY SAVINGS BANK.** Rules of the National Security Savings Bank of Edinburgh... 19p. *8°. Edinburgh,* 1844. *See also* 1836.

33799 **NETHERLANDS.** *Laws, etc.* Wet houdende vaststelling eener buitengewone belasting op de bezittingen, en daarmede gepaard gaande vrijwillige geldleening en bijdrage. Zoo als dezelve na gemaakte wijzigingen en verbeteringen is aangenomen... 36p. *8°. Haarlem,* 1844.

33800 **NEWDEGATE,** C N. Speeches of C. N. Newdegate, Esq. (M.P. for North Warwickshire) in the House of Commons...May 20th...June 13th...June 24th, and...June 27th, on the Bank of England charter Bill... 31p. *8°. n.p.,* 1844.

33801 **NORTHUMBERLAND.** *Finance Committee.* Northumberland. Report of the finance committee on the several petitions presented from the rate-payers upon the subject of the county rates. 11p. *8°. Newcastle-upon-Tyne,* 1844.

33802 **NOUGUIER,** L. Des lettres de change et des effets de commerce en général... 2 vols. *8°. Paris,* 1844. *Vol. 2 contains the texts of enactments in France and other countries bearing on the subject.*

33803 A few **OBSERVATIONS** on the scheme proposed by Government for redeeming the duties on foreign free labor sugar. By a retired East India merchant. 11p. *8°.* 1844. *The copy that belonged to Earl De Grey.*

33804 **PEEL,** SIR ROBERT, *2nd Bart.* Speeches of the Right Honourable Sir Robert Peel, Bart., in the House of Commons, May 6th and 20th, 1844, on the renewal of the Bank charter, and the state of the law respecting currency and banking. 8op. *8°.* 1844.

33805 **PHILLIPS,** JOHN (*fl.* 1844). A comprehensive synopsis of all the monetary systems in the known world. Exhibiting...the comparative value of all the real and imaginary monies, calculated at their intrinsic par... according to the latest assays made at the Mints of London and Paris, and fully explaining the various methods of keeping accounts in all the principal trading places... Second edition. *s.sh.fol.* 1844.

33806 **PORTUGAL.** *Tribunal do Tesouro Publico.* Instrucções regulamentares paro a execução da carta de lei de 10 de Julho de 1843, sobre o imposto do sello. [Dated: 28 de Março de 1844.] 8p. *fol.* [*Lisboa,* 1844]

33807 **POSTSCRIPT.** [On the property tax.] (From the 'Westminster Review' for December. No. 83.) 19p. *8°. n.p.* [1844]

33808 **RAMSAY,** R. The banking system of Scotland considered, in reference to local parliaments. 14p. *8°. Glasgow & Edinburgh,* 1844.

33809 **REASONS** against legislative interference with the present system of circulation, submitted to Sir Robert Peel, Bart. by the committee of private country bankers. 23p. *8°.* 1844.

33810 **REASONS** for dissent from the scheme of reduction of interest on the three-and-a-half per cents. as proposed by Government; and for assent to such reduction only upon an equitable principle. 24p. *8°.* 1844.

33811 REY, C. L. De la refonte des monnaies de cuivre et de billon, d'après le projet de loi présenté à la Chambre des Députés, et discuté dans les séances des 29, 30, 31 mai, 1er et 2 juin 1843. 138p. *8°. Nîmes, 1844.*

33812 RICHELOT, H. A. J. F. Crise du Mont-de-Piété de Paris. 67p. *8°. Paris, 1844.*

33813 RIVES, W. C. Speech of Mr. Wm. C. Rives, of Virginia, on Mr. McDuffie's proposition to repeal the tariff act of 1842. Delivered in the Senate of the United States...May 27, 1844. 29p. *8°. Washington, 1844.*

33814 ROCKWELL, Julius. Speech of Mr. J. Rockwell, of Massachusetts, on the tariff bill. Delivered in the House of Representatives of the U.S., May 3d, 1844. 16p. *8°. Washington, [1844]*

33815 SALOMON, P. M. Mémoire à consulter sur les moyens et opérations métallurgiques à aviser pour obtenir une refonte des monnaies de cuivre, de bronze ou d'airain sans déchet et sur les machines à employer pour effectuer un monnayage suivi et accéléré... 19p. *8°. Paris, 1844.*

33816 SAUNDERSON, C. Suretiship. The dangers and defects of private security, and their remedies... Ninth edition, carefully revised. 26p. *12°. 1844. For other editions, see 1843.*

33817 SCOTT, Sir Walter, *Bart.* Letters of Malachi Malagrowther on the currency. 31p. *8°. Edinburgh, 1844. For other editions, see 1826.*

33818 SCOTUS, *pseud.* Three letters on the Scottish currency question...Originally published in the Edinburgh Evening Post. 24p. *8°. Edinburgh & London, 1844.*

33819 SMITH, Sydney (1771–1845). Letters on American debts...First printed in the "Morning Chronicle." Second edition. 24p. *8°. 1844. For another edition, see 1843.*

33820 SOCIETY FOR THE EMANCIPATION OF INDUSTRY. First report of the Committee of the Society...bringing down their proceedings to the termination of the Parliamentary session of 1844. 35p. *12°. 1844. See also 1846.*

33821 —— Society for the Emancipation of Industry... Address. 8p. *12°. [London, 1844]*

33822 —— [Another edition.] 8p. *12°. [London, 1844]*

33823 SPECTATOR, *pseud.* A plan of banking & currency, to unite the Bank of England, joint-stock, and private banks in one system, without injury to any. 16p. *8°. 1844.*

33824 *SPENS, W. Papers on life and health assurance. Read before the Glasgow Philosophical Society, session 1843–44. 27p. *8°. Glasgow, 1844. The copy that belonged to Augustus De Morgan.*

33825 TABEL van de sommen welke verschuldigd zullen zijn in geval de belasting op de bezittingen doorgaat, van de te doene inschrijvingen in de leening tegen 3 pCt. rente, evenredig aan de bezittingen van f3,000 tot f10,000,000, en van de sommen waarvoor als vrijwillige bijdrage zoude behooren te worden ingeschreven om te kunnen strekken tot voldoening der belasting. 8p. *8°. 's Gravenhage, 1844.*

33826 TAIT, W. Peter Playfair's correspondence with the editor of the Times Journal, on banks of issue. Republished by the author. 53p. *8°. 1844.*

33827 [TAYLOR, John (1781–1864).] Currency fallacies refuted, and paper money vindicated. By the author of "An essay on money"...Second edition. 84p. *8°. 1844. In a volume of the author's pamphlets presented to Sir Robert Peel. For other editions, see 1833.*

33828 [——] Emancipation of industry...To the editor of "the Times." [Signed: M.M., and dated, February 15, 1844.] 8p. *8°. [London, 1844] See note to no. 33827, above. See also 1845 (Currency investigated).*

33829 —— An essay on money, its origin and use... Third edition. 90p. *8°. 1844. See note to no. 33827. For other editions, see 1830.*

33830 [——] The new Currency Bill. A letter to the Premier in reply to his speech on the Bank Charter Act, May 7. 1844. By an enquirer after truth. 26p. *8°. 1844.*

33831 [——] What is a pound? A letter to the Premier on his new currency measures in reply to his speech on the Bank Charter Act, May 6, 1844. Second edition, enlarged. [Signed: An inquirer after truth.] 71p. *8°. 1844. See also 1845 (Currency investigated).*

33832 —— Who pays the taxes?...Second edition. 37p. *8°. 1844. For other editions, see 1841.*

33833 TOOKE, T. An inquiry into the currency principle; the connection of the currency with prices, and the expediency of a separation of issue from banking. 147p. *8°. 1844.*

33834 —— Second edition. [With a supplementary chapter.] 165p. *8°. 1844.*

33835 TORRENS, R. An inquiry into the practical working of the proposed arrangements for the renewal of the charter of the Bank of England, and the regulation of the currency: with a refutation of the fallacies advanced by Mr. Tooke. 66p. *8°. 1844.*

33836 —— Second edition. To which is added, a reply to the objections of the Westminster Review to the Government plan for the regulation of the currency. 104p. *8°. 1844. Presentation copy from the author to T. Spring Rice, Baron Monteagle.*

33837 —— Reply to the objections of the Westminster Review to the Government plan for the regulation of the currency. 40p. *8°. 1844.*

33838 VIDAL, F. Des caisses d'épargne. I. Les caisses d'épargne transformées en institutions de crédit. II. Création d'ateliers de travail, au moyen d'avances fournies par les caisses d'épargne. 75p. *8°. Paris, 1844. The copy that belonged to Victor Considérant.*

33839 VIRGO, W. Sir Robert Peel, and the Bank charter. The monetary system, illustrated in a series of tables...shewing the relative value of bullion, gold and silver...to English standard value. Also, the value of the nominal pound sterling, and the fallacious state of our present system, and the only method of correcting it... and...securing our foreign and domestic trade... 86p. *8°. 1844. For another edition, entitled* A universal monetary system, *see 1847.*

33840 WILSON, Effingham. Wilson's description of the new Royal Exchange, including an historical notice of the former edifices, and a brief memoir of Sir Thomas Gresham, Knt.... 132p. *12°. 1844.*

33841 WOOD, Charles, *Viscount Halifax.* Speech of Charles Wood, Esq. in the debate on Sir R. Peel's resolutions on banking, Monday, May 20, 1844. 64p. *8°. 1844.*

33842 WOODBURY, L. Speech of Mr. Woodbury, of New Hampshire, on the tariff. Delivered in the Senate of the United States, February 7 and 8, 1844. 30p. *8º*. *Washington*, 1844.

33843 WOOLLGAR, J. W. Friendly societies' security. An essay on testing the condition of a friendly society, by valuation of all policies at annual or other short periods, without resorting to a professional actuary. Also observations on the rates of contribution... 32p. *8º*. *Lewes*, 1844.

33844 [WRIGHT, THOMAS B. and **HARLOW**, J.] The currency question. The Gemini letters. xii, 398p. *8º*. *London, Birmingham, &c.*, 1844. *The copy that belonged to Sir Robert Peel.*

33845 [——] "Gemini" in reply to Sir R. Peel. ⟨From the Midland Counties Herald, May 9, 1844.⟩ 3p. *4º*. *Birmingham*, [1844] *See note to no.* 33844, *above*.

33846 *YOUNG, ALEXANDER. A guide to life assurance; containing an account of the origin and progress; an explanation of the system; and pointing out the benefits of life assurance: with directions for effecting a policy. [With prospectuses of companies and 'A correct list of all the fire, life, and annuity insurance offices in London; with the branch offices of the provincial companies'.] 36, [36]p. *12º*. 1844. *The copy that belonged to Augustus De Morgan.*

TRANSPORT

33847 A brief **ACCOUNT** of the rise, and early progress of steam navigation: intended to demonstrate that it originated in the suggestions and experiments of the late Mr. James Taylor of Cumnock, in connexion with the late Mr. Miller of Dalswinton. [With an appendix.] 19, 5p. *8º*. *Ayr*, 1844.

33848 BRIGHTON AND CHICHESTER RAILWAY COMPANY. [*Endorsed:*] Brighton and Chichester Railway. Prospectus. [4]p. *fol. Brighton*, [1844]

33849 CAEN. *Conseil Municipal.* Rapport fait au Conseil municipal de la ville de Caen, dans sa séance du 5 août [11 & 16 novembre] 1844, sur un projet d'embranchement de chemin de fer à diriger sur la Basse-Normandie. 31p. *4º*. *Caen*, 1844.

33850 CHEMIN DE FER D'ORLÉANS. The cahier des charges; or, book of conditions, annexed to the lease for the working of the Orleans and Bordeaux Railway; with a map. Translated from the French, with a notice by W. Page Smith, Esq. 18p. *4º*. [*London*, 1844]

33851 CHEVALIER, M. L'Isthme de Panama... Extrait de la Revue des Deux Mondes 1er janvier 1844. 72p. *8º*. *Paris*, 1844. *Presentation copy from the author to M. Avezal.*

33852 —— L'Isthme de Panama. Examen historique et géographique des différentes directions suivant lesquelles on pourrait le percer et des moyens à y employer; suivi d'un aperçu sur l'Isthme de Suez... 182p. *8º*. *Paris*, 1844. *A greatly revised and expanded version of the work above.*

33853 EASTERN COUNTIES RAILWAY COMPANY. Report. [And resolutions passed at a special general meeting of the shareholders...the 30th April, 1844.] [4]p. *fol. n.p.* [1844] *A covering letter is printed on p. 1.*

33854 EASTERN UNION RAILWAY COMPANY. Report at the first general meeting of shareholders held in Ipswich, 11th December, 1844. 2, [4]p. *fol. Ipswich*, [1844] *See also* 1845, 1846, 1847, 1848, 1849, 1850.

33855 ENGLAND. *Laws, etc.* [*Endorsed:*] Brighton and Chichester Railway. An Act for making a railway from the Shoreham Branch of the London and Brighton Railway to Chichester. ⟨Royal Assent, 4th July, 1844.⟩ 7 & 8 Victoriæ, sess. 1844. ⟨13.⟩ 3, 17, 165p. *fol.* [*London*, 1844] *The Rastrick copy.*

33856 FORRESTER, JOSEPH J. Papers relating to the improvement of the navigation of the River Douro,

from its mouth to the Barca de Vilvestre in Spain; and to the maps of that river and of the wine-district of the Alto-Douro. [20]p. *8º*. *Oporto*, 1844. *In a volume of his pamphlets presented by the author to 'Alex. Young Esqre.'.*

33857 GALE, C. J. A letter to the Right Hon. the Earl of Dalhousie, President of the Board of Trade, on railway legislation. 32p. *8º*. 1844. *The Rastrick copy.*

33858 GALLOWAY, J. A. Communication with India, China, &c. Observations on the proposed improvements in the overland route viâ Egypt, with remarks on the ship canal, the Boulac canal, and the Suez railroad... 24p. *8º*. 1844.

33859 [GALT, W.] Railway reform; its expediency and practicability considered. With...appendix, containing a description of all the railways in Great Britain and Ireland; fluctuations in the prices of shares; statistical and parliamentary returns; financial calculations...Third edition, revised and considerably enlarged. 116p. *8º*. 1844. *The Rastrick copy. For other editions, see* 1843.

33860 GREAT WESTERN & Newbury and South Western and Newbury Railway Bills. The case of the promoters of the Great Western and Newbury Bill. 61p. *8º*. 1844.

33861 The **HAND BOOK** to the Dublin & Drogheda Railway, containing a description of the scenery, towns, villages, and remarkable places lying along...the line from Dublin to Drogheda; with all necessary statistical, historical...information. And also a guide to Drogheda and its environs... 70p. *8º*. *Dublin: N. Walsh*, [1844]

33862 HENDSCHEL, U. Eisenbahn-Atlas von Deutschland, Belgien und dem Elsass. Mit allen Fahrplänen, Tarifen, Betriebs-Verordnungen und sonst dahin gehörigen Nachweisungen sowie den speciallen Karten der bedeutenderen bis jetzt vollendeten Eisenbahnen. Ein Handbuch für Reisende...Nach officiellen Quellen bearbeitet von U. Hendschel. Neu revidirt und mit allen Veränderungen und Nachträgen vervollständigt. [330]p. *16º*. *Frankfurt a M.*, 1844.

33863 JENNINGS, E. Practical hints addressed to seamen, for preventing accidents on board ship, and especially for guarding against hurricanes, collision, fire, &c. [With 'Addenda to "Practical hints to seamen"'.] 2 vols. *8º*. 1844–45. *Presentation copy from the author to Sir George Clerk, Bart. (1787–1867). A reissue of the edition published with the title* Hints on sea-risks, *in 1843 (q.v.).*

33864 LANE, S. The shopkeepers' rebellion; or, the

tollgate war. [A ballad on the opposition to the abolition of tolls on the bridge in New Street, Norwich.] *s.sh.fol. Norwich*, [1844] [*Br.* 608]

33865 LEAHY, E. A practical treatise on making and repairing roads... xvi, 306p. *12°. 1844. See also 1847.*

33866 A LETTER to the Right Hon. W. E. Gladstone, M.P. President of the Board of Trade, on railway legislation. 57p. *8°. 1844.*

33867 MALLET, R. Report on the railroad constructed from Kingstown to Dalkey, in Ireland upon the atmospheric system, and upon the application of this system to railroads in general. 55p. *4°. n.p.* [1844?] *The copy that belonged to George Bidder.*

33868 MORRIS, EDWARD (*d.* 1860). The life of Henry Bell, the practical introducer of the steam-boat into Great Britain and Ireland; to which is added, an historical sketch of steam navigation. 175p. *12°. Glasgow, Edinburgh, &c., 1844. Presentation copy, with inscription, from the author to 'John Wilson Esqr'.*

33869 MURRAY, JOHN (1804–1882). Report of John Murray, Esq., civil engineer, on the proposed west harbour and dock, at Hartlepool. [With 'Extracts from the report of John Urpeth Rastrick, Esq., C.E.'.] [3]p. *fol. Hartlepool,* [1844]

33870 NEW JERSEY. *Legislature.* Report of the Joint Committee, to whom was referred that part of the Governor's message, on the subject of the Delaware Breakwater, at Cape May. Read and ordered to be printed, February, 1844. [With a list of vessels shipwrecked off Cape May during the previous 20 years.] 11p. *12°. Trenton,* 1844.

33871 OBSERVATIONS on the government measures as to railways, being extracts from the leading articles of "The Railway Times." 20p. *8°.* [1844]

33872 PARIS. *Conseil Municipal.* Chemins de fer. Ligne de Paris à Lyon et de Paris à Strasbourg. Rapport fait au Conseil municipal de Paris sur le tracé de Paris à Strasbourg par Victor Considérant. 30p. *8°. Paris,* 1844. *Considérant's own copy.*

For the **RAILWAY CHRONICLE,** 1844–47, *see* vol. III, *Periodicals list.*

For the **RAILWAY REGISTER** and record of public enterprise, 1844–45, *see* vol. III, *Periodicals list.*

For **SOCIÉTÉ INDUSTRIELLE DE MULHOUSE,** Bulletin, *see* vol. III, *Periodicals list,* Bulletin de la Société...

33873 SOUTH WESTERN STEAM PACKET COMPANY. Abstract of report presented by the directors to the third half-yearly general meeting of the shareholders, held at the Nine Elms Station of the London and South Western Railway, 30th December 1843. 3p. *fol. n.p.* [1844]

33874 STEPHENSON, ROBERT (1803–1886). Report on the atmospheric railway system. 44p., 26 plates. *4°. 1844. The copy that belonged to George Bidder.*

33875 TOURNEUX, F. Encyclopédie des chemins de fer et des machines à vapeur, à l'usage des practiciens et des gens du monde. 520p. *8°. Paris,* 1844.

SOCIAL CONDITIONS

33876 ADAMS, WILLIAM (*fl.* 1824–1879). A few words to the owners and occupiers of land, and to the ratepayers in general, of the Buntingford Union. 8p. *8°. 1844.*

33877 The ADMINISTRATION of the Post Office from the introduction of Mr. Rowland Hill's plan of penny postage up to the present time, grounded on parliamentary documents, and the evidence before the Select Committee on postage... To which are added the last returns to the House of Commons. 218p. *8°. 1844.*

33878 ALCOTT, W. A. Vegetable diet defended. viii, 24p. *8°. 1844. Printed at the Concordium Press, Ham Common.*

33879 ALISON, W. P. Observations on the epidemic fever of MDCCCXLIII in Scotland, and its connection with the destitute condition of the poor. 80p. *8°. Edinburgh & London,* 1844.

33880 —— Remarks on the Report of Her Majesty's Commissioners on the Poor-Laws of Scotland presented to Parliament in 1844, and on the dissent of Mr. Twisleton from that report. 302p. *8°. Edinburgh & London,* 1844.

33881 ARCHER, T. Self-culture and its impediment in late hours of business... A lecture delivered at the request of the General Association for effecting an Abridgment of the Hours of Business. 23p. *12°. London, Edinburgh, &c.,* 1844.

33882 ASSOCIATE INSTITUTION FOR IMPROVING AND ENFORCING THE LAWS FOR THE PROTECTION OF WOMEN. Remedies for the wrongs of women. Published by order of the committee of the Associate Institution... Third edition. 64p. *8°. 1844. The compilation of this work was conjecturally attributed by HSF to Thomas Joplin, the honorary secretary of the Institution.*

For ***ASSOCIATION FOR PROMOTING THE RELIEF OF DESTITUTION IN THE METROPOLIS,** First annual [–twenty-first] report of the committee, 1844–66, *continued as* **METROPOLITAN VISITING AND RELIEF ASSOCIATION,** Twenty-second[–ninety-ninth] report..., 1867–1959, *see* vol. III, *Periodicals list,* Metropolitan Visiting and Relief Association.

33883 BAILEY, T. Rights of labour: with proposals for a new basis for the national suffrage. 60p. *12°. London, Nottingham, &c.,* 1844.

33884 BEARDSALL, F., *comp.* Selection of hymns and songs, suitable for public and social temperance meetings. [Third edition.] 204p. *16°. Manchester, London, &c.,* [1844] *The Turner copy.*

33885 BENEVOLENT OR STRANGERS' FRIEND SOCIETY. Report of the... Society... with an account of the cases visited, and a list of subscribers in the year ending September 29 1844. lii, 43p. *12°. 1844. See also* 1816, 1817.

33886 BOOKBINDERS' CONSOLIDATED UNION. To the officers and members of the Bookbinders Consolidated Union. [A letter from the Central Committee, signed: Henry Searson, chief sec., and dated from Dublin, 4 March 1844.] *s.sh.8°. n.p.* [1844]

33887 BRIGHT, John (1811–1889). Speech of Mr. Bright, M.P. in the House of Commons, on Lord Ashley's amendment to Sir J. Graham's Factory Bill, March 15, 1844. 45p. *8°. 1844. The copy that belonged to Victor Considérant.*

33888 —— [Another edition.] 16p. *8°. n.p.* [1844]

33889 BULLER, C. Ten Hours' Factory Bill. The speech of C. Buller, Esq., M.P. in the House of Commons on...March 22nd, 1844, in support of Lord Ashley's amendment, that in the eighth clause the word "ten" be substituted for the word "twelve." 26p. *8°. 1844. Presentation copy from the author to the Hon. Mrs. Stanley.*

33890 BURKE, J. F., *comp.* Cottage economy and cookery. [Compiled... from essays submitted to the Royal Agricultural Society of England; and reprinted from the Journal of the Society, vol. III., part I, 1842.] 20p. *8°. 1844.*

33891 CARPENTER, William (1797–1874). Machinery, as it affects the industrial classes; and the employment of children in factories, etc. 72p. *12°.* [1844?]

33892 COBDEN, R. Tenant farmers and farm labourers. Speech of R. Cobden, Esq., in the House of Commons, on...12th March, 1844, on moving for a Select Committee "to inquire into the effects of protective duties on imports upon the interests of tenant-farmers and farm-labourers." 23p. *8°. Manchester,* [1844]

33893 —— Second edition. 49p. *8°. 1844.*

33894 COMMITTEE APPOINTED TO TAKE THE CHARGE...OF THE SUBSCRIPTIONS...FOR THE RELIEF OF THE DISTRESSED MANUFACTURERS. Report of the Committee to take the charge...of the subscriptions and of the collections made under the authority of the Queen's Letters, dated May 11th, 1842, for the relief of the distressed manufacturers; with an appendix, and lists of individual subscriptions and of congregational collections. 171p. *8°. 1844.*

33895 COMMITTEE OF INHABITANTS OF EDINBURGH AND LEITH. Observations by the Inhabitants' Committee on the report of the meeting of shareholders of the Edinburgh Water Company, held on 2nd January 1844. As reported in Courant of 4th of January. 10p. *4°. n.p.* [1844] *Bound in a volume with other printed and manuscript pieces on the water supply of Edinburgh. For the manuscripts, see vol. III, MS. 470.*

33896 CONSIDÉRANT, V. P. Théorie de l'éducation naturelle et attrayante; dédiée aux mères. 194p. *8°. Paris, 1844. Considérant's own copy.*

33897 COOPER, A. A., *7th Earl of Shaftesbury.* Ten Hours' Factory Bill. The speech of Lord Ashley, M.P. in the House of Commons on...March 15th, 1844... 30p. *8°. 1844.*

33898 —— Ten Hours Factory Bill. The speech of Lord Ashley, M.P. in the House of Commons...10th May, 1844. 18p. *8°. 1844.*

33899 COULTHART, J. R. State of large towns and populous districts. A report on the sanatory condition of the town of Ashton-under-Lyne; with remarks on the existing evils and suggestions for improving the health... of the inhabitants...As communicated to Dr. Lyon Playfair, one of Her Majesty's Commissioners for Enquiring into the State of Large Towns and Populous Districts. 57p. *8°. Ashton-under-Lyne, 1844.*

33900 D., T. The metropolitan charities: being an account of the charitable, benevolent, and religious societies; hospitals, dispensaries, penitentiaries, annuity funds, asylums, almshouses, colleges and schools; in London and its immediate vicinity... 236p. *8°. 1844.*

33901 DAVIES, Thomas (*fl.* 1843). Prize essay on the evils which are produced by late hours of business, and on the benefits which would attend their abridgement... 39p. *8°. 1843[1844] The original paper wrapper (now destroyed) bore the words '7th thousd. 1844'. For another edition, see 1843.*

33902 DAY, William, *Asst. Poor Law Commissioner.* Correspondence with the Poor Law Commissioners, with observations on the working of certain points of the Poor Law and on Sir James Graham's proposed alteration in the law of settlement. 49p. *8°. London, Lewes, &c., 1844. The copy that belonged to Col. C. R. Fox, M.P. (1796–1865).*

33903 DEMETZ, F. A. Résumé sur le système pénitentiaire. 48p. *8°. Paris,* [1844] *The copy that belonged to Victor Considérant.*

33904 DUCPÉTIAUX, E. Projet pour la construction, aux environs de Bruxelles, d'un quartier modèle spécialement destiné à des familles d'ouvriers. 8p. *8°. n.p.* [1844] *Presentation copy from the author to 'Monsieur le Docteur Roeder à Heidelberg'.*

33905 EDINBURGH WATER COMPANY. Report by the Directors of the Edinburgh Water Company to be submitted to the special general meeting of proprietors of stock, to be held within the Royal Hotel, Prince's Street, Edinburgh...8th day of August, 1844. [4]p. *fol. n.p.* [1844] *See note to no.* 33895.

33906 ÉGRON, A. C. Le livre de l'ouvrier, ses devoirs envers la société, la famille et lui-même. 407p. *12°. Paris, 1844.*

33907 ENGLAND. *Commissioners for Inquiring into the State of Large Towns and Populous Districts.* First report of the Commissioners... 2 vols. *8°. 1844.*

33908 —— *Home Office.* Report of the Surveyor-General of Prisons [Joshua Jebb] on the construction, ventilation, and details of Pentonville Prison, 1844. Presented to both Houses of Parliament... 62p., 22 plans. *8°. 1844. See also* 1847.

33909 —— *Laws, etc.* The Poor Law Amendment Act, An Act (7 & 8 Vict. Cap. 101.) for the amendment of the laws relating to the poor in England and Wales. Passed 9th August, 1844. With copious index, by a barrister. 31p. *8°.* [1844]

33910 —— [Another edition.] The Act for the further amendment of the laws relating to the poor in England, with the other statutes affecting the Poor Law passed in the Parliament of 1844. With notes, forms, and index. By William Golden Lumley. 188p. *12°. 1844.*

33911 —— *Parliament.* [*Endorsed:*] Sheffield United Gas Light Company. A (proposed) Bill for uniting the Sheffield gas light companies. 7 Vict. sess. 1844. 58p. *fol.* [*London,* 1844]

33912 —— *Poor Law Commission* [*1834–1847*]. Report of the Poor Law Commissioners on local taxation... 360p. *8°. 1844.*

33913 GLASGOW. *Town's Hospital.* Regulations of the Town's Hospital of Glasgow: with the original constitution of the house, and an appendix. 45p. *8°. Glasgow, 1844.*

33914 GOVERNMENT clerks and their salaries. Facts addressed to the Rt. Hon. Sir Robert Peel...upon the unjust and partial mode of remunerating government clerks, with suggestions for an improvement. Also an outline of a plan for forming a general annuity fund for the benefit of the widows and orphans of those officers who die in the public service. By an old revenue officer. 16p. *8⁰.* [1844]

33915 GREY, H. G., *3rd Earl Grey.* The substance of two speeches delivered in the House of Commons on the factory question, on...May 3, and...May 10. 34p. *8⁰.* 1844. *The copy that belonged to Victor Considérant.*

33916 GRINDROD, R. B. The slaves of the needle; an exposure of the distressed condition, moral and physical, of dress-makers, milliners, embroiderers, slop-workers, &c. 35p. *12⁰. London & Manchester,* [1844]

33917 HANSARD, LUKE J. Remarks in relation to an appeal now before Parliament for the suppression of an intolerable nuisance [prostitution] which has long afflicted the community, by tending to the destruction of their best interests and truest happiness. ⟨The Bill to which this refers was withdrawn in the House of Lords on the 9th July 1844.⟩ 67p. *8⁰.* 1844.

33918 [HARNESS, W.] Visiting societies and lay readers. A letter to the Lord Bishop of London. By Presbyter Catholicus. 55p. *8⁰.* 1844.

33919 The **HEALTH** of the people. A call upon the people of Great Britain to petition Parliament for legislative measures embodying the suggestions contained in two government reports...having for...object the improvement of the public health... 12p. *8⁰. Bath,* [1844]

33920 HEALTH OF TOWNS ASSOCIATION, *London.* Health of Towns Association. Abstract of the proceedings of the public meeting held at Exeter Hall, Dec. 11, 1844. Containing the speeches of the...Marquess of Normanby, chairman; Sir R. H. Inglis, Bart., M.P.... [and others] together with a form of petition [for the improvement of drainage, sewerage and ventilation]. 36p. *12⁰.* [1844]

33921 [HELPS, SIR A.] The claims of labour. An essay on the duties of the employers to the employed. 174p. *8⁰.* 1844. *Presentation copy to Samuel Smiles, when editor of 'The Leeds Times', with his signature on the flyleaf; he afterwards presented it to G. S. Phillips. See also 1845.*

33922 HENSLOW, J. S. Suggestions towards an enquiry into the present condition of the labouring population of Suffolk. 29p. *8⁰. Hadleigh, Ipswich, &c.,* [1844]

33923 HESKETH, R. A synopsis of the Metropolitan Buildings Act, 7 & 8 Victoriæ, cap. 84. Calculated as well for the use of architects, builders...as for that of owners, occupiers and agents... 52p. *8⁰.* 1844.

33924 HICKSON, WILLIAM E. The apologists of City administration. Reprinted from the 'Westminster Review,' for June 1844. (With an appendix upon city freedoms.) [An attack on the Corporation and the City solicitor, Charles Pearson, with special reference to charitable trusts. Signed: W.E.H.] 31p. *8⁰.* 1844. *The identity of the author is disclosed in a footnote. Presentation copy to Richard Monckton Milnes, Baron Houghton.*

33925 HILL, SIR ROWLAND (1795–1879). The state and prospects of penny postage, as developed in the evidence taken before the postage committee of 1843; with incidental remarks on the testimony of the Post-Office authorities; and an appendix of correspondence. 84p. *8⁰.* 1844.

33926 [HOGG, THOMAS.] No. IV. Leeds weekly half holiday in warehouses, &c. To employers. [Dated: February 29th, 1844.] 4p. *12⁰. Leeds,* [1844] *Presentation copy with inscription (cut into), from the author.*

33927 HUCKABACK, HABAKKUK, *pseud.* A letter on early shop-shutting, in reply to the counter cracks, of the shopkeeper of the old school. 16p. *8⁰. Edinburgh,* 1844.

33928 HUTCHINSON, JOHN, *M.D.* Contributions to vital statistics, obtained by means of a pneumatic apparatus for valuing the respiratory powers with relation to health...⟨Read before the Statistical Society of London, June 17th, 1844.⟩ 20p. *8⁰.* [*London,* 1844]

33929 JAMES, SIR WALTER, *Bart.* The poor of London: a letter to the Lord Bishop of the diocese. 75p. *8⁰.* 1844.

33930 JEBB, SIR JOSHUA. Modern prisons: their construction and ventilation...With ten plates. ⟨From 'Papers on subjects connected with the duties of the Corps of Royal Engineers,' vol. VII.⟩ 24p. *4⁰.* 1844.

33931 [LHOTSKY, J.] On cases of death by starvation, and extreme distress among the humbler classes, considered as one of the main symptoms of the present disorganization of society; with a preparatory plan for remedying these evils in the Metropolis and other large cities. By J. L. late of the colonial service. With an introduction by Viscount Ranelagh. 47p. *8⁰.* 1844. *Presentation copy, with inscription, 'To his kind and most successful medical adviser, Dr. de Pratti – his friend the Author'.*

33932 LIVERPOOL. Late hours of business among shopkeepers. Report of a public meeting of the inhabitants of Liverpool..."to consider the most desirable means of bringing into use such an amended system of business, in regard to the hours of attendance, as may give permanent and effectual relief to a...deserving class of persons without injury either to their employers or to the public." Held in the Music-Hall, 10th April, 1844. 24p. *12⁰. London & Liverpool,* [1844]

33933 LIVERPOOL ASSOCIATION OF ASSISTANT TRADESMEN. The third annual report of the...Association...1843. [With officers for 1844, 'List of shops in the principal streets which are closed at seven o'clock', and a short bibliography on late hours of business.] 20p. *12⁰. Liverpool,* 1844. *See also 1845.*

For the **MARINERS' CHURCH GOSPEL TEMPERANCE SOLDIERS' AND SAILORS' MAGAZINE,** *see* vol. III, *Periodicals list.*

33934 MARTIN, WILLIAM (1772–1851). The philosopher's letter to the British Government, in behalf of the poor pitmen, making a struggle to throw off the tyrannical yoke... 2p. *8⁰. Newcastle,* [1844]

33935 MARX, KARL F. H. On the decrease of disease effected by the progress of civilization. By C. F. H. Marx, M.D. Professor of Medicine in the University of Göttingen, etc. and R. Willis, M.D., member of the Royal College of Physicians, etc. 102p. *8⁰.* 1844. *Written originally in German by Dr. Marx, translated and paraphrased by Dr. Willis.*

33936 MASON, H. J. M. History of the origin and

progress of the Irish Society, established for promoting the education of the native Irish, through the medium of their own language. 112p. *8°. Dublin*, 1844. *Presentation copy from the author to Countess De Grey.*

33937 METROPOLITAN DRAPERS' ASSO-CIATION. The late-hour system. A full report of the speeches delivered at a meeting of the Metropolitan Drapers' Association held at Exeter Hall, on...October 9, 1844. With the statement of the committee. Fourth thousand. 32p. *8°.* 1844.

33938 MUNDAY, A. The Fishmongers' pageant, on Lord Mayor's Day, 1616. Chrysanaleia, the golden fishing, devised by Anthony Munday...Represented in...plates by Henry Shaw...from contemporary drawings in the possession of the...Company of Fishmongers. Accompanied with...documents and an historical introduction by John Gough Nichols... 32p. *fol.* [*London:*] *For the Worshipful Company of Fishmongers*, 1844.

33939 NAPER, J. L. W. Suggestions for the more scientific and general employment of agricultural labourers, together with a plan which would enable the landlords of Ireland to afford them suitable houses and gardens with applotments at a fair rent, being observations on chapter x. of Dr. Kane's "Industrial resources of Ireland." 24p. *8°. Dublin & London*, 1844.

For the **NATIONAL TEMPERANCE MAGA-ZINE,** 1844–46, *see* vol. III, *Periodicals list.*

33940 NEW SOUTH WALES. *Legislative Council.* General education vindicated: being the report from the select committee on education, and the appendix...the report of the public meeting at the School of Arts on... September 7th; with report of the Commissioners of National Education in Ireland... 64p. *8°. Sydney*, 1844.

33941 OASTLER is free! Oastler is welcome. [Two ballads printed side by side.] *s.sh.fol. n.p.* [1844] [*Br.* 609]

33942 OBSERVATIONS on the factory system. 31p. *8°.* 1844.

33943 ORPHAN WORKING SCHOOL, *London.* Short account of the Orphan Working School in the City Road...for the maintenance, instruction, and employment of orphans and other necessitous children. With the rules, a list of governors, &c.&c. 68p. *8°.* 1844.

33944 OSBORNE, LORD S. G. A letter to the Right Hon. Lord Ashley, M.P. on the condition of the agricultural labourer. 48p. *8°. London & Blandford*, 1844.

33945 —— A view of the low moral & physical condition of the agricultural labourer. 32p. *8°. London & Blandford*, 1844.

33946 OVERS, J. Evenings of a working man, being the occupation of his scanty leisure...With a preface relative to the author by Charles Dickens. 205p. *8°.* 1844.

33947 OWEN, ROBERT D. Moral physiology; or, a...treatise on the population question. 48p. *8°.* 1844. *For other editions, see* 1831.

33948 PALMER, W. Principles of the legal provision for the relief of the poor. Four lectures, partly read at Gresham College, in Hilary term, 1844. 120p. *8°.* 1844. *With a manuscript addition to the preface by the author.*

33949 PENNSYLVANIA. *General Assembly.* Documents officiels sur le Pénitencier de l'Est, ou de Cherry-Hill, à Philadelphie...extraits des rapports annuels lu au Sénat et à la Chambre des Représentants de l'État de Pennsylvanie depuis l'ouverture du Pénitencier, en 1829, jusqu'au 8 mars 1843; traduits...par M. Moreau-Christophe, Inspecteur général des prisons de France. 130p. *8°. Paris*, [1844]

33950 PUSEY, P. The poor in Scotland; compiled from the evidence taken before the Scotch Poor-Law Commission...Extracted from The Christian Remembrancer, October 1844. [A review of the official report and of three works by W. P. Alison on the poor in Scotland. With an analysis of the report drawn up by Edward Twisleton.] 70p. *8°.* 1844.

33951 RASHLEIGH, W., *ed.* Stubborn facts from the factories, by a Manchester operative. Published and dedicated to the working classes, by Wm. Rashleigh, Esq., M.P. 84p. *8°.* 1844. *The copy that belonged to Victor Considérant.*

33952 A **REPORT** of the special committee appointed by the coal-owners of Northumberland and Durham, respecting the cessation of work by the pitmen, read at a general meeting of the trade, held at Newcastle-upon-Tyne, on the 27th of April 1844, adopted and ordered to be printed. 14p. *8°. Newcastle-upon-Tyne*, 1844.

33953 RITCHIE, R. Observations on the sanatory arrangements of factories, with remarks on the present methods of warming and ventilation, and proposals for their improvement...Abridged from a paper illustrated by drawings, read before the Royal Scottish Society of Arts, March, 1844. 40p. *8°. London & Edinburgh*, 1844.

33954 SALMON, J. C. Assessing cottages to the poor rates. On the justice and fairness of assessing cottages to the poor rates; the unfairness and injustice of making excused lists; and the...impracticability of collecting the assessments from the cottage tenants. Shewing the...necessity of a legislative enactment, authorising the rating of the proprietors... 16p. *8°.* [1844]

33955 [**SEELEY,** R. B.] Remedies suggested, for some of the evils which constitute "the perils of the nation." 472p. *12°.* 1844.

33956 [——] Second edition: revised. 484p. *12°.* 1844.

33957 SENIOR, N. W. Letters on the Factory Act, as it affects the cotton manufacture, addressed in the spring of 1837, to the Right Honourable the President of the Board of Trade...Second edition. 32p. *8°.* 1844. *This edition does not contain the correspondence with Leonard Horner printed in the second of the two editions of 1837 (q.v.), but has a note written in 1844, answering criticism in the Spectator.*

33958 —— Third edition. 33p. *8°.* 1844. *With an addendum to the 1844 note.*

33959 SHAPTER, T. Remarks upon the mortality of Exeter; together with suggestions towards the improvement of the public health. Being a letter addressed to Henry Hooper, Esq....Mayor of Exeter. 32p. *8°.* 1844.

33960 Biographical **SKETCH** of the late William Allen...the benevolent founder of the Lindfield British Schools. [Chiefly extracted from the "Herald of Peace".] 13p. *8°. Lindfield*, [1844] *The copy that belonged to Henry Bradshaw.*

33961 SOCIÉTÉ FRANÇAISE DE BIEN-FAISANCE. Société Française de Bienfaisance. Fondée à Londres en février 1842. Statuts... 4p. *12°.* [*Londres*, 1844]

33962 SOCIÉTÉ POUR LE PATRONAGE DES JEUNES DÉTENUS...DU DEPARTE-MENT DE LA SEINE. Assemblée Générale tenue à l'Hôtel-de-ville, le 14 juillet 1844. [Compte décennal des travaux de la Société.] 135p. *8°. Paris, 1844. See also 1846, 1848, 1849. The annual reports for the years 1848–49, 1850, published in 1851, and for the years 1851–52, published in 1853, are also in the Goldsmiths' Library.*

For **SOCIETY FOR THE IMPROVEMENT OF THE CONDITION OF THE LABOURING CLASSES,** The labourer's friend, 1844–55, *see vol.* III, *Periodicals list*, Labourer's friend.

33963 SPOONER, L. The unconstitutionality of the laws of Congress prohibiting private mails...Printed for the American Letter Mail Company. 24p. *8°. New York, 1844. Presentation copy from the author to 'Hon. Mr. Phelps'.*

33964 STOPFORD, E. A. ⟨Not published.⟩ A report to the Lord Bishop of Meath on the state of elementary schools in the diocese, and the opinions of the clergy respecting the question of national education. 122p. *8°. Dublin, 1844. The copy presented by the Bishop of Meath to the Earl of Ripon; it afterwards belonged to Earl De Grey.*

33965 TAYLOR, WILLIAM C. Factories and the factory system, from parliamentary documents and personal examination. 118p. *8°. 1844. The copy that belonged to Victor Considérant.*

33966 TERME, J. F. Des eaux potables à distribuer pour l'usage des particuliers et le service public. Rapport présenté au Conseil Municipal de Lyon. 259p. *8°. Paris, 1844.*

33967 THOM, WILLIAM (1798?–1848). Rhymes and recollections of a hand-loom weaver. 128p. *8°. London, Edinburgh, &c., 1844. See also 1845.*

33968 THOMAS, V. Refutation of the assertions made by the writer of the article in the Quarterly Review for October, 1844, entitled Report of the Metropolitan Commissioners in Lunacy...as far as they relate to the conduct and practice of the Warneford Asylum...near Oxford, and also an appeal to Parliament on behalf of the non-chargeable poor...Being the substance of the Chairman's observations at the weekly meeting of the Committee of Management...Nov. 12...Nov. 19, and ...Nov. 26, 1844. 52p. *8°. Oxford, [1844]*

33969 THOMPSON, HENRY W. The runaway apprentice; or, his journey to Manchester, in 1795 not by steam, but by Pickford's broad-wheeled waggon. A peep into the factory system. By the author of "Rambles with the British Army...". 94p. *12°. [1844]*

33970 TODD, J. H. University of Dublin. Remarks on some statements attributed to Thomas Wyse... in his speech in Parliament on academical education in Ireland, July 19th, 1844. [Reprinted from the *Irish Ecclesiastical Journal*, October 1844.] 28p. *8°. Dublin, 1844. The copy that belonged to Earl De Grey.*

33971 TORRENS, R. A letter to Lord Ashley, on the principles which regulate wages, and on the manner and degree in which wages would be reduced, by the passing of a Ten Hours Bill. 80p. *8°. 1844. Two copies, one a presentation copy, with inscription, from the author to the editor of The Times, the other that belonged to Victor Considérant.*

33972 VARRENTRAPP, G. De l'emprisonnement individuel sous le rapport sanitaire et des attaques dirigées contre lui par MM. Charles Lucas et Léon Faucher à l'occasion du projet de loi sur la réforme des prisons présenté par le gouvernement. 75p. *8°. Paris & Francfort-sur-Mein, 1844.*

33973 VINCENT, G. G. A letter to the editor of "The Times," in the cause of the poor. 56p. *8°. 1844.*

33974 WILSON, JAMES, *miners' delegate, and others.* An address to the public by the delegates from the coal-miners of Northumberland and Durham, now in London, on the sufferings and wrongs endured by, and the present position of, that body: containing also a few brief remarks on the coal monopoly. [Signed: James Wilson, Nicholas Morgan, Wilson Ritson, and dated, August 29, 1844.] 12p. *12°. [1844]*

33975 WOŁOWSKI, L. F. M. R. Conservatoire Royal des Arts et Métiers. Cours de législation industrielle. Sixième année. Première leçon...De l'organisation du travail. [Extrait de La Revue de Législation et de Juris-prudence. Livraison de novembre 1844.] 32p. *8°. Paris, 1844. Presentation copy, with inscription, from the author to N. W. Senior.*

33976 WOOD, REV. SIR JOHN PAGE, *Bart.* An inaugural address, delivered...at the opening of the Witham Literary Institution...4th November, 1844. Published by, and at the request of the Committee. 22p. *8°. Witham, [1844]*

For the **WORKING MAN'S TEETOTAL JOURNAL,** *see vol.* III, *Periodicals list.*

SLAVERY

33977 EMERSON, R. W. The emancipation of the negroes in the British West Indies. An address delivered at Concord, Massachusetts, on 1st August, 1844. 32p. *8°. 1844.*

33978 ENGLAND. *Admiralty.* Instructions for the guidance of Her Majesty's naval officers employed in the suppression of the slave trade. 684p. *8°. 1844.*

33979 —— *Treaties, etc.* Treaties, conventions, and engagements, for the suppression of the slave trade. 631p. *8°. 1844.*

33980 FRIENDS, *Society of, New York State.* An address of Friends of the yearly meeting of New-York, to the citizens of the United States, especially to those of the southern States, upon the subject of slavery. [Signed: Richard Carpenter, clerk.] 16p. *8°. New-York, 1844.*

33981 HILL, P. G. Fifty days on board a slave-vessel in the Mozambique Channel, in April and May, 1843. 115p. *8°. 1844.*

33982 LAIRD, M. The effect of an alteration in the sugar duties on the condition of the people of England and the negro race considered...Second edition. 86p. *8°. 1844.*

33983 ROPER, M. A narrative of the adventures and escape of Moses Roper, from American slavery... Twenty-eighth thousand. 116p. *12°. 1844.*

33984 TEMPLE, H. J., *Viscount Palmerston*. Speech of Viscount Palmerston in the House of Commons, on Tuesday, July 16th, 1844, on the slave trade. 48p. *8°.* 1844.

33985 ZULUETA, P. DE. Trial of Pedro de Zulueta, jun., on a charge of slave-trading...on...the 27th...the 28th, and...the 30th of October 1843, at the Central Criminal Court, Old Bailey, London. A full report from the short-hand notes of W. B. Gurney...With an address to the merchants, manufacturers, and traders of Great Britain, by Pedro de Zulueta...and documents illustrative of the case. lxxiv, 410p. *8°.* 1844.

33986 —— [Another edition.] Trial of Pedro de Zulueta, jun....Reported by J. F. Johnson...With introductory and concluding remarks, by the committee of the British and Foreign Anti-Slavery Society. Second edition. 95p. *8°.* 1844. *The copy that belonged to Earl De Grey.*

POLITICS

33987 CONSIDÉRANT, V. P. Petit cours de politique et d'économie sociale à l'usage des ignorants et des savants. 50p. *16°. Paris*, 1844. *Considérant's own copy, abridged from his* Débacle de la politique en France.

33988 DENMAN, T., *Baron Denman*. The judgment of Lord Denman in the case of O'Connell and others against the Queen, as delivered in the House of Lords, September 4, 1844. With notes, a preface, and additional observations. Edited by David Leahy, Esq.... 68p. *8°. London & Dublin*, 1844.

33989 HENNEQUIN, V. A., *ed*. Les dogmes, le clergé et l'état. Études religieuses par MM. Aug. Pelletan, Aug. Colin, Hipp. Morvonnais & Victor Hennequin. 95p. *8°. Paris*, 1844. *The copy that belonged to Victor Considérant.*

33990 HILL, WILLIAM. A scabbard for Feargus O'Connor's sword: being a reply to that person's fourpenny pamphlet entitled "A letter from Feargus O'Connor, Esq., to the Reverend Wm. Hill," &c. [Second edition.] 12p. *8°. Hull & London*, [1844] *A printed slip headed 'Second edition. – O'Connor's rejoinder' has been pasted over the advertisements on p. 12.*

33991 JACKSON, JOHN, *of Bradford*. The demagogue done up: an exposure of the extreme inconsistencies of Mr. Feargus O'Connor, showing, from the "Northern Star" itself, that he has justly earned the title of the Political Jim Crow. 68p. *8°. Bradford & London*, 1844.

33992 LOYAL NATIONAL REPEAL ASSOCIATION. Address to the Queen, on the subject of the incarceration of the state prisoners, brought up by William Smith O'Brien, Esq., M.P. and adopted by the... Association, on...June 17th, 1844. 3p. *8°. Dublin*, [1844] *The copy that belonged to Earl De Grey.*

33993 —— Correspondence between Lord Wicklow and the...Association... 9p. *8°.* [*Dublin*, 1844] *The copy that belonged to Earl De Grey.*

33994 —— Report from the Parliamentary Committee of the...Association on the attendance of Irish members in Parliament. Read at a meeting of the Association...on ...the 2nd day of September, 1844. 6p. *8°. Dublin*, [1844] *The copy that belonged to Earl De Grey.*

33995 —— Report from the Parliamentary Committee of the...Association on the opening of Post-Office letters. Read at a meeting of the Association...on...the 26th day of August, 1844. 7p. *8°.* [*Dublin*, 1844] *The copy that belonged to Earl De Grey.*

33996 —— Report from the Parliamentary Committee on the hurrying of Bills through Parliament. Read at a meeting of the Association...on...the 19th August, 1844. 3p. *8°.* [*Dublin*, 1844] *The copy that belonged to Earl De Grey.*

33997 —— Second general report of the Parliamentary Petition Committee of the...Association. 33p. *8°. Dublin*, [1844] *The copy that belonged to Earl De Grey.*

33998 —— Second report of the Parliamentary Petition Committee of the...Association, on Lord Eliot's Registration Bill. 27p. *8°. Dublin*, [1844] *The copy that belonged to Earl De Grey.*

33999 MITCHELL, J., *of Preston*. Letter to W. B. Ferrand, Esq. M.P. and to Mr. Richard Oastler, "Factory child's king;" showing how the former gentleman...made one of the most wanton...attacks on Mr. Alderman Brooks...pointing out how the shamefully partial reduction of the duty on coffee might...have been prevented ...also showing the part that Mr. Oastler took in that infamous affair...(Respectfully recommended to the friends of complete suffrage and the abolition of the corn laws, and to the Chartists.) 32p. *8°. Manchester*, 1844

34000 O'BRIEN, T. A glance at parties. [No. 1.] 44p. *8°.* 1844. *Presentation copy from the author to Earl De Grey.*

34001 O'CONNELL, D. Wood's edition. Trial of O'Connell and others... 95p. *8°.* 1844. *Published in parts.*

34002 PERCEVAL, JOHN T. A letter to the editor of The Times; containing strictures upon the remarks of that journal upon the events which have lately occurred in connexion with our foreign policy. [With particular reference to Tangier.] 12p. *8°.* [*London*, 1844]

34003 The POLITICS of the New Testament. [Reprinted by permission, from Tait's Edinburgh Magazine.] 16p. *12°. Edinburgh*, [1844?] *The copy that belonged to William Lovett, with his signature at the head of p. 1.*

34004 ROUSSELIN CORBEAU DE SAINT-ALBIN, M. P. H., *Comte*. A messieurs les électeurs du septième collége de la Sarthe. [Session de 1844.] 11p. *8°. Paris*, 1844.

34005 THOMASON, W. O'Connorism and democracy inconsistent with each other; being a statement of events in the life of Feargus O'Connor. 17p. *8°. Newcastle*, 1844.

34006 W. Letter-opening at the Post-Office. The article on this subject from no. LXXXII. of the Westminster Review, for September, 1844, entitled, Mazzini and the ethics of politicians. To which is added Some account of the brothers Bandiera, by J. Mazzini. 31p. *8°.* 1844. *The copy that belonged to William Lovett.*

SOCIALISM

34007 A full **ACCOUNT** of the farewell festival given to Robert Owen, Esq., on his departure for America, with reports of the speeches of Messrs. Ellis, Holyoake, Fleming, A. Campbell, Southwell and Mrs. Chappellsmith; also, Mr. Owen's second legacy to the human race. 16p. *8°. London, Edinburgh, &c.,* [1844]

34008 **BRAY,** C. An essay upon the union of agriculture and manufactures, and upon the organization of industry. 114p. *12°. 1844. First issued as the introduction to Mary Hennell's* An outline of the various social systems, *no.* 34020.

34009 **CABET,** E. Les masques arrachés... 144p. *8°. Paris,* 1844.

34010 **COMBE,** ABRAM. The life and dying testimony of Abram Combe in favour of Robt. Owen's new views of man and society. [Edited by Alexander Campbell.] 24p. *12°. London, Edinburgh, &c.,* 1844.

34011 **CONSIDÉRANT,** V. P. Destinée sociale... Tome troisième [1er livraison]. p.353–595. *8°. Paris,* 1844. *The first edition of vol. 3, the text of which was printed with vol. 2 in 1838 but not then published. In this copy 3 leaves following p. 586 were cancelled and replaced by 5 leaves (p. 587–595) apparently printed at the same time as the prelims for this edition. For editions of vols. 1–2, see* 1834.

34012 —— Le sept avril. Banquets commémoratifs de la naissance de Charles Fourier. Année 1843 et 1844. 36p. *12°. Paris,* 1844. *Considérant's own copy.*

34013 **[DAMETH,** C. M. H.] Notions élémentaires de la science sociale de Fourier, par l'auteur de la Défense du Fouriérisme. 300p. *12°. Paris,* 1844. *Presentation copy, with inscription, from the author (identifying himself) to Gustave La Bonninière de Beaumont.*

34014 **ETZLER,** J. A. Emigration to the tropical world, for the melioration of all classes of people of all nations. 24p. *8°. Ham Common, Surrey: The Concordium, & London,* 1844.

34015 —— J. A. Etzler's mechanical system, in its greatest simplicity, for agricultural works, formation of ditches, canals, dams and any excavation...and other works. Patented & practically proved... 15p. *8°.* 1844.

34016 —— Two visions of J. A. Etzler...A revelation of futurity. 15p. *8°. Ham Common, Surrey: The Concordium, & London,* 1844.

34017 Young **GERMANY.** An account of the rise, progress, and present position of German communism; with a memoir of Wilhelm Weitling, its founder: – and a report of the proceedings at the banquet given...in... 1844, to commemorate his escape from the persecution of the Prussian Government, and arrival in England. 24p. *12°.* [1844]

34018 **GIRARD,** S. F. Socialisme. Trois leçons du Professeur E. Cherbuliez sur Fourier, son école et son système, reproduites et réfutées par un ministre du Saint Evangile. 490p. *12°. Paris,* 1844. *Presentation copy, with inscription, from the author to 'Monsieur Gustave Petit-pierre'.*

34019 **GODWIN,** P. A popular view of the doctrines of Charles Fourier. Second edition. 120p. *8°. New York,* 1844.

34020 **HENNELL,** M. An outline of the various social systems & communities which have been founded on the principle of co-operation. With an introductory essay, by the author of "The philosophy of necessity" [C. Bray]. cxiv, 252p. *12°.* 1844. *The copy that belonged to J. M. Ludlow, with his signature on the title-page. First published as an appendix to* The philosophy of necessity, *by C. Bray, in 1841 (q.v.).*

34021 **[HOLYOAKE,** G. J.] A visit to Harmony Hall! (Reprinted from the "Movement"). With emendations, and a new and curious vindicatory chapter...by G.J.H. 27p. *12°.* 1844. *The copy that belonged to William Lovett.*

34022 **JOURNET,** J. La bonne nouvelle ou idée succincte de l'association... 2e édition. 70p. *12°. Paris,* 1844.

34023 ***OWEN,** ROBERT. Manifesto of Robert Owen ...Public paper no. 1, addressed to all governments and people who desire to become civilized, to aid in the adoption of measures now to lay a solid foundation for the peace of the world...and happiness of all individuals... [Signed: Robert Owen, and dated, Washington, December, 1844.] *s.sh.fol. n.p.* [1844] *A galley proof. The FWA copy that belonged to William Pare.*

34024 *—— Manifesto of Robert Owen. Public paper no. 2, addressed to the leading men of all parties in the United States who possess extensive experience in the general business of society. [Signed: Robert Owen, and dated, Washington, December, 1844.] *s.sh.fol. n.p.* [1844] *A galley proof. The FWA copy that belonged to William Pare.*

34025 **PAGET,** A. F. and **CARTIER,** E. Examen et défense du système de Fourier...Édité par la Société pour la propagation et la réalisation de la Théorie de Fourier. 204p. *8°. Paris,* 1844. *The copy that belonged to Victor Considérant.*

34026 **PECQUEUR,** C. N. S. De la république de Dieu. Union réligieuse pour la pratique immédiate de l'égalité et de la fraternité universelles. Rédigé à la démande de ses frères par C. Pecqueur. 320p. *16°. Paris & Leipsig,* 1844.

34027 ***PUBLICOLA,** *pseud.* Socialism exposed, with its baneful tendency, and pernicious effects: containing the origin of its rise and progress, and a brief history of Robert Owen, its founder. [A pro-socialist satire.] 8p. *8°. London, Leeds, &c.,* [1844] *An anonymous edition, entitled* A full and complete exposure of...the Owenites, *was published in 1840 (q.v.).*

34028 ***RATIONAL TRACT SOCIETY.** A new state of society. A diologue [*sic*] between Theophilus and Amida. 4p. *8°.* [*London,* 1844?] *The FWA copy that belonged to William Pare.*

For the **REGENERATOR,** *see vol.* III, *Periodicals list.*

34029 **REYBAUD,** M. R. L. Études sur les réformateurs ou socialistes modernes...Quatrième édition, précédée du rapport de M. Jay...et de celui de M. Villemain... 2 vols. *8°. Paris,* 1844, 1843. *Vol. 1 only is of the fourth edition. For other editions, see* 1841.

34030 **RUGE,** A. and **MARX,** KARL (1818–1883),

eds. Deutsch-Französische Jahrbücher...1ste und 2te Lieferung. 237p. *8°. Paris,* 1844.

34031 SOCIÉTÉ CIVILE DE CITEAUX. Société Civile de Citeaux. Statut constitutif. [With 'Conditions', 'Prospectus', 'Rapport de M. Lefour sur le domaine de Citeaux', 'Budgets' and 'Ménage sociétaire'.] 16, 7, 7, 20, 25, 3p. *8°. Paris,* [1844]

34032 TRISTAN, F. Union ouvrière...Deuxième édition, contenant un chant: La Marseillaise de l'atelier, mise en musique par A. Thys. 136p. *12°. Paris,* 1844.

34033 WRIGHT, F. Biography, notes, and political letters of Frances Wright d'Arusmont. 48p. *16°. Dundee,* 1844. *An autobiography in outline.*

MISCELLANEOUS

34034 BANKS, T. C. Baronia Anglica concentrata; or a concentrated account of all the baronies commonly called baronies in fee...Whereto is added the proofs of parliamentary sitting, from the reign of Edw. I. to that of Queen Anne, also a glossary of dormant English, Scotch, and Irish peerage titles with reference to presumed existing heirs. 2 vols. *4°. Ripon & London,* 1844.

34035 BLOMFIELD, C. J., *Bishop of London.* Religious Trusts and Dissenters' Chapels Bill: a speech delivered by the Lord Bishop of London, in the House of Lords, on the 3rd day of May, 1844, against a motion for going into committee on the Bill. 12p. *8°.* [1844]

34036 CHILD, L. M. The remembered home. 8p. *8°.* 1844.

34037 COMTE, I. A. M. F. X. Discours sur l'esprit positif. 108p. *8°. Paris,* 1844.

34038 FRANCIS FERDINAND PHILIP LOUIS MARY, *Prince de Joinville.* Note sur l'état des forces navales de la France. [Nouvelle édition.] 36p. *12°. Paris,* [1844]

34039 HUDSON, T. Just published, price 2s. "The right use of gold," a new song, written by the late Thomas Hudson, composed by Edward James Loder. [2]p. *s.sh.8°.* [1844] [*Br.* 607] *The verses written for the Goldsmiths' Benevolent Institution dinner. The music is not included.*

34040 LOYAL NATIONAL REPEAL ASSOCIATION. Report of the Committee of the...Association at a meeting of the Association...upon the "Arms (Ireland) returns." Read...on...May 27th, 1844. 8p. *8°.* [*Dublin,* 1844] *The copy that belonged to Earl De Grey.*

34041 —— Report of the Committee of the...Association, on petit juries, County Tipperary. 5p. *8°. Dublin,* [1844] *The copy that belonged to Earl De Grey.*

34042 METCALFE, J. J. The Practical Christian Union. Addenda to the proposals made in the pamphlet entitled Temporal prosperity ensured to mankind by the practice of Christianity. 37p. *8°.* 1844. *The copy presented to H. D. Griffiths for the library of the West-London Anti-Enclosure Association, with a note to this effect by Griffiths on the verso of the title-page.*

34043 The **MILLION COMPENSATION** of the Six Clerks and co. in Chancery. Statute 5 & 6 Victoria, chapter 103. Second edition. 84p. *8°.* 1844.

34044 MONTEM ode for 1844. [Signed: Montem Poet.] *s.sh.fol. Windsor,* [1844] [*Br.* 606]

34045 Some **OBSERVATIONS** on the present state of the Navy. 16p. *8°.* 1844.

34046 PALGRAVE, Sir F. Truths and fictions of the middle ages. The merchant and the friar...Second edition, revised and corrected. 256p. *8°.* 1844. *The copy that belonged to Cliffe Leslie, with his pencil notes and corrections.*

34047 SPENCER, T. What David did: a reply to the Queen's Letter. Containing reasons for declining to urge upon the parishioners of Hinton-Charterhouse a collection in behalf of the Society for the Building of Churches, and pointing out to Her Majesty's ministers a more excellent way...Twenty-sixth thousand. No. 19. 16p. *8°. London & Bath,* 1844.

34048 A **VOICE** to the aristocracy, of the order of the protectionists, usually called monopolists. By a Christian. 19p. *12°. London & Manchester,* 1844.

34049 WALTER, E. How is man's character formed? The question answered in a letter to the Rev. Dr. Redford of Worcester...Third edition. 12p. *12°.* 1844.

34050 WHATELY, R., *Archbishop of Dublin.* Thoughts on church government; being the substance of a charge, delivered at the visitation of the Diocese and of the Province of Dublin, 1844. 50p. *8°. London & Dublin,* 1844.

1845

GENERAL

34051 The new statistical **ACCOUNT** of Scotland. By the ministers of the respective parishes, under the superintendence of a Committee of the Society for the Benefit of the Sons and Daughters of the Clergy. 15 vols. *8°. Edinburgh & London,* 1845. *For* The statistical account of Scotland, *edited by Sir John Sinclair, see* 1791.

34052 [AJASSON DE GRANDSAGNE, J. B. F. E., *Vicomte,* and **PARISOT,** V.] Notions générales sur les sciences; ou, philosophie des sciences. Par Aj. de Gr. et P. 192p. *12°. Paris,* 1845.

34053 An **ANGLOCHINESE CALENDAR** for the year 1845, corresponding to the year of the Chinese cycle aera 4482. [With 'List of foreign residents in Canton, Macao, Hongkong, Amoy, Fuchau, Ningpo, and Shanghai' and 'List of commercial houses, agents, &c.'.] 35p. *8°. Hongkong,* 1845.

34054 An **APPEAL** to the editors of The Times newspaper, in behalf of the working classes. Being a survey of the conduct of that journal during the last autumn on the most important subjects of the day. By two lay members of the Church. 79p. 8°. 1845.

34055 ARND, K. Die naturgemässe Volkswirthschaft, gegenüber dem Monopoliengeiste und dem Communismus, mit einem Rückblicke auf die einschlagende Literatur. 493p. 8°. Hanau, 1845.

34056 ARNOLD, THOMAS (1795–1842). The miscellaneous works of Thomas Arnold, D.D. late Headmaster of Rugby School... Collected and republished. 519p. 8°. 1845. Edited by Arthur Stanley, Dean of Westminster.

34057 BANFIELD, T. C. Four lectures on the organization of industry; being part of a course delivered in the University of Cambridge in Easter term 1844. 96p. 8°. London [& Cambridge], 1845. See also 1848 (The organization of industry explained...).

34058 BARRY, M. J. First prize repeal essay [of the Loyal National Repeal Association]. Ireland, as she was, as she is, and as she shall be. 112p. 8°. Dublin, 1845.

34059 BIANCHINI, L. Della scienza del ben vivere sociale e della economia degli stati... 508p. 8°. Palermo, 1845.

34060 BLANQUI, J. A. Histoire de l'économie politique en Europe, depuis les anciens jusqu'à nos jours, suivie d'une bibliographie raisonnée des principaux ouvrages d'économie politique... Troisième édition. 2 vols. 8°. Paris, 1845. For other editions, see 1837.

34061 The **BRITISH ALMANAC** of the Society for the Diffusion of Useful Knowledge, for... 1845... [With 'The companion to the Almanac; or, year-book of general information'.] 96, 260p. 12°. [1845] For other editions, see 1828.

34062 BROUGHAM, H. P., Baron Brougham and Vaux. Lives of men of letters and science, who flourished in the time of George III... 2 vols. 8°. 1845–46.

34063 BUCKINGHAM, J. S. Plan of an improved income tax and real free trade, with an equitable mode of redeeming the National Debt, and some observations on the education and employment of the people – on systematic colonization – and on the welfare of the labouring classes. 71p. 8°. 1845.

34064 —— ⟨Second edition, corrected and enlarged by a chapter on colonization.⟩ 96p. 8°. 1845.

34065 CAVOUR, C. B. DI, Conte. Considerations on the present state and future prospects of Ireland... Translated from the French, by a friend to Ireland. 138p. 8°. 1845.

34066 COMBE, G. Notes on the new reformation in Germany, and on national education, and the common schools of Massachusetts. 37p. 8°. Edinburgh & London, 1845.

34067 DUNOYER, C. B. De la liberté du travail, ou simple exposé des conditions dans lesquelles les forces humaines s'exercent avec le plus de puissance... 3 vols. 8°. Paris, 1845.

34068 EAST INDIA COMPANY. A catalogue of the library of the Hon. East-India Company. 324p. 8°. 1845. A supplement to the catalogue, published in 1851, is also in the Goldsmiths' Library.

34069 ENGLAND and America contrasted, or, the evils of taxation; in which the superiority of America, as regards climate, produce, commercial facilities, &c. &c., is clearly demonstrated. By a cotton manufacturer. 38p. 12°. 1845.

34070 FAUCHER, L. Études sur l'Angleterre. 2 vols. 8°. Paris, 1845.

34071 FORD, RICHARD. A hand-book for travellers in Spain, and readers at home. Describing the country and cities, the natives, and their manners; the antiquities, religion, legends, fine arts, literature, sports, and gastronomy: with notices on Spanish history. 2 vols. 12°. 1845. The upper cover is lettered: Murray's Hand Book. Spain.

34072 FRAYSSE, C. B. Quelques observations à propos de l'organisation du travail. 32p. 8°. Paris, 1845. The copy that belonged to Gustave La Bonninière de Beaumont.

34073 HEEREN, A. H. L. Ancient Greece. From the German of Arnold H. L. Heeren. By G. Bancroft. Fourth edition. 344p. 8°. 1845. For other editions, see 1824.

34074 KANE, SIR R. J. The industrial resources of Ireland... Second edition. 438p. 8°. Dublin, London, &c., 1845. For another edition, see 1844.

34075 KANKRIN, E. F., Graf. Die Oekonomie der menschlichen Gesellschaften und das Finanzwesen von einem ehemaligen Finanzminister. 346p. 8°. Stuttgart, 1845.

34076 KNIGHT, C. Capital and labour, including the results of machinery. 250p. 12°. 1845. A new version of The working man's companion, the rights of industry no. 1 and The working man's companion. The results of machinery, originally published in 1831 (q.v.).

34077 ——, ed. Mind among the spindles: a selection from the Lowell Offering, a miscellany wholly composed by the factory girls of an American city. With an introduction by the English editor [and a letter to him from Harriet Martineau]. 240p. 12°. 1845.

34078 LHOTSKY, S. Regeneration of society, the only corrective for the distress of the country; or an appeal to the English nation in the cause of humanity reform, religious and political: a restitution for the debt she owes to Germany and France, for the work of "first" reformation and the enactments of the Revolution. 36p. 8°. 1845.

34079 LITTRÉ, M. P. É. De la philosophie positive. 103p. 8°. Paris, 1845. Articles on Comte's Cours de philosophie positive, reprinted from Le National of November–December 1844.

34080 [**LONG,** G., ed.] Political dictionary; forming a work of universal reference, both constitutional and legal; and embracing the terms of civil administration, of political economy and social relations and... of finance and commerce. 2 vols. 8°. 1845–46.

34081 LOYAL NATIONAL REPEAL ASSOCIATION. Report of the Committee of the... Association, on the industrial resources of Ireland; founded on Dr. Kane's treatise on that subject. 63p. 8°. Dublin, [1845] The copy that belonged to Earl De Grey.

34082 McCULLOCH, JOHN R. The literature of political economy: a classified catalogue of select publications... with historical, critical, and biographical notices. 407p. 8°. 1845.

34083 MEERTS, C. Dictionnaire géographique et

statistique du royaume de Belgique... xvii, 830p. *8°.* *Bruxelles,* 1845.

34084 MORIN, E. F. T. Essai sur l'organisation du travail et l'avenir des classes laborieuses. 590p. *8°. Paris & Valence,* 1845. *Presentation copy, with inscription, from the author to 'Monsieur de Bouilhanne Lacoste'.*

34085 NOEL, Hon. B. W. The Catholic claims. A letter to the Lord Bishop of Cashel. 54p. *8°.* 1845.

34086 PARTOUNAU DU PUYNODE, M. G. Des lois du travail et des classes ouvrières. 270p. *8°. Paris,* 1845.

34087 [PELHAM, Hon. D.] Remarks as to measures calculated to promote the welfare and improve the condition of the labouring classes; and to provide for the maintenance of the increasing population, more particularly in connexion with the future prospects and the interests of landed proprietors and agriculturists. By a member of the aristocracy. 94p. *8°.* 1845.

34088 PERCEVAL, Hon. A. P. The amelioration of Ireland contemplated. III. The ecclesiastical and civil grievances of Ireland, with their remedies. 114p. *8°.* 1845. *For the first and second papers in the series, see* 1844.

34089 PITT, William, *Earl of Chatham.* The speeches of the Earl of Chatham. (*The Modern Orator.*) 90p. *8°.* 1845.

34090 POPE, C., *ed.* The yearly journal of trade, 1845 ...Twenty-third edition. [With 'Pope's yearly journal of trade advertiser. 1845'.] 616p. *8°.* [1845] *See also* 1838, 1840, 1842, 1843, 1844, 1846.

34091 PORTER, J. G. V. Some calm observations upon Irish affairs...Letter B. 47p. *8°. Dublin & London,* 1845.

34092 PUTNAM, G. P. American facts. Notes and statistics relative to the government, resources, engagements, manufactures, commerce...manners and customs of the United States of America... 292p. *12°.* 1845.

For **REVUE DE LÉGISLATION,** *see* vol. III, *Periodicals list.*

34093 SIEBOLD, P. F. von. Catalogus librorum et manuscriptorum japonicorum a Ph. Fr. de Siebold collectorum, annexa enumeratione illorum, qui in Museo Regio Hagano servantur...Libros descripsit J. Hoffmann ... 35p. *fol. Lugduni-Batavorum,* 1845.

34094 TAPIÈS, F. de. La France et l'Angleterre ou statistique morale et physique de la France comparée à celle de l'Angleterre sur tous les points analogues. 501p. *8°. Versailles & Paris,* 1845.

34095 URQUHART, D. Wealth and want: or taxation, as influencing private riches and public liberty. Being the substance of lectures on pauperism. Delivered at Portsmouth, Southampton, etc. in February and March, 1845. 111p. *8°.* 1845.

34096 WHITE, William (*fl.* 1826–1870). History, gazetteer, and directory of Norfolk, and the city...of Norwich; comprising...a general survey of the county of Norfolk, and the diocese of Norwich; with separate historical, statistical, & topographical descriptions of all the...boroughs, towns, ports, parishes... 816p. *12°. Sheffield,* 1845.

AGRICULTURE

34097 ALMACK, B. Report on the agriculture of Norfolk. [From the Journal of the Royal Agricultural Society of England, 1845, vol. V, part II.] 51p. *8°.* 1845.

34098 ANTISELL, T. A manual of agricultural chemistry, with its application to the soils of Ireland. 83p. *8°. Dublin,* 1845.

34099 BASS, M. T. The advantages of employing a greater amount of manual labour in agriculture: read at the Burton-on-Trent Farmers' Club, March 20th, 1845 ... 34p. *8°. Burton-on-Trent,* [1845]

34100 BYNG, George, *Viscount Torrington.* On farm buildings; with a few observations on the state of agriculture in the county of Kent. 111p. *8°.* 1845.

34101 COBBETT, W. The English gardener; or, a treatise on the...laying out, of kitchen gardens... 405p. *12°.* 1845. *For other editions, see* 1829.

34102 DAVENPORT, E. D. How to improve the condition of the labouring classes. [By agricultural improvement, increased investment of capital in land, longer leases to tenants.] 28p. *8°.* 1845.

34103 —— Second edition. 28p. *8°.* 1845. *Presentation copy from the author to John Lindley (1799–1865).*

34104 —— Third edition. 37p. *8°.* 1845.

34105 DAVIS, H. The farmers' resources for meeting the reduced prices of their produce...Second edition. 43p. *8°.* 1845.

34106 DUCROQUET, . Coup-d'œil sur les améliorations agronomiques en France, et les questions sociales et financières qui s'y rattachent. 60p. *8°. Arras,* 1845. *The copy that belonged to Gustave La Bonnière de Beaumont.*

34107 The **FLOWER GARDENER'S** manual; containing practical instructions for the cultivation and management of shrubs and flowers, adapted to English gardens. A new edition. 64p. *8°.* [*c.* 1845]

34108 FRANCE. *Ministère de l'Agriculture et du Commerce.* Agriculture française, par MM. les Inspecteurs de l'Agriculture...Département du Tarn. 484p. *8°. Paris,* 1845.

34109 HART, H. An essay on corn rents, by a practical farmer. Being a paper, read at a meeting of the Lewes Farmers' Club, on the 8th of July, 1845. 27p. *8°. Lewes & London,* 1845.

34110 HENSLOW, J. S. An address to landlords, on the advantages to be expected from the general establishment of a spade tenantry from among the labouring classes. 36p. *8°. Hadleigh...& London,* 1845.

34111 LIEBIG, J. von, *Freiherr.* On artificial manures. 36p. *8°.* 1845.

34112 LOYAL NATIONAL REPEAL ASSOCIATION. Report of the Committee of the...Association on the Valuation (Ireland) Bill. 5p. *8°. Dublin,* [1845]

34113 —— Report of the Parliamentary Committee of the...Association on a Bill to promote the letting of field gardens to the labouring poor. Read...on...30th June, 1845. 7p. *8°. Dublin,* [1845]

34114 —— Report of the Parliamentary Committee of the...Association on the Tenants' Compensation Bill, (sessional paper no. 196.) presented to the House of Peers by the Lord Stanley. Read...on...23rd May [June], 1845. 8p. *8°. Dublin,* [1845]

34115 —— Second report of the Parliamentary Committee of the...Association on the land question. Read... on...21st April, 1845. 2p. *8°.* [*Dublin,* 1845]

34116 —— Third report...Read...on...12th May, 1845. 9p. *8°. Dublin,* [1845]

34117 M'ARTHUR, JOHN, *land surveyor.* The roots of plants: their natural tendencies and requirements; or, an investigation of the growth of agricultural plants, as displayed by their roots in different soils and under different modes of cultivation. 38p. *12°. London, Belfast, &c.,* 1845.

34118 [**MACONOCHIE,** ALLAN, *Lord Meadowbank.*] Directions for preparing manure from peat. 31p. *8° Edinburgh,* 1845. *For another edition, see* 1815.

34119 MARTINEAU, H. Forest and game-law tales... 3 vols. *8°.* 1845–46.

34120 MECHI, J. J. A series of letters on agricultural improvement: with an appendix. 122p. *4°.* 1845.

34121 MITCHELL, JOHN, *F.C.S.* Manual of agricultural analysis. 140p. *8°.* 1845.

34122 MURRAY, ADAM. The report on the plantations of the Drapers' Company [in the County of Derry]. 31p. *8°.* 1845.

34123 NATIONAL LAND-DRAINING COMPANY FOR ENGLAND, IRELAND, AND SCOTLAND. Thoughts upon supplying food and employment for the working population of the United Kingdom. Published in connection with the prospectus of the above company. [Extracted from Mr. Blacker's evidence contained in Appendix No. 9 of the first volume of the Irish Land Commission Evidence]. 15p. *8°.* 1845.

34124 NEWMAN, C. Practical hints on land draining, illustrating its importance, with some suggestions on agriculture addressed to the young farmers. 64p. *8°.* 1845.

34125 O'CONNOR, F. A practical work on the management of small farms...Second edition. 192p. *12°. Manchester,* 1845.

34126 The **POTATO DISEASE:** the prospects of scarcity at present, of famine in future years, through this calamity; and the means which reason indicates, and God has provided, for averting it. In a letter to Sir Robert Peel, Bart. &c. &c. By a naturalist. 15p. *8°.* 1845.

34127 RAINY, A. On the transfer of property by public auction and private contract: the reciprocity or allowance system; etc....Being the substance of a statement made at a meeting held on the 8th of July, 1845. 54p. *8°.* 1845.

34128 SAINT PANCRAS ASSOCIATION FOR THE PURPOSE OF PURCHASING REAL AND LEASEHOLD PROPERTY, ETC. The rules of the...Association... 29p. *8°.* 1845.

For the **SCIENTIFIC AND PRACTICAL AGRICULTURIST,** *see vol.* III, *Periodicals list.*

34129 THYNNE, F. An account of the first distribution of the prizes given by the Right Honorable the Earl of Dartmouth for the encouragement of spade husbandry and stall feeding on his Yorkshire estates. November 1844. 43p. *8°.* 1845.

For the **UNITED GARDENERS' & LAND-STEWARDS' JOURNAL,** 1845–47, *continued as* the Gardeners' & farmers' journal, 1847–49, *see vol.* III, *Periodicals list,* Gardeners' & farmers' journal.

34130 [*Begin.*] The **WRITER** of these lines hopes that those for whose perusal they are intended...[Instructions for cultivating green crops in Ireland.] 16p. *8°. n.p.* [*c.* 1845]

CORN LAWS

34131 ASPINALL, J. Speech of the Rev. James Aspinall, Rector of Althorpe, Lincolnshire, delivered at the great free trade meeting, at Hull on...December 15, 1845. 12p. *12°. Liverpool,* [1845]

34132 ASSER, J. A letter to the Right Honorable the Earl of Winchelsea practically proving the importance of a gradual drawback being established upon foreign wheat at Her Majesty's Customs, for protecting British growers, and importers of wheat... 15p. *8°.* 1845.

34133 BASTIAT, C. F. Cobden et la Ligue, ou, l'agitation anglaise pour la liberté du commerce. xcvi, 426p. *8°. Paris,* 1845.

34134 BROWNE, EDMUND H. Stack-guaging, corn returns and annual duties, thus placing the graduated duty on growth, and not on price. 15p. *8°.* 1845.

34135 CAVOUR, C. B. DI, *Conte.* De la question relative à la législation anglaise sur le commerce des céréales. 84p. *8°.* [*Genève,*] 1845. *The copy that belonged to Sir John Boileau* (*1794–1869*).

34136 A **LAWYER'S** letter to the Anti-Corn Law League. 19p. *12°.* [*c.* 1845]

34137 MAYDWELL, I. Now or never. Tracts on the influence of the League, and the operations of the Tariff and Canada Bill. Published at different times. 15, 60, 24, 8p. *8°.* [1845?] *A collection of the author's separately published tracts, reissued with a general title-page.*

34138 MORTON, JOHN (1781–1864) and **TRIMMER,** JOSHUA. An attempt to estimate the effects of protecting duties on the profits of agriculture...Fourth edition. 86p. *8°.* 1845. *See also* 1846.

34139 NATIONAL ANTI-CORN-LAW LEAGUE. National Anti-Corn-Law League bazaar gazette. [Issued during the bazaar held in May 1845.] Nos. 1–17. *8°. Printed in Covent-Garden Theatre,* [1845] *See also* 1842.

34140 What should be the **POLICY** of the Government & the people in the present corn crisis; embodying conclusions deduced from a careful investigation of the extent of our deficiency & the general results of the present harvest. By a true friend of the labouring classes. 18p. *8°*. 1845.

34141 REUBEN, *pseud.* A brief history of the rise and progress of the Anti-Corn-Law League, with personal sketches of its leading members. 51p. *8°*. [1845]

34142 SMITH, Nicholas. The League, the Tory press and the assassins. 16p. *8°*. [*c.* 1845]

POPULATION

34143 *BIENAYMÉ, I. J. Société Philomatique de Paris. De la loi de multiplication et de la durée des familles, probabilités, par M. J. Bienaymé, Inspecteur général des finances. (Séance du 29 mars 1845.) [Extrait du no. 589 de l'Institut, journal universel des sciences...en France et à l'étranger; 1re section...xiiie année, 9 avril 1845.] 4p. *8°*. *Paris,* [1845] *Presentation copy from the author to Augustus De Morgan.*

34144 MALTHUS, T. R. Essai sur le principe de population...traduit de l'anglais par MM. P. et G. Prévost...Précédé d'une introduction par M. Rossi...et d'une notice sur la vie et les ouvrages de l'auteur, par Charles Comte...Avec les notes des traducteurs et de nouvelles notes par M. Joseph Garnier. lx, 687p. *8°*. *Paris,* 1845. *For other editions, see* 1798.

34145 NEISON, F. G. P. Contributions to vital statistics: being a developement of the rate of mortality and the laws of sickness; from...data procured from friendly societies...With an inquiry into the influence of locality on health...Read before the Statistical Society, March 17th, 1845. 148p. *4°*. 1845.

34146 TWISS, Sir T. On certain tests of a thriving population. Four lectures delivered before the University of Oxford in Lent Term, 1845. 107p. *8°*. 1845.

TRADES & MANUFACTURES

34147 FELKIN, W. An account of the machine-wrought hosiery trade: its extent, and the condition of the framework-knitters; being a paper read in the Statistical Section at the second York meeting of the British Association, held September 18th, 1844. Together with evidence given under the Hosiery Commission Inquiry...Second edition. 50p. *8°*. *London & Nottingham,* 1845.

For **FINISHERS' FRIENDLY ASSOCIATION,** The finishers' friendly circular, 1845–50, *see* vol. III, *Periodicals list,* Finishers' friendly circular.

34148 FORRESTER, Joseph J. Observations on the attempts lately made to reform the abuses practised in Portugal, in the making and treatment of port wine... Part first. 80p. *8°*. *Edinburgh,* 1845. *See note to no.* 33856.

34149 —— Mr. Forrester's vindication from the aspersions of the Commercial Association of Oporto; and his answer to the judge, and late member of the Côrtes, Bernardo de Lemos Teixeira de Aguillar. Being the 2.d part of "Observations on the attempts lately made to reform the abuses practised in Portugal, in the making and treatment of port-wine." Published in his own defence. 49p. *8°*. *Edinburgh,* 1845. *See note to no.* 33856.

34150 JOBARD, J. B. A. M. Le Monautopole, ou code complémentaire d'économie sociale, réglant les droits et les devoirs de l'inventeur, présenté à la Société des Inventeurs Français. 54p. *8°*. *Bruxelles,* 1845.

34151 JULLIEN, A. Nouveau manuel complet de sommelier, ou instruction pratique sur la manière de soigner les vins...Ouvrage revu, corrigé et augmenté par C. E. Jullien...Sixième édition. (*Manuels-Roret.*) 245p. *12°*. *Paris,* 1845.

34152 LOYAL NATIONAL REPEAL ASSO-CIATION. Report of the Trade and Commerce Committee of the...Association on the hosiery trade. Read... on...May 5th, 1845. 4p. *8°*. *Dublin,* [1845]

34153 —— To the Trade and Commerce Committee of the...Association. Report of Thomas Matthew Ray... being the result of his inquiries into the state of trade and manufactures in such towns as he visited on the Repeal Mission in 1842–3. Read...on...August 5[–August 25th], 1845. 7, 4, 11p. *8°*. *Dublin,* [1845]

34154 MARTIN, William (1772–1851). A challenge to all great speakers without genius. [With ' The explosion', a verse on the pit explosion at Jarrow.] 2l. *8°*. *Newcastle,* [1845 ?]

34155 —— The explosion of all infidels, and college professors of lies and nonsense. [In verse, with a verse on the mine disaster at Jarrow, caused, according to the author, by the Davy safety lamp.] 2 l. *8°*. *Newcastle,* [1845?]

34156 SCHOOL OF ARTS, *Edinburgh.* Nineteenth report of the Directors of the School of Arts...for the instruction of mechanics in...physical science...October 1845. 19p. *8°*. *Edinburgh,* 1845. *See also* 1822, 1827.

34157 —— School of Arts. – Winter session, 1845–6. [Syllabus of courses.] 4p. *8°*. *n.p.* [1845]

34158 Corrected to 1845. The thirty-fifth edition of **SKYRING'S** builders' prices and weekly journal... Abstract of the new Building Act [Metropolitan Buildings Act, 7 & 8 Vict., cap. 84. Compiled by W. H. Skyring.]... 185p. *8°*. 1845. *See also* 1812, 1818, 1819, 1827, 1831, 1838, 1846.

34159 WARD, John, *operative chemist.* Ward's condensed catalogue of chemical, philosophical, electrical and electrotype apparatus; (manufactured by first rate workmen on the premises,). Sixth edition. 16p. *8°*. 1845.

COMMERCE

34160 CLEMENTS, G. Clements' customs guide [for 1845 & 1846], containing copious extracts of the laws, with tables of the duties payable upon goods imported and exported...to which is added a list of the warehousing ports...together with an appendix, containing an alphabetical arrangement of the different articles of merchandize...also the London waterside practice... [Tenth annual edition.] 364p. *12°. [London,* 1845] *Interleaved, with manuscript notes by James Lloyd, its first owner. See also* 1840.

34161 DROUHIN et Cie, Pouilly-en-Auxois (Côted'Or). Transports de vins par eau. Tarif des prix. [Dated: 10 février 1845.] *s.sh.4°. Dijon,* [1845]

34162 KLOEDEN, K. F. VON. Beiträge zur Geschichte des Oderhandels...Programm zur Prüfung der Zöglinge der Gewerbeschule am 17. März 1845[–29. März 1852]. 120, 111, 91, 88, 83, 80, 78, 80p. *8°. Berlin,* [1845]–52.

34163 LOYAL NATIONAL REPEAL ASSOCIATION. First general report of the Trade and Commerce Committee of the...Association. Read... March 31st, 1845. 7p. *8°. [Dublin,* 1845]

34164 —— Second report...Read...on...21st April, 1845. 3p. *8°. Dublin,* [1845]

34165 —— Observations of the Parliamentary Committee of the...Association, on the report of the Council of the Chamber of Commerce, Dublin, for 1844. Adopted at a meeting...March 3rd, 1845. 4p. *8°. Dublin,* [1845]

34166 MALET, X. Grand diminution sur les prix du fret. [Circular letter with table, dated: 5 janvier 1845.] *s.sh.8°. n.p.* [1845]

34167 A MEMORIAL to the Legislature of the State of New York, upon the effects of the passage of the trade of the western states, through the Welland and Oswego Canals, upon the income of the State and the interests of its citizens. 24p. *8°. Rochester,* 1845. *The Rastrick copy.*

34168 OFFLEY, WEBBER AND FORRESTER. Representation made by Offley, Webber, & Forrester, of Oporto, to their correspondents, respecting the recent discussions on the subject of port-wine. 8p. *8°. Oporto,* 1845. *See note to no.* 33856.

For **PRICES OF COALS AT THE LONDON MARKET,** *Newcastle,* 1845–46, *see vol.* III, *Periodicals list.*

34169 R., P. Commercial policy of England and Germany. (From the 'Westminster Review' for March. No. 84.) 32p. *8°.* 1845.

34170 ROMANET, A. DE, *Vicomte.* De la protection en matière d'industrie et des réformes de Sir Robert Peel. Mémoire lu à l'Académie des Sciences morales et politiques, le 15 mars 1845. 33p. *8°. Paris,* 1845.

34171 WINE TRADE of Portugal. Proceedings at the meeting of the nobility, wine proprietors and publick authorities of the wine-district of the Alto-Douro, held at the quinta of Messrs. Offley, Webber, and Forrester at Pezo-da-Regôa, 8th October, 1844; at the invitation of Joseph James Forrester...Second edition. 31p. *8°.* 1845. *See note to no.* 33856.

34172 [WYLIE, A. H.] American corn and British manufactures. 36p. *8°.* 1845.

COLONIES

34173 Lord **AUCKLAND** and Lord Ellenborough [as Governors-general of India]. By a Bengal civilian. 68p. *8°.* 1845.

34174 BAGSHAW, J. Calcutta & George's Point railway. Remarks on the plan of a railway from Calcutta to Diamond Harbour, with spacious docks at the latter place, as proposed to be carried out by "The Calcutta and Diamond Harbour Railway and Dock Company." By the chairman of the committee of management. [With 'Appendix. Extract from a report drawn up by Major J. T. Boileau...'.] 40p. *8°.* 1845.

34175 *BALFOUR, J. O. A sketch of New South Wales. 139p. *8°.* 1845.

34176 BRODIE, WALTER. Remarks on the past and present state of New Zealand, its government, capabilities, and prospects; with a statement of the question of the land-claims, and remarks on the New Zealand Land Company; also, a description...of its indigenous exports, and hints on emigration... 171p. *8°.* 1845.

34177 DIALOGUES of the living upon our colonies, and upon our colonial and Indian administrations, compared. 19p. *8°.* 1845. *Containing only Dialogue I.*

34178 *DIXON, C. G. Report on tank embankments [for land irrigation] constructed in the Ajmere District, during 1844. 32p. *8°. Agra,* 1845.

34179 ENGLAND. Parliament. *House of Commons.* A corrected report of the debate in the House of Commons, on the 17th, 18th and 19th of June, on the state of New Zealand and the case of the New Zealand Company. 287p. *8°.* 1845.

34180 EYRE, E. J. Journals of expeditions of discovery into central Australia, and overland from Adelaide to King George's Sound, in the years 1840–1; sent by the colonists of South Australia...including an account of the manners and customs of the aborigines... 2 vols. *8°.* 1845.

34181 *FELLECHNER, A., *and others.* Bericht über die im höchsten Auftrage...des Prinzen Carl von Preussen und...des...Fürsten v. Schoenburg-Waldenburg bewirkte Untersuchung einiger Theile des Mosquitolandes, erstattet von der dazu ernannten Commission [A. Fellechner, Dr. Müller, C. L. C. Hesse]. 274p. *8°. Berlin,* 1845.

34182 FRANKLIN, SIR J. Narrative of some passages in the history of Van Diemen's Land, during the last three years of Sir John Franklin's administration of its government. [Relating to his disputes with John Montagu.] 157p. *8°. [London,* 1845]

34183 GAWLER, G. Tranquillization of Syria and the East. Observations and practical suggestions, in furtherance of the establishment of Jewish colonies in Palestine, the most sober and sensible remedy for the miseries of Asiatic Turkey. 48p. *8°.* 1845.

34184 *JACOB, Sir George Le G. Report upon the general condition of the Province of Katteewar in 1842... 96p. *8°. Bombay,* 1845.

34185 NOTES on Canada, with reference to the Act 6–7 Vict. 1843, c. 29, for reducing the duties on Canadian wheat and wheat flour imported into the United Kingdom, comprising statistical and general information relative to the province, statements from official returns...&c. &c. By a member of the Essex Agricultural Protection Society. 43p. *8°. Chelmsford, Colchester, &c.,* 1845.

34186 RAILWAYS in India; being four articles reprinted from The Railway Register for July, August, September, and November, 1845...[The advertisement signed: H.O.] 52p. *8°.* 1845. *The Rastrick copy. See also* 1846.

34187 REMARKS on the right of the landowners of South Australia to the sums withdrawn by Government from the emigration fund; addressed to the Right Hon. Lord Stanley...[Signed: A landowner of South Australia, and dated, Edinburgh, May 1845.] 20p. *8°. n.p.* [1845]

34188 STEPHENSON, Sir Rowland M. Report upon the practicability and advantages of the introduction of railways into British India; with copies of the official correspondence with the Bengal Government, and full statistical data respecting the existing trade upon the line connecting Calcutta with Mirzapore, Benares, Allahabad, and the North-West frontier... 77p. *8°.* 1845.

FINANCE

34189 ALISON, Sir A., *Bart.* England in 1815 and 1845: or, a sufficient and a contracted currency. 94p. *8°. Edinburgh & London,* 1845.

34190 —— Second edition, revised and enlarged, with a postscript containing a reply to the observations of the Right Honourable Sir Robert Peel, Bart. 132p. *8°. Edinburgh & London,* 1845. *See also* 1846, 1847.

34191 ALLAN, J. B. Proposal for the abolition of the present system of taxation. 18p. *8°. Forres,* 1845. *Presentation copy from the author to 'Dr Cumming' of Edinburgh.*

34192 ARNOULD, D. Situation administrative et financière des monts-de-piété en Belgique. Nécessité et moyens de les réorganiser. 365p. *8°. Bruxelles,* 1845. *Presentation copy, with inscription, from the author to M. Silvain van de Weyer, Minister of the Interior.*

34193 ARTICLE on the present state of the insolvency laws. Extracted from "The Bankers' Magazine," by permission. January 1st, 1844 [i.e. 1845]. 7p. *8°.* [1845] *'With Mr. Elliott's compliments' is stamped on the title-page. Conjecturally attributed to Elliott by HSF.*

34194 ASSOCIATED BANKERS OF SCOT-LAND. Report of the proceedings of the Associated Bankers of Scotland in relation to "A Bill to regulate the issue of bank notes in Scotland." Session 1845. 33p. *8°. Glasgow,* 1845.

34195 BRITISH LINEN COMPANY. Edinburgh, 1st March 1845. List of the proprietors of the British Linen Company. *s.sh.fol. n.p.* [1845] [Br. 610] *See also* 1819, 1846.

34196 BRUEGGEMANN, K. H. Der Deutsche Zollverein und das Schutzsystem. Ein Versuch zur Verständigung der Ansichten und für Ausgleichung der Interessen. 195p. *8°. Berlin,* 1845.

34197 BYLES, Sir J. B. Observations on the usury laws, and on the effect of the recent alterations: with suggestions for the permanent amendment of the law, and the draft of an Act for that purpose. 167p. *12°.* 1845.

34198 C., D. G. Observations on the readjustment of taxation, and the substitution of a more simple mode of collecting a revenue than at present pursued: with a view to the extension of commerce and the amelioration of the condition of the "people". [A letter to John Macgregor.] 12p. *8°.* 1845.

34199 CARGILL, W. The currency, showing how a fixed gold standard places England in permanent disadvantage in respect to other countries, and produces periodical domestic convulsions. Reprinted from The Portfolio. 60p. *8°.* 1845.

34200 CARY, T. G. A practical view of the business of banking. [An address delivered before the Mercantile Library Association of Boston, December, 1845.] 16p. *8°. n.p.* [1845]

34201 —— Profits on manufactures at Lowell. A letter from the treasurer of a corporation to John S. Pendleton, Esq., Virginia. 23p. *8°. Boston,* 1845. *Presentation copy from the author to 'Hon. J. Fairbanks'.*

34202 COMMITTEE OF DELEGATES DE-PUTED...TO COLLECT INFORMATION ON THE SUBJECT OF THE WINDOW DUTIES. Report of the Committee...on...the window duties, with a view to their repeal. London, April, 1845. 16p. *8°.* [*London,* 1845]

34203 COMMITTEE OF DEPUTIES FROM THE JOINT STOCK BANKS. Record of the proceedings of the Committee...with the Acts of Parliament affecting joint stock banks, which were passed during the session of 1844. 106p. *8°.* 1845.

34204 CONNECTICUT. *General Assembly. House of Representatives.* Report of the Bank Commissioners to the General Assembly, May session, 1845...Document no. 4. 56p. *8°. Hartford,* 1845.

34205 COXHEAD, W. The immaculate and infallible ready-reckoner; with complete interest tables, and farming and market tables... 248p. *12°.* 1845.

34206 The CURRENCY theory reviewed; in a letter to the Scottish people on the menaced interference by Government with the existing system of banking in Scotland. By a banker in England. 76p. *8°. Edinburgh,* 1845.

34207 DE BODE, C. J. P. P., *Baron.* Statement for counsel's opinion, and opinions of MM. Gressier, Ernest Vincent [and others]...concerning the indemnity due to the Baron de Bode, under Convention no. 7, of the Conventions of 1815 and 1818. 72p. *8°.* 1845.

34208 EAST OF ENGLAND BANK. Copy of certificate by the honourable the Commissioners of Stamps and Taxes, of the partners of the East of England Bank, for the year 1845... 15p. *8°. Norwich*, [1845].

34209 *EAST OF SCOTLAND LIFE ASSURANCE COMPANY. Prospectus of the East of Scotland Life Assurance Company, for the granting of assurances on lives and survivorships; for the sale of annuities, present, deferred, and survivorship, for the granting of endowments to children... Capital £250,000 ... 26p. *8°. Dundee*, [1845?] *The copy that belonged to Augustus De Morgan.*

34210 ELLIOT, JONATHAN. The funding systems of the United States and of Great Britain, with some tabular facts of other nations touching the same subject. xxiv, 1299p. *8°. Washington*, 1845.

34211 ELLIOTT, J. H. Credit the life of commerce: being a defence of the British merchant against the unjust and demoralizing tendency of the recent alteration in the laws of debtor and creditor; with an outline of remedial measures. 220p. *12°*. 1845.

34212 EQUITABLE DEBTOR AND CREDITOR ASSOCIATION. The address of the... Association to the members of the trading and mercantile interests, and to the landlords throughout Great Britain, on the difficulties of conducting business with the present laws between debtor and creditor; and the legislative remedies for those difficulties... 16p. *8°*. 1845.

34213 [EVANS, D. M.] The city; or, the physiology of London business; with sketches on 'change and at the coffee houses. 211p. *8°*. 1845. *Presentation copy from the author to Charles Barker.*

34214 FANE, R. G. C. Limited liability: its necessity as a means of promoting enterprise. 8p. *8°*. [1845]

34215 FRAGUEIRO, M. A. S. J. Fundamentos de un proyecto de banco presentado a la Sociedad de Agricultura i Beneficencia de Chile. [With 'Observaciones sobre el proyecto de estatuto para el Banco Nacional de Chile'.] 121, 51p. *4°. Santiago*, 1845.

34216 FULLARTON, J. On the regulation of currencies; being an examination of the principles, on which it is proposed to restrict, within certain fixed limits, the future issues on credit of the Bank of England, and of the other banking establishments throughout the country ...Second edition, with corrections and additions. 253p. *8°*. 1845. *For another edition, see* 1844.

34217 [GILBART, J. W.] The letters of Nehemiah; relating to the laws affecting joint stock banks, and the effects likely to be produced, by the measures of Sir Robert Peel, upon the system of banking in London, and throughout the country. [Introductory note signed: J.W.G.] 16p. *8°*. 1845.

34218 —— The London bankers. An analysis of the returns made to the Commissioners of Stamps and Taxes by the private and joint stock banks of London in January 1845, pursuant to the Act 7 & 8 Victoria, c. 32. 16p. *8°*. 1845.

34219 GLADSTONE, W. E. Remarks upon recent commercial legislation; suggested by the expository statement of the revenue from customs, and other papers lately submitted to Parliament. 65p. *8°*. 1845.

34220 —— Third edition. 65p. *8°*. 1845.

34221 HANSARD, LUKE J. What is the real value of a government? Let us place the substance before the shadow...Good! A proposition on the National Debt, with the ways and means of the riddance from all oppressive taxes... February 1845. 46p. *8°*. 1845.

34222 —— Second edition. [With 'Supplement to the appendix'.] 56p. *8°*. 1845. *The copy that belonged to Earl De Grey.*

34223 [——] The reviving life of Good! is the moral power of the press. [A collection made by Hansard of opinions of the press on a pamphlet by him entitled 'Good.' Signed: L.J.H.] 28p. *8°. n.p.* [1845] *The copy that belonged to Earl De Grey.*

34224 —— Sources or means of appropriation for the human creature's property of pecuniary possessions or increasings, now offered in lieu of the unsound, the unreal national funding system. A letter to the editor of the Times ...August 16, 1845... 28p. *8°*. 1845.

34225 HEYWORTH, L. On economic fiscal legislation. To the honourable the Members of both Houses of Parliament. 16p. *8°*. 1845.

34226 HODGSON, C. An account of the augmentation of small livings by "The Governors of the Bounty of Queen Anne, for the augmentation of the maintenance of the poor clergy," and of benefactions by corporate bodies and individuals...Second edition...to the end of... 1844. [With an appendix of documents.]... 46, cclvip. *8°. London, Oxford, &c.,* 1845. *The volume also contains the supplement published in 1864.*

34227 HOFMANN, J. G. Die Macht des Geldes. Eine Aufsuchung der Ursachen der Verarmung und des sittlichen Verfalls so vieler unserer Mitmenschen nebst Mitteln zur Abhülfe. 56p. *8°. Leipzig*, 1845.

34228 JOHNSON, WILLIAM (*fl.* 1845). Reduction of price and rate of duty. Remarks on the fallacy of the doctrine that, by reduction of price and rate of duty, consumption can be increased in a greater proportion than price is decreased, and so much so as to produce increased revenue...Reprinted...from Hunt's Merchant's Magazine...New York, July 1842. 22p. *8°*. 1845.

34229 [KNOTT, J. M.] The currency. A letter to the Right Honourable Lord Dunfermline, on his address to the Edinburgh County Meeting, convened to consider the effect of the projected interfering of the Government with the long-established currency of Scotland. By Anglicus. Third edition. 15p. *8°*. 1845. *See note to no.* 33779.

34230 LAWSON, W. J. History of banking in Scotland, embracing a brief review of the revenues of Scotland, with a copy of the Act of the Scottish Parliament establishing the Bank of Scotland. 50p. *8°. London & Newcastle-upon-Tyne*, 1845.

34231 LEE, H. Considerations on the cultivation, production and consumption of cotton, connected with the questions of currency, credit, commerce and banking; addressed to the cotton manufacturers of Massachusetts. p. 9–416. *8°. Boston*, 1845.

34232 Private. Commercial and financial **LEGISLATION.** 30p. *8°.* [*London*, 1845] *Conjecturally attributed to John Macgregor by HSF. The copy that belonged to T. Spring Rice, Baron Monteagle.*

34233 LESLIE, C. An essay concerning the divine right of tithes...Re-printed from the edition of 1700. 192p. *8°. Edinburgh, London, &c.,* 1845. *For another edition, see* 1700.

34234 LINDSAY, John. A view of the coinage of Scotland, with copious tables, lists, descriptions and extracts from Acts of Parliament... 291p. *4°. Cork, 1845. Two supplements, published in 1859 and 1865 respectively, are also in the Goldsmiths' Library.*

34235 LOYAL NATIONAL REPEAL ASSOCIATION. First report of the...Association on the Budget of 1845. Read at a meeting of the Parliamentary Committee, 11th March, 1845. 7p. *8°. Dublin,* [1845]

34236 —— Second report...Read...March 29, 1845. 7p. *8°. Dublin,* [1845]

34237 —— Report of the Parliamentary Committee of the...Association on the provisions of the Bill recently introduced into the House of Commons, to regulate the issue of bank notes in Ireland. Read...at meeting of the Association... 8p. *8°. Dublin,* [1845]

34238 —— Report of the Trade and Commerce Committee of the...Association, on the soap and candle trade. Read...on...April 28th 1845. 7p. *8°. [Dublin,* 1845]

34239 McCULLOCH, John R. A treatise on the principles and practical influence of taxation and the funding system. 504p. *8°. 1845. Presentation copy from the author to Lord John Russell.*

34240 MACFARLAN, John F. Remarks on the Scotch banking system; being the substance of a speech delivered at a meeting of the Town Council of the city of Edinburgh, on Tuesday, 24th December, 1844. 24p. *8°. Edinburgh & London,* 1845.

34241 MAINE. *Secretary of State.* List of stockholders, (with amount of stock held by each, Jan. 1, 1845,) in the banks of Maine... 69p. *8°. Augusta,* 1845.

34242 NATIONAL SECURITY SAVINGS BANK. Outline of an expeditious method for the daily checking and ultimate balancing of the accounts in extensive savings banks [as used in the National Security Savings Bank of Edinburgh and Glasgow]. 20p. *8°. Edinburgh,* [1845]

34243 —— Report on the affairs of the...Bank... prepared by the Committee of Accounts, and presented to and approved by, the annual general meeting of trustees and managers, held on 16th January 1845, for the year ending 20th November 1844. 12p. *8°. n.p.* [1845] *See also* 1838, 1840, 1841.

34244 NORFOLK, W. J. The general principles of banking, bills of exchange, British funds, and foreign exchanges. 342p. *8°. London & Nottingham,* 1845.

34245 OBITER DICTUM, *pseud.* Let us alone: being five letters, addressed to the editor of "The Edinburgh Observer," condemnatory of any tampering with the existing systems of Scotch banking and currency. 15p. *8°. Edinburgh,* 1845. *The copy that belonged to the 3rd Marquis of Lansdowne.*

34246 PEEL, Sir Robert, *2nd Bart.* An accurate and special report of Sir R. Peel's financial statement, delivered in the House of Commons, on...February 14th, 1845. 31p. *8°.* [1845]

34247 —— [Another edition.] Sir R. Peel's financial statement...[With 'Duties of customs [tables]'.] 21, 43p. *8°.* [1845]

34248 PENNSYLVANIA. *Revenue Commission.* Report of the Revenue Commissioners transmitted to the Governor of Pennsylvania, in pursuance of an act of the 29th day of April, 1844. Printed by order of the Legislature of Pennsylvania, March 19, 1845. 30p. *8°. Harrisburg,* 1845.

34249 POLLARD, G. Banking, currency, and taxation. 32p. *8°.* 1845. *Presentation copy from the author to 'Chas. Rugge Price Esqre'.*

34250 PRATT, J. T. Progress of savings banks. An account of the number of depositors and of the sums deposited in savings banks, in Great Britain and Ireland ...on the 20th of November in each of the years from 1829 to 1844, both inclusive... 28p. *8°.* 1845.

34251 The **RAILWAY INVESTMENT GUIDE.** How to make money by railway shares; being a series of hints and advice to parties speculating in the shares of British, colonial, and foreign railways. By one of the initiated, behind the scenes. Second edition. 23p. *8°.* [1845]

34252 REMARKS upon the effects of the alteration in the mode of levying the timber duties in the Port of London. By a sufferer from the change. 16p. *8°.* 1845.

34253 RICHELOT, H. L'Association douanière allemande. 475p. *8°. Paris,* 1845.

34254 RODBERTUS-JAGETZOW, J. C. Die preussische Geldkrisis. 64p. *8°. Anclam & Swinemünde,* 1845.

34255 ROYER, C. E. Rapport sur les institutions de crédit hypothécaire en Allemagne et en Belgique. 453p. *8°. Paris,* 1845.

34256 SAUNDERSON, C. Suretiship. The dangers and defects of private security, and their remedies... Twenty-second edition, carefully revised. 26p. *12°.* 1845.

34257 *——* Twenty-third edition, carefully revised. 26p. *12°.* 1845. *The copy that belonged to Augustus De Morgan. For other editions, see 1843.*

34258 SKOGMAN, C. D. Anteckningar om Rikets Ständers Bank och allmänna laner örelsen i Sverge. 2 vols. *8°. Stockholm,* 1845–46.

34259 SPACKMAN, W. F. An analysis of the railway interest of the United Kingdom; embracing all companies registered to the 31st day of October, 1845, shewing the defects of the present system of railway management, and the necessity for amendments in the law of provisional registration. 54p. *8°.* 1845.

34260 SPOONER, R. The speech of Richard Spooner, Esq., (M.P. for Birmingham,) on Mr Hume's motion relating to light gold – the currency. In the House of Commons, Friday, July 25th, 1845. 16p. *8°.* 1845.

34261 STEWART, A. The tariff. Speech of Mr. A. Stewart, of Pennsylvania, on the portion of the President's message and Treasury report relating to the tariff. Delivered in the House of Representatives of the United States, on...the 9th of December, 1845. 16p. *8°. n.p.* [1845]

34262 T., Q. The Pitt pound versus the Peel pound. An appeal to common sense. *s.sh.fol.* [c. 1845]

34263 [**TAYLOR,** James (1788–1863).] John Bull's letter to Malachi Malagrowther, Esquire, of North Britain, on the Premier's currency projects. 30p. *8°.* 1845.

34264 [——] The silver-plated spade and French-polished mahogany wheelbarrow. [A pamphlet on the currency, illustrated from the opening ceremony of the Trent Valley Railway by Sir Robert Peel. Dated: Dec. 1, 1845.] 4p. *8°. n.p.* [1845]

34265 TAYLOR, John (1781–1864). Currency investigated, with a view to its scientific principles. In a series of essays published between the years 1832 and 1845. 10 parts. *8°. 1845. A reissue, with a general title-page, introduction and list of contents, of editions as published. Contents: An essay on money, 3rd edition, 1844; The standard and measure of value, 2nd edition, 1844; Currency fallacies refuted, 2nd edition, 1844; Who pays the taxes? 2nd edition, 1844; The monetary policy of England and America, 1843; The Minister mistaken, 1843; Currency explained...By Verus, 1843; Emancipation of industry, 1844; What is a pound? 1844; The labourer's protection the nation's remedy, 1845.*

34266 [——] The labourer's protection, the nation's remedy. 66p. *8°. 1845. For another issue, see no. 34265 above.*

34267 UDNY, G. A word on "the currency." 51p. *8°. Calcutta, 1845. The copy presented to HSF by the author's son, Sir George Udny.*

34268 UNION BANK OF LONDON. List of proprietors, returned to the Stamp Office...With the number of votes to which each is entitled, and the names of the directors of the Union Bank of London. 32p. *8°.* 1845.

34269 YOUNGER, S. Strictures on the policy of the Bank of England, with some remarks on the foreign exchanges and the corn laws; the whole suggested by the power of railway and marine steam; respectfully addressed to the First Lord of the Treasury. 42p. *8°.* 1845.

TRANSPORT

34270 ASHURST, W. H. Direct London and Manchester railway. [Letters to the *Manchester Times, Journal of Commerce,* and *Morning Herald* by W. H. Ashurst and George Remington, August 1845.] 17p. *8°.* [1845] *Without a title-page.*

34271 AYLESBURY AND THAME RAILWAY COMPANY. Aylesbury and Thame Railway Company. Provisionally registered. Capital £100,000. [Prospectus.] [4]p. *fol. n.p.* [1845]

34272 [**B.,** H.?] Reminiscences of railway making. Rhymes, &c. 122p. *12°. 1845. Presentation copy to 'Percival Bosanquet Esq.ʳ with H.B.'s best Regards'. 'H.B.' has been conjecturally identified as Henry Barrett.*

24273 BELGIUM. *Ministère des Travaux Publics.* Chemin de fer. Compte-rendu des opérations de l'exercice 1844. Rapport présenté aux Chambres législatives, le 19 février 1843, par le Ministre des Travaux publics. 278p. *fol. Bruxelles, 1845. See also 1839.*

34274 BERMINGHAM, T. [*Endorsed:*] A letter from Thomas Bermingham, Esq., to the people of Ireland, particularly to the inhabitants of the provinces of Leinster & Connaught, on the subject of the Irish Great Western Railway from Dublin to Galway...April 26, 1845. [6]p. *fol.* [*London,* 1845]

34275 BLANCHARD, E. L. L. Bradshaw's Descriptive guide to the London & South Western Railway...To which is added, The tourist's companion to the Isle of Wight. 97p. *12°. London & Manchester,* 1845.

34276 The **BOARD** of Trade and the Kentish railway schemes. 41p. *8°.* 1845.

For **BRADSHAW'S RAILWAY GAZETTE,** 1845–46, *continued as the* Railway gazette, 1846–47, *see* vol. III, *Periodicals list,* Railway gazette and mining chronicle.

34277 BUTTERWORTH, E. Views on the Manchester & Leeds Railway, drawn from nature, and on stone, by A. F. Tait; with a descriptive history, by Edwin Butterworth. 34p. *fol. London & Manchester,* 1845.

34278 CASTLE, H. J. Railway curves... 29p. *8°.* [*London,* 1845 ?] *The Rastrick copy.*

34279 CHEMIN DE FER de Paris à Rennes. Supplément aux pièces administratives, quelques articles publiées par le Courrier de la Sarthe. 36p. *8°. Le Mans,* 1845.

34280 CHEMIN DE FER DE L'ENTRE-SAMBRE-ET-MEUSE. Sambre and Meuse Railway. Grant from the Belgian Government. Report of Mr. Stephenson, and general statement, May 1845. 128p. *8°.* 1845.

34281 DÉNAIN, A. Considérations sur les intérêts politiques et commerciaux qui se rattachent à l'Isthme de Panama et aux différents isthmes de l'Amérique centrale; relation directe de ces isthmes avec celui de Suez. 253p. *8°. Paris,* 1845.

34282 DIRECT LONDON & MANCHESTER RAILWAY. Offices – 48, Moorgate Street, London. Provisionally registered. Capital £5,000,000 in 100,000 shares of £50 each. [Prospectus, dated: July 1845.] 3p. *fol.* [*London,* 1845]

34283 DUBIED, E. Du transport des marchandises sur les canaux au moyen de la vapeur. 15p. *8°. Paris,* [*c.* 1845]

34284 DUNSTABLE RAILWAY COMPANY. First ordinary half-yearly general meeting of the Court of Proprietors...27th August 1845. [4]p. *fol.* [*London,* 1845] *See also 1846.*

34285 EASTERN UNION RAILWAY COMPANY. Eastern Union Railway half-yearly report of the...Company, 12th February [–August 20th], 1845. 2 vols. *fol. n.p.* [1845] *See also 1844, 1846, 1847, 1848, 1849, 1850.*

34286 ENGLAND. Board of Trade. *Railway Department.* Report of the Railway Department of the Board of Trade on the schemes for extending railway communication in Scotland. 23p. *12°.* [*Edinburgh,* 1845]

34287 —— —— —— Reports of the Railway Department...on schemes for extending railway communication, and on amalgamation of railways. Sess. 1845. With a copious index. 269p. *12°. Westminster, Edinburgh, &c.,* 1845.

34288 —— *Laws, etc.* Anno quinto Victoriæ Reginæ, sess. 2. Cap. xxxiv. An Act to alter, amend, and enlarge the powers and provisions of the Acts relating to the London and Blackwall Railway. p.873–880. *fol.* 1845.

34289 —— —— [*Endorsed:*] Middlesbro' and Redcar Railway. An Act for making a railway from Middlesbro' to...Redcar, in the North Riding of the County of York, to be called "The Middlesbro' and Redcar Railway."

⟨Royal Assent 21st July, 1845.⟩ 8 Vict. – sess. 1845. 15p. *fol.* [1845]

34290 —— —— [*Endorsed:*] Wear Valley Railway. An Act for making a railway to be called "The Wear Valley Railway," from...the Bishop Auckland and Weardale Railway, to Frosterley, with a branch terminating at or near Bishopley Crag, in Stanhope in Weardale, all in the county of Durham. ⟨Royal Assent, 31st. July 1845.⟩ 8 Vict. – sess. 1845. 14p. *fol.* [1845]

34291 —— Parliament. *House of Lords.* The Standing Orders of the House of Lords relating to private Bills, as amended the 7th of August, 1845: with an abstract of the Orders respecting Railway Bills, arranged in the order of the proceedings thereon. And a copious index. 98p. *12°. Westminster, Edinburgh, &c.,* 1845.

34292 GARELLA, N. Projet d'un canal de jonction de l'Océan Pacifique et de l'Océan Atlantique à travers l'Isthme de Panama. 233p. *8°. Paris,* 1845.

34293 ⟨Registered provisionally.⟩ **GREAT WESTERN AND WYCOMBE JUNCTION RAILWAY** [to link High Wycombe with the Great Western Railway at Maidenhead]. Capital £150,000 – in 10,000 shares of £15 each...[Prospectus, dated: 29th April 1845.] [4]p. *fol. n.p.* [1845]

34294 The illustrated **GUIDE** to the London and Dover Railway; accompanied by a complete and accurate tourist's and travellers' directory to the counties in communication with the line, Kent, Surrey, and Sussex; visitors' notes to the Metropolis; tables of hackney coach and cab fares from the termini to all parts of London... 72, lxxiip. *12°. J. Mead,* [1845?]

34295 HARDING, WYNDHAM. Railways. The gauge question. Evils of a diversity of gauge, and a remedy... With a map. Second edition. 62p. *8°.* 1845. *One of a collection of pamphlets on railways that belonged to Samuel Smiles, bound in two volumes, one of which bears his signature and the date 1849 on the flyleaf. See also 1846.*

34296 **IPSWICH AND BURY ST. EDMUND'S RAILWAY COMPANY.** First report of the directors ...September 12th, 1845. [With the report of the Engineer, Peter Bruff.] 2, [2]p. *fol. n.p.* [1845] *See also* 1846.

34297 The **ISLE** of Wight system of roads, and system of guardians of the poor, not a model, but a warning to the Legislature; especially as to the abuses arising from the incompatible functions of magistrates; and a proof that the maintenance of the highways is not one of the peculiar burdens on land. 91p. *8°. Southampton & London,* 1845. *The copy that belonged to Sir Richard Simeon, one of the Board of Commissioners controlling the roads of the Isle of Wight, with his signature on the title-page and manuscript notes by him.*

34298 **ITINÉRAIRE** des bâteaux à vapeur de Paris au Havre, avec une description statistique et anecdotique, des bords de la Seine, suivi d'un guide du voyageur, précédé d'une notice historique sur le chemin de fer de Paris à Saint Germain...[Troisième édition.] 244p. *12°. Paris,* [c. 1845]

34299 [JANIN, J. G.] Voyage de Paris à la mer, par Rouen et le Havre. Description historique des villes, bourgs, villages et sites sur le parcours du chemin de fer et des bords de la Seine... 135p. *8°. Paris,* [1845]

34300 **JONES,** WILLIAM, *M.D.* A popular sketch of the various proposed systems of atmospheric railway, demonstrating the applicability of the mechanical properties of the atmosphere, as a motive power...Being the substance of lectures, delivered on the subject, at the Royal Adelaide Gallery. In...February, 1845. With additions and corrections. By the late proprietor, William Jones, Esq. 108p. *12°.* 1845.

34301 LAVELEYE, A. DE. Sambre and Meuse Railway. Central Line. Memoir by Aug. Delaveleye. Translated from the French. 35p. *8°.* 1845. *Two letters to Sir John Phillipart, one from Osmund Lewis accompanying the pamphlet, are bound with it. For these, see vol. III, A.L. 289/1–2.*

34302 [LEVER, C. J.] Tales of the trains: being some chapters of railroad romance. By Tilbury Tramp, Queen's Messenger. [Illustrated by Phiz.] 156p. *8°. London & Dublin,* 1845.

34303 **LOYAL NATIONAL REPEAL ASSOCIATION.** Report of the Parliamentary Committee of the...Association on the subject of having the enquiries connected with Irish railway legislation transacted in Dublin. Read...on...22nd December, 1845. 11p. *8°. Dublin,* [1845]

34304 MALLET, R. Three reports upon improved methods of constructing and working atmospheric railways. 73p., 10 plates. *4°. n.p.* [1845]

34305 MORO, G. Communication between the Atlantic and Pacific Oceans through the Isthmus of Tehuantepec. Additional observations to the report lately given on this subject by the engineer Signor Gaetano Moro. 16p. *8°.* 1845.

34306 MULOCK, T. Railway revelations: being letters on the subject of the proposed Direct London and Manchester railways. 46p. *8°.* 1845.

34307 **NEW YORK AND HARTFORD RAILROAD COMPANY.** Report of the executive committee upon the statistics of business, and of the engineer [Edward H. Brodhead] upon the survey of the several routes for the contemplated New York and Hartford Railroad, via Danbury. [With 'Appendix. Description of bridge for the Naugatuc River', by S. Whipple.] 119p. *8°. Hartford,* 1845. *The Rastrick copy.*

34308 **NEWCASTLE AND CARLISLE RAILWAY COMPANY.** Report of the directors of the Newcastle upon Tyne & Carlisle Railway Company, read to the shareholders at their annual meeting March 27, 1845. 15p. *8°. Newcastle,* 1845. *See also* 1835, 1837, 1838, 1843.

34309 NEWTON, W. E. Notes of the cause tried at the Liverpool summer assizes, before Mr Justice Cresswell and a special jury, August 27th, 1845, between W. E. Newton and the Grand Junction Railway Company, for an infringement of letters patent for the improvements in the construction of boxes for the axletrees of locomotive engines and carriages. 186p. *8°.* 1845.

34310 **NORTH STAFFORDSHIRE RAILWAY COMPANY.** North Staffordshire, or Churnet, Potteries, and Trent Junction Railway. (Registered provisionally.) Capital £2,350,000, in 117,500 shares of £20 each ...[Prospectus, dated: April 30, 1845.] *s.sh.fol.* [1845]

34311 PAGAN, W. Road reform: a plan for abolishing turnpike tolls and statute labour assessments, and for providing the funds necessary for maintaining the public roads by an annual rate to be levied on horses. 336p. *8°*. *Edinburgh & Cupar-Fife*, 1845. *See also* 1846.

34312 PHILADELPHIA AND READING RAILROAD COMPANY. Report of the president and managers of the Philadelphia & Reading Rail Road Co. to the stockholders. January 13, 1845. 20p. *8°*. *Philadelphia*, 1845.

34313 PROUDHON, P. J. De la concurrence entre les chemins de fer et les voies navigables. 48p. *8°*. *Paris*, 1845.

For the **RAILWAY HERALD**, *see vol.* III, *Periodicals list*.

34314 RAILWAYS and the Board of Trade. 32p. *8°*. 1845.

34315 —— Third edition. 40p. *8°*. 1845.

34316 ROBERTSON, JOHN (*fl.* 1845). Suggestions on railway legislation... ⟨From the Railway Review.⟩ 8p. *8°*. *n.p.* [1845]

34317 RUMINATIONS on railways. No. I. Railway speculation. 15p. *8°*. 1845.

34318 —— No. II. The Railway Board of Trade. 32p. *8°*. 1845.

34319 SALT, S. Statistics and calculations essentially necessary to persons connected with railways or canals, containing a variety of information not to be found elsewhere. 116p. *8°*. *Manchester & London*, 1845.

34320 SOCIÉTÉ DES CHEMINS DE FER DE LA FLANDRE OCCIDENTALE. West Flanders Railways. Report of George Stephenson, Esq. with the decree, grant, convention, and the statutes of the Company, September, 1845. 59p. *8°*. 1845.

34321 SOUTH LONDON RAILWAY COM- **PANY.** The South London Railway, from London Bridge to Peckham, Camberwell, Brixton, Clapham, Balham, Tooting & Mitcham; with branches to Dulwich and Norwood, and to the South-Western Railway, near Wandsworth...Capital £850,000 in 42,500 shares of £20 each...[Prospectus, dated: 16th October 1845.] 2, [2]p. *fol. n.p.* [1845]

34322 STEVENSON, DAVID. Remarks on the improvement of tidal rivers...Read before the Royal Society of Edinburgh, at the meeting of 17th March 1845. 36p. *8°*. *London & Edinburgh*, 1845.

34323 TIGHE, R. R. A letter to the Right Honourable the Earl of Lincoln, Chief Commissioner of Her Majesty's Woods, Forests, Land Revenues, etc., on the present state and direction of the roads intersecting the parks and grounds of Windsor Castle...with suggestions for their improvement... 13p. *fol.* [*London,*] *Printed for presentation only*, [1845] *Presentation copy, with inscription, from the author to the Duke of Wellington.*

34324 TRENT VALLEY RAILWAY. Origin and progress of the undertaking. Compiled from official documents. 82p. *8°*. *Manchester*, 1845.

34325 TUCK, H. The railway shareholder's manual; or, practical guide to the railways of Great Britain, completed, in progress, and projected, forming an entire railway synopsis, indispensable to all interested in railway locomotion. 112p. *8°*. 1845.

34326 —— The railway shareholder's manual; or, practical guide to all the railways in the world...Fifth edition. 147p. *8°*. 1845. *See also* 1846, 1847.

34327 WILKINS, C. House of Lords. Wakefield, Pontefract, and Goole Railway. Reply of Mr. Wilkins, as counsel on behalf of the promoters of the Bill...July 23, 1845... 40p. *8°*. *York*, 1845.

SOCIAL CONDITIONS

34328 An **ADDRESS** to the people of Suffolk on incendiary fires. 8p. *8°*. *Bury* [*St. Edmunds*], [1845 ?] *Attributed, in a manuscript note on p. 1, to 'the late Lord Thurlow', i.e. Edward Thomas Hovel Thurlow, the third Baron.*

34329 ADSHEAD, J. Prisons and prisoners... 320p. *8°*. 1845. *Presentation copy from the author to R. B. Armstrong.*

34330 ALCOCK, THOMAS (*fl.* 1845–1848). Remarks on the inclosure of commons and wastes, (not village greens) with recognition of the indefinite rights of the poor, as well as the definite rights of the rich, and the reservation of ample space for recreation for all classes. 11p. *8°*. 1845.

34331 ASSOCIATION OF MILL OWNERS AND MANUFACTURERS ENGAGED IN THE COTTON TRADE. Factory legislation. Report of the central committee of the Association...for the year 1844, as also upon the recent proceedings in Parliament, on the passing of the Factories Act. Agreed upon at a meeting held in Manchester, Dec. 31st, 1844. 17p. *8°*. *Manchester*, 1845.

34332 B., J. M. Temperance and abstinence, or, an attempt to end the controversy. A familiar dialogue between two friends, on the principles, constitution, and objects of teetotal societies. 40p. *8°*. *Leicester & London*, 1845. *The Turner copy.*

34333 BADHAM, L. ⟨Not published.⟩ The annual charity sermon for the year 1845, in aid of the Ferns Diocesan Church Education Society; preached in the church of Gorey. 32p. *8°*. *Dublin*, 1845. *The copy that belonged to Earl De Grey.*

34334 BALFOUR, E. Statistical data for forming troops and maintaining them in health in different climates and localities. [Two papers, read by Joseph Hume, Esq., M.P., before the Statistical Society of London, on the 21st April and 19th May, 1845, and reprinted from the Journal of the Society.] 17p. *8°*. *n.p.* [1845] *The copy presented, with inscription, by Joseph Hume to N. W. Senior.*

34335 —— [Another edition of the first paper.] Observations on the means of forming and maintaining troops in health in different climates and localities...Read [by Joseph Hume] before the Statistical Society of London, on the 21st April 1845. 8p. *8°*. [1845] *The copy presented, with inscription, by Joseph Hume to the Reform Club.*

34336 —— [Another edition of the second paper.] Observations on the means of preserving the health of troops, by selecting healthy localities for their cantonments ...Read by Joseph Hume, Esq., M.P., before the Statistical Society of London, on the 19th of May 1845. 14p.

8°. [1845] *The copy presented, with inscription, by Joseph Hume to the Reform Club.*

34337 **BALY,** W. On the mortality in prisons, and the diseases most frequently fatal to prisoners...Received November 9th, 1844 – Read February 25th 1845. 160p. *8°. n.p.* [1845]

34338 **BRIDEWELL HOSPITAL.** General report of the Royal Hospitals of Bridewell and Bethlem, and of the House of Occupations, for the year ending 31st December, 1844. Printed for the use of the Governors. 112p. *8°.* 1845.

34339 **BURN,** J. An historical sketch of the Independent Order of Oddfellows M.U. 180p. *12°. Manchester,* [1845]

34340 **CALEDONIAN SOCIETY OF LONDON.** Rules of the Caledonian Society... 15p. *8°.* 1845.

34341 [**CARTER,** THOMAS (1792–1867 ?) ?] Memoirs of a working man. [With an introduction by Charles Knight.] 234p. *12°.* 1845. *Also attributed to John Carter.*

34342 **CHARITY FOR THE RELIEF OF POOR WIDOWS AND CHILDREN OF CLERGYMEN.** Report of the Governors...for the year 1845. 46p. *8°.* 1845.

34343 **CHRISTIE,** R. Report regarding the affairs of the Edinburgh Water Company. 4p. *4°. n.p.* [1845] *See note to no. 33895; see also no. 34355.*

34344 **CITY OF LONDON GENERAL PENSION SOCIETY.** City of London General Pension Society, for providing a permanent relief to decayed artisans, mechanics, tradesmen, manufacturers, and the widows of such persons, above 60 years of age. List of officers, rules and subscribers. 1845. 67p. *8°.* [1845]

34345 **COCHRANE,** G. On the employment of the poor in Great Britain & Ireland. 16p. *8°.* 1845.

34346 **COMMITTEE OF INHABITANTS OF EDINBURGH AND LEITH.** Observations by the Committee of Inhabitants of Edinburgh and Leith, upon the "Statement" by the Directors of the Edinburgh Water Company, of date 28th July, 1845. 20p. *8°. Edinburgh,* 1845.

34347 **COMMON SENSE** v. bigotry; or, reasons for supporting the parliamentary grant to Maynooth. By a clergyman of the Church of England. 15p. *8°.* 1845.

34348 **COOPER,** A. A., *7th Earl of Shaftesbury.* Printed for private distribution. Employment of children in calico print works. Corrected report of the speech of Lord Ashley M.P., in the House of Commons, on 18th day of Feb. 1845, on moving "that leave be given to bring in a Bill to regulate the labour of children in the calico print-works of Great Britain and Ireland." 24p. *8°.* 1845.

34349 **CURTIS,** JOHN H. Advice on the care of the health; with remarks on the present state of hygiology; showing the necessity for the adoption of public sanatory measures; on the cure and prevention of disease... 56p. *8°. London & Paris,* 1845.

34350 **DEAN,** JAMES. On the beneficial employment of the surplus labouring classes, more especially the agricultural portion of them, in the winter season of the year; and on the garden allotment system...Being the substance of a correspondence...between...Lord Willoughby d'Eresby – the editor of the "Times" – the Editor of the "Mark Lane Express and Agricultural Journal" – the Editor and a correspondent of the "Gardeners' Chronicle" – Mr. Warner, the philanthropist, and James Dean. 16p. *8°.* [1845]

34351 The **DOCTOR** scrutinized; or, for what purpose do physicians prescribe alcoholic beverages? Extracted from "The Temperance Recorder for the Eastern Counties of England." [With 'Critique of an eminent surgeon...on the annexed medical essay...'.] (*National Temperance Society, New Series,* 3.) 6p. *8°.* [1845 ?] *The Turner copy.*

34352 **DUNCAN,** , *bailie.* Spirit licenses. The following speech was delivered by Bailie Duncan, in the Town Council of Edinburgh, in Feb. last, upon the subject of granting spirit licenses, as reported in the Scottish Herald of February 6th, 1845. [Issued by the Edinburgh Total Abstinence Association, 15th May, 1845.] 12p. *12°. Edinburgh,* [1845]

34353 **EDINBURGH.** *Town Council.* Capital punishments. Report of speeches by Messrs Russell and Cruickshank, in the Town Council...29th July and 26th August 1845, in favour of their entire abolition. 32p. *12°. Edinburgh & London,* 1845.

34354 —— —— Proceedings in the Town Council regarding supply of water. 14th October, 1845. 8p. *8°. n.p.* [1845] *See note to no.* 33895.

34355 —— —— Proposal by the Edinburgh Water Company to transfer their works to a public trust; and reports in relation thereto, by the Lord Provost's Committee, and also by Robert Christie, Esq., accountant. 1845... 14p. *8°. Edinburgh,* 1845. *The copy presented to the Lord Provost of Edinburgh.*

34356 **EDINBURGH WATER COMPANY.** Statement by the Directors of the Edinburgh Water Company, in regard to a report of the Lord Provost's Committee, on the proposal to transfer the affairs of the Company to a public trust. 8p. *8°. Edinburgh,* 1845.

34357 —— Additional statement to the Town Council ... 15p. *8°. Edinburgh,* 1845.

34358 **ENGELS,** F. Die Lage der arbeitenden Klasse in England. Nach eigner Anschauung und authentischen Quellen. 358p. *8°. Leipzig,* 1845. *See also 1848.*

34359 **ENGLAND.** *Commissioners for Inquiring into the State of Large Towns and Populous Districts.* Health of Towns Commission. Report on the state of Birmingham and other large towns. By R. A. Slaney. 46p. *8°.* 1845.

34360 —— —— Health of Towns Commission. Report on the state of large towns in Lancashire. By Dr. Lyon Playfair, one of Her Majesty's Commissioners... 136p. *8°.* 1845.

34361 —— —— Health of Towns Commission. Report on the state of Newcastle-upon-Tyne and other towns. By D. B. Reid. 156p. *8°.* 1845.

34362 —— —— Second report of the Commissioners ... 2 vols. *8°.* 1845.

34363 **FALLAS,** T. The people's rights, and how to get them. By the poor man's friend. [On the effects of machinery, particularly in the woollen industry.] 8p. *8°. n.p.* [c. 1845]

34364 **FELLOWES,** R. Common sense truths proposed for the consideration of the working classes, of the philosophic ultras, and of Henry, Lord Bishop of Exeter. 45p. *8°.* 1845.

34365 **FIELD,** John (1812–1884). Separate imprisonment. Report read at the Berkshire Quarter Sessions by the Chaplain of the County Gaol & House of Correction, at Reading, Michaelmas, 1845. 61p. *8⁰. Reading & London,* [1845]

34366 **FIELDEN,** J. A selection of facts and arguments in favour of the Ten Hours' Bill, as regards its probable effects on commerce and wages, if universally adopted. 56p. *8⁰. Manchester,* 1845. [*phc*] *From the Manchester Public Library copy.*

34367 [**FISH,** S.] A supplicacyon for the beggars. Reprinted from the original edition of 1524 [or rather, 1529. Edited by W. Maskell]. [32]p. *8⁰.* 1845.

34368 **FOX,** William J. Lectures addressed chiefly to the working classes...Published from the reporter's notes. 4 vols. *12⁰.* 1845–49.

34369 **GAUSSEN,** A. Remarks on improving the condition of the agricultural poor, suggested by a pamphlet by the Rev. William Adams, Rector of Throcking. 32p. *8⁰. Royston,* 1845.

34370 **GIRDLESTONE,** C. Letters on the unhealthy condition of the lower class of dwellings, especially in large towns. Founded on the first Report of the Health of Towns Commission. With notices of other documents on the subject, and an appendix, containing plans and tables from the Report (inserted by permission). 92p. *8⁰.* 1845.

34371 **GRAINGER,** R. D. Health of Towns' Association. Unhealthiness of towns, its causes and remedies: being a lecture delivered at the Royal Institution, Liverpool, and the Athenæum, Manchester. 48p. *12⁰.* 1845. *The FWA copy that belonged to William Pare.*

34372 **GRISCOM,** J. H. The sanitary condition of the laboring population of New York. With suggestions for its improvement. A discourse (with additions) delivered on the 30th December, 1844, at the Repository of the American Institute. 58p. *8⁰. New York,* 1845.

34373 [**GROVES,** E. S. D.] Dramatic sketches of the new Poor Law, as administered by guardians; or, reality and fiction identified. By a surgeon. [In verse.] 76p. *12⁰.* 1845. *Presentation copy, with inscription, from the author to the Society of Apothecaries.*

34374 **GUY,** W. A. Health of Towns' Association. Unhealthiness of towns, its causes and remedies; being a lecture delivered at Crosby Hall, Bishopsgate Street. 47p. *12⁰.* 1845. *Presentation copy from the author to H. M. Villiers. *Another, the FWA copy, belonged to William Pare.*

34375 [**HELPS,** Sir A.] The claims of labour. An essay on the duties of the employers to the employed. The second edition. To which is added, an essay on...the improving the health...of the labouring classes. 288p. *8⁰.* 1845. *For another edition, see* 1844.

34376 **HOPE,** afterwards **BERESFORD HOPE,** A. J. B. The new government scheme of academical education for Ireland considered, in a letter to a friend. 23p. *8⁰. London & Cambridge,* 1845. *The copy that belonged to Earl De Grey.*

34377 **HULL,** E. A letter to the House of Lords on the grant to the College of Maynooth. 28p. *8⁰.* 1845.

34378 **KIVETON LODGE BENEVOLENT SOCIETY.** Rules, laws and regulations of the Kiveton Lodge Benevolent Society, held at the Bee-hive Inn, Harthill. Established November 21st, 1843. 7p. *8⁰. Worksop,* 1845.

34379 **KLEINSCHROD,** C. T. von. Der Pauperism in England in legislativen, administrativen und statistischen Beziehungen. Mit einer Uebersicht der Hauptergebnisse der jüngsten Bevölkerungs-Ausnahme in Grossbritannien und Irland nach amtlichen Quellen bearbeitet von C. T. Kleinschrod. 266p. *8⁰. Regensburg,* 1845. *For a continuation,* Die neue Armengesetzgebung Englands und Irlands, *see* 1849.

34380 **LESLIE,** John, *Commissioner of Sewers.* A short address to the representative vestries under Sir John Hobhouse's Vestry Act. 23p. *8⁰.* 1845.

34381 **LINTON,** W. J. Bob-Thin, or the poorhouse fugitive [in verse]...illustrated by T. Sibson – W. B. Scott – E. Duncan – W. J. Linton. 39p. *8⁰. n.p.,* 1845. *Presentation copy, with inscription, from the author to 'J. Franklin, Esq.'.*

34382 **LIVERPOOL ASSOCIATION OF ASSISTANT TRADESMEN.** Fourth annual report of the...Association...1844...[With the committee for 1845 and a list of publications on late hours of business.] 23p. *12⁰. Liverpool,* [1845] *See also* 1844.

For **LIVERPOOL HEALTH OF TOWNS' ASSOCIATION,** Liverpool health of towns' advocate, 1845–47, *see* vol. III, *Periodicals list,* Liverpool health of towns' advocate.

34383 **LOGAN,** William (1813–1879). An affecting story. [A warning to those who are supporting...the drinking customs of the present day.] 2p. *8⁰. Glasgow,* [1845 ?] *The Turner copy.*

34384 **LOYAL NATIONAL REPEAL ASSOCIATION.** Report of the Parliamentary Committee of the...Association on returns of charitable donations & bequests, Ireland...1844. With appendices...and an abstract of the Ecclesiastical Commissioners' reports for 1843 and 1844. Read...on the 21st of July, 1845. 15p. *8⁰. Dublin,* [1845]

34385 **LYNE,** C., *ed.* An old man's wanderings; or an account of a tour through the manufacturing districts. 188p. *8⁰. London & Manchester,* 1845.

34386 **M'GEACHY,** F. L. A speech, delivered in the House of Commons...19th May, 1845, on the third reading of the Maynooth College Bill. 35p. *8⁰.* 1845.

34387 **MARBEAU,** J. B. F. Des crèches, ou moyen de diminuer la misère en augmentant la population... Troisième édition. 139p. *18⁰. Paris,* 1845.

34388 **MARCHAND,** P. R. Du pauperisme. 535p. *8⁰. Paris,* 1845.

34389 **MAURICE,** James. Christian self-denial, in its bearing upon teetotalism. A sermon. 16p. *8⁰. Birmingham,* [1845 ?] *The Turner copy.*

34390 The **MAYNOOTH** endowment vindicated, on the ground of religious principle. By a clergyman of the Church of England. 70p. *8⁰.* 1845.

34391 **METROPOLITAN ASSOCIATION FOR IMPROVING THE DWELLINGS OF THE INDUSTRIOUS CLASSES.** Copy. Charter of incorporation of the Metropolitan Association...1845. 29p. *8⁰.* 1845. *For the* Supplemental charter of incorporation, *see* 1850.

34392 METROPOLITAN WORKING CLASSES ASSOCIATION FOR IMPROVING THE PUBLIC HEALTH. The first address from the Committee... 14p. *8°.* 1845. *See also* 1848.

34393 MITCHELL, JAMES (*d.* 1862). What's the harm in taking a dram? 2p. *8°. Glasgow,* [1845?] *The Turner copy.*

34394 NEWLAND, H. Observations on the past and present condition of the education of the poor in Ireland, with remarks on the Lord Primate and Bishops' address. 98p. *8°. Dublin & London,* 1845. *The copy that belonged to Earl De Grey.*

34395 PARKER, HENRY W. Letters to the Right Hon. Sir James Graham, Bart....on the subject of recent proceedings connected with the Andover Union. 58p. *8°.* 1845. *Presentation copy from the author to 'Edwd. H. Alderson'.*

34396 PARSONS, B. Anti-Bacchus: an essay on the crimes, diseases, and other evils connected with the use of intoxicating drinks...Fourteenth thousand. 136p. *8°.* [1845?] *The Turner copy. For other impressions, see* 1841.

34397 —— Education, the birthright of every human being, and the only scriptural preparation for the millennium; exhibiting the present imperfect state of popular instruction, and the means of rendering it effectual for the salvation of the country and the world. 162p. *8°.* 1845.

34398 PERCEVAL, D. M. Maynooth and the Jew Bill: further illustrations of the speech of the Rt. Hon. Spencer Perceval on the Roman Catholic question, in May, 1805...With four letters to the editor of the "Morning Herald," and a petition against the "Jewish Disabilities Removal" Bill. 64p. *8°. London & Edinburgh,* 1845.

34399 PHILLIPS, M. The duties of property and the rights of labour: original poems, by the author of "Live, and let live". 18p. *8°.* [1845]

34400 PHIPPS, CONSTANTINE H., *Marquess of Normanby.* Speech of the Marquess of Normanby in the House of Lords, on...the 26th of July, 1844, on moving an address to the Crown on the sanatory condition of the people. 24p. *12°.* 1845.

34401 PLUM, T. W. Remarks on the operation of the parochial settlement laws; with suggestions for a new and improved system. 30p. *8°.* 1845.

34402 PROUDHON, P. J. De la célébration du dimanche, considérée sous les rapports de l'hygiène publique, de la morale, des relations de famille et de cité ...Troisième édition. 92p. *12°. Paris & Besançon,* 1845.

34403 READWIN, T. A. An account of the charities of the town and parish of Wokingham, chronologically arranged, and compiled from documents and authenticated sources. 170p. *8°. Wokingham,* 1845.

34404 RELIGIOUS TRACT SOCIETY. No. 1620. John Tomkins: or, the dram-drinker. 8p. *8°.* [*London, c.* 1845?]

34405 RICE, THOMAS S., *Baron Monteagle.* Substance of a speech delivered in the House of Lords by Lord Monteagle, March 12, 1845, on the College of Maynooth. 18p. *8°.* 1845.

34406 SCORESBY, W. American factories and their female operatives; with an appeal on behalf of the British factory population, and suggestions for the improvement of their condition. 122p. *8°. London & Bradford,* 1845.

34407 SCOTTISH ASSOCIATION FOR PROTECTION OF THE POOR. Constitution of the...Association...with relative papers. 32p. *8°. Edinburgh,* 1845.

34408 *[SENIOR, N. W.] Penal jurisprudence of Germany. [A review of P. J. A. von Feuerbach's *Merkwürdige Criminal-Rechtsfälle.*] 49p. *8°. n.p.* [1845?] *Presentation copy from the author to George Grote.*

34409 SOAMES, H. The way to thrive. A sermon preached at Stapleford Tawney, October 19, 1845, when the prizes, awarded by the Ongar Labourers' Friend Society, were distributed to successful candidates, in the parishes of Stapleford Tawney and Thoydon Mount. 16p. *8°. Chipping Ongar,* 1845.

34410 STANILAND, M. Law of settlement. A letter to the Right Hon. Sir James Graham, Bart., on his speech delivered in the House of Commons, February 12, 1845, on bringing in a Bill to amend and consolidate the law relating to parochial settlement, and removal of the poor: with reasons for the entire abolition of the law of settlement. 8p. *8°. London & Boston [Lincs.],* [1845]

34411 Outer House. April 29, 1845. **SUMMONS** of reduction, the Edinburgh Water Company against the Lord Provost of Edinburgh, and others [Commissioners under the Edinburgh Water Company's Acts]. 14p. *4°. n.p.* [1845] *See note to no.* 33895.

34412 SUNDAY SCHOOL SOCIETY FOR IRELAND. Sunday School Society for Ireland. Seventeenth address. To the conductors, superintendents and teachers of Sunday schools in England, Wales and Scotland. [Signed: James Irvine, honorary secretary, and dated, May, 1845.] [4]p. *8°.* [1845]

34413 TALLOW CHANDLERS' BENEVOLENT SOCIETY. Tallow Chandlers' Benevolent Society. [The second annual report, 1844–45.] 35p. *12°. n.p.* [1845]

34414 The **TEMPERANCE MOVEMENT.** 31p. *8°.* [1845?] *The Turner copy.*

34415 THOM, WILLIAM (1798?–1848). Rhymes – and recollections of a hand-loom weaver...Second edition, with additions. 192p. *12°.* 1845. *For another edition, see* 1844.

For the **TRUTH-SEEKER TEMPERANCE ADVOCATE,** *see* vol. III, *Periodicals list.*

34416 VINÇARD, P. Histoire du travail et des travailleurs en France... 2 vols. *8°. Paris,* 1845–46.

34417 VYVYAN, SIR R. R., *Bart.* A letter from Sir Richard Vyvyan, Bt., M.P. to the magistrates of Berkshire, upon their newly-established practice of consigning prisoners to solitary confinement before trial, and ordering that they be disguised by masks whenever they are taken out of their cells. 42p. *8°.* [1845]

34418 WADDINGTON, G. Three lectures on national education, delivered in St. Nicholas Church, Newcastle-on-Tyne. 47p. *8°.* 1845.

34419 WALKER, WILLIAM S. A practical analysis of the Act 8 & 9 Victoriæ cap. 83, for the amendment and better administration of the laws relating to the relief of the poor in Scotland...Third edition. 44p. *8°. Edinburgh & London,* 1845.

34420 —— Fourth edition. 48p. *8°. Edinburgh & London,* 1845.

34421 WHATELY, R., *Archbishop of Dublin.* The Christian duty of educating the poor; a discourse delivered in St. Patrick's Cathedral, 24th November, 1844, in behalf of the National School of Clondalkin. 31p. *8°. Dublin & London,* 1845.

34422 —— Reflections on a grant to a Roman Catholic seminary [St. Patrick's College, Maynooth]; being a charge delivered at the visitation of the Dioceses of Dublin and Glandelough, 26 June, 1845, comprising the substance of a speech delivered in the House of Lords, 3 June, 1845. 64p. *8°. London & Dublin,* 1845.

34423 —— Thoughts on the Sabbath; to which is subjoined an address to the inhabitants of Dublin on the observance of the Lord's Day [1832]...Third edition, enlarged. 52p. *8°.* 1845.

34424 WIGHT, W. Common sense: a word to those who do not think by proxy; or, the temperance movement – the public press – opium eating – the Bishop of Norwich – Father Mathew – Ireland – and English Protestants... Fifty-fifth thousand, much enlarged. 16p. *8°. Glasgow & London,* [1845 ?] *The Turner copy.*

34425 WILLIS, THOMAS. Facts connected with the social and sanitary condition of the working classes in the city of Dublin, with tables of sickness, medical attendance, deaths, expectation of life, &c., &c.; together with some gleanings from the Census returns of 1841. 59p. *8°. Dublin,* 1845. *Presentation copy from the author to Robert Mallet Esq.*

SLAVERY

34426 DOUGLASS, F. Narrative of the life of Frederick Douglass, an American slave. Written by himself. [With a preface by William Lloyd Garrison.] 125p. *8°. Boston,* 1845. *See also* 1846.

34427 An affectionate **EXPOSTULATION** with Christians in the United States of America, because of the continuance of negro slavery throughout many districts of their country, addressed by the minister, deacons, and members of the Congregational Church, joined by the congregation, assembling in Mill-Street Chapel, Perth. 8p. *8°. Glasgow,* [c. 1845]

34428 FRANCE. *Chambre des Pairs et Chambre des Députés.* Exposés des motifs, rapports et débats des Chambres législatives concernant les lois des 18 et 19 juillet 1845 relatives au régime des esclaves, à l'introduction de cultivateurs européens et à la formation d'établissements agricoles dans les colonies françaises. 1024p. *8°. Paris,* 1845.

34429 HISTORY of the slave trade. 32p. *8°. n.p.* [1845 ?] *No. 19 of an unidentified series.*

34430 [JAMESON, D. D.] The sugar question. [Signed in manuscript: D.D.J.] 27p. *8°.* 1845.

34431 MACAULAY, T. B., *Baron Macaulay.* The speech of the Rt. Hon. T. B. Macaulay, M.P. for Edinburgh, on the proposed discriminating duties on sugar, in the House of Commons...February 26, 1845. From Hansard's Parliamentary debates. 23p. *8°.* [1845]

34432 ROUVELLAT DE CUSSAC, J. B. Situation des esclaves dans les colonies françaises; urgence de leur émancipation. 256p. *8°. Paris,* 1845.

34433 SAMPSON, M. B. Slavery in the United States. A letter to the Hon. Daniel Webster. 88p. *8°.* 1845. *Presentation copy, with inscription, from the author to 'John Jones, Esq.'.*

34434 SLAVERY in America. 31p. *8°. n.p.* [1845 ?] *No. 27 of an unidentified series.*

34435 The present **STATE** of the anti-slavery question in Tunis and Algiers: in a letter addressed to Thomas Clarkson, Esq., President of the British and Foreign Anti-Slavery Society; by a correspondent of the same Society. 20p. *8°.* 1845.

34436 STOLLMEYER, C. F. The sugar question made easy. 19p. *8°.* 1845.

POLITICS

34437 BEKE, C. T. Abyssinia. A statement of facts relative to the transactions between the writer and the late British political mission to the court of Shoa. 30p. *8°.* 1845.

34438 BROWN, JOHN, *vicar of Leicester.* Some considerations in favour of the Maynooth grant; intended as a help to tender consciences. Being extracts from a pamphlet of the author's, entitled, "A plea for Ireland," ... 30p. *8°. London & Leicester,* 1845. *The copy that belonged to Earl De Grey.*

For the **CIRCULAR OF THE ANTI-PERSECUTION UNION,** *see* vol. III, *Periodicals list.*

34439 COOPER, THOMAS (1805–1892). The purgatory of suicides. A prison-rhyme... 344p. *8°.* 1845.

34440 GLADSTONE, W. E. Substance of a speech for the second reading of the Maynooth College Bill, in the House of Commons, on...April 11, 1845. 58p. *8°.* 1845. *The copy that belonged to Earl De Grey.*

34441 HATHERELL, J. W. Maynooth: its adoption by the state considered. A letter addressed to the House of Lords. 14p. *8°. London & Southampton,* 1845. *The copy that belonged to Earl De Grey.*

34442 JONES, THOMAS H., *Viscount Ranelagh.* Legal order and constitutional rights, as defined by the Earl of Aberdeen, in a correspondence with the author. [On British policy towards Spain.] 60p. *8°.* 1845.

34443 LOYAL NATIONAL REPEAL ASSOCIATION. Report of the Committee of the... Association on the Bill for the perpetual endowment of the College of Maynooth. Read...on...the 14th April, 1845. 4p. *8°. Dublin,* [1845] *The copy that belonged to Earl De Grey.*

34444 —— Report of Committee of the...Association on the service of process Bills for England and Scotland. Read...on...May 19th, 1845. 5p. *8°. Dublin,* [1845]

34445 —— Report of the Parliamentary Committee of the...Association on the progress of legislation for Ireland during the session of 1845...Read...on...1st September, 1845. 16p. *8°. Dublin,* [1845]

34446 —— Second series of reports of the Loyal National Repeal Association of Ireland. 120p. *8°. Dublin,* 1845. *Originally published in 1840.*

34447 MacDONNELL, E. An appeal to the opponents of the Maynooth grant: to which is added, a publication entitled, "Supplementary memoir," which was printed in June, 1844. 44, xivp. *8°.* 1845. *The copy that belonged to Earl De Grey.*

34448 —— Letter to the Rt. Hon. William Ewart Gladstone, M.P. respecting the Maynooth grant. [With an appendix.] 52, xxiip. *8°.* [1845] *The copy that belonged to Earl De Grey.*

34449 —— A short reply to a long speech [by R. J. M'Ghee] upon the Maynooth question: including testimony furnished by ministers of the Established Church... educated in Maynooth College. [With an appendix.] 10, xiiip. *8°.* 1845. *The copy that belonged to Earl De Grey.*

34450 M'GHEE, R. J. Maynooth. Speech of the Rev. R. J. M'Ghee...at the annual meeting of the Protestant Association, held...on...May 14, 1845... 16p. *8°.* [1845] *The copy that belonged to Earl De Grey.*

34451 MALLALIEU, A. Rosas and his calumniators. The justice and policy of a triple alliance intervention of England, France, and Brazil in the affairs of the River Plate considered in letters to the Right Honourable the Earl of Aberdeen. 111p. *8°.* 1845.

34452 The **MAYNOOTH** question. (Reprinted from the British Magazine for May, 1845.) 16p. *8°. [London,* 1845] *The copy that belonged to Earl De Grey.*

34453 *MAZZINI, G. Italy, Austria, and the Pope. A letter to Sir James Graham, Bart. 136p. *8°.* 1845. *The FWA copy that belonged to William Pare.*

34454 NATIONAL CHARTER ASSOCIA-TION, *Manchester.* Address of the General Council of the National Charter Association, to the inhabitants of Manchester & its vicinity. [Signed: John Murray, chairman. Maurice Donovan, secretary.] 4p. *8°. Manchester,* [c. 1845].

34455 "Perfect edition.⟩... The **PEOPLE'S CHARTER:** being the outline of an Act to provide for the just representation of the people of Great Britain and Ireland in the Commons' House of Parliament...Reprinted from the third edition, revised and corrected, from communications made by many associations in various parts of the Kingdom. 8p. *8°. [London:] A. Dyson,* [c. 1845] *For other editions, see* 1838.

34456 REPORT of the fourteenth anniversary of the Polish Revolution, celebrated at the Crown and Anchor Tavern, on the 29th of November, 1844. Dr. Bowring, M.P. in the chair. 36p. *8°.* 1845.

34457 THIRLWALL, C., *Bishop of St. David's.* Substance of a speech for the second reading of the Maynooth College Bill, in the House of Lords, on...June 4th, 1845. 24p. *8°. [London,* 1845] *The copy that belonged to Earl De Grey.*

34458 [WORDSWORTH, C., *Bishop of Lincoln.*] A review of the Maynooth Endowment Bill, shewing its fatal tendencies, and of the debates in the Commons, on the first and second reading; with a proposal for the conciliation of contending parties in Ireland. By the author of "Maynooth, the Crown, and the country." 149p. *8°.* 1845. *With a leaf before the title-page on which is printed 'With Dr. C. Wordsworth's best respects.' The copy that belonged to Earl De Grey.*

SOCIALISM

34459 BAUDET-DULARY, A. F. Projet de réalisation. 13p. *8°. Paris,* [1845] *With a manuscript inscription, 'à Vinçard – D.B.'.*

34460 BLANC, J. J. L. Organisation du travail... Quatrième édition considérablement augmentée... 283p. *8°. Bruxelles,* 1845. *See also* 1848.

34461 CONSIDÉRANT, V. P. Exposition abrégée du système phalanstérien de Fourier...3e édition: – 3e tirage. 114p. *16°. Paris,* 1845. *See also* 1846, 1848.

34462 ENGELS, F. and **MARX,** KARL (1188–1883). Die heilige Familie, oder, Kritik der kritischen Kritik. Gegen Bruno Bauer & Consorten. 335p. *8°. Frankfurt a. M.,* 1845.

34463 FOREST, P. Défense du Fouriérisme. M. Reybaud et l'Académie Française. MM. Rossi, Michel Chevalier, Blanqui, Wolowski. M. de Lamartine. 90p. *12°. Paris,* 1845. *The author's name is printed only on the wrapper.*

34464 FOURIER, F. C. M. Publication des manuscrits de Fourier. [Extracts from the 10 vols. of the octavo series of *La Phalange.*] 3 vols. *8°. [Paris,* 1845–49] *A second copy has the extracts arranged in the order of their publication in* La Phalange. *It belonged to Victor Considérant and has printed and manuscript additions and insertions, and a fourth volume of miscellaneous extracts.*

34465 GREAVES, J. P. Letters and extracts from the MS. writings of James Pierrepont Greaves...[Edited by Alexander Campbell.] 2 vols. *8°.* 1845. *With a manuscript inscription on the fly-leaf, 'To Robert Owen from his Social Son Alexander Campbell. Concordium Ham Common Surrey January 26th 1844 [sic]'. For another edition of vol. 1, see* 1843.

34466 GRUEN, K. Die soziale Bewegung in Frankreich und Belgien. Briefe und Studien. 471p. *8°. Darmstadt,* 1845.

34467 HOLYOAKE, G. J. Rationalism: a treatise for the times. 47p. *16°.* 1845. **Another, the FWA copy, belonged to William Pare.*

34468 [KING, WILLIAM, *of Charlotte Street, London.*] Money dialogue: or, a catechism on currency, exchanges, &c. By a member of the Bank of Industry. [With 'Currency. Over-trading – over-population – and over-production', from the *Sun* newspaper. Signed: W.K.] 28p. *12°.* 1845. *See note to no.* 28379.

34469 [——] Reasons why orders are not useful in promoting the progressive extention and concentration of banks of interchange. *s.sh.8°. n.p.* [c. 1845]

34470 LONDON BANK OF INDUSTRY. London Bank of Industry, no. 8. Margaret Street, Oxford

Street, is instituted for the interchange of all kinds of useful property...[A prospectus; by William King of Charlotte Street?] *s.sh.fol. n.p.* [1845?] *See note to no.* 28379.

34471 —— To the thinking and reflecting portion of the public. No. 3. [A pamphlet on the beneficial results of establishing banks of industry (issued first in 1821).] All who wish to implement the principles expressed in the pamphlet, are invited to apply to the Bank of Industry, 8, Margaret St., Cavendish Square. [4]p. *8°.* [*London,* 1845?]

34472 **MORGAN,** JOHN M. The Christian commonwealth. [With an appendix.] 40, xp. *fol.* 1845. *See also* 1846, 1850. *Presentation copy, with an accompanying letter, from the author to Professor Adam Sedgwick (1785–1873). For the letter, see vol.* III, *A.L.* 286.

34473 *OWEN, ROBERT. Address by Robert Owen, on leaving the United States for Europe, June 1, 1845. [Dated: New York, 24th May, 1845.] *s.sh.fol. n.p.* [1845] *The FWA copy that belonged to William Pare.*

34474 *—— To the Government of the United States. [An address on 'equal rights for all'. Dated: Washington City, March 12, 1845.] *s.sh.fol. n.p.* [1845] *A galley proof with a manuscript correction in Owen's hand. The FWA copy that belonged to William Pare.*

34475 *—— To the new President of the United States, and to his new cabinet. [Dated: Washington City, March 10, 1845.] *s.sh.fol. n.p.* [1845] *The FWA copy that belonged to William Pare.*

34476 **RENAUD,** H. Solidarité. Vue synthétique sur la doctrine de Ch. Fourier...Deuxième édition. 325p. *8°. Paris,* 1845. *For another edition, see* 1842.

34477 *W., J. A reply to the infidelity and atheism of socialism. By John Brindley. [A refutation of Brindley's work with this title.] 4p. *12°. n.p.* [*c.* 1845] *The FWA copy that belonged to William Pare.*

34478 **WEITLING,** W. C. Die Menschheit, wie sie ist und wie sie sein sollte...Zweite Auflage. 54p. *12°. Bern,* 1845.

MISCELLANEOUS

34479 **BOWES,** J. Second edition. A hired ministry unscriptural. 24p. *12°. Manchester,* [1845?] *See note to no.* 27827.

34480 —— Second edition...Scriptural reasons for giving up the sprinkling of infants, and adopting the immersion of believers, as the only Christian baptism. 16p. *16°. Paisley,* [*c.* 1845] *See note to no.* 27827.

34481 **BROUGHAM,** H. P., *Baron Brougham and Vaux.* Lord Brougham's speech on law reform, May 19, 1845. 34p. *8°.* 1845.

34482 **DALY,** R., *Bishop of Cashel, Emly, Waterford and Lismore.* Primary charge of the...Lord Bishop of Cashel, Waterford, and Lismore, delivered to the three dioceses in July, 1843. Third edition. 23p. *12°.* 1845. *The copy that belonged to Earl De Grey.*

34483 He would not neglect the **DEFENCE** of the country. What Sir R. Peel has to do to fulfill that promise, that word of his, to his country. 60p. *8°.* 1845.

34484 **FACTS** and observations, in reference to masters of the Royal Navy; with a plan for the removal of their disabilities. 15p. *8°.* 1845.

34485 **JONES,** THOMAS H., *Viscount Ranelagh.* Observations on the present state of our national defences. 30p. *8°.* 1845.

34486 **LOYAL NATIONAL REPEAL ASSOCIATION.** Report of the Parliamentary Committee of the...Association, on a Bill to enable town councils to establish museums of art in corporate towns. Read...14th April, 1845. 3p. *8°. Dublin,* [1845]

34487 —— Report of the Parliamentary Committee of the...Association on the general grand jury laws of Ireland. Read...on...December 1st, 1845. 28p. *8°. Dublin,* [1845]

34488 [**MACKIE,** A.] An extinguisher to atheism & infidelity: being a reply to Mr. Southwell's Roland for (what he calls) Dr. Massie's Oliver, proving him and all the "godless infidels" to be, "If atheists, fools; if not, liars." By the author of "A word to the dupes of Mrs. Martin & Co." 24p. *12°. Manchester,* 1845.

34489 —— A word to the dupes of Mrs. Martin, Messrs. Buchanan, Southwell, & Co. of the Hall of Science, Manchester. And a receipt for making money without working. 8p. *8°. Manchester,* [1845]

34490 **MARTINEAU,** H. Dawn island. A tale. 94p. *8°. Manchester,* 1845.

34491 **PHILLIPS,** P. I. The defence of the nation best intrusted to the working classes. Addressed to the common sense of the country. 8p. *8°.* [*London,* 1845?]

34492 **PYE,** J. Patronage of British art, an historical sketch: comprising an account of the rise and progress of art and artists in London from the beginning of the reign of George the Second...Illustrated with notes, historical, biographical and explanatory. 422p. *8°.* 1845.

34493 **SMITH,** SYDNEY (1771–1845). A fragment on the Irish Roman Catholic Church. 32p. *8°.* 1845.

34494 —— Second edition. 32p. *8°.* 1845.

34495 **SPECULATIVE SOCIETY.** History of the Speculative Society of Edinburgh from its institution in M.DCC.LXIV. [With an annotated list of members.] 485p. *4°. Edinburgh,* 1845.

34496 [**TITE,** SIR W.] A garland for the new Royal Exchange: composed of the pieces of divers excellent poets made in memory of the first opening thereof on January the 23rd, Anno Dom. 1571...written in honour of the second opening on September the 28th, 1669. Now first collected and printed complete. 98p. *4°.* 1845. *One of 50 copies printed.*

1846

GENERAL

34497 BAGSHAW, S. History, gazetteer and directory of Derbyshire, with the town of Burton-upon-Trent; comprising a general survey of the county, with... historical, statistical, topographical, commercial, and agricultural information... 702p. 8°. *Sheffield*, 1846.

34498 BANFIELD, T. C. Industry of the Rhine. Series I. Agriculture: embracing a view of the social condition of the rural population of that district. [With 'Series II. Manufactures: embracing a view of the social condition of the manufacturing population of that district'.] 2 vols. *12°.* 1846–48.

34499 BARBET, A. Système social et responsabilité de l'homme, ou de la nécessité du prêt par l'état, troisième force gouvernementale prenant sa base d'action sur les masses dans l'organisation du travail. 343p. 8°. *Paris*, 1846.

34500 The **BATTLE** of the ploughshares. Price, profit, and rent: their mutual relation in... British agriculture. By a landowner and a farmer. 32p. 8°. 1846.

34501 BERRY, C. The theory of trade, showing the operation of rent and tax. 71p. 8°. 1846.

34502 The **BRITISH ALMANAC** of the Society for the Diffusion of Useful Knowledge, for...1846... [With 'The companion to the Almanac; or, year-book of general information'.] 96, 260p. *12°.* [1846] *For other editions, see* 1828.

34503 BUCKINGHAM, J. S. Considerations on certain great social evils which still require to be amended or removed, in the most civilised nations. Discourse delivered in the French language at the Athenée Royale of Paris...the 7th of December, 1846. 40p. 8°. [1846]

34504 BURTON, JOHN H. Life and correspondence of David Hume... 2 vols. 8°. *Edinburgh*, 1846.

34504A CARUS, C. G. The King of Saxony's journey through England and Scotland in the year 1844... Translated by S. C. Davison. 391p. 8°. 1846.

34505 CLIFT, H. W. Elements of political economy: designed as a manual for education...Fourth edition. 221p. *12°. Calcutta*, 1846.

34506 COLTON, C. The life and times of Henry Clay...Second edition. 2 vols. 8°. *New York*, 1846.

34507 Some **CONSIDERATIONS** suggested by the loss of the potato, as a staple of food in Ireland; and its consequences as affecting the moral and domestic position of the peasantry. Addressed to Corry Connellan, Esq.... By a resident rector in...Leinster. 26p. 8°. *Dublin*, 1846.

34508 DAVENPORT, A. Origin of Man and the progress of society. 15p. *12°.* 1846.

34509 DROZ, J. F. X. Économie politique ou principes de la science des richesses...Seconde édition, revue et augmentée. 354p. 8°. *Paris*, 1846.

34510 —— [Another issue.] 354p. 8°. *Paris*, 1846. *For other editions, see* 1829.

34511 DUPONT-WHITE, C. B. Essai sur les relations du travail avec le capital. 444p. 8°. *Paris*, 1846.

34512 [ELLIS, WILLIAM (1800–1881).] Outlines of social economy. 77p. 8°. 1846. *Presentation copy from the author to H. Shaw Lefevre. See also* 1850, *and, for a sequel,* 1849 (Questions and answers).

34513 ENGLAND. Parliament. *House of Commons.* First and second Reports from the Select Committee appointed to inquire into...advances made by the Commissioners of Public Works in Ireland. Ordered... to be printed...1835. And reprinted by the Society for the Improvement of Ireland...200p. 8°. *Dublin*, 1846.

34514 ENSLIN, T. C. F. Bibliothek der Handlungswissenschaft oder Verzeichniss der vom Jahre 1750 bis zu Anfang des Jahres 1845 in Deutschland erschienenen Bücher...Nebst einem Nachtrage enthaltend die wichtigsten Schriften der englischen, französischen, holländischen, italienischen und spanischen Sprache, und eine Uebersicht der Eisenbahnliteratur...Zweite Auflage gänzlich umgearbeitet von Wilhelm Engelmann...255p. 8°. *Leipzig*, 1846.

34515 FITZGERALD, LORD W. Some suggestions for the better government of Ireland, addressed to the Marquis of Kildare. 52p. 8°. 1846.

34516 FLANDERS, *East. Conseil Provincial.* Exposé de la situation de la province de la Flandre-Orientale, pour l'année 1846. 300, cxlviiip. 8°. *Gand*, [1846?] *With the book-plate of the third Marquis of Lansdowne.*

34517 *FORD, RICHARD. Gatherings from Spain. By the author of The handbook of Spain; chiefly selected from that work...(*The Home and Colonial Library.*) 342p. 8°. 1846. *The copy that belonged to George Grote.*

34518 FOSTER, T. C. Letters on the condition of the people of Ireland...Reprinted, by permission, with additions and copious notes, from "The Times" newspaper. 771p. 8°. 1846. *Presentation copy from the author to Lord Hatherley, the Lord Chancellor.*

34519 GARNIER, C. J. Éléments de l'économie politique, exposé des notions fondamentales de cette science. 368p. 8°. *Paris*, 1846.

34520 [GOUGENOT-DESMOUSSEAUX, H. R.] Des prolétaires. Nécessité et moyens d'améliorer leur sort, par l'auteur du Monde avant le Christ. 568p. 8°. *Paris & Lyon*, 1846.

34521 [HARDINGE, H.] Common sense for the people, and facts for every body. 32p. 8°. 1846.

34522 HEEREN, A. H. L. Historical researches into the politics, intercourse, and trade of the principal nations of antiquity...Translated from the German [by D. A. Talboys and others]... 2 vols. 8°. 1846. *For other editions, see* 1824.

34523 [HOWITT, W.] The aristocracy of England: a history for the people. By John Hampden, junr. Second edition. 336p. 8°. 1846.

34524 KUDLER, J. Die Grundlehren der Volkswirtschaft. 2 vols. 8°. *Wien*, 1846.

For the **LATTER-DAY SAINTS' MILLENNIAL STAR**, 1846–54, *see* vol. III, *Periodicals list.*

For le **LIBRE-ÉCHANGE**, 1846–48, *see* vol. III, *Periodicals list.*

34525 M'CULLAGH, W. T. The industrial history of free nations, considered in relation to their domestic institutions and external policy. 2 vols. 8°. 1846.

34526 McCULLOCH, JOHN R. A. supplement to the edition of Mr. McCulloch's commercial dictionary published in 1844. 83p. 8°. 1846. *For editions of the main work, see* 1832.

34527 *[MARWELL, S.] Narrative of voyages to New South Wales and the East Indies, in 1840, 1842, and 1843, and to New York and the West Indies, in 1843 and 1844. 71p. 8°. 1846. *The copy that belonged to George Grote, inscribed in manuscript on the half-title 'by Samuel Marwell late footman in the service of Geo. Grote. Esq. 1846'.*

34528 MILES, H. A. Lowell, as it was, and as it is... Second edition. 234p. 12°. Lowell, 1846.

For the **NATIONAL REFORMER, AND MANX WEEKLY REVIEW**, 1846–47, *see* vol. III, *Periodicals list.*

34529 NICHOLS, JOHN G., *ed.* The chronicle of Calais in the reigns of Henry VII. and Henry VIII. to the year 1540. Edited from MSS. in the British Museum, by John Gough Nichols. (*Camden Society, Old Series*, 35.) xlii, 227p. 4°. 1846.

For the **PENNY SATIRIST AND LONDON PIONEER**, *see* vol. III, *Periodicals list.*

34530 POPE, C., *ed.* The yearly journal of trade, 1846 ...twenty-fourth edition. [With 'Pope's yearly journal of trade advertiser'.] 616p. 8°. [1846] *A reissue of the volume for 1845. See also* 1838, 1840, 1842, 1843, 1844, 1845. *The volume for 1854–5 is also in the Goldsmiths' Library.*

34531 PORTER, J. G. V. Some calm observations upon Irish affairs... 32p. 8°. Dublin & London, 1846.

34532 *QUETELET, L. A. J. Lettres à S.A.R. le Duc régnant de Saxe-Coburg et Gotha, sur la théorie des probabilités, appliquée aux sciences morales et politiques. 450p. 8°. Bruxelles, 1846. *The copy that belonged to Augustus De Morgan. See also* 1849.

For the **REASONER**, 1846–47, 1849–53, 1855–60, *continued as* the Counsellor on secular, cooperative and political questions, 1861, *then* the Secular world, 1862–63, *see* vol. III, *Periodicals list*, Reasoner.

34533 RICARDO, D. The works of David Ricardo, Esq., M.P., with a notice of the life and writings of the author by J. R. McCulloch, Esq., xxxiii, 584p. 8°. 1846. *For a separate edition of McCulloch's introduction, see* 1825.

34534 ST. GALLISCH-APPENZELLISCHE GEMEINNÜTZIGE GESELLSCHAFT. Verhandlungen der... Gesellschaft an der Hauptversammlung in Teufen...den 28. Mai 1846. 312p. 8°. St. Gallen & Bern, 1846.

34535 SAY, H. Études sur l'administration de la ville de Paris et du département de la Seine. 484p. 8°. Paris, 1846. *Presentation copy, with inscription, from the author to Richard Cobden.*

34536 SCHNITZLER, J. H. Statistique générale méthodique et complète de la France comparée aux autres grandes puissances de l'Europe... 4 vols. 8°. Paris, 1846.

34537 SHATTUCK, L. Report to the committee of the City Council appointed to obtain the census of Boston for...1845, embracing collateral facts and statistical researches, illustrating the history and condition of the population, and their means of progress and prosperity. [With an appendix.] 179, 95p. 8°. Boston, 1846.

34538 SLATER, I. I. Slater's national commercial directory of Ireland: including in addition to the trades' lists, alphabetical directories of Dublin, Belfast, Cork and Limerick. To which are added, classified directories of the important English towns...With a...map of Ireland... 9 parts. 8°. Manchester & London, 1846.

34539 SOCIETY FOR THE IMPROVEMENT OF IRELAND. Report of the Committee of the Society...as adopted at the public meeting of the citizens of Dublin...held 21st May, 1846, at the Music Hall, Abbey-street... 43p. 8°. Dublin, 1846. *See also* 1828, 1829.

34540 SOCIETY FOR THE PROTECTION OF AGRICULTURE AND BRITISH INDUSTRY. Tracts. 21 parts. 8°. [*London*, 1846] *A collection of pamphlets originally separately published by other publishers, reissued with a general title-page. Contents: E. S. Cayley, Reasons for the formation of the Agricultural Protection Society; Sir A. Alison, Free trade and protection; G. G. Day, Defeat of the Anti-Corn-Law League in Huntingdonshire. The speech...June 17, 1843; Idem, The farmers and the League. The speech...January 27, 1844; A. S. O'Brien, History of the League. The speech...June 26, 1844; J. B. Sharp, The Anti-Corn-Law League and the cotton trade; Anon., Protection of British agriculture; Humanitas, Free trade; Anon., American notions of free trade; J. Almack, Cheap bread and low wages; Anon., To artisans and labourers; Anon., Corn laws; Anon., A letter from a crow to Mr. Cobden; G. Townsend and J. Tyson, The substance of two speeches...Feb. 20, 1844; J. Haddon, The substance of a speech...15th day of March, 1844; J. Barton, The influence of the price of corn on the rate of mortality; R. Baker, An answer...to Earl Ducie; Opinions of Sir Robert Peel and Sir James Graham on the corn-laws in 1839; R. B. Seeley, The corn laws. Speech...December 29, 1845; Anon., A few words to the industrious classes. By one of themselves; Lord W. G. F. C. Bentinck, Sir Robert Peel's commercial policy. Speech...February 27, 1846. All but the last four were previously issued in a collection published in 1844 (q.v.).*

34541 STIRLING, P. J. The philosophy of trade; or, outlines of a theory of profits and prices, including an examination of the principles which determine the relative value of corn, labour, and currency. 380p. 8°. Edinburgh & London, 1846.

34542 THORNTON, WILLIAM T. Over-population and its remedy; or, an inquiry into the extent and causes of the distress prevailing among the labouring classes of the British Islands, and into the means of remedying it. 446p. 8°. 1846.

For the **TOPIC**, 1846–47, *see* vol. III, *Periodicals list.*

34543 TUCKETT, J. D. A history of the past and present state of the labouring population, including the progress of agriculture, manufactures and commerce... 2 vols. 8°. London & Plymouth, 1846.

34544 WARDELL, J. The municipal history of the borough of Leeds, in the county of York, from the earliest period to the election of the first mayor...on the 1st January, 1836; including numerous extracts from the court books of the Corporation, and an appendix containing copies and translations of charters, and other documents relating to the borough. 96, ccxixp. *8°. London & Leeds*, 1846.

34545 WATERSTON, W. A cyclopædia of commerce, mercantile law, finance, commercial geography, and navigation...New edition, containing the present tariff, and an essay on commerce written for the Society of Promoting Useful Knowledge by J. R. McCulloch, Esq. 128, 684, 21, 39p. *8°. 1846. For another edition, see 1843.*

34546 WHITE, WILLIAM (*fl.* 1826–1870). History, gazetteer, and directory of Leicestershire, and the small county of Rutland; together with the adjacent towns of Grantham & Stamford; comprising general surveys of both counties, and separate historical, statistical, & topo-

graphical descriptions of all their...towns... 704p. *12°. Sheffield*, 1846.

34547 [WILSON, THOMAS, *Chevalier de l'Ordre du Lion Néerlandais.*] Essai sur l'économie politique d'Angleterre, considérée dans ses rapports avec les richesses nationales, son agriculture, son industrie et son commerce, par T.-W. 98p. *8°. Bruxelles, 1846. *Another, the FWA copy, was presented by the author, with a signed manuscript note, to William Pare, whose notes it also contains.*

34548 WYSE, F. America, its realities and resources: comprising important details connected with the present social, political, agricultural, commercial and financial state of the country, its laws and customs, together with a review of the policy of the United States...the Texas and Oregon questions, etc. etc. 3 vols. *8°. 1846.*

AGRICULTURE

34549 AGRICOLA, *pseud.* How to supply the home market from British land and labour, and thereby supersede the corn laws. 26p. *8°. 1846.*

34550 ALMACK, B. Hints to landowners. On tenure, prices, rents, &c. 70p. *8°. 1846.*

34551 BEAMISH, N. L. Remedy for the impending scarcity [the reclamation of waste land]; suggested by a visit to the Kilkerrin estate of the Irish Waste Land Improvement Society. 49p. *8°. Cork, 1846.*

34552 BISHOP, JAMES (*fl.* 1846–1847). A new and popular abstract of the English laws respecting landlords, tenants, and lodgers. Containing...information respecting letting and taking of houses...laws relative to lodgings and lodgers...The sixth edition, improved. The whole re-written from the latest authorities. 54p. *12°. [1846?]*

34553 COLMAN, H. European agriculture and rural economy. From personal observation. Vol. 1. *8°. Boston & London, 1846.*

34554 CONNER, W. Two letters to the editor of The Times, on the rackrent oppression of Ireland, its course – its evils – and its remedy, in reply to The Times Commissioner... xxvii, 36p. *8°. Dublin, 1846. Two copies, one a presentation copy from the author to Sir Robert Peel, the other bound in a collection made by John Stuart Mill of the author's works on the land question in Ireland; see note to no. 27313.*

34555 COOKE, GEORGE W. The Act for the enclosure of commons in England and Wales: with a treatise on the law of rights of commons, in reference to this Act... 331p. *12°. 1846.*

34556 DICKSON, J. H. A series of letters on the improved mode in the cultivation of flax; with various rules...on the...qualities of flax adapted to spin into the different numbers of yarns; also, several tables calculated to guide the merchant in his purchases, and the manufacturer in the...method of giving out yarns to be wove into linens, lawns...and handkerchiefs... 248p. *8°. 1846.*

34557 EDEN, T. E. The search for nitre, and the true nature of guano, being an account of a voyage to the south-west coast of Africa; also a description of the minerals found there, and of the guano islands in that part of the world. 133p. *12°. London, Liverpool, &c., 1846.*

34558 HAMILTON, CHARLES W. Short hints to

the small farmers in Ireland, on the question What shall we substitute for the potato? 30p. *12°. Dublin, 1846.*

34559 [HORNE, THOMAS H.] The complete grazier; or, farmer's and cattle breeder's and dealer's assistant... By a Lincolnshire grazier...Eighth edition: edited enlarged, and partly re-written by William Youatt... 692p. *8°. 1846. For other editions, see 1805.*

34560 KARKEEK, W. F. The report on the farming of Cornwall; to which the prize was awarded by the Royal Agricultural Society of England. 66p. *8°. 1846.*

34561 MAC NEVIN, T. The confiscation of Ulster, in the reign of James the First, commonly called the Ulster Plantation...Second edition. 260p. *12°. Dublin & London, 1846.*

34562 MARYLAND AND NEW YORK IRON AND COAL COMPANY. Charters and by-laws of the Maryland and New-York Iron and Coal Company. [Largely concerned with their right to build a rail road and roads.] 18p. *12°. New-York, 1846.*

34563 MOUNIER, L. De l'agriculture en France, d'après les documents officiels...avec des remarques par M. Rubichon... 2 vols. *8°. Paris, 1846.*

34564 PARKIN, J. The cause of blight and pestilence in the vegetable creation; with suggestions for the development of other supplies of food during the present crisis. 15p. *8°. 1846.*

34565 PASSY, H. P. Des systèmes de culture et de leur influence sur l'économie sociale. [With 'Appendice. De la répartition de la propriété territoriale et des progrès du morcellement en France'.] 177p. *8°. Paris, 1846. See also 1848.*

34566 SEWELL, H. A letter to Lord Worsley, on the burthens affecting real property arising from the present state of the law; with reasons in favour of a general registry of titles. 110p. *8°. 1846.*

34567 SKILLING, T. The science and practice of agriculture. 275p. *12°. Dublin & London, 1846.*

34568 WARNES, J. On the cultivation of flax; the fattening of cattle with native produce; box-feeding; and summer-grazing... 321p. *8°. 1846.*

34569 WELFORD, R. G. The influence of the game laws; being classified extracts from the evidence taken before a Select Committee of the House of Commons on the game laws, and some introductory remarks...With an appendix, and an address to the tenant farmers of Great Britain, by John Bright, Esq., M.P. 429, lxxxip. *8°. 1846.* *The copy that belonged to Sir William Molesworth, with his book-plate.*

CORN LAWS

34570 Some **ACCOUNT** of the corn laws and their operation: designed to elucidate the approaching debates ...Reprinted from "the Daily News," of January 28, 1846. 32p. *8°. 1846.*

34571 **ACRÆUS,** *pseud.* God's laws versus corn-laws. A letter to His Grace the Archbishop of Canterbury. From a dignitary of the English Church. 51p. *8°. London, Edinburgh, &c., 1846.*

34572 **ASPINALL,** J. Speech of the Rev. J. Aspinall, delivered at a meeting held at the Town Hall, Hull, on Monday, May 25th, to petition the House of Lords in favour of Sir Robert Peel's Corn Bill...⟨From the Hull Advertiser of May 29th, 1846.⟩ 11p. *12°. Hull,* [1846]

34573 —— Speech of the Rev. James Aspinall, M.A., Rector of Althorpe, Lincolnshire, delivered at a festival of free-traders, held at the Mechanics' Institute, Hull, on ...July 22, 1846. 11p. *12°. Hull,* [1846]

34574 **BENTINCK,** LORD WILLIAM G. F. C. Protection triumph. Speech of Lord George Bentinck on the Corn Importation Bill, March 26. Corrected by himself. 15p. *8°.* [*London,*] 1846.

34575 **BROWN,** THOMAS, *of Brighton.* Letter from Mr. Brown to W. W. Burrell, Esq., of Knepp Castle, showing the danger that will ensue from free trade in corn. 4p. *8°. Brighton,* [1846]

34576 **C.** An address on the corn laws. By a protectionist. 42p. *8°. 1846.*

34577 **CORN** and consistency. A few remarks in reply to a pamphlet entitled "Sir Robert Peel and the corn law crisis." 54p. *8°. 1846.*

34578 [**CREWE,** H. R.] The repeal of the corn laws, and other measures of these latter days, considered in their relation to the rights of God and the rights of man. By one who fears God, and regards man. 32p. *8°. London & Derby, 1846. The copy presented to T. Perronet Thompson, with a letter written on the verso of the title and the blank leaf at the end, by W. G. Burns. For the letter, see vol.* III, *A.L.* 269.

34579 **DEATH** of the Corn Bill. [A ballad.] *s.sh.fol. n.p.* [1846] [*Br.* 612]

34580 **ENGLAND.** *Parliament.* The battle for native industry. The debate upon the corn laws, the Corn Importation and Customs' Duties Bills, and the other financial measures of the Government, in session 1846. Reprinted...from "Hansard's Parliamentary Debates." ...[The preface signed: A.S.O'B., i.e. A. S. O'Brien.] 2 vols. *8°. The Society for the Protection of Agriculture and British Industry,* [1846]

34581 **GLADSTONE,** SIR J., *Bart.* Plain facts intimately connected with the intended repeal of the corn laws, its probable effects on the public revenue, and the prosperity of this country. Addressed to all classes, in the United Kingdom and her colonies. 31p. *8°. 1846.*

34582 [**GREVILLE,** C. C. F.] Sir Robert Peel and the corn law crisis. 33p. *8°. 1846.*

34583 **HAINWORTH,** W. Free trade fallacies refuted. Remarks on a pamphlet by Mr. John Morton, F.G.S., and Mr. Joshua Trimmer, F.G.S., entitled "An attempt to estimate the effects of protecting duties on the profits of agriculture." 28p. *8°. 1846.*

34584 Upon the probable **INFLUENCE** of a repeal of the corn laws, upon the trade in corn. 46p. *8°. 1846.*

34585 **KING,** PETER, *7th Baron King.* A short history of the job of jobs...Written in 1825. 16p. *8°. 1846.*

34586 **LANE,** S. The landowners thrown overboard; or, Bob Peel coming to his senses. [A ballad on the repeal of the corn laws.] *s.sh.fol. Norwich,* [1846] [*Br.* 613]

34587 **MORTON,** JOHN (1781–1864) and **TRIMMER,** JOSHUA. An attempt to estimate the effects of protecting duties on the profits of agriculture...Fifth edition. 86p. *8°. 1846.*

34588 —— Sixth edition. [With an appendix, containing a letter by C. H. Lattimore to the *Mark Lane Express.*] 92p. *8°. 1846. For another edition, see 1845.*

34589 —— Supplement to An attempt to estimate the effects of protecting duties...bring a vindication of its data and conclusions. 59p. *8°. 1846.*

34590 **NEVILE,** C. Corn and currency...In a letter to A. Alison, Esq. Second edition. 43p. *8°. 1846.*

34591 **P.,** M. Letter to Sir Robert Peel, on the mode of meeting the present crisis. From M.P., a supporter (hitherto) of the League. 34p. *8°. 1846.*

34592 A political **PARODY** on Tubal Cain. [A ballad in praise of Peel and the Anti-Corn-Law League.] *s.sh.fol.* [*London,* 1846] [*Br.* 615]

34593 **POPKINS,** , *pseud.* Corn laws. Popkins' protest: addressed to the House of Lords. 15p. *8°. 1846.*

For **SEELEY,** R. B. The corn laws. Speech of a wholesale trader of London, December 29, 1845, 1846, *see no.* 34540.

34594 **TEMPLE,** H. J., *Viscount Palmerston.* Speech of Viscount Palmerston, in the House of Commons, on Friday, March 27, 1846, on the second reading of the Bill for the repeal of the corn laws. 26p. *8°. 1846.*

34595 **VECK,** TOBY, *pseud.* "Facts and figures." No. I. Ten tables telling of "my landlord" and "the Church"... 31p. *8°. 1846.*

34596 **WHITMORE,** W. W. A third letter to the agriculturists of the County of Salop...January 24, 1846. 13p. *12°.* [1846]

34597 A few **WORDS** on the corn laws. By a landowner. 35p. *8°. 1846.*

34598 A few **WORDS** on the repeal of the corn laws. 44p. *8°. 1846.*

34599 **WYSE,** F. A letter addressed to the Right Honorable Lord Stanley, on the proposed repeal of the corn laws, and its injurious consequence to the well-being and prosperity of Ireland. 14p. *8°. Dublin,* 1846.

POPULATION

34600 DOUBLEDAY, T. The true law of population shewn to be connected with the food of the people. Second edition. 278p. 8°. 1846. *A reissue, without the postscript, of the second edition, 1843 (q.v.).*

34601 VERHULST, P. F. Deuxième mémoire sur la loi d'accroissement de la population. [From *Mémoires de l'Académie Royale de Bruxelles,* vol. 20.] 32p. 4°. n.p. [1846]

TRADES & MANUFACTURES

34601A BABBAGE, C. On the economy of machinery and manufactures...Fourth edition, enlarged. 408p. 8°. 1846. *Presentation copy, with inscription, from the author to the Duchess of Somerset. A reprint, without the preface, of the 4th edition, 1835 (q.v.). For other editions, see 1832.*

34602 BECKMANN, J. A history of inventions, discoveries, and origins...Translated from the German, by William Johnston. Fourth edition...revised and enlarged by William Francis...and J. W. Griffith. (*Bohn's Standard Library.*) 2 vols. 8°. 1846. *For other editions, see 1797.*

34603 BOURNE, JOHN, *C.E., ed.* A treatise on the steam engine in its application to mines, mills, steam navigation, and railways. By the Artizan Club. Edited by John Bourne... 259p. 4°. 1846.

34604 HICK, BENJAMIN, **& SON.** A list of new wheel patterns made on a correct principle, and with perfect mechanical accuracy, belonging to Benjamin Hick & Son, Engineers, Brass & Iron Founders, Soho Iron Works, Bolton, May 1846. 74p. 8°. *Bolton,* [1846]

34605 HINDMARCH, W. M. A treatise on the law relating to patent privileges for the sole use of inventions; and the practice of obtaining Letters Patents for inventions; with an appendix of statutes, rules, forms, &c.&c. 807p. 8°. *London & Dublin,* 1846.

34606 LE PLAY, P. G. F. Mémoire sur la fabrication et le commerce des fers à acier dans le nord de l'Europe, et sur les questions soulevées depuis un siècle et demi par l'emploi de ces fers dans les aciéries françaises. 194p. 8°. *Paris,* 1846.

34607 MARTIN, WILLIAM (1772–1851). On the high level bridge. [In verse.] *s.sh.*8°. *Newcastle,* [1846]

34608 The present **SHIP-BUILDING CONTROVERSY;** or, which is the misrepresented party? Illustrated by a few examples, shewing the difference between "facts" and "fictions." By a naval architect. 48p. 8°. 1846.

34609 Corrected to 1846. The thirty-sixth edition of **SKYRING'S** builders' prices and weekly journal... Enlarged abstract of the new Buildings Act [7 & 8 Vict., cap. 84]...[Compiled by W. H. Skyring.] 185p. 8°. 1846. *See also* 1812, 1818, 1819, 1827, 1831, 1838, 1845.

34610 SOPWITH, T. Reports on the iron works, manufacturing establishments, and mineral property at Couvin, in the district of the Sambre and Meuse, in Belgium. By T. Sopwith and T. Macdougall Smith. 36p. 8°. 1846.

34611 TIZARD, W. L. The theory and practice of brewing...[Second edition.] 591p. 8°. 1846.

34612 URE, A. Recent improvements in arts, manufactures, and mines: being the second edition of a supplement to the third edition of his Dictionary, by Andrew Ure. 311p. 8°. 1846. *For editions of* A dictionary of arts, manufactures, and mines, *see* 1839.

COMMERCE

34613 An **APPEAL** on behalf of the British subjects residing in and connected with the River Plate, against any further violent intervention by the British and French Governments in the affairs of that country. 43p. 8°. [*London,*] 1846.

34614 ASSOCIATION BELGE POUR LA LIBERTÉ COMMERCIALE. Première séance publique de l'Association...tenue en la salle de la philharmonie, 11 octobre, 1846. 27p. 8°. *Bruxelles,* 1846.

34615 Brief **CONSIDERATIONS** with reference to the corn laws, and on the theory of protection generally. 40p. 8°. 1846.

34616 —— Additional remarks [to Brief considerations] on the effect produced on a country's trade by foreign duties on its exports. 22p. 8°. 1846.

34617 DRUMMOND, H. Letter to the Bishop of Winchester on free trade. 44p. 8°. 1846.

34618 DUNN, M. A review of a pamphlet entitled "Observations addressed to the coal owners of Northumberland and Durham, on the coal trade of those counties ...By T. John Taylor, 1846." [With 'Proposed regulation of the coal trade'.] 15p. 8°. *Newcastle-upon-Tyne,* 1846.

34619 EDINBURGH. Edinburgh markets and customs. [Circular letter addressed to Thomas Ker, one of the occupiers of property affected, by the city clerks, C. Cuningham and Carlyle Bell, with a 'Plan of part of the Grassmarket of Edinburgh. Shewing the lands proposed to be acquired for the enlargement of the meal, corn & grain markets'.] [4]p. *fol.* [*Edinburgh,* 1846]

34620 EDINBURGH markets and customs. Heads of a Bill to enlarge and improve the meal, corn, and grain markets of...Edinburgh, and further to amend an Act passed in the third year of the reign of Her present Majesty, for abolishing certain petty and market customs ... 9p. *fol.* n.p. [1846]

34621 EDINBURGH markets and customs. Heads of a Bill to enlarge and improve the meal, corn, and grain markets of...Edinburgh, and for other purposes in relation thereto. 10p. *fol.* [*Edinburgh,*] 1846.

34622 FIFE, *County of.* Fife fiars, from 1619 to 1845 inclusive, reckoned in Scots money from 1619 to 1787, and in sterling money from 1787 to 1845. To which is prefixed the Act of Sederunt, dated December 21, 1723, for regulating the proceedings. 69p. *12°. Cupar,* 1846. *Spaces for continuations for the years 1846–54 have not been filled in. See also 1842.*

34623 FREE TRADE; or, the coalition. [A ballad.] *s.sh.fol.* [*London,* 1846] [*Br.* 614]

34624 Our **FREE TRADE POLICY** examined with respect to its real bearing upon native industry, our colonial system, and the institutions and ultimate destinies of the nation. By a Liverpool merchant. 46p. *8°. London & Liverpool,* 1846. *Sometimes attributed to Henry Arthur Bright. The copy that belonged to T. Spring Rice, Baron Monteagle.*

34625 FREE TRADE TAXATION. The principles of Sir Robert Peel's new tariff examined. 34p. *8°.* 1846.

34626 LEITH. Case for the Provost, magistrates, and town council of Leith [in support of the proposed measure for abolishing the existing petty customs and substituting a small tax upon the tonnage of goods brought into the harbour of Leith. With a covering letter signed: Thos. Hutchison, Provost.] 4, 3p. *fol. n.p.* [1846] *Addressed in manuscript to 'Mr. Thomas Ker, St. Leonards Edin'.*

34627 LIBERTÉ du commerce. Collection de documents, pièces et matériaux, sans commentaires. 59p. *8°. Paris,* 1846.

34628 LIVERPOOL ANTI-MONOPOLY AS- SOCIATION. Progress of free trade in 1845. Fourth annual report of the Council of the...Association, for the year 1845, read at the annual meeting of the members, held March 9, 1846; the treasurers' account, and a list of members. 43p. *8°. Liverpool,* 1846.

34629 MARTIN, Robert M. Reports, minutes and despatches, on the British position and prospects in China. 134p. *8°.* [1846]

34630 OFFLEY, WEBBER AND FORRESTER. Second representation made by Offley, Webber, & Forrester of Oporto, to their correspondents, respecting the recent discussions on the subject of port-wine. 27p. *8°. Oporto,* 1846. *See note to no.* 33856.

34631 —— Third representation... 31p. *8°. Oporto,* 1846. *See note to no.* 33856.

34632 SOETBEER, A. Statistik des hamburgischen Handels. 1842. 1843. 1844. (*Ueber Hamburgs Handel,* dritter Theil.) 322p. *8°. Hamburg,* 1846. *For the original work,* Ueber Hamburgs Handel, *see* 1840; *for an earlier continuation, see* 1842.

34633 SPARKHALL, E. A broad hint to the manufacturers, on the subject of corn, coals, steam, and machinery. Or, a first impression from a seal intended for the lips of the free-trade advocates. 24p. *8°.* 1846.

34634 TAYLOR, Thomas J. Observations, addressed to the coal owners of Northumberland and Durham, on the coal trade of those counties: more especially with regard to the cause of, and remedy for, its present depressed condition. 56p. *8°. Newcastle,* 1846.

For A few **WORDS** to the industrious classes. By one of themselves, 1846, *see no.* 34540.

COLONIES

34635 [**ANDREW,** Sir William P.] Indian railways; as connected with the power, and stability of the British Empire in the East; the development of its resources, and the civilization of its people...By an old Indian postmaster. Second edition. 174p. *8°. London, Dublin, &c.,* 1846. *See also* 1848.

34636 BRAIM, T. H. A history of New South Wales, from its settlement to the close of the year 1844... 2 vols. *12°.* 1846.

34637 BRITISH GUIANA. No. 17...1846. ⟨Court of Policy.⟩ An Ordinance to amend Ordinance No. 18, of the year 1844, entituled "An Ordinance to establish Administrators-General in the colony of British Guiana." 8p. *fol.* [*Georgetown,* 1846]

34638 DESJOBERT, A. L'Algérie en 1846. 118p. *8°. Paris,* 1846.

34639 DUTTON, F. South Australia and its mines, with an historical sketch of the colony, under its several administrations, to the period of Captain Grey's departure. 361p. *8°.* 1846.

34640 HAYDON, G. H. Five years' experience in Australia Felix, comprising a short account of its early settlement and its present position, with many particulars interesting to intending emigrants... 168p. *8°. London & Exeter,* 1846. *Presentation copy from the author to Charles Blake.*

34641 HEAD, Sir F. B., *Bart.* The emigrant... Third edition. 441p. *8°.* 1846.

34642 HISTORY of the campaign on the Sutlej, and the war in the Punjaub, from the most authentic sources, including copious original information, memoirs of many distinguished officers...and official lists of the killed and wounded... 69p. *8°.* 1846.

34643 *JACOB, Sir George Le G. Extract from a report on the District of Babriawar...dated the 15th March 1843. 10p. *8°. Bombay,* 1846.

34644 RAILWAYS in India; being several articles reprinted from The Railway Register. Third edition... 64p. *8°.* 1846. *This edition is without the 'Advertisement' signed 'H.O.' printed in the edition of 1845 (q.v.).*

34645 S., J. The moral and pecuniary evils which the free colonists of Van Diemen's Land are suffering from the conversion of that island into the chief receptacle of British convicts. (For private circulation.) 12p. *8°.* [*London,* 1846]

34646 UNION AGRICOLE D'AFRIQUE. L'Union Agricole d'Afrique; nouveau système de colonisation de l'Algérie. 136p. *8°. Lyon,* 1846. *The copy that belonged to Victor Considérant.*

34647 WEST INDIA PLANTERS AND MERCHANTS. ⟨Printed for the West India Body.⟩ Report of the Acting Committee to the Standing Committee...at their half-yearly meeting, held on the 11th March, |1846. 50p. *8°*. [1846] *See also* 1847, 1848, 1849.

34648 WILLIAMSON, THOMAS, *H.E.I.C.S.* Two

letters on the advantages of railway communication in western India, addressed to the Right Hon. Lord Wharncliffe...[With 'Notes on the cotton traffic of western Berar' by R. H. Fenwick.] 38p. *8°*. 1846.

FINANCE

34649 AKERMAN, J. Y. Ancient coins of cities and princes, geographically arranged and described...Hispania – Gallia – Britannia. 203p. *8°*. *London & Paris*, 1846.

34650 ALISON, SIR A., *Bart.* England in 1815 and 1845; or, a sufficient and contracted currency...Third edition, revised and enlarged, with a postscript containing a reply to the observations of the Right Honourable Sir Robert Peel, Bart. 133p. *8°*. *Edinburgh & London*, 1846. *For other editions, see* 1845.

34651 APPLETON, N. What is a revenue standard? and a review of Secretary Walker's report on the tariff. [From the National intelligencer.] 23p. *8°*. *Boston*, 1846.

34652 ASSOCIATION OF LONDON AND COUNTRY SOAP MANUFACTURERS. Case of the soap duties. Printed for the Committee of the Association... 19p. *8°*. 1846. *The copy given to Col. C. R. Fox, M.P., with accompanying letter, by Richard and John Wheen, soap manufacturers. For the letter, see vol. III, A.L. 256.*

34653 AYRES, H. To landlord and tenant farmers. The repeal of the malt-tax: and its effect on land, labour, and commerce. With an explanation of the art of making malt, and the mode of calculating the duty; also a statistical account of the malting trade for the last hundred years. 32p. *8°*. 1846. *Presentation copy from the author to T. Banister.*

34654 B., W. The comparative merits of direct and indirect taxation. 27p. *8°*. 1846.

34655 Good and cheap **BEER** for the million, by the use of sugar & molasses in public breweries. 35p. *8°*. *London, Liverpool, &c.*, 1846.

34656 BENTINCK, LORD WILLIAM G. F. C. Sir Robert Peel's commercial policy. Speech of Lord George Bentinck, member for King's Lynn, in the House of Commons, on...February 27, 1846. 42p. *8°*. 1846. *For another issue, see no.* 34540.

34657 BRITISH LINEN COMPANY. List of proprietors of stock of the British Linen Company, incorporated by Royal Charter 1746. 17p. *4°*. *Edinburgh*, 1846. *See also* 1819, 1845, *and no.* 34686.

34658 The **BRITISH TARIFF** (formerly edited by Robert Ellis, Esq.)...By Edwin Beedell... 372p. *12°*. 1846. *See also* 1829, 1832, 1834, 1848.

34659 BRODRIBB, E. Published by the Liverpool Association for the Reduction of the Duty on Tea. Abstract of a letter to the Right Hon. Sir R. Peel, Bart. First Lord of Her Majesty's Treasury, etc. on the tea duties. 14p. *8°*. *Liverpool & London*, [1846]

34660 BUELOW-CUMMEROW, E. G. G. VON. Das normale Geldsystem in seiner Anwendung auf Preussen. 75p. *8°*. *Berlin*, 1846.

34661 CARROLL, E. A. Tariff, or rates of duties from and after the first day of December, 1846, on all goods, wares and merchandise imported into the United

States of America...Collated and compiled by E. A. Carroll, Ship and Insurance Broker... 127p. *12°*. *Philadelphia*, 1846. *See also the edition compiled by E. D. Ogden and published in 1850.*

34662 CHARITABLE TRUSTS' BILL. An address to the Lords spiritual and temporal of Great Britain and Ireland, showing cause why the Bill should not pass into a law. 30p. *8°*. 1846.

34663 CLÉMENT, P. Histoire de la vie et de l'administration de Colbert, contrôleur général des finances ...précédé d'une étude historique sur Nicolas Fouquet, surintendant des finances. Suivie de pièces justificatives, lettres et documents inédits. 520p. *8°*. *Paris*, 1846.

34664 COMMITTEE OF MERCHANTS AND TRADERS...APPOINTED TO PROMOTE THE IMPROVEMENT OF THE LAW RELATING TO DEBTOR AND CREDITOR. [*Endorsed:*] Bankruptcy and insolvency law amendment. Proceedings of a public meeting...held at the London Tavern, 16th February, 1846, to receive the report of the Committee thereon. 7p. *fol.* [1846] *See note to no.* 32762.

34665 —— Bankruptcy and Insolvency Law Amendment Act. [*Begin.*] At a public meeting held at the London tavern on the 16th inst...[An appeal for funds.] [2]p. *s.sh.fol. n.p.* [1846] *See note to no.* 32762.

34666 A **CONTRAST** between the rival systems of banking. By a country manager. 43p. *8°*. *London & Nottingham*, 1846. *The copy that belonged to William Hawes (1805–1885).*

34667 CRAWFORD, JOHN, *of Paisley.* The philosophy of wealth...Second edition. 102p. *8°*. 1846. *For other editions, see* 1837.

For **DEUTSCHE VIERTELJAHRES-SCHRIFT** *see vol.* III, *Periodicals list.*

34668 DUNCAN, JONATHAN. How to reconcile the rights of property, capital, and labour. (*Currency Reform Association*, Tract 1.) 55p. *8°*. 1846.

34669 ELLIOTT, W. A plea for building societies; or, a word on their principles and practice. 35p. *12°*. 1846.

34670 ENGLAND. *Poor Law Commission* [*1834–1847*]. The local taxes of the United Kingdom: containing a digest of the law, with a summary of statistical information concerning the several local taxes in England, Scotland, and Ireland. Published under the direction of the Poor Law Commissioners. 280p. *8°*. 1846.

34671 An **EXPOSURE** of the knavery of pawnbrokers, and ample and clear detail of the charges which they ought to make according to law, and to the Act of Parliament...By a barrister at law. 11p. *12°*. 1846.

34672 FANE, R. G. C. A letter to Lord Cottenham, on the present position of Her Majesty's Commissioners of the Court of Bankruptcy, and suggesting a more extended use of that Court in matters of account. 16p. *8°*.

1846. The copy that belonged to T. Spring Rice, Baron Monteagle.

34673 —— [*Endorsed:*] Society for Promoting the Amendment of the Law. Paper on the law of debtor and creditor... 6p. *fol.* [1846 ?] *See note to no.* 32762.

34674 ⟨Extracted from the Law Review, Nov. 1846.⟩ **FRAUDS** under the bankruptcy laws. Mr. Warburton's Bill to restore arrest. 23p. *8º. n.p.* [1846] *See note to no.* 32762.

34675 [**GIBBON,** A.] A familiar treatise on taxation, free trade, etc. comprising facts usually unnoticed in theories of those subjects. With notes on subjects arising incidentally. 324p. *8º.* 1846. *Presentation copy to the editor of the Quarterly Review 'from the author'. The copy afterwards belonged to Cliffe Leslie. A second copy (with an inscription to the Bishop of Llandaff) contains all but p. 1–42, and there is in the library a copy of p. 1–42 with title and 'advertisement' (dated February 16, 1846, and not present in the other copies) which says that this early portion (chapters 1–2) has been published first. On the authorship of this work see note to no.* 33771.

34676 **GOULBURN,** H. Financial statement. Speech of the Right Hon. H. Goulburn, (Chancellor of the Exchequer,) in the House of Commons on...May 29, 1846. Extracted from Hansard's Parliamentary Debates. 27p. *8º.* 1846. *The copy that belonged to T. Spring Rice, Baron Monteagle.*

34677 [**HOLLOWAY,** W. ?] Essay on the repeal of the malt-tax, for which a prize of twenty pounds was awarded by the [Total Repeal Malt-Tax] Association. 28p. *8º.* 1846.

34678 [**HUMPHREYS,** H. N.] The coins of England. 120p. *8º.* [*London,* 1846]

34679 *****HUTCHISON,** J. A popular view of life assurance: embracing a sketch of its origin and progress, its principles, objects, and advantages; with a tabular view of the offices in Great Britain and Ireland... 80p. *8º. Glasgow, London, &c.,* 1846. *The copy that belonged to Augustus De Morgan.*

34680 **INGERSOLL,** J. R. Speech of Joseph R. Ingersoll, on the Subtreasury Bill: delivered in the House of Representatives of the United States, March 31, 1846. 15p. *8º. Washington,* 1846.

34681 **INNES,** JOHN (*fl.* 1830–1849). Equalization of duty on rum and British spirits. 28p. *8º.* [1846] *A new edition of* A letter to the Rt. Hon. Henry Goulburn, *1830* (*q.v.*), *with a prefatory letter to Charles Wood, explaining that its reissue resulted from observations on the differential duty on rum made by him and by Lord John Russell in the House of Commons.*

34682 **JENKINSON,** CHARLES, *1st Earl of Liverpool.* A treatise on the coins of the realm, being a concise account of all the facts relating to the currency, which bear upon the exchanges of Europe, and the principles of political science...Second edition. 283p. *8º.* 1846. *For another edition, see* 1805.

34683 **KENTUCKY.** *Commissioners of the Sinking Fund.* Annual report of the Commissioners...prepared by the Secretary of the Board. 7p. *8º. n.p.* [1846]

34684 [**KUEHNE,** L. ?] Der deutsche Zollverein während der Jahre 1834 bis 1845. Zweite vermehrte Auflage. [The preface signed: L.K.] 87p. *8º.* 1846.

34685 *****LIFE INSURANCE OFFICES,** new and speculative, with a table of the inducements held out by each of the existing offices to insurers. [With a table of companies, arranged by date of foundation, with notes on the inducements offered by each.] 28p. *8º.* 1846. *The copy that belonged to Augustus De Morgan.*

34686 A **LIST** of all the names, contained in the printed lists of proprietors of the Bank of Scotland, Royal Bank, and British Linen Company; and in the returns of the other banks in Scotland...of persons of whom each company or partnership consists. 312p. *8º. Edinburgh,* 1846.

34687 **LIVERPOOL.** Report of the proceedings of the public meeting on the tea duties, held in the Borough Sessions House, Liverpool on the 25th November 1846. Published by the Committee of the Liverpool Association for the Reduction of the Duty on Tea. 70p. *8º. Liverpool,* [1846] *See also* 1848.

34688 Ten **MINUTES'** advice to speculators in railway shares. By an observer, a resident of Manchester. 14p. *8º. London & Manchester,* [1846 ?]

34689 **MOREAU,** M. J. Aperçu statistique des assurances en France, presenté à M. le Ministre de l'Agriculture et du Commerce; suivi d'un plan de centralisation des courtages d'assurances dans l'intérêt des colonies agricoles. 2 vols. *8º. Paris,* 1846.

34690 **NIEBUHR,** M. VON. Bankrevolution und Bankreform. Wort eines Laien für Laien...Mit Zusätzen aus dem Janus, Heft 12–15, abgedruckt. 104p. *8º. Berlin,* 1846. *The copy that belonged to Wilhelm Roscher.*

34691 —— Beitrag zur Feststellung der Urtheile über die heutige Gestaltung des Bankwesens und insbesondere über die Mannheimer Credit- und Giro-Bank...(Besonders abgedruckt aus dem Archiv der politischen Oekonomie und Polizeiwissenschaft. Neue Folge. Bd. v., Heft 2.) 115p. *8º. Heidelberg,* 1846.

34692 **NORTH,** HON. SIR D. Discourses upon trade. 23p. *4º. Edinburgh,* 1846. *For other editions, see* 1691.

34693 **PORTER,** G. R. Sketch of the progress and present extent of savings' banks in the United Kingdom ...⟨From the Report of the British Association for the Advancement of Science for 1845.⟩ p.129–141. *8º.* 1846.

34694 **PRATT,** J. T. A summary of the savings banks in England, Scotland, Wales, & Ireland; with the period of the establishment of each institution, the place where it is held, the days and hours when open, the rate of interest payable to depositors, the number of open accounts, and amount of deposits, &c &c &c. according to the latest official returns. 333p. *8º.* 1846.

34695 **RAMSEY,** A. Speech of Alex. Ramsey, of Pennsylvania, on the bill for the reduction of the tariff. Delivered in the House of Representatives...June 19, 1846. 11p. *8º. Washington,* 1846.

34696 **REMARKS** on the Bill to amend the laws relating to bankruptcy and insolvency. 9p. *fol.* [1846] *See note to no.* 32762.

34697 **RIPLEY,** W. R. The present state of the law of tithes, under Lord Tenterden's Act, and the Act for the limitation of actions and suits relating to real property, with reference to tithe commutations. 155p. *8º.* 1846. *Presentation copy from the author to the Rev. Sutton Watt.*

34698 **ROCKWELL,** JOHN A. Speech of Mr. John A. Rockwell, of Connecticut, on the bill to reduce the duties on imports. Delivered in the House of Representatives, U.S., June 26, 1846. 16p. *8°. Washington*, 1846.

34699 ROWCROFT, C. Currency and railways; being suggestions for the remedy of the present railway embarrassments. 24p. *8°*. 1846.

34700 ROYER, C. E. Des institutions de crédit foncier en Allemagne et en Belgique... 488p. *8°. Paris*, 1846.

34701 SCOTTISH PROVIDENT INSTITUTION. Observations on life assurance, from the Post Magazine Almanack, circulated with prospectus of the Scottish Provident Institution. [4]p. *16°*. [1846?]

34702 —— The Scottish Provident Institution for the assurance of capital sums and annuities on lives and survivorships; and for the purchase and sale of reversions and annuities. Constituted on the principle of mutual assurance without personal liability...Established at Edinburgh in MDCCCXXXVII. [With 'Specimens of the tables'.] 10, [10]p. *8°. Edinburgh*, 1846.

34703 SMEE, W. R. The income tax: its extension at the present rate proposed to all classes; abolishing the malt tax, window tax, duty on hops, on licenses to sell and make beer, the tax on railways, the excise on bricks; and reducing the duty on French wines. 24p. *8°*. [1846]

34704 SMITH, JOHN PRINCE (1809–1874). John Prince-Smith über die englische Tarifreform und ihre materiellen, sozialen und politischen Folgen für Europa. 108p. *8°. Berlin*, 1846.

34705 SMITH, JOSHUA T. ⟨Printed for private distribution only.⟩ Considerations respecting the system of anonymous espionage and search-warrants practised by the Commissioners of Excise as affecting the civil liberties of Englishmen...Second edition. With additional authorities and a copy of petition presented to the House of Commons on the 8th of April, 1846. 32p. *8°*. [*London*,] 1846.

34706 SOCIETY FOR THE EMANCIPATION OF INDUSTRY. Second report of the Committee of the Society...bringing down their proceedings to the commencement of the Parliamentary session of 1846. 59p. *12°*. 1846. *See also* 1844.

34707 SOPER, G. I. On the life assurance offices: their national and social advantages, their principles and practice. [16]p. *8°*. [1846]

34708 STROHM, J. Speech of Mr. John Strohm, of Penn'a, on the tariff. Delivered in the House of Representatives, U.S., June 25, 1846. 14p. *8°. Washington*, 1846.

34709 STURROCK, J. The principles and practice of life assurance. 32p. *8°. Dundee, Edinburgh, &c.*, 1846.

34710 TAUNTON, E. Principle confounding expediency; or, Adam Smith v. Sir Robert Peel...Two petitions to Parliament. Returns of the Calcutta Mint: on my principle. Sir Robert Peel attempting to work the nation's clock with the spring of a lady's watch. 24p. *12°. Birmingham*, 1846.

34711 TAYLOR, H. Observations on the current coinage of Great Britain, as the medium of barter, calculation, and accounts; and on Professor De Morgan's plan for its more convenient and scientific arrangement, on the decimal system, with the advantages that would result from it, exemplified... ⟨Reprinted from the "Bankers' Magazine," and dedicated to the Lords of the Treasury.⟩ 12p. *12°*. 1846.

34712 [**TAYLOR,** JAMES (1788–1863).] The currency question. [Reprinted from the *Pictorial Times* of March 21, and the *Agricultural Advertiser* of March 28, 1846.] 4p. *8°. n.p.* [1846]

34713 THOMASSY, R. Du monopole des sels par la féodalité financière...Extrait de la Démocratie pacifique, augmenté de pièces justificatives et d'une note sur la constitution de la féodalité française. 59p. *8°. Paris*, 1846.

34714 [**WILLIAMS,** S. B.] Thoughts on finance and colonies. By Publius. 141p. *8°*. 1846.

34715 WOENIGER, A. T. Bülow-Cummerow's Zettelbankproject. Ein kritischer Beitrag zur Geschichte der Geldaristokratie. 75p. *8°. Berlin*, 1846.

TRANSPORT

34716 The **AMALGAMATION** of railways considered as affecting the internal commerce of the country. 16p. *8°. London & Manchester*, 1846.

34717 BOURNE, JOHN C. The history and description of the Great Western Railway, including its geology, and the antiquities of the district through which it passes ...and...numerous views of its principal viaducts, bridges, tunnels, stations...from drawings taken expressly for this work... 76[78]p. *fol.* 1846.

34718 BRADSHAW'S monthly railway and steam navigation guide, for Great Britain, Ireland, the Continent and foreign ports, containing a correct account of the hours of departure of the railway trains, Her Majesty's mails, and British and foreign steam vessels...Illustrated with a map ...[6th mo. (June) 1st, 1846. No. 155.] 94p. *4°. London & Paris*, [1846] *See also* 1843.

34719 The **BROAD GAUGE** the bane of the Great Western Railway Company. With an account of the present & prospective liabilities saddled on the proprietors by the promoters of that peculiar crotchet. By £.s.d. Third edition. 57p. *8°*. 1846. *For another issue, see no.* 34724.

34720 CHEMIN DE FER d'Amiens à Boulogne. Ville d'Amiens. Observations sur le projet de voûter le chemin de fer dans le fossé du Boulevard du Mail, et sur les opinions émises à l'occasion de ce projet. 18p. *4°. Amiens*, 1846.

34721 COCHRANE, G. The way to make railroad shares popular. 15p. *8°*. 1846.

For [**COLE,** SIR H.] Dialogues of the gauges. ⟨Reprinted from the "Railway Record."⟩, 1846, *see no.* 34724.

For [——] A few of the miseries of the break of gauge at Gloucester, which occasions the shifting of passengers, luggage, and goods from one carriage to another, [1846], *see no.* 34724.

For [——] Railway eccentrics. Inconsistencies of men of genius exemplified in the practice and precept of Isambard Kingdom Brunel, Esq., and in the theoretical opinions of

Charles Alexander Saunders, Esq. secretary to the Great Western Railway. By Vigil, 1846, *see no.* 34724.

For [——] A railway traveller's reasons for adopting uniformity of gauge addressed to I. K. Brunel, Esq. ⟨Fourth edition.⟩, [1846], *see no.* 34724.

34722 [——] Railway travelling charts; or, iron road books, for perusal on the journey...London and Brighton. *s. sh. fol. Railway Chronicle Office,* [1846] *Folded and enclosed in a printed paper wrapper.*

34723 On the **COMMUNICATIONS** between Europe and India, through Egypt. 73p. *8°.* 1846.

34724 CUNDALL, J., *comp.* Pamphlets in support of national uniformity of gauge and the report of Her Majesty's Gauge Commissioners. Collected, bound, and sold by Joseph Cundall, 12, Old Bond Street, London. 13 parts. *8°.* [1846] *A collection of pamphlets originally separately published by other publishers, reissued with a general title-page. Contents: W. Harding, Uniformity of gauge. Railways. The gauge question, 4th edition; [Sir H. Cole,] Railway eccentrics. Inconsistencies of men of genius exemplified in the practice and precept of Isambard Kingdom Brunel, Esq.... By Vigil; The broad gauge the bane of The Great Western Railway Company... By £.s.d.; Fallacies of the broken gauge. Mr. Lushington's arguments...refuted ...By a Fellow of two Royal Societies, 2nd edition; [K. Morison,] The origin and results of the clearing system, which is in operation on the narrow gauge railways; [Sir H. Cole,] Dialogues of the gauges. ⟨Reprinted from the "Railway Record."⟩; [H. S. Melville,] Narrow gauge speedier than broad gauge railways, as well as cheaper, 3rd edition; [Sir H. Cole,] ⟨Fourth edition.⟩ A railway traveller's reasons for adopting uniformity of gauge addressed to I. K. Brunel, Esq.; T. L. Hunt, Unity of the iron network: showing how the last argument for the break of gauge, competition, is at variance with the true interests of the public, 3rd edition; Reply to "Observations" of the Great Western Railway Company on the report of the Gauge Commissioners; A letter to the Directors of the Great Western Railway Company, shewing the public evils... attendant upon their break of gauge...By an old carrier; [Sir H. Cole,] A few of the miseries of the break of gauge at Gloucester; [Begin.] Travellers between Birmingham and Bristol who would prefer not to have to change the carriage at Gloucester, are informed that the following petition lies for signature at the stations on the line.*

34725 DOUGLAS, SIR H., *Bart.* Metropolitan bridges and Westminster improvements...Second edition. 27p. *8°.* 1846.

34726 DUNSTABLE RAILWAY COMPANY. At an Extraordinary General Meeting of proprietors of the Dunstable Railway, held...on...the 13th November, 1846. [To discuss the offer of the London and North Western Railway Company to buy out the Company.] [4]p. *4°. n.p.* [1846] *A covering letter is printed on the first page.*

34727 —— Second ordinary half-yearly general meeting of the Court of Proprietors...3rd March, 1846. [4]p. *fol.* [*London,* 1846]

34728 —— Third ordinary half-yearly general meeting of the Court of Proprietors...11th August, 1846. [4]p. *fol.* [*London,* 1846] *See also* 1845.

34729 DUPLESSY, J. and **LANDOY,** E. The indispensable guide for travellers on the railroads of Belgium...Translated from the French by M. Asborne de Chastelain... 280p. *12°. Brussels,* 1845-46.

34730 EASTERN COUNTIES RAILWAY COMPANY. Eastern Counties and Norfolk, and Eastern Union railways. [Timetable with map.] Nov. 1st. 1846. [10]p. *16°.* [*London,*] 1846. *See also* 1847.

34731 EASTERN UNION RAILWAY COMPANY. Eastern Union Railway. Half-yearly report of the directors of the...Company, 26th February, [-31st August] 1846. 2 vols. *fol. n.p.* [1846] *See also* 1844, 1845, 1847, 1848, 1849, 1850.

34732 —— Eastern Union Railway. Regulations for the clerks at the different stations. [Signed: James F. Saunders, secretary, and dated, May 1846.] [4]p. *fol. n.p.* [1846]

34733 —— Eastern Union Railway. Report of the directors of the...Company, at a special general meeting at Ipswich, December 8, 1846. [Concerned with negotiations for an amalgamation with the Ipswich and Bury St. Edmund's Railway Company.] 2p. *fol. n.p.* [1846]

34734 ENGLAND. *Laws, etc.* 9 & 10 Victoriæ. – Sess. 1846. An Act for making a railway from London to York, with branches therefrom, providing for the counties of Hertford, Bedford, Huntingdon, Northampton, Rutland, Nottingham, and...Lincoln...to be called "The Great Northern Railway." ⟨Royal Assent, 26 June, 1846.⟩ 150p. *8°. n.p.* [1846]

34735 —— —— Anno nono & decimo Victoriæ Reginæ. Cap. cclxxiii. An Act for widening the line of "the London and Blackwall Railway;" and for amending the Acts relating to the said railway. ⟨27th July 1846.⟩ p.4849-4856. *fol.* 1846.

34736 FALLACIES of the broken gauge. Mr. Lushington's arguments in favour of broad gauge and breaks of gauge refuted. Being a reply to the remarks of a late Fellow of Trinity College, Cambridge, on the report of the Gauge Commissioners. By a Fellow of two Royal Societies. 40p. *8°.* 1846. *See note to no.* 34295. *For another issue, see no.* 34724.

34737 FRASER, JAMES B. The Perth and Inverness railway: its importance as a national and commercial enterprise. 28p. *8°.* 1846.

34738 GEOMETRICUS, *pseud.* Round rail versus T rail; or, the principles of the geometrical railway system examined. 29p. *8°.* 1846.

34739 GLOVER, F. R. A. Harbours of refuge. 68p. *8°.* 1846.

34740 GREAT NORTHERN RAILWAY COMPANY. The Great Northern Railway. At the first ordinary general meeting of the proprietors of this Company, held pursuant to public notice, at the Hall of Commerce, Threadneedle Street, London, on Saturday 25th July, 1846. [Resolutions and directors' report.] 4p. *8°.* [*London,* 1846]

34741 [**HARDING,** WYNDHAM.] The question of the gages [*sic*] commercially considered by a practical man. Second edition, enlarged. 58p. *8°. London & Westminster,* 1846.

34742 —— Uniformity of gauge. Railways. The gauge question. Evils of diversity of gauge, and a remedy... With a map. Fourth edition. 53p. *8°.* 1846. *The Rastrick copy. For another edition, see* 1845, *and for another issue see no.* 34724.

34743 HARTFORD AND NEW HAVEN RAILROAD COMPANY. Eleventh annual report of the

Board of Directors, to the stockholders of the Hartford and New Haven Rail Road Company. 15p. *8°. Hartford, 1846. The Rastrick copy.*

34744 HARVEY, D. W. An address [to the members of the Railway Mutual Protection Society] upon the law and liabilities of railway speculation, with hints for legislative interference. [With 'House of Commons. Metropolitan railroads'. A speech of Mr. Harvey, 12th Feb., 1836.] 32p. *8°. 1846. The Rastrick copy.*

34745 HOPE, . Speech of Mr. Hope, on behalf of the Huddersfield and Manchester Railway Company, in the Select Committee of the House of Commons, on the Huddersfield & Manchester Company's Bradford Branch, and the West Riding Union railways, on Wednesday, 1st July, 1846. 8p. *8°. [Huddersfield, 1846]*

34746 HUNT, THORNTON L. The rationale of railway administration, with a view to the greatest possible amount of accommodation, cheapness and safety. 74p. *8°. 1846. See note to no. 34295.*

For —— Unity of the iron network: showing how the last argument for the break of gauge, competition, is at variance with the true interests of the public... Third edition, *1846, see no. 34724.*

34747 IPSWICH AND BURY ST. EDMUND'S RAILWAY COMPANY. Second report of the directors... January 30th, 1846. [With the report of the engineer, Peter Bruff.] 2p. *fol. n.p. [1846] See also 1845.*

34748 IPSWICH, BURY AND NORWICH RAILWAY COMPANY. Ipswich, Bury and Norwich Railway. First half-yearly report of the directors... 28th July, 1846 [with the report of the engineer, Peter Bruff]. 2p. *fol. n.p. [1846] See also 1847, 1848.*

For a **LETTER** to the Directors of the Great Western Railway Company, shewing the public evils and troubles attendant upon their break of gauge, and pointing out the remedy. By an old carrier, *1846, see no. 34724.*

34749 LONDON, BRIGHTON AND SOUTH COAST RAILWAY COMPANY. At the first meeting of the Company of the London, Brighton, and South Coast Railway, held...on...19th August, 1846. [Containing the report of the Directors and of the engineer, William Cubitt.] 2p. *s.sh.fol. n.p. [1846]*

34750 LUSHINGTON, H. The broad and the narrow gauge; or, remarks on the report of the Gauge Commissioners. 64p. *8°. Westminster, Manchester, &c., 1846.*

34751 McGEACHY, E. Suggestions towards a general plan of rapid communication by steam navigation and railways: shortening the time of transit between the eastern and western hemispheres. 17p. *8°. 1846.*

34752 MARTIN, WILLIAM (1772–1851). A letter to the Queen and Government. [On the advantages of the broad gauge on railways.] *s.sh.8°. Newcastle-on-Tyne, [1846]*

34753 —— To the conductors of railways and the gentlemen of Newcastle-upon-Tyne. *s.sh.8°. Newcastle-upon-Tyne, [1846]*

34754 —— To the Honourable the Lords and Commons of Great Britain and Ireland in Parliament assembled. [A petition, in favour of the broad gauge on railways. Dated: March 5th, 1846.] *s.sh.4°. [Newcastle-upon-Tyne, 1846]*

34755 [MATHER, JAMES.] Ships and railways. 40p. *8°. 1846.*

34756 —— Second edition. [With appendixes.] 55p. *8°. 1846. Presentation copy from the author to Joseph Hume.*

34757 MELVILLE, H. S. Narrow gauge speedier than broad gauge railways, as well as cheaper... Second edition. 15p. *8°. 1846. For the third edition, see no. 34724.*

For [**MORISON**, K.] The origin and results of the clearing system, which is in operation on the narrow gauge railways, with tables of the through traffic in the year 1845, *1846, see no. 34724.*

34758 MORRISON, JAMES (1790–1857). Observations illustrative of the defects of the English system of railway legislation, and of its injurious operation on the public interests; with suggestions for its improvement. 44p. *8°. 1846.*

34759 —— Speech of James Morrison, Esq., M.P., March 20th, 1845, on moving resolutions respecting railways. 39p. *8°. 1846.*

34760 MULLINS, B. and M. B. The origin and reclamation of peat bog, with some observations on the construction of roads, railways, and canals in bog... Extracted, by permission of Council, from the Transactions of the Institution of Civil Engineers of Ireland. 48p. *8°. Dublin & London, 1846.*

34761 NEWTON, W. E. Notes of the hearing and judgment of the cause between W. E. Newton and the Grand Junction Railway Company for an infringement of letters patent for improvements in the construction of boxes for the axletrees of locomotive engines and carriages ...in the Court of Exchequer, Westminster...January 29th, 1846. 78p. *8°. 1846.*

34762 NICHOLSON, P. The guide to railway masonry containing a complete treatise on the oblique arch in four parts...Revised & corrected throughout by R. Cowen...Third edition. 10, lxviii, 57p. *8°. London & Carlisle, 1846. For another edition, see 1839.*

34763 PAGAN, W. Road reform: a plan for abolishing turnpike tolls and statute labour assessments, and for providing the funds necessary for the public roads by an annual rate on horses. [Abridged edition.] 123p. *8°. Edinburgh & London, 1846. Presentation copy from the author to Sir George Strickland, M.P. For another edition, see 1845.*

34764 PEARSON, W. W. Suggestions for improved railway legislation at the present crisis, in Great Britain and Ireland, in a letter to the Committee of the House of Commons. 8p. *8°. 1846.*

34765 QUESTED, J. A treatise on railway surveying and levelling. In which the author has endeavoured to simplify the most approved methods now adopted by surveyors. 73p. *8°. 1846.*

For the **RAILWAY GAZETTE**, 1846–47, *see vol. III, Periodicals list*, Bradshaw's railway gazette.

34766 REASONS in favour of a direct line of railroad from London to Manchester. 35p. *8°. 1846.*

For **REPLY** to "Observations" of the Great Western Railway Company on the report of the Gauge Commissioners, *1846, see no. 34724.*

34767 REPLY to the statement put forth by the directors of the South-Eastern Railway Company. 46p. *8°. 1846.*

34768 RITCHIE, R. Railways, their rise, progress,

and construction: with remarks on railway accidents, and proposals for their prevention. 444p. *8°.* 1846.

34769 ROCKWELL, John A. Comparison between the internal and foreign commerce of the United States, in a speech on the Harbor and River Bill, delivered before the House of Representatives, U.S., March 17, 1846. 20p. *8°. Washington,* 1846.

34770 On the **SELECTION** of projected lines, with description of the railway scale. 23p. *8°.* [1846]

34771 SIDNEY, S., *ed.* Gauge evidence. The history and prospects of the railway system, illustrated by the evidence given before the Gauge Commission... xxxix, 400p. *8°.* 1846.

34772 —— Second edition. lxxi, 400p. *8°.* 1846.

34773 SOUTH-EASTERN RAILWAY COMPANY. South-Eastern Railway. General statement of the position and projects of the Company. 1845–6. 45p. *8°.* [1846]

34774 SYMONS, Jelinger C. Railway liabilities as they affect subscribers, committees, allottees, and scrip-holders inter se, and third parties. 79p. *8°.* 1846.

For **TRAVELLERS** between Birmingham and Bristol who would prefer not to have to change the carriage at Gloucester, are informed that the following petition lies for signature at the stations on the line, [1846], *see no.* 34724.

34775 Experimental **TRIP** of the "Great Western" new locomotive passenger engine, made on the 13th June,

1846. Extracted from the Morning Herald of the 15th June. 16p. *8°.* [1846]

34776 TROUP, J. Railway reform, and rights of shareholders and the public in the railway highways of the United Kingdom. 39p. *8°.* 1846.

34777 TUCK, H. The railway shareholder's manual; or practical guide to all the railways in the world, completed, in progress, and projected... To which is added a correct list of offices and officers of existing and projected railways. Seventh edition. Carefully revised and corrected. 297p. *8°. London, Liverpool, &c.,* 1846. *For other editions, see* 1845.

34778 TURNBULL, George (1809–1889). An account of the drops used for the shipment of coals at Middlesbro'-on-Tees, with a description of the town and port of Middlesbro'-on-Tees... Excerpt minutes of proceedings of the Institution of Civil Engineers. 8p. *8°.* 1846.

34779 National **UNIFORMITY** of gauge: a letter to Lord Dalhousie, submitting reasons for preferring the original recommendations of the Gauge Commissioners, to the recent proposals of the Board of Trade. 16p. *8°.* 1846.

34780 WALTON, William (1784–1857). The facilities and advantages of navigating the Ebro by steam, from the sea nearly as far up as Logroño; and also of making that river the basis of a line of communication, (partly by water and partly overland,) from the point above named to St. Sebastians, or Bilboa, in the Bay of Biscay, so as to form a connecting link between the Atlantic and the Mediterranean Seas. 66p. *8°.* 1846.

SOCIAL CONDITIONS

34781 ALLEN, William (*fl.* 1846). Mutual improvement; or, a scheme for the self-adjustment of the social machine. 16p. *8°.* 1846.

34782 AMOR PATRIAE, *pseud.* Industry, education, and public virtue; or measures for a new Parliament to complete under a liberal and enlightened Government; suggested by Amor Patriæ in three letters to Lord John Russell... 31p. *8°. London & Sherborne,* [1846]

34783 ANDERSON, James S. M. The profitable employment of hours gained from business: an inaugural address, delivered in the Town-Hall, Brighton, on... March 11, 1846, to the members and friends of the Brighton Athenæum, and Young Men's Literary Union... 53p. *8°. London & Brighton,* 1846.

34784 BARNES, A. On the traffic in intoxicating liquors. Showing its immoral and destructive tendency... With preface by the Rev. John Kirk. Thirtieth thousand. 12p. *8°. Glasgow & London,* [1846] *The Turner copy.*

34785 BEECHER, L. Six sermons on intemperance. Delineating its nature, occasions, signs, evils, and remedy... With an introductory preface by the Rev. William Reid. 31p. *8°. Edinburgh, London, &c.,* 1846. *The Turner copy.*

34786 —— Forty-fifth thousand. 32p. *8°. Glasgow & London,* [1846] *The Turner copy.*

34787 —— The nature and occasions of intemperance. (Extracted from Dr. Beecher's Sermons on intemperance.) (*Glasgow and West of Scotland Temperance Society,* 4.) 8p. *12°. n.p.* [1846?] *The Turner copy.*

34788 BEGGS, T. Three lectures on the moral elevation of the people... Reprinted from the National Temperance Magazine. 82p. *8°. London & Leicester,* [1846]

34789 BEITH. *Parochial Board.* Report on the affairs of the poor of Beith. Submitted to the first meeting of the new parochial board, 3rd February, 1846. [Signed: Jas. Dobie.] 22p. *8°. Beith,* 1846.

34790 BLACKER, W. An essay on the best mode of improving the condition of the labouring classes of Ireland. 56p. *8°. London, Edinburgh, &c.,* 1846.

For **BOOKBINDERS' CONSOLIDATED UNION,** Book-binders' Consolidated Union friendly circular, *see* vol. III, *Periodicals list.*

34791 Dear **BREAD!!** A tract for the winter of 1845–6. (*Midland Temperance Tracts,* 87.) 4p. *8°. Leicester, London, &c.,* [1846] *The Turner copy.*

34792 BURGESS, R. A letter to the Rev. W. F. Hook, D.D., Vicar of Leeds, on his proposed plan for the education of the people. 32p. *8°.* 1846.

34793 CATTLEY, S. R. The first stone of a new building: together with some account of the proceedings of the Committee organized to further the establishment of a refuge for persons discharged from custody. 23p. *8°.* 1846.

For **CENTRAL TEMPERANCE ASSOCIATION,** The temperance gazette, 1846–48, *see* vol. III, *Periodicals list,* Temperance gazette.

34794 CHADWICK, Sir E., *ed.* Papers read before the Statistical Society of Manchester, on the demoralisation and injuries occasioned by the want of proper regulations of labourers engaged in the construction & working of railways, viz.: A return of the fatal accidents, wounds and injuries, sustained by workmen engaged in the construction of the Summit Level Tunnel of the Sheffield and Manchester Railway...by John Roberton, Esq., surgeon...Statements on railway contracts and railway labourers, by Robert Rawlinson, Esq., engineer to the Bridgewater Trust. Statements as to some of the effects produced in this country by the past expenditure of capital on labour in the construction of railways...by Edwin Chadwick, Esq.... 51p. *8°. Manchester & London*, [1846]. *See note to no.* 34295.

34795 CHADWICK, R. S. The pleasures of poetry, the purgatory of poets, and other poems. 122p. *8°. Manchester*, 1846. *The Turner copy.*

34796 CHALMERS, T. Churches and schools for the working classes. An address...on the practicability of providing moral and religious education for the working population of large towns, as illustrated by the success which has attended the operations carried on in the West Port of Edinburgh, delivered 27th Dec. 1845. 31p. *8°. Edinburgh & London*, 1846.

34797 CLÉMENT, A. Recherches sur les causes de l'indigence. 359p. *8°. Paris*, 1846.

34798 *COLONIE AGRICOLE. Notice sur l'école préparatoire de Mettray près Tours (Indre-et-Loire). 8p. *8°. Paris*, 1846.

34799 DAWSON, George, *minister.* A lecture delivered in the Manchester Athenæum, on the evil tendency of the late hour system...on...the 8th of May, 1846. Published by authority of the Manchester and Salford Early Closing Association. 18p. *12°. Manchester*, 1846.

34800 DELBRUCK, J. Visite à la crèche-modèle et rapport général adressé à M. Marbeau sur les crèches de Paris... 138p. *12°. Paris*, 1846.

34801 A DIGEST of the evidence taken before the Select Committee of the House of Commons on Andover Union; with some introductory remarks. By a barrister. lxx, 195p. *8°.* 1846.

34802 DOUGLAS, John (*fl.* 1828–1846). Life and property in Ireland assured as in England, by a poor-rate on land, to provide employment for the destitute poor on the waste lands of Ireland. 39p. *8°.* 1846.

34803 The DRESSMAKERS' and milliners' advocate. By the author of "Our female servants," the prize tract of the London Female Mission, etc. 32p. *8°.* 1846.

34804 DUCPÉTIAUX, E. Projet d'association financière pour l'amélioration des habitations et l'assainissement des quartiers habités par la classe ouvrière à Bruxelles ...Mémoire adressé au Conseil communal et au Conseil central de Salubrité publique de Bruxelles. 96p. *8°. Bruxelles*, 1846.

34805 DUNDEE. List of the poor of Dundee, as divided into districts; board of children, nurse-fees, and boarders in asylum; with abstract of the revenue and expenditure, from 1st February 1845, to 1st February 1846. [With 'Roll of assessment for support of the poor of ...Dundee for the year from the 1st day of February 1846, to the 1st day of February 1847'.] 80p. *8°. Dundee*, 1846.

34806 DUTOUQUET, H. E. De la condition des classes pauvres à la campagne; des moyens les plus efficaces de l'améliorer. 112p. *8°. Paris*, 1846.

34807 DYER, John (*fl.* 1846). Teetotalism examined by the light of science; or, an antidote to objections to the practice of total-abstinence. In three lectures. 58p. *8°. Leicester, London, &c.*, 1846.

34808 EDINBURGH AND LEITH WATER COMPANY. Correspondence between the Edinburgh and Leith Water Company and the Edinburgh Water Company, and other documents relative to a transfer of both to a public trust. 16p. *4°. n.p.* [1846] *See note to no.* 33895.

34809 EDWARDS, D. O. A proposal for an agrarian endowment of the population, in lieu of the existing poor law and corn law. In a letter to His Grace the Duke of Richmond. 54p. *8°.* 1846.

34810 EDWARDS, H. An appeal to the public on the late hour system; addressed alike to the Christian, the citizen, the tradesman, and the philosopher. 16p. *8°.* 1846.

34811 ENGLAND. *Laws, etc.* Abstract of an Act for the improvement of the sewerage and drainage of the borough of Liverpool, and for making further provisions for the sanatory regulation of the said borough. 48p. *8°. n.p.* [1846]

34812 —— Parliament. *House of Commons.* Railway labourers and labourers on public works. Report of the Select Committee of the House of Commons appointed to inquire into the condition of the labourers employed in the construction of railways and other public works, and into the remedies which may be calculated to lessen the peculiar evils, if any, of that condition. Together with the passages from the examination of witnesses referred to in the Committees' [*sic*] Report... 44p. *8°. London & Manchester*, [1846]

34813 —— Privy Council. *Committee on Education.* Minutes of the Committee of Council on Education in August and December, 1846. Presented to both Houses of Parliament, by command of Her Majesty. 23p. *12°. Sunday School Union*, [1846]

34814 An ESSAY on the principles of supply and demand, and the results, when applied to labour. [With particular reference to the iron trades.] By a trades' unionist. 16p. *8°. Saint Andrews, Islington, &c.*, 1846.

34815 EXAMINATION and committal of seventeen persons, mechanics and engineers, on the charge of conspiracy [to prevent workmen entering the premises of Messrs. Jones and Potts, of the Viaduct Foundry, Newton, and to persuade workmen in their employ to leave], at the Court-House, Warrington, on the 2nd December, 1846. 12p. *8°. n.p.* [1846]

34816 FIELD, John (1812–1884). Prison discipline. The advantages of the separate system of imprisonment, as established in the new County Gaol of Reading, with a description of the former prisons, and a detailed account of the discipline now pursued. 307p. *8°. London & Reading*, 1846. *See also* 1848.

34817 FITZGERALD, James E. A letter to the noblemen, gentlemen, and merchants of England. [On the famine in Ireland.] 14p. *8°.* [1846]

34818 FIX, T. Observations sur l'état des classes ouvrières. 412p. *8°. Paris*, 1846.

34819 FORTESCUE, HUGH, *3rd Earl Fortescue*. Health of Towns' Association. Unhealthiness of towns, its causes and remedies: being a lecture delivered on the 10th of December, 1845, in the Mechanics' Institute at Plymouth. By Viscount Ebrington, M.P.... 48p. *12°*. 1846. *Presentation copy from the author to N. W. Senior.*

34820 *GARNIER, C. J. Sur l'association, l'économie politique et la misère; position du problème de la misère, ou considérations sur les moyens généraux d'élever les classes pauvres à une meilleure condition matérielle et morale. Extrait du no. 58 du Journal des économistes. 34p. *8°. Paris*, 1846. *The copy that belonged to George Grote.*

34821 GLASGOW COMMERCIAL COLLEGE. Constitution of the Glasgow Commercial College. Instituted 3d. December, 1845. 7p. *8°. Glasgow*, 1846.

34822 GREEN, JOHN O. The factory system, in its hygienic relations. An address, delivered at Boston, at the annual meeting of the Massachusetts Medical Society, May 27, 1846... 34p. *8°. Boston*, 1846. *The copy presented to Lord Ashley by Edward Everett.*

34823 GUY, W. A. On the health of towns, as influenced by defective cleansing and drainage. And on the application of the refuse of towns to agricultural purposes. Being a lecture delivered at the Russell Institution, May 5, 1846...Second edition. 50p. *8°*. 1846. *The copy that belonged to T. Spring Rice, Baron Monteagle.*

34824 HEALTH OF TOWNS ASSOCIATION, *London*. Health of Towns Association. Report of the Committee to the members of the Association, on Lord Lincoln's Sewerage, Drainage, &c., of Towns Bill. 122p. *8°*. 1846. *See also 1847.*

34825 [HICKEY, W.] The labouring classes in Ireland: an inquiry as to what beneficial changes may be effected in their condition by the Legislature, the landowner, and the labourer respectively. By Martin Doyle. 78p. *12°. Dublin, London, &c.*, 1846.

34826 HILL, LORD G. A. Facts from Gweedore. Compiled from notes by Lord George Hill, M.R.I.A. ⟨Second edition.⟩ [With an appendix.] 41, [7]p. *8°. Dublin & London*, 1846.

34827 Practical **HINTS** towards improving the merchant marine service. Dedicated to the Committee of the General Shipowners' Society. By a merchant captain. 39p. *8°*. 1846.

For **IPSWICH SERIES OF TEMPERANCE TRACTS** [1846–60?], *see* vol. III, *Periodicals list*.

34828 JEFFREYS, H. An affectionate appeal to all who love the Lord Jesus Christ in sincerity [on behalf of temperance societies]. 16p. *8°. Glasgow & London*, [1846] *The Turner copy.*

34829 KAY, JOSEPH. The education of the poor in England and Europe. 400p. *8°*. 1846.

34830 LIFE of William Allen, with selections from his correspondence... 3 vols. *8°*. 1846–47.

34831 LIVERPOOL HEALTH OF TOWNS' ASSOCIATION. Second annual report of the committee... 8p. *8°. Liverpool*, [1846] *The first annual report was printed in* The Liverpool Health of Towns Advocate (supplementary no. April 1, 1845), *for which see* vol. III, *Periodicals list*.

34832 LOCK HOSPITAL, *London*. Centenary report of the Lock Hospital and Asylum...Paddington, with the proceedings of the building committee and an abstract of the income and expenditure, and a list of the governors and subscribers. 56p. *8°. Paddington*, 1846.

34833 For private circulation. The **LODGING-HOUSES** of London. Extracted from the "London City Mission Magazine" of August, 1845. 16p. *8°*. 1846.

34834 MACCALL, W. A lecture on the physical and moral evils of protracted hours of labour, published after its second delivery, at the request of the Exeter Association for obtaining an abridgement of the hours of business... Second edition. 47p. *12°. Exeter*, 1846.

34835 The poor **MAN'S** four evils. 12p. *8°. London & Manchester*, [1846] *The Turner copy.*

34836 MARTIN, JOHN, *K.L.* Thames and metropolis improvement plan. First division...[On sewage disposal.] 48p. *8°*. 1846.

34837 MAY, S. J. The rights and condition of women; considered in "the Church of the Messiah," November 8, 1846. 16p. *8°. Syracuse*, [1846]

34838 MILROY, G. Quarantine and the plague: being a summary of the report on these subjects recently addressed to the Royal Academy of Medicine in France; with introductory observations, extracts from Parliamentary correspondence, and notes. 16p. *8°. London, Edinburgh, &c.*, 1846.

34839 NATIONAL TEMPERANCE SOCIETY. The address of the National Temperance Society. 24p. *8°*. 1846.

34840 —— Address of the National Temperance Society to the people of England. ⟨Eighth thousand.⟩ (*Bristol New Series*, 70.) 4p. *8°. Bristol*, [1846] *The Turner copy.*

34841 NEALE, J. M. Songs and ballads for manufacturers and for the people. 24, 24p. *12°*. [1846] *Two separately published collections reissued with a general title on the printed paper wrapper.*

34842 NEISON, F. G. P. Observations on odd-fellow and friendly societies...Fourth edition. 36p. *12°*. 1846. *The author's own copy, with his book-stamp on the title-page. See also 1847.*

34843 NICHOLLS, SIR GEORGE. On the condition of the agricultural labourer; with suggestions for its improvement. Prize essay. [From the Journal of the Royal Agricultural Society of England, 1846, vol. VII., part I.] 32p. *8°*. 1846. *See also 1847.*

34844 NIGHT ASYLUM FOR THE HOUSELESS. Ninth annual report of the Glasgow Night Asylum for the Houseless. Instituted 1838. Incorporated by Seal of Cause 1842. 27p. *8°. Glasgow*, 1846. *See also 1848.*

34845 ODDFELLOWS. Grand United Order of Oddfellows. *Lumley Lodge*. Bye laws of the Lumley Lodge of the Grand United Order of Odd Fellows. No. 658. Tickhill. Established May the 27th, 1839. 16p. *8°. Worksop*, 1846.

34846 PAGE, THOMAS. An earnest appeal to the nation at large, on the mischievous effects of beer houses. 111p. *12°*. 1846.

34847 PALMER, W. Considerations on the Charitable Trusts Bill, in a letter addressed to the Right Hon. Lord Cottenham. With a copy of the Bill. 55p. *8°*. 1846.

34848 PENNIE, J. Temperance and other rhymes. 15p. *8°. Heywood*, 1846. *The Turner copy.*

For the **PEOPLE'S JOURNAL**, 1846–48, *see* vol. III, *Periodicals list.*

34849 PERRY, G. W. The peasantry of England. An appeal to the nobility, clergy, and gentry, on behalf of the working classes, in which the causes which have led to their present impoverished... condition, and the means by which it may best be permanently improved, are clearly pointed out... 217p. *12°.* 1846.

34850 *QUEENWOOD COLLEGE, near Stockbridge, Hants. George Edmondson, principal. [Prospectus.] [4]p. *4°. n.p.* [1846?] *The FWA copy that belonged to William Pare.*

34851 RAY, T. M. Report on the Irish Coercion Bill, the causes of discontent in Ireland, condition of the people, comparative criminality with England, etc. etc....17th March, 1846. 27p. *4°. Dublin,* 1846.

34852 RIBBANS, F. B. Observations on the advantages of general education amongst the youth of the higher ranks... 35p. *8°.* [1846?]

34853 ROBERTS, S. Lessons for statesmen, with anecdotes respecting them, calculated to preserve the aristocracy from destruction and the country from ruin... 90p. *8°. London & Sheffield,* 1846.

34854 ROGERS, JASPER W. Letter to the landlords and ratepayers of Ireland, detailing means for the permanent and profitable employment of the peasantry, without ultimate cost to the land or the nation, and within the provisions of the Act, 10 Vic. Cap. 107. 77p. *8°.* 1846.

34855 SCROPE, G. P. Letters to the Right Hon. Lord John Russell, on the expediency of enlarging the Irish Poor-Law to the full extent of the Poor-Law of England. 91p. *8°.* 1846.

34856 SELWYN, J. M. The servants' companion; comprising the most easy, perfect, and expeditious methods of arranging and getting through their work; rules for setting out tables & side-boards; directions for conducting large and small parties... 48p. *12°. Otley,* 1846.

34857 *SLANEY, R. A. Health of Towns' Association. Suggestions for forming branch associations. 24p. *12°.* 1846. *The FWA copy that belonged to William Pare.*

34858 SMITH, J., *M.A.* The grievances of the working classes; and the pauperism and crime of Glasgow; with their causes, extent, and remedies. 116p. *12°. Glasgow, Edinburgh, &c.,* 1846.

34859 SOCIÉTÉ DE SECOURS MUTUELS DITE DE SAINT-THÉODORE. 184me Société de Secours Mutuels, dite de Saint-Théodore, composée d'ouvriers doreurs sur métaux, autorisée par décision de M. le Ministre de l'Intérieur du 24 octobre 1846, époque de sa fondation... 32p. *8°. Paris,* 1846.

34860 SOCIÉTÉ POUR LE PATRONAGE DES JEUNES DÉTENUS...DU DEPARTEMENT DE LA SEINE. Assemblée Générale tenue à l'Hôtel-de-ville, le 16 août 1846. [Compte-rendu 1845.] 66p. *8°. Paris,* 1846. *See also* 1844, 1848, 1849.

34861 Friendly **SOCIETIES.** [Statutory rules relating to friendly societies.] 7p. *8°. n.p.* [1846]

34862 SOCIETY IN SCOTLAND FOR PROPAGATING CHRISTIAN KNOWLEDGE. Royal Highland School Society. An account of the origin, progress, and present state of the Society...with a list of the officers and subscribers in London. 24p. *8°.* 1846.

34863 SWAINE, E. Equity without compromise; or, hints for the construction of a just system of national education: (second edition:) with remarks on Dr. Hook's pamphlet, and the Letters of Edward Baines... 60p. *8°.* 1846. *For another edition, see* 1843.

34864 TEARE, J. The origin and success of the advocacy of the principle of total abstinence from all intoxicating liquors; including some account of the progress of the temperance reformation. 31p. *8°.* 1846. *The Turner copy. See also* 1847.

For the **TEMPERANCE NEWS,** *see* vol. III, *Periodicals list.*

For the **TEN HOURS' ADVOCATE** and journal of literature and art, 1846–47, *see* vol. III, *Periodicals list.*

34865 TRATTINNICK, C. Darstellung der bestehenden Vorschriften über die Vergütung der Fuhr- und Zehrungskosten für die in Dienste, reisenden öffentlichen Beamten...nebst dem vervollständigten Diäten-Schema für die verschiedenen Dienstes-Cathegorien...der gesammten österr. deutsch, italienisch und ungarischen Erblande, von Emanuel Hünner... 2 vols. *8°. Wien,* 1846.

For the **TRUTHSEEKER** in literature, philosophy and religion, *see* vol. III, *Periodicals list.*

34866 TUKE, JAMES H. The common and free schools of the United States of America, a paper read...at the annual meeting of the Friends' Educational Society, 1846. 31p. *8°. York & London,* 1846.

34867 TURNER, SYDNEY, and **PAYNTER,** T. Report on the system and arrangements of "La Colonie Agricole," at Mettray. Presented to the committee of the Philanthropic Society, St. George's Fields, 19th August, 1846. 46p. *8°. Printed for the use of the committee,* 1846. *Presentation copy from Turner to Macvey Napier.*

34868 —— Mettray. Report on the system and arrangements of "La Colonie Agricole," at Mettray...Second edition, revised. 74p. *8°.* 1846. *The copy that belonged to Victor Considérant.*

34869 WALKER, E. A letter to the Wesleyan Conference appointed to be held in Bristol, on...July 29th, 1846, in which are considered the claims of the temperance reformation on the Wesleyan Methodist connexion, and its bearings on the conversion of the world. 64p. *8°. Hull,* 1846. *The Turner copy.*

34870 WALKER, GEORGE A. Burial-ground incendiarism. The last fire at the bone-house in the Spa-Fields Golgotha, or, the minute anatomy of grave-digging in London. 48p. *8°.* 1846.

34871 WOOD, T. [*Begin.*] The subjoined letter from the honourable Member for Brecon to Lord John Russell, is respectfully submitted to the attentive perusal and consideration of the public, by farmers and other persons attending Uxbridge Market. [A letter suggesting a total abrogation of the law of settlement, and the establishment of a national assessment for the maintenance of the poor.] 7p. *8°.* [*Uxbridge,* 1846]

34872 WORLD'S TEMPERANCE CONVENTION. The proceedings of the World's Temperance Convention, held in London, August 4th, and four following days, with the papers laid before the Convention... [Edited by T. Beggs.] 140p. *8°.* 1846.

SLAVERY

34873 APPLETON, N. Correspondence between Nathan Appleton and John G. Palfrey intended as a supplement to Mr. Palfrey's pamphlet on the slave power. 20p. *8°. Boston,* 1846.

34874 BABINGTON, C. The influence of Christianity in promoting the abolition of slavery in Europe... 199p. *8°. Cambridge & London,* 1846.

34875 BLYTH, . A letter to Her Majesty's Ministers on the Sugar-Bill. No. 1. – 13th August 1846. Pleading the cause of mankind and demanding "protection"; not for the planter, but for the slave. 4p. *8°. Boulogne,* [1846]

34876 DOUGLASS, F. Narrative of the life of Frederick Douglass, an American slave. Written by himself ...Second Dublin edition. 135p. *12°. Dublin,* 1846. *For another edition, see* 1845.

34877 FÉLICE, G. DE. Emancipation immédiate et complète des esclaves. Appel aux abolitionistes. 114p. *8°. Paris,* 1846.

34878 GARRISON, W. L. American slavery. Address on the subject of American slavery, and the progress of the cause of freedom throughout the world. Delivered in the National Hall, Holborn, on...September 2, 1846. [From the *Inquirer* of Saturday, September 5.] 24p. *12°.* [1846]

34879 [LUCKOCK, B.] Jamaica: enslaved and free. (*Religious Tract Society, Monthly Series.*) 192p. *16°.* [1846]

34880 MASSIE, J. W. The slave; hunted, transported, and doomed to toil; a tale of Africa...Published at the request and expense of the teachers and scholars of Chapel Street Independent Sunday School Salford. The entire proceeds to be applied to support a mission in Africa by negroes from the West Indies. 176p. *8°. Manchester,* 1846.

34881 Interesting **MEMOIRS** and documents relating to American slavery, and the glorious struggle now making for complete emancipation. 266p. *8°.* 1846.

34882 PALFREY, J. G. Papers on the slave power, first published in the "Boston Whig." 90p. *8°. Boston,* [1846] *For a supplement, see no.* 34873.

34883 PALMER, HENRY. Letters on the slave trade. 56p. *8°. London & Leicester,* 1846.

34884 The **SUGAR DUTIES.** Free and slave labour. 20p. *8°.* 1846.

34885 WRIGHT, HENRY C. The dissolution of the American union, demanded by justice and humanity, as the incurable enemy of liberty. With a letter...on Christian fellowship with slaveholders: and a letter to the members of the Free Church...Addressed to the abolitionists of Great Britain and Ireland. 46p. *12°. London, Edinburgh, &c.: The Glasgow Emancipation Society and Hibernian Anti-Slavery Society,* 1846.

POLITICS

34886 A fragmentary **CHAPTER** from the most pleasant and delectable history of Robert, the Fox: a newly found apologue of the present age...[A satire on Sir Robert Peel.] 35p. *8°. Westminster: The Chiswick Press,* 1846.

34887 COOPER, THOMAS (1805–1892). The baron's yule feast: a Christmas-rhyme. 123p. *8°.* 1846. *Presentation copy, with inscription, dated 1855, from the author to John Harland.*

34888 The two **DICTATORS** Francia and Rosas. The system of the former as adopted and openly supported by the dictator of Buenos-Aires. 25p. *8°. Monte-Video,* 1846.

34889 The Right Honourable Thomas **GRENVILLE.** Reprinted from the Wakefield Journal, Dec. 31, 1846. 12p. *8°.* [1846]

34890 LITERARY ASSOCIATION OF THE FRIENDS OF POLAND. Address of the Literary Association of the Friends of Poland to the people of Great Britain and Ireland, drawn up by Lord Dudley Stuart. 47p. *8°.* 1846.

34891 ⟨January 22, 1846.⟩ **MORT-AUX-RATS:** or, ministerial ratsbane...No. I. [A satire in verse.] 10p. *8°. n.p.* [1846]

34892 NATIONAL ASSOCIATION FOR PROMOTING THE POLITICAL AND SOCIAL IMPROVEMENT OF THE PEOPLE. An address from the National Association...to the working classes of the United Kingdom, on...the militia.

Adopted by a public meeting...February 11, 1846. [Signed: Wm. Lovett, sec.] 8p. *8°.* 1846.

34893 O'CONNELL, D. Coercion Bill, Ireland. Letters of Daniel O'Connell, Esq., M.P. and Remonstrance of the Loyal National Repeal Association of Ireland. 30p. *8°. Dublin,* [1846] *The copy that belonged to Earl De Grey.*

34894 *OWEN, ROBERT. To the electors of the borough of Marylebone. [Signed: Robert Owen, and dated, 30th July 1846. Thanking those who supported his nomination as Parliamentary candidate.] *s.sh.4°.* [*London,* 1846] *The FWA copy that belonged to William Pare.*

34895 *—— Who are the parties interested in the continuance of peace [between the United States and Great Britain] ? [Signed: Robert Owen, and dated, Washington, March 23, 1846.] *s.sh.fol. n.p.* [1846] *A galley proof. The FWA copy that belonged to William Pare.*

34896 SCROPE, G. P. How is Ireland to be governed? A question addressed to the new administration of Lord Melbourne in 1834, with a postscript, in which the same question is addressed to the administration of Sir Robert Peel in 1846. 65p. *8°.* 1846. *The copy that belonged to Earl De Grey.*

34897 THIERS, L. A. Discours de M. Thiers sur les députés fonctionnaires prononcé dans la séance de la Chambre des Députés du 17 mars 1846. 52p. *8°. Paris,* 1846.

34898 Deutsche **ZEITUNG** ohne Censur. *8°. Mannheim,* 1846.

SOCIALISM

34899 CABET, E. Le vrai Christianisme suivant Jésus-Christ. 636p. *18°. Paris*, 1846.

34900 CONSIDÉRANT, V. P. Exposition abrégée du système phalanstérien de Fourier...3e édition. – 4e tirage. 114p. *16°. Paris*, 1846. *Considérant's own copy. For other editions, see 1845.*

For the **CO-OPERATOR,** *see vol.* III, *Periodicals list.*

34901 HENNEQUIN, V. A. Féodalité ou association. Type d'organisation du travail pour les grands établissements industriels à propos des houillères du Bassin de la Loire. 50p. *8°. Paris*, 1846.

34902 JOURNET, J. Cri suprême, appel aux honnêtes gens. 123p. *16°. Paris*, 1846.

34903 MICHELET, J. The people...Translated, with the author's especial approbation, by C. Cocks... Third edition. 164p. *8°.* 1846. **Another, the FWA copy, belonged to William Pare.*

34904 MORGAN, JOHN M. Colonie chrétienne de 300 familles...Traduit de l'anglais. 74p. *12°. Paris & Londres*, 1846. *For other editions, see 1845, and no. 34905, below.*

34905 *—— Explanation of the design for a self-supporting institution. [With a prospectus, 'Church of England agricultural self-supporting institution for 300 families'.] 8p. *8°. n.p.* [1846?] *The FWA copy that belonged to William Pare. The* Explanation *was also issued with the third edition of* Religion and crime, *1840, q.v.* (SOCIAL CONDITIONS). *For other editions of the prospectus, issued by the Church of England Self-Supporting Village Society, see* 1849, 1850.

34906 —— Letters to a clergyman, on institutions for ameliorating the condition of the people, chiefly from Paris, in the autumn of 1845. 192p. *12°.* 1846. *Presentation copy, with inscription, from the author, to 'Rev^d Dr. Symons'. See also* 1850.

34907 MUIRON, J. Aperçus sur les procédés industriels et l'organisation sociétaire, suivis d'un essai sur l'éducation morale...3e. édition. 233p. *12°. Paris*, 1846. *For another edition, see* 1824.

34908 OWEN, ROBERT D. Wealth and misery. 16p. *8°.* 1846. *The date on the wrapper is 1845. For other editions, see* 1839.

34909 PROUDHON, P. J. Système des contradictions économiques, ou philosophie de la misère... 2 vols. *8°. Paris*, 1846. *See also* 1850.

34910 RUGE, A. Zwei Jahre in Paris. Studien und Erinnerungen... 2 vols. *8°. Leipzig*, 1846.

34911 TAMISIER, A. Coup d'œil sur la théorie des fonctions...Deuxième édition. 32p. *16°. Paris*, 1846. *The copy that belonged to Victor Considérant. For another edition, see* 1841 (Théorie générale de Fourier).

34912 VIDAL, F. De la répartition des richesses ou de la justice distributive en économie sociale...l'examen critique des théories exposées soit par les économistes, soit par les socialistes. 500p. *8°. Paris*, 1846.

34913 VILLEGARDELLE, F. Histoire des idées sociales avant la Révolution Française, ou les socialistes modernes, devancés et dépassés par les anciens penseurs et philosophes, avec textes à l'appui. 219p. *16°. Paris*, 1846.

MISCELLANEOUS

34914 An **ACCOUNT** of the consecration and opening of the new church of St. Giles, at Cheadle, in Staffordshire, on the 1st September, 1846: with a description of the edifice. Extracted from Dolman's Magazine for October. 23p. *8°.* 1846.

34915 BOWES, J. Strictures on "A form of prayer and thanksgiving," for the victories on the Sutlej, used by the episcopalian clergy in England, &c. 4p. *8°. Manchester*, [1846?] *See note to no.* 27827.

34916 BOWLES, SIR WILLIAM. Short remarks on the present state of the Navy. 16p. *8°.* 1846.

34917 GILLIS, J. A discourse delivered at the opening of St. Giles' Catholic Church of Cheadle, on the 1st September, 1846. 15p. *8°.* 1846.

34918 GREGORY, WILLIAM (1803–1858). Phonography, or writing by sound. 3p. *8°. n.p.* [1846]

34919 KINGSCOTE, H. A letter to His Grace the Archbishop of Canterbury, on the present wants of the Church...Fourth edition. 16p. *8°.* 1846.

34920 LAYARD, B. V. Speech in the House of Commons, August 3rd, 1846, on limited enlistment. 16p. *8°.* 1846.

34921 LORD, J. Observations on the mortmain laws, Act of Supremacy, &c. with reference to Bills now before Parliament; or, Popery opposed to national independence, and social happiness. 16p. *8°. London, Dublin, &c.*, 1846.

34922 [LOVETT, W.] Enrolment of the Militia for immediate service!! 2p. *8°.* [*London*, 1846]

34923 MARTIN, WILLIAM (1772–1851). William Martin, philosophical conqueror of all nations. Also a challenge for all college professors, to prove this wrong and themselves right... 32p. *8°. Newcastle-on-Tyne*, [1846]

34924 "Our first **MEN:**" a calendar of wealth, fashion and gentility; containing a list of those persons taxed in the city of Boston, credibly reported to be worth one hundred thousand dollars, with biographical notices of the principal persons. Revised edition. 48p. *8°. Boston*, 1846.

34925 On the **NECESSITY** of a general arming in England, by a permanent system of organization, analogous to that of the Anglo-Saxon period, when every able man was a soldier for home defence, with remarks on the militia. 63p. *8°.* 1846.

34926 THOMAS, F. S. Notes of materials for the history of public departments. 216p. *fol.* 1846. *The copy that belonged to Sir Edwin Chadwick.*

34927 VATTEMARE, N. M. A. Movement of the

international litterary [sic] exchanges, between France and North America, from January, 1845, to May, 1846. With instructions for collecting, preparing, and forwarding objects of natural history written by the Professors Administrators of the Museum of Natural History at Paris. And instructions relative to anthropology and zoology, by M. Isidore Geoffroy St.-Hilaire, (both series translated by an American lady.)... 74p. 8°. Paris, 1846.

1847

GENERAL

34928 ASSOCIATION POUR LA DÉFENSE DU TRAVAIL NATIONAL. Examen des théories du libre-échange et des resultats du systême protecteur. 50p. 4°. [Paris, 1847]

34929 BAGSHAW, S. History, gazetteer, and directory of the County of Kent, comprising a general survey of the county...with a variety of statistical, topographical, commercial, and agricultural information... 2 vols. 8°. Sheffield, [1847]

34930 [BANISTER, T.] Memoranda relating to the present crisis as regards our colonies, our trade, our circulating medium, and railways. [By] Thomas Retsinab. 8p. 8°. 1847. *With the author's manuscript corrections for a second edition.*

34931 BASTIAT, C. F. Sophismes économiques... 3e édition. 188p. 16°. Paris, 1847. *See also* 1849. *For the second series, see* 1848.

34932 BERMINGHAM, T. The Thames, the Shannon, and the St. Lawrence, or the good of Great Britain, Ireland, and British North America identified & promoted: in the development of the vast resources of Ireland and British North America, by the employment, for the next ten years, of 250,000 families of the destitute peasantry of Ireland, improperly called redundant population. xiv, 31p. 8°. [London,] 1847.

34933 BISHOP, D. The constitution of society, as designed by God. 132p. 8°. 1847.

34934 The **BRITISH ALMANAC** of the Society for the Diffusion of Useful Knowledge, for...1847... [With 'The companion to the Almanac; or, year-book of general information'.] 96, 260p. 12°. [1847] *For other editions, see* 1828.

34935 BROWNE, G. J., *3rd Marquess of Sligo.* A few remarks and suggestions on the present state of Ireland. 36p. 8°. 1847.

34936 *Entry cancelled.*

34937 CONGRÈS DES ÉCONOMISTES. Congrès des Économistes réuni à Bruxelles par les soins de l'Association belge pour la liberté commerciale. Session de 1847. – Séances des 16, 17 et 18 septembre. 211p. 8°. Bruxelles, 1847.

34938 DAVIS, THOMAS O. Letters of a Protestant on repeal. Edited by Thomas F. Meagher. (*The Irish Confederation,* 2.) 36p. 12°. Dublin, 1847.

34939 [ELLIOT, JOHN L.] A letter to the electors of Westminster. From a conservative. 68p. 8°. [London,] 1847.

34940 [——] Third edition. 69p. 8°. [London,] 1847.

Presentation copy from the author to the Rev. Thomas Jackson.

34941 FABRONI, G. V. M. Scritti di pubblica economia. (*Raccolta degli Economisti Toscani.*) 2 vols. 8°. Firenze, 1847–48.

34942 FAUVETY, C. Der freie Handel, in staatswirthschaftlicher und industrieller Beziehung. 45p. 12°. Leipzig, 1847.

34943 FEATHERSTONHAUGH, G. W. A canoe voyage up the Minnay Sotor; with an account of the lead and copper deposits in Wisconsin; of the gold region in the Cherokee country; and sketches of popular manners; &c.&c.&c. 2 vols. 8°. 1847.

34944 FORTUNE, R. Three years' wanderings in the northern provinces of China, including a visit to the tea, silk and cotton countries: with an account of the agriculture and horticulture of the Chinese, new plants, etc.... 406p. 8°. 1847.

34945 FRANCE. *Ministère de l'Agriculture et du Commerce.* Statistique de la France...[Industrie.] 2 vols. 4°. Paris, 1847–48. *See also* 1835 (*Ministère du Commerce*), 1837 (*Ministère des Travaux Publics*).

34946 GORE, M. Suggestions for the amelioration of the present condition of Ireland. 70p. 8°. London & Dublin, 1847. *For a postscript, see* 1848.

34947 [GRAYDON, W. ?] Relief for Ireland, prompt and permanent, suggested in a letter to the Right Hon. Lord John Russell, by Agricola. 19p. 8°. 1847.

34948 [GREGORY, SIR WILLIAM H. ?] Paddiana; or, scraps and sketches of Irish life, present and past. By the author of "A hot water cure"... 2 vols. 12°. 1847.

34949 HANCOCK, WILLIAM N. Three lectures on the questions, should the principles of political economy be disregarded at the present crisis? and if not, how can they be applied towards the discovery of measures of relief? Delivered in...Trinity College, Dublin, in Hilary term, 1847. 61p. 8°. Dublin & London, 1847.

34950 HEYWOOD, THOMAS (1797–1866), *ed.* The Moore Rental. [With an appendix.] (*Remains historical and literary connected with the Palatine Counties of Lancaster and Chester, published by the Chetham Society,* 12.) lii, 158p. 4°. Manchester, 1847.

34951 HOFFMANN, JOHANN G. Nachlass kleiner Schriften staatswirthschaftlichen Inhalts. 708p. 8°. Berlin, 1847. *Presentation copy, with inscription, from the author to Professor Schubert.*

34952 HOLMES, R. The case of Ireland stated. 102p. 8°. Dublin & London, 1847. *The copy that belonged to Earl De Grey.*

34953 HOMMAIRE DE HELL, X. Travels in the steppes of the Caspian Sea, the Crimea, the Caucasus, &c. ...With additions from various sources. 436p. 8°. 1847.

34954 A INTERFERENCIA ingleza nos negocios de Portugal. 42p. 8°. *Paris,* 1847.

34955 JOBARD, J. B. A. M. Chacun doit-il être propriétaire et responsable de ses œuvres? 27p. 8°. *Bruxelles,* 1847.

34956 —— Entente cordiale du propriétaire et du prolétaire, dialogue. 15p. 8°. *Bruxelles,* 1847.

34957 —— La force, le capital et le droit, drame industriel. Précédé d'une lettre à M. Wollowski [*sic*] sur la propriété intellectuelle. [With 'Des inventions et des inventeurs. Par M. Gardissal'.] 36p. 8°. *Bruxelles,* 1847.

34958 KELLNER, G. Zur Geschichte des Physiokratismus. Quesnay. – Gournay. Turgot. 241p. 8°. *Göttingen,* 1847.

34959 *LECONTE, C. Étude économique de la Grèce, de sa position actuelle, de son avenir; suivi de documents sur le commerce de l'Orient, sur l'Égypte, etc.... 452p. 8°. *Paris,* 1847. *The copy that belonged to George Grote.*

34960 LESTIBOUDOIS, T. Économie pratique des nations, ou système économique applicable aux différentes contrées, et spécialement à la France. 515p. 8°. *Paris,* 1847.

34961 [LETCHIOT, , Rev.?] The Southampton guide; comprising an account of the ancient and present state of Southampton and its neighbourhood, with a particular account of its trade, the railways, docks, etc. A new edition, with considerable additions and alterations. 154p. 12°. *London & Southampton,* [1847 ?]

34962 McCULLOCH, JOHN R. A descriptive and statistical account of the British Empire: exhibiting its extent, physical capacities, population, industry, and civil and religious institutions...Third edition, corrected, enlarged, and improved... 2 vols. 8°. 1847. *For other editions, entitled,* A statistical account of the British Empire, *see* 1837.

34963 MACGREGOR, JOHN (1797–1857). The progress of America, from the discovery by Columbus to ...1846. 2 vols. 4°. 1847.

34964 MANNIX, , and WHELLAN, W. History, gazetteer, and directory of Cumberland; comprising a general survey of the county, and a history of the diocese of Carlisle; with separate historical, statistical, & topographical descriptions of all the boroughs, towns, parishes ...and villages... 630p. 8°. *Beverley,* 1847.

34965 MARTIN, ROBERT M. China; political, commercial, and social; in an official report to Her Majesty's Government. [With 'Appendix of official and public documents'.] 2 vols. 8°. 1847.

34966 MICHAUD, L. G. and VILLENAVE, T. Histoire du Saint-Simonisme et de la famille de Rothschild, ou biographie de Saint-Simon et de Bazard... Suivie de la biographie de Mayer-Anselme Rothschild et de Nathan son fils. (Extrait de la Biographie Universelle, tomes LVII et LXXX.) [With 'Notice sur Georges-Guillaume de Hesse-Cassel, par M. Lesourd'.] 63p. 8°. *Paris,* 1847.

34967 MICHEL, J., ed. Irish political economy. [Reprints of *A short view of the state of Ireland* and *A proposal for the universal use of Irish manufacture*.] By Jonathan Swift, Dean of St. Patrick's and [Extracts from *The Querist, containing several queries proposed to the consideration of the public*. By] George Berkeley, Bishop of Cloyne. (*The Irish Confederation,* 1.) 39p. 12°. *Dublin,* 1847.

34968 MOREAU DE JONNÈS, A. Éléments de statistique, comprenant les principes généraux de cette science, et un aperçu historique de ses progrès. [With 'Bibliographie statistique de l'Europe'.] 362p. 12°. *Paris,* 1847.

34969 O'CONNELL, J. An argument for Ireland... Second edition. Printed by order of the Loyal National Repeal Association of Ireland. 469[489]p. 8°. *Dublin,* 1847.

34970 PEEL, SIR ROBERT, 2nd Bart. Letter from Sir Robert Peel to the electors for the Borough of Tamworth. [On the policies of the Conservative Government since 1841.] 35p. 8°. 1847. *The copy that belonged to Earl De Grey.*

34971 *—— Second edition. 25p. 8°. 1847.

34972 The PEOPLE'S ALMANACK. 1848. [24]p. 8°. [1847] *See also* 1849.

34973 PLAIN FACTS, pseud. An answer to Lord George Bentinck's address to the electors of the Borough of King's Lynn, on the eve of the general election of 1847. With an appendix, containing remarks on the returns moved for by the noble Lord on the 20th of July. Second edition, with a few words to the "Quarterly Review," &c. 83p. 8°. 1847.

34974 A RELATION or rather a true account, of the island of England; with sundry particulars of the customs of these people, and of the royal revenues under King Henry the Seventh, about the year 1500. Translated from the Italian, with notes, by Charlotte Augusta Sneyd. (*Camden Society, Old Series,* 37.) 135p. 4°. 1847.

34975 ROGERS, JASPER W. An appeal for the Irish peasantry, with facts of paramount advantage to the iron masters, manufacturers, and agriculturists of England, respecting the value of peat, and peat-charcoal, as a fuel and a fertilizer. 116p. 8°. 1847.

34976 —— An appeal for the peasantry of Ireland, and objects of the Irish Amelioration Society. Second edition, with heads of the amended Act. 108p. 8°. 1847.

34977 SENIOR, N. W. A lecture on the production of wealth, delivered before the University of Oxford, in Michaelmas term, 1847. 20p. 8°. *Oxford & London,* 1847.

34978 SIMONDE DE SISMONDI, J. C. L. Political economy, and the philosophy of government; a series of essays selected from the works of M. de Sismondi, with an historical notice of his life and writings by M. Mignet. Translated from the French...with a preliminary essay by the translator. 459p. 8°. 1847.

34979 SPACKMAN, W. F. An analysis of the occupations of the people, showing the relative importance of the agricultural, manufacturing, shipping, colonial, commercial, and mining interests, of...Great Britain and its dependencies...Compiled from the census of 1841 and other official returns. [With an appendix.] 128, 187p. 8°. 1847.

34980 The STATE of Ireland, and the measures of Government for its relief, considered with reference to the interests of the poor. 28p. 8°. 1847.

34981 STRATEN-PONTHOZ, A. VAN DER, *Graaf.* Onderzoek naar den toestand der landverhuizers in de Vereenigde Staten van Noord-Amerika... 124p. *8°. Utrecht, 1847.*

34982 SUTTON, H. G. The necessity of a system of public agricultural & commercial statistics of food, considered...Read before the Literary and Philosophical Society of Liverpool, on...22d February, 1847. 32p. *8°. Liverpool, 1847.*

34983 *TAYLOR, H. Simple arithmetic as connected with the national coinage, weights and measures. Dedicated to the Lords Commissioners of Her Majesty's Treasury...Third edition. [A plea for decimalization.] 36p. *8°. 1847. The copy that belonged to Augustus De Morgan.*

34984 TWISS, SIR T. View of the progress of political economy in Europe since the sixteenth century. A course of lectures delivered before the University of Oxford in Michaelmas term, 1846, and Lent term, 1847. 298p. *8°. 1847.*

34985 WARD, JAMES. How to re-construct the industrial condition of Ireland: a letter to Lord J. Russell. 35p. *8°. 1847. Presentation copy from the author to James Wyld, M.P.*

34986 WATTS, J. The alphabet of political economy. 36p. *12°. London & Manchester, 1847.*

34987 WHATELY, R., *Archbishop of Dublin.* Introductory lectures on political economy, delivered at Oxford in Easter Term, MDCCCXXXI...Third edition, revised and enlarged. 313p. *8°. 1847. For other editions, see 1831.*

AGRICULTURE

34988 AMICUS CURIÆ, *pseud.* Food for the million. Maize against potato. A case for the times: comprising the history, uses, & culture of Indian corn, and especially showing the practicability and necessity of cultivating the dwarf varieties, in England and Ireland. 160p. *12°. London & Ipswich, 1847. With the book-plate of the 13th Earl of Derby.*

34989 *BUELOW-CUMMEROW, E. G. G. VON. Die Taxen und das Reglement der landschaftlichen Creditvereine nach ihren nothwendigen Reformen. 92p. *8°. Berlin, 1847. The copy that belonged to George Grote.*

34990 CHEVALIER, M. Des mines d'argent et d'or du nouveau monde. (Extrait de la Revue des Deux Mondes décembre 1846 et janvier 1847.) 114p. *8°. Paris, 1847. Two presentation copies from the author: one to N. W. Senior, the other to A. Blanqui.*

34991 CLAPPERTON, J. Instructions for the small farmers of Ireland, on the cropping and culture of their farms...Recommended by the Royal Agricultural Improvement Society of Ireland. 35p. *12°. Dublin, 1847.*

34992 CURTIS, JOHN (1791–1862). Observations on the natural history and economy of a weevil affecting the pea-crops, and various insects which injure or destroy the mangold wurzel and beet...Paper XIII. [From the Journal of the Royal Agricultural Society of England, vol. VIII., part II.] 19p. *8°. 1847. Presentation copy from the author to Lord John Russell.*

34993 DUMONT, ARISTIDE F. M. Des travaux publics dans leurs rapports avec l'agriculture. 376p. *8°. Paris, 1847.*

34994 ENDERBY, C. Proposal for re-establishing the British southern whale fishery through the medium of a chartered company and in combination with the colonisation of the Auckland Islands, as the site of the company's whaling station...Third edition. 67p. *8°. 1847.*

34995 ENGLAND. *Commission of Inquiry into the State of the Law and Practice in Respect of the Occupation of Land in Ireland.* Digest of evidence taken before Her Majesty's Commissioners...[With prefatory notes by the Earl of Devon and J. P. Kennedy.] 2 vols. *8°. Dublin, 1847–48.*

34996 —— —— Extracts of evidence taken by the late Commission...on the subject of waste lands reclamation; with a prefatory letter to the Right Hon. Lord John Russell

from G. Poulet Scrope, M.P. 89p. *8°. 1847. The copy that belonged to Earl De Grey.*

For the **GARDENERS' & FARMERS' JOURNAL,** 1847–49, *see vol.* III, *Periodicals list.*

34997 *GOOLD, H. Thoughts on a judicious disposition of land in Ireland. Calculated to promote the best interests of landlord and tenant, while securing remunerative employment for the entire labouring population... 23p. *8°. Dublin & London, 1847. The FWA copy that belonged to William Pare.*

34998 HAMILTON, JOHN (1800–1884). A word from an Irish landowner to his brethren of the United Kingdom. 16p. *8°. Dublin, 1847.*

34999 JOHNSTON, JAMES F. W. Instructions for the analysis of soils. 22p. *8°. Edinburgh & London, 1847.*

35000 LIEBIG, J. VON, *Freiherr.* Chemistry in its applications to agriculture and physiology...Edited from the manuscript of the author, by Lyon Playfair and William Gregory. Fourth edition. Revised and enlarged. 418p. *8°. 1847. For other editions, see 1841.*

35001 LOUDON, J. C. Self-instruction for young gardeners, foresters, bailiffs, land-stewards, and farmers; in arithmetic and book-keeping...mechanics...land-surveying...architectural drawing...With examples... With a memoir of the author [by his wife Jane]...Second edition, with corrections and additions. li, 244p. *8°. 1847.*

35002 LOW, D. Elements of practical agriculture; comprehending the cultivation of plants, the husbandry of the domestic animals, and the economy of the farm... Fifth edition. 811p. *8°. London & Edinburgh, 1847. For another edition, see 1834.*

35003 MACADAM, JAMES. On the cultivation of flax...Prize essay. [From the Journal of the Royal Agricultural Society, vol. VIII., part II.] 40p. *8°. 1847. Presentation copy from the author to T. Spring Rice, Baron Monteagle.*

35004 MECHI, J. J. Mechi's experience in drainage; to which are added his letters XVII., XVIII., XIX. & XX.; likewise his speech on the general subject of agriculture, delivered to the Wickham-Market Farmers' Club, November 2, 1846. 48p. *8°. 1847.*

35005 MEGUSCHER, F. Memoria del Signor Francesco Meguscher in risposta al quesito additare la migliore e piu' facile maniera per rimettere i boschi nelle montagne diboschite dell'alta Lombardia e per conservarli e profittarne, proposto dall' Imp. R. Istituto Lombardo di Scienze, Lettere ed Arti... 402p. *8°. Milano,* 1847.

35006 MORTON, JOHN C. On the maintenance of fertility in new arable land. [From the Journal of the Royal Agricultural Society of England, vol. VII., part II.] 14p. *8°.* 1847.

35007 OSBORN, J. T. The food question: shewing the effects which steam power applied to agriculture would have on increasing the supply of food, throughout Great Britain, Ireland, and the colonies... Second edition... 32p. *8°.* 1847.

35008 ROYER, C. É. L'agriculture allemande, ses écoles, son organisation, ses mœurs et ses pratiques les plus récentes. 541p. *8°. Paris, Alger, &c.,* 1847. *The paper wrapper has a printed slip substituting a Brussels for the Paris imprint.*

35009 SINCLAIR, GEORGE (1786–1834). Library of Useful Knowledge. Useful and ornamental planting... 151p. *8°.* [1847?]

35010 SPEECHES at the agricultural meeting at Drayton Manor. Reprinted from the "Gardener's Chronicle and Agricultural Gazette," of October 11, 1847. 16p. *8°.* [1847]

35011 TRIMMER, JOSHUA. On the improvement of land as an investment for capital... Extracted from the North British Review for May, 1845. 32p. *8°.* 1847.

35012 *＊——* Third edition. 32p. *8°.* 1847. *The copy that belonged to George Grote.*

35013 WASHINGTON, G., *President of the USA.* Letters on agriculture from George Washington, President of the United States, to Arthur Young, Esq. and Sir John Sinclair, Bart., with statistical tables and remarks by Thomas Jefferson, Richard Peters, and other gentlemen, on the economy and management of farms in the United States. Edited by Franklin Knight. 198p. *4°. Washington, Philadelphia, &c.,* 1847. *For another edition, without the letters to Sir John Sinclair, see* 1801.

35014 WASON, R. Letter to the Right Honorable Lord John Russell, M.P. suggesting that the mode adopted for the reclamation of waste land at Corwar, should be pursued in Ireland. 17p. *8°. Edinburgh & London,* 1847.

35015 —— New edition, with preface and postscript. iv, 17, 10p. *8°. Edinburgh & London,* 1847.

35016 WILSON, JOHN M., *ed.* The rural cyclopedia, or a general dictionary of agriculture, and of the arts, sciences, instruments, and practice, necessary to the farmer, stockfarmer, gardener, forester, landsteward, farrier, &c.... 4 vols. *8°. Edinburgh & London,* 1847–49. *See also* 1848.

35017 YOUATT, W. The pig: a treatise on the breeds, management, feeding, and medical treatment, of swine; with directions for salting pork, and curing bacon and hams... 164p. *8°.* 1847.

CORN LAWS

35018 CROSBY, G. Crosby's Parliamentary record of elections in Great Britain and Ireland: with select biographical notices and speeches of distinguished statesmen, &c. [Containing debates in the Lords and Commons on the corn laws, in the memorable session of 1846.] 2 vols. *12°. York [& Leeds],* 1847. *See also* 1848, 1849.

35019 HAYS, J. Remarks on the late crisis in the corn trade; with some suggestions arising therefrom, particularly on the probable advantages of a fixed permanent duty. 48p. *8°.* [1847]

POPULATION

35020 HOWARD, W. The vital question in political economy. 24p. *8°.* 1847.

35021 [KING-NOEL, W., *Earl of Lovelace.*] The true law of population shown to be connected with the food of the people. By T. Doubleday... Over-population and its remedy. By W. T. Thornton... [A review signed: L. Reprinted from the *Westminster Review,* vol. XLVII, no. 1.] p.100–117. *8°. n.p.* [1847]

35022 ＊QUETELET, L. A. J. Bulletin de la Commission Centrale de Statistique. De l'influence du libre arbitre de l'homme sur les faits sociaux, et particulièrement sur le nombre des mariages. [Extrait du tome III.] 21p. *4°.*

n.p. [1847] *The copy that belonged to Augustus De Morgan.*

35023 A THEORY of population deduced from the general law of animal fertility. [An offprint of a review of works on population by T. Doubleday and others.] 35p. *8°.* [1847]

35024 WIGLESWORTH, T. Vital statistics. An essay on the rate of mortality among children. Read before the British Association, Sept. 12, 1846. To which is added tables on the rate of mortality among orphans founded upon... the records of the London and British Orphan Asylums and the Orphan Working School. 32p. *8°.* 1847.

TRADES & MANUFACTURES

35025 CLARKE, HYDE. The high pressure steam engine and Trevithick. [Extracted from the Railway Register.] p.73–96. *8°. [London,* 1847?]

35026 CRADDOCK, T. The chemistry of the steam engine practically considered; being the substance of a course of lectures, delivered in... Birmingham: with a description of the patent universal condensing steam-engine, illustrated by...drawings. 92, 40p. *8°. London & Birmingham,* 1847.

35027 CURR, J. The learned donkeys of eighteen hundred and forty seven. Being a review of the reviewers [in the *Mechanics' Magazine*] of Railway locomotion, and steam navigation: their principles and practice. p.185–198. *8°.* 1847.

35028 [DARLING, G.] Instructions for making unfermented bread. With observations on its properties, medicinal and economic. By a physician. Tenth edition, with additions. 16p. *8°. London, Edinburgh, &c.,* 1847.

35029 EVANS, WILLIAM J. The sugar-planter's manual; being a treatise on the art of obtaining sugar from the sugar-cane. 244p. *8°.* 1847.

35030 GILROY, C. G. The art of weaving by hand and by power: with an account of recent improvements in the art, and a sketch of the history of its rise and progress in ancient and modern times. For the use of manufacturers and practical weavers...Second edition. 537p. *8°.* 1847.

35031 MARTIN, WILLIAM (1772–1851). W. Martin's invention of the high level bridge; height, from high water to railway level, 108 feet 6 inches. *s.sh.4°. Newcastle,* [1847]

35032 PRITCHARD, A. English patents; being a register of all those granted for inventions in the arts, manufactures, chemistry, agriculture, during the first forty-five years of the present century. 411, 91, 67, 70, 162p. *12°.* 1847. *A reissue, with a general title-page, of 5 separately published works, 1841–46.*

35033 ROBERTS, WILLIAM H. The Scottish ale-brewer and practical maltster, a comprehensive digest of the art of brewing ales according to the Scottish system... With a supplement on the relative value of malt and sugar ...Third edition. 251p. *8°. Edinburgh & London,* 1847.

35034 ROLLET, A. Mémoire sur la meunerie, la boulangerie et la conservation des grains et des farines... Précédée de considérations sur le commerce des blés en Europe...Publié sous les auspices de M. Le Ministre de la Marine et des Colonies. 594p. *4°. Paris,* 1847.

35035 THEOPHILUS, called also **RUGERUS.** Theophili, qui et Rugerus...libri III. De diversis artibus ...Opera et studio R. Hendrie. li, 447p. *8°. Londini,* 1847. *The Latin and English texts are printed on opposite pages.*

35036 THOMPSON, BENJAMIN, *colliery engineer.* Inventions, improvements, and practice of Benjamin Thompson, in the combined character of colliery engineer, and general manager. With some interesting particulars relative to Watt's steam engine, and a short treatise on the coal trade regulation. 133p. *8°. Newcastle,* 1847.

35037 TURNER, THOMAS, *barrister.* Remarks on the right of property in mechanical invention, with reference to registered designs. 30p. *12°.* 1847.

35038 URE, A. Observations on fiscal chemistry; in reference to sugar, spirits, and tobacco. Respectfully submitted to the Legislature. 26p. *8°.* 1847.

35039 WATHERSTON, J. H. A familiar explanation of the art of assaying gold and silver; and its bearing upon the interests of the public demonstrated; with considerations on the importance of the Pix Jury; a review of the past and present state of the goldsmiths' trade... 64p. *8°.* 1847.

COMMERCE

35040 ANISSON-DUPERRON, A. J. L., *Comte.* Essai sur les traités de commerce de Methuen (1703), et de 1786, dans leurs rapports avec la liberté commerciale ...Extrait du no. 65 du Journal des Économistes (avril 1847). 19p. *8°. Paris,* 1847.

35041 AYLWIN, D. C. A letter to George Frederick Young, Esq. (deputy chairman of the Shipowners' Association,)...in reply to certain questions regarding the operation of the navigation laws on the trade of Calcutta. 18p. *8°. [London,* 1847]

35042 BIZET, L. C. Du commerce de la boucherie et de la charcuterie de Paris et des commerces qui en dépendent...suivis du Rapport sur le projet de l'organisation de la boucherie par M. H. Boulay de la Meurthe. 537p. *8°. Paris,* 1847.

35043 BROWNE, JOSEPH H. The navigation laws: their history and operation. 45p. *8°. London, Liverpool, &c.,* 1847. *The copy that belonged to Victor Considérant.*

35044 BURN, RICHARD (*fl.* 1845–1870). Statistics of the cotton trade arranged in a tabular form; also a chronological history of its various inventions, improvements, etc., etc. 34p. *8°. London & Manchester,* [1847]

35045 CHEVALIER, M. Des forces alimentaires des états et des devoirs du gouvernement dans la crise actuelle. 59p. *8°. Paris,* 1847. *Presentation copy from the author to N. W. Senior.*

35046 DUNN, JAMES (*fl.* 1847). A view of the navigation laws, briefly shewing the most important points in which those laws regulate the registration, transfer, equipment, manning, and employment of British ships, and of foreign ships trading with Great Britain and the colonies. Compiled from the parliamentary reports of evidence on the navigation laws. With remarks. 16p. *8°. Sunderland,* 1847. *Presentation copy from the author to Thomas Banister.*

35047 ENGLAND. *Laws, etc.* [*Endorsed:*] Edinburgh markets and customs. An Act to enlarge and improve the meal, corn and grain markets of the City of Edinburgh... ⟨Royal Assent, 21st June 1847.⟩ 10 & 11 Victoriæ, sess. 1847. 24p. *fol. Westminster,* [1847]

35048 A frightful EXAMPLE. [4]p. *8°. [London,* 1847] *'A frightful example' is the title of a caricature which occupies p.*[1]*. The caption of p.*[2] *reads: 'The following may be said to exhibit a frightful example of the effects of free trade'.*

35049 GILBART, J. W. Lectures on the history and principles of ancient commerce. 316p. *12°.* 1847. *Presentation copy from the author to W. Kirkman.*

35050 GREENHOW, C. H. Observations on the navigation laws: suggesting their immediate repeal, and unqualified free trade. 39p. *8°.* [1847] *The copy that belonged to Victor Considérant.*

35051 HAMEL, J. VON. Tradescant der aeltere 1618 in Russland. Der Handelsverkehr zwischen England und

Russland in seiner Entstehung. Rückblick auf einige der älteren Reisen im Norden... 264p. *4°. St. Petersburg & Leipzig*, 1847.

35052 LE BASTIER, J. Défense du travail national, ou nécessité de la protection commerciale démontrée à l'aide des principes, des faits et du calcul. 152p. *12°. Paris*, 1847.

35053 MACGREGOR, JOHN (1797–1857). Commercial statistics. A digest of the productive resources, commercial legislation, customs tariffs...shipping, imports and exports, and the monies, weights and measures of all nations. Including all British commercial treaties with foreign states... 5 vols. *8°.* 1847–50. *The copy that belonged to Joseph Hume, with his book-plate.*

35054 MACINTOSH, G. Biographical memoir of the late Charles Macintosh, F.R.S. of Campsie and Dunchattan... 186p. *8°. Glasgow*, 1847.

35055 [MATHER, JAMES.] An address to the electors of the sea-ports of the United Kingdom on the navigation laws: and their duties at this critical juncture. By the author of "Ships & railways." 23p. *8°. South Shields*, 1847.

35056 MONGRÉDIEN, A. Revue du marché de Liverpool de l'année 1846. 59p. *8°. n.p.* [1847]

35057 [MURE, W.] The commercial policy of Pitt and Peel, 1785–1846. 67p. *8°.* 1847. *Also attributed to David Mure.*

35058 [——] Reply to the Quarterly Review. By the author of the "Commercial policy of Pitt and Peel." 37p. *8°.* 1847. *Also attributed to David Mure.*

35059 RICARDO, J. L. The anatomy of the navigation laws. 336p. *8°.* 1847. *The copy that belonged to Sir Robert Peel, with his book-plate.*

35060 WARD, W. Remarks on the commercial legislation of 1846, addressed to the Right Honourable the Lord Mayor and the Livery of London. 82p. *8°.* 1847.

35061 WILLIAMS, A. The crisis and the crash. A letter to the free traders of England. 16p. *8°.* 1847. *Reissued in* Facts for philosophers, *1849, q.v.* (GENERAL).

COLONIES

35062 *ABBOTT, SIR F. Practical treatise on permanent bridges for Indian rivers. 38p. *8°. Agra*, 1847. *See also* 1850.

35063 ACLAND, C. A popular account of the manners and customs of India... 156p. *8°.* 1847.

35064 ALCOCK, THOMAS ST. L. Observations on the Poor Relief Bill for Ireland, and its bearing on the important subject of emigration; with some remarks on the great public works projected in the British North American colonies. 30p. *8°.* 1847.

35065 BALFOUR, T. G. Statistical report on the sickness and mortality among the troops serving in the Madras Presidency. Prepared from official documents ...From the Edin. Med. and Surg. Journal, No. 172. 64p. *8°. Edinburgh*, 1847.

35066 BENNETT, J. W. Letter to Robert William Hay, Esq....setting forth a case of unprecedented oppression and injustice...humbly submitted to the ...public of the United Kingdom and of the colonies. 233p. *8°.* 1847. *The copy that belonged to Earl De Grey.*

35067 [BOURNE, JOHN, C.E.] Railways in India. By an engineer. 127p. *8°.* 1847. *See also* 1848.

35068 BOYD, B. A letter to His Excellency Sir William Denison, &c.&c.&c. Lieut.-Governor of Van Diemen's Land, on the expediency of transferring the unemployed labour of that colony to New South Wales. 20p. *8°. Sydney*, 1847.

For **BRITISH AND FOREIGN ABORIGINES' PROTECTION SOCIETY,** The colonial intelligencer; or, aborigines' friend...Comprising the transactions of the society, 1847–50, 1867–71, *see* vol. III, *Periodicals list,* Colonial intelligencer.

35069 BURKE, J. H. India salt. Scinde versus Cheshire, Calcutta and Bombay. 31p. *8°.* 1847.

35070 CHAMBER OF COMMERCE, *Jamaica.* (Printed for the Chamber of Commerce.) Report of the Standing Committee of the Chamber of Commerce, Jamaica, upon the present condition of that colony; the causes of its depression; and the remedial measures necessary to restore its prosperity. [Signed: William Wright, chairman, and dated, Sept. 4, 1847.] 23p. *8°.* 1847.

35071 CHISHOLM, C. Emigration and transportation relatively considered; in a letter, dedicated, by permission, to Earl Grey. 46p. *8°.* 1847.

35072 CLARKE, HYDE. Practical and theoretical considerations on the management of railways in India. 48p. *8°.* [*London,* 1847]

35072A [COLQUHOUN, J. C.] Claims of the West India colonies. [With a postscript.] 22, 16p. *8°.* [*London,* 1847]

35073 *FRANCE. *Chambre des Députés.* (No. 183.) Chambre des Députés. Session 1847. Rapport fait au nom de la commission chargée d'examiner le projet de loi relatif aux crédits extraordinaires demandés pour l'Algérie. Par M. de Tocqueville...24 mai 1847. 104p. *4°.* [*Paris,*] 1847. *The copy that belonged to George Crote.*

35074 *—— —— (No. 205.) Chambre des Députés. Session 1847. Rapport fait au nom de la commission chargée de l'examen du projet de loi portant demande d'un crédit de 3 millions de francs pour les camps agricoles de l'Algérie. Par M. de Tocqueville...2 juin 1847. 43p. *4°.* [*Paris,*] 1847. *The copy that belonged to George Grote.*

35075 FREE TRADE & the cotton question with reference to India, being a memorial from the British merchants of Cochin, to the Right Hon. Sir John Hobhouse, Bart., M.P. President of the Board of Control; with a letter and appendix. By Francis Carnac Brown, Esq. of Tellicherry. 126p. *8°.* 1847.

35076 HUTT, SIR W. Colonization for Ireland. Speech...4th of February, 1847...on going into Committee on the Irish Destitution Bill. 15p. *8°.* [1847?]

35077 LANDOR, E. W. The Bushman; or, life in a new country. 438p. *8°.* 1847.

35078 LANG, JOHN D. Cooksland in north-eastern

Australia; the future cotton-field of Great Britain: its characteristics and capabilities for European colonization. With a disquisition on the origin, manners, and customs of the aborigines. 496p. *8⁰*. 1847.

35079 A LETTER to the shareholders of the East Indian and Great Western of Bengal Railways, on their present position and future prospects. By one of themselves. [Signed: A shareholder.] 15p. *8⁰*. 1847. *The Rastrick copy.*

35080 MILLS, A. Systematic colonization. 47p. *8⁰*. 1847.

35081 NAPIER, R. Remarks on Lieut-Colonel Outram's work, entitled "The conquest of Sinde, a commentary." 138p. *8⁰*. 1847.

35082 NEW ZEALAND COMPANY. Twenty-second report of the Court of Directors... 19p. *8⁰*. *n.p.* [1847] *See also* 1844.

35083 *OUSELEY, J. R. Reports by the Agent to the Governor General of tours made by him through the districts attached to the Political Agency of the South-West Frontier, in 1840, 1844, 1847. 58p. *8⁰*. *Calcutta*, 1847.

35084 PAYNE, C. W. The Eastern Empire. Crown colonies...(First series.) Ceylon. 20p. *8⁰*. 1847.

35085 REASONS for railways in Madras and Bombay, and against the exclusive favour of Government to those in Bengal and Agra. First edition, July, 1847. 19p. *8⁰*. [1847] *The Rastrick copy.*

35086 RICE, THOMAS S., *Baron Monteagle*. Emigration – Ireland. The speech of the Lord Monteagle...in the House of Lords...June 4th, 1847. Extracted from Hansard's Parliamentary Debates. 19p. *12⁰*. 1847.

35087 ROWCROFT, C. Le colon de Van Diémen ou aventures d'un émigrant. Contes des colonies... Traduit de l'anglais sur la 5e édition, par N. Lefebvre-Duruflé. 3 vols. *12⁰*. *Paris*, 1847.

35088 SAINTHILL, R. Objections to English inscriptions on the coinage of the East India Company. 16p. *8⁰*. [*London*, 1847?]

35089 SOCIÉTÉ ANGEVINE POUR LE PLACEMENT DES COLONS EN ALGÉRIE. Projet de colonisation présenté par M. Lieutaud, notaire à Alger. [A prospectus.] 15p. *4⁰*. *Angers*, 1847.

35090 THOMPSON, GEORGE (1804–1878). Free trade with India: its influence on the condition and prospects of the country, and on the slave systems of America. Speech...delivered before the electors and non-electors of the Tower Hamlets at the Eastern Institution, October 26th, 1847. 24p. *8⁰*. *Kennington*, [1847]

35091 TORRENS, R. Self-supporting colonization. Ireland saved, without cost to the Imperial Treasury. [With 'Substance of a speech delivered...in the House of Commons, 15th February 1827, on the motion of Sir Robert Wilmot Horton, Bart. for the re-appointment of a Select Committee on emigration from the United Kingdom. Second edition'.] 56p. *8⁰*. 1847. *For another edition, see* 1849 (Systematic colonization).

35092 WARD, JAMES. The true policy of organising a system of railways for India. A letter to the Right Hon. the President of the Board of Control. 37p. *8⁰*. 1847. *The Rastrick copy.*

35093 WEST INDIA PLANTERS AND MERCHANTS. Memorandum by the Acting Committee of West India Planters and Merchants. ⟨Transmitted on the 26th October, 1847, to Her Majesty's Government.⟩ 12p. *8⁰*. [*London*, 1847]

35094 —— ⟨Printed for the West India Body.⟩ Report of the Acting Committee to the Standing Committee of West India Planters and Merchants, 13th January, 1847. 56p. *8⁰*. 1847. *See also* 1846, 1848, 1849.

35095 WILBRAHAM, G. Thoughts on the salt monopoly in India. 55p. *8⁰*. 1847.

35096 WINDOW, J. Reasons for the employment of convicts in the British sugar growing colonies in the West Indies, with a view to their moral reformation, and to afford labour to the proprietors of estates in those parts of Her Majesty's dominions. 16p. *8⁰*. 1847.

FINANCE

35097 ALISON, SIR A., *Bart*. England in 1815 and 1845; and the monetary famine of 1847; or, a sufficient and contracted currency...Fourth edition, revised and enlarged. 80p. *8⁰*. *Edinburgh & London*, 1847. *For other editions, see* 1845.

35098 —— Free trade and a fettered currency. 80p. *8⁰*. *Edinburgh & London*, 1847.

35099 [ANDERSON, WILLIAM, *station master*.] Thoughts on the currency, with suggestions for placing it on a new and permanent basis. By a resident in Sunderland. 16p. *8⁰*. *Bishopwearmouth*, 1847. *Attributed to William Anderson in a manuscript note on the title-page.*

35100 ANTI-GOLD-LAW LEAGUE. Anti-Gold-Law League. [Propositions on the formation of the League, 29th September, 1847.] *s.sh.4⁰*. *n.p.* [1847]

35101 AYTOUN, J. The railways and the currency as connected with the present monetary crisis. 36p. *8⁰*. *Edinburgh & London*, 1847.

35102 BANCO DE PORTUGAL. Organisação do Banco de Portugal. [With 'Banco de Portugal. 21 de Novembro de 1846. Relaçao geral dos accionistas'.] 59, 39p. *8⁰*. *Lisboa*, 1847.

For the **BANKERS' MAGAZINE,** *Baltimore*, 1847–1943, *see* vol. III, *Periodicals list.*

35103 BANKRUPTCY and insolvency. Reprinted from the January number of the Westminster and Foreign Quarterly Review. 19p. *8⁰*. 1847. *See note to no.* 32762.

35104 BARING, A., *Baron Ashburton*. The financial and commercial crisis considered. 40p. *8⁰*. 1847. *Presentation copy from the author to T. Spring Rice, Baron Monteagle.*

35105 —— Second edition. 40p. *8⁰*. 1847.

35106 —— Third edition. 40p. *8⁰*. 1847. *The copy that belonged to T. Spring Rice, Baron Monteagle.*

35107 —— Fourth edition. 40p. *8⁰*. 1847.

35108 BARTON, J. The monetary crisis of 1847. Prediction and counter-prediction. 12p. *8⁰*. *Chichester*, [1847]

35109 BIERSACK, H. L. Ueber Differenzialzölle im Verhältniss des deutschen Zollvereins zu andern Ländern. Von H.L.B. 127p. *8°. Frankfurt am Main,* 1847.

35110 BOOTH, H. The rationale of the currency question; or, the plea of the merchant and the shareholder for an improved system of national banking. 23p. *8°. London & Liverpool,* 1847.

35111 BROWNE, WILLIAM J. The real El Dorado; or, true principles of currency developed. 30p. *8°. London & Liverpool,* 1847.

35112 BROWNELL, C. A letter to the Right Hon. the Earl of Clarendon, President of the Board of Trade, on the copper ore duties, in reply to the letter of Sir Charles Lemon, Bart. 34p. *8°. London & Liverpool,* [1847]

35113 CAMPBELL, JOHN, *registrar, and others.* [*Endorsed:*] Bankruptcy and Insolvency Bill. Answer of John Campbell, William Henry Whitehead, and John Fisher Miller, three of the registrars of the Court of Bankruptcy, to the case of William Vizard, the younger, also a registrar...April 1847. 5p. *fol. n.p.* [1847] *See note to no.* 32762.

35114 CAMPO, A. and **BONA,** F. DE. La hacienda y el Banco de San Fernando en 1846. Parte primera... 200p. *4°. Madrid,* 1847. *Presentation copy from Felix de Bona to Baron V. Gülich.*

35115 CARGILL, W. The commercial crisis and the Bank Charter Act. 23p. *12°. Newcastle-upon-Tyne,* 1847.

35116 —— The currency: showing how a fixed price of gold subjects England to loss abroad and to convulsions at home. First published in 1844. 45p. *8°.* 1847.

35117 CHAMBER OF COMMERCE AND MANUFACTURES, *Edinburgh.* Monetary affairs. Resolutions of the Chamber of Commerce and Manufactures of the City of Edinburgh...August, 1847. [On the effects of recent legislation on currency and commerce. Issued with a covering letter, dated September 1847, soliciting support, signed: John F. Macfarlan, secretary.] [4]p. *fol. n.p.* [1847]

35118 CHARD, H. Spanish bonds. A statement of the present position of the Spanish bondholders: with the opinions of eminent counsel and jurists on their case; and petitions...for such interposition with Spain as will obtain a settlement of the claims of the bondholders. 67p. *8°.* 1847.

35119 CHEVALIER, M. De la situation actuelle dans ses rapports avec les subsistances et la Banque de France. 78p. *8°. Paris,* 1847. *Presentation copy from the author to N. W. Senior.*

35120 COCHRANE, G. Opinions on loans of government stock; respectfully addressed to the landed, commercial, and professional world... 15p. *8°.* 1847.

35121 COMMITTEE OF MERCHANTS AND TRADERS...APPOINTED TO PROMOTE THE IMPROVEMENT OF THE LAW RELATING TO DEBTOR AND CREDITOR. [*Endorsed:*] Bankruptcy and insolvency law amendment. [Third] report of the Committee, February 25, 1847. 3p. *fol.* [1847] *See note to no.* 32762.

35122 CRAWFORD, JOHN, *of Paisley.* The philosophy of wealth...Third edition. 102p. *8°.* 1847. *Presentation copy, with inscription, from the author to Lord Denman. For other editions, see* 1837.

35123 On the **CURRENCY.** A letter to the Right Honourable Lord John Russell, M.P., &c. By "One who has seen better days." 8p. *8°.* 1847.

35124 The **CURRENCY QUESTION.** Currency records; being, extracts from speeches, documents, &c.&c.&c., illustrating the character and consequences of the Acts of 1819 and 1844. Second edition. 43p. *8°.* [1847]

35125 [**DAHLMANN,** T.?] New kind of money... A new system of banking, is fully developed in nos. 1 & 2, of Dahlmann's "Monetary Corrector,"...[A prospectus.] [4]p. *4°.* [1847?]

35126 [——] New money advocate. A plan for realising the perfection of money; in which it is demonstrated, that paper is capable of being made a much more perfect, true, and unvarying standard of value than it is possible that either gold or silver can be, which scheme appears to the reviewer to deserve his primary attention...By A.B.C. 45p. *8°.* [1847]

35127 DANSON, J. T. The accounts of the Bank of England, under the operation of the Act 7 & 8 Vict., c. 32. 22p. *8°. n.p.* [1847]

35128 DOUBLEDAY, T. A financial, monetary and statistical history of England, from the Revolution of 1688 to the present time...In seventeen letters to the young men of Great Britain. 414p. *8°.* 1847.

35129 DUNCAN, JONATHAN. The National Anti-Gold Law League. The principles of the League explained, versus Sir R. Peel's currency measures, and the partial remedy advocated by the Scottish banks, in a speech delivered at the City Hall, Glasgow, 7th August, 1847. 16p. *8°.* 1847.

35130 ENDERBY, C. The fallacy of our monetary system, as deduced from its author's, Sir Robert Peel's, definition of a "pound". 16p. *8°.* 1847.

35131 —— Our money laws the cause of the national distress. 46p. *8°.* 1847.

35132 EWART, W. Taxation. Speech in favour of the substitution of a system of more direct taxation. In place of the indirect system now in use...(May 28th, 1847.) Extracted from Hansard's Parliamentary Debates. 22p. *12°.* 1847.

35133 A brief **EXAMINATION** of the proposed Customs' Duties Bill, and a few reasons for it's not passing into a law. [With 'Copy petition of the English corn distillers to the House of Lords'.] 38p. *8°.* 1847.

35134 FALKNER, E. D. The adaptation of the present monetary system of Great Britain to the commerce of the country considered, in a letter addressed to the members of both Houses of Parliament, with suggestions for an alteration in the circulating medium... 24p. *8°. Liverpool & London,* 1847.

35135 FANE, R. G. C. A letter addressed to the Secretary of Bankrupts, on the remuneration of official assignees in bankruptcy. 11p. *8°.* 1847.

35136 FAUCHER, L. Chambre des Députés. Session de 1846–1847. Discours prononcé par M. Léon Faucher Député de la Marne, dans la discussion du projet d'adresse. Séance du 8 février, 1847. [Extrait du Moniteur Universel du 10 février 1847.] 15p. *8°. Paris,* [1847]

35137 —— Chambre des Députés. Session de 1846–1847. Discours prononcé par M. Léon Faucher Député de la Marne, dans la discussion du projet de loi tendant à abaisser à 250 fr. la moindre coupure des billets de la Banque de France. Séance du 13 avril, 1847. [Extrait du Moniteur Universel du 16 avril 1847.] 16p. *8°.* [*Paris,* 1847]

35138 —— (Extrait de l'Industriel de la Champagne.) Du droit sur les fers. Discours prononcé par M. Léon Faucher, Député de la Marne, à la réunion de la Société pour le Libre-Échange, le 30 mars, 1847, à la salle Montesquieu. 31p. *8°. Reims*, [1847]

35139 FOALE, T. A tract for the million. How to build or buy a house on easy terms: an elucidation of the fundamental principles of ordinary building societies; with a series of tables…also, how to build a philanthropic institution by extensive co-operation. 16p. *8°.* [1847]

35140 FRANCIS, J. History of the Bank of England, its times and traditions. 2 vols. *8°.* [1847]

35141 —— Second edition. 2 vols. *8°. 1847. See also* 1848.

35142 FURNIVALL, T. Taxation revised and national progress. 23p. *8°. 1847.*

35143 GILBART, J. W. A record of the proceedings of the London and Westminster Bank, during the first thirteen years of its existence; with portraits of its principal officers. 75p. *4°. 1847.*

35144 GODDARD, S. A. Miscellaneous letters on currency, free trade, &c. 46p. *8°. London, Birmingham, &c.,* 1847.

35145 GRAY, JOHN (1799–1883). The currency question. The confidence of "The Times" in its own monetary doctrines exemplified, by its refusal to give publicity to a free offer of the sum of one hundred guineas to any man who may be able to maintain their validity before a competent and impartial tribunal. A rejected letter to the editor of "The Times" on the subject of the currency. To which is added the above-named offer repeated… 23p. *12°. Edinburgh & London,* 1847.

35146 [**GRAYDON**, W. ?] On the reduction of taxes, and increase of food and revenue for the United Kingdom of Great Britain and Ireland. By Agricola. 12p. *12°.* 1847.

35147 [——?] An oppressed poor in an insolvent nation. A letter to the members of the new Parliament. By Agricola. 27p. *8°.* 1847.

35148 HAGGARD, W. D. Observations on the standard of value and the circulating medium of this country…Second edition. 39p. *8°. 1847. For another edition, see* 1840.

35149 *HILLMAN, W. E. Familiar illustrations of the theory and practice of assurance: being notes of a lecture delivered in various towns of England. 114p. *8°.* 1847. *The copy that belonged to Augustus De Morgan.*

35150 HOWS, W. A. H. A history of pawnbroking, past and present. 102p. *12°.* 1847.

35151 National **INDUSTRY**, the basis of national wealth, being a dissertation on the present state of the currency. 26p. *8°. Liverpool,* 1847.

35152 *JONES, JENKIN. What is life assurance? Explained by practical illustrations of its principles, with observations on each description of assurance, and on the rates of premium charged by the different offices. 48p. *8°. London & Edinburgh,* 1847. *The copy that belonged to Augustus De Morgan.*

35153 KELLY, P. The elements of book-keeping, comprising a system of merchants' accounts, founded on real business…with an appendix on exchanges, banking, and other commercial subjects…The twelfth edition. 240p. *8°. 1847. For another edition, see* 1839.

35154 KINNEAR, G. Banks and exchange companies. A letter to Alexander Blair, Esq. Treasurer of the Bank of Scotland, in answer to the prospectus issued by the proposed British Trust Company. 27p. *8°. Glasgow, Edinburgh, &c.,* 1847.

35155 KINNEAR, J. G. The crisis & the currency: with a comparison between the English & Scotch systems of banking. xv, 69p. *8°.* 1847.

35156 —— Second edition: with a postscript. 104p. *8°.* 1847.

35157 KLETKE, G. M. Die Geldkrisis und der Pauperismus, verbunden mit der Bankfrage und Bankreform im preussischen Staate. Besonderer Abdruck aus dem Janus Heft 14–20 pro 1847. 77p. *8°. Berlin,* 1847.

35158 KNIGHT, JAMES (*fl.* 1847–1857). A review of the private & joint stock banks in the Metropolis; with remarks upon the constitution of a new chartered joint stock bank… 36p. *8°.* 1847.

35159 —— Second edition. 39p. *8°. 1847. Presentation copy from the author to F. G. P. Neison.*

35160 LAMBERT, ALPHONSE, *Baron.* Note adressée à M. le Ministre des Finances sur la Commission des Monnaies. 8p. *4°. Paris,* [1847]

35161 —— Note remise à la Commission du Budget. 4p. *4°. Paris,* [1847]

35162 LEBER, J. M. C. Essai sur l'appréciation de la fortune privée au moyen âge, relativement aux variations des valeurs monétaires et du pouvoir commercial de l'argent: suivi d'un examen critique des tables de prix du marc d'argent depuis l'époque de Saint Louis…Seconde édition revue et augmentée de nouvelles recherches. 340p. *8°. Paris, 1847. A greatly enlarged version of a paper read to the Académie des Inscriptions et Belles-Lettres, Mémoires sur l'appréciation de la fortune privée au moyen âge, 1841 (q.v.).*

35163 LEMON, SIR C., *Bart.* A letter to the Right Hon. the Earl of Clarendon, on the copper ore duties. 35p. *8°.* 1847.

35164 A **LETTER** to Lord Archibald Hamilton, on alterations in the value of money; and containing an examination of some opinions recently published on that subject. Published in 1823; re-printed in 1847. 99p. *8°.* [1847] *Originally attributed by HSF to Thomas Attwood, but later (tentatively) to Thomas Paget. For another edition, see* 1823.

35165 A **LETTER** to the congestive bankerhood of Great Britain, with a proposition for a new currency. By a traveller (not from Geneva.) 20p. *8°.* 1847.

35166 LITTLE, J. The monetary crisis of 1847; its causes, and a proposed new system of paper currency. 16p. *12°.* 1847.

35167 [**LOYD**, S. J., *Baron Overstone.*] The petition of the merchants, bankers, and traders of London against the Bank Charter Act; with comments on each clause. 24p. *8°. 1847. The copy that belonged to T. Spring Rice, Baron Monteagle. HSF records in a note that the work has also been attributed to Torrens.*

35168 MAITLAND, JOHN, *actuary.* National savings banks. Suggestions for rendering such savings banks self-supporting; to increase efforts through them for the promotion of moral and provident habits…and to remove from the Public Funds the present evil influence of savings banks. 31p. *8°. London & Edinburgh,* 1847.

35169 **MARTIN,** William (1772–1851). W. Martin, the philosopher, on money matters. [With 'The philosopher's fourth letter to the Queen and Government on the defeat of the Roman Catholics'. Both in verse.] 4p. *8°. Newcastle,* [1847]

35170 **MASON,** John. An inquiry into the economy, exchange & distribution of wealth. 2 vols. *8°. London* [*& Birmingham*], *1847–49. A second copy of part II is a presentation copy from the author to A. Spottiswoode.*

35171 **MASSEY,** B. The money crisis; its causes, consequences, and remedy. In a letter to the Right Hon. Sir Robert Peel, Bart. 41p. *8°. 1847.*

35172 **MEMORIAL** [dated from Edinburgh, 11th March, 1847, on exchange banks, deposit rates, etc.]. 23p. *8°. n.p.* [1847]

35173 **MICHELL,** W. The National Debt the basis of the national currency. 87p. *12°. Bodmin,* [1847 ?]

35174 **MITCHEL,** J. Report on the levy of rates in Ireland for the repayment of government loans. (*The Irish Confederation,* 4.) 12p. *12°. Dublin,* 1847.

35175 **MORRISON,** W. H. Observations on the system of metallic currency adopted in this country... Third edition, with explanatory notes. 87p. *8°. 1847. For other editions, see* 1837.

35176 **NICHOL,** W. Proposal for the development of the principle of assurance as an instrument for the gradual extinction of pauperism and for the permanent improvement of the condition of the industrious classes. 25p. *8°. Edinburgh,* 1847.

35177 **NOIRON,** L. de. Des banques en France. Leur mission, leur isolement actuel, moyen de les coordonner dans leur intérêt, celui du Trésor et du Pays. 192p. *8°. Paris,* 1847.

35178 **NORTH OF ENGLAND JOINT STOCK BANKING COMPANY.** A list of the shareholders in the North of England Joint Stock Banking Company, Newcastle-on-Tyne. 12p. *12°. Newcastle-on-Tyne,* 1847.

35179 **OBSERVATIONS** on Sir Robert Peel's currency system and taxation. 6p. *8°. n.p.* [1847 ?]

35180 The **OWLS** in Witenagemote, a fable for currency doctors, by one of themselves. 16p. *8°.* 1847.

35181 **PARRY,** John W., *ed.* The yeoman philosophising on his poverty, the cause and the cure; familiarly exhibiting the origin of distress in England and destitution in Ireland, by an atrocious monopoly of the monetary system of coining bank notes...By a Welsh plebeian of the nineteenth century... 80p. *8°.* [1847]

35182 **PHIPPS,** Hon. E. The monetary crisis, with a proposal for present relief, and increased safety in future. 16p. *8°.* 1847.

35183 [**POLLARD,** G.] A plan for a domestic currency, rendered independent of the foreign exchanges, and measured in standard gold. By a banker. (Second edition.) 16p. *8°. 1847. See also* 1848.

35184 **PROPOSAL** for a paper currency, not convertible into gold at the pleasure of the holder, but not liable to depreciation. 9p. *8°.* 1847.

35185 **QUOTEM,** Caleb, *pseud.* The conspiracy of the bullionists as it affects the present system of the money laws. 16p. *8°. Birmingham,* 1847.

35186 **REVANS,** J. A per centage tax on domestic expenditure, to supply the whole of the public revenue: the customs, excise, stamp, legacy, income, and all other government taxes...to be abolished... 42p. *8°.* 1847.

35187 **ROGERS,** J. R. Chapters on country banking ...Part 1. Second edition. 64p. *8°.* 1847.

35188 **ROLDAN,** A. de. Memoria historica y cientifica de tres siglos a esta parte de los valores dados a los metales preciosos de plata y oro, variaciones de sus leyes, y causas de haber desaparecido de España tanta riqueza. Con una critica razonada a los dos proyectos del sistema monetario de los señores Mon y Salamanca. 48p. *8°. Madrid,* 1847.

35189 *New **SCHEME** of taxation. To the editor of the Liverpool Chronicle. [Two letters, signed: A Liverpool merchant, the second dated, 28th January 1847.] [2]p. *s.sh.fol. n.p.* [1847] *Possibly written by John Finch (1783–1857), who used this designation at this period. The FWA copy, that belonged to William Pare.*

35190 *****SCOTTISH PROVIDENT INSTITUTION.** Report of meeting of contributors in London, to the Scottish Provident Institution. Held on 4th October, 1847. [Concerned with the dismissal of Mr. Leifchild, with testimonials enclosed concerning his conduct.] Extracted, with some corrections, from the "Post Magazine." 11p. *8°.* [1847] *The copy that belonged to Augustus De Morgan.*

35191 **SHARPE,** B. Plan for an extension of the currency; proposed in a letter to the Right Hon. Sir Charles Wood, Bart., Chancellor of the Exchequer, &c. &c.&c. 16p. *8°.* 1847.

35192 **SKETCH** of a plan to be submitted to the London bankers, by which it is proposed to economize the funds required by them for clearing-house purposes. 8p. *8°.* 1847.

35193 *****SMITH,** Frederick G. Observations on life assurance, illustrative of the many important benefits resulting...from its practice, to which is added, a brief outline of the Scottish Union Assurance Corporation... Presented to the Directors by their secretary...Third edition. 44p. *8°. n.p.* [1847] *The copy that belonged to Augustus De Morgan.*

35194 **SNOOKS,** *pseud.* A letter to Lord Palmerston, on the "Condition of England question." Elicited by his speech to the electors of Tiverton. 26p. *8°.* 1847.

35195 **SPECTATOR,** *pseud.* Paper versus gold-money; or, a new system of currency and banking, to render paper as secure as specie, and to unite the Bank of England, joint-stock and private banks in one harmonious plan...Second edition. 2 vols. *8°. 1847,* [1843] *Part 1 only is of the second edition. Part 2 was printed for private circulation in 1843.*

35196 The present **STATE** of the currency practically considered; proving the justice and necessity of immediately and effectually revising the currency measures of 1819 and 1844. 76p. *8°.* 1847.

35197 **STATE** of the currency. Facts and arguments, showing the dangers that may be expected from the restrictions imposed upon the operations & circulation of the Bank of England by the Banking Act of 1844. 10p. *fol. n.p.* [1847 ?]

35198 **SUGGESTIONS** for a domestic currency founded upon philosophic and unerring principles: preceded by a few thoughts on the economy of order and industry, the harmony of which becomes permanent only by an equitable measure of exchange. 71p. *8°*. 1847. *Sometimes attributed to G. Harvey. p.56–68 contain extracts from Archibald Alison's pamphlets entitled* Free trade and a fettered currency *and* England in 1815 and 1845 *(nos. 35097–8).*

35199 SUGGESTIONS for an amendment of the currency. 8p. *12°. Liverpool,* 1847.

35200 SUGGESTIONS for the regulation of discount by the Bank of England. 15p. *8°.* 1847.

35201 TAUNTON, E. The six fundamental principles of currency defined & explained, and the three gross mercantile errors in our currency exposed. Second edition. 4p. *12°. Birmingham,* [1847]

35202 [TAYLOR, JAMES (1788–1863).] A correct monetary system essential to a free-trade system. By the author of "No trust, no trade." 32p. *8°.* 1847.

35203 [——] The essential error of "Peel's Bill" [the Currency Act of 1819] pointed out and a prompt and efficient remedy suggested. [Dated: Oct. 7, 1847.] 4p. *8°. n.p.* [1847]

35204 —— Remarks on Mr. Tooke's Letters to Lord Grenville on the currency. Addressed to the Duke of Wellington...First published in December 1829. [With 'Reply to William Cobbett, being the postscript of a letter to the Duke of Wellington...first published in January 1830'.] 112p. *8°.* 1847. *For another edition, see* 1830 (A letter to his Grace the Duke of Wellington).

35205 [——] Remarks on the letter of Mr Gladstone, Sen. on the currency question. Being a vindication of the market price system of cash payments. By the author of "No trust, no trade." [A letter, signed: Iota, reprinted from the *Sun* newspaper, of 5th April, 1844.] 8p. *8°.* 1847.

35206 [——] What constitutes the "pound sterling;" or, remarks on Sir Robert Peel's speech in the debate of April 30, 1847. Addressed to a Member of Parliament by one of his constituents. 8p. *8°.* 1847.

35207 THOMPSON, T. A few words respecting the currency, the Bank of England, and the new banking Act. 18p. *8°.* 1847. *Presentation copy from the author to T. Spring Rice, Baron Monteagle.*

35208 THOUGHTS on the present crisis; with a suggestion for the reform of the currency. 8p. *8°.* 1847.

35209 TORRENS, R. On the operation of the Bank Charter Act of 1844 as it affects commercial credit. 40p. *8°. London & Dublin,* 1847.

35210 —— Second edition. 40p. *8°. London & Dublin,* 1847.

35211 TRYE, TRISTRAM, *pseud.* Tract for the times – No. II. The incubus on commerce; or, the false position of the Bank of England: a practical enquiry. [With an appendix.] 91, xxxixp. *8°.* 1847.

35212 —— Why trade is at a stand-still; or, the influence of the Bank of England on property, commerce, and labour; a practical enquiry. 45p. *8°.* 1847.

35213 URQUHART, D. The Parliamentary usurpation of 1819 and 1844, in respect to money, considered in a letter to the burgesses and electors of Stafford. 19p. *8°.* 1847.

35214 VIRGO, W. A universal monetary system, illustrated in a series of tables, shewing the relative value of bullion, gold and silver coins; between England and all other nations...Also the value of the nominal pound sterling, with suggestions for reviving the...foreign and domestic trade... 114p. *8°.* 1847. *For another edition, see* 1844 (Sir Robert Peel and the Bank charter).

35215 WARD, JAMES. The Bank of England justified in their present course. 35p. *8°.* 1847.

35216 WARD, W. Remarks on the monetary legislation of Great Britain. 73p. *8°.* 1847.

35217 WHICKER, W. G. A national note, proposed to the Right Honourable Sir Charles Wood, Bart., Chancellor of the Exchequer, &c.&c.&c. 8p. *8°.* 1847.

35218 WILSON, JAMES (1805–1860). Capital, currency, and banking; being a collection of a series of articles published in the Economist in 1845, on the principles of the Bank Act of 1844, and in 1847, on the recent monetarial and commercial crises, concluding with a plan for a secure and economical currency. 294p. *8°.* 1847.

35219 WILSON, THOMAS, *Chevalier de l'Ordre du Lion Néerlandais.* De l'influence des capitaux anglais sur l'industrie européenne depuis la révolution de 1688 jusqu'en 1846. 220p. *8°. Bruxelles,* 1847.

35220 WOOD, CHARLES, *Viscount Halifax.* Speech of the Chancellor of the Exchequer, on moving for a select committee to inquire into the causes of the recent commercial distress, etc. on the 30th November, 1847. 60p. *8°.* 1847. *The copy that belonged to T. Spring Rice, Baron Monteagle.*

35221 A few **WORDS** on behalf of the middle classes of England on the subject of the income tax. 21p. *8°.* 1847.

35222 WRIGHT, I. C. The evils of the currency, an exposition of Sir Robert Peel's Bank Charter Act. 21p. *12°. London & Nottingham,* 1847.

TRANSPORT

35223 BENTINCK, LORD WILLIAM G. F. C. Railways in Ireland. The speech of the Rt. Hon. Lord George Bentinck, on moving for leave to bring in a Bill "to stimulate the prompt and profitable employment of the people by the encouragement of railways in Ireland." In the House of Commons, on...February 4th, 1847. Extracted from Hansard's Parliamentary Debates. 34p. *12°.* [*London,* 1847] *The Rastrick copy.*

35224 [BOURDON, E.] Insurrection des agioteurs. [Attacking the estimates of French railway companies.] 8p. *8°.* [*Paris,* 1847] *The copy that belonged to Victor Considérant.*

35225 BRADSHAW, G. Bradshaw's railway companion, containing the times of departure, fares, &c. of the railways in Great Britain and Ireland, and also hackney coach fares... 72[164]p. *32°.* 2nd mo. (February) 1st,

1847. *With a prospectus for no. 1 of The Traveller's miscellany. See also* 1841, 1843.

35226 BREES, S. C. First series of Railway practice: a collection of working plans and practical details of construction in the public works of the most celebrated engineers: comprising roads, tramroads, and railroads; bridges...canals...harbours, docks...drainage of marshes...water-works...Third edition. With additional examples. 164p. *4⁰.* 1847. *For other editions, see* 1837, *and for an appendix,* 1839.

35227 —— Fourth series of Railway practice: a collection of working plans and practical details of construction in the public works of the most celebrated engineers: comprising roads, tramroads, and railroads; bridges...canals ...harbours, docks...drainage of marshes...waterworks... 46, cliip. *4⁰.* 1847. *For editions of the first series, see no.* 35226 *above and* 1837, *and for the second series,* 1840.

35228 BRIDGES, J. The Sunday railways practically discussed. A letter to John James Hope Johnstone, Esq. of Annandale, chairman of the Caledonian Railway Company. 19p. *8⁰. Edinburgh & London,* 1847.

35229 C., E. Voyage en chemin de fer de Paris à Boulogne et à la frontière du nord. Guide du voyageur dans Amiens et description historique de la cathédrale et des principaux monumens de cette ville. 63p. *8⁰. Amiens,* 1847.

35230 [CLARKE, R. Y.] The rail, its origin and progress: with illustrative anecdotes and engravings. By Peter Progress the younger. 60p. *8⁰.* 1847. *The Rastrick copy.*

35231 COCKBURN, Sir A. J. E., *Bart.* Speech of Mr. Cockburn on behalf of the Salisbury and Yeovil, Exeter Yeovil and Dorchester, Exeter and Exmouth, and Blandford and Bruton lines, on the 30th of June and 1st and 2nd of July, 1847. [A statement of the case for the London and South Western Railway Company's scheme for extending the railway from Salisbury to Exeter, in opposition to that of the Great Western Railway.] 175p. *8⁰.* [1847]

35232 E. The overland India mail by Genoa and Switzerland. [Dated: July 21st 1847.] 12p. *12⁰.* [1847]

35233 EASTERN COUNTIES RAILWAY COMPANY. Eastern Counties and Norfolk, and Eastern Union railways. [Timetable with map.] [12]p. *16⁰.* [*London,* 1847?] *For another edition, see* 1846.

35234 EASTERN UNION RAILWAY COMPANY. Eastern Union Railway. Half-yearly report of the directors of the...Company, February 24th [–20th August], 1847. 2 vols. *fol. n.p.* [1847] *See also* 1844, 1845, 1846, 1848, 1849, 1850.

35235 ENGLAND. *Laws, etc.* Anno quarto Victoriæ Reginæ. Cap. xii. An Act for granting further powers to the London and Blackwall Railway Company. ⟨10th May 1841.⟩ p.121–127. *fol.* 1847.

35236 —— —— Anno octavo & nono Victoriæ Reginæ. Cap. cciii. An Act for making a railway from the London and Blackwall Railway at Stepney to the Eastern Counties Railway. ⟨9th August 1845.⟩ p.4893–4911. *fol.* 1847.

35237 —— —— Anno decimo Victoriæ Reginæ. Cap. xii. An Act to enable the Newmarket and Chesterford Railway Company to extend their line of railway to Bury Saint Edmunds, with a branch to the City of Ely. ⟨8th June 1847.⟩ p.133–146. *fol.* 1847.

35238 —— —— Anno decimo Victoriæ Reginæ. Cap. xiii. An Act for repealing certain provisions of the Newmarket and Chesterford Railway Act, 1846. ⟨8th June 1847.⟩ p.149–150. *fol.* 1847.

35239 —— —— Anno decimo Victoriæ Reginæ. Cap. xx. An Act to enable the Newmarket and Chesterford Railway Company to extend their line of railway to Thetford in the county of Norfolk. p.249–254. *fol.* 1847.

35240 —— —— [*Endorsed:*] Wear Valley, Bishop Auckland and Weardale, Weardale Extension, and Wear and Derwent Railways, and Shildon Tunnel amalgamation. An Act for enabling the Wear Valley Railway Company to purchase or lease the Bishop Auckland and Weardale Railway, the Wear and Derwent Railway, the Weardale Extension Railway, and the Shildon Tunnel, and to raise an additional sum of money... ⟨Royal Assent, July 22nd, 1847.⟩ 10 & 11 Victoria. – sess. 1847. 33p. *fol.* [*London,* 1847]

35241 —— —— A collection of the Public General Acts relating to railways in Scotland: including the Companies, Lands, and Railways Clauses Consolidation (Scotland) Acts. 1838–1846. With general index. 232p. *12⁰. Westminster, Edinburgh, &c.,* 1847.

35242 ENTWISLE, W. Government railways. 58p. *8⁰.* 1847.

35243 GARDNER, Edward V. An easy introduction to railway mensuration, illustrated by drawings from original works, that have been carried out upon various English railway lines, showing a plain and easy method of taking out quantities of every description of railway work and estimating them, and setting out work for the making of railways generally. 63p. *fol.* 1847.

35244 GLYNN, H. Reference book to the incorporated railway companies of England and Wales, alphabetically arranged, including a list of their directors, offices and officers, constitution, and capital, shewing also the lines suspended in Session, 1847, and applications for Bills in 1848... 227p. *8⁰. London & Newcastle,* 1847.

35245 —— A reference book to the incorporated railway companies of Ireland, alphabetically arranged, including a list of their directors, offices and officers, constitution, and capital, gauge of way 5 feet 3 inches. 84p. *8⁰. London & Newcastle,* 1847.

35246 —— Reference book to the incorporated railway companies of Scotland, alphabetically arranged, including a list of their directors, offices and officers, constitution, and capital. Gauge of way 4 feet 8½ inches. xl, 60p. *8⁰. London & Newcastle,* 1847.

35247 GREAT NORTHERN RAILWAY COMPANY. The Great Northern Railway. First half-yearly meeting, 27th February, 1847. 9p. *8⁰.* 1847.

For ——, The Great Northern Railway Company's Reporter [containing the reports of the half-yearly meetings], 1847–52, *see* vol. III, *Periodicals list.*

35248 A short and sure **GUIDE** to permanent investments in railways. A few plain rules how to invest and speculate with safety and profit in railway shares, with some remarks on the monetary effect of deposits and calls. By a successful operator. Ninth edition, dedicated to George Hudson, Esq. M.P. 24p. *8⁰.* 1847. *The Rastrick copy.*

35249 IPSWICH AND BURY ST. EDMUND'S RAILWAY COMPANY. [*Begin.*] Ipswich & Bury

St. Edmund's Railway. At an extraordinary general meeting of the proprietors...the 27th day of April, 1847 ...[Extensions to the line and approval of a draft Bill to amalgamate with the Eastern Union Railway.] *s.sh.fol. n.p.* [1847]

35250 IPSWICH, BURY AND NORWICH RAILWAY COMPANY. Ipswich, Bury and Norwich Railway. Half-yearly report of the directors...January 29th, [–July 30,] 1847. 2 vols. *fol. n.p.* [1847] *See also* 1846, 1848.

35251 The **IRISH RAILWAY GUIDE**; containing a correct account of the hours of departure of the railway trains, with a list of coaches, cars, etc. starting from the various railway stations, and a map of Ireland, showing the working lines of railway. 50p. *8°. Dublin: W. Curry,* 1847.

35252 KELLY, WILLIAM, *engineer.* Tables for determining the cubical content of earthwork, in the construction of railways and common roads, whether in level ground or side cutting. 69p. *8°. London & Dublin,* 1847.

35253 KING, GEORGE (*fl.* 1847–1849). Holyhead harbour. Reply to letter addressed by Charles Wye Williams...to the Rt. Hon. Viscount Sandon. 19p. *8°. n.p.,* 1847.

35254 LAING, SAMUEL (1812–1897). Observations on Mr. Strutt's amended Railway Regulation Bill now before Parliament. 32p. *8°. Westminster, Manchester, &c.,* 1847. *See note to no.* 34295.

35255 LAMB, A. Portland breakwater. Letter to the Right Hon. Lord John Russell... 8p. *fol.* 1847.

35256 LEAHY, E. A practical treatise on making and repairing roads...Second edition. 306p. *12°.* 1847. *For another edition, see* 1844.

35257 LIVERPOOL, MANCHESTER, AND NEWCASTLE-UPON-TYNE JUNCTION RAILWAY COMPANY. Report of the ordinary and extraordinary meeting of shareholders, held at the Palatine Hotel, Manchester, on the second day of February, 1847. Also a correspondence with the Secretary, relative to the publication of the report by the Directors, and a requisition to, and correspondence with, George Hudson, Esq., M.P., arising out of the extraordinary disclosures at the above meeting. 51p. *8°. Leeds,* 1847.

35258 LIZARS, W. H. Lizars' guide to the Edinburgh and Glasgow, Glasgow, Paisley, Kilmarnock, Ayr, and Greenock Railways. [With map.] [4]p. *fol.* [*Edinburgh,* 1847?]

35259 LONDON, BRIGHTON AND SOUTH COAST RAILWAY COMPANY. [*Endorsed:*] Kent railway (Tonbridge, Maidstone & Canterbury), promoted by the London, Brighton, and South Coast Railway Company. Statement [including arguments in favour of their line as against that promoted by the South Eastern Railway]. 3p. *fol.* [1847]

35260 NEW YORK AND BOSTON RAILROAD COMPANY. Report of Edwin F. Johnson, C.E. to the Central Committee. August, 1847. [With 'Act of Incorporation of the New-York and Boston Railroad Company'.] 64p. *8°. Middletown, Conn.,* 1847. *The Rastrick copy.*

35261 NEWCASTLE-UPON-TYNE. *Town Council.* Report of the discussion in the Town Council of Newcastle on Tyne...February 3, 1847, on the railways projected through the Team Valley by the Leeds and Thirsk, and York and Newcastle Railway Companies. [Including a report of the special meeting 15 February, 1846, with 'Third discussion in Newcastle Town Council ...on the Team Valley railways', of March 17, 1847.] 47, 12p. *8°. Newcastle-upon-Tyne,* 1847.

35262 OBSERVATIONS on Mr. Strutt's Railway Bill. 56p. *8°. Westminster, Manchester, &c.,* 1847.

For the **RAILWAY RECORD,** *see vol.* III, *Periodicals list.*

35263 SALOMONS, SIR D., *Bart.* Railways in England and in France: being reflections suggested by Mr. Morrison's pamphlet, and by the report drawn up by him for the Railway Acts Committee. 79p. *8°.* 1847.

35264 SHAEN, S. A review of railways and railway legislation at home and abroad. 103p. *8°.* 1847. *The copy that belonged to W. H. Ashurst.*

35265 SIDNEY, S. Speed on railways considered in a commercial point of view. 22p. *8°.* 1847.

35266 SMITH, ARTHUR. The Eastern Counties Railway viewed as an investment: with statistical information taken from Parliamentary Papers, showing the powers possessed by this Company of raising money. With remarks on the present and prospective outlay on the Eastern Counties district... 24p. *8°.* 1847.

35267 [——] The course of the panic traced by facts; its evils, and remedy. Railways as they really are: or, facts for the serious consideration of railway proprietors. No. II. The Dover, or South-Eastern Company. 44p. *8°.* 1847.

35268 [——] Railways as they really are: or, facts for the serious consideration of railway proprietors. No. VII. Lancashire and Yorkshire Railway. Second edition. 40p. *8°.* 1847.

35269 STEPHENSON, ROBERT (1803–1886). The double gauge. Observations by Mr. R. Stephenson on Mr. Brunel's report on the double gauge [with the report]. 27p. *4°.* 1847. *The Rastrick copy.*

35270 TEISSERENC, E. Études sur les voies de communication perfectionnées et sur les lois économiques de la production du transport suivies de tableaux statistiques sur les frais de navigation et d'une analyse raisonnée des comptes des principaux chemins de fer français, belges, anglais et allemands. 944p. *8°. Paris,* 1847.

35271 TUCK, H. The railway shareholder's manual; or practical guide to all the railways of the world, completed, in progress, and projected...To which is added a correct list of the offices and officers of existing and projected railways. Eighth edition. Carefully revised and corrected. 409p. *8°. London, Liverpool, &c.,* 1847. *For other editions, see* 1845.

35272 TURNBULL, W. An essay on the air-pump and atmospheric railway; containing formulæ and rules for calculating the various quantities contained in Mr. Robert Stephenson's report on atmospheric propulsion, for the directors of the Chester and Holyhead Railway Company. 96p. *8°.* 1847.

35273 WARD, JAMES. Railways for the many, and not for the few; or, how to make them profitable to all... Second edition, enlarged. With some remarks on building and other benefit societies. 57p. *8°.* 1847.

35274 WHITEHEAD, J. Railway and government

guarantee. Which is preferable? Facts and arguments to shew that guaranteed railway stock offers a better investment than do government securities...Fourth edition. 54p. *8°. 1847. See also 1849.*

35275 WHITMORE, W. W. Letter to Lord John Russell on railways. 22p. *8°. 1847.*

35276 WILKINSON, SYMONS & WEST, *solicitors.* Evidence and opinions on the harbour of Valencia (Ireland), as to its fitness for a western packet station. Submitted to the Right Hon. Lord John Russell, First Lord of the Treasury. Compiled by the solicitors of the Wexford and Valencia Railway Company. With a map. 51p. *8°. 1847.*

35277 WILLIAMS, CHARLES W. Remarks on the proposed asylum harbour at Holyhead, and the monopoly contemplated by the Chester and Holyhead Railway

Company, in a letter addressed to Lord Viscount Sandon, M.P. 46p. *8°. n.p.,* 1847.

35278 —— Further remarks on the proposed asylum harbour at Holyhead...in a second letter...to... Viscount Sandon... 40p. *8°. n.p.,* 1847.

35279 WILLIAMS, WELLINGTON. Appletons' railroad and steamboat companion. Being a travellers' guide through New England and the middle states, with routes in the southern and western states, and also in Canada... 235p. *8°. New-York & Philadelphia,* 1847. *See also 1848.*

35280 YOUNG, C. D. A short treatise on the system of wire fencing, in its various forms, as applicable to railway purposes, together with a description of simultaneous acting iron gates for railway level crossings...To which is added, a descriptive catalogue of iron and wire work required by railway companies and engineers... 17p., 23 plates. *fol. Edinburgh & Glasgow,* [1847]

SOCIAL CONDITIONS

35281 ABERDEEN MECHANICS' INSTITUTION. The twenty-first report of the Committee...30th April, 1847. 23p. *8°. Aberdeen,* 1847.

35282 ADAIR, ROBERT A. S., *Baron Waveney.* The winter of 1846-7 in Antrim, with remarks on out-door relief and colonization. 70p. *8°. 1847.*

35283 —— Third edition. [With 'Return of the monthly numbers of paupers...in the Ballymenagh Union House for the last twenty-one months'.] 70p. *8°. 1847.*

35284 An **ADDRESS** to the inhabitants of St. James's Westminster, on certain local circumstances affecting the health of rich and poor. By a retired churchwarden. 26p. *8°. 1847.*

For the **ADVISER,** *1847-48, see vol.* III, *Periodicals list.*

35285 Distinguished **ADVOCATES** of the Ten Hours' Bill since the year 1815. [A roll of honour, printed in gold on black glazed paper, including the text of the Bill, resolutions of the Lancashire Central Short-Time Committee, and lists of the members of that committee and of the Yorkshire Central Short-Time Committee.] *s.sh.fol. Manchester,* [1847]

35286 AITKEN, W. An essay on remedies for the relief of the prevailing distress of the labouring population, especially of Scotland...and of Ireland. Also, suggestions to those who have the power and influence of reforming the manners and customs...of the working classes of the United Kingdom... 104p. *8°. Ayr,* 1847. *Presentation copy, with inscription, from the author to Lord John Russell.*

35287 ALISON, W. P. Observations on the famine of 1846-7, in the Highlands of Scotland and in Ireland, as illustrating the connection of the principle of population with the management of the poor. 72p. *8°. Edinburgh & London,* 1847.

35288 ALMSHOUSES for the aged and infirm poor at Bransgore, in the parish of Christchurch, Hants. [An appeal for funds, dated: February 12, 1847.] *s.sh.8°. Christchurch,* [1847] [*Br. 611*]

35289 ARCHBOLD, J. F. The law relative to examinations and grounds of appeal in cases of orders of removal; with forms in all cases which occur in practice. 160p. *12°. 1847.*

35290 ASSOCIATION OF SELF-HELP. General laws of the Association of Self-Help, parent society, established at Edwinstowe, Nottinghamshire, March 8th, 1847 "to elevate the financial, physical, and religious condition of the people." 26p. *12°. Sutton-in-Ashfield,* 1847.

35291 AUSTIN, H. Report of Henry Austin, Esq., C.E. honorary secretary to the Health of Towns Association, on the sanatory condition of the city of Worcester. With an appendix by Edwin Chadwick, Esq. 46p. *8°. Worcester,* 1847.

35292 *BENNETT, WILLIAM (1804-1873). Narrative of a recent journey of six weeks in Ireland, in connexion with the subject of supplying small seed to some of the remoter districts: with current observations on the depressed circumstances of the people, and the means presented for the permanent improvement of their social condition. 178p. *12°. London & Dublin,* 1847.

35293 BENSEN, H. W. Die Proletarier. Eine historische Denkschrift. 495p. *8°. Stuttgart,* 1847.

35294 *BERNE, *Canton of.* Gesetz über das Armenwesen. 16p. *8°. n.p.* [1847] *The copy that belonged to George Grote.*

35295 *—— Verordnung betreffend die Ausführung des Armengesetzes vom 23. April 1847. 6p. *8°.* [1847] *The copy that belonged to George Grote.*

35296 BISHOP, JAMES (*fl.* 1846-1847). A practical guide and popular abstract of the new County Courts Act, for the more easy recovery of small debts and demands... Third edition, corrected...also, the City of London new Small Debts Act. 52p. *12°.* [1847]

35297 *BRAY, C. The education of the body, an address to the working classes...Second edition. 24p. *8°. Coventry,* 1847. *The FWA copy that belonged to William Pare. For another edition, see 1836.*

For the **BRITISH LEAGUE,** *see vol.* III, *Periodicals list.*

35298 BROUGHAM, H. P., *Baron Brougham and Vaux.* Letter to Lord Lyndhurst, from Lord Brougham, on criminal police and national education. 42p. *8°. 1847.*

35299 BROWNING, C. A. The convict ship, and

England's exiles. In two parts...Second edition. 414p. *12°*. 1847.

35300 BROWNLOW, J. Memoranda; or, chronicles of the Foundling Hospital, including memoirs of Captain Coram, &c. &c. 231p. *8°*. 1847.

35301 [BRUCE, JAMES (1806–1861).] Destitution in the Highlands. Letters on the present condition of the Highlands and islands of Scotland. Reprinted from the Scotsman newspaper. 83p. *8°*. *Edinburgh,* 1847.

35302 BURNE, P. The concordance of Scripture and science illustrated, with reference to the temperance cause: being a popular exposition of the original Bible-terms relating to the wine and strong drink question... With a prefatory letter by Dr. Lees, on the philosophy and philology of the question. 116p. *8°*. 1847. *The Turner copy.*

35303 —— The teetotaler's companion; or, a plea for temperance; being an exposition of the personal, domestic, and national evils that result from the present drinking custom of society...With a history of the temperance movement... 510p. *8°*. 1847. *The Turner copy.*

35304 BURRITT, E. A journal of a visit of three days to Skibbereen, and its neighbourhood. [With an introduction by Joseph Sturge.] 15p. *8°*. *London & Birmingham,* 1847.

35305 *CARR, D. The necessity of brown bread for digestion, nourishment, and sound health; and the injurious effects of white bread. 16p. *16°*. 1847. *The FWA copy that belonged to William Pare.*

35306 CENTRAL BOARD FOR THE RELIEF OF DESTITUTION IN THE HIGHLANDS AND ISLANDS OF SCOTLAND. First [–seventh] report by the Central Board of Management of the Fund raised for the relief of the destitute inhabitants of the Highlands and islands of Scotland. 7 vols. *8°*. [*Edinburgh* [*Glasgow*],] 1847. *Each volume contains the reports of the Edinburgh and Glasgow Sections, with the Minutes of the meetings of the Central Board. For later reports of the Edinburgh Section of the Central Board, see 1849.*

35307 CO-OPERATIVE LEAGUE, *London.* Plan of the Co-operative League...Central Hall, King's Arms Yard, Snow Hill. 16p. *8°*. 1847.

35308 COUSINS, D. L. Extracts from the diary of a workhouse chaplain. 303p. *12°*. *London, Bristol, &c.,* 1847.

35309 COXWORTHY, F. The potato disease and bad ventilation: being a correspondence with the Right Honourable the Lords of the Treasury; the directors of the Polytechnic Institution; Professor Faraday; Mr. Barry, the architect to the Houses of Parliament; and the editors of the Philosophical Magazine. 14p. *8°*. 1847.

35310 [CRAIK, G. L.] Sketches of popular tumults; illustrative of the evils of social ignorance. 236p. *12°*. 1847. *For another edition, see 1837.*

35311 DAY, WILLIAM, *Asst. Poor Law Commissioner.* A letter to Lord Viscount Courtenay, M.P. chairman of the Andover Committee. [An attack on Sir James Graham for alledgedly false statements about Day's administration of the poor law in South Wales.] 20p. *8°*. 1847.

35312 [DODD, WILLIAM (*b.* 1804).] The labouring classes of England, especially those engaged in agriculture and manufactures; in a series of letters. By an Englishman. Also, a voice from the factories, a poem, in serious verse. 168p. *12°*. *Boston,* 1847.

35313 EAST LONDON WATERWORKS. Re-

port to the Directors...by Thomas Wicksteed, Esq., (engineer of the Company,) being replies to a series of questions proposed by Dr. Southwood Smith, relative to the practicability...of giving a constant supply. With an appendix, containing Mr. Wicksteed's report to the Health of Towns Commissioners; his letter to J. G. Shaw Lefevre, Esq., of the Board of Trade...Printed by order of the Court of Directors. 48p. *4°*. 1847.

35314 ELLIS, S. The women of England, their social duties, and domestic habits...Twenty-first edition. 356p. *8°*. *London & Paris,* [1847?] *Presentation copy, with inscription, from the author to her sister Mary.*

35315 EMIGRATION, a more humane and more profitable test of destitution than the workhouse. Remarks on the policy of Ministers with respect to the present condition of Ireland, with suggestions for its improvement. 16p. *8°*. 1847.

35316 ENGLAND. *Home Office.* Second report of the Surveyor-General of Prisons [Joshua Jebb]. Presented to both Houses of Parliament by command of Her Majesty. 220p. *8°*. 1847. *See also 1844.*

35317 —— *Laws, etc.* City Small Debts Court, for the recovery of small debts and demands not exceeding twenty pounds. The new Act 10 & 11 Victoria, cap. 71, for the more easy recovery of small debts and demands within the City of London and the liberties thereof. Passed, 2d July, 1847. 40p. *8°*. [1847]

35318 —— *Parliament. House of Commons.* Andover Union. Extracts from the Report of the Select Committee of the House of Commons; and an epitome of the evidence on the cases of Mr. Parker and Mr. Day, late assistant Poor Law Commissioners. 117p. *8°*. 1847.

35319 —— *Poor Law Commission [1834–1847].* Letters addressed by the...Commissioners to the Secretary of State respecting the transaction of the business of the Commission, &c.&c.&c. 67p. *8°*. 1847.

35320 ENGLAND in 1830: being a letter to (the late) Earl Grey, laying before him the condition of the people as described by themselves in their petitions to Parliament. ⟨Reprinted.⟩ [With extracts from the petitions.] xxxii, 122p. *8°*. [1847] *For another edition, see 1831.*

35321 A brief EXPLANATION of the objects of a Bill "for the more effectual suppression of trading in seduction and prostitution, and for the better protection of females." 14p. *8°*. [*London,* 1847]

35322 EXTRACTS from letters to the Rev. Dr. M'Leod, Glasgow, regarding the famine and destitution in the Highlands and islands of Scotland. 72p. *8°*. *Glasgow,* 1847.

35323 FAGAN, J. Waste lands of Ireland: suggestions for their immediate reclamation, as a means of affording reproductive employment to the able-bodied destitute. 36p. *8°*. *Dublin,* 1847.

35324 FORLONG, G. Principles of a bank of character and skill...Second edition. 19p. *12°*. *Glasgow,* 1847.

35325 FRANCE. *Chambre des Pairs.* Impressions No. 136. 1847...Séance du 29 juin 1847. Rapport fait à la Chambre par M. le baron Dupin, au nom d'une commission spéciale chargée de l'examen du projet de loi relatif au travail des enfants dans toutes les manufactures, fabriques, usines, chantiers et ateliers. 121p. *8°*. *n.p.* [1847] *The texts of the Projet de loi and suggested amendments are* *printed in parallel columns following the Report. Presentation copy, with covering letter, from Baron Dupin to Lord Ashley.*

35326 FREE CHURCH OF SCOTLAND. *Destitution Committee.* Destitution in the Highlands and islands of Scotland; with extract returns to schedule of queries. Second statement of the...Committee... 24p. *8°. Glasgow,* 1847.

35327 FRIENDS, *Society of. Central Relief Committee.* Distress in Ireland. Extracts from correspondence published by the Central Relief Committee of the Society of Friends. No. I.[–II.] 31, 63p. *8°. Dublin,* 1847.

35328 GODLEY, J. R. An answer to the question what is to be done with the unemployed labourers of the United Kingdom? 57p. *8°.* 1847.

35329 GUTHRIE, T. A plea for ragged schools; or, prevention better than cure...Third edition. 48p. *8°. Edinburgh, Glasgow, &c.,* 1847. *See also* 1849.

35330 HALFORD, Sir H., *Bart.* A plea for the framework-knitters, with a view to the amelioration of their condition, and the correction of practices in the trade by which they are injured and oppressed. 103p. *8°.* 1847. *Presentation copy from the author to John Walter, M.P.*

35331 [HARRIS, Alexander, *pseud.*] Settlers and convicts; or, recollections of sixteen years' labour in the Australian backwoods. By an emigrant mechanic. 435p. *12°.* 1847.

35332 HEALTH OF TOWNS ASSOCIATION, *London.* Health of Towns Association. Report of the Committee to the members of the Association, on Lord Lincoln's Sewerage, Drainage, &c. of Towns Bill. Fourth thousand. 122p. *8°.* 1847. *For another impression, see* 1846.

35333 —— Report of the...Association, read at a meeting held in the rooms of the Statistical Society, February 24, 1847. 16p. *8°.* 1847.

35334 HILL, Matthew D. Draft report on the principles of punishment, presented to the Committee on Criminal Law appointed by the Law Amendment Society, in December, 1846. [With 'Supplementary observations' dated: Feb. 4 1847.] 19p. *8°.* 1847.

35335 HOUSE of Mercy, Handsworth. [Dated: St. Mary's Convent, July 26, 1847.] *s.sh.4°. n.p.* [1847] *In a volume of newspaper cuttings and printed and manuscript pieces concerning Birmingham, collected by Josiah Allen.*

35336 IRISH IMPROVIDENCE encouraged by English bounty; being a remonstrance against the Government projects for Irish relief, and suggestions of measures by which the Irish poor can be speedily and effectually fed, relieved, employed...without taxing English industry for this purpose. By an ex-member of the British Parliament. 16p. *8°.* [1847?]

35337 JAMES, Sir Walter, *Bart.* Thoughts upon the theory and practice of the poor-laws. Being a series of letters originally written to the editor of "The Spectator." 93p. *8°.* 1847.

35338 JOHN, *ouvrier ébéniste.* Réflexions d'un ouvrier sur l'organisation de la société. [Signed: Un ouvrier.] Projets de réforme sociale. 72p. *12°. Paris,* 1847. *The author's name, as above, is printed only on the wrapper.*

35339 JOHNSON, C. W. and **CRESY,** E. On the cottages of agricultural labourers; with economical working plans, and estimates for their improved construction. 66p. *12°.* [1847] *With the signature of Earl Cowper on the wrapper.*

35340 JONES, Alfred. A few words on the state of Westminster. 24p. *12°.* 1847.

35341 K., W. H. Convict treatment, and national defences. [Signed: W.H.K.] 79p. *8°.* 1847.

35342 LEES, F. R. The teetotal topic, or long-pledge temperance advocate. An organ of correspondence on the criticism, chemistry, and physiology of the temperance question. Conducted by Dr. Frederic Richard Lees. 56p. *4°. Douglas, Isle of Man,* [1847] *The Turner copy.*

35343 LETTER to Lord Morpeth, on the Health of Towns' Bill...showing that it ought to be withdrawn, and an entirely new sanatory measure introduced...By a townsman. 19p. *8°.* [1847]

35344 [LEWIS, Sir George C., *Bart.* ?] The English Poor-Law and Poor-Law Commission in 1847. 56p. *8°.* 1847.

35345 LIVERPOOL HEALTH OF TOWNS' ASSOCIATION. First address of the Committee of the Liverpool Health of Towns' Association. To the working classes. [Dated: February, 1847.] 4p. *8°. Liverpool,* [1847]

35346 —— Second address. [Dated: April, 1847.] 4p. *8°. Liverpool,* [1847]

35347 —— Third address. [Dated: June 1847.] 4p. *8°. Liverpool,* [1847]

35348 LONDON SOCIETY OF COMPOSITORS. Report of the journeymen members of the Arbitration Committee, or Conference of Employers and Employed. To which is added, an appendix, containing the scales of prices regulating news and parliamentary work. 28p. *8°.* [1847]

35349 MABERLY, Hon. K. C. The present state of Ireland, and its remedy. 32p. *8°.* 1847.

35350 MANN, William, *Esq., late of New Zealand.* A plan for relieving the landed interest of the Empire from the necessity of granting out-door relief to able-bodied paupers, &c. in a letter addressed to the Reproductive Labour Committee, College Green, Dublin...⟨Second edition.⟩ 11p. *12°. Dublin,* 1847.

35351 MARSHALL, John (1818–1891). Vaccination considered in relation to the public health: with inquiries and suggestions thereon... 34p. *8°.* 1847.

35352 *MATHEWS, E. H. The philosophy of bread-making: showing the wasting effects of yeast...Together with Elihu Burritt's collection of receipts for making a variety of articles of food from Indian corn meal... ⟨Fifteenth thousand.⟩ 15p. *16°. London, Bristol, &c.,* 1847. *The FWA copy that belonged to William Pare.*

35353 The **MEASURES** which can alone ameliorate effectually the condition of the Irish people. 68p. *8°.* 1847. *The copy that belonged to Earl De Grey.*

35354 METROPOLITAN WORKING CLASSES' ASSOCIATION FOR IMPROVING THE PUBLIC HEALTH. Bathing and personal cleanliness. Tenth thousand. 16p. *8°.* 1847.

35355 —— Drainage and sewerage. Tenth thousand. 16p. *8°.* 1847.

35356 —— Exercises and recreation. Fifth thousand. 16p. *8°.* 1847.

35357 —— On household cleanliness. Fifth thousand. 16p. *8°.* 1847.

35358 —— On the ventilation of rooms, houses, workshops, &c. Twentieth thousand. 16p. *8°.* 1847.

35359 —— The rearing and training of children. Fifth thousand. 16p. *8°.* 1847.

35360 —— Water supply; especially for the working classes. Fifth thousand. 16p. *8°.* 1847.

35361 MOREWOOD, J. J. Letters to the Right Honourable Lord John Russell, M.P. on the subject of the drainage of the Metropolis; state of the Thames, and the waste of fertilizing substances. 16p. *8°. n.p.* [1847]

35362 NAPER, J. L. W. On reproductive employment: being a paper addressed to the Reproductive Committee. 11p. *8°. Dublin,* 1847.

35363 NEISON, F. G. P. Observations on odd-fellow and friendly societies... Seventh edition stereotype. 36p. *12°.* 1847. *For another edition, see* 1846.

35364 —— Statistics of crime in England and Wales, for the years 1842, 1843, and 1844... Read before the Statistical Section of the British Association... 15th of September, 1846. 58p. *8°.* 1847.

35365 NEWLAND, H. An address to the Relief Committee of the Gorey electoral division, on the close of their operations. 11p. *8°. Dublin,* 1847. *The copy that belonged to Earl De Grey.*

35366 NICHOLLS, Sir George. On the condition of the agricultural labourer; with suggestions for its improvement... Second edition, with additions. 76p. *12°.* 1847. *For another edition, see* 1846.

35367 NICHOLSON, A. Ireland's welcome to the stranger; or, excursions through Ireland, in 1844 & 1845, for the purpose of personally investigating the condition of the poor. 442p. *12°.* 1847.

35368 OASTLER, R. Brougham versus Brougham on the new Poor Law, with an appendix consisting of a letter to Lord John Russell. Dedicated to the Duke of Wellington. xxxvi, 43p. *8°.* 1847.

35369 O'BRIEN, W. S. Reproductive employment; a series of letters to the landed proprietors of Ireland; with a preliminary letter to Lord John Russell. 51p. *8°. Dublin & London,* 1847.

For **ODD FELLOWS.** *Grand Lodge of British North America,* The Odd Fellows' record, *see* vol. III, *Periodicals list,* Odd Fellows' record.

35370 ODGERS, W. J. A report on the sanitary condition of Plymouth. 59p. *8°. Plymouth,* 1847. *Issued as nos. 1–6 of a periodical,* The Plymouth Health of Towns' Advocate, *from January 1847. Upon the completion of Odgers' work, the periodical ceased publication.*

35371 PARKER, Henry W. Andover Union. Two letters to the Right Honourable Sir George Grey, Bart. M.P. one of Her Majesty's Principal Secretaries of State. [With 'Extract from Mr. Christie's speech in the House of Commons, on the 28th January, 1847'.] 16p. *8°.* 1847.

35372 [**PARSONS,** W., *3rd Earl of Rosse.*] Letters on the state of Ireland. By a landed proprietor. 26p. *8°.* 1847. *The copy that belonged to Earl De Grey.*

35373 —— [Second edition.] 36p. *8°.* 1847.

35374 PHILLIMORE, John G. Letter to the Lord Chancellor on the reform of the law... Second edition. With a preface. 87p. *8°.* 1847.

35375 A PLAN for the establishment of a general system of secular education in the county of Lancaster. Second thousand. 23p. *12°. London & Manchester,* 1847. *The copy that belonged to William Lovett.*

35376 POCOCK, Z. P. Transportation and convict discipline considered in a letter to the Right Honourable Earl Grey... showing the evils attendant upon the system pursued in Van Diemen's Land, and the remedy for those evils; with suggestions for the profitable employment of convict labour... 29p. *8°.* [1847]

For the **POOR MAN'S GUARDIAN,** *see* vol. III, *Periodicals list.*

35377 POOR MAN'S GUARDIAN SOCIETY. The first annual report of the... Society... 44p. *8°.* 1847.

35378 RIADORE, J. E. On the remedial evils attending the life of the people, engaged in professions, commerce... 130p. *12°.* 1847.

35379 RIBEIRO, J. S. Apontamentos sobre as classes desvalides, e institutos de beneficencia. 72p. *12°. Funchal,* 1847.

35380 ROBERTS, S. A most extraordinary case of disregard of the laws of God and man, and of perversion of judgment. [The trial of Michael Mellon, chimney sweep, for illegally sending a child up a chimney.] 8p. *8°. Sheffield,* 1847.

35381 ROBERTSON, John, *writer on crime.* The progress of crime, and What is crime? Fragmentary essays towards a science of crime... Reprinted from the "Eclectic Review" for January and February, 1847. 24p. *12°.* 1847.

35382 ROGERS, Jasper W. Employment of the Irish peasantry the best means to prevent the drain of gold from England. Originally published in "The Mark Lane Express." With an appendix, containing notes and observations on the letters of... the Lord Lieutenant of Ireland and Sir John Burgoyne, Bart., K.C.B. 32p. *8°.* 1847.

35383 —— Facts for the kind-hearted of England! as to the wretchedness of the Irish peasantry, and the means for their regeneration. 39p. *8°.* 1847.

35384 —— The potato truck system of Ireland the main cause of her periodical famines and of the non-payment of her rents. 16p. *8°.* 1847.

35385 —— Second edition. 18p. *8°.* 1847.

For **SCOTLAND.** *Board of Supervision for the Relief of the Poor,* Annual reports, 1847–53, *see* vol. III, *Periodicals list,* Annual report...

35386 SCROPE, G. P. Address delivered at the opening of the Stroud Athenæum, on Thursday, July 22nd, 1847. By G. Poulett Scrope, Esq. M.P. as first President of the institution. 19p. *8°. Stroud,* 1847.

35387 —— Remarks on the Irish Poor Relief Bill. 32p. *8°.* 1847. *The copy that belonged to Earl De Grey.*

35388 —— Reply to the speech of the Archbishop of Dublin, delivered in the House of Lords... March 26th, 1847, and the protest, signed R. Dublin, Monteagle, Radnor, Mountcashel, against the Poor Relief ⟨Ireland⟩ Bill. 41p. *8°.* 1847. *The copy that belonged to Earl De Grey.*

35389 SEARSON, H. A letter to the members of the Book-binders' Consolidated Union. [Signed: Henry Searson, and dated: Sept. 24th, 1847. A vindication of his conduct as chief secretary of the union.] 4p. *8°. n.p.* [1847]

35390 SELSBY, H. Selsby and others on the prosecution of Jones and Potts. Narrative, introduction, &c. [The proceedings at the South Lancashire Assizes, April 2nd, 1847, against Henry Selsby and 21 other men for conspiring against John Jones and Arthur Potts to prevent them carrying on their trade or business.] 68p. *8°. n.p.* [1847]

35391 The **SETTLEMENT** and removal of the poor considered. [With 'Extract from Adam Smith'.] 58p. *8°.* 1847.

35392 SHAW, W. [*Begin.*] To the Right Honorable the Lords Spiritual and Temporal, and to the members of the House of Commons. [Letters and statements respecting the injurious effects of the contract system upon the social and moral condition of the poorer working classes.] 40p. *8°.* [1847] *The copy that belonged to J. M. Ludlow.*

35393 SIMPSON, William, *surgeon.* Medical reform. The article on medical reform, which appeared in no. xxi. of "The British and Foreign, or European Quarterly Review," for July, 1840; and letters on medical subjects, published in the "Lancet," &c. Also evidence given before the Metropolitan Sanitary Commission... Second reprint, enlarged. 36p. *8°.* [*London*, 1847]

35394 SPEDDING, T. S. Letters on the poor-laws. 81p. *12°.* 1847.

35395 STOPFORD, E. A. The rate-screw for Ireland, considered in reference to the Public Works Act, the Relief Act, and the new Poor Law. In a letter to the most noble the Marquis of Lansdowne... 39p. *8°. Dublin & London,* 1847.

35396 SYMONS, Jelinger C. A plea for schools; which sets forth the dearth of education and the growth of crime, and proves the fallacy of Mr. Baines' statistics... 71p. *8°.* 1847.

35397 TABBERNER, J. L. The past, the present, and the probable future supply of water to London; with observations in respect of improved sanitary measures: accompanied with a financial scheme for carrying the... reform into effect, and entirely subverting water-rates... 50p. *8°.* 1847.

35398 TAYLOR, William C. Notes on a visit to the model schools in Dublin, and reflections on the state of the education question in Ireland, suggested by that visit. 134p. *8°. Dublin & London,* 1847.

35399 TEARE, J. The history of the origin and success of the advocacy of the principle of total abstinence from all intoxicating liquors... Second edition. 37p. *8°.* 1847. *The Turner copy. For another edition, see* 1846.

35400 THOMSON, Alexander. Industrial schools; their origin, rise, and progress, in Aberdeen. 42p. *8°. Aberdeen, London, &c.,* 1847.

35401 THOMSON, Christopher. The autobiography of an artisan. 408p. *12°. London & Nottingham,* 1847.

35402 TUKE, James H. A visit to Connaught in the autumn of 1847. A letter addressed to the Central Relief Committee of the Society of Friends, Dublin. 67p. *8°. London & York,* 1847. *Two copies, one that belonged to Sir Harry Verney, and the other a presentation copy from the author to 'Jno Bell'.*

35403 VINCENT, H. Early closing movement. A lecture delivered...January 14, 1847...at Finsbury Chapel, Finsbury Circus. 8p. *8°.* [*London*, 1847]

35404 WALKER, George A. The warm vapour cure; or, the treatment of disease by moist and dry vapour; with an explanation of the mode in which this powerful agent acts on the human body, and proofs that the cure of rheumatism, gout, indigestion, and many other maladies, may be effected by it in a more speedy and certain manner than by the methods of internal treatment generally employed. 84p. *8°.* 1847.

35405 *WHATELY, R., *Archbishop of Dublin.* Substance of a speech delivered in the House of Lords, on... the 26th of March, 1847, on the motion for a committee on Irish poor laws. 35p. *8°. London & Dublin,* 1847. *Presentation copy from the author to George Grote.*

35406 WILLIAMS, James (*fl.* 1847). The footman's guide: containing plain instructions for the footman and butler, for the proper arrangement and regular performance of their various duties...Fourth edition... 131p. *12°.* [1847]

35407 WILLOUGHBY, Sir H., *Bart.* A few remarks on the Poor-Law Commission and on the necessity of providing an adequate protection for the poor in the workhouses of England & Wales. 18p. *8°.* 1847.

35408 WINDOW, J. A letter addressed to the Right Honourable the Lords, and others, justices of the peace of the several counties in England, proposing to establish asylum farms, for the voluntary reception of discharged prisoners. 8p. *8°.* 1847. *Presentation copy from the author to 'Wm. H. Bond Esq.'*

SLAVERY

35409 ALLEN, George (1792–1883). Resistance to slavery every man's duty. A report...to the Worcester Central Association, March 2, 1847. 40p. *8°. Boston,* 1847.

35410 DOUGLASS, F. Farewell speech...previously to embarking on board the Cambria, upon his return to America...at the valedictory soiree...at the London Tavern, on March 30, 1847. Published, by order of the Council of the Anti-Slavery League... [With 'Mr. Frederick Douglass and the Cambria steam-packet'.] 24p. *8°.* [1847]

35411 FRANCE. *Ministère de la Marine et des Colonies.* Compte rendu au Roi de l'exécution des lois des 18 et 19 juillet 1845 sur le régime des esclaves, la création d'établissements agricoles par le travail libre, etc. 310p. *4°. Paris,* 1847.

35412 [HIGGINS, M. J.] Is cheap sugar the triumph of free trade ? A letter to the Right Hon. Lord John Russell, &c.&c.&c. By Jacob Omnium. 19p. *8°.* 1847.

35413 PARTOUNAU DU PUYNODE, M. G. De l'esclavage et des colonies. 223p. *8°. Paris,* 1847.

For **REVUE ABOLITIONISTE,** *see* vol. III, *Periodicals list.*

35414 **UPHAM,** W. Speech of Mr. Upham, of Vermont, on the three million bill. Delivered in the Senate of the United States...March 1, 1847. [Proposing an amendment '...that there shall be neither slavery nor involuntary servitude in any territory which shall hereafter be acquired...to the United States'.] 8p. *8°. Washington, 1847.*

POLITICS

35415 **ALASTOR,** *pseud.* An address to the Chartists of the United Kingdom, on the attainment of the Charter by means of building societies. [Dated: July, 1847.] 8p. *12°. Printed for gratuitous circulation, 1847.*

35416 **ANGLO-LUSITANIAN,** *pseud.* A letter to Joseph Hume, Esq., M.P., upon the late debate on Portugal, in the House of Commons. 118p. *8°. 1847.*

35417 —— Lettre adressée au Chevalier Joseph Hume, membre du Parlement, sur le dernier débat dans la Chambre des Communes au sujet des affaires de Portugal ...Traduite en Portugais et apostillée par ★★★. ix, 240p. *8°. Lisbonne, 1847. Translated from the Portuguese edition.*

For **ANTI-BRIBERY SOCIETY,** Tracts, *see* vol. III, *Periodicals list*, Tracts...

35418 The black **BOOK** of England; exhibiting the existing state, policy, and administration of the United Kingdom...With lists of the chief recipients of public pay in Church and State. 384p. *12°. 1847.*

35419 **COCHRANE,** ALEXANDER D. R. B., *Baron Lamington.* The state of Greece. 32p. *8°. 1847.*

35420 **DE LA PRYME,** C. The Roman embassy. A letter to Viscount Palmerston, M.P. 15p. *8°. London, Paris, &c., 1847.*

35421 **DUFFY,** SIR C. G. Report on organization, and instructions for the formation and government of Confederate Clubs. (*The Irish Confederation*, 3.) 12p. *12°. Dublin, 1847.*

35422 —— The use and capacity of Confederate Clubs; a lecture delivered at the Dr. Doyle Confederate Club, Dublin. (*The Irish Confederation*, 5.) 17p. *12°. Dublin, 1847.*

For the **LABOURER**...Edited by Feargus O'Connor & Ernest Jones, 1847–48, *see* vol. III, *Periodicals list.*

35423 **METAXÀ,** G., *Count.* A reply to the pamphlet of Alexander Baillie Cochrane, Esq. entitled the "State of Greece." 8p. *8°. 1847.*

35424 **NATIONAL ALLIANCE FOR PROMOTING THE REAL REPRESENTATION OF THE PEOPLE IN PARLIAMENT.** Object and rules of the National Alliance...as resolved at a meeting of the members held at the Guildhall Coffee House, 12th of February, 1847. 4p. *8°. n.p.* [1847]

35425 —— [Another edition.] [4]p. *8°. 1847.*

35426 ★**OWEN,** ROBERT. To the electors of the borough of Marylebone. [An election address, signed: Robert Owen, and dated, 23rd. of July, 1847.] *s.sh.4°. n.p.* [1847] *The FWA copy that belonged to William Pare.*

35427 **PEOPLES' INTERNATIONAL LEAGUE.** Address... 16p. *8°. 1847.*

25428 —— [Another edition.] Address of the Council ... 16p. *8°. 1847.*

25429 ★—— [Another edition.] 16p. *8°. 1847. The FWA copy that belonged to William Pare.*

35430 —— Report of a public meeting, held at the Crown and Anchor Tavern, Strand...November 15, 1847, "to explain the principles and objects of the Peoples' International League." 16p. *8°.* [*London*, 1847]

35431 ★—— No. 1. "Peoples' International League tracts." The Swiss question: a brief statement of facts. 16p. *8°. 1847. The FWA copy that belonged to William Pare.*

35432 **PFEIL,** A. R. The Anglo-French intervention in the River Plate: considered especially with reference to the negociations of 1847, under the conduct of the Right Hon. Lord Howden. 111p. *8°. 1847.*

35433 **SMITH,** , *of the National Alliance.* A proposition to the people of England. 3p. *8°. n.p.* [1847]

35434 **SMYTHE,** G. A. F. P. S., *Viscount Strangford.* Speech of the Honourable George Sydney Smythe, M.P. at Canterbury on July 6, 1847. 19p. *8°. 1847.*

35435 **TEMPLE,** H. J., *Viscount Palmerston.* Speech of Lord Viscount Palmerston, Secretary of State for Foreign Affairs, to the electors of Tiverton, on the 31st July, 1847. An authentic report. 38p. *8°. 1847.*

35436 **THOMPSON,** GEORGE (1804–1878). Address of Mr. George Thompson to the electors of the Tower Hamlets. 20p. *8°.* [1847]

35437 **URQUHART,** D. Europe at the opening of the session of 1847. The Spanish marriages, and the confiscation of Cracow. 168p. *8°. 1847.*

35438 A **VOICE** from the millions! Reasons for appealing to the middle classes on behalf of their unenfranchised brethren. By a Norwich operative...Second thousand. 20p. *8°. London & Norwich,* [1847]

35439 **YOUNG IRELAND PARTY.** Proceedings of the Young Ireland Party, at their great meeting in Dublin, December 2, 1846, with a correct report of the speeches and resolutions. 46p. *12°. Belfast, 1847.*

SOCIALISM

35440 **CABET,** E. Le démocrate devenu communiste malgré lui ou réfutation de la brochure de M. Thoré intitulée Du communisme en France. 31p. *16°. Paris, 1847.*

35441 **CANTAGREL,** F. J. F. De l'organisation des travaux publics et de la réforme des Ponts-et-Chaussées. 91p. *8°. Paris, 1847.*

35442 **CATALOGUE** de la Librairie Phalanstérienne,

Quai Voltaire, N.25, et Rue de Beaune, N.2, Bureaux de La Phalange et de la démocratie pacifique... 10p. *8°. Paris*, *n.p.* [1847]

35443 COMMUNITY of Icarie. [With 'Mr. Cabet's address, inviting his disciples to go to Icarie' and 'Address of the Icarien committee to those who desire to ameliorate the condition of the people'.] [4]p. *8°.* [1847]

35444 [CONSIDÉRANT, V. P.] Bases de la politique positive. Manifeste de l'École sociétaire fondée par Fourier. Troisième édition. 202p. *12°. Paris,* 1847. *Considérant's own copy. For other editions, see* 1841.

35445 —— Destinée sociale...2e édition. 2 vols. *8°. Paris,* 1847–49. *Presentation copy, with inscription dated 1848, from the author to 'mon cher Antony Muray'. For other editions, see* 1834.

35446 —— Principes du socialisme. Manifeste de la démocratie au XIX siècle... Suivi du procès de la Démocratie Pacifique. 143p. *12°. Paris,* 1847. *Considérant's own copy.*

35447 —— Deuxième édition. [With 'Doctrine de l'harmonie universelle. Publications de l'École phalanstérienne' and 'Extrait du catalogue de la Librairie sociétaire'.] 100p. *12°. Paris,* 1847. *This edition does not have the account of the trial.*

35448 DERCSÉNYI, J., *Báró.* Baron Dercsényi's researches for a philanthropical remedy against communism; or, a system of philanthropy applied to national economy, national education, and the political life of the people. Translated from the German. 118p. *8°.* 1947.

35449 [FINCH, JOHN (1783–1857).] Society as it is and society as it ought to be; or, social diseases and social remedies. Part 1. By a Liverpool merchant. 16p. *8°. Liverpool,* 1847. *The copy that belonged to J. M. Ludlow.* *★Another, the FWA copy, belonged to William Pare.*

35450 FOURIER, F. C. M. De l'anarchie industrielle et scientifique. 70p. *12°. Paris,* 1847.

35451 —— Égarement de la raison démontré par les ridicules des sciences incertaines et Fragments... (Extrait de la Phalange...) 128p. *8°. Paris,* 1847. *The copy that belonged to Victor Considérant.*

For the **HERALD OF CO-OPERATION,** 1847–48, *see* vol. III, *Periodicals list.*

35452 JOUVENCEL, P. DE. Du droit de vivre, de la propriété et du garantisme. 90p. *16°. Paris,* 1847.

35453 KRANTZ, S. J. B. Étude sur l'application de l'armée aux travaux d'utilité publique. 116p. *8°. Paris,* 1847.

35454 —— Projet de création d'une armée des travaux publics. 90p. *8°. Paris,* 1847.

35455 LA FARELLE, F. F. DE. Du progrès social au profit des classes populaires non indigentes... suivi de: Plan d'une réorganisation disciplinaire des classes industrielles en France... Deuxième édition revue et corrigée. 504[508]p. *8°. Paris,* 1847. *For another edition, see* 1839.

35456 MARX, KARL (1818–1883). Misère de la philosophie. Réponse à la Philosophie de la misère de M. Proudhon. 178p. *8°. Paris & Bruxelles,* 1847.

For ★the **MORNING STAR,** a journal of progressive literature, *see* vol. III, *Periodicals list.*

35457 N., W. A letter advocating the establishment of equitable banks of interchange; through which, by means of property-notes, symbolically representing the wealth deposited in such banks, an equitable exchange of all kinds of useful goods and services may be accomplished, independently of a scarce and costly metallic currency... ⟨Extracted from the 'Reasoner'.⟩ 16p. *8°.* 1847.

35458 OWEN, ROBERT. Le livre du nouveau monde moral contenant le système social rationnel basé sur les lois de la nature humaine... abrégé et traduit de l'anglais par T. W. Thornton. 72p. *12°. Paris,* 1847. *For other editions, see* 1836.

35459 ★—— Manifesto of Robert Owen to the civilized world: a solution of the great problem of the age. [Dated: New York, April 6 and April 12, 1847.] 8p. *4°. n.p.* [1847] *The FWA copy that belonged to William Pare.*

35460 ★—— Robert Owen on charity, and its effects in politics. [Dated: New York, April 10, 1847.] *s.sh.8°. n.p.* [1847] *A galley proof, with manuscript corrections in Owen's hand. The FWA copy that belonged to William Pare.*

35461 REY, JOSEPH A. Appel au ralliement des socialistes. [With 'Les deux communismes. Observations sur la lettre de M. Rey. Par M. V. Considérant'. Reprinted from *La Démocratie Pacifique* of 27th June and 19th July, 1847.] 30p. *16°. Paris,* 1847.

35462 RODBERTUS-JAGETZOW, J. C. Die neusten Grundtaxen des Herrn v. Bülow-Cummerow. 147p. *8°. Anclam, Berlin, &c.,* 1847.

For the **SPIRIT OF THE TIMES;** or, the social reformer, *see* vol. III, *Periodicals list.*

35463 VERMASSE, C. A mitraille! Sur les agioteurs. Par un paysan. 36p. *12°. Paris,* 1847.

MISCELLANEOUS

35464 Migratory **BIRDS;** or, such as visit Britain at different seasons of the year. A guide to their favourite places of resort... and the benefits which their migrations confer on mankind. 64p. *8°.* 1847.

35465 CARPENTER, R. L. A fast day sermon preached in Christ Church Chapel, Bridgwater. 24p. *12°.* 1847.

35466 FITZGERALD, M., *Knight of Kerry.* Considerations on the establishment of a dockyard and arsenal in Ireland. Submitted to the Treasury, Admiralty and Ordnance departments. 16p. *8°.* [1847] *The copy that belonged to Earl De Grey.*

35467 A brief **HISTORY** of the remains of the late Thomas Paine, from the time of their disinterment in 1819. By the late William Cobbett, M.P. down to the year 1846. 8p. *8°.* 1847.

35468 ★MARKWICK, A. A few remarks on the uses and mode of applying the new epithems lately invented to supersede poultices and fomentation cloths... and a valuable remedy in cases of rheumatism, gout, tic doloureux, etc. etc. etc. 12p. *12°.* 1847. *The FWA copy that belonged to William Pare.*

35469 ★MODE of using the spongio piline, as recommended by Mr. Alfred Markwick. [A handbill.] *s.sh.8°.*

n.p. [1847] *The FWA copy that belonged to William Pare.*

35470 **MULVANY**, G. F. Thoughts and facts concerning the fine arts in Ireland, and schools of design. 60p. *8°. Dublin & London, 1847. The copy that belonged to Earl De Grey.*

For the **SAILORS' MAGAZINE AND NAUTICAL INTELLIGENCER,** *see* vol. III, *Periodicals list.*

35471 **SOCIETY FOR PROMOTING THE AMENDMENT OF THE LAW.** The fourth annual report of the Council. 7p. *8°.* [1847]

35472 **STAPLETON**, A. G. The claims of the Irish priest, the duty of the British people. 33p. *8°. 1847. The copy that belonged to Earl De Grey.*

35473 **STOKES**, WILLIAM. No more war but arbitration. A letter to the Right Hon. Lord John Russell, First Lord of the Treasury. ⟨Reprinted from "The Universe."⟩ 12p. *8°. London & Norwich, 1847. The Turner copy.*

35474 A few **THOUGHTS** upon the present affliction of Ireland. By an Irish lady. 8p. *8°. 1847. The copy that belonged to Earl De Grey.*

35475 **WEALE**, JOHN. Letter to the Right Honorable Lord John Russell, First Lord of the Treasury, &c.,&c., &c., on the defence of the country, and on the expediency of training, as auxiliaries, able-bodied male persons applying for parochial relief. 35p. *8°. 1847. Presentation copy from the author to Lord Brougham, with his library stamp on the title-page.*

35476 **WHATELY**, R., *Archbishop of Dublin.* On instinct. A lecture delivered before the Dublin Natural History Society, 11th November 1842. 32p. *8°. Dublin & London, 1847.*

1848

GENERAL

35477 **ARMISTEAD**, W. A tribute for the negro: being a vindication of the moral, intellectual, and religious capabilities of the coloured portion of mankind... 564p. *8°. Manchester, London, &c., 1848.*

35478 **ASH**, W. C. A voice from the people; or, an inquiry into the cause of our present distress, principally directed to the industrious classes... With an appeal to our rulers on behalf of our suffering fellow-countrymen. 38p. *8°. 1848.*

35479 **BANFIELD**, T. C. The organization of industry, explained in a course of lectures, delivered in the University of Cambridge in Easter Term 1844... Second edition. 166p. *8°. 1848. For another edition, entitled* Four lectures on the organization of industry, *see 1845.*

35480 —— and **WELD**, C. R. The statistical companion. 144p. *8°. 1848. The edition for 1852, by Banfield alone, is also in the Goldsmiths' Library.*

35481 **BASTIAT**, C. F. Propriété et loi. Justice et fraternité... Extrait du Journal des Économistes. Nos. du 15 mai et du 15 juin 1848. 72p. *16°. Paris, 1848.*

35482 —— Sophismes économiques... Deuxième série. 190p. *16°. Paris, 1848. For editions of the first series, see 1847.*

35483 **BETRACHTUNGEN** eines deutschen Proletariers. 80p. *8°. München, 1848.*

35484 **BLACKALL**, S. W. Suggestions for relieving distress, by stimulating private and public employment. 23p. *8°. Dublin, 1848.*

35485 The **BRITISH ALMANAC** of the Society for the Diffusion of Useful Knowledge, for... 1848... [With 'The companion to the Almanac; or, year-book of general information'.] 96, 264p. *12°.* [1848] *For other editions, see 1828.*

35486 **BUCKINGHAM**, J. S. Belgium, the Rhine, Switzerland, and Holland. An autumnal tour. 2 vols. *8°. London & Paris,* [1848]

35487 —— France, Piedmont, Italy, Lombardy, the Tyrol and Bavaria. An autumnal tour. 2 vols. *8°. London & Paris,* [1848]

35488 **BURNESS**, W. Essay on the elements of British industry; comprising remarks on the cause of our present depressed state... Together with suggestions for its removal. 160p. *8°. 1848.*

35489 **BURRITT**, E. Voice from the forge. 134p. *12°. 1848.*

35490 **CAREY**, H. C. The past, the present, and the future. 474p. *8°. Philadelphia, 1848.*

35491 **CHAMBERS**, W. and ROBERT (1802–1871), *eds.* Chambers's information for the people. 2 vols. *8°. Edinburgh & London, 1848–9. Published in 100 parts. For another edition, see 1842.*

35492 **CHEVALIER**, M. La liberté du travail, discours d'ouverture du cours d'économie politique au Collège de France, pour l'année scolaire 1847–48; prononcé le 22 décembre 1847... Réimprimé par l'Association pour la liberté des échanges. (Extrait du Journal des Économistes, no. 74. – 15 janvier, 1848.) 16p. *8°. Paris,* [1848] *Presentation copy from the author to N. W. Senior.*

35493 **CLÉMENT**, P. Le gouvernement de Louis XIV, ou la Cour, l'administration, les finances et le commerce de 1683 à 1689. Études historiques, accompagnées de pièces justificatives, lettres et documents inédits... faisant suite à l'Histoire de la vie et de l'administration de Colbert du même auteur. 348p. *8°. Paris, 1848.*

35494 **COMTE**, I. A. M. F. X. République occidentale. Ordre et progrès. Discours sur l'ensemble du positivisme, ou exposition sommaire de la doctrine philosophique et sociale propre à la grande république occidentale... 399p. *8°. Paris, 1848.*

35495 *****COUSIN**, V. Justice and charity... Being the first of a series of tracts in defence of social order, issued by the Academy of Moral and Political Sciences, with the authority of the French Government. Translated by

William Hazlitt. 36p. *12°. 1848. The FWA copy that belonged to William Pare. See also* 1849.

35496 DÉGÉNÉTAIS, V. La triple réorganisation du crédit, des richesses, du travail, par l'agriculture, l'industrie, la navigation et le commerce, pour plus de 24 millions de travailleurs de 100 professions différentes... 2e édition. 24p. *8°. Paris, Rouen, &c.,* 1848.

35497 DUPIN, F. P. C., *Baron.* Petits traités publiés par l'Académie des Sciences morales et politiques [no. 4]. Bien-être et concorde des classes du peuple français. 141p. *12°. Paris,* 1848.

35498 The **FERMENTATION** of Europe: why we have no hopes for France. Why we have much hope for Italy and Germany. Why we have no fears for England. Public credit and public order, the only guarantees for commercial prosperity, full employment and good wages. From the "Economist." Second edition. 21p. *8°.* [1848]

35499 ***FRANCE**. Bibliothèque Républicaine. No. 7. Constitution française de 1848, précédée d'une notice historique sur les Assemblées législatives de la France (Deuxième édition.) Par J. Lagarde. 100p. *18°. Paris,* 1848. *The copy that belonged to George Grote.*

35500 —— *Gouvernement Provisoire.* Actes officiels du Gouvernement provisoire dans leur ordre chronologique ...revue des faits les plus remarquables précédés du récit des événements qui se sont accomplis les 22, 23 et 24 février, 1848. 207p. *8°. Paris,* 1848. *The copy that belonged to Earl De Grey.*

35501 GORE, M. A postscript to the third edition of Suggestions on the amelioration of the present condition of Ireland; induced by the existing important aspect of affairs. 12p. *12°.* 1848. *For the original work, see* 1847.

35502 —— Thoughts on the present state of Ireland. 27p. *8°.* 1848. *The copy that belonged to Earl De Grey.*

35503 HALBERT D'ANGERS, A. Lettre aux ouvriers sur la question du travail. [2]p. *s.sh.fol. Paris,* [1848]

35504 HANCOCK, WILLIAM N. On laissez faire and the economic resources of Ireland: being a paper read before the Dublin Statistical Society. 17p. *8°. Dublin,* 1848.

35505 ***HAYDEN**, G. T. The present state of Ireland – the causes of that condition – the remedies: being a brief dialogue between an Englishman and Irishman. 21p. *8°. Dublin & London,* 1848. *The FWA copy, presented by the author to William Pare.*

35506 HILDEBRAND, B. Die Nationalökonomie der Gegenwart und Zukunft...Erster Band. 329p. *8°. Frankfurt am Main,* 1848.

35507 The **IRISH DIFFICULTY**: addressed to his countrymen, by an Englishman. 40p. *8°.* 1848.

35508 ITIER, A. V. A. J. Journal d'un voyage en Chine en 1843, 1844, 1845, 1846. 3 vols. *8°. Paris,* 1848–53.

35509 JELLY, T. A cursory glance at the past and present condition of Great Britain; intended as a beacon to the British sugar colonies. 67p. *8°.* 1848.

35510 [**KING-NOEL**, W., *Earl of Lovelace.*] Review of the work of Messrs. Rubichon and Mounier, (De l'action de la noblesse et des classes superieures dans les sociétés moderns [*sic*],) and of the memoir of M. Benoiton de Chateauneuf, "Sur l'extinction des familles nobles en France." 28p. *8°.* 1848.

35511 KINGSFORD, P. Two lectures upon the study of political philosophy; delivered at the College of Preceptors, in November 1848. 43p. *8°.* 1848. *Presentation copy from the author to Joseph King.*

35512 KINGSLEY, C. The saint's tragedy; or, the true story of Elizabeth of Hungary, Landgravine of Thuringia, saint of the Romish Calendar...With a preface by Professor Maurice. 271p. *8°.* 1848.

35513 LAFAURIE, A. Geschichte des Handels in Beziehung auf politische Oekonomie und öffentliche Ethik. 262p. *8°. [Stuttgart,* 1848]

35514 LAMBERT, É. Lettre au futur Président de la République. [2]p. *s.sh.fol. [Paris,* 1848]

35515 LESSONS on political economy. Published under the direction of the committee of general literature and education, appointed by the Society for Promoting Christian Knowledge. 56p. *12°.* 1848.

35516 The social **LESSONS** of the day. Parisian notions of freedom. Some measures of the French Government. From the "Economist" [of 15th April 1848]. 24p. *8°.* [1848] *Presentation copy from the anonymous author to Col. C. R. Fox, M.P.*

35517 Première **LETTRE** à l'Assemblée Nationale par une réunion de prolétaires, sur les changemens à apporter dans nos institutions pour procurer le bien-être à tous les Français. 4p. *4°. [Paris,* 1848]

35518 LOVETT, W. A proposal for the consideration of the friends of progress. [Dated: Dec. 31st, 1847. Suggesting the formation of a 'general association of progress'.] 8p. *8°.* [1848]

35519 M., M. C. Britain's cry for reform, retrenchment, and reduction of taxation. By a middle-class man. 16p. *8°. Manchester, Leeds, &c.,* 1848.

35520 MACGREGOR, JOHN (1797–1857). Germany: her resources, government, Union of Customs, and power, under Frederick William IV. With a preliminary view of the political condition of Europe and America in 1848. lxviii, 317p. *8°.* 1848. *A reissue, with a new introduction, of* The Germanic Union of Customs, *1842 (q.v.).*

35521 —— Sketches of the progress of civilisation and public liberty; with a view of the political condition of Europe and America in 1848. 72p. *8°.* 1848.

35522 MARTIN, ROBERT M. Ireland before and after the Union with Great Britain...Second edition. xxxvi, xii, 424p. *8°. London & Dublin,* 1848.

35523 —— Third edition – with additions. xl, 424p. *8°. London & Dublin,* 1848. *For another edition, see* 1843.

35524 MIGNET, F. A. M. Petits traités publiés par l'Académie des Sciences morales et politiques [7 & 8]. Vie de Franklin, à l'usage de tout le monde... 230p. *12°. Paris,* 1848.

35525 MILL, JOHN S. Principles of political economy with some of their applications to social philosophy. 2 vols. *8°.* 1848.

35526 —— Second edition. 2 vols. *8°.* 1848–9. *Charles Kingsley's copy, with manuscript notes.*

35527 NEWMAN, F. W. An appeal to the middle classes on the urgent necessity of numerous radical reforms, financial and organic. 28p. *8°.* 1848.

35528 PASSY, H. P. Aristocracy, considered in its

relations with the progress of civilization. From the French...With notes and appendix by the translator. 252p. *12⁰*. 1848.

35529 —— Petits traités publiés par l'Académie des Sciences morales et politiques [3]. Des causes de l'inégalité des richesses. 67p. *12⁰*. *Paris*, 1848.

35530 An earnest **PLEA** for Ireland. By an Englishman. 16p. *8⁰*. 1848.

For the **POWER OF THE PENCE**, 1848–49, *see* vol. III, *Periodicals list.*

35531 Nouveau **PROJET** de Constitution. [2]p. *s.sh.fol.* [*Paris*, 1848]

35532 **QUETELET,** L. A. J. Du système social et des lois qui le régissent. 360p. *8⁰*. *Paris*, 1848.

35533 The **REVOLUTION** in France, a warning to the aristocracy and middle classes of England. 40p. *8⁰*. 1848.

35534 **ROUSSEAU,** J. J. An inquiry into the nature of the social contract, or principles of political right. Translated from the French. 148p. *8⁰*. *Manchester & London*, [1848] *For other editions, see* 1762.

35535 [**SCROPE,** G. P.] How to make Ireland self-supporting; or, Irish clearances and improvement of waste lands. [Signed: G.P.S.] From the 'Westminster and Foreign Quarterly Review' for October, 1848. With a postscript. 39p. *8⁰*. 1848.

35536 —— A plea for the rights of industry, in Ireland. Being the substance of letters which recently appeared in the Morning Chronicle, with additions. 94p. *8⁰*. 1848. *The copy that belonged to Earl De Grey.*

35537 **SHEEPSHANKS,** R. [*Endorsed:*] Statement of the means employed for obtaining an authentic copy of the lost imperial standard yard. 6p. *fol.* [1848]

35538 **SIDNEY,** S. Railways and agriculture in north Lincolnshire. Rough notes of a ride over the track of the Manchester, Sheffield, Lincolnshire and other railways... 103p. *12⁰*. 1848.

35539 **SLIDDELL** afterwards **SLIDDELL-MACKENZIE,** A. The American in England. 305p. *12⁰*. *Aberdeen & London*, 1848.

35540 **SMITH,** ADAM. An inquiry into the nature and causes of the wealth of nations...With a life of the author. Also, a view of the doctrine of Smith, compared with that of the French economists; with a method of facilitating the study of his works; from the French of M. Garnier...

404p. *8⁰*. *London & Edinburgh*, 1848. *For other editions, see* 1776.

35541 **SOMERS,** R. Letters from the Highlands; or, the famine of 1847. 203p. *12⁰*. *London, Edinburgh, &c.,* 1848.

35542 **SOMERVILLE,** ALEXANDER. Capital and labour...By "One who has whistled at the plough." (*Somerville's National Wealth Tracts*, 1.) 20p. *12⁰*. [1848]

35543 **SPENCER,** T. Justice to the industrious classes; or the causes of commercial distress and political discontent considered, and suitable remedies suggested... No. 20. 32p. *8⁰*. *London & Bath*, 1848.

For the **SPIRIT OF THE AGE**, 1848–49, *see* vol. III, *Periodicals list.*

35544 **SWITZERLAND.** Constitution fédérale pour la Confédération suisse, du 12 septembre 1848. 40p. *8⁰*. *n.p.* [1848] *The copy that belonged to Earl De Grey.*

35545 **THIERS,** L. A. Discours de M. Thiers prononcés à l'Assemblée nationale dans la discussion de la constitution septembre et octobre 1848. Droit au travail. – Papier-monnaie. Remplacement militaire. 155p. *8⁰*. *Paris*, 1848.

35546 **TOOKE,** T. A history of prices and of the state of the circulation, from 1839 to 1847 inclusive: with a general review of the currency question, and remarks on the operation of the Act 7 & 8 Vict. c. 32...Being a continuation of the history of prices from 1793 to 1839. 500p. *8⁰*. 1848. *For the original work, see* 1838, *and for an earlier supplement, see* 1840.

For the **TRADES' WEEKLY MESSENGER**, *see* vol. III, *Periodicals list.*

35547 **TREVELYAN,** SIR C. E., *Bart.* The Irish crisis...Reprinted from the "Edinburgh Review." No. CLXXV., January, 1848. 201p. *8⁰*. 1848.

35548 **VIGNE-MONTET,** . Projet de loi pour améliorer le sort de l'industrie, présenté à l'Assemblée nationale. 12p. *8⁰*. *Nîmes*, 1848.

For la **VRAIE RÉPUBLIQUE**, *see* vol. III, *Periodicals list*, Journal de la vraie république.

35549 **WHITE,** WILLIAM (*fl.* 1826–1870). History, gazetteer, and directory of the county of Essex; comprising ...a general survey of the county, and separate historical, statistical, & topographical descriptions of all the... boroughs, towns, ports, parishes... 732p. *8⁰*. *Sheffield*, 1848.

35550 **WOŁOWSKI,** L. F. M. R. Études d'économie politique et de statistique...423p. *8⁰*. *Paris*, 1848.

35551 [**ZABRANHI,** L. D. H.] Heaven upon earth. [Essays.] By a Polish exile. 259p. *8⁰*. *Edinburgh*, 1848.

AGRICULTURE

35552 **ALCOCK,** THOMAS (*fl.* 1845–1848). The tenure of land in Ireland considered. 34p. *8⁰*. 1848.

35553 **ALEXANDER,** JAMES. A letter to Sir R. A. Ferguson, Bart. M.P. on the relative rights of landlord and tenant, proposing an adjustment of their interests on the basis of certain principles already recognised in India, and held to be applicable to the present condition of Ireland. By an Irish landowner and member of the Bengal Civil Service. 21p. *8⁰*. 1848.

35554 **BALL,** S. An account of the cultivation and manufacture of tea in China: derived from personal

observation during an official residence in that country from 1804 to 1826...with remarks on the experiments now making for the introduction of the culture of the tea tree in other parts of the world. 382p. *8⁰*. 1848.

35555 **BRABAZON,** W. The deep sea and coast fisheries of Ireland, with suggestions for the working of a fishing company...Illustrated by W. Cooper... 111p. *8⁰*. *Dublin & London*, 1848.

35556 **COLMAN,** H. The agriculture and rural economy of France, Belgium, Holland and Switzerland; from personal observation. 304p. *8⁰*. 1848.

35557 **COLVILE,** C. R. "Impediments to agricultural improvement" considered, in a paper read before the Burton-upon-Trent Farmers' Club, on Thursday, September 23, 1847. 48p. *8°.* 1848.

35558 **CORBET,** H. Tenant right: on the necessity of some legislative enactment to secure the tenant farmer the benefit of his improvements...Prize essay. 16p. *8°. London, Much Wenlock, &c.,* 1848.

35559 **CULLYER,** J. The gentleman's and farmer's assistant; containing...tables for finding the content of any piece of land...tables shewing the width required for an acre in any square piece of land...tables shewing the number of loads that will manure an acre of land...a table for measuring thatcher's work...The twelfth edition. 150p. *24°. Norwich & London,* [1848] *For another edition, see* 1803.

35560 **DAVIS,** H. Farming essays. 107p. *8°.* 1848. *Presentation copy from the author to the editor of the Quarterly Review.*

35561 **HOWARD,** C. Report on the farming of the East-Riding of Yorkshire. [Entered for a prize offered by the Royal Agricultural Society.] 31p. *8°. York,* 1848.

35562 **KING-NOEL,** W., *Earl of Lovelace.* On climate in connection with husbandry, with reference to a work entitled Cours d'agriculture, par le Comte de Gasparin. [From the Journal of the Royal Agricultural Society of England, vol. IX., part 2.] 32p. *8°.* 1848.

35563 [——] Review of the agricultural statistics of France: with a notice of the works of MM. Rubichon, Mounier and Passy, respecting its produce, and the condition of its rural population. 44p. *8°.* 1848.

35564 **LATTIMORE,** C. H. A plea for tenant right, addressed to the tenant farmers of Hertfordshire and of the United Kingdom; shewing the existing obstructions to an improved system of agriculture, and the necessity of legal security for the occupiers of the soil, in a statement of facts connected with the late occupation of Bride Hall Farm, Herts. 19p. *8°. London & Hertford,* [1848]

35565 **McCULLOCH,** JOHN R. A treatise on the succession to property vacant by death: including inquiries into the influence of primogeniture, entails, compulsory partition, foundations, &c., over the public interests. 193p. *8°.* 1848. *Presentation copy from the author to Sir Robert Peel.*

35566 **MITCHEL,** J. Lectures on the land tenures of Europe, delivered in the "Swift" Confederate Club, Dublin, on the 18th and 25th of October, 1847. (*The Irish Confederation,* 6.) 41p. *12°. Dublin,* 1848.

35567 **PASSY,** H. P. On large and small farms, and their influence on the social economy; including a view of the division of the soil in France since 1815...With notes. 173p. *12°. London, Edinburgh, &c.,* 1848. *For another edition, see* 1846.

35568 **RONDEAU,** T. A. Aux travailleurs des villes et des campagnes. [With 'Petition à l'Assemblée nationale'. Concerning a suggested revision of the Code Civil in favour of the lessees of farms.] [2]p. *s.sh.fol.* [*Paris,* 1848]

35569 **SHORT,** THOMAS K. On the cultivation and management of flax, and the best method of consuming the seed. 30p. *12°.* [1848] *Presentation copy from the author to the Duke of Newcastle.*

35570 **SOUTHEY,** T. The rise, progress and present state of colonial wools...with some account of the goat's wool of Angora and India... 333p. *8°.* 1848. *Presentation copy from the author to T. Murray.*

35571 **STEWART,** JAMES (1805–1860). On the means of facilitating the transfer of land. In three lectures. 121p. *8°.* 1848. *Presentation copy from the author to Sir Robert Peel.*

35572 **TAYLOR,** RICHARD C. Statistics of coal. The geographical and geological distribution of mineral combustibles or fossil fuel, including, also, notices and localities of the various mineral bituminous substances, employed in arts and manufactures...embracing from official reports of the great coal-producing countries the respective amounts of their production, consumption and commercial distribution, in all parts of the world; together with their prices, tariffs, duties and international regulations...with incidental statements of the statistics of iron manufactures... cxlviii, 754p. *8°. Philadelphia,* 1848.

35573 **THORNTON,** WILLIAM T. A plea for peasant proprietors; with the outlines of a plan for their establishment in Ireland. 256p. *12°.* 1848.

35574 **TUSSER,** T. Some of the five hundred points of good husbandry...Newly corrected and edited...by H.M.W. 116, 45p. *8°. Oxford,* 1848. *For other editions, see* 1574.

35575 **WALLSEND COLLIERY.** Rules and regulations to be observed by the officers and workmen of the colliery. [Signed: G. Clark, viewer. Dated: April 10, 1848.] *s.sh.fol. Newcastle-upon-Tyne,* [1848]

35576 **WELCH,** J. Tenant-right: its nature and requirements; together with a plan for a legislative act for the re-adjustment of the relationship between landlord and tenant and for the promotion of agriculture. 39p. *8°.* 1848.

35577 **WILSON,** JOHN M., *ed.* The rural cyclopedia, or a general dictionary of agriculture, and of the arts, sciences, instruments, and practice, necessary to the farmer, stockfarmer, gardener, forester, landsteward, farrier, &c.... 4 vols. *8°. Edinburgh & London,* 1848–49. *For another issue, see* 1847.

35578 **WRAY,** L. The practical sugar planter; a complete account of the cultivation and manufacture of the sugar-cane, according to the latest and most improved processes. Describing and comparing the different systems pursued in the East and West Indies and the Straits of Malacca... 415p. *8°.* 1848.

35579 **YULE,** A. The importance of spade husbandry and general manual agriculture as a certain means of removing Irish distress. 82p. *8°. Dublin,* 1848.

CORN LAWS

35580 CROSBY, G. Crosby's Parliamentary record, containing debates in the Lords and Commons on the corn laws, in the memorable session of 1846. Vol. 2. 555p. *12°. Leeds, 1848. For other editions, see 1847.*

POPULATION

35581 *QUETELET, L. A. J. Académie Royale de Belgique. Extrait du tome XXI des Mémoires. Sur la statistique morale et les principes qui doivent en former la base...(Présenté à la séance du 7 décembre 1846.) 112p. *4°. n.p.* [1848] *The work includes two papers, by P. J. F. de Decker and P. F. van Meenen, both with the title 'De l'influence du libre arbitre de l'homme sur les faits sociaux'. The copy that belonged to Augustus De Morgan.*

TRADES & MANUFACTURES

For the **ARTIZAN**, *1848–54, see vol.* III, *Periodicals list.*

35582 CATALOGUE of the exhibition of arts, manufactures, and practical science, at Newcastle-upon-Tyne, 1848. [With 'Advertising sheet'.] 83, [18]p. *8°. Newcastle, 1848. See also 1840.*

35583 FRANCIS, G. W. The dictionary of practical receipts; containing the arcana of trade and manufacture; domestic economy; artistical, ornamental & scientific processes; pharmaceutical and chemical preparations, &c.&c.&c. 348p. *8°.* 1848.

35584 The new **HISTORY** of inventions and origins. 123p. *8°. Dublin & London, 1848.*

35585 *Entry cancelled.*

35586 LE PLAY, P. G. F. Description des procédés métallurgiques employés dans le pays de Galles pour la fabrication du cuivre et recherches sur l'état actuel et sur l'avenir probable de la production et du commerce de ce métal. 496p. *8°. Paris, 1848.*

35587 A Messieurs les membres de l'Assemblée Nationale et du Conseil Général du Département du Doubs. **MÉMOIRE** présenté par les fabricants et ouvriers en horlogerie de Besançon. 37p. *8°. Besançon,* 1848.

35588 REMONSTRANCE by many inventors and others interested in inventors against the bill for altering and amending the patent laws [in the United States]. 16p. *8°. n.p.,* 1848.

35589 ROHART, F. F. Traité théorique et pratique de la fabrication de la bière. 2 vols. *8°. Paris, 1848.*

35590 STATISTICS of Lowell manufactures. January, 1848. Compiled from authentic sources. [A table.] *s.sh.fol.* [*Lowell,* 1848] [*Br.* 618] *See also 1840.*

35591 The **STEAM ENGINE**, familiarly described, with a brief account of its history and uses...A new edition. 56p. *8°.* 1848.

35592 TAYLOR, WILLIAM C. On the changes in the locality of textile manufactures. A paper read before the Dublin Statistical Society. 10p. *8°. Dublin, 1848.*

COMMERCE

35593 BRITISH SPIRITS. Comments upon the evidence affecting the spirit trade, given before the Committee of the House of Commons, upon sugar and coffee planting. By a Scotchman. 82p. *8°.* 1848.

35594 BULL, JOHN, *pseud.* An enquiry into the present state of Smithfield cattle market, and the dead meat markets of the Metropolis... 47p. *8°.* 1848.

35595 COSMOPOLITE, *pseud.* Free trade and no colonies. A letter...to the Right Hon. Lord John Russell, Prime Minister of England. 19p. *8°. Edinburgh & London,* 1848.

35596 DIBS, J. The navigation laws. Three letters to Lord John Russell, M.P., showing the justice, necessity, and economy of protection to British shipping...⟨Reprinted from the "Shipping and Mercantile Gazette."⟩ 60p. *8°.* 1848.

35597 EDINBURGH. New Corn Exchange. Corn market duty, stand and stall dues, &c. payable to the City of Edinburgh, in terms of the Act 10. and 11. Victoria, cap. 48. *s.sh.fol. Edinburgh,* [1848]

35598 [**ELLIOT**, JOHN L.] A letter to the electors of Westminster, from a protectionist. 84p. *8°.* [*London,*] 1848. *The copy that belonged to Col. C. R. Fox, M.P.*

35599 [——] Third edition. 84p. *8°.* [*London,*] 1848.

35600 FRANCE. *Administration des Douanes.* République Française...Tableau décennal de commerce de la France avec ses colonies et les puissances étrangères... 1837 à 1846... 358, 470p. *4°. Paris, 1848. See also 1838.*

35601 FRUITS of the system called free trade, as shown in three letters to the operatives of the manufacturing districts of the United Kingdom. By a London merchant. 8p. *8°. Glasgow & London,* [1848]

35602 FRUITS of the system called free trade. Some remarks upon three letters under the above title, addressed by "A London merchant" to the operatives of the manufacturing districts of the United Kingdom. 10p. *8°. n.p.* [1848]

35603 FRUITS of the system called free trade. A letter to the author of "Some remarks upon three letters under the above title, addressed by a London merchant to the operatives of the manufacturing districts of the United Kingdom." By a London merchant. 12p. *8°. Glasgow & London,* 1848.

35604 HARLE, W. L. The total repeal of the navigation laws, discussed and enforced, in a letter to the Right Honourable the Earl Grey. 34p. *8°. London & Newcastle-upon-Tyne,* 1848.

35605 LABOUCHERE, H., *Baron Taunton.* The speech of the Right Hon. Henry Labouchere, M.P. in the House of Commons on the navigation laws. 54p. *8°.* 1848.

35606 LEFAURIE, A. Geschichte des Handels in Beziehung auf politische Oekonomie und öffentliche Ethik...Aus der "Neuen Encyklopädie für Wissenschaften und Künste" Band v. besonders abgedruckt. 262p. *8°. Stuttgart,* 1848.

35607 [MEEUS-VANDERMAELEN, J. ?] Du gouvernement de l'industrie; pour prévenir une fausse organisation du travail. Par J.M.... 103p. *8°. Bruxelles,* 1844, 1848 [i.e. 1848]

35608 PHILOPATRIS, *pseud.* Commerce and free trade promoted in the Indian archipelago. 23p. *8°.* 1848.

35609 Mr. **RICARDO'S** Anatomy of the navigation laws, dissected. By a barrister. 206p. *12°.* 1848. *Conjecturally attributed to Sir J. B. Byles by HSF.*

35610 [SALT, T. C. ?] Breach of privilege: being the evidence of Mr. John Bull, taken before the Secret Committee on the National Distress in 1847 and 1848. 32p. *8°.* 1848.

35611 SCHLEIER, L. Die Handelswissenschaft. Theoretisch und praktisch dargestellt. 872p. *8°. Leipzig,* 1848.

35612 YOUNG, GEORGE F. Letters on the navigation laws...Originally published in the "Standard" newspaper... 41p. *8°.* 1848.

COLONIES

35613 [AGOULT, M. C. S. D', *Comtesse.*] Les suppliantes. Au Général Cavaignac. [Signed: Daniel Stern. A plea that those condemned for their part in the June uprisings should be sent to Algeria as settlers.] *s.sh.fol. Paris,* [1848]

35614 [ANDREW, SIR WILLIAM P.] Indian railways and their probable results, with maps and an appendix, containing statistics of internal and external commerce of India, by an old Indian postmaster. lviii, viii, 150, xxivp. *8°. London, Edinburgh, &c.,* 1848. *For another edition, see* 1846.

35615 —— A letter to the Chairman of the honourable East India Company, on the position of the East Indian Railway Company, with extracts from the public papers: and remarks. 16p. *8°.* 1848.

35616 ASSOCIATION FOR FOUNDING THE SETTLEMENT OF CANTERBURY, IN NEW ZEALAND. Plan of the Association... 23p. *8°.* 1848.

35617 BALLANTYNE, R. M. Hudson's Bay; or, every-day life in the wilds of North America, during six years' residence in the territories of the honourable Hudson's Bay Company. 328p. *8°. Edinburgh,* 1848.

35618 BARILLON, , *avocat.* Requête au Général Cavaignac sur la transportation des insurgés de juin. [A plea that some with less heavy sentences should be transported to Algeria and settled there.] [2]p. *s.sh.fol. Paris,* [1848]

35619 —— [Another edition.] [2]p. *s.sh.fol. Paris,* [1848]

35620 BARRAULT, P. A. C. E. Paris, septembre 1848...Algérie! Algérie! Lettre au Général Cavaignac. (*Lettres contemporaines,* 4e livraison.) [2]p. *s.sh.fol. Paris,* [1848]

35621 BOURNE, JOHN, *C.E.* Railways in India; with an introduction, illustrative of the practicability of rendering available existing works in diminution of the cost of such undertakings whereby their profits may be greatly increased...Second edition, with a plate of projected lines. 24, 127p. *8°.* 1848. *For another edition, see* 1847.

35622 [BURLEND, R.] A true picture of emigration; or fourteen years in the interior of North America; being a full and impartial account of the various difficulties and ultimate success of an English family who emigrated from Barwick-in-Elmet, near Leeds, in the year 1831. 62p. *12°.* [1848]

35623 CHAMEROVZOW, L. A. The New Zealand question and the rights of aborigines. [With 'Appendix... being the opinions thereupon of J. Phillimore Esq., D.C.L. and S. F. Woolmer, Esq.' and 'Appendix B. Concerning the settlement of Nelson, New Zealand...'.] 418, 53, 16p. *12°.* 1848.

35624 CHEEVER, G. B., *ed.* The journal of the pilgrims at Plymouth in New England, in 1620. Reprinted from the original volume [entitled 'A relation or journall of the beginning and proceedings of the English plantation setled at Plimoth in New England...' edited by G. Mount]. With historical and local illustrations...by G. B. Cheever. 369p. *8°. New York & London,* 1848.

35625 CINNAMON REVENUE. [Against the reduction of the export duty on cinnamon grown in Ceylon.] 20p. *8°. n.p.* [1848 ?] *The caption title (above) on p. 1 is in manuscript lettering.*

35626 DANSON, J. T. Observations on the speech of Sir William Molesworth, Bart., M.P. in the House of Commons...25th July, 1848, on colonial expenditure and government. 87p. *8°.* [1848] *Presentation copy from the author to F. G. P. Neison.*

35627 The **EMIGRANT'S** guide to New Zealand: comprising every requisite information for intending emigrants, relative to the southern settlements of New Zealand. By a late resident in the colony...Third edition. 64p. *8°.* 1848.

35628 ENGLAND. *Colonial Office.* Colonial Land and Emigration Commission. The first seven general reports of the Colonial Land and Emigration Commissioners, 1840 to 1847; to which are prefixed the instructions to the Commissioners from the Secretary of State, dated 14 Jan. 1840...with an index. 7 vols. *8°.* 1848.

35629 GORE, M. Reflections on the present state and prospects of the British West Indies. 40p. *8°.* 1848.

35630 GRAY, M. W. Self-paying colonization in North America: being a letter to Captain John P. Kennedy ... 64p. *8°. Dublin,* 1848.

35631 GREY, H. G., *3rd Earl Grey.* 1848. Grey and Stanley. How the colonies are represented and misrepresented in England. [Speeches on the West Indies.] 21p. *8°.* [1848]

35632 HOFFMAN, D. Views on the formation of a British & American land and emigration company. Addressed to the British public. 36p. *8°.* 1848.

35633 *IMPEY, E. A report on the cultivation, preparation, and adulteration, of Malwa opium. 83p. *8°. Bombay,* 1848.

35634 Is **INDIA** to have railways? Fallacies of an East India merchant exposed, in a letter to Lieutenant-General Sir James Law Lushington, G.C.B., chairman of the Honourable East India Company. By an East India officer (a shareholder in the East Indian Railway Company). 87p. *8°.* 1848. *The Rastrick copy.*

35635 LABOURERS' RELIEF EMIGRATION SOCIETY. Prospectus... 7p. *8°.* [1848]

35636 A **LETTER** to the Right Honourable Lord John Russell, M.P., on the subject of Indian railways. By an East India merchant. [Including correspondence between the East Indian Railway Company, the East India Company and the Board of Control.] 123p. *8°.* 1848.

35637 MOLESWORTH, SIR W., *Bart.* Speech of Sir William Molesworth, Bart. M.P. in the House of Commons...25th July, 1848, on colonial expenditure and government. 40p. *8°.* [1848]

35638 NIGER, *pseud.* A short statement of facts, in reply to the attacks on the policy of the present Government towards the colonies, in a letter to Lord John Russell. 22p. *8°.* 1848.

35639 *NORTH TEXAN COLONIZATION COMPANY. [*Begin.*] Many friends in the country have requested to know what progress the Company is making. [Information for intending district groups and for emigrants to Texas. Signed: John Cameron, secretary.] *s.sh.4°. n.p.* [1848] *The FWA copy that belonged to William Pare.*

35640 [PENNINGTON, JAMES.] The currency of the British colonies. 247p. *8°.* 1848. *Presentation copy, with inscription, from the author to Sir Robert Peel.*

35641 RICE, THOMAS S., *Baron Monteagle.* Colonization of Vancouver's Island. Substance of the speech of the Lord Monteagle in the House of Lords, Thursday, August 24, 1848. Extracted from Hansard's Parliamentary Debates. 15p. *12°.* 1848.

35642 —— The necessity and consequences of colonization. Substance of a speech delivered in the House of Lords by the Lord Monteagle...August 10, 1848...To which are appended, the first report on colonization from Ireland, 1847, and propositions proposed to be submitted to the Committee of the Lords on colonization. Extracted from Hansard's Parliamentary Debates. 60p. *12°.* 1848.

35643 RICHARDSON, G. C. Sugar cultivation. Malacca. [A prospectus for a plantation.] 24p. *8°.* [1848]

35644 *SCHOMBURGK, SIR R. H. The history of Barbados; comprising a geographical and statistical description of the island; a sketch of the historical events since the settlement; and an account of its geology and natural productions. 722p. *fol.* 1848. *The copy that belonged to George Grote.*

35645 [SHAHAMAT ALI, *Mir.*] Notes and opinions of a native on the present state of India and the feelings of its people. 123p. *8°. Ryde, Isle of Wight,* 1848. *Presentation copy, with inscription, from the author to the Reform Club.*

35646 SMITH, JOHN T. Observations on the duties and responsibilities involved in the management of mints; chiefly with reference to the rules and practice of those in India. With suggestions for their improvement. 186p. *8°. Madras,* 1848.

35647 WALLBRIDGE, EDWIN A. The Demerara martyr. Memoirs of the Rev. John Smith, missionary to Demerara...With a preface by the Rev. W. G. Barrett. xxvi, 274p. *8°.* 1848.

35648 WEST INDIA PLANTERS AND MERCHANTS. ⟨Printed for the West India Body.⟩ Report of the Acting Committee to the Standing Committee of West India Planters and Merchants, at their half-yearly meeting, held at the West India Committee Rooms, No. 13, Old Jewry Chambers, on the 26th. January, 1848. 41p. *8°.* 1848. *See also* 1846, 1847, 1849.

35649 WESTGARTH, W. Australia Felix; or, a historical and descriptive account of the settlement of Port Phillip, New South Wales; including full particulars of the manners and condition of the aboriginal natives, with observations on emigration, on the system of transportation, and on colonial policy... 440p. *12°. Edinburgh & London,* 1848.

35650 [WHYTE, R.] The ocean plague; or, a voyage to Quebec in an Irish emigrant vessel. Embracing a quarantine at Grosse Isle in 1847. With notes illustrative of the ship-pestilence of that fatal year. By a cabin passenger. 127p. *12°. Boston,* 1848.

35651 WILKINSON, F. A proposal for, and a few considerations in favour of, the formation of a national colonization and colonial association. 26p. *8°.* 1848.

35652 WILKINSON, G. B. South Australia; its advantages and its resources. Being a description of that colony, and a manual of information for emigrants. 391p. *8°.* 1848.

FINANCE

35653 ALLEMAND, C. Projet de décret adressé au Ministre et au Comité des Finances...le 25 juillet 1848. 11p. *8°.* [*Paris,* 1848]

35654 ANTI-GOLD-LAW LEAGUE. Manifesto of the Anti-Gold-Law League. *s.sh.4°.* [1848]

35655 The **ANTI-PANIC MONETARY SYSTEM.** Relief to the commercial classes, and to shareholders in public works. 15p. *8°. London & Birmingham,* 1848.

35656 AUBERTIN, E. Remède à la crise financière

actuelle déposé au 4e Bureau. 15p. *8°.* [*Paris,* 1848] *Catalogued from the caption on p. 3. This is preceded by a leaf bearing a covering address headed 'Aux représentants du peuple', and signed: D'Olivier.*

35657 AUDIFFRET, C. L. G. D', *Marquis.* La crise financière de 1848. 116p. *8°. Paris,* 1848.

35658 B., R. S. Two letters to a member of Parliament; containing suggestions for a property tax upon an improved basis; with remarks upon the principal speeches in defence of the present income tax during the late debates. 40p. *8°.* 1848. *The copy that belonged to Earl De Grey.*

35659 BABBAGE, C. Thoughts on the principles of taxation, with reference to a property tax, and its exceptions. 24p. *8°.* 1848.

35660 BAILDON, H. C., *comp.* Committee of enquiry into the validity of the monetary principle advocated in Gray's Lectures on the nature and use of money. 28p. *8°. Edinburgh & London,* 1848. *The work consists of 35 reviews of Gray's book, followed by a short note by him. See also* 1849.

35661 BANQUE nationale hypothécaire. 16p. *8°.* [*Paris,* 1848]

35662 BAUDRON DE LAMOTHE, A. Le peuple exempt d'impôts au-dessous de 3,500 fr. de revenu ou de produits... Considérations sur les impôts, un seul à conserver, trois à établir, six à supprimer... 23p. *8°. Belleville,* 1848.

35663 [BEGBIE, SIR M. B.] Partnership "en commandite," or partnership with limited liabilities (according to the commercial practice of the continent of Europe, and the United States of America), for the employment of capital, the circulation of wages, and the revival of our home and colonial trade. 249p. *8°.* 1848. *Presentation copy from the author to Sir Robert Peel. Formerly attributed to Thomas Wilson.*

35664 BERTHÉLEMY, J. F. J. Au citoyen rédacteur du journal Le Commerce. 4p. *8°. Paris,* [1848]

35665 BISHOP, D. A letter to the Right Hon. Sir Robert Peel, on the currency question. 11p. *8°.* 1848.

35666 BLACKER, W. Mr. Blacker's theory of the currency. From the "Bankers' Magazine," June, 1848. 8p. *8°.* 1848.

35667 —— Statement of evidence which would have been given to the Committee of the House of Commons, on commercial distress by William Blacker, Esq. had not a majority of the Committee refused to admit of his being examined. 49p. *8°.* 1848.

35668 BORUCKI, N. P. A. Raisons de la décadence de la concurrence des produits de l'industrie française à l'étranger. 16p. *8°. Troyes,* [1848]

35669 BRESSON, J. Liberté du taux de l'intérêt ou abolition des lois sur l'usure, avec des réflexions sur la Banque de France, et un examen du système de banque d'échange de M. Proudhon. 30p. *8°. Paris,* 1848.

35670 The **BRITISH TARIFF**...By Edwin Beedell ... 394p. *12°.* 1848. *See also* 1829, 1832, 1834, 1846.

35671 BROWN, JAMES (*fl.* 1848). Observations on Mr. Kinnear's "History of the rise of exchange companies in Scotland; and a defence of their proper business." 16p. *8°. Glasgow & Edinburgh,* 1848.

35672 BUCHANAN, I. Jottings on the subject of the currency. [A paper written for a member of the Currency Committee of the House of Commons, dated: New-York, 10th March, 1848.] *s.sh.fol. n.p.* [1848]

35673 [——?] Justice or injustice to fixed property & labour ? or, in other words, Shall we have Pitt, or Peel, money ? [A reprint of letters to the *Glasgow Examiner* during October and November 1848.] 4p. *fol. n.p.* [1848] *Attributed to Buchanan in a manuscript note on the first page.*

35674 A **BUDGET** of two taxes only. A stamp tax, with the legacy duty equalized and extended to real property; and a property tax, applied to all realized property, with an equitable proportion of income. 12p. *8°.* 1848. **Another, the FWA copy, belonged to William Pare.*

35675 BURCHELL, J. Letter to the members of the Mutual Life Assurance Society. 16p. *8°.* [1848]

35676 BUREAU, A. Plus de droits réunis! Plus d'exercice! – Plus d'octroi! Révision des lois de douanes, création de nouvelles ressources pour le budget. [2]p. *s.sh.fol.* [*Paris,* 1848]

35677 CAPPS, E. Currency tracts for the industrious of all classes, no. 1. ['The currency question in a nutshell.' With a letter to both Houses of Parliament, written in 1826, by Sir Robert Peel [1750–1830], and 'Sketch of Sir Robert Peel's financial career'.] 24p. *12°. Birmingham & London,* [1848] *For other editions of* The currency question in a nutshell, *see* 1837.

35678 CLUZEL, J. B. Fusion des intérêts territoriaux et commerciaux, ou nouveau système de crédit applicable, par le commerce, à la propriété foncière et aux industries agricoles et manufacturières...Nouveau mémoire descriptif adressé au Congrès central d'Agriculture. 45p. *8°. Toulouse,* 1848.

35679 COMMITTEE OF MERCHANTS AND TRADERS...APPOINTED TO PROMOTE THE IMPROVEMENT OF THE LAW RELATING TO DEBTOR AND CREDITOR. [*Endorsed:*] Bankruptcy and insolvency law amendment. Summary of measures proposed by the Metropolitan Committee of Merchants and Traders. 1848. 3p. *fol.* [1848] *See note to no.* 32762.

35680 —— To the honourable the Commons of the United Kingdom of Great Britain and Ireland in Parliament assembled. The humble petition of the undersigned merchants, bankers, and traders of the Metropolis [that the law relating to bankruptcy and insolvency be further amended. Presented 5 July 1848]. 3p. *4°. n.p.* [1848 ?] *See note to no.* 32762.

35681 COQUELIN, C. Du crédit et des banques. 424p. *12°. Paris,* 1848.

35682 COULOMBEL, . La crise va cesser et ne pourra plus se reproduire... 16p. *8°. Paris,* 1848.

35683 —— Exposé des motifs suivi de trois projets de décrèt demandant 1° Ouverture d'un grand livre d'inscriptions hypothécaires, 2° Établissement d'une banque nationale foncière, 3° Extension des attributions de la Banque de France actuelle. 8p. *8°. Paris,* 1848.

35684 —— La vérité sur la crise financière et sociale... État de la société et de ses ressources. Le crédit... 8p. *8°.* [*Paris,* 1848]

35685 DANRÉ, C. Problème de l'impôt résolu mathématiquement en théorie et en pratique...Sixième édition... 16p. *8°. Paris,* 1848.

35686 DELCROS, J. B. Suppression de la Banque de France, création d'une banque nationale. 78p. *8º. Paris*, 1848.

35687 DEMESMAY, A. Assemblée Nationale. Session de 1848. De l'impôt du sel en 1848. 16p. *8º. Paris*, 1848.

35688 —— Du sel dans ses emplois agricoles. 32p. *8º. Paris*, 1848.

35689 DEMONCHY, . Quelques idées sur le projet de loi touchant la constitution d'une banque hypothécaire en France. 8p. *8º. Paris*, [1848]

35690 The national **DISTRESS**: its financial origin and remedy. With the proposal of a common principle of union amongst the promoters of an equitable adjustment of the currency; and a vindication of the railways. [With 'Appendix. Propositions for a public Act relating to the issues of the Bank of England and to a national currency'.] 260, 8p. *8º*. 1848. *The copy that belonged to Sir Robert Peel. There is also a proof copy in the Goldsmiths' Library, with the title*: The capricious, usurious, and blighting interest of money.

35691 DRABWELL, W. A short treatise on equitable taxation, and a property tax. Tax capital, not skill and industry. The income tax assimilated to a property tax. With four tables, corroborative of the argument. 16p. *8º*. 1848.

35692 DRUMMOND, H. Elementary propositions on currency. 14p. *8º*. 1848. *For other editions, see* 1820.

35693 DU MÉRIL, E. Organisation financière de la République. 35p. *8º*. [*Paris*,] 1848.

35694 [DUNCAN, JONATHAN.] Letters on monetary science. By Aladdin. ⟨Revised and reprinted from "Douglas Jerrold's Weekly Newspaper."⟩ Second edition. 73p. *8º*. 1848.

35695 DUTREIH, E. Lettre sur la nécessité, le mode de création et les résultats d'une banque immobilière en France... 16p. *8º. Paris*, 1848.

35696 ENGELS, P. H. De geschiedenis der belastingen in Nederland, van de vroegste tijden tot op heden, met eenen beknopten inhoud der tegenwoordig in werking zijnde belastingwetten. 350p. *8º. Rotterdam*, 1848.

35697 ENGLAND. *Commissioners of Excise*. Index to the general orders of the Honorable Board of Excise, from the year 1700 to the year 1847, inclusive. Arranged according to the subjects. Compiled by W. Stones. Published for the sole use of the Excise Establishment. 114p. *8º*. 1848.

35698 —— *Laws, etc.* 11º & 12º Victoriæ, sess. 1847–8. Act of incorporation of the Scottish Provident Institution. Established 1837. 16p. *8º. Edinburgh*, [1848?]

35699 —— *Parliament. House of Commons.* The first report of the Secret Committee of the House of Commons, on the Bank Charter Act of 1844, and the recent commercial distress. With the evidence thereon. ⟨Reprinted from the 'Bankers' Magazine'.⟩ 136p. *8º*. 1848.

35700 —— —— *House of Lords.* The Lords' Report on commercial distress. Report: by the Lords' Committee appointed a Secret Committee to inquire into the causes of the distress which has for some time prevailed among the commercial classes, and how far it has been affected by the laws for regulating the issue of bank-notes payable on demand... 68p. *8º*. 1848.

35701 EVANS, D. M. The commercial crisis 1847–1848; being facts and figures illustrative of the events of that important period, considered in relation to the three epochs of the railway mania, the food and money panic, and the French Revolution. To which is added; an appendix, containing an alphabetical list of the English and foreign mercantile failures, with the balance sheets and statements... 151, lxxxp. *8º*. 1848. *See also* 1849, *and for another, separately published, appendix*, 1850.

35702 *FAUCHER, L. Assemblée nationale. Session de 1848. Discours prononcé...dans la discussion des proposition relatives à l'établissement du crédit foncier. [Extrait du Moniteur Universel du 11 octobre, 1848.] 19p. *8º*. [*Paris*,] 1848. *The copy that belonged to George Grote.*

35703 —— [Another edition.] Du crédit foncier, discours prononcé à l'Assemblée nationale. 35p. *8º. Paris*, 1848.

35704 FISHER, D. Speech of Mr. David Fisher, of Ohio, on the loan bill, delivered in the House of Representatives of the U.S., February 9th, 1848. 16p. *8º. Washington*, 1848.

35705 FOURNIER SAINT-ANGE, F. A. Du rachat de la dette consolidée par l'impôt foncier. 15p. *8º*. [*Paris*, 1848]

35706 FRANCE. *Assemblée Nationale*. No. 588... Rapport fait au nom du Comité des finances, sur la proposition du citoyen Pougeard, tendant à remplacer l'impôt extraordinaire de 45 centimes, l'impôt sur les créances hypothécaires et l'impôt sur les successions par un emprunt forcé de deux cents millions...Par le Citoyen Faucher (Léon), représentant du peuple. Séance du 29 août 1848. 24p. *8º. n.p.* [1848]

35707 —— *Ministère des Finances*. Observations de l'Administration des Finances sur le rapport fait à l'Assemblée Nationale, le 1er septembre 1848, au nom de la Commission chargée d'examiner le projet de décret relatif à l'établissement d'un impôt progressif sur les successions et donations, suivies des amendments au projet de la Commission présentés par le Ministre des Finances. 33p. *8º. Paris*, 1848.

35708 FRANCIS, J. History of the Bank of England, its times and traditions...Third edition. 2 vols. *8º*. 1848. *For other editions, see* 1847.

35709 FRESNEL, R. F. Mobilisation des propriétés immobilières. Cinq milliards de capital mis en circulation. 15p. *8º. Paris*, 1848.

35710 GANNAL, . Abolition de l'impôt sur les boissons... 8p. *8º. Paris*, [1848]

35711 The **GOLD STANDARD**. 28p. *8º*. 1848.

35712 GOUPY, L. Aux citoyens réprésentants du peuple. Projet de loi pour relever nos fonds, accélérer la consommation, développer le travail et libérer le trésor public en même temps que la propriété. 4p. *8º*. [*Paris*, 1848]

35713 GRAY, JOHN (1799–1883). Lectures on the nature and use of money. Delivered before the members of the "Edinburgh Philosophical Institution" during the months of February and March, 1848. 344p. *8º. Edinburgh & London*, 1848.

35714 HANCOCK, WILLIAM N. Two papers read before the Dublin Statistical Society: I. On the effects of the usury laws on the funding system. II. A notice of the theory "that there is no hope for a nation which lives on potatoes." 10p. *8°. Dublin, 1848.*

35715 HEQUET, J. B. Création d'une banque nationale hypothécaire. 15p. *8°. Paris, 1848.*

35716 HERPIN, J. C. Quelques mots sur le crédit agricole et la réforme du régime hypothécaire. [Extrait des Annales de l'agriculture française, juin 1848.] 12p. *8°.* [*Paris, 1848*]

35717 HESELTINE, W. A family scene during the panic at the Stock Exchange, in May, 1835...Second edition. [With 'Reflections at the grave of N. M. Rothschild, Esq.' in verse.] 56p. *8°. Canterbury, 1848. Presentation copy from the author to A. B. Cook.*

35718 HODGSON, A. A letter to the Right Honourable Sir Robert Peel, Bart., on the currency. 19p. *8°. London & Liverpool, 1848.*

35719 HUBBARD, J. G., *Baron Addington*. A letter to the Right Honourable Sir Charles Wood, Bart., M.P., Chancellor of the Exchequer, on the monetary pressure and commercial distress of 1847. 50p. *8°. 1848.*

35720 HUGHES, T. M. Three letters to Senhor Rodrigo da Fonseca Magalhães, on the subject of a purchase of bonds referred to in the Lisbon Chamber of Peers. 64p. *4°. Lisboa, 1848. With a second title in Portuguese, and the text in English and Portuguese printed in parallel columns.*

35721 HYDE, J. Opinions and observations on national and local taxation, on the property of labour, and the application thereof. With suggestions and a general outline for a property tax, in lieu of twenty-two millions of taxes which press unequally on various classes of the community. In a letter to Richard Cobden, Esq., M.P. 24p. *12°.* [*1848*]

35722 JUNGHANNS, C. Der Fortschritt des Zollvereines. [With 'Zweite Abtheilung. Statistik des Zollvereins von 1834–1846'.] 320, 191p. *8°. Leipzig, 1848.*

35723 Fiat **JUSTITIA!** A few plain arguments, derived from considerations of the impolicy and injustice of the present income tax, to prove the policy and justice of supplying the deficit in the revenue by an additional per centage on real property only. 16p. *8°. 1848.*

35724 KINNEAR, G. A history of the rise of exchange companies in Scotland; and a defence of their proper business. 33p. *8°. Glasgow, Edinburgh, &c., 1848.*

35725 —— Second edition. 33p. *8°. Glasgow, Edinburgh, &c., 1848.*

35726 —— Third edition, with a postscript. 33, 10p. *8°. Glasgow, Edinburgh, &c., 1848.*

35727 A **LETTER** to the electors of Great Britain on the income tax, &c.&c. [Signed: A Surrey elector.] 6p. *8°. 1848.*

35728 LETTRE au Citoyen Goudchaux Ministre des Finances par un créancier de la Caisse d'Épargne. [2]p. *fol.* [*Paris, 1848*]

35729 LEVACHER-D'URCLÉ, F. Moyens les plus justes, les plus prompts et les plus faciles que l'on puisse employer en ce moment pour sauver tous les Français et de la banqueroute de leur trésor et de la ruine entière dont ils sont menacés par suite de l'incapacité ou des calculs d'intérêts personnels de tous ces pouvoirs qui se sont intronisés à Paris depuis le 24 février dernier. 8p. *8°.* [*Paris, 1848*]

35730 LIBERT, A. B. Aux représentants du peuple. Considérations sur la position critique des propriétaires, et sur l'inégalité des charges imposées aux propriétés immobilières. 8p. *8°. Paris,* [*1848*]

For ★*the* **LIFE ASSURANCE RECORD,** *see* vol. III, *Periodicals list.*

35731 LIVERPOOL. Reduction of taxes. Speeches at the public meeting held at the Sessions House, Liverpool, on the national expenditure and taxation, May 31, 1848... 42p. *16°. Liverpool,* [*1848*]

35732 —— The tea duties. Report of the second public meeting, held in the Sessions-House, Liverpool, on the 14th January, 1848, Thos. B. Horsfall, Esq., Mayor, in the chair. To which is prefixed the Report of the Parliamentary Committee of last session. Published by the Liverpool Association for the Reduction of the Duty on Tea. 60p. *8°. Liverpool, 1848. See also 1846.*

35733 LIVERPOOL FINANCIAL REFORM ASSOCIATION. Financial reform tracts. Nos. 1–17, 19–20. *8°. Liverpool, 1848–9. Some of the early numbers are in several editions, some of which belonged to Earl De Grey. See also 1849. For a reissue of the series by the Manchester Financial and Parliamentary Reform Association, see 1850.*

35734 LOCKWOOD, J. On the forgery of Bank of England notes, official stamps, and other public documents, being a letter to enlighten the Chancellor of the Exchequer. 16p. *8°. 1848.*

35735 MAHUZIER, H. and **MONTET,** E. Établissement du crédit foncier. Papier-monnaie hypothécaire. 24p. *8°. Périgueux, 1848.*

35736 MARESCHAL, J. Un dernier mot sur la question du sel agricole. 6p. *8°. Paris, 1848.*

35737 —— Mémoire sur l'emploi du sel en agriculture et sur la nécessité de sa franchise d'impôt. 35p. *8°. Paris, 1848.*

35738 MARESTAING, T. and **LAPALME,** L. Banque agricole de crédit et de circulation. 46p. *8°. Paris, 1848.*

35739 MILLER, SAMUEL, *barrister*. Suggestions for a general equalization of the land tax and the abolition of the income and real property taxes, and the malt duty. 34p. *8°. 1848.*

35740 MILNER, T. H. On the regulation of floating capital, and freedom of currency: with an attempt to explain practically the general monetary system of the country. 115p. *8°. 1848. The copy that belonged to C. N. Newdegate.*

35741 MORELLET, C. V. Projet de banque hypothécaire. 8p. *8°. Lyon,* [*1848*]

35742 Mr. **MUNTZ** & the currency. An address to the people of Birmingham, on Mr. Muntz and the currency. By no friend to the new way of paying old debts. 48p. *8°. Birmingham, 1848.*

35743 MURRAY, THOMAS (1792–1872). The incidence of the annuity tax...Second edition. 16p. *8°. Edinburgh, 1848.*

35744 N., L. Projet de décret pour la création d'une banque hypothécaire. 15p. *8°. Moulins,* [*1848*]

35745 NEY, J. N., *Prince de la Moskowa*. Du papier-monnaie et de la démonétisation des espèces considérés dans leurs rapports avec les besoins du pays et les developpements de la fortune publique, par M. de la Moskowa. 80p. *8°. Paris*, 1848.

35746 [NUNN, M.] Great joy for the Marylebone ratepayers. A dialogue between a ratepayer and the vestry. 8p. *8°. [London,]* 1848.

35747 *PECK, A. To the operatives of Great Britain on life assurance. 29p. *8°. [London,]* 1848. *The copy that belonged to Augustus De Morgan.*

35748 PÉTITION des vignerons de la Corrèze à l'Assemblée Nationale Constituante, pour réclamer l'abolition de l'impôt sur les boissons, suivies de quelques observations sur le même sujet, par Camille Planchard. 26p. *8°. Brive,* 1848.

35749 PHIPPS, HON. E. The adventure of a £.1000 note; or, railway ruin reviewed. 32p. *8°.* 1848.

35750 PICKERING, W. The currency, its defects and cure. 18p. *8°. Liverpool & London,* 1848.

35751 POLINO, C. Réfutation des discours des citoyens Goudchaux, Ministre des finances, Thiers, Léon Faucher, représentants du peuple, relatifs à l'établissement d'une banque nationale immobilière...Nouveau projet pour ladite banque... 19p. *8°. [Paris,* 1848]

35752 [POLLARD, G.] A plan for a domestic currency, rendered independent of the foreign exchanges, and measured in standard gold. By a banker. Third edition, with additions. 24p. *8°.* 1848. *For another edition, see* 1847.

35753 PORTER, W. H. Savings banks: their defects – the remedy. The position respectively of the Commissioners for the Reduction of the National Debt, the trustees and managers, and the depositors in savings banks, explained...together with some account of the failure of St. Peter's Parish Savings Bank, Dublin...Part I[-II]. 170p. *8°. Dublin,* 1848.

35754 PROPERTY TAX versus income tax; in a letter addressed to the representatives of the United Kingdom. 16p. *8°.* 1848.

35755 PROUDHON, P. J. Organisation du crédit et de la circulation et solution du problème social... 42p. *8°. Paris,* 1848.

35756 —— Deuxième édition. 43p. *12°. Paris,* 1848.

35757 —— Proposition relative à l'impôt sur le revenu, présentée le 11 juillet 1848, par le citoyen Proudhon; suivie du discours qu'il a prononcé à l'Assemblée Nationale le 31 juillet 1848. (Conforme au Moniteur universel.) 66p. *12°. Paris,* 1848.

35758 REID, H. What should be done for the people? An appeal to the electors of the United Kingdom. 50p. *8°. London, Edinburgh, &c.,* 1848. *Presentation copy from the author to 'Alexr. Wilson Esq'.*

35759 RENÉ, A. Quelques mots sur la crise actuelle et sur les moyens d'y remédier adressés au peuple et à l'Assemblée Nationale par un travailleur. 16p. *4°. Paris,* [1848]

35760 RICE, THOMAS S., *Baron Monteagle.* Financial measures of 1848. Substance of the speech of the Lord Monteagle, in the House of Lords...September 4, 1848, on the third reading of the Bill for raising a loan of £2,000,000. Extracted from Hansard's Parliamentary Debates. 21p. *12°. [London,]* 1848. *See note to no.* 31024.

35761 ROBERTS, WILLIAM (*fl.* 1848). Banking and the currency briefly considered. 16p. *8°.* 1848.

35762 *[ROBERTSON, ALEXANDER, *W.S.*] Defects in the practice of life assurance, and suggestions for their remedy, with observations on the uses and advantages of life assurance, and the constitution of offices. 40p. *8°.* [1848] *The copy that belonged to Augustus De Morgan. See also* 1849.

35763 RODRIGUES, B. O. Théorie des banques. 31p. *8°. Paris,* [1848]

35764 *RYLEY, E. A statement of facts connected with an anonymous circular, and the proceedings at certain meetings lately held of actuaries and others officially connected with life assurance companies [to discuss forming a society of those officially connected with life assurance, and a college of actuaries]. 28p. *8°.* 1848. *The copy that belonged to Augustus De Morgan.*

35765 SARDINIA AND PIEDMONT. *Ministero delle Finanze.* Relazione sulle condizione delle finanze dal 1830 al 1846. Rassegnata a sua Maestà dal Primo Segretario di Stato delle Finanze. [Signed: O. Thaon di Revel.] 102p. *8°. Torino,* 1848.

For the SAVINGS BANK CIRCULAR, 1848-49, *see vol.* III, *Periodicals list.*

35766 SCHOMBERG, J. D. An enquiry into the currency; in which the measures of 1819 and 1844 are fully considered: the schemes of Lord Ashburton and Mr. Caley examined; and suggestions made towards an improvement of the system. 34p. *8°.* [1848]

35767 SCOTTISH PROVIDENT INSTITUTION. Life assurance on the mutual system, combined with moderate premiums. [A leaflet, dated: August 1848.] [2]p. *16°. n.p.* [1848]

35768 SIMS, A. D. Speech of Mr. Sims, of South Carolina, on the loan bill. Delivered in the House of Representatives, February 15, 1848. 16p. *8°. Washington,* 1848.

35769 STEWART, J. C. Facts and documents relating to the affairs of the Union Bank of Calcutta, during his service as secretary to that institution. [With an appendix.] 100, xxiiip. *8°. Calcutta & London,* 1848.

35770 SUGGESTIONS for the repeal of the assessed taxes, and the substitution of an equitable property and income tax. 8p. *8°.* 1848.

35771 TAXATION upon equitable principles: not the poor made to pay for the rich. 4p. *8°. Bristol,* [1848]

35772 [TAYLOR, JAMES (1788-1863).] Is Parliament or Sir Robert Peel responsible for "Peel's Bill"? Being a reply to Sir Robert Peel's speech of the 3rd December, 1847, as reported in the "Times Paper" the following day. By the author of "No trust, no trade," etc., etc. 24p. *8°.* 1848.

35773 —— Printed for private circulation. The repeal of the Act of 1819 and a real restoration of cash payments to the old system demanded by reason, justice, equity and expediency... 28p. *8°. Bakewell,* 1848.

35774 [——] The Scotch currency system and Sir Robert Peel, by the author of "No trust no trade," etc. etc. 8p. *8°.* 1848.

35775 THOMAS, F. S. The ancient Exchequer of England; the Treasury; and origin of the present management of the Exchequer and Treasury of Ireland. 174p. *8°.* 1848.

35776 [THOMPSON, THOMAS P.] A catechism on the currency. By the author of the "Catechism on the corn laws." Second edition, with additions and corrections. 16p. *8°*. 1848. *Presentation copy from the author to George Pryme.*

35777 —— Third edition, containing additions... 16p. *8°*. 1848. *Presentation copy, with an accompanying letter from the author to George Pryme. For the letter, see vol.* III, *A.L.* 117.

35778 TORRENS, R. The principles and practical operation of Sir R. Peel's Bill of 1844 explained, and defended against the objections of Tooke, Fullarton, and Wilson. 177p. *8°*. 1848. *The copy that belonged to S. J. Loyd, Baron Overstone, formerly among his papers, for which see vol.* III, *MS.* 804.

35779 TRANSITION. De l'épargne. 15p. *8°. Paris*, 1848.

35780 VAN SOMMER, J. Tables exhibiting the various fluctuations in three per cent consols, in every month during each year, from 1789 to 1847 inclusive; with ruled pages for their continuance to 1857. To which are annexed the amounts and rate of interest of all the loans contracted since 1788, and the amount of Navy, victualling and Exchequer bills funded. 149p. *4°*. 1848. *Engraved throughout. For another edition, see* 1834.

35781 VINTON, S. F. Speech of Mr. S. F. Vinton, of Ohio, on the loan bill, delivered in the House of Representatives of the U. States, February 8th, 1848. 16p. *8°. Washington*, 1848.

35782 VOORTHUIJSEN, E. VAN. De directe belastingen, inzonderheid die op de inkomsten. Eene Staatshuishoudkundige proeve... 2 vols. *8°. Utrecht*, 1848.

35783 VROLIK, A. De edele metalen en het papier. Twee voorlezingen. 80p. *8°. Utrecht*, 1848. *Presentation copy from the author to the Netherlands Minister for Colonies.*

35784 WALLON, V. Prêt hypothécaire à raison de 5% de la valeur immobilière de la France. Projet de décret présenté à l'Assemblée Nationale. 7p. *8°*. [*Paris*, 1848]

35785 WARD, JAMES. The true action of a purely metallic currency, as the type of the most perfect mixed currency, examined and developed. 101p. *8°*. 1848. *The copy that belonged to T. Spring Rice, Baron Monteagle.*

35786 WATSON, WILLIAM (*fl.* 1848). New system of currency, by which panic is rendered impossible. 12p. *8°. London, Birmingham, &c.*, 1848.

35787 WATT, ROBERT, *of Edinburgh*. A summary practical elucidation of national economy, in support of direct taxation and direct assessment. 240p. *12°. Edinburgh*, 1848.

35788 WATT, ROBERT, *of London*. The principles of insurance applied to mercantile debts; a letter to the Right Honourable Lord Ashburton. 15p. *8°*. 1848.

35789 WELFORD, R. G. The impolicy of the present high duties on tobacco; and their injurious effects on the trade and morals of the country. 68p. *8°*. 1848.

35790 *WOŁOWSKI, L. F. M. R. De l'organisation du crédit foncier. [Extrait de la Revue de Législation et de Jurisprudence, novembre, décembre, 1848.] 126p. *8°. Paris*, 1848. *Presentation copy from the author to George Grote.*

35791 WRIGHT, I. C. The evils of the currency, no. 2. 20p. *12°. London & Nottingham*, 1848. *For the first pamphlet in this series, see* 1847.

TRANSPORT

35792 BARLOW, H. B. A comparative account and delineation of railway engine & carriage wheels. 51p. *8°*. 1848.

35793 BEADON, G. Ten minutes' reading of plain observations upon canals and navigable rivers; showing their vast importance, agricultural, political, & commercial, and upon the question of the national defence of Great Britain from foreign invasion. 38p. *8°*. 1848.

35794 BOGUE, A. Steam to Australia, its general advantages considered; the different proposed routes for connecting London and Sydney compared; and the expediency of forming a settlement at Cape York, in Torres Strait, pointed out in a letter to the Right Honorable Earl Grey... 70p. *8°. Sydney*, 1848.

35795 BOYLE, T. Hope for the canals! showing the evil of amalgamations with railways to public and private interests, and the means for the complete and permanent restoration of canal property to a position of prosperity, upon its present basis of original and independent enterprise. 43p. *8°*. 1848.

35796 BRADSHAW'S railway almanack, directory, shareholders' guide, and manual for 1848: third edition, with emendations... 140p. *12°. London, Manchester, &c.*, [1848] *For the later volumes in this series, see vol.* III, *Periodicals list.*

35797 BROWN, HUMPHREY. Irish wants & practical remedies. An investigation on practical and economical grounds as to the application of a government system of railways in Ireland. 67p. *8°*. 1848. *See note to no.* 34295.

35798 CLEVELAND, R. F. The London and North Western Railway. Are railways a good investment? The question considered by an examination of the last half-yearly statements of the six leading companies. 53p. *8°*. 1848. *See note to no.* 34295.

35799 COURT, M. H. A digest of the realities of the Great Western Railway. 17p. *8°*. 1848. *The Rastrick copy.*

35800 EASTERN UNION RAILWAY COMPANY. Eastern Union Railway. First half-yearly general meeting of the Court of Proprietors [following upon the amalgamation with the Ipswich and Bury St. Edmund's Railway]...25th August, 1848. [2]p. *fol. n.p.* [1848] *See also* 1844, 1845, 1846, 1847, 1849, 1850.

35801 —— Report of the directors proposed to be presented to the general meeting, to be held on the 2nd June 1848. 2p. *fol. n.p.* [1848]

35802 ECKERSLEY, P. Railway management. Observations on two letters to George Carr Glyn, Esq., M.P. by John Whitehead, of the Stock Exchange, London, and Mark Huish, General Manager of the London and North Western Railway. 22p. *8°. London & Manchester*, 1848. *See note to no.* 34295.

35803 ENGLAND. *Laws, etc.* Anno sexto & septimo Gulielmi IV. Regis. Cap. cxxiii. An Act for making a railway from the Minories to Blackwall, with branches, to be called "The Commercial Railway." ⟨28th July 1836.⟩ p.5509–5667. *fol.* 1848.

35804 —— —— Anno undecimo & duodecimo Victoriæ Reginæ. Cap. xc. An Act to amend the Acts relating to the London and Blackwall Railway, and to authorize the Company to alter the gauge of their railway, and to make certain improvements in the approaches to the said railway, and to make branches to the London and Saint Katherine's Docks. ⟨22d July 1848.⟩ p.1001–1010. *fol.* 1848.

35805 —— —— Anno undecimo & duodecimo Victoriæ Reginæ. Cap. cxi. An Act to alter and amend some of the provisions of the Acts relating to the London and Blackwall Railway Company. ⟨25th July 1848.⟩ p.1309–1312. *fol.* 1848.

35806 [**GILL**, THOMAS, *chairman of the South Devon Railway.*] Address to the proprietors of the South Devon Railway. By the Chairman of the Board of Directors. 58p. *8°.* 1848.

35807 HAMPTON, M. Speech of Mr. Hampton, of Pennsylvania, on rivers and harbors, and the policy of protection and free trade. Delivered in the House of Representatives, March 9, 1848. 16p. *8°. Washington,* 1848.

35808 HUISH, M. Letter to George Carr Glyn, Esq. M.P. Chairman of the London & North Western Railway Company, on some points of railway management, in reply to a late pamphlet. 22p. *8°.* 1848. *See note to no.* 34295.

35809 IPSWICH, BURY AND NORWICH RAILWAY COMPANY. Report of the directors at the half-yearly meeting of the shareholders...held at Ipswich, 31st January, 1848. 2p. *fol. n.p.* [1848] *See also* 1846, 1847.

35810 JERNINGHAM, F. Steam communication with the Cape of Good Hope, Australia, and New Zealand, suggested as the means of promoting emigration to those colonies. [With an appendix, consisting of a letter to the author, signed C. D. Hays, refuting attacks on the Cape route put forward by Adam Bogue in his work *Steam to Australia.*] 43p. *8°.* 1848.

35811 MORRISON, JAMES (1790–1857). The influence of English railway legislation of trade and industry: with an appendix of tracts and documents. 187p. *8°.* 1848. *Two copies, one the Rastrick copy, the other a presentation copy from the author to the Marquis of Granby.*

35812 PARRY, E. Parry's railway companion from Chester to Holyhead; containing a narrative of the early and parliamentary history of the project. With a descriptive and historical account of the adjacent towns... 154p. *8°. London & Chester,* 1848.

35813 RAILWAY POLICY. A letter to George Carr Glyn, Esq., M.P., Chairman of the London and North-Western Railway Company, on the correspondence addressed to him, by Captain Huish and Mr. John Whitehead: from a sufferer. 12p. *12°.* 1848.

35814 RAILWAY RESCUE: a letter addressed to the directorates of Great Britain. By a traveller of many lands. 19p. *8°.* 1848. *See note to no.* 34295.

35815 Brief **REMARKS** and description of the iron truss railway bridge, invented by Nathaniel Rider, of New York, U.S. Patented, April, 1847. 11p. *12°. Bradford, Wilts,* 1848.

35816 SALT, S. Facts and figures, principally relating to railways and commerce. 152p. *12°. London & Manchester,* 1848.

35817 SIDNEY, S. The commercial consequences of a mixed gauge on our railway system examined. 47p. *8°.* 1848.

35818 SMITH, ARTHUR. The bubble of the age; or, the fallacies of railway investments, railway accounts, and railway dividends. Third edition. 63p. *8°.* 1848.

35819 STEVENSON, ALAN. Account of the Skerryvore Lighthouse, with notes on the illumination of lighthouses. 439p. *4°. Edinburgh & London,* 1848.

35820 WEBSTER, T. The port and docks of Birkenhead. With maps...and an account of the Acts of Parliament relating to the Mersey and Dock Estate of Liverpool. [Proceedings leading to the establishment of the Birkenhead Dock Company.] 192p. *8°.* 1848.

35821 WHITEHEAD, J. Railway management. Letter to George Carr Glyn, Esq. M.P. Chairman of the London and North Western Railway Company...Second edition. 23p. *8°.* 1848. *See note to no.* 34295.

35822 WILLIAMS, WELLINGTON. Appletons' railroad and steamboat companion. Being a travellers' guide through the United States of America, Canada, New Brunswick, and Nova Scotia... 313p. *8°. New York & Philadelphia,* 1848. *For another edition, see* 1847.

35823 WOODCROFT, B. A sketch of the origin and progress of steam navigation from authentic documents... 140p. *4°.* 1848.

SOCIAL CONDITIONS

35824 ACLAND, P. L. D. A sermon, preached in the Church of the Holy Trinity, Exeter, on...December 10, 1848, on behalf of the Devon and Exeter Female Penitentiary...To which is annexed the twenty-eighth annual report of the Committee, with the list of subscribers and benefactors. 16, 16p. *8°. Exeter,* 1848.

35825 ADAMS, A. M. Report of an inspection of English and Irish workhouses; with observations on the operation of the poor-laws. 38p. *8°. Glasgow,* 1848.

35826 ALISON, W. P. Letter to the chairman of the Edinburgh Parochial Board, on the present position of the question relative to the claim of the able-bodied unemployed to legal relief in Scotland. 32p. *8°. Edinburgh & London,* 1848.

35827 An **APPEAL** to Lord John Russell on behalf of the working population: by a Tory freeholder. 22p. *12°. London, Leeds, &c.,* [1848]

35828 ASSOCIATION OF SELF-HELP. Rules of the Frugal Investment Society of the Association of Self-Help. Established at Edwinstowe, Nottinghamshire,

March 25th, 1848. Enrolled pursuant to Act of Parliament. 22p. *12°. Sutton-in-Ashfield, 1848.*

35829 AUSTIN, H. The claims of the sanitary question on the attention of the directors of life assurance offices. Re-printed from the "Journal of public health." 15p. *8°.* 1848.

35830 BELGIUM. *Ministère de l'Intérieur.* Enquête sur la condition des classes ouvrières et sur le travail des enfants... 3 vols. *8°. Bruxelles, 1848, 1846.*

35831 BENEVOLENT INSTITUTION FOR THE RELIEF OF AGED AND INDIGENT GARDENERS AND THEIR WIDOWS. Rules and regulations... Together with a list of subscribers. 34p. *12°.* 1848.

For **BOOKBINDERS' CONSOLIDATED UNION,** Trade circular, 1848–96, *see* vol. III, *Periodicals list.*

35832 BROUGHAM, H. P., *Baron Brougham and Vaux.* Speech of Lord Brougham in the House of Lords ...May 12, 1848, on legislation and the law. 80p. *8°.* 1848.

35833 BURRITT, E. Ocean penny postage; its necessity shown and its feasibility demonstrated. 32p. *16°.* [1848]

35834 CHALLICE, J. Should the cholera come, what ought to be done? 32p. *8°.* 1848.

35835 CLEFF, J. A. De la ruine du commerce, de la misère de l'ouvrier, des causes qui la produisent, et des moyens de l'atténuer. 24p. *12°. Paris, 1848.*

35836 COCHRANE, C. Speech of Charles Cochrane Esq. at a public meeting in favour of the employment of the poor, held at the Literary and Scientific Institution, Leicester Square, on...October 18, 1848. B. Bond Cabbell, Esq. in the Chair. Second edition... 12p. *8°.* [1848]

35837 COMMITTEE OF METROPOLITAN TRADES. Report of the Committee...appointed at a trades' delegate meeting, held at the Bell Inn, Old Bailey, on...March 16, 1848, "To consider and report on the destitute condition of the London trades, as also to define the causes which have led to that destitution, and to state the remedies considered necessary for its removal." 8p. *8°. [London, 1848]*

35838 COMPETENCE in a colony contrasted with poverty at home; or relief to landlords and labourers held out by Australian colonisation and emigration. A memorial addressed to the Right Hon. Lord John Russell, etc. etc. [Preceded by an account of the inaugural meeting of a committee to further colonization, signed: Henry White, secretary.] 28p. *8°.* 1848.

35839 COUNTY COURTS: or, a letter to Bailey Cochrane, Esq., M.P. By a creditor. Second edition. 19p. *8°.* 1848.

35840 CULVERWELL, R. J. The art of longevity and health; or, how to live 100 years...A few matter-of-fact considerations relating to eating, drinking, sleeping, air, rest, exercise, and occupation... 47p. *12°.* 1848. *The Turner copy.*

35841 DANSON, J. T. ⟨For private circulation.⟩ A contribution towards an investigation of the changes which have taken place in the condition of the people of the United Kingdom...from...1839 to...1847; and an attempt to develope the connexion (if any) between the changes observed and the variations occurring during the same period in the prices of the most necessary articles of food. ⟨Read before the Statistical Society, 21st Feb., 1848.⟩ 40p. *8°.* 1848.

35842 [DELAAGE, H.] Affranchissement des classes déshéritées. Par Henri D***. 102p. *12°. Paris, 1848.*

35843 DUNCAN, G. J. C. Memoir of the Rev. Henry Duncan...founder of savings banks...By his son. 379p. *8°. Edinburgh & London, 1848.*

35844 ELLERMAN, C. F. Sanitary reform and agricultural improvement; or, how to promote health and abundance. In three letters...Letter 1. Drainage, sewerage, urinaria, and cloacae. 70p. *8°.* 1848.

35845 —— Second edition. 70p. *8°.* 1848.

35846 [ELLIS, WILLIAM (1800–1881).] Causes of poverty. (Extracted from the Westminster and Foreign Quarterly Review.) [Signed: W.E.] 15p. *8°. n.p.* [1848]

35847 [——] A few questions on secular education, what it is, and what it ought to be: with an attempt to answer them. Preceded by an appeal to Richard Cobden, Esq., M.P., and the members of the late Anti-Corn-Law League. By the author of "The outlines of social economy." 23p. *8°.* 1848. *The copy that belonged to William Lovett, with his signature on the title-page.*

35848 ENGELS, F. Die Lage der arbeitenden Klasse in England. Nach eigner Anschauung und authentischen Quellen...Zweite Ausgabe. 358p. *8°. Leipzig, 1848. For another edition, see 1845.*

For **ENGLAND.** *Commissioners for Administering the Laws for the Relief of the Poor in Ireland,* Annual reports, 1848–58, *see* vol. III, *Periodicals list,* Annual report...

35849 —— *Metropolitan Sanitary Commission.* First Report of the Commissioners appointed to inquire whether any and what special means may be requisite for the improvement of the health of the Metropolis, with minutes of evidence. 430p. *8°.* 1848.

35850 —— —— Second Report... 144p. *8°.* 1848.

35851 —— *Parliament. House of Commons.* Education in Ireland. Report of speeches in the House of Commons, on Mr. Hamilton's motion on the above subject, August 21, 1848. 54p. *8°. London & Dublin, 1848. The copy that belonged to Earl De Grey.*

For the **FAMILY ECONOMIST,** 1848–60, *see* vol. III, *Periodicals list.*

35852 FAUCHER, L. Du droit au travail. 50p. *8°. Paris, 1848.*

35853 FIELD, JOHN (1812–1884). Prison discipline; and the advantages of the separate system of imprisonment, with a detailed account of the discipline now pursued in the new County Gaol at Reading...[Second edition.] 2 vols. *8°. London & Reading, 1848. For another edition, see 1846.*

35854 FRY, C. and **CRESSWELL,** R. E. Memoir of the life of Elizabeth Fry, with extracts from her journal and letters. Edited by two of her daughters...Second edition. Revised and enlarged. 2 vols. *8°.* 1848.

35855 GAVIN, H. Sanitary ramblings. Being sketches and illustrations, of Bethnal Green. A type of the condition of the Metropolis and other large towns. 118p. *8°.* 1848.

35856 GILLKREST, J. Cholera gleanings, a family

handbook, enabling readers...to judge for themselves of the great error into which governments were unfortunately led by men looked upon as infallible guides, who... maintained the cholera to be a disease during which "the living shall fly from the sick they should cherish." 86p. *8°. Gibraltar,* 1848.

35857 GILLON, P. Rapport sur la Colonie pénitentiaire de Mettray, fait au Comité du Travail, le 20 octobre, 1848. 15p. *8°. n.p.* [1848] *The copy that belonged to Victor Considérant.*

35858 GOBART, F. DE. Du paupérisme. Port de refuge à construire à Blanckenberghe, ou considérations sur la nécessité de quelques travaux puplics [*sic*]... ⟨Publié au profit des pauvres.⟩ 22p. *8°. Bruges,* 1848.

35859 GOLDSMID, SIR F. H., *Bart.* Reply to the arguments advanced against the removal of the remaining disabilities of the Jews. 58p. *8°.* 1848.

35860 GRATRY, A. J. A. Demandes et réponses sur les devoirs sociaux. 110p. *12°. Paris,* 1848.

35861 GUY, W. A. The case of the journeymen bakers: being a lecture on the evils of night-work & long hours of labour, delivered on...July 6th, 1848, at the Mechanics' Institution, Southampton Buildings, Lord Ashley, M.P., in the chair. 20p. *8°.* 1848. *The copy that belonged to J. M. Ludlow.*

35862 HANCOCK, WILLIAM N. On the condition of the Irish labourer: being a paper read before the Dublin Statistical Society. 12p. *8°. Dublin,* 1848.

35863 *HAYDEN, G. T. The right to differ: a lecture introductory to the business of the Original School of Medicine, Peter-Street. Session 1848–49. [On medical education.] 16p. *8°. Dublin,* 1848. *The FWA copy, presented by the author to William Pare.*

35864 HAYWOOD, J. A report on the sanatory condition of the borough of Sheffield. By James Haywood, professional chemist, and William Lee, C.E.; also, an appendix to the first edition, containing a report on baths and wash-houses, &c. Second edition. 161p. *8°. Sheffield & London,* 1848.

35865 HEALTH OF TOWNS' ASSOCIATION, London. Health of Towns Association. Report of the Subcommittee on the answers returned to questions addressed to the principal towns of England and Wales, and on the objections from corporate bodies to the Public Health Bill. 69p. *8°.* 1848. *The copy that belonged to N. W. Senior.*

35866 —— The sanitary condition of the City of London; being a letter to the Lord Ashley from the City Remembrancer [Edward Tyrrell], on the statements of the Sub-committee of the Health of Towns Association; with the Sub-committee's reply and Lord Ashley's letter. 23p. *8°.* 1848.

35867 HILL, MATTHEW D. Report of a charge delivered to the grand jury of the borough of Birmingham, at the Michaelmas Quarter Sessions for 1848: by the Recorder. 16p. *8°.* 1848.

35868 HOMERSHAM, S. C. Report to the directors of the Manchester, Sheffield, and Lincolnshire Railway Company...Comparing the quantity, quality, and price of the water that can be supplied to the inhabitants of Manchester and Salford, by means of the Surplus Water Act obtained last session by the...Company, with that of the water works scheme promoted by the Corporation of Manchester... 88p. *8°.* 1848.

35869 HOSKING, W. A guide to the proper regulation of buildings in towns, as a means of promoting and securing the health, comfort, and safety of the inhabitants. 295p. *12°.* 1848. *Presentation copy from the author to Dr. Guy.*

35870 [HOWARD, JAMES.] The evils of England, social & economical. By a London physician. 152p. *8°.* 1848.

35871 HUOT, P. Trois jours à Mettray. Rapports lus au Congrès Scientifique de Tours et à la Société des Sciences Morales de Seine-et-Oise. 64p. *8°. Paris,* 1848. *The copy that belonged to Victor Considérant.*

35872 JARROLD, J. A comparative statement of the number of labourers employed in the execution of the same quantity of work, if executed by hand or machines, amount of weekly and yearly earnings, the overwhelming difference of indirect taxation evaded, by non-consuming machines. 8p. *12°. Norwich,* [1848]

35873 [JOHNSON, H.] Can things be better? An address to the working classes, in which the present demand for organic changes is calmly considered. By H. J. Mathetes. [With a summary.] 59p. *8°. Manchester,* [1848]

35874 KEBBELL, W. Popular lectures on the prevailing diseases of towns: their effects, causes and the means of prevention. Recently delivered at the Brighton Literary and Scientific Institution... 196p. *8°. Brighton & London,* 1848.

35875 LABOURT, L. A. Recherches historiques et statistiques sur l'intempérance des classes laborieuses; et sur les enfants trouvés...Deuxième édition, revue et augmentée de notes explicatives. 131, 360p. *8°. Paris,* 1848.

35876 LATOUCHE, M. Le Diable et l'amnistie... Vendu au profit des femmes des transportés. [Lithographed poem.] *s.sh.fol. n.p.* [1848]

35877 —— Une sœur des transportés au Général Cavaignac. [A poem.] *s.sh.fol. Paris,* [1848]

35878 LEAVITT, J. Cheap postage. Remarks and statistics on the subject of cheap postage and postal reform in Great Britain and the United States. 72p. *8°. Boston,* 1848. *The copy that belonged to Joseph Hume, with an accompanying letter to him from Thomas M. Webb of Boston, for which, see vol. III, A.L. 234.*

35879 LEFRANC, B. D. République démocratique. – Liberté, égalité, fraternité. Cris de détresse des ouvriers. [A complaint about the usurious rates of monts-de-piété.] [2]p. *s.sh.fol.* [*Paris,* 1848]

35880 LOGAN, WILLIAM (1813–1879). An astounding fact or two for Sabbath school teachers who support the drinking system. 2p. *s.sh.8°. Glasgow,* [1848] *The Turner copy.*

35881 M'KNIGHT, JAMES. The Ulster tenants' claim of right; or, landownership a state trust; the Ulster tenant-right an original grant from the British Crown, and the necessity of extending its general principle to the other provinces of Ireland, demonstrated in a letter to...Lord John Russell. 71p. *8°. Dublin, London, &c.,* 1848.

35882 MARRIOTT, JOSEPH. On ragged scientific institutes: or, societies for diffusing useful information among the poor and miserable. 4p. *8°. Islington,* [1848?] *The copy that belonged to William Lovett.*

35883 METROPOLITAN WORKING CLAS-

SES ASSOCIATION FOR IMPROVING THE PUBLIC HEALTH. The first address from the Committee. 8p. *8°. 1848. For another edition, see 1845.*

35884 **MOODIE,** J. Principles and observations on many and various subjects, for the health of nations and individuals... 8, 38, 67, 79, 104p. *8°. Edinburgh, 1848.*

For **NATIONAL ASSOCIATION OF UNITED TRADES,** The labour league; or, Journal of the National Association of United Trades, *see* vol. III, *Periodicals list,* Labour league.

35885 **NIGHT ASYLUM FOR THE HOUSELESS.** Eleventh annual report of the Glasgow Night Asylum for the Houseless. Instituted 1838... *8°. Glasgow, 1848. See also 1846.*

35886 The model **PARISH;** or, the present state of parishes in Great Britain consequent upon the drinking usages of society; and proposals for the erection of a church, parsonage, schools, and college, to assist in the eradication of these drinking customs. With a notice of Bishop Chase's proposed temperance village. By a clergyman of the Church of England. Third thousand. 36p. *8°. 1848. The Turner copy.*

35887 **PARSONS,** B. Tracts for fustian jackets and smock frocks. Nos. 1–18. *12°. [1848–49] Nos. 2–3 were issued as a double number. In this copy nos. 1–3 are continuously paginated, and may be reprints.*

35888 **PIM,** JONATHAN. The condition and prospects of Ireland and the evils arising from the present distribution of landed property: with suggestions for a remedy. 348p. *8°. Dublin, 1848.*

35889 **PRIMROSE,** ARCHIBALD, *Baron Dalmeny.* An address to the middle classes upon the subject of gymnastic exercises. 53p. *8°. 1848.*

32890 **READ,** G. A brief history of the bread baking trade, from the earliest period to the present time; containing some valuable, and important information on bread, with the evils resulting from the present unnatural system of night work, and unlimited hours of labour, endured by the London journeymen bakers. 20p. *8°. [1848]*

35891 Brief **REMARKS** on employment and recreations; and on the mis-direction of charitable intentions. Written in 1832. 16p. *8°. [1848 ?]*

35892 **ROSS,** *County of.* Report of the Committee appointed to inquire into the expediency of erecting a poorhouse in Easter Ross. [Signed: H. D. Macleod, H. St. V. Rose, C. Robertson, D. Monro, A. Innes, D. Williamson.] 64p. *8°. Inverness, 1848.*

35893 **SAINT GEORGE'S AND SAINT JAMES'S DISPENSARY SAMARITAN FUND COMMITTEE.** Ventilation illustrated: a tract for the schools of rich and poor. Edition for the working classes. ⟨Seventh thousand.⟩ 31p. *8°. 1848.*

35894 **SAINT JAMES,** *Westminster, Parish of.* Saint James, Westminster. Committee of Health and Sanitary Improvement. Report... upon the inquiries made by the visitors as to the sanitary conditions of certain poor istricts of the parish. 15p. *8°. [1848]*

35895 **SALT,** T. C. A letter to the magistrates of the borough of Birmingham. [Objecting to the swearing in of special constables.] 4p. *8°. Birmingham, [1848]*

35896 **SCROPE,** G. P. The Irish relief measures, past and future. 96p. *8°. 1848.*

35897 —— The rights of industry, or, the social problem of the day, as exemplified in France, Ireland, and Britain. 44p. *8°. 1848.*

35898 **SINKS** of London laid open: a pocket companion for the uninitiated, to which is added a modern flash dictionary...With a list of the sixty orders of prime coves...Embellished with humorous illustrations by George Cruikshank. 131p. *8°. 1848.*

35899 **SOCIÉTÉ POUR LE PATRONAGE DES JEUNES DÉTENUS...DU DEPARTEMENT DE LA SEINE.** Assemblée Générale tenue à l'Hôtel-de-ville, le 22 août 1847. Compte-rendu de l'année 1846. 56p. *8°. Paris, 1848. See also 1844, 1846, 1849.*

35900 **STATISTICAL SOCIETY OF LONDON.** Report of a Committee of the Council of the Statistical Society of London, consisting of Lieut.-Colonel W. H. Sykes...Dr. Guy, and F. G. P. Neison, Esq., to investigate the state of the inhabitants and their dwellings in Church Lane, St. Giles's. ⟨Read before the Statistical Society of London, 17th January, 1848.⟩ 24p. *8°. n.p. [1848]*

35901 **STEPHENSON,** ROBERT (1803–1886). The supply of water. Mr. Stephenson's award [concerning the purchase by the Corporation of Liverpool of the Bootle and Harrington water companies]. From the Liverpool Times of Thursday, January 20, 1848. *s.sh.4°. n.p. [1848] [Br. 617]*

For the **SUNDAY-SCHOOL AND YOUTHS' TEMPERANCE JOURNAL,** *see* vol. III, *Periodicals list.*

35902 **TAYLOR,** GEORGE L. On gas works, and the introduction of cannel coal gas (thoroughly purified) into the Metropolis. 24p. *8°. [1848]*

35903 *WADDINGTON,* G. An inaugural address delivered at the opening of the Mechanics' Institute, at Gateshead, on...April 10, 1848. 24p. *8°. [1848] The copy that belonged to George Grote.*

35904 **WALKER,** JAMES (1781–1861), *and others.* City of London Sewers. Report of James Walker, William Cubitt, and Isambard K. Brunel, civil engineers, addressed to the City Remembrancer, dated 28th August, 1848. 43p. *4°. [London, 1848] The copy that belonged to Sir William Cubitt.*

35905 The **WAREHOUSEMAN:** or, a citizen's seven ages. By a commercial man. 82p. *8°. 1848.*

35906 **WESTON,** H. W. The influence of alcohol, or strong drink, on health, morals, and religion. 12p. *8°. 1848.*

35907 [**WILLIAMS,** JANE.] Artegall: or remarks on the Reports of the Commissioners of Inquiry into the state of education in Wales. 62p. *8°. 1848.*

35908 **WHATELY,** R., *Archbishop of Dublin.* A speech ...August 1, 1833, on a Bill for the removal of certain disabilities from His Majesty's subjects of the Jewish persuasion. With additional remarks on some of the objections urged against that measure...Reprinted, by permission...during the progress of Lord John Russell's Bill for removing the remaining disabilities of the Jews. 32p. *8°. 1848.*

35909 A few **WORDS** of remonstrance and advice

addressed to the farming and labouring classes of Ireland, by a sincere friend. 14p. *8°. Dublin*, 1848.

35910 The **WRONGS** of the counter: an appeal for young men employed in shops, against the late-hour system; including a practical suggestion of a remedy. With a recommendatory preface by J. Carlile. 28p. *8°. London & Woolwich*, 1848 [*phc*] *From the BM copy.*

SLAVERY

35911 BUXTON, C. Memoirs of Sir Thomas Fowell Buxton, Baronet. With selections from his correspondence. Edited by his son. 600p. *8°.* 1848.

35912 CASS and Taylor on the slavery question. 23p. *12°. Boston*, 1848.

35913 DENMAN, Hon. J. West India interests, African emigration, and slave trade... Privately printed. 31p. *8°. Worcester*, 1848.

35914 DENMAN, T., *Baron Denman*. A letter from Lord Denman to Lord Brougham, on the final extinction of the slave-trade. Second edition, corrected. 80p. *8°.* 1848.

35915 ENGLAND. Parliament. *House of Commons.* The sugar question: being a digest of the evidence taken before the Committee on Sugar and Coffee Plantations, which was moved for by Lord George Bentinck, M.P., 3rd February 1848. By one of the witnesses. Part I. The East Indies and the Mauritius. [With 'Part II. The British West Indies, and foreign sugar growing countries'.] 2 vols. *8°.* 1848.

35916 [**HIGGINS**, M. J.] Is cheap sugar the triumph of free trade? A second letter to the Rt. Hon. Lord John Russell, &c.&c.&c. By Jacob Omnium. 64p. *8°.* 1848.

35917 [——] The real bearings of the West India question, as expounded by the most intelligent and independent free-trader of the day; edited by Jacob Omnium, and dedicated to the Right Hon. Lord John Russell, &c.&c.&c. 58p. *8°.* 1848.

35918 [——] A third letter to Lord John Russell, containing some remarks on the ministerial speeches delivered during the late sugar debates. With an appendix, containing copies of the despatches of Sir C. Grey and Lord Harris. By Jacob Omnium. 41p. *8°.* 1848.

35919 INCONSISTENCY and hypocrisy of Martin Van Buren on the question of slavery. 16p. *8°. n.p.* [1848 ?]

35920 The **LIBERTY BELL**. By friends of freedom. 292p. *12°. Boston: National Anti-Slavery Bazaar*, 1848. *See also* 1849.

35921 MacNEILE, H. Slave labor versus free labor sugar. Speech...delivered at a public meeting held at Liverpool, 13th June, 1848. 18p. *8°.* 1848.

35922 MANN, H. Speech of Mr. Horace Mann, on the rights of Congress to legislate for the territories of the United States, and its duty to exclude slavery therefrom. Delivered in the House of Representatives, in Committee of the Whole, June 30, 1848. Revised edition. 31p. *8°. Boston*, 1848.

35923 MARTIN, ROBERT M. The sugar question in relation to free trade and protection. By the author of the "History of the British colonies." 21p. *8°.* 1848.

35924 MATSON, H. J. Remarks on the slave trade and African squadron...Fourth edition. 96p. *8°.* 1848. *The copy that belonged to Earl De Grey.*

35925 RESULTS of emancipation, and the immigration scheme. Reprinted from the 'Eclectic Review,' for Feb. 1848. 24p. *8°.* 1848.

35926 WILBERFORCE, S., *Bishop of Winchester.* Cheap sugar means cheap slaves. Speech...in the House of Lords, February 7th, 1848, against the admission of slave labour sugar on equal terms with free labour produce; with an appendix illustrative of the impetus given to the slave trade by the Bill of 1846. 30p. *8°.* 1848.

35927 —— Second edition. 31p. *8°.* 1848.

POLITICS

35928 ALIBAUD, L. Testament d'Alibaud. Contrat d'alliance entre les socialistes et les républicains. ['Avis au lecteur' signed: Raymond Brucker.] [4]p. *fol. Paris*, [1848]

35929 ANDRÉ, JUSTIN. Fragments du programme politique des anciens élèves de l'École polytechnique licenciés en juin 1832. *s.sh.fol.* [*Paris*, 1848] *On the verso a printed form of petition entitled: Pétition à l'Assemblée nationale.*

35930 ARAGO, J. E. V. Aux juges des insurgés. [2]p. *s.sh.fol. Paris*, [1848]

35931 —— [Another edition.] [2]p. *s.sh.fol. Paris*, [1848]

35932 l'**ARC** de triomphe Président. Raisonnement d'un monarchiste. [With 'Observations d'un républicain', by Jean Macé and 'Propagande socialiste', signed: Bernard, Gamet, Jean Macé.] [2]p. *fol. Paris*, [1848]

For l'**ARISTO RÉACTIONNAIRE**, *see* vol. III, *Periodicals list*, Réactionnaire.

35933 B..., FRANÇOIS. Lettre d'un transporté à un détenu de Vincennes [Barbès]. [2]p. *s.sh.fol. Paris*, [1848]

35934 BARKER, JOSEPH. Aristocracy and democracy. The speech of Mr. Barker at the Bolton tea party, on...September 28, 1848. 8p. *4°. Wortley*, [1848]

35935 —— A full account of the arrest, imprisonment, & liberation on bail, of Joseph Barker; together with an account of his triumphant election for the borough of Bolton. 8p. *4°. Wortley*, [1848]

35936 —— The triumph of right over might; or, a full account of the attempt made by the Manchester magistrates and the Whig government to rob J. Barker of his liberty... 8p. *4°. Wortley*, [1848]

35937 —— The Unitarians and Chartism. 32p. *8°. Wortley*, [1848]

35938 BARRAULT, P. A. C. E. Paris, juillet 1848... 1er lettre. Lettre à M. Lamartine. [2]p. *s.sh.fol. Paris,* [1848]

35939 —— Paris, juillet 1848...2e lettre. Lettre à M. Thiers. [2]p. *s.sh.fol. Paris,* [1848]

35940 —— Paris, août 1848...Lettre à M. Rothschild. (*Lettres contemporaines,* 3e. livraison.) [2]p. *s.sh.fol. Paris,* [1848]

35941 —— [Another edition.] [2]p. *s.sh.fol. Paris,* [1848]

35942 [**BESSON,** , *employé au Ministère de la Guerre?*] Les conseils du père Jean, ou un chiffonier de Paris à ses amis des faubourgs. [2]p. *s.sh.fol. Paris,* [1848]

35943 [**——**?] Opinion d'un chiffonier de Paris sur Monsieur Lamartine. [Signed: le Père Jean.] [2]p. *s.sh.fol.* [*Paris,* 1848]

35944 BRENAN, JOSEPH. The only road; or, hints for the reorganization of a national party in Ireland. 15p. *12°. Dublin,* [1848 ?]

35945 BRISEBARRE, E. L. A. and [**DÉADDÉ,** E.] Théâtre de l'Opéra-National. Les barricades de 1848. Opéra patriotique en un acte et deux tableaux. Par MM. Édourd [*sic*] Brisebarre et Saint-Yves...Représenté...le 5 mars 1848. 7p. *8°. Paris,* 1848.

35946 BROUGHAM, H. P., *Baron Brougham and Vaux.* Letter to the Marquis of Lansdowne...on the late Revolution in France. 165p. *8°.* 1848.

35947 BUNSEN, C. C. J. VON, *Freiherr.* Memoir on the constitutional rights of the Duchies of Schleswig and Holstein, presented to Viscount Palmerston by Chevalier Bunsen on the 8th of April, 1848: with a postscript of the 15th of April. Published, with M. de Gruner's essay on the Danish question, and all the official documents, by Otto von Wenckstern... 165p. *8°.* 1848.

35948 CALLAND, V. Aux catholiques républicains: science de la politique. [Extrait de la Théorie du Christianisme...ouvrage inédit par Victor Calland. Dated: le 28 février, 1848.] *s.sh.fol. Paris,* [1848]

35949 CALOMNIE, , *Mme., pseud.* Lettre de Mme Calomnie au citoyen Proudhon pour le recommander aux électeurs. [A satire, signed: Mme Calomnie, J. B. Couré.] *s.sh.fol. Paris,* [1848]

35950 CASTAUD, . Les trahisons de Ledru-Rollin. Révélations faites au Club du Salon de Mars, le samedi 25 novembre, par le cit. Castaud, ancien condamné politique, ancien membre de la Société Républicaine centrale et du Club de la Révolution. *s.sh.fol. Paris,* [1848]

For le **CAUCHEMAR DES INTRIGANTS POLITIQUES,** *see* vol. III, *Periodicals list.*

35951 [**CHARPENTIER,** F.] Armand Carrel et Chateaubriand aux Champs-Elysées. Dialogues d'outre-tombe. [Signed: F. C[harpentier]. de Damery.] [2]p. *s.sh.fol.* [*Paris,* 1848]

35952 [**——**] Paris, 21 juillet 1848...1re lettre. Lettres à M. le Général Cavaignac. Par F. C[harpentier]. de Damery. [2]p. *s.sh.fol.* [*Paris,* 1848]

35953 **The* **CHARTER.** Stop! Read! Unite! Liberty, equality, fraternity. [A handbill addressed to Chartists, in the form of a catechism.] *s.sh.8°.* [1848] *The copy that belonged to Augustus De Morgan.*

35954 Deux **CHEFS** de clubs. Auguste Blanqui,

ordonnance de la Chambre du Conseil, rendue contre lui; Juin d'Allas (dit Michelot), arrêt de la Cour d'Assises de la Seine, qui le condamne à cinq ans de travaux forcés. [2]p. *s.sh.fol. Paris,* [1848]

35955 CHRISTIAN CHARTIST CHURCH. Englishman! [A protest against the prevention of a meeting, and a resolution to refuse to pay all taxes. Signed, by order of the Committee, Arthur O'Neill, secretary.] *s.sh.8°. Birmingham,* [1848?] [*phc*] *From the Lambeth Palace Library copy.*

35956 DARESTE DE LA CHAVANNE, A. E. C. Histoire de l'administration en France et des progrès du pouvoir royal, depuis le règne de Philippe-Auguste jusqu'à la mort de Louis XIV...[With 'Pièces justificatives'.] 2 vols. *8°. Paris,* 1848.

35957 DAWSON, GEORGE, *minister.* A letter to the middle classes on the present crisis. 4p. *8°. Birmingham,* [1848]

35958 [**DÉADDÉ,** E.] and **CHOLER,** A. J. Théâtre des Variétés. Le république de Platon. Vaudeville en un acte, par MM. Saint-Yves et Adolphe Choler, représenté...le 7 juin 1848. 14p. *8°. Paris,* 1848.

35959 DEBRAY, , *ainé.* Citoyens! A vos rangs! [2]p. *s.sh.fol. Paris,* [1848]

35960 DÉFENSE du Citoyen Ledru-Rollin. [Signed: Un misanthrope.] [2]p. *s.sh.fol.* [*Paris,* 1848]

35961 Le grand **DÉGOMMAGE** du Général Cavaignac...Élection du Président. Résultats des votes connus jusqu'à ce jour... *s.sh.fol.* [*Paris,* 1848]

35962 —— [Another edition.]...Élection du Président. Votes connus le 14 décembre... *s.sh.fol.* [*Paris,* 1848]

35963 DESPLANTADES, . Lettre à Louis-Philippe sur la présidence de la République. [A royalist pamphlet in favour of the candidature de M. Larochejacquelein.] [2]p. *fol. Paris,* [1848]

35964 DUFFY, SIR C. G. Confederate principles. The creed of "The Nation," a profession of confederate principles. 15p. *12°. Dublin,* 1848.

35965 DUNCAN, J. E. A scourge for a gag. (No. 2. – Pe-ans for the people; or, rhyme-rays in the fading glooms, and froth-foams on the waves of progress.) [A ballad.] *s.sh.fol. n.p.* [1848] [*Br.* 616(1)]

35966 —— Fourth thousand. Tocsin 'gainst tyranny; or, the British Marseillaise...(No. 1. – Pe-ans for the people; or, rhyme-rays in the fading glooms, and froth-foams on the waves of progress.) [A ballad.] Recited at a meeting of British people in the Hall of the Co-operative League, 2d March 1848. *s.sh.fol.* [*London,* 1848] [*Br.* 616(2)]

35967 ESPIARD, A. Septembre 1848...Feuille no. 1....La loterie démocratique et sociale. Seules chances ouvertes à l'ouvrier...pour devenir propriétaire. [2]p. *s.sh.fol. Paris,* [1848]

35968 GALLOIS, C. A. G. L. Point de Président. Lettre au citoyen Armand Marrast, rapporteur de la Commission de Constitution. [2]p. *s.sh.fol.* [*Paris,* 1848]

35969 GERMANY unmasked; or, facts and coincidences explanatory of her real views in seeking to wrest Schleswig from Denmark. With an appendix, containing remarks on the "Memoir" on Schleswig and Holstein "presented to Viscount Palmerston by the Chevalier Bunsen." xlvi, 90p. *8°.* 1848. *The copy that belonged to Col. C. R. Fox, M.P.*

35970 GUÉNÉE, A. and TANDOU, F. Un voyage en Icarie, à-propos en un acte, mêlé de couplets... représenté...à Paris, sur le Théâtre des Délassements-Comiques, le 26 août 1848. 8p. *8°*. [*Paris*, 1848]

35971 GUESNIER, A. Amnistie! Amnistie! Lettre au Général Cavaignac. *s.sh.fol. Paris*, [1848]

35972 GUIOT, A. Adresse aux démocrates. [Dated: 21 novembre 1848.] *s.sh.fol. Paris*, [1848]

35973 HARTMANN, H. Élection du Président de la République. Appel au peuple français. [2]p. *s.sh.fol. Paris*, [1848]

35974 [HELPS, Sir A.] A letter from one of the special constables in London on the late occasion of their being called out to keep the peace. 23p. *12°*. 1848.

35975 HILBEY, C. Affreuse tentative de corruption dévoilée par Constant Hilbey, rédacteur du Journal des Sans-Culottes. [2]p. *s.sh.fol.* [*Paris*, 1848]

35976 IZAMBARD, H. Presse parisienne. [An annotated list of newspapers published since Feb. 1848.] [2]p. *s.sh.fol.* [*Paris*, 1848]

35977 JERROLD, W. B. A vote for our money and our blood; a pamphlet addressed to all non-voters who pay the income-tax, and are liable to serve as militia-men. 16p. *8°*. 1848.

35978 JONES, Ernest C. Chartist songs and fugitive pieces... 16p. *8°*. *n.p.* [1848 ?]

35979 —— The Queen against Ernest Jones. Trial of Ernest Charles Jones for sedition and unlawful assembly at the Central Criminal Court, before Wilde, C.J. July 10, 1848. 38p. *fol. n.p.* [1848] *Apparently a proof, printed in columns numbered 411–446.*

For les JUDAS DE LA RÉPUBLIQUE, *see* vol. III, *Periodicals list.*

35980 LAGRANGE, C. Supplément au numéro du 22 décembre de La Révolution démocratique et sociale. Discours du citoyen Ch. Lagrange, représentant du peuple, sur l'amnistie. [4]p. *fol.* [*Paris*, 1848]

35981 LATOUCHE, M. Le banquet du vieux Montagnard, ou l'anniversaire du 22 septembre 1792. [A poem.] *s.sh.fol.* [*Paris*, 1848]

35982 LEFEBVRE, *le Père, pseud.* Première lettre du Père Lefebvre. [Dated: le 11 août 1848. An attack on Proudhon.] *s.sh.fol. Paris*, [1848]

35983 LEROUX DE MONTGREFFIER, L. F. Lettre au citoyen E. Delamothe se disant Émile de Girardin sur sa nouvelle candidature à l'Assemblée nationale. [Dated: 12 septembre 1848.] [4]p. *fol.* [*Paris*, 1848]

35984 A LETTER from a rejected member of a late Parliament, to the Earl of Clarendon, the Queen's viceroy. p.72–115. *8°*. 1848.

35985 LETTRE des insurgés déportés au Général Cavaignac chef du pouvoir exécutif. [Dated: août 1848.] 8p. *8°*. *Paris*, [1848]

35986 LETTRE du Pape au Général Cavaignac. [Signed: Mathéi, dit Pie IX, ex-pape, ex-capitaine de dragons. A satire.] *s.sh.fol.* [*Paris*, 1848]

35987 LETTRE sur la Présidence de la République, par un représentant du peuple, à M. de Lamartine. [2]p. *s.sh.fol.* [*Paris*, 1848]

35988 LIBRE-MONT, P. Défense des insurgés de juin, adressée au citoyen Armand Marrast, président de l'Assemblée nationale. 2p. *s.sh.fol.* [*Paris*, 1848]

35989 *LOMBARDY. Governo Provvisorio. Comitato di Pubblica Difesa.* The late melancholy events in Milan: narrated by the Committee of Public Defence. [Signed: Restelli, Maestri. Translated from the Italian by E.A.H.] 52p. *16°*. 1848. *The FWA copy that belonged to William Pare.*

35990 LOVETT, W. Justice safer than expediency: an appeal to the middle classes on the question of the suffrage. 8p. *8°*. 1848.

35991 MACÉ, J. Suspension du Club Chabrol. Lettre d'un homme inquiet au citoyen Pinard, procureur de la République. [2]p. *s.sh.fol.* [*Paris*, 1848 ?]

35992 MACKAY, A. Electoral districts; or, the apportionment of the representation of the country on the basis of its population, being an inquiry into the working of the Reform Bill, and into the merits of the representative scheme by which it is proposed to supersede it. 40p. *8°*. 1848. *The copy that belonged to Earl De Grey.*

35993 MANN, A. Mann's black book of the British aristocracy; or, an exposure of the more monstrous abuses in the state and the church; with black lists of pensioners ... 54p. *12°*. [1848]

35994 MARAT, J. P. Extrait du Publiciste parisien. Document authentique pris à la Bibliothèque nationale. Commandements de la patrie. *s.sh.4°. Paris & London*, [1848 ?]

35995 Les MÉMOIRES d'un insurgé...1re livraison. 8p. *fol.* [*Paris*,] 1848.

For M[ONSIEUR]. PIPELET, *see* vol. III, *Periodicals list.*

35996 MOREAU, E. L., *and others.* Théâtre des Variétés. Les peureux. A-propos-vaudeville en un acte de MM. Moreau, Siraudin et Delacour, représenté...le 16 avril 1848. 9p. *8°*. *Paris*, 1848.

For les MOUSTIQUES RÉPUBLICAINES, *see* vol. III, *Periodicals list.*

35997 [NICOLAIE, L. F. and VAULABELLE, É. T. DE.] Théâtre du Vaudeville. Le club des maris et le club des femmes. Vaudeville en un acte, par MM. Clairville et Jules Cordier, représenté...le 4 juin 1848. 14p. *8°*. *Paris*, 1848.

35998 [——] Théâtre du Gymnase-Dramatique. Les filles de la liberté. A-propos-vaudeville en un acte, de MM. Clairville et J. Cordier, représenté...le 14 mars 1848. 10p. *8°*. *Paris*, 1848.

35999 [——] Théâtre des Variétés. Un petit de la mobile. Comédie-vaudeville en deux actes. Par MM. Clairville et J. Cordier, représentée...le 7 août 1848. 21p. *8°*. *Paris*, 1848.

36000 [——] La propriété c'est le vol. Folie-socialiste en trois actes et sept tableaux par MM. Clairville et J. Cordier, représentée...sur le Théâtre du Vaudeville. Le 28 novembre 1848. 23p. *8°*. [*Paris*, 1848]

36001 NOEL, Hon. B. W. Facts taken from an essay on the union of Church and state. 4p. *12°*. *Darlington*, [1848]

For the PEOPLE: THEIR RIGHTS AND LIBERTIES, 1848–52, *see* vol. III, *Periodicals list.*

36002 The **PEOPLE'S CHARTER,** with the address to the radical reformers of Great Britain and Ireland... 28p. 8°. 1848. *For other editions, see* 1838.

36003 **PEOPLE'S LEAGUE.** The People's League. To the people of London and its vicinity. [Signed: Wm. Lovett, honorary secretary.] 12p. *12°.* [1848]

36004 —— Plan of organization of the People's League. 8p. 8°. 1848.

36005 **PEREDA,** V. M. DE. La situacion contra el deseo nacional. 46p. 8°. *Lóndres,* 1848.

36006 **PETOT,** . Le mémoire de M. Émile de Girardin. Sa correspondence. – Lettres. – Réponses. – Réfutation. [2]p. *s.sh.fol.* [*Paris,* 1848]

For le **PEUPLE SOUVERAIN,** *see* vol. III, *Periodicals list.*

For le **POPULAIRE,** *see* vol. III, *Periodicals list.*

For le **POT AUX ROSES,** *see* vol. III, *Periodicals list.*

36007 **PROPHÉTIES** politiques de Michel Nostradamus, sur les républicains rouges et les socialistes, dernières prédictions sur les terribles événemens qui doivent arriver. [6 quatrains from *Les centuries,* with explanation and comment.] *s.sh.fol. Paris,* [1848]

36008 **PRUDHOMME,** . Lettre au citoyen Proudhon liquidateur de la société française par M. Prudhomme, élève de Brard et Saint-Omer, expert assermenté près les tribuneaux de la Seine, maître d'écriture dans l'Ile Saint-Louis, propriétaire, juré, garde national et père de famille. [2]p. *s.sh.fol.* [*Paris,* 1848]

For **RÉACTIONNAIRE,** *see* vol. III, *Periodicals list.*

36009 The **REFORMER'S** companion to the almanacs. [By Joseph Barker.] Nos. 1–6. January[–May] 1848. *12°. Wortley,* 1848.

For les **RÉPUBLICAINS DE LA VEILLE AU TRIBUNAL,** *see* vol. III, *Periodicals list,* Réactionnaire.

For les **RÉPUBLICAINS DU LENDEMAIN AUX ELECTEURS,** *see* vol. III, *Perodicals list,* Réactionnaire.

For the **REPUBLICAN:** a magazine, advocating the sovereignty of the people, *see* vol. III, *Periodicals list.*

For **RÉVEIL DU PEUPLE,** *see* vol. III, *Periodicals list.*

36010 **RÉVÉLATIONS** d'une somnambule sur l'avenir et les destinées du Général Cavaignac. *s.sh.fol.* [*Paris,* 1848]

36011 **RIVIÈRES LES FOSSES,** . La présidence récompense honnête à celui qui retrouvera notre vraie République Française une et indivisible. [2]p. *s.sh.fol.* [*Paris,* 1848]

36012 **ROUX,** P. M. L. F. No. 1...1848. La misère vaincue par l'œuvre de M. Roux, vicaire des Quinze-Vingts. [With 'No. 1...1848. Le rapport par M. Roux, vicaire des Quinze-Vingts, sur le Faubourg Saint-Antoine'.] [2]p. *s.sh.fol.* [*Paris,* 1848]

36013 **SOCIÉTÉ RÉPUBLICAINE CENTRALE.** La Société Républicaine centrale au Gouvernement provisoire. [On the royalist counter-revolution at Rouen. Signed by L. Auguste Blanqui and 11 other officers of the society.] [2]p. 8°. *Paris,* [1848]

36014 **STAINES,** T. Les adieux lamentables du Général Cavaignac au peuple français. *s.sh.fol. Paris,* [1848]

36015 **STYLES,** THOMAS, *pseud.* The coming era, and the men to figure in it. 32p. 8°. [1848] *In the preface it is stated that the author's name is a pseudonym.*

36016 **TELLIER,** C. J. Plus d'insurrection! Le droit d'insurrection aboli par l'organisation de la souveraineté du peuple. [4]p. *fol. Paris,* [1848]

36017 Dernière **VÉRITÉ** sur E. Cavaignac. [2]p. *s.sh.fol. Montmartre,* [1848]

36018 **VIEIRA,** A. Art de voler. Critique des roueries politiques, administratives et sociales... Traduit pour la première fois... par Eugène Garay-Monglave. 311p. *12°. Paris,* 1848.

36019 [**VILLARD,** B.] Cavaignac au désespoir devant le tribunal du peuple, par le Citoyen B.V*** (de l'Isère). *s.sh.fol.* [*Paris,* 1848]

36020 —— Lettre adressée à l'Assemblée Nationale en faveur des travailleurs et des détenus politiques. *s.sh.fol.* [*Paris,* 1848]

36021 **WARNOD,** V. Lettre au Général Cavaignac. Opinion de M. Sénard, relativement au peuple et au Gouvernement provisoire. [Dated: 14 août 1848.] [2]p. *s.sh.fol. Paris,* [1848]

36022 **WATSON,** H. C. Public opinion: or safe revolution, through self representation. 24p. 8°. 1848. *The copy that belonged to William Lovett.*

36023 A **WORD** to the masses on their right to the franchise, and the means of attaining it. By a Norwich operative. 16p. 8°. *London & Norwich,* [1848?]

36024 **ZAMBELLI,** N. The Ionian Isles, and the anomaly of their present condition, in which after more than thirty years under British protection, they are still without either freedom of the press, or the power of nominating their representatives. A letter to the Right Hon. the Earl Grey, His Britannic Majesty's Secretary of State for the Colonies, by an Ionian. 27p. 8°. [*London,*] 1848. *Translated, with an introduction, by G. D. Papanicolas.*

SOCIALISM

36025 **ALMANACH** phalanstérien pour 1848. [4ᵉ année.] 208p. *16°. Paris,* [1848]

For the **APOSTLE, AND CHRONICLE OF THE COMMUNIST CHURCH,** *see* vol. III, *Periodicals list.*

36026 **BAILEY,** JAMES N. The social reformers' cabinet library. Containing – Life of Lycurgus [1840].

Objects...of the science of society [1840]. Pleasures...of literature and philosophy [1841]. Gehenna...a dissertation on...the kingdom of Hell [1841]. Sophistry unmasked. In reply to John Brindley [1841]. Sketches of Indian character...[1841]. 31, 32, 34, 64, 64, 64p. 8°. 1848. *A reissue of the collection of separately published pamphlets, first issued in Leeds in 1841 (q.v.).*

For le **BAILLON**, *see* vol. III, *Periodicals list*, Réactionnaire.

36027 BANQUET de la République démocratique et sociale du mardi 17 octobre 1848. 8p. *fol. Paris*, [1848]

36028 BARBEU DU ROCHER, . Du partage des terres et du communisme. 16p. *16°. Le Mans*, 1848.

36029 BAUDET-DULARY, A. F. Quelques mots sur l'organisation du travail. 15p. *8°. S.-Germain-en-Laye*, 1848. *The copy that belonged to Victor Considérant.*

36030 BIARD, G. Révolution de 1848. Premier dialogue. Le socialisme dévoilé. (Dialogues entre un socialiste et un bourgeois.) [4]p. *fol.* [*Paris*, 1848]

36031 BLANC, J. J. L. Organisation du travail... Cinquième édition. Revue...et augmentée d'une polémique entre M. Michel Chevalier et l'auteur, ainsi que d'un appendice indiquant ce qui pourrait être tenté dès à présent. La première édition a paru en 1839. 284p. *12°. Paris*, 1848.

36032 —— The organization of labour. 132p. *16°.* 1848.

36033 —— Threatened social disorganisation of France. Louis Blanc on the working classes; with corrected notes, and a refutation of his destructive plan. By James Ward. Second edition. 237p. *8°.* 1848. *A translation of part I of* Organisation du travail. *For another edition of the complete work, see* 1845.

36034 —— Le socialisme. Droit au travail. Réponse à M. Thiers...Deuxième édition. 107p. *18°. Paris*, 1848.

36035 —— Socialism: the right to labour. In reply to M. Thiers...With memoir and portrait of the author. 20p. *8°.* 1848. *The major part of the Memoir is based on the sketch by Goodwyn Barmby, which appeared in Tait's Magazine for April, 1848. *Another, the FWA copy, belonged to William Pare, and is bound with a copy of* Supplement to the Spirit of the Age, *No. 1, August 28, 1848, which consists of the whole of Blanc's work, with the memoir, as above.*

36036 BORDEAUX, H. Conditions de la paix publique. [Socialist theory.] *s.sh.fol.* [*Paris*, 1848]

36037 —— Des droits de la classe populaire. *s.sh.fol.* [*Paris*, 1848]

36038 —— Description de la raison sociale. *s.sh.fol.* [*Paris*, 1848]

36039 —— Principes pour le peuple. *s.sh.fol.* [*Paris*, 1848]

36040 BOURGEOIS, L. Des deux cotés de la barricade. A Jacques Arago, du Fort de l'Est. [With 'Réponse par J. Arago'.] [2]p. *s.sh.fol. Paris*, [1848]

36041 BRIANCOURT, M. Précis de l'organisation du travail extrait de "L'organisation du travail et de l'association". [2e édition, 3e tirage.] 63p. *16°. Paris*, 1846[1848] *The information concerning the edition, and the date 1848 appear only on the printed wrapper.*

36042 —— Visite au phalanstère. 340p. *16°. Paris*, 1848.

36043 CABET, É. La femme, son malheureux sort dans la société actuelle, son bonheur dans la communauté ...Huitième édition. 31p. *16°. Paris*, 1848.

36044 —— L'ouvrier; ses misères actuelles, leur cause et leur remède; son futur bonheur dans la communauté; moyens de l'établir...Publié sur l'invitation des action-naires du Populaire. Quatrième édition. 47p. *16°. Paris*, 1848.

36045 —— Voyage en Icarie...[Cinquième édition.] 600p. *18°. Paris*, 1848. *For another edition, see* 1840.

36046 CHEVALIER, M. Lettres sur l'organisation du travail, ou études sur les principales causes de la misère et sur les moyens proposés pour y remédier. 515p. *12°. Paris*, 1848.

36047 —— [Another edition.] 354p. *12°. Bruxelles, Livourne, &c.*, 1848.

36048 [——] Question des travailleurs. [L'amélioration du sort des ouvriers. – Les salaires. – L'organisation du travail.] 32p. *8°. Paris*, [1848] *Reprinted from Revue des Deux Mondes, 15 March 1848. Presentation copy, with inscription, from the author to N. W. Senior.*

36049 —— [Another edition, revised and enlarged.] 71p. *12°. Paris*, 1848.

36050 —— The labour question. 1. Amelioration of the condition of the labouring classes. 2. Wages. 3. Organization of labour...Translated from the French. 150p. *16°.* 1848.

36051 CHUTE de l'atelier révolutionnaire des tailleurs de Clichy. [2]p. *s.sh.fol. Paris*, [1848?]

36052 COMITÉ DE SALUT PUBLIC. Projets de décrets du Comité de Salut Public. Pièces trouvées chez le citoyen Sobrier...et déposées à la Chambre des Représentants par le citoyen Jeandel, de la 2e légion. 4p. *8°.* [*Paris*, 1848]

36053 CONSEIL CENTRAL DES ÉLECTEURS RÉPUBLICAINS DÉMOCRATES-SOCIALISTES. Le Conseil...aux électeurs républicains-democrates-socialistes. [2]p. *s.sh.fol. Paris*, [1848]

36054 CONSIDÉRANT, V. P. Description du phalanstère et considérations sociales sur l'architectonique ...2e édition, revue et corrigée. 111p. *12°. Paris*, 1848.

36055 —— Destinée sociale...2e édition. 2 vols. *12°. Paris*, 1848–49. *Vol. 2 is of the third edition. For other editions, see* 1834.

36056 —— Exposition abrégée du système phalanstérien de Fourier...Recueillie par P.-C.-E.Mo....e. Troisième édition... 114p. *16°. Paris*, 1848. *For other editions, see* 1845.

36057 —— Le socialisme devant le vieux monde ou le vivant devant les morts. Par Victor Considérant...Suivi de Jésus-Christ devant les conseils de guerre. Par Victor Meunier. 264p. *12°. Paris*, 1848. *Considérant's own copy.*

36058 —— Le socialisme c'est le vrai Christianisme. Payens, convertissez-vous!! [Extrait du Socialisme devant le vieux monde.] [2]p. *s.sh.fol.* [*Paris*, 1848]

36059 *COOPER, Thomas (1805–1892), *ed.* The land for the labourers, and the fraternity of nations: a scheme for a new industrial system, just published in Paris, and intended for proposal to the National Assembly. [Signed: A cosmopolite republican. Translated from the French.] 15p. *8°.* [1848] *The FWA copy, that belonged to William Pare.*

36060 CURIOSITÉS révolutionnaires. Les journaux rouges. Histoire critique de tous les journaux ultra-républicains publiés à Paris depuis le 24 février jusqu'au 1er octobre 1848. Avec des extraits-spécimens et une préface par un Girondin. 138p. *18°. Paris*, 1848.

36061 DARIMON, A. Exposition méthodique des

principes de l'organisation sociale, – théorie de Krause, – précédée d'un examen historique et critique du socialisme. lxviii, 216p. *18°. Paris*, 1848.

36062 DÉCLARATION au peuple. [Signed by 54 'représentants du peuple (montagnards)'.] [2]p. *s.sh.fol. Paris*, [1848]

36063 [DELEUZE, J.] Le droit au travail avec son organisation pratique. [2]p. *s.sh.fol.* [*Paris*, 1848]

36064 DESAGES, L. and **DESMOULINS**, A. Doctrine de l'humanité. Aphorismes. 32p. *8°. Boussac*, 1848.

36065 [DESCHAMPS, N.] Un éclair avant la foudre ou le communisme et ses causes. Par l'auteur de Monopole destructeur de la religion et des lois... 2 vols. *12°. Avignon*, 1848–49.

36066 DUMAS, ALEXANDRE (1802–1870). Révélations sur l'arrestation d'Émile Thomas... Suivi de pièces justificatives. 54p. *18°. Paris*, 1848.

36067 ÉCOLE SOCIÉTAIRE. Doctrine de l'harmonie universelle et de l'organisation du travail. Publications de l'École phalanstérienne fondée par Fourier. 21p. *12°.* [*Paris*, 1848] *The copy that belonged to Earl De Grey.*

36068 ÉGRET, . Organisation du travail par les travailleurs. 108p. *18°. Paris*, 1848.

For the **ENGLISH PATRIOT AND IRISH REPEALER**, *continued as* the English patriot and herald of labour and co-operation, *see* vol. III, *Periodicals list.*

36069 FABRE, JEAN J. A. Solution du problème social, par l'association de l'agriculture et des capitaux. 120p. *8°. Toulouse*, 1848. *Presentation copy, with inscription, from the author to A. F. Gatien-Arnoult.*

36070 FOURIER, F. C. M. Analyse du mécanisme de l'agiotage et De la méthode mixte en étude de l'attraction...(Extrait de la Phalange...) 128p. *8°. Paris*, 1848. *The copy that belonged to Victor Considérant.*

36071 FRANCE. *Assemblée Nationale.* Le droit au travail à l'Assemblée Nationale. Recueil complet de tous les discours prononcés dans cette mémorable discussion ...suivis de l'opinion de MM. Marrast, Proudhon, L. Blanc, Éd. Laboulaye et Cormenin; avec des observations inédites par MM. Léon Faucher, Wołowski, Fréd. Bastiat, de Parieu, et une introduction et des notes par M. Joseph Garnier. 455p. *8°. Paris*, 1848.

36072 FUGÈRE, H. Organisation du travail par la fondation d'une commune modèle...Dédié aux représentants du peuple. *s.sh.fol. Paris*, [1848]

36073 GORGES, É. Organisation de la commune en France. 30p. *8°. Paris*, 1848.

36074 GUINIER, T. Réponse à M. Thiers à propos de son livre De la propriété publié dans le Constitutionnel, le 29 septembre 1848. [2]p. *s.sh.fol. Paris*, [1848]

36075 HENNEQUIN, V. A. Organisation du travail d'après la théorie de Charles Fourier. Exposition faite à Besançon, en mars 1847...Troisième édition. 195p. *12°. Paris*, 1848. *The copy that belonged to Victor Considérant.*

36076 HILBEY, C. Le socialisme et la Révolution française. [An attack on Proudhon. Dated: 1er novembre 1848.] [2]p. *s.sh.fol. Paris*, [1848]

36077 JOBEZ, A. Une préface au socialisme ou le système de Law et la chasse aux capitalistes. 234p. *8°. Paris*, 1848.

36078 KRANTZ, S. J. B. Le présent et l'avenir. Coup d'œil sur la théorie de Fourier. 118p. *18°. Paris*, 1848. *The copy that belonged to Victor Considérant.*

36079 *LEAGUE OF SOCIAL PROGRESS. League of Social Progress: established November 27, 1848. [Membership card.] *n.p.* [1848] *The FWA copy that belonged to William Pare.*

36080 LECHEVALIER SAINT ANDRÉ, L. J. Au peuple. [An open letter dated: le 28 novembre 1848, prefixed to 3 documents intended to show Lechevalier's political opinions and to clear him of charges of treachery to the Republic.] [4]p. *fol. Paris*, [1848] *The copy that belonged to Earl De Grey.*

36081 —— Qui donc organisera le travail? – Les travailleurs eux-mêmes. Organisons-nous. Discours du citoyen Jules Lechevalier prononcé le dimanche 18 juin, dernière séance du Club de l'Organisation du Travail. [2]p. *s.sh.fol. Paris*, [1848]

36082 LEDRU-ROLLIN, A. A. Réponse du citoyen Ledru-Rollin, à ses calomniateurs. [2]p. *s.sh.fol.* [*Paris*, 1848]

36083 LEROUX, P. H. La Commune de Paris par Barbès, Sobrier, Georges Sand et Cahaigne. *s.sh.fol.* [*Paris*, 1848]

36084 —— De l'égalité...Nouvelle édition. 272p. *8°. Boussac*, 1848.

36085 —— De la ploutocratie, ou du gouvernement des riches...Nouvelle édition. 164p. *16°. Boussac*, 1848.

36086 The social **LESSONS** of the day. Parisian notions of freedom. Some measures of the French Government. From the "Economist." Second edition. 24p. *8°.* [1848] *The copy that belonged to J. M. Ludlow.*

For **MANIFESTE DE LA LIGUE SOCIALE**, *see* vol. III, *Periodicals list.*

36087 MERSON, E. Du communisme. Réfutation de l'utopie icarienne. 370p. *8°. Paris & Nantes*, 1848.

36088 MEUNIER, V. La propriété et l'usure devant Jésus-Christ et les Pères de l'Eglise. [Extrait d'un écrit intitulé Jésus-Christ devant les conseils de guerre.] [2]p. *s.sh.fol.* [*Paris*, 1848 ?] *With a list of books for sale at the Librairie phalanstérienne, quai Voltaire 25. For an edition of the complete work, see no.* 36057.

36089 —— Union démocratique et sociale. [2]p. *s.sh.fol.* [*Paris*, 1848]

36090 *NOAKES, J. The right of the aristocracy to the soil, considered...Third thousand. 16p. *8°.* 1848. *The FWA copy, that belonged to William Pare.*

36091 —— Second edition, revised. 16p. *8°.* 1848.

36092 [NOÉ, A. C. H. DE.] Proudhoniana par Cham. Album dédié aux propriétaires. [Cartoons.] 16f. *4°. Paris*, [1848]

36093 *OWEN, ROBERT. Adresse à l'Assemblée Nationale de France. [Dated: Paris, mai 1848.] *s.sh.8°. n.p.* [1848] *The FWA copy that belonged to William Pare.*

36094 *—— Contrast between two states of society, one emanating from the laws of men and the other from the laws of nature or of God. [With 'The proposed improvement of society', and 'Practical measures required to prevent greater political changes in Great Britain and Ireland', all signed by Robert Owen, the first two dated June 1846 and the third March 15 1848.] *s.sh.fol. n.p.* [1848] *A galley proof. The FWA copy that belonged to William Pare. See also no.* 36097.

36095 —— Dialogue entre la France, le monde et Robert Owen, sur la nécessité d'un changement total dans nos systèmes d'éducation et de gouvernement. [With 'Lois des cités'.] 36p. *12°. Paris,* 1848. *The title on the printed paper wrapper reads 'Dialogue sur le système social de Robert Owen'.*

36096 —— Dialogue entre les membres de la Commission exécutive, les ambassadeurs d'Angleterre, de Russie, d'Autriche, de Prusse, de Hollande, des États-Unis, et Robert Owen. 24p. *12°. Paris,* 1848. *The title on the printed paper wrapper reads 'Deuzième dialogue sur le système social par Robert Owen'.*

36097 *—— Practical measures required to prevent greater political changes in Great Britain and Ireland. [Dated: London, March 15, 1848.] *s.sh.8°. n.p.* [1848] *Also printed in the Northern Star, no.* 544, *25 March 1848. The FWA copy that belonged to William Pare.*

36098 *—— A proclamation by Robert Owen. [*Begin.*] It is evident the Government of this country is reposing on a barrel of gunpowder...[A poster, dated: London, March 1, 1848.] *s.sh.fol. n.p.* [1848] *The FWA copy that belonged to William Pare.*

36099 *—— Socialism misrepresented [in The Times], and truly represented [in the 'Address to all classes... containing an official declaration of principles, adapted for practice by the Congress of the Universal Community Society of Rational Religionists...in Leeds, May 1840', signed: Robert Owen, president. With 'The rational state of human existence, and model constitution for the government of Man. By Robert Owen']. 16p. *16°.* [*London,* 1848] *The FWA copy that belonged to William Pare. For another edition of the* Address to all classes, *see* 1840 (Rational Society).

36100 *—— The universal permanent government, constitution, and code of laws, based on the unchanging laws of nature, for the world...and also for each state or nation separately, until they shall have acquired the knowledge and wisdom to unite in federative union. [Signed: Robert Owen, and dated, London, November 25th, 1848.] 4p. *4°. n.p.* [1848] *The FWA copy that belonged to William Pare.*

36101 PARTOUNAU DU PUYNODE, M. G. Organisation du travail. Lettres économiques sur le prolétariat...I. Subsistences. II. Esclavage et émancipation. III. La concurrence et le socialisme. IV. Le prolétariat. 266p. *12°. Paris,* 1848.

36102 PELLARIN, C. The life of Charles Fourier... Second edition with an appendix. Translated by Francis Geo. Shaw. 236p. *12°. New York,* 1848. *For other editions, see* 1839.

36103 PERTUS, C. La capote et la blouse, ou le soldat et l'ouvrier. [A song.] *s.sh.4°.* [*Paris,* 1848 ?]

For le **PEUPLE,** 1848–49, *see* vol. III, *Periodicals list.*

36104 [POITEVIN, P.] Réponse au représentant Proudhon par un de ses disciples. [Accusing him of plagiarism. Signed: Le paysan du Danube.] *s.sh.fol. n.p.* [1848]

For **POLITICS FOR THE PEOPLE,** *see* vol. III, *Periodicals list.*

36105 POLITICS FOR THE PEOPLE. [*Begin.*] On the [*blank*] of [*blank*] will be published (to be continued weekly,) price one penny, no. 1., of Politics for the People. [A prospectus.] 2p. *8°.* [1848] *The copy that belonged to J. M. Ludlow.*

36106 —— [Another edition.] 2p. *8°.* [1848] *The copy that belonged to J. M. Ludlow.*

36107 PROUDHON, P. J. Avertissement aux propriétaires, ou lettre à M. Considérant, rédacteur de La Phalange, sur une Défense de la propriété...Deuxième édition. 100p. *12°. Paris,* 1848. *For another edition, see* 1841.

36108 —— Qu'est-ce que la propriété? Ou recherches sur le principe du droit et du gouvernement...Premier mémoire. 252p. *12°. Paris,* 1848. *For another edition, see* 1841.

36109 —— Qu'est-ce que la propriété? Deuxième mémoire. Lettre à M. Blanqui...sur la propriété... Deuxième édition. 155p. *12°. Paris,* 1848. *For another edition entitled:* Lettre à M. Blanqui, *see* 1841.

36110 —— Solution du problème social. 119p. *8°. Paris,* 1848.

For le **REPRÉSENTANT DU PEUPLE,** *see* vol. III, *Periodicals list.*

36111 SAGRA, R. DE LA. Organisation du travail. Questions préliminaires à l'examen de ce problème. 95p. *8°. Paris,* 1848.

36112 —— Le problème de l'organisation du travail devant l'Académie des Sciences morales et politiques. 15p. *8°. Paris,* 1848.

36113 —— Le problème de l'organisation du travail devant le Congrès des économistes de Bruxelles. 8p. *8°. Paris,* 1848.

36114 SCHEIDTMANN, G. Der Communismus und das Proletariat... 127p. *8°. Leipzig,* 1848.

36115 SCHMIT, J. H. A few words addressed to the labouring classes, by J. H. Schmit, one of themselves. Translated from the French [by Simon Waley. A warning that they should not be misled into thinking that the interests of the labouring classes are opposed to those of employers]. 16p. *8°.* 1848.

36116 SOCIÉTÉ POSITIVISTE. Rapport à la Société Positiviste, par la commission chargée d'examiner la question du travail. 15p. *8°. Paris,* 1848. *With an introduction by Auguste Comte. The copy that belonged to Earl De Grey. See also* 1850.

36117 —— République occidentale...Rapport à la Société Positiviste, par la commission chargée d'examiner la nature et le plan du nouveau gouvernement révolutionnaire de la République française. 33p. *8°. Paris,* 1848. *With an introduction by Auguste Comte. The copy that belonged to Earl De Grey.*

36118 SUE, M. J. E. Le berger de Kravan ou entretiens socialistes et démocratiques sur la république, – les prétendants et la prochaine présidence. 175p. *16°. Paris,* 1848.

36119 TERENCE, *pseud.* A short introduction to the works of Charles Fourier. 26p. *8°.* 1848. *The copy that belonged to J. M. Ludlow.*

36120 THIERS, L. A. De la propriété. 439p. *8°. Paris,* 1848.

36121 —— Édition augmentée des discours sur le droit au travail et sur le crédit foncier. 385p. *12°. Bruxelles, Livourne, &c.*, 1848.

36122 —— Petits traités publiés par l'Académie des Sciences morales et politiques [6]. Du droit de propriété. Deuxième partie. p.[91]-175. *12°. Paris*, 1848. *Chapters 11-14 of* De la propriété. *Wanting the first part, number 5 of the series.*

36123 —— The rights of property; a refutation of communism & socialism. 286p. *8°*. 1848.

36124 THOMAS, É. Histoire des ateliers nationaux considérés sous le double point de vue politique et social ... 395p. *18°. Paris*, 1848.

For le **TOCSIN DES TRAVAILLEURS**, *see vol.* III, *Periodicals list.*

36125 VIDAL, F. Vivre en travaillant! Projets, voies et moyens de réformes sociales. 324p. *12°. Paris*, 1848.

36126 VILLEGARDELLE, F. Accord des intérêts dans l'association et besoins des communes...Deuxième édition...augmentée. 128p. *16°. Paris*, 1848.

MISCELLANEOUS

36127 [**BOWLES**, Sir William (1780-1869).] Thoughts on national defence. [Signed: W.B.] 12p. *8°*. 1848.

36128 BURTON, James R. A letter addressed to the editor of the "Morning Herald," on the national defences. 16p. *8°*. 1848.

36129 COUSIN, V. Philosophie populaire...Suivie de la première partie de la profession de foi du vicaire savoyard, sur la morale et la religion naturelle. [By J. J. Rousseau.] 102p. *12°. Paris*, 1848.

36130 FADDY, P. Essay on the defence and military system of Great Britain, at home and abroad. 36p. *8°*. 1848.

36131 GAWLER, G. Organised special constables, a very efficient bulwark, in this period of serious danger, against internal anarchy, and foreign invasion; with further remarks upon the present duties of Great Britain. 26p. *8°*. 1848.

36132 HAYWARD, A. Report of the proceedings before the judges, as visitors of the Inns of Court, on the appeal of A. Hayward, Esq., Q.C.... 165p. *8°*. 1848.

36133 JUPP, E. B. An historical account of the Worshipful Company of Carpenters of the City of London, compiled chiefly from records in their possession. 338p. *8°*. 1848.

36134 [**KING-NOEL**, W., *Earl of Lovelace.*] Ramée: Architecture du moyen age. [A review.] 23p. *8°. n.p.* [1848?]

36135 LONDON. Livery Companies. *Coopers.* Coopers Company, London. Historical memoranda, charters, documents, and extracts, from the records of the Corporation and the books of the Company, 1396-1848. [Compiled by J. F. Firth.] 135p. *8°*. 1848. *Presentation copy from J. F. Firth to J. Hazard.*

36136 An earnest and respectful **REMONSTRANCE** with the Premier. The three questions: Ought or ought not the Church of Rome in Ireland to be established? Diplomatic relations with the Court of Rome to be resumed? And the Roman version of the Holy Scriptures to be received into our national schools? With a note on educational statistics: considered, in a letter to the Right Hon. the Lord John Russell, M.P....By a beneficed clergyman of the county of Warwick. 40p. *8°*. 1848.

36137 ROME, *Church of*. The Papal Bull, "in coenâ Domini," translated into English. With a short historical introduction; and evidence of its present validity, as part of the Roman law, and of its recognition by the Romish Hierarchy in Ireland. [By G. E. Biber.] 28p. *8°*. 1848.

36138 TAYLER, J. N. Defence of the coast of Great Britain, and other most important matters: with extracts from Rear-Admiral J. N. Tayler's forthcoming work, on naval tactics and gunnery. Suggestions to prevent the horrors of slavery...Plan to abolish flogging...improving the mercantile service...Remarks on the un-English mode of registering seamen... 35p. *8°*. 1848.

36139 TROWER, C. F. The anomalous condition of English jurisprudence. 122p. *8°*. 1848.

1849

GENERAL

36140 *[**AGOULT**, M. C. S. D', *Comtesse.*] Esquisses morales et politiques. Par Daniel Stern, auteur de l'Essai sur la liberté. 397p. *8°. Paris*, 1849. *The copy that belonged to George Grote.*

36141 ANGLICANUS, *pseud*. The state of the nation: or, an inquiry into the effects of free trade principles upon British industry and taxation; in which the arguments of Sir Robert Peel in reply to Mr. Disraeli, in the House of Commons, July 6, 1849, on the question of free trade, are carefully investigated and refuted. 64p. *8°*. 1849.

36142 *[**ARRIVABENE**, G., *Conte.*] Des causes qui ont assuré la tranquillité de la Belgique au milieu des événements de 1848. Lettre adressée à M. Matteuci. 15p. *8°. Bruxelles*, 1849. *The copy that belonged to George Grote.*

36143 BALL, John (1818-1889). What is to be done for Ireland? 125p. *8°*. 1849.

36144 —— Second edition. 125p. *8º*. 1849. *The copy that belonged to Earl De Grey.*

36145 BAMFORD, S. Early days. 312p. *8º*. 1849.

36146 BARHYDT, D. P. Industrial exchanges and social remedies, with a consideration of taxation. 238p. *12º*. *New York & London*, 1849.

36147 BASTIAT, C. F. Popular fallacies regarding general interests; being a translation of the "Sophismes économiques" by M. Frédéric Bastiat, with notes, by G. R. Porter. 192p. *8º*. *London & Belfast*, 1849. *For another edition of the first series, see 1847; for the second series, see 1848.*

36148 [**BATES**, W.] A pictorial guide to Birmingham: being a concise, historical, and descriptive account of the great midland metropolis; with notices of its public buildings, institutions, and manufactures, and topographical notices of the surrounding localities... 198p. *8º*. *Birmingham & London*, 1849.

36149 BEAUMONT, W., *ed.* Warrington in M.CCCC.LXV. as described in a contemporary rent roll of the Legh family, in the possession of Thomas Legh, Esquire, of Lyme Park. (*Remains historical and literary connected with the Palatine Counties of Lancaster and Chester, published by the Chetham Society, 17.*) lxxviii, 151p. *4º*. *Manchester*, 1849.

36150 BERNHARDI, T. VON. Versuch einer Kritik der Gründe, die für grosses und kleines Grundeigenthum angeführt werden. 666p. *8º*. *St. Petersburg*, 1849.

36151 BODINGTON, G. Letters; I. – A New Year's gift to Ireland. II. – Irish prospects. III. – On political expediency, colonial injustice, and Irish misgovernment. IV. – On Irish agriculture and manufactures. The dislocation and misdirection of capital. V. – The defects of the Irish Act of Union. VI. – The effects of free trade on wages. The Irish question solved. VII. – On the principle which should defend or protect the position of the relative interests of any given community from clashing with those of any other. 31p. *8º*. *London & Birmingham*, [1849]

36152 BRATIANU, D. C. Documents concerning the question of the Danubian principalities. Dedicated to the English Parliament. 32p. *8º*. 1849.

36153 BRIDGES, W. Three practical suggestions for the colonization of Ireland. 16p. *8º*. 1849.

36154 The **BRITISH ALMANAC** of the Society for the Diffusion of Useful Knowledge, for...1849... [With 'The companion to the Almanac; or, year-book of general information'.] 96, 264p. *12º*. [1849] *For other editions, see 1828.*

36155 The **BRITISH IMPERIAL CALENDAR** for...1849...or general register of the United Kingdom ...and its colonies... [With 'A companion to the British Imperial Calendar, for...1849'.] 456, 113p. *12º*. [1849] *For other editions, see 1817.*

36156 BURTON, JOHN H. Political and social economy: its practical applications. 345p. *8º*. *Edinburgh*, 1849.

36157 [**BYLES**, SIR J. B.] Sophisms of free trade and popular political economy examined. By a barrister. 220p. *8º*. 1849. *See also* 1850.

36158 CASSOU, C. Simples observations aux paysans. Quelle est leur histoire, quels sont leurs amis naturels. 63p. *8º*. *Paris*, 1849.

36159 CAUSSIDIÈRE, M. La Révolution de février: mémoires de Caussidière ex-préfet de police et représentant du peuple. 386p. *8º*. *Bruxelles*, 1849.

36160 CHERBULIEZ, A. E. Le potage à la tortue. Entretiens populaires sur les questions sociales. 157p. *18º*. *Paris*, 1849.

36161 —— Een portie schildpadsoep. Gemeenzame gesprekken over het maatschappelijk leven. Naar het fransch. 125p. *12º*. *Arnhem*, 1849.

36162 COLTON, C. Public economy for the United States...Second edition. 536p. *8º*. *New York & Cincinnati*, 1849.

36163 COMTE, I. A. M. F. X. Culte systématique de l'humanité...Calendrier positiviste, ou système général de commémoration publique, destiné surtout à la transition finale de la Grande République Occidentale composée des cinq populations avancées, française, italienne, germanique, britanique, et espagnole, toujours solidaires depuis Charlemagne... 35p. *8º*. *Paris*, 1849. *The copy that belonged to Earl De Grey.*

36164 CONSIDÉRANT, V. P. Discours prononcé à l'Assemblée constituante dans la séance du 14 avril, 1849. 173p. *12º*. [*Paris*, 1849] *Considérant's own copy.*

36165 COUSIN, V. Petits traités publiés par l'Académie des Sciences morales et politiques [1]. Justice et charité...Deuxième édition, revue par l'auteur. 66p. *12º*. *Paris*, 1849. *For another edition, see* 1848.

36166 DAVIES, E. American scenes, and Christian slavery: a recent tour of four thousand miles in the United States. 324p. *12º*. 1849.

36167 [**DICK**, T.] The curse removed. A letter to the manufacturers of Manchester, on the state & prospects of England. By a citizen of Edinburgh. 38p. *8º*. 1849.

36168 [**ELLIS**, WILLIAM (1800–1881).] Questions and answers suggested by a consideration of some of the arrangements and relations of social life: being a sequel to the "Outlines of social economy," by the same author. Second edition. 180p. *8º*. 1849. *For* Outlines of social economy, *see* 1846.

36169 ESMÉNARD DU MAZET, C. Nouveaux principes d'économie politique. 456p. *8º*. *Paris*, 1849.

36170 FLETCHER, JOSEPH. Summary of the moral statistics of England and Wales. 216, [26]p. *8º*. [*London*, 1849 ?]

36171 *FRANCE.* Constitution de la République Française accompagnée de notes sommaires explicatives du texte, et suivie de diverses pièces et de quelques discours prononcés dans la discussion du projet, par M. Dupin...[With 'Catalogue des ouvrages de M. Dupin'.] 250p. *12º*. *Paris*, 1849. *The copy that belonged to George Grote.*

36172 GERMANY. *Nationalversammlung.* Grundrechte des deutschen Volks...[27. December 1848.] 16p. *8º*. *Braunschweig*, 1849.

36173 GOODLUCK, W. R. England and her possessions, in 1849: shewing, at one view, the countries and islands, colonies and dependencies, subject to the British flag; with monitory notices to intended emigrants... *s.sh.fol.* [*London*, 1849]

36174 HANCOCK, WILLIAM N. An introductory lecture on political economy. Delivered in the Theatre of

Trinity College, Dublin, in Trinity term, 1848. 36p. *8°*. *Dublin*, 1849.

36175 HOLYOAKE, G. J. The life and character of Richard Carlile. 40p. *8°*. 1849.

36176 HOMUNCULUS, *pseud*. John Bull and his wonderful lamp. A new reading of an old tale...[An attack on Cobden and free trade.] 59p. *4°*. 1849.

36177 IGNORANCE, serfdom, and the worship of the golden image. 31p. *8°*. 1849.

36178 IRELAND imperialised: a letter to His Excellency the Earl of Clarendon. 19p. *8°*. *Dublin*, 1849.

For **JOURNAL DE LA VRAIE RÉPUBLIQUE**, *see* vol. III, *Periodicals list*.

36179 De la **LIBERTÉ** en général, de la liberté du travail et des moyens d'assurer le bien-être matériel et moral des classes laborieuses par un économiste, ami du peuple et des lois. Ce mémoire est suivi d'un éloge de Turgot par le même auteur. 34p. *8°*. *Paris*, 1849.

36180 McCULLOCH, JOHN R. The principles of political economy...The fourth edition. Corrected, enlarged, and improved. 646p. *8°*. *Edinburgh & London*, 1849. *For other editions, see* 1825.

36181 MacDONNELL, E. Address and advice to his countrymen. 16p. *8°*. 1849. *The copy that belonged to Earl De Grey*.

36182 MACKAY, A. The western world; or, travels in the United States in 1846–47; exhibiting them in their latest development social, political, and industrial, including a chapter on California...Second edition. 3 vols. *8°*. 1849.

36183 MARTINEAU, H. The history of England during the thirty years' peace: 1816–1846. 2 vols. *8°*. 1849–50.

36184 MILNES, R. M., *Baron Houghton*. The events of 1848, especially in their relation to Great Britain. A letter to the Marquis of Lansdowne. 70p. *8°*. 1849.

36185 MUGGERIDGE, R. M. Notes on the Irish "difficulty;" with remedial suggestions. 95p. *8°*. *Dublin, London, &c.*, 1849.

36186 NATIONAL ASSOCIATION FOR THE PROTECTION OF BRITISH INDUSTRY AND CAPITAL. Report of the proceedings and speeches at the great public meeting of this association held at the Theatre-Royal, Drury Lane...26th June, 1849 ...48p. *8°*. *London & Chelmsford*, 1849.

36187 O'CONNOR, afterwards **CONDORCET O'CONNOR**, A., *General*. Le monopole cause de tous les maux. 3 vols. *8°*. *Paris & London*, 1849–50. *Translated by O. La Revellière-Lépeaux*.

36188 PECCHIO, G., *Conte*. Storia della economia pubblica in Italia, ossia epilogo critico degli economisti italiani, preceduto da un' introduzione...Terza edizione. 272p. *8°*. *Lugano*, 1849. *With the book-plate of Edith Wharton. For other editions, see* 1829.

36189 PEEL, SIR ROBERT, *2nd Bart*. Speech of Sir Robert Peel, Bart., delivered on...July 6, 1849 on the state of the nation. 60p. *8°*. 1849. *With a manuscript note at the head of the title-page: With Sir Robert Peel's Compts*.

36190 The **PEOPLE'S ALMANACK** for 1850... 24p. *8°*. [1849] *See also* 1847.

36191 [**PERCEVAL**, HON. A. P.] Suggestions for the benefit of the British Navy. 16p. *8°*. 1849.

36192 PRENTICE, A. A tour in the United States with two lectures on emigration, delivered in the Mechanics' Institution, Manchester...Fourth edition. 217p. *16°*. *London & Manchester*, 1849.

36193 QUETELET, L. A. J. Letters addressed to H.R.H. the Grand Duke of Saxe Coburg and Gotha, on the theory of probabilities, as applied to the moral and political sciences...Translated from the French by Olinthus Gregory Downes. 309p. *8°*. 1849. *For another edition, see* 1846.

36194 REMARKS on Ireland; as it is; – as it ought to be; – and as it might be: Sir Robert Peel's plantation scheme, &c. suggested by a recent article in "The Times;" and addressed to the capitalists of England. By a native. 42p. *8°*. *London & Dublin*, 1849.

36195 A brief **REVIEW** of the action of labour, production, commerce, and consumption, under their existing forms and practice; with proposed expedients for improvement... 16p. *8°*. *Philad'a*, [1849] *Addressed in manuscript on the wrapper to 'Hon. William Upham, (U.S. Sen.)'.*

36196 RUSSELL, ROBERT W. America compared with England. The respective social effects of the American and English systems of government and legislation; and the mission of democracy. 289p. *12°*. 1849.

36197 SCROPE, G. P. The Irish difficulty; and how it must be met. From the 'Westminster and Foreign Quarterly Review,' for January, 1849. With a postscript. 37p. *8°*. 1849. *The copy that belonged to Earl De Grey*.

36198 SIRR, H. C. China and the Chinese: their religion, character, customs, and manufactures: the evils arising from the opium trade: with a glance at our religious, moral, political, and commercial intercourse with the country. 2 vols. *8°*. 1849.

36199 SMITH, EDWARD. Account of a journey through north-eastern Texas, undertaken in 1849, for the purposes of emigration. Embodied in a report: to which are appended letters and verbal communications...and the recently adopted constitution of Texas... 288p. *12°*. *London & Birmingham*, 1849.

36200 SMITH, JOSHUA T. Government by commissions illegal and pernicious. The nature and effects of all commissions of inquiry and other Crown-appointed commissions. The constitutional principles of taxation; and the rights, duties, and importance of local government. 380p. *8°*. 1849.

36201 [**STAPLETON**, M. T., *Baron Beaumont*.] Austria and central Italy. 56p. *8°*. 1849.

36202 —— Second edition. 56p. *8°*. 1849.

36203 The **STATE** of the nation considered with reference to the condition of the working-classes. 108p. *8°*. 1849. *With a 14-page manuscript 'appendix (a)', dated: 16 May, 1849*.

36204 [**STONEHOUSE**, JAMES.] The stranger in Liverpool; or, an historical and descriptive view of the town of Liverpool and its environs. 282p. *12°*. *Liverpool*, [1849] *Formerly published, with the title:* Pictorial Liverpool, *in 1844 (q.v.). A different work from that published anonymously earlier in the century, for an edition of which see* 1823.

36205 TVETHE, M. B. Norges statistik. 393p. *8°. Christiania,* 1848[1849]

36206 UHDE, E. W. Die Grundzüge der National-Oekonomik oder socialen Physiologie nach ethischer Anschauung, und mit Bezug auf die Landwirtschaft und ihre Geschichte...Erste Abtheilung: Propädeutik. 199p. *8°. Berlin,* 1849.

36207 VISINET, . Aperçus économiques à propos de l'exposition des produits de l'industrie en 1844; et des doctrines d'organisation du travail de Louis Blanc, en 1847. [With 'Sur le premier volume de L'histoire de la Révolution française de M. Louis Blanc'.] 123p. *8°. Paris & Rouen,* 1849.

36208 WALRAS, A. Théorie de la richesse sociale, ou résumé des principes fondamentaux de l'économie politique. 103p. *12°. Paris,* 1849.

36209 WAYS and means for Ireland. 47p. *8°.* 1849.

36210 WHELLAN, William, **& COMPANY.** History, gazetteer, and directory of Northamptonshire; comprising a general survey of the county, and a history of the diocese of Peterborough: with separate historical, statistical, and topographical descriptions of all the towns, parishes... 962p. *8°. London & Peterborough,* 1849.

36211 WILLIAMS, A. Facts for philosophers. 39, 30, 123, 16, 43, 16, 16p. *8°.* 1849. *A collection of the author's separately-published works reissued with a general title-page. Presented by him to J. M. Knott. Contents: The law or the League? Which?, 1843; Great facts concerning free trade and free trade essays, 1844; Facts upon facts (chiefly historical) against the League, 1845; Titan's letter to Milo, 1846; Curious light on strange anomalies, 1847; The crisis and the crash, 1847; Antagonistic anomalies, 1847.*

36212 WOOD, Charles, *Viscount Halifax.* Speech of the Chancellor of the Exchequer, on Mr. D'Israeli's motion, July 2, 1849, on the state of the nation. 76p. *8°.* 1849.

AGRICULTURE

36213 BACON, Richard N. The history of the agriculture of Norfolk, which obtained the prize of the Royal Agricultural Society...The second edition. 412p. *8°.* 1849. *For another edition, see* 1844.

36214 BOYDELL, James. A treatise on landed property, in its geological, agricultural, chemical, mechanical and political relations. 236p. *8°.* 1849.

36215 CAIRD, Sir J. High farming, under liberal covenants, the best substitute for protection. 32p. *8°. Edinburgh & London,* 1849.

36216 —— Second edition. 32p. *8°. Edinburgh & London,* 1849.

36217 —— Fifth edition. 33p. *8°. Edinburgh & London,* 1849. *See also* 1850.

36218 Mr. **CAIRD'S** pamphlet on "High farming, under liberal covenants, the best substitute for protection," considered. By a Perthshire farmer. 20p. *8°. Stirling,* 1849.

36219 CALVERT, F. A letter to the Right Hon. Sir Charles Wood, Bart., M.P. upon certain laws affecting agriculture...Second edition, with a postscript. 32p. *8°.* 1849.

36220 DUMESNIL, C. De l'abolition des droits féodaux et seigneuriaux au Canada, et sur le meilleur mode à employer pour accorder une juste indemnité aux seigneurs... 52p. *8°. Montreal,* 1849.

36221 DUPIN, A. M. J. J. Des comices agricoles et en général des institutions d'agriculture. 227p. *12°. Paris,* 1849. *With the book-plate of the Dukes of Portland.*

36222 ENGLAND. *Commissioners for the Herring Fishery.* Instructions for an officer of the fishery, under the Act 6° & 7° Victoriæ, cap. 79. 5p. *8°. [Edinburgh,* 1849] *See also* 1809.

36223 GARNETT, W. J. Prize report on the farming of Lancashire...Reprinted...from the Journal of the Royal Agricultural Society...for the Royal North Lancashire Agricultural Society. 47p. *8°. Preston,* 1849.

36224 HASWELL COLLIERY. Cautions and instructions respecting the proper use of the safety lamps, and rules to be observed in conducting the working of the Haswell and Shotton Collieries. [Signed: John Taylor, viewer. Dated: March, 1849.] *s.sh.fol. Newcastle-upon-Tyne,* [1849]

36225 [HICKEY, W.] Agricultural class book; or, how best to cultivate a small farm and garden: together with hints on domestic economy. 317p. *12°. Dublin: Commissioners of National Education in Ireland, London, &c.,* 1849.

36226 HILLARY, Sir A. W. A letter to the Right Honourable Lord John Russell, First Lord of the Treasury, suggesting a plan for the adjustment of the relation between landlord and tenant in Ireland. 55p. *8°. London & Dublin,* [1849]

36227 HOSKYNS, C. W. A short inquiry into the history of agriculture... 160p. *8°.* 1849.

36228 JOHNSTON, James F. W. Contributions to scientific agriculture. [Reprinted from the Proceedings of the Agricultural Chemistry Association of Scotland.] 231p. *8°. Edinburgh & London,* 1849.

36229 —— Experimental agriculture being the results of past, and suggestions for future experiments in scientific and practical agriculture. 265p. *8°. Edinburgh & London,* 1849.

36230 JONES, Ebenezer. The land monopoly, the suffering and demoralization caused by it; and the justice & expediency of its abolition. 28p. *8°.* 1849.

36231 KINNAIRD, G. W. F., *Baron Kinnaird.* Profitable investment of capital, or 11 years practical experience in farming: a letter from Lord Kinnaird to his tenantry; with lecture by W. White, Esq., and a speech of Mr. Finnie, of Swanston, on the application of chemistry to agriculture. [With 'High farming. Mr. Caird's pamphlet'. Signed: A County Down farmer.] 40p. *8°. Dundee, Edinburgh, &c.,* 1849.

36232 LIBRAIRIE AGRICOLE DE LA MAISON RUSTIQUE. Catalogue de la Librairie Agricole de la Maison Rustique, rue Jacob, no. 26... 16p. *8°. Paris,* 1849.

36233 MAHONY, P. Incumbered Estates Act, (Ireland.) Case and opinion. 13p. *8°. Dublin,* 1849.

36234 *[MEDCALF, W.] A plea for Ireland; or a proposal to form an association for the purchase and improvement of Irish lands, and the re-sale thereof...By a member of the Manchester Corporation. 27p. *8°. Manchester*, 1849. *The FWA copy that belonged to William Pare.*

36235 MONRO, DAVID. "Landlords' rents" and "tenants' profits;" or corn-farming in Scotland. 31p. *8°. Edinburgh & London*, 1849.

36236 NEALE, E. V. Thoughts on the registration of the title to land: its advantages and the means of effecting it. With observations upon the Bill to facilitate the transfer of real property brought in by Mr. Henry Drummond and Mr. Wood. 72p. *8°.* 1849.

For the **NEW ENGLAND FARMER,** 1849–62, *see* vol. III, *Periodicals list.*

36237 RAYNBIRD, W. and H. On the agriculture of Suffolk...Including the report to which the prize was awarded by the Royal Agricultural Society of England. 324p. *8°. London, Bury St. Edmund's, &c.,* 1849.

36238 RITCHIE, R. The farm engineer: a treatise on barn machinery, particularly on the application of steam and other motive powers to the thrashing machine...and the extended application of steam as a motive power at farms... 272p. *8°. Glasgow, Edinburgh, &c.,* 1849.

36239 ROSS, T. Lord Kinnaird's letter to his tenantry, on "Profitable investment of capital, or eleven years practical experience in farming," answered by Thomas Ross, farmer, Wardheads. 20p. *8°. Perth, Coupar-Angus, &c.,* 1849.

36240 —— [Another edition.] Revised by Lord Kinnaird. 24p. *8°. Perth, Coupar-Angus, &c.,* 1849.

36241 —— Second answer to Lord Kinnaird. 31p. *8°. Perth, Coupar-Angus, &c.,* 1849.

36242 SCORESBY, W. The northern whale-fishery. [An abridgment of vol. 2 of *An account of the Arctic regions.*] 192p. *16°.* [1849] *For the original work, see* 1820 (GENERAL).

36243 SHELLEY, SIR J. V., *Bart.* A plea for truth, addressed to the tenant farmers of Hertfordshire and of the United Kingdom: exposing the mis-statement of facts advanced by Mr. C. H. Lattimore, in his pamphlet entitled "A plea for tenant right,"...With a few observations on the best mode of carrying out tenant right. 20p. *8°. London, Lewes, &c.,* [1849]

36244 [SMITH, SAMUEL, *vicar.*] A word in season; or, how the corn-grower may yet grow rich, and his labourer happy. Addressed to the stout British farmer. 16p. *8°.* 1849.

36245 THOMSON, JAMES, *of Aberdeen?* The value and importance of the Scottish fisheries, comprehending fully every circumstance connected with their present position. 214p. *12°. London & Aberdeen,* 1849.

36246 [VIZETELLY, H.] Four months among the gold-finders in Alta California: being the diary of an expedition from San Francisco to the gold districts. By J. Tyrwhitt Brooks, M.D. 207p. *12°.* 1849.

36247 WASON, R. Letter to the Right Honourable Lord John Russell, M.P., suggesting a plan for the reclamation of waste lands in Ireland, securing the government from any loss. 20p. *8°. Ayr,* 1849.

CORN LAWS

36248 CROSBY, G. Crosby's Parliamentary record, containing debates in the Lords and Commons on the corn laws, in the memorable session of 1846. Vol. 2. 555p. *12°.* 1849. *For other editions, see* 1847.

POPULATION

36249 HICKSON, WILLIAM E. Malthus. An essay on the principle of population in refutation of the theory of the Rev. T. R. Malthus. [Reprinted from the "Westminster and Foreign Quarterly Review," for October, 1849. Revised and enlarged by the author.] 77p. *8°.* [1849] *Presentation copy from the author to Sir Rowland Hill.*

TRADES & MANUFACTURES

36250 CHIMNEY sweeping by machinery. 14p. *8°. Derby,* [1849] *Publicizing L. W. Wright's patent Vulcan sweeper.*

36251 DOBSON, E. A rudimentary treatise on masonry and stone-cutting; in which the principles of masonic projection and their application to the construction of curved wing walls, domes, oblique bridges, and Roman and Gothic vaulting are concisely explained... 118p. *12°.* 1849.

36252 —— Rudiments of the art of building... 174p. *12°.* 1849.

36253 Les **ENTREPRENEURS** de batimens du Département de la Seine, à Monsieur le Ministre des Travaux Publics. [On the resumption of building projects in Paris in 1849. Signed: Veyret...Delore...] 11p. *8°.* [*Paris,*] 1849.

36254 ESPINASSE, F. Lancashire industrialism. James Brindley and his Duke of Bridgewater, Richard Arkwright. A lecture...(Reprinted from the Roscoe Magazine for July.) 8p. *8°. Manchester,* 1849.

36255 FAIRBAIRN, T. Britannia and Conway tubular bridges. Truths and tubes on self-supporting principles; a few words in reply to the author of 'Highways and dry-ways.' 62p. *12°. London & Manchester, 1849.*

36256 GIFFORD, G. An address on the patent laws, delivered on invitation of the American Institute, in Castle Garden, at its twenty-second annual fair. 23p. *8°. New York, 1849.*

36257 *GUEUVIN BOUCHON ET CIE. Fabrique de meules à moulins de Gueuvin Bouchon et Cie à Laferté-sous-Jouarre. (Seine et Marne.) [An advertisement, the text engraved in French, German and English in parallel columns.] [2]p. *4°. Paris, [1849] The copy that belonged to Augustus De Morgan.*

For the **JOURNAL OF DESIGN AND MANUFACTURES,** 1849–51, *see* vol. III, *Periodicals list.*

36258 KENNEDY, JOHN (1769–1855). Miscellaneous papers on subjects connected with the manufactures of Lancashire...Reprinted from the Memoirs of the Literary and Philosophical Society of Manchester. For private distribution only. [With 'Brief notice of my early recollections'.] 83, 42p. *8°. Manchester, 1849.*

36259 MARTIN, WILLIAM (1772–1851). To the Queen, Lords, and Commons. The philosopher's charge against coal-viewers, for neglecting the means of saving the poor pitmen's lives from 1816 to 1849 [by not using his safety lamp]. 2p. *8°. Newcastle, [1849]*

36260 ORMEROD, RICHARD, **& SON.** A new list of wheel and other patterns, belong to Richard Ormerod & Son, Engineers, Brass and Iron Founders, Coppersmiths, and Millwrights, St. George's Foundry, Manchester... 127p. *8°. Manchester, 1849.*

36261 SOCIÉTÉ TYPOGRAPHIQUE DE PARIS. Tarif des prix de main-d'œuvre discuté et adopté par les délégués patrons et ouvriers le 15 septembre, 1843. Règlement de la Société, suivi d'un itinéraire typographique. 32p. *8°. Paris, 1849.*

COMMERCE

36262 ALLEN, JOSEPH (1810?–1864). The navigation laws of Great Britain, historically and practically considered, with reference to commerce and national defence. 344p. *8°. 1849.*

36263 BENARD, T. N. Lettre à Monsieur le Ministre de l'Agriculture et du Commerce sur le nouvelle acte de navigation anglais et les traités de réciprocité. 27p. *8°. Paris, 1849. The copy that belonged to Victor Considérant.*

36264 BROUGHAM, H. P., *Baron Brougham and Vaux.* Speech of the Rt. Hon. Lord Brougham in the House of Lords, on Monday, May 7, 1849, on the navigation laws. 54p. *8°. 1849.*

36265 C., F. Free-trade a bunya's owl. [Signed: F.C.] To which is added, a literal version of the original Hindee satire to Meerza Rufee-oos-Souda. 24p. *8°. 1849.*

36266 CAMPBELL, WILLIAM F., *Baron Stratheden and Campbell.* Will Mr. Labouchere's navigation measure pass the House of Lords? In a letter to a protectionist peer. 28p. *8°. London & Cambridge, 1849.*

36267 COIGNET, F. Réforme du crédit et du commerce. Appel à tous les producteurs, manufacturiers et agricoles. 236p. *12°. Paris, [1849] The copy that belonged to Victor Considérant.*

36268 DIX, J. A. Speech of Hon. John A. Dix, of New York, in favor of reciprocal trade with Canada: delivered in the Senate of the United States, January 23, 1849. 14p. *8°. Washington, 1849.*

36269 GARDINER, RALPH. England's grievance discovered in relation to the coal-trade...A new edition, with explanatory notes, and some account of the author. 237p. *8°. North Shields, 1849. For other editions, see 1655.*

36270 LAW, E., *Earl of Ellenborough.* Speech of the Right Hon. the Earl of Ellenborough, in the House of Lords, on the navigation laws, May, 1849. 18p. *8°. 1849.*

36271 *LEVI, L. Chambers and tribunals of commerce, and proposed General Chamber of Commerce in Liverpool... 39p. *8°. London, Liverpool, &c., 1849. The FWA copy that belonged to William Pare.*

36272 MITCHELL, JOHN M. On British commercial legislation, in reference to the tariff or import duties, and the injustice of interfering with the navigation laws. Being the substance of a speech at a meeting of the Chamber of Commerce and Manufactures, Edinburgh. 58p. *8°. Edinburgh & London, 1849.*

36273 NEWDEGATE, C. N. A letter to the Right Hon. H. Labouchere, M.P....on the balance of trade, ascertained from the market value of all articles imported during the last four years. [With 'Official and market value (in bond) of all foreign and colonial articles... imported into and exported from the United Kingdom, in the year 1845[–1848]'.] 28, 51p. *8°. 1849. Presentation copy from the author to the Dowager Countess of Hardwicke. For another edition, see no. 36274, below.*

36274 —— Two letters to the Right Hon. H. Labouchere, M.P. &c.&c....on the balance of trade. Ascertained from the market value of all articles imported, as compared with the market value of all articles exported during the last four years. xliii, xxvii, 52p. *8°. 1849.*

36275 OASTLER, R. Free trade "not proven," in seven letters to the people of England. With an introductory address to Richard Cobden, Esq. M.P. 40p. *8°. London, Manchester, &c., 1849.*

36276 REVANS, J. England's navigation laws no protection to British shipping. 28p. *8°. 1849.*

36277 STANHOPE, PHILIP H., *4th Earl Stanhope.* Substance of the speech of Earl Stanhope, in the House of Lords on June 14th, 1849. 14p. *8°. Sevenoaks, [1849] With an inscription recording the presentation of the work by the author to the West London Anti-Enclosure and Social Improvement Society.*

COLONIES

36278 ADDERLEY, C. B., *Baron Norton.* The Australian Colonies Government Bill discussed. 32p. *8⁰.* [*London*, 1849]

36279 BONNYCASTLE, SIR R. H. Canada and the Canadians...New edition. 2 vols. *12⁰.* 1849.

36280 BOURNE, JOHN, *C.E.* Indian river navigation. A report addressed to the committee of gentlemen formed for the establishment of improved steam navigation upon the rivers of India...Illustrating the practicability of opening up some thousands of miles of river navigation in India... 67p. *8⁰.* 1849.

36281 CEYLON and Lord Torrington's administration. ⟨From the Calcutta Review, no. 23.⟩ 30p. *8⁰. n.p.* [1849]

36282 COMPANY OF SCOTLAND TRADING TO AFRICA AND THE INDIES. The Darien papers: being a selection of original letters and official documents relating to the establishment of a colony at Darien by the Company of Scotland trading to Africa and the Indies, 1695–1700. [Edited by J. H. Burton.] (*Bannatyne Club*, 90.) xxxii, 417p. *4⁰. Edinburgh*, 1849.

36283 COOKESLEY, W. G. Colonization. A lecture delivered at the Windsor and Eton Literary, Scientific and Mechanics' Institution...December the 19th, 1849. 25p. *8⁰. Windsor & London*, [1849]

36284 The new **COUNTRY** to the northward. ⟨From the Western Australia Inquirer, September 26, [October 3–10] 1849.⟩ 15p. *8⁰. n.p.* [1849]

36285 EAST INDIA COMPANY. Report of proceedings at a Special General Court of Proprietors...held at the East India House...25th April, 1849. Major General Sir Archibald Galloway...in the chair... 144p. *8⁰.* [*London*, 1849]

36286 GESNER, A. The industrial resources of Nova Scotia. Comprising the physical geography, topography, geology, agriculture...commerce...and resources, of the province. [With two appendixes.] 341, 15, 4p. *8⁰. Halifax, N.S.*, 1849.

36287 [GOODWYN, A. G.] Emigration for the million; being the digest of a plan for more equally locating the population of Great Britain and Ireland throughout the British Empire. By Gershom. 35p. *8⁰. London, Liverpool, &c.*, 1849.

36288 HAWES, SIR B. Speech of Benjamin Hawes, Esq., (M.P. for Kinsale,) on colonial administration. In the House of Commons...April 16, 1849. Extracted from Hansard's Parliamentary Debates. 27p. *12⁰.* 1849.

36289 HINCKS, SIR F. Canada: its financial position and resources. 32p. *8⁰.* 1849.

36290 HURSTHOUSE, C. F. An account of the settlement of New Plymouth, in New Zealand, from personal observation, during a residence there of five years... 160p. *8⁰.* 1849.

36291 INNES, JOHN (*fl.* 1830–1849). Claims of the British West India planters. [A letter to Lord John Russell.] 12p. *8⁰.* [1849]

36292 KENNEDY, JOHN P. A railway caution!! or exposition of changes required in the law and practice of

the British Empire to enable the poorer districts to provide for themselves the benefits of railway intercourse; and to forewarn the Government and the capitalists of British India...that they may avoid those fatal errors which have occurred elsewhere...Illustrated in reports addressed to the proprietors and directors of the Waterford and Limerick Railway Company. 66p. *8⁰. Calcutta*, 1849.

36293 LANG, JOHN D. Remarks on the proposed constitution for the Australian colonies, in a letter to Benjamin Hawes, Esq., M.P. 16p. *8⁰.* 1849. *Presentation copy from the author to Henry James Baillie.*

36294 A LETTER to the Right Honorable Sir John Cam Hobhouse, Bart. M.P. President of the Board of Control, on the existing Indian railway companies, and particularly the Great Indian Peninsula Railway Company; showing that their projects would be useless to the country, expensive to the Government, and unprofitable to the shareholders. By a friend to Indian railways. 15p. *8⁰.* 1849.

36295 MACKAY, A. The crisis in Canada; or, vindication of Lord Elgin and his Cabinet as to the course pursued by them in reference to the Rebellion Losses Bill. 67p. *8⁰.* 1849.

36296 MARTIN, ROBERT M. The Hudson's Bay Territories and Vancouver's Island, with an exposition of the chartered rights, conduct, and policy of the Honble Hudson's Bay Corporation. 175p. *8⁰.* 1849.

36297 MOLESWORTH, SIR W., *Bart.* Speech of Sir William Molesworth, Bart. M.P. in the House of Commons...25th June, 1849, for a Royal Commission to inquire into the administration of the colonies. 32p. *8⁰.* [1849]

36298 [MONTGOMERIE, H. E. and **MORRIS**, A. ?] The question answered: "Did the ministry intend to pay rebels?" In a letter to His Excellency the Right Honourable the Earl of Elgin and Kincardine, K.T., Governor General of British North America. By a Canadian loyalist. [A discussion of the Rebellion Losses Bill, for the indemnification of those who suffered during the troubles of 1837 and 1838.] 23p. *8⁰. Montreal, Quebec, &c.*, 1849.

36299 ROEBUCK, JOHN A. The colonies of England: a plan for the government of some portion of our colonial possessions. 248p. *8⁰.* 1849.

36300 SMITH, SIDNEY. The settler's new home: or the emigrant's location, being a guide to emigrants in the selection of a settlement, and the preliminary details of the voyage...British America, – Canada...the United States ... 106p. *12⁰.* 1849.

36301 SMYTH, R. C. A letter from Major Robert Carmichael-Smyth to his friend the author of "The clockmaker," containing thoughts on the subject of a British colonial railway communication between the Atlantic and the Pacific, from the magnificent harbour of Halifax, in Nova Scotia...to the mouth of Frazer's River, in New Caledonia... 68p. *8⁰.* 1849.

**36302 —— ** The employment of the people and the capital of Great Britain in her own colonies, at the same time assisting emigration, colonization and penal arrangements, by undertaking the construction of a great national railway between the Atlantic and the Pacific, from Halifax harbour, Nova Scotia, to Frazer's River, New Caledonia. 75p. *8°*. 1849. *The Rastrick copy.*

36303 TORRENS, R. Systematic colonisation. Ireland saved, without cost to the Imperial treasury. Second edition. To which is prefixed an introductory letter to Earl Grey, on the results of the emigration branch of the South Australian experiment. 59p. *8°*. 1849. *For another edition, entitled* Self-supporting colonization, *see 1847.*

36304 WAKEFIELD, EDWARD G. A view of the art of colonization, with present reference to the British empire; in letters between a statesman and a colonist... 513p. *8°*. 1849.

36305 WAKEFIELD, F. Colonial surveying with a view to the disposal of waste land: in a report to the New-Zealand Company. 89p. *8°*. 1849.

36306 WEST INDIA PLANTERS AND MERCHANTS. ⟨Printed for the West India Body.⟩ Report of the Acting Committee to the Standing Committee... at their half-yearly meeting, held at the West India Committee Rooms, No. 12, Old Jewry Chambers, on 28th March, 1849. 27p. *8°*. 1849. *See also 1846, 1847, 1848.*

FINANCE

36307 AKERMAN, J. Y. Tradesmen's tokens, current in London and its vicinity between the years 1648 and 1672. Described from the originals in the British Museum and in several private collections. 257p. *8°*. 1849.

36308 AVRIL, V. Histoire philosophique du crédit... Tome premier. 332p. *8°*. *Paris,* 1849.

36309 BAILDON, H. C., *comp.* Committee of Enquiry into the validity of the monetary principle advocated in Gray's Lectures on the nature and use of money. (*Edinburgh Monetary Reform Pamphlet,* 1.) 28p. *8°*. *Edinburgh & London,* 1849. *The work consists of 36 reviews of Gray's book, preceded by a short note by him. For another edition, see 1848.*

36310 BAILLE, A. De l'égalité dans l'impôt, question vinicole, travailleurs, contributions indirectes, octrois, douanes. 144p. *12°*. *Paris,* 1849.

36311 [*Endorsed:*] **BANKRUPT LAW CONSOLIDATION BILL.** Statement in support of the Bill; showing the necessity and importance of a Chief Commissioner; the reasons for the proposed increase in certain of the salaries; the fees abolished; the present charge... and the eventual annual saving to be effected by the Bill. May 1849. (126a.) 6p. *fol.* [1849] *See note to no.* 32762.

36312 [*Endorsed:*] **BANKRUPT LAW CONSOLIDATION BILL.** Statement showing the object of the Bill. June 1849. (126b.) 4p. *fol.* [1849] *See note to no.* 32762.

36313 BONNEVILLE, A. Encyclopédie monétaire; ou, nouveau traité des monnaies d'or et d'argent en circulation chez les divers peuples du monde. Avec un examen complet du tire, du poids, de l'origine et de la valeur intrinsèque des pièces... 220p. *fol. Paris,* 1849. *For a prospectus of this work, see no.* 36341.

36314 *BRENAN, JUSTIN. The National Debt, and public funds, simplified for general comprehension... Second edition, very considerably augmented. 35p. *12°*. 1849. *The copy that belonged to Augustus De Morgan.*

36315 BRITANNICUS, *pseud.* Reduction of taxation. No. 1[–8], of a series of letters... addressed to the landowners and farmers; the manufacturers and tradesmen, the merchants and shipowners; and to all other tax-payers of the United Kingdom – comprising the development of a practicable and equitable means of paying off the National Debt... 132p. *8°*. [1849]

36316 BRITISH LINEN COMPANY. Charter erecting, and warrant of a charter confirming new privileges to the British Linen Company. [With 'Supplementary charter to the British Linen Company, 19th March, 1849'.] 47, 20p. *8°*. *Edinburgh,* 1849. *There is also a proof copy of the supplementary charter in the Goldsmiths' Library. For other editions of the charter, see 1746 (COMMERCE).*

36317 —— Resolutions in reference to increasing the capital stock of the British Linen Company, unanimously agreed to by the general Quarterly Court of Proprietors, held on the 17th September last... and unanimously confirmed... on the 17th December current... 2p. *fol. n.p.* [1849]

36318 *BROWN, S. A few thoughts on commission, divisions of profit, selection of lives, the mortality in India, and other subjects relating to life assurance, contained in a series of letters recently published in the Post Magazine, under the signature of "Crito." 131p. *8°*. 1849. *Presentation copy from the author to Augustus De Morgan.*

36319 BUCHANAN, I. Alteration of the money law. A system desiderated which will retain all the present security which we have for the paper circulation, and at same time provide for the price of gold rising and falling, like other commodities... [Two letters, dated 5th January, 1849, one to the *Witness* and one to the *Weekly Register*.] *s.sh.fol. n.p.* [1849] [*Br.* 619(1)]

36320 —— Legislation on gold. [A letter, dated 24th Feb. 1849, to the *Weekly Register*, on 'The question of money – how it will be affected by large imports of gold from California'.] *s.sh.fol. n.p.* [1849] [*Br.* 619(2)]

36321 BUELOW-CUMMEROW, E. G. G. VON. Beleuchtung des preussischen Staats-Haushaltes und der in diesem vorzunehmenden wichtigen Reformen. 46p. *8°*. *Berlin,* 1849.

36322 *BURT, ALFRED. Life assurance. An historical and statistical account of the population, the law of mortality, and the different systems of life assurance; including the validity and non-validity of life policies; with observations on friendly societies and savings banks... 211p. *8°*. [1849] *The copy that belonged to Augustus De Morgan.*

36323 [**C., S.**] No. 5. The commerce of Malta. A letter to the Right Honorable Earl Grey, Secretary of State for the Colonies, &c.&c.&c. By a British merchant. [On the Maltese currency.] 22p. *8°*. [*London,* 1849]

36324 To CAPITALISTS, miners and others. Important sale of lead mine shares in the Bage, George, Ratchwood, Ran Tor, Wall Close, Philip's, Hopton Rake, and Middle Peak Mines, situate in the Wapentake of

Wirksworth, in the County of Derby. [An announcement of a sale on August 16th 1849.] [4]p. *8°. n.p.* [1849]

36325 COBBOLD, R. K. An address to the members of the Society for Equitable Assurances, on Lives and Survivorships, and especially to such as have become members since the year 1816. 25p. *8°.* [1849]

36326 COMMITTEE OF DEPUTIES FROM SEVERAL METROPOLITAN...PARISHES NOMINATED TO OBTAIN AN EQUALIZATION OF THE LAND TAX. Equalization of the land tax. A statement respecting the present unequal, oppressive and as it is believed illegal assessment of the land tax, in the Holborn division of the county of Middlesex; with a report of the proceedings before the Commissioners of Land Tax for that division in an appeal case... 15p. *8°.* 1849.

36327 COMMITTEE OF MERCHANTS AND TRADERS...APPOINTED TO PROMOTE THE IMPROVEMENT OF THE LAW RELATING TO DEBTOR AND CREDITOR. Bankrupt Law Consolidation Bill. Remarks thereon by the London Committee. [4]p. *fol.* [1849] *See note to no.* 32762.

36328 —— Fifth report of the Committee...[May 1, 1849.] 5p. *fol.* [1849] *See note to no.* 32762.

36329 —— Bankruptcy Law Amendment Act Committee. At a meeting of the Committee and subscribers... the following report was read...Sixth report of the Committee...August 3, 1849. [4]p. *fol.* [1849] *See note to no.* 32762.

36330 DUFRESSE DE CHASSAIGNE, J. E. Nécessité pour le gouvernement d'établir une banque nationale immobilière... 32p. *8°. Angoulême,* 1849.

36331 DUMON, P. S. Histoire financière. De l'équilibre des budgets sous la monarchie de 1830. 70p. *12°. Paris,* 1849.

36332 DUNCAN, JONATHAN. The principles of money demonstrated, and bullionist fallacies refuted. 52p. *8°.* 1849.

36333 EDINBURGH FINANCIAL REFORM ASSOCIATION. Tracts of the Edinburgh Financial Reform Association. [Signed: W.C., i.e. W. Chambers.] Nos. 1–4. *8°. Edinburgh,* 1849.

36334 EDWARDS, EDWARD, *compositor.* The duties on paper, advertisements, and newspapers. Speech of Mr. Edward Edwards, (compositor,) delivered at a meeting of printers, held at the London Mechanics' Institution, May 22, 1849. L. J. Hansard, Esq. in the chair. 8p. *8°.* [1849] *The copy given by Joseph Hume to 'Mr Macfarlane', with an inscription in Hume's hand.*

36335 EVANS, D. M. The commercial crisis, 1847–1848; being facts and figures illustrative of the events of that important period, considered in relation to the three epochs of the railway mania, the food and money panic, and the French Revolution. To which is added; an appendix, containing an alphabetical list of the English and foreign mercantile failures, with the balance sheets ...Second edition, revised and enlarged. 155, cip. *8°.* 1849. *For another edition, see* 1848, *and for a second, separately published appendix, see* 1850.

36336 FANE, R. G. C. [*Endorsed:*] ⟨For consideration.⟩ Bankruptcy. Proposed clauses to enable debtors and creditors to make private settlements, under the sanction and controul of the Court of Bankruptcy. 7p. *fol. n.p.* [1849 ?] *See note to no.* 32762.

36337 FAUCHER, L. Histoire financière. De l'impôt sur le revenu. 36p. *8°. Paris,* 1849.

36338 FRANCE. *Assemblée Nationale.* No. 947... Proposition ayant pour but de rétablir les finances, et de raviver par la même mesure l'agriculture, le commerce et l'industrie, presentée le 14 mars 1849, par le Citoyen Pierre Leroux... 42p. *8°.* [*Paris,* 1849]

36339 FRANCIS, J. Chronicles and characters of the Stock Exchange. 386p. *8°.* 1849.

36340 GILBART, J. W. A practical treatise on banking...Fifth edition... 2 vols. *8°.* 1849. *For other editions, see* 1827.

36341 GROSSET, . Extrait du Moniteur Universel du 9 décembre 1849. Encyclopédie monétaire ou nouveau traité des monnaies d'or et d'argent en circulation sur la surface du globe...par Alphonse Bonneville...un fort volume grand...Paris, 1849. [A prospectus, signed: Grosset, commissaire du gouvernement près la Monnaie de Strasbourg.] 3p. *4°. Paris,* [1849] *For the work, see no.* 36313.

36342 HEADLAM, T. E. A speech on limited liability in joint stock banks delivered by Thomas Emerson Headlam, Esq., M.P., in the House of Commons, May 8, 1849; together with a proposed Act of Parliament on the subject. 28p. *8°.* 1849.

36343 HEATHFIELD, R. Means of extensive relief from the pressure of taxation, on the basis of a charge of five per cent. on all property in the United Kingdom, real and personal...With some prefatory notes upon the early history of taxation by G. P. R. James, Esq. 31p. *8°.* 1849.

36344 HERBERT, H. A. Savings' banks. Speech delivered in the House of Commons, on...April[March] 29, 1849, on moving an amendment to Mr. Reynolds' motion for "a Committee to inquire into the circumstances connected with the failure of Cuffe Street Savings' Bank, Dublin," that instructions be given to the Committee to extend their inquiries to the cases of the Tralee and Killarney Savings' Banks, and that of Auchterarder, in Scotland. 48p. *8°.* 1849.

36345 HUEBNER, O. L. Oesterreichs Finanzlage und seine Hilfsquellen... 228p. *8°. Wien,* 1849.

36346 KELLOGG, E. Labor and other capital: the rights of each secured and the wrongs of both eradicated. Or, an exposition of the cause why few are wealthy and many poor, and a system, which, without infringing the rights of property, will give to labor its just reward. 298p. *8°. New York,* 1849.

36347 KIMPTON, W. Financial reform, currency, &c. A letter to C. H. Lattimore, Esq. 16p. *8°. London & Hertford,* 1849.

36348 LINDSAY, JOHN. Notices of remarkable medieval coins, mostly unpublished... 10p. *4°. Cork,* 1849.

36349 LIVERPOOL CURRENCY REFORM ASSOCIATION. Suggestions for a new system of currency, by which monetary panics will be rendered impossible: submitted to the consideration of the trading community of Liverpool by a committee of gentlemen, who believe that the permanent prosperity of the country depends upon a proper settlement of the money question. 15p. *8°. Liverpool,* 1849.

36350 LIVERPOOL FINANCIAL REFORM ASSOCIATION. Liverpool financial reform tracts. 11 parts. 8°. [*London*, 1849] *A reissue of nos. 1–12 (11–12 being a single number) of* Financial reform tracts, *originally published from 1848 (q.v.).*

36351 M., W. Equalization of taxation. 12p. *12°. n.p.* [1849]

36352 MACGREGOR, JOHN (1797–1857). Financial reform: a letter to the citizens of Glasgow...With an introduction and supplementary notes. 54p. *8°.* 1849.

36353 [MACLEAN, A. W.] Observations on the fundamental principles of monetery [*sic*] circulation, and the necessity for a national bank of issue. 42p. *8°. Glasgow, Edinburgh, &c.,* 1849. *See also* 1850.

36354 MACLEOD, J. M. Remarks on some popular objections to the present income tax. 32p. *8°.* 1849.

36355 MALET, W. W. The Tithe Redemption Trust. A letter to the Lord Lyttelton. [With an appendix.] 28p. *8°.* 1849. *Presentation copy from the author to the Rev. C. B. Pearson.*

36356 MILNER, T. H. Some remarks on the Bank of England; its influence on credit; and the principles upon which the Bank should regulate its rate of interest. 62p. *8°.* 1849.

36357 MOLROGUIER, P. Histoire critique de l'impôt des boissons dans ses rapports avec les intérèts généraux et avec l'intérèt municipal. Suite du Régime municipal de la France, et introduction aux finances municipales. 172p. *8°. Paris,* 1849.

36358 NAPIER, SIR W. F. P. Six letters in vindication of the British Army, exposing the calumnies of the Liverpool Financial Reform Association. [On supplies, payments, etc.] 29p. *8°.* 1849.

36359 —— Second edition. 29p. *8°.* 1849. *Presentation copy from the author to Lord Goderich, afterwards Earl De Grey and Ripon.*

36360 NEWMAN, F. W. On the constitutional and moral right or wrong of our National Debt. 36p. *8°.* 1849.

36361 PHIPPS, HON. E. A few words on the three amateur budgets of Cobden, Macgregor, and Wason. 24p. *8°.* 1849.

36362 PINA, E. DE. Ce que les producteurs vinicoles ont droit d'attendre de l'Assemblée Nationale. 13p. *8°. Paris & Montpellier,* 1849.

36363 Practical financial **REFORM.** 30p. *8°.* 1849.

36364 RICKARDS, H. D. The National Debt; an account of its origin and progress, with an explanation of its nature, and the influence which it exerts upon the physical and moral condition of the community. 31p. *8°.* [1849] *Presentation copy from the author to Cornelius Walford.*

36365 RIVET, J. C. Impôt sur les vins. Note presentée...sur les moyens à employer pour asseoir d'une manière équitable...les différents droits...sur les vins. 2p. *s.sh.8°. [Paris,* 1849 ?]

36366 ROBERTSON, ALEXANDER, *W.S.* (Sixth thousand,) Defects in the practice of life assurance, and suggestions for their remedy, with observations on the uses and advantages of life assurance, and the constitution of offices. Fourth edition. 32p. *8°. London, Edinburgh, &c.,* [1849] *For another edition, see* 1848.

36367 ROYAL BRITISH BANK. The Royal British Bank, incorporated by charter, 17th September, 1849...[A prospectus.] 4p. *8°. n.p.* [1849]

36368 —— The Royal British Bank, incorporated by Royal charter, 17th September, 1849...[With 'Opinions of the press on the proposed new Bank'.] 39p. *8°. n.p.* [1849]

36369 ST. LUKE'S CHURCH, *Chelsea.* Statement shewing the sums received and paid by the trustees, under the Act for building the new church of St. Luke, Chelsea, and for other purposes relating thereto [59 Geo. III., local and personal, c.xxxv.]; and of another Act for amending the same [6 Geo. IV., local and personal, c.lvi.]: from the 31st January 1848, to the 31st January, 1849. [Signed: S. Cornell, clerk.] *s.sh.fol. Chelsea,* [1849]

36370 SAINT-CLAIR DUPORT, . De l'utilité, en France, d'une banque territoriale hypothécaire; discours lu à l'Académie des Sciences, Belles-Lettres, et Arts de Lyon, dans les séances des 16 janvier et 6 février, 1849. 107p. *8°. Lyon,* 1849.

36371 SAVINGS BANK, *Manchester.* On the audit and supervision of accounts in savings banks, with observations on the plan pursued in the Savings Bank at Manchester. Printed from the Manchester Guardian of Dec. 8, 1849 [and published by the Trustees]. 12p. *12°. Manchester,* 1849.

36372 SCOTTISH PROVIDENT INSTITUTION. Laws and regulations of the Scottish Provident Institution, for the assurance of capital sums and annuities on lives and survivorships. Constituted on the principle of mutual assurance without personal liability...Established in 1837. Incorporated by Statute 11th and 12th Vict. chap. 106. 20p. *8°. Edinburgh,* 1849.

36373 —— The Scottish Provident Institution...[An abridged prospectus, dated: January 1849.] [4]p. *8°. Edinburgh,* [1849]

36374 SCRATCHLEY, A. A treatise on benefit building societies containing remarks upon the erroneous tendency of many...and an inquiry into the true causes of their defective operation... 206p. *8°.* 1849.

36375 SMITH, AQUILLA. Catalogue of the tradesmen's tokens current in Ireland between the years 1637 and 1679...From the Proceedings of the Royal Irish Academy, vol. IV. part II. 31p. *8°. Dublin,* 1849.

36376 SOMERVILLE, ALEXANDER. Somerville's financial reform catechism. No. 1. The soldier's kit. 8p. *8°.* [1849]

36377 STANSFELD, H. A remedy for monetary panics and free trade in currency suggested in a brief view of the currency question... 133p. *8°. [Bonn] London,* 1849. *A printed slip with the London imprint has been pasted over the German one.*

36378 STRACHAN, JAMES, *bank manager.* The anatomy and philosophy of banking; or, the true character and value of banks briefly explained to the middle classes of society. 84p. *8°.* 1849.

36379 TATE, WILLIAM (1781 ?–1848). The modern cambist: forming a manual of foreign exchanges, in the different operations of bills of exchange and bullion; with tables of foreign weights and measures...Sixth edition, with extensive alterations and additions [and a 'supplementary appendix']. Edited by his son, William Tate. xvi, 222p. *8°.* 1849. *For other editions, see* 1834.

36380 TAUNTON, E. I challenge all England to confute me! and particularly the sordid idolatrous gold-mongering Peelites. Englishmen! pray read my proofs. 8p. *8°. Birmingham*, [1849]

36381 TAXATION considered: second part. 76p. *8°.* 1849.

36382 [TAYLOR, JAMES (1788–1863).] Printed for private circulation. Instructions, derived from the "Times Paper," for the discovery of a mine of wealth in England far richer than any that has yet been discovered in the golden regions of California. [Dated: April 16, 1849.] 12p. *12°. Bakewell*, 1849.

36383 [——] [Another edition.] (Printed for private circulation.) Instructions, derived from "The Times Newspaper"... 8p. *8°. Liverpool*, [1849]

36384 [——] Printed for private circulation. California surpassed. Instructions, derived from the "Times Paper," for the discovery of a mine of wealth in England ...Third edition, with a preface [dated: June 30, 1849]. 12p. *12°. Bakewell*, 1849.

36385 THIMBLEBY, J. What is money? or, man's birthright "time," the only real wealth; its representative forming the true medium of exchange. 19p. *8°.* [1849] *The copy that belonged to J. M. Ludlow.*

36386 *UNITED GUARANTEE AND LIFE ASSURANCE COMPANY. [Prospectus.] 15p. *8°.* [1849] *The copy that belonged to Augustus De Morgan.*

36387 WASON, R. A budget for the million, in a letter to the inhabitants of the Borough of Ipswich... Second edition. 26p. *8°. Ayr*, 1849.

36388 WESTERN BANK OF SCOTLAND. List of partners of the Western Bank of Scotland. 31p. *8°. n.p.*, 1849.

36389 WILLIAMS, THEOPHILUS. Political equity; or, a fair equalization of the national burdens. Comprised in some intermingled and scattered thoughts, suggesting an anti-destitution policy; a graduated system of taxation on real property and regular incomes... 88p. *8°.* 1849.

36390 WOOD, CHARLES, *Viscount Halifax*. Burthens on land. Speech of the Right Hon. Sir Charles Wood, Bart. Chancellor of the Exchequer, in the House of Commons ...March 14th, 1849, on the motion of Mr. Disraeli, on local taxation. 50p. *8°.* 1849.

36391 X.+Y, *pseud.* Direct taxation. Prize essay; to which has been awarded the premium offered by the National Confederation, for the best essay on the equitable adjustment of national taxation. 60p. *8°. London, Liverpool, &c.*, [1849]

36392 ZOLL-TARIF für Deutschland. Vorge-schlagen vom allgemeinen deutschen Vereine zum Schutze der vaterländischen Arbeit. 119p. *8°. Frankfurt a.M.*, 1849.

TRANSPORT

36393 BOSTON AND PROVIDENCE RAIL ROAD CORPORATION. Report of the directors ...presented at the annual meeting of the stockholders, June 6, 1849. 22p. *8°. Boston*, 1849. *The Rastrick copy. See also* 1832, 1833, 1834.

36394 BREWSTER, P. Sunday trains defended. 18p. *8°. Paisley*, 1849.

36395 [CLARK, JOSIAH L.] General description of the Britannia and Conway tubular bridges on the Chester & Holyhead Railway...By a resident assistant. 34p. *8°.* 1849. *See also* 1850.

36396 CLARKE, HYDE. Contributions to railway statistics, in 1846, 1847 & 1848... ⟨Reprinted from the Civil Engineer and Architect's Journal.⟩ 55p. *8°.* 1849.

36397 The CONSERVATORSHIP of the River Tyne [the plea and defence of the Mayor and Burgesses of Newcastle-upon-Tyne...against the malevolent accusations of Gardiner and his adherents as exhibited by him before Parliament in 1653...now first printed from an original office copy in the Hornby MSS....together with an introduction...]. 108p. *8°. Newcastle-upon-Tyne & London*, 1849. *The preface is signed: M.A.R., i.e. M. A. Richardson, the publisher.*

36398 EASTERN COUNTIES RAILWAY COMPANY. Articles of agreement [for an amalgamation] made this second day of May, one thousand eight hundred and forty-eight, between the Eastern Counties Railway Company...and the Norfolk Railway Company ...[With 'Supplemental agreement made this tenth day of August, one thousand eight hundred and forty-nine...'.] 6p. *fol. n.p.* [1849]

36399 EASTERN UNION RAILWAY COM-PANY. Report of the directors at the annual general meeting...23rd February, 1849. 2p. *fol. n.p.* [1849]

36400 —— Eastern Union Railway. Third half-yearly report of the directors...September 21st, 1849. [6]p. *fol. n.p.* [1849] *See also* 1844, 1845, 1846, 1847, 1848, 1850.

36401 —— Statement of capital and loans to be raised under their Acts of Parliament. [A series of tables, including receipts and disbursements and revenue for the half year ending December 31st 1848.] *s.sh.fol. n.p.* [1849 ?]

36402 ENGLAND. *Laws, etc.* A collection of the Public General Acts for the regulation of railways: including the companies, lands, railway clauses consolidation Acts. 1838–1847. With general index. 251p. *12°. Westminster, Edinburgh, &c.*, 1849.

36403 —— —— Anno nono & decimo Victoriæ Reginæ. Cap. clxxii. An Act for making a railway from Chesterford to Newmarket, with a branch to Cambridge. ⟨16th July 1846.⟩ p.3149–3162. *fol.* 1849.

36404 —— —— Anno duodecimo & decimo tertio Victoriæ Reginæ. Cap. lxxiii. An Act to extend the time for the purchase of lands required for the widening of the London and Blackwall Railway, and to amend the Acts relating to such railway. ⟨28th July 1849.⟩ p.1037–1042. *fol.* 1849.

36405 [FORRESTER, A. H.] How he reigned and how he mizzled. A railway raillery. A. Crowquill delt. [Cartoons on a scandal involving George Hudson, the 'Railway King'.] 8l. *obl.8°.* 1849.

36406 GLYNN, J. A review of the plans which have been proposed for connecting the Atlantic and Pacific Oceans by a navigable canal...With an abstract of the discussion upon the paper. Excerpt minutes of proceedings of the Institution of Civil Engineers... 34p. *8°*. 1849.

36407 GORDON, L. D. B. Railway economy: an exposition of the advantages of locomotion by locomotive carriages instead of the present expensive system of steam tugs. 67p. *8°*. *Edinburgh & London*, 1849. *See note to no.* 34295.

36408 HUNT, JAMES H. L., *comp*. Readings for railways; or, anecdotes and other short stories, reflections, maxims, characteristics, passages of wit, humour, and poetry; etc. Together with points of information on matters of general interest. Collected in the course of his own reading, by Leigh Hunt. 136p. *12°*. [1849]

36409 JACKSON, GEORGE B. W. Description of the Great North Holland Canal, and of the works at Niewediep; with an account of the mode of gaining land from the sea by polders, and of the art of building with fascine work... With an abstract of the discussion upon the paper. Excerpt minutes of proceedings of the Institution of Civil Engineers... 56p. *8°*. 1849.

36410 KING, GEORGE (*fl.* 1847–1849). Uniformity of railway accounts. A few remarks elucidatory and suggestive on the subject of railway economy, also proposal of a method of keeping railway accounts on one uniform plan, and of closing capital accounts in a way that shall not encroach unduly upon present dividends. 84p. *8°*. 1849. *See note to no.* 34295.

36411 KING-NOEL, W., *Earl of Lovelace*. On harbours of refuge... With an abstract of the discussion upon the paper. Excerpt minutes of proceedings of the Institution of Civil Engineers... 52p. *8°*. 1849. *Presentation copy from the author to N. W. Senior.*

36412 LAING, SAMUEL (1812–1897). Railway taxation. 23p. *8°*. *Westminster*, 1849. *See note to no.* 34295.

36413 MARTIN, ROBERT M. Railways – past, present, & prospective. 82p. *8°*. 1849. *See note to no.* 34295.

36414 —— Second edition. ⟨With additions.⟩ 82p. *8°*. 1849. *Presentation copy from the author to Arthur Smith. The Rastrick copy.*

36415 MARTIN, WILLIAM (1772–1851). The philosopher shewing the public an imposition. The Martinian high-level bridge. Containing four river arches and three centres, and not six river arches and five river centres as has been falsely represented... The philosopher's letter to the Queen and Government... [In verse.] *s.sh.fol. Newcastle-upon-Tyne*, [1849]

36416 MOFFAT, A. Scottish railways: their present and future value considered as an investment for capital. 39p. *8°*. *Edinburgh*, 1849.

36417 [NASH, C.] Railways and shareholders; with glances at railway transactions, shareholders' powers, accounts and audits, railway meetings, defective legislation, &c.&c. By an Edinbro' reviewer. 20p. *8°*. 1849.

36418 NORTH WESTERN RAILWAY. Rules and regulations to be observed by officers and men on the North Western Railway. October 1849. 52p. *12°*. *Settle*, [1849]

36419 PARRY, E. The railway companion from Chester to Shrewsbury; containing a description and historical account of the various attractive and interesting objects that present themselves... 138p. *8°*. *Chester*, [1849]

36420 PENFOLD, C. The justice of rating railway companies to the relief of the poor, considered. Addressed to the owners of landed property and the ratepayers of England. 21p. *8°*. 1849.

36421 PÉPIN-LEHALLEUR, E. Observations adressées à l'Assemblée nationale sur le projet de décret relatif à l'expropriation des compagnies des chemins de fer. 15p. *8°*. [*Paris*, 1849]

36422 RAILWAY COMPETITION. A letter to George Carr Glyn, Esq. M.P. Chairman of the London & North Western Railway. 31p. *8°*. 1849. *See note to no.* 34295.

36423 REPORT of the public meeting of railway shareholders, held in the Clarendon Rooms, Liverpool, on... the 16th of April, 1849, to consider the propriety of petitioning Parliament to amend the law in respect to the rating of railways. 21p. *8°*. *Liverpool*, 1849.

36424 SCRIVENOR, H. Government intervention in railway affairs. A letter to the Right Hon. H. Labouchere, M.P. President of the Board of Trade, upon the right, necessity, and duty, of government interference... with especial reference to the establishing a uniform system of railway accounts, and an independent audit... as an effectual remedy for existing evils. 61p. *8°*. 1849.

36425 —— The railways of the United Kingdom statistically considered, in relation to their extent, capital, amalgamations, financial position... concisely arranged from solely authentic documents; together with the railway accounts, rendered upon a uniform plan. [With 'The railways of the United Kingdom, statistically considered. Supplemental part'.] 2 vols. *8°*. 1849–51.

36426 SMILES, S. Railway property: its condition and prospects. 64p. *8°*. [1849] *The Rastrick copy.*

36427 UNITED STATES OF AMERICA. Congress. *House of Representatives*. Official report to the American Congress [of the Committee on Naval Affairs], on the communications between the Atlantic and Pacific. (Reprinted from the "Colonial Magazine".) [A plan for a railway across the Isthmus of Panama.] 16p. *8°*. *London & Liverpool*, [1849]

36428 WEBB, C. L. A letter to the Right Hon. Henry Labouchere, M.P. President of the Board of Trade, etc., etc. on railways, their accounts and dividends, their progress, present position, and future prospects; their effects on trade and commerce, with suggestions for government assistance, and the amendment of the General Railway Acts of 1845. 64p. *8°*. *London & Westminster*, [1849]

36429 WHITE, GEORGE P. Letter to the Right Honourable Lord John Russell on the expediency of promoting railways in Ireland. 40p. *8°*. 1849. *Presentation copy from the author to J. H. Swanton. The Rastrick copy.*

36430 WHITEHEAD, J. Railway and government guarantee. Which is preferable? Facts and arguments to shew that guaranteed railway stock offers a better investment than do government securities... Sixth edition, completely remodelled. 50p. *8°*. 1849. *See note to no.* 34295. *For another edition, see* 1847.

36431 YORK AND NORTH MIDLAND RAILWAY. York and North Midland Railway. Reports of the Committee of Investigation. [Second–fourth report.] 58, 8, 60, xxi, 12, xxvp. *8°*. *York*, 1849.

SOCIAL CONDITIONS

36432 AIKEN, J. Labour and wages, at home and abroad: in a series of newspaper articles. 29p. *8°. Lowell,* 1849.

36433 ALLEN, C. B. Rudimentary treatise. Cottage building: or, hints for improving the dwellings of the labouring classes. 12p. *12°.* 1849–50.

36434 *Entry cancelled.*

36435 B., A. S. The present and the proposed law of marriage in Scotland. 16p. *8°. n.p.* [1849]

36436 BASCOME, E. Prophylaxis; or, the mode of preventing disease, by a due appreciation of the grand elements of vitality: light, air, and water. With observations on intramural burials. 29p. *8°.* [*London,*] 1849.

36437 BEGG, J. Pauperism and the poor laws; or, our sinking population and rapidly increasing public burdens practically considered. 96p. *8°. Edinburgh & London,* 1849.

36438 BEGGS, T. The cholera: the claims of the poor upon the rich. 12p. *12°.* [*London,* 1849 ?]

36439 —— An inquiry into the extent and causes of juvenile depravity... 184p. *8°. London, Dublin, &c.,* 1849.

36440 BIRD, G. Authentic report of the public discussion which took place in the Theatre Royal, Whitehaven, between George Bird...and Philip William Perfitt...on...March 16, 1847. [On temperance.] Third edition. 36p. *12°.* [1849]

36441 BLANQUI, J. A. Petits traités publiés par l'Académie des Sciences morales et politiques [12 & 14]. Des classes ouvrières en France, pendant l'année 1848... 255p. *12°. Paris,* 1849.

36442 BOILEAU, Sir John P., *Bart.* Statistics of mendicancy. [From the Journal of the Statistical Society of London, February, 1849. Read before the Statistical Section of the British Association, at Swansea, 14th August, 1848.] 8p. *8°. n.p.* [1849]

36443 BRITISH ASSOCIATION FOR THE RELIEF OF THE EXTREME DISTRESS IN IRELAND AND SCOTLAND. Report of the... Association...with correspondence of the agents, tables, &c., and a list of subscribers. 191, [45]p. *8°.* 1849. *The copy that belonged to Earl De Grey.*

36444 BROWNE, John C. Friendly societies. A letter to the Rev. C. B. Dalton, M.A., Rector of Lambeth, on the evils of existing friendly societies, to which are added suggestions for the formation of a mutual provident association in this parish. 13p. *8°.* [1849]

36445 BROWNE, Joseph H. and **OGBOURNE,** W. W., *eds.* The new Bankruptcy Act. The Bankrupt Law Consolidation Act, 1849; (12 & 13 Vict., cap. 106;) with a popular explanation of the powers, duties, obligations, and responsibilities of debtors and creditors; the facilities for avoiding bankruptcy, and the provisions for punishing fraud. With a copious index. 123p. *8°.* 1849.

36446 BUTT, I. "The rate in aid." A letter to the Right Hon. the Earl of Roden, K.P. 75p. *8°. Dublin,* 1849.

36447 CARLETON, W. The tithe proctor: a novel. Being a tale of the tithe rebellion in Ireland. 320p. *8°. London & Belfast,* 1849.

36448 CENTRAL BOARD FOR THE RELIEF OF DESTITUTION IN THE HIGHLANDS AND ISLANDS OF SCOTLAND. *Edinburgh Section.* Reports of the Edinburgh Section of the Central Board...for 1848. 90, 100, 120, 67p. *8°. Edinburgh,* [1849] *A reissue of the four separately issued quarterly reports with a general title-page. The two reports for 1850, issued together in 1851, are also in the Goldsmiths' Library. For the 1st–7th reports of the Central Board, see 1847.*

36449 CHACOU, J. B. Feuille d'ordonnance spéciale pour préparer à opérer en commun l'organisation d'un système social instructif... 4p. *fol. Paris,* [1849]

36450 CHADWICK, J. Essay on the use of alcoholic liquors in health and disease. 123p. *12°.* 1849. *Presentation copy from the author to the Rev. W. Roseman. The Turner copy.*

36451 CHURCH EDUCATION SOCIETY FOR IRELAND. Ninth report of the...Society... being for the year 1848. With an appendix, a list of subscribers, and an alphabetical list of schools. 72p. *8°. Dublin,* 1849. *The copy that belonged to Earl De Grey.*

36452 CITY OF LONDON GAS CONSUMERS' GENERAL COMMITTEE. Address of the... Committee. [Signed: Thomas Hall, chairman.] *s.sh.fol. n.p.* [1849]

36453 —— [*Begin.*] Sir, At a meeting of committees of gas consumers of the various wards of the City of London. [Circular letter, dated: Dec. 21, 1849, stating the aims of the Committee. Signed: William Mawby, chairman, Mark Pitt, secretary.] *s.sh.8°. n.p.* [1849]

36454 CITY OF LONDON GAS LIGHT AND COKE COMPANY. [*Begin.*] By direction of the Committee of Management of this Company, I have to acknowledge with thanks the patronage they have hitherto enjoyed at your hands. [Circular letter asking for customers' continued support. Signed: Daniel Benham, secretary.] *s.sh.4°. n.p.* [1849]

36455 —— [*Begin.*] The Committee of Management of the...Company hereby give notice. [Circular letter, dated: 4th Dec. 1849, announcing a reduction in the price of gas to 4s. per 1000 cubic feet. Signed: Daniel Benham, secretary.] *s.sh.4°. n.p.* [1849]

36456 —— [*Begin.*] The Committee of Management of the...Company hereby give notice...[Circular letter, dated: 24 Dec. 1849, stating that the Company will not raise the price of gas above 4s. per 1000 cubic feet. Signed: Daniel Benham, secretary.] *s.sh.4°. n.p.* [1849]

36457 —— To the gas consumers of the City of London. [Circular letter, dated: 18th December 1849, answering charges of profiteering by the Company. Signed: Daniel Benham.] 3p. *fol. n.p.* [1849]

36458 CLAY, Sir W., *Bart.* Remarks on the water supply of London...Second edition. 108p. *8°.* 1849.

36459 COCHRANE, C. How to improve the homes of the people! Address delivered...August 27th, 1849, at the Vestry-Hall of St. Pancras...to a numerous assemblage of householders, shopkeepers, artisans, & labouring persons, as to the means within their own power of rendering their habitations healthful and comfortable. 16p. *8°*. [*London*, 1849]

36460 COX, E. H. The practice of poor removals, as regulated by the recent statutes 9 & 10 Vict. c. 66 and 11 & 12 Vict. c. 31...With observations, forms and all the cases decided...The second edition. 85p. *12°*. 1849.

36461 CREAGH, P. Correspondence between the Irish Poor Law Commissioners and Pierse Creagh, Esq. ..."relative to a crisis being brought about by heavy and destructive poor rates, by the imposition of which the present landlords and tenants could be got rid of." 32p. *8°*. *Dublin*, [1849]

36462 CROLL, A. A. Gas consumers agreement with A. A. Croll. [Memorandum of agreement, dated: 24 March 1849, between A. A. Croll, the promoter of the Great Central Gas Consumers' Company, and intending customers.] *s.sh.fol. n.p.* [1849]

36463 CROSS, T. A discourse on the subject of the Jewish disabilities. 15p. *8°*. *Cambridge*, [1849]

36464 DAILLY. *Parochial Board.* What is the poor-house best calculated to save Scotland from pauperism and degradation? [Report by the Committee appointed by the Parochial Board of the parish of Dailly, in Carrick, Ayrshire.] 29p. *8°*. *Maybole & Ayr*, 1849.

36465 *DAWES, R. Observations on the working of the government scheme of education and on school inspection, suggesting a mode of providing an efficient and more extended inspection for those schools in connexion with the Church, without expense to the country... 59p. *8°*. 1849.

36466 —— Second edition. 59p. *8°*. 1849.

36467 DEAN, G. A. Essays on the construction of farm buildings and labourers' cottages... 32, 14, 14p. *4°*. *Stratford, Essex, London, &c.*, 1849.

36468 DEMPSEY, G. D. Rudimentary treatise on the drainage of towns and buildings; suggestive of sanatory regulations that would conduce to the health of an increasing population. 176p. *12°*. 1849.

36469 The DIACONATE and the poor. The duty of the laity of England, briefly considered with reference to the above two objects. By a parish priest... 15p. *8°*. 1849.

36470 [ELLIS, WILLIAM (1800–1881).] The distressed needlewomen and cheap prison labour. (Extracted from the Westminster and Foreign Quarterly Review [vol. 50, no. 2].) 24p. *8°*. [1849]

36471 ENGLAND. *Commissioners appointed to Inquire into the State and Operation of the Law of Marriage.* Report..."To enquire into the state and operation of the law of marriage as relating to the prohibited degrees of affinity, and to marriages solemnized abroad or in the British colonies;" together with brief extracts from the evidence given before the Commission. 71p. *8°*. 1849.

36472 —— *General Board of Health.* Public Health Act. (11 & 12 Vict., cap. 63.) Report...on a preliminary inquiry into the sewerage, drainage, and supply of water, and sanitary condition of the inhabitants of...Birmingham. By Robert Rawlinson. 99p. *8°*. 1849.

36473 —— —— Public Health Act. (11 & 12 Vict., cap. 63.). Report...on a preliminary inquiry into the sewerage, drainage, and supply of water, and the sanitary condition of the inhabitants of...Leicester. By William Ranger. 37p. *8°*. 1849.

36474 —— —— Public Health Act (11 & 12 Vict., cap. 63). Report...on a preliminary inquiry into the sewerage, drainage, and supply of water, and the sanitary condition of the inhabitants of...Taunton. By George T. Clark. 24p. *8°*. 1849.

36475 —— —— Public Health Act, (11 & 12 Vict., cap. 63.) Report...on a preliminary inquiry into the sewerage, drainage and supply of water, and the sanitary condition of the inhabitants of...Waltham Abbey. By William Ranger. 22p. *8°*. 1849.

36476 —— *Laws, etc.* Anno decimo & undecimo Victoriæ Reginæ. Cap. cclxi. An Act for better supplying with water the Borough of Liverpool...and for authorizing the Mayor, Aldermen, and burgesses...to purchase the Liverpool and Harrington Waterworks and Liverpool Waterworks. ⟨22d July 1847.⟩ p.3765–3808. *fol.* 1849.

36477 —— Privy Council. *Committee on Education.* Published by permission. An account of the King's Somborne school. Extracted from the "Minutes of the Committee of Council on Education, 1847–8." 31p. *12°*. [1849] *The copy that belonged to William Lovett, with his signature on the title-page.*

36478 [FARQUHAR, B. H.] The pearl of days; or, the advantages of the Sabbath to the working classes. By a labourer's daughter. With a sketch of the author's life. Twenty-fifth thousand. 90p. *12°*. *London & Glasgow*, 1849.

For **FORESTERS**, *Ancient Order of*, Foresters' miscellany, 1849–53, 1891, *see* vol. III, *Periodicals list*, Foresters' miscellany.

36479 FRANCE. *Assemblée Nationale.* Rapport et projet de loi sur le patronage des jeunes détenus présentés au nom de la Commission de l'Assistance publique. Par M. Corne...Séance du 14 décembre 1849. 47p. *8°*. *Tours*, [1849] *The copy that belonged to Victor Considérant.*

36480 FRYER, J., *and others.* Labour and wages. Six prize essays on the causes which regulate the wages of labour. By six working men [Jabez Fryer, William Dove, Thomas Goddard, John Smith, Thomas Palmer, William Burden]. 95p. *8°*. *Leicester*, 1849.

36481 GRANTHAM, R. B. Description of the abattoirs of Paris...With an abstract of the discussion upon the paper. Excerpt minutes of proceedings of the Institution of Civil Engineers... 18p. *8°*. 1849.

36482 GREAT CENTRAL GAS CONSUMERS' COMPANY. Cheap and good gas! Address from the Board of Directors, showing the past history – the present position – and the future prospects of the... Company; containing a plain narrative of the antecedents, the relatives, and the consequences of their triumphant victory over the Leviathan gas monopoly of the City of London, Dec. 17th, 1849. [Signed: J. T. Barham.] 15p. *8°*. *n.p.*, 1849.

36483 —— The Great Central Gas Consumers' Company. Capital £150,000 in 15,000 shares of £10 each. [Prospectus.] 8p. *8°*. *n.p.* [1849]

36484 —— The Great Central Gas Consumers' Company, (provisionally registered.) Capital £250,000 to be divided into 25,000 shares of £10 each. [Prospectus.] [4]p. *fol. n.p.* [1849]

36485 —— [*Begin.*] To the Directors of the Great

Central Gas Consumers' Company. [A form of agreement to take the gas provided by the Company at a maximum price of 4 shillings per 1000 cubic feet for five years.] *s.sh.8⁰. n.p.* [1849 ?]

36486 **GUTHRIE,** T. A plea for ragged schools; or, prevention better than cure. 15p. *8⁰. Edinburgh,* 1849. *For another edition, see* 1847.

36487 —— A second plea for ragged schools; or, prevention better than cure...Fourth edition. [With an appendix.] 58p. *8⁰. Edinburgh, Glasgow, &c.,* 1849.

36488 **HARTSHORNE,** C. H. The system of building labourers' cottages pursued on the estates of His Grace the Duke of Bedford, practically examined. 12p. *8⁰. Northampton,* [1849]

36489 **HINDLEY,** C. Ten hours' Act. Speech of Charles Hindley, Esq. M.P. on the evasion of the Factory Act by relays and shifts, delivered to the delegates of Lancashire, in Manchester, April 14, 1849...Together with a report of the delegates as to the effects of the Bill where carried out. 32p. *8⁰.* 1849. *Presentation copy from the author to J. M. Cobbett.*

36490 **HODSON,** J. H. A practical method for the extinction of pauperism and poor-rates, and their necessarily co-existent evils: over-competition in the labour market, crime against property, cost of prosecutions and punishment, expenditure for superabundant police, &c.; by a process...so simple...and economical, that in less than five years they may cease altogether. 36p. *8⁰.* 1849.

36491 *——* Prospectus of a National Philanthropic Self-supporting Emigration Association, or, Colonial Home for the Destitute and Unemployed Poor... 13p. *8⁰.* 1849. *The FWA copy that belonged to William Pare.*

36492 **HOPE,** A. J. B. The report of Her Majesty's Commission on the laws of marriage, relative to marriage with a deceased wife's sister; examined in a letter to Sir Robert Harry Inglis, Bart., M.P. 183[185]p. *8⁰.* 1849.

36493 —— Third edition, revised and enlarged. 94p. *8⁰.* 1849.

36494 **HORSELL,** W. Cholera prevented by the adoption of a vegetarian diet; and cured, by a judicious application of the hydropathic treatment; illustrated by facts and figures. 10p. *12⁰.* 1849.

36495 **HOVENDEN,** R. Crime & punishment; or the question, how should we treat our criminals? practically considered. 128p. *8⁰.* 1849.

36496 **HUTCHINSON,** G. L. Second edition, with considerable additions, new tables, &c.&c. A plan for the equalization of the poor rates throughout the United Kingdom; by abolishing the law of settlement, and the removal of paupers...[With appendixes.] 151, [45]p. *8⁰.* 1849.

36497 **INQUIRY** into the meaning of the phrase "means and substance," and the claim to assess income apart from capital, under the Poor Law Act for Scotland, with a new plan of assessment on just and equal principles. Together with remarks on the qualifications of electors... Also, some general observations on the condition of the working classes...By a merchant burgess of Glasgow. 31p. *8⁰. Glasgow,* 1849.

36498 A statistical **INQUIRY** into the condition of the people of colour, of the city and districts of Philadelphia. 44p. *8⁰. Philadelphia,* 1849.

36499 **IRELAND.** *Commissioners of National Education.* The fifteenth report of the Commissioners...For the year 1848. Presented to both Houses of Parliament by command of Her Majesty. 213p. *8⁰. Dublin,* 1849. *See also* 1836.

36500 **IRISH POOR LAW:** past, present and future 59 p. *8⁰.* 1849.

36501 **JOURNEYMEN BOOKBINDERS OF LONDON AND WESTMINSTER.** An address to the donors, subscribers, and friends of the British and Foreign Bible Society, and the religious public in general, by the Journeymen Bookbinders...in reply to a statement of the contractress of the above society contradictory of certain portions of their "appeal" on the subject of "cheap Bibles." 8p. *8⁰.* [*London,* 1849]

36502 —— Appeal of the Journeymen Bookbinders... to the Committee, members, donors, and subscribers, of the British and Foreign Bible Society...on the subject of cheap Bibles. 8p. *8⁰.* [*London,* 1849]

36503 —— British & Foreign Bible Society and cheap Bibles. [On the wages paid for binding the Society's Bibles.] 2p. *s.sh. 8⁰.* [*London,* 1849]

36504 —— Cheap Bibles, and the British and Foreign Bible Society. [An account of protest meetings and a memorial addressed to the Society, praying that the price of their Bibles may be increased so that the binders may pay their workpeople a living wage. The memorial signed: T. J. Dunning, secretary, and dated, November 13, 1849.] 4p. *8⁰.* [*London,* 1849]

36505 **KLEINSCHROD,** C. T. VON. Die neue Armengesetzgebung Englands und Irlands in ihrem zehnjährigen Vollzuge, als Fortsetzung des "Pauperism in England 1845" nebst allgemeiner Betrachtung über die Arbeiterfrage und Massenverarmung... 138p. *8⁰. Augsburg,* 1849. *For the original work,* Der Pauperism in England, *see* 1845.

36506 **LAMELIN,** , *Madame.* A messieurs les membres de l'Assemblée Nationale, Madame Lamelin, propriétaire du café-estaminet, Chaussée des Martyrs, 10, à Montmartre, pour son mari transporté. 4p. *8⁰.* [*Paris,* 1849]

36507 **LARCHER,** L. J. Le droit au travail. Solution du problème social par un travailleur. [Dated: 18 février 1849.] [2]p. *s.sh.fol.* [*Paris,* 1849]

36508 **LOGAN,** WILLIAM (1813–1879). The moral statistics of Glasgow. 76p. *8⁰. Glasgow & London,* 1849. *The Turner copy.*

36509 [**MALET,** W. W.] The Ardeley petition for alteration in the Poor Law; or, a plan for every parish managing its own poor, police, registration, &c. by means of vestry committees...With a prospect of much more extensive economy, including a...substitute for church rates, in an appendix: being a letter to M. T. Baines, Esq., M.P. president of the Poor Law Board, from the chairman of the Ardeley Vestry. 31p. *8⁰.* 1849.

For the **MANCHESTER TEMPERANCE REPORTER,** 1849–50, *see vol.* III, *Periodicals list.*

36510 A plain **MAN'S** fifty reasons for preferring the system of the National Board [i.e. Commissioners for National Education] to other systems of general education in Ireland. Third edition, revised. 36p. *12⁰. Dublin,* 1849. *The copy that belonged to Earl De Grey.*

36511 **MASSIE,** James W. Social improvement among the working classes, affecting the entire body politic...Second lecture of the course... 32p. 8°. [1849]

36512 **MECHANICS' MUTUAL BENEFIT ASSOCIATION,** *Springfield, Mass.* By-laws of the Mechanics' Mutual Benefit Association. Adopted October 1st, 1849. 8p. 8°. *Springfield*, 1849.

36513 **MOREAU-CHRISTOPHE,** L.-M. Du droit à l'oisiveté et de l'organisation du travail servile dans les républiques grecques et romaine. 336p. 8°. *Paris*, 1849.

36514 **MUDIE,** G. A solution of the portentous enigma of modern civilization, now perplexing republicans as well as monarchs with fear of change. Addressed to Charles Louis Napoleon Bonaparte President of the French Republic and author of a work on the extinction of pauperism... 36p. 8°. 1849.

36515 **NEWLAND,** H. Remarks addressed to W. H. Bellamy, Esq....on the state of education in Ireland, and on the extracts circulated by him from the charge of the Lord Bishop of Ossory and Ferns. 80p. *12°. Dublin, London, &c.,* 1849. *The copy that belonged to Earl De Grey.*

36516 **NOTTINGHAM.** *Town Council.* A report upon the past & present sanitary state of the town of Nottingham: presented by the Sanitary Committee to the Town Council, October 1, 1849. 12p. *12°. Nottingham,* [1849]

36517 **NOTTINGHAM MECHANICS' INSTITUTION.** Rules of the Nottingham Mechanics' Institution; as amended and adopted at a general meeting of members, and also at a general meeting of trustees, and ratified at the general annual meeting, held February 12, 1849. 16p. 8°. *Nottingham,* 1849.

36518 **ODD FELLOWS.** *Nottingham Ancient Imperial United Order of Odd Fellows. Priors' Lodge Benevolent Society.* Laws, rules, and regulations of the Priors' Lodge Benevolent Society [No. 229], held at the Boat Inn, Worksop, Nottinghamshire. 16p. 8°. *Worksop,* [1849]

36519 ***OWEN,** Robert. Narrative of the thirty years' experiments at New Lanark, under the direction of Robert Owen. [Dated: London, 25th Feb., 1849.] *s.sh.fol. n.p.* [1849] *The FWA copy that belonged to William Pare.*

36520 **PALLISTER,** W. A. Essays, chiefly on the temperance question; also poems on various subjects. 218p. 8°. *London & Leeds,* 1849. *The Turner copy.*

36521 **PAUPERISM:** is it the effect of a law of nature, or of human laws and customs which are in opposition to nature? 92p. 8°. 1849.

36522 **PEARSON,** C. Are the citizens of London to have better gas, and more of it, for less money? A dialogue between Charles Pearson, Esq., M.P. and a gas consumer of the City, February 16, 1849... 16p. 8°. 1849.

36523 —— A second dialogue between Charles Pearson, Esq., M.P., and a gas-consumer of the City, April 5, 1849. 30p. 8°. 1849.

36524 —— Synopsis of Mr. Charles Pearson's intended lecture upon prison discipline, on the 15th and 16th January, 1849, and the discussions which will take place on the 22nd and 23rd...To which is appended a report from the daily journals of the proceedings of the preliminary meeting... 16p. 8°. *London, Manchester, &c.,* [1849]

For the **PEOPLE'S ABSTINENCE STANDARD,** 1849–50, *see* vol. III, *Periodicals list.*

36525 Copy of **PETITION** to both Houses of Parliament from the City consumers of gas. [For better and cheaper gas.] 2p. *s.sh.fol. n.p.* [1849]

36526 (Copy of petition to be signed by inhabitants of the City.) To the Worshipful the Court of Commissioners of Sewers of the City of London. The respectful **PETITION** of the undersigned owners, occupiers, inhabitants, and gas consumers within the City of London [that the Great Central Gas Consumers' Company might lay their pipes in the City]. *s.sh.fol. n.p.* [1849]

36527 **PHILLIPS,** Sir T. Wales: the language, social condition, moral character, and religious opinions of the people, considered in their relation to education: with some account of the provision made for education in other parts of the Kingdom. 606p. 8°. 1849.

36528 **PROCTOR,** Sir T. W. B. B., *Bart.* "Attend to the neglected and remember the forgotten." An appeal for the ragged schools. 31p. 8°. 1849. *The copy presented to Sir Culling Eardley by Lady B[eauchamp] Proctor.*

36529 **QUINTON,** J. A. Working men's essays upon the Sabbath. First prize. Heaven's antidote to the curse of of labour; or, the temporal advantages of the Sabbath, considered in relation to the working classes. [Edited by J. Jordan.] 61p. 8°. *London & Glasgow,* 1849.

For the **RAGGED SCHOOL UNION MAGAZINE,** 1849, *continued as* the Ragged School Union quarterly record, 1877–86, *see* vol. III, *Periodicals list.*

36530 On the **RESPONSIBILITIES** of employers. (*Small Books on Great Subjects,* XVI.) 199p. 8°. 1849. *Sometimes attributed to David Power. The copy presented to HSF by Henry Higgs.*

36531 **RICHMOND,** R. B. "Prevention better than cure." Practical remarks on the prevention of cholera... 48p. 8°. 1849.

36532 **ROBERTS,** S. Autobiography and select remains of the late Samuel Roberts. 245p. *12°.* 1849.

36533 **SAINT-GENEZ,** T. and **ROLLET,** P. De l'assistance publique. Son passé. – Son organisation actuelle. – Bases sur lesquelles il conviendrait de l'asseoir à l'avenir. 94p. 8°. *Paris,* 1849. *The copy that belonged to N. W. Senior.*

For **SCOTTISH TEMPERANCE LEAGUE,** [Tracts, 1849–55,] *see* vol. III, *Periodicals list,* Tracts...

36534 **SCROPE,** G. P. Draft report proposed by Mr. Poulett Scrope, to the Select Committee of the House of Commons on the Irish Poor Law. ⟨From the appendix to the last Report of the Committee.⟩ 7p. 8°. *n.p.* [1849] *The copy that belonged to Sir Harry Verney.*

36535 —— The Irish Poor Law. How far has it failed? and why? A question addressed to the common sense of his countrymen by G. Poulett Scrope, Esq., M.P. ⟨With extracts from and references to the evidence given before the Committee of the two Houses of Parliament now sitting on the subject.⟩ 60p. 8°. 1849.

36536 —— A labour rate recommended in preference to any reduction of the area of taxation, to improve the operation of the Irish Poor-Law. In three letters to the editor of the Morning Chronicle. 20p. 8°. 1849.

36537 —— Some notes of a tour in England, Scotland, & Ireland, made with a view to the inquiry, whether our labouring population be really redundant? In three letters to the editor of the "Morning Chronicle." 44p. 8°. 1849.

36538 —— Suggested legislation with a view to the improvement of the dwellings of the poor. 24p. *8°.* 1849.

36539 —— Votes in aid and rates in aid of the bankrupt Irish [poor law] unions. Two speeches delivered in the House of Commons...on...16th February, and...27th March, 1849. 25p. *8°.* 1849. *The copy that belonged to Earl De Grey.*

36540 SHAPTER, T. The history of the cholera in Exeter in 1832. 297p. *8°. London & Exeter,* 1849.

36541 SIMPSON, WILLIAM, *surgeon.* Health of towns. A digest of several reports on sanitary reforms: containing the views of E. Chadwick, Esq. C.B.; Dr. Southwood Smith...and others. 23p. *8°.* 1849.

36542 SMITH, ALBERT R., *ed.* Gavarni in London: sketches of life and character, with illustrative essays by popular writers. 115p. *4°.* 1849.

36543 SMITH, SIDNEY. The mother country: or, the spade, the wastes, and the eldest son. An examination of the condition of England. 163p. *12°.* 1849.

36544 SOCIÉTÉ POUR LE PATRONAGE DES JEUNES DÉTENUS...DU DEPARTEMENT DE LA SEINE. Assemblée Générale tenue rue Taranne, 12, le 20 août 1848. Compte-rendu de l'année 1847. 61p. *8°. Paris,* 1849. *See also 1844, 1846, 1848.*

36545 SOCIETY FOR IMPROVING THE CONDITION OF THE LABOURING CLASSES. Plans and suggestions for dwellings in agricultural districts, etc. etc. 2p., 7 plans. *8°.* [1849]

36546 A plain **STATEMENT** relating to the manufacture and sale of gas, addressed to the Honourable the Commissioners of Sewers for the City of London. By a director of one of the metropolitan gas companies [the City of London Gas Light and Coke Company]. 17p. *8°.* 1849.

36547 STEVENS, JAMES (*fl.* 1842–1879). Remarks on education, including an outline of a practical system of instruction and discipline with synopses of lectures, examinations, and reports or diaries...Second edition, revised and corrected. 27p. *12°. London & Oxford,* [1849]

36548 STEWART, JOHN V. A letter to the Earl of Clarendon, on the subject of poor laws, with an appendix. 44p. *8°. Letterkenny,* 1849.

36549 STIRLING, T. H. The question propounded; or, how will Great Britain ameliorate and remedy the distresses of its workmen, and others out of employment. 25p. *8°.* 1849.

36550 STUART, M., *and others.* The temperance topic. The scriptural view of the wine question, by Moses Stuart, Frederic R. Lees, John Eadie, P. Mearns, Henry Homes. 145p. *8°. Leeds,* 1849. *The Turner copy.*

36551 SUBSCRIPTION FOR THE RELIEF OF BRITISH WORKMEN, REFUGEES FROM FRANCE. Subscription for the Relief of British Workmen...Report, 46p. *12°.* 1849.

36552 SYME, H. Poems and songs. Chiefly for the encouragement of the working classes. 140p. *8°. Dunfermline, Edinburgh, &c.,* 1849. *Presentation copy from the author to 'Miss Brown of Newton'.*

36553 SYMONS, JELINGER C. Tactics for the times: as regards the condition and treatment of the dangerous classes. 245p. *8°.* 1849.

36554 TABRAHAM, R. Twentieth thousand. An appeal to the pious in favour of total abstinence; or love to Man, a powerful motive to abstain from the use, gift, sale, and manufacture of all kinds of intoxicating drinks. 23p. *12°. London & Manchester,* 1849. *The Turner copy.*

36555 UNION SOCIETY, *Worksop.* Rules and regulations of the Union Society, no. 2, held by permission, in the Abbey School Room, Worksop. 23p. *12°. Worksop,* 1849.

36556 UNITED JOINERS AND HOUSE CARPENTERS, *Glasgow.* Rules for the guidance of the United Joiners... 8p. *8°. Glasgow,* 1849.

36557 VAUGHAN, CHARLES J. A letter on the late Post Office agitation. 15p. *8°. London & Harrow,* 1849.

36558 VILLERMÉ, L. R. Petits traités publiés par l'Académie des Sciences morales et politiques [10]. Des associations ouvrières. 103p. *12°. Paris,* 1849.

36559 W., J., *of Bayswater.* Perils, pastimes, and pleasures of an emigrant in Australia, Vancouver's Island and California. 404p. *12°.* 1849.

36560 WALKER, GEORGE A. Practical suggestions for the establishment of national cemeteries. 15p. *8°.* 1849.

36561 WATSON, WILLIAM, *Sheriff-Substitute of Aberdeenshire.* Remarks on the bothie system and feeing markets...Third thousand. 8p. *8°. Aberdeen & Edinburgh,* [1849]

36562 *WORSLEY, H. Juvenile depravity. £100. prize essay...[Attributing juvenile crime particularly to intemperance.] 275p. *8°.* 1849.

SLAVERY

36563 CAVE, SIR S. A few words, on the encouragement given to slavery and the slave trade, by recent measures, and chiefly by the Sugar Bill of 1846. 34p. *8°.* [*London,*] 1849.

36564 DENMAN, T., *Baron Denman.* A second letter from Lord Denman to Lord Brougham, on the final extinction of the slave trade, with remarks on a late narrative of the Niger expedition in 1841. 34p. *8°.* 1849.

36565 HUNTLEY, SIR H. V. Observations upon the free trade policy of England, in connexion with the Sugar Act of 1846, showing the influence of the latter upon the

British tropical possessions, and its direct operation to perpetuate the slave trade... 104p. *8°. London & Leamington,* 1849.

36566 The **LIBERTY BELL.** By friends of freedom. 292p. *12°. Boston: National Anti-Slavery Bazaar,* 1849. *See also* 1848.

36567 STEPHEN, SIR G. A letter from Sir George Stephen to Sir E. F. Buxton, Bart., M.P., on the proposed revival of the English slave trade. 16p. *8°.* 1849.

36568 —— The Niger trade considered in connection

with the African blockade... 71p. *8°. London, Liverpool, &c.,* 1849.

36569 TIFFANY, J. A treatise on the unconstitutionality of American slavery: together with the powers and duties of the Federal Government... 144p. *8°. Cleveland, Ohio,* [1849]

36570 Free **TRADE** in negroes. 51p. *8°.* 1849.

POLITICS

36571 AMARI, M. The Anglo-French mediation in Sicily; or, post-scriptum to "Sicily and the Bourbons." Translated from the French. 20p. *8°.* 1849.

36572 AMNISTIE par le Président de la République de 1228 transportés de juin. [With an account of the celebrations to mark the anniversary of the proclamation of the Republic.] [2]p. *fol.* [*Paris,* 1849]

36573 ANDRÉ, J. A M. Guizot. [On the 'droit d'association'.] *s.sh.fol.* [*Paris,* 1849]

36574 Extrait de la Révolution démocratique et sociale. **ANNIVERSAIRE** du 24 février 1848. Banquet commémoratif de Paris, Salle de la Fraternité. [2]p. *fol. Paris,* [1849]

36575 An **APPEAL** to the Chartists proper, in a series of letters, shewing in what manner the People's Charter may be rendered worthy of being made a reality. Letters I & II. [Dated: December 26, 1848 and Epiphany, 1849.] Second edition. By the Pimlico hermit. 16p. *8°.* [1849]

36576 BARRAULT, P. A. C. E. Lettre au Pape Pie IX. (*Lettres contemporaines,* 6e livraison.) 7p. *fol. Paris,* [1849]

36577 BARTHÉLEMY, A. M. Lamartine. [A poem praising his political courage.] *s.sh.fol. Paris,* [1849]

36578 *BARTHÉLEMY SAINT-HILAIRE, J. Petits traités publiés par l'Académie des Sciences morales et politiques [9]. De la vraie démocratie. 99p. *12°. Paris,* 1849. *The copy that belonged to George Grote.*

36579 BLANC, J. J. L. Appel aux honnêtes gens. Quelques pages d'histoire contemporaine...Deuxième édition... 168p. *18°. Paris,* 1849. *Presentation copy, with inscription, from the author, 'au docteur Travis'.*

36580 [BURMEISTER, J. P. T.] Die Wiener-Ereignisse vom 6. Oktober bis 12. November 1848. Geschildert von einem Augenzeugen. Mit allen während dieses Zeitraums erschienenen Kundmachungen und Proclamationen. [The introduction is signed: J. P. Lyser.] 99p. *8°. Wien,* 1849.

36581 CAMPBELL, WILLIAM F., *Baron Stratheden and Campbell.* Substance of a speech on the Jewish question, delivered in the House of Commons...May 4, 1848. 28p. *8°. London & Cambridge,* 1849.

36582 CHABOUD, H. Les vengeurs du peuple et de l'armée...[In praise of Louis Napoléon Bonaparte as President.] *s.sh.fol. Paris,* [1849]

36583 CHAIS, A. Les fonctionnaires pullics [*sic*] et les dénonciations. Réponse au Rapport fait au nom du Comité de législation, sur la proposition de M. V. Considérant, relativement aux fonctionnaires publics, civils et militaires, par le citoyen Aug. Chais, réprésentant du peuple. [2]p. *s.sh.fol.* [*Paris,* 1849]

36584 CHAMIER, F. A review of the French revolution of 1848: from the 24th of February to the election of the first president. 2 vols. *8°.* 1849.

36585 COGNIARD, T. and **BOURDOIS,** A. Théâtre du Vaudeville. Les grands écoliers en vacances. Folie-vaudeville en deux actes...représentée...le 15 septembre 1849. 17p. *8°. Paris,* 1849.

36586 CONSIDÉRANT, V. P. Simples explications à mes amis et à mes commettants. 19p. *8°. Paris,* 1849. *Considérant's own copy.*

For the **DEMOCRATIC REVIEW,** 1849–50, *see* vol. III, *Periodicals list.*

36587 DUBRUEL, L. Théâtre du Gymnase-Dramatique. Un socialiste en province. Vaudeville en un acte... Représenté...le 5 juillet 1849. 15p. *8°. Paris,* 1849.

36588 *DU VERGIER DE LA ROCHE-JAQUELEIN, H. A. G., *Marquis de la Rochejaquelein.* Situation de la France. Lettre aux électeurs. 32p. *8°. Paris,* 1849. *The copy that belonged to George Grote.*

36589 DUVERT, F. A. and **LAUZANNE DE VAUROUSSEL,** A. T. DE. Théâtre du Vaudeville. La fin d'une république ou Haïti en 1849. A-propos-vaudeville en un acte...réprésenté...le 18 décembre 1849. 13p. *8°. Paris,* 1849.

36590 EDGCUMBE, E. A., *Earl of Mount Edgcumbe.* Extracts from a journal kept during the commencement of the revolution at Palermo, in the year 1848. 50p. *8°.* 1849.

36591 —— Extracts from a journal kept during the Roman revolution. 65p. *8°.* 1849.

36592 ENGLAND. Parliament. *House of Commons.* The question of arbitration in the House of Commons. Being the substance of the debate on Mr. Cobden's motion in favour of arbitration treaties instead of war, for the settlement of international disputes. With an appendix ... 24p. *8°.* [1849]

36593 FAVRE, J. G. C. La liberté de la presse: discours du citoyen Jules Favre. *s.sh.fol. Paris,* [1849]

36594 FLOTTE, B. Les calomniateurs démasqués. Protestation du citoyen B. Flotte accusé devant la Haute-Cour de justice, séant à Bourges. *s.sh.fol.* [*Paris,* 1849]

36595 FRANCE. *Commission du Pouvoir Exécutif.* Histoire de la révolution de février 1848, du Gouvernement Provisoire, et de la République. Commission du Pouvoir Exécutif, 9 mai au 23 juin. [With 'Constitution française de 1848, décrétée le 4 novembre'.] 2 vols. *8°. Bordeaux,* 1849.

36596 IMBERT, J. Antinomie sociale. Première lettre du paysan d'Auteuil. Aux Montagnards. [Dated: 23 juin 1849.] 4p. *fol.* [*Paris,* 1849]

36597 —— Antinomie sociale. Deuxième lettre...Aux modérés. [Dated: 1er juillet 1849.] 4p. *fol.* [*Paris,* 1849]

36598 —— Antinomie sociale. Troisième lettre...Aux républicains. [Dated: 20 juillet 1849.] 8p. *fol.* [*Paris,* 1849]

36599 —— Antinomie sociale. Quatrième lettre...Aux légitimistes. [Dated: 1er août 1849.] 4p. *fol.* [*Paris,* 1849]

36600 —— Antinomie sociale. Cinquième lettre... Déduction rationnelle de l'Antinomie. [Dated: 15 août 1849.] 8p. *fol.* [*Paris*, 1849]

36601 —— Antinomie sociale. Sixième lettre...La Patrie est en danger! [Dated: 10 septembre 1849.] 4p. *fol.* [*Paris*, 1849]

36602 Extrait du journal La Révolution démocratique et sociale, numéro du 4 février 1849. **JEAN-PIERRE** laboureur à la Ville-aux-Bois, à Monsieur le Président de la République. 4p. *fol.* [*Paris*, 1849]

36603 LABICHE, E. M. and **LEFRANC**, A. Théâtre du Gymnase-Dramatique. A bas la famille, ou les banquets, à-propos montagnard en un acte... représenté ...le 16 décembre 1848. 16p. *8°. Paris*, 1849.

36604 LANDOUIN,   . Le loustic de la compagnie. Grand récit détaillé des injustices révoltantes d'un adjudant sous-officier et d'un caporal contre deux soldats de la ligne... *s.sh.fol.* [*Paris*, 1849] *Printed on red paper.*

36605 LEBON, N. Extrait du journal L'Égalité. Rouge ou blanc...Aux voix! [On the election of 13 May 1849.] [2]p. *s.sh.fol.* [*Paris*, 1849]

36606 [**LE ROY DE KERANIOU**, H.] Peuple on te trompe! [Signed: Romulle.] [2]p. *s.sh.fol. Paris*, [1849]

36607 LEVY, A. and **VALLETON**, H. Les émeutiers! Les deux lundis. [2]p. *s.sh.fol. Paris*, [1849]

36608 LOVETT, W. The peace principle, the great agent of social and political progress: being a short review of the peace doctrines of the "Family Herald." 16p. *16°.* 1849.

36609 MAMOZ, P. A ceux qui détestent la République. [An anti-royalist tract.] [2]p. *s.sh.fol.* [*Paris*, 1849]

For le **MONITEUR DE LA RACAILLE**, *see* vol. III, *Periodicals list.*

36610 [**MOREAU-CHRISTOPHE**, L.-M.] Le 13 mai 1849! Pour qui voterons-nous? [Signed: Un délégué au Comité central de l'Union electorale du departement de la Seine, and dated, ce 5 mai 1849.] [2]p. *s.sh.fol.* [*Paris*, 1849]

36611 Au peuple français. Quelques **MOTS** sur la vice-présidence de la République Française. [In favour of General Montholon.] *s.sh.fol.* [*Paris*, 1849]

36612 NATIONAL CLUB, *London*. Address by the Committee of the National Club, to Her Majesty's subjects of the United Kingdom [on the dismissal of Lord Roden for his action with regard to the disturbances at Castlewellan]. 4p. *8°. [c.* 1849] *The copy that belonged to Earl De Grey.*

36613 —— Address by the Committee of the National Club to the British public on the dismissal of Lord Roden. 8p. *8°.* [1849] *The copy that belonged to Earl De Grey.*

36614 NEATE, C. Dialogues des morts politiques... Premier dialogue. Interlocuteurs: MM. Guizot et Louis Blanc. 70p. *12°. Paris*, 1849.

36615 [**NICOLAIE**, L. F., *and others.*] Théâtre du Gymnase-Dramatique. Les grenouilles qui demandent un roi. Vaudeville en un acte de MM. Clairville, J. Cordier et Arthur de Beauplan. Représenté...le 26 février 1849. 15p. *8°. Paris*, 1849.

36616 [——] and **SIRAUDIN**, P. Théâtre du Vaudeville. L'âne à Baptiste ou le berceau du socialisme. Grande folie lyrique en quatre actes et douze tableaux. Par MM.

Clairville et Siraudin...représentée...le 15 mai 1849. 22p. *8°. Paris*, 1849.

36617 [—— and **VAULABELLE**, É. T. DE.] Théâtre du Gymnase-Dramatique. Les partageux. Vaudeville en un acte, par MM. Clairville et J. Cordier, représenté ...le 17 novembre 1849. 12p. *8°. Paris*, 1849.

36618 ***OWEN**, ROBERT. To Her Majesty, Queen of the British Empire, and to her responsible advisors. [Dated: London, July, 1849. On the hitherto misdirected powers of the British Government, which could be used to create prosperity for all.] *s.sh.fol. n.p.* [1849] *The FWA copy that belonged to William Pare.*

36619 To the oppressed and mystified **PEOPLE** of Great Britain. [A Chartist manifesto. Signed: A Chartist (of ten years' standing, and a Christian).] *s.sh.fol. n.p.* [1849 ?] [*Br.* 627]

36620 PERRET, J. B. Le Général Lapique aux électeurs... [2]p. *fol.* [*Paris*, 1849]

36621 PHYSIOLOGIE du réactionnaire. [2]p. *fol. Paris*, [1849 ?]

36622 PLAIN FACTS, *pseud.* Political principles and political consistency. 68p. *8°.* 1849. *The copy that belonged to Earl De Grey.*

For the **PLAIN SPEAKER**, *see* vol. III, *Periodicals list.*

36623 POSTSCRIPT to the further considerations respecting the marriage of the Duc de Montpensier, with reference to the Treaty of Utrecht. 72p. *8°.* 1849.

36624 The **REFORMER'S** almanack and political year-book, 1850... 88p. *8°.* [1849] *With the signature of Francis Place inside the front cover.*

36625 RENARD, L. Anniversaire de la proclamation de la République Française. Paris s'embête. *s.sh.fol.* [*Paris*, 1849]

36626 REPORT of the evidence taken before the government commissioner, Walter Berwick, Esq., Q.C., at a court held in Castlewellan, from 30th July to 4th August, and, by adjournment, on...18th September, 1849. [Concerning an affray at Castlewellan.] 126p. *12°. Newry*, 1849. *The copy that belonged to Earl De Grey.*

For **REYNOLDS'S POLITICAL INSTRUCTOR**, 1849–50, *see* vol. III, *Periodicals list.*

36627 La **SAINT-BARTHÉLEMY** des republicains *s.sh.fol. Paris*, [1849]

36628 STEPHANOPOLI DE COMNÈNE, N., *Prince.* Catéchisme historique et politique des vrais républicains, servant de guide aux électeurs de la France, et à démasquer les faux Mirabeau de la rue de Poitiers, conjurés avec les coalisés étrangers contre la République. *s.sh.fol. Paris*, [1849]

36629 —— L'enfant de la République aux électeurs de la France. Sourdes manœuvres de l'Angleterre; sa vaste conspiration contre la République avec les coalisés reactionnaires de la rue de Poitiers; moyens d'annuler sa puissance navale à l'égard de la France. [2]p. *s.sh.fol. Paris*, [1849]

36630 —— L'enfant de la République aux electeurs de Paris et des autres départements. Mystères, trahisons, calomnies et crimes de la rue Poitiers contre la République révélés aux défenseurs de la République démocratique et sociale. [2]p. *s.sh.fol. Paris*, [1849]

36631 —— Qu'est-ce que le statu quo et ses réactions

contre les républiques. Servant d'éclaircissement aux électeurs et aux défenseurs de la Révolution du 24 février. [2]p. *s.sh.fol. Argenteuil*, [1849]

36632 —— Vaste conspiration de la rue de Poitiers contre la République et ses gloires militaires dénoncée aux electeurs de Paris et des autres départements. [With a list of 8 socialist candidates (including the author) to represent the Departement de la Seine.] [2]p. *s.sh.fol. Paris*, [1849]

36633 SWAINE, E. The political franchise, a public trust, demanding an intelligent and virtuous care for the public good. A lecture to working men...at the request of the Congregational Union. With an appendix, on the exclusion of women and others from the franchise. 36p. *12⁰.* [1849]

36634 TAPIN, . Quatre hommes et un caporal. Entretien de Jean Pichu avec son sergent, au sujet du discours du citoyen Bugeaud. *s.sh.fol. Paris: Lacour & Ce.*, [1849]

36635 —— [Another edition.] *s.sh.fol. Paris: N. Chaix & Ce.*, [1849 ?]

36636 —— Le soldat répresentant. Deuxième entretien de Jean Pichu avec son sergent, au sujet des élections du 13 mai 1849. *s.sh.fol.* [*Paris*, 1849]

36637 —— Boichot, Rattier et Commissaire. Troisième entretien de Jean Pichu avec son sergent, au sujet de la nouvelle Assemblée de 1849. *s.sh.fol.* [*Paris*, 1849]

36638 THIERS, L. A. La répression de la presse, discours du citoyen Thiers. *s.sh.fol. Paris*, 1849.

36639 VALLOU DE VILLENEUVE, T. F., *and others*. Théâtre des Variétés. Lorettes et aristos ou une soirée au Ranelagh. Tableau-vaudeville en un acte par MM. Villeuve [*sic*], Édouard et Siraudin. Représenté... le 31 août 1849. 15p. *8⁰. Paris*, 1849.

36640 VARIN, C. and [**BULLY**, E. R. DE]. Théâtre de la Montansier. Les femmes saucialistes. A-propos mêlé de couplets par MM. Varin et Roger de Beauvoir, représenté...le 21 avril 1849. 15p. *8⁰. Paris*, 1849.

36641 —— and [**ROUSSEAU**, V. A.]. Théâtre du Gymnase-Dramatique. La montagne qui accouche. Vaudeville en un acte, par MM. Varin et Arthur de Beauplan, représenté...le 30 mai 1849. 14p. *8⁰. Paris*, 1849.

36642 VARWIC, S. Du droit de réunion, protestation contre la fermeture des clubs. [Dated: le 28 janvier, 1849.] [2]p. *s.sh.fol. Paris*, [1849]

36643 WADE, JOHN. Unreformed abuses in Church and State: with a preliminary tractate on the continental revolutions. 270p. *12⁰.* 1849.

36644 WILLIAMS, JOHN (1802–1855). Special report of the speech which was delivered in the House of Commons, on...May 24th, 1849, in support of Mr. Fitzhardinge Berkeley's motion, in favor of the adoption of voting by ballot. 48p. *8⁰.* [1849]

36645 WILLIAMS, WILLIAM (1789–1865). An address to the electors and non-electors of the United Kingdom on the defective state of the representative system, and the consequent unequal and oppressive taxation and prodigal expenditure of the public money. 31p. *8⁰.* 1849. *Presentation copy from the author to Henry Drummond.*

SOCIALISM

For l'**AIMABLE FAUBOURIEN**, *see* vol. III, *Periodicals list.*

36646 BANQUE DU PEUPLE. 1er Bulletin. Réunion préparative du dimanche 24 septembre. Rue du Faubourg Saint-Denis, 25. [2]p. *s.sh.fol. Paris*, [1849]

36647 La **BANQUE DU PEUPLE** doit régénérer le monde. Transition de la vieille société au socialisme. Un prolétaire, ami du commerce et de l'industrie, à ses frères du travail, aux riches dans l'intérêt de ceux qui souffrent, aux travailleurs malheureux pour l'éclaircissement de leurs droits et de leur puissance. 62p. *8⁰. Paris*, 1849.

36648 BARRAU, J. J. Les électeurs et les élus. *s.sh.fol. Paris*, [1849]

36649 BERNARD, S. F. Tais-toi, Rodin! Réponse aux calomniateurs du socialisme. Fermons les clubs! Premier pamphlet adressé à Monsieur Léon Faucher, ministre de l'Intérieur. [2]p. *s.sh.fol.* [*Paris*, 1849]

36650 —— Tais-toi, Rodin! Réponse aux calomniateurs du socialisme. Une campagne. [2]p. *s.sh.fol. Paris*, [1849]

36651 —— Tais-toi, Rodin!...Nous les vaincrons! [2]p. *s.sh.fol. Paris*, [1849]

36652 —— Tais-toi, Rodin!...L'union fait la force. [2]p. *s.sh.fol.* [*Paris*, 1849]

36653 —— Tais-toi, Rodin!...Tous ou aucun! [2]p. *s.sh.fol. Paris*, [1849]

36654 BLANC, J. J. L. La Révolution de février au Luxembourg. 157p. *18⁰. Paris*, 1849.

36655 BOITAR, . La corruption. Aux électeurs. [With a list of socialist candidates.] *s.sh.fol. Montmartre*, [1849]

36656 BUCKINGHAM, J. S. National evils and practical remedies, with the plan of a model town... Accompanied by an examination of some important moral and political problems. 512p. *8⁰.* [1849]

36657 BUGEAUD DE LA PICONNERIE, T. R., *Duc d'Isly*. Les socialistes et le travail en commun. 30p. *16⁰. Lyon*, 1849.

36658 CHEVALIER, M. L'économie politique et le socialisme. Discours prononcé au Collège de France, le 28 février, pour l'ouverture du cours d'économie politique. [Extrait du No. 93 du Journal des Économistes (mars 1849).] 20p. *8⁰. Paris*, 1849.

36659 —— [Another edition.] 20p. *8⁰. Montpellier*, 1849.

36660 CHURCH OF ENGLAND SELF-SUPPORTING VILLAGE SOCIETY. The Church of England self-supporting village, for promoting the religious, moral, and general improvement of the working classes, by forming establishments of three hundred families on the land, and combining agricultural with manufacturing employment, for their own benefit. [A prospectus. With 'Explanation of the design for a self-supporting institution', 'Circular to the clergy...1843', and 'Petition...to the House of Commons, March 1844', signed: J. M. Morgan.] 15p. *8°. [London, 1849 ?] The copy that belonged to J. M. Ludlow. See also 1850, and for other editions of the* Explanation *by John Minter Morgan, 1846.*

36661 COLINS, J. G. C. A. H., *Baron de Colins.* Le socialisme ou organisation sociale rationnelle. 18p. *8°. Paris,* 1849.

36662 —— Socialisme rationnel ou association universelle des amis de l'humanité, du droit dominant la force, de la paix, du bien être général pour l'abolition du prolétariat et des révolutions. 32p. *8°. Paris,* 1849.

For la **COMMUNE DE PARIS,** *see vol.* III, *Periodicals list.*

36663 COMMUNISM & free trade, or theory and practice exemplified; being a glance at the Proudhon and Manchester schools. By an attentive observer. 8p. *8°.* 1849.

36664 COURTOIS, E. H. L'urne electorale. (Le socialisme et la constitution, 2e article.) Conseils aux démocrates socialistes. [2]p. *s.sh.fol.* [*Paris,* 1849]

36665 The **DEMOCRATIC AND SOCIAL ALMANAC** for 1850. Presented to the readers of the "Weekly Tribune" of Dec. 8. 1849...[With 'The socialist's catechism. By M. Louis Blanc'.] 24p. *12°.* [1849] *The running title reads: Weekly Tribune almanac. *Another, the FWA copy, belonged to William Pare.*

36666 Le **DROIT** au travail au Luxembourg et à l'Assemblée Nationale. Par MM. de Lamartine, Thiers, Louis-Blanc, Dufaure, Duvergier de Hauranne, de Tocqueville, Wołowski, Ledru-Rollin, etc. etc. Avec une introduction par Emile de Girardin. 2 vols. *18°. Paris,* 1849.

36667 FOURIER, F. C. M. Cités ouvrières. Des modifications à introduire dans l'architecture des villes... (Extrait de la Phalange...) 39p. *8°. Paris,* 1849.

36668 —— L'harmonie universelle et le phalanstère exposé par Fourier. Recueil méthodique de morceaux choisis de l'auteur... 2 vols. *18°. Paris,* 1849.

36669 GRÜN, A. Le vrai et le faux socialisme. Le communisme et son histoire. 56p. *12°. Paris,* 1849.

36670 HENNEQUIN, V. A. Programme de la presse démocratique et sociale interprété au point de vue phalanstérien. [Extrait de la Démocratie Pacifique du 18 avril.] [2]p. *s.sh.fol.* [*Paris,* 1849]

36671 JOUBERT, C. Biographies et portraits d'après nature des candidats socialistes du Département de la Seine. Liste adoptée par le Comité centrale democrate-socialiste...Dessins par le citoyen Ch. Marville... 35p. *16°. Paris,* 1849.

36672 KROLIKOWSKI, L. K., *ed.* Système de fraternité. (Extraits du Populaire.) 284p. *16°. Paris,* 1849–51. *Published in six parts; wanting part 5, p.129–158.*

36673 LECHEVALIER SAINT ANDRÉ, L. J. Haute Cour de Versailles. Procès du 13 juin. Déclaration du citoyen André-Louis-Jules Lechevalier...accusé, ex-membre du Comité de la presse... 16p. *8°. Londres,* [1849] *The copy that belonged to Earl De Grey.*

36674 —— The French Republic before the British people. [An open letter to English newspapers, justifying his political opinions, and including a translation of the declaration read at his trial on 13 June.] 15p. *8°. n.p.* [1849] *Presentation copy presumably to Earl De Grey, in a*

volume of whose pamphlets it is bound. For another edition of the Declaration, see no. 36673, *above.*

36675 LEROUX, P. H. Malthus et les économistes, ou y aura-t-il toujours des pauvres?...Nouvelle édition. 344p. *16°. Boussac,* 1849.

36676 MAURICE, JOHN F. D. Introductory lecture delivered at the opening of the Metropolitan Evening Classes for Young Men. 22p. *12°.* 1849.

36677 [MAURIN, A.] Les petits livres rouges de la science politique, démocratique et sociale. Par un ami du peuple. I. Exposition. La France est démocrate; la grande majorité des Français a tout intérêt à la réforme sociale. 30p. *16°. Paris,* [1849]

36678 —— Les petits livres rouges...II. Situation. Les questions politiques. 32p. *16°. Paris,* 1849.

36679 MERZ, H. Armuth und Christenthum. Bilder und Winke zum christlichen Communismus und Socialismus. 238p. *8°. Stuttgart & Tübingen,* 1849.

36680 [METHIVIER, S.] Donatien ou le socialisme jugé par le bon sens. Aux ateliers, aux chaumières, aux châteaux, à tous; par un campagnard...Deuxième édition. 72p. *12°. Paris,* 1849.

36681 MORELL, J. R. Sketch of the life of Charles Fourier, introductory to his treatise on the human soul... 16p. *8°.* 1849. *The copy that belonged to J. M. Ludlow.*

36682 [MORGAN, JOHN M.] The revolt of the bees ...Fourth edition. (*The Phœnix Library.*) 244p. *12°.* 1849. *For other editions, see* 1826.

36683 —— Tracts: originally published at various periods, from 1819 to 1838. With an appendix. (*The Phœnix Library.*) 217p. *12°.* 1849. *See also* 1850.

36684 MURET, T. C. La vérité. Aux ouvriers. – Aux paysans. Aux soldats. Simples paroles...Trente-unième tirage. 34p. *12°. Paris & Rouen,* 1849.

36685 *OWEN, ROBERT. New Lanark. [Dated: London, Feb. 20th, 1849.] *s.sh.fol. n.p.* [1849] *The FWA copy that belonged to William Pare.*

36686 —— The revolution in the mind and practice of the human race; or, the coming change from irrationality to rationality. 171p. *8°.* 1849. *Three copies: the first has the Royal arms on the binding; the second has an inscription in Owen's hand 'To Mr Duncan from his friend the Author'; *the third, the FWA copy, belonged to William Pare.*

36687 —— A supplement to The revolution in the mind ...Also a copy of the original memorial...which was presented to the...Congress...at Aix-la-Chapelle, in 1818...To which is added a discourse delivered to the socialists of London, on the 25th of October, 1849. 83p. *8°.* 1849. *The copy that belonged to the Literary & Scientific Institution, John Street, Fitzroy Square.*

36688 *—— To Lords John Russell and Stanley, Sir Robert Peel, and Messrs. Cobden and Feargus O'Connor. [Dated: April, 1849.] *s.sh.fol. n.p.* [1849] *The FWA copy that belonged to William Pare.*

36689 PELLARIN, C. Fourier, sa vie et sa théorie... Quatrième édition. 444p. *12°. Paris,* 1849. *A second copy of the second part, 'Théorie sociétaire' (p.213–444), belonged to Victor Considérant. For other editions, see* 1839.

36690 POMPÉRY, É. DE. Despotisme ou socialisme. 32p. *16°. Paris,* 1849.

36691 PROGRAMME électoral des Communistes révolutionnaires. [Signed: Rasetti, Gohé, Turgard.] *s.sh.fol. Paris*, [1849]

36692 PROUDHON, P. J. Banque du peuple, suivie du rapport de la Commission des délégués du Luxembourg. 52p. *12°. Paris*, 1849.

36693 —— Candidature du citoyen Proudhon. Aux électeurs catholiques! *s.sh.fol. Paris*, [1849]

36694 —— Les confessions d'un révolutionnaire, pour servir à l'histoire de la Révolution de février. 288p. *12°. Ixelles lez Bruxelles*, 1849. *See also* 1850.

36695 —— De la création de l'ordre dans l'humanité ou principes d'organisation politique...Deuxième édition. 454p. *12°. Paris*, 1849.

36696 —— Idées révolutionnaires...Avec une préface par Alfred Darimon... 268p. *18°. Paris*, 1849.

36697 —— Résumé de la question sociale, banque d'échange. [The preface signed: Alfred Darimon.] 116p. *12°. Paris*, 1849.

36698 RAGINEL, A. Pourquoi avons-nous la République et la misère? [2]p. *s.sh.fol.* [*Paris*, 1849]

36699 REYBAUD, M. R. L. Études sur les réformateurs ou socialistes modernes...Sixième édition...2 vols. *12°. Paris*, 1849. *For other editions, see* 1841.

36700 RICHARD, J. M. Catéchisme de la Banque du Peuple. 4p. *4°.* [*Paris*, 1849]

36701 SAGRA, R. DE LA. Banque du Peuple. Théorie et pratique de cette institution fondée sur la doctrine rationelle. 157p. *18°. Paris*, 1849.

36702 —— Mon contingent à l'Académie. Sur les conditions de l'ordre et de réformes sociales. Premier mémoire. 78p. *8°. Paris*, 1849.

For the **SOCIAL REFORMER,** *see vol. III, Periodicals list.*

36703 SOCIÉTÉ DES TRAVAILLEURS-UNIS. Société des Travailleurs-Unis. Siège provisoire de la gérance centrale. [With 'Credo des travailleurs-unis'.] [4]p. *4°.* [*Paris*, 1849]

36704 SOCIÉTÉ POSITIVISTE. République occidentale...Rapport à la Société Positiviste, par la commission chargée d'examiner la nature, et le plan de l'École Positive, destinée surtout à régénérer les médecins. 31p. *8°. Paris*, 1849. *With an introduction by Auguste Comte. The copy that belonged to Earl De Grey. See also* 1850.

36705 STEPHANOPOLI DE COMNÈNE, N., *Prince.* L'enfant de la République aux électeurs de la France. Le socialisme selon la loi naturelle et évangélique, selon le progrés social et les republiques. Le dix-neuvième siècle et ses réformes. [2]p. *s.sh.fol. Paris*, [1849]

36706 SUDRÉ, T. R. L. A. Histoire de communisme ou réfutation historique des utopies socialistes...Deuxième édition. 532p. *18°. Paris*, 1849.

36707 —— Nouvelle édition, revue et augmentée... 495p. *8°. Bruxelles*, 1849.

36708 VERMASSE, C. Avril 1849...Mère Duchêne au pilori. [With a list of 26 socialist candidates for the forthcoming election.] Par C. Vermasse, dit Mitraille. [2]p. *s.sh.fol. Paris*, [1849]

36709 —— Avril 1849. Sauve qui veut! [Proposal for an association of workers.] 4p. *fol. Paris*, [1849]

MISCELLANEOUS

36710 A'BECKETT, T. T. Law-reforming difficulties, exemplified in a letter to Lord Brougham and Vaux, accompanied by an analysis of a Bill for the improvement of the law relating to the administration of deceased persons' estates, and a statement showing its existing evils, first submitted to the Government, Dec. 24, 1842. 79p. *8°.* 1849.

36711 An **'ARTICLE'** for Lord Brougham's Bankruptcy Digest; being remarks upon a recent letter [by him]. By a practical man. 27p. *8°.* 1849.

36712 BROUGHAM, H. P., *Baron Brougham and Vaux.* Letter from Lord Brougham to Sir James Graham, on the making and digesting of the law. 42p. *8°.* 1849.

36713 ECKETT, R. Methodist reform. The "Fly sheets" and the Conference condemned. The conference laws of 1835, relative to the rights of the laity, proved to be more despotic than the law of 1835 affecting the preachers. The opinions, on reform, of "the expelled ministers" examined, and a plan of reform suggested... Second edition. 32p. *8°.* 1849. *The Turner copy.*

36714 FARRENC, C. Les amis de collège ou vice et vertu...Deuxième édition. [With 'La cabane du pêcheur. Par Sorel'.] (*Bibliothèque historique et morale.*) 263p. *12°. Lille*, 1849.

36715 [**KING-NOEL,** W., *Earl of Lovelace.*] Villemain. Literature du moyen âge...[A review signed: L. Reprinted from the *Westminster Review*, vol. LI, no. 2.] p.[334]–55. *8°.* [1849]

36716 LONDON. Livery Companies. *Ironmongers.* Rules, ordinances, bye-laws, & customs, of the Worshipful Company of Ironmongers, as settled and confirmed by a special General Court of the Company, held on the 22nd day of May, 1849. With a brief account of the charities of the Company. 61p. *8°.* [*London*, 1849]

36717 MACGREGOR, R. S. A plan for raising a defensive force; remodelled from the disembodied militia, &c....Second edition, revised and enlarged. 20p. *8°. Edinburgh, London, &c.*, 1849.

36718 RAPHALL, M. J. Jewish dogmas. A correspondence between Dr. Raphall, M.A. preacher at the synagogue and head master of the Hebrew National School at Birmingham, and C. N. Newdegate, M.P. 49p. *8°.* 1849.

36719 SENSUS COMMUNIS, *pseud.* The cholera, no judgment! The efficacy, philosophy, and practical tendency of the prayer by the Archbishop of Canterbury, ordered to be used during the prevalence of cholera, examined in a letter, addressed to the Right Hon. the Earl of Carlisle. 19p. *8°.* [1849] *Attributed, in a manuscript note on the title-page, to B. Britten.*

36720 Our great **STATE-CHURCH** Parliament.

Reprinted from the "Standard of Freedom." Corrected and much enlarged. 38p. *8°*. [*London*, 1849]

36721 THOMAS, F. S. A history of the State Paper Office; with a view of the documents therein deposited. 83p. *8°*. 1849.

36722 THOUGHTS on the present state of the legal establishment in Ireland. By a resident in Dublin. 21p. *8°*.

Dublin, 1849. *The copy that belonged to Earl De Grey.*

36723 —— [Another edition.] 21p. *8°*. *London & Dublin*, 1849.

36724 A few **WORDS** on the endowment of the Roman Catholic clergy in Ireland. By an English Protestant. 15p. *8°*. 1849.

1850

GENERAL

36725 A. and B. A run across Ireland, in August 1850 ...Reprinted from the Scotsman. 64p. *12°*. *n.p.* [1850 ?]

36726 [**AGOULT**, M. C. S. D', *Comtesse.*] Histoire de Révolution de 1848 par Daniel Stern. 292p. *8°*. *Paris*, 1850.

36727 BAGSHAW, S. History, gazetteer, and directory of the County Palatine of Chester; comprising a general survey of the county, with a variety of historical, statistical, topographical, commercial, and agricultural information... 711p. *8°*. *Sheffield*, 1850

36728 BASTIAT, C. F. Harmonies économiques. 463p. *8°*. *Paris*, 1850.

36729 BRENTANO, H. Geschichtliche Hauptmomente der Nationalökonomie und Handels-Produktion ...(Besonderer Abdruck des Programms zu dem Jahresberichte der k. Handels- und Gewerb-Schule zu Fürth... 1849/50.) 16p. *4°*. *Fürth*, [1850].

36730 BRIGHT, JOHN (1811–1889). Mr. Bright's speech on Ireland. Meeting of Irish residents in Manchester. Presentation of an address to J. Bright, Esq., M.P. (From the Manchester Examiner and Times of... Jan. 5, 1850.) 8p. *8°*. *Manchester*, [1850]

36731 The **BRITISH ALMANAC** of the Society for the Diffusion of Useful Knowledge, for...1850... [With 'The companion to the Almanac; or, year-book of general information'.] 96, 264p. *12°*. [1850] *For other editions, see* 1828.

36732 BROUCKÈRE, C. DE. Principes généraux d'économie politique. 124p. *12°*. *Bruxelles*, [1850]

36733 [**BYLES**, SIR J. B.] Sophisms of free trade and popular political economy examined. By a barrister. Sixth edition: with corrections and additions. 249p. *8°*. 1850. *For another edition, see* 1849.

36734 CALIFORNIA: its past history; its present position; its future prospects: containing a history of the country from its colonization by the Spaniards to the present time; a sketch of its geographical and physical features...including a history of the...Mormon settlements. With an appendix containing the official reports made to the government of the United States. 270p. *8°*. [1850]

36735 —— [Another impression.] 270p. *8°*. 1850.

36736 CARLYLE, T. Latter-day pamphlets edited by Thomas Carlyle. [Nos. 1–8, February–August, 1850.] 56, 46, 48, 54, 50, 47, 46, 53p. *12°*. 1850. *Contents: 1. The present time; 2. Model prisons; 3. Downing Street; 4. The*

new Downing Street; 5. Stump-orator; 6. Parliaments; 7. Hudson's statue; 8. Jesuitism.

For **CHAMBERS'S PAPERS FOR THE PEOPLE**, 1850–51, *see vol.* III, *Periodicals list.*

36737 COBDEN, R. Speeches of Richard Cobden, Esq., M.P., on peace, financial reform, colonial reform, and other subjects. Delivered during 1849. Printed by permission of, and kindly revised by Mr. Cobden. 252p. *12°*. *London, Liverpool, &c.*, [1850]

36738 Fair and foul **COMPETITION**. To artizans, handicraftsmen, and working men. 8p. *8°*. *Edinburgh: The Scottish Protective Association*, [1850]

36739 What is **COMPETITION?** [A connected summary of the answers given by the boys attending the voluntary Saturday class at the Birkbeck School (London Mechanics' Institution).] 16p. *8°*. [1850 ?] *Compiled by the same hand as no.* 36765.

36740 CONVENTION OF IRON MASTERS. Documents relating to the manufacture of iron in Pennsylvania. Published on behalf of the Convention of Iron Masters, which met in Philadelphia, on the twentieth of December, 1849... 115p. *8°*. *Philadelphia*, 1850. *The copy presented to Richard C. Taylor by Charles E. Smith, one of the secretaries of the Convention.*

36741 CORN and currency: a compilation of arguments and documents, from various sources, [chiefly from the writings of Agrestis in the Derbyshire Courier and the speeches of J. Twells] showing that free trade & a fettered currency are utterly incompatible; and lie at the root of all the national difficulties. 15p. *8°*. *London, Chesterfield printed*, [1850]

36742 [**CRAIK**, G. L., *ed.*] Index to the Pictorial history of England: forming a complete chronological key to the civil and military events, the lives of remarkable persons...By H. C. Hamilton. 280p. *8°*. 1850. *The index to the edition published in 1849. For an edition of the* Pictorial history, *see* 1838.

36743 CRAWFORD, WILLIAM S. Depopulation not necessary. An appeal to the British members of the Imperial Parliament, against the extermination of the Irish people...Second edition. 43p. *8°*. *London & Dublin*, 1850. *The copy that belonged to Earl De Grey.*

36744 DAWSON, GEORGE P. How to live; in a letter addressed to agriculturists. 21p. *8°*. *London & York*, 1850.

36745 DICKENS, C. J. H. American notes for general circulation... 175p. *8°*. 1850.

36746 [DOVE, P. E.] The theory of human progression, and natural probability of a reign of justice. (*The Science of Politics*, 1.) 523p. *8°. London & Edinburgh, 1850. The copy that belonged to Henry Higgs.*

36747 ELLIOTT, E. More verse and prose by the cornlaw rhymer. 2 vols. *8°. 1850.*

36748 [ELLIS, WILLIAM (1800–1881).] Outlines of social economy. Second edition. 116p. *8°. 1850.*

36749 [——] Principes élémentaires d'économie sociale à l'usage des écoles...Traduits de l'anglais par M. C. Terrien, avec une préface du traducteur et une introduction de M. Barthélemy Saint-Hilaire. 171p. *12°. Paris, 1850. For another edition, see 1846.*

36750 FRÉGIER, H. A. Histoire de l'administration de la police de Paris depuis Philippe-Auguste jusqu'aux États Généraux de 1789 ou tableau moral et politique de la ville de Paris durant cette période considéré dans ses rapports avec l'action de la police... 2 vols. *8°. Paris, 1850.*

36751 GARNIER, A. Morale sociale, ou devoirs de l'état et des citoyens en ce qui concerne la propriété, la famille, l'éducation, la liberté, l'égalité, l'organisation du pouvoir, la sûreté intérieure et extérieure. 396p. *8°. Paris, 1850.*

36752 GIBBON, A. Past and present delusions in the political economy and consequent errors in the legislation, of the United Kingdom. 181p. *8°. Edinburgh & London, 1850.*

36753 GREELEY, H. Hints toward reforms, in lectures, addresses, and other writings. 400p. *12°. New-York, 1850.*

36754 GUIZOT, F. P. G. Why was the English revolution successful? A discourse on the history of the English revolution...Translated by William Hazlitt. [Second edition.] 78p. *8°. 1850.*

36755 HAMAL, F. DE, *Graaf.* Beginselen der staathuishoudkunde, ten gebruike van jonge lieden, die zich aan eene staatkundige of administratieve loopbaan willen toewijden. 138p. *8°. Deventer, 1850.*

For **HUNT'S MERCHANTS' MAGAZINE,** *1850–60, see* vol. III, *Periodicals list,* Merchants' magazine and commercial review.

36756 LAING, SAMUEL (1780–1868). Observations on the social and political state of the European people in 1848 and 1849; being the second series of the Notes of a traveller. 534p. *8°. 1850.*

36757 LIST, F. Friedrich List's gesammelte Schriften, herausgegeben von Ludwig Häusser. 3 vols. *8°. Stuttgart & Tübingen, 1850–51.*

36758 The lamented **LOSS** and death of the Right Honourable Sir Robert Peel, Bart, M.P....[A ballad.] *s.sh.fol. [London, 1850] [Br. 624]*

36759 LOW, D. Appeal to the common sense of the country regarding the present condition of the industrious classes; and exposition of the effects of what is called free trade on British agriculture and the classes dependent upon it, as well as on the general prosperity of the Empire. 138p. *8°. Edinburgh & London, 1850.*

36760 M'QUEEN, J. Statistics of agriculture, manufactures and commerce. Drawn up from official and authentic documents...Second edition – with additions. 69p. *8°. Edinburgh & London, 1850.*

36761 [MATHIEU, A.] Mémoires d'outre-tombe d'un peuplier mort au service de la République. 108p. *12°. Paris, 1850.*

36762 Réimpression de l'ancien **MONITEUR,** seule histoire authentique et inaltérée de la Révolution française depuis le réunion des États-Généraux jusqu'au Consulat (mai 1789–novembre 1799) avec des notes explicatives... [With 'Introduction historique' and 'Table...par M. A. Ray.'] 32 vols. *fol. Paris, 1850–54.*

For the **NATIONAL INSTRUCTOR,** *see* vol. III, *Periodicals list.*

36763 NATIONAL REFORM CONFERENCE. Address...to the friends of Parliamentary and financial reform throughout the kingdom. Drawn up in accordance with the unanimous resolution of the Conference by the Business Committee. [Signed: J. Henry Tillett, chairman of the Business Committee, and Joshua Walmsley, chairman of the Conference. Dated: April 27th, 1850.] 2p. *s.sh.8°. n.p. [1850]*

36764 O'CALLAGHAN, E. B. The documentary history of the State of New-York. Arranged under direction of the Hon. Christopher Morgan, Secretary of State ... 4 vols. *4°. Albany, 1850–51.*

36765 Not **OVER-POPULATION,** but undereducation, the cause of destitution: not more emigration, but more education, and of better quality, the remedy for destitution. [The answers of the Birkbeck-boys.] 15p. *8°. [c. 1850] Compiled by the same hand as no. 36739.*

For the **PEOPLE'S REVIEW OF LITERATURE AND POLITICS,** *see* vol. III, *Periodicals list.*

36766 PHILANTHROPOS, *pseud.* A voice from the country, or, the case freely stated...Third edition. 27p. *8°. 1850.*

36767 RAIKES, H. Political economy, as taught by the Bible. A lecture delivered at the Mechanics' Institute, in Chester, February 27, 1850...Published by request. 57p. *8°. Chester, 1850.*

36768 ROGERS, H. Essays, selected from contributions to the Edinburgh Review. 2 vols. *8°. 1850.*

36769 SALVUCCI, F. A few brief observations upon England. 70p. *12°. [1850] Presentation copy from the author to T. Richardson.*

36770 SANDELIN, A. Répertoire général d'économie politique, ancienne et moderne... 6 vols. *8°. La Haye, 1850.*

36771 SAURIAC, X. Un système d'organisation sociale. 246p. *8°. Paris, 1850.*

36772 SENIOR, N. W. Encyclopædia metropolitana: or, system of universal knowledge: on a methodical plan projected by Samuel Taylor Coleridge. Second edition revised. First division. Pure sciences. [6] Political economy. [By Nassau William Senior...Reprinted from the original edition.] 231p. *8°. London & Glasgow, 1850. Originally published with the title* An outline of the science of political economy, *in 1836 (q.v.).*

36773 STRANG, J. The progress of Glasgow, in population, wealth, manufactures, &c. Being the substance of a paper read before the Statistical Section of the British Association for the Advancement of Science, in Edinburgh, on...6th August, 1850. 18p. *8°. 1850.*

36774 Un **SYSTÈME** philosophique. 95p. *8°*. [*Paris, 1850?*]

36775 **THOM'S IRISH ALMANAC** and official directory, with the Post Office Dublin city and county directory, for...1850...Seventh annual publication. 1068p. *8°*. *Dublin, London, &c.,* 1850.

36776 **THUENEN,** J. H. VON. Der naturgemässe Arbeitslohn und dessen Verhältniss zum Zinsfuss und zur Landrente...Erste Abtheilung. 285p. *8°*. *Rostock,* 1850. *For the first part of this work,* Der isolirte Staat in Beziehung auf Landwirthschaft und Nationalökonomie, *see* 1842.

36777 The **TITHE-OWNER'S** tale; or, a bleat from the pastures. By a black sheep. 39p. *8°*. 1850.

36778 **TRACTS** for the million. Nos. 5–10. [A series of papers against free trade.] 6 vols. *8°*. [1850–51?]

For **UNIVERSITY OF DUBLIN,** Transactions of the Dublin University Philosophical Society, *see* vol. III, *Periodicals list,* Transactions...

36779 **URQUHART,** W. P. Essays on subjects in political economy. 124p. *8°*. *Aberdeen, Edinburgh, &c.,* 1850.

36780 **V.,** S. Hoe kan men een volk rijk maken? 26p. *12°. n.p.* [*c.* 1850?] '*S.V.' was probably Simon Vissering.*

36781 **VISSERING,** S. Redevoering over vrijheid het grondbeginsel der staathuishoudkunde, uitgesproken den 23sten maart, 1850...aan de Hoogeschool te Leiden. 28p. *8°. n.p.* [1850]

36782 **WASON,** R. A letter to J. Bright, Esq., M.P., on the remedies he proposed for the relief of Ireland: with a suggestion for the introduction of capital into that country. 16p. *8°. Ayr,* 1850.

36783 **WATKINS,** J. Life, poetry, and letters of Ebenezer Elliott, the corn-law rhymer. With an abstract of his politics. 273p. *12°*. 1850. *With the book-plate of Sir Robert Peel, 3rd Bart.*

36784 **WHEWELL,** W. Mathematical exposition of some doctrines of political economy. Second memoir. [From *Transactions of the Cambridge Philosophical Society.*] 22p. *4°. n.p.* [1850] *The copy that belonged to George Pryme.*

36785 *★——* Mathematical exposition of certain doctrines of political economy. Third memoir. [From *Transactions of the Cambridge Philosophical Society.*] 7p. *4°. n.p.* [1850] *Presentation copy from the author to Augustus De Morgan.*

36786 **WHITE,** FRANCIS, & CO. History, gazetteer and directory of Warwickshire, comprising a general survey of the county, with a variety of historical, statistical, topographical, commercial, and agricultural information ... 915p. *8°. Sheffield,* 1850.

36787 **WHITE,** WILLIAM (*fl.* 1826–1870). History, gazetteer, and directory of Devonshire, and the city and county of the City of Exeter; comprising a general survey of the county of Devon, and the diocese of Exeter; with separate historical, statistical, & topographical descriptions of all the boroughs, towns...parishes... 804p. *12°. Sheffield & London,* 1850.

For the **WORKING MAN'S FRIEND, AND FAMILY INSTRUCTOR,** 1850–52, *see* vol. III, *Periodicals list.*

AGRICULTURE

For el **AGRICULTOR ESPAÑOL,** *see* vol. III, *Periodicals list.*

36788 **ALISON,** W. P. Observations on the reclamation of waste lands and their cultivation by croft husbandry, considered with a view to the productive employment of destitute labourers, paupers, and criminals. 88p. *8°. Edinburgh & London,* 1850.

36789 The useful **ARTS** employed in the production of food. The second edition. 183p. *8°* 1850.

36790 **BARTLETT,** T. A treatise on British mining; with a digest of the cost book system, stannarie and general mining laws. 87p. *8°*. 1850. *Presentation copy from the author to Robert C. May.*

36791 [**BARTY,** J. S.] Caird's high farming harrowed. By Cato the Censor. Reprinted from Blackwood's magazine with an appendix. 38p. *8°. Edinburgh & London,* 1850.

36792 [——] Peter Plough's letters to the Right Honourable Lord Kinnaird, on high farming and free trade. 62p. *8°. Edinburgh & London,* 1850.

36793 **BOURN,** J. A corn rent with tenant-right, a substitute for protection. 15p. *8°. Bewdley, Kidderminster, &c.,* [1850]

36794 **BURRELL,** P. R. D., *Baron Willoughby de Eresby.* Ploughing by steam. [4]p., 2 plates. *4°*. 1850.

36795 **CAIRD,** SIR J. High farming, under liberal covenants, the best substitute for protection...Seventh edition. 33p. *8°. Edinburgh & London,* 1850. *For other editions, see* 1849.

36796 —— High farming vindicated and farther illustrated. 35p. *8°. Edinburgh & London,* 1850.

36797 —— Fourth edition, enlarged, – with notes, and comparative tables of the cost and results of high farming under free trade, and ordinary farming under protection. 47p. *8°. Edinburgh & London,* 1850.

36798 —— The plantation scheme; or, the west of Ireland as a field for investment. 191p. *8°. Edinburgh & London,* 1850.

36799 **CARLTON GARDENING SOCIETY.** Carlton Gardening Society. [Rules.] 8p. *12°*. [*Worksop, 1850?*]

36800 **COTTERILL,** C. F. Agricultural distress, its cause and remedy; with a preliminary inquiry concerning the civil law of the freedom of private enterprise. 151p. *8°*. 1850.

36801 **ENGLAND.** *Laws, etc.* Abstract of an Act of Parliament, (19th Geo. III., Ch. 33, 1779,) "for draining, improving, and preserving the low lands; in the parishes of Altcar, Sefton, Halsall, and Walton-upon-the-Hill, in the County Palatine of Lancaster." And some facts... showing the commencement and progress of the works up to the present period. 162p. *8°. Liverpool,* 1850.

36802 The **FARMERS' ALMANAC** and calendar

for 1850, being the second after bissextile, or leap year. By Cuthbert W. Johnson, Esq., and William Shaw, Esq. 188p. *12°*. 1850.

36803 *FREND, H. T. Outlines of a plan for insuring the stability and reducing the expense of investigating titles to landed property, by means of their official investigation and certification. 23p. *8°*. 1850. *The words 'of investigating' have been altered in manuscript on the title-page to 'of the verification of'. The copy that belonged to Augustus De Morgan.*

36804 HOLDFAST, *pseud.* Mr. Huxtable's sophisms exposed: by Holdfast. Reprinted from the Dorset County Chronicle, with notes and additions. 46p. *8°*. 1850.

36805 HORE, H. F. An inquiry into the legislation, control, and improvement of the salmon and sea fisheries of Ireland. 201p. *8°*. *Dublin,* 1850.

36806 HUXTABLE, A. The "present prices"... Third edition. 34p. *8°*. *Blandford & London,* 1850.

36807 —— Fourth edition. 34p. *8°*. *Blandford & London,* 1850.

36808 —— Fifth edition. 54p. *8°*. *Blandford & London,* 1850.

36809 —— Sixth edition. 54p. *8°*. *Blandford & London,* 1850.

36810 —— Seventh edition. [With an appendix and 'Postscript. Remarks on Porcius's pamphlet, "Mr. Huxtable and his pigs"'.] 64p. *8°*. *Blandford & London,* 1850.

36811 IRELAND. *Board of Public Works.* 10th Vict., Cap. 32; 12th Vict., Cap. 23; 12th and 13th Vict., Cap. 59; and 13th and 14th Vict., Cap. 31. Acts to facilitate the improvement of landed property in Ireland. Instructions [prepared by Sir R. J. Griffith] to owners applying for loans for farm buildings; and to persons employed in reporting on such applications, under the above-mentioned Acts. 46p. *8°*. *Dublin,* 1850.

36812 JOHNSON, WALTER R. The coal trade of British America, with researches on the characters and practical values of American and foreign coals. 179p. *8°*. *Washington & Philadelphia,* 1850.

36813 JOHNSTON, JAMES F. W. The state of agriculture in Europe. An address delivered at the annual exhibition of the New York State Agricultural Society, at Syracuse, September 13th, 1849. 47p. *8°*. *Albany,* 1850.

36814 A LETTER addressed to the country party. By a country gentleman. [On measures to benefit British and Irish agriculture.] 8p. *8°*. 1850.

36815 MANGON, H. Études sur les irrigations de la Campine et les travaux analogues de la Sologne et d'autres parties de la France. 117p. *8°*. *Paris,* 1850.

36816 MEREWETHER, H. A. The speech of Mr. Serjeant Merewether, in the Court of Chancery... December 8, 1849, upon the claim of the Commissioners of Woods and Forests to the sea-shore, and the soil and bed of tidal harbours and navigable rivers; the nature and extent of the claim, and its effect upon such property. 48p. *8°*. *London & Dublin,* 1850.

36817 MILNE, afterwards **MILNE HOME,** DAVID. Report of a visit to the farms of Mr. Rigden, Sussex, Rev. Mr. Huxtable, Dorset, and Mr. Morton, Gloucestershire. With remarks on agricultural improvement...Read to a meeting of the East of Berwickshire Farmers' Club. 63p. *8°*. *Edinburgh & London,* 1850.

36818 MONRO, E. Agricultural colleges and their working. A letter to A. J. B. Hope, Esq., M.P. 72p. *8°*. *Oxford & London,* 1850.

36819 NANT-A'R-NELLE SILVER LEAD MINES. Situate in Carmarthenshire, South Wales. Prospectus. *s.sh.fol.* [c. 1850]

36820 NATIONAL ASSOCIATION FOR THE PROTECTION OF BRITISH INDUSTRY AND CAPITAL. Reports on the state of the agricultural interest of the United Kingdom. Received by the National Association...from the local protection societies. May, 1850. 54p. *8°*. [1850]

36821 PORCIUS, *pseud.* Mr. Huxtable and his pigs. 30p. *8°*. *Edinburgh & London,* 1850.

36822 POWDAVIE, *pseud.* The tenants and landlords versus the newspaper press and the free traders. 30p. *8°*. *Edinburgh, London, &c.,* 1850.

36823 Strictly private. **PROPOSAL** for establishing a small proprietors' society of Ireland. 24p. *12°*. *n.p.* [c. 1850] *The copy that belonged to Earl De Grey.*

36824 RICHMOND, J. New catalogue of James Richmond's agricultural implements. Victoria Bridge & Richmond Square, Salford, Manchester. 38p. *8°*. *Manchester,* [c. 1850]

36825 [RODWELL, J.] The rat! and its cruel cost to the nation. By Uncle James. 47p. *8°*. [1850] *The title on the wrapper reads: Rat!!! Rat!!! Rat!!! a treatise on the nature, fecundity and devastating character of the [rat], etc.*

36826 ROTHWELL, W. Report of the agriculture of the county of Lancaster...Written for the Royal Agricultural Society of England, 1849. Together with an appendix, containing reports of crops...for 1849... 162, 67p. *8°*. *London, Chester, &c.,* 1850.

36827 ROYAL SOCIETY FOR THE PROMOTION AND IMPROVEMENT OF THE GROWTH OF FLAX IN IRELAND. The ninth annual report of the...Society...with an appendix, treasurer's statement of accounts, and list of subscriptions and donations, for the year ending 31st October, 1849. 63p. *8°*. *Belfast,* 1850.

36828 [RUSSEL, A.] ⟨From the Edinburgh Review for April, 1850.⟩ Agricultural complaints. 28p. *8°*. [1850]

For the **SCIENTIFIC AND PRACTICAL AGRICULTURIST,** *see* vol. III, *Periodicals list.*

36829 SEWELL, H. A letter to the Earl of Yarborough, on the burthens affecting real property arising from the present state of the law; with reasons in favour of a general registry of titles...Second edition, with a preface referring to the Irish Sale of Incumbered Estates Act. 110p. *8°*. 1850.

36830 SHELLEY, SIR J. V., *Bart.* Comparative results on a two-hundred-acre farm, at the present time (1850), and 12, 13, or 14 years back. 7p. *8°*. *Lewes,* 1850.

36831 —— Mr. John Ellman's examination and criticism of calculations as to the comparative results on a two-hundred-acre farm, at the present time (1850), and 12, 13, or 14 years back, replied to by John Villiers Shelley, Esq. 16p. *8⁰. Lewes*, 1850.

36832 SMITH, EDMUND J. The error of mistaking net rental for permanent income. 11p. *8⁰.* 1850.

36833 SMITH, HUGH (*fl.* 1850). Free farming to meet free trade. 31p. *8⁰.* 1850.

36834 SMITH, RICHARD (*fl.* 1850). A new treatise on the most profitable system of farming. 57p. *8⁰. Brighton,* 1850.

36835 SPOONER, E. O. The adventures and transformations of nitrogen and ammonia; or, the Rev. A.

Huxtable's great pig-secret analyzed. With notes and comments on Dorsetshire agriculture...An address delivered at the Blandford Farmers' Club on...Feb. 27, 1850. 11p. *8⁰. London & Blandford,* 1850.

36836 STRACHAN, JAMES, *schoolmaster.* A series of tables on draining: showing the number of roods and of rods of drains, in any quantity of land...Second edition, carefully revised, with additions. p.1–[54]. *long 12⁰. Edinburgh & London,* 1850.

36837 WARNES, J. Flax versus cotton; or, the two-edged sword against pauperism and slavery...No. I. 57p. *8⁰.* 1850.

CORN LAWS

36838 BLACKER, W. Pro corn-law tracts...No. III. Is it the producer or the consumer that pays a protecting duty? or is it paid, according to circumstances, partly by each? and if so, by what rules are their respective proportions regulated? 15p. *8⁰.* 1850. *A letter from the author to Lord Monteagle, accompanying the pamphlet, is bound in after the title-page.*

36839 COBBETT, W. Fulfilment of prophecy; or, Cobbett on the corn laws. Dedicated to the landlords and farmers of England. 24p. *12⁰.* 1850.

36840 K., D. A letter to the Right Hon. Lord John Russell, M.P., in favour of a protective duty on the importation of foreign grain. 23p. *8⁰.* 1850. *Presentation copy from the unidentified author to Lord Stanley.*

36841 [PHILLIPS, G. S.] The life, character, and genius, of Ebenezer Elliott, the corn law rhymer. [A lecture delivered before the Leeds Mechanics' Institute and Literary Society.] By January Searle. 184p. *12⁰.* 1850.

POPULATION

36842 SUMNER, J. B., *Archbishop of Canterbury.* A treatise on the records of the Creation...with particular reference to the Jewish history, and to the consistency of

the principle of population with the wisdom and goodness of the Deity...Sixth edition. 445p. *8⁰.* 1850. *For other editions, see* 1818.

TRADES & MANUFACTURES

36843 BARCLAY, JOHN, *iron-broker.* Statistics of the Scotch iron trade...Printed for private circulation. 23p. *12⁰. Glasgow,* 1850.

36844 CHUBB, J. On the construction of locks and keys...Excerpt minutes of proceedings of the Institute of Civil Engineers, vol. IX. by permission of the Council. 36p. *8⁰.* [1850]

36845 DOBSON, E. A rudimentary treatise on the manufacture of bricks and tiles; containing an outline of the principles of brickmaking, and detailed accounts of the various processes employed in the making of bricks and tiles in different parts of England... 2 vols. *12⁰.* 1850.

36846 GORDON, WILLIAM E. A. The economy of the marine steam engine; with suggestions for its improvement, and notes upon various subjects connected with steam...Second edition. [With 'The economy of the marine steam-engine further considered, with an exposure of the errors contained in a review of that work by the "Artizan"'.] 148, 14p. *8⁰.* 1850.

36847 KNIGHT AND WOOD. A list of new wheel patterns, belonging to Knight and Wood, late Stoddart & Knight, Millwrights, Brass and Iron Founders, Victoria Foundry, Garside Street, Bolton. 46p. *8⁰. Bolton,* 1850.

36848 LACROIX, P. and SERÉ, F. Le livre d'or des métiers. Histoire de l'orfévrerie-joaillerie et des anciennes communautés et confréries d'orfévres-joailliers de la France et de la Belgique. 216p. *8⁰. Paris,* 1850.

36849 MONTGOMERY, JAMES (*fl.* 1850). In the Circuit Court of the United State in and for the Eastern District of Pennsylvania, in the third circuit of October sessions, 1850. No. 4. James Montgomery and Thomas Ward vs. the Philadelphia and Atlantic Steam Navigation Company. [A lawsuit concerning infringement of patents on steam boilers.] 23p. *8⁰. n.p.* [1850]

36850 NORMANDY, A. R. The commercial handbook of chemical analysis; or practical instructions for the determination of the intrinsic or commercial value of substances used in manufactures, in trades, and in the arts. 640p. *8⁰.* 1850.

36851 OUIN LA CROIX, C. Histoire des anciennes corporations d'arts et métiers et des confréries religieuses de la capitale de la Normandie. 763p. *8⁰. Rouen,* 1850.

36852 PHILOPONOS, *pseud.* The Great Exhibition of 1851; or, the wealth of the world in its workshops. Comparing the relative skill of the manufacturers, designers, and artisans of England with that of France, Belgium, Prussia, and other continental states. 139p. *8⁰.* 1850.

36853 WATSON, LEE, & COMPANY. A list of spur, mortise, bevel & mitre wheel patterns, belonging to Lee Watson & Compy., Engineers, Brass and Iron Founders, St. Helens Foundry, Lancashire. 27p. *8⁰. n.p.* [c. 1850]

COMMERCE

36854 AUSTRIA. *Direction der administrativen Statistik.* Mittheilungen über Handel, Gewerbe und Verkehrsmittel, so wie aus dem Gebiete der Statistik überhaupt, nach Berichten an das k.k.Handels-Ministerium... Erster Jahrgang. 665p. *8°. Wien,* 1850.

36855 BELL, JOHN (*fl.* 1850). The usurer versus the producer; or, free trade illustrated. 31p. *8°.* 1850.

36856 BERKELEY, HON. G. C. G. F. Two letters addressed to the landed and manufacturing interests of the United Kingdom of Great Britain and Ireland, on the just maintenance of free trade. 14p. *8°.* 1850.

36857 [BOWRING, E. A. and **HOBART,** V. H., *Baron Hobart.*] Free trade and its so-called sophisms: a reply to 'Sophisms of free trade, etc., examined by a barrister.' 90p. *8°.* 1850. *The copy that belonged to E. A. Bowring, with his name on the fly-leaf. The authors' contributions have been identified in manuscript in the contents list.*

36858 —— Second edition, revised and enlarged. 95p. *8°.* 1850.

36859 BRANDON, W. An inquiry into the Freedom of the City of London in connection with trade, and into the laws and ordinances within the city respecting wholesale and retail traders; and the power of the Corporation over persons carrying on trade within the city, not being free. 56p. *8°.* 1850.

36860 BRÉE, P. Traité de correspondence commerciale, contenant des modèles et des formules épistolaires pour tous les cas qui se présentent dans les opérations de commerce...Suivi d'un recueil des termes les plus usités dans le commerce...Avec des notes allemandes par le Dr. E. I. Hauschild. 390p. *8° Leipzig,* 1850.

36861 CITY OF LONDON CENTRAL MARKETS' ASSOCIATION. An appeal to the British public; or, the abuses of Smithfield Market and the advantages of a new central cattle market fairly considered. 16p. *8°.* [1850]

36862 The south **COAST** of England. The means of preserving life and property, and of promoting European trade, by the more general use of Southampton and other ports on the south coast, and the more perfect adaptation to the purposes of commerce, demonstrated. 28p. *8°.* 1850.

36863 DANSON, J. T. From the Journal of the Statistical Society of London, May, 1850. On the fluctuations of the annual supply and average price of corn, in France, during the last seventy years, considered with particular reference to the political periods of 1792, 1814, 1830 and 1848. ⟨Read before the Statistical Section of the British Association, at Birmingham, in September, 1849.⟩ 16p. *8°. n.p.* [1850]

36864 [DICK, T.] The trade of the future, a hint to the merchants & traders of London, and equally important to merchants and traders of every class and description residing in...Great Britain...By a citizen of Edinburgh. 10p. *12°.* 1850.

36865 "Our **DUTY** and our encouragement." An address to the protectionist constituency of these realms. In which is inserted a promissory note to Messrs. Cobden and Feargus O'Connor. By "Pro ecclesia Dei." 16p. *8°.* 1850.

36866 EASTERN ARCHIPELAGO COM- **PANY.** Proceedings at a general meeting of the shareholders of the Eastern Archipelago Company. 24p. *8°.* [1850]

36867 [ELLIOT, JOHN L.] A letter to the electors of Westminster. From an aristocrat. 100p. *8°.* 1850.

36868 FERRAND, W. B. The Farmers' Wool League and the cotton trade. Speech of W. Busfeild Ferrand, Esq., at the Doncaster protectionist meeting, April 20th 1850. 8p. *8°. Reading,* [1850]

36869 FLETCHER, J. W. Free trade and restricted currency. A re-publication of six letters which have appeared in the Worcester Journal...(Reprinted at the request of many of his brother farmers.) 22p. *8°. Worcester,* 1850.

36870 LAIRD, W. The export coal trade of Liverpool: a letter to Thomas Littledale Esq., chairman of the Liverpool Dock Trust...Second edition. 59p. *8°. Liverpool,* 1850.

36871 —— Third edition. 59p. *8°. Liverpool,* 1850.

36872 [LAWRENCE, AMOS A.] The condition and prospects of American cotton manufactures in 1849–50. Reprinted from Hunt's Merchants' Magazine [December 1849 and January 1850]. 29p. *8°. n.p.* [1850]

36873 LEVI, L. Commercial law, its principles and administration; or, the mercantile law of Great Britain with the codes and laws of commerce of...mercantile countries... 2 vols. *4°. London, Edinburgh, &c.,* 1850–51.

36874 LEWIS, JOSIAH. The silk trade and protection. To the editor of the Derby Mercury. [Dated: February 11th, 1850.] 2p. *s.sh.8°. n.p.* [1850] [*Br.* 625]

36875 MATTHYSSENS, H. F. La Hollande, l'Angleterre et la Belgique. Modifications proposées au tarif des douanes et aux lois de navigation des Pays-Bas. Traité de commerce conclu en 1846 entre la Belgique et la Hollande. 103p. *8°. Anvers,* 1850. *The copy that belonged to Victor Considérant.*

36876 Just published...the People's Edition of Richard **OASTLER'S** reply to Richard Cobden's speech at Leeds, December 18th, 1849. [A publisher's circular, quoting from reviews in the British press.] *s.sh.fol.* [1850] [*Br.* 623]

36877 PEARSON, ROBERT. Free trade. A reply to "Sophisms of free trade, and popular political economy examined. By a barrister."... 48p. *8°.* 1850.

36878 PHILLIPS, WILLARD. Propositions concerning protection and free trade. 233p. *12°. Boston,* 1850.

36879 The **PRICE** of wheat in Europe: the past a test for the future. Present prices and stocks of wheat in Europe. Agricultural statistics. Reprinted from "The Economist." 24p. *8°.* 1850.

36880 A lay **SERMON** on the influence of free trade, and the instability of our national prosperity, as based on cotton manufactures. By an old soldier. 48p. *8°.* 1850.

36881 STAUNTON, SIR G. T., *Bart.* Miscellaneous notices relating to China, and our commercial intercourse with that country, including a few translations from the Chinese language...Second edition; enlarged in 1822, and accompanied, in 1850, by introductory observations on the events which have affected our Chinese commerce during that interval. 432p. *8°*. 1822-1850 [i.e. 1850]

36882 —— Observations on our Chinese commerce; including remarks on the proposed reduction of the tea duties, our new settlement at Hong Kong, and the opium trade. 52p. *8°*. 1850.

36883 **T.,** T. H. Fallacies of free trade exposed. In seven letters, reprinted from the "Irish Farmers' Gazette." 37p. *12°*. *Dublin*, 1850.

36884 **TAYLOR,** JOHN (1781-1864). Free trade and protection to British industry. 8p. *8°*. *n.p.* [1850]

36885 **WHITMORE,** W. W. A few plain thoughts on free trade as affecting agriculture. Second edition. 2 vols. *8°*. *Bridgnorth*, [& *London*, 1850]

36886 **WILLIAMS,** A. Collected letters and arguments for and against protection. 54p. *8°*. *Reading*, 1840 [1850]

36887 **YEATMAN,** H. F. A speech in favour of protection to British capital and industry. 42, xxiip. *8°*. [1850]

COLONIES

36888 *****ABBOTT,** SIR F. Practical treatise on permanent bridges, for Indian rivers...Second edition. With a description of the use of wells for foundations, by Captain P. T. Cautley...(From the Journal of the Asiatic Society of Bengal, no. 88, April, 1849.) 64p. *8°*. *Agra*, 1850. *For another edition, see 1847.*

36889 **ADDERLEY,** C. B., *Baron Norton*. Some reflections on the speech of the Rt. Hon. Lord John Russell, on colonial policy...Published for the Society for the Reform of Colonial Government. 30p. *8°*. 1850.

36890 Improved **BRIDGE** from starvation to plenty. Annexation of Great Britain to her colonies by means of the Halifax and Quebec railway, combined with ocean omnibuses. [With 'Appendix. Extracts from the report of Major Robinson...on the Halifax and Quebec Railway, presented to Parliament February, 1849'.] 26p. *8°*. 1850.

36891 **BRITISH COLONIAL POLICY.** Municipalities confederated under a viceroy. With an appendix on military colonization as a government measure of emigration...By an absentee proprietor of land in New Zealand. 32p. *8°*. 1850.

36892 **JOHNSTON,** JAMES F. W. Report on the agricultural capabilities of the province of New Brunswick ...Second edition – – – ten thousand. 95p. *8°*. *Fredericton*, 1850.

36893 **KEEFER,** T. C. Prize essay. The canals of Canada: their prospects and influence. Written for a premium offered by His Excellency the Earl of Elgin and Kincardine... 111p. *8°*. *Toronto & Montreal*, 1850.

36894 **LOWE,** R., *Viscount Sherbrooke*. Speech on the Australian Colonies Bill, at a meeting at...the Society for the Reform of Colonial Government, June 1st, 1850... 32p. *8°*. [*London*, 1850]

36895 **MACKAY,** A. Analysis of the Australian Colonies' Government Bill...Published for the Society for the Reform of Colonial Government. 68p. *8°*. 1850.

36896 **McMURDO,** SIR W. M. C. Sir Charles Napier's Indian baggage-corps. Reply to Lieut.-Col. Burlton's attack. 83p. *8°*. 1850.

36897 **MACPHERSON,** W. The procedure of the civil courts of the East India Company in the Presidency of Fort William, in regular suits. lxi, 523, lviip. *8°*. *Calcutta & London*, 1850. *Presentation copy from the author to 'Rt. Hon. Lord Lindsay'.*

36898 **MOLESWORTH,** SIR W., *Bart*. Speeches of Sir William Molesworth, Bart. M.P. in the House of Commons during the session of 1850, on the Bill for the better government of the Australian colonies. 75p. *8°*. [1850]

36899 **PREMIUM,** BARTON, *pseud*. Eight years in British Guiana; being the journal of a residence in that province, from 1840 to 1848...With anecdotes... illustrating the social condition of its inhabitants; and the opinions of the writer on the state and prospects of our sugar colonies generally. By Barton Premium, a planter of the province. Edited by his friend. 305p. *8°*. *London, Liverpool, &c.*, 1850.

36900 *****The SETTLEMENT** of the land revenue in the North West Provinces of the Bengal Presidency. Reprinted from the Calcutta Review. 55p. *8°*. *Calcutta*, 1850.

36901 **SIDNEY,** S. Female emigration as it is – as it may be. A letter to the Right Honourable Sidney Herbert, M.P. With an appendix. 43p. *12°*. 1850.

36902 **SIRR,** H. C. Ceylon and the Cingalese; their history, government, and religion, the antiquities, institutions, produce, revenue, and capabilities of the island, with anecdotes illustrating the manners and customs of the people. 2 vols. *8°*. 1850.

36903 **SOCIETY FOR THE PROMOTION OF COLONIZATION.** Report of the General Committee. January 1850. 14p. *8°*. 1850.

36904 **STANLEY,** EDWARD H. S., *15th Earl of Derby*. Claims and resources of the West Indian Colonies. A letter to...W. E. Gladstone...Second edition. 111p. *8°*. 1850.

36905 —— Third edition. 111p. *8°*. 1850.

36906 **SULLIVAN,** J. A letter to the Right Honourable Sir John Hobhouse, Bart. M.P. conveying the opinions of Sir Thomas Munro, Sir John Malcolm, and Mr. Elphinstone, on the impolicy of destroying the native states of India. 22p. *8°*. 1850.

36907 **THERRY,** R. Letter to the Right Hon. Wm. E. Gladstone, M.P., with the address to the jury by His Honor Mr. Justice Therry, at the opening of the first Circuit Court, at Brisbane, Moreton Bay, May 13, 1850; and his speech at the dinner given...by the magistracy and gentry of the district. 40p. *8°*. *Sydney & London*, 1850.

36908 **TYRANNY** in India! Englishmen robbed of the blessings of trial by jury and English criminal law. Christianity insulted!!! 106p. *8°*. 1850.

36909 **WILSON,** F. A. and **RICHARDS,** A. B. Britain redeemed and Canada preserved... 556p. *8°*. 1850.

36910 **WYNTER,** J. C. Hints on Church colonization. 31p. *12°*. 1850.

FINANCE

36911 The **ANNUITY-TAX** Black-Book; containing a historical account of the origin, object, and operation of this opprobrious impost!! With details of...the citizens ...suffering imprisonment and loss of means from clerical persecution: and a review of the fraudulent means resorted to by the ministers, in order to get the tax legalised and extended, in 1809, over the inhabitants, without their knowledge or consent!! 24p. *8°. Edinburgh, 1850.*

36912 **AUDIFFRET,** C. L. G. D', *Marquis.* On public accountability and the Court of Accounts of France. [With 'Appendix. No. 1. Extract from the English translation of the history of the Consulate and the Empire of France under Napoleon. By M. A. Thiers. No. 2. On the budget. Extracted from the "Dictionnaire général d'administration," and translated from the French of the Marquis d'Audiffret'.] 104p. *8°. 1850.*

36913 ***BAILY,** F. The doctrine of life-annuities and assurances, analytically investigated and practically explained. Together with...tables...To which is now added an appendix...In two volumes... 621, 68p. *8°. 1813[1850] The copy that belonged to Augustus De Morgan. A copy of the spurious edition, with De Morgan's manuscript note, and a cutting from Notes and Queries, vol. 4, in which he drew attention to this edition. For other editions, see 1813.*

36914 **BANCKS,** W. To the Town Council and burgesses of Liverpool. A proposal for establishing a local currency, to be issued by the Corporation of Liverpool for the erection and completion of the public works of the town, without creating the necessity of any further impost upon the ratepayers for interest of borrowed capital. 8p. *8°. Liverpool, [1850]*

36915 **BANK OF ENGLAND.** A list of the Governors of the Bank of England, from the foundation, 1694. [12]p. *4°. Printed at the Bank of England, 1850.*

36916 Mutual **BANKING.** 94p. *8°. West Brookfield, Mass., 1850.*

36917 **BASTIAT,** C. F. Gratuité du crédit. Discussion entre M. Fr. Bastiat et M. Proudhon. 292p. *8°. Paris, 1850. The copy that belonged to T. E. Cliffe Leslie.*

36918 **BIRMINGHAM FIRE OFFICE.** Birmingham Fire Office, empowered by Act of Parliament... [An advertisement for the company, with an account of 'accidents from fire in Birmingham and its suburbs'.] [8]p. *8°. n.p. [1850] See note to no. 35334.*

36919 **BRODIE,** P. B. Tax on successions, and burdens on land, etc. A treatise on a tax on successions to real as well as personal property, and the revival of the house tax, as substitutes for the income tax; and on burdens on land and restrictions on commerce and loans of money. 92p. *8°. 1850.*

36920 **CANSDELL,** C. S. Solvency guaranteed. An address to the bankers, merchants, landlords, etc. of Great Britain; being the outline of a plan for the application of assurance to debts, bills of exchange, promissory notes, rent and monetary risks of every description...Second edition. 19p. *8°. 1850.*

36921 ***COMMERCIAL DEBT INSURANCE COMPANY.** The Commercial Debt Insurance Company. Provisionally registered pursuant to the Act 7 and 8 Vict., cap. 110...Capital. – £500,000, in 25,000 shares of £20 each...[Prospectus.] 12p. *12°. 1850. The copy that belonged to Augustus De Morgan.*

36922 **ENGLAND.** Parliament. *House of Lords.* An abstract of the Lords' Report on the currency. With facts for all classes. 15p. *8°. [London,] The National Currency Reform Association, 1850.*

36923 **EVANS,** D. M. An appendix to the first and second editions of The commercial crisis, 1847–48. Table of dividends paid by the principal failed London houses, revised up to January, 1850. [3]p. *8°. 1850. For editions of the original work, see 1848.*

36924 ***FAUCHER,** L. Histoire financière. De la situation financière et du Budget [de 1850]. 44p. *8°. Paris, 1850. Reprinted from the Revue des Deux Mondes, 1 Nov. 1849. The copy that belonged to George Grote.*

36925 **FINCH,** JOHN (1783–1857). Town dues & currency, free trade and protection to British industry. 46p. *8°. Liverpool, 1850.*

36926 **FRANCE.** *Louis Philippe, King.* Tarifs des matières et espèces d'or et d'argent publiés en exécution de l'Ordonnance royale du 30 juin 1835...et du decret du 15 septembre, 1849, pour l'argent...[With the texts of the ordonnance and the decree.] 29p. *4°. Paris, 1850.*

36927 Vom **GELDE.** 44p. *8°. Berlin, 1850.*

36928 **GREIG,** G. Are friendly societies, secret orders, &c., safe? No! A lecture delivered in the Corn Exchange, Manchester, on...December 6th, 1850...Lord Erskine, President of the Equitable Provident Institution, in the chair. 11p. *8°. London, Manchester, &c., [1850]*

36929 **GUILD,** J. W. A plea for life assurance. [With 'The Edinburgh Life Assurance Company', a prospectus.] 23p. *8°. Glasgow, 1850.*

36930 **HANCOCK,** WILLIAM N. The usury laws and the trade of lending money to the poor in Ireland. A paper read before the Dublin Statistical Society on the 18th February, 1850. 11p. *8°. Dublin, 1850.*

36931 **HELFERICH,** H. A. Anzeige des Feier des Geburtsfestes Sr. Majestät des Königs Wilhelm von Wurttemberg auf den 27. September 1850 von dem Rector und akademischen Senate des Universität Tübingen. Mit einer Abhandlung über die Frage: Wann ist ein Schutzzoll zu Gunsten solcher Gewerbszweige gerechtfertigt, für welche ein Land natürlich minder gut ausgerüstet ist, als das Ausland? 28p. *4°. Tübingen, [1850]*

36932 **HERON,** D. C. Three lectures on the principles of taxation, delivered at Queen's College, Galway, in Hilary Term, 1850. 110p. *8°. Dublin, 1850. The copy that belonged to T. E. Cliffe Leslie.*

36933 ***HIGHAM,** J. A. On the value of selection amongst assured lives...Read before the Institute of Actuaries, 25th March 1850... 16p. *8°. [1850] Presentation copy from the author to Augustus De Morgan.*

36934 **HUDSON,** G. Report of the evidence of George Hudson, Esq., M.P. on the trial of the cause of Richardson versus Wodson, York Summer Assizes, 1850. Edited by a barrister. Second edition. 44p. *8°. [1850]*

36935 **KEYSER,** H. The law relating to transactions on the Stock Exchange. 335p. *12°. 1850.*

36936 KINGDOM, W. Suggestions for improving the value of railway property and for the eventual liquidation of the National Debt. 15p. *8°.* [1850]

36937 KNIGHT, C. The struggles of a book [the Penny Cyclopædia] against excessive taxation [i.e. the Excise duty payable on the paper]. 15p. *8°.* [1850]

36938 —— Second edition. 15p. *8°.* [1850]

36939 KNOTT, J. M. ⟨For private circulation.⟩ The currency and the late Sir Robert Peel. [Correspondence between J. M. Knott and Sir R. Peel, in 1850, on the currency. With 'Extracts from private memoranda, on the national currency, in relation to taxation and productive industry'.] 23p. *8°.* n.p. [1850]

36940 —— [Another issue.] 23p. *8°.* n.p. [1850] *See note to no.* 33779.

36941 —— ⟨For private circulation.⟩ Extracts from private memoranda, on the national currency, in relation to taxation and productive industry. 7p. *8°.* n.p. [1850] *Another edition, with a collection of letters added, was printed with the author's The currency and the late Sir Robert Peel, nos. 36939–40, above.*

36942 KRAJENBRINK, J. A. Gedachten over eene regeling van het Indische muntstelsel. 31p. *8°. Tiel,* 1850.

36943 LAWSON, W. J. The history of banking; with a comprehensive account of the origin, rise, and progress of the banks of England, Ireland and Scotland. 524p. *8°.* 1850.

36944 A LETTER to the Right Hon. Sir Charles Wood, Bt., M.P. etc. etc. etc. Chancellor of the Exchequer, on the assessed taxes; with suggestions for a general revision of the duties. By an officer of the Tax Department of the Board of Inland Revenue. 42p. *8°.* 1850.

36945 A LETTER to the Right Hon. Sir Robert Peel, Bart. on the establishment of a state bank, the repeal of his currency measure of 1844 and free trade in banking. By a free trade banker. 52p. *8°. Glasgow & Edinburgh,* 1850.

36946 LIFE-ASSURANCE. A familiar dialogue [between Thomson and Jones]. 16p. *8°.* n.p. [1850?]

36947 *LIFE ASSURANCE. How to assure, and where to assure. A statement as to safety. Respectfully addressed to persons desirous of effecting policies with assurance societies, properly so called. By a quiet looker-on. 8p. *8°.* [c. 1850] *The copy that belonged to Augustus De Morgan.*

36948 MACLEAN, A. W. Observations on the fundamental principle of monetery [*sic*] circulation, and the necessity for a national bank of issue. 46p. *8°. Liverpool,* [1850] *Wanting the title-page. For another edition, see* 1849.

36949 MANCHESTER FINANCIAL AND PARLIAMENTARY REFORM ASSOCIA-TION. Financial tracts presented to members... Manchester, June, 1850. 19 parts. *8°. Manchester,* [1850] *A reissue of nos.* 1–20 (11–12 *being one number*) *of the Financial Reform Tracts published by the Liverpool Financial Reform Association in* 1848 *and* 1849 (qq.v.).

36950 MARTIN, SAMUEL (1817–1878). Money. A lecture...delivered before the Young Men's Christian Association, in Exeter Hall, January 22, 1850... 44p. *8°.* [1850]

36951 MERCANTILE GUARANTEE ASSO-

CIATION. Mercantile Guarantee Association. Provisionally registered pursuant to the Act 7 and 8 Vict., cap. 110. [A prospectus.] 12p. *8°.* 1850.

36952 MIDDLETON, H. The government and the currency. New edition, with alterations. 190p. *8°. New-York,* 1850.

36953 NATIONAL ASSOCIATION FOR THE PROTECTION OF BRITISH INDUSTRY AND CAPITAL. Report of the sub-committee on currency to the acting Committee of the National Association...[Compiled by J. M. Knott and E. S. Cayley.] 18p. *8°.* n.p. [1850] *See note to no.* 33779.

36954 NATIONAL CURRENCY REFORM ASSOCIATION. Resolutions adopted by the committee of the...Association for the admission of members, &c. [With 'Principles of money advocated by the National Currency Reform Association'.] [4]p. *8°.* n.p. [1850]

For —— *Tracts, see vol.* III, *Periodicals list, Tract[s]...*

36955 *NORMAN, G. W. An examination of some prevailing opinions, as to the pressure of taxation in this, and other countries. 95p. *8°.* 1850. *The copy that belonged to George Grote.*

36956 —— Second edition. 95p. *8°.* 1850. *The copy that belonged to Earl De Grey.*

36957 —— Third edition. 95p. *8°.* 1850.

36958 OGDEN, E. D. Tariff, or rates of duties payable on goods, wares, and merchandise, imported into the United States of America, from and after the first day of December, 1846...Also, containing all the recent circulars and decisions of the Treasury Department, relating to commerce and the revenue. Revised and corrected by E. D. Ogden, entry clerk, Custom-House, Port of New-York. 31, 51p. *8°. New-York,* 1850. *For another edition of this tariff, compiled by E. A. Carroll, see* 1846.

36959 OHIO LIVE STOCK INSURANCE COMPANY. Charter and by-laws of the Ohio Live Stock Insurance Company, incorporated March 20th, 1850. Capital $50,000... 11p. *12°. Cincinnati,* 1850.

36960 OLDHAM, T. ⟨Private.⟩ A report on the improvement of bank notes; with a plan for facilitating their production and economising their expense. 35p. *8°.* n.p. [1850]

36961 POLINO, C. Credit foncier. Banque nationale: nouveau projet présenté à l'Assemblée législative. 47p. *8°.* [*Paris,* 1850]

36962 [POLLARD, G.] The currency question: a republication of three letters which appeared in "The Times," in December, 1848. Suggesting a plan for a domestic currency to be made independent of foreign exchanges, and to be measured in standard gold. By "a London banker." Reprinted at the request of several members of the Legislature. 16p. *8°.* 1850.

36963 PORTER, J. G. V. Moderate fixed duties, for the sake of revenue, on foreign breadstuffs, cattle, meat, &c. Notes on the present customs' duties on articles of food, which come into competition with similar articles grown by our own farmers. 61p. *8°. Dublin,* 1850.

36964 PROPOSAL for the partial liquidation of the public debt of the United Kingdom. By the author of "A proposal for the relief of the nation from fourteen millions of duties of customs and excise." 22p. *8°.* 1850. *The copy that belonged to Earl De Grey.*

36965 PROPOSAL for the relief of the nation from fourteen millions of duties of customs and excise. 14p. *8°*. 1850. *The copy that belonged to Earl De Grey.*

36966 PROUDHON, P. J. Intérêt et principal. Discussion entre M. Proudhon et M. Bastiat sur l'intérêt des capitaux. (Extraits de La Voix du Peuple.) [With 'Capital et rente. A M. Bastiat', a letter, signed: C.-F. Chevé.] 198p. *12°*. *Paris*, 1850.

36967 [RAE, G.] The internal management of a country bank: in a series of letters on the functions and duties of a branch manager. By Thomas Bullion. 203p. *8°*. 1850.

36968 Brief REMINISCENCES of opinions in 1849, on taxation. 16p. *8°*. [1850]

36969 [RICE, THOMAS S., *Baron Monteagle*.] ⟨From the Edinburgh Review for April, 1850.⟩ British and continental taxation. 28p. *8°*. [1850]

36970 ROYAL BRITISH BANK. The Royal British Bank, incorporated by charter 17th September, 1849...[Lists of directors, managers, terms of business, etc., signed: Hugh Innes Cameron, general manager, and dated, 25th June, 1850.] [4]p. *8°*. *n.p.* [1850]

36971 SABATIER, J. and L. Production de l'or, de l'argent et du cuivre chez les anciens, et hôtels monétaires des empires romain et byzantin. 174p. *8°*. *Saint-Pétersbourg, Paris, &c.*, 1850.

36972 SANDARS, S. Observations on the elements of taxation, and the productive cost of corn, &c.&c. 56p. *8°*. 1850.

36973 SCOTTISH PROVIDENT INSTITUTION. Investment and family provision. [A leaflet, dated: 12th March 1850.] *s.sh.8°*. *n.p.* [1850]

36974 —— Notice to members. [A leaflet, appealing for co-operation in publicizing the benefits of the Institution.] *s.sh.8°*. *n.p.* [1850?]

36975 SHAW, G. J. A practical treatise on the law of bankers' cheques, letters of credit and drafts, comprising the statutes and cases relative thereto, with observations. 220p. *12°*. 1850.

36976 The financial SURPLUS. A claim for the repeal of the paper duty. 8p. *8°*. *n.p.* [c. 1850]

36977 [TASKER, J., *ed.*] Spanish finance from 1820 to 1850. An appeal by the Dutch creditors to the finance junta in Madrid, and to their fellow-sufferers, with a few prefatory remarks referring more especially to Spanish loans contracted in, and circulating in, Great Britain, and a glance at loans by other foreign governments, European and South American, by Henry Dashwood. 103p. *8°*. 1850. *Presentation copy, with inscription on the title-page, from the editor to Louis Kossuth.*

36978 TAUNTON, E. Truth, facts, and figures deride falsity, fiction, & robbery. To the industrious classes of Great Britain... 12p. *12°*. *Birmingham*, [1850] *Presentation copy from the author to 'N. N. Newdigate Esq. M.P.'.*

36979 [TAYLOR, JAMES (1788–1863).] Printed for private circulation. Sir James Graham's remarks on landlords & currency. [Dated: March 1850.] 6p. *8°*. *n.p.* [1850]

36980 TAYLOR, JOHN (1781–1864). Principles of currency. Reprinted from the 'Catechism of the currency', first published in 1835. [With 'The Nation's remedy against unfair competition with foreign countries' in verse.] 7p. *8°*. [*London*, 1850] *For editions of the whole work, see* 1835.

36981 THIMBLEBY, J. A lecture on the currency, in which is explained the represented time note medium of exchange, in connexion with a universal system of banking; delivered at the Barnet Institute. 16p. *8°*. [1850]

36982 THOMSON, WILLIAM T. Statements as to rates of interest which have obtained during various periods in the management of the fund established for a provision for the widows and children of the ministers of the Church...in the management of the Writers to the Signet Widows' Fund...With reference to a paper read to the British Association 1850. 8p. *8°*. *n.p.*, 1850.

TRANSPORT

36983 ADAMS, WILLIAM B. Road progress; or, amalgamation of railways and highways for agricultural improvement, and steam farming, in Great Britain and the colonies. Also practical economy in fixed plant and rolling stock for passenger and goods trains. 76p. *8°*. 1850. *See note to no.* 34295.

36984 BAGSHAW, J. A short account of transactions in the affairs of the Harwich railway and pier, with an appendix. 40p. *8°*. 1850.

36985 BARLOW, W. H. On the construction of the permanent way of railways; with an account of the wrought-iron permanent way laid down on the main line of the Midland Railway...Excerpt minutes of proceedings of the Institution of Civil Engineers, vol. IX... 25p. *8°*. 1850. *See note to no.* 34295.

36986 CERROTI, F. Considerazioni sulla strada ferrata da Firenze a Roma in risposta al Sig. Donato Burroni di Arezzo. 32p. *8°*. *Siena*, 1850. *The volume contains a manuscript map entitled 'Corografia dell' Italia media con le sue principali Linee di Strade ferrate'.*

36987 CLARK, JOSIAH L. General description of the Britannia and Conway tubular bridges on the Chester & Holyhead Railway. Published with the permission of Robert Stephenson, civil engineer...Seventh edition. 40p. *8°*. 1850. *For another edition, see* 1849.

36988 COMMISSIONERS OF THE RIVER WEAR. Signals, sailing directions, and notices relating to the port of Sunderland, issued by authority of the Commissioners of the River Wear. 1850. [Signed: T. Meik, engineer to the Commissioners.] 8p. *8°*. *Sunderland*, [1850]

36989 EASTERN UNION RAILWAY COMPANY. [*Begin.*] At the adjourned meeting of the shareholders...held...on the 22nd day of March, 1850... [Minutes and resolutions.] *s.sh.fol.* *n.p.* [1850]

36990 —— Eastern Union Railway. Fourth half-yearly report of the directors...February 28th 1850. [4]p. *fol.* *n.p.* [1850] *See also* 1844, 1845, 1846, 1847, 1848, 1849.

36991 —— General manager's report. To the chairman and directors of the...Company. [With the report and accounts of James Hutton, accountant, dated: 13th March, 1850.] 2, [4]p. *fol.* *n.p.* [1850]

36992 —— Report of the auditors for the half-year ending June 30[–December 31st] 1850. 2 vols. *fol. n.p.*, 1850.

36993 ENGLAND. *Laws, etc.* Anno decimo tertio & decimo quarto Victoriæ Reginæ. Cap. xxx. An Act for granting facilities for the use of certain portions of the Eastern Counties railways by the London and Blackwall Railway Company; and for amending the Acts relating to the London and Blackwall Railway. ⟨25th June 1850.⟩ p.369–376. *fol.* 1850.

36994 GILLESPIE, W. M. A manual of the principles and practice of roadmaking: comprising the location, construction, and improvement of roads, (common, macadam, paved, plank, etc.) and rail-roads...Third edition, with additions. 372p. *8°. New York,* 1850.

36995 GREAT WESTERN, Bristol & Exeter and South Devon Railways' time & fare tables. London to Plymouth and intermediate lines & branches...April, 1850. 92p. *12°.* [1850]

36996 LARDNER, D. Railway economy: a treatise on the new art of transport, its management, prospects, and relations, commercial, financial, and social. With an exposition of the practical results of the railways in operation in the United Kingdom, on the continent, and in America. 528p. *12°.* 1850. *Two copies, one that belonged to J. U. Rastrick, and the other with a manuscript note by HSF recording its purchase about 1875 for 6d, 'the first step in the formation of my economic collection'.*

36997 LAW, H. Rudiments of the art of constructing and repairing common roads...To which is prefixed a general survey of the principal metropolitan roads. By S. Hughes. 136p. *12°.* 1850.

36998 LOW, W. Letter to the Rt. Hon. Lord John Russell, First Lord of the Treasury, explanatory of a financial system for extending railways in Ireland, and for restoring confidence in railway property generally. 16p. *8°. London & Chester,* 1850.

36999 MACPHERSON, P. I. The law expenditure of railway companies, considered with a view to its speedy and effectual reduction. 24p. *8°.* [1850]

37000 NORTH STAFFORDSHIRE RAILWAY. Time and fare table, on and after February 1st, 1850. *s.sh.fol. n.p.* [1850]

37001 PYM, Jethro. The iron ways, bridges, rails & rolling stock, cheap transit combined with steam farming, or, agriculture self-protected. By a practician. Reprinted from the "Westminster and Foreign Quarterly Review" for January, 1850. 45p. *8°.* 1850.

37002 REMARKS on the conveyance of the mails between London and Paris, shewing the advantages that would result by adopting the shortest route, by Folkestone and Boulogne. 28p. *8°.* 1850. *See note to no.* 34295.

37003 SALT, S. Railway and commercial information. 240p. *12°. London, Manchester, &c.,* 1850.

37004 SMYTH, R. C. A letter to the Right Honourable Earl Grey, on the subjects of transportation and emigration, as connected with an imperial railway communication between the Atlantic and the Pacific. 27p. *8°.* 1850.

37005 The **SOUTH-EASTERN RAILWAY** manual: describing the cities, towns, and villages, the principal seats, the cathedrals, fortified places, and ruins, the scenery in the most picturesque districts, and the bathing and watering places, on or near the line... 243p. *12°.* 1850.

37006 STEPHENSON, Sir Rowland M. Railways: an introductory sketch with suggestions, in reference to their extension to British colonies...Part I. 119p. *12°.* 1850. *The copy that belonged to the first Marquis of Dalhousie.*

37007 STEVENSON, David. Abstract of exposition of inland navigation, given at the request of the Council of the Royal Scottish Society of Arts...February 1850. (From the transactions of the Royal Scottish Society of Arts.) 12p. *8°. Edinburgh,* [1850]

37008 TREDGOLD, T. The principles and practice and explanation of the machinery of locomotive engines in operation on the several lines of railway...Completing Division A. And forming the first volume of the new edition of Tredgold on the steam engine. [10 papers by various authors.] 72, [2], 12, 40, 44, 68, 12, 8, 16, 4p. *fol.* 1850. *For another edition of the original work, see* 1838 (TRADES & MANUFACTURES).

37009 TUCK, H. The railway directory for 1850; containing the names of the directors and principal officers of the railways in Great Britain and Ireland, derived from authentic sources. 162p. *12°.* 1850.

37010 UNITED STATES OF AMERICA. Congress. *House of Representatives.* Report of the Naval Committee...July, 1850, in favor of the establishment of a line of mail steamships to the western coast of Africa, and thence via the Mediterranean to London; designed to promote the emigration of free persons of color from the United States to Liberia...With an appendix added by the American Colonization Society. 79p. *8°. Washington,* 1850.

SOCIAL CONDITIONS

37011 ALEXANDER, Gabriel. The bottle; or, the drunkard's career...With beautiful wood engravings drawn by G. Standfast. 156p. *8°.* [1850 ?] *The Turner copy.*

37012 AMALGAMATED SOCIETY OF ENGINEERS. Minutes of the delegate meeting of the Societies of Engineers, Millwrights, Smiths and Pattern Makers, appointed to draw up rules for the government of the Amalgamated Society of the above-named branches of trade, held at Birmingham, commencing September 9th, and ending on the 26th, September, 1850. 40p. *8°.* [1850]

37013 ANDERSON, Arthur (1792–1868). Revision of taxation – the national reckoning with the protectionists. A speech delivered in the House of Commons, on the 19th of February, 1850, on Mr. Disraeli's motion, for a revision of the poor rates, in favour of the agricultural classes. 18p. *8°.* 1850.

37014 ANDERTON, J. Cheap gas! Joint Stock Companies' Registration Act. (7 & 8 Vict., c. 110) "Who's who;" or, the City philanthropists. A New Year's gift for 1850. Being a complete registration schedule to the deed of settlement of the Great Central Gas Consumers' Company. The names, etc. of the 323 merchants, bankers, gentlewomen...the subscribers to the Company, and shares held by each. 31st December, 1849. Second edition. 16p. *8°. n.p.*, 1850.

37015 —— A warning voice. To the bona fide and honest shareholders of "The Great Central Gas Consumers' Company" and the inhabitants of London. [Dated: January 21st, 1850.] 4p. *fol. n.p.* [1850] *Endorsed: Cheap gas! A warning voice.*

37016 ANECDOTES of the new poor laws. No. 1[–2]. 2 vols. *8°. Birmingham,* [*c.* 1850]

37017 ANTONY, MARK, *pseud.* Great Central Gas Consumers' Company. To the citizens of London. [Letter, dated: 12th February, 1850, challenging some of the statements issued by the Company.] *s.sh.fol. n.p.* [1850]

37018 The **APPEAL** of the distressed operative tailors to the Government, the aristocracy, the clergy, and the public in general. 31p. *8°.* 1850. *The copy that belonged to J. M. Ludlow.*

37019 APPLICATION du système de Mettray aux colonies agricoles d'orphelins et d'enfants trouvés. 7p. *8°.* [*Paris,* 1850?] *The copy that belonged to Victor Considérant.*

37020 BAKER, FRANKLIN. The moral tone of the factory system defended: in a letter to the Lord Bishop of Manchester. Being a reply to the allegations of the Rev. Henry Worsley, M.A., contained in a prize essay, entitled "Juvenile depravity," and dedicated... to the Lord Bishop of Norwich. 30p. *8°. London, Manchester, &c.,* 1850.

37021 BARRAU, T. H. Conseils aux ouvriers sur les moyens qu'ils ont d'être heureux avec l'explication des lois qui les concernent particulièrement. 360p. *8°. Paris,* 1850.

37022 BELL, GEORGE. Blackfriars' Wynd analysed. 44p. *8°. Edinburgh,* 1850.

For the **BOOKBINDER'S TRADE CIRCULAR,** 1850–54, 1865–69, *see* vol. III, *Periodicals list.*

37023 BOWKETT, T. E. The bane and antidote or bad and good associations... Vol. 1. 383p. *8°.* 1850.

37024 —— Selections from a series of tables illustrating the working of freehold provident societies. Third edition. 40p. *8°.* 1850.

37025 BRIGGS, JEREMIAH. Advocate of the poor, for the security of wages. The universal anti-truck. 16p. *8°. Derby,* [1850?]

37026 CALCULATIONS showing the facility with which the paupers and unemployed, or any other portion of the population may be enabled to support themselves within most desirable circumstances, by co-operation. 8p. *8°. n.p.* [*c.* 1850]

37027 CARPENTER, WILLIAM B. On the use and abuse of alcoholic liquors, in health and disease. Prize essay. 283p. *8°.* 1850. *The Turner copy.*

For the **CHAMPION OF WHAT IS TRUE AND RIGHT** and for the good of all, *see* vol. III, *Periodicals list.*

37028 CITY OF LONDON GAS LIGHT AND COKE COMPANY. [*Endorsed:*] Caution. City pavements. Are the citizens prepared to have their streets opened for three additional lines of gas pipes? [A manifesto dated: May 18, 1850, opposing the scheme of the Great Central Gas Consumers' Company. Signed: Daniel Benham, secretary.] [2]l. *fol.* [*London,* 1850]

37029 —— Reply of the City of London Gas Light and Coke Company to the address of the Great Central Gas Consumers' Company, respecting their proposal to compromise. [With 'Report of the surveyor to the City of London, Richard Kelsey, Esq., on the petition of the London and Equitable Gas Companies'.] 23p. *8°. n.p.*, 1850.

37030 —— To the inhabitants of the City of London. [Circular letter, dated: January 1850, putting the case of the City of London Gas Light and Coke Company. Signed: D. Benham, secretary. With 'Great Central Gas Consumers' Company...Case submitted to counsel by the City of London Gas Company, with opinion thereon'.] 2l. *fol. n.p.* [1850]

37031 CITY OF LONDON HOSPITAL FOR DISEASES OF THE CHEST. Second annual report... 34p. *8°.* 1850.

37032 COLWELL, C. Money v. life. A review of colliery casualties showing their cause and extent...the great necessity for government inspection...and an adequate provision for widows and orphans...Further showing the means to provide for the same...without unjust taxation. 106p. *8°.* [1850]

37033 COMBE, ANDREW. On the introduction of religion into common schools. (Extracted from his life and correspondence, page 501.) 8p. *8°. Edinburgh,* [1850]

37034 COMMITTEE OF THE TAILORS OF LONDON. Labour and the poor. Report of the speech of Henry Mayhew, Esq., and the evidence adduced at a public meeting held at St. Martin's Hall, Long Acre... Oct. 28, 1850, convened by the Committee of the Tailors of London, for the purpose of exposing the falsehoods contained in an article that appeared in the Morning Chronicle of...Oct. 4th, 1850, on the sweating, or domestic system... 44p. *8°.* 1850.

37035 The **COMMON-LAW RIGHTS** of ratepayers upheld against the Metropolitan Commissioners of Sewers. 16p. *8°. Westminster,* 1850.

37036 COTTAGE CONVERSATIONS. A new edition. Adapted to the use of the Society. 72p. *12°. The Society for Promoting Christian Knowledge,* 1850.

37037 DANIELL, W. Warminster Common: shewing the steps by which it has advanced from its former state of notorious vice, ignorance, and poverty, to its present state of moral and social improvement...To which is added, an account...of..."medical electricity." 387p. *12°. Warminster & London,* 1850.

37038 DUCPÉTIAUX, É. Mémoire sur le paupérisme dans les Flandres. (*Mémoires couronnés...publiés par l'Académie royale des Sciences, des Lettres et des Beaux-Arts de Belgique.*) 640[340]p. *8°. Bruxelles,* 1850.

37039 E., M. How much longer are we to continue teaching nothing more than what was taught two or three centuries ago? Or, ought not our highest education to embrace the whole range of our present knowledge? And, ought not the education of all classes to have a direct reference to the wants of our...enlightened age? 42p. *8°.* 1850.

37040 Sanitary **ECONOMY:** its principles and practice; and its moral influence on the progress of civilisation. 320p. *8°. Edinburgh: W. & R. Chambers,* 1850.

37041 EDWARDS, EDWARD, *compositor.* Prize essay. The disease and the remedy: an essay on the distressed state of the printing trade, proving it to be mainly attributable to excessive boy labour...Accompanied by an appeal to master printers and newspaper proprietors to aid in the work of reformation. 24p. *12°*. 1850.

37042 ENGLAND. *General Board of Health.* Public Health Act. (11 & 12 Vict., cap. 63.) Report...on a preliminary inquiry into the sewerage, drainage, and supply of water, and the sanitary condition of the inhabitants of ...Banbury and...of Neithrop, in the counties of Oxford and Northampton. By T. W. Rammell. 46p. *8°*. 1850.

37043 —— —— Public Health Act. (11 & 12 Vict., cap. 63.) Report...on a preliminary inquiry into the sewerage, drainage, and supply of water, and the sanitary condition of the inhabitants of...Berwick-upon-Tweed ...including the townships of Tweedmouth and Spittal. By Robert Rawlinson. 50p. *8°*. 1850.

37044 —— —— Public Health Act. (11 & 12 Vict., cap. 63.) Report...on a preliminary inquiry into the sewerage, drainage, and supply of water, and the sanitary condition of the inhabitants of...Bridgend. By George T. Clark. 18p. *8°*. 1850.

37045 —— —— Public Health Act, (11 & 12 Vict., cap. 63.) Report...on a preliminary inquiry into the sewerage, drainage, and supply of water, and the sanitary condition of the inhabitants of...Bristol. By George T. Clark. 224p. *8°*. 1850.

37046 —— —— Public Health Act, (11 & 12 Vict., cap. 63.) Report...on a preliminary inquiry into the sewerage, drainage, and supply of water, and the sanitary condition of the inhabitants of...Darlington...By William Ranger. 74p. *8°*. 1850.

37047 —— —— Public Health Act. (11 & 12 Vict., cap. 63.) Report...on a preliminary inquiry into the sewerage, drainage, and supply of water, and the sanitary condition of the inhabitants of...Merthyr Tydfil, in the county of Glamorgan. By T. W. Rammell. 71p. *8°*. 1850.

37048 —— —— Public Health Act. (11 & 12 Vict., cap. 63.) Report...on a preliminary inquiry into the sewerage, drainage, and supply of water, and the sanitary condition of the inhabitants of...Northowram and Southowram, in the county of York. By W. Ranger. 52p. *8°*. 1850.

37049 —— —— Public Health Act (11 & 12 Vict., cap. 63). Report...on a preliminary inquiry into the sewerage, drainage and supply of water, and the sanitary condition of the inhabitants of...Stockton-on-Tees...by W. Ranger. 83p. *8°*. 1850.

37050 —— —— Public Health Act (11 & 12 Vict., cap. 63). Report...on a supplemental inquiry into the sewerage, drainage, and supply of water, and the sanitary condition of the inhabitants, of the township of Bilston, situated within the...borough...of Wolverhampton, in the county of Stafford. By Robert Rawlinson. 35p. *8°*. 1850.

37051 —— Report by the General Board of Health on the supply of water to the Metropolis. Presented to both Houses of Parliament by command of Her Majesty. [With 4 appendixes.] 5 vols. *8°*. 1850.

37052 —— *Home Office.* Report on the discipline and construction of Portland Prison, and its connection with the system of convict discipline now in operation. By Lieut.-Colonel Jebb, Surveyor-General of Prisons. Presented to both Houses of Parliament by command of Her Majesty. 131p. *8°*. 1850.

37053 ENNIS, J. On the necessity of establishing a court of request for the recovery of small debts. 1850. 30p. *8°*. *Jersey*, 1850.

37054 FEATHERSTONE, T. The rhyming temperance advocate, or old truths in a new dress; being a set of speeches, with verses by which to call on every speaker ... 59p. *12°*. *Leeds*, [1850?] *The Turner copy.*

37055 FERRUS, G. M. A. Des prisonniers, de l'emprisonnement et des prisons. 522p. *8°*. *Paris*, 1850. *Presentation copy, with inscription, from the author to 'Mon[r]. le Capit. O'Brien'. The continuation, published in 1853, is also in the Goldsmiths' Library.*

37056 *FLEWIN, T. and **SALSBURY,** J. To the worthy inhabitants of Camden Town. [A handbill from the local dustmen, asking householders only to give Christmas boxes to authorized collectors.] *s.sh.4°*. [*London*, c. 1850] *The copy that belonged to Augustus De Morgan.*

37057 FOTHERGILL, J. The temperance mother and nurse. 4p. *8°*. *Preston*, [1850?] *The Turner copy.*

37058 FRANCE. *Assemblée Nationale.* Rapport général présenté par M. Thiers au nom de la Commission de l'assistance et de la prévoyance publiques dans la séance du 26 janvier 1850. 156p. *8°*. *Paris*, 1850.

37059 —— [Another edition.] De l'assistance et de la prévoyance publiques...Rapport présenté au nom de la Commission le 26 janvier 1850. 204p. *12°*. *Bruxelles*, 1850.

37060 —— *Ministère de l'Intérieur.* Statistique des établissements. Rapport à M. de Ministre de l'Intérieur sur l'administration des monts-de-piété, par Ad. de Watteville. 166p. *4°*. *Paris*, 1850.

37061 FRIENDLY ASSOCIATION OF LONDON COSTERMONGERS. Friendly Association of London Costermongers, instituted June 23rd, 1850, for the mutual assistance, protection, and mental and moral improvement of all those who sell..."perishable articles" in the streets. 4p. *8°*. [*London*, 1850] *The copy that belonged to J. M. Ludlow.*

37062 Cheap **GAS!** no monopoly! [Circular letter, dated: February 14, 1850, urging the public to support the Great Central Gas Consumers' Company. Signed: One of the late City Gas Consumers' Committee.] *s.sh.fol. n.p.* [1850]

37063 GAS! gas! gas! An address from one of the consumers of gas in Surrey, to his brother consumers. [In support of the Surrey Consumers' Gas-Light Company.] 12p. *8°*. *n.p.* [1850]

37064 GIRARDIN, É. DE. L'abolition de la misère par l'élévation des salaires. Lettres à M. Thiers. 96p. *8°*. *Paris*, 1850.

37065 GREAT CENTRAL GAS CONSUMERS' COMPANY. Address of the Directors of the ...Company [dated: 1st June, 1850], with an appendix containing a synopsis of the evidence in support of the Bill, and the decision of the Committee of the House of Commons, finding the preamble proved. 24p. *8°*. 1850.

37066 —— Address of the Directors of the...Company, to the gas consumers and other inhabitants of the City of London. [Signed: R. M. Massey, secretary, and dated, 4th July, 1850.] 3p. *fol.* [*London*, 1850]

37067 —— Address of the...Company to the inhabitants of London, in answer to the publications of James Anderton, Esq., and the other partisans of the old City gas companies. [Signed: J. T. Barham, secretary, and dated: Jan. 14th 1850.] 4p. *fol n.p.* [1850]

37068 GREEN, S. G. The working classes of Great Britain: their present condition, and the means of their improvement and elevation. Prize essay. 180p. *8°.* [1850]

37069 *[GROTE, H.] The case of the poor against the rich fairly considered. By a mutual friend. 24p. *8°.* [*London*, 1850] *The copy that belonged to George Grote.*

37070 GUTHRIE, T. A plea on behalf of drunkards and against drunkenness... Issued under the superintendence of the Scottish Association for the Suppression of Drunkenness. Fourth thousand. 63p. *8°. Edinburgh*, 1850.

37071 HALL, SPENCER T. Life and death in Ireland, as witnessed in 1849. 90p. *12°. Manchester & London*, 1850.

37072 HALLER, C. L. VON, *Freiherr.* Die wahren Ursachen und die einzig wirksamen Abhülfsmittel der allgemeinen Verarmung und Verdienstlosigkeit. 112p. *8°. Schaffhausen*, 1850.

37073 HAUGHTON, J. Statistics of crime: a paper read before the Dublin Statistical Society on the 23rd April, 1850. 14p. *8°. Dublin*, 1850.

37074 HOARE, W. H. A letter to the Right Hon. Sir George Grey, Bart. H.M. Secretary of State for the Home Department, on the scheme of Mr. W. J. Fox, and the educational question. 27p. *8°.* 1850.

37075 *HODGSON, WILLIAM B. Mr. Cobden and the division of labour. From the Manchester "Examiner and Times" of Saturday, Dec. 14, 1850. [Dated: 11th December, 1850.] 6p. *8°. Manchester*, [1850] *The FWA copy that belonged to William Pare.*

37076 HOLZSCHUHER, A. VON, *Freiherr.* Die materielle Noth der untern Volksklassen und ihre Ursachen. Gekrönte Preisschrift. 148p. *8°. Augsburg*, 1850.

37077 HOMERSHAM, S. C. London (Watford) Spring-Water Company. Report to the Directors... Second edition. 58p. *8°.* 1850.

37078 —— Review of the Report by the General Board of Health on the supply of water to the Metropolis; contained in a report to the directors of the London (Watford) Spring Water Company. 71p. *8°.* 1850.

37079 IRISH AMELIORATION SOCIETY. Prospectus of the... Society [for the purpose of employing the peasantry of Ireland in the preparation of peat fuel and charcoal, etc.]. Incorporated by Royal Charter... 16p. *8°.* [1850]

37080 JAMES, JOHN A. The young man from home ... Third edition. 144p. *12°. The Religious Tract Society*, [c. 1850]

37081 JOURNEYMEN BOOKBINDERS OF LONDON AND WESTMINSTER. Reply to a letter from the Committee of the Southwark Auxiliary Bible Society to the Committee of the British & Foreign Bible Society, embodying the "Report of a Sub-committee appointed by them... to investigate certain statements respecting the binder for the British and Foreign Bible Society, and the female workers in her employ." [Signed on behalf of the Journeymen Bookbinders: T. J. Dunning, sec., and dated, March 25, 1850.] 12p. *8°.* [*London*, 1850]

37082 KAY, JOSEPH. The social condition and educa-

tion of the people in England and Europe... 2 vols. *12°.* 1850.

37083 [KINGSLEY, C.] Cheap clothes and nasty. By Parson Lot. 35p. *12°. London & Cambridge*, 1850.

37084 KITTREDGE, J. Address on the effects of ardent spirits. Originally delivered in Lyme, New Hampshire, 1828. (*American Tract Society*, 221.) 24p. *8°. New York*, [1850] *The Turner copy.*

37085 LABOUR and the poor. Important explanation of the Morning Chronicle "Commissioner." [An account of a public meeting of the tailors of the Metropolis addressed by Henry Mayhew, repudiating any connection with the *Morning Chronicle.*] (From the Morning Herald of October 29th, 1850.) 4p. *8°. n.p.* [1850]

37086 LEDRU-ROLLIN, A. A. The decline of England... Second edition. 360p. *8°.* 1850.

37087 LEE, THOMAS G. A plea for the English operatives: being a competing essay for the prize offered by John Cassell, Esq., in which the means of elevating the working classes are humbly suggested. 123p. *12°. London & Manchester*, [1850]

37088 LEICESTER-SQUARE SOUP-KITCHEN. A plan for preventing destitution and mendicancy in the British Metropolis, by means of an adequate number of institutions... Projected and matured by the Committee of the Leicester-Square Soup-Kitchen, and sanctioned at a meeting of the Present, Vice-Presidents and Committee, October 22nd, 1850: H.R.H. the Duke of Cambridge in the chair. 40p. *8°.* [*London,*] 1850.

37089 A LETTER on the gas agitation: addressed to Mr. Thwaites. By a brother tradesman. 8p. *8°.* 1850.

37090 A LETTER to the Lord Chancellor of England, on the administration of justice in courts of quarter sessions. By a barrister. 8p. *8°. Chester*, 1850.

37091 LEWIS, SIR GEORGE C., *Bart.* Evidence of G. Cornewall Lewis, Esq. M.P. before a Select Committee of the House of Lords, appointed to consider the laws relating to parochial assessments, in the session of 1850. 85p. *8°.* 1850.

37092 LONDON RAGGED DORMITORY AND COLONIAL TRAINING SCHOOL OF INDUSTRY. The first annual report of the London Ragged Dormitory... Read at the public meeting on... May 9th, 1850, in the St. Martin's Hall, Long Acre. The Right Hon. Lord Ashley, M.P., in the chair. 32p. *8°.* 1850.

37093 LOW, S. The charities of London. Comprehending the benevolent, educational, and religious institutions. Their origin and design, progress, and present position... 474p. *8°.* 1850.

37094 MACKENZIE, HENRY, *Bishop of Nottingham.* On the parochial system as a means of alleviating temporal distress in the Metropolis. 11p. *8°.* 1850.

37095 MANAGEMENT and cost of prisons. ⟨From the Law Review for November, 1850.⟩ 12p. *8°.* [1850]

37096 MARTIN, JAMES. The address of the Committee of the Synod of Thurles to the Catholics of Ireland reviewed, and the objections to the Queen's colleges considered. 32p. *8°. Dublin*, 1850.

37097 MARTIN, JOHN, *K.L.* Outline of a comprehensive plan for diverting the sewage of London and Westminster from the Thames and applying it to agricultural purposes, – for improving the navigation of the river, – and for establishing a supply of pure water to the Metropolis. 15p. *8°*. 1850.

37098 MEETING of the journeymen bakers of the Metropolis ['to take into consideration the best means of obtaining redress of the grievances under which the trade suffers, and to establish a society for improving the... condition of the bakers of London']. (From the Morning Herald of July 1st, 1850.) 4p. *8°*. *n.p.* [1850]

37099 METROPOLITAN ASSOCIATION FOR IMPROVING THE DWELLINGS OF THE INDUSTRIOUS CLASSES. Copy. Supplemental Charter of incorporation of the Metropolitan Association...1850. 12p. *8°*. 1850. *For the* Charter of incorporation, *see* 1845.

37100 METROPOLITAN CHURCH UNION. History and present state of the education question: being a collection of documents explanatory of the proceedings of the Committee of Privy Council on Education, from its first appointment, in 1839, to the present time, and of the steps taken for the defence of Church education against the encroachments of the said Committee... 191p. *8°*. 1850.

37101 METROPOLITAN COMMITTEE FOR ESTABLISHING EVENING CLASSES. The prospectus and first year's report of the Metropolitan Committee for establishing evening classes for young men in London, and the suburbs. 16p. *8°*. [*London,*] 1850.

37102 METROPOLITAN TRADES' DELEGATES. Second edition. The address of the Metropolitan Trades' Delegates, to their fellow countrymen, on the interests and present position of the labouring classes of the Empire. 8p. *8°*. [*London,*] 1850. *The copy that belonged to J. M. Ludlow.*

37103 MISREPRESENTATIONS of Mr. Bright. (Extracted from the Morning Herald of August 8th, 1850.) [A letter to disprove John Bright's assertion that pauperism had been much diminished between 1842 and 1846. Signed: *not* an Elector of Manchester.] *s.sh.fol. n.p.* [1850] [*Br.* 620]

37104 MOON, M. A. Intemperence [*sic*] the bane of the working classes. 4p. *8°*. *n.p.* [1850?] *The Turner copy.*

37105 MOORE, ARTHUR (*fl.* 1850). Compendium of the Irish Poor Law: containing the Acts for the relief of the destitute poor in Ireland and abstracts of various statutes connected therewith...and general orders issued by the Commissioners of Poor Law in Ireland, for regulating...boards of guardians...Also, instructional circulars and forms, and a statistical table of unions. To which is added, an appendix of temporary Acts, &c.... With notes, and a copious analytical index...Third edition: revised and enlarged. 992p. *12°*. *Dublin,* 1850.

37106 MULOCK, T. The western Highlands and islands of Scotland, socially considered, with reference to proprietors and people: being a series of contributions to the periodical press. 262p. *8°*. *Inverness, Edinburgh, &c.,* 1850.

37107 [MYLES, J.] Chapters in the life of a Dundee factory boy; an autobiography. 76p. *8°*. *Dundee, Edinburgh, &c.,* 1850.

37108 NATIONAL PHILANTHROPIC ASSOCIATION. Second edition. Sanatory progress: – being the fifth report of the National Philanthropic Association...for the promotion of social and salutiferous

improvements...and the employment of the poor... 242p. *8°*. 1850.

37109 [NEALE, E. V.] Scheme for the formation of the working associations into a general union [to be called the Co-operative Labour Union]. 15p. *12°*. [*London,* 1850] *The copy that belonged to J. M. Ludlow.*

37110 NETHERWAY, R. Suggestions for improving the sanatory state of London & its environs, slightly modified from the scheme submitted to the Metropolitan Commissioners of Sewers in 1849. 72p. *8°*. 1850.

37111 NOTTINGHAM PERMANENT BENEFIT BUILDING SOCIETY. Rules of the...Society ...Commenced May, 1850... 39p. *12°*. *Nottingham,* 1850.

37112 OASTLER, R. The working men. Free trade and Peel's monument. To the working men of England. [A letter, dated: August 26, 1850.] 2p. *s.sh.fol. n.p.* [1850] [*Br.* 621]

37113 O'RORKE, E. Speech of Edward O'Rorke, Esq., on the Bill for relieving Belfast from county cess, for roads and bridges, and for the further improvement of that borough...in the Town Hall...on...the 15th and 16th days of April, 1850, at an inquiry held by George Archibald Leach, Esq....the surveying officer... 154p. *8°*. *Belfast,* 1850.

37114 ORPHAN WORKING SCHOOL, *London.* Orphanhood: free will offerings to the fatherless. [A collection of articles in prose and poetry in aid of the Charity.] 92p. *4°*. [1850?]

37115 PARSONS, B. Anti-Bacchus: an essay on the crimes, diseases, and other evils connected with the use of intoxicating drinks...Sixteenth thousand. 136p. *8°*. [1850] *The Turner copy. For other impressions, see* 1841.

37116 PELHAM, HON. D. Suggestions on the immediate legislative requirements, addressed more particularly to the landed interests. [A plea for the amendment of the poor laws, to do away with the injustices of poor rate assessment.] 15p. *8°*. 1850.

37117 PENNSYLVANIA. *House of Representatives.* Report of the Committee on Domestic Manufactures relative to the Ten Hour Law, made to the House of Representatives. 6p. *8°*. *Harrisburg,* 1850. *The copy that belonged to J. M. Cobbett.*

37118 To the Right Honourable the Lords Spiritual and Temporal of the United Kingdom of Great Britain and Ireland in Parliament assembled. The humble **PETITION** of the undersigned bankers, merchants, traders, and other owners and occupiers of premises within the City of London [in support of the Bill incorporating the Great Central Gas Consumers' Company]. *s.sh.fol. n.p.* [1850]

37119 PHILANTHROPIC SOCIETY. List of subscribers to the...Society, 1st March, 1850. 55p. *12°*. *n.p.* [1850]

37120 —— The Philanthropic Farm School, Redhill, Surrey. [Report of the progress of the Farm School established by the Philanthropic Society in 1849.] 26p. *12°*. *Reigate,* [1850] *The reports of 1851 and 1852 are also in the Goldsmiths' Library.*

37121 PIG SOCIETY, *Mansfield-Woodhouse.* Rules of the Pig Society, held at the house of Mr. D. Slater. The Sign of the Ram Tavern, Mansfield-Woodhouse, Notts. Established Jan. 14th, 1850. 4p. *8°*. *Mansfield,* [1850]

37122 RATCLIFFE, H. Observations on the rate of mortality & sickness existing amongst friendly societies; particularised for various trades, occupations, and localities, with a series of tables, shewing the value of annuities, sick gift, assurance for death, and contributions to be paid equivalent thereto: calculated from the experience of the members composing Manchester Unity of the Independent Order of Odd Fellows, Manchester Unity Friendly Society. 168p. *8°. Manchester,* 1850.

37123 RATE-PAYERS of the City of London! [An attack on the Great Central Gas Consumers' Company. Signed: A citizen.] *s.sh.fol. n.p.,* 1850.

37124 RAWSTORNE, L. Ireland's only safety, the productive employment of its indigent population... Second edition, enlarged. 27p. *8°.* 1850.

37125 REID, WILLIAM (1814–1896). The evils of moderate drinking an argument for total abstinence from all alcoholic liquors: an address...New edition. Fifteenth thousand. 22p. *8°. Glasgow & London,* 1850. *The Turner copy.*

37126 ROBERT, , *professeur de philosophie.* Histoire de la classe ouvrière depuis l'esclave jusqu'au prolétaire de nos jours... 4 vols. *8°. Paris,* 1850, 1847–61.

37127 ROBERTS, HENRY. The dwellings of the labouring classes, their arrangement and construction; illustrated by a reference to the model houses of the Society for Improving the Condition of the Labouring Classes...Being an essay, read January 21, 1850, at the Royal Institute of British Architects... 47[61]p. *8°.* [1850]

37128 RULES and orders to be observed by the members of the friendly society, held at the house of Mr. John Parkin, sign of the White Hart, in Norton, in the parish of Cuckney. Instituted December 7th, 1839, for the purpose of affording relief during sickness or infirmity. 8p. *8°. Worksop,* 1850.

37129 RUSSOM, J. "Drunkenness is madness". 4p. *8°. Middlewich,* [1850 ?] *The Turner copy.*

37130 A SAILOR'S yarn. Spun by an old boatswain. ⟨Eighth thousand.⟩ (*Bristol New Series,* 112.) [2]p. *8°. Bristol,* [1850 ?] *The Turner copy.*

37131 SAINT PANCRAS, *Parish of.* [*Endorsed:*] The Parish of St. Pancras and the Great Central Gas Consumers' Company. Important meeting of the Vestry. [A reprint, dated: January 28, 1850, issued by the Company.] 3p. *fol. n.p.* [1850]

37132 SCOTTISH TEMPERANCE LEAGUE. Anti-cholera. 4p. *8°. Glasgow,* [1850] *The Turner copy.*

37133 SCROPE, G. P. Don't tax, but untax, the dwellings of the poor. 23p. *8°.* 1850.

37134 SHAW, W. An affectionate pleading for England's oppressed female workers: respectfully addressed to my Queen...the Government...the aristocracy... 38p. *8°.* 1850.

37135 SOCIÉTÉ FRATERNELLE DES OUVRIERS FERBLANTIERS. Statuts de la Société... 11, [12]p. *12°. Paris,* [1850] *The copy that belonged to Earl De Grey.*

37136 SOCIETY DUTCH METTRAY. Rule [*sic*] of the Society Dutch Mettray, on the estate of Rijsselt, near Zutphen. 16p. *8°. Rotterdam,* [1850]

37137 STARK, A. G. How to render pauperism self-supporting; with practical hints for developing the system of re-productive employment, as a substitute for idleness and useless tests; suggested by a visit to the Cork Union Workhouse...Extracted, by permission of the author, from "The south of Ireland in 1850," and re-published by the Poor-Law Association. [With 'Poor-Law Association. List of committee and objects'.] 16p. *8°. n.p.* [1850] *The copy that belonged to Earl De Grey.*

37138 STEPHENSON, ROBERT (1803–1886). Report of Robert Stephenson, civil engineer, on the supply of water to the town of Liverpool, March 28th, 1850. 89p. *4°.* [1850]

37139 The general STRIKE. [A ballad.] *s.sh.fol.* [1850 ?] [*Br.* 626]

37140 SWETENHAM, E. Temporary employment for discharged criminals; and trial by jury. A letter to the clergy, magistrates, and rate-payers, of England and Wales. 31p. *8°.* 1850.

37141 TEMPERANCE and teetotalism. 30p. *8°. Glasgow,* [1850 ?] *The Turner copy.*

37142 THIRLWALL, C., *Bishop of St. David's.* The advantages of literary and scientific institutions for all classes. A lecture delivered at the Town Hall, Carmarthen, on December 11th, 1849... 37p. *8°. London & Carmarthen,* 1850.

37143 THOMPSON, JOHN (*fl.* 1850). The law and practice of benefit building societies, terminating and permanent, and of freehold land societies... 258p. *12°.* 1850.

37144 THOMSON, S. Temperance and total abstinence, or, the use and abuse of alcoholic liquors in health and disease. 184p. *8°.* 1850. *The Turner copy.*

37145 TOTAL ABSTINENCE songs. 4p. *8°. Manchester,* [1850 ?] *Two of the songs are signed: J.R. The Turner copy.*

For the **TRADES' ADVOCATE AND HERALD OF PROGRESS,** *see vol.* III, *Periodicals list.*

For the **TRADES UNIONS' MAGAZINE,** 1850–51, *see vol.* III, *Periodicals list.*

37146 *TWEDDELL, G. M. An appeal to the members of the Stokesley Mechanics' Institute, by their late secretary, and now expelled member, George Tweddell. 12p. *12° Middlesbro',* 1850. *The FWA copy that belonged to William Pare.*

37147 TYRRELL, T. Cheap gas agitation. Letter to the citizens of London in answer to an address of the Great Central Gas Consumers' Company, dated Sept. 28th, 1850. 11p. *8°.* [1850]

37148 UNITED PAROCHIAL NATIONAL CHARITY AND SUNDAY SCHOOLS OF ST. MARY, *Newington.* The thirty-fourth annual report of the Committee...together with the annual accounts, list of subscribers, &c. 15p. *8°.* 1850.

37149 VAUGHAN, CHARLES J. A second letter on the late Post Office agitation. 35p. *8°.* 1850.

37150 WALLACE, THOMAS (*fl.* 1850). British slavery, an appeal to the women of England: also, the duty of abolishing the late hour system: and maxims for employers. 80p. *12°.* 1850.

37151 WASON, R. A letter to the Home Secretary in answer to the question, What should be done with our convicts ? 27p. *8°. Ayr,* 1850.

37152 **WHITE,** E. H. Slavery; a poem, in five cantos. The artisan; and other poems. 163p. *12°. 1850. The author was a railway guard on the Great Western Railway.*

37153 **WILLIAMS SECULAR SCHOOL,** *Edinburgh.* First annual report of the Williams Secular School. [Signed: Geo. Combe, James Simpson, promoters.] 20p. *8°. Edinburgh & London, 1850. Presentation copy from George Combe to William Lovett.*

37154 **WILSON,** THOMAS C. Guilty or not guilty? An inquiry into the criminality of the traffic in strong drink, and of the drinking customs...Tenth thousand. 12p. *8°. Glasgow & London, [1850] The Turner copy.*

37155 The **WORKING SHOEMAKERS' ASSOCIATIONS.** Appeal to the public. *s.sh.8°. [London, 1850] The copy that belonged to J. M. Ludlow.*

37156 **WRATISLAW,** A. H. Observations on the Cambridge system. [On the limitations of university education.] Second edition. 18p. *8°. Cambridge & London, 1850.*

SLAVERY

37157 **ANALYSIS** of the evidence given before the Select Committees upon the slave trade. By a barrister. 132p. *8°. 1850. The copy that belonged to Earl De Grey.*

37158 **ANTI-CANT,** *pseud.* India v. America. A letter to the Chairman of the hon. East India Company, on cotton. [On the remedy for dependence on slave-produced cotton.] 8p. *8°. 1850.*

37159 **BLYTH,** G. Means of suppressing the slave trade. Extract from a letter written...lately from Jamaica. 2p. *4°. n.p. [1850]*

For **BRITISH AND FOREIGN ANTI-SLAVERY SOCIETY,** The anti-slavery reporter, 1850-1952, *see* vol. III, *Periodicals list,* The anti-slavery reporter and aborigines' friend.

37160 **CLARK,** R. W. A review of the Rev. Moses Stuart's pamphlet on slavery, entitled Conscience and the constitution... ⟨Originally published in the Boston Daily Atlas.⟩ 103p. *12°. Boston, 1850.*

37161 **CLAY,** H. Remarks of Mr. Clay, of Kentucky, on introducing his propositions to compromise, on the slavery question. In the Senate of the United States, January 29, 1850. 16p. *8°. Washington, 1850.*

37162 **DENMAN,** HON. J. The African squadron and Mr. Hutt's Committee...Second edition, enlarged. (Reprinted from the " Colonial Magazine.") 70p. *8°. [1850]*

37163 **ENGLAND.** *Parliament. House of Lords.* Report from the Select Committee of the House of Lords appointed to consider the best means which Great Britain can adopt for the final extinction of the African slave trade – (Presented Sess. 1850.) 11p. *8°. [1850] The copy that belonged to Earl De Grey.*

37164 **FITZGERALD,** JOHN. Man stealing by proxy; or, the guilt of our countrymen in upholding slavery & the slave trade, by the purchase of slave grown produce...Second edition, enlarged. 37p. *8°. 1850.*

37165 **FOWLER,** O. Slavery in California and New Mexico. Speech of Mr. Orin Fowler, of Massachusetts, in the House of Representatives, March 11, 1850...on the President's message communicating the Constitution of California. 15p. *8°. [Washington, 1850] Presentation copy from the author to 'Wm. Jenks'.*

37166 The **JAMAICA MOVEMENT,** for promoting the enforcement of the slave-trade treaties, and the suppression of the slave-trade; with statements of fact, convention, and law: prepared at the request of the Kingston Committee. 430p. *8°. 1850.*

37167 **MANN,** H. Speech of Horace Mann, of Massachusetts, on the subject of slavery in the Territories, and the consequences of a dissolution of the Union. Delivered in the United States House of Representatives, February 15, 1850. 35p. *8°. Boston, 1850.*

37168 **MARSH,** WILLIAM H. God's law supreme. A sermon, aiming to point out the duty of a Christian people in relation to the fugitive slave law: delivered at Village Corners, Woodstock, Conn., on the day of the annual thanksgiving, Nov. 28, 1850; and subsequently repeated, by request, in Southbridge, Mass.... 30p. *8°. Worcester, [Mass., 1850]*

37169 **OUSELEY,** SIR WILLIAM G. Notes on the slave-trade, with remarks on measures adopted for its suppression. To which are added: a few general observations on slavery, and the prejudices of race and colour, as affecting the slave-trade; and some suggestions on the means by which it may be checked. 75p. *8°. 1850.*

37170 A **QUESTION** of great national importance has lately been much agitated, namely, whether the measures in operation for the suppression of the slave trade, should, or should not, be abandoned...Circular. 4p. *4°. n.p. [1850]*

37171 **SPENCER,** I. S. Fugitive slave law. The religious duty of obedience to law: a sermon, preached in the second Presbyterian Church in Brooklyn, Nov. 24, 1850. 31p. *8°. New York, 1850.*

37172 **STOKES,** R. Regulated slave trade. Reprinted from the evidence of Robert Stokes, Esq., given before the Select Committee of the House of Lords, in 1849... xxp. *8°. 1850.*

37173 **STUART,** M. Conscience and the constitution. With remarks on the recent speech of the Hon. Daniel Webster in the Senate of the United States on the subject of slavery. 119p. *12°. Boston, 1850.*

37174 **VAN DYKE,** J. Speech of Mr. John Van Dyke, of New Jersey, delivered in the House of Representatives of the U. States, March 4, 1850, on the subject of slavery, and in vindication of the North from the charges brought against it by the South. 14p. *8°. Washington, 1850.*

37175 **WEBSTER,** D. Speech of the Hon. Daniel Webster, on the subject of slavery; delivered in the United States Senate, on...March 7, 1850. 39p. *8°. Boston, 1850.*

37176 **WILSON,** JOHN L. The British squadron on the coast of Africa...(Reprinted from the "Colonial Magazine" for September, 1850.) 16p. *8°. 1850. The copy that belonged to Earl De Grey.*

37177 **YULE,** SIR H. The African squadron vindicated...Second edition. 41p. *8°. London, Edinburgh, &c., 1850.*

POLITICS

37178 [BERINGTON, S.] The adventures of Signor Gaudentio di Lucca. Being the substance of his examination before the Fathers of the Inquisition at Bologna... Giving an account of an unknown country in...Africa... With critical notes by...Signor Rhedi...(*The Phœnix Library*.) 297p. *12°*. 1850. *For another edition, see* 1748.

37179 CALIFORNIA. Report of the debates in the Convention of California, on the formation of the state constitution, in September and October, 1849. By J. Ross Browne. [With an appendix.] 479, xlvip. *8°*. *Washington*, 1850.

37180 CLARK, THOMAS, *Chartist*. A letter addressed to G. W. M. Reynolds, reviewing his conduct as a professed Chartist, and also explaining who he is and what he is, together with copious extracts from his most indecent writings. Also, a few words of advice to his brother electors of Finsbury. 35p. *12°*. [1850]

37181 —— Reflections upon the past policy, and future prospects of the Chartist party. Also, a letter condemnatory of private assassination, as recommended by Mr. G. J. Harney. 16p. *8°*. 1850.

37182 CONSIDÉRANT, V. P. La solution, ou, le gouvernement direct du peuple. 63p. *8°*. *Paris*, 1850. *Considérant's own copy.*

For COOPER'S JOURNAL, *see* vol. III, *Periodicals list.*

37183 GUÉRIN, A. Au peuple! La victoire électorale. 10 mars 1850. [In verse.] *s.sh.fol. Paris*, [1850]

37184 JENKINS, R. C. ⟨Not published.⟩ A letter to the Rt. Hon. Henry Goulburn, M.P. on the expediency of making a state provision for the Roman Catholic clergy in Ireland. 16p. *8°*. *Chiswick*, 1850. *Presentation copy from the author to the Earl of Ripon.*

37185 JONES, WILLIAM (1726–1800). A letter to John Bull, Esq. from his second cousin, Thomas Bull. By the late Rev. W. Jones... 38p. *8°*. [1850?]

37186 LA PLATA et le Brésil. Observations sur la discours de M. Thiers, prononcé à l'Assemblée Nationale, à l'occasion de la question du Rio de la Plata, dans les débats de février dernier sur le traité "Le Prédour," ou, réponse de la part des Républiques du Rio de la Plata, et celle du Brésil, aux projets de protectorat, colonisation, et conquête, developpés dans le dit discours, dans la vue de dominer ou exclure le commerce de la Grande-Bretagne, et des États Unis, dans ces contrées... 48p. *8°*. 1850.

37187 MACROBIUS, *pseud*. Theocracy; or, a warning to modern politicians. Addressed to the Right Hon. T. B. Macaulay. 39p. *8°*. 1850.

37188 MORE, SIR T. Utopia; or, the happy republic. A philosophical romance, in two books. Written in Latin ...Translated into English by G. Burnet...(*The Phœnix Library*.) 173p. *12°*. 1850. *For other editions, see* 1750.

37189 NATIONAL REFORM LEAGUE. Propositions of the National Reform League. For the peaceful regeneration of society. [Drawn up by J. B. O'Brien?] 4p. *12°*. [*London:*] *Working Printers' Co-operative Association*, [1850]

37190 —— [Another edition.] 4p. *8°*. *n.p*. [1850]

37191 [NICOLAIE, L. F. and VAULABELLE, É. T. DE.] Théâtre du Vaudeville. Paris sans impôts. Vaudeville en trois actes et six tableaux, par MM. Clairville et J. Cordier, représenté...le 28 décembre 1849. 27p. *8°*. *Paris*, 1850.

37192 [——] Théâtre du Gymnase-Dramatique. Les représentants en vacances. Comédie-vaudeville en trois actes, de MM. Clairville et Jules Cordier. Représentée... le 15 septembre 1849. 29p. *8°*. *Paris*, 1850.

37193 OASTLER, R. Richard Oastler's reply to Richard Cobden's speech at Leeds, 18th December, 1849. 47p. *8°*. 1850.

37194 *PEEL, a mystery, the man and his motives made plain. By one who thinks for himself. 12p. *12°*. [1850] *The FWA copy that belonged to William Pare.*

37195 PHIPPS, HON. E. Memoirs of the political and literary life of Robert Plumer Ward...With selections from his correspondence, diaries, and unpublished literary remains. 2 vols. *8°*. 1850.

37196 QUINET, E. L'état du siége. [A plea for the Departement de l'Ain.] 24p. *12°*. *Paris*, 1850. *The copy that belonged to Earl De Grey.*

37197 ROBESPIERRE, M. F. M. I. DE. Declaration of the rights of man and the citizen. 4p. *8°*. *n.p.* [1850?]

SOCIALISM

37198 ADY, W. B. The condition of the labourer in agricultural parishes [and the plan of the Church of England Self-supporting Village Society]. 44p. *8°*. 1850.

37199 BASTIAT, C. F. Baccalauréat et socialisme. 93p. *16°*. *Paris*, 1850.

37200 —— Propriété et spoliation. 64p. *16°*. *Paris*, 1850.

37201 BLANC, J. J. L. Pages d'histoire de la Révolution de février 1848. 359p. *8°*. *Paris*, 1850.

37202 BONNEMÈRE, J. E. Histoire de l'association agricole et solution pratique, ouvrage couronné par l'Académie de Nantes. 166p. *12°*. *Paris*, 1850.

37203 BREYNAT, J. Les socialistes depuis février... 2e édition. 329p. *8°*. *Paris*, 1850.

For the CHRISTIAN SOCIALIST, 1850–51, *see* vol. III, *Periodicals list.*

37204 CHURCH OF ENGLAND SELF-SUPPORTING VILLAGE SOCIETY. The Church of England self-supporting village, for promoting the religious, moral, and general improvement of the working classes, by forming establishments of three hundred families on the land, and combining agricultural with manufacturing employment, for their own benefit. [A prospectus. With 'Explanation of the design for a self-supporting institution', 'Circular to the clergy . . .1843', and 'Petition. . .to the House of Commons, March, 1844', signed: J. M. Morgan.] 16p. *8°*. [*London*, 1850] *For other editions, in which the* Explanation *by John Minter Morgan was printed as the main part, see* 1846; *see also* 1849.

37205 **CONSIDÉRANT**, V. P. La dernière guerre et la paix définitive en Europe. 13p. *8°*. *Paris*, 1850. *Considérant's own copy.*

37206 **ESQUIROS**, A. De la vie future au point de vue socialiste. 144p. *8°*. *Paris*, 1850.

37207 **FINCH**, W. S. The present circumstances of the poor displayed, and the means suggested for their improvement in accordance with the plans of the Church of England Self-supporting Village Society. 25p. *8°*. 1850.

37208 **FOURIER**, F. C. M. Sur l'esprit irréligieux des modernes et dernières analogies. [Extrait de La Phalange.] 63p. *8°*. [*Paris*,] 1850. *The copy that belonged to Victor Considérant.*

For the **FRIEND OF THE PEOPLE,** 1850-52, *see* vol. III, *Periodicals list.*

37209 **GOURAUD**, C. Socialism unmasked. . . . From the French of Charles Gourard [*sic*]. 56p. *8°*. 1850.

37210 **HALL**, CHARLES (1745 ?–1825 ?). The effects of civilization on the people in European states. . .(*The Phœnix Library.*) 252p. *12°*. 1850. *For other editions, see* 1805.

37211 [**HOLMES**, JOHN, *of Leeds*?] The wealth man made; a parody, by one who loves the man more than the wealth. 12p. *12°*. *Leeds*, [1850] *The copy that belonged to J. M. Ludlow, who attributed it to Holmes in his manuscript index to the volume. ★Another, the FWA copy, belonged to William Pare.*

37212 [**HUGHES**, THOMAS (1822-1896).] Tracts on Christian Socialism. No. II. History of the Working Taylors' Association, 34, Great Castle Street. [Signed: H.] 11p. *12°*. [*London*, 1850]

37213 [**KINGSLEY**, C.] Alton Locke, tailor and poet. An autobiography. . . 2 vols. *8°*. 1850.

37214 **LACOMBE**, F. Études sur les socialistes. . . 532p. *12°*. *Paris & Poitiers*, 1850. *The copy that belonged to the Bibliothèque de la Maison du Peuple, Lausanne.*

37215 **LA VARENNE**, C. DE. Les Rouges peints par eux-mêmes. Biographies intimes. . . 330p. *18°*. *Paris*, 1850.

37216 **LECOUTURIER**, H. La cosmosophie ou le socialisme universel. 350p. *8°*. *Paris*, 1850.

37217 [**LUDLOW**, J. M.] Tracts on Christian Socialism. No. IV. The working associations of Paris. [Signed: J.T.] 22p. *12°*. [*London*, 1850]

37218 [——] Tracts on Christian Socialism. No. VI. Prevailing idolatries: or hints for political economists. [Signed: J.T.] 11p. *12°*. [*London*, 1850]

37219 [—— and **SULLY**, C.] Tracts on Christian Socialism. No. V. The Society for Promoting Working-Men's Associations. [Signed: J.T. and C.S.] 23p. *12°*. [*London*, 1850]

37220 [**MAURICE**, JOHN F. D.] Tracts on Christian Socialism. No. I. Dialogue between Somebody (a person of respectability) and Nobody (the writer). 12p. *12°*. [*London*, 1850]

37221 [——] Tracts on Christian Socialism. No. III. An address to the clergy, by a clergyman. What Canhristi Socialism has to do with the question which is now agitating the Church. 12p. *12°*. [*London*, 1850]

37222 [——] Tracts on Christian Socialism. No. VII. A dialogue between A. and B., two clergymen, on the doctrine of circumstances as it affects priests and people. 11p. *12°*. [*London*, 1850]

37223 **MORGAN**, JOHN M. The Christian commonwealth. . .To which is added, An inquiry respecting private property, and the authority and perpetuity of the apostolic institution of a community of goods. From a periodical of 1827. (*The Phœnix Library.*) 151p. *12°*. 1850. *For other editions, see* 1845.

37224 —— Letters to a clergyman, on institutions for ameliorating the condition of the people: chiefly from Paris, in the autumn of 1845. (*The Phœnix Library.*) 174p. *12°*. 1850. *For another edition, see* 1846.

37225 —— Tracts: originally published at various periods, from 1819 to 1838. With an appendix. (*The Phœnix Library.*) 217p. *12°*. 1850. *For another edition, see* 1849.

For **NEUE RHEINISCHE ZEITUNG,** politisch-ökonomische Revue, redigirt von Karl Marx, *see* vol. III, *Periodicals list.*

37226 **OWEN**, ROBERT. Farewell address to all classes of all nations. . .A lecture delivered at the Scientific Institution, John Street, Fitzroy Square, on the 9th of June, 1850. 4p. *8°*. *n.p.* [1850]

37227 ★—— Letters to the human race on the coming universal revolution. . .(1850.) 152p. *16°*. 1850. *The FWA copy that belonged to William Pare. A new edition of the periodical* Robert Owen's weekly letter to the human race, *for which see* vol. III, *Periodicals list.*

37228 —— Robert Owen's catechism of the rational system of society. 4p. *8°*. *n.p.* [1850]

37229 ★—— [Another edition.] Catechism of the rational system of society, and Proclamation. 7p. *8°*. [1850] *The FWA copy that belonged to William Pare.*

37230 **PROUDHON**, P. J. Les confessions d'un révolutionnaire pour servir à l'histoire de la Révolution de février. 325p. *12°*. *Paris*, 1850. *For another edition, see* 1849.

37231 —— Système des contradictions économiques, ou philosophie de la misère. . .Deuxième édition. . . 2 vols. *12°*. *Paris*, 1850. *For another edition, see* 1846.

For **REASONER TRACTS,** *see* vol. III, *Periodicals list.*

For the **RED REPUBLICAN,** *see* vol. III, *Periodicals list.*

For **ROBERT OWEN'S JOURNAL,** 1850-52, *see* vol. III, *Periodicals list.*

For **ROBERT OWEN'S WEEKLY LETTER TO THE HUMAN RACE,** *see* vol. III, *Periodicals list.*

37232 **SMITH**, HENRY, afterwards **WARLEIGH,** H. S. The destitution and miseries of the poor disclosed, and their remedies suggested: being an exposition of the principles and objects of the Church of England Self-supporting Village Society. 150p. *8°*. 1850.

37233 **SOCIÉTÉ POSITIVISTE.** République occidentale. Ordre et progrès. Rapport à la Société Positiviste, par la commission chargée d'examiner la nature et le plan de l'École Positive, destinée surtout à régénérer les médecins. Seconde édition. 30p. *8°. Paris, 1850. With an introduction by Auguste Comte. The copy that belonged to Earl De Grey. For another edition, see 1849.*

37234 —— République occidentale...Rapport à la Société Positiviste, par la commission chargée d'examiner la question du travail. Seconde édition. 15p. *8°. Paris, 1850. With an introduction by Auguste Comte. The copy that belonged to Earl De Grey. For another edition, see 1848.*

37235 THOMPSON, WILLIAM (1785?–1833). An inquiry into the principles of the distribution of wealth most conducive to human happiness...A new edition by William Pare. 463p. *8°. 1850. For another edition, see 1824.*

37236 THONISSEN, J. J. Encyclopédie populaire. Le socialisme dans le passé. 292p. *12°. Bruxelles: Société*

pour *l'émancipation intellectuelle,* [1850] *According to a printed note on the wrapper, this edition was reserved for members of the Society.*

37237 —— Encyclopédie populaire. Le socialisme et ses promesses... 2 vols. *12°. Bruxelles: Société pour l'émancipation intellectuelle,* [1850] *According to a printed note on the wrapper, this edition was reserved for members of the Society.*

37238 WORKINGTAILORS' ASSOCIATION. Address of the Associative Tailors...to their brother toilers of all trades. [Signed: Walter Cooper, on the part of the Association.] 4p. *8°.* [1850?] *The copy that belonged to J. M. Ludlow.*

MISCELLANEOUS

37239 ADDISON, J. Essays moral and humorous. Also essays on imagination and taste...With a memoir of the author. 194p. *8°. Edinburgh,* 1850.

37240 ANSTEY, T. C. The Queen's supremacy considered in its relations with the Roman Catholic Church in England...Being a supplemental chapter to "A guide to the laws of England affecting Roman Catholics," by the same author. 33p. *8°.* 1850.

37241 BROUGHAM, H. P., *Baron Brougham and Vaux.* A letter to Lord Denham from Lord Brougham upon the legislation of 1850 as regards the amendment of the law. 70p. *8°.* 1850.

37242 BURTON, JAMES R. The past and present state of the Navy. 16p. *8°.* 1850.

37243 CLOSSET, A. DE. Encyclopédie populaire. Éléments de droit civil. Tome premier. 106p. *12°. Bruxelles: Société pour l'émancipation intellectuelle,* [1850]

37244 COBBETT, W. A grammar of the English language, in a series of letters; intended for the use of schools and of young persons in general, but more especially for the use of soldiers, sailors, apprentices, and plough-boys...To which are added six lessons, intended to prevent statesmen from using false grammar... Stereotype edition. 239p. *12°.* 1850. *For other editions, see* 1819.

37245 COLLIER, JOHN (1708–1786). Dialect of South Lancashire, or Tim Bobbin's Tummus and Meary, revised and corrected, with his rhymes, and an enlarged and amended glossary of words and phrases, chiefly used by the rural population of the manufacturing districts of South Lancashire. By Samuel Bamford. 241p. *8°. Manchester & London,* 1850.

37246 DISCOURS veritable d'un usurier de Remilly en Sauoye, lequel c'est pendu & estranglé auec le licol de sa jument, le 16. May 1604...(*Portefeuille de l'Ami des Livres.*) 8p. *4°. Paris,* [c. 1850]

37247 An **EXPOSITION** of the case of the assistant-surgeons of the Royal Navy. By a Naval medical officer... Third edition... 39p. *8°.* 1850.

37248 [F., E., *ed.*] Gems from the spirit mine, illustrative of peace, brotherhood, and progress. [In verse. By various authors. Published to commemorate the opening of the League of Brotherhood Bazaar, held to welcome

Elihu Burritt on his return from America...28th of May, 1850.] 184p. *24°.* 1850.

37249 The **FIRE** of London. A.D.1666. [A facsimile reprint of excerpts from the account printed in the *London Gazette* in 1666.] *s.sh.fol. n.p.* [1850]

37250 GENERAL ASSOCIATION FOR THE SUBDIVISION OF PARISHES, *Staffordshire.* Speeches delivered at Stoke-upon-Trent, January 19, 1850, by Smith Child, Esq. chairman, and the Rev. Frederick Wade... 15p. *8°. Burslem & London,* [1850]

37251 LETTER from the ghost of Sir Edmund Saunders to the Lord Chancellor Cottenham, on the Commission for Law Reform. 24p. *8°.* 1850.

37252 MALET, W. W. The funds of the Church; their appropriation and alienation the cause of ignorance, heresy and schism: and Church self-government the only remedy for these evils. A letter to the Archbishop of Canterbury. 22p. *8°.* 1850.

37253 OPINIONS of modern statesmen on standing armaments. 2p. *8°.* [1850?]

37254 PRAYER BOOK AND HOMILY SOCIETY. Proceedings of the...Society, during its thirty-eighth year – (1849–50.) Containing the annual sermon, by the Rev. Henry Hutton...the report of the Committee, with an appendix; and a list of subscribers and benefactors. 89p. *8°.* 1850.

37255 A **PRESERVATIVE** from infidelity: containing proofs of the authenticity and inspiration of the Holy Scriptures: taken from the Elements of Christian theology...And also, a compendious view of the sacred writings: taken from lectures on the Gospel of St. Matthew [by Bishop Porteus]. 82p. *12°.* [1850?]

37256 RHYMES for the people, about battle, glory, and murder. 2p. *8°. Birmingham,* [1850?] *The Turner copy.*

37257 SIMONS, C. Encyclopédie populaire. Éléments de droit civil. [Seconde partie.] De la propriété et de ses modifications. 95p. *12°. Bruxelles: Société pour l'émancipation intellectuelle,* [1850]

37258 SMITH, JOSHUA T. What is the Corporation of London? And who are the Freemen? 44p. *8°.* 1850. *Bound in a volume of his tracts collected by the author, with his signature on the fly-leaf.*